Oxford Dictionary of National Biography

Volume 15

Oxford Dictionary of National Biography

IN ASSOCIATION WITH

The British Academy

From the earliest times to the year 2000

Edited by

H. C. G. Matthew

and

Brian Harrison

Volume 15

Daly–Dewar

OXFORD

UNIVERSITY PRESS

OXFORD
UNIVERSITY PRESS

Great Clarendon Street, Oxford OX2 6DP

Oxford University Press is a department of the University of Oxford.
It furthers the University's objective of excellence in research, scholarship,
and education by publishing worldwide in

Oxford New York

Auckland Bangkok Buenos Aires Cape Town
Chennai Dar es Salaam Delhi Hong Kong Istanbul Karachi
Kolkata Kuala Lumpur Madrid Melbourne Mexico City Mumbai Nairobi
São Paulo Shanghai Taipei Tokyo Toronto

Oxford is a registered trade mark of Oxford University Press
in the UK and in certain other countries

Published in the United States
by Oxford University Press Inc., New York

British Library Cataloguing in Publication Data
Data available

Library of Congress Cataloging in Publication Data
Data available: for details see volume 1, p. iv

ISBN 0-19-861365-2 (this volume)
ISBN 0-19-861411-X (set of sixty volumes)

Text captured by Alliance Phototypesetters, Pondicherry
Illustrations reproduced and archived by
Alliance Graphics Ltd, UK
Typeset in OUP Swift by Interactive Sciences Limited, Gloucester
Printed in Great Britain on acid-free paper by
Butler and Tanner Ltd,
Frome, Somerset

LIST OF ABBREVIATIONS

1 General abbreviations

AB	bachelor of arts		BCnL	bachelor of canon law
ABC	Australian Broadcasting Corporation		BCom	bachelor of commerce
ABC TV	ABC Television		BD	bachelor of divinity
act.	active		BEd	bachelor of education
A$	Australian dollar		BEng	bachelor of engineering
AD	*anno domini*		bk *pl.* bks	book(s)
AFC	Air Force Cross		BL	bachelor of law / letters / literature
AIDS	acquired immune deficiency syndrome		BLitt	bachelor of letters
AK	Alaska		BM	bachelor of medicine
AL	Alabama		BMus	bachelor of music
A level	advanced level [examination]		BP	before present
ALS	associate of the Linnean Society		BP	British Petroleum
AM	master of arts		Bros.	Brothers
AMICE	associate member of the Institution of Civil Engineers		BS	(1) bachelor of science; (2) bachelor of surgery; (3) British standard
ANZAC	Australian and New Zealand Army Corps		BSc	bachelor of science
appx *pl.* appxs	appendix(es)		BSc (Econ.)	bachelor of science (economics)
AR	Arkansas		BSc (Eng.)	bachelor of science (engineering)
ARA	associate of the Royal Academy		bt	baronet
ARCA	associate of the Royal College of Art		BTh	bachelor of theology
ARCM	associate of the Royal College of Music		*bur.*	buried
ARCO	associate of the Royal College of Organists		C.	command [identifier for published parliamentary papers]
ARIBA	associate of the Royal Institute of British Architects		*c.*	*circa*
ARP	air-raid precautions		c.	*capitulum pl. capitula*: chapter(s)
ARRC	associate of the Royal Red Cross		CA	California
ARSA	associate of the Royal Scottish Academy		Cantab.	Cantabrigiensis
art.	article / item		cap.	*capitulum pl. capitula*: chapter(s)
ASC	Army Service Corps		CB	companion of the Bath
Asch	Austrian Schilling		CBE	commander of the Order of the British Empire
ASDIC	Antisubmarine Detection Investigation Committee		CBS	Columbia Broadcasting System
ATS	Auxiliary Territorial Service		cc	cubic centimetres
ATV	Associated Television		C$	Canadian dollar
Aug	August		CD	compact disc
AZ	Arizona		Cd	command [identifier for published parliamentary papers]
b.	born		CE	Common (*or* Christian) Era
BA	bachelor of arts		cent.	century
BA (Admin.)	bachelor of arts (administration)		cf.	compare
BAFTA	British Academy of Film and Television Arts		CH	Companion of Honour
BAO	bachelor of arts in obstetrics		chap.	chapter
bap.	baptized		ChB	bachelor of surgery
BBC	British Broadcasting Corporation / Company		CI	Imperial Order of the Crown of India
BC	before Christ		CIA	Central Intelligence Agency
BCE	before the common (*or* Christian) era		CID	Criminal Investigation Department
BCE	bachelor of civil engineering		CIE	companion of the Order of the Indian Empire
BCG	bacillus of Calmette and Guérin [inoculation against tuberculosis]		Cie	Compagnie
BCh	bachelor of surgery		CLit	companion of literature
BChir	bachelor of surgery		CM	master of surgery
BCL	bachelor of civil law		cm	centimetre(s)

Cmd	command [identifier for published parliamentary papers]
CMG	companion of the Order of St Michael and St George
Cmnd	command [identifier for published parliamentary papers]
CO	Colorado
Co.	company
co.	county
col. *pl.* cols.	column(s)
Corp.	corporation
CSE	certificate of secondary education
CSI	companion of the Order of the Star of India
CT	Connecticut
CVO	commander of the Royal Victorian Order
cwt	hundredweight
$	(American) dollar
d.	(1) penny (pence); (2) died
DBE	dame commander of the Order of the British Empire
DCH	diploma in child health
DCh	doctor of surgery
DCL	doctor of civil law
DCnL	doctor of canon law
DCVO	dame commander of the Royal Victorian Order
DD	doctor of divinity
DE	Delaware
Dec	December
dem.	demolished
DEng	doctor of engineering
des.	destroyed
DFC	Distinguished Flying Cross
DipEd	diploma in education
DipPsych	diploma in psychiatry
diss.	dissertation
DL	deputy lieutenant
DLitt	doctor of letters
DLittCelt	doctor of Celtic letters
DM	(1) Deutschmark; (2) doctor of medicine; (3) doctor of musical arts
DMus	doctor of music
DNA	dioxyribonucleic acid
doc.	document
DOL	doctor of oriental learning
DPH	diploma in public health
DPhil	doctor of philosophy
DPM	diploma in psychological medicine
DSC	Distinguished Service Cross
DSc	doctor of science
DSc (Econ.)	doctor of science (economics)
DSc (Eng.)	doctor of science (engineering)
DSM	Distinguished Service Medal
DSO	companion of the Distinguished Service Order
DSocSc	doctor of social science
DTech	doctor of technology
DTh	doctor of theology
DTM	diploma in tropical medicine
DTMH	diploma in tropical medicine and hygiene
DU	doctor of the university
DUniv	doctor of the university
dwt	pennyweight
EC	European Community
ed. *pl.* eds.	edited / edited by / editor(s)
Edin.	Edinburgh
edn	edition
EEC	European Economic Community
EFTA	European Free Trade Association
EICS	East India Company Service
EMI	Electrical and Musical Industries (Ltd)
Eng.	English
enl.	enlarged
ENSA	Entertainments National Service Association
ep. *pl.* epp.	*epistola(e)*
ESP	extra-sensory perception
esp.	especially
esq.	esquire
est.	estimate / estimated
EU	European Union
ex	sold by (*lit.* out of)
excl.	excludes / excluding
exh.	exhibited
exh. cat.	exhibition catalogue
f. *pl.* ff.	following [pages]
FA	Football Association
FACP	fellow of the American College of Physicians
facs.	facsimile
FANY	First Aid Nursing Yeomanry
FBA	fellow of the British Academy
FBI	Federation of British Industries
FCS	fellow of the Chemical Society
Feb	February
FEng	fellow of the Fellowship of Engineering
FFCM	fellow of the Faculty of Community Medicine
FGS	fellow of the Geological Society
fig.	figure
FIMechE	fellow of the Institution of Mechanical Engineers
FL	Florida
fl.	*floruit*
FLS	fellow of the Linnean Society
FM	frequency modulation
fol. *pl.* fols.	folio(s)
Fr	French francs
Fr.	French
FRAeS	fellow of the Royal Aeronautical Society
FRAI	fellow of the Royal Anthropological Institute
FRAM	fellow of the Royal Academy of Music
FRAS	(1) fellow of the Royal Asiatic Society; (2) fellow of the Royal Astronomical Society
FRCM	fellow of the Royal College of Music
FRCO	fellow of the Royal College of Organists
FRCOG	fellow of the Royal College of Obstetricians and Gynaecologists
FRCP(C)	fellow of the Royal College of Physicians of Canada
FRCP (Edin.)	fellow of the Royal College of Physicians of Edinburgh
FRCP (Lond.)	fellow of the Royal College of Physicians of London
FRCPath	fellow of the Royal College of Pathologists
FRCPsych	fellow of the Royal College of Psychiatrists
FRCS	fellow of the Royal College of Surgeons
FRGS	fellow of the Royal Geographical Society
FRIBA	fellow of the Royal Institute of British Architects
FRICS	fellow of the Royal Institute of Chartered Surveyors
FRS	fellow of the Royal Society
FRSA	fellow of the Royal Society of Arts

FRSCM	fellow of the Royal School of Church Music	ISO	companion of the Imperial Service Order
FRSE	fellow of the Royal Society of Edinburgh	It.	Italian
FRSL	fellow of the Royal Society of Literature	ITA	Independent Television Authority
FSA	fellow of the Society of Antiquaries	ITV	Independent Television
ft	foot *pl.* feet	Jan	January
FTCL	fellow of Trinity College of Music, London	JP	justice of the peace
ft-lb per min.	foot-pounds per minute [unit of horsepower]	jun.	junior
FZS	fellow of the Zoological Society	KB	knight of the Order of the Bath
GA	Georgia	KBE	knight commander of the Order of the British Empire
GBE	knight or dame grand cross of the Order of the British Empire	KC	king's counsel
GCB	knight grand cross of the Order of the Bath	kcal	kilocalorie
GCE	general certificate of education	KCB	knight commander of the Order of the Bath
GCH	knight grand cross of the Royal Guelphic Order	KCH	knight commander of the Royal Guelphic Order
GCHQ	government communications headquarters	KCIE	knight commander of the Order of the Indian Empire
GCIE	knight grand commander of the Order of the Indian Empire	KCMG	knight commander of the Order of St Michael and St George
GCMG	knight or dame grand cross of the Order of St Michael and St George	KCSI	knight commander of the Order of the Star of India
GCSE	general certificate of secondary education	KCVO	knight commander of the Royal Victorian Order
GCSI	knight grand commander of the Order of the Star of India	keV	kilo-electron-volt
GCStJ	bailiff or dame grand cross of the order of St John of Jerusalem	KG	knight of the Order of the Garter
GCVO	knight or dame grand cross of the Royal Victorian Order	KGB	[Soviet committee of state security]
		KH	knight of the Royal Guelphic Order
GEC	General Electric Company	KLM	Koninklijke Luchtvaart Maatschappij (Royal Dutch Air Lines)
Ger.	German		
GI	government (*or* general) issue	km	kilometre(s)
GMT	Greenwich mean time	KP	knight of the Order of St Patrick
GP	general practitioner	KS	Kansas
GPU	[Soviet special police unit]	KT	knight of the Order of the Thistle
GSO	general staff officer	kt	knight
Heb.	Hebrew	KY	Kentucky
HEICS	Honourable East India Company Service	£	pound(s) sterling
HI	Hawaii	£E	Egyptian pound
HIV	human immunodeficiency virus	L	lira *pl.* lire
HK$	Hong Kong dollar	l. *pl.* ll.	line(s)
HM	his / her majesty('s)	LA	Lousiana
HMAS	his / her majesty's Australian ship	LAA	light anti-aircraft
HMNZS	his / her majesty's New Zealand ship	LAH	licentiate of the Apothecaries' Hall, Dublin
HMS	his / her majesty's ship	Lat.	Latin
HMSO	His / Her Majesty's Stationery Office	lb	pound(s), unit of weight
HMV	His Master's Voice	LDS	licence in dental surgery
Hon.	Honourable	*lit.*	literally
hp	horsepower	LittB	bachelor of letters
hr	hour(s)	LittD	doctor of letters
HRH	his / her royal highness	LKQCPI	licentiate of the King and Queen's College of Physicians, Ireland
HTV	Harlech Television	LLA	lady literate in arts
IA	Iowa	LLB	bachelor of laws
ibid.	*ibidem*: in the same place	LLD	doctor of laws
ICI	Imperial Chemical Industries (Ltd)	LLM	master of laws
ID	Idaho	LM	licentiate in midwifery
IL	Illinois	LP	long-playing record
illus.	illustration	LRAM	licentiate of the Royal Academy of Music
illustr.	illustrated	LRCP	licentiate of the Royal College of Physicians
IN	Indiana	LRCPS (Glasgow)	licentiate of the Royal College of Physicians and Surgeons of Glasgow
in.	inch(es)		
Inc.	Incorporated	LRCS	licentiate of the Royal College of Surgeons
incl.	includes / including	LSA	licentiate of the Society of Apothecaries
IOU	I owe you	LSD	lysergic acid diethylamide
IQ	intelligence quotient	LVO	lieutenant of the Royal Victorian Order
Ir£	Irish pound	M. *pl.* MM.	Monsieur *pl.* Messieurs
IRA	Irish Republican Army	m	metre(s)

m. *pl.* mm.	membrane(s)		ND	North Dakota
MA	(1) Massachusetts; (2) master of arts		n.d.	no date
MAI	master of engineering		NE	Nebraska
MB	bachelor of medicine		*nem. con.*	*nemine contradicente*: unanimously
MBA	master of business administration		new ser.	new series
MBE	member of the Order of the British Empire		NH	New Hampshire
MC	Military Cross		NHS	National Health Service
MCC	Marylebone Cricket Club		NJ	New Jersey
MCh	master of surgery		NKVD	[Soviet people's commissariat for internal affairs]
MChir	master of surgery		NM	New Mexico
MCom	master of commerce		nm	nanometre(s)
MD	(1) doctor of medicine; (2) Maryland		no. *pl.* nos.	number(s)
MDMA	methylenedioxymethamphetamine		Nov	November
ME	Maine		n.p.	no place [of publication]
MEd	master of education		NS	new style
MEng	master of engineering		NV	Nevada
MEP	member of the European parliament		NY	New York
MG	Morris Garages		NZBS	New Zealand Broadcasting Service
MGM	Metro-Goldwyn-Mayer		OBE	officer of the Order of the British Empire
Mgr	Monsignor		obit.	obituary
MI	(1) Michigan; (2) military intelligence		Oct	October
MI1c	[secret intelligence department]		OCTU	officer cadets training unit
MI5	[military intelligence department]		OECD	Organization for Economic Co-operation and Development
MI6	[secret intelligence department]		OEEC	Organization for European Economic Co-operation
MI9	[secret escape service]			
MICE	member of the Institution of Civil Engineers		OFM	order of Friars Minor [Franciscans]
MIEE	member of the Institution of Electrical Engineers		OFMCap	Ordine Frati Minori Cappucini: member of the Capuchin order
min.	minute(s)		OH	Ohio
Mk	mark		OK	Oklahoma
ML	(1) licentiate of medicine; (2) master of laws		O level	ordinary level [examination]
MLitt	master of letters		OM	Order of Merit
Mlle	Mademoiselle		OP	order of Preachers [Dominicans]
mm	millimetre(s)		op. *pl.* opp.	opus *pl.* opera
Mme	Madame		OPEC	Organization of Petroleum Exporting Countries
MN	Minnesota		OR	Oregon
MO	Missouri		orig.	original
MOH	medical officer of health		OS	old style
MP	member of parliament		OSB	Order of St Benedict
m.p.h.	miles per hour		OTC	Officers' Training Corps
MPhil	master of philosophy		OWS	Old Watercolour Society
MRCP	member of the Royal College of Physicians		Oxon.	Oxoniensis
MRCS	member of the Royal College of Surgeons		p. *pl.* pp.	page(s)
MRCVS	member of the Royal College of Veterinary Surgeons		PA	Pennsylvania
MRIA	member of the Royal Irish Academy		p.a.	per annum
MS	(1) master of science; (2) Mississippi		para.	paragraph
MS *pl.* MSS	manuscript(s)		PAYE	pay as you earn
MSc	master of science		pbk *pl.* pbks	paperback(s)
MSc (Econ.)	master of science (economics)		*per.*	[during the] period
MT	Montana		PhD	doctor of philosophy
MusB	bachelor of music		pl.	(1) plate(s); (2) plural
MusBac	bachelor of music		priv. coll.	private collection
MusD	doctor of music		pt *pl.* pts	part(s)
MV	motor vessel		pubd	published
MVO	member of the Royal Victorian Order		PVC	polyvinyl chloride
n. *pl.* nn.	note(s)		q. *pl.* qq.	(1) question(s); (2) quire(s)
NAAFI	Navy, Army, and Air Force Institutes		QC	queen's counsel
NASA	National Aeronautics and Space Administration		R	rand
NATO	North Atlantic Treaty Organization		R.	Rex / Regina
NBC	National Broadcasting Corporation		*r*	recto
NC	North Carolina		*r.*	reigned / ruled
NCO	non-commissioned officer		RA	Royal Academy / Royal Academician

RAC	Royal Automobile Club		Skr	Swedish krona
RAF	Royal Air Force		Span.	Spanish
RAFVR	Royal Air Force Volunteer Reserve		SPCK	Society for Promoting Christian Knowledge
RAM	[member of the] Royal Academy of Music		SS	(1) Santissimi; (2) Schutzstaffel; (3) steam ship
RAMC	Royal Army Medical Corps		STB	bachelor of theology
RCA	Royal College of Art		STD	doctor of theology
RCNC	Royal Corps of Naval Constructors		STM	master of theology
RCOG	Royal College of Obstetricians and Gynaecologists		STP	doctor of theology
RDI	royal designer for industry		*supp.*	supposedly
RE	Royal Engineers		suppl. *pl.* suppls.	supplement(s)
repr. *pl.* reprs.	reprint(s) / reprinted		s.v.	*sub verbo* / *sub voce*: under the word / heading
repro.	reproduced		SY	steam yacht
rev.	revised / revised by / reviser / revision		TA	Territorial Army
Revd	Reverend		TASS	[Soviet news agency]
RHA	Royal Hibernian Academy		TB	tuberculosis (*lit.* tubercle bacillus)
RI	(1) Rhode Island; (2) Royal Institute of Painters in Water-Colours		TD	(1) *teachtaí dála* (member of the Dáil); (2) territorial decoration
RIBA	Royal Institute of British Architects		TN	Tennessee
RIN	Royal Indian Navy		TNT	trinitrotoluene
RM	Reichsmark		trans.	translated / translated by / translation / translator
RMS	Royal Mail steamer		TT	tourist trophy
RN	Royal Navy		TUC	Trades Union Congress
RNA	ribonucleic acid		TX	Texas
RNAS	Royal Naval Air Service		U-boat	*Unterseeboot*: submarine
RNR	Royal Naval Reserve		Ufa	Universum-Film AG
RNVR	Royal Naval Volunteer Reserve		UMIST	University of Manchester Institute of Science and Technology
RO	Record Office		UN	United Nations
r.p.m.	revolutions per minute		UNESCO	United Nations Educational, Scientific, and Cultural Organization
RRS	royal research ship			
Rs	rupees		UNICEF	United Nations International Children's Emergency Fund
RSA	(1) Royal Scottish Academician; (2) Royal Society of Arts			
RSPCA	Royal Society for the Prevention of Cruelty to Animals		unpubd	unpublished
			USS	United States ship
Rt Hon.	Right Honourable		UT	Utah
Rt Revd	Right Reverend		*v*	verso
RUC	Royal Ulster Constabulary		v.	versus
Russ.	Russian		VA	Virginia
RWS	Royal Watercolour Society		VAD	Voluntary Aid Detachment
S4C	Sianel Pedwar Cymru		VC	Victoria Cross
s.	shilling(s)		VE-day	victory in Europe day
s.a.	*sub anno*: under the year		Ven.	Venerable
SABC	South African Broadcasting Corporation		VJ-day	victory over Japan day
SAS	Special Air Service		vol. *pl.* vols.	volume(s)
SC	South Carolina		VT	Vermont
ScD	doctor of science		WA	Washington [state]
S$	Singapore dollar		WAAC	Women's Auxiliary Army Corps
SD	South Dakota		WAAF	Women's Auxiliary Air Force
sec.	second(s)		WEA	Workers' Educational Association
sel.	selected		WHO	World Health Organization
sen.	senior		WI	Wisconsin
Sept	September		WRAF	Women's Royal Air Force
ser.	series		WRNS	Women's Royal Naval Service
SHAPE	supreme headquarters allied powers, Europe		WV	West Virginia
SIDRO	Société Internationale d'Énergie Hydro-Électrique		WVS	Women's Voluntary Service
			WY	Wyoming
sig. *pl.* sigs.	signature(s)		¥	yen
sing.	singular		YMCA	Young Men's Christian Association
SIS	Secret Intelligence Service		YWCA	Young Women's Christian Association
SJ	Society of Jesus			

2 Institution abbreviations

All Souls Oxf.	All Souls College, Oxford
AM Oxf.	Ashmolean Museum, Oxford
Balliol Oxf.	Balliol College, Oxford
BBC WAC	BBC Written Archives Centre, Reading
Beds. & Luton ARS	Bedfordshire and Luton Archives and Record Service, Bedford
Berks. RO	Berkshire Record Office, Reading
BFI	British Film Institute, London
BFI NFTVA	British Film Institute, London, National Film and Television Archive
BGS	British Geological Survey, Keyworth, Nottingham
Birm. CA	Birmingham Central Library, Birmingham City Archives
Birm. CL	Birmingham Central Library
BL	British Library, London
BL NSA	British Library, London, National Sound Archive
BL OIOC	British Library, London, Oriental and India Office Collections
BLPES	London School of Economics and Political Science, British Library of Political and Economic Science
BM	British Museum, London
Bodl. Oxf.	Bodleian Library, Oxford
Bodl. RH	Bodleian Library of Commonwealth and African Studies at Rhodes House, Oxford
Borth. Inst.	Borthwick Institute of Historical Research, University of York
Boston PL	Boston Public Library, Massachusetts
Bristol RO	Bristol Record Office
Bucks. RLSS	Buckinghamshire Records and Local Studies Service, Aylesbury
CAC Cam.	Churchill College, Cambridge, Churchill Archives Centre
Cambs. AS	Cambridgeshire Archive Service
CCC Cam.	Corpus Christi College, Cambridge
CCC Oxf.	Corpus Christi College, Oxford
Ches. & Chester ALSS	Cheshire and Chester Archives and Local Studies Service
Christ Church Oxf.	Christ Church, Oxford
Christies	Christies, London
City Westm. AC	City of Westminster Archives Centre, London
CKS	Centre for Kentish Studies, Maidstone
CLRO	Corporation of London Records Office
Coll. Arms	College of Arms, London
Col. U.	Columbia University, New York
Cornwall RO	Cornwall Record Office, Truro
Courtauld Inst.	Courtauld Institute of Art, London
CUL	Cambridge University Library
Cumbria AS	Cumbria Archive Service
Derbys. RO	Derbyshire Record Office, Matlock
Devon RO	Devon Record Office, Exeter
Dorset RO	Dorset Record Office, Dorchester
Duke U.	Duke University, Durham, North Carolina
Duke U., Perkins L.	Duke University, Durham, North Carolina, William R. Perkins Library
Durham Cath. CL	Durham Cathedral, chapter library
Durham RO	Durham Record Office
DWL	Dr Williams's Library, London
Essex RO	Essex Record Office
E. Sussex RO	East Sussex Record Office, Lewes
Eton	Eton College, Berkshire
FM Cam.	Fitzwilliam Museum, Cambridge
Folger	Folger Shakespeare Library, Washington, DC
Garr. Club	Garrick Club, London
Girton Cam.	Girton College, Cambridge
GL	Guildhall Library, London
Glos. RO	Gloucestershire Record Office, Gloucester
Gon. & Caius Cam.	Gonville and Caius College, Cambridge
Gov. Art Coll.	Government Art Collection
GS Lond.	Geological Society of London
Hants. RO	Hampshire Record Office, Winchester
Harris Man. Oxf.	Harris Manchester College, Oxford
Harvard TC	Harvard Theatre Collection, Harvard University, Cambridge, Massachusetts, Nathan Marsh Pusey Library
Harvard U.	Harvard University, Cambridge, Massachusetts
Harvard U., Houghton L.	Harvard University, Cambridge, Massachusetts, Houghton Library
Herefs. RO	Herefordshire Record Office, Hereford
Herts. ALS	Hertfordshire Archives and Local Studies, Hertford
Hist. Soc. Penn.	Historical Society of Pennsylvania, Philadelphia
HLRO	House of Lords Record Office, London
Hult. Arch.	Hulton Archive, London and New York
Hunt. L.	Huntington Library, San Marino, California
ICL	Imperial College, London
Inst. CE	Institution of Civil Engineers, London
Inst. EE	Institution of Electrical Engineers, London
IWM	Imperial War Museum, London
IWM FVA	Imperial War Museum, London, Film and Video Archive
IWM SA	Imperial War Museum, London, Sound Archive
JRL	John Rylands University Library of Manchester
King's AC Cam.	King's College Archives Centre, Cambridge
King's Cam.	King's College, Cambridge
King's Lond.	King's College, London
King's Lond., Liddell Hart C.	King's College, London, Liddell Hart Centre for Military Archives
Lancs. RO	Lancashire Record Office, Preston
L. Cong.	Library of Congress, Washington, DC
Leics. RO	Leicestershire, Leicester, and Rutland Record Office, Leicester
Lincs. Arch.	Lincolnshire Archives, Lincoln
Linn. Soc.	Linnean Society of London
LMA	London Metropolitan Archives
LPL	Lambeth Palace, London
Lpool RO	Liverpool Record Office and Local Studies Service
LUL	London University Library
Magd. Cam.	Magdalene College, Cambridge
Magd. Oxf.	Magdalen College, Oxford
Man. City Gall.	Manchester City Galleries
Man. CL	Manchester Central Library
Mass. Hist. Soc.	Massachusetts Historical Society, Boston
Merton Oxf.	Merton College, Oxford
MHS Oxf.	Museum of the History of Science, Oxford
Mitchell L., Glas.	Mitchell Library, Glasgow
Mitchell L., NSW	State Library of New South Wales, Sydney, Mitchell Library
Morgan L.	Pierpont Morgan Library, New York
NA Canada	National Archives of Canada, Ottawa
NA Ire.	National Archives of Ireland, Dublin
NAM	National Army Museum, London
NA Scot.	National Archives of Scotland, Edinburgh
News Int. RO	News International Record Office, London
NG Ire.	National Gallery of Ireland, Dublin

NG Scot.	National Gallery of Scotland, Edinburgh
NHM	Natural History Museum, London
NL Aus.	National Library of Australia, Canberra
NL Ire.	National Library of Ireland, Dublin
NL NZ	National Library of New Zealand, Wellington
NL NZ, Turnbull L.	National Library of New Zealand, Wellington, Alexander Turnbull Library
NL Scot.	National Library of Scotland, Edinburgh
NL Wales	National Library of Wales, Aberystwyth
NMG Wales	National Museum and Gallery of Wales, Cardiff
NMM	National Maritime Museum, London
Norfolk RO	Norfolk Record Office, Norwich
Northants. RO	Northamptonshire Record Office, Northampton
Northumbd RO	Northumberland Record Office
Notts. Arch.	Nottinghamshire Archives, Nottingham
NPG	National Portrait Gallery, London
NRA	National Archives, London, Historical Manuscripts Commission, National Register of Archives
Nuffield Oxf.	Nuffield College, Oxford
N. Yorks. CRO	North Yorkshire County Record Office, Northallerton
NYPL	New York Public Library
Oxf. UA	Oxford University Archives
Oxf. U. Mus. NH	Oxford University Museum of Natural History
Oxon. RO	Oxfordshire Record Office, Oxford
Pembroke Cam.	Pembroke College, Cambridge
PRO	National Archives, London, Public Record Office
PRO NIre.	Public Record Office for Northern Ireland, Belfast
Pusey Oxf.	Pusey House, Oxford
RA	Royal Academy of Arts, London
Ransom HRC	Harry Ransom Humanities Research Center, University of Texas, Austin
RAS	Royal Astronomical Society, London
RBG Kew	Royal Botanic Gardens, Kew, London
RCP Lond.	Royal College of Physicians of London
RCS Eng.	Royal College of Surgeons of England, London
RGS	Royal Geographical Society, London
RIBA	Royal Institute of British Architects, London
RIBA BAL	Royal Institute of British Architects, London, British Architectural Library
Royal Arch.	Royal Archives, Windsor Castle, Berkshire [by gracious permission of her majesty the queen]
Royal Irish Acad.	Royal Irish Academy, Dublin
Royal Scot. Acad.	Royal Scottish Academy, Edinburgh
RS	Royal Society, London
RSA	Royal Society of Arts, London
RS Friends, Lond.	Religious Society of Friends, London
St Ant. Oxf.	St Antony's College, Oxford
St John Cam.	St John's College, Cambridge
S. Antiquaries, Lond.	Society of Antiquaries of London
Sci. Mus.	Science Museum, London
Scot. NPG	Scottish National Portrait Gallery, Edinburgh
Scott Polar RI	University of Cambridge, Scott Polar Research Institute
Sheff. Arch.	Sheffield Archives
Shrops. RRC	Shropshire Records and Research Centre, Shrewsbury
SOAS	School of Oriental and African Studies, London
Som. ARS	Somerset Archive and Record Service, Taunton
Staffs. RO	Staffordshire Record Office, Stafford

Suffolk RO	Suffolk Record Office
Surrey HC	Surrey History Centre, Woking
TCD	Trinity College, Dublin
Trinity Cam.	Trinity College, Cambridge
U. Aberdeen	University of Aberdeen
U. Birm.	University of Birmingham
U. Birm. L.	University of Birmingham Library
U. Cal.	University of California
U. Cam.	University of Cambridge
UCL	University College, London
U. Durham	University of Durham
U. Durham L.	University of Durham Library
U. Edin.	University of Edinburgh
U. Edin., New Coll.	University of Edinburgh, New College
U. Edin., New Coll. L.	University of Edinburgh, New College Library
U. Edin. L.	University of Edinburgh Library
U. Glas.	University of Glasgow
U. Glas. L.	University of Glasgow Library
U. Hull	University of Hull
U. Hull, Brynmor Jones L.	University of Hull, Brynmor Jones Library
U. Leeds	University of Leeds
U. Leeds, Brotherton L.	University of Leeds, Brotherton Library
U. Lond.	University of London
U. Lpool	University of Liverpool
U. Lpool L.	University of Liverpool Library
U. Mich.	University of Michigan, Ann Arbor
U. Mich., Clements L.	University of Michigan, Ann Arbor, William L. Clements Library
U. Newcastle	University of Newcastle upon Tyne
U. Newcastle, Robinson L.	University of Newcastle upon Tyne, Robinson Library
U. Nott.	University of Nottingham
U. Nott. L.	University of Nottingham Library
U. Oxf.	University of Oxford
U. Reading	University of Reading
U. Reading L.	University of Reading Library
U. St Andr.	University of St Andrews
U. St Andr. L.	University of St Andrews Library
U. Southampton	University of Southampton
U. Southampton L.	University of Southampton Library
U. Sussex	University of Sussex, Brighton
U. Texas	University of Texas, Austin
U. Wales	University of Wales
U. Warwick Mod. RC	University of Warwick, Coventry, Modern Records Centre
V&A	Victoria and Albert Museum, London
V&A NAL	Victoria and Albert Museum, London, National Art Library
Warks. CRO	Warwickshire County Record Office, Warwick
Wellcome L.	Wellcome Library for the History and Understanding of Medicine, London
Westm. DA	Westminster Diocesan Archives, London
Wilts. & Swindon RO	Wiltshire and Swindon Record Office, Trowbridge
Worcs. RO	Worcestershire Record Office, Worcester
W. Sussex RO	West Sussex Record Office, Chichester
W. Yorks. AS	West Yorkshire Archive Service
Yale U.	Yale University, New Haven, Connecticut
Yale U., Beinecke L.	Yale University, New Haven, Connecticut, Beinecke Rare Book and Manuscript Library
Yale U. CBA	Yale University, New Haven, Connecticut, Yale Center for British Art

3 Bibliographic abbreviations

Adams, *Drama* — W. D. Adams, *A dictionary of the drama*, 1: *A–G* (1904); 2: *H–Z* (1956) [vol. 2 microfilm only]

AFM — J O'Donovan, ed. and trans., *Annala rioghachta Eireann / Annals of the kingdom of Ireland by the four masters*, 7 vols. (1848–51); 2nd edn (1856); 3rd edn (1990)

Allibone, *Dict.* — S. A. Allibone, *A critical dictionary of English literature and British and American authors*, 3 vols. (1859–71); suppl. by J. F. Kirk, 2 vols. (1891)

ANB — J. A. Garraty and M. C. Carnes, eds., *American national biography*, 24 vols. (1999)

Anderson, *Scot. nat.* — W. Anderson, *The Scottish nation, or, The surnames, families, literature, honours, and biographical history of the people of Scotland*, 3 vols. (1859–63)

Ann. mon. — H. R. Luard, ed., *Annales monastici*, 5 vols., Rolls Series, 36 (1864–9)

Ann. Ulster — S. Mac Airt and G. Mac Niocaill, eds., *Annals of Ulster (to AD 1131)* (1983)

APC — *Acts of the privy council of England*, new ser., 46 vols. (1890–1964)

APS — *The acts of the parliaments of Scotland*, 12 vols. in 13 (1814–75)

Arber, *Regs. Stationers* — F. Arber, ed., *A transcript of the registers of the Company of Stationers of London, 1554–1640 AD*, 5 vols. (1875–94)

ArchR — *Architectural Review*

ASC — D. Whitelock, D. C. Douglas, and S. I. Tucker, ed. and trans., *The Anglo-Saxon Chronicle: a revised translation* (1961)

AS chart. — P. H. Sawyer, *Anglo-Saxon charters: an annotated list and bibliography*, Royal Historical Society Guides and Handbooks (1968)

AusDB — D. Pike and others, eds., *Australian dictionary of biography*, 16 vols. (1966–2002)

Baker, *Serjeants* — J. H. Baker, *The order of serjeants at law*, SeldS, suppl. ser., 5 (1984)

Bale, *Cat.* — J. Bale, *Scriptorum illustrium Maioris Brytannie, quam nunc Angliam et Scotiam vocant: catalogus*, 2 vols. in 1 (Basel, 1557–9); facs. edn (1971)

Bale, *Index* — J. Bale, *Index Britanniae scriptorum*, ed. R. L. Poole and M. Bateson (1902); facs. edn (1990)

BBCS — *Bulletin of the Board of Celtic Studies*

BDMBR — J. O. Baylen and N. J. Gossman, eds., *Biographical dictionary of modern British radicals*, 3 vols. in 4 (1979–88)

Bede, *Hist. eccl.* — *Bede's Ecclesiastical history of the English people*, ed. and trans. B. Colgrave and R. A. B. Mynors, OMT (1969); repr. (1991)

Bénézit, *Dict.* — E. Bénézit, *Dictionnaire critique et documentaire des peintres, sculpteurs, dessinateurs et graveurs*, 3 vols. (Paris, 1911–23); new edn, 8 vols. (1948–66), repr. (1966); 3rd edn, rev. and enl., 10 vols. (1976); 4th edn, 14 vols. (1999)

BIHR — *Bulletin of the Institute of Historical Research*

Birch, *Seals* — W. de Birch, *Catalogue of seals in the department of manuscripts in the British Museum*, 6 vols. (1887–1900)

Bishop Burnet's History — *Bishop Burnet's History of his own time*, ed. M. J. Routh, 2nd edn, 6 vols. (1833)

Blackwood — *Blackwood's [Edinburgh] Magazine*, 328 vols. (1817–1980)

Blain, Clements & Grundy, *Feminist comp.* — V. Blain, P. Clements, and I. Grundy, eds., *The feminist companion to literature in English* (1990)

BL cat. — *The British Library general catalogue of printed books* [in 360 vols. with suppls., also CD-ROM and online]

BMJ — *British Medical Journal*

Boase & Courtney, *Bibl. Corn.* — G. C. Boase and W. P. Courtney, *Bibliotheca Cornubiensis: a catalogue of the writings … of Cornishmen*, 3 vols. (1874–82)

Boase, *Mod. Eng. biog.* — F. Boase, *Modern English biography: containing many thousand concise memoirs of persons who have died since the year 1850*, 6 vols. (privately printed, Truro, 1892–1921); repr. (1965)

Boswell, *Life* — *Boswell's Life of Johnson: together with Journal of a tour to the Hebrides and Johnson's Diary of a journey into north Wales*, ed. G. B. Hill, enl. edn, rev. L. F. Powell, 6 vols. (1934–50); 2nd edn (1964); repr. (1971)

Brown & Stratton, *Brit. mus.* — J. D. Brown and S. S. Stratton, *British musical biography* (1897)

Bryan, *Painters* — M. Bryan, *A biographical and critical dictionary of painters and engravers*, 2 vols. (1816); new edn, ed. G. Stanley (1849); new edn, ed. R. E. Graves and W. Armstrong, 2 vols. (1886–9); [4th edn], ed. G. C. Williamson, 5 vols. (1903–5) [various reprs.]

Burke, *Gen. GB* — J. Burke, *A genealogical and heraldic history of the commoners of Great Britain and Ireland*, 4 vols. (1833–8); new edn as *A genealogical and heraldic dictionary of the landed gentry of Great Britain and Ireland*, 3 vols. [1843–9] [many later edns]

Burke, *Gen. Ire.* — J. B. Burke, *A genealogical and heraldic history of the landed gentry of Ireland* (1899); 2nd edn (1904); 3rd edn (1912); 4th edn (1958); 5th edn as *Burke's Irish family records* (1976)

Burke, *Peerage* — J. Burke, *A general [later edns A genealogical] and heraldic dictionary of the peerage and baronetage of the United Kingdom [later edns the British empire]* (1829–)

Burney, *Hist. mus.* — C. Burney, *A general history of music, from the earliest ages to the present period*, 4 vols. (1776–89)

Burtchaell & Sadleir, *Alum. Dubl.* — G. D. Burtchaell and T. U. Sadleir, *Alumni Dublinenses: a register of the students, graduates, and provosts of Trinity College* (1924); [2nd edn], with suppl., in 2 pts (1935)

Calamy rev. — A. G. Matthews, *Calamy revised* (1934); repr. (1988)

CCI — *Calendar of confirmations and inventories granted and given up in the several commissariots of Scotland* (1876–)

CCIR — *Calendar of the close rolls preserved in the Public Record Office*, 47 vols. (1892–1963)

CDS — J. Bain, ed., *Calendar of documents relating to Scotland*, 4 vols., PRO (1881–8); suppl. vol. 5, ed. G. G. Simpson and J. D. Galbraith [1986]

CEPR letters — W. H. Bliss, C. Johnson, and J. Twemlow, eds., *Calendar of entries in the papal registers relating to Great Britain and Ireland: papal letters* (1893–)

CGPLA — *Calendars of the grants of probate and letters of administration* [in 4 ser.: *England & Wales, Northern Ireland, Ireland,* and *Éire*]

Chambers, *Scots.* — R. Chambers, ed., *A biographical dictionary of eminent Scotsmen*, 4 vols. (1832–5)

Chancery records — chancery records pubd by the PRO

Chancery records (RC) — chancery records pubd by the Record Commissions

CIPM	*Calendar of inquisitions post mortem*, [20 vols.], PRO (1904–); also *Henry VII*, 3 vols. (1898–1955)		DWB	J. E. Lloyd and others, eds., *Dictionary of Welsh biography down to 1940* (1959) [Eng. trans. of *Y bywgraffiadur Cymreig hyd 1940*, 2nd edn (1954)]

Clarendon, *Hist. rebellion* — E. Hyde, earl of Clarendon, *The history of the rebellion and civil wars in England*, 6 vols. (1888); repr. (1958) and (1992)

Cobbett, *Parl. hist.* — W. Cobbett and J. Wright, eds., *Cobbett's Parliamentary history of England*, 36 vols. (1806–1820)

Colvin, *Archs.* — H. Colvin, *A biographical dictionary of British architects, 1600–1840*, 3rd edn (1995)

Cooper, *Ath. Cantab.* — C. H. Cooper and T. Cooper, *Athenae Cantabrigienses*, 3 vols. (1858–1913); repr. (1967)

CPR — *Calendar of the patent rolls preserved in the Public Record Office* (1891–)

Crockford — *Crockford's Clerical Directory*

CS — Camden Society

CSP — *Calendar of state papers* [in 11 ser.: *domestic, Scotland, Scottish series, Ireland, colonial, Commonwealth, foreign, Spain* [at Simancas], *Rome, Milan,* and *Venice*]

CYS — Canterbury and York Society

DAB — *Dictionary of American biography*, 21 vols. (1928–36), repr. in 11 vols. (1964); 10 suppls. (1944–96)

DBB — D. J. Jeremy, ed., *Dictionary of business biography*, 5 vols. (1984–6)

DCB — G. W. Brown and others, *Dictionary of Canadian biography*, [14 vols.] (1966–)

Debrett's Peerage — *Debrett's Peerage* (1803–) [sometimes *Debrett's Illustrated peerage*]

Desmond, *Botanists* — R. Desmond, *Dictionary of British and Irish botanists and horticulturists* (1977); rev. edn (1994)

Dir. Brit. archs. — A. Felstead, J. Franklin, and L. Pinfield, eds., *Directory of British architects, 1834–1900* (1993); 2nd edn, ed. A. Brodie and others, 2 vols. (2001)

DLB — J. M. Bellamy and J. Saville, eds., *Dictionary of labour biography*, [10 vols.] (1972–)

DLitB — Dictionary of Literary Biography

DNB — *Dictionary of national biography*, 63 vols. (1885–1900), suppl., 3 vols. (1901); repr. in 22 vols. (1908–9); 10 further suppls. (1912–96); *Missing persons* (1993)

DNZB — W. H. Oliver and C. Orange, eds., *The dictionary of New Zealand biography*, 5 vols. (1990–2000)

DSAB — W. J. de Kock and others, eds., *Dictionary of South African biography*, 5 vols. (1968–87)

DSB — C. C. Gillispie and F. L. Holmes, eds., *Dictionary of scientific biography*, 16 vols. (1970–80); repr. in 8 vols. (1981); 2 vol. suppl. (1990)

DSBB — A. Slaven and S. Checkland, eds., *Dictionary of Scottish business biography, 1860–1960*, 2 vols. (1986–90)

DSCHT — N. M. de S. Cameron and others, eds., *Dictionary of Scottish church history and theology* (1993)

Dugdale, *Monasticon* — W. Dugdale, *Monasticon Anglicanum*, 3 vols. (1655–72); 2nd edn, 3 vols. (1661–82); new edn, ed. J. Caley, J. Ellis, and B. Bandinel, 6 vols. in 8 pts (1817–30); repr. (1846) and (1970)

EdinR — *Edinburgh Review, or, Critical Journal*

EETS — Early English Text Society

Emden, *Cam.* — A. B. Emden, *A biographical register of the University of Cambridge to 1500* (1963)

Emden, *Oxf.* — A. B. Emden, *A biographical register of the University of Oxford to AD 1500*, 3 vols. (1957–9); also *A biographical register of the University of Oxford, AD 1501 to 1540* (1974)

EngHR — *English Historical Review*

Engraved Brit. ports. — F. M. O'Donoghue and H. M. Hake, *Catalogue of engraved British portraits preserved in the department of prints and drawings in the British Museum*, 6 vols. (1908–25)

ER — The English Reports, 178 vols. (1900–32)

ESTC — *English short title catalogue, 1475–1800* [CD-ROM and online]

Evelyn, *Diary* — *The diary of John Evelyn*, ed. E. S. De Beer, 6 vols. (1955); repr. (2000)

Farington, *Diary* — *The diary of Joseph Farington*, ed. K. Garlick and others, 17 vols. (1978–98)

Fasti Angl. (Hardy) — J. Le Neve, *Fasti ecclesiae Anglicanae*, ed. T. D. Hardy, 3 vols. (1854)

Fasti Angl., 1066–1300 — [J. Le Neve], *Fasti ecclesiae Anglicanae, 1066–1300*, ed. D. E. Greenway and J. S. Barrow, [8 vols.] (1968–)

Fasti Angl., 1300–1541 — [J. Le Neve], *Fasti ecclesiae Anglicanae, 1300–1541*, 12 vols. (1962–7)

Fasti Angl., 1541–1857 — [J. Le Neve], *Fasti ecclesiae Anglicanae, 1541–1857*, ed. J. M. Horn, D. M. Smith, and D. S. Bailey, [9 vols.] (1969–)

Fasti Scot. — H. Scott, *Fasti ecclesiae Scoticanae*, 3 vols. in 6 (1871); new edn, [11 vols.] (1915–)

FO List — *Foreign Office List*

Fortescue, *Brit. army* — J. W. Fortescue, *A history of the British army*, 13 vols. (1899–1930)

Foss, *Judges* — E. Foss, *The judges of England*, 9 vols. (1848–64); repr. (1966)

Foster, *Alum. Oxon.* — J. Foster, ed., *Alumni Oxonienses: the members of the University of Oxford, 1715–1886*, 4 vols. (1887–8); later edn (1891); also *Alumni Oxonienses … 1500–1714*, 4 vols. (1891–2); 8 vol. repr. (1968) and (2000)

Fuller, *Worthies* — T. Fuller, *The history of the worthies of England*, 4 pts (1662); new edn, 2 vols., ed. J. Nichols (1811); new edn, 3 vols., ed. P. A. Nuttall (1840); repr. (1965)

GEC, *Baronetage* — G. E. Cokayne, *Complete baronetage*, 6 vols. (1900–09); repr. (1983) [microprint]

GEC, *Peerage* — G. E. C. [G. E. Cokayne], *The complete peerage of England, Scotland, Ireland, Great Britain, and the United Kingdom*, 8 vols. (1887–98); new edn, ed. V. Gibbs and others, 14 vols. in 15 (1910–98); microprint repr. (1982) and (1987)

Genest, *Eng. stage* — J. Genest, *Some account of the English stage from the Restoration in 1660 to 1830*, 10 vols. (1832); repr. [New York, 1965]

Gillow, *Lit. biog. hist.* — J. Gillow, *A literary and biographical history or bibliographical dictionary of the English Catholics, from the breach with Rome, in 1534, to the present time*, 5 vols. [1885–1902]; repr. (1961); repr. with preface by C. Gillow (1999)

Gir. Camb. opera — *Giraldi Cambrensis opera*, ed. J. S. Brewer, J. F. Dimock, and G. F. Warner, 8 vols., Rolls Series, 21 (1861–91)

GJ — *Geographical Journal*

Gladstone, *Diaries* — *The Gladstone diaries: with cabinet minutes and prime-ministerial correspondence*, ed. M. R. D. Foot and H. C. G. Matthew, 14 vols. (1968–94)

GM — *Gentleman's Magazine*

Graves, *Artists* — A. Graves, ed., *A dictionary of artists who have exhibited works in the principal London exhibitions of oil paintings from 1760 to 1880* (1884); new edn (1895); 3rd edn (1901); facs. edn (1969); repr. [1970], (1973), and (1984)

Graves, *Brit. Inst.* — A. Graves, *The British Institution, 1806–1867: a complete dictionary of contributors and their work from the foundation of the institution* (1875); facs. edn (1908); repr. (1969)

Graves, *RA exhibitors* — A. Graves, *The Royal Academy of Arts: a complete dictionary of contributors and their work from its foundation in 1769 to 1904*, 8 vols. (1905–6); repr. in 4 vols. (1970) and (1972)

Graves, *Soc. Artists* — A. Graves, *The Society of Artists of Great Britain, 1760–1791, the Free Society of Artists, 1761–1783: a complete dictionary* (1907); facs. edn (1969)

Greaves & Zaller, *BDBR* — R. L. Greaves and R. Zaller, eds., *Biographical dictionary of British radicals in the seventeenth century*, 3 vols. (1982–4)

Grove, *Dict. mus.* — G. Grove, ed., *A dictionary of music and musicians*, 5 vols. (1878–90); 2nd edn, ed. J. A. Fuller Maitland (1904–10); 3rd edn, ed. H. C. Colles (1927); 4th edn with suppl. (1940); 5th edn, ed. E. Blom, 9 vols. (1954); suppl. (1961) [see also *New Grove*]

Hall, *Dramatic ports.* — L. A. Hall, *Catalogue of dramatic portraits in the theatre collection of the Harvard College library*, 4 vols. (1930–34)

Hansard — *Hansard's parliamentary debates*, ser. 1–5 (1803–)

Highfill, Burnim & Langhans, *BDA* — P. H. Highfill, K. A. Burnim, and E. A. Langhans, *A biographical dictionary of actors, actresses, musicians, dancers, managers, and other stage personnel in London, 1660–1800*, 16 vols. (1973–93)

Hist. U. Oxf. — T. H. Aston, ed., *The history of the University of Oxford*, 8 vols. (1984–2000) [1: *The early Oxford schools*, ed. J. I. Catto (1984); 2: *Late medieval Oxford*, ed. J. I. Catto and R. Evans (1992); 3: *The collegiate university*, ed. J. McConica (1986); 4: *Seventeenth-century Oxford*, ed. N. Tyacke (1997); 5: *The eighteenth century*, ed. L. S. Sutherland and L. G. Mitchell (1986); 6–7: *Nineteenth-century Oxford*, ed. M. G. Brock and M. C. Curthoys (1997–2000); 8: *The twentieth century*, ed. B. Harrison (2000)]

HJ — *Historical Journal*

HMC — Historical Manuscripts Commission

Holdsworth, *Eng. law* — W. S. Holdsworth, *A history of English law*, ed. A. L. Goodhart and H. L. Hanbury, 17 vols. (1903–72)

HoP, Commons — *The history of parliament: the House of Commons* [1386–1421, ed. J. S. Roskell, L. Clark, and C. Rawcliffe, 4 vols. (1992); 1509–1558, ed. S. T. Bindoff, 3 vols. (1982); 1558–1603, ed. P. W. Hasler, 3 vols. (1981); 1660–1690, ed. B. D. Henning, 3 vols. (1983); 1690–1715, ed. D. W. Hayton, E. Cruickshanks, and S. Handley, 5 vols. (2002); 1715–1754, ed. R. Sedgwick, 2 vols. (1970); 1754–1790, ed. L. Namier and J. Brooke, 3 vols. (1964), repr. (1985); 1790–1820, ed. R. G. Thorne, 5 vols. (1986); in draft (used with permission): 1422–1504, 1604–1629, 1640–1660, and 1820–1832]

IGI — *International Genealogical Index*, Church of Jesus Christ of the Latterday Saints

ILN — *Illustrated London News*

IMC — Irish Manuscripts Commission

Irving, *Scots.* — J. Irving, ed., *The book of Scotsmen eminent for achievements in arms and arts, church and state, law, legislation and literature, commerce, science, travel and philanthropy* (1881)

JCS — *Journal of the Chemical Society*

JHC — *Journals of the House of Commons*

JHL — *Journals of the House of Lords*

John of Worcester, *Chron.* — *The chronicle of John of Worcester*, ed. R. R. Darlington and P. McGurk, trans. J. Bray and P. McGurk, 3 vols., OMT (1995–) [vol. 1 forthcoming]

Keeler, *Long Parliament* — M. F. Keeler, *The Long Parliament, 1640–1641: a biographical study of its members* (1954)

Kelly, *Handbk* — *The upper ten thousand: an alphabetical list of all members of noble families*, 3 vols. (1875–7); continued as *Kelly's handbook of the upper ten thousand for 1878* [1879], 2 vols. (1878–9); continued as *Kelly's handbook to the titled, landed and official classes*, 94 vols. (1880–1973)

LondG — *London Gazette*

LP Henry VIII — J. S. Brewer, J. Gairdner, and R. H. Brodie, eds., *Letters and papers, foreign and domestic, of the reign of Henry VIII*, 23 vols. in 38 (1862–1932); repr. (1965)

Mallalieu, *Watercolour artists* — H. L. Mallalieu, *The dictionary of British watercolour artists up to 1820*, 3 vols. (1976–90); vol. 1, 2nd edn (1986)

Memoirs FRS — *Biographical Memoirs of Fellows of the Royal Society*

MGH — Monumenta Germaniae Historica

MT — *Musical Times*

Munk, *Roll* — W. Munk, *The roll of the Royal College of Physicians of London*, 2 vols. (1861); 2nd edn, 3 vols. (1878)

N&Q — *Notes and Queries*

New Grove — S. Sadie, ed., *The new Grove dictionary of music and musicians*, 20 vols. (1980); 2nd edn, 29 vols. (2001) [also online edn; see also Grove, *Dict. mus.*]

Nichols, *Illustrations* — J. Nichols and J. B. Nichols, *Illustrations of the literary history of the eighteenth century*, 8 vols. (1817–58)

Nichols, *Lit. anecdotes* — J. Nichols, *Literary anecdotes of the eighteenth century*, 9 vols. (1812–16); facs. edn (1966)

Obits. FRS — *Obituary Notices of Fellows of the Royal Society*

O'Byrne, *Naval biog. dict.* — W. R. O'Byrne, *A naval biographical dictionary* (1849); repr. (1990); [2nd edn], 2 vols. (1861)

OHS — Oxford Historical Society

Old Westminsters — *The record of Old Westminsters*, 1–2, ed. G. F. R. Barker and A. H. Stenning (1928); suppl. 1, ed. J. B. Whitmore and G. R. Y. Radcliffe [1938]; 3, ed. J. B. Whitmore, G. R. Y. Radcliffe, and D. C. Simpson (1963); suppl. 2, ed. F. E. Pagan (1978); 4, ed. F. E. Pagan and H. E. Pagan (1992)

OMT — Oxford Medieval Texts

Ordericus Vitalis, *Eccl. hist.* — *The ecclesiastical history of Orderic Vitalis*, ed. and trans. M. Chibnall, 6 vols., OMT (1969–80); repr. (1990)

Paris, *Chron.* — *Matthaei Parisiensis, monachi sancti Albani, chronica majora*, ed. H. R. Luard, Rolls Series, 7 vols. (1872–83)

Parl. papers — *Parliamentary papers* (1801–)

PBA — *Proceedings of the British Academy*

Pepys, *Diary*	*The diary of Samuel Pepys*, ed. R. Latham and W. Matthews, 11 vols. (1970–83); repr. (1995) and (2000)
Pevsner	N. Pevsner and others, Buildings of England series
PICE	*Proceedings of the Institution of Civil Engineers*
Pipe rolls	*The great roll of the pipe for . . .*, PRSoc. (1884–)
PRO	Public Record Office
PRS	*Proceedings of the Royal Society of London*
PRSoc.	Pipe Roll Society
PTRS	*Philosophical Transactions of the Royal Society*
QR	*Quarterly Review*
RC	Record Commissions
Redgrave, *Artists*	S. Redgrave, *A dictionary of artists of the English school* (1874); rev. edn (1878); repr. (1970)
Reg. Oxf.	C. W. Boase and A. Clark, eds., *Register of the University of Oxford*, 5 vols., OHS, 1, 10–12, 14 (1885–9)
Reg. PCS	J. H. Burton and others, eds., *The register of the privy council of Scotland*, 1st ser., 14 vols. (1877–98); 2nd ser., 8 vols. (1899–1908); 3rd ser., [16 vols.] (1908–70)
Reg. RAN	H. W. C. Davis and others, eds., *Regesta regum Anglo-Normannorum, 1066–1154*, 4 vols. (1913–69)
RIBA Journal	*Journal of the Royal Institute of British Architects* [later *RIBA Journal*]
RotP	J. Strachey, ed., *Rotuli parliamentorum ut et petitiones, et placita in parliamento*, 6 vols. (1767–77)
RotS	D. Macpherson, J. Caley, and W. Illingworth, eds., *Rotuli Scotiae in Turri Londinensi et in domo capitulari Westmonasteriensi asservati*, 2 vols., RC, 14 (1814–19)
RS	Record(s) Society
Rymer, *Foedera*	T. Rymer and R. Sanderson, eds., *Foedera, conventiones, literae et cuiuscunque generis acta publica inter reges Angliae et alios quosvis imperatores, reges, pontifices, principes, vel communitates*, 20 vols. (1704–35); 2nd edn, 20 vols. (1726–35); 3rd edn, 10 vols. (1739–45); facs. edn (1967); new edn, ed. A. Clarke, J. Caley, and F. Holbrooke, 4 vols., RC, 50 (1816–30)
Sainty, *Judges*	J. Sainty, ed., *The judges of England, 1272–1990*, SeldS, suppl. ser., 10 (1993)
Sainty, *King's counsel*	J. Sainty, ed., *A list of English law officers and king's counsel*, SeldS, suppl. ser., 7 (1987)
SCH	Studies in Church History
Scots peerage	J. B. Paul, ed. *The Scots peerage, founded on Wood's edition of Sir Robert Douglas's Peerage of Scotland, containing an historical and genealogical account of the nobility of that kingdom*, 9 vols. (1904–14)
SeldS	Selden Society
SHR	*Scottish Historical Review*
State trials	T. B. Howell and T. J. Howell, eds., *Cobbett's Complete collection of state trials*, 34 vols. (1809–28)
STC, 1475–1640	A. W. Pollard, G. R. Redgrave, and others, eds., *A short-title catalogue of . . . English books . . . 1475–1640* (1926); 2nd edn, ed. W. A. Jackson, F. S. Ferguson, and K. F. Pantzer, 3 vols. (1976–91) [see also Wing, *STC*]
STS	Scottish Text Society
SurtS	Surtees Society
Symeon of Durham, *Opera*	*Symeonis monachi opera omnia*, ed. T. Arnold, 2 vols., Rolls Series, 75 (1882–5); repr. (1965)
Tanner, *Bibl. Brit.-Hib.*	T. Tanner, *Bibliotheca Britannico-Hibernica*, ed. D. Wilkins (1748); repr. (1963)
Thieme & Becker, *Allgemeines Lexikon*	U. Thieme, F. Becker, and H. Vollmer, eds., *Allgemeines Lexikon der bildenden Künstler von der Antike bis zur Gegenwart*, 37 vols. (Leipzig, 1907–50); repr. (1961–5), (1983), and (1992)
Thurloe, *State papers*	*A collection of the state papers of John Thurloe*, ed. T. Birch, 7 vols. (1742)
TLS	*Times Literary Supplement*
Tout, *Admin. hist.*	T. F. Tout, *Chapters in the administrative history of mediaeval England: the wardrobe, the chamber, and the small seals*, 6 vols. (1920–33); repr. (1967)
TRHS	*Transactions of the Royal Historical Society*
VCH	H. A. Doubleday and others, eds., *The Victoria history of the counties of England*, [88 vols.] (1900–)
Venn, *Alum. Cant.*	J. Venn and J. A. Venn, *Alumni Cantabrigienses: a biographical list of all known students, graduates, and holders of office at the University of Cambridge, from the earliest times to 1900*, 10 vols. (1922–54); repr. in 2 vols. (1974–8)
Vertue, *Note books*	[G. Vertue], *Note books*, ed. K. Esdaile, earl of Ilchester, and H. M. Hake, 6 vols., Walpole Society, 18, 20, 22, 24, 26, 30 (1930–55)
VF	*Vanity Fair*
Walford, *County families*	E. Walford, *The county families of the United Kingdom, or, Royal manual of the titled and untitled aristocracy of Great Britain and Ireland* (1860)
Walker rev.	A. G. Matthews, *Walker revised: being a revision of John Walker's Sufferings of the clergy during the grand rebellion, 1642–60* (1948); repr. (1988)
Walpole, *Corr.*	*The Yale edition of Horace Walpole's correspondence*, ed. W. S. Lewis, 48 vols. (1937–83)
Ward, *Men of the reign*	T. H. Ward, ed., *Men of the reign: a biographical dictionary of eminent persons of British and colonial birth who have died during the reign of Queen Victoria* (1885); repr. (Graz, 1968)
Waterhouse, *18c painters*	E. Waterhouse, *The dictionary of 18th century painters in oils and crayons* (1981); repr. as *British 18th century painters in oils and crayons* (1991), vol. 2 of *Dictionary of British art*
Watt, *Bibl. Brit.*	R. Watt, *Bibliotheca Britannica, or, A general index to British and foreign literature*, 4 vols. (1824) [many reprs.]
Wellesley index	W. E. Houghton, ed., *The Wellesley index to Victorian periodicals, 1824–1900*, 5 vols. (1966–89); new edn (1999) [CD-ROM]
Wing, *STC*	D. Wing, ed., *Short-title catalogue of . . . English books . . . 1641–1700*, 3 vols. (1945–51); 2nd edn (1972–88); rev. and enl. edn, ed. J. J. Morrison, C. W. Nelson, and M. Seccombe, 4 vols. (1994–8) [see also *STC, 1475–1640*]
Wisden	*John Wisden's Cricketer's Almanack*
Wood, *Ath. Oxon.*	A. Wood, *Athenae Oxonienses . . . to which are added the Fasti*, 2 vols. (1691–2); 2nd edn (1721); new edn, 4 vols., ed. P. Bliss (1813–20); repr. (1967) and (1969)
Wood, *Vic. painters*	C. Wood, *Dictionary of Victorian painters* (1971); 2nd edn (1978); 3rd edn as *Victorian painters*, 2 vols. (1995), vol. 4 of *Dictionary of British art*
WW	*Who's who* (1849–)
WWBMP	M. Stenton and S. Lees, eds., *Who's who of British members of parliament*, 4 vols. (1976–81)
WWW	*Who was who* (1929–)

Daly, Denis (1747–1791), politician, was born on 24 January 1747, the eldest son of James Daly (c.1710–1769), landowner and politician, of Carrownakelly and Dunsandle, co. Galway, Ireland, and his second wife, Catherine Gore (b. 1723), of Manor Gore, co. Donegal, whose father, Sir Ralph *Gore, fourth baronet (d. 1733), was one of the dominant politicians of his generation. The son of a convert to the Church of Ireland who laid the foundations of the strong Daly political interest in co. Galway, Daly was elected while still a minor to represent the county borough constituency of the town of Galway in 1767, following which he abandoned his studies at Christ Church, Oxford, where he had matriculated in 1764, to take command of the Daly interest in co. Galway. He proved a formidable political operator and, in 1768, masterminded an alliance of convert and liberal protestant interests to ensure his return to represent the county in the first general election held in accordance with the terms of the Octennial Act. His father secured one of the two seats for the county of the town in the same election, and the Dalys emphasized the strength of their position on Galway corporation following his death by securing the return of Denis's brother Anthony in the resultant by-election in 1771. Resentment at the influence wielded by the nonresident Dalys prompted a campaign headed by Patrick Blake of Drum to regain control of the corporation for resident interests. This was pursued with such intensity during the early 1770s that when the Irish privy council accepted the nomination of Denis Daly as mayor in controversial circumstances in 1772 Blake established a rival corporation. He also inaugurated a legal action that he pursued to the English court of king's bench, and even sought in 1775 to settle the dispute in time-honoured fashion by challenging Daly to a duel. Daly fared best in the ensuing encounter. More important, he secured the return in the 1776 general election poll of family members for both seats in the constituency, and he reinforced his ascendancy in the following year when he inaugurated an unbroken succession of Daly mayors extending over thirty-nine years.

The strength of character Daly demonstrated in Galway was also manifest at national level. Possessed, in the estimation of one contemporary, of a 'rare combination of … genius and industry, of eloquence and sagacity' (Falkland, *Principal Characters*, 2–3), he was one of the most eminent independent country gentlemen in the House of Commons. His convictions drew him towards the patriot interest. He participated in the convivial patriot club known as the Society of Granby Row, and joined with Sir William Mayne, George Ogle, and others in challenging the administration in the House of Commons in October 1773, although his opposition to the proposed absentee tax in November indicates that he did not embrace the patriot line on all issues. In common with most patriots, he was disturbed by the outbreak of war in the American colonies, and he opposed the deployment of troops on the Irish army establishment to aid the war effort. His subsequent active opposition earned him a formidable reputation as a parliamentarian and his stature was enhanced

Denis Daly (1747–1791), by Sir Joshua Reynolds

further when he moved an address to the king calling for the relaxation of the embargo on Irish trade in August 1778. By now an intimate of Henry Grattan, he drafted the amendment to the address to the king approved by the Irish House of Commons in October 1779 urging the concession of 'free trade' to Ireland. However, unlike most of his patriot colleagues, he resisted the attempts that were made in 1780 to advance the cause of legislative independence. This was his right as an independent country gentleman, but Daly also had political motives. The cost of constructing new residences at Dunsandle and Dalystown in co. Galway, of sustaining the intellectual enthusiasms that led him to assemble an impressive private library, and the augmented household expenses resulting from his marriage on 5 July 1780 to Lady Henrietta Maxwell (1761–1852), the only daughter and heir of Robert Maxwell, earl of Farnham (d. 1779), and his first wife, Henrietta Stafford-Howard (d. 1761), rendered him amenable to government offers, and he accepted the position of muster-master-general, worth £1200 per annum, in 1781. As a result Daly was soon to be found defending rather than challenging the Irish administration.

An individual of lesser dignity and poorer judgement would have damaged their reputation in the process, but Daly was enabled to escape relatively unscathed by carefully choosing the issues upon which he spoke and by not allowing himself to be pigeon-holed as a voice for hire. Thus he warmly advocated the concession of 'every indulgence … to Roman Catholics' (*The Parliamentary Register*, 1.265) in February 1782; he refrained from commenting on the subject of legislative independence in the spring and summer of the same year but was prominent in advocating that Henry Grattan should be rewarded for his role in bringing it about; and in June he opposed Henry Flood's attempt to compel the British government to renounce its claim to legislate for Ireland on the grounds that it would generate 'perpetual dissension' (ibid., 1.416). Daly's stand on these and other issues in the early 1780s indicated that there were limits to the political reforms he deemed appropriate. This limit was delineated more starkly in 1783–4, when he strongly opposed every suggestion that the Irish representative system should be reformed to allow for the greater representation of the country's middle classes, and in 1785, when he opposed William Pitt's plan for a commercial union on the grounds that it amounted to 'a palpable encroachment on the independence of our legislature' (NL Ire., Bolton MS 16351, fol. 35). Despite this, Daly remained on 'cordial' if 'reserved' terms with the Irish administration until ill health in the late 1780s obliged him to forsake politics. His death in Dunsandle on 10 October 1791 deprived the House of Commons of one of its 'brightest ornaments' (Falkland, *Parliamentary Representation*, 37), though the eldest son of his family of eight children, James, later Baron Dunsandle, ensured the family remained a force in Galway politics well into the nineteenth century. His widow survived him for many years and died at Bromley, co. Wicklow, on 6 March 1852; their younger son, Robert *Daly (1783–1872), became bishop of Cashel in 1843.   JAMES KELLY

Sources J. Kelly, 'The politics of protestant ascendancy: county Galway, 1650–1832', *Galway history and society: interdisciplinary essays on the history of an Irish county*, ed. G. Moran and R. Gillespie (1996), 229–70 · case of the corporation of Galway, Nov 1774, PRO NIre., Shannon MSS, D 2707/A2/2/15 · UCG, Galway corporation MSS, book K · Falkland [J. R. Scott], *A review of the principal characters of the Irish House of Commons* (1789) · M. J. Blake, 'Families of Daly of Galway with tabular pedigrees', *Journal of the Galway Archaeological and Historical Society*, 13 (1924–5) · Burke, *Gen. Ire.* (1976) · Falkland [J. R. Scott], *Parliamentary representation: being a political review of all the kingdom of Ireland* (1790) · J. Porter, P. Byrne, and W. Porter, eds., *The parliamentary register, or, History of the proceedings and debates of the House of Commons of Ireland, 1781–1797*, 17 vols. (1784–1801) · J. Kelly, *Prelude to Union: Anglo-Irish politics in the 1780s* (1992) · J. Kelly, *That damn'd thing called honour: duelling in Ireland, 1570–1860* (1995) · A. P. W. Malcomson, *John Foster: the politics of the Anglo-Irish ascendancy* (1978) · J. Kelly, *Henry Flood: patriots and politics in eighteenth-century Ireland* (1998) · *A catalogue of the library of … Denis Daly* (1792) [sale catalogue, J. Vallance, Dublin, 1 May 1792] · *DNB* · E. Lodge, *Peerage, baronetage, knightage and companionage of the British empire*, 81st edn, 3 vols. (1912) · Foster, *Alum. Oxon.* · NL Ire., Bolton MS 16351

Archives Representative Church Body Library, Dublin, MSS | NL Ire., Bolton MSS

Likenesses H. D. Hamilton, pastel drawing on paper, NG Ire. · J. Reynolds, portrait; Christies, 9 April 1954, lot 94 [*see illus.*] · F. Wheatley, group portrait, oils (*The Irish House of Commons, 1780*), Lotherton Hall, Leeds · oils (after J. Reynolds), NG Ire.

Daly, Sir Dominick (1798–1868), civil servant and colonial administrator, was born on 11 August 1798, at Ardfry, co. Galway, Ireland, the third son of Dominick Daly of Benmore, co. Galway, and his wife, Joanna Harriet, widow of Richard Burke of Glinsk, and daughter of Joseph Blake of

Ardfry. He was educated at St Mary's College, Oscott, near Birmingham. In 1823, thanks to family influence, he went to Lower Canada as private secretary to the lieutenant-governor Sir Francis Burton. On leave in England on 20 May 1826, he married Caroline Maria (d. 1872), third daughter of Colonel Ralph Gore of Barrowmount, co. Kilkenny, and on his return to Canada the following year, he was appointed provincial secretary. While conservative and thoroughly loyal, he sympathized with the French Canadians, who appreciated his integrity and cordiality, and in 1838 on the strong recommendation of Governor Sir John Colborne, Lord Durham kept him on as secretary.

Upon the union of the Canadas in 1840, Daly became the provincial secretary for Lower Canada (earning himself the nickname the 'perpetual secretary'), with a seat in the council. In 1843, as a non-party official, he supported Governor Sir Charles Metcalfe in his opposition to party patronage and full responsible government; as a result he remained in Metcalfe's emergency council, being appointed provincial secretary for the United Canadas on 1 January 1844. He resigned in 1848, with the return of responsible government. Governor Lord Elgin promised that he would be provided for after his resignation, but the secretary of state, Lord Grey, was unco-operative, and not until September 1851 was Daly appointed lieutenant-governor of Tobago, and 8 May 1854 of Prince Edward Island. Here, as in Canada and later in South Australia, he showed both firmness and sagacity, and, helped by a lack of political passion, he served with distinction if not brilliance. In July 1856 he was knighted. He retired in 1859 but in 1861 was gazetted governor of South Australia, assuming office in March the next year.

The Colonial Office very properly instructed Daly to try and have repealed the Court of Appeals Act of 1861, which had destroyed the separation of the judicial and executive powers in South Australia by establishing the executive council as a court of appeal from the supreme court. This act followed the supreme court's declaring invalid certain acts passed by the local parliament. Daly ignored this instruction, like Sir Charles Darling in Victoria, preferring repeated reproofs from London to opposing local sentiment. Reversing his attitude in Canada, he now firmly supported his local ministers and agreed to take proceedings to dismiss the pedantic Justice Boothby who persisted in ignoring the Imperial Colonial Laws Validity Act of 1865, passed to settle the original dispute. Boothby was amoved in July 1867, before the Colonial Office had considered the matter, and both he and Daly died before it did so. During the last year or two of his life Daly's health began to fail, and he died towards the close of the customary term of office, at Government House, Adelaide, on 19 February 1868, survived by his widow, three sons (one of whom was later lieutenant-governor of Nova Scotia), and two daughters.

When Daly had arrived in South Australia, his past training in administration had enabled him to correct a number of irregularities in government departments. This, and his attitude in the Boothby affair, as well as his accessibility and genial Irish manner, make him a popular governor and did much to dispel anti-Catholic prejudice in the colony.   A. G. L. SHAW

Sources *DCB*, vol. 9 · *AusDB* · *South Australian Register* (20 Feb 1868) · J. Holland Rose and others, eds., *The growth of the new empire, 1783–1870* (1940), vol. 2 of *The Cambridge history of the British empire* (1929–59) · J. Holland Rose and others, eds., *Canada and Newfoundland* (1930), vol. 6 of *The Cambridge history of the British empire* (1929–59) · P. A. Howell, 'Constitutional and political development, 1857–1890', *The Flinders history of South Australia*, ed. D. Jaensch, 2: *Political history* (1986), 95–177 · D. B. Swinfen, *Imperial control of colonial legislation, 1813–1865* (1970) · J. W. Kaye, *Life and correspondence of Charles Lord Metcalfe* (1858) · W. P. Morrell, *British colonial policy in the age of Peel and Russell* (1930) · Burke, *Peerage*
Archives PRO, CO 13/109–123 · State Library of South Australia, Adelaide, South Australian archives, CO 13/111–125 | U. Durham L., corresp. with third Earl Grey

Daly, Sir Henry Dermot (1821–1895), army officer in the East India Company, was born on 25 October 1821 at Carisbrooke, Isle of Wight, the younger son of Lieutenant-Colonel Francis Dermot Daly (d. July 1857), 4th light dragoons, of Daly's Grove, co. Galway, and his wife, Mary Ann McIntosh. He was commissioned ensign in the 1st Bombay European regiment on 1 September 1840, and became successively brevet colonel (19 July 1864), lieutenant-colonel (1 September 1866), major-general (4 January 1870), lieutenant-general (1 October 1877), and general (1 December 1888). He arrived at Bombay on 10 October 1840, and in 1841 was appointed adjutant of the detachment at Ahmednagar. He qualified as interpreter in Hindustani in 1841, in Marathi in 1842, and in Gujarati in 1843, when he was appointed acting adjutant of the provisional battalion at Gujarat. After two years' furlough to Europe he returned to Bombay on 10 May 1846, and on 22 August became adjutant of the 1st Bombay European regiment.

In the Second Anglo-Sikh War Daly took part in the operations at Multan, and in the attack of 27 December 1848 had a horse shot under him. He was mentioned in dispatches for conspicuous gallantry by Brigadier-General Stalker and Brigadier-General Dundas. He joined Lord Gough's army, was present at the battle of Gujrat on 21 February 1849, took part in the pursuit under Sir Walter Gilbert of the Sikh army, and was present at the capture of Attock and the occupation of Peshawar.

On 28 May 1849 Daly was appointed to command the 1st Punjab cavalry with directions to raise it in co-operation with Major George St Patrick Lawrence, the deputy commissioner of the district. Daly raised and trained a fine unit, and in February 1850 marched with it under Sir Charles Napier to punish the Afridis. He took part in the action of the Kohat Pass, and remained to occupy Kohat as an outpost. His regiment and his own services were praised by Napier. In October 1851 he served with the field force under Captain Coke from Kohat to Thal. On 10 May 1852 he joined the force under Brigadier-General Sir Colin Campbell at Abazai, and took part in the operations against the village of Noadand in the Utman Khel country, in the attack and destruction of Prangarh on 13 May, in the attack of the 18 May on the Swattis at Skakot in the Ranizai

valley, and subsequently in the affair at Erozshah, for which he was mentioned in dispatches.

Daly married in 1852 Susan Ely Ellen, daughter of Edward Kirkpatrick. After two years' furlough to Europe he returned to India, and was given the command first of the Oudh irregular force and later of the Queen's Own corps of guides: three cavalry troops and six rifle companies. On the outbreak of the Indian mutiny he was ordered to Delhi, and he marched the guides from Mardan in Yusufzai (580 miles) in twenty-two days, an unparalleled feat. Sir Henry Bernard, commanding at Delhi, observed in a general order that the arrival of the corps in perfect order and ready for immediate service after such a march reflected the highest credit on Daly. Daly was twice wounded at the siege of Delhi and had a horse shot under him. He commanded a regiment of Hodson's Horse at the final siege and capture of Lucknow in March 1858, and after Hodson's death (11 March 1858) commanded the brigade of three regiments of Hodson's Horse throughout Sir Hope Grant's campaign in Oudh in 1858–9, including the actions of Nawabganj and the passage of the Gumti and of the Gogra. He went home on furlough in May 1859, having been made CB the previous year.

On his return to India, Daly was appointed on 31 December 1861 to the command of the Central India horse and political assistant at Angur for western Malwa. On 27 October 1871 he was appointed agent to the governor-general for central India at Indore, and opium agent in Malwa. He was promoted KCB, military division, on 29 May 1875, and CIE on 1 January 1880. He retired from active service in 1882. In the same year, his first wife having died, he married Charlotte Claudine Georgina, daughter of James Coape and widow of Alexander C. Sterling Murray Dunlop. Daly was master of the Isle of Wight foxhounds from 1881 to 1889. He was made GCB on 25 May 1889. He died at his residence, Ryde House, Ryde, Isle of Wight, on 21 July 1895, his second wife surviving him.

R. H. VETCH, *rev.* JAMES LUNT

Sources G. J. Younghusband, *The story of the guides* (1908) · *The history of the guides, 1846–1922*, 1 (1938) · G. MacMunn, *The history of the guides, 1922–1947*, 2 (1950) · W. A. Watson, *King George's own central India horse* (1930) · C. E. Buckland, *Dictionary of Indian biography* (1906) · B. J. Cork, *Rider on a grey horse: a life of Hodson of Hodson's horse* (1958) · Fortescue, *Brit. army*, vols. 12–13 · *The Times* (23 July 1895) · J. W. Kaye, *A history of the Sepoy War in India, 1857–1858*, 9th edn, 3 vols. (1880) · G. B. Malleson, *History of the Indian mutiny, 1857–1858: commencing from the close of the second volume of Sir John Kaye's History of the Sepoy War*, 3 vols. (1878–80) · V. C. P. Hodson, *List of officers of the Bengal army, 1758–1834*, 4 vols. (1927–47) · C. Hibbert, *The great mutiny, India, 1857* (1978) · Boase, *Mod. Eng. biog.*
Likenesses J. Brown, stipple, 1887 (after photograph by Debenham), NPG; repro. in *Baily's Magazine* (1887)
Wealth at death £48,312 9s. 1d.: probate, 1 Nov 1895, *CGPLA Eng. & Wales*

Daly, Ivan de Burgh (1893–1974), physiologist, was born on 14 April 1893 at Pyrmont, 43 Brinswood Avenue, Leamington Spa, Warwickshire, the second son and third of the five children of James Thomas Daly (1853–1928), seaman and engineer, and his second wife, Amy Pritchard. He was educated at Beech Lawn preparatory school, Leamington Spa (1903–5), and at Rossall School, Lancashire (1906–11), where he developed an interest in science and engineering and, encouraged by his father, considered becoming an engineer. Two serious illnesses, and acquaintance with an uncle in the medical profession, however, turned his thoughts towards a career in medicine. When he went to Gonville and Caius College, Cambridge, in 1911 he read physiology, chemistry, and anatomy for the natural history tripos. He passed part one with first-class honours and gained an exhibition in 1914.

In the First World War Daly joined the Royal Army Medical Corps as a stretcher bearer, then worked for nine months at St Bartholomew's Hospital as a clinical clerk and surgical dresser. In 1915 he was commissioned as a flight-lieutenant in the Royal Naval Air Service, and trained at Eastchurch, Kent, as a fighter pilot. He saw a brief period of active service in Belgium before being wounded, and returned to Eastchurch as a gunnery officer. He resigned his commission in February 1917 and completed his medical course at St Bartholomew's, qualifying MB BCh (Cantab.) in August 1918. Assigned to the medical branch of the RAF he completed his three months as a house physician, during which time he worked under Dr John Drysdale and gained experience in electrocardiography.

Eager to pursue this line of research, Daly secured an appointment as assistant to Professor Ernest Henry Starling at University College, London, where he was principally engaged on cardiovascular researches. He was awarded a Beit memorial research fellowship for research in which the Fleming diode was used to investigate electrical changes in living tissue; his use of the thermionic valve to record the frog electrocardiogram was the first such application in England. The results were published by Daly and K. E. Shellshear in 1920. On 1 September of that year Daly married Beatrice Mary (Molly; b. 1897/8), daughter of Alfred Leetham of Shelley, Yorkshire. Their elder son, Michael de Burgh Daly (b. 1922), followed his father into a similar branch of the medical profession; the younger, Peter de Burgh Daly (1926–1959), pursued a military career until his death in a helicopter accident.

Daly graduated MD in 1922. The Beit fellowship was extended in 1923 when he moved to the National School of Medicine at Cardiff. His success in the field of heart-lung preparations led to his appointment in 1927 to the chair of physiology at Birmingham University, where he enlarged the department to include animal physiology. He was also involved in planning the new medical school (which opened in 1938) during which time he went to look at medical schools in the United States. He moved to Edinburgh in 1933, taking over the chair in succession to the retiring incumbent, the eminent professor Sir Edward Sharpey-Schäfer. Daly's main interest was now the pulmonary and bronchial circulations which he had developed in his latter years at Birmingham. As the importance of his work gained recognition Daly received the degree of MD from Birmingham in 1928, was elected fellow of the Royal Society of Edinburgh in 1934, Harvey and Hannah lecturer in the United States in 1936, and fellow of the Royal Society in 1943.

During the Second World War, Daly collaborated with the RAF in experiments on the physiology of high-altitude flying and on poison gases. In 1942 he was seconded to direct the Medical Research Council physiological laboratory attached to the gunnery wing of the Armoured Fighting Vehicle Training School in Dorset, looking into the problems of gun fume poisoning. He returned to Edinburgh in 1945.

The Agricultural Research Council (ARC), deliberating on the best way forward in the post-war years, decided to establish an institute to undertake fundamental research on the physiology of the larger farm animals. Daly was offered the directorship in 1947, his first task being to find a site. His choice fell on the 450 acre Babraham Hall estate, near Cambridge. It was purchased by the ARC in 1948 and named the Institute of Animal Physiology, with the various necessary laboratories, animal accommodation, and housing being built up in successive years as the number of staff rose to 160 by 1956. Daly controlled the institute firmly, knowing precisely what he wanted it to achieve (in this he was not always in agreement with the ARC). However, having chosen his scientific staff with care he let them get on with their chosen work unhindered and was supportive, rather than directive. He meanwhile continued his own pulmonary and bronchial investigations, latterly assisted by his son. His success with heart-lung preparations, in which the greater and lesser circulations were separately maintained and controlled by two blood pumps, undoubtedly stimulated and influenced the later development of open heart surgery.

Daly was appointed CBE on his retirement in 1958, and in 1959 he was awarded the Baly medal of the Royal College of Physicians. He secured funding to continue his research in the physiology laboratory of the University of Oxford until 1965, after which he continued at his home, 25 High Street, Long Crendon, Aylesbury. He was on the editorial board of the *Quarterly Journal of Experimental Physiology* from 1935 to 1968, and with Catherine Hebb wrote *Bronchial and Pulmonary Vascular Systems* (1966). He died suddenly while writing at his desk on 8 February 1974.

ANITA MCCONNELL

Sources H. Barcroft, *Memoirs FRS*, 21 (1975), 197–226 • *The Times* (11 Feb 1974), 16g • *BMJ* (1 March 1974), 397 • private information (2004) [A. Silver] • *CGPLA Eng. & Wales* (1974) • b. cert. • m. cert. • d. cert.
Archives Wellcome L., corresp. and papers | CAC Cam., corresp. with A. V. Hill
Wealth at death £34,938: probate, 18 July 1974, *CGPLA Eng. & Wales*

Daly, James (1811/12–1849). *See under* Rochdale Pioneers (*act.* 1844).

Daly, James (*c.*1840–1911), political activist and newspaper proprietor, was born in Boghadoon, co. Mayo, the son of a bailiff on the Elm Hall estate at Belcarra. He was educated by the Franciscan brothers at Errew monastery, near Castlebar, co. Mayo. A tenant and bailiff of estates in co. Mayo, and one in Kilkenny, he also rented property from the Lucan estate in Castlebar. By the end of the 1860s he had become an important figure in Castlebar as town councillor, poor-law guardian, and agent for Dublin-based firms. In 1876 he bought the *Connaught Telegraph*, an old-established Liberal newspaper, and became its editor and proprietor. He always regarded himself as a tenant farmer first and only by accident a newspaper proprietor.

Daly's initial involvement in local politics came in 1874 when he worked with members of the supreme council of the Irish Republican Brotherhood to elect John O'Connor Power to parliament. He went on to organize tenants' associations, saying that he had purchased the newspaper in order to agitate on behalf of small farmers against their landlords. Daly is best known for his part in organizing the meeting at Irishtown, co. Mayo, on 20 April 1879, which opened the land war and inaugurated the Land League of Mayo, the precursor of the Irish National Land League. Although the meeting was held at Daly's initiative, he was put under pressure by local Fenians. Daly later said that the meeting was held at the request of tenants, who had asked him to publicize a threatened eviction. Here Daly's position as a newspaper proprietor certainly helped him to mobilize local agitation. He co-operated with Michael Davitt, who organized the Dublin-based Fenians who took part, and Daly chaired the meeting; Davitt was not present. Daly was arrested with Davitt and James Bryce Killen at Gurteen, co. Sligo, in November 1879 for using seditious language; he had suggested that if anyone was evicted tenants should gather together and reinstate him. They were later released and the case was abandoned in January 1880. Dublin Castle believed him to be a member of the Irish Republican Brotherhood, but Daly was not a Fenian; he was a constitutionalist. With his background as a tenant farmer his knowledge of local conditions was immense. His evidence to the Bessborough commission inquiring into the operation of the Land Acts influenced their recommendations, and these in turn gave Gladstone the basis for the 1881 Land Act. Daly remained a local politician, not a national parliamentarian; he warned that agrarian outrage would lead to coercive legislation and fought a constant battle against the National League, whom he believed to be incompetent and corrupt, arguing that they acted against the interests of poor tenants. In 1889, at the special commission hearing, Davitt accused Daly of being the agent of a landlord to evict a tenant. This accusation Daly never forgave; he denounced Davitt for what he described as his 'crass ignorance' of Mayo politics, and forced him to amend his account. Despite his position as a grazier, Daly continued to campaign for small farmers and evicted tenants against the large graziers. He supported Parnell in the general election of 1880, but had little faith in Westminster's legislation for Ireland.

In his *Recollections* (1905), William O'Brien described Daly as 'A rough-spoken giant, with an inexhaustible fund of knowledge of the people' (p. 225). Because of his combative relationship with the leaders of the National League, he went unnoticed in their memoirs. Daly was married and had two daughters and a son, James. He died on 22 March 1911 in Castlebar, and was buried there in the Old Church cemetery.   Marie-Louise Legg

Sources D. E. Jordan, *Land and popular politics in Ireland* (1994) • W. Feingold, *The revolt of the tenantry* (1984) • J. J. Lee, *The modernisation of Irish society* (1973) • T. W. Moody, *Davitt and Irish revolution* (1981) • G. Moran, 'James Daly and the land question, 1876–1879', *Retrospect* (1980), 33–40 • *Connaught Telegraph* (25 March 1911)

Daly, Richard (1758–1813), actor and theatre manager, was born in co. Westmeath, Ireland, in 1758, the second son of Joseph Daly, a landowner in co. Galway. He entered Trinity College, Dublin, in November 1773 at the age of fifteen, but left without taking a degree. From his youth he displayed a mercurial and sometimes violent temper, and he gained a reputation as a duellist, gambler, and womanizer.

In 1776, having squandered his patrimony and finding himself destitute, Daly travelled to London, where he was counselled to try his fortune on the stage by a fellow Irishman, the popular actor Charles Macklin. The young Daly, who was considered remarkably handsome despite a severe squint in one eye, made his unsuccessful stage début as Othello at Covent Garden on 4 March 1779. Despite the initial disappointment, he was encouraged by the actress Ann Crawford, recently remarried after the death of her second husband, the Irish actor–manager Spranger Barry. After playing opposite her in several major roles, Daly was soon received enthusiastically by London audiences. At the time of his successful benefit in April 1779 he was living at 8 York Buildings, George Street.

When Mrs Crawford toured Ireland later in the spring of 1779, Daly accompanied her, and made his début on the Irish stage on 15 May. Two days later a critic in the *Hibernian Journal* wrote that 'Mr Daly's person is unquestionably the genteelest I have remembered for many years on the stage'. In August and September Daly was greeted with applause at Limerick and Cork, and in mid-September he married Jane, *née* Barsanti (*d.* 1795), the widow of John Richard Kirwan Lyster. She was a successful and popular actress in London and Dublin, and brought with her an income of £20 per week. Thomas Ryder, then the manager at the Crow Street Theatre, engaged the couple for the 1779–80 season, thus beginning Daly's twenty-year association with the Irish theatre.

The Dalys excelled in genteel comedy, playing the major male and female roles at Crow Street, and quickly became Dublin favourites. Ryder, who was the lessee of both the Crow Street and Smock Alley theatres, had kept the venerable Smock Alley Theatre closed in order to ward off competition, despite being unable to pay the rent on the building. Daly made a secret agreement with the owner to assume Ryder's debt in exchange for the lease, and Smock Alley opened under his management on 1 November 1780—and prospered. Ryder, unable to compete against Daly's popularity and the new Smock Alley manager's deft engagement of major London stars, such as Sarah Siddons and John Philip Kemble, withdrew from the fray at the end of 1780–81 and joined Daly's company. The following three seasons were even more successful for Daly, even in the face of heated competition from a series of rival companies at the Crow Street, Capel Street, and Fishamble Street playhouses.

Daly's success as a manager gave him great power over the women in his company:

> He was said to be the general *lover* in his theatrical company; … the resistance of the fair to a *manager* may be somewhat modified by the danger of offending one, who has the power to appoint them to parts, either striking or otherwise; and who must not be irritated, if he cannot be obliged. (Tomalin, 22)

Elizabeth Inchbald reported rejecting his advances and being instantly dismissed. The great comic actress Dorothy *Jordan worked for Daly at the outset of her career; she gave birth to his child in November 1782, having fled to England. (Jordan and Daly were featured in the *tête-à-tête* portrait series in the *Town and Country Magazine* in January 1787.) Daly's own marriage produced eight or nine children.

In November 1786, after being appointed deputy master of the revels in Ireland, Daly was awarded a patent and a *de facto* monopoly on public theatricals in Dublin by the Irish parliament. He purchased the Crow Street Theatre and closed and then sold the dilapidated Smock Alley Theatre. He also gained control of the theatres in Cork, Limerick, Newry, and Waterford. Fortune smiled on the next three seasons, largely because of his time-tested policy of engaging at Crow Street the most popular performers from the London and Scottish theatres. In January 1789 clouds began to gather: Philip Astley, the London equestrian and circus manager, constructed a permanent Amphitheatre Royal in Peter Street, Dublin. Although Astley's patent prohibited the acting of regular plays, his elaborate and expensive spectacles packed his house, and Daly reacted by serving his audiences similar fare. A more insidious threat to Daly's management was posed by John Magee, editor of the *Dublin Evening Post*. Magee's motives for attacking Daly are unclear, but seem to have stemmed from the latter's association with Francis Higgins, a notorious scoundrel and a bitter enemy of Magee. A series of anti-Daly newspaper squibs was followed by periodic riots at Crow Street. The manager's situation became even worse when he and his brother were convicted of assaulting several of the trouble-makers: they were both fined and jailed, Richard for four months.

Thereafter Daly's fortunes declined. Despite a successful libel suit against Magee, intermittent disturbances continued at the theatre, frightening away the public. In an effort to attract audiences Daly and his wife returned to the Crow Street stage in 1791, acting for the first time in four years, but Daly's relations with his now rebellious actors, seldom good, became worse. Although visiting stars such as Sarah Siddons and Thomas King continued to bring in huge audiences, Daly paid his regular company irregularly and used them shabbily. The cumulative result was an increasing difficulty in luring competent players to Crow Street.

At the beginning of the 1793–4 season letters appeared in the newspapers calling for the establishment of a second patent theatre in Dublin, and in March 1793 Frederick Edward Jones and a group of Dublin gentlemen opened a private theatre in Fishamble Street with the declared aim of providing 'a place of rational public amusement'. In 1796 Jones, supported by many of the principal nobility and gentry, petitioned the government for a patent on the grounds that, owing to Daly's mismanagement, the Crow Street Theatre was no longer a fit venue. The attorney-general agreed, and, rather than face the inevitable ruin such competition would bring, Daly ceded his patent to Jones in August 1797 and sold Crow Street Theatre to him in 1800. In 1798 the crown granted him a pension of £100 per year during his own lifetime and those of his children.

Daly lived out the remainder of his life in Dublin in relative obscurity. On 8 September 1813 the newspapers carried an announcement of his death, at his home at 30 Lower Gardiner Street. JOHN C. GREENE

Sources Highfill, Burnim & Langhans, *BDA* · W. S. Clark, *The Irish stage in the county towns, 1720–1800* (1965) · W. J. Lawrence, notes on the history of the Irish stage, University of Cincinnati · *DNB* · C. Tomalin, *Mrs Jordan's profession* (1994) · Burtchaell & Sadleir, *Alum. Dubl.*
Likenesses line engraving, BM, NPG; repro. in *Town and Country Magazine* (1787)

Daly, Robert (1783–1872), Church of Ireland bishop of Cashel, Emly, Waterford, and Lismore, was the younger son of the politician Denis *Daly (1747–1791) and Lady Henrietta (*d*. 1852), only child and heir of Robert Maxwell, first earl of Farnham. He was born at Dunsandle, co. Galway, on 8 June 1783. He entered Trinity College, Dublin, as a fellow-commoner in 1799, and gained a gold medal as well as graduating BA in 1803. He proceeded MA in 1832 and was awarded his BD and DD in 1843. In 1807 he was ordained a deacon, and was admitted to priest's orders in the following year. From 1808 to 1842 he held the prebend of Holy Trinity in the diocese of Cork and from 1814 to 1842 the prebend of Stagonil and the rectory of Powerscourt in the diocese of Dublin. In 1842 he was declared dean of St Patrick's Cathedral, Dublin, by the court of delegates appointed to try the validity of an election held on 8 December 1840, in which the Revd James Wilson DD (precentor of St Patrick's, and soon after bishop of Cork, Cloyne, and Ross) had been the other candidate. Daly became bishop of the united dioceses of Cashel, Emly, Waterford, and Lismore in 1843, having reportedly been offered the post on the day of his installation as dean of St Patrick's. For many years, both before and after he became a bishop, Daly's was a household name throughout the Church of Ireland. He was a prominent leader of the evangelical wing, and a generous contributor to the funds of various evangelical societies. He was a preacher of considerable force and energy, maintaining his own principles with consistency and zeal.

Daly, adversary of the Tractarians and advocate of such projects as the proselytizing Achill Mission, critic of the national schools, and supporter of the Church Education Society, was the author of several printed sermons and charges. He also wrote tracts on religious and moral subjects, and often contributed articles to religious periodicals. In 1832 he published an edition of *Focalóir Gaoidhilge-Sax-Bhéarla, or, Irish–English Dictionary* by J. O'Brien, Roman

Catholic bishop of Cloyne, in which he described himself as 'zealous for education through the medium of the Irish language' (Daly, v). He edited the *Letters and Papers of Viscountess Powerscourt* in 1839, which passed through many editions. His library included a fine and rare collection of bibles and prayer books, which was sold by auction shortly before his death, the proceeds going to charity. He died, unmarried, at his residence, the bishop's palace, Waterford, on 16 February 1872 and was buried in Christ Church Cathedral, Waterford, on 20 February.

B. H. BLACKER, rev. KENNETH MILNE

Sources H. Cotton, *Fasti ecclesiae Hibernicae*, 6 vols. (1845–78) · W. M. Brady, *Clerical and parochial records of Cork, Cloyne, and Ross*, 3 vols. (1863–4) · [J. H. Todd], ed., *A catalogue of graduates who have proceeded to degrees in the University of Dublin, from the earliest recorded commencements to … December 16, 1868* (1869) · R. Daly, preface, in J. O'Brien, *Focalóir Gaoidhilge-Sax-Bhéarla*, ed. R. Daly, 2nd edn (1832) · D. Bowen, *The protestant crusade in Ireland, 1800–70* (1978) · *Irish Ecclesiastical Gazette* (1872) · W. A. Phillips, ed., *History of the Church of Ireland*, 3 vols. (1933–4) · R. B. McDowell, *The Church of Ireland, 1869–1969* (1975) · Mrs Hamilton Madden, *Memoir of the late Rt Revd Robert Daly DD* (1875)

Archives Representative Church Body Library, Dublin, papers

Likenesses T. Cranfield, photograph, Representative Church Body Library, Dublin, MS 223/8 · portrait, palace, Kilkenny · print, Representative Church Body Library, Dublin

Wealth at death under £25,000: probate, 16 March 1872, *CGPLA Ire.*

Dalyell, Sir John Graham, sixth baronet (1775–1851), antiquary and naturalist, the second son of Sir Robert Dalyell, fourth baronet (1724–1791), an army officer, and his wife, Elizabeth (d. 1825), the only daughter of Nicol Graham of Gartmore, Perthshire, was born at The Binns, Linlithgowshire, on 9 August 1775. When an infant he fell from a table onto a stone floor and was lamed for life. After tutoring at home he attended classes first at the University of St Andrews and then at the University of Edinburgh; he qualified for the Scottish bar, and became a member of the Faculty of Advocates on 31 January 1797.

The work in Parliament House proved too fatiguing for him, but Dalyell acquired a considerable business as a consulting advocate. Although he was a younger son and not wealthy, he made it a rule of his legal practice not to accept a fee from a relative, a widow, or an orphan. In 1797 he was elected a member of the Society of Antiquaries of Scotland, and he was chosen as the society's first vice-president; he also became a member of the Society of Arts for Scotland, and served as its president in 1839–40.

Lack of robust health, doubtless combined with a probing curiosity, led Dalyell to immerse himself in the manuscript treasures of the Advocates' Library. In 1798 he produced his first work, *Fragments of Scottish History*, which included the diary of Robert Birrell, burgess of Edinburgh from 1532 to 1608. This was followed in 1801 by *Scottish Poems of the Sixteenth Century*, in two volumes. In the preface to this work he said that during his preparatory researches he had examined about 700 volumes of manuscripts. In addition to his knowledge of antiquarian lore he had an extensive knowledge of natural history, and in 1814 he published his valuable *Observations on several species of planariae, illustrated, in his own hand, by exquisite coloured*

Sir John Graham Dalyell, sixth baronet (1775–1851), by Sir John Watson-Gordon

figures of living animals (the original illustrations remain in the possession of the Dalyell family at The Binns). On 22 August 1836 he was knighted for his services to literature and science, and on 1 February 1841 he succeeded his elder brother, Sir James Dalyell, as sixth baronet.

In 1847 Dalyell finished *Rare and Remarkable Animals of Scotland, with Practical Observations on their Nature*, in two volumes. The publication of this beautifully engraved work was unfortunately delayed for nearly five years owing to a dispute and lawsuit with the engraver. The delay deprived Dalyell of the full credit for several of his discoveries in connection with medusae (jellyfish and sea anemone). The first volume of his last and great work, *The powers of the creator displayed in the creation, or, Observations on life amidst the various forms of the humbler tribes of animated Nature*, was published in 1851. The second volume was published in 1853, after the author's death, under the superintendence of his sister Elizabeth Dalyell and Professor John Fleming DD, while the third volume was delayed until 1858. Dalyell was a meticulous scholar, often revising his texts four or five times before sending them to the printer.

Dalyell became an enrolled member of the Highland Society of Scotland in 1807 and in 1817 was presented by his fellow members with a piece of plate for the invention of a self-regulating calendar. He was one of the promoters of the original zoological gardens of Edinburgh and served as preses (president) of the board of directors in 1841. He was also vice-president of the African Institute of Paris and represented the fourth district of Edinburgh on the city council.

While his scholarly pursuits extended over a wide field,

as witnessed by his published works, Dalyell's main interest lay in natural history. He had a curio cabinet and collected many specimens for observation. One was a sea anemone, found at North Berwick, known as Grannie because of its great powers of sexual and asexual reproduction: fed on mussels, it produced 230 young in a single night. Grannie outlived Dalyell and, on his death, continued to be looked after, in rota, by his fellow naturalists in Edinburgh. The anemone finally died in 1887, aged sixty-six, thirty-six years after Sir John, and merited a death notice in *The Times* and *The Scotsman*. Dalyell observed:

> The errors which have darkened the beautiful science of Natural History are principally to be traced to superficial observation; and if this be true with regard to the larger animals, how is it to be expected that the smaller have received that scrupulous care and attention, by which alone their habits can be illustrated?

Family history has it that Dalyell was one of the teachers of Charles Darwin during his time at Edinburgh University, where he had gone to study medicine, but, uninspired by the lectures, had changed his specialism to natural history. Darwin, like Dalyell, went out with the fishermen from Newhaven, the fishing harbour of Edinburgh, to collect specimens for observation.

Dalyell's massive contribution to marine science, his work on organisms such as the common leech and the planariae (flat worm—a branch of which was named after him) was recognized in the later twentieth century by Sir Maurice Yonge, who published on him in the *Proceedings of the Royal Society of Edinburgh* in 1971. Dalyell died at his home at 14 Great King Street, Edinburgh, on 7 June 1851 and was buried with his ancestors in Abercorn church, Linlithgowshire. He never married, and his successor in the baronetcy was his brother Admiral Sir William Cunningham Cavendish Dalyell, who had a very different career, which provided C. S. Forester with material for his Hornblower books.

In addition to his major works, Dalyell published widely; he translated works from Italian, compiled three volumes on shipwrecks (1812), and edited and wrote various works on the history of Scotland, including *The Darker Superstitions of Scotland* (1834) and *Musical Memoirs of Scotland* (1849). He left a manuscript on Scottish musical practice and contributed to a variety of reference works, among them the *Encyclopaedia Britannica* and the peerages of Douglas and Burke.   KATHLEEN DALYELL

Sources The Binns, West Lothian, Dalyell MSS · C. M. Yonge, 'John Graham Dalyell and some predecessors in Scottish marine biology', *Proceedings of the Royal Society of Edinburgh*, 72B (1971–2), 89–97 · J. H. Ashworth, 'Charles Darwin as a student in Edinburgh, 1825–1827', *Proceedings of the Royal Society of Edinburgh*, 55 (1934–5), 97–113 · J. H. Ashworth and N. Annandale, 'Observations on some aged specimens of Sagartia troglodytes, and on the duration of life in coelenterates', *Proceedings of the Royal Society of Edinburgh*, 25 (1903–5), 295–308 · Anderson, *Scot. nat.* · bap. reg. Scot., 661/3 [Abercorn, Linlithgowshire]
Archives Royal Highland and Agricultural Society of Scotland, Edinburgh, letters relating to Gaelic dictionary · The Binns, West Lothian, MSS, incl. illustrations · U. Edin. L., notebooks, drawings, and papers | NL Scot., corresp. with Archibald Constable · U. Edin. L., letters to David Laing
Likenesses W. S. Watson, oils, The Binns, West Lothian · J. Watson-Gordon, oils, The Binns, West Lothian [*see illus.*] · oils, The Binns, West Lothian
Wealth at death all personal wealth to sister; estate and title to younger brother: The Binns, West Lothian, Dalyell MSS

Dalyell, Robert. *See* Dalzell, Robert, first earl of Carnwath (*d.* 1654); Dalzell, Robert, fifth earl of Carnwath (*c.*1687–1737).

Dalyell, Sir Robert Anstruther (1831–1890), administrator in India, was born in the parish of St Stephen's, Edinburgh, on 5 May 1831, the elder son of Lieutenant-Colonel John Dalyell (*d.* 1843) of Fife, provost of Cupar, and his wife, Jane (*d.* 1865), eldest daughter of Brigadier-General Robert *Anstruther and great-granddaughter of James Douglas, fourth duke of Hamilton. He was educated at Cheltenham College from 1842 until 1845 and privately by William Gambier Hawtayne of South Road, Blackheath, from 1845 until 1848. In July 1848 he obtained a nomination for a writership in the Madras civil service and entered the East India Company's college at Haileybury, arriving in Madras on 1 January 1851.

The first ten years of Dalyell's career were spent in subordinate positions in the *mofussil*, during which time he reputedly devoted as much time to sport and hunting as to administration. In 1861 he earned the gratitude of his colleagues by distributing to every station in India a letter depicting the constrained career opportunities of the Madras civilian and then organizing three numerously signed memorials of protest to the secretary of state. Also in 1861, and possibly not coincidentally, Dalyell was taken into the Madras secretariat as under-secretary to the board of revenue. In 1866 he published *The Standing Orders of the Board of Revenue, from 1820 to 1865*, and in 1867 was promoted to chief secretary of the board. As secretary of the central relief committee in the famine of 1865–6 he compiled a report, *Memorandum on the Madras Famine of 1866* (1867), which subsequently became the official guide for all similar operations in southern India and which, in urging the government to interfere in the market during a famine, presaged the India-wide abandonment of the laws of political economy at times of dearth which was announced by the famine relief code of 1870. A staunch political economist himself, Dalyell was nevertheless forced by his administrative experience to argue that the laws of political economy were only infallible in Europe. In India, he reasoned, where markets were often localized and capital dispersed, only the government was large enough to take on the role of the enterprising merchant and it was therefore the government's duty to import grain into a stricken area. The repeated refusal of Indian governments to do this had, he argued, greatly exacerbated the suffering of their subject populations.

In 1868 Dalyell was promoted to revenue secretary and in 1873 was made a member of the revenue board and chief secretary to the Madras government. He published a *Report on the Land Tenures of South India* and also, in 1874, the results of an extensive inquiry into excise, extending over

Madras, Mysore, the Punjab, and the North-Western Provinces. From 1873 until 1877 he went annually to Calcutta as the Madras representative in the central legislative council and from 1875 until 1876 served as the chief commissioner of Mysore, a posting which he considered to be the high point of his career.

In 1877 Dalyell returned to England to take up a seat on the Council of India. On the council he was consciously a Madras man, always alert to measures that might affect the fortunes of his old province. He maintained a regular correspondence with Mountstuart Elphinstone Grant Duff during his governorship of Madras (1881–6), and, like him, was a conservative Liberal, combining a fierce anti-protectionism with an opposition to local self-government and constitutional reform in India. Upon his retirement from the council in February 1887 he was created KCIE.

Dalyell was captain of the Royal and Ancient Golf Club and a keen and jovial amateur dramatist. For many years a justice of the peace and deputy lieutenant of Fife, he regularly returned to his family there. He was a member of the Royal Statistical Society of London and in 1885 was awarded an honorary LLD by St Andrews University. Dalyell died on 18 January 1890 at the New Club, Edinburgh, and was buried on 23 January at St Andrews in the cathedral burial-ground. He was unmarried.

KATHERINE PRIOR

Sources *The Englishman* (21 Jan 1890), 4 · *Charivari's album* (1875); repr. in *Madras Mail* (29 May 1877) · BL OIOC, Grant Duff MSS · *The Times* (20 Jan 1890), 6 · *DNB* · R. A. Dalyell, *Memorandum on the Madras famine of 1866* (1867) · BL OIOC, Haileybury MSS
Archives BL OIOC, Grant Duff MSS
Likenesses Isca, coloured lithograph, *c*.1875, repro. in *Charivari's album*, no. 63
Wealth at death £16,647 3*s*. 7*d*. in UK: probate, 29 March 1890, CGPLA Eng. & Wales

Dalyell [Dalzell], **Thomas, of Binns** (*bap.* 1615, *d.* 1685), army officer, was the son of Thomas Dalyell (*c*.1572–1642), an Edinburgh merchant who bought Binns and other lands in Linlithgowshire in 1612, and his wife, Janet Bruce, an illegitimate (but subsequently legitimized) daughter of Lord Bruce of Kinross. Dalyell was baptized at Abercorn on 15 October 1615 and can be traced in Paris, Saumur, Lyons, and Geneva in 1634 in the company of other Scottish gentry, evidently completing his education by travel. He was in Paris again in 1636–7, but by August 1637 was home in Scotland. He and his father both gave their support to the resistance to Charles I's religious policies which was sweeping Scotland, signing the petition to the privy council of 17 October 1637 and, in early 1638, the national covenant.

The bishops' wars and Ireland, 1640–1650 By July 1640 Dalyell was serving as a captain under Major-General Robert Monro in forces in Aberdeen which were keeping the burgh reluctantly obedient to the cause of the covenant in the second bishops' war, and with many other officers he was made a burgess of Aberdeen in September. When most of the covenanters' army was disbanded in 1641,

Monro's regiment remained in arms, and Dalyell accompanied it to Ulster as part of the Scottish army in Ireland in April 1642. Early in 1644, when officers were assembled in Carrickfergus to swear the solemn league and covenant, he is said to have been the only one to refuse. Many of the army's officers had become alienated by neglect and conflicting loyalties, and Dalyell (now a major) was one of those disaffected enough to negotiate in 1645 with the marquess of Ormond, the king's lieutenant in Dublin, about the army transferring its support from the English parliament and its Scots covenanter allies to the royalists. This came to nothing, but when in 1648 the army sent a contingent under Major-General George Monro to join the engagers (an alliance in Scotland of moderate covenanters and royalists) in an invasion of England to help Charles I, Dalyell took part in the venture.

After the defeat of the engagers in England Dalyell joined George Monro in an unsuccessful attempt to shore up the collapsing engager regime. They then attempted to return to Ireland, and when this failed Dalyell probably joined Monro in flight to the Netherlands before returning to Ireland at the start of 1649. He served under Monro in a campaign which briefly restored royalist control to much of Ulster, and after Carrickfergus was seized on 4 July he was made governor of the town. However, after the landing of Cromwell in Ireland in August royalist resistance crumbled. Besieged by forces of the English parliament, Dalyell agreed on 2 November that he would surrender on 13 December unless he was relieved by then. This seemingly generous delay may have been intended to tempt Monro into trying to relieve Carrickfergus, and thus bring him to battle. Monro did indeed attempt to save the town, and was routed on 26 November 1649. Dalyell surrendered Carrickfergus a week later.

Scotland and Russia, 1650–1665 Dalyell remained in Ireland until August 1650, when he received a pass from the English authorities to leave and crossed to Scotland. As an engager he had been banished, but he soon gained permission to stay, for the power of the kirk party regime which had succeeded the engagers was waning as a royalist revival grew in response to the arrival of the exiled Charles II and the invasion of the English under Cromwell. None the less, Dalyell was not allowed to serve in the army until the church had accepted his repentance for his engager past, and for cases of brutal treatment to soldiers under his command in Carrickfergus. As soon as the church was satisfied, 'the stiff Irish Engager' (Dalton, 1.21) was appointed one of two major-generals of foot by Charles II, on the recommendation of Lieutenant-General John Middleton (10 May 1651). He took part in the invasion of England that followed, and shared in the rout of Charles's army at Worcester on 3 September. Captured and imprisoned in the Tower of London, he escaped in May 1652. The order for his apprehension provided a description, wart and all, though his age was overestimated: 'a Scotish man aged betweene 50 and 60 yeares somewhat tall his haire blacke and grey and a wart upon one of his Cheekes' (ibid., opposite p. 18). Having made good his escape to the continent he again offered his services to the exiled Charles II, and he was with Middleton and George Monro when they landed in Caithness early in 1654 to take command of the royalists, who had risen against the English conquerors. As major-general of foot he served in the campaigning that followed until the rising collapsed through internal dissension and English pressure. He had been excluded from the 1654 Scottish act of grace and pardon, but in May the English granted him a pass to go abroad. Charles II no longer being able to offer him employment, he and his colleague Lieutenant-General James Drummond decided to seek their fortunes to the east. They received letters of recommendation in August 1655 from Charles to the king of Poland, Prince Radziwill (chamberlain of Lithuania), and the tsar of Russia.

The tsar, Alexei I, having accepted their services, Dalyell at first held the rank of lieutenant-general, being promoted to general in 1660. His service in Russia's wars against Poland also brought him estates near Polotsk and Smolensk, and he became governor of the latter city. In 1665 Alexei agreed that both Dalyell and Drummond should return home, at the request of Charles II.

Commander-in-chief in Scotland, 1666–1667 Though now restored to his thrones, Charles faced the prospect of war with the Dutch and rebellion by presbyterian religious dissidents in Scotland, and called upon the assistance of these two veterans of proved loyalty. On 19 July 1666 Dalyell was appointed lieutenant-general commanding all the forces in Scotland, with Drummond as his second in command. As commander-in-chief Dalyell had ultimate responsibility for the often harsh and arbitrary treatment of dissidents and suspects which did more to provoke than prevent rebellion. The ill-organized revolt based in the western lowlands that followed was easily crushed by Dalyell at Rullion Green on 28 November 1666.

Both before and after the defeat of the rebels Dalyell revealed himself as a supporter of severity, given to bloodcurdling threats. In December 1666 he wrote of the necessity of having the inhabitants of disaffected areas removed or destroyed. 'Extirpation' (Airy, 1.225, 2, appx lxxv) was necessary, though quite what he meant by such a term was probably as unclear to Dalyell himself as it is to others: he favoured drastic action but gave little thought to actual policies. In June 1667, it was reported, when trial of prisoners was discussed, he answered brusquely, 'ther was noe mor to be doune bot tak them out and hang them' (ibid., 2.11). Gilbert Burnet commented that Dalyell 'acted the Muscovite too grossly. He threatened to spit men, and to roast them: and he killed some in cold blood, or rather in hot blood; for he was then drunk, when he ordered one to be hanged, because he would not tell where his father was' (*Bishop Burnet's History*, 1.435–6).

In the immediate aftermath of his triumph at Rullion Green, Dalyell's severity had full approval, and he was rewarded with membership of the Scottish privy council (January 1667), but the policies of violence were soon relaxed as it was realized that they were counterproductive. This, along with the end of the Second Anglo-Dutch War, led to most of the army being disbanded late in 1667. Dalyell's commission was withdrawn, and for over a decade he was without employment.

Domestic interlude, 1667–1679 When, at the end of 1648, Dalyell had been banished from Scotland for his role in the engagement, he had resigned his lands of Binns and his movable and household goods in trust to his brother-in-law William Drummond of Riccarton. Now in 1667 he reclaimed his property and settled in the House of Binns, surrounded by trophies of past campaigns—Polish boots, Cossack rifles, Polish and Muscovite poleaxes.

Dalyell's private life was complex. His three sons with Elizabeth Ker (niece of the laird of Cavers), Anna Powslie, and Christian (surname unknown) are all referred to as illegitimate ('natural') in 1669 (Dalyell and Beveridge, *Binns Papers*, 62–3). The status (and maternity) of two daughters is left undefined, but as there is no evidence that Dalyell ever married, their illegitimacy may be assumed. His eldest son received letters of legitimization in 1673, the second and third in 1682. He also had several children with Marion Abercrombie, sister of an Edinburgh burgess, who survived him by many years. When, in the early 1680s, the more extreme religious dissidents excommunicated Dalyell, their denunciation of his 'lewd and impious life leading adulteries and uncleanness from his youth, with a contempt for marriage which is the ordinance of God' (ibid., x) was not entirely indiscriminate abuse.

Commander-in-chief in Scotland, 1679–1685 By the later 1670s attempts at compromise with dissidents in Scotland had been abandoned as ineffective. Renewed persecution and violent resistance to it culminated in the murder of the archbishop of St Andrews on 3 May 1679. The response was, predictably, increased repression, believed to be necessary as the murder was seen as likely to spark off a new rebellion. In June Charles II appointed his illegitimate son the duke of Monmouth as commander-in-chief in Scotland, and the privy council recommended that Dalyell be reappointed lieutenant-general as his second in command. The king's agreement was notified to the council on 22 June, and Dalyell resolved to set off immediately to join Monmouth's army. But on the same day Monmouth scattered the rebels at Bothwell Bridge, and it quickly became clear that there was little likelihood of further large-scale fighting. On 1 November the king recalled his commission to Monmouth, leaving Dalyell (who had been granted a pension of £400 sterling a year) as commander-in-chief. Thus, as after the 1666 rising, Dalyell was left to oversee an attempt to stamp out active dissent by military force.

In the years that followed Dalyell reinforced his place in presbyterian demonology. To Robert Wodrow he was 'a man naturally rude and fierce, who had this heightened by his breeding and service in Muscovy, where he had seen little but the utmost tyranny and slavery' (Wodrow, 2.13), and certainly in the 'killing times' of 1681–5 he had no scruple in implementing policies of summary execution for extremists who refused to declare assassinating the king unlawful, and in using torture to extract confessions. It is said that Dalyell had insisted in 1679 on being made answerable only to the king himself, for he 'would not accept it [command in Scotland] otherwayes', so as to have a free hand to impose unrestrained military solutions (*Historical Notices*, 1.243–4). In fact he worked with the privy council and leading officials, and there is no sign that they found his methods unacceptable, though two incidents aroused enough attention to be recorded. In 1681, when a prisoner being questioned before a committee of council 'railed on Generall Dalzeel, calling him a Muscovia beast, who used to roast men, the Generall in a passion struck him in with the pommel of his shable [sword] till the blood sprang' (ibid., 1.332). In 1684 a prisoner who had refused to give satisfactory answers under torture before the council 'was put in General Dalzeill's hands: and it was reported that by a hair shirt and pricking (as the witches are used,) he was five nights keeped from sleip' (ibid., 2.546). Sleep deprivation failed to elicit confession, and the victim stated that further torture would simply drive him mad. Dalyell philosophically concluded, 'then all hopes of confession is gone', so there was no point in continuing, and expressed a wish to return to more honourable work. Opinions differed as to his policies: some complained of his 'Muscovian rigour as to severe in tyme of peace' (Lauder, *Historical Observes*, 28), but others thought his strictness in disciplining his own troops set a good example.

In June 1684 Dalyell favoured concentrating the forces in Scotland, and protested at orders to divide them into small parties, as he feared that, as in 1666 and 1679, a successful attack on some isolated band of soldiers might spark off 'a formidable rebellion' (Napier, 2.398). That even after five years of effort he believed rebellion possible at any moment was a clear sign of the failure of the policy of repression. After the accession of James VII in February 1685 Dalyell's commission as commander-in-chief was renewed, but he was evidently in poor health, spending much of his time at Binns. When crisis threatened in May, with the earl of Argyll's rebellion, a younger man was sent in to take over command in Scotland (as in 1679), the earl of Dunbarton, but command reverted to Dalyell in June when the crisis was over.

On the evening of 23 August 1685 'the good old General died of an apoplexy' (Napier, 3.436n.) at his town house in the Canongate in Edinburgh. As he was still in service, he was entitled to an elaborate military funeral, which took place on 1 September, and he was probably buried in the family vault at Abercorn. 'Some ware observing that few of our generall persons in Scotland had come to the grave, without some tach [blemish] or note of disgrace' (Lauder, *Historical Observes*, 216).

Muscovia beast? How is the 'good old General', the man who died without a stain on his character, to be reconciled with 'the Muscovia beast'? Part of the answer is obvious. To those who feared armed risings, based on religious dissent, by the lower orders Dalyell was the man who had slogged away for years at the unglamorous but essential task of maintaining a precarious military control of areas where protest was strong. He had not achieved victory but he had prevented disaster. If the methods used were sometimes rough, they could be justified as necessary.

Equally, it is easy to see that as the man who presided over repression Dalyell was hated by dissidents and those who sympathized with them. As commander Dalyell had responsibility for the brutality of his subordinates. But when it comes to specific instances of atrocious deeds by this man who was supposed to be habitually violent, the record is surprisingly thin, comprising the incidents already mentioned—brutal treatment of soldiers at Carrickfergus; hitting a prisoner who provoked him; obeying orders to torture a man (which he regarded as not very honourable employment, and gave up without extracting information); and the charge that he had ordered an execution while drunk. It is an unpleasant record, of a harsh, bad-tempered officer ready to justify all he did in terms of obedience and loyalty to the crown. Moreover, the Carrickfergus incident indicates that his reputation for brutality predated his service in Russia. Yet it is not the record of a sadist or a lover of violence—the allegation that he introduced the thumbscrew to Scotland from Russia is an invention. It is hard not to conclude that his notoriety far outweighed his deeds.

This, it seems likely, is not entirely due to the exaggerations of Dalyell's enemies. Dalyell would appear to have deliberately cultivated the 'Muscovia beast' image as part of a wider image of eccentricity. Captain John Creighton, who had known Dalyell, recalled his former commander in his *Memoirs* (1731). He depicts him as strikingly eccentric—though in this he may have had some help from his editor, Jonathan Swift.

> He was bred up very Hardy from his youth, in both Dyet and cloathing. He never wore Boots, nor above one Coat, which was close to his Body, with close sleeves, like those we call Jockey-Coats. He never wore a Peruke [wig], nor did he shave since the Murder of King Charles the First. In my time his head was bald, which he covered only with a Beaver Hat … His Beard was white and Bushy, and yet reached down almost to his Girdle.

The king 'had a great esteem for his Worth and Valour'. When he visited court in London his uncouth appearance led to his being followed by crowds of shouting boys and 'As he was a Man of Humour, he would always thank them for their civilities' (*The Prose Works of Jonathan Swift*, ed. H. Davis, 5, 1962, 156). The sketch is of a man who delighted in shocking people, and though the 'beard never cut since 1649' story is false, it may be a myth he himself fostered.

If the fashion was to be clean-shaven, Dalyell would have a huge beard. If other gentlemen wore wigs, he would flaunt his bald head. That he openly acknowledged and supported his large family of bastard children may show humanity, but it was also perhaps a flaunting of immorality designed to horrify. In one respect this love of unconventionality, combined with fierce loyalty to the crown, can be seen as taking to extremes the mode after the restoration of monarchy in 1660 of demonstrating loyalty by adopting a dissolute lifestyle, like that of the king himself, in defiant rejection of puritan morality. But

Dalyell's eccentricities of dress and appearance go far beyond this, and it seems likely that his violence of language and the stories of his barbarity are part of the same striving for effect. Indulging in displays of bad temper, threatening horrors far beyond anything he ever committed (in Britain at least), had practical value in Dalyell's work as a general—tales of the bloodthirsty monster could be useful in terrifying and demoralizing enemies—but they also entertained Charles II and satisfied a craving for notoriety.

There was, however, a price to pay. Dalyell's cultivated wildness may well have deprived him of the honours that he might otherwise have expected to follow from his seniority. Only when he was safely dead were his 'distinguished services' (Dalyell and Beveridge, *Binns Papers*, 80) recognized by the grant of a baronetcy to his son.

DAVID STEVENSON

Sources *DNB* · J. Dalyell and J. Beveridge, eds., *The Binns papers, 1320–1864*, 1 vol. in 3 pts, Scottish RS, 70 (1936–8) · C. Dalton, ed., *The Scots army, 1661–1688* (1909) · *Bishop Burnet's History* · C. H. Firth, ed., *Scotland and the protectorate: letters and papers relating to the military government of Scotland from January 1654 to June 1659*, Scottish History Society, 31 (1899) · D. Stevenson, *Scottish covenanters and Irish confederates* (1981) · M. D. Young, ed., *The parliaments of Scotland: burgh and shire commissioners*, 2 vols. (1992–3) · *Historical notices of Scotish affairs, selected from the manuscripts of Sir John Lauder of Fountainhall*, ed. D. Laing, 2 vols., Bannatyne Club, 87 (1848) · M. Napier, *Memorials and letters illustrative of the life and times of John Graham of Claverhouse, Viscount Dundee*, 3 vols. (1859–62) · *The Lauderdale papers*, ed. O. Airy, 3 vols., CS, new ser., 34, 36, 38 (1884–5) · E. M. Furgol, *A regimental history of the covenanting armies, 1639–1651* (1990) · A. F. Mitchell and J. Christie, eds., *The records of the commissions of the general assemblies of the Church of Scotland*, 3, Scottish History Society, 58 (1909) · R. Wodrow, *The history of the sufferings of the Church of Scotland from the Restoration to the revolution*, ed. R. Burns, 4 vols. (1828–30) · J. Dalyell and J. Beveridge, eds., 'Inventory of the plenishing of the house of the Binns', *Proceedings of the Society of Antiquaries of Scotland*, 58 (1923–4), 344–70 · S. Murdoch and A. Grosjean, 'Scotland, Scandinavia and Northern Europe, 1580–1707', www.abdn.ac.uk/ssne/ · J. Lauder, *Historical observes of memorable occurrents in church and state, from October 1680 to April 1686*, ed. A. Urquhart and D. Laing, Bannatyne Club, 66 (1840)

Archives NA Scot., letters and papers · The Binns, West Lothian, MSS | BL, letters to duke of Lauderdale, Add. MSS 23125–23135, 23243–23246, 35125 · NA Scot., Thomson and Baxter MSS, GD241

Likenesses attrib. D. Patton, oils, The Binns, West Lothian · attrib. L. Schuneman, oils, Scot. NPG; version, The Binns, West Lothian · P. Vanderbank, line engraving (after D. Patton), BM, NPG

Dalzel [*formerly* Dalziel], **Andrew** (1742–1806), classical scholar and tutor, was born on 6 October 1742 at Gateside of Newliston, a farm where his family had held the tenancy for more than a century, in the parish of Kirkliston, Linlithgowshire. He was the son of William Dalziel (*d.* 1751), a carpenter, and of his wife, Alice Linn of Linnmill. A brother, Archibald *Dalzel (*b.* 1740, *d.* in or before 1811), became an apologist for the slave trade and the historian of Dahomey. Andrew was named after his paternal uncle (*d.* 1755), minister of Stonykirk, Wigtownshire, who adopted him on his father's death.

Dalzel's career offers a fine example of how an able Scot

Andrew Dalzel (1742–1806), by Sir Henry Raeburn

of humble origins could with a little luck rise high in the intellectual circles of enlightened Edinburgh. His education was taken in hand by the minister of Kirkliston, John Drysdale, who also served as principal clerk to the general assembly of the Church of Scotland. A pedantic but influential character who was related by marriage to William Robertson, principal of the University of Edinburgh, and to the political and architectural family of Adam of Blairadam, Drysdale made it his business to bring on bright youngsters likely to be of use to the kirk. Dalzel was sent to the parochial school, then to the University of Edinburgh, with the purpose of qualifying him for the ministry. Though after his graduation in 1778 he followed the course of divinity he never sought a licence to preach.

Instead Dalzel became a private tutor in the aristocratic family of Lauderdale, 'living in great retirement at Dunbar', Haddingtonshire, according to Lady Elizabeth Grant of Rothiemurchus (*Highland Lady*, 2.56). She thought him 'a learned but a singularly simple man' (ibid.). She recounted a monumental faux pas of his during a grand dinner at Lauderdale House, when the conversation turned to some current scapegrace in Scottish politics and Dalzel exclaimed: 'There has not been such a rogue unhanged since the days of the wicked Duke of Lauderdale!' (ibid., 2.75). His pupils were James Maitland (Lord Maitland, later eighth earl of Lauderdale, who was to make a name as a political economist) and his younger brother Thomas, who remained Dalzel's lifelong friend. Whatever his shortcomings Dalzel appears to have given the young Maitlands a progressive education. He took them across to the University of Glasgow to hear the radical lectures of John Millar, professor of civil law; both were to come out in public and controversial support of the French Revolution, the elder gaining the sobriquet Citizen Maitland. In 1774–5 Dalzel accompanied James to Paris and to Oxford, where they resided for a term at Trinity College.

Moves were afoot to make Dalzel professor of Greek at Edinburgh in place of the aged and incompetent Robert Hunter, who was generally held responsible for losing the university's reputation in classics to Glasgow. In 1772 Alexander Adam, rector of the high school of Edinburgh, whom Dalzel had already helped to prepare a Latin grammar, forced matters by himself starting to teach Greek to his boys. Apparently prompted by Hunter, Principal Robertson protested to the town council that this breached an exclusive privilege of the university. But his protest can only have been one of form, for it seems clear that he was in fact wielding his powers of patronage to promote Dalzel, who certainly figured in his network for the future. In the event Hunter was forced to retire from teaching and to give up half his salary and all his fees to Dalzel, now named joint professor. On Hunter's death in 1779 Dalzel became sole professor, with emoluments of £400 a year and a residence in college. He found the standard in his subject low and had to start his junior class by teaching the Greek alphabet, but he gradually improved matters. His student Henry Cockburn recalled: 'He inspired us with a vague but sincere ambition of literature, and with delicious dreams of virtue and poetry' (H. Cockburn, *Memorials of his Time*, 1856, 21). In 1789 he produced a pair of textbooks, *Analekta Hellēnika Hēssona* and *Meizona*, with annotated extracts from Greek literature which became standard in Scotland and beyond; they went through four American editions. He offered little in the way of original scholarship, though he kept abreast of German pre-eminence in his field by correspondence with the reviewer Karl August Böttiger and the philosopher Christian Gottlob Heyne.

Having achieved professional security Dalzel set with deliberation about wooing Anne Drysdale (1751–1829), the daughter of his patron; at the successful conclusion of the courtship it was said that 'with a siege of five years, he has conquered his Helen' (Innes, 58). The marriage, which took place on 28 April 1786, produced three sons and two daughters, on whom Lady Elizabeth Grant later pronounced: 'Mary Dalzel played well on the pianoforte; there was no other talent among them' (*Highland Lady*, 2.74). In 1788 Drysdale died, and Dalzel caused a surprise by applying for succession to the principal clerkship at the next year's general assembly. He had often been a lay commissioner to it but no layman had held that post before. His rival was Alexander 'Jupiter' Carlyle, minister of Inveresk, who, though of the dominant moderate party, struck many colleagues as too subservient to secular authority. While enjoying Robertson's personal support Dalzel shrewdly got himself nominated by a whig commissioner, Henry Erskine, and was thus able to mobilize enough of the opposing evangelical party to win, if only after a close

contest and a recount. The episode prompted the caricaturist John Kay to publish a likeness of 'the successful candidate' which depicts Dalzel as tall, plump, twinkling, and amiable; the caption refers to his popularity. Dalzel commemorated Drysdale in 1793 by publishing an edition of his sermons prefaced by a brief biography.

Dalzel helped to found the Royal Society of Edinburgh in 1783. It set out to unify, for political as well as intellectual purposes, sundry circles in this city of enlightenment and to provide a vehicle for distribution of patronage in acceptable quarters. Dalzel made the ideal factotum for it. The society was divided into two classes, physical and literary, and he became secretary of the literary class, which covered the humanities in general and heard papers on topics as varied as Gothic architecture, linguistic theory, and highland tradition. The transactions of the society contain two items read by Dalzel himself, 'On certain analogies observed by the Greeks in the use of their letters', and 'M. Chevalier's tableau de la plaine de Troye' (*Index to the Transactions of the Royal Society of Edinburgh*, 1890, 27–44). In 1785 Robertson made him secretary of the Senatus Academicus at Edinburgh. In the same year he became joint librarian of the university with James Robertson, professor of oriental languages, and sole keeper on the latter's death in 1795. In 1789 he obtained a grant of arms and a common seal for the university, which it had not possessed before. In 1799 he began a history of the university, which remained unfinished at his death; when it was finally published in 1862 Cosmo Innes contributed a memoir of Dalzel, which included long extracts from his correspondence.

In 1805 Dalzel resigned his chair to his assistant, George Dunbar, complaining of 'haematuria, and a sort of scarlet fever' (Innes, 239). He died on 8 December 1806 in Edinburgh, where he was buried in the graveyard of Old Greyfriars. His son John published in 1821 an edition of his lectures on the Greeks and the revival of Greek learning in Europe. No man of genius, Dalzel all the same deserved well of his university and the other institutions that he worked for.   MICHAEL FRY

Sources C. W. Innes, *Memoir of Andrew Dalzel* (1862) · R. B. Sher, *Church and university in the Scottish Enlightenment: the moderate literati of Edinburgh* (1985) · A. Chitnis, *The Scottish enlightenment and early Victorian English society* (1986) · J. Kay, *Original portraits* (1877) · *Memoirs of a highland lady: Elizabeth Grant of Rothiemurchus*, ed. A. Tod, 2 vols. (1988); repr. (1992) · *DNB*
Archives NL Scot., corresp. with R. Liston
Likenesses J. Kay, caricature, etching, repro. in Kay, *Original portraits* · H. Raeburn, oils, Scot. NPG [*see illus.*]

Dalzel [*formerly* Dalziel], **Archibald** (*b.* 1740, *d.* in or before 1811), historian and slave trader, was born in Kirkliston, Linlithgowshire, Scotland, on 23 October 1740, the eldest of the five children of William Dalziel (*d.* 1751) and his wife, Alice Linn. After being educated as a medical doctor in Edinburgh he served in the Seven Years' War as surgeon's mate (1761–2). His life was dogged by a need for money, partly because he helped support his mother and scapegrace brother William. Having been discharged from the navy in January 1763, and not liking medical practice, he told another brother, Andrew *Dalzel, 'Guinea is the only place that I have a probability of raising myself in' (Akinjogbin, 68). In March he accepted employment as a surgeon by the Company of Merchants Trading to Africa.

Dalziel was stationed at Anoumabu on the Gold Coast, and on account of his meagre salary turned to slave trading. On 26 May 1764 he remarked, 'I have at last come a little into the spirit of the slave trade and must own (perhaps it ought to be my shame) that I can now traffick in that way without remorse' (Akinjogbin, 69). In 1767 he became director of the English fort at Ouidah in the kingdom of Dahomey. Trading with the nearby Dutch and Portuguese, he accumulated capital. However, he aspired to retire in affluence in England, and he departed Ouidah in 1770, made a slave voyage to the West Indies, and returned to England in 1771, possessed of about £2000.

Less affluent than he had anticipated, Dalziel continued in the slave trade. He bought three slave ships, *Little Archie*, *Hannah*, and *Nancy*, and prospered until 1778, when he lost his capital to American privateers. That autumn he declared bankruptcy and altered his name from Dalziel to Dalzel.

During the ensuing thirteen years Dalzel attempted piracy and served as captain of a slave ship, employed by London and Liverpool merchants. The African Committee of Liverpool called him to testify to the privy council in April 1788 when it heard evidence about the slave trade. His testimony minimized mortality on slave ships, asserted that slaves were well fed, and claimed that, while changes in slave ship construction were not necessary, some regulations on behalf of slaves and crew might be adopted. The abolitionist William Wilberforce quoted from Dalzel's testimony in the House of Commons in May 1789: 'the trade, says Mr Dalzel, at this time hangs upon a thread, and the smallest matter will overthrow it' (Rawley, 321).

In 1791 the Company of Merchants Trading to Africa appointed Dalzel governor at Cape Coast Castle, its headquarters on the Gold Coast. In this capacity he resisted Danish efforts to expand territorial possessions and Dutch efforts to monopolize the Portuguese trade. He unsuccessfully urged that the British west African stations be made colonial territories. During the years 1797–1803 the London ship *Governor Dalzel* made successive voyages from Cape Coast to American destinations.

In 1802 Dalzel, having resigned as governor and returned to England, published his *The History of Dahomy*. He drew in part on his experience, but also on William Snelgrave's *A New Account of Guinea* (1754), Robert Norris's *Memoirs of the Reign of Bossa Ahadee, King of Dahomy* (1789), and others. His *History* was both a historical compilation and propaganda against abolition of the slave trade. He argued that the slave trade saved African victims from human sacrifice and slaughter. He also sought to exonerate Europeans from charges that they incited African wars to secure slaves, asserting that Africans had long engaged in wars among themselves. Although it is based on borrowed sources and is biased, the *History* remains important for its contents, pleasant style, and influence.

In his final years Dalzel became the owner of the *Thames*, which voyaged to Africa between 1805 and 1808, and *Chalmers*, which in 1805 went to Jamaica and in 1806, 1807, and 1808 made voyages from London to Africa.

Although he never married, Dalzel had close associations with three women. In 1794 he referred to 'Mrs. D and child' being in 'a favourable' way (Akinjogbin, 76–7). Six years later his son Edward went to Africa with him, employed by the company as a writer. Dalzel's life was marked by loyalty to his family. He died a bankrupt no later than 1811. Active as a mariner, shipowner, officer, and historian, he was a significant figure in the last years of the slave trade, and his *History of Dahomy* earned for him an enduring place in the trade's history.

JAMES A. RAWLEY

Sources A. Akinjogbin, 'Archibald: slave trader and historian of Dahomey', *Journal of African History*, 7 (1966), 67–78 · J. A. Rawley, 'Further light on Archibald Dalzel', *International Journal of African Studies*, 17 (1984), 317–23 · L. K. Waldman, 'An unnoticed aspect of Archibald Dalzel's *The history of Dahomey*', *Journal of African History*, 6 (1965), 185–92 · J. D. Fage, 'Introduction', in A. Dalzel, *The history of Dahomy* (1967), 4–22 · PRO, ADM 68/205; B/T 6/3; CO 142/19 · *Lloyd's Register of Shipping* (c.1760–1808) · *Journal of the commissioners for trade and plantations*, [vols. 13–14]: *From January 1768 to May 1782* (1937–8) · 'Slave trade', *Parl. papers*, vol. 61 · *British Sessional Papers: Accounts and Papers*, 24 (1789) [slave trade] · F. E. Sanderson, 'The Liverpool delegates and Sir William Dolben's bill', *Transactions of the Historic Society of Lancashire and Cheshire*, 124 (1972), 57–84 · C. D. Rice, 'Archibald Dalzel, the Scottish intelligentsia, and the problem of slavery', *SHR*, 62 (1983), 121–36 · bap. reg. Scot.

Archives U. Edin. L., special collections division, letters, mainly to his brother Andrew, DK. 7. 52.

Dalzell, Nicol Alexander (1817–1877), botanist, was born at Edinburgh on 21 April 1817, the son of Alexander Dalzell, a clerk in the exchequer office, and his wife, Marion, *née* Hall. He was educated at Edinburgh high school and in 1830 proceeded to Edinburgh University, graduating MA in 1834. From 1834 to 1837 he studied divinity under Thomas Chalmers, but his love of science induced him to give up the intention of entering the ministry. In 1836 he joined the Botanical Society in Edinburgh, one of its earliest members. In 1841 he was induced to visit Bombay, where, in the same year, he was appointed assistant commissioner of customs, salt and opium, in which capacity he published his *Short Review of Mr George Plowden's Report on the Salt Revenue of Bombay* (1856). He still pursued his botanical studies, contributing frequently to Sir William Hooker's *Journal of Botany* and to the *Proceedings of the Botanical Society of Edinburgh*. Seeking a new challenge, he went to Australia in 1853, but returned two years later to India.

From 1858 to 1860 Dalzell was forest ranger in Sind, and, on the retirement of Alexander Gibson in 1862, became conservator of forests and superintendent of botanic gardens in the Bombay presidency. His 'Contributions to the botany of western India', published through Hooker in the *Journal of Botany* (1850–52), formed the most complete account of the remarkable flora of that district at that time. In 1861 he published *The Bombay Flora*, which bore also the name of Gibson, who volunteered to bear the expense of publication. This work remained the only general descriptive work on the vegetation of western

India for forty years, and contained descriptions and scientific names of upwards of two hundred plants new to science, illustrated with 170 watercolours, the work of a Portuguese–Indian artist. Many of the species were later found to be unreliable. Dalzell's pamphlet *Observations on the Influence of Forests* (1863) was important 'in establishing the theoretical desiccationist and climatic rationales for an all-India forest-conservation system' (Grove, 457). Dalzell suffered progressively from malaria, and he retired to Britain on a pension in 1870. He died at his home, Williamfield House, Portobello, Edinburgh, on 18 December 1877. Some time before his retirement he had lost all his savings in the failure of the Bank of Hindostan, China, and Japan, and when his pension ceased on his death his widow, Emily Harriet (*née* Duthy), and six children were left practically destitute. This prompted his relative Pulteney Mein Dalzell, together with several friends, including Hooker, to petition the secretary of state for India on their behalf for a pension.

Dalzell was described by his contemporaries as a particularly competent and committed forestry officer, and Hooker stated that his knowledge and the fidelity of his botanical descriptions were so remarkable that he was selected as one of the intended authors of the *Flora of British India* (1872–97), a position that Dalzell was forced to decline owing to his failing health. Dalzell was elected a fellow of the Royal Society of Edinburgh in 1862 and was a fellow of the University of Bombay. In addition to the publications already mentioned he published nine papers on botanical subjects, six of which appeared in the *Journal of the Proceedings of the Linnean Society*. A tropical aquatic herb of the Podostemaceae family, *Dalzellia* Wight, was named after him.   ROBERT HUNT, *rev.* ANDREW GROUT

Sources P. M. Dalzell, *The memorial of Pulteney Mein Dalzell … on behalf of the widow and family of the late Nicol Alexander Dalzell* (1878) [copy in library, Royal Botanic Garden, Edinburgh] · H. J. Noltie, *The Dapuri drawings: Alexander Gibson and the Bombay Botanic Gardens* (2002) · *The Athenaeum* (2 Feb 1878), 162 · matriculation rolls, arts and divinity, U. Edin. L., special collections division, university archives · R. H. Grove, *Green imperialism: colonial expansion, tropical island Edens, and the origins of environmentalism, 1600–1860* (1995) · private information (1888) · d. cert.
Archives Botanical Society of Edinburgh, plants · NHM, drawings · RBG Kew, herbarium, specimens · Warwick Archaeological and Natural History Society, plants | RBG Kew, Hooker MSS, archives
Wealth at death £356 14*s*. 0*d*.: confirmation, 28 Jan 1878, *CCI*

Dalzell [Dalyell], **Robert**, **first earl of Carnwath** (*d.* 1654), royalist nobleman, was the eldest son of Robert Dalyell, first Lord Dalyell (*d.* 1635/6), and Margaret, daughter of Sir William Crichton of Clunie. That his parents' marriage contract was dated 1580 indicates the earliest possible date of his birth. He succeeded to the title of Lord Dalyell in 1635 or 1636.

Royalism, 1638–1645 In the revolt against Charles I's religious policies in Scotland that began in July 1637 Dalzell at first supported the dissidents, signing a supplication to the king in November and the national covenant about February 1638. However, he soon switched to support for the king, and was admitted to the Scottish privy council

on 30 June 1638. During the first bishops' war, in 1639, he joined the king in York, being created earl of Carnwath on 21 April for his loyalty. When Charles I came to Scotland in 1641 to make a settlement with the rebel covenanters Carnwath was with him, but on 17 August he was excluded from parliament. None the less, on 17 September he was nominated as a member of a proposed new compromise privy council. He soon revealed himself as one of the wilder royalists. Among the allegations accompanying the Incident, a supposed plot to kidnap or assassinate the marquesses of Argyll and Hamilton for treachery, was testimony that Carnwath had said on 11 October that Scotland had three kings and that two of them—Argyll and Hamilton—ought 'to want the head', meaning be killed (*Historical Works of Balfour*, 3.101). He was therefore left out of the new council, and as the king heaped rewards on covenanters, hoping to buy their future support, Carnwath remarked bitterly that 'he would go to Ireland, and join … the rebels there, and then he was sure the king would prefer him' (*Memoirs of Henry Guthry*, 109).

In January 1643 Carnwath was with Charles at court in Oxford when commissioners from Scotland arrived for talks concerning the civil war between the king and the English parliament. The earl denounced them to the king as men who had rebelled and ruined the king in Scotland, and who now sought to co-operate with English rebels. When in June 1643 the covenanters held a convention of estates to consider intervention in the English war they remembered this insult, and in addition had evidence that Carnwath was involved in royalist plots. Carnwath boldly attended the convention, but on 24 June he was ordered, for having 'maliciouslie traduced the proceedings of this kingdome' (*APS*, 6/1.6), to surrender for arrest within twelve hours. He failed to appear, leading to a fine of £10,000 Scots (about £850 sterling) being imposed on him, and rejoined royalist forces in England. He fought with them against the Scottish army which entered England in January 1644, and in April he took part in the marquess of Montrose's royalist raid on Dumfries. The Scottish parliament began proceedings to forfeit his property and title in July, but agreed to postpone the matter after his son and heir, Gavin Dalzell (Carnwath had married Christian, daughter of Sir William Douglas of Hawick), indicated that he was prepared to co-operate with the covenanters. When Carnwath was forfaulted (forfeited) on 25 February 1645, therefore, his title and lands were transferred to Gavin in return for a payment of 100,000 merks.

The battle of Naseby According to an account written much later by the earl of Clarendon, Carnwath (who in royalist eyes retained his title) played a disastrous role in the battle of Naseby on 14 June 1645. As Charles I was about to charge at the head of the cavalry reserve Carnwath, who was riding beside him, judged that such intervention was too dangerous and

> on a sudden laid his hand on the bridle of the King's horse, and swearing two or three full-mouthed Scots' oaths … said 'Will you go upon your death in an instant?' and, before his majesty understood what he would have, turned his horse round.   (Clarendon, *Hist. rebellion*, 4.45)

Assuming the king's swinging away from action indicated orders to withdraw, his cavalry also turned from the battle, and the king was carried off in what quickly became disorderly flight.

The implication—that this decisive battle was lost through the act of an over-protective (if foul-mouthed) Scot—is perhaps too convenient to be entirely plausible, as it both saves the king from any allegation of fleeing instead of fighting, and suggests that the royalists would have been victorious had it not been for this unfortunate trifle. No other source supports Clarendon's allegation, and even if Carnwath did act as alleged his judgement could be argued to have been sound. The battle was probably already lost, and the king being killed or captured would have turned what was already a major defeat into something far worse.

Later life, 1645–1654 Carnwath served under Lord Digby in the north of England in the autumn of 1645. After defeat in October at Sherborne in Yorkshire, Digby retreated to Dumfries in Scotland, hoping to join up with the marquess of Montrose's army, but on learning that it had been scattered he disbanded his force. Digby, along with Carnwath and other officers, escaped first to the Isle of Man and then to Ireland. Nothing is known of Carnwath's activities during the following five years.

In May 1650 the covenanters, negotiating for the exiled Charles II to come to Scotland, sought to exclude former royalist enemies, and Carnwath was listed among those forbidden to enter the country with the king until they had satisfied church and state for their offences. However, he landed with the king in June, and though he was ordered to leave he probably remained until, faced with English invasion, the crumbling covenanter regime yielded to increasing pressure to allow royalists to serve in the army. On 31 March 1651 the question of restoring him to his title (though not his estates) was raised, and this was agreed to on 3 June. He took part in the invasion of England later in the year which ended in disaster at the battle of Worcester on 3 September, and he was then imprisoned in the Tower of London. The poor state of his health led to Carnwath's being given liberty to walk within the Tower, and in June 1652 he was licensed to go to Epsom for six weeks to drink the waters there. He was still in the Tower in March 1653, and though he was offered bail his place of burial (St Margaret's Church, Westminster) suggests that he was still under restraint when he died in 1654. He was buried on 21 June. It was, presumably, in these last years of semi-imprisonment that Carnwath married Katherine, daughter of John Abington of Gloucester, as his second wife. Six years after his death she remarried, then being still only in her mid-twenties, and she lived on until 1712.

Charles I's favours to Carnwath, and his presence at the king's side at Naseby, suggest that he had that fastidious man's friendship, yet all surviving comments on his character suggest that there was something unsavoury about him. According to his covenanting enemy Robert Baillie, he was 'a monster of profanitie' (*Letters and Journals of Robert Baillie*, 2.78). The royalist Henry Guthry accepted that Carnwath was more faithful to Charles I than many, but added 'whatsoever his personal qualities might be' (*Memoirs of Henry Guthry*, 109). Clarendon attributes foul oaths to him, and his alleged words during the 1641 Incident confirm at least that he was outspoken. Whether his defects went beyond bad language remains a mystery. He is a man only rescued from obscurity by the decisive but disastrous action he is said to have taken at the battle of Naseby.

DAVID STEVENSON

Sources GEC, *Peerage* · *Scots peerage* · *Reg. PCS*, 1st ser. · *APS* · *The historical works of Sir James Balfour*, ed. J. Haig, 4 vols. (1824–5) · Clarendon, *Hist. rebellion* · *The memoirs of Henry Guthry, late bishop*, ed. G. Crawford, 2nd edn (1748) · *The letters and journals of Robert Baillie*, ed. D. Laing, 3 vols. (1841–2) · J. Spalding, *Memorialls of the trubles in Scotland and in England, AD 1624 – AD 1645*, ed. J. Stuart, 2 vols., Spalding Club, [21, 23] (1850–51) · John, earl of Rothes, *A relation of proceedings concerning the affairs of the Kirk of Scotland*, Bannatyne Club, 37 (1830) · D. H. Fleming, 'Scotland's supplication … 18th October 1637', *Proceedings of the Society of Antiquaries of Scotland*, 60 (1925–6), 314–83

Dalzell, Robert (1661/2–1758), army officer, is supposed to have descended from a branch of the Dalzell family, earls of Carnwath, whose estates and titles were forfeited (though later restored) by the sixth earl through his involvement in the rising of 1715. He began his military career in January 1682 as ensign in the foot company of his kinsman Sir John Dalzell of Glenae (see muster rolls of the earl of Mar's regiment). Mar's regiment (later the Royal Scots Fusiliers) came into England in 1688.

In February 1694 Dalzell was commissioned captain in Sir John Gibson's regiment (28th foot), newly formed at Portsmouth where Gibson was lieutenant-governor; Dalzell subsequently married Gibson's daughter, Anne Mary (some time before 1698). After serving in Flanders, the West Indies, and Newfoundland, Gibson's regiment was disbanded in 1698, except for a detachment in Newfoundland. It was raised again in March 1702, Dalzell, like Gibson himself, reverting to his former rank in the regiment.

On 2 July 1702 Dalzell was appointed town-major of Portsmouth, an appointment worth £70 a year, which he retained for many years. Gibson's regiment went from Portsmouth to Ireland in 1702, and in 1704 Gibson sold the colonelcy to Sampson de Lalo, a Huguenot officer in the British service. In the same year Dalzell was promoted lieutenant-colonel of the regiment. De Lalo's regiment, as it was now called, joined Marlborough's army, and under the acting command of Dalzell served at the recapture of Huy and the forcing of the enemy's lines at Neer Hespen in 1705, and at the battle of Ramillies in 1706. De Lalo exchanged the colonelcy with John, Lord Mordaunt, on 26 June 1706, and under the name of Mordaunt's the regiment, still under Dalzell's command, went to Spain, and was one of those cut up at the disastrous battle of Almanza on 24 April 1707. Dalzell reformed the regiment in England, and it returned to Spain in April 1708 where it saw action at Tarragona before being brought home again. In April 1709 Dalzell became colonel of a newly raised regiment for Spain, which was taken prisoner at Brihuega (1710) and disbanded in 1712. He was made brigadier-general in 1711, and major-general 1715, in which year his appointment as town-major of Portsmouth was renewed. Dalzell became lieutenant-general in 1727; colonel of the 33rd regiment of foot in 1730, in succession to General Hawley; commander of the forces in north Britain in 1732; colonel of the 38th foot (in succession to Charles Spencer, third duke of Marlborough) in 1739; and general in 1745. He retired by the sale of his regimental commissions in 1749.

In 1720 Dalzell was appointed treasurer of the Sun Fire Office, the first London insurance house to undertake fire risks. Dalzell was one of a group of Scottish investors who took control of the business following the collapse of the South Sea Bubble, and retained his position as treasurer and later chairman until his death nearly forty years later. He lived at the business's premises at Craig's Court, Charing Cross, from 1726 onwards. His son Gibson Dalzell (b. March 1698) was a director of the company from 1746 until his death in Jamaica in 1755. He was buried at St Martin-in-the-Fields, London.

Dalzell died at Craig's Court, London, on 14 October 1758, aged ninety-six. He too was buried in the church of St Martin-in-the-Fields. Dalzell's wife and children had predeceased him, and his only surviving descendants at his death were the two children of his son Gibson Dalzell: Robert, of Tidmarsh Manor House, Berkshire, and Frances, who married the Hon. George Duff, son of the first Earl Fife.　　　H. M. CHICHESTER, rev. JONATHAN SPAIN

Sources C. Dalton, ed., *English army lists and commission registers, 1661–1714*, 3 (1896) · C. Dalton, ed., *English army lists and commission registers, 1661–1714*, 4 (1898) · C. Dalton, ed., *English army lists and commission registers, 1661–1714*, 5 (1902) · C. Dalton, ed., *English army lists and commission registers, 1661–1714*, 6 (1904) · D. S. Daniell [A. S. Daniell], *Cap of honour: the story of the Gloucestershire regiment* (1951) · P. G. M. Dickson, *The Sun Insurance office, 1710–1860* (1960) · *GM*, 1st ser., 28 (1758), 504 · muster rolls of the earl of Mar's regiment, royal Scots fusiliers (21st), 1689–99, NRA8400
Archives Bodl. Oxf., corresp. with sixth Baron North · Bodl. Oxf., letters to Lord North · GL, records of the Sun Fire Office, incl. board and committee minutes
Likenesses engraving, 1888 (aged eighty-four; after painting at Glenae) · P. Filius, line engraving (after C. Alexander), NPG

Dalzell [Dalyell], **Robert, fifth earl of Carnwath** (c.1687–1737), Jacobite army officer, was the eldest son of Sir John Dalzell, second baronet (d. 1689), of Glenae, Dumfriesshire, and his wife, Harriet, second daughter of Sir William Murray of Stanhope. He was educated at the University of Cambridge. He succeeded his father as third baronet in 1689, and in 1702, on the death of John Dalyell, fourth earl of Carnwath, his second cousin once removed, he succeeded as fifth earl, though the property of Carnwath had previously been sold by the third earl to Sir George Lockhart.

A nonjuring episcopalian by family background, Carnwath was prominent among the Jacobite leadership in southern Scotland and may well have been active before the rising of 1715. In the spring of that year he joined the viscount of Kenmure (his brother-in-law) and the earl of Nithsdale at a race meeting at Lochmaben where they formed a Jacobite association. Though Carnwath appeared on a list of Jacobite leaders who attended the earl of Mar's famous hunt at Braemar (27 August 1715) preparatory to the raising of the Pretender's (James Stuart's) standard, most modern historians doubt his presence there. After wavering, Carnwath joined the rising. Though some attributed his decision to the influence of his mother and his sister, it is likely that his hand was forced by the passage of the Act for Encouraging Loyalty in Scotland. A warrant that accompanied the act named Carnwath and forty-one other suspected Jacobites and required them to report to Edinburgh and post bond for their good behaviour. Facing a choice between imprisonment (the fate of those who did surrender) and participation in the rising, Carnwath chose the latter.

Carnwath's role in the Jacobite rising of 1715 was unspectacular. He raised a troop of horse and joined the forces under Kenmure, which assembled at Moffat on 11 October. On arrival at Kelso, William Irvine, his episcopalian chaplain, preached the same sermon he had given twenty-six years before in the presence of Viscount Dundee. Carnwath and Lord Wintoun were dispatched to take Dumfries; but Kenmure abandoned the attack upon learning the town was well defended and led his forces into England, where they combined with those of the English Jacobites under Thomas Forster and the earl of Derwentwater. Under Forster's overall leadership they moved south but halted, and after a brief engagement surrendered at Preston (14 November 1715).

Carnwath, along with Kenmure and other noble leaders of the rebellion, was imprisoned in the Tower of London and impeached on 18 January 1716 before the House of Lords for high treason. Carnwath pleaded guilty and did not attempt to mitigate his actions, but threw himself on the king's mercy. He was condemned to death but was respited, partly through the intercession of the princess of Wales. Ultimately he was pardoned under the Act of Indemnity passed in 1717. His estates and titles forfeit, Dalzell remained for a while in contact with the Jacobite court. In 1718 he asked that he be allowed to 'come over', but was discouraged because of the state of the Pretender's finances. He remained in Britain and ultimately became a model reprieved prisoner. His situation was made more palatable by his success in recovering his lands (valued at £864 at the time of forfeiture). Originally assigned by the court of session to the administration of his mother, they were eventually sold to his lawyer, who returned the bulk of them to Dalzell in 1734–5.

Dalzell's private life was marked by four marriages: first, on 19 January 1710, to Lady Grace Montgomerie (d. 1713), third daughter of the ninth earl of Eglinton, with whom he had two daughters; second, on 3 June 1720, to Grizel (d. 1723), daughter of Alexander Urquhart of Newhall, with whom he had a son, Alexander, who succeeded to the estates; third, on 15 November 1728, to Margaret (d. 1730), daughter of John Hamilton of Bangour, with whom he had a daughter; and fourth, on 19 June 1735, to Margaret (bap. 1696, d. 1758), third daughter of Thomas Vincent of Bamburgh Grange, Yorkshire, with whom he had a son. Dalzell died on 4 August 1737 at Kirkmichael, Dumfriesshire.　　　WILLIAM C. LOWE

Sources J. Baynes, *The Jacobite rising of 1715* (1970) · A. Tayler and H. Tayler, *1715: the story of the rising* (1936) · *Calendar of the Stuart papers belonging to his majesty the king, preserved at Windsor Castle*, 7 vols., HMC, 56 (1902–23) · *The manuscripts of the House of Lords*, new ser., 12 vols. (1900–77), vol. 12 · *Report on the manuscripts of the earl of Mar and Kellie*, HMC, 60 (1904) · D. Szechi, *The Jacobites: Britain and Europe, 1688–1788* (1994) · B. Lenman, *The Jacobite risings in Britain, 1689–1746* (1980) · C. Sinclair-Stevenson, *Inglorious rebellion: the Jacobite risings of 1708, 1715 and 1719* (1971) · *Scots peerage*, vol. 2 and corrigenda · GEC, *Peerage* · *Letters of George Lockhart of Carnwath, 1698–1732*, ed. D. Szechi, Scottish History Society, 5th ser., 2 (1989) · R. Arnold, *Northern lights: the story of Lord Derwentwater* (1959)
Likenesses J. B. Medina, Indian ink and wash drawing, BM
Wealth at death estates valued at £864 p.a. when forfeited for treason; £11,833 principal claimed against estate: *Manuscripts of the House of Lords*, HMC, new ser., 17 (1977), vol. 12, pp. 4033, 4114 · later reacquired most lands

Dalziel family (*per.* 1840–1905), wood-engravers, established the firm known as the Dalziel brothers, one of the most important providers of illustrations for books and magazines of the mid-Victorian period. The prime source of information about the firm is given in *The Brothers Dalziel: a Record* (1901).

Alexander Dalziel (1781–1832) and his wife, Elizabeth Hills (1785–1853), were the parents of twelve children; seven of their eight sons were artists, four of whom worked in the family firm. Alexander Dalziel 'spent a great part of his time in horticultural pursuits, and in middle life took up art as a profession' (Dalziel and Dalziel, 1), and his talent was inherited by most of the couple's children. William (1805–1873) was a heraldic and decorative painter; Robert (1810–1842) was a portrait painter; Alexander John (1814–1836) worked as a black and white artist; George (1815–1902), Edward (1817–1905), and Thomas (1823–1906) were the core of the London firm; and John (1822–1869) worked for the firm until poor health compelled his retirement in 1868 to Drigg, Cumberland. The youngest son, Davison Octavian (*b.* 1825), devoted himself to commerce. Of the daughters, Margaret Jane (1819–1894) also worked for the firm. **George Dalziel** (1815–1902), draughtsman and wood-engraver, the founder and leader of the London firm, was born on 1 December 1815, at Wooler, Northumberland, and was educated at Newcastle upon Tyne. He went to London early in 1835 as pupil to the wood-engraver Charles Gray, with whom he remained for four years. He then set up independently, and in 1840 was joined by his brother Edward at 48 Albert Street, Mornington Crescent. Work came to them partly through association with more established wood-engravers. Through Ebenezer Landells, they engraved for the early numbers of *Punch* (started in 1841) and the *Illustrated London News* (started in 1842), and were thus well placed to participate in the great flowering of the English pictorial press. Their Tyneside origins led them to engrave for the artist William Harvey, who hailed from Newcastle, and who introduced them to the publisher Charles Knight, another pioneer in the use of wood-engraved illustrations in popular works. Other publishers with whom they worked were Cadell of Edinburgh (on the Abbotsford Edition of Sir Walter Scott's novels), Joseph Cundall of Bond Street, and David Bogue. In 1850 they began an association with the publisher George Routledge, which was to underpin their later success. They were joined in their wood-engraving business by their sister Margaret in 1851, and by their brother John in 1852 and Thomas in 1860. Their business address changed to 4 Camden Street North, Camden Town (thus cited in Post Office directories from 1854). George married Mary Ann, the daughter of Josiah Rumball of Wisbech, in 1846, but they had no children.

The family's range of work was wide, and may be seen in the forty-nine volumes (now in the British Museum) in which they filed proofs of their engravings between 1839 and 1893. Illustrations for magazines, trade catalogues, and technical publications are here (the Dalziels supervised all the illustrations in the *Art Journal Illustrated Catalogue* of the Great Exhibition, 1851), as well as those for the artistic books for which they became famous. They became known as the largest firm of wood-engravers in London. Wood-engraving as a process involves intricate work by an individual engraver on a small block of wood. Inevitably, therefore, the organization of the craft of wood-engraving was small-scale; many wood-engravers were self-employed. The scope for making economies of scale was very limited. It was hardly possible to do more than allow engravers to specialize in, say, figures or foliage, so that blocks could be passed from engraver to engraver as necessary, slightly speeding up the process. In expanding their business from the original family co-operative, then, the Dalziels simply employed more engravers. They also took pupils (fondly remembered in the *Record*) and made a point of teaching them drawing as well as engraving. More venturesomely, in 1857 they set up their own printing shop, the Camden Press, which enabled them better to control their output and to initiate projects. To accommodate this they moved premises to 53 Camden High Street (renumbered 110 in 1863).

As is clear from their *Record*, the Dalziels prided themselves on the artistic illustrations they engraved and on the relationships they established with artists. At the start they engraved work by English caricaturists such as George Cruikshank, John Leech, Richard Doyle, and Kenny Meadows; by established artists such as William Harvey and Sir John Gilbert; and by artists influenced by German style, such as John Tenniel and F. R. Pickersgill. As they entered on 'the Golden Period of Illustration' in the 1860s they became particularly associated with Pre-Raphaelite book illustration. If such a category really exists, it can be said to begin with the edition of Tennyson's *Poems*, published by Edward Moxon in 1857, which included illustrations by Dante Gabriel Rossetti, William Holman Hunt, and John Everett Millais, as well as by other artists who did not attempt the entranced, medievalizing scenes usually regarded as Pre-Raphaelite. The Dalziels engraved some of the blocks for the Moxon Tennyson. Their collaboration with Millais endured, and included his illustrations for Trollope's *Orley Farm* (1861), *Framley Parsonage* (1862), and *The Small House at Allington* (1864). The most notable collaboration with Millais was *The Parables of Our Lord*, a six-year project which was published in 1864. A similar but even more extended project was an illustrated

Bible. The illustrations for this were never completely assembled, but sixty-two that were to hand were published in 1881 as *Dalziel's Bible Gallery*. This included work by Millais, Holman Hunt, Ford Madox Brown, E. J. Poynter, Lord Leighton, Edward Burne-Jones, Simeon Solomon, and Frederick Sandys, and can be seen as a Pre-Raphaelite work rather out of due time. The Dalziels also engraved work by Arthur Hughes, who might be seen as the children's Pre-Raphaelite.

Many of the books with engravings by the Dalziels were conceived primarily as illustrated books, and were commissioned, financed, and produced by the brothers, though they appeared over the names of other publishers. Most prominent among these were Routledge and their partners, Warne, who had a close relationship with the Dalziels, concentrating on the business side of publishing, and leaving the art direction to the engravers. The Dalziels' ventures (usually lavishly produced in gold-blocked, embossed cloth bindings, and called fine art gift books) often took the form of anthologies (of text by various writers and illustrations by various artists, the illustrations sometimes being reused in different contexts), which have been criticized as lacking a unified aesthetic. Among them were *The Home Affections Pourtrayed by the Poets* (ed. C. Mackay, 1858), *Summer Time in the Country* (ed. R. A. Willmott, 1858), *English Sacred Poetry* (ed. Willmott, 1862), *A Round of Days* (1866), *The Spirit of Praise* (1866), *Wayside Posies* (1867), *Golden Thoughts from Golden Fountains* (1867), *Touches of Nature* (1867), and *Picture Posies* (1874). There were also texts by a single author with illustrations from many hands, such as the poems of Wordsworth (1859) and Jean Ingelow (1867). Sometimes a single artist's vision of a whole work was conveyed, as in the edition of Shakespeare (1858–61) illustrated by Sir John Gilbert, Bunyan's *Pilgrim's Progress* (1863) and Defoe's *Robinson Crusoe* (1864), both illustrated by J. D. Watson, and Cervantes' *Don Quixote* (1866), illustrated by Arthur Boyd Houghton.

The Dalziels also contributed engravings of the work of their stable of artists to magazines, such as *Good Words* and the *Cornhill Magazine* (both begun in 1860) and the *Sunday Magazine* (begun 1865), which were important showcases for 'sixties' illustration, and assisted in the emergence of several new artists with marked individual talents: Arthur Boyd Houghton, G. J. Pinwell, Frederick Sandys, M. J. Lawless, J. W. North, Fred Walker, and Frederick Barnard. Most of these contributed to another major project, the Household Edition of Dickens's works, published by Chapman and Hall (1871–9). The Dalziels' publications in the 1860s became esteemed and collectable, and they exhibited wood-engravings at the Royal Academy in 1861–3, 1866, 1869, and 1870.

Like all wood-engravers in the mid-Victorian period, the Dalziels practised facsimile engraving wherever possible: when an artist had provided an original drawing with clear black lines, the engravers reproduced those lines exactly. When artists introduced tone, with pencil or brushwork with Chinese white, the engravers' task was more difficult, and they developed various types of shading, which had their own appeal. If there was anything in common between the later illustrators, it was perhaps a tendency to produce designs which, while fully naturalistic, had a strong element of silhouette and pattern, and which were tight within their frames (almost as if they had been cropped down from larger, more expansive designs). Blocks engraved by the firm were signed 'DALZIEL' in sloping script capitals.

The Dalziels became wealthy and prominent people, living in impressive villas in Hampstead and Primrose Hill. They seem to have conducted a sort of salon for their artists: George Du Maurier, when invited to a swell private party, said (rather disparagingly) that he 'would sooner far be invited to the gin and whisky parties of the brothers Dalziel … where the Queen's English is solemnly murdered every other Saturday, I believe' (*Young George Du Maurier … Letters, 1860–67*, 1951, 150). In due course, however, the kind of illustration which the Dalziels promoted was superseded. More importantly, the rise of photomechanical engraving in the 1880s undermined the wood-engraving trade. In their later years, the Dalziels worked largely for comic magazines, some of which they owned, such as *Fun*, *Hood's Comic Annual*, and *Judy*. The style of illustration in many of the comic papers was not too far removed from the style of the sixties illustrators (as the work of Du Maurier in *Punch* demonstrates), but when the Dalziels brought out *Ally Sloper's Half-Holiday* in 1884 they were undoubtedly falling short of their previous standards. However, these papers did offer scope for the literary talent of George Dalziel, who enjoyed writing verses and stories for them. He published three volumes of poems. By 1893 the Dalziels were bankrupt, but the printing press carried on in business until 1905.

George Dalziel died on 4 August 1902 at Dalkeith, 107 Fellows Road, Hampstead, where he had lived since 1900, and was buried in Highgate cemetery. **Edward Dalziel** (1817–1905), draughtsman and wood-engraver, was the fifth son of Alexander and Elizabeth. He was born at Wooler, Northumberland, on 5 December 1817 and educated in Newcastle upon Tyne. Following his brother George to London in 1839, he joined him in his trade as wood-engraver and helped to create the firm. While George was the senior member of the firm, Edward was the driving force. 'The extension and development of our transactions and the carrying out of many of the fine art works which we published, is unquestionably due to my brother Edward', declared Thomas Dalziel (White, 178). Edward trained as an artist at the life school at Clipstone Street Academy, where his fellow students included his close friend Charles Keene and John Tenniel, who was later to bring to the firm his illustrations for Lewis Carroll's *Alice in Wonderland* (1865) and *Through the Looking Glass* (1871). In his leisure time Edward painted in oils and watercolour, exhibiting at the British Institution in 1841, the Royal Academy in 1865 and 1866, and other galleries. The London addresses from which he sent in were 34 Edward Street, Hampstead Road, in 1841, and 10 St George's Square in the 1860s. In 1847 he married Jane Gurden (*d.* 1873), with whom he had five sons and four daughters.

Dalziel contributed designs to some of the books illustrated by the firm, such as William Cullen Bryant's *Poems* (1857?), *Dalziels' Arabian Nights* (1864), and Robert Buchanan's *Ballad Stories of the Affections* (1866) and *North Coast* (1868). While competent, his designs are slightly stilted and laboured, an effect which is turned to advantage in his illustrations of chubby, doll-like children. He played the part of patron to the newer artists whom the firm launched: his private collection (sold at Christies on 19 June 1886) included substantial groups of work, many obtained 'direct from the artist', by Arthur Boyd Houghton, J. D. Watson, J. W. North, G. J. Pinwell, and Fred Walker. He recorded that his recreations were 'the love of art work' and 'wandering about seeking all that would give a higher appreciation of the beauties of nature' (*Who's Who*). He died on 25 March 1905 at Dalkeith, 107 Fellows Road, Hampstead, where he had lived since 1900, and was buried in Highgate cemetery.

Thomas Bolton Gilchrist Septimus Dalziel (1823–1906), painter and draughtsman, was the seventh son of Alexander and Elizabeth. He was born at Wooler, Northumberland, on 9 May 1823 and educated in Newcastle upon Tyne. He was apprenticed to a copperplate engraver, but preferred to work as an illustrator, independently in London from 1843, and as part of the family firm from 1860 (though he began contributing to the books they illustrated from 1857). On 5 July 1856 he married Louisa, the daughter of Charles Gurden, a cook; they had five sons and three daughters and Louisa survived him.

Thomas was the most talented artist among the Dalziel brothers. His illustrations were more fluent and confident than those of Edward, but he tended to be influenced stylistically by other artists. In *The Poets of the Nineteenth Century* (ed. R. A. Willmott, 1857) and *The Home Affections Pourtrayed by the Poets* (ed. C. Mackay, 1858) his figure designs resemble those of John Gilbert or James Godwin, and his landscapes those of Birket Foster or Harrison Weir. In these illustrations the entire surface of his blocks was intricately worked over, but as bolder effects became more common in the firm's work his style became looser. For example, his landscapes in *A Round of Days* (1866) have more supple lines and more white space. His major work of illustration was for Bunyan's *Pilgrim's Progress* (published by Ward, Lock, and Tyler in 1865), for which he designed all the hundred small, strong engravings. Mostly placed among text and unframed, these put a premium on striking silhouette. His contributions to *Dalziels' Arabian Nights* (1865) are freely drawn and often composed with a poised and pleasing irregularity, rivalling those in the same volume (for which several artists supplied designs) by Arthur Boyd Houghton. Both Thomas and Houghton used Houghton's collection of oriental curios and costume when preparing these illustrations. Thomas was also a painter, exhibiting at the Royal Academy in the 1860s. Included in his son Herbert's studio sale (see below), and illustrated in the catalogue, were some fifteen of his highly finished watercolours of land- and seascapes, as well as many drawings. Thomas died on 17 March 1906 at Wooler House, Beltinge Road, in Herne Bay, where he

had lived since 1893, and was buried in Highgate cemetery.

Edward Dalziel's sons kept the firm going into the second generation. Edward Gurden Dalziel (1849–1888) was a painter, exhibiting often at the Royal Academy, and an illustrator, contributing designs to the Household Edition of Dickens's works (1871–9) and to comic and other magazines. Gilbert (1853–1930) learned wood-engraving with the firm, and studied art at South Kensington and the Slade School, but became more of a journalist than an artist; he worked on the family's comic papers and became the proprietor and editor of *Judy* and several other such publications. Unmarried, he recorded as his recreation 'the collection of art treasures and curios, especially Indiaproofs of the Dalziels' wood-engravings' (*Who's Who*). After the wood-engraving business went bankrupt in 1893, Edward's other two sons, Harvey Robert (*b.* 1855) and Charles Davison (*b.* 1857), carried on the Camden Press as Dalziel & Co. until it closed in 1905.

Thomas Dalziel's sons Herbert (*b.* 1858) and Owen (*b.* 1860) were both painters, contributing frequently to Royal Academy exhibitions in the 1880s and 1890s. Many of Herbert's landscapes were illustrated in the catalogue of the sale of the contents of his studio at Sothebys, Belgravia, on 16 May 1978.

ANTHONY BURTON

Sources [G. Dalziel and E. Dalziel], *The brothers Dalziel: a record of fifty years' work … 1840–1890* (1901) · P. Goldman, *Victorian illustrated books, 1850–1870, the heyday of wood-engraving: the Robin de Beaumont collection* (1994) · *Water-colour drawings and modern pictures of Edward Dalziel Esq.* (1886) [sale catalogue, Christies, 19 June 1886] · G. White, *English illustration, 'the sixties': 1855–70* (1903) · F. Reid, *Illustrators of the sixties* (1928) · R. K. Engen, *Dictionary of Victorian wood engravers* (1985) · *The Dalziel family, engravers and illustrators, from the studio of Herbert Dalziel* (1978) [sale catalogue, Sothebys, Belgravia, London, 16 May 1978] · E. de Maré, *The Victorian woodblock illustrators* (1980) · S. P. Casteras, *Pocket cathedrals: Pre-Raphaelite book illustration* (1991) · Graves, *RA exhibitors* · Graves, *Brit. Inst.* · *CGPLA Eng. & Wales* (1902); (1905–6) · m. cert. [Thomas Bolton Gilchrist Septimus Dalziel] · d. cert. [Thomas Bolton Gilchrist Septimus Dalziel]

Archives BM, Dalziel Brothers collection, proof engravings | LUL, Routledge archive · Museum of Fine Arts, Boston, Harold Harley collection

Likenesses photograph, 1897 (Edward Dalziel), NPG · Elliott & Fry, carte-de-visite (George Dalziel), NPG · carte-de-visite (Edward Dalziel), NPG · carte-de-visite (George Dalziel), NPG · photograph (Edward Dalziel), BM · photograph (George Dalziel), BM · photographs (Edward Dalziel, George Dalziel, Thomas Bolton Gilchrist Septimus Dalziel), repro. in Dalziel and Dalziel, *The brothers Dalziel: a record*

Wealth at death £241 14*s.* 7*d.*—Edward Dalziel: probate, 24 June 1905, *CGPLA Eng. & Wales* · £593 18*s.* 11*d.*—George Dalziel: probate, 11 Oct 1902, *CGPLA Eng. & Wales* · £74—Thomas Bolton Gilchrist Septimus Dalziel: administration, 12 June 1906, *CGPLA Eng. & Wales*

Dalziel, Davison Alexander, Baron Dalziel of Wooler (1852–1928), newspaper proprietor and financier, was born in Camden Town, London, on 17 October 1852, the youngest son of Davison Octavian Dalziel (1825–1875) and his wife, Helen, daughter of Henry Gaulter. He was descended from a Northumbrian family distinguished for both artistic and business ability: of the eight sons of his paternal grandfather, Alexander Dalziel of Wooler (1781–

1832), seven became artists; four of them, George *Dalziel, Edward *Dalziel, John Dalziel, and Thomas Bolton Gilchrist Septimus *Dalziel—the 'Brothers Dalziel' [*see under* Dalziel family (*per.* 1840–1905)]—produced as engravers, draughtsmen, and publishers a large proportion of the woodcut illustrations issued in England between 1840 and 1880. The eighth son, Davison Dalziel's father, became a businessman rather than an engraver.

Dalziel went to New South Wales in his youth and worked as a journalist on the Sydney *Echo.* On 29 January 1876 he married Harriet Sarah (1854–1938), the daughter of John Godfrey Dunning of Edinburgh, at St James's Church, Sydney. Their only child, Helen, died on 21 December 1910.

As a young man Dalziel also spent several years in the United States, where he gained experience of newspaper management. On returning to London in 1890, and with American financial backing, he became one of the founders of Dalziel's News Agency. In 1910, together with Sir Alexander Henderson, he bought a controlling interest in *The Standard* and the *Evening Standard* newspapers from Sir Cyril Arthur Pearson, and was chairman of the board of directors for many years. Under his management, *The Standard* made a name for itself through its 'Woman's platform' page, allowing supporters and opponents of female suffrage to argue their case. Dalziel was also a shareholder in the *Daily Express* from 1912 to 1916. He controlled the *Pall Mall Gazette* from August 1915 until 1917, when he sold it for £10,000.

In 1916 Dalziel disposed of his newspaper interests (*The Standard* ceased publication in 1917 and the *Evening Standard* was sold to Sir Edward Hulton), and became prominent as a director of public companies, chiefly those concerned with overland transport. In 1906 he formed the General Motor Cab Company Ltd, of which he was initially vice-chairman and then chairman, 1907–12. In 1907 he was chiefly responsible for the introduction of motor cabs in London. He was chairman of the Pullman Car Company from its inception in 1915 and was a director of the International Sleeping Car Company, being elected chairman and president of the managing committee in 1919. He became chairman of the International Sleeping Car Share Trust Ltd in 1927, a holding company which he formed with a capital of £5.25 million in order to gain a controlling interest in the International Sleeping Car Company. The next year he negotiated the purchase by the latter company of the touring agency business of Thomas Cook & Son.

Dalziel, who had always put his newspapers at the service of the tory party, was elected to parliament as a Conservative MP for Brixton in January 1910, having been narrowly defeated in 1906. He was an effective speaker and an able advocate of tariff reform. Except for a short interval in 1923–4, he continued to represent Brixton in the Commons until he was raised to the peerage as Baron Dalziel of Wooler in 1927, having already been created a baronet in 1919.

Dalziel was a man of ability and energy: in negotiation he was forceful yet conciliatory, and much of his success was due to personal charm which, combined with business acumen and friends in government, secured to him the loyalty of friends and associates both in Great Britain and elsewhere. He died at his home, 18 Grosvenor Place, Westminster, London, on 18 April 1928. After his death, the peerage and baronetcy became extinct.

A. E. WATKIN, rev. CHANDRIKA KAUL

Sources *The Times* (19 April 1928) · *Newcastle Daily Journal* (19 April 1928) · *North Mail* (19 April 1928) · private information (1937) · R. P. T. Davenport-Hines, 'Dalziel, Davison Alexander', *DBB* · *Dod's Parliamentary Companion*
Archives CAC Cam., Swinton MSS · HLRO, Bonar Law MSS · PRO, Foreign Office papers
Wealth at death £2,274,219 3s. 8d.: probate, 25 May 1928, *CGPLA Eng. & Wales*

Dalziel, Edward (1817–1905). *See under* Dalziel family (*per.* 1840–1905).

Dalziel, George (1815–1902). *See under* Dalziel family (*per.* 1840–1905).

Dalziel, (James) Henry, Baron Dalziel of Kirkcaldy (1868–1935), politician and newspaper proprietor, was born at Borgue, Kirkcudbrightshire, on 24 April 1868, the second son of James Dalziel (d. 1904), shoemaker, of Borgue, and his wife, Margaret Emily Davies. He was educated at Borgue Academy, at Shrewsbury high school, and at King's College, London. He began work as a journalist, and through his employment in the parliamentary press gallery he became known to the Liberal Party whips. Having obtained a financial interest in the old radical paper *Reynolds's News* he was encouraged by Edward Marjoribanks, the chief whip, to stand as a Liberal candidate at the March 1892 by-election in Kirkcaldy, in the hope that he could later 'use his knowledge of the press world in the foundation of a Liberal newspaper' (Gilbert, 159). He won the seat by a large majority and retained it until he entered the House of Lords in 1921.

One of Dalziel's earliest acts in parliament was to introduce a motion (3 April 1894) supporting Scottish home rule to provide a legislature in Scotland for Scottish affairs; this was followed soon afterwards by a resolution calling for the same for each of Scotland, Wales, and Ireland. This brought Dalziel into alliance with the Welsh nationalists and with David Lloyd George, who spoke for the motion. Dalziel remained close to, and an important and loyal supporter of, Lloyd George throughout the rest of his career.

Not particularly successful as a parliamentary performer Dalziel was of most use to the future prime minister as part of his political manipulation of the press. In 1909 he first brought Lloyd George together with the powerful press proprietor Lord Northcliffe. In 1914 Dalziel became sole owner of *Reynolds's News*, and during the Liberal split of late 1916 his paper became a mouthpiece, with support from other areas of the press, for Lloyd George in his successful campaign for leadership of a coalition government. In 1918 Dalziel organized Lloyd George's purchase of the *Daily Chronicle*. Dalziel, who had been knighted in 1908 and sworn of the privy council in 1912, was rewarded with a baronetcy on 25 June 1918 and was made chairman and political director of the paper. Sir George Riddell noted that Lloyd George would have full editorial control of the paper through Dalziel, 'who will in effect be his agent' (Koss, 335). Dalziel had also been increasing his own holdings, including the purchase of the *Pall Mall Gazette* in 1917. But he was not a success in his political role at the paper and was replaced in 1921, the year in which, on 28 June, he was raised to the peerage as Baron Dalziel of Kirkcaldy. In December 1922 he sold all his newspaper interests and effectively retired from business and politics, though he was subsequently recruited as a member of the National Party of Scotland.

On 12 July 1928, at the age of sixty, Dalziel married Amy, daughter of Fossey Thackery and widow of Donald Macrae of Wicklow. Her sudden death on 26 June 1935 greatly affected him, and he died of heart failure at his home, 1 Brunswick Terrace, Hove, Sussex, nineteen days later, on 15 July. He was buried at Borgue on 22 July.

MARC BRODIE

Sources *DNB* · *The Times* (17 July 1935) · *The Times* (19 July 1935) · B. B. Gilbert, *David Lloyd George: a political life*, 1: *The architect of change, 1863–1912* (1987) · S. E. Koss, *The rise and fall of the political press in Britain*, 2 (1984) · A. J. Lee, *The origins of the popular press in England, 1855–1914* (1976) · GEC, *Peerage*, new edn · *WWBMP* · R. J. Finlay, *Independent and free: Scottish politics and the origins of the Scottish national party, 1918–1945* (1994) · *CGPLA Eng. & Wales* (1936)
Archives Bodl. Oxf., corresp. with H. H. Asquith · HLRO, corresp. with Lord Beaverbrook
Wealth at death £23,296 4s. 9d.—additional estate: 1939, *CCI*

Dalziel, Thomas Bolton Gilchrist Septimus (1823–1906). *See under* Dalziel family (*per.* 1840–1905).

Daman [Damon], **William** (d. 1591), composer, probably came to England in 1566 as a servant of Sir Thomas Sackville. According to the 1571 return of aliens for the London parish of St Peter-le-Poer, he was born in 'Lewklande' (that is, Lucca), and was 'of the Italian church'. However, his migration and name suggest that he was Jewish, like several other royal musicians at the time. Presumably he converted to Christianity, for on 24 November 1566 he married Anne Derifield (d. 1593) at St James Garlickhythe. Apart from a brief sojourn in Shoreditch in 1583, Daman appears to have remained in St Peter-le-Poer, where eight of his children were baptized or buried over the period 1572–85. In April 1576 he was appointed to a position in the royal household of Elizabeth I as a member of the recorder consort, a six-part ensemble whose principal function was to provide dance music. He remained in royal service for the rest of his life, receiving 20d. per day and an annual livery of £16 2s. 6d.

Daman's surviving output includes five motets and three instrumental works, some of which are incomplete. Arguably his finest motet is *Confitebor tibi*, a setting of psalm 86, verses 12–13, with concluding alleluia. The instrumental music is of interest in preserving at least one piece—the six-part fantasia 'di sei soprani'—that almost certainly formed part of the repertory of the court recorder consort. Daman is chiefly remembered for his harmonizations of tunes from the Sternhold and Hopkins

psalter, which were published without his leave as *The Psalmes of David in English Meter* (1579) by his friend John Bull, a London goldsmith who had used them in his private devotions. A second collection consisting of two books was issued posthumously in 1591.

Daman died from the effects of an ulcer and was buried at St Peter-le-Poer on 26 March 1591. The funeral service, however, took place in St Botolph, Aldgate, where he was a householder. Administration of his nuncupative will and personal estate, valued at £21 7s. 0d., was granted to his widow on 2 July following.

DAVID MATEER

Sources administration of Daman's nuncupative will, GL, MS 9050/2, fol. 67 · A. Ashbee and D. Lasocki, eds., *A biographical dictionary of English court musicians, 1485–1714*, 2 vols. (1998) · R. Prior, 'Jewish musicians at the Tudor court', *Musical Quarterly*, 69 (1983), 253–65 · M. Frost, *English and Scottish psalm and hymn tunes, c.1543–1677* (1953) · R. E. G. Kirk and E. F. Kirk, eds., *Returns of aliens dwelling in the city and suburbs of London, from the reign of Henry VIII to that of James I*, 4 vols., Huguenot Society of London, 10 (1900–08) · A. Ashbee, ed., *Records of English court music*, 6 (1992); 8 (1995) · P. Scott, 'The life and works of William Daman, queen's musician', MA diss., University College, Cork, 1986 · parish register, St James Garlickhythe, London [marriage] · parish register, St Botolph, Aldgate, London [burial: Anne Daman, wife] · memoranda book, St Botolph, Aldgate, London [death] · parish register, St Peter-le-Poer, London [burial]
Wealth at death £21 7s. 0d.: administration, GL, MS 9050/2, fol. 67

Damascene, Alexander (d. 1719), singer and composer, was born in France. He was a protestant, and presumably it was for this reason that he went to England, where he obtained letters of denization on 22 July 1682. On 22 July 1680 he married Honor Powell at St Matthew's, Friday Street, London. From 1684 songs by Damascene were published in collections such as *Choice Ayres and Songs*, the *Theatre of Musick*, *Vinculum societatis*, the *Banquet of Musick*, *Comes amoris*, the *Gentleman's Journal*, and *Pills to Purge Melancholy*. On 11 April 1689 Damascene, who was a countertenor, sang with the choir of the Chapel Royal at the coronation of William and Mary, and three months later he was appointed composer-in-ordinary in the royal private music. In 1690 he sang in Henry Purcell's birthday ode for the queen *Arise, my Muse*. Later that year he was appointed a gentleman-extraordinary of the Chapel Royal; he is known to have sung in performances of a further four of Purcell's odes. On 10 December 1695, nearly three weeks after Purcell's death, Damascene succeeded him as gentleman-in-ordinary, a post he held for the remainder of his life. He sang at the coronation of Queen Anne and is known to have attended her at Hampton Court and at Windsor, where on 12 July 1702 Thomas Tudway's anthem 'Is it true that God will dwell' was sung for her by Damascene, William Turner, and John Gostling. According to Damascene's will he lived in the parish of St Anne, Soho, London; he left his entire estate to his daughter-in-law and executrix, Sara Powell. He died on 14 July 1719 and was buried at St Anne's three days later.

PETER LYNAN

Sources A. Ashbee, ed., *Records of English court music*, 9 vols. (1986–96), vols. 2, 5 · A. Ashbee and D. Lasocki, eds., *A biographical dictionary of English court musicians, 1485–1714*, 1 (1998), 333–4 · A. Ashbee and J. Harley, eds., *The cheque books of the Chapel Royal*, 2 vols. (2000), vol. 1 · *IGI* · PRO, PROB 11/569, sig. 126

Wealth at death see will, PRO, PROB 11/569, sig. 126, proved 27 July 1719

Damer [*née* Conway], **Anne Seymour** (1749–1828), sculptor and author, was born on 8 November 1749 at Coombe Bank, Sevenoaks, Kent, the only child of the Hon. Henry Seymour *Conway (1719–1795), army officer and politician, and his wife, Caroline Bruce, *née* Campbell, Lady Ailesbury (1721–1803), the daughter of John, fourth duke of Argyll. She was born into an aristocratic whig family with strong literary connections that had a lasting impact upon her life. Her early years were spent at the family home, Park Place, Remenham, near Henley-on-Thames, and it was her father's secretary, David Hume, who is credited with focusing her attention on sculpture by goading her to rival the works of Italian plaster makers. Undoubtedly the most significant figure in her youth was Horace Walpole. In early years he acted as her guardian during her parents' frequent absences abroad, and at his death he bequeathed her Strawberry Hill as his executor and residuary legatee; she lived there from 1797 to 1811. Walpole rated her work exceptionally highly, adding to her terracotta eagle an inscription stating 'Anne Damer made me, not Praxiteles'. He provides the first record of her early development as a sculptor, material upon which James Dallaway and Allan Cunningham drew for their fuller and less laudatory biographical sketches of her (in contrast to Walpole's effusive account of her sculptural talents). Her first surviving works are drawings (*c*.1762), small sketches now preserved along with other Damer memorabilia at the Lewis Walpole Library, Farmington, Connecticut.

On 14 June 1767 Anne married the Hon. John Damer (1743–1776), but after seven years she separated from him; he committed suicide on 15 August 1776, leaving behind large debts. Anne's widowhood encompassed her public career as sculptor, testament of which is found in the thirty-two works exhibited by her as an honorary exhibitor at the Royal Academy during the period 1784–1818. Walpole kept a list of her works between 1784 and 1796, and according to him her training came from a variety of sources: Giuseppe Ceracchi taught her modelling, and she took lessons in marble carving in the workshop of John Bacon the elder. There were also anatomy lessons from William Cumberland Cruikshank, a crucial area of practice to which women then had no formal access. One of Damer's earliest exhibited sculptures is the exquisitely worked marble bust of her friend Lady Melbourne (exh. RA, 1784; priv. coll.) in wig and modern dress—a work singled out for praise in Erasmus Darwin's *Economy of Vegetation* (1791, 2.113).

Damer's sculptural development is demonstrated by the contrast between her early wax sculptures, which are within the category of 'accomplishment' art appropriate to her sex and social standing, and the later, technically more complex, works in terracotta, bronze, and marble, executed in a deliberately severe neo-classical mode, usually signed in Greek—a further indicator of her pursuit of

Anne Seymour Damer (1749–1828), self-portrait, 1778

antiquity. In the first category are the early waxes, a 'shock dog' followed by four portrait medallions representing her mother, her cousin Charlotte Campbell, Voltaire, and the emperor Augustus, probably executed *c*.1777, and all mentioned in the Strawberry Hill catalogue. In the latter are her busts of Nelson (marble, 1803; Guildhall, London) and Joseph Banks (bronze, 1812–13; BM), as well as her own, which forms one of the collection of artists' self-portraits in the Uffizi Gallery, Florence (marble, 1786). She also executed two reliefs (*c*.1786–9) for Boydell's Shakspeare Gallery and a statue of George III (marble, 1790–94; Register House, Edinburgh).

Walpole was instrumental in 1789 in introducing Damer to Mary Berry (1763–1852), with whom she developed a passionate and lasting friendship, recorded in letters and notebooks. Her bust of Berry (terracotta painted bronze, 1793; priv. coll.) is one of her most accomplished portraits and was particularly prized by Walpole. Although Joseph Farington commented somewhat waspishly upon Berry's and Damer's extrovert behaviour in his diary, others commented on her reticence, evident in Sir Joshua Reynolds's chaste portrait of her in a sylvan glade (1773; Yale U. CBA). In contrast are the accounts of her various appearances at Pantheon masques and in amateur theatricals at the London home of the duke of Richmond. During her marriage close friendships with women resulted in public allusions to her Sapphic nature, for example *A Sapphick Epistle from Jack Cavendish to the Honourable and most Beautiful, Mrs D—* (*c*.1770). Whatever her public persona might suggest, she was a bluestocking, avidly studying ancient Greek and Latin.

Damer, a frequent traveller to continental Europe, first visited Italy in 1778–9. During a sea voyage in 1779 she was captured by a privateer but released into her father's care on Jersey. She visited Sir Horace Mann in Florence, recorded in letters between Mann and Walpole, and also Sir William Hamilton in Naples, where she met Nelson in 1798. In 1802 she visited Paris with Mary Berry during the peace of Amiens and was granted an audience with Napoleon, who gave her a diamond-studded snuffbox, now in the British Museum, as a memento of her visit. She presented him with plaster busts of Nelson (1802) and Charles James Fox (1802), followed by a marble version of the latter (1812; Musée du Louvre, Paris). Fox had been a friend of long standing; he broke the news of her husband's death to her and she canvassed for him with Mrs Crewe and the duchess of Devonshire in the Westminster election of 1780.

Damer's literary endeavours included a romantic picaresque novel, *Belmour* (1801; translated into French 1804), and she frequented theatrical and literary circles. Among her friends were Princess Daschow and Joanna Baillie, whose epilogue to Mary Berry's play *Fashionable Friends* she recited in her Strawberry Hill production of 1800. Other women friends were the actresses Elisabeth Farren and Sarah Siddons, whom she portrayed as *Thalia* (marble, exh. RA, 1789; NPG) and *Melpomene* (plaster (?); exh. RA, 1789) respectively. Apart from such works and her own theatrical proclivities, Damer's connections with Drury Lane were writ large in the form of her 10-feet high statue of *Apollo* (c.1792; destroyed), made for the rebuilt theatre. In 1818 she moved to York House, Twickenham, where she continued producing sculpture. She died on 28 May 1828 at her London house, 9 Upper Brook Street, Grosvenor Square, and was buried in the church at Sundridge, Kent, alongside her mother. According to her wishes, she was buried with her sculptor's tools and apron and the ashes of her favourite dog. Her private papers were destroyed.

ALISON YARRINGTON

Sources S. Benforado, 'Anne Seymour Damer (1748–1828), sculptor', PhD diss., University of New Mexico, 1986 · A. Cunningham, *The lives of the most eminent British painters, sculptors and architects*, vol. 3 (1830) · P. Noble, *Anne Seymour Damer: woman of art and fashion* (1908) · H. Walpole, *Anecdotes of painting in England: with some account of the principal artists*, ed. J. Dallaway, [rev. and enl. edn], 5 vols. (1826–8) · A. Yarrington, 'The female Pygmalion: Anne Seymour Damer, Allan Cunningham and the writing of a woman sculptor's life', *Sculpture Journal*, 1 (1997), 32–44 · *The Berry papers: being the correspondence hitherto unpublished of Mary and Agnes Berry, 1763–1852*, ed. L. Melville (1914) · *Extracts of the journals and correspondence of Miss Berry*, ed. M. T. Lewis, 2nd edn, 3 vols. (1865–6) · R. Gunnis, *Dictionary of British sculptors, 1660–1851* (1953); new edn (1968) · M. Whinney, *Sculpture in Britain, 1530 to 1830*, rev. J. Physick, 2nd edn (1988) · will, PRO, PROB 11/1741, sig. 344

Archives RA, letters · Yale U., Farmington, Lewis Walpole Library, commonplace books and letters | BL, corresp. with Mary Berry, Add. MS 37727, fols. 143–275 · U. Hull, Brynmor Jones L., letters to Sir Charles Hotham-Thompson

Likenesses studio of Reynolds, oils, 1772–3, NPG · J. Reynolds, oils, 1773, Yale U. CBA · J. R. Smith, mezzotint, pubd 1774 (after J. Reynolds), BM · G. Ceracchi, marble statue, c.1777, BM · A. S.

Damer, self-portrait, marble sculpture, 1778, Galleria degli Uffizi, Florence [*see illus.*] · G. Romney, oils, 1779, Goodwood House, West Sussex · R. Cosway, miniature, 1785, NPG · H. Carr, watercolour drawing, 1788, Scot. NPG · L. Schiavonetti, stipple, pubd 1791 (after R. Cosway), BM, NPG · T. Ryder, stipple, pubd 1792 (after A. Kauffman, 1766), BM, NPG · J. Hopwood, stipple, pubd 1812 (after G. C.), BM, NPG · S. W. Reynolds, mezzotint, pubd 1836 (after J. Reynolds), BM, NPG · A. S. Damer, self-portrait, marble bust, BM

Damerham [**Domerham**], **Adam of** (*d*. in or after **1291?**), Benedictine monk and chronicler, was presumably born at Damerham, Hampshire, one of the abbey's manors. He probably professed at Glastonbury when Michael of Amesbury was abbot (1235–52). The chronicle attributed to Adam, the *Libellus de rebus gestis Glastoniensibus*, was edited by Thomas Hearne in 1727 from the thirteenth-century manuscript (Trinity College, MS R.5.33, fols. 21–73v), together with the copy of the *De antiquitate Glastonie ecclesie* by William of Malmesbury which precedes it in his edition as in the manuscript (ibid., fols. 1–18v). The *Libellus* refers to Adam twice: in 1255, on the deposition of Abbot Robert Ford, Adam was one of the five monks chosen to elect a new abbot by way of compromise—they elected Robert of Petherton; and in 1274, on the death of Abbot Robert, Adam 'appealed in due form on behalf of the monks' (Damerham, *Historia*, 1.256) for the preservation of the monastery's status against the assumption of rights of patronage by Walter Giffard, bishop of Bath and Wells (*d*. 1279). Adam was successively cellarer and sacrist.

The attribution of the *Libellus* to Adam was made by John of Glastonbury over a century later. John used it as the source of his own chronicle for the years 1126–1291, acknowledging the authority of 'Brother Adam of Domerham, monk of our monastery' in his prologue (*Chronicle of Glastonbury Abbey*, 7). However, the attribution is problematical. The nature of the text in Trinity College, MS R.5.33 makes it improbable that one author alone was responsible. The prologue and narrative to c.1230 is in a hand datable to c.1247. Therefore, if Adam composed the whole he must have started writing c.1247 and still have been at work in 1291, which, though possible, is unlikely. The text in Trinity College, MS R.5.33 has the appearance of a typical monastic chronicle, a genre normally composed by a series of authors. The copy of the *De antiquitate*, Glastonbury's early history, is at least partly in the same hand as the *Libellus* to c.1230. Thereafter there are several changes of hand, suggesting that the monks were producing a continuous history of their house by constantly updating it, abbacy by abbacy. (Another copy of the *Libellus*, in BL, Add. MS 22934, has a further continuation to 1313.) Adam's own contribution cannot be determined on the present evidence. Maybe he had a copy made of the section to 1274 and, having himself added the account of the abbacy of John of Taunton (1274–91), was subsequently accredited with the whole.

The prologue states the work's intention: it was to take up the story of Glastonbury from where William of Malmesbury ended, and also to provide evidence to enable the abbey to defend its property and privileges. The recurrent theme of the *Libellus* is the abbey's conflict with the diocesan, the bishop of Bath—later of Bath and

Wells. It has a detailed narrative, interspersed with copies of papal letters and other documents, of the conflict which began in earnest after Savaric (d. 1205) was consecrated bishop of Bath in 1192. 'In order to augment his bishopric, because he was ambitious and prodigal' (Damerham, *Historia*, 2.353), he obtained patronage of Glastonbury Abbey from Richard I. In 1195 Celestine III licensed him to unite Glastonbury and Bath, and in 1197 Savaric established an episcopal see at Glastonbury. The *Libellus* compares the abbot of Glastonbury, Henry de Soilli, whose removal to make way for Savaric was engineered by his promotion to the bishopric of Worcester, to a hireling who flees at the sight of a wolf. Savaric was succeeded in 1206 by Jocelin of Wells (d. 1242), who from 1213 to 1219 styled himself bishop of Bath and Glastonbury. The monks struggled to restore their church's independence from the bishop's control and in 1219 succeeded in regaining its abbatial status. But, as the *Libellus* relates, the bishop's oppression and the consequent litigation and loss of possessions, continued to disrupt the monks' lives. The *Libellus* describes their next important victory over the bishop. Walter Giffard's high-handed methods precipitated a crisis in 1274. On hearing of the death of the abbot, Robert of Petherton, he sent his steward and bailiffs to Glastonbury. They took control and refused admission to the king's escheator. But when the constable of Bristol Castle arrived, the bishop's men succumbed and hid, and the constable established that the king, not the bishop, was the abbey's patron.

Although the monks' conflict with the diocesan is the main preoccupation of the *Libellus*, it records other matters. For example, the account of each abbot ends with details of his achievements and gifts to the abbey. But especially remarkable are two passages seminal to the growth of the Arthurian legend at Glastonbury. The first describes the discovery of the alleged bones of Arthur and Guinevere c.1190. Abbot Henry de Soilli had ordered an excavation 'between two stone pyramids' in the cemetery. The diggers were shielded from public gaze by a curtain and found two coffins, one 'of amazing size' which contained 'incredibly large bones ... one thigh bone reached from the ground to at least the middle of a tall man's leg'. They also found 'a lead cross inscribed "Here lies the renowned King Arthur in the Isle of Avalon"'. With the skeleton in the other coffin was 'the beautiful golden hair of a woman, most skilfully arranged' (Damerham, *Historia*, 2.340–43). The bones were interred in a tomb in the abbey church. The *Libellus* later describes the opening of the tomb at Edward I's command in 1278, 'at twilight on 19 April'. In it were two coffins, each painted with the respective portraits and arms of Arthur and Guinevere, one containing Arthur's 'immense bones', the other the bones ('of extraordinary beauty') of Guinevere (ibid., 2.588–9).

The *Libellus* is an invaluable record of the domestic history of Glastonbury Abbey. Besides its detailed narrative, it preserves copies of numerous documents, notably papal letters, many otherwise unknown. But it has only passing references to the monks' religious observance and intellectual and cultural attainments, and gives little impression of life in the cloister.

Antonia Gransden

Sources *Adamis de Domerham 'Historia de rebus gestis Glastoniensibus'*, ed. T. Hearne, 2 vols. (1727) · J. Crick, 'The marshalling of antiquity: Glastonbury's historical dossier', *The archaeology and history of Glastonbury Abbey …*, ed. L. Abrams and J. P. Carley (1991), 218–43 · S. Keynes, *Anglo-Saxon manuscripts and other items of related interest in the library of Trinity College, Cambridge* (1992), 45, no. 29 · *The letters of Pope Innocent III (1198–1216) concerning England and Wales*, ed. C. R. Cheney and M. G. Cheney (1967) · D. Knowles, *The monastic order in England* (1940); repr. with corrections (1949), 327–30 · *The early history of Glastonbury: an edition, translation, and study of William of Malmesbury's De antiquitate Glastonie ecclesie*, ed. J. Scott (1981) · *The Chronicle of Glastonbury Abbey: an edition, translation and study of John of Glastonbury's Cronica sive antiquitates Glastoniensis ecclesie*, ed. J. P. Carley, trans. D. Townsend, rev. edn (1985) · A. Gransden, 'The growth of the Glastonbury traditions and legends in the twelfth century', *Journal of Ecclesiastical History*, 27 (1976), 337–58; repr. in A. Gransden, *Legends, traditions and history in medieval England* (1992), 153–74 · A. Gransden, 'The history of Wells Cathedral, c.1090–1547', *Wells Cathedral: a history*, ed. L. S. Colchester (1982), 29–34; repr. (1996)
Archives BL, Add. MS 22934 · Trinity Cam., MS R.5.33, fols. 21–73v

Damerment, Madeleine (1917–1944). *See under* Women agents on active service in France (*act.* 1942–1945).

Damet, Thomas (c.1542–1618), historian, was born in Great Yarmouth; his parents' names are unknown. He is recorded initially as a notary and scrivener, later as a merchant. In 1566–7 he was fined for not being a free burgess, suggesting that he was now aged twenty-four. Town clerk of Yarmouth in 1568–73, he soon became a leading and trusted burgess, being chosen as alderman in 1574, one of the two ruling bailiffs of the town in 1577, 1592, and 1602, JP from 1578 onwards, and MP in 1584, 1586, 1593, and 1604. Local patriotism and the search for precedents during the town's protracted suits with Lowestoft over control of the herring fishery and in connection with applications for government help towards costly harbour works inform his historical writing. This includes a manuscript history of Yarmouth harbour from 1549 to 1567, a transcript of the borough's charters dated 1580, and a brief Yarmouth chronicle. His main work is 'Greate Yermouthe: a booke of the foundacion and antiquitye of the saide towne', completed between 1594 and 1599 and previously attributed to Henry Manship senior (d. 1569). It was first published in 1847. There is no indication that Damet was aware of contemporary historians such as Camden but he draws heavily on the town's archives and projects his vision of the dramatic landscape changes that permitted its rapid post-conquest development on an offshore sandspit. His work was derided by the more sophisticated Henry Manship junior (d. 1625), whose own history of Great Yarmouth was completed in 1619, but was quarried by Thomas Nashe for his *Lenten Stuffe* of 1599. Two manuscript maps compiled under Damet's influence reconstruct the Yarmouth–Norwich region as it was in the year AD 1000.

Damet's three wives were: Anne Ellys of Hemsby, Norfolk (married 1565, *d.* 1590); Alice Bishop, widow, *née* Ylberde, of Yarmouth (married 1590, *d.* 1601); and Grace Humfrey, widow, whom he married in 1602. He fell ill in 1610 and retired to Grace's house at Rishangles in Suffolk; he died in 1618 and was buried at Great Yarmouth on 18 March. By his will dated 4 April 1617 he left four alms-houses for Yarmouth seamen's widows. His daughter Mary married Ralph Owner, town clerk of Yarmouth in 1609–33, but his son Edward had disappeared and was believed dead in 1617. He subsequently reappeared to put in a claim as heir, but was in want in 1625 when the town granted him a small pension. He died in 1628.

PAUL RUTLEDGE

Sources [T. Damet], *A booke of the foundacion and antiquitye of the towne of Greate Yermouthe*, ed. C. J. Palmer (1847) · P. Rutledge, 'Thomas Damet and the historiography of Great Yarmouth [pt 1]', *Norfolk Archaeology*, 33 (1962–5), 119–30 · P. Rutledge, 'Thomas Damet and the historiography of Great Yarmouth [pt 2]', *Norfolk Archaeology*, 34 (1966–9), 332–4 · parish register, Great Yarmouth, 18 March 1618, Norfolk RO, PD 28/1 [burial] · will, Norfolk RO, Great Yarmouth first book of entries, Y/C18/61, fol. 79 · *The works of Thomas Nashe*, ed. R. B. McKerrow, 5 vols. (1904–10); repr. with corrections and notes by F. P. Wilson (1958) · marriage licence, 1565, Norfolk RO, HMN7/314 [Anne Ellys] · parish register, Rishangles, 1593–1652, Suffolk RO, FB 156/D1/1 · H. Manship, *The history of Great Yarmouth*, ed. C. J. Palmer (1854) · R. Tittler, *The Reformation and the towns in England* (1998) · N. M. Fuidge, 'Damet, Thomas', HoP, *Commons, 1558–1603*, 2.10–11

Archives Bodl. Oxf., MS Maps England a.2.f.5 · Norfolk RO, history of Yarmouth harbour, in Y/C28/1 · Norfolk RO, 'Thomas Damet's book of charters', Y/C18/4 · Yarmouth Town Hall, 'Hutch map'

Wealth at death immediate legacies £80; one house and four almshouses; after wife's death and sale of jointure property a further £150 was to be distributed: will, Norfolk RO, Y/C18/61, fol. 79

Damm, Sheila Van (1922–1987), rally driver and theatre director, was born on 17 January 1922 in Gloucester Terrace, Paddington, London, the youngest of three daughters (there were no sons) of Vivian Van Damm (*d.* 1960) and his wife, Natalie Lyons. Although her father had sponsored motor cycle speedway events in the 1920s, before inheriting the Windmill Theatre in London and initiating its format of non-stop revues, Sheila's upbringing in an all-girl Jewish family generated no interest in motoring beyond her training as a Women's Auxiliary Air Force driver. She subsequently trained privately as a pilot and joined the Royal Air Force Volunteer Reserve after the Second World War.

As a promotional stunt for the Windmill Theatre, Sheila Van Damm was persuaded in November 1950 to enter her first motor sporting event, the MCC–*Daily Express* car rally, driving a factory-prepared Sunbeam Talbot, which her father had persuaded the Rootes Group to enter carrying the words 'Windmill Girl' on the side of the car. Navigated by her sister Nona, she claimed third place in the ladies' section—a performance which so impressed the Rootes team manager Norman Garrard that he invited her to join Nancy Mitchell and Bill Wisdom to form an all-women crew of a Hillman Minx in the 1951 Monte Carlo rally. She claimed further success in the 1951 RAC rally, when she

Sheila Van Damm (1922–1987), by Lewis Morley, 1962

won the ladies' prize for closed cars under 1500 cc at the wheel of her own Hillman Minx. This was the only occasion on which she competed as a private entrant. Subsequently, she would drive factory cars entered by the Rootes Group.

Her first major success was in the 1952 Motor Cycling Club rally, when she won the ladies' prize in a Sunbeam Talbot. Despite disappointment in the 1953 Monte Carlo rally, when a series of punctures forced her out of contention, she soon afterwards entered the record books, outpacing her more illustrious team-mate Stirling Moss to set a class record for 2–3-litre cars, driving the prototype Sunbeam Alpine sports car at an average of 120.135 m.p.h. at Jabbeke in Belgium.

Described in a contemporary report as 'a fresh faced woman, possessed of an infectious sense of fun', Sheila Van Damm had an ebullient and outgoing personality which masked a fearsomely competitive and determined approach to her sport. The 1953 alpine rally, one of Europe's toughest events, saw her, co-driven by Anne Hall, win not only the coupe des dames, but also one of the coveted coupes des Alpes, for finishing the event without gaining penalty marks for lateness.

Van Damm competed in the Great American Mountain rally before claiming, with Anne Hall, another coupe des dames in the 1954 Tulip rally of Holland, a performance that also saw her winning outright the ten-lap race around the Zandvoort circuit. Winning a further ladies' award in the 1954 Viking rally in Norway successfully clinched the Ladies' European championship for Van Damm and Hall, a feat that they were set to repeat in 1955, after starting the season in fine style by gaining a coupe des dames after five years of trying, on the Monte Carlo rally.

Despite covering over 14,000 miles a year on rallies, Sheila Van Damm still managed to combine motor sport with helping her father run the Windmill Theatre. However, in October 1955 she asked Sir William Rootes to release her to devote her efforts more fully to the theatre. Her final rally for the Rootes team was the 1956 Monte Carlo, in which she overcame myriad problems to finish, but without award-winning success. She was also invited to partner the Le Mans driver Peter Harper at the wheel of a Sunbeam Rapier in the 1956 Mille Miglia road race. Despite the severity of the event, she maintained intact her record of finishing every event which she started in her five-year career. Averaging 66.37 m.p.h., she and Harper won their class.

Van Damm published her autobiography, *No Excuses*, in 1957. In 1958 she was appointed the first honorary colonel of the Warwickshire and Worcestershire battalion of the Women's Royal Army Corps (Territorial Army). She maintained her contacts with the motoring world as president of the Doghouse Club for motor-racing wives and ladies and later as president of the Sunbeam Talbot Owners' Club. Her first love, however, remained the Windmill Theatre. She continued its wartime reputation as 'the theatre that never closed' and its revue format, supporting young comedians including Peter Sellers, Tony Hancock, Harry Secombe, and Bruce Forsyth. She inherited the Windmill from her father on his death in 1960 and energetically presided over the theatre for a further four years, before relinquishing the battle against the advancing tide of strip shows and permissive cinemas in the Soho area, which forced it to close in 1964.

Sheila Van Damm was well built, with dark hair and a round face. She never married and in later life moved to Broadford Bridge Farm, West Chiltington, Pulborough, in rural Sussex, where with her sister Nona she enjoyed running a small farm and stables, in addition to acting as a fund-raiser for the International Spinal Research Trust. She died of cancer at the London Clinic on 23 August 1987 and was subsequently commemorated by a memorial service at the West London Synagogue.

STEPHEN SLATER, *rev.*

Sources S. Van Damm, *No excuses* (1957) · *The Times* (25 Aug 1987) · *Classic and Sportscar Magazine* (Nov 1987) · personal knowledge (1996) · private information (1996) · *CGPLA Eng. & Wales* (1987)
Likenesses L. Morley, photograph, 1962, NPG [*see illus.*] · photograph, 1964, Hult. Arch. · photograph, repro. in *The Times*
Wealth at death £74,809: probate, 23 Oct 1987, *CGPLA Eng. & Wales*

Damon, William. *See* Daman, William (d. 1591).

Damory [Amory], **Sir Roger** (d. 1322), baron and courtier, was the younger son of Sir Robert Damory, of Bucknell and Woodperry, Oxfordshire, Thornborough, Buckinghamshire, and Ubley in Somerset, who died in or before 1285. Although his family was one of well-established county gentry, Damory's position as a younger son probably justified the description of him in the *Vita Edwardi*

secundi as by origin 'a poor and needy knight' (p. 123). It was initially his elder brother, Sir Richard Damory, who was more prominent. As sheriff of Oxford and Buckingham from 1308 to 1310, forester of Whittlewood Forest in Buckinghamshire from 1308, constable of Oxford Castle from 1311 to 1321, and steward of the royal household from 1311 to 1325, Richard Damory moved from local administration to the centre of power and may have been responsible for introducing Roger to royal service.

Roger Damory first appears in 1309 as the retainer of Gilbert de Clare, eighth earl of Gloucester. It was perhaps as a member of Gloucester's retinue that he fought at Bannockburn in June 1314, where Gloucester was killed; and his performance in the battle, for which he was later rewarded with land worth 100 marks a year, may have brought him to Edward II's notice. From then on his rise was rapid and within three years he had become the supreme influence at Edward's court. The royal grant of the castle and honour of Knaresborough, Yorkshire, in December 1314 was the first favour to come his way. By January 1315 he was a knight of the royal household and in the next two years he received various grants of lands, wardships, and money. Damory's progress was crowned in April 1317 by his marriage to Elizabeth de *Clare (1294/5–1360), one of the three sisters and coheirs of the former earl of Gloucester, for which again he had Edward to thank. His wife's share in the partition of the vast Gloucester estates made him one of the leading territorial magnates and led to his being summoned to parliament from November 1317.

From the later months of 1316 Damory became the leading member of a group of royal favourites, two of whom, Hugh *Despenser the younger and Hugh *Audley, were also married to Gloucester's sisters. The royal patronage lavished on them, at a time of general distress caused by famine and Scottish attacks, brought them the enmity of Thomas, earl of Lancaster, the greatest of the magnates, who was determined to purge the court and to overturn Edward's indulgent grants. From 1316 to 1319 Lancaster's feud with the courtiers dominated English politics. In October 1317 the earl seized the royal castles of Knaresborough and Alton, Staffordshire, then in Damory's custody, and he was later to accuse Damory of plotting against his life. As the most avaricious of the courtiers Damory was put under restraint in November 1317 by Aymer de Valence, earl of Pembroke, and Bartholomew Badlesmere, both of them moderates among Edward's associates, who imposed on Damory a written undertaking not to profit excessively from the king's generosity nor to permit others to do so. After long negotiations a fragile settlement between Lancaster and the king's friends was reached in August 1318 by the treaty of Leake, where Lancaster and Damory were temporarily reconciled. Damory's promise to pay Lancaster just over £600 may help to account for both this reconciliation and a subsequent review of royal grants which allowed Damory to keep virtually all that he had gained.

Within a few months Damory's position came under threat from a new direction. In 1318–19 the rise of Hugh

Despenser the younger gradually displaced Damory from his standing at the centre of the court. Although Edward apparently promised him the captaincy of Berwick in September 1319, during the English siege of the town, and grants continued to come his way during 1320, his allegiance was soon to be severed by the ambitions of Despenser, whose attempts in 1320–21 to enlarge his share of the Gloucester inheritance in south Wales raised the whole march against him. Damory and Audley, the husbands of the other two coheiresses, were vulnerable to Despenser's expansionism and in the early months of 1321 they and the other marchers turned to Lancaster for help. Damory was present at Lancaster's assembly at Sherburn, Yorkshire, in June 1321, when the earl tried to put together a coalition against Despenser and his father. In the brief civil war that followed he took Worcester for the rebels in January 1322, but was captured by the king's forces at Tutbury, Staffordshire, on 11 March. He was tried and condemned to death, but spared because of Edward's former affection for him and because of his marriage to the king's niece. Sick or mortally wounded, he died in Tutbury on 13 or 14 March 1322 and was buried in Ware, Hertfordshire. He left a daughter, Elizabeth, born in May 1318. He had been at the head of the factional politics of Edward II's middle years, and his rapid rise and precipitate fall typified the fate of others who had had the misfortune to enjoy Edward's patronage.   J. R. MADDICOTT

Sources Chancery records · N. Denholm-Young, ed. and trans., Vita Edwardi secundi (1957) · W. Stubbs, ed., Chronicles of the reigns of Edward I and Edward II, 2 vols., Rolls Series, 76 (1882–3) · J. C. Davies, The baronial opposition to Edward II (1918) · J. R. Maddicott, Thomas of Lancaster, 1307–1322: a study in the reign of Edward II (1970) · J. R. S. Phillips, Aymer de Valence, earl of Pembroke, 1307–1324: baronial politics in the reign of Edward II (1972) · GEC, Peerage

Dampier, Sir Henry (1758–1816), judge, was born on 21 December 1758 at Eton, the only son of the Revd Thomas Dampier (d. 1777) from Somerset, a master at Eton College and later dean of Durham Cathedral, and his second wife, Frances Walker. Dampier received his early education at Eton College and entered King's College, Cambridge, in 1776, proceeding BA in 1781 and MA in 1784. He was awarded the members' prize in 1782 and 1783. Meanwhile he entered the Middle Temple in 1781, choosing to follow the law rather than become a clergyman as did his father and two half-brothers from his father's first marriage. He was called to the bar on 6 June 1788, after which he entered upon an extended and successful practice which lasted until he was knighted and appointed a judge on king's bench on 23 June 1813. His judicial career was cut short by his untimely death in 1816.

Dampier was named by Lord Campbell as 'among the best lawyers that have appeared in Westminster Hall in my time' (Campbell, 3.155). Soon after his call to the bar, Dampier established himself as a leader on the western circuit along with others who were to become luminaries in the law, such as Sir Vicary Gibbs and Sir Soulden Lawrence. He served as one of three junior counsel assisting Thomas Erskine and Vicary Gibbs in obtaining the acquittals of Thomas Hardy and John Horne Tooke in their notorious treason trials of 1794. He became the intimate friend of Edward Law (Lord Ellenborough), a kinsman by marriage, who later rose to the very top of the profession as chief justice of king's bench and as lord chancellor.

Possessed of a classical education, a pleasing disposition, a large store of legal learning, and brilliant conversational wit, Dampier was widely respected and his friendship valued. He married, on 27 August 1790, Martha Law, daughter of John Law, archdeacon of Rochester. One of his half-brothers, Thomas *Dampier, became bishop of Rochester and later of Ely. Thomas shared with Henry a love of learning, accumulating a superb library which included many rare books, manuscripts, and prints; when Henry arranged for the sale of the library to the duke of Devonshire on Thomas's death in 1812 its value was almost £10,000. Henry died at Montagu Place, Bloomsbury, London, on 3 February 1816; he was survived by Martha and five of their children.

Dampier served on the bench for too short a time to make a substantial contribution to the growth of the common law, but his disciplined habits throughout his career produced an important legacy to legal historians in the form of manuscript collections held by Lincoln's Inn Library and the Middle Temple Library. The Dampier manuscripts at Lincoln's Inn comprise an extensive collection of pleadings and selected documents involved in cases heard by king's bench across four generations of puisne judges. Starting with William Ashurst in 1770, the manuscripts were passed down through Francis Buller and Soulden Lawrence, ending in the hands of Dampier, with each judge adding his own collection of case papers. The papers were donated to Lincoln's Inn Library by John Lucius Dampier, one of Henry Dampier's sons. The manuscripts at the Middle Temple Library consist of eleven notebooks containing notes of both reported and unreported cases decided by king's bench, plus indexes. The notebooks were originally prepared by Soulden Lawrence and were passed on to, and continued by, Dampier.

JAMES OLDHAM

Sources John, Lord Campbell, The lives of the chief justices of England, ed. J. Cockcroft, [rev. edn], 5 vols. (Northport, NY, 1894–9) · DNB · Lincoln's Inn, London, Dampier MSS · Middle Temple Library, Dampier MSS · Foss, Judges · GM, 1st ser., 39 (1769) · J. Haydn, The book of dignities: containing lists of the official personages of the British empire, ed. H. Ockerby, 3rd edn (1894) · Holdsworth, Eng. law · J. Hutchinson, ed., A catalogue of notable Middle Templars: with brief biographical notices (1902) · W. C. Townsend, The lives of twelve eminent judges, 2 vols. (1846) · The public and private life of Lord Chancellor Eldon, with selections from his correspondence, ed. H. Twiss, 3 vols. (1844) · Venn, Alum. Cant. · R. A. Austen-Leigh, ed., The Eton College register, 1753–1790 (1921)

Archives Lincoln's Inn, London · Middle Temple, London, MSS

Dampier, Thomas (bap. 1749, d. 1812), bishop of Ely and book collector, was born at Eton and baptized there on 14 February 1749, the eldest son of Thomas Dampier (d. 1777), lower master at Eton College and subsequently dean of Durham, and his first wife, Anne Hayes. Sir Henry *Dampier was one of his half-brothers. He was educated at Eton College (1753–66) before going to King's College, Cambridge, where he graduated BA (1771), MA (1774), and DD

(1780). After residing at Eton as private tutor to the earl of Guilford, and holding the vicarage of Bexley in Kent, he succeeded in 1776 to the mastership of Sherburn Hospital, near Durham, a post previously held by his father, who resigned it in his favour. He was prebendary of the twelfth stall of Durham Cathedral (1778–1808), dean of Rochester (1782–1802), and bishop of Rochester (1802–8). The see was poor, and Dampier, unlike many of his predecessors, did not hold the deanery of Westminster concurrently with the bishopric. He was translated to the bishopric of Ely in 1808.

Thomas Dibdin described Dampier's theological standpoint as being that of 'a thorough Church-of-England man. Indeed there were those who said he was too "high-backed" in these matters' (Dibdin, 3.344–53). He was opposed to Roman Catholic emancipation. However, Dibdin also described him as 'thoroughly good-natured and good-hearted' (ibid.), as well as being a great scholar and the most learned of his generation of book collectors. He was a dedicated book lover throughout his life, and the personal library which he began to collect as a student became by the time of his death one of the most celebrated of its time, with extensive holdings of early printed books. Dampier's own manuscript account of some of the rarer items in his collection was used extensively by Dibdin when compiling his *Aedes Althorpianae* (1822). His published output comprised only six sermons, issued at various times between 1782 and 1807. He died suddenly at Ely House, Dover Street, London, on 13 May 1812 and was buried in Eton College chapel. His wife, Elizabeth, daughter of Henry Slack, survived him. After his death, the bulk of Dampier's library was sold *en bloc* to William Cavendish, sixth duke of Devonshire, for about £10,000. Some duplicates from the collection had already been sold by auction in 1804, and in 1844 a further sale of the 'remaining library' of Dampier was held, comprising mostly eighteenth- and nineteenth-century material.

E. S. SHUCKBURGH, rev. DAVID PEARSON

Sources T. F. Dibdin, *The bibliographical decameron*, 3 vols. (1817) · *GM*, 1st ser., 82/1 (1812), 501 · *GM*, 1st ser., 91/2 (1821), 280 · Venn, *Alum. Cant.* · R. A. Austen-Leigh, ed., *The Eton College register, 1753–1790* (1921) · P. Mussett, *List of deans and major canons of Durham, 1541–1900* (1974) · *Lists of catalogues of English book sales 1676–1900 … in the British Museum* (1915) · S. L. Ollard, *Fasti Wyndesorienses: the deans and canons of Windsor* (privately printed, Windsor, 1950) · *Fasti Angl., 1541–1857*, [Canterbury] · *VCH Cambridgeshire and the Isle of Ely*, vol. 3
Archives Bodl. Oxf., corresp. on antiquarian subjects · CUL, corresp. on antiquarian subjects · LPL, corresp. on antiquarian subjects | Bodl. Oxf., corresp. with first earl of Guilford
Likenesses H. Meyer, mezzotint (after J. Northcote), BM, NPG · J. Northcote, oils, King's Cam. · Worthington, engraving (after J. J. Masquerier), repro. in Dibdin, *Bibliographical decameron* · etching (after J. J. Masquerier), BM

Dampier, William (1651–1715), buccaneer and explorer, was born in August and baptized on 5 September 1651 at East Coker, Somerset, the second of six children of tenant farmers George Dampier (1618?–1658) and his wife, Anne (*d.* 1665).

William Dampier (1651–1715), by Thomas Murray, *c.*1697–8

Seaman, 1669–1678 When Dampier was eighteen his guardians, probably including William Helyar, East Coker's lord of the manor, removed him from Latin school and, according to his own wishes, apprenticed him a seaman at Weymouth. His observations of the kinds of soil on his mother's farm indicate an early curiosity about the particulars of nature, and during his first long voyage (aboard the East Indiaman *John and Martha*, 1671–2) he began to collect information about the prevailing winds. After brief service during the Third Anglo-Dutch War in which his ship, *Royal Prince* under Admiral Sir Edward Spragge, saw action against de Ruyter (May and June 1673), Dampier was employed in 1674 at Bybrook, William Helyar's Jamaica sugar plantation, a position he abandoned after violent disputes with the manager, William Waley. Then, after a series of jobs aboard merchant ships, he went, in August 1675, to the Bay of Campeche, Mexico, to trade for logwood, a valuable source of purple dye. His vivid account of the region's exotic wildlife and the unruly society of baymen—British privateers set adrift by the 1670 treaty with Spain—show him a conscientious keeper of journals by his early twenties.

Buccaneer, 1679–1691 Failing to prosper among the logwood cutters, Dampier joined a crew of buccaneers who pillaged the bay's coastal towns, so that when he returned to England in 1678 it was with enough money to marry a servant of the duchess of Grafton. He was to live with his wife, Judith (her family name is unknown), rarely during the next three decades although he often attempted to provide for her financial security. Their union was apparently childless. By 1679 he was once again in Jamaica, where, after encountering a countryman who sold him a small estate back in Dorset, he agreed to go to the Mosquito Coast in a trader commanded by a Mr Hobby. At Negril Bay (now Long Bay), however, he deserted to serve under captains John Coxon, Bartholomew Sharp, and Richard Sawkins in a newly formed buccaneer fleet which, with the aid of the Mosquito Indians, captured Portobello and sent a raiding party across the isthmus to attack Panama City in imitation of Henry Morgan's victories of 1670–71. Failure at Panama City broke up the confederation and completed the pattern of hope, disappointment, and defection that Dampier would endure frequently among the buccaneers. He remained with Captain Sharp aboard a ship seized in Panama harbour, but after defeat in 1681 at Arica, northern Chile, Dampier and a small party including his friend Lionel Wafer recrossed the isthmus, whose rivers would have claimed his journals had he not secured them in a length of bamboo stopped with wax.

On Panama's Caribbean coast Dampier met French and English marauders with whom he raided Costa Rica and enjoyed the freedom of the notorious buccaneer base at Tortuga. He sailed from here in July 1682 to Virginia where he remained for thirteen months until, in August 1683, he joined a second raiding expedition into the Pacific. After rounding the Horn and provisioning at Juan Fernandez and the Galápagos Islands (both carefully inventoried by Dampier), his fleet was augmented by hundreds of French and English freebooters, but in May 1685 they were driven from Panama City by Spanish warships. Shortly thereafter Dampier went from the *Batchelor's Delight* under Edward Davis into the *Cygnet*, not for loot, he claims in a manuscript account, but because the designs of its captain, Charles Swan, would allow him further to explore the Pacific.

The *Cygnet* first searched in vain for the enormously rich galleon sent annually from Manila to Acapulco and then, on 31 March 1686, sailed from Cape Corrientes, Mexico, to Guam where it arrived on 20 May, a feat of seamanship which owed much to Dampier's skills. The voyage of over 6000 miles on short rations had nearly driven the crew to desperation, but now Swan could jest to his lean navigator, 'Ah! Dampier, you would have made them but a poor meal'. Dampier's account of Guam and the Philippines is accordingly rich in descriptions of foods: he is the first to describe the breadfruit, banana, and plantain in English. He concluded that Mindanao, still free of Spanish domination, would make an ideal base for British spice traders. Throughout 1687 the *Cygnet* cruised in the South China Sea and the Gulf of Thailand (then known to Dampier as the Bay of Siam) and from 5 January to 12 March 1688 touched upon the coast of New Holland (Australia), the first English ship to do so. Perhaps Dampier's harsh disparagement of the land and natives in the King Sound area, north of the Great Sandy Desert, expressed disappointment at his failure to confirm the enduring myth of a utopian southern continent, Terra Australis Incognita. Six weeks after departing the coast he and some others left the *Cygnet* at Great Nicobar Island, India, and in May 1688 arrived at Achin, Sumatra, surviving a terrible 130

mile passage in an outrigger canoe. Weakened by dysentery but curious as ever he spent the next eighteen months exploring south-east Asia (1688–9), with trips to Tonquin (what is now Vietnam), Malacca (now Melaka) on the Malay peninsula, and India. After brief service as gunner in the East India Company's fort at Bencoolen (now Bengkulu), Sumatra, he arrived home on 16 September 1691 aboard the East Indiaman *Defence*, the first English circumnavigator since Thomas Cavendish, a century earlier.

Literary success, 1691–1699 Dampier's Dorset estate vanishes from the record so it is likely that his capital now consisted largely of his journals and 'Prince *Giolo' [see under Exotic visitors (act. c.1500–c.1855)]*, a tattooed Philippine prince he acquired at Mindanao. When Gioly died after being displayed in London and Oxford, Dampier went, in August 1693, as second mate of the *Dove*, one of four ships intended to trade with the Spanish West Indies and salvage wrecks in the Caribbean, but a mutiny aboard the flagship led to the notoriously successful pirate cruise of Henry Every (also known as Captain John Avery). Dampier remained with the *Dove* at La Coruña, Spain, until his term of employment ended in February 1695, whereupon he joined in a suit for back wages at London. By dismissing the suit the High Court of Admiralty upheld the owners' charge, later repeated by his enemies, that he had aided the mutineers. Holding loyalty above reputation, however, he testified on behalf of six former shipmates tried in 1696 for piracy with Every.

Instead of being charged with piracy himself, after the appearance of *A New Voyage Round the World* (1697) Dampier was greeted like 'a freelance [hero] in the age of reconnaissance' (Lane, 201). The book was a great success, not principally as a tale of buccaneering but as an objective and useful account of lands unknown—and a revelation of Spain's wealth and weakness; seven printings in English and translations into Dutch, French, and German appeared during his lifetime. His straightforward style, graphic descriptions of the flora, fauna, and peoples he encountered, and detailed navigational information were cited in the popular and learned press and were admired by merchants, statesmen, and scientists. He dined with Samuel Pepys and John Evelyn, was befriended by Hans Sloane and Robert Southwell, and was appointed land-carriage man (at £8 15s. per quarter) at the London Customs House thanks to the influence of Charles Montague, lord of the Treasury and president of the Royal Society. By the end of 1699 he had testified four times before the Board of Trade on piracy in eastern waters and the commercial exploitation of Panama and published a *Supplement of the New Voyage*, which included an account of his life before his joining the buccaneers, a description of Campeche, and 'A discourse of winds, storms, seasons, tides, and currents in the torrid zone'. In the portrait painted of him at this time (now at the National Portrait Gallery in London), Thomas Murray captures something of his complex nature: he appears at forty-six a man of slight build but strong features that suggest at once an open demeanour and a brooding temperament.

Explorer and privateer, 1699–1715 Recognition of Dampier's talents was crowned by command of HMS *Roebuck* on a cruise into the Pacific (1699–1701), 'the first ... voyage planned for the deliberate purpose of scientific exploration' (Shipman, 30). His chief aim was to circumnavigate Terra Australis, which he now thought distinct from New Holland and to the east, and to demonstrate its commercial value. Dampier was hindered from the start by an inexperienced and fractious crew, but he fell short of discovering Australia's bounties by again restricting himself to the barren north-west coast (August–September 1699) and then sailing toward New Guinea, hoping to round the eastern coast of Terra Australis. In what is now called the Bismarck archipelago, however, he found a promising site for a colonial outpost, named the verdant island New Britain, and discovered the passage that separated it from New Guinea. After liberally bestowing English names about these islands, he was forced by the *Roebuck's* condition to sail for home. The *Roebuck* sank at Ascension Island in February 1701, and Dampier, bearing specimens of some forty Australian plants (now part of the Sherardian Herbarium, Oxford) and material for *A Voyage to New Holland* (1703), arrived at London in August aboard an East Indiaman. This and the earlier voyage are commemorated in a number of Australasian place names: the Dampier Strait (as the passage is now known), Roebuck Bay and Dampier Land in the north of Western Australia, and the Dampier archipelago off the west coast of Australia.

Dampier was welcomed home on this occasion not by honours but a court martial (held on 8 June 1702) instigated by a career officer he had assaulted aboard the *Roebuck*. After enduring several insults from George Fisher, who considered him an old pirate and friend of Every, he had exploded in rage, caning and then imprisoning the lieutenant. The court found him unfit for naval command, but his reputation as a brilliant navigator survived this disgrace. In April 1703, at the start of the War of the Spanish Succession, he was introduced to the queen by her husband, Prince George, a fellow of the Royal Society, and in September he sailed once more for the Pacific as commodore of a privateering expedition consisting of his ship, *St George*, and a consort, *Cinque-Ports* (Captain Charles Pickering). He left no memoir of this unfortunate voyage in which he was back at the old game of looting coastal towns and attempting to ambush the Manila galleon. He failed at both, and the two ships were consequently so rent with mutiny and desertion that one crewman jeered before departing, 'Poor Dampier, thy Case is like King James, every Body has left thee' (Dampier, *Voyages*, 2.585). When he returned to England in 1707 after a period of imprisonment at Batavia on suspicion of piracy he was forced to defend himself from the charges of former crewmen William Funnell (*A Voyage Round the World*, 1707) and John Welbe (*An Answer to Captain Dampier's 'Vindication'*, c.1707). Their accounts evidence a pattern of favouritism, ill temper, and abuse of his officers that had also characterized Dampier's command of the *Roebuck*; they further allege that he was a drunken coward who refused to board the Manila galleon (the *Rosario*) and that he took bribes from the captains of his few prizes. His short, irascible *Vindication* (1707) failed to convince Elisabeth Cresswell, heir of one of *St George's* owners, who in 1712 named him in an unsuccessful suit for fraud.

So enduring was Dampier's reputation as authority on the south seas and terror to the Spanish, that he was promptly recruited in 1708 to serve in a new privateering venture under Woodes Rogers. This astute commander took a Manila galleon in December 1709, a feat Dampier had attempted for three decades. If his memory of old haunts seems on occasion to have failed Dampier, there is no doubt that he helped plan the expedition of the *Duke* and the *Duchess* and functioned well as its pilot. His value to the nation was best expressed by the agent in Amsterdam who, upon Captain Rogers's coming into port there in July 1711, gratefully reported to Lord Treasurer Robert Harley that 'Dampier is alive' (Williams, 156). Rogers returned to England in October 1711 with literary as well as material wealth aboard: he rescued Alexander Selkirk, prototype for Defoe's Robinson Crusoe, from Juan Fernandez where Dampier's former consort, the *Cinque-Ports*, had marooned him in November 1704.

Dampier retired to the parish of St Stephen's, Coleman Street, London, where he lived modestly upon his Customs House sinecure and earnings from the privateering cruise, but, true to form, contention followed. Court documents reveal his and his heirs' efforts to recover in full what they believed was due from the owners. (Grace Mercer, his maternal cousin, executor, and chief heir, received £1050 17s. 10d. from the master in chancery in 1717, probably bringing Dampier's total earnings under Rogers to about £1500 although he had claimed considerably more.) Dampier died in 1715 leaving debts of £677 17s. 1d. and a will (dated 29 November 1714, proved 23 March 1715) which, as it makes no provision for his wife, suggests that she had died earlier.

Achievement Thrice a global circumnavigator, Dampier was a man of enormous endurance and resolve. Knowledge was his route out of the brutal world of buccaneers and pirates, but he was out of his element in the subtleties of managing men, 'an honest man, and a good sailor, but a little too positive in his own opinions' (J. Swift, *Gulliver's Travels*, 4.1). His tendency toward combativeness is absent from his books, where he adopts the voice recommended to scientific travellers by the Royal Society, that of an unassuming and detached observer, a literary construct that conveys what Masefield has called his 'calm, equable, untroubled and delighted vision' (Dampier, *Voyages*, 1.11). Indeed, his acute impressions of the physical world led Coleridge to savour the paradox of 'old Dampier, a rough sailor, but a man of exquisite mind' (S. Coleridge, *Table Talk*, in *Collected Works*, 16 vols., 1969–90, 1.268). His focus on natural history and ethnography helped to transform maritime travel writing while his prose style and descriptions of the struggle for survival in exotic places advanced the development of realistic fiction, notably in the novels of Defoe.

Dampier characteristically avoided the systematic interpretation of phenomena, but instead added greatly to the substratum of accurate observation upon which scientists of the next two centuries—such as John Ray, Alexander von Humboldt, and Charles Darwin—founded their own theoretical works. His paramount achievement lies in the usefulness of his books to generations of mariners, who consulted them for the disposition of native peoples as well as the best routes and anchorages. His pioneering work on compass variations in the *Voyage to New Holland* was incorporated a century later in the design of Captain Matthew Flinders's improved ship's compass, and the 'Discourse of winds', a 'classic of the pre-scientific era' (Shipman, 8), was recommended by Cook, Howe, and Nelson and was used in compiling *Admiralty Sailing Directions* as late as the 1930s. Mariners also read Dampier for first-hand advice on maintaining their health and on what was 'pleasant and very wholesome' (Dampier, *Voyages*, 2.391) to eat in the Americas and Indies.

Dampier's wanderings were shaped by the desire to exploit vulnerable points in Spain's overseas empire or to find promising new lands uncontrolled by European powers. Consequently, he was drawn to the Pacific where the Spanish were overextended; as his 'golden dreams' (Dampier, *Voyages*, 1.181) of Spanish treasure began to fade he searched for potential British outposts and shaped a course for Terra Australis. He returned frequently to Darien (the Isthmus of Panama) in part because its natives' resistance to Spanish rule gave the English an opening. Accordingly, he depicts the Mosquito Indians as athletic, skilled, and 'noble' savages worthy of protection (ibid., 1.39–42) while the hostile Australian Aborigines are 'the miserablest People in the world' (ibid., 1.453). Dampier's ethnic biases and colonial ambitions are tempered, however, by his genuine delight in learning about and from native peoples and his sensitivity to their melancholy at 'the loss of their Country and Liberties' (ibid., 1.152).

None of his voyages made him rich, yet by recreating a new world of natural wonders, fetched from afar but bearing the sense of reality, Dampier became the most important explorer before Cook to sustain the nation's interest in the south Pacific. A lifelong treasure hunter, a mercantile visionary, and an insatiable naturalist, his career demonstrates the interconnectedness of personal, commercial, and intellectual enterprise during the early modern period.   JOEL H. BAER

Sources W. Dampier, *The voyages of Captain William Dampier*, ed. J. Masefield, 2 vols. (1906) • A. Gill, *The devil's mariner: William Dampier, pirate and explorer* (1997) • G. Williams, *The great South Sea: English voyages and encounters, 1570–1750* (1997) • J. Baer, 'William Dampier at the crossroads: new light on the missing years, 1691–1697', *International Journal of Maritime History*, 8 (1996), 1–21 • N. Rennie, *Far-fetched facts: the literature of travel and the idea of the south seas* (1995) • B. M. H. Rogers, 'Woodes Rogers privateering voyage of 1708–11', *Mariner's Mirror*, 19 (1933), 196–211 • B. M. H. Rogers, 'Dampier's debts', *Mariner's Mirror*, 11 (1925), 322–4 • B. M. H. Rogers, 'Dampier's voyage of 1703', *Mariner's Mirror*, 10 (1924), 366–81 • W. Dampier, 'The adventures of William Dampier', [n.d.], BL, Sloane MS 3236 • K. E. Lane, *Pillaging the empire: piracy in the Americas 1500–1750* (1998) • W. H. Bonner, *Captain William Dampier: buccaneer–author* (1934) • C. Wilkinson, *Dampier: explorer and buccaneer* (1929) • PRO, PROB 11/545, sig. 43 • *IGI* • J. C. Shipman, *William Dampier: seaman–scientist* (1962)

Archives PRO, ADM 106/516, ADM 1/1692 | BL, account of South Sea voyages, Sloane MS 3236 • Som. ARS, Helyar archive

Likenesses T. Murray, oils, c.1697–1698, NPG [*see illus.*] • C. Sherwin, line engraving, pubd 1787 (after T. Murray), BM, NPG

Dampier [*formerly* Whetham], **Sir William Cecil Dampier** (1867–1952), scientist and agriculturist, was born in South Hampstead, London, on 27 December 1867, the only son (he had one sister) of Charles Langley Whetham, manufacturer, and his wife, Mary Ann, daughter of Thomas Dampier, glove manufacturer, of Yeovil. A shy boy, of indifferent health, he was educated for the most part privately. He became interested in science and entered Trinity College, Cambridge, where he was awarded an exhibition and a scholarship in his second and third years. He obtained first classes in both parts of the natural sciences tripos (1888–9), was Coutts Trotter student (1889), and Clerk Maxwell scholar (1893). Influenced by J. J. Thomson he undertook research at the Cavendish Laboratory which earned him a college fellowship in 1891. He was a college lecturer in physics (1895–1922), tutor (1907–13), senior tutor (1913–17), and remained a fellow for the rest of his life, an active member of the finance and estates committees and an ardent supporter of the Cambridge Preservation Society. An attempt in 1918 to represent Cambridge University in parliament as an independent Conservative proved unsuccessful.

In 1901 Whetham was elected fellow of the Royal Society and in the following year he published a treatise, *Theory of Solution*, which was for some time the standard textbook. He wrote a number of papers on ionic velocities and on electrolysis. Although college duties and other pursuits gradually diverted him from research he retained an interest in the work of other scientists, publishing *The Recent Development of Physical Science* (1904) and *History of Science* (1929), both of which went into a number of editions.

In 1897 Whetham married Catherine Durning, daughter of Robert Durning Holt, shipowner, of Liverpool. They had one son and five daughters, two of whom became scientific research workers. Whetham and his wife became absorbed in the history of his forebears, among whom were Thomas and William Dampier, bishop and buccaneer respectively; they published a biography of the roundhead Colonel Nathaniel Whetham in 1907 and, led on to a general study of heredity and its influence on society, they followed this with *The Family and the Nation* (1909) and *Heredity and Society* (1912).

Whetham inherited the Dampier family property in 1916 and farmed the land on the Hilfield estate in Dorset between 1918 and 1926. He specialized in the making of cheese and took part in the investigation of the possibilities of extracting lactose from whey. So he came to his last and abiding interest in agricultural economics.

Whetham was co-opted a member of council of the Royal Agricultural Society in 1921, received its gold medal in 1936, and became a vice-president in 1948. In 1925–42 he was a member of the Agricultural Wages Board, in 1933–51 a development commissioner, and in 1938–9 chairman of the land settlement committee. He was chairman of the Ministry of Agriculture machinery testing committee (1925–33) and of the committee for the preservation of grass and other fodder crops (1933–9), and acting chairman of the rural industries bureau (1939–45). In 1931 he was knighted for his services to agriculture, and changed his name to Dampier. In the same year he became first secretary of the Agricultural Research Council which he was able to establish on sound lines with freedom to engage directly in research before resigning in 1935 when he felt the technical side of the work had gone beyond his range of knowledge. He remained a member of the council until 1945 and served on many of its committees.

A shrewd and kindly man who found his long life 'interesting and amusing', Dampier was always willing to give his services in the public welfare. He died at the Evelyn Nursing Home, Cambridge, on 11 December 1952, a few months after his wife.

H. M. PALMER, rev. ISOBEL FALCONER

Sources W. Dampier, *Cambridge and elsewhere* (1950) · *The Times* (12 Dec 1952) · *The Times* (18 Dec 1952) · *The Times* (23 Jan 1953) · G. I. Taylor and E. H. E. Havelock, *Obits. FRS*, 9 (1954), 55–63 · private information (1971) · election certificate, RS · *CGPLA Eng. & Wales* (1953)
Likenesses W. Stoneman, photograph, 1943, NPG · G. J. Coates, portrait, repro. in Dampier, *Cambridge and elsewhere* · photograph, repro. in Taylor and Havelock, *Obits. FRS*, facing p. 55
Wealth at death £85,372 5s. 4d.: probate, 21 March 1953, *CGPLA Eng. & Wales*

Damplip, Adam. See Bucker, George (d. 1543).

Dana, Richard (1700–1772), lawyer and public official in America, was born in Cambridge, Massachusetts, on 26 June 1700 to Daniel Dana, a town selectman, and Naomi Croswell. After graduating AB from Harvard College in 1718, he remained in Massachusetts and became a lawyer, practising first in Marblehead, then Charlestown, and finally Boston, where he settled for life in 1745. In 1737 he married Lydia Trowbridge, sister of Judge Edmund Trowbridge and member of a prominent Cambridge family. They had nine children, including the Massachusetts politician Francis Dana. Dana quickly rose to prominence in Boston. He handled much of the town's official legal business, served as an overseer of the poor, and frequently presided over town meetings. Although a justice of the peace, he refused to hold any other public office. As he aged, he was nicknamed Father Dana.

Dana was a virulent opponent of British measures to regulate and tax the colonies. He was an original member of the Sons of Liberty, an American patriot organization, and was chosen to receive the honour on 17 August 1765 of taking the oath of Andrew Oliver, stamp master of Massachusetts, that he would never enforce the Stamp Act. Dana thereafter belonged to many town committees that drew up protests, including the one that 'investigated' the Boston 'massacre' of 5 September 1770. With his colleagues he tried to prove that six of the British soldiers keeping the peace in town had murdered innocent townspeople, ignoring the fact that a large crowd hurled insults,

snowballs, ice, and rocks at them. One of Dana's last public acts was to preside over the second commemoration of the 'massacre's' anniversary. Before his death he ranked with Samuel Adams and John Hancock among the resistance leaders.

Dana was a choleric individual who 'was all on fire, his face was inflated and empurpled, he thundered and lightened' (W. Ellery to Richard Henry Dana, 10 March 1819, Dana papers) when angered. As justice of the peace he frequently heard cases of debt and assault between British soldiers and townsfolk, for he was the most popular Bostonian justice before whom the inhabitants took their grievances. He invariably favoured his countrymen, refusing to bail soldiers and even to listen to evidence that might exculpate them. As his obituary in the *Boston Gazette* of 1 June 1772 noted, he was:

> a passionate opposer of all those (even from the highest to the lowest, but especially the former), who in his judgment were Enemies to the Civil and Religious Rights of his Country, and he very well understood what those Rights were.

He left a sizeable fortune to his children, being 'exemplary in Carefulness, Diligence, and Frugality ... HE HATED FLATTERY' and was 'a most inveterate enemy to Luxury and Prodigality', which he identified with supporters of the crown, especially Thomas Hutchinson, governor of Massachusetts, and his numerous relatives. His reputation among Bostonians for integrity clearly ignored his treatment of British soldiers whose presence in the town could not help but lead to frequent altercations. Dana's partiality encouraged his countrymen to goad the troops, and exacerbated rather than eased this tense situation. He died suddenly on 17 May 1772 in Boston.

WILLIAM PENCAK

Sources C. K. Shipton, *Sibley's Harvard graduates: biographical sketches of those who attended Harvard College*, 6 (1942), 236–9 · H. B. Zobel, *The Boston massacre* (1970) · Mass. Hist. Soc., Dana family MSS
Archives Mass. Hist. Soc., papers
Likenesses portrait, repro. in Shipton, *Sibley's Harvard graduates* · portrait, repro. in Zobel, *Boston massacre*
Wealth at death substantial but uncertain: Shipton, *Sibley's Harvard graduates*

Danby. For this title name *see* Danvers, Henry, earl of Danby (1573–1644).

Danby family (*per.* 1493–1667), gentry, had two main residences in Yorkshire, the ancestral mansion at Thorpe Perrow in the North Riding parish of Well, and Farnley Hall, near Leeds, in the West Riding. Although they were already a family of some consequence in the fifteenth century, it was not until the reign of Henry VIII that they emerged as a county family of the first rank. This development had its origins in the marriage of **Sir Christopher Danby** (d. 1518) and Margaret Scrope, one of the daughters of Thomas, fifth Baron Scrope of Masham, which took place in 1493. The marriage proved a valuable long-term investment: as a result of her brother's death without issue in 1517 Lady Danby inherited the extensive Mashamshire estate in the North Riding together with substantial property in other counties.

The estates of both his parents descended to **Sir Christopher Danby** (1503–1571), who became a ward of the crown following his father's death on 17 May 1518. He married Elizabeth Neville, a daughter of Richard, second Baron Latimer, with whom he had six sons and eight daughters. In 1533 he was knighted shortly before the coronation of Anne Boleyn. During the initial stages of the Pilgrimage of Grace in 1536 he joined the rebel leaders at Pontefract Castle but managed to escape punishment for his disloyalty and even acted as foreman of one of the grand juries involved in the subsequent trials. After this episode he became heavily involved in public affairs, serving as a commissioner for musters and a justice of the peace and securing election to the parliament of April 1554 as one of the Yorkshire knights of the shire. On the other hand he was anxious to avoid the burdensome office of high sheriff, but after being reprieved on several occasions he was finally appointed in 1545. In the reign of Elizabeth his Catholic sympathies caused some concern in official circles. In a report on the Yorkshire justices of the peace which the archbishop of York forwarded to the privy council in 1564 he and his son Thomas were described as men who were no favourers of the established religion. The following year the privy council decided that he should be brought before the council in the north for questioning about a story originating with one of his servants that plans were being made for an uprising in Yorkshire. In the event, however, there appears to have been insufficient evidence to justify the framing of charges against him. He died on 14 June 1571.

Sir Thomas Danby (c.1530–1590) was about forty when his father died. He had been knighted in 1547 while serving his military apprenticeship on an expedition into Scotland. In accordance with a marriage contract negotiated in 1534 he took as his wife Mary Neville, a daughter of Ralph, fourth earl of Westmorland (1498–1549), with whom he had four sons. Despite his Catholic convictions and the Neville connection he took up arms for the crown when the northern uprising of 1569 broke out though, on the other hand, his brother Christopher threw in his lot with the rebels and eventually fled abroad. During the early 1570s Sir Thomas was faced with the unwelcome attentions of the northern high commission, which took a close interest in his religious loyalties. In December 1572 he told the commissioners, somewhat disingenuously, that when he was living near a church he attended the services there, and that otherwise he had services in his house which were conducted by a domestic chaplain in accordance with the laws of the realm. He admitted, however, that he had not communicated for four years. Subsequently, in March 1573, he was ordered to receive communion three times a year, and from then on he seems to have conformed sufficiently to avoid further trouble, though he may also have benefited from his friendship with the Cecils, to whom he was distantly related. When he was appointed sheriff of Yorkshire in 1575 it was a clear sign that the central government considered him to be trustworthy.

During Elizabeth's reign the Danbys reorganized their estates by disposing of their property in other counties and purchasing adjoining manors in the North Riding. Sir Thomas was an efficient and enterprising landowner. He mined coal in Mashamshire and at Farnley and elsewhere in the West Riding, and like his father was heavily engaged in enclosing activities. His enclosures on the commons around Masham often caused hardship among the tenants of neighbouring manors, but they felt powerless to mount a challenge against him. In 1586 he finished building a new mansion at Farnley which was relatively modest in scale. In his will, drawn up on 3 September 1590, he styled himself as of South Cave in the East Riding, where he owned one of the manors, stipulated that he should be buried in the parish church there, and bequeathed the manor to his son Richard, who was later convicted of recusancy. At his death shortly afterwards the estate revenue amounted to some £1500 a year, excluding the lands which his widowed daughter-in-law held as her jointure.

Predeceased by his eldest son, another Thomas, Sir Thomas was succeeded by his eight-year-old grandson **Christopher Danby** (1582–1624). The latter's wardship was granted to Thomas Cecil, the eldest son of Lord Burghley, but it was soon transferred to Christopher's mother, **Elizabeth Danby** (d. 1629). She was a daughter of Thomas Wentworth (d. 1588) of Wentworth Woodhouse and aunt of Sir Thomas Wentworth, the future earl of Strafford. An ardent Catholic, she usually had a seminary priest in her house and also employed a private tutor who was described in 1596 as a non-communicant. For some time she and her son led a peripatetic life, one mainly occasioned by her desire to escape the attention of the authorities (though in the latter part of her life she was indicted for recusancy and heavily fined for harbouring recusants). Between 1602 and 1608 the Danby estate was brought to the verge of ruin by a corrupt steward (also called Christopher Danby) whose basic aim was self-enrichment. In 1610 the court of Star Chamber was informed that during the long absence of his employers he had renewed many leases at the old rents in return for gifts, allowed their mansion houses to decay, and defrauded them of £7000. The young squire proved incapable of meeting the challenge: he borrowed heavily, sold some land, and was outlawed for debt. To add to his troubles he was faced with allegations about his religious loyalties. In 1607 the crown granted the benefits of his recusancy to a courtier, Sir Henry Cary, who no doubt expected to be amply compensated for relinquishing his interest.

Further problems arose from Christopher Danby's marriage, on 6 July 1607. **Frances Danby** [née Parker] (d. 1654) was a daughter of Edward, twelfth Baron Morley. Although he was supposed to receive a portion of £1000 with her, it proved impossible to reach agreement on a marriage settlement. The couple had two sons and a daughter but they often lived apart, and at one stage Danby accused his wife of adultery. In 1617 Sir Thomas

Wentworth urged him to seek a reconciliation while observing that it was generally believed that he had frequently been unfaithful. Frances Danby was convicted of recusancy, but her husband apparently conformed. Shortly before his death in 1624 he sent his son Thomas to a school run by a protestant clergyman, William Greene of South Kirkby, near Barnsley, and instructed the master to deny access to any of his wife's relations and friends.

Sir Thomas Danby (1610–1660) was the first unequivocally protestant head of the family. Two parties bid for his wardship, the mother's party and the grandmother's party. The latter included Wentworth, who took a harsh view of the mother, not least because she had already remarried, her new husband being William Richards. In 1626 the wardship was finally secured by his friend Christopher Wandesford, who was a zealous protestant. The crown's financial exactions consisted of a wardship fine of £800 and a rent of £150 a year. At the time of Christopher Danby's death the estate revenue had amounted to some £2000 a year but there were many encumbrances. Elizabeth Danby had a jointure worth £505 a year, and a further £350 a year was allocated for the dower of Thomas's mother. In the event Wandesford cleared the estate of debt and put it on a much sounder footing.

Thomas Danby was admitted as a fellow commoner to St John's College, Cambridge, in 1627 and placed with a tutor whom his guardian described as a strict puritan. In 1630, after some hesitation, he married Wandesford's daughter Catherine, with whom by the time of her death in September 1645 he had eight sons and two daughters.

During a visit to Dublin in 1633 Danby was knighted by Wentworth in his capacity of lord deputy. Two years later Wentworth made him a deputy lieutenant for the North Riding, where he also sat on the commission of the peace. In 1637 he was appointed sheriff of Yorkshire and was required to collect £12,000 in ship money. Although he executed the ship money writ with some severity, there was a shortfall of £1237 15s. 6d., which according to his grandson he was forced to pay himself to his great damage. In May 1638, while still serving as sheriff, he borrowed £5000 and charged his Mashamshire property with the payment of £400 a year as mortgage interest. In the elections for the Long Parliament he was returned as MP for Richmond through the influence of his former guardian. During Strafford's trial he spoke in his favour, and on 21 April 1641 he voted against the bill for his attainder. In March 1642 the house noted that he had joined the king at York, and in September he was deprived of his seat.

Taking up arms for the king, Danby was captured by Ferdinando, second Lord Fairfax, in January 1643. Eventually he escaped, but in August 1644 he surrendered to the parliamentarian forces. In 1646 he compounded for his estate and was fined £4780, which he found difficult to pay.

Despite his financial problems Danby bought a share in a Virginia plantation, and in 1653 two of his younger sons were reported to have arrived there. At the time of his death the Yorkshire estate was producing an income of £2500 a year, but in his will (which was drawn up on 11 November 1659) he stipulated that property worth £450 a year should be sold for the purpose of discharging the mortgage and raising £5000 for his children's portions. Danby died in London on 5 August 1660 and was buried in York Minster.

In 1659 Danby's son **Thomas Danby** (1631–1667) married Margaret Eure, a cousin and coheiress of William, fifth Baron Eure, who had a portion of £2000 and lands worth £500 a year. MP for Malton for a few months in 1660, in 1661 he was the first mayor of Leeds to be appointed under the town's new charter. He had told his father that he was anxious to keep the family estate intact, and in 1663 he persuaded the trustees to let him have possession of the lands scheduled for disposal on the understanding that he would meet his obligations by other means. In the event his aspirations were never fulfilled. When he raised the rents of his tenants, many of them surrendered their leases and some men actually set their houses on fire. While in the process of negotiating a loan of £16,000, he was killed in a London tavern on 1 August 1667 by a stranger who had picked a quarrel with him. Although he left an estate valued at £2300 a year, he had neither paid the portions nor redeemed the mortgage.

During the remainder of the century the Danbys engaged in protracted litigation, sold considerable property (including the manor of Thorpe Perrow), cleared off the mortgage, and settled at Swinton, near Masham. Despite all their vicissitudes they remained a major Yorkshire family until they expired in the male line in 1833.

J. T. CLIFFE

Sources N. Yorks. CRO, Cunliffe-Lister (Swinton) MSS (Danby family papers) · CSP dom., SP 1 (Henry VIII); SP 10 (Edward VI); SP 11 (Mary); SP 12 (Elizabeth) · wills in the York registry, Borth. Inst., vol. 24, fol. 397; vol. 54, fol. 97 · high commission act books, Borth. Inst., vols. R VII/AB/4, 8, and 10 · star chamber proceedings, James I, PRO, STAC 8/120/2 · J. P. Cooper, ed., Wentworth papers, 1597–1628, CS, 4th ser., 12 (1973) · court of wards, miscellaneous books, PRO, wards 9/118, 207, 209, 565, 567 · chancery proceedings, six clerks' series, PRO, C.5/186/98, C.5/420/6, and C.8/52/15 · chancery decrees and orders, PRO, C.33/237, 253, 257, 261, 265, and 307 · J. T. Cliffe, The Yorkshire gentry from the Reformation to the civil war (1969) · C. Whone, 'Christopher Danby of Masham and Farnley', Thoresby Society, 37 (1936–42), 1–28 · HoP, Commons, 1509–58, 2.10–11 · P. A. Bolton and P. Watson, 'Danby, Thomas', HoP, Commons, 1660–90, 2.187–8 · A. Gooder, ed., The parliamentary representation of the county of York, 1258–1832, 2, Yorkshire Archaeological Society, 96 (1938), 14–15 · H. Aveling, Northern Catholics: the Catholic recusants of the North Riding of Yorkshire, 1558–1790 (1966) · GEC, Peerage
Archives N. Yorks. CRO, Cunliffe-Lister (Swinton) MSS
Likenesses J. Carleton, portrait, 1635 (Thomas Danby); formerly at Swinton Park · oils (Thomas Danby), repro. in E. Hailstone, ed., Portraits of Yorkshire worthies, 1 (1869), no. 80

Danby, Sir Christopher (d. 1518). See under Danby family (per. 1493–1667).

Danby, Sir Christopher (1503–1571). See under Danby family (per. 1493–1667).

Danby, Christopher (1582–1624). See under Danby family (per. 1493–1667).

Danby, Elizabeth (d. 1629). See under Danby family (per. 1493–1667).

Danby, Frances (*d.* 1654). *See under* Danby family (*per.* 1493–1667).

Danby, Francis (1793–1861), landscape painter, was born on 16 November 1793 at Common, Killinick, near Wexford, Ireland, one of the twin sons among the three children of James Danby (*d.* 1807), a minor country gentleman, and his second wife, Margaret Watson of Dublin. The Danby family was caught up in the Wexford rebellion, the bloodiest of the insurrections of 1798; they moved to Dublin, where Francis Danby later attended the Dublin Society School of Drawing. In 1813 he had his first oil painting exhibited at the Society of Artists of Ireland. On the proceeds of its sale Danby, together with his two artist friends George Petrie (1790–1866) and James Arthur O'Connor (1792–1841), travelled to London to visit the Royal Academy's annual exhibition. Danby and O'Connor then walked from London to Bristol hoping to catch a free passage on a packet-boat to Ireland. O'Connor continued but Danby remained, perhaps after discovering that there was a ready market for his watercolours of the local scenery, especially of the Avon Gorge and the Hotwells spa. The following year, on 4 July 1814, at Winscombe parish church, south of Bristol on the edge of the Mendips, he entered into a disastrous marriage with an illiterate Somerset servant girl, Hannah Hardedge or Hardidge (*bap.* 1794, *d.* 1879); until 1817 the growing family lived at nearby Compton Bishop. Once resident in Bristol and in more regular contact with other Bristol artists and such sophisticated amateur artists as George Cumberland (1754–1848) and the Revd John Eagles (1783–1855), Danby's art developed very fast. After the early picturesque watercolours of the Avon Gorge, Danby's local subjects inclined more to such intimate and secluded wooded valleys around Bristol as Nightingale valley in Leigh Woods and along the Frome at Stapleton. Very detailed, intensely observed, and with strong dense colour, these increasingly personal records of local landscape scenes are nevertheless profoundly Romantic in spirit. The small Stapleton paintings, inspired by the narrow and steeply wooded valley of the Frome, reflect his fascination with dark effects and with the contented, self-contained world of childhood, which he depicted without sentimentality. An emphasis on the refreshing innocence of youth echoed the beliefs of the great poet and painter William Blake (1757–1827), of whom Danby would have known through their mutual friend George Cumberland.

Early works Evening scenes with a mood of tranquillity and contemplation increasingly predominated among Danby's local views, and such effects were also often the subject of his purely imaginary landscapes. These poetic landscapes ('poetical' was the word Danby himself used to describe them) are unusual in British art. They often have no literary, classical, or biblical subject matter. The Bristol artists and amateurs at their evening sketching meetings, which were so important to Danby, set no specific theme or subject for the evening drawings, contrary to the practice of the London Sketching Society. This almost certainly encouraged a greater element of fantasy in their

Francis Danby (1793–1861), by unknown photographer

evening landscape drawings in sepia wash and in their subsequent oil paintings and watercolours. Danby's outstanding imaginary landscape was *An Enchanted Island* (priv. coll.) of 1824, exhibited at the British Institution in 1825. Warm evening sunshine falls across a landscape of caverns and rocks familiar on the Avon or the Frome, but the kingfisher and the heron are replaced by a bird of paradise and a flamingo and nymphs and fairies can just be seen in the shadows. It is an original work of rare lyricism that pays inspired homage to Claude Lorrain, whom Danby, like both John Constable (1776–1837) and J. M. W. Turner (1775–1851), admired above all other artists. It was this painting that was the favourite possession of the collector John Gibbons (1777–1851), a midland ironmaster who had lived in Bristol until about 1822. From this time until his death in 1851 he supported Danby with extraordinary patience, forbearance, and generosity, acquiring many paintings in return for innumerable loans and even sending the artist a regular survival allowance when he fled to the continent amid much scandal in 1830.

As early as 1819 Danby had begun the first of his ambitious and calculated exhibition paintings. *The Upas, or Poison Tree in the Island of Java* (V&A) was shown at the British Institution in 1820. The artist Richard Redgrave remembered this vast painting as 'a wonderful first attempt' and he noted that 'to succeed in such a subject required a poetical mind, joined to the powers of the highest order: no mere landscape painting, no mere imitation of Nature, would suffice to picture to us the gloomy horrors of this land of fear' (Redgrave and Redgrave, 439–40).

The Upas Tree failed to sell and Danby's next exhibition painting was *Disappointed Love* (V&A). It depicts a forlorn girl beside a dark recess of the River Frome. It was a less forbidding work and it sold immediately at the Royal Academy in 1821. It was equally gloomy, however, and Danby, while acknowledging the difficulties of selling dark paintings, remained fascinated by rich deep tones, by landscapes in which light is an almost tangible force penetrating the shadows, and by effects of dawn, twilight, sunset, and moonlight.

Move to London In April or early in May 1824 Danby moved suddenly and secretly from Bristol to London leaving substantial debts behind him. A few weeks later *Sunset at Sea after a Storm* (Bristol Museum and Art Gallery) was shown at the Royal Academy and purchased by the president, Sir Thomas Lawrence. Although it is essentially a marine landscape painting rather than a history painting, *Sunset at Sea after a Storm*, with its raft of shipwrecked survivors, was certainly inspired by Géricault's *Raft of the Medusa* (Louvre, Paris). Danby did not see this enormous painting when it went to London in 1820, but he later acknowledged that he knew it well through enthusiastic descriptions by his Bristol friends. Early in 1825 he showed *An Enchanted Island* at the British Institution to general acclaim, and soon afterwards he triumphed at the Royal Academy with *The Delivery of Israel out of Egypt* (Harris Museum and Art Gallery, Preston), which was immediately bought by the marquess of Stafford for £500. The size and concept of this painting and its limitless landscape and innumerable figures may have been encouraged by the biblical epics of John Martin (1789–1854), but the studied naturalism of the lowering clouds and the overwhelming sea have no parallels in Martin's work, and the figures are more reminiscent of the Bristol artist Edward Bird (1772–1819). It may well have been the exhibition arranged in 1814 in Bristol by Samuel Taylor Coleridge of the paintings of the American artist Washington Allston (1779–1843) which first attracted Danby to such large and dramatic works. Allston had come to Bristol in 1813 to be treated by the surgeon John King (born Johann Koenig; 1776–1846). King was to be a close friend of Danby and exemplifies the sophistication of his Bristol acquaintances. King had worked with Thomas Beddoes and Humphrey Davy; he married Maria Edgeworth's sister and he knew Coleridge, Southey, and Wordsworth well. In 1826 John Martin's *Deluge* dominated the British Institution's annual exhibition. Danby immediately accused Martin of plagiarizing his own *Attempt to Illustrate the Opening of the Sixth Seal* (NG Ire.), which was then unfinished and whose completion Danby now purposely delayed. It was finally shown at the Royal Academy in 1828 and purchased by William Beckford, author of *Vathek* and builder of Fonthill Abbey. The price was 500 guineas, but Danby also received £300 for the copyright from Colnaghi and 200 guineas from the British Institution as a prize, all of which elicited the grudging admiration of John Constable, who described it as 'a grand but murky dream' (*John Constable's Correspondence*, ed. R. B. Beckett, 6, 1968, 236). It was the most successful moment of Danby's career. The débâcle

was swift, however. Danby had been elected an associate of the Royal Academy in November 1825. Now, in February 1829, he was defeated by Constable in the election for full membership by one vote; Danby bitterly accused Constable of meanness and intrigue as well as having been elected only because his wife had just inherited £30,000.

Move to the continent By July 1829 Danby was heavily in debt and in December he fled from his creditors to Paris, probably taking with him his pregnant mistress, Ellen Evans (*c.*1810–1837), 'a girl who lived in the house as a sort of governess to his children' (E. V. Rippingille to J. G., 16 Dec 1830, Gibbons papers). In January 1830 Danby returned briefly to London to attend Sir Thomas Lawrence's funeral in the vain hope of salvaging his reputation with the Royal Academy. In May Danby and Ellen Evans moved to Bruges, where they were joined by Danby's seven children, among them James Francis *Danby and Thomas *Danby. They had been deserted by their mother, who was now living with the artist Paul Falconer Poole (1807–1879). The family moved on to Aix-la-Chapelle, to Cologne, and then to Neuwied near Koblenz for the winter. Here Danby concocted plans to construct a raft on which to travel up the Rhine and ultimately on to the Mediterranean coast with Ellen and his children, now eight in number. By May 1831 they had all arrived by more conventional means at Rapperswil on Lake Zürich. Danby sent watercolours to London for sale, John Gibbons made advances of money, and the Royal Academy sent a donation of £50, Constable himself seconding the motion. It was not enough, however, and after a year Danby's landlord refused further credit. In August 1832 the family, now including nine children, arrived in Geneva, penniless and near starvation. The wife of the director of the Academy of Arts raised subscriptions from local patrons and commissioned *The Baptism of Christ* of 1833 (Musée d'Art et d'Histoire, Geneva). Danby executed small watercolours both for collectors' albums and for illustration in the elegant British annuals of the day. Several of his oil paintings were of imaginary scenes inspired by memories of his hurried visit to Norway in 1825, notably *Liensfiord, Norway* (Tate collection), a striking landscape with an impressive sense of remoteness. By November 1834 Danby was supporting ten children aged from five months to eighteen years. He was seriously in debt, partly because he had spent much of the summer building a sailing boat which he proudly claimed to be the fastest on Lake Geneva. The Chambre des Étrangers considered expelling him but within a year Danby had cleared his debts.

Later works By May 1836 Danby and his family had moved to Paris. Here he was much occupied with painting copies of works in the Louvre. William Jones, a dubious picture dealer and painter, commissioned *The Deluge* (Tate collection), an enormous work nearly 3 by 4½ metres. It was eventually exhibited at 213 Piccadilly in London in 1840 with moderate success, but the original intentions of sending it on tour to America and elsewhere were abandoned. Although inspired by both Géricault's *Raft of the*

Medusa and Poussin's *Deluge*, both in the Louvre, the painting's monumental gloom may have been affected by the death in Paris of Ellen Evans in 1837 and of three of his younger children in 1838. Melancholy and loneliness rather than despair characterize the two outstanding works that Danby showed at the Royal Academy in 1841, *Liensfiord Lake, in Norway* and *The Enchanted Castle—Sunset* both in the Victoria and Albert Museum, London. From 1841 until his death Danby once again exhibited almost annually at the Royal Academy, but of nearly fifty works shown at the Royal Academy and at the British Institution only ten are known today. Several were destroyed in the Second World War, while others were ruined by overcleaning. Many may have suffered a similar fate to *The Gate of the Harem*. This was purchased at the British Institution's exhibition of 1845 by Queen Victoria for Osborne House but was destroyed by order of Queen Mary in 1927. A moonlight and sunset scene, it was probably very dark, and with surface dirt, the darkening of the varnish, and some deterioration of the more resinous parts of the medium, it probably appeared to be a blackened wreck.

From 1839 until 1846 Danby lived frugally at various modest addresses in and near London. He then settled in Exmouth, Devon, spending many of his summers boatbuilding and sailing—'for this pleasure is what I most care for in life, and I am content to fag all winter, for its repetition' (Francis Danby to John Gibbons, 22 Nov 1856, Gibbons papers). He now had orders in plenty from both industrialists and dealers. The quiet serenity of *Dead Calm—Sunset at the Bight of Exmouth* (Royal Albert Memorial Museum, Exeter), shown at the Royal Academy in 1855, may reflect the contentment of his last years at Exmouth, just as the late, vivid, and small on-the-spot oil sketches such as *Sunset through Trees* (Bristol Museum and Art Gallery) demonstrate his enduring fascination for extreme effects of light and darkness. In August 1860 Danby was shipwrecked off Axmouth in his new yacht, *Dragon Fly*. Within two months he had applied for a patent for a new kind of single-fluked anchor. The patent was later granted to his son James. That Christmas he visited his old friend Samuel Jackson at Bristol, but on or about 10 February 1861 Danby died suddenly at his home, Shell House on The Maer at Exmouth. He was buried in the churchyard of St John-in-the-Wilderness, Withycombe, Devon.

Danby's obituary notice in *The Athenaeum* began: 'A life more sad has been rarely led by a man of undoubted genius' (1861, 294). The writer may have been expressing his own frustration at Danby's failure to become a full member of the Royal Academy, where, he noted, Danby had exhibited in the 1840s and 1850s 'year after year, a series of pictures, the power, the poetry and romance of which should long ago have won a chair among the Forty' (ibid.). Danby's infidelity and his desertion of his wife in 1829 were not reason enough for his continued rejection, which still remains something of a mystery. However, his stubbornness and his concern for his own dignity—best exemplified by his refusal to accept charity even when his children arrived starving in Geneva in 1832—may have caused the endlessly embittered relationship. It was the

Royal Academy, however, together with the British Institution, that had been the focus of Danby's early ambitions and for which he painted some of the most memorable images of British Romantic landscape painting. These imaginary scenes have often been perceived as succeeding the Bristol landscape views. The recent conservation of *The Upas Tree*, painted in 1819 five years before he moved to London, and its display in 1988 for the first time in over 100 years, has helped to confound this impression. The later Bristol landscapes had shown an increasing emphasis on the portrayal of mood becoming no less imaginative than the imaginary scenes. They recorded not only topographical detail but the sensation of man's delight in nature and of his unusually harmonious relationship with it. Whether directly or indirectly through his Bristol friends, Danby was profoundly affected by the legacy of Bristol's close association with Wordsworth, Coleridge, and Southey, leading poets of Romanticism, and he played as crucial a role in the emergence of the Bristol school of artists as did both Crome and Cotman in the success of the Norwich school.

FRANCIS GREENACRE

Sources E. Adams, *Francis Danby: varieties of poetic landscape* (1973) [incl. bibliography] • F. Greenacre, *Francis Danby, 1793–1861* (1988) [exhibition catalogue, City of Bristol Museum and Art Gallery and Tate Gallery, London, 1988] • H. W. Häusermann, 'Francis Danby in Geneva', *Burlington Magazine*, 91 (1949), 227–9 • E. H. Schiotz, *Itineraria Norvegica: foreigners' travels in Norway until 1900* (1976) • J. Baker, 'Francis Danby and his Somerset connections', 1991, City Museum and Art Gallery, Bristol, fine art artists' files • J. Baker, 'Some descendants of Francis Danby, artist', 1991, City Museum and Art Gallery, Bristol, fine art artists' files • Bristol RO, Gibbons papers, 41197 • M. Anglesea, 'Five unpublished drawings by Francis Danby', *Burlington Magazine*, 117 (1975), 47–8 • F. Greenacre, *William Evans of Bristol* (1987) [exhibition catalogue, Martyn Gregory Gallery, London, 10–28 Nov 1987] • R. Redgrave and S. Redgrave, *A century of painters of the English school*, 2 vols. (1866) • CGPLA Eng. & Wales (1861)

Archives Bristol RO, Gibbons papers, letters to John Gibbons, etc., 41197

Likenesses N. C. Branwhite, photograph, c.1825 (of lost drawing), City Museum and Art Gallery, Bristol • C. Moore, plaster bust, 1827, NG Ire. • J. King, oils, 1828, City Museum and Art Gallery, Bristol • S. P. Jackson, photograph, c.1855, City Museum and Art Gallery, Bristol, Ada Villiers Album • H. T. Munns, oils, c.1860, NG Ire. • J. & C. Watkins, photograph, c.1860, City Museum and Art Gallery, Bristol • F. Danby, pencil drawing, Agnew's, London • photograph, priv. coll. [see illus.]

Wealth at death £800: probate, 26 Feb 1861, CGPLA Eng. & Wales

Danby, Frank. See Frankau, Julia (1859–1916).

Danby, James Francis (1815/16–1875), landscape painter, was baptized at Compton Bishop, near Weston-super-Mare, Somerset, on 27 April 1817. He was the second son of the landscape painter Francis *Danby (1793–1861) and his wife, Hannah Hardedge or Hardidge (*bap.* 1794, *d.* 1879). Of Francis Danby's eleven children, with both his wife and his mistress, it was James who remained closest to his father, handling his estate, diligently inscribing many of his father's remaining sketches and drawings, and following his father's painting style very much more closely than did his younger brother, Thomas *Danby (1821?–1886). As J. L. Roget noted: 'It was a susceptibility of the quieter kind that descended upon Thomas Danby, his brother James taking more kindly to the sunsets of blood and fire' (Roget, 2.421). However, James's landscapes, though painted with considerable technical competence, were prosaic in comparison with his father's more imaginative and dramatic scenes. He concentrated on coastal scenes, working almost exclusively in oils, and exhibited with impressive consistency between 1842 and 1875 at the Royal Academy, the British Institution, and the Society of British Artists.

James Danby was probably with his father on the continent throughout most of the 1830s. He had returned to England by 1839 and in the following year applied unsuccessfully to the Bristol Literary and Philosophical Institution to exhibit his father's painting *The Deluge* (Tate collection). While in Paris in 1838 he had almost certainly assisted his father with this vast work. He married Sophia Elizabeth Carter (1820–1880) on 26 July 1841; they had eight children. Danby died at his home, 54 Park Road, Haverstock Hill, Hampstead, London, on 22 October 1875, aged fifty-nine. One hundred and fifty of his paintings and oil sketches were sold at Christie, Manson, and Woods Ltd, London, on 18 March 1876.   FRANCIS GREENACRE

Sources J. Baker, 'Francis Danby and his Somerset connections', 1991, City Museum and Art Gallery, Bristol, fine art artists' files · J. Baker, 'Some descendants of Francis Danby, artist', 1991, City Museum and Art Gallery, Bristol, fine art artists' files · priv. coll., Worcestershire, Gibbons MSS · E. Adams, *Francis Danby: varieties of poetic landscape* (1973) · F. Greenacre, *Francis Danby, 1793–1861* (1988) [exhibition catalogue, City of Bristol Museum and Art Gallery and Tate Gallery, London, 1988] · F. Greenacre, *The Bristol school of artists: Francis Danby and painting in Bristol, 1810–1840* [1973] [exhibition catalogue, City Museum and Art Gallery, Bristol, 4 Sept – 10 Nov 1973] · *Catalogue of the whole of the remaining pictures & sketches of that accomplished artist, James Danby* (1876) [sale catalogue, Christies, 18 March 1876] · J. L. Roget, *A history of the 'Old Water-Colour' Society*, 2 (1891) · Graves, *RA exhibitors* · Graves, *Artists* · parish register (baptism), Compton Bishop parish church, 27 April 1817 · *DNB*
Likenesses woodcut, 1875, NPG · J. Watkins, carte-de-visite, NPG
Wealth at death under £800: probate, 13 Nov 1875, *CGPLA Eng. & Wales*

Danby, John (1756/7–1798), organist and composer, was a younger son of Richard Danby and Hannah Caffrey, whose marriage on 22 February 1748 is recorded in the registers of the Portuguese embassy chapel, Mayfair, Westminster; both Richard and Hannah were still alive in 1789. Richard Danby may have been related to the Catholic Danbys of Catterick in the North Riding of Yorkshire, one of whom subscribed to John's first book of glees. Richard's eldest son, Charles (1749–1824), became a singer at Drury Lane Theatre by 1776, and both John and their nephew Eustace Danby (1781–1821) followed in his steps.

John Danby, who sang bass parts, was apprenticed to Samuel Webbe the elder, who nominated him for membership of the Society of Musicians on 2 January 1785, saying 'his present engagements are Drury Lane Theatre, Concert of Antient Music, Oratorios, Academy of Antient Music, at all of which he sings in Chorus, has several scholars and a variety of other engagements' (Matthews, 44). In 1781 Danby won the first of ten prizes from the Catch Club for his glees and catches with a cheerful glee, 'When Sappho tun'd the raptur'd strain'. In 1785 his songs sung at Vauxhall Gardens began to be published and the first of his four books of glees, catches, and canons appeared; it was dedicated to the Catholic lawyer Charles Butler and re-issued about 1790. In 1787 he was elected a professional member of the Noblemen's and Gentlemen's Catch Club. This introduced him to people of rank, as evidenced by the list of subscribers to his second book of glees, published in 1789.

On 4 April 1788 at St Mary, Lambeth, Danby married Sarah Goose (1766?–1861), whose sister had married his closest friend, Roch Jaubert, the year before. They lived first at 26 Henrietta Street, Covent Garden, but by 1794 were at 8 Gilberts Buildings on the border of Southwark and Lambeth. On 10 April 1795, after he had been ill for seven months, Danby had a benefit concert at Willis's Rooms; it was advertised to include a work by Haydn 'to be performed under his immediate direction' (*The Times*, 10 April 1795). R. J. S. Stevens two years later described Danby's fingers as 'drawn quite crooked by a paralytic stroke' (Argent, 108), and another benefit concert was held at the same place on 16 May 1798. As it was closing, Danby died at his home, 46 Upper John Street, Fitzroy Square, to which he had moved in 1795.

Danby's third book of glees and catches appeared in 1796 and a posthumous one was published in 1798 by Jaubert. Two textbooks had earlier appeared: *La guida alla musica vocale* (1788) and *La guida della musica instrumentale* (1798). His widow subsisted until her death in 1861 mainly on help from the Royal Society of Musicians, though from about 1800 to 1813 she lived with the painter J. M. W. Turner, with whom she had two daughters. With Danby she had had seven children, of whom four daughters lived to maturity, one married the musician Henry George Nixon (1796–1849), and the youngest married a piano maker, Henry Symondson (1800–1848).

Danby's glee 'Awake, Aeolian lyre!' continued to be sung and published throughout the next century. The conventional lines on his altar tomb in the churchyard of St Pancras Old Church referred to his ability to sadden or cheer the heart

Whether by playful Catch, by serious Glee,
Or the more Solemn Canon's Harmony.

At an unknown date he was appointed organist to the Spanish embassy chapel, for which he composed some sacred music.   SELBY WHITTINGHAM

Sources S. Whittingham and others, *Of geese, mallards and drakes: some notes on Turner's family*, rev. edn, 1: *The Danbys* (2000) · S. Whittingham, 'A letter found', *Music and Letters*, 76 (1995), 68–71 · D. Baptie, *Sketches of the English glee composers: historical, biographical and critical (from about 1735–1866)* [1896] · Recollections of R. J. S. Stevens: an organist in Georgian London, ed. M. Argent (1992) · B. Matthews, ed., *The Royal Society of Musicians of Great Britain: list of members, 1738–1984* (1985) · Highfill, Burnim & Langhans, *BDA* · *Morning Herald* (18 May 1798) · *GM*, 1st ser., 68 (1798), 448 · *European Magazine and London Review*, 33 (1798), 359 · W. A. Barrett, *English glees and part-songs* (1886) · J. C. Kassler, *The science of music in Britain, 1714–1830: a catalogue of writings, lectures, and inventions*, 1 (1979) · *The Mawhood diary: selections from the diary note-books of William Mawhood, woollen-draper of London, for the years 1764–1770*, ed. E. E. Reynolds,

Catholic RS, 50 (1956) • Viscount Gladstone [H. J. Gladstone], *The story of the Noblemen and Gentlemen's Catch Club* (1930) • R. Darby, 'The music of the Roman Catholic embassy chapels in London, 1765–1825', MusM diss., University of Manchester, 1984 • parish register (baptism), Baumber, Lincolnshire, 5 April 1766 • parish register (marriage), St Mary, Lambeth, 4 April 1788

Danby, Sir Robert (*d.* 1474), justice, was one of the six sons of Thomas Danby of Yafforth, North Riding of Yorkshire, and Mary, daughter of Sir Robert Tanfield. He pursued his career both in the north of England and in the courts at Westminster. He was an arbitrator for the prior of Durham in 1431, and prior's serjeant from 1442 until at least 1453/4. Appointed as his attorney-general in 1438 by Robert Neville, bishop of Durham, Danby became chief justice of the palatinate of Durham in 1454. He was also a councillor and executor of the bishop's brother, Richard Neville, earl of Salisbury, was retained by Humphrey Stafford, duke of Buckingham from 1441 to 1447, and was counsel to Hull corporation (1448/9–1452/3), to Margaret of Anjou (1452/3), and to Fountains Abbey (1456–8). At Westminster, where he first appears in the year-books in 1433, he was created serjeant in 1443 and was king's serjeant 1449–53. After an inquiry into hostilities between the Percys and Nevilles in the north in 1453, he became a justice of the common pleas (1453–61). During his career he acted frequently as a commissioned justice, feoffee to uses, and arbitrator, and as an executor of Robert Fitzhugh, bishop of London (*d.* 1436). On the accession of Edward IV, Danby, who had been involved in the political trials following the battle of Towton, became chief justice of the common pleas and was knighted (both in 1461), and in 1464 travelled with the king to Gloucester to deal with unrest there. He received summonses to attend parliament, between 1463 and 1470, but there is no record of a return. At the readeption of Henry VI in 1470 he continued as chief justice, but when Edward IV was restored in 1471 he was not reappointed. This may have been politically motivated and the story circulated that he died soon afterwards, reputedly killed at his own wish by his park keeper (a story also told of Sir William Hankford (*d.* 1423)). However, he was retained by Richard, duke of Gloucester, and records show that royal commissions continued, since he was appointed a justice of the peace for Northamptonshire (February 1472) and Warwickshire (July 1473), and a justice in Kent (August 1473).

Danby's first wife was Catherine, daughter of Ralph Fitzrandolph of Spennithorne (a retainer of Richard Neville, earl of Salisbury); married in 1444, they had no children. His second wife was Elizabeth Aslaby, daughter and heir of William Aslaby, whom he married possibly in 1445 and who brought him lands in Durham, Darlington, and Gateshead. Danby bought the manor of Thorpe Perrow, North Riding of Yorkshire, shortly before 1456, obtaining a licence for the marriage there in 1459 of his daughter Marjory to John, son of Sir John Salveyn, and another in 1463/4 for the marriage of his son Thomas to Agnes Forster. In 1496 Marjory bequeathed what was claimed to be a bone of St Ninian to the Greyfriars, York. Danby's eldest son, James, married Anne, daughter of Sir John Langton of Farnley. In 1445 Danby and his wife were authorized to have a portable altar; he presented priests to Hauxwell church and Scruton chantry, and in 1473 he joined the Corpus Christi Guild of York. He died in 1474, and his widow took the veil shortly afterwards.

NORMAN DOE

Sources A. J. Pollard, *North-eastern England during the Wars of the Roses: lay society, war and politics, 1450–1500* (1990) • R. Somerville, *History of the duchy of Lancaster, 1265–1603* (1953) • N. L. Ramsay, 'The English legal profession, c.1340–1450', PhD diss., U. Cam., 1985 • Baker, *Serjeants* • *Chancery records* • *CEPR letters*, vol. 9 • [J. Raine], ed., *Testamenta Eboracensia*, 2, SurtS, 30 (1855) • A. H. Thompson, 'The registers of the archdeacons of Richmond: 1442–77 [pt 1]', *Yorkshire Archaeological Journal*, 30 (1930–31), 1–132

Danby, Sir Thomas (*c.*1530–1590). *See under* Danby family (*per.* 1493–1667).

Danby, Sir Thomas (1610–1660). *See under* Danby family (*per.* 1493–1667).

Danby, Thomas (1631–1667). *See under* Danby family (*per.* 1493–1667).

Danby, Thomas (1821?–1886), landscape painter, was born in Bristol, the fourth son of the seven children of the landscape painter Francis *Danby (1793–1861) and his wife, Hannah Hardedge or Hardidge (*bap.* 1794, *d.* 1879). James Francis *Danby was his brother. His family moved to London in 1824; in 1828, Thomas was attending a school in Yorkshire, together with his three elder brothers. In 1830 all the children joined their bankrupt father and his mistress on the continent. After some years in Switzerland the family moved to Paris in 1836. There, Thomas Danby is said to have made a living initially by copying old masters in the Louvre; it is possible that he was unwittingly abetting the picture dealer William Jones, who commissioned his father to paint *The Deluge* (Tate collection) in 1837 but who in the same year was caught exporting copies of Louvre paintings to the United States as originals. He probably returned to England in 1839, and he exhibited in London for the first time in 1841. From 1855 to 1866 both he and the artist Paul Falconer Poole gave the same address, Glydder House, Hampstead, when exhibiting at the Royal Academy. Surprisingly, they are said to have been intimate friends, despite the fact that, since 1830, Poole had been living with Thomas's mother, Hannah, who, according to Francis Danby, had deserted her children. In July 1847 Thomas Danby married Ellen Williams (1812?–1872), the daughter of a farmer, Henry Williams, who was the landlord of the inn at Capel Curig, Caernarvonshire, where the painter stayed on his sketching trips to north Wales.

From 1843 to 1866 Danby regularly exhibited oil paintings at the Royal Academy; he is said to have missed election as an associate by one vote. In 1866 his two watercolours of Gwynant Lake in north Wales attracted much attention at the Dudley Gallery, London. Thereafter he concentrated on watercolours, and was elected an associate of the Old Watercolour Society in 1867 and a full member in 1870. He was remembered as 'a painter of marked originality, whose landscapes had lent a charm to nearly every exhibition for twenty years, and infused an element of repose … Danby's colouring was tender, mellow, and harmonious' (Roget, 2.421, 423). Widowed in 1872, he married Helen Ann Muir (1847?–1888), the daughter of the artist Thomas Dunsmore Muir, three years later on 3 May 1875. Thomas Danby died at his home, 11 Park Road, Haverstock Hill, London, on 25 March 1886. A substantial sale of his oils and watercolours was held at Christies on 17 and 18 June of the same year.   FRANCIS GREENACRE

Sources J. Baker, 'Some descendants of Francis Danby, artist', 1991, City Museum and Art Gallery, Bristol, fine art artists' files · letters of Francis Danby to John Gibbons, Bristol RO, Gibbons MSS · E. Adams, *Francis Danby: varieties of poetic landscape* (1973) · J. L. Roget, *A history of the 'Old Water-Colour' Society*, 2 (1891) · *The Times* (30 March 1886) · *Art Journal*, new ser., 6 (1886), 158 · F. Greenacre, *Francis Danby, 1793–1861* (1988) [exhibition catalogue, City of Bristol Museum and Art Gallery and Tate Gallery, London, 1988] · F. Greenacre, *The Bristol school of artists: Francis Danby and painting in Bristol, 1810–1840* [1973] [exhibition catalogue, City Museum and Art Gallery, Bristol, 4 Sept – 10 Nov 1973] · Graves, *RA exhibitors* · Graves, *Artists*, 3rd edn · J. Baker, 'Francis Danby and his Somerset connections', 1991, City Museum and Art Gallery, Bristol, fine art artists' files · m. certs.
Wealth at death £2995 9s. 11d.: probate, 27 May 1886, CGPLA Eng. & Wales

Danby, William (1752–1833), writer, was the only son of the Revd William Danby DD of Swinton Park, Yorkshire, and Mary, daughter of Gilbert Affleck of Dalham, Suffolk. From 20 September 1763 to 1770 he had a private tutor at Eton College. On 24 October 1770 he was admitted as a fellow-commoner to Christ's College, Cambridge. In 1784 he served the office of high sheriff of Yorkshire. He was twice married: first in 1775 to Caroline (*d.* 1821), daughter of Henry Seymour, and second on 5 January 1822 to Anne Holwell, second daughter of William Gater. Danby almost entirely rebuilt his mansion of Swinton from designs by James Wyatt and John Foss of Richmond. It included a handsome library and a richly furnished museum of minerals. Describing a tour which he made in 1829, Southey remarked: 'The most interesting person whom I saw during this expedition was Mr. Danby of Swinton Park, a man of very large fortune, and now very old' (*The Life and Correspondence of the Late Robert Southey*, ed. C. C. Southey, 1850, 6.78). He was an accomplished scholar and wrote some works of interest on moral philosophy. His works include: *Thoughts, Chiefly on Serious Subjects* (1821), *Ideas and Realities, or, Thoughts on Various Subjects* (1827), *Extracts from and observations on Cicero's dialogues De senectute and De amicitia, and a translation of his Somnium Scipionis, with notes* (1829), and *Thoughts on Various Subjects* (1831). Danby died at Swinton Park on 4 December 1833. He left no children.
                              THOMPSON COOPER, *rev.* REBECCA MILLS

Sources J. Martin, *Bibliographical catalogue of books privately printed*, 2nd edn (1854), 274 · *GM*, 2nd ser., 1 (1834), 440 · Venn, *Alum. Cant.* · R. A. Austen-Leigh, ed., *The Eton College register, 1753–1790* (1921), 145 · *IGI*
Archives Bodl. Oxf., corresp. with J. C. Brooke · NA Scot., letters to Lord Balgonie
Likenesses E. Scriven, stipple, pubd 1822 (after J. Jackson), NPG, V&A

Dance, Charles (1794–1863), playwright and civil servant, was born in Marylebone, Middlesex, on 19 December 1794, the son of William *Dance (1755–1840), pianist and violinist, and his wife, Jane. William Dance's uncle was the architect George *Dance the younger (1741–1825). Charles spent more than thirty years of his working life in the court for the relief of insolvent debtors, at first as clerk, then as registrar and auditor in 1851, rising to taxing officer in 1853, and finally as chief clerk from May 1858. He retired in October 1861 (when the court was abolished under the new Bankruptcy Act) on a pension of £800 p.a.

Dance's introduction to dramatic authorship came in collaboration with James Robinson *Planché (who, two years his junior, had already some reputation in the theatre), with the farce *Manoeuvring* (Haymarket, 1829). This tentative beginning to his career developed, within two or three years, into a professional writing partnership with Planché at the Olympic, which lasted almost a decade, from 1830 to 1839, ceasing only in consequence of Dance's first marriage. Under the progressive regime of the actress-manager Madame Vestris at the newly refurbished Olympic, they produced some of their most distinctive and original work, notably in the genre of the burlesque-extravaganza, which was largely their own creation. Their coalition at the Olympic began in the winter of 1830 when, at Planché's invitation, Dance agreed to work on a resurrected piece of the former's, already rejected in its original form at several theatres. In the space of 'two or three evenings [they] brushed up' the piece—a burlesque derived (via George Colman the younger's story *The Sun Poker*) from Prometheus and Pandora—added songs, and gave it the 'locally-allusive' title of *Olympic Revels* (1831) (Planché, 126). With Madame Vestris as a graceful, sweet singing Pandora, it was the final embellishment to the Olympic's triumphant opening night on 3 January 1831. This piece inaugurated a fashion for the burlesque-extravaganza based on classical models, dressed, innovatively, in authentic period costume. In the following year *Olympic Devils* (based on Orpheus and Eurydice)—additionally notable for its ambitious scenery—repeated the previous success and thoroughly established the popularity of the new style, which continued with *The Paphian Bower* (1832), *The Deep Deep Sea* (1833), and *Telemachus* (1834).

Apart from 1835, when Planché was engaged elsewhere, he and Dance continued to provide the Olympic with its Christmas entertainment until the 1839–40 season. During that period the only major change in tactic was from 1836 onward when, following Dance's concern that, for the first time, someone else was 'walking in [their] sky' (Planché, 182)—a reference to Samuel Lover, who produced the Christmas piece in Planché's absence in 1835—Planché seized on the idea of substituting an English fairyland setting in place of overexploited classical mythologies. The first representative of the new model, *Riquet with the Tuft* (1836)—in fact a revamped version of another of Planché's rejected pieces—was well received, and it put to rest the fears of the management that a change in the trusted formula would bring the Olympic to financial

Charles Dance (1794–1863), by Maclure & Macdonald

ruin. Later pieces such as *Puss in Boots* (1837) and *Blue Beard* (1839) were not only instant hits but, with their subtle combining of pantomime with burlesque and extravaganza, helped shape the direction of the early Victorian pantomimic tradition.

Outside the partnership with Planché, Dance wrote several very successful pieces in the 1830s, principally domestic farces, including *The Water Party* (1832), which opened Madame Vestris's new winter season and enjoyed much success with John Liston as the matchmaking, party-giving, retired hairdresser Anthony Charles Fluid. This was followed by *A Match in the Dark* (1833), *The Beulah Spa* (1833), *The Bengal Tiger* (1837), and *Naval Engagements* (1838). The company at the Olympic, which in addition to Liston and Vestris comprised William Farren, the Keeleys, and (latterly) Charles Mathews, was ideally suited to Dance's instinct for light situational comedy and farce. One of his favourite plays was *The Country Squire, or, Two Days at the Hall* (1837), which in the published edition he dedicated to Farren, who appeared as Squire Broadlands: as Dance put it, '[t]here is perhaps no gratification more complete than that which a Dramatic Author experiences in seeing a pet part of his faultlessly performed' (Webster).

Dance (like Planché) owed most, if not all, of his early success to the Olympic Theatre and its talented company. But at this time, rather to Planché's dismay (though not, it appears, causing any rift in their relationship), Dance was often seen as the senior partner in the Olympic plays. As Planché observed, 'the fun was [considered] all Dance's and merely the stage carpentry mine' (Planché, 267).

Indeed, in North America their work was advertised so as to give prominence to Dance's name, some managers even crediting Dance with plays which Planché had written alone. But, as Planché conceded in his autobiography, such distinctions were academic, since neither of them received a penny in payment from American productions.

Dance was also a writer of songs, many of which were composed for Madame Vestris to sing in his own comedies and farces (such as the two ballads included in *The Beulah Spa*, which were always warmly encored). Some temporary cooling of relations with Madame Vestris took place in 1835, coincidentally with Charles Mathews's addition to the team at the Olympic, when Dance found himself charged £20 by Madame Vestris as her fee for singing one of his songs. An outraged Dance unwisely brought the matter to public attention by writing to *The Times*, which printed the song in question and then ridiculed its composer by suggesting that readers should consider 'whether anything short of £1,000, at the very least, could compensate any rational being for exposing himself or herself by singing such trash in public'.

Dance wrote occasionally for the Vestris–Mathews venture at the Lyceum in the late 1840s, one of his successes being *Delicate Ground, or, Paris in 1793* (1849). This work, despite characteristic defects of stilted exposition and sometimes sentimental conception, has been praised because in its rational disdain for false convention 'we have the far-off ancestor of Bernard Shaw' (Nicoll, 4.126). In the 1850s, as his civil service responsibilities became heavier, Dance is credited with only four plays, the last being *Marriage a Lottery* (Strand, 1858). Nowadays in total eclipse, his work was formerly regularly printed (mainly by T. H. Lacy and later also John Dicks) and he retained a foothold in the Victorian repertory until the end of the century: *Delicate Ground* was, for example, revived three times in London in the 1890s. His career as a dramatist has sometimes, in the twentieth century, been confused or partially conflated with that of his namesake George Dance, about whom little is known apart from his having had an independent existence writing plays for the London stage between 1831 and 1844, some of which were published by Duncombe, Barth, Lacy, and others.

Dance was a keen early member of the Dramatic Authors' Society in the 1830s in defence of dramatic copyright and payment of fees, and he also took an active role in membership of the newly formed Garrick Club. Always supportive of his fellow dramatists, he organized, with Planché and others, a very productive benefit at Drury Lane in 1840 for the widow and children of the recently deceased dramatist Thomas Haynes Bayly, who had been left virtually destitute.

Dance was married twice and was predeceased by both wives. His portrait shows him as a large man, with prominent features and a shock of rather unruly hair. For many years he lived in comfortable circumstances (with a staff comprising a cook and another servant) at 64 Mornington Road, near Regent's Park, London, but he suffered heart trouble and towards the end of his life, for health reasons, moved to Lowestoft, Suffolk. It was here, in Marine Parade, that he died on 5 January 1863 in his sixty-ninth year.

JOHN RUSSELL STEPHENS

Sources *The Times* (9 Jan 1863), 7 · Boase, *Mod. Eng. biog.* · J. R. Planché, *Recollections and reflections*, rev. edn (1901) · *The Times* (5 Feb 1835), 3 · B. N. Webster, ed., *The acting national drama*, 1 (1837) · C. J. Williams, *Madame Vestris: a theatrical biography* (1973) · *The extravaganzas of J. R. Planché, esq.*, ed. T. F. D. Croker and S. Tucker, 2 (1879) · A. Nicoll, *A history of English drama, 1660–1900*, 6 vols. (1923–59), vol. 4, pp. 126, 288–9, 578; vol. 5, p. 335 [bibliography and performance data] · census returns for London, 1861 · *DNB* · d. cert. · D. Stroud, *George Dance, architect, 1741–1825* (1971)

Likenesses Maclure & Macdonald, engraving, repro. in Croker and Tucker, eds., *Extravaganzas of J. R. Planché* [*see illus.*]

Wealth at death under £4000: probate, 11 March 1863, *CGPLA Eng. & Wales*

Dance, George, the elder (*c.*1694–1768), architect, was the son of Giles Dance (*d.* 1751), mason and member of the Merchant Taylors' Company, and his first wife. He was probably born in the London parish of St Dunstan-in-the-West. Giles Dance completed his eight-year apprenticeship and was made free of the City of London in July 1693; his son George was probably born soon afterwards. As the son of a freeman, Dance did not need to undergo an apprenticeship in order to obtain the right to work in London. He was admitted to the Merchant Taylors' Company on 2 June 1725, when he was described as 'Stonecutter Moorfields', and to the freedom of the City on 5 July 1725.

On 1 March 1720 Dance married Elizabeth (*d.* 1762), daughter of the surveyor James Gould of Hackney, with whom he and his father worked on a number of occasions. No doubt it was while working with Gould at Carshalton House, Surrey, that Giles Dance met his second wife, Sarah Brett, whom he married in 1722, and who thus became Dance's stepmother. The tightly knit building world was also closely associated with the developing craft of freemasonry: Dance was actively involved; he was listed in 1725 as master of a lodge which met at the Bell tavern, Nicholas Lane, in the City of London. In his will of 1749 Giles Dance recorded that he had already given his architect son 'more than his proportion or share' of his fortune 'for his better advancement and Promotion in the World' and that he and George had been in co-partnership. They had worked extensively together, and Dance would have been trained by his father to conduct every aspect of the business of building.

Dance's early style, as seen in the church of St Leonard, Shoreditch (1736–40), depends most on the traditions of Wren, Hawksmoor, and John James. He spent his childhood in the City while St Paul's Cathedral was rising, and in his early adulthood saw the building of the great East End and City churches by Hawksmoor. Moreover, his own parish church, St Luke's, Old Street, was designed by Hawksmoor and James and built between 1727 and 1733; he appears briefly in its building history in connection with mason's work there, and was active in its affairs as parishioner and vestryman throughout his life.

The most significant event in Dance's career was his appointment on 2 December 1735 as clerk of the City's works. Both Giles and his son were well acquainted with the workings of the City and its corporation. Dance had represented the corporation in its dispute with George Smith, the previous clerk, over his dismissal and had been acting clerk of the works since 19 February 1734. He paid £150 for his clerkship, which gave him the right to all fees, profits, and commodities of the office. His duties included drawing plans, calculating estimates, measuring work, settling bills, and attending committees at the Guildhall. He tackled all sorts of designing and building jobs both large and small, and came to be well respected for his meticulous preparations and competence in technical matters. His work extended to replanning schemes in the City, and a number of his town planning ideas were taken up and developed later by his son George, who was nominated by his father to succeed him in his post just before he died in 1768.

Dance's most important commission was to design a mansion house (1739–52) for the lord mayor of London, which would give the lord mayor of an increasingly powerful City an appropriate setting in which to work and entertain. Although a number of designs were received from other architects, Dance was in a strong position at the corporation, whose members entrusted him with the work in 1737. However, his contemporary civic commissions, such as the new Fleet Market House (1736–7) and repairs and alterations at Skinners' Hall (1737), hardly prepared him for this unique task. His design owed much to the fashionable Palladian style in its classical Corinthian portico, but retained a baroque flavour in its side elevations with their attics at each end. Its plan depended both on Palladio's town houses and on the City tradition of courtyard houses and livery company halls. With interiors richly decorated with rococo carving and plasterwork, imposing and well suited to the City's needs, it stood comparison with other grand town houses, such as Spencer House. It did not go uncriticized, however, particularly for its cramped site and the attics, which were likened to Noah's ark in James Ralph's *Critical Review* of 1783. A portrait of Dance, by his son Nathaniel, shows him aged about seventy years, holding a rolled plan of the Mansion House and modestly clad in plain, dark coat and waistcoat.

Dance's other works were mainly in the City, and included: St Botolph's, Aldgate (1741–4); St Matthew's, Bethnal Green (1743–6); the nave of St Mary's, Faversham, Kent (1754–5); St Luke's Hospital, Old Street (1750–51); and the corn market, Mark Lane (1747–50). A large collection of his drawings survives at Sir John Soane's Museum, and a collection of both drawings and documents is held by the corporation of London, at the City of London Record Office.

Dance was evidently comfortably off and his family was well provided for. His eldest son, James *Dance (1721–1774), became an actor; Nathaniel *Dance, later Sir Nathaniel Holland (1735–1811) trained as an artist with Francis Hayman; while George *Dance the younger (1741–1825), the youngest son, followed in his father's footsteps as an architect. The family lived in Chiswell Street in the parish of St Luke's, Old Street. Here Dance died on 11 February 1768; he was buried in the churchyard at St Luke's on 17 February. His wife predeceased him.

SALLY JEFFERY

Sources D. Stroud, *George Dance, architect, 1741–1825* (1971) · J. Daniels, *George Dance the elder, 1695–1768; the younger, 1741–1825* (1972) [exhibition catalogue] · S. Jeffery, *The Mansion House* (1993) · [W. Papworth], ed., *The dictionary of architecture*, 11 vols. (1853–92) · Colvin, *Archs.* · *GM*, 1st ser., 38 (1768), 94 · J. Ralph and W. Nicholson, *A critical review of the public buildings, statues, and ornaments in and about London* (1783) · will of Giles Dance, PRO, PROB 11/789 · parish register, St John, Hackney, 1 March 1720 [marriage]

Archives LMA, drawings and MSS · RIBA BAL, account book and family corresp. · RIBA BAL, accounts and papers relating to Ashburnham Place

Likenesses F. Hayman, oils, c.1745, FM Cam. · N. Dance, oils, c.1765, Guildhall Art Gallery, London

Wealth at death bank store; money; houses: will

Dance, George, the younger (1741–1825), architect, was born on 20 March 1741 in London, the youngest of five sons born to the architect George *Dance the elder (c.1694–1768) and his wife, Elizabeth Gould. The actor and writer James *Dance was his eldest brother. Educated at St Paul's School, London, Dance was sent in 1758 to Italy, where he joined his elder brother Nathaniel *Dance (1735–1811). He spent six years studying Roman antiquity at first hand and became one of the first British architects to absorb the lessons of the emerging style of neoclassicism. He made the acquaintance of Piranesi and began a lifelong friendship with Robert Mylne (1734–1811). A pupil of Nicolo Giansimone in Rome, Dance won the gold medal of the Accademia di Belle Arti, Parma, in 1763 with a design for a public gallery and, in 1764, was admitted to the Accademia di San Luca in Rome. In addition he was elected a member of the Accademia dell'Arcadia, a select gathering of Roman literati. Such firsthand knowledge of intellectual institutions made a lasting impact on Dance, who was to become a founding member of the Royal Academy in 1768.

The elder Dance's strong City connections stood his son in good stead on his return from Italy in 1765. The younger Dance soon won the commission to redesign the church of All Hallows, London Wall. Its free interpretation of the classical orders, seen in the simplified entablature, demonstrated Dance's knowledge of the Abbé Laugier's rational approach to the language of architecture, and anticipated the stylistic boldness of his most famous pupil, John Soane. On his father's death in 1768 Dance succeeded to the post of clerk of the City works: father and son, they held this office from 1733 to 1815, thereby ensuring continuity of direction in an epoch of great change. As an architect, a legislator, and a planner, the younger Dance did much to determine the changing face of the capital. His metropolitan work divides into two parts: his major public buildings and his town planning schemes.

Dance's major London public building was Newgate prison. Started in 1770, the City's prison, almost completed, was badly damaged in the Gordon riots of 1780, and finally opened in 1784. Its forbidding perimeter of heavily rusticated masonry, drawing heavily on Italian

George Dance the younger (1741–1825), by William Daniell, pubd 1825 (after Nathaniel Dance, 1793)

mannerism and the *Carceri* etchings of G. B. Piranesi, formed one of London's most authoritarian buildings, and was one of the few British buildings of its day to attain European notice. Next to it stood Dance's Old Bailey sessions house (demolished, like the prison, in 1902). He also designed St Luke's Hospital, Old Street (1782–9), and two debtors' prisons. His other principal City commission was at the Guildhall. Having added a daringly capacious top-lit council chamber (dem. 1906) he then designed a new south façade (1788–9), memorable for its fusion of Gothic and 'Hindoo' or Indian styles.

City responsibilities gave Dance little time for other public commissions. The Shakspeare Gallery in Pall Mall was designed for Alderman John Boydell, and featured an allegorical relief by Thomas Banks of Shakespeare between the dramatic muse and the genius of painting, as well as an early deployment of the Ammonite order. The Lincoln's Inn Fields premises of the Royal College of Surgeons (1806–13; largely rebuilt 1835–7) sported a mighty portico reminiscent of Dance's country houses. His northern elevation for the Theatre Royal, Bath (1804–5), was an idiosyncratic fusion of allegory and the Greek revival. Dance's later church work consisted of the rebuilding of the London church of St Bartholomew-the-Less, West

Smithfield (1793; again rebuilt 1825); he repeated the octagonal nave at Micheldever church, Hampshire (1808–10).

Equally significant was Dance's work as a designer of townscape. In planning terms he was the true heir of John Wood of Bath, and helped to make the crescent and circus standard items in the repertory of the late Georgian builder. Finsbury Circus (designed in 1802) is his largest surviving set piece, although St George's Circus, with its obelisk and radiating roads creating a new framework for the area to the south of Blackfriars Bridge, hints at the scale of his vision for London. Much effort went into his never executed schemes for the remodelling of the City's riverside, which aspired to a Roman degree of magnificence but which were not carried forward. His scheme for the Legal Quays consisted of a grandiose double bridge design with drawbridges, embankments, and warehouses, aligned on colossal obelisks: it was submitted to a select committee in 1802 but never proceeded with. Nor did his plans for a grandiose development within the emerging suburb of Camden Town reach fruition. Dance's monumental urban visions were among the most ambitious of his day, but few were ever realized.

Together with Sir Robert Taylor, Dance was one of the principal architects of the landmark London Building Act (1774), which consolidated existing legislation and set the standard for later Georgian domestic architecture: houses were divided into categories or 'rates', according to size, with regulations governing the width of walls, building heights, and elevational treatment. His designs for standard terrace house elevations on City land, with blind arches of brick surrounding the first-floor windows, were built in their hundreds and became the norm for late Georgian London.

Dance's country house practice was never extensive. Much of it was undertaken on behalf of London clients such as Charles Pratt, first earl of Camden (Camden Place, Kent, c.1788). Stratton Park, Hampshire (1803–6; dem. 1960), for the Baring family, was an outstanding neoclassical villa design with a powerful Doric portico, an Ionic entrance hall, and a Pompeian library. For his brother-in-law Thomas Dummer MP he created a dramatically vaulted neo-classical interior at Cranbury Park, Hampshire (c.1780). His most memorable Gothic house was Coleorton House in Leicestershire, built for his friend the connoisseur Sir George Beaumont, bt, in 1804–8. Alterations at Ashburnham Place, Sussex (1813–17), were externally Gothic, but contained a Doric entrance hall. Adept in either style, Dance brought a constant inventiveness to his work, as well as an exceptional awareness of French neo-classical architecture. The grandest of his town house commissions was the library at Lansdowne House, Berkeley Square, London (1788–91; remodelled 1816–19 as a gallery). This lofty apsidal chamber marked the acme of palatial neo-classicism.

Dance once remarked that he wanted architecture 'unshackled' (Farington, *Diary*, 6.2275). He challenged the architectural orthodoxies of his day, and developed a singular approach to design, in which meaning and symbolism interacted with form, space, and precedent. C. R.

Cockerell in a Royal Academy lecture of 1845 described him as 'the most complete poet architect of his day' (Watkin, 62). Dance was a highly respected professional and adept in matters of construction. One of his rare supervisory jobs was overseeing the building of the Darnley mausoleum at Cobham Park, near Rochester, in 1783–6, which had been designed by James Wyatt.

Dance was elected professor of architecture at the Royal Academy in 1798. He failed to deliver any lectures, and accordingly resigned his chair in 1806, but was otherwise at the heart of academy affairs: he served for a considerable period as its auditor, and was regarded as a likely candidate for the presidency at the time of Benjamin West's resignation in 1804. He was also the last of the founding academicians to die. Unlike Soane, Dance never let architecture dominate his life. He was a man of wide-ranging interests, and in later years he gained greater satisfaction from arts other than architecture. He possessed considerable musical skill as an instrumentalist and composer: Haydn became a valued friend. His interest in drawing also grew: his distinctive and highly finished pencil profile portraits constituted a vivid gallery of Regency London's artistic establishment of the day, and etchings after them by William Daniell were published in 1804–14. Dance married Mary Gurnell (b. 1752) on 24 March 1772. Together they had three sons before her death in 1791.

From his late twenties onwards George Dance was at the top of his profession. He held high offices, such as clerk of the City works and master of the Merchant Taylors' Company, and had a considerable impact on the face of Georgian London. He suffered a mild stroke in 1815, and thereupon resigned his offices. He elected for burial in the crypt of St Paul's Cathedral, and was laid to rest there following his death on 14 January 1825 at his home at 29 Gower Street, London.   ROGER BOWDLER

Sources D. Stroud, *George Dance, architect, 1741–1825* (1971) · Colvin, *Archs.*, 289–92 · *George Dance* (1973) [exhibition catalogue, Geffrye Museum] · H. Rosenall, 'George Dance the younger', *RIBA Journal*, 54 (1946–7), 502–7 · D. Watkin, *Sir John Soane: Enlightenment thought and the Royal Academy lectures* (1996), 58–63 · S. Angell, 'Sketch of the professional life of George Dance, architect, RA', *The Builder*, 5 (1847), 333–5 · M. Rogers, 'The "self-portrait" of George Dance the younger', *Georgian Group Journal* (1995), 99–100 · Graves, *RA exhibitors*

Archives CLRO · Sir John Soane's Museum, London | E. Sussex RO, corresp., papers, and accounts relating to work at Ashburnham Place · RIBA BAL, letters to his father, George Dance · Rochester Bridge Trust, corresp. and reports relating to Rochester Bridge

Likenesses N. Dance, double portrait, oils, c.1753 (with Hester Dance), priv. coll. · G. Dance, self-portrait, pencil drawing, 1795, AM Oxf. · T. Lawrence, oils, 1812, Guildhall Art Gallery, London · G. Dance, self-portrait, pencil and chalk drawing, 1814, NPG · J. Jackson, oils, c.1820, Leicester Museums and Art Galleries · W. Daniell, etching, pubd 1825 (after N. Dance, 1793), NPG [see illus.] · J. C. F. Rossi, plaster bust, 1825, Sir John Soane's Museum, London · J. C. F. Rossi, marble bust, 1827, RA · H. Singleton, group portrait, oils (*Royal Academicians, 1793*), RA

Dance, James [*performing name* James Love] (**1721–1774**), actor and writer, the eldest son of George *Dance the elder (c.1694–1768), surveyor to the City of London and architect, and his wife, Elizabeth Gould (d. 1762), was born on 17 March 1721. Among his brothers was the architect George *Dance the younger (1741–1825). He entered Merchant Taylors' School, London, in 1732 and on 1 March 1738 was admitted a member of St John's College, Oxford. He left the university without graduating, and contrived to attract the favourable notice of Sir Robert Walpole by replying, in a smart poem entitled 'Yes, they are; what then?', to a satirical piece, 'Are these things so?', directed against the minister and attributed (wrongly) to Pope. Sir Robert, however, does not seem to have done much more for his advocate than feed him with false hopes. Dance entered Lincoln's Inn on 28 November 1738, but may have spent much of 1739 as a strolling player. In August 1739 he married Elizabeth (d. 1783), the daughter of James Hooper, a customs officer.

Bankrupt and disappointed, Dance took to the stage and to the composition of light comedies. About 1740 he wrote and published a heroic poem, 'Cricket', which is interesting as throwing light upon the history of the sport. He has also been credited with the play *Pamela*, published in 1742, but there were several works of this title performed in 1741 and Dance's role is unclear. He continued to act in London—there was a season at Goodman's Fields with Hallam's company in 1744–5—and perhaps elsewhere.

About 1751 Dance may have abandoned his wife, who was left to take care of their two children with the help of Dance's parents, and began a relationship with a 'Mrs Love', whose first name was probably Catherine and whose surname was, according to the *Biographia dramatica*, de l'Amour. If this is so, Dance took the Anglicized version of her name, first seen in July 1751 at Dumfries, and he managed a company at the Vaults, Belfast, under that name in winter 1751–2.

The Loves continued to perform in Ireland and Scotland. In 1754 Love published his *Poems on Several Occasions* from Edinburgh, where in 1759 he succeeded West Digges as manager of the Canongate Theatre. Following problems with the proprietors he accepted Garrick's invitation in 1762 to migrate to Drury Lane, where he made his début as Falstaff, subsequently regarded as his best role, on 25 September 1762. In 1765 he opened a new theatre at Richmond, and received a full licence on 1 July 1766. Love had by this time repaired the breach with his family with the help of his brother Nathaniel *Dance (1735–1811), and his theatre was financed by Sir Richard Horne, whose nephew had married Love's aunt Hester Dance.

Despite the strain his involvement with the Richmond theatre put on his relationship with Garrick, Love continued to perform at Drury Lane during the winter; he also wrote several pantomimes, as well as a further adaptation of Shadwell's version of Shakespeare's *Timon of Athens* (1768). He is often credited with the poorly regarded adaptation of Beaumont and Fletcher's *Rule a Wife and have a Wife* performed at Drury Lane in the later years of Garrick's management, but authorship was allotted to Garrick (who always denied the charge) by contemporaries and Garrick's twentieth-century editors Bergman and Pedicord.

Love died early in 1774, perhaps on 29 January or on 5 February. He was survived by his wife, Elizabeth, by Mrs Love, who died in 1807, and by his children Nathaniel *Dance (1748–1827), Sarah, who married Thomas Poynder, a plumber, whose business she took over and expanded after his death, and William *Dance (1755–1840), who may have been the son of Mrs Love rather than Elizabeth Dance. C. J. ROBINSON, rev. MATTHEW KILBURN

Sources Highfill, Burnim & Langhans, *BDA* · D. E. Baker, *Biographia dramatica, or, A companion to the playhouse*, rev. I. Reed, new edn, rev. S. Jones, 1 (1812), 462 · C. J. Robinson, ed., *A register of the scholars admitted into Merchant Taylors' School, from AD 1562 to 1874*, 2 vols. (1882–3) · D. Stroud, *George Dance, architect, 1741–1825* (1971) · *N&Q*, 4th ser., 8 (1871), 524
Likenesses J. R. Smith, group portrait, mezzotint, pubd 1774 (after F. Wheatley), BM

Dance, Nathaniel [later Sir Nathaniel Holland, baronet] (**1735–1811**), painter and politician, was born on 18 May 1735 in Chiswell Street, London, the third son of George *Dance the elder (c.1694–1768) and his wife, Elizabeth Gould (d. 1762). His father was clerk of works for the City of London, and his brother George *Dance the younger (1741–1825) was also an architect; James *Dance (1721–1774), the eldest son, was an actor and writer, and another brother, William Dance (*fl.* 1780), was a miniature painter. Nathaniel Dance was educated at Merchant Taylors' School, London (his father was a freeman of that company), from 1743 until 1748. From about 1752 he trained as an artist for approximately two years under the painter Francis Hayman, whom he evidently admired; it was during this period that he came to know the young Thomas Gainsborough. He was in Rome from May 1754, but his activities there remain obscure until summer 1758; however, it is possible that he undertook some further training during this time. In winter 1758–9 he visited Leghorn and Florence, where he met his brother George: the two probably shared an apartment in strada Felice, Rome.

Dance devoted much of his time in Italy to developing his powers of invention, drawing, and colouring: he made copies after old masters, remarked on the development of his use of colour, and sought criticism of his work from the most esteemed painters then in Rome, including Gavin Hamilton. However, this careful approach often delayed the completion of his most important works. Two commissioned works begun in 1760, *Nisus and Euryalus* and *Meeting of Aeneas and Achates with Venus* (exh. Society of Artists, 1766) made slow progress in his studio; the former was not completed by the time Dance left Rome, while the latter was nearing completion only in 1764, the year of his election to the Accademia di San Luca. It was as a history painter that Dance sought to develop: his first recorded such work, *Death of Virginia*, its composition based upon that of Raphael's *Sacrifice of Lystra*, was intended for the Society of Arts exhibition of 1760, and Dance was confident that it would win the £100 premium. However, as it was painted abroad it was excluded, and was exhibited the following year at the Society of Artists.

Dance was also a successful and well-connected portrait

painter. He was engaged in some form of partnership with one of the most fashionable portraitists of British visitors to Rome, Pompeo Batoni; a travel card of 1762 introduced 'Rome, Sigr. Pompeo Batoni & Mr Dance, for Portrait and History Painting' (Ingamells, 275). His portraits in Italy included *Charles, Lord Hope, James, Later Third Earl of Hopetoun, and their Tutor William Rouet*, a conversation piece of 1763 (priv. coll.) and *Lord and Lady Spencer* (1764), but his reputation as a portrait painter was already established by 1760, when he was commissioned to paint four versions of a conversation piece, one for each of the group of gentlemen depicted in front of the Colosseum: James Grant, John Mytton, Thomas Robinson, and Thomas Wynn (Yale U. CBA). His most prestigious commission came from the royal librarian and keeper of pictures, Richard Dalton, on behalf of George III, to paint a full-length portrait of Edward, duke of York (1764; Royal Collection). However, a painting of more personal significance was the portrait of the artist Angelica Kauffman (priv. coll), whom he 'courted at Rome' (Farington, *Diary*, 8 Dec 1797).

By June 1766, Dance had returned to London, where he established himself as a fashionable portrait painter at 13 Tavistock Row, Covent Garden. Kauffman arrived in Britain at this date, but their relationship changed and she married the so-called count Frederick de Horn in 1767. Both Dance and Kauffman were foundation members of the Royal Academy. To its inaugural exhibition of 1769 he sent full-length portraits of George III and Queen Charlotte (Uppark, Sussex), as well as likenesses of a bishop and two gentlemen, and his exhibited work until 1772 was dominated by portraiture. In 1773 both he and Gainsborough refused to exhibit at the Royal Academy after a disagreement with the president, Sir Joshua Reynolds: Dance and Gainsborough are the only foundation members not represented in Johann Zoffany's *The Academicians of the Royal Academy* (1771-2; Royal Collection). However, Dance returned to the academy exhibition in 1774, showing *Orpheus Lamenting the Loss of Eurydice*, and in 1776, showing *The Death of Mark Anthony*.

The rococo style of Dance's early works, apparent, for example, in the portrait of George Dance the younger and his sister Hester (*c*.1753; priv. coll.) and that of the composer and violinist Pietro Nardini and an unknown man (1759; priv. coll.), learned from Hayman, was modified in Italy through the influence of Batoni. Dance criticized his former master's 'colouring and correctness of drawing' (Allen, 59), and it was precisely those elements that apparently altered after his association with Batoni began. Dance worked in the high keys of grand-manner portraiture and the paint became more translucent in quality; however, it has been observed that his manner of painting was 'as dry and closely textured as before' (Goodreau, *Nathaniel Dance, 1735-1811*, introduction).

The opportunities for history painting were very limited in eighteenth-century Britain, and although Dance's name was among those chosen for potentially the most important project of the time, the decoration of St Paul's Cathedral, the scheme never came to fruition. His name was also among those listed to decorate the Great Room of the Society of Arts, but this project was realized by James Barry alone. His most public history painting was ephemeral, a transparency depicting an allegory of architecture and displayed on the Royal Academy's building in Pall Mall in 1770 to mark the king's birthday.

At some time in the 1770s Dance became financially independent. Although he stopped exhibiting professionally in 1776 and produced fewer paintings, he was still active professionally and contributed to running the Royal Academy. However, in 1782 he gave up his studio and moved to Cranbury Park, Hampshire—the home of a widow, Mrs Harriet Dummer (*b. c*.1744), daughter of Sir Cecil Bishopp; she had an income of £18,000 per annum. They were married in London on 17 July 1783; there were no children.

Dance resigned from the Royal Academy in 1790, the year of his election to parliament as member for East Grinstead, Sussex, but continued to exhibit there as an amateur in 1792, 1794, and 1800. On each occasion he showed a landscape, a more fitting subject for a gentleman than portraiture. However, the story circulated by the obituarist in the *Monthly Magazine* (December 1811) that he bought back and then destroyed his work in order to consolidate his position as a gentleman is unfounded, although he did destroy a number of works that remained in his studio with which he was dissatisfied. From about the time of Dance's retirement from professional life he produced a number of political caricatures. *War* and *Neither War nor Peace* were etched by James Gillray and published in March 1783, and four volumes of unsigned caricatures and other comic drawings by Nathaniel and his brother George were sold at auction in 1912. The works were dispersed, but many of these pen-and-ink drawings are in the Tate collection.

On 4 July 1800 Dance took, by royal licence, the name Holland, after his wife's cousin Charlotte. He was created a baronet in November in that same year. He served East Grinstead until 1802 and from 1807 until his death; he was MP for Great Bedwyn in Wiltshire from 1802 to 1806. Both seats were gained through family connections and acts of financial generosity. He was generally a supporter of Pitt, but was not an active member of the house; he served on the select committee on the British Museum appointed in June 1805.

Dance was 'considered a singular man in His manner … on the whole very well liked by the neighbouring aristocracy' (Farington, *Diary*, 2 Nov 1807). According to Farington, he 'always objected to wine … but in company passes the bottle so as to keep up an appearance of drinking some wine' (ibid., 6 June 1807). He was wealthy: by 1794, in addition to savings of £50,000, he had an estate near Dorchester, Oxfordshire, and another in Wiltshire, for which he paid £30,000 and £12,000 respectively. In 1807 he built a house in Piccadilly, London, for his wife. He died, suddenly, at home in Wiltshire on 15 October 1811 'after playing in His garden with some Young Ladies' (ibid., 4 Nov 1811). His wife survived him. The National Portrait Gallery,

London, and Tate collection have a number of his portraits. He is also represented at the Yale Center for British Art, New Haven, Connecticut.

DEBORAH GRAHAM-VERNON

Sources D. Goodreau, *Nathaniel Dance, 1735–1811* (1977) [exhibition catalogue, Kenwood House, London, 25 June – 4 Sept 1977] · D. Goodreau, 'Nathaniel Dance RA (1735–1811)', PhD diss., U. Cal., Los Angeles, 1973 · D. Stroud, *George Dance, architect, 1741–1825* (1971) · J. Ingamells, ed., *A dictionary of British and Irish travellers in Italy, 1701–1800* (1997) · HoP, *Commons, 1790–1820* · Farington, *Diary* · V. Manners, 'Last words on Nathaniel Dance, RA', *The Connoisseur*, 67 (1923), 143–53 · B. Allen, *Francis Hayman* (1987) · M. J. Rosenthal, *The art of Thomas Gainsborough* (1999) · A. Wilton and I. Bignamini, *Grand Tour: the lure of Italy in the eighteenth century* (1996) [exhibition catalogue, Tate Gallery, London] · Graves, *RA exhibitors* · W. T. Whitley, *Art in England, 1800–1820* (1928) · will, PRO, PROB 11/1527, sig. 491
Archives Northants. RO, personal accounts · NRA, priv. coll., household accounts · RIBA BAL, notebook of copy letters
Likenesses N. Dance, self-portrait, oils, *c*.1780, NPG
Wealth at death approx. £200,000: will, PRO, PROB 11/1527, sig. 491; Goodreau, *Nathaniel Dance*

Dance, Sir Nathaniel (1748–1827), merchant navy officer, was born on 20 June 1748; he was the son of James *Dance (1721–1774), who was the elder brother of Nathaniel *Dance and George *Dance the younger. His mother was Elizabeth Hooper (*d.* 1783). He entered the East India Company's service in 1759 and made nine voyages to India between 1759 and 1781, as well as voyages to Antigua and the Malacca Strait. He moved up steadily through the company's marine ranks and was eventually appointed commander of the *Lord Camden* in 1786. After four voyages in the *Lord Camden* between 1786 and 1795, he made his last voyage to the East as commander of the *Earl Camden* in 1802.

In 1804 Dance was, by virtue of his seniority, commodore of the company's homeward-bound fleet, which sailed from Canton on 31 January. Off Pulo Aor, on 14 February, this fleet, consisting of sixteen Indiamen and eleven country ships, fell in with the French squadron under Admiral Linois. Linois believed that he was engaged with ships of the line and did not notice that they were lightly armed merchant ships. The next morning, thinking he was in the presence of a superior force, he fired a few broadsides and fled. The British lost one man killed and one wounded, both on board the *Royal George*; the other ships sustained no damage. Dance made the signal for a general chase, and for two hours a powerful squadron of ships of war fled before a number of merchantmen; then fearing a longer pursuit might carry him too far out of his course, and 'considering the immense property at stake', he recalled his ships, and the next morning continued his voyage. In the Malacca Strait, on 28 February, they met two British ships of the line, which convoyed them as far as St Helena, whence they obtained a further escort to Britain. Generous rewards were voted to the several commanders, officers, and ships' companies. Dance was knighted, and was presented with £5000 by the Bombay Insurance Company, and with a pension of £500 a year

by the East India Company. He seems to have lived for the remainder of his life in retirement, and he died at Enfield on 25 March 1827, aged seventy-nine.

J. K. LAUGHTON, *rev.* H. V. BOWEN

Sources GM, 1st ser., 74 (1804), 963 · GM, 1st ser., 97/1 (1827), 380 · biographical file, BL OIOC · East India Company marine records, BL OIOC, misc. vols. 651–4 · East India Company stock ledgers, BL OIOC, L/AG/14/5/28, 333 · F. Marryat, *Newton Forster, or, The merchant service* (1832) · will, PRO, PROB 11/1724, sig. 228
Likenesses C. Knight, coloured stipple, pubd 1804 (after G. Dance), BM, NPG · portrait, *c*.1804, BL OIOC · C. Turner, mezzotint, pubd 1805 (after R. Westfall), BM · J. Fittler, line engraving (after G. Dance), BM, NPG; repro. in *Naval Chronicle* (1804) · J. R. Smith, mezzotint, BM · chalk drawing, BL OIOC

Dance, William (1755–1840), pianist and violinist, was born in London on 20 December 1755. His grandfather was George *Dance (*c*.1694–1768), the architect, and his father was George's eldest son, the 'Oxford-educated actor, manager and playwright' James *Dance (1721–1774), who 'had assumed the name Love'. His mother may have been 'James's wife the actress Elizabeth, daughter of James Hooper' (Highfill, Burnim & Langhans, *BDA*, 4.133–5), although some scholars believe her to have been the actress Mrs Love, with whom James Dance had formed a company. The family therefore had strong connections with the theatre and the Royal Academy of Arts.

William studied the piano under Theodore Aylward and the violin under K. F. Baumgarten and later with the renowned Felice Giardini. He is said to have played the violin in an orchestra as early as 1767. From 1771 to 1774 he

William Dance (1755–1840), by George Dance, 1800

was at the Drury Lane Theatre, under Garrick's management, and was afterwards a member of the King's Theatre orchestra (1775–93). He led at the Haymarket during the summer seasons (1784–90) and at the Handel commemoration in Westminster Abbey in 1790, in the absence of Wilhelm Cramer. A member of the royal band before 1800, he subsequently gave up performing in public and became a successful teacher in London.

On 17 January 1813 a circular proposing a meeting, signed by J. B. Cramer, P. A. Corri, and Dance, was issued from Dance's house (or perhaps that of his brother Henry), 17 Manchester Street. The meeting on 24 January, in the house of Henry Dance, led to the foundation of the Philharmonic Society. William became a director and the treasurer of the society until his death. Although Dance was not regarded as a soloist on the violin, William Thomas Parke (whom Dance taught the viola) praised his 'great taste and execution' on the piano. Among his published works are *Six Lessons for the Harpsichord or Piano-Forte*, dated about 1780 with several later editions, songs, preludes, fantasias, variations, and numerous piano sonatas, including op. 4 (1805).

Dance died at Brompton, London, on 5 June 1840, having enjoyed 'an almost unparalleled breadth of acquaintance, especially in artistic, theatrical, and musical circles' (Highfill, Burnim & Langhans, *BDA*, 133–5). Haydn and Mendelssohn were friends of the family, and the latter inscribed the manuscript of 'his fourth Song without Words (14 September 1829) to Dance's daughter Sophia Louisa'. He had been an active member of the Royal Society of Musicians, which holds a pencil drawing of him by his brother George. The society also granted his widow, Jane, a pension of £2 12*s*. 6*d*. per month. His son Charles *Dance (1794–1863) became a noted playwright. His great-granddaughter Nellie Curzon Smith, who married Henry J. Watt, was 'a brilliant pianist' (*New Grove*).

DAVID J. GOLBY

Sources Highfill, Burnim & Langhans, *BDA*, 4.133–5 · H. G. Farmer, 'Dance, William', *New Grove* · W. T. Parke, *Musical memoirs*, 1 (1830), 111 · C. Ehrlich, *First philharmonic: a history of the Royal Philharmonic Society* (1995) · S. McVeigh, *The violinist in London's concert life, 1750–1784: Felice Giardini and his contemporaries* (1989) · *GM*, 2nd ser., 13 (1840), 108 · Brown & Stratton, *Brit. mus.*, 115 · [J. S. Sainsbury], ed., *A dictionary of musicians*, 2 vols. (1824) · C. Price, J. Milhous, and R. D. Hume, *Italian opera in late eighteenth-century London*, 1: *The King's Theatre, Haymarket, 1778–1791* (1995)
Likenesses G. Dance, pencil drawing, 1800, NPG [*see illus.*] · G. Dance, pencil drawing, Royal Society of Musicians, London; repro. in Highfill, Burnim & Langhans, *BDA* · lithograph (after W. P. Sherlock), NPG

Dancer, Ann. *See* Barry, Ann (*bap.* 1733, *d.* 1801).

Dancer, Daniel (1716–1794), miser, was born at Harrow Weald to unknown parents, the eldest of four children. His grandfather and father, a prosperous farmer and landowner, were both noted in their time for their parsimonious streak. Following his father's death in 1736, Daniel succeeded to his estate, which consisted of 80 acres of rich meadow land and the adjoining farm of Waldos. There

Daniel Dancer (1716–1794), by Robert Cooper, *c*.1790

Dancer, who previously had given no manifestation of his miserly instincts, lived in seclusion with his only sister as housekeeper. His lands were allowed to lie fallow so that the expense of cultivation might be avoided. He took only one meal a day, consisting invariably of a little baked meat and a hard-boiled dumpling, quantities of which were prepared a week in advance. His clothing consisted mainly of hay bands, which were swathed round his feet for boots and round his body for a coat, but it was his habit to purchase one new shirt every year. On one occasion he brought, and lost, a lawsuit against a tradesman who, he alleged, had cheated him out of 3*d*. over one of these annual transactions. The only person who could be said to be at all intimately acquainted with the Dancers was a Lady Tempest, the widow of Sir Henry Tempest, a Yorkshire baronet. To this lady Dancer's sister intended to leave her own private property, amounting to some £2000, but she died in 1766 before she could sign her will. This prompted a lawsuit among her three brothers as to the distribution of her money, the result of which was that Daniel was awarded two-thirds of the sum on the ground of his having maintained her for thirty years.

To fill his sister's place Dancer engaged a servant named Griffiths, a man whose manner of living was as penurious as his own, and to whom he paid 18*d*. a week as wages. The two lived together in Dancer's ramshackle house until the master's death at Pinner on 30 September 1794. In his last moments he was tended by Lady Tempest, who had shown uniform kindness to the old man, and who was rewarded by being made the sole recipient of his wealth, which amounted to a sum equal to £3000 per annum. However, she too died soon after of a cold contracted while she watched over Dancer's deathbed. Despite his reputation for miserliness, Dancer was also known for his integrity in his business dealings, his gratitude for service rendered to him, his droll sayings, and even occasional acts of generosity. ALSAGER VIAN, *rev.* DAVID TURNER

Sources *GM*, 1st ser., 64 (1794), 964 · H. Wilson, *Wonderful characters*, 3 vols. (1821) · *The strange and unaccountable life of the penurious Daniel Dancer*, 2nd edn (1797)
Likenesses R. Cooper, pencil and chalk drawing, *c*.1790, NPG [*see illus.*] · J. Chapman, stipple, 1801, BM, NPG · R. Page, engraving, repro. in Wilson, *Wonderful characters*, vol. 2 · drawing, NPG · engraving, repro. in *Strange and unaccountable life*
Wealth at death £3000 p.a.: *Strange and unaccountable life*

Dancer, John (*fl.* 1660–1675), translator and playwright, was probably a servant of the duke of Ormond while he was lieutenant of Ireland. To the duke and to his children, Thomas, earl of Ossory, and Lady Mary Cavendish, he dedicated his books, and in 1673 he wrote that he owed to the duke 'all I have and all I am'. Langbaine credits him with the alternative name of Dauncy and identifies him with John Dauncey or Dauncy, a translator living at the same time. But John Dancer and John Dauncey were clearly not the same person.

Dancer's translation of Tasso's *Aminta* (1660) in heroic couplets is praiseworthy. Langbaine considered it superior to Abraham Fraunce's previous translation (Langbaine, 224). Dancer's two translated plays, *Nicomede, a Tragicomedy Translated out of the French of Monsieur Corneille* (1671) and *Agrippa, King of Alba, or, The False Tiberinus, … from the French of Monsieur Quinault* (1675), are in rhyming couplets. Both were performed with some success at the Theatre Royal, Dublin. *Nicomede* was published by Francis Kirkman 'in the author's absence', and dedicated to Thomas, earl of Ossory. Kirkman added a valuable appendix to the play: 'A true, perfect, and exact catalogue of all the comedies, tragedies, tragicomedies, pastorals, masques, and interludes that were ever yet printed and published till this present year 1671'. Dancer also published translations from French: *Judgment on Alexander and Caesar, and also on Seneca, Plutarch, and Petronius* (1672); *The comparison of Plato and Aristotle, with the opinions of the fathers on their doctrine, and some Christian reflections* (1673), by the Jesuit René Rapin; and *Mercury gallant, containing many true and pleasant relations of what hath passed at Paris from January 1st 1672 till the king's departure thence* (1673).

SIDNEY LEE, *rev.* ANTONELLA BRAIDA

Sources G. Langbaine, *An account of the English dramatick poets* (1691), 92, 224 [annotated copy with Oldys's notes, BL, C.45.d14] · Hunter, 'Chorus vatum', BL, Add. MS 24489, fol. 173 · D. J. O'Donoghue, *The poets of Ireland: a biographical and bibliographical dictionary* (1912)

Dancer, John Benjamin (1812–1887), maker of scientific instruments, was born on 12 October 1812 at 52 Great Sutton Street, London, the son of Josiah and Anna Maria Dancer. Josiah Dancer (1779–1835) had worked for some time for the instrument maker Edward Troughton, but at this

John Benjamin Dancer (1812–1887), by unknown photographer

date had his own instrument business in partnership with his father, Michael. In 1816 both Josiah Dancer's wife and his father died, and by 1817 he had moved his business to Liverpool. It was here that John received some basic education at a dame-school and was then tutored in mathematics, French, Latin, and Greek. He later attended lectures at the Liverpool Mechanics' Institute. From an early age he assisted in his father's workshop, and also with the latter's lecture demonstrations. Josiah died in 1835, leaving the business to his son. On 22 March 1836 Dancer married Elizabeth Barrow (*d.* 1889), and the first of their eight children was born in the same year.

In Liverpool, Dancer made important contributions to the development of the Daniel electric cell, is thought to have prompted the initial development of electrotyping, and demonstrated the application of limelight to the magic lantern. In later years he developed a double lantern, which, combined with a gas tap of his own devising, enabled the projection of sophisticated 'dissolving views'. In 1841 he moved to Manchester where he first worked in partnership as Abraham and Dancer. This arrangement lasted until 1845, by which date Dancer was well established in the local community: in 1842 he joined the Manchester Literary and Philosophical Society, and later he was a founder member of the Manchester Photographic Society. Through these societies he maintained close contact with the city's scientists and industrialists, supplying many of them with instruments.

Dancer was one of the first provincial opticians to offer relatively inexpensive achromatic microscopes: an early example went to John Dalton, while another was used by

James Prescott Joule in his determination of the mechanical equivalent of heat. Later Dancer devised a novel binocular microscope, an achievement which ensured continued demand for his instruments. His practical competence as a microscopist enabled him to provide support to the sanitary expert Robert Angus Smith. Dancer pioneered photography in Manchester, and developed what is now considered to have been the first effective stereoscopic camera. For Joseph Whitworth he made a boresight device for the accurate alignment of firearms. At its peak Dancer's workshop is reputed to have provided employment for twelve persons.

In 1852 Scott Archer developed the wet collodion process and this, combined with Dancer's great skill as a microscopist and photographer, enabled the latter to prepare the first 'microscopic photographs' in 1852 or 1853. This involved the capture of a large object as a small photographic image. Significantly, an early Dancer microphotograph (as they were soon known) recorded the lettering on a memorial tablet, thus demonstrating the potential for data storage at reduced dimensions. Dancer mounted the microphotographs on slides for microscopical examination, and public interest in them as curiosities thereafter created an important market for his business. Their first significant application was during the siege of Paris, in 1870, when carrier pigeons were used to carry microphotographed messages.

In 1870 Dancer's sight began to fail, and he had to give up his business in 1878, though the production of microphotographs was carried on for some years by his daughters, Eleanor, Elizabeth, and Catherine. He died in near poverty in Manchester on 24 November 1887, and was buried in Brooklands cemetery in Sale.

Dancer was the most important provincial instrument maker of his time, yet throughout his life he was seldom able to exploit fully his numerous scientific and technological innovations. Indeed, his seminal contribution to the development of microphotography and the microfilm gained full recognition only during the twentieth century. His surviving instruments and microphotographs are now greatly prized.

RONALD M. BIRSE, *rev.* R. H. NUTTALL

Sources F. Luther, 'John Benjamin Dancer (1812–87) a family history', *History of Photography*, 16 (1992), 123–34 · J. Wetton, 'John Benjamin Dancer: Manchester instrument maker', *Bulletin of the Scientific Instrument Society*, 29 (1991), 4–8 · *John Benjamin Dancer, 1812–1887: selected documents and essays*, ed. M. Hallett (1979) · W. Browning, 'John Benjamin Dancer, FRAS, 1812–1887; an autobiographical sketch, with some letters', *Memoirs of the Literary and Philosophical Society of Manchester*, 106 (1964–5), 1–28 · L. L. Ardern, *John Benjamin Dancer: instrument maker, optician and the originator of microphotography*, Occasional Papers, Library Association North Western Group, 2 (1960) · B. Bracegirdle and J. B. McCormick, *The microscopic photographs of J. B. Dancer* (1993)
Archives Manchester Museum of Science and Industry, catalogues, instruments, microphotographs · Ransom HRC
Likenesses J. B. Dancer, microphotograph, *c.*1855, Manchester Museum of Science and Industry · photograph, 1860, Manchester Museum of Science and Industry · group portrait, microphotograph, *c.*1885 (Dancer family), Manchester Museum of Science and Industry · photograph, Ransom HRC [*see illus.*]

Dancer, Thomas (*c.*1750–1811), physician and botanist, was awarded his MD at Edinburgh in 1771 and left for Jamaica in 1773. He was physician to the military expedition which left Jamaica in February 1780 for Fort San Juan, Nicaragua. On his return to Jamaica he published *A Brief History of the Late Expedition Against Fort San Juan* (1781), which dealt with the terrible loss of life among the troops, the result of poor sanitation and hygiene. He was appointed physician to the island's Bath waters in 1781, and in 1784 he published a small book on the virtues of the waters, to which he added a two-page catalogue of the rarer plants cultivated in the garden there. A full *Catalogue of Plants, Exotic and Indigenous, in the Botanical Garden* was published in 1792; from this it can be seen that in the two previous years he introduced many plants, some of which he owed to his correspondence with Sir Joseph Banks. Dancer was appointed curator of the Botanic Garden, Bath, Jamaica, in 1798 and became island botanist in 1797. In 1804 he printed a small tract, *Some Observations Respecting the Botanic Garden*, recounting its history and making suggestions for its better support. His proposals were not adopted by the house of assembly and he resigned his position as island botanist. His most important publication was the *Medical Assistant, or, Jamaica Practice of Physic* (1801). This book, intended specifically for use by families and plantation owners in Jamaica, contains recipes, weights, measures, doses, and an index of diseases, with remedies. It was anonymously attacked, by a former official named Fitzgerald, in a professed reprint in the *Royal Jamaica Gazette* of a critique in the *Edinburgh Review*. Dancer's last literary effort was to expose this fiction in *A Rowland for an Oliver, or, A Jamaica Review of the Edinburgh Reviewers* (1809). He died at Kingston, Jamaica, on 1 August 1811.

B. D. JACKSON, *rev.* CLAIRE L. NUTT

Sources GM, 1st ser., 81/2 (1811), 390 · Desmond, *Botanists*, rev. edn · F. Cundall, *Historic Jamaica* (1915); repr. (New York, 1971)
Archives RBG Kew, plants · RSA, letters to the RSA relating to botanical matters | BL, corresp. with Edward Long and Samuel Moore, Add. MS 22678
Likenesses Holl, stipple, Wellcome L. · portrait, repro. in *Journal of the Institute of Jamaica*, 1 (1891–3), 141

Danckerts [Danckers, Dankers, Danckertszoon], **Hendrick** (*c.*1625–1680), landscape painter and engraver, was born to a Catholic family, allegedly in The Hague. His father was called Jan Danckerts, and likewise his brother, **Jan Danckerts** (*c.*1615–1686), who was a history painter and engraver who joined the Guild of St Luke in The Hague in 1632 and became warden in 1649 and dean in 1651. Hendrick was admitted as an engraver to the same guild in 1651. According to Buckeridge, a landscape painter himself, Hendrick 'was first bred a graver, but upon the persuasions of his brother John took to Painting' (Buckeridge, 367).

The brothers travelled to Italy *c.*1653–1657. Jan Danckerts possibly came to England about 1658/9 because his illustrations (engraved by Wenceslaus Hollar) to the second edition of Sir Robert Stapylton's translation of Juvenal's *Satires* were published in 1660. The first definite record of Hendrick's presence in England was when he married 'Theodosia Hugh's of Staffordshire' on 24 October 1664 in a ceremony witnessed by his brother in St James's Chapel, London (Weale). He revisited the Netherlands at least once, in 1670, but otherwise remained based in England until the increasing threat to Catholics of the Popish Plot drove him back to Holland c.1679. On 10 August 1680 Hendrick, now called 'the widower of Theodosia Hues', married the 28-year-old Elizabeth, daughter of William Boon (Bredius, archival notes). But by 30 October 1680 he had died, in Amsterdam, leaving several thousand guilders, paintings, jewels, and coins to his brother and his new wife, Elizabeth.

Among Danckerts's engravings are nine portraits, some holy figures (several after Titian), and a series of the antiquities of the island of Walcheren (1647). Hollstein gives the full list. His engravings of members of the English royal family include in 1645 Henrietta Maria after Van Dyck, Mary, princess of Orange, in 1646, and her brother Charles II in exile in 1649, both after portraits by Hanneman. Hendrick was probably enrolled as a royalist agent: on 30 June (1650?) Hugh May wrote to Sir Charles Cotterell that 'one Danckers ... is comeing over from the Hague speedily to him' (MS, priv. coll.).

Having moved permanently to England, Danckerts became a successful painter of topographical and idyllic landscapes. His canvases were often inset as over-doors and chimney pieces, or in ceilings. His first task in England was to provide three fine decorative paintings for Eltham Lodge, Kent, the lavish house (1663–5) built by Hugh May for Sir John Shaw. These are almost Claudian in mood. In 1669 Samuel Pepys commissioned four panels for his dining-room from the 'famous lanskip painter'. They were painted in 'distemper' (tempera). Pepys called them 'mighty pretty', though after some consideration he decided he preferred Danckerts's oil paintings (Pepys, vol. 9). The diarist also admired a depiction of the fortress at Tangier which the king had commissioned from Danckerts in 1669, for which Sir Charles Harbord had made the sketches. The earl of Sandwich had requested a copy and Pepys was minded to do likewise (ibid., 9.541).

Danckerts provided many paintings for the gentry and nobility: in 1664 for Sir Stephen Fox for his house in Chiswick; in 1666 five views of Rome as over-doors for Lady Clarendon's house in Piccadilly; between 1669 and 1672 views of two country seats for Henry Herbert, later first duke of Beaufort; and in the latter year two scenes of classical gardens for George Vernon for Sudbury Hall, Derbyshire; idyllic landscapes for the duke of Lauderdale in 1673; a view of Plymouth citadel for the earl of Bedford for Woburn Abbey in 1676; views of Plymouth, Windsor, and Penzance for the earl of Radnor for his house in St James's in 1678; an over-door of Nonsuch Palace for the earl of Berkeley; several views, including Tangier and Pontefract Castle, for the earl of Peterborough; and some ceiling pieces for the duke of St Albans. The lawyer and historian Roger, fourth Baron North, commented wryly on his *capriccio* of Rome by Danckerts: 'if after the life, Creept some Invention upon the foreground' (North's notebook,

BL, Add. MS 32504, fol. 43). Sir Peter Lely owned at least three of Danckerts's landscapes when he died in 1680.

Danckerts's most important patron, however, was Charles II who, in 1665–7, commissioned some large classical landscapes and a view of the recently completed canal works at Hampton Court. The king later commissioned paintings of the palaces and fortresses of his realm, and Danckerts was paid £73 18s. od. on 30 June 1675 (PRO, sub-category PRO 30/32/42, king's warrant book 4, fol. 399), and £34 5s. 6d. on 15 March 1679 (PRO 30/32/44, king's warrant book 6, fol. 204). The Royal Collection in 1688 boasted twenty-nine prospects by Danckerts, eight of which belonged to James II when duke of York (BL, Harley MS 1890, fols. 48–86). One was painted on a sliding panel which covered a portrait of the naked Nell Gwyn. Fifteen of them are still in the Royal Collection, and there is also a *Mystic Marriage of St. Catherine* which may be by both Danckerts brothers.

The British Museum has six drawings by Danckerts (in pen and brown ink with grey wash) of London and Badminton House, two of which featured in the British Museum's exhibition 'Drawing in England from Hilliard to Hogarth' in 1987, along with his fine drawing of Caerphilly Castle from the Yale Center for British Art.

The success achieved by Danckerts may seem unwarranted to modern eyes: his later works occasionally contain feeble figure painting and expanses of dull canvas. His seventy or so paintings are important in their decorative contexts, however, and can be charming. He had an attractive way with sunshine and shadows, and liked to place bird formations in his glowing skies. The Ogdens stated that English landscapes of the period are often permeated with a sense of prosperity and well-being. The paintings of Hendrick Danckerts are no exception. Other examples of his works are held at Sudbury Hall, Derbyshire; Brighton City Museum and Art Gallery; Virginia Museum of Fine Arts, Richmond, Virginia; and in several private collections.   KATHARINE GIBSON

Sources F. D. O. Obreen, ed., *Archief voor Nederlandsche kunstgeschiedenis*, 7 vols. (Rotterdam, 1877–90), vol. 3, p. 261; vol. 4, pp. 9, 32–4; vol. 5, pp. 78–81 · A. Bredius, MS archival notes, Rijksbureau voor Kunsthistorische Documentatie, The Hague · A. Bredius, ed., *Künstler-Inventare*, 8 vols. (The Hague, 1915–22), vol. 6, pp. 1974–8 · A. Bredius, 'Iets over Hendrick Danckerts', *Oud Holland*, 28 (1910), 70–72 · [B. Buckeridge], 'An essay towards an English school', in R. de Piles, *The art of painting, with the lives and characters of above 300 of the most eminent painters*, 3rd edn (1754), 354–439; facs. edn (1969), esp. 367–8 · Pepys, *Diary*, 9.421, 423, 434, 438, 445, 465, 485, 487, 504, 539, 541 · O. Millar, *The Tudor, Stuart and early Georgian pictures in the collection of her majesty the queen*, 2 vols. (1963), vol. 1, p. 153; vol. 2, nos. 397–412 · J. Harris, *The artist and the country house: a history of country house and garden view painting in Britain, 1540–1870* (1979), 17, 42–3; nos. 45–47, 49, pl. 36 · H. V. S. Ogden and M. S. Ogden, *English taste in landscape in the seventeenth century* (1955), 153–4, 159, 162 · F. W. H. Hollstein, *Dutch and Flemish etchings, engravings and woodcuts, c.1450–1700*, 5 (1951), 133–4 · E. Croft-Murray and P. H. Hulton, eds., *Catalogue of British drawings*, 1 (1960), 296–8 · J. C. M. Weale, ed., *Registers of the Catholic chapels royal and of the Portuguese embassy chapel, 1662–1829*, Catholic RS, 38 (1941) · L. Abel-Smith, 'Danckerts and Badminton', *Georgian Group Journal*, [3] (1993), 78–81

Wealth at death relatively wealthy; 10,619/8/12 florins to Johannes Danckerts; 3698/14/8 florins plus pictures, jewels, and coins to wife: legal documents, Oct–Dec 1680, Bredius, *Künstler-Inventare*, vol. 6, pp. 1974–8

Danckerts, Jan (*c*.1615–1686). *See under* Danckerts, Hendrick (*c*.1625–1680).

Danckwerts, Peter Victor (1916–1984), chemical engineer, was born on 14 October 1916 at Emsworth, Hampshire, the eldest of five children (three sons and two daughters) of Rear-Admiral Victor Hilary Danckwerts (*d*. 1943), CMG, and his wife, Joyce Middleton. He came from a family with distinguished naval and legal experience; one of his grandfathers was a highly successful QC and an uncle became a lord justice of appeal. Nevertheless, his own inclination was towards chemistry, and as a boy he constructed his own laboratory in an attic at his home. He was educated at Winchester College and at Balliol College, Oxford, where he obtained first-class honours in chemistry (1939). He held a post in a small chemical company in 1939–40.

Shortly after the outbreak of the Second World War Danckwerts became a sub-lieutenant in the Royal Naval Volunteer Reserve and was trained in bomb disposal. By the beginning of the blitz in September 1940, he had been posted as bomb disposal officer to the Port of London Authority. Although he had learned about defusing bombs his training had not extended to magnetic mines. Nevertheless, when some magnetic mines were dropped on a south London suburb Danckwerts volunteered to try to defuse them, and succeeded in doing so. On one subsequent occasion he worked for two days almost without rest and dealt with sixteen mines. In 1940 he was awarded the George Cross for his bravery. Later in the war he was transferred to bomb disposal work abroad and was wounded in a minefield in Sicily. Following this episode he joined the combined operations headquarters in Whitehall and was subsequently appointed MBE (1943).

At the end of the war Danckwerts entered the field of chemical engineering, which was then much more firmly established in the USA than in Britain. With a Commonwealth Fund fellowship he studied at the Massachusetts Institute of Technology and there obtained a master's degree.

Danckwerts's return to Britain in 1948 coincided with a donation to Cambridge University by the Shell group of companies which enabled the setting up of a new department of chemical engineering under T. R. C. Fox. Danckwerts did much excellent research at Cambridge, but felt that he had insufficient industrial experience to teach effectively. For this reason he joined the Industrial Group of the UK Atomic Energy Authority at Risley in 1954, but left in 1956 to become professor of chemical engineering science at Imperial College, a newly created chair within the department led by D. M. Newitt. In this post Danckwerts continued with research and teaching and also played an active part in the affairs of the college.

In 1959 Fox resigned from the Shell chair at Cambridge and Danckwerts was elected in his place. The following

Peter Victor Danckwerts (1916–1984), by Godfrey Argent, *c*.1970

year he married Lavinia, daughter of Brigadier-General Alwyn Macfarlane. The couple, who had no children, lived at Abbey House, Abbey Road, Cambridge, until Danckwerts's death.

Danckwerts made many innovations in the Cambridge teaching course and also did research of great originality, especially in the fields of mixing phenomena and gas absorption. He became increasingly sought after as an international speaker, and travelled widely. He was elected FRS in 1969 and received honorary degrees from the universities of Bradford (1978), Loughborough (1981), and Bath (1983), and the foreign associateship of the National Academy of Engineering, USA (1978). Danckwerts was president of the Institution of Chemical Engineers (1965–6). He was executive editor of *Chemical Engineering Science* until 1983, six years after he had retired from the Shell chair because of prolonged illness.

Danckwerts had a complex personality and was regarded by contemporaries as reserved, even aloof, yet still having a strong sense of humour. His outstanding talents were combined with personal charm and considerable forcefulness of character. Danckwerts died in Cambridge on 25 October 1984, survived by his wife.

K. G. DENBIGH, *rev.*

Sources K. G. Denbigh, *Memoirs FRS*, 32 (1986), 97–114 • personal knowledge (1990) • private information (1990)
Likenesses G. Argent, photograph, *c*.1970, RS [*see illus.*]
Wealth at death under £40,000: probate, 9 Jan 1985, *CGPLA Eng. & Wales*

Dando, Jill Wendy (1961–1999), journalist and television broadcaster, was born on 9 November 1961 in Weston-super-Mare, the only daughter and younger child of (Herbert) Jack Dando (b. 1918), a compositor on the *Weston Mercury*, and his wife, Jean, *née* Hockey (1927–1986). She was ten years younger than her brother, Nigel (later chief reporter of the *Bristol Evening Post* and then a reporter for the BBC in Bristol). She was a sickly infant and at eighteen months was found to have a hole in the heart. The condition was rectified during surgery at the Bristol Royal Infirmary when she was three, after which her health improved dramatically. She had an unremarkable school career at Worle comprehensive school, Weston-super-Mare, until the age of sixteen, and looking back described herself as, 'rather an ugly little girl, with canine teeth, glasses, and an extremely old-fashioned dress sense' (*Daily Telegraph*, 27 April 1999). Perhaps she was being characteristically modest, for at Broadoak sixth-form college, Weston-super-Mare, she became head girl.

Dando also had early flair for performance. She joined the Weston-super-Mare Amateur Dramatic Society, and as a teenager yearned for a job in television, writing to the *Jim'll Fix it* children's show asking for a break. If not television, then she would follow her father, and her older brother, Nigel, into newspapers. In 1980 she applied for a job on the *Weston Mercury*. As part of the selection process she was required to write an essay called 'My Thoughts on the Year 2000', and though the predictions she made for herself—of married life with children—were not fulfilled she won herself a place as a junior reporter. Six years later, in 1986, her mother died of leukaemia. The two had been especially close, and for a while the bereavement shook Jill's faith. She had been brought up a Baptist, and though in later life not outwardly religious she always retained her quiet Christian convictions.

In that same year Dando applied for a job with BBC Radio Devon and moved into broadcasting. She showed a natural aptitude for the medium, and soon presented the breakfast show. After two years she moved to television, briefly to the local commercial station Westward TV, and thence to the south-west BBC news programme *Spotlight*. Her good looks and ease in front of the camera quickly identified her as a potential presenter of national television. Her break came when the BBC's *Breakfast Time* needed a stand-in. She made such an impression that when the programme was revamped in the following year, 1988, she was taken on as a newsreader full time.

Over the next six years on *Breakfast Time* Dando grew in stature and popularity. She was a televisual natural, extremely capable, unflappable, equally at ease with serious news and lightweight features—a 'professional chameleon', as she put it herself—and with a radiating screen presence. She often presented *The Six O'Clock News* and became the 'Golden Girl' of British television (*The Times*, 27 April 1999), though one of her attractions was that she retained her modesty, was unfailingly generous to colleagues, and seemed genuinely surprised that she should be so popular and successful. In the early 1990s one of the BBC's top-rated series, *Holiday*, needed a new presenter and Dando quickly made the show her own, full of fun and sunshine, flattering and flattered by the camera,

building audiences of up to 9 million. Her gruelling travel schedule was at a far remove from the limited horizons of her childhood, and was equally remote from the superficial glamour of the series.

Dando always admired one show in particular and hoped one day to work on it: the live appeals programme *Crimewatch UK*. In 1995 Sue Cook, who had presented *Crimewatch* with Nick Ross since it had started ten years earlier, decided to leave, and Dando was the natural choice as her successor. She played her part in solving several notorious crimes, finding interviews with victims the most gruelling part of her career. She coaxed the best out of them, not merely because she was good at her job but because she related to them personally, seamlessly combining professionalism and empathy. She also presented the most successful television appeal of its time, raising money for victims of the civil war in Kosovo for an alliance of disaster response charities. She supported many other charities, among them the British Heart Foundation (who named an honorarium after her), Weston Hospicecare (who funded a consultant in her name), the Royal British Legion, the British Academy of Film and Television Arts, Children in Need, and Chain of Hope.

Two years after joining *Crimewatch*, Dando had been introduced to a surgeon, Alan Farthing, a relationship that over eighteen months blossomed into plans for marriage. In the early months of 1999 she was at the peak of her profession, planning a host of new programmes, and excitedly making arrangements for her wedding. She was always diffident about her popularity, and remained unaffected by fame, but her iconic status turned out to be fatal. On a Monday morning, 26 April 1999, she was shot in the head by a lone assailant at point-blank range on the front doorstep of her home, 29 Gowan Avenue, Fulham, London. Her body was cremated at Worle crematorium in Weston-super-Mare on 21 May.

Dando's murder provoked huge news coverage, in Britain and abroad, and public grief. In the wake of her death Nick Ross and Alan Farthing created the Jill Dando Fund to raise money for the Jill Dando Institute of Crime Science, with a mission to find new ways to reduce crime. The institute was formally inaugurated on 26 April 2001 at University College, London, on the second anniversary of her death. Barry George, unemployed, of Fulham, was convicted of her murder on 2 July the same year.

NICK ROSS

Sources *The Times* (27 April 1999) · *The Guardian* (27 April 1999) · *The Independent* (27 April 1999) · *Daily Telegraph* (27 April 1999) · personal knowledge (2004) · private information (2004) [Nigel Dando, brother; A. Farthing]
Archives FILM BBC, London | SOUND BBC, London
Likenesses photograph, repro. in *The Times* · photograph, repro. in *The Guardian* · photograph, repro. in *The Independent* · photograph, repro. in *Daily Telegraph* · photographs, BBC Publicity, London · photographs, Press Association, London
Wealth at death £1,181,207: administration, 1999

Dando, Joseph Haydon Bourne (1806–1894), violinist, was born on 11 May 1806 at Somers Town in London. Nothing is known of his parents. He began to study the violin with his uncle Gaetano Brandi and was then a pupil of

Nicolas Mori for seven years (1819–26). He was page to his teacher at the coronation of George IV, and later performed at the coronations of William IV and Queen Victoria.

After leading some concerts in London, Dando joined the Philharmonic Orchestra (1831–55) and subsequently became a well-known orchestral leader in the capital and the provinces, appearing with orchestras such as those of the Classical Harmonists' and Choral Harmonists' societies. In 1832 he played in the first English performance of Beethoven's *Fidelio* in the Haymarket Theatre. Dando did perform as a soloist, but it was as a chamber musician that he achieved his reputation. He is best known for organizing the first public concert in England with a programme consisting exclusively of string quartets. This benefit concert, with Dando leading, took place on 23 September 1835 at the Horn tavern, Doctors' Commons, and was followed by two more, on 12 and 26 October. The success of these performances led to the establishment of a regular series of quartet concerts involving Dando, at first at the same place, then at the London tavern, and finally at the Hanover Square Rooms. A group for the performance of chamber music was then formed, with Henry Blagrove, Henry Gattie (violins), Charles Lucas (cello), and Dando (viola), which performed together for seven seasons from 17 March 1836 to 29 April 1842, when Blagrove left the group. Dando then became leader and John Fawcett Loder played viola. The newly restored throne room of Crosby Hall in Bishopsgate Street became the venue for the concerts, in place of Hanover Square, until the deaths of Gattie and Loder in 1853. Dando and his colleagues gave first English performances of Haydn's *The Seven Last Words* (15 April 1843), Mendelssohn's quartet in E♭ (op. 44, no. 3), and Schumann's quartet in A minor. He was a friend of Spohr and of Mendelssohn, who played at one of the Crosby Hall concerts (8 June 1844). As a result of a stiffening of the third finger of his left hand, Dando was forced to give up the violin in the early 1870s and in 1875 became music master at Charterhouse School, Godalming, where he worked until a short time before he died, on 9 May 1894, at his home, Attwell Cottage, Peper-Harrow Road, Godalming.

Dando was characterized by Dubourg, who considered him to be a leading contemporary violinist, as a man of 'agreeable manners' and 'professional merits' (Dubourg, 295); his playing was described as combining elegance of expression, neatness, and vigour when required. He was a popular teacher, a conductor of amateur orchestras, and also composed and arranged a small number of pieces.

DAVID J. GOLBY

Sources G. Dubourg, *The violin*, 4th edn (1852), 293–302 · M. Parikian, 'Dando, Joseph (Bourne Haydon)', *New Grove* · Brown & Stratton, *Brit. mus.* · 'City concerts', *The Harmonicon*, 8 (1830), 217–18 · *The Musical Examiner* (1842–4)
Wealth at death £779 2s. 0d.: resworn probate, Dec 1894, CGPLA Eng. & Wales

Dandridge, Bartholomew (*bap.* 1691, *d.* in or after 1754), portrait painter, was baptized on 17 December 1691 in Fetter Lane, London, the second son of the fourteen children of John Dandridge (*b. c.*1654), a house painter, and his second wife, Anne. From 1712 he studied at Sir Godfrey Kneller's academy of painting and later went on to attend the St Martin's Lane Academy following its foundation in 1720 by John Vanderbank and Louis Cheron. On 2 April 1725 Bartholomew married Hannah Answorth at St James's, Duke's Place, Aldgate, London, while both were living in the parish of St Margaret's, Westminster. They had one son. In 1729 Dandridge was living in Lincoln's Inn Fields; he later married Rachel (*d.* 1744).

For more than four decades he ran a successful and fashionable portrait practice but is chiefly of interest to art historians as an early pioneer of elegant conversation pieces in the rococo style. His earliest known extant work is a Knelleresque full-length portrait, *Sir John Clarke* (1717; Apothecaries' Hall, London). *The Price Family* (*c.*1728; Metropolitan Museum of Art, New York), by contrast, shows a family group in a garden setting in the manner of a French *fête galante*. The impressionistic paintwork and delicate colours illustrate a familiarity with the French rococo style most probably learned through engravings and contact with French artists in London. The intricate composition seems to bear out George Vertue's assertion that the artist used lay figures to work out the lighting and arrangement of large figure groups (Vertue, *Note books*, 3.39). He continued to paint conversation pieces throughout his career, of which *The Ladies Noel* (*c.*1740; Manchester City Galleries), with its delicate palette and effervescent drapery, is a fine example. In 1731 Dandridge acquired the studio and house of Sir Godfrey Kneller in Great Queen Street. His ambitions for his practice were amply rewarded in 1732 when he was commissioned by Lord Barington to paint Frederick, prince of Wales, on horseback (1732; NPG), for which the prince sat on three occasions and which is 'vastly like' (Vertue, *Note books*, 3.57). Other equestrian portraits survive, notably *Captain Richard Gifford* (*c.*1725; NAM) and *General Sir John Ligonier* (1752; French Protestant Hospital, London).

During the 1730s Dandridge supplied designs for publication, in particular twelve designs engraved by Louis-Philip Boitard in François Nivelon, *Rudiments of Genteel Behaviour* [London, 1737]. He died some time after his last recorded work in 1754.

EMMA LAUZE

Sources Vertue, *Note books*, vol. 3 · C. H. Collins Baker, 'The Price family by Bartholomew Dandridge', *Burlington Magazine*, 72 (1938), 132–9 · H. Curtis, 'Bartholomew Dandridge, portrait-painter, 1691–*c.*1754', *N&Q*, 165 (1933), 219–22, 236–41 · S. West, 'Bartholomew Dandridge', *The dictionary of art*, ed. J. Turner (1996) · R. Edwards, 'Portraits by Bartholomew Dandridge at Poundisford Park', *Country Life*, 76 (1934), 673–4 · E. Waterhouse, *Painting in Britain, 1530–1790*, 5th edn (1994), 184–5 · E. Einberg, *Manners and morals: Hogarth and British painting, 1700–1760* (1987) [exhibition catalogue, Tate Gallery, London, 15 Oct 1987 – 3 Jan 1988] · E. G. D'Oench, *The conversation piece: Arthur Devis and his contemporaries* (1980), 79 [exhibition catalogue, Yale U. CBA, 1 Oct – 30 Nov 1980] · E. Einberg, *The French taste in English painting* (1968) [exhibition catalogue, Iveagh Bequest, Kenwood, London] · E. Einberg, *The conversation piece in Georgian England* (1965) [exhibition catalogue, Iveagh Bequest, Kenwood, London]

Dane, Clemence. *See* Ashton, Winifred (1888–1965).

Dane, Sir Louis William (1856–1946), administrator in India, was born on 21 March 1856 at Chichester, where his father, Richard Martin Dane (1813–1901), was an army staff surgeon; he later became an inspector-general of hospitals. His mother was Sophia Eliza, daughter of Colonel Charles Griffiths who served in the First Anglo-Afghan War, and granddaughter of Henry Griffiths, a close friend in India of Warren Hastings. The Dane family had long dwelt in co. Fermanagh and, although Dr Dane moved to England, he nevertheless sent Louis, who was his fifth son, and an elder brother, Sir Richard Morris *Dane, to Dr Stackpole's school, Kingstown, Dublin. Both in turn then entered the Indian Civil Service. Louis passed the examination in 1874 and in 1876 was posted to the Punjab. As assistant commissioner in Dera Ghazi Khan he ensured supplies for the Pishin column in the Second Anglo-Afghan War (1878–80). In 1879 he became private secretary to Sir Robert Egerton, lieutenant-governor of the Punjab. He had a successful spell as a settlement officer at Gurdaspur and Peshawar. His brother Richard had served in the former location before him. In 1898 Dane was appointed chief secretary to the Punjab government. On 21 March 1882 he had married Edith (d. 1948), daughter of Sir Francis Booth *Norman. They were to have four daughters and three sons.

In 1900 Dane went on leave and seemed to have ended his Indian career, for he became resident magistrate of Tralee, co. Kerry. In November 1901 however he was recalled to India by Lord Curzon to become resident of Kashmir, and in March 1903 foreign secretary in the government of India. Curzon was especially concerned over Afghan affairs. In 1901 Amir Habibullah had succeeded his father, Abdur Rahman, whose reign of twenty years had been marked by friendship with India, although at its end certain issues were unsettled. In October 1904 Dane headed a mission to Kabul where he gained the young amir's respect. Negotiations were too protracted for the forceful viceroy who wanted to withdraw the mission, but Dane, dissenting, held that the amir's renewal of his father's engagements should be accepted as sufficient. The cabinet in London supported Dane and the treaty was signed in March 1905. Dane, who had been appointed CSI in 1904, was now made a KCIE. The value of his achievement became clear in the First World War when, despite persistent German pressure, Habibullah maintained his country's neutrality in the face of domestic dangers which were tragically underlined by his assassination in 1919.

In 1908 Dane became lieutenant-governor of the Punjab. This was a difficult period following the widespread rural disturbances the previous year. It fell to Dane to oversee the enactment in 1912 of the Punjab Colonization of Land Bill. An earlier ill-judged version of the legislation had caused the 1907 disturbances. His tireless energy in touring his province set a high example to his officers. His linguistic gifts and handsome presence helped to win him general respect and public confidence. In December 1911 he was called upon to arrange the memorable people's fair at the royal durbar. He was promoted GCIE and,

exactly a year later, had to hand over to the government of India the Delhi district as part of the enclave of the new capital. The viceroy, Lord Hardinge of Penshurst, was seriously wounded on his way to the ceremony which nevertheless took place. In this emergency, Dane, after his formal speech, 'laid aside the typescript', wrote his contemporary Sir Henry Sharp, 'and began to talk [in Urdu] .... It swept through the audience like a strong wind. Formality melted in emotion.' In May 1913 Dane's successful period as lieutenant-governor of the Punjab ended and he retired to London.

After his retirement Dane continued to take an active interest in Indian affairs and was for many years on the board of the Attock Oil Company. On 13 March 1940, at a joint meeting of the East India Association and Royal Central Asian Society, he was badly wounded in the arm by the assailant who killed Sir Michael O'Dwyer. He was then nearly eighty-four, and lived to be almost ninety, dying at his home, 24 Onslow Gardens, South Kensington, London, on 22 February 1946. The youngest of his sons, Henry, died in captivity in Japan in 1942 and was posthumously appointed to the DSO in 1946.

EDWIN HAWARD, rev. IAN TALBOT

Sources Burke, *Gen. Ire.* (1976) · C. E. Buckland, *Dictionary of Indian biography* (1906) · P. H. M. van den Dungen, *The Punjab tradition: influence and authority in nineteenth-century India* (1972) · N. G. Barrier, 'The Punjab disturbances of 1907: the response of the British government in India to agrarian unrest', *Modern Asian Studies*, 1 (1967), 353–83 · C. Dewey, *The settlement literature of the Greater Punjab: a handbook* (1991) · H. Banerjee, *Agrarian society of the Punjab, 1849–1901* (1982) · I. Ali, *The Punjab under imperialism, 1885–1947* (1988) · WWW, 1941–50 · CGPLA Eng. & Wales (1946)

Archives BL OIOC, corresp. and papers, MS Eur. D 659 | BL OIOC, Birdwood of Anzac MSS · BL OIOC, Denise Montgomery Dane MSS · BL OIOC, Morley MSS · CUL, corresp. with Lord Hardinge

Likenesses J. St H. Lander, oils, 1914, Lawrence Hall, Lahore, Pakistan

Wealth at death £38,827 8s. 5d.: probate, 15 June 1946, CGPLA Eng. & Wales

Dane, Sir Richard Morris (1854–1940), administrator in India, was born on 21 May 1854, the third of four surviving sons of an Anglo-Irish family that was prominent in service in imperial India. His father was Richard Martin Dane (1813–1901) of the Royal Army Medical Corps, who served in India and eventually became inspector-general of hospitals; his mother, Sophia Eliza, née Griffiths, came from a family long connected with India. His brother Sir Louis William *Dane was also to serve in India, and his own son, also Richard, served in the 1st Punjab cavalry. The bulk of Dane's career was spent in the Indian Civil Service, and it was here that he made a name for himself as an administrator of boundless confidence and exceptional vigour, who was painstaking in attention to detail, and unusual in his effectiveness.

Dane was educated at Dr Stackpole's school, Kingstown, Dublin, before passing the Indian Civil Service examination in 1872. After a probationary period he went out to Punjab province. While Dane was briefly attached to the foreign department of the government of India, his right eye was seriously injured in a polo match at Lahore. The lingering effects of the injury rendered his later accomplishments that much more impressive: although the eye was saved, he could not read for long periods without strain, and in order to continue shooting he taught himself to shoot from the left shoulder. While in England for medical attention following the accident he married, on 24 June 1880, Emily (1861/2–1928), third daughter of Sir Edward Leeds, third baronet, a colonel in the Indian army. They had a son and two daughters, one of whom did not survive infancy. Dane divorced his wife in 1901 and she remarried in the following year.

Throughout the 1870s and 1880s Dane's career advanced with appointments that included under secretary to the government of the Punjab, boundary settlement officer in central India, and assistant commissioner at Ajmer. In 1890 he was promoted to commissioner of excise; from then on his most significant achievements were in the realm of tax, particularly salt tax, administration. He attracted wider attention, not all of it positive, when he aided Lord Brassey's royal commission on opium and contributed two lengthy historical appendices on the production of opium and the opium trade between India and China to the commission's final report (1895). These were an important component of the report, which found that the claims of the then quite vociferous anti-opium lobby were overstated, and that in any case the Indian government could not abolish the trade without instituting new and unpopular taxes in its stead. For his contribution to the final report Dane earned the opprobrium of the anti-opiumists, and was denounced in the House of Commons.

Dane was made CIE in 1896 and continued his administrative career with appointments as secretary in the finance and commerce department, commissioner for salt revenue in north India in 1898, and eventually as the first inspector-general of excise and salt in 1907. During these years he developed and first attempted to implement his ideas on salt tax and administration. He believed that, in the realm of colonial finance, an indirect tax was always more popular than a direct tax, and that with unification of control, rationalization of administration, and the prevention of smuggling, a large revenue to the state and a lower tax on the people could be achieved simultaneously.

Although active as an administrator, and incessant in touring remote areas of India, Dane retired from the Indian Civil Service in 1909, in order to get in some years of hunting while his health remained good. He was made KCIE in the same year. Retirement was short lived. In 1913 the fledgeling post-imperial Chinese government and a consortium of banks then in the process of extending a controversially large loan (the 'reorganization loan') to the Chinese government invited Dane to China to reorganize the salt gabelle and put it on an administrative basis sound enough to service the ensuing annual loan debt. Knowing not a word of Chinese, but a good deal about rationalizing the salt tax administration, Dane arrived in China in 1913. Without preliminaries, he wrested for his newly created salt inspectorate an impressive degree of autonomy and set up a joint Sino-foreign administration that was organized on strict civil service principles of entry by examination and promotion by seniority. The Sino-foreign salt inspectorate was, from the very beginning, so untainted by corruption and so successful in terms of efficient tax collection that even after the reorganization loan debt service was paid, its annual surpluses continued to provide the second highest and most reliable source of tax to the Chinese government long after Dane departed from China in 1919. Indeed, the salt inspectorate, along with the customs administration formed by Sir Robert Hart in the previous century, embodied a set of principles that provided a working model of efficient, effective, and depoliticized administration. As such, it attracted a great deal of admiration from administrative reformers who wished to emulate it, and opprobrium from Chinese nationalists for whom the organization's links to the group banks reeked of imperialism. The salt inspectorate was taken into the nationalist government of Chaing Kai-shek in 1928, and continued to operate successfully along the principles originally articulated by Dane until some years after the outbreak of the Sino-Japanese War of 1937. Dane was rewarded by the Chinese government with the first class of the order of the Excellent Crop (1915) and of the Striped Tiger (1918).

After Dane left China he wrote an affectionate memoir of his hunting expeditions entitled *Sport in Asia and Africa* (1921); he retired to Herefordshire, where he remained active in salmon fishing into his eighties. He died at his home, Morney Cross, Fownhope, Herefordshire, on 13 February 1940.   JULIA C. STRAUSS

Sources *The Times* (14 Feb 1940) · S. A. M. Adshead, *The modernization of the Chinese salt administration, 1900–1920* (1970) · R. Dane, *Sport in Asia and Africa* (1921) · 'Royal commission on opium: final report', *Parl. papers* (1895), 42.28–214, C. 7723-I · O. M. Green, *The foreigner in China* (1942) · Burke, *Gen. GB* (1937) · Burke, *Peerage* (1939) · m. cert. · d. cert.
Archives Number 2 Historical Archives, Nanjing, People's Republic of China
Likenesses photograph, repro. in Green, *Foreigner in China*
Wealth at death £23,121 12s. 5d.: administration with will, 7 May 1940

Danell, James (1821–1881), Roman Catholic bishop of Southwark, the son of Robert and Christina Danell, was born in Hampstead on 14 July 1821. He was educated from 1830 at Dr Kenny's academy in Fitzroy Street, Fitzroy Square, and at St Edmund's College, near Ware (1835–43). In 1843 he was sent to finish his ecclesiastical studies at St Sulpice in Paris. He was ordained priest in June 1846 by Archbishop Affre of Paris, and in August of that year he was appointed to the mission of St George's, Southwark. At Southwark he was appointed canon (1857) and vicar-general (1862), and, after the death of Dr Thomas Grant, he was made bishop of Southwark by Pius IX in 1871. He was consecrated by Archbishop (later Cardinal) Manning on 25 March at St George's Cathedral. During his episcopate he ordained seventy-two priests for service in the diocese and started fifty new missions. He continued the work of his predecessor, Dr Grant, in conducting negotiations with government bodies, particularly over the supply of chaplains to the army and navy. Danell died kneeling at his bedside saying his prayers on 14 June 1881; his death was attributed to a combination of heart disease and a chest infection. He was buried in St George's Cathedral. He was well known for his commanding presence, his sonorous voice when preaching, his care for the poor, and his many fine pastoral letters.

MICHAEL CLIFTON

Sources *The Tablet* (18 June 1881) · *Catholic Directory* (1887), 239 · 'Great Southwark Catholics V: Bishop Danell', *The Shield* [Southwark diocesan magazine] (Aug 1907), 187–91 · G. Albion, 'Bishops of Southwark II: James Danell, 1871–1881', *The Southwark Record* [Southwark new diocesan magazine], 18 (1939), 121–7 · B. Bogan, *The great link: a history of St George's, Southwark, 1786–1848–1948* [1948], 273ff. · B. Plumb, *Arundel to Zabi: a biographical dictionary of the Catholic bishops of England and Wales (deceased), 1623–1987* (privately printed, Warrington, [1987])
Archives St George's Roman Catholic Cathedral, Southwark, London, Southwark Roman Catholic diocese archives, corresp. and papers | U. Leeds, Brotherton L., papers relating to Edith Somerville
Likenesses portrait, archbishop's house, Southwark, London
Wealth at death £757 8s. 7d.: probate, 8 July 1881, *CGPLA Eng. & Wales*

Danett, Thomas (1543–1601?), historian and translator, was the elder son of another Thomas Danett (d. 1569), a Leicestershire man who had settled at Stockland Lovell, Somerset, and his wife, Anne Browne of Betchworth, Surrey. A friend and cousin of Sir William Cecil, and also evangelical in religion, the elder Thomas Danett supported the duke of Northumberland in 1553 and the duke of Suffolk a year later, and consequently fled to the continent in 1554 when the latter's rising against Queen Mary failed. He was accompanied by his family, and the education of Thomas junior was entrusted to John Aylmer, the future bishop of London, with whom he studied in Strasbourg, Basel, Zürich, and probably Italy. Having returned to England after Elizabeth's accession, the younger Thomas Danett was a member of Gray's Inn in 1560, and a student at Jesus College, Cambridge, in 1565. He had entered the service of Robert Dudley, from 1564 earl of Leicester, and perhaps through the latter's influence obtained occasional employment overseas, in France in 1562 and on a diplomatic mission to Spain in 1577. He also had the support of John Aylmer, who was probably instrumental in Danett's becoming MP for Maidstone in 1572, and who wrote to Cecil, now Lord Burghley, in 1582 recommending Danett for the position of clerk to the council. This approach failed, and another in 1586 was no more successful. But Danett may eventually have become maker of pardons and licences to the court of common pleas. He may also have been the Thomas Danett, esquire, of the city of London, who was licensed to marry Mary Sackvyle on 3 October 1582. Danett is reported to have died in 1601.

Danett's years abroad clearly made him fluent in foreign languages and gave him an interest in continental history. While still a student he translated the *Mémoires* of Philippe de Commines into English, with a dedication to the earl of Leicester dated 30 September 1565. His epistle to the reader, which refers scornfully to 'foolishe forged tales suche as are written of Kinge Arthur, the iiij sonnes of Aimon, or Amadis de Gaule', suggests that he saw history primarily in exemplary terms, and those who profit from it as making 'the historie to be a paterne of all their doings, both private and publique, & studie not onelie to have the speculation of histories, but also the practise' (BL, Add. MS 21579, fols. 3v–5v). Danett eventually published his translation in an expanded version in 1596, with a dedication to Burghley. He explains in the preface that Sir Christopher Hatton had read it in manuscript and commended it, while other gentlemen had read it after Hatton's death in 1591, and urged him to publish it. Danett had responded that the secrets of princes should not be published in the vulgar language, but the 'gentlemen' threatened to publish it themselves, and so Danett had proceeded into print for fear that an unauthorized publication would mar his work. He provided his text with sometimes elaborate notes on such matters as his choice of words in translation, English values for French money, and the differences between Commines and English chronicles, and even ventured to disagree with Commines over the latter's belief that the world was going to the dogs.

His translation of Commines was not Danett's first publication, for it had been preceded by *The description of the Low Countreys and of the provinces thereof, gathered into an epitome out of the historie of Ludovico Guicchardini* (1593). This too was dedicated to Burghley, appropriately since Danett regarded him as the greatest 'politique' of the age, as well as 'the onely patron to whome I owe even by discent a peculiar band of all dewty and devotion'. In 1600 Danett published *A continuation of the historie of France from the death of Charles the Eight, where Comines endeth, till the death of Henry the Second* (1559), dedicating it to Thomas Sackville, Lord Buckhurst. In setting out why he did not continue the work up to his own time, Danett explained that in 1577 he had been so shocked by the depredations of the wars of religion in France that he could not bear to take the history of that country beyond 1559. He hoped that his own history would serve 'to teach Princes … to live peaceably at home', occupying themselves with seeing that justice was done among their own people and with serving the purposes of God.

Danett's translation of Commines was his most popular work, with further editions in 1601, 1614, 1665, and 1674. It was reissued in the Tudor Translations series in 1897, edited by Charles Whibley, who praised Danett's prose style, noting that he often supplied lively metaphors for which there was no equivalent in Commines's rather plain prose. He also asserted that even in the translation there was evidence for Danett's historical expertise, since he 'rigorously' corrected his original as well as adding notes. 'No man of his time', Whibley concluded, 'was better inspired with the critical spirit, and he had the courage to specialise in an age devoted to vast enterprises' (*Historie*, 1.xxxix–xl).

CHRISTINA DECOURSEY

Sources HoP, *Commons, 1558–1603*, 2.13 · C. H. Garrett, *The Marian exiles: a study in the origins of Elizabethan puritanism* (1938) · T. Danett, *The description of the Low Countreys and of the provinces thereof, gathered into an epitome out of the historie of Ludovico Guicchardini* (1593) · T. Danett, *A continuation of the historie of France from the death of Charles the Eight, where Comines endeth, till the death of Henry the Second* (1600) · *The historie of Philip de Commines*, ed. C. Whibley, trans. T. Danett, 2 vols. (1897) · BL, Add. MS 21579 · BL, MS 35, fol. 1 · Venn, *Alum. Cant.*, 1/2.8 · J. L. Chester and G. J. Armytage, eds., *Allegations for marriage licences issued by the bishop of London*, 1, Harleian Society, 25 (1887), 112

Danforth, Thomas (*bap.* 1623, *d.* 1699), politician in America, was born at New Street Farm, Framlingham, Suffolk, and baptized on 20 November 1623, the eldest son and fourth of the seven children of Nicholas Danforth (*bap.* 1589, *d.* 1638), yeoman and colonist, and his wife, Elizabeth Barber (*d.* 1629) of Aspall, Suffolk. His widower father, a member of Thomas Shepard's emigrant company, arrived in Cambridge, Massachusetts, in October 1635, and quickly, if only briefly, became a town leader. Thomas showed early maturity and ability. In February 1644 he married Mary, daughter of Henry Withington of Dorchester, Massachusetts. The first of their twelve children was born in 1645. By the age of twenty-three Danforth had been admitted a church member and freeman of the colony (1643), and elected constable (1646) and selectman of Cambridge (1647). His fine penmanship and knowledge of shorthand led to his appointment as Cambridge town clerk (1645–68), recorder of Middlesex county court (1649–86), clerk to the Harvard overseers (1654), registrar of Middlesex deeds (1652–86), and scribe of numerous official letters and reports. Thousands of documents in his hand survive in the Massachusetts and Harvard archives. He continued on the town executive board for twenty-four years, and represented the town at the general court in 1657 and 1658. His long service to Harvard College began in 1650, when he was appointed treasurer, becoming college steward, or bursar, from 1669 to 1682. In 1659 Danforth began his twenty-year service as an assistant (magistrate and member of the upper house of legislature). He acted as Massachusetts representative on the Commission of the United Colonies (1662–78) and organized colonial co-operation in war against both the Dutch and American Indians. He was deputy governor from 1679 to 1686, and from 1689 to 1692, when he was effectively in control of the colony's government. Massachusetts appointed him president of Maine from 1681 to 1686. His public service culminated as judge of the superior court (1692–9); he continued his duties on circuit until a few weeks before he died.

Danforth held forthright, independent opinions. He idolized the 'primitive' faith and unwavering commitment of the founders of Massachusetts Congregationalism. His support of the half-way covenant (1662), which extended baptism to the children of baptized adults who had not experienced conversion, was derived from a wish to bring the younger generation within church discipline. He was a harrier of Quakers and Baptists and was profoundly hostile to later Stuart declarations of indulgence, which extended toleration to Roman Catholics. His will required cancellation of valuable bequests to Harvard 'if any prelatical injunctions should be imposed on the society' (Massachusetts Archives, probate documents). Danforth witnessed one examination in 1692 during the Salem witchcraft trials and was thereafter a strong opponent of the accusations and the trials. After his death his fellow judge Samuel Sewall regretted that 'a great deal of the first ways of New England seem to be buried with him' (*Letter-book*).

In the conflicts between crown and colony between 1660 and 1691 Danforth was a passionate defender of the rights and liberties in the charter of 1629. As spokesman of the 'popular' faction, he advocated evasion, delay, or non-conciliation with the king's commissioners in 1665 and proved a dogged opponent of Edward Randolph from 1676 to 1689. He refused to doff his hat when Charles II's 1676 proclamation was read, and castigated compliance with royal demands as betrayal. The Andros regime in the dominion of New England (1687–9) seemed 'little inferior to absolute slavery' (Massachusetts Archives, 128.142–3) and he was a leader of Massachusetts's extension of the revolution of 1688 in April 1689. His subsequent firmness steadied the colony and prevented serious disorder. As a diehard 'charter-monger' Danforth was omitted from the nominated council in 1691. Rigid localist conservatism offended sensibilities in the new provincial world.

Danforth's independence of mind was best displayed in his ethnic values. Not only did he 'diet' and look after American Indian scholars at Harvard during the 1650s and 1660s, but during King Philip's War (1675–6), fought between the New England colonists and neighbouring American Indians, he was a rare and courageous defender of the 'praying Indians' (American Indian converts to Christianity), who greatly contributed to New England's ultimate victory. His life was threatened in a poster campaign, and he narrowly escaped being drowned and run over by opponents. In his will he freed and endowed his black servant.

Danforth died on 5 November 1699 at his home in Kirkland Street, Cambridge, and was buried in Cambridge five days later. At the time of his death he was a wealthy man. His probate inventory was appraised at £1483 after large gifts during his lifetime. His grants and purchases of land exceeded 16,000 acres. Although his wife of fifty-three years and many of his ten children predeceased him, he was surrounded in his last years by many relatives through his siblings and his surviving daughters. William Brattle preached two long eulogies on Danforth's relentless round of public duties, and an elegy by his nephew John was published. It repeated the apt anagram on his name when he was first elected to high office: 'Handsom for that' (Danforth, *Elegy*).   ROGER THOMPSON

Sources R. Thompson, 'Thomas Danforth', *Transit of civilization*, ed. W. Herget and K. Ortseifen (Tübingen, 1986) · F. Bremer, 'Danforth, Thomas', *ANB* · J. Booth, ed., *Nicholas Danforth and his neighbours* (1935) · J. Booth, *The home of Nicholas Danforth* (1954) · J. J. May, *The Danforth genealogy* (1902) · W. T. Harris, 'Notes on the Danforth family', *New England Historical and Genealogical Register*, 7 (1853), 315–21 · J. Danforth, *A funeral elegy to TD* ([Boston?], 1699) · *The diary of*

Samuel Sewall, 1674–1729: newly edited from the manuscript at the Massachusetts Historical Society, ed. M. H. Thomas, 2 vols. (1973) • L. R. Paige, ed., *History of Cambridge, Massachusetts, 1630–1877* (1877) • S. C. Powell, *Puritan village* (1963) • *Collections of the Massachusetts Historical Society*, 6th ser., 1 (1886), esp. 215 [*Letter-book of Samuel Sewall*, vol. 1] • Massachusetts Archives, probate documents, Middlesex county, 5915, 14/11/1699

Wealth at death £1483: 1699, Massachusetts Archives, probate documents, Middlesex county, 5915

Dangerfield, Edmund (1864–1938), printer and magazine publisher, was born on 15 April 1864 at 22 Bedford Street, Covent Garden, London, the youngest son in the family of four sons and one daughter of Frederick Dangerfield and his wife, Emiline Bruce Walker. His father was the owner of the Dangerfield Printing Company, with a lithographic business in Bedford Street, Strand. Dangerfield became a wages clerk in the family printing works. He was then put in charge of printing the *Friendly Companion* and *Gospel Standard* from premises in Bouverie Street, near the Temple, in the City.

A keen racing cyclist, Dangerfield was a member of several cycling clubs including the Bath Road Club. He won a number of races, including the first Bath Road '100' in 1890. Although several cycling newspapers existed they were mainly interested in attacking each other, and at a time when cycling was becoming a fashionable pastime there was a need for a new sort of paper, concentrating on cycling news and cycling club events. Dangerfield launched *Cycling* in 1891, published weekly in Bouverie Street, edited first by C. P. Sisley, and from 1893 by Walter Groves, both in their twenties and members of cycling clubs. Lavishly illustrated, humorous, and very readable, it was the first paper to devote itself to the sport, pastime, and trade of cycling, and it was an instant success. But relations between Dangerfield and his brothers became difficult, and in 1894 he withdrew from the Dangerfield Printing Company, setting up his own printing company, Temple Press Ltd, at 17½ and 27 Bouverie Street, and severing his connections with the family lithographic business. He moved the Temple Press to Rosebery Avenue in 1895. On 10 September 1896 he married Alice Ada (*b.* 1868/9), daughter of William George Upham: they had one son and one daughter.

The success of *Cycling* encouraged Dangerfield to open an office in Birmingham in 1895, and later that year he launched the *Cycle Manufacturer and Dealers' Review*, posted weekly to manufacturers and suppliers all over the world. This lasted only until 1899, and other early ventures, including *Pictorial Life*, a popular illustrated weekly paper, started in 1900, did even less well, with a run of thirteen weeks. Dangerfield nevertheless continued to acquire or launch new titles, including *The Regiment* in 1901. In 1902 he started *Motor Cycling and Motoring*, whose title was changed to *The Motor* in 1903, and its success led him to expand the business. New titles included the *Motor Boat* (1904), the *Commercial Motor* (1905), *Motor Cycling*, relaunched in 1909 after the success of the first motorcycle TT race in 1907, and the *Cycle Car* (1912). This became the *Light Car and Cycle Car* in 1913. Dangerfield's activities extended to organizing *Cycling* concerts in the Royal

Albert Hall and the Crystal Palace, and opening a motor museum in Oxford Street in 1912. Not all of his publications were confined to cycling and motoring: he commissioned G. Forrester Scott to write a book on gardening for those who did not employ a gardener; but when *The Single-Handed Gardener* (1912) appeared, its title suggested it was written for one-armed gardeners, and it was reissued as *The Best Book on Gardening*. All the journals apart from *The Regiment* kept going during the First World War, and the *Motor Ship* was added in 1920, and the *Oil Engine* in 1933.

Dangerfield retired in 1933 because of ill health, and was succeeded as managing director of the Temple Press by his son, Roland, who had been a director since 1918. Although he gave up racing early on he was a cyclist all his life, and a vice-president of the Bath Road Club. Dangerfield died on 10 May 1938 at his home, Colbry, 7 Belvedere Drive, Wimbledon, Surrey. He was cremated on 13 May at Brookwood, Woking, Surrey. He was survived by his wife.

ANNE PIMLOTT BAKER

Sources A. C. Armstrong, *Bouverie Street to Bowling Green Lane* (1946) • *Cycling* (18 May 1938) • *The Times* (12 May 1938) • *The Times* (4 June 1938) • b. cert. • m. cert. • d. cert. • CGPLA Eng. & Wales (1938)
Likenesses G. Moore, drawing, 1890, repro. in *Cycling*, 700 • photograph (in early forties), repro. in Armstrong, *Bouverie Street*, pl. 3 • photograph (in old age), repro. in *Cycling*, 700
Wealth at death £284,973 19s. 11d.: probate, 1 June 1938, CGPLA Eng. & Wales

Dangerfield, George Bubb (1904–1986), historian, was born on 28 October 1904 at Milton House, London Road, Newbury, Berkshire, the second son and youngest of four children of the Revd George Dangerfield, Church of England clergyman and later rector of Finmere, Buckinghamshire, and his wife, (Ethel) Margaret, *née* Tyrer. His father had changed his surname from Bubb to Dangerfield in gratitude to an aunt who had financed his education. Dangerfield was educated at a preparatory school in Wiltshire before being sent to Forest School in Walthamstow, where his elder brother, John, had gone before him. There he was outstanding academically, in sports, and as an actor, as well as being editor of the school magazine. He next attended Hertford College, Oxford, graduating with a second-class degree in English in 1927. He spent the two years after university teaching English in Prague and then in Hamburg. He was throughout his life a person of great charm and good looks, with an ironic and somewhat quizzical style. On 15 August 1928 he married Helen Mary Deey Spedding (1902/3–1935), daughter of the Revd Trevor Wolfe Deey Spedding, rector of Mixbury, Oxfordshire. They had no children; she died in 1935. In 1930 he moved to the United States. He worked first as an assistant editor for a publishing house, and then from 1933 to 1935 as literary editor of *Vanity Fair*. He also travelled around the country as a lecturer.

Dangerfield published his first historical study, *Bengal Mutiny: the Story of the Sepoy Rebellion*, in 1933. It was interesting that he did not give it the more common title of the Indian mutiny, already indicating the radical mind that was to be found under the external trappings of an English gentleman. From the first he saw himself as a writer who happened to practise his craft through history. His idea of historical writing was that it was 'a combination of taste, imagination, science and scholarship; it reconciles incompatibles, it balances probabilities; and at last it attains the reality of fiction' (*New York Times*). He had no desire to be an academic (although he gave some distinguished lectures at universities and taught at the University of California at Santa Barbara from 1968 to 1972) and he wished for a wide audience. But in no way did he compromise his vision in order to achieve popularity.

In 1935 Dangerfield published *The Strange Death of Liberal England*, his most famous work. (It appeared in England in 1936 without its epilogue.) In it he considered four crucial radical movements to be found in England from 1910 to 1914. Two were on the right: the members of the House of Lords who attempted to prevent the Liberal government of the day from virtually stripping them of their power, and those within and outside parliament determined to prevent home rule for Ireland. On the left there were the labour movement, at its most radical, and the suffragettes who had concluded that only violence might gain them the vote. He wrote about them in a compelling style, rich in colour and imagination, but firmly based on an extensive reading of published sources—manuscript material for the period not yet being available. Dangerfield treated these movements almost as Jungian archetypes of Thanatos and Eros, of an older world dying and a newer one struggling to be born. He was both ironic and admiring, which has meant, particularly in his treatment of the suffragettes, that some have found him patronizing and belittling. The book ended with a paradox. The violence of the period, when some thought that Britain was verging towards civil war, was submerged in the greater violence of the First World War. At the same time, the English characteristic to be calm on the surface no matter what might be happening underneath was present in the epilogue to the book, a discussion of Rupert Brooke and his representation of an 'eternal' England. Dangerfield's book was written with great brio. Its high style and its dramatic nature struck some as excessive but they provided its lasting vitality. Dangerfield's assessment of the importance of the movements he dealt with continues to fuel discussion and disagreement years after publication. The book had a strong, almost cult reputation from the beginning, but its readership did not broaden out until it was reissued in paperback in 1961. It has been in print virtually ever since. A panel of the Modern Library division of the publisher Random House placed it eighty-second in a list of the 100 best books of non-fiction written in the twentieth century, in a survey published in 1999. In 1941 Dangerfield followed up this book with *Victoria's Heir: the Education of a Prince*, a political study of the future Edward VII.

When the Second World War broke out Dangerfield had a choice of being in the British or in the American army. He chose the latter, rising to the rank of sergeant and seeing service in Germany. In 1941 he married Mary Lou Schott; they had one son, Anthony, and two daughters, Mary Jo and Hilary. In 1951 he and his family moved to California, settling in 1961 in Santa Barbara in a splendid house in the hills overlooking the ocean, where he lived for the rest of his life. He became an American citizen in 1943. Now, except for occasional reviews, and his very last book, he became a highly regarded historian of the United States, concentrating on the early nineteenth century, with works that became standard studies of their subjects. In 1952 he published *The Era of Good Feeling*, a discussion of the administrations of James Monroe and John Quincy Adams (1817–29), a comparatively neglected period of American history. Written with his customary vivid style and based on thorough research, the book won the two most important book prizes in American history: the Bancroft and the Pulitzer. He made this period his own, following it with *Chancellor Robert R. Livingston of New York, 1746–1813* in 1960 and *The Awakening of American Nationalism, 1815–1828* in 1965. Two lesser works were the co-editing of a selection from Henry Adams's *History of the United States* in 1963 and *Defiance to the Old World: the Story of the Monroe Doctrine* in 1970. His last book, published in 1976, was *The Damnable Question: a Study of Anglo-Irish Relations*. This covered the period 1800 to 1922, with its primary emphasis on 1912 to 1921. Here he returned to the troubled years he had treated earlier, with their intractable problems that refused to resolve themselves. As in all his work, Dangerfield showed humour and humanity, combined with great literary gifts and thorough historical research. He died in California of leukaemia on 27 December 1986.   PETER STANSKY

Sources personal knowledge (2004) · 'George Dangerfield and *The strange death of liberal England*', *Albion*, 17 (1985), 401–47 · B. Hirschhorn, 'Dangerfield, George', *The Scribner encyclopedia of American lives*, 2 (1986–90) · *New York Times* (6 Jan 1987) · *The Times* (29 Dec 1986) · b. cert. · m. cert.

Dangerfield, John. *See* Crawfurd, (John) Oswald Frederick (1834–1909).

Dangerfield, Thomas (1654–1685), informer, was born in the parish of Holy Cross, Waltham, Essex, on 7 July 1654, the son of Thomas Dangerfield (*d.* 1680) and his wife, Apollina. His father was apparently an honest gentleman of Cromwellian sympathies but, according to a hostile account of his early years, *The Matchless Rogue* (1680) by Elizabeth Cellier, Thomas began his life of crime at an early age, gaining a local reputation as a light-fingered and disruptive child. Resenting the punishments meted out by his father, Dangerfield ran away to London. He was found there three years later and although brought home he soon ran off again with a Scottish servant, the pair having first robbed his father of some horses. The two of them made their way to Scotland, committing further robberies. At the age of fifteen Dangerfield returned to his family in Waltham, where his father apprenticed him to a barber, but he absconded yet again. He went to Spain where he was alleged to have become successively a soldier, a thief, and a counterfeiter, and was marked with a brand on his right hand. After various further adventures over much of Europe, he was, Cellier alleges in *The Matchless Rogue*, condemned for theft in England and transported, ending up in Antwerp where he courted trouble once more and was arrested as a counterfeiter. A more sympathetic account claimed he was mistaken for a French spy. He was saved from the noose by an English priest who, having obtained a pardon for Dangerfield, gave him £30 and sent him back to England.

By 1679 Dangerfield had been convicted of passing counterfeit coins, had broken out of gaol at least twice, and had stood in the pillory at Old Sarum. In March 1679, having been arrested once more for counterfeiting under the alias of Willougby, he was brought to the notice of Elizabeth Cellier in Newgate gaol. Cellier, a Catholic, was almoner for the countess of Powis and spent her time befriending imprisoned Catholics. A 'Proper, Black, handsome fellow' (Dangerfield, *Memoires*, 2), Dangerfield seems to have charmed Mrs Cellier into believing he was a Catholic, although he had in fact little by way of religious belief, and she offered to pay for his release. Once Dangerfield was released, however, he was almost immediately re-arrested and placed in the Counter. Removed to the king's bench prison, at Mrs Cellier's prompting he played the informer with one Stroud, a man who claimed to have evidence that would blast the credit of William Bedloe, one of the main witnesses to the Popish Plot. Dangerfield's failure at this task did not prevent Mrs Cellier from indulging him and he was again released after she had paid his debts. Rumour later had it that they became lovers. Cellier also carried Dangerfield to the countess of Powis and he was then employed by them as a messenger and to spy on various opposition parties.

During his rambles around London, Dangerfield invented evidence of a presbyterian plot, which later came to be known as the Meal-Tub Plot. This spurious plot implicated the earl of Shaftesbury, included rumours of commissions for a rebel army, and spoke of the overthrow of Charles II and the duke of York. Dangerfield brought this 'news' to his sponsors and was consequently introduced to the earl of Peterborough, who in turn introduced him to the duke of York and the king, but they did little to encourage him. James and Charles did give Dangerfield some money and the latter directed him to the secretary of state, Coventry. At which point, despite Dangerfield's request for a warrant against the whig Colonel Roderick Mansell, the scheme faltered. To further his plot Dangerfield had planted some documents behind the bedhead in Mansell's rooms in Axe Yard. Other incriminating documents had been hidden in a meal tub at Mrs Cellier's home. Denied a warrant to hunt for his own planted papers, however, Dangerfield, advised by Mrs Cellier, obtained a bogus customs search of Mansell's rooms instead. When the papers were discovered Mansell was arrested, but he managed to defend himself against such an obvious cheat. Dangerfield was also revealed as a coiner at this point and committed once more, Cellier once again undertaking to bail him from gaol.

Fearful of the collapse of his own fortunes, however, Dangerfield now sought to change sides and directed Sir William Waller to Mrs Cellier's house where the papers hidden in the meal tub were discovered. Cellier and her cronies were soon arrested and Dangerfield now claimed that the 'presbyterian' plot was actually a sham devised by Cellier and other Roman Catholics, including the countess of Powis, to incriminate the whigs while a real popish design was carried out. He also claimed he had been offered money to murder both the king and Shaftesbury. Dangerfield subsequently gave evidence against those persons that he said had employed him. He implicated Roger Palmer, earl of Castlemaine, the earl of Peterborough, the countess of Powis, John Gadbury, and Mrs Cellier. Released from prison, Dangerfield was given a pension and a pardon, although whether by accident or design the latter, issued in November 1679, did not cover his previous felonies. Now one of the king's witnesses, Dangerfield soon went into print relating his story. He also accused Sir Robert Peyton of involvement with Cellier's schemes and testified before the House of Commons on Peyton's relations with the duke of York, leading to Peyton's expulsion from the Commons.

In June 1680 Cellier, Lady Powis, and Castlemaine were brought to trial and Dangerfield appeared as a rather ineffectual witness against them. Once his past history was revealed, and it was discovered that his felonies were not covered by his pardon, Lord Chief Justice Scroggs blasted whatever credit Dangerfield had left. The grand jury threw out the case against Powis, and Dangerfield went to Newgate. Released some days later with a corrected pardon, he acted alongside Titus Oates as a witness against Castlemaine, but was given little credence and Castlemaine was found not guilty. Mrs Cellier, who had faced her own trial and pillorying with some credit, subsequently attacked Dangerfield in print in *Malice Defeated* (1680). Dangerfield responded in kind to this and other such pamphlets. He was also probably responsible for *Don Tomazo, or, The Juvenile Rambles of Thomas Dangerfield* (1680), which purported to give an account of his early life and which contributed to the popular genre of 'rogue' literature. Although Dangerfield continued to act as a priest catcher and witness against a number of Catholics, his tales were given little credence. His last appearance as a witness was in February 1681, against the priest John Attwood.

Within a week of the third Exclusion Parliament in March 1681 Dangerfield's pension was cut off. According to later published accounts he then toured the country as a confidence trickster, passing himself off on a number of occasions as the duke of Monmouth, and even fooled some individuals into letting him touch for the king's evil in return for money. He was eventually arrested in March 1685 and tried in May 1685 for high misdemeanours and libels against the new king, James II, when the latter had been duke of York. At his trial before Lord Chief Justice Jeffreys, Dangerfield performed poorly. His defence was described by one author as 'cant'; he also claimed to be one of the props of the protestant religion, which 'made great Laughter in the Court' and he was found guilty (*A True Narrative*, 2). He was fined £500 and sentenced to be pilloried and whipped from Aldgate to Newgate and two days later from Newgate to Tyburn.

On 2 July the whippings commenced but as Dangerfield

returned to prison in a coach, after the second flogging, he was involved in a confrontation with Robert Francis, a barrister and a former clerk of Sir Joseph Williamson. As the pair argued, Dangerfield spat at Francis, who struck Dangerfield in the face with his cane. The metal point of the cane pierced Dangerfield's eye and he died some two hours later. Francis was subsequently charged with murder, tried, and hanged. ALAN MARSHALL

Sources *A true narrative of the arraignment, tryal and conviction of Thomas Dangerfield* (1685) · *Dangerfield's Memoires digested into adventures, receipts and expences by his own hand* (1685) · E. Cellier, *The matchless rogue, or, A brief account of the life of Don Thomazo the unfortunate son* (1680) · T. Dangerfield, *The case of Thomas Dangerfield* (1680) · *State trials*, 11.503–10 · *Dangerfield's dance, giving an account of several notorious crimes by him committed* (1685) · *Domestick Intelligence, or, News from City and Country* (1679–80) · *The Protestant (Domestick) Intelligence* (1680–81) · T. Dangerfield, *Mr Tho. Dangerfield's particular narrative of the late popish design* (1679) · [T. Dangerfield?], *Don Tomazo, or, The juvenile rambles of Thomas Dangerfield* (1680) · T. Dangerfield, *Mr Tho. Dangerfield's second narrative* (1680) · T. Dangerfield, *More shams still, or, A further discovery of the designs of the papists, to impose upon the nation the belief of their feigned protestant or presbyterian plot* (1681) · T. Dangerfield, *The information of Thomas Dangerfield, gent. delivered at the bar of the House of Commons, Tuesday the twentieth day of October … 1680* (1680) · parish register, Waltham, Holy Cross, 7 Aug 1654, Essex RO, Chelmsford [birth] · will, PRO, PROB 11/364, sig. 162 [will of Thomas Dangerfield's father, also Thomas Dangerfield]
Likenesses engraving, *c*.1685, repro. in *A true relation of the sentence and condemnation of Thomas Dangerfield, at the king's bench bar for his horrid crimes and perjuries* (1685) · engraving, repro. in *Dangerfield's dance*

Daniel. *See* Deiniol (*d.* 584).

Daniel (*d.* 745), bishop of Winchester, was the fourth bishop of that diocese, from 705 or 706 until 744, but the first to control the see after a second West Saxon diocese had been created at Sherborne on the death of Hædde. Some compensation for the reduction of territory was provided by the incorporation of the Isle of Wight into the Winchester diocese. Bede praised Daniel for being 'fully instructed in ecclesiastical matters and in the knowledge of the Scriptures' (Bede, *Hist. eccl.*, 5.18). Daniel was his main informant on West and South Saxon affairs and provided a particularly detailed account of the circumstances surrounding the conquest of the Isle of Wight by King Cædwalla in 685.

Daniel was Boniface's diocesan and provided him with a letter of introduction when he left for Frisia in 718. Boniface continued to seek his help after he was established in Germany. A letter with practical instruction on how best to convert pagans to Christianity may have drawn on Daniel's own experiences in Wessex. Boniface also sought the bishop's advice about what he should do when his visits to the Frankish court brought him into contact with 'false priests', to which Daniel provided a long and considered reply citing biblical and patristic authorities in support of compromising over principles if it led to the greater good. A letter also survives from Daniel to Bishop Forthhere of Sherborne recommending a deacon called Merewalh whom he had ordained outside the canonical

period. Daniel witnessed a number of West Saxon charters, but only one grant (of land in what later became Somerset from King Æthelheard and Queen Frithugyth) is recorded for the church of Winchester during his long episcopate (*AS chart.*, S 254). The Anglo-Saxon Chronicle records a pilgrimage to Rome in 721, the first which is known to have been made by a West Saxon bishop. In 731 he assisted in the consecration of Tatwine as archbishop of Canterbury.

As early as the 720s Daniel had been complaining to Boniface of ill health and in later years he became blind. Such infirmities probably lay behind his resignation as bishop in 744, but may have been causing problems for some time; an account of a vision of the other world in circulation on the continent a few years after his death recorded a multitude of babies in the nether regions who had died unbaptized during his episcopate. Daniel died the year following his retirement, and was presumably buried at Winchester. William of Malmesbury believed he had retired to become a monk at Malmesbury, but that may only have been inference from a list of those commemorated there. However, the chronicler also claimed an earlier association of Daniel with Malmesbury and that there was a spring there called after him, where he had been accustomed to spend whole nights in his youth mortifying his flesh. BARBARA YORKE

Sources Bede, *Hist. eccl.*, preface; 4.16; 5.18 · M. Tangl, ed., *Die Briefe des heiligen Bonifatius und Lullus*, MGH Epistolae Selectae, 1 (Berlin, 1916), nos. 11, 23, 63–4, 115 · C. H. Talbot, ed. and trans., *The Anglo-Saxon missionaries in Germany* (1954) · *Venerabilis Baedae opera historica*, ed. C. Plummer, 2 (1896), 307–8 · *AS chart.*, S 254 · H. Edwards, *The charters of the early West Saxon kingdom* (1988) · *ASC*, s.a. 709, 721, 731, 744, 745 [texts A, E] · *Willelmi Malmesbiriensis monachi de gestis pontificum Anglorum libri quinque*, ed. N. E. S. A. Hamilton, Rolls Series, 52 (1870), 160

Daniel Ddu o Geredigion. *See* Evans, Daniel (1792–1846).

Daniel, Alexander. *See* Daniell, Alexander (1599–1668).

Daniel, Edmund (1541/2–1572), Jesuit and martyr, was born in Limerick. He was related to David *Wolfe, the first Irish Jesuit. On the recommendation of Wolfe, who by then was papal commissary (nuncio) in Ireland and was spearheading the Irish Counter-Reformation, Daniel was received into the Jesuit noviciate in Rome on 11 September 1561 at the age of nineteen. After studies in Florence, Loreto, and Padua he was sent to Flanders because of ill health (probably tuberculosis). Still unwell, he was sent back to Limerick in the hope that his native air would benefit him and that he would assist Wolfe as a teacher.

With some help Daniel and his English Jesuit companion, William Good, conducted a school in the city of Limerick (the first Jesuit school in Ireland) for most of 1565. They closed it when material support failed and their house was raided and looted. They opened a school in nearby Kilmallock. After its closure they reopened the school in Limerick. They taught Latin and English and inculcated Catholic belief and practice, ignoring the ban on teaching petrine and papal primacy and the importance of the mass and sacraments. At the insistence of citizens trying in their fashion to combine religious and political loyalties, to save their mission and with his consent they distanced themselves from Wolfe who was considered an arch-traitor to the crown.

The Limerick mission, truly heroic for temperamentally timid men as were Daniel and Good according to Wolfe, had ended by mid-1568. Daniel quested in Portugal (perhaps also in Spain) for ransom money for the release of Wolfe from Dublin Castle. He became a messenger (to what extent is uncertain) of the leader of the first Desmond rising, James Fitzmaurice Fitzgerald, who presented the rising as a Catholic crusade.

It is clear from English state papers that the crown authorities had Daniel under observation. He was arrested in Limerick in mid-1572 as being disaffected towards the queen. He was tried at Cork by the zealously protestant Sir John Perrot, lord president of Munster. There is no extant record of the trial. In November 1572 Perrot told Burghley that he had just executed twenty for treason. Daniel was surely one of these. Wolfe dates his death to 25 October 1572.

Daniel is the protomartyr of Irish Jesuit tradition. With time his *fama* developed among Jesuits and beyond; he is honourably mentioned in both Jesuit and non-Jesuit martyrologies. His cause for beatification is being considered by the Holy See.   STEPHEN REDMOND

Sources letter of David Wolfe, 29 June 1561, Roman Archives of the Society of Jesus, Rome, MS Germ. 143 · letter of David Wolfe, June 1566, Roman Archives of the Society of Jesus, Rome, MS Ital. 131 · letter of David Wolfe, 7 May 1574, Roman Archives of the Society of Jesus, Rome, MS Lusit. 66 · declaration of Edmund Daniel, 11 Sept 1561, Roman Archives of the Society of Jesus, Rome, MS Rom. 48v · letter of Edmund Daniel to the Jesuit father-general, 19 Jan 1570, Roman Archives of the Society of Jesus, Rome, MS Hisp. 113 · letter of William Good, 8 April 1566, Roman Archives of the Society of Jesus, Rome, MS Anglia 41 · letter of William Good, 8 June 1566, Roman Archives of the Society of Jesus, Rome, MS Anglia 41 · letter of William Good, 29 July 1566, Roman Archives of the Society of Jesus, Rome, MS Anglia 41 · letter of William Good, 1 Nov 1572, Roman Archives of the Society of Jesus, Rome, MS Germ. 141 · letter of Juan Polanco, 1 Sept 1564, Roman Archives of the Society of Jesus, Rome, MS Germ. 105 · Papal grant of absolution from censure to Thomas FitzJohn Arthur, 7 July 1575, Vatican Archives, reg. suppl. 3363 · report on Ireland, *c*.1580, Vatican Archives, A. A. Arm. i–xviii, 4064 · J. Howlin, 'Perbreve Compendium, in quo continentur nonnullorum nomina, qui in Hibernia regnante impia regina Elizabetha, vincula, martyrium et exilium perpessi sunt', *c*.1590, St Patrick's College, Maynooth, Maynooth College Archives, MS, S/XL/4/1 · J. Coppinger, *The theatre of Catholique and protestant religion* (1620) · 16 Oct 1571, PRO, SP/63/34/32ii · 30 March 1572, PRO, SP 63/35/46 · May 1572, PRO, SP/63/36/29 · P. Alegambe, *Mortes illustres et gesta eorum de Societate Jesu qui in odium fidei, pietatis, aut cuiuscunque virtutis ab ethnicis, haereticis, vel aliis, morte confecti sunt*, ed. J. Nadasi (1657) [enl. and ed. by J. Nadasi] · A. Bruodinus, *Propugnaculum Catholicae veritatis* (Prague, 1669) · E. Hogan, *Distinguished Irishmen of the sixteenth century* (1896) · P. Ó Fionnagáin, *The Jesuit missions to Ireland in the sixteenth century* (privately printed, Dublin, [n.d., *c*.1975]) · T. M. McCoog, *The Society of Jesus in Ireland, Scotland, and England, 1541–1588* (1996)
Likenesses woodcut (at his execution), repro. in M. Tanner, *Societas Jesu usque ad sanguinis et vitae profusionem militans* (Prague, 1675)

Daniel, Edward. *See* Pickford, Edward (1601–1657).

Daniel, Evan (1837–1904), Church of England clergyman, educationist, and author, born at Pontypool on 4 September 1837, was the second son of Evan Daniel of Pontypool, builder and architect, and his wife, Sarah Beach. After education at the national school, Pontypool, he entered St John's Training College, Battersea, in 1856. He became lecturer in English literature at the college in 1859 and vice-principal in 1863. In the same year he was ordained deacon, and priest in 1864. He was appointed principal in 1866, a post which he held for twenty-eight years. On becoming principal he began reading for a degree at Trinity College, Dublin; both in 1868 and 1870 he won there the vice-chancellor's prize for English verse, and in 1869 the prize for English prose. He graduated BA in 1870 as senior moderator and gold medallist in English literature, history, and political science, and proceeded MA in 1874.

Daniel was well regarded as an educationist, and published several books on the subject, including *How to Teach the Church Catechism* (1882) and *Elementary Algebra* (2 vols., 1883–5). He edited John Locke's *Some Thoughts on Education* (1880), and made the complex history of the prayer book comprehensible in his popular *The Prayer-Book* (1877), which went through at least twenty editions. From 1873 to 1879 he served on the second London school board, and in 1881 he was appointed practical lecturer on education at Cambridge. In 1879 Anthony Wilson Thorold, bishop of Rochester, made him an honorary canon of his cathedral, and from 1892 he was proctor in convocation for the dean and chapter of Rochester. On his resignation of the principalship of St John's Training College in 1894, Archbishop E. W. Benson nominated him to the vicarage of Horsham, and in 1902 he became rural dean of Storrington. Daniel, who held broad-church views, was known as a powerful preacher. He married in 1863 Elizabeth Mosell of Pontypool, who died in 1901. They had six daughters and three sons. Daniel died at Horsham vicarage on 27 May 1904, and was buried in the churchyard there.

A portrait of Daniel, painted after his death by P. Keelan, was hung in the hall of St John's Training College, Battersea, where he was also commemorated by the establishment of the Daniel Library. A stained-glass window to his memory was installed in Horsham parish church.

G. S. WOODS, *rev.* H. C. G. MATTHEW

Sources *The Times* (28 May 1904) · *The Guardian* (1 June 1904) · *Horsham Times* (4 June 1904) · *The Schoolmaster* (4 June 1904) · *Crockford* (1902)
Likenesses P. Keelan, portrait, after 1904; at St John's Training College, Battersea, London, 1912
Wealth at death £7525 10s. 5d.: probate, 1 July 1904, CGPLA Eng. & Wales

Daniel, George (1616–1657), poet, was born on 29 March 1616 at Beswick, a manor in the parish of Kilnwick in the East Riding of Yorkshire. His father was Sir Ingleby Daniel (d. 1644?), a graduate of Gonville and Caius College, Cambridge, and an active royalist in the first civil war; his mother was Frances, daughter and heir of George Metham of Pollington, in the parish of Snaith. She was Sir Ingleby's second wife. Although Daniel clearly benefited from a humanist training, it is not known where he received his education. His elder brother, William, predeceased Sir Ingleby, so George inherited the manor of Beswick after his father's death. His younger brother, Thomas, was a professional soldier: a captain in the royal army in 1640, he may have served in Europe; an intimate of Prince Rupert, he rose to the rank of lieutenant-colonel of horse in the Prince of Wales's regiment. George and Thomas were firm friends; the frontispiece by Daniel to the manuscript of his poems shows the brothers clasping hands (dated 1647). Daniel described his own humour as phlegmatic. He followed the outdoor pursuits of the country squire and he was addicted to his tobacco pipe. He married Elizabeth, daughter and heir of the wealthy landowner William Ireland of Nostell, Yorkshire, and it was her fortune that saved Daniel's estate from his creditors. They had one son, George, and three daughters, Frances, Elizabeth, and Girarda.

Daniel had a highly developed interest in contemporary poetry but he does not seem to have sought out literary friendships. He was, however, a friend of Sir Thomas Browne, whose *Pseudodoxia epidemica* and *Religio medici* he commended in verse. Daniel shunned print, but we know from the title-pages in his manuscript that he circulated his poems among his neighbours and friends. He repeatedly insisted that his best poems were lost in a fire, but a considerable body of work survives nevertheless, preserved in a magnificent folio volume now in the British Library (Add. MS 19255), erratically edited by A. B. Grosart in 1878. The poems are copied in two separate hands, the second of which may be the poet's.

Daniel painted in oils, and of the five paintings in the manuscript volume, two are of particular interest for what they tell us about Daniel's self-image as a poet and country gentleman. The first is a portrait of Daniel as a Horatian poet, in pseudo-classical dress, wearing slippers (a Horatian motif), with ink and paper to hand, and a rural landscape in the background (Add. MS 19255, fol. 112). This is the author of the 'Pastoral Ode', which celebrates the contentments of rural life. Another self-portrait, from the year of the regicide, shows Daniel seated in his library, dressed like a Muscovite, wearing the massive beard that he refused to trim in memory of Charles I's execution (Add. MS 19255, fol. 152). The pose is modelled on Van Dyck's *Sir Kenelm Digby in Mourning*. The lamp hanging from the ceiling resembles the everlasting lamps that were believed to exist in classical tombs. An open book on his desk is inscribed 'nec in curia nec in carcere melior est' ('neither a court nor a prison is better'): everywhere is alike to the philosopher, whose freedom and contentment come from within.

Daniel was an imitator of Horace and the *Eclogues* of Virgil, a receptive reader of Donne's poetry, and a self-proclaimed 'son of Ben'. In *The Genius of this Great and Glorious Isle* (1637), the genius of Britain appears to the poet and presents a patriotic and royalist account of English history. *Scattered Fancies* (1646) is a collection of fifty-nine odes, predominantly on philosophical subjects; they are the basis for Daniel's reputation as a poet. *Polylogia, or, Several Elogues* (1638–48) form a thinly veiled commentary on political events from a royalist angle. His longest poem, *Trinarchodia* (1649), chronicles the reigns of Richard II, Henry IV, and Henry V, drawing pointed political lessons. Daniel often composed line by line, and he was a stranger to revision, but he was capable of passages of real poetic merit, as in these lines on the end of the universe:

> The mightie Elephant, and Mouse may run
> An equall race;
> And in this case,
> The heliotrope, may live with the last Sun.
> (*The Selected Poems of George Daniel*, ed. T. B. Stroup, 1959, 93)

Daniel died at Beswick on 25 September 1657 and was buried in the churchyard of All Saints, Kilnwick.

Ian William McLellan

Sources G. Daniel, 'The poems of George Daniel', BL, Add. MS 19255 • G. Daniel, *The poems of George Daniel of Beswick, Yorkshire, from the original manuscripts in the British Museum, hitherto unprinted*, edited, with introduction, notes, portraits &c., ed. A. B. Grosart, 4 vols. (1878) • All Saints, Kilnwick, parish records, 1616 • All Saints, Kilnwick, parish records, 1657 • *VCH Yorkshire* • J. W. Walker, ed., *Yorkshire pedigrees*, 3 vols., Harleian Society, 94–6 (1942–4), 1.135 • P. R. Newman, *Royalist officers in England and Wales, 1642–1660: a biographical dictionary* (1981)

Archives BL, MS poems, Add. MS 19255

Likenesses G. Daniel, self-portraits, oils, BL, Add. MS 19255, fols. 112, 152

Daniel, George [*pseud.* P— P—] (1789–1864), writer and book collector, was born on 16 September 1789 and descended from Paul Danieli, a Huguenot who settled in England in the seventeenth century. His father died when he was eight. Educated at Thomas Hogg's boarding-school at Paddington Green, Daniel became clerk to a stockbroker in Tokenhouse Yard, and was engaged in commerce for most of his life, but all his leisure was devoted to literature. He remembered with pride that Cowper the poet had patted him on the head when he visited the Deverells at Dereham, Norfolk, in 1799.

At sixteen Daniel published *Stanzas on Nelson's Victory and Death* (1805), and between 1808 and 1811 contributed many poems to Ackermann's *Poetical Magazine*, notably a mild satire in heroics entitled 'Woman'. In 1811 he issued anonymously a similar poem, entitled *The Times, a Prophecy* (enlarged edn, 1813), and in 1812 under his own name *Miscellaneous Poems*, including 'Woman'. A novel, *Dick Distich*, which Daniel says he wrote when he was eighteen, was printed anonymously in 1812. It is an amusing story of the struggles of a Grub Street author.

Daniel's début in satirical verse late in 1811 turned on a rumour that Lord Yarmouth had horsewhipped the prince regent at Oatlands, the duke of York's house, for making improper advances to the marchioness of Hertford, Yarmouth's mother-in-law. On this he based a sprightly squib entitled 'R—y—l stripes, or, A kick from Yar—th to Wa—s; with the particulars of an expedition to Oat—ds and the sprained ancle: a poem, by P— P—, Poet Laureat'. Attempts by the interested parties to suppress the poem were not entirely successful: although its publication was prevented, it circulated in manuscript. But Daniel was not quieted, although his poem was suppressed. A large placard was issued announcing the issue of 'The ghost of R—l Stripes, which was prematurely stifled in its birth in January 1812'. Under the same pseudonym he published other squibs on royal scandals.

Daniel next satirized the poetasters and petty journalists of the day in *The Modern Dunciad* (1814; 2nd edn, 1816). His denunciations are pointed and vigorous, but his praise of Byron, Crabbe, Cowper, Southey, and Burns showed little critical power. In this work he claimed to live for 'old books, old wines, old customs, and old friends'. His geniality and humorous conversation won him a literary circle, including in 1817 his neighbours at Islington, Charles Lamb and Robert Bloomfield. He also cultivated the society of actors, and John Kemble gave him the white satin bill of his last stage appearance (Covent Garden, 23 June 1817).

On 21 July 1818 Daniel's 'serio-comick-bombastick-operatick interlude', entitled *Doctor Bolus*, was acted successfully at the English Opera House with Fanny Kelly, Chatterley, and Harley who became a close friend. On 1 December 1819 Daniel's musical farce, *The Disagreeable Surprise*, was acted at Drury Lane, followed in 1833 by another farce, *Sworn at Highgate*.

Meanwhile Daniel edited for John Cumberland his *British theatre, with remarks biographical and critical, printed from the acting copies as performed at the Theatres Royal, London* (39 vols., 1823–31), writing a preface for each of its nearly 300 plays, which included most of Shakespeare and eighteenth-century drama. These prefaces show his literary taste, his intimate acquaintance with stage history, and a gift for theatrical criticism. In 1831 and 1832 he added fourteen volumes, known as Cumberland's *Minor Theatre*. He had a hand in further compilations from 1838 up to 1862. He also had a talent for spotting acting ability, as with Mary Ann Stirling in 1838 and Marie Wilton in 1862.

In 1829 Daniel published a scurrilous attack on Charles Kean's domestic life, entitled *Ophelia Kean, a Dramatic Legendary Tale*, but this was suppressed. He also contributed to *Bentley's Miscellany* a long series of gossiping papers on old books and customs, collected as *Merrie England in the Olden Time* (2 vols., 1842), with illustrations by Leech and Cruikshank. His later works included two religious poems, *The Missionary* (1847) and the *Stranger Guest*. His last published work, *Love's Last Labour not Lost* (1863), included his recollections of Charles Lamb and Robert Cruikshank.

Meanwhile Daniel had been making a reputation as a collector of Elizabethan books and of theatrical curiosities. About 1830 he had moved to 18 Canonbury Square, and the house was soon crowded with such rarities as the first four folio editions of Shakespeare, quarto editions of separate plays, and a collection of black-letter ballads. In 1835 he bought the carved casket made out of the mulberry tree of Shakespeare's garden, and presented to Garrick in 1769, and wrote of it in C. J. Smith's *Literary Curiosities* in 1840, together with a sketch of Garrick's theatrical

career. He owned Garrick's cane, a rich collection of theatrical prints, and watercolours by David Cox, Stansfield, Wilkie, and others. The bibliophile F. S. Ellis, who knew him in later life, refers to his:

> portly figure and florid good-humoured countenance … he affected the style and manners of the Regency period in his later days, and there are touches in Dickens's creation of Mr Turveydrop, senr., [*Bleak House*] that strongly remind one of him. His manner was too supercilious, condescending and pompous …

Yet he acknowledges that 'he had a real love for books and could tell many a good anecdote concerning the prize he had secured …' When he bought a first folio of Shakespeare for £100 he insisted on having it wrapped in silk (Ellis, 86).

Daniel died suddenly of apoplexy, at his son's house, The Grove, Stoke Newington, on 30 March 1864. By his will Garrick's cassolette passed to the British Museum. His library was sold over ten days starting on 20 July 1866 by Messrs Sotheby, Wilkinson, and Hodge. The sixth day, allocated to the Shakespeare editions, aroused intense interest, and the atmosphere was, according to Ellis, that of 'the black hole of Calcutta'. His first folio Shakespeare fetched £716 2s., and was bought by the Baroness Burdett-Coutts. In all the sale realized (with the prints, pictures, and porcelain) a total of £15,865, of which the books accounted for over £14,000.

SIDNEY LEE, rev. JOHN D. HAIGH

Sources F. S. Ellis, 'George Daniel, 1789–1864', *Contributions towards a dictionary of English book-collectors*, ed. B. Quaritch, 10 (1897); repr. (1969), 86–9 · *GM*, 3rd ser., 17 (1864), 450–55 · *The Era* (3 April 1864) · *The Athenaeum* (9 April 1864), 512 · *N&Q*, 3rd ser., 5 (1864), 346; 3rd ser., 6 (1864), passim · Daniel sale (1866) [Sothebys, 20–30 July 1866]
Archives LUL, papers | BL, letters, as sponsor, to the Royal Literary Fund, loan no. 96 · U. Edin. L., letters to James Halliwell-Phillipps
Likenesses R. Graves, line engraving, 1835 (after T. Wageman), BM · G. Cruikshank, group portrait, caricature, etching (*Sir Lionel Flamstead and his friends*), V&A
Wealth at death under £18,000: resworn administration with will, 1864, *CGPLA Eng. & Wales*

Daniel, Glyn Edmund (1914–1986), archaeologist and writer, was born on 23 April 1914 at Llanbedr Felffre, Pembrokeshire, the only child of John Daniel, schoolmaster, and his wife, Mary Jane Edmunds. He was educated in his father's school at Llantwit Major (where they moved in 1919), and then at Barry county school, of which he had many happy memories, vividly recorded in his autobiography *Some Small Harvest* (1986). He gained a place for 1932 at St John's College, Cambridge, spending the preceding year at University College, Cardiff, studying geology and the organ. Turning to the archaeology and anthropology tripos at St John's, after getting a first in the qualifying examination for the geography tripos (1933), he graduated with first classes in both section A (1934) and section B (1935, with distinction). He continued as a research student at St John's with a Strathcona studentship, receiving also an Allen scholarship in 1937. The remarkable megalithic monuments of western Europe formed the subject of his research, both in Britain (his doctoral dissertation of

Glyn Edmund Daniel (1914–1986), by Robert Tollast, 1970

1938 being published in 1950 as *The Prehistoric Chamber Tombs of England and Wales*), and in France, where his first visit to Brittany in 1936 resulted eventually in *The Prehistoric Chamber Tombs of France* (1960), with an authoritative overview of the whole subject in *The Megalith Builders of Western Europe* (1958). His doctoral dissertation won him a research fellowship at St John's in 1938, but his tenure was interrupted by the Second World War. He served as an intelligence officer in the RAF (1940–45), during which time he was officer in charge of photo interpretation, India and south-east Asia (1942–5), rose to the rank of wing commander, and was mentioned in dispatches. In India he met his future wife, Ruth (d. 2000), daughter of the Revd Richard William Bailey Langhorne, headmaster of Exeter Cathedral choristers' school. They were married in 1946, and their happy partnership formed thereafter a central part of his life. They had no children.

On his return from India, Daniel resumed his fellowship at St John's, another significant and enduring strand in his life, serving as steward from 1946 to 1955. He was made assistant lecturer in the department of archaeology in 1945, becoming lecturer, then reader, and then, in 1974, Disney professor and head of department until his retirement in 1981. He received a Cambridge LittD in 1962. Already with his first major publication, *The Three Ages* (1943), he showed an acute awareness of the relevance of the history of archaeology to current archaeological research. His *A Hundred Years of Archaeology* (1950), a pioneering study in the history of archaeology, perhaps his

most important contribution, was followed by several others, including *The Idea of Prehistory* (1962).

As a teacher Daniel excelled in kindling the enthusiasm of his pupils, many of whom became also his friends. He held that 'friendship is a conspiracy for pleasure', and while food and drink habitually formed part of that pleasure (a point well documented in *The Hungry Archaeologist in France*, 1963, as also in *Oxford Chicken Pie*, 1965), people mattered more. His keen eye for character is deployed in his two detective novels (*The Cambridge Murders*, 1945, and *Welcome Death*, 1954), and his ebullient sense of humour comes over well in the small, privately published *The Pen of my Aunt* (1961). His love affair with France was consummated in 1964 by the purchase of a house in the Pas-de-Calais, which he and his wife visited frequently until the year of his death.

While Daniel's most influential academic work was in the history of archaeology, his greatest impact on the archaeology of post-war Britain was as a communicator, not least as chairman of the highly successful television panel game *Animal, Vegetable, Mineral?*, which made both Sir Mortimer Wheeler and Glyn Daniel household names and brought them the accolade of television personality of the year in 1954 and 1955 respectively. Daniel was a founding director of Anglia Television from 1959 to 1981. He was a brilliant and entertaining speaker, and his public lectures and broadcasts made him widely known and recognized. As editor of the Ancient People and Places series for Thames and Hudson he commissioned over 100 volumes. He became editor of *Antiquity* in 1958, following the death of its founder editor O. G. S. Crawford the previous year. Yet he was not elected a fellow of the British Academy (where his role as a popularizer may have counted against him) until 1982.

Daniel was a fellow of the Society of Antiquaries from 1942, and served as president of the Royal Anthropological Institute in 1977–9. A corresponding fellow of many learned societies overseas, he became a knight (first class) of the Dannebrog in 1961: Princess Margrethe of Denmark, like the prince of Wales, had been among his many distinguished pupils. His scholarly contributions will be remembered, and yet the sheer humanity and zest that sparkle from his *Antiquity* editorials (of which *Writing for Antiquity*, 1992, forms an anthology), and from the pages of *Some Small Harvest*, give as valid an insight into a remarkable teacher and scholar. A non-smoker, after a short illness he died of lung cancer in Cambridge on 13 December 1986. His ashes were scattered in the fellows' garden at St John's College.   COLIN RENFREW, *rev.*

Sources G. Daniel, *Some small harvest* (1986) · S. Piggott, 'Glyn Edmund Daniel, 1914–1986', *PBA*, 74 (1988), 351–60 · J. D. Evans and others, eds., *Antiquity and man: essays in honour of Glyn Daniel* (1981) · G. Daniel, *Writing for antiquity*, ed. R. Daniel (1992) · *CGPLA Eng. & Wales* (1987) · personal knowledge (1996)
Archives St John Cam. · U. Cam., Museum of Archaeology and Anthropology, corresp., literary MSS, notes, photographs, etc. | Bodl. Oxf., letters to O. G. S. Crawford
Likenesses R. Tollast, pencil drawing, 1970, St John Cam. [*see illus.*] · V. David, charcoal drawing, priv. coll. · photographs, repro. in Daniel, *Some small harvest*

Wealth at death £8389: probate, 13 April 1987, *CGPLA Eng. & Wales* · £103,529: further grant of probate, 15 April 1987, *CGPLA Eng. & Wales*

Daniel, Henry (*fl.* 1379), Dominican friar and horticulturist, was skilled in the medical and natural science of his time. His surviving works include a treatise on diagnosis from urinoscopy, *De judiciis urinarum*, based on the work of Ysaac Judaeus (*d. c.*955), preserved in several manuscripts in the British and Bodleian libraries (among them BL, Royal MS 17 D.i, and Bodl. Oxf., MS Ashmole 1404); an extensive herbal known as *Aaron Danielis* (BL, Arundel MS 42; BL, Add. MS 27329), which includes a virtually complete English translation of the *Circa instans* of Platearius (*d.* 1161); and a translation of a Latin treatise on rosemary with an original supplement dealing with the plant's cultivation (Trinity College, Cambridge, MS O.1.13, fols. 77v–82v; BL, Royal MS 17 A.iii, fols. 13–17; Bodl. Oxf., MS Digby 29, fols. 295v–297).

The clinical book is dated to 1379, when it was finished during the summer after three years of work, hindered by Daniel's obedience as a friar and by serious illness. The herbal was evidently begun soon afterwards and exists in two forms: a detailed but incomplete draft in BL, Arundel MS 42, rich in personal asides; and the regularized but somewhat abridged final version of BL, Add. MS 27329. The latter is divided into two parts, the first covering herbs and the second trees, fruits, and animal and mineral substances used in medicine.

What little is known of Daniel's life is derived from autobiographical remarks in his works. They record that he had in his 'young years … worked seven years to learn', and had possessed a garden at Stepney beside London, in which he grew 252 kinds of herbs. By 1380 he must have reached a considerable age and had over thirty years' experience of growing rosemary. He had detailed knowledge of the region around Stamford and mentions journeys in Wiltshire, to Bristol, and in Kent and East Anglia. Many accounts of plants in the herbal display a remarkably deep interest in plant ecology and include some of the earliest records of individual species. He also distinguished between wild and garden plants and provided vernacular as well as Latin names.   JOHN HARVEY

Sources C. H. Talbot and E. A. Hammond, *The medical practitioners in medieval England: a biographical register* (1965) · J. Harvey, *Medieval gardens* (1990), 118–19; 189–62 · J. H. Harvey, 'Henry Daniel: a scientific gardener of the fourteenth century', *Garden History*, 15 (1987), 81–93
Archives BL, Arundel MS 42 · BL, Add. MS 27329 · BL, Royal MS 17 A.iii, fols. 13–17 · BL, Royal MS 17 D.i · Bodl. Oxf., MS Ashmole 1404 · Bodl. Oxf., MS Digby 29, fols. 295v–297 · Trinity Cam., MS O.1.13, fols. 77v–82v

Daniel, (Charles) Henry Olive (1836–1919), printer and college head, was born on 30 September 1836 at Wareham, Dorset, the eldest son of the Revd Alfred Daniel, curate of Wareham, and his wife, Eliza Anne, daughter of Clement Wilson Cruttwell. In 1838 his father became perpetual curate of Frome, Somerset. Henry, as he was later known, was interested in printing from the age of ten; his first 'book', printed 'by the use of types and thumb and

inking', appeared about 1845. He was educated at Grosvenor College, Bath, King's College School, London, and Worcester College, Oxford, where he was elected scholar in 1854. After taking his degree in 1858, with a first class in *literae humaniores*, he returned to King's College as classical lecturer in 1859. In 1863 he was elected to a fellowship at Worcester College, where he spent the remainder of his life. In 1864 he was ordained deacon. He was dean in 1865, vice-provost in 1866, junior bursar in 1870, and proctor in 1873. On 21 August 1878 he married his cousin Emily Crabb Olive (*b.* 1852/3), an artist, and third daughter of Edmund Crabb Olive; they had two daughters, Rachel (*b.* 1880) and Ruth. Compton Mackenzie, who was engaged to Ruth, painted a vibrant portrait of the Daniels in his novel *Guy and Pauline* (1915).

Daniel began printing at Oxford in 1874, seventeen years before William Morris founded the Kelmscott Press. He exerted considerable influence, largely because of his adoption of the Fell type which had lain unused at the Clarendon Press for 150 years (thirty-six years previously Caslon's old-faced type had been revived by William Pickering and Charles Wittingham 'the nephew', for the Chiswick Press). Fell type was first used by Daniel in *A New Sermon of the Newest Fashion* (1876), the second book which he printed at Oxford. He also used a black letter, of which the first example is *The Growth of Love* (1890) by his friend Robert Bridges. Daniel first used a toy press; from 1850 to 1882 he used a small Albion press, and from 1882 onwards a large Albion hand-press, which was first used to print *Hymni ecclesiae* in 1882.

One of the most interesting productions of the Daniel Press, and perhaps the best-known, was *The Garland of Rachel* (1881), a celebration in verse of the first birthday of his daughter Rachel with contributions by Andrew Lang, Austin Dobson, Robert Bridges, Lewis Carroll, and Edmund Gosse. Emily Daniel contributed capital letters and other designs to the Daniel Press, and this was the first book in which large ornaments and illuminations by her were used. Some of Daniel's books were reprints, including *Desiderii Erasmi colloquia duo* (1880); *Hymni ecclesiae* (1882); *Sixe Idillia* of Theocritus (1883), probably translated by Sir Edward Dyer from the unique copy in the Bodleian Library; *Love's Graduate*, an attempt by Edmund Gosse to separate Webster's work from that of William Rowley in *A Cure for a Cuckold* (1885); William Blake's *Songs* (1885) and *Songs of Innocence* (1893); Robert Herrick's *His Flowers* (1891) and *Christmas* (1891); *Odes, Sonnets, and Lyrics of John Keats* (1895); and Robert Jones's *The Muses' Garden for Delights* (1901). Other books contain the work of contemporaries and friends, particularly the plays and poems of Robert Bridges, later poet laureate, comprising fifteen pieces printed between 1883 and 1903, and *Our Memories* (1893), consisting of personal reminiscences of Oxford by a number of senior members of the university. Richard Watson Dixon, Henry Patmore, Margaret Woods, Herbert Warren, Walter Pater, Laurence Binyon, and others are represented by one or more volumes. The smaller Daniel books are delicate, the larger, such as the *Keats* and Bridges' *Shorter*

Poems, in five parts, are fine and handsome. But typographically none of them rivals the best work from later famous presses. Daniel had admirable taste, but had no serious intention of reforming or improving English printing. He was an amateur who aimed at pleasing himself and his friends by printing as well as his means would allow, rather showing how beautifully a book could be made.

Daniel was connected to Worcester College, Oxford, as provost from 1903 (the first to be elected by the fellows), and he wrote the college's history with W. R. Barker in 1900. He was remembered by J. C. Masterman, a scholar at Worcester when Daniel was provost, and later provost himself, as a 'venerable figure, belonging to the past rather than to the present' (Masterman, 46). In later life he was 'magnificent', his golden beard almost completely white, his complexion 'bright and sanguine', his bearing upright, and with the overall appearance of a 'Viking chief' (ibid., 46–7). He was much loved and admired at Worcester, where he was thought of as a generous bursar and a 'gentle and understanding' provost (ibid.). He was chiefly responsible for the decoration of the college's chapel and hall, carried out from the designs of William Burges; the former is, perhaps, the most important example in Oxford of Pre-Raphaelite influence (Daniel's portrait is incorporated into the fresco on the north wall of the chapel). Daniel also took an interest in municipal affairs, and held office as councillor and alderman. He died at Oddington, near Moreton in Marsh, Gloucestershire, on 6 September 1919, and was buried in Holywell cemetery, Oxford. In 1920 Daniel's large press was presented by his wife to the Bodleian Library, and *The Daniel Press* (1921) was the first book to be printed in the library.

C. H. WILKINSON, rev. JOHN D. HAIGH

Sources F. Madan, *The Daniel Press* (1904) · *The Daniel Press* (1921) [*Addenda and corrigenda* pubd 1922]; repr. (1974) · J. Foster, *Oxford men and their colleges* (1893) · Foster, *Alum. Oxon.* · Crockford (1868) · J. C. Masterman, *On the chariot wheel: an autobiography* (1975) · m. cert. · d. cert.
Archives Worcester College, Oxford, personal and family corresp. and papers
Likenesses C. W. Furse, oils, 1905, Worcester College, Oxford; repro. in Madan, *The Daniel Press*, frontispiece
Wealth at death £6446 11s. 10d.: probate, 20 Nov 1919, *CGPLA Eng. & Wales*

Daniel, John (*bap.* 1564?, *d. c.*1626), lutenist and composer, was the younger brother of the poet Samuel *Daniel. The place and date of his birth are not known for certain, but a John Daniell was baptized on 6 November 1564 at Wellow, near Bath. Likewise, the John Daniel who married an Ethel Bridges at nearby Combe Hay on 6 September 1607 may have been the subject of this article. Thomas Fuller's claim (in *Worthies*) that their father—also said to be named John—was a music master may well be due to a confusion of father with son.

The first sure information available about John Daniel is that he supplicated for the degree of bachelor of music at Christ Church, Oxford, on 16 December 1602, and that he received the degree on 14 July 1603, not 1604, as generally stated. From then on there are records of his employment as musician in various families. In September 1603, when

the earl of Hertford was planning a masque 'against the kinges cumminge', he sent for the 'two danyells', Samuel and John; and in April 1605 John was one of a party of musicians (including Robert Johnson and John Bartlet) who accompanied the earl to the court of Albert, archduke of Austria, at Brussels. In 1606 Daniel published his *Songs for the Lute Viol and Voice*, dedicated to Anne Grene, the daughter of Sir William Grene of Milton, near Oxford. Daniel must have been the Grenes' household musician, for the dedicatory poem explains that the songs were 'privately compos'd, For your delight'. The first song, 'Coy Daphne fled', ends with a reference to the dedicatee— 'Shee rests still *Greene*, and so wish I to bee'—and following the songs there is a set of variations for solo lute, entitled *Mrs Anne Grene her Leaves Bee Greene*, based on the popular tune 'The Leaves be Green'. The dedicatory poem makes passing reference to the composer's poet brother ('him, who is / Both neare and deare to mee'), and two of the songs (nos. 4 and 8) use words from Samuel's sonnet sequence *Delia*.

A 'Mr. Danyell' appears in the accounts of the Petre family for September 1613 and July 1615, and from about Christmas 1616 to July 1617 a 'Mr. Daniell the musicon' was being paid to teach the lute to the family of Sir Thomas Thynne of Longleat. In November 1617 Daniel was appointed one of the musicians of Prince Charles, and he occupied this position until 1625, when his name is last recorded among the 'Musicians for the Lute and voices' (22 December). In this capacity he attended the funeral of James I.

John Daniel was also active in theatrical management. In July 1615 his brother Samuel was given permission to form a company of boy actors at Bristol, under the patronage of the queen; almost immediately, however, the direction of the company was given over to John. He took the company to Norwich in 1616–17, but by April 1618 had assigned the patent to others. In 1618 John again replaced his brother as 'allower of the plays' at Philip Rosseter's Blackfriars playhouse, and in 1622 he and others were granted a further licence to run the Bristol company.

On the death of Samuel in 1619 John was named as the sole executor, and in 1623 he collaborated with the printer Simon Waterson to produce *The Whole Workes of Samuel Daniel*, dedicating the volume to Prince Charles. The date of John's death is not known, but it is presumed to be about 1626, shortly after the last entry of his name in the court records.

The few surviving pieces for solo lute and lute duet by Daniel show him to have been a skilful player with a distinctive variation technique. *Mrs Anne Grene her Leaves Bee Greene* appears to be the first English lute piece to use the French *cordes avalées* tuning. But he is best remembered for the collection of songs published in 1606. His most characteristic ones, such as 'Like as the lute delights', 'Can dolefull notes', and the funeral trilogy 'Griefe, keepe within', are in a deeply melancholic vein, with passages of vivid text expression. In these respects, and in his liking for contrapuntal textures, he resembles his great contemporary John Dowland. The affinity becomes explicit in

'Eyes looke no more', which is modelled on Dowland's famous *Lachrimae* pavan. Dowland in turn may have had a passage from the second part of 'Can dolefull notes' in mind when he composed 'From silent night' (*A Pilgrimes Solace*, 1612). It is appropriate that the two composers' names are linked in Thomas Tomkins's 'O let me live for true love' (*Songs*, 1622), in which the two sections are dedicated to Dowland and Daniel respectively.

DAVID GREER

Sources *New Grove*, 2nd edn, vol. 7, p. 3 · A. Ashbee, ed., *Records of English court music*, 9 vols. (1986–96), vols. 3–5 · A. Ashbee and D. Lasocki, eds., *A biographical dictionary of English court musicians, 1485–1714*, 1 (1998), 334–5 · D. C. Price, *Patrons and musicians of the English Renaissance* (1981) · E. K. Chambers, *The Elizabethan stage*, 4 vols. (1923), vol. 2, pp. 68–9 · E. H. Fellowes, *The English lute-songs*, rev. D. Scott, 2nd ser., 8 (1970) · M. Spring, *The lute in Britain: a history of the instrument and its music* (2001) · private information (2004) [Oxf. UA] · D. Scott, 'John Danyel: his life and songs', *Lute Society Journal*, 13 (1971), 7–17 · A. Rooley, 'The lute solos and duets of John Danyel', *Lute Society Journal*, 13 (1971), 18–27 · J. Rees, *Samuel Daniel: a critical and biographical study* (1964), 2 · Fuller, *Worthies* (1662) · parish register, Wellow, near Bath, 6 Nov 1564 [baptism] · parish register, Combe Hay, near Bath, 6 Sept 1607 [marriage]

Daniel, John (1745–1823), Roman Catholic priest, was probably a member of a branch of the family living at Wittingham, Kirkham, Lancashire, rather than, as is commonly believed, the son of Edward and Mary Daniel of Durton, Preston. He entered the English College at Douai on 20 October 1760, was ordained priest probably in 1771, and thereafter lectured in philosophy and theology at the college, becoming its vice-president in 1786. His appointment as president in 1792 coincided with attacks on British property by the French. In October 1793 the college was seized. Daniel and the remaining staff and students, in company with six monks from the English Benedictine college at Douai, were imprisoned at Doullens, where they were joined some time later by the students of the English College at St Omer and their president Gregory Stapleton. Their return home in March 1795 accelerated the search for a college on English soil. Bishop John Douglass of the London district had already gathered former students at Old Hall Green Academy, Hertfordshire, in November 1793, and Bishop William Gibson of the northern district did likewise at Crook Hall in co. Durham in October 1794. Favouring a site in the north, Daniel paid a visit there in June 1795 and became its president for a few days before resigning at the insistence of those who preferred a college in the south. Thereafter he kept his own counsel, always hoping for a return to Douai. In 1802 he went to live in France in order to protect the interests of his college, but its claims for compensation were gradually taken over by Dr William Poynter, assisted by the Revd Francis Tuite. The president, closeted in a room in the seminary of St Gregory, Paris, spent the time compiling his *Ecclesiastical History of the Britons and Saxons* (1815), a new edition of which appeared in 1824.

In 1818 the French government finally handed over nearly £3 million to the British commissioners to cover all claims against it. The personal ones, including those from Catholic clergy, were quickly settled, but those brought by the Catholic institutions were never awarded, one of the grounds being that the commissioners could not hand over money for purposes considered in law to be superstitious uses. The rumour persists that the money was used instead to pay off the debt on the new Brighton Pavilion or to furnish Windsor Castle. Daniel did not live to suffer this final blow. He died in Paris, probably from hypothermia, on 3 October 1823, and was buried two days later in the Père Lachaise cemetery, Paris. The judgement passed by some of his contemporaries at the time of his appointment that he was too inexperienced and indecisive a man to guide the college through its last turbulent days seems to have been borne out by subsequent events.

D. MILBURN

Sources B. Ward, *The dawn of the Catholic revival in England, 1781–1803*, 2 vols. (1909) · B. N. Ward, *The eve of Catholic emancipation*, 3 vols. (1911–12) · B. Ward, *History of St Edmund's College, Old Hall* (1893) · D. Milburn, *A history of Ushaw College* (1964) · D. Milburn, 'Journey to the promised land: from Douai to Durham', *Ushaw Magazine*, 274 (1993–4), 12–26 · G. Anstruther, *The seminary priests*, 4 (1977) · Gillow, *Lit. biog. hist.* · P. R. Harris, ed., *Douai College documents, 1639–1794*, Catholic RS, 63 (1972)
Archives Westm. DA
Wealth at death £1500: Anstruther, *Seminary priests*, 81

Daniel [*née* Lee], **Joyce Mary** (1890–1985), campaigner for birth control, was born on 10 May 1890 at Redland House, north Malvern, Worcestershire, the third of three daughters of Walter Lee, a Congregational minister, and his wife, Alice Amelia Hyrons. She was educated at Milton Mount College, in Kent, and was employed as a secretary in banks in Worcester and Birmingham until she married Archibald Daniel (*b.* 1874/5), son of William Lewes Daniel, official receiver of bankruptcy. They married on 23 April 1918 and she moved to Pontypridd where he was a solicitor. They had two sons, Noel (*b.* 1919) and Tony (*b.* 1922). She was also guardian to her husband's son, Russell, whose mother had died in childbirth.

In 1930 Joyce Daniel, as a result of her involvement delivering maternity parcels for the Lord Mayor's Distress Fund, was approached by Janet Chance, the founder of the Abortion Law Reform Association, whose attempts to raise money from doctors, councillors, magistrates, and other important local figures to establish a birth control clinic in Pontypridd had failed. Joyce Daniel invited the wives of these officials who did not 'care to be mixed up in it' (Family Planning Association Archives) to a meeting held in her own sitting room. This all woman meeting resolved to set up and finance the clinic and use their domestic influence to overcome their husbands' reluctance. An application to the local authority health committee for permission to hire rooms in the maternity and child welfare premises was also refused, but the decision was reversed after Daniel visited each councillor in person.

Joyce Daniel's resourcefulness and determination did not go unnoticed. Following the government's decision in 1930 to allow local authorities to provide birth control advice to women for whom further pregnancy was deemed detrimental to their health (Memo 153/MCW), Daniel was made local correspondent and later area organizer for the National Birth Control Association (NBCA); this was an amalgamation of various birth control associations and later became the Family Planning Association. Daniel proved to be active, dedicated, and successful. The executive committee minutes of the NBCA frequently noted the amount of unpaid overtime she put in. She approached councils, medical officers of health, health committees, and maternity committees, forced a discussion of birth control on to local authority agendas, and persevered, frequently revisiting areas where she did not meet with immediate success. Such pressure was essential as the government did not publish the new permissive Memo, sending it out, at first, only to local authorities who asked for it. Daniel reported finding the Memo 'lying forgotten in council pigeon holes' (*Western Mail*). In September 1932, after only two years' activity, she had succeeded in increasing the number of clinics in south Wales from one to eight. By 1939 thirteen authorities had set up clinics (Aberdâr, Barry, Caerphilly, Gelli-gaer, Llanelli, Llantrissant and Llantwit Fadre, Mountain Ash, Ogmore and Garw, Penarth, Pontardawe, Pontypridd, Port Talbot, and Rhondda). Maesteg was in the process of setting one up, Merthyr had set up a clinic in co-operation with the NBCA, and Glyncorwg urban district council had made arrangements to send women to the clinic at Pontypridd. She had also established a voluntary clinic in Pontypool. The number of clinics run by local authorities in south Wales was significant and attests to the success of Daniel's campaigns. In 1939 thirteen of the seventy-nine local authority birth control/gynaecological clinics in Great Britain were in south Wales. Elsewhere clinics tended to be set up by voluntary associations and received varying degrees of support from local authorities.

Politically Conservative (she was scornful of the Labour Welsh), religiously active (she had a family pew in the local United Reform church), and with an air of social superiority, Daniel's motives for her involvement in the birth control movement stemmed more from the traditions of Victorian philanthropy than from radical proto-feminism. A 1970s history of general practice in south Wales described her as being saddened by the plight of mothers worn out by successive pregnancies and eager to give them an alternative solution to backstreet abortions. There is no evidence, however, that she shared any of the eugenic motives associated with many supporters of the birth control movement. She was opposed to abortion and refused to remove the words 'married women only' from clinic advertisements in the 1950s despite pressure from the central Family Planning Association (FPA). 'I kept having to tell them … that with the Roman Catholics on one side and the Nonconformist Conscience on the other I just could not do it' (*Western Mail*).

Daniel remained active in the NBCA for thirty years. One FPA worker remembered her as 'tall, autocratic looking and very positive. The people who were associated with her were absolutely devoted to her, and in awe, as she had obviously fought some great battles' (private information). It is for this persistence and formidableness that she is primarily remembered; stories were even told of her personally confronting violent husbands who were opposed to their wives' attending a birth control clinic. Joyce Daniel died on 29 January 1985 of bronchopneumonia during a visit to her niece, at 292 Avery Hill Road, Eltham, London. She was cremated in Kent and her ashes were buried in Glyntaf cemetery, in Pontypridd.

KATE FISHER

Sources Wellcome L., Family Planning Association archives, CMAC SA/FPA/A14/17; SA/FPA/A61E • private information (2004) • b. cert. • m. cert. • *Western Mail* [Cardiff] (12 Oct 1976) • d. cert.
Archives BM • Wellcome L., Family Planning Association archives
Wealth at death £60,303: probate, 10 April 1985, *CGPLA Eng. & Wales*

Daniel, Robert Mackenzie (1814–1847), novelist, was born in Inverness-shire and educated at a school in Inverness, at Marischal College, Aberdeen, and at the University of Edinburgh. Despite studying law for four years, Daniel resolved to pursue a career as a journalist and writer. In 1836 he went to London where he contributed largely to the magazines, and was appointed editor of the *Court Journal*. His first work of fiction, *The Scottish Heiress*, appeared in 1843, and was followed in the same year by *The Gravedigger*. In 1844 he moved to Jersey, where he produced *The Young Widow*, a tale of a young woman's trials after her missionary husband is reported dead in Africa. This novel was favourably received; *The Young Baronet* (1845) sustained his reputation, and he became known as the Scottish Boz. In January 1845 he accepted the editorship of the *Jersey Herald*, a post which he held until September 1846, when he was overtaken by mental illness and removed by his friends to Bethlem Hospital, London, where he died on 21 March 1847. Daniel's wife, Elizabeth, whom he married in 1844, also pursued a career as a novelist. She survived her husband and between 1841 and 1877 published more than twenty novels, the best-known being *Georgina Hammond* (1849).

THOMPSON COOPER, rev. CHARLES BRAYNE

Sources Anderson, *Scot. nat.*, 19–20 • *GM*, 2nd ser., 27 (1847), 671 • Irving, *Scots.* • J. Sutherland, *The Longman companion to Victorian fiction* (1988)
Wealth at death presumed negligible: *GM*

Daniel, Samuel (1562/3–1619), poet and historian, was born either in north Somerset, somewhere between Bath and Frome, or further to the east on Salisbury Plain in Wiltshire. The little that is known about his family and origins suggests a connection with the Daniels of St Margaret's in Marlborough in Wiltshire, and, perhaps more distantly, with families in the north of England. Fuller's claim that Daniel's father was a master of music has not been substantiated; it is quite likely that Fuller confused the father with Daniel's younger brother, John *Daniel, an Oxford graduate in music and a composer for the lute.

Daniel himself was educated at Oxford in the early 1580s (he matriculated at Magdalen Hall in 1581, making it likely that he was born in 1562 or 1563), but he left without taking a degree. Two things Daniel did acquire at Oxford were the friendship of John Florio (his sister may have

Samuel Daniel (1562/3–1619), by Thomas Cockson, pubd 1609

married Florio) and enough French and Italian to get him started in life: first, in 1585, as the translator of a book of *impresa* (emblems with mottoes) by the Italian writer Giovio; then, for a few months in 1586, as a servant of some kind at the English embassy in Paris; and finally, for five years or more, until about 1592, as an above-stairs servant and companion to the Italophile Sir Edward Dymoke, the queen's champion. Daniel lived at Dymoke's home in Lincolnshire in the late 1580s, and accompanied him to northern Italy in 1590, where together they met Guarini, the author of *Il pastor fido*.

It is not known when Daniel started writing poetry (it may have been while he was at Oxford), but certainly by 1590, as Florio confirms, some if not all of his *Delia* sonnets were in manuscript, though perhaps not gathered under that title. In 1591, quite possibly while he was abroad, twenty-eight of the sonnets were printed for the first time, attributed but without a title, at the end of the pirated quarto of Sir Philip Sidney's sonnets, *Astrophel and Stella*. How the publisher Newman obtained the two manuscripts, of unpublished Sidney and Daniel poems, is unclear, but Daniel himself is not above suspicion, nor is Florio who may have wanted to help his friend and protégé by launching him into the world as the disciple of Sidney, England's dead hero and poet.

The gamble, if such it was, paid off. The Sidney set was offended by *Astrophel and Stella* appearing in print and the book was withdrawn, but no blame was attached to Daniel. Indeed, he was permitted the following year to dedicate an authorized edition of the *Delia* sonnets (fifty of them, arranged as a sequence) to Sidney's sister, Mary, countess of Pembroke. In the dedication, in prose, he claimed that the sonnets had been '*consecrated to silence*' (that is, not for publication) and that they had come to light only because of '*the indiscretion of a greedie Printer*'. This edition also introduced a long narrative poem, written in seven-line stanzas of rhyme royal, called *The Complaint of Rosamond*, which was an account by the ghost of Rosamond Clifford of how she was seduced by Henry II and poisoned by his queen. The book, on sale by the spring of 1592 (it was entered in the Stationers' register on 4 February), was an immediate success; Daniel followed up in the same year with a second edition, which supplied four new sonnets to *Delia*, and a revised version of *Rosamond*.

The quality of Daniel's poetry, and in *Delia* his obvious familiarity with (and debts to) the French lyric poets Du Bellay and Desportes, evidently prompted an invitation from Lady Pembroke to join her at Wilton House. No documentary evidence of his time there has survived, but ten years later in 1603—when he dedicated his *Defence of Rhyme* to her son, William, the third earl (whom he may have taught at some stage)—Daniel described Wilton as his 'best Schoole', that is, the place from which he had learned most. One thing it certainly taught him was how to write to commission, since Lady Pembroke set him the task of writing a companion piece to her own *Tragedy of Antony*, the translation she had published in 1592 of the play by Garnier, the French neo-classical dramatist. For his play, *The Tragedy of Cleopatra*, Daniel drew on the same sixteenth-century French Senecan models and conventions (a text for reading not acting, a chorus, much of the action narrated by a messenger), but he caught at something new in English, at least among the Elizabethan writers, the grace and pathos of a great woman who was suffering. *Cleopatra* was entered in the Stationers' register on 19 October 1593 and published the following year as the final piece in the third edition of *Delia* (with sonnets added, replaced, and in many places revised) and *Rosamond* (also much expanded and rewritten).

Civil Wars and Musophilus By 1594 Daniel had established himself as the new poet of the English *dolce stile*—perfect in melody, phrasing, and idiom—and as a writer whom other writers had to keep an eye on. Spenser in 1595, in *Colin Clout's Come Home Again*, described him as surpassing everyone in sight, and Shakespeare had begun to borrow from him freely, especially for his narrative poems and sonnets. The direction Daniel chose next, though, was upwards, away from lyric poetry and neo-classical drama, towards the pinnacle of genres, the epic or, more exactly, the heroic poem. His subject was the medieval civil wars fought between the houses of Lancaster and York; it was to begin with the deposing of Richard II and end with the defeat of Richard III at Bosworth and the accession of the Tudors. Work on *The Civil Wars* must have begun in the Wilton years (the first four books, down to the death of the duke of Somerset in 1455, were entered in the Stationers' register on 11 October 1594 and published late in 1595), but it was not done under Lady Pembroke's auspices. It is not clear why there was a parting of the ways between Daniel and the countess (perhaps they disagreed about how best to commemorate Sidney and to extend his influence on English writing), but the first instalment of *The Civil Wars* appeared without a dedication. This was tactful but also tactical, since Daniel had already secured another patron, Charles Blount, Baron Mountjoy, whom he thanks in the opening stanzas of the first book for saving him, at the last moment, from shipwreck (the metaphor was borrowed from Tasso, but even so his difficulties were probably real enough). Among the younger set of courtiers favoured by the queen, Mountjoy was second only to Robert, earl of Essex, and Daniel's association with him must have provided new, powerful friends and connections, including Essex himself and possibly Greville (though that link may have been made through Florio somewhat earlier). The financial help he received from the nobleman (as he later insisted, in the poem he wrote for Mountjoy's funeral) was not substantial, but Daniel got from him what other authors could barely hope for, the encouragement and intellectual support of a cultivated and scholarly aristocrat, as well as access to a well-stocked library (in this case, at Mountjoy's home, Wanstead House).

The impact of *The Civil Wars*, as with Daniel's other poetry, was felt throughout the literary scene at once. This time, however, it was not just his writing that contemporaries remarked upon, but the depth and subtlety of his exposition of kingship, matters of state, and the causes of rebellion. Shakespeare was drawing on it for aspects of *Richard II* within weeks of the poem going on sale (probably November 1595), and Spenser took notice of it too, if his reference in the *Prothalamion* to a coming 'brave muse' (a writer capable of a heroic poem on Lord Essex) can be read as an allusion to Daniel. Another book of *The Civil Wars*, the fifth, which Daniel wrote quite possibly about the time of Cadiz in 1596 (Camden quotes from it in his drafts for the *Remains*, *c*.1597), was printed and sold separately without a date, but also bound up as an attachment at the end of the first four books. From this point until early in 1599 direct evidence of Daniel's whereabouts, what exactly he was writing, and how he was managing to live, is lacking. The signs are that he was desperately short of money on occasions (in April 1595 Fulke Greville begged the reversion on a parsonage and its tithes for him from Robert Cecil) and that he continued to look for and find new patrons. This much can be concluded from one poem he was definitely working on during this period, the *Letter from Octavia*. Although Daniel did not invent the Elizabethan epistolary poem (Drayton was ahead of him in this), he did in time turn it to great effect, in the *Epistles* of 1603, but in *Octavia*—cast in stanzas of *ottava rima* as a letter of complaint to Mark Antony living in Egypt with Cleopatra—he was still feeling his way in the mode, and there is a tentativeness, even uncertainty, about how far he could go without making the wronged wife, Octavia, seem shrill. Part of the difficulty is that the poem was in some sense a representation of the marital difficulties of

his patron, Margaret Clifford, countess of Cumberland (*d.* 1616), the wife of George, the third earl (*d.* 1605), a notoriously philandering husband. It is conceivable that Lady Cumberland commissioned Daniel to write *Octavia* and to dedicate it to her because she had seen how much sympathy he could evoke for élite women of the past (including her ancestor by marriage, Rosamond Clifford).

The patronage of Lady Cumberland, however Daniel obtained it, was not an unmixed blessing, since it involved the duty (probably an exacting one) of tutoring her formidably intelligent and self-willed daughter and heir, Lady Anne Clifford. Daniel must have started teaching Lady Anne when she was eight or nine, or even younger, probably in one of the Clifford family homes in London or Northamptonshire (certainly not, as is sometimes claimed, in Skipton Castle in Yorkshire where Lady Anne was born in January 1590, but which she never lived in until she was much older). The relationship between Daniel and his pupil later deepened into mutual regard and even friendship (not a common thing across a social divide as great as theirs), but at this date he chafed at being distracted from continuing and completing *The Civil Wars*: 'whilst I should have written the actions of men', he confessed in a letter to another of his patrons, Sir Thomas Egerton, 'I have been constrayned to live with Children' (Pitcher, 'Samuel Daniel's letter', 56).

In the late 1590s, however, there were other distractions for Daniel, notably the work of writing the long colloquy poem *Musophilus*. This is perhaps the single most important poem of Daniel's whole career, and it is certainly the most innovative. The influence of Montaigne (the reflexive, self-probing, revising side of Montaigne) is everywhere in the poem, not always to Daniel's advantage, since it encouraged in him even more self-distrust than he already had. He dedicated the poem to Greville, but again (as with *The Civil Wars*) he acknowledged Mountjoy as a presiding presence in it, giving the reader to understand that the poem flowed out of his continuing conversation with the nobleman about life and letters. It is formally arranged as a dialogue between Musophilus and Philocosmus (the champions, at least at the outset, of the contemplative and active lives), and it deals with matters such as the function and credibility of poetry, and whether political and religious changes can be accommodated without revolution. The over-complexity of the work, and its occasional lapses in coherence, are the result of too many voices in debate (the poet with his patrons, with himself, with contemporary and past writers and others).

Daniel later described the period of *Musophilus* as one of crisis for him, when his doubts about what he was doing nearly made him give up writing poetry altogether. Greville persuaded him to continue, however, and Daniel published the poem early in 1599 as the centrepiece of his first collected edition, a quarto entitled, with a nod to Montaigne, *The Poetical Essays*. He dedicated the collection to Mountjoy, and included in it *Octavia* (addressed to Lady Cumberland), alongside revised versions of *Rosamond* and *Cleopatra*, and unsold copies of the first five books of *The Civil Wars*. The book as a whole is intriguing because it is a physical compilation of old and new printings, and because each of the pieces in it has its own title-page and printer's signature, and could be sold separately (and they were: there are surviving copies of each piece in original vellum covers).

The Poetical Essays is also important evidence of the special business and personal relationship Daniel enjoyed with his publisher and friend, the stationer Simon Waterson (d. 1627). All but one or two of Daniel's editions (more than twenty in thirty years) were published by Waterson, whose support for the poet went well beyond any money he could make out of him. Waterson, a warden of the Stationers' Company, showed little interest in other contemporary poets or dramatists, although he did publish the translation of Montaigne's Essays done by Daniel's mentor, Florio. It was evidently Daniel's literary reputation and character and his association with so many high-born patrons that made him attractive to Waterson, from a business angle and in terms of his own social standing as a publisher. The benefit Daniel derived from the relationship increased over the years, especially when he came to publish his prose histories in 1612 and 1618, but even in 1600 the connection with Waterson was invaluable to him. It was Waterson who asked him, about this date, to publish more of The Civil Wars, and it must have been their joint decision to issue the revised version as part of a second collected edition, this time in an impressive, well-printed folio with the title The Works of Samuel Daniel. This contains six books of The Civil Wars, dedicated to the queen, with revised texts of Rosamond, Cleopatra, Octavia, and Musophilus, and it concludes with a substantially rewritten Delia (now fifty-seven sonnets in total: several new ones, a few dropped, and the rest worked over in great detail in phrasing, rhymes, and lexicon). The edition, with a specially designed title-page, was published as two issues, differentiated by date and by the size and quality of the paper. Most of the large-paper 1601 issue was for Daniel to give away, while the smaller 1602s were for Waterson to sell.

The Works folio, which appeared late in 1601, was intended to establish Daniel's credentials as the leading writer among living English poets, after the death of Spenser. Perhaps it was this unspoken claim, or the unflattering reference in Musophilus to writers bringing the humours on stage, that first set Jonson against Daniel. The quarrel between them had no place to surface until a year or so later, in the new court, but even at this point Jonson had enough to feed his anger on, especially when he thought of the whole constellation of patrons, even the intelligent, knowledgeable ones, who openly admired Daniel. Just how many of the élite Daniel could write to, with respectful assurance, was made obvious only a few months later when he published a set of letters in verse, his Certain Epistles, addressed to Sir Thomas Egerton, Lord Henry Howard, Lucy, countess of Bedford, Margaret, countess of Cumberland, Lady Anne Clifford, and Henry, earl of Southampton. The poems are in effect moral essays, with Daniel drawing freely on Seneca's letters and the sixteenth-century neo-Stoics. Each deals with a large

ethical problem (why God tests us with adversity is one), fashioned to reflect on some aspect of the recipient's circumstances or character: the epistle to Lady Bedford is written in terza rima, for instance, as a compliment to her learning and her interest in Italian. Daniel's manner in the Epistles—even-toned and sagacious—is entirely at one with the quality of thinking and reflectiveness he shows when tackling familiar (not to say conventional) moral topics. Two centuries later Samuel Taylor Coleridge understood, in a way that few have since, just how difficult it is to write in this manner, on the borderline between prose and verse, and how considerable Daniel's achievement was: in this respect, as Coleridge realized, Daniel had anticipated William Wordsworth (who quotes and borrows from the Epistles in various places, including The Excursion).

The Epistles were completed in the months before the queen's death in March 1603, or within days of King James coming to the throne (the occasion for the poem to Southampton was the earl's release from the Tower). One of the houses at which the new king stopped on his way south to London was Burley on the Hill in Rutland, the home of Lord and Lady Harington of Exton, and it was there, on 23 April, that Daniel greeted the king with a poem of praise and advice, A Panegyric Congratulatory (the presentation autograph manuscript survives in the Royal Collection in the British Library). This privilege was due to the influence of Lord Harington's daughter, Lucy, countess of Bedford, who was already in Scotland, establishing herself as chief among the ladies who were to serve the new queen. Daniel acted promptly, bringing out a folio of the Panegyric and Epistles, together with a prose work, A Defence of Rhyme, within eight weeks of the accession (Waterson had the folio designed and printed to be bound with the 1601 and 1602 Works folios). The Defence might at first look out of place in this collection, but it is not. It started life, Daniel explained, as part of an exchange of letters, probably with Greville, in response to Campion's arguments (in his Observations of 1602) that English verse needed to be reformed according to classical principles, especially in its metre and rhyme. Daniel rapidly exposes the silliness of some of these claims (courteously pointing out that Campion, whom he admires, has written his own best lyrics entirely in an English mode), but he then moves on to a general consideration of the place of custom in the history of England, manifested in this case in rhyme. This was of course relevant to the question of how the English constitution and traditions might best accommodate a monarch with new ideas arriving from Scotland.

Royal patronage The new reign brought Daniel his most important patron ever—not, as he may have hoped at first, the king himself, but rather his consort, Queen Anne (or Anna). The opportunities that presented themselves were not always to his taste, though, and he did not excel in them all. The first sign of royal favour was an invitation in September 1603 to perform an entertainment of some kind with his brother John, the musician, when the royal couple, on progress in the west country, stayed for two nights at Tottenham Park, one of the homes of Edward

Seymour, earl of Hertford (*d.* 1621), and his wife, Lady Frances. Hertford, by blood if not by character, was one of the few aristocrats who might have laid claim to the throne at Elizabeth's death. It soon became clear, however, that he presented no threat to the Stuart succession, and the visit to Tottenham Park was the king's way of acknowledging publicly that the earl was a loyal subject. Daniel's connection with the Hertford family was a long-standing one, probably dating back to the 1590s or before. In May 1601 he wrote a sonnet to Lady Frances on her marriage to the earl, and later gave her a printed version of it bound into one of his 1601 *Works* folios. For Hertford himself, about 1602, he wrote a short poem as a response to a *questione d'amore* (part of an Italian court game of questions and answers about love) posed by the earl, and had it printed at the end of the 1603 collection of *Epistles*. No text of the Tottenham Park entertainment survives, but it may well have comprised Daniel's poems set to the lute by his brother (John's *Songs for the Lute*, published in 1606, contains settings for several *Delia* sonnets together with translations of lyrics by Tasso and Guarini, important writers for Daniel at this point).

The next step was taken by the queen herself, when she commissioned Daniel to write a masque to be played at Hampton Court on 8 January 1604. This was *The Vision of the Twelve Goddesses*, a device in which the queen and her ladies, as classical deities, traversed the hall between a rock and a temple, and then danced to music and singing that invoked the Platonic harmonies (for which Daniel drew on Seneca). The commission and carrying out of the masque owed much to two of the accompanying ladies, both of them of the queen's bedchamber, the countesses of Bedford and of Hertford. When Daniel published the masque a few months later, and tried to defend it, in vain, against the scorn heaped on it by Jonson and others (who called it old-fashioned and uninspired), he dedicated the text to Lady Bedford and thanked her for her support (it was she who had ensured that he was the queen's choice). Lady Hertford's contribution was drawn from her husband's huge wealth. Among other payments for work done on the masque, almost £250 was paid to James Kirton, Hertford's steward, for having the rock and the temple set up in the hall, and another £40 went to Daniel himself for preparing the *Vision* over a period of six weeks. The attacks on him by Jonson must have been difficult for Daniel to swallow—not because he wanted to write masques (which he didn't), but because they came from, as he saw it, an opinionated and bullying writer of stage-plays who was bringing the vulgarity of Southwark (greasepaint, whorehouses) into the court itself. His disdain for the public theatre may have been costly to him in other ways too. Even the sinecure of monitoring a few stage-plays—the queen had made him licenser of the Children of the Queen's Revels in February 1604—was something he couldn't bring himself to do with any care. It is not impossible that he let the controversial plays *The Dutch Courtesan* and *Eastward Ho!* get by him simply because he hadn't read them closely enough before they were performed.

The following years were the most difficult of Daniel's life. The first disaster was with *The Tragedy of Philotas*, performed before the king by the Children of the Queen's Revels early in January 1605. Daniel was immediately called before the privy council to answer the charge that his treatment of the subject—the downfall of Philotas, a favourite of Alexander the Great—was seditious comment on the trial and execution of Robert, earl of Essex, in 1601. He protested that he had only written the play 'to reduce the stage from idlenes to those grave presentments of antiquitie used by the wisest nations', and he was sure, he told the council, that his patron Mountjoy, who had seen *Philotas* in manuscript, would speak on his behalf. But Mountjoy, who had just about steered clear of the failed Essex coup, was furious when Daniel dragged in his name like this. The letters of apology that Daniel wrote to Mountjoy and to Robert Cecil in May show how complete was his humiliation. Whether or not he did intend *Philotas* as a comment on behalf of the Essex cause (modern scholars believe that he did), the scandal and the stain on his reputation hurt him deeply. But he cannot have been out of favour for long, if at all, since his pastoral tragicomedy *Arcadia Reformed* (published in 1606 as *The Queen's Arcadia*) was played before the queen and Prince Henry at Christ Church in August when the royal family visited Oxford (the auditorium set up in the hall in Christ Church was designed by Inigo Jones). *Philotas* too, despite Daniel's offer to Cecil to withdraw the play altogether, was judged acceptable; it appeared late in 1605, with a dedication to Prince Henry, in the third collected edition, *Certain Small Poems*. Daniel's spirits were low, however—'the remnant of another time' was how he described himself to the prince (*Tragedy of Philotas*, 98)—and more unhappiness was to come.

Daniel quickly repaired his relationship with Mountjoy (by now earl of Devonshire), but the nobleman was dead within a year. In the long poem he wrote for the funeral, privately printed and distributed among the mourners, Daniel expressed profound regret at having written nothing substantial to commemorate his patron's achievements. In 1607, in his fourth collected edition, *Certain Small Works*, he published a longer version of the funeral poem, the chief addition being an account of Mountjoy's victory over the Spanish and Irish at the siege of Kinsale in 1601. Daniel promised to write more about Mountjoy and Ireland but he never did. His own health had begun to fail (the symptoms he described, a dozen years later, point to a heart condition), and clearly he did not expect to live much longer: when he dedicated the *Certain Small Works* to Lady Anne Clifford he asked her to oversee the legacies (his poems) that he was giving away for the last time.

History in prose Away from London, Daniel recovered, however, in rural seclusion on one of the earl of Hertford's estates in the west country. There he started work on something new: a prose history of the Norman conquest, which eventually formed the first section of his history of medieval England. Cecil may have had some hand in prompting (or permitting) him to begin this work (the 1612 *History* should have been dedicated to him, but he died before it could be published). Daniel's friendships with Camden and Cotton gave him access to documents, and his years of detailed reading for *The Civil Wars* (comparing sources, analysing the motives of this or that baron or bishop, and learning from Bodin and the new French historiography) fitted him perfectly for the task. The work also rekindled his interest in *The Civil Wars* itself. He added new material to the poem, continuing the narrative as far as the marriage of Edward IV to Lady Grey, and he published it, now in eight books, in 1609, with a dedication to one of his earliest patrons, Lady Pembroke. The countess had revived his verse with her eyes, he said—a gallant reminder of the language of love he used in *Delia* in the 1590s—but the revival stopped at this point; henceforth all his history would be in prose.

By now Daniel had arrived at some degree of financial security, from different sources. He first signed himself a groom of the queen's privy chamber in 1607, and the regular annual payments he received from the queen's exchequer probably began not long afterwards. Prince Henry's accounts record payments to him at different dates (1609 appears to be the earliest), and he had a salary and a home as an overseer (not a demanding job in his case it seems) on the Hertford estate. His personal standing with his patrons could not have been higher. In May 1608, when negotiations for a marriage between Lady Anne Clifford and Edward Seymour, one of Hertford's grandsons, began to falter, the earl summoned Daniel to London in the hope that the poet might be able to persuade Lady Cumberland and her daughter to accept the proposed terms (he didn't, but the ladies were gratified to see him).

At court, in spite of the criticism levelled at the 1604 *Vision*, it was Daniel whom the queen commissioned to write a masque celebrating Henry's investiture as prince of Wales in June 1610. This was *Tethys' Festival*, in which (in settings designed by Inigo Jones) Meliades, prince of the Isles (Henry), was given symbols of British power from the sea by his mother, Tethys (Anne), the wife of Oceanus (James). *Tethys' Festival* shows that Daniel had learnt nothing from Jonson about writing masques, because he had not changed his mind about what they could be (for him they were only ephemera). But the political views he expresses through *Tethys' Festival*—advising the prince not to pursue a war of empire and plunder against enemies in the new and old worlds—were important to him, as is clear from their fuller exposition in a verse epistle he wrote to Henry at the same time: no doubt it was his historical studies that compelled Daniel to contradict the court party urging the prince to begin a protestant war. Henry's death in 1612 ended the matter, leaving Daniel, like others, ever more gloomy at the moral decline of the court. In an unfinished and unpublished collection of verse epistles, written between 1610 and 1616, beginning with the one to Prince Henry (the others were addressed to Lady Bedford, to her widowed mother, Lady Harington, and to Sir Robert Carr of Ancrum, Donne's friend), he describes the world of aristocrats and courtiers as frenzied and bankrupt, where an escape through death (even an early one, like the prince's) is preferable to life.

Daniel's own escape was into writing and publishing his history of medieval England, though he still had obligations to the queen and to his patrons and friends. In 1614, for example, he wrote another pastoral tragicomedy, *Hymen's Triumph*, modelled on Tasso, to celebrate both the completion of the queen's palace, Somerset House, and the wedding of her confidante Jean Drummond, who had been a special friend to him. And in February 1616, when he wrote a letter to Lady Cumberland advising her not to confront Lord Dorset, her son-in-law, on his arrival in the north with Lady Anne, Daniel was almost certainly acting on behalf of the queen who didn't wish to show her hand in the matter (it was also a reminder to the countess, by now an old friend, of the counsel of calmness and withdrawal from the world that he had drawn up for her in his prose paraphrase from Petrarch, *The Praise of Private Life*).

Nevertheless, the history was the major preoccupation of Daniel's final years. He published two instalments of it: the first, in 1612, ran from the Saxons immediately before the conquest to the death of Stephen, while the second, in 1618, entitled *The Collection of the History of England*, reprinted 1612 and continued the history to the end of Edward III's reign. The 1612 quarto was dedicated to the king's favourite, Robert Carr, Viscount Rochester (a last-minute replacement for Cecil, to whom manuscript versions had been dedicated). The book was privately printed, 'a few copies for my friends', Daniel said, urging them to comment on what he had done so far (the friends included Camden, Cotton, and Sir Peter Manwood, the antiquarian). The 1612 quarto must have been an immediate success since the Stationers bought the book outright from Daniel (over two hundred copies) and reprinted it in 1613. The *Collection* of 1618, a large folio dedicated to the queen, had attached to it a royal privilege which gave Daniel and his heirs ten years of exclusive rights of publication (the cost of printing the book was met by the queen: Daniel was granted £40 in May 1618). The *Collection* was another success, so much so that it was reprinted at least three times before the ten years were up; by the 1620s the total number of copies sold, all in large-paper folios, may have been as large as two thousand (with perhaps as many again from the 1634 and 1685 reprints).

Daniel's public reputation, whatever knocks it had taken over the masques and court plays, reached a high point again (as high as it had been in the 1590s) because of the history. His contemporaries saw, as have modern historians, that he had broken free of the Tudor chroniclers, the antiquarians, and those who sought the shapes of history in divine providence or a political orthodoxy. Daniel was every inch a new historian, minutely examining sources and citing them for his readers (he would have published an appendix of sources had he lived), and he wrote a prose as lucid as anything the later seventeenth century could manage. Above all, it was his judgement that made him reliable: he could look with sympathy as well as disinterest at individuals and the institutions they had to live with. He had a rare sense of the past, and an even rarer sense of the limits of historical understanding. So great was his fame as a historian in the decades before and after the civil war (when he was read and admired by both sides) that his achievements as a poet were almost forgotten. By the 1660s, he had become Daniel the Historian, who had also written some poems.

Death and reputation Daniel ended his life as he began it, in provincial obscurity. By 1619 his home was in the hamlet of Ridge (now Rudge), part of Beckington in Somerset, where he died and where he was buried on 14 October. Towards the end he told Bishop Montague, a fellow sufferer, that although his own health had been deteriorating for several years it had never been bad enough to stop him from working. His last year must have been filled with sadness: the queen died in March 1619 (he was a mourner at the funeral), and the Mrs Daniel whose burial was recorded in the Beckington register on 25 March 1619 may have been his wife. Little is known about his personal life, other than what can be gleaned from his will (there were bequests to his sister Susan Bowre and her family, but no children of his own are mentioned). He appointed his brother John sole executor, and made both John Phillipps, his brother-in-law, and Simon Waterson, his publisher and 'loving ffriend', overseers of the will. The bequests amounted to £40 and a feather bed and linen, and no doubt his brother received an income from the sale of the *Collection* and its reprints (over the years Daniel had used his connection with the queen to secure several minor offices for John). The will, dated 4 September 1619, makes it clear that Daniel died a protestant, though there were those, according to Fuller, who suspected that he had Roman tendencies—perhaps an unavoidable charge, given his long association with the Catholic Queen Anne.

It was in the 1650s, almost four decades later, that his former pupil Lady Anne Clifford had a monument (a tablet and pediment) erected to Daniel's memory in St George's Church in Beckington where he had been buried (there is an intriguing possibility that this replaced an earlier, less impressive one that she herself had commissioned in the 1620s). The memory that he was a poet rested on the collection (made up of reprints of the poems and plays together with unsold copies of the 1609 *Civil Wars*) that was published by his brother in 1623, *The Whole Workes of Samuel Daniel Esquire*. Ben Jonson's famous remark that Daniel was 'a good honest man, had no children, bot no poet' is more just than might have been expected from such an enemy, but it is still short shrift. Daniel was not a poet in Jonson's terms (gifted with a sublime imagination, that is, and a master of high and low speech), but he was an 'honest' man (honourable, full of integrity), the word Jonson most liked to hear used of himself (*Ben Jonson*, ed. C. H. Herford, E. Simpson, and P. Simpson, 11 vols., 1925–52, 1.132). Daniel 'had no children' by a wife, but also—another Jonson preoccupation shows itself here—he had no successors as a writer, no disciples (or sons or a tribe) as Ben did.

A fairer summing up would allow that Daniel was a major not a minor poet, whose development was marked by a gradual loosening of the ties that bound together literary forms. Daniel began with the *Delia* sonnets, with honeyed rhymes and a cruel lady, but he linked these to *Rosamond*, a hybrid of Ovidian and Gothic lament, in which popular Tudor medievalism (the tradition of *The Mirror for Magistrates*) sat uneasily with his more accurate and sensitive reading of medieval history. From there, through further experiments in vernacular epic, neo-classical drama, Italian lyric, and other genres, Daniel arrived at his greatest but most perturbing achievements, *Musophilus* and the verse epistles of 1603—achievements which, although they have been much praised since Coleridge and Wordsworth first discerned their quality, have few literary precedents and even fewer literary successors. It is true that in *Musophilus* can be discerned the influence of Castiglione and the humanist colloquy, and a bedrock of commonplaces from Seneca, Horace, and Erasmus, but Daniel had few guides (perhaps only Montaigne) in making a poetry that shows the mind actually thinking, analysing, at work. And it might be argued too that Daniel attempted to occupy a space where the self had rarely been, in English poetry before the Renaissance, and where few Elizabethan writers would wish to follow, as he tested out ideas about integrity, in social rank, kingship, virtue, and poetic form. What kept him this side of literary greatness, but made him of immense importance to modern understanding of the 1590s and of the Jacobeans, was that all of this mental work had to be done *in the verse*—as C. S. Lewis put it, meaning it as the highest praise, Daniel always thinks arduously and deeply in his poetry.

JOHN PITCHER

Sources STC, *1475–1640*, nos. 6236–65 • H. A. Sellers, 'A bibliography of the works of Samuel Daniel, 1585–1623', *Proceedings and Papers of the Oxford Bibliographical Society*, 2 (1927), 29–54; supplementary note, 2 (1930), 341–2 [incl. Daniel's will] • P. Beal, *Index of English literary manuscripts*, ed. P. J. Croft and others, 1/1 (1980), 197–206 • Fuller, *Worthies* • A. Wood, *Historia et antiquitates universitatis Oxoniensis*, trans. R. Peers and R. Reeve, 2 vols. (1674) • Wood, *Ath. Oxon.*, 1st edn • A. C. Sprague, *'Poems' and 'A defence of ryme'*, 2nd edn (1965) • J. Rees, *Daniel: a critical and biographical study* (1964) • *The tragedy of Philotas, by Samuel Daniel*, ed. L. Michel (1949) • *'The civil wars' by Samuel Daniel*, ed. L. Michel (1958) • J. Pitcher, ed., *Samuel Daniel: the Brotherton manuscript: a study in authorship* (1981) • J. Pitcher, 'Samuel Daniel, the Hertfords, and a question of love', *Review of English Studies*, 35 (1984), 449–62 • J. Pitcher, 'Samuel Daniel's letter to Sir Thomas Egerton', *Huntington Library Quarterly*, 47 (1984), 55–61 • J. Pitcher, '"In those figures which they seem": Samuel Daniel's *Tethys' festival*', *The court masque*, ed. D. Lindley (1984), 33–46 • S. Daniel, *Hymen's triumph*, ed. J. Pitcher (1994) • J. Pitcher, 'Essays, works and small poems: divulging, publishing and augmenting the Elizabethan poet, Samuel Daniel', *The Renaissance text*, ed. A. Murphy (2000), 8–29 • J. Pitcher, 'Samuel Daniel's occasional and dedicatory verse: a critical edition', 2 vols., DPhil diss., U. Oxf., 1978 • R. B. Gottfried, 'The authorship of "A breviary of the history of England"', *Studies in Philology*, 53 (1956), 172–90 • C. R. Wilson, '*Astrophil and Stella*: a tangled editorial web', *The Library*, 6th ser., 1 (1979), 336–46 • E. Doughtie, ed., *Lyrics from English airs, 1596–1622* (1970) • B. Juel-Jensen, review of J. Pitcher, ed., *Samuel Daniel* (1981), *The Library*, 6th ser., 5 (1983), 428–30 • R. F. Brinkley, ed., *Coleridge on the seventeenth century* (1955), 509–17 • C. C. Seronsy, 'Wordsworth's annotations in Daniel's poetical works', *Modern Language Notes*, 68 (1953), 403–6 • M. McKisack, 'Samuel Daniel as historian', *Review of English Studies*, 32 (1947), 226–43

Likenesses bust on pediment, 1650–59, St George's Church, Beckington • T. Cockson, engraving (after unknown artist), NPG; repro. in S. Daniel, *The civil wars* (1609) [*see illus.*]

Wealth at death bequests of £40; contents of home (bed, etc.); income from sale of books (royal privilege for ten years) not known: will, Sept 1619

Daniel, Thomas. *See* West, Thomas (1720?–1779).

Daniel, Walter (*fl.* 1150–1167), Cistercian monk, hagiographer, and theologian, was a monk of the abbey of Rievaulx from 1150 to his death, and the author of a number of theological, philosophical, and biographical works. The best known of these is his life of *Ailred of Rievaulx. Ailred died in 1167; Walter had lived under his direction for seventeen years; and when he entered Rievaulx in 1150, his father, Daniel, was already a monk of the house, having taken the habit at least three years earlier. It is possible that the family was of knightly origin, but whether, as has been suggested, they were the Daniels of the Balliol fief in Cleveland, Yorkshire, can be regarded as no more than conjecture. Before entering Rievaulx, Walter had been educated in the schools—where is unknown—and it would appear that he had also received professional medical training. He refers to himself as *medicus*, he betrays a specialized knowledge of disease, and he was Ailred's constant attendant during the latter's chronic illnesses. It is therefore possible that he was infirmarian of Rievaulx, though that is not certain.

Apart from being Ailred's *medicus*, Walter was also his amanuensis and one of his closest companions. He himself seems to have been an intelligent, learned, and devout monk, quick to understand and effective in argument, though perhaps somewhat irritable and too easily offended. But whatever his faults, he was a prolific writer and John Leland (*d.* 1552), who visited Rievaulx shortly before the dissolution, saw in the library nine of his works: *Centum sententiae*; *Centum homiliae*; *Epistolae, justum volumen*; *De virginitate Mariae*; *Expositio super 'Missus est angelus Gabriel'*; *De honesta virginis formula*; *De onere jumentorum austri, libri ii*; *De vera amicitia, libri v*; and *De conceptione beatae Mariae contra Nicholaum monachum, libri ii*. Leland does not mention the life of Ailred, and apart from that work only the *Centum sententiae* and four sermons survive. The life of Ailred is prefaced by a defence of the work and of Ailred's own reputation, known as the *Epistola ad Mauricium*: the Maurice in question was probably Maurice of Kirkham. Of the other works nothing is known save their titles and incipits. The *Expositio super 'Missus est angelus Gabriel'* echoes the four sermons on the same verse (Luke 1: 26) by Bernard of Clairvaux; the *De onere jumentorum austri* (Isaiah 30: 6) was clearly indebted to Ailred's sermons on the burdens of Isaiah; the *De vera amicitia* perhaps continued Ailred's dialogue *De spirituali amicitia*, in which Walter was proud to have been one of the participants; and the Nicholas against whom Walter wrote his *De conceptione beatae Mariae* was Nicholas of St Albans, whose treatise in defence of the doctrine of the immaculate conception against Bernard of Clairvaux still survives. Judging from the *Centum sententiae*, Walter's works might have been learned and thorough rather than inspired and original, though Leland thought them worthy of publication.

According to John Bale (*d.* 1563), Walter died and was buried at Rievaulx—there is no reason to doubt the tradition—but the date of his death, as that of his birth, remains unknown.
DAVID N. BELL

Sources *The life of Ailred of Rievaulx by Walter Daniel*, ed. and trans. F. M. Powicke (1950); repr. (1978); repr. with a new introduction by M. Dutton (1994) · *Commentarii de scriptoribus Britannicis, auctore Joanne Lelando*, ed. A. Hall, 1 (1709), 200–01 · C. H. Talbot, 'The *Centum sententiae* of Walter Daniel', *Sacris erudiri*, 11 (1960), 266–383 · Bale, *Cat.*, 1.213

Daniel, William [Uilliam Ó Domhnaill] (*c.*1575–1628), Church of Ireland archbishop of Tuam, was born in Kilkenny. His parentage is unknown. One of the first three scholars of Trinity College, Dublin, in 1592, he was elected junior fellow the following year. He graduated MA in 1595 and was made DD on 24 February 1603. In 1596 Daniel was sent to Galway to assist in improving the state of the Church of Ireland in the city, although he was still reader in Trinity College. Writing to Lord Burghley in September 1596, he says he has spent nine months painfully instructing the people in both English and Irish and 'rooting out their famous idols, which they served'. He also recounts how the Catholic clergy of Galway, displeased with his efforts, incited their flock against him. He was still in Galway in June 1601.

At some time during the 1590s Daniel took upon himself the translation of the New Testament into Irish. This had been begun by Nicholas Walsh, bishop of Ossory. After Walsh's murder in Kilkenny in 1585, it was continued by John Kearnaigh (Seaán Ó Cearnaigh), Miellien Oge Mac Brody (Maoilín Óg Mac Bruaideadha; *d.* December 1602), and Nehemias Donellan (Fearganainm Ó Domhnalláin), who became archbishop of Tuam in 1595. The translation had been requested by the Irish privy council as early as the 1560s. Daniel tells us that by the year 1597 the gospels, as far as the sixth chapter of St Luke, had already been typeset at the expense of Sir Richard Bingham, president of Connaught. The rest of St Luke's gospel and the gospel of St John were in manuscript, and the remainder of the book as yet untranslated. Daniel's New Testament incorporated the work already done. He asserts that he based his translation on the original Greek, and a comparison of the Irish with the *Textus receptus* vindicates his claim. Daniel was assisted by Domhnall Óg Ó hUiginn, who transcribed the remaining portion of the New Testament for the printer.

The book was printed in folio in 1602 in the house of Sir William Ussher, clerk of the council. The printer mentioned on the title-page was John Francke (or Franckton), the earlier portion of the book having apparently been typeset in 1592–7 in Trinity College by William Kearnaigh, a relative of John's. William Kearnaigh was untrustworthy in his business dealings, but a better printer than Francke. The type used had first been employed by John Kearney (*d.* 1572) to publish an Irish catechism (*Aibidil gaoidhilge & caiticiosma*) in 1571. Though not inelegant, the fount is a curious mixture of roman, italic, and Gaelic letters. It seems to have been based on the Anglo-Saxon type designed by John Day for Archbishop Parker in 1567. The

Irish letters were independently cut, however. In February 1603 Daniel went to London to present a copy to the queen, who died the next month. It is not known whether she ever saw the book. Daniel prefixed to all the remaining copies of the 500 printed a dedicatory epistle addressed to the new king.

No reprint of Daniel's New Testament appeared until the quarto edition of 1681, which was published by Robert Everingham, in London, at the expense of Robert Boyle. The type used was a small Gaelic fount cut by Joseph Moxon in 1680. A further edition in roman characters was published together with Bedell's Old Testament in London in 1690, again at Boyle's expense. Numerous reprints of Daniel's New Testament followed, the last revision being that of Earnán de Siúnta, published in Dublin in 1951.

Having produced the Irish New Testament, Daniel was preferred to the treasurership of St Patrick's Cathedral. In 1605, at the insistence of Sir Arthur Chichester, Daniel undertook the translation of the Book of Common Prayer and in the same year went to Connaught to get help with the work. The book was finished by 1608 and Daniel saw the quarto volume, entitled *Leabhar na nUrnaightheadh gComhchoidchiond*, through the press himself. John Francke was again the printer, though by this time he had his own establishment and styled himself 'printer to the king of Ireland'. As a reward for his new translation Daniel was elevated to the archbishopric of Tuam, being consecrated in August 1609. He held his treasurership *in commendam* until his death in 1628. Daniel's dedication to Chichester is dated from 20 October 1609 'from my House in Sainct Patricks Close, Dublin', and in it he begs his patron 'to send [the prayer book] abroad into the Country Churches, together with the elder brother the new Testament, to be fostered and fomented'.

The work begins with a translation of the English Act of Uniformity, rather than the Irish one (which had been passed in the Irish parliament in 1560). The translation follows the English prayer book of 1604, though it omits both the ordinal and the psalter. A cleric using the Irish book would have had to say the psalms in either Latin or English. Daniel was puritan in sympathy as can be seen, among other things, from his translation of 'priest' as *minisdir* ('minister') throughout, and 'Catholick' as *comhchoidchionn* ('universal'). One commentator has described Daniel's Book of Common Prayer as 'one of the monuments of Irish translation, though one greatly ignored' (McAdoo, 253). An inferior translation of the Book of Common Prayer was published in the Moxon type in 1712. Pól Ó Coigligh produced a revised version of Daniel's Book of Common Prayer in 1931.

Daniel's translations were used fairly widely. The Franciscan Hugh Mac Caughwell, disturbed that the two books were seducing the Irish from the Catholic faith, wrote in 1618 that the Irish Book of Common Prayer was not so much a *leabhar aifrinn* ('mass-book') as a *leabhar iffrinn eiriceachda* ('book of heretical hell'). It is clear, none the less, that Mac Caughwell had read his own copy of Daniel's New Testament closely.

In September 1610 Daniel was sworn of the Irish privy council. In 1611 a plan was drawn up to transfer the seat of the archbishop to the collegiate church in Galway, since the cathedral in Tuam was in ruins. The plan was not carried out, however. Tuam became a parliamentary borough in 1612 and the cathedral was repaired. Daniel attended the parliament held in Dublin in 1613 and the convocation of 1615 which adopted the Irish articles of faith, with their strong Calvinist bias.

Little is known about Daniel's family. His sister Elizabeth married Nehemias Donellan, Daniel's predecessor in the see of Tuam. She probably met her future husband when he was resident in the diocese of Kilkenny in 1591. John and Edmund, the sons of Nehemias and Elizabeth Donellan, are both mentioned in Daniel's will, dated 4 July 1628, as are Daniel's wife, Mary, and his daughter Cathleen (Catelin). Nehemias and Elizabeth Donellan had three further sons, James, Teigue, and Murtagh. A third nephew of William Daniel's, Richard Butler, is also mentioned in his will, which suggests that Daniel had at least one other sister. It has been claimed that Godfrey Daniel (born c.1618), who produced an Irish-language catechism in 1652, was a relative of William's. This is unlikely, since Godfrey's surname in Irish was Mac Domhnaill, not Ó Domhnaill. William Daniel died in Tuam on 11 July 1628 and was buried there in the tomb of his predecessor and brother-in-law, Donellan.   N. J. A. WILLIAMS

Sources N. J. A. Williams, *I bprionta i leabhar* (1987) · *CSP Ire., 1600–01; 1603–6; 1625–32* · J. S. Brewer and W. Bullen, eds., *Calendar of the Carew manuscripts, 6: Miscellaneous papers*, PRO (1873), 1603–24 · A. Vicars, ed., *Index to the prerogative wills of Ireland, 1536–1810* (1897) · *DNB* · *The whole works of Sir James Ware concerning Ireland*, ed. and trans. W. Harris, 2 vols. in 3 (1739–45, [1746]) · H. R. McAdoo, 'The Irish translations of the Book of Common Prayer', *Éigse*, 2 (1940), 250–57

Daniel, William Barker (1754–1833), Church of England clergyman and writer on field sports, was born in Colchester, the son of William Daniel. Little is known about his early life except that he was educated at Felsted and that his father was an attorney. In 1771 he went to Christ's College, Cambridge, where he obtained a BA in 1787 and an MA three years later. He was ordained deacon at Lincoln in December 1785 and priest at Gloucester on 12 March 1786, although he was never beneficed. In 1788 he was appointed private chaplain to the prince regent, a position he is believed to have retained until his retirement.

Daniel's notoriety stemmed principally from his authorship of *Rural Sports*, published in 1801. The advertisement for the text led one correspondent in the *Gentleman's Magazine* to conclude contemptuously that 'I can not help thinking that he is fitter to act the character of Nimrod than that of a dignitary in the Church of England' (*GM*, 1st ser., 72/2, 1802, 621). While the comment was firmly rebuked in a note by the editor the caustic critique has been widely cited in subsequent biographical reviews of Daniel's career. His two-volume text dedicated to J. H. Strutt MP was, on his own admission, mainly a compendium; for example, in the section on fishing he reviewed the main species before embarking on an alphabetical review of the different counties and their river systems. Proving very popular among contemporary sportsmen and even naturalists, the volumes describe in detail hunting, coursing, and fishing and contain many impressive plates interspersed with occasional references to Daniel's own exploits. They were reissued as a three-volume set in 1812, with a supplementary fourth volume, dedicated to the marquess of Blandford, published in 1813. The latter, though written in a more careless style, contained a miscellany of anecdotes and receipts. *Rural Sports* provided the basis of many more modern texts and constitutes an early historical record of shooting before the introduction of the revolutionary breach-loading guns in the mid-nineteenth century. The significance of Daniel's text was still being eulogized as late as 1886 on the grounds that it contained:

> one of the earliest, if not the earliest authentic accounts of wild-fowl shooting with punt and gun, beside many incidents connected with fowling, that are of great interest as records of the sport of catching and shooting ducks in past days. (Walsingham and Gallway, p. 314)

Daniel was not only interested in sport but was the author of several other texts, the most detailed of which was an account of the fraudulent export of debenture goods that was published in 1795 together with his proposals for ending such practices. He was also the author of two works that addressed the controversial sale of the rectory at Hanningfield in Essex. His attempts to draw public attention to this local issue coincided with his move in 1813 to Garden Row, London, within the rules of the king's bench. His text *Plain thoughts, of former years upon the Lord's prayer: with deference, addressed to Christians in the present period*, consisting of eight sermons, was published in 1822. He continued to live at Garden Row until his death there in 1833.

Daniel was an enigmatic figure whose rural activities seemed only in retrospect to conflict with his role as a minister in the Church of England. His contemporaries tended to see such sporting activities as integral to the lifestyle of the rural clergy. This tendency to focus on one aspect of his life has caused historians to neglect his other writings. JOHN MARTIN

Sources Venn, *Alum. Cant.* · QR, 118 (1865) · GM, 1st ser., 103/2 (1833), 255 · Lord Walsingham [T. De Grey] and R. P. Gallway, *Shooting*, 2: *Moor and marsh* (1886) · *Annual Register* (1833) · *British Museum general catalogue of printed books … to 1955*, BM, 263 vols. (1959–66) · *DNB*

Likenesses P. W. Tomkins, stipple (after G. Engleheart), BM, NPG; repro. in W. B. Daniel, *Rural sports*, [another edn], 3 vols. (1812)

Daniel, William Thomas Shave (1806–1891), law reformer, was born on 17 March 1806 at Stapenhill, Derbyshire, the eldest son of William Daniel, a cheesemonger in nearby Burton upon Trent, Staffordshire. He went to Repton School in February 1815 and was articled to a solicitor, probably at Atherstone, Warwickshire, on 16 March 1822. Without completing his articles he entered Lincoln's Inn

on 27 January 1825, and was called to the bar on 5 February 1830.

Daniel practised initially as an equity draftsman and went the midland circuit, building up a large assize practice. From May 1842 to November 1848 he was recorder of Ipswich. On 11 July 1851 he was made a QC, and on 3 November of the same year he became a bencher of his inn. He was twice married: first, on 12 September 1830, to Harriet (d. 1838), eldest daughter of John Mayou of Coleshill, Warwickshire; and second, on 11 April 1840, to Sarah (b. 1808), eldest daughter of the Revd Arthur William *Trollope (headmaster of Christ's Hospital and a distant relation of the novelist Anthony Trollope) and his wife, Sarah. Daniel's marriage to Sarah Trollope was one of several between these two families.

In the 1850s Daniel joined the Law Amendment Society. He was a council member of the Association for the Promotion of Social Science from 1858, soon after its foundation, to its dissolution in 1886. Although 'not a political partizan' (*Law Times*, 50, 1872, 213), he twice contested the borough of Tamworth, standing as a Conservative 'on a platform of strict purity' (*Law Times*, 76, 1884, 394); he was soundly defeated by the Peel family in 1859 and 1865.

In 1863 Daniel took up the cause of improving the system of reporting law cases. The defects were widely acknowledged: the productions of the authorized reporters of each court were often dilatory and prolix, while several weekly publications competed vigorously for the market with earlier reports. Competition generated unselective reporting, a proliferation costly to practitioners and offensive to advocates of law as a methodical science. Previous initiatives had foundered largely because opinions differed on whether reporting should be the responsibility of government, courts, bar, or publishers, but Daniel's energy and persistence, encouraged by Roundell Palmer, enlisted enough backing for Palmer, by then attorney-general, to summon a meeting of the bar on 2 December 1863. A committee was established and its proposals were for the most part implemented in 1865 with the creation of an Incorporated Council for Law Reporting. Under its auspices the official series of law reports appeared, supplemented by weekly notes of recent cases. At the end of the twentieth century these were still the most authentic reports, albeit without the privilege of exclusive citation which Daniel advocated. Daniel was vice-chairman of the council until 1869 and also sat on the abortive Law Digest Commission from 1868 to 1870.

On 21 March 1867 Lord Chelmsford made Daniel county court judge for district 11, which straddled the Pennines and had its principal court at Bradford. He declined to move to Leeds in 1875 but took on the equity and bankruptcy work there in exchange for the transfer of two courts from his district. He lived initially at Skipton and later in Bradford, where he was held in high regard. Daniel was one of the best-known of the county court judges, for he ensured that his most instructive judgments were carried by the legal press, and he disseminated his views on the legal topics of the day through speeches, pamphlets, and papers to congresses of the Social Science Association. He also gave oral evidence to select committees on imprisonment for debt (which he supported), bills of sale, county courts, and tribunals of commerce.

Daniel, whose 'very profile and attitude tell you that he is a man of indomitable will' (*Pen and Ink Sketches in Chancery*, 6), was a strong advocate of the fusion of jurisdictions and the decentralization of civil justice. He was keenly interested in bankruptcy and was a prescient critic of Joseph Chamberlain's attempt to create a 'poor man's bankruptcy' in the Bankruptcy Act of 1883. He described himself as 'preferring … the practical to the theoretical—the experiences of the exchange, the market and the workshop to the lucubrations of the library and the scholastic logic of the courts' (*Transactions of the National Association for the Promotion of Social Science*, 1876, 180), and though opposed to businessmen sitting as judges he welcomed proposals for them to sit alongside the judge as assessors in commercial cases.

After some months of poor health Daniel resigned on 12 April 1884 and went to live at Leamington Spa, where he died at his home, 51 The Parade, on 9 June 1891. He was survived by his wife and by a son of his first marriage, the Revd William Mayou (*b*. 1837). The first son of his second marriage, Arthur William Trollope Daniel (1841–1873), a barrister of Lincoln's Inn, was well known as an athlete and sportsman.   PATRICK POLDEN

Sources J. Foster, *Men-at-the-bar: a biographical hand-list of the members of the various inns of court*, 2nd edn (1885) · Boase, *Mod. Eng. biog.* · W. T. S. Daniel, *The history and origin of the law reports* (1884) · Holdsworth, *Eng. law*, 15.248–57 · W. P. Baildon, ed., *The records of the Honorable Society of Lincoln's Inn: the black books*, 4 (1902) · *The records of the Honorable Society of Lincoln's Inn: the black books*, 5, ed. R. Roxburgh (1968) · W. P. Baildon, ed., *The records of the Honorable Society of Lincoln's Inn: admissions*, 2 (1896) · *Pen and ink sketches in chancery … by a lounger in the courts*, 1 [1866], 6 · 'Select committee on the County Courts Jurisdiction Bill', *Parl. papers* (1878), 11.143–54, no. 267 [minutes of evidence] · J. Foster, *The peerage, baronetage, and knightage of the British empire for 1882*, 2 vols. [1882] · F. W. S. Craig, *British parliamentary election results, 1832–85*, 2nd edn (1989) · J. Whishaw, *Synopsis of the members of the English bar* (1835) · M. Messiter, ed., Derby, Repton School register, 1910 · *CGPLA Eng. & Wales* (1891) · *GM*, 2nd ser., 9 (1838), 330 · Venn, *Alum. Cant.* · 'The law of bankruptcy', *Transactions of the National Association for the Promotion of Social Science* (1876), 180 · *Law Times* (20 July 1872), 213 · *Law Times* (3 Feb 1877), 245–6 · *Law Times* (15 Jan 1876), 202–4 · *Law Times* (29 March 1884), 394 · *Law Times* (26 April 1884), 461

Wealth at death £940 6s. 2d.: 1891, *CGPLA Eng. & Wales*

Daniell, Alexander (1599–1668), diarist, was born on 12 December 1599 in North Street, Middelburg, Zeeland, in the United Provinces, the only son of Richard Daniell (1560?–1630), a wealthy merchant adventurer from Cornwall, and his first wife, Jaquelina (1568?–1601), widow of Reignold Coprot and daughter of Jan van Hoergarden of Antwerp, in the Spanish Netherlands, and his wife, Maria. His father lived for twenty-eight years in Middelburg, rising to be the deputy of the Merchant Adventurers' company there. After his wife's death in 1601, he sent Alexander and his half-sister Maria Coprot to stay with their maternal grandmother in Antwerp, where they remained

for several years. Alexander was sent to his uncle, Jenkin Daniell, in Truro, Cornwall, about 1610, and was educated at the grammar school there. His father, now married to Margaretha van Gengen (*b. c.*1590), returned to Truro on James I's dissolution of the Merchant Adventurers in 1614. There he became a burgess and was MP for the town in the 1624 and 1628 parliaments. Alexander matriculated from Lincoln College, Oxford, on 21 November 1617. He became a fellow-commoner, but was removed by his father in 1618 for extravagance. He studied at Leiden University about 1620, and for a few years accompanied his father on journeys to the Netherlands.

By this time Daniell was keeping copies of his correspondence, sometimes in verse to his friends, a practice which later developed into a diary. He had also begun writing poetry, including the poignant 'On the Sight of his Mistress' to his first and thwarted love. He married Grace, daughter of John Bluet of Little Colan, Cornwall, on 20 January 1625, probably at Newlyn. They rented property at Tresillian, near Truro, and had eight sons, of whom five lived to adulthood, and two daughters. On the death of his father, who died intestate in 1630, Daniell inherited all his land and property, despite the claims of his detested stepmother, and five half-brothers and -sisters. The next year he successfully resisted a fine on distraint of knighthood on the ground that he had not yet inherited when Charles I was crowned. In 1632 he moved to Penzance, where he had inherited the manor of Alwarton, Penzance, and Mousehole. He built a house at Laregan in 1639.

By the time his eldest son, Richard, was born, Daniell had a strong Calvinistic faith, expressed in his belief that God had made the child his lifelong servant. He later catalogued 'Certaine … altogether undeserved Favo[u]rs of Almightie God', ranging from his praying for a ship about to run aground, at which the wind dropped, to a dog tearing up a fraudulent lease when the forger was carousing, thus preserving Daniell's title. His piety is conveyed in hundreds of poems which reflect on aspects of Christian life and faith. They are more notable for their feeling than their quality.

Daniell's sympathies in the civil war were royalist, and he raised horse and fought, as did his sons Richard and Alexander, in the siege of Plymouth in 1643. He describes the battle of Stratton as between the Devonians and the Cornish, 'when God gave a wonderful victorie to o[u]r Cornish who stood for a King' (Cornwall RO, AD1239 D/16/2, fol. 257). In 1644 he contributed, with difficulty, £30 to the king, though he later claimed that it was to avoid distraint and imprisonment. He stated that he was forced under threat of sequestration to ride in 1646 with the Cornwall commissioners to confiscate arms, but only noted them, and endeavoured to prevent soldiers 'embezzling' them. Nevertheless, in 1648 he was put under arrest by the parliamentarians, and his own guns were confiscated. His ambiguous activities caused his name to be given to the exchequer in 1662, which he contested. Throughout, retaining his estates was a preoccupation.

By 1665 Daniell was deteriorating in health. He and his friends light-heartedly wrote epitaphs, and following his death on 12 April 1668 his gravestone in Madron churchyard read: 'Belgia me birth, Britain me breeding gave, Cornwall a wife, ten children, and a grave.'

ELIZABETH ALLEN

Sources Cornwall RO, AD567; AD1239 D/16/2, fols. 1, 2, 13, 23–5, 27, 44, 47, 113, 233–5, 237–9, 241–6, 248–52, 256–7, 259, 261, 263 · J. S. Courtney, *Guide to Penzance and its neighbours* (1845), 75–6, 78–9, 87 · Bodl. Oxf., MS Rawl. 789, fols. 1v–3 · *DNB* · *Reg. Oxf.*, 2/2.364 · C. Hill, *The century of revolution* (1961), 35 · Foster, *Alum. Oxon.*
Archives Cornwall RO, family coucher book containing autograph verse and copy letters · Cornwall RO, memorandum book, autobiographical notes, and copy corresp.

Daniell, Edward Thomas (1804–1842), artist and traveller, was born on 6 June 1804 in Charlotte Street, London, the son of Thomas Daniell, attorney-general of Dominica, and Anne, daughter of John Drosier. He was educated first at Norwich School under Edward Valpy, where the drawing master was John Crome, and then at Balliol College, Oxford, which he entered in December 1823. He graduated BA in 1828 and MA in 1831.

Daniell learnt to etch with the Norwich artist Joseph Stannard, and became the friend and patron of John Linnell, the father-in-law of Samuel Palmer and friend of William Blake. In 1829 and 1830 he travelled on the continent. He was ordained deacon in 1832 and priest in 1833; he was a curate at Banham, near Attleborough, from 1832 until 1834, when he was appointed to a curacy at St Mark's, North Audley Street, London.

Daniell lived in London until 1840 and regularly entertained several of the leading artists of the time, including J. M. W. Turner and David Roberts. His letters show his continued encouragement of Linnell; he is said to have given a series of dinner parties at which he seated Linnell opposite Turner so that he could observe and subsequently paint him, since Turner was known to dislike sitting for portraits. Daniell exhibited at the Royal Academy and the British Institution.

Prompted by Roberts's drawings of Egypt and Palestine, Daniell left England in 1840 to travel in the eastern Mediterranean. By September he was in Corfu, travelling from there to Athens and Alexandria. In June 1841 he went on to Sinai and then to Beirut, and in December joined the *Beacon*, a naval vessel which was to convey back to Britain archaeological remains discovered by Sir Charles Fellows at Xanthus. In January and February 1842 Daniell made excursions from Xanthus, but when Fellows departed in March, he remained in Lycia with the naval surveyor T. A. B. Spratt and the naturalist Edward Forbes. Together they explored many ancient cities, including eighteen sites said to be 'unknown to the geographers of antiquity', of which Termessus was the most important. Daniell then left his companions to visit and sketch a number of further sites alone, including Selge, Marmora, and Perge. He contracted malaria and died at the residence of the British consul in Adalia, Syria, on 24 September 1842. An account of his solitary travels forms part of volume 2 of T. A. B. Spratt and Edward Forbes, *Travels in Lycia, Milyas and the Cibyratis* (1847), which also includes details of some of the coins and inscriptions which he discovered.

Although Daniell is generally considered an artist of the Norwich school, he was less a provincial than its other more notable members. His reputation rests chiefly upon his small output of etchings, many of which date from his residence in Norwich, but the bulk of his works (most of which are at Norwich Castle, the Victoria and Albert Museum, and the British Museum) were the product of his final tour. They are free pen sketches on buff paper washed in using a limited range of colours, which have been admired for their freedom, although it is unclear how Daniell intended to develop them.

RICHARD SMAIL

Sources F. R. Beechend, *E. T. Daniell: a memoir* (1889) · T. A. B. Spratt and E. Forbes, *Travels in Lycia, Milyas and the Cibyratis*, 2 vols. (1847) · D. P. Clifford, *Watercolours of the Norwich School* (1965) · *GM*, 2nd ser., 19 (1843), 102
Archives BM · Norwich Castle Museum · V&A
Likenesses J. Linnell, oils, 1835, Norwich Castle Museum; repro. in Beechend, *E. T. Daniell*

Daniell, Georgiana Fanny Shipley (1836–1894). *See under* Daniell, Louisa (1808/9–1871).

Daniell, John Frederic (1790–1845), experimental philosopher and businessman, was born on 12 March 1790 at Essex Street, Strand, London, the eldest son of George Daniell (*c*.1760–1833), barrister, and his wife, Louisa Hahn (*d*. 1833). His mother was of German birth but had long lived in England. Educated at home by tutors, he received a good classical education. He early developed strong scientific tastes, and attended the lectures of Adam Walker which inspired his earliest scientific experimentation and reading. From 1808 to 1821 Daniell worked for a sugar refining establishment which belonged to a relative of his mother. Despite his business activities he was able to pursue his scientific interests. In 1812 he attended lectures delivered by William Thomas Brande at the Anatomical School in Great Windmill Street and they formed a lifelong friendship. Through his association with Brande he became a fellow of the Royal Society (1814), and began a lasting connection with the Royal Institution (where Brande had become a professor in 1813). In 1815, with Brande and another friend, he went on a geological tour of Wales and northern Ireland. In 1816 they toured the alps. In the same year Daniell became one of the managers of the Royal Institution (to 1819) and began to assist Brande in editing the first twenty volumes of the *Quarterly Journal of Science*, which though not a formal publication of the institution was closely connected with it.

On 4 September 1817 Daniell married Charlotte Rule (*d*. 1834); they had two sons and five daughters. They spent most of their married life in Gower Street, London. In 1819 he began work on meteorology; he invented a new dew point hygrometer and improved the methods of maintaining weather records. In 1823 he published *Meteorological Essays* (2nd edn 1827, 3rd edn 1845). The following year he returned to business as a director of the Continental Gas Company. During the first half of 1825, together with William Congreve and George Landsman, he visited many continental cities to investigate the possibilities of lighting them with gas.

Daniell was interested in the dissemination of scientific knowledge: in 1827 he helped to found the Society for the Diffusion of Useful Knowledge, and in 1841 was involved in the foundation of the Chemical Society. With the support of Samuel Taylor Coleridge he was appointed in 1831 the first professor of chemistry at King's College, London. Though he had never delivered a lecture before he quickly became a respected lecturer. From 1836 until his death he also held the professorship of chemistry and geology at the East India Company's military seminary at Addiscombe, where he lectured every August and September. At the Royal Institution he delivered three Friday evening discourses, and during Faraday's illness in 1840–41 he stepped in to deliver the Christmas lectures.

In 1830 Daniell invented a new pyrometer, and started construction of a water barometer that he set up at the Royal Society. His appointment at King's College gave him access to a newly equipped laboratory, and he turned his attention to electricity. In the course of this work he invented the Daniell cell, a battery which gave constant, as opposed to decreasing, current, and which was of great value to electrical researchers. A photograph of Daniell with Faraday shows a Daniell cell between them. Much of his work on electricity and forces he wrote up in his *Introduction to Chemical Philosophy* (1839, 2nd edn 1843), which also contains information on the work of Faraday and others.

By the end of the 1830s Daniell's reputation was such that the government sought his advice on technical issues such as lightning conductors, and why the protectors of the copper bottoms of ships did not work in the tropics. In 1839 he became chemistry examiner for London University and foreign secretary of the Royal Society, both tasks that he continued until his death. He was a visitor of the Royal Institution in the periods 1822–31, 1833–4, and 1839–41. He was one of the few men to win all three medals of the Royal Society: the Rumford medal in 1832, the Copley medal in 1837 (for his cell), and the royal medal in 1842. In 1828 he received the Fuller gold medal of the Royal Institution, and in 1843 Oxford University made him a DCL.

In June 1834 Daniell moved to Norwood, London, for the sake of his wife's health; however, she died in August of that year, a blow from which he never fully recovered. His own health was poor after a lung haemorrhage in 1841. On 13 March 1845, after delivering a lecture at King's College, he attended a meeting of the Royal Society council at Somerset House, where he collapsed and died of apoplexy within five minutes. A devout Anglican, he was buried at Norwood cemetery on 17 March.   FRANK A. J. L. JAMES

Sources 'Life' of J. F. Daniell, King's Lond., Daniell MSS, box 1 · J. F. Daniell, *Elements of meteorology*, ed. W. A. Miller and C. Tomlinson, 3rd edn (1845), memoir of the author xiii–xxxv · *Abstracts of the Papers Communicated to the Royal Society of London*, 5 (1843–50), 577–80 · D. I. Davies, 'John Frederic Daniell, 1791–1845', *Chemistry in Britain*, 26 (1990), 946–9, 960 · V. Gold, 'Samuel Taylor Coleridge and the appointment of J. F. Daniell, FRS, as professor of chemistry at King's College, London', *Notes and Records of the Royal Society*, 28 (1973–4), 25–9 · *GM*, 2nd ser., 23 (1845), 554–5 · *Catalogue of scientific papers*, Royal Society, 19 vols. (1867–1925)

Archives King's Lond., corresp. and papers | LUL, letters to Society for the Diffusion of Useful Knowledge · RS, letters to Sir John Lubbock
Likenesses oils, King's Lond. · photograph (with Faraday), King's Lond. · two engravings, RS

Daniell [*née* Drake], **Louisa** (1808/9–1871), philanthropist, was orphaned soon after her birth. She married Captain Frederic Daniell of the 18th Madras native infantry; they had two children before he died at Kotagiri on 3 April 1837. On returning to England she lived primarily in the midlands, educating her son, Frederick William, at Rugby School. Her daughter, **Georgiana Fanny Shipley Daniell** (1836–1894), philanthropist, born on 20 May 1836 in India, was sent to a school in Brighton. Distressed by the sight of so many vagrants (reportedly 14,000 a year) passing through Rugby, Louisa Daniell established missions for the destitute in the neighbourhood. Over five years she established five village missions, often with financial endowments from local noblemen: reading rooms were opened, religious tracts distributed, and Bible reading and sewing classes held. Her basic aims were to save souls and counteract the spread of Roman Catholicism.

Through this work Louisa Daniell came in contact with the County Towns Mission Society, the secretary of which, a Mr Wilson, urged her to direct her missionary zeal towards Aldershot. By the early 1860s Aldershot had a garrison of nearly 15,000 soldiers. These soldiers had few recreational facilities other than eighteen canteens on site and the twenty-five public houses and forty-seven beer houses that had been built around the camp, many of which were public brothels (approximately one-third of the soldiers were hospitalized each year with sexually transmitted diseases). Aldershot, argued Mrs Daniell, was 'one of Satan's strongholds' (Daniell, 26)—a camp and town desperately in need of spiritual uplift. The Wesleyan Methodist Charles Henry Kelly had already opened the first soldiers' home in a small basement club-house in Chatham in 1861, but Mrs Daniell had access to more substantial funding. Supported by some of the great evangelical philanthropists—the third earl of Shaftesbury, Lord Kinnaird, Stevenson Blackwood, and Robert Baxter—she opened her first soldiers' home in October 1862. Baxter, Lord Radstock, and Captain E. Gardner Fishbourne RN, shared the weekly services and joined the trustees who had agreed to back the foundation of her more permanent Mission Hall and Soldiers' Home and Institute. Begun on 11 February 1863, the hall was officially opened on 11 October 1863. It eventually had a lecture hall seating up to 500 for services, a tea and coffee bar, a smoking and games room, a reading room with newspapers, and a lending library, as well as a classroom capable of holding 150 people, and several bedrooms.

Mrs Daniell and her daughter, Georgiana, who continued her work, regarded their task as primarily a spiritual one. Every evening, save for the weekly temperance meeting, they organized hymn singing and scripture talks in the classroom, with Sunday evening services in the hall. They also founded a mothers' meeting, a women's missionary working party, and a Band of Hope for service children. Yet their activities had a greater social impact at a time when the state (as distinct from some individual regiments) provided relatively few recreational and educational facilities for the rank and file. For those soldiers who were undeterred by the evangelical piety and by the strict prohibition of alcohol, the homes provided respectable meeting places and centres where they could repair deficiencies in their education. For soldiers' and pensioners' wives, the sewing classes taught them a skill from which they could earn as much as 3 to 4s. a week by the late 1870s, while the weekly savings club enabled them to put money aside for clothes, shoes, bedding, and coals. Women married 'off the strength' (and so denied free quarters) received charity and visits from the Bible women of the Aldershot Mission Hall Soldiers' Wife Aid Society, founded a few years before Mrs Daniell's death.

Both Louisa and Georgiana Daniell were convinced that these activities contributed to improving standards of behaviour within the army. In this respect, they invested great hopes in the Total Abstinence Society, established soon after the opening of the hall in 1863. Within a year the society had 500 members and, although many lapsed either temporarily or permanently, it continued to hold regular meetings, monitored its numbers on a weekly basis, and later awarded medals for those who kept their pledge. If these endeavours hardly transformed morals within the army as a whole (for many men were driven away by the proselytizing and the temperance regime), they may have contributed to the improving standards of behaviour within the army in the later nineteenth century.

After Mrs Daniell died from breast cancer in Great Malvern on 16 September 1871 Georgiana continued her work, opening homes at Chatham, Weedon, London, Colchester, Manchester, Windsor, and Plymouth. For another twenty-two years she laboured on behalf of ordinary soldiers, and their wives and children, and also promoted foreign missionary activities. She earned the sobriquet the Soldiers' Friend, and her initiatives were replicated in Ireland by Elsie Sandes, who opened the first soldiers' home at Tralee in 1877, and by some churches. The state moved in a similar direction, building barracks towards the end of the century with many more recreational facilities for the other ranks. Georgiana Daniell died unmarried in the Mission Hall and Soldiers' Home, Aldershot, after a protracted illness brought on by influenza, on 24 June 1894. On 29 June her coffin was carried on a gun carriage for burial in the military cemetery at Aldershot, at which her mother's remains had earlier been interred on 26 September 1871.   EDWARD M. SPIERS

Sources G. Daniell, Aldershot: a record of Mrs Daniell's work amongst soldiers and its sequel (1879) · F. D. How, Noble women of our time (1901) · H. J. Hanham, 'Religion and nationality in the mid-Victorian army', War and society: historical essays in honour and memory of J. R. Western, 1928–1971, ed. M. R. D. Foot (1973) · A. R. Skelley, The Victorian army at home: the recruitment and terms and conditions of the British regular, 1859–1899 (1977) · E. M. Spiers, The late Victorian army, 1868–1902 (1992) · M. Trustram, Women of the regiment: marriage and the Victorian army (1984) · O. Anderson, 'The growth of Christian militarism in mid-Victorian Britain', EngHR, 86 (1971), 46–72 · K. Hendrickson, 'A kinder, gentler British army: mid-Victorian experiments in the management of army vice at Gibraltar and Aldershot', War and Society, 14 (1996), 21–33 · J. H. Y. Briggs, 'Daniell, Georgina', The Blackwell dictionary of evangelical biography, 1730–1860, ed. D. M. Lewis (1995) · 'Aldershot Mission Hall and Soldiers' Institute', Sheldrake's Aldershot and Sandhurst Military Gazette (14 Feb 1863), 3 · Boase, Mod. Eng. biog. · d. cert.
Likenesses photograph, repro. in How, Noble women of our time (1901), frontispiece
Wealth at death under £450: probate, 16 Oct 1871, CGPLA Eng. & Wales · £89 13s. 10d.—Georgiana Daniell: probate, 20 July 1894, CGPLA Eng. & Wales

Daniell [née Carter], **Madeline Margaret** (1832–1906), educationist, was born at Secrole, India, on 19 May 1832, the daughter of Major Henry Carter of the Bengal native infantry and his wife, Helen Gray. She attended the Edinburgh Institution for the Education of Young Ladies and a finishing school in Europe. On her return to India she married on 13 November 1851 Charles Astell Daniell (1833–1855), a cornet in the 18th light cavalry. He died in Lahore on 24 November 1855 leaving her with one son.

Madeline Daniell made her home at 1 Inverleith Terrace, Edinburgh, where, in the 1860s, she played an important role in the campaign for higher education for women. When the Edinburgh Ladies' Educational Association was being formed, the first meeting of the executive committee was held in her house in 1866 and she became honorary secretary. Mary Crudelius (president) and Mrs Ranken (treasurer) were the other office bearers. Their principal university advisers were professors Masson and Laurie and Dr Arthur Mitchell. The initial object of the association was to provide women with the opportunity for advanced post-school education, but specifically not to encourage women to provoke male opposition by attempting to enter the professions. In the first year (1867–8) 263 women enrolled for the programme which commenced in the Hopetoun Rooms as a series of lectures by Masson on the history of English literature. Thereafter other classes were developed in experimental physics and mental philosophy.

Mary Crudelius was an important leader of the group, but she suffered from poor health; in the period 1866–9 much of the work was actually taken on by Madeline Daniell, whose 'devoted labours … are often mentioned' by Mrs Crudelius in her correspondence (Burton, 23). Madeline attended many of the lectures and negotiated with Masson about the examinations which, it was agreed, had to be identical to those undertaken by male university students. She appears to have herself sat some of the first exams. Madeline formed friendly contacts with leaders of the women's movement elsewhere, including Emily Davies and Elizabeth Wolstenholme (Elmy), and was in contact with the organizers of the parallel Glasgow association. Madeline's sister Mrs De Lacy Evans, also the widow of an Indian officer and later wife of the editor of The Scotsman, was one of the group of women who in 1869 joined Sophia Jex-Blake in the unsuccessful attempt to enable women to gain admission to medical lectures at Edinburgh.

About 1870 Madeline Daniell moved to St Andrews to care for her invalid mother. There she played a part in the establishment of St Leonard's School for Girls, which provided middle-class girls with a high-quality education as a foundation for subsequent university-level study. All the teachers were to be women, one principal aim being to provide appropriate professional occupations for educated women. Madeline seems to have been one of the originators of the plan for St Leonard's and, in 1877, she was one of the two founding honorary secretaries of the St Andrews School for Girls Company.

After the deaths of her mother and her son Madeline Daniell moved to London, where she became active in work for the Charity Organization Society. She lived for a time in the East End of London, where she took a particular interest in the plight of impoverished women. In June 1887 she met the brilliant young essayist and poet Constance Naden (1858–1889), and for the next two years the women were close friends and companions. These were years which Madeline described as 'a time of great happiness'. In the autumn of 1887 the two women embarked on an extensive tour of Greece, Turkey, Egypt, and India, before returning to settle at Naden's house in Grosvenor Square. In 1889 Constance Naden died, and when her collection of essays, *Induction and Deduction*, was published in the following year under the editorship of Dr R. Lewins, Madeline contributed an affectionate 'Memoir' as an introduction, in which she described something of the friendship.

The early death of Naden resulted in another move for Madeline Daniell, on this occasion to Southport, where she lived for a period with Miss Kay Shuttleworth. There once again she was active in various women's and charitable organizations, including the Women's Suffrage Society, the Women's Local Government Society, and the University Extension Society. She was also a member of the Women's Liberal Association. From about 1898 she suffered from a prolonged paralysing illness which effectively ended her active career. Her last years were spent at Southsea, Hampshire, where she died at her home, Ashburton, in Ashburton Road, on 21 April 1906.

TOM BEGG

Sources *Englishwoman's Review*, 38 (1906), 207–10 · M. M. Crudelius, *A memoir of Mrs Crudelius*, ed. K. Burton (privately printed, Edinburgh, 1879) · M. M. Daniell, 'Memoir', in C. C. W. Naden, *Induction and deduction (and other essays)*, ed. R. Lewins (1890) · J. Grant and others, *St Leonards School, 1877–1927* (1927) · register of births, marriages and deaths, BL OIOC

Wealth at death £1129 10s. 1d.: probate, 6 July 1906, *CGPLA Eng. & Wales*

Daniell, Samuel (1775–1811), landscape and animal painter and traveller, was the second son of William Daniell (d. 1779), innkeeper of The Swan at Chertsey, and his wife, Sarah. Samuel was the younger brother of William *Daniell RA (1769–1837), and nephew of Thomas *Daniell RA FRS (1749–1840). He was educated at the East India College at Hertford and trained as an artist under the drawing-master there, Thomas Medland. He exhibited his first landscape at the Society of Artists in 1791 and continued to exhibit both there and at the Royal Academy periodically until his death.

Unable to make a living as a landscape painter in London, Daniell travelled to the Cape of Good Hope in 1799 in the suite of Sir George Yonge, governor and commander-in-chief at the Cape. His subsequent friendship with Lieutenant-General Francis Dundas resulted in his appointment as secretary and draughtsman to a mission to visit the country of the Booshuanas (Bechuanaland) under Mr Truter and Dr Somerville, in October 1801, to purchase cattle to replace those lost in the Cape Frontier War. During the perilous 700 mile trek to Lataku, the seat of King Mooliahaben of the Booshuanas, Daniell made a large number of drawings of the landscape, the wild animals, and the inhabitants of the interior. The full account of this journey is given as an appendix to Sir John Barrow's *Voyage to Cochin China* (1805), in which four engravings after Daniell's drawings are included. A year later the second edition of Sir John Barrow's *Travels into the Interior of South Africa* included eight engravings, by Thomas Medland, after Daniell's drawings.

Daniell returned to England in 1803 and immediately began to work up his drawings for publication in his most important work *African Scenery and Animals* (2 pts, 1804–5). This magnificent publication stated on the title-page that the aquatints reproduced were 'drawn and engraved Samuel Daniell'. Despite this it has generally been assumed that the engraving was done by his elder brother, William. This is by no means certain, as after Samuel's death the sale of his equipment reported in the *Ceylon Government Gazette* (May 1812) included copper plates for engraving.

Perennial financial problems and the attraction of exotic environments persuaded Daniell to leave England again in 1806, this time for Ceylon. There he became closely associated with the governor, Sir Thomas Maitland, who appointed him ranger of woods and forests. This gave Daniell the opportunity to explore the island and make numerous drawings of the landscape and animals. He sent a number of these home to his brother for engraving and these were published in 1808 as *A picturesque illustration of the scenery, animals and native inhabitants of the island of Ceylon*. He died of tropical fever in Ceylon on 16 December 1811, and was buried in Pettah burial-grounds. He was unmarried. An obituarist praised him for the accuracy of his drawings from natural history and commented on the esteem in which he was held by his friends in these terms:

> Mr Daniell was ever anxious with his own eye to explore every object worthy of research, and with his own hand to convey to the world a faithful representation of what he saw … His friends have to mourn the death of one who was endeared to them by every social amiable quality and the publick to regret the loss of a traveller, equally intrepid and indefatigable, from whose exertions much both of instruction and entertainment will have already been derived, but from whose skilful eye and practiced hand much more might reasonably have been expected. (*GM*)

After his death his elder brother continued to use his work for his publications on South African natural history, the most important of which were *Sketches Representing the Native Tribes and Scenery of Southern Africa* (1820), and *Twenty Varied Subjects of the Tribe of Antelopes* (1832), of which only five plates appear to have been published.

Many of Daniell's drawings and watercolours survive in various collections. The most important of these are in three albums in the Witwatersrand University, Johannesburg, in the Fehr collection in Cape Town, and in the Victoria and Albert Museum and the British Museum, London. His animal studies are both accurate and original, his landscapes reveal an empathy with wild places, and his figure studies are lively and sympathetic. His worked-up watercolours, with their sense of colour, clarity of light, and animated figures, suggest that the artist was at the forefront of the artistic developments at the beginning of the nineteenth century. Recently two oil paintings by Daniell have come to light. The first, done in South Africa, *A Korah Hottentot Village on the Bank of the Orange River*, is technically less assured and is softer in outline than the work of the elder Daniells, but it conveys a more intimate understanding of his subject. The second, *The Tullipot Tree: View in the Kiribadgoda District, Island of Ceylon*, was exhibited posthumously at the Royal Academy in 1812. It reflects his South African work but it is closer in style to that of his elder brother. Samuel was certainly the most innovative artist of this remarkable family.

H. M. CHICHESTER, *rev.* CHARLES GREIG

Sources T. Sutton, *The Daniells: artists and travellers* (1954) · J. Barrow, *A voyage to Cochin China* (1805) · J. Barrow, *Travels into the interior of south Africa*, 2nd edn, 2 vols. (1806) · Graves, *RA exhibitors* · Graves, *Artists* · *Oriental Annual*, 6 vols. (1834–9) · *GM*, 1st ser., 82/2 (1812), 295–6 · R. K. De Silva, *Early prints of Ceylon (Sri Lanka), 1800–1900: fully illustrated in colour and accompanied by original texts with biographical information* (1985) · BL OIOC · J. W. Bennett, *Ceylon and its capabilities* (1843)

Daniell, Thomas (1749–1840), landscape painter and printmaker, was born at Kingston upon Thames, Surrey, the son of an innkeeper at Chertsey. From 1763 to 1770 he was apprenticed to a Mr Maxwell as a coach-painter and spent the following three years working for Charles Catton RA, coach-painter to George III. In 1773 he entered the Royal Academy Schools and exhibited thirteen pictures at the academy from 1774 to 1784, including paintings from his tours of England through Somerset, Oxfordshire, and Yorkshire and depictions from Spenser's *Faerie Queen* (1780). In 1781 he secured a commission for six paintings of West Wycombe Park, Buckinghamshire, from Lord Le Despencer. In 1784 Daniell received permission from the East India Company to travel as 'engraver' to India with his nephew William *Daniell (1769–1837) as his assistant/apprentice. They left England on 7 April 1785 and arrived in Calcutta via Canton early in 1786. They worked primarily in the British capital of Calcutta, restoring paintings in the Council House and the Old Court House, as well as producing the first topographical series of prints of the city (*Views of Calcutta*, 1786–8, aquatint and etching), which according to contemporary diaries and inventories proved extraordinarily popular among both an Indian and a European clientele. It has been suggested

that Thomas Daniell was among the first British painters to use Indian assistants in printmaking; the influence of his landscape compositions and working techniques are visible in Indian topography, *c.*1790–1850 (including oils after the *Views* in the Victoria Memorial, Calcutta).

Thomas Daniell played an instrumental role in graphically documenting a wide geographical and cultural range of sites across the Indian subcontinent, travelling more extensively than any of his contemporary colonial artists, and earning him the title 'artist-adventurer'. Assisted by his nephew, Daniell made three tours: from Calcutta to Srinagar (1788–91), a circular tour from Mysore to Madras (1792–3), and in 1793 they visited Bombay and its temple sites—always sketching, drawing, and painting intensively as they travelled. A large part of the itinerary and artistic activities of Thomas Daniell are known from the diary kept by William Daniell (on loan to the India Office prints and drawings department, London). They made extensive use of a camera obscura and William Hodges' *Select Views of India* (1785–8) to compare with their own compositions. *En route* they also restored and completed pictures for Europeans, experimented with copperplate engraving, and occasionally made pencil portrait sketches. There is no evidence that they worked for Indian patrons at this time—although the nawab of Oudh, Asaf ud-Daula (1775–97) initially expressed an interest in having a series of views of his capital Lucknow (Uttar Pradesh) done in the same manner as the *Views of Calcutta*. It has been suggested that several 'Company school' pictures in the India Office Library derive from the Daniells' personal collection—indicating their keen interest not only in the architecture but also the painting of northern and southern India.

On return to Calcutta in 1792 Thomas Daniell, again assisted by William, produced 150 oil paintings which they sold by public lottery, thus enabling them to tour Mysore, which had recently been the scene of British battles. A second lottery was drawn in Madras in February 1793 comprising sixty-eight oil paintings and eight drawings, which funded their final tour of western India. It was there that they met James Wales, a Scottish artist based at Bombay and Poona, who with his assistants Robert Mabon and Gangaram Tambat had been producing and commissioning sketches and plans of the temple at Ellora. After Wales's death in 1795 the Daniells adapted his sketches (then in the possession of Wales's patron Sir Charles Malet) for the sixth volume of *Oriental Scenery*.

Thomas Daniell returned to London in September 1794, settling at 37 Holland Street, Fitzroy Square. He began translating his field sketches into exhibition oil paintings (which he showed at the Royal Academy and the British Institution) mainly representing Indian scenery. In 1796 Thomas Daniell was elected an associate of the Royal Academy and in 1799 Royal Academician. He was also a fellow of the Royal Society, the Asiatic Society, and the Society of Antiquaries. From 1800 to 1805 he was patronized by George Wyndham, third earl of Egremont, at Petworth House, Sussex. He also worked for the collector Thomas

Hope—painting *Composite View of Hindoo and Moorish Architecture* for Hope's Indian Room at his Duchess Street mansion in London.

From 1795 to 1808 Daniell, assisted by his nephew, produced his best-known work *Oriental Scenery* (issued in six series) of Indian views making a total of 144 hand-coloured aquatint views of India. These represent Mughal and Dravidian monuments, cityscapes and sublime views of mountains and waterfalls and formed the most extensive work of its kind, finding subscribers throughout Britain as well as in Calcutta and Madras. The large scale, number of plates, and use of colour printing were greatly admired and emulated; J. M. W. Turner, speaking of the plates for his *Liber Studiorum*, reputedly said he would like to have them engraved like Mr Daniell's. Following its success, Daniell also produced a smaller quarto version of *Oriental Scenery* in 1812–16, as well as *A Picturesque Voyage by Way of China* (1810) and *The Oriental Annual* (1834–9). The Daniells' Indian views had an enormous impact on Staffordshire pottery and on French wallpaper (Zuber, *L'Indoustan*, 1806; Dufour, *Paysage indien*, 1815)—samples of which can be seen at Laxton Hall, Northamptonshire (1805–11). Daniell was invited by Major John Osborne to design an oriental garden folly at Melchet Park, Hampshire (based on the porch of the temple in the fort of Rohtasgarh), which he also reproduced as an engraving in 1802. At Sezincote, Gloucestershire, Daniell's old Indian ally Sir Charles Cockerell commissioned him to design the garden (including a temple and bridge), the farm buildings, and the dairy. When the project was finished, Cockerell invited Daniell to paint six oils of the estate (exh. RA, 1818–19). Thomas Daniell rarely painted professionally after 1828 and died, unmarried, at his home, Earl's Terrace, Kensington, on 19 March 1840. Important examples of his oil paintings are in the Victoria Memorial, Calcutta, the India Office, London, and the National Gallery of Modern Art, Delhi. NATASHA EATON

Sources W. Daniell, 'Diary in India', BL OIOC · M. Archer, *Early views of India* (1980) · H. Hardie and M. Clayton, 'Thomas Daniell', 'William Daniell', *Walker's Quarterly*, 35–6 (1932) · M. Shellim, *India and the Daniells* (1979) · M. Archer, *Artist adventurers in 18th-century India* (1974) · G. H. R. Tillotson, *The artificial landscape* (2000) · G. H. R. Tillotson, 'The Indian picturesque', *The raj: India and the British, 1600–1947*, ed. C. A. Bayly (1990) [exhibition catalogue, NPG, 19 Oct 1990 – 17 March 1991] · W. Foster, 'British artists in India, 1760–1820', *Walpole Society*, 19 (1930–31), 1–88 · M. Archer, *British drawings in the India office library* (1969) · P. Conner, *Oriental architecture in the west* (1979) · P. Mitter, *Much maligned monsters* (1977) · *Visions of India* (1998) [sale catalogue, Christies]
Archives BL OIOC, court minutes, marine records, Bengal and Madras European inhabitants · BL OIOC, William Daniell, diary, MSS · BM, Farington diary · RA, Ozias Humphry corresp.
Likenesses R. Home, oils, c.1790, Asiatic Society of Bengal, Calcutta, India · D. Wilkie, oils, 1838, Tate collection · G. Dance, drawing, RA

Daniell, William (1769–1837), landscape painter and engraver, was the eldest son of William Daniell (d. 1779), an innkeeper, and his wife, Sarah. He was the nephew of the renowned landscape painter Thomas *Daniell (1749–1840). Orphaned at an early age, he was adopted by his uncle and at about fifteen accompanied him to India as his assistant. He kept an extensive diary of their travels in India (1786–93) (on loan; India Office Library) which reveals his own sketching strategies and his assistance in the finishing of his uncle's sketches and oil paintings, as well as details of Indian flora and fauna.

On return to London in 1794, Daniell spent the next fifteen years working on the aquatints of *Oriental Scenery* (1795–1808), followed by another collaboration with his uncle—*Voyage to India by Way of China* (1810). From 1795 to 1838 he exhibited 168 pictures at the Royal Academy and sixty-four at the British Institution (1807–36)—including views of India, Scotland, and England. Unlike his uncle, William increasingly produced representations of Indian figures and small, waterside scenes, concentrating less on topography than on oriental fantasy. He joined the Royal Academy Schools in 1799, becoming an associate in 1807 and Royal Academician in 1822. In 1826 he won a prize at the British Institution for *The Battle of Trafalgar*.

William Daniell was an extremely accomplished aquatinter and etcher and at times experimented with the latest printmaking techniques as adopted by J. M. W. Turner, for instance wiping out highlights in his watercolours. In *Oriental Scenery* he used sepia and bluish grey for printing and stained the prints so as to replicate the effects of the original watercolours; colourists were only employed to add small touches to figures or foreground foliage. He was a prolific printmaker, producing a series of high-quality productions that included *A Brief History of Ancient and Modern India* (1802–5); *Interesting Selections from Animated Nature* (1807–12); *A Familiar Treatise on Perspective* (1810); *View of London* (1812); *Illustrations of the Island of Staffa* (1818); *Sketches of South Africa* (1820); *Views of Windsor, Eton and Virginia Water* (1827–30), and the *Oriental Annual* (1835). His most famous independent work was his *Voyage around Britain* (4 vols., 1814–25), which made extensive use of sepia wash. He also collaborated in works with his brother Samuel *Daniell (1775–1811), a topographical artist, and his brother-in-law William Westall, and made prints from the drawings of his old Indian friend Samuel Davis (for example, *View of Bhutam*, 1813) and Colonel Robert Smith. He died, unmarried, in Camden Town, London, on 16 August 1837. Examples of his work including a *View of the Long Walk, Windsor* are in the Royal Collection, the Victoria and Albert Museum, London, and the Victoria Memorial, Calcutta. NATASHA EATON

Sources W. Daniell, 'Diary in India', BL OIOC · *Visions of India* (1998) [sale catalogue, Christies] · M. Archer, *Early views of India* (1980) · H. Hardie and M. Clayton, 'Thomas Daniell', 'William Daniell', *Walker's Quarterly*, 35–6 (1932) · M. Shellim, *India and the Daniells* (1979) · G. H. R. Tillotson, *The artificial landscape* (2001) · C. Stewart, trans., *The travels of Abu Talib* (Calcutta, 1814) · M. Archer, *Company school drawings in the India Office* (1972) · C. Grieg, *Landscape painting in the Victoria Memorial Collection* (Calcutta, 1991) · press cuttings, V&A, Paul Malan centre · microfilm of Calcutta newspapers, BL OIOC
Archives BL OIOC, diaries from India; drawings, journals | RA, Ozias Humphry corresp.
Likenesses R. Home, double portrait, c.1790 (with William Daniell), Asiatic Society of Bengal, Calcutta, India · G. Dance, chalk drawing, 1794, BM

Daniell, William Freeman (1817–1865), surgeon and botanist, was born at Salford on 16 November 1817, one of three sons of George and Mary Daniell. Nothing is known of his early life or education; he became MRCS on 5 November 1841, at which time he gave a Manchester address. In 1845 he left Liverpool at the head of an exploratory expedition to central Africa where, based in Angola, he studied the local botany, corresponding with Sir William Hooker at Kew about his finds. He returned to England in June 1847 with 100 plant specimens. Daniell joined the army medical department on 26 November 1847 as assistant surgeon and spent the next nine years stationed in the Gambia, the Gold Coast, and Sierra Leone, returning periodically to England. On one such visit he married Agnes Sophia Tucker in London (28 August 1852). Their only child, Evelyn Lucy, was born on 27 August 1855. The marriage does not appear to have been a happy one.

Outside his military duties, Daniell engaged in ethnographic study and investigated disease in local Africans, publishing the well-received *Sketches of the Medical Topography and Native Diseases of the Gulf of Guinea* (1849). He was promoted staff surgeon, second class, on 11 March 1853. His main scientific contribution came in the field of economic botany: in articles published in the *Pharmaceutical Journal* between 1850 and 1860 he described various west African plants, and, working from their indigenous uses, discussed their economic and/or medicinal value. A plant from Sierra Leone that produced sweet fruit, which he described in 1855, was identified as a new species named *Phrynium danielli*. His description of the west African frankincense tree led to the establishment of a new genus, *Daniellia*. Daniell channelled his findings on the natural wealth of Africa back to the London scientific community through publications, and by sending specimens to the herbarium of the British Museum and to the Pharmaceutical Society, which made him an honorary member. He was elected fellow of the Royal Geographical Society, fellow of the Linnean Society in 1855, and FRCS on 11 March 1857.

Daniell continued his botanical work while posted to the West Indies in 1857–8, to Colchester in 1858–9, to China in 1860, to Templemore in 1861–2, and to Jamaica in 1862–4. Broken health forced him to return to England in September 1864, where he was diagnosed as having 'disease of the lungs'. With characteristic diligence he worked during his long final illness on the paper announcing his discovery that the cola nut contained caffeine (*Pharmaceutical Journal*, 6, 1865, 450–57). Daniell died at Southampton on 26 June 1865 and was buried at Kensal Green, London, on 3 July.   HEATHER BELL

Sources *Journal of Botany, British and Foreign*, 3 (1865), 294–6 • *Catalogue of scientific papers*, Royal Society, 2 (1868), 146–7 • *Catalogue of scientific papers*, Royal Society, 7 (1877), 483 • Desmond, *Botanists*, rev. edn, 192 • *Army List* (1847–65) • directors' correspondence LIX, Royal Collection, 91–6 • *Pharmaceutical Journal and Transactions*, 2nd ser., 7 (1865–6), 86–7 • R. W. D. Nickalls, 'W. F. Daniell (1817–1865) and the discovery that cola-nuts contain caffeine', *Pharmaceutical Journal*, 236 (1986), 401–2 • V. G. Plarr, *Plarr's Lives of the fellows of the Royal College of Surgeons of England*, rev. D'A. Power, 1 (1930), 320 • A. Peterkin and W. Johnston, *Commissioned officers in the medical services of the British army, 1660–1960*, 1 (1968), 341 • *Proceedings* [Royal Geographical Society], 10 (1865–6), 214–15 • *CGPLA Eng. & Wales* (1865) • will, proved, PR, 26 June 1865 • m. cert. • b. cert. [Evelyn Lucy Daniell]

Archives BM, plant specimens • RGB Kew, Museum of Materia Medica of the Pharmaceutical Society, plant specimens | RBG Kew, letters to Sir William Hooker, African letters; vol. LIX

Wealth at death under £1500: probate, 20 Sept 1865, *CGPLA Eng. & Wales*

Danielli, James Frederic (1911–1984), biologist, was born at 36 Swinderby Road, Alperton, near Wembley, London, on 13 November 1911, the only son and the elder child of James Frederic Danielli, civil servant, and his wife, Helena Mary Hollins. He was educated at Wembley county school to 1928, and University College, London, and held a Commonwealth Fund fellowship at Princeton University in 1933–5, where he began working on the structure of the living cell membrane. In 1935 he returned to University College, London, where he extended this research to the problems of membrane permeability and function. In 1937 he married Mary, a poet and anthropologist, the daughter of Herbert Spencer Guy, an accountant. They had a son and a daughter.

In 1938 Danielli moved to Cambridge University to work on oedema, and became a fellow of St John's College in 1942. During the Second World War he was involved in defence research, initially on the problems of wound healing, and later in finding an antidote to the chemical warfare poison Lewisite. In 1946 he was appointed reader in cell physiology at the Royal Cancer Hospital, London, and in 1949 professor of zoology at King's College, London. There he rapidly assembled a team of talented young scientists, widening the scope of departmental research. Danielli himself extended his work on the cell membrane, developed methods for the quantitative study of cellular chemistry, and jointly with the Chester Beatty Cancer Research Institute became involved in the development of anti-cancer drugs. He was elected FRS in 1957.

In 1962 Danielli became chairman of the department of biological pharmacology in the University of Buffalo. In 1965 he was appointed director of the university's new interdisciplinary centre for theoretical biology, and became involved in exploring the possibility of life on other planets. But the venture began to falter as state funding diminished, and in 1974 he became chairman of life sciences at the Worcester Polytechnic Institute in Massachusetts. He finally retired in 1980. In 1982, when his health was already failing, he began campaigning for a cause that later became fashionable, the preservation of the DNA of endangered species, so that posterity could re-create them if they became extinct.

Danielli's life's work can perhaps be best described as providing a constant stimulus to research over a remarkably wide area. His best-known work on the structure and behaviour of the cell membrane was regarded as seminal, but it was to be extensively amended and refined by others as the years went by. His work on quantitative methods in cell chemistry was a stimulus to others, as was his work on anti-cancer agents. His research on the transplantation of nuclei from one amoeba to another likewise prompted much research that ultimately threw new light on aspects of the living cell, most notably on the function of the nucleus and the mechanisms of developmental biology.

It was, however, not only Danielli's research that provided these stimuli. Many of his young research workers went on to make their mark worldwide. His activity in founding and editing scientific journals meant that his ideas spread out to the whole biological community. These included the *International Review of Cytology*, *Progress in Surface and Membrane Science*, the *Journal of Molecular Biology*, and the *Journal of Theoretical Biology*. The recognition of cell biology as one of the most important new areas of research owed much to his immense energy and constant flow of ideas, invariably stimulating, if often controversial. Danielli was regarded as a kind, generous, imaginative, and quixotic man. He died, after a long illness, at Houston, Texas, on 22 April 1984. He was survived by his wife.   MICHAEL SWANN, *rev.* V. M. QUIRKE

Sources W. D. Stein, *Memoirs FRS*, 32 (1986), 117–35 · personal knowledge (1990) · *WWW*, 1981–90
Archives Bodl. Oxf., corresp. relating to Society for the Protection of Science and Learning · CAC Cam., corresp. with A. V. Hill · CUL, corresp. with Peter Mitchell

Daniels, Henry Ellis (1912–2000), statistician, was born on 2 October 1912 in London, the second child of Morris Daniels (1889–1953), a salesman, and his wife, Hannah, *née* Goldberg (1890–1959). His was a Jewish family of Russian (partly Polish and partly Lithuanian) origin. When he was two the family moved to join the Lithuanian branch in Edinburgh. He enjoyed an excellent Scottish education at the Sciennes School and then at George Heriot's School there. He won a scholarship to read mathematics at Edinburgh University, where he obtained an MA degree in 1933. He published his first paper, a short note on a pure mathematical issue, while a final year student. With the encouragement of the head of department, Sir Edmund Whittaker, for whom he retained a high regard, Daniels went for a further period of study at Cambridge. This began a long and in some respects uneasy association with that university. A young colleague, who had moved from work in fluid mechanics to statistics, suggested that the latter subject was a good one to study, which Daniels duly did.

In 1935 the somewhat unconventional but highly effective director of research of the Wool Industries Research Association (WIRA) in Leeds, B. H. Wilsdon, appointed Daniels to study mathematical and statistical aspects of the wool industries. Except for a break during the Second World War he remained in this appointment for ten years, taking his PhD externally at Edinburgh in 1943. In Leeds he did some of his most wide-ranging work. Wilsdon had appointed a biochemist, A. J. P. Martin, to study the scouring process. In fact Martin, together with R. M. Synge, worked largely on the development of paper chromatography, for which work they were awarded a Nobel prize. Daniels contributed a mathematical appendix to their key

paper, giving a quantitative explanation of why the method works. As a skilled experimenter himself he developed delicate techniques for fibre measurement. He introduced statistical methods at a high level into many aspects of the work at WIRA, made important contributions to statistical theory, and, perhaps most notably, formulated and solved mathematical problems connected with textile physics. In particular his 1944 paper in *Proceedings of the Royal Society* on strength of bundles turned out thirty years later to be key to the theory of fibre composite materials. During 1942–5 he was seconded to the Ministry of Aircraft Production and worked in particular on navigational problems. Some of his results were published in 1952 in a particularly elegant paper on the statistical theory of position finding.

In 1947 Daniels returned to Cambridge as a lecturer in mathematics attached to the newly formed statistical laboratory. While he had few doctoral students, and in fact disapproved of the PhD system, he played a pivotal role in training and encouraging many of the impressive group of students who passed through the laboratory during the following years. There was, however, no professor, and none of the academic staff held a college fellowship—despite the high international reputation of the laboratory, which owed much to Daniels himself. On 31 July 1950 he married Barbara Edith Pickering (*b.* 1916), a teacher. They had a daughter, Catharine, and a son, Peter.

It was no surprise when in 1957 Daniels left Cambridge for a chair at the University of Birmingham, where he established a strong programme in his subject. He clearly found the intellectual climate at Birmingham more to his liking and it caused his friends wry amusement when, after his retirement from the chair in 1978, he returned immediately to live in Cambridge. He resumed his connection with the statistical laboratory, to which he was much attached, and worked there regularly until his death. In 1980 he was elected a fellow of the Royal Society. Although his knowledge of statistical theory and application was broad and deep, his research in later years was at the mathematical end of the subject. In particular he was unsurpassed at deploying classical mathematical techniques to solve, often in strikingly elegant form, very difficult probabilistic problems motivated by scientific issues.

While Daniels was never totally at ease in the general Cambridge environment, in the international and national community of research workers in his field he was regarded with great affection and respect. This was partly because of the beauty of his work, but also because it was clear that behind his occasionally acerbic wit was a man of broad interests and intrinsic kindness and consideration. A significant attraction of Cambridge was the opportunity for musical companionship. As an accomplished pianist he became captivated by the English concertinas he found in junk shops and then repaired. The physicist Wheatstone had developed the instrument to replace the viola in chamber music, and Daniels put this into practice. He was also an expert watch repairer and his much prized position as liveryman of the Worshipful

Company of Clockmakers recognized his mathematical contribution to watch design.

Daniels remained active until the end of his life. On the evening of 14 April 2000, after a difficult journey to an annual conference at Gregynog, Montgomeryshire, he was at supper talking enthusiastically about his latest results, soon to be presented at a meeting in Switzerland. At breakfast the next day he suffered a massive stroke. He died in the Royal Shrewsbury Hospital on 16 April 2000 without regaining consciousness. He was cremated on 2 May 2000 at Cambridge crematorium after a funeral conducted by an official of the British Humanist Association. He was survived by his wife and their two children.

D. R. COX

Sources CUL, Daniels MSS · P. Whittle, 'A conversation with Henry Daniels', *Statistical Science*, 6 (1993), 342–53 · *The Guardian* (4 May 2000) · *The Times* (23 May 2000) · *The Independent* (20 June 2000) · WWW · private information (2004) · personal knowledge (2004)
Archives CUL, MSS |FILM Video conversation. Held by Royal Statistical Society, c. 1980
Likenesses photograph, RS; repro. in *The Guardian*
Wealth at death £161,462—gross; £158,998: probate, 2001, CGPLA Eng. & Wales

Danneley, John Feltham (*bap.* 1785, *d.* 1834x6), writer on music, was baptized on 1 April 1785 in Wokingham, Berkshire, the second son of George Danneley, a lay clerk at St George's Chapel, Windsor, and his wife, Elizabeth. He was taught music by his father, and at the age of fifteen he studied thoroughbass with Samuel Webbe and the piano with Charles Knyvett. Later he learned with Charles Neate, and he is also said to have had some lessons from Joseph Woelfl, but this was probably later still, as Woelfl settled in England only in 1805.

About 1803 Danneley gave up music to live with a rich uncle, but after the uncle died without making a will he went back to studying music. In 1812 he settled in Ipswich as a music teacher, and a few years later he was appointed organist of the church of St Mary of the Tower. In 1816 Danneley visited Paris, where he studied under Reicha, Pradher, and Mirecki and met Monsigny and Cherubini. He returned to Ipswich, and in 1820 published a pedestrian *Introduction to the Elementary Principles of Thorough Bass and Classical Music*. Shortly afterwards he published *Palinodia a Nice*, a set of thirteen vocal duets.

Danneley married in 1822, and about 1824 seems to have settled in London. In 1825 he published his best-known work, *An Encyclopaedia or Dictionary of Music*, which was followed by *A Musical Grammar* (1826). In 1829 he contributed the article on music to *The London Encyclopaedia*. He seems to have ended his career as a publisher and seller of music at 22 Tavistock Place, and, between 1832 and 1834, at 13 Regent Street. His name disappears from the Post Office directories after 1834, in which year he probably died, although many sources give 1836 as the year of his death.

W. B. SQUIRE, *rev.* ANNE PIMLOTT BAKER

Sources Grove, *Dict. mus.* · IGI · [J. S. Sainsbury], ed., *A dictionary of musicians*, 2nd edn, 2 vols. (1827) · [Clarke], *The Georgian era: memoirs of the most eminent persons*, 4 (1834), 531

Dannreuther, Edward George (1844–1905), pianist and writer, was born on 4 November 1844 in Strasbourg, the first of three children of Abraham Dannreuther (1814–1861), cabinet-maker and piano manufacturer, and his wife, Sophie, daughter of George Leonard Fischbacher of Strasbourg. Dannreuther spent his boyhood in Cincinnati, Ohio, whither his father had emigrated in 1846 to establish a piano manufacturing business. There he took music lessons with Frederick Louis Ritter, learning the cello and piano. In the autumn of 1859 he travelled to Leipzig, where he entered the conservatory in 1860 as a piano student with Moscheles, studying theory with Moritz Hauptmann and E. F. Richter, and numbering among his friends Grieg, Sullivan, and August Wilhelmj. In 1863 Henry Chorley, critic of *The Athenaeum*, brought Dannreuther to London, where immediately on his arrival he gave with great success the first complete English performance of Chopin's piano concerto no. 2 in F minor (11 April 1863) at the Crystal Palace; a fortnight later he performed Beethoven's concerto no. 4. In 1865 he made a tour of the United States with Carl Rosa, an account of which he was persuaded to publish by Dickens in his weekly journal *All the Year Round*. At the same time he had also fallen in love with one of his pupils, Chariclea Anthea Euterpe Ionides (1844–1923), sister of Constantine Alexander Ionides, a wealthy patron of the arts. Initial opposition to their marriage from Chariclea's father led to a period of three years in which they did not see each other, but in 1870, after Dannreuther had considered returning permanently to America, they became engaged, and were married in the Greek church at London Wall on 5 August 1871. On settling in London, Dannreuther became a naturalized British citizen.

During the 1870s Dannreuther established a reputation in London as a musical radical, with catholic tastes and wide-ranging interests. As a pianist he continued his career as a virtuoso, giving the first English performances of concertos by Grieg, Liszt (in A), Tchaikovsky (in B♭ minor) and Scharwenka (in B♭ minor), as well as Parry's concerto in F♯ major. At his home at 12 Orme Square, Bayswater, he organized a series of semi-public chamber concerts, which began in 1876 and ceased in 1893, when the lease of the house expired. These concerts soon became known for their contemporary emphasis, with programmes consisting of works by Brahms, Sgambati, Tchaikovsky, Liszt, Wagner, Rheinberger, Richard Strauss, Parry, Stanford, and Mackenzie. But, of all contemporary composers, Dannreuther championed the work of Wagner, who was a close friend. In order to help raise money for the building of the theatre in Bayreuth he founded in 1872 the Wagner Society, two of whose series (1873–4) he conducted. In 1876 he went to Bayreuth for the first performance of *Der Ring des Nibelungen*, attending all the final orchestra and stage rehearsals. In May 1877, during the Wagner Festival in London, the composer was his guest at Orme Square. There, on 17 May, in the company of George Eliot, George Lewes, Parry, Walter Bache, and Alfred Forman, Wagner recited his newly completed poem *Parsifal*. Wagner's theories of opera and drama were the subject of several of

Edward George Dannreuther (1844–1905), by Bertha Wehnert-Beckmann, 1861?

Dannreuther's articles, the most notable being 'Wagner and the reform of the opera'. In addition, he provided a lengthy article for *Grove's Dictionary of Music and Musicians* and translations of three of Wagner's essays: *Das Kunstwerk der Zukunft* (1873), *Beethoven* (1880), and *Über das Dirigieren* (1887). Such was Dannreuther's ardour that he named his first four children—Tristan, Sigmund, Wolfram, and Isolde—after characters in Wagner's music dramas; his fifth child, Hubert, was named after Parry.

Although in the first instance Dannreuther was best known to the public as a virtuoso, it is as a teacher and writer that he is now mainly remembered. He proved to be a vital catalyst in the early career of Parry and numbered among his other pupils Fuller Maitland, Frederick Dawson, William Hurlstone, and James Friskin. In 1895 he joined the staff of the Royal College of Music. He contributed several articles to *Macmillan's Magazine* between 1875 and 1876 and wrote over thirty for *Grove's Dictionary*. For the *New Oxford History of Music* he wrote the sixth volume, *The Romantic Period* (1905), but perhaps his most enduring work was his treatise on *Musical Ornamentation* (2 pts, 1893–5), which remained a standard text for many generations.

Dannreuther died at his home, Chester Studio, Gerald Road, Chester Square, Pimlico, on 12 February 1905, and was cremated at Golders Green.   JEREMY DIBBLE

Sources *MT*, 39 (1898), 645–54 · C. Dannreuther, 'Memories', family MSS · m. cert. · d. cert. · Grove, *Dict. mus.*
Archives Nationalarchiv der Richard-Wagner-Stiftung, Bayreuth, Germany · Richard-Wagner-Gesamtausgabe, Munich, Germany · Shulbrede Priory, Sussex · University of Rochester, New York, Eastman School of Music

Likenesses photograph, 1859, repro. in *MT* (Oct 1898) · B. Wehnert-Beckmann, photograph, 1861?, NPG [*see illus.*] · double portrait, photograph, 1877 (with Richter), Hastings Borough Museum · T. Pall, photograph, 1892, repro. in *The Keyboard* (Sept 1892) · photograph, *c.*1900, priv. coll. · A. Legros, pencil sketch · carte-de-visite, Royal College of Music, London
Wealth at death £967 19s. 9d.: probate, 23 Feb 1905, *CGPLA Eng. & Wales*

Danquah, Joseph Boakye (1895–1965), lawyer and politician in Ghana, was born on 21 December 1895 at Bepong, Kwawu, Gold Coast, the son of Emmanuel Yaw Boakye Danquah (*d.* 1907) and his second wife, Lydia Okom Korantemaa. His royal father had been chief state drummer to the king of Akyem Abuakwa but had become a Presbyterian adherent of the Basel Mission; at great personal risk he had exchanged the palace for evangelism at the age of forty. Danquah was educated in Basel Mission schools and in 1913 was employed as a clerk with a prominent African barrister, Vidal Buckle, in Accra. In 1914 he passed the local civil service examination and became a clerk in the supreme court. In 1915 his older half-brother Nana Ofori Atta, the king or *okyenhene* of Akyem Abuakwa, appointed him first secretary and then in 1916 chief clerk and registrar of the native court in Akyem's capital, Kyebi. In this period Danquah collected the information that he later used in two of his finest books, *Cases in Akan Law* and *Akan Laws and Customs* (both 1928). These contributions to comparative law and anthropology were in the great tradition of Ghanaian legal writing established in the nineteenth century by John Mensah Sarba and continued by J. E. Casely Hayford. Danquah also wrote a celebration of his kingdom and his king, *The Akim Abuakwa Handbook* (1928), *Ancestors, Heroes and God* (1938), and *The Akan Doctrine of God* (1941).

Initially antagonistic to the aims of anti-colonial organizations in the Gold Coast because of his king's hostility to them, Danquah was by 1921 moving closer to the aims of the Aborigines' Rights Protection Society (ARPS). At the suggestion of one of the most prominent leaders of the ARPS, the lawyer and politician Kobina Sekyi, Danquah decided that he should read law. This won the support of his king and in 1921 he left for Britain. He studied philosophy and law at University College, London and ate dinners in the Inner Temple. By 1927 he had managed to graduate as a bachelor of arts, a bachelor of laws, and a doctor of philosophy and had been called to the bar. He was also involved in anti-colonial politics in London, and was one of the founder members of the West African Students' Union and editor of its journal.

In 1927 Danquah returned to the Gold Coast where he established a legal practice. Increasingly committed to nationalism, he founded and then edited the daily *Times of West Africa*. In 1930 he was the moving force behind the new anti-colonial Gold Coast Youth Conference. In 1934 he returned to Britain as secretary to a deputation of chiefs and intellectuals petitioning the secretary of state for the colonies to refuse his assent to a new, restrictive Sedition Bill. The deputation failed. Danquah was now at odds with his royal half-brother whom he suspected of being hostile to the nationalism with which he himself was increasingly identified. He remained in Britain until 1936, spending much of his time in the British Museum's reading room researching African history. That research led him to the conclusion that the Akan, his own ethnic group, were the relicts of the ancient empire of Ghana. This argument gained local currency eventually and led to an independent Gold Coast choosing to be known as Ghana from 1957.

On his return to Accra in 1936 Danquah maintained his nationalism and was one of the most formidable proponents of rapid democratization and the end of British colonial rule. While continuing his legal practice, he also revived his newspaper, wrote plays and innumerable scholarly and more popular articles, and acted, somewhat uncomfortably, as legal adviser to his half-brother. He had also married Mabel, the daughter of one of the country's most eminent lawyers, Frans Dove. Both before and after their later divorce she was among the Gold Coast's most influential women intellectuals and political activists. She also became a lifelong political adversary of Danquah. His second wife, Elizabeth, died in 1987. He had numerous children, both legitimate and illegitimate.

In 1947 the tempo of anti-colonial politics picked up after an unofficial truce during the Second World War. Unpersuaded that the reformed constitution of 1946 amounted to progress and increasingly alienated from the colonial regime, Danquah, a nephew, the husband of one of his nieces, and a cluster of intellectuals and businessmen formed the United Gold Coast Convention (UGCC) in August 1947. The first modern nationalist party in the country's history, the UGCC demanded 'self government in the shortest possible time'. It invited a London-based student, Kwame Nkrumah, to act as its general secretary. Although the evidence shows they played little part in fomenting the pivotal urban riots of February and March 1948, Danquah and other senior figures in the UGCC were illegally detained under emergency regulations. After their release the more conservative nationalists of the UGCC and their more radical, dynamic general secretary began to pull apart. Depending upon which account one believes, Nkrumah and his lieutenants were either expelled or elected to leave the UGCC in June 1949 and founded their own party, the Convention People's Party (CPP).

This brought into public gaze a serious rift in the nationalist movement between gradualists and socialists. Danquah was to remain the most prominent spokesman of conservative nationalism until his death, a tradition which is still evident in modern Ghanaian politics. His antagonist was Kwame Nkrumah. It was a personal as well as an intellectual animosity. Danquah was prominent in a sequence of unsuccessful political alliances which failed to gain significant votes in each of the colonial general elections (1951, 1954, and 1956) which led to independence in March 1957. He lost his parliamentary seat in the 1954 election. Outflanked by the greater organizational skills and popular attraction of the CPP which governed Ghana from 1954 until deposed by a military coup in 1966, Danquah was condemned to watch his arch-enemy flourish.

Although respected professionally—he was elected president of the Ghana Bar Association in 1963 and was a fellow of the Ghana Academy of Arts and Sciences—he remained on the losing side. He stood against Nkrumah in the election for a president when Ghana opted to become a republic in 1960 but polled no more than 10 per cent of the votes in a somewhat suspect electoral process. Ghana's most internationally respected intellectual and a founding father of the nationalist movement had been humiliated.

Suffering from hypertension and asthma, Danquah was detained under Ghana's Preventive Detention Act in 1961 and was released in 1962. He was again detained in 1964 and died in his cell in Nsawam gaol, 80 miles north of Accra, on 4 February 1965, gasping for breath and unattended by a doctor he had begged to see. He was buried in Akyem Abuakwa. He is commemorated in Accra by an imposing statue on that city's ring road. The statue portrays him in traditional cloth leaning on a pile of books.

RICHARD RATHBONE

Sources J. B. Danquah, *The Ghanaian establishment* (1997) • L. Ofosu-Appiah, *The life and times of Dr J. B. Danquah* (1974) • R. Rathbone, *Murder and politics in colonial Ghana* (1993) • D. Austin, *Politics in Ghana* (1964) • *The Times* (5 Feb 1965) • private information (2004) • *DNB*
Likenesses statue, Accra, Ghana

Dansey, Sir Claude Edward Marjoribanks (1876–1947), intelligence officer, was born at 14 Cromwell Place, South Kensington, London, on 10 September 1876, the second child and eldest son in the family of four sons and five daughters of Edward Mashiter Dansey, captain and later lieutenant-colonel in the 1st Life Guards, and his wife, Eleanore, daughter of Robert Francis Gifford, second Baron Gifford. His parents removed him from Wellington College in 1891, following a diphtheria epidemic, to a school in Bruges, whence too he was removed after a homosexual scandal. In childhood he acquired fluent French, a language he often pretended hardly to speak.

In 1895 Dansey went to the new colony of Rhodesia and became a trooper in the Matabeleland regiment of the British South Africa police. He helped suppress the Matabele (Ndebele) uprising in 1896, and learned the elements of scouting and intelligence gathering. In 1898 he returned to England and secured a militia commission in the Lancashire Fusiliers.

Dansey spent ten weeks in the winter of 1899–1900 with the British North Borneo Company police force as a sub-commandant, in operations against Muhammad Salleh, before rejoining his regiment in South Africa in 1900. He took part in the relief of Mafeking, was briefly a fellow-subaltern with Winston Churchill in the South African light horse, and spent the rest of the war in the field intelligence department. In 1900 he received a regular commission as lieutenant in the 6th battalion of the Lancashire Fusiliers. He stayed in South Africa, on intelligence duties, until 1904, and then spent five years in British Somaliland as a political officer, trying to counter Muhammad bin Abdullah, known as the Mad Mullah.

While in England on sick leave Dansey was recruited into the security branch of the secret service. He spent three years in New York state as resident secretary of the

Sir Claude Edward Marjoribanks Dansey (1876–1947), by Elliott & Fry

Sleepy Hollow Country Club, a rich men's recreation park on the Hudson River, whence he could keep an eye on wealthy Irish-Americans.

In August 1914 Dansey was recalled to England, and placed in charge of port security. He revisited the USA in 1917 to play a decisive part in helping to set up the first official American military intelligence service. He was promoted lieutenant-colonel and transferred to the Secret Intelligence Service (SIS) to unravel a disastrous muddle in the Netherlands. He next took over SIS's organization in Switzerland.

In 1919 the service's staff was cut back; Dansey spent most of the 1920s in private business ventures on both sides of the Atlantic. From 1929 to 1936 he was re-employed, under the cover of passport control officer, in Rome. His chief, 'C' (Sir Hugh Sinclair), then realized that German secret police had penetrated several SIS stations. Dansey left Rome in 1936; word seeped out that he had been caught with his hand in the till and sacked. He settled into an export–import office in Bush House in the Strand, and set up parallel networks of secret intelligence agents to cover the penetrated areas, using the code name Z and avoiding the use of wireless.

In September 1939 Z's networks amalgamated with C's, and Dansey went back to Bern. In November C died;

Dansey returned to London, and became assistant chief to his friend Stewart Menzies, the new C. He was in charge of all active espionage until 1945. All the arrangements for stay-behind agents in north-west Europe collapsed, but Dansey was able to charm most of the governments in exile in London into recruiting spies.

Dansey was closely involved with the Special Operations Executive in its early stages—Frank Nelson, its first executive head, had been a Z agent. Dansey did not seek to influence its policy, so long as it kept out of his agents' way. He often used to display there his sharp tongue, as notorious as his charm. He also kept a keen eye on MI9, the secret escape service. At the end of the war he was persuaded to retire, to Bathampton Manor, near Bath.

Dansey was appointed CMG in 1918 and KCMG in 1943. In 1915 he married Mrs Pauline Monroe Cory Ulman, daughter of David Cory, doctor of medicine, of New York. She separated from him in 1929 and later divorced him. His second wife, whom he married in 1945, was Mrs Frances Gurney Rylander, daughter of Dr D. F. K. Wilson. There were no children of either marriage but he had a stepdaughter from each. He died in the Lansdown Grove Hospital, Bath, on 11 June 1947. M. R. D. FOOT, *rev.*

Sources A. Read and D. Fisher, *Colonel Z* (1984) · private information (1993) · *The Times* (13 June 1947) · *WWW* · *CGPLA Eng. & Wales* (1947) · d. cert.
Likenesses Elliott & Fry, photograph, NPG [*see illus.*] · photograph, repro. in Read and Fisher, *Colonel Z*
Wealth at death £15,526 0*s*. 5*d*.: probate, 30 Aug 1947, *CGPLA Eng. & Wales*

Dansey, William (1792–1856), Church of England clergyman, son of John Dansey, a surgeon and apothecary, was born at Blandford, Dorset, and matriculated from Exeter College, Oxford, in 1810. He was elected a scholar of his college in 1811, but resigned the appointment in the following year. He took second-class honours in the classical school and graduated BA in 1814 and MA in 1817. He studied medicine, obtaining his BM from Oxford in 1818, but withdrew his name from the list of inceptor-candidates of the Royal College of Physicians in 1820. In the previous year he had been ordained as a clergyman, and in 1820 was nominated to the rectory of Donhead St Andrew, Wiltshire, of which he was patron. He was presented to a prebendal stall at Salisbury on 10 August 1841 which, together with his rectory, he held until his death. He married on 28 August 1849 Sarah, youngest daughter of the Revd Richard White Blackmore, rector of Donhead St Mary, Wiltshire.

Dansey was best known for his compilation of documents, *Horae decanicae rurales. Being an attempt to illustrate the name, title, and functions of rural deans, with remarks on the rise and fall of rural bishops* (2 vols., 1835; 2nd edn, 1844). A member of a group of high-churchmen active in the diocese of Salisbury, he received encouragement from leading orthodox churchmen including H. H. Norris and Joshua Watson in publishing this lavishly produced work. Its purpose was to offer historical precedents for diocesan reform in contrast to the centralizing activity of the recently appointed ecclesiastical commissioners. Its appearance reflected the revival of the office of rural dean, a movement which was already under way in several dioceses. He also published a translation (1831) of a treatise on coursing (the *Cynegeticus*) by Flavius Arrianus. Dansey died at Weymouth, Dorset, on 7 June 1856.

G. C. BOASE, rev. M. C. CURTHOYS

Sources Boase, *Mod. Eng. biog.* · C. W. Boase, ed., *Registrum Collegii Exoniensis*, new edn, OHS, 27 (1894) · Foster, *Alum. Oxon.* · Munk, *Roll* · R. A. Burns, 'A Hanoverian legacy? Diocesan reform in the Church of England, c.1800–1833', *The Church of England, c.1689–c.1833*, ed. J. Walsh and others (1993), 265–82

Likenesses portrait, Donhead St Andrew church, Wiltshire

Danson, Thomas (*bap.* 1629, *d.* 1694), ejected minister, the son of Thomas Danson of St Mary-le-Bow, London, was baptized there on 9 July 1629. He identified himself as a Londoner: 'I have a large acquaintance with London, being both a native of that city, and a dweller in it, a considerable part of my time', he was to assure Anthony Wood (*Calamy rev.*, 157). He was formidably equipped in languages under two tutors in London: Thomas Wise, who taught him Latin and Greek, and Dr Christian Rave (or Ravis) who taught him Hebrew, Chaldaean, Syriac, and Arab languages. From London he went to Oxford, first as a student of New Inn and then as chaplain of Corpus Christi in 1648. He graduated BA in 1650 and MA in 1652 (the latter degree was incorporated at Cambridge in 1654). He was a fellow of Magdalen College, Oxford, from 1652 to 1657.

In August 1654 Danson was preaching at Berwick. He became vicar of Sandwich in May 1656, from which he was ejected in 1661 on the grounds that his presentation to the living by Cromwell had been illegal. However, he initially survived within the Restoration church, and was instituted to the living of Sibton with Peasenhall in Suffolk on 3 June 1661. He was ejected again, though he seems to have survived there a while: a daughter, Ann, was born there in September 1663 and his successor was instituted only in February 1664. The rest of Danson's life was spent preaching in London and Abingdon. In 1672 he was licensed as a presbyterian to preach at his house in Spitalfields. On the death of Henry Langley in 1679 he moved to Abingdon, Berkshire, where he remained presbyterian minister (with one brief absence) until 1692. The move to Abingdon may in part be explained by family connections: his wife, Anne Garbrand (*d.* 1689), was the daughter of Tobias *Garbrand [see under Garbrand, John (*b.* 1646/7)], the former principal of Gloucester Hall, Oxford, who spent the years after his ejection living and practising medicine in Abingdon. He was excommunicated in 1684 and presented at quarter sessions in 1684 for non-attendance at church. In July 1689 it was certified that the meeting-places of the presbyterians in Abingdon were the market house for Sundays and his home for weekdays. The 1690 survey of dissenting ministers reported of Danson's congregation and his maintenance: 'Att Abington, has a great people, a comfortable Supply, has of his own' (Gordon, 6).

Shortly after the death of his first wife Danson married again, and in his will, made at Abingdon in August 1690, acknowledged his bequests to his wife, Elizabeth, as 'too small an acknowledgement of her greate deserts' (PRO,

PROB 11/421, fol. 258v). In 1692 he moved back to London, where he died on 9 October 1694, and was buried at Bunhill.

Danson began his writing career with an attack on the Quakers in 1659. It earned him a savage put-down by Samuel Fisher, in his *Rusticos ad academicos*, in the following year. His scholastic achievements counted for little with Fisher (himself an Oxford man). Danson was pilloried as a pedantic show-off, who belonged less to the world of academe than to the basic step-by-step learning of the ABC primers. Fisher thus referred scornfully to Danson 'and his fellow ABCDerians in the Schools of Christ' (Fisher, 124). It would be Danson's fate to suffer at the hands of nimbler wits than his own. Danson's self-perception was different. Ousted at the Restoration, he saw himself as part of a protestant rearguard, which included William Jenkyn, Christopher Fisher, and William Cowper. He had identified one enemy in the Quakers, but there were to be others: Socinians, papists, Hobbists, and Arminians. In the manner of the earlier Thomas Edwards, Danson sought to document the theological errors of his day. The Arminian champion whom he singled out to attack in *Vindiciae veritatis* of 1672 and *De causa Dei* of 1678 was John Howe, formerly private chaplain to both Oliver and Richard Cromwell. In a manuscript note Richard Baxter commented on the unfairness of Danson in selecting Howe, rather than himself, as his anti-Calvinist adversary (Baxter treatises, DWL, 18, fol. 73). Baxter had aroused controversy by his lectures on doctrine in 1674 at Pinners' Hall, which challenged the Calvinist line of Independent ministers such as John Owen. They foreshadowed the ultimate secession to Salters' Hall of Arminian presbyterian lecturers under the leadership of Howe in 1694 (Baxter himself having died three years earlier). This was a momentous division in English nonconformity, and Danson's attack on Howe had helped to precipitate it.

It also inspired one of only four prose works written by one of the greatest satirists of the age, Andrew Marvell. His *Remarks upon a Late Disingenuous Discourse* of 1678 is a devastating criticism of Danson's predestinarian writings. In Marvell's eyes Danson's greatest crime was to call Howe a papist simply because he spoke well of free will. In 1677 Marvell was publishing his famous exposé of French papal designs, *An Account of the Growth of Popery and Arbitrary Government in England*. No time could have been, therefore, less propitious for one protestant (Danson) to be name-calling another (Howe) as being 'under a Popish Vizard'. If free will made one man a Jesuit, pointed out Marvell, the opposite made him a Dominican. Marvell posed as the honest broker, treading upon 'Theological Ground' when he would rather not, and insisting on care in the use of words: 'for although we live under a rationall jealousie alwaies of Popery, yet whatever is said by any Author of that persuasion is not therefore to be clamorously rejected'. All then that Marvell was doing, he claimed, was 'hindering one Divine from offering violence to another' (Marvell, 142, 155). Who, we might ask, was writing the disingenuous discourse? This claim to the high moral ground is bogus: it is Danson, not Howe, who is being savaged. And it is done wittily. In his pamphlet T. D. becomes not the initials of the author, but of 'This Discourse', referred to throughout as 'It'. When 'It' makes 'bold with Bishop Davenant', Marvell, despite his supposed unfamiliarity with 'Theological Ground', is deft in showing how Howe's line (it is Baxter's too) chimes with Davenant's doctrinal compromise of 'hypothetical universalism'. Danson doggedly held to a Calvinist predestinarian course—against Fisher the Quaker, against Howe the Arminian, and also against William Sherlock, whose *Discourse Concerning the Knowledge of Jesus Christ* (1673), with its emphasis on the Christian's inherent righteousness, provoked Danson to a not-so-friendly *Friendly Debate between Satan and Sherlock* (1676). All this made Danson seem a somewhat passé figure in the 1670s, although Marvell's prose made him seem to be more so than he was. In that sense Danson was unlucky in his adversary, but when one thinks what Marvell had done earlier to a high-church Anglican, Samuel Parker, in his *Rehearsal Transpros'd*, Danson may in the end have got off relatively lightly.   WILLIAM LAMONT

Sources *Calamy rev.*, 156–7 • E. Calamy, ed., *An abridgement of Mr. Baxter's history of his life and times, with an account of the ministers, &c., who were ejected after the Restauration of King Charles II*, 2nd edn, 2 vols. (1713), vol. 2, p. 648 • Wood, *Ath. Oxon.*, new edn, 4.591 • T. Danson, *The Quakers folly made manifest to all men* (1659) • *The nonconformist's memorial … originally written by … Edmund Calamy*, ed. S. Palmer, [3rd edn], 3 (1803), 287 • T. Danson, *Vindiciae veritatis* (1672) • T. Danson, *A friendly debate between Satan and Sherlock* (1676) • T. Danson, *De causa Dei* (1678) • A. Marvell, *Remarks upon a late disingenuous discourse* (1678) • DWL, Baxter treatises, 18, fol. 73 • J. Howe, *Works* (1938) • S. Fisher, *Rusticos ad academicos* (1660) • A. Gordon, ed., *Freedom after ejection: a review* (1690–1692) *of presbyterian and congregational nonconformity in England and Wales* (1917) • PRO, PROB 11/421, sig. 168, fols. 200v–209r

Wealth at death money to wife 'too small an acknowledgement of her greate deserts': *Calamy rev.*, 157; will, PRO, PROB 11/421, sig. 168

Dant, Joan (1631–1715), pedlar and benefactor, was the wife of a weaver in New Paternoster Row, Spitalfields, London, but little else is known about her early life. She had a half-brother called John Allen.

Left facing destitution on her husband's early death, Joan became a pedlar in mercery, haberdashery, and hosiery, carrying her merchandise on her back. Her major customers were in the countryside around London, and she established her reputation for honest and fair dealing across a wide area. A Quaker, she made good use of her contacts with other members of the Society of Friends. Women figured largely among her clients, and she attracted much business from affluent households in luxury items. Eventually, she was able to enter the wholesale market, and by the end of her life she had customers as far afield as Paris and Brussels.

Joan Dant lived frugally and avoided unnecessary expenditure, so that her growing prosperity went unnoticed until 1714, when she asked a Quaker associate to assist in drawing up her will; when he realized the extent of her wealth, he baulked at the prospect and recommended that she call upon a group of Quakers with greater experience in financial matters, which she did.

Her fortune stood at over £9000. When asked how she wished this to be disposed she replied, 'I got it by the rich, and I mean to leave it to the poor' (Clark, 33). Accordingly she left a total of £110 to the poor of various London parishes and £1800 to Quaker meetings and charities. In addition she established a trust fund to assist poor Friends in London and elsewhere; this was still in existence in 1844. The trustees met twice a year to make grants of under £2 to deserving Quaker individuals or families. Joan Dant died on 29 September 1715, aged eighty-four, at New Paternoster Row, and was buried in the Quaker burial-ground at Bunhill Fields, London. In a letter to her executors Joan declared:

> It is the Lord that creates true industry in people, and that blesseth their endeavours in obtaining things necessary and convenient for them, which are to be used in moderation by all his flock and family everywhere … And I, having been one that has taken pains to live, and have through the blessing of God, with honesty and industrious care, improved my little in this world to a pretty good degree; find my heart open in that charity which comes from the Lord, in which the true disposal of all things ought to be, to do something for the poor—the fatherless and the widows in the Church of Christ, according to the utmost of my ability.   (Clark, 33)

Joan Dant thus embodied the Quaker ideals of piety, hard work, thrift, honesty, and charity; she is also a rare example of a female capitalist from before the industrial revolution. This combination of factors brought her story to the attention of Alice Clark, the pioneering Quaker historian of women's work in early modern England.

PETER FLEMING

Sources *British Friend*, 2 (1844), 113 • will, PRO, PROB 11/549, sig. 235 • A. Clark, *Working life of women in the seventeenth century*, 2nd edn (1982), 32–3

Wealth at death over £9000; bequests indicate considerable wealth: *British Friend*, 113; will, PRO, PROB 11/549, sig. 235

D'Anvers [*née* Clarke], **Alicia** (*bap.* 1668, *d.* 1725), poet, was the daughter of Samuel *Clarke (*bap.* 1624, *d.* 1669), superior beadle of civil law and first architypographus of Oxford University, and was baptized on 5 January 1668 at Holy Cross Church, Holywell, Oxford. On 31 March 1688 she married Knightley D'Anvers (*c.*1670–1740), son of the physician Daniel D'Anvers, at St Pancras Old Church, Middlesex. Knightley had entered Trinity College, Oxford, in 1685, studied law at the Inner Temple, and was admitted barrister in 1696.

Though not a prolific writer D'Anvers's three works of poetry reveal a competent satirist and an astute commentator on political and university life in the reign of William and Mary. Her first work, *A Poem upon His Sacred Majesty, his Voyage for Holland* (1691), is a poetic dialogue between Britannia and Belgia over their claims to Nassau (William III). Licensed shortly before William met his European allies at The Hague, it endorses his foreign policy and calms English anxiety over his divided allegiance.

D'Anvers's second and most popular work, *Academia, or, The Humours of the University of Oxford* (1691; repr. 1716, 1730), is a lengthy burlesque poem written in the octosyllabic doggerel known as hudibrastics. It satirizes young Oxford scholars through the figure of John Blunder, a new university student transformed from over-indulged yokel to ill-educated profligate. Though Oxford University was often the subject of satire or *facetiae* in the period few women poets ventured to publish such works.

A third text, *The Oxford-Act: a Poem* (1693), is attributed to D'Anvers in a contemporary handwritten note on the title-page of a copy of the poem. This satirical work traces the narrator's pilgrimage to Oxford to observe the Act, a ceremony held to confer higher degrees, which included a ribald speech by the *terrae filius*, an academic buffoon. D'Anvers may have published the work anonymously because of bawdy content; the question of attribution, however, has not been settled.

D'Anvers and her husband presumably moved to Northampton when Knightley was employed as deputy recorder in 1705. The burial of Alicia D'Anvers was certified on 19 July 1725 in Holywell parish.

HOLLY FAITH NELSON

Sources A. D'Anvers, *Academia* (1691) [annotated copy with Anthony Wood's MS notes on title page, Bod., Wood 517, pamphlet 6] · G. Greer and others, eds., *Kissing the rod: an anthology of seventeenth-century women's verse* (1988), 376–82 · parish register, St Pancras Old Church, 31 March 1688 [marriage] · chamberlains' accounts of the borough of Northampton, Northants. RO, Northampton borough 8/1 · minutes of the court of the mayor and aldermen, Northants. RO, Northampton borough 4/1 · Foster, *Alum. Oxon.* · Wood, *Ath. Oxon.*, new edn · G. Midgley, *University life in eighteenth-century Oxford* (1996) · *DNB* · E. H. Cordeaux and D. H. Merry, *A bibliography of printed works relating to the University of Oxford* (1968) · A. D. Godley, *Oxford in the eighteenth century*, 2nd edn (1909) · W. R. Ward, *Georgian Oxford: university politics in the eighteenth century* (1958) · M. Feingold, 'Oriental studies', *Hist. U. Oxf.* 4: 17th-cent. Oxf., 449–503

Danvers, Sir Charles (*c.*1568–1601), soldier and conspirator, was the eldest son of Sir John Danvers (1540–1594) of Dauntsey, Wiltshire, and thus heir to extensive estates in Wiltshire, Gloucestershire, and Yorkshire. Through his mother, Elizabeth (1545x50–1630), youngest daughter and coheir of John Neville, fourth Baron Latimer (*d.* 1577), he was connected to the Cecil, Percy, and Cornwallis families. According to family tradition, Lady Danvers exhibited 'prodigious parts for a woman', having 'Chaucer at her fingers' ends' and being fluent in Italian (*Brief Lives*, 1.193). Her interests seem to have strongly influenced Danvers, who spent much of his life abroad. He was a student in Paris by April 1584, but had returned to England by October 1586 when he was named an MP for the Gloucestershire borough of Cirencester, which was owned by his father.

Danvers subsequently became a soldier in the Netherlands, where his younger brother Henry *Danvers had been page to Sir Philip Sidney (*d.* 1586). Danvers served with Dutch forces, but was knighted by the English commander Lord Willoughby at Bergen-op-Zoom in 1588. He had returned to England by February 1589, when he again represented Cirencester in parliament. He was created an MA of Oxford with Sir Charles Blount (later Lord Mountjoy) on 16 July. In September Danvers was one of twelve gentlemen named to accompany the earl of Lincoln to attend James VI's wedding in Scotland. However, James's wedding plans were disrupted and the mission was cancelled. Danvers jousted in the great Accession day tournament at Whitehall of November 1590 which also involved the earls of Essex and Cumberland, Sir Henry Lee, Sir Charles Blount, and other prominent courtiers, many of whom had connections with the late Sir Philip Sidney. By 1593 he was again travelling abroad, visiting Vienna between July and September and passing southwards through Venice in October. A shipment of books sent home indicates that Danvers cultivated intellectual interests during his visit to Italy. However, this trip also reflected his embrace of Catholicism. In Rome he allegedly 'kyst the Pope's toos' (LPL, MS 649, fol. 431r). When he returned to England in December he was promptly arrested and spent a fortnight in the Marshalsea prison before he could convince the authorities of his continuing loyalty to the queen.

During 1594 Danvers became increasingly entangled in his family's feud with their Wiltshire neighbours, the Long family. This quarrel escalated to such an extent that Danvers and his brother Sir Henry led a band of followers to attack their rivals, who were dining with other local JPs at Corsham, on 4 October. Danvers cudgelled Henry Long, but was trapped and injured while trying to escape from Long's men. Sir Henry Danvers then shot Long dead with his pistol. The Danvers brothers immediately sought sanctuary with their friend Henry Wriothesley, third earl of Southampton, who hid them from the authorities and ensured their escape into exile across the channel. This disaster involving his two eldest sons apparently broke Sir John Danvers, who died on 19 December 1594. By contrast Lady Danvers worked steadily towards securing them a pardon, spending heavily and even marrying Sir Edmund Carey in 1598 to bolster support for her suit. The Danvers brothers mounted a similar campaign, regularly reporting news learned while serving as soldiers of fortune with Henri IV of France to correspondents in England. Sir Charles Danvers cemented strong ties with Sir Robert Cecil, his relative by marriage, in this way, whereas Sir Henry usually corresponded with the earl of Essex (who had knighted him in 1591). Sir Charles again travelled to Italy in November 1596 and spent several months in Venice during the first half of 1597. In 1598 he and his brother renewed their acquaintance with Southampton, who spent several months in Paris. Southampton planned to travel to Italy with Sir Henry, but his hopes were dashed when the Danvers brothers finally received a pardon from the queen in June 1598. They returned to London at the end of August.

Even before his return to England, Danvers was sounded out about the prospect of marrying a cousin of Essex, but the match was not pursued. Although he returned with plans to repair his reputation in England by soldiering in Ireland, Danvers found that his estate had been severely depleted in his absence by fines, enormous bribes to facilitate his pardon, and duplicitous servants. Repairing the damage absorbed much of his time and energy over the next two years. Danvers's hopes of pursuing his military career were also foiled by the queen.

When he was nominated a colonel in the army which Essex took to Ireland in early 1599, Elizabeth refused to let him go. Danvers now became increasingly attached to the Essex faction, which strained his previously close relations with Cecil. Southampton, 'to whom', as Danvers later explained, 'I owed my love and life itself' (*State trials*, 1448), had become a firm partisan of Essex, and Danvers's own brother Sir Henry was wounded while serving with Essex in Ireland. When Essex returned to England at the end of September and was arrested, it was therefore inevitable that Danvers would be drawn into the enthusiastic (but ineffectual) plotting of Southampton, Mountjoy, and Sir Henry Danvers to free him. Southampton subsequently told Danvers that he would 'adventure his lyfe' to save Essex and asked him to make the same commitment in late April 1600 (Cecil MS 83/108). Danvers agreed and soon became an intermediary between Essex, Mountjoy, and Southampton. He even visited Mountjoy in Ireland to request that the latter bring his army to England.

By 1601 Danvers was intimately involved in the desperate schemes of Essex and his remaining followers. He attended the final meeting of Essex's co-conspirators, which Southampton chaired at Drury House on 3 February, and was assigned the task of seizing the halberds from the queen's guards and securing the presence chamber if Essex decided to march upon the court. When Essex instead chose to march into the City, Danvers urged him to abandon the plan and to flee abroad or to Wales. When this advice was rejected Danvers dutifully joined the march on the following day and was arrested with Essex and the others when it collapsed in ignominy. He was conducted into the Tower by Sir Walter Ralegh, arraigned at Westminster Hall on 5 March, and beheaded on Tower Hill on 18 March 1601. His body was buried in the church within the Tower, probably St Peter ad Vincula, on the same day.   PAUL E. J. HAMMER

Sources state papers, PRO, SP 12 (Elizabeth: domestic); SP 15 (domestic: addenda, 1547–1625); SP 63 (Ireland); SP 80 (Germany: empire); SP 84 (Holland); SP 85 (Italian states) · *Calendar of the manuscripts of the most hon. the marquis of Salisbury*, 3–14, HMC (1889–1923) · papers of Anthony Bacon, LPL, MSS 647–662 · *Reg. Oxf.* · Cecil MSS, Hatfield House, Hertfordshire · *State trials*, vol. 1 · BL, Lansdowne MSS 82, 94, 827, 830 · Bodl. Oxf., MS Tanner 168 · *The manuscripts of his grace the duke of Rutland*, 4 vols., HMC, 24 (1888–1905), vols. 1, 4 · *Report on the manuscripts of Lord De L'Isle and Dudley*, 2, HMC, 77 (1933) · *The letters of John Chamberlain*, ed. N. E. McClure, 2 vols. (1939) · J. Maclean, 'The armory and merchants' marks in the ancient church of Cirencester', *Transactions of the Bristol and Gloucestershire Archaeological Society*, 17 (1892–3), 268–321, esp. 303 · *Brief lives, chiefly of contemporaries, set down by John Aubrey, between the years 1669 and 1696*, ed. A. Clark, 2 vols. (1898) · *APC*, 1596–1604 · HoP, Commons, 1558–1603

Archives Hatfield House, Hertfordshire, Cecil MSS · LPL, papers of Anthony Bacon · PRO, SP 12, 80

Wealth at death estates in Wiltshire, Gloucestershire, and Yorkshire; wealthy, but heavily encumbered by debt

Danvers, Frederick Charles (1833–1906), civil servant and writer on engineering, was born on 1 July 1833 in Hornsey, London, the second son of Frederick Samuel Danvers, an officer in the East India Company, and his wife, Mary Matilda, daughter of H. Middleton of Wanstead, Essex. He was educated at Merchant Taylors' School, London (1843–6), at King's College, London, and at Addiscombe College, near Croydon; he then studied civil and mechanical engineering for two years. In January 1853 he joined the clerical establishment at East India House. When the India Office was created in 1858 he was made, in September of that year, a junior clerk in its public and ecclesiastical department. The following year he was sent to Liverpool and Manchester to report on the fitness of traction engines for use in India. His technical knowledge led in 1861 to his transfer to the public works department. He became a senior clerk in June 1867 and an assistant secretary in February 1875. On 17 October 1860 he married, at the parish church in Hove, Louisa (1837–1909), daughter of Elias Mocatta. They had three sons and five daughters.

In 1868 Danvers's proposals for a tunnel under the Hooghly River to solve the problem of taking the East India Railway from Howrah into Calcutta were forwarded by Sir Stafford Northcote. Danvers became a busy writer on technical, statistical, and economic matters, chiefly with respect to India, contributing articles on public works to *Engineering*, 1866 to 1875, and an article to Spon's *Information for Colonial Engineers*, in 1877. He compiled memoranda on India's coal 1867–9, and the parliamentary paper 'Statistical papers relating to India' (1869); he wrote *Coal Economy* (1872) and *A Century of Famines, 1770–1870* (1877).

Danvers was an original associate of the Institution of Electrical Engineers, for which he acted as honorary auditor from its foundation in 1872 until his death. He was elected a fellow of the Royal Statistical Society in 1880, later serving on its council (1893–1905). One of the two papers he read to it was 'A review of Indian statistics' in 1901. He was also elected a member of the Society of Arts in 1890, subsequently sitting on its Indian section committee. He read three papers to the society, for two of which he was awarded its silver medal: 'Agriculture in India' (1878) and 'The India Office papers' (1889). The third paper, in 1886, was 'Famines in India'.

In 1877 Danvers transferred, still as an assistant secretary, to the revenue department. In January 1884 he became registrar and superintendent of records to the India Office. His appointment effected greater efficiency in this area which, partly in anticipation of the fourth centenary of Vasco da Gama's first voyage to western India, led to his being sent to Lisbon in 1891–2 to study records of Portuguese rule in the east. His report was published in 1892, followed by *The Portuguese in India … a History of the Rise and Decline of their Eastern Empire* (2 vols., 1894). Although referred to as his *magnum opus*, S. E. Fryer deemed it to be 'marred by want of perspective [with] incomplete reference to authorities' (*DNB*). He was made knight commander of the royal military order of Jesus Christ of Portugal. Danvers similarly studied records in the state archives in The Hague (1893–5). His subsequent report was eventually published in 1945 as 'Dutch activities in the east'. He retired from the India Office in July 1898.

In 1877 Danvers wrote *The covenant, or, Jacob's heritage, being an examination into circumstances connected with ancient Israel, with England, and with other leading nations*. His last work was '*Israel Redivivus*', *being a History of the Tribes of Israel* (1905). Other late works included *Map of the World, Commonly Known as 'the Second Borgian Map'* (1889) and a contribution to *Memorials of Old Haileybury College* (1894) entitled 'An account of the origin of the East India Company's service and of their college in Hertfordshire'. He also wrote the introduction to several works on records of the East India Company.

Danvers died of pneumonia on 17 May 1906 at Broad Oaks, Addlestone, Surrey; he was buried at All Saints' Church, Benhilton, near Sutton, Surrey. His wife died in Sutton on 29 May 1909 and was buried beside him.

ROBERT SHARP

Sources *DNB* · *The Times* (21 May 1906), 7 · *Journal of the Institution of Electrical Engineers*, 37 (1906), 438–9 · *The Engineer* (25 May 1906), 526 · *Journal of the Society of Arts*, 54 (1905–6), 735 · *WWW* · *The Electrician* (25 May 1906), 202 · m. cert. · d. cert. · *CGPLA Eng. & Wales* (1906)
Archives BL OIOC, MSS re his work on Borgian map, 1889, EURB 196 | BL OIOC, corresp. with Evelyn Grant-Duff, 1857–81, EURF 234
Likenesses lithograph, 1879, BL OIOC
Wealth at death £2373 7s. 5d.: administration, 25 Aug 1906, *CGPLA Eng. & Wales*

Danvers, Henry, earl of Danby (1573–1644), army officer and administrator, was born on 28 June 1573 at Dauntsey, Wiltshire, the second son of Sir John Danvers (1540–1594), landowner, of Dauntsey and the Hon. Elizabeth (1545×50–1630), youngest daughter and coheir of John Neville, fourth Baron Latimer (*d.* 1577). Educated at home, he was, from an early age, page to Sir Philip Sidney and was probably present with his master at the battle of Zutphen in 1586 where Sidney was fatally wounded. Danvers then volunteered for service under Maurice, count of Nassau and prince of Orange, who put him in command of a company of infantry when he was eighteen years of age. In 1591 he was distinguished for his bravery in the Normandy campaign under the second earl of Essex and was knighted by him on the field for his part in the siege of Rouen. He and his brother, Sir Charles *Danvers, an equally distinguished soldier, were involved in the long-standing feud with the Long family in Wiltshire which led to the murder of Henry Long on 4 October 1594.

There are two contemporary but conflicting accounts of the incident; according to one, Henry Long was dining with friends at 'one Chamberlaine's house in Corsham' when the Danvers brothers and their retainers burst into the room and shot Long dead (BL, Lansdowne MS 827, fols. 25–9). The other version of events states that Long was 'slain by Sir Henry Danvers while defending his brother Sir Charles against Long and his company' (*CSP dom.*, 1595–7, 34). Both accounts agree that the brothers then fled to Whitley Lodge, near Titchfield, the seat of Henry Wriothesley, third earl of Southampton, a close friend of the Danvers. Southampton was Shakespeare's patron, and some literary critics have suggested that this family feud, ending as it did in duelling and death, may have inspired

Shakespeare's *Romeo and Juliet*. The brothers were outlawed and Southampton helped them flee to France; no indictment was preferred against them by either the Long family or the state.

In France the Danvers joined the military forces of Henri IV and because of their outstanding valour became personally known to the French king, who also interceded for them with Queen Elizabeth. The earl of Shrewsbury also met them in Rouen and in October 1596, commending them to Sir Robert Cecil, wrote: 'Heare is daily with me Sir Charles and Sir H. Davers, two discreet fine gentlemen who cary themselves heare with great discretion, reputacion and respect: God turne the eyes of her Majestie to incline unto them [that] thei shall soon tast of her pittie and mercie' (Lodge, *Illustrations*, 3.78–9). In 1597 Sir Henry Danvers was apparently a captain of a man-of-war in the earl of Nottingham's expedition to the coast of Spain; the earl said of him that he was 'one of the best captains of the fleet'. Danvers's mother Elizabeth, who had by this time married Sir Edmund Carey, cousin to the queen, played a notable part in the campaign for a pardon, and Essex's wife, Frances Walsingham, widow of Sir Philip Sidney, helped in the brothers' rehabilitation. With so much highly placed influential intercession it is not surprising that the Danvers were pardoned on 30 June 1598, though it was not until 1604 that the coroner's inquisition was found to be technically unsound and the verdict of outlawry reversed. Their return to England was delayed until August 1598 because of Sir Henry's illness in Paris.

Danvers soon crossed to Ireland, his patrons Essex, Southampton, and later Charles, eighth Baron Mountjoy, ensuring his employment in the army there. He showed outstanding bravery in the more important engagements of the Nine Years' War, being wounded three times. Under Lord-Deputy Essex in 1599 he was prominent in the reduction of Cahir Castle, and was shot in the face while aiding Essex and Lord Barry near Mallow, co. Cork; in July that year his command of the cavalry near Arklow in Wicklow was significant in the defeat of Feagh McHugh O'Byrne's men. In September 1599 Essex made him lieutenant-general of horse. Danvers was present at the famous parley and truce between Essex and O'Neill, but unlike his elder brother, Sir Charles, he kept clear of the subsequent conspiracy and revolt of the earl of Essex for which both were attainted and beheaded.

Under Lord Mountjoy, Essex's successor, Danvers was prominent in a battle at Moyry Pass (between Dundalk and Newry—the famous Gap of the North) in November 1600 when Mountjoy forced a passage against very strong opposition from O'Neill's forces. He took important rebel leaders prisoner but was shot through the thigh. In the disposal of forces in the summer of 1601 Danvers had command of 100 horse. Mountjoy appointed him governor of the garrison at Armagh in July 1601 and used his cavalry expertise in re-establishing the former fort of Portmore on the Blackwater.

For the decisive siege and battle of Kinsale in the last months of 1601 Danvers, a lieutenant of horse, mobilized detachments of cavalry from the northern garrisons; his troop of horse then made a courageous charge on the rear-guard of O'Neill's forces in their feigned retreat during which Danvers suffered a slight sword cut. In January 1602 he was in England, apparently bringing the good news of the main victory at Kinsale back to the court. He was again in Ireland as sergeant-major-general of the army under Mountjoy during the latter's final campaigns against O'Neill's resistance in Ulster after Kinsale and was much mentioned in dispatches in the taking of Innisloghlin (later Loughinsholin), one of the last major O'Neill fortresses in his own heartlands of Tyrone.

In November 1602 Mountjoy sent Danvers to England 'with a million letters to all my friends there' (Brewer and Bullen, 4.379), and on 4 April 1603 it was Danvers who brought news of the queen's death to Mountjoy in Dublin. James I created him Baron Danvers of Dauntsey, Wiltshire, in the great hall at Hampton Court on 21 July 1603 'for his valiant service at Kinsale in Ireland' (*CSP dom.*, *1603–10*, 23). Furthermore in 1605 by a special act of parliament (3 James I c. viii) Danvers was restored in blood as heir to his father, Sir John, notwithstanding the attainder of his elder brother, Sir Charles. Thereafter he attracted important and lucrative offices. He became lord president of Munster on 14 November 1607, a post he kept until 1615 (though he does not appear to have often resided there), when he sold it to the earl of Thomond for £3200, despite the clamours of Sir Richard Moryson, his vice-president, to succeed to the office. He acquired a grant, in reversion, of the office of keeper of St James's Palace on 15 June 1613, and on 23 March 1621 he became governor of the island of Guernsey for life. He visited the island to present his patent to Guernsey's royal court and to take the oath as the island's 'cappitaine garde et gouverneur' on 25 August 1621 (greffe, 2.313, 315).

Although responsible for the defences of the Channel Islands, and frequently mentioned in this regard in official papers, Danvers was reluctant to reside in Guernsey. Writing to Secretary Coke in August 1627 he thought it was 'not for the king's honour, nor suitable to his own reputation, that he, who was appointed general against anticipated foreign invaders in Ireland, should go to Guernsey to be shut up in a castle'; but, he added, if it was the king's pleasure he would be at Portsmouth before they could bring round a ship for his transport (*CSP dom.*, *1627–8*, 321–2). His residence was not insisted upon, and he visited the island on only two further occasions, in 1629 and in 1636. Under Charles I he was created earl of Danby on 5 February 1626 and sworn a member of the privy council on 20 July 1628. Two years later his mother died and Danby succeeded to her estates. In May 1633 he was made a councillor for Wales and on 7 November installed knight of the Garter. Much trusted by Charles I, Danby was given further commissions, was one of the council of war appointed on 17 June 1637, and acted on the commission for the regency from 9 August to 25 November 1641.

Immensely wealthy and unmarried, Danby became a public benefactor in his foundation of what is now Oxford Botanic Gardens, the oldest surviving physic and botanic gardens in Britain. Probably inspired by his knowledge of the Jardin des Plantes in Paris founded in 1597, Danby first conceived his project in 1621. In 1622 he began to bring it to fruition by buying 5 acres of poor drained meadow and the former Jewish cemetery opposite Magdalen College; he raised the levels, walled the gardens, and commissioned a magnificent gateway of three portals and entrance portico built by Nicholas Stone after a design by Inigo Jones. Danvers's bearded bust crowned the portico, and the entrance was inscribed *Gloriae Dei Opt. Max. Honori Caroli Regis, in usum Acad. Et Reipub. Henricus comes Danby DD. MDCXXXII*. He donated his gardens to the college and university 'for the advancement ... of the faculty of medicine' (Alden, 50): the original financial outlay was in the region of £5000, and he also left in his will the impropriate rectory at Kirkdale, Yorkshire, towards their future maintenance.

The gardens were laid out on the 'living text-book approach' and though Danby failed to get John Tradescant, the king's gardener, he did employ Jacob Bobart, a veteran of the German wars, to collect and propagate plants. In retirement in his country house in Cornbury Park, Oxfordshire, Danby appears to have suffered much ill health; he died there on 20 January 1644 in his seventieth year 'full of honours, wounds and das' (Aubrey, 93), and reportedly worth more than £11,000 per annum. According to his relation John Aubrey, Danby was 'of a magnificent and munificial [generous] spirit ... he was tall and spare; temperate, sedate and solid; a very great favourite of Prince Henry' (ibid.). He was buried in the chancel of Dauntsey parish church, Wiltshire, where a monument of white marble, engraved with some verse written in 1629 by his relative the poet George Herbert (*d.* 1633), was erected to his memory. On his death his titles became extinct.   J. J. N. McGURK

Sources *CSP dom.*, *1603–18*, with *addenda 1580–1625*; *1627–8* · B. Burke, *A genealogical history of the dormant, abeyant, forfeited and extinct peerages of the British empire*, new edn (1883) · F. Moryson, *An itinerary containing his ten yeeres travell through the twelve dominions*, 2–3 (1907–8) · J. S. Brewer and W. Bullen, eds., *Calendar of the Carew manuscripts*, 6 vols. (1867–75), 3: *1589–1600*; 4: *1601–03*; 5: *1603–24* · E. Lodge, *The peerage of the British empire*, 4 (1850), 149–53 · *Calendar of the manuscripts of the most hon. the marquis of Salisbury*, 24 vols., HMC, 9 (1883–1976), vols. 8–9 · *CSP Ire.*, *1600–01* · E. Lodge, *Illustrations of British history, biography, and manners*, 3 (1791) · J. Aubrey, *Brief lives: a selection based upon existing comtemporary portraits*, ed. R. Barber (1975) · *Actes des etats de l'île de Guernesey*, 8 vols. (1851–1907), vol. 1 · Jugements, ordonnances et ordres du conseil, Greffe, Royal Court House, Guernsey, vol. 2, fols. 313v–315v · T. W. M. de Guerin and W. Rolleston, eds., 'Jean de la Marche, 1585–1651', *Transactions of La Société Guernesiase*, 11 (1931), 193–236 · 'William Farmer's *Chronicles of Ireland* from 1594 to 1613 [2 pts]', ed. C. L. Falkiner, *EngHR*, 22 (1907), 104–30, 527–52 · T. Coningsby, 'Journal of the siege of Rouen, 1591', ed. J. G. Nichols, *Camden miscellany, I*, CS, 39 (1847) · A. L. Rowse, *Oxford in the history of the nation* (1975) · A. L. Rowse, *Shakespeare's Southampton* (1965) · GEC, *Peerage*, new edn · E. C. Alden, *Alden's Oxford guide* (1937–8), 50 · HoP, *Commons*, *1558–1603* · will, PRO, PROB 11/194, sig. 123

Archives PRO, letters, state papers domestic, Ireland · PRO, papers, C104/20 42–43, 63–64, 84–91, 109–111, 135–137, 152–153 · Wilts. & Swindon RO, Earl Danby's charity, Dauntsey; deeds and legal papers, estate accounts of Dauntsey (Wiltshire)

Likenesses V. Green, mezzotint, pubd 1775 (after A. Van Dyck), BM; repro. in *Houghton gallery* (1775) · E. Scriven, stipple (after

M. Miereveldt), BM, NG Ire.; repro. in E. Lodge, *Portraits of illustrious personages of Great Britain*, new edn • A. Van Dyck, black chalk study, BM • A. Van Dyck, oils, The Hermitage, St Petersburg; repro. in Aubrey, *Brief lives*, 92 • bust, U. Oxf. Botanic Gardens • portrait; formerly at Dauntsey rectory, Wiltshire, in 1888 • portrait, priv. coll.

Wealth at death over £11,000 p.a.: Aubrey, *Brief lives*; DNB

Danvers, Henry (*b.* in or before **1619**, *d.* **1687/8**), General Baptist preacher and radical, was born at Swithland, Leicestershire, the second son of William Danvers (*d.* 1656), gentleman, and his wife, Elizabeth. A notation on the title-page of his *The Mystery of Magistracy Unvailed* (1663) indicates that he studied at Trinity College, Oxford. Like his father, Danvers supported the parliamentary cause, and in 1647–8 he participated in discussions of the *Agreement of the People* with the radical army officers Thomas Harrison, Hugh Courtney, and others. When the general council of the army debated the state's role in religion on 14 December 1648, Danvers presumably supported toleration, a position he espoused in *Certain Quaeries Concerning Liberty of Conscience* (1649), addressed to Leicestershire ministers. From 1647 to 1652 he served on the Staffordshire committee, and he was an assessment commissioner for Leicestershire (April and December 1649, November 1650, December 1652) and a trustee for sequestered tithes (June 1649). In June 1649 the council of state assigned Danvers and others to oversee the destruction of Belvoir Castle. The council commissioned him a major in the Leicestershire militia (March 1650) and a colonel in the Staffordshire militia (May 1650). From 1650 to 1652 he was governor of Stafford, during which period the council of state praised him for preparing troops to defend against invading Scots. In October 1651 the council ordered him to examine people suspected of helping King Charles and the duke of Buckingham escape. The following year he endorsed Roger Williams's *The Fourth Paper*, protesting against the Rump's proposed denial of toleration to groups whose tenets ostensibly contravened scripture. While at Stafford, Danvers became a General Baptist and was (re)baptized by Henry Haggar.

When Danvers moved to London in June 1653, residing in lodgings provided by the council of state, he became an elder in Edmund Chillenden's General Baptist church. Chillenden may have been the person who persuaded Danvers to become a Fifth Monarchist. A member of the nominated assembly for Leicester, Danvers served on committees for Scottish affairs, prisons, and tithes. From 20 July to 25 October he apparently withdrew from the assembly, but thereafter was prominent in its work. With John James he was a teller for the winning side in the crucial vote of 10 December opposing tithes. Around this time Danvers and others published *Questions about Laying on of Hands*; apparently no copy has survived, but John More replied to it in *A Lost Ordinance Restored* (1654).

Angered by the establishment of the protectorate, Danvers urged gathered churches to protest, but Chillenden successfully opposed his call. In March 1656 Danvers allegedly tried to persuade Baptists to rebel, and in the same year his hostility to the protectorate led him to negotiate with Commonwealthsmen. His father's death in 1656 increased his estate, which was already worth £300 p.a, with property at Swithland and Rothley, Leicestershire. He remained loyal to his Fifth Monarchy principles, supporting the secession of Fifth Monarchists from John Simpson's congregation in 1657, but refusing to support Thomas Venner's planned insurrection the same year. Arrested in April for suspected complicity, Danvers was briefly incarcerated. Following the Rump's recall in May 1659, he received instructions to attend the committee of safety in July, and the same month he was appointed militia commissioner for Leicestershire and Staffordshire. With Hugh Courtney, Henry Jessey, John Vernon, and others he issued a broadside, *An Essay towards Settlement upon a Sure Foundation* (1659), calling for a purge of the protectorate's supporters and the reformation of the ministry and law according to biblical principles. Besides serving on the Staffordshire committee in 1659–60 he became assessment commissioner for Middlesex on 26 January 1660.

At the Restoration Danvers lost his offices. In 1661 he was residing in London with his brother, a merchant, and in nearby Stoke Newington, where Sir John and Lady Elizabeth Hartopp (Charles Fleetwood's daughter) lived. Danvers's circles now included the printer Francis Smith and Jessey, who perhaps taught him how to compose prodigies; Danvers may be the anonymous author of *Mirabilis annus secundus* (1662). In June 1661 Danvers and Clement Ireton were reportedly planning a rebellion. During the autumn of 1662 the informer William Hill and the conspirator Edward Riggs claimed Danvers was on the council responsible for the Tong plot, but the allegations are probably baseless. The government issued a warrant for his apprehension in February, but he eluded arrest. Around this time he married Anne, daughter of Sir John Coke, after she had been widowed in 1662 by the death of her husband, Henry Sacheverell. In addition to preaching at conventicles in 1663, Danvers published *The Mystery of Magistracy Unvailed*, in which he counselled subjection to the government only as a plague and curse, calling for resistance when providence allowed. He fraternized with the astrologer William Lilly, perhaps seeking guidance about such providence. After a visit to the Netherlands, he returned to England with the conspirator Colonel Gilby Carr by 6 November. A warrant for his (or, less likely, Robert Danvers's) arrest was issued on 30 December, but he escaped by going to Rotterdam, where he associated with New Model Army officer George Joyce. Allegedly, Danvers now plotted to enlist men to fight the Turks, though he intended to use this force against the Stuart regime. By April he was back in England, operating at times in disguise, preaching at conventicles, and affiliating with the Independent minister Laurence Wise, the Baptist and former Cromwellian officer John Gladman, and with the Fifth Monarchists Anthony Palmer, George Cokayne, and especially Nathaniel Strange. Danvers was active in London and the midlands. Suspected of complicity in the Rathbone conspiracy to assassinate Charles and re-establish the republic, he was arrested in August 1665, but a crowd rescued him *en route* for the Tower.

After his narrow escape, Danvers went into deeper hiding, though he was reputedly in Ireland with Carr and Thomas Blood in February 1666, plotting to seize Limerick. Another warrant for his apprehension was issued in May 1670, to no avail. Although Danvers did not apply for a licence to preach in 1672, he published an exposition on millenarianism, *Theopolis, or, The City of God*. The following year, his *Treatise of Baptism*, a defence of believers' baptism, joined a rancorous debate triggered by John Bunyan's *A Confession of my Faith* (1672). Having responded to Bunyan's sequel, *Differences in Judgment about Water-Baptism* (1673), Danvers was in turn attacked by Obadiah Wills, Richard Baxter, and Richard Blinman. Danvers responded in the second edition of his *Treatise* (1673) and *Innocency and Truth Vindicated* (1675). To counter-attacks by Wills, Baxter, and Blinman, Danvers retorted in *A Rejoynder to Mr. Wills* (1675), *A Second Reply* (1675), a third edition of the *Treatise* (1675), and *A Third Reply* (1676). Meanwhile, he wrote *A Treatise of Laying on of Hands* (1674), defending the General Baptists' practice. Two years later he published *Solomon's Proverbs*, an alphabetical collection of proverbs intended for students, with Latin translations by S. Perkins on facing pages.

In January 1676, by which time Danvers was again preaching in England, magistrates arrested him on earlier charges of treason and committed him to the Tower. Incapacitated by ill health, he was released on 28 April on £1000 security and confined to his house. Following disclosures of the alleged Popish Plot, Danvers interviewed and managed witnesses for the earl of Shaftesbury; he was also close to Titus Oates and William Radden, a General Baptist attorney associated with Oates. During the election campaign of July–September 1679, Danvers was one of Algernon Sidney's managers at Amersham. With Gladman, Smith, and Radden he was subsequently active in the Salutation Tavern Club, with its links to Buckingham. By 1682 Danvers was preaching to a congregation of approximately 600 in London, which led to his prosecution for holding an illegal conventicle. Around this time he became involved with the fringes of the duke of Monmouth's cabal; he was allegedly present when Thomas Shepherd told Sidney that Scottish dissidents would rebel if they had financial support from England. William Howard reputedly recommended Danvers to Robert West's Rye House cabal for service on a revolutionary council, but the evidence is weak. Not until September 1684, by which time Danvers was in the Netherlands, was the government interested in interrogating him. Incensed by his attempt to prove that the earl of Essex had been murdered, *Murther will out* (1684; republished 1689), the state offered £100 in December for his apprehension.

Although Secretary Middleton made Danvers's arrest in the Netherlands a high priority, he not only eluded capture but secretly returned to London. There he worked with John Wildman and Matthew Meade as a Monmouth agent. The duke wanted Danvers to lead an uprising in London as soon as James ordered his forces to the south-west. After Monmouth landed in Dorset, Danvers, Wildman, and William Disney could not agree on a commander for London, and Meade was in Essex. With neither the stature nor a credible mandate to command, Danvers fled to the Netherlands. Again, the government vainly issued a warrant for his arrest in July 1685. At Middleton's urging, William asked Amsterdam magistrates to apprehend Danvers in December, but they refused. Excepted from James's general amnesty in March 1686, Danvers unsuccessfully sought a pardon. Some of his time was devoted to supporting the former Rye House plotter and Monmouth rebel Joseph Tiley's cloth factory at Leeuwarden, Friesland. He spent his final months in Utrecht, where he died in late 1687 or early 1688. Thomas Macaulay's condemnation of Danvers as a cowardly demagogue is unjust; generally consistent in his commitment to republican and Baptist principles, Danvers is representative of those late Stuart radicals whose religious and political principles moved them to endorse violence as a legitimate means to attain their aims.   RICHARD L. GREAVES

Sources CSP dom., 1649–53; 1656–7; 1659–60; 1663–7; 1682–5 • R. L. Greaves, *Saints and rebels: seven nonconformists in Stuart England* (1985), chap. 6 • PRO, State Papers, 29/44/134; 29/83/28; 29/91/100; 29/97/31 • C. H. Firth and R. S. Rait, eds., *Acts and ordinances of the interregnum, 1642–1660*, 2 (1911) • *JHC*, 7 (1651–9), 285–6, 361 • R. L. Greaves, *Secrets of the kingdom: British radicals from the Popish Plot to the revolution of 1688–89* (1992) • R. L. Greaves, *Deliver us from evil: the radical underground in Britain, 1660–1663* (1986) • Thurloe, *State papers*, 4.365, 629 • B. S. Capp, *The Fifth Monarchy Men: a study in seventeenth-century English millenarianism* (1972) • Pepys, *Diary*, 6.184 • N. Luttrell, *A brief historical relation of state affairs from September 1678 to April 1714*, 1 (1857), 324, 355, 432 • T. B. Macaulay, *The history of England from the accession of James II*, new edn, 5 vols. (1902–5), vol. 1, pp. 408, 459 • R. Ashcraft, *Revolutionary politics and Locke's two treatises of government* (1986) • *The manuscripts of the Marquess Townshend*, HMC, 19 (1887), 43–4 • G. F. Nuttall, 'Henry Danvers, his wife and the "heavenly line"', *Baptist Quarterly*, 29 (1981–2), 217–19 • A. Betteridge, 'Early Baptists in Leicestershire and Rutland [pts 2 and 3]', *Baptist Quarterly*, 25 (1973–4), 272–85, 354–78
Archives PRO, State Papers domestic

Danvers, Sir John (1584/5–1655), politician and regicide, was the third and youngest son of Sir John Danvers (1540–1594) of Dauntsey, Wiltshire, and of Danby Castle, Yorkshire, and his wife, Elizabeth (1545x50–1630), fourth daughter and coheir of John Neville (d. 1577), fourth and last Baron Latimer. His elder brothers were Charles *Danvers and Henry *Danvers. Having attended Winchester College, John matriculated from Brasenose College, Oxford, on 10 July 1601, aged sixteen. According to the gossip of his kinsman John Aubrey, whose grandmother was Rachel Danvers, as a young man John Danvers:

> travelled France and Italy and made good observations. He had in a fair body an harmonicall mind. In his youth his complexion was so exceeding beautiful and fine, that Thomas Bond, esq., of Ogbourne … in Wiltshire, who was his companion in his travells, did say that the people would come after him in the street to admire him. He had a very fine fancy, which lay chiefly for gardens and architecture. (*Wiltshire*, 93)

In 1609, when only in his early twenties, he married a widow, Magdalen Herbert (d. 1627), daughter of Sir Richard Newport. His elder brother Henry disapproved of his marrying a woman fully twice his age and the mother of ten children (her sons included the poet George *Herbert and the diplomat and philosopher Edward *Herbert, first Baron Herbert of Cherbury). According to Aubrey, Danvers married her 'for love of her witt' (*Brief Lives*, 1.195). Magdalen's friend John Donne wrote of Danvers at that time that:

> his birth and youth and interest in great favours at court, and legal proximity to great possessions in the world, might justly have promised him acceptance in what family soever, or upon what person soever he had directed and placed his affections. (*DNB*)

But Donne saw much of their married life, for instance their taking refuge at Chelsea during the plague of 1625 in London, and insists that the inequality of their years was reduced to an evenness by the staid sobriety of their temperaments, and that they lived happily together until Magdalen's death. At an equally youthful age Danvers acquired a fine house and garden at Chelsea: the former he furnished sumptuously and curiously, and the latter he laid out after the Italian manner, which was said to have delighted Danvers's patron, Lord Chancellor Bacon. ''Twas Sir John Danvers of Chelsey', Aubrey wrote, 'who first taught us the way of Italian gardens' (*Wiltshire*, 93). His house, called Danvers House, adjoined the mansion, once the home of Sir Thomas More, which was known in the seventeenth century as Buckingham and also as Beaufort House. Danvers House was pulled down in 1696 to make room for Danvers Street.

Danvers was knighted by James I in 1609 and was admitted to Lincoln's Inn in 1612. Under Charles I he became a gentleman of the privy chamber. He was MP for Arundel in 1610, for Montgomery in 1614, for Oxford University in 1621, and for Newport (Isle of Wight) in 1624, benefiting from the patronage of William Herbert, third earl of Pembroke. He was engaged in mercantile transactions, and particularly the trade with the Americas. In 1624 he learned that the government was contemplating a seizure of the papers of the Virginia Company. With Edward Collingwood, the secretary, he had the whole of the records copied out and entrusted them to Henry Wriothesley, earl of Southampton, a family friend, who deposited them at his house at Titchfield, Hampshire. Danvers was re-elected MP for Oxford University on 16 April 1625, and again on 17 January 1626 and 20 February 1628. On 10 July 1628, a year after the death of his first wife, he married Elizabeth (1604–1636), daughter of the late Ambrose Dauntsey, and granddaughter of Sir John Dauntsey. Through this marriage he came into possession of the estate of Lavington, Wiltshire, where he laid out gardens even more elaborately than at Chelsea. Freely indulging his extravagant tastes, Danvers soon fell into debt, and from 1630 to 1640 was struggling with creditors. He lost his second wife, with whom he had several children, on 9 July 1636; refused to contribute to the expenses of the king's expedition to Scotland in 1639; and was returned to the Short Parliament by Oxford University (for a fifth time), by which time he was the client of Philip Herbert,

fourth earl of Pembroke. In 1641–2 he played a prominent part in the negotiations taking place between factions at Westminster and at Edinburgh. He was also an early patron of Henry Parker, the parliamentarian propagandist. In 1642 he took up arms for parliament, and was granted a colonel's commission but played no prominent part in military affairs. His brother Henry, earl of Danby, a committed royalist, died early in 1644, and left his property to his sister Lady Gargrave. Still in pecuniary difficulties, Danvers resisted this disposition of his brother's property, and his influence with the parliamentary majority eventually led the House of Commons to pass a resolution in 1649 declaring that he was deprived of his brother's estate 'for his affection and adhering to the parliament' (*JHC*, 1648–51, 232), and that Danvers's eldest son, Henry, was entitled to the property. Danvers was ordered by parliament to receive the Dutch ambassadors late in 1644, and on 10 October 1645 was returned to the Commons as MP for Malmesbury in the place of 'Anthony Hungerford, esq., disabled to sit'. Danvers supposedly took little part in the proceedings of the house, but joined the Derby House committee in May 1648.

Danvers married his third wife, Grace Hewett or Hewes (1607/8–1678) at Chelsea on 6 January 1649. Later that month he was appointed a member of the commission nominated to try the king. He was only twice absent from the meetings of the commission, and signed the death warrant. About the same time he was also named to the commission for overseeing fresh parliamentary elections envisaged by the army officers' *Agreement of the People*, which was put before the Commons on 20 January 1649. But Danvers was no social revolutionary. Aubrey called him 'a great friend of the King's partie and a patron to distressed and cashiered Cavaliers' (*Brief Lives*, 1.196). In 1649 he appears to have assisted his son-in-law, the royalist Sir Peter Osborne, to secure his house and a portion of his estates at Chicksands, Bedfordshire.

In February 1649 Danvers was given a seat on the council of state, which he lost a year later after a row with Henry Marten in which Danvers had argued that the council ought to enjoy yet greater autonomy of action independent of parliament. In 1651 it was alleged that Danvers was implicated in a plot against the Rump, but without any solid evidence. In 1651 he was a governor of the Bermudas Company. He died at his house in Chelsea on 16 April 1655, and was buried at Dauntsey on 28 April.

Danvers's family with his second wife consisted of Henry (*bap.* 1633), who inherited much of his uncle Henry's property, and died before his father in November 1654, when the Anglican Thomas Fuller is stated to have preached the funeral sermon; Charles, who died in infancy; Elizabeth (*bap.* 1629, *d.* 1709) who married Robert Wright alias Howard alias Villiers, second Viscount Purbeck [see Danvers, Robert]; and Mary, who died in infancy. Danvers's son Henry bequeathed 'the whole of the great estate in his power' to his niece Ann (his sister Elizabeth's daughter), who married Sir Henry Lee of Ditchley in 1655, and had a daughter, Eleanor, who married James Bertie, first earl of Abingdon, who thus ultimately came into possession of the property at Chelsea. With his third wife, Sir John Danvers had a son, John (*bap.* 10 Aug 1650).

The eighteenth-century historian Laurence Echard makes the remarkable statement, not elsewhere confirmed, that Danvers 'was a professed papist, and so continued to the day of his death, as his own daughter has sufficiently attested' (L. Echard, *The History of England*, 3 vols., 1707–18, 2.647). Clarendon, who describes Danvers as a 'proud, formal, weak man,' writes of his career thus:

> Between being seduced and a seducer, he became so far involved in their [i.e. the parliamentarian] counsels that he suffered himself to be applied to their worst offices, taking it to be a high honour to sit upon the same bench with Cromwell, who employed and contemned him at once. Nor did that party of miscreants look upon any two men in the kingdom with that scorn and detestation as they did upon Danvers and [Henry] Mildmay.   (Clarendon, *Hist. rebellion*, 4.488)

Aubrey's gossip about Danvers gives the impression that he was a man of refinement and geniality. Bate, the royalist biographer of the regicides, was of opinion that Danvers's intimacy with Thomas Fuller, who frequently preached in his presence at Chelsea church, led him to repent of his political action before his death.

SEAN KELSEY

Sources T. Faulkner, *An historical and topographical description of Chelsea and its environs*, 2 vols. (1829), vol. 1, pp. 114, 118–19, 135, 171–2; vol. 2, pp. 50, 125, 130, 140, 142–3, 158, 288 • G. J. Aungier, *The history and antiquities of Syon monastery, the parish of Isleworth and the chapelry of Hounslow* (1840) • F. N. Macnamara, *Memorials of the Danvers family of Dauntsey and Culworth* (1895) • *Letters from Dorothy Osborne to Sir William Temple, 1652–4*, ed. E. A. Parry (1903) • *Brief lives, chiefly of contemporaries, set down by John Aubrey, between the years 1669 and 1696*, ed. A. Clark, 1 (1898), 195–6 • *The parliamentary or constitutional history of England*, 2nd edn, 24 vols. (1762–3), vol. 18, p. 528 • D. Underdown, *Pride's Purge: politics in the puritan revolution* (1971) • B. Worden, *The Rump Parliament, 1648–1653* (1974) • J. J. Slade, 'Yorkshire estates of Danvers of Dauntsey', *Wiltshire Archaeological and Natural History Magazine*, 1, 214–18 • M. B. Rex, *University representation, 1604–1690* (1954) • J. S. A. Adamson, 'The baronial context of the English civil war', *TRHS*, 5th ser., 40 (1990), 93–120, esp. 110 n. • W. A. Shaw, *Knights of England*, 3 vols. (1906), vol. 2, p. 147 • J. Aubrey, *The natural history of Wiltshire*, ed. J. Britton (1847) • J. L. Chester and J. Foster, eds., *London marriage licences, 1521–1869* (1887) • M. Noble, *The lives of the English regicides*, 2 vols. (1798), vol. 1, pp. 163–70 • *N&Q*, 2nd ser., 3 (1857), 495 • *N&Q*, 2nd ser., 8 (1859), 309 • *N&Q*, 2nd ser., 9 (1860), 88–9 • *N&Q*, 2nd ser., 10 (1860), 322 • *N&Q*, 3rd ser., 6 (1864), 148, 334 • *N&Q*, 4th ser., 3 (1869), 225 • G. Bate, *The lives, actions, and execution of the prime actors, and principall contrivers of that horrid murder of our late pious and sacred soveraigne King Charles the first* (1661) • J. E. Bailey, *The life of Thomas Fuller, D.D.* (1874) • GEC, *Peerage*, 7.485 • E. Gosse, *The life and letters of John Donne, dean of St Paul's*, 2 vols. (1899) • R. Brenner, *Merchants and revolution: commercial change, political conflict, and London's overseas traders, 1550–1653* (1993) • will, PRO, PROB 11/248, sig. 264, fols. 2v–3r
Likenesses engraving (after drawing; formerly in possession of Robert Stearne Tighe) • line engraving, BM, NPG; repro. in J. Thane, *British autography*, 3 vols. (1788–93)
Wealth at death see will, PRO, PROB 11/248, sig. 264, fols. 2v–3r

Danvers [*formerly* Wright, Howard, Villiers], **Robert, styled second Viscount Purbeck** (1624–1674), alleged conspirator, was born on 19 October 1624 at Somerset House, London, the illegitimate son of Frances (1600/01–1645), daughter of Sir Edward Coke and his second wife, Elizabeth, widow of Sir William Hatton and daughter of Thomas Cecil, earl of Exeter. The wife of John Villiers, Viscount Purbeck, brother of the duke of Buckingham, Frances had left her husband for Sir Robert *Howard (1584/5–1653) of Clun Castle, Shropshire, fifth son of Thomas Howard, earl of Suffolk. Sir Robert was the presumed father of Robert Wright, as he was baptized on 20 October 1624. Summoned before the high commission in March 1625, the viscountess was eventually found guilty of adultery on 19 November 1627. Raised in France as a Catholic under the surname Howard, Robert returned to England in 1641. After Viscount Purbeck recognized him as his son he took the surname Villiers.

Villiers fought with the royalist forces at Edgehill, and in 1643–4, owing to his mother's influence, he was colonel of a foot regiment and governor of Oswestry. Dismissed by Rupert, he retired to Ludlow, and by 1645 professed to support parliament. Unable to find employment in its service because of his Catholicism, he unsuccessfully sought a position abroad before converting to protestantism under Stephen Marshall's guidance. On 6 January 1646 he embraced the solemn league and covenant before Marshall and soon compounded for his estate, supporting his plea with a certificate attesting his protestantism from Marshall, Herbert Palmer, and Obadiah Sedgwick. Delinquency fines of £2650 on an estate worth nearly £3000 p.a. forced him into debt. On 23 November 1648 he married Elizabeth (*bap.* 1629, *d.* 1709), daughter and coheir of the future regicide Sir John *Danvers of Dauntsey, Wiltshire, and his second wife, Elizabeth, daughter of Ambrose Dauntsey. Elizabeth's inheritance included moieties of various Wiltshire manors, including Malmesbury and Westbury Seymour. Following his father-in-law's death Villiers petitioned Cromwell for a patent to assume the Danvers's surname and arms, citing the Villiers's support of Charles. Lady Danvers protested that this was prejudicial to her family, forcing a hearing in the court of wards chamber on 23 January 1657. After Viscount Purbeck died in February 1658 Danvers renounced his claim to the title. After reportedly plying the electors with alcohol he was elected to represent Westbury in the parliament that convened in January 1659. Opposing factions sought to expel opponents on the grounds of past delinquency and on 12 February the house heard charges that Danvers was a former Catholic and had commanded a regiment of royalist foot. He denied the accusations but Colonel Marvin Touchett, a former officer under Rupert, testified that he had seen Danvers leading a royalist regiment near Bridgnorth. Danvers pleaded his youth and blamed his mother for possibly having raised the troops but the house expelled him and disabled him from sitting in future parliaments, though a vote to consider his incarceration failed by 145 to 112.

Danvers represented Malmesbury in the Convention, though he sat on no committees. On 17 May he denied complaints in the Commons apparently stemming from critical remarks he had made about Charles during his trial. Nothing came of this because the evidence was hearsay, but the Lords took up the charges, summoning Danvers as Viscount Purbeck on 15 June. Kneeling at the bar of the Lords the following day, he averred that he had neither patent nor writ to be a peer, but the Lords proceeded to hear the accusations. Monmouth alleged that Danvers had expressed a willingness to decapitate Charles, and Lord Petre accused him of having praised John Bradshaw as a defender of liberty while castigating Charles as tyrannical. Danvers had also allegedly denied the soul's immortality and scoffed at the last judgment. Rather than responding to the charges he questioned the Lords' right to try an MP, noting that the king was willing to permit him to renounce his peerage upon payment of a fine. The Lords confined Danvers while they gathered evidence, including the earl of Oxford's attestation that Danvers had boasted he 'had rather wash his Hands in the King's Blood, than in the Blood of any Dog in England' (*JHL*, 11.93). Pleading ill health and debts of £5000, Danvers was released on 27 July 1660 after posting a £10,000 bond. He reportedly did not resume his seat in the Convention, claiming he could do his county no good. In Michaelmas term 1660 he paid the fine to renounce his titles of Viscount Purbeck and Baron Stoke and Whaddon. He and his wife petitioned Charles in November for the right to assume the Danvers's surname and arms, explaining that he had received no estate from the Villiers; the licence was granted on 25 March 1662.

Further allegations of disloyal comments led the government to require Danvers to post another bond, for £5000, in December 1660, and he was reputed to have espoused republican principles ahead of Thomas Venner's uprising on 6 January. As a security measure magistrates temporarily seized his horses. By 2 July 1662 he was in the Tower, probably arrested following disclosure of the alleged Yarrington and Nonsuch House conspiracies in late 1661. On 17 February 1663 the government issued a warrant for the apprehension of Robert Danvers or the Baptist Henry Danvers for alleged complicity in the Tong plot. A similar warrant followed on 30 December 1663 in the aftermath of the northern risings. By January Robert Danvers was in the Tower and Henry Danvers in the Netherlands; the government moved Robert to the Isle of Wight and then to York, from where he had escaped by 27 July. He reappears in September 1667 as a prisoner on the Isle of Wight, suspected of treasonable speech. He had been released by 1668, when he obtained the freedom of Chipping Wycombe, Buckinghamshire. After the earl of Arran received Arlington's warrant to arrest Robert or Henry Danvers in May 1671, Arran remarked that both were dangerous. Although Robert had an income of nearly £1000 p.a. in 1660, he was now heavily in debt and fled to France to avoid his creditors. He must have reconverted to Catholicism, for he was buried in the church of Notre Dame at Calais in 1674. His widow returned to their estate at Knighton, Radnorshire, in November, referred to herself as Viscountess Purbeck, and later married Colonel John Duval. Danvers and his wife had five children; his

heir, Robert (*c*.1656–1684), assumed the surname Villiers and unsuccessfully appealed to the Lords for the resumption of the viscountcy in 1675.   RICHARD L. GREAVES

Sources PRO, SP 29/22/191; 29/24/15, 52; 29/28/80; 29/91/91; 29/100/120; 29/217/35; 29/290/65 · *JHC*, 4 (1644–6), 460, 508, 534, 605 · *JHC*, 7 (1651–9), 602–3 · *JHC*, 8 (1660–67), 34, 84 · *JHL*, 10 (1647–8), 360 · *JHL*, 11 (1660–66), 58, 64–6, 75–6, 93–4, 107–8, 166–7, 337 · *JHL*, 12 (1666–75), 673, 679 · Bodl. Oxf., MS Tanner 60, fol. 493r–v · *CSP dom.*, 1656–7, 215; 1661–2, 320; 1663–4, 51, 393, 652–3; 1673–5, 407 · *Diary of Thomas Burton*, ed. J. T. Rutt, 4 vols. (1828), vol. 3, p. 241–53 · *Seventh report*, HMC, 6 (1879), 110, 117, 126–7 · *Ninth report*, 2, HMC, 8 (1884), 58 · GEC, *Peerage*, new edn, 10.684–8 · M. W. Helms and B. D. Henning, 'Danvers alias Villiers (formerly Wright and Howard), Robert', HoP, *Commons*, 1660–90, 2.189–90 · *VCH Wiltshire*, 7.200; 8.150; 9.95; 10.139; 14.122, 139, 142, 166 · R. L. Greaves, *Deliver us from evil: the radical underground in Britain, 1660–1663* (1986)
Wealth at death see will, proved 1676, as Robert Danvers, alias Villiers, GEC, *Peerage*, 10.687–8

Danyell, Thomas (*b.* after **1488**, *d.* **1566**), administrator, probably was born in Suffolk shortly after 1488, the third of five sons of Edmund Danyell, esquire, of Stoke by Nayland, Suffolk (*d.* 1497×1504), and his wife, Grace (*d.* 1509), daughter and heir of Sir Richard Baynard of Messing, Essex. In the will of his mother, dated 6 December 1508, Danyell and his younger brothers were each assigned the annual sum of £5 until they attained the age of twenty on condition that they continue their 'learning'. No information on Danyell's education survives, and his early life is obscure before he entered the service of Thomas Howard (1443–1524), earl of Surrey, duke of Norfolk, and lord treasurer of England. Danyell's paternal grandparents were Sir Thomas Danyell of Rathwire, Ireland, constable of Dublin Castle, and Margaret, sister to John Howard, first duke of Norfolk (*d.* 1485). In 1494 his father was named executor for the duke's widow.

As clients of the Howards, the Danyell family rose within East Anglia and at court. On 16 July 1517 Thomas Danyell was admitted for life by Norfolk to the recently vacated position of writer of the tallies in the receipt of the exchequer. There he joined his cousin Henry Everard, esquire, of Deverston, Suffolk, secretary to the lord treasurer in 1514 and subsequently a teller of the exchequer (1514–40), and other members of the Howard entourage. Danyell's eldest surviving brother, John, esquire, of Messing, had already married a daughter of Edmund Denny (*d.* 1519/20), lord treasurer's remembrancer and baron of the exchequer. Another cousin, John Danyell, gentleman, of Felsted, Essex (*d.* 1518), was in the service of John de Vere, earl of Oxford. Thomas Danyell continued to be active in the private affairs of the Howard family until at least 1540.

The writer of the tallies emerged under the early Tudors as the senior administrative officer in the receipt of the exchequer, below the under-treasurer who was increasingly a non-resident supervisor. Danyell's active tenure of the office for almost thirty-three years before his resignation in May 1550 was highly influential in the development of the administrative structure of the department, and he was the first to be called by the new, at first informal, title of auditor of the receipt, in recognition of the enhanced responsibilities. The auditor supervised the four tellers, composed—in the name of the under-treasurer—the annual declaration of the state of the treasury for presentation to the royal council, and managed the disbursement of crown money. It was Danyell who received Henry VIII's last will, and numerous leagues and treaties, for safe keeping in the treasury of the receipt. And Danyell was the first to establish a gentry family from his substantial profits of office in the department. He had inherited no property from his parents. However, following modest land purchases in the vicinity of his residence in Sudbury, Suffolk, during the 1520s and at Downhall, Essex, in 1530, he purchased five manors in Suffolk and Essex in the 1540s, establishing his seat at Acton Place, Suffolk, about 1546. Danyell's retirement marked the end of significant acquisitions, and at his death in 1566 the landed estate was worth approximately £165 per annum. He was regularly appointed to the Suffolk commission of the peace from 1537 until 1564, and served on commissions for taxation and for oyer and terminer. He was reputed to be a religious conservative who resisted the Edwardian and Elizabethan reforms.

Danyell married first, at an unknown date, Anne, daughter of Sir Edmund Lucy of Suffolk. This marriage produced his only surviving child and heir, Edmund, who married Margaret, daughter and heir of Edmund West, esquire, of Cornard, Suffolk. Danyell married second, by 1550, Frances, daughter of John Butler, recorder of Coventry, and widow of Edmund Felton of Pentlow, Essex (d. 1542). Danyell had long been associated with Felton, and in 1550 he resigned his exchequer post in favour of Felton's relative, Thomas Felton of Clerkenwell, Middlesex, who had served as clerk to the writer of the tallies from 1535.

Danyell died at Acton Place in late 1566; his wife survived him. The elder branch of the family at Messing remained better connected after the fall of the Howards, retaining close ties to Sir Anthony Denny and later Sir Francis Walsingham, but it was Thomas Danyell who through a painstaking bureaucratic career helped to alter irrevocably the ancient course of the exchequer and established a prominent gentry family in his native Suffolk. J. D. ALSOP

Sources J. D. Alsop, 'The exchequer of receipt in the reign of Edward VI', PhD diss., U. Cam., 1978 · W. C. Metcalfe, ed., *The visitations of Suffolk* (1882) · J. D. Alsop, 'The exchequer in late medieval government, c. 1485–1530', *Aspects of late medieval government and society*, ed. J. G. Rowe (1986), 179–212 · PRO, PROB 11/11, fol. 230v · PRO, PROB 11/16, fol. 93 · PRO, PROB 11/19, fols. 102, 235–7 · PRO, PROB 11/30, fols. 45–6 · PRO, PROB 11/49, fol. 37 · PRO, E 36/266, fols. 70v, 73v · PRO, E 368/324, 331 · PRO, E 36/132 · PRO, E 405/115 · PRO, E 405/190–211 · PRO, SP 12/9, fol. 119v · *LP Henry VIII* · W. A. Copinger, ed., *County of Suffolk*, 5 vols. (1904–5) · W. A. Copinger, *The manors of Suffolk*, 7 vols. (1905–11) · *CPR, 1476–1509; 1547–75* · *CIPM, Henry VII*, 3, no. 532 · P. H. Reaney and M. Fitch, eds., *Feet of fines for Essex*, Essex Archaeological Society, 4: 1423–1447 (1964) · D. MacCulloch, 'Power, privilege and the county community: county politics in Elizabethan Suffolk', PhD diss., U. Cam., 1977 · W. Hervey, *The visitation of Suffolk, 1561*, ed. J. Corder, 1, Harleian Society, new ser., 2 (1981), 9–12

Wealth at death approx. £165 p.a.; landed estate: will, PRO PROB 11/49, fol. 37; subsidy assessment for Acton, 1559, PRO, SP 12/9, fol. 119v

Dar Lugdach (d. 525/527). *See under* Brigit (439/452–524/526).

Daranda, Elias Paul. *See* D'Arande, Elié-Paul (*bap.* 1626, d. 1669), *under* D'Arande, Elié (1568–1633).

D'Arande, Elié (1568–1633), Reformed minister, was born, as his will reveals, on 8 May 1568 in or near Lausanne in the Pays de Vaud, Switzerland, of a noble and probably immigrant family: both his parents and grandparents were protestants and he was brought up in the Reformed church 'of the realme of France' (Hants. RO, wills 1634/B/12). He was tentatively linked by Haag to Michel D'Arande, bishop of Saint-Paul-Trois-Châteaux, a member of the Meaux circle, but this seems to lack foundation, as does a claim that the family were of Spanish descent and had fled the Southern Netherlands during the Alvan persecution. By 1603 D'Arande was serving as a Reformed minister at Claye in the Île de France and was recorded at the Synod of Gap. In 1607 he was at Amiens but he had moved by 1617 to serve the Huguenot community of Étaples.

By 1619 D'Arande had succeeded Timothé Blier as the minister of the French-speaking congregation of Southampton. The community, established in 1567 by refugees from the Southern Netherlands, had expanded with the exodus of refugees from the conflicts in northern France. The community's heyday had probably been under Philippe de la Motte and by the early seventeenth century it was in decline, due to the improved European situation, migration from Southampton, and the integration of the exile families into the host community. In 1619 D'Arande represented the congregation at the colloquy of the French churches held in Norwich and was elected as moderator of the meeting. Although the details are unclear, the Southampton congregation seems to have been divided and their relations with the minister were not harmonious. The congregation appealed to the colloquy that year for advice as to how to recover the church's papers. D'Arande's will, begun on 13 October 1624 and concluded on 8 and 9 May 1625, mentions 'the Offences which many and dyvers personnes have committed againste me either through ignorance or mallice', particularly in the Southampton church,

> wherin many which doe boaste themselves to bee the cheefest and moste apparente to have pretexte and couver for theire damnable Avarice, envy, hatred of piety, ingratitude and malignity, have layd to my charge stronge, impudente, secrete, affrontinge and perverse calumniations, and have troubled me by falce and secrete practices and have offended God in divers waies most cruelly in my personne.

Before 1624 D'Arande married Elizabeth Bonhomme (d. 1641); they had two sons who were baptized in Southampton—Paul, who died in infancy, and Elié-Paul D'Arande [*see below*]. D'Arande had already been suffering from gout and other illnesses when he began his will in October 1624; in 1625 he was excused attendance at the colloquy on grounds of ill-health. He died in Southampton on 13

May 1633 and was buried two days later in the town cemetery of St Mary's, Southampton. Although there had been an influx of new refugee members to the French church in 1628, a permanent replacement for D'Arande was not found and in 1635 the congregation succumbed to Archbishop William Laud's assault upon the exile churches.

Elié-Paul D'Arande [Elias Paul Daranda] (*bap.* 1626, *d.* 1669), Reformed minister, matriculated from Merton College, Oxford, on 10 December 1641, aged seventeen. Made a fellow of Pembroke College by the parliamentary visitors in 1648, on 14 April that year he was created MA. He served as assistant to Francis Cheynell, one of the visitors, in his parish of Petworth, Sussex, and on 8 October 1651 was presented under the great seal to the vicarage of Patcham in the same county. He married and had several children, including Paul (1652–1712), later a successful Turkey merchant. An assistant to the Sussex commission of triers and ejectors in 1654, he was instituted rector of Rotherfield on 12 May 1658, but one J. Crawley was admitted in his place the following year. On 2 April 1663 he became pastor of the French church at Canterbury. He married as his second wife, on 25 February 1666, Frances (*d.* 1704x27), daughter of Benjamin Pickering of West Hoathly, Sussex; they had two sons, Benjamin (1667–*c.*1740), later a canon of Salisbury, and Peter. D'Arande died at Canterbury on 17 August 1669.

ANDREW SPICER

Sources E. Haag and E. Haag, *La France protestante*, 2nd edn, 6 vols. (Paris, 1877–88) · A. Spicer, *The French-speaking Reformed community and their church in Southampton, 1567–c.1620* (1997) · H. M. Godfray, ed., *Registre des baptesmes, mariages et mortz, et jeusnes de léglise wallonne et des isles de Jersey, Guernesey, Serq, Origny, etc.*, Huguenot Society of London, 4 (1890) · A. C. Chamier, ed., *Les actes des colloques des églises françaises et des synodes des églises étrangères refugiées en Angleterre, 1581–1654*, Huguenot Society of London, 2 (1890) · wills, Hants. RO, 1634/B/12, 1641/Ad/018 · F. W. Cross, *History of the Walloon and Huguenot church at Canterbury*, Huguenot Society of London, 15 (1898), 137, 208, 234 · *Calamy rev.*, 157 · Foster, *Alum. Oxon.*
Wealth at death £340 19s. 1d.: probate inventory, Hants. RO, 1634/B/12

D'Arande, Elié-Paul (*bap.* 1626, *d.* 1669). *See under* D'Arande, Elié (1568–1633).

D'Arányi, Adila Adrienne Adalbertina Maria. *See* Fachiri, Adila Adrienne Adalbertina Maria (1886–1962).

D'Arányi, Jelly Eva (1893–1966). *See under* Fachiri, Adila Adrienne Adalbertina Maria (1886–1962).

Darbishire, Helen (1881–1961), literary scholar and college head, was born in Oxford on 26 February 1881, the second of the three children of Samuel Dukinfield Darbishire (1846–1892), physician to the Radcliffe Infirmary and coroner to the university, and his wife, Florence Eckersley (*d.* 1917). Both parents were natives of Manchester, where the Darbishires' home in the mid-nineteenth century was a centre of Liberal and Unitarian society, frequented by such distinguished figures as William and Elizabeth Gaskell and James and Harriet Martineau; Helen's grandfather, the elder Samuel Dukinfield Darbishire (1796–

Helen Darbishire (1881–1961), by Lafayette, 1926

1870), a solicitor, befriended J. A. Froude and employed him as tutor to his daughters in 1849.

Helen Darbishire was at first educated privately with her cousins in Penmaen-mawr in Caernarvonshire, where the family lived from 1889 to 1892, during her father's illness. After his death, she went to the Oxford high school. In 1900 she entered Somerville College, Oxford, as a Pfeiffer scholar, and in 1903 graduated with a first class in the recently instituted honour school of English. One of her teachers was Ernest De Selincourt, the first university lecturer in English, and a cousin by marriage of her mother; he became, as she wrote later, 'a lifelong friend … I owe more to his mind and spirit than can be said'. After working as a visiting lecturer at Royal Holloway College, London University, between 1904 and 1907, she returned to Somerville in 1908 as English tutor, and remained there for thirty-seven years. She became a member of the college council in 1913, a fellow in 1921, and she was university lecturer in 1926–31, principal in 1931–45, and honorary fellow in 1946. She was also the first woman to be chair of the faculty board of English. Her only absence from Oxford of more than a few months was as visiting professor at Wellesley College, Massachusetts, in 1925–6.

As a tutor, Helen Darbishire was quick to recognize and foster any genuine response to literature, however immature; and if her teaching was not always immediately stimulating (some pupils found her remote), it was felt as a slow-growing, durable influence, sustained by the continuing example of her own meticulous scholarship. One of the future directions of her own studies is seen in an early publication, the exemplary edition in 1914 of Wordsworth's *Poems in Two Volumes* (1807), which shows her characteristic power of combining close attention to textual matters with sensitive interpretation. She assisted De Selincourt in his work on Wordsworth until his death in 1943, when she took responsibility for the remaining three volumes (1946–9) of the five-volume Clarendon edition of Wordsworth's *Poetical Works*. This may be regarded as her greatest achievement.

Meanwhile Helen Darbishire was laying the foundations of her own monumental edition of Milton, with *The Manuscript of Milton's 'Paradise Lost', Book I* (1931), which broke new ground by demonstrating, through close study of the handwriting of the manuscript, that Milton used spelling and punctuation to emphasize the meaning and the movement of his verse. After *The Early Lives of Milton* (1932), however, publication of work other than articles and reviews was long delayed by her duties as principal—an office unsought, and even unwelcome to her modesty and reserve, but one which was fulfilled loyally and efficiently. Before and during the Second World War she actively assisted displaced foreign scholars. Her tenure of office saw new developments in the college's constitution and additions to its buildings, including the east quadrangle (now named after her) and the college chapel. A selection of her regular addresses was posthumously published in 1962; their keynote was Wordsworth's 'We live by admiration, hope, and love'.

In retirement, after completing the Clarendon edition of Wordsworth, Helen Darbishire returned to her work on Milton. Believing that 'an editor must take his courage in his hands and exercise his critical judgment', she set out to offer a text of *Paradise Lost* 'which represents more nearly than any previous printing … what Milton would have achieved if he had had his sight' (Willey, 410). Although the new text (published in 1952) received criticism, it has remained a foundation for subsequent editions. The second, less controversial volume of *The Poetical Works of John Milton*, containing the rest of his poems, appeared in 1955, and an edition of the complete poems in the Oxford Standard Authors series was published in 1958.

Helen Darbishire expressed the wisdom accumulated from her extensive work on the editions of Wordsworth and Milton in the 1949 Clark lectures at Trinity College, Cambridge, on Wordsworth (published as *The Poet Wordsworth*, 1950), and in the 1951 James Bryce memorial lecture at Somerville, on *Paradise Lost* (published 1951). Further work on the manuscripts of *The Prelude* at the Dove Cottage Museum led to the revision in 1952 of her 1914 edition of *Poems in Two Volumes* and in 1959 of De Selincourt's 1926 edition of *The Prelude*. Her last publication, in 1958, was a World's Classics edition of the *Journals* of Dorothy Wordsworth, with whom she felt a particular sympathy.

Constantly consulted by Wordsworth scholars and eager amateur inquirers from all parts of the world, Helen Darbishire was generous with the fruits of her own researches and with the resources of the Wordsworth Library at Grasmere. As a trustee of Dove Cottage, and, from the death of De Selincourt in 1943 until her own death, chair of the trustees, she greatly developed its facilities as a centre of study. She received many honours for her scholarship. She was twice awarded the Rose Mary Crawshay prize by the British Academy: in 1932 for her work on Milton, and in 1950 for that on Wordsworth. She was elected a fellow of the British Academy in 1947. She received the honorary degree of DLitt from Durham and London, and in 1955 was appointed CBE.

Helen Darbishire was of middle height, fair, with candid blue eyes, and a look of serenity and determination. For the last seven years of her life, Shepherds How, overlooking the Vale of Grasmere, was the 'quiet heart's selected home', which she shared with her friend and 'second sister', Vera Farnell. Age hardly affected her ability to work steadily and unhurriedly, and did not diminish her sense of humour. She died at home, after a short illness, on 11 March 1961.   KATHLEEN TILLOTSON, *rev.* MELANIE ORD

Sources B. Willey, 'Helen Darbishire, 1881–1961', *PBA*, 47 (1961), 401–15 · *BL cat.* · personal knowledge (1981) · private information (1981)

Likenesses B. Meninsky, portrait, 1923, priv. coll. · Lafayette, photograph, 1926, NPG [*see illus.*] · W. Coldstream, oils, 1938–9, Somerville College, Oxford · W. Stoneman, photograph, 1947, NPG; repro. in Willey, *PBA*, 400

Wealth at death £28,930 12*s.*: probate, 21 Aug 1961, *CGPLA Eng. & Wales*

D'Arblay, Frances. *See* Burney, Frances (1752–1840).

Darby [*née* Maude; *other married name* Sinclair], **Abiah** (1716–1794), Quaker minister, was born in Sunderland, co. Durham, the youngest of the thirteen children of Samuel Maude (1665–1730), a Sunderland Quaker and coal fitter, and his wife, Rachel (1667–1734), *née* Warren. Little is known about her upbringing, but by sixteen she was, like her parents, a committed Friend. However, despite a strong inner call to public testimony, she was unable to respond for many years. In 1733 she met John Sinclair, a fellow Friend but apparently of lower social standing. Her widowed mother reluctantly consented (on 10 February 1734) to the marriage. Sinclair died in 1737, shortly after the death from smallpox of their only child, Rachel. Abiah's sister, Jane Nelson of Kendal, tried to bring the young widow into society, but she found this a distraction from the sober religious life to which she felt called.

In 1745, on her way back from London yearly meeting, Abiah Sinclair met Abraham *Darby (1711–1763), himself a widower and a Friend, and they married in Preston Patrick meeting on 9 March 1746. Darby was a partner in the Coalbrookdale ironworks in Shropshire. His improvements to the smelting process in the late 1740s were instrumental in the expansion of the iron industry in that county, which subsequently spread throughout Britain. As a result, the works attracted much attention. Abiah Darby therefore played hostess, not only to Friends, but also to businessmen, described in her journal (67) as 'Company, not Friends' (ibid.), combining this with running a family malting business and bringing up her children. She and her husband had three sons and four daughters; three of the seven died young. Those surviving infancy included two of the daughters, Sarah and Mary, and Abraham *Darby (1750–1789) and his brother Samuel, who were involved in the ironworks and associated ventures.

Shortly after her daughter Mary's birth in 1748 Abiah Darby was 'seized upon with Mighty power to declare the word … the very same words I shoud have opened my mouth with when between fifteen and seventeen years of age' (Darby, journal, 28–9). From then on she often felt strongly called, experiencing spiritual unease, even physical distress, until she responded. Thus she added a tireless ministry of the Word to her other activities, confronting in speech or writing moral laxity wherever she found it. Austere in her demeanour and very outspoken, she nevertheless avoided the hostility some Friends provoked. The range of her ministry is impressive. For example, in a northern tour in 1759 she addressed Friends at Chesterfield, Ambleside, Newcastle, and Shields, three public meetings, and, with their general's consent, the garrison at Berwick. The minister at Morpeth refused to let her use the town hall. Undaunted she handed round books to the crowd and wrote him a letter as his 'well wishing friend', praying he should be 'enlightened by the Glorious Light of the Gospel' (Darby, journal, 64).

Some of Abiah Darby's addresses were subsequently published, such as the *Serious Warning to the Inhabitants of Shrewsbury* (1752) and the *Epistle to the Inhabitants of Hereford* (1754). Her most enduring publication was *Useful Instruction for Children by Way of Question and Answer* (1763). This she wrote 'for the Use of my own Children, … but my Love to all, begot in me a Desire to have it generally spread among the little Children of our Society for their Instruction' (Darby, *Useful Instruction*, iii). As a result of her initiative, stronger links between the women's and the main meetings became part of Friends' practice after 1754 so that each was aware of the others' concerns.

John Fletcher, the evangelical vicar of Madeley, respected rather than merely tolerated the Friends in his parish, and for this Abiah Darby's unfailing courtesy and manifest Christian love were largely responsible, but she regarded attending his meetings 'an exceeding great cross' (Darby, journal, 93) and was distressed that she could not persuade him from his views on doctrine. Her journal reflects her interest in all creation, such as the planets, which she believed might be full of inhabitants, like us capable of glorifying God.

Her husband's death, in 1763, hardly affected Abiah Darby's activities, but growing infirmity from 1783 confined her increasingly to her home at Sunniside, Coalbrookdale, which she shared with her daughter Sarah, her son Samuel, and his family. From 1769 she no longer kept her journal (at least none has survived), and that kept by Samuel's wife, Deborah, only partially fills the gap. As Mother Darby, Abiah was held in affection and esteem by family, Friends, and neighbours. She died at Sunniside on 26 June 1794 and was buried three days later in the Quaker burial-ground at Coalbrookdale. She was perhaps the most remarkable of the Quaker women in the eighteenth century who broke the shackles confining their sex and who lived out actively Friends' ideas on Christian love.

NANCY COX

Sources A. Darby, journal, RS Friends, Lond. · 'Dictionary of Quaker biography', RS Friends, Lond. [card index] · R. Labouchere, *Abiah Darby* (1988) · A. Darby, *Useful instruction for children* (1763)
Archives Dudmaston Hall, Shropshire · RS Friends, Lond. · RS Friends, Lond., Quaker records · Shrops. RRC

Darby, Abraham (1678–1717), iron founder, copper smelter, and brass manufacturer, was born on 14 April 1678 at Old Farm Lodge, Wrens Nest, near Dudley, Worcestershire, the older child and only son of John Darby (d. 1725), farmer and nailer, and his wife, Ann, née Baylies. Nothing is known of Darby's early life before his apprenticeship to the Quaker Jonathan Freeth, malt-mill maker of Birmingham. Just out of his apprenticeship, on 18 September 1699, Darby married Mary Sargeant (1678–1718), the daughter of a linen yarn bleacher. They had ten children, four surviving into adulthood: Abraham *Darby, Mary (who married Richard Ford, a partner in the iron foundry at Coalbrookdale), Edmund (1712–1757), and Ann.

Darby set up business as a malt-mill maker in Bristol, probably in Cheese Lane. In 1702 he went into partnership with three fellow Quakers to set up a brass works at Baptist Mills, Bristol. Darby's contribution to the nascent British brass industry is a matter for speculation, except that, by recruiting foreign workers, he helped to overcome the shortage of expertise.

Baptist Mills used battery, a process of hammering cold brass to make pans. Darby's next enterprise was markedly different; in 1703 he set up an iron pot foundry in Cheese Lane. The two enterprises were distinct, though they were confused by his daughter-in-law, Abiah Darby, who wrote an account of his life. He succeeded in making iron bellied pots using a technique new to iron working, which he patented in 1707 (no. 380). He fought off a challenge to his patent in chancery, thereby acquiring a virtual monopoly in the trade. He probably introduced the reverberatory or air furnace to iron working, using it to remelt iron from the Forest of Dean.

From 1706 Darby seems to have been planning a move to Coalbrookdale in Shropshire. Precise details remain obscure, but the move involved severing links with Baptist Mills and establishing, as well as the Cheese Lane foundry, four distinct new partnerships. The first involved a copper smelter and brass works at Coalbrookdale. The smelter probably survived until Darby's death but the less successful brass works were wound up in 1713. The second was to mine copper. In 1710 Darby signed on behalf of the Company of Bristol an agreement with the countess of Bridgewater's agent for mining rights at Harmear or Middle Hill, just north of Shrewsbury. The subsequent history of mining in this area suggests little was achieved.

The third enterprise was the most ambitious, a substantial works on the confluence of the rivers Severn and Tern to process iron and brass. This 'Joint Works' included battery, nailing shops, the rolling of brass plates and iron hoops, and wire drawing, and was clearly intended to complement the works at Coalbrookdale. Darby was directly involved in the negotiations, but did not sign the lease in 1710. However, the signatories did include his brother-in-law Thomas Harvey and partners in the Coalbrookdale works. The Tern mills provoked the implacable hostility of the landlord and operations had to be scaled down substantially.

The fourth enterprise is the one for which Darby is best known. He leased the semi-derelict blast furnace at Coalbrookdale abandoned by Shadrach Fox some years earlier. His intentions remain obscure, not least because of the inaccurate accounts left by Abiah Darby and by Hannah Rose, the daughter of one of his workmen. However, the account book for 1709–10 shows coke was used in the blast furnace from the first, a major innovation and the culmination of several former attempts to use fossil fuel, including those by Dud Dudley in the previous century.

By January 1710 the Coalbrookdale works were working well, but were still small compared with those at Cheese Lane. However, early promise was not fulfilled; over the next few years shipments to Bristol fell sharply, and by 1712 the partnership was breaking up. One partner, Graffin Prankard, complained about the quality of pots sent to Bristol, urging Darby to use charcoal and 'to sink the copper affair' (Graffin Prankard's letter book, Som., ARS, Dickenson MSS, DD/DN 423). Furthermore, Meshack Fox was suing for the recovery of the supposed estate of his father, Shadrach Fox, including rights to the Coalbrookdale lease. Perhaps in response, Darby and some Bristol backers entered negotiations with the Quaker ironmaster William Rawlinson of Backbarrow in Furness. In terms of pot-founding this proposed partnership makes little sense, although another joint works involving copper and iron is a possibility.

From 1713 the situation improved. The problems with coke firing were resolved, and production increased substantially. A second blast furnace was built in 1715 and Darby gained part control over furnaces at Dolobran near Dolgellau and at Vale Royal in Cheshire. These allowed him to supply his markets in these regions more easily. He also resolved the problems of faulty castings by introducing to iron working the technique of insertion. This involved pressing preformed legs into the sand in the mould, where they became attached to the pot wall in the casting. Although never overcome entirely, his financial difficulties were eased by a mortgage taken out by Thomas Goldney, a substantial Bristol Quaker.

From 1715 poor health caused Darby to leave most of the management to his brother-in-law Thomas Baylies, who nearly caused the collapse of the firm. Darby died at Madeley Court, Madeley, Shropshire, on 5 May 1717, his New House at Coalbrookdale being not quite complete; he was buried three days later in the Quaker burial-ground at Broseley, Shropshire. He was survived by his wife. Darby lived in an age of experiment, in industrial management no less than in technology. He contributed to both, as did many of his less well-known contemporaries; but the firm he founded survived and became a symbol of British industrial success.   NANCY COX

Sources N. Cox, 'Imagination and innovation of an industrial pioneer: the first Abraham Darby', *Industrial Archaeological Review*, 12 (1990), 127–44 · letter by Abiah Darby, c.1779, Dudmaston, Shropshire, Lady Labouchere's collection · H. Rose, Some account of the family of the Darbys, Dudmaston, Shropshire, Lady Labouchere's collection · Coalbrookdale account book, 1709–10, Shrewsbury Borough Library, MS 328 · RS Friends, Lond., Norris papers, esp. vol. 8 · chancery depositions, PRO, C7/89/4, C11/766/8, C11/1379/19 · PRO, Gloucester coastal port books, E190 1252/7–1260/11 · Graffin Prankard's letter book, Som. ARS, Dickenson MSS, DD/DN 423 · A. Darby, letter to Rawlinson, 12 May 1712, NL Wales, MS 10823E · Rawlinson, letter to Darby, c.1712, Cumbria AS, Barrow, BD/HJ 89, Bundle 11/7 · A. Raistrick, *Dynasty of iron founders: the Darbys and Coalbrookdale* (1953) · J. Day, *Bristol brass: a history of the industry* (1973) · R. A. Mott, 'Abraham Darby (I and II), and the coal-iron industry', *Transactions* [Newcomen Society], 31 (1957–9), 49–93 · R. A. Mott, 'Coalbrookdale: the early years', *Transactions of the Shropshire Archaeological Society*, 56 (1957–60), 82–93 · R. A. Mott, 'The Coalbrookdale story—facts and fancies', *Transactions of the Shropshire Archaeological Society*, 58 (1965–8), 153–66 · B. Trinder, *The industrial revolution in Shropshire*, 2nd edn (1981) · legal opinion by Mr Talbott, 1723, Bristol RO, AC/JS 87(5) · J. Pinnell, PRO, PROB 11/434 (168) · case with opinions of Sir Thomas Pengelley, 1719–26, BL, Add. MS 22675, fol. 36 · papers relating to Tern Works, Shropshire, Shrops. RRC, MS 112/15/65–7 · agreement over mining rights, 1710, Shrops. RRC, MS 212, box 105 · U. Newcastle, Misc. MS 32, fols. 313, 323 · *The Quaker burial grounds*, information sheet, no. 3 (Ironbridge Gorge Museum Trust, c.1979) · register of Shropshire monthly meeting

Archives Shrewsbury Borough Library, MS 328 · Shrops. RRC, corresp. and papers | NL Wales, Wilkinson MSS, MS 10823E · RS Friends, Lond., Norris papers, esp. vol. 8 · Dudmaston, Shropshire, Lady Labouchere's collection

Darby, Abraham (1711–1763), ironmaster, was born on 12 May 1711 in Coalbrookdale, Shropshire, the eldest son of Abraham *Darby (1678–1717), ironmaster of Coalbrookdale, and his wife, Mary Sargeant (1678–1718). He was educated at a school at Penketh, Lancashire, kept by a Quaker, Gilbert Thompson. One of his exercise books survives among family papers.

In 1734 Darby married Margaret Smith (d. 1740), of Shifnal. After her death, on 9 March 1746 he married Abiah Sinclair [see Darby, Abiah (1716–1794)], widow of John Sinclair, daughter of Samuel Maude (1665–1730), a Sunderland Quaker, and his wife, Rachel (née Warren) (1667–1734). They had three sons and four daughters, three of whom died young. Of those who reached adulthood, Mary (1748–1807) married Joseph Rathbone (d. 1790) of Liverpool, and Abraham *Darby (1750–1789) and his brother Samuel (1755–1796) were involved in management of the ironworks and associated ventures. Throughout his life Darby was an active member of the Society of Friends.

Darby began to work at the Coalbrookdale ironworks, then managed by the Ford and Goldney families, in 1728. In 1732 new articles of agreement acknowledged that he was to share the profits, and he became a full partner in 1738. During the early part of his career the Coalbrookdale ironworks lay outside the mainstream of the British iron industry. Following the demonstration in 1709 by the elder Abraham Darby that iron ore could be smelted with coke, the two blast furnaces at Coalbrookdale were charged with coke, iron ore, and limestone, which were purchased from local mining partnerships. The resulting pig iron was not, as was usual in the iron trade, sent to forges to be converted to wrought iron, but was used to make castings, principally household utensils. Such wares were sold to ironmongers throughout the west midlands and the borderland, purchases being recorded in the surviving account books for the works from the years 1718 to 1748. The Coalbrookdale works was also the principal manufacturer of cast-iron cylinders for steam engines, which were supplied to every mining area in Britain. Although the Society of Friends eschewed the arms trade, cannon were produced at Coalbrookdale from 1740 until 1748, and probably for some years afterwards.

Darby transformed the iron trade in England. Between 1755 and 1757, with his partner Thomas Goldney (II), he blew in four new coke-fired blast furnaces at Horsehay, about 2 miles from Coalbrookdale, and at nearby Ketley. These ventures represented a new type of integrated ironworking enterprise. Darby and his partners leased mining rights and worked mines through subcontractors. The partners thus became involved in the marketing of coal in brick making and lime burning, as well as in the construction of primitive railways, and the operation of farms to provide horses and fodder. Darby's company continued to make castings at Coalbrookdale, but also sold iron from Horsehay and Ketley, as pig iron from the blast furnace, as blooms of wrought iron from the forge, or as rolled bars or plates of wrought iron. This pattern of organization was copied by other partnerships in Shropshire, and in other ironworking regions.

Darby's role as managerial innovator in iron-making may be compared with that of Richard Arkwright in cotton-spinning and his success was based on two technological innovations. In 1742 he used a steam engine to recirculate the water which had powered the water-wheels of the Coalbrookdale ironworks. Previously blast furnaces ceased operation in the summer for fear of water shortages. Similar systems were used on all the new coke-blast furnace complexes built in the 1750s. It appears also that Darby was responsible for an innovation which made it possible to produce iron which could be forged into wrought iron in a coke-fired furnace. Charles Hyde has argued that coke-blast pig iron was not used for the production of wrought iron before the 1750s because it was more expensive than charcoal-blast pig. Analysis by Lawrence Ince of the accounts of the Knight family, forgemasters in the Stour valley, show conclusively, however, that the coke-blast pig iron which they purchased from Horsehay from 1755 had different characteristics from that which was previously available (Ince). His wife's recollection that about 1753 Darby spent six days and nights experimenting at the Coalbrookdale furnaces further suggests a breakthrough in metallurgical technology.

In 1750 Abraham and Abiah Darby built a three-storey, three-bay mansion above the western side of Coalbrookdale, which they named Sunniside. It was demolished in 1856. None of Darby's personal accounts or diaries survives, but the scale of his home and its landscaped surroundings suggest that he lived in some comfort. He was described as 'small and slight of stature, very active and strong. His eyes were black and very bright and his complexion dark' (Rose, 'Some account'). Darby died on 31 March 1763 at Sunniside, Coalbrookdale, Shropshire, and was buried in the nearby Quaker burial-ground. He was survived by his wife.   BARRIE TRINDER

Sources B. Trinder, *The industrial revolution in Shropshire*, 2nd edn (1981) · R. Labouchere, *Abiah Darby* (1988) · B. Trinder, *The Darbys of Coalbrookdale*, 4th edn (1993) · A. Raistrick, *Dynasty of iron founders: the Darbys and Coalbrookdale* (1953) · L. Ince, *The Knight family and the British iron industry* [1991] · C. K. Hyde, *Technological change and the British iron industry, 1700–1870* (1977) · B. Trinder, ed., *The most extraordinary district in the world*, 2nd edn (1988) · *VCH Shropshire* · B. Trinder, 'The development of the integrated ironworks in the eighteenth century', *Institute of Metals handbook, 1988–89* (1989) · H. Rose, Some account of the family of the Darbys, Dudmaston, Shropshire, Lady Labouchere's collection

Archives RS Friends, Lond., Abiah Darby's journal · Shrops. RRC, financial records of the Horsehay Ironworks · Shrops. RRC, Labouchere collection, letters

Darby, Abraham (1750–1789), ironmaster, was born on 24 April 1750 at Dale House, Coalbrookdale, Shropshire, the eldest son of Abraham *Darby (1711–1763) and his second wife, Abiah *Darby, *née* Maude (1716–1794). He was educated at the school run by James Fell in Worcester. On 3 May 1776 he married Rebecca Smith (1752–1834) of Doncaster. They had seven children, of whom four survived to adulthood, including Francis (1783–1850) and Richard (1788–1860), who were both involved with the Coalbrookdale Company. Like his father and grandfather, Darby was a member of the Society of Friends throughout his life.

Darby inherited from his father shares in the ironworks at Coalbrookdale, Ketley, and Horsehay and in associated mining partnerships. In 1768, at the age of eighteen, he took over from his brother-in-law Richard *Reynolds (1735–1816) the day-to-day management of the Coalbrookdale ironworks, and was a partner with Reynolds in the various concerns of the Coalbrookdale Company for the remainder of his life. In 1776 he purchased the lordship of the manor of Coalbrookdale, and the Madeley Wood (or Bedlam) ironworks, with its associated coalmines. He inherited from his father a half share in Hay Farm on the eastern edge of Madeley, acquired the other half in 1771, and lived there from the autumn of 1780.

Darby was chiefly important as the builder of the Iron Bridge across the River Severn near Coalbrookdale, which was universally acknowledged in the eighteenth century as the first of its kind. Its construction was proposed in 1773 by the Shrewsbury architect Thomas Farnolls Pritchard to the ironmaster John Wilkinson. It appears that Pritchard designed the bridge, but Darby, who was appointed treasurer to the project at the first meeting of subscribers on 15 September 1775, was responsible for its construction. He kept the accounts for the building of the bridge in his personal daybooks and ledgers, and by repute lost considerable sums through his involvement with the project. An act of parliament for the bridge was obtained in 1776, but divisions among the proprietors led to delays, and construction work did not begin until November 1777, and that on a small scale. Pritchard died in December of that year. The project employed about twenty men during most of the summer of 1778, but it was not until the summer of 1779 that the iron ribs of the bridge were raised into place, and not until new year's day 1781 that it was opened to traffic. The costs of construction came to £2737 4s. 4d., a much greater sum than an estimate of 1775, which suggested that only £550 would be needed for this purpose. The costs of the land, the iron-work, and the stone used in the abutments are not recorded. Darby was granted the gold medal of the Royal Society of Arts in May 1788 for the mahogany model of the bridge (later held by the Science Museum, London), which had been constructed by Thomas Gregory in 1785.

Darby was active in many local organizations in Shropshire. He was a trustee of several turnpike trusts, and a subscriber to the Tontine Hotel, the imposing hostelry built in 1784 facing the Iron Bridge. His account books enable his lifestyle to be reconstructed in some detail. His home was comfortably furnished, and he bought luxuries from craftsmen in London and Bristol. He drank wine, as well as chocolate prepared by Joseph Fry of Bristol. He regularly purchased newspapers and magazines, and enjoyed sporting pastimes with two spaniels. He bought apparatus for scientific experiments and was interested in geology, exchanging fossils with Erasmus Darwin.

After the completion of the Iron Bridge, Darby appears to have suffered financial embarrassment, while Richard Reynolds, his partner, and husband of his late step-sister, waxed prosperous. There are no sources which throw significant light on the relationship. Reynolds had scarcely been involved in the Iron Bridge project until he and his son William *Reynolds (1758–1803) purchased Darby's shares in 1781–2. Darby also sold to Richard Reynolds the lordship of the manor of Madeley, and parts of Hay Farm were conveyed to William Reynolds for the building of the canal terminus of Coalport.

Darby died suddenly on 20 March 1789 at Hay Farm, Madeley, Shropshire, following an attack of scarlet fever, and was buried in the Quaker burial-ground at Coalbrookdale. He was survived by his wife. He died intestate and in debt to the partnership, and his farm stock and the contents of his house were sold. The iron-making interests of his descendants were separated in 1796 from those of the Reynolds family, the Darbys keeping control of the Coalbrookdale and Horsehay undertakings. Darby's sons Francis and Richard were both involved in managing the ironworks, but his great-nephews, Abraham Darby (1804–1878) and Alfred Darby (1807–1852), sons of Edmund Darby (1782–1810), were responsible for the great prosperity of the Coalbrookdale concerns in the mid-nineteenth century.   BARRIE TRINDER

Sources B. Trinder, The industrial revolution in Shropshire, 2nd edn (1981) • N. Cossons and B. Trinder, The iron bridge: symbol of the industrial revolution (1979) • R. Labouchere, Abiah Darby (1988) • B. Trinder, 'The first iron bridges', Industrial Archaeology Review, 5 (1979) • A. Raistrick, Dynasty of iron founders: the Darbys and Coalbrookdale (1953) • B. Trinder, The Darbys of Coalbrookdale, 4th edn (1993) • B. Trinder, ed., The most extraordinary district in the world, 2nd edn (1988) • VCH Shropshire
Archives Ironbridge Museum Library, personal ledger • Shrops. RRC, cash books, etc.

Darby, Charles (bap. 1635, d. 1709), poet and clergyman, probably born at Bramford, Suffolk, was baptized there on 1 March 1635, the son of Charles Darby. He was admitted as a pensioner of Jesus College, Cambridge, on 21 April 1652 under the tutorship of Thomas Woodcock, who said that Darby enjoyed 'the best naturall parts of any pupill he ever had, yet extream idle' ('Extracts from the papers of Thomas Woodcock', 84). He was elected a scholar of the college in the following year and took his BA in 1655–6, his MA in 1659. Darby delivered the prevaricator's speech at the commencement of 1660 to great acclaim, but thought that he had 'only shewed that I can play the fool to please Boys', hoping instead that 'God would keep him from such company' (ibid., 84). He was also the author of a number of neo-Latin university poems. To Musarum Cantabrigiensium (1658) he contributed two meditations occasioned by the death of Oliver Cromwell (of which the second was in English) which look to the succession of Cromwell's son Richard as lord protector, but a year after the Restoration his verses on the death of Mary, princess of Orange, eldest sister of Charles II, were published in Threni Cantabrigienses (1661), and in Epithalamia Cantabrigiensia (1662) he celebrated the king's marriage to Catherine of Braganza. He remained a fellow of Jesus College from 1657 to 1666.

Darby was ordained a deacon at Lincoln on 27 September 1662 and a priest at Ely on 19 September 1663. In 1664 Woodcock prevailed on Sir Thomas Barnardiston to present Darby in the rectorship of Kedington, Suffolk. There he remained for the rest of his life. Darby thanked his former tutor for his help and asked for his further assistance in finding a wife, 'with whome he desired not durty mony, but pure vertue, yet in regard vertue was not infallibly certain, he desired 1,000 pounds caution-mony, for vertue should fail' ('Extracts from the papers of Thomas Woodcock', 84). On 8 November 1666 he married Mary Haiward at Sproughton, Suffolk. They had over ten children. Although at least three died in infancy, two daughters, Mary and Elizabeth, lived to marry in Kedington and three sons, Charles (their first child, baptized on 12 October 1667), Edward, and Henry (their last, baptized on 5 November 1683), followed their father to Jesus College. Darby continued to write and to publish during his incumbency, including Bacchanalia, or, A Description of a Drunken Club (1680), a popular Pindaric which had enjoyed four editions by 1698, An Elegy on the Death of the Queen (1695), in memory of Queen Mary, and The Book of Psalms in English Metre (1704), a hymnal prefaced by fourteen pages of familiar melodies to which his renderings are set. 'The tacker[s]: by a Church of England minister', composed about April 1705, a verse satire on those who sought to attach the Bill against Occasional Conformity (1704) to a money bill, has been attributed to Darby (British Library MS Add. 71446, fols. 1v–3v, citing fol. 1v; the manuscript is a copy, not the poet's autograph). Union: a Poem Humbly Dedicated to the Queen (1707) celebrates the Act of Union in figures which tell of his many years of settled rural ministry; 'Thus have I often seen' he comments on the failure to unite the Anglican establishment and the Kirk, 'Two Churches friendly stand in one Church-Yard' (p. 6).

Darby died in Kedington and was buried there, at the church of Sts Peter and Paul, on 19 September 1709.

JONATHAN PRITCHARD

Sources parish register, Bramford, Ipswich, Suffolk RO, Ipswich, FB6/D1/1 · parish register, Kedington, Ipswich, Suffolk RO, Ipswich, FL 595/4/1 · *Boyd's marriage index, Suffolk*, 15: *Grooms, 1651–75: A–K*, 119 · 'Extracts from the papers of Thomas Woodcock', ed. G. C. M. Smith, *Camden miscellany, XI*, CS, 3rd ser., 13 (1907), [49]–89 · Venn, *Alum. Cant.* · *The correspondence of Dr Matthew Hutton, archbishop of York*, ed. [J. Raine], SurtS, 17 (1843), x–xvi · IGI

Wealth at death lands in Suffolk: will, PRO, PROB 11/517, sig. 207

Darby, Sir (Henry) Clifford (1909–1992), geographer, was born on 7 February 1909 at 3 Cross Street, Resolfen, a coal mining village in the upper Neath valley, Glamorgan, south Wales, the only child of Evan Darby, a pit mechanic and blacksmith, and his wife, Janet, *née* Thomas. His father was largely self-taught, and took education seriously, giving lantern slide lectures to men's clubs and church groups on a variety of topics.

Clifford travelled daily to Neath county school, 20 miles from his home. He was a bright pupil, and at sixteen he went to St Catharine's College, Cambridge, on a state scholarship. Although his original intention was to read English, he transferred to geography. Three years later he graduated with first-class honours in both parts of the geographical tripos, and was made a scholar of St Catharine's. When just eighteen Darby deputized for Frank Debenham, the professor of geography, in conducting an enquiry into pioneer settlement in Northern and Southern Rhodesia and Nyasaland. Two substantial chapters came out of the work in 1931–2. Back in Cambridge he completed his doctoral dissertation on the role of the fenland as a physical barrier between East Anglia and Mercia and as a place of refuge in times of turmoil. His supervisor was Bernard Manning, fellow and bursar of Jesus College. Manning was a lecturer in geography and an expert in medieval ecclesiastical history, and he probably stimulated the interest in the medieval world and the Domesday Book as a geographical source which dominated Darby's subsequent professional life. At twenty-two he was awarded the first PhD in geography at Cambridge, and was appointed to a university lectureship in the geography department. A year later he became an Ehrman fellow of King's College, and then an official fellow. For such a young man to succeed so brilliantly in Cambridge immediately after the First World War was a measure of his determination, dedication, and unassuming brilliance. Darby completely reworked the fenland material as an outstanding example of the transformation of the landscape, and his work was published in two volumes, *The Medieval Fenland* and *The Draining of the Fens* (1940).

The intellectual problem posed by the early fenland work was one with which Darby wrestled all his professional life: how to combine successfully place and time, geography and history; in other words, how to write a historical geography rather than a geographical history. The quest to understand the practical and methodological nuances of what he frequently called 'the intellectual borderland between history and geography' epitomized his life's work. He took the view that historical geography was the reconstruction of past human geographies and landscapes, and proselytized with a missionary zeal to establish historical geography as a self-conscious and distinctive discipline.

The opportunity for Darby to put his ideas into practice came with his plan for the volume *An Historical Geography of England before A. D. 1800* (1936), encouraged by his friend and mentor Sir John Clapham. It was begun when he was only twenty-four, and was an extraordinary accomplishment, both personally and intellectually, going through many reprints. Darby also began a long association with the publisher Philip, editing locational and historical atlases. *The University Atlas* (1937) went through twenty-two editions in six languages. It was followed in 1938 by a sister publication, *The Library Atlas*, which ran to fifteen editions. About 600,000 copies of the two titles were produced. Many years later, with the help of Harold Fullard of George Philip & Sons, Darby edited a historical atlas to accompany the *New Cambridge Modern History*. The *Atlas* appeared as volume 14 in 1970, and was still in print some thirty years later.

On 26 December 1941, at the church of St Mary, Tenby, Darby married Eva Constance (*b*. 1911/12), daughter of William Thomson, a doctor of medicine. She was a scholar of Girton College, Cambridge, and one of his students. They had two daughters, Jennifer and Sarah.

Darby's intellectual reputation and record for meticulous and rigorous editing was recognized during the Second World War when he was first commissioned into the intelligence corps, and then, in 1941, became the civilian head of the Admiralty's geographical handbook centre in Cambridge, as editor-in-chief. Each handbook was a sophisticated regional geography (with much historical geography) of the countries concerned, liberally illustrated with maps (many drawn by Gwen Raverat), photographs, and statistical appendices. All the volumes remain excellent sources of information, and examples of synthesis and interpretation. Between 1941 and 1945 thirty volumes were produced in Cambridge by a team of about twenty-five distinguished geographers. As well as carrying out his editorial duties Darby wrote most of volumes 2 and 3 of France; Belgium; the Netherlands; volumes 1 and 2 of Germany; volume 2 of Yugoslavia; and volumes 1 and 3 of Greece. Portions of those on France, Greece, and Yugoslavia were revised after the war as parts of 'a short history' of those countries. For his wartime service he was appointed OBE in 1946.

In 1945 Darby was appointed to the John Rankin chair at Liverpool University. Four years later he became professor of geography at University College, London (UCL), where he spent his most productive years and which he built into one of the major geography departments in the country. At the same time Darby became fascinated with the United States, its historical geography, and its intellectual life. He made many visits to the USA, and offers of chairs flowed in, including invitations from Berkeley and Harvard, the latter resuscitating the subject after a lapse of forty years.

Darby was a powerful figure at UCL but declined administrative positions, preferring to devote his time to scholarship, building up the department, and proselytizing for historical geography. He also served on three government bodies. From 1953 to 1977 he was a member of the Royal Commission on Historical Monuments (England). His knowledge of the history of the English landscape led to his appointment to the National Parks Commission in 1958, and in 1964 he joined the Water Resources Board. There his knowledge of the human impact on hydrological phenomena gained from his study of the fens, of national parks, and of Wales made him a valuable and active member.

Darby's foremost scholarly project was the geographical analysis of the Domesday Book (7 vols., 1952–75). In recognition of this sustained scholarly endeavour, in 1968 the British Academy elected him fellow, the first geographer so honoured. The Domesday work overshadowed his other innovative works on novels, agricultural regions, medieval surveys, early censuses on migration, the relationship between history and geography, the problem of geographical description, and the human fashioning of the landscape, which may have more lasting value than the Domesday project. Darby's other major publications were *A New Historical Geography of England* (1974) and *The Changing Fenland* (1983).

Darby was elected president of the Institute of British Geographers (1961), chairman of section E (geography) in the British Association for the Advancement of Science (1963), chairman of the British national committee for geography (1973–8), and vice-president of the British Academy in 1972 and 1973. He received many honorary degrees, the Victoria medal of the Royal Geographical Society (1975), and the Daly medal of the American Geography Society. He was created CBE in 1978 and knight bachelor in 1988.

On 14 April 1992 Darby died at the Evelyn Hospital, Cambridge, having suffered from bronchopneumonia and Parkinson's disease. His dedication to work was puritanical; he communicated geographical ideas in print and in lectures clearly, succinctly, and unambiguously. He was a towering figure in British geography for sixty years in the mid-twentieth century and was in the first rank of scholars in the country.   MICHAEL WILLIAMS

Sources M. Williams, memorial, *PBA*, 87 (1995), 289–306 · T. J. Coppock, memorial address, King's College Chapel, *Cambridge Review* (1992), 187–91 [revised form of original address] · *Journal of Historical Geography*, 15 (1989) · H. C. Darby, 'Historical geography in Britain, 1920–1980: continuity and change', *Transactions of the Institute of British Geographers*, new ser., 8 (1983), 421–8 · H. C. Darby, *The relations of history and geography: studies in England, France and the United States*, ed. M. Williams (2000) [with contributions by H. Clout, T. J. Coppock, and H. Prince] · H. C. Darby, speech, King's Cam., to mark Darby's 80th birthday, 14 Feb 1989 · A. R. H. Baker, *Transactions of the Institute of British Geographers*, new ser., 17 (1992), 495–501 · H. C. Prince, *Journal of Historical Geography*, 18 (1992), 456–60 · b. cert. · m. cert. · d. cert. · *The Times* (17 April 1992) · personal knowledge (2004) · private information (2004) [Lady Darby]
Wealth at death £329,019: probate, 6 July 1992, *CGPLA Eng. & Wales*

Darby [*née* Barnard], **Deborah** (1754–1810), Quaker minister and traveller, was born on 25 August 1754 at Upperthorpe, near Sheffield, Yorkshire, one of fifteen children born to John Barnard (1723–1789), tanner of Upperthorpe, and Hannah Wilson (d. 1793), of Kendall. Four of their sons and two daughters survived infancy. Little is known about her childhood but she evidently received a sound education and developed a deep spiritual awareness in the Quaker circles in which her family moved.

On 2 August 1776 at the Hartshead meeting in Sheffield Deborah married Samuel (1755–1796), the second son of Abraham *Darby (1711–1763) and Abiah *Darby (1716–1794). Samuel was involved in the family ironworks and related business ventures centred around Coalbrookdale, Shropshire. Samuel and Deborah lived initially in London at George's Yard, near Gracechurch Street, as since 1775 Samuel had had charge of the family's London manufactory. Their life in London was overshadowed by the death of their first baby in 1778, Samuel's poor health, and business difficulties. In 1779 they moved to the family home of Sunniside, Coalbrookdale, which soon became their permanent home as the London business was sold.

On 1 August 1779 Deborah began the journal which she kept until the end of her life. In the same month she began to transcribe the journal of her mother-in-law, a Quaker travelling minister. Deborah's diary contains some personal information, for example about her husband's worsening mental health and her children, Samuel (1779–1808), a daughter who lived for just a few hours in 1780, and Edmund (1782–1810), but is overwhelmingly concerned with spiritual matters. She too became a travelling minister certified by her home meeting and her journal records the lengthy and arduous journeys she made to visit Quaker meetings and homes, schools, and prisons, and sometimes the services of other denominations. She usually travelled with another woman, first Ann Summerland and later Rebecca Young, and her journal records whom and where they visited and their spiritual 'opportunities'. Hers is not a travel journal in the conventional sense: there is scant comment on the character of the places they visited, the landscapes they passed through, or the political events of the times, even in turbulent places such as Ireland. Instead she describes meetings, visits, and opportunities, often judging them 'favoured', 'comfortable', or 'solid', but sometimes finding them 'trying' and 'exercising'.

Deborah's travels began in 1782. She first visited areas in southern England and then made the first of several successful journeys to Wales, despite the difficulties of understanding Welsh Quakers. A tour to Scotland followed in 1786–7 and thereafter she ventured further afield, despite the fact that her children were still very young. She went to Ireland (which she visited three times), France and the Channel Islands, and America (1793–6). She visited almost all the local or monthly meetings known to have existed in America from Tennessee in the south to Maine in the north, ministering to Friends and non-Friends; black, Native American, and white; young and old, in an exhausting schedule which made very few concessions to the harsh climatic conditions or poor transport links. On Long Island she met Stephen Grellet, a refugee from the French Revolution, who became a Friend under her influence. He recalled 'she seemed like one reading the pages of my heart' (Labouchere, *Deborah Darby*, 197) and went on to become an extremely important minister.

Deborah arrived back in England in June 1796 to find her husband very ill. His death on 1 September 1796, though greeted with sorrow, did not change the pattern of her life, much of which continued to be spent away from home, though it did cause her to play a more active role in the affairs of the company on whose board she now sat, representing her own and her sons' interests.

Following a difficult visit in 1797–8 to Ireland, Deborah returned to Coalbrookdale to a memorable meeting with Elizabeth Gurney, later Fry. Elizabeth Gurney was seeking inspiration for a change in her life and found it in Darby, who foretold that she would spend her life in ministry.

Deborah Darby continued her travels, recording all carefully, and finding continued comfort in her friend Rebecca Young and the latter's husband: but she began to feel her age, recording in 1805 'how awfully rapid is the progress of time, how difficult to keep pace with it' (Labouchere, *Deborah Darby* 304). She none the less made her third visit to Ireland in 1807, but afterwards had spells of illness. By 1810 she was housebound and she died on 14 February 1810 at Sunniside, Coalbrookdale, having suffered from 'inflammation on the lungs' (letter of her son; Labouchere, *Deborah Darby*, 337) and was buried on 22 February at the Friends' burial-ground there, beside her husband.

Deborah Darby's ministry had been remarkable. Her manner was said to be gentle and attractive and her voice musical and she held listeners' attention by the power of her own convictions. Her journal provides only rare insights as to what she said, since according to Quaker tradition she did not prepare her words in advance but spoke as she was moved at the moment (or remained silent, though she knew this would disappoint meetings). It does though give a detailed insight into the life of an early Quaker travelling minister and into the famous Darby family. ELIZABETH BAIGENT

Sources R. Labouchere, *Deborah Darby of Coalbrookdale, 1754–1810* (c.1993) • R. Labouchere, *Abiah Darby, 1716–1793* (1988) • B. Trinder, *The Darbys of Coalbrookdale* (1993)
Archives RS Friends, Lond., corresp. and material

Darby, George (c.1720–1790), naval officer, is a man of whose parentage and upbringing nothing is known. He entered the navy as a volunteer per order in the *Sunderland* and served under Edward Boscawen. He was promoted lieutenant on 7 September 1742. After being promoted commander he was posted on 12 September 1747 to the *Warwick* (60 guns). In 1757 he commanded the *Norwich* (50 guns) in the West Indies and in the same ship he served under Rodney in 1759 at the bombardment of Le Havre. In January 1760 Rear-Admiral George Bridges Rodney left him in command of the squadron. Darby then came under Commodore Lord Colvill who brought relief to Quebec in May 1760. In 1761 Darby, backed by Colvill, resisted John Amherst's order to take 0.5 per cent instead of the customary 1 per cent on carriage of money to pay troops in the West Indies. Early in 1762 Darby, in the *Devonshire* (64 guns) participated in Rodney's capture of Martinique. In February Rodney sent Darby, together with Major Horatio Gates, home with the dispatches. Each duly received an award of £500 from the king.

In 1768 Darby married Mary, daughter of Sir William St Quentin, baronet; the couple had two sons before her death on 5 April 1773. At some point before 1777 Darby married the widow of a Thomas Bridges, a sister of the barrister and MP Richard Jackson. On 23 January 1778 Darby was promoted rear-admiral of the white, but he did not go to sea that year. On 19 March 1779 he was advanced to vice-admiral of the blue. He remained apolitical during the Keppel–Palliser affair, though in April he reluctantly presided at Palliser's court martial. As Sir Charles Hardy's second-in-command he sailed in June with his flag in the *Britannia* (100 guns). He commanded the van division of a fleet of thirty ships of the line and had as his flag-captain a youthful Charles Morrice Pole—who later became an admiral of the fleet. In August Hardy countered the advance of a greatly superior allied fleet by retiring, adroitly if ingloriously, to Portsmouth. Lord Sandwich reported to the king that Lord Mulgrave, a commissioner of the Admiralty serving in the fleet as a captain, 'speaks very highly of Admiral Darby and says he is quite adored in the fleet' (5 Sept 1779, George III, *The Correspondence of King George III*, ed. J. Fortescue, 6 vols., 1927–8, 4.424). In the spring of 1780, when the fleet was again preparing for sea, Hardy suddenly died. The chief command in the channel was now refused by Samuel Barrington but was accepted by the seventy-year-old Sir Francis Geary. With Barrington, Darby, Digby, and Ross as his subordinate flag-officers, he cruised during June and July, for the most part off Ushant, with twenty-four of the line. In August Geary saw an important Jamaican convoy clear of the western approaches. A week later the allies intercepted this convoy, a calamitous event which emphasized Britain's relative weakness in home waters. Early in September Geary resigned his command on grounds of ill health. His obvious successor was Barrington but, hoping to lever Keppel back into the chief command, Barrington again refused to serve in that post. On 2 September the king strongly agreed with Sandwich that Darby should now be appointed. On 6 September Darby was made a lord of the Admiralty and on 26 September he was promoted vice-admiral of the white. Between 1780 and 1784 he also served as an MP for Plymouth. If Darby lacked Barrington's experience of high command in action, he had given ample indications of professional ability, steadiness, tact, and dependability. He was determined to lay to rest the political divisions which had hampered the navy since the onset of the American War of Independence.

On 26 October 1780 Darby, in the *Britannia*, sailed from Torbay with twenty-two ships of the line. His second-in-command was Vice-Admiral Francis Samuel Drake with his flag in the *Victory*. Darby cruised in the hope of meeting one of the allied squadrons based at Cadiz. Meanwhile d'Estaing, with thirty-eight French ships of the line, was about to sail from Cadiz. In November Darby cruised off Cape St Vincent. By 10 December he realized that, in limited visibility, he had narrowly missed meeting the French. He lamented to Sandwich having 'been so long at sea without doing the smallest service to the nation' (*Private Papers of … Sandwich*, 3.309). On 21 December he returned to St Helens. D'Estaing did not reach Brest until 3 January 1781.

On 19 February the senior naval lord of the Admiralty, Lord Mulgrave, wrote, on Sandwich's instruction, to defend Darby from criticisms emanating from within the Commons. In particular Mulgrave strongly rejected the tale that he disliked serving under Darby. 'Admiral Darby', he wrote to Sandwich, was

> the last man under whom I would serve with reluctance. From what I have always heard and seen of his behaviour during the two former wars, I had been used to look on him as an officer of great firmness, spirit, knowledge, and experience. That opinion has been much confirmed by serving with and under him. (*Private Papers of … Sandwich*, 4.31)

Having no personal bias in the matter, Mulgrave thought Darby admirably well placed in the chief command of the Channel Fleet.

Meanwhile the country's strategic problems had been further magnified by Dutch membership of the hostile alliance. In some desperation the government decided to give priority during 1781 to two warlike objectives, namely the reinforcement of the West Indies and a second relief to Gibraltar. This last enterprise, which was entrusted to Darby, entailed great risks. With a Channel Fleet inferior in numbers to the French at Brest, he had also to shepherd his convoy past the main Spanish fleet at Cadiz, see the supplies carried, despite local interference, into Gibraltar, and return before the French occupied westerly parts of the English Channel. As it turned out, Córdoba, superior in numbers to Darby, had returned to Cadiz for replenishment while Darby, having had to collect victuallers from Ireland, did not reach Gibraltar until 12 April. He delegated command of the unloading process to Rear-Admiral Sir John Ross who, despite some harassment from Spanish gunboats, performed the task in exemplary fashion. As soon as the wind came easterly Darby, as ordered, sailed for home. None the less he just missed La Motte-Piquet on that admiral's return to Brest. The French had taken eighteen prizes in the defenceless soundings.

During the course of 1781 Darby put to sea on three further occasions but he was never strong enough to be able to control the western approaches. On the second of these occasions his twenty-one of the line faced a Franco-Spanish fleet of forty ships. After conferring with Sir John Ross and Commodore John Elliot, both by nature much inclined where possible to the offensive, he settled on the successful defensive solution of anchoring with the fleet in Torbay on 25 July. He reported to Sandwich that he had arranged his ships 'in the form of a crescent in two lines' (*Private Papers of … Sandwich*, 4.60). The enemy did not dare either to attack or try to move on past him.

On the change of government in March 1782 Darby resigned from his command. He had efficiently performed all the tasks assigned to him, difficult and discouraging though the circumstances were. Nor was he himself exempt from that recurrent scourge of seamen, the scurvy. Darby's second wife died on 12 November 1790 and he himself followed her on 26 November.

RUDDOCK MACKAY

Sources DNB · *The private papers of John, earl of Sandwich*, ed. G. R. Barnes and J. H. Owen, 4 vols., Navy RS, 69, 71, 75, 78 (1932–8) · N. A. M. Rodger, *The insatiable earl: a life of John Montagu, fourth earl of Sandwich* (1993) · W. L. Clowes, *The Royal Navy: a history from the earliest times to the present*, 7 vols. (1897–1903); repr. (1996–7), vol. 3 · A. T. Patterson, *The other armada: the Franco-Spanish attempt to invade Britain in 1779* (1960) · I. R. Christie, 'Darby, George', HoP, *Commons, 1754–90*, 2.299 · N. A. M. Rodger, *The wooden world: an anatomy of the Georgian navy* (1986) · E. H. Jenkins, *A history of the French navy* (1973) · D. Syrett and R. L. DiNardo, *The commissioned sea officers of the Royal Navy, 1660–1815*, rev. edn, Occasional Publications of the Navy RS, 1 (1994)

Archives BL, letter-book and order-book, Add. MSS 38681–38682 · PRO, Admiralty records | NMM, letters to Lord Sandwich · NMM, Sandwich papers, SAN/F/28

Likenesses C. Knight, stipple, pubd 1781 (after C. Sherriff), BM · G. Romney, oils, 1783–6, NMM; repro. in Barnes and Owen, eds., *Private papers*, vol. 4

Wealth at death see will, PRO, PROB 11/1190

Darby, Joan (*d.* 1708/9). *See under* Darby, John (*d.* 1704).

Darby, John (*d.* 1704), printer, was born in Diseworth, Leicestershire, the son of John Darby, a husbandman. Anecdotal sources suggest that he was born in 1625, though no record exists to corroborate this. Similarly nothing else is known about his parents, or indeed his early education. On 6 September 1647, he was apprenticed to a bookbinder, John Hide. He was apparently transferred, about 1654, to a new master, Peter Cole, a bookseller who also diversified into printing. Darby was released from his apprenticeship in 1660.

Darby's precise whereabouts for the next four years are uncertain; but in 1664 he began working in the London printing house of Simon Dover, whose widow, Joan, he married some time between 1664 and 1666. The background of **Joan Darby** (*d.* 1708/9), as she then became, is unclear before 1664; however, she evidently worked with her first husband as a printer in Christopher's Alley, Aldersgate, specializing in the illicit printing of radical texts. Simon Dover's professional activities led to his conviction in 1663, and he died in prison in April 1664. The same year, Joan—together with Darby—relocated to Bartholomew Close, London, where both lived until their deaths. Joan continued to work under the name J. Dover until 1666, by which time she and Darby were married. Thereafter Darby's name appears on the title-pages of works officially printed by the house, and at this point the careers of husband and wife became inextricably related. Joan Darby brought to the marriage one son, James Dover, who also became a printer; she and Darby had three or four further children, including two daughters, Mary and Elizabeth (the latter married a bookseller, Andrew Bell), and a son, John, who succeeded his father in a printing business which, by 1700, had become an extended family enterprise. Roger L'Estrange, surveyor of the presses, described Joan Darby as 'one of the craftiest and most obstinate of the trade' (*CSP dom.*, *1667–8*, 360); the bookseller John Dunton eulogized her as 'chaste as a picture cut in Alabaster' (Dunton, 328).

To all appearances the output of John Darby throughout the 1660s and 1670s was characterized by the scientific and navigational texts, together with almanac work for the Stationers' Company, to which he put his name. In practice, however, his career represents perhaps the most persistent and successful instance of resistance to the strictures of censorship and press surveillance in Restoration England. Blacklisted as a printer who had established himself contrary to the Printing Act of 1662, Darby was constantly investigated by both L'Estrange's men and the Stationers' Company. He was involved from the outset in the printing of Quaker texts and such incendiary works as *A Trumpet Blown in Sion*, and the mid to late 1660s saw a series of warrants against the Darby house, resulting in its master's repeated arrest, charge, and binding upon recognizance. In April 1668 he was arrested for his alleged part in the publication of a libellous broadside, *The Poor Whore's Petition*; released upon recognizance in May, he was imprisoned again in December with William Penn for printing the latter's *The Sandy Foundation Shaken*.

Undeterred by the regular dismantling and confiscation of his presses, Darby acquired replacements and continued apace. In 1670 he printed a series of pamphlets attacking the second Conventicle Act, and while expanding his range of technical and cartographic texts on the one hand, on the other he was involved in the printing of *The Rehearsal Transpros'd* (1672) and, even more controversially, *Mr. Smirke* (1676), both by Andrew Marvell. By the late 1670s Darby's business had expanded considerably to include devotional works by both conformists and nonconformists, and further work for the Stationers' Company. In the early 1680s Darby's professional association with whig radicals brought him again under close governmental scrutiny. Clearly responsible for the printing of seditious works, including the *Julian* texts of Samuel Johnson and a folio edition of *Lord Russell's Speech*, Darby appeared before the privy council in 1683 and was eventually fined and bound to good behaviour. He remained subject to surveillance and searches until the revolution of 1688.

After this time Darby and his professional family continued to print and reprint controversial radical texts alongside accounts of the national land bank and almanacs. Nevertheless, in 1689 Darby was accepted into the livery of the Stationers' Company, at last achieving professional recognition. He died in 1704 (supposedly on 11 December), leaving to his wife and children a thriving business, assets of unknown value deposited in the Bank of England, and the leasehold on two houses in Bartholomew Close. Joan Darby followed her husband to the grave in 1708 or early 1709; alongside bequests to her family she left 20*s.* to Richard Allen, pastor of the General Baptist church at Paul's Alley, Barbican, to be distributed among the poor of his congregation.

Simultaneously condemned and praised as an 'Anabaptist', and associated professionally with radicals, John Darby's faith was, doubtless, strongly nonconformist. No likeness survives of him. However, Dunton characterized him as '*cool and Temperate*' and 'very Happy in all his Relations' (Dunton, 328). L'Estrange lambasted his *bête noire* as 'as dangerous and desperate an Anabaptist as lives', 'bold, cunning and bloody' (*CSP dom.*, *Jan–June 1683*, 336, 346). Yet Dunton pays tribute to 'the *Religious Printer*' who 'goes to Heaven with the *Anabaptists*', portraying him as 'a *True Assertor of English Liberties*', and 'no *Biggot* to any Party' (Dunton, 328). That Darby inspired such extreme representation, by licenser and nonconformist bookseller alike, testifies in some measure to a figure of tenacity, ingenuity, and exceptional success at the heart of nonconformist print culture.

BETH LYNCH

Sources *CSP dom.*, 1663–4; 1666–9; 1671–2; 1675–7; 1683; 1685; 1689–90 • J. S. T. Hetet, 'A literary underground in Restoration England: printers and dissenters in the context of constraints, 1660–1689', PhD diss., U. Cam., 1987 • D. F. McKenzie, ed., *Stationers' Company apprentices*, [2]: 1641–1700 (1974) • Wing, *STC* • P. G. Morrison, *Index of printers, publishers and booksellers in Donald Wing's 'Short-title catalogue of books … 1641–1700'* (1955) • J. Dunton, *The life and errors of John Dunton … written by himself* (1705) • *Fourth report*, HMC, 3 (1874) • *Fifth report*, HMC, 4 (1876) • *Sixth report*, HMC, 5 (1877–8) • *Seventh report*, HMC, 6 (1879) • *Eighth report*, 3 vols. in 5, HMC, 7 (1881–1910) • *Ninth report*, 3 vols., HMC, 8 (1883–4) • H. R. Plomer and others, *A dictionary of the booksellers and printers who were at work in England, Scotland, and Ireland from 1641 to 1667* (1907) • H. R. Plomer and others, *A dictionary of the printers and booksellers who were at work in England, Scotland, and Ireland from 1668 to 1725* (1922) • R. Myers, ed., *Records of the Worshipful Company of Stationers: wardens accounts, 1663–1728* (1985), 7: reel 76: film no. 8520 [microfilm] • will, PRO, PROB 11/496, fols. 352r–352v • will of Joan Darby, PRO, PROB 11/507, fols. 62r–62v • E. Arber, ed., *The term catalogues, 1668–1709*, 3 vols. (privately printed, London, 1903–6) • G. E. B. Eyre, ed., *A transcript of the registers of the Worshipful Company of Stationers from 1640 to 1708*, 3 vols. (1913–14) • C. H. Timperley, *Encyclopaedia of literary and typographical anecdote*, 2nd edn (1842) • Trinity Cam., Jeremy Maule MSS • N. H. Keeble, *The literary culture of nonconformity in later seventeenth-century England* (1987) • G. Kitchin, *Sir Roger L'Estrange: a contribution to the history of the press in the seventeenth century* (1913) • T. Crosby, *The history of the English Baptists, from the Reformation to the beginning of the reign of King George I*, 4 vols. (1738–40), vol. 4 • W. Wilson, *The history and antiquities of the dissenting churches and meeting houses in London, Westminster and Southwark*, 4 vols. (1808–14), vol. 3, pp. 234, 238–41

Wealth at death left £10 apiece to three children; shares and stocks in Bank of England; dividends from business; leasehold on two houses; residue to Joan: will, 19 Feb 1702, PRO, PROB 11/496, fols. 352*r*–352*v* · £5 apiece to surviving children, £30 to grand-children on reaching twenty-one; 20*s*. to pastor and poor of church; 40*s*. to maidservant; residue to son John: will [Joan Darby] 16 April 1708, PRO, PROB 11/507, fols. 62*r*–62*v*

Darby, John Nelson (1800–1882), member of the so-called (Plymouth) Brethren, was born on 18 November 1800 at 9 Great George Street, Westminster, the youngest of six brothers who survived infancy. His father, John Darby of Markly, Warbleton, Sussex, was born in 1751 and was said to have profited as a merchant from naval contracts in the Napoleonic wars. He inherited Leap Castle, King's county, Ireland, in 1823 and died in 1834. His wife, Anne, the daughter of Samuel Vaughan, died in 1847. John Nelson Darby's second name echoes the festivities during the month of his birth, celebrating the arrival in England of the admiral under whom his uncle Sir Henry D'Esterre Darby served at the battle of the Nile. After attending Westminster School (1812–15) and Trinity College, Dublin, where he graduated as a gold medallist in 1819, John Darby was admitted in the same year to Lincoln's Inn, having previously been admitted to King's Inn, Dublin. To his father's displeasure Darby abandoned the law and was ordained in August 1825, going to work among the peasants in Calary, near Enniskerry, co. Wicklow. In late 1827 he was injured in a riding accident and his spiritual experience in the following months, when he was convalescing in the Delgany and Dublin homes of his sister Susan Pennefather, was of crucial importance for his future development. Previously he had been an exact churchman, attaching great importance to sacramental grace, but now he discovered what he later referred to as a 'deliverance from bondage' and the reality of 'union with Christ'.

Darby's growing disillusion, especially with the Erastian tendencies of the Irish establishment, gave rise to his *Considerations on the Nature and Unity of the Church* (1828), in which he deplored the worldliness of many churchmen and dissenters alike, and likewise the divisions between believers. He now resigned his curacy to do itinerant mission work, though he had not yet seceded and still wore his clerical robes. It is not clear how far he was involved at this stage with those such as Anthony Groves (1795–1853) and John Bellett who began in 1829 to 'break bread' informally, and with whom Darby was later to be associated in the Brethren movement.

In 1830 Darby's enthusiasm was rebuffed by the doyen of evangelicalism, Charles Simeon, at Cambridge, but at Oxford he was warmly received in May and June by John Hill and Francis Newman, who had tutored his nephews in Ireland, as also by Henry Bulteel and Benjamin W. Newton; the latter encouraged him to investigate the manifestations of glossolalia near Port Glasgow, and then in December to visit Plymouth. Darby's zest for controversy in these years is well illustrated by his anonymous pamphlet in support of Bulteel's Calvinism and against Professor Edward Burton, published at Oxford in 1831, and by his spirited attack in 1832 on Archbishop Whately and his fellow commissioners on the Irish board of education. By

John Nelson Darby (1800–1882), by Edward Penstone

September he was advocating a decidedly separatist position in the prophetic conference at Powerscourt, and when the ecclesiastical authorities wound up the Irish home mission in 1833 they were throwing away what was, in Darby's eyes, their last saving grace.

By now Darby was closely identified with the Brethren assembly at Plymouth which, he said, had 'altered the face of Christianity for me' (*Letters*, 3.230); and his secessionist preaching, especially in Ireland, where one archiepiscopal biographer described him as 'this Goliath of Dissent' (J. D. Sirr, *Memoir of … Power Le Poer Trench*, 1845, 344), resulted in the establishment of many Brethren meetings similar to the one at Plymouth. Several clergy followed his lead, but by 1837 the work in Ireland was hampered by his notoriety. There are some indications that in the early 1830s Darby and Theodosia Wingfield, the widow of Viscount Powerscourt, considered the possibility of marriage, but his itinerant lifestyle precluded any such union. He had a small private income derived from several family legacies, but he lived simply and was generous in his giving.

Fascinated by the continental *réveil*, Darby had visited Switzerland in 1835 and in 1837. The *dissident* assembly in Geneva, which was in some confusion on questions of ecclesiastical order, welcomed Darby in 1839, as his ministry at this stage emphasized unity rather than separation. Similarly in 1840 the Calvinist emphasis of his teaching was appreciated by the *dissidents* in Lausanne, who were troubled by growing Methodist activity. Darby's lectures, published as *L'attente actuelle de l'Eglise* (1840), in which can be found the earliest systematic exposition of his very distinctive teaching that the church was in ruins, were also well received by certain members of the state church who were apprehensive about the Erastianism of the ecclesiastical constitution which would come into force in 1841. Such was their enthusiasm that some of them began to break bread with Darby in 1840. When, in the following year, certain of the *dissidents* questioned his ecclesiology, Darby called for a general separation from all existing churches in favour of 'non-sectarian groups of believers'. To this call for secession many of his followers responded, and by the end of 1842 the *Darbistes*, as the Exclusive Brethren are still called on the continent, were established as an independent communion—totally separate from the older *dissidents*. In 1843 Darby briefly visited England and then, with help from the Swiss *Darbistes*, established several Brethren assemblies in France, before returning to Switzerland, whence he was compelled to withdraw by the revolution of 1845.

During his time on the continent Darby's ecclesiology had become more radical, his eschatological ideas were formulated more precisely, and he had become accustomed to a position where he enjoyed almost unquestioning respect and compliance from his followers. On his return to England in early 1845 he soon clashed with his former co-worker Benjamin W. Newton, who had acquired a similarly dominant influence in the Plymouth assembly and whose eschatology was very different from Darby's. After an acerbic exchange of letters filled with mutual recriminations and charges of sectarianism, Darby withdrew from the Plymouth assembly in October and began to break bread with another group of Brethren. In 1847 some Christologically heterodox teaching by Newton led Darby to insist that all of Newton's associates and any Brethren assemblies which, like the Bethesda assembly in Bristol, received them should be excluded from communion. The subsequent schism between the Open and Exclusive Brethren left Darby as the undisputed, though unofficial, leader of the latter. In due course the exclusive principle on which Darby had insisted bore its inevitable fruit and the movement suffered further divisions. In 1866 William H. Dorman and Percy F. Hall, who had been associated with Brethren from the earliest days, accused Darby of Christological heresy and separated from him, and in 1881 a further ecclesiastical disagreement led to a rift between him and two other long-standing friends, Edward Cronin and William Kelly.

To the end of his life Darby was almost continuously engaged in an itinerant ministry among his followers. In 1853, at the invitation of Julius van Poseck and Rudolph Brockhaus, he visited Elberfeld in Germany, where several Brethren assemblies had been established, and in the following year he began his translation of the New Testament into German. In 1871 he was in Italy and in 1875 he travelled to New Zealand, where his aim was to strengthen the 'exclusive' principles of some Brethren, such as the emigrant James G. Deck whose ecclesiastical position had become far too liberal for Darby's approval. He made several visits between 1862 and 1877 to Canada, where he regularly taught at the Brethren's summer conference in Guelph, and to the United States, where at first he worked only among his followers but later found an appreciative audience among non-Brethren. Particularly influential was his dispensational interpretation of scripture, in which he maintained that the mode of God's dealings with mankind is not uniform and varies from one era to another. His teaching on this subject was widely adopted among evangelicals, though only a few seceded from their denominations to become Brethren. His expository works, of which the *Synopsis of the Books of the Bible* (5 vols., 1857–67) is the best-known, enjoyed a similarly wide readership on both sides of the Atlantic. His translations of the Bible into English, French, and German were respected for their literal accuracy, but their use was confined to Brethren circles except for his German translation, which was used more widely. On the other hand, although much of his polemical writing was concerned with issues of interest principally to Brethren, he also wrote a number of apologetic and doctrinal critiques of such books as Francis Newman's *Phases of Faith* and *Essays and Reviews*, Colenso's *Examination of the Pentateuch*, and John Henry Newman's *Apologia pro vita sua*, as well as less memorable works.

Darby's character was full of contradictions. Generous and compassionate to a degree, he could be a dynamic and ruthless opponent. The rugged features of his portrait suggest the dedication of a single-minded and tireless worker. As late as 1880 he was still travelling on the continent, but a fall sustained in Dundee early in 1881 seriously weakened his heart and lungs. He died at Sundridge House, Bournemouth, the home of a friend, Henry A. Hammond, on 29 April 1882 and was buried in Bournemouth cemetery. TIMOTHY C. F. STUNT

Sources *Collected writings of J. N. Darby*, ed. W. Kelly, 34 vols. (1867–c.1883); repr. (1956) · *Letters of J. N. D.*, 3 vols. (1886–9) · H. H. Rowden, *The origins of the Brethren, 1825–1850* (1967) · F. R. Coad, *A history of the Brethren movement* (1968) · G. Ischebeck, *John Nelson Darby, son temps et son œuvre* (1937) · T. C. F. Stunt, 'Darby, John (Nelson)', *The Blackwell dictionary of evangelical biography, 1730–1860*, ed. D. M. Lewis (1995) · M. S. Weremchuk, *John Nelson Darby, a biography* (1990) · d. cert. · City Westm. AC · T. C. F. Stunt, *From awakening to secession: radical evangelicals in Switzerland and Britain, 1815–35* (2000)

Archives JRL, corresp. and papers · priv. coll. | JRL, corresp. with B. W. Newton

Likenesses photograph, *c.*1840, repro. in F. C. [F. Cuendet], *Souvenez-vous de vos conducteurs* (1966) · E. Penstone, watercolour drawing, NPG [*see illus.*] · sketches, paintings, and photographs, JRL, Christian Brethren archive

Wealth at death £3553 19*s.* 2½*d.*: probate, 14 Dec 1882, CGPLA Eng. & Wales

Darbyshire, Alfred (1839–1908), architect, was born on 20 June 1839 at 8 Peru Street, Salford, Lancashire, the son of William Darbyshire, manager of a dyeworks, and his wife, Mary Bancroft. He was a nephew of George Bradshaw, originator of the railway guide. Of an old Quaker family, he went to Quaker schools, first that of Charles Cumber at Manchester, then Ackworth School, near Pontefract (1851–4), and finally Lindow Grove Academy at Alderley, Cheshire. He was articled to the architect Peter Bradshaw Alley, of Lane and Alley, Manchester, in 1855 and remained in the office until 1862, when he went into practice for himself. He married on 10 August 1870 Sarah (*d.* 1933), daughter of William Marshall of Westmorland, with whom he had one son and three daughters.

Alfred Waterhouse had been articled to Alley's partner Richard Lane and Darbyshire admired Waterhouse's adaptation of Gothic to modern circumstances. But he was not a committed Goth. In competitions for Macclesfield town hall (1864), Pendleton town hall (1865), and the Manchester exchange (1866) he submitted alternative Gothic and classical designs, and the classical one—'French Italian', as he described it—was successful at Pendleton.

Darbyshire's reputation, however, was chiefly that of a theatrical architect. At one stage he considered becoming an actor, and had many theatrical friends. In Manchester he built the Comedy Theatre (1884; later called the Gaiety) and carried out alterations at the Theatre Royal and the Prince's. He also designed a theatre at Rawtenstall, Lancashire. In London he altered and decorated the Lyceum Theatre in 1878 for Henry Irving, with whom he developed the 'Irving–Darbyshire safety plan', which he described in a publication of 1884. It was intended to make the audience safe from fire by isolating the separate parts of the theatre and providing two fireproof escape routes from every part of the house, and was first fully implemented in his rebuilding of the Exeter theatre (1889) after a disastrous fire in 1887. In his last major theatre, the Palace of Varieties, Manchester, an audience of 3000 people could be cleared in a few minutes. His other buildings include: Alston Hall, Lancashire (1876); the churches of St Cyprian (1899) and St Ignatius (1900) in Salford; and the Carnegie Library in Knutsford, Cheshire (1903–4). Many of these works were designed with Frederick Bennett Smith (*b.* 1863), a pupil of Alley's who joined Darbyshire in partnership from about 1885 to 1905. He also produced designs for temporary exhibitions, including a military bazaar at Manchester in 1884, a great Shakespearian show in the Royal Albert Hall, London, in the same year, and the old Manchester section of the Royal Jubilee Exhibition at Manchester in 1887. 'No job was too small for Darbyshire', wrote Cecil Stewart (*The Stones of Manchester*, 105).

Darbyshire was an amateur actor and a friend of actors, in particular Charles Calvert, whom he assisted in the production of his Shakespearian revivals at the Prince's Theatre, Manchester (1864–74), and Henry Irving, who was a stock actor at the Theatre Royal, Manchester, in the mid-1860s. When he took leave of Lancashire in 1865, Darbyshire played the part of Polonius to Irving's Hamlet. In the Calvert memorial performances at Manchester in October 1879 he was instrumental in obtaining the assistance of Tom Taylor, Herman Merivale, Lewis Wingfield, and Helen Faucit, who gave her last performance as Rosalind, with Darbyshire acting the part of Jacques.

In 1869 Darbyshire was one of the original members of the Brasenose Club, Manchester. He was elected an associate of the Institute of British Architects in 1864, fellow in 1870, and vice-president 1902–5. He was elected FSA in 1894. From 1901 to 1903 he was president of the Manchester Society of Architects, and did much to encourage the

foundation of a chair of architecture at Manchester University. He was a member of the Society of Friends. A keen student of heraldry, his collection of books on that subject is in the John Rylands Library, Manchester. Besides several pamphlets and lectures, Darbyshire published *The Booke of Olde Manchester and Salford* (1887), *A Chronicle of the Brasenose Club, Manchester* (2 vols., 1892–1900), *An Architect's Experiences: Professional, Artistic, and Theatrical* (1897), and *The Art of the Victorian Stage* (1907). He died at Manchester Infirmary on 5 July 1908, and was buried at Flixton church. Even one of his obituarists made the common mistake of confusing him with H. A. Darbishire, another architect, by wrongly crediting him with the design of Columbia market, Bethnal Green, London (dem.). IAN DUNGAVELL

Sources A. Darbyshire, *An architect's experiences: professional, artistic, and theatrical* (1897) · W. B. Tracy and W. T. Pike, *Manchester & Salford at the close of the 19th century: contemporary biographies* (1899), 208 · *The Builder*, 95 (1908), 140–41 · *Building News*, 95 (1908), 41 · *RIBA Journal*, 15 (1907–8), 540 · D. Harbron, 'Alfred Darbyshire: accounted a good actor', *ArchR*, 82 (1937), 31–3 · T. A. Lockett, *Three lives: Samuel Bamford, Alfred Darbyshire, Ellen Wilkinson* (1968) · C. Stewart, *The stones of Manchester* (1956) · C. Cunningham and P. Waterhouse, *Alfred Waterhouse, 1830–1905: biography of a practice* (1992) · *Dir. Brit. archs.* · R. Foulkes, *The Calverts: actors of some importance* (1992) · 'The Comedy Theatre, Manchester', *The Builder*, 47 (1884), 245 · *DNB*

Archives JRL, corresp. and photographs relating to theatre and architecture · JRL, heraldic collection · Man. CL · RIBA, nomination papers · RIBA BAL, biography file

Likenesses J. Ingham, photograph, repro. in Darbyshire, *Architect's experiences* · photograph, repro. in Tracy and Pike, *Manchester & Salford*, 208 · portraits, repro. in Darbyshire, *Architect's experiences*

Wealth at death £691 8s. 5d.: probate, 19 Aug 1908, *CGPLA Eng. & Wales*

Darbyshire, Thomas (1518–1604), Jesuit, was the son of a sister of Edmund *Bonner, bishop of London. He was educated at Broadgates Hall, Oxford, graduating BA in 1544, BCL in 1553 and DCL on 20 July 1556. His uncle collated him to the prebend of Totenhall in the church of St Paul on 23 July 1543. In Mary's reign his ecclesiastical career blossomed, aided both by his uncle's position and his own ability as a canon and civil lawyer. He was collated to the rectory of Hackney on 26 May 1554, to the rectory of Fulham on 1 October 1558, to the archdeaconry of Essex on 22 October 1558, and to the rectory of St Magnus the Martyr, near London Bridge, on 27 November 1558. He was vice-president of London's Jesus Guild at its refoundation in July 1556, and was briefly commissary delegate of the prerogative court of Canterbury late in 1558. He was also chancellor of the diocese of London, in which capacity he was involved in the examination of those brought before Bishop Bonner on charges of heresy.

Under Elizabeth, Darbyshire was deprived of all his benefices. In the early years of Elizabeth's reign there was some doubt among English Catholics as to whether attendance at the religious services established by law was permissible. In 1562 a group of English noblemen acting in concert with the Spanish and Portuguese ambassadors arranged for Darbyshire to travel to Trent to solicit an authoritative statement on the issue from the council and the pope. As a result of his mission a secret committee of the council pronounced a condemnation of attendance at Church of England ceremonies which remained unpublished until 1593.

Darbyshire entered the Society of Jesus in Rome on 1 May 1563, and the following year he was sent to Dillingen. Before the early 1580s, when Robert Persons's establishment of the English Jesuit mission and schools gave some institutional independence and cohesion to the English Jesuits, Darbyshire appears to have worked hard to maintain correspondence and contacts with the Englishmen scattered throughout the various provinces of the society. He was preacher and confessor at the Jesuit college in Dillingen for two years, and was scheduled to travel to Scotland on papal business in 1566, although he may not have done so. He subsequently became master of novices at Billom, in the province of Toulouse. At some point he was transferred to Paris, where he gave Latin lectures to the sodalists. His success as a lecturer in Paris led to his appointment as public catechist in Pont à Mousson in Lorraine. He was solemnly professed of the four vows at Paris in 1572.

In 1574 Darbyshire was apparently in the Low Countries and was involved in the publication by John Heigham of the French edition of a book emanating from the circle of the exiled countess of Northumberland 'against Her Majesty's title and right to the crown' (CSP for., 1572–4, no. 1614). He was certainly back in Paris in 1577, when he was acting as spiritual adviser to a number of English students at the university. Several future members of the Society of Jesus, such as John Gerard, Richard Gibbons, George Gilbert, and Robert Southwell, spent time under his spiritual direction. From Paris he also organized the smuggling of Catholic booklets and letters into England. In 1580 he visited Rome, apparently on business concerning the papal bull of 1570 releasing Elizabeth's subjects from their oath of obedience, a bull which was suspended in 1580 in order to allay antagonism towards the planned Jesuit mission. On his return journey he accompanied William Allen as far as Rheims, spending a week at the English College there before continuing on his way to Paris. He again spent some time at the English College in December 1590. From 1595 he was professor of the catechism at Pont à Mousson, where he remained until his death there on 6 April 1604, still in constant correspondence with other English Jesuits.   PAUL ARBLASTER

Sources T. F. Knox and others, eds., *The first and second diaries of the English College, Douay* (1878) · A. Walsham, *Church papists* (1993) · *The Elizabethan Jesuits: Historia missionis Anglicanae Societatis Jesu* (1660) of Henry More, ed. and trans. F. Edwards (1981) · *DNB* · *CSP for.*, 1571–85 · D. Flynn, '"Out of step": six supplementary notes on Jasper Heywood', *The reckoned expense: Edmund Campion and the early English Jesuits*, ed. T. M. McCoog (1996), 179–92 · M. Questier, 'Like locusts all over the world', *The reckoned expense: Edmund Campion and the early English Jesuits*, ed. T. M. McCoog (1996), 265–84 · T. M. McCoog, *The Society of Jesus in Ireland, Scotland, and England, 1541–1588* (1996)

D'Arci, Chevalier Patrice. See D'Arcy, Patrick, Count D'Arcy in the French nobility (1725–1779).

Darcie [Darcy], **Abraham** (*fl.* 1623–1635), author and translator, called himself, in his work on the Howard family, Abraham de Ville Adrecie, alias Darcie. According to the inscription on his portrait by Delaram he was the son of Peter Darcie and was born in Geneva. He may have been attached to the households of the duke of Lennox, the earl of Derby, and the Howard family, judging from a number of works addressed to members of those families in the 1620s and in 1633, though the sheer number and range of his dedications throughout his career shows him constantly in pursuit of patronage.

Darcie is credited with a range of elegiac works, for which he possessed a not inconsiderable talent. In 1624, for example, he published *Frances, Duchesse Dowager of Richmond and Lenox, &c., her Funerall Teares*. Lady Richmond was well known for her despair on bereavement, to which Darcie gave voice and proper record. In the same year he published a translation of an anonymous French work under the title *The originall of idolatries, or, The birth of heresies … with the true source and lively anatomy of the sacrifice of the masse*. The title went on to attribute the work to Isaac Casaubon. Perhaps because of this false attribution the work was called in that year; it was published again in 1630 with the attribution clearly corrected in the title. The 1624 edition was dedicated to Buckingham and fifteen other courtiers who accompanied Charles to Spain.

In 1625 Darcie published an English translation of the first three parts of Camden's *Annales* (1558–88), not from the original but from the French translation of Paul de Bellegent. The text was dedicated to James I, Prince Charles, two dozen nobles, and a number of lesser figures. The elaborately engraved title-page was made to Darcie's design by R. Vaughan; some copies contain Delaram's valuable portrait of Darcie on the last page. Darcie had also designed the title-page of his 1625 *Honour's True Arbour, or, The Princely Nobility of the Howards*. In 1628 he began to prepare a memorial volume for Buckingham, with engravings of the duke, the assassination, and the hearse, and lost £20 on engravings commissioned before censorship which followed the assassination called a halt to the venture.   JOANNA MOODY

Sources *DNB* · *STC, 1475–1640* · Fuller, *Worthies* (1811) · V. Skretkowicz, 'Abraham Fraunce and Abraham Darcie', *Quarterly Journal of Bibliography*, 31 (1976), 239–42 · J. Hunter, 'Chorus Vatum', BL, Add. MS 24488, fols. 517–18 · W. C. Hazlitt, *Hand-book to the popular, poetical and dramatic literature of Great Britain* (1867) · A. M. Hind, *Engraving in England in the sixteenth and seventeenth centuries*, ed. M. Corbett and M. Norton, 3 vols. (1952–64) · F. B. Williams, 'An index of dedications and commendatory verses', *The Library*, 5th ser., 12 (1957), 11–22

Likenesses F. Delaram, line engraving, BM, NPG; repro. in W. Camden, *Annales* (1625)

Darcy family (*per.* 1086–1333), barons, came to prominence with **Norman (I) Darcy** (*d.* 1116x29), who held lands valued at £63 16*s.* per year in 1086, the most valuable of which lay in Nocton, Lincolnshire. Norman was living in 1115 or 1116, by which time he had slightly expanded his estates. He was succeeded by **Robert Darcy** (*d.* 1148x60), who may have been his son and was probably the Robert Darcy who was a tenant of the Percys, appears in the

1129/30 pipe roll, is said to have founded the Augustinian priory of Nocton, and endowed Kirkstead Abbey and Lincoln Cathedral. Robert married Alice and was succeeded by 1162 by his son **Thomas (I) Darcy** (*d.* 1180) who held just over twenty knights' fees in Lincolnshire in 1166. Thomas endowed Kirkstead Abbey and Nocton Priory, and appears to have augmented his lands with five knights' fees held of the Percys. He married Aelina (*d.* 1182/3), and was succeeded by his son **Thomas (II) Darcy** (1166/7–1206), who attained his majority in 1185.

The Darcys became heavily indebted to the crown and the Jews of Lincoln and York in the late twelfth and thirteenth centuries. This was due initially to Aelina Darcy's proffer of £200 for custody of her son and his lands, the need for money to retain lands at Cawkwell, Lincolnshire, and the increasing demands of the crown for military service. Thomas (II) received several quittances of scutage between 1194 and 1203 which, together with a reference to his serving overseas in 1202, indicates that he often served in person. He was also charged scutage in 1190, 1204, and 1205. In 1203, in return for providing knights, Thomas (II) received a royal pardon of 225 marks owed to the Jews. Despite his debts Thomas endowed the religious houses of Nocton, Kirkstead, Newhouse, and Alvingham.

Thomas married Joan, with whom he had **Norman (II) Darcy** (*d.* 1254), who succeeded him and under whom the family debts mounted. This was owing to the imposition by the king of a fine of over 1100 marks for admitting Norman to the lands of his father, and to scutage demands. These debts may explain why Norman may have preferred to serve in person in Scotland and Wales in 1211 and in Poitou in 1214 (indicated by scutage quittances), and why he established a weekly market at Nocton in 1214. Indebtedness and possibly resentment at having to fight in or pay for overseas wars may have been at least partly responsible for the involvement of the Darcys in the rebellion against King John in 1215–16. Although John deprived Norman and two of his relatives of their lands in 1216, by October 1217 the Darcys had made peace and were restored to their possessions. Later in his career Norman served as a royal justice from 1227 to 1230, in 1234, and in 1245. He was also a benefactor of Bardney Abbey and Lincoln Cathedral. He married Agnes, whose parentage is unknown, and in February 1254 was so ill and weakened by old age that his property, of which his house and land at Nocton were then valued at £26 11s. 8d., was transferred to his son, **Philip (I) Darcy** (*d.* 1264). Norman died shortly before 16 October 1254.

Philip was an experienced soldier by the time his father died, having served in Gascony in 1242–3 and in 1253–4, when he was constable of Meilhan. This brought him into considerable debt, for the relief of which the king requested Philip's men to grant Philip an aid in 1255. It was probably the need for money that led Philip to lease his manor of Conesby to the countess of Lincoln for ten years in 1255, and to secure the right to have an annual fair at Nocton in 1257. Further military demands were made on Philip in 1260 and 1263 when he was commanded to help suppress the raids of Llywelyn ap Gruffudd in Wales, and in 1261 when he was summoned to London with horses and arms to support the king after Henry's repudiation of the control of the council and the rule of the provisional government. Philip was rewarded for his loyalty by the grant of pardons for his debts to the Jews, and perhaps of custody of the Tower of London. As well as continuing the military traditions of his family Philip maintained its religious patronage by endowing monasteries, including Thornton and Bardney. He married Isabel Bertram, sister of Roger (III) Bertram of Mitford, with whom he had at least four sons, one of whom, Roger (*d.* before 12 May 1284), was the father of Sir John *Darcy 'le cosyn' of Knaith (*b.* before 1284, *d.* 1347).

Philip's successor, his son **Norman (III) Darcy** (*c.*1236–1295/6), had been arrested with Roger Darcy at Hull shortly before 4 June 1264, almost certainly for killing William Gorham and for involvement in the rebellion against Henry III. In 1267 the king pardoned Norman and Roger and their uncle Thomas for their actions during the rebellion. The cost of recovering royal favour and his lands probably explains why Norman was heavily in debt to the Jews of London and other creditors from the 1270s to the early 1290s, which led him to alienate important estates in Nocton, Dunston, Stallingborough, and elsewhere to Queen Eleanor, the templars, the abbey of Newhouse, and the bishop of Ely in return for money. His debts were probably also the result of service on royal campaigns in Wales in 1277, 1282, and 1287, and in Scotland in 1291. A banneret by February 1284, Norman married first Julian, who died before 15 June 1281, and second, before 20 January 1293, Margery (*d.* after 19 Feb 1303), widow of Ralph Rastel; he was succeeded by his son with his first wife, **Philip (II) Darcy**, Lord Darcy (*c.*1259–1333).

Philip continued the military traditions of his family, serving in Scotland in 1291 and 1296, and as constable of Durham Castle in 1301, when he led an attack on Durham Cathedral and forcibly removed the prior. He later fought for the contrariants at the battle of Boroughbridge in 1322. In 1299 he succeeded his uncle, Thomas Darcy, lord of Scottlethorpe, Lincolnshire, and in the same year was summoned for the first of many times to parliament. He died shortly before 24 November 1333. The family arms were argent, three sixfoils or cinquefoils (or roses) gules.

PAUL DALTON

Sources GEC, *Peerage*, new edn • *Chancery records* (RC) • Pipe rolls • I. J. Sanders, *English baronies: a study of their origin and descent, 1086–1327* (1960) • C. W. Foster and K. Major, eds., *The registrum antiquissimum of the cathedral church of Lincoln*, 10 vols. in 12, Lincoln RS, 27–9, 32, 34, 41–2, 46, 51, 62, 67–8 (1931–73) • J. H. Round, ed., *Rotuli de dominabus et pueris et puellis de XII comitatibus* (1185), PRSoc., 35 (1913) • F. M. Stenton, ed., *Documents illustrative of the social and economic history of the Danelaw* (1920) • F. M. Stenton, ed., *Transcripts of charters relating to Gilbertine houses …*, Lincs. Rec. Soc., 18 (1922) • D. M. Stenton, ed., *The earliest Lincolnshire assize rolls, A.D. 1202–1209*, Lincs. Rec. Soc., 22 (1926) • H. Hall, ed., *The Red Book of the Exchequer*, 3 vols., Rolls Series, 99 (1896) • C. W. Foster and T. Langley, eds. and trans., *The Lincolnshire Domesday and the Lindsey survey*, Lincs. Rec. Soc., 19 (1924) • *VCH Lincolnshire*, vol. 2 • W. Farrer, *Honors and knights' fees*, 3 vols. (1923–5) • A. Farley, ed., *Domesday Book*, 2 vols.

(1783) • Beresford's plea roll, Durham, Dean and Chapter Muniments, loc. 7, 14

Darcy family (*per. c.*1284–1488), gentry, produced several notable royal servants in the fourteenth century. At the death of Roger Darcy of Oldcotes and Styrrup (*c.*1284) [*see* Darcy family (*per.* 1086–1333)] Sir John *Darcy 'le cosyn' (*d.* 1347) headed the family. He had a distinguished career initially in the service of Aymer de Valence, earl of Pembroke (*d.* 1324), then achieved prominence in the political and military service of Edward II and, particularly, of Edward III. Royal patronage founded the fortunes of his successors with the receipt of considerable gifts of land and office. John's service as justiciar of Ireland provided an enduring connection with the political community there and, although it was with his first wife, Emmeline, heir of Walter Heron of Silkstone, that he had a son and heir, his second wife, Joan (*d.* 1359), daughter of Richard de Burgh, second earl of Ulster, and widow of Thomas Fitzjohn, earl of Kildare, provided Irish lands and founded through their eldest son, William Darcy of Plattyn, co. Meath (*b.* 1330, *d.* before 1362), a noteworthy junior Irish branch of the family.

John Darcy, second Lord Darcy (1317–1356), 'le fitz', was the eldest son of Sir John *Darcy 'le cosyn' (*d.* 1347); he accompanied his father to Ireland as early as 1324 and followed him into royal service. Under Edward III he commanded a company with Walter Mauny in the opening phase of the Hundred Years' War and was rewarded in 1341 by a grant to him and his heirs of £40 a year for his long service. On 15 July 1346, when with the king at La Hogue, he was granted a further £200 a year for life to maintain himself as a banneret and went on to fight at Crécy and Calais. In 1347 he received his father's land and the office of keeper of the Tower of London for life. Outside the military sphere in 1344 he was appointed escheator of Holderness for life. He served on numerous judicial commissions, particularly in Yorkshire, and on the diplomatic commission to negotiate peace with France in September 1347. Although he never held high office in Edward III's household, he was personally summoned to parliaments from 20 November 1348 until his death. John Darcy 'le fitz' married Alianore, daughter of Robert *Holland, Lord Holland (*d.* 1328), of West Derby, Lancashire, before 1332, and then in 1344 Elizabeth (1331–1368), heir of Nicholas, Lord Meynell. The latter marriage required a papal dispensation, granted in 1344, and was licensed by the king to help John finance his royal service. He died at Notton, Yorkshire, on 5 March 1356 and was buried at Guisborough Priory, of which he had held half the advowson. In his lifetime he had given the advowson of the church of Knaith to the impoverished prioress and convent of Heynings, Lincolnshire, perhaps to support a relative, Margery, who was confined there. He left a substantial fortune to his son, John, born on 24 June 1350. During his minority the family estates were taken into royal hands, the bulk being granted for the support of Queen Philippa, and the remainder to Isabella, the king's eldest daughter. The depredations committed by Queen Philippa's tenants of the estate were so severe that a damning inquisition was held in 1360.

On the death of the young John Darcy on 26 August 1362 the estates passed to his younger brother **Philip Darcy**, third Baron Darcy (1352–1399), who received his estate in autumn 1373. Philip successfully adopted his father's mantle. He served with John of Gaunt in Picardy and Caux between July and November 1369 and was active in the royal household, being described as 'de familia regis' in 1372. He served with the earl of Buckingham in the raid on Brittany of July 1380 to April 1381. He was on the commission to take the homage of the count of Flanders on 20 June 1383, served in Scotland under the duke of Lancaster in April 1384, and under the king in August 1385. He was an active admiral of the Thames and northwards (1385–9) and in February 1389 was being retained for the king's intended expedition in Scotland. In the same year he is first recorded as one of the king's knights in the royal household, probably an uncontroversial appointment. Philip was a justice of the peace in Lindsey, Lincolnshire, between 1377 and 1385, and occasionally served in the West Riding of Yorkshire and Northumberland. He was also frequently appointed to judicial commissions and to array men. Philip was summoned to all the parliaments of Richard II's reign until his death, but by the mid-1390s no longer seems to have been active in the royal or local administration. In September 1397 he gave an oath to maintain the statutes of the preceding parliament, but appears to have retired from public life. Philip had married Elizabeth (*d.* 1412), second daughter of Sir Thomas Grey of Heaton, Northumberland. He died on 24 April 1399 and was buried next to his father in Guisborough Priory.

Philip's son **John Darcy**, fourth Baron Darcy (1377–1411), received livery of his father's estates on 12 June 1399. He seems to have been able to make an easy transition to support for Henry IV. He was summoned to all parliaments from August 1399 until his death. In May 1402 he was appointed to suppress sedition and then was with the prince of Wales in 1407. However, he never seems to have aspired to, nor achieved, the prominence of his father or grandfather in matters of war or affairs of state. In part this may reflect the declining financial fortunes of the family exacerbated by the longevity of family widows. At John Darcy's death on 9 December 1411 his estate was valued at barely over £100 a year, although this appears to allow for dowers to his mother and his widow, Margaret, daughter of Sir Henry Grey of Wilton, and was suspected to be a substantial undervaluation.

The Darcy family fortunes were not to revive for the next fifty years: John Darcy was succeeded by his son Philip, born *c.*1398, who never achieved his majority, dying on 2 August 1418. In June 1412 John's widow, **Margaret Darcy** [*née* Margaret Grey of Wilton], Lady Darcy (*d.* 1454), was granted £40 per year from the estate to support herself, her second son, and four daughters. Worse, in 1433 Margaret had to present herself at parliament to prove she still lived and that her Irish estates should not be seized. Philip had married Alianore (*d.* 1469), daughter of Sir Henry Fitzhugh, his guardian. She received a third of his estate in dower in 1421 and the remainder, not entailed in the male line, was left to two infant daughters: Elizabeth (b. c.1417, d. after 1458), who married Sir James *Strangways (d. 1480), and Margery (1418–1469), who married Sir John *Conyers of Hornby, Yorkshire (d. 1490) [see under Conyers family (per. c.1375–c.1525)]. The tomb in Selby Abbey, usually attributed to his father, is more likely to be that of Philip. Intriguingly, in 1427 a commission was sent to the abbey to investigate the documents in a chest supposedly relating to the inheritance of some of the family lands. Those estates entailed in the male line, including the valuable manors of Temple Newsam and Temple Hirst, Yorkshire, passed to **John Darcy** (b. before 1412, d. 1458), brother of Philip Darcy. He married Joan, daughter of Lord Greystoke, without licence and only received a pardon in October 1427 on payment of 200 marks. He achieved little prominence and was succeeded by his grandson **Sir William Darcy** (c.1454–1488), who married Euphemia, daughter of Sir Thomas Langton. The couple are most notable as the parents of Thomas *Darcy (d. 1537). ANTHONY VERDUYN

Sources GEC, *Peerage* · CIPM · CPR, 1321–1488 · CCIR, 1321–1488 · VCH Lincolnshire, vol. 2 · Burke, *Gen. Ire.* · W. H. Bliss, ed., *Calendar of entries in the papal registers relating to Great Britain and Ireland: petitions to the pope* (1896), 1 · CEPR letters, vol. 3, pp. 87, 165; vol. 5, p. 569
Likenesses tomb (Philip Darcy), Selby Abbey
Wealth at death approx. £124—John Darcy: CIPM

Darcy, Abraham. *See* Darcie, Abraham (*fl.* 1623–1635).

Darcy, Brian (d. 1587), witch-hunter, was probably born in Essex, the son of Thomas Darcy of Tolleshunt Darcy, and his second wife, Elizabeth Bedingfield, daughter of John Haydon of Baconsthorpe, Norfolk. Thomas was a lesser member of the family of the barons Darcy of Chiche, and the family seat was St Osyth Priory, Essex. Brian Darcy lived there during the 1580s, though he also lived at Tiptree Priory, and is said to have rebuilt it. With his wife Brigit, daughter of John Corbett of Sprowston, Norfolk, he had eight children; she and two daughters and three sons survived him. Two sons were educated at Gonville and Caius College, Cambridge, and one of them progressed to Lincoln's Inn in London.

Darcy made his first appearance as a justice of the peace at the March assizes of 1581 at Brentwood, Essex. He attended assizes fairly regularly, as his post as a magistrate demanded, and in 1582 did his duty most zealously in questioning and committing for trial a large group of women and a man suspected of witchcraft in St Osyth and the surrounding villages. Darcy publicized his involvement with their pre-trial interrogation in a pamphlet of more than a hundred pages, entitled *A true and just recorde of the information, examination and confession of all the witches, taken at S. Oses*, and published in London by Thomas Dawson in 1582. The pamphlet was written by 'W. W.', perhaps William Lowth. In 1581 Lowth had dedicated a translated devotional book (Bartholomew Batty, *The Christian Mans Closet*) to Brian Darcy with his relative Thomas Darcy. However, Brian Darcy himself clearly inspired *A True and Just Recorde*, and can certainly be described as having written

some of it, for its text is based on transcripts of his examinations of suspected witches and the informations of their alleged victims.

The pamphlet is one of the fullest and most fascinating accounts of the processes of questioning and recording involved in bringing witches (or other felons) to trial. Darcy, working through or with W. W., used the work to argue for the harsher punishment of witches (by burning rather than the existing penalty, hanging), to publicize the idea that witches were in fact devil-worshippers (a notion acquired from European demonologists such as Jean Bodin, whose *Demonomanie* is quoted in *A True and Just Recorde*), and to draw attention to himself. The pamphlet's emphasis suggests that Darcy was particularly proud of his use of trick questions against suspected witches, and of his false promises of favourable treatment of anyone who confessed. He undoubtedly felt that these progressive and imported methods would help rid the country of antichristian workers of public mischief, and that in promoting them he was earnestly doing right. However, his activities led to the execution of two women (Ursley Kempe and Elizabeth Bennett), the remand of three women (Ales Newman, Cysley Selles, and Annis Glascock), and the miscellaneous imprisonment of four other people (Henry and Robert Sylls or Selles, Joan Pechey, and Ales Hunt). Henry and Cysley Selles, Joan Pechey, and Annis Glascock died in gaol, and Ales Newman was not freed until 1588. Brian Darcy would undoubtedly have been disappointed by this lack of official rigour in executing witches, which suggests a failure to endorse his crusade. However, he did become sheriff of Essex in 1586, perhaps because of his involvement with this unusually large prosecution and his related publication.

Darcy was said by Raven, in his 1612 visitation of Essex, to have been knighted in 1587, but there is no evidence elsewhere of this. His will, with its devout preamble, is dated 19 December 1587; he died on 25 December. His will was proved on 10 April 1588. MARION GIBSON

Sources W. W., *A true and just recorde* (1582) · B. Rosen, *Witchcraft in England, 1558–1618* (1991), 103–57 · W. C. Metcalfe, ed., *The visitations of Essex*, 1, Harleian Society, 13 (1878), 46 · will, PRO, PROB 11/72, fols. 195v–196v · J. S. Cockburn, *Calendar of assize records: Essex indictments, Elizabeth I* (1978) · J. S. Cockburn, *Calendar of assize records: introduction* (1985) · GEC, *Peerage* · M. H. Gibson, *Reading witchcraft* (1999) · Venn, *Alum. Cant.*
Wealth at death see will, PRO, PROB 11/72, fols. 195v–196v

D'Arcy, Charles Frederick (1859–1938), Church of Ireland archbishop of Armagh, was born at Rehobeth House, Dublin, on 2 January 1859, the eldest son of John Charles D'Arcy, assistant cashier in the Great Southern and Western Railway Company's service, and Henrietta Anna, daughter of Thomas Brierly. He was descended from John Darcy, lord justice of Ireland in the reign of Edward III. D'Arcy's childhood and youth were passed in Dublin. He attended the high school, and in 1877 entered Trinity College, where he spent seven years, studying chiefly mathematics, philosophy, and divinity, and graduating with a senior moderatorship in logics and ethics. In 1884 he was ordained for St Thomas's Church, Belfast. There he remained for six years. He married on 12 August 1889 Harriet le Byrtt (*d.* 1932), elder daughter of Richard Lewis, of Comrie, co. Down; they had one son and three daughters.

In 1890 D'Arcy was appointed to the country parish of Billy, near the Giant's Causeway, moving in 1893 to the industrial town of Ballymena, co. Antrim. Here he laid the foundation of his career and reputation, publishing *A Short Study of Ethics* (1895), which went through two editions and was reprinted in 1912. In 1899 he published his first set of Donnellan lectures (delivered at Trinity College in 1897–8) under the title *Idealism and Theology*. In it he argued that the current idealism could not bridge the gulf between the self and society, that idealism, if it were to survive, must transcend itself and mere theism, and must accept substance, at once personal and supra-personal, that is the Christian Trinity.

D'Arcy was now recognized as a leading religious thinker of his country, and preferment came his way every three or four years. He returned to Belfast in 1900 as vicar of the city and dean of the newly founded St Anne's Cathedral; three years later he was raised to the bench as bishop of Clogher. In 1907 he was translated to the southern see of Ossory, Ferns, and Leighlin. In 1911 he returned to the north to preside over the populous see of Down, Connor, and Dromore. The home-rule movement was at its height, and the clouds of civil war were gathering. Some indication of D'Arcy's strength of feeling as a unionist is given by the remark attributed to him that there were worse things than civil war. D'Arcy after some hesitation took his stand openly with Sir Edward Carson, and the Ulster Unionist Council, and signed the Ulster covenant (28 September 1912). The bishop called for special services in the churches of his diocese on that day, to the embarrassment of other northern bishops, whom he had not consulted. By the Larne gun-running on 24 April 1914 the Ulster Volunteer Force secured arms; but in August the First World War broke out, and civil war was averted.

D'Arcy's political views were strongly unionist, and he had taken a firm line in the crisis. He also understood well the feelings of southern protestants, and was *persona grata* with members of his church in both north and south. When in 1919 the archbishopric of Dublin fell vacant, he was elected to fill the see; but he was not to serve for long in his native city, for in the following year he was called to the highest office in the Church of Ireland, becoming archbishop of Armagh and primate of all Ireland.

D'Arcy's eighteen years' tenure of the primacy was outwardly uneventful; he was not confronted with any acute crisis, nor called upon to take any far-reaching decision; but the problem of preserving an undivided Church of Ireland in a divided Ireland was present and urgent, if in the background. D'Arcy was an enthusiast for church reunion, especially with the Presbyterian church, though his attitude to Roman Catholicism was one of caution and courteous disapproval. He avoided word or act which might accentuate the acute division of political sentiment consequent on the recent partition of the country. His successor in Armagh, John A. F. Gregg, had immense respect for D'Arcy's intellect but not (according to Gregg's biographer) for his capacity as an administrator.

As primate, D'Arcy soon became well known in England both in ecclesiastical circles and in the learned societies. He was prominent at the Lambeth conferences of 1920 and 1930, and at the Lausanne conference of 1927. In 1927 also he was elected a fellow of the British Academy. In 1936 he was chosen to represent the Anglican communion at the centenary of the consecration of W. G. Broughton as first Anglican bishop of Australia. In the summer of 1937 his health began to fail, and he had thoughts of resignation, but he remained primate to the day of his death, which occurred at the palace, Armagh, on 1 February 1938. He was buried on 3 February in Armagh Cathedral.

D'Arcy's writings fall into two periods. In his younger days he was the metaphysician and moralist, seeking along academic lines to harmonize faith and reason in the spheres of thought and practice. Later in life science in its theoretical aspects occupied his attention, and in a series of books, *Science and Creation* (1925), *The Christian Outlook in the Modern World* (1929), and *God in Science* (1931), he endeavoured to reconcile the doctrine of evolution with Christian faith and practice. His views found their best expression in his last serious work, *Providence and the World-Order* (1932, Alexander Robertson lectures delivered at Glasgow University in that year); here he argued that what to God is creation, to man is evolution, and that the ascending orders of reality—physical, biological, psychical, and so on—constitute 'the splendid epic of creation'.

A. A. LUCE, *rev.* KENNETH MILNE

Sources C. F. D'Arcy, *The adventures of a bishop* (1934) · A. A. Luce, 'Charles Frederick D'Arcy, 1859–1938', *PBA*, 24 (1938), 363–77 · G. F. Seaver, *John Allen Fitzgerald Gregg, archbishop* (1963) · R. B. McDowell, *The Church of Ireland, 1869–1969* (1975) · M. Hurley, ed., *Irish Anglicanism, 1869–1969* (1970) · J. J. Lee, *Ireland 1912–1985, politics and society* (1989) · A. J. Megahey, 'The Irish protestant churches and social and political issues, 1870–1914', PhD diss., Queen's University, Belfast, 1969 · The high school, Dublin, roll book · Church of Ireland records · *Church of Ireland Gazette*

Likenesses F. Whiting, oils, 1920, Synod Hall, Armagh · J. Lavery, oils, 1928, Belfast Museum and Art Gallery · T. Allison & Son, photograph, Christ Church Cathedral, Dublin, chapter house · group portrait, photograph, repro. in Seaver, *John Allen Fitzgerald Gregg, archbishop*, 96 · photograph, NPG

Wealth at death £2777 11*s. od.*: Irish probate sealed in London, 3 May 1938, *CGPLA Eng. & Wales* · £10,000: probate, 24 Feb 1938, *CGPLA NIre.*

D'Arcy, Constance Eleanor Mary Byrne [known as Ella D'Arcy] (1857?–1937), writer, was born in Pimlico, London, one of the nine children of Anthony Byrne D'Arcy (1826–1873), corn factor and maltster, and his wife, Sophia Anne (1833–1891), daughter of John Matthews, town clerk of Gravesend, Kent. Her father's family home was Drummartin Castle, near Dublin, and she had a private income from the estate. Educated at a convent in Clapham and abroad, she studied fine art between 1875 and 1877 at the Slade School of Art, London. Relinquishing art, because, it was said, of poor eyesight, she turned to short-story writing. Her early work, some of it under the pseudonym Gilbert H. Page, was published in *Argosy*, *All the Year Round*, *Blackwood's Magazine*, and *Temple Bar*.

Greater recognition came when 'Irremediable' appeared in the first issue of the *Yellow Book*. Ella D'Arcy acted, at least in an unofficial capacity, as an assistant to the quarterly's founder and editor, Henry Harland (1861–1905), and was a frequent guest at his soirées. She had more work published in the *Yellow Book* than any writer other than Harland himself. Her stories regularly explore bleak lives, brittle and emancipated women, and the misery of marriage to a designing, selfish, or stupid partner, such as Esther in 'Irremediable', who 'evinced all the self-satisfaction of an illiterate mind'. Other stories, including 'The Death Mask' and 'At the Villa Lucienne', are evocations of horror and fear, or, like 'The Web of Maya', of the psychology of the obsessed. A group of stories set in the Channel Islands contrasts peasant superstition with a heartless sophistication among the landed class. Although she was regarded as 'a distinctive voice in fin-de-siècle literature' (Orel, 255), and the 'most astringent writer of her sex in the 'nineties' (Stanford, 63), Ella D'Arcy's output was modest: she was given to polishing and repolishing her work and was regarded by a contemporary, N. Syrett, as the laziest woman she had ever met. Her first collection of short stories, *Monochromes*, was published in John Lane's Keynotes series in 1895. *Modern Instances* followed in 1898, also the year of publication of her sole novel, *The Bishop's Dilemma*, the tale of a weak priest who has a wishy-washy love affair and takes to drink.

Quickened interest in the latter part of the twentieth century in the writers and artists of the 1890s has focused in the case of Ella D'Arcy on the French influence on her work (especially that of Maupassant), and on the short story as a vehicle for the expression of cynicism, discontinuity, and isolation. Her realism has also been analysed, with its depiction of a broader cross-section of society including its failures, its willingness to embrace taboo subjects, and its readiness to detail the commonplace. The quality of her descriptions has also been admired, many of them having a visual appeal held to derive from her training as an artist. In her interest in the supernatural and in the folklore of the Channel Islands, Ella D'Arcy has been held to foreshadow the work of Elizabeth Goudge, Sheila Kaye-Smith, John Ferguson, C. Northcote Parkinson, and G. B. Edwards.

Ella D'Arcy was short in stature, with ginger hair, small greenish eyes, and a large upper lip. Her love of travel and habit of losing touch with her friends for months before turning up unannounced earned her the nickname of Goblin Ella. Frederick Rolfe described her as a 'mouse-mannered piece of sex' (Rolfe, 31), while Constance Smedley, who had failed to persuade her to join a literary coterie, found her 'entirely sincere and unsentimental' (Smedley, 46). She had a zest for life, was amusing and witty, keenly interested in genealogy, sharp and penetrating in her judgements, and with decided views on most subjects. Ella D'Arcy's last years were spent in Paris, where she lived in a single room in the rue Jacob, but she was brought to England in 1937 after a stroke and died in a London hospital on 5 September 1937. She was buried in the Roman Catholic section of the Brookwood cemetery. She is best-known for her short stories, and for her translation into English of André Maurois's *Ariel* (1924), a biography of Shelley.   C. M. P. TAYLOR

Sources K. L. Mix, *A study in yellow: the Yellow Book and its contributors* (1960) · N. Syrett, *The sheltering tree* (1939), 98 · private information (2004) · D. Stanford, ed., *Short stories of the 'nineties: a biographical anthology* (1968) · H. Orel, ed., *The trials of love*, 2 (1990) · I. Fletcher, ed., *Decadence and the 1890s* (1979) · E. Darcy, *Some letters to John Lane*, ed. A. Anderson (1990) · F. R. Rolfe, *Nicholas Crabbe* (1960), 31 · C. Smedley, *Crusaders: the reminiscences of Constance Smedley* (1929) · B. F. Fisher, 'Ella D'Arcy: a commentary with a primary and annotated secondary bibliography', *English Literature in Transition, 1880–1920*, 35 (1992), 179–211 · B. F. Fisher, 'Ella D'Arcy reminisces', *English Literature in Transition, 1880–1920*, 37 (1994), 28–32 · K. Beckson, 'Ella D'Arcy, Aubrey Beardsley and the crisis at the *Yellow Book*: a new letter', *N&Q*, 224 (1979), 331–3 · P. Stubbs, *Women and fiction: feminism in the novel, 1880–1920* (1981) · M. D. Stetz and M. S. Lasner, *England in the 1890s: literary publishing at the Bodley Head* (1990)

Archives U. Cal., Los Angeles, William Andrews Clark Memorial Library, letters

Likenesses photograph, repro. in Mix, *Study in yellow*

D'Arcy, Dame Constance Elizabeth (1879–1950), obstetrician and gynaecologist, was born on 1 June 1879 at Rylstone, New South Wales, the fifth daughter and the youngest of the ten children of Murty D'Arcy, a sergeant of police, and his wife, Bridget Synnott. She passed the senior public examination from Rylstone public school and, after attending Riviere College, Woollahra, matriculated at the University of Sydney, whence she graduated MB and ChM in 1904. As Sydney hospitals did not then accept women doctors, she went to Adelaide for hospital experience before opening a practice in Sydney. She was appointed resident medical officer at the Royal Hospital for Women in 1905, the first woman to hold the post, but resumed private practice in 1908, when she became an honorary surgeon at the hospital.

D'Arcy was one of six women who, worried by the continuing difficulties women experienced in obtaining hospital experience, raised £1000 in 1922 to buy premises for a new hospital for women and children (the Rachel Forster Hospital for Women and Children). She gave her services free to the hospital. D'Arcy had a large private practice and was highly regarded in her profession; she was a member of the Royal College of Obstetricians and Gynaecologists in London and later a foundation fellow of the College of Surgeons of Australasia (the Royal Australasian College of Surgeons).

Renowned for her quick response when called, D'Arcy was chauffeur driven on her rounds. She was a large woman, heavily built, with a hearty, infectious laugh, remembered for her hats and jewellery—on emergency calls the first task of the sister on duty was to lock away the jewellery.

D'Arcy believed that professionally qualified women should help younger women in their careers. She was active in the formation of the Sydney University Women's Union, an executive member of the Catholic University Women Graduates' Association, a long-serving president of the Sydney Women Graduates' Association, and a founder of the Australian Federation of University

Women. She served on the senate of the university from 1919 to 1949 as an elected representative of its graduates. When the Catholic archbishop appealed to Catholic women to raise money for a college for women, D'Arcy responded to the call. She was appointed to the council of Sancta Sophia College when it opened in 1929 and chaired its council from 1946 to 1948.

D'Arcy was professionally concerned to lower the rate of maternal mortality. She blamed, in part, interventionist practices by some doctors: in 1925 she wrote that meddlesome midwifery was bad midwifery. In hospitals where nurses were routinely replaced at the end of a shift there was less pressure for hasty and dangerous practices. She stressed the importance of asepsis—the use of sterilized gloves in particular—and good nursing. As a long-serving vice-president and the first woman president (1927–8) of the Australasian Trained Nurses' Association of New South Wales she was involved in negotiations for a statutory nurses' registration board to take over the responsibility for accreditation of nurses. She encouraged nurses to organize nationally and to change the association's rules to expand their own part in its management. She also saw a need to improve medical training in obstetrics. On the senate of the University of Sydney she helped secure additional clinical training, with recognition of St Vincent's as a teaching hospital, and the creation of a chair in obstetrics. She served as honorary senior gynaecologist at St Vincent's (1923–45) and lecturer in clinical obstetrics at the Royal Hospital for Women (1925–39). She was also a member of the university's cancer research committee and its finance committee and served on the conjoint board of Royal Alexandra Hospital for Children, which she represented on the Australian Council of Hospital Almoners.

D'Arcy had a long association in New South Wales with the National Council of Women—on a sex education committee, as a representative of the Australasian Trained Nurses' Association, and from 1929 as vice-president. The Catholic hierarchy respected her as a leading member of the laity, and she graced many Catholic occasions. When she spoke on moral issues she adhered to Catholic doctrine, and when she addressed gatherings of Catholic women she spoke as if the progression from school to marriage and motherhood was universal and as if her own departure from the pattern was in no way problematic. Her extensive networking among women suggests otherwise. She helped reform the Medical Women's Society, which she served as president (1933–4), she joined the Professional Women's Workers Association, and she was foundation president of the Business and Professional Women's Club (1939–44).

D'Arcy was appointed DBE in 1935, and the pope honoured her in 1940 with the Cross Pro Ecclesia et Pointifice. During the war she was a director of training for Catholic VADs. Also in those years she was deputy chancellor of Sydney University (1943–6), where she took major responsibility for solving wartime problems in a purely secular institution. Among her considerable achievements was her ability to rise above the sectarianism which disfigured Australian public life.

In poor health from 1948, D'Arcy died from cerebrovascular disease in the Sacred Heart Hospice for the Dying, Darlinghurst, on 25 April 1950. After a requiem mass at St Mary's Cathedral, she was buried in Waverley cemetery.　　　　　　　　　　　　　HEATHER RADI

Sources AusDB · U. Bygott and K. J. Cable, *Pioneer women graduates of the university of Sydney, 1881–1921* (1985) · *Catholic Weekly* (4 May 1950) · *Sydney Morning Herald* (26 April 1950) · *Medical Journal of Australia* (12 Aug 1950), 274–5 · *Union Recorder* (18 May 1950) · C. D'Arcy, 'Puerperal infection: its causes and prevention', *Australasian Nurses Journal*, 15 (1925), 265–9 · C. E. D'Arcy, 'The indications for Caesarean section', *Medical Journal of Australia* (1922), 322–5 · C. D'Arcy, 'Problems of maternal welfare', *Medical Journal of Australia* (1935), 385–99 · S. Kennedy, *Faith and feminism* (1985) · L. Cohen, *The Rachel Forster Hospital* (1972) · M. Foley, 'The women's movement in New South Wales and Victoria, 1918–38', PhD diss., University of Sydney, 1985 · *Biennial reports*, National Council of Women, New South Wales, 1921.22–1938.40 · minutes, National Council of Women, New South Wales, ML MSS3739 · University of Sydney, senate minutes, University of Sydney · P. R. Thoms, *The first 25 years B. P. W. Australia* (c.1974) · H. M. Carey, *Truly feminine, truly Catholic* (1987) · E. S. Morgan, *A short history of medical women in Australia* (1969) · A. Sefton and others, *Centenary book of the Sydney University Medical Society* (1992) · M. Little, 'Some pioneer medical women of the University of Sydney', *Medical Journal of Australia* (1958), 348–51 · *Australian Nurses' Journal* (1908–29) · *Australian Nurses' Journal* (1935), 165 · *Sydney Morning Herald* (6 June 1935) · *Sydney University Medical Journal* (1919)
Likenesses photographs

Darcy [*née* Wray; *other married names* Foljambe, Bowes], **Isabel**, **Lady Darcy** (d. 1622), patron of clergymen, was the eldest daughter of Sir Christopher *Wray (c.1522–1592), lawyer, and his wife, Anne Brocklesby, *née* Girlington (d. 1593). Despite, or perhaps because of, the fact that Sir Christopher was a religious conservative and a noted opponent of the puritans his three children were all prominent supporters of radical protestants. Sir William Wray, Sir Christopher's heir, was hailed by the separatist leader John Smyth as the principal patron of godly religion in Lincolnshire. Isabel, along with her sister Frances, financed the university education of Richard Bernard, the eminent puritan minister. In 1586, while married to her first husband, Godfrey Foljambe (1558–1595), a Derbyshire JP and MP, Isabel had Katherine Wright, who was believed to be a demoniac, conveyed to her house at Walton, near Chesterfield, and had godly ministers brought in to treat her. Eventually John Darrell, who later enjoyed a spectacular, if short-lived, career as an exorcist, was credited with curing Wright. He later sent Isabel Foljambe his own accounts of his successful exorcisms and she almost certainly brought him into a circle of puritans led by Arthur Hildersham and centred on Ashby-de-la-Zouch; a leading member of this circle was her former protégé Richard Bernard. Darrell moved to Ashby and these puritans became his staunch supporters.

Godfrey Foljambe died in June 1595, leaving his wife considerable property in Derbyshire and Yorkshire. By 1599 Isabel had married Sir William Bowes (d. 1611), a Durham gentleman who, during Elizabeth's reign, had held several important offices in the north of England and served on embassies to Scotland. Both Sir William and Lady Bowes were angered by opposition to the millenary petition for church reform and they expressed their views in a letter to the earl of Shrewsbury, dated 17 December 1603. Paying what was for the time an unusual tribute to female perspicacity in matters of theology, Sir William wrote that he had consulted his wife before penning his letter because 'she is verie wise, especiallie in thinges of this kind' (LPL, MS 3203, fol. 166r). Sir William then transmitted Lady Bowes's detailed criticisms of the University of Oxford's disparaging *Answer* to the millenary petition. Lady Bowes added her personal postscript to the letter, comparing the *Answer* to Rabshakeh's ultimatum to Hezekiah (see 2 Kings 18: 19–36)—a comparison all the more barbed because 'railing Rabshakeh' was a stock figure of a blasphemer in religious literature. She also prayed that God would turn the king's heart and lead him to favour the petition. Shrewsbury replied to Lady Bowes that 'your indiscrete comparison bewrayes the weaknes of your womanhode, thoughe much disagreeing from the modestie of your sex'. He went on, invoking the example of Eve, to warn Sir William against following his wife's counsel and bewailed the influence puritan ministers had on 'simple women' (LPL, MS 3201, fols. 178v–179r).

Undeterred by such strictures, in 1606 Lady Bowes hosted a conference at her house in Coventry that was attended by many leading puritans, including Hildersham, Bernard, and John Dod; John Smyth, her brother's protégé, also attended, as did Smyth's associate Thomas Helwys. At the conference Smyth and Helwys argued that the Church of England had shunned the reformation necessary to make it part of the true church and that consequently all Christians must separate from it. This position was rejected by an overwhelming majority of those present at the conference, although for a time Richard Bernard seemed ready to embrace it. Eventually, however, he decisively rejected separatism and vehemently attacked the separatists. Like Bernard, Lady Bowes may have been sympathetic to them; in 1611 Helwys dedicated an anti-predestinarian work, *A Short and Plaine Proofe*, to her, stating his gratitude for her past support and hoping that God would reveal to her the truth of his arguments.

There is no evidence that Lady Bowes gave Helwys any further support but her bounty continued to flow out to puritan ministers, particularly to those who had lost their livings for non-conformity. Among those who benefited from her patronage were the eminent preachers Paul Baynes and Richard Rothwell; in fact Lady Bowes was the sponsor of Rothwell's highly successful ministry in Durham and paid Rothwell's salary of £40 a year. Sir William Bowes died in 1611 and six years later, on 7 May 1617, his widow married her third husband, John Darcy, Baron Darcy of Aston (d. 1635). She died on 12 February 1622 at her house in Aldwark, Yorkshire, and was buried at Rawmarsh. THOMAS S. FREEMAN

Sources C. M. Newman, '"An honourable and elect lady": the faith of Isabel, Lady Bowes', *Life and thought in the northern church, c.1100–c.1700: essays in honour of Claire Cross*, ed. D. Wood (1999), 407–19 • S. Clarke, 'The life of Master Richard Rothwel, who dyed anno Christi, 1627', *The lives of thirty two English divines*, in *A general martyrologie*, 3rd edn (1677), 67–74, esp. 69–70 • Sir William and Lady Bowes to the earl of Shrewsbury, 17 Dec 1603, LPL, MS 3203, fol. 166r • earl of Shrewsbury to Sir William and Lady Bowes, LPL, MS 3201, fols. 178v–179r • T. Freeman, 'Demons, deviance and defiance: John Darrell and the politics of exorcism in late Elizabethan England', *Conformity and orthodoxy in the English church, c.1560–1660*, ed. P. Lake and M. Questier (2000), 34–63, esp. 35–6 • T. Helwys, *A short and plaine proofe … that Gods decree is not the cause off anye mans sinne or condemnation* (1611) • E. L. C. Mullins, 'Bowes, William', HoP, *Commons, 1558–1603* • W. J. Jones, 'Foljambe, Godfrey', HoP, *Commons, 1558–1603* • S. T. Bindoff, 'Wray, Christopher', HoP, *Commons, 1558–1603* • GEC, *Peerage*

Darcy, Sir John (b. before 1284, d. 1347), landowner and administrator, of Knaith and Upton, Lincolnshire and Kexby, Yorkshire, was the son and heir of Sir Roger Darcy (d. c.1284) of Oldcoates and Styrrup, Nottinghamshire, and of Isabel, daughter of Sir William d'Aton of West Ayton, Yorkshire. John Darcy was often referred to as 'le neveu' or 'le cosyn' to distinguish him from the senior line of the family descending through his father's brother Norman *Darcy (d. 1295/6) of Nocton, Lincolnshire [see under Darcy family (per. 1086–1333)]; later he was described as 'le piere' to distinguish him from his son. He was born before 1284 and was still a minor in 1292. He married as his first wife Emmeline, the daughter and heir of Walter Heron of Silkstone, Yorkshire.

Darcy was outlawed for felony in 1306, but pardoned on 19 May 1307 at the request of Aymer de Valence, earl of Pembroke. This was the first indication of a relationship that was to be formalized in 1309–10 when Darcy became a life retainer of Pembroke's, albeit with the interesting proviso that he be allowed to serve with whichever lord he wished at tournaments. The connection continued until Pembroke's death in 1323 and helped bring Darcy to prominence in the political and military service of Edward II. He was sheriff of Nottinghamshire and Derbyshire from 5 November 1319 to November 1322 and knight of the shire for Nottinghamshire in parliament in 1320. He served in the Scottish wars, was appointed constable of Norham Castle in 1317, and was present at the rout of the English army by Robert I near Byland in October 1322. He briefly held the strategically important shrievalty of Lancashire between 10 February and 13 July 1323 and was accorded the status of a knight-banneret by 12 August 1323.

On 18 November 1323 Darcy was appointed to replace the earl of Louth as justiciar of Ireland. His appointment indicated the concern of Edward II's government to establish a firmer administrative and political hold on the lordship. Although he later complained that the king had thereby taken him away from 'his good lord and master the earl of Pembroke' (PRO SC8/239/11949), Darcy appears to have been conscientious in fulfilling his new post. Although he continued to support Edward II after the latter's deposition and consequently lost the justiciarship on 12 March 1327, his appointment as sheriff of Yorkshire (from 30 September 1327 to 13 August 1328) signified a speedy reconciliation with the regime of Mortimer and Isabella, and he was re-established as justiciar of Ireland between 21 August 1328 and 27 February 1331. In 1329 he married as his second wife Joan (*d.* 23 April 1359), the daughter of Richard de *Burgh, earl of Ulster, and the widow of Thomas Fitzjohn, earl of Kildare, an alliance that for the first time gave him personal interests in Ireland.

Darcy appears to have established close links with the young Edward III, who summoned him to the parliament of January 1332 as a member of the lords and granted him in April 1332 the manors of Brocklesby and Greetham in Lincolnshire as a reward for his constant service. His reappointment as justiciar of Ireland (from 30 September 1332 to 28 July 1337) was occasioned by the king's concern for the security of the lordship during the impending war with Scotland, and after serving as envoy in negotiations with the Scots at Newcastle in October 1332 Darcy organized and led Irish armies into Scotland in the autumn of 1333 and the summer of 1335. On 12 March 1337 he was appointed steward of the king's household and became closely involved in the preliminaries of the Hundred Years' War, accompanying the king and the royal household on their long sojourn in the Low Countries between 1338 and 1340. The exceptional life grant of the justiciarship of Ireland made to Darcy on 3 March 1340 proved no distraction from this course, since the post was treated as a sinecure to be held *in absentia*; later, in 1344, the king actually redeemed it in return for annuities to the value of £183. Darcy was also one of the beneficiaries of the redistribution of offices occasioned by Edward III's sudden return to England late in 1340; on 15 December he was replaced as steward of the household and took on the post of king's chamberlain.

The quarrel between the king and the former leader of the regency administration, John Stratford, archbishop of Canterbury, during the parliament that met at Westminster between April and May 1341 proved the most difficult episode in Darcy's eventful political career. Along with the new steward, Ralph Stafford, Darcy was charged to prevent Stratford from entering the parliament chamber, and successfully denied him access for a week. The chronicle ascribed to Stephen Birchington identifies Darcy and, more especially, the keeper of the privy seal, William Kilsby, as the archbishop's main enemies at court. In the resulting political crisis, Darcy was certainly listed by the earl of Surrey as one of those 'not worthy to sit in parliament' (Aungier, 90) and had to withdraw from the chamber, after which the king was forced to admit Stratford to his presence. Although Darcy retained the king's favour and remained at his post as chamberlain until at least 13 September 1346, it is noticeable that his career was rather less eventful after the crisis of 1341 than before it. For the remainder of his life he was more fully occupied in local administration within those counties where he had personal interests, serving on commissions of the peace and of oyer and terminer and as a tax assessor in Yorkshire, Nottinghamshire, Lincolnshire, and Hertfordshire.

Darcy received no further personal summonses to parliament after 1334: his presence in the assembly of 1341, as in that of 1344, was warranted only by his official status as chamberlain (though in 1903 the House of Lords judged, a little belatedly, that the latter appearance gave him the status of a peer sitting in right of the barony of Darcy). He saw military service in Brittany in 1342 and on the Crécy campaign of 1346, and was one of the envoys sent home to announce the latter victory to parliament. He was appointed for life to the constableships of Nottingham Castle (1344) and the Tower of London (1346). Darcy died on 30 May 1347, the very day on which he had received a royal pardon for all offences committed during his lifetime. From his first marriage he had a son, John 'le fitz' *Darcy [*see under* Darcy family (*per. c.*1284–1488)], who also served in Edward III's household. W. M. ORMROD

Sources GEC, *Peerage* · Tout, *Admin. hist.* · R. Frame, *English lordship in Ireland, 1318–1361* (1982) · J. R. S. Phillips, *Aymer de Valence, earl of Pembroke, 1307–1324: baronial politics in the reign of Edward II* (1972) · *Chancery records* · [H. Wharton], ed., *Anglia sacra*, 2 vols. (1691) · G. J. Aungier, ed., *Chroniques de London*, CS, 28 (1844) · R. Nicholson, *Edward III and the Scots: the formative years of a military career, 1327–1335* (1965) · J. E. Powell and K. Wallis, *The House of Lords in the middle ages* (1968) · A. Hughes, *List of sheriffs for England and Wales: from the earliest times to AD 1831*, PRO (1898); repr. (New York, 1963) · M. Jones and S. Walker, eds., 'Private indentures for life service in peace and war, 1278–1476', *Camden miscellany, XXXII*, CS, 5th ser., 3 (1994), 1–190

Darcy, John, second Lord Darcy (1317–1356). *See under* Darcy family (*per. c.*1284–1488).

Darcy, John, fourth Baron Darcy (1377–1411). *See under* Darcy family (*per. c.*1284–1488).

Darcy, John (*b.* before 1412, *d.* 1458). *See under* Darcy family (*per. c.*1284–1488).

Darcy, Margaret, Lady Darcy (*d.* 1454). *See under* Darcy family (*per. c.*1284–1488).

D'Arcy, Martin Cyril (1888–1976), Jesuit and theologian, was born on 15 June 1888 near Bath, the youngest of four sons, two of whom died in childhood, of Martin Valentine D'Arcy, a barrister on the northern circuit, and his wife, Madoline Mary Keegan. He was educated at Stonyhurst College from 1898 to 1906, when he followed his brother Edmund Conyers-D'Arcy into the Jesuit noviciate at Manresa College, Roehampton. His career at first took the normal course of two years of noviceship and a year of juniorate devoted largely to the classics, followed by three years of philosophical studies in the scholastic tradition at St Mary's Hall, a Jesuit seminary situated beside his old school. His early promise led his superiors to send him in 1912 to read classics at Pope's Hall, the Jesuit private hall of Oxford University. He had to be content with a second class in moderations in 1914, a setback which made him all the more determined to gain a first in *literae humaniores*, as he duly did in 1916. He also won a series of university prizes: the Charles Oldham prize in 1915, the John Locke scholarship in 1918, and the Green moral philosophy prize in 1923.

On leaving Oxford, D'Arcy returned to Stonyhurst as a

Martin Cyril D'Arcy (1888–1976), by Augustus John, 1939

master, and later as assistant prefect of studies. His teaching methods were unconventional and stimulating. One pupil was encouraged to read Pierre Rousselot, a progressive French theologian killed at the front in 1915, as well as James Joyce and the still relatively unknown Gerard Manley Hopkins.

In 1919 D'Arcy began the four-year course of theology of a Jesuit ordinand. The first year he spent with his exiled French *confrères* at Hastings (where Pierre Teilhard de Chardin had studied a few years before); there he deepened his interest in modern French philosophy and theology. The remaining three years were passed at St Beuno's College, north Wales (where Hopkins had written some of his best poetry), and he was ordained priest there in 1921. In 1923 he returned to Stonyhurst for a further year of teaching before going to Tullamore in Ireland for his tertianship, the third year of probation which concludes a Jesuit's long training.

In 1925 his superiors directed him to doctoral work in philosophy with a view to his teaching the subject to Jesuit students. The first year of these studies he spent in the normal way at the Gregorian University, Rome, but Rome was not his natural scene. His unpublished memoirs record that, while there, he protested to the superior general of his order, Wladimir Ledochowski, at the suspicions of unorthodoxy entertained concerning Rousselot's writings. With remarkable wisdom his superiors allowed him to spend his second year of research at the headquarters of the English Jesuits at Farm Street in London, and then let him have his head at Oxford.

Accordingly D'Arcy returned to Campion Hall (as Pope's Hall had by then become) in 1927, and began lecturing and tutoring in philosophy in the university. The impact he made both at Oxford and more widely over the next twelve years was dramatic. He became the foremost English apologist for Roman Catholicism, and received into that church a stream of distinguished converts, of whom the most articulate was Evelyn Waugh. (Father Rothschild in *Vile Bodies* is said to have been modelled partly on D'Arcy.) Indeed, a character in Muriel Spark's *The Girls of Slender Means* (1966), could 'never make up his mind between suicide and an equally drastic course of action known as Father D'Arcy'. From his fellow Jesuit Cyril Martindale he inherited a prominent position in Christian broadcasting.

A succession of books flowed from D'Arcy, notable among them being *The Nature of Belief* (1931), in which he developed the ideas of Cardinal Newman's *An Essay in Aid of a Grammar of Assent* (1870), *The Pain of this World and the Providence of God* (1935), and *The Mind and Heart of Love* (1945), his favourite among his own works. He wrote in what was, even for his own generation, a rhetorical and decorated style. His writing was always allusive, and, at least in his later years, his reflections on life tended to take the form of books about books. Of his preaching, an obituarist said that 'he would argue that the essence of a good sermon was "magic", that it did not matter, if the emotions were memorably stirred, whether or not anybody could subsequently remember what the preacher had actually been saying' (*Letters and Notices*, 200). Part of the secret of his own magic lay in his very striking and much painted features; a portrait of him by Augustus John is a well-known example of that artist's work.

In 1933 D'Arcy became master of Campion Hall. His predecessor had already begun to make plans for a new building. D'Arcy conceived the vision of a hall worthy of a historic order in a great university. He was advised to approach Sir Edwin Lutyens, who agreed to undertake the task. When the building was completed D'Arcy set about adorning it with a collection of works of sacred art (the famous *objets D'Arcy*), always insisting that the vestments and chalices, however precious, should remain in liturgical use.

Complementary with this ideal of a Jesuit contribution to English Christian humanism was an attachment to an English Catholic past, hazily and romantically conceived, and an addiction to the English Catholic gentry. He took innocent pleasure in an 11 foot long genealogical table, written in 1617 and illuminated with numerous coats of arms and two coronets, which allegedly traced his family back to the Norman conquest.

The 1930s were the golden age of D'Arcy and his hall. His young Jesuits won a succession of firsts and university prizes. His guest nights acquired a reputation for brilliant conversation. In 1935 he paid the first of many visits to the United States to preach in New York and to be made an honorary LLD of Georgetown University. This was the first of several American honours, including the Aquinas-Spellman medal of the Catholic Philosophical Association of America (1967). Over the years he lectured at Georgetown, Fordham, Boston College, and Notre Dame. He continued his visits even during the war, at the request of the

Ministry of Information. December 1942 saw him under the same auspices in Spain and Portugal, later he was in Japan. In 1956 he was elected a fellow of the Royal Society of Literature, and in 1960 he became an honorary member of the American Academy of Arts and Sciences.

In 1945 D'Arcy left Oxford to become provincial of the English Jesuit province. He formed imaginative plans for influencing the life of a country newly restored to peace, though his term of office is sometimes best remembered for his proclivity towards purchasing old houses with Catholic associations. Unfortunately he neglected the routine paperwork of administration, preferring to achieve results by personal contact, and in particular he failed to explain what he was about to the general in Rome. In February 1950 he was relieved of his post, about a year and a half before the normal time. His own province expressed its confidence by electing him its representative at a congregation in Rome, but he took his dismissal hard. He was in his sixty-second year.

The last twenty-six years of D'Arcy's life were something of a protracted dark night. He was out of sympathy with post-war Oxford and England. He saw no merit in the type of analytical philosophy then in the ascendant; the changes in the liturgy and theology of his church left him with a sense of betrayal. The United States, to which he returned nearly every year, came to be the place where he found his ideals most appreciated and where he felt most at home. Death, when it came to him in the Hospital of St John and St Elizabeth, St John's Wood, London, on 20 November 1976, was not unwelcome. He was buried on 29 November at Kensal Green cemetery, London. The art gallery at Loyola University, Chicago, perpetuates his name.

EDWARD YARNOLD

Sources British Society of Jesus, 114 Mount Street, London, records of the Provincial · Archives of the British Province of the Society of Jesus, London · H. J. A. Sire, Father Martin D'Arcy: philosopher of Christian love (1997) · Letters and Notices [Society of Jesus], 82 (1977), 188–202 · The Times (22 Nov 1976) · Laughter and the love of friends: reminiscences of … Martin Cyril D'Arcy, ed. W. S. Abell (1991) · The Tablet (27 Nov 1976) · M. Spark, The girls of slender means (1966)
Archives Archives of the British Province of the Society of Jesus, London · Campion Hall, Oxford, archives | FILM BFI NFTVA, 'Father D'Arcy — a self-portrait', Thames Television, 1971
Likenesses P. W. Lewis, drawing, 1932 · H. Cooke, drawing, 1937, Campion Hall, Oxford · H. Coster, photographs, c.1938, NPG · A. John, oils, 1939, Campion Hall, Oxford [see illus.] · F. Shrady, bronze bust, 1954, Metropolitan Museum of Art, New York · F. Shrady, bronze head, 1954, Campion Hall, Oxford · R. Avedon, bromide print, 1958, NPG · G. Argent, photographs, 1968, NPG · photograph, 1968, NPG · M. Rennell, drawing, 1972, Campion Hall, Oxford
Wealth at death £45: administration with will, 17 Nov 1977, CGPLA Eng. & Wales

Darcy, Mary, Lady Darcy of Chiche (1565/6–1644). *See under* Kitson family (*per. c.*1520–*c.*1660).

Darcy, Norman (**I**) (*d.* 1116×29). *See under* Darcy family (*per.* 1086–1333).

Darcy, Norman (**II**) (*d.* 1254). *See under* Darcy family (*per.* 1086–1333).

Darcy, Norman (**III**) (*c.*1236–1295/6). *See under* Darcy family (*per.* 1086–1333).

Darcy, Patrick (**1598–1668**), lawyer and politician, was the seventh son of Sir James Riveagh Dorsey (*d.* 1603), the third born to his second wife, Elizabeth Martin. The family was of Gaelic extraction, influential in the province of Connaught, and one of several leading Catholic merchant landowning families, both Irish and Old English, with the means and the inclination to send its sons to train in English law in London. Accordingly, Darcy attended the Middle Temple from 1617 until about 1622, as did a number of his family connections, cousins, and brothers-in-law such as Richard Blake, Richard Martin, Roebuck Lynch, and Geoffrey Browne. He and they all came from a stratum of Irish society defined in terms of a patchwork of affinities which overlay, perhaps at times transcended, fundamental divisions along lines of ethnicity or religion. About 1630 Darcy married Elizabeth, widow of Peter Blake and the eldest of Sir Peter French's four daughters. The couple had a son, James, and three daughters, Clara, Mary, and Frances.

First entering the Irish parliament in 1634 as MP for Navan, Darcy was immediately prominent as a leader of the Catholic interest with whom the new lord deputy, Viscount Wentworth, had established a tactical alliance on his arrival in Ireland. However, the relationship was abruptly terminated when the Catholics failed to extract from Wentworth the statutory confirmation of concessions granted by Charles I in the form of certain 'matters of grace and bounty', better known as 'the graces', which had held out the prospect of accommodation for the Catholic élite within the system of political franchises and legal privileges pertaining in an Ireland increasingly dominated by protestant English settlers. Darcy thenceforth led the political counter-attack, using Wentworth's unpopularity among the established protestant interest in Ireland against him. He was counsel for the defence when the lord deputy attempted to prosecute one of the most prominent New English potentates, Richard Boyle, earl of Cork, for illegal ownership of church lands in the diocese of Waterford and Lismore. He was also one of the commissioners sent to London to make representations to the king himself in opposition to Wentworth's planned Connaught plantation, a scheme typical of the arbitrary government with which Wentworth became associated, calling in question the property titles of Catholic landowners with a view to the expropriation of their estates and their resumption to the ownership of the crown. Wentworth, who evidently held Darcy in some esteem as a lawyer and as a man of integrity, sought almost to excuse the Irishman's opposition to him as the result of malign third parties—apparently meaning Cork and others. However, Darcy now took advantage of his presence at court to prosecute a scheme to relieve the lord deputy of his lucrative interest in the farm of the Irish customs, not impossibly at the behest of Cork himself, probably with the support of other New English opponents of the lord deputy such as Mountnorris as well as Wentworth's principal enemies in the English privy council, Hamilton and Holland. Wentworth's patience was now exhausted. When Darcy refused the oath of supremacy on his return to Ireland in May 1636 he was disqualified from practising as a lawyer. He was also imprisoned along with his brother Martin, the sheriff of Galway, who had led the resistance to the western plantation and who died in prison in June.

Darcy was an active and influential member of the House of Commons in the Dublin parliament which first assembled in 1640, to which he was not returned until winning a by-election in May 1641, whereupon he immediately took to the leadership of the Catholic interest. He played a prominent role in the moves to impeach key members of the Straffordian administration in Ireland in June 1641. In the course of so doing he submitted his famous *Argument* in response to the answers made by the Irish judges to a set of twenty-one questions on constitutional matters promulgated in the Irish Commons in assertion of the legal rights of the Irish parliament. Darcy's *Argument* was a powerful restatement of the connection between England and Ireland from a Catholic royalist perspective, devised to take account of the challenge emerging at Westminster to the royal prerogative, linchpin of the Irish and Old English understanding of Anglo-Irish relations. He argued in opposition to the judges that, although Irish subjects might make recourse to common law procedure in England, including trial in any of the king's courts, even before the Westminster parliament, that nevertheless no law made by the English parliament was of force in Ireland unless enacted by the Irish parliament. Although in composing his statement of constitutional theory Darcy was able to draw on numerous family connections from within the Irish legal establishment, *An Argument* remains his most important personal legacy. 'A close study of the text shows that he completed his brief in a masterly manner; alternately sarcastic and passionate, contemptuously dismissive or full of ringing conviction, he left an undeniably personal stamp on the text' (Caldicott, 199). His modern editor has compared the cogency and *élan* of his treatment of topical issues with that of Milton.

On the outbreak of the Ulster rising in October 1641, Darcy was prominent in denouncing the northern insurgents as 'the enemy' (Kearney, 214). But when the rising grew general he became one of the supreme council of confederated Catholics at Kilkenny, in which he played an influential role. In November 1642 Darcy was at the forefront in the formulation of a model of government for the confederation 'wherein care was taken that the former Government might be continued, lest any variation might make the right recontinuance difficult' (Gilbert, 1.lxiii). In many ways a classic statement of the principles inspiring the loyal rebellion of the Catholic Irish, his *Argument* was published in 1643 by Thomas Bourke, printer to the confederation. When constitutional controversy arose once more in relation to the Adventurers Act, passed at Westminster as an attempted English solution to the problem of reconquering rebellious Ireland, a manuscript book was widely circulated in Ireland entitled 'A declaration setting forth how and by what means the laws and statutes of England from time to time come to be in force in Ireland'. Rehearsing many aspects of Darcy's *Argument*, it too was almost certainly written by him.

In 1646 Darcy and his nephew Geoffrey Brown, with five others, were appointed by the general assembly of confederated Catholics to arrange articles of peace with the marquess of Ormond. The treaty, which nominated Darcy and his friends commissioners of the peace throughout Ireland, was signed on 28 March in that year. In 1649 Darcy once again negotiated a peace with Ormond, concluded on 17 January, but it proved just as ill-fated as the first. After the Cromwellian conquest Darcy was put on trial, convicted, banished from the Irish bar once more, stripped of his property, and imprisoned. At the Restoration reward for his loyalty was scant. Ormond secured his return to legal practice but could do nothing to restore his estates. Embittered, Darcy complained of the injustice suffered by Galway at the hands of the royalists. He died at Dublin in 1668, and was buried in the Franciscan friary at Kilconnell, co. Galway, in that year.   SEAN KELSEY

Sources DNB · *History of the Irish confederation and the war in Ireland … by Richard Bellings*, ed. J. T. Gilbert, 7 vols. (1882–91) · H. Kearney, *Strafford in Ireland, 1633–1641* (1959) · A. Clarke, *The Old English in Ireland, 1625–1642* (1966) · T. W. Moody and others, eds., *A new history of Ireland*, 3: *Early modern Ireland, 1534–1691* (1976) · L. O'Malley, 'Patrick Darcy, Galway lawyer and politician, 1598–1668', in D. Ó Cearbhaill, *Galway, town and gown, 1484–1984* (Dublin, 1984), 90–109 · C. E. J. Caldicott, 'Patrick Darcy, an argument', *Camden miscellany, XXXI*, CS, 4th ser., 44 (1992), 191–320 · A. Vicars, ed., *Index to the prerogative wills of Ireland, 1536–1810* (1967), 123
Wealth at death see Vicars, ed., *Index*

D'Arcy, Patrick [*known as* Chevalier Patrice D'Arci], **Count D'Arcy in the French nobility** (1725–1779), soldier and mathematician, was born in Galway on 17 February 1725, the third son of John D'Arcy (*d.* 1743) and his wife, Jane, daughter of Sir Robert Lynch, fourth baronet, of co. Mayo. His father's family, eminent locally, was of French origin and had settled in Ireland during the reign of Queen Elizabeth. Living under protestant domination, D'Arcy's parents, as Catholics and Jacobites, preferred their son to be educated in France. He was sent in 1739 to an uncle in Paris and there taught by the mathematician Jean Baptiste Clairaut, alongside his son Alexis Clairaut (1713–1765), who was to become the pioneer in France of Newtonian mathematics, with a reputation surpassing that of his father. In this environment D'Arcy soon showed a precocious competence in mathematics, applying his knowledge to mechanics and physics. When only seventeen he presented two memoirs on dynamics to the Académie Royale des Sciences.

Influenced by the young military officers whom Clairaut was also tutoring, D'Arcy entered the army, and adopted the name Chevalier Patrice D'Arci, which he henceforth used in his publications. As captain to the duke of Condé's regiment, he campaigned twice in Germany and once in Flanders. In 1746 he sailed as aide-de-camp to Count Fitzjames in command of a French force dispatched to assist Prince Charles Edward in Scotland. The fleet was seized by Admiral Knowles: D'Arcy, as an

Irishman bearing arms against his own government, could have been condemned, but he was repatriated with the other French officers.

After peace was declared, D'Arcy was elected *adjoint mécanicien* at the Académie Royale des Sciences, and rose to higher status as vacancies occurred. He returned to the army as a colonel in 1752 and served for the rest of his life; he attained the rank of field marshal in 1770. He was granted French nationality in February 1756: the pedigree that he submitted showed his connection to most of the crowned heads of Europe, and his title of Count D'Arcy, dating from 1746, was confirmed. In the campaign of 1757 he was under Fitzjames at the battle of Rossbach, where the French were driven back. Promoted to brigadier, D'Arcy was employed for his knowledge of the Irish coast under Count d'Hérouville, who was preparing an invasion of Great Britain, but nothing came of this project.

D'Arcy continued to work on applied mathematics and mechanics as the theme linking science and military matters. He published extensively in the *Mémoires de l'Académie Royale des Sciences* between 1747 and 1765. He took an interest in electricity, and in 1749 collaborated with Jean Baptiste Le Roy in an unsuccessful attempt to develop a floating electrometer. He embarked on a debate with Maupertuis on the principle of least action, published between 1749 and 1753. His memoir of 1751 on the physics and chemistry of gunpowder mixtures, the dimensions of cannon, and the placement of the charge was extended as *Essai d'une théorie d'artillerie*, published in Paris in 1760 and in Dresden in 1766. In measuring the recoil and power of cannon he invented a momentum pendulum that was adopted by the Régie des poudres. D'Arcy's sight had been damaged in an accident and this encouraged him to investigate the persistence of vision where a point light source, moved at speed, is seen as a continuous line. His experiments on this well-known phenomenon, not hitherto measured, were published in 1765.

With an income derived from a Galway estate yielding £2000, an inheritance from his uncle, his military pay, and investments in mines, D'Arcy was able to assist other refugees from Ireland; in 1767 he refused a fortune offered by another uncle to settle there. He maintained good relations with the English scientific community, reserving his hatred for the English king. In 1777 he married his niece Jane D'Arcy, whose education he had supervised; they had no children. Two years later, in Paris, he died from cholera, on 18 October 1779.   ANITA MCCONNELL

Sources 'Eloge de M. le Comté D'Arci', *Histoire de l'Académie Royale des Sciences*, 1779 (1782), 54–70 · DSB · C. E. Lart, *The pedigrees and papers of James Terry, Athlone herald at the court of James II in France* (1938), 1–22 · Burke, *Gen. Ire.* (1976), 323–4 · P. Fagan, ed., *Ireland in the Stuart papers*, 2: 1743–65 (1995), 245

Darcy, Penelope (d. 1660/61). *See under* Kitson family (*per.* c.1520–c.1660).

Darcy, Philip (I) (d. 1264). *See under* Darcy family (*per.* 1086–1333).

Darcy, Philip (II), **Lord Darcy** (1259–1333). *See under* Darcy family (*per.* 1086–1333).

Darcy, Philip, third Baron Darcy (1352–1399). *See under* Darcy family (*per.* c.1284–1488).

Darcy, Robert (d. 1148x60). *See under* Darcy family (*per.* 1086–1333).

D'Arcy, Robert, fourth earl of Holdernesse (1718–1778), politician, was born on 17 May 1718, the second but only surviving son of Robert D'Arcy, third earl of Holdernesse (1681–1722), a landowner, and Lady Frederica Schomberg (1687/8–1751), the eldest surviving daughter and coheir of Meinhardt *Schomberg, third duke of Schomberg (1641–1719). Upon his father's death on 20 January 1722 he succeeded to the title. Educated first at Westminster School and then at Trinity College, Cambridge, where he does not seem to have completed a degree, he was appointed in 1740 lord lieutenant of the North Riding of Yorkshire, a post he retained until 1777. In April 1741 he became a member of George II's court as a lord of the bedchamber, and in this capacity he was present with the king on the battlefield of Dettingen in 1743. Later in the same year, at The Hague (29 October), he married a wealthy heiress, Mary Doublet (1720/21–1801), the daughter of Francis Doublet, a member of the provincial states of Holland, and his wife, Constantia van der Beek. A man of more rank than ability, Holdernesse at this point in his life was a great patron of opera. Horace Walpole, who viewed him with disdain and described him as 'that formal piece of dullness' (Walpole, *Corr.*, 20.202), declared that the earl's 'passion for directing operas and masquerades was rather thought a contradiction to his gravity, than below his understanding, which was so very moderate' (Walpole, *Memoirs*, 1.198).

Birth was the essential springboard for advancement in Hanoverian Britain, and royal service launched Holdernesse into a public career. In the summer of 1744 he secured nomination as ambassador to the republic of Venice, a post of considerable prestige but relatively limited stature, and he took up residence there in mid-October 1744. Venice was a backwater in Britain's eighteenth-century diplomacy. The main purpose of his embassy was to re-establish formal relations, broken off in 1737 because British ministers had resented 'the extraordinary distinctions and honours paid to the Pretender's son' (*Eglinton MSS*, 268) when he visited the republic. Holdernesse remained in Venice for almost two years, returning to Britain in late August 1746. While he was in the republic his first son, George Darcy (1745–1747), was born, but died of smallpox while still an infant. A second son, Thomas, was born on 7 May 1750, but died little more than two months later, on 27 July 1750. A daughter, Amelia, was born on 12 October 1754. Three years after his return from Venice, with the support of George II and the duke of Newcastle, Holdernesse was appointed to the far more important post of minister-plenipotentiary to the Dutch republic. He arrived at The Hague in early June 1749 and departed at the very end of July 1751, though he returned later in the same year on a brief, formal mission of condolence on the death of the stadholder, William IV (1747–51). In the final stages of his mission to the Dutch republic,

Robert D'Arcy, fourth earl of Holdernesse (1718–1778), by George Knapton, 1752

Holdernesse had been appointed (18 June 1751) to be secretary of state for the southern department. The circumstances of his appointment highlight the motive for his elevation, which was sudden and dramatic, particularly for a peer of his relative youth and political unimportance. Until 1782 formal control of British foreign policy was divided on a geographical basis between the southern and northern departments, with each secretary being responsible for conducting diplomatic relations with a particular group of countries. The potential for divisions and clashes within such a system was considerable, and the then northern secretary, the duke of Newcastle, had quarrelled with a succession of fellow secretaries. The latest and in many ways the most serious of these disputes was with the duke of Bedford, southern secretary since 1748. Bedford had criticized the duke's pursuit of continental alliances through the payment of subsidies, and had championed alternative policies; he had also been negligent in carrying out his official duties. Newcastle, a vain, insecure, and secretive man, was determined to have a pliable and subordinate brother secretary in order to facilitate his own complete control of British policy; he may also have understood the drawbacks inherent in the geographical division of control over Britain's diplomacy. When Holdernesse's appointment was first rumoured, in April 1751, George Bubb Dodington rightly noted that Newcastle's intention was 'to curtail the Southern Province' (*Political Journal*, 113). The earl's conduct while at The Hague had suggested that he might be the ideal choice for a subordinate role. He had been reasonably conscientious, if occasionally dilatory in sending his dispatches. More importantly, he had not challenged Newcastle's personal handling of Anglo-Dutch relations, through regular correspondence and occasional meetings with the leading Dutch statesman, William Bentinck. When Bedford was finally dismissed from the southern department in June 1751 Holdernesse, who also had George II's support, was appointed to succeed him.

Holdernesse remained in office for a decade, with the exception of the period between 9 and 29 June 1757, when he resigned temporarily during a period of intense ministerial upheaval. He stayed at the southern department until 23 March 1754, when he changed to the northern secretaryship. His political longevity was not accompanied by commensurate importance, and his impact upon British foreign policy was slight. He was not even a competent minister: his contemporaries thought him 'very incapable' (*Political Journal*, 297), and Walpole never tired of sneering at his incapacity. Largely content to follow orders, he was active but not influential in government, conscientiously carrying out the policy decided by others. The main exception to this came in 1755, when as northern secretary he accompanied the king to Hanover. His role as a link to George II meant that he played a minor part in the negotiations which produced the abortive Convention of St Petersburg (September 1755). This agreement, signed but never ratified, was an Anglo-Russian subsidy convention which was intended to protect the electorate of Hanover from a Prussian or French attack if the war with France which threatened should spread to Europe. This was the single example of Holdernesse's political significance. He was mainly content to handle the day-to-day routine of meetings with foreign diplomats in London and to write the dispatches to those missions which lay within his department. Waldegrave rightly noted that the earl 'had been ready on all occasions to act according to direction' (Waldegrave, 121). He seems to have held no strong personal views on British policy, and was unaffected by the switch from an Austrian alliance to links with Prussia, which was a consequence of the diplomatic revolution of 1756.

Newcastle had at first welcomed Holdernesse exactly because he was the pliable subordinate he had long wished for, but by the mid-1750s this gratitude had been replaced by disdain. In 1757 the duke remarked that 'Poor Holdernesse is a greater cipher than ever' (Yorke, 3.193). Holdernesse's temporary resignation in June 1757 had earned him George II's hostility and destroyed what little political standing he possessed, making him more dependent upon Newcastle's support. During the next two years relations between the two men declined further, as Holdernesse slowly transferred his loyalty to the rising star of William Pitt. His subservient status did not alter. On one celebrated occasion Pitt stood over the northern secretary until 3 a.m., correcting an important dispatch to Andrew Mitchell, Britain's minister in Prussia, line by line. George II famously described the earl as 'Pitt's footman' (ibid., 3.67). By 1759 even Holdernesse was openly resentful of Newcastle's extensive private correspondence with British diplomats, behind the back of his northern secretary, and of the duke's domineering attitude towards his fellow minister. By that autumn the breach between the two men was complete. When Holdernesse complained about Newcastle's correspondence with Sir Joseph Yorke, the son of Lord Chancellor Hardwicke and an influential minister at The Hague, he received a complete snub. His adversary now commented that Holdernesse was 'no more informed than a page of the backstairs' (Middleton, 146). Holdernesse was totally eclipsed, yet he remained in office for two further years: he simply was not important enough to dismiss. By November 1760 he was said to be ready to resign because of the 'slights and ill-usage he daily experienced' (*Political Journal*, 403). Dismissal was finally his fate on 12 March 1761, when he was removed from office to make way for the new king, George III's, ministerial favourite, the earl of Bute, who took his place at the northern department.

On leaving office Holdernesse was compensated with the reversion of the post of warden of the Cinque Ports, which he received in October 1765, together with a pension for life of £4000. His tenure of the wardenship was coloured by scandal when his wife, who had in the past sought to evade customs duties, was accused of exploiting her husband's position by engaging in extensive smuggling. He was an important patron of the poet and Anglican cleric William Mason, although the two men later quarrelled. His links with the royal court, which had earlier helped to keep him in high office, were rebuilt under George III. In 1771 he was appointed governor of the king's two eldest sons, George, prince of Wales, and Frederick, duke of York, but though he was a conscientious tutor he found his young charges to be a handful, and this contributed to a breakdown in his health. In 1774–5 he was forced to spend fifteen months abroad recuperating, and returned 'very lean and very deaf' (Walpole, *Corr.*, 24.207). When he returned he found that his influence with his two young charges was much reduced, and he resigned in 1776. Although he had long been promised the Garter by the king, it was never bestowed upon him. Holdernesse died on 16 May 1778, at Isleworth in Middlesex, and was buried on 1 June at Hornby in the North Riding of Yorkshire. His widow died in Hertford Street, Mayfair, Westminster, on 13 October 1801. Since their only surviving child was their daughter, Amelia (1754–1784), who married Francis Godolphin, marquess of Carmarthen, later fifth duke of Leeds, the earldom became extinct upon Holdernesse's demise. On hearing of his death, Walpole penned a suitable epitaph: Holdernesse, he declared, had been 'not quite so considerable a personage as he once expected to be, though nature never intended him for anything that he was' (Walpole, *Corr.*, 24.385).

H. M. SCOTT

Sources GEC, *Peerage*, new edn, vol. 6 · Walpole, *Corr.* · *The political journal of George Bubb Dodington*, ed. J. Carswell and L. A. Dralle (1965) · P. C. Yorke, *The life and correspondence of Philip Yorke, earl of Hardwicke*, 3 vols. (1913); repr. (1977) · D. B. Horn, ed., *British diplomatic representatives, 1689–1789*, CS, 3rd ser., 46 (1932) · J. Waldegrave, *Memoir from 1754 to 1758* (1821) · H. Walpole, *Memoirs of the reign of King George the Second*, ed. Lord Holland, 2nd edn, 3 vols. (1847) · R. Middleton, *The bells of victory: the Pitt–Newcastle ministry and the conduct of the Seven Years' War, 1757–1762* (1985) · *Reports on the manuscripts of the earl of Eglinton*, HMC, 10 (1885) · DNB

Archives BL, corresp. and papers, Egerton MSS 3401–3497 · BL, corresp. as governor to the princes, Add. MS 39168 · Derbys. RO, corresp. relating to Ireland · W. Yorks. AS, Leeds, Yorkshire Archaeological Society, Syon Hill Library catalogue, letters | BL, corresp. with first earl of Hardwicke, Add. MSS 35590–35596, *passim* · BL, corresp. with Sir Benjamin Keene, Add. MSS 43425–43440 · BL, corresp. with Robert Keith, Add. MSS 6825, 35465– 35483, *passim* · BL, corresp. with Sir Andrew Mitchell, Add. MSS 6804–6819, 6831–6832, 58284–58285, *passim* · BL, corresp. with first duke of Newcastle and others, Add. MSS 32695–33090, *passim* · BL, corresp. with Lord Tyrawly, Add. MSS 23631, 23634 · Chatsworth House, Derbyshire, letters to third and fourth dukes of Devonshire · NL Scot., letters to Lord Tinwald · PRO, letters to first earl of Chatham, PRO 30/8 · PRO, letters to G. B. Rodney, PRO 30/20 · U. Nott. L., department of manuscripts and special collections, letters mainly to Henry Pelham

Likenesses G. Knapton, oils, 1749, Brooks's Club, London, Dilettanti Society · G. Knapton, oils, 1752; on loan to Temple Newsam, Leeds [*see illus.*] · J. Reynolds, portrait, 1755 · R. Cooper, stipple (after J. Reynolds, 1755), BM, NPG; repro. in W. Mason, *Works* (1811) · attrib. J. Huysmans, oils (in youth), Gov. Art Coll.

Darcy, Thomas (I) (*d.* **1180**). *See under* Darcy family (*per.* 1086–1333).

Darcy, Thomas (II) (**1166/7–1206**). *See under* Darcy family (*per.* 1086–1333).

Darcy, Thomas, Baron Darcy of Darcy (*b.* in or before **1467**, *d.* **1537**), soldier and rebel, was born before May 1467, being over twenty-one in May 1488. He was the son of Sir William *Darcy (*c.*1454–1488) [*see under* Darcy family (*per. c.*1284–1488)], landowner, of Temple Hirst, West Riding of Yorkshire, and his wife, Euphemia, daughter of Sir John Langton of Farnley, West Riding. The Darcy family were lesser gentry, long settled at Temple Hirst near Selby. Darcy's exact date of birth is unknown; in depositions made probably in the summer of 1529 he gave his age as about sixty.

Early life and advancement, 1492–1509 Darcy's early reputation appears to have rested on his soldiering skills. He was knighted in 1489. In 1492 he was bound by indenture to serve Henry VII abroad with 1000 men during the Brittany campaign. He attended the king at the reception of the French embassy sent to treat for peace later that year. In 1497 he saw service on the Scottish borders when he marched with Thomas Howard, earl of Surrey, to raise the siege of Norham, Northumberland, and pursued James IV into Scotland and he was rewarded with the title of knight banneret. While this is the first occasion on which he is named in connection with the borders, his service to both Henry VII and Henry VIII was largely to take the form of office-holding in the east and middle marches and in the captaincy of Berwick. By 1500 he was deputy to Henry, duke of York, who was appointed titular warden. The first suggestion that Darcy was captain of Berwick dates from the summer of 1498 when he was granted the stewardship and constableship (with other offices) of Bamburgh Castle, Northumberland. He was named as lieutenant of the east and middle marches in November 1498 and appears to have served continuously as captain of Berwick until the end of 1508. His service as warden was probably more intermittent. He is not named among the deputies of Henry, prince of Wales, in March 1500, but is among those of August 1501. In 1505 he was named as warden of the east marches.

Darcy's service to Henry VII, who advanced him as one of his intimates, was not limited to the north. In 1498 he was named as one of the commissioners sent to assess fines on those implicated in the previous year's west-country revolts and was appointed constable and earl marshal at the trials of any who would not compound. In 1500 he was named a knight of the body. It seems probable that he surrendered the captaincy of Berwick in 1509 to become vice-chamberlain of the royal household and captain of the guard. He was one of the councillors who met on 22 April 1509 at Richmond Palace, Surrey, on the morning after Henry's death to consider precedents for the interment of a monarch. He was enough of a court insider for his recollections to be called upon during the divorce of Henry VIII and Katherine of Aragon in the late 1520s. Through royal patronage, a man who in 1498–9 was satisfied to be steward to Henry Clifford, tenth Baron Clifford, was raised to the first rank of royal servants. As Henry VIII told the commons of Yorkshire in 1536 in a particularly barbed comment, Darcy was among those councillors who were 'scant well born gentlemen and yet of no great lands until they were promoted by us, and so made knights and lords' (*State Papers Published under … Henry the Eighth*, 11 vols., 1830–52, 1.507).

While all this suggests that Darcy was well regarded by Henry VII, the most compelling evidence of the favour the king showed him comes from his second marriage. His first wife was Dousabella (*d.* in or before 1499), daughter and heir of Sir Richard Tempest of Stainforth in Ribblesdale, West Riding. Tempest's family was a cadet branch of the Tempests of Bracewell: there is little to show that he was of either great wealth or standing. Darcy and his wife had two sons, George Darcy (*d.* 1558), first Baron Darcy of Darcy, and Sir Arthur Darcy (*d.* 1561). In 1499 or 1500 Darcy married Edith (*d.* 1529), daughter of Sir William Sandys of the Vyne, Sherborne St John, Hampshire, and his wife, Margaret, sister of William *Sandys, first Baron Sandys; Edith was the widow of Ralph Neville, Baron Neville (*d.* 1498), son and heir of Ralph Neville, third earl of Westmorland. Westmorland died on 6 February 1499 and Darcy's stepson Ralph *Neville (1498–1549) became the fourth earl of Westmorland. It may be assumed that Darcy acquired some or all of the political influence of the earldom. The king's favour, and Darcy's position as the stepfather of an earl, justified his elevation to the peerage. The first references to him as Lord Darcy come from April 1504: it is likely that he was created Baron Darcy of Darcy by writ of parliament on 25 January 1504. The price of the marriage was that Lord and Lady Darcy were compelled to assign a share of her jointure to the king. Darcy also entered into an indenture with Henry whereby, after acknowledging his 'preferment and advancement' at the king's hands, he agreed to be retained exclusively by him and to retain a force of 200 men for the defence of Berwick at his own charges over and above the normal establishment of the town's garrison. This agreement was to remain in force for as long as Darcy was captain of Berwick. He was made steward of the lordship of Sheriff Hutton for life in 1500 and was appointed receiver-general of the lands assigned for the support of Berwick in 1503, although he held this office for only two years. In 1505 he was made steward of all Westmorland's manors during his minority.

Darcy acquired offices in Yorkshire. As Sheriff Hutton Castle was the seat of the northern council, his stewardship of Sheriff Hutton may reflect Darcy's role in the council. In 1497 he was granted the stewardship of Snaith near his house at Temple Hirst and was appointed JP for the West Riding from 1497 onwards. The only real evidence of Darcy playing a role in Yorkshire at this time comes from his intervention in the affairs of the Forest of Knaresborough, West Riding, where riots over new enclosures took place in May 1507. He was instructed to remain at Temple Hirst in order to keep an eye on his tenants. After the death of Sir William Scargill, steward of Knaresborough, Darcy took the opportunity to lobby for the grant of the stewardship, and he received it for life on 30 May 1509 from the hands of the new king.

Loss of favour, 1509–1529 Summer 1509 was the high-water mark of Darcy's career. While he surrendered his household offices, on 18 May he was admitted to the Order of the Garter. On 18 June he was appointed warden of the east marches. In June he had patents for the captaincy, treasurership, and chamberlainship of Berwick, the stewardship and surveyor-generalship of Westmorland's lands during his minority, the stewardship and surveyorship of the lands of Sir Ralph Grey during the minority of Thomas Grey (and Grey's wardship in November), and the chief justiceship of forests beyond the Trent. Darcy was also granted several duchy of Lancaster offices in the West Riding, including the stewardship of Pontefract, the constableship of Pontefract and Knaresborough castles, and new grants of the stewardships of Snaith and Dunstanburgh. And in the reaction against Henry VII's rapacity, the king returned the whole of Lady Darcy's jointure.

Unlike Henry VII, who also employed Darcy as a courtier, Henry VIII used him more for his military abilities on the Scottish borders. In 1511 he allowed Darcy to lead a force to Spain to fight the Moors on behalf of his father-in-law, Ferdinand of Aragon. Darcy's force was at Cadiz by 14 June, but the Spanish had no use for it, and despite his request that they should have a trial with the Moors organized for them, or that he and his captains should serve Ferdinand for a year without pay, they were repatriated as a source of embarrassment. While Thomas Dacre, second Baron Dacre of Gilsland, was authorized to keep the warden courts in the east and middle marches during Darcy's absence, Darcy had a new grant of the captaincy of Berwick on his return. However, Dacre was made warden of the east and middle marches in December, apparently after Darcy had declined the office. In 1512 he was again active on the borders, undertaking to find 2000 men, of whom his neighbours would supply 386. His 'neighbours' were all Yorkshire gentry, at least three of whom had been to Spain with him the previous year. In 1513 he saw service in France and fought at the Battle of the Spurs on 16 August. It seems to have been envisaged that on his return he would proceed immediately to Northumberland to take up the campaign against the Scots which followed the battle of Flodden in September.

There are signs that Darcy craved involvement in Henry's French campaigns and found the borders unrewarding. His determination to participate in the French theatre of war extended to taking men from his Northumberland stewardships to fight with him in France in 1513. In January 1514 he was lobbying Thomas Wolsey for a position in the following summer's projected campaign. In 1515 he surrendered the captaincy of Berwick to another Yorkshire gentleman, Sir Anthony Ughtred. He believed that he was removed by Wolsey, and while promised compensation, the fact that he never received any rankled to the end of his life. However, at the same time Darcy was regranted his duchy of Lancaster offices in Yorkshire, and this suggests that his removal from Berwick was not the result of any disgrace, but a deliberate decision to translate his sphere of activity to Yorkshire, perhaps as part of an abortive reorganization of the government of the county. He seems to have been omitted from the founding membership of the king's council of the north, established in 1525, being admitted only in 1533. In a real sense his career as a leading royal servant ended in 1515: he was offered few opportunities during Wolsey's ascendancy. The occasional references to his service under Wolsey concern ceremonial duties: the receipt of Wolsey's cardinal's hat in November 1516, the reception of Cardinal Lorenzo Campeggi in July 1518. He was one of those named to attend the king at the Field of Cloth of Gold in 1520, but the indications are that he stayed in England during Henry's absence. Darcy served on the Scottish borders in 1523, but under Thomas Howard, earl of Surrey (later third duke of Norfolk). He became an embittered critic of both Wolsey and the divorce. He remained relatively inactive during the late 1520s and concentrated on local affairs. Darcy was now extremely wealthy, with an annual income from land of £1834 4s. in September 1526.

Alienation, 1529–1536 Darcy's re-entry into politics came with the fall of Wolsey. He compiled long and elaborate memoranda itemizing complaints against the cardinal's conduct of government. While it is unclear how far these circulated, they fed into the articles prepared against Wolsey (signed by Darcy, among others) which were presented to parliament on 1 December 1529. It was impossible for Darcy to make any common cause with Henry. He maintained that spiritual men should not be involved in temporal government, a point which he made directly against clerical members of the council of the north, but which equally applied to Wolsey. Conversely he held that matrimonial causes correctly belonged to ecclesiastical jurisdiction. He maintained this principle in the House of Lords in January 1532, and so set his face against the whole direction of royal policy in these years. Darcy was probably particularly hostile to the suppression of the orders of Observant friars in mid-1534, for he had been one of their most notable patrons. Lady Darcy died at Stepney, Middlesex, on 22 August 1529 and was buried in the friary of the Greenwich Observants (a house sponsored by Henry VII) three days later.

In September 1534 Eustace Chapuys, the imperial ambassador, spoke to Darcy at the invitation of another embittered peer, John Hussey, Baron Hussey (with whom Darcy had a long association). Darcy was willing to tell Chapuys of his alienation and to outline his plans for a rebellion against Henry, in which he was confident of the support of other, mostly unnamed, peers. He suggested that Charles V should land a force in the Thames estuary to add to an invasion of the north from Scotland. There were further treasonable conversations between them in the spring of 1535 which led Chapuys to believe that some sort of rising was imminent. None came. Darcy's willingness to talk treason may be connected to the expectation of radical 'Lutheran' reform in the autumn parliament of 1534: this too failed to materialize. He pleaded ill health as an excuse to be allowed to absent himself from future parliaments and Garter feasts. This was conceded on 28 October. He was in financial difficulties at this time, Lady Darcy's jointure lands having reverted to Westmorland. In the autumn of 1533 Darcy sought from Henry a pardon for a debt of £660 for which he was in danger of being outlawed.

The Pilgrimage of Grace, 1536–1537 Given his vocal opposition to the early Reformation and his withdrawal to Temple Hirst, it is all too easy to assume that the Pilgrimage of Grace was the rebellion of which Darcy had talked with Chapuys in 1534–5. The existence of a muster-book of his forces thought (erroneously) to date from 1 October 1536, his willing surrender of Pontefract Castle, West Riding, to Robert Aske, his emergence as one of the captains of the pilgrims who negotiated with Norfolk, and his refusal to defect to the duke when challenged to do so all point to Darcy's complicity. His claims to have been loyal throughout have been long read as being disingenuous.

Darcy's actions are in fact perfectly plausible when taken at face value and especially when the Pilgrimage of Grace is seen as a widespread popular movement in opposition to expected and feared religious innovations. When disturbances broke out in Yorkshire, he sent the king a long and accurate assessment of the situation and sought reinforcements, money, supplies of munitions, and the authority to mobilize. On two further occasions he wrote at length describing a deteriorating situation. On all three occasions his information and advice were ignored. At the outbreak of trouble he moved to Pontefract Castle, which became a refuge for Thomas Lee, archbishop of York, and other refugee gentry, and made it an irresistible prize for Aske. The muster-book actually shows the complete breakdown of Darcy's ability to recruit troops. Pontefract was blockaded and lacked supplies; the garrison was held to favour the commons. While Darcy hoped to be rescued by George Talbot, fourth earl of Shrewsbury, the latter told Darcy by letter of 17 October that he had been told to hold his position at Newark, Nottinghamshire. After Aske came to Pontefract, Darcy sought a truce, but the situation was judged hopeless and the castle was surrendered on 20 October. It was Aske's contention that Darcy could not have resisted a siege, but would have been killed if the commons had stormed the castle.

Darcy then became one of the pilgrims' captains. Yet he

supported the disbandment of both the pilgrims and the royal army at Doncaster (27 October) as a way of avoiding conflict. He maintained order during the truce while Sir Ralph Ellerker and Robert Bowes visited the king. There was some doubt at court about Darcy's motives in surrendering Pontefract. He was given the opportunity to demonstrate his continued fidelity to Henry by capturing Aske. However, he rejected the king's instruction, delivered orally on 10 November, but while he dressed his refusal in the language of honour, it was hardly practical. During the period of truce, he was pushed towards treason by fears of Henry's intransigence. It is certain that he and Aske flirted with the idea of seeking help from Charles, but the messenger they selected never travelled beyond Hull. In common with all the commons' leaders, he accepted the minimal concessions (of a pardon and a future parliament) granted by Norfolk at Doncaster on 6 December as a device to bring peace. As the commons progressively repudiated this agreement in January, Darcy (and Aske) spoke for it and argued against foolhardy new risings, including that by Sir Ralph Bigod. The crown was determined to trap both men: they were arrested on 7 March for offences alleged to have been committed after the uprising, the immediate justification being that they had dealings with a man caught up in Bigod's revolt. Darcy was tried in Westminster Hall and found guilty of treason on 15 May. Having first been degraded from the Order of the Garter on 22 June, he was beheaded at Tower Hill on 30 June 1537 and his remains interred in St Botolph, Aldgate. It was later claimed that Darcy had been found guilty only because Sir Thomas Cromwell, principal secretary, led the peers trying him and persuaded them to believe that he would be pardoned by the king.

Darcy was poorly served by Henry and finally abandoned by him: having been taken by the pilgrims, he worked to secure their disbandment through the use of 'policy'. While there is plenty of evidence for his sympathy for the aims of the commons, his claim that 'I have served above fifty years the king's majesty and his father and should not in my old age enter rebellion with the commons' is correct. In a private memorandum he noted, 'and he [God] be my judge, never lost [a] king a truer servant and subject without any cause but lack of furniture [arms] and by false reports and pickthanks [sycophants]. God save the king: though I be without recovery' (Hoyle, *Pilgrimage of Grace*, 415).

Following his conviction, Darcy's lands were seized. He was posthumously attainted by statute in 1539. The Darcy title was thereby suspended until his eldest son, George Darcy, was restored in blood in 1548 and elevated to the peerage as Baron Darcy of Darcy. He never regained any of his father's estates. Darcy's papers were seized from Pontefract in 1537: some, but by no means all, survive in the Public Record Office. R. W. HOYLE

Sources M. Bush, *The Pilgrimage of Grace: a study of the rebel armies of October 1536* (1996) • *LP Henry VIII* • R. W. Hoyle, *The Pilgrimage of Grace and the politics of the 1530s* (2001) • *DNB* • *Hall's chronicle*, ed. H. Ellis (1809) • R. W. Hoyle, 'Thomas Lord Darcy and the Rothwell tenants, c.1526–1534', *Yorkshire Archaeological Journal*, 63 (1991), 85–107 • *GEC, Peerage* • H. Miller, *Henry VIII and the English nobility* (1986)
Archives PRO, MSS, SC 1 • PRO, MSS, SP 46/187

Darcy, Thomas, first Baron Darcy of Chiche (1506–1558), courtier and administrator, was born on 4 December 1506, the only son of Roger Darcy (*d.* 1508) of Danbury, Essex, and Elizabeth, daughter of Sir Henry Wentworth of Nettlestead, Suffolk. His father, who had been an esquire of the body to Henry VII, died before Darcy was two, and his wardship was granted to Sir John Raynsford of Bradfield, Essex. By September 1521, as soon as he had attained the minimum legal age for cohabitation, Raynsford married Darcy to his daughter Audrey. Nothing is known of his upbringing, but he seems to have been destined for a career as a soldier and courtier. Audrey died soon after Darcy achieved his majority in 1527, and they appear to have had no children. By 1532 he had married Elizabeth, the daughter of John de Vere, fifteenth earl of Oxford, and it was probably de Vere patronage that caused his career to take off at that point. He was knighted on 1 November 1532, and was appointed a knight of the household either then or shortly after. At the same time Darcy began to serve on numerous commissions, and it can be deduced that he enjoyed the favour of Thomas Cromwell, as well as the support of the earl of Oxford. He may have sat in the parliament that met from April to July 1536, and was certainly knight of the shire for Essex in 1539. When the earl of Oxford died in 1540 Darcy's position in Essex was enhanced by the grant of a number of local offices traditionally held by the de Veres. There are a number of references to his serving with 200 men in the French campaigns of 1543–4, which suggests that he was now one of the most important men in the county. On 9 June 1544 he was appointed to the key position of master of the Tower armouries. At court he became a carver of the king's table in 1540 (a position of honour but little substance) and was a gentleman of the privy chamber by the spring of 1544. He sat again for Essex in the parliament of 1545, and received a bequest of £200 in Henry VIII's will.

At what point Darcy became associated with the victorious Seymour–Dudley group at court, or why he did so, is not clear. His subsequent record does not suggest a strong commitment to religious reform. That he did support the coup is evident from his being appointed under the king's 'unwritten will', announced on 15 February 1547, as steward of the liberties of Bury St Edmunds and of all the duke of Norfolk's confiscated lands in Suffolk, and keeper of Framlingham Castle. He had a distant family relationship with the earl of Hertford (subsequently duke of Somerset) and during the Scottish campaign of 1547 he served as captain of the gentlemen pensioners, being wounded at the battle of Pinkie. He sat again as knight of the shire for Essex in the first parliament of Edward VI's reign. Most of the former duke of Norfolk's lands were granted to Princess Mary in 1548, but Darcy clearly remained in favour with Somerset's government, and with his friend Sir John Gates he led one of the duke's enclosure commissions in 1549. Nevertheless in the coup against the protector he sided with the London lords and was appointed on 15

October as one of the four principal gentlemen of the privy chamber specially responsible for the king's safety. By now he was probably in touch with John Dudley, earl of Warwick, for when the earl established his control following the overthrow of the conservatives in December 1549 Darcy was appointed to the privy council on 24 January following, and on 2 February took office as vice-chamberlain of the household and captain of the guard. In December 1550 he was one of those appointed to command a troop of fifty in the proposed gendarmerie. The following spring he was raised to the peerage on 5 April 1551 as Baron Darcy of Chiche in order to become lord chamberlain of the household, following the death of Lord Wentworth. On 6 October he was elected to the Order of the Garter. Darcy's principal political importance at this period was as a vital link between Dudley and the court, controlling the flow of information to Edward and influencing the young king in the required direction. Darcy also served on the jury that condemned Somerset on 1 December 1551, and in March 1552 he was appointed to head the important reform commission 'for the survey and examinacion of the state of all his Majesties Courtes of Revenue'.

When Edward VI died on 6 July 1553, Darcy supported the attempt by Warwick (now duke of Northumberland) to place Lady Jane Grey on the throne, but apparently without great enthusiasm. Nevertheless his closeness to Northumberland brought him into some danger, and he was arrested after the failure of the bid. He was pardoned on 1 November 1553, but lost his offices at court and his membership of the council. Thereafter he abandoned his ostensible support for protestantism, and by 1556 was noted by John Foxe as having been one of the more zealous persecutors among the Essex justices. He was a trier of petitions in the House of Lords in each of the Marian parliaments, and when attack from France was feared after the fall of Calais in January 1558 he was appointed lieutenant to organize the defence of Essex. He died at Wivenhoe on 28 June 1558, and was buried at St Osyth's Priory. With his second wife Darcy had three sons and at least one daughter, but only one son, John, survived him to inherit the title. The second Lord Darcy was knighted at Elizabeth's coronation. DAVID LOADES

Sources GEC, *Peerage*, new edn, 4.78 · HoP, *Commons, 1509–58*, 2.14–16 · *LP Henry VIII* · APC, 1542–58, 1–6 · *CSP dom.*, 1547–53 · A. F. Pollard, ed., *Tudor tracts, 1532–1588* (1903) · M. L. Bush, *The government policy of Protector Somerset* (1975) · J. Foxe, *Actes and monuments*, 4th edn, 2 vols. (1583) · W. K. Jordan, *Edward VI, 1: The young king* (1968) · W. K. Jordan, *Edward VI, 2: The threshold of power* (1970) · D. E. Hoak, *The king's council in the reign of Edward VI* (1976) · D. M. Loades, *John Dudley, duke of Northumberland* (1996)
Archives PRO, state papers, domestic, SP1, SP10

Darcy, Sir William (*c.*1454–1488). *See under* Darcy family (*per. c.*1284–1488).

D'Arcy, William Knox (1849–1917), financier, was born on 11 October 1849 at Highweek, Newton Abbot, Devon, the only son among the seven children of William Francis D'Arcy, solicitor, of Newton Abbot, and his wife, Elizabeth Baker, daughter of the Revd Robert Bradford of Wolborough, Devon. He was educated at Westminster School and in 1866 emigrated with his parents to Australia, where they settled in Rockhampton on the Queensland coast.

D'Arcy qualified as a solicitor in March 1872, initially working with his father, but in 1882 formed a syndicate to exploit a vein of gold that had been discovered close to Rockhampton. With seven other shareholders, D'Arcy formed the Mount Morgan Mining Company. Holding 125,000 shares in his own name, plus 233,000 in trust, D'Arcy became a very rich man. He disposed of his legal practice in 1886, and three years later he returned to England, where he enjoyed high society and sporting pursuits: there were shooting parties on his Norfolk estate, and he held his own private stand at Epsom.

On 23 October 1872 D'Arcy married Elena, daughter of Samuel Bradford Birkbeck, a mining engineer, of Glenmore, Queensland; they had two sons and three daughters. Elena died in 1897, and in 1899 D'Arcy married Ernestine ('Nina') Nutting (*b.* 1867), daughter of the Australian journalist Arthur Leslie Boucicault. Nina Boucicault was the first actress to play the title role in James Barrie's *Peter Pan*. On her husband's death in 1917 she became the only female owner of a private stand at Epsom.

Although still a director of Mount Morgan, and chairman of its London board, D'Arcy remained interested in new financial ventures. Towards the end of 1900 he was approached about funding exploration in Persia, where oil seepages had long been known about. D'Arcy himself never went to Persia, but on 28 May 1901 his representative obtained a concession valid for sixty years. This entitled him to search for and sell 'natural gas, petroleum, asphalt and ozokerite' throughout all of Persia except in the five northern provinces adjoining Russia. Drilling operations began towards the end of 1902 in Chiah Surkh, a likely oil-bearing area near the border with Iraq. D'Arcy's engineer, George Bernard *Reynolds (1852/3–1925), was a man of great experience and tenacity, but the difficulties proved formidable.

After three years without success D'Arcy feared that the venture would fail. 'Every purse has its limits', he wrote, 'and I am beginning to see the bottom of my own.' D'Arcy had invested some £250,000 of his own money in the enterprise, and felt that it was 'money that I shall never see again'. Other financial help was needed, and in 1905 it came in the form of a deal with the Burmah Oil Company—to whom D'Arcy ultimately surrendered his interest in the whole venture, in return for 170,000 Burmah shares and the reimbursement of all his expenses.

Drilling operations had meanwhile been shifted to the south, and oil was finally struck in Masjid-i-Suleiman on 26 May 1908, just as D'Arcy and Burmah were on the point of giving up. The discovery of oil in significant quantities ensured D'Arcy's successful formation of the Anglo-Persian Oil Company on 14 April 1909, and marked the birth of the oil industry of the Middle East. Although D'Arcy sat on the board of the new company he was not disposed to play any further significant role. D'Arcy died on 1 May 1917 at his home, Stanmore Hall, Middlesex, and was buried four days later at Stanmore parish church.

ROBERT BROWN

Sources R. W. Ferrier, *The history of the British Petroleum Company*, 1: *The developing years, 1901–1932* (1982) · R. W. Ferrier, 'D'Arcy, William Knox', *DBB*, 2.12–14 · D. Carment, 'D'Arcy, William Knox', *AusDB*, 8.207–9 · J. Parker, ed., *Who's who in the theatre*, 6th edn (1930) · *The Times* (2 May 1917), 9b · BP Archive, University of Warwick, D'Arcy papers
Archives University of Warwick, BP Archive | priv. coll., Birkbeck-D'Arcy corresp.
Likenesses photographs, University of Warwick, BP Archive
Wealth at death £984,011 18s. 1d.: probate, 12 Sept 1917, *CGPLA Eng. & Wales*

Dare, Phyllis (1890–1975). *See under* Dare, Zena (1886–1975).

Dare, Thomas (*d.* 1685), political activist and rebel, was the son of a civil war cavalier and a goldsmith by occupation. He sat on Taunton's common council following the grant of a new charter to the town in 1677 (the corporation had fallen into abeyance in 1662 following the old members' refusal to comply with the Corporation Act of 1661), and was a member of the whig Green Ribbon Club, which met at the King's Head tavern in Chancery Lane, London. During the exclusion crisis, he was active in promoting a petition in the name of the inhabitants and freeholders of Somerset calling for the sitting of parliament and the prosecution of Catholic recusants, which he presented to Charles II on the stairs of the House of Lords on 26 January 1680 just as the king was about to announce a further prorogation. When the outraged monarch asked 'How he dared do that?', Thomas retorted, 'Sir, my Name is Dare' (North, 543).

It was later alleged that while collecting signatures to the petition, Dare had said 'That the subject has but two ways of redress, by petition or rebellion', and he was indicted at the Taunton assizes at the end of March for dangerous and seditious words against the government. Dare claimed that when he had been challenged about the legality of petitioning, he had simply pointed out that Henry VIII had told the northern insurgents of 1536 'that they ought not to have rebelled, but to have applied to him by petition, the subject having, as the king's words declared, but these two ways of address'. When asked, however, whether he agreed that, 'suppose the King should not hear petitions, must we rebel', he had explicitly said, 'No, God forbid' (*CSP dom.*, 1680–81, 152). The presiding judge, Sir Thomas Jones, refused Dare's request to have the trial postponed so that he could call a material witness in his defence, and advised Dare to plead guilty to the words but deny the seditious intent, promising to intercede with the king on his behalf. Dare agreed, only to be fined £500, bound over to good behaviour for three years, and ejected from his seat on the Taunton common council. At the same time the grand jury made a presentment disowning Dare's petition and bound Dare over to the next assizes to answer another charge, this time for allegedly having said to someone who had advised him

not to meddle in state affairs, because the king had his privy council to advise him, 'that he knew no Council the King had, but the Duchess of Portsmouth, the French ambassador, Lord Duras [Louis Duras, earl of Feversham], and the Duke of Lauderdale' (ibid., 1679–80, 428). On 22 December the House of Commons voted to impeach Jones for his harsh treatment of Dare, though the dissolution of parliament the following month meant that no action was taken. Dare remained in prison for at least ten months because he could not pay his fine, though at length he managed to escape, whereupon he fled to the Netherlands.

Dare attended the earl of Shaftesbury on his deathbed in January 1683 and witnessed his will. By the spring of 1683 Dare was reportedly caballing against the king's interests, and over the next couple of years his house in Amsterdam became a regular meeting-place for English exiles in the Low Countries. John Locke stayed at Dare's house following his flight to the Netherlands, and continued to receive his mail there throughout this period. The duke of Monmouth and the earl of Argyll met at Dare's house in late February 1685 to plan their co-ordinated invasion of England and Scotland, and again in April to finalize details about the two-pronged attack. Dare served as paymaster for Monmouth's invasion force and sailed with Monmouth in June, coming ashore at Chideock, in Lyme Bay, several hours in advance of the main invasion force on Thursday 11 June to gather intelligence. Dare spent the next couple of days scouring the countryside around Lyme for horse, and by Saturday the 13th had managed to create the nucleus of a cavalry force. On that day he got into an argument with his co-conspirator Andrew Fletcher of Saltoun about who should have the best horse, and in the heat of the dispute Fletcher shot him through the head and killed him. His son Thomas was also involved in the Monmouth rebellion, but turned king's evidence. Dare's wife, Ellen, had accompanied him into exile; a few weeks after his death, she was apologizing profusely to John Locke that she was not yet in a position to pay him the money he had asked for.

TIM HARRIS

Sources *LondG* (19 Feb 1679/80–23 Feb 1679/80) · *LondG* (5–8 April 1680) · *Protestant (Domestick) Intelligence*, no. 80 · *CSP dom.*, 1679–81; 1683–4 · Magd. Cam., Pepys Library, Pepysian miscellanies, VII, 465–91 · *Letters of Humphrey Prideaux … to John Ellis*, ed. E. M. Thompson, CS, new ser., 15 (1875) · *JHC*, 9 (1667–87) · J. Oldmixon, *The history of addresses*, 2 vols. (1709–11), vol. 1 · R. North, *Examen, or, An enquiry into the credit and veracity of a pretended complete history* (1740) · M. Cranston, *John Locke: a biography* (1957) · R. Clifton, *The last popular rebellion: the western rising of 1685* (1984) · R. Ashcraft, *Revolutionary politics and Locke's two treatises of government* (1986) · R. L. Greaves, *Secrets of the kingdom: British radicals from the Popish Plot to the revolution of 1688–89* (1992) · M. Knights, *Politics and opinion in crisis, 1678–1681* (1994) · K. H. D. Haley, *The first earl of Shaftesbury* (1968)

Dare, Zena [*real name* Florence Harriette Zena Dones] (1886–1975), actress, was born at 18 Oakley Crescent, Chelsea, London, on 4 February 1886, the eldest daughter of Arthur Albert Dones, a barrister's clerk, and his wife, Harriette Amelia Wheeler. Educated at Maida Vale high school, she alternated schooling with pantomime from

Zena Dare (1886–1975), by Elwin S. Neame, 1905

the age of twelve. Her first appearance was at the Coronet Theatre, understudying in *Babes in the Wood* (1899), after which she appeared in pantomimes in Edinburgh, Manchester, and Glasgow, and Seymour Hicks chose her for the title role in *An English Daisy* (1902). In 1903 she returned from learning French in Brussels to play Cinderella in Liverpool. Her performance in *Sergeant Brue* at the Strand—'Miss Zena Dare … as Mabel Widgett … combines refinement of style with dainty archness and quiet drollery' (*The Era*, 18 June 1904)—set her firmly on her path in musical comedy.

Zena's dramatic style impressed critics: it was praised as 'distinctive and quite original' by the *Play Pictorial* (1904). By casting her opposite himself in a large part Hicks recognized her quality. 'She was remarkably intelligent,' he said; 'her performance … spelt her name in golden letters of success which she has made brighter each year by the whole-heartedness and sincerity of all she undertakes' (Hicks, 259). She created Angela in *The Catch of the Season*, by Seymour Hicks and Cosmo Hamilton, at the Vaudeville in 1904. *The Era* found this modern Cinderella 'positively bewitching, playing with a sweetness and delicacy that are beyond all praise … the gaiety of the young actress is irresistible' (17 Sept 1904). In 1905 she played the title role in *Lady Madcap*, by Paul Rubens and N. Newnham Davis, for George Edwardes. Until 1910 she played leading roles in major shows, including Owen Hall's *The Little Cherub* (1906), *The Beauty of Bath*, by S. Hicks and C. Hamilton (1906), and Hicks's *The Gay Gordons* (1907). On 23 January

1911 she married Lieutenant-Colonel the Hon. Maurice Vyner Baliol Brett (1882–1934), second son of Reginald Baliol *Brett, second Viscount Esher, and a captain in the Coldstream Guards, and retired from the stage. They had one son and two daughters.

Edwardian musical comedy was insouciant and glamorous. Light-hearted to the point of being nonsensical, its ephemeral pleasures relied on the personality and superb technical accomplishments of its stars. When Zena returned to the theatre in 1926 in *The Last of Mrs. Cheyney*, by Frederick Lonsdale, this escapist world had vanished, but her distinguished career was not restricted to a single genre. She worked in London and toured with her own company to South Africa (1928–9). There were musical comedies and reviews with Ivor Novello and Noël Coward. John Gielgud cast her in *Spring Meeting*, by M. J. Farrell and J. Perry (1939), and in J. M. Barrie's *Dear Brutus* (1941). She toured in Lilian Hellman's *Watch on the Rhine* (1943) and played Julia Ward McKinlock in Samuel Taylor's *Sabrina Fair* (1954) and Isabel Sorodin in Noël Coward's *Nude with Violin* (1957). Her sophistication, warmth, and sincerity culminated in the creation of Mrs Higgins in Alan Jay Lerner's *My Fair Lady* (Drury Lane, 1958), a part that she played for over five years, subsequently touring with the company in 1964–5. It seems unjust that when the play was filmed in 1964 her part was played by Gladys Cooper.

Her husband died on 18 August 1934. Zena Dare died on 11 March 1975 in Chelsea.

Phyllis Dare (1890–1975), Zena's younger sister, was born Phyllis Constance Haddie Dones at 18 Landridge Road, Fulham, on 15 August 1890. She played the Brother in *Babes in the Wood* at nine years old. Martin Harvey engaged her to appear in *Ib and Little Christina*, by Basil Hood, in 1900 and she played Mab in *Bluebell in Fairyland* for Seymour Hicks in 1901. Seasons in pantomime, some with Zena, some playing Cinderella herself across the UK, alternated with formal education and the study of stage skills. Her début in musical comedy—*The Catch of the Season*, by S. Hicks and C. Hamilton (1905)—was a great success. In 1906 she went to the Ardennes to complete her education, returning almost immediately to take over the lead in *The Belle of Mayfair*, by C. H. Brookfield and C. Hamilton, with just four days to learn the script as she travelled home. 'Her delightful dancing and winsome manner won all hearts' (*Popular Favourites*, 2, 1922). Her instantaneous success led to a tour with *The Dairymaids*, by A. M. Thompson and R. Courtneidge, and a year's run in *The Arcadians*, by M. Ambient and A. M. Thompson (1909). By 1907, aged sixteen and a star, she was asked to write a short book about herself. In 1909 she played Gonda Van der Loo in *The Girl on the Train*, by V. Leon, and went on to create a series of 'girls' including Prudence in *The Quaker Girl*, by J. J. Tanner (Châtelet Theatre, Paris, 1911), Delia Dale in *The Sunshine Girl*, by Paul Rubens and Cecil Raleigh (1912), and Sally Hook in *Miss Hook of Holland* (1914), by Paul Alfred Rubens and Austen Hurgon.

A talented composer, Rubens (1875–1917) adored Phyllis; only his ill health prevented their engagement from leading to marriage. Her contribution to the tango craze came from his *The Sunshine Girl* (she later filmed *The Argentine Tango and other Dances*, 1913). He wrote notes for his best ballad ('I Love the Moon') for her on his dirty shirt-cuff while at dinner and then had to retrieve it from the laundry. During 1914 she sang his 'Your King and Country Want You' in recruiting campaigns. Rubens died in 1917, leaving her a small fortune.

After the war Phyllis's talent matured. In Frederick Lonsdale's *The Lady of the Rose* (1922) and *Lido Lady*, by Ronald Jeans (1926), she was queen of the romantic musical play. James Agate reported wryly of Lonsdale's *The Street Singer* (1924) that 'she received an ovation never accorded to Bernhardt, Duse or Ellen Terry' (Trewin, 67). A new career might have opened with Edgar Wallace's dramatic *The Yellow Mask* (1928); unfortunately she was generally offered trivial comedies, with the exception of Stella Trent, in *Cheated* (1930), where she acted with 'a depth of feeling that was astonishingly impressive' (B. Oulton, *The Stage*, 8 May 1975). Her last appearance was with Zena in Ivor Novello's *King's Rhapsody* (1949).

The adventurous, compassionate child heroine of her children's book, *Kitty in Fairyland* (1914), reflected its author. Phyllis Dare died on 27 April 1975 at her home, 22 Pembroke Avenue, Hove, Sussex. The Dare sisters were caught up in the picture craze of the early 1900s, signing 300 postcards a week. In these cards one glimpses the casual grace and strong stage presence that they brought to their enthralled audiences.   SUSAN C. TRIESMAN

Sources *Who was who in the theatre, 1912–1976*, 2 (1978) • E. M. Truitt, *Who was who on screen*, 3rd edn (1983) • *Popular Favourites* (*Stage, Concert and Screen*), no. 2, *Phyllis Dare* (1922) • J. P. Wearing, *The London stage … a calendar of plays and players*, 9 vols. (1981–90) [vols. covering 1900–39] • S. Hicks, *Twenty-four years of an actor's life by himself* (1910) • W. Macqueen-Pope, *Carriages at eleven: the story of the Edwardian theatre* (1947) • E. Short, *Sixty years of theatre* (1951) • *Play Pictorial*, 1–17 (1904–12) • *The Stage* (20 March 1975); (8 May 1975) • J. C. Trewin, *The gay twenties: a decade of theatre* (1958) • P. Dare, *Kitty in fairyland* (1914) • P. Dare, *From school to stage* (1907) • b. certs. [Zena Dare; Phyllis Dare] • m. cert. [Zena Dare] • d. cert. [Phyllis Dare] • K. Gänzl, *The encyclopedia of the musical theatre*, 2 vols. (1994) • CGPLA Eng. & Wales (1975) [Zena Dare]
Archives Jerwood Library of the Performing Arts, London, Mander and Mitchenson Theatre Collection
Likenesses E. S. Neame, photograph, 1905, PRO [*see illus.*] • Rotary photo, photograph, c.1905 (Phyllis Dare), NPG • tinted photograph, c.1908, NPG • portrait, 1922 (Phyllis Dare), repro. in Trewin, *The gay twenties* • C. Buchel and Hassall, lithograph (Phyllis Dare), NPG • J. Ross, coloured woodblock (Phyllis Dare), NPG • J. Ross, wash caricature (Phyllis Dare), NPG • Rotary photo, photograph, NPG • group portrait (with Phyllis Dare), repro. in W. Macqueen-Pope, *Gaiety: theatre of enchantment* (1949), 332 • group portrait (with Phyllis Dare), repro. in S. Naylor, *Gaiety and George Grossmith* (1913), 48 • photograph (in *Sergeant Brue*), repro. in *Play Pictorial*, 1/4 (1904–12) • photograph (in *Catch of the season*), repro. in *Play Pictorial*, 1/6 (1904–12) • photograph (in *The little cherub*), repro. in *Play Pictorial*, 7/43 (1904–12) • photograph (in *The gay Gordons*), repro. in *Play Pictorial*, 10/63 (1904–12) • photograph (Phyllis Dare), repro. in *Play Pictorial*, 28/107 (1904–12) • photograph (Phyllis Dare), repro. in *Play Pictorial*, 16/96 (1904–12) • photographs, Hult. Arch. • portrait, repro. in Short, *Sixty years of theatre*, 56 • portraits (Phyllis Dare), repro. in W. Macqueen-Pope, *The footlights flickered* (1959), 97
Wealth at death £63,373: probate, 1975, CGPLA Eng. & Wales • £8238—Phyllis Dare: administration with will, 8 July 1975, CGPLA Eng. & Wales

Darell, William (*d.* in or after **1580**), Church of England clergyman and antiquary, was related to the Darells of Calehill, Little Chart, Kent, who adhered to Rome after the Reformation. Otherwise nothing is known about his family or early life before 1546, when he was presented to Little Chart rectory. He acquired several other livings, including St Andrew's, Droitwich, Worcestershire (by 1548), Milton next Gravesend, Kent (1549), and Chawton, Hampshire (1553). On 23 September 1553 and again on 24 March 1554 he was appointed by the crown to the third prebend in Canterbury Cathedral, vacated by Robert Goldeston, a married cleric. Darell graduated BA from Oxford on 24 April 1554 and proceeded MA on 29 May following. At the time of Elizabeth's accession he was resident at Lenham, Kent.

In 1559 Darell was one of five members of the chapter of Canterbury Cathedral who elected Matthew Parker as archbishop. It was he who, as the chapter's proxy, announced the election in the cathedral choir and presented it to Parker for his assent. In 1560 he was subdean of Canterbury, from 1565 to 1570 chancellor of Bangor, and in 1568 he briefly held the prebend of Flixton in the diocese of Lichfield. By 1564 he was one of Queen Elizabeth's chaplains, and in 1569 she appointed him a commissioner for Berkshire. Darell was also rector of various parishes in the dioceses of Canterbury, Rochester, Norwich, and Bath and Wells.

Darell was one of the circle of antiquaries encouraged by and united under Archbishop Parker. This connection perhaps accounts for the MA he received for residency at Corpus Christi College, Cambridge, in 1564. Darell is chiefly known for his unpublished treatise on Kentish castles, now held by the College of Arms, 'Castra in campo Cantiano ab antiquo aedita nobilium ope et diligentia'. This was dedicated to William Brooke, sixth Lord Cobham, constable of Dover and lord warden of the Cinque Ports, from whom Darell had received favours. Parts of the text were printed in an English translation by Alexander Campbell as *The History of Dover Castle*, in London in 1786; it was reprinted in 1797. Darell is perhaps of more significance as a collector, however, than as a writer. In 1566 he came into the possession of a copy of the late thirteenth-century 'Flores historiarum'; with early fourteenth-century additions, it had previously belonged to John Bale (Lambeth Palace Library, MS 1106). Other manuscripts Darell owned included 'Chronicle of the brute' (BL, Stowe MS 69), and a heraldic collection relating to the Irish nobility (College of Arms, MS B 22), both also dating from the fifteenth century.

In 1567 Darell appointed Henry Style of Westminster as his attorney in case he should leave England, styling himself 'Deane of Fernes in Irelande' (Canterbury Register V2, fol. 72). He can therefore be identified conclusively as the 'Mr. Dorrell' whose proposed election as archbishop of Armagh was vehemently opposed by Edmund Grindal, bishop of London. Writing to Cecil in November 1567, Grindal agreed with the 'poor scholar' from Ireland who thought the appointment would 'hinder the course of religion in that country', since 'the said Dorrell hath been heretofore convented before me and other commissioners for sundry his misdemeanours, and therefore I know him to be an unfit man for so high an office' (Nicholson, 292).

Darell's 'misdemeanours' were not at an end. Despite his benefices he acquired debts which the cathedral chapter eventually paid, confiscating his prebend's salary in recompense. In 1575 Darell became the subject of much local gossip and was brought before the ecclesiastical courts when Clemence Ward, a lady of 'suspect behaviour', was apprehended by a lay clerk of the cathedral while being smuggled into Darell's residence in a laundry basket. In November 1579 the privy council wrote to the commissioners for causes ecclesiastical in the diocese of Canterbury 'to cite peremptorily William Darrell, Prebendary of the Church of Canterbury, before them for certain horrible offences committed by him' (*APC, 1578–80*, 315). Nothing more of the matter is known, although Darell did relinquish the rectory of Monkton, Kent, in 1579, and had been deprived of his Canterbury prebend by 16 February 1580. It is not known when he died.

PETER SHERLOCK

Sources Foster, *Alum. Oxon., 1500–1714*, 1.373 · Venn, *Alum. Cant.*, 1/2.12 · P. Collinson, N. Ramsay, and M. Sparks, eds., *A history of Canterbury Cathedral* (1995), 167–9 · W. Stubbs, ed., *Chronicles of the reigns of Edward I and Edward II*, 2 vols., Rolls Series, 76 (1882–3) · J. Strype, *The life and acts of Matthew Parker*, new edn, 3 vols. (1821), vol. 1, pp. 103–5 · general register, 1567–9, Christ Church Cathedral, Canterbury, Register V2 · *CSP dom., 1547–80*, 302 · *Fasti Angl., 1541–1857*, [Canterbury] · *CPR, 1547–72* · *APC, 1578–80*, 315 · J. Strype, *The history of the life and acts of the most reverend father in God Edmund Grindal*, new edn (1821) · W. Nicholson, ed., *The remains of Edmund Grindal*, Parker Society, 9 (1843) · W. Urry, *Christopher Marlowe and Canterbury*, ed. A. Butcher (1988) · *DNB*

Archives Coll. Arms, 'Castra in campo Cantiano'

Dargan, William (1799–1867), railway contractor, the son of a farmer whose name is not known, was born in the county of Carlow, Ireland, on 28 February 1799. Having received an English education he was trained as a surveyor. His first important contract was under Thomas Telford in constructing the embankments linking Holy Island to Anglesey on the Holyhead road in 1819; on its completion he returned to Ireland and took small contracts on his own account, the most important of which was the road from Dublin to Howth. In 1833 he became the contractor for the construction of the railway from Dublin to Kingstown, the first line made in Ireland. He next constructed the Ulster Canal between Lough Erne and Belfast, a signal triumph of engineering. Other great works followed—the Dublin and Drogheda Railway, the Great Southern and Western, and the Midland Great Western lines.

By 1853 Dargan had constructed over 600 miles of railway, valued at £2 million, and he had then contracts for 200 more. He paid the highest wages with the greatest punctuality, and his credit was unbounded. In total he undertook nearly sixty major contracts, the overwhelming majority for railways, and became the largest railway contractor in Ireland and one of its greatest capitalists. He made arrangements in 1853 for the Dublin Exhibition. He began by placing £30,000 in the hands of the organizers, and before the exhibition was opened on 12 May 1853, his advances reached nearly £100,000, of which he ultimately lost £20,000. At the close of the exhibition the Irish National Gallery on Leinster Lawn was erected, as a monument to Dargan. Queen Victoria, who had visited Dargan and his wife, Jane, at their residence, Dargan Villa, Mount Annville, on 29 August 1853, offered him a baronetcy, but this he declined.

Between 1850 and 1860 Dargan tried to establish a linen industry. He took a tract of land near Rathcormack, co. Cork, where he grew flax, and established linen mills at Chapelizod, near Dublin, but the business did not prosper. After 1860 he became increasingly involved in railway finance. He devoted much effort to the Dublin, Wicklow, and Wexford Railway, of which he was chairman.

In 1866 Dargan was seriously injured by a fall from his horse. While he was unable to work his affairs became disordered and he stopped paying out money, though it was believed that his assets would more than cover his liabilities. These problems, however, affected his health and spirits. He died at 2 Fitzwilliam Square East, Dublin, on 7 February 1867, and was buried in Glasnevin cemetery. His widow was granted a civil-list pension of £100 on 18 June 1870. They had no children.

G. C. BOASE, rev. MIKE CHRIMES

Sources *The Times* (8 Feb 1867) · *GM*, 4th ser., 3 (1867), 388–9 · *The Engineer*, 23 (1867), 134 · *Irish Builder* (15 Feb 1867) · *Irishman* (9 Feb 1867) · 'The Great Industrial Exhibition of Ireland', *ILN* (14 May 1853), 390 · 'The Dargan Villa, Mount Anville: visit of Her Majesty', *ILN* (10 Sept 1853), 205–6 · J. Sproule, ed., *The Irish Industrial Exhibition of 1853* (1854), ix–xiv · *Irish tourists' illustrated handbook* (1853), 12, 14, 148 · L. Popplewell, *A gazetteer of the railway contractors and engineers of Ireland, 1833–1914* (1987) · 'Mr Dargan', *Railway Times*, 15/52 (25 Dec 1852), 1368b

Archives PRO NIre., notes, etc. | PRO NIre., Irish Railway Records Society

Likenesses coloured lithograph, pubd 1853, NG Ire. · J. E. Jones, marble bust, 1854, NG Ire.; plaster copy by B. Cheverton, NG Ire. · G. Mulvany, portrait, 1855, Irish Rail headquarters, Heuston station, Dublin · S. C. Smith, oils, 1862, NG Ire. · T. Farrell, bronze statue, 1863, NG Ire. · W. J. Edwards, stipple and line engraving (after G. F. Mulvany), NPG; repro. in Sproule, ed., *The Irish Industrial Exhibition of 1853*, frontispiece · J. Mahony, watercolour, NG Ire. · W. Woodhouse, medal, National Museum of Ireland · engraving, repro. in *Irish tourists' illustrated handbook* · portrait, NG Ire.

Dark, Sidney Ernest (1872–1947), newspaper editor, was born on 14 January 1872 at 35 St John's Wood Road, St Marylebone, London, the eldest son of Henry Sidney Dark, of Lord's Cricket Ground, and his wife, Mary Jane Burns. His birth certificate gave his father's occupation as bat maker. Following a short period in Paris where he worked as a clerk in the business of a friend of his father's, and a time as a professional actor and singer, Dark began his journalistic career as correspondent for green room gossip at the *Daily Mail* in 1900. He married Helen Sarah, daughter of Henry Anders, a journalist, on 26 February 1895. He and Nellie, as she was known, had one son and one daughter. In 1902 Dark moved to the *Daily Express*, initially as a theatre critic. Immediately after the First World War Dark was sent to France to report on the reception of the peace settlement and President Wilson's visit to France and as the paper's special correspondent during the Paris Peace Congress. From 1919 to 1924 Dark was joint editor of *John O'London's Weekly* owned by Sir George Newnes. Dark became editor of the *Church Times* in 1924. He was a member of the original committee of the PEN Club and in 1927 was elected a fellow of the Institute of Journalism.

Dark was the first layman to be editor of the *Church Times* since its founder, J. B. Palmer, as well as the first Fleet Street journalist to become editor of this distinctly Anglo-Catholic weekly. Dark had held sympathies with Anglo-Catholicism for some time and in 1924 went on the Anglo-Catholic pilgrimage to the Holy Land. As editor Dark changed the political position of the paper towards a more left-wing stance without entering a party political alliance. In addition to his journalistic work Dark wrote more than thirty books. There were two novels, *The Man who would not be King* and *Afraid*; a number of children's books, including *The Child's Book of England* (1922), *The Child's Book of Scotland* (1923), and *The English Child's Book of the Church* (1925); books on recent Anglican church history, such as *Five Deans: John Colet, John Donne, Jonathan Swift, Arthur Penrhyn Stanley, William Ralph Inge* (1925), *Archbishop Davidson and the English Church* (1929), and *The Lambeth Conferences, their History and their Significance* (1930); and anthologies on literature and theatre of his time. He also edited the letters of W. S. Gilbert and wrote biographies of the newspaper proprietor Sir Arthur Pearson (1922) and Lord Halifax (1934).

Sidney Dark commented on the danger of an overstated anti-communism, which in his view had resulted in the fatal alliance between the churches and fascism in both Spain and Germany. During the Spanish Civil War he attempted to use his influence to prevent the Church of England from backing Franco. Dark became increasingly critical of the Roman Catholic church and argued in his autobiography, *Not such a Bad Life* (1941), that its alliance with Franco had made a reunion of the churches impossible and intolerable.

> The Roman Catholic Church is compromised in a world that is half enslaved and half fearful of being enslaved. I did not realise that the Spanish Civil War was the prologue of Hitler's bid for world supremacy. I did, however, accurately foretell what the Vatican-Franco alliance would mean for Christendom, and the anger of my Roman Catholic critics was evidence of their uncomfortable consciences. (Dark, *Life*, 239)

From an early stage Dark also commented on 'the Jewish question'. Antisemitism for him was not so much a question of race but rather a political, social, and economic issue; and he depicted it as part of the anti-bourgeois agenda of fascism. He regarded the fact that both the Church of England and the British government largely ignored the plight of German Jewry and maintained political and economic relations with Hitler's Germany as 'the moral abdication of Christendom' (Dark, *Life*, 261). In a work entitled *The Folly of Anti-Semitism* (1939) he wrote:

> Anti-Semitism is not merely a Jewish concern: it is a concern of all men who care for justice, decency and kindness, and all who value their individual freedom won by centuries of struggle against tyranny and privilege. When the Jew is persecuted, all minorities, and, indeed, even majorities, disliked by the controllers of the state, are in danger. (Dark, *Folly*, 90)

Persecution of the Jews, he insisted, put democracy and Christian civilization as a whole in irreparable danger.

In *The Church Impotent or Triumphant* (1941) Dark criticized the Munich agreement of 1938. He argued that the church 'encouraged the fear that made Munich possible. Christian and democratic Europe was terrorised into peace until Hitler was ready for war' (Dark, *Church*, 25). In order to fulfil its mission the church must engage with all aspects of society: 'If we are to build Jerusalem on England's green and pleasant land, the Bloomsbury intellectuals will have to be reckoned with in company with the Blimps and the Stock Exchange' (ibid., 62).

In 1941 the proprietors of the *Church Times* were no longer able to afford Dark's salary and he worked as a freelance writer from his home in Sonning, Berkshire, until his death. This took place on 11 October 1947 at Greenlands, Redlands Road, Reading.   NATALIE K. WATSON

Sources S. Dark, *Not such a bad life* (1941) • *WWW* • B. Palmer, *Gadfly for God: a history of the Church Times* (1991) • S. Dark, *The folly of anti-Semitism* (1939) • S. Dark, *The church impotent or triumphant* (1941) • b. cert. • m. cert. • d. cert.
Archives Lambeth Archives, London, papers relating to natural history of Streatham | JRL, letters to the *Manchester Guardian*
Wealth at death £3423 19s. 9d.: probate, 9 Jan 1948, CGPLA Eng. & Wales

Darley, George [*pseud.* John Lacy] (1795–1846), poet and writer, was born in Dublin, the eldest of the seven children of Arthur Darley (1766–1845), a grocer who, after about 1815, enjoyed independent means, and his wife and second cousin once removed, Mary (*d.* 1833), daughter of John Darley, collector of customs at Newry in the north of Ireland. Darley's parents left for a prolonged stay in America shortly after his birth and he consequently spent much of his childhood with his paternal grandfather, George Darley of Springfield, co. Dublin. He appears to have been privately educated (latterly by a Mr Falloon) until his admission as a pensioner at Trinity College, Dublin, on 3 July 1815.

Darley graduated in 1820 (being placed third in his year) and began reading for a fellowship, but quickly abandoned the attempt and, assisted by a small allowance, moved to London to begin a literary career in 1821. His first book, *The Errors of Ecstasie*, was published in April 1822 and attracted little notice, but by the end of the year Darley had become a contributor to the *London Magazine* and in 1823 he made his mark with a series of 'Letters to the dramatists of the day', written under the pseudonym John Lacy, in which he vigorously denounced the mediocrity of contemporary theatrical writing. His work on the *London* also established a number of lasting friendships with other writers, including Charles Lamb, Henry Francis Cary, Allan Cunningham, and John Clare, but the journal itself declined after John Taylor relinquished the editorship, and Darley's last contribution appeared in March 1825.

Darley did not immediately attach himself to another periodical, but instead wrote (under the *nom de plume* Guy Penseval) a collection of vapid prose tales entitled *The Labours of Idleness, or, Seven Nights' Entertainments* (1826), which was greeted with general indifference on its publication. Rather more successful and remunerative, however, was *A System of Popular Geometry* (which went into five editions), the first of five popular textbooks on mathematics and astronomy that he produced between 1826 and 1830. Labour on these educational projects was alleviated by the composition of *Sylvia, or, The May Queen*, published in November 1827, a verse play abounding in metrical ingenuity, fairies, and pseudo-Elizabethanism. Although *Sylvia* attracted some attention (Coleridge confessed that he 'sometimes liked to take up the poem'; Abbott, *Life and Letters*, 65), it was not calculated for popular success and, in the month of its publication, Darley sought to eke out his literary earnings by applying—unsuccessfully—for the first chair in English literature at the University of London, a surprising ambition given his introspective habits and the disabling stammer from which he had suffered since childhood.

In 1830 Darley completed his last textbook, *Familiar Astronomy*, and in the following year he began an extended European tour. Between 1831 and 1835 he travelled (with a brief interlude in London) through France, Italy, Germany, and Belgium, familiarizing himself with most of the major galleries and writing perceptive articles on art for *The Athenaeum*, to which he now became, and remained, a regular contributor of reviews and occasional papers. In 1835, after his return to England, Darley published at his own expense, and distributed to his friends, the first two cantos of *Nepenthe*, the achievement on which his reputation now chiefly rests. Although the projected third canto was never completed, the two extant parts of this post-Romantic philosophical allegory show respectively (as Darley wrote in a letter to his new friend Richard Monckton Milnes) 'the deleterious effects of ultra-natural joy' and those of 'ultra-natural melancholy'; the intended purpose of the whole was 'to show the folly of discontent with the natural tone of human life' (Abbott, *Life and Letters*, 125). The poem's opacity baffled even Darley's close friends, so that he found himself 'forced to write a series of headings for each page' (ibid., 146), and, despite expressions of enthusiasm from Mary Russell Mitford, it followed his other literary works into near-oblivion.

In 1837 and again in 1838, Darley returned to Germany, and in 1839 he paid a visit to Ireland, where he formed a close attachment to the three granddaughters of his uncle Henry Darley (Mary Jane, Laura, and Henrietta); their correspondence was to become a great comfort to him in his last years. While in Ireland, Darley worked on a closet historical drama called *Thomas à Becket*, which was published in 1840 and immediately sank without trace (overfreighted with its cargo of debts to Shakespeare); this was followed by the still more ponderous *Ethelstan, or, The*

Battle of Brunanburh in 1841. Darley's close knowledge of Jacobean drama was more profitably employed in his introduction to an edition of Beaumont and Fletcher, published by Edward Moxon in 1840.

For the remaining years of his life, Darley maintained a steady output for *The Athenaeum* (reviewing, among much else, the first two volumes of Ruskin's *Modern Painters* in 1844 and 1846), and contributed verse and short stories to *Bentley's Miscellany* and the *Illuminated Magazine*. His health, however, was fast deteriorating, and in September 1845 he visited Paris for an unspecified operation. In debt, and working incessantly to remain solvent, he stayed in London for most of the hot summer of 1846 (paying a brief visit to Surrey in July) and died of a 'decline' (Abbott, *Life and Letters*, 270) in his lodgings at 2 Lower Belgrave Street, South Eaton Square, on 23 November 1846. He was buried in Kensal Green cemetery.

In his surviving letters Darley repeatedly pleads his stammer as a reason for refusing social invitations. But although this impediment was certainly severe (Beddoes described him as 'almost inconversible'; Abbott, *Life and Letters*, 39), it did not altogether preclude close friendships with chosen companions and was perhaps as much alibi as source for a more deep-seated impulse of withdrawal. In a letter of 1833 Darley claimed that writing was his sole means of communicating 'freely and unpainfully' (ibid., 102), but writing also enabled him to construct a series of personae behind which he could remain discreetly concealed.

Darley's defensive reticence is also apparent in his work. Both the imitativeness of much of his lyrical poetry (for some of which he even adopted an archaic orthography) and the dense obscurity of more extended works like *Nepenthe* seem wilfully self-effacing (as does their deliberately restricted dissemination). The paradox of Darley's achievement is encapsulated in his decision to write his most ambitious poem about the perils of ambition. Even so, Darley's finest writing (like that of Beddoes, whom he admired) is at the same time distinctive and significantly representative of a transitional phase between Romantic and early Victorian poetics. Impelled by its intensity of local sensory response and parading its metrical and linguistic inventiveness, Darley's verse nevertheless seems disabled by an ultimate lack of confidence in its own value and purpose, unable to direct its incidental brilliance to any coherent objective and ultimately uncertain of its cultural role.　ROBERT DINGLEY

Sources C. C. Abbott, *The life and letters of George Darley: poet and critic* (1928) · C. C. Abbott, 'Further letters of George Darley', *Durham University Journal*, new ser., 2 (1940), 25–45 · E. M. Curran, 'George Darley and the London English professorship', *Modern Philology*, 71 (1973–4), 29–38 · A. Ridler, 'Introduction', *Selected poems of George Darley* (1979), 11–48 · R. Colles, 'Introduction', *Complete poetical works of George Darley* (1908), ix–xxxvii · M. R. Mitford, *Recollections of a literary life*, 2nd edn, 2 vols. (1853) · L. Brisman, *Romantic origins* (1978) · J. Heath-Stubbs, *The darkling plain: Romanticism in English poetry from Darley to Yeats* (1950)

Archives Trinity Cam., papers · U. Durham L., corresp. and papers | Bodl. Oxf., letters to Allan Cunningham · Trinity Cam., Houghton MSS

Darley, Henry (*c*.1596–1671), politician, was the eldest son of Sir Richard Darley (*d. c*.1654) of Buttercrambe, Yorkshire, and his wife, Elizabeth (*b*. 1576, *d*. after 1657), daughter of Edward Gates of Seamer. Although resident in Yorkshire since the twelfth century, the Darleys exercised little influence in county affairs before the Stuart period. Darley matriculated at Trinity College, Cambridge, in 1611, and was admitted to Gray's Inn on 26 October 1614. In the autumn of 1619 he married Margery (*d. c*.1630), daughter of Ralph Hungate of Sand Hutton, and towards the end of 1631, Elizabeth (*d*. before August 1642), daughter of William Wattes of the Inner Temple. Darley was the first of his line to enter parliament, securing election for Aldborough, Yorkshire, in 1628.

The Darleys were one of Yorkshire's leading godly families and gave shelter to the future New England divine Thomas Shepard and other ministers silenced by the Laudian church authorities. They also possessed a wide network of godly intimates that included gentlemen from Essex (Nathaniel Bacon, Richard Harlakenden), Warwickshire (Godfrey Bosevile), and Yorkshire (John Alured, Sir William Boynton, Sir William Strickland). Darley's godly zeal lay behind his involvement in all three major colonizing ventures of the Caroline era. He was an original investor in the Massachusetts Bay Company; served twice as deputy governor of the Providence Island Company; and was on the executive committee of the Saybrook project. Through these enterprises he became a close friend of several leading opponents of the personal rule, notably Viscount Saye and Sele, Lord Brooke, and John Pym.

Darley was allegedly pro-covenanter by the late 1630s (CUL, MM.1.45, 107), and there is strong evidence that he acted in concert with Saye and Brooke in 1640 to encourage a Scottish invasion and thus compel the king to summon parliament. In January 1641 he was elected for Northallerton, Yorkshire, and by late 1642 had joined those at Westminster urging the vigorous prosecution of the war. A leading supporter of Pym's policy of a military alliance with the Scots, he was part of the parliamentary delegation to Edinburgh that negotiated the solemn league and covenant in September 1643. Like his fellow commissioner the younger Vane he was probably a religious Independent by this stage and only accepted the adoption of the covenant as the necessary price of Scottish support.

Darley spent much of the next two years in northern England liaising with the covenanter forces. With the disintegration of the war party–covenanter alliance late in 1644, however, his relations with the Scots cooled, and from the summer of 1645 he played a leading role in apprising Westminster of the Scots' 'oppressions' in the north. In the Commons he was firmly aligned with the Independent interest, and he was among those MPs who fled to the army in July 1647. A leading member of the Independent-dominated committee for advance of money, he was also active on the committees for compounding and for indemnity. The evidence suggests that, like Saye, he supported a negotiated settlement with the king in 1648. He was absent from the house from late September 1648 until May 1649, and, in contrast to his brother Richard, had no hand in the king's trial. Despite his apparent misgivings concerning the purge and regicide, he was named to numerous committees in the Rump, and was an active member of the third council of state, to which he was elected in February 1651. He also acquired former church lands under the Commonwealth, and allegedly amassed £15,000 through manipulation of the 'state-clockwork' (*Mercurius Pragmaticus*, 5–12 Sept 1648, sig. Gg2v; *The Countrey Committees Laid Open*, 5). On the death of his father he inherited £4000 and an estate worth between £700 and £1000 per annum.

Darley's hostility to army rule pushed him further towards the republican camp during the mid-1650s. In 1656 he and his brother were returned for the East Riding to the second protectorate parliament, but were excluded as opponents of the major-generals. Admitted to the Commons early in 1658, he supported the republicans' attack upon the protectoral settlement, although his main objective was to secure religious toleration. He was an active member of the restored Rump during 1659 and early 1660, but apparently withdrew from parliament following the readmission of the secluded members in February 1660. His estate was temporarily confiscated after he was implicated (probably falsely) in the 1663 northern rising, and in 1665 he was briefly imprisoned on suspicion of 'seditious practices' (*Various Collections*, 2.120). He died intestate and was buried at Buttercrambe on 6 August 1671.   DAVID SCOTT

Sources 'Darley, Henry', HoP, *Commons* [draft] · D. Scott, 'Yorkshire's godly incendiary: the career of Henry Darley during the reign of Charles I', *Life and thought in the northern church*, ed. D. Wood (1999), 435–64 · N. Yorks. CRO, Darley of Aldby papers · D. Scott, '"Hannibal at our gates": loyalists and fifth-columnists during the bishops' wars—the case of Yorkshire', *Historical Research*, 70 (1997), 269–93 · JHC, 2–7 (1640–59) · *Diary of Thomas Burton*, ed. J. T. Rutt, 4 vols. (1828), vol. 2 · *CSP dom.*, 1640–64 · *The queens proceedings in Yorkshire*, 1643, BL, E93(2) · *The countrey committees laid open*, 1649, BL, E558(11) · Thomason tract [E 453(11)] · Thomason tract [E 462(34)] · M. Y. Ashcroft, ed., *Scarborough records, 1600–1640: a calendar* (1991) · M. Y. Ashcroft, ed., *Scarborough records, 1641–1660: a calendar* (1991) · *God's plot: the paradoxes of puritan piety, being the autobiography and journal of Thomas Shepard*, ed. M. McGiffert (1972) · J. T. Peacey, 'Seasonable treatises: a godly project of the 1630s', *EngHR*, 113 (1998), 667–79 · A. P. Newton, *The colonising activities of the English puritans* (1914) · Venn, *Alum. Cant.* · PRO, C 10/466/6, C 54/3290/6 · C. B. Norcliffe, ed., 'Paver's marriage licences [pt 14]', *Yorkshire Archaeological Journal*, 14 (1896–8), 458–513, esp. 497 · *Dugdale's visitation of Yorkshire, with additions*, ed. J. W. Clay, 3 vols. (1899–1917) · Borth. Inst., PR/BUT 2, fol. 21 · *Report on manuscripts in various collections*, 8 vols., HMC, 55 (1901–14), vol. 2

Archives N. Yorks. CRO, Darley of Aldby MSS

Wealth at death £700–£1000 p.a.: private information; N. Yorks. CRO, Darley of Aldby MSS

Darley, John Richard (1799–1884), schoolmaster and bishop of Kilmore, Elphin, and Ardagh, a member of a mercantile family long connected with the city of Dublin, was the second son of Richard Darley of Fairfield, co. Monaghan, and his wife, Elizabeth, daughter of B. Brunker of Rockcorry, in the same county. He was born at Fairfield in November 1799. From the Royal School,

Dungannon, he entered Trinity College, Dublin, in 1816, and soon distinguished himself in classics, mathematics, and Hebrew; in 1819 he was elected to a foundation scholarship, and he graduated BA 1820, MA 1827, and BD and DD 1875.

In early life Darley was a schoolmaster and was successively headmaster of the grammar school at Dundalk, from 1826, in which year he was ordained, and headmaster of the Royal School of Dungannon, from 1831. He published two classical works—on Greek drama (1840) and Horace (1848).

In 1850 Darley became rector of Drumgoon in the diocese of Kilmore. He married, on 18 November 1851, Anna (d. 1900), daughter of John, third Baron Plunket, and sister of William Conyngham Plunket, the fourth baron, archbishop of Dublin. In 1866 he became archdeacon of Ardagh, and rector of Templemichael. An evangelical, Darley sought to reunite the Primitive Methodists in Ireland with the Church of Ireland. On the death of Thomas Carson LLD, he was elected by the joint synods, 23 September 1874, to the bishopric of Kilmore, Elphin, and Ardagh, and was consecrated in Armagh Cathedral on 25 October 1874, being the second bishop appointed under the new constitution of the Church of Ireland. At the time of his election comments were freely made that he was too old for the position, but he proved equal to the duties of the episcopate. He died at Kilmore House, co. Cavan, on 20 January 1884.   B. H. BLACKER, *rev.* M. C. CURTHOYS

Sources Irish Ecclesiastical Gazette (26 Jan 1884) · Annual Register (1884), 113 · H. Cotton, *Fasti ecclesiae Hibernicae*, 6 (1878), 102 · Boase, *Mod. Eng. biog.* · *Men of the time* (1875)

Wealth at death £9343 4s. 5d.: probate, 20 Feb 1884, CGPLA Eng. & Wales

Darling, Sir Charles Henry (1809–1870), army officer and colonial governor, was born at Annapolis Royal, Nova Scotia, on 19 February 1809, the eldest son of Major-General Henry Charles Darling, formerly lieutenant-governor of Tobago, and his wife, Isabella, the eldest daughter of Charles Cameron, former governor of the Bahamas. He was educated at the Royal Military College, Sandhurst, and on 7 December 1825 obtained an ensigncy without purchase in the 57th foot. In 1827 he was appointed assistant private secretary to an uncle, Lieutenant-General Ralph *Darling, governor of New South Wales, and in 1830 became his military secretary. After Ralph returned home in 1831, Charles joined the senior department at Sandhurst. Between 1833 and 1836 he served in the West Indies as military secretary to Sir Lionel Smith, with whom he moved to Jamaica in 1836. He left the staff in 1839 when he obtained an unattached company. In 1835 he had married the eldest daughter of Alexander Dalzell of Barbados; she died in 1837, and two years later he married the eldest daughter of Joshua Bushell Nurse, a member of the legislative council of Barbados.

In 1841 Darling retired from the army and settled in Jamaica. Two years later the governor, Lord Elgin, appointed him agent-general for immigration and adjutant-general of the militia. A member of the legislative council

and various executive boards, he served as governor's secretary during the interim administration of Major-General Sackville, and retained that post under Sir Charles Grey from 1846 to 1847. In 1847 he became lieutenant-governor of the Cape Colony during Sir George Cathcart's absence. Darling's second wife, who had borne one daughter, died in 1848, and in 1851 he was married again, this time to Elizabeth Isabella Caroline, the only daughter of Christopher Salter of Buckinghamshire. After Cathcart's departure he administered the colony from May to December 1854, presiding over the introduction of parliamentary government. Offered the governorship of Antigua and the Leeward Islands, he chose instead to administer Newfoundland. He was appointed governor after responsible government was introduced, and remained there until February 1857. He then became governor of Jamaica, which included Honduras and the Bay Islands.

Up to that time Darling's career had been highly successful, and in 1862 he was appointed KCB in recognition of 'his long and effective public services'. On 11 September 1863, however, a new and controversial phase of his career began when he was appointed governor of Victoria, one of the most flourishing Australian colonies. Responsible government had been established in 1856, midway through the gold-rush era, which brought a vast influx of newcomers and unprecedented wealth. The aftermath of the gold rushes was marked by tension between the conservative landed interest and the more progressive, largely urban-based population, much of which had only recently arrived. Conflict broke out between the conservative legislative council and the legislative assembly, which represented the more progressive forces. Darling sided with the assembly, thus creating problems for himself and his superiors in London. Matters came to a head when the reformist premier, James McCulloch, sought to impose a protective tariff, designed to stimulate industry and provide employment for workers. The legislation, which he first introduced in July 1865, was finally passed in April 1866, but only after he had used tactics of dubious legality. Darling was accused by a group of former cabinet ministers of having sanctioned financial and constitutional irregularities. A petition complaining of his actions and accompanied by his own adverse comments on his critics and their criticisms was sent to Britain in December 1865. He had earlier been censured for allowing his ministers undue latitude in their dealings with other colonies and for his involvement in the controversy surrounding the decision to continue sending convicts to Western Australia. After receiving the petition, Edward Cardwell, the colonial secretary, decided that Darling was unfit for office. News of his recall prompted widespread public protests in Victoria, and the assembly, unable to make a direct gift to Darling, voted £20,000 for his wife. This action provoked a further crisis and was eventually disallowed. Angered by this decision and by the government's refusal to acknowledge that he had done no more than follow his ministers' advice, Darling resigned from the colonial service in April 1867. However, he withdrew his resignation in May 1868 and was given a retrospective pension after the McCulloch government, backed by strong popular support, protested. But the set-backs Darling had experienced proved too much, and after retiring to Cheltenham he died, on 25 January 1870, and was buried there. The McCulloch government voted funds for the education of his children and a pension for his widow. The latter, with whom Darling had four sons, lived for another thirty years, and died on 10 December 1900.

Darling led an interesting life and occupied an unusually large number of colonial posts. His behaviour after arriving in Victoria forms a curious contrast to that elsewhere. His actions were out of character, but stemmed from a genuine belief that he had the best interests of the colony at heart. Unfortunately, by becoming embroiled in politics, he stepped outside the bounds within which governors were expected to remain. In doing this he blighted an otherwise unblemished career.

H. M. Chichester, *rev.* Brian H. Fletcher

Sources PRO, CO 309/66–89 · *Correspondence of Lieut.-General the Hon. Sir George Cathcart* (1856) · J. Hatton and M. Harvey, *Newfoundland: its history, present condition and prospects* (1883) · F. Crowley, 'Aspects of the constitutional conflicts between the two houses of the Victorian legislature, 1864–1868', MA diss., University of Melbourne, 1947 · D. P. Clarke, 'The colonial office and the constitutional crises in Victoria, 1865–68', *Historical Studies: Australia and New Zealand*, 5 (1951–2), 160–71 · F. Crowley, 'Darling, Sir Charles Henry', *AusDB*, vol. 4
Archives NRA, priv. coll., letters to Sir George Cathcart · PRO, Colonial Office MSS · Wesley College, Bristol, corresp. with Dumaresq family
Wealth at death under £1500: probate, 12 Feb 1870, *CGPLA Eng. & Wales*

Charles John Darling, first Baron Darling (1849–1936), by Charles Wellington Furse, 1890

Darling, Charles John, first Baron Darling (1849–1936), judge, was born at Abbey House in Colchester on 6 December 1849, the elder son of Charles Darling, a farmer and estate manager, later of Langham Hall, Essex, and his wife, Sarah Frances, daughter of John Tizard, of Dorchester. Educated at home, he read voraciously and acquired an impressive command of French language and literature. He never went to university, but, obtaining an inheritance from an uncle, he commenced articles with a firm of solicitors in Birmingham. Transferring to the bar, he was admitted to the Inner Temple in 1872, where he read in the chambers of John Welch. He was called in 1874 and became a bencher in 1892. He 'devilled' for John Huddleston in Crown Office Row and joined the Oxford circuit. He combined legal practice with journalism, contributing notably to the *St James's Gazette*, the *Pall Mall Gazette*, and the *Saturday Review*. His career at the bar was not particularly noteworthy but he took silk in 1885. The same year, he married Mary Caroline (*d.* 1913), elder daughter of Major-General William Wilberforce Harris *Greathed, RE, a veteran of the Indian mutiny, and granddaughter of Caroline Clive. They had one son, who predeceased his father, and two daughters.

In December 1885 Darling contested South Hackney as a Conservative, and after a further unsuccessful contest there in July 1886 against Sir Charles Russell he was returned at a by-election in February 1888 for Deptford,

having defeated Wilfrid Scawen Blunt, and retained the seat until his elevation to the bench in 1897. His years in the Commons were undistinguished. A competent party man rather than a politician with any original contributions to make, he spoke on legal matters and on home rule for Ireland, and occasionally on social and economic issues such as the operation of the Fair Wages Resolution and matters pertaining to the dockyard victualling depot in his constituency.

In the autumn of 1896 Darling was appointed commissioner of assize on his own circuit and did his work competently and for no payment, thus thwarting the Liberal Party's demand that he vacate his seat on assuming an office of profit under the crown. In October 1897 rumours spread that the lord chancellor, Lord Halsbury, was intending to appoint Darling to the High Court bench. On 26 October *The Times* devoted a leading article to the rumours and stated, without mentioning a name, that the subject of the rumour was a man of 'acute intellect and considerable literary power', but that he had given 'no sign of legal eminence … if he is raised to the Bench, it will be on political grounds'. Two days later Darling's appointment to the Queen's Bench Division was announced. *The Times* returned to the charge; H. H. Asquith gave expression to his doubts, and much indignation was expressed in the Temple. The *Solicitors' Journal* charged that the 'way to the High Court bench is once more shown to be through contested elections and general service as a political hack', to the exclusion of learning, practical experience, and appropriate moral qualities. Yet despite the almost universal condemnation of Darling's appointment, the *Law Journal* wrote: 'He will prove a far better judge than some of his critics believe.' In respect to his long judicial tenure which lasted until 1923, it may be said in his favour that his summing-up in criminal cases and his judgments in the court of criminal appeal were on the whole excellent, his judgments being particularly characterized by close reasoning and admirable English. Indeed, he often had to deliver judgments in cases where each side's evidence seemed hopelessly irreconcilable. In other cases, including Official Secrets Act prosecutions, the evidence was frequently bizarre. In a murder trial he was very good. Unfortunately, in charges of less gravity he often allowed himself to behave with a levity quite unsuited to the trial of a criminal case, thinking erroneously that he could thereby induce the jury to bring in the right verdict by an eventual careful and accurate summing-up. In fact he had frequently lost the respect of the jury to such an extent that they ignored or paid little attention to the judge. The Pemberton Billing case (1918), with its sensational and absurd disclosure of a German 'black book' naming 47,000 English moral degenerates, including R. B. Haldane, the Asquiths, and even Darling himself, was a shocking example and went far to lower the status of the bench. Darling often allowed himself as a judge to be grossly insulted by witnesses and laughed with them and at them. He presided over the notorious Steinie Morrison (1911) and Armstrong (1922) cases, *Douglas* v. *Ransome* and *Wootton* v. *Sievier* (1913), the Romney picture case (1917), and the Mond libel case (1919) among others, and was much concerned with the court career of Horatio Bottomley. In the court of criminal appeal Darling presided over the Crippen (1910) and Casement (1916) appeals. Few of his judgments, however, constituted precedents. One exception was *Chester* v. *Bateson* (1920) on the legality of subordinate legislation (albeit in wartime) with its fine quotation, in French, from Montesquieu's *De l'esprit des lois*. The case became familiar to many generations of constitutional law students and practitioners.

As an overall assessment of Darling's judicial career, the view of a later observer that it were better he had not been appointed to the bench is unduly harsh. No doubt he was, as some have suggested, a 'professional oddity', whimsical and given to 'inveterate facetiousness'. Yet his literary sense and rapidity of literary allusion were due to a vast reading and a deep appreciation of English and French literature. Despite this, he was to some extent a 'populist' judge who enjoyed entertaining his audience and receiving their plaudits in court. In that respect, the dignity which he lent to his office was perhaps less than appropriate on occasions. But many of his cases, meat and drink to the popular press of the day, deserved no better.

When R. D. Isaacs, Lord Reading, went to the United States of America as ambassador during the First World War, Darling as senior puisne of the King's Bench Division

served as his deputy and his work was recognized by the distinction, unusual in the case of a serving judge, of being sworn of the privy council (1917). During the machinations by Lloyd George in 1922 to prevent the attorney-general, Sir Gordon Hewart, from vacating for the moment his Commons seat in order to succeed Reading as lord chief justice, Darling was mooted as a possible stop-gap appointment. Indeed, he had written to Hewart stating that he would be willing gladly to take the office for a little time—'even for ten minutes'—and to give it up when asked to do so. But to no avail. On being passed over in favour of the 77-year-old A. T. Lawrence, Lord Trevethin, he is said characteristically to have remarked that he supposed he was not old enough. Darling retired from the bench in November 1923, an event which was marked by a public farewell in court. In January 1924 he was raised to the peerage as Baron Darling of Langham. He spoke in the House of Lords on matters of legal interest, proposing unsuccessfully a modification to the MacNaughton rules on insanity by the inclusion of a new category of 'irresistible impulse'. He took part in privy council cases as a member of the judicial committee, and as late as 1931 he returned to the King's Bench Division in order to assist in reducing arrears. In 1926 he made a six weeks' tour of Canada as guest of the Canadian Bar Association. His last three years were lived quietly. He died at the age of eighty-six at the Cottage Hospital, Lymington, Hampshire, on 29 May 1936 and was buried on 31 May at Beaulieu. He was succeeded as second baron by his grandson, Robert Charles Henry Darling.

Darling was a member of the royal commission on the working of the King's Bench (1912), and chairman of the committees of courts martial (1919), on the Moneylenders Bill (1925), and on national marks (1928). Given the controversy in subsequent years surrounding the First World War capital courts martial, it is unfortunate that the courts martial commission recommended that the evidence presented to it should not be published (it never was), and that Darling's ruling as chairman meant that it was prevented from fully investigating alleged miscarriages of justice.

Physically, Darling was small, gaunt, and somewhat short-sighted. He none the less affected to present a patrician hauteur in court. As a conversationalist, particularly in the benchers' room of the Inner Temple, he was pleasant, amusing, and often really witty, and was a delightful companion on a walk. He wrote *Scintillae juris* (1877), rich in gnomic wisdom and sharp satire, and *On the Oxford Circuit and other Verses* (1924), among other works of literary, although at times somewhat slight and precious, character. NEVILLE LASKI, *rev.* G. R. RUBIN

Sources The Times (30 May 1936) • Law Journal (6 June 1936) • D. Walker-Smith, *The life of Lord Darling* (1938) • E. Graham, *Lord Darling and his famous trials* (1929) • D. Barker, *Lord Darling's famous cases* (1936) • R. F. V. Heuston, *Lives of the lord chancellors, 1885–1940* (1964) • R. Jackson, *The chief: the biography of Gordon Hewart, lord chief justice of England, 1922–40* (1959) • Earl of Birkenhead, 'Lord Darling', *Contemporary personalities* [1924] • C. Andrew, *Secret service: the making of the British intelligence community* (1985) • A. Babington, *For the sake of* *example: capital courts-martial, 1914–1920* (1983) • *CGPLA Eng. & Wales* (1936)

Archives NRA, papers

Likenesses C. W. Furse, oils, 1890, NPG [*see illus.*] • A. Savage, portrait, 1924, priv. coll. • E. I. Halliday, oils, 1928, Inner Temple, London • R. G. Eves, oils, Arts Club, Dover Street, London • G. C. Jennis, sketch, V&A • B. Partridge, cartoon, V&A; repro. in *Punch's Almanack* (1922) • A. P. F. Ritchie, cigarette card, NPG • Spy [L. Ward], cromolithograph caricature, NPG; repro. in *VF* (15 July 1897) • Spy [L. Ward], drawing, NPG • Spy [L. Ward], mechanical reproduction, NPG; repro. in *VF* (8 May 1907); related watercolour study, NPG • photograph, repro. in *The Times* • photograph, repro. in *Law Journal* • photograph, repro. in Walker-Smith, *Life of Lord Darling*

Wealth at death £22,288 7s. 8d.: probate, 22 June 1936, *CGPLA Eng. & Wales*

Darling, Sir Frank Moss Fraser (1903–1979), ecologist, was born Frank Moss Darling, on 23 June 1903 at 3 Soresby Street, Chesterfield, Devon, the son of Harriet Ellse Cowley Darling. No father's name was entered on his birth certificate. However, on his first and third marriage certificates Fraser Darling (as he was by then known) claimed that his father was Frank Moss, variously described as a decorator and as a captain in the South African army. Darling attended the Midland Agricultural College, and in 1924 began work with Buckinghamshire county council. On 5 September 1925 he married Edith Marian, *née* Fraser. The couple had one son, but the marriage was ultimately dissolved. Despite the dissolution, he continued to use the name Fraser Darling.

In 1928 Fraser Darling became a research student in the Institute of Animal Genetics in the University of Edinburgh, and in 1930 he was appointed chief officer of the Imperial Bureau of Animal Genetics. However, Fraser Darling hankered after a post in the field, and in 1933 was successful in obtaining a Leverhulme research fellowship to work on red deer.

For the next twenty years, precariously supported by further grants from the Carnegie and Rockefeller foundations, and by his writing, Fraser Darling lived and worked in the wildest parts of Scotland. Under the name Frank Fraser Darling he produced several popular books, including *A Herd of Red Deer* (1937) and *A Naturalist on Rona* (1939). His more rigorous *Bird Flocks and the Breeding Cycle* (1938) was less well received; Fraser Darling was considered too 'popular' to obtain the approval of the contemporary scientific establishment.

From 1944 to 1950 Fraser Darling served as director of the west highland survey. He hoped that the government would implement his proposals, which included preserving the wild countryside for posterity, and which were published under the title *West Highland Survey* in 1955; he was deeply disappointed when none of his recommendations was implemented.

On 24 March 1948 Fraser Darling married ornithologist Averil, *née* Morley (d. 1957). They had two sons and a daughter. Following her death, Darling married on 2 July 1960 Christina Macinnes Brotchie, children's nurse, daughter of Alexander Brotchie, joiner.

In 1953, at the age of fifty, Fraser Darling returned to academic life as senior lecturer in ecology at Edinburgh University, a post he held until 1958, when there was an unhappy parting. He advised the Nature Conservancy on red deer research, and saw work started on the island of Rhum. However, Fraser Darling felt rather out of the academic stream in Britain, and in 1959 he accepted an invitation from Dr Fairfield Osborn to become vice-president of the World Conservation Foundation in Washington, DC. He held this post until 1972, travelling widely and publishing several works, including *Alaska: an Ecological Reconnaissance* (with A. S. Leopold, 1953), *Wild Life in an African Territory* (1960), and *The Nature of a National Park* (1968).

After Fraser Darling moved to America, his reputation in Britain, particularly for his contribution to the ecology of wildlife conservation, began to rise. Indeed, there was widespread approval of his appointment by the BBC in 1969 as Reith lecturer. His lectures, and the subsequent publication, *Wilderness and Plenty* (1970), made a considerable impact on a community that had just discovered the meaning of the word 'conservation'.

From then on Fraser Darling enjoyed much greater recognition in his own country. He was knighted in 1970, and was invited to be one of the first members (1970–73) of the royal commission on environmental pollution. He was much in demand as a speaker, particularly by student bodies. It is somewhat ironic that as his reputation grew, so his health declined, and that in later years sickness often prevented him from presenting his views to an audience which was finally receptive to them.

Fraser Darling was a fellow of the Royal Society of Edinburgh and had honorary degrees from Glasgow University, Heriot-Watt University, the New University of Ulster, and Williams College, Massachusetts. He died on 22 October 1979, in Leanchoil Hospital, Forres, Morayshire.

KENNETH MELLANBY, rev. V. M. QUIRKE

Sources J. M. Boyd, *Fraser Darling's islands* (1986) • V. Martin and M. Inglis, eds., *Wilderness: the way ahead* (1984) • *The Times* (19 Nov 1979) • d. cert.

Archives NL Scot., journals, MSS, and papers | Rice University, Houston, Texas, Woodson Research Center, corresp. with Sir Julian Huxley • U. Reading L., letters to George Bell & Sons

Darling, George (1779/80–1862), physician, was born at Middletown, Stow, near Galashiels, on 21 September 1779 or 1780, the son of Thomas Darling and Betty Anderson. He was educated at the University of Edinburgh, and, having made two or three voyages as a surgeon in the East India Company's service, settled in London in general practice as a partner of Dr Neil Arnott. He left this and in 1815 was awarded his MD degree by Marischal College, Aberdeen. In London he settled in Russell Square and began to practise as a physician, having become in 1819 a licentiate of the Royal College of Physicians.

Darling was associated with a number of artists including David Wilkie, Benjamin Haydon, Thomas Lawrence, and Francis Chantrey, as both physician and friend. In 1814 he published *An Essay on Medical Economy*, which addressed the whole question of medical reform as regards the education, practice, and status of medical practitioners, and which anticipated many of the changes that later took place in the profession, such as the establishment of a university in London and the conjoint scheme of medical examination. Darling was of a retiring disposition, and published this essay anonymously. He later became interested in the making of bread using sodium bicarbonate rather than yeast, and printed a pamphlet on the subject in which he argued that brown bread was more nourishing than white. This was also published anonymously, and it reached many editions.

Darling died at his home, in 6 Russell Square, London, on 30 April 1862. He left a son, the Revd Thomas Darling, rector of St Michael's Royal, London.

JAMES DIXON, rev. PATRICK WALLIS

Sources Munk, *Roll* · private information (1888) · *Fasti academiae Mariscallanae Aberdonensis: selections from the records of the Marischal College and University, MDXCIII–MDCCCLX*, 2, ed. P. J. Anderson, New Spalding Club, 18 (1898) · CGPLA Eng. & Wales (1862) · Boase, *Mod. Eng. biog.* · parish register (birth), Stow, Midlothian, 15 Oct 1779–1780 · b. cert. · d. cert.
Archives U. Cam., Centre of South Asian Studies, papers
Likenesses T. Bridgford, lithograph, 1839, Wellcome L. · G. Zobel, photogravure, 1855 (after W. Hilton, 1832), Wellcome L.
Wealth at death under £35,000: probate, 9 July 1862, CGPLA Eng. & Wales

Darling, Grace Horsley (1815–1842), heroine, born at Bamburgh, Northumberland, on 24 November 1815, was the daughter, and the seventh of nine children, of William Darling and his wife, Thomasin, *née* Horsley. William Darling in 1815 succeeded his father as keeper of the lighthouse on Brownsman island, one of the lonely Outer Farne Islands off the Northumbrian coast; in 1825 he took over the new Longstone lighthouse there. He was a man of strong religious principles, who brought up his children puritanically; he objected to light literature and regarded cards as the devil's books, but he had a taste for music and natural history. Grace Darling helped her father, effectively acting as assistant keeper and often sharing the watch. She sometimes slept in the lighthouse in the room below the lantern. In the early morning of 7 September 1838 the steamer *Forfarshire*, sailing from Hull to Dundee, was wrecked on one of the rocks, and forty-three of the sixty-three persons aboard were drowned. At about 5 a.m., as dawn broke at the lighthouse, Grace Darling spotted the wreck and several survivors huddling on a rock; she called her father. Bad weather prevented action until 7 a.m. The Victorian story—that Darling acted only on Grace's passionate entreaties—is a legend; it was at once clear to him that, with the lifeboat unable to leave the shore, he had the chance of sole salvage rights if he could reach the ship. Darling launched a coble more than 20 feet long and he and his daughter rowed the heavy vessel to the wreck, knowing that it would be impossible to return without the help of some of the endangered survivors. Four men and a woman were successfully taken off by Grace and her father and brought to the lighthouse. Darling then returned with two of the rescued men and brought off four men who had been left: nine people were rescued.

The reports of this gallant exploit produced an outburst of enthusiasm. The Humane Society voted gold medals to Darling and his daughter. The Treasury gave £50 to Grace. A sum of £750, produced by subscription, was invested for the benefit of Grace, and £270 for the benefit of her father. Applications for locks of hair came in until Grace was in danger of baldness. Her dress was cut to pieces and sold. The proprietor of Batty's circus tried to engage her, and advertised her appearance on the stage. Darling wrote to the papers complaining that he and his daughter had had to sit for their portrait seven times in twelve days. Summer visitors came to the Farne Islands to see her and the site of the rescue, 'Grace's deed', as it came to be called. William Wordsworth celebrated the 'deed' in some embarrassing verses; A. C. Swinburne's are little better.

In some respects Grace welcomed her fame. It gave her a wider dimension to her life and she gained from good advice from her senior trustee, the duke of Northumberland. She remained at the lighthouse: a national heroine but also a curiosity. Her rare visits to the mainland posed many problems, and there are some indications that she began to find her reputation oppressive. She was always rather delicate and was beneath average height. She suddenly developed a bad cough, and died on 20 October 1842. She was buried in St Aidan's churchyard, Bamburgh, with an elaborate cenotaph. When St Cuthbert's Chapel on Great Farne Island was restored in 1848, a plain stone monument to Grace Darling was erected in it. Her mother died in 1848; her father, who had been allowed to retire on full pay in 1860, died on 28 May 1865.

Grace Darling, 'the girl of the windswept hair', caught the nation's imagination. Her famous 'deed' occurred just as national press reporting had begun to look for copy of this sort. Unsatisfactory lives written by Eva Hope (1880) and by Thomas Arthur (1885) for the Religious Book Society reinforced the errors and romance of the story. Her sister, Thomasin, arranged the publication of the more satisfactory *Grace Darling, her True Story: from Unpublished Papers in Possession of her Family* (1880) and of *The Journal of William Darling, Grace Darling's Father* (1887). Constance Smedley's biography (1932) was the first scholarly account, followed by that of Richard Armstrong (1965). One of the series of paintings by William Bell Scott at Wallington House, Northumberland, attractively depicts the 'deed'.

H. C. G. MATTHEW

Sources C. Smedley, *Grace Darling and her times* (1932) · R. Armstrong, *Grace Darling: maid and myth* (1965)
Archives Northumbd RO, letters, notes, and cuttings
Likenesses L. Corbaux, lithographs, 1838 (after drawing by E. Hasting), NPG · D. Dunbar, marble bust, 1838, NPG · M. Gauci, lithograph, pubd 1838 (after G. Harrison), BM · H. McCulloch, portrait, 1838, Shipley Art Gallery, Gateshead · H. McCulloch?, oils, 1838, Grace Darling Museum, Bamburgh, Northumberland · H. P. Parker, portrait, 1838, Grace Darling Museum, Bamburgh, Northumberland · H. P. Parker, two pencil and watercolour drawings, 1838, NPG · J. Reay, portrait, 1838, Grace Darling Museum, Bamburgh, Northumberland · R. Watson, watercolour sketch, 1838, Grace Darling Museum, Bamburgh, Northumberland · T. M. Joy, oils, 1839, Dundee City Art Gallery · R. Smith, recumbent effigy, 1846, Bamburgh cemetery, Northumberland · J. W. Carmichael, two watercolours, Grace Darling Museum, Bamburgh, Northumberland · C. Cook, stipple (after G. Cook), BM, NPG; repro. in *New Monthly Belle Assemblée* (1843) · D. Lucas, mezzotint (after oil painting by H. P. Parker and J. W. Carmichael), Grace Darling Museum, Bamburgh, Northumberland · H. P. Parker, oil sketches, Grace Darling Museum, Bamburgh, Northumberland · H. P. Parker and

J. W. Carmichael, oils, Grace Darling Museum, Bamburgh, Northumberland · W. Taylor, lithograph (after J. Reay), Grace Darling Museum, Bamburgh, Northumberland

Darling, James (1797–1862), bookseller and bibliographer, was born in Edinburgh. He was apprenticed to the Edinburgh publisher Adam Black in 1809 and became active in the Scottish Presbyterian church. On moving to London in 1818, Darling entered the theological bookselling business of Ogle, Duncan, and Cochran. On 28 December 1820, at St Pancras Old Church in London, he married Sarah Ann (*bap.* 1793), the daughter of John Ward and his wife, Sarah Edwards. They had a daughter and a son, his daughter later assisting in his editorial work, and his son, James Dolling Darling, eventually inheriting the business.

Darling took advantage of the opportunity to read and catalogue the books that surrounded him, and in 1825 opened his own shop at Little Queen Street, Lincoln's Inn Fields. About 1830 he joined the Church of England. He established the Clerical Library (later called the Metropolitan Library) in 1840 for students of theology, who could subscribe 1 guinea to borrow from his extensive collection of theological works as well as use the reading room for conversation and to consult contemporary newspapers and reviews. As part of this service he compiled in 1843 the *Bibliotheca clericalis: a Catalogue of the Books in the Clerical Library and Reading Rooms*, which included abstracts of all principal works in the library. When the library failed financially, the books being sold by auction, he returned to business as a bookseller and began to compile and solicit subscribers to his *Cyclopaedia bibliographica: a Library Manual of Theological and General Literature*. His first volume, *Authors* (1854), provided names, biographical notes, principal titles, and sometimes review notices of all major theological authors; volume 2, *Subjects* (1859), gave an account of works about the scriptures, arranging commentaries and even published sermons by book, chapter, and verse. A projected third volume, 'General subjects in theology', remained unpublished despite Darling's pleas for more subscribers. James Darling died at his home, 7 Fortess Terrace West, Kentish Town, London, on 2 March 1862.

LESLIE HOWSAM

Sources *The Bookseller* (29 March 1862) · *GM*, 3rd ser., 12 (1862), 512 · J. Darling, preface, *Cyclopaedia bibliographica: a library manual of theological and general literature*, 1 (1854) · J. Darling, preface, *Cyclopaedia bibliographica: a library manual of theological and general literature*, 2 (1859) · IGI · DNB · CGPLA Eng. & Wales (1862) · d. cert.

Wealth at death under £1500: probate, 1 April 1862, CGPLA Eng. & Wales

Darling, Sir Kenneth Thomas (1909–1998), army officer, was born in India on 17 September 1909, the eldest of the three sons of George Kenneth Darling (1879–1964), Indian Civil Service, of Dial House, Aldeburgh, and his first wife, Mabel Eleanor, *née* Burgess (*d.* 1952). Having become interested in military life while at Eton College, he entered the Royal Military College, Sandhurst, with friends. From school he carried forward the nickname 'Katie'—a play on his initials—into the Royal Fusiliers, which he joined in 1929. From the outset he entered fully into the military life. He excelled at games and in the hunting field. His only

shortcoming, of which he was quite unaware, was a brusque manner, fortunately relieved by a strong sense of humour. On home service when the Second World War began, he was rapidly promoted to command the 11th battalion of his regiment. On 1 March 1941 he married Pamela Beatrice Rose Denison-Pender (1913–1990), of Hook, Hampshire. They had no children.

Anxious to see service in battle, Darling volunteered in 1943 to join the growing corps of airborne forces. He was selected to command the 1st battalion of the Parachute regiment, recently returned from campaigning in north Africa, Sicily, and Italy, but suffering from underemployment. Its veterans were inclined to rate themselves superior in arms to a newcomer who had never seen action of any sort. Darling pointed out their faults unsparingly. He was right to do so but failed to motivate and draw upon their strengths. He ruffled so many feathers that, with the invasion of Europe apparently imminent, it was decided to replace him.

This was a serious setback to a devoted regular officer. Offered a command elsewhere, he asked to be kept in airborne forces, accepting reversion to a lower rank, an attitude which persuaded the commander of 6th airborne division to post him as second-in-command of the 12th battalion, the Parachute regiment. Darling soon earned the respect of that unit for his skills in training. He accompanied them in the airborne assault into Normandy in June 1944, in which the commanding officer was killed and Darling was wounded. In December, when fit again, he was appointed commanding officer of the 12th battalion.

He found that after the high losses in Normandy some among the remnant of the battalion had become dispirited, and he roundly berated them. This time Darling was speaking to men who were not strangers, as the 1st battalion had been to him in the previous year, but comrades bound by the trials of the battlefield. He had their respect and confidence. Within days, the 12th recovered their high morale to plunge with vigour into the Ardennes 'battle of the bulge' and subsequently to cross the Rhine by airborne assault towards a meeting on the Baltic with the advancing Russian Red Army. For his fighting leadership he was awarded the Distinguished Service Order.

After the war Darling succeeded to command of the 5th Parachute brigade in Java until it was caught up in the reduction of airborne forces to a single brigade group, a formation to be retained in the post-war order of battle. But it lacked a settled base or a headquarters for the Parachute regiment. Darling was appointed to remedy these omissions. His structure has maintained the demands upon it for more than fifty years.

In 1950 Darling took command of the brigade, then in Egypt, poised—though never committed—to intervene in the Iranian oil crisis, and became involved again with the Middle East as chief of staff of the British corps ill-advisedly dispatched with others to reopen the Suez canal, blocked by President Nasser in 1956. A posting to the War Office followed as deputy director of staff duties.

Promoted major-general in 1958, Darling was appointed

director of operations in Cyprus under the governor, Sir Hugh Foot, the military agent of the political chief. He found 40,000 troops employed to bring about the defeat of the EOKA organization seeking to seize power in the island by terrorism. He judged this number to be excessive. A brigade was sent home. 'Brains not brawn' was the theme General Darling communicated to his soldiers as he toured their camps and posts to tell them how they were going to win the engagement. Within three months of his arrival his strategy—and dynamic tactics—persuaded EOKA to accept a Christmas truce. Progressively the EOKA leadership was brought under pressure until it accepted the terms of a political settlement offered by the British government early in 1959. Of all his many services to the crown, Darling's contribution to the defeat of terrorism in Cyprus was outstanding.

Still, almost ten years of service awaited him. He became director of infantry (1960–62); commander of the 1st British corps in Germany (1962–3), and of the southern command—the army strategic reserve—(1964–6); and finally commander-in-chief of allied forces northern Europe, a component of NATO (1967–9). He was made knight commander of the Bath (1963) and knight grand cross of the Order of the British Empire (1969). During the last two years of his service he was an aide-de-camp to the queen.

Regimental responsibilities and interests continued in the late years of his service and in retirement. He was colonel-commandant of the Parachute regiment (1965–7), and of the Royal Fusiliers (1963–8), when he was influential in the amalgamation of the four fusilier regiments of the army, recognizing that if they did not accomplish this change themselves, other options, less acceptable, would shortly be imposed upon them by the War Office. It was a task involving much patience on his part. He became colonel of the amalgamated body from 1968 to 1974.

Sir Kenneth Darling retired to hunting country at Chesterton in Oxfordshire with his wife; they had long shared a love of horses and hounds. Here she fell ill and was nursed by her husband until her death in 1990. He died on 31 October 1998 in the John Radcliffe Hospital in Oxford, and his funeral took place on 9 November at St Mary's, Chesterton, Oxfordshire. ANTHONY FARRAR-HOCKLEY

Sources Parachute Regiment and Airborne Forces Museum archive, Aldershot [scrapbooks, press cuttings] · army records (1998, 2001) · personal knowledge (2004) · J. Thompson, *Ready for anything: the parachute regiment at war, 1940–82* (1989) · *Daily Telegraph* (3 Nov 1998) · *The Independent* (12 Nov 1998) · *The Times* (4 Nov 1998) · *WW* · Burke, *Peerage* (1999) · d. cert.

Archives IWM, papers

Likenesses photograph, *c.*1958, repro. in *Daily Telegraph* · photograph, 1969, repro. in *The Times* · photograph, *c.*1970, repro. in *The Independent* · painting, Parachute Regiment and Airborne Forces Museum archive

Wealth at death £1,130,068: probate, 1999, *CGPLA Eng. & Wales*

Darling, Sir Ralph (1772–1858), army officer and colonial governor, was born in January or February 1772 at an unknown location in Ireland, the eldest in a family of three sons and two daughters. His father, Christopher, was a sergeant in the 45th regiment, and the only known information about his mother is that her name was Ann.

Sir Ralph Darling (1772–1858), by John Linnell, 1825

Christopher Darling rose to be adjutant and later quartermaster of the 45th regiment, but bringing up a young family strained his limited resources. He was away from home for long periods, and in May 1785 his wife and children were allowed to accompany him to the West Indies. Ralph was forced to find employment when still young, and between June 1786 and June 1788 his name appeared on the regimental muster list as a private.

Military career Darling's military career indicates that he possessed considerable ability. He also appears to have received some form of education, possibly at a school for children of the rank and file run by the 45th regiment. What happened to him after June 1788 is not clear, but he certainly stayed in the West Indies, and in April 1793, following the outbreak of the war between Britain and revolutionary France, secured an ensigncy in the 45th regiment. The commanding officer, in recommending him, wrote of Darling's father as a 'man with a large family' who deserved an 'act of charity' (PRO, WO 31/4/62). Darling had now been given the chance he needed and from this time steadily advanced. He remained in the West Indies when his regiment sailed for England in 1794 and was recorded as serving in Grenada as acting comptroller of customs. Early in 1795 he had his first taste of action when he was posted to the 15th regiment to help suppress an uprising in Grenada. In January 1796 he became adjutant of the 15th regiment, and in August he was appointed military secretary to the distinguished soldier Sir Ralph Abercromby, who was in command of British forces in the West Indies. He served in a similar capacity under General Graham while Abercromby was in England. Abercromby returned in January 1797, but there was no vacancy on his staff. Darling, by this stage a captain in the 27th Inskillings, obtained permission to join the 2nd Queen's regiment in the attack on Trinidad on 17 February 1797. In July 1797 he rejoined the headquarters staff and served as military secretary to a succession of commanders until 1802, when he sailed for England with Sir Thomas Trigge, whom he had accompanied on expeditions against Surinam in 1799 and the Danish and Swedish West Indian islands in 1801. He had risen steadily, and on 17 July 1801 became lieutenant-colonel in the 69th foot.

Darling had carried out his onerous duties with distinction and was praised by Trigge as 'an officer uncommonly well acquainted with the military details, especially the financial part' (Hobart MSS, D/MH/Wa-y). In June 1802, after reaching England, he joined the staff of Lord Harrington as temporary assistant quartermaster-general. The resumption of war, following the short-lived peace of Amiens, resulted in Darling's being sent to take command of his regiment in March 1804. He sailed for India a month later, but in mid-1806 was invalided home. After recovering he was transferred to the 51st regiment, and in August 1806, on the recommendation of the adjutant-general, Major-General Henry Calvert, he was appointed principal assistant adjutant-general. He saw two further periods of active service, first as commander of the 51st regiment at Lugo and Corunna in the Peninsular War, then as deputy adjutant-general to the Walcheren expedition, which sailed for the River Scheldt on 28 July 1809. He distinguished himself on both occasions, but it was in the administrative sphere, rather than as a fighting soldier, that he excelled. In August 1810, following his return from the Scheldt, and again on Calvert's recommendation, the duke of York placed him in charge of the recruiting service as deputy adjutant-general. He served in this capacity at the Horse Guards until 1818, rising to the rank of major-general on 4 June 1813.

Promotion was followed by Darling's appointment to the clothing board and to the boards of the Royal Military College, Sandhurst, and the Royal Military Asylum, Chelsea. His main task, however, was to ensure that there was an adequate supply of troops. This called for the 'most vigilant and unremitting attention' as well as a detailed knowledge of the 'Resources of the different Recruiting Stations throughout the United Kingdom' (PRO, WO 3/199). Darling devoted himself wholeheartedly to his task. He reorganized his department with a view to improving its efficiency and introduced reforms affecting the whole recruiting service. By this means he greatly enhanced his reputation and won the praise of his superiors. Operating at the centre of affairs, he was also able to widen his contacts and make influential friends. By the end of the war he had left his humble beginnings far behind. Among his circle of friends was the marquess of Queensberry, who shared his taste for high living. Conscious of the need to elevate his social standing, he obtained a grant of armorial bearings on 13 July 1813.

Darling's future, once peace returned, however, was no longer assured. The war had provided continuous opportunities for advancement, but after 1815 the openings became fewer and the competition greater. Life changed in one important direction on 13 October 1817, when, at the parish church of St Mary, Cheltenham, he married Elizabeth (Eliza) Dumaresq (1798–1868), the fourth of the six children of Ann and the late Colonel John Dumaresq. Darling was twenty-six years older than his wife, but despite this age gap their marriage proved extremely happy. It linked Darling to a family of considerable standing, exposed him to the influence of an Anglican of deep religious conviction, and increased his prospects of advancement. In August 1818, assisted by the patronage of the duke of York, he was appointed acting governor and commandant of the garrison at the Indian Ocean island of Mauritius, which had been taken from France in December 1810.

Governing Mauritius Thus opened a new and controversial phase of Darling's career. His administration, first of Mauritius, then of New South Wales, generated much criticism. Opponents saw his appointments as illustrating the defects of a patronage system which rewarded military officers with civil posts for which they were unsuited by temperament and training. Darling made numerous personal and political enemies, among whom he won a reputation for being harsh, tyrannical, vindictive, and reactionary. It is true that he shared the duke of Wellington's brand of conservatism, and he was also authoritarian in outlook. A life devoted solely to the army had bred such attitudes and accustomed him to being obeyed by those under his command. Years of fighting against revolutionary and Napoleonic France turned him against progressive ideas. In public his manner was formal, and he often appeared cold and aloof. Yet to focus exclusively on these characteristics would be to reduce him to a mere caricature. As a number of contemporaries and historians recognized, there was another side to Darling and his work. This needs to be appreciated if he is to be treated justly.

Darling's initial task, on reaching Mauritius in February 1819, was to heal the rifts created by Major-General Gage Hall, whom the governor, Sir Robert Farquhar, had left in charge when he temporarily returned to England. Hall's ill-advised measures and intemperate manner had alienated the settlers and divided the public service. Darling introduced more moderate policies, dismissed a number of officials whom he considered incompetent, and placed the administration on a more efficient footing. After restoring harmony he took steps to promote economic development by encouraging trade, diversifying agriculture, and improving communications. He also took steps to improve the cleanliness of the capital, Port Louis, and to provide better educational facilities for children.

The slave trade More difficult was the task of curbing the slave trade, which had been banned by the British government. In this, Darling was opposed by the planters, principally French and well represented in the judiciary and the public service. Darling objected to slavery on moral grounds and acted vigorously to prevent more slaves being landed and to register those already on the island.

His measures were resisted by the French, who resented British rule. Tension mounted, and was made worse by a serious outbreak of cholera that began on 19 November 1819 and lasted for some two months. Blame was placed on a British frigate, the *Topaze*, which had been sent to Mauritius as a patrol vessel. Members of the crew were said to have brought the disease, and Darling was criticized for allowing the ship to land. The port officer was unable to find any trace of the disease on board, and Darling was convinced that the French sought only to embarrass him and rid the island of the *Topaze* so that they could continue to import slaves. His anger increased when members of the elective *conseil générale* refused to come to Port Louis for a meeting on 13 January 1820 to review the situation. Darling had earlier accused them of complicity in the slave trade and he now admonished them for lack of fortitude. When the *conseil* finally assembled on 14 February, after the epidemic was over, it censured Darling, prompting him to dissolve it and suspend local officials who had criticized him. His actions also brought him into conflict with the *Mauritius Gazette*, the colony's only newspaper. Tension died down only after the return of the placatory Farquhar, who resumed command in July 1820. Darling remained on the island in charge of the garrison until 28 July 1823, when he sailed for England.

Governing New South Wales Although disliked by the French, Darling was highly praised by his superiors, who strongly supported his policies. He was considered to have been a success and, despite some misgivings on the part of Lord Bathurst, secretary of state for the colonies, he was appointed on 12 November 1824 to succeed Sir Thomas Brisbane as governor of New South Wales. Administering this colony posed problems more formidable than those which Darling had faced at Mauritius. New South Wales existed in part as a receptacle for convicts, who continued to arrive in large numbers. Yet the colony was also in the process of becoming a free society and contained a growing population of migrants, emancipists, and local-born inhabitants. The task of reconciling 'the discipline required of a Gaol, with the freedom of … action essential to a remote and increasing Colony' (PRO, CO 323/74), as James Stephen described it, presented all the early governors with considerable difficulties. Fortunately, Darling had loyal subordinates, among them his brother-in-law and private secretary, Henry Dumaresq, and Alexander Macleay, the new colonial secretary. The three men formed a tight-knit group that was said to constitute 'the real cabinet of the colony' (Forbes MSS, A1819 p. 117).

By the time of Darling's arrival the importance of New South Wales as a source of wool for Yorkshire manufacturers was widely recognized, and the colony was already closely linked to the English industrial system. Pastoralism expanded considerably during the Darling era, despite a three-year drought and a commercial slump that marked its early years. The frontiers of settlement were pushed steadily further afield, migrants with capital continued to arrive, and wool exports grew at a rapid rate. Darling did much to promote these developments. He opened new roads into the interior, encouraged exploration, and introduced more regularity into the distribution of crown land, not least through the proclamation of the nineteen counties on 14 October 1829, which defined the area in which settlement could take place. In addition he established new townships in the interior, insisting that they be laid out on a grid pattern and that buildings be neatly arranged and properly constructed. Darling paid great attention to town planning and took steps to improve facilities in Sydney. His passion for order and symmetry was further reflected in his reform of the public service, which was placed on a new and more efficient basis that was not fundamentally changed until the 1850s.

Penal policy in New South Wales These reforms included improvements to the running of the penal system. British policy had earlier moved towards making convict transportation more punitive with a view to increasing its deterrent effect. Darling immediately took steps to implement these objectives, both in relation to the convicts who were assigned to private settlers and to the much smaller proportion who remained in government hands. The office of the superintendent of convicts was reorganized, discipline was tightened, and concessions, such as tickets-of-leave, were made more difficult to obtain. Convicts found guilty of committing further offences were flogged, or worked, sometimes in chains, in road gangs. The recalcitrant were sent to the isolation of penal settlements, of which the most feared was Norfolk Island, which Darling reopened. Yet the governor sought to reform as well as punish, and in this was encouraged by his wife, who showed great interest in the plight of convicts, particularly females. He ensured that convicts were exposed to the teachings of the church and, with Eliza Darling's help, did much to improve conditions at the female factory, which housed women who were awaiting assignment, as well as those who had misbehaved after reaching the colony. Efforts were also made to ensure that convicts who had been sent out as children were properly educated.

These and other measures have been overlooked by those who described Darling as excessively severe and cruel. He was, in fact, genuinely interested in the welfare of the convicts, and his humanitarianism was further illustrated in his treatment of the Aborigines. He sought to ensure that their rights under British law were protected and that they were treated compassionately. That he was unable fully to achieve such ends was more a reflection of the difficulty of controlling race relations in so farflung a territory than of shortcomings on his own part.

'Exclusives' and 'emancipists' in New South Wales Darling handled his administrative duties with considerable success. A man of great dedication and a high sense of duty, he devoted himself unstintingly to his task, working such long hours that his health eventually suffered. He effectively discharged his social duties, entertaining at Government House on a scale not previously witnessed. He had the misfortune, however, to be present in the colony at a

155

time when it was divided politically between the 'exclusives', who favoured the existing constitution, and the 'emancipists', who sought to liberalize it by introducing trial by jury and representative government. Darling sought to heal rifts and keep aloof from faction, but this proved impossible. His conservative leanings and his belief that authoritarianism was essential in a penal colony led him to oppose the reformers, who were more than usually active in the early part of his administration. A new Constitution Act was due in 1828, and the emancipists used every opportunity to advance their cause through public meetings, petitions to London, and the press. The atmosphere became highly charged, and Darling himself was vilified with a view to discrediting the existing system of government.

Events played into the hands of Darling's opponents in November 1826, following the death of a soldier, Joseph Sudds, who, along with Patrick Thompson, had committed a crime to obtain discharge from the army. Darling, unaware that Sudds was ill, and anxious to check crime of this kind, ordered the two men to be stripped of their uniforms and placed in irons at a regimental parade before being sent to a road gang. Sudds died shortly after and, although at first there was little criticism, liberal opinion later turned against Darling. William Charles Wentworth, one of his leading opponents, threatened impeachment proceedings. Wentworth's actions, like those of the liberal press, were politically motivated and resulted in Darling's taking steps to curb the press, as he had earlier been ordered to do by the British government. His actions aroused a furore and undermined his relations with the chief justice, Francis Forbes, who declared two of his proposed measures invalid. The harmony and mutual understanding that had characterized the opening of Darling's administration gave way to conflict and recrimination. Sections of the judiciary, progressives disappointed at the limited constitutional reforms introduced in 1828, and colonists who considered themselves to have been wronged by Darling joined forces in making life difficult and unpleasant for him. He was, however, supported by the *Sydney Gazette*, by leading officials, and by John Macarthur and the exclusives. The British government became alarmed by the growing tension and used new regulations, limiting the tenure of governors to six years, as a reason for recalling him. Darling considered this an injustice, and there were grounds for his protests. He had proved himself to be an upright, loyal, and extremely efficient administrator. He was also caught in an unusually volatile political situation. Yet he lacked urbanity and grace and possessed an abrasive personality, as well as a degree of inflexibility, that counted against him. Divisions within the community could only grow worse while he was governor.

Retirement, exoneration, and death Darling left the colony on 22 October 1831 amid unprecedented scenes of rejoicing orchestrated by his opponents. His troubles did not cease following his arrival in England in May 1832. He was pursued by a small group of foes who won the ear of the liberal press and parliamentary radicals. Constant pressure resulted in the appointment of a House of Commons select committee, which met between June and 29 August 1835, to inquire into a number of allegations. Ably defended by Sir Thomas Hardinge, Darling was completely exonerated and on 30 August, while attending a levee, was unexpectedly invested by the king as a knight grand cross of the Royal Guelphic Order. He was not again, however, given an appointment, although he retained his army connections, including a commissionership of the Royal Military College. In September 1837 he became colonel of the 41st Welsh regiment and on 11 February 1848 colonel of the 69th South Lincolnshire regiment.

These posts involved Darling in only minor duties and left him free to devote his attention to his wife and their young family of three sons and four daughters. In September they moved from Cheltenham to Brighton, where they lived initially at Hampton Lodge, then, from 1850, at 39 Brunswick Square. Deeply attached to his wife and children, Darling led a contented existence in their company, displaying a degree of warmth and softness that he never revealed in public. The household was deeply religious, and Elizabeth Darling engaged in philanthropic work, besides pursuing her interests in music, literature, and art. Darling encouraged her, watched over the well-being of his children, spent time in the company of friends, and made occasional trips to Europe. He died peacefully at his home on Good Friday, 2 April 1858, and was buried on the following Thursday at St Andrews Old Church, Hove. His wife and seven children survived him.

BRIAN H. FLETCHER

Sources B. H. Fletcher, *Ralph Darling: a governor maligned* (1984) · A. G. L. Shaw, *Heroes and villains in history: Governors Darling and Bourke in New South Wales* (1966) · *AusDB* · C. H. Currey, *Sir Francis Forbes* (1968) · C. M. H. Clark, *A history of Australia*, 2 (1968) · A. McMartin, *Public servants and patronage: the foundation and rise of the New South Wales public service, 1786–1859* (1983) · A. C. V. Melbourne, *Early constitutional development in Australia* (1934) · L. N. Rose, 'The administration of Governor Darling', *Royal Australian Historical Society Journal and Proceedings*, 8 (1922–3), 49–176 · A. G. L. Shaw, *Convicts and the colonies: a study of penal transportation from Great Britain and Ireland* (1966) · A. Pitot, *L'Ile Maurice: esquisses historiques*, 1 (Port Louis, 1910) · J. Waldersee, *Catholic society in New South Wales, 1788–1860* (1974) · PRO, Colonial Office MSS · PRO, War Office MSS · Bucks. RLSS, Hobart papers · Mitchell L., NSW, Chief Justice Forbes MSS · d. cert. · census returns for Brighton, 1851
Archives Mauritius Archives · Mitchell L., NSW, family corresp. · NL Aus., papers · NRA, priv. coll., corresp. and papers · PRO · State Archives of New South Wales, Sydney · State Library of New South Wales, Sydney, Dixson Wing, papers | Allport Library, Hobart, Dumaresq MSS · Derbys. RO, letters to R. J. Wilmot-Horton · Mitchell L., NSW, Dumaresq MSS · priv. coll., Dumaresq MSS
Likenesses J. Linnell, portrait, 1825, NL Aus. [*see illus.*]
Wealth at death under £50,000: probate, 17 April 1858, *CGPLA Eng. & Wales*

Darling, William (1802–1884), anatomist, was born at Demse in Scotland, in 1802. He was educated at Edinburgh University and in 1830 went to America and began to study medicine in the university medical school in New York, where he took his MD in 1842, having devoted the whole of his time during the intervening years to the teaching as well as the study of anatomy. He went to England in the same year, and in November 1856 was made a member of the Royal College of Surgeons of England; he became a fellow in 1866. He also held the degrees of MA, LLD, Vermont. In 1862 he returned to New York and was soon afterwards appointed professor of anatomy in the medical school in which he had been a student. His anatomical collection was considered one of the finest in the city. Besides his knowledge of anatomy Darling had a good knowledge of mathematics, and had a taste for poetry, which he occasionally wrote himself. His only publications are *Anatomography, or, Graphic Anatomy* (1880), *A Small Compound of Anatomy*, and *Essentials of Anatomy*. He also edited Professor Draper's work. Darling died at the University of New York on Christmas day 1884.

ROBERT HARRISON, *rev.* MICHAEL BEVAN

Sources *The Times* (7 Jan 1885) · V. G. Plarr, *Plarr's Lives of the fellows of the Royal College of Surgeons of England*, rev. D'A. Power, 2 vols. (1930)
Likenesses portrait, RCS Eng.

Darlington. For this title name *see* Kielmansegg, Sophia Charlotte von, *suo jure* countess of Darlington and *suo jure* countess of Leinster (1675–1725).

Darlington, Cyril Dean (1903–1981), cytogeneticist and evolutionist, was born on 19 December 1903 in Chorley, Lancashire, the younger son (there were no daughters) of Henry Robertson Darlington, a schoolmaster, and his wife, Ellen Frankland. He attended Heathside elementary school, 1909–10, and Boteler Grammar School, 1910–11, both in Warrington, Lancashire. In 1911 the family moved to Ealing, London, where his father became secretary to Dr K. E. Markell, chief chemist of Crossfields Soap Ltd. Following the move Darlington enrolled at Mercers' School, Holborn, London. In 1917 he won a foundation scholarship to St Paul's School, London, and attended the school as a day boy until 1920, when he entered South Eastern Agricultural College at Wye with the aim of becoming a farmer in Australia.

In 1923 Darlington obtained a BSc in agriculture (London), but instead of leaving for Australia he applied for the Empire Cotton Corporation scholarship. Unsuccessful, he accepted a position as a volunteer unpaid worker at the John Innes Horticultural Institution (JIHI), Merton Park, London, from its director, William Bateson. During his early years there he worked under W. C. F. Newton, the head of the cytology department. Following Newton's untimely death, Darlington was appointed cytologist in 1928, and rose to head the cytology department. From 1939 he also served as its director.

Darlington's interest in genetics began in 1921 as the result of reading the influential 1915 book *The Physical Basis of Mendelian Heredity* by American geneticists T. H. Morgan, A. H. Sturtevant, and C. B. Bridges. Although he had little or no training in cytology or genetics he learned the necessary cytological techniques and genetical principles from Newton and through self-tuition. During 1931–2 Darlington was in the United States and Japan, and in 1932 he married Kate Pinsdorf (1901–1975), a history lecturer at Vassar College, New York. The marriage was short-lived; when he

returned to England she was unwilling to join him, and in 1934 they obtained a divorce in the state of Nevada. This annulled the marriage within the United States but was not legally valid within the UK.

By 1932 Darlington's expertise had become so well developed that he formulated cytogenetics, his own synthesis of the new sciences of cytology and genetics which was discussed in his book *Recent Advances in Cytology* (1932). Although many of Darlington's interpretive statements in this book were praised for their boldness and imagination, they also earned more than their share of criticism. Geneticists like John Belling charged against its speculative and insupportable claims. Cytogeneticist Hampton L. Carson, a student at the time, recalls the response to *Recent Advances in Cytology* as follows:

> The book was considered to be dangerous, in fact poisonous, for the minds of graduate students. It was made clear to us that only after we had become seasoned veterans could we hope to succeed in separating the good (if there was any) from the bad in Darlington. Those of us who had copies kept them in a drawer rather than on the tops of desks. (Carson, 91)

Despite the controversy, Darlington's widespread influence drew many graduate students and workers to his institute, making it one of the leading centres of cytogenetics research. The controversy diminished with his book *The Evolution of Genetic Systems* (1939), which both synthesized and clarified the earlier work and received general praise. One of Darlington's postgraduate students was Margaret Blanche, daughter of Sir Gilbert Giles Upcott, a senior civil servant in the Treasury, and a graduate of Royal Holloway College, London. During 1934 a relationship began between them, and in 1937 they underwent an irregular marriage under Scottish law, an arrangement which left Margaret with no marital rights under English law. Darlington persuaded her that his career prospects would be wrecked by the scandal of a divorce in the English courts; she changed her name by deed poll. Margaret went on to publish a number of distinguished papers as a postdoctoral research worker at JIHI, and raised their two sons and three daughters, although she suffered from ill health in the late 1940s, after the births of the last two girls.

Darlington recognized that chromosomes and their behaviour in states like meiosis could be seen as genetic systems, which themselves were subject to evolutionary forces. This insight was a critical contribution to evolutionary theory, which at the time was incorporating genetical principles within a Darwinian selectionist framework. As a result Darlington is considered one of the most important individuals in bringing cytogenetics to the modern synthetic theory of evolution. His work was especially critical to the understanding of evolutionary mechanisms of plants at the genetic level, and was used heavily by American botanical geneticist G. Ledyard Stebbins jun. in his own synthesis of plant evolution, *Variation and Evolution in Plants* (1950).

In addition to making numerous observations on chromosome behaviour such as pairing, describing chromosome pattern and number in various horticultural species of plants, and developing new cytological techniques, Darlington contributed to the science of cytogenetics a more precise vocabulary of terms. Additional books in cytogenetics included the compendium *Chromosome Atlas of Cultivated Plants* (1945) written with E. K. Janaki-Ammal, followed by *Chromosome Atlas of Flowering Plants* (1956) with A. P. Wylie, and *The Handling of Chromosomes* (1942), a book describing preparation of the chromosomes for microscopical study, with L. F. La Cour.

Darlington's interest in the sciences of genetics and evolution was extended in mid-career to more general societal concerns. In 1953 he left the institute to accept the Sherardian chair of botany at Oxford University and become a keeper of the Oxford Botanic Garden. In 1971 he became emeritus professor. His interest in genetics, humans, and society occupied a significant part of his career at Oxford. In 1953 he addressed these issues in *The Facts of Life*, later revised and expanded into *Genetics and Man* (1964), and in 1969 he wrote *The Evolution of Man and Society*. His penchant for making bold statements also characterized his conclusions with respect to the genetic understanding of humans. His reasoning was that as biological creatures they were subject to biological understanding. He believed that racial, class, and sex differences had a strong genetic basis, as did human practices like marriage, homosexuality, and fertility. Darlington had no qualms about the application of knowledge from genetics to human improvement and was an outspoken advocate of eugenics. His understanding of genetics also led him to appreciate differences between different groups of humans as it was a source of genetic and evolutionary novelty.

Darlington was a keen organizer of conferences, especially on chromosome biology, and was a guiding force of the JIHI during the Second World War. In 1949 he eased a difficult transition when the institute moved from Merton to Bayfordbury, Hertfordshire. In 1947 he founded *Heredity* with geneticist R. A. Fisher. He later gave the profitable journal as a gift to the Genetical Society.

Darlington's attitude to scientific work was well known among his colleagues, and his quotation that 'work not published is not done' (Lewis, *Heredity*, 167) has served as a maxim to numerous followers. His publication output was not only prodigious but covered a broad spectrum of topics. These included not only cytogenetics and the application of genetical principles to humans and their society but also the teaching of genetics and the history and philosophy of biological science. In 1959, the centenary of the publication of Darwin's *Origin of Species*, Darlington contributed his own historical reflections on Darwin in *Darwin's Place in History*.

A tireless advocate of scientific research, Darlington led the exposure of Soviet atrocities against geneticists led by Trofim Lysenko in the 1940s. He was an outspoken individual, who frequently took difficult positions on politically important matters, and who frequently denigrated establishment values and bureaucracies. Numerous contemporaries commented on his confident, if not sometimes arrogant, demeanour, amplified no doubt by the combination of a flamboyant personality and a handsome appearance. He was a patron of the arts and literature, and was especially fond of gardening, to which his home at South Hinksey, Oxford, was a monument. While plans were being made for the JIHI to move from Merton, Darlington began an affair with a close family friend, Gwendolen Mabel, *née* Adshead (1901–2000), the former wife of his cousin Jack Harvey. Six weeks after his last child was born Darlington announced his intention of moving in with Gwendolen. Margaret and her children found themselves on the wrong side of the law, and considerable pressure was put on Darlington to persuade him to pay maintenance. Margaret regretted losing the camaraderie of the institute and struggled to make ends meet. Darlington and Gwendolen did not marry, but the partnership lasted until his death.

Darlington received many honours: he was elected FRS in 1941, and received the royal medal in 1946 and the Trail award of the Linnean Society in 1951. In 1956 he was recipient of DSc from Oxford, and became honorary fellow of Magdalen College, Oxford, in 1971. From 1953 to 1971 he was fellow of Wye College. He served as president of the Genetical Society (1943–6) and the Rationalist Association (1948). Darlington died of a heart attack on 26 March 1981 in Oxford.
VASSILIKI BETTY SMOCOVITIS

Sources H. L. Carson, 'Cytogeneticists and the neo-Darwinian synthesis', *The evolutionary synthesis: perspectives on the unification of biology*, ed. E. Mayr and W. B. Provine (1980), 86–95 · D. Lewis, *Memoirs FRS*, 29 (1983), 113–57 · D. Lewis, 'Cyril Dean Darlington (1903–1981)', *Heredity*, 48 (1982), 161–7 · R. C. Olby, 'Darlington, Cyril Dean', *DSB*, suppl., 17.203–9 · V. B. Smocovitis, 'Botany and the evolutionary synthesis: the life and work of G. Ledyard Stebbins Jr', PhD diss., Cornell University, 1988 · Carnegie Mellon University, Pittsburgh, Pennsylvania, USA, Hunt Institute for Botanical Documentation · *CGPLA Eng. & Wales* (1982) · O. Harman, 'A life of controversy, or, Darlington's place in history', DPhil diss., U. Oxf., 2001 · private information (2004) [Clare Passingham, daughter; P. D. A. Harvey, stepson]

Archives Bodl. Oxf., personal, family, and professional corresp. and papers · John Innes Centre, Norwich, corresp. and papers, incl. MSS of several of his books | Rice University, Houston, Texas, Woodson Research Center, corresp. with Sir Julian Huxley

Likenesses W. Bird, photograph, repro. in Lewis, *Memoirs FRS* · photograph, repro. in Lewis, 'Cyril Dean Darlington (1903–1981)', *Heredity*

Wealth at death £115,757: probate, 9 March 1982, *CGPLA Eng. & Wales*

Darlington, John of (d. 1284), archbishop of Dublin, was a Dominican friar and confessor to Henry III. Presumably he took his name from Darlington in co. Durham. His early life is obscure, but it is probable that he studied at the Dominican priory of St Jacques at Paris, for he was associated with the production of a well-known biblical concordance which was compiled at that house. A first concordance to the Bible, known as the concordance of St Jacques, had been compiled at Paris in the years 1235–47 by a team of friars under the direction of the famous biblical theologian Hugues de St Cher. A second and more elaborate version of the work, which became known as the English concordance, was undertaken at the priory a few years later. This, unlike its predecessor, supplied the scriptural context in which words occurred as well as the biblical references. The Dominican chronicler Nicholas Trevet represents John of Darlington as the sole author of this work; but it was evidently a collaborative enterprise; and a number of manuscripts name another English scholar, Richard of Stainsby, as one of the helpers.

It is uncertain at what stage of his career Darlington was appointed King Henry's confessor; but early in 1256 he was made a member of the king's increasingly professional council and a member of the royal household. In the spring of 1256 money was disbursed to London merchants for cloth to make habits for Darlington and his Dominican companions resident at court, and to provide them with three palfreys, saddles, and harness. The position of confidence he enjoyed with the king is attested from 1256 onwards by a series of royal pardons and privileges that were issued to various people at his request. He was also instrumental in obtaining royal gifts of land for the Friars Preacher to build priories at Bamburgh and Ipswich, and he probably inspired the numerous gifts made by the king to the Dominican priory at Holborn, Middlesex.

Darlington's closeness to the king made it inevitable that he should be involved in the political turmoil of the years 1258 to 1265. As Henry's mentor and trusted councillor, he cannot wholly escape the suspicion that he approved, or at least complied with, the king's foolish plan to underwrite the debts of the papacy in an attempt to obtain the crown of Sicily for his son Edmund. At the crisis parliament of June 1258 Darlington was one of the twelve, or as it emerged eleven, chosen to represent the king's interests on the committee of twenty-four, which was entrusted with drafting the provisions of Oxford. In the spring of 1260, when the king was in France and the Lord Edward appeared to have sided with Montfort's party against his father, Darlington acted as mediator, travelling to France to assure the king of Edward's loyalty: his efforts paved the way for the formal reconciliation between father and son in May of that year. It is possible that his election to the headship of the London priory in 1261 indicates that his order was concerned to withdraw Darlington from the political arena. If so, it was unsuccessful. In July 1263, after Montfort had gained control of London and the south-east, Darlington played an important part in an attempt to arrest the drift into civil war. Together with the bishops of London and Lichfield he was empowered by the king to negotiate with the Montfortian barons, and reached an agreement that the provisions of Oxford should be upheld after the deletion from them of anything prejudicial to the king, and that unacceptable aliens should be dismissed from the royal counsels. In December of that year Darlington assisted at the drawing-up of an instrument by which the king and magnates submitted the dispute arising from the provisions of Oxford to the arbitration of Louis IX of France and swore to observe whatever he ordained.

During the conflict that followed Louis's arbitration,

given in January 1264, Darlington appears to have withdrawn from the royal household: in a letter dated 11 September 1265 the king asks the Dominican provincial, Robert Kilwardby, for Darlington's return to counsel the king as he had done previously. From November of that year his presence at court is indicated by a resumption of royal pardons to rebels and others and gifts made expressly at his instance. A mandate of December 1267 refers to his chamber, close to that of the king, in Winchester Castle.

Early in the reign of Edward I, Darlington became absorbed by the thorny duties of a papal tax collector. In 1274 the Second Council of Lyons had, at the instance of Pope Gregory X, levied a tax of a tenth on the incomes of all beneficed clergy for six years to finance a crusade for the recovery of the Holy Land. Papal letters of 20 September 1274 appointed Darlington an assessor and collector of the tax in England in association with the existing papal nuncio, Raymond de Nogaret. Their task was made heavier by a requirement that the assessment for tax should be based upon a fresh and more stringent valuation of benefices than the previous valuation of Norwich, made in 1254. In the teeth of much protest from the clergy, they undertook this reassessment in 1276. Over the years, as the money was collected by sub-collectors in each diocese, Darlington and his colleague had to deal with a number of churches and monastic bodies that had incurred ecclesiastical sanctions for falling into arrears with their payments. He and the new nuncio, Ardicio, acted throughout under the protection of a safe conduct from the king, who had a financial interest in their work, for the pope had promised the yield of the ecclesiastical tenth to any ruler who undertook the crusade. In fact, although King Edward had not taken the cross, in June 1276 the collectors allowed him 2000 marks from the sums raised in the dioceses of Winchester and Chichester, for his own purposes. Early in the spring of 1278 Darlington was dispatched by the king to Rome, together with William of Louth and Master Henry of Newark, to seek financial concessions from Pope Nicholas III. They presented a request that responsibility for payment of the annual tribute of 1000 marks due from England to the apostolic see be assigned to certain abbeys, which would be granted lands for the purpose; they also requested immediate delivery to the king of the proceeds of the tenth already collected in England. The pope refused the first proposal, but declared his willingness to grant Edward the proceeds of the tenth if and when he took the cross.

Darlington's embassy to the papal curia had brought him to the notice of Pope Nicholas and it was possibly this, as well as the fact that he enjoyed the confidence of King Edward, that resulted in his provision to the archbishopric of Dublin on 8 February 1279, only a few months after his return from Rome. The see had been vacant since the death of Archbishop Fulk of Sandford in 1271, owing to a dispute between its two contending chapters. Dublin, like the see of Bath and Wells, was served by both a chapter of secular canons, that of St Patrick's, and also a monastic chapter, that of Holy Trinity, consisting of Augustinian canons regular. On receiving the royal licence to elect a successor to Sandford, the former had elected William de la Cornere, one of their canons and a papal chaplain; but the latter had instead elected the royal chancellor of Ireland, Master Fromund le Brun, who was also a papal chaplain. The double election resulted in prolonged litigation and a reference to the pope, who ultimately quashed both nominations and provided Darlington to the archbishopric instead. His elevation, only a few days after the pope's provision of the Franciscan John Pecham to Canterbury, was one of many indications of a marked preference of the papacy for choosing bishops from the mendicant orders. He was obviously acceptable to the king, and Edward received his homage and fealty on 27 April 1279, and released to him the temporalities of his see on the following day. He was consecrated by Pecham at Waltham Abbey on Sunday 27 August. The unfinished business involved in collecting the tenth and coercing reluctant ecclesiastical bodies into payment kept him in England, and the king allowed him to be represented by attorney in Ireland. Not the least of his problems were the pressing financial demands of the king, who in March 1283 seized a portion of the proceeds of the tax from deposit in monastic houses and was only induced to disgorge it by a menacing letter from the pope. When at length in 1284 Darlington set out for Ireland to take up his see, he was struck down by illness, and died, still in England, on 28 March. He was buried in the choir of the church of the Blackfriars in London.

                                    C. H. LAWRENCE

Sources Paris, *Chron.*, vol. 5 · *Ann. mon.* · *Gesta abbatum monasterii Sancti Albani, a Thoma Walsingham*, ed. H. T. Riley, 3 vols., pt 4 of *Chronica monasterii S. Albani*, Rolls Series, 28 (1867–9) · N. Trevet, *Annales sex regum Angliae, 1135–1307*, ed. T. Hog, EHS, 6 (1845) · *Willelmi Rishanger … chronica et annales*, ed. H. T. Riley, pt 2 of *Chronica monasterii S. Albani*, Rolls Series, 28 (1865) · *Chancery records* · H. S. Sweetman and G. F. Handcock, eds., *Calendar of documents relating to Ireland*, 5 vols., PRO (1875–86) · R. F. Treharne and I. J. Sanders, eds., *Documents of the baronial movement of reform and rebellion, 1258–1267* (1973) · *CEPR letters*, vol. 1 · J. Gay, ed., *Les registres de Nicolas III* (1938) · *Registrum epistolarum fratris Johannis Peckham, archiepiscopi Cantuariensis*, ed. C. T. Martin, 3 vols., Rolls Series, 77 (1882–5) · W. A. Hinnebusch, *The early English Friars Preachers* (1951) · T. Kaeppeli and E. Panella, *Scriptores ordinis praedicatorum medii aevi*, 4 vols. (Rome, 1970–93) · W. E. Lunt, *Financial relations of the papacy with England to 1327* (1939) · R. H. Rouse and M. A. Rouse, 'The verbal concordance to the scriptures', *Archivum Fratrum Praedicatorum*, 44 (1974), 5–30

Darlington, William Aubrey Cecil (1890–1979), theatre critic and author, was born at Taunton on 20 February 1890, the only son and eldest of four children of Thomas Darlington (1864–1908), principal of Queen's College, Taunton, a notable scholar who became an inspector of schools for Wales, and his wife, Annie Edith Bainbridge. Darlington was educated at Shrewsbury School and at St John's College, Cambridge, where he obtained a second class in the classical tripos (1912) and a third in the medieval and modern languages tripos (1913). He was devoted to cricket and rowed in his college boat. He was commissioned in the 7th battalion of the Northumberland Fusiliers in 1915, and served in the trenches (being wounded at Arras) during the First World War, at the end of which he

was a captain. He enjoyed himself even in such conditions, and in 1916 he began sending humorous sketches to *Punch* from the trenches. On 3 October 1918 he married Marjorie (1889/90–1973), daughter of Sydney Sheppard, a member of the stock exchange; they had two daughters, one of whom predeceased him.

After the war Darlington took up journalism as a profession and was editor for a brief period of *The World*. He wrote a successful novel, *Alf's Button* (1925), which was equally successfully dramatized. He followed these up with other Alf stories, and a burlesque of *The Streets of London* (1932) by Dion Boucicault. He also wrote an autobiography with the expressive title *I Do What I Like* (1947). But his life work was his drama criticism for the *Daily Telegraph*.

This covered a forty-eight-year period, from 1920 to 1968, and a series of theatrical developments unparalleled in the career of any other metropolitan critic. Darlington came into professional London criticism with the last plays of John Galsworthy; he followed the philosophical plays of J. B. Priestley during the 1930s, the poetic drama of Christopher Fry and T. S. Eliot after the Second World War, and the theatrical revolution brought about by John Osborne and the Royal Court dramatists after the production of *Look Back in Anger* in 1956. He retired in 1968 after the opening night of *Hair*, which was the first play to introduce nudity to the public stage, and was the first public production after the abolition of censorship. Many people thought it symbolic that Darlington and the authority over the theatre of the lord chamberlain should leave the stage simultaneously.

Darlington's preference was always for the well-made, well-bred type of drama, but he was by no means intolerant. Greatly as the young lions of the kitchen sink drama affronted his convictions, Darlington did his best to be fair to them. He regarded them with the benevolent air of a genial uncle giving the benefit of the doubt to a group of nephews and nieces who had suddenly become unruly. Curiously and dramatically, it was only on the very last night of his professional career that his attitude of friendliness to the young (whom he lived to see grow to middle age) became acerbic. The first night of *Hair* was the only dramatic event to disturb the peaceful, even flow of Darlington's years of gentle activity. *Hair* was presented by young people who were briefly known as flower children. Members of the revolutionary youth of the 1968 movement which began in the Latin quarter of Paris, they believed in brotherly love in a boisterous way, and at the end of the performance, just as Darlington was hurrying from the theatre to catch his last deadline, several of them leaped from the stage and together embraced Mrs Darlington, who was frightened and called out to a colleague for help. Thus a disillusioned Darlington finished his professional career.

Darlington had a streak of hardness which sometimes showed itself in his behaviour to his subordinates, but he was a well loved figure, and influential in his low-keyed, lucid, middle-of-the-road reviews. His long life was distinguished by his eminence in his profession, his delight in it, and the happiness of his disposition and his marriage. He was appointed CBE in 1967, and he was unique in his profession in that, whenever a colleague received any honour, he never failed, even up to his ninetieth year, to send his congratulations. His generosity of mind was shown also in his criticisms, which exactly hit the taste of the large majority of middle-class theatregoers. Yet beneath the smooth surface of his work there was a stern moral and social conviction, which sometimes revealed itself in a sudden flash of ruthless condemnation. Of a fellow critic with whom he regularly played golf he once remarked, 'He was a very wicked man'; and he meant it. Darlington died on 24 May 1979 at Seaford, Sussex.

HAROLD HOBSON, *rev.*

Sources *Daily Telegraph* (25 May 1979) · *Daily Telegraph* (28 May 1979) · *The Times* (23 Nov 1979) · personal knowledge (1988) · m. cert. · *CGPLA Eng. & Wales* (1979)

Wealth at death £3502: probate, 2 Nov 1979, *CGPLA Eng. & Wales*

Darly, Mary (*fl.* 1760–1781). *See under* Darly, Matthew (*c.*1720–1778?).

Darly, Matthew [Matthias] (*c.*1720–1778?), designer and printseller, is of obscure origins: nothing is known of his parents, his early life, or by which name he was baptized. He used Matthias about as frequently as Matthew. In 1735 he was apprenticed to the clockmaker Umfraville Sampson, implying that he was probably born about 1720. In 1749 he was one of several printsellers rounded up by the government for questioning about several satirical prints which ridiculed the duke of Cumberland. At that time Darly had a shop in Duke's Court, St Martin's Lane, London, opposite Old Slaughter's Coffee House. Shown *The Agreeable Contrast*, he admitted acquiring a hundred, of which 'his Wife has sold several' (Atherton, 80), in exchange for a book of ornament—presumably his own freshly published *New Book of Ornament* (1749). In 1749, then, Darly was probably married (although he may have been the Matthias Darly who married Elizabeth Harold at St George's, Mayfair, Westminster, on 15 April 1750), publishing designs for carved furniture and, through his wife, retailing political satires. This was to be the pattern of his career, although he had trained as an engraver and undertook jobbing engraving such as visiting cards and shop bills and was also a drawing-master, later styling himself 'professor and teacher of ornament'.

As a designer Darly was a central figure at a time when English craftsmen were struggling for a distinct identity and for preference over foreign rivals. In 1751 he issued *A New-Book of Chinese, Gothic and Modern Chairs* intended for hermitages and garden temples. A second book containing prints of 'parlour chairs' is known only from reissued impressions in Robert Manwaring's *The Chair-Maker's Guide* (1766). He took William Darling as apprentice in 1752 and in 1753 he took over Thomas Chippendale's lease in Northumberland Court, sharing a house with the furniture designer and his family while engraving 98 out of 147 of the signed plates in Chippendale's *The Gentleman's and Cabinet-Maker's Director* (1754), which he then helped to sell. A trade card in the British Museum advertises his

Matthew Darly (*c.*1720–1778?), self-portrait, pubd 1771

'Manufactory for Paper Hangings' with 'Modern, Gothic or Chinese' designs. In partnership with the ornithologist George Edwards he published *A New Book of Chinese Designs* (1754). These designs were widely adopted by manufacturers to decorate porcelain, delftware, and printed cotton.

In 1756 Edwards and Darly took a shop at the Golden Acorn opposite Hungerford market in the Strand and published a burst of caricatures, several of which were designed by their near neighbour, the politician George Townshend. Significantly, this was the first occasion on which caricature—exaggeration of facial features—was fused with political satire, of which it later became a characteristic element. Another innovation was the small but hard-wearing caricature card.

In 1762 Darly's wife assumed responsibility for this aspect of their business. At what point **Mary Darly** (*fl.* 1760–1781) joined Matthew is uncertain. She described herself as 'Fun Merchant, at the Acorn in Ryder's Court, Fleet Street' (Clayton, 215). She may have been the wife mentioned in 1749. On the other hand, the fact that Matthew and Mary Darly had five children between 1761 and 1770 and not (apparently) earlier suggests that she may have been his second wife. When, in early 1762, a new shop at the Acorn in Ryder's Court near Leicester Fields began to advertise caricatures, it was Mary Darly who was named as publisher. Her principal targets were the dowager princess of Wales, her alleged paramour the earl of Bute, and his allegedly locust-like Scottish friends and relations, of whom the Darlys promised prints 'as fast as their Needles will move, and Aqua fortis Bite' (*Public Advertiser*, 28 Sept 1762). To this end Mary welcomed contributions from the general public: 'Gentlemen and Ladies may have any Sketch or Fancy of their own, engraved, etched &c. with the utmost Despatch and Secrecy' (ibid.). That she herself was the etcher of these designs was established by her offer to 'have them either Engrav'd, etched, or Dry-Needled, by their humble Servant' (ibid.). In October she published the first part of *Principles of Caricatura* (1762) which according to the title-page provided guidance in drawing caricatures and which reinforced her offer to give exposure in the capital to the ideas of provincial amateurs: 'any carrick will be etched and published that the Authoress shall be favoured with, Post paid'. Styling herself 'fun merchant', Mary Darly fostered enthusiasm for graphic satire, cultivated a polite audience, and increased sensitivity to caricature as an artistic convention.

In 1766 the Darlys moved to 39 Strand, the shop depicted in *The Macaroni Print Shop* (1772). It continued to supply not only caricature and ornament, but a range of equipment for the amateur artist and decorator—'materials of every kind used in the Polite Arts of Drawing, Etching, &c with all Sorts of Drawing books for young Ladies and Gentlemen' (*Public Advertiser*, 1 Jan 1779), borders and decorations for print rooms and screens, as well as 'Ladies Stencils for painting Silks, Linens, Paper, &c, by Mary Darly' (ibid., 13 June 1769). It also sold portraits and history prints.

Meanwhile Matthew Darly had continued his respectable career as a designer with *A New Book of Ceilings* (1760). He contributed to Robert Sayer's *Household Furniture in Genteel Taste* (1760) and engraved the plates for William Ince and John Mayhew's *Universal System of Household Furniture* (1762). He was also responsible for forty-one of the plates in volume 4 of *Vitruvius Britannicus* (1767) by John Woolfe and James Gandon. He exhibited four of these with the Society of Artists, as well as some of his designs for vases and ornaments for print rooms, between 1765 and 1770 and with the Free Society in 1771. His later publications included *Sixty Vases* (1769), *The Ornamental Architect* (1769–71), *A New Book of Ornaments* (1772), and *A Compleat Body of Architecture* (1773).

In the early 1770s after the Wilkesite disturbances the Darlys relinquished political satire and instead published satires of fashion, manners, and well-known individuals. Inviting sketches and ideas, they warned that 'illiberal and indelicate Hints, such as one marked A. Z. [were] not admissible' and that 'low or political Subjects will not be noticed' (*Public Advertiser*, 15 and 22 Oct 1772). Contributions were received from a variety of amateurs, including the talented William Henry Bunbury, Edward Topham, and Richard St George Mansergh. Prints mocking affected macaronis and extremes of dress and coiffure were characteristic. In 1773 they held an exhibition of 233 original drawings for prints. Collected sets were offered from 1772 with a portrait of Matthew Darly dated 1771 as frontispiece (BM 4632).

The decline of the Darlys is as obscure as their rise. A hostile caricature of Matthew Darly (BM 5367) showed him old, corpulent, and gouty, standing beside an ass and proclaiming 'We are Professors of Design'. Musgrave's *Obituary Prior to 1800* records his death in 1775 but Atkins notes an apprentice taken in 1778. All prints published after 1775 are signed 'MDarly' except one by 'Mathina' (BM 5441). The collected volume of *Darly's Comic Prints of Characters: Caricatures, Macaronies etc. Dedicated to D. Garrick* (1776) was published by Mary Darly. Characteristically, she advertised it as 'the most entertaining Work ever published in Europe' (*Public Advertiser*, 1 Jan 1779). She (or they) continued to publish caricatures regularly to the end of 1779 but then output declined sharply. The last prints, dated 1781, were published from a new address, 159 Fleet Street. Examples of the Darlys' prints are in the Bodleian Library, Oxford; the British Museum, London; the Lewis Walpole Library, Farmington, Connecticut; the Library of Congress, Washington; and the New York Public Library.

TIMOTHY CLAYTON

Sources F. G. Stephens and M. D. George, eds., *Catalogue of prints and drawings in the British Museum, division 1: political and personal satires*, 11 vols. in 12 (1870–1954) · F. G. Stephens and M. D. George, eds., *Catalogue of political and personal satires preserved … in the British Museum*, 5–11 (1935–54) · *Public Advertiser* (2 Sept 1762) · *Public Advertiser* (28 Sept 1762) · *Public Advertiser* (13 June 1769) · *Public Advertiser* (15 Oct 1772) · *Public Advertiser* (22 Oct 1772) · *Public Advertiser* (1 Jan 1779) · W. Musgrave, *Obituary prior to 1800*, ed. G. J. Armytage, 6 vols., Harleian Society, 44–9 (1899–1901) · H. Atherton, *Political prints in the age of Hogarth* (1974) · E. Harris and N. Savage, *British architectural books and writers, 1556–1785* (1990) · T. Clayton, *The English print, 1688–1802* (1997) · C. Gilbert, 'The early furniture designs of Matthias Darly', *Furniture History*, 11 (1975), 33–9 · C. Gilbert, *The life and work of Thomas Chippendale* (1978) · M. D. George, *Hogarth to Cruikshank: social change in graphic satire* (1967) · D. Donald, *The age of caricature: satirical prints in the reign of George III* (1996) · C. Atkins, *Register of the apprentices of the Worshipful Company of Clockmakers* (1931) · J. Döring, *Eine Kunstgeschichte der frühen englischen Karikatur* (Hildesheim, 1991)

Likenesses M. Darly, self-portrait, etching, 1771, BM; repro. in M. Darly, *Darly's comic prints of characters* (1776), frontispiece · M. Darly, self-portrait, etching and line engraving, pubd 1771, BM, NPG [*see illus.*] · etching, pubd 1772, NPG · caricature, 1775, BM · line engraving medallion, pubd 1775, NPG · M. Darly, caricature (Mary Darly?), BM; repro. in *The female connoisseur* (1772)

Darnall, Sir John (d. 1706), lawyer, was the son of Ralph Darnall of Loughton Hope, near Pembridge, Herefordshire, and of Gray's Inn, who was clerk to the parliament during the protectorate. Darnall's date of birth is unknown, but he matriculated at King's College, Cambridge, in 1662 and was admitted to Gray's Inn on 2 December 1662. He was admitted to the Middle Temple on 7 June 1670 and was called to the bar on 22 November 1672. He had married his wife Mary by September 1671 when his son Herbert, was baptized at Canon Pyon, Herefordshire. Another son, Sir John *Darnall, was baptized there in 1673. Darnall first came to prominence in 1680 after being assigned to argue an exception taken by the earl of Castlemaine to the evidence of Dangerfield, on the grounds that the witness had been convicted of felony. Lord Chief Justice Scroggs inclined for a while in favour of the exception, but eventually overruled it. Darnall also defended John Giles, tried for the murder of a justice of the peace named Arnold in the same year.

In June 1690 Darnall was assigned by special grace of the

court to show cause why one Crone, who had been found guilty of raising money for the service of the exiled James II and sentenced to death, should not be executed. The alleged grounds were that the indictment was bad because the endorsement contained a clerical error, 'vera' being spelt 'verra'. Darnall was made a serjeant-at-law in April 1692. He defended Peter Cooke from the charge of conspiring to assassinate the king in 1696. He was made a king's serjeant on 30 January 1699, and was knighted on 1 June. In the same year he appeared with the attorney-general Trevor for the crown on the information brought against Charles Duncombe, for falsely endorsing exchequer bills and paying them into the Excise Office with intent to defraud the revenue, although the case broke down. In June 1700 there were rumours that Darnall would be made a judge. In November 1701 he was employed in one of the actions involving the Kentish petitioner David Polhill; however, in the following month he was reported to be very ill. He was reappointed a queen's serjeant in 1702, and that year he was employed in the prosecution of William Fuller, an informer. Darnall was engaged in the prosecution of John Tutchin, the author of *The Observator*, for seditious libel in 1704. In the same year he prosecuted Nathaniel Denew and others for an assault against William Colepeper. Darnall died at his house in Essex Street, the Strand, on 14 December 1706, and was buried on 20 December in the chancel of St Clement Danes. His will, made on 23 November 1706, referred to his 'satisfaction' that the 'entire confidence between my wife and our only son', John (PRO, PROB 11/492/6), would mean that his wife would be well provided for. His eldest son, Herbert, had committed suicide in 1694.

J. M. RIGG, *rev.* STUART HANDLEY

Sources *Le Neve's Pedigrees of the knights*, ed. G. W. Marshall, Harleian Society, 8 (1873), 467 · Sainty, *King's counsel*, 24 · Baker, *Serjeants*, 451, 508 · will, PRO, PROB 11/492, sig. 6 · *IGI* · Venn, *Alum. Cant.* · J. Foster, *The register of admissions to Gray's Inn, 1521–1889, together with the register of marriages in Gray's Inn chapel, 1695–1754* (privately printed, London, 1889), 294 · H. A. C. Sturgess, ed., *Register of admissions to the Honourable Society of the Middle Temple, from the fifteenth century to the year 1944*, 1 (1949), 181 · *State trials*, 8.1085–6, 13.311–98, 1061–1106, 14.903, 1099, 1110 · N. Luttrell, *A brief historical relation of state affairs from September 1678 to April 1714*, 3 (1857), 512; 4 (1857), 652–3; 5 (1857), 112, 116; 6 (1857), 117

Darnall, Sir John (*bap.* 1673, *d.* 1735), lawyer, was baptized on 17 September 1673 at Canon Pyon, Herefordshire, the son of Sir John *Darnall (*d.* 1706), serjeant-at-law, and his wife, Mary. He was admitted to the Middle Temple on 26 October 1689, and was called to the bar on 24 May 1695. In 1710 he defended Dammaree, Willis, and Purchase, charged with high treason for organizing a riot near Lincoln's Inn Fields in support of Dr Sacheverell. Dammaree was found guilty and sentenced, but was later pardoned.

In 1715 Darnall was created a serjeant-at-law, and he was knighted in 1724. The same year he was appointed a judge of the court of Marshalsea. In 1717 Darnall was asked his opinion on whether the king was entitled to the custody of his grandchildren, when the prince of Wales appealed to have his children returned to his care after he had been expelled from court. Although he advised that everyone had the right to the custody of his own children, the decision went against the prince, and it was ruled that according to English law the royal grandchildren belonged to the crown. In 1719 Darnall appeared for the crown in the case of the Revd William Hendley, indicted at Rochester for using children to collect money for the Pretender during a church service by pretending to be raising money for a charity school. Other cases included the defence of Thomas Bambridge, warden of the Fleet Prison, tried at the Old Bailey in 1724 for murdering a prisoner by putting him in a cell with a man suffering from smallpox so that he would catch the infection and die. Bambridge was acquitted. In 1733 Darnall was put on a commission appointed to inquire into the fees charged in the courts of justice.

Darnall married Margaret (*d.* 1741), daughter of Sir Thomas Jenner. They had two daughters and lived in a large house in Petersham, Surrey. He died on 5 September 1735, at Petersham, and was buried in Petersham churchyard. J. M. RIGG, *rev.* ANNE PIMLOTT BAKER

Sources H. W. Woolrych, *Lives of eminent serjeants-at-law of the English bar*, 2 vols. (1869) · Baker, *Serjeants*, 508 · R. Hatton, *George I: elector and king* (1978) · J. Hutchinson, ed., *A catalogue of notable Middle Templars: with brief biographical notices* (1902) · *GM*, 1st ser., 5 (1735), 559 · *IGI*

Darnell, George (1799?–1857), schoolmaster, was born at Barton in the Beans near Market Bosworth, Leicestershire, probably in 1799, the son of Samuel Darnell and his wife, Sarah. He ran a preparatory school at Market Harborough and then established, and conducted for many years, a large classical day school at Islington, where he was living by 1851. With a somewhat feeble body, but an active and shrewd mind and a kind heart, he attempted to make the beginnings of school work less uninviting to the pupil.

Darnell's principles underlay his educational writings, *Short and Certain Road to Reading* (1845), *Grammar Made Intelligible to Children* (1846), and *Arithmetic Made Intelligible to Children* (1855), which for many years had an enormous sale. The prefaces to these short works contained practical suggestions, which were new at the time but which came to be widely adopted by teachers. His series of copybooks were long and widely used in elementary schools, and for many years 'Darnell's copybooks' was a household name. They were started about 1840, and Darnell was the first to introduce the plan of giving a line of copy in pale ink to be first written over by the pupil, then to be imitated by him in the next line, the copy being thus always under the young writer's eye. Darnell, who was unmarried, died at 70 Gibson Square, Islington, on 26 February 1857, aged fifty-eight. He had at least two sisters, Esther and Anne, and two brothers, John and Thomas, the latter of whom was a teacher and educational writer in Islington.

CHARLES WELSH, *rev.* M. C. CURTHOYS

Sources *GM*, 3rd ser., 2 (1857), 499 · Boase, *Mod. Eng. biog.* · will, PRO, PROB 11/2247/186 · d. cert.

Darnell, Sir Thomas, baronet (*d.* in or before 1638), landowner, was the son of Sir Thomas Darnall (*d.* in or before

1609) of Thornholme, Yorkshire, and Stickford, Lincolnshire, and his wife, Helen (d. 1638), daughter of Sir John Stanlow of Stickford. Darnell was admitted to Lincoln's Inn in London in May 1613 having, possibly, matriculated at St John's College, Cambridge, at Easter in 1610. He succeeded his father in 1609 and was created a baronet on 6 September 1621. He married Sarah, daughter of Sir Thomas Fisher of Islington, Middlesex. Darnell's main properties were in Lincolnshire and London.

Darnell's chief claim to fame is as one of the defendants in the celebrated *Five Knights case*, a landmark in the history of *habeas corpus* and a direct cause of the petition of right. This was a rather unexpected role for Darnell: unlike the other defendants he did not have any prior reputation as a 'country patriot', nor was he active in local government or politics. He appears to have lived for the most part in London and, this episode apart, to have maintained a low public profile. His involvement in the case stemmed from his appointment as a forced loan commissioner for Lincolnshire in February 1627. Since he had not paid the loan on his property in Middlesex, the privy council ordered him to travel north with the earl of Rutland, the lord lieutenant of Lincolnshire, to help to relaunch the service in the county. At the meeting at Lincoln on 7 March Darnell and five other commissioners refused to lend the king the money required. When told that 'such as refuse doe incurre the king's high displeasure' he answered that 'he hoped he should have the libertie of a subject to dispose his money and estate at his pleasure' (PRO, SP 16/56/39).

On the privy council's orders, Darnell was committed to the Fleet prison, where he became part of a network of gentry loan refusers in various London prisons who kept up a campaign of protest over their treatment. In June it was reported that he and his fellow Lincolnshire refusers, William Anderson and Sir William Armine, were refusing to accede to the council's request that they leave London for confinement in the shires, 'lest by that means they should bar themselves of the benefit of a *habeas corpus*'. They were also said to be seeking 'a judicial trial in Kings Bench, whether they have committed any offence or no' (*Fairfax Correspondence*, 1.68–9).

The case finally came to trial in November 1627, when the five loan refusers—Sir John Corbet, Sir Walter Earle, Sir Edmund Hampden, Sir John Heveningham, and Darnell—were given leave to sue for a writ of *habeas corpus* from the king's bench. The defendants' counsel cited Magna Carta and ancient statutes to demonstrate that the privy council had imprisoned them without due process of law. In response, Attorney-General Heath claimed that in previous cases involving national security the king had been allowed to keep prisoners confined without having to show cause. The judges largely accepted Heath's argument and refused to grant the prisoners bail. Darnell and his fellow refusers remained in prison until 2 January 1628, when the king gave orders for their release in preparation for the coming parliament.

Little is known about Darnell after this. He was called before the 1628 parliament to testify about a sermon he had heard preached in London by Roger Mainwaring, and during the 1630s he was involved in a lawsuit concerning the property of his mother-in-law. His own mother made her will in October 1638, by which date he had died, leaving one daughter.   RICHARD CUST

Sources S. R. Gardiner, *The history of England, 1603–1642*, 10 vols. (1904), 6.213–17 · R. P. Cust, *The forced loan and English politics, 1626–1628* (1987) · C. Holmes, *Seventeenth-century Lincolnshire* (1980) · A. R. Maddison, ed., *Lincolnshire pedigrees*, 4 vols., Harleian Society, 50–52, 55 (1902–6), vols. 1, 3 · state papers, domestic, Charles I, PRO, SP 16 · *APC, 1627–8* · R. C. Johnson and others, eds., *Proceedings in parliament, 1628*, 6 vols. (1977–83) · G. W. Johnson, ed., *The Fairfax correspondence: memoirs of the reign of Charles the First*, 1 (1848), 68–9 · PRO, SP 16/56/39 · Venn, *Alum. Cant.* · W. P. Baildon, ed., *The records of the Honorable Society of Lincoln's Inn: admissions*, 1 (1896), 162 · IGI

Darnell, William Nicholas (1776–1865), Church of England clergyman and antiquary, was born in Newcastle upon Tyne on 14 March 1776, the only son of William Darnell (1731/2–1813), a wine merchant, and his wife, Frances, daughter of Michael Dawson and widow of William Cook. Educated at the Newcastle grammar school under the auspices of two able scholars, the Revds Hugh and Edward Moises, uncle and nephew, successively headmasters, he was elected to the Durham scholarship at Corpus Christi College, Oxford, where he matriculated in 1792. Graduating BA in 1796, MA in 1800, and BD in 1808, he became a fellow and tutor of his college. He was appointed university examiner in 1801, 1803, and 1804, and select preacher in 1807. Among his more distinguished pupils at Corpus was John Keble, who long afterwards, in 1847, dedicated to his former tutor a volume of sermons 'in ever grateful memory of invaluable helps and warnings received from him in early youth'.

Darnell left Oxford in 1809, having been presented by Archdeacon Robert Thorp to the rectory of St Mary-le-Bow in Durham, which he held until 1815. In that year he was collated to the vicarage of Stockton upon Tees by Bishop Barrington, and married Elizabeth (d. 1864), daughter of Revd William Bowe, headmaster of Scorton School. On 12 January 1816 Barrington gave him the ninth stall, and on 12 October 1820 translated him to the sixth stall in Durham Cathedral.

From 1820 to 1827 Darnell was perpetual curate of St Margaret's in Durham, and from 1827 to 1831 vicar of Norham, both of these livings being in the gift of the dean and chapter. Together with his stall and incumbency in the diocese of Durham, he held for several years previously to 1828 the vicarage of Lastingham, in the North Riding of Yorkshire, one of the most widely scattered parishes in England, a preferment which he owed to Lord Chancellor Eldon, his fellow townsman and a relation, by marriage, to Darnell's sister Lucy. Darnell was of necessity non-resident at Lastingham, but when he visited the place he considerably raised the stipend of the curate in charge. In 1831, on the advancement of Darnell's Corpus friend Henry Phillpotts to the see of Exeter, he exchanged his stall at Durham for the valuable rectory of Stanhope, co. Durham, reputedly worth £6000 a year, which he continued to hold until his death there on 19 June 1865. He was buried on the 24th in the churchyard of Durham Cathedral, leaving a large family.

Darnell printed some occasional discourses, including a sermon preached at the archdeacon's visitation at St Mary-le-Bow in 1810, one on the death of George III, preached at Stockton, one on the death of Princess Charlotte, also preached at Stockton, one on the death of Archdeacon Bowyer in Durham Cathedral in 1826, and one on the death of his friend and schoolfellow Henry Burrell of Lincoln's Inn, preached at Bolton Chapel in Northumberland. He was also the author of *Two charges delivered in the years 1828 and 1829 to the clergy of the officialty of the dean and chapter of Durham* (1829). In 1816 he issued a volume of sermons dedicated to his patron, Bishop Barrington, and in 1818 an abridgement of Jeremy Taylor's *Great Exemplar of Sanctity*. In 1831 he edited from the manuscripts in the Dean and Chapter Library the *Correspondence of Isaac Basire*, archdeacon of Northumberland and prebendary of Durham in the reigns of Charles I and Charles II. He also published an edition of the *Book of Wisdom, with a Short Preface and Notes*, and in 1839 *An Arrangement and Classification of the Psalms*. His *Lines Suggested by the Death of Lord Collingwood*, another distinguished pupil of the Newcastle grammar school, were reprinted by John Adamson in 1842. A well-written ballad from his pen entitled 'The king of the Picts and St Cuthbert' was published in James Raine's *History and Antiquities of North Durham* (1852). A popular ballad, 'On the Loss of a Vessel called the Northern Star', was said to have been written by him in 1810.

In 1804 Darnell became a fellow of the Society of Antiquaries, and was a founder member of the kindred society of Newcastle upon Tyne. In 1812 he was one of the committee appointed to administer the funds raised by subscription for illustrating Robert Surtees's *History of Durham*. He was chosen in 1826 to be a trustee of the charities of Lord Crewe, bishop of Durham, which 'enabled him to exchange occasionally the leafy shades of Stanhope for the bracing breezes of Bamborough Castle, and thus his life was prolonged beyond the usual span' (Welford). Among other useful works he built a church at Thornley, in the parish of Wolsingham, where he had an estate, and instituted the Darnell School Prize Fund for the encouragement of the study of the prayer book in parochial schools. GORDON GOODWIN, *rev.* M. C. CURTHOYS

Sources R. Welford, *Men of mark 'twixt Tyne and Tweed*, 3 vols. (1895) · Boase, *Mod. Eng. biog.* · Foster, *Alum. Oxon.* · R. Surtees, *The history and antiquities of the county palatine of Durham*, 4 vols. (1816–40)

Archives U. Newcastle, Robinson L., letters to Sir Walter Trevelyan

Wealth at death under £60,000: probate, 11 Sept 1865, *CGPLA Eng. & Wales*

Darnley. For this title name *see* Stewart, John, Lord Darnley (*c*.1531–1563); Stewart, Henry, duke of Albany [*known as* Lord Darnley] (1545/6–1567); Bligh, Ivo Francis Walter, eighth earl of Darnley (1859–1927).

Darnton, (Philip) Christian (1905–1981), composer and writer, was born on 30 October 1905 in Leeds, the third son

(Philip) **Christian Darnton** (1905–1981), by Howard Coster, 1940

and third among the three children of John Edward Darnton, formerly von Schunck (1869–1940), landowner, and his wife, Mary Gertrude (1871–1952), daughter of Henry Illingworth and his wife, Mary. In the eighteenth century the von Schuncks had been raised to a barony of the holy Roman empire, but the change of name was effected in 1913 in response to the will of Darnton's paternal grandmother, Kate Schunck. Darnton was educated privately and at Chilverton Elms School and Down House, Rottingdean, before attending Gonville and Caius College, Cambridge, from 1923 to 1926. He studied composition under Charles Wood but took no degree, then spent a year at the Royal College of Music, London, studying the bassoon and conducting. His compositional style was epigrammatic, strongly contrapuntal, and ruthlessly dissonant. In March 1927, at the Grotrian Hall, his parents mounted a complete concert of his principal works to date, including his first string quartet, op. 23, and first piano sonata, op. 33 (both composed in 1925). The project was almost universally criticized in the press and prompted a further course of study in Berlin with Max Butting from 1928.

During his time in Germany Darnton met the artist Joan Mary Bell (1905–2001), daughter of Charles Bell, formerly Zimmermann, merchant: the name was changed in 1916 to avoid anti-German sentiment. They were married on 20 November 1929 at Kensington register office and had two sons: John Nicholas (1933–2002) and Charles Leigh (*b.* 1942), the latter named after Darnton's fellow composer and close friend Walter Leigh, who had been killed in action at Tobruk a few months before the child's birth.

In 1931, after a brief and unsuccessful appointment at Stowe School, Darnton embarked on a journalistic career, becoming assistant editor of a new paper, the *Music Lover*, under Edwin Evans, a notable supporter of his. Some of Darnton's articles were published after the magazine's demise as *Chats with the Orchestra* (British Continental Press, 1934). In 1936, with Benjamin Britten, Alan Rawsthorne, and the pianist Adolph Hallis, Darnton became a founder member of the Hallis Concerts Society, a body dedicated to promoting contemporary composers as well as reviving the works of earlier masters. His *Suite concertante* for violin and orchestra was one of the earliest of the compositions to be written for the society, but the première of his *Five Orchestral Pieces* at the International Society for Contemporary Music Festival in Warsaw in 1939 constituted his first major success and aroused the admiration of the musical administrator and composer Edward Clark. Extremely brief but teeming with colour, they were one of the most advanced works by any English composer of the time. At this time he also published *You and Music* (1940), a flawed but readable introduction to the subject. Clark remained a staunch friend, and Darnton acted as a character witness for him in court in 1953 when Clark was accused by the composer Benjamin Frankel of embezzling the funds of the International Society for Contemporary Music.

Darnton had joined the Communist Party by early 1941 and was soon persuaded that his avant-garde harmonic language ought to be simplified in order to get his work more widely understood. An early result of this new approach was the rousing cantata *Ballad of Freedom* (1941–2) to words by a close friend, the left-wing poet Randall Swingler, which the BBC declined to broadcast for reasons of national security. In general, this change of direction also proved unsuccessful from a musical point of view. It may, however, have assisted the provision of incidental music for documentary films, which Darnton undertook from 1944 to 1946 (notably *A Harbour Goes to France* of 1944), and for productions by the Old Vic Theatre Company, including Peter Ustinov's *The Tragedy of Good Intentions* (1945). Darnton's major success at this time was his third symphony (1944), but *Cantilena* for string orchestra (1946) and the Stravinsky-influenced *Epic Suite* for violin and piano also received several performances, being among the handful of his works to be published.

During the Second World War Darnton worked in civil defence, but he was injured in a fall and was left partially paralysed. This was probably a suicide attempt and certainly exacerbated a profound personality change and the end of his marriage, although the divorce was not finalized until 1952. Before meeting his future second wife, Vera, Darnton had a wild affair with Elisabeth Balchin [see Ayrton, Elisabeth Evelyn (1910–1991)], then still the wife of the novelist Nigel Balchin, who caricatured him quite viciously in at least three of his books, principally *Mine Own Executioner* (1945). Darnton's unfinished second symphony, 'The anagram', was dedicated 'to my memory of

E.B.' and was constructed around the musical notes C-D and E-B (his own initials and those of Elisabeth). On 2 October 1953 he married Vera Blanche Martin, *née* Anstee (1900/01–1988), a dancer and teacher, at Caxton Hall; his cantata *Jet Pilot* was written in memory of Vera's son, who was killed in a Meteor jet accident in 1951. Although this work had some success in 1953, Darnton had placed greater hopes in his allegorical opera *Fantasy Fair*, written with Swingler for the opera competition promoted by the Arts Council to mark the Festival of Britain. His discovery that the opera was not even seen by the judges caused his resignation from composition, and following the Soviet invasion of Hungary in 1956 he also renounced politics, turning instead to poetry, essay writing, and extensive travel.

It was almost twenty years before Darnton's next musical work appeared: a virtuosic concerto for orchestra (1973), founded on the pattern of ancient Greek drama. It was followed in 1978 by *A Twenty-Minute Symphony*, subtitled 'Diabolus in musica' in acknowledgement of the 'forbidden' interval of a tritone on which it was based. Darnton did not live to hear the first performance of this work, which was given on 23 September 1981 by the BBC Northern Symphony Orchestra under Edward Downes. He died on 14 April that year in Hove, Sussex, having failed to recover from a bladder operation. In accordance with his wishes, no religious ceremony was performed after his death, and he was cremated at Brighton and Hove crematorium, where his ashes were scattered.

ANDREW PLANT

Sources music MSS, corresp., and papers, BL, Christian Darnton collection, Add. MSS 62717–62774 · J. E. Darnton, *The von Schunck family: a history of the Hanau branch and connections* (privately printed, 1933) · D. ApIvor, 'Christian Darnton', *Composer*, 74 (1981–2), 13–19 · A. Plant, '(Philip) Christian Darnton', *New Grove*, 2nd edn · A. Plant, 'The life and music of Christian Darnton', PhD diss., U. Birm., 2002 · m. certs. · private information (2004) [Nicholas Darnton]
Archives BL, music MSS, corresp., and papers, Add. MSS 62717–62774 | BL, corresp. with Nancy Cunard, Add. MS 62763 · McMaster University, Hamilton, Ontario, ApIvor MSS, letters to D. ApIvor | FILM BFI NFTVA · IWM FVA · National Archives of Canada | SOUND BL NSA
Likenesses photograph, 1924, Gon. & Caius Cam. · H. Coster, five photographs, c.1940, NPG · H. Coster, photograph, 1940, NPG [*see illus.*]

Darracott, Risdon (1717–1759), Independent minister, was born at Swanage on 1 February 1717. His father, Richard Darracott (1688–1727), was the Independent minister there, having trained at Taunton Academy, and his mother, married in 1714, was Hannah Risdon (1693–1717). Both parents were descended from families long connected with Bideford, Devon. Their first child, a daughter, married Isaac Clark, a dissenting minister at Bow, Devon. Hannah died on 10 February 1717, at the age of twenty-three, after giving birth to Risdon Darracott, her second child. When the boy was about five years old his father moved to Chulmleigh, Devon. He was taught at first by his father, but then educated under William Palke, the dissenting minister of South Molton. In 1732, aged fifteen, having decided to enter the nonconformist ministry, he went to the academy of Philip Doddridge at Northampton. As a student Darracott preached in villages near Northampton, once, at Brixworth, being attacked in a riot. He left the academy in August 1737 with a certificate of proficiency. For a short time in 1738 he preached at Chulmleigh, but the congregation was divided in its choice of minister, and Darracott's first charge was at the Market Jew Street Chapel, Penzance, Cornwall. He was there from the autumn of 1738 to the beginning of the following year, resigning when he became ill and moved to Barnstaple to recover.

Early in 1741 Darracott became minister of the dissenting congregation at Wellington, Somerset, succeeding Humphrey Berry. He was ordained there on 11 November 1741 by twelve local ministers. He married, on 15 December 1741, Katherine Besley (d. 1799) of Barnstaple. He remained in Wellington until he died, labouring in that town and neighbourhood and increasing his congregation from 28 to over 300. He was the friend and correspondent of Doddridge, Whitefield, Samuel Walker of Truro, Benjamin Fawcett, and James Hervey. Doddridge described him as 'Absolutely the most successful Minister I have known amongst us for many years' (Calendar, ed. Nuttall, 151), while Whitefield called him a 'Star in the West' (Bennett, 81).

Darracott's bodily constitution was not strong, and after many attacks of illness he died at his South Street home in Wellington on 14 March 1759. He was buried at 1 a.m. on 19 March 1759 at Wellington. His funeral sermon was preached there on 15 April by his old friend the Revd Benjamin Fawcett of Kidderminster, who had also trained under Doddridge and from 1741 to 1745 had been assistant at Pauls Meeting, Taunton. The sermon was printed, passing through four impressions at least. Darracott's tract entitled Scripture Marks of Salvation was published in 1756. Over 70,000 copies were circulated in many editions, dedicated to his friends at Wellington. In 1813 James Bennett of Romsey published a memoir of Darracott, entitled The Star of the West, which was reprinted in a slightly enlarged second edition in 1815.

Darracott, in his will, left his house and property in South Street to his wife, who died on 28 December 1799, aged eighty-six. Her body was removed from Romsey to Wellington to be buried near her husband. Risdon and Katherine had six children, but only two survived, Katherine and Richard. Katherine married John Comley of Romsey in 1765 at Taunton. They had a daughter, who married the Revd James Bennett, the author of the memoir. Richard became a minister, training at Daventry Academy and afterwards preaching around Taunton; he died on 23 March 1795. In 1972 Darracott's church in Fore Street became Wellington United Reformed Church.

W. P. COURTNEY, rev. BRIAN W. KIRK

Sources J. Bennett, The star of the west, 2nd edn (1815) [incl. 'Extracts from correspondence', 176–224, and 'Scripture marks of salvation' as a sep. appx (24 pp.)] • A. L. Humphreys, Materials for the history of the town and parish of Wellington in the county of Somerset, 1 (1908) [abstract of will, 34] • A. L. Humphreys, Materials for the history of the town and parish of Wellington in the county of Somerset, 3 (1913), 341–53 • Calendar of the correspondence of Philip Doddridge, ed. G. F. Nuttall, HMC, JP 26 (1979) • C. Stanford, Philip Doddridge D.D. (1880) • B. Fawcett, Christian steadfastness: a sermon occasioned by the death of the Revd. Mr. Risdon Darracott. Including Darracott's 'Solemn farewell' as a postscript, 4th edn (1774) • Protestant Dissenter's Magazine, 2 (1795), 216 • register of marriages, St Mary Magdalene Church, Taunton, 22 May 1765 [John Comley and Katherine Darracott] • Boase & Courtney, Bibl. Corn., 3.1148, 1358 • C. Surman, index of dissenting ministers, DWL • IGI
Likenesses Blood, engraving (after J. Sharp), repro. in Bennett, Star of the west
Wealth at death messuage with garden and orchard in South Street: will, 11 July 1758, abstracted Humphrey, Materials, 34

Darrell [Darrel], **John** (b. c.1562, d. in or after 1607), exorcist, was born in Nottinghamshire, probably in the area of Mansfield, the son of Henry Darrell. He became a sizar of Queens' College, Cambridge, in June 1575 and graduated BA in 1579. He subsequently left Cambridge and studied law at the inns of court in London before returning to Mansfield to take up farming. He married at some stage, though his wife's name is unknown.

In the next few years Darrell must have acquired a reputation as a spiritual healer, since in 1586 Katherine Wright, a demoniac, was sent to him by a neighbour of hers, who had heard that Darrell was 'a man of hope, for the releeving of those that were distressed in this sort' (Harsnett, 299). After two sessions with Wright, held several weeks apart, Darrell was credited with having expelled the demons from her. He also attempted to prosecute a local woman whom Wright had accused of bewitching her; according to Samuel Harsnett, who was to become Darrell's chief polemical adversary, this embroiled Darrell in a confrontation with Geoffrey Fouljambe, the local magistrate (Harsnett, 304, 310–12). If this is true, it is remarkable that Isabel Fouljambe, the magistrate's wife, received a written account by Darrell himself, of Wright's exorcism. Isabel Fouljambe was the patron of later puritan preachers and exorcists such as Richard Bernard and Richard Rothwell. She was also closely associated with a coterie of puritan clergy, led by Arthur Hildersham, centred in Ashby-de-la-Zouch. These puritans were to become Darrell's most important supporters and it is likely that Isabel Fouljambe introduced Darrell to them.

Some time after Wright's exorcism, Darrell moved first to Bulwell, near Nottingham, and then to Ashby-de-la-Zouch, where he settled. He was an enthusiastic participant in godly exercises throughout the midlands and is known to have preached at Ashby-de-la-Zouch. During this period he led an exemplary life, and he later produced testimonials to his good character from the townspeople of Mansfield, Bulwell, and Ashby-de-la-Zouch. Even Abraham Hartwell, in attacking Darrell, was still forced to admit 'the Stoicall conversation and holy life' of the exorcist (Marescot, A2r).

Darrell's rise to more than local fame began with his exorcism of Thomas Darling, an adolescent demoniac of Burton upon Trent, on 28 May 1596. As was the case in Wright's exorcism, a local woman was accused of causing the possession by means of witchcraft; this time the accused was convicted and died in prison, though there is no evidence that Darrell had anything to do with her prosecution. Darrell capped his success by exorcizing seven demoniacs in the household of Nicholas Starkey, a Lancashire gentleman, on 17 and 18 March 1597. The Darling and Starkey exorcisms were sensational triumphs in which Darrell, assisted by other godly ministers, had succeeded in curing demoniacs while the remedies of both physicians and folk healers had been ineffective.

In an effort to build on these successes, Darrell and his followers began to broadcast his achievements in print. Notes of Darling's possession, taken by Jesse Bee, a kinsman of the demoniac, were edited by John Denison, then sent to Darrell and Hildersham for their approval, and finally published in June 1597 as *The most Wonderfull and True Storie* (Harsnett, 2, 266–9). Furthermore, a note at the end of Bee's book promised readers that an account of Darrell's exorcism of the Starkey demoniacs would soon be printed (pp. 32–3). A few months later, in August 1597, an account of the Starkey exorcisms was printed. It was written by John Dickens, a local minister who had participated in these exorcisms. (There are no surviving copies of this book; it should not be confused with later works by Darrell and George More on the Starkey exorcisms.) There apparently was a planned effort to publish accounts of Darrell's exploits, written by godly witnesses to them.

In November 1597 Darrell, at the invitation of the town authorities, arrived in Nottingham to cure William Somers, an apprentice musician who claimed that he was possessed. On the evening of 7 November, Darrell exorcized Somers before an enthusiastic crowd. Shortly afterwards, Darrell was appointed preacher at St Mary's, Nottingham. Somers, however, soon claimed that he had been repossessed by demons; he was again exorcized by Darrell, but again repossessed; and the cycle of Somers's possessions, exorcisms, and repossessions continued for several weeks. By the end of November, Somers, along with his sister, Mary Cooper, who also maintained that she was possessed, were denouncing specific individuals as witches responsible for their being possessed. Acting on these denunciations, Darrell had thirteen people arrested, though eventually all but two were released. Alice Freeman, one of the two suspects who was not released, was a relative of William Freeman, a JP and alderman of Nottingham. The magistrate had Somers arrested on a countercharge of witchcraft. In February, Somers confessed to fraud, not witchcraft; to support his confession he feigned convulsions before the mayor and certain aldermen. A commission was established by Matthew Hutton, archbishop of York, to investigate the case. Hutton's commission convened in Nottingham on 20 March 1598. Composed of a mixture of prominent local lay and clerical figures, the commission was heavily biased in Darrell's favour—an indication of the depth of Darrell's support in Nottingham. The commission declared that Somers had been genuinely possessed and cleared Darrell of any wrong-doing. Darrell's opponents pressured Hutton and he deprived the exorcist of his licence to preach on 20 April. They also complained to John Whitgift, archbishop of Canterbury, who summoned Darrell to Lambeth in London, where he was imprisoned along with George More, a minister who had assisted him in the Starkey exorcisms.

After being imprisoned for more than a year, Darrell and More were found guilty of fraud by the commissioners for ecclesiastical causes, in late May 1599. The two ministers were deprived of their livings and returned to prison to await sentencing. An acrimonious controversy ensued which lasted for four years and provoked more than a dozen books. Darrell's opponents, led by Richard Bancroft, the bishop of London, and his chaplain Samuel Harsnett, were well placed to sponsor sermons and printed attacks on Darrell and to suppress works defending him. But Darrell clearly enjoyed well-organized support, since works championing him poured from foreign and clandestine presses. Although Darrell was quietly released in the summer of 1599, he went underground and by the end of 1602 had published five works on his own behalf. His career as an exorcist, however, was finished, and he eventually returned to the area around Mansfield. Along with his wife and household, he was presented at Teversal, in 1607, for not receiving communion. In the autumn of the same year Darrell preached without a licence in at least two churches in the area. After this there is no further record of him, unless (as is highly probable) he was the John Dayrell who wrote a book attacking the Brownists in 1617.

Darrell was the most spectacularly successful and celebrated (or notorious) of the puritan exorcists, who included Edward Nyndge, John Foxe, Richard Rothwell, and Robert Balsom. His career, and the difficulty Bancroft had in ending it, largely inspired the seventy-second canon, which forbade exorcism without episcopal permission.

THOMAS S. FREEMAN

Sources S. Harsnett, *A discovery of the fraudulent practises of J. Darrel* (1599) · J. Darrel, *A detection of that sinnful, shamful, lying and ridiculous discours of S. Harshnet* (1600) · *The triall of Mast. Dorrell* (1599) · I. D., *The most wonderfull and true storie, of a certaine witch named Alse Gooderige* (1597); [2nd edn] (1984) · J. Darrell, *The replie of John Darrell … concerning the doctrine of the possession and dispossession of demoniakes* (1602) · J. Darrel, *A true narration of the strange and grevous vexation by the devil of 7 persons in Lancashire, and W. Somers* (1600) · G. More, *A true discourse concerning the certaine possession and dispossession of 7 persons in one familie in Lancashire* (1600) · J. Darrel, *An apologie, or defence of the possession of William Sommers* (1599?) · R. Marchant, *The puritans and the church courts in the diocese of York, 1560–1642* (1960) · Venn, *Alum. Cant.* · M. Marescot, *A true discourse upon the matter of Marthe Brossier*, trans. A. Hartwell (1599) · *N&Q*, 171 (1936), 94 · T. Freeman, 'Demons, deviance and defiance: John Darrell and the politics of exorcism in late Elizabethan England', *Conformity and orthodoxy in the English church, c.1560–1660*, ed. P. Lake and M. Questier (2000), 34–63

Darrell, Thomas (*b.* 1538/9), Roman Catholic priest, was born at Turweston in Buckinghamshire, the son of Henry Darrell, who came from the gentry family who lived in nearby Lillingstone Dayrell. His mother's surname was Martial. He was admitted as a scholar of Winchester College in 1551, aged twelve, and then matriculated in 1555 at

New College, Oxford, graduating BA on 30 May 1559 and becoming a fellow of his college. In 1562 he was ejected from the university for refusing the oath of supremacy. He went to the Spanish Netherlands, and received the bachelor's degree at Douai in 1572, later becoming a doctor of theology at either Louvain or Douai. He was at some point ordained priest. In 1568 he had assisted William Allen, the leading Catholic academic exile, in founding the English College at Douai. He was able to help in providing funds for this new seminary. He followed a clerical career in France, and was noted as a preacher. There is a story that at some unknown date he travelled to Rome and met a bishop who persuaded him to return with him to Gascony, where he became his chaplain and was provided with a valuable benefice. Evidence from 1593 and 1600 places him as dean of Agen, France. In 1590 he was sent two young students from Douai so that he could help educate them at his own expense in his household. In 1593 he wrote to Anthony Bacon in England offering a place to any young English scholar who wanted to improve his French. In 1600 a 'John' Darrell wrote a letter attacking the archpriest George Blackwell, which was published by Christopher Bagshaw as part of the appellant controversy, and it seems reasonable to identify this as the work of Thomas Darrell. The date of his death is not known.

PETER HOLMES

Sources DNB · G. Anstruther, *The seminary priests*, 1 (1969) · Foster, *Alum. Oxon.* · C. Dodd [H. Tootell], *The church history of England, from the year 1500, to the year 1688*, 2 (1739), 64 · T. F. Knox and others, eds., *The first and second diaries of the English College, Douay* (1878), 4, 229, 273 · E. H. Burton and T. L. Williams, eds., *The Douay College diaries, third, fourth and fifth, 1598–1654*, 1, Catholic RS, 10 (1911), 198 · T. G. Law, ed., *The archpriest controversy: documents relating to the dissensions of the Roman Catholic clergy, 1597–1602*, 1, CS, new ser., 56 (1896), 7ff., 207, 237; 2, CS, new ser., 58 (1898), 241 · C. Bagshaw, *A true relation of the faction begun at Wisbech* (1601), 83–90 · *VCH Buckinghamshire*, 252 · A. Wood, *The history and antiquities of the University of Oxford*, ed. J. Gutch, 2 (1796), 144 · N. Sanders, *De visibili monarchia ecclesiae* (Louvain, 1571), 700 · J. A. Bossy, 'Elizabethan Catholicism: the link with France', PhD diss., U. Cam., 1960, 41 · T. G. Law, ed., *A historical sketch of the conflicts between Jesuits and seculars in the reign of Queen Elizabeth* (1889), 126–33 · T. F. Kirby, *Winchester scholars: a list of the wardens, fellows, and scholars of … Winchester College* (1888), 130 · LPL, MS 649

Archives Inner Temple, London, MS 538, fols. 233–4 · LPL, letters to A. Bacon, MS 649, fol. 93 (n. 61), fol. 198 (n. 128)

Darrell, William (1651–1721), Jesuit, was the younger son of Marmaduke Darell of Fulmer, Buckinghamshire, and nephew to Roger Palmer, earl of Castlemaine. He was born in Buckinghamshire and entered the Society of Jesus on 7 September 1671. He entered the novice college at Watten in November 1672, and studied philosophy at the English College, Liège, from 1673 to 1675. He arrived at the English College, St Omer, in 1676. He was ordained in 1680 and returned to Watten in 1681. He taught at Liège (1683–6), was reported in England, in the College of St Ignatius (London area) in 1687, and was professed of the four vows on 25 March 1689. In 1696 he was procurator of the province in Paris. He was prefect of studies in the college at St Omer in 1696, and subsequently filled the same office at Liège (1699–1700). He was also professor of casuistry at Liège, and rector of the college from 17 November 1708 to 29 January 1712. In 1712 he again became procurator of the English province in Paris. Some of the funds of the province were invested there and Darrell looked after its financial affairs and tried to secure payment by the French government of the annual pension of 6000 livres, often in arrears.

Described as 'a man of superior merit' whose 'pen was always ready' (Oliver, 80), Darrell wrote a number of controversial works, including *A Letter on King James the Second's most Gracious Letters of Indulgence* (1687) and *The Lay-Man's Opinion* (1687), in which he poses as an Anglican worried about the future of the Church of England, and which elicited a published response. His *Letter to a Lady* (1688) discussed purgatory, indulgences, good works, and papal power, in reply to Charles Bancroft's *Letter to a Lady* (1688). In the same year Darrell published *A vindication of St. Ignatius … from phanaticism, and of the Jesuites from the calumnies laid to their charge in a late book entitul'd the Enthusiasm of the Church of Rome* in reply to Henry Wharton. His most popular work was *The Gentleman Instructed in the Conduct of a Virtuous and Happy Life*, the second edition of which was published in 1704. It was published with a supplement, 'A word to the ladies', in 1708 and was in its tenth edition by 1731. According to Dodd it was 'much admired and often reprinted' (*Dodd's Church History*, 3.494). It was translated into French by P. de Mareuil SJ in 1728 and also into Hungarian and Italian. His most controversial work was *The case reviewed, or, An answer to the case stated by Mr. L—y*, in which it is clearly shewed that he has stated the case wrong between the Church of Rome and the Church of England, a reply to Dr Charles Leslie's *Case Stated between the Church of Rome and the Church of England* (1711), which was first published by the St Omer's College press in 1715; it passed through at least three editions and occasioned much correspondence, to be found among the correspondence of the St Omer's rector, Lewis Sabran. The work was published with a second part, the *Treatise of the Real Presence*, in 1721, and reprinted in 1724. The reprint embodies a refutation of Archbishop Ussher's 1624 'Answer to a challenge of a Jesuit [W. Malone] in Ireland'. Darrell was appointed rector of St Omer's in 1720, and died in the college on 28 February 1721.

THOMPSON COOPER, *rev.* RUTH JORDAN

Sources G. Holt, *The English Jesuits, 1650–1829: a biographical dictionary*, Catholic RS, 70 (1984), 77 · J. Gillow and R. Trappes-Lomax, eds., *The diary of the 'blue nuns' or order of the Immaculate Conception of Our Lady, at Paris, 1658–1810*, Catholic RS, 8 (1910), 43–4, 346 · Gillow, *Lit. biog. hist.*, 5.417 · T. H. Clancy, *English Catholic books, 1641–1700: a bibliography*, rev. edn (1996), 52 · *The letter book of Lewis Sabran*, ed. G. Holt, Catholic RS, 62 (1971), 3, 44 · G. Oliver, *Collections towards illustrating the biographies of the Scotch, English and Irish members of the Society of Jesus* (1885), 80 · A. de Backer and others, *Bibliothèque de la Compagnie de Jésus*, new edn, 2, ed. C. Sommervogel (Brussels, 1891), 1374; 9 (Brussels, 1900), 1826–30 · *Dodd's Church history of England*, ed. M. A. Tierney, 5 vols. (1839–43), vol. 3, p. 494 · T. Jones, ed., *A catalogue of the collection of tracts for and against popery*, 1, Chetham Society, 48 (1859), 77 · S. Halkett and J. Laing, *Dictionary of anonymous and pseudonymous English literature*, ed. J. Kennedy and others, new edn, 7 vols. (1926–34) • H. Chadwick, *St Omers to Stonyhurst* (1962), 256–7, 275, 259

Dart, John (*d*. 1730), antiquary, trained as an attorney, but met with little success in that profession, and later entered the church. Although apparently not of exemplary lifestyle, in 1728 he became perpetual curate of Yateley, Hampshire, at the gift of the master of St Cross Hospital, Winchester, and served the church there from the neighbouring village of Sandhurst, Berkshire. His literary output comprised a modernized version of Chaucer's suppositious poem *The Complaint of the Black Knight* (1718), an unreliable life of the poet prefixed to John Urry's *The Works of Geoffrey Chaucer* (1721), and the inaccurate translation *The Works of Tibullus* (1720). Of similarly little merit is *Westminster Abbey: a Poem* (1721), which Dart later included in his *Westmonasterium, or, The history and antiquities of the abbey church of St. Peter's, Westminster*, published posthumously in two volumes in 1742. Together with his *The history and antiquities of the cathedral church of Canterbury* (1726), it received as little acclaim as his literary works, as both were more notable for the quality of their engravings, which were by J. Cole, than their antiquarian content. Richard Gough considered the former 'a pompous, but very inaccurate work' (Gough, 1.763), and William Gostling, in his *A Walk in and about the City of Canterbury* (1774), wrote of the latter that 'Mr Dart came to see our cathedral, and did see it, most certainly; but it is one thing to see and another to observe' (Gostling, 164). Dart died in December 1730 at Sandhurst and was buried at Yateley on 20 December 1730.

GORDON GOODWIN, rev. NICHOLAS DOGGETT

Sources *A biographical history of England, from the revolution to the end of George I's reign: being a continuation of the Rev. J. Granger's work*, ed. M. Noble, 3 (1806), 353–4 • *N&Q*, 5th ser., 3 (1875), 28, 96, 197 • *N&Q*, 5th ser., 12 (1879), 15 • R. G. [R. Gough], *British topography*, [new edn], 1 (1780), 452–3, 763 • W. Gostling, *A walk in and about the city of Canterbury, with many observations not to be found in any description hitherto published* (1774) • Nichols, *Lit. anecdotes*, 1.198n.
Likenesses J. Faber junior, mezzotint, BM, NPG; repro. in J. Dart, *Westmonasterium, or, The history and antiquities of the abbey church of St. Peter's, Westminster*, 2 vols. (1742) [*see illus.*]

Dart, Joseph Henry (1817–1887), lawyer, was born at India House, Leadenhall Street, London, the eldest son of Joseph Dart of St Andrew Undershaft, London, and Tidwell, Devon, secretary to the East India Company. From 1834 he was educated at Exeter College, Oxford, where he gained the Newdigate prize for English verse with his poem 'The Exile of St Helena'; he graduated BA in 1838 and proceeded MA in 1841. He was admitted a student at Lincoln's Inn on 25 January 1836, and was called to the bar on 28 January 1841. On 15 September 1842 he married Adeline Pennal, eldest daughter of Richard Humber.

In 1851 Dart published *A Compendium of the Law and Practice of Vendors and Purchasers of Real Estate*, which went through several editions. It was also published in America. In the later editions Dart was assisted by William Barber QC. The book became the standard work on the subject. In 1860 Dart was appointed one of the six conveyancing

John Dart (*d*. 1730), by John Faber junior, pubd 1742

counsel to the court of chancery, and, on the passing of the Judicature Act of 1875, he became senior conveyancing counsel to the High Court of justice. He held both posts until 1886, when he retired because of ill health.

In 1877 Dart was elected one of the verderers of the New Forest, on the borders of which he had an estate—Beech House, Ringwood, Hampshire; he was also a justice of the peace for the county. Although he never took silk, he was elected a bencher of his inn in 1885. He died on 27 June 1887 at his house at Ringwood at the age of seventy, survived by his wife and their family. Besides the legal work already mentioned, Dart translated Homer's *Iliad* into English hexameters (1862–5).

J. M. RIGG, rev. BETH F. WOOD

Sources *The Times* (1 July 1887), 8 • *Law Journal* (2 July 1887), 373, 381 • *Solicitors' Journal*, 31 (1886–7), 596 • J. Foster, *Men-at-the-bar: a biographical hand-list of the members of the various inns of court*, 2nd edn (1885), 115 • Allibone, *Dict.* • *Law List* (1886), 57
Wealth at death £25,030 14s. 7d.: probate, 17 Aug 1887, *CGPLA Eng. & Wales*

Dart, (Robert) Thurston (1921–1971), musicologist and harpsichordist, was born at Surbiton, Surrey, on 3 September 1921, the only child of Henry Thurston Dart, metal merchant's clerk, and his wife, Elizabeth Martha Orf. He was educated at Hampton grammar school and was a chorister at the Chapel Royal, Hampton Court, subsequently studying at the Royal College of Music in 1938–9 and then at University College, Exeter, where he read mathematics and took the London external degree of BA in 1942. He became ARCM in the same year. He served in the RAF from 1942 to 1945, using his mathematics training

(Robert) Thurston Dart (1921–1971), by unknown photographer

within the field of operational research. He was mentioned in dispatches. A minor hand injury caused him some concern but fortunately did not affect his subsequent performing career. His ex-service gratuity enabled him to study in Brussels in 1945–6 with Charles van den Borren. After returning to England he established himself quickly as a harpsichordist, and as one knowledgeable in early music, English particularly, and in early musical instruments. In 1947 he was appointed assistant lecturer in the Cambridge music faculty, and in 1952 university lecturer in music.

Dart had a prodigious capacity for work. From 1947 to 1955 he was editor of the *Galpin Society Journal*, the society having been founded the previous year by Dart and others to commemorate and continue the work of Canon Francis Galpin (1858–1945) on early musical instruments. From 1948 onwards he was a regular broadcaster for the BBC's new Third Programme, equally at home speaking or performing. He was secretary to the editorial board of the series Musica Britannica (1950–64) and remained a vigorous member of its committee until his death, seeing thirty-three volumes through the press, a number of which were edited by young scholars he himself had trained.

Dart was a fellow of Jesus College, Cambridge, from 1953 to 1964, visiting lecturer at Harvard University in 1954, and recipient of the Cobbett prize in 1957. His book *The Interpretation of Music* appeared in 1954, incorporating many of his discoveries and hypotheses relating to early music. About 1950 he began his long association with the

firm of L'Oiseau-Lyre, Monaco, both as editor of music publications and as performer on L'Oiseau-Lyre recordings. He became a lifelong friend of the proprietor, Mrs Louise Hanson Dyer, and her husband; their patronage was undoubtedly influential in furthering his career.

From 1955 to 1959 Dart was artistic director of the newly formed Philomusica of London (formerly the Boyd Neel Orchestra). With Granville Jones and then Neville Marriner as concert-master, he directed numerous performances and recordings from the harpsichord (and latterly as conductor). The recordings were based on editions he had prepared from autographs and other prime sources and in some cases tested certain hypotheses; they thus remain a valuable testament to Dart's scholarship and musicianship. He made about ninety recordings in all of solo, chamber, and orchestral music.

In addition Dart undertook the editing of a large amount of music and the re-editing of the monumental series on English madrigalists and the works of William Byrd (first prepared by E. H. Fellowes). Yet his work as university lecturer and teacher was by no means neglected. His lectures were memorable for their meticulous preparation, excellent delivery, and stimulating content; and his influence as a teacher was perhaps his most considerable contribution, a whole generation of students (for whom Dart and Cambridge were virtually synonymous) being affected by him, not a few becoming in turn influential in the field of English music.

In 1962 Dart became professor of music at Cambridge and, as ever, he brought fresh thinking to bear upon old problems and conventions. He found it virtually impossible to change established customs, however, and resigned the chair in 1964 to take up the challenge of establishing a new faculty of music at King's College, London, which he did most successfully as King Edward professor of music, a post he held until his death.

Dart was a complete musician, an instinctive performer (he played the harpsichord, the clavichord, viols, the recorder, and other woodwinds, and sang) and one whose intellect and imagination were unusually well matched. Indeed, despite his reputation as solo performer his most outstanding performances were probably those in which he played harpsichord or organ continuo (often directing the ensemble at the same time), for it was in such performances that his perfect sense of rhythm, his self-discipline, his scholarly approach, and at the same time his creative flair for musical improvisation were most fully matched and realized.

As a scholar Dart was concerned chiefly with English music of the sixteenth to eighteenth centuries, but also with aspects of French music of the period and, especially, Handel and J. S. Bach. (He was engaged in recording a particularly controversial account of Bach's 'Brandenburg' concertos at the time of his final hospitalization resulting from the cancer of which he died.) He had a wide and practical knowledge of earlier musical notations, Western and non-Western, and wrote on the subject in the fifth edition of *Grove's Dictionary of Music and Musicians* (1954). He also had an unusual knowledge of music printing, past and present. However, he by no means confined himself to early music. He often played Chopin for private relaxation, he commissioned a harpsichord concerto from Roberto Gerhard, and his music syllabus at London paid due attention to the nineteenth and twentieth centuries, and to electronic and non-Western music.

In person Bob Dart was large and somewhat formidable. He did not suffer fools gladly, particularly as demands on his time increased. His hobby-horses were not always securely stabled. However, to those who had worked with him and knew him well he was brilliant and amusing (with a delightful sense of the absurd) and generous in spirit and deed. He had a large library of books and scores and possessed many early instruments, most of which he gave away. He collected paintings and enjoyed the good things of life.

Dart was unmarried. He died in London on 6 March 1971. To honour Dart, King's College, London, created in 1996 the Thurston Dart chair of performance studies in music.

GERALD HENDRIE, *rev.*

Sources I. D. Bent, 'Dart, (Robert) Thurston', *New Grove* · *The Times* (8 March 1971) · *The Times* (12 March 1971) · *The Times* (24 March 1971) · I. D. Bent, *Source materials and the interpretation of music: a memorial volume to Thurston Dart* (1981) · *DNB* · personal knowledge (1986) · private information (1986) · *CGPLA Eng. & Wales* (1971) · N. Marriner, 'Robert Thurston Dart: an English musicologist', *The Gramophone*, 49/580 (Sept 1971), 423–4 · S. Jeans, 'Robert Thurston Dart, 1921–1971: an appreciation by a friend', *Galpin Society Journal*, 24 (1971), 2–4
Archives SOUND BL NSA, *The BBC archive*, BBC Radio 3, 19 Oct 1997, H9316/2 · BL NSA, oral history interview · BL NSA, 'Orpheus Britannicus – a tribute to Thurston Dart', BBC Radio 3, 7 March 1981, T3806 BW BD1 · BL NSA, performance recordings
Likenesses photograph, repro. in Bent, *Source materials* [see illus.]
Wealth at death £47,322: probate, 24 Sept 1971, *CGPLA Eng. & Wales*

Dartasso, Janico (d. 1426), adventurer, was born in Navarre, of Basque descent; he is first mentioned in 1367–8, while serving in the garrison of Cherbourg, then in the possession of Charles d'Évreux, king of Navarre. It seems likely that he remained at Cherbourg for some years, for it was there that, in collaboration with the English forces commanded by Sir John Arundel, he captured Olivier du Guesclin, brother of the constable of France, in January 1379. The garrison of Cherbourg was, by this time, a joint Anglo-Navarrese one, and Dartasso's determined pursuit of du Guesclin's ransom, set at 40,000 gold francs, led him to transfer permanently from Navarrese to English service. By December 1380 he had moved from Cherbourg to the pale of Calais, serving in the garrison of Guînes, and he continued in similarly unglamorous military employment for several years. By 1384, however, Dartasso had attracted the attention of an influential new patron, Henry Percy, first earl of Northumberland. He came to be particularly identified with the service of Northumberland's eldest son, Henry (Hotspur), commanding a company on Hotspur's naval expedition in August 1387, and falling into Scottish hands, together with his master, after Hotspur's defeat at Otterburn in 1388. During this period of Percy service, Dartasso also made himself useful to the ruling junta of lords appellant, who twice employed him on confidential missions to Calais.

During the following decade, Dartasso advanced his reputation as a tough and experienced soldier and substantially augmented the level of his rewards. In March 1390 he travelled to the Calais marches, together with many other English knights and esquires, in order to participate in the jousts of St Inglevert, and then joined the crusade of Louis, duc de Bourbon, against the Hafsid city of Mahdiyya. When mounting casualties obliged Bourbon to lift his siege, Dartasso immediately journeyed northward to join Henry, earl of Derby, in Prussia, where he was campaigning with the Teutonic knights against the Lithuanians. Such exploits brought his virtues to the attention of a new group of patrons. One of them was John Waltham, bishop of Salisbury and treasurer of England, whose household esquire Dartasso now became. Soon afterwards, at Michaelmas 1392, he was retained by the king, initially at a fee of 40 marks p.a. Richard put his new esquire's cosmopolitan experience to repeated use, sending him on a series of confidential missions: to the city states of northern Italy in 1392–3; to Paris, in October 1396 and March 1397; and to the Rhineland, to consult with the archbishop of Cologne regarding the possibility of Richard's election as Holy Roman emperor. In the intervals between these employments, Dartasso's long military experience continued to prove valuable. He distinguished himself during the king's expedition to Ireland in 1394, and was rewarded for his good service with a large grant of confiscated land in the south of co. Dublin. On Richard's return to the lordship in 1399, Dartasso acted as field commander for the new lieutenant of Ireland, Thomas Holland, duke of Surrey. This promising campaign was cut short, however, by the news of Henry of Lancaster's invasion of England. Dartasso accompanied the king back to Wales and remained with him, while the rest of his household dissolved, until Richard's final surrender to the Lancastrian forces at Conwy. His defiant conduct, in refusing to take off the king's livery badge when ordered to do so, caused him to be confined in Chester Castle.

Nevertheless, Dartasso soon made his peace with the new Lancastrian regime, swiftly regaining his position in the royal household and establishing himself as an intimate of Henry IV. A stream of grants and favours followed, many of them drawn on the lordship of Ireland, where he had recently acquired substantial private estates by virtue of his marriage to an Anglo-Irish heiress, Joan Rowe, *née* Taafe (d. in or before 1413). Accordingly, when Dartasso travelled to the lordship once more in April 1401, in the suite of the new lieutenant, Thomas of Lancaster, the king's second son, it marked the start of a more permanent residence in Ireland. As constable of Dublin, deputy to the king's admiral in Ireland and, from c.1407, steward of Ulster, Dartasso played an important part in the defence of the lordship. He defeated a Scottish raiding party at sea in May 1405, and launched an effective campaign into Ulster in June 1409. His success in this role was recognized by his appointment as one of three 'governors of the king's wars' in Ireland in January 1414.

The resumption of full Anglo-French hostilities promised richer rewards than Ireland could provide, however, and Dartasso was quick to join Henry V's first expedition to northern France, contracting to serve with a company of ten men-at-arms and thirty mounted archers. By January 1416 he was part of the garrison at Harfleur, where, drawing upon his long experience of warfare along the Norman coastline, he played a significant part in the escape of Thomas Beaufort, earl of Dorset, from the superior French forces that confronted him at Valmont. It seems that Dartasso spent much of the rest of Henry V's reign in Normandy, for he was active throughout the siege of Rouen (July 1418 – January 1419) in mustering the besieging forces, and took out letters of protection for the king's third and final French campaign in 1421. On his eventual return to Ireland he was able to regain his old prominence within the lordship, which had been briefly thrown into question by the hostility of the new lieutenant, John, sixth Lord Talbot, and acted once again as steward of Ulster until his death on 20 November 1426. He was survived by his second wife, Elizabeth, whom he had married in or before 1414.

Janico Dartasso's career demonstrates the enduring significance of military service as a vehicle for social advancement in later medieval England. His successful cultivation of a chivalric reputation, as 'a noble man of arms among the esquires of all England and France' (*Itineraries*, 348), kept him closely in touch with the centres of cultural influence and political authority and allowed this Navarrese garrison soldier to move with facility at the highest social level.   SIMON WALKER

Sources PRO · *Chancery records* · E. Tresham, ed., *Rotulorum patentium et clausorum cancellariae Hiberniae calendarium*, Irish Record Commission (1828) · S. Walker, 'Janico Dartasso: chivalry, nationality and the man-at-arms', *History*, new ser., 84 (1999), 31–51 · E. Curtis, 'Janico Dartas, Richard the second's "Gascon esquire": his career in Ireland, 1394–1426', *Journal of the Royal Society of Antiquaries of Ireland*, 7th ser., 3 (1933), 183–205 · M. D. Legge, ed., *Anglo-Norman letters and petitions from All Souls MS 182*, Anglo-Norman Texts, 3 (1941) · E. Izarn, ed., *Le compte des recettes et dépenses du roi de Navarre en France et en Normandie de 1367 à 1370* (1885) · [J. Creton], 'Translation of a French metrical history of the deposition of King Richard the Second … with a copy of the original', ed. and trans. J. Webb, *Archaeologia*, 20 (1824), 1–423 · A. M. Chazaud, *La chronique du bon duc Loys de Bourbon* (Paris, 1876) · *Itineraries [of] William Worcester*, ed. J. H. Harvey, OMT (1969) · [J. Hardiman], ed., *Inquisitionum in officio rotulorum cancellariae Hiberniae asservatarum repertorium*, 2 vols., Irish Record Commission (1826–9), vol. 1
Wealth at death Irish lands: *Inquisitionum cancellariae*, vol. 1

Dartiquenave, Charles (*bap.* 1664?, *d.* **1737**), epicure and courtier, was rumoured to be the illegitimate child of Charles II, though there is no substantial evidence for a claim that was subsequently derided in later eighteenth- and nineteenth-century accounts of his life. It is elsewhere suggested that he was the pupil of a French émigré family, whose name he adopted (Caulfield, 223). However, parish registers also record the baptism of a Charles, son

Charles Dartiquenave (*bap.* 1664?, *d.* 1737), by Sir Godfrey Kneller, 1702

of John Jacob and Anne Dartiquenave, at St Martin-in-the-Fields, Westminster, on 13 October 1664, though it is unclear that this is the subject of this article. Certainly Dartiquenave was educated in London at a school in Oxenden Street, Haymarket, where he penned a slender volume of Greek and Latin exercises—printed but not published—which he dedicated to Charles II. On 18 June 1713 he married Mary (1684–1756), daughter of John Scroggs and Mary Cuntiffe of Albury, Hertfordshire, at St Lawrence Jewry, London; the couple had at least two sons and one daughter.

Though politically non-partisan, Dartiquenave had an enduring sympathy for the whigs which resulted in his acquisition of several offices connected to the courts of Queen Anne and George I. Between 1707 and 1726 he was paymaster of the royal works (with a daily salary of 6*s.* 6*d.* in 1709, rising by £200 a year in 1717). In June 1726 he became surveyor-general of the king's gardens, and in March 1731 he was expected to receive the surveyorship of the king's private roads, an office that eventually went in May to the MP for Knaresborough, Richard Arundel.

During his lifetime, however, Dartiquenave's reputation was less that of a courtier than of a witty and convivial man about town. His tendency to 'say very good things' (Caulfield, 223) made him a regular dining and drinking companion of Jonathan Swift, who described Dartiquenave in October 1710 and March 1711 as 'the greatest punner of this town next to myself' and 'the man that knows everything and that everybody knows' (Swift, 1.36, 221).

For others Dartiquenave was remarkable for his seemingly ceaseless appetite for fine food and drink.

> Each Mortal has his Pleasure: None deny
> *Scarsdale* his Bottle; *Darty* his Ham-Pye

wrote Alexander Pope in the second epistle in book 2 of his *Imitation of Horace* (lines 45–6). Lord Lyttleton's *Dialogues of the Dead* (1760) likewise identified Dartiquenave as a contemporary epicure of sufficient taste and appetite to challenge the Roman gourmand Apicius in a debate over the merits of cuisine ancient and modern (dialogue 19). Dartiquenave himself may have been the author of a *Tatler* paper on drink (no. 252, 18 November 1710) in which he encouraged readers in 'moderate Use of the Grape' as a means of improving conversation and bringing 'to Light agreeable talents which otherwise would have lain concealed under the Oppression of an unjust Modesty' (Bond, 3.281–3).

A member of the whig Kit-Cat Club, Dartiquenave appears in a portrait by Godfrey Kneller, later engraved by John Faber, as a man of gently rounded face and girth, though no more so than other less overtly epicurean club members. As a man connected with the court throughout his life, Dartiquenave lived in quarters at St James's Palace, Westminster, where he died on 19 October 1737. He was buried on 26 October at Albury church, Hertfordshire, where he is commemorated by a plaque. Survived by his wife, who died on 31 August 1756, Dartiquenave passed his estate at Albury, Patmere, part of which was bought from his sister-in-law Judith Scroggs, to his son before it was sold by his grandson, Charles Peter, in 1775.

PHILIP CARTER

Sources DNB · J. Caulfield, *Memoirs of the celebrated persons comprising the Kit-Cat Club* (1821) · J. Swift, *Journal to Stella*, ed. H. Williams, 2 vols. (1948) · J. E. Cussans, *History of Hertfordshire*, 1/2 (1872), 162–8 · *GM*, 1st ser., 1 (1731), 127, 175 · *GM*, 1st ser., 7 (1737), 638 · D. F. Bond, ed., *The Tatler*, 3 vols. (1987) · IGI · will, PRO, PROB 11/686, fols. 249r–251r
Likenesses G. Kneller, oils, 1702, NPG [*see illus.*] · J. Faber junior, mezzotint, 1734 (after G. Kneller), BM, NPG · oils (*Kit-Cat Club* portrait; after G. Kneller), NPG

Dartmouth. For this title name *see* Legge, George, first Baron Dartmouth (*c.*1647–1691); Legge, William, first earl of Dartmouth (1672–1750); Legge, William, second earl of Dartmouth (1731–1801); Legge, George, third earl of Dartmouth (1755–1810); Legge, Augusta, countess of Dartmouth (1822–1900).

Darton, Frederick Joseph Harvey (1878–1936), publisher and writer, was born on 22 September 1878, the eldest of the two sons and one daughter of Joseph William Darton (1843–1916), partner in the publishing firm of Wells Gardner, Darton & Co., and his wife, Mary (*d.* 1934), eldest daughter of Dr Charles Schooling of Milton, Kent. Darton was educated at Sutton Valence School and Dover College, and won a scholarship to St John's College, Oxford, taking a second class in classical moderations in 1899 and in *literae humaniores* in 1901. He then joined the family firm, which had been established in the eighteenth century by William Darton (1755–1819). He remained until 1928 when it was sold to Love and Malcomson. During his time at the

firm, Darton brought a more scholarly approach to its general editorial policy, as befitted the only member of the firm ever to have had a university education; at the same time he was closely involved with its two juvenile magazines, *Chatterbox* and *The Prize*. (He wrote an amusing account of his experiences with these in the *Cornhill Magazine*, May 1932.)

Darton was also engaged in his own literary work. From 1901 onwards he produced many retellings of stories from old legends and romances, published by his firm. He contributed book reviews to the *Daily News*, short monographs on Arnold Bennett and J. M. Barrie to the Writers of the Day series, and in 1910 edited the life of Mary Martha Sherwood, some of whose later children's books had been published by the Darton firm. He also wrote two pseudonymous novels touching on his own life, *My Father's Son* (under the name William W. Penn, 1913) and *When: a Record of Transition* (under the name John L. Pole, 1929). He edited the Bankside Acting Edition of Shakespeare from 1927 to 1929. On 2 October 1906 he married Emma Lucretia Bennett (*b.* 1876), daughter of George Lovett Bennett, headmaster of Sutton Valence School, but the marriage was annulled on grounds of non-consummation. At this period he was living in Cheyne Walk, Chelsea, London, the centre of a convivial circle of friends, but after the death of his father he left London and lived variously in Kent and Dorset, writing several books about these localities. A gregarious and genial man, he loved the country and its people and, as *The Times* obituary said of him, 'country sports and all recreations, from shove-halfpenny to cricket and fox-hunting: he knew a good deal of archaeology; and he was at home in any decent public house' (*The Times*, 28 July 1936). (His last address was a Dorset pub, and he was to die of cirrhosis of the liver.)

The work for which Darton is remembered is the ground-breaking and influential *Children's Books in England* (1932), which remains a vital resource for historians and general readers. This survey of children's reading, from Caxton to the later Victorians, written as 'a minor chapter in the history of English social life' (Alderson, vii), stands out for the wealth of its material, its benign, Olympian viewpoint, and lightly carried learning—the product of a cultivated, widely read but non-specialist bibliophile with a classical education. Darton had in 1914 contributed the chapter on children's books to volume 11 of the *Cambridge History of English Literature*, having already written on the same subject in the tenth edition of the *Encyclopaedia Britannica* (1902–3). He had also acquired an impressive collection of books, games, and illustration material from the Darton firm's publications. However, as he said in the preface to *Children's Books*, this had gone to America 'in the stress of the Peace' (ibid., viii)—it is now housed at the teachers college of Columbia University—and when he settled down to write in 1931 he was working from his catalogue of the collection, and from memory, augmented by research at the British Museum. 'With these facts to hand', said Brian Alderson, who revised the original for a third edition in 1982, 'he was able to write the book with concentrated energy, and it is this which gives it the homogeneity of style and viewpoint that are its personality' (ibid., xiii). Darton produced a handful more books after this, but died of alcoholism on 26 July 1936, in Dorchester County Hospital, and was buried on 28 July at Cerne Abbas, Dorset.

GILLIAN AVERY

Sources Lawrence Darton's family archives · *The Times* (28 July 1936) · m. cert. · d. cert. · *Oxford University Calendar* · B. Alderson, preface, in F. J. Harvey Darton, *Children's books in England: five centuries of social life*, rev. B. Alderson, 3rd edn (1982)
Archives Col. U., Teachers College, book collection and catalogue · priv. coll., family archives

Darton, Nicholas (1602/3–1649×52), Church of England clergyman, was born in Cornwall. He matriculated at Exeter College, Oxford, on 14 December 1618, aged fifteen, and graduated BA on 22 October 1622. Presented by John Rudyard to the living of Kilsby, Northamptonshire, he was instituted on 31 January 1628. In 1641 he published *The True and Absolute Bishop*, dedicated to Lord Saye and Sele, 'an especiall Member for Gods Glory and Great Britaines safety, among the Right Honourable Lords in the Parliament now assembled', although personally unknown to him. The work aimed to show that 'Christ is our only Shepheard, As well as our truest Bishop', and explores the thirteen scriptural criteria for such office that he fulfilled, but does not venture direct comment on the contemporary debate on episcopacy.

In 1643 Darton became vicar of Bibury-with-Winston, Gloucestershire, and by 1645 he had ceased to hold the Kilsby living. For a while he was apparently a preacher at St Peter-in-the-East in Oxford but by 1649, when he addressed his *Ecclesia Anglicana, or, Darton's Clear and Protestant Manifesto* to the governor of Oxford, he had been excluded from the pulpit. Complaining not only of his own fate but also of that of John Prideaux, Gilbert Sheldon, Henry Hammond, and another, named Heywood, 'rare men with hundreds more outed for I know not what' (Darton, 3), he railed against 'our Antiepiscopists … [who] take upon them now to governe (I will not say tyrannize over) the weake and tender consciences of the most pious and conscientious christians' (ibid., 4), the 'Calvinistical Directors' who were no better than the bishops and deans and chapters they had replaced. Denying charges of meddling in state matters or being the 'ring-leader of any sect in the Universitie' (ibid., 12), he called for peace, liberty of conscience, and the right of people to attend their parish churches.

Darton's subsequent movements are unknown, as is the date of his death. A nuncupative will of Nicholas Darton 'DD' of West Wycombe, Buckinghamshire, was registered on 23 July 1652, and letters of administration granted on 20 August to the sole legatee, a cousin and namesake described as a mercer in Oxford. This Nicholas Darton had been apprenticed to William Cornishe on 15 September 1651, and the bequest was specifically destined 'towards the setting him up in his trade' (PRO, PROB 11/224, 199).

VIVIENNE LARMINIE

Sources Foster, *Alum. Oxon.* · G. Baker, *The history and antiquities of the county of Northampton*, 1 (1822–30), 402–3 · Wood, *Ath. Oxon.*, new edn, 3.263 · N. Darton, *Ecclesia Anglicana, or, Darton's clear and protestant manifesto* (1649) · will of Darton, PRO, PROB 11/224, 199 (219 Bowyer, 1652) · M. G. Hobson and H. E. Salter, eds., *Oxford council acts, 1626–1665*, OHS, 95 (1933), 184

Darton, William (1755–1819), publisher and writer, was born at the Coach and Six Horses, Tottenham, Middlesex, where he was baptized at the parish church on 14 November 1755. He was the second of three children (two boys and one girl) of John Darton (d. 1774), an innkeeper, and of Ann Bramton (1717–1804), who had been a widow when John Darton married her in 1750/1751. He was apprenticed for seven years to Thomas Dent, a London engraver, and following the death of his father in 1774 returned to Tottenham, where he ran a village store. In 1777 he joined the Society of Friends, and on 2 July 1778 he married Hannah Pace (1755–1822) of Spitalfields, herself a Quaker; they were to have eleven children (five girls and six boys). In 1787 he moved to London and set up as engraver, stationer, and printer in White Lion Alley, Birchin Lane. In this year he published what seems to be his first book, *Little Truths Better than Great Fables*, which blends information with moral teaching in the then approved style for children. He moved to 55 Gracechurch Street, London, in the next year, and in 1791 formed a partnership with Joseph Harvey (1764–1841). Harvey, also a Quaker, was primarily a printer, while Darton saw to the publishing side, and in some thirty years, starting from nothing, a flourishing business had been built up with a distinctive house style. The firm's adult publications were mostly of Quaker origin, and included anti-slavery literature, but it was best known for juvenile books, several of which, like *Little Truths*, were written and probably illustrated by Darton himself. Among the firm's more famous authors were Maria Hack, Priscilla Wakefield, the grammarian Lindley Murray, and Jane and Ann Taylor, whose two volumes of *Original Poems, for Infant Minds* were published in 1804 and 1805. In 1810 William Darton's son Samuel Darton (1785–1840) became a partner in the firm, and Darton sen., though still a partner, went to live in Plaistow, Essex, where he died on 13 August 1819.

William Darton (1781–1854), publisher, the eldest son and second child (of eleven) of William and Hannah Darton, was born at Tottenham on 2 February 1781. He was educated at the Friends' school, Clerkenwell, London, and at Ackworth (Quaker) school, Yorkshire, and from 1795 was apprenticed to his father. In 1804 he set up his own business in Holborn Hill, London, and like his father specialized in children's books. He also published jigsaw puzzles and table games notable for their decorative detail. Among the firm's authors were the unidentified Arabella Argus, Mary Belson Elliott, and Mary Robson Hughs. He was a skilled engraver, and finished the work on *A Complete Atlas of the English Counties*, begun by Thomas Dix and published from Holborn Hill under their joint names in 1822. On 3 May 1808 he married Phoebe Harvey (1777–1860) of Maldon, Essex. There were five children of whom the eldest, John Maw Darton (1809–1881), became a partner in the Holborn Hill firm. William Darton retired in 1836 and died on 28 July 1854 at 47 Hemingford Terrace, Islington, London.   GILLIAN AVERY

Sources priv. coll., Lawrence Darton's family archives • L. David, ed., *Children's books published by Wm Darton and his sons* (1992) [exhibition catalogue, Lilly Library, Indiana University, Indiana] • 'Dictionary of Quaker biography', RS Friends, Lond. [card index]
Archives priv. coll., family archives
Likenesses portrait (William Darton, 1781–1854), priv. coll.

Darton, William (1781–1854). *See under* Darton, William (1755–1819).

Darusmont, Frances. *See* Wright, Frances (1795–1852).

Darwin, Bernard Richard Meirion (1876–1961), writer on golf, was born at Downe in Kent on 7 September 1876, the only son of Sir Francis *Darwin (1848–1925), botanist, and his first wife, Amy, daughter of Lawrence Ruck, of Pantlludw, Machynlleth, north Wales. Amy died in childbirth in 1876. Bernard was the grandson of Charles Darwin, a piece of information with which he sometimes greeted strangers, so often had he been asked his relationship to the author of *On the Origin of Species*. He was educated at Summer Fields School (Oxford), at Eton College (1889–94), to which he won a scholarship, and at Trinity College, Cambridge. He played for three years in the university golf team and captained it in his third year, 1897. In the law tripos he took third-class honours in the first part (1896) and second-class honours in the second part (1897). In 1903 he was called to the bar of the Inner Temple but his heart was not in law. In 1908, a year after being engaged to contribute occasional articles to the *Evening Standard*, *Country Life*, and *The Times*, he began to devote himself full-time to the world of golf. It was almost as though he had deliberately turned his back on the scholarship and literary talent by which he was surrounded in his family, including two relatives, Berta Ruck and Gwen Raverat, who became established literary figures.

The links that were forged with Fleet Street that year endured. Darwin continued to write about golf for *The Times* until 1953 and for *Country Life* until shortly before his death. The only time his weekly article for *The Times* failed to appear was on his first visit to the United States in 1913, when the *Mauretania* containing his dispatch was held up by fog in New York harbour. War intervened between what were for Darwin two important visits to the United States. That first one in 1913 enabled him to cover for *The Times* the appearance of Harry Vardon and Edward Ray in the United States open championship. The contest resulted in victory for an unknown American youth, Francis Ouimet, a historic event since it marked the turning of the tide in the direction of American ascendancy in the game. Darwin was the only daily British correspondent present and marked the card for the winner in the three-way play-off.

In the First World War Darwin served in the Royal Army Ordnance Corps as a lieutenant (acting major). He spent two and a half years in Macedonia. For some time he was deputy assistant director of ordnance services for the 26th division. His second visit to the United States was in 1922, when he accompanied the British amateur team which played in the first Walker cup match against the United States. The British captain fell ill and Darwin replaced him. The match was lost but Darwin won his single. He was well qualified to fill that gap for he had just reached the semi-finals of the British amateur championship for the second time (1921 and 1909). He had also to his credit achievements which in his time ranked second in importance only to the amateur championship: eight England caps against Scotland, and victory in the *Golf Illustrated* golf vase (1919) and in the President's Putter (1924). In 1934 he received golf's greatest honour when he was elected captain of the Royal and Ancient Golf Club. He continued writing through the Second World War, both golf articles and fourth leaders, his supply of raw material coming from his own personal experience and from the letters of friends who wrote to him from all corners of the world. Because of the restrictions on newsprint he was never given full rein after the war, and in 1953 he retired from *The Times*. His departure was marked by a dinner given to him not by *The Times*, whose staff scarcely knew him apart from his writings, but by a host of golfing friends which included not only golfers and writers but a governor-general, members of parliament, and judges.

Golf has always had its eloquent apologists but nobody before had attempted to submit his or her thoughts on the subject to the glare of daily journalism. Blandly expressing ignorance of the workings of Fleet Street, Darwin succeeded in making his reports acceptable to a wide public through the milder qualities of scholarship, humour, and urbanity. When he began to write, golf reporting in the daily press was little more than a list of figures at the bottom of a column; by the time of his retirement he had turned it into a branch of literary journalism. That Darwin was something of a snob few would deny, but this seldom showed in his writings, and when it did the point was so delicately made that it was almost impossible to take offence. More important from the golfing point of view was the fact that whereas his keen, experienced eye could instantly detect a weakness he was uniformly kind to the perpetrators of it. Because he himself had suffered at the highest level, not perhaps from a lack of nerve but from an overheated temperament, he was long-suffering in print about all except bores.

Partisanship was the key to Darwin's outlook on life. A taste for murder trials, to which he readily confessed, may be attributed to his legal background, but what fascinated him most was the contest between the accuser and the accused, and the insight which such trials gave him into the lives of others. He was fascinated by prize-fighting to the extent of writing a book on it, and this pugnacious streak in his temperament may have accounted for his love of Dickens and his battling characters. Darwin quoted freely and without affectation from his favourite authors Stevenson, Thackeray, Hazlitt, Borrow, and Trollope, but in the case of Dickens he seemed hardly able to help himself; quotations spilled over from his abundant knowledge of and deep affection for his characters. He was an entirely suitable choice for the formidable task of writing a foreword to the *Oxford Dictionary of Quotations* (1941), and it occasioned little surprise when the citation for the CBE which he was appointed in 1937 spoke of his contribution to both literature and sport. In a thousand small ways he must have kindled in others an appreciation of the joys of good reading.

Darwin married in 1906 Elinor Mary (*d.* 1954), daughter of William Thomas Monsell; they had one son and two daughters. His son, Sir Robert Vere (Robin) *Darwin, became principal of the Royal College of Art (1948–67) and was knighted in 1964. Darwin's wife provided the illustrations for some children's books he wrote, the first of which, *The Tale of Mr. Tootleoo*, appeared in 1926. Outside the realm of golf his writings reflected his own interests—a book on the English public school (1929), another on London clubs, and another on W. G. Grace (1934). It was in his autobiographical writing that he scored most heavily. In *Green Memories* (1928), *Pack Clouds Away* (1941), and *The World that Fred Made* (1955) his style was nostalgic without becoming sentimental. It brought vividly to life the gentle pleasures of childhood and family life. Darwin died at Filsham House Nursing Home, St Leonards, Sussex, on 18 October 1961.   PETER RYDE, *rev.*

Sources B. Darwin, *Green memories* (1928) · B. Darwin, *Pack clouds away* (1941) · B. Darwin, *The world that Fred made: an autobiography* (1955) · P. Ryde, ed., *Mostly golf* (1976) · *The Times* (19 Oct 1961) · *The Times* (24 Oct 1961) · *The Times* (25 Oct 1961) · private information (1981) · personal knowledge (1981) · *CGPLA Eng. & Wales* (1962)
Archives News Int. RO, papers | BL, corresp. with Sir Sydney Cockerell, Add. MS 52712
Likenesses G. C. Beresford, photograph, 1921, NPG · G. C. Beresford, photograph, 1927, NPG · P. Evans, pen-and-ink drawing, *c.*1930, NPG · H. Coster, photographs, *c.*1936, NPG
Wealth at death £85,003 16*s.* 2*d.*: probate, 16 Jan 1962, *CGPLA Eng. & Wales*

Darwin, Sir Charles Galton (1887–1962), physicist, was born on 19 December 1887 at Newnham Grange, Cambridge, the eldest of the two sons and two daughters of Sir George Howard *Darwin, FRS (1845–1912), and his wife, Maud (1861–1947), daughter of Charles du Puy, of Huguenot descent, from Philadelphia. He was a member of the widespread Darwin–Wedgwood family; Charles Robert *Darwin was his great-grandfather. One of his sisters, Margaret, married Sir Geoffrey Keynes, surgeon and writer, and the other, Gwen *Raverat, described in *Period Piece* (1952) the family's happy early life when five Darwin first cousins, including Frances, later Cornford, the poet, were especially close Cambridge companions.

Darwin was a scholar at Marlborough College (1901–6) and at Trinity College, Cambridge (1906–10), where he read for the unreformed mathematical tripos, becoming fourth wrangler in part one in 1909 and obtaining a first class in part two in 1910. He joined Ernest Rutherford in Manchester as Schuster lecturer in mathematical physics in 1910, the period of the discovery of the atomic nucleus. Darwin wrote, *inter alia*, a paper on the collision of alpha particles with light nuclei which helped Rutherford in

Sir Charles Galton Darwin (1887–1962), by Elliott & Fry, 1942

work which led to the discovery of artificial nuclear disintegration. He then worked with H. G. J. Moseley on the diffraction of X-rays and in 1914 published two papers which were described as landmarks in the history of X-ray analysis of crystals.

In the First World War Darwin commanded a section in one of the royal engineer units organized to detect enemy guns by sound ranging and won the MC. Late in 1917 he was attached to the Royal Flying Corps for work on aircraft noise. From 1919 to 1922 he was fellow and lecturer at Christ's College, Cambridge, and in this period he and R. H. Fowler wrote joint papers about the basis of classical atomic statistics and their relation to thermodynamics, introducing the useful concept of 'the partition function'. In 1922 he was elected a fellow of the Royal Society. In the same year, while a visiting professor at the California Institute of Technology, he began work on optical properties, especially those involving magnetic fields. In 1924 he was appointed first Tait professor of natural philosophy at Edinburgh University, but, although an outstanding lecturer, he did not establish a school of theoretical physics.

Darwin himself worked on the applications to magneto optics of the then new Bohr–Sommerfeld quantum theory of atomic structure. When he spent short periods at Niels Bohr's institute in Copenhagen in 1927 and 1928 he was excited by the ferment of ideas there and returned to write important papers. The first, in 1927, usefully suggested the way free electrons behave. Then, on 1 February 1928, Paul A. M. Dirac's first paper on his new relativistic electron appeared. Darwin immediately realized its significance and a month later had produced a paper which made Dirac's theory accessible to ordinary physicists and greatly hastened its general acceptance. He also used the theory to derive for the first time the correct explanation of the fine structure of the hydrogen spectrum. Two further papers analysed the magnetic moment, and the diffraction, of the relativistic electron. Subsequently he worked out in detail for non-relativistic Schrödinger electrons the very important case of a collision between two electrons and then considered other examples of the uncertainty principle. At intervals over the years he continued to spend time on a purely classical problem concerning the effective electric field acting on an electron in an ionized medium. In 1925 Darwin married Katharine, daughter of Francis William Pember, a lawyer, who was the warden of All Souls College, Oxford, from 1914 to 1932. She was the granddaughter of Edward Henry Pember and was herself a mathematician. They had one daughter (a crystallographer) and four sons (an electronic engineer, a civil engineer, a Foreign Office lawyer, and a zoologist).

Darwin returned to Cambridge in 1936 as master of Christ's College but in 1938 he became director of the National Physical Laboratory (NPL). He successfully reorganized the NPL for urgent war work and in 1941 was seconded to Washington for a year as first director of the British office set up to improve Anglo-American scientific war co-operation—a crucial post which he filled with energy, sound scientific judgement, and diplomatic skill. He was involved in liaison over the atomic bomb, and was one of the few to realize that it presented problems different in kind, as well as in explosive power, from conventional weapons. On returning to Britain he became scientific adviser to the War Office. When he went back full time to the NPL Darwin was concerned with the reconversion for peace and with reorganization and new creations among the laboratories of the Department of Scientific and Industrial Research. Foreseeing the great potentialities of electronic computers, he created in the NPL two new divisions, mathematics and electronics. The successful collaboration of these divisions produced Pilot ACE, the first electronic digital computer available to British industry.

Darwin retired from the NPL in 1949. Thereafter he continued to write some scientific papers but his chief interest became population problems and eugenics. In his book *The Next Million Years* (1952) he considered the long-term future of mankind. He contributed the notices of Sir W. H. Bragg and D. R. Hartree to the *Dictionary of National Biography*. Before and after retirement he was in demand for committee work. For example, he was a member of the University Grants Committee for a double term, from 1943 to 1953. From 1941 to 1944 he was president of the Physical Society and from 1953 to 1959 president of the Eugenics Society. He and his wife enjoyed foreign travel and among his missions was a visit as scientific adviser to Thailand in 1953 on behalf of the United Nations Educational, Scientific and Cultural Organization.

Darwin was knighted in 1942. He received honorary degrees from Bristol, Manchester, St Andrews, Trinity College (Dublin), Delhi, Edinburgh, Chicago, and California. He was an honorary fellow of Christ's College (1939) and of Trinity College, Cambridge (1953). He received the royal medal of the Royal Society in 1935 and was a vice-president in 1939. He also received the Makdougall Brisbane prize from the Royal Society of Edinburgh. He was a foreign member of the Hollandsche Maatschappij der Wetenschappen of Haarlem, and an honorary member of the French Physical Society and of the American Philosophical Society.

Sir George P. Thomson, who wrote the Royal Society memoir of Darwin, suggests that Darwin's most useful work was as an interpreter of the new quantum theory to experimental physicists and that he was especially fitted for this because of his exceptionally wide range of understanding and a most unusual capacity for seeing the essential idea in a maze of complicated mathematics or conflicting experiments. This capacity of seeing essentials equally helped him at the National Physical Laboratory and in his work in the two wars.

Darwin was physically large, cheerful, and tolerant. The two portraits of him are very similar and were painted by his cousin Robin Darwin. He was warm and sympathetic to those who knew him well but students and some of his staff at the National Physical Laboratory felt awe as well as admiration for him. He had wide curiosity. He was proud of his family connections and devoted to his immediate family. He died on 31 December 1962 at Cambridge in the house where he was born, which subsequently became part of Darwin College. His wife survived him.

MARGARET GOWING, rev.

Sources G. P. Thomson, *Memoirs FRS*, 9 (1963), 69–85 · N. G. Annan, 'The intellectual aristocracy', *Studies in social history: a tribute to G. M. Trevelyan*, ed. J. H. Plumb (1955), 241–87 · G. Raverat, *Period piece* (1952) · private information (1981) · *CGPLA Eng. & Wales* (1963)

Archives American Philosophical Society, Philadelphia, corresp. and papers relating to quantum physics · Medical Research Council, London, corresp. | Bodl. Oxf., letters to O. G. S. Crawford · CAC Cam., corresp. with A. V. Hill · CUL, corresp. with Eugenics Society · ICL, corresp. with Dennis Gabor · Rice University, Houston, Texas, Woodson Research Center, corresp. with Julian Huxley · University of Copenhagen, Niels Bohr Institute for Astronomy, Physics, and Geophysics, corresp. with Niels Bohr

Likenesses W. Stoneman, photographs, 1926–53, NPG · Elliott & Fry, photograph, 1942, NPG [*see illus.*] · W. Stoneman, photograph, 1946, RS · R. Darwin, oils, 1949, Darwin College, Cambridge · R. Darwin, oils, 1949, RS · photograph, repro. in Thomson, *Memoirs FRS*, facing p. 69

Wealth at death £135,731: probate, 25 March 1963, *CGPLA Eng. & Wales*

Darwin, Charles Robert (1809–1882), naturalist, geologist, and originator of the theory of natural selection, was born on 12 February 1809 at The Mount, Shrewsbury, the fifth child and second son of Robert Waring Darwin (1766–1848), Shrewsbury's principal physician, and Susannah Wedgwood (1765–1817). His sisters were Marianne, Caroline, Susan, and Emily Catherine, his brother Erasmus Alvey. His grandfathers, the potter Josiah *Wedgwood

Charles Robert Darwin (1809–1882), by John Collier, 1881

(1730–1795) and the evolutionist poet and physician Erasmus *Darwin (1731–1802), were leading lights of the industrial revolution; his grandmothers were respectively Sarah Wedgwood (1734–1815) and Mary Howard (1740–1770). Charles's mother died in 1817, when he was eight, and in later life he had no distinct recollection of her beyond the 'black velvet gown' she wore on her deathbed and her 'curiously constructed work-table' (*Autobiography*, 22). She was buried in St Chad's Church, Montford, near Shrewsbury, where Darwin's father also rests.

Darwin's three older sisters took on maternal responsibility and he remembered his childhood with great affection. The nature of the relationship between father and son is disputed. Robert Waring Darwin was a talkative man of strong principles, freethinking, and an enthusiastic gardener. In later life Charles frequently referred to cherished medical and scientific opinions of his father, and he appreciated his father's powers of observation and intuitive understanding of human nature, qualities that enabled him to read 'the characters, and even the thoughts of those whom he saw even for a short time' (*Autobiography*, 32). Shrewd investments in canals and property made Dr Darwin prosperous, and through private mortgages and loans he kept a tight grip on the financial affairs of several Shrewsbury families. He was also a noted philanthropist. With a large medical practice and many friends, his life as a whig gentleman-physician was comfortably full, varied, and respectable, even if some nephews and nieces felt him to be domineering.

Charles Darwin's childhood is mainly known from his own recollections, where he portrays himself as a simple, docile, and happy child, with a liking for long solitary walks. He showed an early habit of fabricating adventures to seek attention. In 1817 he went to a day school run by George Case, minister of the local Unitarian chapel, where his mother (in keeping with her Wedgwood heritage) had taken him to services. At Shrewsbury School, which he attended as a boarder from 1818 to 1825, the teaching was narrow and classical. Darwin hated it and claimed that his daily facility in Latin verse was forgotten by the next morning. Later he recalled benefiting from little except private lessons in Euclid, although he did enjoy reading Shakespeare in private hours at school; at home he dabbled in chemistry in a small laboratory fitted up by his brother in an outhouse, but such science had no place in public schools, and when he repeated experiments in the dormitories he was publicly reproved by the headmaster, Dr Thomas Butler, for wasting time. The boy was an inveterate collector, of franks, seals, coins, birds' eggs, and minerals, and from early adolescence his passion became game shooting.

University education, 1825–1831 Robert Darwin intended both his sons to become physicians. Charles, unsuccessful at school, was removed in 1825, two years early, and spent the summer accompanying the doctor on his rounds. In the autumn he was sent with his brother Erasmus to Edinburgh University (1825–7), which offered the best medical education in Britain. Here English dissenters, barred from taking degrees at Oxford and Cambridge universities, kept abreast of continental work in the extramural schools and studied a suite of new sciences. The Darwins had studied medicine here for three generations, and Erasmus Darwin's grandsons found easy entrée to intellectual society. Leonard Horner took Charles to the Royal Society of Edinburgh, where he saw Sir Walter Scott. Diplomatic socializing with the professors, not least the elder Andrew Duncan, the octogenarian joint professor of the theory of physic (whose family vault contained Darwin's uncle), preceded the term's work. However, after a diligent start, Darwin recoiled at the early mornings: anatomy disgusted him, and his letters home criticized the professors. Civic politics had allowed some to treat their chairs as family property, and he was appalled at the case of the anatomist Alexander Monro tertius—the third generation to hold the seat. While the younger Andrew Duncan's winter lectures on materia medica left Darwin with the enduring memory of spending 'a whole, cold, breakfastless hour on the properties of rhubarb' (*Correspondence*, 4.36), this probably said more about Darwin's youth and restlessness than about Duncan's abilities. Duncan was widely versed in European learning and at the forefront in teaching Augustin de Candolle's 'natural system' of classification (it was Candolle who emphasized the 'war' among species, so important to Darwin later). Most of all, Darwin was sickened by surgery (this was before the introduction of anaesthesia), and he fled during an operation on a child in the Royal Infirmary. All of this determined him to forsake the dead house and dissection, a decision he would later on occasion regret.

There were diversions: Thomas Hope's theatrical chemistry classes, coastal walks, and bird stuffing lessons, a craft taught to Darwin by a freed slave from Guiana, John Edmonstone, in the university natural history museum. After hiking through Wales during the summer of 1826, inspired by Gilbert White's *Natural History of Selborne* which taught him to see birds as more than targets, he returned to Edinburgh. His interest in medicine gone, he joined the thriving student Plinian Society. Here he heard the tyros talk on classification and cuckoos, and he even spoke himself. There was sometimes a frisson in these basement meetings in 1826, generated by a handful of young radical freethinkers using a deterministic science against the Church of Scotland. Darwin was nominated for the Plinian by the anti-clerical phrenologist William A. F. Browne, among others, and he petitioned to join on 21 November 1826, the day that Browne announced that he would refute Charles Bell's *Anatomy and Physiology of Expression* (which argued that the human facial muscles were specially created to express mankind's unique emotions). Darwin joined a week later, with the Unitarian W. R. Greg, who read a paper on lower animals' possessing every human mental faculty. Darwin himself was on the council of the Plinian Society by 5 December 1826.

Darwin's fascination for the local sea pens and sea mats on the Firth of Forth coast brought him briefly under the wing of his most influential mentor at Edinburgh, the physician and sponge expert Robert Edmond Grant, who guided Darwin's invertebrate studies in this rich North Sea environment. A Francophile and friend of Étienne Geoffroy Saint-Hilaire, Grant was a deist and materialist, and Darwin in old age recalled his bursting out with praise for the transformist Jean-Baptiste Lamarck. Indeed, Grant, like Lamarck, believed that the simple tissues of sponges and polyps could elucidate the primitive origin and primal function of complex human organs. Beneath Grant's stern crust Darwin found an enthusiast for this microscopic life, and Darwin made his own observations in March 1827 on the larvae of molluscs, the sea mat *Flustra*, and sea pens, confirming Grant's belief that sponge and sea-mat larvae could swim by means of cilia. Grant pushed Darwin into consulting continental books, including Lamarck's *System of Invertebrate Animals*, to check his *Flustra* findings. From late 1826 Grant took Darwin to meetings of the Wernerian Natural History Society, to which, on 24 March 1827, Grant announced Darwin's discovery that the black bodies inside oyster shells were the eggs of the skate leech *Pontobdella*. Three days later Darwin made his public début, presenting his findings on swimming *Flustra* larvae and *Pontobdella* eggs before the Plinian Society.

Darwin had read his grandfather Erasmus's book on the evolutionary laws of life and health, *Zoonomia*. Grant approved of it and exposed the grandson to the latest ideas on transmutation, endorsing Geoffroy's view that all animals showed a 'unity of plan'; from people to polyps, they shared similar organs that differed only in complexity. Thus life could be threaded into a chain, which for Grant represented a real blood line. His belief that the common origin of the plant and animal kingdoms lay just below the simplest algae and polyps, whose eggs were analogous to the 'monads', or elementary particles of living tissue, would provide a launch point for Darwin's own speculations a decade later. However, Grant's zoology was out of step with the safe taxonomic preoccupations of the age, and Darwin was exposed to the passions that such subversive science aroused. Browne's talk on the material basis of mind at the 27 March 1827 Plinian meeting so inflamed listeners that Darwin's début was probably overshadowed. Browne's propositions were struck out of the minute book in an act of censorship typical in the long tory years following the French Revolution (during which Darwin's own grandfather had been vilified). A sensitive eighteen-year-old student could have been left in little doubt of the fate awaiting ideas that threatened to undermine spiritual and political authority.

Darwin remembered his Edinburgh years as a sterile period, but he was in rich scientific surroundings. He sat Robert Jameson's lectures in zoology and geology and heard Jameson explain rocks as sedimentary precipitates in opposition to Hope's view of granites as cooled crystals. Darwin, taking Hope's chemistry course, was teased to take his side in this old-fashioned debate. Jameson's course required Darwin to attend practical sessions three times a week in the magnificent museum, newly refurbished in 1826 and the fourth largest of its kind in Europe. Here budding civil engineers and East India Company men learned mineral types and colonial flora, while field trips taught them how to read strata sequences. This was an ideal training for a future imperial traveller.

Young and homesick, and loathing medicine, Darwin left Edinburgh in April 1827 without a degree. His father, a freethinker, fearing that he would become a wastrel on the family fortune, shrewdly decided on a clerical career. The complacent Church of England was ideal for an aimless son addicted to field sports, and once again Darwin followed his brother Erasmus, this time to Cambridge (where Erasmus had just finished his medical requirements) to read for the ordinary degree, the usual precursor to taking holy orders. His schoolboy Greek had to be revised, and he was tutored at home, not entering Christ's College until January 1828. Here Darwin found a cousin also preparing for the church, William Darwin Fox, who soon became his close friend. Though the idea of a comfortable parish appealed, Darwin had doubts about his faith, but he found nothing in Bishop John Pearson's *Exposition of the Creed* and the Revd John Bird Sumner's *Evidences of Christianity* that he could not believe.

The contrast between Edinburgh and Cambridge was total. Cambridge was a market town dominated by a medieval university, ruled by clergymen and their proctors. Darwin avoided the horsey set at Christ's and Fox introduced him to beetle collecting in the local fens. For Darwin this sport was compulsive and competitive. He identified his catches from standard texts, including Lamarck's, and was thrilled to see his name in print, in an instalment of J. F. Stephens's *Illustrations of British Entomology*. Expert advice was also available at the Friday soirées held by the young botany professor, the Revd John Stevens Henslow, which were attended by other reverend professors, such as the geologist Adam Sedgwick and the polymathic William Whewell. The dons' brilliant conversation inspired Darwin to make a name for himself in natural history; he attended Henslow's botany course in 1829, and again in 1830 and 1831.

Formal studying became a desultory affair. Darwin's mathematics suffered (as it always would) and in the summer of 1828 he admitted not feeling sufficiently inwardly moved by the Holy Spirit to enter the church. His brother Erasmus, already a freethinker, now lived in London on the family purse, and when Fox left Cambridge, Darwin latched on to Erasmus during the vacations. Back in college he idled away his time, ran up bills, drank, rode, and gambled. There were greater temptations for the students. In spring 1829 the radicals Richard Carlile and the Revd Robert Taylor started an 'infidel home missionary tour' at Cambridge. They challenged the divines to a debate and sought converts before being hounded out of town. Taylor, a Cambridge graduate in holy orders, had been dubbed the Devil's Chaplain, and years later, as Darwin prepared to publish on evolution, he remembered the name and exclaimed 'What a book a Devil's chaplain might write on the … horridly cruel works of nature!' (*Correspondence*, 6.178). He feared that he himself might be similarly reviled, an outcast from respectable society.

In March 1830 Darwin passed his first major exam, the 'little go', which included questions on the Revd William Paley's *Evidences of Christianity*, a book that Darwin relished. He became Henslow's walking companion, excelling himself on the professor's botany field trips and turning up early for lectures. Henslow's course was far removed from anything that Darwin had experienced at Edinburgh; it introduced him to plants as living organisms. Darwin employed his microscopical skills on plant fertilization processes, making good use of Henslow's knowledge of the recent work of French physiologists and the British botanist Robert Brown. Henslow taught Darwin about the properties of life and the dividing line between animals and plants. Darwin came to idolize his professor and said that their friendship was one of the most influential circumstances in his early life.

With Henslow as his tutor in 1830, Darwin studied mathematics and read Paley's *Principles of Moral and Political Philosophy* just as the agricultural unrest, or 'Swing riots', sweeping southern England reached Cambridge and 800 special constables were sworn in to protect the colleges. It was probably from this period that Darwin would remember how Henslow rejected Paley's utilitarian rationale for the established church. In the final BA examination in January 1831 Darwin ranked tenth in the pass-list of 178, surprising even himself. His residence requirement kept him in Cambridge, and he continued to seek Henslow's guidance. 'I do not know', Darwin confessed, 'whether I love or respect' him more (*Correspondence*, 1.123). He read the last of Paley's trilogy, the *Natural Theology*, with its argument for a designer God from the adaptation of living species to their environments. This was the cornerstone of Cambridge science, along with John Herschel's *Preliminary Discourse on the Study of Natural Philosophy*, which inspired Darwin further in his scientific career. After reading Alexander von Humboldt's *Personal Narrative* of his voyage to the tropics, Darwin began planning a month's expedition with friends to Tenerife. In preparation he attended Sedgwick's geology lectures in spring 1831 and in August accompanied Sedgwick (at Henslow's request) to north Wales for two weeks in the field. It was the best possible training, much more effective than the dry lectures at Edinburgh, which had made Darwin vow never to 'attend to Geology' (*Autobiography*, 53). Sedgwick built up Darwin's expertise and self-confidence, introducing him to some of the most perplexing geological issues of the day. Then, on returning to Shrewsbury, Darwin found a letter from Henslow offering him passage on a ship headed round the world.

The Beagle voyage, 1831–1836 Henslow's letter referred to a proposed two-year trip to 'Terra del Fuego & home by the East Indies', explaining that the position was 'more as a companion than a mere collector'. Henslow had recommended Darwin, 'not on the supposition of yr. being a finished Naturalist, but as amply qualified for collecting, observing, & noting any thing worthy to be noted in Natural History' (*Correspondence*, 1.128–9). This was not an official vacancy open to all. It was a private arrangement originating with the captain, Robert FitzRoy, a nephew of the duke of Grafton, who asked Francis Beaufort, hydrographer to the navy, to find a well-educated gentleman with scientific interests who could make good use of such a voyage. The search thus made its way through a network of Cambridge professors and their Admiralty friends, via Henslow and his brother-in-law, the Revd Leonard Jenyns (both of whom would have accepted but for family commitments), and on to Darwin. At first Darwin's father objected so strongly that he felt obliged to refuse, but his uncle Josiah Wedgwood II was in favour and Dr Darwin relented. Afterwards he provided every assistance, including the cost of equipping his son and covering all of his considerable expenses during the voyage.

On 1 September 1831 Darwin accepted and went to Cambridge to consult Henslow. In London he met FitzRoy and was approved by him. Darwin was also taken with the captain. The *Beagle* had recently returned from South America after a two-ship expedition (1827–30) commanded by Phillip Parker King, which had surveyed a large part of the eastern coast, a region significant in naval and commercial terms for Great Britain during Canning's ministry. On that voyage FitzRoy had assumed temporary command of the *Beagle* after the suicide of Captain Pringle Stokes. FitzRoy was appointed overall commander for a second voyage to complete the survey. Darwin now prepared himself, visiting naturalists at the British Museum and Zoological Society, learning preserving techniques, getting his equipment in order, and visiting the *Beagle*, under refit at the naval base of Devonport in Plymouth. He sought advice from Robert Brown about travelling microscopes and worried about the lack of room on board. The *Beagle* was a converted 10-gun brig, only 90 feet long, capacity 242 tons, popularly known as one of the 'coffin' class. Arriving at Devonport in October, Darwin found that departure was delayed. He grew anxious, with heart pains, and feared that he might have to abandon the voyage. When the ship did sail, it was forced to return to port twice because of storms. The *Beagle* left finally on 27 December 1831, by which time much of Darwin's initial excitement had disappeared.

The voyage, which lasted five years, was the key formative event in Darwin's life. It 'determined my whole career' (*Autobiography*, 76), giving him an unrivalled opportunity to make observations, collect animals and plants, and explore some of the most beautiful, desolate, and isolated places in the world. Under FitzRoy the voyage's objectives extended to include geophysical measurements, and the *Beagle* was equipped with a variety of instruments and devices, including a lightning conductor and a large number of marine chronometers for measuring longitude. The Admiralty intended the officers to make a chain of exceptionally accurate measurements round the globe. The ship also carried out trials on Beaufort's wind scale. Supernumeraries in FitzRoy's private employment were appointed, including an artist, Augustus Earle (replaced *en route* by Conrad Martens in 1833), and an instrument-tender, George Stebbing. The voyage was also to be more of a Christianizing and civilizing mission than most imperial cruises: a novice missionary, Richard Matthews, was on board, accompanied by three native Fuegians who had been taken hostage by FitzRoy on the previous voyage, carried to England, and briefly educated with a view to establishing an Anglican mission in Tierra del Fuego. Darwin was independently financed but on the Admiralty books for victuals. He was the only member of the ship who held any intimacy with the captain; they usually dined together, and they shared a number of adventures. FitzRoy at times seemed as unstable as his uncle Lord Castlereagh, who had committed suicide, and he and Darwin occasionally argued, once in Plymouth and again in Brazil, over slavery (which Darwin abhorred), when Darwin nearly left the ship. But FitzRoy wanted Darwin aboard, not least perhaps to allay his own fears about mental instability and spare him Pringle Stokes's fate. Although the young tory aristocrat and Darwin became friends, even publishing a short paper on missionary activity together in 1836, their views and temperaments were at root incompatible, and afterwards they drifted apart.

Darwin slept and worked in the poop cabin, which he shared with the mate and draughtsman, John Lort Stokes, and midshipman Philip Gidley King, son of the former commander. He befriended the officers, especially second lieutenant Bartholomew Sulivan, and one or another often joined him in his natural history ventures. In 1833 FitzRoy gave Darwin permission to employ as a personal assistant one of the cabin boys, Syms Covington (who would remain with him afterwards until 1839). Darwin's collecting activities amused the sailors and earned him the nickname Philos, meaning ship's philosopher.

The *Beagle* visited the Cape Verde Islands (January 1832), Brazil (April–July 1832), Montevideo and Buenos Aires (July–November 1832), Tierra del Fuego and Cape Horn (December 1832–January 1833, February 1834), the Falkland Islands (March–April 1833, March–April 1834), Patagonia (April 1833–January 1834), the west coast of South America (Chiloé, Valparaiso, Lima: June 1834–July 1835), the Galápagos Islands (September–October 1835), Tahiti (November 1835), New Zealand (December 1835), Australia (Sydney, January 1836; Tasmania, February; King George's Sound, March), the Cocos Islands (April 1836), Mauritius (April–May 1836), Cape Town (May–June 1836), and St Helena and Ascension (July 1836). Darwin participated in all the excitements of the voyage. He joined the carnival in Brazil, witnessed revolutions in Montevideo and Lima, and saw gauchos exterminating the natives on the pampas. He watched Mount Osorno erupting on 26 November 1834 while on the island of Chiloé and experienced an earthquake in the woods outside Valdivia. He walked through the ruins of the town of Concepción, destroyed by the same earthquake, on 20 February 1835, and declared them to be 'the most awful yet interesting spectacle I ever beheld' (*Diary*, ed. Keynes, 296). It was a humbling vision that revealed the powerlessness of people and impermanence of their works before the awesome forces of nature. He proved a stalwart member of inland expeditions and a good shot, often helping to supply fresh meat for the crew. After a dangerous escape from an enormous wave created by a calving glacier, when Darwin's quick action saved lives, FitzRoy named an expanse of water and a mountain in the Beagle Channel in his honour. His shipmates all warmly vouched for his even humour, resilience, and likeable manners, and he similarly remembered them with affection. The only exception was the ship's surgeon, Robert McCormick, who left the voyage at Rio de Janeiro in 1832, apparently annoyed at the preference given to Darwin's collecting over his own. The privileges of a self-financed captain's companion showed too in the invitations Darwin received to join polite society ashore.

Playing no part in the ship's daily orders, Darwin often travelled overland. In Patagonia he made several expeditions, riding over 70 miles from Maldonado in May 1833, from Patagones to Bahia Blanca that August, and in September–October 1833 he rode 700 miles from Bahia Blanca, via Buenos Aires, to Santa Fe. In November he set off again, from Montevideo to Mercedes, to see the Rio Uruguay. On the west coast he rode to the base of the Andes in August–September 1834, and in March–April 1835 trekked across the cordilleras, from Valparaiso through the Portillo Pass to Mendoza. On another occasion he was seriously ill with a fever, brought on, he thought, by sour wine, and recuperated for five weeks in the house of an old school friend, Richard Corfield, who lived in Valparaiso. Always he studied the local geology and natural history, whether travelling or more permanently based in lodgings. For three months in 1832 he rented a cottage on Botofogo Bay near Rio de Janeiro, where he hunted, dredged, and collected corallines and plants. The pleasure he took in tropical vegetation and alpine scenery was both aesthetic and scientific. It fuelled his growing sense of purpose as a naturalist.

Darwin's geological achievements mounted up. Using Charles Lyell's radical new *Principles of Geology* (1830–33) as a guide, he grew bold in interpreting the earth's crust by causes now in operation. (The first volume was a gift from FitzRoy, the other two reached him during the voyage.) He was captivated by Lyell's grand theoretical scheme— 'when seeing a thing never seen by Lyell, one yet saw it partially through his eyes' (*Correspondence*, 3.55)—and confirmed many of Lyell's observations with careful field-work. On other points Darwin expanded innovatively, especially in understanding the piecemeal formation of the Andes and the origin of coral reefs on sinking mountain rims. There was an immediacy to it all. After experiencing the Concepción earthquake in 1835, Darwin found the shoreline raised a few feet and mussel beds lifted out of the sea, confirming his Lyellian incremental upthrust theory. As he trekked through the Portillo and Uspallata passes of the Andes, the coloured rocks seemed almost like a geological diagram, and in the Cocos Islands he waded over the reefs to confirm his theory of the formation of coral atolls. His geology was dynamic, with continents slowly rising and sea basins sinking, and it formed the basis of all his later views. He endorsed Lyell's belief in an earth gradually shaped over countless ages: time enough—as he later grasped—for evolution by natural selection to occur.

Darwin's collections were extensive. At Punta Alta near Bahia Blanca he found fossilized remains of gigantic extinct mammals, which at the time he thought must belong to mastodons, armadillos, and megatheriums (ground sloths). The fossils were later identified as belonging to previously unknown giant species. The cause of their extinction puzzled him because the remains were embedded with species of shells still in existence. In the far south of Patagonia he collected a new species of rhea (well known to local inhabitants), which he afterwards used to illustrate the geographical differentiation of species. He collected a great number of insects, birds, molluscs, small vertebrates, invertebrates, and plants, recording their provenance, living appearance, and behaviour in field notebooks and diaries. Crates of specimens were periodically shipped back to Henslow for storage. Henslow encouraged William Buckland and William Clift to exhibit some of the megatherium remains at the Cambridge meeting of the British Association for the Advancement of Science in 1833, and in 1835 Henslow published extracts on natural history topics from Darwin's letters. These were read at meetings of the Cambridge Philosophical Society and the Geological Society of London.

Ironically, what proved to be the most famous collection of all, the birds from the Galápagos Islands, was carelessly labelled. Darwin did not notice the diversification of finch species on separate islands during the *Beagle*'s five-week visit, although the English resident on Charles Island informed him that the giant tortoises were island-specific, and Darwin realized that the mockingbirds were too.

Thus, identifying the finch skins proved difficult when he returned to London. Even so, the Galápagos Islands impressed him greatly. He was fascinated by the iguanas, giant tortoises, mockingbirds, and other birds, as well as the volcanic geology. The relations between the species on different islands, and between the island species and those of continental South America, were, however, sufficiently puzzling for him to allude to them in his ornithological notes on the return voyage. He seems to have wondered about the possibility of transmutation at this time.

Darwin was stirred by the diverse human populations he met, ranging from expatriate Europeans to indigenous tribes. His writings contain colourful references to gauchos, with whom he travelled across Argentina, the Patagonian 'Indians', Tahitians, Maori, and Australian Aborigines, as well as missionaries, colonists, slaves, and emigré Cornish miners. He met General Rosas (leading the war to exterminate the native Patagonians) in August 1833 and was caught up in military blockades. The most unsettling of all Darwin's encounters was with the native inhabitants of Tierra del Fuego. He was stunned by their naked 'savage' state, particularly in comparison with the three fine-clothed Fuegians on board. 'I would not have believed how entire the difference between savage & civilized man is.—It is greater than between a wild & domesticated animal' (*Diary*, ed. Keynes, 122). Yet the fact that Fuegians could be 'civilized' (as Darwin saw it) confirmed his belief that, under the skin, humans were all one species, and this remained a lasting influence on his later evolutionary theories. During the *Beagle*'s time in the far south Darwin and FitzRoy were sad to note that the three Anglicized Fuegians soon returned to the aboriginal state.

Darwin suffered from sea-sickness throughout, and his longing for home grew with his maturity as a naturalist. As the voyage ended, his love of nature was ousting the church: 'your situation is above envy', he wrote to his clerical cousin Fox; 'to a person fit to take the office, the life of a Clergyman is a type of all that is respectable & happy' (*Correspondence*, 1.460). But Darwin himself now had other plans. The voyage had fostered an intellectual ferment and fortified him to re-evaluate all of natural history. His future, he believed, lay in the élite world of London science. He disembarked at Falmouth on 2 October 1836 and arrived at Shrewsbury two days later, where his sister Caroline realized that he had gained an 'interest for the rest of his life' (ibid., 1.505).

Theorizing in London, 1836–1842 After visiting Cambridge to consult Henslow about experts to describe his *Beagle* specimens, and calling on his Wedgwood relatives in Staffordshire, Darwin stayed with his brother in London for a few weeks. During the five-year voyage the whigs had established a new workhouse regime for the losers in a Malthusian competitive economy. Erasmus was intimate with the poor-law propagandist Harriet Martineau, which put him at the heart of the whig machine, and Darwin's cousin Hensleigh Wedgwood, whose wedding to Frances Mackintosh had been attended by Thomas Robert Malthus's daughter as a bridesmaid, completed the two brothers' dining circle. The landlubber had moved straight into an aggressively Malthusian, reforming environment.

On 29 October 1836 Darwin first met Lyell in person. They became close friends, and Lyell introduced him to the comparative anatomist Richard Owen. In December and January 1837 Owen received Darwin's pampas fossils at the College of Surgeons; Thomas Bell accepted the *Beagle* reptiles, Leonard Jenyns the fish, George Robert Waterhouse the mammals, and John Gould the birds. After obtaining a £1000 Treasury grant through Henslow's government contacts, Darwin arranged for the naturalists' technical descriptions to be published in nineteen numbers as *The Zoology of the Voyage of H.M.S. Beagle* (1838–43; reissued in five parts, 1839–43). The plants and insects, which Darwin planned to include, and the marine invertebrates that he intended to tackle himself, were described piecemeal in other publications. Henslow, to whom Darwin gave the plants, later sent them to Joseph Dalton Hooker for identification.

Darwin lived in Cambridge until March 1837, working on his manuscripts and specimens, and lecturing at the Cambridge Philosophical Society on the lightning-fused glass tubes in the Maldonado sand dunes. On 4 January he read his first scientific paper, 'Observations of proofs of recent elevation on the coast of Chile', as a new fellow of the Geological Society of London. Lyell's influence showed in Darwin's discussion of the slowly rising Chilean coastline, compensated by a sinking Pacific, but some of his views were unLyellian, notably that coral reefs crowned mountains disappearing undersea. Darwin soon established himself as a gentleman geologist, at one with the urban gentry and clerical dons: he became a council member of the Geological Society in 1837 and a secretary in 1838. He was also vice-president of the Entomological Society in 1838.

Living on £400 a year from his father, Darwin enjoyed independence. He turned his *Beagle* diary into a book of travels. It was finished by June 1837 and published in May 1839 as *Journal and Remarks, 1832–1836*, the third volume of FitzRoy's *Narrative of the Surveying Voyages*, and again separately on 15 August 1839 as *Journal of researches into the geology and natural history of the various countries visited by H.M.S. Beagle under the command of Captain Fitz-Roy, R.N., from 1832–1836*. Meanwhile Darwin continued sorting the *Beagle* collections for distribution to specialists and sometimes bought in expert help, such as that of the engraver George Sowerby. Bit by bit, his collections ended up in major scientific institutions.

The expert reports on his collections surprised him. Darwin had initially thought that his pampas fossils were huge extinct forms allied to rhinoceroses and mastodons (both found on other continents), as well as megatheriums, but Owen diagnosed a capybara relative, *Toxodon*, an anteater-like *Scelidotherium*, ground sloth *Mylodon*, armadillo *Glyptodon*, and llama-like *Macrauchenia*. These identifications suggested that some 'law of succession' had caused the previous South American mammals to be replaced by others of their own kind. On 4 January 1837

Darwin presented the Zoological Society museum with eighty preserved mammals and 450 birds. Within days Gould discovered that the Galápagos birds, misunderstood by Darwin as a mixture of finches, wrens, 'Grossbeaks', and blackbird-relatives, were in fact a closely related (and new) group of differentially adapted ground finches. Gould also distinguished the small rhea that Darwin had collected as a new species, *Rhea darwinii* (subsequently renamed).

On 6 March 1837 Darwin moved from Cambridge to London lodgings, at 36 Great Marlborough Street, close to his brother. Here the secular milieu was more conducive to his private musings on extinction and repopulation arising from Owen's, Gould's, and his own geological findings. In Erasmus's freethinking circle Martineau believed in the natural predetermination of human life and Wedgwood interested himself in the genealogy of languages (itself a sort of evolution). Darwin attended Charles Babbage's soirées. Babbage's in-press *Ninth Bridgewater Treatise* made God a legislator, working pre-eminently through grand laws rather than miracles. This was the rational whig answer to what John Herschel had called the 'mystery of mysteries' (Cannon, 'Impact'), the cause of the replacement of species through time. By early 1837 Darwin too accepted that 'the Creator creates by … laws' (Barrett and others, *Notebooks*, B98).

In March that year Gould recognized Darwin's four Galápagos mockingbirds (which, unlike the finches, Darwin had labelled by island) as three separate species. The island-specific types suggested to Darwin that they were mainland South American castaways that had changed to meet local conditions. Darwin belatedly examined FitzRoy's labelled finches to confirm that each too was island-specific. Bell's work on the giant Galápagos tortoises and Waterhouse's on the rodents further confirmed that representative species were the rule on these islands.

Inured, perhaps, to transmutation by the works of his grandfather Erasmus and Grant, Darwin came to accept the idea unquestioningly early in 1837, even though 'evolution' (an anachronistic word, 'descent' he called it from 1838) was detested by his Cambridge mentors and assailed in Lyell's *Principles of Geology*. This was a year and a half before he devised a definite causal mechanism. Owen, preparing his first Hunterian lectures at the College of Surgeons, stimulated Darwin's search for the laws of living matter. Unlike Henslow, who had taught that the matter inside pollen granules was inert, and that life was impressed from without, Owen accepted that the embryonic germ had an intrinsic 'organizing energy' that directed its development and waned as the tissues grew. Darwin would stretch this 'organizing energy' to transmutational (and to Owen illicit) lengths. Like Grant's radical anatomists, Darwin in his most radical phase (1837 to mid-1838) considered living atoms to be self-organizing. He now returned to the intense questioning monologues started in his 'Red' notebook during the last months of the *Beagle* voyage. Were extinctions due to species senescence? If island isolation on the Galápagos was necessary for species formation (to stop back-blending with mainland parents), how to explain the overlapping ranges of the two species of Patagonian rhea? Were changes produced *per saltum*, with no blending intermediates? Were new species 'monsters' from the womb, the sort then being mooted by Owen?

In July 1837 Darwin opened his first notebook on transmutation, which he labelled 'B' (his 'A' notebook was mostly concerned with geology). Thus began two years of secret telegraphic jottings on the mechanics of organic change. He first toyed with Lamarck's and Grant's idea of the spontaneous generation of monads driving the escalator of life 'upwards', and his joke, 'If all men were dead then monkeys make men.—Men make angels' (Barrett and others, *Notebooks*, B169), showed his defiance of clerical fears of a simian ancestry. Then his thoughts became relativistic, radically departing from Lamarck's. He foreswore any unidirectional change; life merely adapted to local habitats. He developed a non-human orientation and found it 'absurd to talk of one animal being higher than another', for humans and bees would have different criteria of 'highness' (ibid., B74). He conceived life rather as a branching tree, and he jettisoned a continuous spontaneous generation of life in favour of a single Precambrian emergence. He rejected, too, his own former idea of species senescence, which would cause all the creatures on a branch to die out together. A species died out, he now thought, because conditions changed too fast.

Faltering health accompanied these disturbing conclusions. Darwin led a double life, mixing with the Oxford and Cambridge divines at the respectable Geological Society while secretly plumbing a materialistic transmutation. He read papers to the Geological on the pampas fossils and coral reefs in May 1837, on the formation of mould through the action of worms in November, and on the earthquake and volcanic causes of Andean uplift in March 1838. The worms, corals, and incremental uplift expressed his belief in small causes producing large results, as would come to be the case in his secret evolutionary views. Behind this façade his contempt for the anthropocentric divines grew. He privately scoffed at the Geological Society's president, William Whewell, who 'says length of days adapted to duration of sleep of man!!! whole universe so adapted!!! … instance of arrogance!!' (Barrett and others, *Notebooks*, D49). Darwin's acceptance by the geological élite, which decried materialistic science as morally corrupting and politically seditious, only exacerbated his inner plight.

As the tory–Anglicans were ousted from town halls in countrywide reforms, Darwin was evicting their providential God from a reformed biology. Of Unitarian stock himself, he expressed radical dissenting sentiments in his notebooks, sentiments of equality, anti-slavery, and anti-privilege to sustain a levelling kinship with all life: 'Animals—whom we have made our slaves we do not like to consider our equals.—Do not slave holders wish to make the black man other kind?' (Barrett and others, *Notebooks*, B231). He also saw pain run through the whole creation:

'animals our fellow brethren in pain, disease death & suffering … they may partake, from our origin in one common ancestor we may all be netted together' (ibid., B232). But whatever his sanction from dissenting political gains in the country, he knew that his speculations would alienate the Anglican establishment, which saw evolution as a threat to belief in human accountability in the next world and with it their paternalistic control of this one.

In 1838 Darwin filled three notebooks ('C', 'D', and 'E') on transmutation, and parallel 'M' and 'N' notebooks on the behavioural, psychological, and metaphysical implications of evolution for mankind. Evolution from the first was designed to explain human morality no less than body form. Darwin's first sight of an ape, an orang-utan, at London Zoo, on 28 March 1838, led him to make notes on her human-like emotions. He began studying the expressions and behaviour of monkeys. More and more a cultural and genetic determinist (dismissing free will at this time), he accepted that morality was culture-relative and saw its origin in the social instincts of troop animals. To Plato's claim that 'our "necessary ideas [of good and evil]" arise from the preexistence of the soul', Darwin responded, 'read monkeys for preexistence' (Barrett and others, *Notebooks*, M128). Other remarks left no doubt that he grasped the implications, such as 'whole [miraculous] fabric totters & falls' (ibid., C76).

Darwin explained the inheritance of instincts by means of their coding in the nervous system, and considered even the 'love of deity [an] effect of organization. oh you Materialist!' (Barrett and others, *Notebooks*, C166). In an age when science was expected to underpin traditional values, such materialism, had it been made public, would have been anathema to conservatives. Darwin, an anomalous theorizer in an age primarily concerned with describing and classifying, was not about to expose himself. His rising career—he was elected to the Athenaeum in 1838, the Royal Society in 1839, and the council of the Royal Geographical Society in 1840—served to emphasize how much he stood to lose. He had seen the Plinian Society censorship and was familiar with the anatomist William Lawrence's disgrace for holding materialist ideas. On one occasion Darwin had a nightmare of execution, which he recorded in his notebook, and he began conceiving disarming tactics: 'Mention persecution of early Astronomers' (ibid., C123).

Overwork and ill health drove Darwin to the Scottish highlands in summer 1838, where he visited the parallel 'roads' of Glen Roy. These he compared to the terraced beaches in Chile, in accordance with his theory of rising mountains and sinking sea basins. The roads were the subject of his 1839 'Observations on the parallel roads of Glen Roy', published in the *Philosophical Transactions of the Royal Society*. He would later characterize the paper as 'one long gigantic blunder' (*Correspondence*, 9.255) because it had taken no account of the effects of glaciation. Of no other part of his life's work was he ever so frankly self-critical.

Early in 1838 Darwin's thoughts turned to marriage. By now an inveterate cataloguer, he drew up a cost-benefit analysis (*Correspondence*, 1.443–5). To his mind, the advantages materially outweighed the disadvantages and he became engaged to his first cousin Emma Wedgwood (1808–1896) a few months later, almost routinely. She considered him the most 'transparent man I ever saw' (*Emma Darwin*, 2.6) and, going against his father's advice, Darwin confided to her his secret beliefs. Probably she was shocked, for while visiting her at her home in Maer, Staffordshire, Darwin noted that he must disguise 'stating how far, I believe, in Materialism' (Barrett and others, *Notebooks*, M57). Nevertheless, the two became warmly devoted to each other. About that time he also sensed the importance of his work. In the summer of 1838 he began recording the events of his life in a journal, starting with a 1700-word recollection of his childhood (this also formed part of his research into the nature of mind and memory). Emma was devout, an Anglican by baptism, with Unitarian convictions, and although her fears for Charles's eternal salvation became a sad undercurrent during the early years of the marriage, she remained steadily sympathetic towards his work.

In September 1838 Darwin studied books on human statistics. With distress rising round him and the workhouses going up, Malthus was highly topical; Darwin read his *Essay on the Principle of Population*. From it he quickly came to appreciate that overpopulation must be the factor driving competition and selection, for:

> being well prepared to appreciate the struggle for existence … it at once struck me that under these circumstances favourable variations would tend to be preserved, and unfavourable ones to be destroyed. Here, then, I had at last got a theory by which to work. (*Autobiography*, 120)

Malthus's doctrine that human population tends to double every twenty-five years (if there is no check or restriction) struck Darwin in his primed state, even as he planned to marry and reproduce. The numbers of animals and plants were not stable, as he had thought; too many individuals were born, in nature as in society. Competition left only the best adapted, those most able to leave offspring. Each stage in the genealogical ascent was 'the surviving one of ten thousand trials' (Barrett and others, *Notebooks*, Mac58v); millions must die so that the species remained fitted to changing conditions. Darwin recorded this new insight in his 'D' notebook in an entry dated 28 September. With its kernel of Malthusian overpopulation and struggle, Darwin's private view synchronized with the social theories of the whig grandees and was divorced from those of the anti-Malthusian radicals. But even though Paley's happy nature gave way to Malthus's bleaker image, Darwin, retaining his creedless rational faith, still saw 'descent' as God's mechanism for this 'production of higher animals' (ibid., OUN37).

Darwin's faith was too slim even for Emma. She took him to King's College Church, London, but he had ceased to believe in divine revelation. With £10,000 from Dr Darwin and Emma's dowry of £5000, plus an allowance of £400 a year, the couple were wealthy. Married by a cousin, the Revd John Allen Wedgwood, on 29 January 1839 at St Peter's Church, Maer, they moved into a rented house in Upper Gower Street, London, where Emma soon became pregnant.

By now Darwin accepted that mental as well as bodily variations arose by chance. Selection worked on randomly altering instincts. It became irrelevant whether or not instincts were coded in the brain, and this allowed Darwin to play down his mental materialism, with its overtones of atheistic radicalism. However, the randomness of Darwin's new nature made it even more irreconcilable to a higher design, although he still portrayed nature anthropomorphically as a sort of omnipotent breeder who selected the most useful traits. Having grown up among the agricultural gentry, he studied livestock husbandry as a matter of course. He discussed fancy breeds, particularly dogs, with William Yarrell and learned how breeders picked the desired traits from each litter; he talked with agriculturists and gardeners at every opportunity. Although Darwin opened a 'Questions and experiments' notebook in 1839 on husbandry issues and sent country gentlemen of his acquaintance a list of 'Questions about the breeding of animals', the analogy between natural and artificial selection that was to underpin all his subsequent work was already complete. On 10 July 1839 Darwin closed his 'E' notebook—his last major transmutation notebook.

The Darwins began to withdraw, giving up parties and the old circles. The man who saw contingency rule biology led a routine life, his days alike 'as two peas' (*Correspondence*, 2.236). Stomach troubles, flatulence, and nausea began to plague him, marking the onset of the illness that would dog his life. But he was delighted by the birth of their first child, William Erasmus (1839–1914), on 27 December 1839. The child's expressions fascinated Darwin, who took notes comparing them to those of animals. An extended period of vomiting in 1840 forced Darwin to reduce his workload and seek medical help from a distant cousin, the society physician Henry Holland. He spent two summers seriously ill, cared for by his wife at her family home. Back in London he shunned unnecessary contacts and resigned as secretary of the Geological Society in 1841. When his paper on the distribution of the erratic boulders and their transport by ice-floes in South America was finished, he asked Hensleigh Wedgwood to read it to the society, delegating in a way that was to increase over the years.

The Darwins' second child, Anne Elizabeth (1841–1851), was born on 2 March 1841. Darwin finished his *Structure and Distribution of Coral Reefs* (1842), the first volume in a trilogy on the geology of South America, and studied humble-bees boring through the corollas of flowers (publishing a note in the *Gardeners' Chronicle*). His theoretical isolation was soon accompanied by the physical: he persuaded his father to lend him the money to buy a rural retreat in Down, Kent. Before moving he wrote a 35-page sketch of his evolution theory, completed in June 1842, which enumerated the arguments for descent and his Malthusian mechanism of natural selection but skirted the origin of morality and the ancestry of mankind. He had no intention of publishing immediately, certainly not that summer, with industrial Britain riot-torn and suffering a general strike.

Parish naturalist of Down, 1842–1856 In September 1842 Darwin moved the family to Down, a parish of about 400 inhabitants on the North Downs, 16 miles from London. Here, at 'the extreme verge of the world' (*Correspondence*, 2.352), he found security in an old parsonage with 15 acres of land. Down House would be his refuge for the next forty years. Much of his life here resembled that of a prosperous country parson, the sort of man he had once intended to be.

Finding that going to London 'so generally knocks me up, that I am able to do scarcely anything' (*Correspondence*, 2.355), he increasingly dropped out of metropolitan society. He undertook his major works at home, fitting out his estate as a place for natural history researches of a gentlemanly kind. He had the house renovated and extended, the lawns landscaped, gardens dug, and the road outside his study window lowered to keep passers-by from peering inside. A grove of trees was planted where he laid out his thinking path, the 'Sandwalk', and he began (but abandoned) a country diary, following in the footsteps of the Revd Gilbert White. Over the winter of 1843–4, with the second volume of his *Beagle* geology, *Volcanic Islands*, going into print, Darwin transformed the pencil sketch of his species theory into a coherent essay, but he only rarely broached the subject of transmutation with friends, and then with trepidation, fearing that his ideas would appear as 'the merest trash'. 'I am almost convinced (quite contrary to the opinion I started with) that species are not (it is like confessing a murder) immutable', he wrote to the young Kew botanist Joseph Dalton Hooker: 'You will groan, & think to yourself "on what a man have I been wasting my time …"' (ibid., 3.2). Hooker, however, was not put off. Buoyed by his response, Darwin finished the 231-page manuscript in February 1844. He had it copied out neatly by a local schoolmaster and entrusted it to his wife with a letter to be opened in the event of his 'sudden death', stating as his 'most solemn & last request' that she should engage an editor to publish his theory posthumously. 'If it be accepted even by one competent judge, it will be a considerable step in science' (ibid., 3.43).

Darwin's motives for not publishing at this point undoubtedly involved prudence mixed with great anxiety. His *Journal* had given him an entrée into scientific society worldwide and a reputation among travellers; animals and plants were now named after him; among London's savants he was also rated highly—he served as a Geological Society vice-president in 1844; and, not least, there were his clerical friends, determined to keep science responsible and supporting the creationist *status quo*: an ill-spoken word and Darwin's reputation would be in peril. Indeed, he watched as a popularization of evolution, *Vestiges of the Natural History of Creation* (1844), shocked intellectual society only weeks after he finished his essay. He read the reviews uneasily, knowing that the anonymous book—by the publisher Robert Chambers—had even been attributed to him, 'at which', he admitted, 'I ought to be much flattered & unflattered' (*Correspondence*, 3.181).

Vestiges attracted considerable scientific and theological abuse, particularly from conservatives. Darwin would not expose his own theory and risk enduring the same fate, but at the same time he felt driven to amass more and more authoritative evidence to support it.

Hooker, though sceptical of transmutation, became Darwin's sounding board and sparring partner, a trusted friend whose encyclopaedic knowledge of plants was constantly at his disposal. It was Hooker who inadvertently goaded him into his next project by remarking that only one who had studied many species was qualified to discuss their origin. Thus after finishing his last book based on the *Beagle* voyage, *Geological Observations on South America* (1846), Darwin turned to barnacles. He intended only to describe an anomalous tiny species he had brought back from southern Chile, *Arthrobalanus*, but ended up dissecting and describing all known species, living and extinct. What he found confirmed his ideas about the origin of the sexes from hermaphrodite invertebrate ancestors and strengthened his belief in transmutation. Every part of every species was subject to change, and he worked out how barnacles had descended from their crab-like relatives.

During this period the family grew and prospered. Emma, constantly pregnant for the first twelve years of marriage, bore eight more children: Mary Eleanor, who died three weeks old in 1842; Henrietta Emma (1843–1929), George Howard *Darwin (1845–1912), Elizabeth (1847–1926), Francis *Darwin (1848–1925), Leonard *Darwin (1850–1943), Horace *Darwin (1851–1928), and Charles Waring (1856–1858). With his father's help Darwin planned carefully for their future, buying land in Lincolnshire and reinvesting the income from his and Emma's portfolios. Prosperous respectability would be the children's legacy. Following his friend Henslow's example Darwin became a pillar of the parish. He subscribed towards church improvements and advised the incumbent, the Revd John Innes, on educational and charitable matters. Darwin became treasurer of the village Coal and Clothing Club, and in 1850 he and Innes founded the Down Friendly Society, with Darwin serving as guardian and treasurer. He also discussed charitable and village business with Sir John Lubbock, the mathematician and banker, whose house, High Elms, was nearby.

Darwin's stomach continued to plague him. He experimented on himself, giving up snuff and trying faddish electrotherapies, to no avail. His father, whom he revered, was a constant source of medical advice. After his death in 1848, Darwin's health deteriorated sharply, with vomiting fits, flatulence, fainting sensations, and black spots before his eyes, and he again placed himself in the hands of Dr Holland. He grew despondent, expecting his own imminent death, and was tortured by anxiety. He had even been too ill, he said, to reach Shrewsbury in time for his father's funeral (although he had arrived later in the day). With Emma's support, he turned to religious literature, but by now he was unable to believe 'in the same spirit … that ladies do believe on all & every subject' (*Correspondence*,

3.141). Just after his fortieth birthday in 1849 he fled in desperation for four months—his longest absence from Down—to a water-cure establishment at Malvern run by the fashionable hydropathist James Manby Gully. The water cure seemed to work and Darwin kept up the energetic cold-water regime when he returned home, with Joseph Parslow, the Down House butler, sluicing him down. He shivered with cold, plodding to and from a specially built outside shower-house throughout the winter. Darwin varied the treatment according to Gully's instructions and recorded his daily symptoms obsessively, and elliptically, for six years in a foolscap health diary. After many relapses, and fearing that his ailment was a heritable defect, he gave up 'all hopes of ever being a strong man again' (ibid., 4.369).

In 1850 Anne, his eldest daughter and favourite, became ill. Just before Easter 1851 Darwin took her to Malvern, confident of Gully's care, but here she developed a virulent fever and died. Emma, pregnant, stayed at Down, praying in vain. Afterwards neither of them could 'see on any side a gleam of comfort' (Correspondence, 5.27). Darwin himself found no consolation in Christianity for what he called 'our bitter & cruel loss' (ibid., 5.32). He composed a moving threnody, portraying 'Annie' as an example of human nature in its physical and moral perfection. 'Formed to live a life of happiness' (ibid., 5.542), she had fallen in the amoral struggle for existence, and Darwin now came to believe that all of his children had inherited his poor constitution. 'My dread is hereditary ill-health. Even death is better for them' (ibid., 5.84).

The Darwins were wealthy from his £50,000 inheritance, interest on mortgages, and rent from Lincolnshire farms at Beesby and Sutterton Fen (bequeathed by his father). There was also Emma's £25,000 trust fund, and her interest in the Wedgwood firm inherited on her father's death in 1843. By investing in the Leeds and Bradford Railway, the London and North Western, and in 1854 putting £20,000 in the Great Northern Railway, Darwin's income in the 1850s reached £5000 a year. Secure and self-financed, his days ran like clockwork, with set times for working, walking, lunching, napping, reading, letter writing, and nightly backgammon. His health remained precarious in the 1850s, and trips to London or social events brought on flatulence and vomiting.

Family duty for Darwin meant overriding his own dislike of the traditional public-school classical education and sending William (who until twelve was privately tutored in Latin by Henry Wharton, vicar of Mitcham, Surrey) to Rugby School in 1852. The family also had its duty: to support the patriarch, whose study became a sacred place. Nevertheless its boundary was often crossed by exuberant children asking for string or sticking plaster, or when a child was ill and settled on a sofa beside Darwin as he finished his barnacles. The younger children had never known him do anything else and must have supposed that all fathers were similarly employed, for one reportedly enquired about a neighbour, 'Then where does he do his barnacles?' (More Letters, 1.38).

Darwin's first results appeared in 1851 in two volumes on the stalked barnacles, A Monograph of the Fossil Lepadidae, or, Pedunculated Cirripedes of Great Britain, published by the Palaeontographical Society, and the 400-page A monograph on the sub-class Cirripedia, with figures of all the species: the Lepadidae, or, Pedunculated cirripedes, published by the Ray Society. The latter reported Darwin's discovery of tiny 'complemental males', as well as more contentious points, particularly his view of the cement glands as modified ovaria (which Thomas Henry Huxley and, later, August Krohn were to disprove). For his geological and barnacle volumes the Royal Society awarded Darwin its royal medal in 1853, and in 1854 he was elected to the Royal Society's Philosophical Club and the Linnean Society. By then he was finishing his work on the acorn-shell barnacles, fascinated by abnormal types such as the parasitic Alcippe, whose tiny males were little more than reproductive organs in an envelope, twelve of which could be found cemented to a female. These results were contained in the 684-page A monograph on the sub-class Cirripedia, with figures of all the species: the Balanidae (or sessile cirripedes); the Verrucidae, etc. (1854), and the shorter A Monograph on the Fossil Balanidae and Verrucidae of Great Britain (1854). In eight years Darwin had overhauled the entire subclass of fossil and living Cirripedia. He emerged not just an accredited geologist, but as a zoological specialist with authority to speak, when the time was ripe, on variability and transmutation.

This work brought Darwin into closer contact with Huxley, who had sent Darwin his early scientific papers and received from him a reference for a professorial chair. They probably first met in April 1853 at the Geological Society. Huxley, with Herbert Spencer, was part of a growing meritocratic, secularist network in London which was to make the world safe for Darwin's theories. These men, marginal to the Oxbridge–Anglican power structure, were recasting society and nature as a competitive market-place in the relaunched Westminster Review, seeking to claw power from a church establishment. The Westminster displayed the age's growing interest in laws of progress, division of labour, and questions of population and perfectibility, in society as in nature. Huxley, like Hooker, came round to transmutation after mid-decade, and Darwin recognized the importance of recruiting such men. However, although totally committed to natural selection, Darwin would still disarm correspondents by declaring that when he finally published, he would 'give all arguments & facts on both sides' (Correspondence, 5.294).

Late in 1854, after he finished the barnacles, Darwin returned to collating his notes on species. He resolved one outstanding problem some time after November: how natural selection could force the branching of genera to give life's metaphorical 'tree'. Darwin explained this diverging of species as if it were the result of a division of labour; he proposed that natural selection favours those variants which diversify most from the original form. This was an industrial analogy, common in a decade of specializing workforces (personally familiar to Darwin from Wedgwood production-line practices) but also given meaning by the French zoologist Henri Milne-Edwards, whom Darwin cited. More directly, he came to this insight from statistical study of the relative proportions of species and genera in certain geographical areas, a study that led him to dwell on the problem of diversification and the maximum number of individuals that a plot of land could support. For Darwin, selection in nature's 'more efficient workshops' (Darwin, *Origin*, 1859, 380) would increase the 'physiological division of labour' over time. Competition for an overcrowded niche would favour variants that could exploit new opportunities. Dense populations would thus fan out on the spot, and in so doing mitigate the blending effects of back-breeding with the parent stock. Adding this 'principle of divergence' to his existing theories constituted a major intellectual shift for him, the most important alteration to his evolutionary scheme since writing the 1844 essay.

He tackled contemporary assumptions inimical to his theory. From 1855 he experimented to prove that seeds, plants, and animals could reach oceanic islands where they might produce new species in geographical isolation (in opposition to Hooker's belief in overland migration across former continental connections and land bridges, whose existence Darwin never accepted). To test the common notion that seeds were killed by seawater, he steeped kitchen garden seeds in brine and grew samples periodically to check their fertility. Then he attempted similar work with seeds specially chosen from lists of island plants supplied by Hooker and others. In the first of a series of notices in the *Gardeners' Chronicle*, Darwin announced that seeds germinated after forty-two days' immersion, which, given Atlantic currents, might see them floating 1400 miles, the distance to the Azores. He asked correspondents to watch for seeds or snails stuck to birds' feet; he floated dead pigeons bloated with seeds, raised seeds from bird droppings, and fed seed-stuffed sparrows to the snowy owl and Bateleur eagle at London Zoo in order to test the pellets for seed survival.

Like these dispersal experiments, Darwin's study of fancy pigeons from 1855 assumed a life of its own. Darwin joined the Philoperisteron and Borough pigeon clubs in London, corresponded with experts such as William Bernhard Tegetmeier and Bernard Brent, and built lofts at Down to house every fancy breed (in 1856 he had about ninety birds). His new contacts, and old friends such as his cousin Fox, gave him much practical help. Darwin himself became adept at dissecting nestlings and used natural selection to explain their embryonic similarity. The earlier in development the embryos were observed, the more they resembled the ancestral dove. He suggested that only dispositions to vary were inherited, the variations themselves appearing later when selection could operate. Embryos in the womb, untouched by selection, would thus look more alike than the divergent adults, such as pouters and runts. The way fanciers produced novel strains by accentuating chance variations through selective breeding (artificial selection) served as a powerful analogy for understanding Malthusian mechanisms in nature. Pigeons became part of Darwin's presentation strategy. Soon he was dissecting ducks and dogs. With

Tegetmeier's advice he began a long-term programme of experimental crossing among different breeds of fowl, hoping to produce adults that reverted to the ancestral wild form. Darwin's use of animal husbandry, horticultural, and livestock manuals again set him apart from conventional specialists, whose descriptive, taxonomic enterprise disdained the farmyard.

The *Origin of Species* For support Darwin was now looking primarily to the rising London men of science rather than Cambridge clerics. In April 1856 he invited Huxley to Down for a weekend party of naturalists, during which he hoped to ensure that his theory could overcome Huxley's objection to life's progressive specialization. After this meeting Darwin began writing for publication. He was encouraged by Lyell, who feared for Darwin's priority after reading Alfred Russel Wallace's 'On the law which has regulated the introduction of new species' in the *Annals and Magazine of Natural History* for 1855. It was an opportune moment to publish, with the last radical scares—the Chartist marches and European revolutions of 1848—a fading memory, and with society liberalizing and the social basis of science shifting towards Huxley's professionals and secularists.

Darwin began writing on 14 May 1856, planning an extended technical treatise aimed at his peers. Within months his chapters were running to 100 pages. He suffered much anxiety and illness. He continued as Emma, aged forty-eight, gave birth to their last child, Charles Waring Darwin (1856–1858), who, according to Darwin's daughter Henrietta, lacked a 'full share of intelligence' and 'never learnt to walk or talk' (*Emma Darwin*, 2.162). During the period 1857–8 Darwin made four trips to Edward Lane's hydropathic establishment at Moor Park in Surrey, where he found a temporary respite from vomiting. He asked Hooker, Huxley, and John Lubbock to read parts of 'Natural selection', as he planned to call the book, and sent a summary dated 5 September 1857 to the Harvard University botanist Asa Gray. One aspect of his theory was now more pronounced: he no longer accepted organic beings as well adapted until conditions changed; rather, new variants were all to some degree imperfect and thus constantly struggling.

Still finding time to experiment and make natural history observations, Darwin studied the flight paths of humble-bees and tried to induce plant variations by rearing seeds under coloured glass or over-manuring the ground. He also solved, to his satisfaction, the problem of the evolution of the instincts of sterile worker bees. These left no offspring, so their instincts could not be selected. Darwin originally assumed that the sterile bees had been working queens that retained their instincts, but by 1857 he settled on another long-standing idea of his, 'family' selection, to explain the neuter castes. This assumed that the whole colony would benefit from any new adaptive instinct that appeared by chance among the sterile workers.

By March 1858 'Natural selection' was two-thirds complete, at 250,000 words, with the whole book projected to run to three volumes. It would carry the full weight of Darwin's scientific and social authority, which had increased in 1857 as the Academia Caesarea Leopoldino-Carolina Naturae Curiosum (the German academy of naturalists in Leipzig) elected him a member and the Kent commission of the peace swore him in as a justice of the peace. However, on 18 June he stopped abruptly, after receiving a letter from Wallace which enclosed an essay detailing Wallace's own seemingly identical theory. Wallace had corresponded with Darwin occasionally and sent him a few bird skins from the Malay archipelago. In previous letters they had touched on the species problem and Wallace enquired whether Darwin's book would tackle human origins (it would not, directly at least). Wallace had evidently singled Darwin out as potentially sympathetic to his own Malthusian explanation, devised in the spice islands in February 1858. More immediately, Wallace hoped that his essay would be passed on to Lyell, who had expressed interest in his earlier work. Although fearing loss of priority, Darwin did this and accepted Lyell's solution to the dilemma, which was to announce their theories jointly. Sick with worry—his infant son Charles Waring had developed scarlet fever and died on 28 June—Darwin left the arrangements to Lyell and Hooker. They presented extracts from Darwin's 1844 essay and excerpts from a copy of his 1857 letter to Gray, followed by Wallace's paper, at the Linnean Society on 1 July 1858. This joint paper was published later that year as 'On the tendency of species to form varieties; and on the perpetuation of varieties and species by means of selection' in the *Journal of the Proceedings of the Linnean Society* (*Zoology*). Events had moved so fast that Wallace was not notified until afterwards. Darwin, greatly relieved by Wallace's courteous response, thereafter considered him one of the most generous of men: 'too modest, & how admirably free from envy or jealousy.—He must be a good fellow' (*Correspondence*, 8.218). This was the first public presentation of the theory of natural selection.

Darwin now moved quickly. On the Isle of Wight (where he had taken the ailing family), he started, at Hooker's urging, an 'abstract' of 'Natural selection' on 20 July 1858. First intended as an essay, it soon turned into a book. Recurrent stomach complaints and severe vomiting led to more bouts of water cure as Darwin passed his fiftieth birthday, but he pressed on to finish a manuscript of 155,000 words in April 1859. The book, stripped of references and academic paraphernalia, was aimed not at the specialists, but directly at the reading public. John Murray agreed to publish it sight unseen on Lyell's recommendation, although he did subsequently read the first three chapters and ask two respected friends to assess the completed manuscript. Darwin finished revising the proofs of *On the Origin of Species by Means of Natural Selection, or, The Preservation of Favoured Races in the Struggle for Life* 'as weak as a child' (*Correspondence*, 7.328) and retreated to Ilkley Wells House spa, on the Yorkshire moors. He arranged with Murray to send out a large number of complimentary copies, and from his spa posted self-deprecating letters to many recipients of these copies, exclaiming typically,

'how you will long to crucify me alive' (*Correspondence*, 7.368). He described his time there, awaiting the outcome, covered in rashes and 'fiery Boils', as like 'living in Hell' (ibid., 7.362). He remained at the spa while Murray organized the trade sale of *Origin of Species* on 22 November 1859. The 1250 print-run was oversubscribed, requiring Murray to initiate a reprint. This permitted Darwin immediately to start collating corrections for a second edition. He was in Yorkshire on the presumed date of publication, Thursday 24 November (Freeman, *Works*, 75), returning home a fortnight later.

Darwin called the book 'one long argument', which he summarized thus:

> If during the long course of ages and under varying conditions of life, organic beings vary at all in the several parts of their organization, and I think this cannot be disputed; if there be, owing to the high geometrical powers of increase of each species, at some age, season, or year, a severe struggle for life, and this certainly cannot be disputed; then, considering the infinite complexity of the relations of all organic beings to each other and to their conditions of existence, causing an infinite diversity in structure, constitution, and habits, to be advantageous to them, I think it would be a most extraordinary fact if no variation ever had occurred useful to each being's own welfare, in the same way as so many variations have occurred useful to man. But if variations useful to any organic being do occur, assuredly individuals thus characterised will have the best chance of being preserved in the struggle for life; and from the strong principle of inheritance they will tend to produce offspring similarly characterised. This principle of preservation, I have called, for the sake of brevity, Natural Selection ... Amongst many animals, sexual selection will give its aid to ordinary selection, by assuring to the most vigorous and best adapted males the greatest number of offspring. Sexual selection will also give characters useful to the males alone, in their struggles with other males ... Natural selection ... leads to divergence of character; for more living beings can be supported on the same area the more they diverge in structure, habits, and constitution, of which we see proof by looking at the inhabitants of any small spot or at naturalised productions. Therefore during the modification of the descendants of any one species, and during the incessant struggle of all species to increase in numbers, the more diversified these descendants become, the better will be their chance of succeeding in the battle of life. Thus the small differences distinguishing varieties of the same species, will steadily tend to increase till they come to equal the greater differences between species of the same genus, or even of distinct genera ... On these principles, I believe, the nature of the affinities of all organic beings may be explained.   (Darwin, *Origin*, 1859, 127–8)

The *Origin of Species* was applauded by Lyell, Hooker, Huxley, and others, and it impressed many younger men of science. Huxley's secular professionals and the literary radicals welcomed its thoroughgoing naturalism. For these reformers the *Origin* provided a dynamic biology to replace the old static, creationist hierarchy, while its progress through open competition defied Anglican Oxbridge privilege. The chief Malthusian apologist, Harriet Martineau, talked of her 'unspeakable satisfaction' at the way Darwin had 'collected such a mass of facts, to transmute them by such sagacious treatment into such portentous knowledge' (*Harriet Martineau's Letters*, 186).

But anti-Malthusians such as Karl Marx and Friedrich Engels were aghast at the way the *Origin* shadowed English political economy, however liberating its naturalism. On the other side, Adam Sedgwick was shocked that Darwin ignored providential design, although Henslow was more magnanimous. And the Christian socialist Charles Kingsley was content to follow Darwin's argument to some extent, believing that God had 'created primal forms capable of self-development into all forms needful pro tempore & pro loco' (*Correspondence*, 7.380). Others respected Darwin's evident sincerity and acknowledged his mass of factual material, while rejecting the argument wholesale.

In general Darwin's support within Anglicanism came from advanced liberals, often those who backed the broad-church manifesto *Essays and Reviews* (1860); indeed, they included one of the essayists, the Oxford geometry professor the Revd Baden Powell. Such support rested on the twin convictions that Darwin did not intend to subvert religious faith and that his work was based on genuine research. On the other hand, many critics drew the one conclusion that Darwin had avoided mentioning—that mankind was descended from apes—and castigated the book as dangerously irresponsible. Moreover the 'chance' appearance of variations and their utilitarian preservation, while horrifying detractors, were difficult concepts even for many supporters, including Huxley. One of those best qualified to judge Darwin's work, Richard Owen, delivered a crushing rebuttal in the April 1860 *Edinburgh Review*, turning Darwin's own words and facts against the *Origin*'s conclusions. This review caused a permanent breach in their relationship; Darwin felt personally offended as well as angry that his book had not been given the serious assessment he thought it deserved.

Darwin still believed in a distant deity and could speak of evolution being the result of 'designed laws' (*Correspondence*, 8.224), although he did not mean the phrase providentially, but rather in the Unitarian sense of a succession of material causes running back to creation. But he abstained from public controversy, preferring that Huxley should tackle the *Origin*'s critics. Huxley was confrontational; by alienating Owen and the conservative clergy, he polarized the debate. Darwin backed him none the less, even while excusing himself from combat because of illness. During Huxley's famous contretemps with Bishop Samuel Wilberforce on 30 June 1860 at the Oxford meeting of the British Association for the Advancement of Science, Darwin was recuperating at Lane's new water-cure establishment at Sudbrook Park in Surrey.

Variation of Animals and Plants and the Descent of Man Darwin's theoretical work remained controversial among men of science. Thus, although he was nominated three years running for the Copley medal of the Royal Society, he was awarded it only in 1864. Even then it was amid furious politicking because, to Huxley's and Hooker's anger, the president, Edward Sabine, deliberately omitted the

Origin of Species from the grounds of the award. But after 1866 'Darwinism' began to dominate the relevant sections of the British Association, where Darwin's chief scientific supporters, Hooker and Huxley, were presidents respectively in 1868 and 1870. However withdrawn, Darwin was adept at self-publicity, particularly to counteract hostile criticisms. He persuaded John Murray to publish a translation of Fritz Müller's *Für Darwin* (1864), subsidizing the project himself and targeting the review copies. This was a strategy that Darwin had already used successfully in arranging republication in Britain of Asa Gray's favourable reviews (*Natural Selection not Inconsistent with Natural Theology*, 1861), and encouraging Henry Walter Bates to publish his evidence of natural selection among tropical butterflies. Darwin's attention also turned quickly towards overseas editions of the *Origin of Species*. The book was translated into French in 1862 by Clémence Royer (Darwin resented her alterations), and then by J. J. Moulinié in 1873 and Edouard Barbier in 1876; into German in 1860 by Heinrich Bronn (again disappointing Darwin) and 1862 by J. V. Carus; into Dutch in 1860 by T. C. Winkler, and then into Italian and Russian in 1864; Swedish in 1869; Danish in 1872; Hungarian and Polish in 1873–4; Spanish in 1877; and Serbian in 1878. After three pirate reprintings in New York before July 1860, Gray intervened and negotiated Appleton's official American editions with Darwin's blessing. The accounts for these transactions were carefully recorded by John Murray and Darwin.

Darwin's health deteriorated again, beginning in September 1861. Lyell's failure to support evolution in his *Geological Evidences of the Antiquity of Man* (1863) provoked a further crisis, putting Darwin 'in despair' (*More Letters*, 1.241) and sending him back to Dr Gully at Malvern. Darwin's vomiting was now accompanied by severe headaches, which increased his isolation. At times he was too weak even to walk in the garden or write, and he dictated to Emma. From April 1865 he suffered eight months of appalling illness and was bedridden for some of the time. His symptoms remained primarily gastro-intestinal, including extensive nausea, indigestion, skin inflammations, flatulence, and vomiting, often accompanied by headaches, tiredness, irregular sleeping patterns, occasional giddy spells, and faintness. He became a recluse for several years and developed the fixed habits of an invalid. Doctors came and went, sometimes overlapping. One was the rationalist John Chapman, editor of the *Westminster Review* and a specialist in psychological problems among the intelligentsia, who treated Darwin with ice-bags on the spine; this was to no avail and Darwin again looked elsewhere. His physicians ranged from eminent metropolitan doctors to water-cure practitioners and purveyors of popular remedies. Most of them prescribed special diets or medications to make Darwin's stomach fluids more alkaline. Henry Bence Jones diagnosed 'suppressed gout' and advised brisk exercise. Darwin complied for a year or two by horse-riding, but this ceased in 1869 after his horse fell on Keston Common, throwing Darwin.

A ruddy complexion and sturdy physique often masked

Darwin's suffering. In middle life he was about 6 feet tall, with a slight stoop. His son Francis records that he had an average build and long thin legs, which he crossed completely when seated (*Life and Letters*, ed. Darwin, 1.108–60). His eyes were blue-grey and he wore pince-nez spectacles in later years for reading and experimenting. Though hirsute, he became quite bald, with only a fringe of dark untidy hair behind. After 1862 he grew a full beard, partly to soothe recurrent facial eczema, and this so altered his appearance that friends failed to recognize him when he briefly appeared in society in 1864. His voice was a thin tenor, rather like his father's, and his laugh a hearty peal. When excited he became thoroughly animated, gesturing frequently, especially when explaining a complex point, and he tended to speak in fragmentary sentences. He often complained about the difficulties he experienced in writing connected scientific prose and gratefully received help from family members and friends. From boyhood he had a habit of moving his fingers rapidly in parallel and, if very excited, raising both hands to the sides of his face, fingers still fidgeting. To control this, when seated, he would hold one wrist with the other hand, but even in later life the habit would take over as he paced the Sandwalk.

In October 1866 Darwin met his chief German supporter, Ernst Haeckel of Jena University. For Haeckel the trip to Down House was like a religious pilgrimage. Gray and his wife, visiting in 1868, commented on the house's frayed and workaday interior and Darwin's rhythmical daily routine, ending in the obligatory evening game of backgammon, but not even their host's 'merriest laugh' could disguise the ravages of 'suffering and disease' (J. L. Gray to S. L. Jackson, 28 Oct 1868, Gray Herbarium, Harvard University). The same year, while holidaying on the Isle of Wight, Darwin was introduced to Alfred Tennyson, the American poet Henry Wadsworth Longfellow, and the photographer Julia Margaret Cameron, for whom Darwin sat for a fine set of portraits. With the *Origin of Species* in half a dozen foreign translations, Darwin had the order of merit conferred on him by the king of Prussia and was elected a corresponding member of the Imperial Academy of Sciences at St Petersburg. In 1870 Oxford University offered him an honorary doctorate of civil laws, but this was rejected by Darwin on grounds of ill health, and the Imperial Society of Naturalists in Moscow made him an honorary member. The Church of England's South American Missionary Society did the same, recognizing that Darwin, keen to see civilization spread in Tierra del Fuego, had made small donations for several years.

In later editions of the *Origin of Species* Darwin somewhat tempered the power of natural selection. The physicist William Thomson (Lord Kelvin) calculated the age of the earth as 100 million years or less since crustal condensation, while Darwin mooted 300 million years since Cretaceous times. With natural selection relying on the rare appearance of minute advantageous variations, the new shorter term required an acceleration of the evolutionary process. In the fifth edition of the *Origin* (1869), Darwin

allowed that a number of useful variations might have been induced by changing environments and that 'use-inheritance', or the inheritance of beneficial characteristics acquired during an individual's life, played a larger part in adaptive change. These *ad hoc* devices also helped to meet the engineer Fleeming Jenkin's objection about the swamping effects of blending inheritance, but, for bringing them into play in the *Variation* as well as the *Origin*'s later editions, Darwin was accused of resorting to Lamarckian causes, even though, in reality, he had never entirely foresworn them. The words 'I am convinced that Natural Selection has been the main [or 'most important'] but not exclusive means of modification' conclude the introductory chapter in each edition of the *Origin of Species* (1859, 1860, 1861, 1866, 1869, 1872). For all the changes in detail, overall its main thesis stood firm.

After the *Origin*'s publication Darwin embarked on two broad lines of research: botanical experiments, and studies of variation, sexual selection, and emotional expressions in humans and mammals. In 1860 he began recycling the early, as yet unpublished, chapters of 'Natural selection' and studying the osteology of domestic pigeons, ducks, and geese for a book on how breeders and horticulturists modify species. This was *The Variation of Animals and Plants under Domestication* (1868), which progressed only slowly. Its two volumes were intended to provide overwhelming evidence for the ubiquity of variation, although they would also incidentally answer Lyell and Gray, who maintained that variations had not occurred purely by chance but were providentially directed. Darwin showed that breeders indeed selected from a vast array of minute random variations. He gave numerous instances of the causes of variability, including the direct effect of the conditions of life, reversion, the effects of use and disuse, saltation, prepotency, and correlated growth.

The *Variation* also addressed a key criticism of the *Origin of Species*: that it lacked an adequate understanding of inheritance. Darwin's 'provisional hypothesis of pangenesis' was constructed to explain how changes were passed from parents to offspring. He supposed that each part of a parent organism throws off minute particles, or 'gemmules', which circulate in the body and collect in the sexual organs to be transmitted in reproduction. Because gemmules are received from two parents, the offspring develop to resemble them both more or less. 'The child, strictly speaking, does not grow into the man, but includes germs which slowly and successively become developed and form the man' (Darwin, *Variation*, 1875 edn, 2.398). Darwin's hypothesis was roundly criticized, most tellingly by his cousin Francis Galton, who transfused pure-colour rabbits with the blood of other varieties to show that gemmules were not present in the blood. However, Darwin denied that his hypothesis required blood to bear the gemmules. On a different question Jenkin argued in 1867 that natural selection was powerless to preserve individual favourable variants if characteristics were always blended in inheritance. Any variants appearing in a freely interbreeding population would soon be swamped and disappear. This argument gave Darwin considerable trouble, his pangenesis hypothesis notwithstanding. It was only later, with Moritz Wagner's insistence on geographical isolation in the evolutionary process (a notion itself developed from Darwin's work), that the blending problem looked as if it was solved.

The term 'survival of the fittest' (borrowed at Wallace's insistence from Herbert Spencer's 1866 *Principles of Biology*) first appeared in the *Variation* and in the fifth edition of the *Origin of Species* (1869). It was a partial substitute for Darwin's more anthropomorphic 'natural selection', which many critics took to imply the existence of a 'selector'. Mistaking Darwin's metaphor, they concluded that intelligence lay as much behind nature's selecting as behind a pigeon fancier's. Nevertheless Darwin defended his use of 'natural selection' while conceding that he had personified it too much.

The *Variation* was a full statement of the facts on which the theories of the *Origin* were based. Darwin, 'taunted that I concealed my views' (*Life and Letters*, ed. Darwin, 3.98) on human origins, had at first intended to include a chapter on mankind, fleshing out his old notebook conviction that humans had evolved like other animals. But long before *Variation* was published he gave up this plan and decided to treat the topic separately. Still reluctant to speak out, he had hoped that either Lyell, Huxley, Lubbock, or Wallace would publish a full-blooded account of human evolution, but none came up to expectation. Accordingly, in February 1868, he started sorting his huge collection of notes and began a two-volume treatise, *The Descent of Man, and Selection in Relation to Sex* (1871).

While writing Darwin differed sharply from Wallace over mental development and sexual selection. Wallace, a convert to spiritualism, in 1869 explained the savage's expansive brain as a spiritually guided preadaptation for civilization, thus limiting natural selection to the earlier physical origin of human races. Darwin, dismayed, wrote to him, 'I hope you have not murdered too completely your own and my child' (Marchant, 1.241). Similarly, Wallace denied the existence of sexual selection, the adjunct cause that Darwin had introduced to account for characteristics with no physically adaptive functions, such as human beards or humming-bird iridescence. Wallace's critique went to the heart of the arguments in the *Descent of Man*, for Darwin believed that sexual selection also accounted for the differentiation of human races.

Other critics had to be answered. The Catholic comparative anatomist St George Mivart published articles in *The Month* in 1869 denying that natural selection could explain the independent 'convergence' of animal forms (such as a placental dog and Australian thylacine) or that the intermediate stages of certain structures (such as a wing) could be functional and thus formed by selection. Moreover, the duke of Argyll in *Primeval Man* (1869) argued that mankind had more likely fallen from some higher state than risen from animals. He questioned how selection could have produced a weak-framed, hairless human, at least without morality and reason having been bestowed first. But

Darwin turned the logic around: it was this physical vulnerability, he said, that had forced humans into social groups whose cohesion and altruism were themselves responsible for the continuing evolution of morality.

Cautiously, Darwin asked his daughter Henrietta to check the proof sheets, but the *Descent of Man* could safely be published by 1871. Darwinism had become a byword among intellectuals and the preceding decade had seen the public habituated to writings on ape ancestry by Huxley, Wallace, Karl Vogt, and Haeckel, and on the evolution of civilization by Galton, Lubbock, Edward Tylor, W. R. Greg, and Walter Bagehot. Much of their work—which reinforced conventional racial, national, and sexual prejudices—was incorporated into the *Descent of Man*. Darwin also extended his notebook themes of the natural origin of morality, religious belief, and society from animal instincts and savage superstitions.

The *Descent*, understood by Darwin as a sequel to the *Origin*, was written with a maturity and depth of learning that marked Darwin's status as an élite gentleman of science. Despite its title, less than half of the book dealt with mankind. Some two-thirds was devoted to a description of sexual selection in the animal kingdom, leading Wallace to complain that it was really two books. Yet sexual selection was an answer to those critics who saw peacock tails as an expression of divine aesthetics—beauty as an end in itself and incapable of natural explanation. Darwin also set out a definite family tree for humans, tracing their affinity with the Old World monkeys. He provided a survey of aboriginal societies to establish that each held its own ideal of beauty. For he believed that, during prehistory, such distinct ideals of beauty, when preserved with other useful traits by long-continued sexual selection, had led to the divergence of the human races. Darwin laid out his views on the evolutionary origins of morality and religion, and illustrated those aspects in which 'Man still bears in his bodily frame the indelible stamp of his lowly origin'. Indeed, he gave a graphic description of ancestral humans, shocking to Victorian eyes:

> The early progenitors of man were no doubt once covered with hair, both sexes having beards; their ears were pointed and capable of movement; and their bodies were provided with a tail, having the proper muscles … The foot, judging from the condition of the great toe in the foetus, was then prehensile; and our progenitors, no doubt, were arboreal in their habits … (Darwin, *Descent*, 1.206)

While perhaps causing less of an outcry than the *Origin*, the *Descent of Man* brought the full force of evolutionary proposals directly into the heart of ordinary Victorian life. It sold more than 5000 copies within a year and provoked numerous press caricatures, cartoons, articles, and commentaries. A second edition appeared in 1874 and eight translations were published during Darwin's lifetime.

Darwin was sensitive to Mivart's renewed criticism in *On the Genesis of Species* (1871) and determined to break off communication with him. (He did so in 1874 after Mivart accused Darwin's son George of advocating the loosening of marriage bonds in cases where there was a threat to the 'fitness' of offspring.) In 1871 Darwin arranged for an article by the American philosopher Chauncey Wright rebuking Mivart to be reprinted as a pamphlet under the title *Darwinism*. At this time the *Origin* was also extensively rewritten to answer Mivart. The sixth and last edition explained how, for instance, swim bladders were preadapted to function as lungs, obviating the need to talk of half-formed organs. In this edition the word 'evolution', used in its modern sense, first appeared.

One batch of material proved too bulky for incorporation in the *Descent of Man* and Darwin held it over for separate treatment. This derived from his research into human and animal expressions. The subject had fascinated him since his London days, and had drawn him many times to the zoological gardens to watch the monkeys and apes. Later he had recorded his children's behaviour, investigated facial expressions of the insane, consulted artists and photographers, and collected material on the exterior manifestation of emotional states such as happiness or rage. The material was sophisticated for its day. Darwin invited the photographer Oscar Reijlander to make comparative studies of laughter and crying; he obtained photographs of lunatics from asylum director James Crichton-Browne; and he consulted the French physiologist Guillaume Duchenne about his electrical research on facial muscles. Believing that learned expressions could be 'fixed' by habit, Darwin also formulated his clearest statement to date on the inheritance of acquired characteristics. Though much of his analysis has been superseded, and was for modern scientific purposes marred by much unconscious anthropomorphism, he was convinced that an evolutionary continuity existed between the expressions (and hence mental life) of animals and humans, and that animals experience traces of every human emotion, including the moral feelings. In this sense, *The Expression of the Emotions in Man and Animals* (1872) completed his great cycle of evolutionary writings. It proved popular, not least because of its accessible subject matter and plentiful illustrations, including some of the earliest commercially reproduced photographs in a printed book.

Botanical observations, 1861–1880 During the controversy over the *Origin of Species* Darwin increasingly turned to botanical observations. He had always considered plants as important to his theories as animals: many of the arguments for adaptation, variation, and descent in the *Origin* hinged on his early botanical work, particularly in plant geography. He was a regular contributor to *Gardeners' Chronicle* and sent papers on botanical topics to the Linnean Society of London. After publishing the *Origin* he carried out a wide range of investigations into the living processes of plants and their adaptations. He usually characterized these researches as a pleasant rest or amusement, apparently feeling that they interrupted the hard work of compiling his big book on variation. He often remarked that he was not a 'proper' botanist, by which he meant a taxonomic expert like his friends Hooker and Gray, but his pleasure in experimenting with plants was

obvious. The stream of books and papers that he published during the last twenty years of his life was greatly admired by botanists, earning him a reputation as a gifted observer and ingenious botanical thinker. When Darwin was elected a corresponding member of the Académie des Sciences in Paris in 1878, it was specifically to the botanical section. From 1873 he was helped by his son Francis who wrote several works with him. (Francis continued various projects after his father's death, and produced amended editions of some of Darwin's books.) Despite Darwin's humorous protestations, every aspect of his botanical work, however trivial it appeared, bore closely on adaptation, variation, and the origin of species by natural selection.

Many of Darwin's research projects began with observations made in his garden or while on holiday. In 1860 he experimented on the sundew, an insectivorous plant that he noticed while resting in Sussex. He continued the work intermittently until 1875 when he published *Insectivorous Plants*, which discussed the whole range of such plants, their adaptations and evolutionary relationships, and their specialized digestive processes. On holiday at Torquay in 1861 he took up the fertilization of orchids, a subject that had long intrigued him; this resulted in *On the Various Contrivances by which British and Foreign Orchids are Fertilised by Insects* (1862). Darwin called the book a 'flank movement' (*Correspondence*, 10.331) on the enemy, meaning that it tackled the question of design in nature. He maintained that the ornate ridges and horns of orchid flowers, and the complex internal arrangements, were not beauty for its own sake, or created for the delight of humans, but adaptations to facilitate reproduction. They existed to ensure cross-pollination by insects. If they were regarded as functional flowers, rather than beautiful ones, natural selection could explain their origin. Among Darwin's striking discoveries was his revelation that three well-known species of the orchid *Catasetum* were actually a single species existing in three forms, male, female, and hermaphrodite. He distinguished such relationships by comparing the gradual separation of the sexes with a similar process he had described in barnacles.

Examples of mutual adaptation between insects and flowers tantalized Darwin and he continued to research into orchids and many other plant–insect relationships, especially those involving bees. He had first read C. K. Sprengel's *Das entdeckte Geheimniss der Natur im Bau und in der Befruchtung der Blumen* (1793) on the advice of Robert Brown in 1841 and he thought it 'a wonderful book' (*Autobiography*, 127). His own work involved many small experiments in his garden, masking and unmasking flowering plants during the summer season. In the winter of 1862–3 his orchid research led him to build the first of several hothouses in which he could keep delicate research specimens obtained from Hooker at Kew and other specialists in Britain and abroad.

From the late 1830s he had suspected that cross-pollinated plants tended to leave more vigorous offspring than those which were self-fertilized. One long-term aim was to show how far plants had adapted to ensure this crossing. After the *Origin* he performed experiments on dozens of species and hundreds of plants, sometimes to the tenth generation, to establish that crossing conferred selective advantage, which he usually measured by counting or weighing seeds. In this work he relied on the experimental plant-hybridizing results of K. F. von Gaertner, J. G. Koelreuter, and latterly K. W. Nägeli. In *The Effects of Cross and Self-Fertilisation in the Vegetable Kingdom* (1876) he showed statistically that the offspring of crosses are more vigorous than seedlings of self-fertilized parentage and thus more likely to survive. The advantage in developing mechanisms that prevented selfing or in transforming hermaphroditic systems into bisexual structures was quantified for the first time. Darwin's further work on the evolution of two sexes expressed a similar interest. He investigated the two forms of primula, long styled and short styled, which he concluded in 1862 were more fertile when crossed. In 1865 he published on *Lythrum salicaria*, the purple loosestrife, which has three forms of flower: having experimented to induce 'illegitimate unions' (*Collected Papers*, 2.120) among them, he assessed the increased sterility of the offspring and showed how the flowers functioned to effect cross-pollination. These and other experiments were reported in papers at the Linnean Society and then in *The Different Forms of Flowers on Plants of the Same Species* (1877), which was dedicated to Gray in gratitude for decades of encouraging correspondence.

There was perhaps more to Darwin's lifelong fascination with in- and out-breeding than met the eye. Married himself to a first cousin, and both of them from a line with its share of perceived physical or mental anomalies, he feared that he carried a weakness, most evident in his chronic ill health. After his daughter Anne's death in 1851, and long years of sickness among his remaining children, he became convinced that his 'detestable constitution' (*Correspondence*, 7.60) had been passed to the next generation. So urgent was the subject to him, with its social-evolutionary implications, that he tried—unsuccessfully—to get a question on first-cousin marriages and their offspring placed on the 1871 national census return through the good offices of his friend Lubbock, who had become MP for Maidstone the previous year.

Darwin was also intrigued by the more energetic aspects of plant physiology. While ill in 1863 he studied the circular movements of pea tendrils as they searched for an object to twine around. He went on to examine over 100 species of climbers, publishing the results in 1865 as a Linnean Society monograph and in 1875 under the same title, *The Movements and Habits of Climbing Plants*. In the wild, he surmised, the climbing adaptation aided survival in dense vegetation. Assisted by his son Francis he widened the research to survey the movements of stems, leaves, and roots under the influence of gravity, moisture, and light. Darwin believed that in plants an inherent tendency to move had been intensified and diversified by natural selection. His interpretation of geotropism (the response of roots to gravity) in *The Power of Movement in Plants* (1880) contradicted the results of Julius Sachs, stimulating a fierce argument that disintegrated into a nationalistic

contest between Darwin's old-style country-house observations and the new laboratory-based physiological research emerging in the German states. Despite Sachs's criticism, Darwin never wavered in his belief that a substance in the tip of a shoot was activated by light, a belief that gave impetus to subsequent studies on plant hormones. His experimental equipment in all these investigations was makeshift and rudimentary. Darwin took pride in the *ad hoc* nature of his practical researches, frequently praising his simple apparatus over the fine gadgetry available to younger university workers. All the same, he purchased several expensive microscopes, justifying the expense as 'essential'.

Although Darwin's achievement in botany was long underestimated, his chief aim was to show the power of evolutionary theory for understanding plant morphology and physiology. Many people who might have shied away from ape-ancestry were prepared to accept natural selection and evolution among plants. His botanical books, however, were not as widely read or appreciated as the others.

Final years, 1873–1882 Solidly wealthy, in the 1870s Darwin was reinvesting over half of his annual income of £8000. His affection for his closest friends remained intense: he felt Lyell's death in 1875 keenly, and played a leading part in arranging a collection of funds in 1873 to permit an exhausted Huxley to take a rest from his duties. He enthusiastically supported the foundation of the zoological station at Naples, under Anton Dohrn, and donated £100 for equipment in 1879. In his will he provided £250 annually for the completion of a catalogue of all known plants, the *Index Kewensis*. Darwin continued his parish duties until the early 1870s, donating funds to the church and vicarage, but after 1871 a new vicar at Downe (as it was increasingly being spelled) turned the school committee and parish education towards the Thirty-Nine Articles, causing Darwin to withdraw his support.

In 1881 the impecunious Wallace received a civil-list pension of £200 at Darwin's instigation and with the Liberal government's approval. Nevertheless, the two old men never fully appreciated one another's political and cultural views; while remaining friends, they moved apart intellectually. Darwin deplored Wallace's spiritualism. With seances all the rage he and Emma Darwin did attend one in 1874 at his brother Erasmus's house, along with Galton, Henrietta and Richard Litchfield (Darwin's son-in-law), Hensleigh and Fanny Wedgwood, and George Lewes and Marian Evans (George Eliot). Darwin's son George hired the medium, Charles Williams. Darwin retired upstairs before the performance, denouncing it all as 'rubbish' (*Life and Letters*, ed. Darwin, 3.187).

Though a rationalist, Darwin was cautious of mooting his religious views lest he offend or be offended in turn. He did give an endorsement to the freethinking platform of Francis Abbot's American newspaper *The Index* in 1871, only to regret his public support when atheism became an issue in Britain with Charles Bradlaugh's case in 1880. He had the endorsement removed. While admitting 'I do not believe in the Bible as a divine revelation, & therefore not in Jesus Christ as the Son of God' (Darwin to F. McDermott, 24 Nov 1880, CUL), Darwin also confessed that he had 'never been an atheist in the sense of denying the existence of a God', and 'that generally (& more & more as I grow older), but not always, that an agnostic would be the most correct description of my state of mind' (*Life and Letters*, ed. Darwin, 1.304). Thus Edward Aveling's request in 1880 to dedicate a book to Darwin was turned down on the grounds that:

> though I am a strong advocate for free thought on all subjects, yet it appears to me (whether rightly or wrongly) that direct arguments against christianity & theism produce hardly any effect on the public; & freedom of thought is best promoted by the gradual illumination of men's minds, which follow[s] from the advance of science.   (Feuer, 2–3)

Darwin disapproved of socialists, ultra-radicals, and neo-Malthusians (that is, birth-controllers) no less than atheists, spiritualists, and bishops. When Bradlaugh and Annie Besant subpoenaed him in 1877 to appear at their trial for publishing contraceptive advice, Darwin threatened to denounce their views. A Malthusian struggle was the cornerstone of natural selection, and he opposed those who diminished it by 'any means' (Darwin, *Descent*, 2.403). 'The rule insisted on by all our Trades-Unions, that all workmen,—the good and bad, the strong and weak,—sh[ould] all work for the same number of hours and receive the same wages' rather than be paid by 'piece-work' was, he insisted, 'opposed … to all competition. I fear that Cooperative Societies … likewise exclude competition. This seems to me a great evil for the future progress of mankind' (Weikart, 611).

For all his antipathy to extremes, Darwin in his autobiography, 'Recollections of the development of my mind and character', written for the family in stages through 1876, 1879, and 1881, frankly stated his conviction that the doctrine of eternal damnation for unbelief was itself 'damnable'. (This passage, and others, were omitted for Emma's sake when the autobiography was first published in *The Life and Letters of Charles Darwin*.) In 1876 Francis Darwin moved back into Down House with his infant son Bernard after the death of his wife, so that Darwin's last years were spent with a grandchild, the only one born during his lifetime, in whom he took great delight. In 1879 Darwin also wrote an introduction to Ernst Krause's biography of his grandfather Erasmus Darwin on its translation into English, which elicited a sharp attack from Samuel Butler.

The Liberal press, led by John Morley, long supported Darwin, and he remained a staunch Gladstonian Liberal himself. From 1865 he supported Lubbock (later the first Lord Avebury) when he stood at Maidstone as Liberal MP, and he took intense political and humanitarian interest in the American civil war, discussing it vigorously in letters to Gray. In 1876 Darwin signed up as one of the convenors of the St James's Hall demonstration against the massacre of 15,000 Bulgarian rebels by Turkish troops (the 'Bulgarian horrors'), and agreed with Gladstone that the Russians should secure Christian Bulgaria against the Turks. Darwin also supported professional science, backing the comparative anatomists and medical men in their fight for vivisection. He helped draft a bill enabling vivisection under licensed conditions, which he sent to Lord Derby. At Huxley's request, he appeared as a witness in 1875 before the royal commission on the practice of subjecting live animals to experiments.

During these autumn years Darwin's health improved and his honours multiplied. In 1877 Cambridge University bestowed an honorary doctorate of laws on him. When he did not go into the world, it came to him: Gladstone visited Down House in 1877, accompanied by the Liberal lights Lyon Playfair, Morley, Lubbock, and Huxley. No archive sources have been found to show that Darwin was suggested for a knighthood (despite an unsubstantiated rumour that his name had been put forward before the publication of the *Origin of Species*). Many thought it shameful that the British establishment signally failed to honour him. Only in 1881 did Gladstone belatedly offer him a trusteeship of the British Museum. It was a rare, and minor, show of state recognition, and one of the very few official duties ever offered to him, but Darwin turned it down. He sat for the artist John Collier (1881), the oil portrait being commissioned by the Linnean Society. By special invitation he dined with the prince of Wales and leading physicians at the seventh International Medical Congress in 1881. By then he had returned to a subject that he had mulled over since the 1830s, the action of earthworms in causing great earth movements. It was his leitmotif, explaining vast changes by minute incremental events: mountain uplift, evolving life, and now worms transforming the soil. More ingenious experiments—including testing worms' sensitivity to sound, light, and shape—culminated in *The Formation of Vegetable Mould through the Action of Worms* (1881).

In June 1881 an attempt at a mountain walk on holiday in the Lake District left Darwin feeling faint, and angina was diagnosed. Enforced idleness made him miserable; insatiably curious, he needed some new intellectual peak, but he had climbed them all. At Christmas that year he had a minor heart attack on the steps of his protégé George Romanes's house in Regent's Park, London. Another seizure followed on 7 March 1882 as he hobbled round the Sandwalk, with a further series on 4 and 5 April. He died, in great suffering, at Down House on 19 April 1882, aged seventy-three. On his brother Erasmus's death the previous year (and burial in Downe churchyard), Darwin had inherited half of his estate and became personally worth over a quarter of a million pounds. His new will bequeathed £34,000 to each of his daughters, £53,000 to each son, and £1000 each to Hooker and Huxley. His oldest son, William, a banker, was the executor.

Following agitation by Galton and Huxley among the cultural and scientific élite, and with a petition raised by Lubbock in the House of Commons, plans were made to bury Darwin in Westminster Abbey, although he himself had expected to lie in Downe churchyard. A press campaign compared Darwin to Newton and evoked imperial and patriotic feelings, and Darwin's intellectual conquests were seen to equal the great Victorian geographical annexations: 'we owe it to posterity to place his remains in Westminster Abbey, among the illustrious dead who make that noble fane unrivalled in the world' (*The Standard*, 22 April 1882). On 26 April 1882 Darwin was buried in the abbey, close to the monument to Newton at the north end of the choir screen, in a ceremony attended by the elders of science, state, and church.

Darwin's legacy Agnostic scientists, Liberal politicians, and broad-churchmen joined in paying homage to one who, though an unbeliever, symbolized England's success in conquering nature and civilizing the globe during Victoria's reign. They consolidated Darwin's most enduring image. In their speeches, sermons, and memoirs, the Kentish squire and patriarch became the iconic scientist—detached, objective, a lone seeker after truth, released by personal wealth and stoic dedication in the face of long-continued illness to bestow priceless truths on humanity. By the end of the century everyone wanted this Darwin as an ally. From secularists to salvationists, from Prussian nationalists to Russian anarchists, efforts continued to enlist his authority by appealing to his life and works.

Darwin's personal reputation did not guarantee the success of his ideas. The *Origin of Species*, never out of print, was translated into at least thirty-six languages, but its theories were often too materialistic for idealists and too capitalistic for socialists, too empiricist for Germans and too English for the French. Not even his key belief, the one he himself most emphasized, 'change of species by descent' (*Correspondence*, 11.402–3), was accepted *in toto*. Many of his avowed disciples, including scientists, exempted 'man' from evolution by supposing that the human mind or soul was added to an animal body. More ironically, for over half a century the distinctive core of Darwin's science, his arguments for natural and sexual selection, came under sustained fire. Natural selection, if anything, was construed as a negative force rather than creative, a purging of unfit organisms shaped by Lamarckian use-inheritance, macromutation, or evolution's inner directing energy. Sexual selection was explained away or found inapplicable to human beings. Even among Darwin's closest allies, Huxley never allowed that natural selection had been proved, but evolution *per se* became an academic commonplace, and in 1909 leading scientists gathered on both sides of the Atlantic to mark Darwin's centenary with speeches and public celebrations.

So 'Darwinism', a term first publicized by Huxley, and increasingly used during Darwin's lifetime, was contested from the start. Efforts to restrict its meaning to natural selection pure and simple or 'what Darwin taught' proved futile as later critics and commentators exploited the textual changes in the *Origin*'s six editions. Soon after Darwin's death publications brought his private letters to the fore. Everywhere Darwinism became synonymous with naturalism, materialism, or evolutionary philosophy. It stood for competition and co-operation, liberation and subordination, progress and pessimism, war and peace.

Its politics could be liberal, socialist, or conservative, its religion atheistic or orthodox. At the turn of the twentieth century European social scientists, then American, began using 'social Darwinism' as a shorthand for biological theories that impinged on their professional domain. The phrase all but disappeared at the end of the First World War but in the 1940s American liberals revived it as a label for *laissez-faire* ideology as found in the works of Darwin's contemporary, the English philosopher Herbert Spencer, and his latter-day followers. Social Darwinism then became a sin from which Darwin himself had to be absolved. Great pains were taken during the cold war to show that the sources of his science, no less than his own motives and beliefs in writing the *Origin*, were ideologically pure.

The issue was made more urgent by what the early twentieth century saw perpetrated in Darwin's name. While in Britain his cousin Galton's campaign for national eugenics had only marginal political impact, events took a sinister turn on the continent: from Ernst Haeckel to Adolf Hitler, German imperialist readings of the *Origin*'s subtitle, 'the preservation of favoured races in the struggle for life', sanctioned unthinkable suffering and played into anti-Darwinian hands. In communist Russia from the late 1930s, no less than in fundamentalist America after the First World War, Darwin's theories were vilified for their degrading effects. (Only much later was the full extent of eugenic practices, East and West, revealed.) Thus besieged liberals in the mid-twentieth century maintained that Darwin had been persistently misread, his theories misapplied, his science 'misused' by partisans on all sides, and that, properly understood, Darwin had taught nothing politically untoward.

Many defenders of a non-ideological Darwin also saw themselves as his true successors. This placed them in awkward company. From the time of Darwin's death, natural selection had been upheld chiefly by biometricians such as W. F. Weldon and Karl Pearson, whose experimental and statistical researches buttressed Galton's eugenics. Darwin's sons George, Leonard, and Horace also supported Galton and the eugenics movement; Leonard specially encouraged the young R. A. Fisher, who in 1918 showed that Darwinian selection could harness Mendelian genetics to solve eugenic problems. It was Fisher's *The Genetical Theory of Natural Selection* (1930) and the collateral work of J. B. S. Haldane in England and Sewall Wright in the United States that made possible the 'evolutionary synthesis' of the 1930s. With further contributions by Theodosius Dobzhansky, Julian Huxley, Ernst Mayr, G. G. Simpson, and G. Ledyard Stebbins, natural selection was then reformulated in terms of mathematical population genetics, and a generation of evolutionists in the 1950s happily positioned themselves 'closer … to the Darwin of 1859 than at any other period in the last 100 years' (Mayr, 'Introduction', viii). In centenary celebrations they hailed the *Origin*'s first edition for precipitating a 'Darwinian revolution' in which natural selection had in principle defeated all competing evolutionary mechanisms. Darwin the iconic scientist, whose theories had long been attacked and politically abused, was revalued as the founder of an ascendant 'neo-Darwinism' and the patron saint of modern biology.

Yet this apparent vindication of a non-ideological Darwin was inextricably bound up with moral and metaphysical issues, as indeed Darwin's own work had been from the start. In the 1970s and 1980s, with the hardening of the neo-Darwinian synthesis in the new fields of sociobiology and evolutionary psychology, the pattern persisted. Despite the efforts of Stephen Jay Gould, the most popular and historically minded of Darwinian scientists in the late twentieth century, biologists' attachment to Darwin's theories assumed a quasi-theological character. Natural selection to them became a deity *manqué*, a 'blind watchmaker' that fills 'design space' with marvellous adaptations. After the collapse of Soviet communism ended the cold war in the 1990s, some sympathizers and many pundits urged political progressives to seek fresh inspiration for the new millennium, not from Karl Marx, but from Darwin.

Historiography A large and increasingly technical literature has grown up around Darwin's life and works. From the outset, interpreters were indebted to his family for preserving and publishing key manuscripts—Darwin's memory was well served by his children. The seven who reached adulthood survived to see his 1909 centenary celebrations in London and Cambridge, in which the sons were honoured guests. Francis Darwin edited an exceptional three-volume *Life and Letters* (1887), two further volumes of his father's correspondence with the assistance of A. C. Seward (1903), and the two unpublished early drafts of the theory of natural selection (1909). Francis also published a one-volume *Life* (1892) and Henrietta Litchfield, the eldest daughter, prepared two volumes of her mother's family letters, which were printed privately in 1904 and published in 1915.

While the children lived their memories and opinions shaped Darwin's public image. They adored him, and interpreters deferred to their authority. The Darwins were conspicuous among the intermarried extended families that dominated British intellectual life and politics at the end of the nineteenth century. They held sway in Cambridge, where George Darwin became Plumian professor of astronomy, Francis a reader in botany, and Horace a founder and director of the Cambridge Scientific Instrument Company and later mayor. All married well and had families. In 1964 the George Darwin family residence, Newnham Grange, became the home of Darwin College, the first Cambridge college for postgraduates. Of the nine grandchildren, all but one survived past mid-century. Nora Barlow, the youngest child of Horace Darwin, published five important transcripts of Darwin's manuscripts, including his *Beagle* diary (1933) and ornithological notes (1963), and the full autobiography (1958), of which only the expurgated *Life and Letters* version had been known. A great-grandson descended through George Darwin, Richard Darwin Keynes, re-edited the *Beagle* diary (1988) and published the zoological notes and specimen lists from the *Beagle* voyage (2000). From the 1920s family

members were also active in helping to preserve the Down House estate as a national shrine. The house was rented by Down House School (1907–22), then (through the bequest of Sir George Buckston-Browne) passed to the British Association in 1929. In 1953 it was given to the Royal College of Surgeons of England, from whence it was transferred to the Natural History Museum, and from 1996 it was restored and run as a public museum by English Heritage.

For the first half of the twentieth century scholars studied Darwin primarily as a thinker who had 'forerunners' or 'precursors' and whose ideas were either 'revolutionary' or 'in the air'. His life was treated as an episode in intellectual history. Scientists made him a reference point in debates about evolutionary theory, humanists portrayed him as a great (though perhaps dangerous) moralist, and religious commentators as a theological saint or satan. In the 1940s the Darwin family began depositing a wealth of manuscripts and other biographical material, including Darwin's working library, at Cambridge University Library, but for years this went almost untapped as interpreters dwelt on Darwin's published work and its place in the history of ideas. At its best, this concentration yielded authoritative studies such as Ellegård's *Darwin and the General Reader* (1958), about the reception of Darwin's ideas in the British periodical press. The most widely read and evocative study of Darwin from this period was William Irvine's *Apes, Angels, and Victorians* (1955).

Reassessments of Darwin's life accompanied the neo-Darwinian re-evaluation of natural selection celebrated on the centenary of the *Origin of Species* in 1959. Much of the enthusiasm surrounding this centenary and its publications rested on the assumption that a theory recognized as true must have a history different from one written when its status was in doubt. Scientists dealt severely with a professional historian, Gertrude Himmelfarb, whose important *Darwin and the Darwinian Revolution* (1959) failed sufficiently to recognize the new status of natural selection. But much interest was also focused on Darwin because, to mark the 1859 centenary, Gavin De Beer, the retired director of the British Museum (Natural History), began publishing Darwin manuscripts, including the private notebooks that recorded his earliest thoughts about transmutation. This was a watershed. A generation of historians of science, professionalizing themselves since the Second World War, then began to exploit the Darwin papers at Cambridge. The 'Darwin industry' was born.

De Beer's concise biography (1963) was the last major attempt by a working scientist to interpret Darwin's life as history. Although efforts continued to enlist Darwin's authority in debates about evolution—the most tenacious and influential scientist–commentator into the twenty-first century was Ernst Mayr, an architect of the evolutionary synthesis—within two decades the field was crowded with historical specialists. A strong shift in approach was signalled by the vigorous work of Young, published from 1967 onwards. Philosophers and philosophically minded historians such as Ghiselin, Hull, R. J. Richards, and Ruse analysed Darwin's logic, methodology, and metaphysics, but most crucially historical specialists led by Kohn, Hodge, Gruber, Barrett, Herbert, Manier, and Schweber offered particularly fruitful readings of Darwin's early manuscripts. Darwin's debts to Grant and the 'Grantian' social and scientific context were elucidated by Sloan and Desmond, while Sloan demonstrated how Darwin's first evolutionary theorizing in 1837 took shape in response to Owen's work. Sulloway carefully reconstructed Darwin's ornithological collections from the Galápagos and thereby re-evaluated the timing of Darwin's appreciation of island speciation. Limoges wrote carefully about natural selection and Ospovat's *The Development of Darwin's Theory* (1981) studied its relations with mid-nineteenth-century biology. Vorzimmer traced the theory's vicissitudes through the six editions of the *Origin of Species* into the *Descent of Man*.

Much of the historians' interest lay in the discovery of natural selection, but their research held little for the champions of Darwin's methodological rectitude. The notebooks revealed the young Darwin reaching out in all directions, to physics, philosophy, political economy, and theology, as well as to collectors, breeders, museum keepers, and field naturalists. 'Conjecture run wild' (Barrett and others, *Notebooks*, B232) or 'mental rioting' (*Correspondence*, 4.40), he called it. By the 1980s historians had shown that natural selection was no classic 'discovery', but rather a slow, painstaking 'construction' (La Vergata, 917) from diverse cultural resources. Their work—in particular the detailed reconstructions of Darwin's zig-zagging path to natural selection by Kohn and Hodge—marked an epoch in Darwin research. No longer could it be claimed that Darwin was the iconic scientist conforming to methodological ideals past or present. His originality lay in his idiosyncrasy.

Central to Darwin's theorizing was his effort to explain the descent of human beings—body, mind, and society—from ape-like animals on the basis of a materialist or monist metaphysics and using Malthus's 'principle of population'. This was clear from De Beer's edition of the transmutation notebooks, and from early work by Herbert, and in 1974 Gruber and Barrett published further manuscripts, including two notebooks ('M' and 'N') in which he speculated about 'metaphysics', 'morals', and 'expression'. Here at last was compelling evidence that 'man' lay at the core of his work from the start. Darwin did not first formulate natural selection and then apply it to human beings; he drew the theory directly from contemporary (and ideologically loaded) assessments of human behaviour and afterwards concealed its implications for over three decades, until the *Descent of Man*.

Much historical ink was spilt in the mid-twentieth century (surveyed by Oldroyd in 1984) over the question of Darwin's debt to Malthus. Thanks to the notebooks, particularly the monumental new edition published in 1987 by Barrett, Gautrey, Herbert, Kohn, and Sydney Smith, and to commentators such as Gruber, Schweber, and Ospovat, interpretations once dismissed as externalist or even Marxist were found more congenial. Few now could doubt that (as Greene first demonstrated) Darwin was as

much a social evolutionist as Spencer, with whom he had often been contrasted. Moreover, the emergence in the late 1970s and 1980s of sophisticated social studies of science, fortified by Desmond's re-evaluation of the medical and scientific context of Darwin's key creative period in the 1830s, permitted greater flexibility in understanding the meaning of Malthusian science in Darwin's day, his potential audience, and his reluctance to publish his theory. As Darwinian studies proliferated, historians turned to re-examine other figures in the history of evolutionary theory, notably Chambers, Huxley, Spencer, and Lamarck. Their analyses in turn cast important new light on Darwin's Victorian context.

Moore reassessed Darwin's religious faith, showing that while he remained a pillar of his rural parish, the deaths of his father in 1848 and daughter Annie in 1851 finally led him to give up Christianity. Brown offered a different view, while Ospovat, Kohn, and Gillespie traced the vicissitudes of Darwin's theology. Beddall and Kottler re-examined Darwin's relations with Wallace, analysing differences and the question of illicit borrowing. Browne, Kohn, and Ospovat reinterpreted his 'principle of divergence' and Secord recast Darwin's breeding work as social history. Browne analysed his biogeography and Ekman assessed his research on expression. Barrett, Herbert, Rudwick, and Secord offered new interpretations of Darwin's geology. Darwin's non-evolutionary and non-geological research also came in for detailed study, including his insect collecting by K. G. V. Smith, his barnacle taxonomy by Sydney Smith, Ghiselin, and Newman, and his plants by Porter. Legends were laid to rest: Gruber and Burstyn disposed of Darwin as the *Beagle*'s official naturalist (he was the captain's gentleman companion); Sulloway demoted Darwin's Galápagos finch-collecting from its previous evolutionary eureka-point status; P. Thomas Carroll, Colp, Feuer, and others showed that it was not Marx's offer of the dedication in volume two of *Das Kapital* that Darwin refused in a famous letter; and Moore exposed the fundamentalist story that Darwin gave up evolution and professed Christianity on his deathbed. Detailed studies of Darwin's reception in France, Italy, Germany, Russia, Spain, China, North America, and the Arab world were also published, including comparative works edited by Glick, and Numbers and Stenhouse.

So from the 1970s, revisionist views proliferated on every aspect of Darwin's life and work. His long post-*Beagle* illness was much debated but its nature never fully resolved. Early complaints such as eczema and heart palpitations possibly foreshadowed a permanent disorder, and some later symptoms certainly suggest the possibility of an underlying physical defect such as an ulcerated gut, allergies, or a neurological or metabolic malfunction. In any case, both before and during the *Beagle* voyage Darwin displayed hearty good health. Only after 1837, when he moved to London and began theorizing about transmutation, does his correspondence chart an increasingly persistent series of nausea-related conditions. These lifted during his last decade, after the *Descent of Man* appeared, and he died of heart failure brought on by old age.

Interpretations of the illness broadly support either physical or psychosomatic causation and thus themselves chart controversies in medical knowledge. Pickering's influential suggestion in 1974, that Darwin's condition should be regarded as a 'creative malady' that allowed him time to get on with his work, was a view partly expressed by Darwin himself and mooted by his younger contemporaries. As an invalid needing peace and privacy, he chose to conduct much of his scientific work through correspondence. He withdrew from the administrative side of science at an early age and constantly found excuses to avoid society. During the mid-1860s, when he was severely ill, colleagues visited Down House only infrequently and Emma forbade them to linger. Yet Darwin's symptoms were real enough and he regularly complained that sickness was keeping him from his work. Over the years he offered so many excuses that even his own words must be interpreted with caution.

Medical authorities joined the debate, particularly after the 1959 centenary. The parasitologist Saul Adler's suggestion that Darwin contracted Chagas's disease while in Chile was repeatedly discounted on archival grounds. In a full review of the literature, Colp, a psychiatrist, proposed in 1977 that Darwin suffered from stress-related conditions induced by his private study of transmutation and his fears about the public controversy it would provoke. At one point Darwin himself declared, 'my abstract [the *Origin of Species*] is the cause, I believe of the main part of the ills to which my flesh is heir' (*Correspondence*, 7.247). This psychosomatic aetiology has been widely accepted, and in 1998 Colp acknowledged Chagas's disease as a likely predisposing cause. Bowlby, a child psychiatrist, considered the death of Darwin's mother when he was eight years old highly significant for his future health. Many other interpretations have been offered, all more or less likely. The subject's endless interest may be partly explained by the traditional association of creative genius with intense mental agitation. Darwin's personal equanimity and calm private life, however, stand in marked contrast to the social and intellectual turmoil provoked by his work.

When scientists and historians marked the centenary of Darwin's death in 1982 their views of Darwin were as disparate as their commemorative publications. Kohn's 1000-page collection, *The Darwinian Heritage* (1985), surpassed all others as the most tangible evidence to date that responsibility for shaping Darwin's image had passed to historians. The study of his life and works was now a specialism as rigorous and exacting as any in the life sciences, and indeed by 1990 scholars possessed an array of sophisticated tools for constructing an entirely fresh portrait of Darwin: the newly edited *Beagle* diary (1988) and transmutation notebooks (1987); the 'big book' ('Natural selection') from which the *Origin of Species* was condensed (1975); a variorum *Origin* edited by Peckham (1959); Darwin's collected papers (1977); his marginalia transcribed by Di Gregorio and Gill (1990); concordances to the *Origin*

(1981), *Descent of Man* (1987), and *Expression of the Emotions* (1986) supervised by Barrett; a bibliographical handlist (1977; supplement 1986) and biographical 'companion' (1978) compiled by Freeman; and a calendar of some 15,000 letters to and from Darwin (1985; revised edn 1994) together with *The Correspondence of Charles Darwin* (1985–), edited by a transatlantic team under the guidance of Burkhardt and, until his death, Sydney Smith. The thirty-two projected volumes of the *Correspondence*, due for completion about 2012, will keep biographers busy well into the twenty-first century.

In 1990 new biographies based on these rich resources began to appear. Though they differ (often sharply) from one another, and none should be called definitive, they mark the abandonment of intellectual hagiography. Scholars now concern themselves less with Darwin as a heroic thinker than as a Victorian gentleman-naturalist who had the time, income, and nerve to touch the untouchable and make evolution culturally acceptable. This turn towards histories that offer more deeply informed, socially embedded explanations of Darwin's career and influence is clear evidence that the study of Western science, its history and social relations, reached new levels of professionalism by the end of the twentieth century.

ADRIAN DESMOND, JANET BROWNE, and JAMES MOORE

Sources BIOGRAPHIES J. Browne, *Voyaging* (1995), vol. 1 of *Charles Darwin* • A. Desmond and J. Moore, *Darwin* (1991) • P. J. Bowler, *Charles Darwin: the man and his influence* (1990) [with historiographic survey] • J. Bowlby, *Charles Darwin: a biography* (1990) • G. Himmelfarb, *Darwin and the Darwinian revolution* (1959) • P. Brent, *Charles Darwin: a 'man of enlarged curiosity'* (1981) • G. De Beer, *Charles Darwin: evolution by natural selection* (1963) • W. Irvine, *Apes, angels, and Victorians: the story of Darwin, Huxley, and evolution* (1955) TEXTS AND TOOLS P. H. Barrett, P. J. Gautrey, S. Herbert, D. Kohn, and S. Smith, eds., *Charles Darwin's notebooks, 1836–1844: geology, transmutation of species, metaphysical enquiries* (1987) [transcription of Darwin's notebooks; with index and bibliography] • *The correspondence of Charles Darwin*, ed. F. Burkhardt and S. Smith, [13 vols.] (1985–) • *The collected papers of Charles Darwin*, ed. P. H. Barrett, 2 vols. (1977) [Darwin's periodical articles, omitting only a few; with index and bibliography] • *The autobiography of Charles Darwin, 1809–1882, with original omissions restored*, ed. N. Barlow (1958) • *Charles Darwin's Beagle diary*, ed. R. D. Keynes (1988) [annotated transcription] • C. Darwin, *The works of Charles Darwin*, ed. P. H. Barrett and R. B. Freeman, 29 vols. (1986–9) [with bibliography] • F. Burkhardt and S. Smith, eds., *A calendar of the correspondence of Charles Darwin, 1821–1882* (1985); rev. edn (1994) • T. Junker and M. Richmond, eds., *Charles Darwins Briefwechsel mit deutschen Naturforschern: ein Kalendarium mit Inhaltsangaben, biographischen Register und Bibliographie* (1996) • *The life and letters of Charles Darwin*, ed. F. Darwin, 3rd edn, 3 vols. (1887) • *More letters of Charles Darwin*, ed. F. Darwin and A. C. Seward, 2 vols. (1903) • *Emma Darwin: a century of family letters, 1792–1896*, ed. H. Litchfield, 2 vols. (1915) [privately printed, 1904] • H. E. Gruber and P. H. Barrett, *Darwin on man: a psychological study of scientific creativity … together with Darwin's early and unpublished notebooks* (1974) • S. Herbert, ed., *The Red notebook of Charles Darwin* (1980) • *Charles Darwin's 'Natural selection': being the second part of his big species book written from 1856 to 1858*, ed. R. C. Stauffer (1975) • M. A. Di Gregorio and N. W. Gill, *Charles Darwin's marginalia*, 1 (1990) [transcription of annotations in Darwin's scientific library] • *Charles Darwin's diary of the voyage of H.M.S. 'Beagle'*, ed. N. Barlow (1933) • *Charles Darwin's zoology notes and specimen lists from H.M.S. 'Beagle'*, ed. R. D.

Keynes (2000) • N. Barlow, ed., 'Darwin's ornithological notes', *Bulletin of the British Museum (Natural History)*, Historical Series, 2 (1963), 201–78 • C. Darwin, *On the origin of species by means of natural selection, or, The preservation of favoured races in the struggle for life* (1859) • C. Darwin, *The descent of man, and selection in relation to sex*, 2 vols. (1871) • C. Darwin, *The variation of animals and plants under domestication*, 2 vols. (1868); rev. edn (1875) • *The foundations of 'The origin of species': two essays written in 1842 and 1844*, ed. F. Darwin (1909) • R. B. Freeman, *The works of Charles Darwin: an annotated bibliographical handlist*, 2nd edn (1977); suppl. (1986) [standard bibliography] • R. B. Freeman, *Charles Darwin: a companion* (1978) • R. B. Freeman, *Darwin pedigrees* (1984) • M. Peckham, ed., *The 'Origin of species' by Charles Darwin: a variorum text* (1959) • P. H. Barrett, D. J. Weinshank, and T. Gottleber, eds., *A concordance to Darwin's 'Origin of species', first edition* (1981) • P. H. Barrett, D. J. Weinshank, P. Ruhlen, and S. J. Ozminski, eds., *A concordance to Darwin's 'The descent of man, and selection, in relation to sex'* (1987) • P. H. Barrett, D. J. Weinshank, P. Ruhlen, S. J. Ozminski, and B. M. Berghage, eds., *A concordance to Darwin's 'The expression of emotions in man and animals'* (1986) • L. Huxley, *Life and letters of Joseph Dalton Hooker*, 2 vols. (1918) • L. Huxley, *Life and letters of Thomas Henry Huxley*, 2 vols. (1900) • J. Marchant, *Alfred Russel Wallace: letters and reminiscences*, 2 vols. (1916) • R. H. Keynes, *Annie's box: Charles Darwin, his daughter and human evolution* (2001) • E. Healey, *Emma Darwin: the inspirational wife of a genius* (2001) • R. B. Freeman, 'The Darwin family', *Biological Journal of the Linnean Society*, 17 (1982), 9–21 • parish register, Shrewsbury, St Chad's, 17 Nov 1809 [baptism] • parish register, Maer, St Peter's, 29 Jan 1839 [marriage] • d. cert.

INTERPRETATIVE STUDIES D. Kohn, ed., *The Darwinian heritage* (1985) • D. Kohn, 'Theories to work by: rejected theories, reproduction, and Darwin's path to natural selection', *Studies in History of Biology*, 4 (1980), 67–170 • F. J. Sulloway, 'Darwin and his finches: the evolution of a legend', *Journal of the History of Biology*, 15 (1982), 1–53 • F. J. Sulloway, 'Darwin's conversion: the *Beagle* voyage and its aftermath', *Journal of the History of Biology*, 15 (1982), 325–96 • P. R. Sloan, 'Darwin's invertebrate program, 1826–1836: preconditions for transformism', *The Darwinian heritage*, ed. D. Kohn (1985), 71–120 • P. R. Sloan, 'Darwin, vital matter, and the transformism of species', *Journal of the History of Biology*, 19 (1986), 367–95 • D. Ospovat, *The development of Darwin's theory: natural history, natural theology, and natural selection, 1838–1859* (1981) • M. J. S. Hodge, 'Darwin and the laws of the animate part of the terrestrial system (1835–1837): on the Lyellian origins of his zoonomical explanatory program', *Studies in History of Biology*, 7 (1983), 1–106 • A. Desmond, *The politics of evolution: morphology, medicine, and reform in radical London* (1989) • J. Moore, 'Darwin of Down: the evolutionist as squarson-naturalist', *The Darwinian heritage*, ed. D. Kohn (1985), 435–81 • R. Colp jun., *To be an invalid: the illness of Charles Darwin* (1977) • J. Secord, 'Darwin and the breeders: a social history', *The Darwinian heritage*, ed. D. Kohn (1985), 519–42 • D. Kohn, 'Darwin's ambiguity: the secularization of biological meaning', *British Journal for the History of Science*, 22 (1989), 215–39 • E. Richards, 'Darwin and the descent of woman', *The wider domain of evolutionary thought*, ed. D. R. Oldroyd and I. Langham (1983), 57–111 • J. C. Greene, 'Darwin as a social evolutionist', *Journal of the History of Biology*, 10 (1977), 1–27 • B. G. Beddall, 'Darwin and divergence: the Wallace connection', *Journal of the History of Biology*, 21 (1988), 1–68 • J. Moore, 'Of love and death: why Darwin "gave up Christianity"', *History, humanity and evolution: essays for John C. Greene*, ed. J. Moore (1989), 195–229 • D. Kohn, 'The aesthetic construction of Darwin's theory', *The elusive synthesis: aesthetics and science*, ed. A. I. Tauber (1996), 13–48 • M. J. S. Hodge and D. Kohn, 'The immediate origins of natural selection', *The Darwinian heritage*, ed. D. Kohn (1985), 185–206 • M. J. S. Hodge, 'Darwin as a lifelong generation theorist', *The Darwinian heritage*, ed. D. Kohn (1985), 207–43 • M. J. S. Hodge, 'The structure and strategy of Darwin's "Long Argument"', *British Journal for the History of Science*, 10 (1977), 237–46 • R. Colp jun., '"To be an invalid", redux', *Journal of the History of Biology*, 31 (1998), 211–40 • R. Colp, '"Confessing a murder": Darwin's first revelations about

transmutation', *Isis*, 77 (1986), 9–32 • J. A. Secord, 'Nature's fancy: Charles Darwin and the breeding of pigeons', *Isis*, 72 (1981), 163–86 • J. Browne, 'Darwin's botanical arithmetic and the principle of divergence, 1854–1858', *Journal of the History of Biology*, 13 (1980), 53–89 • D. Kohn, 'Darwin's principle of divergence as internal dialogue', *The Darwinian heritage*, ed. D. Kohn (1985), 245–57 • J. Moore, 'Freethought, secularism, agnosticism: the case of Charles Darwin', *Traditions* (1988), vol. 1 of *Religion in Victorian Britain*, ed. G. Parsons, 274–319 • E. Manier, *The young Darwin and his cultural circle: a study of the influences which helped shape the language and logic of the first drafts of the theory of natural selection* (1977) • C. Limoges, *La sélection naturelle: étude sur la première constitution d'un concept (1837–1859)* (1970) • S. Herbert, 'The place of man in the development of Darwin's theory of transmutation, part 1, to July 1837', *Journal of the History of Biology*, 7 (1974), 217–58 • S. Herbert, 'The place of man in the development of Darwin's theory of transmutation, part 2', *Journal of the History of Biology*, 10 (1977), 155–227 • G. Jones, 'The social history of Darwin's "Descent of man"', *Economy and Society*, 7 (1978), 1–23 • M. Kottler, 'Charles Darwin and Alfred Russel Wallace: two decades of debate over natural selection', *The Darwinian heritage*, ed. D. Kohn (1985), 367–432 • S. S. Schweber, 'Darwin and the political economists: divergence of character', *Journal of the History of Biology*, 13 (1980), 195–289 • S. S. Schweber, 'The origin of the "Origin" revisited', *Journal of the History of Biology*, 10 (1977), 229–316 • H. L. Burstyn, 'If Darwin wasn't the *Beagle*'s naturalist, why was he on board?', *British Journal for the History of Science*, 8 (1975), 62–9 • J. W. Gruber, 'Who was the *Beagle*'s naturalist', *British Journal for the History of Science*, 4 (1968–9), 266–82 • F. W. Nicholas and J. M. Nicholas, *Charles Darwin in Australia, with illustrations and additional commentary from other members of the Beagle's company, including Conrad Martens, Augustus Earle, Captain FitzRoy, Philip Gidley King, and Syms Covington* (1989) • P. Armstrong, *Charles Darwin in Western Australia: a young scientist's perception of an environment* (1985) • P. Armstrong, *Darwin's desolate islands: a naturalist in the Falklands, 1833 and 1834* (1992) • P. Armstrong, *Under the blue vault of heaven: a study of Charles Darwin's sojourn in the Cocos (Keeling) Islands* (1991) • P. Armstrong, *Charles Darwin's last island: Terceira, Azores, 1836* (1992) • J. A. Secord, 'The discovery of a vocation: Darwin's early geology', *British Journal for the History of Science*, 24 (1991), 133–57 • M. Rudwick, 'Charles Darwin in London: the integration of public and private science', *Isis*, 73 (1982), 186–206 • S. Herbert, 'Darwin the young geologist', *The Darwinian heritage*, ed. D. Kohn (1985), 483–510 • J. Browne, 'Darwin and the expression of the emotions', *The Darwinian heritage*, ed. D. Kohn (1985), 307–26 • J. Browne, 'I could have retched all night: Charles Darwin and his body', *Science incarnate: historical embodiments of natural knowledge*, ed. C. Lawrence and S. Shapin (1998), 240–87 • J. Moore, 'Charles Darwin lies in Westminster Abbey', *Biological Journal of the Linnean Society*, 17 (1982), 97–113 • L. S. Feuer, 'Is the "Darwin–Marx correspondence" authentic?', *Annals of Science*, 32 (1975), 1–12 • R. Colp jun., 'The myth of the Darwin–Marx letter', *History of Political Economy*, 14 (1982), 461–82 • R. Weikart, 'A recently discovered Darwin letter on social Darwinism', *Isis*, 86 (1995), 609–11 • M. J. S. Rudwick, 'Darwin and Glen Roy: a "great failure" in scientific method?', *Studies in the History and Philosophy of Science*, 5 (1974), 97–185 • P. H. Barrett, 'The Sedgwick-Darwin geologic tour of north Wales', *Proceedings of the American Philosophical Society*, 118 (1974), 146–64 • J. Browne, *The secular ark: studies in the history of biogeography* (1983) • J. Browne, 'The Charles Darwin–Joseph Hooker correspondence: an analysis of manuscript resources and their use in biography', *Journal of the Society of the Bibliography of Natural History*, 8 (1976–8), 351–66 • W. A. Newman, 'Darwin and cirripedology', *Crustacean Issues*, 7 (1993), 349–434 • K. G. V. Smith, ed., 'Darwin's insects: Charles Darwin's entomological notes', *Bulletin of the British Museum (Natural History)*, Historical Series, 14 (1987), 1–143 • D. M. Porter, ed., 'Darwin's notes on *Beagle* plants', *Bulletin of the British Museum (Natural History)*, Historical Series, 14 (1987), 145–233 • D. R. Stoddart, 'Darwin, Lyell, and the geological significance of coral reefs', *British Journal for the History of Science*, 9 (1976), 119–218 • P. Ekman, ed., *Darwin and facial expression: a century of research in review* (1973) • S. de Chadarevian, 'Laboratory science versus country-house experiments: the controversy between Julius Sachs and Charles Darwin', *British Journal for the History of Science*, 29 (1996), 17–41 • F. B. Brown, *The evolution of Darwin's religious views* (1986) • D. Amigoni and J. Wallace, eds., *Charles Darwin's 'The origin of species': new interdisciplinary essays* (1995) • P. J. Vorzimmer, *Charles Darwin, the years of controversy: the 'Origin of species' and its critics, 1859–82* (1970) • E. Mayr, 'Introduction', in C. Darwin, *On the origin of species by natural selection: a facsimile of the first edition, with an introduction by Ernst Mayr* (1964) • S. Smith, 'The origin of the "Origin" as discerned from Charles Darwin's notebooks and his annotations in the books he read between 1837 and 1842', *Advancement of Science*, 16 (1960), 391–401 • H. Atkins, *Down, the home of the Darwins: the story of a house and the people who lived there*, rev. edn (1976) • J. H. Ashworth, 'Charles Darwin as a student in Edinburgh, 1825–1827', *Proceedings of the Royal Society of Edinburgh*, 55 (1934–5), 97–113 • G. Shepperson, 'The intellectual background of Charles Darwin's student years at Edinburgh', *Darwinism and the study of society*, ed. M. Banton (1961), 17–35 • J. J. Parodiz, *Darwin in the New World* (1981) • W. F. Cannon, 'The impact of uniformitarianism: two letters from John Herschel to Charles Lyell, 1836–1837', *Proceedings of the American Philosophical Society*, 105 (1961), 301–14 • N. C. Gillespie, *Charles Darwin and the problem of creation* (1979) • M. Ruse, *The Darwinian paradigm: essays on its history, philosophy, and religious implications* (1989) • E. Mayr, *One long argument: Charles Darwin and the genesis of modern evolutionary thought* (1991) • M. Ruse, *The Darwinian revolution* (1979) • M. T. Ghiselin, *The triumph of the Darwinian method* (1969) • S. Adler, 'Darwin's illness', *Nature*, 184 (10 Oct 1959), 1102–3 • G. Pickering, *Creative malady: illness in the lives and minds of Charles Darwin, Florence Nightingale, Mary Baker Eddy, Sigmund Freud, Marcel Proust, Elizabeth Barrett Browning* (1974) • *Harriet Martineau's letters to Fanny Wedgwood*, ed. E. Sanders Arbuckle (1983)

DARWIN'S INFLUENCE A. Ellegård, *Darwin and the general reader: the reception of Darwin's theory of evolution in the British periodical press, 1859–1872* (1958) • R. M. Young, *Darwin's metaphor: nature's place in Victorian culture* (1985) • G. Beer, *Darwin's plots: evolutionary narrative in Darwin, George Eliot, and nineteenth-century fiction* (1983) • J. Gayon, *Darwinism's struggle for survival: heredity and the hypothesis of natural selection* (1998) • P. J. Bowler, *The eclipse of Darwinism: anti-Darwinian evolution theories in the decades around 1900* (1983) • T. Glick, ed., *The comparative reception of Darwinism* (1974) • R. L. Numbers and J. Stenhouse, eds., *Disseminating Darwinism: the role of place, race, religion, and gender* (1999) • D. C. Bellomy, '"Social Darwinism" revisited', *Perspectives in American History*, new ser., 1 (1984), 1–129 • S. Shapin and B. Barnes, 'Darwin and social Darwinism: purity and history', *Natural order: historical studies of scientific culture*, ed. S. Shapin and B. Barnes (1979), 125–42 • P. Crook, *Darwinism, war and history: the debate over the biology of war from the 'Origin of species' to the First World War* (1994) • M. Hawkins, *Social Darwinism in European and American thought, 1860–1945: nature as model and nature as threat* (1997) • P. Tort, ed., *Darwinisme et société* (1992) • R. J. Richards, *Darwin and the emergence of evolutionary theories of mind and behavior* (1987) • D. Oldroyd and I. Langham, eds., *The wider domain of evolutionary thought* (1983) • J. Moore, *The post-Darwinian controversies: a study of the protestant struggle to come to terms with Darwin in Great Britain and America, 1870–1900* (1979) • J. Moore, 'Deconstructing Darwinism: the politics of evolution in the 1860s', *Journal of the History of Biology*, 24 (1991), 353–408 • J. Roberts, *Darwinism and the divine in America: protestant intellectuals and organic evolution, 1859–1900* (1988) • R. L. Numbers, *Darwinism comes to America* (1998) • P. Corsi and P. J. Weindling, 'Darwinism in Germany, France, and Italy', *The Darwinian heritage*, ed. D. Kohn (1985), 683–729 • T. Junker, *Darwinismus und Botanik: Rezeption, Kritik und theoretische Alternativen im Deutschland des 19. Jahrhunderts* (Stuttgart, 1989) • Y. Conry, *L'introduction du darwinisme en France au XIXᵉ siècle* (1974) • G. Pancaldi, *Darwin in Italy: science across cultural frontiers* (1991) • A. Kelly, *The descent of Darwin: the popularization of Darwinism in Germany, 1860–1914* (1981) • D. P. Todes, *Darwin without Malthus: the struggle for existence in Russian evolutionary*

thought (1989) • A. Vucinich, *Darwin in Russian thought* (1988) • R. MacLeod and P. Rehbock, eds., *Darwin's laboratory: evolutionary theory and natural history in the Pacific* (1994) • T. Glick, *Darwin en España* (1982) • A. A. Ziadat, *Western science in the Arab world: the impact of Darwinism, 1860–1930* (1986) • J. R. Pusey, *China and Charles Darwin* (1983) • P. J. Bowler, *Evolution: the history of an idea* (1984) • P. J. Bowler, *The non-Darwinian revolution: reinterpreting a historical myth* (1988) • D. L. Hull, *Darwin and his critics: the reception of Darwin's theory by the scientific community* (1973) • E. Mayr and W. B. Provine, *The evolutionary synthesis: perspectives on the unification of biology* (1980) • V. B. Smocovitis, *Unifying biology: the evolutionary synthesis and evolutionary biology* (1996) • V. B. Smocovitis, 'Celebrating Darwin: the Darwin centennial celebration at the University of Chicago', *Osiris*, 2nd ser., 14 (1999), 1–66 • J. Moore, *The Darwin legend* (1994) • D. S. Bendall, ed., *Evolution from molecules to men* [Cambridge 1982] (1983) • Y. Conry, ed., *De Darwin au darwinisme: science et idéologie* [Paris, Chantilly 1982] (1983) • S. Tax and C. Callender, eds., *Evolution after Darwin: the University of Chicago centennial*, 3 vols. (1960) • A. C. Seward, ed., *Darwin and modern science: essays in commemoration of the centenary of the birth of Charles Darwin and of the fiftieth anniversary of the publication of 'The origin of species'* (1909) • American Association for the Advancement of Science, *Fifty years of Darwinism: modern aspects of evolution: centennial addresses in honour of Charles Darwin before the American Association for the Advancement of Science, Baltimore, Friday, January 1, 1909* (1909) • W. G. Ridewood, ed., *Memorials of Charles Darwin: a collection of manuscripts, portraits, medals, books and natural history specimens to commemorate the centenary of his birth and the fiftieth anniversary of the publication of 'The origin of species'* (1909)

LITERATURE SURVEYS A. La Vergata, 'Images of Darwin: a historiographic overview', *The Darwinian heritage*, ed. D. Kohn (1985), 901–72 • I. Bohlin, 'Through Malthusian specs? A study in the philosophy of science studies with special reference to the theory and ideology of Darwin historiography', PhD diss., University of Göteborg, 1995 • D. Oldroyd, 'How did Darwin arrive at his theory? The secondary literature to 1982', *History of Science*, 22 (1984), 325–74 • J. Moore, 'Socializing Darwinism: historiography and the fortunes of a phase', *Science as politics*, ed. L. Levidow (1986), 38–80 • J. Moore, 'On revolutionizing the Darwin industry: a centennial retrospect', *Radical Philosophy*, no. 37 (1984), 13–22 • I. Bohlin, 'R. M. Young and Darwin historiography', *Social Studies of Science*, 21 (1991), 597–648 • R. Colp jun., 'Charles Darwin's past and future biographies', *History of Science*, 27 (1989), 167–97 • F. B. Churchill, 'Darwin and the historian', *Biological Journal of the Linnean Society*, 17 (1982), 45–68 • T. Lenoir, 'The Darwin industry', *Journal of the History of Biology*, 20 (1987), 115–30 • J. C. Greene, 'Reflections on the progress of Darwin studies', *Journal of the History of Biology*, 8 (1975), 243–73 • M. Ruse, 'The Darwin industry: a critical evaluation', *History of Science*, 12 (1974), 43–58 • D. C. Bellomy, '"Social Darwinism" revisited', *Perspectives in American History*, new ser., 1 (1984), 1–129

Archives American Philosophical Society, Philadelphia • CUL, corresp. and papers • Darwin Museum, Down House, Downe, Kent • Hunt. L., letters • John Murray, London, letter-books • Lincs. Arch., estate corresp. • Linn. Soc., letters • NHM, letter-book • NRA, priv. coll., corresp. and papers | American Philosophical Society, Philadelphia, letters to Sir Charles Lyell • American Philosophical Society, Philadelphia, letters to George Romanes • Bath Royal Literary and Scientific Institution, letters to Leonard Blomefield • BL, John Lubbock papers • BL, letters to Philip Sclater, M/441 [some copies] • BL, letters to Richard Strachey, Add. MS 60631 • BL, A. R. Wallace papers • BL, corresp. with Alfred Russel Wallace, Add. MS 46434 • Case Western Reserve University Library, Cleveland, Ohio, letters to Henry Walter Bates • Case Western Reserve University Library, Cleveland, Ohio, letters to J. B. Innes • Christ's College, Cambridge, letters to William Darwin Fox • Elgin Museum, letters to George Gordon • Harvard U., Arnold Arboretum, letters to Asa Gray • Hunt. L., letters to Ernest Krause • ICL, letters to Thomas H. Huxley • John Innes Centre, Norwich, letters to Sir W. H. Flower • Keele University, Wedgwood-Mosley collection • Linn. Soc., letters to Lord Farrer • New York Botanical Garden Library, letters to Albany Hancock · New York Botanical Garden Library, corresp. with W. Tegetmeier · NHM, corresp. and notebooks incl. journal of a voyage in HMS *Beagle* [copies] · NHM, letters to Andrew Murray [copies] · NHM, letters to Osbert Salvin [copies] · Norwich Castle Museum, letters to Robert Fitch · Oxf. U. Mus. NH, letters to John Phillips · Oxf. U. Mus. NH, corresp. mainly with Ralph Medola [some copies] · RBG Kew, corresp. with Sir Joseph Hooker · RBG Kew, letters to Sir William Thiselton-Dyer · RGS, letters to Royal Geographical Society · Royal Entomological Society, London, letters to Roland Trimen and related papers · Royal Institution of Great Britain, London, letters to John Tyndall · RS, letters to Sir John Lubbock · Shrewsbury School, letters to Albert Gunther · U. Cam., department of zoology, letters to Alfred Newton · UCL, letters to Sir Francis Galton · University of British Columbia Library, Woodward Biomedical Library, corresp. with Sir John Burdon-Sanderson

Likenesses R. Sharples, double portrait, pastel drawing, 1816 (with his sister Emily Catherine), Darwin Museum, Down House, Downe, Kent · G. Richmond, pencil sketch, *c.*1839, U. Cam., botany school · G. Richmond, drawing, 1840, Darwin Museum, Down House, Downe, Kent · double portrait, daguerreotype, 1842, Darwin Museum, Down House, Downe, Kent · T. H. Maguire, lithograph, 1849, BM; repro. in *Ipswich Museum portraits* (1851) · S. Laurence, chalk drawing, 1853, Darwin Museum, Down House, Downe, Kent · S. Laurence, drawing, 1853, Sedgwick Museum of Geology, Cambridge · Maull & Polyblank, photograph, *c.*1854, Literary and Scientific Portrait Club; copy, NPG · Maull & Polyblank, photograph, *c.*1855, NPG · Maull & Polyblank, carte-de-visite, *c.*1857, CUL, Darwin archive · W. E. Darwin, photograph, 1861, Harvard U., Gray Herbarium · London Stereoscopic Co., carte-de-visite, *c.*1864, Wellcome L. · E. Edwards, photograph, 1866, NPG; repro. in L. Reeve, ed., *Portraits of men of eminence* (1863-7) · J. M. Cameron, photograph, 1868, NPG; version, RS · photograph, *c.*1868, Darwin Museum, Down House, Downe, Kent · T. Woolner, marble bust, 1869, U. Cam., botany school · O. G. Reijlander, photograph, *c.*1871, CUL, Darwin archive · caricature, 1873 · L. Darwin, photograph, *c.*1874, repro. in *Transactions of the Shropshire Archaeological and Natural History Society*, 8 (1884) · C. H. Jeens, stipple, 1874 (after carte-de-visite by O. G. Reijlander, *c.*1871), BM; repro. in *Nature* (1874) · W. W. Ouless, oils, 1875, priv. coll.; copy, Christ's College, Cambridge · P. Rajon, engraving, 1875 (after Ouless, 1875) · Barraud, cartes-de-visite, 1876-9, NPG · Elliott & Fry, cartes-de-visite, 1876-9, NPG · M. Collier, pencil drawing, *c.*1878, NPG · M. Huxley, pencil drawing, 1878, NPG · Lock & Whitfield, photograph, *c.*1878, Wellcome L.; repro. in T. Cooper and others, *Men of mark, a gallery of contemporary portraits*, 3rd ser. (1878) · W. B. Richmond, oils, *c.*1879-1880, U. Cam., department of zoology · Elliott & Fry, photographs, *c.*1880, CUL · A. Goodwin, double portrait, oils, 1880 (with his wife), Darwin Museum, Down House, Downe, Kent · J. Collier, oils, 1881, Linn. Soc. [*see illus.*] · A. Legros, bronze medallion, 1881, Man. City Gall. · J. E. Boehm, marble statue, 1883, BM · L. Flameng, engraving, 1883 (after Collier, 1881) · caricature, 1883 · G. Kruell, engraving, 1884 (after photograph by Maull & Polyblank, *c.*1857) · J. E. Boehm, medallion, 1887, Westminster Abbey · J. E. Boehm, terracotta bust, 1887, NPG · G. Kruell, engraving, 1887 (after photograph by Elliott & Fry, *c.*1880) · T. Woolner, green Wedgwood ware plaque, *c.*1887, Christ's College, Cambridge · A. Wyon, bronze medallion, 1890, BM · H. R. H. Pinker, stone statue, *c.*1896, Oxf. U. Mus. NH · H. Montford, statue, exh. RA 1898, Shrewsbury; terracotta copy, NPG · Ape [C. Pellegrini], lithograph, repro. in *VF* (30 Sept 1871) · L. Baker, drawing, Darwin Museum, Down House, Downe, Kent · F. Betlader, lithograph, NPG · J. Collier, engraving, NPG · J. Collier, oils, other versions, NPG, RS · Dalziel, caricature, repro. in *Fun* (22 July 1871) · Dalziel, caricature, repro. in *Fun* (16 Nov 1872) · E. Eustafieff, paintings, Darwin Museum, Down House, Downe, Kent · M. Klinkicht, woodcut, BM · Lock & Whitfield, photographs, NPG · L. A. Nash, washed Indian ink drawing, priv. coll. · G. Pilotell, drypoint etching, BM · J. Reily, oils, Darwin

Museum, Down House, Downe, Kent · L. Sambourne, caricature, repro. in *Punch* (1875) · L. Sambourne, caricature, repro. in *Punch's Fancy Portraits*, 54 (1881) · J. J. Tissot, chromolithograph caricature, NPG; repro. in *VF* (30 Sept 1871) · A. Wyon, wax sculpture, Darwin Museum, Down House, Downe, Kent · caricature, repro. in *The Hornet* (22 March 1871) · caricature, repro. in *Figaro* (28 Oct 1871) · caricature, repro. in *Punch's Almanack* (6 Dec 1881) · lithograph, repro. in *London Sketch Book* (1874) · paintings, Darwin Museum, Down House, Downe, Kent · prints, NPG

Wealth at death £146,911 7*s.* 10*d.*: CGPLA Eng. & Wales, 1882

Darwin, Ellen Wordsworth (1856-1903). *See under* Darwin, Sir Francis (1848-1925).

Darwin, Erasmus (1731-1802), physician and natural philosopher, was born on 12 December 1731 at Elston Hall, near Nottingham, the seventh child of Robert Darwin (1682-1754), a lawyer of independent means who had retired early, and his wife, Elizabeth (formerly Hill; 1702-1797). Darwin had three brothers and three sisters. He was sent to the Chesterfield School in 1741 and in 1750 became a student at St John's College, Cambridge, where he studied classics and mathematics. He held the Exeter scholarship there and wrote a poem on the death of Frederick, prince of Wales, in 1751 (which was published in the *European Magazine* in 1795). While a student at Cambridge he travelled to London to attend the lectures of the surgeon William Hunter. From 1753 to 1756 Darwin studied medicine in Edinburgh which was, at that time, a major centre for medical education in Europe. He took his MB degree from Cambridge in 1755. There is no record of Erasmus Darwin's taking his BA at Cambridge (although Charles Darwin claimed that he did), nor of the award of an MD (although this appears on some of his books and papers).

Early career, marriages, and family Darwin established his first medical practice in Nottingham in 1756, with little success. In November 1756 he moved to Lichfield, where his practice flourished. He married Mary Howard (*b.* 1740), the daughter of Penelope (*née* Foley) and Charles Howard, a Lichfield solicitor, in 1757. Mary died in 1770 leaving three surviving children: Charles (1758-1778), who died at the age of nineteen, from an infection sustained while dissecting, when he was a medical student; Erasmus (*b.* 1759), who became a lawyer and died in 1799; and Robert Waring (*b.* 1766) who became a successful physician and father of Charles *Darwin, the author of *Origin of Species* (1859). In the early 1770s Darwin formed an attachment to Mary Parker (later Day; 1753-1820), with whom he had two illegitimate daughters, Susan and Mary Parker. In 1775 Darwin met Mrs Elizabeth Pole (1747-1832), wife of Colonel Edward Sacheverel Pole, and she brought her children to his home for treatment. Colonel Pole died in 1780 and Darwin married Elizabeth in 1781; she was the daughter of Elizabeth Collier and the earl of Portmore, Charles Colyear. Darwin and Elizabeth took up residence a few miles outside Derby at Radburn Hall, moved into Derby in 1783, and to Breadsall Priory, north of Derby, in 1802. They had six children who survived beyond infancy.

While establishing his medical practice Darwin also

Erasmus Darwin (1731–1802), by Joseph Wright of Derby, 1792–3

pursued his interests in natural philosophy and mechanical invention. In 1757 the first of his six papers in the *Philosophical Transactions* appeared. He presented an experiment which proved that electricity did not affect the mechanical properties of air, thereby disproving Henry Eeles's contention that vapours rise only if they are electrically charged. A second paper, on his treatment of a patient who was spitting up blood, was published in the *Philosophical Transactions* in 1760. In 1761 Darwin became a fellow of the Royal Society. During the 1760s to early 1770s he was not only treating patients but also experimenting on gases and studying chemistry, designing carriages and speaking machines, developing an interest in geology, and exploring the potential of steam engines. Between 1776 and 1786 Darwin kept a commonplace book which records medical case notes, reflections on meteorology, and mechanical designs such as spinning machines, water pumps, and canal locks. A keen inventor, among his many other mechanical contrivances were a new steering mechanism for carriages, a copying machine, and even a mechanical bird.

Botanical practice, theory, and poetry Botany became an absorbing practical and theoretical interest for Darwin in the late 1770s. He constructed his own botanic garden outside Lichfield and undertook the translation of writings of the Swedish naturalist Carl Linnaeus (1707–1778). These appeared as *A System of Vegetables* (1783, the thirteenth edition of *Systema vegetabilium*), and *The Families of Plants* (1787), comprising the *Genera plantarum* and *Mantissae plantarum* of the elder Linnaeus and the *Supplementum plantarum* of Carl Linnaeus the younger (1741–1783). Although Darwin was the main executor of these translations they were

attributed to the Botanical Society at Lichfield, which included two further members who assisted him: Brooke Boothby and William Jackson. Darwin sought the advice of many contemporary botanists, as well as Samuel Johnson. He aimed for clear, frank language, taking issue with William Withering and others who favoured more euphemistic renderings of Linnaeus's sexual classificatory system. *A System of Vegetables* was dedicated to the president of the Royal Society, Joseph Banks, who supported this undertaking.

While cultivating his botanic garden and translating Linnaeus, Darwin began a poetic work designed to introduce a wider public to the Linnaean mode of plant classification. Anna Seward, Darwin's friend and fellow poet at Lichfield, encouraged his poetic venture and some of her verse was incorporated into the resulting volume without acknowledgement. Fearing that his reputation as a physician might suffer through identification with poetry Darwin delayed publication and *The Loves of the Plants* appeared anonymously in 1789. This lengthy didactic poem in heroic couplets has four cantos, narrated by the goddess of botany, and consists of dramatized representations of eighty-three species of plants, interspersed in the interludes with dialogues about the nature of poetry. The extensive footnotes and further notes display Darwin's knowledge of natural philosophy. He offers his first public speculation on the development of the natural world here: 'Perhaps all the products of nature are in their progress to greater perfection? an idea countenanced by the modern discoveries and deductions concerning the progressive formation of the solid parts of the terraqueous globe'. Poetry, Darwin contended, should be directed towards the visual sense. His pictorial representations and use of personification and pathetic fallacy intensified the Linnaean view of plant sexuality in which stamens are represented as men and pistils as women: lovers, brides, husbands, courtships, and pregnancies abound. *The Loves of the Plants* was Erasmus Darwin's first substantial exploration of what he considered to be key features of the natural world: the importance of reproduction and the continuities or analogies between the functioning of the vegetable and the animal worlds.

The Loves of the Plants was well received and was conceived of as a two-part project. Darwin brought this to completion with the publication of *The Botanic Garden* in 1791, including *The Economy of Vegetation* (part 1) and a reprint of *The Loves of the Plants* (part 2). He beckoned his readers in the advertisement:

> The general design of the following sheets is to inlist Imagination under the banner of Science; and to lead her votaries from the looser analogies, which dress out the imagery of poetry, to the stricter ones which form the ratiocination of philosophy.

The Economy of Vegetation is a lengthy didactic poem in four cantos, one on each of the classical elements—fire, earth, water, and air. Footnotes accompany the verse and there are 115 pages of additional notes on natural history theories and experiments.

In *The Economy of Vegetation* Darwin celebrated the

achievements of contemporary natural philosophers and industrialists, including Josiah Wedgwood, William Herschel, Henry Cavendish, Benjamin Franklin, Joseph Priestley, James Watt, Matthew Boulton, James Brindley, Thomas Savery, and John Whitehurst. Besides observing the introduction of steam power he welcomed new forms of mechanization, such as Boulton's coin production machinery. Vivid representations of industrial processes such as the manufacture of steel and the operations of steam engines and coining machinery are juxtaposed with poetic descriptions of the natural world. Supernatural agents such as nymphs, gnomes, sylphs, and salamanders, and men of industry and science (referred to as 'immortal' and 'ingenious') appear in equal measure. The products of new industrial processes, such as Wedgwood's cameos of the Slave and of Hope, are also on display, with an extensive additional note on the Portland vase, reproductions of which Wedgwood was producing. *The Economy of Vegetation* presented an integrated panorama of nature and industry across a broad temporal sweep. Darwin suggested that 'philosophers of all ages seem to have imagined, that the great world itself had likewise its infancy and its gradual progress to maturity' (canto 1, fn. 101), citing monstrous births as evidence of this progress.

The Lunar Society and industrialization Darwin was a founder of provincial scientific societies in late eighteenth-century Britain: the Botanical Society at Lichfield, the Lunar Society based in Birmingham, and the Derby Philosophical Society. The Lunar Society was the most important of these, incorporating Darwin into a network which included Boulton, Thomas Day, Richard Lovell Edgeworth, Samuel Galton jun., Robert Augustus Johnson, James Keir, Priestley, William Small, Jonathan Stokes, Watt, Wedgwood, Whitehurst, and William Withering. These innovating men of science and industry were drawn together by their interest in natural philosophy, technological and industrial development, and social change appropriate to these concerns. The society acquired its name because of the practice of meeting once a month on the afternoon of the Monday nearest the time of the full moon, but informal contacts among members were also important. Launched around 1765 the Lunar Society was most active between 1781 and 1791.

The Lunar Society constituted a formidable force in the industrialization of provincial England and, as a leading member, Darwin was at the forefront of these changes. In 1763–4 he launched a venture with John Barker, a Lichfield draper, merchant, and banker, Samuel Garbett, a Birmingham merchant, and Robert Bage, a local paper manufacturer, for a mill for slitting and rolling iron at Wychnor. As a mechanical inventor of such devices as a horizontal windmill which was used to grind pigments for Wedgwood's pottery production at Etruria, Darwin was an expert on, and advocate of, technological innovation. Enthusiastic about steam power he encouraged Boulton and Watt to extend its uses. He recognized the need for good transport systems to facilitate industrialization and, as well as designing canal lifts, he campaigned for canals

including the Grand Trunk Canal, built between 1766 and 1777, and the Birmingham Canal, which was completed in 1771. Darwin became embroiled in one of the many disputes about patenting during this period: he and James Watt appeared as witnesses on behalf of the cotton manufacturer Richard Arkwright in 1785. Darwin's poetry offers vivid, triumphal representations of the industrialization of Britain. He focused on industrialists and innovators and made no mention of manual labour.

Medical theory and practice As a physician Darwin was highly regarded. Anna Seward attributed the launch of his successful career to his treatment of 'a young gentleman of family, fortune and consequence' (William Inge) (Seward, 8), and his patients included the countess of Northesk. George III reputedly sought Darwin's services. Seward and others commented on his 'professional generosity' (ibid., 5), and he tried unsuccessfully to establish a dispensary for the poor in Derby. Nevertheless, most of Darwin's medical practice was conducted within the middle ranks of midlands society, including industrialists and their families.

Darwin's medical practice dominated his life. He travelled extensively to treat patients and maintained a lively medical correspondence, providing advice and reflecting on specific cases. Innovative in his treatments, he experimented with drugs (including digitalis), gases, and exercise regimes, as well as unsuccessfully attempting inoculation of his own children. He was concerned with illnesses of both the body and mind, with heredity, and with broad public health issues, including improving nutrition and ventilation.

The first volume of what Darwin described as his medico-philosophical work, *Zoonomia*, appeared in 1794. As the preface explains, it is both a taxonomy, designed 'to reduce the facts belonging to animal life into classes, orders, genera and species' and a more ambitiously physiological synthesis of the 'laws of organic life' designed to establish a sound basis for medical practice. The key locus of the animal economy, for Darwin, was the sensorium which, he contended, was not concentrated in one location but distributed throughout the body (effectively including the sense organs, nervous structures, and muscles), processing the 'subtile fluid', which he called the 'spirit of animation'. He delineated the laws of animal motion which he categorized as: irritative (resulting from the stimulation of organs of sense and muscular fibres by external bodies), sensitive (caused by pleasure or pain), voluntary (caused by desire or aversion), or associative (caused by succession of fibrous contractions). For Darwin the power of contraction of the muscles and the stimulation of the organs of sense were equivalent to the mechanical principle of attraction, and the laws of animate beings could be similarly charted. He considered that there were three elements involved in any single animal function: the stimulus, the sensorial power, and the contractile fibre, and that this combination made organic motions distinctive.

Drawing on the work of John Locke, David Hartley, David Hume, and Priestley, *Zoonomia* offered a theory of biological learning which included both mind and body. Opposed to notions of innate ideas, Darwin showed that ideas resulted from mental development through habits, often based on imitation. Hence he attributed the link between the wavy line and the sense of beauty, proposed by William Hogarth, to the infant's experience of the mother's breast. Darwin's contribution to associationist psychology was to sketch a sequential development of the faculties, through animal interaction with their environment, that fully integrated body and mind: from simple irritative responses to those of volition and association.

Volume 2 of *Zoonomia* appeared in 1796, incorporating a catalogue of diseases, classified according to their proximate causes, together with a materia medica listing substances for use in medical treatment. Darwin regarded diseases as disorders in animal motion and the healthy body as self-regulating. *Zoonomia* presented a grid: the classes of diseases were irritative, sensitive, voluntary, and associative; the orders were identified as increased, decreased, or retrograde motions of each of these faculties. Common names of diseases appeared only as species of disease. Darwin felt he was offering a more natural classification than those hitherto available, facilitating a better understanding of the nature of diseases and appropriate treatment.

Darwin's nosological views were close to those of the influential Edinburgh physicians William Cullen and John Brown. Like Brown, Darwin tended to favour strong interventions, such as the use of bark, steel, and opium, as well as the use of mechanical devices, including swinging machines. He took issue with Sydenham and others who advocated that fevers were simply the 'healing hand of nature'. Often experimental in his treatments, late in his life Darwin became an advocate of the new 'pneumatic medicine', developed by Thomas Beddoes and James Watt, which involved the mechanical administration of gases. Darwin generally treated mind and body as a unit, and this has led to his reputation in the twentieth century as an early advocate of psychosomatic medicine.

Innovation in medical treatment was one strand in Darwin's disputes with William Withering. In 1780 Darwin edited and published an essay, referring to the medical use of digitalis (deriving from foxglove), which had been written by his son Charles. A paper by the elder Darwin, recounting the successful employment of digitalis in treating pulmonary consumption, appeared in *Medical Transactions* (1785). These publications undermined Withering's claim to be the initiator of the therapeutic use of this drug. The antagonism between these two doctors was further fuelled by Erasmus Darwin's support for his son Robert Waring in a dispute with Withering over a case in 1788–9.

Theory of reproduction and evolution The first volume of *Zoonomia* contained a long section on reproduction, entitled 'Of generation'. Darwin rejected ideas of preformation, which had been supported by animalculists such as Boerhaave and by the ovists Bonnet, Haller, and Spallanzani. Instead, Darwin posited that generation involved a continuous development process: irritative, sensitive, voluntary, and associative capacities were passed on to the new living creature and subsequently developed. His account of embryological growth showed the sequential and interrelated development of organic properties, functions, and structures.

Initially Darwin regarded the new organism as primarily an extension of the male parent since the male secreted the 'embryon' in his blood. As the parental extension, the primordium inherited the habits and propensities its male parent had acquired during his lifetime. Darwin secularized David Hartley's theological view that habits of this life were carried into afterlife, contending that habits and characteristics developed during the organism's life were passed on in a natural extension, to the offspring. In parallel with Linnaeus's view of vegetable species, Darwin tentatively suggested that all the species of animals may have arisen from the mixture of a few natural orders: 'Would it be too bold to imagine, that in the great length of time, since the earth began to exist … that all warm-blooded animals have arisen from one living filament, which the great first cause endued with animality' (505). Although Darwin emphasized paternal lineage he contended that exposure to the environment of the maternal womb enabled the emergence of non-paternal traits.

Three editions of *Zoonomia* appeared in Darwin's lifetime and the third, four-volume edition of 1801 incorporated notable revisions to his theory of generation. In a new appendix Darwin distinguished various levels of organic reproduction. Unilinear development was identified with simple organisms, while complex animals were shown as developing through simultaneous transformations in several locations. He explained that paternal fibrils and maternal molecules, possessing propensities towards union, coalesced in the uterus. This revised theory was pangenetic, allotted equal roles to the paternal and maternal organisms, and differentiated between primary and secondary embryological development. Because he attributed 'appetencies' to matter and offered a vision of a self-sufficient, autonomous nature, Darwin was labelled a materialist by contemporary critics like William Paley, who strongly objected to what they saw as his denial of the role of a designing divine mind.

Educating young women Darwin's concern with women's roles was expressed not only in his theories of reproduction, but also through his prescriptions for girls' education. He helped his illegitimate daughters, Susan and Mary Parker, to establish a boarding-school in Ashbourne in 1794. The Misses Parker also sought their father's advice on the education of young women and *A Plan for the Conduct of Female Education, in Boarding Schools* (1797) resulted from their urging him to make this advice publicly available. Regretting that a good education had not been generally available to women in Britain during his time Darwin drew on the theories of Locke, Rousseau, and Genlis in assembling his own educational precepts. Oriented to women in the middle ranks of the social order, the treatise reinforced contemporary conventions linking the female character to 'the mild and retiring virtues'. Darwin argued that amorous romance novels were inappropriate for young women and that they should seek simplicity in dress. Nevertheless he also proposed some reforms of contemporary practices, contending that young women should be educated in schools rather than privately at home, learn physiognomy as a basic social skill, take vigorous exercise, cultivate some knowledge of botany, chemistry, mineralogy, and experimental philosophy, familiarize themselves with recent achievements of arts and manufactures through visits to sites like Coalbrookdale, and Wedgwood's potteries, learn how to handle money, and study modern languages. Darwin's educational philosophy amplified the view that men and women should have different, but complementary capabilities, skills, spheres, and interests. His educational innovations seemed designed to make middle-class women better wives, mothers, and companions to men of industry, commerce, and natural philosophy.

Agricultural theory: *Phytologia* Darwin consolidated his interests in yet another field with the publication, in 1800, of a major treatise on agriculture, *Phytologia, or, The Philosophy of Agriculture and Gardening*. His intention was to systematize agricultural knowledge, informed by his conviction that plants were inferior animals, providing a theoretical framework that could sustain better agricultural and horticultural practices. *Phytologia* opens with a section on plant physiology, followed by one on the economy of vegetation, and then a final section on agriculture and horticulture, oriented around production of various plant parts (fruits, roots, barks, flowers, seeds, leaves, and woods). Darwin provided a confident overview of the prospects for improving agricultural production and an imaginative range of innovations, including methods for forwarding the production of seeds and their ripening, for perfecting and enlarging fruit, and for growing timber with appropriate flexibility for use in the shipbuilding industry. A strong interest in the chemical aspects of agriculture was obvious throughout the volume: he recognized the use of ammonia in vegetation, understood the importance of nitrate and phosphate in plant growth, and considered the possibility of a chemical insecticide (a lime–sulphur mixture). Like the contemporary chemist Richard Kirwan, Darwin emphasized the importance of manures in increasing agricultural productivity. In *Phytologia* Darwin also proposed what came to be regarded as ecological controls, such as the regulation of insects by increasing the numbers of their predators.

Darwin's agricultural theory was linked to eighteenth-century Scottish and English agricultural reform. *Phytologia* was dedicated to John Sinclair, president of the board of agriculture in the 1790s. It demonstrated Darwin's familiarity with technical innovations realized by Tull, Bakewell, Coke, and other key figures in eighteenth-century agriculture. He even proposed his own improvements on the drill plough in an appendix. Labelled by the *Monthly Magazine* as a 'philosophical agricultor' (1802, 13.460), Darwin, like his friend the geologist James Hutton, regarded scientific agriculture as a sign of human progress.

Appearance, character, and death A large man inclined to corpulence Darwin was apparently awkward in stature and movement, but very energetic. He sported a large wig and, according to Anna Seward, his face had been marked by smallpox, although this is not evident in his portraits. As the result of an accident in 1768, while riding in one of the carriages he had designed, Darwin was lame thereafter. He had a wide circle of friends and correspondents. A man of wit and sociability, Darwin was a lauded conversationalist, despite his stammer. He displayed considerable sympathy and benevolence to patients and friends. Nevertheless, he had strong views and some found him domineering. Darwin became convinced that alcohol consumption was injurious to health and was a teetotaller for much of his life. Tending towards deism and scepticism in his religious views, he was dismissed by some contemporaries as a materialist or atheist.

In spring 1801 Darwin became seriously ill from pneumonia. After this he effectively retired from medical practice, although he continued work on another poetic volume and his correspondence. He and his family moved out of Derby in March 1802 to Breadsall Priory, which had been purchased by his son Erasmus. Darwin died there, apparently of a lung infection, on 18 April 1802 and was buried in Breadsall church.

The Temple of Nature Darwin's final work, which he titled 'The origin of society', published posthumously in 1803 as *The Temple of Nature, or, The Origin of Society*, was his poetic paean to evolution. He sought to 'amuse by bringing distinctly to the imagination the beautiful and sublime images of operations of Nature in the order' in which, he believed, 'the progressive course of time presented them' (preface). Adorned with figures drawn from Eleusinian and Egyptian mysteries, *The Temple* presented a poetic panorama of the operations of the natural world. Ideas first aired in *Phytologia*, especially notions of spontaneous generation, the transmigration of matter, utilitarian calculations of organic happiness, and modifications of his theories of reproduction rehearsed in the revised edition of *Zoonomia*, were prominent. In *The Temple of Nature* Darwin explored the implications of and the evidence for his early vision that the entire natural world developed and progressed over time.

The Temple was a showcase for human achievements as the culmination of the progressive ways of nature. In the first canto, which some contemporary critics condemned as materialist, Darwin contended that life originated from the chemical operations of the forces of heat, repulsion, attraction, and contraction on brute matter. He followed with a sketch of the physiological faculties of irritation, sensation, volition, and association, as laid out in *Zoonomia*, showing organic forms developing from primitive forms in the sea, moving onto land, and ultimately evolving into human form. Reproduction, the theme of canto 2 and the subject of an additional note, was presented as facilitating not just the increase of organic life, but, through the inheritance of acquired characteristics and through the potential emergence of new traits in sexual reproduction, evolution in organic forms. In the third canto, Darwin showed how 'human science … builds on Nature's base' as he celebrated the triumph of human reason linked to the accomplishments of natural philosophers and technological innovators such as Newton, Herschel, Savery, and Arkwright. In the final canto he reflected on the moral dimensions of his vision: accounting for death and destruction, including natural checks on human population growth, as necessary components in nature's progressive ways.

Jacobin scares and the reception of Darwin's work Darwin's ideas were forged in the cauldron of the British reaction to the French Revolution, and fears of Jacobinism were crucial in the response to his books. Like most members of the Lunar Society, Darwin applauded the challenging of the old order in France:

> Long had the Giant-Form on Gallia's plains
> Inglorious slept, unconscious of his chains;

His poetic welcome to the revolution from *The Economy of Vegetation* (canto 2, lines 377–94) was reprinted in a popular radical pamphlet, Daniel Eaton's *Politics for the People* (1794).

As advocates of social and political change, members of the Lunar Society were linked to the revolutionary cause. Darwin also espoused support for the campaign against the slave trade, for religious toleration, and for freedom of the press. To many of their contemporaries the hallmarks of Jacobinism were evident in Lunar Society interests and activities. The presence of dissenters in their ranks and the support for dissenters' rights were further signs of this link. Darwin, like many supporters of the revolution, assumed that knowledge would lead automatically to power and morality: he set out to unveil nature and society in charts, portraits, or pictures of various facets of the natural world. The heady faith in reason and progress, which Burke and other critics of the French Revolution regarded as insidious and foreign, animated Darwin's writing.

The members of the Lunar Society paid a high price for their sympathy with the French revolutionary cause. This was exacted most obviously in the Birmingham riots of July 1791, sparked by a dinner held to celebrate the capture of the Bastille, in which the city establishment seems to have pitted a mob against members of the commercial and industrial (and largely dissenting) middle class. A main target for this attack was Joseph Priestley, who lost his home and scientific equipment and fled Birmingham, but other Lunar Society members were also threatened. Darwin suffered a related form of persecution. He was subjected to political satire in a publication by Pitt's under-secretary for foreign affairs, George Canning, in collaboration with Hookham Frere and George Ellis, titled 'The Loves of the Triangles: a Mathematical and Philosophical Poem, Inscribed to Dr. Darwin', which appeared in the *Anti-Jacobin, or, Weekly Examiner* in 1798. Darwin's *Botanic Garden* and Godwin's *Enquiry Concerning Political Justice* (1793) were the combined targets of this conservative attack. Despite the popularity of *The Botanic Garden*, Darwin's later work, especially *The Temple of Nature*, came under attack as reviewers condemned his theories as atheistic and materialistic.

Influence and reappraisals Darwin's ideas and writing have been widely disseminated. His major poetic and scientific works were republished in other European languages during his lifetime or shortly after his death. Irish editions were issued of all of his books, except *The Temple*, as well as American editions of all volumes, except *Phytologia*. As late as 1954 a Russian translation of *The Temple* was published. Facsimile editions of *Female Education*, *The Botanic Garden*, and *The Temple* have appeared since 1968.

Darwin's literary legacy is ambiguous but crucial. His long, visually oriented didactic poems were designed to 'enlist the imagination under the banner of science'. In the 1790s many of the young Romantic poets, including Wordsworth and Coleridge, admired Darwin. However, his gaudy visual images, contrived imagery, personification, and Augustan heroic couplets quickly fell out of favour, as the *Lyrical Ballads* (1798) indicated. William Blake's struggle against the mythical figure of Urizen, who was portrayed as a tyrant threatening to destroy the universe and human imaginative capacities, indicated his sense of the dangers in trying to enlist the imagination under the banner of science. Nevertheless, traces of Darwin's ideas, language and imagery have been identified across the range of Romantic literature. So, for example, Wordsworth's story of 'Goody Blake and Harry Gill' in the *Lyrical Ballads* probably derived from *Zoonomia*. Darwin's theories and experiments have also been linked to Mary Shelley's *Frankenstein* (1818), since Shelley was exposed to Darwin's ideas about the time when she was composing her Gothic tale. Beyond his specific influence on Romantic literature, Darwin's poetic, epistemological, and aesthetic theories continued to cast a diffuse, but recurring, influence well into the twentieth century.

Since the late nineteenth century, Erasmus Darwin has been identified with J. B. Lamarck and a generalized notion of organic development through acquired characteristics. The assessment of his evolutionary theory has been overshadowed by the achievements of his grandson Charles. However, late twentieth-century research on Erasmus's writing and on Charles's biography has shaken previous adjudications. The complexity of Charles's relationship to his grandfather has been exposed. It is now known that Charles's draft 'Preliminary notice' for Krause's (1879) essay on Erasmus's scientific work was substantially edited by Charles's daughter Henrietta in such a way as to underplay Charles's admiration for, and intellectual debt to, his grandfather. Early exposure to the ideas of *Zoonomia* was crucial in Charles's formulation of his theory of evolution and the connections between these two evolutionary theorists may have been underestimated. His grandfather's reputation is likely to have provided Charles with some powerful lessons about the formulation of his theory of evolution: political and religious controversy should be avoided; materialism and speculation abhorred; human evolution was to be downplayed. Moreover, late twentieth-century scholars tried to move out of the shadow cast by Charles—focusing more intently on the elder Darwin's theories and observations of the natural world, particularly around reproduction, heredity, and breeding.

Exploration of the connections between Erasmus Darwin's views and his social and political context has been another direction of this research. Attention has been drawn to Darwin's role as a spokesman for the innovating bourgeois 'men of ideas' in late eighteenth-century provincial England: heralding their achievements as the manifestation of human progress, and expressing their new found influence as the universal expansion of human powers. Likewise, Darwin's fascination with sexual reproduction, his popularizing of Linnaean sexual taxonomy, and his vivid erotic representations of plant life have been situated in the gender politics of his period. His endorsement of a mode of botanical classification which prioritized male parts, his stereotypical representations of masculine and feminine characteristics, and his pictures of a feminine nature seen through masculine eyes comprise a view typical of gentlemen of his era. Yet he did break with the Linnaean convention of portraying plants exclusively within marriage, provide images of extramarital sexual liaison, and propose some reforms in education for young women. Darwin endorsed notions of complementary gender differences associated with Rousseau and other Enlightenment thinkers, but he also demonstrated an interest in assuring that his professional and industrial peers would have appropriately educated wives and daughters.

While interpretations have varied, Erasmus Darwin continues to be a figure to be reckoned with across a wide range of fields, including the history of literature, biology, botany, psychology, education, mechanization, transportation, meteorology, agriculture, and medicine.

MAUREEN MCNEIL

Sources The letters of Erasmus Darwin, ed. D. King-Hele (1981) • D. King-Hele, Erasmus Darwin: a life of unequalled achievement (1999) • M. McNeil, Under the banner of science: Erasmus Darwin and his age (1987) • R. Porter, 'Erasmus Darwin: doctor of evolution?', History, humanity and evolution: essays for John C. Greene, ed. J. R. Moore (1989), 39–69 • J. Browne, 'Botany for gentlemen: Erasmus Darwin and The loves of the plants', Isis, 80 (1989), 593–621 • R. Colp jun., 'The relationship of Charles Darwin to the ideas of his grandfather, Dr. Erasmus Darwin', Biography, 9/1 (1986), 1–24 • R. E. Schofield, The Lunar Society of Birmingham (1963) • C. Darwin, 'Preliminary notice', in E. Krause, Erasmus Darwin, trans. W. S. Dallas (1879) • A. Seward, Memoirs of the life of Dr Darwin (1804) • N. Garfinkle, 'Science and religion in England, 1790–1800: the critical response to the work of Erasmus Darwin', Journal of the History of Ideas, 16 (1955), 376–88 • D. King-Hele, Erasmus Darwin and the Romantic poets (1986) • M. T. Ghiselin, 'Two Darwins: history versus criticism', Journal of the History of Biology, 9 (1976), 121–32 • J. Harrison, 'Erasmus Darwin's view of evolution', Journal of the History of Ideas, 32 (1971), 247–64 • I. Primer, 'Erasmus Darwin's Temple of nature: progress, evolution, and the Eleusinian mysteries', Journal of the History of Ideas, 25 (1964), 58–76 • R. N. Ross, '"To charm thy curious eye": Erasmus Darwin's poetry at the vestibule of knowledge', Journal of the History of Ideas, 32 (1971), 379–94 • E. Posner, 'William Withering versus the Darwins', History of Medicine, 6 (1975), 51–7 • C. Emery, 'Scientific theory in Erasmus Darwin's The botanic garden, 1789–91', Isis, 33 (1941–2), 315–25 • D. G. King-Hele, 'Erasmus Darwin, man of ideas, and inventor of words', Notes and Records of the Royal Society, 42 (1988), 149–80 • D. M. Hassler,

Erasmus Darwin (1973) • T. Brown, Observations on the Zoonomia of Erasmus Darwin, M.D. (1798) • H. Pearson, Doctor Darwin (1930)
Archives FM Cam., corresp. and papers • priv. coll., commonplace book of poems • RS, essays read at the Royal Society • UCL, corresp. and papers • Wellcome L., medical notes | Birm. CA, corresp. with Matthew Bolton • Birm. CA, letters to James Watt • BL, letters to Charles Francis Greville, Add. MS 42071, fols. 48–64b • NHM, letters to Dryander and Banks • Royal Society of Medicine, London, letter to Withering
Likenesses J. Wright of Derby, group portrait, 1768 (An experiment on a bird in the air pump), National Gallery, London • J. Wright of Derby, oils, c.1770, Darwin College, Cambridge • J. Wright of Derby, portrait, 1770, NPG • W. Hackwood, medallion plaque, 1780 (of Darwin?; after oil painting by J. Wright of Derby, c.1770), Wedgwood Museum, Barlaston; copy, Down House, Downe, Kent • attrib. F. Torond, silhouette, c.1785, RCS Eng. • J. Wright of Derby, portrait, 1792–3, priv. coll. [see illus.] • J. Wright of Derby, oils, 1792–3, Wolverhampton Art Gallery • J. R. Smith, mezzotint, 1797 (after J. Wright of Derby, 1792–3), Wellcome L.; two copies, Down House, Downe, Kent • B. Pym, mezzotint, pubd 1801 (after S. J. Arnold), BM, Wellcome L. • J. Rawlinson, oils, before 1802, Derby Corporation • J. Rawlinson, oils, 1802, High View community school, Breadsall, Derby • attrib. W. Coffee, alabaster bust, 1804, Darwin College, Cambridge • J. Heath, stipple, 1804 (after J. Rawlinson), Wellcome L. • M. Haughton, stipple, pubd 1807 (after J. Rawlinson), NPG • M. Alpin, stipple, 1825 (after oil painting by J. Wright of Derby, c.1770), Wellcome L. • bronze bust, 1967 (after bust attrib. W. Coffee), Down House, Downe, Kent • attrib. W. Coffee, plaster bust, Derby Museum and Art Gallery • H. Meyer, stipple, Wellcome L. • J. Rawlinson, portrait, RCS Eng. • J. Sharples, pastel drawing, Bristol City Art Gallery • A. Tardien, stipple (after Moll), Wellcome L.
Wealth at death £33,930: Pearson papers (576), UCL

Darwin, Sir Francis (1848–1925), botanist, was born on 16 August 1848 at Downe, Kent, the seventh of the ten children of Charles Robert *Darwin (1809–1882), the naturalist, and his wife, Emma (1808–1896), daughter of Josiah Wedgwood (1769–1843) and granddaughter of Josiah Wedgwood (1730–1795). He was educated at home and then at Clapham grammar school, where Charles Pritchard, who later became Savilian professor of astronomy at Oxford, was headmaster. In 1866 he went to Trinity College, Cambridge, where he graduated with first-class honours in the natural sciences tripos in 1870. He then studied medicine at St George's Hospital, London, with the intention of becoming a physician. In 1875 he obtained the MB degree in Cambridge. However, he never practised medicine, turning instead to botany. From 1874, except for brief periods of research, he spent the next eight years working as secretary and assistant to his father; in 1876 he went to the University of Würzburg for some months to learn laboratory methods from Julius Sachs, and in 1881 he spent a short time working with Heinrich Anton de Bary at the University of Strasbourg. In 1874 he had married Amy Ruck, who died in 1876 giving birth to their son, Bernard Richard Meirion *Darwin. After the death of his wife he lived at Down with his parents and child.

Darwin's first major contributions to botany were inspired by the collaboration with his father. The results of their observations and experiments were published in 1880 in The Power of Movement in Plants, whose title page reads 'By Charles Darwin assisted by Francis Darwin'. The book was an extension of Charles Darwin's work on

Sir Francis Darwin (1848–1925), by Sir William Rothenstein, 1905

botany moved away from the purely taxonomic tradition towards a more experimental and physiological approach. Darwin's experience in holding a practical class in this new subject for many years encouraged him to publish *Practical Physiology of Plants* (1894). Written together with E. H. Acton, it was the first book of its kind in the English language. One year later a more elementary botanical textbook, *The Elements of Botany*, followed, in which he presented the lectures he had given to medical students.

In his own original research Darwin began to focus on the distribution and function of stomata and on the transpiration of plants in general. To analyse the control of loss of water by plants he invented or developed a variety of special instruments. In 1897 he introduced the horn hygroscope for the study of stomatal function and in later years the porometer, in which air was drawn through a leaf and its velocity measured, and other apparatus.

An additional focus of Darwin's scientific work was his editions of the letters and manuscripts of his father. In 1887 he published the three-volume *Life and Letters of Charles Darwin*, which included an autobiographical chapter and many annotations, as well as a delicately observed chapter of family reminiscences. He further produced one-volume versions of these in subsequent years. In 1903 a sequel, *More Letters of Charles Darwin*, followed, which was edited jointly with A. C. Seward. As a last important contribution to Darwin studies the edition of the two earliest evolutionary essays written by Charles Darwin (1842 and 1844) has to be mentioned (*The Foundations of The Origin of Species*, 1909). These books have provided the basis for all subsequent scientific biographies and papers on Darwin, and only recently have new editions of manuscripts and letters started to supersede Francis Darwin's editions.

After the death of his second wife in 1903 Darwin resigned from the readership in botany and moved to London, but after only about a year returned to Cambridge and continued his botanical research. In 1913 he married Florence, *née* Fisher (*d.* 1920), the widow of Professor F. W. Maitland. His later publications consisted mainly of collections of earlier essays and lectures on a variety of subjects, including musical instruments, which had been a lifelong interest. Darwin's publications, which are dated from 1872 to 1921, include, besides several scientific books, lectures, and addresses, some sixty papers.

For his contributions to science Darwin received many honours. He became a fellow of the Royal Society in 1882, served on its council in 1894–5 and 1902–8, and as foreign secretary in 1903–7. He was made an honorary ScD of Cambridge in 1909, at the time of the Darwin centenary, and, in 1912, received the Darwin medal of the Royal Society. He received honorary degrees from the universities of Dublin, Liverpool, Sheffield, St Andrews, Uppsala, Prague, and Brussels. He was knighted in 1913. He died at his home, 10 Madingley Road, Cambridge, on 19 September 1925.   THOMAS JUNKER

climbing plants and it showed that the same mechanisms can be observed in plants in general. By extending the idea of irregular circumnutation the Darwins analysed the growth movement of plants in response to factors of the environment such as light, gravity, and wounds. In addition, they demonstrated that the mechanism of curvature in both roots and shoots was the result of differential growth rates. They could also confirm that the effect of the stimuli on the growth movement was indirect and that light and gravity act on some substance in the tip of the root and the shoot, which is transmitted to other parts of the plant. Francis Darwin later refined some of the experimental techniques and modified their theoretical conclusions. Between 1880 and 1908 Darwin published a dozen papers and some public lectures he had given on growth movements in plants.

After his father's death in 1882 Darwin moved to Cambridge. In 1883 he married Ellen Wordsworth Crofts [**Ellen Wordsworth Darwin** (1856–1903)], a lecturer in English literature at Newnham College (where she had been a student in 1874–7), with whom he had a daughter, Frances, who became known as a poet under her married name of Frances *Cornford. In 1884 he became university lecturer in botany in Cambridge, co-operating with S. H. Vines in teaching plant physiology. In 1886 he was elected to a fellowship at Christ's College. After the appointment of Vines to the chair of botany at Oxford, Darwin became reader in botany (1888), a position which he held until 1904. During these years Darwin's academic interests were the teaching of botany, the editing of his father's letters, and the study of the control of water loss by plants.

When Darwin began teaching in Cambridge, British

Sources A. C. S. [A. C. Seward] and F. F. B. [F. F. Blackman], *PRS*, 110B (1932), i–xxi · *DNB* · F. O. Bower, 'Francis Darwin', *Sixty years of botany in Britain, 1875–1935* (1938), 78–9 · *The Times* (21 Sept 1925) · *Nature*, 116 (1925) · *CGPLA Eng. & Wales* (1925)

Archives BL, corresp. and papers, Add. MSS 58375–58380, 38394–38397 · CUL, corresp. and papers | American Philosophical Society, Philadelphia, letters to Charles Edward Sayle · American Philosophical Society, Philadelphia, letters to Thomas Stebbing · BL, letters to Alfred Russel Wallace · Harvard U., letters to Sir William Rothenstein · ICL, letters to Thomas Huxley · NRA, priv. coll., letters to Sir Norman Moore · Oxf. U. Mus. NH, corresp., mainly letters and postcards to Sir E. B. Poolton · U. Edin., letters to Sir Archibald Geikie · U. Glas., Archives and Business Records Centre, corresp. with Frederick Bower · UCL, letters to Sir Francis Galton · UCL, letters to Karl Pearson

Likenesses W. Rothenstein, oils, 1905, U. Cam., department of botany [*see illus.*] · J. Palmer Clarke, photograph, *c.*1907, NPG · W. Stoneman, photograph, 1918, NPG · photograph, repro. in Seward and Blackman, *PRS* · photograph, RS; repro. in Bower, 'Francis Darwin'

Wealth at death £37,747 14*s.* 3*d.*: probate, 3 Nov 1925, *CGPLA Eng. & Wales*

Darwin, Sir George Howard (1845–1912), mathematician and geophysicist, was born on 9 July 1845 at Down House, Downe, Kent, the fifth child (the third of seven to survive childhood) of Charles Robert *Darwin (1809–1882), the naturalist, and his wife, Emma Wedgwood (1808–1896), granddaughter of the potter Josiah Wedgwood of Etruria.

Education George Darwin was reared in a scientific environment and his earliest education was at his father's side. In 1856 he was sent to the nearby Clapham grammar school owned and directed by the Revd Charles Pritchard FRS, later Savilian professor of astronomy at Oxford. There, among the Airys, Herschels, and Hamiltons, he studied mathematics and science at a level higher than that found at the public schools. At that time the young Darwin exhibited no profound aptitude for mathematics but, as might be expected, he took an interest in natural history, especially in the study of lepidoptera.

In both 1863 and 1864 Darwin failed to gain entrance scholarships at Cambridge, but he matriculated at Trinity College in 1864. There he became friends with the Balfour brothers, Arthur, Frank, and Gerald, and with J. W. Strutt (later Lord Rayleigh). He also quickly joined Fletcher Moulton (later a lord justice of appeal) and William Christie (later astronomer royal) in the mathematics classes of E. J. Routh, the most successful coach of his generation. These studies paid handsome dividends, for in 1866 Darwin won a foundation scholarship at Trinity, and in 1868 he was placed second wrangler in the tripos and won the second Smith's prize, both behind Moulton. Later that autumn he was elected a fellow of Trinity.

Although offered the mathematical mastership at Eton, Darwin decided to make the law his profession, and he studied in London from 1869 to 1872. He was called to the bar in 1874 but never practised, for it was during those years that he developed (apparently inherited) symptoms of serious digestive troubles that would ail him for the rest of his life. He took cures at Malvern, Homburg, and Cannes, but to no avail. The bouts of illness apparently persuaded him to give up the legal profession, and he settled back at Trinity in October 1873, gradually turning to scientific pursuits.

Sir George Howard Darwin (1845–1912), by Gwen Raverat

Geodesy Darwin's first major scientific paper, 'On the influence of geological changes on the earth's axis of rotation', was read before the Royal Society in 1876 and published the following year (*Philosophical Transactions*, 167, 1877, 271–312). Darwin was animated by recent speculations of geologists that great changes in the obliquity of the ecliptic and in the positions of the earth's poles could explain glacial periods. He proved analytically that 'thus throughout geological history the obliquity of the ecliptic must have remained sensibly constant' (ibid., 303). However, he did find that changes of position of the earth's axis of symmetry due to geological deformations were possible, although limited, for large-scale deformations could produce a geographical displacement of the pole of at most 1° to 3°. Nevertheless, because Darwin thought that the earth exhibited plasticity by making rough readjustments to a figure of equilibrium, perhaps through earthquakes, he suggested that the pole might actually have wandered up to some 10° or 15°. Since Darwin had proved that the obliquity of the ecliptic itself could not have shifted, here he had found a way to explain the geologists' problem of the glacial epoch: the glacial period may only appear to have been a period of great cold, for, if the north pole were in Greenland, then Europe and much of North America would have been glaciated. But he backed off, modestly, but rhetorically, asking: 'If, then, geologists are right in supposing that where the continents now stand they have always stood, would it not be almost necessary to give up any hypothesis which involved a very wide excursion of the poles?' (ibid., 305).

This paper was reviewed for the Royal Society by William Thomson. Soon afterwards, in the spring of 1877, Thomson invited Darwin to Glasgow to discuss the issues. That dialogue profoundly altered Darwin's life. It was the beginning of a very intimate friendship between Darwin and Sir William and Lady Thomson, the Thomsons later becoming the godparents of Darwin's first son. Given the traditional portrayal of the confrontational relationship between Thomson and Charles Darwin concerning the age of the earth and its impact on the theory of natural selection, George's position is all the more surprising.

That discussion, and many similar ones, convinced Darwin to investigate the geophysical history of the earth. In particular he determined that if he treated the earth as a viscous body, instead of as an elastic one as Thomson had done—mathematicians and astronomers heretofore had only treated it as rigid—then an analysis of tidal reactions, especially of the frictional resistance to the tides, might prove illuminating. Consequently Darwin was the first to find that Thomson's own path breaking work on the strain of an incompressible elastic sphere could be adapted to the flow of an incompressible viscous fluid, he was the first to treat the earth as a wholly viscous body, and he was the first to develop a theory of viscous tides in the body of the earth.

Study of tides   Darwin began to develop the consequences of this line of thought in his seminal paper, 'On the precession of a viscous spheroid, and on the remote history of the earth' (*Philosophical Transactions*, 170, 1879, 447–538). The paper is ostensibly an investigation of how the rotation of a homogeneous viscous spheroid is altered by the tides raised in it by external disturbing bodies. But it is really about tides in the earth's body caused by the moon and sun and the reaction of such tides on the moon, for, indeed, it was Darwin's desire to fathom the physical history of the earth that led him to apply his mathematical talents along this vein in the first place.

Darwin analysed the tidal friction due to bodily tides in the earth. The result was the development of his theory of the tidal evolution of the earth–moon system, resulting from the effects of tidal retardation. If the earth is now being retarded and the moon receding, then in the remote past the earth must have been rotating much more swiftly and the moon must have been much closer. Darwin calculated that a minimum of 57 million years ago (he believed the actual lapse of time was magnitudes greater) the day would have been 6 hours 45 minutes, the month would have been about 1 day 14 hours, the obliquity would have been 9° less, and the moon's distance from the earth would have been 36,000 miles. Darwin did not believe this whole process had to be pre-geological, and he saw much to aid the geologist: the change in obliquity could affect climate, the trade winds would be augmented and the ocean currents affected, the shorter days and nights would lead to more violent storms, and the higher and more frequent tides would increase oceanic denudation.

From dynamical principles, it is clear that as long as the day and month are not equal, tidal friction must act, and Darwin was determined to find the initial condition of the earth and moon. Using the principle of the conservation of moment of momentum, Darwin altered his analysis to find a day-month equal to 5 hours 36 minutes, but this was a position of dynamically unstable equilibrium, for if the month were ever less than the day, then the moon would fall into the earth. Since the moon exists, something caused the equilibrium to tip in the other direction. At first, Darwin suggested that the contraction of the earth as a cooling body may have been the deciding circumstance. But with a day-month of 5 hours 36 minutes, only 6000 miles separated the surfaces of the two bodies. This clearly indicated to Darwin a rupture into at least two bodies of a primeval planet rotating in about 5 hours. Darwin hypothesized that the resonance of the enormous solar tides with the gravitational oscillation of an inhomogeneous earth could rupture the primeval planet. Thus was born Darwin's fission theory of the genesis of the moon, a theory largely accepted for the next fifty years.

Mathematician   This initial series of papers catapulted Darwin into the scientific elite. In 1879 he was elected a fellow of the Royal Society, and by the mid-1880s he was well on his way to becoming a central figure of the scientific aristocracy of late Victorian and Edwardian Britain. In 1883 he succeeded James Challis as Plumian professor of astronomy and experimental philosophy at Cambridge and won the Telford medal of the Institution of Civil Engineers. On 22 July 1884 he married Maud du Puy (1861–1947) of Philadelphia; in the same year he was awarded the royal medal, which he jokingly referred to as a wedding present. The couple soon moved into Newnham Grange (later Darwin College), Cambridge. Their four children included the artist Gwen *Raverat (1885–1957) and the physicist Sir Charles Galton *Darwin (1887–1962).

As his eminence grew, so did Darwin's scientific responsibilities. He spent significant amounts of time on committee and government work. His work on oceanic tidal theory, through which he became the government clearing-house for the organization and reduction of tidal observations throughout the British empire, led to his being recognized as the world's leading authority on the tides. In turn, he wrote the standard reference articles (for example, 'Tides', in the *Encyclopaedia Britannica*), assisted foreign governments, and developed a tide predictor and a tidal abacus. His book, *The Tides and Kindred Phenomena in the Solar System* (1898)—a semipopular account of nearly the whole compass of his scientific work, based on the Lowell lectures he gave at Boston in 1897—became a scientific bestseller and was translated into German, Hungarian, Spanish, Italian, and other languages. In addition Darwin was an influential member of the Seismological Congress and the meteorological council to the Royal Society.

Darwin's theory of tidal evolution also led to three other important series of papers containing some of his most significant and sophisticated mathematical work. In the first of these series the changes in the earth–moon system led him to consider what the figure of the earth must have been in past times, and this in turn led him later to consider the whole theory to the second order of small quantities. By the 1890s Darwin was considered Britain's leading geodesist, and he urged his country's membership in the International Geodetic Association, of which he later became vice-president. In the second series Darwin considered the initial conditions of stability of a primeval planet preceding rupture. These studies of the figures of equilibrium of rotating fluid masses brought Darwin into a close relationship with Henri Poincaré. Darwin's researches elucidated the pear shaped figure of equilibrium Poincaré had shown to exist. In the third series Darwin began by attempting to discover how a Laplacian ring could coalesce into a planet but was quickly diverted to a study of periodic orbits. In these papers, also involving the work of Poincaré as well as of the American astronomer G. W. Hill, Darwin calculated numerous classes of orbits by a complex numerical procedure, and, even more importantly, attempted to determine their stability.

Darwin's researches laid the groundwork for the startling growth of the geophysical sciences. If this period saw the emergence of geophysics in Britain, then the following half-century saw the discipline's consolidation into a vibrant and vital aspect of twentieth-century science. Geophysicists of the second and third generations knew well the guiding influence of Darwin. Sir Harold Jeffreys paid his tribute by dedicating the first great classic in the field, *The Earth* (1924), to the memory of Sir George Howard Darwin, 'Father of Modern Geophysics and Cosmogony'.

Physically, Darwin was of average height but slight in build. His personality was marked by a childlike naïvety and unassuming modesty. A romantic streak suffused his interests and activities. He keenly loved heraldry, history, and travel and was fluent in several languages and odd dialects. Although traditional in morals, Darwin was delighted by the new consumer technologies. For example, he made sure his family was among the first in Cambridge to ride bicycles with pneumatic tyres and to become connected to the telephone system. He was an avid tennis player in his younger days, and he took up archery late in his life, joined the Royal Toxophilite Society and even won the Norton cup and medal in 1912.

By the end of his career Darwin had been honoured with numerous presidencies, vice-presidencies, medals, and memberships in the leading scientific societies of the world. In 1911 he was awarded the Copley medal of the Royal Society, the country's highest scientific distinction. Darwin was particularly pleased at being made a knight commander of the Bath in 1905 after his successful presidency of the British Association for the Advancement of Science on its tour of south Africa following the Second South African War, and by Cambridge University Press's decision to publish his collected *Scientific Papers* (5 vols., 1907–16).

Darwin died at Newnham Grange on 7 December 1912 of cancer of the pancreas and was buried at Trumpington. He was survived by his wife and their four children.

DAVID KUSHNER

Sources D. Kushner, 'The emergence of geophysics in nineteenth century Britain', PhD diss., University of Princeton, 1990 · D. Kushner, 'Sir George Darwin and a British school of geophysics', *Osiris*, 2nd ser., 8 (1993), 196–223 · F. Darwin, 'Memoir of Sir George Darwin', in G. H. Darwin, *Scientific papers*, 5 (1916), ix–xxxiii · G. Raverat, *Period piece* (1952) · S. S. H. [S. S. Hough], *PRS*, 89A (1913–14), i–xi · F. J. M. S. [F. J. M. Stratton], *Monthly Notices of the Royal Astronomical Society*, 73 (1912–13), 204–10 · E. W. Brown, 'The scientific work of Sir George Darwin', in G. H. Darwin, *Scientific papers*, 5 (1916), xxxiv–lv · M. E. Keynes, *A house by the river: Newnham Grange to Darwin College* (1976) · d. cert.

Archives CUL, corresp. and papers | CUL, corresp. and papers relating to Cambridge University · CUL, corresp. with Lord Kelvin · CUL, corresp. with H. Middleton · CUL, letters to Sir George Stokes · King's AC Cam., letters to Oscar Browning · NA Scot., corresp. with Arthur Balfour · priv. coll., letters to Sir Norman Moore · RAS, letters to Royal Astronomical Society · RGS, letters to Sir David Gill · RGS, corresp. and papers relating to International Geodetic Conference · U. Glas. L., corresp. with Lord Kelvin and Lady Kelvin · UCL, corresp. with Sir Francis Galton · UCL, letters to Karl Pearson

Likenesses M. Gertler, oils, 1912, NPG · Elliott & Fry, cabinet photograph, NPG · D. Pertz, watercolour (after G. Raverat), Trinity Cam. · G. Raverat, pen-and-ink drawing (after photograph, 1883), repro. in Raverat, *Period piece* · G. Raverat, watercolour, NPG [*see illus.*] · photograph, repro. in P. E. B. Jourdain, 'Sir George Darwin: a biographical sketch', *The Open Court* (April 1913), frontispiece

Wealth at death £47,108 12s. 9d.: probate, 21 Feb 1913, CGPLA Eng. & Wales

Darwin, Sir Horace (1851–1928), civil engineer and manufacturer of scientific instruments, was born at Downe, Kent, on 13 May 1851, the ninth child of Charles Robert *Darwin (1809–1882), the naturalist, and his wife, Emma (1808–1896), daughter of Josiah Wedgwood. Their father's poor health and his writing activities left the boys to find their own entertainment in their quiet rural surroundings. Their mother employed governesses for all her children's primary education and in due course Horace followed his brothers to Clapham grammar school. He found the teaching there, apart from mathematics, dull and old-fashioned, so his father sent him to study under a private tutor at Southwold, from where he went to Trinity College, Cambridge. He graduated BA in 1874, with the accolade of senior optime in the mathematical tripos. He served a three-year apprenticeship with Easton and Anderson, engineers, of Erith, Kent, where his lasting interest in scientific instruments was first aroused. On completion of this training he returned to Cambridge, where he remained for the rest of his life.

Darwin began earning his living as a consulting engineer on land reclamation and drainage schemes but his university friends were soon asking him to design and construct new types of instruments and apparatus which they needed, particularly in the natural sciences school, where research techniques were becoming more dependent on precision measurements and recording of events. After working with various scientists and mechanics on different projects, Darwin entered into a formal partnership in 1878 with A. G. Dew Smith to establish the Cambridge Scientific Instrument Company. This became a limited company in 1880 with Darwin as its chief shareholder, and from 1891 he was in sole control. When, in response to its success, larger premises were needed, money was forthcoming from shares taken up by Darwin's family and friends. The company was associated from the outset with prominent figures in the university; it specialized in constructing apparatus for their individual needs and underpinned this with the production of basic apparatus for schools and colleges, and for industry. It became widely known as 'Horace Darwin's shop' and its reputation grew apace, supported by Darwin's flair for design and the skilled workforce who served him. Darwin himself contributed in large part to the marked improvement in British scientific instrument design which took place between 1880 and 1930, as industry came to rely on instruments for process control. Darwin frequently aired his strong views on the place of the designer in industry, in lectures and in print: he argued that the designer should be a mechanical engineer with much scientific knowledge and well acquainted with the available methods of manufacture.

In 1880 Darwin married the Hon. Emma Cecilia (Ida), daughter of Thomas Henry *Farrer, first Baron Farrer; they had one son (killed in action in 1915), and two daughters. Darwin became an associate member of the Institution of Civil Engineers in 1877 and a member of the Institution of Mechanical Engineers in 1878. He served on numerous local and university boards and committees, and as a JP, and held office as mayor of Cambridge in 1896–7. In 1903 he was elected FRS.

Darwin was one of the founder members of the advisory committee for aeronautics set up in 1909 and his company soon became involved in this new industry, building the apparatus needed for wind-tunnel and other airframe tests, and designing and making aircraft instruments. During the First World War he also served as chairman of the inventions committee. He was created KBE in 1918. Darwin died at his home, The Orchard, Huntingdon Road, Cambridge, on 22 September 1928, and was buried in St Giles's cemetery, Cambridge.

R. T. GLAZEBROOK, rev. ANITA McCONNELL

Sources M. J. G. Cattermole and A. F. Wolfe, *Horace Darwin's shop: a history of the Cambridge Scientific Instrument Company, 1878–1968* (1987) · *The Times* (24 Sept 1928) · R. T. G., *PRS*, 122A (1928–9), xv–xviii · *Cambridge Review* (26 Oct 1928) · d. cert. · *IGI*
Archives CUL, corresp., letter-books, notebook, etc. · CUL, CSIC MSS | UCL, letters to Sir Francis Galton · UCL, corresp. with Karl Pearson
Likenesses A. C. Cooper, negative, RS · photograph, repro. in Cattermole and Wolfe, *Horace Darwin's shop* · photograph, RS
Wealth at death £100,919 8s. 5d.: probate, 19 Dec 1928, *CGPLA Eng. & Wales*

Darwin, Leonard (1850–1943), scientist and eugenicist, was born on 15 January 1850 at Down House, Downe, Kent, the fourth son and eighth child of Charles Robert *Darwin (1809–1882) and his wife, Emma Darwin, *née* Wedgwood (1808–1896). He was educated privately and at Clapham grammar school, but his happy and privileged home environment in the countryside of the North

Downs was the strongest influence on his early development. At the age of eighteen he passed into the Royal Military Academy, Woolwich, claiming in characteristically self-effacing fashion that he chose the army as his profession because he thought himself the stupidest member of the family. He was commissioned in the Royal Engineers in 1871 and worked at the School of Military Engineering at Chatham until, in 1874, he was chosen by Captain Abney, instructor of chemistry and photography, as the photographer on an expedition to New Zealand to observe the transit of Venus on 9 December. The day, however, was cloudy. After a two-year posting in Malta he returned to Chatham to succeed Captain Abney.

In 1882 (the year of his father's death) Darwin married Elizabeth Frances Fraser (11 July), and with her and two Royal Engineers officers he set off once again to observe a transit of Venus, this time from Australia on 10 December. The day was cloudy once more. He returned at the end of April 1883, spent two years at the Staff College at Camberley as instructor in chemistry, and then moved to London on his appointment to the War Office intelligence department, where he was concerned with African questions.

In 1886 the weather at last smiled on an astronomical expedition undertaken by Darwin, this time to Grenada in the West Indies to photograph a total eclipse of the sun. Soon after his return he joined the Royal Geographical Society; he was elected to its council in 1890 and served as president from 1908 to 1911. He resigned his commission in 1890, having attained the rank of major. He then entered the second phase of his long life, serving first on the London county council and then, in 1892, as the member of parliament for Lichfield. He was elected by a majority of only four, and lost the seat in the 1895 election. His experiences in parliament led to an interest in economics and thence to his book *Bimetallism* (1897), of which Maynard Keynes wrote after Darwin's death:

> His book appeared towards the end of the long controversy [on the use of both gold and silver as the basis for currencies]. But his statement of the conflicting arguments was so clear and unbiassed that it remained the standard text-book … until questions on bimetallism had disappeared from the examination papers on economic theory. (*Economic Journal*, Dec 1943)

A similarly balanced approach marked Darwin's next work, *Municipal trade: the advantages and disadvantages resulting from the substitution of representative bodies for private proprietors in the management of industrial undertakings* (1903).

In 1898 Darwin's first wife died, and in 1900 he married Charlotte Mildred Massingberd, the eldest daughter of his first cousin Edmund Langton (she had changed her name from Langton). There were no children of either marriage. The third and most important phase of his life did not start until he was sixty-one, when he was persuaded to succeed his father's cousin Sir Francis Galton as president of the Eugenics Education Society upon the latter's death in 1911. He held the presidency until 1928 (by which time the word 'Education' had been dropped). In 1926 his book *The Need for Eugenic Reform* had appeared, shortly followed by the more popular *What is Eugenics?* His greatest influence was through his support and encouragement of the young R. A. Fisher. The friendship between the two men, forty years apart in age, formed the intellectual link between Charles Darwin and Francis Galton on the one hand and Fisher on the other, and thus to neo-Darwinism and the foundations of modern statistics. Leonard suggested the topic of Fisher's classic 1918 paper 'The correlation between relatives on the supposition of Mendelian inheritance', and saw to its publication, personally defraying some of the cost. In 1930 Fisher dedicated *The Genetical Theory of Natural Selection* to him, and when Darwin died in 1943 Fisher described him as the kindest and wisest man he ever knew. In 1912 the University of Cambridge conferred the honorary degree of doctor of science on Darwin.

Darwin and his wife moved from London to West Hoathly, near Forest Row, Sussex, in 1921. Mildred Darwin died in 1940. Darwin died from bronchial pneumonia at home on 26 March 1943. He was buried at Forest Row cemetery. A. W. F. EDWARDS

Sources M. E. Keynes, *Leonard Darwin, 1850–1943* (1943) · R. A. Fisher, *Natural selection, heredity, and eugenics*, ed. J. H. Bennett (1983) · *Eugenics Review*, 34 (Jan 1943), 109–16 · *WWW* · *Cambridge University Reporter* (11 June 1912), 1265 · J. M. Keynes, *Economic Journal*, 53 (1943), 438–48
Archives Scott Polar RI, corresp. · U. Sussex, corresp. and papers | Adelaide University, Barr Smith Library, letters to R. A. Fisher · Bodl. Oxf., short history of Basutoland MS · UCL, corresp. with Sir Francis Galton · UCL, corresp. with Karl Pearson
Likenesses photographs, priv. coll.
Wealth at death £62,924 17s. 5d.: probate, 18 June 1943, *CGPLA Eng. & Wales*

Darwin, Sir Robert Vere [Robin] (1910–1974), landscape and portrait painter, was born in Chelsea, London, on 7 May 1910, the second of the three children and the only son of Bernard Richard Meirion *Darwin (1876–1961), golf correspondent, and his wife, Elinor Mary (d. 1954), daughter of William Thomas Monsell, herself a painter and sculptor of distinction. He was the great-grandson of Charles Darwin, author of *The Origin of Species*, and a descendant of the physician Erasmus Darwin. Educated at Eton College, he went on to study painting at the Slade School of Fine Art, London, in 1929. He began his professional career as art master at Watford grammar school and in 1933, at the age of only twenty-three, was appointed to Eton in the same capacity. There he quickly proved himself an inspiring teacher and within a year had turned the drawing schools from a scene of discrete activity in drawing from the cast and painting in watercolour into a vital centre of the college's daily life. In 1931 he married (Margaret) Yvonne, daughter of Herbert James Darby, solicitor; they divorced in 1949.

Soon after the outbreak of war in 1939 Darwin went to the camouflage directorate of the Ministry of Home Security at Leamington Spa, Warwickshire (of which he became secretary), having lately taken a characteristically bold gamble in throwing up his job at Eton so as to live in a

Sir Robert Vere [Robin] **Darwin** (1910–1974), by Ruskin Spear, 1961

small, grand manor house in Gloucestershire, with which he had fallen in love, and to concentrate on painting. Towards the end of the war he moved to the Ministry of Town and Country Planning and in 1945 was appointed education officer in the newly formed Council of Industrial Design, where his important contribution was a report on the training of industrial designers in which he examined in particular the proper role of the Royal College of Art, commenting that the appointment of the next principal would be of pivotal importance to the future of the college.

In 1946 Darwin was appointed director of the King Edward VII School of Art in Newcastle upon Tyne and professor of fine art at Durham University, but in 1948 he returned to London to take up the principalship of the Royal College of Art—the very appointment whose vital importance his own report foreshadowed. All his previous experience now fell into place and combined with his huge energy and gusto to fit him perfectly to plot a new course for the college in full knowledge of what to aim for and how to achieve it. To that end he widened the range of disciplines taught to match the industries the college ought to serve, developed academic and administrative systems that would win respect for the place and its products among those most sceptical of the art student's value in an industrial society, and attracted many of the leading practitioners of the day to organize and staff the various schools.

Within fifteen years of Darwin's appointment the Royal College of Art, which had rather lost direction in its wartime exile from London, had become by general consent the foremost institution of its kind in the world, and its influence spread through the whole edifice of art education in Britain. Its academic stature was recognized by the grant of a university charter in 1967, when Darwin became its first rector and vice-provost, retiring in 1971 to devote himself to his friends, to painting and travel, and the affairs of the Royal Academy. In 1962 he married Ginette, the former wife of Lieutenant-Colonel Kenneth Morton Channer Evans, and daughter of Captain Francis W. Hewitt and his wife, Adriana, *née* Pelliccioni, who in 1941 had married (Arnold) John Hugh Smith, of Hambro's Bank and treasurer of the National Art Collections Fund.

Darwin's painting was an expression of the exuberance of his own nature, and his love of paint marked him as the heir of Constable, Gustave Courbet, and André Derain. His realism was decisive and he attacked his subject with generosity which showed his instinctive largeness of vision. He painted many fine and sympathetic portraits, among them a small gallery of his colleagues at the Royal College of Art (which owns a characteristic portrait of him by Ruskin Spear), but it is his landscapes that particularly reveal his sense of breadth and personal feeling for place. His originality was never better expressed than in his watercolours, where his remarkable skill combined strength, tenderness, and spontaneity. He exhibited regularly at the Redfern Gallery and Leicester Galleries, at Agnew's, and at the Royal Academy, and his pictures were bought by the Contemporary Art Society, public galleries, and many private collectors. He was elected ARA in 1966 and RA in 1972.

As a young man Darwin seemed slight and apparently vulnerable, an impression which he adjusted by the menacing black moustache and heavy spectacles which he retained when maturity had built up his frame and bearing into a figure of formidable weight and proportions. His character was full of contradictions. He was a man of outward gravity and inner gaiety; he made working for him seem of the greatest importance but also the greatest fun, and yet on the very rare occasions when his judgement was at fault in making an appointment he could hardly forgive the victim of his own mistake. He could be fierce and domineering, but behind the imperious manner was a shy man who did not easily establish personal relationships. He made enemies among those who did not understand the gentle character he concealed behind the stern façade, yet he was a warm and constant friend to very many and a marvellous travelling companion.

At the end of his life Darwin was president of the Royal West of England Academy and served, during his time at the Royal College of Art, on virtually all the councils and committees which modelled Britain's system of art education and encouraged excellence in art and design, as also on the advisory councils of the Science and Victoria and Albert museums and the governing body of the Imperial College of Science and Technology. He was elected honorary fellow of the Society of Industrial Artists and Designers (1950), fellow of University College, London (1962), and senior fellow and honorary doctor of the Royal College of Art (1971), and was awarded the honorary degree of DLitt

at Newcastle upon Tyne University (1964) and Birmingham University (1966). In 1962 he was awarded the bicentenary medal of the Royal Society of Arts. He was appointed CBE in 1954 and knighted in 1964. He died, childless, in Chelsea, London, on 30 January 1974.

R. Y. GOODDEN, *rev.*

Sources *The Times* (1 Feb 1974) · personal knowledge (1986) · private information (1986) · *CGPLA Eng. & Wales* (1974)
Likenesses R. Spear, portrait, 1961, Royal College of Art, London [*see illus.*]
Wealth at death £72,119: probate, 9 July 1974, *CGPLA Eng. & Wales*

Das family (*per. c.*1750–*c.*1820), bankers in India, known in the later days of its influence as the Shah family, were Purbiya or eastern Agarwals. Agarwals were one of the main communities of commercial castes indigenous to northern India. With the decline of the Mughal central government after 1707, Agarwal and Khattri financiers became more important, and the previously dominant Gujaratis declined. The family firm appears to have originated in the small town of Amroha, near Delhi, and to have moved to the pilgrimage and commercial centre of Benares in northern India in the seventeenth century. According to one tradition the family rose to importance as a member of the Naupatti (or group of 'nine sharers') who helped the city of Benares pay off a large forced loan to the nawab of Oudh.

This cross-caste association of families hereafter played an important role in financing and advising Balwant Singh and Chet Singh, rajas of Benares. They took farms of land revenue from the rulers, moved specie from Benares to Lucknow (and later Calcutta), and financed the burgeoning pilgrim traffic. At some point in the later eighteenth century the Bhaiaram family settled in a large *haveli*, or mansion, in the Chaukhamba district of Benares, close to the holiest of the sites for ritual bathing on the banks of the Ganges. They also played an important part in the patronage of the Vallabhacharya Hindu temples of the locality.

In the mid-eighteenth century the firm's principal was **Bhaiaram Das** (*fl.* 1750–1770), banker (*mahajan*) and money dealer (*sarraff*, or *shroff*). Despite directing some fifty-two branches of his house throughout northern India, Bhaiaram Das remains a shadowy figure. His son **Gopal Das** (d. 1787), along with a second son, Bhavani Das, began to figure prominently in the East India Company records when, after 1769, the British received the grant of the revenues of Benares from the nawab of Oudh, Asaf ud-Daula. In succession to his father, Gopal Das became the principal of the firm, now renamed Bhaiaram Gopal Das, during the period when the East India Company was consolidating its power in the post-Mughal kingdom of Oudh.

The Benares bankers, and the Naupatti in particular, became intermediaries in the remittance of the Benares revenue to the East India Company's treasury in Calcutta. They also helped move company funds from Lucknow to Calcutta and from Calcutta to Bombay via the city of Surat. These funds provided the financial muscle behind the military power of the East India Company. Despite this, Bhaiaram and the other bankers appear initially to have been regarded as impediments to the growth of British influence in Benares. After the revolt and expulsion of Maharaja Chet Singh in 1781, when the commercial wealth of the city generally rallied behind the company, the firm fully came to terms with the British presence. Gopal Das died in 1787 and the business passed to his son **Manohar Das** (*fl.* 1780–1800); Gopal Das was survived by his wife, of whom further details are unknown.

During the period when Jonathan Duncan was resident at the Benares court (1787–95), Manohar Das was regularly interviewed on the movements of money markets across India and on political developments bearing on the company's finances. These reports were sent on to Calcutta and London. Gopal Das Manohar Das (as the firm was now titled) purchased large quantities of company paper in 1787–90 and aided it during the Second Anglo-Mysore War. It had opened further *kothis*, or branches, at Cuttack, in central eastern India, and latterly at Madras, thus contributing to the creation of a network of indigenous financial support for the British across the whole subcontinent. Manohar Das was succeeded by his son Mukund Lal, under whom the firm's fortunes began to falter. During the opening decades of the nineteenth century the family declined in importance as a commercial interest, edged aside by newcomers and by British banks. By mid-century some family members had secured *zamindaris*, or landholdings, in the Benares region, and a few had entered the new professions, though others had fallen into poverty. Their history reveals, nevertheless, the extent to which the rise of the East India Company depended on Indian occupational élites through to the time of the later Indian middle class.

C. A. BAYLY

Sources *Calendar of Persian correspondence: being letters, referring mainly to affairs in Bengal, which passed between some of the company's servants and Indian rulers and notables*, 11 vols. (1911–69) · K. P. Mishra, *Banaras in transition (1738–1795): a socio-economic study* (Delhi, 1974) · C. A. Bayly, *Rulers, townsmen and bazaars: north Indian society in the age of British expansion, 1770–1870* (1983); new edn (Delhi, 1993) · V. Dalmia, *The nationalization of Hindu traditions, Bharatendu Harischandra and nineteenth-century Banaras* (Delhi, 1997) · K. Chatterjee, *Merchants, politics and society in early modern India: Bihar, 1730–1820* (Leiden, 1996) · L. Subramanian, *Indigenous capital v. imperial expansion: Bombay, Surat and the west coast* (Delhi, 1996) **Archives** BL OIOC | National Archives of India, New Delhi, foreign department misc. serial 12, 1, 1832 · Uttar Pradesh Central RO, Allahabad, India, Duncan records, resident's proceedings **Wealth at death** property in Calcutta and elsewhere, incl. market called Bara Bazar, tanks at Sita Rund and opposite Indica Museum; also a *dharmsala* at Gomati Manohar Das: H. R. Nevill, *District gazetteers of the United Provinces of Agra and Oudh: Benares* (Allahabad, 1909), 119

Das, Bhaiaram (*fl.* 1750–1770). *See under* Das family (*per.* c.1750–c.1820).

Das, Chittaranjan (1870–1925), Indian nationalist and barrister, was born on 5 November 1870 in Calcutta, the second child and eldest son of Bhuban Mohan Das, a solicitor of the Calcutta high court, and his wife, Nistarini Devi. His youngest brother, P. R. Das, became a judge of the Patna high court.

Das was educated at the London Missionary Society Institution, Bhowanipore, Calcutta, and then at Presidency College, Calcutta, one of the foremost colleges of India. He sailed to England in 1890 to take the Indian Civil Service examination. However, he failed in this effort, and changed course and entered the Inner Temple. He was called to the bar in 1893 and upon his return to India enrolled as a barrister at the Calcutta high court. After paying off large debts left by his father he gradually became one of the highest-paid Indian barristers, and amassed considerable wealth.

In 1897 he married Basanti Devi, the daughter of Barada Nath Haldar, diwan of Bijni estate in Assam. Basanti Devi played some part in nationalist politics and she, along with her son Chitta Ranjan Das, her husband, and many political activists, was arrested during the 1921 non-cooperation movement. Basanti Devi lived until May 1974.

As a lawyer Das made his early successes in the *mofussil*, or local courts, outside Calcutta. He took up civil and criminal cases, but became famous in India at first for his passionate and shrewd defences of Indian nationalists charged with terrorism in political cases, the most famous of which was the Alipore bomb case of 1908. In this case he defended Aurobindo Ghose, public political leader and secret revolutionary theorist. Das gained an acquittal for Ghose, who two years later flew to Pondicherry and later became known as the guru and philosopher Sri Aurobindo.

Das participated in politics from his student days in England and was linked to the extremist party in the Indian National Congress from 1905 onwards. However, the moderate group was more successful in outlasting the extremists, who fell into disarray from about 1910. Das continued his legal work and sporadic political participation and re-emerged in 1917 as a leader of a revitalized Indian National Congress in Bengal.

By 1919 he became the foremost nationalist in the Bengal Congress at about the time that M. K. Gandhi came to the leadership of the national Congress. Das at first opposed Gandhi's call for non-co-operation, but then, as Gandhi demonstrated his political skill and wide support, Das joined with him in energizing the national non-co-operation campaign of 1920 to 1922. Das was arrested in 1921 and was in gaol when Gandhi called off the campaign because of acts of violence by Indian nationalists.

Angered by what he believed was short-sightedness and incorrect strategy by Gandhi, Das, together with Motilal Nehru, father of India's first prime minister, Jawaharlal Nehru, founded the Swaraj party. This party operated within the Congress as an opposition group to Gandhi's loyal supporters, and outside the Congress as a party participating in the elections to the provincial legislative councils and the central legislative assembly from 1923. Their strategy was to deadlock the councils from within, and both Das in the Bengal legislative council and the elder Nehru in the central legislative assembly had considerable success.

Das was also elected mayor of Calcutta in 1924 under the revised Calcutta Municipal Act. He flourished from 1923 to

1925 as leader of the Bengal Congress, leader of the opposition in the Bengal legislative council, mayor of the second city of the British empire, and national president of the Swaraj party. Part of his effort in all these roles was to have Hindus and Muslims work together and to this end he formulated the Bengal pact of 1924. The pact specified how this co-operation was to be achieved, *inter alia*, through additional places for Muslims in public employment. It was utilized in Bengal, but not accepted by the national Congress. As the political leader of a province in which Muslims had a slight majority, Das believed he needed Muslim help to achieve the goals he sought, and for this brief period he had a good deal of Muslim support.

At the height of his political success his health began to fail and he retreated to his mountain home in Darjeeling in May 1925. Gandhi visited him there. On 16 June 1925, succumbing to severe fever, he died. Gandhi led the enormous funeral procession in Calcutta, and said:

> Deshbandhu [friend of the country] was one of the greatest of men … He dreamed … and talked of freedom of India and of nothing else … His heart knew no difference between Hindus and Mussalmans and I should like to tell Englishmen, too, that he bore no ill-will to them.   (Gandhi, *Collected Works* 27.250)

Throughout his life Das was religious, and was attracted to the emotional Vaishnava Hinduism of Bengal which stressed the centrality of the principle of love. He wrote several books of religious poetry in Bengali, one of which was translated into English by Aurobindo Ghose as *Songs of the Sea* (1920). As a passionate Bengali who loved his country and was himself non-violent, he opposed, but did not disown, some of the Bengalis who turned to acts of violence. He preferred open political work inside and outside government institutions aiming for the independence of his country.   LEONARD A. GORDON

Sources H. D. Gupta, *Deshbandhu Chittaranjan Das* (1960) · P. C. Ray, *Life and times of C. R. Das* (1927) · L. A. Gordon, *Bengal: the nationalist movement, 1876–1940* (1974) · J. H. Broomfield, *Elite conflict in a plural society: twentieth century Bengal* (1968) · N. C. Chatterjee, 'Chitta Ranjan Das', *Dictionary of national biography*, ed. S. P. Sen (1972–4) [India] · D. K. Chatterjee, *C. R. Das and Indian national movement* (1965)
Archives Gandhi Memorial, New Delhi, M. K. Gandhi MSS · Nehru Memorial Library, New Delhi, All-India Congress Committee MSS | FILM BFI NFTVA, news footage
Likenesses portrait, Mahajati Sadan Hall, Calcutta, India · statue, near West Bengal Legislative Assembly, near Maidan Park, Calcutta, India

Das, Gopal (*d.* **1787**). *See under* Das family (*per. c.*1750–*c.*1820).

Das, Manohar (*fl.* **1780–1800**). *See under* Das family (*per. c.*1750–*c.*1820).

Dasent, Sir George Webbe (1817–1896), Scandinavian scholar, was born on 22 May 1817 at St Vincent, in the West Indies. He was the third son of John Roche Dasent (1773–1832), attorney-general of St Vincent, and his second wife,

Charlotte Martha, younger daughter and coheir of Captain Alexander Burrowes Irwin of the 32nd foot, who settled in the island and died there in 1806. The Dasent family had long been prominent in the West Indies, and included early settlers and administrators of St Kitts, Nevis, and Antigua.

George Dasent was educated at Westminster School (1830–34), at King's College, London, and at Oxford. He matriculated in 1836 from Magdalen Hall (where John Delane was a fellow pupil, and friend), and graduated BA in 1840, MA in 1843, and DCL in 1852. In 1840 he went to Stockholm as secretary to the British envoy, Sir Thomas Cartwright. The encouragement of Jacob Grimm led him to an interest in Scandinavian literature and mythology, and his four years at Stockholm led to an intensive study of the sagas, by which his whole career was animated. The first-fruits of this labour were *The Prose or Younger Edda* (1842), which he inscribed to Thomas Carlyle, and a *Grammar of the Icelandic or Old-Norse Tongue* (1843), from the Swedish of Erasmus Rask.

Dasent returned to England in 1845, and joined John Delane as assistant editor of *The Times*. On 4 April 1846 he married John's sister, Fanny Louisa, third daughter of W. F. A. Delane of Old Bracknell, Easthampstead. Dasent's intimacy with the Prussian ambassador, C. K. G. Bunsen, proved of great service to Delane in connection with the foreign policy of *The Times*. Together with his demanding journalistic duties he worked hard at translations from the Norse. The first of the stories so translated appeared in *Blackwood's Magazine* in November 1851, and the collective edition, *Popular Tales from the Norse* (derived from the collection by M. M. Asbjörns and Moe), was published in 1859 with a substantial introductory essay, which Dasent considered his best piece of work. He was encouraged in such independent work at the Sterlings' house in South Place, Knightsbridge, London, where he met John Stuart Mill, Julius Hare, and Thackeray. In January 1852 he was called to the bar from the Middle Temple (to which he had been admitted in 1844), and became an advocate in Doctors' Commons (2 November). In 1853 he accepted, under Richard William Jelf, the post of professor of English literature and modern history at King's College, and did some examining for the civil service commissioners, and he was elected a member of the Athenaeum in 1854. Simultaneously he was writing for the reviews, and was approached regarding the editorship of *Fraser's Magazine*.

Njáls saga, which since 1843 Dasent had planned to translate, was completed and issued in 1861, with valuable introductory matter by Guðbrandur Vigfússon. In that year and in 1862 he visited Iceland in the company of John Campbell of Islay. He was warmly received at Reykjavík, where he was entertained at a public banquet. He rode across the Vatna Jökull and visited nearly every place of interest in the island. The adventures of the party were humorously described by Sir Charles Clifford in his privately printed *Travels by 'Umbra'* (1865), in which Dasent figures as 'Mr Darwin'. In 1863 Dasent visited the Ionian Islands as the guest of Sir Henry Storks, the British high commissioner. Then came *Gisli the Outlaw* (1866), the best of his Icelandic translations, and a second series of popular stories, *Tales from the Fjeld* (1874). In 1864 Dasent was approached by the representatives of Richard Cleasby, who had long been engaged in collecting materials for an Icelandic dictionary prior to his death in October 1847. Dasent, unable himself either to complete the etymologies or undertake the laborious task of minute revision, persuaded Guðbrandur Vigfússon to come to England to work on the dictionary. Financed by the Clarendon Press (largely owing to the good offices of Dean Liddell) *An Icelandic–English Dictionary* was published in 1873, Dasent having provided a lengthy introductory memoir of Cleasby.

In 1870 Gladstone, on the advice of Lowe, who had an interest in Icelandic studies, offered Dasent a civil service commissionership under Sir Edward Ryan, and the acceptance of the post led to Dasent's resignation from *The Times*. He now frequented the Athenaeum and the Cosmopolitan Club in Charles Street, Berkeley Square, and became a well-known figure in London society, numbering Lord Granville, Matthew Arnold, Dean Stanley, Lord Houghton, and Baron Meyer de Rothschild among his friends. With Baroness Rothschild he took a leading part in the movement for the oral instruction of deaf people. He devoted his leisure between 1870 and 1875 to writing lively semi-autobiographical novels, including *Annals of an Eventful Life* (1870), and also *Jest and Earnest: a Collection of Essays and Reviews* (1873). He was already a knight of the Danish order of the Dannebrog, and on 27 June 1876, on Disraeli's recommendation, he was knighted at Windsor Castle. He was also appointed one of the original commissioners of historical manuscripts in 1870. In 1890 he sustained a severe loss when his library and other collections at Tower Hill, Ascot, were destroyed by fire. He was a connoisseur of antique silver and an early student of hallmarks, of which he had a fine collection (a portion of which he had sold in June 1875).

Dasent retired from public service in 1892 on a gratuity of £1200 p.a. From the house which he had rebuilt at Ascot he wrote his last work, a masterly translation for the Rolls series, *The Orkneyinger's Magnus and Hacon's Sagas* (1894), with the assistance of his elder son, John Roche Dasent CB. This occupies the third and fourth of the four volumes of *Icelandic Sagas Relating to the British Isles*; the Norse text was edited by Vigfússon in the first two volumes. Dasent's contemplated life of Delane, whose vast correspondence passed into his hands, was ready for publication, but was left in the hands of his literary executors. Dasent died at Tower Hill, Ascot, on 11 June 1896, and was buried near John Delane in the churchyard of Easthampstead, Berkshire. His wife survived him with two sons and one daughter. THOMAS SECCOMBE, *rev.* JOHN D. HAIGH

Sources private information (1901) [Arthur Irwin Dasent] • *The Times* (13 June 1896) • *The Athenaeum* (20 June 1896), 811–12 • *Saturday Review*, 11 (1861), 429–30 • *Men and women of the time* (1895) • J. K. Laughton, *Memoirs of the life and correspondence of Henry Reeve* (1898), vol. 1, pp. 284–5, 338 • *Travels by 'Umbra'* (privately printed, Edinburgh, 1865) • Boase, *Mod. Eng. biog.* • G. W. Dasent, *Annals of an eventful life*, 3 vols. (1870) • G. W. Dasent, 'Introduction', *Popular tales from the Norse* (1859), ix–lxxxviii • J. Foster, *Men-at-the-bar: a biographical hand-list of the members of the various inns of court*, 2nd edn (1885), 115 • *Letters of John Sterling to George Webbe Dasent, 1833–1844* (privately printed, Edinburgh, 1914)
Archives News Int. RO, papers | Bodl. Oxf., letters to Guðbrandur Vigfússon • NL Scot., letters to William Blackwood & Sons • NL Scot., letters to J. F. Campbell
Wealth at death £2102 11s. 11d.: probate, 15 Aug 1896, CGPLA Eng. & Wales

Dash, Jack O'Brien (1907–1989), political activist and unofficial dockers' leader, was born on 23 April 1907 in Southwark, south London, the youngest of four sons of Joseph Thomas Dash, a stagehand, and his wife, Rose Gertrude Johns, an actor. According to Dash's own account, his upbringing was one of great material hardship. His mother died of tuberculosis when he was seven and his father, who then had an even greater struggle to support the family, also died of a lung complaint a few years later. After an elementary schooling, his skill at drawing led to a trial period with an engraving firm, but pressure to take home a better wage resulted in a series of menial jobs, starting in a J. Lyons café, followed by spells as an office boy and then as a carrier of books for a wholesaler. After being unemployed for several weeks at the age of nineteen he signed up for two years in the Royal Army Service Corps.

On 22 June 1931 Dash married Ellen Elizabeth Frett (d. c.1980); they had a daughter, Kathleen. After leaving the army, he found it hard to get regular work, though by the mid-1930s he was most often employed on building sites as a hod-carrier. An already strong commitment to trade unionism, further stimulated by the reading of left-wing literature, encouraged him to persuade other building workers on the site to join a trade union, for which he was awarded the Trades Union Congress's Tolpuddle medal. In his autobiography, Dash claimed that he thanked Walter Citrine and Herbert Morrison, the signatories of a citation that accompanied the medal, while pointing out that he had recently joined an organization of which they disapproved, the Communist Party of Great Britain. He remained a loyal, active, and uncritical member of the party for the rest of his life.

In the late 1930s Dash took part in some of the publicity stunts organized by Wal Hannington and others in the National Unemployed Workers' Movement. These included a visit in December 1938 to the Ritz Hotel by a group of the unemployed who attempted to order afternoon tea. It was after the war (in which he volunteered for the fire service) that his political activities became notorious. In the summer of 1945, when non-registered men were being taken on in the Port of London, he became a docker in the Royal Group of Docks. That he was neither born into the industry nor able to boast dock work as his first and only trade was sometimes held against him, but he soon showed an understanding of the peculiar conditions of the industry and their effects on the workforce. He was most able to influence the actions of his fellow dockers by expressing the grievances that arose from issues of piece-work rates, compulsory overtime, the unloading of dirty or dangerous cargoes, and, even after the Dock Labour Scheme of 1947, the existence of casual employment. Though an ardent trade unionist—in his autobiography he wrote warmly of workers 'bound in the finest brotherhood of man, the trade union movement' (Dash, 163)—he was frequently at odds with the officials of his own union, the Transport and General Workers.

In 1949 Dash and five other dockers were questioned by Arthur Deakin (1890–1955), general secretary of the union, about their agitation to 'black' the unloading of the Canadian cargo of the *Beaver Brae*, in support of a strike of Canadian seamen. Three of the six were expelled from the union while Dash and two others received a two-year suspension from holding office—although communists had recently been debarred by the union from official positions. The exclusion of militants from the councils of the Transport Workers' Union strengthened a separate body claiming to represent rank-and-file workers of which Dash became the chairman in 1958, the London Docks Liaison Committee. This unofficial group, usually numbering five men informally elected at dock-gate meetings, was at the centre of several disputes with employers. Typically on these occasions dockers would leave their work to hear Dash address them, a stocky, pugnacious speaker who usually stood on an old chair and opened with the words he later used for the title of his autobiography, 'Good morning, brothers!'

In 1966 Dash's notoriety became more widespread when during the seamen's strike he was named in the House of Commons by the prime minister, Harold Wilson. In a controversial speech which drew on evidence gathered by the secret services, Wilson argued that members of the Communist Party were intent on extending the dispute to trade unions beyond the National Union of Seamen. After identifying Dash as a member of 'the unofficial liaison committee in the London docks', he added: 'Mr. Dash … took a more moderate line because he was torn between his loyalty to the party and his loyalty to his union, which was resisting all pressures to take the Communist line' (*Hansard 5C*, cols. 1619–20). In turn, Dash held that Wilson was 'the greatest man in the con business', one of Labour's 'unholy trinity'—in the 1960s the other two were George Brown and Ray Gunter, by the 1970s his derided trinity comprised Wilson, Roy Jenkins, and James Callaghan (Dash, 155, 33).

Dash's standing as unofficial leader was recognized by Lord Devlin who met him when gathering evidence for his report of 1965 into the port transport industry and took up his suggestion that dockers should have shop stewards. In 1968 Dash was elected as a shop steward, which caused the Transport Workers' Union, then led by the left-winger Frank Cousins, to end its ban on communist officials. Though Devlin's report proposed an end to the system whereby the docks were run on casual labour, the militants argued that decasualization would result in a smaller labour force and the end of restrictive (or, according to Dash, protective) practices. As an alternative, the liaison committee pressed for improved conditions for dockers and the nationalization of the industry. Dash maintained that Devlin's proposals were designed to protect the employers' profits. He could readily quote figures

to show how the capitalist system as a whole and the port employers in particular exploited the workers. As he humorously stated in an obituary he composed for a television programme, the epitaph he wished for was:

Here lies Jack Dash
All he wanted was
To separate them from their cash.
(Dash, 188)

Dash's penchant for colourful phrases, along with a largely hostile portrayal in the press, helped to make him a public figure. In the course of his leadership of an eight-week unofficial strike against the Devlin proposals in late 1967 he received much attention. Yet his personality made it difficult for critics to demonize him. His cockney wit and charm could be disarming. In addition to politics and the docks he talked freely about his enthusiasm for painting and drawing, his fondness for animals (in his younger days he bred dogs), his fitness regime (he was a vegetarian, had boxed and given instruction in physical training), his tastes in music and poetry, and his interest in the history of London. He frequently spoke to audiences of students and occasionally to such groups as rotary clubs. Roy Thomson invited him to a dinner at Claridge's Hotel to address a meeting of millionaires.

Early in 1970, nearing the age of sixty-three and affected by a back complaint that had kept him off work for some time, Dash decided to accept a severance payment of £1500 and to leave the docks. For the rest of his life he followed his hobbies and welcomed opportunities to further his views, travelling widely to address meetings. He remained an uncompromising communist, unreconstructedly repeating the old slogans associated with the party's Stalinist period. Visits to Poland and the USSR had reinforced his beliefs and he expressed support for Soviet policies, including the invasion of Czechoslovakia in 1968.

In his retirement Dash was saddened by the redevelopment of dockland—he observed many of the changes that took place from his top-storey flat in a high-rise council block—and by the level of unemployment, especially of young people, in the East End. During the last few months of his life, despite the onset of what was to be a fatal attack of cancer, he kept up his political work, regularly attending and speaking at meetings. He died on 8 June 1989 in the London Hospital, Whitechapel. The hundreds of mourners at his funeral, held on 14 June at the East London crematorium, were accompanied by trade union banners and sang the 'Internationale' as his coffin was draped with the flag of the shop stewards' committee of the Royal Group of Docks.

D. E. MARTIN

Sources D. F. Wilson, *Dockers: the impact of industrial change* (1972) • J. Dash, *Good morning, brothers!* (1969) • *The Guardian* (9 June 1989) • *Morning Star* (9 June 1989) • *Morning Star* (15 June 1989) • *Daily Telegraph* (9 June 1989) • *The Times* (9 June 1989) • H. Wilson, *The labour government, 1964–1970: a personal record* (1971) • *Hansard 5C* (1966), 730.1619–20 • S. Barnes, 'What makes Jack Dash?', *The Sun* (29 April 1966) • D. Ballard and D. E. Martin, 'Dash, Jack O'Brien', *DLB*, vol. 9 • B. Hunter, *They knew why they fought: unofficial struggles and leadership* on the docks, 1945–1989 (1994) • J. Phillips, 'Decasualization and disruption: industrial relations in the docks, 1945–79', *A history of British industrial relations, 1939–1979*, ed. C. Wrigley (1996) • m. cert.

Archives priv. coll., scrapbook

Likenesses photographs, *c.*1965–1967, Hult. Arch. • R. Case, photograph, 1967, Hult. Arch. • J. Minihan, photograph, 1967, Hult. Arch. • S. O'Meara, photograph, 1967, Hult. Arch. • M. Hart, photograph, People's History Museum, Manchester • photographs, repro. in Dash, *Good morning, brothers!*

Dashwood [*née* de la Pasture], **Edmée Elizabeth Monica** [*pseud.* E. M. Delafield] **(1890–1943)**, novelist, was born on 9 June 1890 at 6 Walsingham Terrace, Aldrinton, near Hove, Sussex, the elder of the two daughters of Comte Henry Philip Ducarel de la Pasture (1840/41–1908) and his wife, Elizabeth Lydia Rosabel, *née* Bonham (1866–1945). Her father was directly descended from the maharaja of Purnea, and his French grandfather had fled to England in 1791. He occupied himself with country pursuits and Catholicism, while her mother, whose father was a diplomat, wrote lucrative fiction under the name Mrs Henry de la Pasture. Edmée, as she was called until adulthood, thereafter Elizabeth or E. M. D., was brought up in both London and Devon and later in Monmouthshire. Educated by French governesses and at several schools, she was bilingual but was 'allowed to read for only an hour a day' (Delafield, *Beginnings*, 66); unsurprisingly, tyrannical mothers appear often in Elizabeth's novels. In 1910 her mother married for a second time. Her new husband was Sir Hugh Charles Clifford (1866–1941), colonial administrator, and later high commissioner for the Malay States and British agent in Borneo. Edmée, who had failed to ensnare a husband, entered a convent in Belgium, which she left after nine months, an experience she wrote about while recuperating (in a manuscript published in Powell's *Life*).

Elizabeth became a nurse in Exeter in 1914 and 'in the odds and ends of time permitted to VADs [voluntary aid detachments]' (Delafield, *Beginnings*, 73) wrote her first novel, *Zella Sees Herself* (1917), the first of five novels with a strong Catholic element which also endorse the comment that 'in women novelists, the analysing habit is very frequently devoted to the study of egoism' (Johnson, 178). Like all the novels to follow, it was published under the pseudonym E. M. Delafield, a loose translation of her maiden name. *The War Workers* appeared in 1918, as did *The Pelicans* (in fact written first), which centred on the suffocating love between two sisters. Meanwhile, Elizabeth worked at the Ministry of National Service in Bristol, continuing to write 'as a matter of course, regardless of interruptions. … All that I have tried to do is to observe faithfully, and record accurately, the things that have come within my limited range' (Delafield, *Beginnings*, 73, 78). The next year came *Consequences*, about a girl who enters a convent and then cannot adjust to life outside.

On 17 July 1919 Elizabeth was married, at St James's, Spanish Place, London, to Major (Arthur) Paul Dashwood (1882–1964), the second son of Sir George Dashwood, and left for Malaya, where her husband worked as a civil engineer. In 1920 she gave birth to a son. But an expatriate

Edmée Elizabeth Monica Dashwood [E. M. Delafield] (1890–1943), by Howard Coster, 1930s

life based on the club proved uncongenial and the Dashwoods returned to Britain in 1922, moving to Croyle House near Kentisbeare in Devon. A daughter was born in 1924 and her husband became a land agent, although Elizabeth's earnings were always to be essential. By now her witty, incisive style of writing was fully established, as she continued to follow her mother's advice to write 'about something of which I had personal experience' (Delafield, *Beginnings*, 68). Thus *The Way Things Are* (1927) concerned a woman not unlike herself, married to a husband not unlike Paul Dashwood; this was described by a contemporary as 'her *completely* perfect novel' (Ferguson, 166). In 1924 Elizabeth became president of the local Women's Institute, a post she retained until the end of her life. Criminology had always been an interest, and in the same year she became the first woman to sit on her local bench; *A Messalina of the Suburbs* (1924) was based on the Thompson Bywaters trial.

By now Elizabeth was writing a great deal of journalism—'she was valued for her ability to see everyday life in terms of comic desperation' (Powell, 69)—and was always at work on a novel, publishing over thirty, as well as several other books of sketches, essays, short stories, and parodies, in the years between 1917 and 1943. She was on the board of *Time and Tide*, to which she contributed, and in late 1929 filled a space in the magazine by beginning the hugely successful *The Diary of a Provincial Lady* (1930), so characteristic of its author's self-deprecating humour and lightly satiric observation. That year, too, Elizabeth's play

To See Ourselves was produced in London and the novel *Turn Back the Leaves* appeared. In 1932 she published probably her best book, *Thank Heaven Fasting*, 'an almost unbearably poignant account of the struggles of a young girl of respectable family in Edwardian times to find a husband—any husband—as a passport to some kind of grownup life' (Colegate). In 1937 E. M. Delafield wrote *Nothing is Safe*, a novel about the tragic effect of divorce upon children, as well as a travel book on Russia, where she had been the year before. On the outbreak of the Second World War, she lectured for the Ministry of Information and spent some weeks in France. But the death of her newly called-up son in late 1940, most probably by his own hand, was something from which she never recovered.

Elizabeth was described as 'a witty, extremely soignée person, with a gift for laughter' (Kunitz and Haycraft), and her friend Lady Rhondda 'used to wonder how that frail looking creature could stand the strain of the unending round of never ceasing work. I suppose it would be true to say that in the end she did not' (*Time and Tide*). E. M. Delafield, a warm, kind, and generous woman completely without personal vanity, died of cancer at her home, Croyle House, near Kentisbeare, Devon, on 2 December 1943 and was buried on 6 December in Kentisbeare churchyard.   NICOLA BEAUMAN

Sources V. Powell, *The life of a provincial lady: a study of E. M. Delafield and her works* (1988) · E. M. Delafield, *Beginnings*, ed. L. A. G. Strong (1935) · D. K. Roberts, ed., *Titles to fame* (1937) · 'Introduction', E. M. Delafield, *The diary of a provincial lady* (1984) · 'Introduction', E. M. Delafield, *The way things are* (1988) · 'Introduction', E. M. Delafield, *Thank heaven fasting* (1988) · J. Gawsworth [T. I. Fytton Armstrong] and others, *Ten contemporaries: notes toward their definitive bibliographies* [1933] · R. Brimley Johnson, *Some contemporary novelists (women)* (1920) · *Time and Tide* (11 Dec 1943), 1019–20 · I. Colegate, review of *Life*, *The Spectator* (8 Oct 1988), 34–5 · S. J. Kunitz and H. Haycraft, eds., *Twentieth century authors: a biographical dictionary of modern literature* (1942) · R. Ferguson, *Passionate Kensington* (1939) · b. cert. · m. cert. · d. cert.
Archives University of British Columbia, literary MSS and MSS · University of Exeter, MSS | BL, corresp. with Macmillans, Add. MS 54972 · Harvard U., Houghton L., letters to Theodora Bosanquet · Newberry Library, Chicago, Illinois, letters to Arthur Meeker
Likenesses D. A. Wehrschmidt, portrait, 1909; known to be in family possession in 1959 · H. Coster, photograph, 1930–39, NPG [*see illus.*] · H. Coster, photographs, NPG · photograph, repro. in Roberts, ed., *Titles to fame*, facing p. 126 · portrait, repro. in Powell, *Life of a provincial lady*, following p. 82
Wealth at death £11,548 16s. 11d.: probate, 13 March 1944, CGPLA Eng. & Wales

Dashwood, Sir Francis, first baronet (*c.*1658–1724), merchant, was the third son of Francis Dashwood (1619–1683), a member of the Saddlers' Company and Turkey merchant, and his wife, Alice (1621–1693/4), daughter of Richard Sleigh of Derbyshire. Francis and his elder brother Samuel (*d.* 1705) were educated at home before joining their father in his silk business, which they inherited at his death.

Samuel soon rose to power in the City of London, which he represented as MP in 1683–7 and 1690–95. During the 1680s both brothers invested in the Levant, Royal African,

and Old East India companies (they held seats on the governing body of the last named company); Samuel was knighted in 1684. Francis was made free of the Vintners' Company in 1680. He married on 13 April 1683 Mary (*d.* 1694), daughter of John Jennings of Westminster, a marriage which produced a son and two daughters. By the time of the revolution Francis's success in trade had enabled him to accumulate a sizeable fortune, and in 1690 he loaned the government £1000. To Sir Samuel he expressed a wish to obtain a government post, in which he was not successful. He established a residence at Wanstead, Essex, and in 1698 the brothers spent £15,000 on the manor of West Wycombe, Buckinghamshire. Queen Anne knighted Francis during the feast held for Sir Samuel's inauguration as lord mayor in October 1702.

Dashwood's first involvement in politics came before the general election of 1705, when he was considered as a possible whig candidate for Coventry, standing in partnership with or in place of either of his sons-in-law, Sir Fulwar Skipwith, second baronet, or Sir Orlando Bridgeman. Dashwood, however, imprudently sought to intercede with Lord Brooke, the tory patron, on Skipwith's behalf, and although he then contributed to Bridgeman's electoral expenses, the whigs were defeated at both Coventry and the county polls.

The year 1705 was a turning point in Francis's life. Samuel died, and on 30 May Francis married Mary (1674–1710), daughter of Vere Fane, the fourth earl of Westmorland and lord governor of the Cinque Ports, who brought with her title to the barony of Le Despencer. This union enhanced Dashwood's personal and political standing. It brought him another son, Francis *Dashwood, eleventh Baron Le Despencer (1708–1781) and best known as a member of the notorious Hellfire Club, and a daughter, Rachel (*d.* 1788), who married the politician Sir Robert Austin. In 1706 Dashwood was able to purchase for £15,000 from his nephew George Dashwood, who had inherited it, Sir Samuel's share of the manor of West Wycombe, and having transferred his Wanstead estate to Sir Orlando Bridgeman, he settled his family at West Wycombe. The following year a baronetcy was conferred upon him.

Dashwood finally entered parliament without a contest in 1708 as whig MP for the Cinque Ports town of Winchelsea, where he contributed little beyond voting in 1709 for the naturalization of the 'poor Palatines' (German protestants) and in 1710 supporting the impeachment of Henry Sacheverell. He also voted in favour of the merger between the Old and New East India companies. The resulting merger opened up not only the oriental trade, but also that of the West Indies and America, to all English merchants. He had to dig into his purse to hold the contested seat again at the 1710 election, successfully defending accusations of bribery of the electorate. His allegiance wavered at this point, and he was one of those who uncovered the mismanagement of the previous whig government, but he came back into the fold to vote in 1713 against the French Commerce Bill, which would have affected his trading interests. He did not stand at the election held that year and retired from active political life.

Following the death of his second wife, Dashwood married on 17 June 1712 Mary (d. 1719), the daughter of Major (Charles?) King, who bore him two sons and two daughters. His fourth marriage, on 21 July 1720, to Elizabeth (1666?–1736), daughter of Thomas Windsor, first earl of Plymouth, was childless. About 1720 he bought the manor of Halton in Buckinghamshire, on the improvement of which he spent lavishly, at the same time beautifying his home at West Wycombe. He died at his town house in Hanover Square, Westminster, on 4 November 1724 and was buried at West Wycombe. Despite the expenditure of his latter years, Dashwood's personal estate was valued at over £34,000. The baronetcy passed to his son Francis, then aged fifteen.   DOROTHY M. MOORE

Sources Burke, *Peerage* (1967) · F. Dashwood, *The Dashwoods of West Wycombe* (1987) · K. G. Davies, *The Royal African Company* (1970) · private information (2004) [P. Gauci] · G. Holmes and W. A. Speck, eds., *The divided society: parties and politics in England, 1694–1716* (1968) · J. R. Jones, *Country and court: England, 1658–1714* (1978) · *Le Neve's Pedigrees of the knights*, ed. G. W. Marshall, Harleian Society, 8 (1873) · *VCH Buckinghamshire*, vol. 3 · C. Roberts, *Schemes and undertakings: a study of English politics in the seventeenth century* (1985) · L. S. Sutherland, *The East India Company in eighteenth century politics* (1952) · J. R. Woodhead, *The rulers of London, 1660–1689* (1965) · H. Horwitz, 'The East India trade, the politicians and the constitution', *Journal of British Studies*, 17/2 (1977–8), 1–18 · C. Jones, 'A fresh division lately grown up amongst us: party strife, aristocratic investment in the Old and New East India companies and the vote in the House of Lords on February 23, 1700', *Historical Research*, 68 (1995), 302–17 · H. R. Snyder, 'Party configurations in the early eighteenth century House of Commons', *BIHR*, 45 (1972), 38–72 · J. G. Sperling, 'The division of 25 May 1711 on an amendment to the South Sea Bill: a note on the reality of parties in the age of Anne', *HJ*, 4 (1961), 191–217 · R. Walcott, 'The East India interest in the general election of 1700–1701', *EngHR*, 71 (1956), 223–39

Archives Yale U., James Marshall and Marie-Louise Osborn collection, Osborn manuscript files: D 4162 portraits and unprocessed folder

Likenesses portrait, Yale U., James Marshall and Marie-Louise Osborn collection, Osborn manuscript files: D 4162

Dashwood, Francis, eleventh Baron Le Despencer (1708–1781),

politician and rake, born in Great Marlborough Street, London, in December 1708, and baptized at St Botolph without Bishopsgate on 23 December 1708, was the only son of Sir Francis *Dashwood, first baronet (c.1658–1724), merchant and MP, of West Wycombe, Buckinghamshire, and the second of his four wives, Mary Fane (1674–1710), the eldest daughter of Vere Fane, fourth earl of Westmorland and seventh Baron Le Despencer. On his father's death on 4 November 1724 the baronetcy and estates passed to Dashwood, who was just short of his sixteenth birthday. Dashwood was to prove a curious but colourful character. His range of interests and achievements was unusual and highlighted his intelligence, discriminating taste, and inquisitive interest in new ideas. Contemporaries with whom he worked noted his capacity for diligent administration, his generosity of spirit, his honesty, and his courage, which rendered him careless of popularity. He consequently made powerful political enemies, whose attempts to discredit him were facilitated

Francis Dashwood, eleventh Baron Le Despencer (1708–1781), by Nathaniel Dance, 1776

by the manner in which he flaunted his lecherous proclivities.

Traveller and dilettante Dashwood was a contemporary of the elder Pitt at Eton College. Between January and September 1726 he made his first visit abroad, staying in France and then returning via Germany. From 1729 to 1731 and from 1739 to 1741 he was again in Italy, visiting Leghorn and the excavations at Herculaneum and staying in Florence and Rome, where he began a friendship with the philosopher and theologian Niccolini which lasted until the latter's death in 1769. Through him he met Montesquieu and other scholars and antiquaries. In 1733 Dashwood accompanied George, Lord Forbes, envoy-extraordinary, to St Petersburg, stopping *en route* at Copenhagen. His intelligent and discriminating diary of this expedition offers important first-hand descriptions of both capitals at this date.

Such travel further stimulated Dashwood's passionate interest in antiquity and the arts. In 1732 he took a leading role in founding the Dilettanti Society to promote a knowledge and understanding of classical art and taste in England. An active member for more than thirty-five years, he sat on nearly all the society's important committees, often acting as chairman, and was elected archmaster on 2 March 1746. He presented to the king various petitions when the society was seeking to acquire a permanent home. He was elected FRS in June 1746 and FSA in June 1769. He became a member of the Lincoln Club in the mid-1740s and of the Society for the Encouragement of Arts, Manufactures, and Commerce in 1754. He had connections with the Spalding Society and became vice-president of both the Foundling Hospital and the General Medical Asylum.

Dashwood's other pursuits were more dubious. In 1725 he joined the Beefsteak and Hellfire clubs and the 'Bucks' or 'Bloods', and in the mid-1740s he was a leading light of the Divan Club. Horace Walpole's testimony is not unprejudiced, but his memoirs record how on his travels Dashwood earned a 'European reputation for his pranks and adventures' as he 'roamed from court to court in search of notoriety' (Cust, 9). Dressed as a watchman, he secreted himself in the Sistine chapel before the penitential scourging ceremonies of holy week and emerged from the darkness at the most sacred part of the ceremony, lashing out severely with an English horsewhip. In Russia he 'masqueraded as Charles XII, and in that unsuitable character aspired to be the lover of Tsarina Anne' (ibid., 9). In 1742 George Knapton painted Dashwood's portrait for the Dilettanti, indecorously representing him as 'St Francis of Wycombe', holding a goblet inscribed 'Matri Sanctorum', and in an attitude of devotion before a figure of the Venus de' Medici. Unsurprisingly, Walpole denigrated the society in 1743 as 'a club for which the nominal qualification is having been to Italy, and the real one, being drunk'. Dashwood, he maintained, was 'seldom sober' the whole time he was in Italy (Walpole, *Corr.*, 18.211).

Entry into politics On his return to England in 1741 Dashwood determined to enter parliament. His brother-in-law Sir Robert Austen obligingly stood down for him at New Romney, where Henry Furnese supported him, and he served the borough until 1761. In parliament he followed Samuel Sandys, first Baron Sandys, becoming 'one of the most inveterate' of Robert Walpole's opponents (Walpole, *Corr.*, 17.249). Wounded family pride sharpened his hostility: in 1737 his maternal uncle John Fane, seventh earl of Westmorland and tenth Baron Le Despencer, had been dismissed from the army for supporting an increase in the prince of Wales's allowance.

Dashwood soon emerged as an able speaker and one of the most prominent independent members of the Commons. From the outset he was a regular member of committees on public works, and he introduced a bill providing for voluntary public works in order to relieve unemployment in 1747. However, his politics were considered suspect. Following Walpole's downfall in 1742 rumours circulated that Dashwood's delighted accounts of the ministry's death throes had reached the Pretender in Rome via an intermediary. His opposition to the prevailing political system continued unabated, and he supported moves to tax places and pensions and pushed for an inquiry into corruption. In February 1744 he spoke against a loyal address to the king on the threatened French invasion, causing grave offence by drawing unfortunate parallels with 1688: 'a weak, avaricious, narrow-minded Prince on the throne, a great part of the nation proscribed and forced into disaffection, the daily encroachments made upon the constitution—no wonder there was an unwillingness in the people to support the government' (Cobbett, *Parl. hist.*, 13, 1743–7, 647).

On 19 December 1745, at St George's, Hanover Square,

Dashwood married Sarah Ellys (*d.* 1769), the widow of Sir Richard *Ellys, third baronet (1682–1742), and the daughter and coheir of George Gould of Iver, Buckinghamshire. To Walpole she was 'a poor forlorn Presbyterian prude' (Walpole, *Corr.*, 19.224), but the marriage strengthened Dashwood's existing political interest in Lincolnshire and gained him access to Ellys's books, pictures, and antiquities.

Before the general election of 1747 Dashwood published an anonymous *Address*, essentially a country party political programme, that called for an end to corruption and exhorted voters to extract a pledge from candidates to repeal the Septennial Act, introduce a place bill, and establish a numerous and effective militia. Soon afterwards the last two aims were included in the terms for an alliance unsuccessfully offered to the tories by Frederick, prince of Wales, who used Dashwood as one of his intermediaries. In April 1749 the University of Oxford showed its approval of Dashwood's politics by conferring on him the degree of DCL at the opening ceremony of the Radcliffe Camera. Throughout the 1747 parliament Dashwood found himself courted as the leading member of a small group of independents, not least by Bubb Dodington, who was acting under Frederick's banner. The prince promised that at his accession Dashwood would become either treasurer of the navy or cofferer. Dashwood declined to take the bait and followed his own instincts. He once again raised his uncle's dismissal 'after much disclaiming of Jacobitism' (Walpole, *Memoirs of the Reign of George II*, 1.10). In January 1751 he was one of the few who opposed the burning of the Jacobite pamphlet *Constitutional Queries* and after Frederick's sudden death, on 21 March 1751, he criticized the proposed Regency Bill in the Commons.

At the start of the 1754 parliament Walpole reckoned Dashwood among the thirty best speakers in the Commons: 'a man who loved to know, and who cultivated a roughness of speech [and] affected to know no more than what he had learned from a very unadorned learning' (Walpole, *Memoirs of the Reign of George II*, 2.143). While Dodington was busily making his peace with the administration Dashwood continued to remain aloof, and he voted against the subsidy treaties on 13 November 1754. In December 1755 Henry Fox initially considered him a possibility for the Admiralty, but then offered the post of controller of the household, which Dashwood declined, explaining that he did not wish to compromise his opinions on constitutional and great national points.

Dashwood now marked himself out by his interest in the vexed question of the militia, which he saw in terms of patriotic self-defence. He had already been on the committee appointed in October 1745 to prepare a bill for the better regulation of the militia, and his papers contain a draft bill and two draft pamphlets on the subject. He spoke in favour of the two militia bills of 1756 and from 1757 until 1762 served as first colonel of the Buckinghamshire militia. In February 1757 he was also prominent in the unsuccessful attempts to save Admiral Byng. His feeling that 'at most he could impute only misjudgement to Mr. Byng' (Walpole, *Memoirs of the Reign of George II*, 2.328) led him to believe that the court martial had acted 'unjustly' (ibid., 312). This drew praise from Walpole, who noted that Dashwood was normally 'a man distinguished by no milkiness of temper' (ibid., 318).

In office In the years immediately preceding George III's accession, the royal favourite Bute courted Dashwood's support. He was now more receptive, believing that the new reign heralded a favourable change in the political climate. Bute therefore indicated to Newcastle that he would join him in government only if Dashwood and certain others were given office. Accordingly, Dashwood was appointed as treasurer of the chamber and privy councillor on 20 March 1761. At the general election Dodington and Bute now readily obliged Dashwood with a seat at Weymouth and Melcombe Regis. This extricated him from his problems at New Romney, where Furnese's death in 1756 had triggered a vicious struggle for control of the corporation between Edward Dering and Rose Fuller. Dashwood's attempt to remain impartial had irritated both sides, and the triumphant Derings took revenge by effectively driving him out of the borough.

In May 1762 Bute took over at the Treasury, choosing Dashwood as his chancellor of the exchequer. Although Dashwood declared that 'he knew nothing' of his new responsibilities (Harris, 'Parliamentary memorials', Malmesbury MSS, 16 June 1762), he instigated moves against fraud that foreshadowed the proposals of economical reformers in the early 1780s: enquiries were launched into the fees of revenue officials, the methods of obtaining contracts, and the gross and net produce of taxes. On 7 March 1763 Dashwood opened the first peacetime budget after the Seven Years' War. He proposed to fund a large floating ordnance and navy debt with 4 per cent annuities and to secure a loan of £3,500,000 by additional duties on both imported wine and cider and on domestic cider. However, his speech was poor. According to Walpole, he:

> performed so awkwardly, with so little intelligence or clearness, in so vulgar a tone and in such mean language, that he, who had been esteemed a plain country gentleman of good sense, said himself afterward: 'People will point at me, and cry: There goes the worst Chancellor of the Exchequer that ever appeared!' (Walpole, *Memoirs of the Reign of George III*, 1.198)

Informed contemporary opinion considered these measures sensible, but displaced old corps whigs and metropolitan radicals alike ferociously attacked them. Allegations of profiteering over the annuities were rife, but the domestic cider duty became the focus of the most severe storm of protest since Walpole's ill-fated excise scheme in 1733. In an attempt to defuse criticism from west country MPs, Dashwood unwisely altered his original proposal for an additional duty of 10s. per hogshead to be paid by the retailer to one of 4s. per hogshead to be paid by the maker. The poor were to receive exemptions, while those producing cider purely for their own household consumption would be permitted to pay 5s. per head composition. Administration and collection of the duty was to be in the hands of the excise department. The fact that officers

would have the right of entry into cider-makers' homes handed the government's opponents a spectacular propaganda gift: the scheme was unscrupulously portrayed as the first stage of a Machiavellian scheme of despotism. Wilkes eagerly devoted no. 43 of the *North Briton* to the issue. However, the ministry successfully rode out the storm and the tax received the royal assent on 8 April 1763. Bute, who had been determined for some months to stay in office only until peace was secured, now resigned. His successor, George Grenville, as a commoner, followed tradition by combining the positions of first lord of the Treasury and chancellor of the exchequer. A disappointed Dashwood therefore agreed for technical reasons to resign with Bute, receiving the sinecure keepership of the great wardrobe instead. The true reasons behind these ministerial changes were rapidly masked by gleeful opposition claims that Bute and Dashwood had been unnerved by the recent furore.

Dashwood's uncle John Fane had died on 26 August 1762, and the consequent abeyance of the English barony of Le Despencer was terminated in Dashwood's favour on 19 April 1763. He thus inherited Mereworth Castle, Maidstone, and was shortly afterwards appointed lord lieutenant of Buckinghamshire, in which capacity he served until his death. As eleventh Baron Le Despencer he regularly attended the House of Lords, but his interest in high politics began to wane and he rarely spoke in debate.

West Wycombe and the Medmenham monks Le Despencer generally supported Grenville's administration and in late 1763 joined in Lord Sandwich's denunciation of the *Essay on Woman*. This made him a prime target for the metropolitan radicals, who saw him as a hypocrite, and their attack soon escalated into one of the major scandals of the age. Long-established stories of his youthful escapades were matched by more recent rumours, but John Wilkes's first-hand knowledge of his entourage proved the devastating trump card. Since the 1740s Le Despencer had rented from Francis Duffield the former Cistercian abbey of Medmenham, situated on the banks of the Thames near Marlow and not far from West Wycombe. Wilkes is known to have visited on 21 June 1762, and even this full-blooded rake later confessed himself astonished and disgusted by what he witnessed. Le Despencer was now portrayed as a blaspheming, libidinous rake that had used the restored abbey to engage in black magic, outlandish orgies, and obscene parodies of the rites of Rome. The exposé began in the satirical print *The Saints of the Convent* (April 1763), which depicted him in a monkish gown raising a chalice to a naked Venus. The onslaught continued with Charles Churchill's *The Conference* (May 1763), the *Public Advertiser* (June 1763), Churchill's *The Candidate* (May 1764), Charles Johnstone's fanciful *Chrysal* (1760–65), and the *Town and Country Magazine* (1769). Even allowing for politically inspired exaggeration, there is abundant evidence to confirm the basic charge. About 1745 Le Despencer had founded the brotherhood of the knights of St Francis, or the Franciscans of Medmenham. The members included Lord Sandwich, Dodington, Thomas Potter, the son of the archbishop of Canterbury, and the poet Paul

Whitehead, who acted as secretary and steward. Their motto was 'love and friendship', and 'St Francis' emblazoned the grand entrance with the inscription 'Fay ce que voudras', copied from Rabelais's abbey of Thelème. He acted as grand master of the order, used a communion cup to pour out libations to heathen deities, and even administered the sacrament to a baboon. According to Wilkes, he had also positioned suggestive statues and thickets in the gardens in such a way that the initiated could enjoy the lewd imagery. To a sympathetic apologist they were simply 'a set of worthy, jolly fellows, happy disciples of Venus and Bacchus' (E. Thompson, *Life of Paul Whitehead*, 1777, xxxviii), but others considered the initiation ceremony 'subversive of all decency' (Wraxall, 1.348), while Le Despencer himself 'far exceeded in licentiousness of conduct any model exhibited since Charles II' (ibid., 2.18).

Shortly after his marriage Le Despencer had begun making extensive alterations to West Wycombe House to reflect his interest in Greek architecture. Nicholas Revett designed much of the work, and in September 1771 a jubilee fête was held in the park to celebrate the completion of his west portico. The remodelling by John Donowell of West Wycombe church in a picturesque Italianate style was completed in 1763. Superimposed on the tower was a golden ball made of copper. Shortly afterwards construction of a hexagonal mausoleum began on the hill at the east side of the church, the situation being carefully chosen for the sight available from the London road for High Wycombe. Dodington's ashes were the first to be placed in the mausoleum. In 1774 Le Despencer arranged an impressive ceremony for the deposit of a marble urn containing Whitehead's heart. Opponents insinuated that the church had more secular purposes. Churchill referred to:

> Temples which built aloft in air
> may serve for show, if not for prayer.
> (*The Poetical Works of Charles Churchill*, ed. W. Tooke, 2 vols., 1871, 2.87)

Wilkes meanwhile noted that it was 'built on the *top* of a hill for the convenience and devotion of the town at the *bottom* of it' (*Correspondence of … John Wilkes*, 3.57–9), and later he related how, before its completion, he and Churchill had joined Le Despencer inside the golden ball to drink punch (*Letters between the Duke of Grafton … and John Wilkes*, 1769, 42–3). Gossips saw this as evidence that the Medmenham excesses had found a new venue, and similar suggestions circulated about the prehistoric chalk caves hollowed out of West Wycombe Hill.

Ministerial changes and the Post Office In their ministerial negotiations with George III in the summer of 1765 the Rockingham whigs insisted on Le Despencer's dismissal. Newcastle's inaccurate reference on 29 June 1765 to 'Lord Bute's most intimate friend' (*A Narrative of the Changes*, 28) explains their revulsion. The king was so desperate to rid himself of Grenville that he reluctantly acquiesced, while acknowledging to Le Despencer his faithful and sincere service. In February 1766 Le Despencer opposed the Rockinghams over the repeal of the Stamp Act.

Following the formation of the Chatham administration in July 1766, the new ministry attempted to strengthen its support base. Accordingly, Le Despencer became joint postmaster-general in December 1766, a position he retained until his death. He remained aloof from parties and connections, but was on good terms with Bute and Chatham and gave general support to Grafton and North. His concern over the American crisis led him to draft a 'Plan of reconciliation between the two countries', which won Benjamin Franklin's praise in July 1770.

On 24 December 1766 Anthony Todd, secretary of the Post Office, reported to Bute Le Despencer's 'earnest desire to gain knowledge of the business' (Bute MSS), but his own domination of that institution allowed Le Despencer to remain in affable semi-retirement. Todd looked after Le Despencer's dependants and their promotion and in return received any required support for a series of reforms designed to improve both the speed and the safety of mail carriage. Le Despencer also championed the Post Office in its attempts to free itself from the claims of political interest.

Religion and final years Le Despencer was sympathetic to religious dissent and subscribed to the building of the Unitarian chapel in Essex Street in the Strand, which opened in September 1774. He was also interested in the controversy over subscription to the Thirty-Nine Articles and compiled *An Abridgement of the Book of Common Prayer*, which was printed on his private printing press at West Wycombe in 1773. Franklin contributed sections on the psalms and catechism and advised him to omit his description of the Old Testament as 'a Jewish book very curious' (Kemp, *Dashwood*, appx 3). Le Despencer none the less stated that the Old Testament was best left to private study because it did not teach Christ's doctrine. Throughout, he emphasized clarity, intelligibility, and brevity, the elimination of all Catholic remnants, and the unacceptability of tithe payments.

Lady Le Despencer had been in continuously poor health since 1763 and died on 19 January 1769, leaving no children. Her husband subsequently lived at West Wycombe with a Mrs Barry 'on the most friendly and affectionate terms' (Lee, 11), and a daughter, Rachel Fanny Antonina, was born about 1774. Within a few years Le Despencer succumbed to a 'tedious illness' (*GM*, 594); he died at West Wycombe on 11 December 1781 and was buried in his mausoleum seven days later. He was succeeded as third baronet by Sir John Dashwood-King (1716–1793), his half-brother from his father's third marriage, to Mary King. The barony of Le Despencer again fell into abeyance, but became the focus of a sharp family dispute. His daughter claimed that her father had secretly married Mrs Barry, but the papers proving this had been stolen. Meanwhile, his sister Rachel, the widow of Sir Robert Austen, third baronet, of Bexley, Kent, illegally assumed the title. On her death without heirs on 16 May 1788 the abeyance was terminated in favour of her cousin Thomas Stapleton (1766–1831), who became twelfth Baron Le Despencer.

PATRICK WOODLAND

Sources B. Kemp, *Sir Francis Dashwood: an eighteenth century independent* (1967) · R. R. Sedgwick, 'Dashwood, Sir Francis', HoP, *Commons, 1715–54* · B. Kemp, 'Dashwood, Sir Francis', HoP, *Commons, 1754–90* · H. Walpole, *Memoirs of the reign of King George the Second*, ed. Lord Holland [H. R. Fox], 2 vols. (1846) · H. Walpole, *Memoirs of the reign of King George the Third*, ed. G. F. R. Barker, 4 vols. (1894) · Walpole, *Corr.* · H. Walpole, 'Horace Walpole's journals of visits to country seats', *Walpole Society*, 16 (1927–8), 9–80 · *The correspondence of the late John Wilkes*, ed. J. Almon, 5 vols. (1805) · N. W. Wraxall, *Historical memoirs of my own time*, 2nd edn, 2 vols. (1815) · *A narrative of changes in the ministry, 1765–1767*, ed. M. Bateson, CS, new ser., 59 (1898) · *GM*, 1st ser., 51 (1781), 594 · R. F. A. Lee, *A vindication of Mrs. Lee's conduct* (1807) · 'Parliamentary memorials of James Harris's', Hants. RO, Malmesbury papers · Cardiff Central Library, Bute MSS · F. G. Stephens and M. D. George, eds., *Catalogue of prints and drawings in the British Museum, division 1: political and personal satires*, 4 (1883), pp. 306–8, no. 4072; pp. 309–12, no. 4075 · L. Cust and S. Colvin, eds., *History of the Society of Dilettanti* (1898) · C. Harcourt-Smith, *The Society of Dilettanti* (1932) · R. Fuller, *Hell Fire Francis* (1939) · D. McCormick, *The Hell-Fire club: the story of the amorous knights of Wycombe* (1958) · A. H. Plaisted, *The manor and parish records of Medmenham* (1925) · P. T. M. Woodland, 'The cider excise, 1763–1766', DPhil diss., U. Oxf., 1982 · *The political journal of George Bubb Dodington*, ed. J. Carswell and L. A. Dralle (1965) · GEC, *Peerage* · K. Ellis, *The Post Office in the eighteenth century: a study in administrative history* (1958) · P. H. Ditchfield, *Memorials of old Buckinghamshire* (1901) · *DNB* · *IGI* · Cobbett, *Parl. hist.*, 13.647

Archives BL, corresp., Egerton MSS 2136–2137 · Bodl. Oxf., corresp. and papers · Bucks. RLSS, papers relating to army and navy costs · CKS, original will and family accounts | American Philosophical Society, Philadelphia, Franklin MSS · BL, corresp. with earl of Liverpool, Add. MSS, 38200–38216, 38304–38308, *passim* · BL, Newcastle MSS · BL, letters to Wilkes, Add. MS 30867 · Bodl. Oxf., letters to Lord Guilford · Cardiff Central Library, Bute MSS · CKS, Fane MSS · Hants. RO, Malmesbury papers · Mount Stuart, Isle of Bute, Bute MSS · PRO, Chatham MSS, 3018 · S. Antiquaries, Lond., Dilettanti Society minute books and committee book

Likenesses J. Faber, mezzotint, 1739 (after A. Carpentier), BM, NPG · G. Knapton, oils, 1743, Brooks's Club, London, Society of Dilettanti · attrib. W. Hogarth, line engraving, 1760, BM, NPG · print, 1763, BM · attrib. N. Dance, oils, 1776, NPG · N. Dance, oils, 1776, priv. coll. [*see illus.*] · W. Hogarth, portrait; known to be in possession of Viscount Boyne in 1901 · Platt, line engraving (after W. Hogarth), BM, NPG · portrait; known to be at West Wycombe House in 1901 · portrait, repro. in Walpole, *Memoirs*, ed. Barker (1894), vol. 1, 204; known to be in possession of Viscount Dillon at Ditchley in 1901

Wealth at death extensive estates centred on West Wycombe, Buckinghamshire, and property holdings in Lincolnshire

Dashwood, George Henry (1801–1869), antiquary, son of James Dashwood (1740–1815), rector of Doddington, Cambridgeshire, and vicar of Long Sutton, Lincolnshire, and his wife, Sarah, daughter of the Revd David Lloyd LLD, was born at Downham Market, Norfolk, on 21 October 1801. His grandfather George Peyton Dashwood of Bury St Edmunds inherited Peyton Hall at Boxford in Suffolk. After five terms at Christ's College, Cambridge (1818–20), Dashwood migrated to Lincoln College, Oxford, where he graduated BA in 1824. The following year he proceeded MA and was ordained; he served his first curacy at Wellesbourne, Warwickshire. He was curate at Stow Bardolph, Norfolk, from 1840, and was presented to this rich living, combined with Wimbotsham, in 1852 by his friend Sir Thomas Hare, bt, whose Stow Hall muniments had already given Dashwood a taste for antiquarian study. He married Marianne (1800–1855), the daughter of W. H.

Turner and the widow of Dr Henry Job of the 13th light dragoons, but there were no children of the marriage.

In 1843 Dashwood exhibited a book of Elizabethan swan marks of the Ouse to the Society of Antiquaries, of which he was elected a fellow the following year. On his own press he printed for publication small editions of documents and engravings of seals he found at Stow Hall, all of local interest, and starting in 1845, wrote articles for the first six volumes of *Norfolk Archaeology*, the proceedings of the newly founded Norfolk and Norwich Archaeological Society. Marianne Dashwood died on 28 April 1855 and was buried in a vault in Stow Bardolph chancel three days later. In 1863 Dashwood promised the society *Pedes finium, or, Fines Respecting the County of Norfolk* from 1191, but Walter Rye found only sixteen pages extant when he completed the edition for publication in 1881. Of another later work by Dashwood, a selection of pedigrees from the Warwickshire visitation of 1682, only twelve copies were printed; there is no copy in the British Library. Dashwood made more impression by his editing for publication of about half of the earliest *Visitation of Norfolk* with many additions to the pedigrees. But it fell to others to complete the first volume (1878) and compile the whole of the second (1895), for Dashwood died on a visit to Captain W. E. G. Lytton Bulwer at Quebec House, East Dereham, on 9 February 1869. He was buried beside his wife at Stow Bardolph on 18 February. Bulwer, Dashwood's executor in all matters, led the team of writers who brought both volumes of the *Visitation* to fruition. Dashwood's substantial library formed a large part of a sale by Sotheby, Wilkinson, and Hodge in London, which ran for six days from the following 22 November. G. C. BOASE, *rev.* J. M. BLATCHLY

Sources preface, W. Harvey, *The visitation of Norfolk in the year 1563*, ed. G. H. Dashwood and others, 1 (1878) · *Register and Magazine of Biography* (April 1869), 310–12 · *Proceedings of the Society of Antiquaries of London*, 2nd ser., 4 (1867–70), 302–3 · *Report of the Norwich and Norfolk Archaeological Society* (1868–9), iii · Venn, *Alum. Cant.* · Foster, *Alum. Oxon.* · register of burials, archdeaconry of Norfolk, 1 May 1855 [wife's burial]

Archives Norfolk RO, corresp. and papers, incl. many of an antiquarian nature, MSS Bul. 4/321–342, 13/1–8, 16/238–241; 12637, 30 E4 · Norfolk RO, pedigrees, genealogical notes · priv. coll., extracts, genealogical notes, pedigrees, etc.

Wealth at death under £1500: probate, 10 April 1869, *CGPLA Eng. & Wales*

Dassier, Jacques-Antoine [James Anthony] (1715–1759), medallist, was born on 15 November 1715 in the place de la Madeleine, Geneva, the son of the medallist John (Jean) *Dassier (1676–1763). After early instruction from his father he went to Paris about 1732 for training under the goldsmith Thomas Germain. Four years later he travelled to Italy, where, in Rome, he executed a medal of Clement XII and then, in Turin, modelled a head of the king of Sardinia, from which he struck a medal on his return to Geneva. Following a period assisting his father he moved in 1740 to London, where on 9 April 1741 it was recorded that 'James Anthony Dassier is to be instructed and employed in graving at the Mint with an allowance of 80£ per an' (W. A. Shaw, *Calendar of Treasury Books and Papers, 1729–1745*, 5 vols., 1897–1903, vol. 4). In the same year George Vertue noted that he had published 'proposals for cutting several medals or Dies—the portraitures of famous men Living in England', the subscription being 4 guineas for thirteen medals (Vertue, *Note books*, 3.101). Among the first of those to be represented (along with Alexander Pope and the mathematician Abraham de Moivre) was the numismatist and antiquary Martin Folkes. Folkes had a connection with Dassier's father through his uncle and fellow numismatist, Archbishop William Wake, and his interest may indeed have prompted Dassier's scheme. As Vertue notes, the medal is 'done very like him—but was struck at Geneva. From the Die done here. because here is not engines allowd for that purpose. or because it is cheaper' (ibid.). Executed between 1740 and 1744, the complete series combines figures involved with the Royal Society and the Society of Antiquaries, including Sir Andrew Fountaine, with whig politicians such as Sir Robert Walpole, John Campbell, second duke of Argyll, and William Pultney, each with an obverse showing a head and shoulders in profile, 'done from the life … free and boldly cutt', and a simple reverse bearing only a legend (ibid., 3.104). These were perhaps the most accomplished medals produced in England during the eighteenth century. With their fluent modelling, suggesting momentary effects of light and drapery, they frequently resemble Roubiliac's busts of the same sitters, though Dassier's medals generally predate the marbles. The admiration of both sculptor and sitters for Dassier's work is evident from the way in which the socles of Roubiliac's busts of both Folkes and Fountaine reproduce the reverses of the medals. A further medal, of Frederick, prince of Wales, was produced outside this series.

While employed at the Royal Mint and producing medals such as these, Dassier evidently returned periodically to Geneva, although his precise commitments there are unclear. It was on one of these journeys that he visited Paris and executed from life a wax model of Montesquieu, who, despite his refusal to sit to painters, could not 'resist the burin of Dassier' (F. Mazerolle, *Revue Suisse de Numismatique*, 1895, 96). On 23 July 1756 he was engaged by Prince Galitzin, Russian ambassador in London, to take up a position at the St Petersburg mint, and on his return journey in 1759 he died at Copenhagen. However, a reference in the mint records of 20 February 1771 to Thomas Pingo being employed instead of Dassier suggests that he had left the mint fairly recently, so casting doubt on the death date of 1759. Whatever his date of death, there is no question that he was important in the history of the medal in England and in the sculptural portraiture of this period. Following the success of his father's medals of English monarchs and 'worthies', Dassier took advantage of the interest in medals in the mid-eighteenth century by producing examples that were unrivalled in England for their subtlety as portraits and their quality of finish. They continued to be admired for the rest of the century.

MALCOLM BAKER

Sources Vertue, *Note books*, 3.100–02 · H. Walpole, *Anecdotes of painting in England … collected by the late George Vertue, and now digested and published*, 4th edn, 5 vols. (1786) · L. Forrer, *Biographical dictionary of medallists* (1904), 511 · M. Baker, 'Rococo styles in eighteenth-century English sculpture', *Rococo: art and design in Hogarth's England*, ed. M. Snodin, 283–4 [exhibition catalogue, V&A, 1984] · T. Murdoch and others, *The quiet conquest: the Huguenots, 1685–1985*, 220 [exhibition catalogue, Museum of London, 1985] · W. Eisler, *The Dassiers of Geneva: 18th century European medallists*, 1: *Jean Dassier and sons: an artistic enterprise in Geneva, Switzerland and Europe, 1733–1759* (Geneva and Lausanne, 2002) [Société des amis du Musée d'art et d'histoire de Genève and Association des amis du Cabinet des médailles]

Archives Burgerbibliothek, Bern, A. Dassier and J. Dassier II, 'Mémoire abrégé de la vie de Jean Dassier et de Jacques-Antoine Dassier', MS Hist. Helv. III 189, fols. 132–9

Dassier, John [Jean] (1676–1763), medallist, was born on 17 August 1676 in the place de la Madeleine, Geneva, the son of Domaine Dassier (d. 1720), a silversmith and engraver to the Geneva mint. After learning die-sinking from his father, Dassier travelled to Paris to work with Jean Mauger and Norbert Roettiers. On his return to Geneva he was appointed assistant engraver at the mint on 23 June 1711. When his father died, in 1720, he was made chief engraver to the republic of Geneva, a post he held until his death, sharing it with his younger brother Paul (1681–1768). Although he executed his first medal for an academic prize in 1707, Dassier seems in the early part of his career to have been concerned largely with the cutting of dies for the Geneva coinage, along with the multiple production of watch-cases and boxes purportedly made by hand. Using dies engraved mainly by Jérôme Roussel, he executed a set of sixty counters (for use in a card game) with scenes from Ovid's *Metamorphoses*. But the production of those series of medals that were to secure his reputation as one of the outstanding medallists of the eighteenth century began only in 1723 with the seventy-three small medals of illustrious men from the century of Louis XIV, dedicated to Philippe d'Orléans. The drawings for most of these were executed by Dassier's cousin Jacques-Antoine Arlaud, a painter specializing in miniatures at the French regent's court. Two years later Dassier was commissioned by the Genevan professor of theology Jean-Alphonse Turrettini to make, in a less richly baroque manner, a set of twenty-four medals representing the protestant reformers from John Wycliffe to Calvin's successor, Theodore Beza. Most of these portraits were based on the woodcuts in Beza's *Icones* (1580). As a theologian dedicated to protestant unity, Turrettini had earlier elicited the support of William Wake, archbishop of Canterbury, who shared the Genevan divine's interest in numismatics. A set of the reformers was sent to Lambeth Palace by Dassier.

Following the enthusiastic reception by Wake of what was a far more ambitious series of medals than any struck in England, Dassier travelled there in the summer of 1728. He was, however, disappointed in his hopes of obtaining a post at the mint in London because of John Croker's position there, and by August 1728 had returned to Geneva. His second visit made in 1731 was more successful. Having being presented to Queen Caroline, perhaps through the good offices of Wake, Dassier set out proposals for a set of thirty-three medals of English sovereigns from William I to George II, to whom the series was dedicated. Based on engravings by George Vertue for Paul Rapin de Thoyras's *History of England*, these were advertised in the prospectus published in 1730 for purchase by subscription at 6 guineas for sets in copper and at 15 guineas for silver. During his second stay in England Dassier also planned, according to Vertue,

> to engrave many remarkable persons noted for great Actions in the government of this nation in Times passd. and learned men of all degrees lately or formerly or of the present time which he proposes to grave at his own expence. (Vertue, *Note books*, 3.51–2)

Medals of Milton, Bacon, and Selden were included in this set. Together these two medallic series belong to those series of historicizing portraits in different media that were being formulated at Stowe and elsewhere during the 1730s to represent figures from the national past.

On his return to Geneva, Dassier continued in his role of chief engraver and in 1738 became a member of the city's Council of Two Hundred. As well as supervising the minting of the Geneva coinage, he continued to produce medals, the most notable being a subscription series of sixty small medals representing scenes from Roman history, executed between 1740 and 1743; an *Explication* of these was published in Paris in 1778. Dassier died on 15 October 1763, leaving two sons, Antoine (1718–1780), who succeeded him at the Geneva mint, and the medallist Jacques-Antoine (James Anthony) *Dassier. His medals continued to be collected and esteemed later in the century, and some of his medals were restruck in England from Dassier's dies by Thomason. Along with his son Jacques-Antoine and Jean Varin, he was one of only three modern medallists to be mentioned in the entry 'graveur' in Diderot and d'Alembert's *Encyclopédie … des sciences, des arts et des métiers* (Paris, 1757): '[ils] sont digne d'être comptés parmi les plus célèbres *graveurs*' (p. 867).

MALCOLM BAKER

Sources Vertue, *Note books*, 3.52–3 · J. K. Füssli, *Geschichte der besten Künstler in der Schweiz*, 4 (Zürich, 1774) · G. E. von Haller, *Schweizerisches Münz- und Medaillenkabinet* (Bern, 1780–81) · H. Fatio, 'Les jetons représentant les hommes illustres de siècle de Louis XIV gravés en 1723 par Jean Dassier', *Revue suisse de numismatique*, 18 (1912), 202–13 · L. Forrer, *Biographical dictionary of medallists*, 1 (1904), 512 · T. Murdoch and others, *The quiet conquest: the Huguenots, 1685 to 1985* (1985), 218–21 [Museum of London exhibition catalogue] · W. Eisler, 'The medal and protestant diplomacy: Jean Dassier and his ecclesiastical patrons in Geneva and England, 1725–1731', *The Medal*, 39 (2001), 16–23 · W. Eisler, *The Dassiers of Geneva: 18th-century European medallists, 1700–1733*, 1: *Jean Dassier, medal engraver: Geneva, Paris and London* (Geneva and Lausanne, 2001) [Société des Amis du Musée d'Art et d'Histoire de Genève and Association des Amis du Cabinet des Médailles] · M. Baker, 'Jean Dassier: Geneva', *Burlington Magazine*, 144 (2002), 119–20

Archives Christ Church Oxf., MS Arch. W. Epist. 26/318–19, 31/198, 202

D'Assigny, Marius [Marie] (*bap.* **1643**, *d.* **1717**), author and translator, was baptized Marie at St Helier, Jersey, on 15 March 1643, the younger surviving son of Pierre *D'Assigny (*fl.* 1635–1660), the rector there, and of his second wife, Elisabeth or Elizabeth (*d.* 1652×4), daughter of Nathaniel *Marie, minister of the French church, Threadneedle Street, London. The family fled Jersey in November

1643, settling for a period in Norwich, before returning to Jersey, where Pierre D'Assigny became minister of St Martin's in 1652. 'After long and painful study in foreign universities' (Venn, *Alum. Cant.*), a period at Tangier as an army chaplain, and a year as vicar of Penrith, Cumberland (1667–8), in 1668 Marius D'Assigny was awarded the degree of BD at Cambridge.

Thereafter, during the course of a clerical career, D'Assigny published (as Marius D'Assigny, the version of his name apparently always adopted) a variety of works. *The Assurance of the Faithful, or, The Glorious Estate of the Saints in Heaven* (1670) was followed by a translation of the Jesuit Galtruchius or Gautruche's *L'histoire poétique* as *The poeticall histories … a compleat collection of all the stories necessary for a perfect understanding of the Greeke and Latine poets* (1671). Dedicated to Sir Orlando Bridgeman, the latter contained treatises on 'the Curiosities of old Rome' and the 'most remarkable Hieroglyphicks of Egypt' written by D'Assigny himself. Explaining his intent to render these stories 'fit for the perusal of judicious men, as well as of young students' (p. 6), he dismissed attempts to 'find in the ignorance of Paganism the knowledges of the Gospel' (p. 1v); rather, the heathen gods were 'devils or apostate angels' (p. 3v) and stories of them 'ingenious Fables, contrived by the Devil, and delivered to Poets to discredit Virtue' (p. 6).

Appointed vicar of Cutcombe, Somerset, in 1672, D'Assigny held the living for the next twenty-seven years. By this time he was married; a son, Samuel, was born in 1673 or 1674. In 1679 he published *The History of Tamerlan the Great*, his translation of a French work by the Sieur de Sainctyon. Prompted by the needs of his 'Countrey Neighbours, they being in a Wilderness, and at a distance from other like Books of Devotion', his *The Divine Art of Prayer* (1691) provided, in avowedly 'easie and plain' language, 'open to the apprehension of the Vulgar sort', prayers for various people and occasions. Dedicated to William and Mary, among more domestic concerns it remembered particularly the army, the fleet, and the fight for 'true Religion' against the forces of Antichrist.

The same year Samuel D'Assigny matriculated at Trinity College, Oxford, subsequently making a career in Ireland and publishing in Dublin, as 'a well-wisher to the Church of England', *An Antidote Against the Erroneous Opinions of some People* (1698), a rejection of double predestination. Meanwhile Marius D'Assigny celebrated the created soul and explored the bodily conditions affecting memory in his popular *The Art of Memory* (1697), 'a treatise useful for such as are to speak in publick', directed at young men aiming to serve in church and state and dedicated to 'the Young Students of Both Universities'. A complementary book of oratorical exercises, *Rhetorica Anglorum*, appeared in 1699, while in contrast two years later 'the late war in Flanders' inspired his *A History of the Earls and Earldom of Flanders* (1701), dedicated to the duke of Ormond. An Irish connection also underpinned his most successful work, a translation of Charles Drelincourt's *Les consolations contre les frayeurs de la mort*, undertaken at the request of Drelincourt's son Peter Drelincourt, dean of Armagh, published in 1701 as *The Christian's Defence Against the Fears of Death*, and reissued in many subsequent editions.

In 1702 D'Assigny became rector of Tidmarsh, Berkshire, and published his *Seasonable Advice to Protestant Non-Jurors*. Claiming to have been 'the first who writ … in Vindication of the Revolution and of the Reasonableness of the Oaths of Allegiance and Supremacy' (p. 33), he entered the lists again to persuade those still unreconciled to the government to join forces against the 'French Tyrant and Persecutor' (p. 23). Asserting the great obligations owed to William III, 'Deliverer of the Nation and Protector of our true Interests' (pp. 1, 8–9), D'Assigny poured scorn on the manner of James II's 'son's' birth in 1688 and on those who thought they might 'live quiet under the government of a Papist' (p. 12). Even 'Kings and Princes who have the clear Title and undoubted claim to the Dignity and Government, may render themselves unworthy, or dangerous … In such a case, 'tis no Injustice to remove them' (p. 19).

Having become vicar of Aveley, Essex, in 1706 D'Assigny turned his attention to other enemies of the Church of England. In *The Mystery of Anabaptism Unmask'd* and *The Divine Institution of Infant Baptism*, both published in 1708, he defended it against Robert Morgan 'and other the Principal Leaders of the Dipping Sect'. They 'may be good moral and well-meaning men' he conceded in the former, dedicated to Bishop Henry Compton of London, but they had abused toleration and struck at the whole ministerial order in God's church.

D'Assigny's final parish, from 1712, was Blackmore, Essex. He died on 14 November 1717 and was buried at Woodham Walton in the same county.

VIVIENNE LARMINIE

Sources Venn, *Alum. Cant.* · Foster, *Alum. Oxon.* · W. J. C. Moens, *The Walloons and their church at Norwich: their history and registers, 1565–1832*, Huguenot Society of London, 1 (1887–8), 233–5 · M. D'Assigny, *The poeticall histories* (1671) · M. D'Assigny, *The divine art of prayer* (1691) · M. D'Assigny, *The art of memory* (1697) · M. D'Assigny, *Seasonable advice to protestant non-jurors* (1702) · M. D'Assigny, *The mystery of Anabaptism unmask'd* (1708)

D'Assigny, Pierre (*fl.* 1635–1660), ejected Church of England minister, was described at his marriage as a native of Authon in Perche (in central France) and the son of the late Daniel D'Assigny. Nothing else is known of his life before his marriage: William Prynne's statement that he 'was late a zealous popish monk' who left his orders 'some say for incontinency' (Prynne, 42) is unsubstantiated. D'Assigny married Marguerite, daughter of Jacques Courtois, native of Valenciennes, at the French church, Threadneedle Street, London, in December 1635. She died within the year and he married again at Threadneedle Street, in December 1636; his second wife was Elisabeth or Elizabeth (*d.* 1652×4), the daughter of Nathaniel *Marie (1577–1642), minister there. Her brother, also Nathaniel, had been minister of St Clement, Jersey, in 1631–4, and it may have been that connection which led D'Assigny to Jersey.

D'Assigny, who was called to the ministry some time between his first and second marriages, became rector of St Helier, the town parish in Jersey, following the death of his predecessor on 14 July 1638. It is likely that, as Prynne claims, Sir Philippe De Carteret helped him secure this appointment, for which episcopal ordination was in theory required. Certainly De Carteret was godfather to D'Assigny's son Philippe, baptized at St Helier on 2 January 1639; Philippe and Marius *D'Assigny, baptized Marie at St Helier on 15 March 1643, were the only two of the four known children of the marriage to survive to adulthood. D'Assigny's good relations with De Carteret were not to last long, for D'Assigny soon became a leading member of the parliamentarian party in Jersey and his commitment to the parliamentarian cause was to shape the rest of his life. It is recorded in the St Helier registers that he fled with the rebels on 21 November 1643, the day on which the news of the royalist Captain George De Carteret's landing at Mont Orgueil reached the town of St Helier. On 15 October 1645 D'Assigny was condemned in his absence by the royal commissioners to be hanged.

D'Assigny went from Jersey to the French church at Norwich, which sided with the parliamentarian cause and deposed its pastor Pierre De Laune (a maternal uncle of D'Assigny's wife) in favour of D'Assigny, who seems to have had the unanimous support of the church. The meeting of the colloquy of the stranger churches in England in 1646 decided in favour of De Laune as the legitimate pastor of the church in Norwich. D'Assigny and his party refused to submit to the colloquy's judgment and the matter came before successive colloquy meetings in the following years, D'Assigny being repeatedly condemned. Only in June 1650 was the matter settled. The Norwich church recognized De Laune as its pastor and D'Assigny was forced to flee.

In 1652, after parliament had recovered Jersey, D'Assigny returned to the island and became rector of St Martin. The youngest child of his second marriage was baptized there on 9 May 1652. His wife died before 20 September 1654, when he married his third wife, Marguerite, daughter of Richard Nicolle and his wife, Susanne Mallet. They had three children baptized in the parish in the following years, one of whom died in infancy. At the Restoration D'Assigny was deprived of his functions as rector of St Martin and order given for the sequestration of the living, by letter dated July 1660 of the count of St Albans, governor of Jersey. It seems that he left Jersey then: nothing is known of his later life. A Jersey court record of 1674 implies that he was dead by then. His widow was buried at St Martin on 23 December 1688.

HELEN M. E. EVANS

Sources G. R. Balleine, *A biographical dictionary of Jersey*, [1] [1948] · *The registers of the French church, Threadneedle Street, London*, 2, ed. W. J. C. Moens, Huguenot Society of London, 13 (1899) · W. J. C. Moens, *The Walloons and their church at Norwich: their history and registers, 1565–1832*, Huguenot Society of London, 1 (1887–8) · Channel Islands Family History Society, transcripts of Jersey parish registers, Jersey Archive, Clarence Road, St Helier, Jersey, D/E/A · Channel Islands Family History Society, indices to Jersey parish registers, Société Jersiaise, St Helier, Jersey, Lord Coutanche Library · *Ile de Jersey: ordres du conseil et pièces analogues enregistrés à Jersey*, 1 (Jersey, 1897) · W. Prynne, *The lyar confounded* (1645) · *Journal de Jean*

Chevalier, ed. J. A. Messervy, 9 parts (1906–14) • B. Cottret, *The Huguenots in England: immigration and settlement, c.1550–1700* (1991)

Dastin, John (*fl. c.*1288–*c.*1334), alchemist, is a somewhat mysterious author, although a number of treatises have been assigned to him. He is set in time by one of these, addressed to Pope John XXII (*r.* 1316–34), and by two others, addressed to Cardinal Napoleon Orsini, cardinal deacon of St Adrian (1288–1342) and scion of the famous Roman Orsini family. The abundance of manuscripts bearing his name in Britain suggests that Dastin was a British alchemist.

Twelve different works attributed to John Dastin have been uncovered. Some of them were printed in seventeenth-century collections of alchemical writings by Zetzner and Manget and two have been edited in modern times, but the majority are accessible only in medieval manuscripts. Important collections of Dastin's works are to be found in Bodl. Oxf., MS Ashmole 1416 and BL, Sloane MS 2476. In some copies, however, the same works are also ascribed to such authors as Arnald de Villanova, Ramon Lull, and John of Damascus.

Judging from the number of extant manuscripts, Dastin's most important treatise is a *rosarius*, identified by the incipit 'Desiderabile desiderium, impretiabile pretium'. According to Thorndike, this rosary adheres to a new doctrine that the metals and the elixir are formed from combining 'quicksilver' with gold and silver, instead of with sulphur. The old theory held that the six known metals, gold, silver, tin, lead, copper, and iron, are composed of the two principles mercury and sulphur. William Newman has convincingly demonstrated that all proponents of this new 'mercury alone' theory (among whom was John Dastin) had been influenced by the *Summa perfectionis* of pseudo-Geber. The same theory, that only mercury is necessary for alchemical success in transmuting metals, is also prominent in two other works attributed to Dastin, the letter to John XXII, with the incipit 'Hoc est secretum secretorum impretiabile pretium opus verissimum et infallibile', and the *Libellus aureus* (incipit 'Testificatur ad credendum meditationum experimentum'). These might well be summaries of the rosary's main contentions, as Thorndike suggests. The *rosarius*, furthermore, gives a description of several alchemical processes, often veiled in allegories and figures, and with occasional analogies to human bodily functions, such as digestion.

Two other works which, according to Thorndike, bear a certain resemblance to the *rosarius* are the tracts addressed to Cardinal Orsini. One of these is usually called *Liber philosophiae* (incipit 'Scito igitur mi domine quod hec scientia'), whereas the other has been variously referred to as *Verbum abbreviatum*, *Liber de cognitione*, *De transmutatione metallorum*, and *Speculum secretum alkimiae*; its incipit is 'Converte ergo quadrangulum in rotundum'. These tracts, too, restrict themselves to mercury as the essential element for the production of metals and of the philosophers' stone; and both are further characterized by their frequent citations of authorities such as Aristotle, Plato, Hermes, al-Razi, Avicenna, and Geber. In particular,

the influence of Geber upon Dastin's views seems great and openly acknowledged.

In addition to the rosary opening 'Desiderabile desiderium', two others with different texts are ascribed to Dastin. One of them, with the incipit 'Sciendum itaque quod lapis philosophorum', mentions sulphur (called *kybrit*, derived from Arabic) as the father of mercury and of all liquefiable bodies. This view does not concur well with the theory, expressed in other works presumably by Dastin, that 'quicksilver' is the essential ingredient in alchemical transformations. Possibly the conflicting doctrines are the result of confusions with respect to the interpretation of the terms 'quicksilver', 'mercury', and 'sulphur', rather than of different authorship.

The *Super arte alcumistica* (incipit 'Deus igitur gloriosus cui sit laus') is a very brief treatise in which the author draws a parallel between the creation of the soul and the creation of the philosophers' stone. According to Theisen, this view of alchemy as a sacred activity is consistent with the attitude found in other works attributed to Dastin, in particular the *Epistola boni viri* (incipit 'Omne datum optimum'), extant in three different versions. Here Dastin presents alchemy as a discipline established 'to bring to perfection what is incomplete in the metals, and to preserve their perfection undiminished' (Theisen, 'John Dastin's letter', 85). The work is a compilation of authoritative quotations from, among others, Aristotle, Geber, al-Razi, Albebekar, Albumasar, al-Kindi, Avicenna, Euclid, and Plato. J. M. M. H. THIJSSEN

Sources L. Thorndike, *A history of magic and experimental science*, 8 vols. (1923–58), vol. 3, pp. 85–102 • G. Sarton, *Introduction to the history of science*, 3 (1947), 752–3 • C. H. Josten, 'The text of John Dastin's "Letter to Pope John XXII"', *Ambix*, 4 (1949–51), 34–51 [Lat. text with Eng. trans.] • W. Theisen, 'John Dastin's letter on the philosopher's stone', *Ambix*, 33 (1986), 78–87 [Lat. text with introduction and Eng. trans. of *Epistola boni viri*] • W. Theisen, 'John Dastin: the alchemist as co-creator', *Ambix*, 38 (1991), 73–8 • *The Summa perfectionis of Pseudo-Geber: a critical edition, translation and study*, ed. and trans. W. R. Newman (1991), 193–210 • D. W. Singer and A. Anderson, *Catalogue of Latin and vernacular alchemical manuscripts in Great Britain and Ireland, dating from before the XVI century*, 3 vols. (1928–31) • L. Thorndike and P. Kibre, *A catalogue of incipits of mediaeval scientific writings in Latin*, rev. edn (1963) • *Jo. Jacobi Mangeti … bibliotheca chemica curiosa*, 2 vols. (Geneva, 1702), vol. 2, pp. 119–33, 309–26 • L. Zetzner, *Theatrum chemicum*, [new edn] 6 vols. (1659–61), vol. 3 p. 659–65

D'Athequa, George (*d.* 1545), bishop of Llandaff, took his name from Athequa, west of Saragossa in Aragon. Nothing is known of his early life. A Dominican friar, he travelled to England, probably in 1516, to replace Fra Diego Fernandez as Katherine of Aragon's confessor and spiritual adviser. On 18 January 1517 Henry VIII nominated him for the see of Llandaff. He was formally provided in February and consecrated by the bishop of Hereford in St Paul's on 8 March. The temporalities were restored on 22 or 23 April.

It seems unlikely that D'Athequa's duties to Katherine allowed him to visit his diocese often, or perhaps ever. It was presumably ignorance which in 1521 led him to lease the episcopal manor of Nash to Howell Carne in perpetuity at a very low rent. In the 1520s Wolsey arranged for

D'Athequa's duties to be performed by a suffragan, John Smart, abbot of Wigmore and bishop of Pavada *in partibus*. The choice does not seem to have been a happy one, since Smart was accused of ordaining unworthy persons in return for money. In 1535 the absence of both bishop and archdeacon from Llandaff was said to have led to 'great ruin and decay in their mansions' (*LP Henry VIII*, vol. 9, no. 806).

D'Athequa attended Queen Katherine at the Field of Cloth of Gold in June 1520, and was among those who greeted Charles V at Canterbury in June 1522. Otherwise he is largely invisible until the time of the royal divorce. Made essential to Katherine by his ability to hear her confession in Spanish, he was one of the small number of servants permitted to join the queen in her exile from court, and travelled with her first to Ampthill, Bedfordshire, and then in July 1533 to Buckden, Huntingdonshire. For the next two and a half years he shared his mistress's virtual captivity and felt the effects of her estranged husband's considerable displeasure.

In mid-December 1533 Charles Brandon, duke of Suffolk, descended upon Buckden to demand that Katherine renounce her title as queen. When she refused and withdrew to her bedchamber, Suffolk had all her servants, including D'Athequa, locked up. After several days he relented somewhat and allowed the queen's confessor access to her, perhaps in the hope that he would persuade her to relent. When this ploy failed Suffolk left the damp and draughty palace, making it even less hospitable by removing furniture, hangings, and plate. He had dismissed several of Katherine's servants, but permitted D'Athequa to remain, despite Henry's instructions to the contrary—he justified himself to the king by assuring him that the confessor was 'the man of most simplicity, and will do little harm' (*LP Henry VIII*, vol. 6, no. 1541). He may have been reluctant to deny Katherine the comfort of being able to make her confession in her native tongue, or simply fearful of the likely public response to his doing so. In May 1534 Katherine understandably refused to take the oath demanded by the Act of Succession (it illegitimated her own daughter), and she and her household were transferred to Kimbolton manor. D'Athequa kept her company in this secluded and fortresslike house, remaining with her throughout her final illness. At 10 a.m. on 7 January 1536 he gave Katherine extreme unction; she died four hours later.

If D'Athequa mourned the death of the queen he had served for twenty years, he soon had troubles of his own to distract him. In November 1535 royal officials criticized the state of his diocese, and not least his own failure to preach the word of God to the people. As a result the revenues of the see were taken into the king's hands. This blow was followed up by a royal admonition, sent on the day of Katherine's death, that D'Athequa must make greater efforts to stop the preaching of sedition in his diocese. Well aware of Henry's disinclination if not to forget than certainly to forgive, in February 1536 D'Athequa attempted to flee England disguised as a sailor. Betrayed by a loquacious servant he was arrested and imprisoned in the Tower. But the imperial ambassador Chapuys made representations on the bishop's behalf, and in September obtained a passport for him to leave the country. Once back in Spain D'Athequa's loyal service to Queen Katherine was recognized by her nephew Charles V, who on 5 June 1538 made him bishop of Ampurias and Tempio. He died in possession of that see early in 1545.

LUKE MACMAHON

Sources P. G. Bietenholz, ed., *Contemporaries of Erasmus*, 3 vols. (Toronto, 1985) · *LP Henry VIII*, vols. 2–11 · G. Mattingly, *Catherine of Aragon* (1942) · F. Eubel, ed., *Hierarchia Catholica medii et recentioris aevi*, 6 vols. (1923), vol. 3 · *CSP Spain, 1509–25* · *Fasti Angl., 1300–1541*, [Welsh dioceses] · G. Williams, *The Welsh church from conquest to Reformation* (1962) · G. Williams, *Wales and the Reformation* (1997) · W. E. Wilkie, *The cardinal protectors of England* (1974)

Dathí mac Fiachrach. *See* Nath Í mac Fiachrach (*supp. d.* 445?).

Datta, Sukha Sagar [Sukhsagar] (1890–1967), medical practitioner and political activist, was born in Bengal, the youngest son in the family of three sons and two daughters of Dwijadas Datta (*b.* 1856), professor of agriculture, and his wife, Muktakeshi, daughter of a Mr Nandi. Dwijadas Datta had studied at Calcutta University and the Royal College of Agriculture, Cirencester: he attended the latter with a scholarship from the imperial government from 1886 to 1888. On his return to India he taught at Bethune College, Calcutta, and was then principal of Shibpore Engineering College, and a deputy magistrate. Later he wrote two books, *Landlordism in India* (1931) and *Peasant Proprietorship in India* (1933), in which he argued, from both Hindu and Islamic sources, that historically it was the cultivating peasant who was the true proprietor of land. He advocated the abolition of landlordism and its replacement by a system of peasant co-operatives. A convert in youth to Brahmo Samaj, he also published *Rig Veda Unveiled* (1934), in which he argued that 'true Christianity, true Islam and true Hinduism are in essence one' (p. 341).

Dwijadas Datta's second son, Ullaskar Datta (1885–1965), was a member in the early 1900s of the Juganter movement, which aimed to end British rule in India through violent means. On 2 May 1908 he and a number of associates were arrested for the murder in a bomb attack of two British ladies in Alipore, in an attempt on the life of an unpopular local magistrate, Mr Kingsford. Ullaskar Datta, who had made the bomb, was sentenced to death. On appeal his sentence was reduced to life imprisonment in the Andaman Islands; he was released after twelve years in a general amnesty.

Ullaskar Datta's involvement in what came to be known as the Alipore conspiracy case deeply affected the lives of the rest of his family. Dwijadas Datta (in whose house Ullaskar was said to have prepared explosives) was immediately dismissed from government service without a pension, though his pension was later restored. The eldest brother, Mohini Mohan Datta, had sent chemistry books to Ullaskar from the USA. Ullaskar had used them for preparing explosives and this implicated (albeit unwittingly) Mohini Mohan. As a consequence, he lost a promised government post and had to turn to business to support his family. Sukhsagar Datta's life was also transformed by his brother's actions. Still a teenager, he was at the time sharing a boarding-house with his brother. Fearing that the police would arrest him as well, his mother gave him some money, saying, 'Please go away to England. I do not wish to lose another son to the Raj' (Barot, 15). Datta arrived in London shortly afterwards.

In London, Datta enrolled at the London Tutorial College, where he met the writer David Garnett. The latter recalled Datta as 'a brown young man with a head of luxuriant black ringlets': he at first mistook him for a Madagascan (Garnett, 140). Datta also mixed with revolutionaries such as Vinayak Damodar Savarkar and Madan Lal Dhingra, who were committed to the violent overthrow of British rule in India. After Dhingra had assassinated Sir William Curzon Wyllie in 1909, the police closed down India House, the base of the India Home Rule Society, and shadowed all those associated with it, including Datta. Later Savarkar asked Datta to join Abdul Karim, who was resisting the Spanish occupation of Morocco. Borrowing a Winchester rifle from Garnett, Datta set off, but his rifle was impounded at Gibraltar, and he was unable to proceed further than Algiers. Not long after his return he ended his contact with Savarkar and others committed to violence. His brother's actions and their consequences had already, as Garnett noted, 'set [him] profoundly against terrorists and terrorism' (ibid.).

In 1910 or 1911 Datta met Ruby Sarah Elizabeth Young (1895–1977), daughter of John Young (1860–1932), dairyman, of Bristol, and his wife, Sarah Strange (1866–1949). She was brought up in a strict Seventh Day Adventist household. One of her sisters married a Jamaican, and eventually left Britain to live with him in Jamaica; another married Pastor Sammy Joyce, an Irishman who led the Seventh Day Adventist church in California. She and Datta married on 25 September 1911 at the Paddington register office, London. They had two sons, David and Albion Ajit Kumar. After their marriage they travelled to Milan, where Datta studied operatic singing with Maestro Sabatini while his wife worked for Fratelli Münster. A singing career seemed distant, however, while Ruby Datta became pregnant with the first of their two sons. They returned to the St Paul's area of Bristol, where they lived with and were supported by her parents.

Datta enrolled at Bristol's Merchant Venturers' Technical College about 1913 or 1914. He passed his matriculation examination in 1914 and then joined the University of Bristol medical school, where he qualified as a doctor on 22 October 1920. He joined Bristol General Hospital as a house physician in 1920 and then Southmead Infirmary in 1921, at a salary of £300 per annum. In 1922 he became senior medical officer at Manor Park Hospital, where he worked until he retired in 1956. He also volunteered his medical skills to St John Ambulance Brigade from 1937. He became surgeon of Fishponds ambulance division in 1949, a serving brother in 1951, and an officer brother in 1959. This marked his lifelong dedication to the brigade. During the war years he also played an important part in the civil defence programme in Bristol.

Like his brother Ullaskar, Datta also committed himself to the cause of Indian independence, but through less violent means. He believed that the British labour movement and the Labour Party represented that part of British society most likely to accept the idea of independent India. Socialist ideas attracted him, and he joined the Labour Party in 1926 both to advance socialist politics and to argue for India's independence. He became chair of Bristol North Labour Party in 1946 and was later chair of Bristol borough Labour Party. He also served as president of the Bristol Trades Council, and led the Co-operative Party as its first president.

Once the momentum for Indian independence gathered, Datta had an opportunity to promote the cause of Indian freedom. He succeeded in getting his local party to support a National Union of Railwaymen motion at the national conference of the Labour Party in 1944, calling on the government to consider granting self-rule to India as part and parcel of the fight against fascism, and urging the British authorities to release all imprisoned political leaders in order to assist the formation of an Indian national government. Datta seconded this motion. The conference chairman had referred to India as a 'vast prison house'. Datta said:

> When Labour stands at the threshold of power, the key to the unlocking of that prison house is lying on the floor of this conference. You, as men who stand by the faith which you profess, who stand by the brotherhood of men, irrespective of colour and race, you should take up that magic key, you have the power to unlock those gates. (*Labour Party Annual Report*, 185–9)

The motion was passed, and, with a Labour government in power, on 15 August 1947 India became independent.

Datta founded the Bristol Indian Association in 1947, to mark the birth of independent India. The association was launched at the Grand Hotel, Bristol, with both British and Indian supporters. In 1956, on his first visit to India after fifty years, Datta noted, 'Fifty years ago, the dream of a free Indian nation seemed to be just a cry of the heart. Here I am treading the soil of free India by the side of my wife' (private information). After a brief illness Datta died of heart failure at Southmead Hospital, Bristol, on 3 November 1967. He was survived by his wife, Ruby, and their two sons.

ROHIT BAROT

Sources S. Nandi, 'Datta, Ullaskar, 1885–1965', *Dictionary of national biography*, ed. S. P. Sen (1972–4) [India] · U. Datta, *Twelve years of prison life* (Calcutta, 1924) · D. Garnett, *The golden echo* (1953) · R. Barot, *Bristol and the Indian independence movement* (1988) · *Labour Party Annual Report* (1944), 185–9 · Ullaskar Datta's undated autobiographical notes (in Bengali), priv. coll. · Sukhsagar Datta's personal notes, priv. coll. · private information (2004) [David Datta and Dr Jyoti Berra] · m. cert. · d. cert.

Archives priv. coll., personal notes | priv. coll., Ullaskar Datta's autobiographical notes

Likenesses photographs, *c.*1907–1969, repro. in Barot, *Bristol* · photographs, *c.*1913, priv. coll.

Wealth at death £2899: probate, 14 Feb 1968, *CGPLA Eng. & Wales*

Daube, David (1909–1999), jurist, was born in Freiburg im Breisgau, in Baden, Germany, on 8 February 1909, the younger son of Jakob Daube (1875–1954), a wine merchant, and his wife, Selma, *née* Ascher, from Nördlingen.

Both parents were Orthodox Jews. Throughout his life he remained a loyal Badener and a loyal Jew, rigidly Orthodox in his youth and middle years, though with some relaxation in later life. The family was comfortably off. In Freiburg he attended the Berthold Gymnasium and studied law at Freiburg University. At a seminar organized by Fritz Pringsheim he met and became friendly with the octogenarian Otto Lenel. Lenel had revolutionized the study of Roman law by reconstructing the praetor's edict and fixing the original setting of the texts that form part of Justinian's sixth-century codification. Daube became expert in the Lenel method. He applied it, and insights derived from Hempel and from form criticism, to Roman, biblical, and rabbinic sources, and later to the New Testament. He qualified with distinction for a doctorate with Hempel at Göttingen in 1932 but, because it was on Old Testament law, his thesis could not be published in the Third Reich and the degree was not awarded until 1962. Besides his expertise in these areas, Daube's armoury included a dozen or more ancient and modern languages and a deep knowledge of classical, German, French, and English literature.

Daube had heard Hitler speak and was impressed by the menace he presented. When the Nazis came to power in 1933 Lenel, himself of Jewish stock, regretfully concurred in Daube's decision to leave, at least temporarily, for England. Daube left later that year with an introduction from Lenel to the Roman lawyer Herbert Felix Jolowicz in London and from Pringsheim to William Warwick Buckland, professor of civil law at Cambridge. This led to his working with Buckland for a doctorate on Roman law in Cambridge, which he obtained in 1936. With Buckland's sponsorship Daube taught Roman law at Cambridge first as a fellow of Gonville and Caius College from 1938 to 1946 and then, from 1946 to 1951, as a university lecturer. His English, rudimentary when he first arrived in England, became witty and idiomatic. From then on he wrote mainly in English, though in speech he retained a strong Baden accent. In 1936 he married Herta Aufsesser (b. 1914) in Munich. They had three sons: Jonathan (b. 1937), Benjamin (b. 1946), and Michael (b. 1948). With the help of Philip Grierson, a young fellow of Gonville and Caius College, and others he was able to arrange for his brother Benjamin and his own and his wife's parents to come to England in 1938.

Daube was briefly interned in 1940 but was soon released. He worked in London during the war on school and hospital evacuation. After the war he quickly resumed contact with most of his German colleagues, particularly his lifelong friend Wolfgang Kunkel, who had never compromised with Nazism. He helped to put the *Savigny Zeitschrift*, the most prestigious legal history periodical, on its feet again. In the 1940s, on account of his knowledge of Aramaic and the Talmud, he was invited to attend the New Testament seminar run by Charles Harold Dodd in Cambridge. It aroused in him an absorbing interest in the rabbinic background to Christianity and he learned to use the technique of form criticism. New Testament studies was the area in which he was to make his

most original contribution to scholarship, in his eyes also a contribution to Jewish–Christian relations. He reinterpreted many New Testament texts in the light of Talmudic scholarship. The Christian scriptures could be reappraised as a form of Jewish literature, New Testament Judaism.

After the war Daube and his wife became British subjects, and Daube retained his new nationality thereafter. In 1947 he published his first book, *Studies in Biblical Law*. Turned down for a chair of Roman law at Edinburgh, and refusing one at the Hebrew University of Jerusalem, he became professor of jurisprudence at Aberdeen in 1951 and regius professor of civil law at Oxford from 1955 to 1970. Like some other Jewish refugees, Daube helped to introduce new standards of scholarship to British universities. His most lasting contribution to Roman law was a long paper (1959), written in a sober German, that carried forward Lenel's work of restoring legal texts to their original setting. He was a learned and entertaining lecturer, and his pyrotechnics could captivate the most unlikely students. At the doctoral level his rigorous supervision fostered a school of researchers in both Jewish and Roman law. His pupils were devoted to him, and he in return was good at securing them posts, even if this involved overstating their merits. During his Oxford period he published many papers and three books: *Forms of Roman Legislation* (1956), *The New Testament and Rabbinic Judaism* (1956), his most substantial work, and the highly original *Roman Law: Linguistic, Social, and Philosophical Aspects* (1969). They sparkle with original insights, along with some mirages. His virtuosity extended to a talk on the origins of Humpty Dumpty: not an egg but a 'tortoise'—a siege engine used in the English civil war. He was a master of the pithy phrase.

Though now the most eminent Roman lawyer in Britain, Daube during the 1960s became restless. He grew disillusioned with Oxford and All Souls College, of which he was a fellow. The compulsory study of Roman law was being eroded. The climate did not, he claimed, suit his asthma. He was a 'rotten husband' (Jonathan Daube, funeral eulogy, Berkeley law faculty website), as he would have been the first to admit, and his divorce in 1964 was followed by bitter and protracted litigation. He travelled round the world and spent much time in California with Helen Smelser, *née* Margolis, whom he eventually married in 1986. Reinforcing his German links, he had a flat in Constance, where he was a visiting professor from 1966 to 1976. In 1970 he resigned the Oxford chair and from then until 1981 was professor in residence at Boalt Hall school of law, at the University of California, Berkeley, and joint director of the Robbins Hebraic and Roman law collections in the library there. He gave exciting and well-attended lectures, but spent most of his time, then and after retirement, studying and writing in a cramped room in the Boalt Library. He lived in a run-down area of North Beach, San Francisco.

Of Daube's books, only *The New Testament and Rabbinic Judaism* (1956) was lengthy and none of his writing was systematic. His essays—the word that best fits his favoured genre—nearly always began from a text or word and spread outwards to illuminate, often with panache, an area of human experience. Many had contemporary echoes: *Collaboration with Tyranny in Rabbinic Law* (1965), *Civil Disobedience in Antiquity* (1972), *Johann ben Beroqua and women's rights* (1982), *Appeasement and Resistance* (1987). Though apparently disjointed, the essays often centred on a recurring type, such as the Jewish collaborator Flavius Josephus. Many of his pieces were short, but together they mounted up. His collected works include not only two volumes of *Collected Studies in Roman Law* (1991) and a volume on Talmudic law (1992), but others on the New Testament and biblical law, along with a collection of miscellaneous pieces, *Varia*.

Daube received, and greatly enjoyed receiving, many honours. He was a fellow of the British and Bavarian academies. His range of learning was such that for his sixty-fifth birthday three Festschriften were published, one each on Jewish and Roman law and the New Testament. Cambridge, Paris, and Munich, among other universities, awarded him honorary degrees, but that conferred in 1990 by Aberdeen, where he held his first chair, gave him as much pleasure as any.

Daube liked to startle. It was not always easy to know how seriously to take what he said or wrote. He loved puzzles, chess, limericks, and dodges, such as the dodge of the high-born Roman lady who registered as a prostitute to avoid being punished for adultery. But despite a cover of playfulness, he was both deeply serious and unsure of ultimate truth. Even the pope had doubts, he said: he knew, because he had asked him. In California he affected a hippyish lifestyle. But though on the surface empathizing with rebellious students, he remained at core a meticulous German scholar. His timely emigration from the Third Reich bore fruit in his adopted countries. It gave them a fresh spurt in the study of Talmudic and Roman law and of the New Testament.

Tall, with hawklike eyes, jet-black hair (when young), and a waxen complexion, Daube looked the Jewish scholar that he was. A father who insisted on his children being taught Hebrew in German before breakfast was hardly an easy person to live with. He did not mean to be easy. But, though maddeningly unbusinesslike, he had a gift for friendship, entertained generously, and in later life established good relations with his children and grandchildren. Supported by his Boalt Hall colleagues he continued in his eighties to publish challenging articles. His last papers, published in 1994–5, were about Judas, the betrayer of Jesus, whose repentance, he argued, is to be taken seriously and whose suicide contemporary Judaism would not have condemned out of hand. After some years of ill health Daube died at Pleasant Hill Nursing Home, Pleasant Valley, California, on 24 February 1999. He was buried in Oakland cemetery, California. He was survived by his first wife, Herta, their three sons, and his second wife, Helen.   TONY HONORÉ

Sources A. R. Rodger [Lord Rodger of Earlsferry], 'David Daube', *Savigny Zeitschrift*, 118 (2001) · www.law.berkeley.edu/library/daube [incl. eulogies by Jonathan Daube, Michael Daube, and W. D. Davies, 'A gentle hawk'] · *WWW* · *The Scotsman* (10 March 1999) · *The Independent* (5 March 1999) · *The Guardian* (12 March 1999) · *The Times* (28 April 1999) · *Frankfurter Allgemeine Zeitung* (1 March 1999) · D. Nörr, *Nachruf, Bayerische Akademie der Wissenschaften* (1999), 264–70 · private information (2004) · personal knowledge (2004) · P. Stein, 'David Daube, 1909–1999', *PBA*, 111 (2000), 429–44
Archives Bodl. Oxf., corresp. · priv. coll., papers | Bodl. Oxf., corresp. relating to Society for the Protection of Science and Learning · U. Southampton L., corresp. with James Parkes
Likenesses photograph, repro. in *The Independent* · photograph, repro. in *The Guardian* · portrait, priv. coll.; copy, U. Aberdeen
Wealth at death a few hundred dollars

Daubeney family (*per. c.*1225–*c.*1510), gentry, of Somerset and Bedfordshire, came originally from Brittany, their name deriving from the town of Aubigné in the diocese of Rennes. By the 1220s, in addition to their Breton estates, the family held property in Lincolnshire, around South Ingleby. At some time before 1225, King Henry III granted the Somerset manor of South Petherton to Philip Daubeney, seigneur de Landal (*d.* 1236). This manor soon became their main English seat. In 1236 Philip died in the Holy Land, leaving as his heir a nephew, Sir Ralph Daubeney (*d.* 1292). Sir Ralph was in turn succeeded by his two sons: Sir Philip Daubeney (*d.* 1294) and **Elis Daubeney**, Lord Daubeney (*c.*1270–1305). Elis made two significant contributions to the family's interests. First, he determined that their attentions would focus on England rather than his own birthplace of Brittany, their primary sphere of influence hitherto; and in 1295 Edward I granted a charter naturalizing Elis and his heirs in perpetuity. Second, Sir Elis was the first member of the family to rise to a position of national prominence. After serving in Edward I's campaign against the Welsh rebel Madog ap Llywelyn in 1294–5, he received personal summonses to parliament until his death in 1305. He also took an active part in King Edward's campaigns against the Scots. He married Joan, with whom he had twin sons, **Sir Ralph Daubeney** (*c.*1304–1378) and Sir William Daubeney (*c.*1304–*c.*1372). On Sir Elis's death, the crown took possession of most of his lands during Ralph's minority, his Lincolnshire properties being assigned to Joan as her dower.

In 1326 Ralph Daubeney was granted livery of his family's English estates, while his brother, William, took possession of the Breton properties, becoming seigneur de Landal. Thereafter, these two spheres of Daubeney interest remained separate. Following the outbreak of hostilities with France in 1337, William's branch of the family ran into difficulties as a result of their English associations, and in 1373 Edward III granted Sir William's widow, Phillipa, £50 per annum until she recovered her Breton lands, which had been confiscated owing to her alleged English allegiance. Ralph, by contrast, had no such difficulties and went on to carve out a successful career. Like his father he served in the wars in Scotland, where he was knighted and appointed a knight banneret. At some time after 1330 he was taken prisoner by the Scots and was not released until October 1337. Despite this setback, Ralph resumed his career upon release and in February 1342 was admitted to the royal council, though he apparently never received an individual writ of summons to parliament. In 1346 he fought in the bishop of Durham's retinue at Crécy, and he subsequently took part in the successful siege of Calais. Ralph was married twice: his first wife was Alice, daughter of William *Montagu, second Lord Montagu, of Shepton Montague, Somerset (*d.* 1319), and his second was Katherine, daughter of Marmaduke (III) *Thwing, first Lord Thwing (*d.* 1323) [*see under* Thwing, Sir Robert (III) (*d.* 1245×57)].

Sir Ralph Daubeney was succeeded by **Sir Giles** [i] **Daubeney** (*c*.1333–1386), his son from his first marriage. Even before his father's death, Giles had begun building up his own estates, in 1357 purchasing the manors of Kempston, Bedfordshire, and Tottenham, Middlesex, for 200 marks from his uncle, Sir William Daubeney. These properties subsequently provided the descendants of Giles [i] with an important secondary sphere of influence, and in the years before his father's death Giles was active in Bedfordshire administration, serving as a justice of oyer and terminer there several times in the 1370s, and as sheriff in 1379–80. Thereafter, having received his inheritance in 1378, his interests returned to his native Somerset, and he served as MP from 1382 to 1384. He died in June 1386 at his manor of Barrington, near South Petherton. His commitment to his midland estates is, however, suggested by the fact that he was buried at Kempston.

If the Daubeneys' decline from the heights of influence which Sir Elis had scaled was relatively slow during the seventy years after his death, in subsequent decades it accelerated, largely owing to the minorities and early deaths which beset the family from the late fourteenth century. In 1358 Sir Giles [i] Daubeney had married Alianore, daughter of Sir Henry Willington of Umberleigh, Devon. The marriage produced a son, **Sir Giles** [ii] **Daubeney** (1370–1403), aged sixteen at his father's death. During his minority his lands were farmed by Margaret Courtenay, countess of Devon, while his marriage was granted to Thomas Lee, one of the king's esquires. In 1390 Giles [ii] was assigned £20 per annum from his lands for his maintenance, and at the end of 1391 he was granted livery. Over the following years he was active in Bedfordshire, where he served as sheriff in 1394–5 and again in 1400. He died in 1403 at Kempston, where he was buried. From his marriage to Margaret, daughter of Sir John Beauchamp (*d.* 1388?), Giles had two sons. The elder was **John Daubeney** (*c*.1394–1409), whose wardship the king granted to his consort, Joan of Navarre. John married Elizabeth, daughter of the Yorkshire knight Roger Scrope, but died in 1409 before he could produce any offspring. His heir was his younger brother, **Sir Giles** [iii] **Daubeney** (1399–1446).

By the time Giles [iii] Daubeney took possession of his inheritance, minorities had deprived his family of more than twenty years' estate income and prevented them from playing the active role in local and national affairs which, a century before, had enabled Sir Elis and Sir Ralph temporarily to elevate the Daubeneys above the county gentry. By these minorities they had also been denied the opportunity to benefit from royal patronage, or to profit in the land and marriage markets. Their position began to improve after Sir Giles [iii] took possession of the family lands in 1416. Within two years he was in France, and campaigned there until 1421, but was apparently not among the beneficiaries of the Lancastrian land settlement in Normandy and returned to England in order to enhance his existing interests. Most of his official activities were connected with Somerset, where he served as sheriff in 1426, MP in 1424–5 and 1429, and on a variety of *ad hoc* commissions from the late 1420s. He was also active in the administration of Bedfordshire (where he had been born), serving as sheriff there in 1431–2. He also expanded his estates. After the death of his first wife, Joan, daughter of Philip, Lord Darcy (*d.* 1399), Giles married Mary, daughter and coheir of Simon Leke of Cotham, Nottinghamshire, thereby acquiring the manors of Cotham and Hawton and tenements in Newark.

Upon his death in 1446, Sir Giles [iii] Daubeney was succeeded by his eldest son with his first wife, **Sir William Daubeney** (1424–1461), who followed his father in marrying an heiress, in his case Alice (*b.* 1432), daughter and coheir of John *Stourton (*d.* 1438) of Preston Plucknett, Somerset [*see under* Stourton family]. As a result of this marriage, considerable estates in Somerset, worth in excess of £80 per annum and including the manors of Yeovilton, Speckington, and Bridgehampton, came to the family. Having been knighted, William served as MP for Bedfordshire in 1448–9 and as sheriff of Cornwall in 1452–3, but does not appear to have been personally involved in the factional strife then besetting the government of Henry VI. Indeed, after 1453 Sir William performed no further official service, perhaps being content to keep his head below the parapet.

Sir William's son and heir was altogether less reticent, and raised the family's fortunes to their medieval pinnacle. Giles *Daubeney, first Baron Daubeney (1451/2–1508), was brought up a Yorkist and served Edward IV, but rebelled against Richard III in 1483 and fled to Brittany where he joined Henry Tudor. Having fought at Bosworth, he became one of Henry's closest associates and, through a series of grants, the dominant magnate in the southwest. In March 1486 Henry created him a baron. He served as a councillor, administrator, diplomat, and, from 1495, as lord chamberlain. Contemporary accusations of wavering loyalty during the western rebellion of 1497 (which he nevertheless helped to put down), and the fine imposed on him by the king in 1506, suggest that there were some strains in his relations with Henry. Nevertheless, on his death in May 1508 he was given a splendid funeral in Westminster Abbey, where alabaster effigies of him and his wife survive. He had married, by 1476, Elizabeth, daughter of John Arundel of Lanherne and his second wife, Katherine Chidiock. They had one daughter, Cecily, who married John Bourchier, Lord Fitzwarine, later second earl of Bath (*d.* 1539), and a son, Henry Daubeney, who was created earl of Bridgewater by Henry VIII.   Dominic Luckett

Sources *CPR* • *VCH Somerset* • *CClR* • PRO, C82 [warrants for the great seal] • PRO, E101 [Accounts various] • *RotP* • D. A. Luckett, 'Crown patronage and political morality in early Tudor England: the case of Giles, Lord Daubeny', *EngHR*, 110 (1995), 578–95 • R. E.

Horrey, *Richard III: a study of service* (1989) • J. Collinson, *The history and antiquities of the county of Somerset*, 3 vols. (1791) • King's bench, PRO, KB 27 [*coram rege* rolls] • PRO, SC I [ancient correspondence] • will, PRO, PROB 11/16, sig. 16 [Giles Daubeney]
Wealth at death over £2000: will, PRO, PROB 11/16, sig. 16 [Giles Daubeney]

Daubeney, Elis, Lord Daubeney (*c.*1270–1305). *See under* Daubeney family (*per. c.*1225–*c.*1510).

Daubeney, Sir Giles (*c.*1333–1386). *See under* Daubeney family (*per. c.*1225–*c.*1510).

Daubeney, Sir Giles (1370–1403). *See under* Daubeney family (*per. c.*1225–*c.*1510).

Daubeney, Sir Giles (1399–1446). *See under* Daubeney family (*per. c.*1225–*c.*1510).

Daubeney, Giles, first Baron Daubeney (1451/2–1508), administrator, soldier, and diplomat, was the elder son and heir of Sir William *Daubeney (1424–1461) [*see under* Daubeney family] of South Petherton, Somerset, and his wife, Alice (*b.* 1432), third daughter and coheir of John Stourton of Preston Plucknett, Somerset. Born on 1 June 1451 or 1452, Daubeney was made ward on 10 January 1461 to Sir Thomas Kyriell, a grant confirmed to Kyriell's widow, Cecily, in April 1461 and again in 1463. Daubeney had licence of entry on his father's lands on 25 August 1473 and soon became a successful courtier of Edward IV. He led a company of four men-at-arms and fifty archers on the French campaign of 1475 and was an esquire of the body by 12 July 1477 when appointed keeper of Petherton forest. Edward knighted him on 18 January 1478 and by 1480 he was a knight of the body. The king's confidence brought him local offices, as sheriff of Somerset and Dorset in 1474–5 and 1480–81 and of Devon in 1481–2, and as a JP for Somerset from 1475. It also inspired the confidence of others, as he was granted the constableships of Taunton and Bridgwater castles by Bishop Waynflete of Winchester and Cecily, duchess of York, in 1477 and 1483, admitted to Lincoln's Inn in 1478, and chosen knight of the shire for Somerset for the parliament of that year.

Daubeney continued to be appointed to local commissions under Edward V and Richard III, but like many of Edward IV's household men, and in company with a number of his relatives, he rebelled against Richard in October 1483. He may well have been plotting revolt as early as 20 August when he began to settle some of his lands jointly on himself and his wife, Elizabeth, whom he had married by 1476, the daughter of Sir John Arundel of Lanherne and his second wife, Katherine Chidiock. When his section of the revolt, centred on Salisbury, failed, he fled with six of his servants from Devon to Brittany in the company of John Cheyne and John Halwell. His lands were seized and granted away by Richard, who allowed Elizabeth an annuity of £40 for her keep. He was attainted in the parliament of 1484, but in 1485 he returned with Henry Tudor, fought at Bosworth, as deputy chamberlain helped the king to

Giles Daubeney, first Baron Daubeney (1451/2–1508), tomb effigy

dress on his coronation day, and had his attainder reversed.

Daubeney soon emerged as one of Henry's leading courtiers, councillors, and military commanders. At court he became master of the king's harthounds on 12 October 1485, attended on the king frequently, and succeeded Sir William Stanley as lord chamberlain in 1495. He was a regular attender at the king's council and was appointed joint master of the mint on 2 November 1485, a chamberlain of the receipt of the exchequer on 29 December 1487, and joint warden and chief justice of the king's forests south of Trent on 24 November 1493. On 7 March 1486 he was appointed lieutenant of Calais, and on 12 March he was created a baron, a rare honour in Henry's reign. By May 1487 he was also a knight of the Garter. In the early years of the reign he regularly spent time at Calais, and once led a small fleet against the king's enemies at sea.

In 1486 Daubeney negotiated at Calais with the ambassadors of Maximilian (*r.* 1486–1519), king of the Romans, and in 1489 led an expedition of some 1800 English troops to assist Maximilian against the Flemings and their French allies. On 13 June he attacked the Flemish siege lines outside Dixmude, wading through ditches in water up to his armpits to defeat the besiegers and capture many of their guns. In June 1492 he led negotiations with the French together with Bishop Fox, and later that year he accompanied the king to the siege of Boulogne. His part in the battle of Dixmude and the making and ratification of the treaty of Étaples with the French brought him pensions from Maximilian and Charles VIII of France (r. 1483–98) respectively.

In 1497 Daubeney was to have led a vanguard of 7000 men, 918 of them from his own retinue, into Scotland, but the invasion was aborted because of a major rebellion in the south-western counties, sparked by the heavy taxation levied for the war. Daubeney's absence and that of his troops enabled the revolt to take hold, but he may also have contributed to its provocation. Henry's favour brought him a steady flow of grants of land, wardships, and offices on the crown estates in Devon, Dorset, Hampshire, Wiltshire, and, above all, Somerset. As under Edward IV, such royal confidence attracted grants of pensions and offices from local landowners such as the bishops of Bath and Wells, Salisbury, and Winchester, and the earls of Devon and Northumberland. The king's favour also made Daubeney an influential patron at court for others in the west. In Somerset in particular his virtual monopoly of benefits in the king's gift left many of the gentry sufficiently discontented with Tudor rule to assist the rebel cause. At Blackheath on 17 June Daubeney helped to rout the rebel forces, but some contemporaries suggested that he had been reluctant to deal harshly with a movement comprising several of his neighbours and relations by marriage and even his own brother James Daubeney; reports that the rebels sought his mediation with the king and released him when he was wounded and captured during the fighting might reinforce such suspicions. None the less, Henry gave him command of the van of the army assembled in September to deal with Perkin Warbeck's renewal of the Cornish revolt. With it he took Taunton and relieved Exeter from rebel siege.

Daubeney considerably expanded his landed patrimony by purchase and royal gift. By his death he held lands in eight counties, and in his will he allocated income of £666 13s. 4d. to his wife's jointure and the payment of his debts. He also made careful provision for the marriage of his children. He bought the wardship of John Bourchier, Lord Fitzwarine, from Edward IV in 1480 and married him to his only daughter, Cecily. From Henry VII he sought consent for a marriage between his son and heir Henry, born in December 1493, and a daughter of Sir John Basset, for whom he had exerted great efforts to secure an inheritance which would pass to the couple. This marriage did not take place, but the arrangements Daubeney had made were to cause trouble between Henry and the Bassets in the next reign.

Daubeney remained influential in the last years of Henry VII's reign: Katherine of Aragon told her father that he was the man who could do most in private with the king. He was often at court, and made attendance there easier by securing a lease in 1505 of the manor of Hampton Court. In May 1508 he fell ill with a strangury; he made his will on the 19th and died on the 21st. In his will and on his deathbed he protested his loyalty to Henry, perhaps in some irritation at the harsh fine of £2000 and the surrender of his French pension imposed on him by the king in

1506 for claiming excessive payments for the Calais garrison. After a splendid funeral on 26 May, he was buried in St Paul's Chapel, Westminster Abbey, where alabaster effigies survive of him and his wife. She was alive in November 1510 when granted her son's wardship, but how long she survived thereafter is unclear. Daubeney was succeeded by his son Henry, who was later created earl of Bridgewater.　　　　　　　　　　　　　　S. J. GUNN

Sources GEC, *Peerage* · D. A. Luckett, 'Crown patronage and political morality in early Tudor England: the case of Giles, Lord Daubeny', *EngHR*, 110 (1995), 578–95 · S. J. Gunn, 'The courtiers of Henry VII', *EngHR*, 108 (1993), 23–49, esp. 28–30 · *Chancery records* · PRO, PROB 11/16/16 · R. Horrox, *Richard III, a study of service*, Cambridge Studies in Medieval Life and Thought, 4th ser., 11 (1989), 151, 159, 172, 262 · M. St C. Byrne, ed., *The Lisle letters*, 6 vols. (1981), vol. 4, pp. 1–11, 95–103 · C. L. Kingsford, ed., *Chronicles of London* (1905), 279 · I. Arthurson, 'The king's voyage into Scotland: the war that never was', *England in the fifteenth century*, ed. D. T. Williams (1987), 1–22 · R. Horrox and P. W. Hammond, eds., *British Library Harleian manuscript 433*, 1 (1979), 150, 277 · borough chamberlains' accounts, Canterbury RO, FA7 · BL, Stowe MS 440, fol. 78v · register Blythe, Wilts. & Swindon RO, fol. 43v · W. Waynflete, bishop's register, Hants. RO, Winchester diocesan records, 21M65/A1/14, vol. 2, fol. 39r–v · A. F. Sutton and P. W. Hammond, eds., *The coronation of Richard III: the extant documents* (1983) · B. André, *Historia regis Henrici septimi*, ed. J. Gairdner, Rolls Series, 10 (1858) · *An inventory of the historical monuments in London: Westminster Abbey*, Royal Commission on Historical Monuments (1924) · earl of Northumberland's receiver-general's accounts, 1488–9, Suffolk RO, Bury St Edmunds, Hengrave Hall MSS, Ac 449/E3/15.53/2.8
Likenesses alabaster tomb effigy, Westminster Abbey, St Paul's Chapel [*see illus.*]
Wealth at death £666 13s. 4d. left to wife and for payment of debts: will, PRO, PROB 11/16/16

Daubeney, Sir Henry Charles Barnston (1810–1903), army officer, born at Ripon, Yorkshire, on 19 December 1810, was eldest son of Lieutenant-General Henry Daubeney KH, and his first cousin, Elizabeth, daughter of Charles *Daubeny, archdeacon of Sarum. After education at Sandhurst he was commissioned ensign in the 55th foot (later 2nd battalion Border regiment) in 1829. He served in it for thirty years, until promoted colonel. In the Coorg campaign, in south India (1832–4), he served with his regiment with the northern column under Colonel Waugh; he was present at the assault of the stockade of Kissenhully, and at the attack on that of Soamwarpettah. There he was in charge of one of the two guns attached to the column, and he saved it from capture during the retreat. The British losses were three officers and forty-five men killed and 118 men wounded, but the raja of Coorg, who was opposing the British advance, was defeated and deposed on 10 April 1834.

Daubeney served with his regiment during the Chinese War of 1841–2, and as a captain commanded the light company at the repulse of the enemy's night attack at Chinhai (Zhenhai), and at the storm and capture of Chapu (Zhapu) (18 May 1842). He was on the staff as major of brigade to Major-General Schoedde at Wusang, Shanghai, and Chinkiang Fu (Zhenjiang fu), and was mentioned in dispatches. He was promoted brevet major on 23 December 1842, and was made CB on 24 December 1842.

Daubeney was promoted major (25 November 1845) and

went through the Crimean campaign of 1854. On 26 October 1854 he helped to repulse the sortie of the Russians from Sevastopol. At Inkerman, on 5 November 1854, Daubeney, at the head of thirty men of his regiment, made a flank charge; without firing a shot he forced his way through the attacking Russian column, compelling the enemy to fall back in confusion. He was commended in dispatches and was gazetted to a substantive lieutenant-colonelcy on 12 December 1854 for his services at Inkerman, but he declined a promotion which would have removed him from the seat of war and placed him on half pay, while his regiment was serving in the field. General Sir John Pennefather recommended him for the Victoria Cross, but being a regimental field officer he was held to be ineligible. He received the next year the reward for distinguished service, the Légion d'honneur, and the fourth class of the order of the Mejidiye. From 1858 to 1869 he was inspector of army clothing. Promoted major-general on 6 March 1868 and lieutenant general on 1 October 1877, he was made KCB on 30 May 1871, was appointed colonel of his regiment on 3 February 1879, became general on 4 March 1880, and was made GCB on 24 March 1884.

On his retirement in 1880 Daubeney resided at Osterley Lodge, Spring Grove, Isleworth, Middlesex, where he died on 17 January 1903. He was married three times: in 1840, to Amelia (d. 1857), only child of Samuel Davy Liptrap of Southampton, with whom he had two sons; in 1859 to Henrietta Anne (d. 1876), only daughter of Charles Jacomb of Upper Clapton, Middlesex; and in 1878 to Eliza, second daughter of Charles Carpenter of Brunswick Square, Brighton, who survived him.

H. M. VIBART, rev. JAMES LUNT

Sources Hart's Army List · Burke, Gen. GB · A. W. Kinglake, The invasion of the Crimea, [new edn], 6 (1877), 49, 336 · Fortescue, Brit. army, vol. 12 · E. G. Phythian-Adams, History of the Madras regiment (1952) · W. J. Wilson, ed., History of the Madras army, 4 (1888) · WWW · CGPLA Eng. & Wales (1903)

Archives Border Regiment, Carlisle, museum, commonplace book and diaries · LMA, family papers

Wealth at death £18,585 10s. 2d.: resworn probate, July 1903, CGPLA Eng. & Wales

Daubeney, John (c.1394–1409). See under Daubeney family (per. c.1225–c.1510).

Daubeney, Philip. See Aubigny, Philip d' (d. 1236).

Daubeney, Sir Ralph (c.1304–1378). See under Daubeney family (per. c.1225–c.1510).

Daubeney, Sir William (1424–1461). See under Daubeney family (per. c.1225–c.1510).

Daubeny, Charles (bap. 1745, d. 1827), Church of England clergyman and religious controversialist, was baptized on 16 August 1745 in Bristol, the second son of George Daubeny, a wealthy Bristol merchant. He was educated at a private school at Philip's Norton, Somerset, and from 1760 to 1762 at Winchester College, where despite a serious illness he became head boy. He matriculated from Oriel College, Oxford, on 17 December 1762 and gained an exhibition at New College, Oxford, in 1763, where he obtained a fellowship in 1774 after taking holy orders. He was

awarded the degree of BCL in 1773, and in 1822 obtained a DCL by a degree of the Oxford convocation.

Accompanied initially by his brother, the Revd James Daubeny of Stratton, Gloucestershire, Daubeny travelled widely in northern, central, and eastern Europe between 1770 and 1772, visiting Paris, Lausanne, Aix-en-Provence, the courts of Dresden and Berlin, and also German spas for medical reasons, on account of his poor health. His sojourn in Russia in 1771–2 proved to be a formative influence on his emerging high-churchmanship. He was introduced at court in St Petersburg through the medium of the Princess Dashkova, whose acquaintance he had made in Paris, and made a study of Orthodox theology and ecclesiology. He concluded that, while lacking the 'vital spirit of true religion', the Greek church was not as 'degraded' or corrupt as that of the Church of Rome. In 1773, shortly after his return to England, he was ordained deacon by Dr Robert Lowth, bishop of Oxford, and priest the following week by Bishop Richard Terrick of London. Daubeny vacated his New College fellowship in 1776, when he was offered the college living of North Bradley, Wiltshire, which, due to dilapidations, yielded him an average annual income of a mere £50. In 1784 he was appointed by Bishop Shute Barrington to the prebend of Minor Paris in Salisbury Cathedral, and in 1804 he was appointed archdeacon of Salisbury.

On 19 July 1778 Daubeny married Elizabeth (d. 1823), the eldest of three daughters of William George Barnston (d. 1784), banker, and his wife, Mary Sawbridge. The marriage took place in Bath at the house of Thomas Meade (1753–1845), who had married Daubeny's only sister, Mary (d. 1786), two years earlier. Daubeny and his wife lived in Clifton, Bristol, together with Elizabeth's unmarried sister Catherine, until the vicarage of North Bradley was made habitable. Daubeny later became embroiled in a bitter family feud with Meade, who after the death of his wife claimed that Daubeny had prevented him from marrying Catherine Barnston. A trial ensued, in which Meade was awarded costs against Daubeny; intemperate pamphlets were written on both sides and the opposing parties became irreconcilable after Catherine Barnston married Meade in 1792. Daubeny and his wife had two sons and one daughter.

Once Daubeny had moved to North Bradley he introduced weekday services at his church, raised the income of the living to above £180 per year, and supported a Sunday school. In 1790, while wintering in Bath, he began to promote the erection of a free church (with space for 1300 free sittings) for the local poor. His sermon in aid of the first free and open church in the country raised over £1200. The first stone of the new building, Christ Church, Walcot, was laid in 1795, and the church was opened and consecrated by Bishop Charles Moss of Bath and Wells in 1798. In 1808 Daubeny endowed an almshouse for four poor inhabitants of North Bradley and built a school at his own expense, and in 1817 he built a poorhouse in the parish. In 1822 he commenced plans for a new church at Road, in his parish. On 25 June 1823 the foundation stone was laid; the church was completed in the autumn of 1824 and consecrated by Bishop John Fisher of Salisbury on 2 September. The cost, with the endowment and parsonage, exceeded £13,000, of which Daubeny contributed nearly £4000.

In spite of his generous benefactions and the publication of *A Friendly and Affectionate Address to his Parishioners* (1785) Daubeny initially made himself unpopular in his parish, especially among dissenters, on account of his rigidly high-church principles. In 1785–6, in correspondence with Bishop Shute Barrington, he even contemplated an exchange of livings because of the intensity of dissenting hostility to him. His subsequent high-church publications were shaped mainly by the context of his parochial experience. A series of lectures and discourses on schism and the unity of the church, which he delivered from time to time to his parishioners at North Bradley, were published under the title *A Guide to the Church, in Several Discourses* (1798). This influential publication, along with a second volume, *An Appendix to the Guide to the Church* (1799), sealed his high-church credentials; both works, while winning him numerous Anglican admirers in the episcopal churches of Scotland and North America as well as in the Church of England, were warmly attacked by nonconformists. His high-churchmanship also found expression in *Lectures on the Church Catechism* (1788), originally delivered to the children of his Sunday school, in *Vindiciae ecclesiae Anglicanae* (1803), and most notably in *Reasons for supporting the Society for Promoting Christian Knowledge in preference to the new Bible Society* (1812), in which he warned against the latitudinarian protestant principle of private judgement in religious matters. Daubeny employed the high-church argument that the Bible needed to be rightly interpreted in order to guard against 'an almost continued state of agitation from every wind that blows' (C. Daubeny, *The Substance of a Discourse*, 1814, 4). He also opposed the Bible Society because of his perception that it promoted the aims of dissenters 'at the expense of the Establishment' (ibid., 23).

Daubeny was a conventionally complacent pre-Tractarian high-church upholder of the protestant constitution in church and state, who defended his repeated references to political themes, as in his 1807 archidiaconal charge, on the ground that it was necessarily 'interesting to a Protestant clergy' to be reminded of 'that happy connection between church and state to which we owe our present estimable establishment' (C. Daubeny, *A Charge*, 1807, 24). He regarded the established church as 'the most perfect specimen of primitive discipline in reformed Christendom' (C. Daubeny, *A Charge*, 1805, 12) and his numerous archidiaconal charges (published at regular intervals between 1805 and 1827) were imbued with high-church rhetoric and the dangers of 'lukewarmness' in defending the doctrine of the church.

The main focus of Daubeny's polemic was the dangers to the integrity of the establishment posed by the forces of protestant sectarianism and fanaticism. His strictures against 'Evangelical preaching', for being a revival of puritanism and presenting 'a mutilated sketch of the Gospel

system' (C. Daubeny, *Vindication*, 2), earned him evangelical and dissenting antipathy, and led to his being branded a 'doctrinal dissenter' from this quarter (Hill, *Reformation Truth Restored*, xvii). Daubeny was no less critical, especially in his later charges, of the threat from what he termed popery. In 1797 he had applauded the fall of papal Rome to Bonaparte's forces in apocalyptic terms, and he lauded the protestant reformers for effecting 'our deliverance from Popish thralldom, with all its baneful consequences' (C. Daubeny, *A Charge*, 1821, 10–11). His anti-Catholicism, no less than his antipathy to protestant dissent, was a reflection of his anti-latitudinarianism. Denying motives of political expediency he opposed Catholic emancipation on religious grounds, lamenting that the issue was debated without the idea being set forth 'that the Church of England constituted an integral branch of the constitution, or, that the Faith, which the Church has in her keeping, stood upon any broader ground than that of mere human opinion' (ibid., 14–15).

Daubeny's high-church principles and adherence to the 'branch theory' predisposed him to be sympathetic to the misfortunes of the unestablished Episcopal church in Scotland; contacts with its leading figures, such as Bishop John Skinner and Bishop William Abernethy Drummond, were promoted by the impact of Daubeny's *Guide to the Church* and Bishop Drummond's abridged version of that work (1799). The fruitful interaction was also reflected in Daubeny's authorship of *A Letter to the Earl of Kinnoul on the Subject of Ecclesiastical Unity*, which was annexed to *A Layman's Faith and Practice as a Member of the Episcopal Church of Scotland* (1801).

In later life Daubeny was described as 'above the middle height, erect, rather stout' and as 'manly in appearance', with 'a keen and penetrating eye'. Regarded by critics as a 'haughty dignitary' and 'high priest' (H. Daubeny, xlvii) he was handicapped by extreme nervousness, rigidity of manner, and 'constitutional shyness' (ibid., lii). His circle of private friends was small and he was vulnerable to domestic affliction, never having recovered from his wife's death in January 1823. George III favoured his preferment and Queen Charlotte approved of his sermons but his retiring personality and precarious health (in 1816 he suffered a paralytic stroke which affected his left side and impaired his speech) were the main reasons for his repeatedly turning down offers of a bishopric. His self-effacement, however, co-existed with a warm temper and a reputation as an acerbic controversialist. His private verdict on those with whom he disagreed could be severe; the mild-mannered bishop of London, Beilby Porteus, being described as 'neither sound nor honest' (Daubeny correspondence, B/5/14, C. Daubeny to John Bowdler, 27 Feb 1800). In public and in print his controversial temper sometimes got the better of his judgement. In the so-called Blagdon controversy with the popular Evangelical churchwoman Hannah More, to whom he referred as 'the great idol of half informed divines' (ibid., B/5/16, C. Daubeny to John Bowdler, 7 Nov 1800) he criticized her foundation of Sunday schools in the Somerset village of Blagdon for being 'schismatical' in tendency (C. Daubeny,

Letters to Mrs Hannah More on her Strictures on Female Education, 1799). Daubeny's attack on Hannah More, along with that on the historical reputation of the seventeenth-century puritan divine Richard Baxter, was greeted with dismay by liberal churchmen, one of whom claimed that 'Mr Daubeny was predestined, like the Wolf in Aesop, to pick a quarrel at all events, and afterwards to find a pretext, the best way he could' (*A Brief Confutation*, 13).

While hostile to what he termed enthusiasm in religion, Daubeny's private diaries and compilations of prayer manuals reveal a rich and vibrant spirituality rooted in the Caroline and nonjuring tradition of Anglican devotion; his favourite spiritual works included Jeremy Taylor's *Holy Living and Holy Dying*, Bishop Thomas Ken's *Manual for Winchester Scholars*, Bishop Thomas Wilson's *Sacra privata*, and the sermons of Bishop Lancelot Andrewes, a collection of which he edited and had published in 1821. Daubeny died on 10 July 1827, after experiencing chest pains; he left several thousands of pounds for charitable causes.   PETER B. NOCKLES

Sources H. Daubeny, 'Some account of the author's life and writing', in C. Daubeny, *Guide to the church*, 3rd edn, 2 vols. (1830), 1 · Daubeny corresp., University of Virginia, Charlottesville, Locker–Lampson collection · J. Overton, *Four letters to the editor of the Christian Observer* (1805) · T. J. Brown, *A letter to the Very Rev. Archdeacon Daubeny* (1826) · *A brief confutation of the Rev. Mr Daubney's strictures on Mr Richard Baxter in the appendix to his 'Guide to the church'* (1801) · R. Hill, *Reformation truth restored* (1800) · R. Hill, *Daubenism confuted and Martin Luther vindicated* (1800) · *A letter to the Rev. Charles Daubeny … on some passages contained in his 'Guide to the church' and his 'Letter to Mrs Hannah More'* (1799) · *DNB* · *Thomas had two wives. Taken from the diaries of Thomas Meade (1753–1845)* (1956) · C. Daubeny, *A vindication of the character of the pious and learned Bishop Bull, from the unqualified accusations brought against it by the archdeacon of Ely* (1827)

Archives LPL, letters and papers | Bodl. Oxf., corresp. with Thomas Burgess · College of William and Mary, Williamsburg, Virginia, letters to J. Boucher

Likenesses J. S. Agar, stipple, pubd 1828 (after C. Jagger), BM · engraving, repro. in C. Daubeny, *Guide to the church*, 3rd edn, 2 vols. (1830), frontispiece

Wealth at death several thousands of pounds

Daubeny, Charles Giles Bridle (1795–1867), chemist and botanist, was born at Stratton, Gloucestershire, on 11 February 1795, the third and youngest son of the Revd James Daubeny, rector of Stratton, and of Helena, third daughter of Andrew Daubeny of Bristol. From Winchester College (1808–10) he won a scholarship to Magdalen College, Oxford. He was awarded a BA in 1814 and in 1815 won the chancellor's prize for the Latin essay. Daubeny's curiosity led him to attend chemistry and mineralogy lectures by John Kidd, and geology lectures by the charismatic William Buckland; they inspired him. In 1815 Magdalen offered him a fellowship, but Daubeny had decided to avoid the church, and, without means, needed a livelihood. In 1815–18 he studied medicine in Edinburgh, where he followed the geological controversy between Huttonians and the Wernerians.

Daubeny graduated a BM of Oxford in 1818 and gained his MD in 1821. In 1819 he travelled through France and his report on the volcanic region of the Auvergne was noted by the London savants. Further research led to his publication of *A Description of Active and Extinct Volcanoes* in 1826, a detailed exposition of the chemical theory of volcanic action earlier postulated by Davy, a description upon which Daubeny's fame as a chemist chiefly depends.

Academic scientist In 1820 Daubeny sought and was elected to the nominal office of Magdalen's praelector of natural philosophy. As a fellow he had a college room and small income. He practised medicine at the Radcliffe Infirmary, but did not enjoy it. In 1822 Kidd secured Daubeny's election to the prestigious but not lucrative Aldrichian chair of chemistry; at that time he studied the chemical composition of mineral waters for the information they could reveal about natural earth processes, and he later reported on the current state of knowledge of mineral and thermal waters for the British Association for the Advancement of Science (1836–7). In 1829 Daubeny made the very unusual decision to follow the example of James Bradley and Thomas Hornsby and make a career as an academic scientist. He resigned his position at the infirmary so that he could attend the Geneva lectures of Augustin de Candolle, the Swiss botanical authority with whom he developed a close friendship.

Daubeny knew that George Williams, the professor of botany at Oxford, was ailing, and that Sibthorp's intended endowment of a new chair of rural economy would be held concurrently by his successor. The electors were the Royal College of Physicians, of which, as an MD, Daubeny was a fellow; his botanical study in Geneva then London qualified him as a candidate. His important paper, 'The degree of selection exercised by plants with regard to the earthy constituents presented to their absorbing surfaces', in the *Transactions of the Linnean Society*, enabled him to lobby the electors. In 1834 he was appointed to the Sherardian chair of botany (which he held in addition to the chemistry chair), and moved to the Physic Garden where he lived for the rest of his life. During his occupancy, the garden was transformed, largely at his expense, and opened to the public. In 1840 Daubeny was duly appointed to the Sibthorpian chair of rural economy, and gained the stipend of £200. As he explained at his 1834 inaugural lecture, only the combined income enabled him to devote himself to teaching the mutual relations of the several departments of natural knowledge.

It took Daubeny twenty-eight years to break chemistry free of the medical incubus. *Volcanoes* made his international reputation. Then by championing John Dalton's atomic theory he insisted that Oxford acknowledge the utility and intellectual rigour of chemistry, and its potential to link the sciences. He lectured constantly so as to influence convocation, and enabled his students to make practical experiments; meanwhile as a benefactor, he applied half his income to improving facilities. Then as soon as government legislation in 1854 compelled Magdalen to increase the praelectorship stipend to £250, Daubeny resigned the chemistry chair to make it available to new talent, which made it a lever on the university to provide properly at the new university museum then being planned.

Botanical research There is a strong chemical underpinning to the geological and botanical work for which Daubeny is particularly noted, well illustrated in the important research that he undertook into plant growth and soil analysis. He investigated the reasons why the continuous growth of crops on the same ground brought about a diminution of yield (which necessitated crop rotation) by means of a series of controlled plot experiments. In the 1830s it was widely held that the superiority of rotation over the continuous growth of the same crop was accounted for by toxic secretions from plant roots, a theory that was promulgated by Macaire of Geneva, who was himself strongly influenced by Candolle. Daubeny's research, the subject of his 1845 Bakerian lecture, led to a rejection of that explanation and instead directed attention to the rate of removal of essential plant nutrients in the course of plant growth. He also made the important distinction between available and unavailable plant nutrients, which was a highly significant contribution to the developing specialization of agricultural science. He contributed to the early volumes of the *Journal of the Royal Agricultural Society of England* on the links between science and agriculture, and was an advocate of a formal system of agricultural education. Much of his advice was adopted in creating Cirencester College in 1845. He was one of the few pioneers of agricultural science in Britain who researched independently of the leading agricultural societies or the Rothamsted research station that had been established by J. B. Lawes, who had attended Daubeny's chemistry lectures in the late 1830s. Daubeny was a strong advocate of the ideas of Justus von Liebig (1803–1873) as was demonstrated in his 1856 presidential address to the British Association in which he presented Liebig's view that soil organic matter had little importance for plant nutrition and that plants would obtain all their nitrogen requirements from the atmosphere if the soil contained sufficient minerals. Lawes's field experiments on the value of nitrogenous fertilizers had by this time helped to discredit Liebig's 'mineral theory'; characteristically, Daubeny attempted to reconcile the two opposed viewpoints.

Daubeny served on the botanical committee of the British Association and his other botanical work included an investigation of the process by which plant roots absorb nutrients, and the distribution of potash and phosphates in fruit and leaves. His 'Essay on the action of light upon plants and of plants on the atmosphere' (*PTRS*, 1836) was very influential. In 1855 Daubeny published a paper, 'On the influence of the lower vegetable organisms in the production of epidemics', which is a statement of the fungal theory of epidemics. It was perceptive in that, predating the science of microbiology, it gave reasons for believing that the organisms which cause disease are extremely minute. Daubeny's experimental plot, the basis for his rural economy lectures, was purchased and entirely supported by his own funds. He made the botanic garden (as he had renamed the Physic Garden) the leading centre for the study of botanical and vegetable physiology. Following the publication of Darwin's *Origin of Species*, Daubeny gave him strong support with a paper on the sexuality of plants which he gave in Oxford to the British Association in 1860.

Daubeny was elected a fellow of the Royal Society in 1827, and was a member of its dining club in 1841–64; he was a founder of the Chemical Society in 1841, and its president in 1853, and was a member of the Royal Irish Academy and a foreign associate of the Academy of Science of Munich. He was one of the first members of the British Association, and participated in its inaugural meeting in 1831; his spontaneous initiative brought the association to Oxford the following year, and its return in 1847 helped to demonstrate the increasing value put on experimental science in the university, largely as the result of Daubeny's own efforts.

Although not now remembered for his original experimental scientific work, Daubeny published some eighty-one scientific papers. Apart from *Volcanoes* (expanded edn, 1848), his significant output included *An Introduction to Atomic Theory* (1831 and 1850), *Lectures on Roman Husbandry* (1857), *Lectures on Climate* (1863), *Trees and Shrubs of the Ancients* (1865), and reprints of his own papers in *Miscellanies on Scientific and Literary Subjects* (2 vols., 1867).

Reforming education Daubeny is characterized principally by his lifelong zeal for reforming the Oxford University curriculum. He did not deny the benefit of training in classical and logical studies, but knew that Edinburgh, London, Paris, and Geneva led Oxford in natural sciences. In his 1822 inaugural lecture as professor of chemistry, at a time when there was no British Academy, when the Royal Society was unreformed, and when there were no natural history societies, museums, or public lectures to any but registered students, he made the fanciful proposal that natural science should be included among the ordinary studies for all undergraduates. He argued relentlessly that elementary science was indispensable to a liberal education.

Daubeny had suggested in 1825, and by 1847 was chiefly responsible for, a new effort to build a museum to house the six professors of natural knowledge, founded on the ideal of unity of knowledge, and an examined status for science. It was that ideal rather than his own preference for specialization which in 1847 young Henry Acland took up as the museum cause. In 1848 Daubeny, Robert Walker, and Acland pressed for the establishment of an honour school in natural science, and Daubeny defined the detailed framework of the statute of 1850. It gradually dawned on a reluctant convocation that the statute made the museum a necessity, and by 1860 the University Museum in Parks Road was built. But Daubeny knew that effectiveness depended on involving college tutors in encouraging their students to attend elementary courses in 'chemical physics' as distinct from professorial advanced lectures for those who would take a physical science school. In 1865 he was still arguing for it against his old friend the provost of Oriel by public letters. A letter of Daubeny's to *The Times* (24 February 1864) helped to bring about a further liberalization of the university regulations regarding prescribed study requirements to make natural science a credible option, though the classicists managed to circumscribe its effectiveness. That he was able to do this was a reflection of the fact that Daubeny was not a radical *per se* but part of the university 'establishment', and viewed science as a complement to literary and classical studies in which he was himself well versed. Similarly, although he was interested in theological questions he viewed the study of science as being entirely compatible with established religious orthodoxy.

The Daubeny Laboratory Daubeny's professorial lectures in chemistry were delivered in the dismal basement laboratory of the old Ashmolean Museum, which was very outdated. When the university would not provide a modern chemistry lecture room and laboratory, Daubeny in 1848 built one to house his extensive geological and chemical collections at his own expense beside the botanic garden, and opened it to all students.

Short in stature, rather rotund with age, Daubeny retained a mischievous humour and a versatile intellect ever open to new ideas and to act upon them. His lectures were full of ingenuity but his lecturing style appears to have been mildly eccentric and his character has been termed almost Pickwickian in nature. Generous and hospitable, kindly to juniors, always involved in college matters, his personal qualities enabled him to persuade 'as no mere man of science could have done' (Baxter, 6). In later years Daubeny suffered from increasing ill health which led him to spend part of the winters in Torquay. There he took close interest in the climate and atmospheric conditions of the resort and one of his last public addresses was in 1865 as president of the Devonshire Association for the Advancement of Science, Literature, and Art. Daubeny died on 13 December 1867 at the botanic garden after a few weeks' illness. A member of Magdalen for fifty-seven years, and fellow for fifty-two, he never married. He was buried in a vault in front of Magdalen's chapel in order to meet his wish not to be separated in death from the institution that had been central to his life and work.

Before his death Daubeny ordered his affairs. He republished his scientific papers, but apparently destroyed all personal correspondence except a collection of autograph letters. In 1861 he catalogued his historical and modern apparatus worth £3000, and his geological specimens, and left them to the college along with endowment for a curator's stipend. (Robert T. Gunther later saved the collection in his new Museum of the History of Science.) Daubeny's old wines, pictures, monkeys and cage, and other effects were put to auction.

Daubeny spent his life eroding active opposition, passive indifference, and incredulous obstinacy in Oxford. His legacies were his role in founding the museum, the school of natural science, and his influence upon science at Magdalen. He and Chapman led a revolution from the advanced base of the Daubeny Laboratory and its extension; fourteen subjects at different levels were taught or researched for varying periods there by at least twenty-six individuals between 1848 and 1929. Through his influence scientific scholarships were started at Magdalen: his successors, Edward Chapman and J. J. Manley, also left bequests to further scientific education in the college. The

tradition Daubeny started produced a galaxy of Magdalen talent before 1939—Tizard, Florey, J. Z. Young, and Medawar.   NICHOLAS GODDARD

Sources [J. Phillips], *PRS*, 17 (1868–9), lxxiv–lxxx · *GM*, 4th ser., 5 (1868), 108–9 · E. J. Russell, *A history of agricultural science in Great Britain, 1620–1954* (1966), 86–8, 136–42 · R. T. Günther, *A history of the Daubeny Laboratory, Magdalen College Oxford* (1904) · D. R. Oldroyd and D. W. Hutchings, 'The chemical lectures at Oxford, 1822–1854, of Charles Daubeny', *Notes and Records of the Royal Society*, 33 (1978–9), 217–59 · N. A. Rupke, 'Oxford's scientific awakening and the role of geology', *Hist. U. Oxf.* 6: *19th-cent. Oxf.*, 543–62 · R. Fox, 'The University Museum and Oxford science, 1850–1880', *Hist. U. Oxf.* 6: *19th-cent. Oxf.*, 641–91 · R. Hutchins, 'Charles Daubeny, 1795–1867: the bicentenary of Magdalen's first modern scientist', *Magdalen College Record* (1995), 81–92 · N. I. Miller, 'Chemistry for gentlemen: Charles Daubeny and the role of a chemistry education at Oxford, 1800–1867', pt two chemistry thesis, U. Oxf., 1986, MHS Oxf., MS Museum B09 · A. P. Willsher, 'Daubeny and the development of the chemistry school in Oxford, 1822–1867', pt two chemistry thesis, U. Oxf., 1961, Magd. Oxf., MS 392 (B) · W. H. Baxter, 'Dr Daubeny', notebook collection, 1867, U. Oxf., department of plant sciences, MS Sherard 412 · C. G. B. Daubeny, *Inaugural lecture on the study of chemistry, read at the Ashmolean Museum, 2nd November 1822* (1823) · C. G. B. Daubeny, *An inaugural lecture on the study of botany, read at the Physic Garden, May 1 1834* (1834)

Archives Bodl. Oxf., diaries, journals · Magd. Oxf., commonplace book I and II, MS 377 · Magd. Oxf., letters, MS 400 · Magd. Oxf., register of lectures, MSS 393–394 · Oxf. U. Mus. NH, notes relating to volcanoes · U. Oxf., department of plant sciences, diaries, journals, notebooks, and papers | Bodl. Oxf., letters to Thomas Burgess · RBG Kew, letters to Sir William Hooker · RS, corresp. with Sir J. F. W. Herschel · U. Newcastle, Robinson L., letters to Sir Walter Trevelyan

Likenesses lithograph, c.1819 (as geologist), repro. in *Hist. U. Oxf.* 6: *19th-cent. Oxf.*, no. 33 · oils, 1820?, U. Oxf., department of plant sciences · watercolour, c.1830, U. Oxf., department of plant sciences · M. Haughton, drawing, 1836, Magd. Oxf. · lithograph, pubd 1836 (*Athenaeum portraits*; after M. Haughton), BM · oils, c.1850–1859, Magd. Oxf. · attrib. T. Phillips, oils, Botanic Gardens, Oxford · photographs, MHS Oxf.

Wealth at death under £25,000: probate, 18 Jan 1868, *CGPLA Eng. & Wales*

Daubeny, Sir Peter Lauderdale (1921–1975), theatre impresario, was born on 16 April 1921 in Wiesbaden, Germany, the youngest of the three children and only son of Lieutenant-Colonel Cyril James Brooke Daubeny, a regular soldier, and his wife, Margaret Duncan. On retirement Cyril Daubeny served as military attaché to the Low Countries and Scandinavia, from a base in Brussels. Neither he nor his wife had any special interest in the theatre, but they provided a cosmopolitan background to their son's early years and he was fluent in French when he went to boarding-school (Selwyn House, Broadstairs) in 1930. There, in his own words, he was 'hopelessly unsporting, a small stage-struck bookworm'. Marlborough College followed, and by now his obsession with the theatre was complete.

Daubeny's life work was to be built on a foundation of wide-ranging, but discriminating, practical—and largely requited—hero-worship. His first idol was Hugh Walpole, who did not disappoint. Daubeny, aged thirteen or so, having read all his novels, invited him to lunch at the Ritz. Walpole moved the rendezvous to his own house. 'It was one of the most important events of my life,' Daubeny says in his autobiography; the boy was listened to and spoken to without condescension. Alec Guinness and Walpole recommended the London Theatre Studio, run by Michel Saint-Denis and George Devine, as the only worthwhile drama school; he enrolled but hated it, finding it 'more suitable for psychiatric therapists than drama students'. In 1937 Walpole again came to the rescue with an introduction to William Armstrong, distinguished director of the well-known Liverpool Repertory Company. Daubeny's first part was a monkey; this was followed by the trauma of going on (for Alan Webb) at a day's notice at the age of eighteen as an elegant man of the world in a suit that did not fit and a 'dickey' which 'popped out with rude assertiveness' whenever he approached the heroine.

In 1940 Daubeny joined the Coldstream Guards, and after training in Syria and a visit to the tomb of a crusader ancestor, Sir Philip d'Aubigny, in the church of the Holy Sepulchre in Jerusalem, he took part in the battle for Tunisia, and the Salerno landing, where he lost his left arm. He was invalided out of the army in 1943. While convalescing in Tripoli he confessed to a sympathetic Noël Coward his determination to become a theatre manager. His qualifications were 'a brazen confidence, an unquenchable enthusiasm, an ardent desire to learn everything and … an army of carefully cultivated contacts and some genuine friends'. For money he had formed a syndicate with a few fellow officers.

In the thirty years of his managerial career Daubeny put on 200 productions in London without a penny of Arts Council support. In the first phase (1945–51) successes were few. They included *But for the Grace of God* (1946), which he had to dragoon Frederick Lonsdale into completing; *We Proudly Present* (1947), written for him by Ivor Novello, and in which he gave his only post-war performance in a part based on himself; and *The Late Edwina Black* (1949), which ran for a year. Meanwhile in May 1948 he had married Mary (Molly) Vyvyan, daughter of Vyvyan Kempster, of Durban, Natal, a businessman and farmer. They had one son and one daughter.

Ironically, it was through a resounding flop—*The Gay Invalid* (1951), from Molière's *Le malade imaginaire* (starring A. E. Matthews and Elisabeth Bergner, with choreographer Walter Gore responsible for the mime)—that Daubeny discovered a passion for the dance. Between 1951 and 1955, starting with the Spanish dancers Antonio and Rosario, he presented companies from France, India, America, Yugoslavia, and Russia, and at least six other ensembles from Spain. In 1955 Edwige Feuillère's *La dame aux camélias* signalled the return of drama, and thereafter the range of Daubeny's offerings expanded. He presented drama from Russia, China, East Germany, Sweden, and Italy; dance from Africa, Hungary, and Poland; opera from Austria—together with return visits of previous favourites. This unique achievement (to which his wife made an incalculable contribution as supporter, confidante, and diplomatic hostess) turned him into 'the most discerning and knowledgeable connoisseur of the theatre arts' (Ronald Bryden). It was also the exciting overture to the eleven World Theatre seasons at the Aldwych.

In the first season Daubeny presented the Comédie Française; Schiller-Theater; Peppino de Filippo's Italian Theatre; Abbey Theatre, Dublin; Polish Contemporary Theatre; Greek Art Theatre; and Moscow Art Theatre. The playwrights included Molière, Feydeau, Goethe, Sean O'Casey, Aristophanes, Gogol, and Chekhov. And so the World Theatre seasons went on, from 1964 to 1975, for two or three months every year, bar one. The choice, the organization, the negotiations, the languages, the travelling, the temperaments (artistic and governmental), and the triumphs and disasters—all rested ultimately on the shoulders of one man. He was a man moreover fighting ill health from 1965 and mortally sick from 1973.

Daubeny wrote two volumes of autobiography, *Stage by Stage* (1952) and *My World of Theatre* (1971). The latter contains an eloquent foreword and afterword by Ronald Bryden, who makes a strong case for the influence of Daubeny's imports not only on his audiences but also on Laurence Olivier, Peter Hall, Peter Brook, and Trevor Nunn when they were creating the National Theatre and Royal Shakespeare Company, and on the ensemble playing which is a feature of both companies. Daubeny was made a consultant director of the Royal Shakespeare Company. His honours included OBE, 1961; CBE, 1967; Légion d'honneur (officer 1957, chevalier 1971); gold cross of the Royal order of King George I of the Hellenes, 1965; gold medal of Czechoslovakia, 1967; order of merit of the Italian republic, 1966; and order des lettres et des arts (France), 1974. He was knighted in 1973. He died in London on 6 August 1975.　　　　　　　　MICHAEL DENISON, *rev.*

Sources P. Daubeny, *Stage by stage* (1952) · P. Daubeny, *My world of theatre* (1971) · J. Parker, ed., *Who's who in the theatre*, 15th edn (1972) · *The Times* (7 Aug 1975) · *The Times* (13 Aug 1975) · personal knowledge (1986) · private information (1986) · CGPLA Eng. & Wales (1976)
Archives SOUND BL NSA, 'Man for all theatres', T3363W C1
Likenesses photograph, Hult. Arch.
Wealth at death £21,294: administration, 29 Jan 1976, *CGPLA Eng. & Wales*

Daubuz, Charles (1673–1717), Church of England clergyman and theologian, was born in France in July 1673 at Agen, in the province of Guienne, the eldest son of Isaye Daubuz (1637–1685), a Huguenot minister at Nérac, and his wife, Julie (*c*.1639–1714). In October 1685 Louis XIV's revocation of the edict of Nantes gave Protestant ministers a fortnight in which to leave France, on pain of death or imprisonment if they delayed. Isaye obtained from the king, through a friendly courtier, a letter authorizing him to leave with his wife and four children. At Calais he died; he was buried at night in the garden of an inn, the innkeeper helping Julie to dig the grave. By posing as the minister, Isaye's brother, who was already in England, managed to bring the family over. He then helped them to settle in Yorkshire.

On 11 September 1686, aged thirteen, Charles Daubuz went to Merchant Taylors' School in London, and thence, in January 1689, to Queens' College, Cambridge; as a sizar he received a college allowance. After graduating BA in March 1693 he became college librarian. In 1696 he was appointed headmaster of Sheffield grammar school. He proceeded MA at Cambridge in 1697. In 1699 he was presented by the dean and chapter of York to the vicarage of Brotherton, a village near Ferrybridge in the West Riding of Yorkshire. To supplement a modest stipend Daubuz taught the sons of neighbouring gentry. At a time when many parsons were slack he was devoted. One of his successors at Brotherton, John Law, recorded in a manuscript note his parishioners' memories: 'a tall, stout, strong, hale man, of a swarthy black complexion, wore his own strong, black curled hair, and had a very loud voice. He was a worthy, good man—a man beloved and respected by all' (*DNB*). He was also described as 'Pious, humble and benevolent' (Hames).

Probably in 1703 Daubuz married Anne Philota, with whom he had eight children. She was the daughter of Philippe Guide MD, a friend of the Huguenot theologian Claude La Mothe, author of *The Inspiration of the New Testament* (1694). That work may have aroused Daubuz's own interest in the book of Revelation, which appealed especially to persons in uprooted or persecuted communities but could lead to delusions. For La Mothe, the orthodox Calvinist, and Daubuz, the Anglican priest, the remedy lay in scholarly appraisal. Daubuz wrote *A Perpetual Commentary on the Revelation of St John* (1720) and on its 1068 closely printed folio pages would be founded later dictionaries of prophetic symbols. The work's subtitle revealed the author's purpose *concerning the certainty of the principles upon which the Revelation of St John is to be understood*. The task of mastering its dense and richly allusive material was to be aided by the abridgement of Peter Lancaster, published in 1730. Through this abridgement and the new enlarged edition prepared by Matthew Habershon in 1842, the *Commentary* enjoyed a continuing influence.

Daubuz unfortunately did not live to see his *Commentary* published. According to John Law, soon after travelling to London with the manuscript, showing it to the renowned Dr Richard Bentley, and receiving a discouraging response, 'poor Mr. Daubuz returned home unhappy in mind and weary in body, sickened of pleuritic fever, and died in a few days' (Law). His death occurred on 14 June 1717 at his vicarage at Brotherton. His wife survived him. Law further maintained that Bentley feared that 'Mr Daubuz would outshine him in learning, and eclipse his glory' (ibid.). Dr Richard Zouch, commending the *Commentary* to fellow clergy in 1792, was more realistic: 'works of that kind, however excellent they might be, were little relished in those times' (Zouch, 4). In an age of rationalism tending to deism, Daubuz's concern with the nature of the 'Prophetick Stile' and the use of 'Symbolical and Mystick terms' verged on the esoteric. It reflected, however, a view characteristic of the Enlightenment: 'enthusiasm' should be tempered with scholarship.

GEOFFREY TREASURE

Sources D. C. A. Agnew, *Protestant exiles from France in the reign of Louis XIV, or, The Huguenot refugees and their descendants in Great Britain and Ireland*, 2nd edn, 2 (1871), 219; 3 (1874), 73, 214 • S. W. Kershaw, *Protestants from France in their English home* (1885) • G. Holmes, *Augustan England* (1982) • R. D. Gwynn, *Huguenot heritage* (1985) • *DNB* • E. La Brousse, 'Great Britain as envisaged by the Huguenots of the seventeenth century', *Huguenots in Britain and their French background, 1550–1800*, ed. I. Scoloudi (1987), 143–57 • R. D. Gwynn, 'Patterns in the study of Huguenot refugees in Britain', *Huguenots in Britain and their French background, 1550–1800*, ed. I. Scoloudi (1987), 217–35 • R. L. Poole, *History of the Huguenots of the dispersion at the recall of the Edict of Nantes* (1880) • M. Hames, *Life and times of the church and people of Brotherton* (1986) • Nichols, *Lit. anecdotes* • note by John Law, Brotherton Church, Yorkshire • R. Zouch, *An address to the clergy of the deaneries of Richmond, Catterick and Boroughbridge* (1792)

Archives Cornwall RO, dissertation

Dauglish, John (1824–1866), physician and bread manufacturer, was born on 10 February 1824, in Bethnal Green, London, the third son of William Dauglish and his wife, Caroline. His father, who was Scottish, was employed in one of the large East India merchant houses ruined by the commercial panic of 1847. His mother was a descendant of the Jacobean writer, Sir Richard Baker.

Dauglish was educated at Dr Alexander Allen's school at Hackney. There and during his later studies, he had great difficulty in mastering languages, and this suggests that he was probably dyslexic. However, at an early age he demonstrated his mechanical ability by constructing a model steam engine and inventing a paddle-wheel. His parents were unable to provide either a technical education or to finance him as pupil in a large Liverpool engineering firm; in consequence Dauglish began work in his father's office. Deeply unhappy, he immersed himself in the study of philosophy. He published a short sketch and contributed an article to the *British Quarterly*, and then in 1852 he decided to study medicine at Edinburgh University. His practical abilities were again evident; a skilled dissector, he worked as assistant to Professor Hughes Bennett and Professor Henderson. In 1855 he took his MD degree and was the joint winner of the gold medal for his thesis.

In 1848 Dauglish married Selina, the second daughter of William Consett Wright of Upper Clapton, London. Nothing is known about their children. In November 1855 they moved to Brighton, where Dauglish immediately began experimenting with new techniques for the commercial manufacture of bread. His interest in bread making stemmed from the poor quality of Scottish bread, which had prompted him to make the bread for his household. Based on his practical experience and knowledge of chemistry, he developed a method of producing aerated bread without fermentation by yeast. Instead, the dough was aerated by the injection of carbon dioxide in a closed cylinder. He took out his first patent for 'an improved method of making bread' in 1856. The process offered several advantages: it greatly reduced production time and labour requirements and was suitable both for the more nutritious wholemeal flours and for the white flours of high extraction rates. But the main benefit was that throughout manufacture the dough was untouched by hand. Previously, as the sanitary reformer, Benjamin Richardson, had illustrated, most bread had been produced with little regard either for hygiene or for the conditions of labour. Dauglish proposed to remedy this by the use of his machinery.

Dauglish's ideas were not entirely original, although he appears to have been unaware of the fact. As early as 1816, Professor Thomas Thompson of Glasgow had demonstrated that the only purpose of fermentation in bread making was the production of carbon dioxide, which could also be achieved by using carbonate of soda and muriatic acid. In 1836 Luke Herbert patented machinery for manufacturing bread, in which he used carbonic acid to raise the dough. Problems of practical application and his inability to overcome conservative attitudes resulted in failure. Dauglish faced similar difficulties. In 1856 he secured the co-operation of the Carlisle biscuit makers, Carr & Co., and erected a model machine for the manufacture of aerated bread in their factory. The first experiments were successful and were taken up by other firms. But problems were encountered with larger-scale production and the project was abandoned.

Dauglish then briefly practised as a physician, but in 1859, determined to try again, he set up a bakery at Islington. The following year he presented a paper to the Society of Arts (for which he was awarded a silver medal) and convinced several leading physicians and sanitary reformers of the benefits of his process. The Aerated Bread Company was formed, and its products introduced into London hospitals. Despite these advances, the high capital costs of mechanized bread making remained a major barrier, and by 1862 there were only six aerated bakeries throughout the country. Only after the widespread adoption of the joint-stock limited liability company after 1880 did leading bakers such as George Macfarlane shift to factory production. Dauglish's work had, however, provided the foundations for the mechanization of the British baking industry.

Dauglish was a quiet, reserved man who was never robust. After 1859 his health began to fail, and he spent much of his time at health resorts in Switzerland and France. He died on 14 January 1866 at his home, Furze Bank, Great Malvern, and was survived by his wife. Dauglish was buried at Malvern Wells.

W. J. HARRISON, rev. CHRISTINE CLARK

Sources B. W. Richardson, *On the healthy manufacture of bread* (1884) · J. Burnett, 'The baking industry in the nineteenth century', *Business History*, 5 (1962–3), 98–108 · L. Mirabile, ed., *International Directory of Company Histories*, 2 (1990), 592–4
Likenesses engraving, repro. in Richardson, *On the healthy manufacture of bread*
Wealth at death under £25,000: administration, 6 Feb 1866, *CGPLA Eng. & Wales*

Dauncey, John (*fl.* 1660–1663), author and translator, wrote two histories of recent events in England from a royalist standpoint. These were *A History of His Sacred Majesty Charles II*, from 1649, published in 1660 before the Restoration and dedicated to Henry Pierrepoint, marquess of Dorchester, and *An Exact History of the Several Changes in Government in England*, which appeared in July the same year

and which recapitulated and updated events. Dauncey's interests comprehended continental history, which he explored in *The History of the Thrice Illustrious Henrietta Maria de Bourbon, Queen of England* (1660), dedicated to the duchess of Albemarle, and *A Compendious Chronicle of the Kingdom of Portugal* (1661), which arose from the negotiations surrounding the marriage of Charles II and Catherine of Braganza and was dedicated to the earl of Clarendon. He also translated from the French a work by Péréfixe de Beaumont, bishop of Rodez, published as *The History of Henry IV*.

Dauncey must be distinguished from the poet and translator John *Dancer, and though he styled himself a gentleman there is similarly no reason to connect him to the Dauntsey family of West Lavington, Wiltshire, or its branch in south-east Lancashire. Elizabeth, Lady Bloundell, to whom Dauncey dedicated *The English Lovers* (1661), might have been either the first or the second wife of Sir George Blundell (1622–1689) of Cardington, Bedfordshire. A preface by the printer in *A History*, to the lord mayor and colonels of the London militia, notes that the work 'must expect to meet with the hard censures and calumnies of many' and asks for protection from their 'zealous frenzy … under the shadow of your wings'. Perhaps Dauncey was then also living in London. In its 'preface to the general reader', he divides presbyterians into patriotic royalists, 'moderate folk who are as truly loyal as they are godly', and others 'like wolves in sheep's clothing', which suggests that he wished to be numbered among the former (McGillivray, 49). This is consistent with his attack upon Edmund Cooper MD, a candidate of the College of Physicians in 1653, whom he accused of abusing Smectymnuus. His references to the king, Lords, and Commons as three estates of the realm also suggest that Dauncey may have had a parliamentarian past. In comments on the protector's death, he stressed that Oliver Cromwell should be celebrated only for his valour, but conceded that through this quality he had raised 'the nation to that glory, that foreign princes both feared and envied it' (*Exact History*, 275). *The History of Henry IV* was reissued in 1672, but there is no direct evidence of Dauncey's survival after 1663.

STEPHEN WRIGHT

Sources R. Macgillivray, *Restoration historians and the English civil war* (1974)

Daunt, Achilles (1832–1878), dean of Cork, was born at Rincurran, near Kinsale, co. Cork, on 23 August 1832, the eldest son of Achilles Daunt (*d.* 1871) of Tracton Abbey, co. Cork, and Mary, third daughter of John Isaac Heard, MP for Kinsale. He was educated at Kinsale endowed school and, from 1848, at Trinity College, Dublin, where he gained a classical scholarship in 1852, having won the vice-chancellor's prize for English poetry in 1851. At the degree examination in 1853 he came out second senior moderator and gold medallist in classics. He graduated BA in 1854, MA in 1866, BD in 1872, and DD in 1877.

Daunt was curate of St Matthias, Dublin, for seven months in 1855, and was then presented by his maternal grandfather to the vicarage of Rincurran. Here his preaching attracted large congregations, and he soon had to enlarge the church. Among other activities started and carried out by him were confirmation classes for servants and the chaplaincy to the garrison at Charles Fort. He married Catherine Mary, daughter of the Revd John Leslie, rector of Kilcredan, Cloyne, on 24 February 1863. They had a son and two daughters. On 11 January 1867 he resigned Rincurran, was for a short time rector of Ballymoney, co. Cork, and then became rector of Stackallen, co. Meath, and private chaplain to his friend and diocesan, Samuel Butcher. In August 1867 he left Stackallen for the vicarage of St Matthias, Dublin.

While this Dublin church was being rebuilt, Daunt had to use the large concert hall of the exhibition palace. His sermons were so popular that his congregations averaged 3000 or more people. The last service in the concert hall was held on 31 July 1870, by which time the new church was ready. As well as preaching, Daunt also worked with students and organized evening lectures and classes for young women. As soon as the new constitution of the 'disestablished' church came into being, Daunt was elected to the office of diocesan nominator. He was also chosen as the representative canon in St Patrick's Cathedral for the united diocese of Dublin and Glendalough, and was named a member of the committee to revise the prayer book. The pressure of work in Dublin began to affect Daunt's health, which inclined him (in 1875) to accept the deanery of Cork and the rectory of St Fin Barre from his old friend John Gregg, the bishop of Cork. But he soon became ill and died, of heart and lung disease, at St Anne's Hydropathic Clinic, St Anne's Hill, Blarney, co. Cork, on 17 June 1878. He was buried at Mount Jerome cemetery, Dublin, on 21 June; his wife survived him. Daunt was the author of only a few works as he devoted most of his time to his parish. He was one of Dublin's leading evangelical preachers.   G. C. BOASE, rev. DAVID HUDDLESTON

Sources F. R. Wynne, *Spent in the service: a memoir of the Very Rev. Achilles Daunt* (1879) · *The Times* (18 June 1878), 9 · J. H. Cole, *Records of the united diocese of Cork, Cloyne and Ross* (1903), 120 · [J. H. Todd], ed., *A catalogue of graduates who have proceeded to degrees in the University of Dublin, from the earliest recorded commencements to … December 16, 1868* (1869), 144 · *A catalogue of graduates of the University of Dublin … from the year 1868 to … 1883* (1884), 40 · Burtchaell & Sadleir, *Alum. Dubl.*, 2nd edn, 30 · J. Daunt, *Some account of the family of Daunt* (1881), 25–8 · R. B. McDowell, *The Church of Ireland, 1869–1969* (1975) · H. E. Patton, *Fifty years of disestablishment* (1922)

Archives TCD

Likenesses photograph, repro. in Wynne, *Spent in the service* · portrait, repro. in Daunt, *Some account of the family of Daunt*

Wealth at death under £2000: administration, 12 Oct 1878, *CGPLA Ire.*

Daunt, William Joseph O'Neill [*pseud.* Denis Ignatius Moriarty] (1807–1894), politician and author, was born at Tullamore, King's county, Ireland, on 28 April 1807, the oldest of five children of Joseph Daunt (1779–1826) of Kilcascan, co. Cork, landowner and militia captain, and his first wife, Jane Wilson (*d.* 1816), daughter of the Revd Thomas Wilson, rector of Ardstraw, co. Tyrone. The

William Joseph O'Neill Daunt (1807–1894), by unknown photographer

Daunts, English protestants, had acquired land in co. Cork in the late 1500s; in 1828, breaking with family and class traditions, young Daunt became a Roman Catholic. He attributed his conversion to the influence of his tutor and his perusal of Catholic literature, although complicated psychological reasons involving his family may have played a more significant role.

A protégé of Daniel O'Connell, Daunt was MP for Mallow in 1832–3, until unseated on petition. A charter member of the Repeal Association from 1840, he was field director successively for Leinster, Ulster, and Scotland. In 1841–2, he was O'Connell's secretary while the latter was lord mayor of Dublin. In 1842 Daunt collaborated with Thomas Davis, John Blake Dillon, and Charles Gavan Duffy to found the Dublin *Nation*. He contributed occasionally to *The Nation*, but later distanced himself from it and the associated Young Ireland movement. Daunt was close to O'Connell during the repeal leader's declining years in 1844–7, but after his death retired from politics.

Daunt re-emerged in 1856 to help found the Irish church disestablishment movement, and remained active until the Disestablishment Act became law in 1869. Although Catholic, Daunt worked closely on disestablishment with the intensely protestant English Liberation Society. In 1862, the liberationists invited him to join their executive council, but he declined. After Daunt and other Irish disestablishmentarians founded the National Association of Ireland in 1864, the liberationists supported it on the basis of 'uncompromising voluntarism' for religious bodies; this alliance would have been impossible if Daunt had not persuaded the Irish Catholic hierarchy to renounce the British government's grant to Maynooth College for training priests.

Daunt deprecated papal and episcopal denunciations of secular republican organizations such as the Fenians, and generally urged complete separation of church and state. From his connection with the Liberation Society he became friendly with John Bright and other English Liberals, but was distrustful and critical of W. E. Gladstone. In 1870 Daunt joined Isaac Butt's Home Government Association. As one of the few important surviving O'Connellites he exerted considerable behind-the-scenes influence in what became the Home Rule League, until Butt's death in 1879. He supported Butt against the Parnellites, but unlike Butt he saw the value of parliamentary obstruction as a tactical weapon against English politicians. Although never a Parnellite, Daunt viewed home rule as the best attainable goal short of full repeal of the union.

In July 1839 Daunt married Ellen Hickey (d. 1897), daughter of Daniel Hickey. The couple had one son and one daughter. Daunt in his last years rarely left his estate at Kilcascan, co. Cork, but contributed prolifically to the press, especially concerning Irish finance, on which he was an acknowledged expert.

Daunt wrote numerous books on political and economic issues and Irish history, and four novels, three of them under the pseudonym Denis Ignatius Moriarty. His *Personal Recollections of Daniel O'Connell* (2 vols., 1848) is an important record of the Liberator's political conversations and non-political anecdotes. *A Life Spent for Ireland* (1896) is a selection of extracts from Daunt's voluminous journals kept between 1842 and 1888, edited by his daughter, Alice Ismere Daunt. His writing style is dry, pithy, and readable, although frequently rambling. Daunt died at Kilcascan, Ballyneen, co. Cork, on 29 June 1894.

Too introverted and reclusive, and possibly too scrupulous to be a successful politician, Daunt was nevertheless important as a link between the repeal and home-rule movements, and as an observer and chronicler of Irish nationalist politics for over sixty years. His unpublished journals and letters to scores of correspondents, as well as his many published works, are major historical sources, significant for their factual accuracy and broadmindedness. D. M. CREGIER

Sources *A life spent for Ireland: selections from the journals of W. J. O'Neill Daunt*, ed. A. I. Daunt (1896) · *The Times* (2 July 1894) · E. R. Norman, *The Catholic church and Ireland in the age of rebellion, 1859–1873* (1965) · D. Thornley, *Isaac Butt and home rule* (1964) · R. Davis, *The Young Ireland movement* (1988) · B. McKenna, *Irish literature, 1800–1875: a guide to information sources* (1978) · O. MacDonagh, *The emancipist: Daniel O'Connell, 1830–47* (1989) · L. J. McCaffrey, *Daniel O'Connell and the repeal year* [1966] · *Correspondence of Daniel O'Connell, the liberator*, ed. W. J. Fitzpatrick, 2 vols. (1888) · C. G. Duffy, *My life in two hemispheres*, 2 vols. (1898) · E. Larkin, *The Roman Catholic church and the home rule movement in Ireland, 1870–1874* (1990) · J. Loughlin, *Gladstone, home rule and the Ulster question, 1882–93* (1987) · Burke, *Gen. Ire.* (1976) · Boase, *Mod. Eng. biog.*

Archives NL Ire. | Cashel archdiocese archives, Thurles, Archbishop Patrick Leahy MSS · NL Ire., Isaac Butt MSS · University College, Dublin, Daniel O'Connell MSS

Likenesses photogravure, repro. in Daunt, ed., *A life spent for Ireland*, frontispiece [see illus.]

Wealth at death £250: probate, 2 Oct 1894, CGPLA Ire.

Daus, John. *See* Dawes, John (c.1516–1602).

D'Auvergne, Edward (1665–1737), historian and army chaplain, belonged to the ancient D'Auvergne family of St Ouen, on the island of Jersey. He was the third son of Philip D'Auvergne (d. 1690) and Madeleine le Maistre (d. c.1712). At his baptism on 17 February 1665 he was presented by Edward de Carteret, cup-bearer to Charles II, and Anne Dumaresq, the widow of Sir Philippe de Carteret, seigneur of St Ouen. He entered Pembroke College, Oxford, in Michaelmas term 1679, one of the first Channel Islanders to benefit from Bishop Morley's Foundation, which provided for five scholarships each worth £10 with chambers valued at 40s. It was a condition that Morley scholars promised to return to the islands 'to serve the publick as preacher, schoolmaster or otherwise' (D. Maclean, *History of Pembroke College*, 1900, 157–8). He graduated BA in 1683 and MA in 1686.

In 1692 D'Auvergne went to Flanders as chaplain to the earl of Bath's regiment. His patrons, the de Carteret family, were connected by friendship and marriage to John Grenville, first earl of Bath, colonel of the regiment. At the end of the year's campaign he returned to London with the purpose of writing a short account of events for private circulation. A decision was taken to publish, and this account became the first of D'Auvergne's series of contemporary histories of the campaigns, usually written up in winter quarters at Bruges and published every year between 1692 and 1698. In March 1693 he was appointed rector of St Brelade, Jersey. However, he quickly returned to Flanders with the earl of Bath's regiment. He was assisted in producing a fuller and more polished account of the 1693 campaign by his friend and fellow Jerseyman Philip Falle, who edited and published it. Falle, who was at that time also preparing his *Account of the Island of Jersey* (1694), retained his literary association with D'Auvergne, editing and preparing the narrative of the 1696 campaign with assistance from Lord Cutts, to whom D'Auvergne had dedicated the volume.

In 1694 D'Auvergne transferred to the regiment of Scots guards, under Colonel Ramsay, where he remained chaplain until the conclusion of the war in 1697. In his preface to the history of the campaign of 1694 he gave thanks to the dean of Winchester, John Wickart, for recommending him to Colonel Ramsay. D'Auvergne's literary efforts brought him a wider and influential audience. In June 1699 he was appointed one of the royal chaplains and accompanied King William to the Netherlands. Although he was absent from his native island, his position at court enabled him to assist with the affairs of Jersey: in 1700 he and Falle were granted 415 livres by the general meeting of the Jersey states for the redemption of islanders who were being held as slaves in Morocco.

In December 1701 the king granted D'Auvergne the rectory of St Giles at Great Hallingbury, Essex. He married Susanna (or Susan) Sabenone (d. 1740) at Westminster Abbey on 4 May 1704. It is likely that the de Carteret influence was again important, for the family had strong historical connections with the abbey. D'Auvergne had accepted the rectory of Great Hallingbury without giving up the benefice of St Brelade. His continued absence from Jersey, together with that of Falle and another absent rector, Philippe de la Place, led to the assembling of the island's ecclesiastical court in January 1706, where all three were stripped of their benefices—these votes being confirmed by the bishop of Winchester in 1709.

D'Auvergne is listed as chaplain to Major-General Roger Eliott's regiment between 1703 and 1713, when the regiment was disbanded. This would not appear to have been an 'active' commission—it was becoming a common practice for regimental chaplaincies to be held while absent. The regiment served as the garrison at Gibraltar for much of the period. In 1713 D'Auvergne began a second term as chaplain of the Scots guards, although, again, it seems clear that he did not serve with the regiment. In fact, he remained at Great Hallingbury for the rest of his life, and missed only four Easter vestries between 1701 and 1737. In 1728 he hoped to be made a dean. G. R. Balleine reports that Lord Newcastle wrote to Lord Cobham, saying that D'Auvergne had obtained a promise from the late King William of a deanery when a vacancy should occur, and had been strongly recommended. However D'Auvergne was to be disappointed.

In 1735, still in his capacity as chaplain of the Scots guards, D'Auvergne published an account of the campaign in Flanders for 1691, the first in which King William had taken part, with the intention of completing his history of William III's war. Dedicated to John Murray, earl of Dunmore, colonel of the regiment, this account was based upon published memoirs rather than D'Auvergne's own recollection.

D'Auvergne died at Great Hallingbury on 7 November 1737, aged seventy-two. He was survived by his wife, Susan, and only son, Barrington D'Auvergne, of Enfield, Middlesex, joint beneficiaries of his last will, dated 13 October 1737.

D'Auvergne's clear and detailed narratives of the campaigns in Flanders soon became established as a principal historical and literary source. Sterne makes specific reference to the histories in *Tristram Shandy* (vol. 2, chap. 1): Uncle Toby and Corporal Trim's meticulous re-creations of Landen and the siege of Namur were undoubtedly based upon the contemporary eyewitness accounts provided by D'Auvergne; and so too the works of modern historians of the period.

While D'Auvergne was at pains to stress his impartiality, reminding the reader that as a clergyman he could do no other, in the preface to the history of the 1693 campaign he added that he 'should be very sorry to have writ this account so as to leave the reader in suspense whether I am for French Slavery or English Liberty' ('Preface' to *The History of the Last Campaign in the Spanish Netherlands, a.d. 1693*, 1693). For, as the war in Flanders dragged on, he came to see his role more directly as a protagonist in the Williamite cause, providing a narrative of events which would 'inform the people of England, (that have a share in the burdens of this present war), of the Truth; and to disabuse them of many stories imposed upon them … by the enemies of the present government' ('Preface' to *History of the Campaign in the Spanish Netherlands, a.d. 1694, with a Journal of the Siege of Huy*, 1695). Thus D'Auvergne's histories quickly evolved from a straightforward eyewitness account of the actions of the British forces into a wider study of the conflicting parties, not only to refute French accounts, but also to defend the role of the allied forces in the confederate army from domestic political foes who sought to undermine the alliance and bring the war to an end.

D'Auvergne's literary efforts quickly gained him royal patronage. William III was well served by his regimental chaplains: George Story had previously written a favourable account of the Williamite wars in Ireland. The duties of a regimental chaplain were not onerous, and a small salary (£120) provided an additional financial inducement to put time, education, and experience to literary account, opening up new avenues of influence, patronage, and income.   JONATHAN SPAIN

Sources G. R. Balleine, *A biographical dictionary of Jersey*, [1] [1948] · J. A. Messervy, 'Notes on some ancient Jersey families: D'Auvergne', *Annual Bulletin* [Société Jersiaise], 6 (1906–9), 44–73 · list of rectors of St Brelade, *Annual Bulletin* [Société Jersiaise], 8 (1915–18), 104–5 · R. Lemfriere, 'Channel Islands links with Westminster Abbey', *Annual Bulletin* [Société Jersiaise] (1971), 262 · C. Walton, *History of the British standing army, A.D. 1660 to 1700* (1894) · J. C. R. Childs, *The British army of William III, 1689–1702* (1987), 39 · J. C. R. Childs, *The Nine Years' War and the British army, 1688–1697: the operations in the Low Countries* (1991), 4 · F. Maurice, *The history of the Scots guards, from the creation of the regiment to the eve of the Great War*, 2 vols. (1934) · C. Dalton, ed., *English army lists and commission registers, 1661–1714*, 6 (1904), 59–60 · C. Dalton, *George the First's army, 1714–1727*, 1 (1910), 130–31 · [L. Sterne], *The life and opinions of Tristram Shandy, gentleman*, 9 vols. (1759–67) · Foster, *Alum. Oxon.* · P. Morant, *The history and antiquities of the county of Essex*, 2 (1768), 515 · *VCH Essex*, vol. 8 · letter to Lord Cutts, 1697, BL, Add. MS 61686, fol. 99 · J. L. Chester, ed., *The marriage, baptismal, and burial registers of the collegiate church or abbey of St Peter, Westminster*, Harleian Society, 10 (1876), 41 · PRO, PROB 11/697

Archives BL, letters to Lord Cutts, Add. MS 61686, fols. 99, 103 · BL, letters to J. Ellis, Add. MS 28880, fols. 186, 190; Add. MS 28904, fol. 48

D'Auvergne, Philippe (*bap.* 1754, *d.* 1816), naval officer and claimant to the duchy of Bouillon, was born in St Helier, Jersey, Channel Islands, and baptized at St Helier parish church on 13 November 1754. He was the only surviving child of Charles Dauvergne, retired army officer, and his first wife, Elizabeth (*d.* 1754), daughter of Philippe Le Geyt, lieutenant-bailiff of the island. His mother died shortly afterwards and Philippe Dauvergne, as he was known until the mid-1780s, was subsequently raised by his stepmother, Elizabeth Bandinel, daughter of the seigneur of Meleches. He had six half-brothers and half-sisters.

Educated at St Mannelier School in Jersey and later in England and France, Dauvergne showed early interest in mathematics and in 1769 his father secured him a place, with the aid of the influence of his friend Vice-Admiral Lord Howe, as captain's servant in the yacht *Mary*. In this capacity he was able to complete his studies, and gain the necessary sea time for advancement to midshipman. In 1772 he was appointed midshipman in the frigate *Flora*, during one of whose voyages to the Baltic he was presented to the Russian empress, Catherine II. Interested in navigational calculations and the development of accurate sea compasses, he went as midshipman on the ketch *Racehorse* that in 1773 sailed with the *Carcass* to the Arctic to attempt, unsuccessfully, to navigate a north-eastern passage to the Orient. Service followed during the American War of Independence, initially in the warship *Asia* and the frigate *Chatham*, and then as lieutenant in the sloop *Kingfisher*. Dauvergne was present with a naval landing party at the battle of Bunker Hill in June 1775, and was subsequently engaged in small-boat raids along the Virginia coast. In September 1778 he was court martialled for the loss of his armed galley the *Alarm*, when trapped by French warships off Rhode Island, and was honourably acquitted.

Dauvergne joined the frigate *Arethusa* as first lieutenant in 1778 and was captured by the French when she was wrecked off Ushant in 1779. Imprisoned at Carhaix in Brittany, he became closely acquainted with Charles Godefroy de La Tour D'Auvergne, the duke of Bouillon, who was charmed with the young man and by the similarity of their family names. Upon his release Dauvergne was appointed in 1782 to command the sloop *Lark* and he spent many months on the barren island of Trinidada off the coast of Brazil on the eccentric orders of his flotilla commander to found a colony there with his crew and a group of French prisoners. A rescuing ship took him to Madras, but in April 1783 he was court martialled for the loss of the sloop *Rattlesnake* on the island; he was acquitted once again. Before his return to England he championed the cause of the nawab of Arcot over unsubstantiated claims that the governor, Lord Macartney, was misusing his tax revenues. There were reports of an 'unfortunate' marriage in Madras to Mlle Damprecourt, but research by George Balleine has thrown doubt on this.

Dauvergne was made post captain in January 1784. Between 1784 and 1787 he stayed in France for his health and resumed contact with the duke of Bouillon who in 1786 assumed parental rights over D'Auvergne, as he now styled himself, and the following year recognized him as his adopted son. D'Auvergne had a further reason for his prolonged stay in France, having been recommended by Lord Mulgrave, a lord of the Admiralty, to reconnoitre the French ports and coasts of the Channel and the Bay of Biscay. Returning to Britain during the 1787 crisis with France over control of the United Provinces, he presented his notes to Lord Howe, first lord of the Admiralty, who gave him command of the frigate *Narcissus*, ostensibly on antismuggling duty in the channel, but in reality to reconnoitre the French ports, particularly Cherbourg. He relinquished his command on the grounds of ill-health in 1790 and returned to France to repeat his tour of the maritime

provinces, directing his attention from 1792 to the means of obtaining information from the principal ports. In 1792 the duke of Bouillon died, having perhaps injudiciously named D'Auvergne as prince successor to the duchy of Bouillon and his other estates at the Château de Navarre in Normandy, upon the eventual demise of his own disabled and childless heir. Despite questions on the validity of adoption in France at this time, this son, Jacques, ratified the recognition before his death in 1802.

After the outbreak of war with revolutionary France, D'Auvergne returned to his native Jersey in 1794 as commodore in command of the old battleship *Nonsuch* (shortly replaced by *Bravo*) and a gunboat flotilla tasked with the defence of the Channel Islands. He was extensively engaged in coastal operations, raiding French shipping and protecting convoys, but his principal role became that of main government spy-master on the western coasts of France. Within months of his arrival he pressed for control of the communications which had been established from the Channel Islands to the royalists of western France, and backed strongly by the first lord of the Admiralty, Lord Chatham, and by the Jersey-based leader of the Breton royalists, Count Joseph de Puissaye, he was entrusted with what became known as *La Correspondance*. Networks linked Jersey to royalists in Brittany and the Vendée, conveying money and arms in one direction and intelligence in the other. Agents established at Brest reported on movements of the French fleet. Connections were also established with royalist, anti-revolutionary and later anti-Bonapartist networks in Paris. D'Auvergne's energetic and skilful handling of these activities enabled *La Correspondance* to continue until 1808 when one of his main agents, Noel-François Prigent, was captured and betrayed its organization and agents in an unavailing effort to save himself from execution.

Following the peace of Amiens in 1802 D'Auvergne rashly visited Paris, intent on pressing his claim to his inheritance. He was arrested by Fouche's secret police, despite having a valid passport, but after brief imprisonment in the Temple was deported to Jersey. Upon the resumption of hostilities in 1803 D'Auvergne, who had now taken the title duke of Bouillon, was again in command of naval and intelligence operations from Jersey, under Admiral Sir James Saumarez who led the Channel Islands flotilla from Guernsey. In 1808 D'Auvergne assumed that command, but continued to base himself in Jersey. Having become rear-admiral in 1805, he progressed to vice-admiral of the blue in 1810. The strain of hazardous operations had taken its toll, and he was obliged by ill health to retire in January 1813. D'Auvergne's dedicated work off the coasts of the Channel Islands in a campaign lasting nearly twenty years was a significant effort to limit the power of revolutionary and Napoleonic France. He was placed on the half pay list as vice-admiral of the white and became vice-admiral of the red in 1814.

Philippe D'Auvergne was a tall and handsome man possessing great personal charm, and speaking English with a pronounced French accent. He assumed a rather grand manner, and was a firm disciplinarian at sea, but he had little difficulty in getting Jerseymen to man the ships under his command. An accomplished mathematician, he was a doctor of law (1785), a fellow of the Royal Society (1786), a fellow of the Society of Antiquaries (1793), and a member of the Society of Arts (1793). His work on the improvement of navigational instruments was widely known, and he published *An Account of the New Improved Sea Compasses Made by K McCulloch* (1789). Although D'Auvergne is now believed never to have married he was fond of the company of women, and acknowledged three illegitimate children—two daughters born in 1794 and 1800 (the latter to one Mary Hepburn), and a son born in 1799. All were accepted in Jersey society and both daughters made good marriages but the son, Philippe, died in 1815 while in Royal Naval service.

Upon the abdication of Napoleon in 1814 D'Auvergne went to Paris to press his claim to the duchy of Bouillon. He was proclaimed duke in the duchy shortly afterwards, and in December 1814 the French garrison withdrew. D'Auvergne proceeded to issue decrees for the duchy and to mint his own coinage, but a rival claimant to the title came forward, and he declined to take residence in Bouillon until the inheritance question was settled. However, in June 1815 the congress of Vienna awarded the sovereignty of the duchy to the newly enlarged kingdom of the Netherlands. D'Auvergne expended great sums of money and much energy in unsuccessfully attempting to overturn this decision. In continuing poor health, and burdened by debts, he died at Holmes Hotel, 17 Parliament Street, Westminster, London, on 18 September 1816, and was buried in St Margaret's churchyard, Westminster, on 22 September. Ultimately a rather tragic figure, broken in health by hard campaigning and in fortune by his efforts to secure his title to the duchy of Bouillon, D'Auvergne was nevertheless an enterprising naval officer entrusted with missions of the most daring and difficult kind.

JAMES FALKNER

Sources *Navy List* · 'Biographical memoir of Philippe D'Auvergne', *Naval Chronicle*, 13 (1805), 169–91 · G. R. Balleine, *The tragedy of Philippe D'Auvergne* (1973) · *GM*, 1st ser., 86/2 (1816) · H. Kirke, *From the gunroom to the throne* (1904) · G. R. Balleine, *A biographical dictionary of Jersey*, [1] [1948] · P. Le Geyt, 'Phillipe D'Auvergne', *Annual Bulletin* [Société Jersiaise], 14 (Oct 1946), 301–10 · A. Cobban, 'The beginning of the Channel Isles correspondence, 1789–94', *EngHR*, 77 (1962), 38–52 · M. Hutt, 'Spies in France, 1793–1808', *History Today*, 12 (1962)
Archives PRO, corresp. and papers, PC1, FO95, HO69, WO1 · Société Jersiaise, St Helier, Jersey, Channel Islands | BL, letters to W. Windham and E. J. A. Woodford, Add. MSS 37851–37872, *passim*
Likenesses oils, *c*.1790, Société Jersiaise, St Helier, Jersey, Channel Islands

Davall, Edmund (1763–1798), botanist, was born in August 1763 in Holborn, London, the son of Edmund Davall, keeper of a navy clothing store in Crutched Friars, and Charlotte Thomasset (*d.* 1788). Little is known of his education and early life, but on the death of his father about 1786 he moved with his mother, who was Swiss, to Orbe, canton Bern. About this time he first became interested in botany, making the acquaintance of Edward Forster and of James Edward Smith, and becoming one of the original fellows of the Linnean Society. On 4 September 1789 he married Henriette-Louise-Stephanie Grinzos de Cottens (1762–1839), with whom he had a daughter and son who died in infancy, and two sons, Edmond (1793–1860) and Charles-Edouard (*b.* 1795), who survived him. Davall himself died at Orbe on 26 September 1798, leaving an unfinished work, *Illustrations of Swiss Plants*. His botanical papers and herbarium were bequeathed to Smith. Davall is credited with many additions to the Swiss flora; his name was perpetuated in a genus of ferns, *Davallia*, by Smith, his constant correspondent and dearest and best friend.

G. S. BOULGER, rev. P. E. KELL

Sources G. R. de Beer, 'Edmund Davall, FLS: an unwritten English chapter in the history of Swiss botany', *Proceedings of the Linnean Society of London*, 159th session (1946–7), 42–65 · *Memoir and correspondence of the late Sir James Edward Smith*, ed. Lady Smith, 1 (1832), 313; 2 (1832), 1–7, 70
Archives Linn. Soc., journal and papers | Linn. Soc., corresp. with Sir James Smith

Davenant, Charles (1656–1714), government official and political economist, was born in London on 17 November 1656, the eldest son of Sir William *Davenant (1606–1668), the poet and playwright, and his third wife, French-born Henrietta Maria du Tremblay (*d.* 1691). He went to school in Cheam and matriculated at Balliol College, Oxford, on 21 July 1671. He left Oxford without a degree, but in 1675 was awarded an LLD from Cambridge, obtained by incorporation from Oxford. In November 1675 he was admitted to Doctors' Commons, although there is no evidence of him practising civil law. Indeed, he had already inherited his father's interest in one of London's two patent theatres, taking over active management in 1673, and obtaining full possession of his shares and rights in 1677, the same year his operatic *Circe: a Tragedy* was produced. In or before 1678 he married Frances, daughter of James Molin, physician, of St Bride's, London.

Although *Circe* went through several editions it was Davenant's only work of literature and in the following year he became an excise commissioner. In this post he was notably active, frequently travelling widely across southern and western Britain investigating this vital new element of the state's bureaucracy. The post suited him admirably and gradually he gave up his interest in the theatre, finally in 1687 selling up all of his interests to his brother Alexander for £2400. It is possible, however, that he was driven to this by financial desperation, for with two partners he had in 1683 lent the crown £30,000 which was probably only ever repaid in part. This loan, his position in the excise (he also had a post in the hearth tax administration for most of the period 1684–9), his seat as MP for St Ives, Cornwall, in the 1685 parliament, and his appointments as a commissioner of the lieutenancy of the City of London in 1687 and a deputy lieutenant of Herefordshire in April 1688 powerfully demonstrated his attachment to the government of James II. Consequently, although he stood against the king's favouring of Roman Catholics, he was very perilously placed at the revolution of 1688 and lost all his positions with the advent of the new regime of William and Mary in 1689. Unemployed and deep in debt, he now turned towards the career for which he is best known, as a writer on economics, public finance, and politics.

For much of the 1690s Davenant was on the payroll of the out-of-favour East India Company. His attempts to return to the government service all being unsuccessful, but his interest in government finances appears to have been kept alive as the burdens of paying for the Nine Years' War (1688–97) mounted. In 1695 he published his first major work, *An Essay upon Ways and Means of Supplying the War*, which established him as an important commentator on financial and economic questions—although published anonymously its authorship was quickly and widely known. There he adumbrated in characteristically clear prose several of his fundamental tenets: that England could most easily become wealthy and powerful by expanding overseas trade, that the burdens of the war upon landed society should be just and proportionate (socially and geographically), and that the excise rather than debt or customs duties was the best means of finding large amounts of extraordinary revenue. Central to Davenant's analysis were some simple exercises in 'political arithmetic', which elsewhere he crisply defined as 'the art of reasoning by figures, upon things relating to government' (*Political and Commercial Works*, 1.128). Here he was much influenced by Gregory King.

Although the 1695 *Essay* brought Davenant to the attention of a wider public, it was still office he craved and there quickly followed six unpublished works that sought to show his worth both to government and patrons. These memorials made important contributions to discussions over the major recoinage of 1696, the founding of the Board of Trade in the same year, and the state of trade with India. Yet though these pieces appear to have been used at the heart of government their impact on policy was slight. Office continued to elude him and his next published work, *An Essay on the East-India Trade* (1696), was probably designed to secure him a position with the East India Company, which was then engaged in a bitter political struggle to retain its privileges. If there was partisanship in that work, there also appeared the important argument that because international trade was multilateral it was nonsensical to consider whether the balance between just two nations was positive or negative, an argument he later extended when considering trade between England and Holland, Holland and France, and England and her colonies. Davenant also made some valuable points about the difficulties of regulating trade, stating that 'Trade is in its nature free, finds its own channel, and best directith its own course' (*Political and Commercial Works*, 1.98), although he cannot be described as an unqualified 'free trader'. These points, among other cogently expressed ideas about economic well-being, he developed in *An Essay upon the Probable Methods of Making a People Gainers in the Ballance of Trade* (1699). From at least 1696 he had had access to unpublished writings and calculations by Gregory King, and in the *Essay* he published some of King's more important findings, including the so-called King–Davenant 'law of demand', which related variations in harvest yield to prices.

With the conclusion of the Nine Years' War, Davenant still apparently had no means of support other than his pen, and his writings now became rather more overtly partisan. As his positions in the 1680s suggest, by nature and temperament Davenant was in many (though not all) respects a tory and, as with many tories between 1697 and 1701, he was also happy to put his weight behind aspects of the 'country programme' that sought to limit the executive power of William III and the whig junto, notably by looking to reduce the 'standing army' and limiting the crown's right to dispose of forfeited estates in Ireland. This took its most obvious form in his election as MP for Great Bedwyn in 1698 and again early in 1701—parliaments which subjected William to close critical scrutiny. If in his writings Davenant was able to adopt a high moral tone, developing executive arguments about civic virtue, political responsibility, the distribution of power, and accountability, he could also be shrill and foolish. For example, in his *Essays upon I. The ballance of power, II. The right of making war, peace and alliances, III. Universal monarchy* (1701) he accused leading ecclesiastics of having an enmity towards Christ's divinity, although when pressed he did not name those he had in mind. There was also gossip that he was in the pay of Jacobites, and certainly there were attempts to recruit him into the service of the French. He had, indeed, the misfortune in 1701, with Britain and France once again at the brink of war, to be discovered dining with Poussin, the French *chargé d'affaires* in London, by officers serving an expulsion order on the latter. Probably largely as a consequence of this Davenant lost his seat in parliament once and for all.

Davenant's more overt posturing also found notable voice in *The True Picture of a Modern Whig Set Forth in a Dialogue between Mr Whiglove and Mr Double* (1701), an imaginative satire on the whigs' drift towards the political mainstream, cronyism, and corruption. This notably successful work (going through six editions in just four months) was followed up early in 1702 with *Tom Double Returned out of the Country*. There is no question that in the early years of the new century Davenant was at the peak of his renown. His work helped to set some of the terms of debate over political obligation, definitions of the public good, executive responsibility, and the sociology of power, with his arguments used by both tory and country politicians, even though his enthusiasm for overseas trade sat somewhat awkwardly with their obsession with land and agriculture as the basis of national well-being.

The accession of Queen Anne in March 1702, with her instinctive Englishness, Anglicanism, and toryism, introduced a political climate much more conducive to the likes of Davenant. It is notable that during Anne's reign his political pamphleteering became much more infrequent. And at long last he found favour with the government—Sidney Godolphin, lord treasurer from 1702 to 1710, appears to have had a high opinion of his abilities. In September 1702 he was appointed secretary to the commissioners considering a union between England and

Scotland. Although this short-lived post brought him little financial reward it marked a clear change in his fortunes, for in the following June he was made inspector general of exports and imports on an annual salary of £1000, a post he held until his death. This post, which had been created in 1696, required Davenant to oversee the compilation of statistics on customs duties and trade, a task for which he was admirably qualified. His administrative and arithmetical abilities ensured that the customs service functioned effectively during the War of the Spanish Succession (1702–13). Certainly Godolphin continued to turn to him for advice, sending him on a mission to Holland in the autumn of 1705 to consider the delicate question of that ally's continued trade with France. In 1712 he published in two parts *A report to the honourable the commissioners for putting in execution the act, intituled, an act for the taking, examining, and stating the public accounts of the kingdom.*

Superficially, from 1703 until he died, Davenant led a life of quiet endeavour and modest success. Only occasionally did he take up his pen again and then in conspicuously more moderate spirits, even at the cost of the loss of respect and admiration among earlier ideological bedfellows. It may be, as his critics charged, that with office he compromised his principles, but it is clear that office solved few of his problems. He continued to feel himself undervalued (the tone of self-pity in his correspondence is marked) and despite his handsome salary he remained deep in debt for the rest of his life. The reasons for this are unclear, but in 1708–9 he lived in Whitehall in order to avoid his creditors, some of his goods were seized, and later he estimated his debts at nearly £4000. Consequently he continued to press his patrons and friends for further office and funds: letters to Electress Sophia of Hanover, the duke of Marlborough, and James Brydges, the future duke of Chandos, show a sycophant desperate to impress, and in 1705 he wrote a memorial to Godolphin probably designed to obtain a place in and rewards from the union negotiations (he was overlooked).

The clarity of Davenant's thinking, the powerful organization of his writing, the ability to assimilate the best of the ideas of others, and his (rather rarely exercised) capacity to judge from beyond the fray gave his voice and his writing some authority. But he was no original thinker and his natural capacities were those of the able administrator. Moreover, he conspicuously lacked political acumen and foresight, damaging his prospects by the commitments he made under James II and the later years of William III. It is perhaps not surprising that he appears, for much of his life, to have been a frustrated or disappointed man. Perhaps his large family of two sons and four or five daughters provided some solace. Little is known of them: although he often pressed the claims of his second son, Henry, born in 1679, for prestigious diplomatic postings, he was no more successful on Henry's behalf than he usually was on his own.

Davenant died on 7 November 1714 and was buried on 9 November in St Bride's, Fleet Street, London. His wife survived him. For a while he was little remembered, but ever since Charles Whitworth brought out his edition of The

Political and Commercial Works of ... Charles D'Avenant in five volumes in 1771 his true worth has been widely acknowledged. JULIAN HOPPIT

Sources D. A. G. Waddell, 'The career and writings of Charles Davenant (1656–1714)', DPhil diss., U. Oxf., 1954 · *The political and commercial works of that celebrated writer Charles D'Avenant*, ed. C. Whitworth, 5 vols. (1771) · D. A. G. Waddell, 'The writings of Charles Davenant (1656–1714)', *The Library*, 5th ser., 11 (1956), 206–12 · D. A. G. Waddell, 'Charles Davenant (1656–1714)—a biographical sketch', *Economic History Review*, 2nd ser., 11 (1958–9), 279–88 · *Two manuscripts by Charles Davenant*, ed. A. P. Usher (1942) · D. Coombs, 'Dr Davenant and the debate on Franco-Dutch trade', *Economic History Review*, 2nd ser., 10 (1957–8), 94–103 · D. A. G. Waddell, 'An English economist's view of the Union, 1705', *SHR*, 35 (1956), 144–9 · R. M. Lees, 'Parliament and the proposal for a council of trade, 1695–6', *EngHR*, 54 (1939), 38–66 · G. Davies and M. Schofield, 'Letters of Charles Davenant', *Huntington Library Quarterly*, 4 (1940–41), 309–42 · J. Creedy, 'On the King–Davenant "law" of demand', *Scottish Journal of Political Economy*, 33 (1986), 193–212 · A. H. Nethercot, *Sir William D'Avenant: poet laureate and playwright-manager* (1938)

Archives BL, corresp. with his son, Add. MSS 4291, 4297, *passim* · BL, notebooks as an excise commissioner, Harley MSS 4077, 5120, 5121, 5123 · LUL, papers, MSS 59–60, 110, 136, 210 | BL, letters to Henry Davenant, Lansdowne MS 773

Likenesses oils, priv. coll.; repro. in Waddell, 'The career and writings of Charles Davenant (1656–1714)'

Davenant, John (*bap.* 1572, *d.* 1641), bishop of Salisbury, was born in Watling Street, London, and baptized at All Hallows, Bread Street on 25 May 1572, the second of at least four sons of John Davenant (*d.* 1597?), wealthy citizen and merchant tailor. He attended Merchant Taylors' School before matriculating in Michaelmas 1587 as a pensioner from Queens' College, Cambridge, from where he graduated BA in 1591 and proceeded MA in 1594. According to Thomas Fuller, son of Davenant's sister Judith, Davenant was forbidden to accept a fellowship by his father, 'as conceiving it a bending of those places from the direct intent of the Founders, when they are bestowed on such as have plenty' (quoted in Twigg, 81). However, he was admitted a fellow in 1597, after his father's death, and remained so for the next seventeen years. He proceeded BD in 1601, and proceeded DD and was appointed Lady Margaret professor of divinity in 1609, holding the position until 1621. Although instituted rector of Fleet, Lincolnshire, in 1609 and of Leake, Nottinghamshire, in 1612, his home was Cambridge, where he became known as a staunch defender of Calvinist orthodoxy.

Davenant had enjoyed a powerful patron in the earl of Salisbury. Other high-placed patrons like the earl of Rochester helped him in 1614 to gain the presidency of Queens'. Apparently through the quick thinking of another fellow, John Preston, he was able to wrest the election from George Mountain, also a Salisbury protégé, who had been confidently expecting the reversion since 1608. As president he presided over building work, lending the college £172 to complete the project; five years after his departure in 1621, he gave £100 for the library. However, his growing reputation as a theologian and duties at court increasingly took his attention from college affairs.

By 1618 Davenant had become a royal chaplain. At this stage established, despite his brush with Mountain, more

John Davenant (*bap.* 1572, *d.* 1641), by unknown artist, 1640

as a Calvinist anti-papist than as an overt anti-Arminian, he was chosen along with his friend Samuel Ward, master of Sidney Sussex, as one of the British delegation to the Synod of Dort. Briefed by the king at Royston just before their departure in October 1618, he and Ward took careful notes of the proceedings once they arrived at the conference. After painstaking analysis of the issues dividing conservative Calvinists from remonstrants, the two men joined with ministers from Bremen in arguing a moderate position, that of 'hypothetical universalism', which held that while Christ died for all men, not just for the elect, not all would receive salvation. The other British representatives were persuaded to accept this view, and maintained it in the conflicts which followed, 'decisively' (Patterson, 276) influencing the synod's final decrees. Although the decrees which were read out at Dort on 6 May 1619 were not universally to British taste, on the whole they represented a judicious compromise such as generally reflected Davenant's, Ward's, and also James I's own attitudes.

Davenant was soon rewarded. In 1620 he acquired the rectory of Cottenham, Cambridgeshire. Following the death on 15 May 1621 of his sister Margaret's husband, Robert Townson, Davenant was elected on 11 June to succeed him as bishop of Salisbury. Resigning his presidency of Queens', he was consecrated on 18 November. Interpretations of his stance as bishop have varied, but it seems evident that, although like fellow delegate at Dort George Carlton he accepted divine right episcopacy, he was at least uncomfortable with much ceremonial change. While he adopted Bishop John Overall's innovative 1619 visitation articles as the basis of his own of 1622 and 1628,

he made successive modifications to particular clauses, retaining a general thrust towards observance of the prayer book and the canons, but omitting or pruning sections related to particular nonconformist practices. In his 1635 articles he introduced some such clauses and two years later Archbishop William Laud claimed he approved the official policy on positioning the communion table altarwise, but in the latter case at least he seems to have been acting under duress from the king. In the Elizabethan tradition, he wrote that he considered the placing of the table 'a thing indifferent' (Tyacke, 211); in a letter to Ward of October 1639 he expressed himself nostalgic for 'that doctrine and those rites which our predecessors have left unto us. I can see nothing altered, or augmented, for the better' (ibid.). It was perhaps in this spirit that Davenant duly sanctioned but did not enforce the Book of Sports when it was reissued by Charles I. His own sabbatarianism was revealed, according to Fuller, when he declined to travel to Newmarket on Sunday to preach before the king.

Davenant's continued commitment to doctrinal Calvinism is more immediately evident. By the mid-1620s he was all too aware of the growing influence of the Arminians. In 1626, with Ward, Carleton, and others, he issued the defensive *Joynt Attestation* that what they had assented at Dort conformed to the official doctrine and discipline of the Church of England. That June he expressed himself worried as to how repressively Bishop Richard Neile's circle, 'those of Durresme House' (Tyacke, 107), would interpret the recent proclamation against controversy over predestination, and by 1628 he was concerned about the extension of the label 'puritan' to those who, like himself, considered themselves conformists. His sermon to parliament on 5 April that year, later published as *One of the Sermons Preached at Westminster* (1628), talked of 'a general calamity which out of doubt hangs over us' (p. 13) and of mutual and to a degree justified dissatisfaction of clergy and laity with each other. Yet he seemed confident that repentance and acceptance of God's sanctifying grace, not by means of superstitions like 'your proud Papisticall merit-mongers' (p. 30), but by means of prayer, Word, and sacraments, would restore the nation. In February 1629 he was convinced that the majority in convocation would reject the arguments of Richard Mountague and reaffirm core Calvinist doctrines. Events the following year undermined such confidence. In 1630 Davenant was brought before the privy council for having disobeyed the injunction against preaching the doctrine of predestination when he preached his Lent sermon at court, although the only penalty was a personal warning from the king against repeating the offence. His *Prælectiones de duobus in theologia controversis capitibus* (1631) indicates that his taste for controversy was not quenched. However, although he was included in the list of Lenten court preachers in the later 1630s, he was carefully watched.

Away from court Davenant and Ward spent much of their energies in the 1630s countering writings by Arminians at home and abroad, becoming convinced that they were opening the door to Pelagianism and that much

Laudian innovation 'was inspired by foreign protestant heterodoxies' (Milton, 406). To counter this threat, it was vital that Calvinists present a united front, and to that end, like Thomas Morton and Joseph Hall, the two men corresponded with foreign Calvinists and worked with John Dury on plans for a union of Reformed churches. Davenant's contributions to the scheme were published in the collected work *Ad fraternam communionem inter evangelicas ecclesias restaurandam adhortatio* (1640) and separately in *An Exhortation to Brotherly Communion* (1641).

With the return of parliament in 1640 Davenant argued fruitlessly in convocation for a canon suppressing Arminianism, although the Lords later gave to him and to Morton the task of composing the retractions of some of its more notorious proponents. On the other hand he assented to the canons in May 1640, and played a role in inducing the reluctant Bishop Godfrey Goodman to do the same. Like Joseph Hall, he registered assent to the 'etcetera oath', answered its critics, and administered it despite regrets about its wording. However, he had been ailing as early as 1639, and did not live to see the final fate of the policy. He died on 20 April 1641, unmarried but leaving in his kin a flourishing clerical dynasty. Among the many beneficiaries of his will, dated 29 January 1638, were his brothers Edward and William, his sister Ellen (wife of the future bishop Humphrey Henchman), and his many nephews and nieces, including Thomas Fuller, who had joined him at Salisbury as a prebendary, and John Townson. VIVIENNE LARMINIE

Sir William Davenant (1606–1668), by William Faithorne the elder, pubd 1673 (after John Greenhill)

Sources Venn, *Alum. Cant.* · IGI [parish register of All Hallows, Bread Street, London] · will, PRO, PROB 11/186, sig. 101 · T. Fuller, *The church history of Britain*, ed. J. S. Brewer, new edn, 6 vols. (1845) · Fuller, *Worthies* · J. Twigg, *A history of Queens' College, Cambridge, 1448–1986* (1987) · A. Milton, *Catholic and Reformed: the Roman and protestant churches in English protestant thought, 1600–1640* (1995) · N. Tyacke, *Anti-Calvinists: the rise of English Arminianism, c.1590–1640* (1987) · K. Fincham, *Prelate as pastor: the episcopate of James I* (1990) · K. Fincham, ed., *Visitation articles and injunctions of the early Stuart church*, 1 (1994), xx–xxi · W. B. Patterson, *King James VI and I and the reunion of Christendom* (1997) · J. Davies, *The Caroline captivity of the church: Charles I and the remoulding of Anglicanism, 1625–1641* (1992) · C. Russell, *The fall of the British monarchies, 1637–1642* (1991) · Bodl. Oxf., MS Tanner 290, fol. 86r

Archives York Minster, exhortation for restoring communion between evangelical churches | Bodl. Oxf., corresp. with Ward and papers, MS Tanner 67

Likenesses oils, 1640, Queens' College, Cambridge [*see illus.*] · T. Trotter, line engraving (after oils, Queens' College), BM, NPG; repro. in E. Middleton, *Biographia Evangelica* (1783)

Wealth at death see will, PRO, PROB 11/186, sig. 101

Davenant [D'Avenant], **Sir William** (1606–1668), poet, playwright, and theatre manager, was the second of four sons of John Davenant, vintner, and Jane, daughter of Robert and Elizabeth Sheppard.

Origins and early life The Davenants had long been settled in north Essex, near London; the Sheppards were from much further north, co. Durham. During the sixteenth century some members of both families were drawn to London by the growing wealth and expansionist policies of Tudor England, culminating in the long reign of Elizabeth I. Relatives of Sir William became merchant adventurers and freemen of the related Merchant Taylors' Company (Edmond, pedigree facing p. 1), while some Sheppards entered royal service. Davenant's mother was baptized at St Margaret's, Westminster, in 1568. His grandfather and father, both named John, were merchant vintners, importing wines from the continent, and also brokers—licensed agents operating between merchants of all kinds. The elder John became a freeman of the new Muscovy Company, trading with Russia and Persia, and married Judith Sparke, daughter of a founder member: their first child—Sir William's father—was born in 1565.

Davenant's parents would have been married about 1593 (date and place unknown). They lived in the parish of St James Garlickhythe, close to the river and Vintners' Hall, and directly opposite the playhouses on the south bank. John Aubrey, in his long (and, for him, fairly neat) 'brief life' of Sir William (Bodl. Oxf., MS Aubrey 6, fols. 46–47v) describes his mother, Jane—or Jennet, as she was known in the family—as beautiful and highly intelligent ('of a very good witt'). Anthony Wood adds that her husband was 'an admirer and lover of plays and playmakers, especially Shakespeare'. The Davenants' first six children did not long survive, and they left London, presumably hoping for better fortune elsewhere. In 1600 or 1601 the experienced wine merchant took over a wine tavern in the centre of Oxford, where he and his wife successfully reared a family of seven. Their home has been described as 'obscure', but it was called simply 'the tavern' because it was so *well*-known. Aubrey states that Shakespeare stayed at John Davenant's establishment—where he was 'exceedingly respected'—on annual visits to Stratford. The tavern was owned by New College, and the leasebooks show that it had about twenty rooms (the rear of the old tavern, now 3 Cornmarket, was demolished in 1934). Inns offered beds to the travelling public, wine taverns did not, so Shakespeare was staying as a friend. He and Mrs Davenant's eldest brother, Thomas, royal glover and perfumer, were professional colleagues in London, and as members of the royal household were granted cloth for liveries to attend the old queen's funeral in Westminster Abbey in 1603, and to walk in the progress of James I through the City in 1604 (PRO, LC2/4(4), LC2/4(5)). The notion that Shakespeare and his Oxford hostess shared a bed in the 'painted chamber' of the tavern, and that William was the result of their union, is highly improbable. In later life, says Aubrey, William Davenant (whom Aubrey knew) sometimes remarked that he felt he wrote with Shakespeare's spirit, and was ('seemed' cautiously inserted above) happy enough to be 'thought his Son': what poet or playwright would not? There is no compelling reason to reject near-contemporary reports that Shakespeare stood *god*father when young William was baptized at St Martin's, Carfax, on 3 March 1606.

In autumn 1621 John Davenant, already in failing health, was elected mayor of Oxford. Jennet was buried on 5 April 1622, John died on the 19th, and was given an impressive funeral on the 23rd. He left a long and meticulous will planning for his motherless children, and bequeathed the handsome sum of £1200 overall. He intended his lively and gregarious son William, then sixteen—who had been educated at Oxford by a schoolmaster, Edward Sylvester—to be apprenticed to a London merchant, and left him extra money for 'double apparell'. William hastened to the capital, acquired a tailor called Urswick (to whom he would later be constantly in debt), ordered elegant attire, and almost immediately became a page in the household of Frances Howard at Ely House in Holborn. She was the third wife of Lodovic Stuart, a kinsman of James I, created duke of Richmond in 1623. Soon after he arrived in London, Davenant had married someone called Mary (details unknown), and the first of his many sons was baptized at St James's, Clerkenwell, on 27 October 1624. Richmond had died early that year and Davenant entered the household of Fulke Greville, Lord Brooke, who was stabbed to death by a servant in 1628.

Plays and masques The first play of Davenant's to be performed was *The Cruel Brother: a Tragedy*, an old-fashioned revenge piece, put on by the King's Men at Blackfriars, having been licensed in 1627; it was obviously important to the budding playwright that the Shakespeare first folio and John Webster's *The Duchess of Malfi* were published in

1623, shortly after his arrival in London, and there are echoes of both playwrights in his early work. His play *The Tragedy of Albovine, King of the Lombards*, probably written at about the same time, was not performed. It was published, however, in 1629, when the author introduced an apostrophe into his name as part of a fanciful claim that his family had originally come from Lombardy, a claim that aroused much mirth. In 1630 he contracted a venereal disease, probably syphilis, which nearly cost him his nose and his life. Aubrey says that he had been infected by 'a black [dark] handsome wench' of Axe Yard, Westminster. In his play *The Wits* (1634), Davenant has Lucy speak lightly of 'lewd gallants/That have lost a nose' (III. i). In the only known portrait of Davenant, by John Greenhill, surviving in an engraving by William Faithorne that forms the frontispiece to his *Works* of 1673, the nose is somewhat disfigured. The subject prompted ribald comment, some wits linking nose and name, for example:

> *Will*, intending *D'Avenant* to grace,
> Has made a Notch in's name like that in's face.
> (Nethercot, 90 and n.1)

The only treatment for syphilis was quicksilver—'Devill Mercurie', as Davenant called it. He sought help and comfort from Dr Thomas Cademan, physician to Queen Henrietta Maria (whose widow he later married), and from his loyal friend, the courtier Endymion Porter; he was profoundly grateful to them for his survival. That gratitude was expressed not with pounds but 'Poesie': he advises Cademan to concentrate on wealthy patients rather than:

> such as pay like mee
> A Verse, then thinke they give Eternity.
> ('To Doctor Cademan')

Davenant was nearly always short of money, and it must be a tribute to his talent and charm, and the generosity of his friends, that he achieved so much.

Davenant probably left London in summer 1632 to recuperate after his illness, succinctly describing the capital as a place of 'smoke, diseases, law and noise' (*The Wits*, I.ii). But in *The Wits* there is much too about the horrors of country life, recalling the recent reluctant exile of the young London playwright. This, his fifth play, written at the age of twenty-seven, was his first comedy, and marks a significant advance: it is assured, lively, and set in an authentic seventeenth-century London. The theme is not courtly love, but people living on their wits in the big city; it owes much to the example of Ben Jonson.

The playwright soon became a servant of the queen, and most of his future work was for the court. The next two plays, *Love and Honour* (1634) and *The Platonic Lovers* (1635), were prompted by the queen's liking for romantic comedy and interest in Neoplatonism. It is clear that in the second half of the 1630s he became a valued member of Henrietta Maria's circle.

The brilliantly gifted Inigo Jones, surveyor of the king's works and principal creator of court masques, had collaborated with several writers from 1605, beginning with Ben Jonson and including Davenant's friend Thomas Carew. The Jones–Carew *Coelum Britannicum* (1634) has been described as the best of all Caroline masques, the two men combining to give full expression to Stuart autocratic ideals. The queen invited her servant William Davenant to write the words spoken or sung for the next masque, *The Temple of Love* (1635). He was as yet unfamiliar with the conventions of the genre, and the entertainment owed its success to Jones's creation of an Asian fantasy for Henrietta Maria and her ladies. The queen wore a feathered Indian costume—one of many which Jones designed for masques—and was seen banishing Lust, in the persons of three Asian magicians, from the realm. *The Temple of Love* was the last masque performed in Jones's great Banqueting House in Whitehall; it was then closed to allow the installation of Rubens's paintings in the ceiling, which remain in place. The last three Jones–Davenant masques, in 1638 and 1640, were staged in a temporary 'masking room' which King Charles had instructed his surveyor to build in a courtyard behind the hall. Smoke from the huge numbers of candles required to light performances would have endangered the paintings.

In late summer 1637 William Davenant visited the west of England with Sir John Suckling and Jack Young: 'Twas as pleasant a journey as ever men had; in the height of a long peace and luxury, and in the venison season'. The trip included a week's stay with Davenant's brother, Parson Robert of West Kington near Chippenham in Wiltshire—'mirth, witt and good cheer flowing' says Wood in his brief life of Suckling. This belies Wood's statement that John Davenant and his eldest son were 'of a melancholic disposition and … seldom or never seen to laugh' (Wood, *Ath. Oxon.*, 3rd edn, 3.802–9).

Davenant's first masque for the king, staged in February 1638 in the new hall, was entitled *Britannia triumphans*, title and theme bearing no relation to political realities. King Charles appeared as Britanocles, 'glory of the western world', whose hated ship money tax had allegedly cleared the seas of piracy. One painted scene showed a formidable British fleet sailing into harbour: only at sea was the navy's real weakness apparent. The queen's masque following her husband's, as usual, was put on three or four times in February, and was entitled *Luminalia, or, The Festival of Light*, an idea derived from a Florentine entertainment. Inigo Jones devised a haunting night-scene giving way to dawn, symbolizing the triumph of light over darkness—the triumph of monarchical rule. Songs, with words by Davenant, praised Henrietta Maria's benevolent effects upon the nation as 'queen of brightness', with much use of platonic imagery.

Also in 1638 Davenant published a collection of poems with the overall title *Madagascar*. The first and longest poem was addressed to Prince Rupert, and related to a tentative plan—never carried out—for him to lead an expedition to colonize the island. More than forty shorter poems were included, many reflecting Davenant's court connections and friendships, and he dedicated the volume to his beloved Endymion Porter and Henry Jermyn. His standing as a poet was confirmed in the same year, when he was recognized as the unofficial laureate, succeeding Jonson who had died in 1637.

Court masques required a great deal of preparation, and rehearsals for the last Caroline masque—generally regarded as among the best, and Davenant now writing with more assurance—were in full swing by the beginning of December 1639. Its title (*Salmacida spolia*) meant the trophies of the king's peace: the earlier triumphalist tone had been abandoned, and King Charles—Philogenes, 'lover of his people'—although still claiming victory over his opponents, was now a saddened and patient monarch enduring adverse times. The masque, spectacular as ever, was staged on 21 January 1640 and on three days in February. For the only time, the king and queen took part together. It was a final desperate appeal to the court for understanding and support, but put on far too late to influence events. The continuing opposition of parliament to the king's policies led to the outbreak of war in August 1642.

War, exile, and imprisonment During the civil war the king campaigned in England while the queen, often on the continent, worked hard to raise money, arms, and munitions, with Davenant helping her from time to time. He did much to keep the royal couple in touch, and served for some months, with apparent competence, as lieutenant-general of the ordnance. In 1643 at Gloucester the king knighted him for his 'loyalty and poetry'. When the royalist armies had been defeated, Davenant joined the exiled court at St Germain-en-Laye near Paris, later becoming a guest of Lord Jermyn at the Louvre. The compulsive writer, cut off from his country and with theatres closed, was forced to become 'an Author', as distinct from poet and playwright. He wrote two books of a long rambling work called *Gondibert*, which he described as a new kind of heroic poem, based on earlier writers, but modelled on a five-act tragedy without dramatic action. He sent his long preface, and then the first two books of the poem, to his friend Thomas Hobbes, who was also living in Paris at the time; Hobbes replied with some qualified praise, and commended Davenant's choice of verse form. Davenant incautiously published the preface on its own in Paris, prompting predictable scoffing by exiled courtiers: 'A Preface to no Book, a Porch to no house: Here is the Mountain, but where is the Mouse?'. John Dryden, who succeeded Davenant as laureate at his death, described the poem as 'rather a play in narrative … than an heroic poem': later readers have generally found it extremely dull. The first two books were published in London in 1651, but Davenant abandoned the project after the third book, which was published posthumously in 1685.

King Charles had been executed in Whitehall in January 1649. In January 1650 there were plans, probably initiated by the widowed queen, for Davenant to take up an appointment in Virginia or Maryland. In May he sailed from Jersey, but he was intercepted by a parliamentary frigate, and imprisoned in Cowes Castle on the Isle of Wight, on orders from the new council of state in London, 'having been an active enemy of the commonwealth'. Soon he was moved to the Tower of London, and there was talk of a treason trial with a possible death penalty. But there was probably no real intention to take drastic action against 'Davenant the poet', as he was usually then called, although he was not released, on bail, until October 1652. He seems to have been a victim of bureaucracy and muddle. Within the month he married Anne Cademan, the widow of the doctor who had cured his illness, and she provided money from the estate of a first husband (Davenant was her third), but also four stepsons. Soon the poet was arrested again, for debt; early in 1654 he appealed for fair treatment, and was finally pardoned and released on 4 August. His second wife died in March 1655. In August he secured a pass to visit France, and returned with a third and last wife, Henrietta Maria du Tremblay (d. 1691), of 'an ancient family' in Anjou. They had nine sons, including Charles *Davenant, government official and political economist, and the translator William *Davenant. His wife was a capable business partner during his years as a theatre manager, a role she continued after his death.

The opera Sir William Davenant was a man of great resilience and enterprise, and after his release from the Tower he pursued a cautious plan aimed at promoting operatic drama, as a first step towards restoring drama proper. By May 1656 he was ready to offer an 'entertainment', with 'declamations' and music, to run for ten days; he put this on at the back of Rutland House in Aldersgate Street near the Charterhouse and the present Barbican Centre, where he was living at the time. A prologue apologized for the 'narrow room', and those present were invited to regard it as a way 'to our Elyzian field, the *Opera*'—the first appearance of the crucial word. The figures of Aristophanes and Diogenes the Cynic declaimed for and against the value of public entertainments by 'moral representations'; then, after a song, a Parisian and a Londoner debated the merits of their respective capital cities. The debates were interspersed with appropriate instrumental music. The entertainment (titled *The First Days Entertainment at Rutland-House*) was quite unlike a stage play, with seated declaimers, and no dialogue, elaborate costumes, or props. An anonymous observer reported that at the end there were 'songs relating to the Victor [Oliver Cromwell]' (PRO, SP 18/128/108). No official criticism resulted, and in the autumn Davenant put on and published *The Siege of Rhodes*, part 1, which is generally regarded as the first English opera (Pepys, 2.130 and n. 2). Again he avoided all theatre terms: the show is described on the title-page as a 'Representation by the Art of Prospective [sic] in Scenes, And the Story sung in *Recitative* Musick': but this time there was also a 'small narrative' delivered by 'seven persons'. Davenant prudently sent an advance copy to Bulstrode Whitelocke, lord commissioner of the treasury, whom he had known in their youth, and soon followed this up with a memorandum to Cromwell's secretary of state, John Thurloe, arguing the value of 'entertainments' to divert people's minds from 'melancholy that breeds sedition'. Davenant was now emboldened to move to a theatre, the Cockpit in Drury Lane (dismantled in 1649, but refitted in 1651). He transferred *Rhodes* from Rutland House, and put on two more operas, one relating to Cromwell's anti-Spanish policy, entitled *The Cruelty of the Spaniards in Peru* (1658), the other a history of Sir Francis Drake (1659). *Drake*

was certainly more like a play than an opera, with several characters, and some dialogue, action, and plot. Criticism of Davenant's activities had sharpened after Cromwell's death in September 1658, and Cromwell's son Richard and the council of state ordered him to say by whose authority he was staging opera publicly at Drury Lane. But sentiment in favour of the exiled king was increasing, and on 29 May 1660—his thirtieth birthday—Charles II entered his capital. Soon the poet laureate, whose role had been in abeyance during the Commonwealth, produced a long panegyric on his 'happy Return to his Dominions'.

Restoration theatre manager On 9 July 1660 Thomas Killigrew, who was six years younger than William Davenant and personally on good terms with Charles II, secured a warrant to form the King's Company of players. Davenant had long intended to become a theatre manager, and as early as March 1639 (the year before he and Jones staged the last court masque, *Salmacida spolia*) he had successfully secured from Charles I a warrant to build a playhouse on the north side of Fleet Street, between Fetter and Shoe lanes and behind the Three Kings ordinary (eating house); there he planned to stage 'Action, musical Presentments, Scenes, Dancing and the like'. But the time was not propitious. Now, twenty-one years later, on 19 July 1660—ten days after Killigrew's warrant—he drafted an updated one for the attorney-general, to grant a monopoly to both Killigrew and himself (PRO, SP 29/8/1; and plate in Davenant's hand, Edmond, 136). They planned to put on tragedies, comedies, plays, operas, and all other similar entertainments, setting reasonable admission charges to meet 'the great expences of scenes, musick and new decorations as have not bin formerly used' (Edmond, 143–4). The draft, somewhat added to, passed the privy signet, the final stage before the great seal, on 21 August 1660.

The two men recruited the best actors available from Drury Lane and the Red Bull in Clerkenwell. Samuel Pepys, a man totally in love with the theatre, had begun keeping his *Diary* (without which knowledge of stage history at the time would be very much the poorer), on 1 January 1660; it records that from 8 October until 4 November the Cockpit was used by a short-lived troupe called His Majesty's Comedians. The diarist did not fail to go there; on 11 October he saw '*The Moore of Venice* [Othello] … well done' (Pepys, 1.264). The cast included Thomas Betterton from the former Cockpit group who was presumably playing the title role; he later became Davenant's leading player. On 5 November the two companies were formally established, with Killigrew's under the patronage of the king, and Davenant's under the duke of York; henceforth Davenant's company and theatre would be known as the Duke's. The managers made use of former tennis court buildings: Killigrew's was in Vere Street near Lincoln's Inn Fields, Davenant's at the Salisbury Court, Whitefriars, between Fleet Street and the river. Killigrew opened almost immediately.

Davenant did not open his new playhouse in Lincoln's Inn Fields to the public until 1661. Killigrew was less cautious. He initially retained almost all existing plays (including Davenant's), on the ground that his King's

Company was the automatic successor to the pre-war and pre-Commonwealth King's Men. It was not until 12 December 1660 that Davenant was able to secure from the lord chamberlain a somewhat fairer distribution of plays. Those he received included *The Tempest, Romeo and Juliet, Twelfth Night, Henry VIII, King Lear, Macbeth*, and *Hamlet*; also John Webster's *The Duchess of Malfi* and his own works. From then on he had a great deal of rehearsing to do. Pepys went to see Davenant's company for the first time on 29 January 1661, and it may be presumed that this devotee of the theatre went on or near the opening date. The manager was having teething troubles: the performance started late, and Pepys had to exercise 'great patience' and endure 'poor beginnings'. He did eventually, to his 'great content' see three acts of *The Maid in the Mill* by Fletcher and Rowley; on 9 February he saw Fletcher's *The Mad Lover* for the first time, and liked it 'pretty well', and on the 23rd, *The Changeling* by Middleton and Rowley: 'the first time it hath been acted these 20 yeeres—and it takes exceedingly'. On 1 March Pepys watched Thomas Betterton's performance in the title role of Philip Massinger's tragi-comedy *The Bondman*: 'an excellent play and well done—but above all that ever I saw, Baterton [*sic*] doth the Bondman the best' (Pepys, 2.34, 41, 47, and n. 2). Thomas Betterton, then aged twenty-five, is generally considered to have been the greatest actor of the Restoration period, and Pepys, like Davenant, immediately recognized his quality.

The diarist paid his last visit to Davenant's Whitefriars theatre on 6 April 1661. By then the conversion of the new location for the Duke's Theatre at Lincoln's Inn Fields must have been completed, allowing the company to move in and concentrate on final intensive preparations before the opening in June. The important articles of agreement (Edmond, 153–4, 156), which Davenant signed with his ten leading players on 5 November 1660, the date on which the Duke's company was formally constituted, ensured that the manager was in complete control, and closely involved in day-to-day operations. He lodged at his theatre, unlike Killigrew, who lacked his rival's professional experience and delegated most of his functions to his leading players.

The Duke's Theatre Shakespeare and Davenant were supremely fortunate in their leading men: Shakespeare wrote for the first great English actor, Richard Burbage (1568–1619), Davenant employed and directed the second, Thomas Betterton (1635–1710). Betterton once paid a notable tribute to his former master as a disciplinarian:

> When I was a young Player under *Sir William Davenant*, we were obliged to make our Study our Business, which our young Men do not think it their duty now to do, for they now scarce ever mind a word of their Parts but only at *Rehearsals*. (Edmond, 156)

—a stricture not unheard in the theatre world of today. After a month or two, said Betterton, young actors imagined themselves masters of an art which required a lifetime of application.

Pepys had first seen women on the stage at Killigrew's theatre, on 3 January 1661, as he noted without comment.

Davenant's articles of agreement with his players show that he too had decided to use actresses: but he wisely did not deploy them until he opened at the Duke's Playhouse, where he would have rehearsed them with special care. He had recruited eight, and boarded the four principals, mistresses Davenport, Saunderson, Gibbs, and Norris, in his own part of the building. With them too he was fortunate: Mary Saunderson was the first leading English professional actress.

It is generally agreed, on the strength of Pepys's evidence, that the new theatre opened on Friday 28 June 1661 with Davenant's *The Siege of Rhodes*, part 1, dating from 1656 but now enlarged: it was repeated on 29 June and 1 July and was followed by the first gala performance of part 2, now in play form, on Tuesday 2 July. This became the standard version. The theatre had a small stage and proscenium arch; the scenery consisted of wings fronting pairs of large painted flats, which could be moved along grooves set in the floor and flies of the stage. Davenant's was the first public playhouse in England to use this system continuously. King Charles, making his first visit to a public theatre, was present on 2 July, with the duke of York. *Rhodes* had an exceptional run of twelve days (omitting a Sunday), and was greeted with great applause. Pepys considered the scenery 'very fine and magnificent', and the play 'well acted'. Betterton played Solyman the Magnificent, and Mary Saunderson was Ianthe. (In 1665 Pepys spent a winter afternoon setting to music some lines of Solyman beginning 'Beauty, retire! Thou dost my pity move!' He was very proud of his composition, and later commissioned John Hayls to paint his portrait holding it (NPG).) Next Davenant put on a successful revival of his own early play *The Wits*—with scenes, of course, for the first time, which Pepys considered 'admirable'. The king and the duke and duchess of York were at the first performance on 15 August.

As the cast were familiar with *Rhodes* and *The Wits*, the manager had been able to devote most of the morning rehearsal-times, during the first hectic weeks at his new theatre, to preparing his first ambitious production, his adaptation of *Hamlet*. The play returned to the London stage on the afternoon of Saturday 24 August.

Davenant and Shakespeare Sir William's father, the devotee of Shakespeare, had probably left London just before the first performance of *Hamlet* at the Globe on Bankside; he would certainly have seen it at Oxford by 1603 (title-page, first quarto). Later on he no doubt told his young son about the production: thus William Davenant, the man mainly responsible for the return of Shakespeare's plays to the London stage at the Restoration, would have had the unique advantage of hearing a firsthand account of how Richard Burbage played the prince. By 1661 Shakespeare had been dead for nearly half a century; his language would have seemed old-fashioned, his plots were unfamiliar, and tastes had changed. Davenant's version of *Hamlet* (printed 1676) was severely cut—largely of course because of its length—and some of its diction altered in the supposed interest of clarity and intelligibility. However, the power of the play prevailed.

Pepys, who was at the first performance, wrote that it was 'done with Scenes very well. But above all, Batterton [*sic*] did the Prince's part beyond imagination' (Pepys, 2.161). Mary Saunderson, then aged about twenty-five, played Ophelia, her first Shakespearian role in a career which, to quote Colley Cibber, 'was to the last, the Admiration of all true Judges of Nature and Lovers of Shakespeare' (Edmond, 167). John Downes reports in his *Roscius Anglicanus* that 'No succeeding Tragedy for several Yeares got more Reputation, or Money to the Company'.

In October 1661, between a few more presumed showings of *Hamlet* in the summer and following winter, the manager revived his *Love and Honour* of 1634, no doubt having in mind those who did not care for tragedy but loved 'spectacle'. Downes reports that the production was 'Richly Cloath'd': Betterton and two other leading players were allowed to wear the coronation suits of King Charles, the duke of York, and the earl of Oxford respectively—a not uncommon practice. The quality of Davenant's productions demonstrates how much he had benefited from working with Inigo Jones on the court masques of the 1630s.

Thomas Killigrew must have been alarmed at his rival's continuing success: he had never used moveable scenery at Vere Street, and badly needed a larger and better-equipped playhouse to compete. On 20 December 1661 he secured a plot of ground between Drury Lane and Bridges (now Catherine) Street: on this was built the first of the Theatre Royals that have stood to the present day. Work continued throughout 1662—a year in which, on 30 September, Davenant revived one of the great plays of the past, John Webster's *The Duchess of Malfi*. Mary Saunderson played the title role, and Betterton was Bosola: it became one of the most popular tragedies in the company's repertoire (Pepys, 3.209 and n. 1). On the following Christmas eve, Betterton and Mary Saunderson found time to marry before the afternoon performance—making the company even more popular.

Thomas Killigrew finally opened at the Theatre Royal 'with scenes' on 7 May 1663, the cost having risen from an estimated £1500 to £2400. To counter any opposition, Davenant spared no expense on a production in December of Shakespeare's *Henry VIII*, a play in which the element of pageant has always been exploited. The Bettertons played the king and his first wife, Katherine of Aragon, the cast were all 'new cloath'd in proper Habits', and the play ran for fifteen days (Pepys, 4.411 and n. 5).

The date of Davenant's production of *Macbeth* is debatable, but it seems probable that it was launched in 1664. His version would have included music, and marked a further step towards the development of English opera. It would have been a variation on the theme of Shakespeare's play: it was not until 1744 that David Garrick staged it purportedly 'as written by Shakespeare'. Davenant once tried to stage *King Lear*, no doubt with Betterton in the title role, but it evidently did not 'take' until put on at the Dorset Garden Theatre (the company's new playhouse) built shortly after Davenant's sudden death: it was then given a happy ending by Nahum Tate. Davenant's

last brief engagement with Shakespeare was in 1667, when *The Tempest* as altered by him and John Dryden was made into an opera.

Last years Between 1664 and 1668 Davenant launched several new plays and playwrights. In the spring of 1664 he staged with success *The Comical Revenge, or, Love in a Tub*, by George Etherege, a lively prose piece with a realistic underplot, which 'got the Company more Reputation and Profit than any preceding Comedy, and took a thousand pounds in a month' (Edmond, 187). On 6 February 1668 the king was present at another new play by the same author, *She Would if she Could*, and there was a command performance at court on his birthday, 29 May. On 13 August 1664 Davenant staged a play by another new author, Roger Boyle, earl of Orrery: this was a rhymed tragedy, *Henry V*, which had one of his leading players, Henry Harris, in the title role. Again, the three principals wore royal coronation suits. The earl, of a prominent Anglo-Irish family, was the elder brother of Robert Boyle the scientist. In April 1665 Davenant put on a second play by Orrery, *Mustapha, the Son of Solyman the Magnificent*—clearly a follow-up to his own *Siege of Rhodes*. A play called *The Villain*, by Tom, son of Davenant's old friend Endymion Porter, had unexpectedly attracted full houses for ten days in 1662, and had at least one command performance at court in 1667.

In June 1665 a severe bout of plague erupted in the capital; all theatres were closed, and they did not reopen until November 1666. Now began Davenant's short-lived collaboration with Dryden, and in August 1667 he staged Dryden's comedy *Sir Martin Mar-All*. Pepys was unable to get into the first performance, but saw it eight times in whole or in part, in a matter of months: 'It is the most entire piece of Mirth, a complete Farce from one end to the other … I never laughed so in all my life.' In October the Duke's Theatre was so full that the Pepyses had to go to the Theatre Royal: there the diarist heard Nell Gwyn cursing because there were so few people in the pit—the other house was 'said nowadays to have generally most company, as being better players' (Pepys, 8.463–4). This is one of seven references in the *Diary*, from 1663 to 1667, to the superiority of Davenant's players, both men and women, over Killigrew's.

In the first months of 1668 Davenant was as active as ever. On 26 March the king was at his playhouse to see the manager's new play, *The Man's the Master*, based on a French work. There are some shrewd digs at 'Town-Gallants' who put 'Half-Crowns of Brass' into the box instead of 'true Coyne', or pretend 'but to speak to a friend' and get in for nothing. On 7 April Pepys was at the Theatre Royal for a play by James Howard, and went down afterwards to call on his favourite actress, Mrs Knepp, in her dressing room; while they were chatting, news came that 'Sir W Davenant is just now dead' (Pepys, 9.155–6). He had died at his home in the Duke's Playhouse, Lincoln's Inn Fields.

The funeral took place two days later. Pepys went to the Duke's Playhouse to see the cortège leave for Westminster Abbey: 'many coaches, and six horses and many hackneys, that made it look, methought, as if it were the burial of a poor poett' (Pepys, 9.158–9). John Aubrey, at the west door of the abbey, heard the choir sing 'the Service of the Church (I am the Resurrection &c)', and accompanied the coffin to what is now called Poets' Corner. Both observers remarked upon the many young boys, Davenant's sons, in the first mourning coach. Aubrey noted that the marble paving stone above the grave bore the words 'O rare Sr Will: Davenant', echoing the nearby inscription to Ben Jonson, whom Davenant had succeeded as unofficial laureate.

In a long career through great social change, William Davenant kept abreast of and sometimes advanced the tastes of the day: in the 1630s he wrote city comedies in the Jonsonian manner, and tragicomedies of statecraft, love, and intrigue; in the circle of Henrietta Maria he provided entertainments to meet the vogue for Neoplatonism, and wrote poetry in the stylish cavalier manner, honouring the conduct and taste of Caroline courtiers. With Inigo Jones he put on the final court masques, vainly attempting to promote Charles I as a benevolent autocrat, seeking the support of the ruling élite against a surge of discontent. In exile Davenant attempted to create a new style of heroic poetry, Christian, stoical, and high-minded. He returned to London in the dying days of the Commonwealth and surreptitiously introduced a form of English opera while playhouses were still banned: on the restoration of Charles II he opened a modern theatre with scenery, built up a distinguished company of players of both sexes, revived old plays and promoted writers of new ones, and exercised a virtual stage monopoly until his sudden death. His leading players, Betterton and Harris, carried on as directors without a break, until the opening three years later of their new playhouse, then the finest in the capital (Edmond, 204–6).   MARY EDMOND

Sources M. Edmond, *Rare Sir William Davenant* (1987) · *DNB* · Pepys, *Diary* · *Sir William Davenant: the shorter poems and songs from the plays and masques*, ed. A. M. Gibbs (1972) · J. Orrell, *The theatres of Inigo Jones and John Webb* (1985) · S. Orgel and R. Strong, *Inigo Jones: the theatre of the Stuart court*, 2 vols. (1973) · W. A. Pantin and E. C. Rouse, 'The Golden Cross, Oxford', *Oxoniensia*, 20 (1955), 46–89 · *LCC survey of London*, 35 (1970) [on Theatre Royal, Drury Lane and Royal Opera House, Covent Garden] · J. Downes, *Roscius Anglicanus*, ed. M. Summers, [new edn] (1928) · A. H. Nethercot, *Sir William D'Avenant: poet laureate and playwright-manager* (1938) · *Sir William Davenant: dramatic works*, ed. J. Maidment and W. H. Logan, 5 vols. (1872–4) · Wood, *Ath. Oxon.*, new edn, 3.802–9 · Bodl. Oxf., MS Aubrey 6, fols. 46–47*v* · C. Gildon, *The life of Mr Thomas Betterton* (1710) · Essex RO, Chelmsford · testamentary records, marriage licences, etc., Oxon. RO · testamentary records, marriage licences etc., Victoria Library, London · PRO · testamentary records, marriage licences etc., Family Records Centre, Myddelton Street, London EC1 · testamentary records, marriage licences, etc., LMA · testamentary records, marriage licences, etc., GL · leasebooks, New College, Oxford · draft council minutes, 1615–34, Oxon. RO · GL, Merchants Taylors' Company MSS · exchequer records, PRO, E351 series · will, PRO, PROB 11/61/39 [William Sheppard]
Likenesses W. Faithorne the elder, line engraving (after J. Greenhill), Bodl. Oxf., NPG; repro. in *The works of Sir William Davenant* (1673) [*see illus.*]

Davenant, William (1656/7–1681), translator, was the fourth son of the playwright Sir William *Davenant

(1606–1668) and his third wife, Henrietta Maria du Tremblay (*d.* 1691). When plague struck London in 1665 he was probably sent to school at Cheam, Surrey, with his elder brother Charles (Manning and Bray, 2.467). Davenant was 'a youth of very pregnant hopes in learning' ([? June] 1676, Dame Mary Davenant to Charles II, SP, dom., Chas. II 382, no. 175). He studied the Latin and Greek authors under the poet John Milton, who had been released from the Tower of London through the influence of Davenant's father. After Milton died in 1674, Davenant and his close friend the bookseller and publisher Jacob Tonson tried to see Milton's books, but were turned away because Mrs Milton was absent.

Davenant matriculated at Magdalen Hall, Oxford, on 1 August 1673, aged sixteen, and continued his studies under Mr Pullen. He was also admitted to Gray's Inn on 12 February 1676. In June 1676 his mother, a widow since 1668 and unable to maintain him any longer, petitioned the king and her late husband's patron Henry Jermyn, earl of St Albans, unsuccessfully, for Davenant to have a fellowship at All Souls College (28 June 1676, Sir Thomas Clarges to Williamson, SP, dom., Chas. II 382, no. 176). Nevertheless he obtained his BA on 19 July 1677 and his MA on 5 July 1680. His embellished translation of a work by François La Mothe Le Vayer was published in Oxford in 1678, presumably as a means of funding his education. Entitled *Notitia historicorum selectorum, or, Animadversions upon the antient and famous Greek and Latin histories*, it was dedicated to James, earl of Doncaster.

Davenant became tutor to Robert Wymondsold of Putney, who presented him with a living in Surrey and whom he accompanied on a tour of France. He drowned in 1681 while swimming in the Seine near Paris.

ANTHONY R. J. S. ADOLPH

Sources *DNB* · Foster, *Alum. Oxon.* · A. H. Nethercot, *Sir William D'Avenant: poet laureate and playwright-manager* (1938) · W. R. Parker, *Milton: a biographical commentary*, rev. G. Campbell, 2nd edn, 2 · H. Darbishire, ed., *The manuscript of Milton's 'Paradise lost', book 1* (1931) · O. Manning and W. Bray, *The history and antiquities of the county of Surrey*, 3 vols. (1804–14)

Davenport, Allen (1775–1846), radical, was born on 1 May 1775 in Ewen, Gloucestershire. One of a hand-loom weaver's ten children, he was entirely self-educated. At nineteen he enlisted in the Windsor foresters, a light cavalry regiment, with which he served mainly in Scotland. After being discharged in 1801, he spent four years working in Cirencester as a shoemaker (a trade he had learned in the army) before moving to London. Here he spent the remainder of his life, married his wife, Mary, a shoebinder, in 1806, and around the same time fell under the influence of the radical land reformer Thomas Spence.

Davenport was a women's shoemaker, and a member of the union executive of the 'women's men'. In 1813 the union was ruined by a strike, which Davenport opposed, and from this stemmed his lasting scepticism about trade unionism. He concentrated instead upon politics and journalism, mainly for Richard Carlile's *The Republican* but also independently. His first two publications in his own right were poems: *Kings, or, Legitimacy Unmasked* (1819), a spirited republican drama, and *Claremont* (1820?), a contribution to the Queen Caroline affair. Like many Spenceans, he was actively prepared for revolution, and in 1819 followed Wedderburn in forming a Spencean splinter group in Soho. Not surprisingly, he later chose to obscure his activities at this time.

From 1822 to 1828 Davenport left shoemaking to become a watchman at Tollington Park (Holloway), Middlesex. Here he concentrated upon his poetry (a collection, *The Muse's Wreath*, appeared in 1827) and, more notably, political journalism. His return to shoemaking coincided with the rise of Owen's influence among the London trades, and Davenport became an enthusiastic socialist and lecturer to Owenite and adult education groups throughout the capital. More than anyone he was responsible for the revival of interest in Spence (of whom he published a biography in 1836), and he extended the case for public ownership to include not only land but machinery as well. He also advocated birth control and women's rights.

Davenport's wife died in 1816, and Mary Ann, their only known child, around 1824. Dogged by ill health and deteriorating eyesight, he none the less threw himself into the Chartist movement. He was the founding president of the East London Democratic Association, mentor of the young George Julian Harney, and a supporter of the Chartist land plan. During Chartism's doldrum years after 1842 Davenport concentrated on secularism, educational causes, and writing, sustained by public subscriptions organized by Harney and G. J. Holyoake. His poem *English Institutions* (1842) extolled adult education, which was also the main theme of his 1845 autobiography. *The Origin of Man and the Progress of Society* (1846) drew together his popular lecture series tracing the development of private property. Davenport died at Goswell Road, Finsbury, London on 30 November 1846, and was buried in an unconsecrated common grave in Kensal Green cemetery. The graveside oration was delivered by the freethinker W. D. Saull. 'Had he been less poor he would have been more famous' wrote Holyoake in an obituary (Holyoake, 18). However, it was as an educator and agrarian polemicist, rather than as a political leader, that Davenport influenced English radicalism.   MALCOLM CHASE

Sources *The life and literary pursuits of Allen Davenport…written by himself*, ed. M. Chase (1994) • M. Chase, 'Davenport, Allen', *DLB*, vol. 8 • I. Prothero, 'Davenport, Allen', *BDMBR*, vol. 1 • M. Chase, *The people's farm: English radical agrarianism, 1775–1840* (1988) • A. Janowitz, *Lyric and labour in the Romantic tradition* (1998) • I. J. Prothero, *Artisans and politics in early nineteenth-century London: John Gast and his times* (1979) • G. J. Holyoake, *The Reasoner* (29 Jan 1847) • *Northern Star* (5 Dec 1846) • *Utilitarian Record* (Jan 1847)
Likenesses portrait, repro. in A. Davenport, *Life, writings and principles of Thomas Spence* (1836), frontispiece
Wealth at death costs of funeral met by public subscription

Davenport, Christopher [*name in religion* Franciscus à Sancta Clara] (*c.*1595–1680), Franciscan friar and religious controversialist, was born in Coventry in or about the year 1595, the eldest of three children of Barnabas Davenport and Mary Glover. He is often wrongly taken to be the

brother of John Davenport, the puritan, who was his uncle. Wood says that he was educated at the free grammar school of Coventry (Wood, *Ath. Oxon.*, 3.1222). In 1613 he was admitted to Merton College, Oxford, where he studied under Samuel Lane, but he appears to have transferred to Magdalen Hall, taking his degree in 1614. No details are known of his introduction and conversion to the Roman Catholic church. Most biographers assume that this happened at Oxford but it is possible that he converted while at Atherstone grammar school in Warwickshire, where he taught from 1614 until 1616.

Davenport was admitted to the English College at Douai on 28 August 1616 under the name Christopher Davenport, alias Lathroppe. About this time the English Franciscans were being revived, particularly under John Gennings, who was involved in recruiting men from his old college. Among the first of these was Davenport, who entered the Franciscan order at Ypres in October 1617. He now became known as Franciscus à Sancta Clara. He returned to Douai and received the four minor orders, the subdiaconate, and the diaconate in 1619 and was raised to the priesthood on 14 March 1620. According to Wood he then went to Salamanca, where others claim that he gained a reputation as being one of the most able divines. However, if indeed he did go it was only for a short time and he did not receive a doctorate. He returned to Douai where 'he first read philosophy and afterwards became chief reader of Divinity at St. Bonaventure's' (Wood, *Ath. Oxon.*, 3.1222). He then became professor of theology. In 1622 he left the convent at Brussels, where he had also been confessor, to take up his new teaching appointment. With the appointment of Sancta Clara teaching at St Bonaventure's 'began to stumble and slowly bloom again. It produced, in a miraculously short time, men of great learning' (*Fragmenta, vel, Historia Minor*, Douai, 1644, 128). He visited Rome in 1625 to make a request for the restoration of the English province, which was granted fully in 1629.

Davenport returned to England in the early 1630s as a missionary and lodged near Somerset House with Queen Henrietta Maria's Capuchin priests, whom he knew from time he had spent at St Omer. He styled himself as 'theologian' or 'confessor' to Henrietta Maria and though he is often described as her chaplain he does not appear to have been directly employed by her (Dockery, 36–7). Somerset House was a focus of Catholicism in England and Sancta Clara's presence there enabled him to be at the centre of a number of the high-profile conversions of the 1630s, including those of Windebank and Walter Montagu. He was in close contact with Goodman, bishop of Gloucester. From this position Sancta Clara, protected from imprisonment, pressed for reconciliation between the English and Roman churches. He was encouraged by King Charles, who expressed his desire that George Con, the papal agent, 'induce the Pope to meet me halfway' (R. T. Petersson, *Sir Kenelm Digby*, 1956, 93). Sancta Clara was the constant adviser to Panzani in his mission of 1634–6 and it was in the context of possible reconciliation with Rome that he published his most important work, *Deus, natura, gratia*, in 1634.

This book, printed in Lyons, was a bold attempt to prove that the Thirty-Nine Articles were not incompatible with the doctrines of the Roman church, an argument similar to that of the Tractarians in the nineteenth century. It consists of thirty-seven problems, such as predestination and salvation by good works, followed by an explanation of the Thirty-Nine Articles and an attempt to reconcile them with the doctrine of the Catholic church, especially the decrees of the Council of Trent. It was dedicated to the king who was said to be much pleased with it. Panzani wrote that it

> was highly esteemed by His Majesty the King as being full of complaisance for the Protestant systems in several points and discovering an inclination of approaching nearer to them by concessions, where the Catholic cause would permit it to be done. (Berington, 166)

An edition appears to have been printed in England in 1646 and, though it does not survive, other references seem to confirm its existence (Dockery, 64). The book received a hostile reception from many contemporaries, Catholic and protestant. In Rome it was not officially banned, perhaps through the work of the Benedictine procurator, Wilfred Selby (Bodl. Oxf., MS Clarendon 6/394, Selby to Jones, 23 Oct 1634). The Jesuits, especially in Venice, were alarmed at the pre-eminence of the Franciscans and circulated rumours that it had been censured. In Spain it was placed on the *Index expurgatorius*. In England opinion was split on both sides. The Minim friar Francis Maitland declared it 'a devouring fire in God's house in this realm, indeed everywhere' (Dockery, 66). However, the support of King Charles meant that it was not banned. The controversial reputation it gained was not easily forgotten. The seventh article of Laud's impeachment was that he had conferred with Sancta Clara to further popery. Laud denied meeting Sancta Clara more than five times, denied licensing his book, and denied holding the same views as him on the Thirty-Nine Articles, saying that 'the Church of England would have little cause to thank him for it' (Laud, 379).

None the less the book may have increased Sancta Clara's reputation among his own order, who elected him as their provincial in 1637. He continued writing books for the next forty years, publishing works of history, theology, and philosophy, the most important of which was the theological work *Systema fidei* (Liège, 1648), which used ancient authorities to state the essence and authority of a council. He may have left London in the troubles of the civil wars, living under the name of Hunt in Arundel, Sussex, in 1642 before leaving to teach again at Douai in 1647. He returned to live in England for much of the 1650s, visiting Thomas Barlow, Bodley's librarian, in Oxford. Amid calls for toleration he presented to Cromwell in 1656 his 'Explanation of the Roman Catholic belief'. At the Restoration he returned to London and became chaplain to Catherine of Braganza and lodged at the Savoy. From 1667 he lived with the Portuguese Franciscans in London and concentrated on the internal affairs of his order, particularly

raising funds and receiving converts, most notably Anne Hyde, duchess of York, in 1670. His friends in his last years included Anthony Wood, Thomas Blount, and John Belson. He described himself in 1665 as 'already whitehaired and broken with age and study' (Dockery, 130) and died at Somerset House, having moved back there, on Whitsunday, 26 May 1680. Wood states that Sancta Clara had desired to return to Oxford to be buried in St Ebbe's Church. However, despite a further request to be buried under Somerset House, which was refused by the queen, he was buried at the Savoy Chapel. His epitaph in the Capitular register declares him

> a most prudent and loving father to his brethren and children … a vigilant pastor and a faithful labourer for fifty-seven years; making himself all to all, he gained both rich and poor; his name is held in veneration at home and abroad. (Trappes-Lomax, 274)

A. P. CAMBERS

Sources J. B. Dockery, *Christopher Davenport: friar and diplomat* (1960) · Wood, *Ath. Oxon.*, new edn, 3.1221–8 · R. Trappes-Lomax, ed., *The English Franciscan nuns, 1619–1821, and the Friars Minor of the same province, 1618–1761*, Catholic RS, 24 (1922) · J. Fendley, 'William Rogers and his correspondence', *Recusant History*, 23 (1996–7), 285–317 · C. M. Hibbard, *Charles I and the Popish Plot* (1983) · N. Tyacke, *Anti-Calvinists: the rise of English Arminianism, c.1590–1640* (1987) · C. Dodd [H. Tootell], *The church history of England, from the year 1500, to the year 1688*, 3 (1742) · W. Laud, *The history of the tryals and troubles* (1695) · Foster, *Alum. Oxon.* · J. Berington, *History … including the memoirs of Gregorio Panzani* (1763), 166 · W. Camden, *The visitation of the county of Warwick in the year 1619*, ed. J. Fetherston, Harleian Society, 12 (1877) · E. H. Burton and T. L. Williams, eds., *The Douay College diaries, third, fourth and fifth, 1598–1654*, 1, Catholic RS, 10 (1911), 132, 136–7

Archives Bodl. Oxf., Wood MSS, corresp. with Wood

Davenport, Ernest Harold [*pseud*. Nicholas Davenport] (1893–1979), journalist and economist, was born on 10 August 1893 at 10 Ivanhoe Terrace, Ashby-de-la-Zouch, Leicestershire, the youngest in the family of three sons and one daughter of Thomas William Davenport (*d.* 1905/6), a brewer and high Anglican lay preacher of Ashby-de-la-Zouch, and his wife, Florence Elizabeth Lowe; his father died when he was twelve. He was educated at Cheltenham College (1907–12), where he proved an outstanding scholar and athlete—an all-rounder from the start—and then at Queen's College, Oxford, where he obtained a first-class honours degree in modern history (1915) and won the Lothian historical prize (1914).

Barred for medical reasons from military service Davenport worked in the War Office and Ministry of Supply: his experience of government, and of wasteful expenditure, was reflected in his second book, *Parliament and the Taxpayer* (1918); he had already written *The False Decretals* in 1916. After the war he was called to the bar (Inner Temple, 1919), and he contemplated with some uncertainty a conventional career of law and politics, even canvassing the mining village where his father had his mission. But instead he entered the City: his earliest venture, with a British-American oil company, was an abrupt failure but crucially instructive. These were struggling times, financially and domestically. He had married Ada Constance Winifred Wood (*d.* 1946), the daughter of Ernest Wood, businessman; they had one child, a son, born in 1922. The marriage was shadowed by the collapse of her health, and they were divorced.

Meanwhile, somewhat in desperation, Davenport turned to journalism and there found his destiny. His success was instant. His first articles, on the politics of the oil business, were given centre-page prominence in *The Times*—his long and influential career as a writer had begun. He became oil correspondent for *The Guardian* in 1920, and from 1930 to 1953 City columnist for the *New Statesman and Nation*; during these years he contributed to *The Economist* and wrote leaders for the *Investors' Chronicle* (as Candidus). By now he had begun to use the name Nicholas. Then for twenty-five years he wrote the City column for *The Spectator*; he survived nine editors and was asking for more space than usual in the issue of the week of his death. The consistent quality of his commentaries was a matchless achievement in economic journalism. Under weekly pressure for almost six decades, his flow of ideas and elegant prose lost neither wit nor boldness, neither originality nor radicalism.

Davenport's writings were rooted in the reality of his own City career. A broker in the 1920s, he was appointed in 1931 to the board of the National Mutual Life Assurance Society, of which J. M. Keynes was chairman; he became its deputy chairman from 1960 to 1969. His own business ventures ranged beyond institutional commitments, and included the funding of films with Gabriel Pascal in the first *Pygmalion* of G. B. Shaw (1938). Later he worked with Sir Alexander Korda. He served on the short-lived National Investing Council (1946–7), and briefly on the National Film Finance Corporation, founded by Harold Wilson in 1947. At the time of his death he was still a consultant of the internationally respected stockbrokers, L. Messell & Co. So, despite the awkward independence of his views, he enjoyed a lifetime of diverse City affairs and sustained a remarkably wide circle of relationships.

Among these Davenport's work and association with John Maynard Keynes were decisive. His own interpretation of Keynes became central to the purpose of all his writing. It was Keynes who encouraged him to write *The Oil Trusts and Anglo-American Relations* in 1923 (with S. R. Cooke), and to join *The Nation*, where he worked with other socially minded economists and mixed actively with the leading Fabians of the Labour Party. But above all it was the Keynesian challenge to the established ideas of the City that inspired his radicalism: the sheer humanity and gaiety of Keynes chimed with Davenport's own spirit. He became dedicated to making a mixed economy work harmoniously.

Not that Davenport was ever a tidy 'party-liner'. He was certainly close to the Fabian leadership of the Labour Party in the 1930s and 1940s, but at the same time he was also a friend of R. J. G. Boothby and close to Winston Churchill and the non-appeasers. He never ceased his mental fight with both sides of 'the split society'. In 1932 he was one of the founders of the XYZ Club to advise the Labour Party on economic and financial matters, but he despaired of the party's indifference to wealth creation.

He described its post-war government as the 'second puritan revolution', and Labour's 1964–70 period as the 'socialist miscarriage'. Equally, he belaboured the Conservative Party for its alienation of the working class: 'economics without psychology' was meaningless, in his judgement, and it would end in explosion.

Davenport's strategies for the reconstruction of capitalist society were developed in two books, *Vested Interests or Common Pool?* (1942) and the more elegant and cogent diagnosis, *The Split Society* (1964). This latter work showed a disenchantment with revolutionary Marxism of the left: its flexibility repudiated his earlier, wartime, optimism about planning—such as the proposal for a national investment board. Davenport argued that it must be possible to reconcile the imperatives of vigorous private enterprise with the inevitable commitment in any advanced industrial society to a degree of public enterprise.

Davenport never succeeded in persuading any government with his particular strategies: the theme, however, of unity through a wider spread of shares in results and of shared commitment has continued to grow in influence. And his contribution to the build-up of that momentum was unique.

Davenport's individuality found a special focus in his happiness at his Oxfordshire home, Hinton Manor, Hinton Waldrist, a superb Tudor house; in the seventeenth century this had belonged to Henry Marten, republican and regicide, but no leveller, with whose free spirit Davenport felt a lively affinity. His second marriage took place on 27 September 1946, to the actress and painter Olga Florence Baerlein (*b.* 1914/15), who had taken the lead in his one venture into theatre, the play *And so to Wed*, written that year. She was the daughter of J. M. Solomon, distinguished architect in South Africa, and stepdaughter of Hugh Edwards, company secretary, also of South Africa, and the widow of Anthony Baerlein, who was killed in action in 1942. Davenport's sheer joy in their life at Hinton shines through his *Memoirs of a City Radical* (1974) and his last work, about the house itself, *The Honour of St. Valery: the Story of an English Manor House* (1978). He was appointed CBE in 1977 and died at Hinton Manor on 26 May 1979.

PETER PARKER, rev.

Sources N. Davenport, *Memoirs of a City radical* (1974) · *The Spectator* (2 June 1979) · *The Spectator* (9 June 1979) · personal knowledge (1986) · b. cert. · m. cert. [Olga Baerlein]
Wealth at death £89,926: probate, 18 July 1979, *CGPLA Eng. & Wales*

Davenport, Harold (1907–1969), mathematician, was born on 30 October 1907 in Huncoat, near Accrington, Lancashire, the elder child and only son of Percy Davenport, a clerk, and, later, the company secretary, at Perseverance Mill, and his wife, Nancy, daughter of John Barnes, the owner of the mill. From Accrington grammar school Davenport won scholarships to Manchester University where, in 1927 at the age of nineteen, he graduated with first-class honours in mathematics. In Manchester he came to the notice of E. A. Milne, who encouraged him to

Harold Davenport (1907–1969), by Walter Stoneman, 1940

enter for a scholarship at Trinity College, Cambridge. He was successful and in 1929 was classed as wrangler in part two of the mathematical tripos and declared by the examiners to have deserved special credit in the most advanced subjects.

When Davenport first went to Manchester he had an interest in the history of mathematics and thought up the so-called 'birthday paradox' to calculate the number of people needed for a fifty-fifty chance that two share the same birthday. There were no signs of an early commitment to arithmetical questions—he even considered seriously a career in chemistry—but in 1929 all doubts had vanished, and Davenport became Professor J. E. Littlewood's research student, with number theory as his chosen field. Littlewood was then at the height of his fame and Cambridge was soon to become, thanks to his celebrated partnership with G. H. Hardy, a world centre for mathematics. Davenport used his opportunity to the full. His first investigations, into the distribution of quadratic residues, involved pioneering studies of character sums and exponential sums; the skills he acquired then he put to good use in many subsequent researches. Indeed, Davenport assimilated his mathematical experiences so well that they were always readily available for his own and his students' use. By the summer of 1930 his first two papers were in the course of publication, in 1931 he was Rayleigh prizeman, and in 1932 he was elected to a Trinity fellowship.

A long visit to Helmut Hasse in Marburg in 1931 taught Davenport the power of modern algebra in the study of arithmetical questions, as well as giving him a fluent command of German, and their joint work proved to be notably influential. In Germany, Davenport met H. Heilbronn in Göttingen, and, by the time Heilbronn arrived in Cambridge as a refugee in 1933, the two had formed a friendship which led to a successful and lifelong collaboration. Several of their earliest papers were skilful applications of the celebrated circle method of Hardy and Littlewood to novel additive problems, and Davenport himself at this time made several highly original contributions to Waring's problem. He was, for example, the first to prove the best possible result that every sufficiently large integer is representable as the sum of sixteen fourth powers of integers. Years later the mastery he thus gained in all aspects of the circle method was to stand him in good stead in his work on values taken by quadratic and cubic forms in many variables. This work, whether done alone, with collaborators such as B. J. Birch and D. J. Lewis, or by students under his direction, is perhaps the most enduring part of Davenport's mathematical testament.

However, that was still in the future; in 1937, after the expiry of his fellowship, Davenport joined L. J. Mordell as an assistant lecturer in Manchester and set himself to study the geometry of numbers. Although Davenport was by now a scholar of international renown—in 1938 he received the Cambridge ScD, in 1940 he was elected to a fellowship of the Royal Society and won the Adams prize of the University of Cambridge—the Manchester period completed his mathematical education. In 1941 Davenport went to the chair of mathematics at the University College of North Wales in Bangor, where in 1944 he married a colleague from the modern languages department, Annie, daughter of James J. Lofthouse, engineer; there were two sons of the marriage.

In 1945 Davenport became Astor professor of mathematics in University College, London. He drew to him scholars and students from all parts of the world, and when, in 1958, he moved to the Rouse Ball chair of mathematics at Cambridge he recreated there the vitality of his London seminar. Many of his former students demonstrated awe-inspiring qualities; three were winners of Fields medals, 'the Nobel prize of mathematics', and Davenport was proud of them but careful of his many other less able students. He corresponded tirelessly with yet more students (in his beautiful handwriting), giving freely of his enthusiasm, wisdom, and patience.

In 1956 Davenport embarked on his important researches on quadratic forms and his success released a new vitality. From now until his death, and especially after his return to Cambridge, the scale and range of his mathematical activities increased. At the time of his death he was the unquestioned leader of the important British school of number theory.

Davenport was shy and reserved and in later years could put a slight deafness to good use. He was very conservative by temperament, and one of his favourite sayings was that all change was for the worse. He was always accessible, entirely without arrogance, and genuinely modest. While he admired talent enormously, he thought his own achievements more the result of tenacious study and perseverance. He was an outstanding lecturer and exceptionally lucid writer, and his book *The Higher Arithmetic* (1952) is a minor classic.

Davenport was awarded the senior Berwick prize of the London Mathematical Society in 1954, and in 1957–9 he was president of the society. He received the Sylvester medal of the Royal Society in 1967. In 1964 he had been elected an ordinary member of the Royal Society of Science in Uppsala, and in 1968 he received an honorary DSc from the University of Nottingham. He spent the summer term of 1966 at the University of Göttingen, as Gauss professor, the first Englishman to hold this distinguished visiting appointment. He died at Addenbrooke's Hospital, Hills Road, Cambridge, on 9 June 1969. His wife survived him.   HEINI HALBERSTAM, *rev.*

Sources C. A. Rogers, D. A. Burgess, and others, *Memoirs FRS*, 17 (1971), 159–92 · personal knowledge (1981) · private information (1981) · d. cert.
Archives Trinity Cam., corresp. and papers
Likenesses W. Stoneman, photograph, 1940, NPG [*see illus.*] · two photographs, RS
Wealth at death £24,739: probate, 17 Nov 1969, *CGPLA Eng. & Wales*

Davenport [*married name* Hoet], **Hester** [*known as* Roxalana], **styled countess of Oxford** (1642–1717), actress, was born on 23 March 1642. Late in 1660 she was living in Lincoln's Inn Fields, with three other actresses, as a protégée of Sir William and Lady Davenant. During 1661, as a member of Davenant's company, she appeared as Lady Ample in his play *The Wits*, as Gertrude in *Hamlet*, and as Evandra in *Love and Honour*; at some point she seems also to have played Clerora in *The Bondman*. From June 1661 she played her most famous role, Roxalana, in the revival of Davenant's 1656 play, *The Siege of Rhodes*; she was still remembered by this name decades later.

By 18 February 1662, as Samuel Pepys noted with evident regret, Roxalana had left the stage. Popular report was that she had gone to live with Aubrey de *Vere, twentieth earl of Oxford (1627–1703); Hester herself subsequently asserted that she married him in good faith. Depositions in a lawsuit brought by the earl in 1686 to refute her claims are partly based on hearsay evidence so that the exact status of their relationship remains unclear. It was alleged that a marriage had been performed (by implication at some time in 1662 or 1663, at which date the earl was a widower) on a Sunday morning, between ten and eleven, in the dining room of one Elizabeth Farlow, who kept a chandler's shop in Harts Horn Lane, London. The officiant was a man 'in a Minister's Habit' (London, Metropolitan Archive, DL/C/241, fol. 435*v*), considered by some to have been the earl's groom or one of his soldiers. Thereafter Oxford and Hester lived together as man and wife at Jane Price's house in Drury Lane until, Hester being pregnant, they moved to Covent Garden. A son, Aubrey, was born on 17 April 1664 and baptized on 15 May at St Paul's, Covent Garden, with acknowledgement of his paternity, and Oxford eventually paid Hester a pension and assumed responsibility for her debts. Pepys depicted a distinctly disorderly household. On 4 January 1665 he visited and found 'his Lordshipp was in bed at past 10 a-clock: and Lord help us, so rude a dirty family I never saw in my life' (Pepys, 6.3). However, the earl claimed in the lawsuit that Hester had later married one Barber, alias (or possibly as well as) one Radcliffe; he himself contracted an officially recognized marriage with Diana Kirke shortly before 12 April 1673.

Hester lost the case but continued to call herself countess of Oxford. She developed an international reputation as an innocent victim: the memoirs of the count de Grammont, published in English in 1714, asserted that Oxford was attracted by her proud virtue and deceived her into a fake marriage. When she protested she was threatened with violence and appealed to Charles II for redress, including a dowry of 1000 ecus. While no evidence has yet emerged of the appeal to the king, stories of a staged marriage seem to have been widely current.

On 25 July 1703, four months after Oxford's death and as 'dowager countess of Oxford', Hester married Peter Hoet of Gray's Inn at St Benet Paul's Wharf. He was probably significantly younger than his bride for he had been admitted to the inn, as of Debden, Essex, esquire, only on 21 November 1696. Hester's son was buried at St Andrew's, Holborn, on 4 June 1708 as 'earl of Oxford, from Grays Inn'. Hoet died in 1717, probably at his lodgings in Compton Street, and was buried on 8 May at St Dionis Backchurch. 'Hester Oxford' signed her will on 16 November of that year, cutting off her widowed sister, Anne Walker, with the proverbial shilling and leaving the rest of her estate to her friends and executors John Hardy, baker, and Dorcas Magenis, both of the parish of St Anne's, Soho. She died within hours, the will being proved on 18 November, and was buried on 20 November at St Anne's.

V. E. CHANCELLOR

Sources GEC, *Peerage* · Count de Grammont [A. Hamilton], *Memoirs of the life of count de Grammont*, trans. A. Boyer (1714) · J. H. Wilson, 'Lord Oxford's Roxolana', *Theatre Notebook*, 12, 14–16 · LMA, DL/C/240, fols. 141*v*–142*v*; DL/C/241, fols. 288, 435–9 · BL, MS Sloane 1684, fol. 6 · PRO, PROB 11/561, fol. 23 · W. A. Littledale, ed., *The registers of St Bene't and St Peter, Paul's Wharf, London*, 2, Harleian Society, register section, 39 (1910), 57 · W. H. Hunt, ed., *The registers of St Paul's Church, Covent Garden, London*, 1, Harleian Society, register section, 33 (1906), 22 · Pepys, *Diary*, vol. 3 · J. Foster, *The register of admissions to Gray's Inn, 1521–1889, together with the register of marriages in Gray's Inn chapel, 1695–1754* (privately printed, London, 1889), 348 · *Registers of St Dionis Backchurch*, 286 · Highfill, Burnim & Langhans, *BDA*, 4.194–5 · W. Van Lennep and others, eds., *The London stage, 1660–1800*, 5 pts in 11 vols. (1960–68), vol. 1
Likenesses W. MacQueen Pope, portrait, BM · drawings, BM · prints, BM

Davenport, Sir Humphrey (*c.*1566–1645), judge, was the third son of William Davenport of Bramhall, Cheshire, and Margaret, daughter of Richard Asheton of Middleton, Lancashire. Having entered Balliol College, Oxford, in 1581, Davenport progressed to London and the inns of court and chancery, entering Gray's Inn from Barnard's Inn in 1585. An active participant in the life of the inn, Davenport was called to the bar in 1589 and to the bench in 1611; he was Lent reader of the inn in 1613. Created serjeant-at-law in June 1623, Davenport was knighted in 1624, served as king's serjeant-at-law from 1625 to 1630, justice of the court of common pleas from 1630, and chief baron of the exchequer from 1631 until shortly before his death in February or March 1645. Davenport's career was marked by constitutional tensions which led to his parliamentary impeachment in 1641.

Davenport belonged to a Cheshire gentry family with puritan and Catholic branches—but in the ecclesiastical dispute known as *Peter Smart's case* (1628) he supported the Arminians, labelling the puritan Smart 'as wicked a man as any lived in the world' (*Articles of Accusation*, 30), and he served on the 1633 high commission. He married Mary, daughter of Francis Sutton, and they had three sons and two daughters. Davenport was elected MP for Brackley in 1589 through the patronage of the earl of Derby, and introduced a motion in parliament which rebuked clerical actions 'contrary ... to the minds and meanings of the law-makers' (HoP, *Commons, 1558–1603*, 2.21). Davenport lived at Bramhall in Cheshire until about 1597, when he moved to Manchester to become steward of the manors of Christ's College, thereafter settling at Sutton Hall near Macclesfield about 1601. He maintained a presence in the border counties while building up a successful practice in the court of exchequer, almost certainly aided by his uncle, Chief Baron Sir Lawrence Tanfield. By 1619 Davenport was serving as counsel to the earl of Derby in Chester and Flintshire.

Chamberlain considered Davenport the principal accuser in the *Earl of Oxford's case* (1622) and one of the 'prime men' in the great call of serjeants in 1623 (*Letters of John Chamberlain*, 2.433, 518). As king's serjeant Davenport represented the crown in the first stages of *Sir John Eliot's case* (1630), emphasizing 'the great respect which the law gives to the commands of the king' (*State trials*, 2.251). Possessed, in Aylmer's estimation, of a neutrality which 'inclined, if at all, in the royalist direction' (Aylmer, 386), Davenport was raised to a puisne judgeship in the court of common pleas on 2 February 1630, and on 10 January 1631 became the first chief baron of the exchequer to hold his patent at the king's pleasure rather than for as long as he should discharge the office well (*durante bene placito* rather than *quam diu se bene gesserint*); Sir William Jones suggested that Sir James Whitelocke 'in the life of Sir John Walter had promise of the place, but missed of it' (82 ER 121).

In 1633 Davenport was removed from the northern circuit after reiterating in open court Coke's dictum that the council at York in session was not a court of record. In *Hampden's case* (1637–8) he found, upon the basis of a legal technicality, that the king had the power to command payment of ship money, but not in this instance to receive payment—but at the Gloucester assizes in the summer of 1636 he instructed the grand jury to return a bill against a defendant who had spoken against this imposition, and then imprisoned him without showing cause. Condemning his support of royal impositions parliamentary articles of impeachment were presented against Davenport on 6 July 1641, but were subsequently dropped. Davenport

spent the final stage of his life with the king at Oxford. On 11 January 1645 he resigned office; he was buried on 4 March 1645 at Macclesfield. D. X. POWELL

Sources Foss, *Judges*, 6.297–9 · HoP, *Commons, 1558–1603*, 2.21 · Baker, *Serjeants*, 56, 181, 333, 376, 438, 508 · *Articles of accusation, exhibited by the Commons House of parliament now assembled* (1641), 25–35 · W. R. Prest, *The rise of the barristers: a social history of the English bar, 1590–1640* (1986), 42, 65, 355 · *State trials*, 3.250–51 · W. J. Jones, *Politics and the bench: the judges and the origins of the English civil war* (1971), 37, 39, 126–7, 139 · C. Russell, 'The ship-money judgments of Bramston and Davenport', *EngHR*, 77 (1962), 312–18 · *The letters of John Chamberlain*, ed. N. E. McClure, 2 (1939), 433, 518 · *The diary of Sir Richard Hutton, 1614–1639*, ed. W. R. Prest, SeldS, suppl. ser., 9 (1991), 70, 79–81, 91, 111, 132, 137 · J. S. Cockburn, *A history of English assizes, 1558–1714* (1972), 42, 235, 271–2, 287 · J. Rushworth, *Historical collections*, 5 pts in 8 vols. (1659–1701), vol. 2, p. 166 · J. H. Baker, *The legal profession and the common law: historical essays* (1986), 455 · G. E. Aylmer, *The king's servants: the civil service of Charles I, 1625–1642*, rev. edn (1974), 386 · W. R. Prest, *The inns of court under Elizabeth I and the early Stuarts, 1590–1640* (1972), 206 · *Report on records of the city of Exeter*, HMC, 73 (1916), 196 · *Calendar of the manuscripts of the dean and chapter of Wells*, 2, HMC, 12 (1914), 409 · *Child v. Baylie*, Cro Jac 459, 79 ER 393 [CD-ROM] · *Rex v. executors of Daccombe*, Cro Jac 512, 79 ER 437 [CD-ROM] · *Hobert and Stroud's case* (1631), Croke Car 209, 79 ER 784 · *Lord Digby's case*, Hutton 131, 123 ER 1152 [CD-ROM] · *Colledge de Physitians case*, Littleton 349, 124 ER 280 [CD-ROM] · *Kinge v. Loder*, Jones W 230, 82 ER 121 [CD-ROM] · *Symons v. Smith*, Jones W 218, 82 ER 116 [CD-ROM] · *mayor of Kingston upon Hull v. Horner*, 1 Cowper 102, 98 ER 989 [CD-ROM] · *Tanfield v. Davenport*, 2 Cooper T Cottonham 244, 47 ER 1151 [CD-ROM]
Archives CUL, MSS Dd.3.46, fol. 196r; Ee.3.55, fols. 74v–80r; Ee.5.17, fol. 128v; Ii.v.27, fol. 254; CUA Collect. Admin. 38, fols. 247v–249r · BL, MS 4206, fol. 26 | BL, Harley MS 786, fol. 9; 859, fol. 2; 6231, fol. 1; 6810, fol. 12 · BL, Lansdowne MSS 93, fol. 67; 514, fol. 30; 616, fol. 7 · CUL, C. Pell papers, 7, 27; 12, 1r–2v · Hunt. L., ship money, unnumbered piece, MS HA
Likenesses oils, Capesthorne Hall, Cheshire

Davenport, James (1716–1757), Congregationalist minister in America, was born in Stamford, Connecticut, the son of the Revd John Davenport (1668–1731), a Congregational minister, and Elizabeth Morris Maltby, and a descendant of the founder of New Haven colony. A precocious young man, he graduated from Yale College in 1732. He studied theology, was licensed to preach in 1735, and three years later was ordained for a respectable position as Congregational minister at the First Church at Southold, Long Island, New York.

Evangelical preachers, including the transatlantic itinerant George Whitefield, influenced Davenport's style. In his own parish Davenport held services for twenty-four hours without a break, whereupon he collapsed. Soon thereafter he claimed that he could distinguish between the converted and the unconverted, whom he excluded from communion. After meeting Whitefield and Gilbert Tennent in 1740, he became an itinerant revivalist who incorporated extemporaneous, open-air preaching and an extensive use of music, including his own songs. Absenting himself from his Long Island parish, he toured both with Whitefield and on his own in New England.

In his Connecticut travels Davenport exhibited extreme, controversial emotionalism. In New London, observers noted women fainting and in hysterics, while he alternately sang, prayed, and preached. Elsewhere he counted Indians among his converts. Other revivalists had offered general warnings about uninspired ministers, but Davenport specifically named local ministers he felt were not among the saved, including Joseph Noyes of the First Church in New Haven and Thomas Clap, rector of Yale. His anti-clerical warning was that it might be better to eat rat poison than listen to the sermon of an unconverted minister. Also disturbing was his practice of leading crowds late at night through the city streets singing in loud voices. Such activities led to the Connecticut general assembly's charging him in 1742 with disturbing the peace under a new colonial law that outlawed itinerancy. The judgment, which deported him to Southold, New York, claimed that he was 'under the influences of enthusiastical impressions and impulses, and thereby disturb'd in the rational faculties of his mind' (Bushman, 46).

Davenport, who was becoming a most radical revivalist, resumed his itinerancy, and within weeks was preaching in Boston Commons using extravagant, theatrical gestures. In early July 1742 ministers of Boston and Charlestown had agreed not to invite him to preach in their churches, despite their general approval of revivalism, for they opposed his judging ministers, encouraging lay preaching, and street singing. Predictably, Davenport denounced his critics as unworthy, and in August faced charges of slanderous speech against ministers, many of whom interceded with the court to urge leniency. For the second time in 1742, he was declared *non compos mentis* and therefore not guilty. By October he was back in Long Island, where an ecclesiastical council censured him for neglect of his parish.

In New London in March 1743 Davenport exhibited his most extreme fanaticism by encouraging his followers to purify themselves by participating in a book-burning of many classic puritan texts. The next day they built another bonfire of worldly luxury items, such as wigs, jewellery, and clothing. He even cast his own breeches onto the pile, but they were retrieved. This episode resulted in a conviction of profaning the sabbath, and followers lost confidence. From home he solicited opinions of friends, whose letters he published in 1744, as well as his own *Confession and Retractions*, in which he apologized for the New London bonfires, street singing, and denunciations of ministers by name. He confessed doing 'much Hurt to Religion' (Heimert and Miller, 260) by encouraging lay preaching, and lamented his previous reliance on impulses and impressions.

Relations with his Southold parish had long been strained and, as the official relationship dissolved, Davenport began supply preaching for the New Side (evangelical) Presbyterians in New York and New Jersey, and in 1750–51 toured Virginia with Samuel Davies. Upon his return he supplied for Gilbert Tennent's Philadelphia church, and in 1754 became pastor of the New Side Church of Hopewell and Maidenhead, New Jersey. It was a more modest parish than Southold but his reputation improved among the Presbyterians, for he was moderator for the 1754 annual synod meeting and delivered the opening sermon the following year. Yet he faltered with his parish: in his final days he faced petitions for removal. Davenport died on 10 November 1757 in Hopewell, and was buried near Pennington, New Jersey. He was survived by his wife, Parnel (1738/9–1789), with whom he had three children.

Fanatics such as Davenport provided ample evidence for anti-revivalists who claimed that enthusiasm distracted sinners and led to serious errors, but even fellow revivalists feared that his excessive emotionalism threatened to bring disrepute to the whole movement. Ultimately such enthusiastic extremists heightened interest in revivalism but also contributed to its decline.

NANCY L. RHODEN

Sources H. S. Stout and P. Onuf, 'James Davenport and the Great Awakening in New London', *Journal of American History*, 70 (1983), 556–78 · R. E. Cray jun., 'James Davenport's post-bonfire ministry, 1743–1757', *The Historian*, 59 (1996–7), 59–73 · M. R. McCoy, 'Davenport, James', *ANB* · R. L. Bushman, ed., *The Great Awakening: documents on the revival of religion, 1740–1745* (1970) · A. Heimert and P. Miller, eds., *The Great Awakening: documents illustrating the crisis and its consequences* (1967) · J. Tracy, *The Great Awakening: a history of the revival of religion in the time of Edwards and Whitefield* (1845), esp. 230–55 [repr. 1969] · F. B. Dexter, *Biographical sketches of the graduates of Yale College*, 6 vols. (1885–1912) · J. W. T. Youngs, *The Congregationalists* (1990) · E. S. Gaustad, *The Great Awakening in New England* (1965) · C. C. Goen, *Revivalism and separatism in New England, 1740–1800: strict Congregationalists and Separate Baptists in the Great Awakening* (1962) · H. W. Bowden, ed., *Dictionary of American religious biography*, 2nd edn (1993), 139–40 · C. A. Dinsmore, 'Davenport, James', *DAB*, 5.84–5 · J. G. Wilson and J. Fiske, eds., *Appleton's cyclopaedia of American biography*, 2 (1887), 83–4 · *Who was who in America: historical volume, 1607–1896* (1963), 136

Davenport, John (*bap.* 1597, *d.* 1670), minister in America, was born in Coventry, Warwickshire, and baptized at Holy Trinity Church there on 9 April, the son of Henry Davenport (*d.* by 1627), a merchant and alderman of that city, and Winifred Barneby. Probably educated initially at the free school, Coventry, in 1613, shortly after having experienced a religious conversion, he matriculated at Merton College, Oxford. Two years later he transferred to Magdalen College, Oxford, which was known at that time for its puritan sympathies. Shortly thereafter, and before graduating, he left the university in order to accept a chaplaincy at Hylton Castle, co. Durham. He had married Elizabeth Wooley (*d.* 1676), about whom little is known, in or before 1619 when he became curate at St Lawrence Jewry in the City of London. He earned a reputation there as an inspiring preacher and in 1624 was elected vicar of St Stephen, Coleman Street. Because of doubts about his orthodoxy the influence of prominent puritans was needed to persuade the bishop of London to accept his election, but at this stage of his career Davenport conformed to the liturgical practices of the church, convinced that differences over such matters must be subordinated to the need for a united Calvinist front against Catholicism and Arminianism. On 28 June 1625 he was awarded both the BD and MA degrees of Oxford. In that same year he garnered favourable notice for ministering to his flock during a severe outbreak of plague.

The spread of anticalvinism in the church, coupled with the rise of a new ceremonialism, drove Davenport and other puritans towards nonconformity, while the failure of James I and Charles I to support the protestant cause on the continent led them to become critics as well of the government's foreign policy. In 1626 Davenport helped formally to organize the feoffees for impropriations, a corporation that sought to spread puritan influence by purchasing church livings and awarding them to zealous preachers. The same year he joined with Richard Sibbes, Thomas Taylor, and William Gouge in circulating a letter calling for contributions to aid protestant refugees from the Thirty Years' War. In a sermon preached before the London Artillery Company, 'A royal edict for military exercises' (1629), he called for English support for the international protestant cause.

In 1633 the trustees of the feoffees for impropriations were called before high commission and the enterprise was quashed, but none the less that year Davenport joined with Thomas Goodwin, Philip Nye, William Twisse, and other conforming puritans in a meeting at Ockley, Surrey, at the home of Henry Whitfield, where they endeavoured to persuade John Cotton and Thomas Hooker of the need to make what compromises were necessary to maintain their livings in the church. The outcome, however, was that Cotton persuaded a number of his friends, including Davenport, that the demands of the church had become too great and that nonconformity was required of puritan consciences. In consequence, Davenport left England for the Netherlands in December 1633. There he was called by the congregation of the English church in Amsterdam to serve as an assistant to John Paget but the latter, who had previously clashed with Hooker over issues of church government, blocked Davenport's appointment. The dispute in the Amsterdam church anticipated the tensions that would later divide puritans into congregationalists and presbyterians. Davenport's *Church Government and Church-Covenant Discussed* (1643) and *The Power of the Congregational Churches Asserted and Vindicated* (1672) were based on manuscripts that he circulated in the 1630s setting forth his position in opposition to Paget. Blocked from a formal call, he ministered to unofficial congregations in Amsterdam and Rotterdam for a time; his only child, John, was born and baptized on 15 April 1635 at The Hague.

In 1636 Davenport returned secretly to England to prepare to migrate to America. Together with other members of his former congregation of St Stephen, Coleman Street, Davenport arrived in Boston, Massachusetts, in June 1637. He participated in the Cambridge synod and the examination of Anne Hutchinson, and advised on the formation of Harvard College. In 1638 he and his followers founded the town and colony of Quinnipiac, later renamed New Haven. The new colony closely reflected Davenport's belief in congregations rigorously restricted to the elect and in civil affairs strongly controlled by the godly.

Davenport closely followed the course of political and religious change in England. He was invited to sit in the Westminster assembly of divines, convened in 1643 to propose a reform of the national church, but chose to stay in America and offer advice from afar. He was the spokesman for the New England clergy in *An Answer of the Elders of Severall Churches in New England* (1643) which responded to queries from England about colonial polity. He wrote other tracts on church reform in the 1640s and 1650s, defending congregationalism from both presbyterian and sectarian attacks. When the Cromwellian regime collapsed he was instrumental in providing refuge for the proscribed regicides Edward Whalley and William Goffe. His *The Saints Anchor-Hold, in All Storms and Tempests* (1661) was a series of sermons preached to the New Haven faithful urging them to remain committed to their mission despite the Stuart Restoration.

Davenport continued to cling to the model of reform created by his generation of founders. He unsuccessfully opposed the merger of New Haven with the more liberal Connecticut colony in 1662, and he was the foremost opponent of the liberalization of colonial church membership referred to as the half-way covenant. His career ended in controversy following his acceptance in 1667 of a call to replace the deceased John Wilson as pastor of the First Church of Boston. His claim to have been released for the new post by his New Haven church led to charges of deception, and his strong conservative stand caused a split in his new congregation, triggering a highly charged debate over the autonomy of local congregations, a debate that was further inflamed by his election sermon to the Massachusetts legislature in 1669. He died at Boston on 15 March of the following year of a paralytic stroke, and was buried in what became King's Chapel burial-ground; he was survived by his wife, who died on 15 September 1676. Less renowned as a preacher and theologian than Cotton or Hooker, Davenport's longevity and more mainstream views allowed him to have a longer and more profound role in the shaping of New England religion than his two famous contemporaries.

FRANCIS J. BREMER

Sources *Letters of John Davenport, puritan divine*, ed. I. M. Calder (1937) · I. M. Calder, *The New Haven colony* (1934); repr. (1962) · F. J. Bremer, *Congregational communion: clerical friendship in the Anglo-American puritan community, 1610–1692* (1994) · M. Peterson, *The price of redemption* (1998) · F. J. Bremer, 'Davenport, John', *ANB* · T. Webster, *Godly clergy in early Stuart England: the Caroline puritan movement, c.1620–1643* (1997) · *DNB* · W. B. Sprague, *Annals of the American pulpit*, 1 (1857)
Archives American Antiquarian Society, Worcester, Massachusetts, sermons, essays, papers · BL, letters to Lady Vere, Add. MS 4275 · Mass. Hist. Soc. · Yale U.
Likenesses oils, Yale U., New Haven, Connecticut; repro. in Calder, ed., *Letters*, frontispiece

Davenport [*née* Harvey], **Mary Ann** (1759–1843), actress, was born at Launceston, Cornwall. Her stage début took place at Bath on 21 December 1784, when she appeared as Lappet in Henry Fielding's *The Miser*. After two seasons at Bath she performed in Exeter and Bristol, where in 1786 she married George Gosling Davenport (1758?–1814), a provincial actor. The pair were itinerant strollers before they were engaged at the Crow Street Theatre, Dublin, in 1792. She opened as Rosalind in *As You Like It*, and continued to specialize in juvenile heroines. In an emergency, however, she undertook the part of an old woman. The

Davenport died at her house, 17 St Michael's Place, Brompton, on 8 May 1843, aged eighty-four, and was buried seven days later at St Paul's, Covent Garden. Her obituary in the *Gentleman's Magazine* (July 1843) recorded that she lived alone, and that her children, a daughter, and a son with a post in India, had predeceased her. Their names are unknown: the Maria Gosling Davenport of Hammersmith, who was buried at St Paul's, Covent Garden, on 1 February 1838, aged forty-seven, is presumed to have been her daughter. JOSEPH KNIGHT, *rev.* K. A. CROUCH

Sources Highfill, Burnim & Langhans, *BDA* · C. B. Hogan, ed., *The London stage, 1660–1800*, pt 5: *1776–1800* (1968) · *Dramatic Magazine*, 2 (1830), 155, 163 · *GM*, 2nd ser., 20 (1843) · *Oxberry's Dramatic Biography*, 2/26 (1825), 159–63 · J. W. Cole, *The life and theatrical times of Charles Kean … including a summary of the English stage for the last fifty years*, 2 vols. (1859) · T. Gilliland, *The dramatic mirror, containing the history of the stage from the earliest period, to the present time*, 2 vols. (1808) · T. Bellamy, 'The London theatres: a poem', *Miscellanies in prose and verse*, 2 vols. (1794–5) · *Monthly Mirror* (Oct 1794)
Likenesses S. De Wilde, drawing, 1802, V&A · S. De Wilde, watercolour drawing, 1809 (as Fiametta in *The tale of mystery*), Garr. Club · B. Burril, watercolour, probably exh. RA 1818, Garr. Club · C. Cork, engraving (as Mrs Peachum in *The beggar's opera*; after G. Clint) · S. De Wilde, oils, Garr. Club [*see illus.*] · W. Leney, engraving (as Winifred Evans in *The school for rakes*; after J. Roberts), repro. in *Bell's British theatre* (1795) · W. Ridley, stipple (as "Mrs Grundy" (actually Dame Ashfield) in *Speed the plough*; after S. De Wilde), BM; repro. in *Monthly Mirror*, 19 (1805), 73 · G. Romney, oils · prints, BM, NPG · six prints, Harvard TC · stipple (as Nurse in *Romeo and Juliet*), BM; repro. in *Dramatic Magazine* (June 1830)
Wealth at death bequests of 10 guineas and £100 to relatives and/or servants: Highfill, Burnim & Langhans, *BDA*

Mary Ann Davenport (1759–1843), by Samuel De Wilde [as Dame Ashfield in *Speed the Plough* by Thomas Morton]

experiment was a success, and she was never able to return to her former line.

The next season, the Davenports were engaged at Covent Garden, each earning £2 a week. On 24 September 1794 Mary Ann appeared as Mrs Hardcastle in Goldsmith's *She Stoops to Conquer*. In the course of the season she played Lady Wronghead in Vanbrugh's *The Provoked Husband*, the Nurse in *Romeo and Juliet*, and the title role in Sheridan Knowles's *The Duenna*. She remained at Covent Garden for the next thirty-six years, though she spent some summer seasons at the Haymarket, and proved a well-respected favourite. By 1824–5 she was making £12 a week. Original parts included Deborah Dowlas in Colman's *The Heir-at-Law*, Dame Ashfield in Thomas Morton's *Speed the Plough*, Mrs Brulgruddery in Colman's *John Bull*, and Monica in William Dimond's *The Foundling of the Forest*.

Davenport was complimented in *Oxberry's Dramatic Biography* (1825) for her private character as 'a hospitable, generous, kind-hearted creature' and described as 'of the common size', with a light complexion and blue eyes. Her husband also acted at Covent Garden, but was perceived as the lesser performer and was the object of some banter in the theatrical records. However, he was a useful member of the company and served as secretary to the Covent Garden Theatrical Fund until his retirement in 1812. After his death, on 13 March 1814, Mary Ann lived in seclusion with her daughter, and contemporary sources commend her continued reliability on the stage. She retired on 25 May 1830, appearing for the last time as the Nurse in *Romeo and Juliet*.

Davenport, Nicholas. *See* Davenport, Ernest Harold (1893–1979).

Davenport, Richard Alfred (1776/7–1852), author and publisher, is of unknown parentage. His first venture into publishing appears to have been the (notionally) annual *Poetical Register*, which first appeared in 1801. This featured often coruscating reviews of other poetical compilations, and numerous examples of his own verse which, even allowing for romantic affectation, showed a depressive streak. 'An admonitory epistle', an attack on alarmist anti-Jacobinism from 1809, betrayed political sympathies with the whiggery of moderate reform. In June of the same year he tried a begging letter to the politician William Windham, addressed from Twickenham, Middlesex, in which he pleaded his inability to provide for his family. A son, Theodore Alfred Davenport, later became professor in the college of Boulogne (Davenport, will). No further details of Davenport's personal circumstances have been discovered beyond his shifts of address; by September 1810 he was at Perry Hill, Sydenham, Surrey. The *Poetical Register* ceased in 1814, with the belated publication of the volumes for 1810–11. By 1809 Davenport was also styling himself in correspondence as editor of the *Annual Register* (the title published by the Rivingtons, which ceased about 1812), to which he had previously been a contributor.

Subsequently Davenport found a niche as a prolific writer of books and articles on history, biography, and criticism: he was a contributor to *The British Poets*, published by Charles Whittingham (1822), and among his own compilations of ephemera were *New Elegant Extracts* (1823–7) and *The Commonplace Book of Epigrams* (1825). By May 1830 he had evidently moved to Camberwell, Surrey, where he resided from about 1841 at Brunswick Cottage, Park Street. His energy for written composition never flagged, and his works contain internal evidence of hard toil and a painstaking attention to detail: his *Dictionary of Biography* (1831) featured 4000–5000 entries and international coverage. While in its preface he regretted that his *History of the Bastille* (1835) was not comprehensive, he was none the less pleased to denominate it 'the only work in the English language to have the slightest pretension' to cover the subject, and was vindicated by reprints in 1838, 1876, and 1883. Among his revisions and continuations of existing works were editions of William Mitford's *History of Greece* (1835) and two revised editions of Matthew Pilkington's *General Dictionary of Painters* (1829 and 1851).

In 1850 the author John Britton wrote of Davenport:

This laborious, critical and acute writer is scarcely known to the public, nor even to the literati of the present time. A devoted student and lover of books, he has lived in the midst of these fascinating companions, and has neglected to cultivate an intimacy with the world, which owes him much. (*GM*, 525)

Davenport died on 25 January 1852 at Brunswick Cottage, in circumstances that lent a savage irony to the title of his 1841 potboiler, *Lives of Individuals who Raised themselves from Poverty to Eminence and Fortune*. A passing policeman heard moans, and inside found Davenport semi-conscious, clutching a bottle of laudanum, and surrounded by empties. He was beyond medical assistance; a coroner's jury found that he had died of an accidental overdose. At Brunswick Cottage they found all the windows broken, and the interior 'crowded with books, papers, pictures, coins and curiosities, but all covered in dust, for no one remembered that the house had been cleaned in the eleven years he had occupied it' (ibid.). This squalid yet picturesque scene of artistic poverty was lovingly dwelt upon by contemporary obituaries and memoirs. Davenport's library was sold in April. He left his house and meagre personal estate to his son, and requested burial at Nunhead cemetery, in the plot next to a Mrs Manison or Mannion, 'one of the most amiable and kind hearted of human beings' (Davenport, will). His erroneous identification as Robert Davenport on his death certificate bore further testimony, if it were needed, to his thorough estrangement from society at large.   H. J. SPENCER

Sources *GM*, 2nd ser., 37 (1852), 525 · *DNB* · correspondence between R. A. Davenport and Mary Russell Mitford, 1810–30, BL, Add. MS 35341 · R. A. Davenport, letter to William Windham, 5 June 1809, BL, Add. MS 37916, fol. 158 · will of R. A. Davenport, 27 May 1847, PRO, PROB 11/2147/112 · d. cert.
Archives BL, corresp. with Mary Russell Mitford, Add. MS 35341
Wealth at death £193 17s. 4d.: PRO, death duty register IR26/1925/67 (proved 5 Feb 1852)

Davenport, Robert (*fl.* 1624–1640), playwright, is one of the most obscure dramatists of the Caroline era. In 1639 he dedicated a poem to two actors, and so he may have been the Robert Davenport, gentleman of St Botolph, London, who was arrested in 1612 along with William Stratford of Prince Henry's men for wounding Henry Saunders at Hoxton.

The first certain record of Davenport comes on 10 April 1624, when *The Historye of Henry the First, Written by Damport* was licensed for the King's Men by the master of the revels. This play is lost but it was entered in the Stationers' register in 1653 along with another lost play, *Henry the 2nd*, as a work of 'Shakespeare, & Davenport' and it also appears in William Warburton's eighteenth-century list of play manuscripts burnt by his cook. The attribution to Shakespeare has been generally dismissed by scholars. On 14 October 1624 another play of Davenport's, *The City Night-Cap*, was licensed for Lady Elizabeth's men at the Cockpit, and this work was eventually printed in 1661. This moral comedy contains contrasting plots of a virtuous wife and a jealous husband (taken from Robert Greene's *Philomela*), and a faithless but witty wife and a foolish husband (taken from Boccaccio's *Decameron*).

Davenport's next known play, *King John and Matilda*, is a reworking of Chettle and Munday's *Death of Robert Earl of Huntington* (1598); although it was first mentioned in 1639 and not printed until 1655 it can be dated 1628–34 from the cast list provided in the quarto. In 1630 'A Comedy called The Pedler by R: Davenport' was entered in the Stationers' register, which may be either a lost play or a misattribution of Thomas Randolph's *Conceited Pedlar*. About 1634 Davenport wrote a manuscript, 'Dialogue between Policy and Piety', dedicated to John Bramhall, bishop of Derry, and containing veiled commentary on Irish affairs. Since Davenport signed the dedication 'a servant and poore neighboure' (Folger Shakespeare Library, Washington, Folger MS V.a.313) he may have been living in Ireland at the time. Another manuscript of the 'Dialogue', dedicated to Sir John Kaye, was noted by Hunter in *Chorus vatum Anglicanorum* as belonging to John Wittern of Broomhead. Davenport's manuscript poem 'A Survey of the Sciences' (now at Cambridge) was probably written about the same time; it is dedicated in similar terms to Dr John Oldesworth, contains a nearly identical exhortation 'To the Booke', and has the same closing line. A third manuscript by Davenport, datable to 1629–43 and dedicated to William Cavendish, earl of Newcastle, contains a prose character and four poems expressing conventional moral sentiments.

In 1639 Davenport published a volume containing two religious poems in dialogue form, *A Crowne for a Conqueror* and *Too Late to Call Back Yesterday*. It was dedicated to two actors of the King's Men, Richard Robinson and Michael Bowyer, and in the dedication Davenport calls the poems 'some expence of my time at Sea' (Bullen, 311). The same year saw the publication of a moral comedy attributed to Davenport, *A New Trick to Cheat the Devil*, in which the Devil appears dressed as a gentleman. However, Lake has cast doubt on Davenport's authorship on stylistic grounds; furthermore, the address from the publisher calls the play 'an Orphant, and wanting the Father which first begot it' (Bentley, 235), even though the following year Davenport prefixed commendatory verses to Nathaniel Richards's *Tragedy of Messalina* and to Thomas Rawlins's *The Rebellion*.

In 1651 Samuel Shepard addressed an epigram 'To Mr. Davenport on his Play called the Pirate' (Monie, vii) and the address to the reader in the 1655 quarto of *King John and Matilda* is signed R. D., both further suggesting that Davenport was still alive. In 1653 *The Woman's Mistake* (now lost) was attributed to Davenport and Drew in the Stationers' register, and in 1660 *The Fatal Brothers* and *The Politic Queen* (also lost) were attributed to Davenport alone. Several extant anonymous plays have been attributed to him on dubious grounds.   DAVID KATHMAN

Sources G. E. Bentley, *The Jacobean and Caroline stage*, 7 vols. (1941–68), vol. 3, pp. 225–38 · W. J. Monie, 'Introduction', 'Sources', *A critical edition of Robert Davenport's 'The city night-cap'* (1979) · J. O. Davis, *Robert Davenport's 'King John and Matilda': a critical edition* (1979), iii–lxxiv · A. H. Bullen, 'Introduction', *The works of Robert Davenport* (1890), xi–xix · M. Eccles, *Brief lives: Tudor and Stuart authors* (1982), 36 · G. Thorn-Drury, ed., *A little Ark containing sundry pieces of seventeenth-century verse* (1921) · 'A dialogue betweene Pollicy and Piety by Robert Davenport', ed. A. H. Tricomi, *English Literary Renaissance*, 21 (1991), 190–216 · D. J. Lake, *The canon of Thomas Middleton's plays* (1975), 233–8

Davenport, Samuel (1783–1867), engraver, was born in the parish of St John, Bedford, on 10 December 1783, and was baptized on 14 May 1784 at St Paul's Church, Bedford, the son of Samuel and Jemima Davenport. His sister Maria was baptized on 22 August 1788 at St Mary's, Bedford. His father was a land surveyor and architect, and the family moved early in Samuel's life to London. From about 1797 to 1804 he was apprenticed to the engraver Charles Warren, following him in the illustration of books. He later specialized in outline portrait work, much of which appeared in contemporary publications: Redgrave records that 700 were done for a single work, possibly one of the serials then popular.

On 31 May 1819 at St Pancras Old Church London, Davenport married Sarah Castle with whom he had a son, Samuel Thomas Davenport, who worked for the Royal Society of Arts from 1843 to 1875. In 1839 Pigot's *Directory of London* gave his address as 38 Myddleton Street, Clerkenwell, London (Pigot, 111). Owing doubtless to Charles Warren's influence, Davenport was an early exponent of steel-engraving, which he used for his major series of engravings for the British annual *Forget-me-Not* in the volumes published between 1828 and 1842 after artists such as Henry Corbould and H. C. Shenton, who was Warren's pupil and eventually son-in-law. Davenport contributed four plates to a new edition of William Hogarth's *Works*, published in 1833. A departure from his previous work came with the production of forty-eight views to accompany the four volumes of the Revd G. N. Wright's *New and Comprehensive Gazetteer* (1834–8). He contributed the ten illustrations on steel to George Cruikshank's *Eighty-Two Illustrations on Steel, Stone and Wood* (c.1870), finely engraved and remarkably preserving the artist's sense of caricature, formerly achieved through etching. Most of his plates were in line on copper or steel and signed Davenport, but S. Davenport and S. Devonport are also known. He was almost certainly the author or part-author of an article on book illustration in the *Journal of the Society of Arts* (January 1865), and was also the author of *Engraving*, a pamphlet published in the series British Manufacturing Industries by Edward Stanford, edited by G. Phillips Beavan, some parts of which were issued in the 1870s. Davenport died on 14 or 15 July 1867 at his home, 38 Myddleton Street, Clerkenwell, London, of senile decay, leaving a widow, his second wife, Frances. His death certificate described him as a historical line engraver.

B. HUNNISETT

Sources Redgrave, *Artists* · IGI · d. cert. · B. Hunnisett, *An illustrated dictionary of British steel engravers*, new edn (1989) · J. Pigot & Co., *Directory of London* (1822–39), 111 · CGPLA Eng. & Wales (1867)

Wealth at death under £50: administration, 29 Aug 1867, *CGPLA Eng. & Wales*

Davenport, William (*bap.* 1584, *d.* 1655), landowner and diarist, was baptized in Stockport, Cheshire, on 25 March 1584, the son and heir of Sir William Davenport (1563–1627) of Bramhall and Dorothy Warren (*fl.* 1566?–1615), the daughter of a neighbouring gentleman. William Davenport is an especially well-documented example of someone who refused to take sides in the English civil war and who suffered for it. He was the head of a cadet line of a cadet branch of a Domesday family, a one-manor gentry family with an income of perhaps £400 p.a. in the 1630s, in the top fifty but not the top thirty families in Cheshire. His ancestors in the fourteenth and fifteenth centuries had been chief foresters of the royal forest of Macclesfield, and his family served continuously from the first Cheshire commission of the peace in 1543 to the death of his father in 1627. Sir William had rebuilt the family home—Bramall Hall—at the turn of the sixteenth century as a magnificent timber-framed mansion—a 'fair house and a park and all things fit for a worshipful seat' (W. Webb, *Perambulation*, 1656, 70). The marriage of his daughters to mere merchants suggests that Sir William may have overextended himself in this rebuilding.

Davenport himself married twice into families higher in the Cheshire rank order of wealth and status than himself; first, in 1599, he married Frances (*d.* 1620), daughter of Thomas Wilbraham of Woodhey, and second, in 1637, he married Margaret (*d.* 1653), daughter of Thomas Legh of Adlington. His father's brother Humphrey was—as chief baron of the court of exchequer—at the centre of legal controversy in the 1630s; his mother's brother was a Jesuit but his own religion seems to have been staunchly conformist Anglican. His younger brother Humphrey was killed in the duke of Buckingham's failed Île de Ré expedition in counter-productive support of the French Huguenots in 1627; he was a country squire with intriguing connections.

Between 1613 and 1650 Davenport kept one of the most interesting of all gentry commonplace books. The first half covers events at court, at Whitehall, and at Westminster, and contains accounts of the failure of English arms abroad down to 1641. It then becomes a chronicle of Davenport's experiences during the lead up to, and through, the civil wars. The first half demonstrates just how much information about matters of public concernment was circulated in manuscript by the 1610s and 1620s; it ranges from scabrous accounts of the divorce of the earl and countess of Essex and the ensuing Overbury scandal (1612–15), and of the earl of Castlehaven's trial for sodomy (1631), to copies of the speeches of all eight managers in the impeachment of the duke of Buckingham (1626), a speech allegedly made by Archbishop Abbott in council against a greater tolerance of Catholic practice (1623), and details of the marriage negotiations (1622–3) between the then Prince Charles and the Spanish court for the hand of the Spanish infanta. Disapproval of royal fiscal policy, of a bungled royal foreign policy, and of corruption at court did not make this unpuritan man a parliamentarian in the civil war. But conventional Anglican piety and a distaste for local sectarian activity did not make him a royalist either.

After 1640 Davenport's book changes and becomes an account of his own experiences. It records the petition—humble in tone, determined in purpose—presented to him by a group of his tenants on 17 September 1642. It explains why, despite his own misgivings, they felt bound in conscience to enlist as soldiers in a parliamentarian regiment being raised by a neighbouring gentleman. It records his decision to remain neutral and to obey all lawful commands (which he took to mean warrants in due form from both sides) and it lays out the various contributions that he made to royalist and parliamentarian commanders. It also records various raids and the pillaging of his house by both sides, and his formal protests (for instance, when he was forced by a file of parliamentarian soldiers to dismount, hand over his horse, and walk home; a subsequent strong protest to their gentleman-captain brought an apology and the return of the horse). His even-handedness did not prevent a local committee from confiscating his estate on account of the assistance he had given to the royalists, and he then fell foul of an internal feud within the parliamentarian bureaucracy; he had to pay fines totalling £995 to two different bodies (the local sequestration committee and the committee for compounding with delinquents in London). Davenport demonstrates that an unwillingness to take sides in the civil war and a willingness to obey whoever was in power in his area was no guarantee of a quiet life. He was buried at the parish church, Stockport, on 24 May 1655.

JOHN MORRILL

Sources J. S. Morrill, 'William Davenport and the "silent majority" of early Stuart England', *Journal of the Chester Archaeological Society*, 58 (1975), 115–29 · R. Cust, 'News and politics in early modern England', *Past and Present*, 112 (1986), 79–87 · J. S. Morrill, *Revolt in the provinces* (1998), 31–4, 63, 125 · J. S. Morrill, *Cheshire, 1630–1660: county government and society during the English revolution* (1974), 21–4, 27, 47, 78, 213 · J. P. Earwaker, *East Cheshire: past and present, or, A history of the hundred of Macclesfield*, 1 (1877), 432–9 · W. Davenport, commonplace book, Ches. & Chester ALSS, CR 63/2/19

Archives Ches. & Chester ALSS, commonplace book, CR 63/2/19
Likenesses portrait, repro. in Earwaker, *East Cheshire: past and present*, vol. 1, p. 438

Wealth at death £400 p.a.: M. A. E. Green, ed., *Calendar of the committee for compounding with delinquents*

Davenport, William (1725–1797), merchant and slave-trader, was born in Red Lion Square, London, in October 1725, the fourth of the eleven children of Davies Davenport (1696–1740), a gentleman, of Woodford and Marton, near Nantwich, Cheshire, and his wife, Penelope (c.1700–1737), the daughter and heir of John Ward, a gentleman, of Capesthorne, near Macclesfield, Cheshire. Both of his parents died before he was sixteen. In 1741 he was apprenticed to William Whaley, a merchant, of Liverpool. Eight years later he became a freeman of the city, being described as a 'grocer, now merchant'.

Davenport dedicated his adult life to commerce. In company with Whaley, he began investing in trading ventures in the late 1740s, and he continued to be involved in overseas trade with various Liverpool merchants, including members of the Earle and Heywood families, until five years before his death. He traded to Venice and Leghorn and was also a partner in a firm of wine merchants in Harrington Street, Liverpool. It was, however, the African slave trade which dominated Davenport's career. From his office in Drury Lane (after 1789, Mathew Street), he invested in no fewer than 160 voyages to Africa for slaves between 1748 and 1792. Furthermore, as co-owner of a bead warehouse, he was a leading supplier of goods to other merchants involved in slave trafficking. Three of his brothers—Christopher, Richard, and Thomas—also invested in slaving voyages, but William clearly dominated the family's trading activities. Surviving accounts suggest that during his career he invested at least £120,000 in the slave trade, and that at the peak of his involvement in the trade—from 1763 to 1775—his investments totalled about £90,000. Returns on this investment fluctuated sharply, but averaged about 8 to 10 per cent per annum. Moreover, records relating to his bead business show that, in the period 1766–70 alone, he supplied some £39,000 of goods to slave ships. Interestingly, Davenport seems rarely, if ever, to have been involved in political lobbying on behalf of the slaving interest at Liverpool. Nor does he seem to have sought election to the city council or political office. There is, nevertheless, little doubt that he was one of the most dedicated of Britain's slave traders in this period.

Davenport was, however, more than simply an investor in slaving voyages; he was also an architect of important changes in patterns of British trade in west Africa and the West Indies between 1750 and 1775. As a managing owner of slave ships, he was instrumental in promoting the growth of British slave trading with the Cameroons. Before 1750 very few ships traded with this region, but from the mid-1750s slaves began to be exported from the region, and ships owned and managed by Davenport were crucial to its entry into the transatlantic slave trade. The records suggest that the ventures to the Cameroons were among the most profitable of Davenport's overseas enterprises, yielding returns up to twice as high as those achieved elsewhere. At the same time, a high proportion of the ships managed by Davenport delivered their slaves to Dominica and Grenada. These colonies came under British rule only in 1763 but, under the stimulus of buoyant demand in Europe for sugar, developed rapidly during the following three decades. In supplying these islands with African slaves, Davenport's ships helped to open up a new frontier of British plantation agriculture after 1763.

A bachelor, Davenport died in August 1797 and was buried at St Nicholas Church, Prescot, Lancashire. The value of his estate is unknown, but he is reputed to have left the bulk of his fortune to his brother Richard, of Marlow, Buckinghamshire, and his nephew Davies Davenport, of Woodford, Marton, Capesthorne, and Calveley, Cheshire.

DAVID RICHARDSON

Sources D. Richardson, 'Profits in the Liverpool slave trade: the accounts of William Davenport, 1757–1784', *Liverpool, the African slave trade, and abolition*, ed. R. Anstey and P. E. H. Hair (1976), 60–90 · Burke, *Gen. GB* · *Gore's Liverpool Directory* (1766–90) · *Bailey's western and midland directory* (1783) · apprenticeship enrolment books, freemen's registers, Lpool RO · *Billinge's Liverpool Advertiser* (28 Aug 1797) · R. Craig and R. Jarvis, *Liverpool registry of merchant ships*, Chetham Society, 3rd ser., 15 (1967) · L. Bromley-Davenport, *The history of Capesthorne*, rev. edn (privately printed, 1974)
Archives Keele University, Raymond Richard collections, Davies-Davenport MSS · Liverpool Museum, accounts of *Calveley, Chesterfield*, and *Eadith*
Wealth at death see obit., *Billinge's Liverpool Advertiser* (28 Aug 1797)

Davey, (James) Ernest (1890–1960), theologian, was born on 24 June 1890 in the manse of the First Presbyterian Church, Castle Street, Ballymena, co. Antrim, the eldest of the seven children (four boys and three girls) of the Revd Charles Davey (1857–1919), Presbyterian minister, and his wife, Margaret (1864–1945), daughter of James Beatty, chemist and druggist, of Ballymena. Ernest's father, whose biography he wrote in 1921, was a preacher of almost mesmerizing power, generous, highly-strung, and perpetually overworked; his mother was quieter and more mystical in spirit. Both left their stamp on their son's adult personality. The family moved to Belfast when Ernest was one.

After an outstanding career at Campbell College, Belfast (1903–9), and at King's College, Cambridge (1909–13), Davey graduated BA in 1912 with first-class honours (third division) in classics (another first, in theology, followed in 1913), proceeded MA in 1916, and was a fellow of King's from 1916 to 1922. He prepared for the Presbyterian ministry at Edinburgh University (1913–15) and at the Presbyterian college, Belfast (1915–16), graduating BD from the former (1917) with among the highest marks recorded in a generation. He also studied briefly at Heidelberg University in 1914. Three months before his ordination in September 1917, he was appointed to the staff of the Presbyterian college, Belfast, where he remained until his death, occupying in succession the chairs of church history (1917–22), biblical literature and Hellenistic Greek (1922–30), Hebrew and Old Testament (1930–33), and New Testament language, literature, and theology (1933–60). In Belfast on 30 April 1927 Davey married Georgiana Eliza (1896–1975), daughter of Henry O'Neill, medical practitioner and barrister; they had a son and two daughters.

Davey came to prominence when, in *Our Faith in God* (1922) and *The Changing Vesture of the Faith* (1923), and in his college lectures, he suggested that certain external forms of Christian belief and practice (including some of the doctrines and credal statements of his own church) were outmoded or inadequate for contemporary needs and experience. Such views disturbed many Ulster Presbyterians, whom the conflict associated with the birth of Northern Ireland in 1921 had already left unsettled and anxious for certainty. Suspicions of 'rationalism' and 'modernism' at the Presbyterian college were voiced in a series of blistering evangelistic rallies by the Revd W. P. Nicholson and led to the formation of the Presbyterian Bible Standards League, which published a series of allegations against the professors by the Revd James Hunter and a young licentiate, W. J. Grier. Finally, late in 1926, five charges of heresy were laid against Davey by over forty signatories. He was accused of denying the literal inerrancy of the Bible and the perfection of Christ; asserting that the doctrine of the Trinity was not set forth in scripture; teaching that God became guilty through bearing the sin of man; and disparaging the doctrine of imputation.

None of the accusers had Davey's gifts of scholarship or expression, and the charges themselves were often poorly formulated and inadequately supported. Both at the trial before the Belfast presbytery in February–March 1927, and at the accusers' appeal to the general assembly of the Irish Presbyterian church in June, Davey defended himself with ability and resolution, unswayed by repeated public misrepresentation and abuse (and incidentally proving himself to be more conservative than anyone had suspected), and he was acquitted on every count by overwhelming majorities. Shortly after, Hunter and Grier seceded to form the Irish Evangelical (later the Evangelical Presbyterian) church.

The Davey trial was a pivotal event for the Irish Presbyterian church, much as the trial of William Robertson Smith had been over forty years earlier in Scotland. To conservative evangelicals (notably, in a later generation, the Revd Ian Paisley), Davey's acquittal marked the moment when the church apostatized; to others, when it declared itself for freedom of scholarly enquiry and liberty of conscience. The truth may be that more people disliked the spirit and methods of his accusers than followed the characteristic sinuosities of Davey's thought and expression. Certainly, despite the verdict, Irish presbyterianism remained, on the whole, conservative in religious outlook.

Davey's career did not suffer from the trial. He was elected principal of the Presbyterian college in 1942, served as moderator of the general assembly in 1953–4, and was awarded an honorary DD by the universities of St Andrews (1928), Edinburgh (1947), Belfast (1953), and Dublin (1954). Its psychological effect on him, however, is less clear. He did not publish another book for over thirty years, and both *The Jesus of St John* (1958) and *Religious Experience: its Nature and Validity* (1964) were based (though sometimes distantly) on much earlier work. But some have thought that it was an increasing burden of teaching, administration, and broadcasting, not the strain of the trial, that made him reluctant to undertake fresh research; he was unsympathetic to the Barthianism which (in his view) came to dominate protestant scriptural exegesis; and in any event he perhaps needed a more bracing intellectual climate than his community, at that time, could offer.

Ernest Davey's transparent integrity and fineness of spirit disarmed almost everyone who met him. Donnish, slightly unkempt, and apparently abstracted in manner (he was always equipped with an overcoat, a waterproof, and an umbrella, whatever the weather), a music lover and a golfer, with an immense circle of friends of all religious persuasions and none, he seemed to many an unlikely rebel; but other contemporaries regarded his calm perseverance in following his own way in a society where, in his words, difference was 'something of a crime' (Fulton, 41), as a lifelong act of uncommon courage.

Davey died of carcinoma of the colon at the Musgrave and Clark Clinic, Grosvenor Road, Belfast, on 17 December 1960, and was buried three days later in the city cemetery.   PETER JACKSON

Sources A. Fulton, *J. Ernest Davey* (1970) • *Record of the trial of the Rev. Prof. J. E. Davey by the Belfast presbytery, and of the hearing of appeals by the general assembly, 1927* (1927) • R. Allen, *The Presbyterian College, Belfast, 1853–1953* (1954), 255–61 • W. J. Grier, *The origin and witness of the Irish Evangelical church* [1946] • S. Bruce, *God save Ulster: the religion and politics of Paisleyism* (1986) • I. Paisley, 'The trial of Professor J. E. Davey for heresy, and its consequences', *The Revivalist* (June 1983), 19–32 • J. Thompson, 'The theology of J. E. Davey: an evaluation', *Biblical Theology*, 21 (1971), 20–24 • J. E. Davey, *A memoir of the Reverend Charles Davey of Belfast* (1921) • *Belfast News-Letter* (19 Dec 1960) • *The Times* (20 Dec 1960) • web.ukonline.co.uk/epc [Evangelical Presbyterian church website] • private information (2004) • *CGPLA NIre.* (1961) • parish register, Ballymena, First Presbyterian Church, 7 Sept 1890, PRO NIre., MIC 1P/114/3 [baptism] • m. cert. • d. cert.
Archives BBC WAC, corresp. and scripts • priv. coll., papers • Union Theological College, Belfast, typescripts, transcripts, photocopies, etc.
Likenesses L. Stuart, photograph, 1950–59, Union Theological College, Belfast; repro. in Fulton, *J. Ernest Davey* • photograph, 1953, repro. in Allen, *Presbyterian College, Belfast*
Wealth at death £4683 12s. 1d.: probate, 7 March 1961, *CGPLA NIre.*

Davey, Francis Noel (1904–1973), Church of England clergyman and publisher, was born on Christmas day 1904, at 227 Whitehorse Lane, South Norwood, Surrey, son of Edward Octavius Davey (d. in or before 1939), artist in watercolours and oils, and his Scottish wife, Mary Eleanor McMaster. In 1909 the family moved to Great Dunmow in Essex. Noel was educated at first privately, then at a preparatory school at Littlehampton and finally at Brighton College. He was musical and played the piano from the age of six; a piano and harpsichord were in all his subsequent homes. He obtained a post at a private school at Ealing and felt called to ordination. When at home he would cycle to Conrad Noel's Anglo-Catholic church at Thaxted. One Sunday, being late, he stopped at the Revd Percy Widdrington's church at Great Easton and was conscripted to play the organ, which began a great friendship. This led him to join Maurice Reckitt's Christendom Group and

years later, on 26 September 1939, to marry Widdrington's daughter, Grizelle Margaret. The couple had three sons and two daughters.

Funded by an uncle, Davey entered Corpus Christi College, Cambridge. He obtained a first in theology and became associated with Sir Edwyn Hoskyns, the biblical theologian. Hoskyns did not find writing easy and *The Riddle of the New Testament* (1931), destined for worldwide influence with its insistence that the Jesus of history and the Christ of faith cannot be disentangled, was written by Davey. He would read each section to Hoskyns, who often made radical criticisms. The same happened with *The Fourth Gospel* (1940), which Davey completed after Hoskyns's untimely death, and *Crucifixion—Resurrection*, which he did not succeed in finishing.

Davey left Cambridge for two periods at St Deiniol's Library, Hawarden, in 1929 and again in 1932, and a curacy at St John Chrysostom, Manchester. He returned to Cambridge in 1933 as vicar of St Benet's in the shadow of Corpus, and two years later was elected into an assistant lectureship in the theology faculty. This carried no security of tenure.

Tall, somewhat shy, monkish in his priest's cloak, he was a brilliant supervisor of abler students, and could intoxicate his pupils with his learning and originality, as he did those who knew him to the end of his life. But he represented the theology of Hoskyns with its Barthian affinities, which the regius professor Charles Raven regarded as the blight on his attempts to reconcile science and religion. Davey preached a demanding university sermon in March 1942, remarkable in the depths of its theological understanding. Developed, it could have made him a creative theologian. It was a tremendous affirmation of the finality of Jesus Christ crucified and risen, the end, ground, subject of our hope, who cannot be kept out of this world, though not through the supposed triumph of science. Time and space are finally related to God 'in the perfect and acceptable moment of the Son's loving response to the Father' (Hoskyns and Davey, 26).

Raven disapproved of the sermon and Davey's lectureship was not renewed. He became rector of Coddenham in Suffolk but in 1945 succeeded, without any great enthusiasm, Lowther Clarke as director of the Society for Promoting Christian Knowledge. His long years there produced some seminal books by younger scholars. He himself wrote scripts for film strips, helped to propagate the *New English Bible* and was much involved in liturgical publication, in which he had great knowledge and interest. He also reorganized the society and transferred its headquarters from Northumberland Avenue to Holy Trinity Church, Marylebone. He continued his priestly ministrations. Davey had a gift with children and in 1947 wrote *The Good Shepherd and his Flock*, a book of Sunday school lessons. He was made CBE and awarded a Lambeth DD.

Rather distant in his relations with people, Davey had a great sense of propriety and discerned the pretensions of others. He died in Norwich at the Norfolk and Norwich Hospital on 3 March 1973 after a short illness. His wife survived him.   GORDON STEVENS WAKEFIELD

Sources personal knowledge (2004) · G. S. Wakefield, 'Francis Noel Davey', in E. C. Hoskyns and F. N. Davey, *Crucifixion—resurrection: the pattern of the theology and ethics of the New Testament*, ed. G. S. Wakefield (1981), 3–15 · F. N. Davey, 'University sermon', in E. C. Hoskyns and F. N. Davey, *Crucifixion—resurrection: the pattern of the theology and ethics of the New Testament*, ed. G. S. Wakefield (1981), 16–26 · F. N. Davey, 'The hope of Christendom authentic', *Prospect for Christendom*, ed. M. B. Reckitt (1945), 11–26 · F. N. Davey, 'Sin, righteousness and judgement', *Good Friday at St Margarets* (1957), 62–79 · D. M. Mackinnon, 'Crucifixion—resurrection', *Themes in theology, the three-fold cord: essays in philosophy, politics and theology* (1987), 196–207 · *CGPLA Eng. & Wales* (1973) · b. cert. · m. cert. · d. cert.

Wealth at death £33,506: probate, 23 May 1973, *CGPLA Eng. & Wales*

Davey, Horace, Baron Davey (1833–1907), judge, was born in Camberwell, Surrey, on 29 August 1833, the third son of Peter Davey (d. 1879) and his wife, Caroline Emma, daughter of William Pace, rector of Rampisham-cum-Wraxall, Dorset. He entered Rugby School in August 1848, being placed in Mayor's house, and won an open scholarship to University College, Oxford, in 1852. Davey matriculated on 20 March of that year, and went on to enjoy a highly distinguished academic career. Having gained a double first class in classics and mathematics, in both moderations (1854) and the final schools (1855–6), Davey was elected Johnson's mathematical scholar in 1857, senior mathematical scholar in 1858, and Eldon law scholar in 1859. He graduated BA in 1856 and proceeded MA in 1859. He was a fellow of University College from 1856 to 1864.

Early years at the bar Davey had been admitted a student of Lincoln's Inn on 19 January 1857 and was called to the bar on 26 January 1861. On 5 August 1862, at St George's, Camberwell, he married Louisa Hawes, daughter of John Donkin of Ormond House, Old Kent Road, London, a civil engineer; they had two sons and four daughters. In his first few years of practice, Davey served on the staff of a short-lived series of law reports—the *New Reports*. He was an equity reporter from November 1862 to August 1863 and a House of Lords reporter from November 1863 to August 1864. His colleagues at the *New Reports* included Farrer Herschell (subsequently lord chancellor) and Roland Vaughan Williams and James Stirling (both subsequently lord justice of appeal). Davey joined the chambers of John (later Sir John) Wickens at 8 New Square, Lincoln's Inn, regarded at the time as the most distinguished school of equity pleading, and subsequently devilled for Wickens himself, who was junior counsel to the Treasury in Chancery matters. Ashton recounts in his memoirs that during this time Davey would slave over the numerous briefs which had been assigned to Wickens, while the latter 'lay on his stomach before the fire and read novels of every kind in various languages'. Wickens was clearly impressed with his devil's work, confiding in Edward (later Lord) Macnaghten that in Davey he had at last found a pupil of whose success he felt assured. Davey acquired a substantial junior practice in the Chancery courts, and when Wickens was raised to the bench in 1871 Davey succeeded to a considerable portion of his practice. He was appointed secretary to his old master, Vice-Chancellor Wickens, in 1871, and was later secretary to Vice-Chancellor Hall from 1873 to 1874.

Leading the chancery bar Davey took silk, 'with strange misgiving and much hesitation' according to Lord Macnaghten, on 23 June 1875, electing to practise in the court of Sir George Jessel MR, where his main opponent was Joseph Chitty. He elected to 'go special' in 1881. Davey's reputation as a senior is generally regarded to have been unrivalled. He was the acknowledged leader of the chancery bar for well over a decade—Lord Macnaghten said that from about the time of Davey's speech in the Lord St Leonards will case until his promotion to the bench, 'there was no case of importance in the Court of Chancery in which he was not retained.' He also had a strong House of Lords practice, Viscount Alverstone later recalling that, 'of all the men who were largely engaged in appeal cases before the House of Lords, I think Sir Horace Davey ... was among the most brilliant.' Further, given his wide knowledge of numerous foreign legal systems, he was much in demand as counsel before the judicial committee of the privy council. The cases of note—many of them still good law—in which Davey appeared as senior counsel are simply too numerous to list, although it might give some indication of his great versatility and importance as counsel to note that *Speight* v. *Gaunt* (1883), *Learoyd* v. *Whiteley* (1887), and *Derry* v. *Peek* (1889) were all argued by him.

Davey's outstanding success at the bar was due to the classic combination of remarkable intelligence, great versatility, and sheer hard work: Viscount Haldane, one of Davey's pupils, thought him 'the finest advocate on pure points of law that I have ever seen ... [i]n legal matters he had a mind like a razor, and was accurate to the last degree' (Haldane, 35); Lord Macnaghten said that he seemed 'as much at home in arguing a point of practice as he was in explaining a complicated invention or illustrating and applying one of the great principles of equity or dealing with the mysteries of ecclesiastical law or some constitutional question before the Privy Council'; and he would usually begin work at four or five in the morning, and thought nothing of working solidly through the weekend. Perhaps his success before the privy council was further attributable to his belief that cases before that tribunal 'should be drawn in such a form that old gentlemen could read them in their libraries after dinner without referring to anything else' (Ashton). His success did not, however, stem from gifts of oratory or forensic advocacy. The anonymous author of *Pie Powder* wrote that 'the intellectual effort necessary to follow his utterances was always considerable; and the absence of anything like animation in his voice and delivery was so ostentatious, that one sometimes wondered how he had forced himself into prominence at all'—even his former pupil Haldane accepted that 'he could not cross-examine well, nor could he address a jury.' But these were not the characteristics necessary to achieve success at the chancery bar or before the highest appeal courts—what mattered there was detailed knowledge of the law and clarity of argument, and in those fields Davey excelled. Haldane writes of his being retained in an 'almost overwhelming' number of cases, and at the peak of his success he earned in excess of £25,000 per annum (Haldane, 36).

Politics Davey also harboured political aspirations, but here success largely eluded him. He was elected MP for Christchurch, in the Liberal interest, in April 1880, but lost his seat in the general election of November 1885. In spite of his poor parliamentary performances, and indeed despite his not at the time having a seat in the Commons, he was appointed solicitor-general by Gladstone on 16 February 1886. He received the customary knighthood on 8 March of that year. His tenure of this office was again undistinguished, and he was obliged to relinquish it when the Gladstone administration fell in August 1886. In that same year, Davey sought re-election to the Commons, unsuccessfully contesting both Ipswich and Stockport. Eventually, he won a seat in Stockton-on-Tees in a by-election of December 1888, but despite his large majority he failed to retain the seat in the July 1892 general election. Davey soon afterwards acquired judicial office, and the 1892 election marked the end of an undistinguished political career. Davey's lack of political success is widely acknowledged. Haldane wrote of his 'deficiencies in the House of Commons', and the *Law Journal* noted that 'Sir Horace Davey was … not of the stuff of which successful politicians are made'. One obvious reason for this lack of success was Davey's inability to court the electorate. His public manner was somewhat austere, and just as he lacked the urbanity to succeed at *nisi prius* work in the lawcourts, so he was unsuited to the showmanship of the hustings. His poor powers of oratory must also have impeded his political advancement—someone of Davey's oratorical shortcomings could simply not have hoped to make a name for himself as a parliamentarian. Haldane recalls, for instance, his old master's speech on the Irish Crimes Bill—although he set aside all other work to prepare for it, on the day 'it went off', according to John Morley, 'like a magnum of soda water that has stood for two days with the cork out'. There is no doubt that Davey very much desired political success, but it was not to be. He had to be content with making his mark on legal, rather than political history.

On the bench Given his almost unrivalled reputation at the bar, it should have occasioned little surprise when Davey was raised to the bench. He was appointed directly to the Court of Appeal on 23 September 1893, in place of his friend Sir Charles Bowen who had been created a lord of appeal-in-ordinary. He was sworn of the privy council one month later, on 23 November. Davey spent less than a year sitting as a lord justice of appeal, although in that time he heard some notable cases, such as *Monson* v. *Tussauds Ltd* (1894), and acquired a reputation for both patience and urbanity in the execution of his judicial role. His intellectual abilities, never in doubt at the bar, he applied with similar success on the bench.

Davey was appointed a lord of appeal-in-ordinary on 13 August 1894, taking the place of Lord Russell of Killowen who had accepted an invitation to become lord chief justice. On the same day he was created a baron for life by the style of Baron Davey of Fernhurst, in Sussex. Davey was to sit in the appellate committee of the House of Lords and in the judicial committee of the privy council from 1894 until his death some thirteen years later. His judicial output was consequently prolific, and involved matters ranging from legal technicalities to some of the great *causes célèbres* of the day. Among the latter were *Russell* v. *Russell* (1897), where Davey formed part of a bare majority of law lords who refused to grant Lord Russell a judicial separation on the grounds of Lady Russell's cruelty (she having made certain allegations, which she continued to make after she no longer believed them to be true, to the effect that Lord Russell had engaged in homosexual activity), and *General Assembly of the Free Church of Scotland* v. *Lord Overtoun* (1904), a major case concerning the fundamental doctrines of the Free Church and some £2 m. worth of its property.

Davey was also involved in a number of legal, rather than social, *causes célèbres*, cases which continue to be recognized instantly by modern legal practitioners. Examples of such cases include *Salomon* v. *Salomon* (1896), the seminal authority on the nature of incorporation; and *Allen* v. *Flood* (1898), a landmark decision on the propriety of the activities of trade unions (and one that led to considerable infighting between the Liberal and Conservative factions of the law lords, not the first or last time that the Liberal Davey would clash with staunchly Conservative colleagues like the lord chancellor, Halsbury).

But perhaps the finest testament to Davey's judicial abilities is the considerable number of his judgments which, despite their being a century old, remain good law. Cases like *Walter* v. *Lane* (1900) (the major ruling on reporters' copyright); *Burland* v. *Earle* (1901) (concerning the fraud on the minority exception to the rule in *Foss* v. *Harbottle*, 1843); *Noakes & Co Ltd* v. *Rice* (1901) and *Bradley* v. *Carritt* (1903) (both concerning the rules governing collateral benefits in mortgage law); and *Ruben* v. *Great Fingall Consolidated* (1906) (establishing the effect of a forged share certificate on a company) continue to be studied and cited by legal students and practitioners, guaranteeing Davey a degree of immortality among successive generations of lawyers.

In 1905, towards the end of his life, Davey pressed a claim to the woolsack in the Campbell-Bannerman administration, although nothing came of this. Edmund Gosse (the librarian of the House of Lords) attributed this lack of success at least partly to Davey's long absence from active party politics and to the cold personality which had earlier worked against him in his efforts to forge a reputation in parliament. He cannot have been helped by the fact that his ally Lord Spencer was prevented by ill health from advising on the appointment of the Campbell-Bannerman cabinet.

Assessment and death Davey the judge was, like Davey the barrister, almost peerless in his time. Atlay considered him and his colleague Lord Lindley to be 'two of the very greatest judicial intellects of [their] generation', while Lord Macnaghten wrote of 'how much he added to the strength of the House of Lords and the Privy Council', referring to his 'weight of authority' and 'wealth of learning', and adjudging him 'the most accomplished lawyer of his day'. Davey sat alongside some very strong and very eminent judges, not the least of whom were Lindley, Macnaghten, and Herschell, but it is fair to say that his immense knowledge, carefully weighed judgments, and incisive legal mind fully entitle him to be ranked alongside those and other great names of the Victorian and Edwardian bench. Arguably the very greatest barrister of his day, Davey was certainly also one of the greatest judges.

Davey's cold public persona has already been highlighted—it cost him dear in his efforts to establish a political career. This reputation is not ameliorated by Edmund Gosse's diary entries, the author noting, in reference to Davey, that '[h]is long, melancholy nose is drawn up in a perpetual sneer', while 'his parchment cheeks and stealthy hyena-like tread freeze conversation whenever he makes an appearance'. Davey was, nevertheless, a member of the Athenaeum, Oxford and Cambridge, and National Liberal clubs, and was apparently a fine companion to those of his intimate acquaintance, and greatly loved by his family. Harrison also refers to the 'inexhaustible culture' of Horace Davey—he had always a particularly keen interest in classical and modern European literature, and also formed a small collection of contemporary paintings.

Davey received many accolades in addition to those already mentioned. He was made an honorary fellow of University College, Oxford, in 1884, and was awarded an honorary doctorate of civil law ten years later (he had been standing counsel to the University of Oxford from 1877 to 1893). He was elected a fellow of the Royal Society on 24 January 1895, was chairman of the Incorporated Council for Law Reporting for England and Wales, and was elected treasurer of Lincoln's Inn in 1897. The following year he chaired the royal commission appointed to make statutes for the reconstituted University of London, and in 1905 he was elected a fellow of the British Academy.

Lord Davey died of acute bronchitis at his London residence, 86 Brook Street, on Wednesday 20 February 1907. He was survived by his wife, and was buried on 23 February at Forest Row, East Grinstead. His position on the appellate committee of the House of Lords was taken by Lord Collins, the former master of the rolls.

NATHAN WELLS

Sources Law Journal (23 Feb 1907) • Lord Macnaghten, 'The late Lord Davey', Journal of the Society of Comparative Legislation, new ser., 8 (1907), 10 • R. B. Haldane, Richard Burdon Haldane: an autobiography (1929) • D. Sommer, Haldane of Cloan: his life and times, 1856–1928 (1960) • R. F. V. Heuston, Lives of the lord chancellors, 1885–1940 (1964) • GEC, Peerage, new edn, vol. 4 • Law reports • [J. A. Foote], Pie powder: being dust from the law courts, collected and recollected on the western circuit by a circuit tramp (1911) • A. J. Ashton, As I went on my way (1924) • Viscount Alverstone [R. E. Webster], Recollections of bar and bench (1914) • [F. Temple], ed., Rugby School register from 1675 to 1867 inclusive (1867) • Sainty, Judges • Sainty, King's counsel • J. B. Atlay, The Victorian chancellors, 2 (1908) • New Reports • Foster, Alum. Oxon.
Archives Bodl. Oxf., corresp. with H. H. Asquith
Likenesses S. J. Solomon, oils, exh. RA 1906, University College, Oxford • oils, Lincoln's Inn, London

Wealth at death £172,398 14s. 6d.: probate, 3 April 1907, CGPLA Eng. & Wales

David. See also Dafydd.

David [St David, Dewi] (d. **589/601**), patron saint of Wales and founder of St David's, is known from written sources dating from no earlier than the eighth century and an inscription which may be of the seventh.

The earliest cult and its sources By the ninth century David's cult was sufficiently well established for him to be one of three Welsh saints included in the early ninth-century Irish martyrology of Tallaght, in which he is placed under 1 March; the same feast day is given in the later Welsh calendars. Even earlier he is named in two lives of Irish saints which probably belong to the eighth century, those of Ailbe of Emly and Mo Lua of Clonfertmulloe in the Codex Salmanticensis. A ninth-century manuscript, probably relying proximately on a Breton source, contains 'certain excerpts from a book of David'. These belong to a group of texts purporting to be of early British origin; the early date of the group is confirmed by their use in early Irish penitentials; but whatever the ultimate origin of the text, its preservation in this collection under the name of David suggests that the saint may have been of considerable repute in ninth-century Brittany as well as Ireland. This is confirmed by Wrmonoc's ninth-century life of St Paul de Léon, in which St David is described as Aquaticus ('Waterman'), a title given him on account of his ascetic practice of standing in cold water up to his neck. The written texts prior to the late-ninth century life of King Alfred by Asser reveal, therefore, the wide extent of his reputation rather than details of his life or his churches.

The inscription commemorates a man slain when plunder was taken from one of St David's churches, presumably Llanddewibrefi in Ceredigion, where the inscription is situated. The forms of the letters are consistent with a date in the early seventh century rather than with the early ninth-century date which has also been proposed. It belongs to a group of inscriptions whose principal letter forms are Roman capitals, but which have one or two letter shapes taken over from book scripts (usually half-uncial); these are attributed to the years around 600. The epigraphic evidence for dating probably outweighs the contrary testimony of a single late feature in the form of a name. The significance of this inscription lies in its confirming that the naming of the church after St David has a background going back to the pre-viking period, and that the cult had this important centre in Ceredigion, whereas St David's lay in Dyfed. The earliest direct evidence that St David's (in Welsh Tyddewi, 'The house of David', or Mynyw; in Latin Menevia or Vallis Rosina) was the outstanding church associated with the saint is Asser's life of King Alfred. Asser says that he himself belonged to the church, explicitly situated on the western extremity of Britain; he also writes of 'the monastery and parochia of St David' and of his kinsman, Nobis, also of St David's, as archbishop. The other reference of pre-Norman date to a Welsh archbishopric is in the Annales Cambriae, in which

Elfoddw is termed 'archbishop of the land of Gwynedd' in his obit, under the year 809. The archiepiscopal claims mentioned by Asser may be to pre-eminence among the bishops of Dyfed (as opposed to Gwynedd), or, more widely, to pre-eminence among the bishops of south Wales (so that Wales would be divided between two archbishoprics, north and south, on the model of England).

The earliest evidence that David might have been regarded, not merely as a leading, but as the outstanding, Welsh saint is in a tenth-century poem, *Armes Prydein vawr* ('The great prophecy of Britain'). This was composed when either Æthelstan or his brother Edmund was threatened by a viking-led alliance; the purpose of the poem was to encourage the Welsh to benefit by the opportunity offered by this attack on West Saxon hegemony and to take up arms against their English overlord. One argument deployed in the poem is that the English had violated the rights of the Welsh saints and that the Welsh would be victorious under the patronage of St David. The saint was thus made into a patron in war as well as in peace, and furthermore a patron of the Welsh cause against English overlordship. St David was receiving the treatment given, at the same period, to such Irish saints as Brigit (made into a patron of Leinster against the Uí Néill).

The context of Rhigyfarch's life of David Written evidence only becomes reasonably plentiful from the late eleventh century, when Rhigyfarch ap Sulien wrote the first surviving life. Rhigyfarch (*d.* 1099) belonged to a family established in the church of Llanbadarn Fawr, close to Aberystwyth, and thus in the north of Ceredigion. His father, Sulien, however, had been bishop of St David's (at the western extremity of Dyfed) for two periods (1071–8 and 1080–85). Rhigyfarch claimed to have written sources for his life

> in the oldest manuscripts of our country, and chiefly from his own monastery. These, though eaten away along the edges and the backs by the continuous gnawings of worms and the ravages of the passing years, and written in the manner of the elders, have survived till now.   (*Rhigyfarch's Life*, 48)

It has been claimed that the *Life* was written to defend the reputation of the saint and the rights of St David's in the aftermath of the Norman invasion of Dyfed in 1093. This followed shortly after the destruction of St David's by a Hebridean fleet in 1091, which in turn was only two years after the shrine of St David was stolen from the church and its gold and silver covering removed. The supposition that Rhigyfarch wrote the life to defend the reputation of the saint in the face of the Norman invasion of Ceredigion and Dyfed is plausible but by no means necessary.

Not only may Rhigyfarch's life of David have been a reaction to one or other of the earlier disasters, it was also a reaction to more long-term problems. The eleventh and twelfth centuries were a period in which the number of churches in Wales that could claim episcopal status was reduced to four: St David's, Llandaff, Bangor, and St Asaph. In the ninth century, however, there had been a bishop based at Llandeilo Fawr (in Ystrad Tywi, a semi-detached

portion of the old *civitas* of the Demetae). In the early tenth century there had been another, Cyfeilliog, who appears in the Anglo-Saxon Chronicle as bishop in Ergyng (Archenfield, now in south-west Herefordshire). In 1005 Æthelred II granted land at Over in Gloucestershire to the bishopric at Dewstow; although it has been thought that Dewstow was simply an English name for St David's, it has more plausibly been identified with Dewstow near Chepstow. In the middle years of the eleventh century an old bishopric attached to the community of Cynidr (in the valleys of the Usk and Wye) came to an end, when the last of the sequence of bishops became attached to Hereford. It is unlikely that, at any point in the period 600–1000, there was only one bishop in Dyfed, let alone in the whole of south Wales: Aldhelm (*d.* 710), in his letter to Geraint, king of Dumnonia, refers to the bishops of Dyfed as well as to the bishops of Dumnonia. One difference between Britain and Gaul seems to have been that, in Britain, the old rule of one bishop to each *civitas* did not apply. Much later than Aldhelm, a probably eleventh-century text, embedded in the twelfth- and thirteenth-century Welsh laws, names seven 'bishop-houses' in Dyfed, chief of which was St David's (Mynyw), to which it ascribes a supremacy over all the churches of Wales. The text does not imply that all seven were currently the sees of bishops, and they are likely to have been churches in which bishops were known to have resided and to have been buried.

One crucial issue for the community of St David's in the late eleventh century was to ensure that their church became the single episcopal see for as much of south Wales as possible. Their ability to attract Sulien from Llanbadarn to be their bishop is one sign that they were succeeding; the attempt by Rhys ap Tewdwr and Gruffudd ap Cynan to associate their causes with St David's is another; a third is the pilgrimage of William the Conqueror to St David's in 1081. This may have been the occasion on which William reduced Rhys ap Tewdwr to that condition of acknowledged tributary clientship in which he appears in Domesday Book; but it was still worthwhile for the much feared conqueror to make the pilgrimage to Dyfed's leading saint, when he brought the kingdom under his overlordship. In the event, St David's would embrace Dyfed, Ceredigion, Brycheiniog, Gower and Cydweli, Elfael, Maelienydd, and the neighbouring lands between the Severn and the Wye, effectively everything outside Glamorgan and Gwent. One of the principal purposes of the Rhigyfarch life was, therefore, to assert David's claim to be the leading bishop of Wales. Asser's reference to Archbishop Nobis indicates that Rhigyfarch may well, as he himself implied, have found useful ammunition in the remnants of the church's archive.

Yet even the particular issue of the primacy of St David's is far from exhausting the significance of Rhigyfarch's life of David. Quite as important was the necessity of setting out the position of St David within a body of traditions about the early saints of Ireland and Wales. Incidents from the life can be paralleled in the contemporary life of St Cadog of Llancarfan in Glamorgan, written by Lifris, and also in the lives of Máedóc of Ferns, Ailbe of Emly, Cainnech of Aghaboe, and Finnian of Clonard. Of these, the lives of Cainnech and Ailbe are likely to belong to the eighth century. A particular incident can be attributed in one life to St David's, in another to Llancarfan. Even if the location of a story were undisputed, its significance could vary: in the lives of Ailbe and David, the Munster saint is agreed to have baptized St David, but Rhigyfarch's text has no place for the further claims made in the life of St Ailbe to some kind of superiority over St David's. The hagiographical tradition was, therefore, contentious and fluid. In such circumstances, a well-written life was likely to be essential for the continuing strength of the cult. This was what Rhigyfarch supplied, and his success is illustrated by the way his original text (best preserved, contrary to some modern views, in BL, Cotton MS Vespasian A. xiv) spawned daughter versions in the course of the twelfth century.

Rhigyfarch's life of David: structure and content The life of St David (*Vita sancti Davidis*) is a carefully constructed text, with a much clearer structure than most of the earlier lives with which Rhigyfarch is likely to have been familiar. Although some sections, such as the account of the saint's death, are in close accord with standard Irish hagiographic practice, others, notably that describing the manner of life, *conversatio*, of the monastery, stand out as exceptional. But even those passages which follow a pre-existing norm have important variations on standard themes. The plan of the *Life* may be conveniently summarized as follows: prophecy, conception, birth, infancy, and education (chapters 1–11); pastoral work and the foundation of churches (12–14); the foundation of St David's and the conflict with Baia or Boia (15–19); the manner of life (*conversatio*) at St David's in the time of the founder (20–32); miracles connected with wells (33–4) and with three Irish saints (35–43); the pilgrimage to Jerusalem (44–8); synods and the archbishopric of Britain (49–58); death; concluding remarks on sources, ending with a request for readers' prayers. In the Vespasian version, the life proper is followed by the saint's genealogy (on his father's side only) and the proper for his feast day.

Rhigyfarch's narrative begins thirty years before David's conception with the prophecy of his birth by an angel to his father, Sant, king of Ceredigion (*fl.* 6th cent.), and to St Patrick. The angel warned Patrick against settling at St David's (here given the Latin name Vallis Rosina), while Sant received a dream in which symbols of David's virtues appeared. Thirty years later he was sent by divine power to Dyfed, where he raped a beautiful nun, **Non** [Nonnita, Non Fendigaid] (*fl.* 6th cent.); as the mother of St David she became known as Non Fendigaid (Non the Blessed). Miracles attended the pregnancy, and David was born during a thunderstorm, supposedly on the cliffs near St David's. An Irish bishop, Ailbe, baptized the boy. He was brought up by his uncle Guistlianus and ordained to the priesthood. David then moved on for further study to 'Winctilantquendi', where his teacher was one Paulens, who encouraged him towards monasticism. He therefore founded twelve *monasteria*, nine of which Rhigyfarch

names: Glastonbury, Bath, Crowland, Repton, Colfa, Glascwm, Leominster, Raglan, and Llangyfelach. David returned to his uncle, but, following an angelic warning, then moved to Vallis Rosina (Mynyw), with a few companions, where he founded his chief monastery, in the teeth of opposition from the local ruler. Rhigyfarch outlines the manner of life (*conversatio*) at the monastery, where the monks held all property in common and performed manual labour. David's miracles are then recounted: two concern the creation of wells, the others involve Irish saints, Máedóc of Ferns in Leinster, here said to be one of David's disciples, Barre (probably the patron saint of Cork in Munster), and Mo Domnóc of Tibberaghny in Osraige. An angel then transported David and two companions to Jerusalem. The story then moves back to Wales, where David addressed the Synod of Llanddewibrefi, when a dove came down and rested on his shoulder, and the so-called synod of victory. David died at his own monastery, allegedly at the age of 147, and was buried there. Various efforts were subsequently made to calculate his date of death, of which 589 and 601 carry most plausibility, though without finality.

Themes of Rhigyfarch's narrative The plan of the life balances chronology with other considerations. Thus the manner of life at St David's follows the account of its foundation; once the asceticism of David's rule of life has been set out, his miracles follow; and, when his sanctity has been demonstrated by his miracles, it is recognized, even as far as Jerusalem, where the patriarch elevates David to the dignity of an archbishop. This recognition of David's primacy in the East foreshadows his effective elevation at the Synod of Llanddewibrefi. Sections are linked where possible: the second part of David's miracles concerns three Irish saints, Máedóc, Barre, and Mo Domnóc; the ensuing pilgrimage to Jerusalem sees David as the leader of a group of three south Welsh saints: himself, Teilo, and Padarn.

The life's opening prophecy has a dual function: on the one hand it serves to make it clear that, while St Patrick was British and belonged to an older generation than St David, God had already allocated Britain to David and Ireland to Patrick. Since Patrick was already long-established by the eleventh century as the patron saint of the Irish, David is here presented as his counterpart—as patron saint of Britain and the Britons. A further prophecy from St Gildas—likewise an older British saint, who had been unable to preach in the presence of St Non, then carrying David in her womb—confirms this picture. David, therefore, was predestined to be an even greater preacher than the notoriously eloquent Gildas.

The beginning of the life is concerned with the primacy of St David among all the saints of Britain; and this theme resurfaces at intervals until the end of the work. Yet the declaration that David was predestined to sanctity was also designed to confirm the Augustinian orthodoxy of the hagiographer, Rhigyfarch, and to foreshadow the culmination of David's career at the Synod of Llanddewibrefi (section 7), when he preached against the Pelagian heresy. These two themes, David's primacy and his orthodoxy, were intimately linked: it was as an immediate consequence of his triumph in preaching the orthodox faith at the synod that all agreed that he should immediately be made archbishop and that St David's should be recognized as the metropolis of Britain. Similarly, in the section on his education, Rhigyfarch expressly notes that Paulens was a disciple of St Germanus of Auxerre, who had earlier preached against Pelagianism before a British audience.

The narrative of the saint's conception and birth had much more local, south Welsh preoccupations. There might be nothing very surprising in it: as the letters of St Boniface illustrate, illicit sexual intercourse with nuns was far from being a rare activity among early medieval kings in Britain. What is more surprising is that all this occurs in the text after Sant has been introduced as 'Sant by name and merits', *sant* being the Welsh form of *sanctus* ('holy'). True, it is emphasized, once Sant has been brought into the narrative, that he subsequently resigned his earthly kingdom in order to gain a heavenly one. Sant, however, having been king of Ceredigion, had been the ruler of Henfynyw (Old Mynyw), where David was first educated, while the outraged nun is said in the saints' genealogies to have been the daughter of Cynyr of Caer Gawch in Mynyw; and from Rhigyfarch's text it is clear that Non did indeed belong to Dyfed, in which the new Mynyw was situated. Father and mother seem to represent two kingdoms, each with a site called Mynyw, and, moreover, each with a special connection with Rhigyfarch and his family: they themselves were attached to Llanbadarn, while Rhigyfarch's father, Sulien, had been bishop of St David's.

There are further oddities about the relationships of Sant and Non. Sant was a king to whom an angel revealed the birth and the character of his son some thirty years before David was born; yet Non was the daughter of a local noble. The kings of Dyfed are mentioned only in passing, when the narrative relates that Non entered a church in which Gildas was accustomed to preach 'in the time of King Triphunus and his sons' (*Brut: Peniarth MS 20*, xxxvi). When David was born, and also when he founded Mynyw, he had to deal with secular powers, but these were presented by Rhigyfarch as local strong men in the neighbourhood of Mynyw, quite separate from the royal dynasty. The effect is that the kings of Dyfed are not given any credit whatsoever for the foundation of Mynyw. The result is all the odder, because the first local strong man, at least, is quasi-royal even though unnamed. He is a tyrant (and ever since Gildas British writers had called evil kings tyrants); also he attempts to kill the child when his magi tell him that a boy would be born 'whose power would expand over the whole country' (ibid., 31). This tyrant, then, was Herod to a Christ-like David. Many years later, when David came to found his chief monastery, Mynyw, another wicked chieftain, Boia or Baia, whom Rhigyfarch calls a 'satrap' and identifies as a magus and an Irishman, attempted to repel the holy man. Boia, however, Ahab to his wife's Jezebel, was upstaged by someone even more implacable in hatred than he was. Not merely did she send her slave-girls to seduce the monks, but she went on to

decapitate her stepdaughter, Dunod. The site of the decapitation was marked by the appearance of a spring, enjoying miraculous powers of healing, and by the construction of a chapel called Merthyr Dunod.

Merthyr Dunod illustrates another central theme of this part of the life. As the monks took possession of the site of Mynyw, so incidents associated with David attached themselves to the surrounding landscape. Ailbe of Emly, the leading saint of Munster, who baptized David, was commemorated at Llaneilfyw (St Elvis), 4 miles to the east-south-east of Mynyw. Within the parish of St David's itself, by the end of the middle ages several chapels commemorated other persons associated with the saint: apart from Merthyr Dunod, already mentioned, there were Capel Non, Capel Padrig, Ffynnon Faiddog (his principal Irish disciple, Máedóc of Ferns), and Capel Stinan (a disciple, St Justinian). An element in the cult, therefore, was the provision of sites, with explanatory narratives attached, that a pilgrim might visit. The topographical grip of the cult was more than matched by the extension of the bishop's local authority. The whole cantref of Pebidiog was, by the twelfth century, in the lordship of the bishop; in the later middle ages it would be the hundred of Dewisland, 'the land of St David'.

The extent of David's cult From Rhigyfarch's time onwards it becomes evident that there was a difference between those areas within Wales in which there are churches dedicated to St David and a more general acknowledgement of his status as the premier saint of the Britons. The latter emerges from support given by the rulers of Gwynedd to the campaign to have St David's recognized by the papacy as an archiepiscopal see. About 1140 Owain Gwynedd and Cadwaladr his brother wrote to Bishop Bernard of St David's to acknowledge his authority as metropolitan of Wales. At the end of the century Gerald of Wales again attracted support from Gwynedd when he renewed the campaign begun by Bernard. On the other hand, dedications to St David are from south, not north Wales; even in Ceredigion they are confined to the south of the River Aeron, while none is to be found in most of Glamorgan. If church dedications were to be taken as the principal evidence for the extension of the cult, it would have to be said that St David was far from being a saint for the Welsh as a whole. The most likely answer to this question is that church dedications sometimes had more to do with belonging to the *familia* of the saint—the body of churches and individuals formally attached to the principal church of that saint—rather than with the extent of the popular cult. This is attested by the fact, demonstrated by the careers of Rhigyfarch and his father, Sulien, that there was a cult of St David at Llanbadarn Fawr, in the north of Ceredigion, outside the area in which there are old dedications to the saint. On the other hand, not all dedications signified a formal attachment to St David's. Those in Cornwall (Davidstow) and in Brittany, centred on Dirinon to the east of Brest, were independent of any Welsh church. Yet the vigour of the late medieval cult in Brittany is attested by the miracle play entitled *Buez Santes Nonn hac he* *map Deuy* ('The life of St Non and her son David'). This situates Non's death at Dirinon and presents highlights of her son's career in a version influenced by Geoffrey of Monmouth's reconstruction of early British ecclesiastical history. Dedications therefore attest the existence, at some period or other, of a cult, sometimes associated with a formal attachment to St David's, sometimes sustained by a story linking the saint to the place; but the absence of dedications does not prove that there was no cult.

The later medieval cult On the far south-eastern border of Wales there were dedications to David in Ergyng, now part of Herefordshire and of the diocese of Hereford (such as Much Dewchurch and Little Dewchurch), and these survived. Llanddewibrefi, on the other hand, became the premier church of St David still usually within territory ruled by Welsh princes. Here the cult can be traced from the twelfth century through into the later middle ages. Gwynfardd Brycheiniog composed a poem in honour of St David (*c*.1175) in which Llanddewibrefi was the focus; the earliest copy of the Welsh vernacular life of St David was written in 1346 by the anchorite of Llanddewibrefi, who was also one of the scribes who wrote the White Book of Rhydderch, which belonged to Rhydderch ab Ieuan of Parc Rhydderch a few miles to the north-west of Llanddewibrefi. Rhydderch's son, the poet Ieuan ap Rhydderch, composed a poem in praise of the saint, which demonstrates knowledge of the life, probably in its vernacular version.

David's cult survived the Anglo-Norman conquest of much of Dyfed, the settlement of Flemings in what is now southern Pembrokeshire by Henry I, and also the imposition, also by Henry I, of his chaplain Bernard as the first Norman bishop. How well the new arrivals took to the old cult is demonstrated by the *Song of Dermot and the Earl*, a Norman-French *geste* about the conquest of Ireland: the war-cry used by the invaders was 'St Dewi!' Bishop Bernard (bishop from 1115 to 1147) became a fervent convert to the cult of St David. It was he who, so it was said, gained a privilege for St David's from Pope Calixtus II and thus secured its future as a successful pilgrimage centre. In the same interest, Bernard also spent years looking for the corporeal relics of the saint. As a result of his expedition to Ireland, Henry II twice visited St David's, at Michaelmas 1171 and on Easter Monday 1172, on the second occasion dressed as a pilgrim. No mention is made by Gerald of Wales, the *Annales Cambriae* or the *Brut* of any shrine, but the king made an offering to God and St David of two choral copes and 10s. of silver.

A shrine was built in 1275, following a dream by John de Gamages, prior of Ewenni. Its stone base may still be seen between two pillars on the north side of the presbytery of the cathedral. John's vision revealed that digging on a spot a certain number of steps outside the south door of the cathedral would uncover the bones of the patron saint. The bones thus disinterred were unhesitatingly identified as those of St David and enshrined. It was this shrine which was visited by Edward I and Queen Eleanor in 1284, while by the time of his death Edward appears to have possessed an arm claimed to be that of St David; as with William the Conqueror in 1081, a king of the English who wished to subdue the Welsh wisely paid attention to their patron saint. The bones themselves appear to have been placed inside a portable shrine or feretory, since the Black Book of St David's, a rental of the bishop's lands dating from 1326, demands that the bishop's tenants follow the relics on a day's march when the bishop, as lord marcher, went to war. Towards the end of the fifteenth century William Worcester, who observed that St Justinian (David's disciple) was buried near the tomb of St David, recounted a number of miracles dating from his time and from the previous centuries. A life of Justinian was incorporated into John Tynemouth's legendary in the fourteenth century.

St David and the Reformation The shrine of St David, decorated by three mural paintings, of the saint himself, of St Patrick, and of St Denis of France, and surmounted by a painted wooden coving, was destroyed in 1538. It was despoiled of its gold and jewels by the canons of the cathedral, but its destruction took place not only as a result of state policy, but also of the protestant inclinations of William Barlow, bishop of St David's (1536–47). In a letter to Thomas Cromwell, of March 1538, he reveals that, having forbidden the canons

> to set forth fayned reliques for to allure people to supersticion … on saint Davids daye, the people wilfully solemnysinge the feest, certain reliques were set forth which I caused to be sequestred and taken awaye, detayninge them in my custody untill I may be advertised of your lordships pleasour, the parcels of the reliques are these: two heedes of sylver plate enclosing two rotten skulles stuffed with putrified clowtes; Item, two arme bones, and a worm eaten boke covered with sylver plate. (Wright, 184)

This first glimpse of what was in the shrine—and the second skull may well have been that of St Justinian—was also the last, since the likelihood is that these, as with so many other Welsh relics, perished in the fires of Smithfield. The presence of the book is intriguing: perhaps it was the incomplete gospel book mentioned by Gerald of Wales.

Although one of the very first steps in the protestant reformation of Wales was the destruction of the shrine and relics of its patron saint, the seeds of a revival in St David's reputation lay in one of the intellectual arguments for reform. It was crucial to maintain that the early British church was the forerunner of the reformed sixteenth-century church: that it was independent of Rome and undefiled by popish superstitions and accretions. While the shrine was unhesitatingly identified as part of those superstitions, the historical figure of the saint was important for the protestant case. This situation produced a somewhat paradoxical stance: popular devotion for St David was suspect and needed to be discouraged; the great figures of the early British church, however, needed to be recruited to the protestant cause. This was the stance adopted by Richard Davies, bishop of St David's (1561–81), in the 'Address to the Welsh nation' prefixed to the translation of the New Testament by William

Salesbury and Davies himself, for whom St David was 'Archbishop David', and his countrymen only adopted the papistical 'faith of the English' at the point of the sword. It was expounded with most learning by Archbishop Ussher in his *Britannicarum ecclesiarum antiquitates* (Dublin, 1639); like Davies before him, Ussher was concerned (probably also with one eye on the Arminian question) to invoke the Augustinian orthodoxy of St David and the Synod of Llanddewibrefi.

St David and St David's in the modern age By the nineteenth century the situation had been further complicated. In 1811 the Welsh Calvinistic Methodists seceded from the established church, which was soon in the position of being a minority denomination in Wales. One argument deployed by Anglicans against the nonconformists was that the Church of England represented the lineal and faithful successors of the great figures of 'the age of the saints'. St David's College, Lampeter, was founded in 1827 to train a parochial clergy capable of withstanding the nonconformist onslaught. In 1853 the lives of the saints, that by Rhigyfarch included, were printed for the first time since the seventeenth-century Bollandists, by William Jenkins Rees, a clergyman of the diocese of St David's in a volume dedicated to its then bishop, after his nephew Rice Rees, a fellow of Jesus College, Oxford, had written a scholarly account of the Welsh saints as an eisteddfod essay (published in 1836). Members of the Anglican clergy continued to be active in the study of the sources for St David and the propagation of the notion of 'an ancient British Celtic church' right up to the time of Welsh disestablishment (passed in 1914 but suspended until the end of the war). In 1923 the Society for the Propagation of Christian Knowledge published an annotated translation of the life by Rhigyfarch by Arthur Wade-Evans, who associated the composition of the life with 'the end of an epoch in Welsh history, that of the "Ancient British Church of Wales"' (Wade-Evans, *Life of Saint David*, xvi). This, in turn, was identified as the moment when the Welsh church fell under the sway of Canterbury. St David could now have a new future, as the patron of a disestablished yet independent Welsh church; the enemy without was now not so much Rome as Canterbury, perceived not as the leading church of the Anglican communion but as a symbol of English hostility towards Welsh liberties.

It was in the 1920s that interest in the corporeal relics of St David resurfaced. During Gilbert Scott's restoration of the cathedral from 1865 onwards, a niche was discovered in the wall of Holy Trinity chapel. It was opened out revealing an open-armed cross facing out into the presbytery behind the high altar, and surrounded by four other crosses. It seemed to belong to the cathedral of 1181 and was located on what was once the outer west wall of the building. Those who cleared the niche noticed that the lower part had been edged by a line of ashlar blocks behind which there were bones. In the nineteenth-century accounts no especial interest was displayed in the bones; they were simply buried beneath the floor of Holy Trinity chapel. At the beginning of the twentieth century, however, it began to be felt, on no good evidence, that the bones might have been those of St David and St Justinian, rescued at the destruction of the shrine in 1538 and hidden to prevent desecration. They were disinterred from the floor of the chapel and placed in an oak casket within the niche as part of the restoration of Holy Trinity chapel in 1923. In 1996 these bones were carbon dated resulting in dates ranging from the mid-twelfth to the fourteenth century.

In the modern period, therefore, St David has been a figure invoked in controversy rather than the unquestioned symbol of a nation. The Welsh national anthem, composed in 1856, in the heyday of nonconformist Wales, presented an image of a glorious Welsh past in which the bard, the language, and even the warrior received due acclamation, but not the saint. In the twentieth century the decline of Welsh nonconformity has left the church in Wales in a relatively stronger position. Yet the nonconformists were never much concerned to lay claim to the inheritance of St David, and it is the cultural shift represented by secularization that constitutes the greatest threat to the reputation of the patron saint of Wales, one more potent even than the iconoclasm of Bishop Barlow. It is a small but telling sign of the times that the name of St David no longer graces his college at Lampeter.

J. WYN EVANS

Sources *Rhigyfarch's Life of David*, ed. J. W. James (1967) · A. W. Wade-Evans, ed., *Vitae sanctorum Britanniae et genealogiae* (1944), 156–70 · A. W. Wade-Evans, *Life of St David* (1923) · D. S. Evans, ed., *The Welsh life of St David* (1988) · M. E. Owen, 'Gwaith Gwynfardd Brycheiniog', *Gwaith Llywelyn Fardd I ac eraill o feirdd y ddeuddegfed ganrif*, ed. K. A. Bramley, N. A. Jones, M. E. Owen, and others (1994), 435–78 · J. Williams ab Ithel, ed., *Annales Cambriae*, Rolls Series, 20 (1860); repr. (1965) · T. Jones, ed. and trans., *Brut y tywysogyon, or, The chronicle of the princes: Peniarth MS 20* (1952) · Williams, ed., *Armes Prydain, o, Lyfr Taliesin* (1964) · *Gir. Camb. opera* · T. Wright, ed., *Three chapters of letters relating to the suppression of the monasteries*, CS, 1st ser., 26 (1843); repr. (1968), 183–6 · *Asser's life of King Alfred*, ed. W. H. Stevenson, repr. (1959) · D. S. Evans, ed., *Historia Gruffud vab Kenan* (1977) · J. W. Willis Bund, ed., *The Black Book of St Davids*, Cymm Rec. Ser., 5 (1902) · S. Baring-Gould and J. Fisher, *The lives of the British saints*, Honourable Society of Cymmrodorion, Cymmrodorion Record Series, 2 (1908), 285–322 · E. G. Bowen, *The Saint David of history* (1981) · G. Gruffydd and H. P. Owen, 'The earliest mention of St David?', *BBCS*, 17 (1956–7), 185–93 · G. Gruffydd and H. P. Owen, 'The earliest mention of St David: an addendum', *BBCS*, 19 (1960–62), 231–2 · S. M. Harries, *St David in the liturgy* (1940) · E. R. Henken, *Traditions of the Celtic saints* (1987), 31–74 · E. R. Henken, *The Welsh saints: a study in patterned lives* (1992) · *Gildas: the ruin of Britain and other works*, trans. M. Winterbottom (1978) · A. C. Thomas, 'The Llanddewi Brefi Idnert stone', *Peritia*, 10 (1996), 136–80 · H. James, 'The cult of St David in the middle ages', *In search of cult: archaeological investigations in honour of Philip Rahtz*, ed. M. Carver (1993), 105–12 · N. Rees, *St David of Dewisland* (1992) · F. G. Cowley, 'A note on the discovery of St David's body', *BBCS*, 19 (1960–62), 47–8 · *Gerald of Wales: the journey through Wales / the description of Wales*, trans. L. Thorpe (1978) · O. T. Edwards, *Matins, lauds and vespers for St David's day* (1990) · Y. le Berre, B. Tanquy, and Y. P. Castel, eds., *Buez Santez Nonn: mystère breton, vie de Sainte Nonne* (1999)

David (*d.* 1137×9), bishop of Bangor, is usually identified with David the Scot, the celebrated scholar who wrote an account of the emperor Henry V's Italian expedition of 1111. If this is right, then David was the scholar described in the anonymous *Kaiserchronik* later used by Ekkehard of

Aura, according to which David Scotigena had become a master at the cathedral school of Würzburg, at the shrine of St Kilian, the Irish apostle of Franconia, some time before 1110. The Irish connections of Würzburg remained strong in these years, and Abbot Tritheim of Würzburg, writing at the end of the fifteenth century in part on the basis of sources now lost, describes David as a kinsman of the Irish-born Macarius. Much earlier Orderic Vitalis seems explicit in calling him Irish, and at the beginning of the twelfth century, in German sources at least, 'Scot' most usually meant Irish too.

In 1110 David came to the attention of Henry V, who foresaw the need for learning as well as arms in his forthcoming expedition into Italy, and made him his chaplain. He joined other scholars with the imperial army in its march on Rome, which ended in 1111 with the dramatic surrender of Pope Paschal II over investitures and Henry's imperial coronation. At the emperor's command David wrote an account of the expedition in three books, composed in a style so easy that it differed little from common speech, adapted to the use of laymen or other less learned readers. The work is lost, but some extracts from the text and the documents it included were used by William of Malmesbury in his *Gesta regum*, and it is also said to be a source by the *Kaiserchronik*, and, much later, by Johannes Aventinus (working in the years 1519–21). Orderic too seems to have known the work, of which he speaks only generally, though favourably. Malmesbury disapproved sharply of its partisan character, rebuking David for his defence of lay investiture and for his comparison of the emperor's capture of the pope to Jacob's forcible extortion of a blessing from the angel, yet he excused the fault of a good man by his purpose in writing a panegyric, not a history.

Nothing more is heard of David until the beginning of 1120, when Gruffudd ap Cynan, prince of Gwynedd, and 'all the clergy and people of Wales' elected one David as bishop of Bangor. Bangor had long been vacant, formally since the Breton Bishop Hervey, installed there with Norman support in 1092, had been translated to the new see of Ely in 1109. In fact, however, Hervey had fled his impoverished and unruly diocese after the murder of his brother and several of his men many years earlier. The Welsh sent their bishop-elect to Archbishop Ralph of Canterbury for consecration; the letter he brought was respectful, though it included a threat to seek a bishop from Ireland, or some other barbarous region, if the archbishop refused to act. Ralph entertained David for a time while he instructed him in some matters of divine learning, before consecrating him bishop at Westminster on 4 April 1120 with the consent of King Henry and the assistance of bishops Roger of Salisbury, Richard of London, and Robert of Lincoln, all leading royal servants, and Urban of Llandaff. The new bishop dutifully professed his obedience to Canterbury. Only the strictly contemporary testimony of William of Malmesbury identifies the new bishop as the scholar of Würzburg. The European sources say nothing of David's Welsh bishopric and the other English sources know nothing of his earlier career (and the late derivative annals of Worcester call him a Welshman), but on such a

point William's authority cannot be lightly set aside. Although Bangor was a surprising destination for a celebrated scholar, the event is not inexplicable; Prince Gruffudd himself had a Norse Irish mother and had spent much of his youth in Ireland, while the emperor was already moving towards a settlement of his dispute with the papacy. In the world of papal–imperial relations which developed after 1112 so relentless an imperial partisan may have become an embarrassment.

Little is known of David's career as bishop. He appears to have taken up his duties at once, for his consent is asserted for the translation of the body of St Dyfrig and the teeth of St Elgar from Bardsey to the new cathedral at Llandaff on 7 May 1120. After that he can be seen from time to time in England: he was at Lambeth twice in 1121 and at Lambeth and Canterbury in 1125. Later that year the king and Giovanni da Crema, the papal legate, drew up an abortive scheme to settle the primacy dispute between Canterbury and York by ceding the dioceses of Bangor, St Asaph, and Chester to York in exchange for a profession of obedience; David's view of the matter is unknown. In May 1127 he attended Archbishop William of Canterbury's legatine council at Westminster with his brother bishops of St David's and Llandaff, but after that he is not recorded in England again. He is last heard of in Wales with his archdeacon at the deathbed of Prince Gruffudd in 1137. His successor, Maurice (or Meurig), had been elected before 3 December 1139, so David may have died a little earlier. It is striking that Maurice at first refused to swear fealty to King Stephen, on the grounds that his predecessor's archdeacon had forbidden him to do so. Perhaps, particularly after the great Welsh rising of 1136, David too had come to support a greater measure of Welsh independence. However, Tritheim asserts that he became a monk of St James of Würzburg (the 'Schottenkloster' or Irish monastery) where his kinsman Macarius became first abbot in 1138. If the two Davids are indeed one, and Tritheim rightly understood his source, then David retired to Würzburg shortly after the death of his prince and the date of his death is unknown.

Besides his book on Henry V's Italian expedition, the earlier English bibliographers claimed that he wrote some further works, and Tritheim listed a quite different set. None of these survives, and none of the attributions suggested by more recent scholars has been widely accepted. At almost every point David's career is uncertain or disputable, and only his history seems to have enjoyed any substantial renown. MARTIN BRETT

Sources *Frutolfs und Ekkehards Chroniken und die anonyme Kaiserchronik*, ed. and trans. F.-J. Schmale and I. Schmale-Ott (Darmstadt, 1972), 40–42, 254 · J. Trithemius, *Annales Hirsaugensis* (1690), vol. 1, pp .349, 403–4 · *Eadmeri Historia novorum in Anglia*, ed. M. Rule, Rolls Series, 81 (1884), 259–60, 298 · William of Malmesbury, *Gesta regum Anglorum / The history of the English kings*, ed. and trans. R. A. B. Mynors, R. M. Thomson, and M. Winterbottom, 2 vols., OMT (1998–9) · John of Worcester, *Chron.* · Bale, *Cat.*, 2.211 · J. C. Davies, ed., *Episcopal acts and cognate documents relating to Welsh dioceses, 1066–1272*, 2, Historical Society of the Church in Wales, 3 (1948), 550–53 · A. Gwynn, 'The continuity of the Irish tradition at Würzburg', *Herbipolis Jubilans: 1200 Jahre bistum Würzburg. Festschrift* zur Säkularfeier der Erhebung der Kiliansreliquien (Würzburg, 1952), 57–82 • I. Schmale-Ott, 'Untersuchungen zu Ekkehard von Aura und zur Kaiserchronik', Zeitschrift für bayerische Landesgeschichte, 34 (1971), 403–61 • W. Wattenbach and R. Holtzmann, Deutschlands Geschichtsquellen im Mittelalter: die Zeit der Sachsen und Salier, 3 vols. (Köln, 1967–71), vol. 2, pp. 364, 476; vol. 3, pp. 118, 153–4 [prev. edns as Deutschlands Geschichtsquellen im Mittelalter: Deutsche Kaiserzeit] • I. Gropp, Collectio novissima scriptorum et rerum Wirceburgensium, 1 (Frankfurt and Leipzig, 1741) • I. Auentino [J. Aventinus], Annalium Boiorum libri septem, ed. H. Ziegler (Ingolstadt, 1554), 601, 611–13 • E. O. Blake, ed., Liber Eliensis, CS, 3rd ser., 92 (1962) • M. Richter, ed., Canterbury professions, CYS, 67 (1973) • Reg. RAN, 2.1243 • Hugh the Chanter: the history of the church of York, 1066–1127, ed. and trans. C. Johnson, rev. edn, rev. M. Brett, C. N. L. Brooke, and M. Winterbottom, OMT (1990) • A. Jones, ed. and trans., History of Gruffydd ap Cynan (1910) • J. Hemmerle, Die Benediktinerklöster in Bayern, Germania Benedictina, 2 (1970), 349–53

David, earl of Huntingdon and lord of Garioch (1152–1219), magnate, was the youngest in the family of three sons and three daughters of Prince *Henry of Scotland (c.1115–1152) and his wife, *Ada de Warenne (c.1123–1178). His grandfather *David I, in whose honour he was named, and his elder brothers, *Malcolm IV and *William the Lion, were successive kings of Scots from 1124 to 1214. He enthusiastically adopted Anglo-Norman values and played an ample supporting role in transforming Scotland into a stronger, European-style kingdom. Sent as a hostage to the English court in July 1163, he returned to Scotland as heir apparent to William the Lion immediately after his accession in 1165. Although never formally designated William's successor, David regularly attested royal charters as chief lay witness, and was occasionally named with his brother in the exercise of authority. His responsibilities were substantially increased by grants of extensive territories in outlying regions where William vigorously sought to consolidate and extend his control.

In 1174 David gained the earldom of Lennox, which he held in the king's name until it was restored to its native house, perhaps in 1185. It has been suggested that David was formally granted Lennox in custody during a minority, but it seems more likely that his role was to enforce royal authority following a pronouncement of forfeiture (later rescinded) against the earldom's rulers. By 1182 he had taken charge of imposing estates on Tayside and in mid-Aberdeenshire, where he controlled the 'frontier' district of Garioch, his principal Scottish power base, important as a centre of operations, defensive and offensive, against the men of Moray and Ross to the north. These acquisitions, centred on the castle-burghs he established at Dundee and at Inverurie (the caput of Garioch), guaranteed his place as one of the kingdom's greatest magnates; and as he strengthened his local influence through innovations on the Anglo-Norman model, so he contributed in good measure to the increasing might of the crown, especially by reinforcing its dominance north of the Mounth (the eastern Grampians). But Scotland was scarcely his entire world. From 1163 his career had continued to unfold under the influence of Anglo-Scottish relations, often in the context of the difficulties raised by Scottish claims to the northern English counties, and by English counter-claims to the overlordship of Scotland. He was knighted by Henry II at Windsor on 31 May 1170 and, together with William the Lion, pledged allegiance to the English king's son, the young King Henry, on 15 June, the day after the latter's coronation. Apparently with some reluctance, David returned to England as his brother's ally in April or May 1174 in aid of young Henry's rebellion, begun the year before. In 1173 William had offered David the honour and earldom of Huntingdon; but only the additional grant of Lennox seems to have secured his intervention in this doomed venture. In the event he acquitted himself well: operating from Huntingdon and Leicester he rallied the midland insurgents, imposed his lordship on the Huntingdon honour, and defied Henry II until news of William's capture at Alnwick reached him late in July 1174.

David was a principal party to the treaty of Falaise in December 1174, and in August 1175 went with William the Lion to York, where they publicly acknowledged Henry II as Scotland's lord superior. The Huntingdon honour, confiscated in 1174, was restored to William in March 1185. With Henry II's approval and perhaps at his bidding, William at once transferred it to David with the title of earl. This was the outstanding landmark in his life. As the most powerful Anglo-Scottish magnate of his day, he became a major focus for the increasing Normanization (or Anglicization) of Scottish society, forged 'cross-border' property ties that in smaller ways reflected his own, and was conspicuous in Anglo-Scottish diplomacy. Despite his dual allegiance, he never entirely lost William's trust. Admittedly, in 1195 William planned to marry his eldest daughter, Margaret, to Otto von Brunswick (the future emperor Otto IV), on the understanding that Margaret would inherit the kingdom, thus excluding David from the succession. But William's main aim seems to have been not so much to marginalize David as to regain Northumberland and Cumberland, with which King Richard I, Otto's uncle, promised to endow the couple. In any event, William quickly withdrew his proposals when an influential noble faction in Scotland spoke up on David's behalf, and no lasting damage was done to the brothers' friendship. David long remained prominent in Scottish governance, and in February 1206 possibly acted as regent during William's absence.

From 1185, however, David was tenaciously committed to moderating warlike Scottish policies, a stance determined by more than self-interest. His experiences in 1174–5 had impressed on him that peace with the stronger English state was essential to Scotland's well-being—though, ironically, the greater the English government's fears of Scottish belligerence, the more he would profit from English royal favour. He gave unquestioned loyalty to Richard I, who rewarded him with an advantageous marriage to Maud (or Matilda; d. 1233), sister of Ranulf (III), earl of Chester, whom he wed on 19 August 1190. It is possible, though perhaps unlikely, that he joined Richard on crusade; and he besieged Richard's enemies at Nottingham in March 1194. He was a war captain in Normandy in July 1194, and served there again in 1197. He was frequently at the English court for discussion of Anglo-Scottish affairs, as on 5 December 1189, when Richard released Scotland from English overlordship. When David's prospects of kingship receded with the birth of William the Lion's long-awaited son, Alexander, in 1198, his standing became more firmly dependent on Anglo-Scottish peace. He worked energetically to this end after King John's succession in 1199, when William demanded the border shires with renewed persistence. Regularly employed by John as an emissary to the Scots between 1199 and 1209, he also supported him in Normandy, Maine and Anjou from 1199 to 1203. During a fresh Anglo-Scottish crisis in 1209 his presence at the Scottish court strengthened the hand of those who urged William to seek an agreement with John at Norham. John's punitive terms undermined the moderates' credibility; but this treaty removed for some time the threat of Scottish aggression.

Since David's usefulness to John had diminished, he now began to fall foul of the English king's arbitrariness and rapacity. In August 1212 they were sufficiently estranged for John to suspect David of conspiring with other magnates apparently to kill him. An implausible assassin, David nevertheless had to surrender Fotheringhay Castle, his chief English seat. The decline of his political influence was accelerated by advancing years and illness. His frailty was noted when, aged sixty-two, he attended Alexander II's inauguration banquet (6–7 December 1214), and he does not appear among the young king's counsellors. He took no known part in the baronial opposition to John at the time of Magna Carta; and his rebellion, half-hearted at best, was delayed until after the Scots had invaded in October 1215. He began to make his peace with the English crown in September 1217 and finally received letters of reseisin on 13 March 1218. Praised by Jordan Fantosme for his wisdom and compassion, he was no doubt a conciliator by nature as well as by necessity. He had the grim satisfaction of being proved right when Alexander II's war effort in 1215–17 collapsed. His influence on royal policy making must not be overstated; yet his career demonstrated the possibility of serving Scottish and English interests alike, as well as the personal rewards to be gained from membership of a cross-border élite. He thus helped to pave the way for the continuous peace and often friendly contact that characterized Anglo-Scottish relations from 1217 to 1296.

Countess Maud survived her husband and did not remarry, dying in 1233. They had three sons and four daughters. The first and second sons, Henry and David, died in infancy, predeceasing their father. The third son, John of Scotland (1206–1237), became a ward of his uncle, Earl Ranulf (III), was married to Helen, daughter of Llywelyn ab Iorwerth, in 1222, and on attaining his majority had livery of the earldom of Huntingdon on 25 April 1227. He was created earl of Chester on 21 November 1232, shortly after the death of Earl Ranulf, whose senior coheir he was, and died childless at Darnhall, Cheshire, in June 1237. He was buried in the chapter house of Chester Abbey. Margaret, the eldest daughter, married in 1209 *Alan, lord of Galloway; Isabel married Robert (IV) de Brus (d. 1226x33); Maud (or Matilda) married John of Monmouth (d. 1257);

and Ada married Henry Hastings (d. 1250). It was from Margaret and Isabel respectively that the houses of Balliol— through the marriage of Margaret's daughter Dervorguilla to John de *Balliol (d. 1268)—and Brus (Bruce) inherited their claims to the throne of Scotland. David also had four known illegitimate children, three sons and a daughter. Earl David died at Yardley Hastings, Northamptonshire, his later English home, on 17 June 1219. He was interred in Sawtry Abbey, Huntingdonshire, though it had apparently been his long-standing wish to be buried in Lindores Abbey, Fife, a monastery of the Tironensian order founded by him c.1190, and colonized from Kelso Abbey.   Keith Stringer

Sources K. J. Stringer, *Earl David of Huntingdon, 1152–1219: a study in Anglo-Scottish history* (1985) · K. J. Stringer, 'The charters of David, earl of Huntingdon and lord of Garioch: a study in Anglo-Scottish diplomatic', *Essays on the nobility of medieval Scotland*, ed. K. J. Stringer (1985), 72–101 · *Jordan Fantosme's chronicle*, ed. and trans. R. C. Johnston (1981)
Likenesses seal, repro. in Stringer, *Earl David of Huntingdon, 1152–1219*, frontispiece · seals, BL, NA Scot., NL Scot., PRO

David I (c.1085–1153), king of Scots, was the sixth and youngest son of *Malcolm III (d. 1093) and his second wife, *Margaret (d. 1093).

The royal brother, c.1085–1124 Despite the violent reaction which followed Malcolm III's death in 1093, when the succession of his eldest son, *Duncan II, was opposed by the conservative Scottish nobles who wished to make Malcolm's brother, *Donald III, king in accordance with older custom, there was strong support, perhaps mainly in southern Scotland, for the novel practice of linear father-to-son succession. The direct heirs of Malcolm III were supported by William the Conqueror's sons William Rufus and Henry I. Although one of David's elder brothers, Edmund, allied himself to their uncle Donald, the other brothers, *Edgar and *Alexander I, along with David himself, fled for safety to England. While Edgar, with Rufus's backing, strove to make himself king of Scots (successfully from 1097), David was attached to the household of the future *Henry I and may have been granted a small estate in western Normandy where Henry had lands and a sizeable following of lords and knights. It must have been known that Edgar would have no children, but his heir was the next brother, Alexander, married to a bastard daughter of Henry I. David's prospects might have lain in England or on the continent, although his descent would entitle him to some share of royal lordships after Alexander I's accession in 1107. From 1100 his elder sister Edith, her name altered to Maud, had been the wife of Henry I. His association with the English court doubtless gave added force to the appeal which David was later said to have had to make to the baronage of northern England, for assistance in compelling Alexander I to hand over the appanage in Scottish Cumbria and eastern Scotland south of Lammermuir which had apparently been bequeathed to David by King Edgar. Precisely when this transfer of regional authority was made is not known, but

ALCOL
falunt
quan
pro f
S₃ po
uenera
locuf it

fita eft fup ripam flummis ṭyebę. in loco qui di
pah fubiectione hb́am ę̃ conceffrc. Jta fcilicet ut a

David I (c.1085–1153), illuminated initial, c.1159 [left, with his
grandson Malcolm IV]

it may have been a little before David's conspicuous promotion south of the border.

At the end of 1113 David, who had hitherto enjoyed only
the style of 'the queen's brother', was given by King Henry
the prize of a rich, highly born heiress, Maud de Senlis.
Maud [Matilda] (d. 1131) was the daughter of *Waltheof,
earl of Northumbria (d. 1076), son of Earl Siward who had
helped to put Malcolm III on the Scottish throne, and
Judith (d. in or after 1086), a niece of William the Conqueror. Maud's first husband was Simon (I) de Senlis (or St
Liz; d. 1111x13), a knight who had served the Conqueror
and Rufus, under whom he gained the rank of earl. With
Simon, Maud had two sons, and she would have been
nearly forty when she married David of Scotland, her junior by almost ten years. The lands acquired by David on his
marriage, stretching from south Yorkshire to Middlesex
but chiefly concentrated in the shires of Northampton,
Huntingdon, Cambridge, and Bedford, formed what came
to be known as the 'honour of Huntingdon'. Its possession
made David an important figure in Anglo-Norman court
circles. As late as 1130, after he had become king, he is
recorded as presiding over the treason trial of Henry I's
chamberlain, Geoffrey Clinton. Acquisition of this great
lordship was marked by King Henry's grant of an earldom,
but to assign the names Huntingdon or Northampton to
this estate before the mid-twelfth century is anachronistic. When in Stephen's reign the Senlis family and the
Scottish royal house vied for control of the honour, which
was never partitioned, the former preferred the title earl
of Northampton (given by Stephen), while the Scots simply spoke of the honour of Huntingdon without using any
territorial style.

In southern Scotland, David quickly showed what was
to prove the overriding passion of his life, reform of ecclesiastical institutions and revival of religion. Between 1110
and 1118 he restored the ancient see of Glasgow, of which
he made his chaplain John bishop, consecrated by Pope
Paschal II (r. 1099–1118) at David's request. In the early
1120s an inquest was held to ascertain the ancient landed

endowments of the see, many of which had been seques-
trated. Fresh endowments were provided and a new cathedral was begun, dedicated in 1136. David brought to Selkirk a community of monks from Tiron, north of Chartres. In 1128 the convent migrated to Kelso, beside the
flourishing centre of Roxburgh, where their abbey grew
into the richest in Scotland. The Tironensians, outstand-
ingly successful in Scotland, were the earliest of the congregations of reformed Benedictines (which were the
dominant feature of monastic life in north-west Europe in
this period) to establish themselves north of the channel.

David I and the Scottish nobility David's sister Queen Maud
died in 1118, by which date it may have seemed probable
that their brother Alexander I would die childless. Soon
after Alexander's death on 23 April 1124, David was inaugurated king of Scots at Scone. It is reported by Ailred of
Rievaulx (d. 1167) that the attendant bishops had difficulty
persuading the new king to undergo the essentially pagan
ceremony of inauguration, at which the earl of Fife, as
head of a junior segment of the royal lineage, placed the
king on the famous stone of Scone (or stone of destiny),
while the royal bard bestowed the rod or wand of kingship.

David I's achievements as king are most easily understood if the secular and ecclesiastical spheres are treated
separately. It must, however, be emphasized that the division is modern and artificial. There is no evidence, and it
seems improbable, that David himself drew any sharp distinction between his roles as guardian of the realm and
protector of holy church.

Given the king's upbringing and marriage and his
lengthy experience of the Anglo-Norman court it was
inevitable that he perceived lordship in feudal terms.
Probably already while ruler of southern Scotland, during
his brother's reign, he established followers from Normandy and England, such as Robert (I) de Brus (d. 1142),
Hugh de Morville and Ranulf de Soulles as lords of substantial portions of the princely demesne of Cumbria.
Such men were trained in cavalry warfare and the use of
motte-and-bailey castles. By the 1140s the greater part of
southern Scotland, with the exception of Galloway and
Nithsdale, had been allotted to incoming followers of the
king. In the west they were given extensive lordships (for
example, Annandale, Kyle Stewart), while in the east
smaller, discrete, estates were the norm for newly created
fiefs. Many (probably all) of these fiefs were held for military service, including the duty of garrisoning the king's
castles.

Although David I was willing to repeat this pattern of
fief-creation in Scotia, north of the Forth–Clyde line, the
outstanding fact of his reign in secular affairs was the continued and peaceful coexistence of a newly established
military feudalism with the older arrangement of provinces ruled by hereditary dynasties of mormaers (literally
'great officers', 'chief stewards'). These were territorial in
character, probably a legacy of the pre-ninth century Pict-
ish kingdom. An exception to the rule of peaceful coexistence was the revolt in 1130 by Angus, mormaer of Moray.

Angus was the son of a daughter of Lulach Mac Gillachom-gan, who had been briefly king of Scots in 1057–8. Taking advantage of the king's absence in the south of England, Angus led an army south by the east coast route. Just south of the crossing of the River North Esk near Stracathro, the men of Moray were met by a force under the command of King David's constable Edward and suffered a decisive defeat, Angus himself being killed. Had the battle gone the other way, the course of Scottish history might well have been significantly different. As it was, David annexed the province of Moray to the crown and established followers of continental origin, notably Flemings, in estates which had presumably belonged to the mormaers. In all the provincial earldoms or mormaerdoms the king possessed rights, for example, military service, justice, and certain types of revenue, while in some, especially Fife, Gowrie, and Angus, as well as in Moray after 1130, he had extensive lands in demesne. These were exploited to create and support the castles and trading towns ('burghs') which in David I's time were established at Perth, Forfar, Montrose, Aberdeen, Elgin, Forres, and Inverness. A mixture of the old and the new, in which the crown held the initiative, characterized the political entity coming to be known as the kingdom of the Scots in the earlier twelfth century.

The transformation of the church However powerfully he had left his mark on Scottish secular government, David I was to be remembered, not without reason, as the king who almost single-handedly transformed the church within his realm, with a generosity which is said to have prompted King James I (r. 1406–37) to observe ruefully that David's grants to the religious had made him 'a sair sanct to the croun' (Ritchie, 337). He was personally responsible for founding monasteries of the Tironensian, Cistercian, and Augustinian orders, while he enlarged the Benedictine priory of Dunfermline to form the second richest abbey in Scotland, and established Benedictines of the Cluniac observance on the Isle of May. He was largely responsible for founding an Augustinian cathedral priory at St Andrews, and he welcomed the military orders of the Hospital and the Temple. Such a rich infusion of monastic life, closely tied as it was to forms of regular observance universal throughout western Christendom, would have altered the Scottish church almost beyond recognition. But David went much further, imposing a territorially defined system upon the Scottish bishoprics. This involved strengthening the authority of the two largest dioceses of St Andrews (which he strove unsuccessfully to have recognized as metropolitan) and Glasgow. Almost certainly David created the dioceses of Caithness and Moray, while he re-established the see of the bishop of north-east Scotland at Old Aberdeen, close to the royal castle and burgh of Aberdeen. Within the dioceses, whose boundaries were now relatively well defined, the king encouraged the formation of parish churches with fixed territories, served by priests supported by tithes (Scottish, 'teinds'), payment of which was enforced by the secular power.

Anglo-Scottish relations Scotland's relations with England remained peaceful and even friendly as long as Henry I was alive. Not only was there a close personal tie between the two kings, but it is clear also that Henry's plan to have his daughter, the Empress Matilda (d. 1167), recognized as his heir—even though a woman and married to the count of Anjou—was fully accepted by the king of Scots, who in 1127 was first among the lay magnates to swear an oath of fealty to Matilda as prospective successor to her father. David enjoyed a special position within the English kingdom, being entrusted by Henry with important administrative roles and judicial decisions. The Anglo-Scottish peace was shattered by Stephen of Blois's bid for the crown at the end of 1135, when David took possession of Carlisle and Cumberland, as his father had held them, enforcing a Scottish restoration which he had never attempted as long as Henry I was king of England. The Scots were compelled to recognize Stephen's authority, at least *de facto*, and by David's first treaty with Stephen (February 1136) he retained Cumbria, relinquished Northumberland, and had his son and heir *Henry recognized as lord of the honour of Huntingdon. Relations with Stephen broke down in 1137, however, and by 1138 the Scots were invading Northumberland and pushing even further south, towards Yorkshire, probably with the aim of establishing Scottish authority over the whole of England north of Lancashire and the Tees. But David's strategy received a setback on 22 August 1138, when a well-disciplined force of English barons and knights met a large but unruly Scottish host on Cowton Moor near Northallerton, and in the battle of the Standard inflicted a severe defeat.

Stephen's difficulties in southern England prevented him from exploiting this English victory, and by his second treaty with the Scots (Durham, 9 April 1139) he was forced in effect to cede to David control over England between Tees and Tweed, as well as continued enjoyment of the honour of Huntingdon. After Stephen was captured by his enemies in 1141, David and his son joined forces with the empress when she made her unsuccessful bid for the English throne. Even though the rout of the empress's forces at Winchester, on 14 September 1141, sent David and Henry northward again in undignified flight, their discomfiture did not affect their position north of Tees, where they remained in control until David's death. The honour of Huntingdon, however, was now lost. Indeed, at this period the Scottish king even exercised lordship over the honour of Lancaster, while in 1149 he entertained the young Henry of Anjou, son of the empress, at a splendid ceremony at Carlisle, where David conferred knighthood upon the future king of England and extracted a solemn promise, soon to be broken, that after Henry's accession the Scots would be left in undisturbed enjoyment of the English northern counties. Contemporary English writers reproached David for allowing his followers to commit many atrocities during the invasions of 1137–8, but at least one of them, William of Newburgh, gives the Scottish king credit for enforcing a twelve-year peace throughout northern England when it was conspicuously absent in the south.

The achievements of David I David I was driven by a clear and consistent vision, pious and authoritarian, of what his kingdom should be: Catholic, in the sense of conforming to the doctrines and observances of the western church; feudal, in the sense that a lord–vassal relationship, involving knight-service, should form the basis of government; and open, in the sense that external (especially continental) influences of all kinds, religious, military, and economic, were encouraged and exploited to strengthen the Scottish kingdom. Alongside his eclecticism, David's strong sense of the autonomy of his realm and of his own position within it must be acknowledged. The surviving numbers of his charters, compared with those of his predecessors, surely point to an increase in the sophistication, and probably also in the activity, of government. During David's reign the administration of royal justice became more firmly established and was organized more effectively. Those who enjoyed their own courts were told that the king would intervene if they failed to provide justice. The addresses of royal charters and writs (Scottish 'brieves') show that from c.1140 justiciars were appointed. Although none is known by name, these officers were clearly the predecessors of the named justiciars of succeeding reigns.

David prevented his bishops (save only Galloway) recognizing any claims by York or Canterbury to ecclesiastical authority over the Scottish church, and he refused homage to Stephen, only allowing his son to do homage for Northumberland and Huntingdon. He restored the southern border of his kingdom west of the Pennines to Westmorland, where it had run before 1092. He was the first king of Scots to have a coinage struck in his name, in the form of silver sterlings minted at Carlisle, Berwick, Edinburgh, and elsewhere, from c.1139 onwards. His greatest failure, for which he cannot be blamed, lay in the succession. From c.1136, when his son Henry (understandably, in view of Maud's probable age at her second marriage, the only son to survive to adulthood) would have been about twenty, David had begun to associate his heir with himself in royal government. From 1139 onwards, indeed, it is not misleading to speak of joint kingship in Scotland. But Henry died tragically young in 1152. David himself died a year later, on 24 May 1153 at Carlisle Castle; he was buried in early June before the high altar of the church of Dunfermline Abbey. His heir, Henry's eldest son, *Malcolm IV, was only twelve and no match for the vigorous Henry of Anjou who succeeded to the English throne at the end of 1154. Yet Malcolm succeeded comparatively peacefully and the greater part of his grandfather's legacy remained to the Scottish kingdom as it was to develop, on foundations which David had largely laid, during the remaining medieval centuries.   G. W. S. BARROW

Sources G. W. S. Barrow, ed., *The charters of King David I: the written acts of David I king of Scots, 1124–53, and of his son Henry earl of Northumberland, 1139–52* (1999) • A. C. Lawrie, ed., *Early Scottish charters prior to AD 1153* (1905) • Ailred of Rievaulx, 'Eulogium Davidis', *Vitae antiquae sanctorum qui habitaverunt in ea parte Britanniae nunc vocata Scotia vel in ejus insulis*, ed. J. Pinkerton (1789) • Symeon of Durham, *Opera* • R. Howlett, ed., *Chronicles of the reigns of Stephen, Henry II, and Richard I*, 3, Rolls Series, 82 (1886) • G. W. S. Barrow, ed., *Regesta regum Scottorum*, 1 (1960) • R. L. G. Ritchie, *The Normans in Scotland* (1954) • G. W. S. Barrow, 'The charters of David I', *Anglo-Norman Studies*, 14 (1991), 25–37 • G. W. S. Barrow, *David I of Scotland (1124–53): the balance of new and old* (1985) • A. O. Anderson and M. O. Anderson, eds., *The chronicle of Melrose* (1936) • *A Scottish chronicle known as the chronicle of Holyrood*, ed. M. O. Anderson (1938) • GEC, *Peerage* • *Johannis de Fordun Chronica gentis Scotorum*, ed. W. F. Skene (1871) • *Johannis de Fordun Chronica gentis Scotorum / John of Fordun's Chronicle of the Scottish nation*, ed. W. F. Skene, trans. F. J. H. Skene, 2 (1872), 224

Archives Durham Cath. CL, charters • NA Scot. | NL Scot., Edinburgh Advocates MSS

Likenesses illuminated initial, c.1159, NL Scot., charter of Malcolm IV for Kelso Abbey [*see illus.*]

David II (1324–1371), king of Scots, was the elder son of *Robert I (1274–1329) and his second wife, *Elizabeth (d. 1327), daughter of Richard de Burgh, earl of Ulster.

Childhood and youth David was born in Dunfermline Abbey on 5 March 1324, apparently the elder of twins. His younger brother, John, died, probably in infancy, and was buried at Restennet Priory. David had two older sisters surviving, both, like himself, children of Robert's second marriage: Matilda, who married Thomas Isaac, of whom little is known, probably in 1342, and died in 1353; and Margaret, who married William *Sutherland, fifth earl of Sutherland [*see under* Sutherland family], in or before 1345. She had died by 1360. His half-sister by Robert's first marriage, Marjorie, was married to Walter, the steward of Scotland, and died, probably in 1317 or 1318, leaving a son, Robert, who succeeded his father as steward in 1327. He was therefore David's nephew, though some eight years older, and ultimately succeeded him as Robert II in 1371.

From the moment of his birth David was recognized as the heir of his father, Robert I, and this was formally declared by a tailzie, or entail, in 1326, perhaps as a result of the death at an unknown date of his twin brother and the need to reassert the position of Robert the Steward as heir to David, a position which would have been held by John while he lived. David succeeded his father at the age of five on 7 June 1329. He was the first Scottish monarch to be anointed, by virtue of a bull of John XXII granted on 13 June 1329. This followed the treaty of Edinburgh of 1328, by which the independent status of the rulers of Scotland was acknowledged. As part of that treaty David had on 17 July married *Joan (1321–1362), the second daughter of Edward II, king of England. He was four years old, she had just turned seven. The young king and queen were crowned at Scone on 24 November 1331.

David was too young to have any influence on events during the difficult years which followed his father's death in 1329. There is no evidence of his reaction to the invasions by Edward Balliol in 1332, the disastrous defeat at Dupplin, the temporary ejection of Balliol in the winter of 1332–3, and the even more disastrous invasion of Edward III in 1333, after which Balliol, as king of Scots, held Scotland as a fief from Edward III. David and his queen were at first kept safe in Dumbarton, one of the few castles that remained out of English hands, and in May

David II (1324–1371), illuminated initial [left, with Edward III]

1334 were sent to France, where they were well received by the French king, Philippe VI, who maintained his support for Scottish independence and gave David and Joan a refuge at Château Gaillard in Normandy. They continued to receive a pension from Philippe throughout their stay.

Little is known of David's activities in France at this time. In 1335–6, when he was eleven, he was almost certainly involved in the abortive negotiations between Philippe VI and Edward III, which attempted to resolve the respective claims of David and Edward Balliol to the Scottish throne; and in 1339, during the siege of Perth by the Steward, there is evidence that Sir William Douglas visited Château Gaillard and obtained the services of some French knights and sailors who helped in the siege. This may have been financed by David or Philippe. David is said by the chronicler Froissart to have been present with the French king on campaign in Picardy in 1339, and at the siege of Tournai in 1340. Meanwhile, his claim to Scotland was maintained during this period by a series of king's lieutenants, including his nephew, Robert the Steward, and these seem, naturally enough in view of his age, to have handled affairs with little reference to David. It may, however, have been through his influence with Philippe that the French king brokered the release in 1340 of the captive John Randolph, earl of Moray, in exchange for the earl of Salisbury, recently captured in France. By 1341 the Steward, by then king's lieutenant, was satisfied that the situation in Scotland was secure enough for David to return. He and Joan landed at Inverbervie, north of Montrose, on 2 June 1341.

First reign, 1341–1346 David's return was greeted with rejoicing: 'All Scots were delighted beyond belief at his arrival, and held feasts with joy and dancing' (Bower, 7.151). Yet the problems which faced him were grave, and

he was only in his eighteenth year. In his absence his country had been repeatedly invaded and destabilized. Most of the nobles at one time or another had come to terms with Balliol, even if only briefly. Part of the kingdom had been ceded into direct English rule; and there had been recurrent guerrilla warfare which had caused widespread destruction. The processes of administration had been disrupted: at times in the southern counties there had been an English administration which found itself unable to collect more than nominal revenues, but which excluded any Scottish authority, while elsewhere there had been two rival administrations, neither of which could achieve much. Regular exchequer audits been resumed in the north-eastern parts only relatively recently, and in other areas apparently not until just before David's return. It was a situation to daunt someone much older than the young king. His lack of experience may have showed: the *Liber pluscardensis*, written in the mid-fifteenth century, comments that he 'did little with mature deliberation and wise counsel but acted without advice headstrongly and following his own ideas' (*Liber pluscardensis*, 291).

Nevertheless the mechanics of government were rapidly put back in place. A new chamberlain, William Bullock, who, curiously, had held the same office under Edward Balliol, soon restored financial order, collecting revenues and dealing with claims efficiently. A number of charters were immediately issued, confirming rights which had been held from David's predecessors; parliaments and councils were convened.

David's relations with the nobility who had been managing affairs independently for so long proved more difficult, especially his dealings with Sir William Douglas, a cadet of the immensely powerful Douglas family and at this point its only prominent and active member. He had been one of the outstanding leaders of Scottish resistance against Edward III and Edward Balliol, and had gained a strong landed position in the borders, particularly the lands of Liddesdale, from which he was henceforth known as William Douglas of Liddesdale. He expected power and reward, and was prepared to take them if not given. In the central borders David was anxious to rely on another equally notable fighter for Scottish independence, Sir Alexander Ramsay, who had just in 1342 recovered the important castle of Roxburgh. David made him sheriff of Teviotdale, a position which had allegedly already been given to Douglas. Douglas's reaction was to capture Ramsay, imprison him in Hermitage Castle in Liddesdale, and starve him to death. In the face of noble pressure David could do nothing but accept the situation, allowing Douglas to hold the sheriffdom he had seized. It was not an auspicious beginning.

It was also natural that David should have wanted to assert himself against Edward III, whom he was bound to regard as his enemy. He was encouraged by the young knights by whom we are told he was surrounded, and invaded England three times, apparently with declining success after his first raid in 1341, when he devastated the town of Penrith, and provoked a retaliation from Edward

III, who celebrated Christmas that year at Melrose. However, Edward's attention was by now concentrated in France, and David's later raids, if not notable triumphs, brought no disasters.

David remained conscious of his debt to Philippe VI of France; and, when the latter was facing Edward's great invasion in 1346 and asked for a counter-invasion by the Scots, David agreed. He entered the English west march early in October, and began well by capturing Liddel Strength in Cumberland and executing its captain, Sir Walter Selby. But the expedition was marred by divisions among the Scots. When their army had mustered at Perth, the earl of Ross took his chance to contrive the assassination of his northern enemy, Ranald MacRuairi, leader of a contingent from the Isles, and then departed. After the capture of Liddel, William Douglas argued that enough had been done, and that in view of Ranald's murder it would be wise to return to Scotland and reconsider their plans. This probably sound advice was opposed by many of David's commanders, who believed that the north of England was ripe for plunder while Edward's attention was given to France. The result was substantial ravaging, particularly of monastic lands; but ultimately an army assembled by the archbishop of York confronted David's force near Bearpark outside Durham, and on 17 October, in what has became known as the battle of Nevilles Cross, the Scots were routed. Many of their leaders were killed, and David himself was captured, having been wounded in the head by two English arrows. One of these was extracted with great difficulty after the battle, the other remained embedded until it allegedly sprang out automatically while the king was at prayer during a pilgrimage to the church of St Monance in Fife, probably some time after 1365. Other Scottish captives included Sir William Douglas, Duncan, earl of Fife, and Malcolm Fleming, earl of Wigtown. The Steward and Patrick, earl of Dunbar, fled before the disaster had gone too far, the Steward to become for the second time lieutenant during the king's absence.

Captivity, 1346–1357 David's captivity lasted for eleven years. Much of it was spent in the Tower, though he was at Windsor for the St George's day festivities of 1348; he also went north for negotiations with the Scots in 1351–2, and perhaps again in 1353. During these negotiations he was allowed to return to Scotland for a few months in 1352. From March 1355 he was in more relaxed quarters at Odiham Castle in Hampshire, where he remained until his eventual release. He seems to have been on reasonably good terms with Edward III. During this period there is no evidence of any contact with his wife, Joan, who apparently remained in Scotland despite a safe conduct to visit her husband in 1348, and David is thought to have begun his relationship with one Katherine Mortimer (d. 1360), whose origin is unknown. She is described as 'Welsh' in Bower's *Scotichronicon* (7.321), though this does not exclude the possibility that she belonged to the prominent Mortimer family, many of whose lands were on the Welsh march. She accompanied David when he eventually returned to Scotland, and was openly treated as his mistress.

Most of what we know of David's actions at this time concerns his attempts to secure his release. For long, the chief problem was Edward's determination to establish a permanent English supremacy over Scotland. In 1350 David presented a petition to the pope, asking him to use his influence with Philippe VI of France to ensure that David's release was included in any peace between Philippe and Edward. To reinforce the appeal, the petition recites the terms demanded by Edward for David's release, which probably date from negotiations in 1348. The essence was that the king of Scots should hold Scotland as a fief from the king of England, with all normal feudal liabilities; and that, if David died without an heir, he should be succeeded by the king of England or his son. By the early 1350s the argument seems to have moved on, though we depend on difficult texts which have often been misdated and misinterpreted. It appears that David himself achieved a breakthrough by suggesting the possible succession not of the king of England, but of one of Edward's sons, other than the heir to England. The object was to make certain that Scotland remained a separate kingdom, not directly subject to the king of England. This proposal was apparently acceptable to Edward, and by 1351–2 it was formally put to the Scots. David, who hoped to persuade them to accept, was allowed to return for some months to Scotland to see if he could.

There appear to have been two sticking points. If David had no other heir, the heir under the entail of 1326 was Robert the Steward, now lieutenant in David's absence. The arrangement with Edward would have disinherited him, so his opposition could be assumed. There also seems to have been a more general opposition to an English succession, even if the separate kingdom was preserved. We have no evidence of the balance of opinion in Scotland beyond the fact that the proposals being supported by David were rejected. There exist from this period the texts of some letters from Jean II of France offering support to the Scots in the event of an attempt by David to invade his own country with English backing. There is no evidence at all that he contemplated this; but perhaps it was considered a possibility by the Steward, who may have envisaged recourse to desperate measures if it looked like coming to pass.

David returned to captivity, accepting the rejection of the scheme. By 1354 Edward was facing difficulties in France, and was prepared to contemplate a simpler solution: to release David in return for a ransom, by a treaty which left quite unresolved the question of English claims to superiority. This was rejected by the Scots at the time, probably because they were inclined once more to join the French in the war against England, to which end they were offered French support. During this period the Steward seems to have favoured a French alliance in preference to a settlement with England. But the Black Prince's triumph at Poitiers in 1356 and the capture of Jean II changed the position again. Edward was now triumphant and bent on exploiting his advantage as the captor of two kings. As far as the Scots were concerned, he was prepared to offer more or less the terms proposed in 1354, which were now accepted. In September 1357 David was brought from Odiham to London; he paid a brief visit to Canterbury and by 29 September was at Berwick, where on 3 October he formally confirmed the text of the treaty of Berwick, by which he was to be released in return for a ransom of 100,000 merks, payable over ten years.

Second reign, 1357–1371 On his return David faced serious problems, some of them personal. His open attachment to his mistress, Katherine Mortimer, no doubt alienated his wife; in 1358 she retired to England under a safe conduct, and remained there until her death in 1362. His mistress was treacherously murdered in 1360, possibly at the instigation of the earl of Angus, who was later imprisoned and died in captivity. In 1363 David married *Margaret (*née* Drummond) (*d.* in or after 1374), widow of Sir John Logie, whom he divorced probably early in 1369; and he was clearly contemplating a further marriage, to Agnes Dunbar, apparently the sister of the earl of March, when he died in 1371. It is likely that David still sought an heir; but neither of his marriages produced one. Nor, as far as is known, did he have any illegitimate issue.

The treaty of Berwick also left David with a large ransom to pay, on which he soon defaulted, after only 20,000 merks had been paid. This inevitably complicated relations with England and imperilled the position of the nobles who were being held in England as hostages for the payments. The result was a series of negotiations which tried to win better terms. In 1363, when Edward III was ready to consider a permanent settlement, it was suggested that all other English claims and the ransom would be abandoned provided the Scots agreed that if David died without a legitimate heir, the king of England should succeed him. If this happened, Scotland was to remain a separate kingdom, and there were detailed provisions to ensure that this would be so. This proposal was firmly rejected by a Scottish parliament in 1364. Subsequent negotiations concentrated on possible reschedulings of the ransom. In 1365 Edward felt in a strong position, and the only terms on offer were severe. But he was much more generous in 1369, when renewed war with France threatened, and hence Scottish friendship was more important to him. He conceded a fourteen-year truce to the Scots, and fixed the residue of David's ransom at only 56,000 merks. This much more favourable settlement was in force when David died.

David's captivity and the English reoccupation of parts of the south of Scotland after 1346, even if temporary, had seriously disrupted Scottish government. Until the mid-1350s there was a state of war over much of the border region; and more generally the Steward, as lieutenant during the king's absence, seems to have done little to keep the routine processes of government in operation. Audits of accounts were not held, and after David's release there had to be a laborious effort to catch up, which revealed that the sheriffs had been able to do little and that judicial administration was in confusion.

When David returned in 1357, he held a general council which brought into the open many complaints about public order during his absence. It urged the king to hold a justice ayre in person to strike terror into wrongdoers: no one was to levy private wars against their neighbours, and churches were to enjoy their liberties as they had in times of good peace. There is enough evidence on record that David took the enforcement of justice seriously, and that good order and effective administration were restored. Royal charters and other documents were sought and issued in profusion, and the exchequer accounts were regularly audited; a reassessment of taxation, and above all a substantial increase in customs revenues, made it possible for David to make regular payments towards his ransom, while still enjoying a marked increase in his income. A rather curious result of the collapse of authority in his absence was that, erratically in the relatively few texts issued, acts were dated by a regnal year one year less than was mathematically correct, a practice which became regular after his return. The cause of this error is still under debate. None the less, David's second reign was to prove a period of strong and determined government in which his authority was enforced throughout the realm.

The most serious consequence of the king's absence, and indeed of developments during and since the wars of independence, was the growing power of a small group of the greater nobles whose ancestors had fought against English domination under Robert I, notably Robert the Steward, Patrick, earl of March, and William, lord of Douglas. These three inherited and added to great estates during David's minority and early rule, and had held power during his captivity. Effective government depended on being able to work with these men, and David clearly grasped this, for he supported and rewarded them for what they had done: the Steward received the earldom of Strathearn, and Douglas became the first earl of Douglas. March was now elderly and perhaps less influential; and was in any case already an earl.

But David clearly wanted to establish his own adherents. In his first reign he was said to be surrounded by a group of young chivalric knights to whom he gave much favour. This pattern continued after 1357, when he combined his recognition of the great nobles with steady reward of a group of younger men who became his personal following. Among these, Robert Erskine had worked consistently for the king's release during his captivity, and rapidly became a key figure in his administration. The king extended considerable patronage to the family of his second wife, both her Drummond and Logie relatives, and, it seems, favoured the Drummonds in a serious dispute with the Steward [*see* Drummond family]. He also enforced the marriage of another of this group, Walter Lesley, to the heiress of the elderly fifth earl of Ross, and compelled the entail of Ross's lands on Lesley and his wife. This provoked an elaborate but futile complaint by Ross to Robert II after David's death and shortly before Ross's own; the latter occurred in 1372, whereupon Lesley duly inherited the earldom.

These policies may have been one of the causes of an

obscure revolt by Douglas, the Steward, and March in 1363; the rebels may have been alarmed by the king's apparently severe treatment of the earl of Mar, whose castle of Kildrummy David seized early in 1363, and by his failure to pay his ransom to Edward III, which might have led to their being sent into captivity in England, as hostages for its payment. It is also possible that the king's plans for a second marriage aroused hostility. Whatever the exact causes, the revolt rapidly collapsed: only Douglas seemed anxious to proceed, and David very wisely was content simply to exact submissions. He continued his policy of recognizing the claims of the greater nobles, while building up his own following on which he could rely.

In the late 1360s David was concerned to enforce law and order, especially in the highland areas where much depended on powerful local lords, given to the reset (harbouring) of malefactors. David required men such as the Steward, whose earldom of Strathearn made him an important highland lord, and the lord of the Isles, publicly to give sureties for the behaviour of their followers. Later writers give David credit for some success in this matter, and these policies may have provoked another temporary clash with the Steward, who was briefly imprisoned in 1369 and for a short time ceased to be described in witness lists as earl of Strathearn.

Yet there remained the problem of the succession. David may still have hoped for an heir; but it seems that he was taking account of the possibility of a Stewart succession. It looked unlikely that the Steward himself would succeed, since he was eight years older than the king; in 1366 or 1367, while Margaret was still in favour, and no doubt with her support, David forced the marriage of the Steward's son and heir, John, to Margaret's niece Annabella Drummond; and in 1368 he gave him the title of earl of Carrick, which David himself had held as heir to the throne. This suggests that he was trying to preserve the influence of his inner ring of supporters in the event of a Stewart succession by establishing a connection between Margaret's family and the likely heir. But on 22 February 1371 David died suddenly at Edinburgh Castle; he was buried in Holyrood Abbey. Consequently it was the Steward who succeeded, to rule as Robert II until his death at the age of eighty-four in 1390. Annabella's influence was not sufficient to preserve the power of the Drummonds and others of David's supporters with the new monarch.

Reputation and achievements David's reputation has suffered many vicissitudes. The nearest to a contemporary judgement, that of the chronicler Andrew Wyntoun, writing probably early in the fifteenth century, is also one of the most favourable: 'his land in realté he led, and rewlyt in equité … He was manly, war and wys. Thus in al forme of justris he left his land at his ending' (Andrew of Wyntoun, 2.506–7). Walter Bower, in the middle of the fifteenth century, follows the same line:

> King David reformed his kingdom with excellent laws, he punished rebels, he calmed his subjects with undisturbed peace, and he united to their fatherland by means of one legal contract Scots speaking different tongues, both the

wild caterans and the domesticated men with skills. (Bower, 7.359)

The last comment refers to his pacification of the highlanders. Writers of the sixteenth century remain favourable, if perhaps more qualified. John Mair, whose history was published in 1521, observes: 'I can only compare David to middling rulers. He had little experience of war, was unfortunate in worldly matters, but showed patience rather than fear. In the end he gave his realm peace and subdued the wild Scots' (Mair, 256–7). Hector Boece, in his *Scotorum historiae* (published 1527), commented simply that he was 'no less great in spirit than his father [Robert I] but less fortunate' (Boece, citing *Scotorum regum catalogus*, no. 98). George Buchanan, whose *Rerum Scoticarum historia* was published in 1582, is of a similar opinion: 'a man to be remembered for every sort of virtue, and primarily for justice and clemency; having endured both good and evil, he seemed throughout to have lacked good fortune rather than diligence' (Buchanan, 301).

It was in the century after the Act of Union of 1707 that David's reputation suffered; and primarily because of his negotiations with Edward III, in which he was thought to have been willing to surrender the independence of Scotland in order to secure his liberty and subsequently peace with England and release from the ransom he owed. David Dalrymple, Lord Hailes, in the second volume of his *Annals of Scotland*, first published in 1779, wrote:

> the defects in his character were many, and all of them were prejudicial to the public: he was weak and capricious, violent in his resentments and habitually under the dominion of women … We ought not to forget that he degenerated from the magnanimity of his father and that, through the allurement of present ease or through motives of base jealousy, he was willing to surrender the honour, security and independence of that people whom God and the laws had entrusted to his protection.   (Dalrymple, 2.321–2)

Hailes's view has been repeated by generations of historians down to the present century, who have all condemned David as the degenerate son of a noble father.

A final judgement on David II is still very difficult, and there remain many uncertainties about his motives and plans. The only narrative written by a contemporary, that of John Fordun, is extremely sketchy about the years of David's second reign. Although substantial documentation survives from his government, it tells us little that is known for sure about David himself and his personality; and the crucial texts about his relations with England are few, mostly undated or misdated in many accounts, and hard to interpret. He was certainly anxious to achieve a permanent peace with England, which would undoubtedly have been for the benefit of his country; it remains unclear how far he was prepared to go to secure that peace, or what his own attitude was to the proposals of 1363, for the succession of Edward III in the event of his own death without an heir.

In spite of these interpretative difficulties, since the 1960s there has been something of a reversion to the views of the earliest writers concerning David II. He has come to be generally seen as a strong and capable ruler, not to be trifled with, determined to assert himself and generally successful in doing so. His marriages are more likely to have been the result of his search for a direct heir than, as Hailes suggested, because he was dominated by women, while he left the finances of his kingdom in a better state than they had been in for generations.

BRUCE WEBSTER

Sources Johannis de Fordun Chronica gentis Scotorum, ed. W. F. Skene (1871) • Andrew of Wyntoun, *The orygynale cronykil of Scotland*, [rev. edn], 2, ed. D. Laing (1872) • W. Bower, *Scotichronicon*, ed. D. E. R. Watt and others, new edn, 9 vols. (1987–98), vol. 7 • G. W. S. Barrow and others, eds., *Regesta regum Scottorum*, 6, ed. B. Webster (1982) [incl. texts of all David's surviving *acta*] • R. Nicholson, *Scotland: the later middle ages* (1974), vol. 2 of *The Edinburgh history of Scotland*, ed. G. Donaldson (1965–75); repr. (1989) • A. A. M. Duncan, 'Honi soit qui mal y pense': David II and Edward III, 1346–52', *SHR*, 67 (1988), 113–41 • J. Campbell, 'England, Scotland and the Hundred Years' War in the fourteenth century', *Europe in the Middle Ages*, ed. J. R. Hale, J. R. L. Highfield, and B. Smalley (1965), 184–216 • R. Nicholson, 'David II, the historians and the chroniclers', *SHR*, 45 (1966), 59–78 • B. Webster, 'David II and the government of fourteenth-century Scotland', *TRHS*, 5th ser., 16 (1966), 115–30 • S. I. Boardman, *The early Stewart kings: Robert II and Robert III, 1371–1406* (1996), 1–38 • A. A. M. Duncan, ed., 'A question about the succession, 1364', *Miscellany … XII*, Scottish History Society, 5th ser., 7 (1994), 1–97 • B. Webster, 'Scotland without a king, 1329–1341', *Medieval Scotland: crown, lordship and community: essays presented to G. W. S. Barrow*, ed. A. Grant and K. J. Stringer (1993), 223–38 • F. J. H. Skene, *Liber pluscardensis*, 2 vols. (1877–80) • J. Mair, *Historia majoris Britanniae* (1740) • H. Boece, *Scotorum historiae a prima gentis origine* (Paris, 1527) • G. Buchanan, *Opera omnia*, 1: *Rerum Scoticarum historia*, ed. T. Ruddimanno (1725) • D. Dalrymple of Hailes, *Annals of Scotland*, 3rd edn, 3 vols. (1819) • *Scalacronica: the reigns of Edward I, Edward II and Edward III as recorded by Sir Thomas Gray*, trans. H. Maxwell (1907) • A. A. M. Duncan, 'The regnal year of David II', *SHR*, 68 (1989), 105–19 • A. A. M. Duncan, 'The laws of Malcolm MacKenneth', *Medieval Scotland: crown, lordship and community: essays presented to G. W. S. Barrow*, ed. A. Grant and K. J. Stringer (1993), 239–73
Likenesses illuminated initial (confirmation of a grant of Robert I to the Carmelite friars of Aberdeen), U. Aberdeen, Marischal College, charter chest 1/4 • illuminated initial, BL, Cotton MS Nero D.vi, fol. 61v [*see illus.*]

David ap Gwilym. *See* Dafydd ap Gwilym (*fl.* 1330–1350).

David fitz Gerald (*c.*1103x9–1176), bishop of St David's, was the son of Gerald of *Windsor (*d.* 1116x36) and *Nest (*b.* before 1092, *d.* *c.*1130), daughter of the Welsh prince, *Rhys ap Tewdwr (*d.* 1093). His eldest brother, William, was lord of Carew; Maurice, a younger brother, had a small local endowment; his sister, Angharad, married William de Barry of Manorbier. He also had half-brothers who were established in south Wales and, after 1170, Ireland. The distinction of this ambitious group was greatly enhanced by Gerald of Wales (*d.* 1220x23), David's nephew, whose works promoted both the most successful members of his family and himself.

By 1148, David was a canon of St David's and archdeacon of Cardigan. In that year, the canons of St David's were divided over his election as bishop, and two different motives were suggested. One, recorded by Gerald of Wales, was that some wanted a Welshman as bishop, while others opposed such an appointment. The other was that some wished to defend the metropolitan claims of St David's and others accepted Canterbury's primatial authority. Summoned to Lambeth for the election, a group of canons was persuaded by Theobald, archbishop of Canterbury, to elect David as a bishop who would not oppose the archbishop's claims to primacy in Wales. The unusually detailed promise of obedience which he gave Theobald lends credence to this view. The election has been seen as a valuable tactical victory for the archbishop.

Although his connections with the Welsh dynasty and Anglo-Norman settlers made him potentially an important political figure, David rarely exercised political influence. He intervened with Rhys ap Gruffudd in 1167 to secure the release from prison of his half-brother, Robert fitz Stephen. This family matter had wider significance because Robert, at liberty, was obliged to join the Anglo-Norman forces preparing to invade Ireland.

David was essentially a local bishop, appearing rarely on major ecclesiastical occasions affecting the church in Britain. In twenty-six years he assisted at the consecration of a fellow bishop only once, that of Archbishop Thomas Becket. He attended the Council of Tours summoned by Alexander III in 1163. Late in life, prompted by personal interests, he attended the Council of Westminster convened by Richard of Dover, archbishop of Canterbury, in 1175. The council enacted legislation for the Welsh dioceses; the status of St David's was again being discussed by some of his canons; and his chapter had prepared an indictment of his conduct to present to the archbishop. His links with the royal court were likewise minimal. He was at Clarendon early in 1164 to give assent to Henry II's constitutions for the church. When, in September 1171, Henry was preparing to embark for Ireland, he made a brief formal visit to the shrine of St David. To spare the bishop expense, he accepted an invitation to dinner but refused to stay with his retinue at St David's.

David seems to have discharged his episcopal functions, though not with any great distinction. He was greatly hampered by the poverty of his diocese, compounded in turn by the spoliation of the episcopal estates by barons such as Mahel of Hereford. The problem was further exacerbated by the demands of his own family. His brother, Maurice, was promoted to be steward of the diocese and given episcopal estates. Bishop David himself, in flagrant contravention of the church's teaching for the higher clergy, had a family. He used the episcopal lands to endow his daughters, and his son (formally acknowledged as such), Miles, took part in the invasion of Ireland. David died on 8 May 1176, and was buried at St David's.

Gerald of Wales admired David and wrote about him in a number of his works, but was nevertheless commissioned by the archbishop of Canterbury to deal with moral laxity among the diocesan clergy. An account of David's episcopate by an anonymous author, which has in the past been attributed to a canon of St David's and sometimes to Gerald himself, is much sharper in its criticism.

DAVID WALKER

Sources *De rebus a se gestis, Gir. Camb. opera*, vol. 1 • *De jure et statu Menevensis ecclesie, Gir. Camb. opera*, vol. 3 • *Expugnatio Hibernica, Gir. Camb. opera*, vol. 5 • Giraldus Cambrensis, *Expugnatio Hibernica / The conquest of Ireland*, ed. and trans. A. B. Scott and F. X. Martin (1978) •

Itinerarium Kambriae, Gir. Camb. opera, vol. 6 · *Vita Davidi II, Gir. Camb. opera*, vol. 3 · M. Richter, 'A new edition of the so-called vita Dauidis secundi', *BBCS*, 22 (1966–8) · J. C. Davies, ed., *Episcopal acts and cognate documents relating to Welsh dioceses, 1066–1272*, 1, Historical Society of the Church in Wales, 1 (1946) · A. Saltman, *Theobald, archbishop of Canterbury* (1956) · T. Jones, ed. and trans., *Brenhinedd y Saesson, or, The kings of the Saxons* (1971) [another version of *Brut y tywysogyon*]

David, Sir, fitz Walter (d. 1375×8). *See under* Hamilton family (*per.* 1295–1479).

David Gam. *See* Dafydd Gam (d. 1415).

David, Albert Augustus (1867–1950), bishop of Liverpool and headmaster, was born in Exeter on 19 May 1867, the second son of the Revd William David, then principal of the Exeter Diocesan Training College for schoolmasters and afterwards priest-vicar of the cathedral, and his wife, Antonia Altgelt. After attending Exeter School he won a classical scholarship to Queen's College, Oxford, where he took a first in both classical moderations and Greats. He was successively a lecturer at his college, a master at Bradfield College and Rugby School, and then a fellow of his college. He was ordained priest in 1895. David married Edith Mary, daughter of the late Thomas William Miles, of the public works department, India, in 1909, and they had three sons and one daughter.

In 1905 David became headmaster of Clifton College. A tall and imposing presence, he was a great success with masters, boys, and the school's trustees. He introduced physical drill into the curriculum, expanded the chapel and grounds, and increased pupil numbers. But when he moved back to Rugby as headmaster in 1909, he did not repeat this success. He had become interested in the progressive educational theories of a controversial American psychologist, Homer Lane, some of which he now sought to implement. He was concerned that the public schools did nothing for the less able boy, and sought to reform the curriculum to promote creativity and free expression. He later expanded on these ideas in his book *Life and the Public School* (1932). David encouraged masters at Rugby to experiment with new teaching methods, and allowed one of them, J. H. Simpson, to institute a system of self-government for his class, in which boys were constituted into a court to discipline their peers. Such innovations went too far for many of his older masters, who felt that he was jeopardizing the discipline and reputation of the school, and one of them, G. F. Bradby, wrote a comic novel, *The Chronicles of Dawnhope* (1921), satirizing David's progressive regime.

David, who had been made DD in 1910, had already refused four offers of bishoprics when he was appointed bishop of St Edmundsbury and Ipswich in 1921. He had barely made a start in his new diocese before being translated to Liverpool in 1923. As only the third Anglican bishop of Liverpool, he inherited an unfinished cathedral, consecrated in 1924. David also had to confront the city's sectarian divisions, which erupted into violent attacks by protestant mobs on Anglo-Catholic churches and on the Anglican cathedral in 1932.

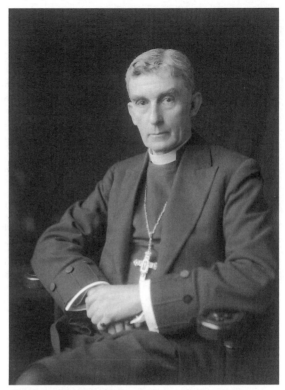

Albert Augustus David (1867–1950), by Lafayette, 1930

But the most serious sectarian controversy of his episcopate came from an unlikely source, Unitarianism. David was a liberal churchman, and during the First World War he had been prominent in Life and Liberty, the campaign for church self-government which was led by his old pupil from Rugby William Temple. But in 1933–4 David found himself in conflict with Temple, who was by then archbishop of York, over whether Unitarians should preach in Anglican churches. David was a proponent of reunion with the nonconformists, and to this end gave permission for the prominent Unitarian L. P. Jacks to preach at a special service in Liverpool Cathedral in 1933. This was a controversial move. Many Anglicans held that Unitarians were not Christians because they denied the Trinity. David defended his action on the narrow grounds that Jacks had preached at a special service, and when the dean, F. W. Dwelly, invited another Unitarian, Lawrence Redfern, to preach at a regular cathedral service, the bishop reproved him. But this legalistic distinction did not satisfy critics like Lord Hugh Cecil, who accused David of promoting heresy. In 1934 the bishops of the northern province, led by William Temple, rebuked David for inviting non-Christian ministers to preach at Anglican services.

David remained bishop until 1944, raising £85,000 for his diocese before retiring to Cornwall. He was elected an honorary fellow of Queen's College, Oxford, in 1920, and received an honorary DD from Glasgow University in 1937. Besides his work on the public schools, he published a number of devotional books, and a pamphlet, *Who are*

Christians? (1934), justifying his conduct in the unitarianism controversy.

David died at Trebetherick, Cornwall, on 24 December 1950. His wife survived him.   MATTHEW GRIMLEY

Sources *The Times* (27 Dec 1950) • P. J. Waller, *Democracy and sectarianism: a political and social history of Liverpool, 1868–1939* (1981) • O. Chadwick, *Hensley Henson: a study in the friction between church and state* (1983) • F. A. Iremonger, *William Temple, archbishop of Canterbury* (1948) • H. H. Henson, *Retrospect of an unimportant life*, 3: *1939-1946, the years of retirement* (1950) • J. B. H. Simpson, *Rugby since Arnold* (1967) • O. F. Christie, *A history of Clifton College, 1860–1934* (1935) • A. A. David, *Life and the public school* (1932) • G. F. Bradby, *The chronicles of Dawnhope* (1921) • D. Winterbottom, *Clifton after Percival* (1990) • J. Gathorne-Hardy, *The public school phenomenon* (1979) • *CGPLA Eng. & Wales* (1951)
Archives LPL, papers incl. corresp., sermons, and literary MSS
Likenesses Lafayette, photograph, 1930, NPG [*see illus.*] • K. Kennet, bronze bust, *c.*1939, diocesan house, Liverpool • W. Stoneman, photograph, 1939, NPG • H. Coster, photographs, NPG • H. G. Riviere, portrait, Clifton College, Bristol • W. Russell, oils, Rugby School, Warwickshire
Wealth at death £4368 0s. 2d.: probate, 7 April 1951, *CGPLA Eng. & Wales*

David, Sir (**Tannatt William**) **Edgeworth** (1858–1934), geologist, was born at the rectory at St Fagans, Glamorgan, on 28 January 1858, the eldest child of William David (*c.*1823–1897), rector of St Fagans, and his wife, Margaret Harriette, *née* Thomson (*c.*1834–1903). He was a descendant of the David family of Radyr Court, Cardiff, and on his mother's side from James Ussher, archbishop of Armagh, the Abbé Edgeworth de Firmont, Richard Lovell Edgeworth, and Maria Edgeworth. He received his early education from his father, attended Magdalen College School, Oxford, and then became a scholar at New College, Oxford; he obtained a first class in classical moderations in 1878.

David's decision not to take holy orders prompted a bout of ill health which caused him to break his studies and travel to Canada and Australia. In 1880 he graduated in the pass schools, being particularly influenced by John Ruskin and the geologists Joseph Prestwich, Charles Tanfield Vachell, and his relative William A. E. Ussher. He continued to study geology at the Normal School of Science and Technology (later the Royal College of Science), under John Wesley Judd. In 1882 he was appointed assistant geological surveyor in New South Wales, under the direction of Charles S. Wilkinson. While travelling to Australia he met his future wife, Caroline Martha (Cara) Mallett (1856–1951), whom he married in Sydney on 30 July 1885. David remained with the Geological Survey for nine years and produced highly praised reports and maps on tin mining, fossil occurrences, petrology, underground water, and particularly coal deposits of the Hunter River region; the last ensured that a source of gas-coal was kept in government rather than private control.

In 1891 David was appointed to the chair of geology at the University of Sydney, where he quickly became famous for his teaching ability, especially on his field excursions. Above medium height, he was tough and wiry, good at ice skating and skiing, and untiring in the field. With Thomas Anderson Stuart, David became involved in the preparations for the first expedition (1896) of the Royal Society to Funafuti in the Ellice Islands. When this proved unsuccessful he gained support for two further expeditions; he led the second (1897), accompanied by his wife, and planned the third (1898). The drilling to a depth of more than 1000 feet on the island went a long way towards supporting Darwin's theory of the origin of coral atolls. For this work David received the Bigsby medal of the Geological Society of London, and was elected FRS in 1900. He was known as Tavita by the inhabitants of Funafuti, a name he used for some publications in 1897 and 1898.

David's interest in glaciation, initiated in Wales, and the subject of his first publication, was stimulated with the recognition of late Palaeozoic glaciation in Australia. He pursued this matter in India in 1906, *en route* for Mexico for a meeting of the International Geological Congress, and continued to publish on this subject until his death. In 1907 he seized the opportunity to visit Antarctica with Ernest Shackleton's expedition, having used his influence to obtain Australian funding for it. He then applied retrospectively for university permission to remain in Antarctica and led the successful expeditions to the summit of Mount Erebus and to the south magnetic pole. These exploits and the popular lectures he gave around Australia to pay the expenses of the expedition made him widely known, and he was appointed CMG in 1910. David was instrumental in gaining funding and personnel and advising for various Antarctic expeditions up to 1930.

During the early years of the First World War, David gave patriotic lectures, and in 1915 persuaded the Australian government to use Australian miners by raising a battalion of Australian tunnellers. He enlisted, aged fifty-seven, and in 1916, with the rank of major, travelled to France, where he used his expertise in underground water and drilling with great success. He was particularly responsible for the great mining operation under Messines Ridge, which destroyed a German vantage point on 7 June 1917. Despite a fall down a mine shaft he remained active, and was mentioned in dispatches three times. In June 1917 he was appointed chief geologist and attached to the inspector of mines at general headquarters, British expeditionary force. He was awarded the DSO in 1918 and promoted lieutenant-colonel. In 1920 he was appointed KBE, but rather against his will.

After returning to Sydney, David began a serious attempt to compile a comprehensive *Geology of the Commonwealth of Australia*, which he had begun some years earlier. His offer to resign in 1922 to concentrate on the book was rejected by the university, which obtained funding to allow him to take leave for several years. He travelled widely in Australia to check important localities and discuss material with colleagues, but was deflected from his writing by involvement in the Pan-Pacific Congress held in Australia in 1923. He retired in 1924.

Despite travelling to England in 1925–6 to write, David continued to be deflected from his proposed book by other interests, notably Precambrian life. He believed he had found evidence of both small and large forms in Precambrian rocks near Adelaide and worked on these until his death, but was particularly disappointed when the Royal Society rejected his paper on the subject.

David's *Geological Map of the Commonwealth of Australia* was published in 1931 (and reprinted in 1932 with accompanying notes) to general acclamation. The notes summarized his knowledge and ideas about Australian geology. Written in just a few weeks, it was an extraordinary achievement, and the culmination of an outstanding career. David realized he would never complete his much larger proposed work, which was taken over after his death by W. R. Browne and finally published in 1950, being essentially Browne's work rather than David's.

After a fall when he was alighting from a tram at Sydney University, David collapsed and died, on 28 August 1934 at the Prince Alfred Hospital in Sydney. His death produced an extraordinary reaction around Australia. The commonwealth and state governments moved unprecedented acts of sympathy and provided a state funeral at Sydney (Church of England) Cathedral on 30 August, which was attended by thousands. He was cremated at the Northern Suburbs crematorium, Sydney. He was survived by his wife, his son, and two daughters.

From his earliest days in Australia, David was heavily involved in the scientific societies, particularly the Royal and Linnean societies of New South Wales and the Australian Association for the Advancement of Science. He was first president (1921–2), and councillor until his death, of the independent Australian National Research Council, the forerunner of the Australian Academy of Science, which supported the development of the government-sponsored Council for Scientific and Industrial Research (CSIR) and later Commonwealth Scientific and Industrial Research Organisation (CSIRO). He received many awards, including the Wollaston medal of the Geological Society of London (1915), the patron's medal of the Royal Geographical Society, and honorary degrees from the universities of Oxford, Manchester, Cambridge, Wales, Sydney (all DSc), and at St Andrews (LLD).

Despite these activities and awards, David had contacts with farmers and railway navvies as well as premiers and generals, and his word was highly regarded by all. He combined in a rare way aspects of the romantic and the practical, but was essentially an interpretative rather than a creative genius. Although he contributed nothing original to the principle or method in geology, he saw order in complexity and the relations between things unlike or far apart, which led him to support the theory of continental drift of Alfred Wegener.   D. F. BRANAGAN

Sources University of Sydney, David MSS · M. E. David, *Professor David* (1937) · M. E. David, *Passages of time: an Australian woman, 1890–1974* (1975) · L. A. Cotton, unpublished biography of Edgeworth David, priv. coll. · D. Branagan, 'Putting geology on the map: Edgeworth David and the geology of the Commonwealth of Australia', *Historical Records of Australian Science*, 5/2 (1981), 30–57 · *Sydney Morning Herald* (Aug–Sept 1934) · *Daily Telegraph* [Sydney] (Aug–Sept 1934) · *Sydney Mail* (Aug–Sept 1934) · W. R. Browne, 'Tannatt William Edgeworth David, 1858–1934', *Proceedings of the Linnean Society of New South Wales*, 61 (1936), 341–57 · S. W. Carey, *Sir Edgeworth David memorial oration: 'knight errant of science'*, ed. D. F. Branagan (Parkville, Vic., 1990) · D. Mawson, *Obits. FRS*, 1 (1932–5), 493–501 · private information (2004) · *DNB*

Archives Mitchell L., NSW, family papers · NHM, letters concerning Precambrian fossils · NL Aus., family corresp. · University of Sydney, division of geology and geophysics | Australian Academy of Science, Canberra, Basser Library · Scott Polar RI, letters to Raymond Priestley | SOUND University of Sydney, tape from gramophone disc, dictated letter

Likenesses W. Stoneman, photograph, 1927, NPG · N. Carter, oils, Royal Society of New South Wales, Australia · N. Carter, oils, NMG Wales · J. Longstaff, oils, University of Sydney, Australia · photographs, University of Sidney, Australia · portrait, repro. in *Obits. FRS*

David, Edward. *See* Edward Dafydd (*c*.1602–1678?).

David [*née* Gwynne], **Elizabeth** (1913–1992), cookery writer, was born on 26 December 1913 at Wootton Manor, near Polegate, Sussex, the second of four daughters of Rupert Sackville Gwynne (1873–1924), politician, and his wife, the Hon. Stella, *née* Ridley (*d.* 1973), daughter of Matthew White *Ridley, first Viscount Ridley. Her father was the Conservative MP for Eastbourne from 1911 until his death, and she was baptized in the chapel of the House of Commons on 22 January 1914. She and her sisters were educated at home until their father's sudden death in 1924, when they were sent to boarding-school. She attended Godstowe preparatory school and then St Clare's Private School for Ladies, Tunbridge Wells. At the age of sixteen her mother sent her to Paris to study art and French, and it was there that she had her first taste of good French food.

Restless and independent, Elizabeth Gwynne tried (without much success) to become an actress during the mid-1930s, and for a brief time she worked as a junior vendeuse at the fashion house of Worth. She taught herself to cook, collected recipes, and bought a refrigerator with money given for her twenty-first birthday. Yet she also wanted adventure. In early 1939 she and her lover Charles Gibson Cowan—another social rebel, though from the East End rather than the home counties—bought a boat, the *Evelyn Hope*, and set off for Greece. The outbreak of the Second World War found them in the south of France, and they were forced to spend the winter of 1939–40 in Antibes. There Elizabeth Gwynne met her most important mentor, the writer and traveller Norman Douglas, who inspired her love of the Mediterranean. She and Cowan set off again in the spring of 1940, and had reached the Strait of Messina when the Italians entered the war on 10 June. The *Evelyn Hope* was impounded, they were briefly interned, and they reached Athens—boatless and penniless—in July 1940. In September Cowan found a job teaching English on the island of Syros in the Cyclades. There, living in primitive conditions in the village of Vari, Elizabeth Gwynne learned how to cook with the basic staple foods of the Mediterranean. The German invasion of Greece in the spring of 1941 forced them to flee to Egypt, where she spent the rest of the war—first in Alexandria and then in Cairo, where between 1942 and 1945 she ran the ministry of information's reference library. On 30 August 1944, in Cairo, she married Lieutenant-Colonel Anthony David (1911–1967), an officer in the

Indian army (Royal Deccan horse regiment), later a club manager and shop owner, and son of Ivor David. She followed him to India after the war, fell ill, and returned to England alone in 1946. That winter, which was exceptionally harsh, she began writing out her yearning for the food she had grown to love in France, Greece, and Egypt. Her husband returned to England in 1947, and in 1949 they bought the house she was to live in for the rest of her life, at 24 Halsey Street, Chelsea, London.

In 1949, encouraged by a friend who worked on the magazine, Elizabeth David began writing a cookery column for *Harper's Bazaar*. Her first book, *A Book of Mediterranean Food*, was published in 1950 by John Lehmann. It proved an immediate success, and was followed by *French Country Cooking* (1951). Her next book was *Italian Food*, for which she made an extensive research trip to Italy which took up most of 1952. Of all her books it was the one in which she felt she had put the best of herself, though it was by far the most difficult. It was published in 1954, and was followed a year later by *Summer Cooking*. She had not stopped writing for *Harper's*, but in 1956 she was easily persuaded to move to *Vogue*, which offered her more money and more prominence. *Vogue* also gave her the opportunity to visit many different areas of France, during which she completed her research on the book for which she would be best remembered: *French Provincial Cooking* (1960). The book was dedicated to 'PH', a man with whom she had been in love since the early 1950s. The affair coincided with her separation from Tony David, from whom she was divorced in 1960. There were no children of the marriage.

The publication of *French Provincial Cooking* marked the end of a decade of strenuous work, during which David had written for a number of newspapers, including the *Daily Express*, the *News Chronicle*, and (from 1955 to 1960) the *Sunday Times*. She left the paper in 1960 and soon after was taken on by *The Spectator*. Her professional career was at its height. She was hailed not only as Britain's foremost writer on food and cookery, but as the woman who had transformed the eating habits of middle-class England. To her editors she was a stickler for detail, but to her readers she was a joy. Her books and articles were filled with historical anecdote and irreverent wit, and she could describe food in a way that inspired people to cook—though her recipes took no short cuts, and demanded time and trouble. 'To one reader who totted up the deadly total of bowls, sieves, spoons and forks needed to make a smoked haddock soufflé, she wrote back: "You forgot the plates"' ('Profile of Elizabeth David', *New Statesman*, 9 Aug 1968).

Tall and well-built, with a long neck and slanting black eyes, David's feline grace was accentuated by the severe, well-cut suits she wore with crisp white shirts in her professional life. Some people found her cold and daunting, but around the kitchen table at Halsey Street her friends saw a very different person. She loved to sit and talk for hours over a bottle of wine and a packet of Gauloise cigarettes, with her back to her old gas cooker. Every now and again she would lean round to peer into the oven or twiddle with a knob, but her attention was on the conversation—which was colourful, wide-ranging, and punctuated by gales of laughter. When the food was ready it was served in the dishes it had cooked in, without fuss or comment.

Yet for all David's success, she was not happy. Her longstanding affair with PH ended, and a combination of misery, alcohol, sleeping pills, and overwork resulted in a cerebral haemorrhage, in the spring of 1963. She

Elizabeth David (1913–1992), by unknown photographer, c.1960

recovered, but her sense of taste was impaired for a time, and she felt that she could never write another book. Instead, she and four other partners decided to set up a kitchen shop. Elizabeth David Ltd opened at 46 Bourne Street, Pimlico, in November 1965. It pioneered a new generation of shops devoted exclusively to kitchenware. David chose the stock and compiled the catalogues, and Bourne Street became the centre of her life. She wrote four little booklets, for sale on the premises: *Dried Herbs, Aromatics and Condiments* (1967), *English Potted Meats and Fish Pastes* (1968), *The Baking of an English Loaf* (1969), and *Syllabubs and Fruit Fools* (1969). She even found time to write another full-length book, *Spices, Salt and Aromatics in the English Kitchen* (1970), which she saw as one of the first of a series of volumes on English cookery. But she was not a businesswoman. Tensions between her and her partners became intolerable, and in 1973 she severed all connection with the shop—which continued trading under her name. Over the years she tried repeatedly to get her name back, but without success.

In 1977 David was badly injured in a car accident, from which she took a long time to recover. She was still in hospital for the publication of *English Bread and Yeast Cookery* (1977), which was hailed as a masterpiece of scholarship. Once on her feet again she immersed herself in researches for her next project, *Harvest of the Cold Months: the Social History of Ice and Ices* (1994). This book developed slowly, as a series of essays. It was still far from completion when she published a book of her journalism, *An Omelette and a Glass of Wine* (1984). Although she made several visits to California in the 1980s, David's health was failing. A series of falls resulted in long periods in hospital, and she never got over the death in 1986 of her sister Felicité, with whom she had shared her house for the previous thirty years. She was seventy-eight when she suffered a severe stroke, followed two days later by another. She died at her Halsey Street home on 22 May 1992, and was buried on 28 May at the family church of St Peter's, Folkington. On 10 September 1992 a memorial service was held at St Martin-in-the-Fields, followed by a 'memorial picnic' in the Nash Room at the Institute of Contemporary Arts.

Elizabeth David appeared on *The Food Programme* with Derek Cooper on Radio 4, broadcast on 24 October 1982, and a few years later she agreed to take part in a documentary about herself presented by Jancis Robinson—*A Matter of Taste*, broadcast by Channel 4 on 26 December 1989. These were exceptional: she usually shunned publicity, rarely gave interviews, and never spoke about her private life. However, she was much photographed, by Cecil Beaton and Anthony Denney among others. There is also a portrait of her by John Ward now in the National Portrait Gallery, showing David in the kitchen of her house in Halsey Street.

David was the best writer on food and drink this country has ever produced. When she began writing in the 1950s, the British scarcely noticed what was on their plates at all, which was perhaps just as well. Her books and articles persuaded her readers that food was one of life's great pleasures, and that cooking should not be a drudgery but an exciting and creative act. In doing so she inspired a whole generation not only to cook, but to think about food in an entirely different way.   ARTEMIS COOPER

Sources *The Times* (23 May 1992) · *The Independent* (25 May 1992) · *The Times* (1 June 1992) · *The Independent* (3 June 1992) · priv. coll. · Elizabeth David MSS · private information (2004)
Archives NRA, priv. coll. | FILM 'A matter of taste', film by Jancis Robinson, Channel 4, 26/12/1989 | SOUND 'A matter of taste', Radio 4, 1/1987 · *The food programme*, Derek Cooper (interviewer), 10/1982
Likenesses A. McEvoy, watercolour drawing, c.1923–1924, priv. coll. · Madame Hassia, Cairo, photograph, 1943–4, NPG · A. Daintrey, pen-and-ink drawing, 1954, NPG · J. Ward, drawing, 1956, NPG · photograph, c.1960, NPG [*see illus.*] · photograph, repro. in *The Times* (23 May 1992) · photograph, repro. in *The Times* (1 June 1992) · photographs, repro. in L. Chaney, *Elizabeth David: a Mediterranean passion* (1998) · photographs, repro. in A. Cooper, *Writing at the kitchen table: the authorized biography of Elizabeth David* (1999)
Wealth at death £571,632: probate, 25 Sept 1992, CGPLA Eng. & Wales

David, Jacob (c.1640–1689), merchant, born in Darnetal near Rouen, France, was the son of David David (d. 1677), a clothier. Vouched for as a devout protestant of good character, he was invited to England in 1668 by the London merchant Charles *Marescoe (1633?–1670), who conducted a large-scale trade with Sweden. Employed as bookkeeper at £40 per annum, David was left £25 in his master's will and shortly after was taken into a quadripartite partnership by the widow, Leonora Marescoe, née Lethieullier [**Leonora David** (c.1637–1715?)], who provided his £1000 capital investment. In 1673 the partnership, worth over £15,000, was re-formed between Leonora and David alone; their marriage in the autumn of 1675 brought him into the Huguenot merchant aristocracy of London.

David thus acquired a share of responsibility for the three surviving daughters of Leonora and the management of their inheritance, which entitled them to marriage portions of some £7100 each. The eldest daughter, Leonora II (b. 1659), had been recently married in lavish style to Thomas Frederick (1650–1720), son of a former lord mayor of London, but quarrels between mother and daughter soon degenerated into serious allegations of fraud against the Davids. Leonora's gross extravagance, which is amply recorded in her ledgers, and her concealment of some profitable East India Company shares, laid the Davids open to proceedings in the City of London's court of orphans and between 1679 and 1687 a chancery suit on behalf of the daughters was dragged out to a crushing conclusion. Another daughter, Jane (b. 1661), was married off in 1679 to John Lewknor (1658–1707), a member of parliament for Sussex, from whom she eloped in 1685 with another member, William Montagu (1652–1691), and in July 1681 an unlicensed marriage of the youngest daughter, Anne (b. 1666), to the allegedly penniless Frenchman, David Gansel of Rouen, led to Jacob David's arrest by the City authorities and a £2000 fine. This was paid off by his wife's aldermanic kinsmen, Sir John Lethieullier and Sir William Hooker, but on 9 October 1685, faced with the final judgment of the court of chancery, Jacob and Leonora fled to Amsterdam, where they were eventually joined by their own children, Isabella (*b.* 1676) and a son (*b.* 1678). Early in 1689 both children died of smallpox and in May, after a violent illness, David followed.

At the height of his prosperity in the 1670s David had been a respected and generous member of the French Protestant church in Threadneedle Street, of which he was a deacon in 1676–8 and an elder in 1684. Acting as banker for some of the church's investments he was also actively involved in the church's efforts to relocate newly arrived Huguenot refugees. He had secured denization for himself on 14 October 1675 and his naturalization by private bill obtained royal assent on 16 April 1677. There is no record of his London citizenship but he was made free of the East India Company by redemption on 5 December 1679 and he was admitted to the Eastland Company in 1681. Nevertheless his controlling grasp on imports of Swedish pitch and tar and his close liaison with Dutch entrepreneurs laid him open to suspicion from a government which felt it could not trust such vital strategic goods in an alien's hands. His arrest by the City and subsequent travails were noted with some satisfaction by an anti-French public.

Despite her influential connections with rich and powerful merchants and aldermen, such as her brothers Sir John, Christopher, and William Lethieullier, Leonora remained an embittered exile, corresponding infrequently with the incumbent of Low Leyton parish, the distinguished antiquarian John Strype (1643–1737), about erecting a memorial to her first husband, 'dear Mr Marescoe'. With him, in the 1660s, Leonora had run a thrifty household on about £10 per week, but her second marriage had liberated an extravagant nature, which lavished £500 on her eldest daughter's wedding and established £50 per week as her average 'fraits des mesnage'. It was undoubtedly her initiative which devised the concealment of assets in her first husband's inventory and, in collusion with David, schemed to evade the consequences. Although still pursued by lawsuits with her daughters, she remained unrepentant and lived on in Amsterdam, probably until 1715, when responsibility for the suits passed to her executors.   H. G. ROSEVEARE

Sources *Markets and merchants of the late seventeenth century: the Marescoe–David letters, 1668–1680*, ed. H. Roseveare, British Academy, Records of Social and Economic History, new ser., 12 (1987); repr. (1991)
Archives CUL, Strype MSS · PRO, chancery masters exhibits, C 114/63–78 · Riksarkivet, Stockholm, Momma–Reenstierna Sammlung

David, Leonora (*c.*1637–1715?). *See under* David, Jacob (*c.*1640–1689).

David, Sir Percival Victor David Ezekiel, second baronet (1892–1964), financier and collector of Chinese art, was born in Bombay on 21 July 1892, the fifth and youngest child in the family of three sons (the elder two of whom died at the age of two) and two daughters of Sir Sassoon Jacob David, first baronet (1849–1926), cotton and yarn merchant, mill owner, and later founder and chairman of the Bank of India, and his wife, Hannah (*d.* 1921), daughter

of Elias David *Sassoon [*see under* Sassoon family] of Bombay. He was educated at Elphinstone College and Bombay University (BA, 1909), and succeeded his father as baronet in 1926. He married his cousin, Vere Mozelle, daughter of Abraham (Aubrey) David, financier, on 26 January 1913. They had two daughters, the younger of whom died in infancy.

David was always reticent about his personal history, but his public renown grew with his status as collector of Chinese art and promoter of art study as a key to the understanding of the Chinese intellect. Active in his family's business, he visited China in 1927 and there resolved to devote his life to Chinese connoisseurship. His frequent presence in Peking (Beijing) afforded him unprecedented opportunities of acquisition among the art objects released on the market as the old social order of China broke down.

After joining in 1930 the Oriental Ceramic Society, founded in London a decade earlier, David began a career of scholarship with papers read to that body, distinguishing himself by identifying the imperial *ru* ware made between AD 1107 and 1127. In 1930 he funded a lectureship in Chinese art and archaeology at the then School of Oriental Studies at the University of London. In 1931 central funding was made available by the university for a chair; however, in 1932 this was moved to the newly established Courtauld Institute of Art. David was the chief instigator and director of the international exhibition of Chinese art held in London at Burlington House in 1935–6. It fulfilled his ambition of showing items from the Chinese imperial collection together with the best of Western collections. For the safety of transport from China the request of protection by the British navy was not thought inappropriate. The exhibition may be said to have motivated the adoption of Chinese art studies in Western universities.

The porcelains, stonewares, and books David had collected in China provided the contents of the Percival David Foundation of Chinese Art which he gave to the University of London in 1950 and which was attached as his exclusive benefaction to the School of Oriental and African Studies in 1952, housed in a building, also his gift, at Gordon Square, Bloomsbury. A condition of the donation was that the university chair in Chinese art and archaeology should again be filled. The David collection has no rival outside China for post-Tang ceramics.

Captured by the Japanese in 1941, David was interned in Shanghai for nine months, and contracted the sclerosis which caused him difficult last years and finally ended his life.

David was made a DLitt by London University in 1950, became a fellow of the Society of Antiquaries, and was an officer of the Légion d'honneur. Following a divorce in 1953, David married on 15 October of the same year Sheila Jane Yorke, daughter of Arthur Yorke Hardy, mining engineer, of Harrow. They had no children and the baronetcy became extinct when David died on 9 October 1964 at 53 Gordon Square, London, of the sclerosis he had contracted in Shanghai. His last work, *Chinese Connoisseurship:*

the *Ko Ku Yao Lun*, was published posthumously in 1971, and saw the first translation of the fourteenth-century album of connoisseurship *Gegu yaolun*.

WILLIAM WATSON, *rev.*

Sources personal knowledge (1993) · private information (2004) · *WWW* · www.soas.ac.uk/PDF/home.html · Burke, *Peerage* · m. cert. · d. cert.
Wealth at death £36,721: probate, 28 June 1966, *CGPLA Eng. & Wales*

Davids, James. *See* Dixwell, John (*c.*1607–1689).

Davids, Thomas William (1816–1884), ecclesiastical historian, born at Swansea on 11 September 1816, was the only child of William Saunders Davids, minister of the Congregational church meeting in Providence Chapel, Swansea, and his wife, Bridget, daughter of Thomas Thomas of Vrowen in the parish of Llanboidy, Carmarthenshire. He was a descendant of David *Jones (1736–1810), rector of Llan-gan, Glamorgan, the 'Wesley of Wales'. Thomas's father died in December 1816, and his mother in 1831; the orphan was adopted by his uncle, Thomas Thomas of Llanbedr Felffre, a man of considerable means. For some years Davids was educated for the medical profession, but in 1835 he decided to become an Independent minister. In 1836 he entered the old college at Homerton, then under John Pye Smith, and there studied for the ministry, until in 1840 he was invited to become minister of the Congregational church meeting in Lion Walk at Colchester in Essex.

In 1841 Davids married Louisa, the daughter of Robert Winter, solicitor, of Clapham Common. They had ten children, among them the orientalist Thomas William Rhys *Davids. Under her superintendence the Sunday school attached to his church soon became known as a model, and after its transfer to new and extensive premises she published in 1847 an essay entitled *The Sunday School*. It was awarded a prize offered by the committee of the Sunday School Union, passed rapidly through four editions, and was for some years regarded as the standard textbook on the management and organization of similar institutions among all denominations. Following Louisa's death in 1853, Davids remarried, on 28 April 1859; his new wife was Mary, the daughter of William Spellman of Norwich.

Davids had marked success as a minister. The church became too small for the congregation, and it was through his efforts that the new Gothic church in Lion Walk was built. He also devoted much attention to the organization of his denomination within the county, and for many years was secretary of the Essex Congregational Union and the Home Missionary Society.

Meanwhile Davids had given such time as he could spare to the study of the religious history of Essex. In connection with the bicentenary celebration of the eviction of the nonconforming clergy in 1662, he was asked in 1862 to prepare a memorial of those who were evicted in Essex. He devoted immense labour to this volume, searching the Essex parish registers, the Public Record Office, the British Museum, Dr Williams's Library, and elsewhere, for all references to the puritans settled in Essex at the time of the eviction and to the previous religious history of each parish in the county. The more important results of his researches appeared in the *Annals of evangelical nonconformity in the county of Essex from the time of Wycliffe to the Restoration, with memorials of the Essex ministers ejected or silenced in 1660–1662* (1863). But the bulk of his genealogical, parochial, and other collectanea remained unpublished in six folio volumes, which, frequently added to and carefully indexed, were purchased, after his death, for the library of the Congregational Memorial Hall (now administered by Dr Williams's Library). The minute details of the personal and family history of the early puritans contained in the published volume were of special interest in America, and the author was elected an honorary corresponding member of the New England Historic Genealogical Society.

A larger question, however, began increasingly to occupy Davids's time. While searching in each case for the direct or indirect sources of the puritan belief held by the evicted clergy, the author was led to the opinion that there had been an unbroken tradition of so-called evangelical belief stretching back to a period long before the time of Wyclif and Hus, and probably even to the earliest beginnings of Christianity. The task of tracking this undercurrent of belief throughout Europe occupied his retirement after his resignation from ministerial work in 1874. His *Annals of Reformers before the Reformation* were never completed. However, Davids did contribute numerous articles to Smith's *Dictionary of Christian Biography*, and a paper entitled 'Evangelical nonconformity under the first of the Plantagenets' was published in the *British Quarterly Review* (September 1870).

Davids died at 4 St George's Square, Upton, Essex, of heart disease on Good Friday, 11 April 1884, and was buried in Colchester.

T. W. R. DAVIDS, *rev.* DAVID HUDDLESTON

Sources *Congregational Year Book* (1885) · personal knowledge (1888)
Archives Congregational Library, corresp. and papers mainly relating to nonconformity in Essex · DWL | Essex RO, letters to Philip Benton
Wealth at death £2128 10s. 2d.: probate, 5 July 1884, *CGPLA Eng. & Wales*

Davids, Thomas William Rhys (1843–1922), orientalist, was born at Colchester on 12 May 1843, the eldest son of Thomas William *Davids (1816–1884), ecclesiastical historian and Congregational minister at Colchester, and his wife, Louisa Winter. He was educated at Brighton School, Colchester, before a period of private tuition. He then went to New College, Finchley Road, London, from 1860 to about 1861, and finally studied Sanskrit under A. F. Stenzler at Breslau University until 1863. He went to Ceylon in 1864 and joined its civil service in 1866. In Ceylon he studied the Pali language and early Buddhism under native teachers. Here he found his vocation. He published articles on local inscriptions, and in 1870 became a member of the Archaeological Commission. In August 1871 he was appointed assistant government agent at Anuradhapura, but soon fell out with his superior and after less than a year was forced to leave. Though his offence amounted to little worse than slovenly bookkeeping, he was dismissed from the service (after appeal) in 1873. He returned to England in 1874. He was called to the bar by the Middle Temple in 1877 but practised little.

Rhys Davids's first major publication was *Ancient Coins and Measures of Ceylon* (1877); but it is as a scholar of Pali and of early Buddhism that he is remembered. In 1877 he wrote *Buddhism* for the Society for Promoting Christian Knowledge. This can claim to be the first book in English on Buddhism to meet modern scholarly standards. Reprinted more than twenty times, it has been influential, not least for its implied analogies between Theravada Buddhism and protestantism on the one hand as against Mahayana Buddhism and 'popery' on the other. In 1880 the publication of Victor Fausböll's *Jātakas* in Pali led Rhys Davids to contemplate a translation, but he abandoned this idea (after a notable first volume—*Buddhist Birth Stories*, 1880) in order to produce, for the series of Sacred Books of the East (published by the Clarendon Press), *Buddhist suttas from the Pali* (1881), which was followed by three volumes of translations (in collaboration with Hermann Oldenberg) of *Vinaya texts* (1881–5) and *Questions of King Milinda* (1890–94). These translations have stood the test of time. Rhys Davids married in 1894 Caroline Augusta (d. 1942), daughter of John Foley, vicar of Wadhurst, Sussex; they had one son, killed in action during the First World War, and two daughters. Caroline Rhys Davids herself wrote many books on Buddhism.

In 1881 Rhys Davids founded the Pali Text Society on the model of the Early English Text Society. It soon became the world's foremost publisher of Pali texts, translations of those texts, and auxiliary works. At the end of the twentieth century it was still publishing the journal of Pali studies which he founded, and kept about 300 volumes in print. Rhys Davids himself edited, with Joseph Estlin Carpenter, the text of the *Dīgha Nikāya* (3 vols., 1899–1910) and volume 1 of the commentary thereon. He also began a translation, finished by his wife, of the same text (3 vols., 1899–1921); its title, *Dialogues of the Buddha*, recalled Plato's Socratic dialogues, with which he believed the *Dīgha Nikāya* to rank. His introductions to the individual dialogues are notable for their cultural sensitivity, while his translations, though not wholly free from error, are perhaps as fluent and appropriate as any yet made of Buddhist scriptures.

Of Rhys Davids's books about Buddhism not already mentioned, the chief are *The Origin and Growth of Religion as Illustrated by … the History of Indian Buddhism* (Hibbert lectures, 1881), *Buddhist India* (1903), and (his own favourite) *Early Buddhism* (1908). He contributed many articles to Hastings's *Encyclopaedia of Religion and Ethics*, and the chapter on early Buddhism to volume 1 of the *Cambridge History of India*. He began his Hibbert lectures by condemning the tendency of western scholarship to examine other religions merely with a view to discovering where they agreed with Christianity; and in his conclusion he compared the western discovery of oriental civilizations to the discovery that the earth is not the centre of the universe. As a historian of religion he was an evolutionist and owed much to E. B. Tylor. His interpretation of Buddhism stressed its rational and humanistic aspects.

Rhys Davids was honorary professor of Pali and Buddhist literature at University College, London, from 1882 to 1912. From 1904 to 1915 he was professor of comparative religion at the University of Manchester; the post was the only one of its kind in Britain, perhaps (as he claimed) in the world. He was secretary of the Royal Asiatic Society of Great Britain and Ireland from 1888 to 1904, and was an original fellow of the British Academy, which he helped to found. In 1894 he was granted a civil-list pension of £200 a year.

In 1902 Rhys Davids suggested an international project to produce a Pali–English dictionary. When the First World War finally put paid to this plan, he decided to launch a provisional dictionary himself. Leaving Manchester, he secured William Stede as a full-time co-editor, and issued the first volume in 1921, and the second in 1922, the year of his death. The final instalment was published by Stede in 1925. Without Rhys Davids's energy this result could not have been achieved. He died at his home, Middleshaws, at Chipstead, Surrey, on 27 December 1922.

Rhys Davids was a lifelong Liberal. He combined enthusiasm with a keen sense of humour, and was at his best when discussing religion, politics, and the historical evolution of ideas. He delighted in placing his materials and ideas at the disposal of his friends.

CHALMERS, *rev.* RICHARD F. GOMBRICH

Sources L. A. Wickremeratne, *The genesis of an orientalist* (1984) · J. E. Carpenter, 'The passing of the founder', *Journal of the Pali Text Society, 1920–23* (1923), 1–21 · private information (1937) · personal knowledge (1937) · *CGPLA Eng. & Wales* (1923)
Archives U. Cam., faculty of oriental studies
Likenesses W. Stoneman, photograph, 1917, NPG · photographs, U. Cam., Oriental Faculty Library
Wealth at death £4612 14s. 3d.: administration with will, 17 Feb 1923, *CGPLA Eng. & Wales*

Davidson. *See also* Davison.

Davidson, Alexander Dyce (1807–1872), Free Church of Scotland minister, was born in Aberdeen on 8 May 1807, the son of George Davidson, a superintendent in the Devantia Brewery. He was educated at the Aberdeen grammar school and the Marischal College, before becoming a tutor in the family of James Blaikie, an advocate and provost of Aberdeen. He was licensed as preacher in March 1830, and was ordained minister of South Church on 3 August 1832. On 11 August 1840 he married Elizabeth Blaikie (d. 1842); both she and their only child died early, but Davidson never remarried.

Davidson was a devoted minister, who sought neither promotion nor a role in public life: 'if ever a minister spent his whole time and strength on a congregation, Dr Davidson did' (Wylie, 212). The transformation of religious opinion in Aberdeen from moderate to evangelical can be attributed largely to his influence; at the Disruption of 1843 Davidson led his own congregation into the Free Church, ministering to it from January 1844 in Belmont Street and from February 1869 at a newly built church in Union Street. Davidson devoted himself particularly to preaching, spending many hours in his study carefully preparing his sermons. In 1859 he published a series of sermons on the book of Esther, and at his death he left 1800 completed lectures and sermons, a selection of which were published posthumously in 1872. He was awarded a DD in 1854 by the University of Aberdeen; he died in Aberdeen on 27 April 1872.

ROSEMARY MITCHELL

Sources Fasti Scot. · A. W., 'Alexander Dyce Davidson', in J. A. Wylie, Disruption worthies: a memorial of 1843 (1881), 211–14 · F. Edmond, preface, in A. D. Davidson, Lectures and sermons (1872), v–x
Archives U. Aberdeen, lectures and sermons
Likenesses E. Burton, mezzotint (after J. W. Gordon), BM · J. W. Gordon, oils, Aberdeen Art Gallery

Davidson, Andrew Bruce (1831–1902), Hebraist and theologian, was born on 25 April 1831 in the farmstead at Ellon, north Aberdeenshire, the son of Andrew Davidson (d. 1863) and Helen Bruce (d. 1876). His parents were keenly interested in the ecclesiastical and theological controversies that were to lead to the Disruption of 1843 and the founding of the Free Church of Scotland, and Davidson was consequently brought up, from the age of twelve, in the Free Church, which he served for the whole of his life. He went to Aberdeen grammar school in 1845, and in 1846 he entered Marischal College, Aberdeen; he graduated in 1849.

After teaching at the Free Church school in Ellon, Davidson entered the Free Church college in Edinburgh, New College, in 1852, and during his four years there he visited the University of Göttingen, where he studied under H. G. A. Ewald. In 1856 he was licensed as a preacher and in 1858 he became an assistant at New College to the professor of Hebrew, John Duncan (1796–1870), whom he succeeded as professor of Hebrew and oriental languages in 1863. He held the post until his death. From 1870 to 1884 he was a member of the committee that produced the Revised Version of the Bible. His scholarship was recognized by the award of several honorary degrees: LLD, Aberdeen (1868); DD, Edinburgh (1868) and Glasgow (1901); and LittD, Cambridge (1900).

While in some ways enigmatic, Davidson was an important transitional figure in the history of biblical scholarship in Britain. His views on critical matters were sufficiently traditional and orthodox in their account of recent criticism to allay any suspicions about his suitability for the chair at New College. At the same time he did not close the door to biblical criticism, and the first volume of his commentary on Job (1862) was a landmark in British scholarship. It was a profound exegesis of the text rather than a doctrinal tract, and it was mildly critical in tone. However, the rapidly moving tide of criticism in the 1860s and 1870s raised considerable problems for Davidson, who was

quoted as saying, 'I dislike the old, I distrust the new' (Strahan, 108).

Several of Davidson's pupils published the notes taken at his lectures, but the most interesting are the unpublished notes of his most distinguished and most controversial pupil, William Robertson Smith. These show that in 1868–9 Davidson was combining elements of traditional Scottish orthodoxy with the mildly critical positions of German scholars such as G. F. Oehler and F. A. G. Tholuck. Davidson also mentioned more radical critical views and clearly kept in touch with the latest developments, but he taught within a theological framework shared by Oehler, Tholuck, and his teacher, Ewald. This presented the Old Testament as a record of God's progressive self-revelation, each stage of which was suited to the receptive ability of the Israelites. However, the version of this position adopted by Davidson could not easily contain the radical implications of the theories of K. H. Graf and Abraham Kuenen, and, later, Julius Wellhausen, which placed the prophets before the law, and when Robertson Smith was put on trial by the Free Church for advocating such views Davidson failed to declare himself openly to be on Smith's side.

Towards the end of his life Davidson became cautiously more critical, especially in articles for James Hastings's Dictionary of the Bible; but by then the critical cause had been largely won. Davidson's apparent ambivalence has occasioned sharply differing verdicts. To some he was a disappointment, left behind by the tide of criticism that he had helped to begin. For others his caution in distrusting the new was justified, and he was praised for having helped to produce a generation of younger critical scholars.

Davidson was a consummate Hebraist and his Introductory Hebrew Grammar (1874) and Hebrew Syntax (1894) have taught generations of students, with revised editions, for more than a hundred years. His great love of Hebrew prophecy was exemplified in his commentaries on Ezekiel (1892), Nahum, Habakkuk, and Zephaniah (1896), and the posthumously published Old Testament Prophecy (1903). This last work, together with his Theology of the Old Testament (1904), was not prepared for publication by Davidson himself, and the value of these as a guide to his thought has been disputed.

In appearance Davidson was small and slight, needing spectacles for long distances and able without them to read the smallest print. His genuine modesty was epitomized by the fact that he constantly reminded his friends that he was not the great Dr Samuel Davidson but only A. B. Davidson of New College, Edinburgh. However, for all his modesty and his undemonstrative nature he was a riveting lecturer, and in his quiet, unassuming way he helped to change the face of Old Testament scholarship in Britain. He died, unmarried, in Edinburgh, on 20 January 1902.

J. W. ROGERSON

Sources A. Taylor Innes, 'Introduction', in A. B. Davidson, The called of God, ed. J. A. Paterson (1902), 1–58 · J. Strahan, Andrew Bruce Davidson (1917) · W. R. Smith, lecture notes of A. B. Davidson, 1868–

9, CUL • A. S. Peake, *Recollections and appreciations* (1938) • *The Scotsman* (27 Jan 1902) • *British Weekly* (30 Jan 1902) • *British Weekly* (6 Feb 1902) • *British Weekly* (20 Feb 1902) • J. Y. Simpson, 'Professor A. B. Davidson', *The Expositor*, 6 ser., 27 (March 1902), 161–9 • J. Skinner, 'Professor A. B. Davidson', *Expository Times*, 13 (1901–2), 248–50 • *CCI* (1902) • *DNB*

Likenesses photogravure, 1901, repro. in Davidson, *Called of God* • G. Reid, oils, New College, Edinburgh • photogravure, repro. in Davidson, *Called of God*

Wealth at death £5734 18*s*. 11*d*.: confirmation, 15 Nov 1902, *CCI*

Davidson, Charles (1824–1902), watercolour painter, was born on 30 July 1824 in London, the son of John Davidson, a tailor. Both parents, who were Scottish, died when he was a baby. After leaving school in Fulham, he was apprenticed to a seedsman and market gardener in Brompton, but left after a year to study music. He turned to painting and studied for some years with John Absolon, a member of the New Watercolour Society. On 8 December 1842 he married Ann Topham, daughter of Richard Topham, pawnbroker, and sister of the painter Francis William Topham. They had two sons and four daughters, one of whom, Annie Laura, married the painter Frank Holl.

Davidson was elected an associate of the New Watercolour Society in 1847 and a member in 1849, but he left it for the Old Watercolour Society; he was elected an associate in 1855 and a member in 1858. A friend of John Linnell, Samuel Palmer, and the Varleys, he soon built up a reputation for his English landscapes and domestic rural scenes. He exhibited over 800 paintings at the Old Watercolour Society between 1844 and 1902, and 114 at the New Watercolour Society. Four of his paintings were shown at the Royal Academy between 1844 and 1854, including *Bolton Abbey on the River Wharfe* (1846) and *Walmer Church in Sunshine after Rain* (1854), and he also exhibited at the British Institution and the Society (later Royal Society) of British Artists. Prince Albert bought his *Haymaking at Priory Park, Near Reigate* as a Christmas present for Queen Victoria in 1856. Eight of his watercolours are in the Victoria and Albert Museum in London.

Davidson lived for many years near Samuel Palmer in Redhill, Surrey, and also painted a lot in Wales. In 1882 he moved to Trevena, Falmouth, Cornwall, where he died on 19 April 1902.　　　B. S. LONG, rev. ANNE PIMLOTT BAKER

Sources S. Wilcox and C. Newall, *Victorian landscape watercolors* (1992) [exhibition catalogue, New Haven, CT, Cleveland, OH, and Birmingham, 9 Sept 1992 – 12 April 1993] • Wood, *Vic. painters*, 3rd edn • J. Johnson, ed., *Works exhibited at the Royal Society of British Artists, 1824–1893, and the New English Art Club, 1888–1917*, 2 vols. (1975) • A. M. Reynolds, *The life and work of Frank Holl* (1912), 36–40 • Mallalieu, *Watercolour artists*, vols. 1–2 • Graves, *RA exhibitors* • *The Times* (22 April 1902) • private information (1912) • m. cert.

Likenesses J. Watkins, carte-de-visite, NPG • photograph, repro. in *The year's art* (1890), facing p. 32

Wealth at death £7806 6*s*. 6*d*.: probate, 28 May 1902, *CGPLA Eng. & Wales*

Davidson, Harold Francis (1875–1937), Church of England clergyman and circus performer, was born on 14 July 1875 at Sholing House in the suburbs of Southampton, the son of the Revd Francis Davidson and his wife, Alice Selina Augusta Hodgkin. From the age of six he attended Banister Court School, Southampton, going on to Whitgift School, Croydon, early in 1890. Despite his father's desire that he should become a clergyman, Davidson wanted to go on the stage, and got his first role in a comedy sketch at the Steinway Hall in London in 1895. He nevertheless decided to seek ordination and gained admission to Exeter College, Oxford, despite a lack of formal qualifications.

Davidson's academic performance continued to be disappointing: forced to leave Exeter College in March 1901, he was nevertheless allowed to persevere with his studies at Grindle's Hall, Oxford, and finally obtained a degree. Contemporaries noted that he had pictures of actresses on the walls of his room, and that he continued to undertake occasional theatrical engagements. His connections were undoubtedly excellent, however, as he served as curate in prestigious parishes; first, Holy Trinity, Windsor, and then from 1905 at St Martin-in-the-Fields, London. In May 1906 Davidson was appointed to the living of Stiffkey-with-Morston in Norfolk. With an income of perhaps £800 p.a. he was able on 9 October 1906 to marry an Irish actress, Moyra (Molly) Cassandra (*b*. 1878/9), the daughter of Michael James Joseph Saurin. They had two boys and two girls.

Molly Davidson had a strong temper, and made her feelings known about the 'waifs and strays' with whom Davidson increasingly populated the large vicarage. Their fourth child was born while Davidson was serving as a naval chaplain during the First World War: he later admitted knowing that the child was not his. In addition, despite the income of the rectory, it never proved enough to fund all of Davidson's activities; and he unfortunately fell into the clutches of a swindler called Arthur John Gordon, whose dubious financial schemes continued to cast a shadow over the vicar of Stiffkey until his death. In October 1925 Davidson was forced to file for bankruptcy: the settlement with his creditors disposed of much of the income of the rectory for years to come.

In the early 1920s Davidson began spending more time in London. With his bishop's permission, he undertook a ministry as a chaplain, accredited to the Actors' Church Union, in and around the theatres of the West End of London. In that twilight world he seems to have been especially drawn to vulnerable women, often as young as fifteen or sixteen years old. He realized that such girls, working as assistants in shops or as 'nippies' in Lyons teashops or ABC restaurants, were easily led into casual prostitution. He later recalled having saved such a teenager from drowning herself in the Thames, adding that 'I have ever since, whenever I had any spare time in town, kept my eyes open for opportunities to help that type of girl, namely, the country girl stranded on the alluring streets of London' (Cullen, 32). It became a consuming, if, perhaps, innocent, passion; but his need to seek out and maintain such relationships increasingly dominated his life. Living in rented rooms and battling with suspicious landladies over unpaid rent, Davidson would often return to Stiffkey only at the weekend; but he remained a popular incumbent.

'I was picking up roughly, as my diaries show, an average of 150 or 200 girls a year', Davidson later recalled (Cullen, 129). There is no doubt that Davidson actively approached likely girls (many of whom gave him the brush-off, as he did not always wear his clerical collar). He may at times have seemed a pest, but there is little evidence of wrongdoing: he would take them for a cup of tea and get them theatre tickets; would listen to their problems, and through his influential contacts, help them with accommodation and employment. Davidson found places in domestic service for some of those he befriended: others successfully made careers on the stage before marrying. He paid for Rose Ellis—later his chief accuser—to receive medical treatment for syphilis.

In the summer of 1931, for reasons which are still not entirely clear, the bishop of Norwich decided to take action: a firm of private detectives was hired to collect evidence of Davidson's 'slackness'. Rose Ellis, who was to be the key prosecution witness, proved willing to testify that for several nights they had slept in the same room, and that he had once tried to have 'connection' with her. Presented with the evidence, the bishop of Norwich decided to press charges that Davidson had offended against public morality under the 1892 Clergy Discipline Act by adultery and accosting young women in London. Supported by his wife and family, Davidson determined to fight the case. It is hard not to believe him when he protested to his bishop that his activities, if not perhaps seemly in the eyes of 'the icebergs of chastity', were still worthy of a man in holy orders (Cullen, 141). 'For years I have been known as the Prostitute's Padre', he wrote, and it was 'the proudest title that a true priest of Christ can hold' (ibid., 13).

The consistory court hearing, which opened at Church House, Westminster, on 29 March 1932, was given immense coverage in the press. Newspaper articles were filled with salacious details of Davidson's dealings with young women: the fact that he had keys to their rooms, and often called to see them late at night, being especially heinous in the eyes of the prosecution. Most of the evidence proved to be inconclusive and, but for a startling *coup de théâtre*, the prosecution might have failed. However, a shocking photograph was produced of Davidson with a fifteen-year-old girl standing with her back to the camera: although clutching a black shawl, it revealed she was naked.

One newspaper led with the headline 'Nude photo bombshell', and it turned opinion against Davidson. His protestations that he had been 'entrapped' by two press photographers were in all likelihood true. Offered money for posing with one of his young fifteen-year-old friends, he may naïvely have believed that publicity photos would be beneficial after the trial. The verdict of the court on 8 July surprised no one: guilty on all five counts of immoral conduct. Although formally deprived of his holy orders, Davidson continued to protest his innocence, and appealed twice to the privy council. He also tried to state his case at a meeting of the church assembly in 1936: Cosmo Gordon Lang, the archbishop of Canterbury, told him he had no right to speak.

Notoriety unfortunately dogged Davidson until his tragic death. Faced with the need for another source of income, and showing how deep-seated was his theatrical bent, Davidson decided to use his reputation to draw the crowds at fairgrounds and circuses. He was first employed as part of the freak show on Blackpool's golden mile, and was exhibited in a barrel or roasted in a glass oven while a devil prodded him with a pitchfork. 'While I am in the barrel I shall be occupied in preparing my case' he told the press (Parris, *The Times*). In 1937, as his popularity was starting to wane, Davidson was forced to sign up with a menagery at Skegness amusement park. Billed as 'A modern Daniel in a lion's den', he was expected to enter a cage holding two lions, and talk for ten minutes about the lack of justice in his case. Unfortunately, Davidson was badly mauled by one of the lions on 28 July. He was rescued, but died on 30 July 1937, in Skegness. He was buried in the churchyard at Stiffkey.

What exactly motivated the vicar of Stiffkey will never be known. A judicious leading article in the *Church Times*, soon after the verdict, criticized the way the trial was handled, but also stressed that Davidson was 'foolish and eccentric' (Cullen, 171). Recent studies suggest he suffered from 'multiple personalities', but do not entirely do justice to the curious mixture of the sacred and profane in his life. A. J. P. Taylor remarked in *English History, 1914–1945* (1975) that the case was 'the sensation of the decade', and that he attracted more attention while he lived than Archbishop Cosmo Gordon Lang. 'Which man deserves a greater place in the history books?', asked Taylor (p. 316). What is still clear is that the vicar of Stiffkey was indeed foolish and eccentric, both in his life and in the manner of his death.

ROBERT BROWN

Sources T. Cullen, *The prostitutes' padre: the story of the notorious rector of Stiffkey* (1975) · M. Parris, *The great unfrocked: two thousand years of church scandal* (1998) · A. J. P. Taylor, *English history, 1914–1945* (1975) · b. cert. · m. cert. · d. cert. · *The Times* (2 Aug 1937) [report of inquest on his death] · M. Parris, *The Times* (7 Nov 1998)
Likenesses photographs, repro. in Cullen, *Prostitutes' padre* · photographs, repro. in Parris, *Great unfrocked*

Davidson, Harriet Miller (1839–1883), writer, was born on 25 November 1839 at Cromarty, Scotland, the second but eldest surviving child of Hugh *Miller (1802–1856) and his wife, Lydia Falconer Fraser [see Miller, Lydia Mackenzie Falconer (*bap.* 1812, *d.* 1876)]. She had two brothers, the elder of whom was three years her junior. While Hugh Miller, the son of a shipowner who had served in the British navy, had received no formal training in science, he was a self-taught expert in geology, and during his daughter's childhood he became a popular writer and lecturer. Lydia Miller, who shared her husband's intellectual interests, was a teacher and writer, and published a novel, *Passages in the Life of an English Heiress*, in 1847. Harriet Miller, who is said to have been a very beautiful and highly gifted child, with a remarkable talent for improvisation in verse and song, was educated at Edinburgh, where she won a prize for poetry (Allen, 107), and London, where she travelled with her parents. Her life changed dramatically when on Christmas eve 1856 her father, who had been subject to fits of severe anxiety and depression for several years, committed suicide in what was described in the post-mortem report as an 'impulse of insanity' (*Scottish Nation*, 3.167). According to Margaret Allen, Hugh Miller's suicide 'always haunted' his daughter and 'the remembrance of it visited her again and again' (Allen, 107). None the less, Miller continued her London education in the years following her father's death. On 14 April 1863 she married the Revd John Davidson (1834/5–1881), minister of the Free Church of Scotland at Langholm in Dumfriesshire.

Davidson began her literary career by contributing poems to local journals, but she soon turned to fiction. The British Library catalogue attributes the anonymous *Lines for Little Life* (1856) and *The Two Babies* (1859) to her, but the attribution is almost certainly incorrect, as the latter, published four years before Davidson's marriage, proclaims itself to be 'by a Mother' and is signed with the initials H. D. Davidson's first novel, *Isobel Jardine's History*, is a temperance tale and was published under the auspices of the Scottish Temperance League in 1867. This story was very popular and ran through several editions. An advertisement for a later edition quotes *The Scotsman* as observing that while many 'would be inclined off-hand to dismiss a work put out by a Temperance League', the work transcended its didactic purpose and could be read for its 'simple and attractive' style and its 'naturally sketched' characters (Davidson, 331). *Christian Osborne's Friends* (1869) followed, a story suggesting several references to Davidson's seafaring ancestors.

In 1869 Davidson emigrated to Australia with her husband, who had been appointed minister of Chalmers's Church in Adelaide, South Australia. He was later appointed to a chair in English literature and mental philosophy at the University of Adelaide. For a time Harriet Davidson ran a small private school at her house in Adelaide, and she also became a contributor to the local newspapers, publishing articles, poems, and stories until shortly before her death. Among these stories she considered *A Man of Genius*—a temperance tale serialized in the *Adelaide Observer*, but not subsequently reprinted—the best of her prose writings. *Sir Gilbert's Children*, the last of her stories, was left unfinished, but was completed from her instructions to a friend. Margaret Allen sees both these novels as quasi-autobiographical; long after Hugh Miller's suicide, Davidson continued to explore the subject of daughters abandoned by brilliant, charismatic fathers (Allen, 115–16, 122). Davidson also contributed to *Chambers's Journal*, where 'Daisy's Choice' appeared in 1870, and 'The Hamiltons', a story of Australian life, in 1878. Her short stories were never collected, and none of her writing has been republished since the nineteenth century. Harriet Davidson was in a precarious state of health from at least 1877, when she visited Europe for medical treatment, and from 1880 she was a confirmed invalid. She died in Adelaide on 20 December 1883.   W. G. BLAIKIE, *rev.* PAM PERKINS

Sources *The Scottish nation*, 3 vols. (1875), 3.158–69 · Boase, *Mod. Eng. biog.* · H. Davidson, *Christian Osborne's friends* (1869) · IGI · M. Allen, 'The author's daughter, the professor's wife—Harriet Miller Davidson', *Journal of the Historical Society of South Australia*, 27 (1999), 103–24
Archives State Library of South Australia, Adelaide, McKenzie Jonston family papers

Davidson, James (1793–1864), antiquary and bibliographer, was the eldest son of James Davidson (*b. c.*1748, *d.* after 1802) of Tower Hill, London, a stationer and printer and deputy lieutenant of the Tower, and Ann, his wife, only daughter of William Sawyer of Ipswich. He was born at Postern Row, Tower Hill on 15 August 1793. On 6 March 1823 he married Mary, the only daughter of Thomas Bridge of Frome St Quentin, Dorset; they had two sons and three daughters.

When nearly thirty years old Davidson bought the estate of Secktor, near Axminster in Devon, and enlarged the small cottage there. Here he lived for the rest of his life, interesting himself in Devon antiquities in general, but concentrating especially on the topography and history of the parishes in and around the valley of the Axe. His works on this district were: *The British and Roman Remains in the Vicinity of Axminster* (1833); *History of Axminster Church* (1835); *History of Newenham Abbey, Devon* (1843), an abbey about a mile south of the town of Axminster; and *Axminster during the Civil War* (1851). Davidson's sole excursion into general literature consisted of *A glossary to the obsolete and unused words and phrases of the holy scriptures in the Authorised English Version* (1850), a valuable compilation in its time. He published in 1861 a selection of *Notes on the Antiquities of Devonshire, from before the Norman Conquest*, and he left behind in manuscript four volumes of notes on almost every church in Devon, the results of many country rambles. His most significant work was, however, the *Bibliotheca Devoniensis: a Catalogue of the Printed Books Relating to the County of Devon* (1852) and its supplement (1861). It did not include a bibliography of the works of Devon authors but within the limits of Davidson's scheme it was an accurate and complete catalogue. Davidson spared neither pains nor expense, and the libraries in London and the universities were fully checked. His extensively annotated copy of the bibliography is in the Westcountry Studies Library, Exeter. He was a regular contributor to *Notes and Queries*. In 1859 he published a series of antiquarian papers in *Pulman's Weekly News*, and an article by him entitled 'British antiquities at Winford Eagle, Dorset' appeared in the *Gentleman's Magazine* in 1827. George Oliver acknowledged his assistance with the section on Newenham Abbey in his *Monasticon diocesis Exoniensis* (1846).

Davidson died at Secktor House, Axminster, on 29 February 1864, and was buried in the cemetery of that town; his wife survived him. Many of his manuscript compilations passed into the hands of Joshua Brooking Rowe, who bequeathed them to Exeter City Library. Davidson's eldest son, **James Bridge Davidson** (1824–1885), a lawyer, who shared his antiquarian interests, was called to the bar at Lincoln's Inn in 1850 and from 1865 worked as a law reporter for chancery and equity cases. He died unmarried at 1 Raymond's Buildings, Gray's Inn, London, on 8 October 1885, aged sixty-one. He was the author of many papers, but did not publish any work separately. Many of the books included in the Secktor House library, which was formed by the father and the son, were sold by William George of Bristol in 1887. The extensive collection of Devon pamphlets was bequeathed to the Plymouth Institution. A catalogue was published in 1894 but the collection was destroyed during the Second World War.

W. P. COURTNEY, rev. IAN MAXTED

Sources Pulman's Weekly News (8 March 1864), 3 · N&Q, 3rd ser., 5 (1864), 206 · G. P. R. Pulman, The book of the Axe, 4th edn (1875), 12, 67, 677 · Report and Transactions of the Devonshire Association, 18 (1886), 58–60 [obit. of James Bridge Davidson] · Catalogue of the Davidson collection of pamphlets etc. in the library at the Athenaeum (privately printed, Plymouth, 1894) · private information (1888) · CGPLA Eng. & Wales (1864) · CGPLA Eng. & Wales (1885) [James Bridge Davidson] · Boase, Mod. Eng. biog.

Archives Bodl. Oxf., commonplace book · Devon RO, collections relating to history of Axminster, Bideford, etc. · Exeter Central Library, Westcountry Studies Library, antiquarian, heraldic, and literary collections

Wealth at death under £3000: probate, 11 April 1864, CGPLA Eng. & Wales · £10,695 0s. 7d.—James Bridge Davidson: probate, 19 Dec 1885, CGPLA Eng. & Wales

Davidson, James Bridge (1824–1885). See under Davidson, James (1793–1864).

Davidson, James Leigh Strachan- (1843–1916), classical scholar, was born at Byfleet, Surrey, on 22 October 1843, the eldest son of James Strachan (who took the additional name of Davidson in 1861), and his second wife, Mary Anne Richardson. His father came from a Dundee family, and worked as a merchant in Madras. His mother was the daughter of a Yorkshire land agent who lived at Kirkby Ravensworth; she died when her eldest son was only four years old. Her husband married again in 1853 and retired to Leamington Spa, where he resided until his death in 1867. James Leigh Strachan became a day boy at Leamington College in 1854. He went on from there to Balliol College, Oxford, as an exhibitioner in 1862; among those who entered the college at the same time were William Reynell Anson, Evelyn Abbott, Paul Ferdinand Willert, and Francis de Paravicini, who became and remained his close friends. Strachan-Davidson (as he was called by then) obtained first classes in classical moderations (1864) and literae humaniores (1866). In 1864 he was elected to the Jenkyns exhibition (the chief college prize for classical men), and in 1866 to a fellowship. As an undergraduate he read with three remarkable tutors, Edwin Palmer, Benjamin Jowett, and William Lambert Newman; by the last of these three he was inspired to make ancient history his principal study. He was a frequent speaker at the Union Society, of which he was successively secretary (1863), librarian (1866–7), and president (1867).

In his early years as a fellow Strachan-Davidson was much abroad, owing to the weakness of his health. He began to lecture regularly in 1874, but for many years wintered habitually in Egypt. In 1875 he accepted the office of senior dean, which he held for thirty-two years. In this capacity he was Jowett's right-hand man. His own personality, which though elusive was singularly charming, made him the social centre of the senior common room and the idol of those undergraduates to whom he acted as a tutor or friendly adviser. The subjects which he habitually taught were political economy and Roman history. He assembled a large collection of Greek and Roman coins.

In 1880 Strachan-Davidson contributed a study of Polybius to a volume of Hellenica, edited by Evelyn Abbott, and in 1888 he published Selections from Polybius with substantial prolegomena and appendices. In 1886 and 1890 he contributed to the English Historical Review two articles entitled respectively 'The growth of plebeian privilege at Rome' and 'The decrees of the Roman plebs'. In 1890–91 he wrote articles on Roman subjects for the third edition of William Smith's Dictionary of Greek and Roman Antiquities. His small but learned volume entitled Cicero and the Fall of the Roman Republic (1894) was a brilliant vindication of his favourite Roman statesman and an effective rejoinder to Mommsen's eulogy of Julius Caesar. In 1901 he criticized Mommsen's Römisches Strafrecht at some length in the English Historical Review; and out of this article developed his own searching examination and most elaborate and ambitious work, Problems of the Roman Criminal Law (2 vols., 1912), in recognition of which he was awarded the degree of DCL by Oxford in 1916.

Learning, however, was only a recreation for Strachan-Davidson. Though essentially a scholar he gave his best energies to the service of his university—whose interests in connection with the Indian Civil Service he defended strenuously and successfully on more than one occasion, but especially in 1903–4 and 1913—and of his college, which he loved with a monastic patriotism most appropriate in one of the last representatives of the race of celibate life-fellows.

In 1893, on Jowett's death, many former members of the college hoped that Strachan-Davidson would succeed him. But the electors (the fellows) preferred Edward Caird, a great philosophical teacher, and Strachan-Davidson loyally placed himself at the service of the new master, who was also an old friend. Their alliance was fortunate for the college, and in 1907, when Caird resigned, Strachan-Davidson was unanimously elected in his place—but at the age of sixty-three, with his naturally weak health impaired by a recent accident and operation. His tenure of office was quiet, prosperous, and uneventful until the outbreak of the First World War in 1914. With the help of only three fellows he kept the teaching organization in being; and he did his utmost to make the college useful for the chief purpose that it then served, the training of officer-cadets. He died suddenly of a cerebral haemorrhage at the master's lodgings, on 28 March 1916, and was buried in the cemetery of Holywell church, Oxford.

H. W. C. DAVIS, rev. RICHARD SMAIL

Sources J. W. Mackail, James Leigh Strachan-Davidson (1925) · I. Elliott, ed., The Balliol College register, 1833–1933, 2nd edn (privately printed, Oxford, 1934) · L. E. Jones, An Edwardian youth (1956) · The Times (29 March 1916) · J. Jones, Balliol College: a history, 1263–1939 (1988) · CGPLA Eng. & Wales (1916)

Archives Balliol Oxf., diaries, corresp., and papers

Likenesses G. Reid, oils, 1910, Balliol Oxf. · H. von Herkomer, watercolour drawing, Balliol Oxf.

Wealth at death £13,702 19s. 11d.: probate, 4 Aug 1916, *CGPLA Eng. & Wales*

Davidson [*née* Dickinson], **(Frances) Joan**, Viscountess Davidson and Baroness Northchurch (1894–1985), politician, was born in Kensington, London, on 29 May 1894, the younger daughter and second of three children of Willoughby Hyett Dickinson, first Baron Dickinson (1859–1943), barrister and Liberal MP, and his wife, Minnie Elizabeth Gordon Cumming (*d.* 1967), daughter of General Sir Richard John Meade, who served in India for forty-six years and raised Meade's horse in the Indian mutiny of 1857. She was educated at Kensington high school, at Northfields, and in Germany.

In the First World War, Joan Dickinson served in the wounded and missing department of the Red Cross. She was appointed OBE in 1920. Stanley Baldwin introduced Joan Dickinson to John Colin Campbell *Davidson (1889–1970), the son of James Mackenzie Davidson, surgeon. He was then parliamentary private secretary to Andrew Bonar Law. A few months later, on new year's eve 1918, they became engaged in the Baldwins' house, and they married in April 1919. Baldwin remained friendly with them until his death, and he wrote on average three times a week for twenty-five years to Joan Davidson (Mimi to many of her friends and family).

In 1920 John Davidson was elected MP for Hemel Hempstead, and at once his wife took on his constituency, releasing her husband for his work in parliament and government, as well as giving him time for special work with Baldwin, whose parliamentary private secretary he became.

When Joan Davidson's husband became first Viscount Davidson in 1937 the Hemel Hempstead constituency unanimously asked her to stand as their MP. Duly elected, after canvassing on horseback, she became the only Conservative woman to hold her seat in the general election of 1945. She also retained it in February 1950, October 1951, and May 1955. Possessing much warmth, enthusiasm, and personal charm, she was greatly loved by her Labour women colleagues and respected by her fellow members and the House of Commons staff.

Davidson was a member of the kitchen committee of the House of Commons during the war years of 1939–45. She started parties in Westminster, to which the leader of the Conservative Party always came, for the wives of Conservative candidates in order to interest them in their husbands' work. She was the only woman MP to be a member of the national expenditure committee throughout the Second World War. After the war she served continuously on the estimates committee of the House of Commons until the beginning of 1957, when she was obliged, through pressure of work, to resign. She was the first woman to be a member of the executive of the 1922 committee of the House of Commons, and was re-elected to it in June 1955. She was also an elected member of the Inter-Parliamentary Union executive committee. Senior officials of her party frequently sought her advice.

In 1955 Joan Davidson became a member of the council of the National Union of Conservative and Unionist Associations, a position she held until her death. She started the Young Britons, the junior branch of the Young Conservatives, and she also served on the policy committee of the Conservative Party. In 1964–5 she was president of the National Union of Conservative and Unionist Associations, and chairman of the party conference. She piloted the Anaesthetics for Animals Bill through the House of Commons in 1955, the first act of parliament making it compulsory for anaesthetics to be used when research and experiments were carried out on animals.

Lady Davidson decided to stand down in the 1959 election, after twenty-two years in the Commons (and a period of forty years when she and her husband had represented Hemel Hempstead). She had been appointed DBE in 1952, and in 1963 she was created a life peer, as Baroness Northchurch of Chiswick. The Davidsons were the first husband and wife both to be made peers and to be able to sit together in the Lords. John Davidson died in 1970.

All Joan Davidson's life in London was spent in Westminster. She lived first in an eighteenth-century house in Great College Street for some forty years, and then in a smaller but equally attractive house in Lord North Street. This meant she was a short walking distance from the houses of parliament, and also almost within the precincts of Westminster Abbey, where she attended services every Sunday when she was in London. The Davidsons were an exceptional partnership, in public and in private life. They had two sons and two daughters. Baroness Northchurch died on 25 November 1985 at Great Leighs, near Chelmsford, Essex.　　ELLIOT OF HARWOOD, *rev.*

Sources personal knowledge (1990, 2004) · Burke, *Peerage* (1967) · *The Times* (28 Nov 1985) · *Memoirs of a Conservative: J. C. C. Davidson's memoirs and papers, 1910–37*, ed. R. R. James (1969)

Wealth at death £307,979: probate, 13 March 1986, *CGPLA Eng. & Wales*

Davidson, John (*c.*1549–1604), Church of Scotland minister, was born in Dunfermline to unknown parents. Educated at St Leonard's College, St Andrews, where he matriculated in 1566, aged about seventeen, he served as a regent in the college after graduating MA in 1570 and acted as examiner before entering the ministry at Liberton in 1579. When teaching in the university, he heard Knox preach there during the latter's residence in St Andrews, wrote a play which Knox attended for the marriage of a minister, and followed it with his first poem, *Ane Breif Commendatioun of Uprichtnes*, printed in 1573, in praise of Knox; he also prepared a shorter poem on Knox's death in 1572. He incurred the hostility of Regent Morton in 1574 by writing *Ane Dialog or Mutuall Talking Betuix a Clerk and ane Courteour Concerning Foure Parische Kirks till ane Minister*, a satirical attack on Morton's reorganization of stipends by grouping several adjacent parishes together under the oversight of one minister, for which he was prosecuted by the privy council. Forced to flee to Argyll and then abroad, Davidson was aided by the early Ayrshire reformer Robert Campbell of Kingzeancleuch, who advised him to contact Christopher Goodman (once minister of St Andrews) in England who would find him safe passage to La Rochelle in France. His indebtedness to Campbell is reflected in his poem composed in 1574 (and printed in 1595) *A Memorial of the Life and Death of Two Worthye Christians, Robert Campbel of Kyneancleugh and his Wife Elizabeth Campbell.*

Davidson pursued his academic interests by proceeding to Switzerland, matriculating at the University of Basel in 1575 or 1576, and before returning home to serve as minister was recommended as chaplain in 1577 for the English Merchant Adventurers at Antwerp, but unsuccessfully, for the man appointed was his fellow presbyterian, Walter Travers. Expelled from England for offending Elizabeth by his preaching, Davidson was permitted by Morton to return home and was appointed minister of Liberton in 1579. He executed the church's sentence of excommunication in 1582 against Robert Montgomery, promoted by the crown to the archbishopric of Glasgow, for which he was threatened with assassination. He strongly opposed the government's efforts to remove John Durie from his ministry in Edinburgh, and was active in defending ecclesiastical independence and a presbyterian polity. In the general assembly of June 1582, Andrew Melville as moderator had to ask Davidson 'to moderat his zeale' and in 1583 David Ferguson feared that Davidson would presume too far in his criticism of King James (Calderwood, 4.623–4). He made common cause with the English puritan leader John Field, with whom he corresponded in 1583 on whether the general assembly might intervene on behalf of the English presbyterians. Field's response was positive, and when the general assembly met, representations were made to King James that he urge Queen Elizabeth to 'disburdein their brether of Ingland of the yocke of ceremonies imposed upon them against the libertie of the Word' (Thomson, 2.613–14).

With the onset of Arran's anti-presbyterian administration at home, Davidson was one of the presbyterians who fled to England in 1584, serving for a spell as minister to the exiled ultra-protestant lords who had assembled at Newcastle, before proceeding south to London. He visited Oxford and Cambridge universities and in London he attended the funeral of James Lawson, minister of Edinburgh, who had died in exile in London on 12 October 1584. Encouraged by his fellow exiles to refute Cardinal William Allen's *A True, Sincere and Modest Defence of English Catholiques* (1584), in which Allen had condemned the Scottish ministers as seditious and rebellious, Davidson prepared a short vindication in 1584. He was active, too, in preaching twelve or thirteen sermons in St Olave Jewry, in London, on Sundays and holy days, beginning on 8 November 1584, and 'so railed against the king of Scots in the pulpit' that he was known 'at court and among the bishops as a thunderer' (Laing, 428–9; Calderwood, 4.247). Commanded to cease preaching by the bishop of London in January 1585, Davidson ministered to the banished Scottish nobles at Westminster in May 1585. By November the lords were back in Scotland and, following their *coup d'état*, an invitation was extended from those ministers who had arrived at Stirling with the nobles to Davidson and fellow exiles to return home. He is known to have

'remained a long tyme in Ingland' where he saw for himself 'the corruption of the Bishops there' and on returning home he denounced 'that corruption at all tymes as occasion offered' (Row, 420).

Davidson may have returned by 1586, when the general assembly appointed a minister of that name to a committee to investigate the character and conduct of certain bishops and commissioners, though this more probably was the minister of Hamilton who shared his name. In any event, he did not return to a settled ministry, and it is tempting to identify him with 'Daverson, a Skott, who preached at Aldermanbury church on St Peters day' in London on 29 June 1588 (Donaldson, 79). In that year, too, he declined an invitation to return to his old congregation at Liberton, and in June 1589 was chosen to preach first in Edinburgh and then in the Canongate, until such time that he obtained a particular charge. Nothing came of a proposal in September 1589 to appoint him minister of Dalkeith, but, at the request of Edinburgh presbytery he wrote a reply that year to Richard Bancroft's sermon at Paul's Cross in London against the polity of the Scottish church. His tract *D. Bancroft's Rashnes in Rayling Against the Church of Scotland* was printed in Edinburgh by Waldegrave in 1590, despite James's efforts to have it suppressed. He also addressed a letter, at the request of ministers, to Queen Elizabeth in 1590 defending the polity of the Scottish church against Bancroft's attack.

Davidson opposed Queen Anne's coronation on the sabbath in 1590, and in 1591 admonished the king for his 'contempt of our ministrie' (Calderwood, 5.130–31). In a sermon in 1592 he succeeded in offending the king once again; and in 1593 quarrelled with the moderate David Lindsay, minister in South Leith, who was susceptible to royal influence. To Archbishop John Spottiswoode, he was the maddest man he ever knew, but presbyterians saw him in a different light, as 'a man of authoritie in the Word and Spreit of God' and 'a zealus grave father' (*Autobiography and Diary of … Melvill*, 172, 357), as 'a free rebuker of sinne' (Calderwood, 5.238), and as 'a learned man, and a worthie preacher, yea, a verie prophet of God' (Row, 420). Opposed to ecclesiastical representation in parliament, he firmly believed in the doctrine of the 'two kingdoms' and in 1598 went so far as to inform the king that he sat in assemblies not 'as *Imperator*, but as a Christian' (Calderwood, 5.683). When James complained in 1598 that Davidson spoke 'anabaptisticall-like' and was too friendly with the English puritan John Penry, who spent some time in Scotland between 1589 and 1592, Davidson responded that 'he was no Anabaptist, and agreed not with Mr Penrie' (ibid., 698). He voiced a strong protest when the king discharged Andrew Melville from attending the assembly in 1598, and he himself was warded in 1601 for a letter sent by him to the general assembly at Burntisland.

Inducted to the parish of Prestonpans in Haddingtonshire in January 1596, Davidson founded a school and built a church and manse largely at his own expense. There he prepared a catechism, printed in 1602 by Waldegrave in Edinburgh under the title *Some Helpes for Young Schollers in*

Christianity, in which he quoted scriptural passages from the Bishops' Bible produced in England by Archbishop Matthew Parker in 1568 instead of the Geneva Bible of 1560 which had proved more popular in Scotland. Before his death, which occurred in August or September 1604, he wrote *De hostibus ecclesiae Christi* wherein he affirmed that 'the erecting of Bishops in this Kirk is the most subtill and prevalent mean to destroy and overthrow religion that ever could be devysed' (Row, 421). He was also the author of several other texts.   JAMES KIRK

Sources T. Thomson, ed., *Acts and proceedings of the general assemblies of the Kirk of Scotland*, 3 pts, Bannatyne Club, 81 (1839–45) • D. Calderwood, *The history of the Kirk of Scotland*, ed. T. Thomson and D. Laing, 8 vols., Wodrow Society, 7 (1842–9) • J. Row, *The history of the Kirk of Scotland, from the year 1558 to August 1637*, ed. D. Laing, Wodrow Society, 4 (1842) • J. Spottiswood, *The history of the Church of Scotland*, ed. M. Napier and M. Russell, 3 vols., Bannatyne Club, 93 (1850) • *CSP Scot.*, 1547–1603 • D. Laing, ed., *The miscellany of the Wodrow Society*, Wodrow Society, [9] (1844) • H. G. Waekernagel, ed., *Die Matrikel der Universität Basel* (1956) • J. Kirk, ed., *The records of the synod of Lothian and Tweeddale, 1589–1596, 1640–1649*, Stair Society, 30 (1977) • A. F. S. Pearson, *Thomas Cartwright and Elizabethan puritanism, 1535–1603* (1925) • A. I. Dunlop, ed., *Acta facultatis artium universitatis Sanctiandree, 1413–1588*, 2 vols., Scottish History Society, 3rd ser., 54–5 (1964) • G. Donaldson, 'Scottish Presbyterian exiles in England, 1584–8', *Records of the Scottish Church History Society*, 14 (1960–62), 67–80 • R. M. Gillan, *John Davidson of Prestonpans* (1936) • J. M. Anderson, ed., *Early records of the University of St Andrews*, Scottish History Society, 3rd ser., 8 (1926) • *The autobiography and diary of Mr James Melvill*, ed. R. Pitcairn, Wodrow Society (1842)
Archives Denbighshire RO, Ruthin, treatise on grace and peace

Davidson, John (*c.*1724–1797), antiquary and lawyer, was the son of James Davidson of Haltree, an Edinburgh bookseller, and Elizabeth, sister of William Brown, Church of Scotland minister, also of Edinburgh. He was educated for the law, being apprenticed to George Balfour, writer to the signet, and was himself admitted as writer on 3 April 1749. He was deputy keeper of the signet from 1778 until his death. He was for many years crown agent, and was also agent for a number of Scottish noblemen and landowners, having a successful and lucrative practice.

Davidson lived in Edinburgh with his wife, Helen Gibson (*d.* 1796), and their one son. He knew many of the city's eminent literati and antiquarians, including Lord Hailes, William Tytler, George Paton, David Herd, and Callander of Craigforth; he frequently located rare books for Bishop Percy. Davidson's specialism was Scottish legal history and antiquities. He printed several works on these subjects for private circulation, and was understood to have superintended the 1797 edition of Lord Hailes's *Annals of Scotland*. The third and fourth appendices of this edition were taken entirely from work previously published by Davidson, which is acknowledged in the preface. William Robertson acknowledged Davidson's assistance in the preface to his highly successful *History of Scotland*, published in 1759.

Davidson died at Castle Hill, Edinburgh, on 29 December 1797. His son having died young he left his estate of Haltree to Lord Glenlee, a younger son of Sir William

Miller, bt, and his farm, Cairntons, near Edinburgh, to Henry Dundas, Lord Melville. His legal practice was left to Hugh Warrender, his first clerk, who also received Davidson's house in Edinburgh.

W. W. WROTH, *rev.* ALEXANDER DU TOIT

Sources J. Kay, *A series of original portraits and caricature etchings … with biographical sketches and illustrative anecdotes*, ed. [H. Paton and others], new edn, 2 vols. (1877) • [F. J. Grant], *A history of the Society of Writers to Her Majesty's Signet* (1890) • *N&Q*, 4th ser., 1 (1868), 47–8, 115 • L. R. Timperley, ed., *A directory of landownership in Scotland, c.1770*, Scottish RS, new ser., 5 (1976) • Nichols, *Illustrations* • *Williamson's Edinburgh Directory* (1788) • J. Gilhooly, ed., *A directory of Edinburgh in 1752* (1988) • *Scots Magazine*, 59 (1797), 931 • *Letters from Thomas Percy … John Callander … David Herd, and others, to George Paton*, ed. J. Maidment (1830)
Archives NL Scot., letter-book • U. Edin. L., special collections division, corresp. and papers incl. many relating to the history of the family of Stuart | BL, letters to Thomas Birch, Add. MS 4304 • BL, letters to Lord Hardwicke, Add. MSS 35615–35622, *passim* • NL Scot., letters to George Paton • NL Scot., corresp. with Allan Ramsey • NL Scot., corresp. with Andrew Stuart
Likenesses J. Kay, caricature, etching, BM, NPG
Wealth at death £581 11s. 8d.—Haltree estate and Cairntons farm; also house on Castle Hill, Edinburgh: Midlothian valuation roll, 1771

Davidson, John (1797–1836), traveller, the son of an opulent tailor and army clothier in Cork Street, London, originally from Kelso, Roxburghshire, was born on 23 December 1797. He was educated at a private academy near London, and in 1814 was apprenticed to Savory and Moore, chemists and druggists, a firm in which he ultimately purchased a partnership. Later he became a pupil at St George's Hospital, and entered the University of Edinburgh with the intention of becoming a doctor. His health failed, however, and he gave up the study of medicine to travel. He went first to Naples in 1827 and thence through much of central Europe. He went to Egypt at the end of 1829, visited the pyramids, and passed overland to Quseir on the Red Sea coast where he embarked for India on his way to China and Persia. An attack of cholera, however, drove him back to Quseir. He made an excursion through Arabia, and visited Palestine, Syria, the Greek Isles, Athens, and Constantinople, collecting much geographical information, which he afterwards communicated in papers read at the meetings of the Royal Society and the Royal Institution of London. In 1831 he went to America, travelling in the United States, and in Spanish America where he visited and surveyed the pyramids of Choluteca; he then settled down for a time to the study of Egyptology. On 13 July 1833 he delivered an address on embalming at the Royal Institution, when he unrolled a mummy in the presence of a deeply interested audience; he later published a pamphlet describing the occasion. He was elected a fellow of the Royal Society in 1835. His craving for travel was, however, irresistible. He decided to explore in Africa, planning to go by way of Fez and, after examining the southern slopes of the Atlas Mountains, to Nigritia and across the Sahara to Timbuktu. He left England in September 1835, accompanied only by a black companion,

Edward Donnelan or Abú Bekr. From Gibraltar he crossed the straits into Morocco, where his medical knowledge was so highly valued by the sultan that he had great difficulty in obtaining permission to depart. He estimated that he treated twelve hundred patients in Morocco, and he also gave instruction to local physicians. When leaving he was obliged to plead that his stock of medicine was exhausted, and at his request a medicine chest was forwarded to the sultan from England. He started for the Sahara at the end of November 1836 after numerous delays, but while stopping at a watering-place called Swekeza he was robbed and murdered on 17 or 18 December 1836 by a party from the tribe El Harib, who are thought to have been bribed by the merchants of Tafilelt to seize the traveller and his goods. The findings of his travels were recorded in letters, published later in the *Journal of the Royal Geographical Society* (1836 and 1837). After Davidson's death his brother printed privately a book of pathetic interest entitled *Notes Taken during Travels in Africa* (1839).

ROBERT HARRISON, *rev.* ELIZABETH BAIGENT

Sources *Journal of the Royal Geographical Society*, 6 (1836), 429–33 [letters to the RES] · *Journal of the Royal Geographical Society*, 7 (1837), 144–72 [extracts of letters] · [T. T. Shore], ed., *Cassell's biographical dictionary* (1867–9) · *The Athenaeum* (20 July 1833), 481–3
Archives S. Antiquaries, Lond., notes relating to Egyptian antiquities
Likenesses C. Puy, bust, 1858, RGS · M. Gauci, lithograph (after E. U. Eddis), BM

Davidson, John (1857–1909), schoolteacher and writer, was born on 11 April 1857 at Barrhead, Renfrewshire, the son of Alexander Davidson, a minister of the Evangelical Union, and his wife, Helen Davidson, *née* Crockett. When he was nine the family moved to Greenock, Renfrewshire, where his father had been appointed to the ministry of the church in Nelson Street. Greenock, an industrial town and port on the Firth of Clyde, is undoubtedly the setting of Davidson's major autobiographical poem, 'A Ballad in Blank Verse of the Making of a Poet' (*Ballads and Songs*, 1894).

From 1870 to 1871 Davidson was employed in the chemical laboratory of Walker's, the Greenock sugar firm, and subsequently became an assistant in the office of the town's public analyst. Such employment contributed to the making of a poet whose subject matter would draw on science. In 1872 he returned to his old school at Greenock, Highlanders' Academy, as a pupil teacher. Intellectually restless, with no academic cast of mind, he spent only one year (1876–7) as a student at Edinburgh University. He was subsequently a teacher of English at Alexander's charity school, Glasgow (1877–8), Perth Academy (1878–81), Kelvinside Academy, Glasgow (1881–2), and Hutchinson's charity school, Paisley (1883–4). After a year as a clerk in the Glasgow office of a thread firm, he returned to teaching at Morrison's academy, Crieff, Perthshire (1885–8), where he protested at the rector's cruelty to the pupils; his short story 'The Schoolboy's Tragedy' is an indictment of petty authoritarianism in Scottish education. Although in his play *Smith: a Tragic Farce* (1888) Davidson called school-teaching 'mental boot-blacking', he was remembered as an inspirational instructor, particularly in his classes on poetry.

On 23 October 1885 Davidson married Margaret Cameron McArthur, daughter of John McArthur, dean of guild of Perth, and his wife, Menzies Grant McArthur, *née* McDonald. They had two sons, Alexander and Menzies. Davidson's last teaching post was at a private school in Greenock (1888–9); this also marked the virtual end of his residence in Scotland, with the subsequent move to London and the south of England. He was to return to Scotland for brief writing retreats in the early 1900s, most notably to Blairlogie at the foot of the Ochil hills near Stirling, another part of Scotland much celebrated in his writing.

The bulk of Davidson's early work, composed while he was still in Scotland, is in the form of verse-drama: *Diabolus amans* (1885); *Bruce* (1886), a historical play based on the warrior-king of Scotland, Robert the Bruce; and *Smith: a Tragic Farce* (1888), concerning a Nietzschean-style 'Overman' who despises the constraints of bourgeois mediocrity. In deploying drama Davidson allowed his characters to articulate ideas to which he could avoid making his own overt commitment; nevertheless, and although he rejected his father's Christianity, his quasi-autobiographical characters display an evangelical fervour in their quest for personal and intellectual fulfilment as against conventional pieties. Existential assertiveness animates the protagonists of 'Thirty Bob a Week', the monologue of a poor but proud clerk, and 'A Ballad of a Nun'; these are two of the most notable (and in the latter case notorious) poems of Davidson's *annus mirabilis*, 1894.

Davidson's Victorian earnestness is offset by a premodernist, carnivalesque humour, seen in such novels as *The North Wall* (1885; reprinted in 1891 together with a selection of short stories in *The Great Men, and A Practical Novelist*), *Perfervid: the Career of Ninian Jamieson* (1890), and the play *Scaramouch in Naxos* (1890), which looks forward to twentieth-century reworkings of *commedia dell'arte*. *A Full and True Account of the Wonderful Mission of Earl Lavender* (1895) is a spirited spoof on 1890s high camp. He evolved a concept of irony which delighted in the coexistence of extreme opposites; accordingly, he could deny that he subscribed to any one-sided set of beliefs. For example, although influenced by Nietzsche, he disclaimed discipleship. Even so, it is missionary zeal rather than transcendent irony which characterizes such later work as the five blank verse *Testaments* published between 1901 and 1908, and the unfinished trilogy of plays, *God and Mammon* (1907–8). Such deeply philosophical poetry expounds a scientific materialism and atheistic humanism: man is matter evolved to its highest form, and the individual of the species must assert his or her will.

For most of the period between 1890 and 1907 Davidson and his family lived in London where he worked as a journalist, contributing regularly to *The Speaker* and also to *The Star*, the *Yellow Book*, and the *Glasgow Herald*. He was a publisher's reader for two houses: John Lane during the 1890s, and Grant Richards from 1907 to 1909. He became a member of the Rhymers' Club but maintained a typical aloofness; he was ambivalent in his attitude to nineties decadence, and his fellow poets (notably W. B. Yeats) regarded him as a serious, tough-minded Scot. Journalism, like teaching, he viewed as an economic necessity, distracting him from his vocation as a poet; however, it did provide him with raw material for his poetry, as in *Fleet Street Eclogues* (1893; 2nd ser., 1896). Financial, family, and professional problems led to a breakdown late in 1896, followed by two years' recuperation at Shoreham on the Sussex coast. In 1899 he received a grant from the Royal Literary Fund and in 1906 was awarded a civil-list pension. His last two years were spent in Penzance, Cornwall, where the family had moved in 1907 to escape the pressures of London; this did not stop him becoming ill and depressed. On 23 March 1909 he failed to return from his customary coastal walk. Six months later his body was recovered from the sea, at Mousehole harbour, near Penzance, and although the coroner returned a verdict of 'accidental death', Davidson's own final utterances had demonstrated an inclination towards suicide. On 21 September he was, according to his own wishes, buried at sea, 7 miles off Penzance.

Davidson influenced the careers of two of the greatest English-language poets of the twentieth century: T. S. Eliot acknowledged his discovery of Davidson's urban images, so crucial to the making of the poet of *The Waste Land*; C. M. Grieve (Hugh MacDiarmid) responded to the scientific materialism and its paradoxically mystical possibilities. The standard edition of Davidson's verse is *The Poems of John Davidson*, edited by Andrew Turnbull in two volumes and published by the Scottish Academic Press in 1973. His fiction is far from negligible, and his essays reinforce his position as an early modernist; above all, however, it is his poetry which has secured his reputation.　　　　　　　　　　　　　　　　 Tom Hubbard

Sources J. B. Townsend, *John Davidson: poet of Armageddon* (1961) · M. O'Connor, *John Davidson* (1987) · 'Introduction' and notes, *The poems of John Davidson*, ed. A. Turnbull, 2 vols. (1973) · 'John Davidson', *Twentieth-century literary criticism*, ed. D. Poupard, 24 (1987), 156–96 · *DNB* · R. D. Macleod, *John Davidson: a study in personality* (1957) · T. Royle, *The Macmillan companion to Scottish literature* (1983), 81–2 · *Glasgow Herald* (20 Sept 1909) · m. cert. · d. cert. · *CGPLA Eng. & Wales* (1909)

Archives Morgan L., corresp. and literary papers · NL Scot., letters to various publishers · Princeton University Library, corresp., literary MSS, and papers | BL, letters to William Archer, Add. MS 45291 · BL, letters to George Bernard Shaw, Add. MS 50533 · NL Scot., letters to John Lane, literary MSS · Ransom HRC, corresp. with John Lane · U. Leeds, Brotherton L., letters to Edmund Gosse · U. Reading L., letters to Charles Elkin Mathews

Likenesses W. Rothenstein, pastel drawing, 1894, BM; repro. in W. Rothenstein, *Men and memories: recollections of William Rothenstein, 1872–1900* (1931), 186–7 · M. Beerbohm, cartoon, 1925, AM Oxf. · M. Beerbohm, caricature, repro. in *The chapbook* (1907) · M. Beerbohm, cartoons, Ransom HRC · R. Bryden, portrait · Elliott & Fry, cabinet photograph, NPG · W. Sickert, pencil?, repro. in M. Lindsay, ed., *John Davidson: a selection of his poems* (1961)

Wealth at death £319 19s. 3d.: administration, 19 Oct 1909, *CGPLA Eng. & Wales*

Davidson, John Colin Campbell, first Viscount Davidson (1889–1970), politician, was born in Aberdeen on 23 February 1889. He was the second child and only son of Sir James Mackenzie Davidson (1856–1919), ophthalmic surgeon and pioneer of radiology, and his wife, Georgina Barbara Watt (*d.* 1927), daughter of the Revd William Henderson of Aberdeen. The family originated as farmers near Scone in Perthshire, but Davidson's grandfather John Davidson (1808–1893) emigrated to Argentina in 1825 and prospered there; the income from the family's estates enabled Davidson to follow his interests and refuse payment for the various positions which he held. The family were staunchly Church of Scotland, and Davidson's early years imbued him with a strong faith and the ethic of 'your work always comes first' (Davidson, 5). He was educated at Fretherne House preparatory school, Westminster School (1903–7), and Pembroke College, Cambridge, graduating with a third in part one of the law tripos in 1911. He was called to the bar at the Middle Temple in 1913 but never practised, for by this time he had already begun a different career.

On 10 April 1919 Davidson married (Frances) Joan Dickinson (1894–1985) [*see* Davidson, (Frances) Joan]. Always known as Mimi, she was an attractive and popular personality who shared her husband's outlook and supported his work. She succeeded him as MP for Hemel Hempstead from 1937 to 1959, and became a life peer as Baroness Northchurch in 1963. It was a close and happy marriage and resulted in two sons and two daughters.

Relations with Bonar Law and Baldwin In May 1910 Davidson became an unpaid assistant private secretary to the colonial secretary, Lord Crewe. He continued to serve his successor, Lewis Harcourt, from November 1910 to May 1915, when the formation of the first coalition brought Davidson into the orbit of the new colonial secretary and Conservative Party leader, Andrew Bonar Law. The latter was swiftly impressed by Davidson's industry, and he became more than a trusted aide. A close friendship developed based upon a paternal relationship. Law dissuaded Davidson from leaving Whitehall for military service, and when he became chancellor of the exchequer in the Lloyd George coalition in December 1916 insisted that Davidson move with him to the Treasury. Davidson continued as Law's private secretary until the latter's patronage smoothed his entry into the House of Commons as MP for Hemel Hempstead in November 1920. This was not a change of course, for immediately Davidson became Law's parliamentary private secretary (PPS), discharging the same tasks but with better political access and contacts.

When Law retired on health grounds in March 1921 Davidson became parliamentary private secretary to Stanley Baldwin, which was almost a case of staying in the family. Baldwin was also close to Law and knew Davidson well from having served—initially at Davidson's suggestion—as junior minister at the Treasury in 1916–19. During 1921–2 Davidson shared with Baldwin and a range of junior ministers an increasingly negative view of the Lloyd George coalition. The revolt against this was a movement

John Colin Campbell Davidson, first Viscount Davidson (1889–1970), by Bassano, 1926

his friendship with Baldwin was to keep him there for the next fourteen years in a variety of roles. This was also a filial relationship across generations—indeed, Davidson met his wife through Baldwin, as she was a friend of one of his daughters. Baldwin spent much time in the Davidsons' company; Mimi was a frequent companion in his favourite relaxation of long country walks, and they regularly holidayed with the Baldwins as well. Davidson shared his leader's political aims and moral vision, while being willing to devil on the detail and take care of confidential matters. In Baldwin's first ministry he became chancellor of the duchy of Lancaster; this was outside the cabinet, but an ideal position from which to advise and assist. He combined this office with the position of chief civil commissioner, responsible for preparing plans to cope with a paralysing industrial stoppage; later, in the general strike of 1926, he served as deputy chief civil commissioner with responsibility for government publicity, overseeing the activities of Winston Churchill and the *British Gazette*.

Conservative Party chairman In the general election of 1923 Davidson was defeated at Hemel Hempstead but he recovered the seat in 1924. In Baldwin's second government he was given junior office as parliamentary secretary at the Admiralty. Davidson played a part in the dispute over the naval budget in 1925 between Bridgeman, the first lord of the Admiralty, and Churchill, the chancellor of the exchequer. In this, as on other occasions, his constant vigilance for signs of disloyalty and intrigue led to a distorted picture which added to existing tensions. From 1922 onwards Davidson was almost paranoid in suspecting that the former coalitionists were seeking to reverse their defeat, and he saw hidden plots behind almost anything which they did or said, a reflection of his own tendency to intrigue. His loyalty and dedication were absolute, and in November 1926 Baldwin moved Davidson to the position where this was of paramount importance, as chairman of the Conservative Party organization. From then until his departure in June 1930 Davidson's aim was to serve his leader: he had no thought of promoting his own career, regarding the office as a thankless task and 'a blind alley' (Davidson to Hoare, 30 Dec 1929, CUL, Templewood MS VI/1).

Davidson's period as party chairman was the most important and visible phase of his career. Although there were difficulties, his tenure is considered to have been one of the most significant in the development of the Conservative electoral machine in the twentieth century—a period in which it had been an important factor in the party's success. Davidson was not the founder, for the basis had been laid by his predecessors after the creation of the party chairmanship in 1911–14 and in the early 1920s. His achievements were therefore not quite as sweeping as he later tended to suggest, but he reshaped and energized the central organization after a period of electoral turmoil and haphazard evolution. He made a significant contribution in three main areas: rationalizing the basic structure, developing new areas, and expanding the scale of operations.

The reorganization of the central office which Davidson

at many levels within the Conservative Party involving constituency pressure, back-bench MPs, junior ministers, and restive peers. The range of dissent gave it weight, but its greatest weakness was the lack of a credible leader. Davidson played an important role by helping to persuade Law to come out of retirement and attend the Carlton Club meeting on 19 October 1922 at which Lloyd George and the existing Conservative leaders were overthrown.

Law resumed the Conservative leadership and became prime minister, and with Baldwin's approval Davidson at once returned to his side as Law's PPS. It was in this position that a few months later Davidson played a significant—and controversial—historical role. When Law's terminal illness forced him to retire in May 1923 he declined to recommend whether Curzon or Baldwin should be his successor. At the request of the king's private secretary, Lord Stamfordham, Davidson wrote a memorandum which came down firmly in favour of Baldwin. This document accompanied Law's resignation letter and was handed over by its bearer, Law's private secretary Ronald Waterhouse. Although the latter suggested that it represented Law's own undisclosed view, Stamfordham and the king were aware of its authorship. It played a smaller part in the choice of Baldwin as prime minister than was once supposed, but nevertheless had some influence—if only because it provided arguments for the choice which the crown was disposed to take.

Davidson's relationship with Law had brought him into the inner counsels of the Conservative Party by 1923, and introduced in 1928 laid down the basic structure which continued, with cosmetic changes, for the next six decades. The active departments of central office were drawn together into two main groups. The first embraced all the traditional organizational services, and was headed by the principal agent; the second dealt with publications and propaganda, and the new post of director of publicity was created to oversee it. This reform was intended to establish clear lines of authority and ensure better co-ordination between related sections, and also to emphasize the importance of publicity—for new methods were the key to reach the vastly enlarged electorate. Davidson was adept at securing able individuals, and appointed the three men who held the key posts until 1945: Robert Topping, Joseph Ball, and Patrick Gower.

The priority which Davidson gave to new areas of organization resulted from the democratic electorate created in 1918 and the equalization of the franchise for both sexes at the age of twenty-one in 1928. He was strongly committed to further strengthening the women's side of the party organization, recognizing their importance both as voters and active fund-raisers in the constituency associations. This had been developing since the early 1920s, and Davidson continued to enhance it, giving more resources and seeking to raise its prestige and professionalism. To underline this, in 1928 he appointed the head of the women's department, Marjorie Maxse, to be deputy to the principal agent. He also continued the attempts to promote the trade unionists' wing, the labour advisory committees; this was much more difficult ground, but significant in view of the industrial strife of the 1920s and the rise of the Labour Party. His more original initiatives lay in three other areas: youth, publicity, and political education. The employment of organizers at central office and in the regions led to a considerable expansion of the junior imperial league. The publicity budget was more than doubled, links with the provincial press improved, new party journals founded, and a torrent of leaflets produced. He was open to new methods, using a professional advertising firm and introducing the effective travelling cinema vans. He encouraged political education at local and regional level, and raised £200,000 to provide a national centre which party members could attend; this opened in 1930 at Ashridge in Hertfordshire as the Bonar Law Memorial College. His final contribution came in his last months as chairman, and is often identified with others. However, after much discussion over the previous years, it was Davidson who established the Conservative Research Department in October 1929—he secured Baldwin's approval, raised the funds, found the premises, and appointed Ball as its director—though Neville Chamberlain was more important in making the department a success.

Davidson presided over a huge expansion of staff and spending. By 1928 central office employed 296 persons in London and the regional offices, a level attained again only at the peak of the Woolton machine in 1949–51. Although Davidson did not hold the formal post of party treasurer in fact he did much of the fund-raising. This was an area at which even his critics admitted he was effective, and he raised £1 million before the general election of 1929. In his memoirs Davidson identified himself with having stamped out political corruption through the sale of honours, a scandal which had tarnished the Lloyd George coalition. In practice what this meant was not an end to rewards for faithful contributors, but a return to the former discreet and indirect methods.

Not everything in Davidson's tenure was positive, and the problems mounted after the defeat in 1929. He faced his share of criticism over its timing and over the uninspiring campaign themes of 'Safety first' and 'Trust Baldwin'. In its wake concern grew that Davidson was too close to the leader to act as an effective channel of communication. This was all the more important as the party chairman was also chairman of the executive committee of the national union—a link which was severed on Davidson's departure. He could be prickly and tended to engage in clumsy manoeuvres against Baldwin's critics on the right. By 1930 he had alienated a range of figures, including his own deputy chairman, the otherwise inoffensive Lord Stanley. These problems came to a head as Baldwin came under pressure from Lord Beaverbrook's 'empire crusade' campaign in 1930. A truce was negotiated in March, but collapsed during May partly owing to Davidson's misjudgements over tactics and publicity. He had by now become a liability who was weakening Baldwin's position, but the latter was reluctant to drop him. The nettle was grasped by Neville Chamberlain, who told Davidson bluntly in April that he had to go; after further delay, Chamberlain pressed again and Davidson resigned on 29 May.

India, Argentina, and memoirs Although Davidson felt he had been sacrificed he soon resumed his position as a key figure in Baldwin's inner circle. He remained a trusted adviser and friend during the rest of Baldwin's leadership, but most of his work was behind the scenes and is difficult to assess. In March 1931 he helped at a vital moment to persuade Baldwin not to resign the party leadership. In the National Government Davidson served outside the cabinet as chancellor of the duchy of Lancaster from November 1931 until May 1937. He was knighted in 1935. Much of his attention in the early 1930s focused upon the India question, as this was the most divisive issue within the Conservative Party. He worked to secure support for the bipartisan policy which Baldwin had endorsed since 1929, and to defeat the diehard critics led by Winston Churchill. He took a public part as chairman of the Indian States inquiry committee, visiting India in early 1932. This examined the relationship between the princely states and the proposed federal structure, and he was able to secure a cautious agreement which assisted progress without alarming Conservative opinion at home. In general, his role was not to influence Baldwin's decisions, but to encourage and support him in the path which he had chosen. This was illustrated in the abdication crisis in 1936, when he was a key voice close to Baldwin urging the need for decisive action. When Baldwin retired in May 1937 Davidson also left active politics. The closeness of the relationship was underlined when Davidson was given a viscountcy, the peerage normally given to those of cabinet rank; he took the title of Viscount Davidson of Little Gaddesden, Hertfordshire.

Business concerns, and especially the family's Argentine estates, occupied much of Davidson's time from 1937 until the Peronist government broke the connection in the 1950s. In the Second World War he was an adviser and then controller of production at the Ministry of Information from October 1939 to July 1941. After this he was an honorary adviser on commercial relations with South America, making an official tour there in 1942. On his return in 1943 he founded the Hispanic and Luso-Brazilian councils, which led to the establishment of Canning House in London as a centre to promote closer links with South America. Davidson continued to work for this, and made frequent visits to the continent in the late 1940s and 1950s. His contribution was recognized by honours awarded by several countries and the presidency of the Anglo-Argentine Society. In 1960 he began compiling material for a volume of memoirs, including a number of tape-recorded conversations. However, a cerebral atheroma in 1962 and further serious illness at the end of 1963 meant that he could not complete this. His memory was not affected, and a volume which blended the incomplete memoirs with documents from his extensive archive was edited by Robert Rhodes James. It appeared in 1969, shortly before Davidson's death on 11 December 1970 at his London home, Said House, Chiswick Mall, Chiswick.

The publication of the memoirs drew attention to Davidson's role behind the scenes, in particular as aide and confidant to Bonar Law and Baldwin. Throughout his career Davidson did not seek any independent position, and he was most comfortable with a place in the background as the loyal lieutenant. His role as the perennial insider raised concerns that he was an *éminence grise*; doubt and resentment about the extent of his influence meant that he collected enemies, and his fortunes depended upon his patron. Discreet and industrious, he devoted his efforts to persons and causes that he regarded as greater than himself. His most prominent position, as chairman of the Conservative Party from 1926 to 1930, was simply an extension of this role as the leader's right hand, while his fall from this office illustrated his defects as a politician. In character and appearance Davidson seemed more of an administrator than a politician: he possessed a certain stuffiness and tendency to focus upon detail, and was not an imposing figure either in the House of Commons or in public. He was of medium height, and in his middle years gained weight while his hair thinned; he was normally seen in public as a bland and owlish figure whose most distinctive feature was his round black spectacles.

STUART BALL

Sources DNB · *Memoirs of a Conservative: J. C. C. Davidson's memoirs and papers, 1910–37*, ed. R. R. James (1969) · HLRO, Davidson papers · K. Middlemas and J. Barnes, *Baldwin* (1969) · CUL, Baldwin MSS · U. Birm. L., Neville Chamberlain MSS · J. Ramsden, *The age of Balfour and Baldwin, 1902–1940* (1978) · C. Petrie, *The powers behind prime ministers* (1958) · S. Ball, *Baldwin and the conservative party: the crisis of 1929–1931* (1988) · A. Seldon and S. Ball, eds., *Conservative century: the conservative party since 1900* (1994) · C. Bridge, *Holding India to the empire: the British conservative party and the 1935 constitution* (New Delhi, 1986) · G. R. Searle, *Corruption in British politics, 1895–1930* (1987) · CGPLA Eng. & Wales (1971)

Archives Bodl. Oxf., MSS · HLRO, corresp. and papers | Bodl. Oxf., corresp. with Geoffrey Dawson · Bodl. Oxf., letters to Lewis Harcourt · Bodl. Oxf., Indian States Enquiry Committee papers · Bodl. Oxf., corresp. with Sir W. L. Worthington-Evans · CUL, Baldwin MSS · HLRO, corresp. with Lord Beaverbrook · Shrops. RRC, Bridgeman MSS

Likenesses Bassano, photograph, 1926, NPG [*see illus.*] · W. Stoneman, two photographs, 1936–49, NPG · T. Cottrell, cigarette card, NPG

Wealth at death £69,510: probate, 3 Jan 1971, CGPLA Eng. & Wales

Davidson, Sir John Humphrey (1876–1954), army officer and politician, was born in Mauritius on 24 July 1876, the son of a merchant, George Walter Davidson, and his wife, Johanna Smith Humphrey. He was educated at Harrow School from 1890 to 1893, and at the Royal Military College, Sandhurst, before joining the 1st battalion of his regiment, the King's Royal Rifle Corps, in Mauritius in 1896. The battalion was in South Africa when war broke out against the Boer republics in October 1899. Davidson had a good war, serving with his battalion at the battle of Talana and in the operations around Ladysmith in Natal, and later on attachment to locally raised irregular cavalry units pursuing the Boer commandos. By the end of the war he had won the DSO and been mentioned in dispatches, and had been promoted captain.

After the war Davidson served in Malta, and with the international force in Crete, before being nominated for entry to the Staff College, Camberley, in 1905. On 12 December 1905 he married Margaret, daughter of John Peter Grant, of Rothiemurchus, Inverness-shire. They had one daughter. In a succession of staff appointments before the First World War, Davidson (or Tavish, as he was known universally throughout the army on account of his Scottish origins) demonstrated his considerable talent for staff work: as general staff officer, grade 3, in the directorate of military training at the War Office from 1908 to 1910; as brigade major of the 5th infantry brigade between 1910 and 1912; and as instructor in training and tactics and general staff duties at the Staff College from 1912 to 1914.

On the outbreak of war Davidson, now holding the rank of major, took up his duties as general staff officer, grade 2 (intelligence) for the 3rd army corps and took part in the principal engagements of the 1914 campaign: the battles of the Marne, the Aisne, and first Ypres. Towards the end of that year his talent for staff work was brought to the attention of Sir Douglas Haig, the commander of the First Army corps, when, on attachment to that corps, Davidson organized the relief of the Indian corps from their difficult position on the River Lys. On the formation of the First Army under Haig's command in January 1915 Haig selected Davidson as his principal operations officer. In this capacity Davidson took part in the planning of the principal British engagements of the 1915 campaign, Neuve Chapelle, Aubers Ridge, and Loos.

When Haig replaced Sir John French as commander-in-chief of the British armies in France and Flanders in

Sir John Humphrey Davidson (1876–1954), by Walter Stoneman, 1936

it is impossible to quantify the influence Davidson exercised over the details of operational planning, it would be naïve to assume that he was entirely innocent of the charges subsequently levelled against GHQ of tactical inflexibility and poor strategic judgement. Yet Davidson's measured and thorough approach to operational planning stands out; it is perhaps unfortunate that in the planning of the third battle of Ypres in the summer of 1917 his argument for a steady succession of limited offensives did not prevail over the more ambitious schemes of Haig and the commander of the Fifth Army, General Sir Hubert Gough. Unlike Charteris, Davidson remained secure at GHQ until the end of the war, and so must take some credit for the new combined arms operational methods which swept the British army to success in the Last Hundred Days of war. By 1918 Davidson had risen to the rank of major-general. Among numerous British and foreign honours and decorations for his war service Davidson was awarded the Légion d'Honneur in 1916, and appointed CB in 1917 and KCMG in 1919. He left the army in 1922.

At the end of the war Davidson entered parliament unopposed as MP for the safe Unionist seat of Fareham in Hampshire. As a member of parliament he took an active interest in service questions, taking a leading role on the House of Commons army committee. He was a determined advocate of the reorganization of Britain's peacetime defence administration to create a unified Ministry of Defence, and led the army committee's 1920 deputation to the prime minister advocating such a ministry. In and outside parliament Davidson took an active interest in ex-servicemen's welfare; in parliament as chairman of the parliamentary select committee on the training and employment of ex-servicemen; and outside parliament as a founder and chairman of the King's Roll National Council and president of the Union Jack Club.

Davidson resigned his parliamentary seat in 1931 to concentrate on his business interests. He held a number of company directorships, including a seat on the board of the armaments manufacturer Vickers. Between 1937 and 1949 he was chairman of the Bank of Australia. He was colonel commandant of his regiment from 1937 to 1945. Yet his most formative experience remained his period of service at GHQ in the First World War. In later life he published *Haig: Master of the Field* (1953), a belated but impassioned defence of his former chief, and indirectly of his own part in the British army's victory.

Davidson died at Glack, Daviot, Aberdeenshire on 11 December 1954. He left a small collection of private papers, which were deposited at the National Library of Scotland.   WILLIAM PHILPOTT

Sources G. de Groot, *Douglas Haig, 1861–1928* (1988) · T. Travers, *The killing ground* (1987) · D. Winter, *Haig's command: a reassessment* (1991) · King's Lond., Liddell Hart C., J. E. Edmonds MSS · E. L. Spears, *Prelude to victory* (1939) · W. J. Philpot, 'The campaign for a ministry of defence between the wars', *Government and the armed forces in Britain, 1856–1990*, ed. P. Smith (1996), 109–154 · R. Prior and T. Wilson, *Passchendaele: the untold story* (1996) · P. Griffith, *Battle tactics of the western front: the British army's art of attack, 1916–1918* (1994) · PRO, CAB 45 · *The private papers of Douglas Haig, 1914–1919*, ed.

December 1915 Davidson accompanied him to general headquarters (GHQ) as director of military operations. Like Colonel John Charteris, Haig's much maligned director of military intelligence, Davidson, as one of Haig's trusted inner circle, had unrestricted access to his chief and was in a position to influence his decisions. Davidson's task was, after strategic consultation with the French commander-in-chief, to put his chief's tactical intentions into concrete form and pass them on to subordinate army commanders and executive field officers. In such a role Davidson was a key link in the operational chain of command, accompanying his chief to most allied and army commanders' operational conferences. Yet Davidson was more than a mere messenger, for it was his tactical appreciations and operational instructions that formed the basis of British military doctrine and action during Haig's period of command. Although identified by one of Haig's biographers as among the 'circle of simpering awestruck admirers' surrounding the commander-in-chief (de Groot, 220), Davidson was more than a mere cipher for his chief's views. He was not afraid to incur Haig's wrath, as when, during the preparations for the Anglo-French offensive of spring 1917, he reported his unfavourable impression of the military situation on the French front.

Like his fellow officers Davidson was learning his trade in the testing school of battle on the western front. While

R. Blake (1952) · J. H. Stogdon, ed., *The Harrow School register, 1845–1925*, 4th edn, 2 vols. (1925) · *CGPLA Eng. & Wales* (1955) **Archives** NL Scot., papers · PRO, corresp. and MSS, WO 158 | CAC Cam., corresp. with Sir Edward Spears | FILM IWM FVA, documentary footage **Likenesses** W. Stoneman, photograph, 1936, NPG [*see illus.*] **Wealth at death** £37,655 9*s*. 11*d*.: confirmation, 25 Feb 1955, *CCI*

Davidson, John Morrison (1843–1916), radical and journalist, was born in a roadside house in the parish of Old Deer, Aberdeenshire, the younger son of the unmarried Mary Warrender, farm labourer, and Thomas Davidson, farm labourer, of Hatton, Aberdeenshire. Thomas *Davidson (1840–1900) was his elder brother. He was sickly as a child and unable to walk to school until he was nine, when his education began at the parish school at Deer. He then went to the grammar school of Old Aberdeen. He won a Campbell bursary to Aberdeen University, at which he matriculated in 1860, attending the art class; he felt that he learned little, and he quarrelled with his professors. In 1863 he left the university without a degree and made an abortive attempt to join the Polish revolution. At about that time he married Rose Fowlie, a former schoolmate, with whom he had eleven children. After teaching in Glasgow and Edinburgh he read for the bar in Edinburgh; in 1874 he transferred to London and was called to the English bar from the Middle Temple on 17 November 1877. He had chambers at 6 Pump Court in the Middle Temple from 1878 to 1887, but then ceased to practise.

Davidson's real interest had always been in radical politics and journalism. In the 1860s he wrote for many Scottish newspapers, and was later the London editor of the *Edinburgh Daily Review*. He was an uncompromising republican and democrat, and was secretary of the Advanced Liberal Association in Edinburgh, seceding from it as an opponent of all religious teaching in schools. He was corresponding secretary of the Edinburgh Republican Club from 1870.

In London Davidson was correspondent for the *Bradford Observer* and *Leeds Mercury*, and wrote for many other papers, including *Reynolds News*. He met Henry George and quarrelled with him about usury. In 1885 he stood for election for Greenock, at very short notice, as the candidate of the Scottish Land Restoration League, receiving sixty-five votes. His journalism was amplified by many pamphlets and books, which show him as an energetic and individualistic socialist, but always writing within the British radical tradition and with a strong emphasis on the Norman yoke and Saxon freedoms and institutions. He took Gerrard Winstanley as his model, as evidenced by his *Concerning four precursors of Henry George and the single tax, as also the land gospel according to Winstanley the Digger* (1899). Other characteristic works, from a large output, are *The New Book of Kings* (1884), *Scotia rediviva: Home Rule for Scotland* (1891?), *The Annals of Toil* (4 pts, 1899) (dedicated to Michael Davitt and Prince Kropotkin), and *The Book of Lords* (1884), which reflect a Saxon anti-feudalism. Less polemical is *Eminent Radicals in and out of Parliament* (1879). The biography of him by Autolycus in Davidson's *Politics for the People* is probably, in fact, his autobiography. Davidson was brought up as a Presbyterian but became an Arian, sometimes preaching in Unitarian churches. His anti-clericalism is recorded in *That Great Lying Church of England* (1906), and his ethicalism in *The Son of Man: Standard-Bearer of Humanity* (1906). Davidson died at 56 Marmora Road, Peckham, London, on 18 December 1916, a largely forgotten figure of the British radical tradition.   H. C. G. MATTHEW

Sources Autolycus, 'Grand old man of Fleet Street', in J. M. Davidson, *Politics for the people* [1892] · *The Times* (20 Dec 1916) · Middle Temple, London · U. Aberdeen · d. cert.

Davidson, John Thain (1833–1904), minister of the Presbyterian Church of England, was born on 25 April 1833 at Broughty Ferry, near Dundee, one of the twin sons of David Davidson (*d*. 1843), parish minister of Broughty Ferry, and his wife, Mary, daughter of Dr Ireland of Leith. His grandfather, Dr David Davidson of Dundee, and his great-grandfather were also ministers of the Church of Scotland. John's father left the established church in 1843, and, after his death a few months later, his mother moved to Edinburgh, where many leaders of the Free Church visited their house. Davidson was educated at Edinburgh high school and at Edinburgh University, and studied for the ministry at the Free Church Theological College.

After a few months in charge of a mission station at Craigmill in Perthshire, and as a probationer in Free St George's, Montrose, Davidson was ordained on 19 February 1857 a minister of the Free Church at Maryton, near Montrose, and remained there until 1859, when he was inducted minister of the Presbyterian church at Salford. On 4 October 1859 he married Isabella, daughter of M. M'Callum of Glasgow. They had two sons and six daughters.

In 1862 Davidson moved to the Presbyterian church, Colebrooke Row, Islington, where he greatly increased the size of the congregation. He then turned his attention to non-churchgoers, and from 1868 held services in the Agricultural Hall every Sunday afternoon, for twenty-three years. Speakers included the earls of Shaftesbury, Aberdeen, and Kintore, the bishops of Ballarat and Bedford, Canon Fleming, the vicars of Islington, Holloway, and Clerkenwell, Dr Guthrie, and Dr Talmage; the meetings were soon attracting regular attendances of 4000. From 1878 he also delivered monthly sermons to young men in Islington, and published some of these in *Talks with Young Men* (1884), *Forewarned, Forearmed* (1885), *The City Youth* (1886), *Sure to Succeed* (1888), *A Good Start* (1890), and *Thoroughness* (1892).

In 1872 Davidson was elected moderator of the synod of the Presbyterian church of England, and was awarded a DD by Montgomery College, Alabama. After nearly thirty years in Islington, in 1891 he became minister of St Andrew's Presbyterian Church, Ealing. Davidson died at his home, 23 Park Hill, Ealing, on 7 November 1904, and was buried in the churchyard at Stoke Poges.

C. H. IRWIN, *rev.* ANNE PIMLOTT BAKER

Sources *John Thain Davidson: reminiscences by his daughter* (1906) · *British Weekly* (9 July 1891) · *British Weekly* (17 Sept 1891) · private information (1912) · *CGPLA Eng. & Wales* (1905)

Likenesses photograph, repro. in *John Thain Davidson*, facing p. 114

Wealth at death £5913 5s. 7d.: probate, 4 Feb 1905, *CGPLA Eng. & Wales*

Davidson, Katherine Helen (1845–1925), Church of Scotland deaconess, was born on 5 July 1845 at 237 Union Street, Aberdeen, one of the ten children of Patrick Davidson (1809–1881), advocate and professor of civil law at King's College, Aberdeen University, and his wife, Mary Anne Leslie (1817–1898), eldest daughter of William Leslie of Warthill, Rayne. As a young woman she went to Surrey and worked for four years under the auspices of the Prisongate Mission at the Princess Mary Village Homes, caring for prison inmates' children. From there she became a house deaconess at the Mildmay Centre in London. She then moved to Guernsey, where she spent several years as the head of an institution there caring for young women.

While Katherine Davidson worked at Mildmay she met Professor A. H. Charteris, who was so impressed by her that he immediately asked her to be one of his first deaconesses. She was later set apart as a deaconess at a special service at Old St Cuthbert's Church, Edinburgh, on 13 January 1889. It is clear that the example of Katherine Davidson led to a greater acceptance of women in public and official roles within the Church of Scotland.

Davidson's first assignment was as temporary head of a training centre for future deaconesses at 33 Mayfield Gardens, Edinburgh. Only six months later she was appointed the first deputy of the recently formed Women's Guild. She worked tirelessly and very effectively for the guild's future success. In just one year she visited 100 parishes by pony and cart. On her appointment the guild had some 2000 members, representing thirty-three branches. By the time of her death the guild had mushroomed into a society with 52,000 members and 879 branches. 'Her enthusiasm was so infectious', wrote a fellow guildswoman, 'that she everywhere started new branches of the Guild' (Thomson, 303).

Davidson had two particular interests. She was genuinely concerned for the spiritual and bodily welfare of the many thousands who travelled with the Scottish fishing fleets: she herself financed the building and equipping of a rest-house in Yarmouth for the workers. She also played a major part in the care and management of the Robertson Orphanage at Musselburgh.

In 1918 Davidson was severely injured in a street accident in Edinburgh. For many years she suffered greatly from the injuries she sustained, until she finally died on 12 May 1925 at her home, 14 Craiglockhart Terrace, Edinburgh. A large funeral was held at St Giles's Cathedral in Edinburgh, and the following day her body was returned to the north-east of Scotland to be buried in the old churchyard of Banchory.   MICHAEL D. McMULLEN

Sources D. P. Thomson, *Women of the Scottish church* (1975) · L. O. Macdonald, 'Davidson, Katherine Helen', *DSCHT* · M. Magnusson, *Out of silence: the Woman's Guild, 1887–1987* (1987) · A. Gordon, *The life of Archibald Hamilton Charteris* (1912) · Aberdeen RO · d. cert.

Wealth at death £4262 14s. 11d.: confirmation, 12 Aug 1925, *CCI*

Davidson, (James) Norman (1911–1972), biochemist, was born on 5 March 1911 in Edinburgh, the only child of James Davidson (1873–1956), then treasurer of the Carnegie Trust of Scotland, and his wife, Wilhelmina Ibberson (1874–1970), the sixth of seven children of the Revd James Foote, minister of Bath Street Congregational Church in Dunfermline. From 1919 to 1929 Davidson was educated at George Watson's Boys' College, Edinburgh, where he was dux gold medallist. He then entered Edinburgh University, where he combined the study of chemistry and medicine. He obtained a first-class honours degree in chemistry in 1934 and graduated MB ChB with honours in 1937.

On the completion of his medical course Davidson joined the laboratory of Otto Warburg in Berlin–Dahlem. In 1938, on his return from Germany, Davidson was appointed lecturer in biochemistry in the University of St Andrews. In the same year he married Morag, a fellow Edinburgh student, a chemist and bacteriologist, and daughter of Alexander Mathers McLeod, an Edinburgh lawyer whose family came from Skye. The couple later had two daughters, both of whom were prominent in the University of Glasgow: Rona, as professor of dermatology, and Ailsa, as senior lecturer in biochemistry.

Gaining his MD in 1939, Davidson became a lecturer in the University of Aberdeen in 1940. He gained his DSc in 1945 and went to London as a member of staff of the Medical Research Council: a year later in April 1946 he was appointed to the chair of biochemistry at St Thomas's Hospital medical school. In 1947 he accepted the Gardiner chair of physiological chemistry at Glasgow. Davidson had an intense loyalty to Scotland and he therefore felt compelled to accept the Glasgow post. He spent the rest of his life in Glasgow.

Davidson's early researches were on the metabolism of fructose, the purification and mode of action of uricase, and the intestinal absorption of monosaccharides, but his most important contribution to biochemistry was in the field of nucleic acids. At the time when Davidson started his work in this field it was known that there were two types of nucleic acid: deoxyribonucleic acid (DNA), which was then wrongly assumed to be found exclusively in animal tissues, and ribonucleic acid (RNA), which was considered to be characteristic of plant tissues. By applying quantitative and improved methods for the measurement and isolation of the two types of nucleic acid from a variety of biological material, Davidson and Charity Waymouth demonstrated that both types of nucleic acid occur in almost all types of living matter.

Davidson's work displayed considerable chemical rigour. His isolation and full chemical characterization of ribonucleic acid from mammalian liver was an important milestone in the development of modern nucleic acid research. With the aid of isotopic traces he demonstrated that DNA was metabolically stable, but that RNA turned over at an appreciable rate. He also showed that the nucleolus contained RNA and that cytoplasmic RNA was heterogeneous. In addition, Davidson carried out pioneering work in applying quantitative chemical methods for investigating changes which occur in cells grown in tissue culture. Davidson's book, *The Biochemistry of the Nucleic Acids* (1950), became a classic and was translated into many languages. He was also joint editor of the annual publication *Progress in Nucleic Acid Research*.

Davidson created one of the largest departments of biochemistry in the United Kingdom, and he was a powerful member of the court and senate of his university. He played an important part in the foundation of the International Union of Biochemistry and he was one of the two secretaries of the Royal Society of Edinburgh, becoming its vice-president in 1955–8 and president in 1958–9 and 1964–7. He became a fellow of the Royal Society in 1960 and was appointed CBE in 1967.

Davidson had two outstanding loyalties: one was to biochemistry and the other to Scotland. He was an active member of the Church of Scotland. His somewhat austere personality was largely due to intense shyness. He died on 11 September 1972 at Bearsden, Glasgow.

ALBERT NEUBERGER, *rev.*

Sources A. Neuberger, *Memoirs FRS*, 19 (1973), 281–303 · personal knowledge (1986) · *WWW*, 1971–80
Archives U. Glas., Archives and Business Records Centre, scientific papers · U. Glas., scientific papers | CUL, corresp. with J. S. Mitchell

Randall Thomas Davidson, Baron Davidson of Lambeth (1848–1930), by John Singer Sargent, 1910

Davidson, Randall Thomas, Baron Davidson of Lambeth (1848–1930), archbishop of Canterbury, was born at 15 Inverleith Place, Edinburgh, on 7 April 1848, of pure Scottish blood. He was the eldest son of Henry Davidson (1810–1889), timber merchant of Leith, and his wife, Henrietta (*d.* 1881), third daughter of John Swinton, formerly an army officer, who added the name of Campbell when he inherited estates at Kimmerghame, Berwickshire, from a maternal aunt. Henry's father, the Revd Thomas Randall, had changed his name to Davidson in 1794 as a condition of inheriting an estate at Muirhouse, near Edinburgh. Henry's father, grandfather, and great-grandfather were presbyterian ministers, the last being a chaplain to Queen Anne. Both Henry and his wife were devoutly religious, though this did not prevent Henry enjoying hunting and music, nor operating a modestly profitable business, which enabled him to leave £4145.

Education, ill health, marriage Henry had been educated at the high school in Edinburgh, and then the famous Edinburgh Academy, where a lifelong friendship had been forged with Archibald Campbell Tait, subsequently to be archbishop of Canterbury. It was the Tait, lowland Scots connection which was to be decisive for Henry's son. Randall Thomas Davidson was baptized at home on 18 May 1848 according to the presbyterian form. He was to be reminded of this in 1905 when Princess Victoria Eugenie's baptism at Balmoral was discounted by the Spanish Roman Catholic bishops. Young Randall enjoyed the lowland countryside, narrowly escaping drowning on one occasion. In 1862 he entered Harrow School, where he came under the influence of two Anglican clergy: Henry Montague Butler, and Brooke Foss Westcott, later to be bishop of Durham. He was confirmed into the Church of England at the age of fourteen by his father's old friend A. C. Tait, then bishop of London.

In the school holidays in 1866 Davidson narrowly escaped death while returning from an expedition to shoot rabbits. A friend accidentally pulled his trigger and blasted a hole the size of an orange in Davidson's lower back. A large portion of the pelvis and the muscles of his hips were damaged. For the rest of his life Davidson had to disguise his disabilities. The damage to the hip muscles meant that he was always liable to attacks of lumbago. More difficult to cope with was the need to wear a truss to hold a hernia on the right side. The rupture often came down when Davidson was preaching but he devised cunning coping strategies.

After school Davidson had a dismal three years at Trinity College, Oxford, where his poor physical condition culminated in a breakdown in 1871 in the middle of his final examinations. On the basis of the few papers he had done he was awarded a third class in law and modern history. Davidson had never been drawn to any other life work than the ordained ministry, and seems to have been totally unaffected by the intellectual and theological battles which were being passionately fought in Oxford. After more foreign travels he began his ministerial studies as one of the lodgers of Charles John Vaughan, master of the temple, who also directed his reading and criticized his sermons. Another breakdown in health led to a tour of Egypt and Palestine with three old Oxford friends, one of whom was Crauford Tait, the archbishop's son. Largely through Crauford's influence Davidson was accepted for ordination in the diocese of Canterbury, as curate of Dartford. The archbishop's only requirement seems to have been the removal of his heavy moustache, and he was ordained deacon in 1874 and priest in 1875. Davidson now aspired to succeed at the centre of the ecclesiastical and national life of England. The year after ordination he put his name down for the Athenaeum, and declined all offers of advancement which would take him away from the home counties. In 1877 he was invited, at Crauford's suggestion, to succeed him as private secretary and resident chaplain to the archbishop. The following year Crauford died and on 12 November Davidson married his sister, Edith Murdoch Tait (*b.* 1858), the nineteen-year-old second daughter of the archbishop. Mrs Davidson was a charming hostess and devoted clergy-wife. The marriage was described by his successor, Cosmo Gordon Lang, as a 'perfect union of mind and spirit'; they had no children. For the next four years Davidson occupied an increasingly influential role at Lambeth Palace where the archbishop, reeling under the double blow of the deaths of both son and wife in six months, came to rely heavily on his judgement of men and situations. Tait now found the palace unbearably claustrophobic and took to drafting letters with his secretary as he paced round the gravel paths of Lambeth, once insisting on assessing diocesan statistics while they rode together on horseback along the Embankment on a breezy day. Gradually Davidson found himself suggesting courses of action and forms of words which he knew from experience reflected the mind of the archbishop, who came to place total confidence in his son-in-law. It was in this position that Davidson largely took over the correspondence generated by the ritualism controversy in 1881, and played a significant role in torpedoing Anglican overtures to the Salvation Army in 1882, which he thought concentrated too much power in the office of the general. When Tait died in 1882 it was to Davidson that Queen Victoria turned for an account of the deathbed scene. An invitation to Windsor followed; the queen was much impressed by the young Scot, confiding in her journal the belief that 'Mr. Davidson is a man who may be of great use to me' (Barker, 397). The 34-year-old chaplain quickly became the trusted confidant of the 63-year-old queen.

Adviser to the archbishop and the queen Soon Davidson was steering the queen into the choice of Edward White Benson, bishop of Truro, as new archbishop, who, recognizing Davidson's competence and sound judgement of people, retained him as chaplain until he was in 1883, at the queen's request, appointed dean of Windsor, and her domestic chaplain. Queen Victoria soon turned to him for spiritual consolation, beginning in 1884 when her youngest son, Leopold, duke of Albany, died. Davidson, though attentive, was more than a tame chaplain–courtier. He incurred the royal wrath in the same year when he counselled the queen against the publication of further *Leaves from a Highland Diary*, which would have contained revelations about her servant John Brown that were open to satire. That she trusted his judgement can be seen from her unfailing consultation with him between 1883 and 1901

about senior ecclesiastical appointments. Until Benson's death in 1896 Davidson had a unique influence in shaping the attitudes and decisions of both sovereign and primate. Benson wrote to him almost every day, and particularly depended on his advice in 1888–90 during the trial of Edward King, high-church bishop of Lincoln, for alleged ritual illegalities. King was largely exonerated: Davidson's role was to shape church and public opinion through writing leading articles for *The Times*, and in liaising with Lord Halifax, the Anglo-Catholic lay leader.

Davidson's grasp of Anglican affairs and key personalities was consolidated by his work as assistant secretary of the Lambeth conference of 1881, attended by 100 bishops from the Anglican dioceses of the British empire, United States, and elsewhere. His *Life of Archbishop Tait* (1891), written with William Benham, showed a mastery of recent developments in the Church of England and a sure judgement in their interpretation.

Bishop of Rochester, then Winchester In 1891 the queen reluctantly consented to Davidson's appointment to the bishopric of Rochester, which then included south London. The muck-raking *Pall Mall Gazette* described her choice as 'a royal job'. About ten days after his consecration Davidson vomited blood and was confined to his house in Kennington for six months. He suffered three more spells of illness during his four years in south London. In 1893 he attended a meeting of leaders from all religious traditions called by the editor of the *Daily Chronicle* to discuss the coal strike, in which he urged the importance of a living wage. In 1894–5 he largely drafted Archbishop Benson's rejection of the project hatched by Lord Halifax and the Abbé Portal to ask the pope to recognize the validity of Anglican orders.

In 1895 Davidson accepted translation to the diocese of Winchester, which involved less evening work, as well as renewing his access to the queen, who spent much time, and ultimately died, at Osborne House on the Isle of Wight. The country air restored his health. He was almost immediately drawn into controversy with Robert William Radcliffe Dolling, a fervent Anglo-Catholic priest in charge of Winchester College's mission at Landport. Dolling had a long history of provoking bishops, which came to a head with the dedication of the large, new St Agatha's church. Davidson, whose appointment had been publicly criticized by Dolling because of his health problems, discovered only three days before the opening that it contained a third altar to be used for masses for the dead. Davidson immediately saw Dolling and tried to reach a compromise which would bring his practices within Anglican rules. But compromise was impossible and Dolling resigned immediately and left the diocese. His supporters castigated Davidson, and the episode led one high-church journalist to conclude that it left its mark in forming his determination not to be the archbishop who drove the high-church party out of the Church of England.

When Archbishop Benson died in 1896 Davidson lost his influence at Lambeth Palace and had to endure the sarcasm of the new archbishop, Frederick Temple, who suspected him of having wanted the appointment himself.

The queen vetoed the offer of the bishopric of London in 1897, on the grounds that his health would not stand it, and when Lord Salisbury offered it again in 1901, Davidson himself refused for the same reason. He now divided his time between the diocese, the House of Lords where he was a frequent speaker (especially on licensing and education), and national church policy. Between 1898 and 1901 Davidson was actively involved in seeking a way through the ritual controversy and corresponded at length with Sir William Harcourt, the elderly former Liberal politician, who was an Erastian in church matters and resented any deviations from the Book of Common Prayer. (Harcourt lived at Malwood which was in the Winchester diocese.) Davidson devoted his episcopal charge of 1899 to a comprehensive treatment of the whole subject. His grasp of the issues led in 1901 to his first meeting with the prime minister, A. J. Balfour, who recorded that 'the Bishop has the art of stating with great clearness and sympathy the gist of opinions from which he differs' (Bell, 3rd edn, 349). His advice on public primary education was sought and valued by Balfour in framing the Education Act of 1902. Once the bill had been introduced Davidson was on hand to suggest tactics as well as to defend principles. To counter the vehement nonconformist opposition, led by the Baptist minister Dr John Clifford, he suggested to Balfour 'that it would be well to let Clifford publish his letters as a pamphlet and thus commit himself more deliberately to them before any attempt is made to show their falsity' (Bell, 3rd edn, 377). When Temple died Balfour nominated Davidson as his successor and he was enthroned at Canterbury on 12 February 1903.

Archbishop of Canterbury Davidson saw his task as holding the Church of England together, maintaining its historic position in the national life, and providing a Christian witness in moral, social, and political matters. Through his membership of the House of Lords, and of Grillions and 'the Club', Davidson gave time to making friendships with men of weight. He particularly cultivated the friendship of leading politicians with a Scottish background: Lord Rosebery, Sir Henry Campbell-Bannerman, and A. J. Balfour. His constant presence in the Lords, at official dinners, and in small gatherings of the governing élite was a continuation of the policy of Archbishop Tait.

Within a month of his appointment Davidson was challenged by 100 Unionist members of parliament to take firm action against clergy who were ignoring the law and introducing Roman Catholic ceremonial practices. Davidson's reply was resolute. The actual number of flagrant lawbreakers was, he thought, small, but for them 'the sands [of time] have run out' (Bell, 3rd edn, 399). Feeling in the Commons was such that Balfour felt he would be obliged to appoint a select committee of the House of Commons. Davidson feared that such a step would infuriate even moderate high-churchmen by asserting the authority of the Commons over the church. Only someone steeped in parliamentary procedures would have realized the advantage of persuading Balfour instead to

appoint a royal commission on ecclesiastical discipline, which met from 1904 to 1906. After amassing evidence the commissioners were unanimous in concluding that certain specific illegalities should be made to cease, but also that the law of public worship was 'too narrow for the religious life of the present generation' (*Report of the Royal Commission on Ecclesiastical Discipline*, 1906, 75–6). The commission thus opened the door for the revision of the prayer book which was to cause such controversy in 1927 and 1928.

In his first public utterances as archbishop on matters of national controversy Davidson was criticized by nonconformists and Liberals for appearing to provide Christian underpinning for his tory patron. In February 1904 he showed concern over the compounds set up in the Transvaal in which imported Chinese indentured labour was to be confined. But against opposition cries of 'Chinese slavery' Davidson seemed to moderate his concerns when in a later speech he described imported labour as a 'regrettable necessity'. This last phrase, plucked from its context, was used in speeches and newspaper cartoons to vilify the archbishop. In June 1905 further criticism came when Davidson, who disliked public demonstrations, refused to receive a delegation of unemployed working men who had marched to London from Leicester led by a Christian socialist clergyman, Lewis Donaldson. Even dutiful Anglican clergy bridled in the spring of 1906 when it was announced that the king's niece, Princess Victoria Eugenie, was to marry King Alfonso X of Spain. The public silence of the archbishop at the conversion of the eighteen-year-old granddaughter of Queen Victoria to the Roman Catholic faith, in order to marry into what to British popular protestant prejudice seemed a degenerate Spanish Catholic court, gave the impression of lamentable weakness. In fact Davidson was privately outraged by the insistence of the Spanish Catholic hierarchy that the princess should not only convert but also receive Catholic baptism. He was indefatigable in his advice to the royal family but unwilling publicly to oppose the evident wish of the young princess.

In 1907 Davidson maintained the traditional Anglican opposition to the Deceased Wife's Sister Marriage Bill. When it was carried he noted that for:

the first time in the history of the Church of England, has the law of the State been brought on one specific point into direct open, overt contrast with, and contradiction of, the specific and divine law laid down in the authoritative regulations of the national church.   (Bell, 3rd edn, 552)

His advice to clergy was that such marriages should not be held in Anglican churches, but that those in such marriages should not, on that ground, be refused holy communion, or otherwise deprived of the church's ministrations.

Davidson's leadership was severely tested by the new Liberal government's attempts to pass an education bill which would remove those features of the 1902 act considered unjust by nonconformists. The bill introduced by Augustine Birrell in 1906 seemed to Davidson to violate the deep-seated Anglican conviction that the Church of England had a God-given duty to provide a national system of church schools for the nation. Although unwell with gastric influenza he left his bed to attend three private meetings with Conservative leaders at Lord Lansdowne's house to consider tactics. Balfour wanted the peers to insert amendments which would be unacceptable to the Liberal majority in the Commons, but Davidson wrote from his bed to urge caution and compromise. Rumours that the archbishop was willing to make concessions enraged the National Society, the organization that provided and controlled Church of England schools. In December, Davidson voted with the Conservative peers to defeat the bill, but during the following year he worked hard for a settlement with Walter Runciman, who had taken over the government's attempts to get an agreed solution through parliament. This time Davidson could not deliver the agreement of his church. Though supported by the bishops, the Representative Church Council voted overwhelmingly to reject the measure, and it was abandoned by the government.

Davidson presided at the Lambeth conference of 242 Anglican bishops in 1908, and the unofficial Pan-Anglican Congress which immediately preceded it. Throughout the summer groups of overseas bishops and their wives were invited by the archbishop and Mrs Davidson to spend two nights at Lambeth Palace, where networks were forged and local knowledge transmitted. It was to Davidson at Lambeth that Anglican bishops invariably turned when confronted by difficulties. He had been the first archbishop of Canterbury to cross the Atlantic and pay an official visit to the United States of America and Canada in 1904.

In 1910 Davidson, after much hesitation, was persuaded to attend the World Missionary Conference at Edinburgh under the chairmanship of the American Methodist layman Dr John R. Mott. Though called to consider missionary difficulties, the conference has come to be regarded as the birthplace of the modern ecumenical movement. Mott had been determined that it should be as carefully balanced and, as far as possible, genuinely representative of all the Christian bodies in the world. The archbishop of Canterbury was an obvious adornment for such a gathering, but Mott knew that Davidson's natural caution was likely to prevent his acceptance of an invitation. Therefore Mott first secured the attendance of two high-church bishops, Gore and Talbot, whose judgement was known to be respected by Davidson. Once assured that he would be joining such company he agreed to attend, and was ultimately inspired by the occasion into delivering an uncharacteristically prophetic speech.

The debates over Lloyd George's 'people's budget' and the Parliament Act exposed Davidson to more charges of political partisanship. When the Finance Bill was rejected by the House of Lords in November 1909 Davidson and most of the bishops abstained, thereby incurring the odium of supporters of both government and opposition. In that debate he expressed the belief that the bishops could, and should, speak with authority on religious, educational, social, and moral questions, but were wise to avoid more overtly party political issues. However the new archbishop of York, Cosmo Lang, and Bishop Gore had supported the government, and Bishop Browne of Bristol had voted with the Unionists. After the two general elections in 1910 Davidson played an important part in the consultations in August 1911 preceding the final division on the Parliament Bill, limiting the powers of the House of Lords. When it was announced that the new king George V had agreed to the creation of sufficient peers to secure the passing of the bill Davidson, after taking the advice of Sir William Anson, led most of the bishops in support of the bill, primarily to prevent the creation of 500 new Liberal peers, which might have resulted in a weakening of the prestige of the House of Lords as a platform for episcopal pronouncements. 'Beaten by the bishops and the rats' was Unionist MP George Wyndham's comment (*Life and Letters of George Wyndham*, ed. MacKarl and Wyndham, 1925, 2.699).

In the years before the First World War, Davidson had taken a restrained interest in the efforts of the Anglo-German friendship movement. He was, not surprisingly, jittery about the number of Lutheran pastors making a visit to London in 1908, which he feared might cause a high-church commotion if they were admitted to communion at Anglican altars. In 1909 he urged Bishop Boyd Carpenter to join the British delegation to Berlin because 'it would be disastrous were it to appear as if the Nonconformists were anxious for friendliness with Germany, while we Churchmen were only anxious to build more Dreadnoughts' (Bell, 3rd edn, 592). Another issue of the day was the disestablishment of the church in Wales, which was enacted in 1914, and operative from 1920. Davidson firmly resisted this both in and out of parliament.

Intercommunion between Anglicans and Christians belonging to other denominations became a contentious issue early in the twentieth century. The beginnings of the ecumenical movement both in Britain and overseas at a time when the Anglo-Catholic tradition was gaining in influence in the Church of England opened new possibilities for doctrinal conflict. Davidson's gifts for conciliation were stretched to the limit in the ecclesiastical implosions provoked by the Kikuyu controversy of 1913–14. Two sets of questions about Christian belief and church order came together. Increasing scepticism about the plausibility of biblical miracles found some support in new developments in biblical criticism. This seemed to have implications for the foundations of Christian belief. Bishop Charles Gore of Oxford wanted the whole matter to be thrashed out in the public arena of the convocation of Canterbury, and he sought the repudiation of books by Anglican clergymen which denied or cast doubt on the virgin birth and physical resurrection of Jesus. The archbishop knew that biblical scholarship in the universities could not be restricted, and that attempts to pre-empt academic conclusions would show the church up as myopic, pedestrian, mindlessly dogmatic, and anti-intellectual. He took counsel with Bishop F. H. Chase of Ely and Bishop E. S. Talbot, who both supported the safer course of a discussion at a private meeting of bishops. Gore was dissatisfied with the refusal of the bishops to take his view, and in 1913 alarmed Davidson by talking of resignation.

A year later this theological debate was absorbed into a wider church conflagration. Ignited by a small gathering of missionaries from various denominations at Kikuyu in east Africa to plan a more effective deployment of missionary forces, and concluding with a service of holy communion, conducted by the bishop of Mombasa, the event came to be invested with symbolic significance by all discontented with the present state of the Church of England. The bishop of Zanzibar, Frank Weston, emerged as champion of Anglo-Catholic hardliners. He confronted the archbishop with a fierce denunciation of the participation of the bishops of Mombasa and Uganda in a communion service with free churchmen, raising the huge question of what the Church of England really stood for. Was it primarily a national church, offering its ministry to all the peoples of the British empire, or was it a eucharistic community, presided over by episcopally ordained priests and restricted exclusively to those baptized and confirmed?

Davidson had already set out his position in February 1912 when he delivered a visitation charge, which was published under the title of *The Character and Call of the Church of England*. Chapter 3 answered those who asked, 'What does our Church stand for?' In reply, Davidson emphasized 'the historical continuity of the Church's corporate and organic life' which he interpreted as 'a sacramental, governmental, ministerial, and even ritual system which, with adaptation to local requirements has come down to us from Apostolic days'. The archbishop went on to legitimize New Testament scholarship by asserting that 'we stand for the unfettered study of Holy Scripture, for the liberty of private judgement'.

The first stage of what became an increasingly acrimonious controversy revealed the immense gap between the clerical and lay mind and showed that the sacerdotal concept of ministry which had been gaining ground among the clergy was alien to the thinking of the laity. Anglo-Catholic realization of the situation produced a strategic switch from questions of church order to doctrine. In insisting on the historicity of the virgin birth and the physical resurrection of Jesus, high-churchmen and evangelicals could stand together, and many followed Bishop Gore in wanting to require Anglican clergymen to affirm unequivocally the historical statements in the creed about the virgin birth and physical resurrection of Jesus. But Davidson persuaded convocation in April 1914 instead to support a motion which declared only that 'the denial of any of the historical facts stated in the Creeds goes beyond the limits of legitimate interpretation'. This resolution was amplified a few months later when Davidson expressed the opinion that the most recent speculations of the distinguished Oxford theologian William Sanday

did not fall outside those limits. Three years later Davidson was forced to reconsider those limits by the indignation aroused by the appointment of Hensley Henson to the bishopric of Hereford.

The church and the First World War The outbreak of war with Germany in 1914 swept Kikuyu from the public mind. Davidson, who valued his contacts with German theologians such as the Berlin professor Adolf von Harnack and had always considered war between the two great protestant powers 'unthinkable', found it difficult at first wholly to remain detached from the unbalanced emotions of war. When the spy mania was at its height even the archbishop felt it his duty to pass on to the Metropolitan Police his suspicions that a tobacconist with a shop near Woolwich might be a German spy. Anxiety about the outcome of military engagements led in 1914 to hourly telephone calls from Mary Benson's house in Sussex, where illness turned a short break into a three-week stay. In 1915 Lord Bryce's report apparently authenticating German war crimes led Davidson to claim that 'we are at this moment fighting against what is veritably the work of the Devil'. But while he shared the nation's patriotic concerns and did not hesitate to take the lead, when requested by the government, in the production of a response by British religious leaders to the manifesto of the German church leaders in support of the war, Davidson generally rose above the narrow chauvinism of many of his clerical colleagues. He rebuked a clergyman who insulted a royal princess for her German family ties, and held out against conscripting the clergy for combatant service until the final manpower shortage of 1918. He then told the government that the Church of England no longer opposed clerical conscription, but the clause was dropped following the refusal of the Irish Catholic hierarchy to allow their clergy (unlike priests in France) to become soldiers. Throughout the war years Davidson believed that it was the duty of the church to steady the nation and prevent any sudden swings of national mood or moral lurches. In July 1915 he set up a small group to assess the spiritual needs of the nation and suggest an appropriate way forward. This led to the National Mission of Repentance and Hope in 1916, but uncertainty about its aims and objectives and the subdued public mind produced a disappointing response. Davidson was anxious to prevent the deterioration of moral standards. He questioned the wisdom of the amount of money being given in separation allowances to soldiers' wives, and succeeded in preventing unmarried partners receiving the same amount as of right. In this matter Lloyd George considered his attitude 'a piece of blatant hypocrisy', though he was glad to have the archbishop's support for the even more hypocritical 'king's pledge' to abstain from alcohol for the duration of the war. In 1918 Davidson raised with the War Office and in the House of Lords the toleration of brothels close to army camps.

Davidson was to protest every year of the war 'quietly but firmly' (his chaplain George Bell's words) against the British government's methods of warfare. In February 1915 Asquith was, according to Davidson, 'taken aback by the bluntness' of his criticism, in a conversation, of the false information put out to hide British military reverses. In May 1915 the use of poisoned gas was forthrightly condemned by the archbishop in a private letter to Asquith. The bombing of Freiburg in April 1917 in retaliation for the sinking of two hospital ships appalled tender consciences. Louise Creighton, a bishop's widow, and formidable leader of churchwomen, implored Davidson 'in the name of the Church' to denounce 'these horrible and futile reprisals against Germany'. But the archbishop's instinctive reaction was to shrink from publicly embarrassing the wartime government. 'It often happens that private pressure is more useful, although it does not appease our public sympathisers who prefer to say that we are doing nothing', he replied to her. 'I have been familiar with that difficulty through all my public life.' Eventually he put down a question in the Lords. 'One must be very considerate for the Government,' he wrote, 'remembering that they have to carry with them the Allies as well as to decide for themselves. Heroics on such a question, though very tempting, are not very practicable and not very fair to the Government.' But even to question the policy of reprisals was interpreted as hampering the war effort, and the duke of Argyll was given much newspaper coverage for his injunction to the bishops to 'stick to their belfries' (Bell, 3rd edn, 832). Two months later Davidson responded to the ferocious public mood created by the bombing of London by a public exchange of letters with his doctor, Sir Thomas Barlow. The archbishop reminded him of a resolution earlier passed by the bishops objecting to 'a policy of reprisal which has, as a deliberate object, the killing and wounding of non-combatants' (Bell, 3rd edn, 833). By October Davidson could write: 'I am regarded apparently as the representative mouthpiece of those who object to reprisals undertaken with the deliberate object of injuring non-combatants' (ibid., 837). The hate mail flooded into Lambeth Palace.

The First World War exacerbated tensions within the church, particularly between Anglo-Catholics and liberal thinkers. The determination of Lloyd George in 1917 to nominate Dean Hensley Henson to the see of Hereford was against Davidson's advice and caused an angry agitation. Henson had a reputation as a provocative preacher. He had defended scholars such as J. M. Thompson, B. H. Streeter, and William Sanday, who had questioned the literal interpretation of the virgin birth and resurrection. Bishop Charles Gore called on the bishops to refuse to join in Henson's consecration, and yet again threatened his resignation. All the alarm bells in Davidson's mind were set ringing. He feared that this might be the moment of disruption which he had spent his life trying to avoid. He went behind the smears of the fearful and turned to Henson's published writings, which he found far less heterodox than expected. He then composed a short statement to reassure Gore, which Henson accepted but did not sign. An exchange of letters was then made public in which Henson confirmed that he could join wholeheartedly in the saying of the creed, and had no wish to alter it. Henson later considered that Davidson had been panicked by a

report from his secretary that men on the London underground had been overheard making ribald remarks about 'some kind of an atheist' being made a bishop. He considered that excessive moral pressure had been applied by Davidson to get him to sign, which he had done with much reluctance, and only with the addition of a statement that he stood by his published work. Gore now withdrew his protest and Henson became an outstanding bishop.

The war had shown up the gap between church and nation, and gave rise to demands for a more effective and imaginative effort for religious renewal. In 1916 Dick Sheppard gathered together a group of young enthusiasts under the banner of 'Life and liberty' with William Temple at their head. The archbishop was wary of impetuous raw enthusiasm and in its early days distanced himself. Private correspondence with Temple reassured him, and with masterly skill Davidson arranged a partnership between the new movement and the highly respectable but half-baked Church Self-Government Association set up following a report prepared for the archbishops by a committee chaired by the earl of Selborne. By this means energies were diverted into campaigning for the establishment of a church assembly with limited devolved powers. Through undertaking to pilot the measure through parliament Davidson kept ultimate control of the movement and its outcome, which though disappointing to Sheppard, brought into being bureaucratic structures which took further the archbishop's goals for the more effective management of the church.

Post war: the general strike, prayer book controversy In 1920 Davidson presided again over the Lambeth conference which made an 'Appeal to All Christian People' and in the mood of post-war optimism invited dialogue between Christians of different traditions. As chief pastor of the nation which had won the war he had tremendous international prestige, which was recognized by his unopposed election as president of the World Alliance for the Promotion of International Friendship through the Churches. Church leaders in nations which had not done well out of war now looked to Davidson as a kind of protestant pope, who was thought to have significant influence on the British government. Appeals for support came from Christian minorities in eastern Europe, the Near East, and from the Orthodox in Soviet Russia. In 1922 the Greek Orthodox ecumenical patriarch of Constantinople, Melitios Metaxarchis, recognized Anglican orders, cynics said as part of a desperate bid to save St Sophia from the Turks. Anglo-Catholics, encouraged by their growing strength at home, expanded conversations between Viscount Halifax and the French Abbé Portal into an unofficial exchange of views between Anglican and Roman Catholic theologians led by the Belgian Cardinal Mercier at Malines. Archbishop Davidson agreed to take note of the conversations, after learning that Pope Pius XI was already doing so.

In 1923 Davidson thought seriously about resigning, because he did not feel comfortable 'with the modern social interpretation of Christianity'. His offers to mediate in strikes on the railways in 1919 and the coalmines in 1921 had not been taken up. His immediate reaction to the general strike in 1926 was to follow Asquith's denunciation in the Lords, but to add that every effort should still be made to reach a settlement. This left open the possibility of conciliation, and the archbishop was besieged by concerned individuals as disparate as R. H. Tawney and Lord Londonderry, who saw him as possibly the last hope in breaking the deadlock. Prodded by Henry Carter, a Wesleyan leader, and Prebendary P. T. R. Kirk of the Industrial Christian Fellowship, Davidson worked with them and others on 6 May to produce an appeal for the resumption of negotiations, involving 'simultaneously and concurrently' the cancellation of the strike; the government subsidy of the coal industry to be continued temporarily; the cancellation of the wage reductions. That afternoon Davidson had secured the agreement of Ramsay MacDonald for the Labour Party but the prime minister, Stanley Baldwin, insisted that the strike must be called off before any talks could begin. Davidson's lame response was that he could not make any alterations without the approval of the parties who had agreed the statement, and that they could not be contacted in time. The BBC, on the advice of J. C. C. Davidson, deputy civil commissioner, refused to allow the archbishop to make a broadcast. 'This was the low-water mark of the power and influence of the BBC,' commented its historian, Asa Briggs. The archbishop was criticized by those who feared appearing to give in to the unions, but he was cheered in the streets, and in many places workers marched to church for services of thanksgiving. In fact the appeal was important in overcoming the long-standing suspicion among many trades unionists that the Church of England was part of the establishment, but Davidson preferred to play down its significance: 'I think myself that the direct importance of the Appeal to which I gave expression has been somewhat exaggerated but its indirect importance has evidently been very great'. A part echo of this episode can be seen in the actions of Davidson's old schoolmaster, B. F. Westcott, who in 1893, as their bishop, had given the Durham miners the opportunity to return to work with dignity.

Davidson's final years as archbishop were preoccupied with the unfinished business of the royal commission of 1904. Letters of business had been issued to the convocations in 1906 requiring them to report on the desirability of changes in the law relating to the conduct of worship. These proposals were brought before the crown and the newly created church assembly in 1920. Immense interest was generated by the variety of proposals put forward for consideration. In 1925 Davidson reported that he had received 800 memorials on the subject. In June 1927 the church assembly voted to authorize the permissive use of a revised prayer book, alongside the prayer book of 1662. Controversy centred on the reserved sacrament, which been introduced into many parishes during the war, and on the alternative order for holy communion. Critics of the revision were not convinced by Davidson's judgement that the changes were only differences of emphasis and not of doctrine. Nor did he reassure those feared that the revisions would not be enforced by the bishops as the only permissible alterations. On 15 December 1927 the House of Commons, swayed by the cry of 'No Popery', rejected the measure by thirty-three votes. Davidson commented that the arguments against were 'of the sort which are to be found in *Barnaby Rudge*' (Bell, 3rd edn, 1346).

The archbishop and bishops decided to reintroduce the measure with minor modifications to meet protestant objections. Reservation was now rigorously limited to times and places of special need, but the new measure carried even less support in both church and Commons, and on 14 June 1928 was once again defeated.

Retirement Davidson resigned on 12 November 1928, his golden wedding anniversary, and two days later he was created Baron Davidson of Lambeth. His resignation was not a consequence of the defeat of his policy on the prayer book, to which he had not been vitally committed, but to enable his successor to prepare for the Lambeth conference of 1930. He died at his home, 10 Cheyne Walk, Chelsea, London, on 25 May 1930, and was buried on 30 May in the cloister of Canterbury Cathedral.

As archbishop of Canterbury for longer than anyone since the Reformation, Randall Davidson presided over the denominationalization of the Church of England. Dependent for his own advancement on the patronage of royalty and family friends, he pushed forward the professionalization of the clergy and transformed Lambeth Palace and Church House into the bureaucratic centres of a world communion. Archbishop William Temple, who regarded himself as a surrogate son, formed the view that he was 'not in the least mystical' and was unlikely ever to have spent much time in private prayer, but he was regular, direct, and sincere in his religious observances. Temple also commented that Davidson's 'power of work was astonishing'. Information was processed by him at amazing speed, and filed in the memory for recall at will. Temple always remembered watching him work through the report of a royal commission for a Lords debate. 'He turned over the pages with a steady, slow swing, giving to each about the time required for reading aloud two sentences of average length.'

Davidson's achievement was to maintain the comprehensiveness of the Church of England and to ensure liberty of thought. He maintained a Christian vision in British society at a time when international and class conflict could have obliterated institutional religion. Yet in 1927, the year after his intervention in the general strike, the figures for Easter communion were higher than they have ever been, before or since. Before the First World War, Davidson was regularly invited to comment on national political matters by national leaders, but afterwards ecclesiastical business left little time, and the rise of the Labour Party gave him fewer opportunities. Davidson's great skill was as a chairman, where he usually managed to secure unanimity. He was a naturally cautious man, inclined to worry; it was once said of him that 'he saw the shadows of tigers behind all the bushes in the jungle'. Again it was said that he elevated expediency into a principle. For nearly fifty years he exercised more influence in Anglican affairs than anyone else.

STUART MEWS

Sources G. K. A. Bell, *Randall Davidson, archbishop of Canterbury*, 2 vols. (1935); 3rd edn (1952) · M. Barker, ed., 'Randall Davidson: a partial retrospective', *From Cranmer to Davidson: a Church of England miscellany*, ed. S. Taylor (1999) · R. T. Davidson and W. Benham, *Life of Archbishop Tait*, 2 vols. (1935) · *DNB* · A. C. Benson, *The life of Edward White Benson*, 2 vols. (1900) · *The letters of Queen Victoria*, ed. G. E. Buckle, 3 vols., 3rd ser. (1930-32) · E. G. Sandford, ed., *Memoirs of Archbishop Temple, by seven friends*, 2 vols. (1906) · P. Adam, *The ancestry of Randall Thomas Davidson* (1903) · H. H. Montgomery, *Church Quarterly Review*, 111 (1931), 1-14 · I. H. F. Peile, 'Three great churchmen', *Church Quarterly Review*, 121 (1936), 282-8 · R. Davidson, 'Some Canterbury reminiscences', *Canterbury Cathedral Chronicle*, 17 (1934), 11-19

Archives LPL, corresp. and papers · LPL, travel journal · NL Scot., letters · St George's Chapel, Windsor, corresp. and papers as dean of Windsor · Westminster Abbey, London, corresp. and papers relating to Westminster Abbey sacristy | BL, corresp. with Arthur James Balfour, Add. MS 49788 · BL, corresp. with Sir Henry Campbell-Bannerman, Add. MSS 41222-41242 · BL, letters to W. E. Gladstone, Add. MSS 44478-44519, *passim* · BL, corresp. with Macmillan & Co., Add. MS 55110 · BL, letters to Albert Mansbridge, Add. MS 65254 · BLPES, corresp. with E. D. Morel · Bodl. Oxf., corresp. with Herbert Asquith · Bodl. Oxf., letters to Bickersteth family · Bodl. Oxf., corresp. with Sir William Harcourt and Lewis Harcourt · Bodl. Oxf., letters to Sir James Marchant · Bodl. Oxf., corresp. with second earl of Selborne and third earl of Selborne · Borth. Inst., corresp. with Walter Frere · Borth. Inst., corresp. with Lord Halifax · CAC Cam., corresp. with Alfred Lyttelton · Derbys. RO, letters to W. H. Arkwright · LPL, corresp. with Edward Benson · LPL, corresp. with George Blyth · LPL, corresp. with John Douglas · LPL, corresp. with Arthur Cayley Headlam · LPL, corresp. with Athelstan Riley · LPL, corresp. with Joseph Robinson · LPL, letters to H. R. L. Sheppard · LPL, letters to Blanche Sitwell [copies] · LPL, corresp. and papers incl. some relating to biography of A. C. Tait · LPL, corresp. with Tissington Tatlow · LPL, corresp. with Frederick Anthony White · NA Scot., corresp. with Arthur Balfour · NL Scot., letters to Sir Charles Dalrymple · NL Scot., letters to Lord Haldane · NL Scot., corresp. mainly with Lord Rosebery · U. Newcastle, corresp. with Walter Runciman · Wellcome L., corresp. of Davidson and his wife with Barlow family · Westminster Abbey, letters to Joseph Robinson | FILM BFI NFTVA, news footage

Likenesses L. Graham Smith, watercolour drawing, 1893, Scot. NPG · J. H. F. Bacon, oils, 1903, NPG · H. G. Riviere, oils, 1905, Trinity College, Oxford · J. S. Sargent, oils, 1910, LPL [*see illus.*] · Spy [L. Ward], caricature, watercolour study, 1910, NPG · W. Stoneman, photograph, before 1917, NPG · engraving, 1919 (after F. Dicksee), NPG · P. A. de Laszlo, oils, 1926, Church House, Westminster · N. Trent, bronze bust, 1927, Harrow School, Middlesex · C. Thomas, effigy, 1934, Canterbury Cathedral · O. Edis, two photographs, NPG · F. C. Gould, cartoon, sketch, NPG · S. P. Hall, group portrait, watercolour (*The bench of bishops, 1902*), NPG · Le Marco, bronze bust, LPL · C. B. Leighton, engraving, NPG · J. Russell & Sons, chromolithograph caricature, NPG; repro. in *VF* (19 Dec 1901) · N. P. Zarokilli, etching, BM · etching, BM · two photographs, NPG

Wealth at death £34,946 6s. 5d.: probate, 22 July 1930, *CGPLA Eng. & Wales*

Davidson, Samuel (1806?–1898), biblical scholar, was the son of Abraham Davidson, and Margaret-Measha. He was born at Kellswater, near Ballymena, co. Antrim, Ireland, probably in September 1806, but possibly in the following year. His parents were of Scottish descent and Presbyterians by religion. He attended first the village school and then a school at Ballymena until 1824, when he became a student of the Belfast Academical Institution, with a view to becoming a Presbyterian minister. His college course was distinguished with first prizes in Hebrew and theology, but interrupted by teaching at Londonderry and Liverpool and was therefore not completed until 1832. In November 1833 he was licensed to preach by the Ballymena presbytery, then in 1835 the General Synod of Ulster offered Davidson the newly created chair of biblical criticism at the Belfast Academical Institution.

On 21 September 1836 Davidson married Anne Jane Kirkpatrick of Belfast. They had a daughter and four sons. In 1838 Davidson received from Marischal College, Aberdeen, the degree of LLD. His first book, *Lectures on Biblical Criticism* appeared in 1839. He resigned from his professorship in 1841, having moved from the Presbyterian to the Congregationalist viewpoint. He accepted in 1842 the chair of biblical literature, oriental languages, and church history at the newly founded Lancashire Independent college in Manchester.

Before he left Ireland Davidson finished his monumental work *Sacred Hermeneutics Developed and Applied* (1843), in which an extensive knowledge of German systems of thought was revealed. In the summer of 1844 he made the first of a series of visits to Germany, beginning many friendships that lasted all his life. His knowledge of German biblical scholarship was unrivalled during this period. Through the recommendation of F. A. G. Tholuck and H. Hupfield he received an honorary DTheol from the University of Halle in 1848.

In 1848 Davidson published the first volume of his *Introduction to the New Testament* (the second volume appeared in 1849 and the third in 1851). He also rewrote his first work and republished it in two volumes in 1852 as *A Treatise on Biblical Criticism, Exhibiting a Systematic View of that Subject*. In 1855 he published *The Hebrew Text of the Old Testament, Revised from Critical Sources*. In 1854 Davidson had agreed to rewrite the volume on the Old Testament for the tenth edition of T. H. Horne's *An Introduction to the Critical Study and Knowledge of the Holy Scriptures* (1856), but only on condition that he could cover 'new ground'; that is, 'such ground as the subject has been brought to … especially in other countries' (*Autobiography*, 37). His contribution appeared in October 1856 as part of the second volume of the tenth edition of Horne's *Introduction*. It was entitled *The text of the Old Testament considered; with a treatise on sacred interpretation, and a brief introduction to the Old Testament books and the Apocrypha*. In the November after its publication, the Lancashire College committee were made aware of dissatisfaction felt in orthodox circles with the religious views expressed in the volume, one letter having been sent to the *Record* by Dr S. P. Tregelles, whom Davidson had originally recommended to rewrite the volume on the New Testament. A committee appointed to examine whether certain views in Davidson's volume were 'unsound' reported in February 1857. He was then called upon to justify areas of his work which might have caused offence. Thus Davidson produced in May 1857 his pamphlet *Facts, Statements and Explanations*. The committee did not find his explanations satisfactory, and after some correspondence Davidson resigned from his post.

Davidson's request to the committee for specific charges against his orthodoxy was not met, but criticisms tended to focus around his attitude towards the Mosaic authorship of the Pentateuch, prophetic authorship and inspiration, and his doctrinal views. There was also a charge, to some extent justified, of plagiarism from German authors. These charges were summed up in a pamphlet written by E. Mellor and J. G. Rogers and published in October 1857 as *Dr Davidson: his Heresies, Contradictions, and Plagiarisms. By Two Graduates*. In his support appeared *Dr Davidson's removal from the professorship of biblical literature in the Lancashire Independent college, Manchester, on account of alleged error in doctrine* (1860) by Thomas Nicholas, which cited Bishop Thirlwall, Dean Alford, and Canon Cureton in Davidson's favour. J. A. Picton's account of the proceedings seemed to Davidson to be the most fair, and he included it in his own *Autobiography* of 1899. But he did not offer an account of the story himself, perhaps because he never lost the feeling that he had been treated unjustly. In his later years, from about 1870, he attended services of the Unitarian church, and sometimes the Church of England.

After his resignation many friends gathered round Davidson, and a large testimonial, which finally reached £3000, was presented to him. He retired to Hatherlow, in Cheshire, where he worked as a private tutor. He moved to London in 1862, having been elected scripture examiner in the University of London. His life then was taken up with writing, and visits to the continent; it was also punctuated by domestic bereavements. He and Anne lost three sons before Anne's own death in 1872. After his retirement from Manchester, further publications included *An Introduction to the Old Testament, Critical, Historical, and Theological* (3 vols., 1862–3), a work more radical in tone than similar projects published before the controversy, and *An Introduction to the New Testament* (2 vols., 1868). His essay *On a Fresh Revision of the English Old Testament* (1873) was written for a projected second volume of *Essays and Reviews* which never saw the light. Other work included contributions to Kitto's *Cyclopaedia* and to the ninth edition of the *Encyclopaedia Britannica*. In 1862 he became an occasional contributor to *The Athenaeum*, and for three years from 1871 he reviewed philosophical and theological books in the *Westminster Review*. He died at his home, 14 Belsize Crescent, Hampstead, on 1 April 1898, and was buried in Hampstead cemetery on 5 April. For his courage in presenting biblical-critical ideas Davidson paid a heavy price in his dismissal. He was later commemorated by the foundation of the chair of Old Testament studies at King's College, London, which was named after him.   JOANNA HAWKE

Sources *The autobiography and diary of Samuel Davidson*, ed. A. J. Davidson (1899) • J. Rogerson, 'Samuel Davidson and his dismissal in 1857', in J. Rogerson, *Old Testament criticism in the nineteenth century: England and Germany* (1984), 197–208 • J. F. Waller, ed., *The imperial dictionary of universal biography*, 3 vols. (1857–63) • P. Schaff and S. M. Jackson, *Encyclopedia of living divines and Christian workers of all denominations in Europe and America: being a supplement to Schaff-Herzog encyclopedia of religious knowledge* (1887) • J. Thompson, *Jubilee memorial history of the Lancashire College* (1893) • J. Davson, 'Critical and conservative treatments of prophecy in nineteenth-century Britain', DPhil diss., U. Oxf., 1991 [see chap. 'Samuel Davidson and the historical critical approach']

Likenesses Crellin, carte-de-visite, NPG • M. Sharpe, chalk drawing, NPG • photograph, repro. in Davidson, ed., *Autobiography and diary*, frontispiece

Wealth at death £10,101 12s. 1d.: resworn probate, Sept 1898, CGPLA Eng. & Wales

Davidson, Sir Samuel Cleland (1846–1921), inventor of tea processing machinery and manufacturer, was born on 18 November 1846 at Ballymachan Farm, near Belfast, the youngest of the seven children of James Davidson (1799–1869), corn miller, and his wife, Mary Taylor (1808–1896), also of Irish stock. Until the age of fifteen Samuel was educated at the Royal Academical Institution, Belfast. Then, after two years of private tuition, he entered the offices of William Hastings, a Belfast surveyor and civil engineer, where he acquired his lifelong love of scientific experimentation. As a younger son, he could not hope to inherit the family business. Therefore, in 1864, through a cousin's influence, he found employment on an Indian tea plantation. Later, helped by his father, he purchased the estate.

Thereby enjoying independence and financial security, Davidson spent the rest of his life gratifying his taste and talent for mechanical invention. From 1869 until 1881 he lived in India mapping tea plantations and investigating ways of improving the processing and packaging of tea, becoming a consultant in tea production to the Indian government. He took a leave in Belfast to marry Clara Mary Coleman (1851–1918) on 30 January 1873. Together they had five children; three predeceased their parents. In 1881 Davidson returned permanently to Ireland and established a small engineering business. The demand for quality tea was rising rapidly at this time. The main difficulty in bulk production lay at the drying stage. The old method, using charcoal fires, was slow, and frequently produced inferior tea. Most of Davidson's inventive activity after 1864 was devoted to solving that problem by perfecting the use of fans. In 1898 he finally achieved success, and made the business a limited company trading under the name of Sirocco, called after the hot east wind that blows north from Africa. By 1914 the firm employed over a thousand people. Although Davidson's work on fans was his most enduring contribution, he also revolutionized other aspects of tea manufacture, from the receiving of the leaf at the factory to the packaging of the final product. The fan he had initially invented for drying tea proved adaptable for other purposes such as ventilating mines and ships, and later, after Davidson's death, for use in air-raid shelters, power stations, meat and vegetable dehydration plants, and aircraft.

By the time Davidson died he had registered more than 120 patents. Most were for tea processing machinery and fans, but he also invented the hand howitzer, a predecessor of the anti-tank bazooka. In addition, he held patents for belt rivets, steam engines, the manufacture of peat briquettes, and machinery for processing rubber. Although Davidson never held political office, he was a staunch loyalist and a generous supporter of the Ulster Volunteer Force. But his devotion to unionism did not prevent his fierce opposition to the expulsion of Roman Catholic workers from his factory during rioting in 1912 and 1920. On 22 June 1921 he was made a KBE and on 18 August of the same year he died at his home, Seacourt, Bangor, co. Down. He was buried in Belfast city cemetery two days later. DAVID JOHNSON

Sources E. D. Maguire, *The Sirocco story: the birth and growth of an industry* (1958) · PRO NIre., Davidson & Co. MSS, D 3639/1/A–H [incl. pamphlets, newspapers, cuttings, and letters] · *Belfast Telegraph* (18 Aug 1921) · *Belfast Telegraph* (20 Aug 1921) · *Belfast News-Letter* (19 Aug 1921) · private information (2004) · IGI
Archives PRO NIre., D 3639/1/A–H
Likenesses photograph, repro. in *Belfast Telegraph* (18 Aug 1921) · photograph, repro. in *Belfast Telegraph* (20 Aug 1921) · photograph, repro. in *Belfast News-Letter* · photographs, repro. in Maguire, *Sirocco story*
Wealth at death £185,817 13s. 3d.: probate, 21 Nov 1921, CGPLA NIre. · £65,028 2s. 3d. in England: Northern Irish probate sealed in England, 1 Dec 1921, CGPLA Eng. & Wales

Davidson, Sir (Leybourne) Stanley Patrick (1894–1981), physician and university professor, was born in Ceylon on 3 March 1894, the second son in the family of three sons and one daughter of Sir Leybourne Francis Watson Davidson, coffee, tea, and rubber planter, later of Huntly Lodge, Aberdeenshire, and his wife, Jane Rosalind Dudgeon Brown. He was educated at Cheltenham College and went to Trinity College, Cambridge, as a pensioner in 1913 to read medicine. His studies were interrupted at the outbreak of the First World War and he served for three years with the Gordon Highlanders in France and Belgium, where he was seriously wounded. He went to Edinburgh University in 1917, and graduated MB, ChB with first-class honours in 1919. He held house-physician appointments in Edinburgh hospitals and in 1923 became lecturer in bacteriology at Edinburgh University. He obtained a gold medal for his MD thesis (1925), 'Immunization and antibody reactions', and he became a fellow of the Royal College of Physicians of Edinburgh in 1926 (MRCP 1921) and of the Royal Society of Edinburgh in 1932. He returned briefly to Cambridge in 1925, and graduated BA in 1926. Although athletic by nature, he was advised to seek a warm climate in the winter months and made several voyages on cargo boats to New Zealand, where he enjoyed fishing for shark and swordfish. In 1927 Davidson married Isobel Margaret (Peggy; d. 1979), daughter of Andrew Macbeth Anderson (Lord Anderson; 1862–1936), senator of the college of justice and solicitor-general for Scotland (1911–13), and his wife, Kate, née Mackay. They had no children.

Davidson was appointed as assistant physician at the Royal Infirmary in Edinburgh and decided to pursue research in haematology. He believed that pernicious anaemia was related to a disturbance in the gastrointestinal tract and wrote a monograph on the subject with G. L. Gulland in 1930, summarizing the knowledge of the time. To the surprise of some of his close friends, and with limited clinical experience, in 1930 he was appointed regius professor of medicine at Aberdeen University, where he collected around him a number of talented young colleagues. He applied vital stains to blood films, drew attention to the reticulocyte response in the correction of anaemia, established the role of iron deficiency in the condition then referred to as 'chlorosis', and showed the importance of Weil's disease among fish workers in Aberdeen. In 1942 he wrote *A Textbook of Dietetics* with I. A. Anderson; its successor, *Human Nutrition and Dietetics* (1959), ran into many editions. He collaborated closely with Derrick Melville Dunlop and John W. McNee on the *Textbook of Medical Treatment* (1939 and many later editions), whose success emphasized Scotland's dominance in clinical medicine at that time.

With an established reputation in clinical research, and with his rapidly acquired clinical and teaching skills, Davidson was appointed to the chair of medicine in Edinburgh in 1938. Initially he conducted almost all the undergraduate lectures himself. At the request of the secretary of state he organized the Emergency Medical Service (in six new hutted hospitals of over 1000 beds each) throughout Scotland during the Second World War. He also served on many national committees on food production with John Boyd Orr.

In 1946 Davidson turned his considerable administrative abilities to the upgrading of several local authority hospitals in Edinburgh. Anticipating the shape of modern medicine, he encouraged the development of major medical specialities such as cardiology, gastro-enterology, nutrition, rheumatology, respiratory medicine, and neurology, as well as general medicine. He became a fellow of the Royal College of Physicians of London in 1940, was awarded an honorary MD from Oslo University in 1946, was a distinguished president of the Royal College of Physicians of Edinburgh from 1953 to 1957, received a knighthood in 1955, and was president of the Association of Physicians of Great Britain and Ireland in 1957. In 1946 and 1947 Davidson had tried, unsuccessfully, to establish a Royal College of Physicians of Scotland. He also became physician to King George VI (1947–52) and to the queen in Scotland (1952–61). He had an honorary LLD from the universities of Edinburgh (1962) and Aberdeen (1971).

Davidson had a remarkable personality which all who met him were quick to appreciate. Not an intellectual, he depended largely on his younger colleagues to keep abreast of scientific advances. He possessed a penetrating mind which brushed jargon aside and quickly grasped the essentials of diverse problems. He loved to talk with specialists who were astonished at his capacity to simplify and uncover contradictions in their accounts of their own specialities. He was an excellent editor of undergraduate texts, the *Principles and Practice of Medicine*, first published in 1952, running into nine editions before he retired. His success was due largely to his tireless efforts to put into uncomplicated English the tortured drafts submitted by the members of his staff. He was unaffected and sincere with all who met him and had a remarkable capacity to select young doctors of talent, many of whom later occupied chairs of medicine in Britain and overseas. Firm and scrupulously fair in his decisions, he was occasionally ruthless but his decisions were always accompanied with a charming smile. He was a keen fisherman, golfer, and shot. He retired in 1959. Famously cautious in money matters of a small kind, Davidson before his death gave substantial donations to the medical schools of the chief Scottish cities and to the Royal College of Physicians of Edinburgh. He died in Edinburgh on 22 September 1981.

J. S. ROBSON, rev. H. C. G. MATTHEW

Sources Royal Society of Medicine Year Book (1983), 142–8 · BMJ (10 Oct 1981), 993 · R. H. G., The Lancet (10 Oct 1981), 819–20 · senate minutes, 18 Nov 1959, U. Edin. · personal knowledge (1990) · private information (1990)
Likenesses R. Dobson, oils, c.1957, Royal College of Physicians of Edinburgh

Davidson, Thomas (1817–1885), natural history artist and palaeontologist, was born in Edinburgh on 17 May 1817, the eldest of the three children of William Davidson, the wealthy owner of Muirhouse and other Midlothian estates, and his wife, Jane, daughter of Alexander Horsebrugh of Peeblesshire. From the age of six he was educated in France, Italy, and Switzerland, developing a natural artistic talent as well as a strong interest in natural history. His inclination for the fine arts was encouraged by attending classes in Paris, and then as a pupil of Paul Delaroche and Horace Vernet. Access to the lectures of leading scientists at the major French institutions also widened Davidson's understanding of natural history. From 1832, under the guidance of Constant Prévost, he concentrated on geology and palaeontology, returning to Scotland briefly in 1835–6 to study at Edinburgh University, then carrying out further fieldwork on the continent from 1836. After meeting Leopold von Buch during 1837 he was persuaded to undertake a comprehensive study of both living and fossil Brachiopoda. While studying in France Davidson met Caroline Charlotte Pittar, daughter of Isaac Pittar, of East Brixton, Surrey; there followed a distant and hesitant, but constant, courtship. Once they were engaged Davidson could no longer endure their frequent separations and within a few months they were married, on 29 November 1841. Shortly afterwards they went to Rome, where Davidson concentrated on art.

An adequate private income allowed Davidson to devote his life to brachiopod research. In describing the wealth of British fossil taxa his artistic talent assisted him in the illustration of their distinctive features, and his genuine enthusiasm encouraged many British palaeontologists to assist him in building up an extensive research collection. His great knowledge of the phylum resulted in numerous publications. The Palaeontographical Society monograph on British Fossil Brachiopoda became his *magnum opus*; the first part was issued in 1851 and, with successive parts published over the next thirty-five years, formed six volumes containing 2280 pages and 234 lithographed plates of his drawings; the last part, A Bibliography of the Brachiopoda (1886) was only completed in 1884. He also published a description of the *Challenger* expedition material (1880), and started a monograph on the Recent species.

The substance of Davidson's classification of the Brachiopoda has endured and confirms his thorough understanding of that phylum. His diary records his enormous capacity for work; his research on Elizabeth Gray's collection of Girvan Brachiopoda began on 11 February 1882 and was completed by 22 May, during which he distinguished 118 species. Professor Lapworth considered that the resulting 'table of Girvan brachiopods was the most useful piece of work' he had encountered (see T. Davidson, letter-book 27, NHM). Others subsequently acknowledged Davidson's devotion and energy as he persevered with this research throughout his life, and fellow workers later maintained that he had left very little for future students to accomplish. On his death he was considered to have been one of the most single-minded naturalists of the century.

Davidson's role and scientific achievements were widely acknowledged during his lifetime. He was elected FRS in 1857 and made the first honorary member of the Geological Society of Glasgow in 1858. He served on the council of the Geological Society of London in 1858–60 and as its secretary in 1858–9. He was awarded that society's Wollaston medal in 1865; a 'Silurian medal' by Murchison in 1868; and one of the gold medals of the Royal Society in 1870. In 1880 he was the British representative at the fiftieth anniversary meeting of the French Geological Society, and he was awarded an honorary LLD by St Andrews University in 1882.

After moving to Brighton at the end of 1856, Davidson was involved in the foundation of the 'free' library and museum, becoming chairman of the museum committee until his death. He died at his home, 9 Salisbury Road, Brighton, on 14 October 1885 following a long illness. He left several virtually completed manuscripts that were published posthumously over the next three years. His library, collections, and manuscript notebooks were bequeathed to the British Museum (Natural History), London. R. J. CLEEVELY

Sources 'Eminent living geologists: sketch of the scientific life of Thomas Davidson', Geological Magazine, 7 (1871), 145–9 [incl. bibliography] · R. J. Cleevely, R. P. Tripp, and Y. Howells, 'Mrs Elizabeth Gray, 1831–1924: a passion for fossils', Bulletin of the British Museum (Natural History) [Historical Series], 17 (1989), 167–258, esp. 180–83, 241–4 · J. Young, 'Biographical notice', History of the Geological Society of Glasgow, 1858–1908, ed. P. Macnair and F. Mort (1908), 215–19 · M. O. Mancenido and L. R. M. Cocks, 'Thomas Davidson, 1817–1885', Les Brachiopodes fossiles et actuels, ed. P. R. Racheboeuf and C. Emig, Biostratigraphie du Paléologie, 4 (1986) · 'Unveiling of memorial to Thomas Davidson', Brighton Herald (18 Feb 1888) · R. E. [R. Etheridge], PRS, 39 (1885–6), viii–lxi · L. R. M. Cocks, A review of British Lower Palaeozoic brachiopods, including a synoptic revision of Davidson's monograph (1978), 2–4 · Geological Magazine, new ser., 3rd decade, 2 (1885), 528 · A. Ramsey, 'Thomas Davidson', The English cyclopaedia: biography, 5 (Aug 1870), 447 · T. G. Bonney, Quarterly Journal of the Geological Society, 42 (1886), 39–40 · The correspondence of Charles Darwin, ed. F. Burkhardt and S. Smith, 6 (1990), letter, Dec 1856 · bap. reg. Scot. · d. cert. · m. cert.
Archives Booth Museum Library, Brighton · Brighton Museum · E. Sussex RO, family MSS · GS Lond., papers relating to geology ·

NHM, papers relating to brachiopods | BGS, letters to George Maw • BL, corresp. with Spencer Perceval, Add. MSS 41495–41496 • Booth Museum, Brighton, Crane collection • CUL, letters to Charles Darwin • NHM, corresp. with Robert Owen and William Clift • Norwich Castle Museum, letters to Robert Fitch • U. Edin. L., special collections division, letters to Sir Archibald Geikie • U. Edin. L., special collections division, letters to Sir Charles Lyell

Likenesses R. A. Brock, medallion memorial plaque; formerly at Brighton Museum [now destroyed] • photograph, NHM; repro. in Cleevely, Tripp, and Howells, 'Mrs Elizabeth Gray', 182 • portrait (after photograph), repro. in A. Geikie, *Memoir of Sir Roderick Murchison*, 2 (1875), facing p. 167 • portrait, repro. in 'Eminent living geologists'

Wealth at death £12,980 12s. 5d.: confirmation, 15 Feb 1886, CCI

Davidson, Thomas (1838–1870), poet, was born at Oxnam Row, near Oxnam Water, a tributary of the Teviot, about 4 miles from Jedburgh, Roxburghshire, on 7 July 1838, the son of Jonah Davidson, a shepherd from Wooler, Northumberland. His mother, of whom further details are unknown, came from Belford in the same county. He was educated at various village schools and, having displayed a passionate love of books along with an interest in writing poetry in his early years, he was sent in 1854 to the Nest Academy at Jedburgh. He studied at the University of Edinburgh from 1855 to 1859. In 1859 he won the second prize in his rhetoric class for the poem 'Ariadne at Naxos', which one of his friends sent without his knowledge to Thackeray, who published it with an illustration in the December 1860 issue of the *Cornhill Magazine*.

Davidson had early formed a resolution to enter the ministry and in 1859 began the first of the prescribed five autumnal sessions of the theological course of the United Presbyterian church. Between sessions he was assistant schoolmaster at Forres (1859–61) and later in Dr Douglas's School, Edinburgh (1861–3). During this period he continued writing poetry, and his songs and poems were published in *The Scotsman*. Davidson was licensed as a preacher on 2 February 1864, and in accordance with church regulations spent the next few years travelling extensively and preaching at various churches in Scotland, England, and Ireland. Many poems resulted from his travelling experiences, such as the humorous 'Yang-Tsi-Kiang' used by the supporters of Carlyle in the contest for the lord rectorship of the university, and popular as a students' song.

A cold caught in June 1866 seriously affected Davidson's health and he retired to Jedburgh in December to recuperate. He was an invalid for more than three years, during which he wrote memorable, mournful songs such as the love ballad 'Myspie's Den' and 'Auld Ash Tree', many of which were published in *The Scotsman*. He died of consumption on 29 April 1870 at Bank End, Jedburgh, and was buried at the new cemetery, Jedburgh. Some of his poems were republished in his memoir by John Brown in 1877.

T. F. Henderson, rev. Sayoni Basu

Sources J. Brown, *The life of a Scottish probationer, being a memoir of Thomas Davidson with poems and extracts from his letters* (1877) • C. Rogers, *The modern Scottish minstrel, or, The songs of Scotland of the past half-century*, 6 vols. (1855–7)

Davidson, Thomas (1840–1900), philosopher and adult educationist, was born on 25 October 1840 in Old Deer, Aberdeenshire, the elder child of the unmarried Mary Warrender, a farm labourer, and Thomas Davidson, a farmer. His brother, John Morrison *Davidson, journalist and radical, was born in 1843. When his grandfather died, his grandmother, by now widowed mother, and aunt moved to the nearby village of Fetterangus. Despite the poverty of his family, after attending the village school in Fetterangus Davidson won a scholarship to King's College, Aberdeen, where he graduated in 1860. He then taught at Aberdeen grammar school and later in Tunbridge Wells. He remained an orthodox Christian until early manhood, when he flirted successively with German idealism, Comtean positivism, and a secular republicanism. In 1861 he became engaged to Maye McCombie, eldest daughter of William *McCombie (1809–1870), founder and editor of the *Aberdeen Daily Free Press*. When he denied the divinity of Christ, however, her family became unhappy about the proposed marriage. He yielded a bit, but when the dispute flared up again in 1865, he emigrated and taught briefly in Toronto before settling in the United States. He never married, but corresponded with Maye McCombie until her death in 1873.

Davidson had an excellent command of Greek and Latin, and was at home in Arabic, Hebrew, and Sanskrit. He could converse in most modern European languages, and had a photographic memory. He was a kind and modest man, who kept every letter and document sent to him by others, but would lend his manuscripts to people without bothering much if they were not returned. In the United States, his learning found an initial home among the transcendentalists and radicals of Boston. Before long, however, he moved to St Louis, where he taught classical languages in public secondary schools. Although he joined the St Louis Hegelians, writing in the *Journal of Speculative Philosophy* and translating works by German idealists, he was an Aristotelian with limited sympathy for their views. After eight years in St Louis, he went to live in Greece, and, from 1878 to 1883, in Italy, where he had a private audience with Pope Leo XIII. Reading Aristotle had convinced him there was a faculty above reason, expressed in religion. His youth had shown him the protestant church did not embody this faculty, so now he looked for it in the Greek Orthodox and Roman Catholic churches. Although neither offered what he wanted, he found a pure spiritual community at the Rosminian monastery in Domodossola, Italy. He lived there for eighteen months, writing *The Philosophical System of Antonio Rosmini-Serbati* (1882).

The key features of Davidson's philosophy remained fairly stable. He believed that the divine is immanent in humanity, the telos of the individual is perfection, and the way to perfection is a democratic society and an appropriate education. Later in life, he wrote a series of books outlining his ideal of a popular, democratic education designed to develop the whole self. More immediately, however, he wanted to develop a spiritual philosophy akin to Rosmini's, and embedded in an organization akin to the monastery at Domodossola, but free from Catholic dogma. In 1883 he moved to London to help his disciples form the Fellowship of the New Life. The fellowship set out to cultivate a perfect character in all by subordinating the material to the spiritual and by recognizing the communal nature of our being. Its more specific commitments emphasized the simple life and manual labour. Soon, however, the fellowship split in two, with the New Life constructing a socialist ethic on the foundation of Davidson's spiritual and ethical beliefs, and the Fabian Society turning to social and political matters. Although Davidson always opposed socialism as too material, he was a keen supporter of a more moral economy. He returned to the United States in 1884.

Although Davidson formed an American branch of the New Life, and thereby played an important role in the ethical culture movement, the main organizations he established in America were educational ones. He began to host summer schools in the cultural sciences at his Glenmore retreat in the Adirondack Mountains. Famous philosophers such as John Dewey, William Harris, William James, and Josiah Royce discoursed here with visitors from the Educational Alliance, or Breadwinners' College, that Davidson started on the lower east side of New York city, a slum populated by Jewish immigrants from eastern Europe. This college was his greatest achievement, and one of the best examples of adult education in the history of the United States. It did much to transform a community, helping many second-generation immigrants become lawyers, teachers, and philosophers. One of its alumni recalled that when Davidson gave his first lecture, it was 'as if from nowhere a Moses appeared' (Kovar, 6). From those he taught and inspired Davidson took a love that made his final years happy ones. He died a year after an operation for appendicitis, in the General Hospital, Montreal, Canada, on 14 September 1900.   MARK BEVIR

Sources W. Knight, ed., *Memorials of Thomas Davidson* (1907) · T. Davidson, 'Autobiographical sketch', *Journal of the History of Ideas*, 18 (1957), 529–36 [introduction by A. Lataner] · *New York Times* (18 Sept 1900) · *New York Times* (22 Sept 1900) · A. Kovar, *Thomas Davidson: pioneer in adult education* (1949) · M. R. Cohen, *A dreamer's journey* (1949) · E. R. Pease, *The history of the Fabian Society* (1916) · W. A. Knight, *Some nineteenth century Scotsmen* (1903) [incl. bibliographical appx] · parish register (baptism), Old Deer, Aberdeenshire, 7 Nov 1840

Archives Yale U., Beinecke L., papers | Harvard U., Houghton L., William James MSS · Missouri Historical Society, St Louis, Harris Collection

Davidson, Thomas Randall (1747–1827), Church of Scotland minister, was born Thomas Randall at Inchture, Perthshire, in July 1747, the son of Thomas Randall [see below] and his wife, Mary (d. 1775), daughter of Thomas Davidson, minister at Dundee. The elder **Thomas Randall** (1711–1780), Church of Scotland minister and religious writer, was minister first at Inchture and then at Stirling. He compiled an important collection of tracts on the subject of ecclesiastical patronage, and wrote a significant pamphlet on church communion and a noted sermon (1763) on Christian benevolence, all major subjects of discussion within the popular or evangelical party within the church. Through his father, the younger Thomas thus

inherited a considerable standing among leading ministers of the popular party. He was educated at the University of Leiden, and on 14 June 1769 he was licensed at Rotterdam, where his maternal uncle William Davidson was a prominent merchant within the large Scots commercial community. When his father was translated to Stirling, Thomas the younger succeeded him at Inchture on 21 February 1771. He was translated to the Outer High Church of Glasgow on 18 November 1773, to Lady Yester's in Edinburgh on 26 November 1778, and to the Tolbooth Church in Edinburgh on 9 June 1785, where he remained for the rest of his career. Upon the death of William Davidson in 1794, he inherited his uncle's property of Muirhouse in Cramond, near Edinburgh, and assumed his surname.

Compared to the writings of his father, Davidson's were neither prolific nor especially influential. He was the author of three sermons preached on public occasions between 1775 and 1802, as well as a funeral sermon preached in 1803 upon the death of his fellow minister John Erskine. These sermons were known more for their polish and the benevolence of their sentiments than for any striking originality.

Davidson married twice. His first wife was Christian, daughter of John Rutherford of Edgerton, whom he married on 29 January 1772; she died on 6 July 1797. His second wife was Elizabeth, daughter of Archibald Cockburn, baron of the exchequer, whom he wed on 20 August 1798. He had three children with his first wife and six with his second. Davidson died on 25 October 1827; Elizabeth lived on until 30 March 1850.

Davidson was described in a contemporary publication as 'a sound, practical and zealous preacher' (Kay, 1.388–90). He was known to contemporaries as an evangelical and benevolent clergyman who put forth a cultured and respectable image for the popular party. His reputation for benevolence secured for him an honorary doctorate of divinity from Harvard University in 1793. Davidson's career is notable for illustrating the extent to which evangelical ministers of the later eighteenth century, including such contemporaries as Henry Moncreiff Wellwood, were able to transcend an earlier reputation for crudeness and a lack of polish, and establish themselves as polite men of letters and well-connected gentlemen.

NED C. LANDSMAN

Sources *Fasti Scot.*, new edn · J. Kay, *A series of original portraits and caricature etchings … with biographical sketches and illustrative anecdotes*, ed. [H. Paton and others], 1 (1837), 388–90 · G. Muirhead, *Sermon on the death of Thomas Davidson, D.D.* (1827)

Archives NA Scot., Church of Scotland records

Likenesses J. Kay, etching, NPG; repro. in Kay, *Series of original portraits*, vol. 1, facing p. 388

Davidson, William (c.1756–1797), privateer, was born in Scotland; further details of his family and upbringing are unknown. In 1791 he was serving as an able seaman on the *Niger*, then commanded by Sir Richard Keats. Davidson was noted as a comparatively well-educated man of gloomy and silent disposition, but liable to sudden outbursts of temper. While the ship was at Deal he was condemned to be flogged for drunkenness and insolence to his superior officer. The punishment caused him excessive agony, and at the fifth stroke he fell into convulsions. The sentence was then remitted, but he later struck an officer and was again condemned. While being brought to the gangway he attempted to cut his throat and, this failing, he tried in vain to throw himself overboard. His punishment was not proceeded with, but he was ordered into confinement.

The whole circumstances of the case led to an inquiry into Davidson's past life, which gave rise to a rumour that he possessed a journal (as yet not authenticated) giving an account of singular atrocities in which he had been engaged. Davidson's chest was ransacked, and the journal was found, and laid before the officers. It claimed that on 1 December 1788 Davidson had enlisted on the *Saint Dinnan*, a Russian privateer, which on 3 December had sailed from Leghorn for Messina. He and the other Englishmen on the ship were discharged at Trieste on 6 September 1789 with wages and prize money amounting to £230 per man. During the period at sea the *Saint Dinnan* cruised in the Levant, took a large number of Turkish ships, robbed them, murdered the crews, and burnt the vessels. The privateers also attacked and plundered some of the smaller Grecian islands. On one occasion they had a terrible combat with another pirate, whose crew of over 300 was brutally murdered on capture. These and other horrors Davidson, if the genuine author, narrated in plain methodical order.

'The Bloody journal', as it was called, came to have considerable renown with sailors, among whom it was probably current in manuscript versions. A copy was procured for Sir Walter Scott, who had heard of it, and thought it might form a good subject for a poem. 'On perusal he pronounced it too horrible for versification' but later he printed it in the *Edinburgh Annual Register* (published in 1812, vol. 3, part 2). Copies of the work, of which the full title is *The Bloody Journal Kept by William Davidson on Board a Russian Pirate in the Year 1789*, exist in the library of Corpus Christi College, Oxford, and the library of the National Maritime Museum, Greenwich. The book is full of errors of composition. Whatever its true provenance, Davidson probably found his position on the *Niger* very uncomfortable. He deserted from her at Portsmouth some time in 1793, was afterwards pressed on the *Royal George*, where he became a gunners' mate, and was accidentally drowned in January 1797.

FRANCIS WATT, rev. CHRISTOPHER DOORNE

Sources W. Davidson (?), 'A pirate's journal', NMM, Anderson MSS · *Niger* pay books, 1792–5, PRO, ADM 35/1165–6 · *Niger* muster list, 1790–91, PRO, ADM 36/11040 · *Niger* captain's log, 1791, PRO, ADM 5/631 · *Royal George* muster lists, 1793–5, 1797, PRO, ADM 36/11697; 36/11701; 36/11704 · *Royal George* captain's log, July 1796–June 1797, PRO, ADM 51/1171 · *Royal George* pay book, 1793–4, PRO, ADM 36/1455

Davidson, William (1786–1820), conspirator, was born in Jamaica, the second son of the attorney-general of Jamaica and an unnamed black woman. Educated there until age fourteen, William was sent to England, despite his mother's protests, to complete his education. Arriving

William Davidson (1786–1820), by R. Cooper, pubd 1820 (after Abraham Wivell)

in a country seething with revolutionary fervour, William gave up his studies of mathematics to go to sea. He was impressed into the Royal Navy from his merchant vessel. Once returned to England he was apprenticed, through the agency of his father, to a Liverpool lawyer and probably attended the University of Edinburgh for a while. However, he abandoned this to become apprenticed to a cabinet-maker. After an unhappy love affair in Lichfield, he moved to Birmingham where, with his mother's financial help, he set up his own business. This failed, however, probably due to the dire economic circumstances.

In London, where he must have taken up residence some time before 1816 (when his first son was born), Davidson married a widow, Sarah Leigh (possibly Lane), who had four children. The couple probably lived in Walworth, where Davidson taught at a Wesleyan Sunday school. He worked as a journeyman with a cabinet-maker named Cox, who found him an excellent workman. It was probably after he had been accused of molesting a young woman at the Sunday school—an accusation against which his wife defended him—that the couple moved to Marylebone and Davidson attempted again to set up his own business.

Times were hard and Davidson was soon penniless—and in the thick of the London radical movements. He read the works of Thomas Paine and joined the Marylebone Union Reading Society. Meetings were held at his home and he formed a shoemaker's society. (Such societies were formed in the hopes of mobilizing the metropolis to overthrow the government; a provisional government would then introduce parliamentary and other reforms.)

One of the main speakers at a radical meeting in Finsbury Square, Davidson a few weeks later helped to guard the banner at the Smithfield meeting in November 1819. The flag, of a death's head, was emblazoned with the words 'Let us die like Men and not be sold like Slaves'.

Informers reported that Davidson and his colleagues guarding the flag were well armed.

It is possible that Davidson met George Edwards, a government spy and agent provocateur, at the procession of some 200,000 people and dinner given to honour 'Orator' Hunt (of Peterloo fame) when he arrived in London in September 1819. Edwards apparently introduced him to Arthur Thistlewood, a prison-hardened radical who had witnessed the revolution in France. Davidson joined the group around Thistlewood, which, most likely at Edwards's instigation, decided that the quickest route to reform was to blow up the cabinet in what became known as the Cato Street conspiracy [*see* Cato street conspirators (*act.* 1820)]. When a (false) date for a cabinet dinner was publicized, the men collected arms and ammunition. Raided by the police and the military in their Cato Street loft, the street entrance to which was guarded by Davidson, all but three of the conspirators were arrested. One policeman was killed upstairs in the loft. Thistlewood escaped, but Edwards 'found' him the next day, and claimed the £1000 reward for his capture.

Eleven men were tried in April 1820. Despite quoting Magna Carta (and Alexander Pope) in his defence, Davidson was among the five who were hanged, decapitated, and then buried in quicklime under a prison passage. After the hanging, which took place outside Newgate Prison on 1 May 1820 and was witnessed by one of the largest crowds ever assembled in London, there was a public subscription for the dead men's wives and children, and to bring Edwards to court for high treason. Despite the intervention of Alderman Wood, this was unsuccessful: Edwards (one of many spies and provocateurs employed by the government) had been spirited out of the country by his masters.   MARIKA SHERWOOD

Sources P. Fryer, *Staying power: the history of black people in Britain* (1984), 214–20 · G. T. Wilkinson, *An authentic history of the Cato Street conspiracy* (1820) · V. S. Anand and F. A. Ridley, *The Cato St. conspiracy* (1977) · *State trials*, 33.1337–1566 · I. McCalman, *Radical underworld: prophets, revolutionaries, and pornographers in London, 1795–1840* (1988) · D. Johnson, *Regency revolution* (1974) · C. Oman, *The unfortunate Colonel Despard and other studies* (1922) · H. Mackey, 'Davidson, William', *BDMBR*, vol. 1 · I. J. Prothero, *Artisans and radicals in early 19th century London* (1981) · *GM*, 1st ser., 89 (1819) · *GM*, 1st ser., 90 (1820) · 'Horrible conspiracy and murder', *GM*, 1st ser., 90/1 (1820), 165–8 · 'Commitment of the conspirators', *GM*, 1st ser., 90/1 (1820), 269–70 · 'Trial of the Cato Street conspirators for high treason', *GM*, 1st ser., 90/1 (1820), 454–9 · 'Execution of the conspirators', *GM*, 1st ser., 90/1 (1820), 459–60 · *Annual Register* (1820) · J. Belchem, *Orator Hunt* (1985) · 'Letter to Mr James Paul Cobbett on the death, amongst others, of William Davidson', *Cobbett's Weekly Political Register* (6 May 1820), 537–667

Likenesses R. Cooper, engraving (after A. Wivell), AM Oxf.; repro. in Wilkinson, *Authentic history of the Cato Street conspiracy*, facing p. 339 [*see illus.*]

Davie, Cedric Fredric Thorpe (1913–1983), composer, was born on 30 May 1913 at 4 Eliot Vale, Lewisham, London, the elder of the two sons of Thorpe Davie (*d. c.*1954), singing teacher and a Glaswegian, and his wife, Gladys Louise Butcher (*d. c.*1954). From his earliest years Thorpe Davie, as he too was known, showed his father's artistic

commitment and determination; he won a Caird scholarship to the Scottish National Academy of Music, Glasgow, where he gained the first-year piano prize. His development and promise were recognized through a second Caird award in 1932, which enabled him to study initially with Harold Craxton at the Royal Academy of Music, London. Thorpe Davie, however, nurtured creative ambitions and moved to the Royal College of Music in 1933 to study theory, orchestration, and composition with R. O. Morris, Gordon Jacob, and Ralph Vaughan Williams while continuing piano tuition with Egon Petri. He then used his scholarship for further studies with Zoltán Kodály in Budapest and Yryö Kilpinen in Helsinki, with a visit to Sibelius when in Finland.

Some of Thorpe Davie's early pieces were performed by his father's choir. A student piano trio constituted his official opus 1, but in 1935 the *Phantasie quartet* for strings (winner of the Cobbett prize) and the choral and orchestral *Dirge for Cuthullin* (awarded the Sullivan prize) first established his reputation as a composer. The latter work was dedicated to Margaret Russell Brown (*d.* 1974), whom he married on 23 March 1937.

In 1936 Thorpe Davie was appointed to teach music theory at the Scottish National Academy of Music. While there he affirmed his love of Scotland, a lifelong passion traced through diverse work from the *Fantasy No. 1 on Scottish Tunes* (1937) to the treatise *Scotland's Music* (1980). Thorpe Davie became a leader in Glasgow's musical life, supporting contemporary work and encouraging adventurous programming. The war years saw him in the city's fire service and establishing contact with the Orcadian author Robert Kemp, then seeking a score for a BBC radio programme, *Scotland at War*. Their collaboration in 1943 encouraged Thorpe Davie to write further for radio broadcasts and for films, a field in which he was frequently to provide—with characteristic integrity—music of a Scottish flavour.

Thorpe Davie's links with the composer and musicologist Howard Ferguson, dating from their student days, can be attributed to shared Celtic roots as well as shared academic and practical musical interests. Thorpe Davie's concerto for piano and string orchestra (1944) predates that of Ferguson by seven years and must have exerted an influence in its form and spirit. Through Ferguson, he met Gerald Finzi: their friendship led to regular correspondence and musical liaison, leading St Andrews University eventually to acquire Finzi's manuscript eighteenth-century editions (for which Thorpe Davie compiled a scholarly catalogue).

In 1945 Thorpe Davie's career began to blossom. His symphony, placed second in the *Daily Express* victory music competition, was premièred at the Royal Albert Hall, and he was appointed master of music at St Andrews University. Here he became a pivotal figure, founding the department of music in 1947 and becoming reader in 1956 and professor in 1973. In common with Finzi, Thorpe Davie showed active interest in eighteenth-century music. Arrangements of songs for productions of the ballad operas *The Gentle Shepherd* and *The Highland Fair* (staged at the Edinburgh Festival in 1949 and 1952 respectively) established his partnership with the director, Tyrone Guthrie. In 1948 their renowned production of Sir David Lindsay's play *Ane Satyre of the Thrie Estaitis* made Thorpe Davie's name as a theatre composer. Commissions followed for Shakespeare productions—*Henry VIII* (1949), *King Lear* (1950), and *A Midsummer Night's Dream* (1951). In addition, Thorpe Davie was a prolific composer in the film world, completing twenty-four scores, including four for Walt Disney. Further recognition followed with *Flowers from the Rock*, written for the twenty-first birthday of Princess Margaret, and a coronation march, 'The royal mile', as a result of which he was appointed OBE in 1954.

Enthused by his Scottish heritage, Thorpe Davie composed *Variations on a Theme of Sir Alexander Mackenzie* (1949) and a choral work, *Ode for St Andrew's Night* (1950). He also wrote music for Robert Burns's dramatic cantata *The Jolly Beggars* (1954). Thorpe Davie considered another of his choral works—a setting of verse by the Scots poet Alastair Reid (*Directions for a Map*, 1955–6)—to be perhaps his best work. In 1964 he composed a second *Fantasia on Scottish Tunes* (the title using the traditional spelling) to commemorate the opening of the Forth road bridge, and he was joint compiler of *The Oxford Scottish Song Book*. His last major work, a suite based on eighteenth-century Scots fiddle tunes, celebrated the bicentenary of Edinburgh's New Town (1967). By then—in common with the previous experience of Ferguson—Thorpe Davie felt his essentially tonal expressive idiom had grown outmoded, and so determined to concentrate his energies on his academic work.

From his university base Thorpe Davie exerted wide influence, demonstrating the dedication to amateur and youth music-making that had been revealed in his earlier writing for the National Youth Orchestra of Great Britain and the National Youth Brass Band of Scotland. He chaired the music panel of the Scottish Certificate of Education Examination Board (1966–71) and the music committee of the Scottish Arts Council, also acting as a member of the Arts Council of Great Britain (1968–73). Awards in tribute to his work included honorary fellowships from the Royal Academy of Music (1949) and the Royal Scottish Academy of Music and Drama (1978) and an LLD degree from Dundee University (1969).

Predeceased by his wife in 1974, Thorpe Davie lived from 1978 in retirement at Dalry, Kirkcudbrightshire, pursuing his enthusiasm for hillwalking. A lover of cats, crosswords, malt whisky, and Scottish country dancing, and possessed of a great (if slightly eccentric) sense of humour, he died, following a heart attack, on 18 January 1983 at Dalry. He was cremated at Ayr.

ROBERT GOWER

Sources C. Scott-Sutherland, 'Cedric Thorpe Davie', *British Music*, 21 (1999), 49–62 • M. Lindsay, 'Thorpe Davie, Cedric', *New Grove*, 2nd edn • private information (2004) [Antony Davie, son] • C. Gascoigne, catalogue of Thorpe Davie's works, U. St Andr. L. • b. cert. **Archives** U. St Andr., corresp. and papers incl. scores • U. St Andr., letters | SOUND Scottish Music Information Centre, Glasgow, recordings • U. St Andr. L., recordings

Likenesses J. Finzi, pencil drawing, 1946, repro. in J. Finzi, *In that place: the portrait drawings of Joy Finzi* (1987); priv. coll.

Davie, Donald Alfred (1922–1995), poet and literary critic, was born on 17 July 1922 in Barnsley, Yorkshire, the son of George Davie (d. 1965), a shopkeeper and deacon of the local Baptist chapel, and his wife, Alice, *née* Sugden (d. 1968), a schoolteacher. He was educated at Holgate grammar school, Barnsley, and at St Catharine's College, Cambridge, where he won a scholarship to read English in 1940. His university education was interrupted by wartime service in the Royal Navy, which took him to Ceylon, India, Iceland, and Russia. On his return home with the navy to Plymouth in 1944 he met Doreen John (b. 1920), whom he married on 13 January 1945; they had two sons and a daughter. He resumed his studies at Cambridge, where he graduated in 1947 (MA, 1949) and stayed on as a research student; he was awarded his PhD in 1951.

From 1950 until 1957 Davie was a lecturer in English at Trinity College, Dublin; he spent the academic year 1957–8 as a visiting professor at the University of California before returning to Cambridge as a lecturer and, from 1959, fellow of Gonville and Caius College. In 1964, after a second visit to the USA as a visiting lecturer at the University of Cincinnati, he joined the new University of Essex as professor of literature, and became pro-vice-chancellor a year later: it seemed an ideal opportunity to counter what he saw as the cultural insularity of Cambridge, but the student riots of 1968, and the university's tepid response to them, completed his disillusionment with English academic life. In 1968 he succeeded Yvor Winters, one of his literary mentors, as professor of English at Stanford University, California; ten years later he moved to Vanderbilt University, Tennessee, where he remained until 1988. He and Doreen then retired to the Devon village of Silverton, near Exeter.

Donald Davie belongs to that small and distinguished company of poet–critics (such as Matthew Arnold, William Empson, and Yvor Winters) who are equally poets and critics; the restless concerns of the creative writer and the academic continually reinforce one another. His first two critical books, *Purity of Diction in English Verse* (1952) and *Articulate Energy* (1955), seem respectively to define and to extend the literary principles of those poets who became known as the Movement, just as his own first collection of poems, *Brides of Reason* (1955), despite its ironic intelligence and metrical orthodoxy, already hints at impatience with the Movement's limited agenda: 'A neutral tone is nowadays preferred', he writes (*Collected Poems*, 1990, 35), but the passive voice fails to endorse the preference as his own. Inclusion in Robert Conquest's influential anthology *New Lines* (1956) brought Davie's poetry to a wider public, while his second collection, *A Winter Talent* (1957), contains some of the outstanding English poems of the 1950s, such as the haunting 'Time passing, beloved' and the wry 'Heigh-ho on a winter afternoon': 'Yes, I have "mellowed", as you said I would' (ibid., 74).

But 'mellowing' was not quite Davie's style, and his literary career proved as unpredictable as his academic one. Instead of producing another conventional slim volume of verse, he now wrote *The Forests of Lithuania* (1958), a version of Adam Mickiewicz's epic poem *Pan Tadeusz*, and a series of poems about American history, *A Sequence for Francis Parkman* (1961); meanwhile, his *New and Selected Poems* (1961), including the ambitious and enigmatic 'With the grain'—a poem which, like some of his major essays, worries at the vexed question of poetry's relationships with the other arts—appeared in the USA. His next critical work was equally unexpected, but *The Heyday of Sir Walter Scott* (1961) views its subject, like Mickiewicz and Parkman, as an explorer of the wilderness. Davie was also already engaged in a lifelong tussle with the work of Pound; *Ezra Pound: Poet as Sculptor* (1964) was the first of his three books on the poet (the others appeared in 1975 and 1991). Drawing on his travels both in Europe and in America, his next collection of poems, *Events and Wisdoms* (1964), was thematically and formally his most wide-ranging so far: 'Touched by that wand of transit, / Californian, hopeful …' (*Collected Poems*, 131), he playfully embraces American idioms and looks back with guarded nostalgia to his Barnsley childhood.

In 1964 Davie could not have foreseen the unhappy conclusion of his Essex years nor the fraught circumstances of his more permanent self-exile; nor, indeed, that this difficult period would produce outstanding poetry. For *Essex Poems* (1969) matches bleak East Anglian (and, in a postscript, Iowan) landscapes with a finely pared-down diction. When, in 'Ezra Pound in Pisa', he writes 'Excellence is sparse' (*Collected Poems*, 142), it could stand as epigraph for the entire collection, as could a heartfelt couplet from the final poem, 'Or, solitude': 'The metaphysicality / Of poetry, how I need it!' (ibid., 155). But *Essex Poems* is far from being a farewell to England: once in America, Davie became even more preoccupied with his home country, not only bombarding it with acerbic poems and articles, but publishing *Thomas Hardy and British Poetry* (1972), in which he argued that Hardy (rather than Yeats, Eliot, or Pound) was the most influential figure in twentieth-century British poetry, and *The Shires* (1974), an edgily reflective county-by-county sequence of poems.

A conservative, pipe-puffing and sometimes blunt-speaking Yorkshireman, Davie might have been an incongruous figure on a 1970s, west-coast campus; but he got on well with America, as his teasingly elliptical autobiography, *These the Companions* (1982), demonstrates, and he was an enthusiastic advocate of American poets such as Lorine Niedecker and Edward Dorn. In 1976 he returned temporarily to Cambridge to give the Clark lectures, on 'The literature of the English dissenting interest', and these were published as *A Gathered Church* (1978): this also marked a return to the theological concerns he had touched on as long ago as 1958 in his anthology *The Late Augustans* and which he further explored in his *New Oxford Book of Christian Verse* (1981). He had been received into the Anglican communion in 1972, and his later poetry became increasingly Christian in its focus. Meanwhile, *In the Stopping Train* appeared in 1977: the long, disturbing title poem analyses a divided self, the 'I who has to be punished' and 'the man going mad inside me' (*Collected Poems*, 285). To

Scorch or Freeze (1988) is a sequence of fragmented psalms, to which the ten-part meditation 'Our father' in the posthumously published *Poems and Melodramas* (1996) forms a coda; his Penguin Classics edition of *The Psalms in English* also appeared in 1996.

Although Davie published no entirely new full-length critical books after *A Gathered Church*, he remained a prolific, often controversial, essayist and reviewer. Many of his occasional pieces were collected in *The Poet in the Imaginary Museum* (1977) and *Trying to Explain* (1979), and in the late 1980s he began to reorganize his shorter critical pieces into a series of thematic volumes, starting with *Under Briggflatts: a History of Poetry in Great Britain, 1960–1988* (1989). The project continued after his death with volumes edited by his widow and Clive Wilmer. Donald Davie died of cancer at the Royal Devon and Exeter Hospital in Exeter on 18 September 1995; he was buried on 22 September in the churchyard of St Mary the Virgin, Silverton.

NEIL POWELL

Sources T. Chevalier, ed., *Contemporary poets*, 5th edn (1991) · N. Powell, 'Donald Davie', *British writers*, ed. J. Parini, Suppl. VI (2001), 105–18 · private information (2004)
Archives State University of New York, Buffalo, corresp. and literary papers
Likenesses photograph, repro. in C. Barker, *Portraits of poets* · photographs, repro. in D. Davie, *These the companions* (1982)
Wealth at death under £145,000: administration with will, 30 Nov 1995, *CGPLA Eng. & Wales*

Davie [*née* Dryer], **Elspeth Mary** (1919–1995), short-story writer and novelist, was born in Kilmarnock Infirmary, Ayrshire, on 20 March 1919, the daughter of Oliver Dryer, a Church of Scotland minister, and his Canadian wife, Lilian McFarlane. Her father had a Norwegian grandfather, and Elspeth was always conscious of Norse affinities. Her mother was of old loyalist stock, while her father—who was something of a womanizer—was a strong pacifist; before Elspeth's birth he served in London as secretary of the pacifist Fellowship of Reconciliation. When Elspeth was nine he returned to Scotland, to a parochial charge in Bonnyrigg, Midlothian. Elspeth attended the esteemed George Watson's Ladies' College, in Edinburgh, but would say that she learned less there than in her dame-school in London, where she was bowled over by *Beowulf*. However, she made some mark at Watson's, as a winning high-jumper. Her elder sister, Lois, who married the distinguished theologian Donald McKinnon, was a brilliant philosophy student at Edinburgh University. Elspeth followed her there, and she too did well in philosophy, while also studying English and fine art, but her maths was not good enough for her to complete an MA, so she moved to the city's famous college of art, where she took a diploma.

Walking in the borders with a friend on 11 July 1938 Elspeth met in a youth hostel 'a dark, heavy sort of fellow … dark brooding eyes behind glasses'. They talked all evening and carried on after breakfast the next day, 'both hungering to talk and discuss real things … I felt we could, in the end, have spoken about anything', as she recorded in her diary (*Chapman 81*, 12–13). Her new friend was

George Elder Davie (*b.* 1912), a legend for conversational erudition in Edinburgh student circles, a philosopher just returned from postgraduate study in Germany. His most famous book, *The Democratic Intellect: Scotland and her Universities in the Nineteenth Century*, published in 1961, made an enormous and enduring impact on serious Scottish thinking. He and Elspeth married on 5 October 1944; their daughter, Anne, was born in 1946.

Elspeth taught art in schools in Aberdeen and the borders. By 1946 she was in Belfast, where George was teaching at Queen's University. There she painted *en plein air*, quickly, in a style that echoed French post-impressionism, and sold her canvasses. (She set little store by them, and did not paint after George returned to Edinburgh University in 1959.) She also befriended a general practitioner, Pat Strang, then intimately involved with Philip Larkin. She met Strang for serious discussion of literature once a week, and Larkin took an interest in Strang's quiet friend. She was cautious in forming relationships, having seen in her own family the consequences of over-free 'giving'. She could impress people as shy and retiring, yet she talked well; once, when George Davie visited his friend Hugh MacDiarmid at his cottage near Biggar, the poet saw him out with 'Next time you come bring Elspeth with you—she will aerate the conversation.' She kept up with old friends from college days but did not go out much to court new ones. She read voraciously, deep into the night. The significant record of the last four decades of her life is simply that of her writing.

Elspeth Davie had composed short stories at school. Published excerpts from her diaries of 1938 show that she arrived at an alarmingly mature prose style extremely early. But her gift did not begin to emerge into public view until *The Observer* launched a short-story competition in 1951. The winner was Muriel Spark, from Edinburgh, who thus began her own impressive career in fiction. Elspeth Davie was runner-up. From then her rise to eminence was gradual. Notable magazines began to take her stories. She attracted the attention of a fellow Scot, John Calder, who had been the prime publisher of Samuel Beckett in English. He introduced in translation other experimental European writers, including the French novelist Robbe-Grillet, theorist of the *nouveau roman*, with whom Elspeth felt an especial affinity. In his world human beings are, up to a point, dominated by objects. Calder and Boyars were therefore the natural publishers for the first novel by this quiet *avant-gardiste*. *Providings* appeared in 1965. Three more novels followed: *Creating a Scene* (1971), about art teaching; *Climbers on a Stair* (1978); and *Coming to Light* (1989).

But it was Davie's short stories that provided the basis for mounting critical esteem, represented by her winning the prestigious Kathleen Mansfield prize in 1978. Calder and Boyars published her first collection, *The Spark*, in 1969. Four more followed, from other publishers: *The High Tide Talker* (1976), *The Night of the Funny Hats* (1980), *A Traveller's Room* (1985), and *Death of a Doctor* (1992). Three title-stories represent her range and preoccupations. In 'The High Tide Talker' a man who claims to be an actor appears every day on the beach of a popular resort and preaches to holiday-makers up to the point where the high tide drowns his words, so that his ultimate message is not revealed. This highly original fable displays Davie's interest in 'acting', and also her abiding theological concerns. The latter emerge also in 'The Night of the Funny Hats', in which a coachload of travellers and tourists progress through the great southern desert of Australia. 'Death of a Doctor' is confined to at most an hour in one place. As a nurse moves through a crowded waiting room, breaking to each patient in turn news that their doctor has just died, watchers from windows across the street are jealous because they imagine that some kind of social occasion is in progress. Breaking a simple scene into discrete particles, each dwelt on unemphatically in turn, and changing it into a kind of performance, Davie compels the reader to brood with her on what she called 'the secret side of life' (Gordon, *Beyond the Words*, 87).

Davie believed that meaning could not be abstracted, validly, from a good story; the whole story was its meaning. Her meanings are conveyed by unusual methods. Her stories are copiously populated but remarkably few persons are named. It has been noted, astutely, that 'unlike many excellent woman novelists' she does not 'discriminate in favour of female characters' (Todd, 179); general humankind attends like a Greek chorus the quiet agonies of male principals. She is absorbed with precise visual and aural detailing, but is usually uninterested in smells or sexuality. She offers a vision of humanity transiently and sadly engaged with life under enduring stars, with the arts (music as well as drama and painting) offering the reader, as they did her, purpose.

Elspeth and George Davie lived for many years at 15 Leven Terrace, Edinburgh—a flat at the top of a handsome mid-Victorian block. From one side the view was across the meadows, past the Royal Infirmary and the university, to the ominous grandeur of Arthur's Seat. On another side, over Bruntsfield Links, was James Gillespie's School—the original of Marcia Blane's in Muriel Spark's *The Prime of Miss Jean Brodie*. The flat was the venue of Davie's novel *Climbers on a Stair*. By 1982 a hundred stairs were too much for the ageing couple. George had just retired from the university and Elspeth had suffered a mild brain haemorrhage. But when they moved to a modern block in north Edinburgh they chose another top flat (albeit one reached by a lift). They shared a taste for the long view. Elspeth did not discuss her reading with George, and he found her almost aggressively indifferent to his obsession with the history of Scottish education. To a reader though, the overlapping of their philosophical concerns is amply apparent. Their outwardly quiet lives suggested mutual devotion.

After her first stroke Elspeth, who had never cared for housework, gave it even less attention, but she kept on writing, very well. The second blow fell in 1992. She could still put up a show for visitors, but she was finished. George nursed her as long as he could but at last had to put her in a home. She died at Queensbury House Hospital, Edinburgh, on 13 November 1995, as quietly as she had lived. She had never been a best-seller, but the brilliant younger generations of more flamboyant Scottish fiction writers who had followed in her wake included many who admired her craftsmanship and deep intelligence. Her ongoing and increasing reputation was indicated by the appearance in 2001 of a large selection of her stories, *The Man who Wanted to Smell Books*, published as a Canongate Classic. Introducing it, Giles Gordon evoked her appearance in a certain notable photograph:

> The stern, severe, intelligent face—intense searchlight eyes; prominent nose; tight jaw wide lips; compassionate strong chin—is topped by a sensible fringe and Mrs Davie wears a black, halter-neck jumper. Here is a latter-day Presbyterian visage with a vengeance. (p. vii)

Her Presbyterian vision was certainly not a matter of routine adherence to the kirk, in which her father had reared her. It derived more broadly from the overarching protestant traditions and grey starkness of Edinburgh, and from a rigorous intellectualism tempered by devotion to kindliness and beauty.   ANGUS CALDER

Sources G. Gordon, introduction, in E. Davie, *The man who wanted to smell books* (2001) · 'Elspeth Davie and the gap', *Chapman 81* (1995) · G. Gordon, ed., *Beyond the words: eleven writers in search of a new fiction* (1975) · *The Times* (16 Nov 1995) · J. Todd, ed., *Dictionary of British women writers* (1989) · private information (2004) [George Elder Davie] · b. cert. · d. cert.

Likenesses M. Knowles, oils, Scot. NPG · photograph, repro. in A. Catlin, *Natural light: portraits of Scottish writers* (1985)

Davie, Thomas Benjamin (1895–1955), pathologist and university principal, was born on 23 November 1895 at Prieska, Cape Colony, the fifth of the six children of Thomas Benjamin Davie, law agent and auctioneer, and his first wife, Caroline Charlotte Halliday (d. 1900). With Scottish ancestry on both sides, Davie spoke English at home but, after attending Prieska junior school from about 1901 to 1906, had an Afrikaans education at Paarl Boys' High School and Victoria College, Stellenbosch, Cape of Good Hope. At Stellenbosch he attained a BA in chemistry (1914) and a teachers' certificate (with distinction, 1916). His subsequent career as a secondary school science teacher in the Orange Free State and the Transvaal was interrupted by two years' training in Britain as a Royal Flying Corps pilot during the First World War. As an army volunteer suppressing labour militancy in Johannesburg during the Rand Revolt of 1922, he sustained a serious injury and, during a long hospital bound recuperation, he decided to give up schoolteaching for medicine. The previous year he had married Vera Catherine Roper (1893–1976), daughter of Thomas Roper, a Wesleyan minister; they had one daughter who died in infancy.

Like a number of young South Africans before him, Davie chose Liverpool University for his medical studies. Enrolling as a 28-year-old, his commitment, intellectual ability, and relative maturity soon won him many distinctions, as well as the ready confidence of patients. He graduated MB ChB (1928) and MD (1931). He received his MRCP in 1931, the same year that he became pathologist to the Walton Hospital, Liverpool. Thus did Davie begin his career in pathology, which culminated in chairs at Bristol University (1935–8) and Liverpool University (the George

Holt chair of pathology, 1938–45, and the chair of applied pathology, 1945–7). During this time he co-authored a standard pathology textbook with his mentor at Liverpool, Professor J. H. Dible, entitled *Pathology: an Introduction to Medicine and Surgery* (1939), and published a number of articles on the pathology of various diseases and on the storage of blood for transfusion. His view of pathology as the 'grammar of medicine and surgery', a process which was the subject of living, rather than morbid, anatomy, informed his emphasis on clinical training and research.

A gifted and popular teacher, Davie also showed particular aptitude for organization and administration at Bristol and Liverpool, where he reorganized the pathology departments and fostered greater contact between them and local hospitals. During the Second World War he worked tirelessly to improve blood transfusion and clinical pathology services for the Ministry of Health, notably establishing the first blood bank at Liverpool in 1939. He was elected FRCP in 1940. As the first full-time dean of the medical faculty at Liverpool (1945–7), he worked on post-war reorganization and expansion within the faculty. His qualities as a tactful and outstanding administrator secured his appointment as principal and vice-chancellor at the University of Cape Town in March 1948. Acute rheumatoid arthritis and other medical problems, which began to manifest themselves shortly after his return to South Africa, hampered Davie's work. Nevertheless, he applied himself energetically to the development of the university, which had been hindered by the war. Davie fostered academic and commercial contacts, raising money to expand research and teaching, initiated a scheme whereby the medical school staff became part-time employees of provincial hospitals too, and encouraged the establishment of new, interdisciplinary departments. In a broader sphere, he was instrumental in creating the South African Committee of University Principals.

The issue which loomed largest in Davie's principalship was, however, an attempt by the newly-elected National Party government to bar black students from the few 'open' universities which admitted them. Davie opposed this, initially because he objected to state intervention in university policy per se and later from a broader philosophical position which defined true universities as necessarily open to all—they had to make available 'the whole of knowledge to every one who can benefit by it'. In doing this, Davie hoped that universities would encourage better relations between English, Afrikaans, and black South Africans by fostering 'that toleration to ideas which characterizes the really educated man'. He led the opposition to university apartheid by the 'open' universities, a campaign which was ultimately unsuccessful: the Nationalist government passed legislation in 1959 to bar black students from entering these universities.

By 1955, seriously ill yet determined as ever not to yield to adversity, Davie travelled to England to represent his university and receive honorary doctorates from Oxford and Liverpool universities. This opportunity did not arise, however, as he died in London on the night of 13/14 December 1955. His body was cremated at Golders Green crematorium, Middlesex. He was survived by his wife. Before path-breaking cortisone treatment for his illness swelled his features, he had been a tall, distinguished looking man who was dynamic, genial, and approachable. He inspired affection, loyalty, and admiration: as a contemporary observed, 'One always felt that life was good when one was in his company.' Davie is remembered today chiefly for his role in defining and upholding the ideal of academic freedom, the freedom for institutions to decide 'who shall teach, what we teach, how we teach and whom we teach'. This vital contribution has been commemorated in an annual T. B. Davie memorial lecture at the University of Cape Town since 1959 which reaffirms the university's commitment to the principle of academic freedom.   HOWARD PHILLIPS and HARRIET DEACON

Sources University of Cape Town Library, Cape Town, manuscripts and archives division, T. B. Davie Collection · University of Cape Town Library, Cape Town, manuscripts and archives division, L. Marquard collection · University of Cape Town Administration Archives, Cape Town, principal's corresp. and MSS · *BMJ* (24 Dec 1955), 1567 · *The Lancet* (31 Dec 1955), 1395 · *Journal of Pathology and Bacteriology*, 72 (1956) · *University of Liverpool Recorder*, 10 (Jan 1956), 6–7 · A. van de Sandt Centlivres, Thomas Benjamin Davie (1961) · L. Marquard, 'University education: Thomas Benjamin Davie', *Better than they knew*, ed. R. M. de Villiers, 2 (1974), 121–47 · 'Report of the selection committee for the George Holt chair of pathology', U. Lpool L., special collections and archives, University Report Book · T. B. Davie, *Education and race relations in South Africa* (1955) · T. Kelly, *For advancement of learning: the University of Liverpool, 1881–1981* (1981) · private information (2004) · *DNB* · b. cert.
Archives U. Lpool · University of Cape Town Library, collection | University of Cape Town, principal's corresp. and papers · University of Cape Town Library, L. Marquard collection
Likenesses I. Mitford-Barberton, bronze head, 1951, University of Cape Town, Jagger Library · E. Roworth, oils, 1959, University of Cape Town, Bremner Administration Building · photographs, University of Cape Town Library, manuscripts and archives division · sketch, University of Cape Town Library, manuscripts and archives division

Davies. *See also* Davis, Davys.

Davies. For this title name *see* individual entries under Davies; *see also* Kennedy, Margaret [Margaret Davies, Lady Davies] (1896–1967).

Davies, Sir Alfred Thomas (1861–1949), solicitor and civil servant, was born on 11 March 1861 at Oak Lane, West Derby, Lancashire, the son of William Davies, a master linen draper, and his wife, Ann Thomas. He was educated at Waterloo high school, Liverpool, and the University College of Wales, Aberystwyth. He was admitted a solicitor in 1883, and became notary public in 1887 and cursitor of the county palatine of Lancaster in 1895. On 6 June 1888 he married Margaret Esther (1861/2–1892), daughter of Thomas Christian Nicholas, a cashier, at the Presbyterian church, Canning Street, Liverpool. They had two sons. After her death he married, secondly, on 6 April 1893 at the Baptist tabernacle, Southport, Mary (1858/9–1947), daughter of Charles Colton, an estate agent, of Liverpool, with whom he had a son and a daughter.

Davies practised as a solicitor in Liverpool for over twenty-five years and played a leading role in the city's Liberal Party. A committed member of the Calvinistic Methodist denomination (the Presbyterian Church of Wales), he was an advocate of the temperance movement. He developed a speciality in the licensing laws and published extensively on the subject. For Davies the issue was a moral responsibility resting on the shoulders of those in public life and he maintained that progressive social reform could only come about after drunkenness had been overcome. He served briefly as a member of Denbighshire county council from 1903 until 1907.

The main focus of Davies's activities, however, was education. He contributed to the development of technical classes and adult education lectures in both Liverpool and Wales and took a keen interest in the implementation of the Welsh Intermediate and Technical Education Act (1889), which provided a means of overcoming the nation's serious lack of post-elementary schools. At that time he became increasingly critical of the Board of Education under Conservative administrations during the late 1890s, and was an active opponent of Balfour's Education Act.

In 1907 Davies was appointed permanent secretary to the Welsh department of the Board of Education. Many in Wales had expected the Liberal government to establish a national council for education, a democratic body which would give Wales considerable autonomy over both policy and administration. The limited measure of administrative devolution which was actually granted failed to meet these anticipations, and throughout his period as permanent secretary Davies faced, and resisted, recurring demands for a national body to control education in Wales.

Davies also became embroiled in conflict with the Central Welsh Board (CWB), which was set up in 1896 to examine and inspect schools created under the 1889 act. The situation was complicated by the fact that under the terms of the Education Act (1902) local education authorities in England and Wales were empowered to establish secondary schools, which derived a grant from the Board of Education and were subject to its inspection regime. This meant that intermediate schools in Wales were subject to two sets of inspection—one from the CWB and the other from the Welsh department. The result was a long period of rivalry and sometimes open conflict between the two authorities. Davies was determined to extend the Welsh department's control over all secondary education in Wales, and his methods did little to promote harmonious co-operation with the CWB, not least because of his contempt for the priorities and administrative competency of the board.

Within the Board of Education, Davies proved equally determined in promoting his department's autonomy. Its remit was unclear and he faced considerable opposition as he sought to extend its influence over all aspects of education in Wales at a time when experienced colleagues were unwilling to depart from the principle of a common education policy for England and Wales. At the same time arguments over the school curriculum highlighted the divergence of opinion over the role of secondary education in Wales. The Welsh department—largely because of the influence of its chief inspector Owen Morgan Edwards—maintained that the intermediate schools focused too heavily on academic subjects, that they were too preoccupied with ensuring that pupils passed the array of examinations set by the CWB, and that little attention was given to broader notions of the purpose of education, including the role of the Welsh language in the nation's schools. Both Edwards and Davies were convinced of the need to establish central and technical schools in Wales offering a more vocational form of post-elementary secondary education and filling serious deficiencies in Welsh school provision. Their efforts were hampered mainly by the determination of the Welsh education authorities, which insisted that their schools should provide academic instruction—a view supported by most parents. After Edwards's death Davies was for five years (1920–25) acting chief inspector of education for Wales in addition to holding the permanent secretaryship.

Davies's activities ranged widely during this period. He was director of a scheme to supply books for British prisoners of war in 1914–18, and he also supported the campaign to prevent a reservoir being built at the Ceiriog valley in Denbighshire, a campaign that later led to the movement to establish a permanent memorial to the community. He was made a CB in 1917 and knighted in the following year.

After his retirement in 1925 Davies continued an active public life, holding a number of legal and public appointments in Buckinghamshire, where he lived at Medmenham, and in Denbighshire. He occasionally pronounced on matters of public policy in Wales. He opposed proposals to transfer the Welsh department to Cardiff and was not enamoured of the idea that the post of secretary of state for Wales should be established as a further measure of devolution. He devoted much time to writing, publishing works on O. M. Edwards (1926), John Calvin (1946), Robert Owen (1948), and David Lloyd George (1948). He died at his home, Flat 2, Calthorpe House, 12 Lewes Crescent, Brighton, Sussex, on 21 April 1949.

ROBERT V. SMITH

Sources G. E. Jones, *Controls and conflicts in Welsh secondary education, 1889–1944* (1982) · *Y bywgraffiadur Cymreig, 1941–1950* (1970) · *WWW* · b. cert. · m. cert. [Margaret Nicholas] · m. cert. [Mary Colton] · d. cert. · K. O. Morgan, *Rebirth of a nation: Wales, 1880–1980* (1982) · *CGPLA Eng. & Wales* (1949)
Archives NL Wales, corresp. and papers | NL Wales, Thomas Jones MSS · NL Wales, corresp. with Sir John Herbert Lewis
Wealth at death £43,084 10s. 2d.: probate, 12 Aug 1949, *CGPLA Eng. & Wales*

Davies, Aneirin Talfan [Aneirin ap Talfan] (1909–1980), author and broadcaster, was born on 11 May 1909 at Islwyn, Felindre, near Newcastle Emlyn, Carmarthenshire, the second of the four sons of William Talfan Davies (1873–1938), Calvinistic Methodist minister, and his wife, Alys, née Jones (1878–1948). He was educated at Gowerton grammar school. He left in 1923 and became a pharmacist,

working in London, in Watford, and in his own pharmacy in Swansea until it was destroyed by bombing in 1941. By the mid-1930s his chief interests were literary. On 1 June 1936 he married Mary Anne (Mari) Evans (1912–1971), a native of Barry who taught in Hoxton. During that year Davies produced (with Dafydd Jenkins) the first number of *Heddiw*, a small literary magazine which, together with *Y ddau lais* (1937) and *Y wawr* (undated, but written in 1938), signalled many of his later achievements.

Heddiw shows Davies's determination to create a medium for other writers. *Y ddau lais*, a book of poems published jointly by Davies (under the name Aneirin ap Talfan) and W. H. Reese, became noted for the critical stance and substance of Davies's foreword, which reveals the early but lasting influences of T. S. Eliot and Saunders Lewis. Here he first criticized the poets of the older generation for letting their work 'degenerate into sorry pessimism and escape', for confining poetry to certain subjects, and for ignoring *vers libre*, 'the only measure that gives the poet that freedom necessary to interpret modern life as it is' (ap Talfan, *Y ddau lais*, ix). In later essays he contrasted their 'nonconformist agnosticism' with the more cerebral 'dark gospel' of some of his contemporaries (Davies, *Y tir diffaith*, 20, 23). *Y wawr* is a pageant-play that mainly depicts the labours of the great Welsh Anglican translators of scripture in the sixteenth century: in 1944 Davies was received into the Church in Wales.

Throughout his life Davies remained deeply committed to the Welsh Anglican tradition that predates the establishment of the Calvinistic Methodist church in 1811. Some of his anthologies and his later essays, in *Sylwadau* (1957) and *Astudio byd* (1967), bear witness to the well-known and the neglected classics of that era. He also continued to extend the knowledge of Welsh readers of modern European literary movements and figures. His studies of Eliot (1942, 1946) and Joyce (1944) were designed to resist what he called 'our unyielding parochialism and our narrow puritanism' (Davies, *Yr alltud*, 11). At the same time he worked assiduously on Welsh literature—editing *Gwŷr llên* (1948), a fine collection of critical essays on contemporary writers; compiling the biannual *Llafar* from 1951 to 1957; selecting *Englynion a chywyddau* (1958); writing essays and verse (his later poems, *Diannerch erchwyn a cherddi eraill*, were published in 1975); and contributing substantial works on his native Carmarthenshire (1958) and on his adopted Glamorgan (1972, 1976) to the excellent series of county travel books published by Llyfrau'r Dryw, a company established by him and his youngest brother, Alun. He also championed Welsh authors who wrote in English, most notably David Jones and Dylan Thomas. In these activities, as in his non-literary work, he was the personification of cultured, seemingly leisured, urbanity.

In 1942 Davies joined the BBC. In 1957 he became deputy head of programmes, and in 1965 head of programmes, Wales. His work as broadcaster mirrored much of his work as author and editor. In his production of feature programmes and in his commissioning of plays, talks, and librettos he reflected and enriched Welsh life, but he also sought 'to broaden the ideas' of Welsh listeners

(J. Davies, 196). For a quarter of a century much of Welsh broadcasting was Talfanism aired.

Davies was made MA *honoris causa* by the University of Wales in 1958 and appointed OBE in 1970. His wife died in 1971. Their eldest child, Owen (*b.* 1938), was killed in a car accident in 1963, and they had two other children, Geraint (*b.* 1943) and Elinor (*b.* 1946). Davies died of a stroke at Ysbyty Priordy, Carmarthen, on 14 July 1980, and was buried in the graveyard of Llandaff Cathedral.

DEREC LLWYD MORGAN

Sources J. Davies, *Broadcasting and the BBC in Wales* (1994) · I. Rees, ed., *Bro a bywyd: Aneirin Talfan Davies, 1909–1980* (1992) · private information (2004) [G. T. Davies]
Archives NL Wales, corresp., diaries, and papers | NL Wales, corresp. with Kate Davies · NL Wales, corresp. with Norah Isaac · NL Wales, letters to Thomas Iorworth Ellis and to Annie Hughes-Griffiths | FILM BBC Wales, Llandaff, Cardiff | SOUND BBC Wales, Llandaff, Cardiff
Likenesses photographs, repro. in Rees, ed., *Bro a bywyd*
Wealth at death £60,427: probate, 29 Aug 1980, *CGPLA Eng. & Wales*

Davies, Annie Patricia [Pat] **Llewelyn-** [*née* Annie Patricia Parry; *other married name* Annie Patricia Rawdon Smith], **Baroness Llewelyn-Davies of Hastoe** (1915–1997), politician, was born on 16 July 1915 at 8 Knowsley Road, Wallasey, Birkenhead, the daughter of Charles Percy Parry, mechanical engineer, and his wife, Sarah Gertrude, formerly Allan, *née* Hamilton. She was educated at Wallasey high school, Birkenhead high school, and Liverpool College, Huyton. On 4 October 1934 she married Alexander Francis Rawdon Smith (*b.* 1911/12), research physiologist, son of George Francis Rawdon Smith, physician, of Mossley Hill, Liverpool. They had no children. Shortly after the marriage she went to Girton College, Cambridge.

Petite, attractive, and both fun-loving and intellectual, Pat Rawdon Smith bowled for her college cricket eleven and joined the university Labour Club, having been a Labour supporter since her youth. She also moved among Victor Rothschild's circle and became friendly with Tessa Mayor, Rothschild's future wife, and Anthony Blunt. She was embarrassed by the later revelation that Blunt had been a Soviet spy. In 1935 she was placed in the third class in the intercollegiate examination in English; she remained at Girton until the following year, but did not proceed to a degree. In 1940 she joined the Ministry of War Transport. She later moved to the Foreign Office and the Air Ministry. Meanwhile, her first marriage having ended in divorce, on 3 June 1943 she married Richard Llewelyn *Davies, later Baron Llewelyn-Davies (1912–1981), architect and town planner. They had three daughters.

In 1947 Pat Llewelyn Davies became secretary at the Commonwealth Relations Office to her lifelong friend Philip Noel-Baker. A promising career in the civil service lay ahead, but in 1951 she resigned to contest Wolverhampton South-West for the Labour Party at the general election. A self-declared Bevanite, she was defeated by the Conservative, Enoch Powell. After two narrow defeats at Wandsworth Central, in 1955 and 1959, she did not stand for parliament again. From 1960 to 1969 she was director of the Africa Educational Trust. Although she was active in

public life, by mid-decade her political career had stalled. In 1964 Wandsworth Central was won by Labour and it appeared that she had given up on the seat too soon. Meanwhile the life peerage given to her husband in 1963 made it more difficult for her to enter parliament by the upper house. It was a problem that vexed her close friend R. H. S. Crossman. He was conscious of the irony in Richard Llewelyn Davies having been made a Labour peer, when it was his wife who was 'the *real* politician' (Crossman, *Diaries*, 1.496).

Llewelyn-Davies (her name was hyphenated following her husband's elevation to the peerage) nevertheless had supporters in Wilson's cabinet. They included Anthony Greenwood, as well as Crossman, and with important backing from the latter she was created a life peer, as Baroness Llewelyn-Davies of Hastoe (the village near Tring, Hertfordshire, where she and her husband lived) in 1967. Thereafter her career flourished. She was a government whip in 1969–70 and deputy opposition chief whip in 1972–3, and in 1973 easily defeated two male rivals to be elected chief whip: the first woman to take charge of a whip's office in either house. In March 1974 she became government chief whip, a post she held until Labour's defeat in the general election of 1979. She was sworn of the privy council in 1975. With her new office went the ceremonial role of 'captain of the Honourable Corps of Gentlemen at Arms', but it was considered inappropriate that she should wear the customary military uniform, and after consultation with the queen she wore instead a badge designed by the royal jeweller. When required, though, she exercised her right to salute the monarch, rather than curtsey.

Llewelyn-Davies's concern as government chief whip was with questions of function rather than form. She tried to deploy to best effect the relatively thin ranks of Labour peers nominally under her control. This required an intimate knowledge of the arcane workings of the house, and the intentions of the government, and considerable powers of persuasion. Her 'sex appeal and charm' were an undoubted advantage, and she once remarked: 'You can't whip a lord like an MP. You can only appeal to his reason, and praise him if he turns up' (*Daily Telegraph*). During her second tenure as chief opposition whip, from 1979 to 1982, she began an era, continued by her successor Lord Ponsonby, in which a record number of defeats were inflicted on the government. Although she retained her radicalism on social issues she moved towards the centre as she grew older. She became a defender of the upper house, though not of titles themselves.

The onset of ill health in 1982, the year after her husband's death, caused Llewelyn-Davies's resignation as opposition chief whip. From 1982 to 1987 she was principal deputy chairman of committees, and chairman of the select committee on the European Communities in the House of Lords. She was a member of the board of governors of Great Ormond Street Hospital from 1955 to 1967, and chairman from 1967 to 1969; chairman of the Women's National Cancer Control Campaign from 1972 to

1975; and co-chairman of the Women's National Commission from 1976 to 1979. In 1979 she became an honorary fellow of Girton College, Cambridge. During her last two years she was nursed devotedly by Cuthbert James McCall (Cubby) *Alport, Baron Alport, of Colchester (1912–1998), a widower, and former Conservative minister. They had shared a clandestine love affair for some fourteen years, kept secret largely because of her fear that it would compromise him politically. She died at his home, Cross House, Layer de la Haye, near Colchester, Essex, on 6 November 1997 of bronchopneumonia and arteropathic cerebrovascular disease, and was cremated. She was survived by Lord Alport and by her three daughters.

MARK POTTLE

Sources WWW · *Daily Telegraph* (8 Nov 1997) · *The Times* (9 Nov 1992) · *The Times* (10 Nov 1997) · *The Times* (15 Nov 1997) · *The Times* (29 Oct 1998) · *The Guardian* (15 June 1990) · *The Guardian* (8 Nov 1997) · *The Guardian* (8 March 1999) · D. Healey, *The time of my life* (1989) · R. H. S. Crossman, *The diaries of a cabinet minister*, 1 (1975) · R. H. S. Crossman, *The diaries of a cabinet minister*, 2 (1976) · F. W. S. Craig, *British parliamentary election results, 1950–1970* (1971) · M. Garnett, *Alport: a study in loyalty* (1999) · K. T. Butler and H. I. McMorran, eds., *Girton College register, 1869–1946* (1948) · b. cert. · m. certs. · d. cert.
Likenesses photograph, repro. in *The Guardian* (8 Nov 1997) · photograph, repro. in Garnett, *Alport*, facing p. 139

Davies, Ann Lorraine [known as Ann Lindsay] (1914–1954), actress and translator, was born on 2 October 1914 at 125 Woodville Road, Cardiff, one of the five children of Morgan Davies (b. 1872), a master draper, and his wife, Sarah Ann, née Phillipps. She was a descendant of 'peasant shopkeeping and non-conformist forebears' (Rickword and Lindsay, 7). Like her mother, Ann loved singing, acting, and drama; at eight she played the harp, and she was active in the Tabernacle Welsh Baptist Church. She attended Wentworth School, Bournemouth, from the age of eleven, and in 1932 went to University College, Cardiff, where she studied music, economics, and modern languages. Well liked for her debating skills and 'rascal laugh' (ibid., 16), she became vice-president of the students' union, played in the hockey eleven, and toured America with the Welsh ladies' hockey team in 1936. In that same year she graduated with honours in French and moved to London, where she cared for Basque children and volunteered for work with the League of Nations. While a clerk at Harrods, she became principal boy for the Unity Theatre at St Pancras, playing Robin Hood (and Fairy Wishfulfilment) in Robert Mitchell's *Babes in the Wood*. The play sharply satirized Chamberlain's appeasement at Munich and, with 48,000 paid subscriptions, ran from November 1938 to May 1939, its revisions supervised by the Communist Party. In the last act Robin wore the uniform of a Soviet soldier, supposedly representing the rescuing popular front. The play's lyricist, Geoffrey Parsons, admired Davies's 'low musical Welsh' voice and 'buoyant charm', while Arnold Rattenbury described her as an 'emblem of the communist left … [its] almost pin-up' (private information). Montagu Slater declared that *Babes in the Wood* 'had more direct effect on current politics than any other single production in the history of the English stage'.

While leading a quasi-bohemian existence, Davies early in 1939 became administrative assistant to Randall Swingler, who had closed *Left Review* and was merging *Poetry and the People*, which he co-edited with Jack Lindsay, into his Fore Publications, founded in September 1938. Swingler had an open marriage with Geraldine Peppin, a pianist, and he and Davies embarked on an affair.

Early in 1940 Davies played Vera in the Unity production of Afinogenov's *Distant Point*, but the play received mediocre reviews. During the blitz she worked in air-raid shelters for Unity's mobile group, which was supported by the Council for the Encouragement of Music and the Arts. She also sat on the arts and entertainment committee of the People's Convention, held by the Communist Party of Great Britain to initiate a 'People's government and a people's peace', which took place in Manchester in February 1941.

In order to secure *Poetry and the People*'s paper rations for the literary journal *Our Time* (February 1941), Swingler created Newport Communications, with Davies as secretary and organizer. In June Davies took Humphrey Swingler's place as director and became its 'chair and administrator' (A. Croft, *A Weapon in the Struggle*, 1998, 149). Randall Swingler departed for army service in September and Davies left before March 1942. In October that year she was elected the first woman president of the Unity Theatre; she later became general secretary.

Meanwhile Jack *Lindsay (1900–1990), who had been serving with the signals corps, had been posted to the War Office in London, where he was working as a scriptwriter for the Army Bureau of Current Affairs and was living with Edgell Rickword. He became involved with Davies in 1943 when she was producing Mulk Raj Anand's *India Speaks*, a play about Bengal's famine. In November 1943 Lindsay found accommodation with his army friend Arnold Rattenbury, now invalided out of service, and Davies moved in with him, despite the fact that Lindsay was still married to a woman he had left behind in his native Australia. Soon afterwards Lindsay and Davies made their 'marriage' public, but it was never legally ratified.

Davies now joined Unity's general purposes committee, its *de facto* governing body. As councilwoman of the British Drama League (1944–53), Davies worked indefatigably in conjunction with the People's Entertainment Society to unify various (mostly London-based) drama groups. She pushed the league to create a play encouragement committee to develop topical pieces—Jack Lindsay's forte—and as secretary of Lindsay's script centre she helped obtain plays for labour-related projects. She also sat on the arts committee of the National Council of Social Service and acted in film documentaries, including one for the BBC.

Jack Lindsay wrote *Robin of England* for her; it was produced by Unity in 1945. Later in that year, for the People's Entertainment Society, Davies produced and performed in J. Grigson's *Men of Rochdale*, which went on tour. In the following year she became secretary of Theatre '46, a consortium initiated by Montagu Slater involving Bernard Miles (as producer), Lindsay, and the trade unions. Uniquely, sponsorship came largely (if briefly) from the Amalgamated Engineering Union, then celebrating its centenary, and Davies maintained creative unity within this diverse grouping. The company's first production was Lindsay's Face of Coal, dramatizing the need to nationalize the industry. When Miles began running a deficit, Davies and Lindsay contributed most of their assets to bail him out. Throughout they entertained intellectuals at a flat in Wellington Road, St John's Wood. During this period Davies also organized the Unity production of Lindsay's 'Voice of Greece', a declamation (1947) against the suppression of communist EAM/ELAS resistance, which was being promoted by the Truman doctrine with British support, and worked with the St Pancras People's Players.

After Fore sold its New Developments series to the Bodley Head, Jack Lindsay became editor (1947–8) and published The Theatre (1948), which he had co-written with Davies. Adopting left-wing theatre policy, The Theatre decried the 'suffering English stage' (p. 27), which was then torn between art and business; instead, Davies and Lindsay welcomed the 'unifying clue' (p. 29) created by labour and the grass roots movement. Committed to the movement to ban the bomb, she accompanied Lindsay to both the Wrocaw Peace Congress in 1948 and the Authors' World Peace Appeal in Paris. They were subsequently forced by exhausted finances into the humble Quarry Cottage near Penshurst in Kent, offered them by the publisher Tony Adams, then to a forester's cottage in Ashour Woods. During this period Davies translated a work by Claude Aveline as The Double Death of Frederic Belot (1949). In the spring of 1949 they returned to Paris for the Peace Congress, then spent six weeks in the Soviet Union for celebrations marking the 150th anniversary of Pushkin's birth, meeting Pablo Neruda, Nikolai Tikhonov, and Paul Robeson. This trip, during which Davies, who was a heavy smoker, sometimes felt weak, was chronicled in Lindsay's A World Ahead (1950).

From 1950 to 1951 Davies was secretary of Tunbridge Wells Peace Council. She and Lindsay made further foreign trips in 1951, meeting Brecht in Poland and Aragon and Tzara in Paris. On their return Davies underwent surgery for breast cancer. With her father's underwriting and the Swinglers' help they moved into Bangslappers, an old tollhouse in Castle Hedingham, Halstead, Essex, where she edited Lindsay's monumental Byzantium into Europe (1952). As members of the British-Rumanian Friendship Society they were invited to Bucharest in 1952, where they were shown a model gaol and introduced to President Groza and General Secretary Gheorghieu-Dej. Although troubled by reported persecution of minorities, they failed to penetrate the façade of these hardliners, both of whom had imprisoned thousands.

From 1952 to 1953 Davies worked on translating Zola's La terre, a task she finished on her deathbed, having had her ovaries removed in the winter of 1953 after a recurrence of cancer. She died at Bangslappers on 9 January

1954. Earth was published posthumously, with Davies and Lindsay depicted as French peasants on the dust jacket. Although the translation was fine, it was panned by the critics for its supposed salaciousness.

Lindsay wrote 'Elegy of Ann—the return', one of his Three Elegies (1957), in her memory. He cherished her as 'the finest woman' he ever knew, and Edith Sitwell called her a 'saint' (Lindsay, Life Rarely Tells, 806).

JAMES M. BORG

Sources E. Rickword and J. Lindsay, Nothing is lost: Ann Lindsay, 1914–1954 (1954) [for the Writers Group of the communist party] · J. Lindsay, Life rarely tells (1982) · Daily Worker (13 Jan 1954) · J. Lindsay, A world ahead (1950) · J. Lindsay and M. Cornforth, Rumanian summer (1953) · J. Lindsay and others, 'A month in Rumania', c.1953 · O. Anderson, 'Jack Lindsay', Dictionary of Literary Biography Yearbook (1984), 294–307 · private information (2004) · Jack Lindsay: faithful to the earth, ed. P. Gillen (1993) · C. Hobday, Edgell Rickword: a poet at war (1989) · d. cert. · A. Croft, 'Randall Swingler' (typescript), 1996
Archives NL Aus., papers of Jack Lindsay, MS 7168
Likenesses photographs, repro. in Lindsay, 'A month in Rumania' · photographs, repro. in Rickword and Lindsay, Nothing is lost
Wealth at death £4850: administration, 10 April 1954, CGPLA Eng. & Wales

Davies, Benjamin (1814–1875), Hebrew scholar, was born at Wern, near St Clears, Carmarthenshire, on 26 February 1814. He studied for the Baptist ministry in Wales at the Bristol Baptist college (1830), at Glasgow, and at Leipzig, where he was awarded a PhD degree in 1838. He then moved to Montreal where he trained missionaries for the Canada Missionary Society. While there Davies married Eliza Try, from Portland, Maine, with whom he remained for thirty years. They had several children. In 1844 he returned to England as president of Stepney Baptist college, but stayed only two and a half years, returning to Canada in 1847 to take up a professorship at McGill College in Montreal. He went back to London in 1857 to become professor of oriental and classical languages at his former college, which had just moved to Regent's Park from Stepney. Davies is best known for his published translation of Gesenius's Hebrew grammar and lexicon, which became a standard reference work; he also translated several epistles for the Paragraph Bible, which was issued by the Religious Tract Society, and edited various other scholarly works. He died at Frome in Somerset on 19 July 1875.   W. R. NICOLL, rev. GERALD LAW

Sources Baptist (30 July 1875) · 'Memoirs of Baptist ministers deceased', Baptist Hand-Book (1876), 341–4 · CGPLA Eng. & Wales (1875)
Wealth at death under £4000: probate, 11 Aug 1875, CGPLA Eng. & Wales

Davies, Benjamin Grey [Ben] (1858–1943), singer, was born on 6 January 1858 in Pontardawe, near Swansea, the eldest son of an engineer who died when the boy was seven. Having learned to read music by the tonic sol-fa system, he sang alto in choirs competing in eisteddfods, and in Caradoc's Choir at the Crystal Palace. His voice broke when he was fifteen, and he worked as a shop assistant in Swansea until he won first prize at the 1877 Swansea eisteddfod. This enabled him to study at the Royal Academy of Music with Fiori and Randegger (1878–80), where he won the Evill Prize. A student success in Mendelssohn's *Hymn of Praise* led to an engagement to sing the tenor solo in *St Paul* in Dublin, while another student performance, in Gounod's *Faust*, resulted in his operatic début at Birmingham on 11 October 1881, with the Carl Rosa Opera Company, as Thaddeus in Balfe's *The Bohemian Girl*; in 1885 he married Clara Perry, a soprano in the company. He continued to sing small parts, notably in J. W. Turner's company.

Davies's first leading part came on 20 December 1886 at the Prince of Wales Theatre in London as Geoffrey Wilder in Alfred Cellier's *Dorothy*. By now he was one of the rising stars among English tenors, beginning to succeed Edward Lloyd and Sims Reeves in public affections. He went on to sing the title role in the première (31 January 1891) and on alternate nights of the opening run of Sullivan's *Ivanhoe*, at £70 for four performances a week, according to the composer's diary. In 1891 he also sang Clément Marot in Messager's *La Basoche*, and the following year performed with Augustus Harris's company. Thereafter he turned his attention increasingly to oratorio, both in Britain (Cardiff Festival, 1892, in Dvořák's *Stabat mater*) and in America (where he made his début at the 1893 Chicago World Fair); he returned to America almost annually. He made his Covent Garden début on 25 July 1892 as Gounod's Faust. His many festival appearances included those at Norwich (1893–6), Leeds (1895), and Bristol (1896). He sang in Berlin in 1894. Davies was always a particularly welcome guest in his native Wales, where he sang at eisteddfods, notably in Joseph Parry's oratorio *Saul of Tarsus* at Rhyl in 1892. In 1916 he became vice-president of the newly formed Society of English Singers. His fine natural gifts, which included an attractive timbre and clear enunciation, disciplined by an excellent technique, enabled him to continue his career well into his sixties. In the 1920s he participated in Albani's benefit at Covent Garden (25 May 1925) and at the Handel Festival (1926). He died at Clifton Court, Clifton Hill, Bristol, Gloucestershire, on 28 March 1943.

JOHN WARRACK

Sources *New Grove* · *Grove, Dict. mus.* · *MT*, 40 (1899), 513–8 · A. Jacobs, *Arthur Sullivan: a Victorian musician*, pbk edn (1986) · G. B. Shaw, *Music in London, 1890–94*, 3 vols.; repr. (1949–50) · H. Klein, *Thirty years of musical life in London* (1903) · S. D'Amico, ed., *Enciclopedia dello spettacolo*, 11 vols. (Rome, 1954–68) · Brown & Stratton, *Brit. mus.* · WWW · d. cert.
Archives SOUND BL NSA
Likenesses photograph, repro. in P. Scholes, *The mirror of music* (1947)

Davies, Catherine (*b.* 1773, *d.* in or after 1841), governess and author, was born at Beaumaris, Anglesey, one of a family of thirty-three children of a twice-married father. At fifteen she went to Liverpool to work in a merchant's family and subsequently to London to live with her sister, who she said was 'married to an eminent artist'. In 1802 she was engaged as a governess to a family who were moving to France, but they shortly returned to England because of the tension between the French and the English at that time. However she was engaged by Madame Murat, Napoleon's third sister, who was looking expressly for Englishwomen to take care of her three, and later four, children. Davies was apparently treated with kindness and considerable familiarity in the true sense of the word, maintaining firmly her Welsh origins. Napoleon's visits to his sister were generally secret, but on one occasion at Fontainebleau, when the children greeted their uncle, Miss Davies had a conversation with him and he asked her if she preferred the English to the French and congratulated her on the honesty of her somewhat evasive reply.

In 1808 Murat was made king of Naples by Napoleon and the family took up residence there, visiting the Princess Borghese in Turin on the way after coming through the Mont Cenis Pass. It was then that Davies started to write the book which is her claim to fame, entitled *Eleven Years' Residence in the Family of Murat, King of Naples* (1841). The details which she gives of life in this court from the vantage point of the nursery contain anecdotal, but probably reliable, information. Her health was not good and she sought cures for an affliction of the neck at Ischia and Portici, eventually returning to Wales in 1818 to settle in Beaumaris. She was to be called as a witness at the trial of Queen Caroline, but never took the stand.

In 1841 Davies's book was published by How and Parsons at 12s. 6d. 'for her sole benefit', the preface being dated May of that year. Reviews appeared in both the *Monthly Review* and the *Literary Gazette*. A friendly letter from her charge, Prince Achille, by then postmaster in Lipona, Florida, formed one of the appendices to the book. The date of her death is not known but is thought to have been shortly after the publication of the book in 1841.

WILLIAM ROBERTS, *rev.* J. GILLILAND

Sources C. Davies, *Eleven years' residence in the family of Murat, king of Naples* (1841) · *Monthly Review*, 4th ser., 3 (1841), 349–54 · *Literary Gazette* (8 Oct 1841), 651–3

Davies, Cecilia (1756/7–1836), singer, was the daughter of the flautist and composer Richard Davies (*d.* 1773) and his wife, Cecilia, and sister of the glass armonica player Mary Ann *Davies, who was her first singing teacher. In August 1767 she joined her sister and father in three concerts at the Swan and Hoop tavern, London, singing music by Handel and Arne, after which the family travelled to the continent. In Vienna they lived in the same house as the composer Hasse, who taught Cecilia singing, while she and Mary Ann taught his daughters English. The sisters performed together, becoming favourites at court; Empress Maria Theresa commissioned a cantata for soprano and armonica from Hasse and Metastasio for Archduchess Maria Amalia's wedding in June 1769. Metastasio wrote in praise of Cecilia's pleasing and flexible voice, which imitated the armonica 'so exactly, that it is sometimes impossible to distinguish one from the other' (Burney, *Metastasio*, 3.83). In January 1772, although Hasse felt her unready, Cecilia sang as prima donna in his *Ruggiero* at Naples. Mary Ann wrote that her sister was a success, despite her youth (she was fifteen) and the cabal against her. 'L'Inglesina' sang also at Florence, becoming the first Englishwoman to perform leading roles in Italian opera houses.

The family returned to London, where Signora Davies sang at the Italian Opera in the 1773–4 season, receiving 'thundering shouts of applause' on her début (*General Evening Post*, 23 Nov 1773). She failed to charm Horace Walpole, but Charles Burney praised the flexibility and clarity of her voice, not loud but perfectly in tune, and admired the accuracy of her rapid divisions. David Garrick told James Harris that Cecilia Davies was the best opera actress he had ever seen. Her father died in December 1773 and it was Mary Ann whom Fanny Burney blamed for the disputes in which Cecilia, 'a sensible, well bred & engaging Girl' (*Early Journals*, 2.106), became involved at the Opera. In 1775 Cecilia was engaged in a law suit against the Opera managers and, although she won her case and received £2000 plus expenses, she sang again at the Opera only from January to July 1777, when she replaced the inexperienced Anna Pozzi as prima donna. During these four years she sang at a number of London concerts, mainly for charitable foundations, and at several provincial festivals.

The sisters were in Paris by January 1778 and in 1779–80 Cecilia sang leading roles in opera houses in Venice, Florence, Genoa, and Leghorn. In 1784 she appeared at Florence, having earlier refused engagements because of her sister's serious illness. Mount Edgcumbe later found them at Florence 'unengaged and poor' (Edgcumbe, 17) and assisted their return to England. Cecilia sang in the 1787 Professional Concerts in London and in oratorios at Drury Lane in 1791, still described as 'L'Inglesina'. By 1797 she and Mary Ann were supporting themselves by giving music lessons. Cecilia was seriously ill after Mary Ann's death in December 1818, and by the mid-1820s she was dependent on charitable donations. The publication by subscription in 1829 of six pieces composed for her by Hasse and others raised little money. She grew increasingly frail and became nearly blind, but remained alert and communicative about the successes of her youth. She died at her lodgings at 58 Great Portland Street, on 3 July 1836, and was buried at St Marylebone on 7 July as Cecilia Anglecina Davies.

OLIVE BALDWIN and THELMA WILSON

Sources G. W. Stone, ed., *The London stage, 1660–1800*, pt 4: 1747–1776 (1962) · C. B. Hogan, ed., *The London stage, 1660–1800*, pt 5: 1776–1800 (1968) · S. McVeigh, *Calendar of London concerts, 1750–1800* [unpublished computer database, Goldsmiths' College, London] · B. Matthews, 'The Davies sisters, J. C. Bach and the glass harmonica', *Music and Letters*, 56 (1975), 150–69 · C. Sartori, *I libretti italiani a stampa dalle origini al 1800*, 7 vols. (Cuneo, 1990–94) · *Public Advertiser* (10 Aug 1767) · *General Evening Post* (20–23 Nov 1773) · S. H. Hansell, *Works for solo voice of Johann Adolph Hasse* (1968) · C. Burney, *Memoirs of the life and writings of the Abate Metastasio*, 3 (1796) · Burney, *Hist. mus.*, vol. 4 · *The journals and letters of Fanny Burney (Madame D'Arblay)*, ed. J. Hemlow and others, 12 vols. (1972–84), vol. 12 · *The early journals and letters of Fanny Burney*, ed. L. E. Troide, 2: 1774–1777 (1990) · Madame D'Arblay [F. Burney], *Memoirs of Doctor Burney*, 2 (1832) · *Music and theatre in Handel's world: the family papers of James Harris, 1732–1780*, ed. D. Burrows and R. Dunhill (2002) · *The papers of Benjamin Franklin*, 25, ed. W. B. Willcox and others (1986) · *The papers of Benjamin Franklin*, 27, ed. C. A. Lopez and others (1988) · letters from Marianne [Mary Ann] Davies to Franklin on 26 April 1783 and 17 Oct 1783, American Philosophical Society, Philadelphia, Franklin

MSS · two volumes of airs from various Italian operas collected and partly written in manuscript by 'Signora Cecilia Inglesina Davies', Newberry Library, Chicago · *Musical World* (1836), 1.29, 47; 2.143–4 · 'On the harmonica, or musical glasses', *The Harmonicon*, 6 (1828), 126–7 · *The Harmonicon*, 10 (1832), 184 · R. Edgcumbe, *Musical reminiscences of an old amateur: chiefly respecting the Italian opera in England for fifty years, from 1773 to 1823*, 2nd edn (1827) · *The letters of Mozart and his family*, ed. and trans. E. Anderson, rev. S. Sadie and F. Smart, 3rd edn (1985) · Walpole, *Corr.*, vols. 23, 39
Archives Dorset RO, Solly MSS D/RAC 79, 102, 103, 108, 113, 115, 140

Davies, Charles Maurice (1828–1910), author, was of Welsh origin. In 1845 he entered Durham University as a scholar of University College and graduated BA in 1848 with a second class in classical and general literature, MA in 1852, and DD in 1864. He was elected a fellow of the university on 1 November 1849 and was ordained deacon in 1851 and priest in 1852. After serving various curacies he settled down to educational work in London. Meanwhile, his religious views underwent a change. Once an active supporter of the Tractarian movement, he soon adopted broad church principles and published anonymously a series of sensational novels attacking high-church practices, among them *Philip Paternoster* (1858), *Shadow Land* (1860), and *Verts, or, The Three Creeds* (1876). He also published translations of Sophocles' *Antigone* and *Oedipus tyrannus*, and Plautus's *Captivi*.

After holding the headmastership of the West London collegiate school (1861–8) Davies devoted himself mainly to journalism. In 1870 he represented the *Daily Telegraph* in France on the outbreak of the Franco-Prussian War and was arrested as a suspected spy while searching Metz for his colleague, George Augustus Sala. Among his other contributions to the *Daily Telegraph* was a series of independent studies of religious parties in London, which attracted attention. His articles were collected into a volume entitled *Unorthodox London* (1873; 2nd edn, 1875). This was followed by *Heterodox London, or, Phases of Free Thought in the Metropolis* (1874), *Orthodox London, or, Phases of Religious Life in the Church of England* (1874–5), and *Mystic London, or, Phases of Occult Life in the Metropolis* (1875), all of which were on the same lines. On leaving the service of the *Daily Telegraph* he went to Natal in South Africa to work under Bishop J. W. Colenso. After 1882, however, he abandoned holy orders. On his resettling in London, he was employed after 1893 in superintending a series of translations, undertaken at the instance of Cecil Rhodes, of the original authorities used by Edward Gibbon in his *Decline and Fall of the Roman Empire*. Nearly thirty scholars worked under his supervision and over a hundred volumes were completed. Davies retired from active work in 1901, and died at his home, 50 Connaught Road, Harlesden, London, on 6 September 1910. His funeral service was held at All Souls Church, Harlesden, on 10 September.

G. S. WOODS, rev. NILANJANA BANERJI

Sources *The Times* (9 Sept 1910) · *Durham University Calendar* (1850) · T. E. Fuller, *The right honourable Cecil John Rhodes: a monograph and a reminiscence* (1910), 133 · private information (1912)

Davies [*née* Cavenaugh], **Christian** [Catherine; *alias* Christopher or Richard Welsh; *called* Mother Ross] (**1667–1739**), female soldier, was, according to *The Life and Adventures of Mrs. Christian Davies* (1740), born Christian Cavenaugh in Dublin. She was raised by her parents on a farm at Leixlip, co. Kildare until, seduced by a cousin at the age of seventeen, she moved to Dublin to live with an aunt. Her father, a brewer and maltster, died in the service of the Jacobite cause in 1691, whereupon the family property was seized. Inheriting a Dublin public house upon the death of her aunt, she managed the business for several years, marrying Richard Welsh, an employee, about 1688 and giving birth to two sons. Her husband disappeared in 1692 and, in a letter she received a year later, revealed that he was in the army in Flanders.

After arranging settlement of her business and children, Welsh began the search for her husband, enlisting as a foot soldier under the name of Christopher Welsh. Wounded before the battle of Landen in 1693, she recovered and was taken prisoner and then exchanged in 1694. Passing the winter of 1694–5 with her regiment in Gorkhum, she courted a burgher's daughter for whom she fought a duel. Bidding farewell to the girl under pretence of seeking a commission, she enlisted as a dragoon under Lord John Hay, fighting until the treaty of Ryswick ended hostilities in 1697, when she returned to Dublin, maintaining her disguise as Richard Welsh.

With the renewal of war in 1701 Welsh re-enlisted and, according to the *Life*, fought in most of the battles of Marlborough's campaign, evading discovery of her masquerade even when she was wounded. Following the battle of Blenheim in 1704, she recognized her husband faithlessly courting a Dutch woman, chastised and then forgave him, and arranged with him to serve together (in celibacy), passing as brothers. Wounded at the battle of Ramillies, Welsh was discovered to be a woman by the surgeons and was reported to her officers, who responded with surprise and commendation. Christian and Richard Welsh then wed a second time in the camp, and she continued in the campaign as his acknowledged wife, serving as a sutler foraging for the troops. With the death of Richard Welsh at the battle of Malplaquet (1709), Christian's lamentations earned her the sobriquet Mother Ross from one Captain Ross, a sympathetic bystander. Several months later she married a grenadier named Hugh Jones who was soon killed at the siege of St Venant (1710). In 1712 Christian returned to England where, commended by the duke of Argyll, she was presented to the queen who awarded her, as pension, a shilling a day for life. Having returned to Dublin and been unable to claim the property she had settled in the 1690s, Jones set up a pub and pie house, married another soldier, named Davies, followed him to England, and eventually used her influence to have her husband admitted as a pensioner in the Royal Hospital at Chelsea, where she lived with him until she died of a fever on 7 July 1739. According to the *Life and Adventures* she was buried in Chelsea College burial-ground.

Brief accounts of her life, such as that in *London Magazine* (July 1739), appeared at the time of Christian's death. In 1740 a first-person account, *The Life and Adventures of Mrs. Christian Davies*, was published in London, purportedly 'taken from her own Mouth'. This narrative appeared in several editions, including a third-person abridgement of 1742 ascribed to 'J. Wilson, formerly a Surgeon in the Army'. A biographical 'history' in the picaresque mode, the *Life and Adventures* clearly mixes, in an ultimately undeterminable ratio, elements of fact with legends and motifs conventional in early modern popular ballads and prose narratives about masquerading heroines. Often cited, paraphrased, and reprinted, the *Life and Adventures* was mistakenly included among the works of Daniel Defoe until the twentieth century. A separate strand of traditions about Davies surfaces in histories of Chelsea and the military facilities there. From a 'list of old admissions into Chelsea Hospital', G. R. Gleig quotes in 1838: '19th Nov.1717. Stair's Dragoons: Catherine Welch, a fatt jolly-breast woman, received several wounds in the service, in the habit of a man;—from the 19th July 1717' (Gleig, 2.227). In some fifty pages of 'A tradition of King William's wars' Gleig then recounts the 'life' of 'Catherine Cavenaugh, otherwise Catherine Welch, otherwise Catherine Davies, otherwise Mother Ross' (ibid., 228) in a narrative which parallels the popular 1740 account but includes as well a number of episodes not found in it.

The legendary Christian (or Catherine) Davies poses a challenge to the biographer. A remarkable person who did exist, Davies supplies a glimpse of the lower social ranks which remain largely invisible to history. But events of her picaresque 'life' as variously recounted are controvertible and contradictory. Documentation in a patronymic culture is difficult to trace for any multiply married woman, especially a woman of the underclasses. In addition, the masquerading Davies specialized in fabrication in her actions and undoubtedly in her reporting of those actions. Furthermore, her 'life and adventures' took on larger cultural significance as a legend which contributed to established narratives of early modern cross-gender masquerade. Stories of Davies's soldiering thus predictably conform more to the preoccupation with crossdressing women in seventeenth- and eighteenth-century European popular songs and prose accounts than to heretofore identified records of military history. Her masquerading experiences were wrought into widely known stories which, however apocryphal, accrued imaginative force and cultural meaning for several generations of readers.

DIANNE DUGAW

Sources A. Boyer, *The political state of Great Britain*, 58 (1739), 90 • D. Dugaw, *Warrior women and popular balladry, 1650–1850* (1989) • K. Easton, 'Bad habits: cross-dressing and the regulation of gender in 18th-century British literature and society', PhD diss., Princeton University, 1990 • T. Faulkner, *An historical and topographical description of Chelsea and its environs interspersed with biographical anecdotes*, 2 vols. (1829), 2.226 • G. R. Gleig, *Chelsea hospital and its traditions*, 3 vols. (1838), 2.227–79 • *The life and adventures of Mrs. Christian Davies, commonly call'd Mother Ross* (1740) • *The life and adventures of Mrs. Christian Davies, the British Amazon, commonly call'd Mother Ross*, 2nd edn (1741) • *London Magazine*, 8 (1739), 361 • *N&Q*, 5th ser., 7 (1877), 92–3 • J. Wheelwright, *Amazons and military maids* (1989) • J. Wheelwright, '"Amazons and military maids": an examination of female military heroines in British literature and the changing construction of gender', *Women's Studies International Forum*, 10 (1987), 489–502 •

J. Wilson, *The British heroine, or, An abridgment of the life and adventures of Mrs Christian Davies* (1742)
Likenesses line engraving, BM, NPG; repro. in J. Caulfield, *Portraits, memoirs and characters of remarkable persons*, 4 vols. (1819–20) · two-part engraving, repro. in *Life and adventures of Mrs. Christian Davies, the British Amazon*, frontispiece

Davies, Clement Edward (1884–1962), lawyer and politician, was born on 19 February 1884 at Llanfyllin, Montgomeryshire, the youngest of the seven children of Moses Davies, auctioneer, and his wife, Elizabeth Margaret Jones of Llanerfyl, Montgomeryshire. Clement Davies was sent to the local English school, but won a scholarship to Llanfyllin county school when it was founded in 1897. He went on to Trinity Hall, Cambridge, where he was a senior foundation scholar, obtained first-class honours in both parts of the law tripos (1906–7), and was law student (1907–11). He won prizes in criminal law, constitutional law, and the law of real property, and was awarded the bar prize and certificate of honour in the bar finals in 1909, when he was called by Lincoln's Inn. Shortly before this he had been a lecturer at Aberystwyth University College, but in 1909 he joined the north Wales circuit before transferring in 1910 to the northern circuit. In that year he moved to London and rapidly developed a successful commercial practice. He had the capacity to read quickly and accurately, once mastering twenty-five briefs in a morning. He also published works on agricultural law and the law of auctions and auctioneers.

In 1913 Davies married Jano Elizabeth (1881–1969), daughter of Morgan Davies, a Welsh surgeon with a practice in London. She was a graduate in classics and modern languages of the University of Wales, and had studied in Paris before becoming a teacher; she was the youngest headteacher of her time in London. She was a linguist and an excellent public speaker and was to bring valuable support to her husband's political work. They had three sons and one daughter. Three of the children each died at the age of twenty-four; one son and the daughter were both accidentally killed while on active service.

On the outbreak of war in 1914 Davies volunteered for military service, but was posted instead to the office of the procurator-general as adviser on enemy activities in neutral countries and on the high seas. He was later seconded to the Board of Trade's department concerned with trading with the enemy. After the war he was successively secretary to the president of the Probate, Divorce, and Admiralty Division (1918–19) and to the master of the rolls (1919–23). From 1919 to 1925 he was a junior counsel to the Treasury. He took silk in 1926 and in 1935 he was appointed chairman of the Montgomeryshire quarter sessions, a post that he held, and was most assiduous in filling, until his death. He gave up practice in 1930 when he joined the board of Unilever, and remained a board member until 1941, when he resigned in order to concentrate on his political work.

From his youth onwards Clement Davies had been fascinated by radical politics. One of his forebears had voted for the Reform Bill of 1832. Politics were in the air he breathed as a young barrister when he worked as junior

Clement Edward Davies (1884–1962), by Elliott & Fry, 1954

counsel with John Simon and F. E. Smith, both destined to become lord chancellor; and quite late in life Davies would speak of the Asquith government as though he had been in parliament at the time. But it was not until 1929 that he felt able to contest a seat and was returned at the general election as a Liberal for Montgomeryshire, which he represented for the rest of his life. He was rooted in the county of his birth and made his home there at Meifod. Inevitably, he became entangled in the party disputes which followed the formation of MacDonald's National Government in 1931. At the general election of that year he held his seat unopposed as a Liberal National. He did so again at the election of 1935, although by this time the Liberal Party, led by Sir Herbert Samuel, had withdrawn its support of the government and was in opposition.

It was in his Liberal National phase that Davies did his most valuable work as a back-bencher, serving on a number of committees, and especially as chairman of an inquiry into the incidence of tuberculosis in Wales. Between 1937 and 1938 he made the most searching inquiries and found grave inadequacies in the provision of public health services and housing. His legal training and political sense here complemented each other perfectly. His report was not published until 1939, and most of the remedies had to await the post-war period, but it nevertheless represented a landmark in the development of health administration in Wales.

At the beginning of the war in 1939 Clement Davies became the chairman of an action committee in the

House of Commons which sought the most effective prosecution of the war and which was supported by members of the three main parties in the house. Davies was among an increasing number who had become convinced that there must be a coalition government in which all three parties should be represented, and his action group was important in mobilizing opposition to the Chamberlain government. In the critical debate on the Norwegian campaign, 7–8 May 1940, it was Clement Davies who, on the second day, persuaded Lloyd George to speak—a speech which Churchill described as Lloyd George's 'last decisive intervention in the House of Commons'. The concluding vote was a moral defeat for the government, and on 10 May 1940 Churchill became prime minister. Lord Boothby, who worked closely with Davies in the action committee as its secretary, later described him as 'one of the architects—some may judge the principal architect' of the Churchill coalition government. But this assessment exaggerates Davies's importance and there was to be no place for him in the coalition, which Boothby took as proof of his own belief that Churchill 'did not treat his friends well' (James, 245–6).

In 1942 Davies rejoined the independent Liberal Party and, notwithstanding his Liberal National past, became its leader in 1945 in succession to Sir Archibald Sinclair, who had been defeated in Caithness and Sutherland. With Frank Byers as his chief whip, Davies planned an ambitious programme of recovery for the party after the débâcle of 1945. He was determined to maintain Liberal independence and dismissed as 'unworthy subterfuge' Churchill's appeal for an electoral arrangement with the Conservatives before the general election of 1950, which the Liberals contested on a wide front (Gilbert, 505). But in the absence of an electoral pact only nine Liberals were returned, the number falling to six in 1951, when the Liberal vote fell to a mere three-quarters of a million—a performance that was barely improved upon in 1955. At the party conference the following year, Davies surprised the assembly by announcing his intention of 'handing over the wheel and going below' (Grimond, 188). Jo Grimond was his designated successor. Davies's difficulties had been made greater by a debilitating struggle with alcoholism, which he managed mostly to keep from public view. By 1960, though, he had made the decision not to contest the next election.

As leader Davies had to contend with deep divisions within Liberal ranks. The need to reconcile such disparate elements as Hopkin Morris and Lady Megan Lloyd George led him to adopt contradictory positions, and Lady Violet Bonham Carter, who ultimately held considerable affection for Davies, thought him 'a jelly fish who drifts on every tide … & goes wherever he is pushed or pulled' (V. Bonham Carter to Gilbert Murray, 6 April 1950, Lady Asquith MSS). She was critical, too, of his decision not to seek an electoral alliance with the Conservatives when it was offered—he had even refused office in Churchill's 1951 government. But by maintaining Liberal independence in the party's darkest hour he may also have ensured its future. Emlyn Hooson, who succeeded him as member for Montgomeryshire in 1962, believed that his 'greatest contribution was to hand over the Party to Grimond as a still recognized political entity, with all the trappings and organization of a much larger Parliamentary Party' (private information). From this basis Grimond effected a significant Liberal revival after 1956.

Clem Davies was a kindly man who made friends in all parties in the House of Commons. He was devoted to parliament as an institution, and his respect for it, with his awareness of the chafings of poverty, made him a sturdy advocate of a decent standard of pay for all members. Liberal organization during his leadership was not taut and he was a radical evangelist by temperament rather than a party boss, but he would spread the gospel of Liberalism anywhere with zeal. He had an agreeable voice and spoke frequently in the country, and particularly liked to talk to students at the universities. The ease with which he found himself in his public speeches developing Patrick Henry's theme 'Give me liberty, or give me death!' almost endeared him to his critics, though some bemoaned his 'chapel' oratory. Such causes as social reform, collective security, and world government enthused him, and towards the end of his career he found deep satisfaction in his work as president of the Parliamentary Association for World Government. He was nominated, unsuccessfully, in 1955 for a Nobel peace prize.

Davies was sworn of the privy council in 1947. He was elected an honorary fellow of Trinity Hall in 1950 and a bencher of Lincoln's Inn in 1953. In that year he received the freedom of Welshpool and in 1955 an honorary LLD from the University of Wales. He died at the London Clinic, 20 Devonshire Place, London, on 23 March 1962.

His widow, Jano Davies, survived him. She was involved in women's movements, attending the International Women's Congress in Istanbul in 1935 as a delegate. In 1939 she was a founder of the Women's Voluntary Services for Wales, and from 1941 to 1945 was a member of the commission on reconstruction for Wales. In 1947 she was appointed high sheriff of Merioneth.

FRANCIS BOYD, rev. MARK POTTLE

Sources *The Times* (24 March 1962) · *The Times* (31 March 1962) · J. Grimond, *Memoirs* (1979) · R. R. James, *Bob Boothby* (1991) · Lord Boothby [R. J. G. Boothby], *My yesterday, your tomorrow* (1962) · F. Owen, *Tempestuous journey* (1954) · Bodl. Oxf., MSS Lady Asquith · J. C. Rasmussen, *The liberal party* (1965) · private information (2004) [Lord Hooson] · M. Cowling, *The impact of Hitler* (1975) · *The Times* (27 Dec 1969) [J. Davies] · d. cert. · b. cert. · M. Gilbert, *Winston S. Churchill, 8: Never despair, 1945–1965* (1988)

Archives NL Wales, corresp. and papers · U. Sussex, corresp. and papers relating to World Government Associations | HLRO, corresp. with Lord Beaverbrook · HLRO, letters to David Lloyd George · JRL, letters to *Manchester Guardian*

Likenesses W. Stoneman, photograph, 1948, NPG · Elliott & Fry, photograph, 1954, NPG [*see illus.*] · W. Bird, photograph, 1962, NPG · J. Harvey, bronze bust, priv. coll. · G. Kelly, portrait, priv. coll.

Wealth at death £61,241 18s. 4d.: administration, 27 June 1962, CGPLA Eng. & Wales

Davies, David (1742–1819), Church of England clergyman and writer on social issues, was born on 9 February 1742 of Welsh parentage. His origins and early life are obscure, although his will suggests that his family originated in the border area of Merioneth and Denbighshire and came from a background of small farmers and country craftsmen. In 1755 he entered Codrington College, Barbados, as a foundation or charity scholar, and late in 1760 was appointed temporary usher, following the departure of the previous incumbent. He continued in that post until his resignation from the college on 14 June 1766. Between February 1762 and the autumn of 1763 he also acted as temporary headmaster, following the sudden death of the previous head. At that time he refused to take holy orders because of a reluctance to subscribe to certain of the Church of England's doctrines, and it was because of this that he left the college to become manager of a local sugar plantation. He remained there for three years, but clearly disliked the slavery associated with it. In early March 1791 he gave evidence before a select committee on the African slave trade in which he condemned the cruel treatment accorded the slaves.

About 1769 Davies returned to England and by March 1771 was engaged as tutor to Arthur Fowke, a nephew of Colonel John Walsh, a nabob and close friend of Robert Clive. He remained in Walsh's service as tutor and later secretary until at least the end of 1777. By March 1780 he had become tutor to the only surviving son of Lord Dartrey, an Anglo-Irish banker, who was raised later to Viscount Cremorne. In April 1782, while still in the Dartrey household, Davies was offered the rectory of Barkham, Berkshire, although as yet he had not taken holy orders.

On 28 April 1782 Davies was ordained deacon by the bishop of Chester on letters dimissory from the bishop of Salisbury, in whose diocese Barkham lay. On 26 May he was ordained priest and the following day was instituted into the benefice of St James, Barkham. He remained incumbent until his death. Despite this change of career, his links with both his previous employers in England remained strong and Viscountess Cremorne was a beneficiary under his will.

Davies's importance as a social commentator lies in his painstaking survey *The Case of Labourers in Husbandry Stated and Considered* (1795). It was based initially on researches into the living conditions of the labouring poor of Barkham but was extended to include labourers' budgets from many English counties, as well as a few from Wales and Scotland. The work was dedicated to the board of agriculture, since Davies considered that it possessed powers to investigate the economic plight of rural householders and to recommend pay increases where necessary. The book was well received, the *Gentleman's Magazine* of December 1795 expressing a hope that it would 'attract a degree of attention proportioned to the importance of the subject, and the merit of the execution' (*GM*, 65, 1795, 1023). A second, abbreviated version was published in 1828, when the anonymous editor detailed some of the changes which had occurred in Barkham since the rector's death in 1819. Davies was also contacted by some of the leading poor-law reformers of his day, including the radical MP Samuel Whitbread.

Davies died on 6 February 1819 at the rectory, Barkham;

his estate was valued at about £4700, the bulk of it in stocks held at the Bank of England. Apart from legacies to his three servants and to Viscountess Cremorne and some of her servants, he bequeathed £2127 to various Welsh relatives and acquaintances. The remainder of his estate went to charity (including the poor of Barkham, to whom he had given frequent help in his lifetime), and to English friends. In an obituary the *Reading Mercury* paid tribute to his 'humility of manner and attention to the wants of his poorer brethren' (15 Feb 1819), an indication that he had applied the theories advanced in his book to his daily duties as rector.

PAMELA HORN

Sources R. C. B. Oliver, 'David Davies, rector of Barkham in Berkshire, 1782–1819', *National Library of Wales Journal*, 19 (1975–6), 362–94 • P. Horn, *A Georgian parson and his village: the story of David Davies, 1742–1819* (1981) • *Reading Mercury* (15 Feb 1819) • 'Select committee … respecting the African slave trade', *British Sessional Papers: Accounts and Papers*, 34 (1790–91), 185–9, nos. 745–8 [minutes of evidence] • will of David Davies, PRO, PROB 11/1614/6430, fols. 132ff. • probate duty records, PRO, IR 26/774, fol. 266 • Davies MSS, Nuffield Oxf., Cole Collection • Minutes of the Society for the Propagation of the Gospel in Foreign Parts: Barbados committee minute book, 1760–1767, Society for the Propagation of the Gospel, London • BL OIOC, Fowke MSS • clergy visitation returns, Salisbury diocese, 1783 and 1801, Wilts. & Swindon RO • Berkshire parish records, Berks. RO • *GM*, 1st ser., 65 (1795), 1020–23

Archives Nuffield Oxf., accounts, corresp., estimate of the net profits of living of Barkham, etc. • Society for the Propagation of the Gospel in Foreign Parts, London, Codrington College records and Barbados committee minute books | Berks. RO, Ditchfield MSS, insurance policy/ building and contents, text of two sermons, R/D 134, box 6, envelope 2

Wealth at death approx. £4700: will, PRO, PROB 11/1614/6430, fols. 132 ff.; PRO, death duty registers, IR 26/774, fol. 226; Bank of England, Museum and Historical Research Section

Davies, David (d. 1807), Independent minister and journal editor, is a figure whose parentage and date of birth are unknown, but he was probably born at Llanybydder in Carmarthenshire. A student at the dissenters' academy in Swansea in 1786, he was ordained in 1787. His ministry began with two Independent churches, Capel Sul in Kidwelly and Pen-y-graig, near Carmarthen. In 1790 he moved to Holywell, Flintshire, to be the minister of the Independent church there.

Davies is remembered as the publisher and editor of the most radical Welsh language periodical of the 1790s: *Y Geirgrawn, neu, Drysorfa Gwybodaeth* ('The Magazine, or, Treasury of Knowledge'), a fourpenny monthly. Nine numbers were published between February and October 1796. The periodical covered the debate on the *Seren tan gwmmwl* ('Star under a Cloud'), a pamphlet written by John Jones in 1795 influenced by Thomas Paine's *Rights of Man* (1791). David Davies participated in the debate and defended the work of John Jones against its detractors. Paineite influence may also be seen in Davies's summary of the causes of the French Revolution. The poetry in the periodical had a distinct Jacobin tone, most notably 'Can Rhyddid' ('Poem on Liberty'), a Welsh translation of the 'Marseillaise', which appeared in the May number. In a prefatory note, the author (probably Thomas Evans, Glyn Cothi) claimed that the song had inspired the 'invincible' French forces and had wafted to Britain on the wings of a breeze. This was at a time when Britain and France were at war. The *Geirgrawn* was a well-produced periodical and there were no indications of financial problems. Its sudden end in late 1796 was almost certainly the result of threats from the authorities.

Davies was forced to leave Holywell for a few months during the winter of 1796–7. His church may also have been perturbed by the political implications of their minister's work. They complained to the Independent Association at Denbigh in 1797 that his ministry had been ineffective for years, and 'the hearers are becoming thinner' (Jenkins, 30). Davies left Holywell in October 1800. His movements are not known between October 1800 and 1802. Some time in 1802 he became a minister at Welshpool. He was there for a short while and in 1803 he moved to the Stoneway church in Bridgnorth, Shropshire, where he ministered and also kept school. He was held in esteem by his congregation, and when he died at Bridgnorth in 1807 he was buried in the walls of his church.

HYWEL MEILYR DAVIES

Sources J. E. Lloyd, R. T. Jenkins, and W. L. Davies, eds., *Y bywgraffiadur Cymreig hyd 1940* (1953) · R. T. Jenkins, *Hanes Cymru yn y bedwaredd ganrif ar bymtheg*, 2nd edn, 1972 (1933) · J. J. Evans, *Dylanwad y chwyldro Ffrengig ar lenyddiaeth Cymru* (1928) · T. Rees and J. Thomas, *Hanes eglwysi annibynol Cymru*, 4 (1875) · *Y Geirgrawn, neu, Drysorfa Gwybodaeth* (1796)
Archives U. Wales, Bangor, Scorpion MS

Davies, David (1818–1890), industrialist and politician, was born at Drain-Tewion, Llandinam, Montgomeryshire, on 18 December 1818, the eldest of the nine children of David Davies (d. 1846), farmer and timber sawyer, and his wife, Elizabeth (probably *née* Felix). He left the village school at the age of eleven, and helped his father in farming and sawing timber; in later life he sometimes boasted that he was always 'top sawyer'. When his father died in 1846 he had to support the family, but his career took a dramatic new turn when he was asked to undertake a contract to build a bridge over the River Severn near his home. He showed talent as both engineer and entrepreneur, and other bridges and roads followed. He then turned to building railways. In 1855 he built the first section of the Llanidloes–Newtown line, and later extended his operations all over Wales. By the early 1860s he had supplied much of mid-Wales with a network of railway lines, many of which he built in partnership with Thomas Savin, with whom he later fell out. In 1862 he travelled to the island of Sardinia to advise on developing the railway system there.

He embarked on a new career in 1864 when he took a lease of mineral property between Tonpentre and Treorci in the upper Rhondda valley, not hitherto a coal-producing area. After two years of anxiety for Davies, one of the finest seams of steam coal in the world was struck in the Maendy pit, Cwmparc, and the Ocean Collieries Company was set up in 1867 with an authorized capital of £240,000; new pits were later sunk at Dare (1870) and Bwllfa (1877). By 1900 the Ocean company had four collieries producing more than 1.5 million tons of coal annually, and many other pits had also been profitably established.

In 1887 Davies set up a limited liability company, the Ocean Coal Company, with a nominal capital of £536,000. The Rhondda valleys were now a booming industrial area, Davies was a millionaire, and Ocean stood second only to Powell Duffryn as a mass producer of quality Welsh steam coal.

Davies's rivalry with the Bute estate, which controlled Cardiff docks and the Taff Vale railway that served it, led him into another dramatic new venture—the building of new docks at Barry, 10 miles to the west of Cardiff—as a rival entrepôt for Rhondda coal. After a fierce struggle, a private act of parliament was passed in 1884, and the Barry docks came into being a year later. They grew rapidly and by 1913 Barry had outstripped even Cardiff as the major coal-exporting port in the world.

A devout Calvinistic Methodist and a strict advocate of temperance, Davies became a patron of nonconformist and other charitable and educational causes. He backed the movement for Welsh higher education and became a governor of the newly formed University College of Wales, Aberystwyth, founded in 1872. In 1875 Davies became treasurer of the college and fulfilled this role until 1886. He also took a close interest in Liberal politics. He stood unsuccessfully for Cardigan district against a local whiggish landowner, Sir Thomas Lloyd, in 1865, but in 1874 won the seat and was returned unopposed in 1880. He was elected for Cardiganshire in 1885, but he opposed the first Irish Home Rule Bill introduced by W. E. Gladstone in June 1886. At the resulting general election he was defeated by nine votes by a fellow Liberal, Bowen Rowlands, who backed Irish home rule. He was elected to the first Montgomeryshire county council in 1889.

Davies was a rugged, frugal, self-made capitalist, a relentless business competitor, who remained close to his chapel roots. Severely puritanical and sabbatarian in outlook, he also had a great fund of homely anecdotes about village mores, in both Welsh and English. He was a public-spirited philanthropist, and was perhaps the most influential Welshman of his time.

In 1851 Davies married Margaret Jones of Llanfair Caereinion, the daughter of Edward Jones, a local farmer. They had one son, Edward, who was to die in 1898. David Davies died on 20 July 1890 in Llandinam, and was buried there on 24 July. His grandson, David *Davies, became first Baron Davies. KENNETH O. MORGAN, rev.

Sources I. Thomas, *Top Sawyer* (1938) [new edn, 1988] · E. D. Lewis, *The Rhondda valleys* (1959) · D. Moore, ed., *Barry, the centenary book* (1985) · Boase, *Mod. Eng. biog.* · D. S. M. Barrie, 'Davies, David', *DBB* · E. H. Rowland, *A biographical dictionary of eminent Welshmen who flourished from 1700 to 1900* (privately printed, Wrexham, 1907) · *DWB*
Archives NL Wales, business papers
Likenesses statue, c.1893, Barry docks, Cardiff · statue, Llandinam, Montgomeryshire, Wales

Davies, David, first Baron Davies (1880–1944), politician and philanthropist, was born on 11 May 1880 at Llwynderw, Llandinam, Montgomeryshire, the only son of Edward Davies (1852–1898) and his wife, Mary (d. 1888), daughter of the Revd Evan Jones of Llandinam. He was educated at Merchiston Castle, Edinburgh, and at King's

College, Cambridge, where he was placed in the third and second classes respectively of the two parts of the historical tripos in 1901 and 1903. His father, Edward, died young in 1898, and David inherited the vast industrial empire created by his grandfather David *Davies (1818–1890), 'top sawyer', in railway construction, coalmining in the Rhondda valleys, and building the docks at Barry. The grandson took over these immensely profitable concerns, to which he added directorships of the Great Western Railway and the Midland Bank. From the outset, he was a multimillionaire.

Early on, Davies followed the family tradition of public service and benefaction mainly in Wales. He was a prominent member of the councils of the university colleges in Wales and of the court of the national university, and from 1926 served as president and chairman of the University College of Wales, Aberystwyth. The college owed much to him, with his funding of an imposing new chemistry laboratory named after his father, Edward (opened by H. H. Asquith in 1907), and later purchases of land and property. Davies was also much involved with the founding of the National Library of Wales at Aberystwyth in 1911, and he served as its president from 1927. His munificence extended also to housing development and support of his own Calvinistic Methodists in the Presbyterian Church of Wales, while his two sisters, Gwendoline Elizabeth *Davies and Margaret Sidney *Davies [see under Davies, Gwendoline], made Gregynog Hall a rare centre of culture and the arts in the inter-war years.

Davies's most striking initiative, however, was the Welsh National Memorial Association, in memory of Edward VII, launched by Davies in 1911 with a gift of £150,000 and with Thomas Jones appointed as its executive secretary, in order to combat the scourge of tuberculosis in Wales. There followed a research centre in Cardiff and the David Davies chair of tuberculosis at the Welsh National School of Medicine in 1921. The association set up residential sanatoria throughout Wales and was credited with a significant drop in the mortality rate from the disease. However, the Clement Davies committee in 1939 found that tuberculosis was still more serious in Wales than anywhere else in Britain. The association's limitations, for instance in not dealing with aftercare, later became clear, for all its commendable role in heightening public consciousness.

Like his grandfather, Davies hankered after a political career, and he was returned unopposed as Liberal member for Montgomeryshire in the general election of January 1906. Most unusually, he was nominated by both Liberals and Unionists in the constituency, and was indeed far from radical in his social and political views. Socially, as a large landowner who rode enthusiastically with the Llandinam hunt, he had traditional views on landlord–tenant relations and opposed many of Lloyd George's land reform proposals. At his election he was a tariff reformer who disliked Irish home rule and who had opposed the Welsh Liberals' 'revolt' against the 1902 Education Act. However, he gave broad support to Lloyd George's 'people's budget' and subsequent welfare measures. In general, however, Davies was an inactive MP during his tenure of the Montgomeryshire seat until 1929. He was returned unopposed in both elections in 1910 and in 1918, 1922, and 1923, and the local Liberal association went into decay while Davies busied himself with his industrial and philanthropic interests.

Davies's career, like that of many others, entered a quite new phase with the outbreak of war in August 1914. He fought in France as commander of the 14th Royal Welch Fusiliers and was made a major. However, in July 1916 he became parliamentary private secretary to Lloyd George, newly appointed to succeed Kitchener as secretary for war. In the complex political manoeuvres of autumn 1916 he was prominent in urging his fellow Liberal members that Lloyd George replace Asquith as prime minister. When Lloyd George became premier in December 1916 he made his fellow Welshman Davies one of the five initial members of his private secretariat or 'garden suburb'. Davies's responsibilities included war strategy and munitions, and he accompanied Lord Milner on his visit to Russia in January 1917. However, he proved a dissatisfied aide to Lloyd George and produced a stream of unsolicited criticisms from 'Dafydd Pob Man' ('David Everywhere'), as he called himself. The prime minister sacked him with singular brutality in June 1917.

Thereafter Davies was a frequent critic of Lloyd George. Although he received the coalition's 'coupon' of endorsement in 1918, he attacked the post-war government on many fronts, including the disendowment settlement for the Welsh church. By contrast, he voiced support for the Irish peace treaty and offered up to £1 million to purchase *The Times* in August 1922 as a pro-Lloyd George newspaper. However, he strongly attacked Lloyd George's radical land proposals in the 'green book' in 1925 as rank socialism and announced thereafter that he would not stand at the next election. He tried unsuccessfully to nominate a successor, but Clement Davies was chosen in the face of the sitting member's hostility and succeeded him as Liberal member for Montgomeryshire at the general election of 1929.

By this time David Davies was consumed by a mighty cause, which dominated the remainder of his life: the League of Nations, established after the Versailles peace settlement in 1919. Created Baron Davies of Llandinam on 21 June 1932, he campaigned ceaselessly for the league in speeches and writings, through the National Press Agency which controlled the *Review of Reviews* and *Everyman*, and in two books, *The Problem of the Twentieth Century* (1930) and *Force* (1934). Above all, there was a powerful pressure group, the League of Nations Union, of which he was founder and trustee, along with figures such as Lord Robert Cecil and Professor Gilbert Murray. Davies passionately championed the effective pursuit of collective security by giving the backing of force to the league covenant and giving new authority to the International Court. His particular theme was the creation of an international police force, especially an air force. However, critics felt his vision of nation states merging their sovereignty in a new world order to be a pipe dream. Many members of the union were far less enthusiastic than Davies for military sanctions, and in 1932, after the ineffective world disarmament conference, he founded the New Commonwealth movement to promote his ideas for an international equity tribunal whose decisions would be enforced by an international police force. He was much disillusioned at the failure of the league to stop the Italian invasion of Abyssinia and the Japanese invasion of China, and in the Lords and on the public platform expressed his feelings of 'humiliation and dismay' (*Hansard 5L*, 110, col. 1422, 4 Oct 1938) over Chamberlain's and Halifax's appeasement policies and especially Munich.

Davies's passion for the league extended into his public activities in Wales. In 1919 he endowed the Woodrow Wilson chair of international politics at Aberystwyth, which was first held by Sir Alfred Zimmern; in 1936 he protested bitterly when the college appointed E. H. Carr, a mordant critic of the 'utopianism' of league supporters like Davies. Thereafter, although he remained president of the college, he steadily withdrew from active involvement in its affairs. More positively, in 1938 he provided the Temple of Peace and Health in Cathays Park, Cardiff, as a centre for both the Welsh League of Nations Union and the National Memorial Association. It was to continue as an educational agency for world citizenship. During the war he wrote in favour of a federated Europe.

On 13 April 1910 Davies married Amy (*d.* 1918), the daughter of Lancelot Penman of Broadwood Park, Lanchester. They had a daughter who died in infancy and a son, David, known as Michael. On 9 December 1922 Davies married again, his second wife being Henrietta Margaret (*d.* 1948), daughter of James Grant Fergusson of Baledmund, Pitlochry, Scotland. They had two sons and two daughters. Davies died suddenly at Deildre, Llandinam, on 16 June 1944. He was succeeded as second baron by his son from his first marriage, David, who was killed in action in Holland three months later.

Davies was an imperious, impatient idealist who stamped his personality on Welsh, and to a degree on British, life over three decades. An active freemason, he was generous and public-spirited, given to embracing great crusades for causes such as health or world peace. He was also passionately committed to temperance. But he was liable to assume that his wealth alone would decide outcomes and that colleagues and opponents could be steamrollered into submission, whether in the parliamentary or the university world. He was a prickly colleague, who almost inevitably fell out with Lloyd George, but Thomas Jones and many others found themselves drawn by his charisma and vision. His positive impact on the public life of Wales was immense.

KENNETH O. MORGAN

Sources NL Wales, Davies of Llandinam papers · HLRO, Earl Lloyd-George of Dwyfor papers · NL Wales, Clement Davies papers · BLPES, League of Nations Union papers · NL Wales, Thomas Jones papers · NL Wales, Montgomeryshire Liberal Association papers · cabinet papers, 1916–17, PRO · council etc. minutes, U. Wales, Aberystwyth · NL Wales, Welsh National Memorial Association papers · E. L. Ellis, *The University College of Wales, Aberystwyth, 1872–1972* (1972) · E. L. Ellis, *T. J.: a life of Dr Thomas Jones* (1992) · G. J. Jones, *Wales and the quest for peace* (1970) · K. O. Morgan, *Wales in British politics, 1868–1922*, 3rd edn (1980) · K. O. Morgan, *Modern Wales: politics, places and people* (1995) · *CGPLA Eng. & Wales* (1944)
Archives NL Wales, corresp. and papers · PRO, memoranda on war aims, INF 1/303 | BL, corresp. with Lord Cecil, Add. MS 51138 · BLPES, League of Nations Union papers · Bodl. Oxf., corresp. with Herbert Asquith · Bodl. Oxf., corresp. with Gilbert Murray · HLRO, letters to David Lloyd George with related papers · King's Cam., letters to Oscar Browning · King's Lond., Liddell Hart C., corresp. with Sir B. H. Liddell Hart · NA Scot., corresp. with Lord Lothian · NL Wales, Clement Davies papers · NL Wales, corresp. with and papers relating to Gwilym Davies · NL Wales, letters to Thomas Iorwerth Ellis and Annie Hughes–Griffiths · NL Wales, Thomas Jones papers · NL Wales, corresp. with Sir John Herbert Lewis · NL Wales, letters to Daniel Lleufer Thomas · NL Wales, corresp. with Sir John Herbert Lewis
Likenesses W. Stoneman, photograph, 1921, NPG · W. Goscombe John, bust, 1935, Gregynog Hall, Montgomeryshire · W. Goscombe John, bust, c.1937, NL Wales · S. Morse-Brown, oils, 1939, NMG Wales; on loan to Gregynog Hall, Montgomeryshire · M. Urquhart, oils, 1950, NL Wales · A. John, portrait, Berthddu, Llandinam, Montgomeryshire · photographs, NL Wales
Wealth at death £506,445 7s. 4d.: probate, 11 Dec 1944, *CGPLA Eng. & Wales*

Davies, David Charles (1826–1891), Calvinistic Methodist minister and college head, was born at Aberystwyth on 11 May 1826, the eldest son of Robert Davies (1790–1841), a draper, and Eliza, daughter of David *Charles of Carmarthenshire. His father was one of the leading laymen among the Calvinistic Methodists of Wales during the first half of the nineteenth century, and it was at his house in Great Darkgate Street, Aberystwyth, that their articles of faith (*Cyffes ffydd*) were drawn up in March 1823.

Davies was educated first at Aberystwyth under the noted mathematician John Evans (1796–1861), who had also taught Lewis Edwards. He then went to Bala, where Lewis Edwards had opened an academy in 1837, later a theological college. In 1841 he went to Hanley as a private pupil of the Revd William Fletcher, a Congregational minister. At Hanley his occasional addresses to the Welsh colony prepared the way for the Welsh churches subsequently established in the Potteries. In November 1844, he became a student at University College, London, where his contemporaries included Walter Bagehot, Isaac Todhunter, Richard Holt Hutton, and Sir William Roberts. He graduated BA in 1847. After a short period at New College, Edinburgh, where he was taken ill, he returned to University College, London and graduated as MA in 1849, being placed second on the list. His parents had originally intended him for the bar but deep religious convictions led him to choose a ministerial career.

Davies began his career as a preacher in August 1848, at his home church, Tabernacl, Aberystwyth. Two years later he became minister of an English church at Newtown, Montgomeryshire. In 1850 he was admitted a member of the South Wales Association and was appointed its assistant secretary for two years. In 1852 he became pastor of the bilingual church of Alpha at Builth Wells and was fully ordained at the Llanelli Association on 4 August 1852. In November 1853 Davies left Builth Wells for the English church of Windsor Street, Liverpool, where he remained until March 1856. On 20 May 1857 he married Jane, third daughter of Ebenezer Cooper, a currier in Llangollen.

They had no children. Davies resumed his old charge at Builth until May 1858, when he returned for a year to the English church at Newtown. In 1858 he moved to the Welsh church at Jewin Crescent, and remained there until 1876. Owing to failing health he returned to Wales and took charge of the English church at Menai Bridge, though he retained a connection with London until 1882.

Despite poor health, Davies contributed widely as a preacher, lecturer, author, and teacher, publishing several volumes of sermons, commentaries, lectures, and articles in the Welsh language. Much of his work was prepared for the press by friends or pupils, in some cases from shorthand notes taken at his lectures; a series of lectures 'Darlithiau ar Gristionogaeth', delivered in Welsh at London (1879–1883), was published in *Y Traethodydd* (1881–8) from the notes of Sir E. Vincent Evans. For many years Davies held a unique position, among Welsh nonconformists generally, owing to powers of analysis and abstract reasoning unrivalled among his contemporaries. A powerful and influential preacher and teacher, his sermons and writings made a strong appeal to both Welsh and English congregations of all ages. During his years as a preacher, repeated efforts were made to induce him to undertake educational work at one of the denominational colleges. As early as 1861 he was offered a tutorship at Trevecca College, while the principalship was offered to him in 1863 and 1864. Twelve years later, in 1873, he was invited to succeed John Parry as principal at Bala. In 1888, he eventually agreed to accept the principalship of Trevecca, following the death of William Howells. However, his tenure of the post lasted only three years, for he died on 26 September 1891, at his house, Bronhwfa, Bangor, and was buried on 30 September at the cemetery, Aberystwyth. His wife survived him.   D. L. THOMAS, rev. MARI A. WILLIAMS

Sources E. W. Parry, *Cofiant a phregethau y diweddar Barch David Charles Davies* (1896) · *DWB* · J. P. Jones, 'Y Prifathraw David Charles Davies', *Y Drysorfa*, 61 (1891), 734 · T. R. Roberts, *Eminent Welshmen: a short biographical dictionary* (1908) · *Y Traethodydd*, 49 (1893), 181 · E. Davies, 'Parch David Charles Davies', *Ceninen Gŵyl Dewi*, 10 (March 1892), 1–6 · *Bye-Gones Relating to Wales and the Border Counties*, 2nd ser., 2 (1891–2), 180
Archives NL Wales, Calvinist Methodist archive · NL Wales, corresp., papers, diary, and preaching register · NL Wales, sermons and papers | NL Wales, letters to Lewis Edwards · NL Wales, letters to T. C. Edwards
Likenesses H. Hughes, oils, c.1833–1834, NL Wales · Humphreys, photograph, c.1890, NL Wales · Sawyer and Bird, engraving (after photograph), repro. in *Y Drysorfa* (1877) · J. Thomas, photograph, NL Wales · J. Wickens, photograph, NL Wales · photograph, repro. in Parry, *Cofiant a phregethau y diweddar Barch David Charles Davies* · photograph, repro. in Roberts, *Dictionary of eminent Welshmen*
Wealth at death £3157 15s. 2d.: probate, 19 Dec 1891, *CGPLA Eng. & Wales*

Davies, David Christopher (1827–1885), geologist and mining engineer, was born on 13 September 1827 at Oswestry, the son of Edward Thomas, labourer of Pentre Clawdd, and Elizabeth Davies, servant, of Leg Street, Oswestry. He was probably illegitimate and was orphaned at an early age; he had little or no formal education. When he was eleven he was apprenticed to Mr Minshall, a local ironmonger. However, an article on geology in Chambers's *Information for the People* stimulated a lifelong passion for the subject, and he gradually devoted most of his efforts to geology.

Davies was working as a tin-plate worker in Upper Brook Street, Oswestry, when he married Ellen Davies, daughter of a whitesmith of Ellesmere, on 5 July 1849. By 1855 he had set up in business as a brazier in Leg Street, and within a few years he was writing papers on geology. Thereafter his contributions appeared in the *British Architect*, *British Quarterly*, the *Colliery Guardian*, *Iron*, the *Geological Magazine*, and the journals of the Liverpool Geological Society, the Powysland Club, the Geologists' Association, and the Geological Society, to which he was admitted as fellow in 1872. Even such humble outlets as the *Youths' Play-Hour and Boys' Journal* attracted his notice, and he was for many years the north Wales correspondent to the *Mining Journal*.

All the while, Davies was preparing his major work, 'The geology of the north Wales border', but the manuscript was never quite finished, and its fate, like that of his extensive geological collection, is unknown. He gained several eisteddfod prizes including one of 30 guineas in 1880 for a paper entitled 'Metalliferous deposits of Flintshire and Denbighshire', and another in 1884 of 20 guineas for 'The fisheries of Wales'.

Davies led the British Association for the Advancement of Science to the Llangollen area in 1870, and became associated with many prominent geologists including Robert Etheridge, Joseph Jukes, John Phillips, Joseph Prestwich, and Andrew Grantie Ramsay, whom he found overbearing. In 1872 he began to turn his knowledge to account and in the next few years opened up bedded phosphate deposits in the Berwyn Mountains for F. C. Hills of Deptford. This was followed by an important paper on the phosphorite deposits of north Wales.

Davies also promoted coal enterprises near home, and for a time managed the Ifton colliery near Chirk, but for much of his life he walked a financial tightrope, often borrowing from his bachelor friend William Whitwell FGS (1839–1920). The failure of a new pit at Ifton Rhyn, with which he was also concerned, came as a sore disappointment although his judgement was vindicated by events: the mine eventually developed into the biggest in Shropshire, and lasted until 1968.

In 1874 growing consultancy work enabled the Davies shop to be disposed of, and a year later the family moved from Coneygreen House to Ebnal Lodge, a small-holding near Gobowen, which helped to supplement their income. Further commissions involved examining and opening many metal mines and quarries both at home and in France, Germany, and Norway. Between such activities Davies found time to write three textbooks on mining and quarrying which received widespread acclaim at the time and later proved valuable to industrial archaeologists and historians. Easy to read, clear, and inviting to the layman, they were published by Crosby Lockwood—*Slate and Slate Quarrying* (first published 1878; it ran to five edns),

Metalliferous Minerals and Mining (1880, six edns), and *Earthy and other Minerals and Mining* (1884, two edns).

Davies was also a compulsive and devoted Congregationalist lay preacher for forty years; much of his correspondence with Whitwell concerned religious matters. His volume of sermons, *The Christ for All Ages* (1871), has fallen into obscurity.

Davies and his wife, who was seven years his senior and who predeceased him, had five children. George Christopher (1849–1922) became clerk to Norfolk county council and was author of many popular titles on adventure and natural history. Edward Henry (*b.* 1858) worked closely with his father and illustrated his books before setting up independently as a geologist and mining engineer. His book, *Machinery for Metalliferous Mines* (1894), formed a companion to his father's titles. It was a favourite of W. H. Auden, who as a boy had a passion for abandoned lead mines, and it was still in his library when he died.

From his earliest years Davies had driven himself unceasingly, but found time to serve on Oswestry town council and to take an active interest in its public library. He died suddenly of heart failure while on board the SS *Angelo* returning from a mining visit to Norway; he was found dead in his berth on 19 September 1885. He was buried at Oswestry cemetery. In an age when mining was rife with fraud and ignorance of even basic geology, Davies's experience, good judgement, and integrity stood out, and served as an example to others of how Christian principles might be applied to the world of business and commerce. To him, God, geology, and mining were all part of a great and indivisible unity. His books were sermons, and his readers, the congregation. DAVID BICK

Sources D. C. Davies and G. C. Davies, letters to William Whitwell, NL Wales, Minor Deposit 1350A · *Bye-Gones Relating to Wales and the Border Counties*, [7] (1885), 292 · *Youths' Play-Hour and Boys' Journal*, 3 (1872), 161–5 · I. Watkin, *Oswestry* (1920), 266–7 · *The Times* (24 Sept 1885) · D. Bick, *The old copper mines of Snowdonia* (1982), 105–10 · *DNB*

Archives NL Wales, letters to William Whitwell, Minor Deposit 1350A

Wealth at death £1166 12*s.*: administration, 23 Nov 1885, *CGPLA Eng. & Wales*

Davies, David Ivor. *See* Novello, Ivor (1893–1951).

Davies, David Lewis (1911–1982), psychiatrist, was born on 16 April 1911 at 11 Sycamore Street, Cheetham, Manchester, the son of Harry Davies (*d.* 1956), a tailor's machinist, and his wife, Annie Ribatzkie (*d.* 1968). Davies attended Manchester grammar school and from there he won a scholarship to St John's College, Oxford, where he obtained a BA degree in animal physiology with first-class honours in 1933. After qualifying MB BCh at Oxford in 1936 Davies went to Leeds the next year as lecturer in physiology with the intention of making that his career. He gave up physiology at Leeds because he considered it to be too biochemical, and for a while he considered going into general practice. During the Second World War Davies was an officer in the Royal Army Medical Corps. He had obtained the diploma in psychological medicine in 1943, but was initially posted to a field ambulance for two years. During the later years of the war he commanded a 300-bed psychiatric hospital in India with the rank of major.

After the war Davies obtained a position as 'class III medical registrar' at the Maudsley Hospital in London. The hospital and the associated Institute of Psychiatry were being shaped under the influence of Aubrey Lewis to provide a scientific basis for British psychiatry. After obtaining his MD (Oxford) in 1948 with a thesis on Friedreich's ataxia, he was appointed to the consultant staff, and in 1950 was selected by Lewis as dean of the Institute of Psychiatry, a post which he held until 1966. Here his influence was exerted as 'a superbly creative administrator', who facilitated new developments and identified trainees to be groomed for academic stardom. He led by personal example as an exacting clinical teacher. A careless case formulation would produce 'a state of agonised withdrawal … Too much discussion of psychodynamics would certainly produce pained silence. Someone once remarked that he had the clinical acumen of the best sort of old fashioned family solicitor' (*British Journal of Addiction*, 98). Many subsequently distinguished psychiatrists were indebted to Davies for their early start and for his support for their research.

Davies's other important achievement lay in his work on alcoholism. Here his influence helped to bring the study of drinking firmly within the remit of psychiatry and his publications began the reorientation of psychiatric approaches. From the early 1950s, Davies had begun to take a clinical interest in alcoholism, and alcoholic patients were admitted to his wards. There was no separate alcoholism unit on the model which was subsequently, if briefly, to form part of government alcohol policy during the 1960s. These patients were part of the general life of Davies's 'firm'. In 1956 he, with Michael Shepherd and Edgar Myers, published, in the *Quarterly Journal of Studies on Alcohol*, a two-year follow-up of fifty alcoholics, together with an analysis of prognostic factors. In the developing world of post-war alcohol research this paper was a turning point, dealing, for example, with the nature of 'outcome' as a concept. But his international reputation rested on the paper 'Normal drinking in recovered alcohol addicts' which he published in the *Quarterly Journal* in 1962. Here he reported on seven 'alcohol addicts' who appeared to have returned to normal drinking. This was a revolutionary claim at a time when the belief was that alcoholism was a lifelong disease. A revisionist article in the 1980s suggested that Davies's findings were based on faulty evidence, but the paper was nevertheless of fundamental importance in opening the way for new thinking about 'alcohol problems' and for the modification and rejection of the idea of alcoholism as a disease. Whatever its faults, its importance lay in providing research justification for a new conceptual direction in alcohol studies.

Davies created the highly successful summer schools on alcoholism, and in 1972 he was responsible for the setting up of the Alcohol Education Centre (AEC), located on the Maudsley campus on Denmark Hill, London; a voluntary organization, it became the fulcrum of interdisciplinary alcohol education. It did much to expand medical and lay knowledge of alcoholism. Davies began a dialogue with the drinks industry, which supported some of the AEC's education work. Although his view of other psychiatric disorders was a medical one, Davies increasingly moved towards a psychosocial view of alcoholism, and to the inclusion of political and economic factors as well. He collected around him a group of psychologists and sociologists, who 'found themselves championing the ideas of a man who had essentially regarded himself as a physician and who had invariably worn a white coat for his clinical work' (Murray, 33).

Davies's retirement was marked by his involvement in the AEC, by private practice, and by his chairmanship of the Attendance Allowance Board, for which he was appointed CBE in 1982. Davies was a student of psychotic art, a keen gardener, and supporter of Chelsea Football Club. 'He had a special sort of canniness and an innate sense of judgement' (*British Journal of Addiction*, 99). His public life was founded on a long and happy marriage to Marjorie, a consultant anaesthetist (they had married in Bombay on 12 December 1945), and a warm relationship with their three sons. He died on 24 October 1982 in the Maudsley Hospital, Camberwell, London. He was survived by his wife.   VIRGINIA BERRIDGE

Sources *The Lancet* (20 Nov 1982), 1169 · *BMJ* (13 Nov 1982), 1435 · *British Journal of Addiction*, 78 (1983), 97–9 · Munk, *Roll* · *The Times* (30 Oct 1982) · G. Edwards, ed., *Addictions: personal influences and scientific movements* (1991) · G. Edwards, 'D. L. Davies and "normal drinking in recovered alcohol addicts", the genesis of a paper', *Drug and Alcohol Dependence*, 35 (1984), 249–59 · V. Berridge, 'The Society for the Study of Addiction, 1884–1988', *British Journal of Addiction*, 85/5 (1990), whole issue · B. Thom and V. Berridge, 'Special units for common problems: the birth of alcohol treatment units in England', *Social History of Medicine*, 8 (1995), 75–93 · R. Murray, 'Dr D. L. Davies', *Bethlem and Maudsley Gazette* (winter 1983), 31–3 · private information (2004) · *Medical Directory* (1962) · b. cert. · d. cert.
Likenesses photograph, repro. in Berridge, 'The Society for the Study of Addiction, 1884–1988' · photograph, repro. in *The Times*
Wealth at death £73,286: probate, 7 Jan 1983, *CGPLA Eng. & Wales*

Davies, Dilys Lloyd. *See* Jones, Dilys Lloyd Glynne (1857–1932).

Davies, Donald Watts (1924–2000), computer scientist, was born on 7 June 1924 at 102 Dumfries Street, Treorci, Glamorgan, with a twin sister; they were the only children of John Watts Davies (1899–1925), a colliery pay clerk, and his wife, Hilda, *née* Stebbens (1900–1988). When John Davies died, his young widow returned with the twins to her home town of Portsmouth, where they lived with her mother and sister. At Portsmouth's Southern Secondary School for Boys Donald's progress was unremarkable up to the age of fifteen, but then his talent for mathematics and science suddenly flowered, and after a wartime two-year course in physics at Imperial College, London, he was awarded his BSc degree with first-class honours in 1943.

Davies then joined a group at Birmingham University under Professor Rudolf Peierls, working on the design of a uranium 235 separation plant, part of the atomic weapons

project code-named Tube Alloys; his supervisor was the later notorious Klaus Fuchs. The separation plant was developed by Imperial Chemical Industries (ICI) in Billingham, and after the end of the war he continued working on various projects for ICI and at Birmingham University, before deciding in 1946 to use the remaining third year of his state scholarship by returning to Imperial College to study mathematics. This led to another first-class BSc degree, and he was awarded the Lubbock memorial prize as the leading mathematician of his year at London University in 1947. During this year he heard about the current early development of computers from a lecture by John Womersley of the National Physical Laboratory (NPL). Excited by the potential of this new technology, he applied successfully to join the NPL group, and moved to Teddington in September 1947. There he worked briefly with Alan Turing, whose remarkable pioneering plans for a computer to be called the ACE had not yet been realized because of a lack of staff with appropriate skills in digital electronics. In 1948, after Turing's departure, his group was reconstructed as a balanced team of mathematicians and engineers including Davies, J. H. Wilkinson, and E. A. Newman, led by F. M. Colebrook. The result was the successful Pilot ACE computer which ran its first program on 10 May 1950, one of the first four or five electronic stored-program digital computers in the world.

Recommending Davies for a Commonwealth Fund fellowship in 1954, Colebrook wrote:

> D. W. Davies is one of the most brilliant young men I have ever met; outstanding not only in intellectual power but also in the range of his scientific, technical and general knowledge. He is equally unusual in his ability to apply this knowledge to mechanical and electrical design and even to the actual construction of complex equipment. He is, for example, one of the very small number of persons who could draw up a complete logical design of an electronic computer, realise this design in actual circuitry, assemble it himself (with a high probability that it would work as designed) and then programme it and use it for the solution of computational problems. (Yates, 296)

This breadth of both interest and ability was to remain a feature of his later distinguished career.

Davies married Diane Lucy Erita Burton (*b*. 1931) on 17 May 1955; they lived in Sunbury-on-Thames for the rest of his life. They had two sons and a daughter. Davies was a devoted family man: his children remember particularly his talent for communicating his wide-ranging enthusiasms, which made visits to museums and galleries, for example, fun for all concerned.

During the 1950s Davies turned his attention from computer design to applications, developing a road traffic simulator for Pilot ACE, and in 1958 initiating a project to use full-scale ACE to translate technical Russian into English. In 1963 he was appointed technical manager of the advanced computer techniques project, responsible for government support for the UK computer industry.

With a technical ability matched by growing organizational skills, Davies made rapid progress through the grades of the scientific civil service. In 1966 he succeeded

Albert Uttley as superintendent of NPL's autonomics division, and soon turned it into a division of computer science with new and more practical objectives. His flagship project was based on an idea he had originated in 1965: that to achieve efficient communication between computers a fast message-switching communication service was needed in which long messages were split into chunks sent separately to minimize the risk of congestion. These chunks he called packets and the technique became known as packet-switching. His network design was received enthusiastically by the US Advanced Research Project Agency (ARPA), and the Arpanet and the NPL local network became the first two computer networks in the world using the technique. The internet can be traced back directly to this origin.

In 1979 Davies was able to relinquish most of his managerial responsibilities to concentrate on technical work. Realizing that computer networks would be used widely only if techniques could be developed to combat malicious interference, he started a group to work on data security, concentrating on the new method of public key cryptosystems. The group built a strong consultancy role around his expertise; all the major UK clearing banks, for instance, used their services. He retired from NPL in June 1984, but continued his work as a data security consultant, travelling widely and acting as an expert witness in court cases involving computer security and credit card fraud.

Davies's contributions to UK computer development, in particular his work on packet-switching, were recognized by the British Computer Society, who gave him their John Player award in 1974 and a distinguished fellowship in 1975; he also became their technical vice-president in 1983. He was appointed CBE in 1983, fellow of the Royal Society in 1987, and visiting professor at Royal Holloway and Bedford New College in 1987, and received an honorary DSc from the University of Salford in 1989. He was author or joint author of four influential books in his areas of expertise, notably *Computer Networks and their Protocols* (1973), and over 140 technical reports and papers. He was a first-rate public speaker, confident and expert with a lively incisive style.

His versatility and his fascination with intellectual challenges and puzzles are evident in Davies's private interests as well as in his official work. Over the years these interests included: the design and construction of noughts-and-crosses machines, which in the days before home computers were considerable attractions at the annual NPL children's parties (this game was the subject of his first published paper, in 1950); historic cryptographic machines, particularly the German machines of the Second World War; ball lightning; and all puzzles and games capable of mathematical analysis. His last project showed that his technical skills remained undiminished: he developed for fun a simulator of the Pilot ACE for a modern personal computer. Although a confirmed workaholic, regularly bringing his secretary on Monday mornings a pile of tapes he had dictated over the weekend, Davies had many intellectual interests outside work: after his retirement from NPL he took annual Open University courses in various subjects including astronomy, human biology, oceanography, and the history of art. He enjoyed music, mainly classical, and the extensive opportunities for world travel offered by his lecturing and consultancy work. He died at the Princess Alice Hospice, Esher, Surrey, from malignant melanoma, on 28 May 2000, and was cremated at Leatherhead crematorium on 6 June. He was survived by his wife and their three children.

DAVID M. YATES

Sources *The Times* (31 May 2000) · D. M. Yates, *Turing's legacy: a history of computing at the National Physical Laboratory, 1945–1995* (1997) · personal knowledge (2004) · private information (2004) · M. Campbell-Kelly, 'Data communications at the National Physical Laboratory', *Annals of the History of Computing*, 9 (1988), 221–47 · M. Campbell-Kelly, *The Independent* (7 June 2000) · J. Schofield, *The Guardian* (2 June 2000) · b. cert. · m. cert. · d. cert. · b. cert. [John Watts Davies, father] · b. cert. [Hilda Stebbens, mother] · d. cert. [John Watts Davies, father] · d. cert. [Hilda Davies, mother]

Archives SOUND Sci. Mus., 'D. W. Davies', *Pioneers of computing*, undated, tape no. 1 in a series of interviews with computer pioneers recorded in the late 1970s

Likenesses photograph, 1966, National Physical Laboratory, Teddington, Middlesex

Wealth at death £269,459—gross; £267,246—net: probate, 8 May 2001, *CGPLA Eng. & Wales*

Davies, Duncan Sheppey (1921–1987), chemist and industrialist, was born in Liverpool on 20 April 1921, the only child of Duncan Samuel Davies, stockbroker, and his wife, Elsie Dora, *née* May. He grew up in Liverpool and was educated at Liverpool College. He went to Oxford as a scholar at Trinity College, read chemistry, and graduated with first-class honours in 1943. His postgraduate research was supervised by Cyril Hinshelwood, a polymath and an internationally respected physical chemist. Unusually for that period he studied the kinetics of growth of bacterial cells, which was a field pioneered by Hinshelwood and a precursor to modern biotechnology. His DPhil was awarded in 1946. The years at Oxford formed him as a gifted scientist, a bounding spirit, and a warm and tolerant human being. The principal part of his career was spent in Imperial Chemical Industries (ICI). In 1945 he joined the research department at the dyestuffs division in Blackley, Manchester, at a time when it teemed with chemical talent and spawned the fibres division and pharmaceutical division. He worked for ten years on the mechanism of organic reactions related to the manufacture and use of colours and fine chemicals. His exceptional talents began to be revealed when he took over an experimental section in the colours department at Grangemouth works. Laboratory-derived techniques were applied with considerable ingenuity and success to full-scale operations. As research director of ICI general chemicals division at Runcorn (1959–62) he followed up this work, and was involved in the initiation of major changes in the business portfolio and its associated research. The rebuilding of university relationships with the division proved to be a stepping-stone to his next post: director of the ICI petrochemical and polymer laboratory, 'charged with the creation of new innovative opportunities (products and processes) for ICI'. The hour and the man were well suited. He recruited about four hundred scientists and managers from ICI, other companies, and universities all over the world. He introduced new ways of using the economics of the chemical industry to direct the choice of research programmes. He was one of the first people in the chemical industry to think automatically of it as a global business. Not surprisingly he introduced biotechnology into the laboratory.

Those around Davies, especially the young, were inspired to considerable achievement. Ideas of all sorts poured forth. He became a superb and challenging communicator, in both speech and writing. In this period he extended his influence to the universities and research councils. With Callum McCarthy he wrote *An Introduction to Technological Economics* (1967). He was one of the instigators of the much valued co-operative awards in science and engineering (CASE), in which a PhD student was supervised by an industrial and an academic supervisor. In 1967 he became deputy chairman of Mond division in Runcorn and in 1969 became general manager, research and development, at ICI headquarters. In this post he worked directly with the main board research and development director, and was responsible for group research and development policy and connected matters, such as long-term future business and government contracts. After a career spanning thirty-two years with ICI, Davies became chief scientist in the British Department of Industry in 1977. He was the senior permanent civil servant responsible for policy in science, engineering, and technology. He gave renewed importance to the role of engineering in the UK and brought refreshing vigour to science in Whitehall. He championed biotechnology as an exploitable technology. Davies himself became deeply attached to information technology, and when he retired from the department in 1982, he was an addict of personal computers.

Davies was a European and a member of the Club of Rome. As chairman he breathed new life into the British Ceramics Association. He was an ebullient president of the Society of Chemical Industry. Davies wrote, lectured, consulted, argued, and travelled. He was witty, erudite, loving, and lovable. His two great passions were Wagner and Shakespeare. He was appointed CB in 1982, was an honorary fellow of the University of Manchester Institute of Science and Technology, and received honorary degrees from the universities of Stirling (1975), Surrey (1980), and Bath (1981), and from the Technion in Haifa (1982), and he was a foreign associate of the US Academy of Engineering (1978).

Davies was a large bulky man, with a bluff cheerful face, a warm welcoming personality, and an abundance of energy. In 1944 he married (Joan) Ann, daughter of Edward Noel Frimston, cotton broker, and Caroline Ethel Martin, a Liverpool artist. They had a son and three daughters. Davies died in Paris on 25 March 1987.

GEOFFREY ALLEN, rev.

Sources *The Times* (2 April 1987) · *WWW* · personal knowledge (1996) · private information (1996) · *CGPLA Eng. & Wales* (1987)
Wealth at death £74,619: probate, 2 June 1987, *CGPLA Eng. & Wales*

Davies, Edmund Frank (1900–1951), army officer, was born on 3 September 1900 at Wellington, India, the son of Edmund Oliver Davies, bandmaster of the 4th Queen's Own hussars. After Magdalen College School, Oxford (1911–18), he entered the Royal Military College, Sandhurst, where he gained the name by which most knew him for the rest of his life. As one Sandhurst instructor, an officer of Davies's regiment, recalled: 'He displayed even then the characteristics which we in the Regiment came to know so well: independence, intolerance, robustness, a keen sense of humour and a kind of disciplined bolshevism which earned him the nickname of Trotsky' (*Quis separabit*, 64). Few, even of his closest friends, ever learned his real forenames.

In 1919 Davies was commissioned into the Royal Irish Rifles (from 1921 known as the Royal Ulster Rifles, or RUR), and early in 1920 he joined the 2nd battalion on active service in Mesopotamia. Within months he had made his mark on the regiment by winning his first Military Cross. Long service in Egypt and India followed, during which he established his reputation as a stickler for physical training and as an all-round athlete, excelling particularly at soccer and captaining the battalion team.

Short, prematurely bald, and full of enthusiasm and fun, at heart Davies always remained a 2nd battalion man: 'undoubtedly the "beau ideal" of the Regimental Officer both in peace and war' (*Quis separabit*, 63). Popular, too, with the soldiers' families, in 1924 he was himself married, in India, to Gladys Clare, the daughter of Albert William Henry Bruford and his wife, Mary, of Eastbourne, Sussex. They had a daughter and son. In 1936, after a three-year tour with the London Irish Rifles, Davies rejoined the 2nd RUR at Catterick, and the following year he went with it to Palestine. There he was wounded, received two mentions in dispatches, and, for his command of a mobile column in action at Um-el-Fahm, was awarded a bar to his MC.

The outbreak of war found Davies a chemical warfare staff officer in France. Later evacuated from Dunkirk, he took command in January 1941 of the 70th young soldiers battalion of the RUR. In the summer of 1942, after a short period commanding the 10th battalion of the Durham light infantry, he was appointed to command his old battalion, the 2nd RUR. In August 1943, while at Hawick, Davies was asked to volunteer to lead a Special Operations Executive (SOE) mission into the occupied Balkans. Though disappointed to leave his battalion, he agreed to go, was promoted brigadier, and in due course flew to the Middle East to organize his mission and undergo specialist training. In October 1943 he parachuted into Albania to work with the local resistance.

Despite being much older than the SOE personnel under his command, Davies performed his mission with characteristic vigour, endurance, and application, often in conditions of appalling hardship, and worked hard to achieve a degree of co-operation between the rival guerrilla bands—though ultimately with little success. He was due to make for the coast and evacuation when, at the end of December 1943, he and his mission were forced by a

German offensive to disperse into the snow-bound mountains. On the run and off the air, in January 1944 he was ambushed, grievously wounded, and captured by a group of Albanian quislings, then handed over to the Germans. In Tirana, clinging to life, he was operated on by a German surgeon, then, as his health improved, moved to Belgrade. After rough interrogation by the Gestapo, and several more moves including a brief but unpleasant spell at Mauthausen concentration camp, which ended after a typically robust Davies demanded that he and his party be moved to a regular camp, he ended up, in August 1944, at Colditz. The highest-ranking inmate, though closely guarded he nevertheless helped in causing all kinds of mischief until he was liberated and repatriated in April 1945.

In October 1945, after further operations and a spell of sick leave, Davies returned to work, despite the concern and advice of his friends. A month later he received the DSO for his activities in Albania. Following spells commanding infantry brigades in Greece and later Palestine, he returned to Greece as colonel of the British military mission. In December 1948 he took over his last command, that of 160 infantry brigade at Cardiff. He suffered a stroke, undoubtedly brought on by the strain of his wartime wounds, and died of heart failure at the County Hospital, Haverfordwest, on 14 August 1951. The final draft of his memoir, *Illyrian venture: the story of the British military mission to enemy-occupied Albania, 1943–44*, reached the publishers accompanied by a note informing them of the author's death. It was published in 1952.

RODERICK BAILEY

Sources *Quis separabit: the regimental journal of the royal Ulster rifles* (1952) · private information (2004) [incl. special operations executive adviser] · d. cert.
Archives PRO, SOE archive (HS class), records relating to special operations executive service

Davies, Edward (1756–1831), antiquary and author, was born on 7 June 1756 at a farm called Hendre-einon, in the parish of Llanfaredd, Radnorshire, the eldest son of Edward Davies and Elizabeth, daughter of Richard Owens. He came from farming stock; various members of his family owned ten farms in the neighbourhood. His sight was impaired when he met with an accident at the age of six, and this weakened him for the rest of his life and resulted in blindness in his old age. His knowledge of the Welsh language was probably more competent than some commentators have suggested (he wrote a hymn in Welsh, completed by August 1776). He spent only one year as a pupil at Christ College, Brecon, in 1774. Undeterred, he opened a school of his own in the Methodist meeting-house at Hay in 1775. In 1779 he was ordained deacon, and between 1779 and 1783 served as a curate in several parishes in Herefordshire. About this time he produced three five-act plays: two comedies, *The Gold Mine* and *The Guardian*, and a tragedy, *Owen, or, The Fatal Clemency*.

From 1783 to 1799 Davies was a master at the endowed grammar school at Chipping Sodbury and was appointed to the curacy of the neighbouring parish of Badminton. In 1783 he married his first wife, Margaret Smith (*d.* 1814) of

Whittington. During the last decade of the eighteenth century he devoted himself, in spite of failing health and anxiety neurosis, to a variety of interests connected with Celtic antiquity and with the transcription from manuscript sources of early and medieval Welsh poetry. He made the acquaintance of William Owen Pughe and Edward Williams (Iolo Morganwg). Many of his transcripts were published in *The Myvyrian Archaiology* (3 vols., 1801–7), to the editors of which he had lent his huge collection.

Davies was a self-educated scholar and prolific author who was, by and large, poorly qualified, misguided, and uncritical, although at times he could show considerable care, sagacity, and a good instinct for new and valuable interpretation. His enthusiasm for writing appears to have been fired by a polemical spirit, in part reacting to jibes made by his Chipping Sodbury parishioners who ignorantly claimed that the Welsh language was a 'barren jargon'.

Davies's earliest significant work was *Aphtharte, the Genius of Britain* (1784), a mannered and patriotic poem that reflected his conviction of a connection between Greek and Celtic mythology. *Vacunalia, Consisting of Essays in Verse*, which showed the influence of Virgil's *Bucolics* and a knowledge of Ossianic literature, appeared in 1788. He also wrote an early novel, now an extremely rare book, *Elisa Powell, or, Trials of Sensibility* (1795). An overambitious attempt at studying, *inter alia*, the origin of speech and the fundamental principles of language came to fruition in *Celtic Researches, on the Origin, Traditions and Language of the Ancient Britons* (1804). In 1809 he published *The Mythology and Rites of the British Druids* (1809), which ranged from a consideration of classical sources to false suppositions concerning cromlechs and Stonehenge and 'British' superstition. Another work, *The Claims of Ossian Examined and Appreciated* (1825), was an attack on Macpherson, not least for disparaging the Welsh bards.

In 1799 Davies was appointed to the less demanding curacies of Elberton and Olveston in Gloucestershire, enabling him to combine more effectively his pastoral duties and his insatiable interest in early Celtic history. Theophilus Jones, the Brecon historian who had been his contemporary at school, supported him in his quest for preferment and for subscribers to his publications. In 1802 he secured the perpetual curacy of Llanbedr in Radnorshire and in 1805 became rector of Bishopston in Gower. He continued to live in Olveston until 1813, when he moved to Bishopston. From that year until his death he made his home at Bishopston. In 1816 he married his second wife, Susanna Jeffreys. He died on 7 January 1831 at Bishopston rectory and was buried in Bishopston cemetery.

Edward Davies is remembered today chiefly for his extensive works the *Celtic Researches* and the *British Druids*. Yet his ability to cope with a complex range of sources relating to ancient mythology, patriarchal religion, and linguistic variation was too limited for tackling the tasks on which he worked so assiduously. However, even though his knowledge was too inadequate for producing a reliable interpretation of early and medieval Welsh poetry, his enthusiastic activity was important for the transmission, publication, and study of much of this literature. It is to his credit that he was one of the first to query the authenticity of fallacious claims made by Iolo Morganwg with regard to the Gorsedd of Bards.

D. ELLIS EVANS

Sources DNB · [W. J. Rees], 'Memoir of the Rev. Edward Davies', Cambrian Quarterly Magazine and Celtic Repertory, 3 (1831), 408–36 · Theophilus Jones, FSA, historian: his life, letters, and literary remains, ed. E. Davies (1905) · G. J. Williams, Iolo Morganwg (1956), xxix, 204–5 · DWB · F. R. Lewis, 'Edward Davies, 1756–1831', pt 1, 'The early career of Edward Davies', Transactions of the Radnorshire Society, 39 (1969), 8–23 · G. R. Orrin, 'Edward "Celtic" Davies, rector of Bishopston, 1805–1831', Gower, 31 (1980), 65–71 · M. Stephens, ed., The Oxford companion to the literature of Wales (1986), 128 · D. R. Davis, 'Edward Davies and paradigm shift in nineteenth century Celtic Studies', Proceedings of the Seventh International Conference on the History of Linguistics (1996)
Archives NL Wales, corresp. with John Davies

Davies [née Touchet; other married name Douglas], **Lady Eleanor** (1590–1652), prophetess, was the fifth daughter of George Touchet, eleventh Baron Audley (1550/51–1617), and his first wife, Lucy Mervyn (d. 1609/10), daughter of Sir James Mervyn of Fonthill Gifford, Wiltshire. She had two younger brothers. Her father's barony was recalled in one of the variants of her name which she was to deploy in her writings: Eleanor Audeley. She was to be fluid in the use of the names which birth and marriage gave her, deploying them in pamphlet and petition according to context and the identity she was presenting. Audley was a soldier; he served successively as governor of Utrecht in the Netherlands and governor of Kells in co. Meath. In 1616 he was created Baron Audley of Orier, co. Armagh, and earl of Castlehaven, co. Cork. Eleanor Touchet probably spent much of her childhood at the family home in Stalbridge, Dorset. She was literate in Latin as well as English, and had a good understanding of theology and the law (she administered her father's estate after his death). Some time between the ages of ten and fifteen she moved with her family to Ulster.

At the age of nineteen, in March 1609, Touchet married the poet and attorney-general for Ireland Sir John *Davies (bap. 1569, d. 1626), who was not only more than twice her age but also had a violent temper and was, according to his contemporaries, ugly and exceedingly overweight. The couple had three children. Their daughter Lucy Davies [see Hastings, Lucy] was born in Dublin in 1613. In her eleventh year Lucy was married to the son and heir of the earl of Huntingdon, but continued to reside with her mother for another two years and remained her close friend and supporter throughout her life. Of the two sons, one, Richard, died in infancy, and the other, Jack, who may have been autistic, drowned in Ireland in 1617 or shortly thereafter. In 1619 Sir John Davies was relieved of his position by the king, and the family moved to London. Some three years later, Eleanor Davies became involved in at least two personal disputes, one of which was brought to Star Chamber. By 1623 she was living in the manor of Englefield in Berkshire.

In 1625 Davies took a thirteen-year-old Scottish boy, George Carr, into her protection. Carr, who was deaf and mute, had impressed London society by his fortune-telling abilities. Under Davies's care, he began to speak and to utter prophecies, but when his talents failed him he ran away to sea. None the less, he had a profound effect on his patron. On 28 July 1625 Davies was awakened by a heavenly voice which declared, 'There is Ninteene yeares and a halfe to the day of Judgement and you as the meek Virgin' (E. Douglas, The Lady Eleanor, her Appeale to the High Court of Parliament, 1641, 15). That same year of 1625 she published her first pamphlet, A Warning to the Dragon and All his Angels, in which she interpreted political developments in Europe as a fulfilment of the books of Daniel and Revelation. Her husband's anger at her activities prompted him to burn her prophecies. Davies responded by dressing in widow's weeds and predicting that he would die in less than three years. One day in December of the following year, she began to weep uncontrollably during dinner, and three days later her husband died. There followed a protracted legal dispute over Sir John Davies's estate between his widow and the family of their son-in-law, and Lady Eleanor temporarily lost possession of Englefield and also her estate at Pirton in Hertfordshire (purchased by her husband as her jointure). This was only the first of many court cases involving Davies's ownership of these properties.

In the spring of 1627 Davies remarried. Her second husband was a professional soldier, Sir Archibald Douglas (d. 1644). Lady Eleanor gained increasing renown for her prophecies, many of which were anagrammatic; she read into her own name of Eleanor Audelie the exhortation 'Reveale O Daniel'. She was even consulted about Henrietta Maria's first pregnancy, first by a royal servant and then by the queen herself. However, she also encountered hostility from Charles I's household, especially for her prognostication concerning the death of the duke of Buckingham and her personal warnings to the king. Sir Archibald, possibly in the hope of regaining royal favour, proceeded to follow his predecessor's example in destroying her papers. On this occasion Lady Eleanor announced that her husband would be judged by God, arguing that the prophecy was fulfilled when he became afflicted by a mental disorder.

If the encounter with Carr signals one turning point in Lady Eleanor Davies's prophetic career, a second is marked by the trial of her brother Mervin *Touchet, second earl of Castlehaven, in 1631. Castlehaven was indicted for sodomy and for abetting the rape of his wife by a servant. Sir Archibald and Lady Eleanor's sisters petitioned unsuccessfully for his release, while she continued to protest his innocence for many years. But the tide of public opinion was against him after he was found guilty and executed. In 1633 she travelled abroad on the pretence of accompanying her husband to the Spa. In Amsterdam she organized the printing of more of her prophecies, but after smuggling them back into England she presented a hand-written paper to Archbishop Laud, 'to give him a taste or warning of his judgment at hand, the hand writing (Dan. 5) served on him in his gallery' (Cope, Handmaid,

65). He had the illicitly printed books publicly burned. She was arrested, brought before high commission, fined £3000, and imprisoned. At this point her second marriage effectively ended.

A year after her release from the Gatehouse in 1635 Davies, accompanied by two friends, Marie Noble and Susan Walker, caused a series of disturbances in Lichfield Cathedral by claiming the right to sit in the seats reserved for the wives of cathedral dignitaries. Then, on a subsequent occasion, Davies entered the cathedral, sat on the bishop's throne, and declared that she was primate and metropolitan. This gesture was followed by one equally shocking: she poured tar over the altar, telling worshippers that she was sprinkling it with holy water as preparation for their next communion. In her 1652 tract *Bethlehem Signifying the House of Bread*, Davies explained that she had been driven to her act by the erection of a giant crucifix in the cathedral and by the installation of a purple woollen altar hanging which obscured the ten commandments on the wall. She saw her spectacular attack on these profane objects as the fulfilment in the Last Age of Exodus 32:20, in which Moses destroyed the golden calf worshipped by the Israelites. She was immediately re-arrested and committed to Bethlem Hospital (Bedlam). In April 1638 she was moved to the Tower, from which she was released in September 1640. She was imprisoned for debt and infringements of the publishing laws on at least two more occasions, and in 1651, the year before her death, she was again jailed for a short period.

Despite her imprisonments, Davies published extensively during the 1640s. She was convinced that the end of the world was imminent, originally claiming that the day of judgment would occur in 1644. Her periodization of history and her predictions of the apocalypse fit into established traditions of prophetic writing, and, indeed, her tract entitled *The Everlasting Gospel* (1649) takes its name from the famous work attributed to Joachim of Fiore. Despite her attacks on the authority and corruption of the church, and her opposition to Arminianism, ritual, and ceremony, which she described as sinful idolatry, Davies's religious beliefs bear some affiliation to not only Anglicanism but also Catholicism. She often dated her tracts according to the liturgical calendar, and increasingly her writings dwelled on the importance of the Virgin Mary, not only as intercessor but also as a new redeemer. She had, for a time, some sympathy with the Calvinist doctrine of absolute predestination, but later in her life she developed a strong belief in the ultimate salvation of all humankind. Davies does not seem to have been part of any specific religious sect or movement, and she formulated her own interpretations of scripture and opinions on theological matters. None the less, her writings reveal that she was acquainted with the ideas of the Coleman Street preacher John Goodwin and of the Digger leader, Gerrard Winstanley. She was as preoccupied with matters of politics as with matters of religion, denouncing the reign of Charles I and declaring her support for the protectorate of Oliver Cromwell. In her poem 'To Sion most Belov'd I Sing', which was first printed in 1633 and republished at least four more times before her death, she likened Charles to the Old Testament king Belshazzar, whose downfall was predicted in the writing on the wall. However, her opinions on social matters, and especially the importance of hierarchy and property, were far from revolutionary and may be understood as a reflection of her aristocratic status (she was preoccupied with her own exalted lineage). She certainly did not share Winstanley's beliefs concerning communal ownership and the abolition of wage labour.

Throughout her life, Davies seems to have made enemies easily. In 1622 Christopher Brooke likened her to Jonson's Lady Wouldbe, calling her an 'abominable stinking greate Symnell face excrement', and describing her 'scurvy contracted purse mouth', 'black patches of ugly deformitie', and 'hoodwynkt and clouded' eyes (PRO, SP 14/130/135). This description is contradicted by the much more flattering portrait miniature of a young woman, identified as Davies, painted by Sir Isaac Oliver. Although her father settled £6000 on her at the time of her wedding, the civil war, Irish rising, and her disputes with authority all had an impact on her personal wealth. Davies was an extremely litigious woman, who battled to see her properties restored to her possession. She repeatedly claimed to be destitute and refused to pay what she owed, coming into conflict with Gerrard Winstanley in 1650 after employing the Diggers to work her land. Up to her final months, she continued to rely on her daughter for financial assistance. She died in London on 5 July 1652 and was buried next to her first husband in St Martin-in-the-Fields.

In total, Davies published almost seventy tracts. Although her works are extremely difficult to read, recent historians and critics have reassessed her life and achievements, arguing for her importance as one of the most prolific seventeenth-century prophets, and as one of the first English women to see her works through the press.

DIANE WATT

Sources *Prophetic writings of Eleanor Davies*, ed. E. Cope (1995) [sel. of works] · E. S. Cope, *Handmaid of the Holy Spirit: Dame Eleanor Davies, never soe mad a ladie* (1992) · D. Watt, 'Alpha and Omega: Eleanor Davies, civil war prophet', in D. Watt, *Secretaries of God: women prophets in late medieval and early modern England* (1997), 118–54 [incl. comprehensive work list] · E. S. Cope, '"Dame Eleanor Davies never soe mad a ladie"', *Huntington Library Quarterly*, 50 (1987), 133–44 · T. Feroli, 'The sexual politics of mourning in the prophecies of Eleanor Davies', *Criticism*, 36 (1994), 359–82 · T. Feroli, 'Sodomy and female authority: the Castlehaven scandal and Eleanor Davies's *The restitution of prophecy* (1651)', *Women's Studies*, 24 (1994), 31–49 · B. Nelson, 'Lady Eleanor Davies: the prophet as publisher', *Women's Studies International Forum*, 8 (1985), 403–9 · R. Porter, 'The prophetic body: Lady Eleanor Davies and the meanings of madness', *Women's Writing*, 1 (1994), 51–63 · T. Spenser, 'The history of an unfortunate lady', *Harvard Studies and Notes in Philology and Literature*, 20 (1938), 43–59 · M. Matchinske, 'Gender formation in English apocalyptic writing', *Writing, gender and state in early modern England: identity formation and the female subject* (1998), 127–55 · C. Berg and P. Berry, 'Spiritual whoredom: an essay on female prophets in the seventeenth century', *1642: literature and power in the seventeenth century*, ed. F. Barker, J. Bernstein, J. Coombes, P. Hulme, J. Stone, and J. Stratton (1981), 37–54 · M. Matchinske,

'Holy hatred: formations of the gendered subject in English apocalyptic writing, 1625–1651', *ELH: a Journal of English Literary History*, 60 (1993), 349–77 · GEC, *Peerage* · J. Matthews and G. F. Matthews, eds., *Abstracts of probate acts in the prerogative court of Canterbury, 1620–24* (1911, [1914]), 51 · *The complete poems of Sir John Davies*, ed. A. B. Grosart (1876), 1.lv–lvi

Archives BL, MSS · Bodl. Oxf., MSS · Folger, MSS · Worcester College, Oxford, MSS | Hunt. L., Hastings MSS

Likenesses I. Oliver, portrait, *c.*1610 (of Davies?), repro. in G. Reynolds, *Nicholas Hilliard and Isaac Oliver* (1971), no. 173

Davies, (Sarah) Emily (1830–1921), suffragist and promoter of higher education for women, was born on 22 April 1830 in Southampton, the fourth child and second daughter of John Davies DD (1795–1861) and his wife, Mary Hopkinson (*d.* 1886), the daughter of a businessman from Derby. At the time of her birth her father was acting as a locum in Southampton for a vicar who was seeking a cure for gout at Droitwich. John Davies was himself an invalid, who regularly moved his family's home in his search for bracing air to relieve his nervous disability. In her early childhood Emily's father was a parish priest in Chichester, where he also ran a school. He gave up both to concentrate on his writing, a luxury funded by Mary Hopkinson's allowance from her father. The family moved to Normandy in 1836, and then returned to settle near Chichester.

Family and home life John Davies was a respected scholar whose work *An Estimate of the Human Mind* (1828; new edn, 1847) had led to his name being proposed in 1830 for the chair of moral and political economy at the newly established London University. An evangelical Anglican and a strict sabbatarian, his publications included *Splendid Sins* (1830), an attack on wealthy sabbath-breakers. In 1839 the bishop of Durham, Edward Maltby, appointed him rector of Gateshead, co. Durham, where the family lived until 1861.

Emily Davies's three brothers were all formally educated along conventional upper-middle-class lines: (John) Llewelyn *Davies and William Stephen Davies both attended Repton School before proceeding to Cambridge in preparation for the church, and the third brother was articled to a solicitor. Emily and her elder sister Jane were denied any serious schooling either at home or outside it, and were expected to content themselves with home duties such as needlework and, later, good works in their father's parish. In later life Emily stated that she resented the strict division between the education and privileges given to her brothers and the dull, repetitive, restricted life she and Jane were required to endure. Her two escapes seem to have been wandering about the slums of Gateshead and visiting her neighbours. Through two friends, Annie and Jane Crow, she met one of her lifelong allies, Elizabeth Garrett.

The demands of family duties fell heavily on Emily in the 1850s, when she was the companion to two of her siblings who were suffering from tuberculosis. She nursed Jane at Torquay from 1855 until her death in 1858. She was then sent to Algiers to join her younger brother, Henry. There she met another lifelong ally, Barbara Bodichon (*née* Leigh Smith), who was wintering there with her sister

(Sarah) Emily Davies (1830–1921), by Rudolph Lehmann, 1880

Annie. Her encounter with the Leigh Smith sisters appears to have been Emily Davies's first exposure to feminist ideas and to female political campaigning. Her inchoate and disorganized distaste for the traditional life of a clergyman's daughter and for the injustice of gender inequalities in the upper-middle-class family were crystallized and directed into what became the campaigns for women's suffrage and women's higher education.

The Langham Place group The deaths in 1858 of Emily's brothers Henry and William, the latter a naval chaplain who died in China of wounds previously sustained in the Crimea, left Emily alone with her parents in Gateshead. She visited Llewelyn and his wife in London in the spring of 1859, and returned for a longer visit in September. Llewelyn, the sibling to whom Emily seems to have been closest, was a member of F. D. Maurice's circle and one of the earliest members of the National Association for the Promotion of Social Science, the platform for launching many mid-Victorian feminist campaigns. While in London Emily encountered the women who formed the Langham Place group, the *English Woman's Journal* (founded by Barbara Bodichon and Bessie Rayner Parkes in 1858), and the Society for Promoting the Employment of Women (SPEW, founded in 1859). With Elizabeth Garrett she attended the lectures of Elizabeth Blackwell, the first woman doctor of medicine, who was visiting England; a meeting with Blackwell inspired Garrett to seek the opening of the medical profession to women.

Back in Gateshead during 1860–61, Emily founded a Northumberland and Durham branch of the SPEW, and letters from her advocating women's education and employment were published in a Newcastle newspaper. Following the death of her father, Emily and her mother moved to London in January 1862. From then until her death Emily was involved with campaigns to raise the status of middle-class women in Britain. In June 1862 her paper 'Medicine as a profession for women' was presented at the congress of the Social Science Association (it was read for her by Russell Gurney). In the same year she canvassed support for the efforts of Elizabeth Garrett and her father to open London University degrees to women. Between 1862 and 1864 she wrote for the *English Woman's Journal*, acting as editor during 1863, and was a founder of the *Victoria Magazine*—though she and her friends broke with this new journal when its publisher, Emily Faithfull, was named in the Codrington divorce case. Rigorous avoidance of women with questionable reputations was normal practice among early feminists, who were careful not to expose their campaigns to accusations of immorality.

Admission of women to examinations The first success which Emily Davies achieved as a feminist campaigner was as secretary (from October 1862) to the committee set up to secure the admission of women to university examinations. As a first step, admission was sought to the local examinations for schoolboys established at Oxford and Cambridge five years earlier. In October 1863 the committee, chaired by Henry Alford, dean of Canterbury, and supported by prominent women educationists such as Frances Mary Buss and Elizabeth Bostock, persuaded the Cambridge local examination syndicate to open its examinations to girls on an experimental basis. Given only six weeks' notice, Emily Davies found eighty-three girls to present themselves (twenty-five from Miss Buss's North London Collegiate School). While not all were proficient (especially in arithmetic), many passed and none was hysterical or seized by brain fever and there was no scandal. In October 1864 a memorial organized by Emily Davies and signed by nearly a thousand teachers and more than a hundred 'ladies of rank and influence' requested that the Cambridge examinations be permanently opened; the proposal was accepted in the following year.

Davies then successfully lobbied the schools inquiry commission (the Taunton commission), set up in December 1864, to include girls as well as boys in its investigations of middle-class education. She gave oral evidence to the commission on 30 November 1865, the first of nine female witnesses (the others were Frances Buss, Mary Eliza Porter, Frances Martin, Eleanor Elizabeth Smith, Susan Kyberd, Gertrude King, Dorothea Beale, and Elizabeth Wolstenholme). Her appearance was significant: it was the first time women had given evidence in person to a royal commission as expert witnesses, and she and Miss Buss, who gave evidence on the same day, were nervous, but impressed the commissioners with their 'perfect womanliness'. The report of the commission, signed in December 1867, was a landmark in the feminist campaign for a serious secondary education for middle-class girls.

The Kensington Society and women's suffrage In March 1865 Davies's allies in these successful campaigns formed a ladies' debating group, the Kensington Society, so called

because it met at the Kensington home of Charlotte Manning. Emily Davies was secretary of the society, whose other members included Helen Taylor, Sophia Jex-Blake, Barbara Bodichon, Dorothea Beale, Frances Buss, Frances Power Cobbe, Elizabeth Garrett, Isa Craig, and Elizabeth Wolstenholme. Through this group Emily Davies began for the first time to work for women's suffrage, helping to obtain nearly 1500 female signatories to a petition in its favour, which John Stuart Mill presented to the House of Commons on 7 June 1866. The group later quarrelled over the issue of votes for married women, with Davies and Bodichon wanting to campaign, initially, for the vote for single women and widows only, while Helen Taylor and Mill wished to include married women, on the principle of making suffrage equal for women and men. When a permanent suffrage committee was formed in November 1866, Emily Davies acted briefly as secretary, having refused to hold the position on a permanent basis. She was concerned that her involvement in the suffrage question might damage what had become her chief personal interest: that women should have access to a university education.

The higher education of women In 1866 Emily Davies published her first and most influential book: *The Higher Education of Women* (new edn, 1988), probably an extended version of a paper which she had intended to read at the Social Science Association congress in 1865. Pressing the case for opening both professional careers and university courses to women, it was well received in the press and by reviewers; it challenged the medical and religious arguments against degrees for women, and argued, like Mill, that many differences between men and women were matters of convention, not of biology.

In the same year Davies founded, at a meeting in her home, the London Schoolmistresses' Association, to which she was secretary until its dissolution in 1888; among its first members were Frances Buss, Jane Chessar, Charlotte Manning, and Fanny Metcalfe. It was at a meeting of schoolmistresses in Manchester, on 6 October 1866, that she reached the conclusion that there was a strong demand for a college for women. The transformation of Queen's College, Harley Street, in London, into an institution for preparing women over eighteen to take London degrees appeared the most easily available option. When this proved impossible to achieve, Davies formed an executive committee, which met for the first time on 5 December 1867 to raise £30,000 to build a college for women in Cambridge. The earliest members were Lady Augusta Stanley, Henry Alford, Emilia Gurney (wife of Russell Gurney), Charlotte Manning, Henry Richard Tomkinson, Fanny Metcalfe, G. W. Hastings, James Heywood, H. J. Roby, J. R. Seeley, and Sedley Taylor. Barbara Bodichon joined in 1869 and Lady Stanley of Alderley in 1872.

Rejecting the idea of separate lectures for women, and obsessively focused on a residential college where young women would take the same courses and exams as men, Emily Davies set out on a controversial and lonely course. Her policy stood apart from that promoted by another group at Cambridge headed by Henry Sidgwick and Anne

Jemima Clough, who successfully petitioned the Cambridge senate to institute special examinations for women over the age of eighteen. During the discussions on the constitution of her proposed college, in August 1868, Davies was adamant that the students should follow the ordinary Cambridge course taken by male students, even though the existing Cambridge curriculum and examination system were acknowledged to be archaic and in need of change. Here she was uncompromising: curricular and examination reform could not be pioneered by women without devaluing both the women and the reform. She was, it is now clear, right; but she made some enemies and lost many potential supporters by insisting that women students should be subjected to the existing Cambridge curriculum and system of assessment.

Girton College, Cambridge By July 1868 the executive committee had obtained promises of only £2000 and the prospect of a new building seemed distant. Later in that year Davies found a villa (Benslow House) to rent at Hitchin, Hertfordshire, and the first five students came into residence there in October 1869. Thus began Girton College, Emily Davies's most enduring memorial.

While the first students were staying in the house at Hitchin, reliant on men coming from Cambridge to teach them, Emily Davies and her committee were concentrating on building the real college at Girton, a village outside Cambridge. A physical separation from the male students, and from the city of Cambridge itself, where there were still considerable numbers of prostitutes, was seen as essential to protect the respectability of the young women embarking on their university studies. An alternative institution for women in city premises, however, supported by Henry Sidgwick, opened with Miss Clough as its head in October 1871. It later became Newnham College. Despite her increasing isolation and her difficult position as an 'outsider' in Cambridge, Emily Davies persisted with her plans. The target to be raised for the proposed college was lowered to £10,000 of which £7200 was donated, the rest having to be borrowed. She obtained the services of Alfred Waterhouse, architect of the Manchester assize court, to draw up plans, and the now famous red-brick edifice rose from a muddy field in Girton.

The new building opened in October 1873, though in a raw state with piles of sawdust and lit by candles; the first winters were bleak and cheerless. Emily Davies, who supervised the move from Hitchin, had in 1872 become resident mistress—a post earlier held by her friends: Charlotte Manning (until 1870), Emily Shirreff (1870), Annie Crow (Mrs Austin), (1870–72), and, briefly, after Annie Crow fell ill, by Barbara Bodichon and Lady Stanley of Alderley. Emily Davies herself resigned as mistress in 1875, and was succeeded by Marianne Frances Bernard. Emily Davies resumed the secretaryship of the executive committee, but ill health forced her to resign in 1877. She continued as treasurer until 1882, and became honorary secretary from then until 1904. Adamantly opposed to the mistress joining the executive committee, Emily Davies often experienced uneasy relations with the younger women who were tutors or mistresses of Girton. With Louisa Lumsden, Constance Maynard, Elizabeth Welsh, and Constance Jones, all better educated than Emily herself, she had personality clashes, and disagreements over the rules and procedures that should govern the students' lives, the place of religion in the college, and spending priorities between research and further building. She continued to regard increasing the accommodation of the college, to give more women the opportunity of a university education, as having first claim on funds. Between 1875 and 1902 she pushed through an ambitious programme of expansion.

Emily Davies remained committed to opening university degrees to women on the same terms as men. Her manifesto *Women in the Universities of England and Scotland* (1896) condemned the attempts to create separate arrangements for women, together with women's continued exclusion from Oxford and Cambridge degrees. But she praised the civic universities in England, and the Scottish and Welsh universities, which granted degrees to women on the same terms as men. In 1901 the University of Glasgow conferred on her the honorary degree of LLD. Her collected essays with a preface by Constance Jones were published as *Thoughts on some Questions Relating to Women* (1910).

Later public work and death Emily Davies had been elected to public office as a member of the London school board, representing Greenwich, in the first election held under the Education Act of 1870. She did not stand for re-election in 1873, concentrating instead on Girton. After giving up formal office at Girton in 1904, she returned to active suffrage work and became secretary in London of the National Society for Women's Suffrage, whose committee she joined in 1889. She led a suffrage deputation to Henry Campbell-Bannerman on 19 May 1906, but broke with the London society in 1912 when the National Union of Women's Suffrage Societies, to which it was affiliated, came out in support of the Labour Party. She then joined the Conservative and Unionist Women's Franchise Association and became one of its vice-presidents.

In 1912 Girton celebrated the jubilee of Emily Davies's move from Gateshead to London, fearing that she would not live to see the college's own jubilee. In 1914 she moved to Hampstead, where she was a neighbour of her brother Llewelyn until his death in 1916. By then she had outlived most of her friends. The death in 1917 of Elizabeth Garrett Anderson left Emily Davies as the sole surviving member of the original Langham Place group; she was the only one still alive to cast a vote in the general election of December 1918, the first after women won the parliamentary franchise. She died at her home at 17 Glenmore Road, Belsize Park, London, on 13 July 1921, and was buried two days later at St Marylebone cemetery, East Finchley.

Reputation and assessment During her lifetime Emily Davies was a controversial figure among both opponents of and enthusiasts for the higher education of women. Her uncompromising position on Girton (insisting on exactly the same curricula and examinations for women as for men, and very strict conformity to the conventions of ladylike dress and deportment) alienated many one-time supporters in her lifetime and led to her posthumous excoriation by twentieth-century eugenicists and Freudians such as Meyrick Booth and Arabella Kenealy. Her obsession with buildings rather than scholarship, and her uneasy relations with the tutors and mistresses of Girton, led early historians of the college to react against her. However, subsequent writers have taken a more sympathetic view of her adoption of an uncompromising position, her stubbornness, and her fiery rhetoric, and she has been presented as the heroine of a speculative popular biography. Late twentieth-century historians of Cambridge have similarly been rather more enthusiastic in their evaluations of Emily Davies's contribution to the modern university than were writers in the first half of the century.

While Emily Davies's practical achievements are now recognized, her contribution to the history of ideas remains controversial. While some see her as essentially an activist and committee woman, others see her as an original thinker who combined radical ideas on gender with an inherent social conservatism. Central to this dispute is the question of beliefs and tactics. Davies's tactics were clearly to work with 'establishment' figures. Whether she shared their beliefs about society, or merely paid lip-service to them to achieve her feminist goals, must remain a point of contention.   SARA DELAMONT

Sources B. Stephen, *Emily Davies and Girton College* (1927) · K. T. Butler and H. I. McMorran, eds., *Girton College register, 1869–1946* (1948) · B. Caine, *Victorian feminists* (1992) · O. Banks, *The biographical dictionary of British feminists*, 1 (1985), 59–62 · L. Holcombe, 'Davies, Emily', *BDMBR*, vol. 2 · J. Howarth, introduction, in E. Davies, *The higher education of women*, new edn (1988), vii–liii · R. Strachey, *The cause: a short history of the women's movement in Great Britain* (1928) · A. Rosen, 'Emily Davies and the women's movement', *Journal of British Studies*, 19/1 (1979–80), 101–21 · M. Forster, *Significant sisters: the grassroots of active feminism, 1839–1939* (1984) · G. Sutherland, 'The movement for the higher education of women: its social and intellectual context', *Political and social change in modern Britain*, ed. P. J. Waller (1987) · R. McWilliams-Tullberg, *Women at Cambridge* (1975) · M. Bradbrook, 'That infidel place': a short history of Girton College, 1869–1969 (1969) · S. Fletcher, *Feminists and bureaucrats: a study in the development of girls' education in the nineteenth century* (1980) · P. Hollis, *Ladies elect: women in English local government, 1865–1914* (1987) · D. Bennett, *Emily Davies and the liberation of women, 1830–1921* (1990) · J. Manton, *Elizabeth Garrett Anderson* (1965) · *The Times* (16 July 1921)
Archives Girton Cam., corresp. and MSS
Likenesses A. Mason, drawing, 1851, Girton Cam. · photograph, c.1866, Girton Cam. · R. Lehmann, oils, 1880, Girton Cam. [*see illus.*] · two photographs, 1901, Girton Cam.
Wealth at death £5440 17s. 2d.: probate, 8 Sept 1921, *CGPLA Eng. & Wales*

Davies, Evan (1805–1864), Congregational minister, was born at Hengwm in the parish of Lledrod, Cardiganshire, in 1805. He was educated in the academy at Neuadd-lwyd and in the Western Academy at Exeter; on the completion of his collegiate course he settled at Great Torrington, Devon. In 1835 he was ordained at Wycliffe Chapel, London, as a missionary to the Chinese, and was sent to Penang (the base for Chinese missionary activity) under the auspices of the London Missionary Society. After four years, ill health compelled him to return home. In 1842 he was appointed superintendent of the Boys' Mission School at Walthamstow, and in 1844 he moved to Richmond, Surrey, where he officiated as pastor of the Congregational church for thirteen years. He died at Llansteffan, near Carmarthen, on 18 June 1864.

Davies published *China and her Spiritual Claims* in 1845, and *Memoirs of the Rev. Samuel Dyer, Sixteen Years Missionary to the Chinese* in 1846. He also wrote on revivals in Wales (1859) and on theological subjects.

THOMPSON COOPER, *rev.* H. C. G. MATTHEW

Sources *Congregational Year Book* (1865), 234

Davies, Frances Mary Jemima Woodhill [Fanny] (1861–1934), pianist, was born at Bouët, St Peter Port, Guernsey, on 27 June 1861, the first child of Alfred Arnold Davies (*b.* 1829/30), a schoolmaster, and his wife, Mary Jemima Woodhill (*b.* 1830), the daughter of a gifted amateur cellist. At an early age Fanny was sent to Birmingham to live with her aunt, Eliza Woodhill, who ran a thriving girls' school. Fanny began piano lessons there and gave her first public performance in Birmingham town hall at the age of six, but otherwise was exempt from the life of a prodigy. She later studied the piano and harmony with noted local teachers Charles Flavell and Alfred Gaul; she also learned the violin with Henry Hayward ('the Wolverhampton Paganini'), who instilled in her a love of chamber music.

Owing to delicate lungs Davies spent two winters indoors, studying music. Pianistically she was first inspired by Arabella Goddard, whom she heard in Birmingham in 1870. Encouraged by Charles Hallé, she went to Leipzig in 1882 to study with Carl Reinecke and Oscar Paul, but a year later she fulfilled her dream of studying with Clara Schumann, enrolling at the Hoch Conservatorium in Frankfurt in September 1883.

Returning to England in 1885, Davies made her London début at the Crystal Palace on 17 October, performing Beethoven's fourth piano concerto and some solos by Schumann and C. H. Graun. A month later she made her first appearance in the Monday Popular Concerts, playing solo and chamber music. At a time when pupils of Liszt such as Sophie Menter were dazzling audiences with muscular virtuosity, Davies's more restrained manner caused the *Musical Times* to hail her as 'a legitimate, as opposed to phenomenal or eccentric' pianist (*Musical Times*, 26, 1885, 656–7). She went on to enjoy a successful career as a soloist and a chamber musician in England and abroad, performing extensively in Europe both before and after the First World War. An important influence in her early career was the violinist Joseph Joachim; with the cellist Alfredo Piatti they formed a trio, giving six performances in the 'Popular' concerts of 1885–6. Fanny Davies also performed in the Joachim Quartet concerts in 1906. She remained committed to the music of Schumann and Brahms, regularly performing their concertos and major solo works. She gave the first performance of Brahms's D minor violin sonata, op. 108, in Berlin with Joachim and introduced the *Klavierstücke*, opp. 116 and 117, to English audiences. In addition, she took part in the first performances of Brahms's

Frances Mary Jemima Woodhill Davies (1861–1934), by Sasha

clarinet trio, op. 114, and the clarinet sonatas, op. 120, with their dedicatee, Richard Mühlfeld (1856–1907).

Davies also championed music by English composers: in 1886 she performed Sterndale Bennett's piano concerto at a Philharmonic Concert, and she was the dedicatee of Elgar's bravura *Concert Allegro*, op. 46. She explored both early and contemporary English repertory, as well as early Netherlandish and Italian keyboard music. According to Benton Fletcher (*The Times*, 4 Sept 1934) she owned a 1762 Tschudi harpsichord, though she did not perform publicly on it.

As a chamber musician Fanny Davies performed with some of the greatest artists of the day. In 1907 she undertook a concert tour of Germany with the tenor Gervase Elwes, whose singing of Brahms lieder was well received. She played with the Rosé Quartet in Vienna in 1897 and later joined forces with the Bohemian String Quartet, championing music by Czech composers. In Prague she was hailed as 'the Daviesová' by an enchanted critic. She was also a friend of the cellist Pablo Casals, who invited her to play with his orchestra in Barcelona in 1923.

A protégée of Clara Schumann, Davies maintained her teacher's principles throughout her life, despite a rift with the family in 1893–4. She maintained warm friendships with fellow Schumann pupils such as Leonard Borwick and Mathilde Verne, and with them and others marked the Schumann centenary in 1910 with a gala concert. She also contributed articles on Schumann and Brahms to *Cobbett's Cyclopedia of Chamber Music* (1929).

Davies was also a sought-after teacher. Pupils found her demanding but supportive, and a former headmistress of the Francis Holland School, London, which still has a Fanny Davies prize, remembered the pianist as 'a sparkling raconteuse with an inexhaustible fund of anecdotes' (*Daily Telegraph*, 6 Sept 1934). She was president of the Society of Women Musicians from 1925 to 1926—an apt choice as she had played with most of the leading women instrumentalists of the day. She had connections with Steinway from fairly early on, and was invited by them to record on piano rolls for the Welte-Mignon Company in 1909. They continued to support her, supplying pianos even in remote places, a privilege granted to only a select few. She later recorded for the Columbia Graphophone Company.

A popular performer at private concerts, Davies was famous for her party trick of imitating the mannerisms of contemporary pianists. Edward Speyer, who knew her from the beginning of her career, commented on her formidable memory which had so impressed Casals, and her ability to play for hours in private and congenial company without fatigue. Dorothy Mayer recalled 'the dreamy warmth' of her playing, as well as her 'lively sense of the ridiculous, and combination of whimsy and dignity' (Mayer, 776–9). Never married, she lived for some time with her companion Harriette Grist and had a wide circle of friends. A warm-hearted and exuberant woman, she was undaunted by her small stature, and 'small hands not ideally suited to piano playing' (*The Times*, 3 Sept 1934).

Davies remained professionally active until near the end of her life, when she suffered a stroke and was moved into a west London nursing home at 25 Leinster Square, where she died on 1 September 1934. The obituarist in the *Birmingham Post* (3 September 1934) described her as a 'personal messenger for Schumann and Brahms', which was perhaps her main legacy to twentieth-century pianism, though she was also an exponent of later composers such as Debussy and Granados. In an interview published in the *Musical Times* of June 1905 she stated that 'Clara Schumann's aim was to be technically perfect but never to think too much of the instrument and too little of the music' (46.370). It was a tradition she maintained to the end.

DOROTHY DE VAL

Sources 'Miss Fanny Davies: a biographical sketch', *MT*, 46 (1905), 365–70 · D. Mayer, 'Fanny Davies', *Recorded Sound*, 70–71 (1978), 776–9 · D. McVeagh, 'Elgar's *Concert allegro*', *MT*, 110 (1969), 135–8 · *Birmingham Post* (3 Sept 1934) · *The Observer* (9 Sept 1934) · *The Times* (3 Sept 1934) · *Daily Telegraph* (4–6 Sept 1934) · *Monthly Musical Record*, 64 (1934), 174–5 · *MT*, 75 (1934), 899–900 · E. Speyer, *My life and friends* (1937) · 'Davies, Fanny', Grove, *Dict. mus.* (1927) · *WWW*, 1929–40 · Royal College of Music, London, Marion Scott MSS · autograph letter collection; letters from Fanny Davies to D. Armitage and M. Smith; catalogued by J. Kersey, Royal College of Music, London · Fanny Davies box: a collection of letters, programmes, and ephemera relating to Fanny Davies, partly catalogued by J. Kersey, Royal College of Music, London · b. cert. · d. cert. · m. cert. [Mary Jemima Woodhill]

Archives Royal College of Music, London, box of letters, programmes, and other ephemera | Royal College of Music, London, autograph letters, letters to D. Armitage and M. Smith re musical matters · Royal College of Music, London, Marion Scott MSS, material relating to Davies's estate, solicitor's papers, etc. | SOUND BL NSA, performance recordings

Likenesses Sasha, photograph, Royal College of Music, London [*see illus.*]

Wealth at death £3500: Royal College of Music, London, Marion Scott MSS, solicitor's letter dated 5 Nov 1934

Davies, Francis (1605–1675), bishop of Llandaff, was born on 14 March 1605 of non-gentry parentage in Glamorgan, probably in the border vale of that county. He matriculated from Jesus College, Oxford, on 10 November 1621, graduated BA on 26 February 1625, and proceeded MA on 14 March 1628. He became rector of Pen-tyrch and Radur, in his native part of Glamorgan, in 1630, and rector of Llan-gan, which he held with Llantrithyd, in 1638. He received preferment to the prebendary of St Andrews, in Llandaff Cathedral, in 1639. At some point soon after this he gave up the living of Llantrithyd. He took the degree of BD on 22 June 1640, after election to a fellowship at Jesus College.

As one who was making rapid progress in the Anglican hierarchy in Llandaff diocese Davies was opposed to church reforms of the 1640s, and was ejected from Pen-tyrch and Llan-gan some time between 1646 and 1650. His offence, according to his sympathizers, was having refused to accept the directory of worship produced by the presbyterian Westminster assembly. An even more compelling reason for his ejection was that he was among the Laudian clergy who had helped lead a revolt in Glamorgan in summer 1647 against the county committee of parliament. Even so, after the introduction of the Act for the Propagation of the Gospel in Wales in 1650 there was evidently more local sympathy towards him than towards some other Anglican ministers. He enjoyed a number of concessions: he retained the fourth part of the valuable living of Llan-gan, and the tithes there were let to his brother, Maurice Davies; and in 1655 it was ordered that even though unmarried he should receive the allowance to ejected ministers' families, known as 'fifths', from the vicarage of Pen-tyrch. Another clergyman brother of his, Rice Davies, received small sums from the state-controlled tithes, and occasionally officiated at Pen-tyrch using the outlawed Book of Common Prayer. Despite threats by Major John Gawler, of the Cardiff Castle garrison, Francis Davies 'received the small tithe of Radur for the space of ten years without any molestation' (Bodl. Oxf., MS Walker c. 4). It was said that because of Davies's 'great piety, learning and excellent parts' (Jenkins, 38), his discreet benefactor during these years was Colonel Philip Jones, prominent among the lay propagators. As another way of augmenting his income during the 1650s Davies kept a school in one of the parishes where he had influence. Evidently the arrangements for his maintenance collapsed around 1656, according to Davies's nephew because Philip Jones tired of them, but more probably because Jones lived virtually continuously in London during the protectorate, and others were by then responsible for running the state church in Glamorgan. To secure an income Davies, through the good offices of friends, moved to London to become for three or four years the chaplain of Penelope, countess of Peterborough, whose husband, Henry Mordaunt, second earl of Peterborough, was a prominent royalist.

At the Restoration Davies was thus well placed to recover his livings. In August 1660 he petitioned for the archdeaconry of Llandaff, pleading his attempts to maintain the king's cause and the prayer book liturgy, and was supported by Gilbert Sheldon, the cleric closest to Charles II. Having been restored to his livings Davies was made archdeacon of Llandaff on 6 August 1660 and was installed in October. He took the degree of DD on 21 May 1661. A local ally of Davies's was Sir John Aubrey of Llantrithyd, a leading high-church royalist. While archdeacon he had the whip hand over ministers of the king who had ousted him in the previous decade, but was sufficiently conciliatory to offer a living to Samuel Jones of Brynllywarch, Llangynwyd, who in return propounded a series of questions to Davies on the validity of the liturgy and orders of the Anglican church. On 24 August 1667 Davies was consecrated bishop of Llandaff and gave up his other livings except a Llandaff prebendary which he held *in commendam* with the bishopric. Although well connected with the dominant party in church and state he was content to devote himself to restoring the fabric and reputation of his cathedral. He remained resident in the diocese, at Matharn, re-established the cathedral library, broken up during the Commonwealth, and installed what became the largest bell in the Llandaff bell-tower. He never married, and in his will dated 6 March 1675 disposed of a very small estate to his brother Rice and several servants, nephews, and a niece. He died on 14 March, his seventieth birthday. He was buried before the altar in his cathedral; having been long lost the gravestone came to view again after enemy bombing of Llandaff in 1941. Davies's nephew, another Francis Davies, provided John Walker with material on east Glamorgan for his 1714 martyrology, *The Sufferings of the Clergy*.   STEPHEN K. ROBERTS

Sources Bodl. Oxf., MS Tanner 58 · Bodl. Oxf., MSS J. Walker c. 4, e. 7 · bills and answers of defaulting accountants, PRO, E 113/2 · LPL, MS Comm. XII 6/1 · *Fasti Angl.* (Hardy), 2.254, 260, 267 · B. Willis, *A survey of the cathedral church of Llandaff* (1719) · *CSP dom.*, 1660–61; 1667 · Foster, *Alum. Oxon.* · P. Jenkins, '"The sufferings of the clergy": the church in Glamorgan during the interregnum', *Journal of Welsh Ecclesiastical History*, 3 (1986), 1–17; 4 (1987), 9–41 · T. Rees, *History of protestant nonconformity in Wales*, 2nd edn (1883) · *DWB* · will, PRO, PROB 11/347, sig. 37
Archives Bodl. Oxf., MSS Tanner, letters

Davies, Francis Thomas (1906–1988), intelligence officer and industrialist, was born on 9 December 1906 at 39 Melville Street, Edinburgh, the son of General Sir Francis John Davies (1864–1948) and his wife, Madalen Augusta Lavinia Scott. The family home was Elmley Castle, near Pershore, Worcestershire. He was educated at Broadstairs and at Eton College, which he entered in the lowest form. When he departed his house captain wrote that Davies:

> was a very good footballer, immensely strong and quite unstoppable when really roused … He has left rather young to go into an Insurance office. Though not brilliant in work, we feel sure that he will have a great aptitude for persuading people to insure their lives, for his harrowing tales of various deceases [*sic*] were enough to terrify anyone.   (private information, Eton College archivist)

Davies worked for different firms in France, Germany, and London before joining Courtaulds Ltd in 1929, where he became a director in 1937, with responsibility for exports and for factories in France and Germany. In September 1938 he wrote to the under-secretary of state for war, volunteering for intelligence work. He was interviewed in the War Office and asked to report on Germany's economic preparations for war. This led to espionage within Germany on behalf of the War Office and section D of the Secret Intelligence Service (SIS). During 1939 he was drawn into the work of a new War Office department, military intelligence (research), known as MI(R). On 7 August 1940 he married Eileen Cynthia Millicent Eva (*b*. 1912), daughter of Henry Charles Brougham, third Baron Brougham and Vaux. They had at least one child.

In August 1939, while training with the 1st battalion, Grenadier Guards, Davies was called up from the Territorial Army reserve to serve as a staff officer in the British military mission to Poland. A colleague recalled how Davies 'in a Brigade of Guard's tie, stood disapproving and aloof' amid the hearty mêlée of departing officers at Victoria Station (Wilkinson, 68). Early in September 1939 General Adrian Carton de Wiart, the head of mission, sent Davies back to Britain with urgent requests for assistance in view of the disastrous situation developing in Poland. Davies left Poland on 5 September in a civil aircraft that was fired at by both Germans and Poles during its journey. On arrival in London he summarized Carton de Wiart's concerns in a report discussed by the chiefs of staff at their meeting on 9 September. Carton de Wiart urgently requested sufficient fighter aircraft to ward off the German medium bombers that prevented the Poles from mustering formations to carry out counter-attacks. Carton de Wiart also wanted light machine-guns and ammunition forwarded immediately before Poland's frontiers were sealed off. Davies reported that 'General Carton de Wiart asked me to impress upon everybody I met the absolute urgency for immediate action; there must be no delay' (Davies). But the concern and energy of Carton de Wiart and Davies could achieve virtually nothing for the Poles in the face of British impotence and inertia.

Davies resumed work for MI(R) and travelled widely to seize objects of economic value in Europe before the Nazis marched in. Perhaps his most notable mission came in May 1940, when he made a hurried trip to Amsterdam and successfully removed or destroyed securities held in the national bank. Later in 1940 staff from MI(R) were absorbed into a new organization, the Special Operations Executive (SOE). Labour minister Hugh Dalton was chairman; he chose Sir Frank Nelson as his executive director and was given Gladwyn Jebb, by the Foreign Office, as chief executive officer. In his diary entry for 25 July Dalton noted that he saw Davies, 'who makes a good impression on me … [he] says there has been a lack of drive and direction. He obviously wants me to begin to supply these deficiencies' (*War Diary*, 65). Davies joined SOE on 23 September 1940 as personal assistant to Nelson, with the remit of advising his chief on SOE's resources of staff and supplies. On 12 October he completed a report on training that established a programme for the provision of schools. His plan envisaged four stages: preliminary schools, where agents would be assessed without taking them very far into the secrets of the organization; paramilitary schools; finishing schools, which were to teach subversive warfare and would hold agents until required for operations; and lastly the final briefing of agents in London flats.

Davies was the first to see the need for SOE representation in America. This was duly achieved through the British security co-ordination (BSC), under Sir William Stephenson, established in December 1940 to represent British intelligence in North America. BSC became important as a source of supplies, recruits, and training facilities for SOE—matters at the core of Davies's role in the organization. In September 1941 Davies visited the USA for discussions with Colonel Donovan, head of the office for strategic services (OSS), the new American organization for subversion and espionage overseas. This crucial meeting established friendly relations and the basis for a relatively free exchange of information and facilities between SOE and OSS. Davies committed SOE to establishing a school in Canada to train both British and American personnel, and in return Donovan promised SOE supplies of materials and staff. In autumn 1941 Davies became director of research and supply, and held that post until the end of his SOE career. It gave him considerable influence behind the scenes, not least during the SOE palace revolution of 1942. In February of that year Lord Wolmer succeeded Dalton as minister for SOE, and the involuntary departure of Gladwyn Jebb soon followed. Dalton believed that Davies threw his weight in the scales against Jebb, who was resented by some SOE staff due to a tactless deployment of superior intellect—an unfortunate trait that he shared with Dalton. In contrast, according to one contemporary, 'Davies didn't have much upstairs' (private information). Indeed he was a man of action rather than an intellectual, and so worked easily with the business and military men who formed the core of SOE. He was appraised by Colin Gubbins as 'an officer of great drive and personality, most efficient in his duties. He has any amount of initiative and willingly accepts responsibility … An outstanding officer' (private information, SOE adviser). Davies's work for SOE was not as adventurous as his earlier role in MI(R); rather, he played a vital part in strengthening the logistics of a new and sometimes chaotic organization. This was the most important contribution that he made during a life that was vigorous, versatile, and effective.

In May 1945 Davies left SOE and returned to the business world. He rejoined the board of Courtaulds and, together with its chairman, Sir John Hanbury-Williams, was largely responsible for re-establishing its prestige overseas, especially in the USA. From 1948 he spent much of his time in the United States, overseeing projects there. At Courtaulds he was always referred to as Colonel Davies; he has been described by the company's historian as 'a vigorous and assertive man who liked issuing orders and getting things done' (Coleman, 88) and had a reputation for plunging in without thinking a problem out. An overseas business acquaintance described him as 'très bousculant' (ibid.). Ill health forced him to resign from Courtaulds in January 1954 but he later served as a director of Gulf Oil (GB) and as chairman of British Enkalon. He died on 8 September 1988 at his home, Hill House Farm, Elmley Castle.

E. D. R. HARRISON

Sources W. J. M. Mackenzie, *The secret history of SOE* (2000) · private information (2004) [Eton College archivist, SOE adviser, foreign and commonwealth office] · F. T. Davies, reports, War Office 216/47, PRO · *The Second World War diary of Hugh Dalton, 1940–1945*, ed. B. Pimlott (1986) · b. cert. · d. cert. · *WW* (1941) · P. Wilkinson, *Foreign fields* (1997) · M. R. D. Foot, *SOE: an outline history of the Special Operations Executive, 1940–46* (1984) · D. C. Coleman, *Courtaulds: an economic and social history*, 3 vols. (1969–80) · Burke, *Peerage* (2000)
Archives PRO, War Office 216/47 · PRO, HS, SOE files
Wealth at death £734,944: probate, 13 July 1989, *CGPLA Eng. & Wales*

Davies, Griffith (1788–1855), actuary, son of Owen Davies (1761–1854), farmer and quarryman, and his wife, Mary William, was born at Tŷ Croes, at the foot of Cilgwyn Mountain, in the parish of Llandwrog, Caernarvonshire, on 28 December 1788. He was taught to read and spell in Welsh at the Sunday school of Brynrodyn Chapel, Llandwrog. At the age of seven he began learning English at an English school at Llanwnda. He subsequently discovered a special aptitude for arithmetic, but his parents' poverty obliged him to work as a farm labourer, horse driver, and quarryman. He was often seen with an iron pen, covering slates with arithmetical calculations, and he attended elementary school, though only for short periods.

Desirous of improving his English, which was still very limited, Davies sailed for London in September 1809. There he attended a school to perfect his writing and grammar, and in January 1810 secured an appointment as a teacher of arithmetic at a salary of £20 p.a. In his spare time he started calculating the times of the eclipses and exhibiting their mode of occurrence by diagrams. He opened a school of his own in the summer of 1811 in James Street, Old Street; in the following year he moved into a better house in Lizard Street, Bartholomew Square, in the parish of St Luke, and joined the Mathematical Society in Crispin Street, Spitalfields. Davies published, in 1814, his *Key to Bonnycastle's Trigonometry*, which made his name as a mathematician and brought many pupils to his school; these included the explorer John Franklin, who was keen to increase his knowledge of the mathematics of navigation, and also several employees of insurance offices. This led to actuarial work and contact with William Morgan, the actuary of the Equitable, who furnished him with a certificate of actuarial competency. In 1820 Davies was awarded the large silver medal of the Society of Arts for an ingenious sundial which he had constructed.

In 1821 the projectors of the Guardian Assurance Company applied to Davies for advice and assistance when drawing up their constitution, and he was engaged to construct the necessary life tables. Towards the end of 1823 he was appointed the regular and permanent actuary of the Guardian at an annual salary of £150, an appointment which he held for the rest of his life. He constructed the

first of many life tables for the newly established Reversionary Interest Society in 1823. Two years later he published *Tables of Life Contingencies*, which provided an extensive scale of premiums for life assurance. He also introduced a pioneering remodelling of the columnar method of constructing mortality tables devised by George Barrett.

In 1812 Davies married Mary Holbut, the sister of one of his pupils. They had four daughters, but only one survived childhood. Mary died in 1836, and in February 1841 Davies married Mrs Mary Glynne (d. 1848), a widow, daughter of Euan Owen; they had a son, also called Griffith, who became an actuary like his father.

Davies's fame spread and on 16 June 1831, on the recommendation of Benjamin Gompertz, the astronomer and actuary, he was elected a fellow of the Royal Society. In 1843 he was one of the proponents of the publication of mortality tables based on data collected from all the life offices. When the Institute of Actuaries was founded in 1848 Davies declined the honour of being its first president (he was already then becoming something of a recluse), but the institute recognized him as 'the father of the present race of actuaries' (Chambers, 70). The actuarial consultancy work that Davies undertook during the latter part of his career added to his reputation. In 1829 the directors of the East India Company submitted the documents concerning the Bombay military fund for his investigation and report, for which he was paid £3000. From that time until 1851 his actuarial advice was regularly sought on the various Indian funds. He wrote no fewer than twenty reports on them, each containing extensive insurance tables. He was also engaged from time to time for the Bank of England. This private practice was extremely lucrative; Davies also received £850 p.a. from the Guardian company and £150 p.a. from the Reversionary Interest Society.

Griffith Davies was a man of deep religious feelings, and belonged to a chapel of Welsh Calvinistic Methodists in Jewin Street, Cripplegate. In his final years he absented himself from all society save that of the chapel and his office. On 5 December 1854 he was seized with a paralytic stroke, and he died at 25 Duncan Terrace, Islington, London, on 21 March 1855. He was survived by a son and a daughter, and was buried at Abney Park cemetery, Stoke Newington.

G. C. BOASE, rev. ROBERT BROWN

Sources L. G. Chambers, 'Griffith Davies, 1788–1855, FRS, actuary', *Transactions of the Honourable Society of Cymmrodorion* (1988), 59–77 · T. Barlow, 'Memoir of the late Griffith Davies', *Assurance Magazine and Journal of the Institute of Actuaries*, 5 (1855), 337–49 · W. J. Pinks, *The history of Clerkenwell*, ed. E. J. Wood, 2nd edn (1881), 706–8 · C. Walford, *The insurance cyclopaedia*, 6 vols. (1871–80) [see also 'Columnar method [Commutation method]'] · *The Times* (26 March 1855), 7 · *GM*, 2nd ser., 43 (1855), 534 · E. H. Rowland, *A biographical dictionary of eminent Welshmen who flourished from 1700 to 1900* (privately printed, Wrexham, 1907) · T. Sibett, 'Griffith Davies, F.I.A., F.R.S.', *Fiasco*, 107 (1988), 6–9 · R. C. Simmonds, *The Institute of Actuaries, 1848–1948* (1948) · A. W. Tarn and C. E. Byles, *A record of the Guardian Assurance Company Limited* (1921) · Boase, *Mod. Eng. biog.* · General Register Office for England

Archives Institute of Actuaries, London, manuscripts · NL Wales, corresp. and notes, MSS 12747–12751 | GL, board minutes of Guardian Assurance Company, MS 14281
Likenesses portrait, NL Wales

Davies, Gwendoline Elizabeth [Gwen] (1882–1951), philanthropist and patron of the arts, was born on 11 February 1882 at Plas Dinam, Llandinam, Montgomeryshire, the second of the three children of Edward Davies (1852–1898) and his wife, Mary (d. 1888), daughter of the Calvinistic Methodist minister the Revd Evan Jones. Gwen Davies's paternal grandfather was the Liberal MP David Davies (1818–1890), who had made his fortune through railways, coal, and dock-building. Together with her younger sister, **Margaret Sidney** [Daisy] **Davies** (1884–1963), who was born on 14 December 1884, she was educated at home and at Highfield School, Hendon. Gwen became a talented amateur violinist, while Daisy studied painting at the Slade School of Fine Art, London, and in Paris. After their mother's death, in 1888, their father married her sister, a dominating person with strict Methodist convictions. The sisters grew up shy and ill at ease in company, and neither married.

The Davies sisters' lives remained somewhat circumscribed until the outbreak of the First World War. Having in 1914 assisted Belgian refugee poets and artists to settle in Wales, in 1916 they opened a canteen in Troyes for French troops. Their ideas about establishing a Welsh centre to further art and design began to take shape early in 1919, when the Davies family were contemplating selling Gregynog, a country house included in an estate near Newtown purchased by their brother, David *Davies, later first Baron Davies of Llandinam (1880–1944). On his second marriage, in 1922, the sisters unwillingly left Plas Dinam and moved into Gregynog, whose name soon became synonymous with fine printing, music-making, and art. Under Gwen Davies's supervision the gardens, with their walks and landscaped grounds, provided a fitting setting.

The appointment in 1921 of the artist Robert Ashwin Maynard (1888–1966) as controller marked the beginning of the Gregynog Press, which published forty-two volumes, eight of them in Welsh, in limited editions between 1923 and 1942. It quickly established high standards in design, printing, illustration, and binding and provided training and employment for local people. However, there were constant tensions, not least because the artists employed found life at Methodist, teetotal Gregynog constricting, and Daisy's heart was not in the venture, for her interests were narrower than Gwen's. The sisters relied heavily for advice on the civil servant Thomas Jones (1870–1955) and were assisted by a friend from the Troyes canteen, Dora Herbert Jones, a singer and collector of Welsh folk songs. Music was central to Gregynog and owed much to the sisters' connections with Sir (Henry) Walford Davies, professor of music at Aberystwyth, where University College benefited from their financial support. At Gregynog a music room was built and a choir established, composed of servants as well as family, friends, and neighbours; rumour had it that a good singing voice was the best qualification for any job on the estate. From 1933 to 1938 a major festival of music and poetry was held each summer, featuring musicians such as Sir Adrian Boult, Ralph Vaughan Williams, and Gustav Holst. The house also became the meeting place of the National Council of Music.

Visual art was another lifelong passion for both Gwen and Daisy Davies. Although Daisy was herself a competent artist in oils the sisters' lasting contribution is as collectors, especially in French art, their interest in which can be traced back to their travels in France before the First World War. From 1908 until the early 1920s they bought regularly, with the assistance of Hugh Blaker, brother of their former governess turned companion. They acquired a remarkable collection of oils, watercolours, etchings, engravings, and bronzes, including old masters, contemporary British works, and, most notably, French impressionists, among them works by Corot, Renoir, Cézanne, and Monet. After Gwen Davies's death, in 1951, her sister resumed buying, selling some of the older works in order to invest in those of living artists. The sisters bequeathed the main collection to the National Museum in Cardiff.

The sisters' commitment to the arts was paralleled by their determination to direct some of their considerable financial resources to relieving living conditions for the poor, especially during the years of the depression, when the plight of industrial south Wales, the source of the family fortune, caused them great distress. As early as 1911 they had helped their brother to set up the King Edward VII Welsh National Memorial Association to establish sanatoria throughout Wales and thereby curb the national scourge of tuberculosis; Daisy Davies later left a large bequest to the Welsh National School of Medicine at Cardiff. Youth and social service organizations were regularly invited to Gregynog, as were staff of clubs and settlements for the unemployed. The sisters' Methodist beliefs strengthened their conviction that wealth brought great responsibility, and the constant demands for charitable donations from all directions became a burden to them.

In 1937 Gwen Davies was made a Companion of Honour. The Second World War brought an end to the sisters' book publishing and large-scale music-making ventures at Gregynog, which became a Red Cross convalescent home. When peace came Gwen Davies's deteriorating health prevented a return to the former activities. She died of leukaemia on 3 July 1951 at the Radcliffe Infirmary, Oxford. Daisy Davies, who was made an honorary LLD in 1949, conveyed Gregynog, after much thought, to the University of Wales, living quietly as tenant there until her death, on 13 March 1963, at the Hospital of St John and St Elizabeth in London. Both sisters were cremated (Gwen in Oxford) and their ashes buried in Llandinam churchyard.

CERIDWEN LLOYD-MORGAN

Sources E. White, *The ladies of Gregynog* (1985) · E. D. Jones and B. F. Roberts, eds., *Y bywgraffiadur Cymreig, 1951–1970* (1997) · D. Harrop, *A history of the Gregynog Press* (1980) · J. Ingamells, *The Davies collection of French art* (1967) · P. Hughes, *French art from the Davies bequest* (1982) · H. I. Parrott, *The spiritual pilgrims* (1969) · G. T. Hughes, P. Morgan, and J. G. Thomas, eds., *Gregynog* (1977) · CGPLA Eng. & Wales (1963)

Archives NL Wales, family and financial papers, 'Coffr Gregynog' · NL Wales, MSS 22319–23320B, 22321–23322C · NL Wales, MS 17743E · priv. coll. | NL Wales, papers relating to Hugh Blaker · NL Wales, Gregynog Press archives · NL Wales, Thomas Jones CH papers · NMG Wales, papers relating to Davies bequest **Likenesses** photographs, repro. in White, *The ladies of Gregynog* **Wealth at death** £863,662 4*s.* 1*d.*: probate, 5 Oct 1951, *CGPLA Eng. & Wales* · £590,904 13*s.* 11*d.*—Margaret Sidney Davies: probate, 29 April 1963, *CGPLA Eng. & Wales*

Davies, Dame Gwen Lucy Ffrangcon- (1891–1992), actress, was born on 25 January 1891 at 195 Finchley Road, Hampstead, London, the daughter of David Thomas Ffrangcon-Davies (1855–1918), choral singer, and his wife, Annie Frances, *née* Rayner. Her father was said to have taken the name Ffrangcon from a Welsh beauty spot. She was educated at South Hampstead high school and then studied for the stage under Mrs L. Manning-Hicks and Agnes Platt. As a child she saw Irving act, auditioned for Ellen Terry, and later played Tess of the d'Urbervilles at a private performance given at his home for its author, Thomas Hardy. A lifelong Christian Scientist, she never married but lived for many years in both England and South Africa with the actress Marda Vanne; together in the Second World War they ran a notable South African theatre management.

Ffrangcon-Davies made her stage début as a fairy in a 1911 staging of *A Midsummer Night's Dream*. She subsequently toured for some time, playing Kiki in *The Glad Eye*, Sombra in *The Arcadians*, and other roles. From 1917 to 1918 she worked in the censor's office. She sang the soprano lead in such choral dramas as *The Immortal Hour* and *The Birth of Arthur* at the Glastonbury festival (1919–20) and subsequently at the Old Vic. She joined the Birmingham Repertory Company in 1921, and won critical acclaim for her acting in such J. M. Barrie plays as *Quality Street* (1921) and *The Admirable Crichton* (1922). She first made her name in London in 1923, creating the roles of Eve and the Newly Born in the first staging of Shaw's *Back to Methuselah*.

In 1924 Ffrangcon-Davies first played Juliet to John Gielgud's Romeo, thereby starting a stage partnership that was to last for almost half a century; during that time she was to be the Queen to his *Richard of Bordeaux* (1932) and Gwendolyn in his classic 1940 revival of *The Importance of being Earnest*, though two years later they had a rare joint failure in *Macbeth*. One of her longest-lasting roles was as Elizabeth Browning in *The Barretts of Wimpole Street*, which she played intermittently throughout the 1930s at home and abroad. While living in Marda Vanne's native Johannesburg from 1943 onwards she also scored considerable successes in such comedies as Noël Coward's *Blithe Spirit*.

After returning to England in 1946, Ffrangcon-Davies played the Queen Mother in Terence Rattigan's unsuccessful *Adventure Story* (1949), but soon reclaimed her reputation at home with the 1950 Stratford season, where she succeeded Peggy Ashcroft as Beatrice to Gielgud's Benedick in *Much Ado about Nothing* and also played Portia in *Julius Caesar* and Queen Katharine in *Henry VIII*. She continued to tour at home and abroad, returning to the West End in 1954 to remind audiences of her considerable comic talent as Donna Lucia to the Charley's Aunt of John

Dame Gwen Lucy Ffrangcon-Davies (1891–1992), by Walter Sickert, *c.*1932–4 [in *The Lady with a Lamp* by Reginald Berkeley]

Mills. That same year she was an unforgettable Ranevskaya in *The Cherry Orchard* at the Lyric, Hammersmith, and two years later she became a founder member of the new English Stage Society at the Royal Court, where she played Rose Padley in the opening production by Nigel Dennis, *The Mulberry Bush*, going straight from there to play Agatha in T. S. Eliot's *The Family Reunion* at the Phoenix. Later she again replaced Peggy Ashcroft, a lifelong friend—in Enid Bagnold's *The Chalk Garden* at the Haymarket (1957)—before giving what many believe was her greatest performance, as the doomed, drug-ridden Mary Tyrone in the first London staging of Eugene O'Neill's *Long Day's Journey into Night* (1958) opposite Anthony Quayle.

Ffrangcon-Davies became a founder member of a great theatrical company, Peter Hall's Royal Shakespeare Company, which she joined for its first London season in 1961 at the Aldwych, playing with Leslie Caron in *Ondine* and also as the Queen Mother in Jean Anouilh's *Becket*. In 1963 she made her Broadway début (well into her seventies) as Mrs Candour in *The School for Scandal*. Back home she played Amanda Wingfield in Tennessee Williams's *The Glass Menagerie* at the Haymarket (1965) and Madame Voynitsky in Chekhov's *Uncle Vanya* at the Royal Court (1970).

Often rather too theatrical for film or television cameras, Ffrangcon-Davies was also unlucky perhaps in coming of the same unique theatrical generation as Peggy Ashcroft, Edith Evans, and Sybil Thorndike; all the same, her longevity ensured her a place in theatrical history, and her Shakespearian memory remained in such good shape that for a BBC television documentary, *A Juliet Remembered* (1988), she recited lengthy extracts from *Romeo and Juliet* without faltering. She also gave many memorable masterclasses in acting, and was a regular BBC radio broadcaster from the very early 1930s until a few months before her death. Asked by Nigel Hawthorne (who as a teenager had been inspired by her performances in South Africa) if she was frightened at all of dying, she merely replied 'One is always afraid of something new, dear.' As Hawthorne noted, 'Gwen had the ability to express wonder and girlish rapture even in old age' (*The Independent*, 28 Jan 1992). Her career may well, in her own phrase, have 'come and gone a bit' (ibid.), but it was never less than remarkable, even when, in old age, both her sight and her hearing diminished so that she was, at the last, almost always playing from memory. Her last performance was as an elderly dowager in an ITV *Sherlock Holmes* special, recorded in 1991; she was, belatedly, created a dame in the birthday honours of the same year. She died on 27 January 1992, two days after her 101st birthday, at her home for many years, Tagley Cottage, Dyers End, Stambourne, Essex, of bronchopneumonia. A memorial service was held at St Martin-in-the-Fields on 18 June 1992.   SHERIDAN MORLEY

Sources *The Times* (28 Jan 1992) · *The Times* (1 Feb 1992) · *The Times* (19 June 1992) · *The Independent* (28 Jan 1992) · *The Independent* (19 June 1992) · *WWW*, 1991–5 · b. cert. · d. cert.
Likenesses L. Knight, watercolour, 1922 (as Juliet), Theatre Museum, London · photographs, 1924–42, Hult. Arch. · W. Sickert, oils, 1932, Tate collection · W. Sickert, oils, *c.*1932–1934, priv. coll. [*see illus.*] · A. McBean, group photograph, 1950 (*King Lear, Royal Shakespeare Theatre*), NPG · H. Knight, oils, NMG Wales · H. Leslie, silhouette drawing, NPG · photograph, repro. in *The Times* (28 Jan 1992) · photograph, repro. in *The Independent* (28 Jan 1992)
Wealth at death £146,994: probate, 18 March 1992, *CGPLA Eng. & Wales*

Davies, Harry Parr (1914–1955), songwriter and composer, was born on 24 May 1914 at 15 Grandison Street, Briton Ferry, Glamorgan, the son of David John Davies, a bootmaker, and his wife, Rosina Parr, a teacher. He was playing the chapel organ and composing musical pieces by the age of twelve, and while attending Neath county grammar school his work came to the notice of Sir Walford Davies, who urged him to study at Oxford. At fourteen he had published six songs, and three years later he left Wales to 'seek his musical fortune'.

Gracie Fields, in her autobiography, tells how one day in 1931 a 'long, lanky lad of seventeen, looking half-scared' edged his way into her dressing-room (he had been let in through the stage-door only because he was thought to be a messenger-boy) and pleaded for the chance to play her

one of his compositions (Fields, 106). Having heard him play she engaged him at once, as her accompanist. He spent the next decade playing the piano for her stage act (mostly from the orchestra pit because of his acute shyness), accompanying her performances all over the world, and writing many of the ballads and march songs that she featured. 'Sing as we Go' became the anthem of hope in the depression years and was followed by 'The Sweetest Song in the World', 'Smile as you say goodbye', and—most famous of all—'Wish me luck as you wave me goodbye'. Parr Davies was able to accommodate Fields's unpredictable changes of key and pace through his faultless 'ear' and piano technique, and because his short sight deterred him from relying on sheet music. He also wrote some songs for George Formby films ('It's in the air' and 'In me little snapshot album') before an altercation with Formby's wife and manager, Beryl, terminated the arrangement.

Parr Davies's prodigious songwriting talent led him inevitably towards the musical theatre. He contributed songs to several George Black revues (notably the cleverly ambiguous 'Wind Round my Heart', performed effectively by Beatrice Lillie) and to a Sonnie Hale musical, *The Knight was Bold*. Wartime found him joining a guards regiment. He toured with Gracie Fields in Entertainments National Service Association concerts, but a London posting enabled him to team up with schoolteacher Harold Purcell, who wrote book and lyrics for Parr Davies's score for *The Lisbon Story*, presented at the Hippodrome from June 1943. This was a courageous attempt to break away from the flimsy comic genre of pre-war musicals and link strong, soaring melodies to a contemporary story of espionage and sacrifice set in Second World War Europe. 'Someday we shall meet again', 'Never say goodbye', and 'Somewhere the sunrise is waiting to be born' echoed the sentiments of the time, but the biggest hit of the show was a late addition inserted to cover a scene-change—the extended narrative and infectious whistling chorus of 'Pedro the Fisherman'—a piece that became a classic of the musical theatre. *The Lisbon Story*, a considerable landmark in the maturity of the stage musical, ran for thirteen months in wartime London; forced out only by theatre closures caused by V-1 raids, it returned for a further run some months later.

A year later, at the Hippodrome, George Black staged *Jenny Jones*, a show amalgamating a set of stories from the Welsh poet Rhys Davies. This had all the elements of success, with Parr Davies, as composer, working in his own boyhood milieu, but the ingredients obstinately failed to come together and the show's success was muted. Parr Davies went on to enhance his reputation in film music (with *Maytime in Mayfair* in 1949) and four post-war stage shows. In 1950 a charming score for Christopher Hassall's *Dear Miss Phoebe* (an adaptation of Barrie's *Quality Street* and the first of many post-war shows based on literary classics) featured notably the song 'I leave my heart in an English garden'. In the same year Parr Davies's music also contributed to the surprise long run of the light comedy *Blue for a Boy*.

Parr Davies's score for a show featuring Cicely Court-neidge, *Her Excellency*, was followed by music to comple-ment traditional English airs in a coronation year vehicle for Anna Neagle, *The Glorious Days*. Though his lyrical, melodic style (often using 3/4 time) was becoming increas-ingly out of tune with the rock-influenced pop scene he planned to write a score for another musical based on the 'Peg o'my Heart' story and had been invited back to Holly-wood to write film music. He died, unexpectedly, on 14 October 1955, alone in his London flat—11 Harriet Walk, Chelsea—his collapse caused by the effect of alcohol on a gastric ulcer. He was buried in Oystermouth cemetery, in south Wales, his life having provided an eerie parallel to the career and early end of his exact contemporary and south-Walian compatriot Dylan Thomas, who had died two years earlier. He never married.

Though less famous in his lifetime than his extrovert performing contemporaries Noël Coward and Ivor Nov-ello, Harry Parr Davies has some claim to be counted with them as one of the major British composers of popular music in the mid-twentieth century. REX WALFORD

Sources archive material, Neath Borough Museum, Glamorgan [permanent exhibition of Parr Davies's life and work] · K. Gänzl, *The British musical theatre*, 2 (1986) · D. Parker and J. Parker, *The story not the song* (1979), 135–8 · G. Fields, *Sing as we go* (1960) · D. Bret, *Gracie Fields: the authorised biography* (1995) · b. cert. · d. cert. · *CGPLA Eng. & Wales* (1955)

Archives Neath Borough Museum, Glamorgan

Likenesses J. Flanagan, 1935, Neath Borough Museum, Gla-morgan

Wealth at death £7633 14s. 10d.: probate, 1955, *CGPLA Eng. & Wales*

Davies, Henry (1782–1862), physician, was born in London. His father was of Welsh descent; after leaving the navy, where he had been a surgeon, he set up practice in St Mar-tin's Lane, London. Henry was apprenticed to Mr Ham-mond, a surgeon at Malling, Kent, and after attending lec-tures by George Pearson, Joseph Carpuc, and Joshua Brodres, he was admitted a member of the College of Sur-geons in 1803. Davies became a surgeon in the army, and after serving for several years, in various parts of Europe and America, he resigned his commission and took a house in London in 1817. He made visits to Paris, Dublin, and Edinburgh, where he attended the hospitals and med-ical schools, before obtaining his MD from the University of Aberdeen in 1823 and becoming a licentiate of the Royal College of Physicians on 22 December 1823. He gave up all practice but midwifery, became physician to the British Lying-in Hospital, and was also for some years lec-turer on midwifery and the diseases of women and child-ren in the medical school of St George's Hospital. Davies was described as 'a man of kindly disposition, and great shrewdness and tact at the bedside' (Munk, 280). He edited a tenth edition of Michael Underwood's *Treatise on the Dis-eases of Children* in 1846. His additions are marked by his initials, but his contemporaries considered that he had spoiled the original work by numerous interpolations from other authors. He also published *The Young Wife's Guide* (1844). Deafness made it increasingly difficult for

Davies to practise and in 1851 he was forced to retire to the country, but returned to London after a year, and died there following an attack of 'fever' on 9 January 1862 at his home, 6 Duchess Street, Portland Place. He was survived by at least one son and two daughters.

NORMAN MOORE, rev. SUSAN SNOXALL

Sources Munk, *Roll* · H. T. Davies, *The Lancet* (25 Jan 1862), 106 · *CGPLA Eng. & Wales* (1862)

Wealth at death under £8000: probate, 5 March 1862, *CGPLA Eng. & Wales*

Davies, Herbert (1818–1885), physician, son of Thomas *Davies (1792–1839), a physician, was born in London on 30 September 1818. After education at North End House School, Hampstead, in 1836 Davies entered the London Hospital where his father was assistant physician. He matriculated at Gonville and Caius College, Cambridge, in 1838, was a scholar in 1839–40, but migrated to Queens' College on 6 March 1840 and graduated BA as thirty-first wrangler in 1842. He took the degree of MB in 1843, was elected a fellow of Queens' College in 1844, and graduated MD in 1848, his thesis being 'On the origin of gout'. During these years he also studied medicine at Paris and Vienna as well as in London, and on 5 August 1845 he was elected assistant physician to the London Hospital. In 1850 he was elected a fellow of the Royal College of Physicians, and in 1854 he became full physician to the London Hospital, an office which he held for twenty years. He lectured in the medical school of that hospital, first on materia medica and afterwards on medicine; in addition he was examiner for medical degrees and assessor to the regius professor of physic at Cambridge University.

Davies married Caroline Templar, daughter of John Wyatt, on 24 August 1850. They had three sons and four daughters. Their second son, A. T. Davies, also became a physician. Davies lived in Finsbury Square, London, was physician to the Bank of England, and had a considerable practice in the City. His practice among the Jewish com-munity was so large that he was nicknamed 'the king of the Jews' (Clark-Kennedy, 31). He also acted as physician to the Royal Hospital for Diseases of the Chest, and to the National Assurance Society. His research included obser-vations on the relative magnitude of the areas of the four orifices of the heart, and he advocated the application of blisters to the swollen joints in acute rheumatism.

Besides several papers in the *London Hospital Reports* and in the *Transactions of the Pathological Society*, Davies pub-lished a manual entitled *Lectures on the Physical Diagnosis of the Diseases of the Lungs and Heart* (1851), which reached a second edition in 1854 and was translated into German and Dutch; and *On the Treatment of Rheumatic Fever in its Acute Stage, Exclusively by Free Blistering* (1864). His papers on the form and areas of the heart's orifices were published in the *Proceedings of the Royal Society* in 1870 and 1872.

Davies died at his address at Vale Mount, Hampstead, London, on 4 January 1885, and was buried in Hampstead cemetery. He was survived by his wife and children.

NORMAN MOORE, rev. MICHAEL BEVAN

Sources Munk, *Roll* · Venn, *Alum. Cant.* · private information (1888) · personal knowledge (1888) · A. E. Clark-Kennedy, *The London: a study in the voluntary hospital system*, 2 (1963) · *The Lancet* (17 Jan 1885), 135–6

Wealth at death £17,478 6s. 3d.: resworn probate, Aug 1885, *CGPLA Eng. & Wales*

Davies, Howell (1717?–1770), Methodist leader, was of unknown origins, though historians usually refer to him as a Monmouthshire man. His family connections and his early employment as a schoolteacher at Talgarth suggest that he could have been brought up in Brecknockshire, where, in 1737, he was converted by Howel Harris. On Harris's advice, in 1738 Davies went to Llanddowror to study under Griffith Jones. After his ordination in 1740 he served as curate at Llandeilo Abercywyn, but he could not resist the urge to preach in the Methodist way far outside his curacy, a practice Jones severely criticized: 'it is the cry of the crowd that he will be governed by, which grieves me very much for his own sake' (D. Jones, *Life and Times of Griffith Jones of Llanddowror*, 1902, 252). In 1741 he became curate of Llys-y-frân, near Haverfordwest. The parish soon became the chief meeting-place for Pembrokeshire Methodists.

From 1743 until his death, Davies was the undisputed leader of the Pembrokeshire Methodists: his power as a preacher (a power not discernible in his only printed sermon, *Llais y priodfab*, 1768), his standing as an ordained clergyman, and his financial independence gave him a rare combination of spiritual and social advantages. Ill health was his main disadvantage. He worked in both the English and Welsh parts of the county; in 1755 he opened, at Woodstock, the first chapel built especially for a Welsh Methodist society. His staunch Calvinism allied him to George Whitefield, whose pulpits in London and the west country he sometimes filled, and made him 'violent against John Wesley' (T. Benyon, *Howell Harris, Reformer and Soldier* (1714–1773), 1985, 161). Through Selina Hastings, countess of Huntingdon, he became one of the countess of Walsingham's chaplains.

Davies married, first, in 1744, Katherine (daughter of John Poyer) of Parke, Henllan Amgoed, 'a wife with a thousand dracmas', as Lewis Morris sarcastically noted (H. Owen, 'The Morrises of Anglesey and the Methodists of the 18th century', *Transactions of the Anglesey Antiquarian and Field Society*, 1943, 55). She died in childbirth a year later. The daughter who was born died before the age of two. Then, some time before the summer of 1747, he married Elizabeth, daughter and only surviving child of Philip and Luce White (née Phillips) of Prendergast. A son born to them died in infancy; their daughter Margaret (Peggy) survived both, and in 1776 married Nathaniel, son of Daniel Rowland.

Several of his contemporaries describe Davies as tender and gentle, modest, shy even. No doubt he was, in private. The public man who earned for himself the title Apostle of Pembrokeshire must have been tenacious and fearless, like most of the Methodist revivalists. On the title-page of Williams Pantycelyn's elegy to Davies, the poet notes that he died on 13 January 1770, 'in the fifty-third year of his age' (W. Williams, *Marwnad ar y parchedig Mr H. Davies*, 1770). He died in Parke and was buried in Prendergast cemetery. DEREC LLWYD MORGAN, rev.

Sources W. T. Watson, 'Rev. Howell Davies, Woodstock', *Cylchgrawn Cymdeithas Hanes Eglwys Methodistiaid Calfinaidd Cymru*, 20 (1935), 74–80 · W. T. Watson, 'Revd. Howell Davies, Pembrokeshire', *Cylchgrawn Cymdeithas Hanes Eglwys Methodistiaid Calfinaidd Cymru*, 23 (1938), 128–30 · W. T. Watson and W. T. Morgan, 'A note on Howell Davis', *Cylchgrawn Cymdeithas Hanes Eglwys Methodistiaid Calfinaidd Cymru*, 32 (1947), 109–11 · DWB

Archives NL Wales, corresp.

Davies, Hugh (1739–1821), botanist and Church of England clergyman, was born on 3 April 1739 in Llandyfrydog, Anglesey, the youngest of six children of the Revd Lewis Davies, rector of Llandyfrydog, and his wife, Mary Knight. Only Hugh and two sisters survived their childhood. The father also died early, in 1750, but nevertheless the son was well educated at the free grammar school at Beaumaris and followed his father to Jesus College, Oxford, where he matriculated in 1757 and gained his BA in 1762. He took holy orders, being ordained deacon in 1763 and priest in 1764. From 1763 to 1787, he was a cleric in Anglesey. He served curacies at Llangefni (1763–6), Llan-faes and Penmon (1766–75), and Penmynydd (1775–8). At Llan-faes and Penmon he also held the post of usher at his old school at Beaumaris. In 1778 he was inducted rector of Llandegfan with Beaumaris. Even when he left Anglesey in 1787, he did not stray very far, merely crossing the Menai Strait to take up his ultimate appointment as rector of Aber, Caernarvonshire. About 1801, suffering from a nervous condition, he returned to live at Beaumaris, though he did not resign his benefice at Aber until 1816.

Davies's interest in natural history is first noted through his association with Thomas Pennant. Their friendship dated at least from the period when he was a young curate at Llan-faes and Penmon, sending specimens to his fellow naturalist. In 1774 he accompanied Pennant on his tour of the Isle of Man and returned the following summer to make a second review of the plant life on his behalf. From 1776 onwards Davies regularly helped authors, supplying them with details of the natural history of north Wales, particularly the botany of Anglesey and Caernarvonshire. He provided data for Pennant's *British Zoology* (4th edn, 1776–7), for the same author's *Journey to Snowdon* (1781), and for William Hudson's *Flora Anglica* (2nd edn, 1788). In 1790 the second edition of Pennant's *Indian Zoology* was published; Davies made a considerable contribution to this volume, compiling most of the 'Indian faunula' included therein. Other contributions were to *English Botany* by James Sowerby and James Edward Smith (1790–1814) and to Smith's *Flora Britannica* (1800–04), as well as to *The Botanist's Guide through England and Wales* (1805) by Dawson Turner and Lewis Weston Dillwyn.

In 1790, Davies was elected a fellow of the Linnean Society. He was an active member and four of his papers were read at its meetings and subsequently published in the *Transactions*. Undoubtedly his main achievement was the publication of *Welsh Botanology* in 1813. This volume is important in several respects. It was the first published correlation of Welsh plant names with their binomial equivalents. The first part, a flora of Anglesey, has further importance as the first detailed flora of any of the Welsh counties. The second part ('Llysieuaeth Gymreig') is also of special significance as it is considered, even today, as the most complete listing of Welsh plant names.

Specializing as he did in the detailed accumulation of the plant records of one area—Anglesey—Davies's achievements marked a big step forward from the random plant-hunting expeditions which so characterized botany in eighteenth-century Wales. He died, unmarried, at Beaumaris on 16 February 1821, and was buried in Beaumaris churchyard on the 21st. The genus *Daviesia* (Leguminosae), named by J. E. Smith in 1798, commemorates his services to botany.   RAYMOND B. DAVIES

Sources R. B. Davies, 'The Rev. Hugh Davies (1739–1821): an outline of his literary life', *Journal of the Society of the Bibliography of Natural History*, 9 (1978–80), 147–55 · T. J. Owen, 'Hugh Davies: the Anglesey botanist', *Transactions of the Anglesey Antiquarian Society and Field Club* (1961), 39–52 · P. W. Carter, 'Some account of the botanical exploration of Anglesey', *Transactions of the Anglesey Antiquarian Society and Field Club* (1952), 44–68 · G. Ellis, 'Plant hunting in Wales - II', *Amgueddfa: Bulletin of the National Museum of Wales*, 13 (1973), 37–51 · *DWB* · R. R. Hughes, 'Biographical epitomes', NL Wales, Misc. MSS, vol. 74

Archives NHM, notes and drawings · NL Wales, botanical notes · NL Wales, corresp. and papers · NMG Wales, corresp. and papers · RBG Kew · RS | Linn. Soc., letters to Sir James Smith · NHM, letters to members of Sowerby family

Likenesses silhouette, priv. coll.

Wealth at death bequeathed £300 to nephew: Owen, 'Hugh Davies'

Davies, Idris (1905–1953), poet and schoolteacher, was born on 6 January 1905 at 16 Field Street, Rhymni, Monmouthshire, the elder child of Evan Davies (1881–1947), a colliery winderman, and his wife, Elizabeth Ann, née Williams (1884–1971). In their home they spoke Welsh, as did some two-thirds of the town's population at that time; although most of Davies's work was written in English, which he learned at the local primary school, he read widely in Welsh, having studied it at evening classes, and wrote a little in the language, both verse and prose. An early influence on the young boy was his uncle Edward, a Calvinistic Methodist and liberal, who spoke very little English and introduced him to the Bible and contemporary politics. In later life Davies rejected Christianity in favour of an idealistic humanism, but as a boy he attended a Baptist chapel.

Davies left school at the age of fourteen, against his parents' wishes, to become a miner at the McClaren colliery in Abertyswg, Monmouthshire; he later regretted this decision not to receive secondary education. In the summer of 1920 he moved to the Maerdy pit in nearby Pontlotyn. Having been introduced to the work of Shelley by a workmate named Eddie Balman, he quickly perceived that poetry could relate to politics, particularly socialism. At this time, too, the shy, introverted, but humorous young man began what was to become a lifelong habit of wandering the moorlands above the town of Rhymni, the wild beauty of which contrasted sharply with the dereliction of the valley, and in which he was to find escape from the grim industrialism which he denounced so vehemently in his poetry. His first experience of industrial conflict came with the miners' strike of March–July 1921 and the 'black Friday' (15 April) on which the miners considered their cause to have been betrayed. Early in 1926, shortly before the general strike of that year, he lost the little finger of his left hand in an accident underground, and had barely resumed work after the seven-month stoppage when the closure of the pit forced him to consider other ways of earning a living. Although he was deeply committed to the miners' cause, he and his family were spared much of the hardship of the strike because his father remained in work as a safety man.

Now unemployed, Davies used his new-found leisure to attend lectures at the town's workmen's institute, where his political awareness was sharpened further, and he then took a correspondence course. After matriculating, he went on to study at Loughborough College and the University of Nottingham, qualifying as a teacher. In 1932 he began teaching at Laysterne junior school in Hoxton, in the East End of London. He remained in London for fifteen years (with the exception of the years of the Second World War) and, by now an avid reader of the work of both Welsh and English poets (particularly R. Williams Parry and A. E. Housman), was one of the expatriate Welsh writers who frequented Griff's Bookshop in Charing Cross Road. One of his closest friends at that time was Tom Buchanan, from Ayrshire, a fellow teacher with whom he went on walking holidays in Scotland, Ireland, and France.

A few of Davies's poems were published in newspapers in south Wales during the early 1930s, but his emergence as a poet coincided with the launch of the magazine *Wales*, edited by Keidrych Rhys, to which he became a regular contributor; he also contributed to London magazines such as the *Poetry Review* and *The Adelphi*. His first volume, *Gwalia deserta* (1938), took as its theme the desert of industrial south Wales during the depression of the inter-war years and established him as the voice of his generation; it includes 'The Bells of Rhymney', a poem which was set to music and made famous by the singing of Pete Seeger. In the year of its publication Davies gained a diploma in history from the University of London. At the outbreak of the Second World War his school was evacuated to Pytchley in Northamptonshire, and then to the villages of Meesden and Anstey in Hertfordshire; it was at Anstey, in June–July 1941, that he wrote *The Angry Summer* (1943), 'a poem of 1926', which is regarded as his finest work. In April 1942 he returned to London, and taught at a school in Shoreditch. Later in the year he was moved again, this time to Treherbert in the Rhondda valley, where he stayed for two years and completed his third book, *Tonypandy and other Poems* (1945), which includes the long autobiographical ballad 'I was Born in Rhymni'. In Treherbert he formed a close relationship with Morfydd Peregrine, a fellow teacher at Dunraven School. They never married, because she had an invalid mother whom she could not leave; the relationship was sometimes strained, as his diaries reveal, but they remained devoted to each other to the end of his life. Despite his sympathy with the working class, Davies was appalled by the materialism and vulgarity of the people in the Rhondda, and was not happy there. To his great relief, he was directed to a school in Llandysul in Cardiganshire at the beginning of 1945, where he was again in charge of a group of London evacuees, and was impressed by the high standard of the district's Welsh-speaking culture. He nevertheless had to return to London, to teach at Whitmore primary school and then at Wordsworth School in Stoke Newington. After many applications for a permanent post, in 1947 he obtained one at Cwmsyflog junior school, not far from his home in the Rhymni valley; he also taught English in evening classes at nearby Bargoed and Merthyr Tudful. His homecoming was something of a disappointment, however, for he found that Rhymni, having been for so long ravaged by unemployment, emigration, and social deprivation, now had a cultural life that compared unfavourably with the one he had known as a young man.

A volume of Davies's *Selected Poems* was published by Faber and Faber, on the recommendation of T. S. Eliot, less than a month before his death. In January 1952 he underwent an unsuccessful operation for cancer of the colon at Tredegar Hospital. After his convalescence, he remained in the care of his mother at 7 Victoria Road, Rhymni, until his death just after midnight on 6 April 1953. His ashes were buried in Rhymni cemetery a few days later. Plaques were erected to Davies's memory on the wall of the house in Victoria Road and in Rhymni Public Library. His *Collected Poems*, edited by Dafydd Johnston, was published by the University of Wales Press in 1994. MEIC STEPHENS

Sources *The complete poems of Idris Davies*, ed. D. Johnston (1994) • I. Jenkins, *Idris Davies of Rhymney* (1986) • I. Jenkins, *Idris Davies*, Writers of Wales (1972) • A. Conran, introduction, in I. Davies, *The angry summer: a poem of 1926*, ed. A. Conran (1993) • J. Harris and E. J. Davies, *A bibliographical guide to twenty-four modern Anglo-Welsh writers* (1994) • b. cert. • d. cert.
Archives NL Wales, corresp., literary MSS, and papers
Likenesses photograph, repro. in Johnston, ed., *Complete poems of Idris Davies* (1994) • photograph, repro. in Jenkins, *Idris Davies of Rhymney* (1986) • photograph, repro. in Jenkins, *Idris Davies* (1972) • photograph, repro. in Conran, 'Introduction'
Wealth at death £3077 12*s*.: administration, 19 Aug 1953, *CGPLA Eng. & Wales*

Davies, James. See Iaco ab Dewi (1647/8–1722).

Davies [*formerly* Banks], **James** (1820–1883), classical scholar, was born in Kington, Herefordshire, on 20 May 1820, the second son of Richard Banks and his wife, Esther, niece of James Davies of Moor Court, Herefordshire. Educated at Repton School, he matriculated as James Banks at St Mary Hall, Oxford, in 1841, but migrated to Lincoln College, where he held a scholarship, graduating BA in 1844 (taking third-class honours in classics) and MA in 1846. In 1847 he married Frances Helen, daughter of Abraham Henry Young. From 1847 to 1852 he was incumbent of Christ Church, Forest of Dean, and was headmaster of Ludlow grammar school from 1852 until 1857; he was also diocesan inspector of schools.

In 1858 Banks changed his name to Davies by royal licence on succeeding to his uncle's property at Moor Court, where he resided, combining the functions of

squire, clergyman, and banker, becoming a partner in his brother's bank. He erected a church in his own grounds for the convenience of his neighbours, for whom the parish church was too remote. He was made a prebendary of Hereford in 1875. His time, however, was principally devoted to literature, especially the pursuits of classical scholarship.

For many years Davies wrote the majority of the classical articles in the *Saturday Review*, and he was the author of a lengthy essay entitled 'Epigrams' in the *Quarterly Review* for January 1865. In 1860 he published a metrical translation of the *Fables* of Babrius, from the text of his friend Sir George Cornewall Lewis. This version included the apocryphal second part, the spuriousness of which was not then generally recognized. He produced several editions and translations of classical authors, including prose versions of Hesiod, Theognis, and Callimachus for Bohn's Classical Library, and in 1873 and 1876 wrote volumes on Hesiod and Theognis, and on Catullus, Tibullus, and Propertius, for Collins's series Ancient Classics for English Readers. A volume of original verse entitled *Nugae* was published in 1854. Davies also wrote on architecture, archaeology, topography, and horticulture. He revised several of Murray's Guides for the press, and contributed many articles to *Blackwood's Magazine*, the *Contemporary Review*, and the *Quarterly Review*. He died after a prolonged decline of health at Moor Court, Herefordshire, on 11 March 1883. RICHARD GARNETT, *rev.* RICHARD SMAIL

Sources Boase, *Mod. Eng. biog.* • Walford, *County families* (1875) • Foster, *Alum. Oxon.* • *Wellesley index* • personal knowledge (1888) • *CGPLA Eng. & Wales* (1883)
Archives Hergest Trust, archives, corresp. and papers | Hergest Trust, archives, papers and corresp. with Banks family
Wealth at death £5886 6*s*. 11*d*.: probate, 7 Aug 1883, *CGPLA Eng. & Wales*

Davies, James [*known as* Kitchener Davies] (1902–1952), Welsh-language writer, was born on 16 June 1902 in Pant Afallen, Cardiganshire, the third son of Thomas Davies, smallholder and miner, and his first wife, Martha, *née* Davies. About a year later, the family moved the short distance to the smallholding of Y Llain, Llwynpiod, where a fourth child, Laetitia, was born.

Situated on the edge of the Red Bog of Tregaron, the poor soil of Y Llain was insufficient to support the family, and Thomas Davies followed the established pattern of moving to work as a miner at Nantgarw, returning home at intervals to work on the smallholding. The death of Martha Davies split the family for the first time when James was seven, and he was sent to stay for a year with an aunt in Banbury until Mary Davies, their mother's sister, came to Y Llain to keep house for the family. That traumatic experience developed a precocious self-consciousness in the seven-year-old which fundamentally affected his later development. From Y Llain he travelled the short distance to the church school in Tregaron, and later to the county school, where he came under the influence of the charismatic history teacher S. M. Powell. In the county school he acquired the nickname Kitchener, because of a supposed resemblance between his father and the field marshal. The name stuck, and even appears on his death certificate, although he never assumed it legally; it is as Kitchener that he continues to be known, in preference to his baptismal name.

Two years before Davies left the county school to go as a pupil teacher to Blaengwynfi, his father sold Y Llain and moved to Blaengarw, where he married the woman with whom he had been lodging. Davies later referred to this event as the second great sadness of his life, the third coming when he learned that Mary Davies, his 'aunt/mother', who had moved to Tonypandy when the family split up, was dying of cancer. After taking a general arts degree and training as a teacher in Aberystwyth between 1922 and 1925 Davies established himself as a teacher in the Rhondda valley, where he spent the rest of an active life. On 15 April 1940 he married Mair Irene Rees (1911–1990) of Ffos-y-Ffin, Cardiganshire, the daughter of Evan Rees, schoolmaster. They had three children: Megan, Mari, and Manon.

In the Rhondda Davies was active as a political campaigner on behalf of Plaid Cymru, and threw his weight behind the movement to establish Welsh-medium education in an area where the language was under the severest pressure. He stood for election to the county council and for parliament (1945 and 1950), and was active within the party. He was a member of the Calvinist Methodist chapel, Bethania, in Tonypandy, and was an active lay preacher. He also wrote regularly for the periodical press, and broadcast on literary and cultural topics.

In spite of all of this, however, it is for his poetical and dramatic work that Davies is now chiefly remembered. In 1934–5 he achieved notoriety as the author of a naturalistic play, *Cwm Glo* ('Coal valley'), originally entitled *Adar y to* ('Sparrows'), which investigated the relationship between social conditions, manners, and morals in the coal-mining valleys of the south with a frankness and honesty quite unparalleled in Welsh literature up to that time. Other less important poetic and dramatic works followed, but his next major achievement was the poetic drama *Meini gwagedd* ('Stones of emptiness'), whose title echoes a phrase in Isaiah 34: 11. The inspiration for his final and greatest work was his experience of the cancer which killed him. While in hospital recovering from an operation he dictated to his wife his introspective radio poem *Sŵn y gwynt sy'n chwythu* ('The sound of the wind which blows'), again of biblical inspiration. In all of these works Davies brought a sharply critical consciousness to bear on his own formative experiences and on the myths central to Welsh culture. His work was simultaneously critical, revisionary, and constructive, and although he wrote comparatively little, he has a clear claim to being one of the most important Welsh writers in the twentieth century.

Davies died of cancer at his home, Aeron, Brithweunydd Road, Trealaw, Glamorgan, on 25 August 1952, and was buried at Llethr Du, Trealaw. He was survived by his wife and three daughters. On 3 September 1977 a plaque in his memory was placed on the wall of Llwynpiod Calvinist Methodist Chapel. His widow published a volume of his works in 1980, but many of his papers were destroyed in a fire in her home in Llangwyryfon, Cardiganshire, in 1990, in which she also died.

IOAN WILLIAMS

Sources E. D. Jones and B. F. Roberts, eds., *Y bywgraffiadur Cymreig, 1951–1970* (1997) · I. M. Williams, *Kitchener Davies, llên y llenor* (1984) · M. Davies, ed., *Gwaith James Kitchener Davies* (1980) · J. K. Davies, 'Adfyw', *Cardi* (3 Aug 1968), 14–18 · m. cert. · d. cert. · private information (2004) [family]

Archives BBC WAC, MSS · NL Wales, MSS | SOUND BBC Sound Archives, London · BBC Sound Archives, Cardiff

Likenesses photographs, priv. coll.

Wealth at death £3711 16*s*. 7*d*.: administration with will, 10 Oct 1952, *CGPLA Eng. & Wales*

Davies, John. *See* Rhys, Siôn Dafydd (*b.* 1533/4, *d.* in or after 1620).

Davies [Davis], **Sir John** (1560x63–1625), administrator and conspirator, was the son of John Davies of London. He was born in London about 6 a.m. on 8 February 1560 according to Anthony Wood; the precision suggests that Wood may have seen a copy of Davies's horoscope. An enemy later made much of (and no doubt quite likely exaggerated) Davies's humble origins. However, Davies's funeral monument, which recorded that he died in the sixty-third year of his life, suggests that he was born in 1562 or 1563. He was educated in 'grammaticals' in London before being admitted to Gloucester Hall, Oxford, where his tutor was the mathematician and astrologer Thomas Allen (Wood, *Ath. Oxon.*, 2.373). Gloucester Hall had a reputation as a centre for sheltering church papists nominally conforming to the Church of England, and Davies later owned that Allen had instructed him in the Catholic faith. He graduated BA on 1 July 1577 and proceeded MA on 4 July 1581, continuing at the college for a while thereafter. William Camden considered Davies 'an excellent mathematician' and he reportedly wrote much on mathematics and astrology, none of which had survived by the late seventeenth century, and compiled with John Dee and Matthew Gwinne a volume of letters 'concernyng chymical and magical secrets' (ibid.).

Davies went to London, where he learnt more of astrology from Simon Forman. Their connection was parodied in the title of a pamphlet which appeared in 1590 at the time of the Marprelate controversy: *Sir Martin Mar-people: his collar of esses. Workmanly wrought by Maister Simon Soothsaier, coldsmith of London. And offered to sale upon great necessitie, by John Davies*. In 1595 Davies spoke ill of Forman to the latter's mistress's husband and the following year Forman dreamed that Davies stood by watching while a crowd fired arrows at him.

In February 1588 Davies made his entrance at the royal court, where he seems soon to have come to the notice of the earl of Essex. He may already have embarked on a military career: in 1598 he claimed to have served four years in the Low Countries. In 1589 he served with Essex on the expedition to Portugal and may also have gone to France, as Wood claimed. Wood's comment, 'whereby he advanced his knowledge, as to men, and the languages of those countries very much', perhaps hints that Davies had an intelligence, as well as a military, role (Wood, *Ath. Oxon.*,

2.374). He certainly served with Essex and his brother Walter Devereux in 1591 when they fought in Normandy in support of Henri of Navarre. He was at the taking of Cadiz in 1596, where he was one of thirty-three men knighted on 15 September by the earl. He was also on the expedition the following year to the Azores. About 1593 Davies married his first wife, the widow of Sir Henry Rowse of Devon.

By 1590 Davies had acquired a gunner's place at Sandown Castle. From there in November 1598 he wrote to Essex, then master of the ordnance, seeking the post of surveyor of the ordnance, the third place in the hierarchy of the department, 'the principal military storehouse in the kingdom', after the lieutenant and the clerk (Ashley, 'War in the ordnance office', 338). To support his application he enclosed a three-page treatise 'On the perfection of artillery', together with

> some short collections of my former studies in artillery wherein if I had that practice as this place doth of necessity draw a man unto I would not doubt but in short time to discover the true effect of artillery more sufficiently than hitherto hath been by any of our nation.   (*Salisbury MSS*, 8.440–41)

Davies was duly appointed surveyor on 31 January 1599 through the earl's offices.

Later that year Davies went 'as a prime officer' with Essex to Ireland (Wood, *Ath. Oxon.*, 2.374). The earl issued a warrant to the master of the ordnance in Ireland, Sir George Bouchier, to appoint Davies his lieutenant of the ordnance. Later, during Essex's brief lieutenancy of Ireland, Davies was also a factor of the purveyors of victuals for his forces. Davies and his superior Sir Robert Newcomen, the victualler-general for Ireland, were ordered to produce all books and reckonings, 'whereby Her Majesty may have a perfect knowledge and account of the matters of victuals in Ireland which now lies wrapped in the folds of much confusion' (*CSP Ire.*, 1599–1600, 312). Davies accompanied Essex in his apparently unexpected return to England: leaving Dublin on 24 September 1599 they arrived at Nonsuch Palace, Surrey, four days later. Essex was suspended from all his offices, and bitter conflict ensued in the ordnance office where the lieutenant, Sir George Carew, hastened to fill key places with his clients, his kinsman George Harvey and Richard Palfreyman, to Davies's outrage. He physically ejected Palfreyman as being 'no officer', and in front of the lieutenant of the Tower rounded on Harvey as 'insolent and no deputy' (*Salisbury MSS*, 10.100–01).

In the submissions to the committee of inquiry that followed, a flood of defects and frauds in the conduct of the officers of the ordnance was revealed, not to speak of the sea of mutually recriminatory allegations. Harvey described Davies as 'a shepstar's son, hatched in Gutter Lane'—that is, the son of a dressmaker, or indeed simply the woman who cuts cloth up for dressmaking—and one 'who plots that no man shall serve her Majesty in the office but himself and such as depend upon him'. Were not reforms undertaken, the queen could lose and yet again 'be deceived of almost 100,000l.' (*Salisbury MSS*,

10.399). Legal proceedings and further enquiries were overtaken by the Essex conspiracy.

At the final planning meeting of 3 February 1601 Davies produced the most realistic of the various plans discussed for Essex's attempt to seize the court, the city of London, and the Tower, advising taking the Tower and its munitions at the outset, then carrying out a methodical plan to take the court. Sir Charles Danvers, Sir Christopher Blount, Sir Ferdinando Gorges, and their followers would be stationed at strategic points in Whitehall Palace and at a given signal would seize control and open the way for Essex to approach the queen and present a petition on behalf of himself and the realm. Gorges refused to co-operate and the earl of Southampton angrily dissolved the meeting. In the event the carefully contrived plan was replaced by an ill-organized and hot-headed escapade which misguidedly relied on Essex's popularity with the London citizenry but which ended in the earl's surrender and the siege of Essex House where Davies was left guarding the key government hostages, Lord Chief Justice Popham and Lord Keeper Egerton. The rebellion was over the day it began, 8 February 1601.

In the aftermath the authorities made much of Davies's Oxford past and of his Catholicism: 'that traitor knave Sir J. Davies, a conjuror and Catholic, who at Oxford occupied himself in the idle art of figure casting', according to Sir Robert Cecil, 'a traitor now in hold, brought up in Oxford, and by profession a setter of figures' in the words of the official 'Directions for the preachers' (*CSP dom.*, 1598–1601, 555, 566). At his trial Davies owned that his early instruction in Catholicism at Oxford had been confirmed in Ireland by his fellow conspirator Sir Christopher Blount, carefully explaining (when Blount became angry at the claim) that this had been achieved by Blount's example rather than by any direct attempt at conversion. Davies was convicted and sentenced to death on 5 March 1601, but was subsequently pardoned and 'saved his life by telling first who was in the deepest' (Ashley, 'War in the ordnance office', 343–4). Davies suffered but six months' imprisonment and was restored to his forfeited property in St Leonard Shoreditch in 1610, and in 1613 purchased the erstwhile monastic property of Bere Court in Pangbourne, Berkshire.

Controversy and suspicion continued to dog Davies. In 1610 he sought an act of parliament to restore him to the blood. His recusancy remained a cause of concern. The bill was lost in the Commons but not before it had been debated in the Lords. The bishop of St Asaph noted that he had heard Davies

> confess that when he was to die and was required to have a minister, he answered that he did willingly embrace the minister, but required to have a priest. So then he halted between two opinions. Since that time he hath continually refused to receive the sacrament ... I think it is not fit to restore him to his own blood that refuseth to receive the Lord's blood.   (Foster, *Proceedings*, 1.206)

Other peers and bishops, including Cecil, were more sympathetic, seeing his promising signs in his willingness to come to Anglican church services and in his taking the oath of allegiance at a time when most recusants were refusing it. The bishop of London was all the more optimistic about Davies's conformity, 'because he is forward to finish the holy and good work of founding a college begun by Mr Wadham' (ibid., 1.207).

However, Davies's part in managing Wadham's trust for establishing an Oxford college led to bitter contention with Dorothy Wadham, the widow and executrix. Davies was possibly related to Nicholas Wadham through his second wife, Elizabeth White of Fiddleford, Dorset, whom he had married by 1609. Summoned to Wadham's deathbed in October 1609, he had induced him to make out an instrument making him jointly responsible with Dorothy for establishing the college, 'even in a manner at my husbondes last gaspe' (Briggs, 61). Accusations and counter-accusations of misappropriation of funds ensued. Angrily rebutting his charge that she was herself backward in the business, she bitterly complained that, 'his zeale is greater to compasse his owne endes, then benefit the Colledge' (ibid., 62). Davies perhaps intended to benefit the interests of Gloucester Hall as well as his own. He was excluded from the trust established in July 1610 under a collusive action in chancery directed against him.

Davies died at Bere Court on 14 May 1625. He was buried with his two wives in St James the Less, Pangbourne, where an elaborate tomb, 'large of grey stone, three recumbent effigies, coupled Tuscan columns left and right' (Pevsner), commemorates the Davies family. His son John succeeded as a minor; he also went to Gloucester Hall and was knighted in 1662. The manor at Pangbourne was sold in 1671.

J. J. N. McGURK

Sources Wood, *Ath. Oxon.*, new edn · Foster, *Alum. Oxon.* · *Calendar of the manuscripts of the most hon. the marquis of Salisbury*, 24 vols., HMC, 9 (1883–1976), vols. 7–10 · *CSP dom.*, *1598–1610*, with *addenda*, *1580–1625* · R. Ashley, 'War in the ordnance office: the Essex connection and Sir John Davis', *Historical Research*, 67 (1994), 337–45 · N. Briggs, 'The foundation of Wadham College, Oxford', *Oxoniensia*, 21 (1956), 61–81 · E. R. Foster, ed., *Proceedings in parliament, 1610*, 2 vols. (1966) · R. Ashley, 'Getting and spending: corruption in the Elizabethan ordnance', *History Today*, 40 (Nov 1990), 47–53 · *CSP Ire.*, *1599–1600* · J. S. Brewer and W. Bullen, eds., *Calendar of the Carew manuscripts*, 4: *1601–1603*, PRO (1870) · L. Stone, ed., 'Catalogue of the muniments of Wadham College, Oxford University' [NR: typescript 1962] · E. Ashmole, *The antiquities of Berkshire*, 3 vols. (1719), vol. 2 · W. H. Rylands, ed., *The four visitations of Berkshire*, 2 vols., Harleian Society, 56–7 (1907–8) · *VCH Berkshire*, vol. 3 · Berkshire, Pevsner (1966) · M. E. James, 'At a crossroads of political culture: the Essex revolt, 1601', *Society, politics and culture: studies in early modern England* (1986), 416–65 · J. Cook, *Dr Simon Forman, a most notorious physician* (2001)

Archives Berks. RO, Pangbourne deeds, rel. to Bere Court, Maidenhatch and Pangbourne, D/EAt–NRA 5186

Likenesses tomb effigy, St James the Less, Pangbourne, Berkshire

Davies, John (1564/5–1618), poet and writing-master, was born at Hereford (his birthplace was always noted on his title-pages—'John Davies of Hereford'—apparently to distinguish him from the prominent contemporary poet Sir John Davies). He was probably born a Roman Catholic and was certainly identified as one in 1611 (Peck, 461), but nothing in his voluminous religious poetry suggests a strong adherence to Catholicism. Of his early life it is known only that he was of Welsh descent and that he had two brothers and two sisters. He had no higher education, but because he resided for a time at Oxford as a teacher of handwriting, some (notably Anthony Wood) mistakenly thought he had studied there. By 1605 at the latest, Davies took up residence in London.

It is not certain how Davies acquired his handwriting expertise, although a hint from Pepys's calligraphical collection suggests that he was tutored by a London writing-master named Daniel Johnson. Thomas Fuller in his *Worthies of England* called Davies 'the greatest master of the pen that England in her age beheld' (Fuller, *Worthies*, 2.79), and his renown reached as far as Germany according to a commendatory poem in Davies's *Microcosmos* (Davies, 104). His book *Writing Schoolmaster, or, The Anatomy of Fair Writing* (earliest surviving edition, 1633) exhibits engraved specimen-copies of his handwriting together with a set of practical directions for learners. His writing students included royalty (Prince Henry) and the highest nobility. If his incessant complaints are to be trusted, Davies was not richly rewarded for his teaching. The earl of Northumberland's book of household expenses would seem to confirm this, recording in 1607 a payment 'To John Davis for teaching Lord Percy to write, for a year, 20 l.' (*Sixth Report*, HMC, 229). None the less, his teaching put him in contact with many of the most important families in the country including (in addition to the Percys, with whom he resided in 1607 and 1609–10) the Herberts, the Pembrokes, Thomas, Lord Ellesmere, and his wife, the countess dowager of Derby. He was also friendly with many of the great artists of the period. Even if Davies's links to Sir Philip Sidney are questionable, he was on the periphery of the brilliant circle of wits (among them Donne and Jonson) who wrote panegyric verses for the 1611 edition of 'Coryat's Crudities', Lord Herbert of Cherbury wrote a prefatory poem to him, and he was an acquaintance of Inigo Jones.

This constant contact with the great and famous must have given Davies the social mobility that explains his marriages to women distinctly above him socially. Mary Croft (d. 1612), his first wife, was a relative of the family that owned Croft Castle, Shropshire. With Mary he had his only child, a son named Sylvanus. In 1613, when he was aged forty-eight, he married Dame Juliana Preston (d. 1614), the widow of Sir Amyas Preston, the naval commander and keeper of the stores and ordinance in the Tower of London. While only the first name of Davies's third wife, Margaret, is known, the mention in his will of the 'plate and jewells as were hers before marriage' suggests that she too was well placed. About such marriages, he passed on some apparently hard-earned wisdom:

> He that would faine reduce an high-borne Wife
> Unto the Compasse of his meane estate,
> Must not at first, stick for a little Strife.
> ('Wittes Pilgrimage', Davies, 1.xvi)

Anthony Wood declared that 'finding not a subsistence by poetry', Davies earned his living as a writing-master

(Wood, *Ath. Oxon.*, 3rd edn, 2.260). Nevertheless, throughout his teaching career Davies published vast quantities of poetry. He attempted every kind except the dramatic, but his main efforts were religious, moral, and psychological treatises or sermons. The seriousness of his ambition is suggested by the title to his first separately published poem, *Mirum in modum: a Glimpse of Gods Glorie and the Soules Shape* (1602). His second and longest poem, *Microcosmos* (1603), is similarly ambitious, a 6000 line treatise on the passions and affections with many digressions on human affairs in general. There were ten more weighty volumes, most of them the sort of didactic religious poetry then much in vogue. Patrons of poetry like the Sidneys and King James wrote such poems themselves; literary theory (for example, Sidney's *Defense*) called for such subjects, and Guillaume du Bartas's *Divine Works and Days*, especially in Josuah Sylvester's version, served as a highly esteemed model.

But Davies never gained any recognition or financial profit for his poetry; only one of his works ever reached a second edition. The reason would seem to be distressingly clear. As Douglas Bush put it, 'the master (in Fuller's words) of fast, fair, close, and various handwriting was as a poet slow, laborious, diffuse, and flat' (Bush, 86). Davies's creative method was to versify prose tracts like Pierre de la Primaudaye's *L'Academie Francoise* (1577), Sir Philip Sidney's translation of Mornay's *Verité de la religion chriestienne*, and Puttenham's *Art of Poesie*. Davies condensed, simplified, and omitted much from his sources, and the product was an incoherent and clumsy patchwork of philosophical fragments, often in unreadable technical language. Davies may have been one of the most voluminous didactic poets of the age; he was also one of the most tedious.

While the bulk of Davies's poetry was religious, he also wrote love sonnets, satires, epigrams, panegyrics, eclogues, among other kinds. In the *Wittes Pilgrimage* volume (1610–11?) there is a sonnet sequence about a frustrating love affair that is much superior to his religious poetry. Unfortunately it was written at a moment nearly saturated with dazzling Petrarchan sonnet sequences and, refreshingly, he seems to notice the mediocrity of the 101 sonnets he has been creating. In sonnet 102 he suddenly asks:

> Busie Invention, whie art thou so dull
> And yet still doing?

It is a question he should have asked more frequently. With his 'The triumph of death or the picture of the plague … [of] 1603' in *Humours Heav'n on Earth* (1609), Davies had a compelling subject in plague-stricken London. It led unavoidably to some effective descriptions, but his inveterate prolixity and comparison with such vivid accounts as Dekker's 'The wonderful year 1603' once again make his version forgettable.

In fact, of all Davies's work only his volume of epigrams *The Scourge of Folly* (1610) is mentioned today. It is not because he had discovered in epigrams the natural medium for his muse—they too are relatively lame—but because he addresses many of the 292 epigrams to the greatest writers and most important figures of the period: the king, Francis Bacon, Sir John Davies, Fulke Greville, Thomas Campion, Samuel Daniel, Ben Jonson, William Shakespeare, John Fletcher, John Marston, Joseph Hall, Herbert of Cherbury, Francis Beaumont, Michael Drayton, and George Chapman, among others. It is unclear how many of them he knew personally, but the fact that he says to Chapman, 'I know thee not (good George) but by thy pen' suggests some personal knowledge of the others. Unfortunately, Davies's writing is so vague that little is gained from whatever intimacy he

John Davies (1564/5–1618), by unknown engraver, pubd 1633

might have had with his subjects. This is particularly disappointing in the case of Shakespeare, who is promisingly addressed as 'our English Terence', but in maddeningly cryptic language Davies tells Shakespeare that:

> hadst thou not played some kingly parts in sport,
> Thou hadst been a companion for a king.

With all the vast ingenuity spent on Shakespearian biography, no one has come close to explaining those lines.

Davies did have one respectable contemporary admirer, William Browne of Tavistock, who in his *Britannia's Pastorals* enthusiastically linked him with the poet George Wither:

> by whose Muses' power
> A natural day to me seems but an hour
> (*Poems*, 1.240)

Few subsequent readers have had Browne's endurance. Davies died on 6 July 1618 and was buried that day near his first wife in the church of St Dunstan-in-the-West, London. His wife Margaret survived him.

P. J. FINKELPEARL

Sources C. D. Murphy, 'John Davies of Hereford', PhD diss., Cornell University, 1940 · *Complete works of John Davies of Hereford*, ed. A. B. Grosart, 2 vols. (1878) · H. Heidrich, *John Davies of Hereford (1565?–1618) und sein Bild von Shakespeare's Umgebung* (Leipzig, 1924) · J. N. D. Bush, *English literature in the earlier seventeeenth century, 1600–1660* (1945) · Fuller, *Worthies* (1840) · J. Doelman, 'The accession of King James I and English religious poetry', *Studies in English Literature*, 34 (1994) · A. Heal, *The English writing-masters and their copybooks, 1570–1800* (1931) · F. Peck, ed., *Desiderata curiosa*, new edn, 2 vols. in 1 (1779) · *The poems of William Browne of Tavistock*, ed. G. Godwin, 2 vols. (1894) · T. K. Whipple, 'Martial and the English epigram from Sir Thomas Wyatt to Ben Jonson', *University of California Publications in Modern Philology*, 10/4 (1925), 279–414 · *Sixth report*, HMC, 5 (1877–8)

Likenesses line engraving, BM, NPG; repro. in J. Davies, *Writing schoolmaster* (1633) [see illus.]

Davies, Sir John (*bap.* 1569, *d.* 1626), lawyer and poet, third son of Edward Davies (*d.* 1580), a Welshman settled at Chisgrove in the parish of Tisbury, Wiltshire, and his wife, Mary, daughter of John Bennett of Pitt House, Wiltshire, was baptized at Tisbury on 16 April 1569. He is described by Anthony Wood as the son of a 'wealthy tanner'. At his entry to Middle Temple it was recorded in the register that his father was a gentleman. Apparently first educated at Winchester College, Davies matriculated from Queen's College, Oxford, on 15 October 1585. It does not appear that he graduated. After a brief spell at New Inn, London, he was admitted to the Middle Temple on 3 February 1588, and was called to the bar in July 1595.

Poetic works In the previous year Davies had registered with the Stationers a poetic work entitled *Orchestra, or, A Poeme of Dancing*, the earliest extant edition of which is dated 1596. It was dedicated to Richard Martin, Davies's contemporary at the Middle Temple. At Bridgewater House 100 years ago was preserved a copy of the first edition, with a manuscript dedicatory sonnet to Sir Thomas Egerton, written by Davies in 1600 on the death of the lord chancellor's second wife. About the same time as he wrote and published *Orchestra*, Davies went into print with a number of epigrams, notorious for their 'roughness, even

coarseness' which their modern editor ascribed to 'the "Wild Oats" sowing, of the Poet's youthful period' (*Complete Poems*, 1.21). Manuscript transcripts of certain 'Gullinge Sonnets', addressed to Sir Anthony Cooke and kept in Chetham's Library, Manchester, were probably also written by Davies the lawyer. *Nosce teipsum*, a poem on the immortality of the soul and its relation to the body, much commended by contemporaries and modern critics alike, was written about 1594. A manuscript copy was preserved at Holkham Hall, Norfolk, as late as 1888, with dedicatory verses 'To my honorable patron and frend Ed. Cooke, Esq., her Maties Attorney-Generall' (*DNB*). Another manuscript copy has a dedication to the earl of Northumberland. In 1594 Charles Blount, Lord Mountjoy, presented Davies at court, where the queen had him sworn as servant-in-ordinary. Davies then went as one of the official party sent to the baptism of Prince Henry in Scotland, where he first came to the attention of James VI as the author of a poem already well regarded.

Although clearly an able student of the law, Davies was evidently no model citizen. His 'flamboyant and tempestuous personality' is attested by numerous infractions of the disciplinary code at the Middle Temple, not all of which can be adduced to the ritualized 'misrule' of Candlemas (Pawlisch, 16). He and his friend Richard Martin were temporarily expelled in 1591 for unruly behaviour. In February 1598 Davies was disbarred permanently from the society for a violent assault on the same Martin, and he returned to Oxford, apparently spending some time at New College, where it was once believed he composed *Nosce teipsum* in a fit of remorse. In Trinity term 1601 Davies secured the support of no lesser personages than Sir Robert Cecil and Sir Thomas Egerton for his readmission to the Middle Temple, which was secured by his public apology to Martin. In the same year he was returned to parliament as one of the representatives for Corfe Castle. He attained prominence in the Commons by his insistence on legislative redress to the abuse of the queen's prerogative of monopoly, much to Cecil's distaste. Yet by this time Davies's talents seem to have commended themselves to the secretary of state. When Cecil entertained the queen in 1602 at his new house in the Strand, London, Davies composed for the occasion *A Contention betwixt a Wife, a Widdow and a Maide*.

On the queen's death in March 1603 Davies may have accompanied Sir Robert Carey in his journey to the Scottish court, and he was certainly recorded as present during the new king's progress south. The tale that James now took Davies to his bosom as the author of the much admired *Nosce teipsum* is almost certainly apocryphal.

Solicitor-general for Ireland Although nine years earlier James had indeed delighted to meet the author of the *Nosce teipsum*, Davies was not among the 906 new knights created in the first month of the reign. On 18 September 1603 the king did, however, write to Lord Mountjoy to cause a grant of the office of solicitor-general for Ireland to be passed under the great seal to Davies, and in the following November Davies arrived in Dublin to assume the office; he received his knighthood there at the hands of the lord deputy the following month. A few days after his arrival he sent to Cecil a graphic account of the state of Ireland. Pestilence and famine were raging, and 'the face of things appeared very miserable' (*DNB*). But his first gloomy impressions were dissipated when he observed that the law courts were commanding respect. 'I conceave', he wrote, 'a very good hope that after a parliament wherein many mischiefs may be removed and prevented, and after the people ar acquainted with the forms of justice … this kingdom will grow humane and civile' (ibid.).

This view of the civilizing power of the law and its institutions was one by which Davies set great store throughout his association with Ireland. On 20 February 1604 he sent to Cecil from Castle Reban another long letter, in which he complained of the slothfulness and ignorance of the protestant clergymen, whom he described as 'meer idols and cyphers, and such as cannot read their neckverse if they should stand in need of the benefit of their clergy' (*DNB*). He found churches ruined and preaching neglected, and he asked that commissioners might be sent from England to inquire into these abuses. He also protested at the ease with which royal pardons were obtained in cases of robbery and murder, recommended the holding of quarter sessions, and condemned the debased quality of the coinage. That spring he went on the Leinster circuit. In April 1605 he travelled to England with Sir Richard Cooke, chief baron, to report on the state of Ireland, taking with him a letter to the lords of the council in which his 'industrious pains' and 'toilsome travels through most part of the kingdom' were highly commended by the lord deputy, Sir Arthur Chichester (ibid.). He returned to Dublin in July 1605, the lords of the council showing their own appreciation of his services by ordering that Chichester pay the arrears of his allowance. In 1606, on the elevation of Sir Charles Calthorpe to the bench, Davies succeeded to the post of attorney-general for Ireland, and was afterwards called to the degree of serjeant-at-law.

Land reform in Ireland Davies firmly believed that the successful government of Ireland could not be achieved through military conquest alone, but depended instead on laying the legal foundations for a civil society. He once wrote to Cecil saying that 'the multitude was ever made conformable to edicts and proclamations' (*DNB*). From 1606 he was busy with the management of the work deriving from the establishment of the commissions for defective titles and the implementation of arrangements for the surrender and regrant of lands by tenants of the crown. This was a crucial element in his long-standing campaign to entrench the full-scale operation of property law in Ireland as the bulwark of English rule, and was designed specifically to undermine and finally to abolish Gaelic paralegal forms of land tenure and inheritance which were much more fluid, based on kinship and the sept, and the tribal allegiances underpinning them. Religious reform was also integral to the 'new English' project of establishing 'civility' in Ireland, and Davies was a strong advocate of the expulsion of Catholic priests from Ireland and the firm establishment of the protestant religion. The punishment of recusancy was a political football in early seventeenth-century Ireland, but Davies was consistent in his support for the levying of penal exactions on those who failed to attend protestant churches. He also agitated for the reconstruction of the Irish polity from the ground upwards, recommending that reform of the Dublin corporation, and in particular the proscription of Catholics from the government of the city, would serve the purpose of encouraging reform in urban centres across the kingdom. Davies showed immense energy in the task of legal administration in Ireland, in the conduct of which his lifestyle was highly peripatetic, in and out of term. In May 1606 he was in Munster on assize. That summer he travelled through Monaghan, Fermanagh, and Cavan, recording observations in a long letter to Cecil. In 1607 he went on circuit through the counties of Meath, Westmeath, and Longford, and King's and Queen's counties, and reported to Cecil that it was almost a miracle to see the quiet and conformity that everywhere prevailed.

All was not equally well everywhere else. In September Davies sent Cecil a full report of the flight of the northern earls, and the following January he went himself to Ulster to indict Tyrone and Tyrconnell. In July he returned thither, this time with the lord deputy and the other commissioners appointed to view the escheated lands in the province. A letter from Davies to Cecil, dated 5 August 1608, gives a picturesque account of the journey, describing how the 'wild inhabitants' of the remoter districts 'wondered as much to see the king's deputy as the ghosts in Virgil wondered to see Æneas alive in hell' (*DNB*). Davies was long absorbed in the establishment of the new plantation, which made at least one false start, and profited not a little by it as one of the principal servitors in the only category (councillors of state) permitted also to undertake for estates. In all he obtained 5500 acres. It was also his counsel that secured the seizure of the upper Bann fishery, the richest in Ulster and a key means for the enticement of investors in the province.

> In the absence of fully adequate common law precedents, Davies fortified his brief … by citing 'divers rules of the civil law and the customary law of France agreeable to our law in this point' … Although the dictates of natural geography tell us that rivers flow towards the sea, Davies' application of the civil law led to the government's seizure of the Bann fishery because the sea flows into rivers. (Pawlisch, 173)

It is open to question whether Davies ever really saw his posting in Ireland as anything more than a means to the advancement of a legal career in England. As early as 1610 he petitioned his patron, Salisbury, for a new appointment elsewhere. In doing so he detailed aspects of his record of reform in Ireland, citing 'the assimilation of the autonomous gaelic lordships to the crown, the reduction of medieval corporate liberties, the implementation of religious conformity and the reinvigoration of the Irish revenues' (Pawlisch, 30). There may have been personal reasons for his staying there, however. About March 1609, probably while in England on business connected with the Ulster plantation, Davies married Eleanor Touchet (*d*.

1652), the fifth daughter of George, Baron Audley, future earl of Castlehaven. This was not a felicitous match. The attorney-general's in-laws enjoyed unsavoury reputations. He died five years before the family's ultimate disgrace, the execution of the second earl for gross sexual misconduct against his wife the countess and her daughter, his own stepdaughter. But his own married life had been less than happy. His wife's religious exuberance was frequently aimed aggressively at her husband, the exact timing of whose demise she cheerfully prophesied. 'From that time until his death in 1626, Davies suffered the uncomfortable experience of staring across the breakfast table at a hopelessly insane wife dressed in mourning' (ibid., 29). The marriage produced no surviving male heirs, two sons, one an idiot, having died in minority. Davies's daughter, Lucy, was married at the age of eleven to Ferdinando Hastings, the sixth earl of Huntingdon, on condition that his estate pass to Lucy rather than his somewhat unpredictable wife. Perhaps partly in avoidance of her, Davies remained in the thick of things in Ireland for some years yet. In 1610 he defended at law the crown's plantation of Cavan against counsel under instruction from dispossessed natives. In 1612 he published his *Discoverie of the true causes why Ireland was never entirely subdued nor brought under obedience of the crown of England until his majesties happie reigne*, which argued for the full establishment of a system of law based on land rather than blood.

Irish and English parliamentary duties In 1613 the king himself picked Davies as the best-qualified candidate to take the speaker's chair when parliament opened at Dublin in May. Davies played a crucial role in contriving the first ever protestant majority in the Irish parliament, based on the enfranchisement of new boroughs created during the plantation of Munster and Ulster. The Catholic Old English disputed the validity of many returns, and contested the election of the speaker. Nominated by Sir Thomas Ridgeway, Davies, who sat as knight of the shire for Fermanagh, was chosen by the protestant majority. Thereupon Sir James Gough, as champion of the Catholic party, proposed Sir John Everard, former second justice of the king's bench, whom Davies had forced to resign on grounds of his recusancy. Everard was installed in the chair, which he then refused to vacate to make way for Davies. Therefore, Ridgeway and Sir Oliver St John 'took Sir John Davys by the arms, lifted him from the ground, and placed him in the chair, in Sir John Everard's lap, requiring him still to come forth of the chair' (*DNB*). Eventually Everard was ejected, and he and his party withdrew, angrily insisting that they would seek redress at the hands of the king himself. However, the commission of inquiry that arrived the following September confirmed Davies's election. In 1615 the attorney-general published *Le primer discours des cases et matters in ley resolues et adiudges en les courts del roy en cest realme*, translated in 1762 as *A Report of Cases and Matters in Law*, 'elaborating step by step the innovative judicial measures he had employed to consolidate the Tudor conquest of Ireland' (Pawlisch, 31). If it was written in the same trumpet-blowing spirit as the letter Davies had sent Salisbury in 1610, then it had precisely the

same effect. A few years later Davies petitioned Buckingham for leave to lay down his commission in Ireland. On 30 October 1619 he was finally replaced by Sir William Ryves.

King's serjeant During his Irish service, Davies had spent a lot of time in England on business, and evidently maintained important political contacts. He is said to have been elected to sit for the borough of Newcastle under Lyme in the 1614 parliament, and he certainly represented the Staffordshire town in 1621. Back in 1609 the king had conferred on Davies the dignity of king's serjeant, and it was in this capacity that he now continued his professional practice in England, where he also went on circuit as a judge. The historian of his legal career in Ireland has said that Davies's charge to the jurors at York in 1620 'represents a classic contemporary exposition of the jurisprudence on assize justice' (Pawlisch, 32). In 1622 Davies published a revised edition of his three major poems, *Nosce teipsum*, *Astrea*, and *Orchestra*. At some point he also abridged Coke's reports, although his labours were not published until 1651. In 1624 he translated the Psalms; a manuscript copy, with several poems appended, was noted by the *Dictionary of National Biography* as being in the Laing collection in Edinburgh University Library. These, like all his other writings, were published by Alexander Grosart in three volumes for the Fuller Worthies' Library between 1869 and 1876, dedicated, with his permission, to William Gladstone. The accession of Charles I in 1625 cheered Davies, who wrote that he believed the new king was 'like to restore the glory of our nation by his wisdom and valor' (ibid.). The author of a manuscript tract, not published until 1656, on the prerogative right to levy impositions without parliamentary consent, building his argument on the Roman-law concept of *ius gentium*, or the law of nations, Davies evidently also commended himself to the new king. In 1626 Charles appointed him chief justice of the king's bench in place of Randolph Crew, who had refused to declare the legitimacy of the forced loan.

Early in December 1626 Davies prepared for his new judicial appointment by purchasing the robes of office. On the night of 7 December he was at a supper party given by Lord Keeper Coventry in Westminster, and on the following morning he was found dead of apoplexy; this was the very day he was due to be installed as chief justice—an act of God, wrote the English judge James Whitelocke, that prevented 'so inconvenient an intention to the commonwealth' (Pawlisch, 33). The funeral oration was preached by John Donne, and on 9 December Davies was interred in St Martin-in-the-Fields, Westminster. His wife survived him and remarried, visiting on her new husband, Sir Archibald Douglas, sufferings almost identical to those undergone by her first, who himself failed to elude her for very long, she being buried beside him in 1652.

Reputation Davies's contemporary and posthumous influence was signal. As well as a poet noted in his time, he was an enthusiastic antiquary, and in 1592 had travelled to Leiden to meet the famous Dutch jurist and professor of civil law Paul Merula, with letters of introduction from William Camden. Davies, Sir Robert Cotton, and others were jointly engaged in re-establishing the Society of Antiquaries early in the seventeenth century. Davies's immersion in civil- and canon-law traditions was no doubt deepened during his brief association with New College, Oxford, and possibly by continental study under Merula (printed editions of Davies's youthful epigrams having allegedly originated at Middleburg). It has been cited as prima facie evidence for the need to question the hegemonic grip of common-law insularity and the ancient constitution over the minds and imaginations of early modern English lawyers. Davies's view, expressed only fleetingly, but forcefully, during the 1621 parliament, that 'Ireland is a member of the crown of England … [and] that this kingdom here cannot make laws to bind that kingdom, for they have a parliament of their own', raised a problem which recurred at different stages, and in differing guises, in the seventeenth and eighteenth centuries. But it is his contribution to English 'imperialism' in Ireland which constitutes the most substantial portion of his legacy, and in particular his expansion of the use of civil law there in an attempt to justify and consolidate English sovereignty. His assertion of an English title to Ireland by right of conquest after the conclusion of Tyrone's rising in 1603 effectively reduced the entire kingdom to the condition of virgin territory over which none but the crown could claim any proprietary right, and simultaneously eradicated the jurisdiction of ancient Brehon law. This later proved a pivotal stage in the collapse of Gaelic society in Ireland. It did much to help provoke both the flight of the northern earls and the rising of Sir Cahir O'Doherty (the first of which Davies seems to have connived at quite deliberately), events which themselves cleared the way for the plantation of Ulster. Conquest doctrine continued to serve as a justification for English sovereignty over Ireland until shortly before home rule. But Davies had an altogether more subtle impact on Anglo-Irish legal institutions and culture than his pronouncements on the extirpation of Gaelic traditions might suggest. Aspects of the Brehon code he effectively attempted to assimilate to the customary practice of the Tudor kingdom. And given the insistence of his campaign to reduce Ireland to protestant conformity, it is ironic to note, for example, that his application of canonical law in cases such as the right of ministers to hold plural livings *in commendam* had the effect of ascribing to the popish canons of Catholic Europe the status of English customary law. In this, Davies perfectly embodied some of the more fruitful contradictions of his age. SEAN KELSEY

Sources DNB • P. Robinson, *The plantation of Ulster: British settlement in an Irish landscape* (1984) • H. S. Pawlisch, *Sir John Davies and the conquest of Ireland: a study in legal imperialism* (1985) • A. R. Hart, *A history of the king's serjeants at law in Ireland* (2000) • W. J. Jones, 'Davies, John', HoP, *Commons, 1558–1603*, 2.22–3 • *The complete poems of Sir John Davies, with memorial-introduction and notes*, ed. A. B. Grosart, 2 vols. (1876) • parish register, Westminster, St Martin-in-the-Fields, 9 Dec 1626, City Westm. AC [burial]

Archives Harvard U., Houghton L., MS relating to Ireland • Hunt. L., corresp. and papers • Hunt. L., letters; literary MS • LUL, MS

treatise | BL, Add. MSS; Hargrave MSS • Bodl. Oxf., MSS Carte 61, 62

Wealth at death £100 for poor in parishes of Englefield, Berkshire, and Tisbury, Wiltshire; £500 left to wife for clearing debts: will, PRO, PROB 11/150, fol. 282*v*

Davies, John (*c.*1570–1644), Church of England clergyman and Welsh scholar, was born at Llanferres, Denbighshire, the son of Dafydd ab Ieuan ap Rhys, said to have been a weaver, and his wife, Elizabeth ferch Lewis ap Dafydd Lloyd. It was within a few miles of his birthplace that he came in contact with two men who set the course for his life and achievements. The first, the Gamaliel (the teacher of St Paul) at whose feet he was brought up, as he described him in the preface to his 1632 dictionary, was William Morgan, translator of the Bible into Welsh, and, at the time, vicar of a neighbouring parish. The second was Richard Parry, future bishop of St Asaph, then headmaster of the grammar school at Ruthin, which Davies attended. Davies graduated from Jesus College, Oxford, in 1594. During the following decade his movements are not known: he is speculated to have returned to teach in Ruthin or to have joined Morgan at Llandaff.

Davies was appointed rector of Mallwyd, Merioneth, in 1604 (the living of Llanmawddwy was added in 1613). The following year he became chaplain to Parry (elevated to St Asaph in 1604), and became a canon of the cathedral in 1612. About 1609 he married Jane Price, daughter of Llwyn Ynn, in the parish of Llanfair Dyffryn Clwyd, Denbighshire. She was a granddaughter on her mother's side of Baron Lewis Owen of Dolgellau, and her sister was the wife of Richard Parry. In 1608 he resumed his studies, as a student of Lincoln College, Oxford, where he was in residence as reader of the sentences. He graduated BD the same year, and DD in 1615 (relinquished in 1621 for Llanfor). He became chancellor of St Asaph in 1617 with the prebendal stall of Llanefydd, Denbighshire.

Davies's achievements touched on many fields but were united by a common purpose, to propagate the faith to the people in their native tongue. The unavailability of sufficient numbers of Morgan's Bible of 1588 resulted in a plan to produce a new translation, one which could take into account the Authorized Version of 1611. The 1620 Welsh Bible appeared under Parry's name, but is generally regarded to have been the work of Davies. Davies is also credited with revising the Book of Common Prayer, republished the following year, again under Parry's name.

Further works focusing on the Welsh language itself were an attempt to provide materials through which English-speaking clergymen could learn Welsh in order to communicate with their Welsh-speaking parishioners. Davies's Welsh grammar in Latin, *Antiquae linguae Britannicae … rudimenta* appeared in 1621. In 1632 he published a Welsh–Latin dictionary, *Antiquae linguae Britannicae … dictionarium duplex*. Davies wrote the Welsh–Latin section of the dictionary himself, and used Thomas Wiliems's work for the Latin–Welsh sections, abridged and revised. He was forced to spend almost a year in London while the work was in the press in order to oversee its production. His dictionary was subsequently used and cited as an authority in the English dictionaries of Thomas Blount (1656) and Edward Philips (1658), and Dr Johnson had a copy of the *Dictionarium duplex* in his library.

In addition to his scholarly works Davies also published pastoral materials. He translated *The First Book of the Christian Exercise Appertayning to the Resolution*, the Jesuit Robert Parsons's introduction to Christian truths (as revised by Bunney), as *Llyfr y resolusion* (1632). He edited *Y llyfr plygain a'r catechisme* (1633), a mix of secular almanac and abridgement of the Book of Common Prayer. It was uncommon in being pocket-size at a time when editions of the Book of Common Prayer were normally folio. *Yr articulau* (1664) appeared posthumously.

From 1594 onwards Dr Davies copied a vast quantity of poetry of various periods, often hiring scribes to work for him. This extensive study of the Welsh language, and poetry in particular, informs all his published work. In 1710 Dafydd Lewys of Llanawddog printed a collection of some of Dr Davies's extracts of Welsh poetry under the title *Flores poetarum Britannicorum*.

Davies is said to have died at Harlech on 15 May 1644, and was buried at Mallwyd four days later. His widow later married his curate and successor, Edward Wynn.

Davies's achievements in propagating both the Bible and the Welsh language deeply influenced Welsh culture. Rowland Vaughan, a contemporary, described him as 'the only excellent Plato of our tongue', and Sir Glanmor Williams continues to see Davies as 'the greatest Welsh scholar of his age, if not of all time' (Williams, *Recovery*, 476).   MIHAIL DAFYDD EVANS

Sources G. Williams, *Wales and the Reformation* (1997) · G. Williams, *Recovery, reorientation and Reformation* (1987) · J. W. James, 'Dr John Davies of Mallwyd, 1570–1644', *Journal of the Historical Society of the Church in Wales*, 1 (1947), 40–52 · R. Geraint Gruffydd, 'Richard Parry a John Davies', *Y traddodiadd rhyddiaith*, ed. G. Bowen (1970) · R. F. Roberts, 'Dr John Davies o Fallwyd', *Llên Cymru*, 2 (1952) · C. Davies, *Rhagymadroddion a chyflwyniadau Lladin, 1551–1632* (1980) · De W. T. Starnes and G. E. Noyes, *The English dictionary from Cawdrey to Johnson, 1604–1755* (1946); new edn, ed. G. Stein (1991)
Archives NL Wales, papers

Davies, John (1625–1693), translator, was born at Kidwelly, Carmarthenshire, on 25 May 1625. He was the son of William Davies, yeoman of Kidwelly, and his wife, whose maiden name was Griffiths. He attended school in Carmarthen and entered Jesus College, Oxford, on 16 May 1641, matriculating on 4 June. When the civil war broke out he was removed from Oxford by relatives, and placed in St John's College, Cambridge, as a sizar on 14 May 1646. Wood claims that there he was trained up by presbyterians which 'made him ever after, till his majesty's restoration, keep pace with the times of usurpation' (Wood, *Ath. Oxon.*, 382). At Cambridge he became acquainted with the Durham poet John Hall, who was at St John's in 1645/6. Davies wrote the preface to Hall's book of essays, *Horae vacivae* (1646), claiming that this work represented not only the learning of the university but that of the more serious sort of men in three nations. It was through Hall that Davies acquired the manuscript of *The Ancient Rites, and Monuments of the Monastical, Cathedral Church of Durham*,

which he translated from the Latin and published in 1672, dedicating it to another native of Durham, James Mickleton, of the Inner Temple. Davies's fluency in French came from the years he spent in France during the interregnum. After the Restoration, Davies wrote *The civil warres of Great Britain and Ireland: containing an exact history of their occasion, originall, progress, and happy end* (1661), which he dedicated to the duke of Richmond and Lennox. Davies claims that this work is an unbiased and impartial account of the wars, although it contains a hagiographical account of Charles I's execution:

> Then after some short discourse with Doctor Juxon, his Majesty with an Heroick patience submitted his Head to the Block, which after the Sign given, was at one blow cut off ... Thus fell Charles ... the Martyr of the People, a Prince certainly endowed with much piety, magnanimity and patience, as any that ever this kingdom could boast. (pp. 280, 282)

A Scottish edition of the work was published in 1664.

It appears that Davies earned his living by translating works from French, Spanish, and Latin. The first of these was *The Extravagant Shepherd* from the French of C. Sorel (1653). He translated an esoteric selection of works, which included *The Art of How to Know Men* (1665), originally by De La Chambre, dedicated to Charles Howard, earl of Carlisle, recommending it to him for the use of ambassadors. Other works Davies translated also had a practical function, such as *The voyages & travels of the ambassadors sent by Frederick duke of Holstein, to the great duke of Muscovy, and the king of Persia*, dedicated to the 'English Merchants in Muscovy', which was published together with the *Travel of John Albert de Mandelslo* in 1662. Davies also translated novels and pseudo-scientific works such as *The History of Magick* (1657).

Davies hoped to gain the patronage of well-connected men through his translations. *Observations on the Poems of Homer and Virgil* (1672), translated from the French of René Rapin, was dedicated to Sir John Berkenhead, *The History of Appian* (1679), a translation of the work of Appianus, to the earl of Ossory, and *The History of Henry IV* (1663), from the French of the bishop of Rodez, to Charles II. Davies did not forget his countrymen or his relatives. It is from the dedications to his translations that the few details known about his life can be reconstructed. Murtada's *The Egyptian History* (1672) was dedicated to his uncle John Griffith, of Llangwendraeth, Carmarthenshire, whom Davies had entertained with stories from the book, and to whom it was now dedicated as recompense for Griffith's having lost his collection of papers and books on Wales. *Political and Military Observations* (1679) was dedicated to Sir Thomas Davies, a bookseller and mayor of London. Davies was acquainted with Nahum Tate and Richard Lovelace, the latter writing a prefatory verse for *Letters of Affaires of Love and Courtship* (1657), translated from the French of Vincent de Voiture. The translations were workmanlike. Davies hoped they were pure, simple, and sensible. Davies was buried in Kidwelly church on 22 July 1693.   E. LORD

Sources Wood, *Ath. Oxon.*, new edn, 4.382 · Foster, *Alum. Oxon.* · Venn, *Alum. Cant.* · A. G. Prys-Jones, *The story of Carmarthenshire*, 2 (1972), 109 · *DNB*

Davies, John (1679–1732), college head, was born in London on 22 April 1679 and baptized on 13 May at either St Vedast, Foster Lane, or St Michael-le-Querne, London. He was the son of John Davies, merchant, who died while Davies was young, and Elizabeth, daughter of Sir John Turton, justice of the court of king's bench. He was educated at the Charterhouse School, and in 1695 matriculated from Queens' College, Cambridge. He graduated BA in 1699, was elected fellow of his college on 7 July 1701, and commenced MA in 1702. In 1709 he was junior proctor of the university. He was ordained deacon at Ely on 21 September 1711, and priest on 23 September, and in that year was collated by Dr John Moore, bishop of Ely, to the rectory of Fen Ditton, near Cambridge, and to a prebend in the church of Ely; he also took the degree of LLD. From 1712 to 1718 he held the rectory of Glemsford, Suffolk, another living in Moore's patronage.

On the death of Dr Henry James, president of Queens' College, Davies was elected to succeed him on 23 March 1717. A fervent whig and supporter of the Hanoverian succession, he was created DD when George I visited Cambridge in the same year. In 1726 he was elected vice-chancellor of the university. At some stage he married Sarah, who is mentioned in his will, but nothing more is known of his marriage.

Davies was a close friend and ally of the eminent classical scholar Richard Bentley. Bentley's scholarly influence can be seen in Davies's correct editions of works by Caesar, Lactantius, and Minucius Felix; his second edition of *Maximi Tyrii dissertationes* (1703; 2nd edn, 1740) contained material supplied by Bentley. Davies projected new and beautiful editions of Cicero's philosophical treatises to supplement Graevius's edition of Cicero's works, and accordingly published the first, *Tusculanarum disputationum libri quinque*, at Cambridge in 1709; five more volumes were published in the series, and most went to a second edition. Davies had got as far as editing the middle of the third book of Cicero's 'Offices' when he died, on 7 March 1732 at Fen Ditton. He was buried in Queens' College chapel. In his will he entrusted his unfinished edition of the 'Offices' to the care of Dr Mead, who gave it to Bentley's grandson Dr Thomas Bentley to prepare for the press. All Davies's notes and emendations were lost in a fire at the house where Bentley lodged, in the Strand, London, caused by his carelessness while reading in bed.

THOMPSON COOPER, *rev.* S. J. SKEDD

Sources Venn, *Alum. Cant.* · J. Twigg, *A history of Queens' College, Cambridge, 1448–1986* (1987) · Nichols, *Illustrations*, 3.520 · Nichols, *Lit. anecdotes*, 1.343, 706; 2.134, 142; 4.276, 328–9, 508 · M. L. Clark, *Greek studies in England, 1700–1830* (1945) · will, PRO, PROB 11/674, sig. 225 · IGI
Likenesses Faber, engraving · oils, Queens' College, Cambridge

Davies, John Emerson Harding (1916–1979), business executive and politician, was born on 8 January 1916 at Blackheath, London, the younger son and second of the two children of Arnold Thomas Davies, a chartered accountant, and his wife, Edith Minnie Malchus Harding. John had Welsh, Scottish, and Armenian ancestry. He boarded at Windlesham House School, Washington Pulborough, Sussex, and St Edward's School, Oxford, while home was Paris, where his father worked.

Davies, an articled clerk from 1934, qualified as the youngest chartered accountant in Britain in 1939. An officer during the Second World War with the Royal Army Service Corps, he married (Vera) Georgina (Georgie) Bates on 8 January 1943. In 1946 he left the combined operations experimental establishment after a year and joined the marketing division of the Anglo-Iranian Oil Company, later British Petroleum (BP). Spells at its Stockholm and Paris offices preceded his promotion to the posts of general manager BP marketing (1956–60) and director BP trading (1960–61). Then, as managing director of Shell-Mex and BP Ltd (1961–5), he ran a national chain of petrol stations.

From 1962 Davies served on the grand council of the Federation of British Industry, where his accomplished chairmanship of its technical legislation committee impressed Norman Kipping. After the Federation of British Industry amalgamated with the British Employers' Confederation and the National Association of British Manufacturers in July 1965, he was appointed director-general of the Confederation of British Industry (CBI).

Davies wanted the new business pressure group to have a higher profile than its predecessors. Viewing the CBI as the counterpart of the Trades Union Congress (TUC), he welcomed continuous dialogue with the government through such tripartite bodies as the National Economic Development Council, the British National Export Council, and the National Joint Advisory Council of the Department of Employment and Productivity. Incomes policy and economic planning, he believed, were cornerstones of national survival. At his urging, the CBI called for British entry into the European Economic Community (EEC) in 1966 and instituted a CBI–TUC joint committee in 1967.

The demise of the national plan and the devaluation of sterling meanwhile soured the CBI's relations with the Labour government, of which Davies became a famous critic. Wrangles about wage and price restraint seemed endless, and he lambasted the Industrial Reorganization Corporation's work as back-door nationalization. There was a certain amount of shadow-boxing here: the director-general would give Wedgwood Benn and Barbara Castle a tongue-lashing on television, because rebellious right-wingers in the CBI demanded nothing less. In Whitehall he negotiated affably with ministers, since he saw close partnership as the best way forward. This supple performance reflected the two contrasting sides of his character. There were people who said that Davies was a bumptious little man; others found him remarkably modest and gentle. Close friends being comparatively few, family life meant much to him, especially his children, Francis and Rosamund.

When Davies described Harold Wilson's 'solemn and binding' accord with the trade unions to curb strikes in June 1969 as useful only in the lavatory, he was burning his bridges: he desired to become a Conservative MP. Despite failing to secure the candidature for City of London or Louth, he left the CBI on 15 October and worked for the bankers Hill Samuel until the safe seat of Knutsford returned him to the House of Commons at the general election of 18 June 1970. A mere forty days on, Edward Heath asked him to join the cabinet in the reshuffle caused by the death of Iain Macleod.

Davies became minister of technology knowing that his role in the government would be enlarged when 'MinTech' merged with the Board of Trade to form the Department of Trade and Industry (DTI). From 15 October 1970 he was secretary of state for trade and industry and president of the Board of Trade. The appointment excited much discussion. The right recalled his corporatist past; Enoch Powell talked about Caligula's horse. Loyalists reacted by overselling Davies as a great captain of industry with the managerial skills required to modernize administration.

Anxious to be accepted as a 'real' Conservative, Davies delighted the party conference with a promise not to prop up failing firms indefinitely. In parliament on 4 November 1970 he baited Labour MPs by warning of national decadence if the state treated everyone as a lame duck. The speech caused such an outcry that Davies likened himself to the sorcerer's apprentice, bewildered at the hostile forces which he unleashed. To the left he embodied the capitalist bosses; free-marketeers hailed him as the evangelist of 'disengagement', the current buzzword for ending government interference in industry.

In practice, the DTI sent out mixed signals. Davies declined to rescue the bankrupt Mersey Docks and Harbour Board. He scrapped the Industrial Reorganization Corporation and switched regional aid from investment grants to tax allowances. On the other hand, he persisted with Concorde despite soaring costs, ruled out the denationalization of British Steel, and took Rolls Royce's aero-engine division into public ownership in 1971. Interventionist by temperament, the secretary of state struggled to master his sprawling department. His team of five, then seven, and finally nine subordinate ministers did not pull together; right-wingers Sir John Eden and Nicholas Ridley often sounded out of control. In the Commons, moreover, Davies proved an ineffective debater.

Upper Clyde Shipbuilders (UCS) comprised four unprofitable yards, combined by Benn in 1968, which repeatedly sought government aid. In June 1971 the DTI decided to wind it up: two shipyards would have to close if the other two were ever again to be viable. The left denounced this 'butchery', and UCS became its *cause célèbre* after communist shop stewards began a work-in. Davies, painted as the villain of the piece, was fortunately away when the Angry Brigade bombed his flat in Fulham on 31 July. After unemployment exceeded a million in the new year and the police forecast civil disorder in Glasgow, Davies paid up £35 million to keep all four UCS yards in business. He offered no commercial rationale.

Davies was not part of Heath's inner circle. The industry white paper of March 1972 was prepared outside his department, if not behind his back, but it fell to him to announce its provisions: chief among them, a system of regional development grants and a new Industrial Development Executive (with a strong resemblance to the old Industrial Reorganization Corporation). The Industry Bill which followed gave unprecedentedly wide powers to the DTI to aid firms in 'non-culpable decline'. Henceforth Davies could not speak in the chamber without Labour MPs cheering ironically and affecting convulsions of mirth. He was called 'the minister for lame ducks' or—worse—'the lame duck minister'. When the CBI complained about back-door nationalization, his humiliation was complete, though some felt sorry for an unlucky politician, promoted too fast and burdened with more than his share of the government's embarrassment. Peter Walker supplanted him at the DTI on 5 November 1972.

Davies continued to sit in the cabinet as chancellor of the duchy of Lancaster, with special responsibilities for EEC affairs. Very keen on the Common Market, he helped co-ordinate British policy in the Council of Ministers and formulate community regional development strategy—all well out of the public eye. The oil crisis and the miners' strike made him fear the worst. He left office with the rest of the government on 5 March 1974.

Excluded from the shadow cabinet, Davies gradually recovered his political credibility from May 1974 as a hardworking chairman of the select committee on European secondary legislation (the scrutiny committee). It perused every published paper submitted by the EEC Commission to the Council of Ministers and picked out the ones which warranted debate by the House of Commons. Most of its recommendations never won parliamentary time, but all shades of opinion respected the new-model Davies: scrupulously fair and courteous, and almost above party. He canvassed for a 'yes' vote in the Common Market referendum of 1975, when Labour blocked his nomination as an EEC commissioner.

Margaret Thatcher named John Davies as shadow foreign secretary after dismissing Reginald Maudling on 19 November 1976. He was a privy councillor with useful European credentials to whom she never felt constrained to defer. How many people took very much notice of the silver-haired gentleman with half-moon glasses who sat beside the 'iron lady' at press conferences? Their views on the Soviet challenge coincided well enough, but, on domestic questions, Davies inclined to the Heathite faction. He seemed more sceptical than Thatcher of the internal settlement in Rhodesia, and his ill-judged speech to the party conference on 11 October 1978 provoked jeers. Severe headaches were robbing him of sleep; within the week, surgeons removed a malignant brain tumour. His retirement was announced on 6 November 1978.

Davies was ready to resume part-time work with the Hill Samuel group in the spring. Offered a life peerage, he intended to be known as Baron Harding-Davies, but before letters patent were completed he suffered a fatal relapse and died, at St Thomas's Hospital, London, on 4 July 1979.

A figure so controversial in 1970–72 might have been expected to feature prominently in later debate about the

Heath ministry. In fact, for wets intent on playing down the U-turn the best that could be said of Davies at the DTI was as little as possible. The dries exonerated him as a hapless placeman in an effort to pin more blame on Heath. Notwithstanding his work with the CBI, John Davies, a painstaking and honourable man, was chiefly remembered as a textbook example of the perils of parachuting a manager into government.

JASON TOMES

Sources Daily Telegraph (5 July 1979) · Hansard 5C · S. Ball and A. Seldon, eds., The Heath government, 1970–1974: a reappraisal (1996) · S. Blank, Industry and government in Britain (1973) · 'Ted Heath's fall guy', New Statesman (20 Nov 1970), 672 · E. Heath, The course of my life (1998) · J. Davies, Industry and government (1966) · J. Bruce-Gardyne, Whatever happened to the quiet revolution? (1974) · T. Benn, Office without power: diaries, 1968–72 (1988) · W. Grant and D. Marsh, The Confederation of British Industry (1977) · C. King, The Cecil King diaries, 1970–1974 (1975) · G. Turner, Business in Britain (1969)
Archives U. Warwick Mod. RC, CBI archive, papers as director-general of CBI
Wealth at death £10,825: probate, 4 Dec 1979, CGPLA Eng. & Wales

Davies, John Scarlett. See Davis, John Scarlett (1804–1845).

Davies, Jonathan (bap. 1737, d. 1809), schoolmaster, was born at Eton College, where he was baptized on 26 June 1737, the son of John and Sarah Davies. He was nicknamed by his pupils Barber, which may indicate his father's job. He was a scholar at Eton and proceeded to King's College, Cambridge, whence he matriculated at Easter 1756. Elected a Craven scholar in 1757, he graduated BA in 1760 and proceeded MA in 1763. He returned to Eton as assistant master, appointed by Edward Barnard, in 1760. On the resignation of the very unsuccessful John Foster in 1773 he became headmaster. The following year he became rector of Scaldwell in Northamptonshire. As headmaster he somewhat restored Eton's fortunes, and the number of boys rose from below 250 to above 400, and many subsequently distinguished men were educated there in his time. Memoirs recall his loud voice and fondness for good living. He had his troubles too, though in general he proved more acceptable to the boys than to the masters. He was an exacting headmaster and his staff collectively offered their resignations in 1783; in their absence from duty the boys became rebellious, which compelled the masters to return to re-establish order. Davies prudently closed the school early for the Christmas holidays.

When Provost Barnard died in 1781 Davies might have expected to succeed him, but George III appointed his personal favourite, William Hayward Roberts, and Davies was made a canon of Windsor as a consolation. He did, however, succeed Roberts in December 1791 and continued until his death at Eton on 5 December 1809; he was buried at Eton. He had already restored some prizes which had lapsed, and by his will he created a scholarship for Eton scholars who were not elected to King's, and left £1000 to found a classical scholarship in his name at Cambridge, similar to the Craven scholarship which he had won. He also left £2000 to King's College.

ROBERT HARRISON, rev. TIM CARD

Sources Venn, Alum. Cant. · H. C. Maxwell Lyte, A history of Eton College, 1440–1910, 4th edn (1911) · J. H. Jesse, Memoirs of celebrated Etonians, 2 vols. (1875) · T. Harwood, Alumni Etonenses, or, A catalogue of the provosts and fellows of Eton College and King's College, Cambridge, from the foundation in 1443 to the year 1797 (1797), 31 · GM, 1st ser., 80 (1810), 87–8 · R. A. Austen-Leigh, ed., The Eton College register, 1753–1790 (1921)
Archives Eton, papers

Davies, Kitchener. See Davies, James (1902–1952).

Davies, (John) Llewelyn (1826–1916), theologian, was born at Chichester on 26 February 1826, the eldest son of the Revd John Davies DD (1795–1861), an evangelical divine, rector of Gateshead from 1840 to 1861, and his wife, Mary Hopkinson (d. 1886). (Sarah) Emily *Davies, the educationist, was his sister. Davies was educated at Repton School and at Trinity College, Cambridge (1844–8). In 1848 he was bracketed fifth in the classical tripos with his friend David James Vaughan, also of Trinity, with whom he had been elected to a Bell university scholarship in 1845; in 1850 the friends were elected fellows of their college together, and they subsequently (1852) collaborated in translating Plato's Republic. As an undergraduate Davies was already interested in political and social questions, and he was president of the union in 1847 and 1849. After taking his degree he for a time taught private pupils, among whom was Leslie Stephen. About this time he came under the influence of Frederick Denison Maurice, whose teaching Davies's clear mind was to make acceptable to many who found Maurice himself elusive. Taking orders in 1851 Davies first held a curacy, unpaid, at St Anne's, Limehouse, and was then for four years (1852–6) incumbent of St Mark's, Whitechapel. At this time he became closely associated with Maurice's circle, especially Thomas Hughes, Charles Kingsley, and John Malcolm Forbes Ludlow, in the work of the co-operative movement, and in the establishment of the Working Men's College in Great Ormond Street in 1854. In 1856 he was appointed to the crown living of Christ Church, Marylebone, which he held for thirty-three years. It was mainly a poor parish, but the rector's preaching drew hearers from other parts of London.

In 1859 Davies married Mary (d. 1895), the eldest daughter of Sir Charles John *Crompton and his wife, Caroline, née Fletcher. They had six sons (three of whom were fellows of Trinity College, Cambridge) and one daughter, Margaret Caroline Llewelyn *Davies, who, after attending Girton College, Cambridge, played an important part in the working men's co-operatives.

Davies combined other public activities and interests with his clerical work. He was a warm friend of the movement for the higher education of women, in which his sister, Emily, played a prominent part. From 1873 to 1874 and again from 1878 to 1886 he was principal of Queen's College, Harley Street, which had been founded by Maurice in 1848 for the advancement of women's education. He supported the extension to women of university degrees and of the parliamentary franchise. He was a member of the first London school board; he favoured unsectarian religious teaching in elementary schools, and he suggested the formula known as the 'Cowper-Temple clause', which was embodied in the Elementary Education Act of 1870. In politics Davies was a strong but independent Liberal: he was opposed to Gladstone's home-rule measures, but rejoined the Liberal Party when free trade was threatened. He was strongly in sympathy with trade unionism, and raised his voice to vindicate the movement at a time when it was far from popular. Thus in 1872 he addressed a great meeting at Exeter Hall in support of combinations among agricultural labourers, and the next year at the church congress he vigorously combated clerical prejudice against trade unions.

Like many of his Cambridge friends, Davies was an enthusiastic walker and an original member of the Alpine Club, making the first ascents of the Dom and the Täschhorn. He wrote several articles for the *Alpine Journal* and for *Peaks, Passes, and Glaciers*. It was chiefly, however, as a broad churchman that Davies was known. *St Paul and Modern Thought* (1856), his commentary on St Paul's epistles (1866), and his *Order and Growth* (Hulsean lectures, 1891) exemplify his thinking. He joined in establishing the National Church Reform Union (1870), which aimed at making the Church of England more truly national and comprehensive. His views on the relation between church and state probably stood in the way of ecclesiastical preferment, for which he seemed marked out by his practical ability, his earnestness, moderation, and fairness of mind, as well as by the position which he held in the religious and social life of London. There he was esteemed by many who held widely differing opinions. His marriage brought him into close relation with the English advocates of positivism, two of whom, Henry Crompton and Edward Spencer Beesly, were his wife's brother and brother-in-law respectively. Davies held strongly that Christian theology should seek instruction 'from the progressive development of life and knowledge' (preface to his *Theology and Morality*, 1873). While he gave his allegiance especially to Maurice, his standpoint was in general that of his friends B. F. Westcott, J. B. Lightfoot, and F. J. A. Hort, the contemporary leaders of liberal theology at Cambridge. His preaching was not rhetorical and made no parade of learning, the qualities which rendered it remarkable being depth of conviction, independence of thought, and an unfailing clearness of exposition. When Davies left London in 1889, on being presented to the Trinity College living of Kirkby Lonsdale, Westmorland, a valedictory address, to which was attached a remarkable list of signatures, recognized the combination in him of a 'clear and firm assertion of Christian truth with a generous appreciation of all earnest thought and feeling' and a 'habitual sympathy with rich and poor alike'.

Davies held his Westmorland living for twenty years, adapting himself successfully to the new conditions of life and work, and throwing himself vigorously into the educational business of the town and county. He was also chaplain to the queen (1876–1901) and to the king (1901–16). In 1895 his wife died. He retired in 1908 at the age of eighty-two, and passed the remaining eight years of his life with his daughter at Hampstead. He died there on 18 May 1916.   A. F. HORT, *rev.* H. C. G. MATTHEW

Sources *The Times* (19 May 1916) · *Modern Churchman* (July 1916) · *Contemporary Review* (June 1916) · C. P. Lucas, 'Llewelyn Davies and the Working Men's College', *Cornhill Magazine*, [3rd] ser., 41 (1916), 421–30 · *Cambridge University Magazine* (May 1879) · Venn, *Alum. Cant.* · C. L. Davies, ed., *From a Victorian post-bag: being letters addressed to the Rev. J. Llewelyn Davies* (1926)
Archives NRA, priv. coll., corresp. | BL, corresp. with Macmillans, Add. MS 55108 · LPL, corresp. with Frederick Temple
Likenesses wood-engraving, NPG; repro. in *ILN* (8 Oct 1892)
Wealth at death £20,629 4s. 8d.: resworn probate, 6 July 1916, *CGPLA Eng. & Wales*

Davies [*née* Drummond de Melfort], **Lady Lucy Clementina** (1795–1879), author, was born at the château of St Germain, France, on 21 November 1795. Her father, commonly called Lord Leon Maurice Drummond de Melfort (1761–1826), was the fourth son of James Drummond, third duke of Melfort in the Jacobite peerage and in the peerage of France, who would have been earl of Melfort in the peerage of Scotland but for the attainder of his ancestor. Her mother (*d.* 1824) was Marie Elizabeth Luce de Longuemare. The attainder was reversed in favour of her brother, George Drummond, sixth duke of Melfort, who became fifth earl of Perth and second earl of Melfort, in 1853, and she was granted a patent of precedence as an earl's daughter. She was educated in Edinburgh under Miss Playfair, sister of Professor Sir Lyon Playfair, and her time was divided between England and France. She married, on 8 September 1823, at Marylebone, Middlesex, Francis Henry Davies, a registrar of the court of chancery, who died at Koblenz on the Rhine on 22 October 1863, aged seventy-two. They had one son and two daughters, including Lucy Elizabeth Drummond Sale-*Barker.

She died on 27 April 1879 at 22 Palace Gardens Terrace, Kensington, London, the home of John Sale-Barker, barrister, the second husband of her daughter Lucy Elizabeth. In 1872 she published two volumes entitled *Recollections of Society in France and England*, containing her family history and particulars of the court of France under the Bourbons and the Bonapartes.   G. C. BOASE, *rev.* K. D. REYNOLDS

Sources Boase, *Mod. Eng. biog.* · GEC, *Peerage* · Burke, *Peerage* · *The Times* (10 May 1879), 7
Wealth at death under £100: administration, 23 June 1879, *CGPLA Eng. & Wales*

Davies, Margaret [Marged Dafydd] (*c.*1700–1785?), Welsh-language poet and copyist, was the daughter of Dafydd or David Evans (*d.* 1729) of Coetgae-du, Trawsfynydd, Meirioneth, and his wife, Ann Dafydd (*c.*1664–1726). Little is known about the early life of Margaret Davies but that she mastered the rules of Welsh prosody, a skill then rarely associated with women. So high was her reputation that by 1728 she was acting as bardic teacher to Michael Pritchard (*c.*1709–1733), of Llanllyfni, Caernarvonshire. Some twenty poems are attributed to her in surviving manuscripts, but some of the anonymous works in her manuscripts may also be hers.

Davies never married and, following the death of her

parents, she seems to have enjoyed considerable independence for a woman of her time. Although she had two brothers, John, an Oxford graduate, and Evan, her father named her as his executor and left her the bulk of his estate. Thanks to these unusually favourable circumstances she was able to pursue her career as a collector, copyist, and poet. She is the first documented woman compiler of Welsh manuscripts, and collected Welsh poetry from the middle ages to her own day, being active from about 1725 to 1776, judging by dates found in her manuscripts. Five volumes entirely in her own hand survive (Cwrtmawr MSS 128–9 and 448 and NL Wales, minor deposit, MS 56B; Cardiff MS 64) while at least three others (NL Wales, MS 653B, Cwrtmawr MS 27, and Cardiff MS 65) include portions in her hand. She owned older manuscripts too, notably Cardiff MS 66, a late seventeenth-century compilation in the hand of John Davies of Bronwion, Brithdir, probably a relative. She and her older contemporary, the poet Angharad James, are the only two women named in a list of owners of Welsh manuscripts compiled about 1740 by Lewis Morris. She also collected printed works, and was one of the few women subscribers to Huw Jones of Llangwm's important anthology of Welsh poetry *Dewisol ganiadau yr Oes hon* (1759).

Perhaps Davies's most valuable contribution was as a collector and copyist of women's poetry, recording, in Cwrtmawr MS 128 in particular, work by five women, including her niece Margaret Rowland, whose poems would otherwise be unknown. Letters preserved in her manuscripts reveal that she regularly paid visits to Brithdir, Dolgellau, and Llanelltyd in Meirioneth, and even to Llanllyfni, staying with friends and relatives. These often protracted visits provided opportunities for copying older material from written exemplars and for collecting orally transmitted poems. Into the latter category may fall the women's poems she collected, judging by their intimate, informal, and relaxed tone and the fact that they are composed mainly in the free metres and often patterned on popular tunes. It is not known for certain whether she ever met Angharad James: no documentary evidence has come to light to support J. H. Davies's contention (*Cymru*, 25 1903, 203–4) that they corresponded. But the copyist knew Angharad James's work, for the copy of the latter's elegy on the death of her son is in Margaret Davies's hand in Cardiff manuscript 64.

Davies probably spent her last years, from about 1766 onwards, with relatives at Y Goetre, Llanelltyd. She was still living in 1776, and it is possible, but not certain, that she was the Margaret Davies buried at Llanelltyd on 10 March 1785.   CERIDWEN LLOYD-MORGAN

Sources G. J. Williams, ed., 'Llythyrau at Dafydd Jones o Drefriw', *National Library of Wales Journal*, 3/2 (1943), 1–46 [suppl.] • C. Lloyd-Morgan, 'Oral composition and written transmission: Welsh women's poetry from the middle ages and beyond', *Trivium*, 26 (1991), 89–102 • [O. M. Edwards], 'Michael Pritchard o Llanllechid a Margaret Davies y Goetre', *Cymru*, 25 (1903), 93–8 • J. H. Davies, 'Margaret Davies o Goed Cae Du', *Cymru*, 25 (1903), 203–4 • NL Wales, Cwrtmawr MSS 27, 128–9, 448 • NL Wales, minor deposit MS 56B • Cardiff City Library, Cardiff MSS 64–65

Davies, Margaret Caroline Llewelyn (1861–1944), campaigner for women's causes, was born on 16 October 1861 in Marylebone, London, the youngest of seven children and only daughter of (John) Llewelyn *Davies (1826–1916), a Christian socialist, for many years rector of Christ Church, Marylebone, London, and later of Kirkby Lonsdale, Westmorland, and his wife, Mary (d. 1895), daughter of Sir Charles John *Crompton, justice of the queen's bench. She was educated at Queen's College, London, and Girton College, Cambridge (1881–3), which her aunt (Sarah) Emily Davies had helped to found.

Reared in the idealism of the Christian socialists, Margaret Llewelyn Davies became convinced that the theory of co-operation of the Rochdale Society of Equitable Pioneers provided an ideal basis for society, and joined the Marylebone branch of the Women's Co-operative Guild, which had been formed in 1883. With her Girton friend Rosalind Mary Shore Smith she investigated in 1888 profit-sharing workshops. In 1889 she became general secretary of the guild, which then had fifty-one branches and a membership of between 1700 and 1800. When she retired in 1922 there were 1038 branches with 52,000 members. In her thirty-two years of office, she never accepted a salary.

In 1889 her father moved to the parish of Kirkby Lonsdale and it was from his vicarage in this small town that Margaret, with the help of her lifelong friend Lilian Harris (d. 1950), ran the guild until 1908. Lilian was the daughter of Alfred Harris, a wealthy banker from Bradford. Margaret maintained close contact with the branches, especially in the north, and inspired many campaigns. In 1904 she published *The Women's Co-Operative Guild, 1883–1904*. In 1907 the central committee campaigned for a minimum wage for all women co-operative employees. By 1912, 200 retail societies and the Co-operative Wholesale Society had complied.

In 1909 Margaret Llewelyn Davies gave evidence to a royal commission on divorce law reform, and the guild began its advocacy for divorce on the same terms as men. In 1912 the guild annual congress passed a resolution that divorce should be available after two years' separation. Objections to this, particularly by Roman Catholic members of the co-operative movement, caused the central board of the Co-operative Union to decide to withdraw its £400 annual grant to the guild unless the divorce law campaign were dropped. Margaret Llewelyn Davies was adamant that in no circumstances would the guild surrender its independence and the branches raised sufficient funds to carry on the guild's work until a compromise was reached four years later. From 1904 the guild joined in the non-militant suffrage campaign. It also campaigned for maternity benefit to be paid to the mother and for maternity care to be improved, and, under Margaret Llewelyn Davies's leadership, took a strongly pacifist line. During the First World War she was elected to the general council of the Union of Democratic Control, which called for a negotiated peace.

In 1915 Margaret Llewelyn Davies compiled a deeply moving book, *Maternity: Letters from Working Women*, from the letters of 400 guild officials about their experiences of

Margaret Caroline Llewelyn Davies (1861–1944), by unknown photographer

childbirth and child-rearing. It had a preface by Herbert Samuel, then president of the Local Government Board, and made a considerable impact. In 1931 a similar compilation, *Life as we have Known it*, was published; it had an introduction by Margaret Llewelyn Davies's close friend Virginia Woolf.

The first woman president of the Co-operative Congress, Margaret Llewelyn Davies in the year of her retirement, 1922, declared:

> Our programme transfers the power of capitalism into the hands of the people organised democratically as consumers; makes capital the servant of labour; allows for a partnership with the workers; abolishes profit, socialises rent, and will ultimately get rid of the present wages system.

It is not for such radical views, strongly held though they were, that she is remembered, but for the understanding support she gave to thousands of working-class women, giving them the confidence to venture into public life. She was tall and gracious, with a deep voice and a strikingly vivid personality.

In 1921 Davies helped to found the International Women's Co-operative Guild. A supporter of the Russian Revolution, she was chair of the Society for Cultural Relations with the USSR from 1924 to 1928. She was a lifelong pacifist and throughout the 1920s was regarded as an outstanding campaigner in this field. She regarded the new methods of war then being developed as an example of capitalist exploitation which lined the pockets of the armaments manufacturers at the expense of the common man. She was an ardent supporter of the Peace Pledge Union (founded in 1934 by Canon Dick Shepherd), and

there is no doubt that her pacifism strongly influenced the co-operative guildswomen and must have led to the enthusiastic support of the 'white peace poppy', launched by her successor Eleanor Barton.

After moving from Kirkby Lonsdale in 1908 Davies settled in Hampstead, where she made a home for her father until his death in 1916. She continued to live there with her friend Lilian Harris before they settled at Hillspur, Punchbowl Lane, Dorking, Surrey. She died there on 28 May 1944.   MARY STOTT

Sources DLB · O. Banks, *The biographical dictionary of British feminists*, 1 (1985) · K. T. Butler and H. I. McMorran, eds., *Girton College register, 1869–1946* (1948) · *The Labour who's who* (1927)
Archives McMaster University, Hamilton, Ontario, corresp. with Bertrand Russell · U. Sussex, corresp. with Virginia Woolf and Leonard Woolf; letters to Leonard Woolf | SOUND BL NSA, documentary recording
Likenesses photograph, c.1922, repro. in *Report of the Co-operative Congress* (1922), frontispiece · photograph, U. Hull Archives [*see illus.*] · photographs, repro. in M. L. Davies, *The Women's Co-operative Guild, 1883–1904* (1904)
Wealth at death £23,081 8s.: probate, 14 July 1944, CGPLA Eng. & Wales

Davies, Margaret Sidney (1884–1963). *See under* Davies, Gwendoline Elizabeth (1882–1951).

Davies, Sir Martin (1908–1975), art gallery director, was born at Cheyne Walk, London, on 22 March 1908, the younger son and younger child of Ernest Woodbine Davies CBE, who worked at the stock exchange and later as chief inspector of aliens at the Home Office, and his wife, Elizabeth Eleanor, daughter of the Revd Isaac Taylor. Having attended Rugby School, he went up to King's College, Cambridge, in 1926. He obtained a third class in mathematics part 1 in 1927, and first class in parts 1 and 2 of the modern languages tripos, in 1928 and 1930. He joined the staff of the National Gallery, London, as an attaché in October 1930 and became part of that institution's permanent establishment on 1 January 1932, as assistant keeper.

From an early point in his career Davies played a significant role in developing a new critical approach to the study of the gallery's collection. In an issue of the *Burlington Magazine* of 1937 he announced the National Gallery's new objective: 'A proposed re-edition of the National Gallery catalogues to embody a scholarship more ample and more up-to-date has forced the staff to consider many difficult problems' (Davies, 88). The detailed, scholarly results of such research, both into the physical status of the paintings and their documentary contexts, were to be expressed by developing the catalogue entry, which Davies was to make into an exemplary discipline in itself. Of almost equal importance—and perhaps his first interest—were Davies's critical biographies of artists and their *œuvres*; he was always dismissive of inherited wisdom and speculative theory.

Davies's early concern with the Netherlandish school was interrupted from 1938 to 1941 by the task of finding a safe refuge where the collection could be housed to escape the bombardment of London. But as a result of his industry and dedication he had by the end of the Second World

War prepared catalogues of the Netherlandish, French, and British schools of painting; these were published in 1945 and 1946. In 1951 there followed his acclaimed catalogue *The Earlier Italian Schools*. He was responsible for revised editions of all these catalogues, which saw a new, exacting standard to which other institutions would aspire. His contribution to *Les primitifs Flamands: corpus de la peinture des anciens Pays Bas*, volume 3 (National Gallery, London), which updated his study of the gallery's Netherlandish holdings, was published in 1970.

Davies was made deputy keeper of the National Gallery in 1947 and keeper in 1960; in 1968 he was appointed director, a post that he held for five years. He followed the policies of his predecessor, Sir Philip Hendy; the remodelling of the display rooms and the programme of cleaning and restoration of paintings in the collection were both continued. He developed the educational services provided by the gallery, and in addition he was confronted by the inherited project of the building of a northern extension, which opened to the public three months after his death.

As director Davies insisted on the gallery's role in Britain as the prime public purchaser of masterpieces. The policy was put to the test in 1971, when he mounted the first public appeal made by the National Gallery itself for the outstanding amount of money required to purchase Titian's *Death of Actaeon*. The appeal was a success. Other notable acquisitions—of works by Duccio, G. B. Tiepolo, Rubens, Rogier van der Weyden (now attributed to the artist's workshop), and Henri Rousseau—were made during his directorship. His monograph on Rogier van der Weyden (1972) displayed many of his idiosyncrasies as both scholar and connoisseur.

Davies was a civil servant in the old mould—a precise, fastidious, and unobtrusive administrator. He never married, and his social life—at least in later years—centred on the Reform Club. Otherwise his life and career were bound up with the institution that he had joined as a young man. Indeed, the National Gallery and its staff were the chief beneficiary of his will. His unfailing courtesy, disdain for publicity (and those who sought it), and his retiring demeanour concealed a sharp view of human affairs that could be expressed with a marked, if oblique, wit.

Davies was elected a fellow of the British Academy in 1966, and in 1968 made an honorary DLitt of Exeter University. He was appointed CBE in 1965 and knighted in 1972. He died in St Stephen's Hospital, London, on 7 March 1975.   GREGORY MARTIN

Sources *Sir Martin Davies*, Trustees of the National Gallery (1975) · *Annual Report of the Council* [King's College, Cambridge] (1975) · M. Levey, 'Sir Martin Davies', *Burlington Magazine*, 117 (1975), 729–31 · E. Waterhouse, 'Martin Davies, 1908–1975', *PBA*, 61 (1975), 561–5 · personal knowledge (2004) · M. Davies, 'National Gallery notes', *Burlington Magazine*, 70 (Feb 1937), 88–92 · *CGPLA Eng. & Wales* (1975)

Archives National Gallery, London, personal papers | Harvard University, near Florence, Italy, Center for Italian Renaissance Studies, letters to Bernard Berenson

Wealth at death £109,308: probate, 3 June 1975, *CGPLA Eng. & Wales*

Davies, Mary Ann [Marianne] (1743/4–1818), instrumentalist and singer, was the daughter of the flautist and composer Richard Davies (*d.* 1773) and sister of the soprano Cecilia *Davies. She is often found in reference books as Marianne Davies, the form of her name that she used when writing in French. At her first public appearance at the age of seven at Hickford's Great Room, London, on 30 April 1751 she played a harpsichord concerto by Handel and two flute concertos (one composed by herself) and sang. Two songs composed by her father in praise of her musical skills were published in the early 1750s. Mary Ann had annual benefit concerts in London until 1761; she continued to perform on both flute and harpsichord but was not advertised as singing again until 1760, when she also played an organ concerto. In autumn 1755 she went with her father to Dublin, where she played the flute between the acts at the Smock Alley Theatre. Back in London, she played the Irish tune 'Ellen a Roon' at Covent Garden on 23 March 1756.

Mary Ann was the first to play Benjamin Franklin's new version of the musical glasses, his glassychord or armonica, introducing the instrument to the public at Bath and Bristol in January 1762. It became the family's main means of livelihood. For several weeks a venue was hired where Mary Ann gave performances on the armonica, sometimes accompanied by her father on the flute; she sang to her own armonica accompaniment and played the flute and harpsichord. Private demonstrations of the armonica were given and Mary Ann taught the harpsichord and singing. Such series took place in London in 1762–4. Mary Ann played the armonica at the Crow Street Theatre, Dublin, in the winter of 1763–4 and then gave armonica demonstrations and sang in Dublin oratorio performances organized by Passerini. The Davies family travelled to Paris after their 1764 London concerts and Mary Ann next played the armonica in London between June and August 1767. Her young sister, Cecilia, sang at the last three of these concerts.

The Davies family then began a European tour, armed with letters of recommendation from J. C. Bach and others stressing their musicality, virtue, and Roman Catholicism. In Vienna the sisters found favour with Empress Maria Theresa and lodged in the same house as Johann Adolf Hasse, who composed *L'armonica*, a cantata with words by Pietro Metastasio, for them to perform at a royal wedding in June 1769. Metastasio praised Mary Ann's skill and the 'uncommonly sweet, and celestial tones' of her instrument (Burney, *Metastasio*, 83). The family went on to Italy, and had a joyful reunion with the Mozart family at Milan in September 1771. (The date of their first meeting is not known.) In 1772 Cecilia sang at opera houses in Naples and Florence, after which the family returned to London.

With Cecilia's success Mary Ann no longer needed to give armonica performances. In her journal Fanny Burney blamed Mary Ann for Cecilia's problems at the Italian Opera in London. She described her as 'short, crooked &

squat' (*Early Journals*, 106). Mary Ann became ill and the sisters returned to the continent, meeting Franklin in Paris in 1778. In April 1783, after a further lengthy illness and the loss of their money through a failed investment, Mary Ann wrote from Florence to Franklin, her 'worthy Friend and Benefactor', unsuccessfully seeking his help in obtaining a pension from Marie Antoinette. The sisters were enabled to return to England in 1786 by the proceeds of a concert, at which they both performed, arranged by English residents of Florence at the instigation of the second earl of Mount Edgcumbe. Cecilia obtained a few more engagements but they later supported themselves by giving music lessons. Mary Ann was in poor health by 1813 and died in London, in late December 1818. She was buried on 5 January 1819 at St Marylebone. Cecilia remained devoted to her memory.

OLIVE BALDWIN and THELMA WILSON

Sources *General Advertiser* (30 April 1751) · *General Advertiser* (24 April 1752) · *Public Advertiser* (19 March 1753) · *Public Advertiser* (5 Feb 1754) · *Public Advertiser* (18 March 1755) · *Public Advertiser* (23 March 1756) · *Public Advertiser* (15 April 1756) · *Public Advertiser* (28 Feb 1757) · *Public Advertiser* (27 Feb 1758) · *Public Advertiser* (9 Feb 1759) · *Public Advertiser* (28 Jan 1760) · *Public Advertiser* (2 March 1761) · *Public Advertiser* (18 Feb–13 Aug 1762) · *Public Advertiser* (10 Feb–29 Aug 1763) · *Public Advertiser* (9 July–8 Sept 1764) · *Public Advertiser* (1 June–14 Aug 1767) · *Dublin Journal* (1x5 Nov 1763–5x8 May 1764) · *Bath Journal* (11 Jan 1762) · *Felix Farley's Bristol Journal* (23–30 Jan 1762) · B. Boydell, *A Dublin musical calendar, 1700–1760* (1988) · B. Matthews, 'The Davies sisters, J. C. Bach and the glass harmonica', *Music and Letters*, 56 (1975), 150–69 · *The papers of Benjamin Franklin*, 10, ed. L. W. Labaree (1966) · *The papers of Benjamin Franklin*, 25, ed. W. B. Willcox and others (1986) · *The papers of Benjamin Franklin*, 27, ed. C. A. Lopez and others (1988) · *The papers of Benjamin Franklin*, 31, ed. B. B. Oberg and others (1995) · Marianne [Mary Ann] Davies to Franklin, 26 April 1783 and 17 Oct 1783, American Philosophical Society, Philadelphia, Franklin MSS · S. H. Hansell, *Works for solo voice of Johann Adolph Hasse* (1968) · C. Burney, *Memoirs of the life and writings of the Abate Metastasio*, 3 (1796) · *The Harmonicon* (1828), 126–7 · *The Harmonicon* (1832), 184 · E. Anderson, ed., *The letters of Mozart and his family* (1985) · R. Edgcumbe, *Musical reminiscences of an old amateur: chiefly respecting the Italian opera in England for fifty years, from 1773 to 1823*, 2nd edn (1827) · *The early journals and letters of Fanny Burney*, ed. L. E. Troide, 2: *1774–1777* (1990) · *Musical World* (1836), 1.47
Archives Dorset RO, Solly MSS, D/RAC 79, 102, 103, 108, 113, 115, 140

Davies, Myles (*b.* 1662, *d.* in or after 1719), bibliographer, was born at Tre'r Abad, in the parish of Whitford, Flintshire, the son of George Davies and Elizabeth Blount. The family were Roman Catholics, and on 28 September 1686 Davies was admitted into the English College at Rome; he took the oath on 10 May 1687 and was ordained priest on 17 April 1688. He left on 15 October 1688 with a letter from Cardinal Philip Howard, protector of the college, to the bishop who had jurisdiction in Wales. According to the dedication of his recantation of 1705, he had been educated in the seminaries of St Omer, Douai, Liège, Paris, and Rome; after his return he acted as 'missioner and popish emissary in Worcestershire, Glocestershire, Herefordshire, Flintshire, &c. and popish confessor and chaplain to the Roman catholick families at Hill-End, at Malvern and Blackmore Park, and others, near the city of Worcester' (Davies, *Recantation*, title-page). He explains in the preface

that when abroad he had gone under his mother's family name of Blount, but that in Britain he had been known as Pollet. The recantation, embodying a sermon on Revelation 18:4, is dedicated to William Beveridge, later bishop of St Asaph, as a result of whose ministry at St Peter Cornhill Davies eventually conformed to the Church of England. His career for the next ten years is obscure, but he seems to have taught French and Italian, and taken part in religious controversy (from an extreme anti-Catholic and anti-Jesuit angle), though this gained him no advancement in the church. He also refers to himself on the title-pages of his later publications as a barrister-at-law or a counsellor, but there is no evidence that he was a member of any of the inns of court. His education had, however, equipped him to write adulatory verse in Latin, which, like his later books, he dedicated to persons of eminence (including royalty after 1715), often without receiving any money in return, but rather ridicule and humiliation.

Davies began the series of volumes later entitled *Athenae Britannicae* in 1715, with *Eikōn mikro-biblikē, sive, Icon libellorum, or, A Critical History of Pamphlets ... by a Gentleman of the Inns of Court*. It was reissued in the following year under the author's name, with the title *Athenae Britannicae*, and this title, an allusion perhaps to the author's origins, recurs spasmodically in the subsequent volumes. In total there are six volumes, all except volume 4 in octavo format; the imprint suggests that they were issued at Davies's expense, from the corner of Little Queen Street, Holborn, London, which was perhaps where the author was living. They contain a great deal of bibliographical information about pamphlets and controversial writings, evidently gleaned from libraries in London, and perhaps Oxford, which Davies frequented. Rancour against the Church of Rome, and against the Jesuits in particular, is omnipresent. The fourth volume, in substantial quarto format, collects several series of educational 'posts', in the newly popular periodical form, notably a *Lawyer's Post* in fourteen numbers, though whether these were separately distributed is unclear. Volume 6, 'Containing the present and former state of physick, diseases, patients, quacks and doctors', with dedications to eminent members of the profession, may indicate that Davies, having exhausted the benevolence of the church and the law, was cultivating medicine. The latest date in any part of the *Athenae Britannicae* is 1719, and Davies may have died about that time or shortly after, presumably in London.

The incoherence of Davies's method and presentation have obscured the true bibliographical merits and lively style of his books, which are not as rare as they have been thought to be. Isaac D'Israeli, to whom Davies's biography was otherwise unknown, drew a colourful picture of Davies as a 'Mendicant Author, the hawker of his own works' (D'Israeli, 1.67), whose life was passed in the study of languages and the sciences, who was 'not only surrounded by his books, but with the more urgent companions of a wife and family' (ibid., 1.70), 'while his faculties appear to have been disordered from the simplicity of his nature, and driven to madness by indigence and insult' (ibid., 1.67).

R. JULIAN ROBERTS

Sources R. G. Thomas, 'Myles Davies of Tre'rabbat: a candidate for Pope's *Dunciad*?', *Transactions of the Honourable Society of Cymmrodorion* (1963), 33–47 · M. Davies, *Athenae Britannicae, 1716–1719*, ed. R. G. Thomas (1962) · M. Davies, *Recantation of Mr Pollet, a Roman priest* (1705) · H. Foley, ed., *Records of the English province of the Society of Jesus*, 6 (1880), 43–7 · [I. D'Israeli], *Calamities of authors*, 1 (1812), 66–80 · *DNB*
Wealth at death nothing: *Athenae Britannicae*, ed. Thomas

Davies, Owen (1752–1830), Welsh Wesleyan Methodist minister, was one of twin sons born in Wrexham to Owen Davies (*b.* 1724/5), a tailor; he was baptized on 28 March 1752. He went to London in his youth and then moved to Brentford, where he became a Wesleyan Methodist. There he married a widow, Mrs Hemans, who was a schoolmistress at Ealing, and whose son Thomas also entered the Methodist ministry. In 1789 Davies was appointed an itinerant preacher, and, in 1800, on the establishment of the Welsh Wesleyan Mission, he was sent to Wales as superintendent to work alongside John Hughes (1776–1843).

Davies was a capable administrator and a persuasive preacher. Although he was unable to preach fluently or write in Welsh, several of his works were translated from English. These include a defence of Wesleyan Methodism, a criticism of Calvinism, a catechism for children, and collections of sermons. He died in Liverpool on 12 January 1830 and was buried there at the Brunswick Methodist Chapel; his main achievement was to have done much to lay the foundations of Wesleyan Methodism in Wales.

THOMPSON COOPER, *rev.* DYLAN FOSTER EVANS

Sources J. Hughes, 'Memoir of the Rev. Owen Davies', *Wesleyan Methodist Magazine*, 55 (1832), 389ff. · A. H. Williams, *Welsh Wesleyan Methodism* (1935), 85–7, 140–42 · E. Rees, ed., *Libri Walliae: a catalogue of Welsh books and books printed in Wales, 1546–1820*, 1 (1987), 194–5 · O. Thomas, *Cofiant y Parchedig John Jones, Talsara* (1874), 281–4
Likenesses W. Holl, engraving (after N. Branwhite), repro. in *Methodist Magazine* (1809)

Davies, Rhys [Rees Vivian] (1901–1978), novelist and short-story writer, was born on 9 November 1901 at 6 Clydach Road, Blaenclydach, a village in a tributary valley of the Rhondda, near Tonypandy in Glamorgan. The district was dominated by the presence of two large collieries which were to become the focus of industrial strife during the Tonypandy riots of 1910. Davies's father, Thomas Rees Davies (1872–1955), kept a grocer's shop known rather grandly as the Royal Stores; his mother, Sarah Ann, *née* Lewis (1877–1956), was an uncertificated teacher. Rhys (the Welsh form of his name which he used for all his writing) was the second of three sons, the eldest of whom was killed in the closing weeks of the First World War, and the fourth of six children. His parents were Welsh-speaking, but they did not pass the language on to their children, and he grew up with only a few Welsh phrases at his command. As a boy he attended a nonconformist chapel, and later an Anglican church, but in later life was to declare himself an atheist. At the age of twelve he became a pupil at Porth county school, but was not happy there and did not distinguish himself academically. He left two years later, much to the chagrin of his parents for whom education seemed to be the surest way of avoiding the pits, and

Rhys Davies (1901–1978), by Howard Coster, 1940

began helping behind the shop counter. His parents' status as shopkeepers set them apart from a community dependent on coalmining, and some of his attitudes were distinctly *petit bourgeois*, but in the shop's daily routine he came into contact with local people, particularly the womenfolk, for whom he felt a deep sympathy; many of his stories are written from a woman's point of view. For the next five years, having resisted parental ambition for him to work in a bank, he read avidly, mainly the French and Russian classics, and made his first attempts at writing. A growing awareness of his own homosexuality, however, eventually made life in the male-dominated society of the Rhondda valley unbearable, and, daunted by what he saw as the narrowness of its chapel culture, he went to live for a while in Cardiff, where he found work in a corn merchant's warehouse. He was never to live permanently in south Wales again, but its ethos had marked him indelibly and provided him with an inexhaustible source of material for his writing.

Soon afterwards, drawn to London, Davies embarked on his literary career. On a wet Sunday in 1924 he sat down in his lodgings in Manor Park, near Ilford, and wrote three short stories which were published in a small, left-wing, avant-garde magazine, the *New Coterie*, distributed by Charles Lahr, a German-born bibliophile and owner of the Progressive Bookshop in Holborn. Davies's first collection of stories, *The Song of Songs*, and his first novel, *The Withered Root*, were published in 1927. The public response to these books was favourable, and he now found himself taken up as an original new talent, especially among those who admired the work of D. H. Lawrence. With an advance on a second novel, he was able to give up the menial jobs on which he had subsisted and become a full-time writer.

The rest of Davies's life was without great incident. His habits were sedentary and abstemious, though he was not averse to the social life of Fitzrovia and going to the theatre occasionally. During a visit to the south of France in the winter of 1928–9, he was invited to spend some time with Lawrence and his wife Frieda at Bandol, near Toulon; their friendship is described in Davies's autobiography, *Print of a Hare's Foot* (1969). Although his literary output throughout the 1930s was prolific—he published seven collections of stories, six novels, and three novellas during the decade—financial success eluded him. Unable to settle at any one address, he lived a peripatetic life until he was offered accommodation at the home of Vincent Wells, a wealthy homosexual, in Henley-on-Thames, an arrangement which lasted until 1945, when the house caught fire and Davies's papers were destroyed. He also shared a small house with the Scottish writer Fred Urquhart (1912–1995) near Tring in the Chilterns, and later with other male friends in Brighton. The finest of his stories written during the 1930s and 1940s appeared in *The Things Men Do* (1936) and *A Finger in every Pie* (1942), and the best of his novels from this period are *Jubilee Blues* (1938) and *Black Venus* (1944). His *Selected Stories* was published in 1945 and his *Collected Stories* in 1955.

After the Second World War, when the popularity of the short story declined, Davies sought a new market for his work in the United States, publishing stories in the *New Yorker* and the *Saturday Evening Post*; they included 'The Chosen One', which won the Edgar award for crime fiction in 1966. Honours came his way, too. In 1968 he was made an OBE and, two years later, the Welsh Arts Council made him a financial award in recognition of his contribution to the literature of Wales. Two more of his novels appeared: *Nobody Answered the Bell* (1971), an account of a lesbian relationship, and *Honeysuckle Girl* (1975), about a heroin addict. His last years were made more comfortable by a legacy from the estate of the writer Anna Kavan, and, a year before his death, his patron, Louise Taylor (the adopted daughter and heir of Alice B. Toklas, the companion of Gertrude Stein), left him money in her will. He contemplated a world cruise, but was found to have lung cancer. He died at St Pancras Hospital, London, on 21 August 1978 and a few days later, after a brief secular service, his body was cremated at Golders Green in the presence of his brother Lewis and a few friends. *The Best of Rhys Davies* (1979), the novel *Ram with Red Horns* (1996), and *Collected Stories* (ed. M. Stephens, vols. 1–2, 1996; vol. 3, 1998) were published posthumously. The Rhys Davies Trust, a charity founded in 1990 and endowed by the writer's brother Lewis, promotes Welsh writing in English.

MEIC STEPHENS

Sources M. Stephens, introduction, in R. Davies, *Collected stories*, ed. M. Stephens, 3 vols. (1996–8) · R. Davies, *Print of a hare's foot* (1969); new edn (1998) · D. Callard, 'Rhys Davies', DLitB · personal knowledge (2004) · private information (2004) · R. Mathias, *Contemporary novelists*, ed. J. Vinson, 2nd edn (1976) · J. Harris and E. J. Davies, *A bibliographical guide to twenty-four modern Anglo-Welsh writers* (1994) · D. Rees, *Rhys Davies* (1975) · G. F. Adam, *Three contemporary Anglo-Welsh novelists: Jack Jones, Rhys Davies and Hilda Vaughan* (1948) · R. L. Mégroz, *Rhys Davies: a critical sketch* (1932) · b. cert. · d. cert. · M. Stephens, ed., *Decoding the hare: critical essays to mark the centenary of the writer's birth* (2001)

Archives NL Wales, papers · Ransom HRC, corresp. and literary papers | LUL, literary MSS and letters to Charles Lahr · NL Wales, letters to R. B. Marriott · NL Wales, letters and cards to Louis F. Quinain | FILM BBC Wales

Likenesses H. Coster, photograph, 1940, NPG [*see illus.*] · photographs, priv. coll.

Wealth at death £81,346: administration, 15 March 1979, *CGPLA Eng. & Wales*

Davies, Richard (*c.*1505–1581), bishop of St David's and biblical translator, was born at Plas y Person, Gyffin, Caernarvonshire, the son of Dafydd ap Gronw, curate of Gyffin in the diocese of Bangor, and his 'wife', Sioned, daughter of Dafydd ap Richard; such clerical marriages were common in Wales before the Reformation. Both parents were of gentle stock; Davies's father was descended from the line of Ithel Felyn and his mother from Ednowain Bendew. He was reputedly born in either 1501 or 1509, although a date of about 1505 would best fit other facts known about him. No certainty exists concerning his early education, but his kinsman, a leading poet, Gruffudd ab Ieuan ap Llywelyn Fychan (*c.*1485–1553), seems to have given him the run of his library. He entered New Inn Hall, Oxford, about 1522 or 1523, where he graduated MA in 1530 and BTh in 1536. He was created DTh at London on 30 October 1566 by virtue of a commission from the University of Oxford.

It was at Oxford in his youth that Davies appears to have been converted to his reforming beliefs. His movements between 1536 and 1549 are obscure; but he may have remained at the university and may also have been the canon called Richard Davies preferred at St Asaph in 1540. He was certainly presented by Edward VI to the living of Maidsmorton, Buckinghamshire, in 1549 and to neighbouring Burnham, a traditional stronghold of Lollardy, in 1550. Such royal patronage strongly suggests protestant sympathies on his part. This is further attested by his taking advantage of the act of parliament of 1549 to marry Dorothy, the daughter of Thomas Woodforde, gentleman, of Brightwell, Burnham. Following the accession of Queen Mary, Davies was summoned to appear before the privy council on 17 September 1553—presumably on account of his heretical opinions. By December 1553 he had been replaced as vicar of Burnham. Richard Davies may also be the married cleric of that name ejected from Northales, Suffolk, in 1555. In the same year, he and his wife and family withdrew into exile in Europe. His name is found in the city records of Frankfurt am Main in 1555 and 1557, but not in those of Geneva, where Sir John Wynn believed that Davies had taken refuge, a claim that has been followed by many later historians. While he was in Frankfurt Davies sided with the more conservative wing of the exiles who stood by the Book of Common Prayer. His contacts with exiles like Richard Cox and Edmund

Grindal, both to be influential leaders of the Elizabethan church, may well have been of considerable influence in shaping his later career.

Davies returned from Europe in 1559 following Elizabeth I's accession in the previous November. In July 1559 he was appointed to lead the panel of royal visitors entrusted with enforcing the Elizabethan church settlement in the four dioceses of Wales and those of Worcester and Hereford. Simultaneously, contemporary visitors in the county of Buckingham restored his living of Burnham to him. In the course of his own visitation, begun at Llandaff in August 1559, Davies was elected as bishop of St Asaph on 4 December 1559. He was consecrated at Lambeth on 21 January 1560 by Archbishop Parker and was allowed to retain *in commendam* his two Buckinghamshire livings, the rectory of Llansanffraid-ym-Mechain, Montgomeryshire, and a canonry at St Asaph. His tenure at St Asaph was short, but not without significance. In response to an enquiry from Archbishop Parker of November 1560, he dispatched a valuable report on the state of his clergy: how many were resident, in orders, married, learned, and able to preach. He also established friendly relations with a circle of learned humanists in his diocese, of whom the most notable were William Salesbury, Humphrey Llwyd, and Gruffudd Hiraethog.

On 21 May 1561 Davies was moved to St David's to succeed Thomas Young, who had been translated to York as archbishop. For the next twenty years he would be the leading figure in the Welsh church. His new diocese was much the largest and most lucrative bishopric in Wales. It sprawled over about three-quarters of south Wales, was mountainous and thinly populated (about 80,000–90,000 inhabitants in 1563), had poor communications, and was difficult to administer. It had been the scene of fierce conflicts, religious and personal; most of its livings were poorly remunerated; there was a shortage of clergy, particularly of educated men who could preach; and a majority of its population was Welsh-speaking and conservative by religious inclination, but no provision had yet been made in the way of Welsh bibles or prayer books. Davies's sole surviving register, dating from 1561 to 1565, although giving evidence of his diligence in seeking, ordaining, and installing suitable clergy, also reveals the very slow improvement being achieved.

More important was the lead Davies gave in seeking a Welsh translation of the scriptures, his countrymen's most pressing religious need. It was he, William *Salesbury, and Humphrey *Llwyd who were probably responsible for securing the private act of parliament of 1563, which authorized the translation into Welsh of the Bible and the Book of Common Prayer and their use within all parishes where the language normally spoken by the population was Welsh. Davies also appears to have steered the passage of the act through the House of Lords. To expedite work on the translation he invited Salesbury to the episcopal palace at Abergwili. Salesbury undertook the bulk of the work, being responsible for translating the Book of Common Prayer and most of the New Testament.

Davies's share consisted of translating 1 Timothy, Hebrews, James, and 1 and 2 Peter, while the precentor of St David's, Thomas *Huet, translated the book of Revelation. Both the prayer book and the New Testament were published in 1567, the prayer book appearing first.

Davies was an accomplished author, writing Welsh with greater ease and fluency than his more celebrated collaborator, Salesbury. He also prefaced the New Testament with a highly influential letter addressed to the Welsh nation ('Epistol at y Cembru'). This rewrote Welsh church history from a protestant standpoint from the time of the ancient Britons onwards. It maintained that the island of Britain had first been converted to Christianity by Joseph of Arimathea in apostolic times. It emphasized two cardinal points in order to rebut central criticisms usually levied against the Reformation in Wales: that it was new-fangled heresy; and that it was the faith of Saxons. Conversely, Davies contended that it was the religion of the earliest forefathers of the Welsh, and that superstitious Roman beliefs and practices had been introduced into Wales at the point of the sword by the papal emissary, Augustine of Canterbury, and his Anglo-Saxon minions. This revamping of traditional history was to be extremely influential for centuries to come. Davies also participated in the English Bible of 1568 known as the Bishops' Bible. At Parker's invitation he translated the books of the Old Testament from Joshua to 2 Samuel. He and Salesbury had originally intended to translate the Old Testament into Welsh, and they continued with their task after 1567, but never succeeded in completing it. According to Sir John Wynn, their failure to do so was caused by a quarrel between them over a single word, but it may very well have been due to a difference over the wider issue of how best to present the Welsh language in print.

Davies was, without doubt, one of the most active and vocal champions of the Reformation in Wales. His 'Letter to the Welsh nation', his comprehensive diocesan report (1570), and the *Funeral Sermon* (1577) on the earl of Essex are some of the most forthright statements in favour of protestant reform issued by any Welshman during the period. He condemned the 'great number' in his diocese who were 'slow and cold in the true service of God, some careless for any religion and some that wish the Romish religion', while others indulged in 'pilgrimages to wells and watchings in chapels and desert places' and were 'bearers of superstition and idolatry' (Thomas, 33, 43). He was unsparing in his criticism of the clergy's inadequacies and their failure to preach regularly, and urged the privy council to take appropriate remedial steps. He further drew the council's attention to the desperate poverty of many livings and how this inevitably led to pluralism, non-residence, and failure to hold services regularly. He criticized the tendency among clergy to 'serve three or four, yea sometimes five livings, but never one aright', and to 'come hither galloping from another parish' (ibid., 43), so that the parishioners were little or nothing the better for it.

Himself a learned man, and praised by contemporaries not only for his knowledge of Latin, Greek, and Hebrew but also for his familiarity with French and German, Davies was anxious to maintain his own contacts with scholarly circles. He was in correspondence with Matthew Parker and Sir William Cecil on topics of mutual interest, and kept up his links with the humanist circle around Edmund Grindal and the poet Spenser. In the latter's *Shepherd's Calendar* Davies is very probably the original on whom one of the shepherds, Diggon Davie, is based. He maintained at Abergwili a lively and bountiful household, the subject of much praise by some of his contemporaries. Regular preaching of the gospel was heard there, and he hosted a wide range of scholars, clerics, and men of letters. Davies also recognized the pressing need to raise the level of education among the clergy. To this end he was associated with his friend Walter Devereux, first earl of Essex, whom he praised so warmly in the *Funeral Sermon* to him as an outstanding embodiment of the virtues of protestant aristocratic humanism. In 1576 they joined together to take a leading role in founding Queen Elizabeth Grammar School at Carmarthen, which was to make an invaluable contribution to the education of the clergy in the diocese for centuries to come. On the other hand, Davies was himself censured for bestowing valuable benefices on friends and relatives. He placed Philip Sidney, son of his friend Sir Henry Sidney, as a prebendary when only ten years of age. His own sons, Peregrine and Gerson, also benefited from their father's solicitude. The former became archdeacon of Cardigan at the age of ten, and the latter received preferment worth £110 a year when he was seventeen. Davies's successor at St David's, Marmaduke Middleton, accused him of alienating the bishop's rights of advowson over all livings worth more than £10 per annum, although the chapter records show him to have granted only 38 out of about 150 within his gift.

Davies blamed the laity for many of the deficiencies apparent in the contemporary church and among its clergy. He was appalled by the 'insatiable covetousness and ambition' that reigned on all sides: the 'whole world seeketh to be made blessed by worldly goods and possessions' (Davies, ciii). He accused the office-holding gentry of being responsible for conniving at pluralism and simony and highlighted their reluctance to impose discipline on clerics and laymen: 'they continue the kingdom of Antichrist, defend papistry, superstition and idolatry, pilgrimages to wells and blind chapels', 'procure the wardens of churches to perjury, to conceal images, rood lofts and altars' (Davies, ciii–civ). He unreservedly condemned the absence of scruple on the part of what he described as the 'insatiable cormorants' with which his diocese abounded. The most damaging loss inflicted by these predators was occasioned by George Cary, groom of the queen's chamber, who procured a commission of concealment to inquire into the state of the church of Llanddewibrefi, which he claimed to be a collegiate church being unlawfully withheld from the crown. There ensued a prolonged legal battle which did not end until after Davies's death, with Cary victorious. The victor was then permitted by the queen to lease the church and its prebends for £40 a year, which he promptly sublet for £140 a year. The outcome

was that the annual revenues of St David's diocese were reduced from £457 to £263.

Davies's talents as an administrator were freely employed on secular as well as religious affairs. He attended the House of Lords and the upper house of convocation regularly, though without playing an outstanding role in either. He served as a justice of the peace and as a member of the council in the marches, which commissioned him to act on its behalf to execute a variety of administrative tasks. The most taxing of the duties assigned to him was to act as the privy council's representative in dealing with piracy along the south Wales coast in 1565, 1572, and 1578. Piracy was increasingly prevalent in south-western Wales and was made all the worse by the complicity of the local population. Coping with it was a thankless and burdensome task, which led to friction between the bishop and two prominent local landowners, Sir John Perrott and Richard Vaughan. Another neighbour with whom Davies quarrelled was a fellow member of the council in the marches, Fabian Phillips, who took him to task for his laxity over moral delinquency in the diocese and for blatantly siding with his son-in-law, William Penry, in a dispute between the latter and Phillips's kinsmen.

Davies was the subject of a number of tributes by contemporaries. He was, as might be expected, lavishly applauded by the Welsh poets Wiliam Llŷn, Wiliam Cynwal, Hywel ap Syr Mathew, and Robert Middleton, all of whom had been recipients of his generosity. Two leading antiquaries also testified enthusiastically to his merits. Sir John Wynn described him as a 'rare scholar and especially an Hebrician', and spoke of how his heart warmed 'in recording the memory of so worthy a man' (Wynn, 64–5). George Owen, for his part, declared that Davies was a:

> man no less in his time much reverenced for his rare virtues and excellency in learning … than honoured for his public hospitality and liberality … bearing himself as he was inwardly affected of the good, and never detracted but of the bad. (Owen, 1.240)

Davies made his will on 13 September 1581, in which he provided for his widow, three sons, and two daughters. He died on 7 November 1581 at the bishop's palace in Abergwili, Carmarthenshire, and was buried in the churchyard at Abergwili, as requested in his will. His original gravestone has disappeared, but he is commemorated as one of the translators of the Welsh Bible in the national memorial erected at St Asaph in 1888.

GLANMOR WILLIAMS

Sources DNB · DWB · D. R. Thomas, *Life of Richard Davies and William Salesbury* (1908) · F. O. White, *Lives of the Elizabethan bishops* (1908) · G. Williams, *Bywyd ac amserau'r Esgob Richard Davies* (1953) · G. Williams, *Welsh Reformation essays* (1967) · G. Williams, *Wales and the Reformation* (1997) · C. Ashton, *Bywyd ac amserau'r Esgob William Morgan* (1891) · [W. Whittingham?], *A brieff discours off the troubles begonne at Franckford* (1575); repr. with introduction by [J. Petheram] as *A brief discourse of the troubles begun at Frankfort* (1846) · R. Davies, *A funerall sermon preached the xxvi. day of November MDLXXVI … at the buriale of the … Earl of Essex* (1577) · E. Yardley, *Menevia sacra*, ed. F. Green (1927) · W. B. Jones and E. A. Freeman, *The history of St. David's* (1856) · *Willis' survey of St Asaph, considerably*

enlarged and brought down to the present time, ed. E. Edwards, 2 vols. (1801) · *Testament Newydd, 1567* (1840) · A. O. Evans, *Memorandum on the legality of the Welsh Bible* (1925) [incl. trans. of 'Epistol at y Cembru'] · J. Wynn, *The history of the Gwydir family*, ed. J. Ballinger (1927) · C. H. Garrett, *The Marian exiles: a study in the origins of Elizabethan puritanism* (1938) · E. Spenser, *The shepherd's calendar*, ed. W. L. Renwick (1930) · G. Owen, *The description of Penbrokshire*, ed. H. Owen, 4 vols., Honourable Society of Cymmrodorion, Cymmrodorion Record Series, 1 (1892–1936), pts 1–3
Archives NL Wales, St David's bishop's register
Likenesses memorial, 1888, St Asaph Cathedral
Wealth at death see will, Thomas, *Life*, appx E, 53–6

Davies, Richard (*bap.* 1635, *d.* 1708), Quaker preacher and autobiographer, was baptized on 22 March 1635 at Welshpool, Montgomeryshire, the son of Edward Davies. The name of his mother is unknown.

Richard Davies's parents had a small estate and he was given 'a little learning' (Davies, 13). Brought up an Anglican, at twelve or thirteen he was troubled concerning the state of his soul. He attached himself to the Independents (fairly numerous in the area), attended their meetings in various parishes, and even wrote some of their sermons. He was bound apprentice to a felt maker of the same persuasion but he soon eagerly espoused the beliefs of a visiting Quaker. His lifelong convincement had begun. The fury of the Independents was unabated (for Davies's apostasy was not exceptional), especially that of his master's wife, who severely assaulted him because he addressed her in 'the pure language of *Thee* and *Thou*' (ibid., 25). Ostracized by relations, neighbours, and former friends, he was overwhelmed by depression and he long remembered sitting 'under an ash tree, weeping and mourning' (ibid., 35). A handful of kindred spirits, widely scattered and without a home of their own, held meetings on the sheltered side of a hill. As occasionally happened to Friends, they were looked upon as witches.

Apprenticeship completed, Davies settled in his trade in London, where he married a Quaker at the Horselydown meeting, Southwark, on 26 June 1659. She died in 1705, and may be the Tace Davies who signed the Quaker women's petition against tithes in 1659. However, Davies became convinced that God intended him to bear witness in Wales and to Welshpool he returned with his wife. They were later compared to Zacharias and Elisabeth 'walking in all the commandments and ordinances of the Lord blameless' (Davies, 52). There speedily followed bouts of imprisonment, for instance in Montgomery in 1660 and in Shrewsbury in 1661. They did not, however, last long in his case. Seldom a 'close' prisoner, he was usually allowed almost unlimited freedom, which he used to great effect.

Davies was a central figure in the monthly meetings of north Wales Quakers, notably at Dolobran, Meifod parish, Montgomeryshire, where Quakers were relatively strong. He was one of the foremost apostles of Quakerism in Wales, often preaching in Welsh, an indispensable requirement if Quakerism was to prosper in Wales. At Whitehall he spoke Welsh to his countryman, the querulous secretary of state, Sir Leoline Jenkins, concerning the first appearance of Christianity in the British Isles. He was one of two selected to distribute devotional books sent to Wales from Devonshire House and it was he who successfully pressed for a measure of devolution whereby Welsh Friends had their own yearly meetings.

In confrontations with high and low, Davies avoided the self-righteous admonitions not infrequently delivered with gusto by some early Quakers. His calm, courteous demeanour tended to disarm antagonists, but there was more to it than sanctified tact. It was his shining sincerity. He may not have entirely won the day with Edward, third Baron Herbert of Cherbury, but he was on the best of terms with Bishop William Lloyd of St Asaph (later one of the 'Seven Bishops'). Although his exchanges at Whitehall with Leoline Jenkins began badly, they concluded cordially, Jenkins thereafter apparently moderating his asperity towards Quakers. At Oxford in 1706 unruly students interrupted a Quaker meeting, but having heard Davies they sobered down, some remaining until the end of the proceedings.

Davies consulted lawyers in order to discover loopholes in the law. Thomas Corbet, 'the Welch counsellor' (Davies, 104), as he became known, a barrister who lived in Davies's neighbourhood, often advised him. Corbet was largely instrumental in securing George Fox's release from Worcester gaol in 1675, having argued in Westminster Hall before Sir Matthew Hale and others that no one should be imprisoned upon the writ of *praemunire*, which had long oppressed Quakers. Fox acknowledged Davies's role in arranging for Corbet to act on his behalf.

Davies was well known to English Friends. He attended meetings in the Severn and the Thames valleys, frequently accompanied, as elsewhere, by his daughter Tace. On one occasion he was away from home for three months. To London Friends he was a familiar figure. His reputation was such that the yearly meeting of Friends in England appointed him one of twelve to wait upon Queen Anne at Windsor to thank her for the continued protection of Friends. Davies, it seems, was the chief spokesman. He was one of thirteen who signed the frame of government for Pennsylvania drawn up by Penn.

In his autobiography Davies says little concerning the exodus of Quakers from Wales to Pennsylvania, much in the minds of Friends from 1681 onwards. Yet we know that he bought 5000 acres there, subsequently reselling them to Friends in small parcels. Presumably he was acting as agent for prospective emigrants. Why he did not himself leave cannot now be determined. Perhaps, like other Friends, he was hostile to the migration which denuded Welsh Quakers at home of several of their sturdier members.

Another matter invites speculation. Quakers and Roman Catholics were not natural allies, especially when also divided by a social chasm. Nevertheless, Richard Davies spoke of the first marquess of Powis, the premier Catholic aristocrat, and his wife as 'my particular friends' (Davies, 98). At Powis Castle he sought the aid of the marquess, who allowed him to use his name to curb the excesses of a justice of the peace who had maltreated

Friends. Davies called upon him, too, at his home in Lincoln's Inn Fields in 1685 to be advised concerning the sufferings of Friends. This he did after 'I had ended my country business with him' (ibid., 127), which may mean that Davies had some oversight, hitherto unrevealed, of Powis's estate. Even so, it was an intriguing relationship.

There is no known likeness of Davies, but one Friend recalled 'his gravity and grey hairs, his manly presence, and lovely countenance, especially when he stood up in a meeting' (Davies, 11). A 1667 halfpenny trade token of his as felt maker has survived. Glowing testimonies to his memory by Friends provide few hard facts. A brief tribute by his daughter Tace is more informative, indicating, in addition, that sweetness of disposition had been transmitted from one generation to another. Davies's true memorial is his autobiography, which first appeared in 1710; nine editions followed and a translation into Welsh in 1840.

At an unspecified date, Davies moved a short distance from Welshpool to Cloddiau Cochion. He died at his home there on 22 March 1708 and on 25 March was laid to rest close to his wife in the nearby burial-ground which he had helped to secure for Friends.   J. GWYNN WILLIAMS

Sources R. Davies, *An account of the convincement ... of ... Richard Davies*, 6th edn (1825) · J. G. Williams, 'The Quakers of Merioneth during the seventeenth century', *Journal of the Merioneth Historical and Record Society*, 8 (1978), 122–56; (1979), 312–39 · J. Besse, *A collection of the sufferings of the people called Quakers*, 1 (1753) · C. H. Browning, *Welsh settlement of Pensilvania* (1912) · Records of the Society of Friends, Glamorgan RO, D/DSF · yearly meeting minutes, 1668–1693; epistles received, 1683–1706, vol. 1, RS Friends, Lond. · *The journal of George Fox*, rev. edn, ed. J. L. Nickalls (1952) · P. Mack, *Visionary women: ecstatic prophecy in seventeenth-century England* (1992), 418 · Welshpool parish register, 22 March 1635 [baptism]

Davies, Richard (*d.* 1761), physician, was a native of Shropshire, of whose early life nothing is known. On 19 August 1726 he entered Queens' College, Cambridge, at that time under the presidency of his relative, John Davies (1679–1732). He graduated there as BA in 1730, MA in 1734, and MD in 1748. He was a fellow between 1730 and 1740. He was also elected a fellow of the Royal Society on 8 June 1738, but withdrew two years later. He went on to practise in Shrewsbury, and later in Bath.

Davies's main professional interest was the analysis of human blood, and he published several works on this subject. He died in Bath at the end of 1761, leaving a widow, Jane. He was buried there on 25 December.

GORDON GOODWIN, *rev.* KAYE BAGSHAW

Sources H. Talon, *Selections from the journals and papers of John Byrom, poet, diarist, shorthand writer, 1691–1763* (1951) · K. Dorrington, 'More on the history of the ESR', *The Lancet* (18 April 1987) · Venn, *Alum. Cant.*
Archives BL, Add. MSS 6210, fol. 32, 6181, fol. 21

Davies, Richard (1818–1896). *See under* Davies, Robert (1816–1905).

Davies, Richard Llewelyn, Baron Llewelyn-Davies (1912–1981), architect, was born on 24 December 1912 in London, the elder child and only son of Crompton Llewelyn Davies, solicitor, and his wife, Moya, daughter of James O'Connor. After attending a private school in Ireland, he studied at Trinity College, Cambridge, and took the mechanical sciences tripos in 1934. His interest in engineering also drew him to architecture: he attended summer sessions at the École des Beaux-Arts in Paris, and obtained its certificate in architecture soon after his Cambridge degree.

Having decided to become an architect, Llewelyn Davies enrolled on the diploma course at the Architectural Association (AA) in London. There he joined a set of students who adhered to the principles of modern architecture pioneered in continental Europe during the 1920s. The emphasis was on the use of industrial technology, such as reinforced concrete and steel, and on the pursuit of architecture as a social crusade. Politics had played an important part in Llewelyn Davies's thinking ever since his time at Cambridge, where he had been acquainted with left-wing sympathizers such as Lord Rothschild and Anthony Blunt. Radical views were also in vogue among students at the AA, and Llewelyn Davies became a leader of their revolt against old-fashioned methods of teaching. After completing the AA diploma in 1937, his first commission was for a large house near Chichester (Harbour Meadow, Birdham), which he designed with a talented contemporary, Peter Moro. He qualified and joined the RIBA in 1939, the same year as this project was completed.

Like so many of his generation, Llewelyn Davies was profoundly influenced by his experiences during the Second World War. His contribution to the war effort began in the engineering practice of Sir Alexander Gibb & Partners, where he worked on the design of standardized factory buildings. In 1942 Llewelyn Davies switched to the architectural department of the London Midland and Scottish Railway Company. As well as designing prefabricated railway stations, his time with the company's research division gave him the opportunity to meet ambitious and like-minded architects such as Leslie Martin. Wartime contingencies confirmed Llewelyn Davies's belief in the need to unite architecture and engineering. Equally important was the example set by state control and patronage during a condition of 'total war': he believed that what had been necessary to defeat fascism should be turned to the fight at home against inequality. The welfare system inaugurated by the landslide Labour government in 1945 offered the opportunity, and Llewelyn Davies rose to become one of the great establishment figures of post-war British architecture.

In the first few years after the war, Llewelyn Davies continued to work with the London Midland and Scottish Railway Company. One of the young architects who joined his team during this period was John Weeks; the two were to become lifelong collaborators. Llewelyn Davies also began to expand his interests into other avenues of architecture opened up by the nascent welfare state. He was invited in 1945 to serve on a commission which went to defeated Germany in order to see what might be learned from building technology there. He was involved in promoting modular design systems and, together with John Weeks, he adapted the Hills prefabricated school system for multi-storey use. Yet Llewelyn

Davies's first significant contribution towards social architecture was in hospital research. In 1948 he joined the Nuffield Provincial Hospitals Trust, and soon progressed to the Nuffield Foundation. There he became a member of multi-disciplinary study groups which campaigned for flexible and functional layouts for modern hospitals. Systems of planning and construction were developed that owed much to the innovative school-building programmes in Britain and California. It was an area of expertise that culminated in an influential text which he co-authored for the World Health Organization, entitled *Hospital Planning and Administration* (1966).

The experience of working alongside medical and scientific specialists in the 1950s led Llewelyn Davies to the conclusion that architecture was intellectually undeveloped compared with the physical and social sciences. His view was that the subject could only be redeemed by a technocratic élite, who could combine a broad-based approach with a capacity for systematic research. It was a typical fantasy of the rationalist, scientific version of modernism of which Llewelyn Davies was one of the high priests. Such was his intellectual conviction and diplomatic skills that soon he was highly regarded within government circles.

The 1960s was the key decade for Llewelyn Davies. He pursued his ambitions on two parallel fronts, education and practice, with exceptional success. In 1960 he was appointed to the chair of architecture at University College, London, having been a leading player in the RIBA's influential conference on architectural education held two years before in Oxford. His aims were clearly spelt out in his inaugural lecture, published as *The Education of an Architect* (1961). While he invoked the educational model developed by Walter Gropius at the Bauhaus in the 1920s, he was actually more sympathetic to the better-funded and more academic versions that Gropius and other German émigrés had set up after the war in élite American universities. He soon swept away the sterile Beaux-Arts course at University College, London, and set the standard for a modernist system of architectural education in Britain. Collaborative teamwork was encouraged, and to counter the potential subjectivity of architecture, students were taught the essential principles of physical and social sciences. Above all, research was conceived as the dynamic component of the school. Specialists in engineering and building services were drafted in to teach, and a strong postgraduate research wing was formed. The courses in town planning and architecture were incorporated under a new school of environmental studies, and he himself held the chair of urban planning from 1969 to 1975.

A similar belief in multi-disciplinary teamwork and research also characterized the private architectural firm which Llewelyn Davies established in 1960 with John Weeks (who had also been engaged in the Nuffield Hospital research programme during the 1950s). The practice grew large on medical and commercial projects. They won international attention as specialists in the design of hospitals, of which one of the earliest and most prestigious was at Northwick Park in Harrow, Middlesex (1961–5). Also notable were the offices designed for *The Times* newspaper (1960–64) and the stock exchange (1964–9) in the City of London. Another intriguing early project was an estate village built in a modernist style in the early 1960s for Lord Rothschild at Rushbrooke in Suffolk.

In 1964 the practice was augmented by the arrival of Walter Bor, an expert in urban planning. At the peak of its prestige the firm was called Llewelyn-Davies, Weeks, Forestier-Walker, and Bor. The practice's workload by the 1970s was truly international, and it had managed to establish town planning as yet another of its specialisms. The first significant scheme in the mid-1960s was for Washington New Town in north-east England, but the major achievement was undoubtedly the layout for Milton Keynes, the last of the post-war new towns (built from 1972 onwards). This model, exhaustively explained in *The Plan for Milton Keynes* (1970), represented the importation of the car-based, dispersed American city typified by Los Angeles. However, it was also given the crucial British improvements—at least in theory—of mixed-tenure housing, tight social regulation, and a public transport system. Milton Keynes exemplified Llewelyn Davies's design approach: the master plan was deliberately open-ended, flexible, and repetitious, and consequently lacked any clear aesthetic vision.

Llewelyn Davies's first marriage, to Ann Stephen, ended in divorce. He was married on 3 June 1943 to (Annie) Patricia Rawdon-Smith, daughter of Charles Percy Parry, engineer [see Davies, Annie Patricia Llewelyn-(1915–1997)]. They had three daughters, and owned homes in Tring, Hertfordshire, and Belsize Park, London. His wife became an influential figure in her own right. In 1967 she was created Baroness Llewelyn-Davies of Hastoe, and served as a Labour whip in the House of Lords. Llewelyn Davies died in St Bartholomew's Hospital, London, on 27 October 1981. His second wife survived him.

The cerebral, research-based approach to architecture that brought Llewelyn Davies his rise to fame was also the reason for his eclipse. He earned many prestigious honours during his life. He was created a life peer in 1963; he was founding chairman of the Centre for Environmental Studies in 1967; he served on the Royal Fine Arts Commission from 1969 to 1975; and he was made an honorary fellow of the American Institute of Architects in 1970. Yet the certainty of Llewelyn Davies's scientific approach proved difficult for subsequent architects to share. His commitment to team collaboration and indeterminate design also had the consequence that, although he was an influential figure in British modern architecture, if one looks around there are few monuments in which to seek him.

MURRAY FRASER

Sources R. Llewelyn Davies, *The education of an architect* (1961) · A. Lee Morgan and C. Naylor, eds., *Contemporary architects*, 2nd edn (1987), 538–9 · M. Crinson and J. Lubbock, *Architecture: art or profession ?* (1994) · A. Saint, *Towards a social architecture: the role of school-building in post-war England* (1987) · *DNB* · private information (2004) · L. Esher, *A broken wave: the rebuilding of England, 1940–1980* (1981), 246–71 · m. cert. [Annie Patricia Rawdon-Smith]

Wealth at death £754,764: probate, 21 May 1982, *CGPLA Eng. & Wales*

Davies, Robert (1658–1710), naturalist and antiquary, was born on 15 March 1658, probably at Gwysane, Flintshire, one of eight children of Mutton Davies (1634–1684) and his wife, Elizabeth Wilbraham (*d.* 1678). His father was a great traveller and significantly improved his house and gardens at Llannerch, Denbighshire. Davies matriculated at Christ Church, Oxford, on 2 April 1677 and became a member of the Inner Temple. He subsequently served as an alderman of Denbighshire (1685) and high sheriff both of Denbighshire (1687) and of Flintshire (1704). He married Letitia, daughter of Edward Vaughan and a granddaughter of Sir John Vaughan of Trawsgoed, Cardiganshire, on 2 December 1681. They had at least three children. He continued a family tradition of scholarly enquiry. His great-grandfather Robert Davies (1581–1633), or perhaps his grandfather Robert Davies (1616–1666), prepared 'A catalogue of ye British names of plants', a list of some 250 Welsh names of plants which was printed in the second edition of John Gerard's *The Herball, or, Generall Historie of Plants* (1636). His great-grandfather also seems to have been actively interested in his library, judging from a few references to books and manuscripts in his correspondence. His grandfather Robert Davies was called upon to assist the genealogist Randle Holmes in his work.

Robert Davies (1658–1710) built upon the foundation collections which he had inherited to create at Llannerch one of the major libraries of seventeenth-century Wales and one which, to their great credit, he and his heirs opened to Welsh scholars. A catalogue compiled in 1740 listed 42 Latin manuscripts (including *Liber Landavensis*), 30 English manuscripts, and 16 Welsh manuscripts (including the translations made by their kinsman Bishop Richard Davies for the 1567 New Testament in Welsh). Robert Davies was but one of a circle of antiquaries and naturalists in north Wales: these included Thomas Price, William Maurice, and later Humphrey Humphreys and Josiah Babington, with whom Edward Lhuyd formed close links and who gave the Oxford scholar information and practical support.

Most of Davies's correspondence with his wife deals with personal and family matters, but a few of her letters refer to their gardens at Llannerch. Other letters refer to the purchasing of books and manuscripts and to the repair of his telescope. His correspondence with Edward Lhuyd, and indirectly with Josiah Babington, reveals more of his serious interest in contemporary Welsh scholarship. He gave Lhuyd informed views on manuscript collections, Welsh history, local antiquities, seals, heraldry, inscriptions, and natural history, and also consulted manuscripts at the Ashmolean Museum in Oxford. Though little of their correspondence has survived, it is clear that the two were on friendly terms. Davies contributed generously to the costs of Lhuyd's research tour of the British Isles and Lhuyd listed some of the contents of his library in *Archaeologia Britannica* (1707). Davies died on 8 July 1710 at Llannerch, Denbighshire, and was buried at Mold church, Flintshire.

His son, **Robert Davies** (1685/6–1728), pursued similar interests and was acknowledged as a serious antiquary. He studied at Brasenose College, Oxford, matriculating on 27 June 1702. He died on 22 May 1728. A notable effigy of him by Henry Cheere was erected in Mold church, showing him attired in Roman costume, and a portrait of him is at Gwysane. Robert senior's grandson Robert Davies (1710–1763) continued the tradition of scholarly patronage. He was a friend of the Welsh scholar and poet Evan Evans (Ieuan Fardd), who referred to him warmly and composed an elegy to him. His son, Peter Davies, died unmarried and intestate in 1785, and the estate and the library were divided and passed to his two sisters.

BRYNLEY F. ROBERTS

Sources D. G. Jones, *Un o wŷr y medra: bywyd a gwaith William Williams, Llandygái, 1738–1817* (1999) · J. Y. W. Lloyd, 'History of the lordship of Maelor Gymraeg [pt 5]', *Archaeologia Cambrensis*, 4th ser., 6 (1875), 32–53, esp. 47–51 · H. D. Emanuel, 'The Gwysaney manuscripts', *National Library of Wales Journal*, 7 (1951–2), 326–43 · D. Williams, 'Rhestr gynnar o enwau planhigion yn Gymraeg', *Y Gwyddonydd*, 17 (1979), 73–8 · T. A. Glenn, *The family history of Griffiths of Garn and Plasnewydd* (1934) · G. A. Usher, *Gwysaney and Owston: a history of the family of Davies-Cooke of Gwysaney, Flintshire and Owston, West Riding of Yorkshire* (1964), 100–28 · T. Jeffreys, *A catalogue of the manuscripts in Llannerch Library taken June 21st 1787* (1787) · *Cambrian Register*, 1 (1796), 320–28, 374–6 · *IGI* · Foster, *Alum. Oxon.* · R. T. Gunther, *Early science in Oxford*, 14: *Life and letters of Edward Lhwyd* (1945)

Archives BL, Add. MS 14948 · Bodl. Oxf., Ashmolean MS 1814, fols. 394–9 | NL Wales, MSS 1551, 1588, 1593, 2025, Gwysaney 49A, 60 A

Likenesses H. Cheere, statue, 1728, Mold, Clywd, Wales · H. Cheere, effigy (Robert Davies), Mold church, Flintshire, Wales · portrait (Robert Davies), Gwysane

Davies, Robert (1685/6–1728). *See under* Davies, Robert (1658–1710).

Davies, Robert [*pseud.* Bardd Nantglyn] (1769–1835), Welsh-language poet, was born in the parish of Nantglyn, Denbighshire. He was a tailor by trade, and for four years (1800–04) lived in London, where he filled at intervals the offices of bard and secretary to the Gwyneddigion Society. He was a warm supporter of the eisteddfods patronized by the society at the end of the eighteenth century, and of the provincial eisteddfods of the early nineteenth century. On returning to Wales he settled at Nantglyn, near Denbigh, from which he took his bardic name, Bardd Nantglyn. He occupied the bardic chair for Powys at the Wrexham eisteddfod in 1820 by reason of his prize elegy on the death of George III, which contains his famous line 'Beibl i bawb o bobl y byd' ('A bible for everyone in the world'), although this has also been attributed to Robert Williams (1744–1815). On different occasions he obtained eleven medals for his prize poems, including several awards given at Beaumaris in 1832. He also acted as adjudicator in some of the competitions, including the controversial Denbigh eisteddfod of 1819, in which Edward Hughes of Bodfari was given the prize instead of Dewi Wyn (David Owen).

Most of Davies's compositions are published in his work entitled *Diliau barddas* (1827). He also wrote an excellent Welsh grammar, *Leithiadur neu ramadeg Cymraeg* (1808), which had run into five editions by 1848, and which had a profound effect on poets throughout the century. Davies died on 1 December 1835 and was buried at Nantglyn, where he had been for some years the parish clerk.

THOMPSON COOPER, rev. M. CLARE LOUGHLIN-CHOW

Sources DWB · GM, 2nd ser., 5 (1836), 327–8 · R. Williams, *Enwogion Cymru: a biographical dictionary of eminent Welshmen* (1852), 111 · M. Stephens, ed., *The Oxford companion to the literature of Wales* (1986)

Davies, Robert (1793–1875), antiquary, eldest son of Peter Davies and his wife, Ann, daughter of Robert Rhodes, was born at York on 19 August 1793, and educated there at St Peter's School. Having qualified as a solicitor in 1814, he practised for many years in York. He married in 1826 Elizabeth, youngest daughter of George Cattle of York.

As town clerk from 1828 until 1848, Davies was active in local implementations of the Municipal Reform Act, and left his legal partnership in 1834 to serve the new corporation. He was a member of the Yorkshire Philosophical Society from 1824 and his legal and antiquarian interests resulted in an edition of *The Freeman's Roll of the City of York* (1835) and publication of *Extracts from the Municipal Records of the City of York* (1843). After his retirement he was elected a magistrate and continued his scholarly work, concentrating on more recent history. His *Memoir of the York Press* (1868) remains an important source for the history of printing, and his posthumously published *Walks through the City of York* (1880), edited by his widow from papers read to the Yorkshire Philosophical Society, adopted an approach to topographical and historical writing that has often been copied. He contributed to publications of the Surtees Society and other local societies, and was elected a fellow of the Society of Antiquaries on 22 December 1842. Davies died at his residence in The Mount, in the city of York, on 23 August 1875, and was buried in York cemetery on 29 August. WILLIAM JOSEPH SHEILS

Sources *Law Times* (4 Sept 1875), 333 · *Solicitors' Journal*, 19 (1874–5), 858 · J. M. Biggins, *Historians of York* (1956)
Archives Bodl. Oxf., corresp. · York Minster, heraldic papers relating to chapter house of York Minster | W. Yorks. AS, Leeds, Yorkshire Archaeological Society, letters to Fairless Barber
Wealth at death under £25,000: probate, 15 Sept 1875, CGPLA Eng. & Wales

Davies, Robert (1816–1905), benefactor, born at Llangefni, Anglesey, on 1 April 1816, was the second son of Richard Davies (1778–1849), a general storekeeper at Llangefni, and his wife, Anne, daughter of Owen Jones of Coed Hywel, near Llangefni. He was educated at the national school, Llangefni, and at a private school in Chester. As he and his two brothers grew up, their father extended his business, opening a branch for importing timber and iron at Menai Bridge, which he placed under the management of his eldest son, John, who died unmarried in 1848 and to whose business ability the successful development of the family firm was largely due. An iron foundry at Caernarfon was put under Robert's charge, while a store at Redwharf Bay was entrusted to the youngest son, Richard. The shipping and freight business which the brothers operated at Menai Bridge was extremely successful, and as

the firm established itself as one of the largest shipowning concerns in the district, the other businesses were disposed of and the three brothers settled in the area.

While at Caernarfon Davies had taken an active part in the work of a ragged school in the town and in subsequent years he had charge of a class of children in a Sunday school of which he was for a short time superintendent. With these exceptions, and that of serving as high sheriff of Anglesey for 1862, he took no part in public work. About 1862 he settled at Bodlondeb, a house overlooking the Menai Strait, near Bangor, and here he led a somewhat eccentric and parsimonious life, letting his share of the profits of the business accumulate. After 1885 he began giving money, generally anonymously or under assumed names, towards liquidating the debts of his own denomination, the Calvinistic Methodists. He was popularly credited with giving £½ million towards chapel debts, although his donations probably did not much exceed £150,000. His other benefactions were £177,000 to endow the Welsh Methodist mission in India, £10,000 to an orphanage (of the same connection) at Bontnewydd, near Caernarfon, and £10,000 to the British and Foreign Bible Society (of which he was a vice-president). At a cost of £5000 he built an English chapel for the Calvinistic Methodists at Menai Bridge (where he was commemorated by a window and tablet), and gave £1200 towards restoring the Welsh chapel at the same place, to the building of which he and his brother had contributed generously. His gifts to educational institutions included £1000 to the founding of the normal college at Bangor in 1856 and £1000 to the University College, Bangor (1884), and financial assistance in the establishment and maintenance of a British School at Menai Bridge. His almsgiving for many years took the eccentric form of a weekly distribution of 12 pounds of flour to between seventy and a hundred people, who personally collected this dole from Bodlondeb every Tuesday.

Davies died unmarried and intestate at Bodlondeb on 29 December 1905, and was buried on 2 January 1906 with his parents in the parish churchyard of Llangefni. His estate was valued at more than £400,000.

His younger brother, **Richard Davies** (1818–1896), politician, was born at Llangefni, Anglesey, on 29 November 1818, and married Annie Rees (1836–1918), daughter of the nonconformist minister Henry *Rees, in 1855. He was possessed of business acumen and public qualities of a high order. A Liberal in politics, he unsuccessfully contested the tory seat of Caernarfon Boroughs in 1852, but in 1868 he was granted a historic victory when he was returned as the first nonconformist member of parliament for his native county of Anglesey, a seat which he held until 1886. Davies was appointed high sheriff of Anglesey in 1858 and its lord lieutenant in 1884, being the first nonconformist to hold those offices in Wales. He died at his residence, Treborth, near Bangor, on 27 October 1896, and was buried at Llandysilio cemetery, Anglesey, on 31 October.

D. L. THOMAS, rev. MARI A. WILLIAMS

Sources J. Jones, *Adgofion am Mr Robert Davies, Bodlondeb* (1906) · T. C. Williams, 'Y diweddar Mr Robert Davies, Bodlondeb', *Y Drysorfa*, 76 (1906), 101–7 · J. Jones, 'Mr Robert Davies, Bodlondeb', *Y Geninen*, 24 (1906), 117–21 · *DWB* · R. Thomas, *Cartre'r plant yn y Bontnewydd ger Caernarfon* (1951) · *Trysorfa y Plant* (April 1906), 85–7 · E. A. Williams, *The day before yesterday: Anglesey in the nineteenth century*, trans. G. W. Griffith (1988) · *Baner ac Amserau Cymru* (11 Nov 1896) [Richard Davies]

Likenesses Sprague & Co., ink photograph, repro. in Williams, 'Y diweddar Mr Robert Davies, Bodlondeb' · ink photograph, repro. in Jones, *Adgofion am Robert Davies, Bodlondeb* · ink photograph, repro. in Thomas, *Cartre'r plant yn y Bontnewydd ger Caernarfon*

Wealth at death £425,501 3s. 6d.: administration, 31 Jan 1906, *CGPLA Eng. & Wales*

Davies, (William) Robertson (1913–1995), writer and university teacher, was born on 28 August 1913 in Elizabeth Street, Thamesville, Ontario, the third of the three sons of (William) Rupert Davies (1879–1967), newspaper publisher and broadcaster, and Florence McKay (1870–1948). His father had arrived in Canada from his native Wales, penniless but determined to flourish as a printer, first in the rural village of Thamesville in south-western Ontario. So successful was Rupert Davies that in time he became the owner of several Ontario newspapers, a partner with Roy Thomson (later Lord Thomson of Fleet) in radio and television stations, a Liberal senator, and the owner of a large Victorian pile in south Wales to which he frequently retreated with unfailing enthusiasm. Robertson Davies remained grateful to his affluent father throughout his life, but relations with his mother, nine years older than her husband, were never easy. Florence McKay, a descendant of united empire loyalists who had made their way, with great hardship, to the wilderness of Upper Canada following the American War of Independence, appeared to her three sons as frequently cantankerous, caustic, and distant. It was a troubled relationship that Davies was to explore in his novels.

Placed in Canada's leading boys' school, Upper Canada College, by his increasingly prosperous father, Davies soon demonstrated a love for the theatre, happily participating in student productions there and later at Queen's University in Kingston, Ontario, and at Balliol College, Oxford (where he also joined enthusiastically in college music with Edward Heath). Throughout the 1930s, during his school and university years, Davies sought in drama the fulfilment of his mounting literary ambitions, studying and writing about the English theatre of the eighteenth and especially the nineteenth century and, in Oxford and London, collaborating with his dynamic wife-to-be, the Australian Brenda Mathews (b. 1917). During their subsequent two years at the Old Vic, Tyrone Guthrie, who became a lifelong friend, saw in Robertson Davies a valued literary assistant and a likely Shakespearian actor and in Brenda Mathews a highly competent—and his first female—stage manager. Brenda Mathews and Robertson Davies married on 2 February 1940, but the war effectively ended their still uncertain theatrical prospects in Britain. Rejected by the Canadian army because of his weak eyesight—it was not for nothing that he had affected a monocle during his more flamboyant days at Oxford—Davies

(William) Robertson Davies (1913–1995), by Paddy Cook

sought the safety of Ontario, where a fledgeling career in journalism awaited him. There he wrote regularly for two of his father's provincial newspapers. A tireless reader since schooldays, he soon became the literary editor of the national periodical *Saturday Night* and, at his father's invitation, editor of the *Peterborough Examiner*. Wartime Peterborough, 135 kilometres north-east of Toronto, with a population in 1940 of no more than 25,000, was unappreciative of—if not faintly hostile towards—the intellectual attainments and literary imagination of both Brenda and Robertson Davies. The small-town Ontario experience did, however, lead to Davies's first books, two collections of his provocative and frequently comic 'Samuel Marchbanks' columns from the *Examiner*. Such were their quality that they induced Roy Thomson to offer him the editorship of *The Scotsman*.

Following the end of the Second World War, Davies continued as literary editor of *Saturday Night*, while writing reviews and articles for the *Kingston Whig Standard* and the *Peterborough Examiner*. All the while he continued to help foster with Brenda the modest theatrical life of Ontario. He offered a series of short plays to the annual dominion drama festival, but they challenged Canada's uncertain post-war self-perceptions and were largely unsuccessful despite their easy way with fantasy and humour. Davies's own lack of success as a dramatist did not, however, diminish his commitment to the theatre. He made a major contribution to the launch of the highly successful annual Shakespearian festival in Stratford, Ontario, not far from his birthplace, a festival presided over by his old friend Sir Tyrone Guthrie.

In 1951, increasingly impatient at the continuing cool reception given his plays in Canada and at the Edinburgh festival in 1949, Davies, then aged thirty-eight, attempted his first novel, *Tempest-Tost*. Finally free of the frustrating dependence on cast and producers, he adopted his new literary form with enthusiasm, letting his imagination in *Tempest-Tost* re-create his undergraduate days at Queen's University—and his tense relations with his difficult mother—while offering a memorable and highly amusing account of a bungled student production of Shakespeare's late play. Theatre and, eventually, opera were never distant from his novels. His next two, *Leaven of Malice* (1954) and *A Mixture of Frailties* (1958), soon completed the Salterton trilogy, the first of several trilogies. (Davies later maintained that he had never intended to write trilogies: he simply had more to say about the varied experience and understanding of his principal characters than he could encompass in a single volume.) Davies always wrote rapidly. Drawing on his experience as editor of the *Peterborough Examiner*, the Salterton trilogy reviewed, in a light-hearted and witty way, the part played by a newspaper in a small Ontario community and the diversity of meaning that subscribers read into newspapers. *Leaven of Malice* was awarded the Stephen Leacock prize for humour. *A Mixture of Frailties* reflected the growing interest and conviction of both Brenda and Robertson Davies in the teachings of Carl Jung. Like the major characters in Davies's novels, the Davieses were engaged in a quest for greater self-knowledge and were increasingly captivated by what they read of the Swiss psychoanalyst. He was to them satisfyingly optimistic, flexible, and exploitive of legend in a constructive and illuminating way. They embraced his teachings as 'both safer and more lastingly effective than Freud's', which the Davieses had found restrictive (R. Davies, 'The individual and the mass', *Saturday Night*, 24 May 1958, 26). 'Jung's thought is very expansive, a sort of opening out of life whereas so much psychoanalytical thinking is reductive', Davies said (*New York Times*, 4 Dec 1995). His teachings seemed comprehensive, asserting that wholeness in life can be achieved through a process of integration beyond one's own consciousness to embrace that of the traditions and collective consciousness of a whole race. As one who described his writing as having at its centre 'the isolation of the human spirit' (ibid.) in its progress from innocence to experience, Davies came to accept myths as part of the Jungian understanding of archetypes. Myths also contributed to the richness of his juxtaposed comedy and melodrama, realism and illusion. That Davies, by the 1950s, had been heavily influenced by Jung was even more evident in a final play, *General Confession*. Although a failure in New York City, it is of significance for the close reader of Davies since it reflects in detail his understanding of Jung's 'collective unconscious' and the archetypes that populate it.

By the age of forty-seven Davies had turned decisively from writing plays to writing novels. He knew that he had already achieved much, being recognized, in Canada at least, as an able and witty journalist, a competent playwright, and increasingly as a committed novelist, but not yet more. In a book of essays about reading, *A Voice from the Attic* (1960), he extolled 'the values of the humanist—curiosity, the free mind, belief in good taste, and belief in the human race … an informed, rational and intellectually adventurous individuality must take precedence over all else' (R. Davies, *A Voice from the Attic*, 1960, 39). That understanding was to be the bedrock of Davies's novels and more immediately of the literary columns he wrote for the Toronto *Star* syndicate. Concurrently, he became a part-time lecturer in drama at Trinity College in the University of Toronto, having completed in 1960 a total of twenty-five years with the *Peterborough Examiner*, first as a columnist, then as editor, and later as publisher. The Davies family moved from Peterborough to Toronto with their three daughters when a yet greater involvement in academe arrived in the form of an invitation from Vincent Massey, the former high commissioner for Canada in Britain and later governor-general, to become the first master of Massey College, at the University of Toronto. The college was modelled on Balliol, the beloved Oxford college of both Massey and Davies. As the first master Davies proved an inspired choice, despite criticisms of the penchant he and Massey shared for the traditional trappings of an Oxbridge college and their desire to transpose these to the markedly different terrain of Ontario. The combined experience of Trinity and Massey enriched Davies's subsequent novels, but it also fuelled his critics' charges that he was pretentious and pedantic and preoccupied with cerebral analysis at the expense of emotional understanding. His presence at the university was visually inescapable: no one else had the theatrical appearance of his great silver mane and beard, hats, and capes, all as easily worn as if he were still at the Old Vic.

Davies had long known that criticism is integral to university life and was not unduly distracted from his commitment to create in Massey College a vibrant and productive community, but the price was initially a reduction in the pace of his story-telling. In 1971, ten years after his appointment as master, *Fifth Business* was published. It was, to a degree, an autobiographical novel, but it was also heavily informed by his understanding of Jung's psychoanalysis—as were also, to a greater or less extent, all his subsequent novels. *Fifth Business* also triggered another trilogy, the Deptford trilogy, named like the Salterton after a fictional Ontario village. It launched the journeys of self-discovery of individuals, corresponding to Jungian archetypes, who were also to people the subsequent *The Manticore* (1972), which won the governor-general's award, and *World of Wonders* (1975). *Fifth Business*, among other matters, deals broadly with the nature of mothers; *The Manticore* considers fathers. But the Deptford trilogy as a whole, uneven as it is, embraces much more: the eternal question of what is good and what is evil—or what is God and what is the devil—with the artist as the purveyor of interpretations, analysis, and wonders. For some, the Deptford trilogy, completed in 1975, remains Davies's best work, rich in characterization, elaborate in plot. Certainly its critical and commercial success in the United States brought him continental instead of merely Canadian accolades—and was the beginning of the burgeoning international recognition that was to mark the last two decades of his life (with sales rapidly increasing in Britain as well as in the United States and Canada).

When Davies retired as master of Massey College and ceased teaching at Trinity College in the University of Toronto in 1981, he embarked on what became a third trilogy, completed in 1988, the Cornish trilogy, named after its principal character. *The Rebel Angels* (1981), centred in a Canadian university and narrated largely by a female graduate student, draws heavily on Davies's years at the two colleges (as well as a backward glance at Queen's and Balliol). *The Rebel Angels* was received with acclaim by critics across North America as, variously, baroque, esoteric, mystical, and whimsical. In Britain, Anthony Burgess greeted it with the observation that 'Among Canadian WASP novelists who have remained loyal to the culture of the Commonwealth, Robertson Davies, at age 69, stands out as internationally important and undoubted Nobel material' (A. Burgess, 'Maple leaf Rabelais', *The Observer*, 4 April 1982, 33). Despite Davies's loyalty to the culture of the Commonwealth, the Booker prize for Commonwealth authors eluded him, as did the Nobel prize for literature. Yet an honorary doctorate from Oxford and his honorary fellowship at Balliol as well as the award of the order of Canada gave him great pleasure. He was also the first Canadian to be made an honorary member of the American Academy and Institute of Arts and Letters.

The second and third novels of the Cornish trilogy, *What's Bred in the Bone* (1985) and *The Lyre of Orpheus* (1988), continued Davies's explorations of the magical and mystical, reflecting his Jungian understandings but also confirming, as one critic put it, his conviction that 'the modern habit of baring and telling all to be the most abysmal lack of good taste and manners' (C. Ford, *Calgary Herald*, 5 Dec 1995). Curiosity and intelligence are the major traits of his characters in the Cornish fables. The central figures, an artist and an opera singer, both ambiguous in their very natures, travel through Europe and North America in their pursuit of edification and ultimately salvation. At age seventy-four Davies had one or two new novels already in mind, but the third of the Cornish trilogy, *The Lyre of Orpheus*, was an occasion for drawing together the concerns of his highly symbolic novels—mystical, comic, reflective, and didactic—as well as a comment on the variety of life. The trilogy also furthered the translation of Davies into a dozen or more languages, reflecting the fact that although mainly Canada-centred, they draw on the full range of shared civilization in a deeper kind of measure.

Davies's lifelong fascination with the occult culminated in the novel *Murther and Walking Spirits* (1991) in which the principal character, Connor Gilmartin, is murdered in the first line. While Gilmartin initially sets out, as a ghost, to achieve his revenge, he ends up acquiring self-knowledge as he moves through his ancestral homeland of Wales and through North America, viewing incidents of his family history. Although it was undeniably both entertaining and illuminating, the novel failed to live up to the standards of Davies's trilogies. George Woodcock was especially unappreciative: 'Robertson Davies' theatrical past hangs heavy over his novels, which tend to combine saucily implausible plots with a good deal of creaking stage machinery, a romantic realist manner, and a shameless display of knowledge in some mildly esoteric field' (G. Woodcock, 'Attwood's dark parables, Davies' ballad of bankruptcy', *Quill and Quire*, August 1991, 14).

Davies's final novel, *The Cunning Man*, was published in 1995. The title character, a Toronto physician whose life from his childhood in northern Ontario is formed in part by mysticism as much as by science, eventually achieves notable diagnostic insights that are unconventional and unparalleled. With some of the same characters as *Murther and Walking Spirits*, *The Cunning Man* is liberally sprinkled with asides about Anglican ritual, ageing, medieval art, hagiography, Burton's *Anatomy of Melancholy*, and yet more arcane matter.

Davies lived long enough to see *The Cunning Man*, which he regarded as the second volume of yet another trilogy, receive the now well-established acclaim of his critics and his ardent enthusiasts. Following a brief illness, Robertson Davies died on 2 December 1995 in Orangeville, near his country house, Windhover, north of Toronto, leaving the third volume of his projected trilogy incomplete. He was cremated and his ashes were scattered over his farm at Windhover.

Davies left a remarkably rich legacy, including a posthumous volume of speeches, essays, book reviews, and articles in newspapers and periodicals. *Merry Heart* (1996) embraces the store of wit and wonder that informs all his writing. His love for humankind, with all its remarkable foibles, expressed in his great good humour, patient understanding, and elaborate plots, has given to literature, and not just Canadian literature, a dimension that is both rare and durable. His lifelong rollicking sense of fun found reflection in the wry wit that informs so much of what he wrote and in the richness of his characters. Not surprisingly, Robertson Davies became in his lifetime something of a Canadian literary icon. He did so late in life and within little more than a decade. By the time of his death he had achieved widespread international recognition. The popularity of his novels continues unabated among a large and devoted following, both within Canada and without.

ROY MACLAREN

Sources J. Skelton Grant, *Robertson Davies, man of myth* (1994) · E. Cameron, ed., *Robertson Davies, an appreciation* (1991) · S. Stone-Blackburn, *Robertson Davies, playwright* (1985) · J. Madison Davies, *Conversations with Robertson Davies* (1989) · M. Peterman, *Robertson Davies* (1986) · P. Morley, *Robertson Davies* (1977)
Archives NA Canada, papers, MG 30 D 362
Likenesses P. Cook, photograph, priv. coll. [*see illus.*] · portrait, NA Canada · portrait, University of Toronto, Massey College

Davies, Rosina (1863–1949), evangelist, was born on 2 September 1863 at Bute Street, Treherbert, Glamorgan, the third of six children of David Davies (*d.* 1902), coal haulier, and his wife, Hannah, *née* Jones (*d.* 1929), formerly the wife of William Watkins. Owing to a serious childhood illness her elementary education was interrupted and she was taught at home. She came under the influence of the Salvation Army at an early age and began preaching and singing in their meetings. Aged fourteen she left home, against the will of her parents, to assist the Salvation Army with their missionary work in the Maesteg area. Public reaction to her early appearances was extremely mixed, however, and she encountered much prejudice on account of her age and gender. Despite this her evangelical faith was deepened and she was received as a full member at Libanus Calvinistic Methodist chapel, Garth, near Maesteg, although she later declared that all denominations could lay claim to her.

About 1881, in the company of Mary Charlotte Phillips, Davies began the first of several preaching tours of Wales. During the coming years she conducted several hundred missionary meetings and became well known throughout Wales as an evangelical preacher and singer. Encouraged by her benefactors she attended a short course in voice training at the Royal Academy of Music, London, in 1886. Her services as a preacher and singer were much in demand, and during a ten-month period in 1887 she took part in religious meetings on an almost daily basis. However, this gruelling itinerary took its toll and she was frequently forced to rest on account of ill health.

In 1893 Davies accepted an invitation to tour the Welsh churches in the United States of America and visited chapels from New York to California. During her fifteen-month stay she took part in the Welsh eisteddfod held as part of the Chicago World Fair. In 1897 she embarked on a second tour of the United States but the visit was curtailed on health grounds. Back home in Wales she continued preaching but recurring bouts of illness and the burden of additional domestic responsibilities, following the death of her father in 1902, made it difficult for her to carry out all her public engagements. By 1903, however, she had resumed her evangelical duties and held a series of successful missions across Wales and parts of England.

In 1904 the Welsh Congregational Union requested Davies's assistance in conducting missions at their weaker causes, and she continued with this work until 1916. She played a prominent role in the meetings associated with the religious revival of 1904–5, particularly in north Wales, but was compelled to rest during the early months of 1905, when the revival reached its peak. She was particularly concerned with conducting missionary work among women, and during the First World War she held meetings with female munitions workers. In 1916 she was elected organizing secretary of Undeb Dirwestol Merched y De (the South Wales Women's Temperance Union), a post which she filled until 1930. She also took a keen interest in politics and assisted the Liberal Party during parliamentary elections held in the constituency of Carmarthenshire, where she lived from 1914.

Following the death of her mother in 1929 Davies undertook her third American tour, in 1930–31, and travelled as far as Canada. Her later years were dogged with financial difficulties, and she retired from active missionary work in the early 1940s. In 1942 she published her autobiography, *The Story of my Life*; largely based on her personal diary entries, this work provides both a detailed account of her life and a fascinating insight into the social and religious life of Wales from the late nineteenth century onwards. Davies died at her home in Cliff Lea, Ferryside, Carmarthenshire, on 18 October 1949 and was buried at Treorci cemetery on 21 October. She never married.

MARI A. WILLIAMS

Sources R. Davies, *The story of my life* (1942) · R. Tudur Jones, *Yr undeb* (1975) · W. Jones, 'Rosina Davies, yr Efengyles', *Y Gymraes*, 1 (1896–7), 129–31 · *Tywysydd y Plant* (Jan 1925) · *South Wales Echo* (19 Oct 1949) · b. cert.
Likenesses G. F. Harris, oils, 1896, NL Wales · G. and W., photograph, repro. in Jones, 'Rosina Davies, yr Efengyles' · E. Morgan, photograph, NL Wales · photograph, repro. in Davies, *Story of my life* · photograph, repro. in *Tywysydd y Plant*

Davies, Rowland (1649–1721), dean of Cork, was born at Gille Abbey, near Cork, the son of Rowland Davies, a customs officer of Bandon, co. Cork, and Mary Smith (*née* Scudamore). He was descended from an ancient Herefordshire family and, having received his early education in Cork under Mr Scragg, he entered Trinity College, Dublin, on 23 February 1665; he graduated BA in 1671, and proceeded MA in 1681 and LLD in 1706. Initially he planned to enter the medical profession but on 9 April 1671 priest's orders were conferred upon him, and on 11 May he was admitted to the prebend of Kilnaglory, in the diocese of Cork. He was collated on 26 October 1673, and in 1676 granted the prebend of Iniscarra, in the diocese of Cloyne. In 1674 he exchanged his prebend of Kilnaglory for that of Iniskenny, in the same diocese; and he was instituted on 10 February 1679 to the deanery of Ross by the archbishop of Cashel. To these benefices was added the prebend of Liscleary, in the diocese of Cork, on 20 October 1679. He composed a detailed manuscript 'Account of the state of the diocese of Cork in 1682'. In 1674 he married Elizabeth (*d.* 1715), daughter of Captain Robert Stannard and granddaughter of Archbishop Boyle of Armagh, lord chancellor of Ireland.

Dreading the arrival of James II in Ireland, Davies left Cork in company with many others in March 1689, and sought employment in the ministry in England. Initially he was curate of Camberwell, Surrey, of which his fellow countryman Dr Richard Parr was vicar. Though he applied repeatedly for livings he was disappointed, but at Camberwell he faithfully discharged the duties of his profession. In July 1689, through the interest of friends, he was appointed by the corporation of Great Yarmouth to a lectureship there, which, however, in a few months he resigned.

When William III sailed for Ireland Davies obtained an appointment as chaplain to one of his regiments, and he landed again in his native country on 11 May 1690. His arrival at Belfast and the active part he took at the battle of the Boyne, the siege of Limerick, and generally through the whole Irish campaign, are particularly recorded in his journal. He was, with many more, attainted by King

James, but after the close of the war he regained his preferments. In 1693 he became vicar-general of Cloyne, an office for which from his knowledge of canon law he was well qualified. In 1695 the county of Cork publicly acknowledged his 'great services against the torys' (Bishop Downes's manuscripts, TCD). In 1707 he became precentor of Cork and, resigning the deanery of Ross in 1710, he succeeded to that of Cork, on the death of Dean Pomeroy, by patent dated 17 February. In the same year he was also presented to the rectory of Carrigaline, near Cork, which he resigned in 1717.

Davies died at Dawstown, co. Cork, on 11 December 1721, and was buried in the family vault in Cork Cathedral, where there is an inscription to his memory and to those of three descendants. A fine portrait of him in his doctor's gown, and some of his manuscripts, were in the possession of his descendants in 1857. With his wife, who predeceased him on 28 February 1715, he had four sons who reached manhood, besides other sons who died young, and several daughters. One of his sons was preferred to the archdeaconry of Cloyne in 1742.

B. H. BLACKER, rev. WILLIAM GIBSON

Sources *Journal of the Very Rev. Rowland Davies*, ed. R. Caulfield, CS, 68 (1857) · G. T. Stokes, *Some worthies of the Irish church* (1900) · memorial, north wall, Cork Cathedral

Likenesses portrait; in possession of Rowland Davies of Cork in 1857

Wealth at death £50 annuity to son and £20 each to other sons and daughters: *Journal of Rowland Davies*, ed. R. Caulfield

Davies, Rowland (1740–1797), composer and Roman Catholic priest, was born on 9 May 1740 in London, son of Rowland Davies and his wife, Jane Nicholas. He was a pupil of George Frideric Handel, and is said to have played the organ at the coronation of George III in Westminster Abbey in 1760. He converted to Catholicism and in December 1765 took the college oath at the English College at Douai, where he was ordained priest in 1772. While he was there he taught classics and philosophy. After returning to England he was stationed in turn at Cliff in Yorkshire, Warwick Street in London, and Bosworth Hall, the residence of Francis Fortescue Turville. He died on 16 March 1797, probably at Bosworth Hall. He composed a number of masses, a Te Deum, a Magnificat, and responses for the dead; none appears to have been published.

DAVID BURCHELL

Sources J. Kirk, *Biographies of English Catholics in the eighteenth century*, ed. J. H. Pollen and E. Burton (1909) · Gillow, *Lit. biog. hist.* · D. A. Bellenger, ed., *English and Welsh priests, 1558–1800* (1984) · *The Catholic Annual Register* (1850)

Davies, Rupert Eric (1909–1994), Methodist minister and scholar, was born on 29 November 1909 at 261 Goldhawk Road, Hammersmith, London, the second of the three children of Walter Pierce Davies, solicitor and sometime mayor of Hammersmith, and his wife, Eliza Miriam, *née* Emmett, civil servant. He was educated at St Paul's School, where he was a foundation scholar and school captain. He read classics at Balliol College, Oxford, and became senior denyer and Johnson scholar. He gained a first class in honour moderations and a second in *literae humaniores* in 1932.

His Oxford recreations included tennis, walking, and golf, and he was an active member of the Wesley Society. He trained for the Methodist ministry at Wesley House, Cambridge, and gained first-class honours in the theological tripos in 1934. He then spent a year (1934–5) as Finch scholar in the University of Tübingen, studying the continental reformers, and had first-hand experience of the Nazi regime. On his return to England he was appointed chaplain of Kingswood School, Bath, John Wesley's foundation, where he served for twelve years (1935–47), a period which included the school's wartime evacuation to Uppingham. In addition to religious studies he taught German and coached the junior soccer team. On 7 August 1937 he married Margaret Price Holt (b. 1911), a secondary schoolteacher and daughter of Arthur Edward Holt, a headmaster. They had met at Oxford, where she had studied history at St Hugh's College. They had two sons, John and Stephen, and two daughters, Mary and Judith, together with a foster daughter, Barbara, who was a refugee from Nazi Germany.

Davies served as a minister in pastoral charge in the Methodist circuits of Bristol (South) in 1947, Bristol (Bedminster) in 1948–9, and Bristol (King Street) in 1950–52. In 1952 he became tutor in church history at Didsbury College, Bristol, and began a career in theological education which was to last more than thirty years. When Wesley College, Headingley, Leeds, joined Didsbury in 1967, Davies became principal of the united college and tutor in theology. He was elected president of the Methodist conference in 1970. In the 1970s the college was threatened with closure as part of a reorganization of Methodist theological training, and he fought valiantly and successfully for its retention. With typical magnanimity, after the college's continuance was assured, he made it clear that he had been motivated by no personal ambition by resigning his principalship and resuming circuit ministry at Bedminster, Bristol, in 1973. He retired from full-time ministry in 1976, and served as warden of John Wesley's Chapel, Bristol (the New Room), from 1976 to 1982. The whole of his ministry was spent in the Bristol district, but he was widely travelled and, like John Wesley, looked upon the whole world as his parish. After retirement he made several extensive lecturing and preaching tours overseas.

Davies was a lifelong and convinced ecumenist, and formed strong friendships across the denominational lines. In particular he worked closely with Oliver Tomkins, bishop of Bristol, and was an ardent advocate of Anglican–Methodist unity. He was a member of the Anglican–Methodist unity commission (1965–8), and was grieved when its proposals failed to carry. On the wider ecumenical scene he served on the executive committee of the World Methodist Council (1956–76), the British Council of Churches, the Joint Liturgical Group, and the World Council of Churches faith and order commission (1965–75). He also made a notable contribution as convenor of the Methodist faith and order committee, on which he served from 1958 to 1970. He was a gifted teacher and educationist, with a rare ability to express complex ideas simply, and to lighten both lectures and sermons with his special brand of lively wit. His educational activities included the chairmanship of the governors of Kingswood School (1975–83), and of Redland High School for Girls (1976–83), and membership of the Bristol education committee. He was instrumental in making Kingswood a co-educational school.

Davies was a prolific author, whose published works included *The Problem of Authority in the Continental Reformers* (1946), which earned him a Cambridge BD, *Methodists and Unity* (1962), *Methodism* (1963), a classic introduction to the subject, *Religious Authority in an Age of Doubt* (1968), and *The Church in our Times: an Ecumenical History from a British Perspective* (1979). He was also both contributor and co-editor of the four-volume *A History of the Methodist Church in Great Britain* (1965–88). He was for many years a recognized teacher in the department of theology of Bristol University, which in 1992 awarded him the honorary degree of DLitt. He was select preacher at both Cambridge (1962) and Oxford (1969) universities. In his writing and teaching he conveyed his own enthusiasm for his subject, and stimulated insight by his probing questions. He was never satisfied with glib or shallow answers to serious problems, nor would he allow his students to take refuge in them. Yet he remained to the end of his life a convinced Christian who enjoyed life to the full, and relished the joys of study and debate, music and theatre, friendship and conversation, and the family life he and his wife, Margaret, cherished. They formed an exceptionally strong partnership and shared numerous reforming causes in church and society. Together they worked tirelessly for the ordination of women in Methodism, which was achieved in 1974, and for the fuller participation of women in the wider society.

Davies was short of stature but great of heart. He walked briskly, spoke quickly, and thought rapidly. His eyes were bright with intelligence and a puckish humour. Sartorial elegance was not his forte, but he had a tidy mind and was a good administrator. He continued to write poetry until the end of his life. Only a few weeks before he died he wrote a letter in support of the disestablishment of the Church of England, and was eager to know whether the Methodist conference, then in session, would agree to a new round of Anglican–Methodist conversations. That was typical of his eager, forward looking spirit, and of his zest for life which so endeared him to his many friends. He died at his home, 6 Elmtree Drive, Bishopsworth, Bristol, on 4 July 1994, in the eighty-fifth year of his age and the sixty-first year of his ministry. He was survived by his wife, sons, daughters, and foster daughter.

JOHN A. NEWTON

Sources personal knowledge (2004) · private information (2004) · minutes of the Methodist conference, 1995 · *The Times* (12 July 1994) · *The Independent* (25 July 1994) · *WWW*, 1991–5 · b. cert. · m. cert.

Archives JRL, Methodist Archives and Research Centre, corresp., diaries, and papers

Likenesses photograph, repro. in *The Times* · photograph, repro. in *The Independent* · tempera painting, Wesley College, College Park Drive, Henbury Road, Bristol

Wealth at death £3246: probate, 20 Oct 1994, *CGPLA Eng. & Wales*

Davies, Samuel (1723–1761), Presbyterian minister and college head, was born on 3 November 1723 in the Welsh tract in Pencader hundred in New Castle county, Delaware, the first son of David Davies, a farmer, and his second wife, Martha Thomas. Both his parents were Welsh. Nothing in his background indicated that he would become a popular evangelist, prolific writer, and innovative educator. His parents were simple people who lacked education. His mother, however, placed her son in a school taught by the local Baptist minister, Abel Morgan, and later sent him to another in St Georges, Delaware, conducted by the Reverend William Robinson, a popular Presbyterian minister. At about the age of fifteen he was awakened spiritually and prayed that he be prepared for the ministry.

Because Presbyterians insisted on an educated ministry, Samuel Davies continued his schooling at Fagg's Manor, Chester county, Pennsylvania, not far from his Delaware home. Here he came under the influence of the school's founder, Samuel Blair, a graduate of William Tennent's 'log college' in Neshaminy, Bucks county, Pennsylvania, where a significant number of evangelistic Presbyterian ministers had received their training. It is likely that at Blair's academy Davies received a traditional classical education, and it is certain that frequently he heard Blair preach a moderate Calvinism, including the necessity of repentance, 'new birth' in Christ, and pious living. Davies later included these emphases in his ministry.

Having completed his studies, Davies was licensed by the presbytery of New Castle, Delaware, in 1746, served his six-month probationary period by preaching to pastorless congregations in Delaware and Pennsylvania, and was ordained in 1747 as an evangelist to vacant congregations in and around Hanover county, Virginia, where he served for over a decade.

Before going to Virginia, Davies married Sarah Kirkpatrick (d. 1747) on 16 October 1746. She died in childbirth. Shortly after beginning his ministry in Hanover, he married Jane Holt of Williamsburg on 4 October 1748. They had six children, three sons and three daughters; one daughter died shortly after birth. Although Davies frequently expressed his love for his wife and children, only one child shared his religious interests.

Because the Church of England was legally established in Virginia, Davies had to apply for and obtain a licence to preach there. Throughout his ministry in Virginia he attempted to advocate toleration of religious dissenters. Nevertheless, Davies refused to criticize the ecclesiastical establishment, explaining that he cared not whether people went to heaven from an Anglican or a Presbyterian church. Nevertheless, many Anglicans must have considered their chances better as Presbyterians for hundreds of them joined the seven congregations that Davies served. These were located in five counties in rural southeastern Virginia. Frequently other groups of people there and in North Carolina invited Davies to preach to them, which resulted in the formation of additional congregations. So many had emerged by 1755 that they petitioned the synod of New York to form the Hanover presbytery. Davies was elected its first moderator. During the French and Indian War (1754–63), Davies equated Christianity with patriotism and encouraged men to enlist in the Virginia militia. He preached also to slaves, baptized many, brought them into his congregations, taught them to read, and gave them books on Christianity. American Indians also attracted his attention. He helped to raise money for American Indian missions and served on a committee to manage a fund to send a young Indian to the College of New Jersey.

Many of Davies's compositions were published and circulated widely in America and Great Britain, including not only his sermons but also his hymns and poems. Davies explained that after he had prepared a sermon, he often expressed its essence, or a description of his mood while writing it, in a poem. He wrote approximately 100 such poems, 50 of which appeared in print before his death and more later. Always sensitive to music, Davies set many of his poems to familiar tunes for his congregations to sing. Some were published as appendices to collections of his sermons. He was one of the first American hymn writers.

In 1753 the synod of New York appointed Davies to accompany Gilbert Tennent to Britain to raise funds for the Presbyterians' fledgeling College of New Jersey. The expedition was a financial success which, no doubt, raised Davies in the trustees' estimation. He accepted their invitation to become president in 1759. He was strong in the office. He raised admissions standards, encouraged more rigorous examinations, required seniors to present monthly lectures which he supervised and critiqued, and increased the solemnity of the commencement exercises. In addition to his college responsibilities, he served as minister of Princeton's Presbyterian congregation and as moderator of the synod in 1760. Davies's health, never robust, weakened by tuberculosis and overwork, failed in late 1760. He died on 4 February 1761 in Princeton, and was buried there. Surviving were his wife, three sons, and two daughters.

JOHN B. FRANTZ

Sources W. B. Sprague, 'Samuel Davies, 1746–1761', *Annals of the American pulpit*, 3 (1859), 140–46 · G. W. Pilcher, *Samuel Davies: apostle of dissent in colonial Virginia* (1971) · R. S. Alley, 'The Reverend Mr. Samuel Davies: a study in religion and politics, 1747–1759', PhD diss., Princeton University, 1962 · W. M. Gewehr, 'Samuel Davies and the consolidation of Presbyterianism in eastern Virginia', *The Great Awakening in Virginia* (1930), 68–105 · G. H. Bost, 'Samuel Davies: preacher of the Great Awakening', *Journal of the Presbyterian Historical Society*, 26 (1948), 65–86 · C. A. Gilborn, 'Samuel Davies' sacred muse', *Journal of the Presbyterian Historical Society*, 41 (1963), 63–79 · G. W. Pilcher, 'Samuel Davies and religious toleration in Virginia', *The Historian*, 28 (1965–6), 48–71 · G. W. Pilcher, 'Samuel Davies and the conversion of negroes in early Virginia', *Virginia Magazine of History and Biography*, 74 (1966), 293–300 · L. F. Benson, 'President Davies as a hymn writer', *Journal of the Presbyterian Historical Society*, 2 (1903), 280 · L. J. Trinterud, *The forming of an American tradition: a re-examination of colonial Presbyterianism* [1949] · T. J. Wertenbaker, *Princeton, 1746–1896* (1946) · M. J. Coulter, 'Davies, Samuel', *ANB*

Archives Presbyterian Historical Society, Philadelphia · Princeton University, New Jersey · Virginia Historical Society | Dartmouth College, Hanover, New Hampshire, Eleazar Wheelock MSS · Hist. Soc. Penn., Ebenezer Hazard MSS · Hist. Soc. Penn., Benjamin Rush MSS · L. Cong., William Dawson and Thomas Dawson MSS · NYPL, William Richardson MS
Likenesses print, repro. in Wertenbaker, *Princeton, 1746–1896*, facing p. 68
Wealth at death small: Pilcher, *Samuel Davies*, 186 and n. 52

Davies, Scrope Berdmore (1782–1852), dandy and friend of Lord Byron, was born towards the end of 1782 in Horsley, Gloucestershire, and baptized there on new year's day 1783, the second son in the family of six sons and four daughters of the Revd Richard Davies (1747–1825), vicar of Horsley (and later Tetbury), and his wife, Margaretta, daughter of the Revd Dr Scrope Berdmore, vicar of St Mary's, Nottingham. Like his maternal uncle Scrope Berdmore, who was warden of Magdalen College, Oxford, from 1790 to 1810, Davies was elected to a king's scholarship at Eton College. To his life as a colleger his biographer, Tim Burnett, attributes 'to a large extent the formation of Scrope Davies' (Burnett, 13):

> Eton turned the … clergyman's son into a wit, dandy and a scholar with an entreé into the grandest rooms in London. At the same time it made him into a gambler, a drunkard and a spendthrift who ended his days in ruin. (ibid.)

He entered Eton in September 1794 at eleven. After fulfilling his duty there in Montem 1802 as college salt bearer—an office which although it entailed the wearing of a splendid costume can hardly have prepared him for the rigorous sartorial demands of life as a Regency dandy—Davies was admitted to King's College, Cambridge, on 8 July. On the following day, being the end of term, 'his gown was sewn up in front, and he presented himself to the Provost, who, taking a knife, ripped the gown in two': he was no longer an Etonian (ibid., 27).

Of the group of four friends (including, probably, himself) that Davies caricatured in a pen and ink sketch in a letter to Byron of 1809 (MS, priv. coll., repr. in Burnett, facing 37), he had met John Cam Hobhouse and Charles Skinner Matthews at Trinity College, and it was through them that he met Byron when the latter returned there, after almost a year's absence, in 1807. Becoming a member of this coterie, witty, intellectual, freethinking, interested in poetry and politics, was the reason for Byron's decision to remain at Cambridge; he and Davies rapidly became intimate friends. When debts prevented Byron's return to Cambridge in 1808, the two headed for London where, unable to borrow money with the same ease as his noble friend, the lure of the gaming table formed the greatest attraction for Davies. In his 'Detached thoughts' Byron recalled:

> One night Scrope Davies at a Gaming house—(before I was of age) being tipsy as he mostly was at the Midnight hour—& having lost monies—was in vain intreated by his friends one degree less intoxicated than himself to go home.—In despair—he was left to himself and to the demons of the dice-box.—Next day … he was found in a sound sleep— … a Chamber-pot stood by the bed-side—*brim-full* of—*Bank Notes!*—all won—… and to the amount of some thousand pounds. (*Byron's Letters and Journals*, 9.38–9)

Evocative of his friend's success as a gambler—Davies's good fortune climaxed in 1815 when he estimated that he was worth £22,000 in addition to his college scholarship—Byron's account of Scrope's night of hazard needs to be balanced against the careful book keeping and financial calculations that underlay his friend's play for high stakes. A trunk of Scrope Davies's papers was discovered in the vaults of Barclays Bank in Pall Mall in 1976. It contained notebooks, bills, and receipts, deposited there before his hasty departure to the continent in 1819, and revealed that he kept a detailed financial record of his gambling strategies. These papers (which were found with an original manuscript of *Childe Harold's Pilgrimage*, Canto 3, early versions of Shelley's 'Hymn to Intellectual Beauty' and 'Mont Blanc', and many letters by Byron) form the principal source of Tim Burnett's *The Rise and Fall of a Regency Dandy: the Life and Times of Scrope Berdmore Davies* (1981). When Byron went abroad in 1809 it was Davies who guaranteed the loan of about £5000 that financed his grand tour, a debt he eventually took over himself and which Byron discharged in 1814.

Captain Gronow, himself a former dandy, recalled of Davies that:

> His manners and appearance were of the true [Beau]
> Brummell type: there was nothing showy in his exterior. He
> was quiet and reserved in ordinary company, but he was the
> life and soul of those who relished learning and wit.
> (Burnett, 51)

Less exquisite in his pursuits, perhaps, than Brummell, Davies shared Byron's enthusiasm for pugilism and was 'besides being a profane Jester … a very good shot', a skill that, in a society where fortunes were won and lost at the gaming table, caused others to pause before issuing a challenge (*Byron's Letters and Journals*, 9.25). In the 'two or three duels' (ibid.) that he fought, Byron acted as his second. Following their affairs with Byron, Lady Caroline Lamb, Lady Oxford, and Lady Frances Wedderburn Webster were all taken up by Scrope Davies.

With his life arranged around the racing calendar, the gaming tables, and the requirements of his fellowship at King's College, Davies resided during the autumn months at Cambridge (convenient for the October meetings at Newmarket) and was in London during the season, leaving in August for a variety of watering places. While in London he resided in Limmer's Hotel in Conduit Street (1808 and 1811), and then in lodgings in Jermyn Street (1810), at 3 Little Ryder Street, off St James's Street (1814), and 11 Great Ryder Street (1816). He was a member of several clubs including Watiers, a favourite among the dandies; Brooks's, populated by whigs and where he could play only for small stakes; the Union Club, largely a gaming house where huge gains and losses could be made; and the Cocoa Tree, which he often frequented with Byron.

Party, with Lady Melbourne, to Byron's passionate feelings for his half-sister Augusta Leigh, Davies gave much support to Byron during the breakdown of his marriage in 1816, and visited him during the summer of 1817 at Geneva from where he returned with several of Byron's manuscript poems for John Murray. Following his involvement

with Hobhouse in 1819 in the election campaign of Francis Burdett and Douglas Kinnaird in Westminster, Davies was in increasing financial trouble, and, to escape his creditors, he went into exile in January 1820. In September 1824 he wrote to Augusta Leigh offering consolation for the death of Byron, giving his address as 10 place d'Armes, Ostend. In 1849 the writer Thomas Grattan who had met him several times in the intervening years encountered Davies in Boulogne 'looking so old, so bent, but so spruce, so neatly-dressed, so gentlemanlike in air, so lively and fresh in conversation … still flourish[ing] according to his fashion … but no longer a diner-out' (Burnett, 213). Byron recalled that:

> One of the cleverest men I ever knew in Conversation was
> Scrope Beardmore [*sic*] Davies … When [Beau] Brummell was
> obliged to retire to France—he knew no French & having
> obtained a Grammar for the purpose of Study—our friend
> Scrope Davies was asked what progress Brummell had made
> in French—to which he responded—'that B[rummell] had
> been stopped like Buonaparte in Russia by the *Elements*'.
> (*Byron's Letters and Journals*, 9.21-2)

At the end of May 1852 Edward Hawtrey, headmaster of Eton, wrote to Francis Hodgson, whom he succeeded as provost later that year:

> I am sure you will be sorry to hear that our old friend, Scrope
> Davies, was found dead in his bed at Paris a few days since.
> He was a most agreeable and kind-hearted person … He
> seemed quite broken down when I had a glimpse of him a
> few months since at Eton. I hardly knew him again, and
> should not have done so had he not mentioned his name.
> (Burnett, 216)

Davies had died in the night of 23–24 May in his lodgings in the rue Duras, Paris; he was buried in the cemetery at Montmartre in a plot provided by one John Lyon. The *Gentleman's Magazine* recorded that:

> For some time his constitution had evinced marks of decay.
> On the day previous to his dissolution he complained of cold,
> and retired early to his bed. He was found on the following
> morning lifeless upon the ground; it was evident that he had
> got up in the night, and had been seized by something
> approaching to apoplexy. (Burnett, 216-17)

Although Byron 'wish[ed] that he would marry & beget some Scrooples—it is a pity that the dynasty should not be prolonged—I do not know anyone who will leave such "a gap in Nature"' (*Byron's Letters and Journals*, 5.168), Davies, mindful, perhaps, of the statutes of King's College, under which marriage would have entailed forfeiture of his fellowship and the dividends this brought him, never married.   ANNETTE PEACH

Sources T. A. J. Burnett, *The rise and fall of a Regency dandy: the life and times of Scrope Berdmore Davies* (1981) · *Byron's letters and journals*, ed. L. A. Marchand, 12 vols. (1973–82); suppl. (1994) · A. Peach, 'Portraits of Byron', *Walpole Society*, 62 (2000), 1–144, esp. 35–6, fig. 13 · *IGI*
Archives BL, corresp. and papers | Bodl. Oxf., corresp. with Bruce family
Likenesses S. Davies, self-portrait?, pen-and-ink caricature, 1809, repro. in Peach, 'Portraits of Byron', fig. 13; priv. coll. · J. Holmes, watercolour on ivory miniature, 1815–16; Christies, 5 Dec 1906, lot 33

Davies, Sneyd (1709–1769), poet, was born on 30 October 1709 and baptized the next day in St Mary's Church,

Sneyd Davies (1709–1769), by Henry Hoppner Meyer, pubd 1817

Shrewsbury. His father, John Davies (1668/9–1732), was rector and patron of Kingsland, Herefordshire, and prebendary of Hereford and St Asaph. His mother, Honora (*b.* 1668), daughter of Ralph Sneyd of Keele Hall, Staffordshire, was second cousin to John Dryden, the poet, and was the widow of Thomas Ravenscroft (*d.* 1698). By her marriage to Davies she had three boys and a girl: Sneyd was the second and favourite son. Honora died before her second husband; he took as his second wife Isabella Hartstonge, widow of the bishop of Derry.

Davies was king's scholar at Eton College (1724–9), was admitted as scholar at King's College, Cambridge, on 4 July 1729, and was fellow of King's (1732–3; BA, 1733; MA, 1737). His Eton friends included Charles Pratt (also a fellow of King's, Cambridge), afterwards Lord Camden, and Frederick Cornwallis, future archbishop of Canterbury.

John Davies died in December 1732. He had quarrelled with his eldest son, John (1704–1735), so he bequeathed his rectory to Sneyd, who promptly took orders as deacon; he was ordained priest (Ely diocese) in December 1733. As a bachelor recluse at Kingsland, Davies amused himself with English and Latin poetical compositions and found a congenial crony in Timothy Thomas (*d.* 1751), rector of nearby Presteigne, who shared his tastes as far as superior age and fatness permitted. Davies's letters to Camden and other old college friends express contentment with his humble rectory, but he was pleased when Cornwallis, on becoming bishop of Lichfield, made him his domestic chaplain in February 1750 and, over the next five years, appointed him canon residentiary, master of St John's Hospital, Lichfield (2 July 1751), prebendary of Longdon, and archdeacon of Derby (5 May 1755).

In the 1750s Davies resided mainly in Lichfield, where he

became known in literary circles. The young Anna Seward (1742–1809) wept 'tears of delight' at his 'voice of tremulously pathetic softness' and 'religious energies, struggling through constitutional timidity' (*Letters of Anna Seward*). No sermons of his are extant. He obtained a Cambridge DD degree in 1759 as a step to possible further preferment, and dropped hints to his old friend Lord Camden who, however, was unable or unwilling to oblige until Davies was too old and ill to care.

Sneyd Davies was a poor horseman, except on a chamber-horse; he was fond of smoking his pipe, and had a passion for bowling. He was never married, and was singularly simple, modest, and unworldly. A lady having once taken a seat in his carriage, he showed his discretion by pulling up the blinds as he passed through the town.

Davies never collected his poems. They include Latin verses, imitations of Horace's epistles, serious and burlesque imitations of Milton, whom he specially admired, and verses in the manner of Swift. Some appeared, initialled S. D., in collections (1732 and 1745) by his school and college friend John Whaley; nine were reprinted in Dodsley's *Collection* (vols. 5 and 6, 1758). Davies helped to edit the Duncombes' *Works of Horace in English Verse* (1757), contributed imitations to it anonymously, and received the dedication of the fourth volume. His 'Caractacus' (written in 1757 for an annual meeting of admirers of that hero on Caer Caradog) was first printed in Pennant's *A Tour in Wales* (vol. 2, 1783). More poems appeared in 1780–81 in the *Gentleman's Magazine* and Nichols's *Collection* (vols. 6 and 7); more again were printed in a rambling life of Davies by George Hardinge (1743–1816) in Nichols's *Illustrations* (vol. 1, 1817). There are manuscript copies of his verses in Nottingham University and the British Library (Stowe MSS 5832, 5845). By 1761, in Bath for his health, Davies was weak and paralytic and suffered from irritable nerves; in 1763 he had a stroke. He died on 20 January 1769 and bequeathed Kingsland rectory (income £800 p.a.) to the Revd Richard Evans (1710–1797).

LESLIE STEPHEN, *rev.* BRIDGET HILL

Sources Nichols, *Illustrations*, 1.481–709; 3.130–44 · G. Hardinge, *Biographical memoirs of the Rev. Sneyd Davies, DD ... in a letter to Mr. Nichols* (privately printed, 1816) · R. A. Austen-Leigh, ed., *The Eton College register, 1698–1752* (1927) · Venn, *Alum. Cant.*, 1/1–4 · T. Harwood, *Alumni Etonenses, or, A catalogue of the provosts and fellows of Eton College and King's College, Cambridge, from the foundation in 1443 to the year 1797* (1797) [annotated copy in the library of King's College, Cambridge, 319, 323. Under Ashton] · *Fasti Angl.*, 1541–1857, 577, 615 · *Letters of Anna Seward: written between the years 1784 and 1807*, ed. A. Constable, 1 (1811), 194–5 · T. Pennant, *A tour in Wales*, 2 (1783), 422–4 · R. Churton, *Lives of ... the founders of Braze Nose College* (1800), 488

Likenesses H. H. Meyer, stipple engraving (after unknown artist), BM, NPG; repro. in Nichols, *Illustrations* [see illus.]

Wealth at death bequests of at least £350; advowson of a rectory with income of £800 p.a.: will, 27 Aug 1768, proved 1 Feb 1769

Davies, Stephen Owen (1886–1972), miners' leader and politician, was born at 39 John Street, Abercwmboi, Glamorgan, probably on 9 November 1886, the fourth of six children of Thomas Davies, miner and union organizer, and his wife, Esther. However, there is some uncertainty over the exact date of his birth.

After attending Capcoch School in Abercwmboi Davies started work in local coal mines at the age of twelve, but subsequently studied mining engineering at night classes, and in 1908 secured sponsorship from Brecon Memorial College to study for a BA at University College, Cardiff, with the ultimate intention of entering the nonconformist ministry. Conflict with Brecon over the precise nature of his religious beliefs led to withdrawal of support, but Davies nevertheless obtained his degree in 1913.

Davies's plans to become a minister were superseded by growing activism in socialist politics and trade unionism—two factors inextricably linked in the south Wales coalfield. In 1918 Davies became full-time agent for the Dowlais district of the South Wales Miners' Federation (SWMF) and entered into a formidable partnership with his counterpart in the neighbouring district of Merthyr, Noah Ablett (1883–1935). On 23 August 1919 he married Margaret Eley (d. 1932) of Cardiff; they had three daughters.

Adopting almost a syndicalist position, Davies maintained implacable opposition to post-war demands for nationalization of the industry as well as unsuccessfully advocating affiliation of the Miners' Federation of Great Britain to the Red International of Labour Unions (RILU) formed in Moscow in 1921. In 1922 Davies paid a visit to the Soviet Union as delegate of the Dowlais district of the SWMF to the Second World Congress of the RILU. This visit furnished him with a lifelong but often uncritical admiration for the Soviet system. Despite this, and although sympathetic to many of its aims, Davies did not join the Communist Party of Great Britain, preferring to remain within the Labour Party throughout the coalfield struggles of the 1920s. In 1934 Davies was elected Labour MP for Merthyr. The same year he remarried, his first wife having died two years earlier. His second wife was Sephora Davies from Carmarthenshire, with whom he had two sons.

At Westminster Davies consistently proved himself of independent mind, as prone to oppose the policies of a Labour government as those of a Conservative administration. Ever the watchdog for socialism, in its purest sense, as well as a rigid apologist for Soviet domestic and foreign policy whatever the excesses, he lost the whip on three occasions between 1953 and 1961 on issues relating to American bases in Britain, West German rearmament, and opposition to the Polaris submarine programme. A thorn in the side of the Wilson government between 1966 and 1970, he disagreed with its policy on public spending, wage controls, and trade union legislation. His support for the idea of Welsh self-government also often found him at variance with party policy.

Unsurprisingly, Davies was never offered government office but proved himself an excellent constituency MP. His concerns included reformation of the national insurance law in 1967, giving additional compensation to former miners afflicted with dust-related diseases. Such successes gained him a popular affection which transcended his admission to the Aberfan disaster tribunal in 1966 that he had entertained misgivings about the safety of local coal tips but remained silent, fearing that raising concern might cause closure of nearby collieries.

The Aberfan disaster also led to Davies's final estrangement from the Labour Party. Harold Wilson's support for the idea of using the disaster fund to contribute towards removal of the tips led Davies to boycott the ceremony bestowing freedom of the borough of Merthyr on the prime minister in 1970. His constituency party consequently replaced him as its candidate in the general election later that year. Refusing to accept that his political career was over, he stood as an independent socialist and, campaigning on his record, won by more than 7000 votes over the official Labour candidate. While this may say something about the historically individualistic nature of Merthyr politics, it also testified to his reputation and the local esteem in which he was held.

S. O. Davies died at Merthyr Tudful's general hospital on 25 February 1972, following a chest infection, and was buried at Maesyrarian cemetery, Mountain Ash, in his native Cynon valley on the 29th. He was survived by his second wife.   KEITH DAVIES

Sources R. Griffiths, *S. O. Davies: a socialist faith* (1983) · R. P. Arnot, *South Wales miners / Glowyr de Cymru: a history of the South Wales Miners' Federation*, [2] (1975) · WWBMP · *Merthyr Express* (3 March 1972) · *The Times* (26 Feb 1972) · d. cert.
Archives Glamorgan RO, papers · U. Wales, Swansea, corresp. and papers
Wealth at death £1945: administration, 30 May 1972, CGPLA Eng. & Wales

Davies, (Edward) Tegla (1880–1967), Wesleyan Methodist minister and author, was born on 31 May 1880 at Hen Giât, Llandegla, near Wrexham, Denbighshire, the fourth of the six children of William Davies, a slate quarryman, and his wife, Mary Ann (née Thomas), a domestic servant before her marriage. After elementary education at Llandegla and Ffrith, and serving as a pupil-teacher at a nearby school for seven years, he attended Didsbury College, Manchester (1902–5). On 19 August 1908 at Wrexham he married Jane Eleanor (1879–1948), the daughter of John Evans, a shopkeeper. They had two daughters, Dyddgu and Gwen, and a son, Arfor. Because of his wife's ill health Tegla retired in 1946, and they both moved to their daughter Dyddgu's home at Bangor.

Until 1931 Methodist ministers served a particular pastorate for three years only before moving to another. Tegla served in several areas in north Wales and the north and midlands of England. To his contemporaries he was a striking figure in the pulpit, tall and erect with meditative blue eyes beneath a high forehead and a cloud of auburn curls. In later life he looked even more impressive, his hair then a snowy white. He stood quite still, one hand resting motionless over the other on the open Bible. His voice was somewhat thin, monotonous but mesmeric. He abhorred the *hwyl*, the rousing sing-song of popular Welsh preachers, and himself avoided all pulpit gimmickry. He was theologically orthodox, but his opposition to scriptural literalism aroused hostility during his early ministry. Nevertheless he gradually earned respect as a preacher and writer. Despite frequent house removals and busy pastorates, he somehow found time to write more than forty books as well as editing three prestigious journals and a series of authoritative volumes by distinguished writers.

Tegla's first book, *Hunangofiant Tomi* ('Tommy's autobiography', 1912), was an instant success and was followed by three other amusing stories of boys and three fantasies for children, including the magical *Tir y dyneddon* ('The land of the little men', 1921). He continued to write for children but soon turned to adult fiction. His only full-length novel, *Gŵr Pen y Bryn* ('The master of Pen y Bryn', 1923), received wide critical acclaim until adverse criticism from Saunders Lewis caused the lesser critics to rethink, and disheartened the author. Tegla, with no university education, lacking self-confidence, and hurt by criticism, did not attempt another full-length novel. His farewell to adult fiction was his collection of short stories, *Y llwybr arian* ('The Silver Path', 1934), which contained stories that were well received in English translation.

Tegla's volumes of essays and published sermons contain some of his best writing. His rugged style in fastidiously correct Welsh, his flair for epigram, and his biting satire all contribute to an image of an Old Testament prophet chastising an errant people, but also comforting and encouraging when necessary. Although critics old and new hesitate to acknowledge him as a major writer, he was much honoured during his life. He was once elected moderator of the Welsh Methodist conference. He characteristically declined an OBE, writing to a friend, 'I could not imagine myself an "Officer of the British Empire" when I had committed my life to serving One who died on a cross'. But he did accept two honours from the University of Wales, the honorary degrees of MA in 1924 and DLitt in 1958, both for his contribution to Welsh literature.

After the death of his wife in 1948 Tegla continued to live at Bangor with his daughter and son-in-law in a self-contained flat on the upper floor of a handsome three-storeyed house. His later years were plagued by ill health. He died on 9 October 1967 at the local hospital, and was buried at Y Gelli cemetery in his beloved Tre-garth, near Bangor. He had always said that all his writings were a part of his religious work and it was for this alone that he wished to be remembered. On his gravestone is carved simply, 'E. TEGLA DAVIES, Gweinidog yr Efengyl' ('minister of the gospel'). ISLWYN FFOWC ELIS

Sources P. Davies, *E. Tegla Davies* (1983) · E. T. Davies, *Gyda'r blynyddoedd*, 3rd edn (1956) [autobiography] · H. Ethall, *Tegla* (1980) · I. Ff. Elis, ed., *Edward Tegla Davies, llenor a phroffwyd* (1956) [incl. full bibliography to 1956] · D. Jenkins, 'Tegla', *Taliesin*, 42 (July 1981), 9–24 · T. G. Jones, 'Tegla', *Yr Eurgrawn*, 127, 95–101 · W. E. Powell, 'Diwinyddiaeth Tegla', *Diwinyddiaeth*, 31, 66–75 · G. Ruddock, 'Gŵr Pen y Bryn', *Barn*, 37–48 (1965–6), 314–15, 339–40; 49–60 (1966–7), 23 · P. Davies, 'Tegla a'i Feirniaid', *Yr Eurgrawn*, 146 (July 1954), 180–82 · personal knowledge (2004) · private information (2004)

Archives NL Wales, corresp. with Norah Isaac | FILM BBC, 'Dylanwadan', Tegla Davies interviewed by Aneirin Talfan Davies; part only, No. 003389/02 · Hel Straeon Unit for S4C, 'Hel Straeon', various incl. 'E. Tegla Davies's family watch lost' (missing), No. 002009/04 · NL Wales, Audio-visual archive, 'Hel Straeon' incl. brief item on E. Tegla Davies, No. 002593/02 | SOUND NL Wales, Audio-visual archive, Mrs Eluned Thomas Collection, 'John Morris-Jones' by several, incl. E. Tegla Davies, No. 001519/01 · NL Wales, Audio-visual archive, 'Wedi'r Oedfa', radio talks by several, incl. E. Tegla Davies, No. 000431/01

Likenesses photograph

Wealth at death £3343: probate, 31 Oct 1967, CGPLA Eng. & Wales

Davies, Theophilus Harris (1834–1898), businessman and consul, was born on 4 January 1834 in Coalbournbrook, Stourbridge, Worcestershire, the second of the five children of the Revd Theophilus Davies (c.1798–1879?), a Welsh Congregational minister, and his wife, Mary Ann (c.1798–1849?). By 1837 his father had moved to Ludlow, Shropshire, where he combined his ministry with private tutoring. Davies was educated by his father.

At the beginning of 1851 Davies was employed as a book-keeper by a relative in Manchester, the commission merchant and agent Henry Beecroft Jackson. Davies could not do the job, and after six months he was redeployed as a shipping clerk. In 1856 Jackson's associate Robert Chesshyre Janion, a Liverpool merchant and agent of the Northern Assurance Company, appointed Davies as a clerk at his Honolulu office; thus in November Davies set sail for Hawaii, where he arrived in spring 1857.

In 1867 Janion's partner was in severe financial difficulties, and Davies—who had accumulated some capital—became Janion's new partner in Hawaii. In February 1868 Davies also established his own business, Theo. H. Davies & Co., with which he remained involved until his death. (His business was subsequently incorporated in 1894.) It made a number of very profitable investments in Hawaii's rapidly expanding sugar industry. On 5 October 1870 his father married Davies to Mary Ellen (1849?–1907), daughter of George Cocking, a Ludlow chemist and one-time mayor. They were to have five sons and two daughters.

Davies's partnership with Janion was dissolved following the latter's death in 1881. Davies retained an interest in many of the former partnership's investments, of which the most profitable was to be the Honolulu iron works. By the 1880s he had become one of the wealthiest businessmen in Hawaii. In addition to his business interests Davies found time to be treasurer of the Honolulu Cathedral building committee and to promote a Hawaiian branch of the YMCA. He also served as British vice-consul from 1872 to 1888. He acted as commissioner consul-general from 1872 to 1874 and was acting consul from 1877 to 1878. In 1888 the Hawaiian government considered appointing Davies as its consul-general in London. As a result Davies was required to resign his position of vice-consul in order to avoid a potential conflict of interest. However, King Kalakaua's dislike of Davies meant that the latter did not secure the appointment in London; none the less, Davies had already decided to retire to England that year.

Davies moved with his family to his new home, Sundown, in Southport, Lancashire, where he remained actively involved in the Liverpool branch of his business. During the Hawaiian political crisis of 1893–8 Davies was a strong supporter of Hawaiian sovereignty; he sought to protect the interests of his god-daughter and ward, Princess Kaiulani, the heir to the Hawaiian throne; and he unsuccessfully opposed the campaign by the Republic of Hawaii for annexation to the United States.

During his eleven years in Southport, Davies was an active and generous philanthropist who supported in particular the borough's young men and the parish of All Saints. He became a member of the committee of the YMCA in 1887 and served as its president in 1891, 1892, and 1897. Davies also served as president of the Southport Working Lads' Club from its foundation in 1891. An active supporter of the British and Foreign Bible Society and the Church Pastoral Aid Society, he was a member of the council of the Church Missionary Society, of the executive of the Church of England Temperance Society, and of the diocesan temperance committee for Liverpool. Davies supported the Conservative Party and later, in the 1890s, the Liberal Unionists. While in Southport he served as a justice of the peace. However, though he was offered the position of mayor of Southport, Davies did not seek political office. During his time both in Hawaii and in his retirement, he sought to promote both the commercial and the wider interests of the British empire. He was a fellow of the Royal Geographical Society, and also a fellow of the Imperial Institute.

In 1897 Davies moved to his new home, Ravensdale, in Pembury Road, Tunbridge Wells, Kent, because of his wife's poor health. His philanthropy and parochial work was transferred to the Tunbridge Wells parishes of Trinity and St James. Davies died after a winter visit to Honolulu. He caught a cold that led to his death, at Ravensdale, from what may have been typhoid fever or cholera on 25 May 1898. He was buried in the Tunbridge Wells new cemetery on 27 May. He died a very wealthy man, with real estate in Britain, Canada, and Hawaii, as well as investments in Hawaiian, European, Indian, and Canadian stocks and bonds.   RICHARD A. HAWKINS

Sources E. P. Hoyt, *Davies: the inside story of a British-American family in the Pacific and its business enterprises* (1983) · *Tunbridge Wells Gazette and Fashionable Visitors List* (27 May 1898) · *Southport Visiter* (26 May 1898) · *The Tunbridge Wells Advertiser* (27 May 1898) · 'The late Mr Theo. H. Davies: pulpit references', *Southport Guardian* (1 June 1898) · 'The late Mr Theo. H. Davies: tributes from the pulpit', *Southport Visiter* (31 May 1898) · 'Mr Davies' will', *Pacific Commercial Advertiser* (13 Sept 1898) · G. C. Davies, 'A portrait of Theo. H. Davies', *Davies Today* (May–June 1965), 3–6 · T. H. Davies, 'The Hawaiian situation', *North American Review*, 156 (1893), 605–10 · T. H. Davies, *Letters upon the political crisis in Hawaii, January 1893 to January 1894* (1894) · T. H. Davies, *Letters upon the political crisis in Hawaii: January and February 1894*, 2nd ser. (1894) · *CGPLA Eng. & Wales* (1898) · m. cert.

Archives Bishop Museum, Honolulu, archives · PRO, Foreign Office MSS, FO 58 and FO 331

Likenesses ten photographs, Bishop Museum, Honolulu, archives

Wealth at death £97,158 19s. 1d.: probate, 5 July 1898, *CGPLA Eng. & Wales*

Davies, Thomas (*c.*1511–1573), bishop of St Asaph, was born possibly at Llanbedr-y-cennin, Caernarvonshire, the son of Dafydd ap Robert, a gentleman of substantial means of Caerhun in Arllechwedd Isaf and descendant of

Sir Gruffudd Llwyd of Dinorwig and Tregarnedd, and Margaret, daughter of Rhys ap Wiliam, a descendant of Iarddur. He came from a family that served prominently in local administration, and was educated at Oxford, where he was influenced by religious reforms and obtained sinecure benefices in the dioceses of Bangor and St Asaph. He graduated LLD from St John's College, Cambridge, in 1548.

Davies was appointed chancellor of Bangor Cathedral (1546), archdeacon of St Asaph (probably in 1558–61), and, on Bishop William Glyn's death in 1558, was granted by Cardinal Pole the custodianship of the spiritualities of Bangor diocese until 21 December 1559 when Rowland Meyrick was elected to the see. He accepted Mary I's changes and kept his preferments on her death. On Richard Davies's removal from St Asaph to St David's in 1561 he was elected bishop of that see. He was confirmed on 23 May, consecrated at Croydon on 26 May, and the temporalities were restored on 2 April 1562. Davies made sixteen presentations to livings, most of them of resident, hospitable, and scholarly Welsh clergy, such as Thomas Powell, rector of Llanfechain (1562) and the historian and antiquary David Powel, vicar of Rhiwabon (1576).

Thomas Davies proceeded to establish a learned ministry in his diocese and emphasized the need to educate children in the protestant faith. In 1561 he issued diocesan council orders which stipulated that the catechism, the epistles, and the gospel were to be read in English and then in Welsh every Sunday to educate parishioners and children. The litany was to be sung or said on Wednesdays and Fridays and all 'feyned relyques and other superstycyons' were to be discarded. Also, after the ordination of priests and deacons on 31 October 1568, it was ordered that they were not to minister outside the diocese without the bishop's licence and were to use the New Testament in Latin and English and Erasmus's paraphrase of them. They were also required to learn chapter 1 of St Paul's epistle to the Romans and chapter 6 of the gospel of St John, to recite them in the bishop's presence, and to say morning and evening prayers daily.

In 1563 Davies informed the privy council of the poor condition of his diocese owing to an ill-endowed clergy, non-residence, and pluralism, but proceeded to improve clerical standards and appoint schoolmasters. In 1570 he informed William Cecil that he had succeeded in reorganizing the diocese but requested that an ecclesiastical commission be appointed to review it. He held several sinecures but kept the rectories of Llanbedr-y-cennin and Trefriw, the comportory rectory of Llandinam, and the living of Caerhun. He also retained the archdeaconry of St Asaph and the chancellorship of Bangor. These preferments were necessary in order that he might maintain a standard of living worthy of a bishop and be able to offer hospitality. Although William Salesbury lived in the diocese Davies seems not to have befriended him nor to have taken any part in his translation of the scriptures. However, with Bishop Richard Davies of St David's and Humphrey Llwyd, MP for Denbigh borough, he formed a Welsh lobby in parliament and was present in the House of Lords for the first two of three readings of the bill for a Welsh Bible in 1563. He supported the Thirty-Nine Articles in convocation (1563) and the disciplinary canons (1571).

Thomas Davies was an administrator rather than a theologian and contributed significantly to the organization of his see under the new protestant order. In 1565 he sat on a commission for the suppression of piracy on the Flintshire coast, and on the Lords' committee dealing with the bill for keeping records in the shires of Wales (1563). He was bequeathed books in the will of Arthur Bulkeley, bishop of Bangor, and in turn left books and £10 in his will (19 April 1570) to Friars School, Bangor, and to Queens' College, Cambridge. He bequeathed his interest in a mill and lands at Abergele to that college towards maintaining a scholarship which, however, was not administered. His estate was divided between his wife and executor, Margaret (of whom no other details are known), and his daughter Katherine, wife of William Holland of Abergele. He was a supporter of the classical bards, and laudatory odes were composed for him by Robert ap Dafydd Llwyd, Siôn Tudur, and Wiliam Cynwal. So highly regarded was hospitality at his palace that Siôn Tudur and Siôn Phylip disputed in verse their respective claims to enjoy his bountiful patronage. Davies died a rich man at Abergele, Denbighshire, on 16 October 1573, after completing his will, and was probably buried there.   J. GWYNFOR JONES

Sources NL Wales, Mostyn MS 1,324,486 · BL, MS 50, fol. 29a · BL, Harley MS 594, fols. 1–15 · will, PRO, PROB 11/55, sig. 33 · Wood, *Ath. Oxon.*, new edn, 2.823–4 · *APC, 1558–70*, 286 · Cooper, *Ath. Cantab.*, 1.319 · *Fasti Angl.* (Hardy), 1.75, 119 · D. Wilkins, ed., *Concilia Magnae Britanniae et Hiberniae*, 4 (1737), 228–9 · J. Wynn, *The history of the Gwydir family and memoirs*, ed. J. G. Jones (1990), 61 · J. E. Griffith, *Pedigrees of Anglesey and Carnarvonshire families* (privately printed, Horncastle, 1914), 213, 233 · B. Willis, *A survey of the cathedral church of St Asaph* (1720), 81, 110 · B. Willis, *A survey of the cathedral church of Bangor* (1721), 160 · *Gwaith Siôn Tudur*, ed. E. Roberts, 1, no. 121 (1980), 473–5 · D. R. Thomas, *Esgobaeth Llanelwy: the history of the diocese of St Asaph*, rev. edn, 1 (1908), 89–92, 225 · J. G. Jones, 'Thomas Davies and William Hughes: two Reformation bishops of St Asaph', *BBCS*, 29 (1980–82), 320–35 · J. G. Jones, 'The Reformation bishops of St Asaph', *Journal of Welsh Ecclesiastical History*, 7 (1990), 17–40 · *DWB*
Wealth at death approx. £600–£700

Davies, Sir Thomas (1631/2–1680), bookseller and lord mayor of London, was born between March 1631 and February 1632, one of the five children of John Davies (*d.* 1652) of Old Jewry in the City of London, merchant adventurer and member of the Drapers' Company, and his wife, Mary (*d.* 1665), daughter and heiress of Stephen Pecock and his wife, Elizabeth, sister of the 'infinitely rich' Hugh Audley. His grandfather was a Leicestershire man. Educated at St Paul's School, Davies was apprenticed to a bookseller in April 1648 and to his father in November 1648. The latter apprenticeship was probably a formality; John Davies died in a debtors' prison four years later, and Thomas was made free of the Stationers' Company in April 1655. He set up as a bookseller at the Sign of the Bible, St Paul's Churchyard, and entered into several joint publishing agreements between 1656 and 1662, apparently specializing in books in or translated from French and Latin. In 1662, Hugh Audley, who had made and changed a number of testamentary dispositions, finally gave his valuable

property in Middlesex to Thomas and his brother Alexander Davies, and made Thomas one of his executors and residuary legatees. Alexander bought Thomas's share of the Middlesex land, and died in 1665, leaving his fortune to his daughter Mary, who married Sir Thomas Grosvenor; there were disputes as to whether Alexander had left money to Thomas, or died in his debt, but Thomas was, at any rate, a rich man.

Davies became less active in the book trade (although as late as 1672 the copyrights of Milton's *History of England* and the second part of *Hudibras* passed through his hands), and entered civic life as alderman of the ward of Farringdon Without in 1667. As sheriff in the same year, he was present when the foundation stone of the new Royal Exchange was laid, and was knighted on that occasion, 'a strange turn methinks', as his old schoolfellow Samuel Pepys observed in an unfriendly note (diary, 23 Nov 1667); he also became a member of the governing body of his livery company. This entailed a payment of money to the company, which he did not make for many years. He became its master in 1668 and 1669, and neglected or refused to make the appropriate payment of venison on his election. In February 1669 he married Elizabeth, daughter of an alderman, William Ridges, with whom he had four sons.

In 1676 Davies became lord mayor of London, which necessitated his transferral to the Drapers' Company, of which he became master in the following year. His mayoralty is commemorated by inscriptions on Lamb's Conduit (rebuilt, like the Royal Exchange, after the great fire) and the Monument, and his life by a monument in St Sepulchre's Church, where he was buried in 1680. He died about March or April 1680, leaving property in Yorkshire, and a house at Cressing in Essex, where his eldest son shot himself. He was survived by his wife. A report said to have been prepared for Charles II in 1672 described Davies as 'A mean spirited person; when he was Sheriff of London he would (in a blind tavern) be drunk with his bailiffs and sergeants … He seldom appears in any business but his own' (*GM*, 516).   JOHN CONSIDINE

Sources C. Rivington, 'Sir Thomas Davies: the first bookseller lord mayor of London', *The Library*, 6th ser., 3 (1981), 187–201 · 'Sir Thomas Davies, lord mayor, 1676–7', *Herald and Genealogist*, 6 (1871), 356–9 · C. T. Gatty, *Mary Davies and the manor of Ebury* (1921) · A. L. Reade, *Audley pedigrees*, 2 vols. in 1 (privately printed, London, [1929–32]), vol. 2 · 'The character of the lord mayor of London and the whole court of aldermen', *GM*, 1st ser., 39 (1769), 515–17 · Pepys, *Diary*, 3.264; 8.497
Wealth at death lands in Yorkshire and Essex: Rivington, 'Sir Thomas Davies', 195

Davies, Thomas (*c.*1712–1785), bookseller and actor, is of unknown origins. He attended the University of Edinburgh between 1728 and 1729 to prepare for one of the learned professions, but left, presumably to become an actor. His first known appearance on the stage was at the theatre in the Haymarket, London (then under the management of Henry Fielding), where on 26 May 1736 he originated the role of Young Wilmot in George Lillo's domestic tragedy *The Fatal Curiosity*. Although the reviewer in the *Daily Advertiser* (28 May) observed that the play was acted 'with the greatest applause that has been shewn to any tragedy for many years' and that the 'scenes of distress were so artfully worked up, and so well performed, that there scarce remained a dry eye among the spectators' (Van Lennep and others, 3/1.588), the performance did not enable Davies to find steady work as an actor. Shortly afterwards he attempted bookselling at Duke's Court and Round Court, but when the business failed he once more turned to the theatre, and for several years belonged to various companies in York, Dublin, and Edinburgh. While in York he met and married Susanna (d. 1801), actress and daughter of Joseph Yarrow, an actor and writer; her 'beauty was not more remarkable than her private character', which 'has ever been unsullied and irreproachable' (*European Magazine*, 5). The couple returned to London and for the 1753 season were engaged at Drury Lane Theatre, 'where they remained for several years in good estimation with the town, and played many characters, if not with great excellence, at least with propriety and decency' (ibid.).

Believing that Davies and his wife earned £500 a year from the stage Samuel Johnson considered it 'folly' when Davies left the profession to return to bookselling in 1762. Johnson believed that Davies had been driven from the stage by a line in Charles Churchill's *The Rosciad* (1761)— 'He mouths a sentence, as curs mouth a bone'—and wondered 'what a man is he, who is to be driven from the stage by a line?' (Boswell, *Life*, 3.223). An early biographer of Davies thought that 'Churchill's indiscriminate satire' had 'endeavoured to fix some degree of ridicule on Mr. Davies's performance; but the pen of a satirist is not entitled to implicit credit' (*European Magazine*, 5). Davies himself blamed his leaving the stage on Garrick's 'warmth of temper' (*Letters*, 1.385n.). Whatever the cause he set up as a bookseller at 8 Russell Street, Covent Garden, where he lived until his death. There, in the back parlour of the bookshop, James Boswell first met Johnson, on 16 May 1763. When Boswell published his *Life of Samuel Johnson*, twenty-eight years later to the day, he added a note to the passage, describing the first meeting: 'No. 8.— The very place where I was fortunate enough to be introduced to the illustrious subject of this work, deserves to be particularly marked. I never pass by it without feeling reverence and regret' (Boswell, *Life*, 1.390n.).

In conversation with John Nichols, Davies described how he had published 'a silly pamphlet' in 1742 and then 'was smit with the desire of turning author' (Nichols, *Lit. anecdotes*, 9.665), but it was not until the 1770s that he turned seriously to writing. Johnson's remark that 'the biographical part of literature … is what I love most' (Boswell, *Life*, 1.425) applies equally to Davies, all of whose writings—apart from *Love Poems* (1761), *Miscellaneous and Fugitive Pieces* (1773-4), and his catalogues of books for sale—are biographies, contain biographies, or provide materials for future biographies. Davies edited important editions of the works of William Browne (1772), Sir John Davies (1773), Dr John Eachard (1774), George Lillo (1775), and Philip Massinger (1779), all with biographies of varying lengths. In addition he wrote *The characters of George the*

First, *Queen Caroline, Sir Robert Walpole, Mr. Pulteney, Lord Hardwicke, Mr. Fox, and Mr. Pitt, reviewed. With royal and noble anecdotes: and a sketch of Lord Chesterfield's character* (1777) and *A genuine narrative of the life and theatrical transactions of Mr. John Henderson, called the Bath Roscius* (1777). His most important biography was *Memoirs of the Life of David Garrick* (1780), in two volumes, which had gone through three editions by the following year. It is a wide-ranging 'life and times', but with important information, not only about Garrick but also about Johnson and other contemporaries. Johnson himself contributed the opening sentence, information on Garrick's early life in Lichfield and London, and many anecdotes.

Johnson's assistance to Davies with the memoir was part of a larger attempt to help him to recover from bankruptcy in 1778. Nichols reports that Davies's 'great and good friend Dr. Johnson … exerted all his power on his behalf' (*GM*), rallying friends to contribute to make it possible for Davies to recover his household belongings and prevailing on Richard Brinsley Sheridan, patentee of Drury Lane Theatre, to allow him a benefit. On 27 May 1778 Davies returned to the stage one last time, after an absence of sixteen years, to play Fainall in William Congreve's *The Way of the World*.

Davies's financial problems appear to have been of long standing, and one of his schemes for making money has become legendary. In autumn 1773, when Johnson was touring the Hebrides with Boswell, Davies published the first two volumes of *Miscellaneous and Fugitive Pieces*, which he advertised as 'By the Authour of the Rambler' (Boswell, *Life*, 2.270-71), without Johnson's knowledge or consent. The volumes included some early, uncollected writings by Johnson but also pieces with which he had no connection. Johnson reported to Mrs Thrale (Hester Lynch Piozzi) that when he confronted Davies 'I was a fierce fellow, and pretended to be very angry, and Thomas was a good-natured fellow, and pretended to be very sorry: so *there* the matter ended: I believe the dog loves me dearly' (Piozzi, 78).

The success of the memoir of Garrick encouraged Davies to publish the three-volume *Dramatic miscellanies: consisting of critical observations on several plays of Shakespeare … with anecdotes of dramatic poets, actors, &c.* (1783-4), which drew on a lifetime of experience and interest in the theatre. After Johnson's death, on 13 December 1784, Davies was thought to be among those undertaking a life. Although his own death would preclude such a project he did provide information for Boswell's life, as well as for William Shaw's *Memoirs of the Life and Writings of the Late Samuel Johnson* (1785). He also, according to Nichols, continued to produce miscellaneous writings, 'fugitive pieces without number, in prose and verse, in the St. James's Chronicle, and almost all the public newspapers' (*GM*).

Davies was a member of the club of major booksellers that met monthly at the Shakespeare tavern, where, according to Nichols, 'the germ of many a valuable publication' originated, including the life of Garrick, the *Dramatic Miscellanies*, and the ideas that led to the publication in 1779 of *Works of the English Poets with Prefaces, Biographical and Critical, by Samuel Johnson* (Nichols, *Lit. anecdotes*, 5.325).

Davies was one of three booksellers who had visited Johnson to propose the project. Nichols, who 'knew Mr. Davies well; and for several years passed many convivial hours in his company at a social meeting; where his lively sallies of pleasantry were certain to entertain his friends by harmless merriment', describes him as 'a man of uncommon strength of mind, who prided himself on being through life a companion for his superiors' (*GM*). Boswell described him as 'a man of good understanding and talents, with the advantage of a liberal education. Though somewhat pompous, he was an entertaining companion; and his literary performances have no inconsiderable share of merit' (Boswell, *Life*, 1.390–91). Johnson praised him as having 'learning enough to give credit to a clergyman' (ibid., 4.13) but also thought that no one could 'bring more amusement on his tongue, or more kindness in his heart' (ibid., 4.231).

On Davies's last visit to the club 'he wore the appearance of a spectre; and, sensible of his approaching end, took a solemn benediction' (*GM*). He died on 5 May 1785 and was buried in the vault of St Paul's, Covent Garden. He was survived by his wife, who died on 9 February 1801.

O. M. BRACK

Sources G. Blanton, 'Thomas Davies', *The British literary book trade, 1700–1820*, ed. J. K. Bracken and J. Silver, DLitB, 154 (1995), 93–6 · Boswell, *Life*, 1.390–95; 2.270–71; 3.223; 4.139, 231 · ESTC · J. D. Fleeman, *A bibliography of the works of Samuel Johnson*, 2 vols. (2000) · *The letters of David Garrick*, ed. D. M. Little and G. M. Kahrl, 1 (1963), 382–5 · W. Van Lennep and others, eds., *The London stage, 1660–1800*, 5 pts in 11 vols. (1960–68), pt 3, vol.1, p. 588; pt 5, vol. 1, p. 177 · I. Maxted, *The London book trades, 1775–1800: a preliminary checklist of members* (1977) · Nichols, *Lit. anecdotes*, 4.421–43; 5.325; 9.665 · *GM*, 1st ser., 55 (1785), 404 · J. Nichols, 'Thomas Davies', *Minor lives: a collection of biographies*, ed. E. L. Hart (1971), 237–49 · W. Over, 'Thomas Davies', *Eighteenth-century British literary biographers*, ed. S. Serafin, DLitB, 142 (1994), 69–77 · H. L. Piozzi, *Anecdotes of the late Samuel Johnson*, ed. A. Sherbo (1974), 78 · *Thraliana: the diary of Mrs. Hester Lynch Thrale (later Mrs. Piozzi), 1776–1809*, ed. K. C. Balderston, 2nd edn, 2 vols. (1951), 164, 624n., 625 · H. R. Plomer and others, *A dictionary of the printers and booksellers who were at work in England, Scotland, and Ireland from 1726 to 1775* (1932) · *European Magazine and London Review*, 5 (1784), 199 · *European Magazine and London Review*, 7 (1785), 388 · W. Shaw, 'Memoirs of the life and writings of Samuel Johnson', *The early biographies of Samuel Johnson*, ed. O. M. Brack and R. E. Kelley (1974), 137, 321 · C. H. Timperley, *Encyclopaedia of literary and typographical anecdote*, 2nd edn (1842), 754
Likenesses L. Schiavonetti, stipple, pubd 1794 (after T. Hickey), BM, NPG

Davies, Thomas (1792–1839), physician, was born in Carmarthenshire, and, after some schooling in London, was apprenticed to his maternal uncle, Mr Price, then apothecary to the London Hospital. He became an apothecary, and practised in the East End of London, but after two years had symptoms of phthisis. He went to Montpellier for his health, and afterwards to Paris, where he learned the then new art of auscultation under R. H. T. Laënnec, at the Necker Hospital. This led to him being known later as 'the man with the horn' among his patients in London. Davies graduated MD at Paris on 8 December 1821. After returning to London he was admitted a licentiate of the Royal College of Physicians, on 30 September 1824, and began practice at 30 New Broad Street, London, as a physician. In 1825 he was elected physician to the Infirmary for Asthma (later the Royal Hospital for Diseases of the Chest). Davies lectured at his house on diseases of the lungs and heart, and explained all he had learned from Laënnec. The lectures brought him professional recognition, and he was elected the first assistant physician to the London Hospital on 5 December 1827. He became a fellow of the Royal College of Physicians on 4 July 1838.

Davies's next post was as a lecturer on the practice of physic at the London Hospital. He published a course of lectures on the diseases of the chest in the *London Medical Gazette*; these appeared as a book entitled *Lectures on the Diseases of the Lungs and Heart* (1835). The book shows that its author had understood and tested for himself all the observations of Laënnec and of James Hope, but he added nothing to what they had taught, and though he writes at length on pericarditis, and had examined many examples *post mortem*, he was unaware of the existence of a pericardial friction-sound in such cases. Davies also gives an account and description of the exploring needle, which he introduced as a means of diagnosis in certain thoracic conditions.

Davies was married and had several children, one of whom was the physician Herbert *Davies (1818–1885). His chest disease returned, and it caused his death, at New Broad Street on 30 May 1839. Davies was fond of telling his patients, 'Keep up your spirits', and needed to take his own advice during his last illness, when he suffered from depression. He was buried in the churchyard of St Botolph without Bishopsgate, London.

NORMAN MOORE, rev. MICHAEL BEVAN

Sources *GM*, 2nd ser., 12 (1839), 98 · A. T. Davies, 'A note on Thomas Davies, introducer of the exploring needle', *Proceedings of the Royal Society of Medicine*, 16 (1922–3), 19–22 [section of the history of medicine] · Munk, *Roll* · *Physic and Physicians*, 2 (1839), 266

Davies, Thomas (1837–1892), mineralogist, was born on 29 December 1837 in the parish of St Pancras, London, the only son of William *Davies (1814–1891) of the geological department of the British Museum and his first wife, whose maiden name was Bradford. He left school and went to sea at the age of fourteen, visiting parts of Asia and South America. In 1858 he was appointed third-class attendant at the British Museum, working on the mineral collection under Professor Story-Maskelyne and, the following year, he married Jane Sabey of St Pancras. They later had four sons and five daughters.

At the British Museum, Davies developed an ability readily to identify mineral specimens and his capacity to determine the localities of minerals from their associated matrices was renowned. More than 140 years later many thousands of the museum's specimens retained his characteristic hand-written labels. In 1880 he was promoted to the grade of first-class assistant; by coincidence, his father obtained the same promotion on the same day.

An indefatigable worker, Davies was for a time editor of the *Mineralogical Magazine* and, latterly, foreign secretary of the Mineralogical Society. He was elected fellow of the Geological Society in 1870 and was awarded the Wollaston fund by the council in 1880 'as a testimony of the value of his researches in Mineralogy and Lithology' (*Quarterly Journal of the Geological Society*, 36, 1880, 31). Yet his recorded publications amount to only nine items, several on mineralogical topics and others on Precambrian rocks of Wales and Scotland. They appear in the *Quarterly Journal of the Geological Society*, *Geological Magazine*, and *Mineralogical Magazine*.

Davies spent the latter part of his life at 14 Perryn Road, Acton, where he died on 21 December 1892 after several years of failing health. He was survived by his wife and their nine children.   A. M. CLARK

Sources *Mineralogical Magazine*, 10 (1892–4), 161–4 · W. H. Hudleston, *Quarterly Journal of the Geological Society*, 49 (1893), 54–5 · W. T. Stearn, *The Natural History Museum at South Kensington: a history of the British Museum (Natural History), 1753–1980* (1981), 263–4, 266–8 · d. cert.
Archives NHM, diaries and notebooks
Likenesses wood-engraving (after photograph by J. Perryman), NPG; repro. in *ILN* (14 Jan 1893)
Wealth at death £693 2s. 10d.: probate, 28 Jan 1893, *CGPLA Eng. & Wales*

Davies, Thomas Stephens (1794?–1851), mathematician, was probably born in 1794, but little else about his early life is known. A formative influence was the mathematician William Trail (1745–1831), best known for his *Account of the Life and Writings of Robert Simson* (1812). It was Trail who instilled in Davies a lifelong fascination for geometry and a profound interest in its history. Davies began his career as a schoolmaster in Bath. His first scientific communications were published in the *Leeds Correspondent* in July 1817, and the *Gentleman's Diary* for 1819, and he subsequently contributed largely to the *Gentleman's and Lady's Diary*, to Clay's *Scientific Receptacle*, and to the *Monthly Magazine*, the *Philosophical Magazine*, the *Bath and Bristol Magazine*, and the *Mechanics' Magazine*. These papers earned him a considerable reputation as a mathematician and scientific writer. He became a fellow of the Royal Society of Edinburgh in 1831, and contributed several original and elaborate papers to its *Transactions*. That on the 'Geometrical character of the hour-lines upon the antique sundials' (*Transactions of the Royal Society of Edinburgh*, 12, 1832, 77–122) led to the discussion of the 'Equations of loci traced upon the surface of the sphere' (ibid., 259–362; 379–428) and the development of a new system of spherical geometry, by means of spherical co-ordinates. This system, more general than its predecessors, deserves more recognition than it has subsequently received. Further research on this subject was published as a supplement to John Radford Young's *Elements of Plane and Spherical Trigonometry* in 1833. On 18 April that year, Davies was elected a fellow of the Royal Society of London, and served on that body's mathematical committee until 1844.

Davies's principal area of research was geometry, in which he exhibited equal skill in both ancient and modern methods and acquired a reputation as 'the first of British geometers' (*Westminster Review*, 55, 1851, 83). Among the numerous subjects which engaged his attention were the properties of the trapezium, Pascal's *hexagramme mystique*, Brianchon's theorem, symmetrical

properties of plane triangles, the geometry of three dimensions, and stereographic projection. However, he also wrote on many other areas of science and literature, contributing papers on the 'Phenomena of terrestrial magnetism' to the Royal Society's *Philosophical Transactions* (1835, 1836) and on 'Determination of the law of resistance to a projectile' to the *Mechanics' Magazine*, as well as many other papers in the *Cambridge and Dublin Mathematical Journal*, the *Civil Engineer*, *The Athenaeum*, the *Westminster Review*, and *Notes and Queries*. Many such contributions were anonymous or published under a pseudonym such as 'Pen-and-Ink', 'Peter Twaddleton', or 'Knickerbocker'. He also edited, with William Rutherford and Stephen Fenwick, the first volume of *The Mathematician* (1845).

In 1834 Davies was appointed one of the mathematical masters in the Royal Military Academy at Woolwich. While there, he helped to publish several useful textbooks for the use of its students. The eleventh edition of Charles Hutton's *Course of Mathematics* (1837) was principally Davies's work. In 1840 he produced *Solutions of the Principal Questions in Dr Hutton's 'Course of Mathematics'*, containing 4000 solutions to problems in nearly all mathematical subjects and at every degree of difficulty. Next appeared the twelfth edition of Hutton's *Course* (2 vols., 1841–3) 'with considerable alterations and additions' by Davies—so considerable, in fact, that it contained 'not a single line of the original work'. Finally, his geometrical part of *An Elementary Course of Mathematics Prepared for the Use of the Royal Military Academy* was published as volume 2 in 1852.

Davies's deep interest in the history of geometry led to his election as a fellow of the Society of Antiquaries on 19 March 1840. He was also a council member of the short-lived Historical Society of Science, founded by James Orchard Halliwell in 1840. The last six years of his life were plagued by bronchitis. His death, following an attack of influenza, took place at his home, Broomhall Cottage, Shooter's Hill, Kent, on 6 January 1851, when he was in his fifty-seventh year.   G. C. BOASE, *rev.* ADRIAN RICE

Sources review, *Westminster and Foreign Quarterly Review*, 55 (1851), 70–83 [incl. notes on Davies's *Solutions of the principal questions* in Dr. Hutton's *A course of mathematics*; and *The Mathematician*] · 'Determination of the law of resistance to a projectile', *Mechanics' Magazine*, 54 (1851), 33–5 · *The Athenaeum* (11 Jan 1851), 53 · *The Expositor: a Weekly Recorder of Inventions, Designs, and Art-Manufactures*, 1 (1850–51), 284 · *ILN* (18 Jan 1851), 38 · *GM*, 2nd ser., 35 (1851), 559–60 · election certificate, RS
Archives BL, corresp. with C. Babbage · BL, corresp. with J. Hunter · Chetham's Library, Manchester, letters to Thomas Turner Wilkinson · CUL, letters to Hugh Godfrey · RS, letters to Royal Society · U. Edin. L., letters to James Halliwell Phillipps · UCL, Brougham MSS
Likenesses engraving, repro. in *The Expositor*

Davies, Sir (Henry) Walford (1869–1941), composer and organist, was born on 6 September 1869 in Willow Street, Oswestry, Shropshire, the seventh child and fourth surviving son of John Whitridge Davies (d. 1885), accountant, and his wife, Susannah, daughter of Thomas Gregory, jeweller. After attending Mr Owen's school in Willow Street, Oswestry, he was admitted a chorister at St George's

Sir (Henry) Walford Davies (1869–1941), by Walter Stoneman, 1936

Chapel, Windsor, in January 1882 under Sir George Elvey (who was succeeded only months later by Walter Parratt). In February 1885 he left the choir when his voice broke, but he quickly returned in May as assistant organist and secretary to Dean Randall Davidson. In order to eke out a living he secured a series of organist appointments in London—Park Chapel (1885–90), St George's, Campden Hill (1890), St Anne's, Soho (1890–91) and Christ Church, Hampstead (1892–7)—which culminated with the Temple Church in 1898. In 1885 he became acquainted with Mr and Mrs Thomas Matheson of 15 Cannon Place, Hampstead, the venue of the Hampstead Popular Concerts. A lifelong friendship developed, notably with Mrs Matheson (the 'M. G. M.' of many dedications), who, as mentor, undertook Davies's education in earnest. He entered for the Cambridge MusB in 1889, but his exercise (a cantata, *The Future*, to words by Matthew Arnold) failed the following year. However, Sir Charles Stanford strongly urged him to re-enter and the exercise was passed in 1891. In 1890 he gained a composition scholarship at the Royal College of Music, where he studied composition under Sir Hubert Parry (with a brief interlude under Stanford in 1893), modal counterpoint under W. S. Rockstro, piano with Herbert Sharpe, and the violin (later) with Haydn Inwards. Owing to the tuition he had enjoyed under Parratt at Windsor he declined to study the organ. When his scholarship ended in March 1894 he undertook some counterpoint teaching for Gladstone, and when Rockstro died in 1895 he was appointed teacher of counterpoint, a

post he retained until 1903, though not without some scruple. In 1896 he failed the counterpoint paper for the Cambridge MusD, and though he passed it in 1897, Stanford (professor of music at the university) had nevertheless informed him of its shortcomings. Davies thought of offering his resignation to Parry (who was by now director of the Royal College of Music), but he was persuaded to reconsider. Matters did not improve when his doctoral exercise, a short oratorio *The Days of Man*, was initially rejected. Davies was openly critical of Cambridge, which naturally infuriated its professor, Stanford. On the acceptance of Stanford's corrections Davies was forced to apologize, but his relations with Stanford remained strained for some years to come. He proceeded to the MusD in 1898.

On his appointment as organist at the Temple Church in 1898, one which he held for the next twenty-one years, Davies's position in British musical life began to assume greater prominence. He conducted the London Church Choirs' Association (1901–13), succeeded Stanford as conductor of the London Bach Choir (1902–7), and became well known as an organist (particularly as an exponent of Parry's late organ works) and as a teacher (his most famous pupil being Leopold Stokowski). During the war years he was initially involved with the Music in Wartime movement, but gave this up for a more musically active role, organizing concerts for the troops in France and assisting with musical events for the Fight for Right movement (which included the commissioning of Parry's choral hymn 'Jerusalem'). In 1918 he was raised to the rank of major in the RAF.

Davies's connection with Wales began in 1919 when he was appointed professor of music at University College, Aberystwyth, and chairman of the National Council of Music for the University of Wales. He resigned the former in 1926 but retained the latter post until his death. The resignation of his position at the Temple in 1923 opened the way the following year for further career opportunities, including his appointment as Gresham professor of music (succeeding Sir Frederick Bridge) and a long association with radio, marked by the Cramb lectures from Glasgow, broadcast for the first time from Savoy Hill. Moreover, at the age of fifty-four, on 4 September 1924, he married (Constance) Margaret Isabel Evans (*b.* 1898), daughter of William Evans, canon of St David's and rector of Narberth; she was twenty-eight years his junior. On his appointment as a musical adviser for the BBC in 1926 Davies became well known for his programmes such as *Music and the Ordinary Listener* (1926–9), his wartime children's broadcasts (1939–41), and *Everyman's Music* (1940–41). Between 1927 and 1932 he was organist at St George's Chapel, Windsor, after which he retired from full-time work, though he continued to be active as a lecturer, broadcaster, writer (his book *The Pursuit of Music* was published in 1935), conductor, and adviser, not least in his role as master of the king's musick after Elgar's death in 1934. In recognition of his services to music in Britain he was knighted in 1922, having already been made OBE in 1919. He was created CVO in 1932 and was promoted to KCVO in 1937, in part owing to his role in the musical organization of the coronation of King George VI. He also accepted honorary degrees from Leeds (LLD, 1904), Glasgow (LLD, 1926), Dublin (MusD, 1930), and Oxford (DMus, 1935) and was made a fellow of the Royal College of Organists (1904), the Royal Academy of Music (1923), and the Royal College of Music (1926). At the outbreak of the Second World War he moved to Bristol to be with the BBC's department of religion. He died at Glencairn, Wrington, near Bristol, on 11 March 1941, and after a funeral service at Bristol Cathedral on 14 March his ashes were laid in the cathedral garden.

As a composer Davies was profoundly influenced by Brahms (whom he met at Ischl in 1896) and even more so by Parry, who lies behind the corpus of chamber works and a symphony from Davies's student days, and whose neo-Bachian, ethical preoccupations can be felt in the series of large-scale choral works—namely *The Temple* (Worcester, 1902), *Everyman* (Leeds, 1904), *Lift up your Hearts* (Hereford, 1906), *Noble Numbers* (Hereford, 1909), and the *Song of St Francis* (Birmingham, 1912)—written during the heyday of his career as a festival composer before the First World War. Yet Davies did not live up to his early promise (which enjoyed its zenith in *Everyman*) and his career as a composer fell away after the war. His name is still familiar to church musicians and to educators, but he is best remembered today as a miniaturist, for his *Solemn Melody* (1908), written for the Milton tercentenary celebrations, the introit 'God be in my head' (from *Songs of Church and Home*, 1908), an attractive version of 'O little town of Bethlehem', a frequently sung carol arrangement of 'The holly and the ivy', and the *RAF March Past* (1921). These pieces best show Davies as the professional composer of *Gebrauchsmusik*, but the intensity of expansive lyricism, organic construction, and harmonic adventure, such as one finds in his sadly neglected early setting for baritone and string quartet of Browning's 'Prospice', op. 6 (written after a life-threatening attack of peritonitis in 1890), provides a glimpse of a powerful symphonic imagination that he failed to consolidate in his later works.

JEREMY DIBBLE

Sources H. C. Colles, *Walford Davies* (1942) · H. Ottaway, 'Walford Davies', *New Grove*, 2nd edn, vol. 6 · *RCM Magazine*, 65/3 (1969) · J. Dibble, *C. Hubert H. Parry: his life and music* (1992); pbk edn (1998) · *DNB* · b. cert. · m. cert. · d. cert.
Archives NL Wales, letters · Royal College of Music, London, archive · St George's Chapel, Windsor, MSS | BL, corresp. with Society of Authors, Add. MSS 56687–56688 · Elgar Birthplace Museum, Worcester, letters to Edward Elgar · NL Wales, letters to T. G. Jones · NL Wales, corresp. with Thomas Jones · NL Wales, letters to R. Guy Harland · St George's Chapel, Windsor, letters to E. H. Fellowes | FILM BFI NFTVA, home film footage | SOUND BL NSA, documentary recording · BL NSA, performance recording
Likenesses W. Stoneman, photograph, 1936, NPG [*see illus.*] · E. Walters, charcoal drawing, NMG Wales · photographs, Royal College of Music, London
Wealth at death £3572 12s. 5d.: probate, 9 July 1941, *CGPLA Eng. & Wales*

Davies, Walter [*pseud.* Gwallter Mechain] (1761–1849), antiquary and poet, was born on 14 July 1761 at Y Wern, near Tomen y Castell, Llanfechain, Montgomeryshire, one of the seven children of William Davies, a labourer, and his wife, Catherine Bennett (*b.* 1733). He developed an early passion for books from his mother, who was respected in the area for her learning. As a boy he spent much of his time in the company of local poets and was educated by the parish priest until the age of twelve. He was thereafter apprenticed to a cooper and practised his craft in a barn near Tomen y Castell.

In 1789, taking the bardic name Gwallter Mechain, Davies became an eager competitor for prizes at the local eisteddfods, which were being fostered in north Wales by the Gwyneddigion Society of London. This brought him to the attention of Owen Jones (Owain Myfyr), a literary patron, whose financial assistance enabled him to obtain a place at St Alban's Hall, Oxford, in 1791. He subsequently obtained a clerkship at All Souls College, and in 1792 worked as curator at the Ashmolean Museum, where he gained access to some of the manuscripts of the Welsh scientist and philologist Edward Lhuyd. He read widely during this period, taking an interest in medicine and astrology as well as in literature and antiquities. He graduated BA from Oxford in 1795, and shortly afterwards was appointed curate at Meifod in Montgomeryshire. He proceeded MA as a member of Trinity College, Cambridge, in 1803. In 1797 he was invited by the board of agriculture to compile a survey of agriculture and the domestic economy in north Wales. This was published in two volumes in 1810 and 1813, and followed in 1815 by a second report on south Wales, on which he collaborated with Edward Williams (Iolo Morganwg). On 15 October 1799 Davies married a widow, Mary Pryse of Rhosbrynbwa, at Meifod. They had four children.

In 1807 Davies was appointed rector of Manafon in Montgomeryshire, where he became associated with a group of antiquaries later known as *yr hen bersoniaid llengar* (literally 'the old literary parsons'). From 1818 onwards, together with John Jenkins (Ifor Ceri), William Rees of Cascob, and others, Davies sought zealously to promote regional eisteddfods and to encourage the publication of Welsh literary and historical manuscripts, thus, in effect, continuing the work of Owain Myfyr and the Gwyneddigion Society. He also worked with Daniel Rowland of Llanddewibrefi to found provincial societies throughout Wales to stimulate interest in literature and antiquarian scholarship.

Davies was greatly respected by his contemporaries as an adjudicator of poetry at eisteddfods. He insisted upon the classical canons of criticism favoured by Goronwy Owen and other poets of the mid-eighteenth century. His own obsessive urge to compete for literary prizes continued into old age, yet his work has little merit and is seldom read today. His most enduring work was as an editor of the works of major poets such as Huw Morus (1823) and Lewis Glyn Cothi, whose work he edited in collaboration with John Jones (Tegid) in 1837. On 18 November 1837 Davies became vicar of Llanrhaeadr-ym-Mochnant, in Denbighshire. He died there on 5 December 1849 and was buried in the churchyard.

GERAINT PHILLIPS

Sources J. T. Owen, 'Gwallter Mechain', MA diss., U. Wales, 1928 · NL Wales, MSS 1641–1952 · BL, Owain Myfyr MSS, Add. MSS 14962–

15089 · marriage bonds, St Asaph, NL Wales [W. Davies and C. Bennett] · marriage bonds, St Asaph, NL Wales [W. Davies and M. Pryse]

Archives NL Wales, corresp. and papers; papers | BL, Owain Myfyr MSS, Add. MSS 14962–15089

Likenesses H. Hughes, oils, 1825, NMG Wales

Wealth at death see NL Wales, Gwallter Mechain deeds, copy of his will; probate, 15 Nov 1850

Davies [Dai], **William** (d. 1593), Roman Catholic priest and martyr, was born at Croes-yn-eirias in the parish of Llandrillo-yn-rhos (now Colwyn Bay), son of William Dai and grandson of Dafydd (Dai) Nantglyn, the most distinguished harpist of his day. His mother (or stepmother) was Katherine Evans, wife of 'William Day o'r Groes'; she was listed as a recusant in Llandrillo-yn-rhos in 1587–8. His father was a protestant, however. William Davies, possibly he who matriculated at St Edmund Hall, Oxford, in 1575 and graduated in 1578, was admitted to the English College, Douai (at Rheims), in 1582, ordained in 1585, and in the same year arrived as a missionary in north Wales, on home ground. His centre of activity was probably Plas Penrhyn, the home of Robert Pugh. Both he and Robert Pugh were in 1587 of the company of recusants obliged to flee overnight from the cave at Rhiwledin, near Penrhyn, where they had established themselves with a printing press; the one book incompletely produced on this press (the first known book to be printed in Wales) was the anonymous *Y drych Cristianogawl* ('The Christian mirror').

In 1592, again in the company of Robert Pugh, in Holyhead, while arranging the passage of four Welsh seminary students to Valladolid, Davies was arrested (Pugh escaped). He was imprisoned in Beaumaris Castle, with the four students. Condemned at his first trial, he was removed to Ludlow, to Bewdley, and to other prisons, but, refusing to recant, was brought back to Beaumaris and tried again. On 27 July 1593 he was hanged, drawn, and quartered in Beaumaris Castle. During his time at Beaumaris he became the focus of fervent local support; executioners, and even the material for the execution, had to be brought from afar. His one surviving letter describes his first trial; there are three accounts of his martyrdom. He was declared venerable by Pope Leo XIII in 1886, and beatified by Pope John Paul II in 1987. A single poem by him survives, in Welsh: a meditation on Lent, it echoes poems of Richard Gwyn.   DANIEL HUWS

Sources DWB · P. J. Crean, *Sir William Dai* (1958) · D. A. Thomas, *The Welsh Elizabethan Catholic martyrs* (1971) · R. G. Gruffydd, '"Carol santaidd i'r grawys" o waith y Tad William Davies', *Transactions of the Caernarvonshire Historical Society*, 28 (1967), 37–46 · R. G. Gruffydd, *Argraffwyr cyntaf Cymru* (1972) · NL Wales, Peniarth deed 259 · PRO, E 377/14 membr. 63

Davies, William (fl. 1598–1614), traveller, was born in Hereford, and states himself to have been a barber–surgeon, although no trace can be found of him in the register of admissions to the freedom of that company. He states that he was a gentleman by birth and had served in many naval and military operations. His family may have had Cornish connections since he sailed from there and his brother settled there. On 28 January 1598 he sailed in a trading ship (the *Francis*) from Saltash, Cornwall, and

reached Civita Vecchia, the port of Rome. He subsequently visited Algiers and Tunis. On leaving Tunis his ship was attacked by six galleys of Ferdinand de' Medici, grand duke of Tuscany. Davies was captured and taken to Leghorn, where he worked as a slave for eight years and ten months. For much of his time he was a galley slave and he recounts the extreme miseries of such a state. Indeed, of thirty-six men taken with him only thirteen remained alive nine years later.

In 1608 an Englishman, Robert Thornton, who had entered the duke's service after absconding with his English ship, was appointed captain of the *Santa Lucia*, one of three ships fitted out by the duke for an expedition to the West Indies. The voyage seems to have been conceived by Robert Dudley, the illegitimate son of the earl of Leicester, who provided Thornton with maps and charts. Thornton asked the duke's permission to take Davies with him as surgeon and physician, in which capacities he was said to be experienced. The duke demanded 500 crowns as security for Davies's working under Thornton's orders, and the money was paid by William Mellyn of Bristol, who happened to be in Italy.

Davies spent ten weeks in the Amazon delta area, mainly on the north shore, but his description of it is tantalizingly brief. The explorers found none of the silver or gold that the duke hoped for and Davies evidently considered the region more of a curiosity than a place which would repay further exploration or exploitation or settlement.

On returning to Italy in June 1609 Davies's ship was attacked by an English pirate, and an English sailor, Erasmus Lucas of Southwark, was fatally wounded. Davies landed with the body at Leghorn, and finding that Lucas would be denied burial in sacred ground because he was not a Roman Catholic, Davies proceeded to bury the body himself according to protestant rites. While thus engaged he was arrested by agents of the Inquisition. He lived on bread and water in an unlighted underground dungeon for sixteen days, and after a first examination was moved to a large open prison, the charge against him, that he had buried a Catholic according to protestant rites, having been dropped. An English shipowner, Richard Row of Milbroke, Cornwall, who knew Davies's brother in Plymouth, helped him to escape, and after sailing in the Mediterranean in the *Porrion* he reached London in 1614 and wrote an account of his travels, published that year as *A True Relation of the Travailes … and Captivitie of William Davies*. It was reprinted in 1746 in Osborne's *Travels and Voyages*, volume 1. This was the fullest account of the voyage, though only two brief chapters concern the Amazon and the Caribbean. Other information brought back by Thornton was recorded by Robert Dudley on a manuscript map, which was a revised version of that which Dudley had supplied him at the outset. The voyage did not stimulate further Tuscan interest, Ferdinand having died while the expedition was underway, although it may have helped to keep English interests in the area alive. Nothing further is known of Davies.   ELIZABETH BAIGENT

Sources W. Davies, *A true relation of the travailes and most miserable capitivitie of William Davies* (1614) • J. Lorimer, ed., *English and Irish settlement on the River Amazon, 1550–1646*, Hakluyt Society, 2nd ser., 171 (1989) • *DNB* • *Register of admissions to freedom of the Barber-Surgeons' Company*

Davies, William (d. 1820), bookseller, of obscure origins, was assistant to the elder Thomas *Cadell (1742–1802), bookseller and publisher, when he was chosen by him in 1793 as a partner for his youthful son Thomas *Cadell the younger (1773–1836) [*see under* Cadell, Thomas] in the management of his business. From that time the business traded as Cadell and Davies, and Cadell the younger left the management of the business to his partner until Davies fell ill in 1813. During these years the firm continued its reputation for generosity to authors. Regardless of G. Steevens's comment to Bishop Percy in 1797 that Cadell and Davies, 'in spite of all their boasts, are not allowed to be at the head of their trade in the line of publication' (Nichols, *Illustrations*, 7.30), the business seems to have been thriving at the end of the century. In 1800 the United States congress commissioned Cadell and Davies to supply 5000 dollars' worth of books, journals, and maps which would form the basis for the Library of Congress. The firm continued to publish Burns's poetical works, as well as Boswell's *Life of Johnson*, although in 1797 they declined the opportunity to publish what became Jane Austen's *Pride and Prejudice*. A contemporary bookseller noted in the *Aldine Magazine* that while some in the book trade found Davies somewhat 'haughty', he was in truth a 'straightforward man of business' who was 'possessed of superior abilities', although he later 'became too adventurous and liberal in his literary purchases' (Besterman, xi). Davies was a yeomanry stockkeeper of the Stationers' Company in 1800 and 1803 and a livery stockkeeper in 1812 and 1818. He and his wife, Jessy (or Jesse; 1777/8–1854), had eight children. He died on 28 April 1820, leaving his family less well provided for than might have been expected. His wife died at Bushey, Hertfordshire on 14 October 1854.   H. R. TEDDER, rev. CATHERINE DILLE

Sources T. Besterman, *The publishing firm of Cadell and Davies: select correspondence and accounts, 1793–1836* (1938) • Nichols, *Lit. anecdotes*, 6 (1812), 442 • Nichols, *Illustrations*, 7.30, 126–7, 132, 139, 152–3, 190–91; 8.320, 492–3 • *Aldine Magazine*, 1 (1839), 309–10 • C. Guidici, 'Cadell, T. Cadell and W. Davies, and Cadell, jr', *The British literary book trade, 1700–1820*, ed. J. K. Bracken and J. Silver, DLitB, 154 (1995), 33–8 • R. Myers, ed., *Records of the Stationers' Company, 1554–1920* [1984–6] [microfilm; with guide, *The Stationers' Company archive: an account of the records, 1554–1984* (1990)]
Archives NL Scot., corresp., MSS 1653–1655 | Yale U., Beinecke L., corresp. with T. Cadell
Wealth at death 'The family of Mr Davies was, at his death, not left so well provided for as might have been hoped, from his large business concerns': Nichols, *Illustrations*, vol. 8, pp. 492–3

Davies, William (1814–1891), palaeontologist, was born at Holywell, Flintshire, on 13 July 1814, the son of Thomas Davies and his wife, Elizabeth Turner. After going to school in his native town he studied botany, and on 19 December 1843 obtained a post as an attendant in the British Museum in London, working at first on the mineral collections. He became a competent general mineralogist, and was subsequently employed to work on the fossil vertebrate collections. In this field he not only acquired great technical knowledge as to the best methods of developing and preserving delicate specimens, but also was pronounced to be 'one of its most accomplished students'. He was so skilled in reconstructing the remains of extinct specimens that in 1875 he was made responsible for the whole fossil vertebrate collection.

Davies took an active part in the rearrangement of the natural history collections in 1880, when they were transferred from Bloomsbury to the new buildings in South Kensington. He gave most valuable assistance to Sir Antonio Brady in collecting a series of Pleistocene mammal remains from the Thames valley brickearth, which he later described and figured. He was also responsible for the excavation and preservation of the Ilford mammoth head.

In 1880 Davies was promoted to assistant, first class, having been made assistant five years earlier. He retired in 1887 and was pensioned by the museum, which he continued to provide with revised proofs of palaeontological works. He died at his home, 66 Antill Road, Bethnal Green, London, on 13 February 1891, from epilepsy and syncope. He was twice married, and with his first wife (*née* Bradford) had a son, the mineralogist Thomas *Davies (1837–1892), and a daughter.

The Geological Society made Davies the first Murchison medallist in 1873 and elected him a life fellow in 1877. He disliked literary composition, so his scientific papers were not numerous. He was the author of about fifteen important papers, mostly contributed to the *Geological Magazine*, and published a *Catalogue of the Pleistocene Vertebrata in the Collection of Sir Antonio Brady* (1874).

T. G. BONNEY, rev. YOLANDA FOOTE

Sources *Geological Magazine*, new ser., 3rd decade, 8 (1891), 144, 190–92 • A. Geikie, *Quarterly Journal of the Geological Society*, 47 (1891), 56 • private information (1901) • W. T. Stearn, *The Natural History Museum at South Kensington: a history of the British Museum (Natural History), 1753–1980* (1981) • *DWB* • d. cert.
Wealth at death £2394 8s. 3d.: resworn probate, Sept 1891, CGPLA Eng. & Wales

Davies, William Edmund (1819–1879), bookmaker, was born in London. His father was a carpenter and Davies too entered the building trade, working for Cubitt & Co., contractors and builders, Gray's Inn Road, London. On one occasion he was sent to Newmarket to help repair the inside of the subscription rooms. Whether this influenced him to begin taking bets from his fellow workers is a matter for conjecture, but his success as a petty bookmaker enabled him to give up working as a carpenter. He was a major pioneer of the betting list, in which the names of horses and the odds against them would be displayed openly, often in public-house windows. His first list was at the Salisbury Arms in Durham Street, Strand, London, and his second at a house known as Barr's Windsor Castle, 27 Long Acre, Covent Garden. At these places he and his clerks stood at huge bankers' ledgers and entered the bets.

By the time the Betting House Act of 1853 made such lists illegal, on the grounds that they tempted working people into crime to finance their gambling, Davies had become a wealthy man.

Davies also moved up the betting market, abandoning his 'silver' book and setting a minimum bet of £1. At the other end of the scale he appears to have set no limit and earned himself the sobriquet Leviathan for the size of the bets he accepted, both individually and in aggregate. He established himself at the head of the profession by betting with the earl of Strafford £12,000 to £1,000 on the Cur for the Cesarewitch in 1848; he paid the money on the day after the race. From that moment he enjoyed the chief patronage of all heavy backers of horses, and his lists ruled the market. In 1850, when Lord Zetland's Voltigeur was the winning Derby favourite, Davies had to pay out nearly £40,000 over his list counter to his humbler clients who had put their sovereigns on the race. In the previous Derby, when Hotspur was beaten by the Flying Dutchman, he had lost a similar sum. The victory of Daniel O'Rourke in the 1852 Derby resulted in his having to pay more than £100,000. Yet despite his losses he opened the season of 1853 with £130,000 to his credit at the London and Westminster Bank. His constant habit was to go to Tattersall's after the Derby, however great his losses, and pay on the Monday instead of waiting until the conventional settling Tuesday; and while his lists were in force he returned every night from Newmarket to attend to them and provide the money for paying next day. In an era of turf corruption he was an honest man, one of a small number of bookmakers of whom Admiral Rous, doyen of the Jockey Club, said he would accept their word of a £10,000 bet without a written undertaking. The certainty that claims on him would be paid on demand made his winning tickets as negotiable among his customers as banknotes.

A muscular, powerful man, who once fell through the dilapidated stand at Rochester, Davies opted for early retirement and wound up his business on the Friday of the Houghton meeting in 1857, and took his final leave of Newmarket. On his retirement he lived first at the King and Queen Hotel, Brighton, but soon moved to 18 Gloucester Place, Brighton, where he died on 4 October 1879. In his will he left property in railway shares valued at £60,000 to the Brighton corporation, subject to the payment of certain annuities. His widow, Ann Davies, gave notice to dispute the will, but on 21 January 1880 an arrangement was made by which the greater part of the property went to the corporation on her death. Preston Park, Brighton, which cost £50,000 and was opened on 8 November 1884, was purchased with this money.

G. C. BOASE, rev. WRAY VAMPLEW

Sources T. H. Bird, *Admiral Rous and the English turf* (1939) · W. Vamplew, *The turf: a social and economic history of horse racing* (1976) · J. Rice, *History of the turf* (1879) · *The Field* (Oct 1879) · *The Times* (22 Jan 1880) · J. Fairfax-Blakeborough, *The analysis of the turf* (1927) · The Druid [H. H. Dixon], *The post and the paddock: with recollections of George IV, Sam Chiffney, and other turf celebrities* (1895) · *CGPLA Eng. & Wales* (1880)

Wealth at death under £90,000: probate, 16 Aug 1880, *CGPLA Eng. & Wales*

Davies, William Henry (1871–1940), poet and writer, was born at his paternal grandfather's public house, Church House inn, Portland Street, Newport, Monmouthshire, on 3 July 1871, the younger son of Francis Boase Davies (1843–1874), an iron-moulder, and his wife, Mary Ann Evans (*b.* 1839/40). William Davies's father died when his son was three, and on his mother's swift remarriage he, his sister, and his mentally disabled brother were adopted by their grandparents. His grandfather, a native of Cornwall, had been master of a small schooner. Davies attended the Temple Street School and Alexandra Road School in Newport; he was an unruly schoolboy, but had a passion for reading. Later on, in *Who's Who*, he chose to describe himself as having 'picked up knowledge among tramps in America, on cattle boats, and in the common lodging-houses in England'.

On leaving school Davies was apprenticed to a picture-frame maker, but having been left an allowance of 10s. a week by his grandmother, at the age of twenty-two he obtained from his trustee an advance of £15 for passage-money to the USA, reaching New York with only a few dollars. He then began that career which he later described in his *Autobiography of a Super-Tramp* (1908; many subsequent impressions): tramping thousands of miles in the United States in five or six years, most often begging, but sometimes working at fruit-picking; riding illicitly on freight trains; and making eight or nine trips to England as a cattle-man. He then returned home for a few months, in which time he spent half of his allowance, none of which he had touched since he had been in America, and which had accumulated to £120. He then decided to go to the gold-diggings in the Klondike; at Renfrew, Ontario, while attempting to board a moving train, he fell, and the wheel severed his right foot at the ankle. It was found necessary to amputate the leg at the knee, but he was well nursed and was able to return to Wales within five weeks. He soon moved to London, where he lived in common lodging houses on his allowance, less 2s., which he sent back every week to Newport. After more than two years in London, which continued to be his base, he made several walking tours as a pedlar of laces, pins, and needles, sometimes varying this life by preaching on street corners.

By 1905 Davies's poems had been rejected by several publishers, until he approached C. A. Watts & Co., with a letter of recommendation from George R. Sims. Recognizing the merit of the poems, they agreed to pay for the printing of *The Soul's Destroyer, and other Poems*, partly on the assurance that Davies would do his utmost to dispose of copies among likely purchasers. He sent them to various people, requesting each of them either to send him a half-crown or to return the book. Among the recipients was (George) Bernard Shaw, who became actively interested. At his suggestion Davies sent copies to Philip Edward Thomas, Israel Zangwill, Edward Garnett, St John Adcock, editor of *The Bookman*, and others. Favourable reviews appeared; Davies mentions with especial gratitude notices by Arthur Symons and Arnold Bennett. Edward Thomas, he says, 'gave me a fine boom in several

William Henry Davies (1871–1940), by Sir William Nicholson, 1927–8

influential papers … and became a practical friend, finding me a small cottage in the Weald of Kent [at Sevenoaks] … my rent, coal and light being paid mysteriously by Thomas and his friends'. In *Who's Who* Davies stated briefly: 'became a poet at the age of thirty-four; been one ever since'. Between 1905 and 1939 he produced a score of slim volumes of verse: the *Collected Poems* of 1943, with an introduction by Osbert Sitwell, contains 636 pieces. Following on the early reviews, one newspaper wrote up Davies's story.

At Sevenoaks Davies wrote his *Autobiography*, which was published with a preface by Shaw at the suggestion of Garnett and Thomas. Shaw's wife, Charlotte, paid for the typesetting and the casting of the plates, of which she made a present to Davies. It was no doubt the preface that made Davies known to a large public, but Shaw states that it was for the sake of the poems that he wrote the preface to the *Autobiography*. He had recognized at once that Davies was a poet: it was with some amusement that he wrote of the placid style of the prose book, in which tramps 'argue with the decorum of Socrates, and narrate in the style of Tacitus', and in which Davies's loss of a leg is mentioned with the utmost casualness. Davies also wrote four novels, two of which, *The True Traveller* (1912) and *The Adventures of Johnny Walker, Tramp* (1926), are semi-autobiographical, bridging the gap between the *Autobiography* and *Later Days* (1925). In 1924 he wrote an introduction to Defoe's *Moll Flanders*, which is generically related to his other novels. In 1923 he published *True Travellers: a Tramp's Opera in Three Acts*, in prose with interspersed lyrics. This was to be produced at the Lyric Theatre, Hammersmith, where *The Beggar's Opera* had been successfully revived, but the scheme fell through. Davies's other prose works are *Beggars* (1909), *Nature* (1914), and *My Birds and my Garden* (1933). He selected and edited two anthologies, *Shorter Lyrics of the Twentieth Century, 1900 to 1922* (1922) and *Jewels of Song* (1930, reissued 1938). He was joint editor, with Austin Osman Spare, of a monthly magazine called

Form (October 1921 to January 1922), to which he contributed the editorials, each with incidental poems.

In 1919 Davies was granted a civil-list pension, which was twice increased. In 1926 the University of Wales conferred on him the honorary degree of LittD. On 5 February 1923 he married Helen Matilda (d. 1979), daughter of William Payne, farmer, who came from Sussex: his happiness with her is recorded and reflected in *The Lover's Song-Book* (thirty poems, 1933), reprinted as *Love Poems* (1935), with the number of poems increased to fifty. The story of his search, at the age of over fifty, among the poorer areas of London, for a suitable wife, and of his first meeting with Helen Payne, aged twenty-three and pregnant, at a bus stop, is told with engaging frankness in *Young Emma*, published in 1980, after his wife's death. This account was read with much admiration by Shaw in 1924; he wished to retain the manuscript a while longer for his wife to read, but he advised Davies's publisher, Cape, that to publish at that time would be damaging to the author's reputation. *Young Emma* is also of particular interest to social historians of London after the First World War.

Davies died, childless, at Nailsworth, Gloucestershire, on 26 September 1940. Since the publication of *The Essential W. H. Davies* (1951), and *The Complete Poems of W. H. Davies* (1963), his poetry has become the subject of several re-evaluations. Following D. H. Lawrence's early remark that Davies is 'like a linnet that's got just a wee little sweet song' (DLitB, 19, 1983, 108), Davies's poetry has been compared with that of the Elizabethans, with Blake's *Songs of Innocence*, with the poetry of Robert Burns, and with Wordsworth's work. The publication in 1985 of *W. H. Davies: Selected Poems* led to a further resurgence of interest, when a reviewer in the *Times Literary Supplement* (25 January 1985, 79) described Davies as an 'undercover poet' with an 'instinct for conjuring disquietingness from the seemingly banal'.

FREDERICK PAGE, *rev.* ANNETTE PEACH

Sources S. Harlow, *W. H. Davies: a bibliography* (1993) • L. Hockey, *W. H. Davies* (1971) • W. H. Davies, *The autobiography of a super-tramp* (1908) • W. H. Davies, *Young Emma* (1980) • W. H. Davies, *Later days* (1925) • D. E. Stanford, ed., *British poets, 1880–1914*, DLitB, 19 (1983) [with a sel. bibliography incl. American works not listed in Harlow's bibliography (1993).] • *The Times* (27 Sept 1940) • *TLS* (5 Oct 1940) • [N. C. Nicholson], 'A dedicated poet', *TLS* (10 Aug 1951), 500 • [N. C. Nicholson], 'The nature of a super-tramp', *TLS* (12 April 1963), 247 • J. Bayley, 'The undercover poet', *TLS* (25 Jan 1985), 79

Archives Newport Central Library, Monmouthshire • NL Wales, letters; letters to various correspondents, draft poems, and related papers; papers • priv. coll. • Ransom HRC, corresp. and literary papers • State University of New York College, Buffalo, E. H. Butler Library, corresp. • U. Reading L., corresp. | King's School, Canterbury, letters to Edward Thomas | SOUND BBC WAC, performance recordings • BL NSA, oral history interview • BL NSA, 'Time to stand and stare', BBC Radio 4, 20 Dec 1980; documentary recordings; performance recordings

Likenesses A. L. Coburn, collotype, 1913, NPG • J. Epstein, bronze bust, 1916, NPG; identical version, Newport Art Gallery, Monmouthshire, Wales • A. John, pencil drawing, 1918, NPG • J. Wheatley, pen-and-wash drawing, 1919, BM • A. John, oils, c.1921, NMG Wales • P. Evans, pen-and-ink drawing, c.1922, NPG • T. Spicer-Simson, plasticine medallion, 1922, NPG • W. Nicholson, oils,

1927–8, NPG [*see illus.*] · H. Knight, oils, NMG Wales · L. Knight, portrait · H. Murchison, photograph, NPG · W. Rothenstein, portrait · W. Sickert, portrait

Davies, William John Abbott (1890–1967), rugby player, was born on 21 June 1890 in Pembroke, the eldest of the four children and the only son of William George Davies, a shopkeeper, of Pembroke, and his wife, Florence Meyrick. Davies, who was known by the nickname Dave, was educated at Pembroke Dock grammar school, the Royal Naval College, Keyham, and the Royal Naval College, Greenwich. He was a Pembroke dockyard apprentice in 1905 and went to Greenwich College in 1910. He proved himself to be a gifted athlete and games player at Greenwich, but he did not take up rugby football seriously until he was nearly twenty years old. As a boy, he played more soccer than rugby, and he was about to play a game of hockey when he was pressed into service to play a game of rugby instead. His playing career quickly developed with the United Services Club, Portsmouth, and, within three years, he was capped for England as a fly-half.

Davies played a full international season for England in 1913, when he won five caps, before the outbreak of the First World War, in which he served in the Grand Fleet, first in the *Iron Duke*, and then in the *Queen Elizabeth*. After the war he returned to Admiralty work in Portsmouth as assistant constructor and was appointed OBE in 1919. He resumed playing rugby football for the United Services Club, Portsmouth, and began his club and international half-back partnership with C. A. Kershaw. The two played together for England for four seasons after the First World War, and were so successful that England never lost a match when they were in the team. Indeed, when Davies retired from regular first-class rugby at the end of the 1922–3 season, he had never appeared in a losing England team in the international championship, even though he had won twenty-two caps over a period of eleven years spanning the war. England's only defeat in that time in a match in which Davies played was against South Africa in 1913.

Wavell Wakefield of Kendal, one of England's greatest rugby forwards, who played half his distinguished international career in the same team as Davies, said of him:

> As 'Dave' was born in Wales, I am pretty sure he was qualified to play for Wales, even though I believe his parents came originally from the West Country. However, he chose to play for England instead, and that was a happy decision for us, because no international team can function properly without a sound partnership at half-back, and Kershaw and Davies were wonderfully effective. … 'Dave' was always immaculate. He was always calm, and always appeared to be in control of the situation. He never had a hair out of place, his boots shone, and his playing kit was impeccable. It was an enduring ambition of his opponents, particularly the forwards, to disturb that calm by dumping him unceremoniously on his backside in the mud, but I cannot remember that they ever succeeded! Some of Kershaw's passes were pretty erratic, but 'Dave' had such a fantastic pair of hands that he picked them up without any fuss. He was perfectly happy to do so, because the length of 'K's pass enabled him to stand so far away from the forwards that he had great flexibility of operation. 'Dave' had the ability to wait for his chance, too, and by doing so, he often lulled the opposition into a false sense of security. He usually made only one break in each half, but when he did so, it was decisive. He and Kershaw were both in the Navy and they were firmly established as the best half-backs in England when I won my first cap in 1920. I have often thought since how much easier it made the game for the rest of us.

In 1923 Davies married Margaret Bleecker, daughter of Major Ernest Glanville Waymouth, of the Royal Artillery. They had a son and a daughter, both of whom became medical doctors. Davies's widow, who in 1979 was still living only 2 miles from the Rugby Football Union's ground at Twickenham, recalled that her husband used to practise with C. A. Kershaw almost every day when they were playing for the United Services at Portsmouth. 'What they did may have looked easy, but it was born of long and hard practice', she said. Davies captained the Royal Navy and Hampshire and he became an England selector for three years when he retired. In the year of his retirement (1923) he played in the centenary match at Rugby School, exactly 100 years after William Webb Ellis had supposedly first picked up the ball and run with it, 'thus originating the distinctive feature of the Rugby game'. This assertion is open to some doubt, but few would dispute that Davies was one of the best fly-halves who played for England.

When his playing days were over, Davies continued his work at the Admiralty. He was attached to the staff of the commander-in-chief of the Mediterranean Fleet at Malta between 1935 and 1938, and in 1939 was appointed by the Admiralty as chief constructor. He was assistant director of warship production in 1942, superintendent of warship production on the Clyde in 1946, and director of merchant shipbuilding and repairs between 1949 and 1950.

Davies was president of the civil service football club between 1937 and 1966. In 1951 he became a liveryman of the Worshipful Company of Shipwrights. He wrote two books on rugby football: *Rugby Football* (1923) and *How to Play Rugby Football* (1933). He died at home at 109 Cambridge Road, Teddington, Middlesex, on 26 April 1967.

JOHN REASON, *rev.*

Sources records of the Rugby Football Union, Twickenham · private information (1981) · *The Times* (29 April 1967) · *The Times* (2 May 1967) · CGPLA Eng. & Wales (1967)
Wealth at death £9749: probate, 4 July 1967, CGPLA Eng. & Wales

Davies, Sir William Llewelyn (1887–1952), librarian, was born at Plas Gwyn schoolhouse, near Pwllheli, on 11 October 1887, the third child and younger son of William Davies and his wife, Jane Evans, both natives of Llanafan, Cardiganshire. His father, formerly the earl of Lisburne's gamekeeper, was then similarly employed at Broom Hall, near Pwllheli, but joined the staff of Sir Arthur Osmond Williams, of Castell Deudraeth, when his son was five years old. Davies was brought up at Minffordd, near Penrhyndeudraeth. He was educated at Porthmadog county school (1900–03), Penrhyndeudraeth pupil–teacher centre (1903–6), and the University College of Wales, Aberystwyth, where he graduated BA (1909) with upper second-class honours in Welsh and proceeded MA (1912) following research on a family of sixteenth- and seventeenth-century Ardudwy poets. He held various teaching posts

Sir William Llewelyn Davies (1887–1952), by Bassano, 1947

from 1909 until the beginning of 1917; during a period in Cardiff (1914–17) he also lectured part-time in Welsh at the university college there in 1916. Subsequently he served in the Royal Garrison Artillery, and later as a commissioned officer in the army education service.

In September 1919 Davies was appointed first assistant librarian under John Ballinger at the young National Library of Wales at Aberystwyth. When Ballinger retired in 1930, Davies succeeded him as chief librarian, a position which he held until his death. He continued the work, so successfully begun, of building up in Wales a national library which would rank among the great libraries of the world. His experience as Ballinger's deputy, his interest in Welsh history and literature, and his ability to communicate in both Welsh and English served him in good stead. He proved to be an effective organizer and a conscientious worker. During his period as librarian Davies was able to complete the construction of the first library building. The first stage was opened in 1937 but he did not live to see the opening of the completed building in 1955.

Davies was convinced from the outset that one of the library's most important functions was to collect and preserve the mass of manuscript and documentary material relating to Wales which was scattered (often in a state of neglect) throughout the principality and farther afield. His task was made easier by changing economic conditions, which brought about the disintegration of large estates and the vacating of old country houses. The list of individual owners, institutions, and official bodies who responded to his diplomatic persuasion to transfer their

records to the library, either absolutely or on permanent loan, is a notable one. Of particular importance was the housing at the library of the Calvinistic Methodist archive (1934), a number of Baptist and Congregationalist records, and the Church in Wales records (1944–5). Of the approximately 3.5 million documents housed in the library when Davies died, all but 200,000 or so were acquired during his period of administration. Collection and preservation, however, were only the beginning: he also aimed to make the records available to researchers without undue delay. This was achieved by substituting handy, typewritten, brief-entry schedules and handlists for printed detailed calendars, and by the compilation of subject indexes: the printed *Handlist of Manuscripts* began to appear in 1940. Equally anxious to persuade other authorities to preserve the records in their custody, he urged the various county councils of Wales to establish records committees and he gave to municipal, ecclesiastical, and other bodies and to individuals valuable advice and practical assistance. He kept the National Library of Wales in close touch with other institutions with similar aims through his membership of the Historical Manuscripts Commission, the Society of Antiquaries, the executive committee of the Council for the Preservation of Business Archives, and the British Records Association, of which he was a vice-president representing the interests of Wales.

The preservation of records was only part of Davies's service to Welsh culture. He was also responsible for organizing the lending of books to adult study classes throughout Wales, for operating in eleven counties the regional libraries scheme for Wales and Monmouthshire, and for the selection, acquisition, and distribution of books for patients in the sanatoria of Wales. During the Second World War he established a national committee to provide Welsh books for those serving in the forces. During the war also he undertook the responsibility of housing some of the manuscripts and books of the British Museum in a specially constructed tunnel in the library grounds, as he described in an article in the *Transactions of the Honourable Society of Cymmrodorion* in 1946. Davies missed no opportunity, through lectures, broadcast talks, and publications, of bringing his library into closer contact with the Welsh people. In 1937 he published *The National Library of Wales: a Survey of its History, its Contents, and its Activities*, and two years later he launched the *National Library of Wales Journal*, which he edited for fourteen years. He was also honorary editor of the journals of the Welsh Bibliographical Society (1932–49), the Cardiganshire Antiquarian Society (until 1951), and the Merioneth Historical and Record Society (1949–51). In addition he was associate editor (from 1947 until his death) of *Y bywgraffiadur Cymreig*, the Welsh biographical dictionary published in 1953 by the Honourable Society of Cymmrodorion, to which he contributed some 200 entries on gentry families, antiquaries, and bibliophiles. A member of numerous academic and other cultural bodies, he was a leading spirit in every organization promoting the intellectual life of the principality.

Most of Davies's published work relates to his work as

librarian and he had little opportunity to follow his research interests. Parts of his MA dissertation appeared in the *Transactions of the Honourable Society of Cymmrodorion* (1931) and an article on David Samwell (*d.* 1799), an eighteenth-century poet, in the *Transactions* for 1938.

Davies had married in 1914 Gwen, daughter of Dewi Llewelyn, grocer and baker, of Pontypridd, and afterwards adopted the additional name of Llewelyn; the couple had one daughter. Davies was knighted in 1944 and received the honorary degree of LLD from the University of Wales in 1951. In the year of his death he was high sheriff of Merioneth. He died at home at Sherborne House, Aberystwyth, on 11 November 1952, and his ashes were scattered in the grounds of the library following cremation at Pontypridd on 14 November. His wife survived him.

GILDAS TIBBOTT, *rev.* BRYNLEY F. ROBERTS

Sources *Transactions of the Honourable Society of Cymmrodorion* (1953), 112–14 • *Journal of the Welsh Bibliographical Society*, 7 (1950–53), 172–3 • *Cambrian News* (21 Nov 1952), 73 • D. Jenkins, *A refuge in peace and war: the National Library of Wales to 1952* (2002), chaps. 11–12
Archives NL Wales, letters to Thomas Iowerth Ellis and Annie Hughes-Griffiths • NL Wales, letters to T. G. Jones • NL Wales, Henry Lewis MSS
Likenesses Bassano Ltd, two photographs, *c.*1930–1950, NL Wales • Elliott & Fry, photograph, 1944, NL Wales • W. Stoneman, photograph, 1944, NPG • Bassano, photograph, 1947, NPG [*see illus.*] • D. Bell, pencil sketch, 1947, NL Wales • R. L. Gapper, bronze relief, 1963, NL Wales
Wealth at death £1062 5s.: probate, 11 April 1953, *CGPLA Eng. & Wales*

D'Avigdor-Goldsmid, Sir Henry Joseph. *See* Goldsmid, Sir Henry Joseph D'Avigdor-, second baronet (1909–1976).

Davin, Daniel Marcus (1913–1990), writer and publisher, was born on 1 September 1913 in Invercargill, New Zealand, the fourth of the six children of Patrick Davin (1877–1958), railwayman and smallholder, and his wife, Mary Magdalen, *née* Sullivan (1878–1944), daughter of Daniel Sullivan and his wife, Nora. The Davins were Irish Catholic smallholders in Galway, their name coming from either the Gaelic *damh*, meaning an ox or a stag, or from *dáhm*, a poet. Young Dan always favoured the author over the animal. Although his father and his maternal grandparents had fled the poverty and superstition of the 'old country' at the turn of the century, he would always remain an Irish New Zealander rather than a British subject. This inheritance underlay his lifelong love of the soil and its produce—the five-year-old's delight in his mother's nasturtiums, the seventy-five-year-old's in his own potatoes. It underlay also an unswerving sympathy for the underdog, the underpaid and underprivileged, manual workers, authors, and soldiers.

From the age of five, when Dan Davin taught himself to read, he was aware of all these occupations. The First World War took its toll of the menfolk of Gore, the small town to which the family had moved in 1914. Those who survived brought death home to that and many other households in the form of the flu virus whose victims included Daniel and Nora Sullivan and their younger daughter, Nora. These and other deaths—among them,

those of a favourite dog and bull calves routinely slaughtered by his father—may have exacerbated a tendency to depression, inherited from his mother, that began to manifest itself in Davin's adolescence.

In 1920 the family moved again, this time to Invercargill, where the following year Davin began as a pupil at the Marist Brothers' School. The conventional Catholic Irish education he received there was supplemented by the myths and legends of an itinerant Irish story-teller, and by the discovery of a cache of books (many of them literary) discarded by a retired schoolteacher.

Matriculating in 1929, Davin came first in Southland and fifteenth in New Zealand overall 'with special distinction in English, French and Latin' (Brother Egbert's testimonial, 2 Aug 1933, Davin papers). He won scholarships to Sacred Heart College in Auckland and, later, to Otago University, whose Presbyterian traditions he frequently challenged, emerging with formidable debating skills, a first-class degree in English, another in Latin, and—after a prolonged battle with the custodians of respectability—a Rhodes scholarship. He was by then in love with a lively fellow student. Winifred (always known as Winnie) Gonley [*see below*] was the daughter of Irish Catholic parents, with ambitions as a writer, and more widely read than her Rhodes scholar fiancé with the 'wonderful dark-brown voice' (Denys Hawthorne, quoted in Wilson, 205) to whom she waved farewell from an Auckland wharf in August 1936.

Davin's introduction to England was London's Cable Street riot of 4 October, which he witnessed: an early flickering of the conflagration soon to engulf Spain and, eventually, the world. A natural republican and freethinker, he was dismayed by the Catholic church's support for Franco, and during his years at Oxford finally lost the faith that had begun to fray in Otago. Its loss and the bitterness of Adam unparadised found eloquent expression in his poem 'Knowledge' that begins:

God blazed in every gorsebush
When I was a child.
Forbidden fruits were orchards,
And flowers grew wild.

God is a shadow now.
The gorse blooms pale.
Branches in the orchard bow
With fruits grown stale.

For his first term or two at Oxford, a depressed Davin 'hated Balliol and hated everybody' (Davin papers) but a first visit to Ireland made a deep impression on him, and with Winnie's arrival in Europe in summer 1937 his spirits rose. He enjoyed the classical texts he was reading for the honour school of *literae humaniores*; drafted his first novel; was at the centre of a circle of scintillating friends; and learned to love Paris, which nourished his bohemian instincts. In July 1939 he was awarded a first-class degree and, aware that they might soon be separated by war, he and Winnie were married in Oxford on 22 July 1939.

Hitler invaded Poland on Davin's twenty-sixth birthday. A recruitment board assigned him to the infantry and, in May 1940, he emerged from an officer cadet training unit as a second lieutenant in the 2nd New Zealand expeditionary force, the principal fighting component of which, 2nd New Zealand division, was known as 'the Div'. He saw action as a platoon commander in Greece and as battalion intelligence officer in Crete, where he was wounded. Released from hospital, he was transferred to the intelligence staff of army headquarters in Cairo, there revelling in the effervescent company of such other poets and scholars as Paddy Costello, Lawrence Durrell, G. S. Fraser, Bernard Spencer, Bill Williams, and Reggie Smith. Many would play a part in his post-war life, as would a young German woman, Elisabeth Berndt, with whom he also revelled.

In autumn 1942 Davin served with an intelligence unit from the battle of Alamein to the fall of Tripoli; then, after three months at staff college and three on leave, in January 1944 rejoined the Div. as its intelligence officer at the siege of Monte Cassino. He worked closely with General Freyberg in the battle for Monastery Hill and the more successful assault on Monte Lignano. On Freyberg's recommendation, he was then transferred to the War Office in London as a New Zealand representative on the Allied Control Commission for Germany, set up to administer the dismantling of Nazi institutions.

Reunited with Winnie and two daughters, Anna and Delia, born while he was on active service, he was able to balance an administrative with a literary career, a difficult balance to be maintained—at some cost to the latter—for the rest of his working life. A darkly Dostoevskian, long-delayed novel, *Cliffs of Fall*, was published in 1945 and, at the war's end, he was appointed an editor at the Clarendon Press and returned with his family to Oxford.

There he was greeted with the dismaying news that in 1943 Elisabeth Berndt had given birth to his child, a daughter to be known as Patty, and now wanted him to help them settle in England. Nothing better illustrates the loyalty characteristic of both Dan and Winnie Davin than their solution to this problem: Elisabeth would join their household, ostensibly as housekeeper, and the four unwitting half-sisters (Brigid Davin was born in 1945) would be brought up together. They lived in commendable harmony for almost four years, their Southmoor Road house becoming a famous oasis for writers and scholars from 'the round earth's imagined corners' (John Donne, 'Holy Sonnet', 7).

Under the tutelage of Kenneth Sisam, a distinguished medievalist and secretary to the delegates of Oxford University Press, Davin became by day an expert editor. His evenings and weekends he would spend as a writer, at his own desk or a bar in Fitzrovia, then the failing heart of literary London. Both by day and in the evenings he was extraordinarily productive. A volume of his short stories, *The Gorse Blooms Pale* (1947), was followed over the years by six novels: *For the Rest of our Lives* (1947), *Roads from Home* (1949), *The Sullen Bell* (1956), *No Remittance* (1959), *Not Here, Not Now* (1970), and *Brides of Price* (1972). There were three other collections of his short stories: *Breathing Spaces* (1975), *Selected Stories* (1981), and the *Salamander and the Fire: Collected War Stories* (1986). Davin's fiction has its

strengths—evidenced, most notably, in his autobiographical war novel, *For the Rest of our Lives*, and in his short stories—but technical innovation is not one of them, and his most lasting contribution as a writer may prove to be two non-fiction works in which the novelist's eye for detail and ear for dialogue assist the historian trained in the school of Thucydides: his volume, *Crete*, in the Official History of New Zealand in the Second World War (1953); and the biographer modelling a memoir on Johnson's *Lives of the Poets*. Davin once wrote: 'In my arrogant youth, I had wanted to be a "universal writer"—poet, historian, novelist. It was only gradually that I realized that, after one's twenties, life is a fighting withdrawal' (Davin, 'My language and myself', *Round Table*, 262, 1976, 22). His memoir, *Closing Times* (1975), chronicles the fighting withdrawals of seven of his friends: the writers Julian Maclaren-Ross, Bertie Rodgers, Louis MacNeice, Enid Starkie, Joyce Cary, Dylan Thomas, and Itzik Manger. The most memorable presence, however, in this gallery of ebullient, funny, tender portraits is that of the artist himself, cigarette-holder in hand, eyes half closed against the smoke.

When Sisam retired from Oxford University Press in 1948, to be succeeded as secretary by Arthur Norrington, Davin had become assistant secretary with special responsibility for the Clarendon Press. Over the next thirty years his mastery of the arts of friendship, as much as his intellectual attainments, made him the greatest academic publisher of his time. DMD (as he was always known at the press) could read five languages; knew everyone the press needed to know; knew the book that needed to be written or edited—and knew how it should be done—often before its eventual author or editor. His support was absolute, his workload legendary: eighty letters dictated at a sitting. No editorial pencil moved so swiftly or with such surgical precision, and no academic publisher before him initiated and saw to completion so many major projects. He had his eccentricities: 'an uncommon gift for enjoying his own aversions—parties, dining out, travel, committees, formal social occasions, other people's problems. No man who longed so much for the quiet of his own fireside has been so often out' (Peter Sutcliffe, quoted in Wilson, 156).

DMD had his weaknesses, some that would have an impact on the history of Oxford University Press. In 1967 Oxford University's hebdomadal council instituted a committee, under the chairmanship of Sir Humphrey Waldock, to report on the structure and operations of the university press. Davin was much involved with this. In 1970 his designation changed from assistant secretary to deputy secretary and academic publisher. The Waldock report was published that year, and as a consequence of its recommendations and the press's poor financial results in 1971 and 1972, management consultants were called in. Davin had already seen the writing on the wall, which he correctly translated as 'Management, Marketing, Money', and did not like what he saw. Last of the scholar-publishers, he was not prepared to lower his standards. He was not a good manager, and disliked delegating and supervising. He was a good officer, a natural leader, generating a loyalty in his staff as absolute as his to them. The handsome lieutenant had become a stocky veteran, wary-eyed and bulldog-jawed, who continued to think, and speak, in military terms—of tactics, strategy, lines of communication—and never lost his own tactical sense: in crowded rooms, always taking up a defensive position, backed into a corner with good sight-lines to warn him of the approach of 'difficult' authors. He himself warned the delegates of the press of the qualitative consequences of management decisions taken in the light of the Waldock report, but once they were adopted, he worked to make a success of them.

The professional disappointments of those years helped prepare Davin for retirement in 1978, the five-hundredth anniversary of printing in Oxford, but he was not prepared for the personal disappointments that followed. Dreams of novels, essays, and stories to be written in a Dorchester-on-Thames cottage—long his refuge from the world 'of telegrams and anger' (E. M. Forster, *Howards End*, chap. 19)—were wrecked by bad health and 'writer's block'. He fought them bravely, but was worn out by hard work and hard drinking. The creative capital that might have supported his own writings he had spent too generously refining the writings of others. Failing to make progress with a second volume of memoirs, to be called *Soldiers and Scholars*, he managed nevertheless to write a few stories and more than 100 reviews for the *Times Literary Supplement*. He was created CBE in 1987 and died at his home, 103 Southmoor Road, Oxford, on 28 September 1990. He was cremated at Oxford on 1 October, and his ashes were scattered in Port Meadow, Oxford, with his wife's, in 1996.

Davin's last book, *The Salamander and the Fire* (1986), a collection of his war stories, opened with a characteristic dedication: 'To those who, out of principle, refused to fight, and suffered for it. And to those who fought so that, among much else, that principle should be safeguarded'. This, in its humanity as in its style, expresses the essence of a man worthy to dine at journey's end, as he would have wished, with Boswell and with Johnson.

Davin's wife, **Winifred Kathleen Joan Davin** [née Gonley] (1909–1995), writer and editor, was born on 27 July 1909, in Otautau, New Zealand, the third of the five children of Michael Gonley (1869–1935), merchant seaman and later shopkeeper, and his wife, Winifred, née Crowe (1878–1934). She was educated at St Dominic's, a Dominican convent in Dunedin, and at Otago University, where in 1931 she met her future husband and introduced him to works of Joyce, Proust, Mansfield, Lawrence, and other writers who became important to them both. Winnie followed Dan to Europe and they were married on 22 July 1939, at the end of his Rhodes scholarship. She spent the war in Britain, while he served overseas, and later wrote a memoir of that time, 'A soldier's wife', published in *Women in Wartime: New Zealand Women Tell their Story*, edited by Lauris Edmond and Carolyn Milward (Wellington, 1986).

Although busy with her three daughters in the post-war years, she was involved in everything Davin wrote and in making the choices for his World's Classics editions of Katherine Mansfield's *Short Stories*, *New Zealand Stories*

(both 1953), and *English Short Stories of Today* (1958). She was volume editor of the 'Home and health' volume of *The Oxford Junior Encyclopaedia* (1955) and worked on many of its other volumes. Later she took a full-time job with the education department of Oxford University Press.

Winnie Davin had a genius for friendship. She nursed the novelist Joyce Cary (1888–1957) through his long last illness and, as his literary executor, edited his incomplete final novel, *The Captive and the Free* (1959). Friends of the family—among them writers, artists, teachers, students, many from overseas—thronged the Davins' house. Winnie was always ready to feed, entertain, listen, and advise. Dan's dedication of *Closing Times* (his memoir of some important friends) 'to W.K.D. without whom there would have been neither friends nor book' acknowledges this important aspect of their partnership. Winnie made her last visit to New Zealand at eighty-two for Christmas 1991. She remained the centre of an increasingly large family, much loved, respected, and visited by daughters, grandchildren, and friends until her death at the Churchill Hospital, Headington, Oxford, on 26 March 1995; she was cremated on 30 March at Oxford.   JON STALLWORTHY

Sources K. Ovenden, *A fighting withdrawal: the life of Dan Davin* (1996) · J. Wilson, ed., *Intimate stranger: reminiscences of Dan Davin* (2001) · personal knowledge (2004) · NL NZ, Turnbull L., Davin MSS

Archives NL NZ, Turnbull L. · priv. coll. | U. St Andr. L., letters to Sir Thomas Malcolm Knox | SOUND IWM, tape of Davin talking about the battle of Crete

Likenesses A. Stones, bust, priv. coll. · A. Stones, bust, Invercargill Public Library, New Zealand · G. Sutherland, drawing, priv. coll.

Wealth at death £197,630: probate, 1990, CGPLA Eng. & Wales

Davin, Maurice (1842–1927), sportsman and farmer, was born on 29 June 1842 at Deerpark House, Carrick-on-Suir, co. Tipperary, the first of five children of John Davin (1814–1859), farmer, and his wife, Bridget Walsh (d. 1884). His parents were both natives of Carrick-on-Suir and the Davin family had long-standing connections with the area. Davin received a basic education in the pay schools of Carrick-on-Suir, before completing his education at the O'Shea Academy in the town. His education was cut short by his father's death in 1859; as the eldest son, he was expected to take over the family's farm. In his early years of adulthood Davin spent his spare time training as a boxer. His skills were such that he was quickly able to establish his superiority over local contestants and the regimental champions from among the soldiers stationed in the area. With no further challenges in the boxing sphere, he turned his vast sporting appetite to rowing. In 1865 the revived Carrick regatta allowed him to compete for money against other rowers. He beat all the other competitors and repeated his success in the 1866 Waterford regatta. For the next five years, racing in various canoes, gigs, and wherries, he was able to dominate all the local regattas.

In 1869 Davin took part in his first athletic competition at Gurteen, co. Waterford, where he won the high jump and came second in the 100 yard sprint. Throughout the late 1870s he excelled in athletic competition. He was a specialist at throwing events. Between 1875 and 1879 he won every Irish national championship for throwing the 16 lb hammer, as well as gaining three championship titles for slinging the 56 lb weight, and a further three for the 16 lb shot event. Hurt by criticism in *The Field* of the standard of Irish athletics, he and his brother Pat travelled to the English championships held in Birmingham on 16 July 1881. He answered his English critics by winning both the 16 lb shot and the hammer events in style.

In 1884 Davin played a key role in the foundation of the Gaelic Athletic Association. Formed as part of the revival in Irish culture, the association became Ireland's most important sporting body. As its president from 1884 to 1887 and again from 1888 to 1889, Davin brought to the new association his reputation as one of the greatest sportsmen of his generation. Well versed in the development and codification of sport, he played a central part in drawing up the rules of Gaelic football and hurling, which were crucial to their success. The importance of Davin within the Gaelic athletics movement was reflected in the playing of the 1904 All-Ireland hurling final on fields at his home in Carrick. He died there, unmarried, at Deerpark House, on 27 January 1927, and was buried three days later, after a funeral service at St Nicholas's, Carrick.

MIKE CRONIN

Sources S. Ó Riain, *Maurice Davin (1842–1927): first president of the GAA* (1997) · M. de Búrca, *The GAA: a history of the Gaelic Athletic Association* (1980) · W. F. Mandle, *The Gaelic Athletic Association and Irish nationalist politics, 1884–1924* (1987)
Archives NRA, priv. coll.
Likenesses photograph, 1906, NL Ire.; repro. in *Irish Athletic Record*
Wealth at death £882: probate, 23 April 1927, CGPLA Éire.

Davin, Winifred Kathleen Joan (1909–1995). *See under* Davin, Daniel Marcus (1913–1990).

Davis. *See also* Davies, Davys.

Davis, Miss (*b. c.*1736, *d.* in or after **1755**), musician and singer, was the daughter of Mr Davis (*fl.* 1735–1745), an organist, harpsichordist, and composer, and the singer Mrs Davis (*fl.* 1730–1751), sister of the violinist John Clegg and the singer Miss Clegg. Both parents were active in Dublin concert life. Miss Davis—whose forename is unrecorded—was a child prodigy, first advertised in Dublin in November 1742 with notice of a forthcoming 'Concert of Vocal and Instrumental Musick' for her benefit and described as 'a Child of 6 years old' (Highfill, Burnim & Langhans, *BDA*). The concert (postponed from December 1742 to February 1743) featured her accompanying her mother in a song as well as playing a concerto and other pieces on the harpsichord. Thereafter she generally held at least one benefit concert each year up to 1750, at either the Crow Street Musick Hall or the Fishamble Street Musick Hall in Dublin. At her début on 5 February 1743, which took place at Crow Street, both her mother and aunt sang; subsequently Mrs Davis frequently sang at her daughter's benefits. Her benefit concert on 5 February 1745 received an enthusiastic critical notice:

> Last Tuesday … (a child of 8 Years old) … played several of Mr Handel's most difficult Grand Lessons and Concertos upon

the Harpsichord, to a numerous and polite Audience[;] there were present some of the best Judges, who unanimously expressed their great Admiration of her extraordinary and masterly Performance. (*Faulkner's Dublin Journal*, 9 Feb 1745, quoted in Boydell, *Musical Calendar*, 102)

Miss Davis's London début was at Hickford's Room (then London's foremost concert venue) on 10 May 1745, when she was described as 'a child of eight years … lately arrived from Ireland' (Boydell, *Musical Calendar*, 276); on this occasion she again accompanied her mother. On 6 February 1748, now described as 'a child of eleven' (ibid., 114), besides playing the harpsichord at her annual benefit, Miss Davis sang 'some fine Italian songs' (ibid.) of her own composition. By 1750 the notice of her benefit concert advertised her talents in hyperbolic terms: 'Miss Davis, a Native of this Town … is by all Judges of the Harpsichord, both in England and in Ireland, allowed to have arrived at a greater Perfection on the Instrument than any one ever of her age' (*Faulkner's Dublin Journal*, 30 Jan 1750, quoted in Boydell, *Musical Calendar*, 136). Some 'Ladies of Quality' (ibid.) had encouraged her to think of teaching the harpsichord to young ladies; she hoped with her benefit performance to attract the 'Nobility and Gentry' (ibid.) that they might judge her qualifications 'for that Purpose' (ibid.). She took part in a benefit concert for Signor Marella at Crow Street in December 1751, playing a solo on the harpsichord with Marella playing the violin. In October 1753 it was noted in the *Dublin Journal* that 'Miss Davis, who has been many years distinguished … for her fine Performance on the Harpsichord … proposes to attend young Ladies to teach them' (ibid., 187). In November 1755 a further notice in the *Dublin Journal* stated that she had given up harpsichord playing in public but continued to teach. Nothing further seems to be known of her life and career.

SUSAN WOLLENBERG

Sources B. Boydell, *A Dublin musical calendar, 1700–1760* (Dublin, 1988) · Highfill, Burnim & Langhans, *BDA* · B. Boydell, 'Davis [Davies]', *New Grove*, 2nd edn

Davis, Arthur Joseph (1878–1951), architect, was born on 21 May 1878 at 25 Leinster Square, London, one of the four gifted sons of Montague Davis (*d.* in or before 1923), a merchant, and Ada, *née* Moss. His father and mother, both of Jewish descent, were of Canadian and Australian origin respectively. The family moved to Brussels, where Arthur was educated privately from about 1888 to 1893, before going to Paris at the early age of sixteen to study architecture in the preparatory atelier of J.-A. Godefroy and J.-E. Freynet. In 1895 he entered the atelier at the École des Beaux-Arts of Jean-Louis Pascal, winner of the Prix de Rome in 1866. Davis won the first-class prize in the *concours* of 1896 and entered the office of Charles Mewès (1858–1914) in 1898, assisting him in his competition designs for the Grand and Petit Palais at the Paris Exhibition of 1900.

Trained, like Davis, under Pascal, Mewès combined the mastery of planning for which the Beaux-Arts was celebrated, with knowledge of French eighteenth-century interior design and decoration. Mewès's brilliant creation of the Ritz Hotel in 1898–1900, behind façades of the 1690s

Arthur Joseph Davis (1878–1951), by Bassano, 1947

in the place Vendôme, Paris, led César Ritz to employ him and Davis in London: first, to design the Palm Court and restaurant of the Carlton Hotel, Haymarket (1898–1901; dem.), and then to build the Ritz Hotel, Piccadilly (1903–6). In 1898 Mewès sent Davis to London to take charge of work on the Carlton Hotel at the astonishingly young age of twenty. The bursts of febrile creative activity of this youthful genius seem associated with his condition as a manic depressive. In 1898 he left the École des Beaux-Arts without graduating, partly because, as a British subject, he was debarred from entering for the Prix de Rome.

Having joined Mewès's practice as junior English partner in 1900, Davis collaborated with him from 1902 on the design of the Ritz Hotel in London. As always, they worked so closely together that it is impossible, stylistically, to separate their respective contributions. Despite its Parisian arcade and high mansard roof, the Ritz is one of the first steel-framed structures in England, the steelwork made in Germany from designs by the Swedish engineer Sven Bylander, who had worked in Chicago, home of the skyscraper. Much of the internal decorative work in a sophisticated Louis XVI style was provided by French craftsmen, the finest being in the dining-room, which has been described as the most beautiful in Europe.

The elegant and light interiors of Mewès and Davis's hotels led to the commissions for Inveresk House, designed as offices for the *Morning Post*, in Aldwych (1906–7; alt.), and for the Royal Automobile Club, Pall Mall (1908–11), with a magnificent Pompeian swimming-bath. They also carried out much domestic work in both London and

the country for the kind of wealthy patrons, often with South American or South African connections, who were welcomed at the court of Edward VII. One of the finest was their remodelling in a lavish French manner of Luton Hoo, Bedfordshire (1902–4), for Julius Wernher, for whose first employer and subsequent friend Jules Porgès Mewès had built the château of Rochefort-en-Yvelines in 1898. In Surrey they remodelled Coombe Court for Lord de Grey, treasurer of the household to Queen Alexandra, and Polesden Lacey for Mrs Ronald Greville, the leading Edwardian hostess.

Albert Ballin, head of the Hamburg-Amerika Line, now decided to install Ritz-style restaurants in his fleet of luxury ships, then being built in Hamburg and Belfast. Mewès and Davis thus worked on interiors in 1905–6 for the *Amerika* and the *Kaiserin Auguste Victoria*. The revolution which they effected in the layout and decoration of liners, echoing what they had already done for hotels, led to Davis receiving the commission from the Cunard Line for the design of the *Aquitania* in 1913. With the Liverpool architects Willink and Thicknesse, Davis also designed the Cunard Building, Pierhead, Liverpool (1914–16), a memorable contribution to the waterfront, recalling some massive Florentine palazzo.

Mewès died suddenly, under surgery, in August 1914. After dealing with uncompleted projects in the office, Davis joined HM forces in April 1916, serving as a temporary second lieutenant attached to a hospital unit behind the French lines, until he was invalided out, with the rank of captain, with a severe breakdown in November 1917. After convalescence at Craiglockhart Hospital, he returned to practice, continuing the firm of Mewès and Davis in partnership with Charles H. Gage.

In 1910 Mewès and Davis had designed the first overseas branch bank for the Westminster Bank in Brussels, which led to commissions for banks in Antwerp, Nantes, and Valencia, and, after the war, to Davis's Threadneedle Street branch of the Westminster Bank in 1922 and London headquarters of the bank in Lothbury in 1925. Recalling Peruzzi's Palazzo Massimo, the former won him the RIBA London architecture bronze medal in 1930. It was followed by his Morgan Grenfell's Bank, Great Winchester Street (1925), and offices in Bishopsgate for the Hudson's Bay Company (1928–9). He designed the exquisite interiors of the Cunard liners *Franconia* (1922) and *Laconia* (1923), as well as Cunard House, Leadenhall Street, London (1930; dem.).

An unexpected work was Davis's Armenian church of St Sarkis, Iverna Gardens, Kensington (1928), commissioned by Calouste Gulbenkian, for whom the partners had designed houses in both Paris and London. The design of St Sarkis was inspired by study of churches in Armenia, including that in the cloisters at Haghbat. On 1 November 1923 Davis married Rona Jean Duncan (1898/9–1940), the daughter of Ernest Alfred Lee, a marine engineer; the couple had a daughter, Ann, and a son, Ronald. His friends included the architects Sir Edwin Lutyens, A. E. Richardson, Charles Reilly, Oliver Hill, and Herbert Austen Hall. His long residence in Paris had given him a perfect command of the French language, and this, combined with his distinguished appearance and friendly personality, made him for many years a welcome and influential figure at international conferences of architects and similar gatherings.   (*The Builder*, 27 July 1951)

He was a trustee of Sir John Soane's Museum, and a member of the faculty of architecture at the British School in Rome, the Royal Fine Arts Commission, and the Royal Society of Arts. He became a chevalier of the Légion d'honneur and was awarded the Belgian order of the Couronne, but considered his election to the Royal Academy, as an associate in 1933 and a Royal Academician in 1942, as the highest honours conferred upon him, particularly as they were reserved to so few members of his profession.

Distressed by the insistence of the directors of the Cunard Line that his interiors for the *Queen Mary* should be in an art deco style of which he disapproved, Davis suffered a nervous breakdown on their completion in 1935. He died suddenly on 22 July 1951 at home at 35 Hornton Court, Campden Hill Road, Kensington, his last years having been overshadowed by the rejection in the modern movement of what he saw as the civilized values inherent in traditional classical architecture. He regarded this as wholly unnecessary, since he and Mewès had shown how the classical language was entirely compatible with new building types such as modern hotels and liners.

DAVID WATKIN

Sources *The Builder*, 181 (1951), 127 · *RIBA Journal*, 59 (1951–2), 35–6 · *The Builder*, 107 (1914), 184 [obit. of C. Mewès] · b. cert. · m. cert. · d. cert. · C. Anderson, 'Ship interiors: when the breakthrough came', *ArchR*, 141 (1967), 449–52 · H. Massingberd and D. Watkin, *The London Ritz: a social and architectural history* (1980) · A. Service, *Edwardian architecture and its origins* (1975) · *The parish of St James, Westminster*, 1, Survey of London, 29–30 (1960) · A. S. Gray, *Edwardian architecture: a biographical dictionary* (1985) · C. H. Reilly, *Representative British architects of the present day* (1931) · R. Trevelyan, *Grand dukes and diamonds: the Wernhers of Luton Hoo* (1991) · J. Maxtone-Graham, *The only way to cross* (1972) · J. Maxtone-Graham, *Crossing and cruising* (1992) · private information (2004)
Archives École des Beaux Arts, Paris · Metropolitan Museum of Art, New York · Musée d'Orsay, Paris · RIBA BAL, working drawings for Royal Automobile Club · V&A | CAC Cam., corresp. with Sir E. L. Spears
Likenesses Bassano, photograph, 1947, NPG [*see illus.*]
Wealth at death £27,103 0s. 4d.: probate, 13 Dec 1951, *CGPLA Eng. & Wales*

Davis, Belle (1873/4–1930s?), dancer and singer, was born in New Orleans between June 1873 and September 1874, the daughter of George Davis. Of European and African ancestry, she spent most of her adult life abroad, largely in Britain, where she arrived in mid-1901 with two boys who were billed as 'Piccaninny Actors'. Her performance style changed from 'coon shouting' and 'ragtime singing' in the 1890s to a more decorous manner, where prancing children provided the amusement. She directed their stage act, and with two, sometimes three or four, black children the act was a vigorous and popular entertainment in British and continental theatres.

Davis's troupe appeared on the reputable Empire Theatre circuit in late 1901, recorded in London in 1902 (including the song 'The Honey-Suckle and the Bee'), continued touring London and the provinces in 1903, and ventured to the continent. Dozens of other African-Americans were entertaining the British at this time, and on 9 June 1904 Davis married one of the more successful, Henry Troy, in London. Following her marriage the act continued to tour, and was filmed, for commercial distribution. The Empire circuit continued to employ the group, as did other leading theatres. They presented their ten-minute stage act in Dublin, Cardiff, Swansea, Manchester, Birmingham, Nottingham, Leicester, Edinburgh, Liverpool, and Sheffield between May 1906 and August 1909, and appeared in Berlin, The Hague, Paris, Vienna, St Petersburg, and Brussels during the same period. Some leading performers had their apprenticeship as dancers in Davis's act; when they grew too large she recruited younger boys from America.

The act had been seen by hundreds of thousands of Britons by 1914, when war prevented continental touring and so exposed more Britons to 'Belle Davies [*sic*] and Her Cracker Jacks'. She and the children performed in major cities as well as Ayr, Doncaster, Portsmouth, Ilkeston, and Weymouth during the war years. Her last known performance in Britain was in 1918. From 1925 to 1929 she directed the dancing in the revues at the Casino de Paris, and it is likely that she died in France in the 1930s.

Sometimes billed as a 'creole', Davis was a soprano whose songs were not from the minstrel show or spiritual traditions, but were graceful melodies. By contrast the children were energetic dancers who combined suppleness with comedy. Their well-dressed director's elegance was praised, and is evidenced by surviving promotional material. The mercurial entertainment business had few acts for whom top theatres provided employment for the length of time she worked in Britain. Her qualities both as a singer and as dance director, combined with her professionalism in travelling from town to town, country to country, in charge of boisterous children, were solid, and enabled her to have success at her chosen profession for three decades. Stately, well dressed, and showing faint African features, she presented American dance and song to countless Britons and kept top employers anxious to take her act for their shows.

JEFFREY GREEN and RAINER E. LOTZ

Sources R. E. Lotz, *Black people: entertainers of African descent in Europe and Germany* (1997), 65–87 [with audio CD] · m. reg., London, St Pancras, 9/6/1904
Likenesses photographs, repro. in Lotz, *Black people*, 74, 83, 85

Davis, Brian [*pseud.* Michael ffolkes] (1925–1988), cartoonist and illustrator, was born on 6 June 1925 at 36 St John's Park, London, the only child of Walter Lawrence Davis (1900–1973), typographer, and his wife, Elaine Rachel Bostock (1899–1987), theatre singer. His paternal grandfather was a master carpenter with strong socialist convictions.

From the age of thirteen Brian Davis spent two years at a boarding-school, Leigh Hall in Essex, whose headmaster was a Nazi sympathizer. In his autobiography he described this period of his life as 'excruciating' (ffolkes). He left school to attend evening classes at St Martin's

Brian Davis [Michael ffolkes] (1925–1988), by Howard Coster, 1956

School of Art, London, for a few months, his teacher being the wood-engraver John Farleigh, and to do odd jobs in his father's commercial art studio and elsewhere. During this time he started to draw cartoons, one of which was published in *Punch* when he was seventeen.

Conscripted in 1943, Davis served as a telegraphist in the Royal Navy, mostly in Australia and the Far East. On his demobilization in 1946 John Farleigh helped him to obtain a grant to study at Chelsea School of Art. In spite of the amount of time he spent playing snooker, he gained a diploma after four years. During this period he changed his name (though never by deed poll) to Michael ffolkes, having discovered the name in Burke's peerage and supposing that it reflected the aristocratic, racy image he was cultivating. While still a student he exhibited at the Royal Academy summer show.

During the late 1940s ffolkes's cartoons started to appear in *Lilliput* and the *Strand Magazine* and from 1948 in *Punch*. In the next year he became a *Punch* regular, and remained so for the rest of his days. He described *Punch* as 'my life and home' and election to the *Punch* 'table' as 'my most prized honour' (ffolkes).

In 1953 the first collection of ffolkes's drawings, *ffanfare*, was published by 'ffaber'. At this stage ffolkes revelled in the decorative past, especially the staterooms of noblemen's seats. His style was a little reminiscent of Emett, occasionally of Steinberg. R. G. G. Price in 1957 called his humour 'light, fantastic, often very funny indeed' (Price, 298).

As a freelance cartoonist mainly dependent on the favours of *Punch*, a married man, and a father, he received the opportunity in 1955 to earn a regular income by illustrating the column 'The Way of the World' in the *Daily Telegraph* as a godsend. For over thirty years, four days a week, first with Colin Welch and afterwards with Michael Wharton, he worked sympathetically; in Wharton he found 'a writer who can think in pictures … a rare talent' (ffolkes) as well as a man who shared some of his unorthodox right-wing views. In 1961 he emerged as a caricaturist, illustrating Richard Mallet's film reviews in *Punch*.

From the point of view of his mature style and his enduring reputation, ffolkes's employment by *Playboy*, starting about 1960 and lasting for more than twenty years, was crucial. For the first time his work was excellently reproduced, especially the full pages in colour. The loosening of his style suited the subject matter. Voluptuous ladies romping in bedrooms with satyrs of distinction became his trademark. Wit and charm robbed the *Playboy* cartoons of the power to offend, to the extent that by 1972 even *Punch*, for so long anti-salacious, was publishing spreads with titles like 'ffull Ffrontal Ffolkes', and *Private Eye*, which had no problem with sex, was giving him free rein.

The female form by no means monopolized ffolkes's energies. In 1977 *ffolkes Ffauna* was published and in 1978 *ffolkes Companion to Classical Mythology*, wherein he frisked with animals and gods respectively. In 1982 his cinema caricatures were exhibited at the National Film Theatre in London. Two years later he was the guest on *Desert Island Discs*. His autobiography (in which he revealed a dissatisfaction with the British public's sense of humour) was published in 1985 and coincided with exhibitions at the Palace Theatre and the Royal Festival Hall.

As a cartoonist and the illustrator of more than fifty books, ffolkes was notable for his free-flowing, sensual line. His captions were often delightful—such as the man being rescued from drowning who gasps 'my whole life flashed before my eyes and I wasn't in it', or the duke of Wellington addressing an aide-de-camp at Waterloo with 'Up Guards and at 'em will do for the moment, we'll polish it up later'.

As a young man, living up to his adopted name, ffolkes drank champagne, smoked cigars, and drove a Bentley. Later he wore a battered hat and dressed out of Oxfam. All his life he loved women, wine, movies, and betting on horses. He was twice married, first on 14 March 1953 to Miriam Boxer (dissolved in 1971), with whom he had two sons. With his second wife, Irene (Sophie) Kemp (married 1972; dissolved in 1981), ffolkes had a daughter. His companion for the last nine years was Elfa Kramers. Michael Wharton in an obituary described him as 'highly talented, amusing, moody, troubled, lovable, outrageous, energetic' (*Daily Telegraph*, 20 Oct 1988). ffolkes died on 18 October 1988 at the Lister Hospital, London, of acute pancreatitis and cirrhosis of the liver.   SIMON HENEAGE

Sources M. ffolkes, *ffundamental ffolkes* (1985) [pp. unnumbered] · M. Bateman, *Funny way to earn a living: a book of cartoons and cartoonists* (1966) · R. G. G. Price, *A history of Punch* (1957) · P. Skene Catling,

'An outsider's view of ffolkes', *Punch*, 249 (1965), 534–5 · W. Grundy, 'Who is ffolkes?', *Punch*, 273 (1977), 114–15 · T. Davies, 'ffundamental ffolkes', *Covent Garden Courier* (Nov 1985) · *Daily Telegraph* (19–20 Oct 1988) · *The Guardian* (20 Oct 1988) · *The Independent* (20 Oct 1988) · *The Times* (20 Oct 1988) · private information (2004) · *CGPLA Eng. & Wales* (1989)

Archives *Playboy*, Chicago, archives, papers · *Punch*, 100 Brompton Road, London, archives, papers · Cartoon Art Trust, London, papers · University of Kent, Canterbury, Centre for the Study of Cartoons and Caricature, papers | FILM BFI

Likenesses H. Coster, photograph, 1956, NPG [*see illus.*] · R. Johnson, photograph, *c.*1985, repro. in ffolkes, *ffundamental*, jacket

Wealth at death £126,894: probate, 10 March 1989, *CGPLA Eng. & Wales*

Davis, Charles (*bap.* 1693, *d.* 1755), bookseller, the fifth son of James Davis, a chandler in Hatton Garden, London, and his wife, Mary, was baptized at St Andrew's, Holborn, London, on 5 February 1693. He was bound as an apprentice to the London bookseller Nathaniel Nowell on 8 November 1708 but was not freed as a member of the Stationers' Company until 3 October 1727; he was elected to the livery of the company on the same day. However, Davis was active as a bookseller from as early as 1723 when, based in Covent Garden, London, he published his earliest surviving book catalogue *Bibliotheca literaria, seu, Librorum maxime insignium catalogus: containing a very curious and uncommon collection of books in most languages … to be sold very cheap* (the price mark'd in each book) on 3 December. Still in London, in 1726 he was recorded in Hatton Garden and by 1728, when he took his first apprentice, he had a shop in Paternoster Row. He was also based in Holborn, opposite Gray's Inn and later against Gray's Inn Gate, and was a parishioner of St Andrew's, Holborn, at his death.

At least until 1730 Davis may have had some working relationship with the printer Henry Woodfall, since the evidence of type ornaments in five surviving catalogues suggests that Woodfall was Davis's printer. Altogether ten catalogues pertaining to Davis's business have survived, demonstrating that he was one of the earliest booksellers to retail libraries by priced catalogues. He also sold libraries by auction, including part of the extensive and valuable library of Thomas Rawlinson.

By the date of Davis's death on 31 August 1755 he had achieved considerable eminence as a bookseller. He was unmarried, and on 17 September his estate was granted to his two bookselling nephews, Lockyer *Davis and Charles Reymers (respectively sons of his eldest brother James and younger sister Elizabeth), both of whom had served apprenticeships with Davis. Davis also left a brother, Daniel. Davis's stock was sold off at auction on 21 April 1757; a unique copy of the sale catalogue, annotated with purchasers and prices in an unidentified hand, survives in the British Library.   O. M. BRACK

Sources ESTC · *GM*, 1st ser., 25 (1755), 428 · D. F. McKenzie, ed., *Stationers' Company apprentices*, [3]: *1701–1800* (1978), 102, 251 · I. Maxted, *The London book trades, 1775–1800: a preliminary checklist of members* (1977) · Nichols, *Lit. anecdotes*, 1.364, 434; 2.122; 3.616, 624; 5.489; 6.436; 8.461 · H. R. Plomer and others, *A dictionary of the printers and booksellers who were at work in England, Scotland, and Ireland from 1726 to 1775* (1932) · C. H. Timperley, *Encyclopaedia of literary and* *typographical anecdote*, 2nd edn (1842), 695 · IGI · private information (2004) [M. Treadwell, Trent University, Canada] · administration, PRO, PROB 6/131, fol. 202v · *A catalogue of the remaining part of the quire-stock of the late Mr. Charles Davis* (1757) [sale catalogue, London, 21 April 1757]

Davis, Charles Alfred (1923–1999), theologian, was born on 12 February 1923 in Swindon, the first son and second of the four children of Charles Lionel Davis (1893–1968), sign painter, and his wife, Agatha Ellen Lapham (1893–1979). As a Roman Catholic he was educated at St Brendan's Grammar School, Bristol, and entered St Edmund's Seminary, Ware, aged fifteen. Davis was ordained priest on 15 June 1946 and, after two years of study at the Gregorian University, Rome, where he received the licentiate in sacred theology in 1948, began teaching fundamental theology and apologetics at St Edmund's in 1949. After three years he became professor of dogmatic theology there, a position he held from 1952 until he moved to Heythrop College, Oxfordshire, in 1964. Also in 1964 he attended the third session of the Second Vatican Council and was responsible for briefing the British press at the council. In 1966 Davis was the first Roman Catholic to present the Maurice lectures at King's College, London (published in 1968 as *God's Grace in History*).

On 21 December 1966 Davis announced publicly that he had resolved to break with the Roman Catholic church and to leave its priesthood as he thought the hierarchical institution of the Roman Catholic church no longer represented the intentions of its founder, Jesus Christ. In a press release he outlined the main reasons for leaving:

> I remain a Christian, but I have come to see that the Church as it exists and works at present is an obstacle in the lives of the committed Christians I know and admire … For me Christian commitment is inseparable from concern for truth and concern for people. I do not find either of these represented by the official Church … I do not think that the claim the Church makes as an institution rests upon any adequate biblical and historical basis. The Church in its existing form seems to me to be a pseudo-political structure from the past. It is now breaking up, and some other form of Christian presence in the world is under formation.   (Davis, *Question*, 16)

Davis was at that time regarded as the foremost Roman Catholic theologian in Britain. His theology was seen as moderately progressive. He had been editor of the periodical the *Clergy Review* since 1960. His departure from the official church, precipitated by his conviction that Pope Paul VI was lying about the issue of birth control, caused a major stir and was a turning point in the history of postconciliar Roman Catholicism in Britain. Davis described his break with institutional Roman Catholicism as 'creative disaffiliation' which led him to search for the church of Christ not in other denominations but in informal small gatherings of Christians both inside and outside the church; these, he thought, provided a more credible mode of Christian presence in the modern world. He outlined his reasons for leaving and his plans for his future theological work in *A Question of Conscience* (1967). Written in a popular and polemical style, this book challenged a variety of responses, ranging from anger and disgust to those who found in Davis someone who voiced their own hesitations and doubts about the Roman Catholic church and its priesthood. Its impact on the Roman Catholic church in Britain has been described as similar to that of Bishop John A. T. Robinson's *Honest to God* on the Church of England. In *A Question of Conscience* Davis outlined a programme for his future theological work which represented a significant departure from his hitherto rather traditional and conformist theological thought.

On 4 February 1967 Davis married his old friend the lecturer, writer, and member of the International Grail, Florence Mary Henderson (*b.* 1927), who shared his conviction and left the Roman Catholic church with him. On 8 May 1968 their son, Charles Anthony, was born, followed by their daughter, Claire Susanna, on 26 June 1970. After a short period at Clare College, Cambridge, where he was later made a life member, Davis was appointed head of a new religious studies department at the University of Alberta, Edmonton, where he taught from 1967 to 1970. In 1970 Davis moved to Concordia University, Montreal, where he was professor of religious studies until he retired in 1991. During a sabbatical at the University of Cambridge in 1976/7 Davis presented the Hulsean lectures, published as *Theology and Political Society* in 1980. In 1981 Davis received a Killam research award of the Canada Council. From 1987 until 1991 he was also principal of Lonergan University College in Montreal. In 1986–7 he spent a sabbatical year at the Tantur Ecumenical Institute for Advanced Theological Research in Jerusalem. Davis was president of the Canadian Society for the Study of Religion and editor of the periodical *Studies of Religion / Sciences Religieuses* from 1977 until 1985.

Davis dedicated his theological work to the search for the place of critical Christian theology in a secular world, and this involved a constructive dialogue with the social sciences and especially with the work of the Frankfurt school and Jürgen Habermas. Theology has to move beyond religious orthodoxy, he argued. It must enter into a reciprocal relationship with its cultural context if it wants to find its place as public discourse in the modern world: 'Theology loses its boundaries as an independent discipline, because the only appropriate context for the conscious articulation of *praxis* is a theory of the development of society in its total reality' (Davis, *Religion*, 91). In *Theology and Political Society* (1980) Davis developed a concept of critical theology as having a twofold task, that of developing a theory of history and society, and that of initiating a process of self-reflection within the ecclesial community. In order to be true to itself and its vocation, he argued, the church had to become a community of moral discourse in which the meaning and purpose of all human endeavour could be made explicit and celebrated. Theology is to be done in community and essentially in the public of the secular world.

Following his departure from the Roman Catholic church Davis became interested in sociology and, most important, in the question of the secularization of society. In order to be credible in this context theology has to acknowledge its dependence on human reason and its essential fallibility: 'Theology as public discourse must appeal to methods and modes of rational argumentation and rules of argument' (Davis, 'Theology for tomorrow', 28). This does not, however, mean a total surrender of religion but rather its fulfilment as faith rather than a mere set of beliefs. 'Faith as distinct from beliefs is love ... Faith is the drive towards transcendence, the thrust of human beings out of and beyond themselves, out of and beyond the limited orders and human certainties under which they live' (ibid.).

Davis returned to Britain in 1993 and lived initially in Cambridge, then from 1997 in Edinburgh, where he died at his home, 27 Spottiswoode Road, of Parkinson's disease on 28 January 1999. He was buried at St Catherine's Convent of Mercy, Edinburgh, on 6 February. Despite his official and highly public departure from the Roman Catholic church, Davis was never formally laicized. He celebrated the liturgy in his home and he and his wife hosted many informal small groups of like-minded and different people. It is in them that they saw the realization of the church of Christ. Davis's life and work are the realization of his understanding of theology as a public and dialogical discourse.   NATALIE K. WATSON

Sources private information (2004) [family] · *The Independent* (5 Feb 1999) · *The Guardian* (25 March 1999) · C. Davis, *A question of conscience* (1967) · C. Davis, 'Why I left the Roman Catholic church', *The Observer* (1 Jan 1967) · M. P. Lalonde, *The promise of critical theology: essays in honour of Charles Davis* (1995) · C. Davis, 'Theology for tomorrow', *The promise of critical theology: essays in honour of Charles Davis*, ed. M. P. Lalonde (1995), 23–31 · C. Davis, *Religion and the making of society: essays in social theology* (1994) · *CCI* (1999)
Archives Heythrop College, London
Likenesses C. Henderson Davis, photograph, repro. in Lalonde, *Promise of critical theology* · M. Mann, photograph, repro. in Lalonde, *Promise of critical theology* · photograph, repro. in Davis, *A question of conscience*
Wealth at death £10,653.65: confirmation, 27 April 1999, *CCI*

Davis, Charles Edward (1827–1902), architect and antiquary, was born on 29 August 1827 near Bath, the son of Edward Davis, architect, and his wife, Dorothy (*née* Walker), the widow of Captain Johnston. His father practised in Bath, and had been a pupil of Sir John Soane. In 1833 he restored Prior Birde's Chapel in Bath Abbey church, and in 1834 he published a series of engravings entitled *Gothic Ornaments, etc. of Prior Birde's Oratory*, from drawings by Stephen Burchell. He also designed several houses, including Twerton House, near Bath (1838), and laid out the Victoria Park at Bath, which was opened in 1830.

Charles Edward Davis began the study of architecture as his father's pupil. In 1858 he married Selina Anne, the eldest daughter of Captain Howarth. They had no children. In 1863, having won a competition for the cemetery buildings on the Lower Bristol Road, Davis was appointed city architect and surveyor to the corporation of Bath. He held these offices for nearly forty years. In 1863 he designed an escritoire, Bath's wedding gift to the princess of Wales, which was presented in 1869.

Davis is particularly noted for his work on the mineral baths. In 1869 he started an exploration of the site of the hot springs of the old King's bath; he found extensive remains of Roman thermal work and later published *The Excavations of the Roman Baths at Bath* (9th edn, 1887; first published in *Transactions of the Bristol and Gloucestershire Archaeological Society*, 8, 1883–4, 89–113). In 1877–8 he was successful in exposing the Roman well beneath the King's bath. In 1880–81 he discovered the Great bath and in 1884–6 the Circular bath, both Roman.

With a view to collecting information on the nature and management of spas, in 1885 Davis made a tour of the chief continental springs. He applied the knowledge he gained to various improvements which were made at Bath, and he was also consulted by other English corporations who owned natural baths, such as those at Harrogate and Droitwich. He remodelled the spa baths at Woodhall, Lincolnshire, in 1887.

The old Queen's bath, which had been constructed in 1597 and named after Anne, wife of James I, was removed in the course of the Roman discoveries of 1885. Davis's principal new design was for the new Queen's bath (1886–9). This work, and the incidental restoration, met with criticism on structural as well as archaeological grounds. Reports were made on behalf of the Society of Antiquaries by J. H. Middleton and W. H. St John Hope. An independent opinion was sought from Alfred Waterhouse, whose report, dated 14 January 1887, decided that the new works, though somewhat slender in construction, were not likely to be unstable and that on the whole Davis had struck the right balance between utility and antiquarian values.

Besides his work for the corporation, Davis had an extensive private practice. He designed the church dedicated to St Peter and the schools at Twerton, restored several churches, including Northstoke, Somerset (1888), and St Thomas à Becket at Widcombe, Somerset, and was architect of the Imperial Hotel, Bath, which was opened in 1901. He was elected a fellow of the Society of Antiquaries in 1854, and published *Mineral Baths of Bath: the Bath of Bathes Ayde in the Reign of Charles II* (1883) as well as several pamphlets on the same subject.

The rank of major by which Davis was generally designated was due to his commission in the Worcestershire militia; he had also been a member of the Bath volunteer rifles. He died at his home, Dinmore, 18 Bathwick Hill, Bath, on 10 May 1902. His wife survived him.

PAUL WATERHOUSE, *rev.* JOHN ELLIOTT

Sources *The Builder*, 82 (1902), 504 · *Building News*, 82 (1902), 696 · *Dir. Brit. archs.* · Colvin, *Archs.* · *Lincolnshire*, Pevsner (1964) · *Proceedings of the Society of Antiquaries of London*, 2nd ser., 19 (1902–3), 269–70 · *CGPLA Eng. & Wales* (1902)
Likenesses L. Skeates, oils, Grand Pump Room, Bath
Wealth at death £6567 3s. 7d.: probate, 14 Aug 1902, *CGPLA Eng. & Wales*

Davis, David (1745–1827), dissenting minister and poet, was born on 14 February 1745 at Goetre-isaf, in the parish of Llangybi, near Lampeter, Cardiganshire, where his father, Timothy Jacob (1711/12–1795), a farmer, and his wife, Elinor, were zealous members of the presbyterian church at Cilgwyn. David was the eldest of five brothers, all of whom subsequently adopted the surname of Davis.

A manuscript once in the possession of Davis's eldest son, David, calls him Dafydd ab Ieuan Rhydderch, which was possibly his bardic style. His early religious impressions, as Davis acknowledged in one of his poems, were due to the influence of his pastor, Philip Pugh of Cilgwyn, a notable Independent preacher, in sympathy with the Methodist movement, who had been trained under Samuel Jones, one of the ejected presbyterians of 1662. Davis was accepted as a member at Cilgwyn in 1763.

Having passed through preparatory schools at Leominster (where he spent a year and a half with his uncle, Joshua Thomas, the Baptist historian), Llanybydder, and Llangeler, Davis was sent in 1763 to the grammar school at Carmarthen under Jenkin Jenkins. At the beginning of 1764 he was admitted as a divinity student on the foundation at the Carmarthen Academy, under Samuel Thomas (*d.* 1766). This institution, supported by the London Presbyterian Board, had been aided also by the London Congregational Board until 1755, when the theological teaching of Thomas began to be regarded as heterodox. Yet until Samuel Horsley became bishop of St David's (1788), not only dissenters of all classes but candidates for Anglican orders received their training in this academy. Under Thomas's successor (from 1765), Jenkin Jenkins, the academy was in high esteem for classical learning. Among Davis's contemporaries and lifelong friends were Archdeacon Thomas Beynon and Josiah Rees, editor of *Trysorfa Gwybodaeth*, the first Welsh periodical (1770), and father of Owen Rees, who became a partner in Longmans, the London publisher, in 1794.

After leaving the academy, Davis accepted (1 January 1769) a call to be co-pastor with David Lloyd (Dafydd Llwyd) at Llwynrhydowen, Cardiganshire, where he received presbyterian ordination on 15 July 1773. His stipend was very small and his duties were somewhat laborious, as he had to minister to four or five presbyterian churches of Arian and Unitarian tendencies at some distance from each other. He married on 15 November 1775 Anne Evans (1745/6–1832) of Foelallt, daughter of John Evans, of Llysfaen, Llanwnnen, and they had five sons and four daughters. As a preacher in Welsh he was both powerful and very popular, having a fine voice and great command of his native language. He usually took a comprehensive view of his subject, but at times his sermons lacked preparation and he relied too much on his extempory powers. He excelled in pathos, but this was sometimes taken to extremes. His great theme was the love of God to all his creatures.

In addition to his pastoral work Davis conducted a school at Castellhywel from 1783, and over a period of thirty years he became distinguished as one of the most successful schoolmasters and classical teachers in Wales. The school attracted pupils from all parts of Wales and beyond. Candidates for Anglican holy orders were educated here until about 1790, when Bishop Samuel Horsley declared that he would not ordain such candidates because of Davis's theological and political views. The managers of the Carmarthen Academy were desirous of securing him as tutor, but he declined their overtures.

Lloyd died on 4 February 1779, and a few years later Richard Lloyd, his son, was for a short time colleague with Davis (until 1784). Subsequently Davis's second son, Timothy, was his colleague (1799–1810).

When he began his ministry Davis had already departed from the theological views of his earlier years. The fact that he had become Arian in his theology appears in his friendly controversy with the Revd D. Saunders, a Calvinistic Baptist, of Merthyr Tudful. But he remained more conservative in his theology than most Arians and he retained a good deal of evangelical sentiment, the fruits of Philip Pugh's ministry, as is indicated by his Welsh translation of Henry Scougall's *God's Life in Man's Soul* (1779). As showing the latitudinarian tendencies of his time it is worth noting that, at the instance of Archdeacon Beynon, he began a Welsh translation of John Taylor's work on the epistle to the Romans, but this was not completed. By 1801–2 it was clear that he was not radical enough for some members of his congregations. The dissension led to the seceding of some eighty members, who established three Unitarian churches in the area.

In politics Davis was a radical and openly supported the French Revolution. He was friendly with Richard Price, Edward Williams (Iolo Morganwg), John Jones of Glan-y-gors, Thomas Roberts of Llwyn'rhudol, and Thomas Evans (Tomos Glyn Cothi), all active propagandists in Wales and London, and he published a number of poems voicing his support for the ideals of the revolution. In 1791 he initiated resolutions of condolence offered to Joseph Priestley by the Cardiganshire dissenters after the Birmingham riots; but he never had any intellectual sympathy with thinkers of the Priestley school, and proposed the following epitaph in Welsh and English in response to his ideas of materialism and the mortality of the soul for their leader:

Here lie at rest
In oaken chest,
Together packed most nicely,
The bones and brains,
Flesh, blood, and veins,
And soul of Dr. Priestley.

This choice sample of Welsh humour was repeated by Price to Priestley, who is said to have been 'much pleased with it'.

Davis's poems were collected and published by his son David as *Telyn Dewi* in 1824. The poems were warmly received and rather extravagantly praised by his contemporaries, so much so that Davis regretted that he had not paid more attention to his poetry writing. Some of the poems are occasional pieces, and his hymns are far removed in tone from the emotion of those of contemporary Methodist hymn writers. A number of poems celebrating the French Revolution, however, became popular, but his most common theme is the frailty of human life and the transience of mortal glory. He is best remembered for his free translation of Gray's 'Elegy in a Country Churchyard' and for his classical *englynion* (strict metre quatrains); his poetic references to the ruins of nearby Peterwell House presage the later Romantics.

An engraving of Davis by Bond, from a painting by Harvey, presents a rather heavy countenance, with a forehead high but receding. He was of gentle and genial manners, though a strict disciplinarian at his school, fond of society and the idol of his circle, full of anecdote and sportive in conversation. He retired in 1820. He reached a mellow and venerable age, dying at Llwynrhydowen on 3 July 1827. He was buried on 7 July in the churchyard of Llanwenog, Cardiganshire, where a monument with an inscription in Welsh was erected to his memory. His widow died in 1832 aged eighty-six. Three of his sons entered the ministry; his second son, Timothy, the translator into Welsh of a portion of the commentary of Thomas Coke, died at Evesham, Worcestershire, on 28 November 1860, aged eighty.

ALEXANDER GORDON, *rev.* BRYNLEY F. ROBERTS

Sources T. Griffiths, *Cofiant am y Parch. David Davies* (1828) · W. J. E. [W. J. Evans], 'Memoirs', in *Lloyd letters, 1754–1796*, ed. G. E. Evans (1908), liv–lxi · *Yr Ymofynydd* (Oct 1927) · W. J. Davies, *Hanes plwyf Llandyssul* (1896), 102–8 · J. J. Evans, *Cymry enwog y ddeunawfed ganif* (1937), 172–8 · J. J. Evans, *Dylanwad y chwyldro Ffrengig ar lenyddiaeth Cymru* (1928), 103–9 · J. G. Jenkins, *Hanfod duw a pherson Crist* (1931), 188–90 · T. Rees, *History of protestant nonconformity in Wales* (1861), 473–5 · D. Davis, *Telyn Dewi*, ed. G. R. [G. Rees] (1927), ix–xv · NL Wales, Rees Jenkin Jones MS 4364A

Archives NL Wales, journals, 5487–5494 · NL Wales, other items, 5495–5499 · NL Wales, 3201, 6238, 11138, 13486, 12364–12365, 13484 | NL Wales, Rees Jenkin Jones MSS, 4361–4370

Likenesses W.? Bond, engraving (after W.? Harvey), NL Wales; repro. in Davis, *Telyn Dewi*, frontispiece · miniature, NL Wales

Davis, David Daniel (1777–1841), physician, the son of Daniel Davies, was born on 15 June 1777 at Llandyfaelog, Carmarthenshire. He was educated at Carmarthen grammar school, and at Northampton under John Horsey. Born David Davies, he later altered his surname and added his father's Christian name to his own. He entered the University of Glasgow in 1797, and graduated MD there in 1801. In 1802 he was in Mansfield where he acted as a minister to a nonconformist congregation. He settled in practice at Sheffield in 1803, where he was physician to the infirmary from 1804 to 1813. He was also an active lay preacher in the city and a founder of the Sheffield Literary and Philosophical Society which flourished between 1804 and 1806. During his time in the city he also contributed to the *Edinburgh Review*. On 5 April 1806 he married Catherine, daughter of Henry Hall, a merchant.

Davis moved to London in 1813, was admitted a licentiate of the Royal College of Physicians on 25 June 1813, and practised midwifery. In January 1814 he was appointed physician to Queen Charlotte's Lying-in Hospital, and became physician accoucheur to the Royal Maternity Charity in 1816. As was then customary, he delivered lectures on midwifery, which proved popular, at his house, 4 Fitzroy Street, London. He attended the duchess of Kent at the birth of Queen Victoria but, contrary to later legend, did not take an active part. He was professor of midwifery and diseases of women and children in London University (University College since 1836) from 1828 to 1841 and obstetric physician to University College Hospital from 1834 to 1841. While in London Davis became a member of radical medical circles. He was a friend of Thomas Wakley and was a member of the original committee of the London College of Medicine, formed to oppose the existing 'corrupt' medical colleges.

Davis's first publication, in 1806, was a translation, the *Treatise on Insanity* by Phillipe Pinel (1745–1826), with an introduction by himself, compiled from standard authors. Davis's interest in obstetrics seems to have arisen following the birth of his son Henry Hall Davis in 1807. The child was harmed by the instruments used in the delivery and died in infancy. Davis then set out to improve the design of the obstetric forceps by enlarging the blades and altering the curve. He published his ideas on the subject in his *Elements of Midwifery* (1825). He was also aware of the risk of contagion in cases of childbed fever and insisted that his pupils changed their clothes after dealing with such cases. His most important book, *The principles and practice of obstetric medicine, in a series of systematic dissertations on midwifery and on the diseases of women and children* (2 vols., 1836), was a work of compilation rather than original research but was well done and widely read. In 1840 Davis published *Acute hydrocephalus*. His cures for the condition were large doses of mercury, emetics, and bleeding, but amid many pages of quotation he describes only four cases seen by himself. After a short illness Davis died at his home, 17 Russell Place, Fitzroy Square, London, on 6 December 1841.

Davis had a son, John Hall Davis (1811–1884), who studied medicine under his father at University College and acted as a clinical assistant to his father, before developing a successful career in obstetrics and gynaecology.

NORMAN MOORE, rev. ELIZABETH BAIGENT

Sources Munk, *Roll* · Munk, *Roll* [John Hall Davis] · J. Dewhurst, *Royal confinements* (1980) · C. Woodham-Smith, *Queen Victoria: her life and times*, 1: *1819–1861* (1972) · S. Snell, *Sheffield General Infirmary, 1797–1897* (1897) · A. Desmond, *The politics of evolution: morphology, medicine and reform in radical London* (1989)
Likenesses J. Jackson, portrait, 1825, priv. coll.

Davis, Dorothy Beatrice. *See* Spiers, Dorothy Beatrice (1897–1977).

Davis, Sir Edmund Gabriel (1861–1939), mining financier and art collector, was born on 3 August 1861 at Tintern, Gardiner's Creek Road, Toorak, Melbourne, Australia, the second of the four children of Samuel Davis, merchant, and his wife, Josephine, daughter of Jacob Bensusan. He had two brothers and one sister. At the age of eight Davis moved to Paris with his parents. He was educated at Highburn House, St Leonards, and at the Collège Chaptal in Paris, where he studied painting at the studio of Victor Leclaire. In 1879 he left for the Cape Colony, where he was employed by his uncle's firm, M. L. Bensusan & Co. of Cape Town. Here Davis laid the basis of his later fortune, initially by leasing guano islands off the Cape Coast, and soon afterwards by acquiring copper and railway interests in South-West Africa. The beginning of 1888 found him on the goldfields of Barberton and the Witwatersrand, from where he left for Paris in order to raise capital for his Transvaal ventures. When none of them proved successful, Davis shifted his operations to London, becoming a partner in the firm of Jacob Picard & Co. in 1889. In the same year he married his cousin, Mary Zillah Halford (1866–1941). They had no children.

Davis's South African contacts brought an unending stream of speculative mining ventures to his attention. In the 1890s these were in two areas: central Africa, where Cecil Rhodes's British South Africa Company was ruthlessly establishing its authority under the auspices of a royal charter; and west Africa. By 1904 Davis had acquired sufficient notoriety through his vigorous promotion of dubious concerns on the fringes of the City's capital market for *The Economist* to denounce him by name. Holding more than fifty directorships, and chairman of twelve companies, Davis had interests spanning the globe. At this stage of his career they included gold- and diamond-mining companies in Africa and South America, as well as tramway companies in Hong Kong and Singapore. In the decade before 1914, Davis and Herbert Hoover, later president of the United States of America, became embroiled in controversy when they successfully manipulated the share ownership of the Chinese Engineering and Mining Company in order to wrest control of the Kaiping collieries from their Chinese owners. To many of his Edwardian contemporaries, Davis seemed to be merely the latest in a long line of shady company promoters.

But although a faint air of sharp practice clung to him for the rest of his life, this was also the period in which Davis first displayed his unequalled talent for winning control of business involved in important base minerals. He increasingly devoted his time to constructing cartels. Monopoly or near monopoly control over large sections of the base mineral industry was the key to much of his subsequent success. It was a strategy which he employed to marked effect in coal, chrome, asbestos, manganese, copper, tungsten, tin, and vanadium mining. 'I have ever had a leaning towards base metals in preference to the more precious ores', insisted Davis. 'They have always interested me. I like tonnages' (*African World Annual*, 1933, 40).

During and after the First World War the fortunes of Davis's enterprises soared. His control over the production of chrome, a commodity regarded as vital to the allied war effort because of its steel-hardening qualities, allowed him to repair his battered reputation. From 1915 onwards Davis worked closely with the Admiralty and the Ministry of Munitions in securing supplies of key minerals for Britain and France, while simultaneously denying them to the central powers. Because of Davis's intervention, so *The Times* claimed on 22 February 1939, 'Germany found herself practically "frozen out" from chrome ore, as was indicated by the erratic firing of some German guns towards the end of hostilities'.

The coming of peace saw Davis presiding over an international network of companies and mines that between them controlled about 90 per cent of world chrome production. Although he was never able to replicate the same degree of control over other base minerals, he none the less steadily expanded the scope of his asbestos and copper mining interests in the course of the 1920s and 1930s. In 1929, after successfully waging a savage price-cutting war against Canadian producers, Davis was invited by Turner and Newall, the largest British company in the field, to merge his interests with theirs. Sealed just before the great depression caused prices to tumble, the deal enormously strengthened Turner and Newall's hand in winning an important share of the dwindling world market for asbestos products.

Over the same two decades Davis played a crucial role in the development of the Northern Rhodesian copperbelt. Together with Sir Chester Beatty and Sir Ernest Oppenheimer, he was instrumental in raising the huge sums of capital required to bring mines to the point of production in a part of the world remote from major markets. In all of this, Davis occupied a pivotal position on the board of the British South Africa Company, which he had joined in 1925. The net result made him an extremely powerful figure in the economy of central Africa. Not surprisingly, Davis loomed large in the calculations of settler politicians. 'Everybody knows that the economic dictator of this country is Edmund Davis', the Southern Rhodesian house of assembly was told. 'There may be a case for monarchy; but the King should not sit in an office in London, he should be a Rhodesian' (*Debates of the Legislative Assembly*, 1930).

Despite his financial success, Davis was fond of saying that he could have made as much out of art as he did in business. A noted connoisseur and collector, pictures were with him a passion. With the help of Charles Ricketts, Davis and his wife launched themselves into the art market as major collectors in the late 1890s. Their purchases included paintings of the old masters, and Victorian and modern works. They also owned a collection of major Rodin sculptures. As active patrons of the arts, the Davises' inner circle of artist friends included Ricketts himself, Charles Shannon, James Pryde, and George Lambert. All of them at one time or another lived at Lansdowne House, a block of artists' studios designed for Davis by William Flockhard.

Davis's magnificent art collection was displayed in his Holland Park home, 13 Lansdowne Road, which was designed for him in 1896; and at Chilham Castle in Kent, which he acquired in November 1918. Situated near Canterbury, Chilham was repaired by Sir Herbert Baker. As part of the renovations an enclosed swimming pool was constructed, and here Davis liked to exercise surrounded by Rodin statues. Lesser pictures filled his houses in Venice and the French riviera. Davis's hospitality was famously lavish. Known as a big earner and a big spender, he entertained frequently. Favoured artist friends were taken on Mediterranean cruises on his yacht, the *Catania*; and his musical evenings regularly employed entire orchestras. Davis was said particularly to enjoy fancy-dress balls.

In 1915 Davis presented a major collection of contemporary British paintings to the Luxembourg gallery in Paris, for which he was decorated by the president of France, Raymond Poincaré. In 1935 and again the following year he donated paintings and bronzes to the South African National Gallery, but in 1938 his collection suffered a major loss when thieves broke into Chilham Castle and made off with five paintings. These included *Saskia at her Toilet* by Rembrandt, and portraits by Reynolds, Van Dyck, and Gainsborough. The two Gainsboroughs were found abandoned in a local wood, but the other paintings were never recovered. Davis's collection did not outlive him; the Rodins were sold privately, and the remaining paintings auctioned. At his death his estate was valued at £394,518 4s. 4d.

Davis brought to his art collection the energy and conscientious attention which also characterized his business operations. Renowned for his astonishing memory, he was widely recognized as having a genius for finance as well as a gift for intense concentration on detail. At shareholders' meetings he invariably spoke without notes. Always busy, he was reputed by his associates to be one of the most difficult men in the City with whom to make an appointment at short notice. Short and, in later life, increasingly stout, Davis was thought to bear more than a passing resemblance to Napoleon. Certainly he relished being known as the 'Napoleon of finance', and the 'Napoleon of Northern Rhodesia'. He was knighted in 1927. His sudden death on 20 February 1939 at Chilham Castle left his contemporaries as divided in their opinion of him as they had been during his life. While some celebrated the lightning quickness of his brain and his generosity towards friends, others remembered him for his bluntness and irascibility.

IAN PHIMISTER

Sources G. H. Nash, *The life of Herbert Hoover: the engineer, 1874–1914* (1983) · J. Hamill, *The strange career of Mr Hoover under two flags* (1931) · R. P. T. Davenport-Hines, 'Davis, Sir Edmund Gabriel', *DBB* · R. Murray-Hughes, 'Edmund Davis, 1854–1939', *The Zambia (Northern Rhodesia) Journal*, 6 (1965), 1–12 · 'Death of Sir Edmund Davis', *African World* (25 Feb 1939) · 'Millions made from base metals', *African World Annual* (1933), 40–42 · I. R. Phimister, *An economic and social history of Zimbabwe* (1988) · S. Reynolds, 'Sir Edmund Davis, collector and patron of the arts', *Apollo*, 111 (1980), 459–63 · *The Times* (21 Feb 1939) · *The Times* (22 Feb 1939) · S. E. Katzenellenbogen, 'British businessmen and German Africa, 1885–1919', *Great Britain and her world, 1750–1914*, ed. B. M. Ratcliffe (1975) · *Debates of the Legislative Assembly* [Southern Rhodesia] (21 March 1930), col. 144

Archives PRO, Colonial and FO MSS | BL, Curzon MSS · BL, Charles Ricketts MSS, Add. MSS 58085–58109, 61713–61724 · Bodl. RH, George Cawston MSS · Derbys. RO, Gell MSS · National Archives of Namibia, Windhoek, SWA Company MSS · National Archives of Zimbabwe, Harare, H. U. Moffat, W. Leggate, and F. Newton MSS

Likenesses G. Lambert, drawing, 1903, National Archives of Zimbabwe · E. Dulac, two paintings, *c*.1911–1915 · J. Oppenheimer, drawing, 1936, National Archives of Zimbabwe · M. Lambert, sculpture, National Archives of Zimbabwe

Wealth at death £394,518 4s. 4d.: probate, 1 June 1939, CGPLA Eng. & Wales

Davis, Edward (*fl.* 1682–1693), buccaneer, about whom no details concerning his birth and education are known, was embarked in the late autumn of 1682 in a French privateer operating in the Caribbean under the command of Captain Yanky. Davis transferred into Captain Tristian's ship, Yanky's consort, before being embroiled in a mutiny at Petit Guaves, near Port-au-Prince. Davis sailed under a new captain, John Cook, arriving in Chesapeake Bay in April 1683 where William Dampier and other veteran buccaneers resident in Virginia were recruited for a voyage to the South Sea. On 23 August Cook sailed with Davis as quartermaster. Off the coast of Guinea they seized a Danish prize, 36 guns, which they renamed the *Batchelor's Delight*, before sailing in her to South America in late November.

In March 1684 the *Batchelor's Delight* joined the *Nicholas* (Captain John Eaton) off Valdivia. Together they sailed to the Juan Fernandez Islands to be greeted by a Moskito Indian who had been stranded accidentally by Captain Bartholomew Sharpe in January 1681. Dampier's description of this man's meeting another Moskito Indian, whom they had on board, probably inspired Daniel Defoe's account of Friday's reunion with his father in *Robinson Crusoe* (1719). On 3 May 1684 the buccaneers overhauled a Spanish ship whose crew informed Cook that the authorities were aware of his presence in the South Sea. Cook and Eaton decided to head for the Galápagos Islands. Theirs were the first English vessels to visit the archipelago. After Cook's sudden death Davis was elected commander on 19 July 1684. Davis quarrelled with Eaton and on 2 September they parted, Davis sailing for Port St Helena. On 2 October the *Batchelor's Delight* joined the *Cygnet* (Captain Swan), both crews combining to mount raids ashore. On 1 January 1685 Davis seized a packet-boat bound for Lima with orders concerning the departure of the plate fleet for Panama. On 7 January Davis and Swan sailed for the Pearl Islands to intercept the consignment. By 15 February the treasure had still not arrived. The Spanish fleet was finally sighted on 28 May but it had already detoured to land its cargo at La Villa, and had redeployed to engage a growing number of buccaneer vessels in the Bay of Panama. Battle was joined on 29 May and, despite being outnumbered by three to one, the buccaneers avoided defeat in an indecisive action. Shortly afterwards the buccaneers' alliance fell apart. Davis and Swan combined their forces with those of two other vessels for an attack on Léon after which, on 25 August 1685, they separated. Swan, with Dampier on board, sailed westwards across the Pacific to the East Indies.

Davis spent the remainder of the year cruising, attacking ports in Peru and Chile with Captain William Knight. The pickings were poor, and food was as much sought after as gold. When Knight departed for the West Indies Davis decided to spend Christmas at Juan Fernandez. While approaching the islands the crew felt the shock of the earthquake which destroyed Callao and damaged Lima. Lionel Wafer records they were 450 miles off the mainland when, about four in the morning

> our Ship and Bark felt a terrible Shock [which] made the Guns of the Ship leap in their Carriages, and several of the Men were shaken out of their Hammocks. Captain *Davis*, who lay with his Head over a Gun, was thrown out of his Cabbin.

They learned later that the 'rowling Mountains of Water

… drowned Man and Beast for 50 Leagues along Shore' (Wafer, 213).

Davis resumed cruising in the new year, but by the autumn he had decided to return home. He attempted the Horn late in the season and suffered appalling weather as a result. Sailing south for three weeks, Davis never sighted Tierra del Fuego and never knew when, after turning north, he entered the Atlantic. He made his landfall near the hill of Montevideo just north of the River Plate, almost the same latitude from which he had embarked, on the west side of the continent. To Davis's credit there appears to have been no mutiny, sickness, or death among the crew. From Montevideo the *Batchelor's Delight* headed for the Caribbean, and into obscurity. Davis, Wafer, and John Hingson transferred into a vessel bound for Pennsylvania. On 22 June 1688, after a brief spell in Philadelphia, all three were arrested on suspicion of piracy as they attempted to cross from Port Comfort to the Elizabeth River in a small boat. The inventory of Davis's effects included three bags of Spanish money, and a small chest containing silver weighing 142 pounds.

At a board of inquiry on 26 June Davis claimed to have been a trader, resident in Jamaica for about seven years. He denied ever having been a privateer but his black servant, Peter Cloise, gave contradictory evidence. On 16 August 1688 Davis petitioned for immunity from prosecution under a proclamation by James II concerning privateers, issued the previous year; and in October Lord Sutherland of the council of trade and plantations sent instructions that Davis and his men were to be prosecuted, but these orders seem to have been ignored.

In April 1689 the council of Virginia ordered the buccaneers to be returned to England. They arrived home in November, without their possessions. In March 1692 it was agreed that Davis's property should be restored to him but a royal order withheld £300, plus a quarter of the amount still in Jamestown. The moneys forfeited may have been applied to the building of the College of William and Mary in Williamsburg, Virginia. In November 1693 the council of Virginia invited creditors of the three men to come forward, perhaps indicating that full restitution had still not taken place at that date. Nothing further is known about Davis. There is no evidence to link him with Nathaniel Davis, author of a narrative entitled 'Expedition to the gold mines' which appeared in the second edition of Wafer's *A New Voyage and Description of the Isthmus of America* (1704). Edward Davis signed his depositions in Virginia with a mark, indicating that he may have been illiterate anyway.

Davis's modern fame chiefly rests on his dubious 'discovery' of a Pacific land mass in December 1687. According to Wafer, the *Batchelor's Delight* was in latitude 27°20′ S, some 500 leagues south of the Galápagos archipelago, when a small flat island was encountered to the east of 'a range of high Land, which we took to be Islands, for there were several Partitions in the Prospect' (Wafer, 214). Herman Moll showed 'Davis's Land' in this position on his world map which formed the frontispiece to Dampier's *A New Voyage Round the World* (1697). In 1721 the Dutch West

India Company fitted out three ships under Jacob Rogge-veen to search for 'Davis Land', and half a century later French and British discovery ships were still looking for it. The true identity of 'Davis Land' remains a puzzle. It may have been Easter Island, but it is equally possible that Davis and his men were deceived by a bank of cloud.

JAMES WILLIAM KELLY

Sources PRO, CO 1/65, 136/6, 136/7 · W. Dampier, *A new voyage round the world* (1697) · L. Wafer, *A new voyage and description of the isthmus of America* (1699) · A. Cowley's journal, PRO, Sloane MS 1050 [after 1686] · W. Hacke, ed., *A collection of original voyages* (1699) · G. Williams, *The great South Sea: English voyages and encounters, 1570–1750* (1997) · D. Howse and N. J. W. Thrower, eds., *A buccaneer's atlas: Basil Ringrose's atlas, Basil Ringrose's South Sea waggoner* (Berkeley, CA, 1992) · L. E. Elliot Joyce, 'Introduction', in L. Wafer, *A new voyage and description of the isthmus of America*, ed. L. E. Elliot Joyce (1934), xi–lxvii · P. K. Kemp and C. Lloyd, *The brethren of the coast* (1960) · J. Masefield, *On the Spanish main, or, Some English forays on the isthmus of Darien* (1906) · G. Williams, '"The inexhaustible fountain of gold": English projects and ventures in the south seas, 1670–1750', *Perspectives of empire: essays presented to Gerald S. Graham*, ed. J. E. Flint and G. Williams (1973), 27–52
Archives BL, Sloane MSS · PRO

Davis, Edward (1833–1867), genre painter, was born at Worcester and learned drawing there before attending the Birmingham School of Design, then under the man-agement of J. Kyd. When Kyd transferred to the Worcester School of Design Davis accompanied him, studying there for three years and winning several prizes. He first exhib-ited at the Royal Academy in 1854, giving his address as 22 Foregate Street, Worcester. He showed *Meditation*, depict-ing an old villager sitting by a fireside, and *Parting Words*, a deathbed scene. In the following year he sent *A Cottage Scene* to the academy and by 1856 he was living in London, at 16 Russell Place, Fitzroy Square. Among his most highly regarded works were *On the Way to School* (engraved by Wil-liam Ridgway), *Granny's Spectacles*, *Doing Crochet Work*, *Words of Peace*, and *The Little Peg-Top*, which was presti-giously placed on the line at the Royal Academy. He died young, while studying in Rome, on 12 June 1867. Examples of his paintings, which show careful draughtsmanship and a fondness for chubby figures, are in the Ashmolean Museum in Oxford. An album of his drawings was sold at Christies in 1951.

L. A. FAGAN, *rev.* SUZANNE FAGENCE COOPER

Sources *Art Journal*, 29 (1867), 188 · Redgrave, *Artists* · Graves, *RA exhibitors* · Mallalieu, *Watercolour artists* · Wood, *Vic. painters*, 3rd edn · *Victorian painting* (1962) [exhibition catalogue, Arts Council of England]

Davis [*née* Cadwaladr], **Elizabeth** [Betsy] **(1789–1860)**, trav-eller and nurse, was born on 24 May 1789 at Penrhiw near Bala, Merioneth, the fifth child of Dafydd Cadwaladr (1752–1834), small-holder and Methodist preacher, and his wife, Judith (*d.* 1800), *née* Humphreys, the daughter of a Montgomeryshire farmer. Dafydd Cadwaladr, a self-educated man, was a highly regarded poet and preacher, and a close friend of the Welsh Methodist leader Thomas Charles.

Betsy spent her early years on the hill farm at Penrhiw.

Elizabeth [Betsy] **Davis** (1789–1860), by unknown engraver, pubd 1857 (after Messrs Day)

She attended school in Bala, where she learned to read and write in Welsh and acquired 'a pennyworth of Eng-lish' (*Autobiography*, 8). Life was harsh, and Dafydd Cadwa-ladr imposed a puritanical regime on his lively and extro-vert daughter. She was devastated by the death of her mother, which took place when Betsy was about ten (not, as she later recorded, five) years of age (ibid., 6), and, since she did not get along with her older sister, she moved to the neighbouring Plas-yn-dre, the household of Simon Lloyd, her father's landlord, an Oxford-educated Anglican clergyman who had become a Methodist. Although she was trained in domestic skills at Plas-yn-dre, she was treated more as a family member than a servant, and there she learned English. Though happy with the Lloyds, when she was about fourteen or fifteen she suddenly abandoned the security of Plas-yn-dre and set out on her travels: typically, she left because 'a sudden thought occurred to me not to stay there any longer, and that I must see more of the world' (ibid., 15).

Betsy was a striking-looking woman. Tall, dark, and physically strong, she was proud of her strength and used it to good effect whether in tackling burglars in Liverpool or escaped convicts in the Australian bush. On at least one occasion she successfully masqueraded as a man. She had a strong personality, characterized by courage, enter-prise, honesty, and a great capacity for hard work. She remained throughout her life a devout Christian and a patriotic Welshwoman. She changed her name to Eliza-beth Davis because the English could not pronounce Cad-waladr, but whenever on her world travels she met people who did not understand English she always spoke to them in Welsh.

After first leaving home Betsy worked as a servant in Liverpool and in London, but her desire to see more of the world, coupled with the vagaries of her employers, took her further afield. She toured the continent in 1814–15 and sailed to the West Indies, where she visited the plantations. For many years she served as ship's steward aboard the vessel *Denmark Hill*, sailing to Australia, India, China, the Far East, South America, and many other destinations. Her travels were accompanied by a series of amazing adventures and life-threatening dangers, all of which she managed not only to survive but often to emerge from with glory. Amorous suitors dogged her across the globe (one even kidnapped her and attempted to push her into a forced marriage in Rio de Janeiro), but Betsy resisted all their charms and remained single. A full and fascinating account of all her travels is given in her autobiography published in 1857.

By 1835 Betsy was back in London, and, having lost the money which she had accumulated on her travels at the hands of an unscrupulous property dealer, she was compelled to return to domestic service. She acted as housekeeper to various families and individuals in London, though no employer ever lorded it over Betsy. As a domestic servant, she had often been called on to nurse family members who were ill. Drawing on her sick-room experience, she obtained a position as a nurse at Guy's Hospital in London, where she remained for almost a year during 1850–51. She gained the reputation of being 'steady and sober' (*Autobiography*, 152), but left because she did not want to work nights, and returned to nursing private patients. There is no evidence that she received any formal training at Guy's, and in fact she noted 'I did not like nursing as well as being in service' (ibid., 152), but despite this statement her greatest claim to fame lies in the field of nursing.

In 1854, when Betsy was already sixty-five years old, she embarked upon a new phase of her nursing career. Having read reports in *The Times* of the Crimean War, of the appalling conditions at the barracks hospital at Scutari, and of the proposed departure of a party of nurses under Florence Nightingale, Betsy volunteered her services. She travelled with Mary Stanley's party first to Therapia and then to Scutari on the Black Sea, where the main British hospital was located and where the nurses were under Nightingale's control. Far from being welcomed, their help was only grudgingly accepted, and when Betsy insisted on going to the hospital at Balaklava, in the Crimea itself, she did so without Nightingale's blessing. Once there, she set to work with her accustomed vigour in providing bedding for the wounded, nursing the men, and ensuring that they were well fed. She criticized Florence Nightingale for over-adherence to bureaucracy and for maladministration of resources, and alleged that she had a French cook and lived very well on three-course meals, while the wounded servicemen starved.

Ill health forced Betsy to return to London. She had no means of support, and the autobiography which she related to Jane Williams at this stage ends with an appeal for employment or for subscriptions towards her maintenance. She died at 22 Herbert Street, Hoxton New Town, London, on 17 July 1860. The whereabouts of her grave is unknown. DEIRDRE BEDDOE

Sources *The autobiography of Elizabeth Davis, Betsy Cadwaladyr: a Balaclava nurse*, ed. J. Williams (Ysgafell), 2 vols. (1857); 2nd edn (1987) [incl. introduction by D. Beddoe] · M. Jones, *Elizabeth Davies, 1789–1860* (1960) · d. cert. · F. B. Smith, *Florence Nightingale: reputation and power* (1982)

Likenesses engraving (after Messrs Day), NPG; repro. in *Autobiography of Elizabeth Davis* [*see illus.*]

Wealth at death appealed for employment or subscriptions towards 'the comfort of her latter years': *Autobiography*, ed. Williams

Davis, Francis [*pseud.* the Belfast Man] (1810–1885), poet and Young Irelander, was born at Ballincollig military station, co. Cork, on 7 March 1810, the son of Francis Davis (*d. c.*1825), a Royal Artillery soldier, and Jane M'Fee (*d.* 1822), sister of Daniel M'Fee, a United Irishman. His parents were originally from Ulster and moved back when Francis Davis was a child. Since his father's decision to join the army had resulted in the loss of the family farm near Hillsborough, the family had to move frequently to look for work. Consequently, Davis was mainly taught by his mother. He attended school in Hillsborough when he was seven or eight, but had to leave when he was ten. Two years later his mother died and he was sent to a wealthy relative in Hillsborough. After the death of his father a few years later, he went to Belfast to train as a muslin weaver, and worked in Belfast, Glasgow, and Manchester, before finally settling in Belfast in 1845.

Davis was a self-taught man, often working at the loom with an English grammar beside him (*Morning News*, 13 Oct 1885, 7). Although he had written some street ballads on the subject of Catholic emancipation, he only became known as a poet when he wrote nationalist and radical poetry in *The Nation* as the Belfast Man, for instance 'Kathleen Ban Adair', 'The Minstrel of Mallow', 'The North is Up', and 'A Song of Ulster'. His support for the Young Ireland movement remained artistic, however, and he was not involved in the revolutionary activities of 1848. Davis's first collection of poems, *Miscellaneous Poems*, appeared in 1847, followed by *Lispings of the Lagan* in 1849. These works were very well received in Ireland, England, and America, and a banquet was given in his honour in the Music Hall, Belfast. In 1850, he began the short-lived *Belfast Man's Journal*, which was aimed at enhancing the self-respect of the Irish, and gaining the respect of other nations. It was intended to educate the working classes of Ireland, England, and Scotland, in order to eradicate any form of prejudice among people, 'hoping by such means, if we cannot be induced to love, we may at least live without hating each other' (*Belfast Man's Journal*, 1, 5 Jan 1850, 1–2). Davis, who was often compared with Robert Burns, also published his poetry in the *Dublin University Magazine*, and other journals. Praised by critics for its imagery, power, passion, and harmony, his work expressed Davis's strong independence of mind, his deep religious beliefs, and his passionate sense of justice.

In 1855 Davis published *Belfast, the City and the Man*, which was dedicated to the unveiling of the statue of Frederick Richard Chichester (1826–1852), the young earl of Belfast. In 1861, his *The Tablet of Shadows: a Phantasy; and other Poems* appeared. He also wrote a eulogy in memory of Prince Albert, *Leaves from our Cypress and our Oak* (1863), which earned him a gold medal from Queen Victoria, and a public dinner in Belfast. In 1869 he published *Funeral Voices*, in memory of the Revd Henry Cooke. Davis led a hand-to-mouth existence, and to support his family he worked at several jobs: as a proof-reader in Messrs Simms and M'Intyre, a publishing house in Belfast; as a newspaper reporter; and as an assistant librarian at the Queen's College, Belfast. At the same time, he taught himself Greek, Latin, French, and Irish. Friends obtained him a pension of £50 a year from the literary fund of the civil list.

Not much is known about Davis's personal life. He was never a public figure, but from 1865 he totally disappeared from public life. Davis was married, and his wife, also a Presbyterian, died in 1873. Five children, three sons and two daughters, survived their parents. In November 1874, Davis converted to Catholicism, and this alienated many of his friends and patrons, who believed that this step had completely changed him (*Morning News*, 13 Oct 1885, 7). During his last five or six years he lived as a recluse, devoting himself totally to religion. At that time he was described as 'a little, thin, low-set man with a grey beard and dark hair; stooped in the shoulders; head bent forward … very weak-looking, and his whole appearance and walk suggesting deep thought or prayer' (McGrath, 602).

In 1878 Davis's friends organized the publication of *Earlier and Later Leaves, or, An Autumn Gathering*, a collection of his poetry, to raise funds for the poet. Francis Davis died a poor man on 7 October 1885 at his home in Alloa Street, Clifton Park Avenue, Belfast, and was buried on 10 October 1885 at Milltown cemetery, Belfast. In 1886, the Belfast Young Ireland Society erected a Celtic cross over his grave.   BRIGITTE ANTON

Sources J. McGrath, '"The Belfastman": a forgotten bard', *Dublin University Review*, 2 (1886), 569–604 • D. Stewart, 'Francis Davis: "The Belfast Man"', *Irish Book Lover*, 5 (1913–14), 133–5 • M. Russell, 'Francis Davis: the "Belfast Man"', *Irish Monthly*, 5 (1877), 569–76 • 'Francis Davis: "The Belfast Man"', *The Nation* (24 Oct 1885), 9f, cols. 4–11 • 'Death of Francis Davis: "The Belfast Man"', *Morning News* [Belfast] (8 Oct 1885), 5, col. 3 • 'The late Francis Davis', *Morning News* [Belfast] (9 Oct 1885), 5, col. 5 • 'Funeral of the late Francis Davis', *Morning News* [Belfast] (12 Oct 1885), 5, col. 2 • 'Recollections of Francis Davis (by an old weaver)', *Morning News* [Belfast] (13 Oct 1885), 7, col. 1 • 'Francis Davis—to the editor', *Morning News* [Belfast] (14 Oct 1885), 6, col. 1 • 'Death of Mr Francis Davis, "The Belfast Man"', *Northern Whig* (9 Oct 1885), 5, col. 6 • *The Belfast Man's Journal*, 1–12 (Jan–March 1850) • T. F. O'Sullivan, *The Young Irelanders*, 2nd edn (1945) • R. S. J. Clarke, ed., *Friar's Bush and Milltown graveyards* (1984), vol. 2 of *Gravestone inscriptions: Belfast* (1982–91) • J. Hewitt, '"The northern Athens", and after', in J. C. Beckett, *Belfast: the making of the city, 1800–1914* (1983), 71–82 • F. Davis, *Earlier and later leaves, or, An autumn gathering* (1878) • list of converts, Holycross Church, Belfast, 1868–80, PRO NIre., entry no. 94, mic ID/65 • G. N. B. M'Bean, *Review of Francis Davis's 'Tablet of shadows and other poems', with a general description of his mental characteristics* (1862) • J. Vinycomb, 'Francis Davis', *Ulster Journal of Archaeology*, new ser., 7 (1901), 109 • A. Poplar, 'An autumn ecologue', *Dublin University Magazine*, 48 (1856), 493–7 • N. J. G., 'A quartette of Irish poets', *Irish Quarterly Review*, 5/20 (Dec 1855), 697–731 • T. W. Moody and J. C. Beckett, *Queen's, Belfast, 1845–1949: the history of a university*, 1 (1959)

Likenesses drawing, repro. in Davis, *Earlier and later leaves*

Wealth at death never earned much from poetry; £50 p.a. pension from literary fund of civil list; *Earlier and late leaves* collection organized to provide funds: 'Francis Davis: "The Belfast Man"', *Nation*; Stewart, 'Francis Davis: "The Belfast Man"'; O'Sullivan, *Young Irelanders*, p. 379; Russel, 'Francis Davis: "The Belfast Man"', p. 573; 'Death of Francis Davis: "The Belfast Man"', *Northern Whig*

Davis, Fred (1913–1998), billiards and snooker player, was born on 14 August 1913 at The Moor, Newbold, Whittington, Derbyshire, the youngest of the six children of Fred Davis, innkeeper, and his wife, Ann Eliza Clark. He learned to play snooker on a miniature table at home, and then in the billiard hall in Chesterfield owned by his parents. His ability was overshadowed by that of his eldest brother, Joseph (Joe) *Davis, who won his first world championship in 1928. Fred Davis won his first major title the following year, at the age of sixteen, when he became world junior professional billiards champion (a title he held on two further occasions). Joe was critical of his younger brother: Fred, he believed, did not take the game seriously enough, and smiled too much in practice and in competition. But Joe recognized Fred's inherent skill: 'Fred was the greatest technician in the profession', he said.

> His cue action and stance was near perfect and when in form he never batted an eyelid or moved his head or body so much as a millimetre … if he had a flaw in his make up it was a tendency to be temperamental, at times giving the impression he could not care less.   (Davis, 176)

But, as Fred's opponents often testified, this easy manner and ever present smile concealed a steely determination to succeed: the (unrelated) snooker player Steve Davis remarked that 'He'd be smiling while kicking you in the teeth. He'd smile when concentrating on his shot' (*The Independent*).

Fred Davis arrived on the billiards scene just as the sport was losing its popularity, and did not compete again until 1937, when he reappeared as a snooker player at the world professional snooker championships; he lost 17–14 in the first round to Bill Withers. His performance was undermined by his myopia, which made it difficult for him to focus on the balls for any length of time; the condition was later remedied with the use of a revolutionary pair of swivel-lensed spectacles. His playing improved immediately, and in the world championships of 1940 he lost to his brother Joe in the final by only one frame. On 15 July 1940 Davis married Sheila Goodacre (*b.* 1913/14); they had two daughters. During the Second World War Davis served in the army with the 3rd airborne division.

After the war Joe went into semi-retirement; although Fred no longer had to compete directly with his brother, Joe's status as the undefeated world champion continued to cast a shadow over Fred's achievements. Fred Davis won the first of his eight world championship titles in 1948 by beating Walter Donaldson 84–61. He won again in the following year, and in every year between 1951 and 1956. The world championships were dropped after 1957, when only four players entered the competition. Television saw no future in snooker as a televised sport. The championships were revived in 1964, and from 1969 took the form of a knock-out tournament: Fred Davis, in his late fifties, continued to compete strongly with the best of the new generation of players and reached the semi-finals in 1969, 1974, and 1978. During this last match Joe Davis was taken ill; he died a few weeks later. Despite heart attacks in 1974 and 1977, Fred Davis continued on the professional circuit, and in 1980 he won the world billiards title, which he defended successfully later that year. He published *Snooker* (1977) and *Talking Snooker* (1979), which both had second editions. He retired from professional competition in 1992; at seventy-eight he was probably the oldest active professional sportsman in the world. He died in the Denbigh Infirmary, Denbigh, on 16 April 1998. His wife predeceased him.   RACHEL CUTLER

Sources J. Davis, *The breaks came my way* (1976) · *The Guardian* (18 April 1998) · *The Independent* (18 April 1998) · *The Times* (18 April 1998) · *Belfast News-Letter* (17 April 1998) · b. cert. · m. cert. · d. cert.
Archives SOUND BL NSA, Davis v. Pulman, World Professional Snooker Championship, Blackpool, 17 March 1955, PC 12
Likenesses A. J. O'Brien, double portrait, photograph, 1939 (with Joe Davis), Hult. Arch.; *see illus. in* Davis, Joseph (1901–1978) · double portrait, photograph, 1976 (with Cliff Thornburn), Hult. Arch. · double portrait, photograph, 1976 (with John Pulman), Hult. Arch. · photograph, repro. in *The Guardian* · photograph, repro. in *The Independent* · photograph, repro. in *The Times*

Davis, George Edward (1850–1907), chemical engineer, was born at Eton on 27 July 1850, the eldest son in the family of three sons and two daughters of George Davis, bookseller, and his wife, Lucy (*née* Smith). Little is known of his early education and at the age of fourteen he was apprenticed to a local bookbinder. However, after two years he abandoned this trade to pursue his interest in chemistry. He went to work at the local gasworks and studied part time—initially at the Slough Mechanics' Institute and later (for one year) at the Royal School of Mines. He was a great believer in practical experience and to this end, at the age of nineteen, went to Manchester, then one of the main centres of the British chemical industry. He worked as a chemist at Brearley & Sons where he stayed for three years. In early 1872 he was engaged as manager at the Lichfield Chemical Company in Staffordshire, where his initiative and inventiveness were given full rein by an indulgent proprietor. Davis planned and built a number of new chemical plants, designing both the equipment and the buildings in which it was installed. Thus he became a largely self-taught engineer; his works included the (then) tallest chimney in the UK, with a height of more than 200 ft. He also appreciated the value of economics applied to industry and, in his early writings, was clearly concerned with the costs of materials and products. This concern was reflected at a personal level when, in his letters to his parents, he remarked that he was considering getting married in order to save money and live comfortably.

Davis's years in Lichfield appear to have been a fruitful period professionally. He was contributing papers to scientific journals and also engaged in debate with other industrial scientists, whose work on certain engineering projects he regarded as sadly inadequate. His only complaint (in nearly every letter he wrote) was of the dullness of his existence outside work. He obviously missed the opportunities provided by a big city and journeyed to Manchester as frequently as he was able on business trips. Ultimately his increasing frustration at Lichfield led him about 1875 to return to the north-west, to work at the St Helens factory of J. G. Gamble, pioneers in the Weldon chlorine process.

On 10 December 1878 Davis married Laura Frances Miller (*b.* 1846/7), daughter of Charles Miller, tailor; they had at least one son. Earlier in the same year he had entered private practice, but by the time of his marriage had been recruited into the new chemical inspectorate by its first director, Angus Smith. Davis visited many chemical works, and inspected their arrangements for pollution control. The visits led him to realize that any chemical process could be considered as a sequence of particular operations, the fundamental concept behind the modern field of chemical engineering. Although he did not coin the term 'unit operations' his writings show an awareness of the concept. He argued that all processes could be broken down into a relatively small number of operations which, when studied in the abstract, revealed certain general principles which were applicable to any process.

In 1884 Davis returned to private practice, this time in partnership with his brother Alfred. Although their business as bleach manufacturers was not successful, the consulting business flourished. In addition, Davis continued to develop his ideas on chemical engineering. In 1887 he founded the *Chemical Trade Journal* which, in addition to encouraging and spreading commercial and technical information, also served to publicize Davis's own ideas on chemical engineering. He developed these ideas sufficiently to present a series of lectures at Manchester Technical College in 1887. These were published in the *Chemical Trade Journal* and became the basis of the *Handbook of Chemical Engineering*, published in 1901. In his introduction to the latter, Davis outlines his philosophy, that 'Chemical Engineering deals with the construction of plants … for the utilization of chemical reactions on the large scale without in any way specifying the industry in which such plants are to be used'. This was a revolutionary idea, and it was not widely accepted in the UK until after the Second World War. However, in America it was exploited with great commercial success in the early 1900s.

Davis was for some years the leader of a group of chemists and engineers who met together under the title of the Faraday Club. From this little group sprang the Society of Chemical Industry in 1881; Davis was a founder member and its first honorary secretary (1881–3). He subsequently set up a Manchester section of the society and was its chairman from 1895 to 1898.

Davis was a short, stout, bearded man with a dry sense of humour. He once said:

> Never be in too much of a hurry to give answers to a client. If you are too quick he will think the problem easy and worth

little. If you make a mistake he will not be pleased. In any case, you will make plenty of mistakes without being overhasty. (Swindin, *Engineering*, 30)

His many interests included microscopy and, feeling the lack of any journal on the subject, he founded the *Northern Microscopist* in 1881. He also wrote a book, *Practical Microscopy*, published the same year. He had sixty-seven patents granted, and in addition to his books published numerous scientific papers and prosecuted a successful consultancy business. He was widely considered the father of chemical engineering. He died at his home, 151 Croxted Road, West Dulwich, on 20 April 1907. DON FRESHWATER

Sources N. Swindin, 'George E. Davis memorial lecture', *Transactions of the Institution of Chemical Engineers*, 31 (1953), 189–200 · G. E. Davis's letters to his parents, Institution of Chemical Engineers, Rugby · N. Swindin, *Engineering without wheels: an autobiography* (1962) · private information (2004) · D. C. Freshwater, 'George E. Davis, Norman Swindin and the empirical tradition in chemical engineering', *Advances in Chemistry*, 190 (1980) · m. cert. · d. cert. · *CGPLA Eng. & Wales* (1907)

Archives Institution of Chemical Engineers, Rugby, letters to his parents · Sci. Mus., corresp. and papers

Likenesses photograph, c.1880, Institution of Chemical Engineers, Rugby · · oils (after photograph, c.1880), Institution of Chemical Engineers, Rugby

Wealth at death £9307 12s. 5d.: probate, 13 June 1907, *CGPLA Eng. & Wales*

Davis, Henry David (1839–1915), architect, was born on 1 June 1839 at 121 High Holborn, London, the son of Abraham Davis, and his wife, Emma Moses. Nothing is known about his education or early life, but he became an architect. On 23 October 1879 he married Sara Lindo Baber Isaacs, daughter of Michael Baber Isaacs, a merchant. They had a daughter, Mabel Kate Davis. He was elected associate of the Royal Institute of British Architects (RIBA) on 18 March 1872, one of his proposers being David Mocatta, the first professing Jewish architect in Britain. He became a fellow of the RIBA on 27 January 1879.

Davis set up in independent practice in the mid-1860s and by 1867 was a partner in the City architectural practice of Davis and Emanuel, and this working relationship with his slightly younger contemporary **Barrow Emanuel** (1842–1904) proved enduring, lasting for about thirty years. Emanuel was born on 4 February 1842 in the High Street, Portsmouth, the second son of six children of Alderman Emanuel Emanuel (d. 1888), JP of Portsmouth, the first Jewish mayor of Portsmouth (1866–7), and his wife, Julia Moss of Plymouth. He was a brother of Katie *Magnus, Lady Magnus (1844–1924), and the pair were very close, Barrow remaining a bachelor all his life. In 1889 the two of them erected a memorial fountain in honour of their father on the seafront at Portsmouth. He received his early education in Portsmouth followed by Trinity College, Dublin, where he graduated MA. He became a civil engineer and his first job was as an assistant government inspector of factories. He later became a JP for the county of Middlesex.

Davis and Emanuel's earliest commissions arose out of Emanuel's Portsmouth connections: the Clarence Pier (Emanuel's father had initiated the draining of Southsea

Common on which the Esplanade was constructed); two board schools, jointly with the firm of Mileham and Kennedy; and Portsmouth grammar school. Working out of offices in London at 32 Moorgate Street (1867) and afterwards at 2 Finsbury Pavement, Davis and Emanuel's success was founded largely on commercial work, building offices, banks, and warehouses in the City and East End. They also specialized in schools, welfare institutions, especially convalescent homes, and social housing projects. They won the competition for the City of London School on the Victoria Embankment in 1879, perhaps their best-known building. They developed Finsbury Circus, in the immediate vicinity of their offices, and Lloyds Avenue, Fenchurch Street. They came top in competitions held for the Gosport town hall in 1883 and for the Corporation of London Freemen's almshouses, Brixton, in 1884, in the year that they were selected architects to the Revd Samuel Barnett's newly formed East End Dwellings Company. Between 1885 and 1906 they laid out small estates and built workers' flats in Whitechapel (Katherine and Lolesworth Buildings), Bethnal Green, Spitalfields, and Stepney Green, and in north London at Stoke Newington, Barnsbury, and St Pancras, executed in a somewhat less austere style than those of their rival Nathan S. Joseph, who worked for the Four Per Cent Industrial Dwellings Company.

The beneficiaries of Davis and Emanuel's work in the East End were largely poor immigrant Russian Jews. From 1862 Emanuel was a member and a quiet but generous benefactor of the Jewish Board of Guardians. He showed his business acumen in acquiring on excellent terms a potentially valuable freehold site at Widegate Street, close to the Liverpool Street end of Middlesex Street (Petticoat Lane) in 1896 on which new offices were constructed for the board, the architects giving their services gratis. One of Emanuel's last projects was the new Joel Emanuel Almshouse in Stamford Hill (c.1904). The partners also undertook alteration work on private villas for wealthy English-born Jewish clients, such as G. C. Raphael and Sir Joseph Sebag-Montefiore, who had inherited the estate of his uncle Sir Moses Montefiore at East Cliff Lodge, Ramsgate. Indeed, one of Davis's earliest commissions had been to design the Judith, Lady Montefiore College at Ramsgate, built by Sir Moses in memory of his late wife in 1865–9. The result was a confident essay in mock-Elizabethan red brick, built in a crescent around a courtyard, sadly demolished in 1965. Unlike Emanuel, however, Davis does not seem to have involved himself in Jewish communal life.

Davis and Emanuel designed three major London synagogues, all in individual and distinctive styles characterized by fashionable orientalizing embellishments. West London Synagogue, in Upper Berkeley Street (1870) is still the 'cathedral' of Reform Judaism in Britain. The partnership landed this commission in limited competition, the outcome of which was acrimoniously disputed in the pages of *The Builder* by Hyman Henry *Collins, and the resulting building no doubt helped establish the practice.

Emanuel, like his sister, Lady Magnus, was a member of the Reform congregation. So, too, was Davis. The plain, economical brick exterior of East London Synagogue, Stepney Green (1876–7), disguised a gloriously polychromic internal space, the only 'cathedral' synagogue ever built east of Aldgate for the edification of the immigrant community. It barely survives today, internally divided into expensive flats. The Spanish and Portuguese Synagogue, Maida Vale (1896), has an impressive central dome that, unlike that at west London, can be viewed from the street. They were perhaps the best of the synagogue architects of their generation.

Davis retired from practice in 1898 and from the RIBA in 1903 through ill health, and Emanuel became senior partner. However, the latter died suddenly from a ruptured abscess on the windpipe, on 14 February 1904 at home at 147 Harley Street, London. He had apparently been upset by the death of his nephew Frederick Emanuel a few months previously. At his own request, the funeral was postponed for three days (highly unusual among Jews, whose custom is burial within twenty-four hours). He was laid to rest on 18 February at Kingsbury Road Jewish cemetery, Dalston, the old cemetery of the West London Synagogue (Reform).

The architectural practice was continued by Henry C. Smart, who had worked in the office for fifteen years prior to being made a partner on 1 January 1902. Davis himself died on 30 June 1915 at his home, 32 Portsdown Road, Maida Vale, west London, and was buried two days later in the Reform section of the Jewish cemetery in Golders Green Jewish cemetery, whose red-brick Romanesque chapel and gateway complex Davis and Emanuel had designed in 1895–7. The beneficiaries of the heirless Emanuel's estate inherited almost £59,000, the largest fortune accumulated by any of the group of Jewish architects practising in the second half of the nineteenth century (exceeded in real value only by that of David Mocatta in an earlier generation), but which perhaps reflected inherited wealth accumulated by his family in Portsmouth. Davis, by contrast, left a more modest sum.

SHARMAN KADISH

Sources biographies file, RIBA BAL · *The Times* (17 Feb 1904) · *The Times* (1 July 1915) · *The Builder* (9 July 1915), 26–7 · *RIBA Journal*, 3rd ser., 22 (1914–15), 506 · *The Builder* (13 July 1867) · *The Builder* (3 Aug 1867) · *The Builder* (17 Aug 1867) · *The Builder* (Feb 1904) · *Jewish Chronicle* (4 Jan 1889) · *Jewish Chronicle* (19 Feb 1904) · *Jewish Chronicle* (2 July 1915) · *Dir. Brit. archs.* · *Jewish Year Book* (1901) · L. Fraser, '"Four Per Cent Philanthropy": social architecture for East London Jewry, 1850–1914', *Building Jerusalem: Jewish architecture in Britain*, ed. S. Kadish (1996), 166–92 · R. H. Harper, *Victorian architectural competitions: an index to British and Irish architectural competitions in The Builder, 1843–1900* (1983) · E. Jamilly, 'Anglo-Jewish architects, and architecture in the 18th and 19th centuries', *Transactions of the Jewish Historical Society of England*, 18 (1953–5), 127–41 · *CGPLA Eng. & Wales* (1904) [Barrow Emanuel] · *CGPLA Eng. & Wales* (1915) · b. cert. [Barrow Emanuel] · d. cert. [Barrow Emanuel] · b. cert. · d. cert. · m. cert. · A. Weinberg, 'Portsmouth Jewry', *Portsmouth Papers*, 41 (Feb 1985) [Barrow Emanuel] · burial register, West London synagogue [Barrow Emanuel] · architects directory, 1868

Archives RIBA BAL, biographies file, papers · U. Southampton, Hartley Library, MSS 116/163, 116/176 [Barrow Emanuel]
Likenesses photograph, *c.*1904 (Barrow Emanuel), repro. in *Jewish Chronicle* (19 Feb 1904)
Wealth at death £18,647 2s. 1d.: probate, 11 Aug 1915, CGPLA Eng. & Wales · £58,908 16s. 4d.—Barrow Emanuel: resworn probate, 19 March 1904, CGPLA Eng. & Wales

Davis, Henry Edwards (1756–1784), historian, was the son of John Davis of Windsor. He was born on 11 July 1756, and educated at Ealing. On 17 May 1774 he entered Balliol College, Oxford, and graduated BA early in 1778. On 2 May 1778 he published *An Examination of the Fifteenth and Sixteenth Chapters of Mr Gibbon's 'History'*, in which the historian's alleged plagiarisms and other misdemeanours with evidence were set out at length. Edward Gibbon affected to despise Davis, concluding in his *Memoirs* that 'victory over such antagonists was a sufficient humiliation' (*Miscellaneous Works*, 1.153). Nevertheless, although Davis made some embarrassing blunders when censuring Gibbon's use of classical authors, he was altogether more acute and sure-footed when analysing Gibbon's debts to moderns such as Middleton and Beausobre. In his *Vindication* (1779) Gibbon concentrated on Davis's weaker side and largely passed over his shrewder perceptions. It was a legitimate enough procedure, but it perhaps explains the complicated tone (half chastened, half defiant) of Davis's *Reply to Mr Gibbon's 'Vindication'* (1779). Gibbon states that Davis was rewarded for the attack by a 'royal pension'. He took priest's orders in 1780, and became fellow and tutor of Balliol College. His health broke down and he died, after a lingering illness, on 10 February 1784. His friends praised 'the cheerfulness and vivacity of his conversation [and] the warmth and benevolence of his heart' (Chalmers, 11.325); he is said to have been very amiable, poetical, and patient under suffering.

LESLIE STEPHEN, *rev.* DAVID WOMERSLEY

Sources E. Gibbon, *A vindication of some passages in the fifteenth and sixteenth chapters* (1779) · *Miscellaneous works of Edward Gibbon*, ed. J. Holroyd [Lord Sheffield], 2 vols. (1796) · *Public Advertiser* (2 May 1778) · *Gazetteer and New Daily Advertiser* (2 May 1778) · A. Chalmers, ed., *The general biographical dictionary*, new edn, 11 (1813), 325 · Foster, *Alum. Oxon.*

Davis, Henry George (1830–1857), topographer, born on 14 August 1830 at 4 Mills Buildings, Knightsbridge, London, was the son of J. Davis, master of the parochial schools of St Paul's, Knightsbridge. He was educated at the Marylebone Philological School. Davis became a writer for the local journal, the *West Middlesex Advertiser*, to which he contributed a series of articles entitled 'Our local associations', and prepared for the press *Memorials of the Hamlet of Knightsbridge, with Notices of its Immediate Neighbourhood*. This was published in 1859, two years after his death, by his brother Charles Davis. Two other works by Davis were left in manuscript unfinished, namely 'Pimlico' and 'Recollections of Piccadilly'. He bequeathed his collections to the London and Middlesex Archaeological Society. Many antiquarian papers written by him appeared in *Notes* *and Queries.* Davis suffered all his life from chronic pleurisy, which was worsened in 1850 by rheumatic fever. He died at St Paul's parochial school, Wilton Place, Belgravia, on 30 December 1857.

ROBERT HARRISON, *rev.* JOANNE POTIER

Sources C. Davis, preface, in H. G. Davis, *The memorials of the hamlet of Knightsbridge*, ed. C. Davis (1859) • Boase, *Mod. Eng. biog.* • *GM*, 3rd ser., 6 (1859), 327

Davis, Henry William Carless (1874–1928), historian, was born at Ebley, near Stroud, Gloucestershire, on 13 January 1874, the eldest of the five children—three sons and two daughters—of Henry Frederick Alexander Davis, solicitor, of Ebley, and his wife, Jessie Anna, third daughter of William Carless MD, of Stroud. He and his brothers and sisters were brought up in somewhat straitened circumstances by their mother, who was a woman of character and ability. She removed in 1884 to Weymouth, opened there a school for young children, including her own, and managed it so successfully that she was subsequently (1903) appointed first headmistress of Weymouth College preparatory school. Henry Davis entered Weymouth College in 1886, made his mark there as a boy of unusual capacity, and in 1891 proceeded to Balliol College, Oxford, with a Brackenbury history scholarship. Except to his close friends, who admired his qualities, and to his tutors, who recognized his promise, he was not well known in college; but he came to the front when, after gaining first classes in classical moderations (1893) and *literae humaniores* (1895) as well as the Jenkyns exhibition, he was elected in 1895 to a fellowship at All Souls College.

Davis's interest in history had been awakened at school by the teaching of the Revd Thomas Brace Waitt; and at Oxford, under the guidance of Arthur Lionel Smith, of Balliol, he found in that subject his true bent. He therefore abandoned his intention of entering the civil service, and settled down to the career of a student and teacher of history and especially of medieval history. Save for a short spell of teaching at University College, Bangor (1896–7), he lived in All Souls from 1895 to 1902, where among his friends and contemporaries were Herbert Hensley Henson, afterwards bishop of Durham, John Simon, and C. Grant Robertson. In 1897 he won the Lothian prize. In the same year he was appointed to a lectureship at New College, and thus began his twenty years' experience as a college tutor at Oxford, in the course of which he built up a great reputation as a scholar and teacher of the most exacting standard. In 1899 he exchanged his post at New College for a lectureship at Balliol, and on the expiry of his All Souls fellowship in 1902 he was appointed an official fellow of his old college.

Davis had already published *Balliol College* (1899) in the series College Histories, *Charlemagne* (1900), a life for the Heroes of the Nations series, as well as articles, from 1901, in the *English Historical Review*. But it was the appearance in 1905 of his book *England under the Normans and Angevins* which revealed the full measure of his gifts as a historian and made his name. The book at once became a standard authority and by 1930 had reached a tenth edition; but it

Henry William Carless Davis (1874–1928), by Lafayette

was the only substantial contribution to narrative medieval history which Davis made. He wrote in 1911 a masterly little summary, *Medieval Europe*, in the Home University Library series, and many articles and reviews in historical journals, but after 1905 he devoted a great part of his literary energies to editorial work, preparing an edition of Jowett's translation of Aristotle's *Politics* (1905), a revision of William Stubbs's *Select Charters* (1913), and embarking upon a valuable, if ambitious, calendar of royal charters, *Regesta regum Anglo-Normannorum* (vol. 1, 1913), which, as events proved, he was never able to complete, though it was later finished by others.

Davis's influence as a teacher, however, was of greater moment than his reputation as a writer. Few Oxford tutors can have inspired in their pupils more genuine respect and regard. If his austere manner, steady gaze, and precise speech compelled attention and a touch of awe, closer acquaintance revealed behind the reserve a friendly soul, much quiet humour, and above all an unstinting devotion to his pupils' needs. He lacked entirely the infectious enthusiasm of a teacher like A. L. Smith, but he set an example of hard work and fine scholarship which won immediate response from almost everyone whom he taught. His lectures were very carefully prepared and delivered, and largely attended, but he made no effort to draw big audiences. With his writing and teaching he combined much examining and administrative work. He was junior dean of Balliol from 1906 to 1910, an examiner in the final school of modern history from 1907 to 1909 (and again 1919–21), and Chichele lecturer in foreign history in 1913; he served on the board of his faculty from 1905, on the general board of the faculties from 1913, and became a curator of the Bodleian Library in 1914. He was much interested in women's education and joined the council of Somerville College in 1908.

Davis married in 1912 Jennie Rosa, only daughter of Walter Lindup, of Bampton Grange, Oxfordshire; three sons were born of the marriage, including Ralph Henry Carless *Davis (1918–1991), medieval historian, and Godfrey Rupert Carless Davis, secretary to the Royal Commission on Historical Manuscripts.

The First World War made a complete break in Davis's university activities and came near to deflecting the whole course of his career. After collaborating in the production of the series of Oxford Pamphlets on the war, and publishing a dispassionate analysis, *The Political Thought of Heinrich von Treitschke* (1914), he went to London early in 1915 and helped to organize the 'trade clearing house', a bureau of commercial intelligence arising out of the postal censorship, sponsored by the Admiralty and the Board of Trade. By the following summer the trade clearing house had expanded into the war trade intelligence department, forming a constituent part of the ministry of blockade under the ultimate control of the Foreign Office. Of this department Davis was the vice-chairman for three and a half years. Davis himself wrote subsequently an official, but unfinished, *History of the Blockade* (1920), which describes in detail the elaborate departmental machinery which was devised to put the blockade of the enemy powers into execution. In his own department his organizing ability, power of rapid decision, and almost limitless capacity for work, backed by his fine personal qualities, were a source of inspiration to his colleagues, and attracted the notice of the cabinet. After the armistice he served on the large British delegation to the peace conference in Paris from December 1918 until March 1919, and then for a few weeks, at the invitation of Sir Arthur Steel-Maitland, undertook the duties of acting director of the department of overseas trade in London. He was made CBE in the new year honours of that year.

An opportunity of high appointment in the public service was now presented to Davis, had his ambition lain in that direction; but he decided otherwise, and in April 1919 returned to Oxford, where for two years he resumed the routine of college and university work. It was at this time that he undertook the editorial direction of the *Dictionary of National Biography*, which had been conveyed in 1917 to the University of Oxford to be continued by the Clarendon Press [see Smith, Reginald John]. Arrangements had to be made for the continuation of the dictionary from 1911, to which year it had been brought down by the previous editor, Sir Sidney Lee. The names to be included in the dictionary, and contributors of the biographical notices, were selected by Davis and his co-editor, J. R. H. Weaver, in consultation with an Oxford committee and a number of external advisers. Alike in his dealings with contributors and in his conscientious treatment of the material Davis was an exemplary editor. He had a deft and skilful touch,

and although he worked with great rapidity he never spared himself the more laborious part of the routine. The volume for which he was responsible appeared in 1927, bringing the dictionary down to the end of the year 1921. He wrote a short preface and contributed several articles. The volume reduced by almost a half the number of entries for a decade, as compared with Lee's volume on the 1900s, and reflected the view of the delegates of Oxford University Press that Lee's plans for the twentieth-century coverage of the dictionary were too expensive.

In 1921, shortly after he had embarked on the editorship of the dictionary, and in the midst of the heavy routine of Oxford teaching after the war, Davis accepted an invitation to occupy the chair of modern history at Manchester University. His health had suffered from the strain of his war work, and the new post promised him more leisure for his own studies. He settled at Bowdon, and spent there three and a half busy but quiet years. His studies now took a modern turn—owing partly to the requirements of his professorship and partly to his interest in post-war political questions. When, therefore, he was elected Ford's lecturer at Oxford for 1924–5, he took as his subject *The Age of Grey and Peel* (posthumously published in 1930). He gave the lectures in Hilary term 1925, and in the course of that term he was appointed to succeed Sir Charles Firth as regius professor of modern history at Oxford. He thereby became a fellow of Oriel College. In the same year he was elected an honorary fellow of Balliol College and a fellow of the British Academy.

Davis returned to Oxford as regius professor in the summer of 1925. In addition to the duties of his chair he undertook much committee work, both for his new college and for the university. As a curator of the Bodleian Library he was called upon to take a prominent part in the discussions on the question of the extension of the library and to move in congregation, in May 1928, the official proposals for Bodleian extension in their earliest form (subsequently modified by the report of the Bodleian commission, and finally adopted by the university in 1931). Outside his university activities he was appointed in 1925 to serve on the unemployment insurance committee under the chairmanship of Lord Blanesburgh, and in 1927 he went to Geneva as British representative on a committee of experts charged by the International Labour Organization to investigate and report upon factory legislation in several European countries. These public services—the aftermath of his wartime reputation—made heavy demands on his time and energies during 1926 and 1927.

Davis succeeded to the regius chair of modern history at Oxford at a time when changes in the syllabus were deemed desirable, but as it turned out he had not time to initiate reforms. His ideas on the needs of the school would probably have taken shape in accordance with the views expressed in his inaugural lecture, *The Study of History*, delivered in November 1925. For the moment his commitments were heavy enough. He was getting ready for press his Ford lectures, the *Dictionary of National Biography, 1912–1921*, and the *Report* of the Blanesburgh committee, editing *Essays in History Presented to Reginald Lane*

Poole (1926), and preparing his Raleigh lecture for the British Academy, *The Great Game in Asia* (delivered in November 1926)—one of the liveliest of his writings. In the midst of such activities, while engaged in examining at Edinburgh University, he died of pneumonia, at 19 Great King Street, Edinburgh, after a few days' illness, on 28 June 1928. He was buried at Wolvercote cemetery, Oxford.

Davis was a young-looking man, whose features and reddish hair changed little during middle age. His expression was rather grave, his manner reserved but modest, his gaze singularly penetrating, in spite of short sight, and his words ever to the point. His learning, never paraded, was very great in range and depth. But, as his career shows, he was not in the least the don or scholar of convention. People of the most diverse types found his qualities of mind and heart peculiarly attractive, and his circle of friends in Oxford and outside was very large. Few who met him failed to feel the impress of his high intelligence and unsullied character. His influence upon the Oxford of his time was very great; yet his comparatively early death seemed to many to have left his fullest powers unrevealed and his greatest work unaccomplished.

J. R. H. WEAVER, *rev.* H. C. G. MATTHEW

Sources The Times (29 June 1928) · F. M. Powicke, 'H. W. C. Davis', *EngHR*, 43 (1928), 578–84 · J. R. H. Weaver and A. L. Poole, *Henry William Carless Davis: a memoir, and a selection of his historical papers* (1933) [with portrait and bibliography] · H. C. G. Matthew, *Leslie Stephen and the 'New Dictionary of National Biography'* (1997) · *CGPLA Eng. & Wales* (1928)

Archives Bodl. Oxf., corresp., notebooks, and papers | All Souls Oxf., letters to Sir William Anson

Likenesses Lafayette, photograph, NPG [*see illus.*] · portrait, repro. in Weaver and Poole, *Henry William Carless Davis*

Wealth at death £10,579 2s. 4d.: probate, 15 Sept 1928, *CGPLA Eng. & Wales*

Davis, Hewitt (1804–1884), farmer and agricultural writer, was born on 16 August 1804 to Isaac Davis and his wife, Mary, *née* Kennard. He was baptized on 10 November 1804 at St Mildred Poultry, in the City of London.

In his twenties Davis managed the 2000 acre estate of his former employer, a merchant who recognized his ability for sorting out the accounts of the farm bailiff. By 1829 he had moved to Croydon, the address he gave for a letter, written on 1 April 1830, to *The Times* about the free importation of corn, later elaborated into a pamphlet, *On Foreign Corn Importation*, dedicated to Viscount Milton. On 13 September 1833 he married Maria Husbands, *née* Mennie (1805–1884). They had at least eight children, including a daughter named Ann Marie and a son named Hewitt. He became the land agent for George Smith, and later for his son, George Robert (of the City bankers Smith, Payne, and Smith) of Selsdon Park, south of Croydon, whose Selsdon Farm was a 149 acre chalk hill farm.

Davis's model farm was the nearby Spring Park Farm at Addington, which he tenanted from 1834 to 1849, a 500 acre farm of former heathland, originally known as Coldharbour, which the radical MP John Temple Leader had bought in 1834. Davis farmed 200 acres as arable land, improving it by deep drainage, deep ploughing, and thin

sowing, the increased yields of which he discovered accidentally in 1840 when his drill man sowed half the required quantity of seed corn. He farmed the 149 acre Oaks Farm for the see of Canterbury at Shirley, where he also farmed for the second earl of Eldon.

Spring Park Farm attracted many visitors from throughout Britain but few from Surrey. The most publicized visits were those made by the Maidstone Farmers Club. Davis wrote many articles, little more than letters, for the agricultural press and the county newspapers; about eighty were published in three series of 'Farming essays' brought out in 1848, 1850, and 1855 and collected in *Practical Essays for the Improvement of Farming* (1860). He wrote for tenant farmers, matter-of-fact men like himself. In the late 1830s he was joint managing director, with Dr Augustus Bozzi Granville, of the ill-fated Thames Improvement Company, formed in 1836 to use town manure for agricultural purposes. Davis blamed the City and the commissioners of sewers for its failure.

From 1840 Davis was an inspector of works for the inclosure commissioners, whose sphere of responsibility was much enlarged by the Public Money and Private Money Drainage Acts passed between 1840 and 1850. He promoted the interests of the Land Improvement Company which facilitated private loans. In 1849 or 1850 he gave up tenant farming to become a partner in Messrs Davis and Vigers, surveyors, of 3 Frederick's Place, Old Jewry, probably because his new career was more profitable.

Davis gave evidence to two select committees of the House of Lords, in 1845 and 1849, about improving entailed estates. His advice to landowners helped to restore the profitability of their estates. His firm acted as surveyors to the Rent Guarantee Society, founded in 1850 to assist landlords manage their estates. His publisher, James Ridgway, was one of its trustees. Davis owned shares in the society.

Davis died at his home, 17 Nottingham Place, Marylebone, on 19 July 1884, his wife predeceasing him early in the same year. They had lived there for the previous twenty years and were buried in Highgate cemetery. He advocated economical and scientific farming at a time where agriculture was threatened by the loss of protection; the *Agricultural Gazette* in its obituary praised his clear and simple prose and said that none since William Cobbett and Arthur Young had written more truthful criticism or given sounder advice. BRIAN LANCASTER

Sources Agricultural Gazette, new ser., 20/552 (28 July 1884), 120–21 · The Times (22 July 1884) · C. W. Johnson and W. Shaw, The Farmers' Almanac and Calendar, from 1840 · 'Select committee of the House of Lords on entailed estates', Parl. papers (1845), 12.111, no. 490 [charges for drainage] · 'Select committee of the House of Lords on … entailed estates', Parl. papers (1849), 12.281, no. 350 [charges for drainage] · G. E. Fussell, The old English farming books: 1840–1860 (1984), vol. 4 of The old English farming books (1947–91) · A. B. Granville, Autobiography of A. B. Granville, ed. P. B. Granville, 2 vols. (1874) · The Times (9 April 1830) · PRO, IR 3543 · parish register, London, St Mildred Poultry, 16/8/1804 and 10/11/1804, GL [birth, baptism] · parish register (birth), 17 Oct 1805, St Botolph's, Bishopsgate [Maria Mennie] · parish register (marriage), 13 Sept

1833, St Martin-in-the-Fields · Highgate cemetery records, Holborn Library
Likenesses sketch, repro. in *Agricultural Gazette*
Wealth at death £46,010 5s. 9d.: probate, 23 Aug 1884, *CGPLA Eng. & Wales*

Davis, James (1706/7–1755), satirical writer and physician, was the son of Walter Davis of Chepstow, Monmouthshire. He matriculated at Jesus College, Oxford, on 18 February 1723, aged sixteen, and graduated BA on 13 October 1726 and MA on 9 July 1729. He then decided to study medicine, and graduated MB on 7 December 1732. He practised as a physician in Devizes, Wiltshire, until his death.

Davis is remembered for the publication of *Origines Divisianae, or, The antiquities of the Devizes in some familiar letters to a friend wrote in the years 1750 and 1751* (1754). It is described as a 'very humourous collection' by Nichols who none the less perpetuates 'upon authority which I cannot resist' a wrong ascription of the work to Dr Sneyd Davis (Nichols, *Illustrations*, 1.682). This work is a vigorous and well-sustained caricature of the antiquarian and etymological studies of Musgrave, Stukeley, and others. It has a playful sense of the absurd:

> An old woman, who shew'd Lord Bathurst's fine place by Cirencester, was ask'd by a Gentleman that came to see it— Pray what building is that?—Oh Sir, that is a ruin a thousand years old, which my Lord built last year; and he proposes to build one this year half as old again.   (Davis, 9)

Similarly, the letters end with:

> The foregoing papers were wrote by no man living,—for the Author dy'd some months ago. He long entertain'd a disrelish for the modern sort of scholarship and was not unwilling for these papers to go to the press to prevent many larger from going there.   (ibid., 89–90)

The erudite solemnity of Davis's jokes deceived later writers who took his fancies as facts of local history.

Davis died in Devizes on 13 July 1755, but was buried in the parish church at Chepstow on 17 July.

WILLIAM R. JONES

Sources [J. Davis], *Origines Divisianae, or, The antiquities of the Devizes, in some familiar letters to a friend wrote in the years 1750 and 1751* (1754) · Nichols, *Illustrations*, vol. 1 · S. G. Perceval, ed., 'Journal of an excursion to Eastbury and Bristol, etc, in May and June, 1767', *Proceedings of the Bristol Naturalists' Society* (1900), 6–37 · J. Waylen, *The annals of the royal and ancient borough of Devizes* (1908) · *GM*, 1st ser., 25 (1755), 333 · Foster, *Alum. Oxon., 1715–1886*

Davis [Davys], **John** (c.1550–1605), explorer, was apparently a Devon man living at Sandridge in the parish of Stoke Gabriel near Dartmouth. He may indeed have been born there, but his baptism is not recorded in the parish register. Almost all the details of his early life—his parentage, date and place of birth, and upbringing—are unknown; it is unfortunate that his name can be spelt in different ways and that there are records of others of the same name, of equivalent or higher rank, in the same vicinity. His evident education, indicated by his journals, other publications, and navigational skills, is wholly unrecorded. It was at Stoke Gabriel on 29 September 1582 that he married Faith Fulford, who had been baptized there on 29 May 1561; her local origins make it highly unlikely (as alleged by J. Prince in his *Worthies of Devon*, 1701, 286) that she was from a county family, the daughter of Sir John Fulford, sheriff of Devon in 1535. Their first recorded child, Gilbert, baptized at Stoke Gabriel on 8 June 1589, almost certainly took his name from the Gilbert family of seamen and explorers, who were Davis's closest and earliest recorded maritime associates. His other two sons, Arthur and Philip Davis, were apparently born in the next two years; Faith's adultery effectively ended his marriage in 1593.

The location of Stoke Gabriel on the Dart estuary was conducive to a naval career. John Davis reputedly spent his youth in maritime pursuits, the necessary training for a professional seaman, almost certainly in subordinate and unrecorded capacities on the Gilberts' major voyages. He was never one of the gentlemen so prominent in Elizabethan seafaring—unlike his associates and near neighbours, the Gilberts and Raleghs, with whom his connections certainly antedate by some years the first formal references in 1579 and 1580. By that time he was described as a friend of Adrian Gilbert, brother of the more famous Sir Humphrey Gilbert (d. 1583). Both were visited at their homes in Devon by the astrologer Dr John Dee (1527–1609). On 24 January 1583 all three met with Sir Francis Walsingham at the house of Robert Beale, then acting secretary of state, where they floated their proposal to search for the north-west passage, supporting it with detailed reference to charts. Several further meetings followed up to 18 March, when Davis returned to Devon. At two years' remove these conferences were the gestation of the three Arctic voyages in search of the north-west passage on which Davis's reputation principally depends.

The Arctic voyages   The three voyages seem to have been funded principally by the London merchant William Sanderson (1547–1638), to whom Davis reported by letter and in person, but also by Adrian Gilbert, Walsingham, and some other London merchants; only once did the merchants of Exeter make a significant contribution. Though small in scale and comprising only the smallest of ships, which had the shallow draughts most suitable for unknown shoal waters, such expeditions were expensive. Although they were ambitious in their long-term aims, it appears that the immediate objectives of each voyage were actually quite limited, to discover routes that could be exploited more fully later.

Davis's first expedition consisted of two barks, the *Sunshine* of London, of 50 tons and 23 crew, and the *Moonshine* of Dartmouth, of 35 tons. After departing from Dartmouth on 7 June 1585, they were delayed for twelve days at the Isles of Scilly, an opportunity that Davis characteristically used to chart the archipelago for navigation, and arrived on 20 July at the east coast of Greenland. Blocked by ice to the north, he sailed first southwards down the eastern coast and then northwards up the west coast as far as 66° of latitude, whence he sailed across the open sea to the north-west until he reached Cumberland Gulf, a broad strait which he pursued for 100 miles or so, finding only open waters filled with islands. At this point, late in August 1585, he abandoned exploration for the summer and returned home, arriving safely at Dartmouth on 30

September. *Sunshine* and *Moonshine* were also involved in Davis's second voyage in 1586, together with the *Mermaid* of 120 tons and the pinnace *North Star* of 10 tons. After departing on 7 May 1586, he made his landfall at 60° on 15 June and departed on 11 September. This second voyage was more difficult, relations with the native inhabitants being more troubled and violent, his crew more easily daunted, and the weather not merely foggy but stormy. Never proceeding as far north as on the previous voyage, he investigated the inlets and islands of the east coast of Canada, without either definitely finding a passage to the west or discrediting the notion—hence his third voyage 'for the discovery of a passage to the Isles of the Molucca or the coast of China' (*Voyages and Works*, 39), for which he had the barks *Sunshine* again and the *Elizabeth* of London, and the clincher-built *Helen* of London. After departing from Dartmouth on 19 May 1587, Davis left two ships at the cod fishery, while he pressed northwards through the Davis Strait into Baffin Bay as far northwards as latitude 73° and then westwards to the pack ice, whence high winds forced him to retire southwards. He intended to join his other vessels, on which he depended for supplies. Not finding them, 'having in our ship but litle wood and halfe a hogshead of fresh water' (ibid., 48), he tackled the Atlantic unaccompanied and returned successfully to Dartmouth on 15 September. His brief initial report states that he had proceeded 60 leagues further than he had originally intended and that, at 73°, there were no obstacles, 'the sea all open … The passage is most probable [and] the execution easier' (ibid., 59). The sequel that he evidently planned, a fourth voyage, did not happen.

The three voyages are recorded respectively by journals of the merchant John Janes, Davis himself, and Janes again. Janes's first journal is full of the wonders of unknown lands and seas, of such unfamiliar creatures as the porpoises, whales, seals, and polar bears that they saw and generally slew and ate, the Inuit they encountered and traded with, and the floating wood, tides, soundings, sea colour, and seabed that Davis employed as navigational aids. The latter journals are more balanced, the result of greater familiarity with both the phenomena and the actual locations and people who were encountered. For the second voyage Davis's own journal records a genuine interest in the native population, whose language, diet, and customs he recorded and with whom he dealt—at times they actually outnumbered the explorers and proved extremely acquisitive of iron—and in the local flora and fauna, and reveals his own diplomatic skills and strong sense of divine providence.

These voyages carried Davis to locations in north-east Canada and west of Greenland, where no known Europeans had been before, and to which Davis gave names reminiscent of his west-country origins and of his backers: some, such as Gilbert Sound, Cumberland Sound, Exeter Sound, Totness Road, Cape Dyer, Cape Walsingham, and Sanderson his Hope, still endure. Conditions were inhospitable, foggy, icy, and stormy; water and victuals were several times in short supply. Crewmen died both

naturally and by violence. It was an enormous achievement to penetrate as far as Davis did and to return safely, not once but three times, with almost all his ships and men. Apart from the discoveries (which were not the long-term objective), the voyages were unsuccessful. Davis did not reach the spice islands or East Indies by this route. The north-west passage was not discovered, although Davis remained convinced that it existed. He wrongly supposed that the seas were everywhere navigable and did not freeze, and that the north pole itself must have a delightful climate. Moreover he found none of the treasure sought by Elizabethan investors.

These voyages are nevertheless the foundation for Davis's enduring distinction. The Elizabethan poet Michael Drayton wrote in his *Polyolbion*:

And Davies, three times forth for the North west made,
Still striving by that course, t'inrich the English Trade:
And as he well deserv'd, to his eternall fame,
There, by a mightie sea, Immortalliz'd his name.
(Drayton, XIX.291–302)

Privateering interlude The 'mightie sea' remains the Davis Strait. Davis was never to resume his search as he had intended in 1587 and may have continued to hope a decade later. In 1595, on the latest geographical information, he argued that 'Virginia'—the main North American land mass—extended less far west than was supposed and that an approach from the Pacific end near California was feasible. Obviously it would have been much more expensive. Davis then claimed, somewhat improbably, such an investigation to have been the intended sequel of his voyage with Thomas *Cavendish (*bap.* 1560, *d.* 1592) in 1591–3. If so, circumstances ensured that it did not happen. Davis's three voyages, with hindsight, fall early in a maritime career, which had another eighteen very different years to run until its premature end. Never again was Davis to return to the Arctic, whatever he may have professed. Never again was he in command: he features instead as a subordinate, not always a captain, on larger expeditions. After trying his hand at privateering, he was instead to involve himself on larger enterprises to the south and east, generally as a pilot. To contemporaries it was his navigational skills that marked him out: Davis was 'very well grounded in the principles of the art of navigation', William Sanderson declared in 1585 (*Voyages and Works*, 205). The ancient astrolabe was further developed by him into the Davis backstaff or English double quadrant, which enabled navigators to measure the height of the sun more precisely. His *Seaman's Secrets* (1594), virtually a treatise on practical navigation, ran through eight editions, the last in 1657. His *World Hydrographical Survey* was published in 1595. So, too, with modern historians: if understandably to his biographer Davis was 'the foremost English navigator' (ibid., 23), to Professor Kenneth Andrews he was also 'perhaps the finest navigator of his day' (Andrews, *Drake's Voyages*, 154).

An intended further expedition was delayed by the Spanish Armada and then permanently thwarted the following year by the death in 1590 of Davis's key patron, Secretary of State Walsingham. However important from the perspective of exploration, Davis's voyages were financially unsuccessful, and were no incentive for anyone else to invest in any more. For the Armada campaign Davis may have captained the *Black Dog*, a tender of Admiral Howard of Effingham, and the next year he briefly tried his hand at privateering, with fair success, joining George, earl of Cumberland, off the Azores with the *Drake* of Plymouth (60 tons), a pinnace, and a boat in August 1589, but parting company in November ahead of the disastrous end to the expedition. In 1590 he was part of a squadron that took a Spanish vessel supposedly called the *Urcha Salvagina*, a capture the legitimacy of which was still being contested in 1593. It is not clear how these events relate to the capture by the *Advantage* of Lyme Regis of a prize cargo of sugar and cotton wool worth £700 that he and John Hazard were recorded as selling. Hence perhaps the £1100 of his money that Davis alleged that he had invested in his next expedition, logically not for altruistic exploration, but for his own further profit.

The failed circumnavigation Such a substantial investment renders improbable Davis's later claim that he had to be persuaded to join in the next voyage of Thomas Cavendish (or Candish, as Davis usually spells it), whose highly profitable circumnavigation of 1586–8, when he was unable to carry away all the treasure that he had captured, was the inspiration for the further expedition to China and Japan via Cape Horn. Davis needed to make his own fortune. It is significant that the bark *Delight* or *Dainty*, which Davis owned jointly with Adrian Gilbert, returned home prematurely: just possibly Davis did not share in the losses that others suffered. There were five vessels in all, three tall ships and two smaller ones; Davis was rear-admiral commanding the *Desire*, Cavendish's former flagship of 140 tons. After sailing from Plymouth on 26 August 1591, they were first becalmed and then diverted at Santos in Brazil and thus missed the southern summer, the optimum time to clear the Magellan Strait, where they arrived only on 8 April 1592. Beset by storms, frost, and high mortality on the biggest ships, Cavendish was unable to pass the strait, was confined to harbour, and then gave up, planning instead to take the Good Hope route to the East Indies. Davis, more accustomed to Arctic conditions, was not deterred. He disagreed. The atrocious conditions, he considered, could not last and the squadron was not equipped for the alternative route. When Cavendish withdrew northwards to Santos, Davis remained at Port Desire, perhaps because of a misunderstanding, perhaps (as the paranoiac and dying Cavendish supposed) from self-interested betrayal. Contrary to Davis's later testimony, Cavendish did specify a rendezvous. Bereft of all kind of stores, Davis was not in an enviable situation; he nevertheless made three further efforts to pass the strait, but storms beat him back each time. He is praised by Andrews as 'faithful to the point of disaster to his general's instructions' (Andrews, *Privateering*, 70), which was Davis's own version as set out by Janes, but a recent commentator has found some justification in Cavendish's charge against him that 'onely [his] treacherie hath beene the utter ruine of all' (Hitchcock, 'Charges against Davis', 264). As Davis was well aware, Cavendish desperately needed the smaller vessels, which alone were able to enter shallow waters; without them he was predestined for disaster. Evidently this was appreciated also by Davis's own crew, only a little over half of whom backed him when he sought their approval for his actions, while others mutinied and perhaps tried to kill him. Nine later deserted and were slain by the natives: among them were the principal mutineers. After returning to Port Desire on 27 October 1592 from his fruitless attempts to reach the Pacific, Davis provisioned the ship with no fewer than 14,000 dried penguins for the journey home. Despite losses to Patagonian Indians, the Portuguese, and privations, Davis himself was among the fourteen survivors of an original seventy-six who arrived home on 11 June 1593. Arrested, apparently at the instance of the disreputable lover of his adulterous wife, and subjected to an inquiry ordered by the privy council into his conduct on the evidence of Cavendish's last letter, Davis successfully defended himself against the charges—'were I faulty of so foul a crime, I were worthy of ten thousand torments' (ibid., 268)—and was released at the intercession of his friend Sir Walter Ralegh. His reputation may nevertheless have suffered.

East Indies voyages That little is known of Davis over the next two years may be accounted for by the two books that he published in 1594–5. He was at sea again in 1596–7, most probably at Cadiz and the Azores as master of Ralegh's own ship, and was then recommended by the earl of Essex to the Dutch for the first of three voyages to the East Indies that took up the rest of his life. The first such voyage was as pilot of the Dutch ship *Leeuw*, or *Lion*, captained by Cornelius Houtman, which sailed with the *Lioness* from Flushing on 15 March 1598 and arrived on 21 June 1599 at Acheen in Sumatra, where it remained for three months lading with pepper and other spices. Davis himself had traded on his own account, building up stock for sale in Europe and other 'things which I had provided to show my dutie and love to my best friends' (*Voyages and Works*, 146), all of which were lost with the main cargo in the ensuing disaster. The local potentate launched a treacherous attack on both ships, capturing the *Lioness* and killing Houtman and many others, but Davis, in his own account, with a handful of others successfully defended the *Lion*, cleared it of attackers, and then recaptured the *Lioness*. So many of the assailants were slain that most of the Dutchmen on shore were put to death. 'We lost in this misfortune', wrote Davis, 'three-score and eight persons, of which we are not certain how many are captived; only of eight wee have knowledge' (ibid., 145). After a further clash with the Portuguese, the crew determined to return home, arriving at Middelburg on 29 July 1600. Much more commercially successful, if with similar loss of life, was his next voyage as pilot-major of the first East Indies Company fleet on board the *Red Dragon* (600 tons) of Captain James Lancaster (d. 1618), which sailed from Woolwich on 13 February 1601 and returned on 11 September 1603.

At this point in his career Davis's considerable estate comprised leases, merchandise, money, and debts due. He contracted as pilot for a further voyage to China on the *Tiger* of London (240 tons, captained by Edward Michelbourne) by 12 October 1604. In the meantime he had betrothed himself to Judith Havard, 'my espoused love'—evidently a love match—'unto whom I have given my faith in matrimony to be solemnised on my return': his wife Faith was presumably dead. 'Uncertain of my return' (PRO, PROB 11/109 sig. 4), Davis sensibly made his will, bequeathing his possessions equally to Judith and his three sons, with remainder in the event of all their deaths to the poor and to the children of his brother Edward. The *Tiger* actually sailed from Cowes on 5 December 1604 and arrived at Bantam in Sumatra in October 1605, whence they set off on 2 November for Patany, making but poor progress. The Japanese pirates on board a captured junk, which they encountered peacefully near Bintang, treacherously attacked the *Tiger* off the coast of Borneo on 29 or 30 December 1605 and were repulsed only after a desperate struggle, in which Davis was slain in hand-to-hand combat. Soon afterwards the voyage was abandoned, the *Tiger* returning to Portsmouth on 9 July 1606. Although Davis's will was technically invalid, since no executor was named, it was nevertheless proved on 10 January 1607, when administration was granted to his eldest son, Gilbert.   MICHAEL HICKS

Sources K. R. Andrews, *Drake's voyages: a re-assessment of their place in Elizabethan maritime expansion* (1967) · K. R. Andrews, *Elizabethan privateering* (1964) · E. K. Cooper, 'The Davis back-staff or English quadrant', *Mariner's Mirror*, 30 (1944), 59–64 · *DNB* · M. Drayton, *Polyolbion*, ed. J. W. Hebel (1933), vol. 4 of M. Drayton, *Complete works* · R. Hakluyt, *The principal navigations, voyages, traffiques and discoveries of the English nation*, 2nd edn, 3 vols. (1598–1600); repr. 12 vols., Hakluyt Society, extra ser., 1–12 (1903–5), vol. 11 · R. F. Hitchcock, 'Cavendish's last voyage: the charges against Davis', *Mariner's Mirror*, 80 (1994), 259–69 · R. F. Hitchcock, 'Cavendish's last voyage: purposes revealed and concealed', *Mariner's Mirror*, 87 (2001), 5–14 · parish register, Stoke Gabriel, Devon RO [marriage; baptism: Faith Fulford, wife] · *The voyages and works of John Davis*, ed. A. H. Markham, Hakluyt Society, 59 (1880) · will, PRO, PROB 11/109, sig. 4 · T. K. Rabb, *Enterprise and empire: merchant and gentry investment in the expansion of England, 1575–1630* (1967)

Davis, John (d. 1621), sailor, was one of at least four children of unknown parentage. He sailed as pilot on the *Ascension* on the first East India Company voyage under Lancaster in 1601–3, a voyage on which his namesake, John Davis 'of Sandridge' was pilot major. He was pilot of the *Expedition*, then master, in the company's third voyage in 1608–9. As master on the East India Company's ship *James*, 1612–15, Davis refers to his first sighting of Martin Vaz: 'I saw this island when I was with Michelborne' (Purchas, bk 4.440)—indicating that he had sailed on Sir Edward Michelborne's interloping voyage to the East Indies, 1604–6, during which John Davis of Sandridge had been killed, in 1605, and the captain had also been killed, leaving Davis to bring the ship home. He sailed again in 1616 as master of the *Swan*, which with the *Defence* was bound for Banda under Sir Nathaniel *Courthope's command. The expedition ran into severe difficulties, contesting trading rights and possession of the islands with the Dutch forces, leading to Courthope's death in October 1620. Davis defied Courthope's orders and went ashore for water at Wayre.

He was one of a number of sailors captured by the Dutch and imprisoned at Pularoon where they 'were used very basely ... kept in irons night and day' (letter, Nash to David, 3 Oct 1618, Purchas, bk 5.674). Davis was one of the survivors; he returned home in the *Unicorn* in 1619.

Back in England Davis wrote 'A ruter or briefe direction for readie sailings into the East India, digested into a plaine method by master John Davis of Limehouse, upon experience of his five voyages thither and home againe'. The rutter, now at BL, Sloane 3959, was inserted by Samuel Purchas in his record of voyages published in 1625 (Purchas, bk 4.444). Like his contemporaries Davis gave longitudes not from a prime meridian, but by reckoning from the meridian of some well-known location, such as the Lizard or the Cape of Good Hope. He was well aware of the compass variation experienced as a ship traversed the Atlantic from Europe to Brazil and back to Africa, and used this as an additional guide to longitude. He remarks on the tidal streams, and describes the profiles of islands and coasts as seen on approach, and on the depth and nature of the adjacent sea bed, both as hazard and as good ground for anchoring.

Despite his experience Davis was never promoted to captain, possibly because of his quarrelsome nature and his addiction to strong drink. In January 1621 he sailed as pilot on the *Lesser James*, and succumbed to disease later that year, describing himself in his will written on 14 December 1621 as 'weake of body' (PRO, PROB 11/141, 439r). He died before the year's end, while the *Lesser James* was making for Jambi in Sumatra. After bequests to his brothers Simon and Robert, his sister Elizabeth, and various kinsmen, he gave instructions for the sale of his goods aboard the *Lesser James* and ashore at Batavia, the major portion of his estate going to his wife, Jane. He also mentions that he had been to Amsterdam to demand restitution of the goods seized when he was captured by the Dutch, and was hoping that the Dutch promise to restore his possessions, made in the presence of Gabriel Towerson, would be made good on his arrival in the East Indies. When news of his death reached England Jane petitioned the East India Company directors on 9 July 1623 for his wages owing, and compensation for his imprisonment in 1618. The directors rejected her appeal, but made a token payment to relieve her poverty.   ANITA MCCONNELL

Sources S. Purchas, *Hakluytus posthumus, or, Purchas his pilgrimes*, 1 (1625), bks 4–5 · G. Birdwood and W. Foster, eds., *The register of letters of the governour and company of merchants of London trading into the East Indies, 1600–1619* (1893) · *CSP col.*, vols. 3–4 · D. W. Waters, *The art of navigation in England in Elizabethan and early Stuart times* (1958), 289 · Jane Davis's petition, BL OIOC, B/8, court minute bk 6, 14 · log of the *Lesser James*, 1621, BL OIOC, L/MAR/A/xxxiii · will, PRO, PROB 11/141, fol. 439

Davis, John Bunnell (1777–1824), physician, was one of the eleven or more children of Timothy Davis, a surgeon-apothecary at Thetford in Norfolk, who later moved to London, becoming surgeon-general to the customs. Davis was born in June 1777 at Clare, Suffolk, and was baptized on 17 July 1777 there. He studied surgery at Guy's Hospital and St Thomas's Hospital, London, and became a member of the Company of Surgeons.

Because of severe illness, after receiving his diploma Davis served as medical attendant to a family travelling in France during the peace of Amiens, but had the misfortune to be detained in France as a prisoner of war. He made the best of his circumstances, continuing his medical studies at Montpellier, and graduating MD there in 1803, having completed a dissertation on cancer. Confined later at Verdun, he published *Observations on Precipitate Burial and the Diagnosis of Death* (1806). He sent a copy of the work to J. N. Corvisart, Napoleon's first physician, along with a petition for his release. Permission for Davis's release was granted soon after, and he returned to England in May 1806. Influenced by his detention in France, in 1807 Davis published *More Subjects Than One*, a two-volume collection of essays and reflections on France, and an account of the climate of Nice and its suitability for invalids.

Davis proceeded to Edinburgh University and graduated MD on 24 June 1808, reading a dissertation on phthisis. In September 1809 he was appointed hospital mate for general service in the army and was sent to a hospital at Ipswich to attend to the troops invalided home from Walcheren. As a result, he published an account entitled *A scientific and popular view of the fever at Walcheren and its consequences, as they appeared in the British troops returned from the late expedition: with an account of the morbid anatomy of the body and the efficacy of drastic purges and mercury in the treatment of this disease* (1810). The book contained an account of the symptoms of the fever, and a collection of postmortem records. They show that what was called Walcheren fever included several kinds of dysentery, enteric fever, and enteric fever complicated with malarial fever.

Davis resigned in 1812 and settled in practice in London, having become a licentiate of the Royal College of Physicians in 1810. He was physician to the Northern Dispensary and Surrey Dispensary, and in 1816 was the joint founder of, and physician to, the Universal Dispensary for Sick Indigent Children at St Andrew's Hill, Doctors' Commons. This was the first large-scale institution devoted to the care of sick children, and it accepted children from any locality.

In 1817 Davis published *A Cursory Inquiry into some of the Principal Causes of Mortality among Children*, based on and containing an account of his experiences at the dispensary. The publication of *Annals, Historical and Medical, of the Universal Dispensary for Children* followed in 1821, the year in which the dispensary was renamed the Royal Universal Dispensary for Children.

Davis died suddenly on 28 September 1824 at the age of forty-seven, leaving a widow and three children. He was buried at Kensington.

NORMAN MOORE, *rev.* CLAIRE E. J. HERRICK

Sources Munk, *Roll* · I. S. L. Loudon, 'John Bunnell Davis and the Universal Dispensary for Children', *BMJ* (5 May 1979), 1191–4 · A. Peterkin and W. Johnston, *Commissioned officers in the medical services of the British army, 1660–1960*, 1 (1968), 203 · *GM*, 1st ser., 95/1 (1825), 88 · P. J. Wallis and R. V. Wallis, *Eighteenth century medics*, 2nd edn (1988)

Archives St Thomas's Hospital, London

Likenesses commemorative bust and tablet, Royal Waterloo Hospital; repro. in Loudon, 'John Bunnell Davis and the Universal Dispensary for Children'

Davis, John Ford (1773–1864), physician, was born at Bath and educated at the school of the Revd Edward Spencer. He then studied medicine, first in London and afterwards in Edinburgh, where he graduated MD on 24 June 1797. His whereabouts between that date and 30 September 1808, when he became a licentiate of the Royal College of Physicians in London, are not known, but there is indirect evidence that he was back in Bath, perhaps in dispensary practice, for at least part of the time. Certainly, very soon after he obtained his licence, he set up in practice in that city.

Davis's first hospital appointment was as consulting physician to the Bath Eye Infirmary in 1811, the year of its foundation. He was elected physician to the General Hospital at Bath in 1817 and held the office for seventeen years; he retired in 1834 as senior physician. His main published works were his graduation thesis, *Tentamen chemico-medicum inaugurale de contagio* (1797) and *An Inquiry into the Symptoms and Treatment of Carditis or the Inflammation of the Heart* (1808). The thesis was based upon Y. Van Diemerbroeck's treatise on the plague, on James Carmichael Smyth's *Description of the Jail Distemper* (1795), and on several of the chemical works of the period. It contained no original observation on fever, and, excepting two or three chemical conjectures, was a mere compilation.

Davis's book on carditis, published very early in his career, described three cases of which Davis himself had seen only one; presumably he had been told about the others by friends and colleagues at Bath—one of the patients had been under the care of John Haygarth, probably at Chester, more than twenty years before. The case histories were supplemented by an extensive review of previous writing, some as far back as the twelfth century, on inflammation of the heart. This somewhat slight publication is significant for two reasons. First, it was an early recognition that inflammation could involve the whole substance of the heart, resulting not only in pericarditis, a familiar pathological finding for centuries. Second, it was an example of the wrong choice being made in the debate, current at the time, on the cause of carditis. The possibility that this disease could be due to rheumatic fever had been under consideration in Britain for ten years or more, and some Bath physicians were familiar with the idea. Davis, however, and despite a suggestion by a colleague, John Sherwen, that his cases could be rheumatic, regarded this as no more than 'doubtful'. His book was quite widely quoted in the following years but was rather roughly treated by reviewers; one wrote, in the *Edinburgh Medical and Surgical Journal*, 'Dr Davis has seen but one case of carditis and, out of it he has manufactured a book' (*EMSJ*, 354–5). By 1832 the situation was much clearer and that year Davis published a second short volume, entitled *Pericarditis or Rheumatism of the Heart*.

A third subject on which Davis wrote was the composition of the Bath waters. He has been quoted as describing, for the first time, vegetable matter floating on the surface of the water at certain seasons of the year. There is no suggestion in a publication on the Bath waters by R. W. Falconer that this finding was of any therapeutic—or toxicological—significance.

Davis was also active in the affairs of his native city. He was elected councillor for the first time in January 1811 and held several civic offices—as chief constable, bailiff, and alderman. He was a justice of the peace from 1827 to 1830, and in the latter year was elected mayor. His last appearance at the council was in December 1835. Davis and his wife, Louisa, lived for many years at 13 Royal Crescent, Bath, where he died, on 1 January 1864, aged ninety.

PETER R. FLEMING

Sources Munk, Roll · Catalogue of the Evan Bedford Library of Cardiology (1977), 57 · P. R. Fleming, 'Recognition of rheumatic heart disease', British Heart Journal, 39 (1977), 1045–50 · R. W. Falconer, The baths and mineral waters of Bath, 3rd edn (1860), 34 · Bath city council, minutes · minute book of the General Hospital, Bath · private information (2004) [Dr Roger Rolls] · census returns for Bath, 1851 · review, Edinburgh Medical and Surgical Journal, 5 (1809), 354–8 · DNB

Wealth at death under £10,000: probate, 3 Feb 1864, CGPLA Eng. & Wales

Davis, Sir John Francis, first baronet (1795–1890), colonial governor and Chinese scholar, born in London on 16 July 1795, was the eldest son in the family of four sons and seven daughters of Samuel *Davis (1760–1819), magistrate of Benares and a director of the East India Company, and his wife, Henrietta, daughter of Solomon Boileau of Dublin.

In 1813 Davis was appointed writer in the East India Company factory at Canton (Guangzhou), where he early showed marked linguistic and diplomatic aptitude. In consequence he was chosen to accompany Lord Amherst on his ineffectual embassy to Peking (Beijing) in 1816. On 9 April 1822 he married Emily (d. 1866), daughter of Lieutenant-Colonel Richard Humfrays of the Bengal Engineers; they were to have one son and six daughters. He remained at the East India Company's factory at Canton, becoming its president in 1832. Two years later he was appointed joint commissioner in China with Lord Napier, acting as second superintendent of trade. Following Napier's departure and death in the autumn of 1834 Davis was appointed superintendent of trade by the British government, which was now anxious to reverse Napier's aggressive policy in favour of quiet acquiescence to Chinese prejudices. This policy, along with his Company-bred prejudices against free trade, met with little favour among the British traders in Canton, and he resigned on 21 January 1835 and returned to England.

Davis had already acquired a reputation as a Chinese scholar with his translations of Chinese novels, maxims, and plays (1817, 1822) and The Fortunate Union (1829), and his vocabulary of Chinese words found in the Canton and Macao areas (1824). Now he published The Chinese: a General Description of China and its Inhabitants (2 vols., 1836) and Sketches of China (2 vols., 1841), both of which were very

well received and ran through many editions, and in 1844 Vizier Ali Khan, or, The Massacre of Benares, an account of the action in which his father had been involved in 1799.

On 9 February 1844 Davis was appointed plenipotentiary and superintendent of trade at Canton, and, on 23 February, governor and commander-in-chief of Hong Kong, which had been ceded to Britain under the 1842 treaty of Nanking (Nanjing). The central issue facing Davis was that of the British right of entry into Canton, which, despite the terms of the treaty of Nanking, had not thus far been granted. In April 1846 he agreed with the imperial commissioner, Qiying, to delay British entry into the city in exchange for an agreement not to alienate the Chushan Islands. Attacks on the British in Canton multiplied, and in April 1847 Davis retaliated by sending an armed force which captured the Bogue (Humen) ports and occupied the Canton factories. Qiying reached a rapid agreement with Davis to open Canton in two years' time and punish those who had offended the British, and conceded the right to build warehouses and churches.

Despite the apparent success of this venture, Davis was censured for his actions and resigned in November 1847, although he did not leave his post until the following March. Furthermore, an 1847 parliamentary select committee inquiry into British commercial relations with China, without naming Davis, succeeded in condemning his administration of Hong Kong and supporting the views of the British merchants who had consistently opposed his policies.

Davis, who had been created a baronet in 1845, returned to England and took up residence at Hollywood Tower, Westbury-on-Trym, Gloucestershire. On 26 November 1867 he married again; his second wife was Lucy Ellen (d. 1904), daughter of Thomas James Rocke, vicar of Exmouth, with whom he had a son. He continued to publish works on China, China during the War and since the Peace appearing in 1852 and Poeseos Sinensis commentarii: on the Poetry of the Chinese in 1870. Oxford University created him a DCL in 1876, and the following year he endowed a Chinese scholarship at that institution. He died at Hollywood Tower on 13 November 1890, and was succeeded in the baronetcy by the son of his second marriage.

K. D. REYNOLDS

Sources Burke, Peerage · I. C. Y. Hsü, The rise of modern China, 5th edn (1995) · E. J. Eitel, Europe in China (1895); repr. (1983) · FO List (1864) · Boase, Mod. Eng. biog. · C. Hibbert, The dragon wakes: China and the West, 1793–1911 (1970) · The Times (14 Nov 1890)

Archives BL, corresp. with Lord Aberdeen, Add. MSS 43161–43162, 43198 · Lpool RO, letters to Lord Stanley · NL Scot., letters to Sir T. J. Cochrane · NL Scot., corresp. with Admiral Charles Graham · UCL, letters to Society for the Diffusion of Useful Knowledge

Likenesses W. Drummond, lithograph, BM; repro. in The Athenaeum, 2 (1836), pl. 13

Wealth at death £167,898 6s. 6d.: probate, 3 Dec 1890, CGPLA Eng. & Wales

Davis, Sir John Henry Harris (1906–1993), businessman, was born on 10 November 1906 at 148 Monega Road, East Ham, Essex, the son of Sidney Myring Davis, a schoolmaster, and his wife, Emily, née Harris (christened John Henry,

Sir John Henry Harris Davis (1906–1993), by Godfrey Argent, 1970

Davis later adopted his mother's maiden name as a further forename). He was educated at the City of London School, which he left in 1924 to become a chartered secretary. In later years he liked to refer to himself as a chartered accountant, but there is no record that he ever qualified as such.

Davis married his first wife, Kathleen Blanche Mary Coryn (b. 1904/5), daughter of Bertram Coryn, a merchant, on 29 November 1930. This was the first of six marriages, though in later life Davis preferred to omit two of them—the first and the third—from the records (he also gave a false date for the second marriage). With Kathleen Coryn he had a son, Michael, and a daughter, Barbara. On 23 January 1937 he married Joan Grace Buckingham (b. 1916/17), daughter of Frank Henry Buckingham, a clerk in the Paymaster-General's Office; they had a son, Christopher. On 22 December 1941 he married Jeanne Beryl Stephens (b. 1918/19), daughter of William James Stephens, a company director; this marriage lasted only three months. His fourth wife was Marion Louise (b. 1918/19), daughter of Thomas Sydney Gaved, an antique dealer. She had already changed her surname to Davis by the time of their marriage, on 21 April 1947; they had two daughters, Janet and Susan. On 3 March 1954 Davis married Dinah Sheridan (b. 1920), the film actress and star of *Genevieve*, daughter of James Arthur Sheridan, a photographer, and former wife of Jimmy Hanley, the actor. His final marriage, on 5 March 1976, was to Felicity Mary Rutland (b. 1937/8), a company director, divorcee, and the daughter of

Colonel Mathew Arnold Drew, army officer. All Davis's marriages except the last ended in divorce.

In 1932 Davis joined the British Thomson-Houston Electrical Group as an accountant. Even at this early stage of his career he was gaining a reputation for ruthlessness; it is said that one employee of the company killed himself as a result of Davis's abrasive methods. Thomson-Houston was a leading manufacturer of cinema equipment, much of it supplied to the Odeon theatre chain founded by Oscar Deutsch. In 1938 Davis joined Deutsch as his chief accountant. In 1942, following Deutsch's untimely death, the Odeon chain was absorbed by the rapidly expanding Rank empire, well on its way to becoming the dominant force in the British film industry. Davis was appointed managing director of Odeon, and in 1946 became managing director of the whole Rank Organisation under the chairmanship of flour millionaire and devout Methodist (Joseph) Arthur *Rank. Over the next few years Davis's power within the combine grew steadily. Rank, a well-meaning but rather naive man with scant knowledge of film-making, looked increasingly to his right-hand man to take the tough decisions, a role for which Davis's temperament ideally fitted him. He too had little knowledge of the movie industry, nor much taste for it; but he understood money, and he understood figures.

With his austere financial training, Davis regarded the risky, unpredictable business of film-making with implacable mistrust. Film-makers, in his eyes, were mostly temperamental prima donnas, and financially irresponsible, while actors were spoilt children who needed to be kept in line. One of his first goals at Rank was to oust Filippo del Giudice, the flamboyant moving spirit behind Two Cities Films, makers of such classics as *In Which We Serve*, *The Way Ahead*, *Henry V*, and *Odd Man Out*. Ebullient, extravagant, convivial, a great nurturer of talent, del Giudice represented everything Davis detested in the film world and was determined to expunge from the Rank operation. In 1949, soon after del Giudice's dismissal, the Rank Organization hit a financial crisis, with losses of £16 million. Davis applied to the National Provincial Bank, who lent the money but in return insisted on a new regime of financial stringency. J. Arthur Rank, increasingly preoccupied with the family flour business after the death of his elder brother, withdrew from the day-to-day running of the organization, leaving Davis in effective control.

For the next quarter of a century, Davis was by far the most powerful man in the British film industry. His attitude to film-making was starkly simple: it was—or should be—exactly like any other manufacturing process. 'The cinemas are the retail trade', he explained, 'the distributors are the wholesale, and the film-makers are the equivalent of the factory' (private information). Following this principle he cracked down on anything he regarded as waste, imposed a ceiling of £150,000 on feature-film budgets, and instituted an internal accounting and supply system called Production Facilities Ltd, known to disaffected film-makers as 'Piffle'. Even Davis's most severe critics—whom he never lacked—agreed that he pulled the Rank Organization back from the brink of disaster and re-established it on a sound financial footing. It was a feat that few other men could have achieved. But some would add that while he saved Rank, it was at the cost of its soul. In place of the charismatic del Giudice he installed a former exhibitor, the American Earl St John, as head of production. Amiable and bibulous, terrified of displeasing his boss, St John was contemptuously regarded as Davis's yes-man. Sensing how the wind was blowing, several of the company's most talented film-makers, including David Lean, Carol Reed, and the symbiotic team of Michael Powell and Emeric Pressburger, decamped to more aesthetically minded producers such as Alexander Korda. With the departure of these and other gifted artists, the quality of the Rank cinematic output during the 1950s declined steadily towards mediocrity. This rarely seemed to trouble Davis, who favoured the production-line style of film-making: films devised to formula, whose costs and yield could be readily predicted—the *Doctor* series, the *Carry on* films, and the comedies of Norman Wisdom. Wisdom, indeed, was one of the few actors for whom Davis ever expressed admiration, describing him as 'a great artist' (private information).

Occasionally, though, Davis showed signs of what the critic Alexander Walker called 'a hankering for quality' (*The Independent*, 3 July 1993). At his instigation Rank ventured into more ambitious areas of film-making, with expensive international stars cast in storylines aimed to capture worldwide audiences. Unfortunately, they rarely did. Few of Rank's big-budget ventures even recouped their costs and many of them, such as *Ferry to Hong Kong* (1958) and *The Singer not the Song* (1960), flopped disastrously, to the malicious amusement of the rest of the industry. It may have been films like these that Davis had in mind when, asked years later just what he did on Rank's production side, he responded ruefully, 'Far too much' (ibid.). Such failures confirmed Davis in his belief that the best policy the Rank Organization could adopt towards film production was to extricate itself as smoothly as possible.

During the 1950s and 1960s Rank concentrated increasingly on the distribution and exhibition side of the industry while busily diversifying into other, supposedly more dependable, areas of activity. The company's famous logo, the man with the gong, came to adorn ten-pin bowling, ballroom dancing, gramophone records, service stations, hotels, catering services, bingo—and, above all, photocopying. Inspiration for the company's most lucrative sideways move came from a Rank engineer, Tom Law, who brought glowing reports of a copying process developed in America by the Haloid Corporation, but Davis deserves credit for embracing the venture with such alacrity. Rank Xerox was launched in 1956; by 1969 it was contributing 90 per cent of the group's pre-tax profits.

Not all Rank's diversification projects proved so profitable, however. Some, such as the music label, failed badly, and when this happened the luckless executives in charge could expect little mercy from Davis. JD, as he was universally known in the organization, accepted no excuses for failure, and the casualty rate among Rank personnel was

legendary. Fridays were particularly feared: executives returning from lunch would find on their desks a curt note, signed JD, telling them to collect a month's salary in lieu and be out within the hour, no reason given. So numerous were those summarily fired by Davis that they formed a club, the Rank Outsiders.

Davis ruled by fear, in a style which *The Spectator* of 27 September 1975 compared to that of Josef Stalin. Those entering his office at South Street, in London's Mayfair, would find him ensconced at a high, massive desk at the further end, and had to walk 40 feet under his baleful gaze—a technique borrowed from Mussolini. When the director Lewis Gilbert was making *Reach for the Sky* (1956) a senior Rank executive came to tell him that Davis wanted a scene excised. Gilbert refused, and was amazed to see the man burst into tears, sobbing, 'But you *must*! You don't know what he'll do to me!' (private information). Not even leading film stars were safe from Davis's wrath. The star of *Reach for the Sky*, Kenneth More, was Britain's biggest box-office attraction during the 1950s. About to be loaned out to play a lead role in Carl Foreman's wartime action film *The Guns of Navarone* (1961), More got drunk at a Rank Christmas dinner and passed some unguarded remarks. Davis banned him from appearing in *Navarone*, and More's film career never recovered.

Although Davis was vindictive and arrogant, no one questioned his integrity. He never went back on his word, and a verbal agreement with him was as secure as a written contract. And while his harshness was notorious, his numerous acts of charity, especially to colleagues who had fallen on hard times, were less well known. Even film-makers sometimes experienced his generosity. When Richard Attenborough was struggling to find backing for *Gandhi* (1982), he was surprised to receive a small but useful sum from Davis as a personal gift—though the Rank boss characteristically added that the project was an utter waste of time, as the world knew nothing of Gandhi and cared less.

During the week, Davis lived at the Dorchester Hotel, a hundred yards from South Street. Tireless and workaholic, he was invariably at his desk by 7.30 a.m., and rarely left before 8.00 p.m. at night. In a typical year he would travel 60,000 miles visiting far-flung outposts of the Rank empire. He expected similar dedication from his employees, along with scrupulous timekeeping. 'Punctuality', he once remarked, 'is being ten minutes early' (private information). In appearance he was thickset and bullet-headed, with slightly protuberant blue eyes whose cold stare intimidated many. The film-maker Roy Boulting, no admirer, described him as looking 'like a malevolent pork butcher' (private information).

When J. Arthur Rank retired in 1962, Davis took over as chairman of the organization. He was knighted in 1971. Under his chairmanship the organization accelerated its withdrawal from film production, a policy that had a devastating effect on the British film industry as a whole. His achievement was inexorable and startlingly absolute. In 1949, the year when Davis gained effective control of Rank, the company produced 67 feature films, two-thirds of the British industry's output. In 1977, the last year of his chairmanship, the Rank Organization financed not a single film.

Age scarcely mellowed Davis. The rate of attrition among his underlings never abated, and he openly relished his formidable reputation. 'I eat managing directors for breakfast', he once remarked (*The Times*, 29 May 1993). In 1975 he fired his second in command, Graham Dowson, when Dowson jilted his long-term mistress. The resultant row, along with some unimpressive profit figures, hit the headlines and loosened Davis's hold over the Rank trustees, who had hitherto supported him unquestioningly. (It was also said to have cost him his expected peerage, since Dowson was a friend of the then prime minister, Harold Wilson.) In 1977 Davis was persuaded to step down as chairman, but he appointed himself Rank's president for life—too optimistically, as it proved; in 1983 he was ousted from his post and he retired in dudgeon to his 600 acre estate near Lingfield in Surrey, where he kept a dairy herd, made cheese, and liked to drive a tractor.

Davis sold his farm in 1986, when tractor driving became too risky for an eighty-year-old, and moved to Selwood Terrace in Brompton, west London. In his later years he took up religion, becoming a 'born-again' Christian, and regularly attended Holy Trinity, Brompton. His work for the Westminster Abbey Appeal Fund earned him a CVO in 1985. He died of bronchopneumonia in a private nursing home, Beaumont House, Beaumont Street, Westminster, London, on 27 May 1993, his wife Felicity surviving him. PHILIP KEMP

Sources G. Macnab, *J. Arthur Rank and the British film industry* (1993) · C. Drazin, *The finest years: British cinema of the 1940s* (1998), 43–54 · A. Wood, *Mr Rank: a study of J. Arthur Rank and British films* (1952) · *The Times* (29 May 1993) · *Daily Telegraph* (29 May 1993) · *The Independent* (1 July 1993) · *The Independent* (3 July 1993) · *WWW, 1991–5* · b. cert. · m. certs. · d. cert. · private information (2004)
Likenesses G. Argent, photograph, 1970, NPG [*see illus.*] · photograph, repro. in *The Times* · photograph, repro. in *Daily Telegraph* · photograph, repro. in *The Independent*
Wealth at death £140,220: administration, 4 Oct 1993, *CGPLA Eng. & Wales*

Davis, John Philip [*called* Pope Davis] (**1784–1862**), portrait painter, of whose parents nothing is known, first exhibited at the Royal Academy in 1811. Then, and for ten years following, his contributions consisted of portraits in oil. In 1824 he went to Rome, where he painted a large picture, *The Talbot Family Receiving the Benediction of the Pope* (hence his nickname, Pope Davis). In the year following he was awarded a premium of £50 by the directors of the British Institution. In 1826, after his return to London, he exhibited at the Royal Academy *Canova Crowned by the Genius of Sculpture*. Thenceforward until 1843 he was an occasional exhibitor from a variety of London addresses. With his friend B. R. Haydon, Davis was a vigorous opponent of the Royal Academy. In 1843 he published *Facts of Vital Importance Relative to the Embellishment of the Houses of Parliament*; in 1858 *The Royal Academy and the National Gallery: what is the State of these Institutions?* Davis died on 28 September 1862

at 67 Great Russell Street, Bloomsbury, London. A volume of his essays, *Thoughts on Great Painters*, was published posthumously in 1866. ERNEST RADFORD, *rev.* ANNETTE PEACH

Sources Graves, *RA exhibitors* · Boase, *Mod. Eng. biog.* · Redgrave, *Artists*
Likenesses J. P. Davis, self-portrait, pencil and wash drawing, 1818, V&A

Davis, John Scarlett (**1804–1845**), painter, was born on 1 September 1804 at 2 High Street, Leominster, Herefordshire, the second of the five children of James Davis (1775–1828), silversmith and watchmaker, and Ann Scarlett, a distant relative of Sir James Scarlett (1769–1844), the attorney-general (later Lord Abinger). His Davis forebears had moved from Neath in Glamorgan, Wales, to Leominster at the end of the sixteenth century. At the age of five he demonstrated enthusiasm and talent for drawing; at eleven he copied an anatomical engraving seen in the surgery of the family physician, for which he received a silver palette (awarded by the Society of Arts) from the duke of Sussex, and was declared by the *Hereford Journal* of 5 June 1816 to be 'a young self-taught genius'. In presenting the prize, the duke observed that Davis was so much younger than the other candidates that at first the duke could not see him—but that his merit was soon apparent.

While at school in Leominster, Davis made a number of pencil portraits of the town's leading citizens, receiving £1 for each. Possibly he was among the private pupils of the landscape watercolourist David Cox, who then lived in Hereford. From early 1818 until December 1819 he boarded at Paul De La Pierre's academy in Well Street, Hackney, Middlesex, and in July 1820 he entered the Royal Academy Schools; in 1822 he first exhibited at the Royal Academy itself, and undertook a sketching tour in Wales, producing a group of drawings now in the National Museum and Gallery of Wales, Cardiff.

Of the twenty-seven works exhibited in Davis's lifetime at the major London venues, most were oil paintings; and he enjoyed a successful practice as a portrait painter. Yet his modern reputation rests almost entirely on his watercolours—and above all on his interior views, in which his particular genius was revealed. In his freedom and facility of touch he can be regarded as a worthy follower of Richard Parkes Bonington, and the draughtsmanship in some of his interior scenes owes an apparent debt also to Rembrandt.

In 1824 Davis made a series of copy-drawings of the paintings in the Royal Collection and in the marquess of Stafford's gallery at Cleveland House in London. In October 1825 he went to Yorkshire, where he spent the next three years painting portraits (often through introductions supplied by Sir Thomas Lawrence) and showing his work at the Northern Society exhibitions in Leeds. In the 1830s he gained more and more commissions for his interior views of galleries, churches, and (sometimes) palaces. He now toured the continent regularly, often in the company of his wife, Elizabeth Jane Abbott, whom he married on 12 July 1832. He fulfilled a large commission for Lord Farnborough, which included work in the Grande Galerie of the Louvre. His principal patron, however, was the merchant and naval agent John Hinxman, who at his death in 1846 owned 489 of the artist's works. These included *The Long Gallery of the Uffizi, Florence* (oils, 1833; exh. RA, 1834; ex-Sothebys, London, 14 July 1993), and his last and probably largest oil, *The Interior of St Peter's, with Figures* (7 ft 2 in. x 9 ft 10 in.), painted in Rome in 1842. A version is in the City Museum and Art Gallery, Hereford, which holds a diverse collection of his work.

After several years of illness Davis died of 'diseased lungs' at 11 Bedford Street, Bloomsbury, London, on 29 September 1845, aged forty-one; he was buried at All Souls, Kensal Green, Middlesex. According to the 1874 edition of Samuel Redgrave's *Dictionary of Artists of the English School*, Davis 'became drunken and of demoralised habits, got into prison, and died before the age of 30' (113)—a characterization entirely at odds with his surviving papers (discovered in 1928), which indicate a man settled in his domestic life and dedicated to his art.

PATRICK CONNER

Sources G. W. Williams, 'The life and works of John Scarlett Davis (1804–1845)', *Old Water-Colour Society's Club*, 45 (1970), 8–28 · A. Sandford, *The works of John Scarlett Davis (1804–1845)* (1995) · H. F. Finberg, 'Scarlett Davis as a portrait painter', *Apollo*, 17 (1933), 150–52 · *Catalogue of an exhibition of the works of John Scarlett Davis, a native of Leominster, Herefordshire* [1937] [exhibition catalogue] · M. H. Spielmann, 'Pictures of picture galleries', *The Connoisseur*, 33 (1912), 215–22 · Redgrave, *Artists* · M. Hardie, *Water-colour painting in Britain*, ed. D. Snelgrove, J. Mayne, and B. Taylor, 2: *The Romantic period* (1967), 187–8
Archives Hereford and Worcester County Libraries, family MSS
Likenesses J. S. Davis, two self-portraits, oils, *c*.1820–*c*.1830, Hereford City Museum and Art Gallery · J. S. Davis, self-portrait, pencil, 1828, NPG · J. S. Davis, self-portrait, pencil and sepia, 1829, BM · J. S. Davis, self-portrait, oils, *c*.1830, Leominster Museum

Davis, Joseph [Joe] (1901–1978), billiards and snooker player, was born on 15 April 1901 at Low Pit Lane, Whitwell, Derbyshire, the eldest in the family of three sons and three daughters of Fred Davis, coalminer and publican, and his wife, Ann-Eliza Clark. While he was still at elementary school at Newbold, he spent virtually every spare moment in the billiard room of his father's public house, the Queen's Hotel, in Whittington Moor, another Derbyshire village, developing the skill which was to enable him to win the world professional billiards championship four times and hold the world professional snooker title continuously from 1927 until he relinquished it in 1946. The youngest child of this family, Fred *Davis junior (1913–1998), was the only other player to hold the world title at both games though, unlike Joe, he never did so simultaneously.

Davis was only thirteen when he won the Chesterfield and district amateur billiards championship. He practised assiduously at the home of his coach, Ernest Rudge, who also staged exhibitions in the area featuring leading exponents whom his protégé might thus study at first hand. He managed various billiard halls in which his family or Rudge had an interest and after very few professional engagements won the midland professional billiards championship in 1922 and also the (later defunct) second

Joseph [Joe] Davis (1901–1978), by A. J. O'Brien, 1939 [right, with Fred Davis]

division championship, which gave him right of entry to the world championship.

Davis was well beaten by Tom Newman, as happened again when, much more experienced, he next entered in 1926, but after losing narrowly to Newman in 1927 he beat him by a small margin to win the title in 1928. After retaining the title in 1929, 1930, and 1932, he was beaten in 1933 and 1934 by the Australian Walter Lindrum, the only player in the history of the game whom either statistics or informed opinion rated above Davis. No other sport has been so thoroughly conquered by its leading practitioners as billiards was in the late 1920s and early 1930s by Lindrum, Davis, Newman, and the New Zealander Clark McConachy. Their very mastery killed billiards as a public spectacle. Among the scoring feats of this era which now seem more appropriate to the realms of fantasy, Davis himself was prouder of the break of 1247 with which, having occupied the non-striker's chair for two and a half sessions, he immediately responded to Lindrum's world record of 4137 than he was of such efforts as 2501 in the championship against Newman, 2002 under a new baulk line rule designed to limit the potency of nursery cannons, and 1784 under an even more stringent baulk line rule.

From his days managing billiard halls around Chesterfield, however, Davis knew that snooker was increasingly becoming the people's game. The establishment was slow to appreciate snooker's possibilities but Davis and a Birmingham equipment trader, Bill Camkin, prevailed on the then governing body, the Billiards Association and Control Council, to sanction a professional snooker championship in the 1926–7 season. Davis, who won the title with ease, pocketed £6 10s. 0d. for his trouble. Davis was an innovator in that, in the time he could spare from billiards, he evolved the positional and break-building shots, sequences, and techniques which are taken for granted nowadays but which were then far in advance of the rudimentary assets of his rivals. In January 1928 he made the first public snooker century break (exactly 100) of the 687 he made in public before his retirement in 1964. He retained the world title annually with little apparent difficulty until his younger brother Fred extended him to 17–14 in the 1939 semi-final and 37–35 in the 1940 final. By this time snooker had become the premier billiard-table game. The world professional billiards championship had lapsed and the British professional billiards championship, won annually by Davis from 1934 until 1939, did not attract a level of public interest commensurate to the skill displayed. By 1938 he had gradually increased the record snooker break to 138.

During the war Davis raised over £125,000 for war charities and appeared on various variety stages, including the London Palladium, with a trick shot performance involving the use of a large tilting mirror. In 1946 he won the last of his fifteen world professional snooker titles. His skill and personality had brought snooker to its first peak of popularity but his decision to retire from world championship play while continuing to compete in other tournaments devalued the game's premier event and contributed to a decline which reached its nadir in the suspension of the championship from 1957 until 1964. As the best player (even when he was not officially champion), the chairman of the players' body, the partner with the biggest say in who played at Leicester Square Hall, then the showcase of professional snooker, Davis virtually ran the game. He also wrote several books on the techniques of playing. Outside the world championship, professional tournaments were conducted on a handicap basis, with Davis inevitably the back marker. Victory confirmed his superiority, defeat did not threaten his pre-eminence. In his entire career he lost only four matches on level terms, all of them to his brother Fred. In 1951 and 1954 he made century breaks in three consecutive frames and in 1955, having just made a break of 146, he achieved his dearly held ambition of a break of 147, the first time a player had potted fifteen reds, fifteen blacks, and all the colours in one break in record conditions. He was appointed OBE in 1963 shortly before his retirement.

On 8 June 1921 Davis married Florence Enid Stevenson (b. 1898/9), daughter of Francis Stevenson, farmer; they had a son and a daughter. This marriage was dissolved in 1931 and on 6 April 1945 he married Juanita Ida Triggs (b. 1914/15), who sang under the stage name of June Malo; she was the daughter of William Warren Triggs, a consultant engineer and patent agent. Davis died on 10 July 1978 at Grayshott Hall, Grayshott, Hampshire, and was survived by his wife.   CLIVE EVERTON, rev.

Sources J. Davis, *The breaks came my way* (1976) · C. Everton, *The story of billiards and snooker* (1979) · personal knowledge (1986) · private information (1986) · b. cert. · m. cert. · d. cert.
Archives FILM BFI NFTVA, documentary footage · BFI NFTVA, sports footage
Likenesses J. Capstick, photograph, c.1939, C. Capstick portrait archive; repro. in J. Huntington-Whiteley, *The book of British sporting heroes* (1998), 82 [exhibition catalogue, National Portrait Gallery, London, 16 Oct 1998–24 Jan 1999] · A. J. O'Brien, photograph, 1939, Hult. Arch. [see illus.]
Wealth at death £87,308: probate, 26 Oct 1978, CGPLA Eng. & Wales

Davis, Joseph Barnard (1801–1881), physician and craniologist, second child of Joseph Davis, draper, and his wife, Marianne, was born on 13 June 1801 and was baptized next day in York. In 1820, while still studying surgery, he went as surgeon on a whaling ship to the Arctic. He qualified LSA in 1823, and on 25 September that year married Elizabeth Haslam in Shelton, Hanley, Staffordshire, where he settled for the rest of his life. They had three children.

Soon after his arrival there Davis was appointed medical officer for the Stoke upon Trent district, and acted as parish medical officer in Shelton until his death. He qualified MRCS in 1843, became FSA in 1854, and graduated MD at St Andrews in 1862. As a Methodist of the New Connexion he was concerned for the underprivileged and with the betterment of social conditions, and his religious beliefs were matched by a liberal outlook on life. The small fee he received as a medical officer meant a reduced lifestyle but despite this he doggedly pursued learned interests. In 1828 he offered to write a history of cholera for the Society for the Diffusion of Useful Knowledge, and in 1839 was revising a previous article for them. His commitment to disseminating information was also reflected in *A Popular Manual of the Art of Preserving Health* (1836) which dealt with the activities common to most nineteenth-century health regimens—air, diet, exercise, and bathing.

For many years Davis devoted himself to craniology, and gradually accumulated a huge number of skulls and skeletons of various races, most with carefully annotated histories. Although it is unclear if Davis was influenced by the phrenological enthusiasm of the 1820s, like a number of other scientists he thought that significant information could be extracted from the study and measurement of skulls and other skeletal remains. He was elected into the Ethnological Society in 1856, and joined the Anthropological Society on its commencement in 1862. While members of the Ethnological Society had genuinely scientific interests, many of those in the Anthropological Society mixed science with politics in the shape of the behaviour and abilities of living races. Davis seems not to have ventured into print on this aspect, possibly because he was somewhat isolated from the main body of members in London. Besides a valuable memoir on osteology of the Tasmanians, he published numerous papers in *Anthropological Review* and the *Journal of the Anthropological Institute*. From 1870 he was a joint editor of the *Journal* and of *Anthropologia*. He was elected FRS in 1868.

In 1856 Davis and John *Thurnam commenced work on their *Crania Britannica*, in two volumes, completed in 1865. Supported by a grant from the Royal Society they travelled abroad to gather material to compare with British specimens, many excavated from burial mounds, seen as representing the various races which made up the British population. Davis's own collection of skulls was published in 1867 as *Thesaurus craniorum* (1867), delineating many examples and providing 25,000 careful measurements with copious bibliographical references. Davis spared no time or expense in his collecting: he made contact with travellers and collectors throughout the world, amassing eventually a collection larger than the combined material held in other museums. He was very clubbable and by the end of his life had joined almost thirty medical, anthropological, and general scientific societies and associations in America, Italy, Holland, Spain, Russia, Germany, and Austro-Hungary, as a full or corresponding member. These contacts provided him with information and ample opportunity to publish his own work and ideas.

After the death of his first wife Davis married, on 31 July 1878, Emma Moorhouse (b. 1851), a woman who was fifty years his junior. This led to friction with his son Joseph, and in his will he provided that this son of his first marriage should receive his annuity only if he resided outside the county of Staffordshire, and that the executors must ensure that his debts were not charged to the estate.

In 1880 Davis conveyed to the Royal College of Surgeons fourteen complete articulated skeletons, representing various races, and a large quantity of bones, casts, and other objects. He died at his home, 4 Albion Street, Shelton, on 19 May 1881.   G. T. BETTANY, rev. NICK HERVEY

Sources W. H. Flower, Nature, 24 (1881), 82–3 · letters to SDUK, 1839–41, UCL · St Crux, York, bishops' transcripts · Boase, Mod. Eng. biog. · London and Provincial Medical Directory (1847–81) · census returns for Shelton, Staffordshire, 1881 · parish register, Ashton under Lyne, St Michael, 25 Sept 1823, marriage · Z. Cope, The Royal College of Surgeons of England: a history (1959), 292 · J. Lenhossék, Emlékbeszéd Davis József Bernát (1886) · N. Stepan, The idea of race in science: Great Britain, 1800–1960 (1982) · Journal of the Anthropological Institute of Great Britain and Ireland, 11 (1882), 484–5 · R. Rainger, 'Race, politics and science: the Anthropological Society in the 1860s', Victorian Studies, 22 (1978–9), 51–70 · m. cert. [E. Moorhouse] · d. cert. · B. M. Marsden, The early barrow diggers, [new edn] (1999)

Archives RCS Eng., collection of skulls and skeletons · Royal Anthropological Institute, London, historical, archaeological, and medical notebooks and papers | Auckland Public Library, letters to Sir George Grey · NHM, letters to Sir Richard Owen · UCL, letters to Society for the Diffusion of Useful Knowledge · University of Bristol Library, corresp. with John Beddoe

Likenesses J. B. Davis, portrait, RCS Eng. · R. J. Lane, lithograph, Wellcome L. · photograph, repro. in Lenhossék, Emlékbeszéd Davis József Bernát · plaster bust, RCS Eng.

Wealth at death £7658 6s. 6d.: probate, 22 Aug 1881, CGPLA Eng. & Wales

Davis, Lockyer John (1717–1791), bookseller, was baptized at St Bartholomew-the-Great, London, on 14 November 1717, the son of James Davis, salesman of that parish, and his wife Elizabeth. His father was the eldest brother of the bookseller Charles *Davis (bap. 1693, d. 1755), to whom Lockyer was apprenticed on 1 August 1732, by which time James Davis had already died. Lockyer Davis was freed on 2 December 1746 and was elected to the livery of the Stationers' Company on the same day; from 1753 he was in business over against Gray's Inn Gate, in Holborn. Two years later he succeeded to his uncle's business, and from 1757 until 1768 he was in partnership with his first cousin Charles Reymers, son of his father's youngest sister, Elizabeth. On 9 November 1769, in her forty-eighth year, his wife, Mary, died; she was buried in St Bartholomew-the-Great. A year later Davis had moved his business to 326 High Holborn.

Like his uncle Davis bought and sold libraries, and he

issued numerous catalogues, fifteen of which have survived. As a 'cataligist' (one who 'distributes books at fixed prices for ready money') he is ranked by Nichols second only to Thomas Osborne (Nichols, Lit. anecdotes, 3.625). Davis was a member of the club of major booksellers that met monthly at the Shakespeare tavern, where, according to Nichols, 'the germ of many a valuable publication' originated, including the ideas that led to the publication in 1779 of The Works of the English Poets with Prefaces, Biographical and Critical, by Samuel Johnson, in the imprint of which Davis's name appears (ibid., 5.325). He had earlier been involved in the publication of various editions of Johnson's Dictionary and Plays of Shakespeare.

Davis was bookseller and nominal printer to the Royal Society, and one of the nominal printers of the votes of the House of Commons. His wide knowledge of scholarship and books contributed to his becoming a consultant to many of the literary figures of the day. Fewer men 'knew more of books', Nichols observes, 'or more of the world; and fewer still were equally willing to advantage others by a free communication' (Nichols, Lit. anecdotes, 6.436). The recognition of his integrity as a man and as a tradesman, coupled with his amiable manners, made him a sought-after social companion. Among the legacies of the printer William Bowyer the younger in 1777 was one of £100 to Davis. He was a master of the Stationers' Company for 1779–80 and an honorary registrar of the Literary Fund for the Relief of Distressed Authors, founded in 1790. He contributed light, occasional pieces to the newspapers, particularly the St James's Chronicle, but his only acknowledged book, published in 1775 and again in 1781, was 'a new edition, revised and improved' of Maxims and Moral Reflections by the Duke de la Rochefoucault. The 1775 edition contains a dedication, signed with the name Lockyer Davis, to David Garrick, 'whose various and inimitable representations display a knowledge of the human heart not inferior to that of Rochefoucault these maxims … are gratefully inscribed by one less ambitious of patronage than proud of his friendship' (sig. A3r).

Davis died suddenly at his house in Holborn on 23 April 1791, in his seventy-fourth year. He was buried in St Bartholomew-the-Great, where a tablet to the memory of Davis and his wife was placed under the organ loft.

O. M. BRACK

Sources private information (2004) [M. Treadwell, Trent University] · ESTC · GM, 1st ser., 61 (1791), 390–91 · I. Maxted, The London book trades, 1775–1800: a preliminary checklist of members (1977) · Nichols, Lit. anecdotes, 2.297, 3.207, 281, 625, 636–40, 646, 759, 5.325, 6.436–7, 9.278 · H. R. Plomer and others, A dictionary of the printers and booksellers who were at work in England, Scotland, and Ireland from 1726 to 1775 (1932) · C. H. Timperley, Encyclopaedia of literary and typographical anecdote, 2nd edn (1842), 746, 771–2

Davis [Davies; married name Paisible], **Mary** [Moll] (c.1651–1708), actress and royal mistress, was said to be 'a bastard of Collonell Howard, my Lord Barkeshire' (Pepys, 9.24), a phrase which is more likely to refer to Thomas Howard (bap. 1619, d. 1706), the future fourth earl, than his father, Thomas (c.1590–1669), the then earl. A later account stated that she was the daughter of a blacksmith from Charlton,

Wiltshire, the family seat of the earls of Berkshire. In the early 1660s she was one of the actresses in the Duke's Theatre Company, who were boarded in the house of the company's patentee and manager, Sir William Davenant. She was almost certainly the little girl whose dancing and singing in Davenant's *The Law Against Lovers* Pepys admired when he first saw her on 18 February 1662. A year later her dancing in boy's clothes pleased him, 'she having very fine legs' (Pepys, 4.56). In the season of 1663–4 she played Violinda in Robert Stapylton's *The Step-Mother* and Aurelia in George Etherege's *The Comical Revenge, or, Love in a Tub*; on 8 March 1664 Pepys admired her in *Heraclius*: 'the little guirle is come to act very prettily and spoke the epilogue most admirably' (Pepys, 5.78–9). Etherege wrote the role of Gatty for her, the madcap girl of *She Would if She Could*, giving her a song and a jig. Pepys considered her much superior to Nell Gwyn as a dancer, and the company's prompter, John Downes, praised her dancing at the end of John Dryden's *Sir Martin Mar-All*, in which she created the role of Millisent. In November 1667 the company had a great success with a revival of Davenant's *The Rivals*, in which Moll Davis, as the mad Celania, sang 'My lodging it is on the cold ground'. Downes remembered that she 'perform'd that so Charmingly, that not long after, it Rais'd her from her Bed on the Cold Ground, to a Bed Royal' (Downes, 55). On 11 January 1668 Pepys learned that Miss Davis was leaving the company because the king, who was in love with her, had given her a ring worth £600 and was furnishing a house for her. Three days later Mrs Pearce told him that the 'homely jade' was showing the ring to everyone, that the house was in Suffolk Street, and that Lady Castlemaine, the king's mistress, was jealous. On 31 May 1668 Pepys recorded that she was 'quite gone' from the theatre and had appeared in a play at court, when the queen left before she danced her jig (Pepys, 9.24, 219).

The School of Venus (1716) recounts the story that Nell Gwyn gave her rival sweetmeats laced with a laxative before she visited the king, with the result that Moll was pensioned off with £1000 a year. However, Mary, her daughter with *Charles II and the last of the king's offspring, was not born until 16 October 1673 and Moll certainly continued as a performer in court entertainments. In his 1673 *Epigrams* Richard Flecknoe added his poem 'On her Excellent Singing' to his 1669 effusion 'To M. M. Davies. On her Excellent Dancing'. Between February and April 1675 she was the principal singer in the performances of John Crowne's court masque *Calisto*. The young princesses Mary and Anne had the leading acting roles, while Moll Davis portrayed the River Thames in the sung prologue and the shepherdess Sylvia in the musical interludes. Crowne defended his unorthodox casting of a woman as the River Thames, saying that his purpose was to delight the court: 'and the graceful motions and admirable singing of Mrs. *Davis*, did sufficiently prove the discretion of my choice' (Crowne, sig. a3). A satire of 1681 implied that Moll Davis was the mistress of Baptist May, the keeper of the privy purse, who kept her at the king's expense. In the 'Masque for the Entertainment of the

King', John Blow's opera *Venus and Adonis* (BL, Add. MS 22100), she created the role of Venus, while her daughter, Lady Mary Tudor, sang Cupid. The performance took place after 10 December 1680, when her daughter received her title, and before April 1684, when the opera was performed by a cast of young gentlewomen at Josias Priest's school at Chelsea. The king granted his daughter an annuity of £1500 in September 1683 and she was married to Edward, Viscount Radcliffe, later earl of Derwentwater, in August 1687. Two of their three sons were to be executed for their parts in the Jacobite risings of 1715 and 1745.

In December 1686 Mary Davis (flatteringly described on the marriage allegation as aged about twenty-five) married the instrumentalist and composer James *Paisible (d. 1721), a fellow performer in *Calisto*. Paisible was a member of James II's private musick and became a performer in his Catholic chapel. The Paisibles appear to have spent some time at James's exiled court in St Germain-en-Laye, although in February 1692 they began a chancery suit in England to recover money owed to Mrs Paisible. During 1693 both James and Marie Paisible obtained French passports to return to England. Paisible re-established himself in London's musical life, and in January 1698 he and his wife were granted a licence to remain in England. 'James Paisible now in London', who received £50 in Paisible's will, was probably not her son, but the 'James Peasable of James & Eliz. born 8 July Bastard' who was baptized at St Anne's, Soho, on 19 July 1702. Mary Paisible died probably at her home in Dean Street, Soho, and was buried at St Anne's, Soho, on 24 February 1708.

OLIVE BALDWIN and THELMA WILSON

Sources Pepys, *Diary* · W. Van Lennep and others, eds., *The London stage, 1660–1800*, pt 1: *1660–1700* (1965) · J. Downes, *Roscius Anglicanus*, ed. J. Milhous and R. D. Hume, new edn (1987) · E. Boswell, *The Restoration court stage (1660–1702): with a particular account of the production of 'Calisto'* (1932) · J. Crowne, *Calisto* (1675) · J. Blow, *Venus and Adonis*, BL, Add. MS 22100 · R. Luckett, 'A new source for *Venus and Adonis*', *MT*, 130 (1989), 76–9 · R. Flecknoe, *Epigrams of all sorts* (1669); (1670); (1671) · R. Flecknoe, *A collection of the choicest epigrams and characters* (1673) · A. Smith, *The school of Venus* (1716) · Bishop Burnet's *History of his own time*, 1, ed. G. Burnet and T. Burnet (1724) · G. de F. Lord and others, eds., *Poems on affairs of state: Augustan satirical verse, 1660–1714*, 7 vols. (1963–75), vol. 2 · GEC, *Peerage*, new edn, vols. 12–16 · G. J. Armytage, ed., *Allegations for marriage licences issued by the vicar-general of the archbishop of Canterbury, July 1679 to June 1687*, Harleian Society, 30 (1890) · A. Ashbee and D. Lasocki, eds., *A biographical dictionary of English court musicians, 1485–1714*, 2 (1998) · E. T. Corp, 'The exiled court of James II and James III: a centre of Italian music in France, 1689–1712', *Journal of the Royal Musical Association*, 120 (1995), 216–31 · baptismal and burial registers, St Anne's, Soho · PRO, PROB 11/585, quire 124 [will of James Paisible]

Likenesses P. Lely, oils, c.1670, priv. coll. · G. Valck, mezzotint, 1678 (after P. Lely), BM, NPG · Schiavonetti, print, 1792 (after P. Lely), repro. in A. Hamilton, *Mémoires du comte de Grammont* [1793] · W. N. Gardiner, print, 1793 (after S. Harding; after G. Kneller), repro. in A. Hamilton, *Mémoires du comte de Grammont* [1793] · E. Scriven, print, 1810 (after P. Lely), repro. in A. Hamilton, *Mémoires du comte de Grammont*, new edn, 2 vols. (1811) · R. Earlom, print, pubd 1815 (after G. Valck; after P. Lely), BM, Harvard TC · C. Allard, print (after reversed copy by Tompson), BM · A. De Blois, print (after G. Valck; after P. Lely), BM · G. Kneller, oils (Mary Davis?), Audley End House, Essex · P. Lely, oils (Mary Davis?; as St Mary Magdalen), NPG · R. Tompson, mezzotint (after P. Lely), BM, NPG, Harvard TC · print, Harvard TC

Davis, Morris Harold (1894–1985), local politician, was born on 7 November 1894 at 47 Langdale Street, in the heart of the Jewish East End of London, the son of Joseph Davis (1868–1940) and his wife, Bertha (d. 1954). His father, variously described as a boot maker and a licensee of public houses, hailed from Minsk; his mother was also of eastern European origin. Having married abroad, they appear to have settled in London at the end of the 1880s. Educated at various London county council schools, Davis was apprenticed within the ladies' tailoring trade, but later assisted his father in the running of a public house, and later still ceased regular employment, living, it would seem, off his own wealth and that of his parents.

Davis grew up in a staunchly Orthodox Jewish household, and followed his father in interesting himself in the governance of a variety of Jewish communal bodies in east London. He was also, like many members of the Yiddish-speaking Jewish immigrant community, a passionate Zionist and a man of very left-wing views. In 1887 the banker Samuel Montagu, first Baron Swaythling, had induced the numerous small 'conventicles' which Russian and Polish Jewish immigrants had established in the East End to form themselves into the Federation of Synagogues, which rapidly became the largest Jewish communal body in the United Kingdom. On Montagu's death in 1911 the leadership of the federation had passed to his son, the second baron, Louis Montagu, who in common with many members of the Anglo-Jewish gentry evinced a strong antipathy to Zionism. Louis was one of the ten signatories of an infamous letter, published in the *Morning Post* on 23 April 1919, implicating foreign-born Jews in the spread of Bolshevism in England. Louis's action outraged the impoverished Yiddish-speaking members of the federation's affiliated congregations, and Davis (who spoke fluent Yiddish but also impeccable English) put himself at their head. On 25 November 1925 Davis persuaded the board of the federation to permit delegates to speak in Yiddish. Louis Montagu acknowledged that he could not understand Yiddish and resigned. On 20 March 1928 Davis succeeded to the presidency of the federation, a move which symbolized and signalled the first major transfer of power within Anglo-Jewry from the moneyed Anglicized aristocracy to the sons of the immigrant generation.

Meanwhile Davis had risen in the ranks of the Stepney central Labour Party. Founded in 1918, its creation owed much to its Jewish secretary, the immigrant chemist Oscar Tobin. It was to Tobin's pharmacy in Harford Street, Mile End, that the young Major Clement Attlee had come on his discharge from the army, there to learn the politics of the East End and to take the first steps in his own political career. Tobin had studied the demography of political power in Stepney, and had reached the simple conclusion that a party which retained the support of the Jews and the Irish was bound to win control of the borough council. Tobin forged an alliance with the Irish Catholic community in the borough, and in November 1919 Labour, never having held a single seat on the council, swept to power; Attlee became the borough's first Labour mayor.

Davis appointed himself Tobin's protégé and heir. He made friends with Attlee, who was instrumental in arranging for his election as an alderman of the borough in 1921. That November Tobin became the first Jewish mayor of Stepney. The following year Davis was elected vice-president of the Stepney Labour Party, and within a few years he had succeeded in gaining election to the key committees of the council, becoming in 1928 chairman of its finance committee. In 1930 Davis became mayor, and in 1935 he succeeded to the council leadership. Meanwhile, in 1925, he had secured election to the London county council.

Davis's leadership of Stepney borough council, like that of the Federation of Synagogues, became highly controversial. He steered the federation along the Zionist course its rank and file wished it to go, but at the same time he turned his presidency into (literally) an unelected dictatorship. His political alliance with the Irish Catholics on the borough council was unshakeable. But with the outbreak of the Spanish Civil War in July 1936 this alliance became a source of weakness rather than of strength. On the whole, East End Jewry adopted a position sympathetic to the Spanish republicans. Irish support for General Franco acted, therefore, as a powerful solvent of the Jewish–Irish dialogue that had characterized East End politics hitherto. Davis took very little active part in combating the fascist menace in Jewish Stepney in 1936–7; in February 1937 he and three other Jewish councillors voted to permit the British Union of Fascists to hold a meeting in Limehouse town hall.

Meanwhile, apparently well-founded allegations of wholesale corruption surfaced against Davis and his Irish allies on Stepney council. In October 1940 Herbert Morrison, then minister of home security in Churchill's wartime coalition government, bowed to local pressure by stripping Davis of his role as air raid precautions controller in the borough. These events brought Labour in Stepney into disrepute, and were in part responsible for the growing popularity of communism in the borough. They also impinged on Davis's presidency of the federation. Davis had been able to dispense with elections for offices in the federation, and his retainers saw to it that opponents of his dictatorship were cowed into silence. But the reputation of the federation fell as a result, and it was under Davis that it began its long decline within the communal structure of Anglo-Jewry.

To his enemies Davis was utterly ruthless. To his friends, and to those whom he befriended, no act of kindness was too small for him to undertake. But in the second half of 1944 his careers came to an abrupt end. Attempting to avoid prosecution for alleged non-payment of a railway fare by inciting a Stepney council employee to provide him with a false national identity card, he was sentenced to a term of imprisonment. On his release from gaol he became a recluse, perhaps mentally unstable, and died (of heart disease) in West Heath, a private nursing home in north-west London, on 15 March 1985. He was buried next to his parents at the Federation Jewish cemetery, Edmonton. He never married and left no heir.

GEOFFREY ALDERMAN

Sources G. Alderman, 'M. H. Davies: the rise and fall of a communal upstart', *Jewish Historical Studies*, 31 (1988–90), 249–68 • *CGPLA Eng. & Wales* (1985) • b. cert. • d. cert. • personal knowledge (2004) **Archives** LMA, archives of the Federation of Synagogues **Likenesses** photograph, repro. in G. Alderman, *The Federation of Synagogues* (1987) **Wealth at death** £157,368: probate, 21 Aug 1986, *CGPLA Eng. & Wales*

Davis, Nathan (1812–1882), traveller and excavator, was born in 1812. Nothing is known of his education, save that he is referred to as Dr Davis. He was an American who for many years lived in an old Moorish palace, 10 miles from Tunis, where he extended his hospitality to various travellers. He published his experiences of northern Africa in: *Tunis, or, Selections from a Journal during a Residence in that Regency* (1841); *A voice from North Africa, or a narrative illustrative of the … manners of the inhabitants of that part of the world* (1844); and *Evenings in my tent, or, Wanderings in Balad, Ejjareed, illustrating the … conditions of various Arab tribes of the African Sahara* (2 vols., 1854). In 1852 he edited the *Hebrew Christian Magazine*, and afterwards became a nonconformist minister. From 1856 to 1858 he was engaged on behalf of the British Museum in excavations at Carthage and Utica and between 1857 and 1860 numerous cases of antiquities were sent by him to that museum where the chief antiquities discovered—Roman mosaic pavements—were preserved. His benefactions were particularly appreciated by the museum since he was an American. Davis described his explorations in *Carthage and her Remains* (1861) which, although rather unscholarly in presentation, was widely circulated. It was followed by *Ruined Cities within Numidian and Carthaginian Territories* (1862). He also published *Israel's True Emancipator* (two letters to Dr Adler, 1852), and, with Benjamin Davidson, *Arabic Reading Lessons* (n.d. [1854]). Shortly before his death Davis revisited Tunis, but the journey tried his strength, and he died at Florence on 6 January 1882 of congestion of the lungs. W. W. WROTH, *rev.* ELIZABETH BAIGENT

Sources E. Edwards, *Lives of the founders of the British Museum* (1870) • Boase, *Mod. Eng. biog.* • Allibone, *Dict.* • *Men of the time* (1875) • *The Athenaeum* (14 Jan 1882), 65 • *Inscriptions in the Phoenician character now deposited in the British Museum…discovered by Nathan Davis…in 1856, 1857 and 1858*, BM (1863) **Archives** BM

Davis, Pope. *See* Davis, John Philip (1784–1862).

Davis, Ralph Henry Carless (1918–1991), historian, was born at 11 Fyfield Road, Oxford, on 7 October 1918, the third and youngest son of Henry William Carless *Davis (1874–1928) and his wife, Jennie Rosa, daughter of Walter Lindup of Bampton Grange, Oxfordshire. His father was regius professor of history in the University of Oxford and a fellow of Balliol College. Ralph's older brothers, Patrick (1914–1996), later a city solicitor, and Godfrey Rupert Carless (1917–1997), secretary of the Royal Commission on Historical Manuscripts, both attended the Dragon School, Oxford, and Highgate School, but on his father's sudden death in 1928 Ralph was transferred from the Dragon to the Quaker school at Leighton Park, Reading. He matriculated from Balliol in 1937 to read history; his tutors were R. W. Southern and Denys Hay.

There was an unconformable quality in Ralph Davis which his education had at least done nothing to quell. Under the threat of the Second World War, and despite a visit to Germany in 1939, he refused to register for military service, and after appearing before a tribunal he chose to join a Friends' Ambulance Unit. He served in Finland and was briefly interned in Sweden before being posted to the Middle East, where he moved with the Hadfield-Spears mobile hospital from Lebanon through the western desert to Tunisia, Italy, and southern France. A stay in Cairo enabled him to add *The Mosques of Cairo* (1944) to his publications, which had begun with an undergraduate paper on masons' marks in the Oxfordshire Archaeological Society's *Journal* for 1938. He was demobilized in 1945 and returned to Balliol with the Croix de Guerre to set beside (though he never chose to do so) his brother Patrick's mention in dispatches. He graduated BA with first-class honours in modern history in 1947, and was appointed to an assistant mastership at Christ's Hospital, Horsham. In 1948 he was offered an assistant lectureship at University College, London (UCL), by Sir John Neale. At UCL he met and in 1949 married Eleanor Megaw, who had been tutor to women students since 1946, when she left the Women's Royal Naval Service. Their two sons were born in 1952 and 1955.

The essential elements of Davis's career were now in place. He stayed at UCL until 1956 when he was elected to a fellowship at Merton College, Oxford, and in those years he had revealed a wide range of talents. Neale's expectation that every member of his department would devote two and a half days each week to research, both in term and in vacation, was not burdensome to him. At the same time, however, he was delivering first-year lectures to a mixed and enthusiastic audience of students of both science and the humanities, which issued in a beguilingly popular text book, *A History of Medieval Europe from Constantine to Saint Louis* (1957). He also instituted and maintained an introductory week at Cumberland Lodge—a connection which he owed to a friend of Eleanor's—for history freshmen, who could then meet not only other members of a large and vigorous department, but speakers from elsewhere. From 1956 onwards he pursued similar policies at Merton. As tutor for admissions he established visiting fellowships for schoolteachers and had the satisfaction of seeing the college rise to the top of the Norrington Table, a prize for which he would not have striven but which it was gratifying to receive. In 1970, however, following the retirement of H. A. Cronne, the University of Birmingham appointed Davis to its chair of medieval history and he retired from Oxford, congenial to him in respect of his family's tradition, to the familiar challenge of a great civic university.

Since Davis's later years at UCL his interests had turned from the social structure of medieval Suffolk—studies in the rich archives of St Edmund's Abbey to which V. H. Galbraith had originally drawn his attention—to the broader issues examined in *King Stephen, 1135–1154* (1967) and in the critical work on a variety of historical sources, notably charters and chronicles, which followed it. Most of those works rested on his collaboration with H. A. Cronne upon the third volume of the *Regesta regum Anglo-Normannorum*. The *Regesta* had been launched by H. W. C. Davis, Ralph's father, in 1914, when it fell foul of J. H. Round, a scholar of morbid sensitivity who consistently looked for faults in the work of others. The second volume, containing the writs and charters of Henry I, appeared in 1956, edited by Charles Johnson in collaboration with Cronne.

Cronne then proceeded to a third volume, joined by Ralph Davis, to whom an increasing proportion of the work fell as Cronne resisted and triumphed over a malignant disease. There was much of filial piety in Davis's approach to Stephen's reign, and his preliminary work led to an assault on J. H. Round's conclusions on the nature of Stephen's relations with the baronage, and in particular with Geoffrey de Mandeville. In the event, controversy over the dating of Stephen's and Matilda's charters to Geoffrey continued for the rest of Davis's life, ending with a long-drawn-out sequence of articles and notes in the *English Historical Review* initiated by John Prestwich. The exchanges were ultimately inconclusive, but Ralph's arguments were always cogent. The third volume of the *Regesta* was followed in 1969 by a fourth, with facsimiles. The completed work surpassed H. W. C. Davis's original intentions, with full texts, not only of Stephen's writs and charters, but also those of Matilda and the young Henry of Anjou, all edited to a high standard.

Ralph Davis's own talents lay less in the minutiae of charter dating than in the imaginative reconstruction of society and the lives of individuals which can now be reached only through such formal documents. His identification of Robert of Lewes as the author of the *Gesta Stephani*, perhaps the most significant by-product of his work on the *Regesta*, is a notable example of his skills in research and his serendipitous gift in noting connections. A different, wider-ranging example can be found in *The Normans and their Myth* (1976).

Davis's years in Birmingham from 1970 to his retirement in 1984 gave full play to his abilities in enthusing colleagues and defining common goals. As it happened, the interval between Cronne's retirement in 1968 and Ralph Davis's arrival eighteen months later was a time of disruption and general unease in all universities, but he was not given to finding or making difficulties, and he achieved as much in excitable as others might in more tranquil times. He reorganized undergraduate teaching on the lines with which he had first experimented in UCL, with fortnightly tutorials and seminars. As at UCL, and supported at all turns by his wife, he took every occasion to emphasize the identity and interests of his colleagues and their students. He made no attempt, beyond the adequately formidable business of defining such interests, to create common studies, but he promoted the west midlands as a field of research, and brought colleagues from other universities with an interest in medieval history into annual meetings

to dine and discuss general or particular themes in a congenial atmosphere. He continued to edit *History*, which he had taken up in 1968, and was elected president of the Historical Association in 1981. He was elected fellow of the British Academy in 1975 and remained closely involved in the academy's work until his death.

Much as they had enjoyed their time in Birmingham, the Davises returned to Oxford on Ralph's retirement in 1984. There he spent seven productive years in studying the Normans, medieval warfare—discussed felicitously in *The Medieval War-Horse* (1989)—and the promotion of history as a field of study in schools and universities. He also sought ways of diminishing common strife in Northern Ireland, where Eleanor's family ties with both the Unionist and the home rule camps gave him an insight. He died in Oxford on 12 March 1991, after a sudden illness, and was buried on 17 March. The width of his interests and the warmth with which the whole community of his colleagues regarded him were attested at his funeral and at a memorial service at Merton College in July 1991. He had a rare ability to convey the intensity of his own vision of the past, by a combination of documentary evidence and the physical remains, on the one hand in Cairo and the Krak des Chevaliers, and on the other in the signs and marks of medieval masons in the Cotswolds, and his hearers were always enjoyably aware of and partakers in the zest with which he both pursued and presented his perceptions.

G. H. MARTIN

Sources G. W. S. Barrow, *PBA*, 82 (1993), 381–97 · *WWW* · E. Lemon, ed., *The Balliol College register, 1916–1967*, 4th edn (privately printed, Oxford, 1969) · N. P. Brooks and R. I. Moore, *The Independent* (25 March 1991)
Likenesses photograph, repro. in *The Independent* · photograph, repro. in Barrow, *PBA*
Wealth at death £174,732: probate, 1 July 1991, *CGPLA Eng. & Wales*

Davis, Richard (1617/18–1693×1700), bookseller, was baptized at All Saints' Church in Oxford on 16 August 1618, the third of eight children of William Davis (*fl.* 1609–1651), bookseller, and his wife, Mary (*d.* 1651). In December 1639 Richard followed his father by becoming a licensed university bookseller ('stationer'), as later did his brother Nicholas; their elder brother Thomas graduated from the university. Over the next few decades Richard Davis became Oxford's leading bookseller. Besides large holdings in theology, medicine, law, and the sciences, his stock—which included works from many continental presses—ranged from the esoteric (a Turkish grammar, a Syro-Chaldean dictionary, histories of Lapland and Barbados) to books on cookery or the propagation of vegetables. Aeschylus and Eusebius shared shelf space with Chaucer, Shakespeare, Milton, and Restoration drama. Among his customers were the antiquaries William Fulman (who bought and borrowed books by courier) and Anthony Wood.

From 1646 onwards Davis also made a major contribution to academic publishing, being solely or partly responsible for over 250 books; many, including works by Boyle, were scientific. Such was his reputation that when plague prevented the Royal Society from publishing three numbers of its *Philosophical Transactions* in London, they turned to Davis to produce them.

Davis's shop and home—the present 14–15 Oriel Street, Oxford—were leased him by Lincoln College, but in 1663 he also rented the old Congregation House from the university as a warehouse for his expanding stock. Soon afterwards drunken undergraduates on their way home late one night were puzzled to see a light in the building at that hour, and suspected an illegal conventicle; they thought these suspicions confirmed when, listening at the window, they heard Davis say 'O the bible! I had almost forgot the bible'. A proctor and other dons were hastily summoned, but they 'going with great speed and bursting open the doors … found none but Mr. Richard Davis the bookseller and his wife and boy looking out books to exchange at London' (*Life and Times of Anthony Wood*, 1.509).

Davis's first wife was dead by 21 April 1685, when he married Susannah Adams (1627/8–1700), widow—probably a connection, though not the relict, of his friend the bookseller John Adams. Wood sourly implies that this explains the subsequent collapse of Davis's business, since the following August he 'shut up his shopwindows for debt' (*Life and Times of Anthony Wood*, 3.157), but the expenses of Davis's publishing ventures are a more likely cause. His stock of over 40,000 books was sold off in four great sales (the catalogues of which survive) from 1686 to 1692. A contemporary pamphlet describes the interest these aroused, libraries and lecture halls emptying as scholars flocked to the saleroom. In spite of his reissue of three works in 1690, the bankruptcy effectively marked the end of Davis's career. In March 1693, when he was seventy-five, he was summoned as a witness in a libel suit; his signature is found in the records of the trial, but he had little information to give. Probably by February 1695 he was dead, for another tenant rented his house. He was certainly dead by 1700, when his widow died at the age of seventy-two.   MARGARET FOREY

Sources The life and times of Anthony Wood, ed. A. Clark, 5 vols., OHS, 19, 21, 26, 30, 40 (1891–1900) · parish register, Oxford, All Saints', 16 Aug 1618, Oxon. RO [baptism] · parish register, Oxford, All Saints', 20 April 1651, Oxon. RO [mother's burial] · parish register, Oxford, St Michael-by-the-North-Gate, Oxon. RO [burial, Susannah Davis] · Foster, Alum. Oxon. · Hist. U. Oxf. 4: 17th-cent. Oxf. · G. Smalridge, Auctio Davisiana Oxonii habita (1689) · C. L. Shadwell and H. E. Salter, Oriel College records, OHS, 85 (1926) · A. Wood, letters to W. Fulman, transcribed by A. Clark, 3 vols., Bodl. Oxf., MS Top. Oxon. e 101–3 · will, 20 Feb 1685, Oxf. UA, chancellor's court [J. Adams] · chancellor's court administration, 17 Sept 1668, Oxf. UA [N. Davis] · P. G. Morrison, Index of printers, publishers and booksellers in Donald Wing's 'Short-title catalogue of books … 1641–1700' (1955)
Wealth at death bankrupt in 1685, stock sold off 1686–92

Davis, Richard (1658–1714), Independent minister, was born probably in Cardiganshire, of unknown parents. He was educated in Wales, and at the age of eighteen moved to London to teach at a grammar school. During this time he lived with the family of John Langston (1640?–1704), under whose care and influence he remained for several years. Langston kept a school in London, perhaps the one at which Davis taught, before moving to Bedfordshire some time after 1679. Having experienced a religious conversion, Davis sought the advice of the celebrated John Owen, after which he resolved 'to follow the Lord fully' and became a member of the Independent church in Silver Street where Thomas Cole was minister (Maurice, 60). In or before 1689 he married Rosamund Williams (c.1644–1725).

In February 1690 Davis was called by the church at Rothwell, Northamptonshire, to be their minister and left the Silver Street church. A strict Independent, he soon caused offence amongst the neighbouring ministers by refusing them any part in his ordination. He quickly caused far greater offence by his aggressive itinerant preaching, his use of lay preachers, and his high Calvinism, described by his enemies as Antinomianism. Accused of 'Infecting and Disturbing the Country' and of 'dividing all Societies where he goes' (Rehakosht, 3, 4), Davis in a remarkably short time aroused the opposition of the neighbouring ministers in Northamptonshire and adjoining counties, who appealed to the united ministers in London. An attempt to prosecute him at the Northampton spring assizes in 1692 failed. Advised by his friends to defend himself from these attacks, Davis attended a meeting of the united ministers in London in summer 1692 when, he admitted, 'they treated me very civilly', but at the close of the conference Daniel Williams declared that 'he had many things against me in matters of Faith' (Davis, 38). Davis's offer to attend further meetings to clear himself was ignored. Williams was the principal opponent of high Calvinism, and his *Gospel-Truth*, published in May 1692, was intended to refute the Antinomian teachings of Tobias Crisp. Davis, however, recognized 'this plausible book, lashing not only at us, but at Religion itself, and the Orthodox Professors of it, over the Shoulders of Dr Crisp' (ibid., 6). At the same time a virulently personal attack, *A plain and just account of a most horrid and dismal plague begun at … Rothwell … which hath infected many places round about*, was published against Davis under a pseudonym by John King, Independent minister at Wellingborough. In autumn 1692 the united ministers deputed some of their number, including Williams, to examine witnesses against Davis at Kettering, but Davis refused to co-operate, dismissing the investigation as the 'Ketterin Inquisition'. The consequences of Davis's activities proved far-reaching, leading to the collapse of the 'happy union', the scheme to unite Presbyterians and Independents. The Independent ministers opposed the efforts to discipline Davis and in protest withdrew from the union.

During his first three years at Rothwell Davis exercised an extraordinarily active evangelical ministry. The first church book records that 109 members were admitted in 1690, 332 in 1691, and 198 in 1692. Thereafter admissions rarely exceeded twenty a year. After beginning in parishes close to Rothwell, by the early summer of 1691 Davis was actively preaching in Huntingdonshire. He reached Cambridgeshire later that year and was at Elsworth in September, Guyhirn by October, and Ely in January 1692. In

November he was admitting members from Wisbech. Davis was to burn himself out. By 1700 he was in poor health, rarely able to travel or preach. Although the revival he inspired was extraordinary in both scale and intensity, during the early 1690s dissenters experienced considerable growth and expansion elsewhere. Nevertheless, Davis stands apart from most of his contemporaries by the number of new churches he established: at Wellingborough, Northamptonshire, in October 1691; at Burwell, Cambridgeshire, in 1692; at Kimbolton, Huntingdonshire, in 1693; and at Ringstead, Northamptonshire, in 1714. He was also involved in helping others to establish churches, notably the church at Guyhirn under David Culy. The fervour of the early years is evident from the references to hysterical fits during meetings. Henry Sampson found Davis's preaching 'very affectionate but very rambling' (*Christian Reformer*, 1862, 245), but to Joseph Perry, one of those converted, he had 'a good Voice and a thundering Way of preaching' and 'his words seemed to stick like arrows in my soul' (Glass, 100, 103). Besides *Truth and Innocency* he published *Hymns Composed on Several Subjects* (2nd edition, 1694), *True Spring of Gospel, Sight and Sense of Sin* (c.1691), and *Faith, the Grand Evidence of our Interest in Christ* (1704), where the evangelical strain of his writing is particularly evident. He died at Rothwell on 11 September 1714 and was buried there in the parish church. His wife survived him. DAVID L. WYKES

Sources N. Glass, *Early history of the Independent church at Rothwell* (1871) · P. Rehakosht [J. King], *A plain and just account of a most horrid and dismal plague begun at Rowel, alias Rothwell, in Northamptonshire which hath infected many places round about* (1692) · R. Davis, *Truth and innocency vindicated, against falshood & malice* (1692) · M. Maurice, *Monuments of mercy* (1729) · G. F. Nuttall, 'Northamptonshire and The modern question: a turning-point in eighteenth-century dissent', *Journal of Theological Studies*, new ser., 16 (1965), 104–8 · R. Thomas, 'The break-up of nonconformity', *The beginnings of nonconformity: the Hibbert lectures* (1964), 33–60 · A. Gordon, ed., *Freedom after ejection: a review* (1690–1692) *of presbyterian and congregational nonconformity in England and Wales* (1917), 76, 184–7 · T. Coleman, *Memorials of the Independent churches in Northamptonshire; with biographical notices of their pastors, and some account of the puritan ministers who laboured in the county* (1853) · Northants. RO, probate inventory 1714/148A

Wealth at death £124 7s. 6d. personal estate: will, Northants. RO, probate inventory 1714/148A

Davis, Richard (1750–1814), surveyor, was baptized at Windsor on 22 July 1750, the second of four sons of John Davis (d. 1762), clockmaker and locksmith, and his wife, Anne (d. 1764). He entered Eton College on 24 May 1757 and left in 1761. The family had a long association with the college, maintaining the school clock and doing other small building works. His name next appears in a notice in *Jackson's Oxford Journal* of 6 October 1781, advertising his services in selling a gentleman's property in Stokenchurch, Oxfordshire, in which he describes himself as 'Land-Surveyor at Lewknor'. Another notice throws some light onto his missing years: 'RICHARD DAVIS, of LEWKNOR … (removed from Hammersmith) Surveys and Plans ESTATES, and transacts every other Kind of Business with respect to the Purchasing, Selling, or Letting of Estates, Houses &c. on the most reasonable Terms' (*Jackson's Oxford*

Journal, 23 March 1782, 3). Davis generally referred to himself as 'Richard Davis of Lewknor', as here, to avoid confusion with Richard Davis of nearby Bloxham, also a surveyor. In 1784 Davis secured his first commission; this was as surveyor to the enclosure in Stanford in the Vale and he prepared a map of the enclosure (now lost). In 1785 he undertook the survey and valuation of the manor of Stutteridge, near Stokenchurch, Oxfordshire. In 1786 Davis was appointed topographer to his majesty King George III by the earl of Salisbury, lord chamberlain of the household, and he retained this designation until his death. The royal appointment is not readily explicable although his grandfather had been clockmaker to George II and his father received the royal warrant as locksmith to Windsor Castle: but the appointment certainly gave a major impetus to Davis's career, and from then on his services were frequently sought as surveyor of estates as far afield as Wales; he was also commissioner to the enclosure in Oxfordshire and in Berkshire.

Davis's home at Lewknor was close to Oxford and he gained numerous commissions from Oxford colleges, including Merton College and New College, as well as from the university itself. In 1787 Davis was asked by Christ Church to survey the open fields and old enclosures in the parish of Benson, for which he also produced a beautifully penned terrier, with the titles highlighted in gold leaf, in which he used decimal fractions for both acreages and shilling values. This was one of several surveys he did for the college. Davis also worked for the board of agriculture, who in 1794 published his *General view of the agriculture of the county of Oxford with observations on the means of its improvement*, the forerunner of Arthur Young's edition of 1813. In his *View* Davis included a small-scale map of the county compiled by himself.

Davis's 'New map of the county of Oxford from an actual survey' was produced in response to the Society of Arts' encouragement of large-scale county mapping. In 1790, when the first advertisement for the map appeared, publication was planned for August 1792, but this turned out to be far too optimistic. The price for each map was to be 2½ guineas with 1 guinea to be paid at the time of subscribing. The map was finally published on 1 August 1797 by John Cary of the Strand, London, in sixteen sheets, at a scale of 2 inches to the mile (1:31,680), in an edition estimated to have been of no more than 200, of which 34 are known to be extant. The scale of 2 inches to the mile was chosen as it had been used by John Rocque for his map of neighbouring Berkshire. Subscribers' copies were numbered in the upper left-hand corner of the title sheet and signed by Davis. The map shows the Oxfordshire landscape before enclosure in most instances. An inset plan of the city of Oxford gives detailed and up-to-date information about changes in the city since previous maps were published. A facsimile edition by Oxfordshire County Libraries was published in 1975 under the editorship of Philip Riden.

Davis lived the comfortable existence of the country gentleman. He was fond of hunting and his name regularly appeared on the Oxfordshire game duty lists. As the owner of a sizeable estate Davis was active in local affairs and he frequently attended parish meetings. He was also head of a large family; with his wife, Anne—of whom nothing beyond her name is known—he had three sons and four daughters. Surveying various estates belonging to Oxford colleges and acting as commissioner to the enclosures provided Davis with a handsome income. By 1790 he could afford to buy an estate at Aston Rowant, Oxfordshire. He built a comfortable *cottage ornée* there called Grove Cottage where, on 10 January 1814, he died. He was buried in Lewknor churchyard on 15 January. Davis's wife and son Thomas managed the estate until 1832 when it was sold. Davis's other goods were divided between his surviving two daughters, Elizabeth and Caroline; the latter received also the copper plates of his survey of Oxfordshire. Davis is a good example of a successful estate and county surveyor who was simultaneously involved in the business of agricultural improvements.

LÁSZLÓ GRÓF

Sources L. Gróf, 'Richard Davis of Lewknor: land surveyor, estate agent and enclosure commissioner', *Map Collector*, 71 (1995), 32–7 · R. A. Austen-Leigh, ed., *The Eton College register, 1753–1790* (1921) · *Jackson's Oxford Journal* (1781–1814) · S. J. Barnes, *A handlist of inclosure acts and awards relating to the county of Oxford* (1975), 64–9 · R. Davies, ed., *Estate maps of Wales, 1600–1836* (1982), 11 and 47 · calendar of estate papers, typescript, Christ Church Oxf., vol. 6, 217 · 'Survey and terrier of Benson field', 1787, Christ Church Oxf., VIII.b.69–70 · overseer's minutes book, 1797–1814, parish of Aston Rowant, Oxfordshire archives · land tax assessments, Lewknor parish, 1790–1832, Oxfordshire archives, QSD L.184 · land tax assessments, Aston Rowant, 1790–1817, Oxfordshire archives, QSD L.16 · A. M. Lambert, 'Early maps and local studies', *Geography*, 41 (1956), 167–77 · parish register (burial), Lewknor, Oxfordshire archives, MS d.d.Par.Lewknor, b.3 · PRO, PROB 11/1553 · F. W. Steer and others, *Dictionary of land surveyors and local map-makers of Great Britain and Ireland, 1530–1850*, ed. P. Eden, 2nd edn, 2, ed. S. Bendall (1997), 136 · register of baptisms, New Windsor, Berks. RO, D/P 149/1/3 (17) · P. Ashworth, 'Davis of Windsor: a family business', *Windlesora*, 9 (1990), 2–9
Archives Bodl. Oxf., MS estate maps, terriers · Christ Church Oxf., MS estate maps, terriers · NL Wales, MS estate maps · Oxon. RO, Oxfordshire archives, MS estate maps, terriers
Wealth at death estates at Lewknor and Aston Rowant, Oxfordshire; also dwelling house with stable and coach house in Holywell Street, Oxford; three sums of mortgages totalling £2500; 'my copper plates containing the engravings of my survey of the county of Oxford'; also a herd of deer: will, PRO, PROB 11/1553

Davis, Richard Barrett (1782–1854), landscape and animal painter, was born at Watford, Hertfordshire, and baptized on 25 July 1782 at Hemel Hempstead, the eldest of the nine sons of Richard Davis (1750–1825), who became huntsman to George III's private harriers in 1789, and his wife, Sarah. At the end of the eighteenth century the hunt moved to Windsor, and it was here that the king saw and admired some drawings by the young Davis. Sir Francis Bourgeois RA, landscapist to the king, did not take pupils but, when told it was the royal wish, he became Davis's tutor in 1804. It is also said that Davis studied under Sir William Beechey RA. Subsequently the young artist studied at the Royal Academy Schools, although he was not registered as a pupil. Davis had already exhibited a landscape at the Royal Academy in 1802, and two landscapes

with cattle the following year. His progress and aptitude for animal painting was demonstrated by his picture *His Majesty in his Travelling Chariot Returning to Town from Windsor*, which was shown at the Royal Academy in 1805, and *Mares and Foals in his Majesty's Stud at Windsor* the following year. He started exhibiting at the British Institution in 1808 and at the Society (later Royal Society) of British Artists in 1827. At the last venue he regularly exhibited the maximum number of nine paintings allowed annually for the next ten years. He held various offices in the society, including briefly being president in 1832, ceasing to be a member in 1843. In 1828 he was made animal painter to George IV, and later held similar appointments to William IV and Queen Victoria. In 1831 he painted an enormous panoramic frieze (128 ft 4 in. long) of the coronation procession of William IV (Royal Collection).

William Henry Davis (*c*.1795–1885), a younger brother of R. B. Davis, initially painted similar subjects to his brother, but later turned to scenes from Shakespeare. W. H. Davis exhibited paintings at the Royal Academy and British Institution between 1803 and 1849. He was appointed animal painter to William IV in 1837 and to Queen Victoria in 1839. R. B. Davis's daughter, Sara, painted portraits and six of her miniatures were shown at the Royal Academy between 1846 and 1854. The majority of R. B. Davis's paintings shown at the Royal Academy were of horses including, in 1840, *Portrait of the Hermit, Celebrated in the Royal Hunt, the Property of her Majesty*, followed in 1842 by *Portrait of Mr Davis, her Majesty's Huntsman, on the Hermit*. This was Charles Davis, another younger brother, who became huntsman to the royal buckhounds in 1822, and held that post for forty-four years until his death in 1866. Without doubt the royal patronage and associations with hunting brought many commissions to the industrious R. B. Davis. Despite exhibiting regularly at the Royal Academy for fifty years, he was never elected as an associate of the academy. His output was variable but his honest, if slightly dull, portraits of horses and riders set in recognizable landscapes and of other animals (his painting of hounds was particularly fine) afforded him a comfortable income at this stage of his life. In 1836, in conjunction with the print publishers A. H. Bailey & Co., Davis started producing a series of prints of different hunts: *The Hunter's Annual*. This comprised pages of letterpress describing four contemporary packs of hounds, each with a hand-coloured lithographic equestrian portrait after paintings by the artist of their principal huntsman. These sets of four plates continued, in the series in 1838 and 1839, and in what was described as a second series, in 1841, *The Hunter's Annual* was in aquatint. A number of Davis's engagingly composed shooting scenes were also engraved, and he contributed thirty subjects for the *Sporting Magazine*. Towards the end of his life when Victorian morals led to hunting becoming less fashionable, commissions became fewer, as did the number of his paintings shown at the Royal Academy and the Society of British Artists. When he died on 13 March 1854, at his home, 9 Bedford Place, Kensington, London, as a result of a tetanus infection, he was a poor man, and left a widow, Lucy.

CHARLES LANE

Sources H. A. Bryden, 'Sporting pictures by R. B. Davis', *Country Life*, 62 (1927), 811–15 · M. H. Grant, *A chronological history of the old English landscape painters*, 3 vols. (1926–47), vol. 2, pp. 535–6 · S. Mitchell, *The dictionary of British equestrian artists* (1985) · Graves, *RA exhibitors* · Graves, *Brit. Inst.* · M. Bradshaw, ed., *Royal Society of British Artists: members exhibiting, 1824–1892* (1973) · Farington, *Diary*, 6.2222–3 · private information (2004) · will, PROB 6/230, fol. 352v · IGI · W. Gilbey, *Animal painters of England*, 3 vols. (1900–11)
Wealth at death £200: administration, PRO, 6/230, fol. 352v

Davis, Sir Robert Henry (1870–1965), inventor of diving and breathing apparatus, was born in London on 6 June 1870, the eldest son of Robert Davis, a detective in the City of London police force. In 1882, aged eleven, Davis entered the firm of Siebe, Gorman & Co. Ltd at Lambeth, manufacturers of diving equipment. His neat handwriting was noticed by Gorman, who placed him in the main office. He studied hard to complete his education out of office hours, and, still in his twenties, was promoted assistant manager. In 1900, when Davis married Margaret (d. 1952), daughter of William Tyrrell of Kildare, Gorman gave his gifted assistant a house and a gold watch as wedding presents. There were four sons and two daughters of this marriage. Davis rose successively to become general manager, managing director, governing director, and, in 1959, life president.

Siebe Gorman had long specialized in various types of diving and safety apparatus, but Davis vigorously developed and expanded the company's activities. In 1906 he perfected an oxygen breathing apparatus for mining rescue, and when, in April 1915, the German army launched its first gas attack on allied troops he immediately devised an emergency respirator, persuading friends, relations, and local families to manufacture it in great quantities, which were dispatched to France within 48 hours. Later Davis worked largely with the Royal Navy. He was a member, with Professor J. B. S. Haldane, Sir Leonard Hill, and Captain G. C. Damant, of the Admiralty deep sea diving committee which, in 1933, published decompression tables allowing safe ascents from depths down to 300 feet. Davis again co-operated with the Royal Navy on experiments which culminated in a record 'hard hat' dive to 540 feet in 1948. The submariners' escape method after 1929 was based on the Davis submerged escape apparatus, which incorporated a breathing bag with an oxygen supply from a small bottle and a chemical agent for absorbing carbon dioxide before exhaled breath was returned to the bag. The apparatus incorporated the hazard of breathing more or less pure oxygen under pressure. Siebe Gorman next proposed built-in breathing equipment for supplying a safe mixture of air to escapers—until the moment of exit—from large bottles attached to the submarine. In 1951 this equipment, used with immersion suits, started to replace the earlier apparatus for free ascent from submarines.

During the Second World War, Siebe Gorman, relocated at Chessington, Surrey, assisted in the development of 'chariots'—the so-called human torpedoes, also X-craft, and other midget submarines, human mine clearance units, and anti-blast clothing. In 1951 the firm helped to pioneer the use of underwater television to investigate the sinking of the submarine *Affray* and the Comet aircraft disasters, and in 1953 it provided oxygen sets for the successful British climbing expedition to Mount Everest.

Davis devoted his life to the study of problems confronting those called on to work in unbreathable atmospheres. Among several publications his most important and comprehensive was *Deep Diving and Submarine Operations* (1920), which had run to six editions by 1955. His total absorption for sixty-two years with Siebe Gorman, in a field where his expertise was unrivalled, virtually precluded other interests. Knighted in 1932, and awarded an honorary DSc by Birmingham University, he attended the office regularly until 1964, although he had formally retired in 1960. He died at his home, San Toi, Jackson Close, Epsom, on 29 March 1965. RICHARD COMPTON-HALL

Sources *The Times* (3 April 1965), 10g · *WWW* · personal knowledge (2004) · D. Young, *The man in the helmet* (1963) · d. cert. · CGPLA Eng. & Wales (1965)
Wealth at death £112,930: probate, 15 June 1965, CGPLA Eng. & Wales

Davis, Sir Rupert Charles Hart- (1907–1999), publisher and writer, was born on 28 August 1907 at 79 Victoria Road, Kensington. Through his mother, Sybil Mary (1886–1927), daughter of Sir Alfred *Cooper FRCS and Lady Agnes Duff, he was directly descended from the duke of Clarence—later King William IV—and his mistress Dorothy Jordan, the famous actress and singer. The paternal line was more uncertain: ostensibly he was the son of Sybil's husband Richard Vaughan Hart-Davis (d. 1964), a stockbroker, for whom he never greatly cared; but he himself gradually became certain that his true father was Gervase Beckett (1866–1937), brother of the second Lord Grimthorpe, and his contemporaries among the Beckett family tended to agree with him.

After four years at Stanmore Park in Middlesex, in April 1921 Hart-Davis went on to Eton College; but five months later he fell gravely ill with what he described as an 'internal abscess' in the abdomen. He remained a semi-invalid for most of 1922, undergoing two operations and returning to school only in September. The next two years were blighted by continued ill health and homesickness; only during the last two, when he found congenial friends, was he happy. In October 1926 he went up to Balliol College, Oxford; but his first term was clouded by anxiety for his mother, to whom he had written every day throughout his schooldays and who had sunk into a severe depression. She died on 3 January 1927. 'I realised', he wrote, 'that my life, as I had known it so far, was over' (Hart-Davis, *Arms of Time*, 145). Two months later he left Oxford for good, without a degree.

Hart-Davis loved the theatre, and had acted both at Eton and with the Oxford University Dramatic Society (OUDS); he now became a student at the Old Vic. His stage career—'brief, almost mute and wholly inglorious' (Hart-Davis, *Power of Chance*, 23)—lasted only just long enough for him

Sir Rupert Charles Hart-Davis (1907–1999), by unknown photographer

to meet the actress Peggy Ashcroft [*see* Ashcroft, Dame Edith Margaret Emily (1907–1991)]. They were married on 23 December 1929; already two months before, however, he had joined the publishing firm of William Heinemann, finally embarking on the profession that would occupy him for most of his working life. He left Heinemann in 1932 for a brief spell with the Book Society, and in the following year became a director of Jonathan Cape Ltd.

Hart-Davis's first marriage soon ended in divorce (though the two remained firm friends). On 25 November 1933 he married Catherine Comfort Borden-Turner (1910–1970), with whom he had a daughter, Bridget, in 1935 and a son, Duff, in the following year. A happy family life followed until the war—when, in 1940, he joined the Coldstream Guards and Catherine sailed with the children to America. She returned in 1941; their younger son, Adam, was born in July 1943.

Demobilized in 1945, in January 1946 Hart-Davis founded with his friend David Garnett the firm of Rupert Hart-Davis Ltd, which enjoyed immediate critical—though not financial—success; but this was countered by much domestic unhappiness. Probably during her year in America his wife had contracted Huerger's disease, a rare condition brought about by excessive smoking, which eventually reduced her to what he described as a 'benevolent automaton' (Hart-Davis, *Halfway to Heaven*, 13). From 1946 her place in his affections was taken by Ruth Simon, *née* Ware (d. 1967), and he would spend the working week

in London; unwilling, however, to break up a young family, he returned home—Bromsden Farm, near Henley-on-Thames—every weekend.

In March 1952, after six years' work, Hart-Davis published his biography of Hugh Walpole which received enthusiastic reviews both in Britain and America; and in October 1955 there began his correspondence with his old Eton master George Lyttelton, which was to continue—with some 600 letters altogether—until Lyttelton's death in 1962. By now, however, his firm's fortunes were causing serious concern. He published distinguished books, all superbly produced, but he was no businessman; late in 1955 he sold his firm to Heinemann—keeping, however, his name, premises, and editorial authority. It was a decision he soon had reason to regret.

Succeeding Harold Nicolson as chairman of the London Library in 1957, Hart-Davis inherited a crisis: the library, hitherto exempt, was called on to pay rates of some £5000 a year. A sale at Christies, for which he collected items which included manuscripts of *A Passage to India* and *The Waste Land*, raised £25,000 and saved the day. Meanwhile, however, his relations with Heinemann had reached breaking point; this time the saviour was—or appeared to be—Bill Jovanovich, president of the New York publishers Harcourt Brace, who bought the firm in 1962; but scarcely a year later he decided to liquidate it. Hart-Davis was threatened with ruin, and several London publishers cut off all relations with Jovanovich; fortunately the business was sold to Granada Television in the nick of time.

The Letters of Oscar Wilde, on which Hart-Davis had worked for the past seven years—and the quality of whose footnotes set new standards for all subsequent editors—was published in 1962. In 1964 his wife agreed to a divorce and on 19 October, 'after eighteen years of longing' (Hart-Davis, *Halfway to Heaven*, 65), he and Ruth Simon were married, settling at the Old Rectory in the Yorkshire village of Marske in Swaledale; but little more than two years later, on 31 January 1967—a week before he received his knighthood for services to literature—she died of a sudden heart attack. It was the greatest blow of his life: his family and friends wondered whether he would survive. On 12 April, however, his old friend June Williams, *née* Clifford, a widow who had been his secretary in the early 1950s, came to help him with his correspondence, and on 13 June 1968 they were married.

Hart-Davis's bluff, military bearing concealed a character of deep sensitivity. The remaining years of his life were spent happily in Yorkshire, writing, editing, and watching cricket. *The Catalogue of Max Beerbohm's Caricatures* was published in 1972, on Beerbohm's hundredth birthday; the six volumes of the Lyttelton–Hart-Davis correspondence between 1978 and 1984; and the first volume of autobiography, *The Arms of Time*, in 1979. In 1981 he published the first volume of the diaries of Siegfried Sassoon and was awarded a DLitt by Durham University; two years later he sold his library of some 17,000 volumes to the University of Tulsa, Oklahoma—keeping it, however, until his death. In 1991 came his second autobiographical volume, *The Power of Chance*. The third, *Halfway to Heaven*, appeared in

1998. He also edited *More Letters of Oscar Wilde* (1985) and—with Wilde's grandson Merlin Holland—*The Complete Letters of Oscar Wilde* (2000), which he did not live to see published. Hart-Davis died at the Friarage Hospital, Northallerton, on 8 December 1999 and was buried at Marske churchyard on 20 December.   JOHN JULIUS NORWICH

Sources WW · R. Hart-Davis, *The arms of time* (1979) · R. Hart-Davis, *The power of chance* (1991) · R. Hart-Davis, *Halfway to heaven* (1998) · personal knowledge (2004) · private information (2004) · *The Lyttleton–Hart-Davis letters: correspondence of George Lyttleton and Rupert Hart-Davis*, 6 vols. (1978–84)
Archives priv. coll., personal and family MSS · University of Tulsa, Oklahoma | BL, corresp. with Sir S. Cockerell, Add. MS 52718 · CUL, papers relating to S. Sassoon · Harvard U., Houghton L., letters to T. Bosanquet · JRL, letters to *Manchester Guardian* · U. Sussex, corresp. with Leonard Woolf · University of Bristol Library, corresp. and statements relating to trial of *Lady Chatterley's lover*
Likenesses A. John, drawing, 1923, priv. coll. · D. Hankinson, drawing, priv. coll. · photograph, Camera Press, London [*see illus.*]
Wealth at death £920,000: probate, *CGPLA Eng. & Wales*

Davis, Samuel (1760–1819), East India Company servant and orientalist, was born in the West Indies, the younger son of John Davis, who held the post there of commissary-general, and his Welsh wife (*née* Phillips). He went to England with his mother and two sisters after the death of his father. Despite the evident poverty of the family, Davis appears to have received a good education, although the details are lost.

In 1778 he was nominated a cadet for Madras by Laurence Sulivan, a director of the East India Company, and sailed for India in the *Earl of Oxford*, arriving at Madras in 1780. In 1783 he was selected by Warren Hastings to accompany a second mission to Bhutan and Tibet as 'Draftsman and Surveyor'. The purpose of the mission, led by Hastings's kinsman Samuel Turner, was to renew British contact with the court of the Panchen Lama first established in 1774 by George Bogle. The Tibetan authorities, however, refused to allow a greater number into their territory than had accompanied the Bogle mission. Davis, whose surveying skills may have excited Tibetan suspicions, was left behind in Bhutan and returned to India alone, though not before he had made a very careful documentation in watercolour and pencil of Bhutanese architecture and topography. The qualities of visual accuracy and warm sympathy apparent in his drawings are found also in the diary he kept in Bhutan, extracts of which appeared posthumously in *Remarks on the Religious and Social Institutions of the Bouteas, or Inhabitants of Boutan* (1830). In this he provided a useful account of 'the handsomest race I ever saw', their theocratic government, and many aspects of their Buddhist culture and society. (He was far less happy with the appearance of Bhutanese women and their customary treatment by men.)

In August 1783 Davis was appointed to a writership in Calcutta, and this was soon followed by the post of assistant to the collector of Bhagalpur and registrar of the *adalat* there. He was promoted first assistant in 1787 and factor in 1788, before becoming collector of Burdwan in 1793. It was at the beginning of his career at Bhagalpur

that he first made the acquaintance of the brilliant scholar and lawyer, Sir William Jones, whose intimate friend and collaborator he now became. Davis was an active member of the Asiatic Society of Bengal, founded by Jones, and he emerged in due course as the acknowledged expert of the period on Indian astronomy (*jyotisa*). Basing himself mainly on the modern *Suryasiddhanta* and its commentary, he produced two papers of a superb technical quality in the society's *Asiatick Researches*: 'On the astronomical computations of the Hindus' (1790) and 'On the Indian cycle of sixty years' (1792). Among Jones's surviving letters there are more addressed to Davis than to any other individual, and it is clear that it was only in their close relationship that the main purpose of the Asiatic Society, as envisioned by Jones, in encouraging systematic, collaborative research was actually achieved. In 1792 he was elected a fellow of the Royal Society at the initiative of Sir Joseph Banks. He also became friends at this time with Thomas Daniell and his nephew William, perhaps the greatest of British painters in the East in this period, whom he had earlier known in London. Much later, in 1813, William Daniell produced six aquatints based on Davis's Bhutan paintings, and a further six in 1816 based on his views of the island of St Helena. While sketching with the Daniells at the ancient city of Gaur, Davis was attacked by a bear and left lame for life. (He shot the bear as soon as he had recovered sufficiently from his wounds.) While still at Burdwan, in August 1794 Davis married Henrietta Boileau, who was from an aristocratic French family that had settled in England as refugees early in the century. They were to have four sons and seven daughters. The eldest son, Sir John Francis *Davis (1795–1890), became the first governor of Hong Kong. During Davis's next posting as magistrate at Benares, 1795–1800, he had to face an insurrection by the deposed nawab of Oudh, Wazir Ali. On finding his house attacked, he placed his family on the roof and, unaided, guarded the only access to it with the aid of a pike. (His protégé Mountstuart Elphinstone would visit Davis's widow every year in London on the anniversary of the insurrection to do puja to the pike.)

The remainder of Davis's Indian career was spent in a succession of posts in Calcutta, ending as accountant-general of India in 1804. In 1806 he retired and left with his family for England. He was elected a director of the East India Company in 1810 and re-elected in 1814 and 1819. As co-author (with James Cumming) of the fifth report on East India Company affairs (1812), Davis's talents and reforming zeal were fully employed in the attempt to reconsider the foundations of the company's rule of India. He died at his home, Birdhurst Lodge, near Croydon, on 16 June 1819.   MICHAEL ARIS

Sources M. Aris, ed., *Views of medieval Bhutan: the diary and drawings of Samuel Davis, 1783* (1982) · S. Turner, *An account of an embassy to the court of the Teshoo Lama in Tibet* (1800) · J. F. Davis, *Vizier Ali Khan, or, The massacre of Benares, a chapter in British India* (1871) · W. F. B. Laurie, 'Samuel Davis, BCS, FRS, and the domestic Thermopylae at Benares', *Sketches of some distinguished Anglo-Indians*, 2nd ser. (1888) ·

G. H. Jones, *The letters of Sir William Jones*, 2 vols. (1970) • W. Daniell, *Views in India* (1813) • M. Archer, *Early views of India: the picturesque journeys of Thomas and William Daniell, 1786–1794* (1980) • T. Sutton, *The Daniells: artists and travellers* (1954) • N. R. Ray, 'Samuel Davis in the Victoria memorial collection', *Bulletin of the Victoria Memorial* [Calcutta], 6–7 (1972–3), 36–42 • B. Stein, *Thomas Munro: the origins of the colonial state and his vision of empire* (1989) • K. Ballhatchet, 'The authors of the fifth report of 1812', *N&Q*, 202 (1957), 477–8 • BL OIOC, N/1/4, 163
Archives BL OIOC, letters to the board of revenue from Burdwan, MSS Eur. B 90–91

Davis, Thomas (1749–1807), estate steward and agriculturist, was born on 11 July 1749 at Penton Mewsey, Hampshire, son of Thomas Davis, an itinerant excise officer then based there, and his wife, Elizabeth. Davis received a good classical education at a school in Devizes, Wiltshire, and in December 1763 he was taken into the estates offices of Thomas Thynne, third Viscount Weymouth, later first marquess of Bath. These were in the west front of Longleat House, Warminster, under the chief steward, Simon Jude Cole (1703–1787). On 9 June 1772 Davis married Mary Coombs (1744–1814) at Longbridge Deverill. They had six surviving children, three sons and three daughters. In 1777 Cole was superannuated and moved to nearby Horningsham. Davis took over his apartments and offices at Longleat, after fourteen years as Cole's assistant, and became chief steward to the first and second marquesses, serving their houses in Wiltshire and London and their extensive estates in England and Ireland. Davis's salary was an annual £100, which was considerably supplemented by receipts from the sale of timber, from lands he leased nearby, and from his other occupations. He proved a wonderful manager, having in 1787 improved accountability by introducing separate household and land accounts. In November 1796, after the death of the first marquess of Bath, Davis moved from Longleat House into offices in Horningsham.

Davis also started a notable career as an agriculturist. He had joined the Bath and West of England Agricultural Society by 1782, and started contributing to their published *Letters and Papers* from volume 3 (published 1786). In 1793 he was asked by the board of agriculture to contribute the volume on Wiltshire to their series of county agricultural reports. This was one of the first to be delivered to members, in January 1794, and has ever since been regarded as 'perhaps the best of all the agricultural *Reports*' (R. E. Prothero, Baron Ernle, *English Farming, Past and Present*, 1961, 233). It divided Wiltshire between the north-west vale lands lying under the chalk hills and the south-east Wiltshire chalk downs. These were divided by geology along the foot of the chalk hills.

In 1792 Davis had surveyed the enclosure of Bagendon, near Cirencester, with the surveyor Edward Webb (1751–1828), an estate which then belonged to the marquess of Bath. At a meeting of the Bath Society, Davis met the geologist William Smith, a recent pupil of Webb's. In 1796 Davis introduced Smith to the Revd Benjamin Richardson (1758–1831), who started to champion Smith's remarkable geological results, as did Davis, who, as soon as he heard of Smith's pioneering work on strata, had commented that 'the only way to know the true value of land' was in the light of such geological knowledge (J. Phillips, *Memoirs of William Smith*, 1844, 16). At some early point during his stewardship a shaft in search of coal was put down on an outlying part of the Longleat estate; geological enquiry would help to prevent similar unprofitable investments.

Davis started to make use of Smith's results in his other careers as land agent and valuer. The best example of this work is the discreet and careful way he negotiated the purchase of the Eastbury and Gunville estates in Dorset for the Wedgwood family between 1800 and 1806. Davis also encouraged Smith with his work on water meadows, published in 1806. Their connections had been cemented in 1802 when Smith took on as his Bath partner Jeremiah Cruse (1758–1819), whose son of the same name (1781–1861) served the Longleat estates under four stewards for more than sixty-seven years. Davis's own gratitude to him is shown by the £100 he left in his will to the younger Cruse, 'his faithful clerk as a token of my esteem and regard for him'.

Many agricultural papers flowed from Davis's prolific pen between 1786 and 1808. These were on woodland and marshland management, dairy and arable farming, planting, wool, sheep, oak for the navy, grassland, blight in wheat, compensation for tithes, leasing on lives, plans for labourers' cottages, and other philanthropy, including the supply of milk to the poor. Davis's papers went not only to the Bath Society, but to other publications of the board of agriculture, to William Nicholson's *Journal of Natural Philosophy*, and to Arthur Young's *Annals of Agriculture*, though he was not always on good terms with Young because of 'a very rude illiberal attack' which Young made on him concerning sheep management at a public meeting of the Bath Agricultural Society in the 1790s (Stone, 196).

Davis was also long active as an independent land surveyor throughout the western counties, from the duchy of Cornwall's lands into Gloucestershire. He also served as clerk, surveyor, commissioner, and solicitor (although not in the modern legal sense) in enclosure work from 1763. Here he was regarded as 'a Commissioner of great reputation' (Sinclair, 331), particularly in Wiltshire. The words on his monumental inscription in Horningsham church, Wiltshire, which Davis composed himself, reveal his pride that such 'works have contributed so much to the beauty of [that] country and the comfort of its inhabitants'. Davis was a notable improver who became active in the affairs of his local canal, the Dorset and Somerset Canal, sadly one of the least successful after its promotion in January 1793. He served on its first committee (1793) and in 1803 became a proprietor. Davis was also active as a botanist and a historian, contributing to the work of his fellow Wiltshire historian John Britton, and for a short time (1802–04) he was a member of the London-based Society of Arts.

On 9 November 1807, at a meeting of the court baron at

Frome, Somerset, Davis suffered a paralytic stroke. He died the next day and was buried inside Horningsham church on 16 November 1807. The extent of the loss his sudden death created can be gauged from this, from the printed funeral sermon issued in 1807, from the fine monument by Henry Westmacott (1784–1861) put up to his memory in Horningsham church, and from the attendance at his funeral by the second marquess and both his brothers, Lord George Thynne (1770–1838) and Lord John Thynne (1772–1849). This was a solemn occasion which 'testified how much their departed friend was beloved in life, and lamented in death' (*Monthly Magazine*, 24.511). The wording of a tablet which the Bath Society intended to erect was equally impressive. Its secretary William Matthews (1747–1816) paid his own tribute: 'whoever was personally acquainted with Thomas Davis, and *thousands* were, cannot fail to regret his removal, as a kind and warm-hearted associate; as a skilful arbiter of human rights; as a peace maker and as a good example in civil and social life' (Matthews, 271).

After his death Davis's agricultural report on Wiltshire was improved and re-issued in enlarged second (1811) and third editions (1813) by his eldest son Thomas Davis (1777–1839), who succeeded him as steward of the Longleat estates and retained the post until his own death. William Marshall, 'not finding this any improvement', could still write that he 'preferred the original' version in 1818 (W. Marshall, *Review and Abstract of the County Reports*, 1818, 184). H. S. TORRENS

Sources D. P. Gunstone, 'Stewardship and landed society: a study of the stewards of Longleat', MA thesis, University of Exeter, 1972 · R. C. Hoare, *The history of modern Wiltshire*, 1/2: Hundred of Heytesbury (1822), 53, 266 · *Letters and papers on agriculture, planting, &c.*, Bath and West of England Agricultural Society, 3–11 (1786–1808) · D. Burnett, *Longleat: the story of an English country house* (1978) · K. R. Clew, *The Dorset and Somerset canal* (1971) · T. Stone, *A review of the corrected agricultural survey of Lincolnshire* (1800), 196–200 · J. Sinclair and A. Young, *General report on enclosures: drawn up by order of the board of agriculture* (1808) · L. Blomefield, 'Letter from Mr Stephens to Mr Davis', *Proceedings of Bath Natural History and Antiquarian Field Club*, 3 (1877), 12–20 · E. Meteyard, *A group of Englishmen, 1795–1815* (1871) · T. Bunn, *Answers to inquiries respecting Frome Selwood* (1851), 33–5 · W. Matthews, 'Notice of Thomas Davis', *Letters and papers of Bath Agricultural Society*, 11 (1807), xii, 271–2 · *Farmers Magazine*, 9 (1808), 137 · *GM*, 1st ser., 77 (1807), 1084 · *Monthly Magazine*, 24 (1807), 511 · will, PRO, PROB 11/1473, fol. 103
Archives Keele University, Wedgwood archives, letters · Longleat House, letters
Likenesses Neele, engraving, repro. in T. Davis, *General view of the agriculture of Wiltshire*, ed. T. Davis, 2nd edn (1811), frontispiece

Davis, Thomas Osborne

Davis, Thomas Osborne (1814–1845), politician and journalist, was born at Mallow, co. Cork, on 24 October 1814, not on 16 October as has sometimes been asserted. His father, James Thomas Davis, held a commission in the British army, and as a surgeon in the Royal Artillery was for many years stationed in Dublin. Appointed head of the British ordnance medical department in Portugal, he was on his way there when he died at Exeter, Devon, in September 1814, a month before Thomas, his sixth child, was born. Of these children only four lived to adulthood: the

Thomas Osborne Davis (1814–1845), by Sir Frederic William Burton [posthumous]

three brothers John, James, and Thomas, and their sister Charlotte. Dr Davis's family was of Welsh origin, long settled in England. Davis's mother, Mary Atkins, traced her ancestry to a Cromwellian settler whose descendants, though occasionally intermarrying with Irish families, continued protestants in the English interest. On a fragment of his remaining papers Davis had written that he was brought up a high tory and episcopalian protestant. In his maternal ancestry there was a great-grandmother who belonged to the Gaelic O'Sullivan Beare family of co. Cork. Davis's eldest brother, John Nicholas Atkins Davis, like his father a medical doctor, was also a famous genealogist, known in Dublin as 'pedigree Davis'. Of him Davis once wrote that 'there is no family in Munster but he knows the pedigree of' (Duffy, *Davis*, 174). Davis's mature ambition to bring Irishmen of whatever origin to work for their common country may well be traced to this knowledge of his own mixed ancestry.

When Davis was four his mother moved her family to Dublin, settling first at Warrington Place and later at 61 (now 67) Lower Baggot Street, where Davis lived his brief life, and where he died in 1845. Some of his early education was at a school on Lower Mount Street kept by a Mr Mongan, from which he entered Trinity College in 1831. There is little evidence of Davis's early years except that he was dreamy, self-absorbed, and quickly emotional. Of his knowledge of Ireland during his youth little is known, except that he spent holidays in co. Tipperary, where an aunt was the wife of the Anglican rector in Templederry. At Trinity he was known as a steady plodding student, reading on a wide variety of subjects—history, law, political philosophy—and works of travel. In his own eyes he was filling the gaps he found in the Trinity curriculum. After graduation in 1836, Davis went to London to keep his terms as a law student, and was called to the bar in 1838. He did not practise. In 1837 he had privately printed a pamphlet, *The Reform of the Lords*, arguing for an elected upper house, though leaving it with an absolute power of rejecting bills.

A succession of authors commenting on the origins of Davis's nationalism have suggested that it was the result of a journey before 1840 to Germany, where he was influenced by the writings of Lessing, Herder, Fichte, and the Schlegels. No solid evidence of any continental or German visit exists, but rather more telling is the statement in Duffy's biography that Davis had never travelled. A manuscript in Davis's own hand states that his ideas of national independence and national policy had been formed in the historical societies of Trinity College, Dublin, and came from Trinity College protestants and a few Roman Catholics. Moreover, there was Davis's own early admiration for Daniel O'Connell. In the debates in the Trinity College Historical Society Davis played a prominent part and as president in 1840 delivered an address on 'The utility of debating societies in remedying the defects of a university education'. This address ranged widely over many subjects, and its famous sentence 'Gentlemen, you have a country' has been seen as Davis's public début as an Irish nationalist. It was also an appeal for reform, for the improvement of education at all levels, and for the responsibilities of the educated classes in an age of growing democracy. It indicates the influence on Davis's thinking of Alexis De Tocqueville's *Democracy in America* (1835).

In 1841, with his Trinity friend John Blake Dillon, Davis joined O'Connell's recently formed Loyal National Repeal Association. Journalism rather than law attracted him and between 1839 and 1843 he wrote articles for *The Citizen*, a monthly journal later called the *Dublin Monthly Magazine*, founded by members of the Trinity College Historical Society. These articles—on Grattan's parliament, on India, on Afghanistan, on the Irish parliament of 1689 and on peasant proprietorship—suggested Davis's promise as journalist, politician, and historian. In the spring of 1841 both Davis and Dillon wrote for the Dublin *Morning Register*, an engagement which ended after six months. An acquaintance with Charles Gavan Duffy, the successful editor of the *Belfast Vindicator*, led to discussions on Irish journalism and in 1842 a decision on the part of all three to found a weekly journal to be called *The Nation*. Its first issue appeared on 15 October 1842. The prospectus, written except for one sentence by Davis, had renewal as its theme: emancipation from old and tired issues and the direction of the popular mind and the sympathies of educated men to nationality and the blessings of domestic legislation. The journal endeavoured to bring all Irishmen of whatever origin to patriotic action for their common country. *The Nation* was at once successful, its circulation soon far higher than that of any other Dublin paper. Although Duffy was an outstanding editor, *The Nation* was very much Davis's paper in its intellectual qualities, and in the number of essays, editorials, book reviews, and smaller pieces written by him. During the first year, Davis had written about 210 essays and editorials; and between 1842 and 1845 he published about eighty poems. Duffy was the second most frequent contributor, and sometimes he and Davis wrote most of the paper. For his work Davis received £500 a year—a considerable sum for those days.

At Duffy's urging Davis tried his hand at poetry, and his first effort, 'Lament for the Death of Owen Roe O'Neill', was followed by other poems recalling famous incidents, military engagements, tragedies, and disasters in Irish history. There were songs and love poems as well. Critics of Davis have noted the disparity between *The Nation's* editorial advocacy of non-violence, following O'Connell, and the martial and military cast of so much of Davis's poetry; but the poems were meant to give Irishmen the history they would never hear in the national schools, and to arouse pride in their country's past. *The Nation* was very much a part of the heated atmosphere surrounding O'Connell's mass meetings for repeal during the spring and summer of 1843. After Peel proscribed O'Connell's planned monster meeting at Clontarf in October 1843, followed in 1844 by O'Connell's trial for conspiracy and by his brief imprisonment, *The Nation* entered a new phase, keeping up enthusiasm for a now distant repeal of the union.

During 1844, while O'Connell and Duffy were imprisoned, Davis, acting with William Smith O'Brien, who had become a repealer, prepared reports on various governmental issues, and assumed heavy responsibilities for *The Nation*. In the newspaper he urged the election to parliament of men of character and ability who would stand together for Irish reform. He was also editing the speeches of John Philpot Curran which were published in 1845. His biography of Wolfe Tone was to remain unfinished, indeed hardly begun, at his death. Working in the general committee of the Repeal Association, Davis rarely spoke in public. In May 1845, however, he encouraged the association to welcome Peel's bill for Irish higher education, and to rejoice in the three projected colleges where Catholic and protestant students would be educated together. Despite his endorsement of amendments which would protect the faith and morals of students, Davis was harshly attacked by O'Connell for his stand for secular education. The quarrel was made up, though opinions did not change.

By 1845 Duffy, Davis, and Dillon had become the centre of a group of young men who contributed to *The Nation* and who talked and planned together. A journalist called them Young Ireland, and the name remained. Their history would be written in the 1880s by Gavan Duffy. Close to *The Nation's* founders were John Pigot, John O'Hagan, and Denny Lane of Cork. But Duffy, in his historical works, left no doubt that Davis was their true leader. His wide knowledge, his frank, unpretentious manner, his good nature and fairness attracted friends who would remember him with affection. Writing in 1890, John O'Hagan recalled in him 'a grace of nature and manner which never failed to attract'. Among Dublin's intellectual circles there were many, notably Samuel Ferguson, who disagreed with Davis's nationalist politics but remained his friends.

In the late summer of 1845 Davis became engaged to marry Annie Hutton, whom he had first met in 1843. In early September he became ill with what he described in a note to Duffy as 'some sort of cholera, and perhaps a slight scarlatina'. Dr Stokes was in attendance. A few days later Davis wrote of 'a horrid sore throat'. Improvement was followed by a relapse and on 16 September Davis died at his home in Lower Baggot Street. He was buried in Mount Jerome cemetery. A public funeral attended by those prominent in Dublin's political and cultural life attested to the regard which he had won from all shades of opinion. Commemorative articles in The Nation, where his poems had appeared under the name The Celt, revealed his life and identity to a wider public. In 1846 Gavan Duffy edited Davis's prose articles, and in the same year Thomas Wallis published a collection of his poems. Both volumes went through many editions. A statue by the sculptor John Hogan now stands in the foyer of the Dublin city hall across from that of O'Connell.

Davis was politically moderate, even though unwavering in his ultimate goals. He wanted true independence for Ireland, but was at one point prepared to accept as a step on the way a subordinate parliament. Probably his goal was the responsible representative government which Canada in the 1840s was attaining and which Duffy was to endorse in 1848. Peasant proprietorship on the land must come, but not by violent means. The fervour with which he wrote sometimes concealed his moderation. His hostility to England and to the landlords was a bitter legacy, but in the case of the landlords he could also see their problems. Much of Davis's patriotism was non-political. Preservation and improvement are themes which thread their way through his Nation essays. There must be no road through New Grange; old buildings and older ruins must be saved; Irish music and the Irish language should be cherished. The Irish language, a precious cultural inheritance, was necessary for writing the early history of the country, and for understanding its nomenclature and place names as well as its soul and spirit. He advocated education at every level and set great store by repeal reading-rooms, public lectures, and provision for healthful amusements. Often cited as opposed to modernization, he urged industrial education, hoping that in Ireland, should industrialization come, its worst effects might be avoided.

If Davis has affinities with English Victorian reformers, in Ireland he also belongs, outside political nationalism, in a line of descent going back to the Royal Dublin Society (1731) and to the Royal Irish Academy (1785), and forward to the work of George Russell and Horace Plunkett. His own deepest ambition was to write a history of Ireland, and at one time he sought a leave of absence from The Nation to begin it. He was much attracted to the romantic historical writing of Augustin Thierry. His Citizen essays on the 1689 parliament of James II won high praise from the historian Lecky, but were republished only in 1893 (as The Patriot Parliament). In all the cultural, artistic, and historical activities of Dublin in the 1840s Davis was deeply involved, and in January 1845 he became a member of the Royal Irish Academy. His untimely death caused much speculation, both then and since, on what his life might have become. The dedicated patriotism of Davis's life made him ever afterwards an example and an inspiration to Irishmen of widely different political views.

HELEN F. MULVEY

Sources The Nation (1842–5) · K. MacGrath, 'Writers in The Nation, 1842–5', Irish Historical Studies, 6 (1948–9), 189–223 · T. W. Moody, 'Thomas Davis and the Irish nation', Hermathena, 103 (1966), 5–31 · C. G. Duffy, Young Ireland: a fragment of Irish history, 1840–1845, 2nd edn (1880) · C. G. Duffy, Thomas Davis: the memoirs of an Irish patriot (1890) · The Citizen (1839–43) [later the Dublin Monthly Magazine] · T. S. C. Dagg, College Historical Society: a history, 1770–1920 (privately printed, [Cork], 1969) · The voice of the nation: a manual of nationality by the writers of the 'Nation' newspaper, 5th edn (1844) · J. M. Hone, ed., The love story of Thomas Davis, told in the letters of Annie Hutton (1945) · [S. Ferguson], 'Our portrait gallery, no. XLII: Thomas Davis', Dublin University Magazine, 29 (1847), 190–99 · J. O'Hagan, 'Irish patriotism: Thomas Davis', Contemporary Review, 58 (1890), 592–608 · D. J. O'Donoghue, ed., Essays, literary and historical by Thomas Davis (1914) · D. G. Boyce, Nationalism in Ireland (1982) · parish register (baptism), Mallow, co. Cork

Archives NL Ire. · Royal Irish Acad., notebooks, literary MSS, and corresp. · TCD | NL Ire., J. Atkins Davis MSS · NL Ire., papers relating to collaboration with Sir C. G. Duffy · NL Ire., Gavan Duffy MSS · NL Ire., Smith O'Brien MSS · NL Ire., letters to Thomas Wyse · Royal Irish Acad., Gavan Duffy MSS · TCD, love poems to Annette Hutton

Likenesses J. P. Haverty, group portrait, lithograph with watercolours, pubd 1845 (after drawing, exh. 1854), NG Ire. · J. S. Templeton, lithograph, pubd in or after 1845 (after pencil drawing by F. W. Burton), NG Ire. · F. W. Burton, drawing, repro. in Duffy, Thomas Davis · F. W. Burton, pencil drawing, NG Ire. · F. W. Burton, pencil drawing, NG Ire. [see illus.] · J. Hogan, statue, Dublin city hall · H. MacManus, portrait, Phoenix Park, Dublin, Ireland; repro. in C. G. Duffy, Young Ireland, rev. edn (1896), 33

Davis, William (d. 1689). See under Bennet, John (d. 1690).

Davis, William (1771/2–1807), mathematician and publisher, probably made his early career as a surveyor and teacher of mathematics. He is first known in 1796 and 1797, as a contributor to mathematical periodicals. About this time he must have issued his first publication, An Easy and Comprehensive Description and Use of the Globes, in an edition which is as yet untraced. In 1798, the year in which the second edition of this work was published, he was a bookseller at 2 Albion Buildings, Aldersgate Street, London; and he described himself as a member of the Mathematical and Philosophical Society of London. In the same year he published A Complete Treatise of Land Surveying, a popular work which went through five editions by 1813; it has a five-page subscription list in which many of the provincial names are from Cheshire, Denbighshire, and Flint, from which it may be hazarded that he had worked in those parts before establishing himself in London. In 1798 he also launched the Companion to the Gentleman's Diary, a mathematical annual renamed in the following year the

William Davis (1771/2–1807), by J. S. Dickson, pubd 1813 (after W. Allen)

Gentleman's Mathematical Companion after objections from Charles Wildbore, the editor of the *Gentleman's Diary*.

Davis was married; his wife's name was Anne. His publishing business produced a steady flow of essential mathematical texts. In 1803 he brought out a three-volume edition of Andrew Motte's English translation of Newton's *Philosophiae naturalis principia mathematica*, which he dedicated to the astronomer royal, Nevil Maskelyne. Motte's 1729 translation is still regarded as the best, and Davis's edition made this available to a number of generations of nineteenth-century students. In 1805 Davis revised Thomas Simpson's *The Doctrine and Application of Fluxions*, which he published together with a life of the author. He also issued 'Keys' to a number of John Bonnycastle's elementary mathematical textbooks, a new edition of Daniel Fenning's *The Young Algebraist's Companion*, and, on a more advanced level, brought out a new edition of Colin MacLaurin's *Treatise of Fluxions*, as well as of John Rowe's *Introduction to the Doctrine of Fluxions*.

Davis continued to edit his annual *Mathematical Companion* up to his death at the age of thirty-five, on 8 February 1807. Considering that he had simultaneously attended to his business, his mathematical output over the space of ten years was quite remarkable. After his death the *Mathematical Companion* was edited by John Hampshire, who died in 1825, and it ceased with the number for 1827. Davis's 'mathematical and philosophical book warehouse' at Aldersgate was continued by his widow, who published the fifth edition of his *Complete Treatise* in 1813, with a portrait of her husband opposite the title-page. Anne Davis remarried: her second husband was a London bookseller and printer by the name of J. S. Dickson, and in 1814 the name of the firm was changed to Davis and Dickson. She died on 15 October 1822, when the business was wound up. The stock was auctioned in November and December 1834, and in May 1836. Its sale catalogue was of considerable interest to mathematical antiquaries.

G. J. GRAY, *rev.* RUTH WALLIS

Sources W. Davis, ed., *A Companion to the Gentleman's Diary* (1798); *Gentleman's Mathematical Companion* (1799–1807) · J. Hampshire, ed., *Gentleman's Mathematical Companion* (1808–25) · R. C. Archibald, 'Notes on some minor English mathematical serials', *Mathematical Gazette*, 14 (1928–9), 379–400, esp. 392 · P. J. Wallis and R. V. Wallis, *Newton and Newtoniana, 1672–1975* (1977), 15–16

Likenesses J. S. Dickson, stipple (after W. Allen), BM, NPG; repro. in W. Davis, *A treatise on land surveying*, 5th edn (1813), frontispiece [*see illus.*] · portrait, UCL, Graves Collection, 7 e 2 · portrait, BL

Davis, William (1812–1873), landscape painter, was born in Dublin in August 1812, the son of a solicitor. His family was socially well connected, but found themselves in reduced circumstances. He first intended to train for the law, but later turned to art, attending drawing and modelling lessons at the Royal Dublin Society. In 1833–5 he exhibited portraits at the Royal Hibernian Academy. In 1837 he moved to England, living first in Sheffield and settling in Liverpool about five years later. He enrolled as a probationer in the Liverpool Academy Schools in 1846 and as a student in 1848. He was elected an associate of the same institution in 1851 and a full member in 1853. Between 1856 and 1859 he served as professor of drawing at the Liverpool Academy. Davis maintained his connection with the Liverpool Academy until its final dissolution in 1867. He sent works to exhibitions from a succession of addresses in Liverpool, until 1863 when he used addresses in London. By 1870 he was permanently settled in South Hampstead, London.

William Davis's first patron was John Miller, merchant and shipowner in Liverpool, who had in his collection distinguished Pre-Raphaelite paintings including works by Millais, Ford Madox Brown, and Holman Hunt. H. C. Marillier believed that Miller encouraged Davis to abandon figure painting in favour of landscape. The Liverpool artist Robert Tonge (1823–1856) seems also to have led Davis towards pure landscape subjects. In 1853 the two shared a painting expedition to Ireland, where Davis met his wife.

Davis found his landscape subjects in the countryside around Liverpool, on the Wirral peninsula, and on the north shore of the Mersey towards Runcorn. On occasions he ventured further afield into Cheshire and north Wales, and he also painted on the island of Bute in Scotland, where John Miller had a house. Among his early works as a landscape painter is *Bidston Moss at Wallasey* (Walker Art Gallery, Liverpool), of 1855, showing a view westwards from the Wirral across the Dee estuary towards the Flintshire coast. Davis returned to Ireland in 1857, and it was perhaps on this occasion that he painted *Rye Water Near Leixlip, County Kildare* (National Gallery of Ireland, Dublin).

Davis exhibited at the Royal Academy from 1851, in the first place showing still lifes. In 1855 he sent a landscape painting—a view in Cheshire entitled *Early Spring Evening*—a work that caught the eye of D. G. Rossetti, who mentioned it in a letter to William Allingham as one of 'the four best landscapes in the place' (*Letters of Dante Gabriel Rossetti*, 1.252). Rossetti also drew Ruskin's attention to Davis's painting. In a first reference to *Early Spring Evening* in a supplement to the 1855 *Academy Notes* Ruskin explained that 'my friend [had said that] it contains the "unity of perfect truth with invention"', but subsequently he gave a more qualified account of the painting, judging it as 'merely good Pre-Raphaelite work' (*Works*, 14.30, 32).

That Davis's landscapes were particularly admired by fellow artists is demonstrated by Ford Madox Brown's rapturous comments on *Wallasey Mill, Cheshire*, shown at the 1856 Royal Academy, as a painting of 'leefless [sic] trees & some ducks which is perfection'. He went on: 'I do not remember ever seeing such an english landscape, it is far too good to be understood' (*Diary*, 175). In September 1856 Brown met Davis at John Miller's house in Liverpool, describing him as 'one of the most unlucky artists in England … crushed by disappointment & conscious dependency of Millar [sic] who has entirely kept him for years' (ibid., 190). In 1873 Davis's obituarist in *The Athenaeum* (probably F. G. Stephens) wrote of him: 'No man saw further than Mr Davis into the opportunities of a quiet rural subject: a hedge, a stream, a drenched autumnal pasture, a flitting of light and shadow over an English sky' (*The Athenaeum*).

In 1857 Davis sent six works to the Russell Place exhibition of Pre-Raphaelite art, the titles of which indicate that they were landscapes and paintings of animals. Ruskin saw these and took it upon himself to give advice. In a letter which was apparently never sent, Ruskin told Davis to treat landscapes with more prominent subjects and with more obvious associations: 'Your work … cannot become popular unless you choose subjects of greater interest.' (Ruskin had taken particular exception to a painting of Davis's that he described as 'that "ditch and wheatfield"'.) Furthermore, Ruskin felt that Davis was too dependent on a technique of allowing oil colour, opaque as well as loosely diluted with glazes, to mix and coalesce over a ground of pure flake white. This was the method by which Davis and his contemporaries in Liverpool achieved effects of dense texture and vibrant colour, but Ruskin warned against 'too great trust to the liquidity of the vehicle in blending your colours'. He explained: 'Good use has been made of this quality by the masters of the Pre-Raphaelite school, but it is a dangerous temptation: the highest results in oil-painting depend on judicious and powerful use of dryer, in no wise *floating* colour' (Rossetti, *Ruskin*, 169–70).

Davis operated on the fringe of the Pre-Raphaelite circle, and as such participated in the American travelling exhibition of Pre-Raphaelite art in 1857–8 and in 1858 was invited as one of a group of Liverpool painters to join the Hogarth Club. A total of sixteen paintings by him were shown at the Royal Academy, the last in 1872, but according to Marillier the selectors turned many others of his works away. A painting entitled *Harrowing*, shown first in Liverpool in 1859 but later rejected at the Royal Academy, was exhibited at the 1862 International Exhibition in London and described by W. M. Rossetti in his review of the exhibition as 'profoundly actual in its broadly realized facts, and poetical in its impression and suggestiveness' (Rossetti, *Fine Art*, 160).

Like J. W. Inchbold, Davis worked slowly and struggled to sell his paintings. William Michael Rossetti described him as a 'modest hard-working man, and an artist of uncommon gifts'. Rossetti further observed that Davis was 'greatly admired in a circle too strictly limited. He had a large family, and always found difficulty in "making the two ends meet"' (Rossetti, *Ruskin*, 168). He compounded his problems by consistently refusing commissions from dealers. Gradually, however, his work came to be appreciated by certain Pre-Raphaelite collectors, including George Rae and Joseph Beausire, both of Liverpool, James Leathart of Gateshead, and Humphrey Roberts of London.

In his last years Davis suffered from angina. He died in London on 22 April 1873, it was said as a result of the nervous strain brought on by seeing two of his paintings badly hung at the 1873 International Exhibition. A memorial exhibition was organized by Ford Madox Brown to raise an annuity to support his widow. Two of Davis's sons, Valentine (1854–1930) and Lucien (1860–1951), followed him in becoming painters. CHRISTOPHER NEWALL

Sources F. G. Stephens, 'William Davis, landscape painter, of Liverpool', *Art Journal*, new ser., 4 (1884), 325–8 · H. C. Marillier, *The Liverpool school of painters: an account of the Liverpool Academy from 1810 to 1867, with memoirs of the principal artists* (1904), 99–113 · 'Mr William Davies', *The Athenaeum* (3 May 1873), 573 · *Art Journal*, 35 (1873), 177 · A. Staley, *The Pre-Raphaelite landscape* (1973), 139–44 · *Merseyside painters, people and places: catalogue of oil paintings*, Walker Art Gallery, Liverpool, ed. M. Bennett (1978) · N. Johnson, *Paintings and drawings from the Leathart collection* (1968), 16–17 [exhibition catalogue, Laing Art Gallery, Newcastle upon Tyne, 7 Oct – 18 Nov 1968] · *Letters of Dante Gabriel Rossetti*, ed. O. Doughty and J. R. Wahl, 4 vols. (1965–7) · *The works of John Ruskin*, ed. E. T. Cook and A. Wedderburn, library edn, 39 vols. (1903–12) · *The diary of Ford Madox Brown*, ed. V. Surtees (1981) · W. M. Rossetti, ed., *Ruskin: Rossetti: Preraphaelitism* (1899) · W. M. Rossetti, *Fine art, chiefly contemporary* (1867)

Likenesses W. Davis, self-portrait, oils, Walker Art Gallery, Liverpool

Davis, William John (1848–1934), trade unionist, was born on 6 August 1848 at 263 Bradford Street, Birmingham, the son of Thomas Davis, a brass-founder, and his wife, Tharzia. As a child he received only two and a half years' education at a dame-school, though he made up for this in his teens and twenties by attending Sunday school and then a wide range of evening classes when he entered the local brass trade. He married Mary Jane Cooke (*d*. 1914) in 1869; they had six children.

Foundry men were the least well-organized among skilled metalworkers, partly because of the unusual mixture of highly skilled and laborious tasks the trade entailed, partly because of the wide range of materials and products handled in small workshops. Thus, although Davis was present at the second Trades Union Congress in 1869, he went as the representative of his local reform association. Two years later he was present at the meeting which founded the Amalgamated Society of Brassworkers, was then unanimously chosen as its general secretary, and effectively held this post until his retirement in 1921.

Davis was an outstanding organizer and his first period in office was a very successful one: within the space of a year he had established branches in a dozen towns and recruited 6000 members, and by 1883 the union was well enough established to allow him to take up an appointment as one of the first factory inspectors drawn from the ranks of working men. However, the depression of the 1880s led to the loss of members and serious financial difficulties, so he was recalled to the general secretaryship in 1889: within the space of a year he had once again boosted recruitment from 2000 to 8000 members. Both in the early 1870s and in the late 1880s Davis was clearly assisted by economic prosperity, but in addition he was able to develop craft union tactics in a direction which suited the peculiarities of his members' situation. This involved first focusing on standard wage increases rather than regulation of the trade's highly diverse working conditions, and second targeting employers in specific branches of the trade, beginning with the most prosperous and working outwards. Davis also placed a strong emphasis on negotiations: in the 1870s he persuaded employers in some branches of the trade to adopt a structure of joint conferences, and in 1891 he was successful in getting all the employers to agree to a board of conciliation, eventually leading to the recognition of a minimum wage for brassworkers. This willingness to institutionalize collective bargaining found expression on a wider scale through his involvement in setting up 'alliances' in a wide range of other Birmingham trades, under which the employers offered better conditions in return for a union pledge to work only for those firms in the employers' association, and thus push the cheaper firms out of the market. However, it should be stressed that this willingness to co-operate with the employers was conditional on improved conditions for the men: the 'alliances' themselves included closed-shop agreements, and when necessary Davis showed as much determination in pursuing strike action as he did in negotiations, for example supporting a major strike of brass-bedstead makers in the winter of 1889 until a satisfactory settlement was reached.

This classic craft combination of negotiation and assertion was accompanied by an equally classic commitment to radical Liberalism, and Davis was very active in Birmingham local politics from the 1870s onwards. In 1876 he was one of the first working-class representatives elected to the school board as one of the Birmingham Liberal Caucus nominees, and, with Liberal support, he went on to become the first Labour member of the town council in 1880. In 1906 he was appointed as a JP, acting as a vigilant defender of trade union rights and pressing successfully for the appointment of a further sixteen Labour JPs to the Birmingham bench in 1911. Davis also played an important role in labour politics at the national level, particularly from the 1890s onwards. Within the TUC he was a member of the group of craft unionists, including Robert Knight and Alexander Wilkie, which co-operated with the 'new unionists' in setting up the General Confederation of Trade Unions in 1899, and which co-operated with the Independent Labour Party in setting up the Labour Representation Committee in 1900. Davis's one divergence from the mainstream of the radical-Liberal tradition was in his stronger sense of patriotism, both during the Second South African War and the First World War, in the latter case leading to his brief involvement with the movement for a 'trade union party' during the 1918 general election due to dissatisfaction with official Labour Party policy on a negotiated peace.

Davis was an imposing man with a trim beard and piercing eyes, but he was well liked by his friends and family. He had unusually wide intellectual interests for a trade unionist of his period, lecturing and writing actively on labour affairs, and publishing a two-volume history of the TUC, *The British Trades Union Congress: History and Recollections* (1910–16); he also collected token coinage, on which he published two works (1896, 1904), and played chess to a good standard. On his retirement in 1921 he moved to France with his daughter Mabel. He died at 2 rue de Graviers, Rueilville, near Paris, on 20 October 1934.

ALASTAIR J. REID

Sources *DLB* · W. A. Dalley, *The life story of W. J. Davis, J. P.* (1914)

Davis, Sir William Wellclose (1901–1987), naval officer, was born in Simla, Punjab, India, on 11 October 1901, the elder son and eldest of the three children of Walter Stewart Davis, of the Indian political service, and his wife, Georgina Rose. Having been to Summer Fields School in Oxford, he joined the Royal Navy as a cadet in May 1915 and attended the Royal Naval College at Osborne, Isle of Wight and Dartmouth. He first went to sea as a midshipman in the battleship *Neptune* in 1917. He specialized in torpedoes in 1926 and quickly showed his ability as a staff officer. He was fleet torpedo officer to Admiral Sir Frederic Dreyer on the China station and was promoted commander in 1935. He then became fleet torpedo officer and staff officer, plans, to the commander-in-chief, Home Fleet, and was subsequently appointed executive officer of the battle cruiser *Hood* in January 1939. He served in her for the first eighteen months of the Second World War and was mentioned in dispatches. In 1934 he married Lady (Gertrude) Elizabeth Phipps (d. 1985), second daughter of Constantine Charles Henry Phipps, third marquess of Normanby, canon of St George's Chapel, Windsor, and his wife, Gertrude Stansfeld, née Foster. They had two sons and two daughters.

Promoted captain in December 1940, Davis went to the Admiralty as deputy director of plans. He was for a time seconded to the staff of admiral of the fleet Sir Roger Keyes, director of combined operations. Davis displayed his tact in his handling of Operation Workshop—the projected seizure of the Mediterranean island of Pantelleria, a plan proposed by Keyes and espoused by Winston Churchill, but fiercely resisted by the chiefs of staff and Admiral Sir Andrew Cunningham, the commander-in-chief in the Mediterranean. Operation Workshop never took place, but Davis himself emerged with credit, Keyes calling him 'the admirable staff officer'. In March 1943 Davis took command of the cruiser *Mauritius*, a ship in a very sensitive state of discipline which was aggravated in January 1944 when she arrived in Plymouth Sound with her ship's company expecting to pay off. In spite of Davis's representations to the Admiralty, proper leave was not granted and the ship had to return almost at once to the Mediterranean. Her sailors believed, not unreasonably, that they were being punished for previous acts of indiscipline and there was further unrest, with outright refusals of duty. It was a discouraging start, but Davis, with his gift for making people work together, turned the commission into a triumph. *Mauritius* was the only major British warship to take part in the four invasions, of Sicily, Salerno, Anzio, and Normandy, bombarding enemy shore positions on more than 250 occasions. Later in 1944 *Mauritius* destroyed two enemy convoys in the Bay of Biscay. Davis himself was mentioned in dispatches three more times and appointed DSO with bar (1944).

After the war Davis was director of the underwater weapons division at the Admiralty, where he helped to form the new electrical branch, and then he became chief of staff to the commander-in-chief, Home Fleet (1948–9). Promoted rear-admiral in 1950, he was naval secretary to three first lords of the Admiralty. From 1952 to 1954 he was flag officer, second in command, Mediterranean Fleet, when the first Earl Mountbatten of Burma was commander-in-chief. It was made clear to Davis that he was to run the fleet while Mountbatten dealt with the numerous political and strategic problems in the Mediterranean.

A tall man, and extremely good-looking in his youth, Davis had great personal charm and a good brain. There was nothing bombastic or dramatic about him; he was no fire-eater. But when he went to the Admiralty in 1954, as vice-chief of the naval staff, he provided the competent, imperturbable staff work which ably supported the much more flamboyant Mountbatten, then first sea lord, during a seemingly interminable series of crises in the late 1950s, notably the 'Crabb affair', when Commander Crabb, a naval frogman, disappeared while allegedly inspecting the propellers of the Soviet cruiser which had brought Nikolay Bulganin and Nikita Khrushchov to Portsmouth in 1956; the Suez operation, later that year, which Mountbatten himself deplored; and the navy's response to the swingeing cuts proposed by the 1957 white paper of Duncan Sandys, a man whom Davis privately thought had little grasp of the strategic needs of the country.

Davis's last appointment, as a full admiral, was from 1958 to 1960 as commander-in-chief, Home Fleet, and NATO commander-in-chief in the eastern Atlantic. He was by then the only senior naval officer still serving who had served in the First World War. He was also the first commander-in-chief to haul down his flag afloat and hoist it again ashore over the 'Führer Bunker', the NATO headquarters at Northwood in Middlesex. He was appointed CB in 1952, KCB in 1956, and GCB in 1959. After he retired in 1960 he devoted much time to county affairs in Gloucestershire. To the end of his life he took a close interest in naval history and naval affairs. William Davis died in hospital in Gloucester on 29 October 1987.

JOHN WINTON, *rev.*

Sources *Daily Telegraph* (2 Nov 1987) · unpubd autobiography, priv. coll. · private information (1996) · *CGPLA Eng. & Wales* (1988) **Archives** CAC Cam., MS autobiography **Wealth at death** £157,710: probate, 15 Aug 1988, *CGPLA Eng. & Wales*

Davison. *See also* Davidson.

Davison, Alexander (1750–1829), government contractor, was born at Lanton near Wooler, Northumberland, on 2 April 1750, the third son of Alexander Davison, a farmer at Lanton, and Dorothy Neal of the next parish of Yeavering. As a young man he travelled to London, where he started work in the counting-house of Robert Hunter, but after several years in his service he was sent by Hunter to Canada. Together with his younger brother, George, he steadily built up his wealth as a merchant and shipowner in the Canada trade during the American War of Independence.

While in Quebec Davison joined the freemasons and was appointed to the legislative council, which was composed of crown nominees, one of whom was his brother George. The two brothers appear to have had the monopoly of the Canadian 'posts' and were of considerable assistance to the governor, General Frederick Haldimand. It was Haldimand who recommended Alexander Davison to Evan Nepean, an under-secretary of state, as a man who could be useful to Pitt's government as a government contractor. After his return to Britain Davison settled in London and was commissioned in 1784 by the duke of Northumberland as a lieutenant in the Northumberland militia. On 18 February 1788 Davison married Harriett (1770–1826), daughter of John Gosling, banker, of Lincoln's Inn Fields, London. They had six children: three sons and three daughters. The eldest two were twin boys born on 19 December 1788: Major-General Hugh Percy Davison (1788–1849), who was named after the duke of Northumberland and who served in the 18th hussars, and Lieutenant-Colonel Sir William Davison (1788–1873), who served in the Northumberland militia, the 2nd or Queen's Royal regiment and, unattached, in the Hanoverian army. For many years Sir William was aide-de-camp and equerry to the first duke of Cambridge, when he was viceroy of Hanover. A daughter, Harriett, died in infancy on 9 April 1796, as did another son (*d.* 2 November 1806), who had been baptized Alexander Horatio Nelson Davison in honour of his godfather, the great admiral.

Government contractor and friend of Nelson For more than twenty years, from 1784, Davison worked for the government in providing army uniforms, weapons, transports, and general supplies. He supplied both the earl of Moira's expedition to support the French loyalists in western France in 1793 and the duke of York's army in Flanders in 1793–4. He also acted as commissary-general to the army at Southampton and the Isle of Wight for two years, supplied large orders for the government of Portugal, and acted as supply agent for all the marines in Britain. By the 1790s he had built up a very successful and wide-ranging business in London as a merchant, government contractor, and prize agent. He later also joined a banking house. He was soon very well connected with leading political figures and his government contacts enabled him to build up a lucrative business. The profits from this helped him to buy a substantial house in St James's Square, London, where he regularly entertained Horatio Nelson and other notable figures of the day, including the prince of Wales, the duke of Clarence, William Pitt, and various cabinet ministers and admirals. He was soon wealthy enough to purchase, in 1795, Swarland Hall and Park, 7 miles south-west of Alnwick in Northumberland. Over the next decade or so he spent a fortune improving the house and grounds, and buying adjacent land. He also built up a superb collection of paintings on English historical subjects by British artists, as well as fine collections of plate, porcelain, jewels, and books. He regularly lent money to his friends and numerous contacts, no doubt increasing thereby his influence in government and naval circles.

Davison first met Nelson at Quebec in 1782, when Nelson was captain of the frigate *Albemarle*. According to Robert Southey he was instrumental in saving Nelson from a rash and imprudent marriage to the sixteen-year-old daughter of the provost-marshal of the garrison. Although irritated by his interference at the time, Nelson later established a close relationship with Davison, who acted as his financial adviser as well as confidant, and they corresponded regularly thereafter until very shortly before Nelson's death. Davison became prize agent for Nelson and his whole fleet after the battle of the Nile in 1798, which he commemorated by spending about £2000 to pay for medals for all those who participated in this great victory. When Napoleon threatened to invade in 1803–4 Davison established a volunteer corps, the Loyal Britons, at a cost of nearly £3000; he served as its lieutenant-colonel. A correspondent of both Nelson's wife and his mistress, Davison was a leading mourner at Nelson's funeral and he repaid the admiral's friendship by giving financial assistance to Emma Hamilton after Nelson's death. To commemorate their friendship he erected an impressive obelisk on his estate at Swarland Park, beside the road from Morpeth to Alnwick.

Supplier to the barrack office Late in December 1794 Lieutenant-General Oliver De Lancey, barrack-master-general, approached Davison to offer him a virtual monopoly to supply all new barracks with both a wide range of supplies (including beds, bedding, utensils, and candles) as well as a separate contract to supply them with coal. After securing a commission of two and a half per cent on all his costs, Davison agreed to what proved to be his most lucrative contract. In the absence of a detailed agreement with De Lancey, Davison took advantage of the public purse by supplying poor quality goods and charging inflated prices. After agreeing a separate contract with De Lancey in April 1795 to supply coal, Davison provided coal in winter, when it was more expensive, despite having bought it at the cheaper summer rates, and under-

supplied the weight of coal paid for, by weighing the coal when wet, and therefore heavier. Furthermore he charged the Treasury in advance far in excess of the goods he supplied in the succeeding six months when he submitted his half-yearly accounts. As a result he had very large sums of public money in hand which he could use and invest to his own advantage. Given that Davison was paid over £1 million in cash, and provided accounts for provisions much less than this, it is hardly surprising that the commissioners of inquiry in 1807 calculated that he had built up a fortune at the expense of the public purse and that the barrack office really ought to have procured its supplies by competitive bidding and open contracts as was the case in other public departments.

The government did not become suspicious of Davison's business practices until his enemies, including commercial and political rivals, began to raise complaints against him. It may have been his ill-judged attempt to enter parliament that led to a more serious examination of his business activities. In 1802 Davison was persuaded that he might be able purchase a parliamentary seat at Ilchester in Somerset. He was encouraged to build properties (known as 'Davison's Folly'), which would confer the vote on the householders put in them, and to offer to pay £30 per vote to all those electors who would support his candidacy. His willingness to use bribery and corruption to win the election became so notorious that Sir William Manners, who hoped to gain control of the borough himself, warned him that his conduct would lead him into serious trouble. Davison withdrew from the contest well before the poll, but two other candidates (also rich London merchants) employed agents using similar practices in order to corrupt the voters. When Manners and his ally, James Graham, petitioned against these two candidates who had been returned for the borough, a parliamentary committee of inquiry eventually concluded, in March 1803, that Davison and the two parliamentary agents working for the successful candidates had been involved in corrupting the voters at Ilchester and ought to be prosecuted. Although some leading MPs, including Richard Brinsley Sheridan, tried to save Davison from prosecution, he was arraigned at Taunton in April 1804, convicted and imprisoned for a year in the Marshalsea prison.

Mounting accusations of fraud In 1802 the secretary at war was first alerted by another merchant that Davison might be defrauding the barrack office. Although a strict inquiry was not made for some time, the government put the management of barrack supplies under the commissary-general. In May 1803, after Davison had been criticized by parliament for his electoral malpractices, George III refused to let him stand proxy for Lord Nelson at his installation as a knight of the Bath. In November and December 1805 two correspondents to *The Times*—Aristides and Verax—urged an inquiry into what funds Davison had collected from the public to erect a monument to the nation's naval heroes and to what use he had put these unused funds. Davison was forced to defend himself in a letter to *The Times* on 22 January 1806, in which he claimed that not enough money had yet been subscribed to build the proposed naval pillar and what had been collected had been invested at interest. This dispute may have led him to build the obelisk to Nelson on his own estate.

When General De Lancey retired as barrack-master-general in November 1804 it soon became obvious that the financial accounts of the barrack office were in a very confused state and a commission of military inquiry was appointed by act of parliament in 1805 (45 Geo. III, c. 47). Davison was called upon to give evidence before it in December 1805 and May and June 1806. The commissioners concluded quite early that 'it was impossible for us to ascertain the loss to the public, or the gain to Mr Davison, through the improvidence of the late Barrack Master General in the bargain made with him, and the inattention of the Barrack Office' ('Commissioners of military enquiry', 2.224). Nevertheless on 19 May 1806 the attorney- and solicitor-general agreed that Davison ought to be charged with fraud over the supply of coal to the barracks (ibid., 2.297). In that month Davison repaid the government £6047 17s. 11d. because he admitted he had received more money than he was owed; but no criminal proceedings were taken against him for many months. His career was not immediately ruined since the 'ministry of all the talents' appointed him to serve as treasurer of the ordnance in 1806–7. He sought to defend himself by bringing out a pamphlet, *A Reply to the Committee of Military Enquiry Respecting Barrack Supplies* (1807).

Early in 1807 Lord Archibald Hamilton MP, a vigorous opponent of corruption, urged the House of Commons to press the attorney-general to prosecute Davison, but Lord Henry Petty, the chancellor of the exchequer, persuaded him to withdraw the motion so that the Treasury could be given a chance to recover money from Davison. At the end of 1807 *The Times* expressed surprise that Davison had still not been brought to justice as a 'notorious peculator' (*The Times*, 28 Dec 1807) and suggested that he was being protected by friends in high places. It pointed out that he had recently left London for Yarmouth in the company of Sir Home Popham, a naval officer who had himself recently faced a parliamentary inquiry and a court martial. Six months later Lord Archibald Hamilton again asked Spencer Perceval, chancellor of the exchequer, why, so long after parliament had received such a damaging report on Davison's activities, he had still not been prosecuted, yet received the same explanation as before.

Downfall, and final years Davison may well have been trying to negotiate a financial settlement with the Treasury yet, once General De Lancey was fit enough to attend the trial as a key witness, Davison was finally brought to trial at the court of king's bench, before Lord Ellenborough and a special jury, on 7 December 1808. He was charged with falsifying his vouchers and receipts between 1798 and 1802, and thereby implying that two men who were working in his own warehouse were independent merchants. This allowed him to supply the barracks with goods from his own army clothing warehouse in Bedford Street, while still receiving a commission of two and a half per cent. His defence argued that he did nothing that had not been agreed in advance with De Lancey, though the latter

denied all knowledge of a commission being agreed on goods supplied directly by Davison, rather than being purchased from other merchants. His defence also argued that he had abandoned the claim for commission once he realized he was not entitled to receive it. Lord Moira, Evan Nepean, the earl of Chatham, William Huskisson, and others testified to Davison's probity and public spirit over many years, but he was still found guilty on 6 February 1809. On 27 April he was ordered to pay £18,883 13s. 1d. commission back to the exchequer and was sentenced to twenty-one months' imprisonment in Newgate.

This conviction ruined Davison's career as a government contractor and his finances were seriously embarrassed for a time as he disputed with the government over his accounts. He claimed that the government owed him over £17,000, but the Treasury counter-claimed in February 1814 with a demand for two sums totalling just over £65,000. Not until 25 November 1826 was this amount finally reduced on appeal and Davison paid up and was finally discharged from responsibility for any further payments. While in prison in November 1810, he mortgaged Swarland Hall to the duke of Northumberland for £25,000; he redeemed it on 13 January 1811. He remained a wealthy man for some years, however, though no doubt to meet his debts to the Treasury he sold his house in St James's Square and his plate, porcelain, gems, and books by auction in 1817 and his splendid collection of British paintings by auction in 1823. When he died 'after a short illness' in fashionable Regency Square, Brighton, on 10 December 1829, in his eightieth year, he still owned his Northumberland estate (*The Times*, 12 Dec 1812). His extensive will made substantial bequests, and included gifts given to him by Nelson. He was buried in the same massive vault as his wife in St Gregory's churchyard at Kirknewton, Northumberland, within a mile or so of where he had been born. His son William later raised an obelisk to his memory on a hill overlooking the church.

Assessment Davison was a man of great energy, efficiency, and ambition. He clearly had a good head for business, a great capacity for making friends and for building up business and government contacts, and a love for the good life that great wealth could buy. He was loyal to and financially supportive of his friends and allies, and they clearly regarded him as a man of probity, but his business success undoubtedly alienated rival merchants and aroused the hostility of the press. He was probably fraudulent in his dealings with the barrack office, though he made very little money from the particular offences for which he was convicted in 1809 and undoubtedly profited much more from other aspects of his decade-long and loosely drawn contract to supply the army's barracks with coal and a wide range of other goods. He may not have been any more guilty of robbing the public purse than many other government contractors of the day, but at a time when the public was alarmed by military setbacks and shocked by the revelations of corruption in high places he suffered the penalty when his actions came to the attention of a rattled government and parliament, and an aroused press. Davison is probably the original model for Alexander Willemott, an army contractor, in Captain Frederick Marryat's *The Way to be Happy* (1837). H. T. DICKINSON

Sources *A history of Northumberland*, Northumberland County History Committee, 15 vols. (1893–1940), vol. 7 · 'Commissioners of military enquiry: third report', *Parl. papers* (1806–7), vol. 2, pp.1–312, 402–7 · *State trials*, 31.99–250 · *JHC*, 58 (1802–3) · *The Times* (1803–8) · *The Times* (1829) · *The Times* (1873) · R. G. Thorn, 'Ilchester', HoP, *Commons, 1790–1820* · R. Southey, *The life of Nelson*, repr. (1953) · J. S. Clarke and J. M'Arthur, *The life of Admiral Lord Nelson*, 2 vols. (1809) · C. Oman, *Nelson* (1947) · T. Pocock, *Horatio Nelson* (1987) · *Annual Register* (1807–8) · BL, Add. MSS 21705, fols. 157, 191–2; 21737, fol. 349 · records of court of king's bench, 48 Geo. III, PRO, KB 28/426 · A. T. Mahan, *The life of Nelson*, 2nd edn (1899) · C. O. Davison, *Davison, Alexander, and his descendants*, priv. printed (1998) · *DNB* · *The dispatches and letters of Vice-Admiral Lord Viscount Nelson*, ed. N. H. Nicolas, 7 vols. (1844–6); repr. (1997–8) · *Nelson: the Alexander Davison collection* (2002) [auction catalogue, Sothebys, London, 21 October 2002]

Archives Birm. CA, letters to Boulton family · BL, letters to Sir Frederick Haldimand, Add. MSS 21705, 21733, 21737 · BL, corresp. with Horatio Nelson, Egerton MSS 2240, 2241, fol. 1 · BL, letters to Viscount Nelson and Earl Nelson, Add. MSS 34907–34920, 34992, *passim* · NMM, letters to Lord Nelson

Likenesses W. Barnard, mezzotint, pubd 1804 (after L. F. Abbott), BM, NPG

Davison, Charles (1858–1940), mathematician and writer on seismology, was born on 1 May 1858 in Bishopwearmouth, co. Durham, the second son of Edwin Charles Davison (1818–1902), fleet paymaster, Royal Navy, and his wife, Elizabeth, daughter of Joseph L. Spence of Swayfield, Lincolnshire. He went to the College of Physical Science, Newcastle upon Tyne (1874–7), and then to Emmanuel College, Cambridge (1877–81), where he became a scholar in 1879. He obtained a BA in mathematics (thirteenth wrangler) in 1881 and an MA in 1885.

In January 1884 Davison became senior mathematics master at Blairlodge School, Stirlingshire; in January 1885 he was appointed mathematical master (later head of mathematics) at King Edward's High School, Birmingham, where he remained until his retirement in March 1920. On 14 April 1886 he married Margaret Blanche (1855–1948), daughter of James Harris, schoolmaster, of Great Chart, Ashford, Kent; they had one son and two daughters.

Between 1892 and 1931 Davison wrote nine mathematical textbooks for schools (one as co-author with R. Levett and one with C. H. Richards), covering aspects of plane and solid geometry, trigonometry, algebra, and calculus. He was, however, best known for his work as a writer on the history of British earthquakes and seismology in general, and his books on these topics remain useful sources of reference. He also published numerous papers in *Nature*, the *Philosophical Magazine*, the *Philosophical Transactions of the Royal Society*, and the *Bulletin of the Seismological Society of America*. Always on the lookout for periodicity in the frequency of shocks, Davison was one of the first to apply the analytical technique of Fourier analysis but his claim to find evidence of diurnal and lunar effects, in addition to one-, eleven-, and nineteen-year periods, was not supported when sensitive, continuous, recording techniques became available.

Despite a shy and diffident manner, Davison was a hardworking and gifted teacher of endless patience, from whose classes many able mathematicians went on to university. In 1895 he became secretary to the British Association seismological committee for study of earth tremors and the following year he and the seismologist John Milne, newly returned from his pioneering work in Japan, became joint secretaries of its newly established subcommittee for seismological investigation, until Davison retired from this position in 1899. He had become ScD (Cambridge) in 1896.

Davison died at his home, 70 Cavendish Avenue, Cambridge, where he lived following his retirement, on 28 April 1940. He was survived by his wife. He was buried on 1 May at St Andrew's Church, Cherry Hinton.

RICHARD J. HOWARTH, rev.

Sources E. Tillotson, *Nature*, 145 (1940), 805 · C. H. Richards, *Nature*, 145 (1940), 805 · 'H. J.', *Proceedings of the Geological Society of London* (1940), lxxxv–vi · *Old Edwardian Gazette* (30 June 1920), 6–7 · *The Times* (29 April 1940), 9e · *The Times* (4 May 1940), 9d · archives, King Edward's High School, Birmingham · *CGPLA Eng. & Wales* (1940) · b. cert. · d. cert.

Likenesses portrait, photograph, Cambridge Central Library, Cambridgeshire Collection, PC19.12

Wealth at death £9034 0s. 4d.: probate, 2 Sept 1940, *CGPLA Eng. & Wales*

Davison, Edward (1788–1863), Church of England clergyman, born in Durham in April 1788, was the only son of Edward Davison BA (1760–1839), mayor of Durham in 1815 and incumbent of the church of St Nicholas, Durham, and his wife, Hannah Hopper. He matriculated from Corpus Christi College, Oxford, in 1803, graduating BA in 1807 and MA in 1810, the latter as a member of University College, where he was a fellow from 1807 to 1816. He was ordained in 1817, and was presented by his father to the rectory of Harlington, Middlesex, in 1822. He succeeded his father in 1825 to the living of St Nicholas, which he retained for thirty-one years. He was an eloquent preacher and a diligent parish priest. He was the author of *Tentamen theologicum, or, An attempt to assist the young clergyman of the Church of England in the choice of a subject for his sermon on any Sunday throughout the year* (1850). He was married twice: firstly to Isabella White and secondly, on 11 May 1824, to Margaret Pearson Wolfe, with whom he had two sons. The elder son, John Robert Davison (1826–1871), was Liberal MP for Durham, 1868–71. Davison died at his home in Church Street, Durham, on 22 May 1863.

ROBERT HARRISON, rev. M. C. CURTHOYS

Sources GM, 3rd ser., 14 (1863), 108 · Foster, *Alum. Oxon.* · Burke, *Gen. GB* · Boase, *Mod. Eng. biog.*

Wealth at death under £30,000: probate, 18 Aug 1863, *CGPLA Eng. & Wales*

Davison, Emily Wilding (1872–1913), suffragette, was born on 11 October 1872 at Roxburgh House, Vanbrugh Park Road, Greenwich, the second of the three children of Charles Edward Davison (1822–1893), retired merchant and 'gentleman', and his second wife, Margaret Caisley (1848–1918). Her mother ran a shop in Longhorsley, Northumberland, after the death of her husband left the family in straitened circumstances.

Emily Davison was educated by a resident governess at her family home, Gaston House, near Sawbridgeworth, Hertfordshire, and at Kensington high school (1885–91) and Royal Holloway College (1891–3). After the death of her father she worked as a governess in order to complete her studies, and in 1895 finally gained her London BA, achieving a first-class honours degree in English language and literature. She subsequently taught at the Church of England College for Girls at Edgbaston (1895–6), the Seabury School, West Worthing (1896–8), and privately thereafter until 1908 or 1909.

In 1906 Emily Davison joined the Women's Social and Political Union (WSPU) and in June 1908 acted as chief steward at Marylebone Station for the union's first major procession to Hyde Park. By April 1910 she was working for the WSPU and contributed articles and reviews to their newspaper, *Votes for Women*, until December 1911. However, in keeping with her consistent rejection of authority, she soon fell out of favour with the WSPU leadership over her independent and unauthorized programme of militant actions.

Davison notably hid in the House of Commons three times, including in April 1911 when she spent the night in a cupboard near the crypt chapel in order to avoid participating in the census. She was imprisoned eight times, for offences including obstruction, assault, stone-throwing, breaking windows, and setting fire to pillar boxes, during which she went on hunger strikes, suffered solitary confinement and force feeding, barricaded herself in her cell, had a hosepipe turned on her, and attempted suicide as a protest against the mistreatment of her fellow suffragette prisoners.

Emily Davison's writings consist mainly of letters to the press and accounts of her militant activities, although she also wrote speeches, articles, and scenes for plays. Most remain unpublished, although her essay 'The price of liberty', in which she reveals her Christian feminist faith, was published posthumously in *The Suffragette*. She was 'an active and involved' member of the Workers' Educational Association and the Central Labour College (Morley and Stanley, 170), and her socialist sympathies are evident in the tone of the memorial leaflet produced on her death, as well as in the significant socialist and Labour presence at her funeral procession.

Among Emily Davison's close friends were Rose Lamartine Yates, Elinor Penn-Gaskell, Edith Mansell-Moullin, and Mary Leigh—all prominent and active members of the suffrage movement. Sylvia Pankhurst, in *The Suffragette Movement* (1931), describes her as 'tall and slender, with unusually long arms, a small narrow head and red hair. Her illusive, whimsical green eyes and thin, half-smiling mouth, bore often the mocking expression of the Mona Lisa' (Crawford, 160). She never married and had no children.

On 22 June 1912, after throwing herself onto a staircase at Holloway prison, Emily Davison told the medical officer that she had done so because she felt 'that a tragedy was wanted' (*Hansard 5C*, 25 June 1912, 216). She is usually remembered as the 'suffragette martyr' for her last protest at the Epsom Derby in June 1913. As the horses rounded Tattenham Corner she ducked under the railing and ran out onto the course in front of the king's horse, Anmer, which struck her with its chest and knocked her down. Among the articles found in her possession were two WSPU flags, a racecard, and a return train ticket to Victoria. She remained unconscious for four days and died on 8 June 1913 at Epsom Cottage Hospital as a result of a fracture to the base of the skull. The coroner recorded a verdict of death 'due to misadventure'. It is not known whether she intended to commit suicide. Queen Mary's

Emily Wilding Davison (1872–1913), by Mrs Albert Broom, 1910 [on a suffragette march in Hyde Park; right, with (left to right) Emmeline Pethick-Lawrence, Christabel Pankhurst, and Sylvia Pankhurst]

first thought was for 'poor Jones', the jockey, and she referred to Davison as 'the horrid woman' (Pope-Hennessy, 467).

A public funeral was held in London on 14 June 1913. Emily Davison's body was taken from Epsom and escorted, by a large and spectacular procession, from Victoria to St George's Church, Bloomsbury, where a memorial service was held, and afterwards to King's Cross where the body was entrained for Northumberland for burial at the parish church of St Mary's, Morpeth, on 15 June.

VERA DI CAMPLI SAN VITO

Sources A. Morley and L. Stanley, *The life and death of Emily Wilding Davison* (1988) · Emily Wilding Davison papers, Women's Library, London, 7/EWD · A. J. R., ed., *The suffrage annual and women's who's who* (1913), 221 · E. W. Davison, 'The price of liberty', *The Suffragette* (5 June 1914), 129 · E. Crawford, *The women's suffrage movement: a reference guide, 1866–1928* (1999), 159–63 · J. Sleight, *One-way ticket to Epsom: a journalist's enquiry into the heroic story of Emily Wilding Davison* (1988) · G. Colmore, 'Miss Davison's funeral', *Votes for Women* (20 June 1913), 553–4 · E. S. Pankhurst, *The suffragette movement: an intimate account of persons and ideals* (1931) · 'A night in Guy Fawkes cupboard', *Votes for Women* (7 April 1911), 441 · register of students, Royal Holloway College, Egham, Surrey, RHC AR/200/1 · *Hansard 5C* (1912), 40.216 · J. Pope-Hennessy, *Queen Mary, 1867–1953* (1959) · b. cert. · d. cert.

Archives Women's Library, London, corresp. and papers, 7/EWD | PRO, metropolitan police archive, MEPO/2/1551 · PRO, prison commission archive, PCOM/8/174 · Royal Holloway College, Egham, Surrey, register of students, RHC AR/200/1, p. 14 | FILM British Pathe Library, footage of the Derby, 1913

Likenesses Mrs A. Broom, group photograph, 1910, NPG [*see illus.*] · F. Kehrhahn & Co., photograph, Women's Library, London · photographs, repro. in Sleight, *One-way ticket to Epsom*

Wealth at death £186 1s. 7d.: probate, 1913, CGPLA Eng. & Wales

Davison, Francis (1573/4–1613x19), poet and anthologist, was the eldest, or eldest surviving, son of William *Davison (d. 1608), secretary of state, and his wife, Catherine, daughter of Francis Spelman (who was the nephew of Sir John Spelman (1495?–1544)) and his wife, Mary, and cousin of the earl of Leicester. He matriculated as a fellow-commoner at Emmanuel College, Cambridge, in 1586. He was a clever young man: in 1589 his cousin George Cranmer wrote him a formal Latin letter congratulating him on his learning. In 1593 he was admitted to Gray's Inn, and over the winter of 1594–5 he took part in the revels which culminated in the performance before the queen of the 'Masque of Proteus', which he wrote. It was well received, and was in one very important respect innovative: being performed on a stage, it was 'the first English masque to conceive, in however small a way, of the masquing hall as a theater' (S. Orgel, *The Jonsonian Masque*, 1965, 9), thus anticipating the masque designs of Inigo Jones.

In May 1595 Davison and his tutor Edward Smyth were given a licence to travel in Europe, procured by the earl of Essex, who gave him 400 crowns towards his expenses, and presumably hoped to use him to gather information. The tour was not a success. Davison and Smyth lived expensively and ran into debt: by the beginning of 1596 Smyth was asking William Davison to extend the allowance he was making them, commenting that Francis could not eat inexpensive food. Although in 1596 Davison sent a treatise on the state of Saxony to Anthony Bacon, who commended it and forwarded it to Essex, a proposed sequel on the state of Tuscany never materialized. He quarrelled with Essex's agent in Venice, and with Smyth. In May 1597 he entered his name to study law at the University of Padua, but by summer 1598 he was back in England, quarrelling more seriously: in or shortly before mid-July he killed one Richard Thornell in a duel. In 1600 he received a pardon from the branding which was the usual penalty for manslaughter.

By that year Davison was nearly thirty. His father was neither rich nor influential. Essex's patronage had not extended far, and was not to be relied on. Davison needed an income. He looked elsewhere for patronage, beginning a treatise on the annulled first marriage of the earl of Bath which was designed to ingratiate him with the Russell family (the countess of Bath was a Russell), and appearing as one of the secretaries whom Sir Thomas Parry engaged in the first half of 1602. The treatise, however, remained unfinished, and the secretaryship lasted only a couple of months.

Davison's next move was to publish a collection of poetry. It is for this, *A Poetical Rapsody* (1602), that he is remembered. It is the last of the series of printed poetry collections which begins with *Tottel's Miscellany* in 1557. It is made up from groups of poems by Francis Davison himself, his brother Walter, and an anonymous third writer or group of writers, to which a few poems by Philip Sidney, the countess of Pembroke, Edmund Spenser, and others are added at the beginning and end of the volume. Davison claimed, perhaps disingenuously, that these additions were the printer's responsibility. They certainly accord with his invocations of Sidney in his dedicatory sonnet to the earl of Pembroke and elsewhere, and with the nostalgic, backward-looking quality of the collection, with its Spenserian pastorals and experiments in quantitative metre, as a whole. Some of Davison's contributions are highly conventional; but they also include sharp political commentary, such as a poem in which the lamentations of a grave shepherd called Eubulus who has been harshly treated by his mistress Astraea dramatize the fall from favour of William Davison, and another in praise of the recently executed earl of Essex.

After *A Poetical Rapsody* Davison continued to write, publishing a broadsheet of Latin anagrams on the names of various noblemen, beginning a translation of the psalms, and planning a 'Relation of England'. He owned a manuscript of Donne's satires, and attempted to obtain more poetry by Donne and others in manuscript, perhaps with a second anthology in mind. He added material to the second edition of the *Rapsody* in 1608, but does not seem to have had any connection with the third in 1611. The last work of his which can be dated is a racy poem called 'The Counterskuffle', about a fight in a debtors' prison in February 1613, which claims to be based on firsthand observation. Another poem, the epigram 'On Painted Ladys', whose main point is a pun on fucus (the name of a cosmetic) and 'fuck us', is dated 1615 in a commonplace book, but may have been written earlier.

The antiquary Ralph Starkey possessed a number of

Francis Davison's manuscripts as well as the state papers of William Davison which were confiscated from him in 1619. All these manuscripts presumably came to him as a single collection, probably after Francis's death, which can therefore be dated between 1613 and 1619.

Walter Davison (1581?–1602x8), Francis's younger brother, wrote eighteen of the poems printed in the first edition of *A Poetical Rapsody* when he was in his late teens. Seventeen of these comprise a competent but unmemorable sequence of amatory poems; the last is a translation from the Latin of a misogynistic epigram. In 1602 Francis described him as a professional soldier, then serving in the Low Countries; since he is not mentioned in the will of his father in 1608, he had presumably died before then.

JOHN CONSIDINE

Sources F. Davison and others, *The poetical rhapsody*, ed. N. H. Nicolas, 2 vols. (1826) · R. C. McCoy, 'Lord of liberty: Francis Davison and the cult of Elizabeth', *The reign of Elizabeth I: court and culture in the last decade*, ed. J. Guy (1995) · *The letters of John Chamberlain*, ed. N. E. McClure, 2 vols. (1939) · T. Ferrers, 'Letter to Sir Henry Ferrers', 19 Sept 1598, BL, Stowe MS 150, fol. 114 · *CSP dom., 1581–1601* · P. E. J. Hammer, 'Essex and Europe: evidence from confidential instructions by the earl of Essex, 1595–6', *EngHR*, 111 (1996), 357–81 · K. Duncan-Jones, 'Prentices and prodigals: a new allusion to the *The hogge hath lost his pearl*', *N&Q*, 242 (1997), 88–90 · A. F. Marotti, *Manuscript, print, and the English Renaissance lyric* (1995) · Venn, *Alum. Cant.* · M. Eccles, *Brief lives: Tudor and Stuart authors* (1982) · *CSP for., 1577–80* · R. Hatchwell, 'A Francis Davison/William Drummond conundrum', *Bodleian Library Record*, 15 (1994–6), 364–7 · F. Davison, *A poetical rhapsody, 1602–1621*, ed. H. E. Rollins, 2 vols. (1932)

Archives BL, Harley MSS 249, 290, 296, 298, 304, 347, 541 · PRO, state papers | LPL, letters to A. Bacon [transcripts by Thomas Birch in BL, Add. MSS 4120–4122]

Davison, George (1855–1930), photographer, political activist, and patron of the arts, was born in Kirkley, Suffolk, on 19 September 1855, the fourth child of William Davison (1816–1889), a shipwright and carpenter originally from Sunderland. His mother, Eliza, née Miller (1825–c.1900), supplemented the family income by taking in boarders, and his sisters Annie and Lizzie helped their mother as they expanded this business to the house next door. George, early recognized as the most promising child, did well at elementary school in Lowestoft before going on to the church foundation secondary school, St John's, Lowestoft. He continued his studies at evening classes and had passed the second-division civil service examination for boy clerk before he was twenty.

In 1874 Davison moved to work at the Exchequer and Audit Office in Somerset House, and lodged in north London. He met Susannah Louisa Potter (b. 1858?), the daughter of James Potter, a manufacturer, probably at an Islington church function, and they married in Finsbury Chapel in the City of London on 2 June 1883. They set up home at 10 Battersea Rise, near Clapham Junction, with his sister Annie and brother William occupying the ground floor. A son, Ronald, was born in 1884 and a daughter, Ruby, in 1889.

Davison seems to have taken up photography in 1885; in the same year was started the prestigious Camera Club, of which he shortly became assistant honorary secretary. Evidently his work was well regarded, for the club voted

him a testimonial in November 1887. He was a member of the Photographic Society of Great Britain (PSGB), later—from 1886—the Royal Photographic Society. He was soon elected to its executive council and became deeply involved in the artistic debates about photography then current. In 1887 he attacked the notion of photographic composition by rules, and over the next couple of years espoused the cause of naturalism, as proposed by his then friend Philip Henry Emerson and opposed by Henry Peach Robinson. Relations deteriorated when Emerson, irked at the increasing praise for Davison's work, rubbished his pictures in a review of November 1889; Davison's cause was thereupon taken up by Robinson. In November 1890 Davison read a paper to the Society of Arts entitled 'Impressionism in photography'; Emerson, who had by this time repudiated his earlier naturalistic views, replied in vitriolic and personally offensive terms, calling Davison a 'clerkly personage' who should be 'cut' by any gentleman. In the meantime Davison's picture *An Old Farmstead* (1888), taken with a pinhole camera to produce a 'soft focus', had won a prize at the PSGB exhibition of 1890. Retitled *The Onion Field*, it became his most famous photograph, and was fairly typical of his impressionist style.

More controversy followed, and with further-reaching results. Davison was invited to show examples of his work at the PSGB exhibition of 1891, but they were removed on a technicality after six days by the organization's secretary. Davison, Robinson, and ten other members resigned to form a 'bohemian club' that later became the renowned photographers' collective the Linked Ring. This was run along democratic lines with no president and a rotating chairman; as honorary secretary, Davison was the Ring's sole official. In February 1894 he resigned for business reasons and was presented with another testimonial.

The turning point in Davison's professional life came in 1889 when George Eastman—impressed with his organizational abilities and, very probably, with the dignity with which he emerged from his spat with Emerson—appointed him a director of the British branch of the Emerson Photographic Materials Company. In 1897 he became a full-time assistant manager, in 1899 he was appointed deputy managing director, then the following year took over as managing director. The initial salary of £1000 was modest, but Davison took full advantage of share options, becoming the second largest shareholder in Kodak (as the company became) after Eastman himself. By the time Eastman asked him to resign in 1912, Davison was a millionaire, and he used his wealth to promote his leftist political ideals as well as to enhance his personal comfort. He had by then given up photography; examples of his work are preserved at George Eastman House, Rochester, New York state, and at the National Museum of Photography, Film, and Television in Bradford (including the collection of the Royal Photographic Society).

In 1906 Davison commissioned George Walton, a Linked Ring connection who had designed the PSGB exhibition of 1897, as well as Kodak exhibitions and shop interiors, to draw the plans for a mansion, Wern Fawr, to be built at Harlech, north Wales. In 1907–8 Walton designed for Davison a luxurious houseboat called the *Log cabin*, which was used for excursions for Linked Ring members, as well as the White House at Shiplake, near Henley-on-Thames. This Davison made over to his wife, along with an ample income, when they parted in 1913; his anarchist–socialist views and boundless hospitality were never appreciated by his family.

Davison retreated to Wern Fawr, taking with him as housekeeper Florence Annie Austin-Jones, known as Joan (1897?–1955), who had been the secretary of the Liverpool-based Linked Ring member and Kodak representative Malcolm Arbuthnot. They were later married. Wern Fawr became an extraordinary centre for the arts; it had a much-admired music room, and Davison's hospitality to many of the leading English musicians of the period was unstinting. Visitors included the composer Sir Granville Bantock and his students from Birmingham, the composer and conductor Sir Eugene Goossens, and the pianist Cyril Smith. Davison owned an array of player pianos and aeolian organs, which were played by the photographer Alvin Langdon Coburn, another Linked Ring member, and by the composer and pianist Josef Holbrooke. To the surprise and consternation of the locals he also played host to the Margaret Morris dancers, who floated over the sand dunes in filmy costumes.

Davison aided several socialist projects, including the study centre at the White House, Ammanford, south Wales; the Central Labour College in London, a breakaway from Ruskin College, Oxford; and the famed Chopwell Communist Club in co. Durham (which was Labour rather than Marxist). He allegedly handed out leaflets at the meetings of George Ballard's Workers' Freedom Group, and at one such assembly met the great revolutionary Peter Kropotkin. In 1912 he funded the launch of a magazine, *The Anarchist*, in premises near the Glasgow offices of Kodak. It failed, closing in the following year, and thereafter Davison kept his philanthropic activities under direct control.

At Wern Fawr Davison played host to various political groups; the Whiteway Commune from near Stroud came for holidays and there were summer schools for the Freedom group and visitors from Fabian schools nearby. A story is related that, at one such gathering, the concert pianist Harriet Cohen played 'Chopsticks' with George Bernard Shaw. Davison also arranged free holidays in Harlech for deprived children from the vicinity of his latterly acquired London home, at 32 Holland Park.

Davison's own health—and that of his young daughter Doreen (*b.* 1921)—led him to relocate his family to a new house, Château des Enfants, near Antibes, France. Wern Fawr was sold in 1924 and became Coleg Harlech, a local education centre. In Antibes, Davison continued to welcome his musical friends and children for holidays; four were officially adopted. His house in Holland Park was also sold, but he continued to visit Britain. In 1930 he was taken ill at Exeter and, provoking the outrage of the *Evening News*, to which wealthy left-wingers were anathema,

hired a train to take him to London, where he was reconciled with his son. Thence he proceeded on a special coach on the Blue Train to Antibes, where he died at Château des Enfants on 26 December 1930. Following the cremation at Marseilles, his ashes were interred at Antibes.

One of the most influential photographers before the First World War, Davison is often remembered for the wrong reasons. The journalist and independent MP Horatio Bottomley attacked him as a Bolshevik corrupter of youth, yet nothing was further from the truth: he was an anarchist who abhorred the use of violence and a communist before the word was associated inevitably with Marxism.   COLIN OSMAN

Sources M. Weaver, ed., *British photography in the nineteenth century* (1989) · M. Harker, *The Linked Ring* (1979) · R. Davison, 'The family record', priv. coll. [David Davison] · papers and corresp., priv. coll. [Colin Osman] · J. Griffiths, 'Recollections of George Davison', *c.*1970, Coleg Harlech Archives · A. L. Coburn, *Autobiography*, ed. H. Gernsheim and A. Gernsheim (1966) · *British Journal of Photography*, 2 (9 Jan 1931) · J. Quail, *The slow burning fuse: lost history of British anarchists* (1978) · G. Barrett, *The first person* (1963) · C. Rosen, *The Goossens: a musical century* (1993) · K. Moon, *George Walton, designer and architect* (1993) · b. cert. · m. cert. [Susannah Potter] · d. cert.

Likenesses F. Daniels, portraits, NPG · F. Hollyer, portrait · A. Langdon Coburn, portrait, National Museum of Photography, Film and Television, Bradford, Royal Photographic Society collection

Davison, James William (1813–1885), music critic, was born on 5 October 1813 in London, the son of James Davison (*d.* 1858) and his wife, the actress and singer Maria Rebecca *Davison, *née* Duncan (1780x83–1858). He was given his first lessons in singing and the piano by his mother, and was then educated at University College School. Abandoning plans for the bar, he went to the Royal Academy of Music, where he studied the piano with W. H. Holmes and composition with George Macfarren. He wrote some orchestral music (including an overture that was played at a concert of the Society of British Musicians), some piano music (notably a duet overture, *Fortunatus*), and songs, especially settings of Keats and Shelley. However, he soon abandoned composition for criticism. His first writings appeared in the *Musical Magazine*. He was founder and first editor of the weekly *Musical Examiner* (1842–4), later merged into the *Musical World*, which he edited for the rest of his life. In 1846 he became music critic of *The Times*, a post he retained until 1879. Other journals to which he contributed included the *Saturday Review*, the *Pall Mall Gazette*, and (until 1884) *The Graphic*. His further activities included writing programme notes for the concerts at St James's Hall, where in 1844 he persuaded Louis Jullien to improve the content of the programmes; he also wrote notes for Charles Hallé's recitals. His only book was *An Essay on the Works of Frederic Chopin* (London, n.d. [1849]). He was one of the founder members of the Purcell Society (1876).

For many years Davison wielded an almost despotic sway as a critic. He was not a highly educated or cultured writer, though his style was terse and energetic. He was celebrated for his attachment to Sterndale Bennett and

Mendelssohn, whose popularity in Victorian England owed much to his advocacy, and was personally acquainted with Rossini, Auber, Spohr, Meyerbeer, and Halévy. He was also, unexpectedly for so conservative a critic, one of the first to recognize the merits of Berlioz, including as a conductor, and did much to champion him in England; with Liszt and D'Ortigue, he was the only person outside Berlioz's family to be addressed as 'tu'. However, he was bitterly hostile to Schumann, Gounod, Liszt, Wagner, and Brahms, and initially even to Schubert, all of whom he regarded as dangerous innovators, not least because they seemed to threaten the composers whose cause he espoused. He thought Spohr 'a dream—an ideal being', and that 'a more overrated man never existed' than Schubert. He once wrote: 'Robert Schumann has had his innings, and been bowled out—like Richard Wagner. *Paradise and the Peri* has gone to the tomb of the *Lohengrins*.' He moved in literary as well as musical circles, numbering Dickens, Thackeray, and Théophile Gautier among his friends. Sir George Grove, another friend, wrote that 'his knowledge and his extraordinary memory were as much at the service of his friends as the keen wit and humour—often Rabelaisian enough—with which he poured them forth. He was very much of a Bohemian.' On 12 May 1859 he married Arabella Goddard, who had been his pupil since 1850; they had two sons, Henry, who wrote his father's memoirs, *From Mendelssohn to Wagner* (1912), and Charles. Latterly he suffered from ill health, and went to live first in Malvern, then in Margate, where he died on 24 March 1885.

Davison's wife, **Arabella Goddard** (1836–1922), pianist, was born at St Servan, near St Malo, France, on 12 January 1836, the daughter of Thomas Goddard. At the age of four she played in her village, and went to Paris to take lessons from Frédéric Kalkbrenner when she was six. She studied further with Lucy Anderson, and in 1844, at the age of eight, played before another of Mrs Anderson's pupils, Queen Victoria, and in the same year published *Six Waltzes* for piano. She made her début at the Grand National Concerts at Her Majesty's Theatre on 23 October 1850. She was then recommended by Sigismond Thalberg, who had given her some lessons, to study interpretation with J. W. Davison, and also had composition lessons with George Macfarren. Much influenced by Davison, she was one of the first to study and perform Beethoven's late works, playing his B♭ sonata, op. 106, from memory at a concert of the Quartet Association at Willis's Rooms on 14 April 1853; and on 11 May she performed Sterndale Bennett's third piano concerto at the New Philharmonic Concerts. She then toured Germany and Italy, playing Mendelssohn's D minor concerto at the Leipzig Gewandhaus in October 1855.

Back in England, her stature now widely recognized, Goddard played Bennett's concerto at the Philharmonic Society on 9 June 1856, and also performed at the Crystal Palace and at the Monday Popular Concerts. In 1857 and 1858 she played all Beethoven's late sonatas (opp. 106 to 111), as well as a wide repertory of new music, and in 1859 gave his 'Eroica' symphony as a piano solo at the Bradford festival; she also appeared at festivals in Leeds (1858), Birmingham (1861–70), and Gloucester (1865). She married Davison on 12 May 1859. From 1873 to 1876 she toured America, Australia, and India; before leaving, she gave a farewell concert in March 1873, accompanying some of the most distinguished soloists of the day as well as playing solos. She virtually retired in 1880, though her last concert was with Sims Reeves on 21 March 1882; she was given a benefit concert at St James's Hall on 9 March 1890. The latter part of her life was lived at Tunbridge Wells in failing health and comparative obscurity. She died in Boulogne on 6 April 1922.   JOHN WARRACK

Sources *From Mendelssohn to Wagner: being the memoirs of J. W. Davison, forty years the music critic of The Times*, ed. H. Davison (1912) · Brown & Stratton, *Brit. mus.* · *The Times* (26 March 1885) · Grove, *Dict. mus.* · [S. Morison and others], *The history of The Times*, 2 (1939), 65, 443, 594 · *Correspondance générale: Hector Berlioz*, ed. P. Citron, 3 (Paris, 1978) · *Correspondance générale: Hector Berlioz*, ed. P. Citron, 4 (Paris, 1983) · A. W. Ganz, *Berlioz in London* (1950) · *MT*, 26 (1885), 221 · m. cert. · d. cert.
Archives News Int. RO, papers
Wealth at death £3651 5s. 8d.: resworn administration, July 1885, *CGPLA Eng. & Wales*

Davison [Davidson], **Jeremiah** (c.1695–1745), portrait painter, was born in England of Scottish parents. He copied the works of Sir Peter Lely before setting up in practice with the assistance of the well-known drapery painter Joseph van Aken. Frederick, prince of Wales, sat to him in 1730 (location of portrait unknown) and Admiral Byng, Viscount Torrington, was among his sitters the following year (portrait in National Maritime Museum, Greenwich).

Having met James, second duke of Atholl, at a masonic lodge in London, Davison painted his portrait and presented it to the lodge. Subsequently he painted another portrait of the duke, together with that of the duchess, and under their patronage went to Scotland about 1737. There he painted a large number of the duke's Murray relatives, remarking afterwards that he had made nearly £1500 sterling on his Scottish trip (Vertue, 3.129). Not long after his arrival he produced a handsome pair of full-length portraits of James Moray of Abercairney and his wife, Christian, he in tartan, she in a satin dress and elegant plumed hat, apparently to commemorate their marriage in February 1737. One of the most accomplished works from this period is his charming family group showing James, fourteenth earl of Morton, with his countess and their children, dated 1740, and formerly at Dalmahoy, the Morton family seat near Edinburgh (Scottish National Portrait Gallery, Edinburgh).

Davison returned to London about 1740, set up his studio in his house in Leicester Fields, and prospered, charging 8 guineas for a quarter-length picture, 16 for a half-length, and 32 for a full-length. He made his will on 13 November 1745, leaving about £1000, the residue of his estate, to his seven-year-old daughter Frances. He died, presumably at his home, between 24 and 29 December of that year.   ROSALIND K. MARSHALL

Sources Vertue, *Note books*, 3.129 · H. Walpole, *Anecdotes of painting in England: with some account of the principal artists*, ed. R. N. Wornum, new edn, 2 (1849) • R. K. Marshall, 'James, 13th earl of Morton and family, 1740', *National Galleries of Scotland Bulletin*, 2 (1977) • J. J. H. H. Stewart-Murray, seventh duke of Atholl, *Chronicles of the Atholl and Tullibardine families*, 5 vols. (privately printed, Edinburgh, 1908), vol. 2 • will, proved 30 Dec 1745, London; codicil, 24 Dec 1745, PRO, PROB 11/743

Archives NA Scot., Abercairney Muniments, GD 24/1/627 | Blair Castle, Atholl corresp., Jac.C. I (6) 54, 55 • Scot. NPG, letter of librarian and curator, United Grand Lodge of England to E. Stuart Falconer, Grand Secretary, Grand Lodge of Scotland

Wealth at death £1000: will, PRO, PROB 11/743; NA Scot., CC 8/8/116/1; W. T. Whitley, *Artists and their friends in England, 1700–99* (1928), 1.61

Davison, John (1777–1834), theologian, was born on 28 May 1777 at Morpeth, Northumberland, the eldest son of John Davison and his wife Mary. He was brought up at Durham, to which his father, a schoolmaster, had moved shortly after his birth, and was educated there, either at the grammar school or the cathedral school. In 1794 he proceeded to Christ Church, Oxford, where in 1798 he gained both a Craven scholarship and his BA. In 1800 he was elected a fellow of Oriel College, shortly afterwards becoming a private tutor outside the university. He was ordained in 1803. In 1810 he returned to Oxford as one of the tutors at Oriel, and served occasionally as public examiner and Whitehall preacher until November 1817, when Lord Liverpool presented him to the vicarage of Sutterton, near Boston in Lincolnshire. In 1818 the bishop of Durham, Shute Barrington, appointed him rector of Washington, near Gateshead. On 20 July 1819 he married Mary, daughter of Robert Thorp, elder brother of Charles Thorp: they had four sons and six daughters. In 1824 he became prebend of Sneating in St Paul's Cathedral, and in 1826 Lord Liverpool appointed him a prebendary of Worcester Cathedral and subsequently rector of Upton upon Severn.

Davison was the theological scholar of the early Noetics, the group of Anglican clergymen at Oriel College, Oxford, who defended Christianity on the grounds of its reasonableness. It is perhaps significant that he was the tutor of Renn Dickson Hampden, the theologian of the later Noetics whose controversial Bampton lectures Davison both read and approved. However, unlike Hampden, he achieved neither notoriety nor university office; the consequence is that he has been unjustly forgotten.

Davison's earliest publications were occasional contributions to the *Quarterly Review* which began to appear after his return to Oriel. Like his fellow Noetics, Davison did not confine himself to religious themes. In 1811 he supported Edward Copleston in his defence of an educationally reformed Oxford University against the calumnies of the *Edinburgh Review*. He recognized the importance of educating country gentlemen in the performance of their duties by giving them a broadly based Christian education through the medium of the classics, so that they should have some better pursuit than that of partridges. Like Richard Whately, he also supported educating the poor by preaching in favour of National Society schools: there was, he believed, no necessary connection between knowledge and insubordination. Again like Richard Whately,

although no liberal (in his dialogue between the Christian and the Reformer, published in 1819, he was on the side of the anti-radical Christian), he supported the whig Sir Samuel Romilly's campaign for the abolition of capital punishment for minor property offences.

In Davison's *Considerations on the Poor Laws* (1817), his principal publication of this period, he advocated the strengthening of relief for the infirm and the gradual abolition of automatic relief for the able-bodied over the course of a decade: such relief encouraged dependence and denied a man his self-respect. Abolition was possible on the assumption that able-bodied persons were capable of acting responsibly by making provision for themselves in good times to tide them over the bad. In the case of manufacturing workers, this would be by savings, and in the case of agricultural labourers, by cultivating smallholdings and other sources of income. Although some provision for the destitute would be required, this would be supplied by the rich making voluntary donations to a fund to assist the poor. However, independence had its limits: although not opposed to free trade, in his *Letter to Mr Canning* of 1826 Davison opposed the sudden abolition of duties on the importation of silk, which had caused misery to the domestic industry.

Davison's principal works of theological scholarship did not appear until after he had become a parish priest. The chief of these—much admired by his Oriel colleagues, Thomas Arnold and John Henry Newman, among others—were his Warburtonian lectures on prophecy (1824), which were characteristically Noetic. They emphasized the primacy of revealed religion in view of the insufficiency of natural religion, and considered prophecy as one of the evidences of Christianity. They also endorsed the Noetic theme that such evidences were adapted to the minds of those to whom they were addressed, and thus presented the reader with difficulties and mysteries just as the natural world did. The novelty of the work lay in its discussion of the progressive nature of revelation, a doctrine which influenced Davison's fellow Noetic, Baden Powell, and in Davison's view that prophecy was a preparatory revelation of Christianity, the principal age of prophecy having passed. The polemic was obvious: it was a scholarly attack both on the prophetic interpretation of contemporary political events by millenarian evangelicals and on the advocates of rational religion.

These themes were continued in Davison's work on the origins of primitive sacrifice (1825), a subject touched on in the earlier work. He attacked the evangelical Archbishop Magee's view that primitive sacrifice was divinely ordained, at the same time as he contended that this did not undermine the divine nature of the doctrine of the atoning power of blood as stated in the Mosaic law. This was a wholly new doctrine, and an instance of the progressive nature of revelation that he had outlined in his earlier work. He expressly attacked Unitarians for denying the doctrine of the atonement. According to him, such a denial was possible only if they also ignored or disputed the divine inspiration of the Bible.

Davison did not enjoy good health at Upton, the preferment that his theological writings had obtained, and in January 1834 became ill enough to have to move to Cheltenham, where he died on 6 May of the same year. He was buried in the chancel of Worcester Cathedral.

W. G. BLAIKIE, rev. RICHARD BRENT

Sources J. Davison, *Remains and occasional publications* (1841) · R. Brent, *Liberal Anglican politics: whiggery, religion, and reform, 1830–1841* (1987) · P. Corsi, *Science and religion: Baden Powell and the Anglican debate, 1800–1860* (1988) · H. Hampden, ed., *Some memorials of Renn Dickson Hampden* (1871)
Archives Keble College, Oxford, corresp. with John Keble · Oriel College, Oxford, letters from John Keble

Davison, Sir John Alec Biggs- (1918–1988), politician, was born in Boscombe, Bournemouth, on 7 June 1918, the son of John Norman Biggs-Davison, a major in the Royal Garrison Artillery, and his wife, Sarah, *née* Wright. He was brought up as a Catholic, and remained a devout member of his church until the end of his life. However, he had a strong Ulster Presbyterian background: his grandfather wrote a pamphlet suggesting that the pope was Antichrist. Biggs-Davison, when he came to adulthood, retained strong elements of the family's Ulster tradition. He was a rarity in being an argumentative and committed Catholic Ulster Unionist. Indeed his last book, written with George Chowdharay-Best, was *The Cross of St. Patrick: the Catholic Unionist Tradition in Ireland* (1985).

Biggs-Davison was educated at Clifton College preparatory school and Clifton College itself. He went as an exhibitioner to Magdalen College, Oxford, but his studies were interrupted by the war. Having been commissioned in the Royal Marines in 1939, and promoted lieutenant in 1940, he entered the Indian Civil Service in 1942, being the last British officer appointed to the Punjab Commission in that year. From 1943 to 1944 he was forward liaison officer at Coxs Bazar, in a somewhat irregular military unit operating on the north-west frontier of India, similar in make-up to, if less prominent than, Orde Wingate's Chindits in Burma. He was political assistant and commandant in the border military police, and later deputy commissioner in Dera Ghazi Khan, before and after the transfer of power to Pakistan, from 1946 to 1948. He then returned to England, where he was awarded his Oxford BA under war regulations in June 1948. He was employed as an information officer at Conservative central office from 1948 to 1950. He joined the Conservative Research Department in 1950, where he stayed until 1955. He fought but lost Coventry South in the general election of October 1951. On 27 November 1948 he married Pamela Mary, second daughter of Ralph Hodder-Williams, chairman of Hodder and Stoughton, publishers, and army officer. They had two sons and four daughters.

Biggs-Davison entered parliament as the Conservative MP for Chigwell, Essex, in May 1955. He retained that seat and, following boundary changes in 1974, that of Epping Forest, until his death in September 1988. He was knighted in June 1981. Although he never held ministerial office, he had a bewildering variety of political interests,

and every cause which he espoused was pursued with ferocious tenacity. He was one of nature's rebels. When Anthony Eden went to war with Egypt in 1956 over the Egyptian nationalization of the Suez Canal, Biggs-Davison was one of the few tory MPs who rebelled over the British and French withdrawal from the battle. Along with seven other MPs he resigned the tory whip on this issue in May 1957, and it was more than a year later (in June 1958) that he resumed his Conservative allegiance in the House of Commons. Later, when Margaret Thatcher became leader of the Conservative Party in 1975, he was appointed as a junior front bench spokesman on African affairs, with particular reference to what was then Southern Rhodesia, later Zimbabwe. In 1978, along with Winston Churchill—grandson of the wartime prime minister—he resigned his post in protest against the Conservative policy of opposition to the white-dominated government then in power in that country, although that government was led—in form, at least—by Bishop Abel Muzowera.

Like some fellow Conservatives who were strongly in favour of preserving imperial links, Biggs-Davison also believed passionately in developing closer ties between the United Kingdom and continental Europe. While at the Conservative Research Department he acted as secretary to the British Conservative delegation to the Council of Europe in Strasbourg in 1952 and 1953. He manifested his interest in imperial affairs by acting as an observer at the Malta referendum in 1956. Moreover, he demonstrated his interest in Britain's international relations by serving on various international parliamentary committees and delegations between 1956 and 1984: in addition to Malta, these were to west Africa in 1956, Austria in 1964, France and Ottawa (as a member of the Inter-Parliamentary Union) in 1965, Malawi in 1968, Gibraltar and Tunisia in 1969, Zambia in 1975, the Republic of Ireland in 1981, the Falkland Islands in 1982, Cyprus in 1983, and Canada in 1984.

Biggs-Davison's great passion, however, was Northern Ireland. He served as chairman of the Conservative parliamentary Northern Ireland committee, and between 1976 and 1978 was an opposition front bench spokesman on Northern Ireland. In addition to his journalism—and he had a prolific output—he wrote a number of books and pamphlets, most of which were concerned with the affairs of that troubled province. They included *The Hand is Red* (1974), *Rock Firm for the Union* (1979), and *The Cross of St. Patrick* (1985). He also founded the Friends of the Union. His brother-in-law was George Wyndham and, as an act of filial piety, Biggs-Davison also wrote a biography of George Wyndham (1951), his brother-in-law's father, who had been chief secretary for Ireland in the days when the whole of Ireland was united under the British crown. This was typical of Biggs-Davison. A man immoveable in his opinions, he had a great deal of the sentimental about him. He was the most friendly and avuncular of souls in his attitude to his fellow human beings, even to those with whom he had the most profound differences of opinion. Moreover, his fundamental devotion to his large family and his manifold causes could never be held in doubt.

He died of cancer on 17 September 1988 at Musgrove Park Hospital, Taunton, Somerset. He was survived by his wife and six children.   PATRICK COSGRAVE

Sources A. Roth, *Parliamentary profiles, A–D* (1988) · *Dod's Parliamentary Companion* (1988) · *WWW, 1981–90* · *The Times* (19 Sept 1988) · *The Guardian* (19 Sept 1988) · *The Independent* (19 Sept 1988) · d. cert.
Archives BL OIOC, diaries, letters, and reports, MS Eur. D 844 · Bodl. Oxf., papers · HLRO, papers | BLPES, corresp. with Lady Rhys Williams · Bodl. RH, corresp. with Sir R. R. Welensky · CAC Cam., corresp. with H. M. Belgion
Likenesses photograph, repro. in *The Times* · photograph, repro. in *The Independent*
Wealth at death £29,714: probate, 15 Dec 1988, *CGPLA Eng. & Wales*

Davison [*née* Duncan], **Maria Rebecca** (1780x83–1858), actress, is reputed to have been born in Liverpool, where her parents were provincial performers. From an early age she played children's parts (hobgoblins, fairies, cupids, and so on) in Dublin, Liverpool, and Newcastle, and her first recorded appearance in a speaking part was in Newcastle in 1794–5 as the duke of York to the Richard III of George Frederick Cooke; she also played there Tom Thumb. Elizabeth Farren, by whom she was seen in *The Woodman*, is said to have recognized in her a talent similar to her own, and referred to her as 'a little wonder'. In 1796 she appeared in Dublin as Rosetta in Isaac Bickerstaff's *Love in a Village* and Priscilla Tomboy for her father's benefit. Her first regular engagement was from Tate Wilkinson, as a member of whose company she appeared in York, playing on her first appearance Sophia in Thomas Holcroft's *The Road to Ruin* and Gillian in Charles Dibdin's *The Quaker*. With her reputation increasing, she acted in Edinburgh, Glasgow, and Liverpool. At Margate in 1804 she was seen by a Mr Graham as Widow Cheerly in Andrew Cherry's *The Soldier's Daughter*, and he recommended her to Richard Wroughton for Drury Lane, where she appeared on 8 October 1804, billed as Miss Duncan from Edinburgh, playing for fifteen nights Lady Teazle to the Sir Peter of Charles Matthews and the Charles Surface of R. W. Elliston. She took many leading parts during her first season, including Rosalind, Lady Townly, Lydia Languish, and Letitia Hardy in Hannah Cowley's *The Belle's Stratagem*. On 31 January 1805 she created the role of Juliana in John Tobin's *The Honeymoon*, which ran for twenty-eight nights: her song at the end of act v was constantly encored, and the part finally made her name. She remained with the Drury Lane company for fourteen years, and migrated with it to the Lyceum and elsewhere. The presence of Dorothy Jordan was somewhat of an obstacle to her career as Maria Duncan played similar parts, but she enjoyed considerable popularity, even in roles associated particularly with Mrs Jordan, such as Peggy in Garrick's *The Country Girl*.

On 31 October 1812 Maria Duncan married James Davison (*d.* 1858), and on 5 November she played, as 'Mrs Davison, late Miss Duncan', Belinda in *All in the Wrong*. The marriage was not happy and it was said that her husband deserted her for the gaming tables. They had two sons, the

Maria Rebecca Davison (1780x83–1858), by Henry Singleton, exh. RA 1805 [as Juliana in *The Honeymoon* by John Tobin]

elder being James William *Davison, music critic of *The Times*. She continued on the stage, and appeared in November 1816 in Birmingham, where her 'increasing embonpoint' was remarked upon. On 8 September 1819 she reappeared in London as Lady Teazle to W. C. Macready's Joseph Surface at Covent Garden. The following year she returned to Drury Lane as Julia in *The Rivals*. At Covent Garden on 14 June 1821 she again played, for her benefit, Lady Teazle. She then moved to the Haymarket to take leading business, but was once more at Drury Lane until 13 June 1829, when she played Mrs Subtle in *Paul Pry*, probably her last performance there.

Maria Davison was rather tall, a full, handsome person, with extremely black hair, dark hazel eyes, strongly formed features, and a rich, sweet voice, which was heard at its best in Scottish ballads and in duet with John Braham. She was noted for her 'breeches parts', such as Macheath: Leigh Hunt observed that 'she wears the breeches much better than becomes her'. As a successor to Elizabeth Farren, she was regarded by J. W. Cole as the first high-comedy actress of the London stage for many years. She was said to have made 'a nice little fortune' on a final salary of £15 a week. She lived for many years in retirement and died shortly after her husband, on 30 May 1858, at 5 Alfred Place, Brompton.

JOSEPH KNIGHT, *rev.* J. GILLILAND

Sources L. Hunt, *Critical essays on the performers of the London theatres* (1807) · T. Gilliland, *The dramatic mirror, containing the history of the stage from the earliest period, to the present time*, 2 vols. (1808) · Mrs C. Baron-Wilson, *Our actresses*, 2 vols. (1844) · *Oxberry's Dramatic Biography*, 1/4 (1825), 51–7 · J. W. Cole, *The life and theatrical times of Charles Kean … including a summary of the English stage for the last fifty* *years*, 2 vols. (1859) · *The biography of the British stage, being correct narratives of the lives of all the principal actors and actresses* (1824) · *Theatrical Inquisitor* · Mrs N. Crosland [C. Toulmin], *Landmarks of a literary life, 1820–1892* (1893) · Boase, *Mod. Eng. biog.* · Adams, *Drama* · Genest, *Eng. stage* · A. Davies and E. Kilmurray, *Dictionary of British portraiture*, 4 vols. (1979–81) · Hall, *Dramatic ports.* · W. C. Lane and N. E. Browne, eds., *A. L. A. portrait index* (1906) · d. cert.

Likenesses H. Singleton, oils, exh. RA 1805, Garr. Club [*see illus.*] · C. Turner, mezzotint, pubd 1809 (after G. H. Harlow), BM, NPG · M. Sharp, oils, V&A · prints, BM, NPG · prints, repro. in *Oxberry's Dramatic Biography* · prints, Harvard TC · prints, repro. in *The London stage*, 3

Davison, Richard (1796–1869), lawyer and politician, was born at Knockboy, Broughshane, co. Antrim, the son of Alexander Davison of Knockboy and his wife, Mary, daughter of McKillop of Glenarm. Trained in the law, he became a solicitor in 1818 and a founder member and senior partner of the firm of Davison and Torrens, a successful Belfast legal practice with important individual clients as well as substantial public companies (including several railways) and the Belfast Harbour Commissioners. Described as 'a rentier of rather refined tastes' (Budge and O'Leary, 59), Davison was a noted conchologist, with a fine collection of shells, and a supporter of charitable institutions, including the General Hospital and the Deaf and Dumb Institute. A sincere Anglican, he was a founder member in 1854 of the Christ Church Protestant Association, a body dedicated to turning back the advances made by the Catholic community in Ireland since the Act of Union, not least the 1829 Catholic Emancipation Act, which had at last permitted Catholics to sit in parliament.

In July 1852 Davison stood successfully for Belfast, on the basis of his long business experience and his well-known commitment to the protestant cause and the Conservative interest. In his maiden speech, in December 1852, he confessed that he was not a speech-maker, exemplifying this by speaking less than a dozen times during the eight years of his representation. He was joined in 1852 by another new Conservative candidate, H. M. Cairns, and though both were successful, with Davison topping the poll, it was Cairns who was to become the eminent parliamentarian, rising to the lord chancellorship of England, while Davison contented himself with conscientious voting and attention to the needs of his constituents. Successful in the elections of 1857, and unopposed in 1859, Davison resigned his seat on health grounds in April 1860.

Described by his opponents as having 'no special aptitude for Senatorial pursuits' and as 'not a success in the House of Commons', his 'genial and amiable disposition' was nevertheless conceded, while his supporters expressed warm regard for the 'untiring zeal' with which he devoted himself 'to the business of the House', doing 'more real work of legislation than many' (*Belfast News-Letter*, 2 June 1860, leader) and gaining the respect of both sides. On his retirement he boasted that he 'never asked for personal favour from any government ... never gave a vote that either compromised [his] own political principles or betrayed the trust' of his electors. His interests

had included support for free trade and for 'unrestricted competition', for tenant right as it existed in Ulster, for the extension of education (but with religious and secular instruction combined), and for the extension of railways and inland navigation. He had supported, also, the extension of trade in China but opposed warmongering, being unable to shut his eyes 'to the fact that a cruel and disproportionate revenge has been inflicted on a semi-civilised people' (*Belfast News-Letter*, 11 March 1857). He also opposed the extension of the Maynooth grant, but he was no bigot, and throughout he seems to have conducted himself with level-headed good sense and tolerance. He was a member of the Carlton Club.

In 1822 Davison married Margaret, daughter of George Casement MD of Larne. They had seven children, four of whom predeceased him: Matilda, the first-born, who died in infancy; George (1830–1848); Jane (1837–1852); and Mary (1826–1862), who married Henry Harrison of Holywood. The eldest son, Alexander (b. 1825), seems to have been banished to farm in Canada in 1854, while the two surviving daughters were Margaret Davison (b. 1824) and Matilda Greatorex, widow (b. 1828). Davison's wife, Margaret, died in 1847. For much of his professional life he resided at The Abbey, Whiteabbey, co. Antrim, until shortly after his retirement from parliament, when he moved to Mertoun Hall, Cultra, co. Down. There he died on 20 February 1869, and was buried on 25 February in the family burial-ground of the First Presbyterian Church, Broughshane.

DAVID HARKNESS

Sources *Dod's Parliamentary Companion* · *Belfast News-Letter* (11 March 1857) · *Belfast News-Letter* (2 June 1860) · *Hansard 3* (1832–60) · will, PRO NIre., MIC 15c/2/10, p. 457 · J. Emerson Tennent, correspondence, PRO NIre., D 2922/B/9/1–18 · A. Jordan, *Who cared? Charity in Victorian and Edwardian Belfast* [1993] · *Northern Whig* (22 Feb 1869) · I. Budge and C. O'Leary, *Belfast: approach to crisis. A study of Belfast politics, 1613–1970* (1973)

Wealth at death under £12,000: probate, 9 April 1869, *CGPLA Ire.*

Davison, Walter (1581?–1602x8). *See under* Davison, Francis (1573/4–1613x19).

Davison, William. *See* Davisson, William (c.1593–1669).

Davison, William (d. 1608), diplomat and administrator, presents a number of biographical problems. Sir James Melville of Halhill recorded that Davison told him that he 'was com of Scotismen and was a Scotiman at hart', but hardly anything is known about his background or his personal life (*Memoirs of His Own Life*, 328). His parents cannot be identified, although a brother is mentioned in a letter of 1583, and he left his sister Anne, who married a John Carpenter, an annuity in his will. He is found in no extant university or inns of court records, and all that can be said of his education is that he was fluent in French as well as Latin.

About 1570 Davison married Catherine, daughter of Francis Spelman, a minor Norfolk squire, and his wife, Mary Hill, daughter of Elizabeth Isley, who married first Richard Hill and then Sir John Mason. Elizabeth Isley was also first cousin to Jane Guildford, the mother of Robert Dudley, earl of Leicester (1532/3–1588), who always addressed Davison as 'cousin Davison'. Davison's wife predeceased him, but they had six children who lived to adulthood—two daughters and four sons. His eldest son, Francis *Davison (1573/4–1613x19), enjoyed a contemporary reputation as a poet, while a younger son, Walter *Davison (1581?–1602x8) [see under Davison, Francis (1573/4–1613x19)], followed a military career.

The Davison papers There is also a technical reason why Davison the man remains relatively obscure. In 1619 the keeper of the state paper office, Sir Thomas Wilson, discovered that Davison's papers had been sold to the manuscript collector Ralph Starkey. Since Starkey obtained papers of Francis Davison as well, it has been assumed that Francis was the seller. However, Wilson recorded that Starkey bought them from Davison's son-in-law W[illiam] Duncombe. Wilson claimed that the papers were Davison's secretarial papers and therefore belonged in the paper office. He obtained a warrant from the privy council to seize them on 10 August 1619, and four days later he removed 'a sackfull of papers to the number of 45 pacquets' from Starkey's house, which he later had bound 'into bookes with the rest' (BL, Harley MS 286, fol. 286r, PRO, SP 45/20/99). However, not all the papers he obtained were Davison's, nor did he obtain all of Starkey's Davison papers, for a sizeable body is now found among the Harley manuscripts. Together with the rest of Starkey's collection they were bought by Symonds D'Ewes in 1628. D'Ewes's library in turn was purchased by Humfrey Wanley on behalf of Robert Harley in 1703–6.

Elizabethan diplomatic practice was largely a matter of personal preference. Davison does not appear to have used letter-books, but he retained drafts (minutes) of his out-letters as well as the original letters received, and his papers form one of the richest sources for Elizabethan diplomacy between 1575 and 1586. Without them the state papers for that period (particularly the state papers, foreign) would be greatly reduced. However, the papers have also been weeded of the more obviously personal material, presumably when they were sold to Starkey. Some of Davison's surviving correspondence can legitimately be described as private, but for all its size the collection sheds relatively little light on his personal life.

Initial diplomatic career, 1574–1576 By 1574 Davison was one of Francis Walsingham's confidential men of business. Thanks to the disappearance of Walsingham's own private papers, the origin of their association (and whether Davison served with him during his embassy to France in 1570–73) is unknown. The relationship is nevertheless the key to Davison's career. Melville recorded that he first met Davison when he 'was at my house in company with Sir Harry Killigrew, my auld friend, when he was resident in Scotland' (Memoirs of His Own Life, 360). Nicholas Harris Nicolas, unaware of Killigrew's later embassies to Scotland when writing his biography of Davison, assumed the meeting occurred during Killigrew's embassy in June and July 1566, a date that has been accepted since. However, this is an error, not least because

in June 1566 Melville was sent to Elizabeth I to announce the birth of James VI.

The association between Davison and Killigrew began when Walsingham attached Davison to Killigrew's embassy to Scotland in May 1574, and this was undoubtedly the occasion when Davison met Melville. Killigrew was effusive in his thanks to Walsingham for Davison's services, and he and Davison became close friends as a result. When Davison returned to London in July with a confidential memorandum Walsingham described him as 'a man of his whom he lent Mr. Killigrew' (CSP Scot., 1574–81, art. 25). Davison accompanied Killigrew to Scotland again in the following summer. This time Killigrew was instructed to leave Davison as resident agent in Scotland if he considered one necessary. However, this embassy never got beyond Berwick, for its arrival coincided with the border incident known as the Reidswire raid, of 7 July 1575. Davison did little more than act as a messenger for Killigrew, who nevertheless brought him to Leicester's attention, as 'a gentleman who has married a kinswoman of your lordship's, though unknown, I think, yet to you' (CSP Scot., 1574–81, arts. 179, 184).

Six months later Davison was sent on his first independent mission. In January 1576 Elizabeth had been offered the sovereignty of Holland and Zealand, which she was unwilling to accept if a broader settlement in the Netherlands could be arranged. Philip II's governor-general, Don Luis de Requesens, died on 5 March, and at the end of the month Elizabeth sent Davison to the council of state in Brussels to see if it would now grant a ceasefire. If it was willing he was then to obtain William of Orange's adherence. When he arrived at Brussels in April, Davison was informed that the council could not offer a ceasefire without Philip's prior approval. His own assessment was that it was interested only in bringing the siege of Zierickzee to a successful conclusion. On 23 April, Walsingham informed him that in view of the attitude in Brussels he may as well return, and he left early in May.

The Netherlands embassies of 1577–1579 At the beginning of 1577 the most mysterious of Davison's embassies took place. Thanks to a single reference in February 1577 to Davison's coming from Zealand with Orange's agent Charles de Liévin, sieur de Famars, Professor G. M. Bell has suggested that he may have undertaken a short mission to Orange then. His surmise is confirmed by a letter from Leicester to Orange of 7 March, which notes that, in sending Famars, Orange had followed advice from Leicester passed to him by Davison, 'l'advis que je vous ay donné par Monsr Davison' (Kervyn de Lettenhove, 9, art. 3383). There are numerous other references to Davison's acting as an intermediary between Orange and England in spring 1577, and he is not known to have met him on any prior occasion. The mission also marked the beginning of Davison's association with Leicester, and it is just possible that he was sent privately by the earl rather than officially by the queen. In May, Leicester asked Davison to draft letters in French to Orange and his wife thanking them for naming him godfather to their daughter.

In August 1577 Davison was sent to the Netherlands as

resident agent with a daily allowance of £1 6s. 8d., a post he held until May 1579. Dr Thomas Wilson had served as agent between November 1576 and June 1577, but it is not clear whether he was to be replaced as a matter of course. Davison was appointed in July after the news of Don Juan of Austria's seizure of Namur was received. His instructions (26 July, finalized 2 August) provided a cover story that he had been appointed before Namur to replace Wilson as resident with Don Juan. However, his real purpose was to assure the states general that Elizabeth would support them if Don Juan attempted a reconquest by force and 'covertly as of yourself' advise them to accept the leadership of Orange (BL, Harley MS 285, fols. 44r–45r). He was also expected to co-ordinate the still vague plans for English military assistance to Orange under Leicester's command. Leicester later wrote, 'my desire of your going was chiefly to deal with him [Orange] therein' (CSP for., 1577–8, 308).

Davison arrived in Antwerp on 10 August and immediately reported that Don Juan was determined on reconquest with the enterprise of England as his ultimate aim. In this and later assessments Davison consistently argued that the Netherlands was the key to English security, and that he was confident that the strength of the Dutch cities would make reconquest difficult. An embassy under Charles Philippe de Croye, marquis de Havré, was sent to Elizabeth in September and negotiated the terms for English assistance. At that point it was feared that Henri Guise, third duc de Guise, might come to Don Juan's aid. It was decided that the Leicester expedition would be sent if Guise intervened. At the end of September, Leicester asked Davison to arrange for Orange to request his expedition immediately in order to capitalize on Elizabeth's willingness to act. However, in early October the states general decided that they would not need the English army until the following spring.

On 19 September, Orange arrived in Antwerp, and Davison accompanied him on his famous entry into Brussels three days later. He now argued that Orange offered an opportunity to create a friendly Netherlands government that should not be missed. Yet he also noted the impending arrival of the Archduke Mathias of Austria. Davison was careful in his reporting—once a week was expected—but delays in communication, the apparent rejection of English aid, and the preference for Mathias over Orange as a replacement governor-general for Don Juan made London fretful. On 27 October, Davison supplied a calmly argued assessment that the appointment of Mathias might have its advantages. However, on 15 November he attributed the rejection of English aid to jealousy of Orange.

On 4 November the states general complained to Davison that according to Havré (who had remained in England) his reports of dissension in the Netherlands had discouraged Elizabeth. Later in the month Leicester warned him of complaints (probably also from Havré) that 'you only follow the prince', while still noting that Davison was 'my especial agent to him' (CSP for., 1577–8, art. 453). Davison replied that his original commission was not to the

states general, and 'there is scarce any other with whom I may frankly deal' (ibid., art. 461).

In December, Elizabeth tried for a final time to arrange a mediated settlement with Philip, while at the same time returning Havré to Brussels with proposals for military assistance if necessary. Her efforts at mediation were conducted by a series of special envoys, and Davison could only pass on Orange's opinion that they would be fruitless. His own embassy was now reshaped by three events: the queen's decision in late January to postpone the Leicester expedition in favour of more indirect forms of financial and military assistance, Don Juan's defeat of the army of the states at Gembloux on 31 January 1578, and the intervention of François, duc d'Anjou, in February. On 8 March he sent Walsingham a long analysis of the situation, in which he attributed Dutch interest in Anjou to Elizabeth's hesitation. Elizabeth could not abandon the Dutch, and it made more sense to aid them openly. Walsingham showed the memorandum to Elizabeth, and it was 'greatly approved by her touching the manner, but as for the matter she takes daily less taste thereof' (CSP for., 1577–8, arts. 676, 714).

Davison's position now became awkward. He informed Leicester privately that he would make sure it was known that 'this change succeeded againste the desire of your lordship' (Kervyn de Lettenhove, 10, art. 3820). On 18 April the states general informed him officially that they were negotiating with Anjou, and he warned them Elizabeth would react badly. At the same time he faced further accusations that he had not defended Elizabeth's decisions over military aid but had agreed with her Dutch critics, that he had complained that the instructions he received were 'fonde and childish', and that he was too much in Orange's pocket (CSP for., 1577–8, art. 835). Walsingham advised him to cease sending his own opinions and confine himself to reporting the facts. Thomas Wilkes also warned him that his criticisms had alienated men he thought were his friends. One may have been William Cecil, Baron Burghley, for in December 1578 Davison was concerned that the lord treasurer had not answered his letters for six months.

Elizabeth's response to the Anjou negotiations was to send Walsingham and William Brooke, tenth Baron Cobham, as special envoys to the Netherlands. They arrived at the end of June, and until Walsingham returned to England in early October, Davison was very much his subordinate. In mid-March, Davison had been sent the authority to raise loans to the value of £100,000, which Elizabeth had agreed to supply to the states general. In May he was sent an instalment of £20,000 in bullion. However, he was not to disburse it until the result of the negotiations with Anjou was known, and in July he was ordered to retain custody of both the authority and the bullion until instructed by Walsingham and Cobham.

After Walsingham's departure Davison became involved in the clash between Orange and the Calvinist radicals of Ghent, in which John-Casimir of the Palatinate (whose army Elizabeth had funded) supported the gantois. Worried both by rumours that Casimir was acting on the queen's behalf and the possible effects of an open rebuke to Casimir from Elizabeth herself, Walsingham instructed Davison on his own authority to persuade Casimir to withdraw. Davison's encounter with Casimir took place in Ghent on 8 November; it was a stormy one and Casimir immediately complained to London. Although London backed Davison, Leicester in December sent Casimir's friend Daniel Rogers to calm him down. On the night of 10 January 1579 Davison, Orange, and Casimir were formally reconciled—though with more carousing than Davison would have liked.

The future of Davison's posting appears to have depended on the imperial offer to mediate between the states general and Philip, which resulted in the Cologne conference of summer 1579. On 19 January Walsingham informed Davison that if Elizabeth sent a delegation he would be included. Davison was now exhausted and ill and looking forward to his recall. Elizabeth hesitated for several months, but finally (after Davison had been deliberately excluded from the Cologne conference) she sent him his recall in mid-April. His last months were spent in tidying up and forwarding the paperwork over her loans to the states general. When he returned in May, he brought with him the Burgundian jewels that the states general had deposited as security with him and Walsingham in summer 1578.

Sufficient correspondence survives from this embassy to give some idea of Davison's personal circumstances. His wife joined him in Antwerp with his son 'Frank' in November 1577 (*CSP for.*, *1575–7*, art. 1367). Another child (possibly a daughter) was born there in summer 1578. Most of his private correspondence consists of letters received, chiefly from Henry Killigrew, but also his wife's cousin Edward Cheke, Walsingham's secretary Laurence Tomson, John Stubbe, and Thomas Randolph. Together they arranged for the appointment of the presbyterian Walter Travers as chaplain to the Merchant Adventurers in Antwerp in early 1578. This now celebrated affair embittered Davison's relations with Nicholas Loddington, the governor of the Merchant Adventurers, who complained to Walsingham. Walsingham in turn ordered Davison firmly 'to forbear further proceeding therein' (*CSP for.*, *1577–8*, art. 852). Davison's letters reveal a dry and sardonic humour, but also a somewhat fastidious disapproval of Dutch drinking habits, even those of his hero Orange.

Scottish embassies, 1582–1584   Although he kept up his correspondence with his friends in the Netherlands, Davison was not employed there again until 1584. In July 1580 Elizabeth proposed to send him to Orange, but then changed her mind. On 19 January 1579 he was appointed clerk of the treasury and *custos brevium* (keeper of the writs) of the court of king's bench for life. He had sued for this office in mid-1578, but Elizabeth took some persuading because she did not think it would 'serve your present necessity' (*CSP for.*, *1578–9*, arts. 356, 459). A further preferment was discussed with his friends in the winter of 1582–3, but it was not specified. Of his other personal affairs, all that is known is the birth of his son Christopher in December 1581 and the appointment of Sir Christopher Hatton

and the baby's maternal great-grandmother, Lady Mason, as godparents.

In 1582 and 1584 Davison was employed in two special missions to Scotland, both dealing with the aftermath of the Ruthven raid of 20 August 1582, in which a group of protestant nobles had separated James VI from his favourite, Esmé Stewart, first duke of Lennox. Elizabeth's government was anxious to stabilize the new Scottish administration and prevent the French from trying to restore Lennox. The situation was made particularly awkward by the apparent Anglo-French co-operation in support of Anjou in the Netherlands. In November, Henri III sent the former ambassador to England, Bertrand de Salignac, sieur de la Mothe-Fénelon, first to London and then Edinburgh, with instructions to free James if he was a captive (as Mary, queen of Scots, claimed), negotiate a general reconciliation, and arrange for Lennox to retire to France. Although Elizabeth could not refuse him a passport, the English were suspicious that his purpose was to revive French influence. Although these fears were exaggerated, in December, Davison was given the task of escorting him to Scotland.

This mission had its comic aspects. Initially Davison was to try to delay Fénelon until Lennox had left Scotland. As it turned out they encountered Lennox on his way south between Topcliffe and Northallerton, Yorkshire, on 27 December. The day was so stormy that Lennox and Fénelon spoke only briefly and Davison could not follow all they said. He also spent much time surreptitiously checking Fénelon's baggage for hidden money, as it was believed that he was bringing funds to bribe the Scots nobility. They entered Scotland in early January 1583, and Fénelon had his audience with James on the 18th. Robert Bowes was already in place in Scotland and Davison, considering himself superfluous, expected to return to London with Fénelon at the end of the month. However, under instructions now missing, he was ordered to remain with Bowes, thanks presumably to the arrival of a second French agent, François de Roncherolles, sieur de Maineville, who had sailed directly to Scotland. At the beginning of March, Davison pressed again for his revocation, as he considered that Bowes, even if he could not speak French, was able to handle Maineville on his own. His recall was finally granted on 14 March, and he left Scotland at the beginning of April.

Davison's second Scottish embassy was a more serious affair. James escaped from the Ruthvenites on 29 June 1583 and turned to the protestant, if mercenary, James Stewart, earl of Arran. During the winter of 1583–4 a number of the nobles and clergy associated with the Ruthven regime organized a conspiracy to overthrow Arran. They were forced into action prematurely, and on 17 April some of the lords took possession of Stirling Castle, only to abandon it on the 23rd and retire to England. On 25 April, Davison was instructed to mediate between them and James, but he was also provided with £2000 to disburse if he found them in 'reasonable probability' to 'prevayle ageynst thos that does now abuse bothe the kings eare and his authority' (BL, Harley MS 286, fol. 48r). By the time he reached Berwick he had learned of the surrender of Stirling and did not enter Scotland. James now demanded that Elizabeth return the fugitives, and on 15 May, Davison was instructed to inform him that she considered the lords victims rather than rebels and would not hand them over. On 5 June he had an inconclusive audience with James at Falkland Palace in Fife and then retired to Edinburgh. In Edinburgh he was informed that the constable of Edinburgh Castle, Alexander Erskine, the master of Mar, was sympathetic to the exiled lords, and he became involved in an ultimately abortive scheme to persuade Erskine to rebel.

In the face of this stalemate Elizabeth now permitted Henry Carey, first Baron Hunsdon, the captain of Berwick, to revive what was known as the 'by-course', a scheme of his own devising to reach an understanding with Arran. At the end of June a meeting between the two was agreed. Davison, who was convinced that the by-course was a waste of time, wanted to be relieved, not least because he was worried that his own involvement with Erskine might be exposed. Walsingham was willing but the queen, who had doubts about the by-course, preferred that he stay and keep an eye on things. Davison was not present at Hunsdon's meeting with Arran at Foulden, near Berwick, on 13 August, but his open scepticism came to the notice of Hunsdon, who accused him of trying to sabotage the by-course out of jealousy. However, on 1 September, Davison was granted his recall, and he left Edinburgh on the 15th.

Netherlands embassies, 1584–1586 Less than a month after his return from Scotland, Davison was sent on the most important embassy of his career. Following the assassination of Orange in July, Elizabeth had rejected a Dutch request for unilateral aid in favour of joint action with France. The Dutch had then agreed to accept Henri III as their sovereign, but he showed little interest either in co-operation with England or in the Dutch cause in general. On 10 October the privy council formally debated Netherlands policy and advised Elizabeth that she could not allow them to be reconquered. As a preliminary measure a 'man of skill' was to be sent to assess the situation, and on the 11th Walsingham informed Davison that he had been chosen. As it turned out he did not leave for a month, possibly owing to the queen's illness at the end of October. His letters of credence were signed on the 31st, but his instructions were not ready until 13 November. His main task was to discover the state of the Franco-Dutch negotiations. If Henri 'hath undertaken the action for their defence ether as protector or possessioner', Elizabeth would proceed no further. If he had not, then Davison was to assure them of her assistance upon reasonable conditions. If asked about the 'particularities of the cautions [security] desired by us' he was to let them know off the record that she would expect at least the occupation of Flushing and the Brill (PRO, SP 83/23/115–7).

Davison left London about 13 or 14 November, but owing to bad weather did not reach Middelburg until the 21st. When he had his audience with the states general on the 28th he was greeted with suspicion in the belief that he had been sent to disrupt the French negotiations. At a later private meeting with some of the leading deputies, he told them he was not ordered to 'brouiller' the French treaty, but Elizabeth had reason to believe that Henri was not serious (Algemeen Rijksarchief, The Hague, 1.01.01.01.90A, art. 4). On 27 December, Walsingham instructed him to wait in The Hague until the Franco-Dutch negotiations were concluded. The states of Holland (who were not very enthusiastic about the French treaty) provided him with generous accommodation in the Wassenaar Hof on the Kneuterdijk. In the absence of his personal papers the composition of his household in The Hague is unknown, with one very interesting exception— William Brewster, the future leader of the Pilgrim Fathers of Plymouth, Massachusetts. Brewster was a protégé of Davison; he was the 'young Bruster' for whom he sought to obtain the postmastership at Scroby, Nottinghamshire, in 1590 (CSP dom., 1581–90, 686).

The Dutch embassy to France had left just before Davison arrived, but they had a difficult journey and did not reach Paris until 1 February 1585. On the 18th the privy council informed him that the Dutch were not making any headway, and 'as of yourself' he was to encourage them to look to England (CSP for., 1584–5, 287–8). News that Henri had rejected the proposed treaty reached London on 6 March. Walsingham informed Davison on the following day, and two days later (9 March) he sent Edward Burnham with an outline of the terms of Elizabeth's assistance. Burnham reached Davison on the 17th, and on the 30th the terms were presented to the states general. By 10 May most of the provinces had agreed to send an embassy to England but Zealand proved awkward, and it was only on the 21st that it was brought round. Davison had intended returning with the Dutch embassy, but in view of the delays the states suggested he go first, and he left about 27 May. The Dutch embassy received its instructions only then; it had a difficult passage and did not reach Margate until 24 June.

When the Dutch arrived Davison was summoned to court, and during July he played an important subordinate role in the negotiations as translator, escort, and resident expert. His translating appears to have been purely into French—how much Dutch he knew remains a mystery. The negotiations launched him into the most complicated of his embassies. There was a large gap on both military and political levels between what the Dutch wanted and what Elizabeth would give. The Dutch held an advantage because they would not cede Flushing—the main town Elizabeth wanted as a caution—for an army of fewer than 5000 foot and 1000 horse. The stalemate was broken by an initial compromise, a provisional treaty for the relief of Antwerp, signed on 2 August. Under this treaty, Elizabeth would supply 4000 foot for three months to help to break the siege of Antwerp. She was to be repaid six months after Antwerp was relieved, or within a year if it was not. Immediately afterwards there was a panic that Antwerp had surrendered, and Zealand let it be known that it was prepared to cede Flushing for less than its original demand. This inspired a second provisional treaty (10 August) for aid during the war. Under this the 4000

English were to serve for the duration of the war. The treaty for Antwerp was still in force, but repayment of English expenditure subsequent to the initial three months was to be postponed until a year after the end of the war. Flushing and Brill were to be ceded as cautions a month after the treaty was ratified. The treaty also outlined the political and military role of the governor-general, the assumed commander of the English force.

There was considerable doubt whether the states general would ratify this treaty, but on 20 August it was learned that Antwerp had actually surrendered. Two days later Walsingham invited Davison to discuss the Netherlands with him in advance of a meeting with the Dutch deputies the following day. The Dutch reported on the 23rd that Elizabeth had decided to increase her troops to the desired 1000 horse and 5000 foot and Leicester had been invited to serve as the 'heere van qualiteyt en respect' ('nobleman of rank and reputation'), if Flushing and Brill were handed over immediately (Algemeen Rijksarchief, 1.01.01.01.92). On the 25th it was decided to send an English envoy to The Hague. The initial choice was William Waad, but Davison replaced him. Davison's instructions (over which he was allowed considerable discretion) stated that out of concern over the possible moral effects of the surrender of Antwerp, Elizabeth had decided to concede what the Dutch wanted, but Flushing and Brill were to be handed over first. Once they were in English hands, he could return.

Davison reached Flushing on 3 September and made his way quickly to The Hague. However, just after he left, London had a new idea: an 'instrument' signed by the commissioners for the 10 August treaty that would include both a ratification of the treaty and Elizabeth's recent concessions. This became known as the Act of Ampliation. A copy was sent to Davison on the 3rd, but the Dutch deputies in England then obtained a further concession that the garrisons of the cautionary towns would be supplementary to the 5000 infantry—a point which had not been clear in the 10 August treaty. The Act of Ampliation was redrafted and the new version sent to Davison on the 18th.

Davison had only received the first version of the act when he had his initial audience with the states general on the 11th. On the 20th the states general decided to draft its own act of ratification, to which he agreed in order to save time. On the recommendation of Holland two revisions were introduced. The first was the exclusion of the garrisons of the cautionary towns from the 5000 (to which, they had heard from London, Elizabeth had agreed), and the second the absorption of the 2 August treaty into the 10 August treaty. The result of this was that the repayment of all the costs of the English troops was delayed until the end of the war. Davison was shown a draft on the 22nd; he noted that there were problems, but to save time he was prepared to sign it. As he informed London, his primary concern was the quick and peaceful surrender of the cautionary towns. He considered that the concession over their garrisons fell within his discretion,

but curiously he did not comment on the amalgamation of the treaties.

Davison then moved speedily to obtain possession of Brill (1 October) and Flushing (19 October). To provide their garrisons he requested the English military commander, John Norris, to supply the best of the English companies. Norris wished to use them on a short campaign near Arnhem. Davison publicly stated that this was a mistake given the season, and their relations suffered. He now intended to delay his return until Sir Philip Sidney arrived in Flushing, but on 19 October he was instructed to wait for Leicester and help him settle in; he could return a month after the earl arrived. On the 23rd Elizabeth finally received the Dutch Act of Ratification. She was outraged by what she regarded as sharp practice in the revisions, but Davison was informed that no blame was attached to him.

Leicester did not arrive until 10 December. Davison was among the reception party that greeted him in Flushing, and he then accompanied him into Holland. On the 27th Walsingham informed him that Elizabeth had agreed to his recall for she 'meaneth to use your service otherwise', rumours Davison had already heard over a month before (*CSP for.*, *1585–6*, 155, 241). Before he left, however, he became involved in one of the more controversial episodes in his career. The treaty of 10 August had set out the political and military role of the governor-general in some detail, and Davison was aware during November and December that the Dutch were discussing what form this should take. How much he knew about the debates in England is not clear, although Leicester later claimed he had shown him all his commissions and instructions. It would be a key point in his own future defence that he had received no formal instruction that Leicester was not to hold any office other than command of the queen's troops.

On 31 December the states general agreed on a proposal for the governor-generalship to offer Leicester, and this was delivered to him verbally in his bedchamber at The Hague on the following day. Leicester then had Davison answer for him in French. Davison and Sidney were Leicester's main representatives in the debates with the states general over the terms of the offer between 7 and 16 January 1586. Agreement was reached on the 16th, and Leicester was formally sworn in as governor-general on the 25th. Leicester, Davison, and numerous others informed London that negotiations over the governor-generalship were in train from mid-January, though Leicester did not write to Elizabeth directly. Instead on 14 January he informed Walsingham that Davison would be returning shortly and would explain all. He wrote fulsomely in Davison's praise, urged that the queen give him 'countenance', and despite the rumours of a promotion at home requested that he be returned to the Netherlands where his experience was invaluable (*Correspondence*, ed. Bruce, art. 26).

For reasons that are not entirely clear, Davison did not leave The Hague until 5 February; he was then caught at Brill by adverse winds and did not arrive at the court at Greenwich Palace until the 12th. Leicester's letter of 14

January had reached the court by 26 January, when the privy council sent him a strong expression of Elizabeth's displeasure at the offer of the governor-generalship and ordered him not to accept the office. This letter reached him by 8 February while Davison was trapped at Brill. Leicester wrote to inform Davison on the 10th, but he left for England on that very day. Davison arrived at court apparently unaware that Elizabeth had been fuming over the subject for well over a fortnight and that on learning by the 10th that Leicester had actually assumed office she had prepared Sir Thomas Heneage to go and demand that he resign it.

Davison brought with him a (now missing) letter from Leicester to Elizabeth and a prepared defence on grounds of necessity; if Leicester had rejected the Dutch offer they might have sought a peace with Spain. Elizabeth retorted that Leicester had disobeyed her express command. Having heard that Davison 'of whom she had conceaved better opinion and towardes whom she had intended more good then now she found me woorthy of' and Sidney were 'perswadors thereof', she also attacked him for not having opposed Leicester (*Correspondence*, ed. Bruce, art. 43; BL, Cotton MS Galba C. viii, fol. 30r). Davison's personal defence was the absence of any instruction on the subject, but he considered Leicester's action politically justified anyway.

Thereafter Davison retired from court with a cold he had picked up on his return and spent most of the next few months in bed. However, there was an unpleasant sequel. Leicester does not appear to have learned of Davison's interview until he met Heneage in Harlem on 8 March. On one level he then took the blame 'that I dyd not first acquaint her highness before I dyd accept this office', but he then claimed that he was dissuaded from doing so by Davison 'and others'. Davison had argued 'the extremity of the cace to be such as he thought himself full hable to satysfie her majesty'. He also stood to Davison's defence: 'I say not this to worke any blame to Mr Davyson, whose most sincere honest minde toward hir servyce I must acknowledge'. Yet Leicester also sent him a savage private letter on the 10th, basically blaming him for the whole business, which Davison equally furiously annotated (*Correspondence*, ed. Bruce, arts. 59, 61).

Several months later Leicester and Davison cautiously began corresponding again, but the warmth had left their relations. On 2 July, Davison wrote to deny rumours that he had told Elizabeth that Leicester had proceeded against his objections, and that he was the author of the 'hard procedinges offered to your excellency' (*Correspondence*, ed. Bruce, art. 125). Davison's defence of Leicester to Elizabeth was in some senses not the real issue, for by the time he arrived at court the damage had been done. The mystery lies in the responsibility for the way of proceeding. Why Leicester, who knew better than anyone else how to handle Elizabeth, failed to write to her directly and gambled all on Davison's providing his defence is still to be explained.

Secretary of state, 1586–1587 Davison had intended going to Bath 'for an ache that hath continued in my knees' since he returned from Scotland in 1584, but his cold meant that he did not leave until July (*CSP for.*, *1585–6*, 592). It was in Bath in August, after all the hints, that he was finally informed that Elizabeth intended to appoint him a principal secretary of state. When he returned in February 'it is objected against Mr Davison's being Secretary that he is very poure, as in trewth he is not rych and also that Mr Secretary [Walsingham] is now in perfaict health so there nedeth no haste' (*Rutland MSS*, 1.190). In his letter to Leicester of 2 July, Davison hinted at a concern that he might see any promotion as a reward for having undercut him. However, although Walsingham informed him in July that Elizabeth 'seemethe to be dysposed to make Mr Davison my assystaunt' there is no evidence Leicester had any involvement in the appointment one way or the other (*Correspondence*, ed. Bruce, art. 129).

Davison was formally sworn secretary and a member of the privy council on 30 September, though his letters patent did not pass the great seal until 12 December. His four months' service was dominated by major events. Once appointed a privy councillor he was added to the commissioners for the trial of Mary, queen of Scots, and (for the first time) elected an MP for the duchy of Lancaster borough of Knaresborough in Yorkshire in the parliament that met in October. However, he took no part in either. In October, while Walsingham and Burghley went to Fotheringhay Castle in Northamptonshire, and in November, while they were involved in the parliament, he was in attendance on Elizabeth at Windsor Castle and then Richmond Palace. The correspondence between the three during these months reveals him as an active messenger and co-ordinator, but very much a junior. In December the proroguing of the parliament and the remove of the court to Greenwich brought the council together again, but by the middle of the month Walsingham retired ill, and he did not return until the middle of February 1587. On 10 December, Davison asked him to send him the signet and the privy seal. Burghley remained at Greenwich but a riding accident in mid-January kept him in bed well into February.

Davison's attendance on Elizabeth in these months (he was present at almost every recorded privy council meeting) is the key to his prominence in Mary's last days. Most of what is known of the events surrounding the dispatch of the warrant for Mary's execution comes from the three accounts he drafted later. Two of them, a discourse and a relation of the events of 1 to 14 February 1587, he prepared for Walsingham in the Tower on 20 February. They agree on most of the circumstances, but the relation omits some important issues (*CSP Scot.*, *1586–8*, arts. 284–5). The third is an undated paper defending his innocence that appears to have been drafted after his trial on 28 March 1587 (ibid., art. 360). The last paper reflects the resentment Davison shared with Robert Beale at being singled out as the instruments of Mary's death and the possible targets of James's revenge when he succeeded Elizabeth. He emphasized that he played no role in either her trial or the parliamentary proceedings. He was responsible only for the custody of the warrant for her execution after Burghley drafted it about 10 December 1586, so that it would be on hand when Elizabeth wanted it. He had no particular interest in Mary's death. In this context he made some interesting claims: he had refused to sign the bond of association despite pressure from Elizabeth (presumably just before he left for the Netherlands in 1584), he had gone to Bath deliberately to avoid involvement in the investigation of the Babington plotters, and he had been instrumental in preventing the sentence being pronounced at Fotheringhay. With regard to the last, he was not entirely honest. When he forwarded to Walsingham the queen's instruction to delay pronouncing sentence until the commissioners had returned to London on 14 October 1586, he had expressed the hope that his letter would arrive too late.

Davison's narrative of the events between 1 and 14 February is straightforward and very detailed. He had retained the warrant for six weeks because he would not present it to Elizabeth until 'she sent a greater councillor to him for the same'. This took place at Greenwich on 1 February when the lord admiral, Charles Howard, second Baron Howard of Effingham, told him Elizabeth was ready to sign. Elizabeth signed the warrant having specifically asked for it; it was then to go to the lord chancellor, Sir Thomas Bromley, to pass the great seal. Davison attended to this later that day, telling Burghley (who had Leicester with him at the time) and Walsingham (who was at home) on the way. On the 2nd Elizabeth told him to delay the sealing of the warrant, but he replied that it had already passed. This was a key point, for according to Davison she said nothing further. He then went to see Sir Christopher Hatton to tell him it was signed, that he feared Elizabeth would behave as she had done over the execution of Thomas Howard, fourth duke of Norfolk, and that he was unwilling to proceed on his own. Together they saw Burghley, who then decided to summon the privy council for the following day. On the 3rd the privy council met and Burghley proposed that they take the burden from Elizabeth by sending the warrant under their authority, and to appoint Beale to carry it. Nine privy councillors (presumably all those present), including Davison, signed the letter accompanying the warrant, together with Walsingham, to whom it was sent for signature in his sickbed. From then until news of the execution arrived from Fotheringhay on the 9th Davison saw Elizabeth on several occasions about other business, but did not mention the dispatch of the warrant, on the assumption (so he claimed in the discourse) that she knew about it from more senior privy councillors.

The relation differs from the discourse in two key areas. First, it greatly abbreviates Elizabeth's discussions with Davison over the assassination rather than execution of Mary. Second, it omits a long denial by Davison that the queen had ever told him on the 2nd to retain the sealed warrant in confidence until she ordered him otherwise and not to inform the rest of the privy council. The latter was to be another crucial point. Burghley told Elizabeth about the execution in the evening of the 9th, and after brooding on it overnight she announced to Hatton the next morning in 'some heat and passion' that Davison had abused her trust by allowing the sealed warrant to leave his possession (*CSP Scot.*, 1586–8, 293). Davison himself was told at a privy council meeting later that morning and advised to make himself scarce for a day or two. He was not in good health anyway and returned home. There he learned on the 11th that Elizabeth had decided to send him to the Tower. Owing to his illness this was put off until the evening of 14 February.

The course of events between 14 February and Davison's trial on 28 March is more confusing. He was tried before an *ad hoc* court in the star chamber composed of three privy councillors (John Whitgift, archbishop of Canterbury, Sir Walter Mildmay, and Sir James Croft), who had not signed the letter of 3 February, and a miscellany of bishops, peers, and judges, under the presidency of the lord chief justice, Sir Christopher Wray, who was appointed lord privy seal for the occasion. The trial lasted for four hours between ten in the morning and two in the afternoon. The main charge against Davison was that he had disobeyed Elizabeth's command to retain the warrant and had then misled the privy council by not informing them of this. If Davison was being honest in the discourse, then it was his word against Elizabeth's. This, however, was not the defence he put forward. He specifically stated he was not going to contest the facts, and did not wish 'to utter the private speeches that passed between the queen and him'. He had put the warrant in execution out of concern for Elizabeth's safety and may have mistaken what she told him 'not having been long acquainted with her manner of speech' (despite being in attendance for nearly four months). On the lesser issue of concealing the dispatch of the warrant from Elizabeth after the 3rd, he stated that the privy council had agreed together not to 'let the Queen understand until it [the execution of Mary] was despatched' (*CSP Scot.*, 1586–8, art. 328).

Although Davison received a fairly rough handling by the crown's lawyers, the judgment was delivered in a different tone. The first commissioner to pronounce was Mildmay, whose verdict was that Davison had abused Elizabeth's trust by making the warrant known to the privy council, but that he did it with a good intent. He was to be fined £6666 13s. 4d.—admittedly too much for him to afford—and imprisoned at pleasure, though Mildmay considered that Elizabeth 'might be moved upon humble submission to remitt the extremitie of them both' (*CSP Scot.*, 1586–8, 350). The other commissioners, although expressing greater or lesser condemnation of Davison's actions, fell into line with the punishment. According to an unfortunately anonymous eyewitness, after the trial, when they all dined in the star chamber, Davison dined apart 'thanking Sir W. Mildmay by Swanne his man for his good chere but not the sharpe sauce that he had mixed therewith' (PRO, SP 12/199, fol. 138v–139r).

Davison was quietly released from the Tower—where he spent some of the time writing a description of Ireland—on 23 October 1588. It was shown nearly a century ago that he continued to be paid his salary as secretary of state until the end of his life and the various other emoluments and profits of office until the death of Walsingham in 1590. In 1594 Elizabeth granted him lands worth £200 per annum, possibly in compensation for the loss of the profits; these he sold for £5000. There is no evidence that any part of his fine was ever paid. He was never formally dismissed and he continued to be addressed as Mr Secretary—he was simply suspended from office.

There is a definitely orchestrated tone to Davison's trial. Elizabeth at least was consistent. For all her anger with the ten privy councillors involved, Burghley in particular, Davison was a special case for disobeying her order on 2 February not to reveal the sealed warrant. The trial judgment was thus a vindication of her technical innocence. How Davison was brought to co-operate is an interesting question. Immediately after the execution Burghley had stood up for Davison and offered to resign his own offices. On 11 March, Thomas Randolph visited Davison in the Tower, where he found him ill and depressed, yet determined to maintain his innocence and deny any fault or error, expecting that the other privy councillors would stand with him. On 12, 14, and 16 March, Hatton and Sir John Woolley interviewed him, specifically about what Elizabeth had or had not said to him on 2 February. On the day before the trial the other privy councillors involved were also interviewed and a written statement taken from Burghley—which was mentioned in the trial (and may be BL, Add. MS 48027, fol. 702)—along the lines that Davison had misled him about the queen's intentions.

A story circulated later that Elizabeth had considered imprisoning Burghley as well, but decided against it because she was afraid it would kill him. On 25 February, Burghley became very worried that the lord chief justice of the common pleas, Sir Edmund Anderson, had told Elizabeth she had the power to hang Davison under the royal prerogative. He considered this illegal and warned the other judges against concurring. Davison later said that Mildmay had told him that the attorney-general, Sir John Popham, and the solicitor-general, Thomas Egerton, had threatened to resign if he was tried other than in star chamber (which could not pass capital sentences) and in such a way as would both satisfy Elizabeth yet make it possible for her to remit any punishment. Lastly, the anonymous witness (who wrote from Leicester House) gave Leicester credit for having engineered a successful compromise. It looks very much as though Davison was persuaded to forgo his innocence, justify Elizabeth at his trial, and suffer only nominally. Unfortunately the agreement was a bit too neat, and Davison was rapidly seen as an unconvincing scapegoat, either for the queen or for Burghley.

Yet Davison may have been more of an actor than he claimed. He expressed his conviction that Elizabeth would behave as she had done over Norfolk to Walsingham as early as 10 October 1586, several months before he mentioned it to Hatton. There is also his role in the des Trappes affair or Stafford plot of early January 1587, in which William Stafford and Leonard des Trappes, a gentleman servant of the French ambassador, were accused of plotting to assassinate Elizabeth. It was widely believed at the time that it was a put-up job to discredit the French ambassador, Guillaume de d'Aubespeine, baron de Châteauneuf, or to frighten Elizabeth into action. After Davison's arrest Walsingham admitted to Châteauneuf that the accusation was a mistake, which he attributed to Davison's inexperience. This has been seen as another example of Davison's being used as a scapegoat, but Walsingham may have been right. Davison was deeply involved in the investigation of the 'plot' and may have believed that assassination to prevent Mary's execution was a very real threat.

Yet if Davison was to be rewarded for co-operating, the issue of his restoration to office remained. Amid the considerable sympathy for him, one champion in particular emerged, Robert Devereux, second earl of Essex, who from spring 1587 made his restoration a matter of principle. Walsingham's death in April 1590 initiated a flurry of speculation on the subject. Essex worked hard on Davison's behalf with both Elizabeth and James, and Davison himself petitioned the queen on 7 December 1590. Elizabeth hesitated, but in 1593 she finally informed Essex that, while she appreciated Davison's qualities, restoring him was out of the question. Some years later, in a very bitter paper written after Burghley's death, Davison blamed him for deliberately preventing his 'restitution to his place' in the interests of his son Robert Cecil (*CSP Scot.*, *1586–8*, art. 426). He said nothing about the events of 1587, but whether he considered that Burghley had reneged on an understanding made then is an interesting point.

Davison's last years were spent in possibly deliberate obscurity. Whatever fears he may have had about James's revenge were unfounded, and his secretary's salary continued to be paid to him after 1603. On 25 July 1607 he was granted the reversion of his office of treasurer of king's bench and allowed to assign it to trustees in the interests of his children. He was then living in Stepney, Middlesex, where he died on 21 December 1608. He was buried in St Dunstan's Church, Stepney, on 24 December but no monument was erected. He drew up his last will on 18 December. It contains a predestinarian preamble, but is chiefly concerned with the sharing of the income from his office between his two daughters (referred to only by their married names Duncombe and Townley) and three surviving sons.

By the time of his death Davison had become a Tacitean hero, the honest man destroyed by the deviousness of the court. William Camden even insinuated that he was appointed secretary with the intent of using him as a scapegoat over Mary. The very obscurity of his background and his openly puritan allegiances have given him an attractively homespun image. The comparison of his fate with that of Edmund Grindal, archbishop of Canterbury, first made by R. B. Wernham seventy years ago, is still valid. Yet if he was thrust into some of the trickiest episodes of mid-Elizabethan diplomacy and politics, he also lived dangerously. He held strong views, expressed them publicly, and did not suffer those he considered fools gladly. Throughout his career he urged the seizing of opportunities by decisive action. His behaviour in February 1587 was very much in character, however much he may have wished in retrospect to portray himself as a mere unfortunate instrument. SIMON ADAMS

Sources BL, Harley MSS 285–286 · BL, Cotton MSS Galba C.vii–xi · BL, Add. MSS 48027, 48116 · BL, Egerton MS 1694 · PRO, SP 12 [domestic, Elizabeth I] · PRO, SP 15 [domestic, addenda] · PRO, SP 45 [State Paper Office] · PRO, SP 52 [state papers, Scotland] · PRO, SP 83 [Holland and Flanders] · PRO, SP 84 [Holland] · De regeringsarchiven van de Geünieerde en van der Nader-Geünieerde Nederlandse Provinceën, 1576–88, Nationaal Archief, The Hague, Eerste Afdeling, 1.01 · *CSP Scot., 1571–1603* · *CSP for., 1569–95* · *CPR, 1558–1582* · *CSP dom., 1547–1610*, with *addenda, 1566–1625* · *APC* · *Resolutiën van de Heeren Staten van Holland en Westvriesland*, 276 vols. (The Hague, [n.d.]) · N. Japikse, ed., *Resolutiën der Staten Generaal van 1576 tot 1609*, 4–5 (The Hague, 1919–21) · Baron Kervyn de Lettenhove [J. M. B. C. Kervyn de Lettenhove] and L. Gilliodts-van Severen, eds., *Relations politiques des Pays-Bas et de l'Angleterre sous le règne de Philippe II*, 11 vols. (Brussels, 1882–1900) · J. B. A. T. Teulet, ed., *Relations politiques de la France et de l'Espagne avec l'Écosse au XVIème siècle: papiers d'état, pièces et documents inédits*, new edn, 5 vols. (Paris, 1862) · J. Bruce, ed., *Correspondence of Robert Dudley, earl of Leycester*, CS, 27 (1844) · S. Adams, ed., *Household accounts and disbursement books of Robert Dudley, earl of Leicester, 1558–1561, 1584–1586*, CS, 6 (1995) · *Correspondentie van Robert Dudley graaf van Leycester en andere documenten betreffende zijn gouvernement-generaal in de Nederlanden, 1585–1588*, ed. H. Brugmans, 3 vols. (Utrecht, 1931) · *Calendar of the manuscripts of the most hon. the marquis of Salisbury*, 24 vols., HMC, 9 (1883–1976) · *The manuscripts of his grace the duke of Rutland*, 4 vols., HMC, 24 (1888–1905) · N. M. Sutherland, 'Davison, William', HoP, *Commons, 1558–1603*, 2.23–6 · N. H. Nicolas, *Life of William Davison, secretary of state and privy councillor to Queen Elizabeth* (1823) · B. M. Ward, 'Queen Elizabeth and William Davison', EngHR, 44 (1929), 104–6 · R. B. Wernham, 'The disgrace of William Davison', EngHR, 46 (1931), 632–6 · *Memoirs of his own life by Sir James Melville of Halhill*, ed. T. Thomson, Bannatyne Club, 18 (1827) · G. M. Bell, *A handlist of British diplomatic representatives, 1509–1688*, Royal Historical Society Guides and Handbooks, 16 (1990) · A. C. Miller, *Sir Henry Killigrew* (1963) · C. Read, *Mr Secretary Walsingham and the policy of Queen Elizabeth*, 3 vols. (1925) · C. Read, *Lord Burghley and Queen Elizabeth* (1960) · J. E. Neale, *Queen Elizabeth and her parliaments, 1584–1601* (1957) · F. G. Oosterhoff, *Leicester and the Netherlands, 1586–1587* (1988) · P. E. J. Hammer, *The polarisation of Elizabethan politics: the political career of Robert Devereux, 2nd earl of Essex, 1585–1597* (1999) · W. Camden, *Annales: the true and royall history of the famous Empresse Elizabeth*, trans. A. Darcie (1625) · S. Adams, 'The papers of Robert Dudley, earl of Leicester II', *Archives*, 20 (1993), 131–44 · S. Adams, 'The decision to intervene: England and the United Provinces, 1584–1585', *Felipe II (1527–1598): Europe y la monarquía católica*, ed. J. M. Millán, 5 vols. (Madrid, 1999), vol. 1, pp. 19–31

Archives BL, Harley MSS 285–287, 290 · Bodl. Oxf., MSS Tanner 78–80 · PRO, state papers, Elizabeth I, SP 12, SP 15, SP 45, SP 52, SP 83, SP 84

Wealth at death estate mortgaged for £700: will, PRO, PROB 11/113/29; Nicolas, *Life of William Davison*, 205–12

Davisson [D'Avissone], **William** (c.1593–1669), chemist and physician, was born in Aberdeen, the youngest of the three sons of Duncan Davissone of Ardmakrone (d. c.1600) and Jonet Forbes. Shortly after the death of his father, his mother's holdings were seized by relatives, and after her early death suits for restitution continued for many years. In connection with these proceedings, Davisson obtained a patent of nobility from Charles I in 1629. Davisson entered Marischal College in 1614, obtained an MA in 1617, and, owing to his family's difficulties, declared it better 'to

live industriously and honestly among foreigners, than to live in poverty and degradation amongst my own countrymen and illustrious relatives' (*Prodromus*, 1660, 407), and emigrated to France. There he married a fellow Scot, Charlotte de Thynny (Thégny), with whom he had one child, Charles.

During his first years in France, Davisson may have become qualified as a doctor of medicine at Montpellier. He was befriended by Jean Bapiste Morin, succeeding him as physician to Bishop Claude Dormy, a devotee of chemistry with a laboratory at Beauchamps, near Bourbon-Lancy. After the bishop's death in 1626, Davisson began lecturing on chemistry at Paris, and published his most important work, *Philosophia pyrotechnica* (1633–5), a wide-ranging textbook on chemistry incorporating classical authors, sacred scripture, alchemical authorities, neoplatonic ideas, and experimental data, into a grand Paracelsian chemical system. (In all his publications he used the Gallicized form of his name, D'Avissone, and his descendants used this form exclusively.) He also wrote a curious work on salt, dedicated to Cardinal Richelieu, and entitled *Oblatio salis, sive, Gallia lege salis condita* (1641), which treated the properties of common salt alongside its metaphorical meanings and its (supposed) relation to Salic law. In 1644, through the patronage of Henrietta Maria and François Vautier, first physician to Louis XIII, Davisson became physician to the king, circumventing a recent parliamentary decree forbidding the Parisian practice of physicians who did not belong to the Paris faculty. In 1647, a chair of chemistry was created at the Jardin du Roi, which at Vautier's recommendation was offered to Davisson; this was the first chair of chemistry in France. Davisson became intendant of the Jardin du Roi in 1647, and began lecturing there on 23 July 1648.

In 1651 Davisson resigned his posts, possibly owing to the intrigues of Bouvard, whom he had displaced as intendant. It seems equally possible he resigned because of the controversy about his 1651 tract *Observations sur l'antimoine* which upheld the pharmaceutical use of antimony and sharply criticized physicians who rejected chemical medicine, thus siding with Paracelsian protestants of Montpellier against Galenist Catholics of Paris in their long-waged 'antimony wars'. None the less, in the same year, helped by the Polish Queen Marie-Louise and his friend Morin, Davisson took up similar posts in Warsaw as first physician to King Jan Kazimierz and keeper of the royal garden. In 1663 he completed a lengthy commentary on *Idea medicinae philosophicae* of the Paracelsian physician Peter Severinus (he had published a prodromus in 1660 with Severinus's text). After Marie-Louise's death in 1667 Davisson left Poland, returning briefly to his native Aberdeen where he had a tract on scalp disease printed under the pseudonym Theophrastus Scotus; this work, entitled *Plicomastix* (1668), was sold in Danzig. In 1669 he returned to Paris, where Louis XIV ratified his patent of nobility, guaranteeing nobility to his descendants.

Davisson enjoyed a high reputation in courtly circles. Lord Scudamore, the English ambassador at Paris, wrote of Charles I's 'gracious favour' towards Davisson, and noted that the king 'has been rightly informed concerning the worth of this man, and the benefit his Majesty's subjects receive by him' (*CSP dom.*, 1635–6, 321). His lectures in Paris were well attended; Evelyn visited on 21 October 1649, and Aubrey asserted that Hobbes 'went through a Course of Chymistrie with him' (Read, 77). Sir Thomas Urquhart wrote that Davisson's 'excellency … in alchemy is above all the men now living in the world' (Small, 265). Davisson died at Paris in 1669.

LAWRENCE M. PRINCIPE

Sources J. Read, 'The first British professor of chemistry', *Ambix*, 9 (1961), 70–101 · E. T. Hamy, 'William Davisson, intendant du Jardin du Roi et professeur de chemie, 1647–51', *Nouvelles Archives du Muséum d'Histoire Naturelle*, 3rd ser., 10 (1898), 1–38 · J. Small, 'Notice of William Davidson, MD (Gulielmus Davissonus), first professor of chemistry, and director of the Jardin des Plantes, Paris, afterwards physician to the king of Poland', *Proceedings of the Society of Antiquaries of Scotland*, 10 (1872–4), 265–80 · H. Metzger, *Les doctrines chimiques en France* (1923), 45–51 · J. R. Partington, *A history of chemistry*, 3 (1962), 4–7 · A. G. Debus, *The French Paracelsians* (1991), 124–5 · *CSP dom.*, 1635–6 · L. Thorndike, *A history of magic and experimental science*, 8 vols. (1923–58), vol. 8, pp. 123–6
Likenesses P. Lombart, engraving (after D. Schultz, 1662), repro. in Debus, *The French Paracelsians*, 125

Michael Davitt (1846–1906), by Sir William Orpen, 1906

Davitt, Michael (1846–1906), Irish nationalist, was born in Straide, co. Mayo, on 25 March 1846, the second child of Martin Davitt and his wife, Catherine. Both parents were of peasant origins, but Davitt's father received a good early education and spoke English and Irish. The family survived the great famine of 1846–9, but emerged impoverished and in arrears of rent. They were evicted in 1850, Michael Davitt always claiming a 'remembrance' of the event. The family emigrated to Haslingden, east Lancashire, in November 1850, and Davitt was brought up in the closed world of the poor immigrant Irish community, with its strong nationalist values and, in his case, with a deep hatred of landlordism. After attending infant school Davitt began work in a mill at the age of nine, but lost his right arm in an accident on 8 May 1857, when he was ordered to tend a machine normally supervised by a seventeen-year-old boy. He then attended the local Wesleyan school, where he received a good education from a liberal-minded schoolmaster. In August 1861 he went to work again, this time as an errand boy with a local postmaster and printer, and later became a book-keeper and typesetter. He attended evening classes at the mechanics' institute and came under the influence of Ernest Jones, the veteran Chartist leader, whose radical ideas included land nationalization, and the support of Irish independence.

Work with the IRB In 1865 Davitt joined the Irish Republican Brotherhood (IRB), or 'Fenian' movement, which enjoyed strong support among working-class Irish immigrants. Davitt soon became a 'centre' of the Rossendale 'circle' of the IRB (a group of some ten to a hundred men, under the command of their 'centre'). He was involved in the abortive plot to seize Chester Castle to obtain weapons on 11 February 1867 as a prelude to a Fenian uprising in Ireland, but evaded the law. He helped organize a body of young men to defend Roman Catholic churches against protestant attacks in 1868 in the Haslingden area, and in the same year he became organizing secretary and arms agent for the IRB in England and Scotland, acting as a link between the 'centres' and the supreme council of the IRB. He used his job as a 'hawker' (travelling salesman) as a cover for his activities. He first came to the attention of the police in 1867, and was arrested at Paddington Station on 14 May 1870. At his trial for treason-felony a letter was cited to prove his complicity in planning murder, though in fact Davitt had written it to another member of the IRB to dissuade him from an assassination attempt on the life of a young member of the organization seen talking to a detective. Davitt was sentenced to fifteen years' penal servitude, feeling that he had received neither a fair trial nor the best effort from his defence lawyer.

It was while in prison, in Millbank, Dartmoor, and Portsmouth, that Davitt revealed the tenacity of his character, and his ability to express his views even in the most trying circumstances. In August 1872 he managed to smuggle a letter out of prison criticizing the prison regime, which was published in several Irish and English newspapers, and which led to an inquiry by the home secretary into Davitt's allegations of harshness and cruelty. Upon his release in 1877 he prepared a pamphlet (published in 1878) which was the basis of his evidence before the royal commission on the working of penal servitude. Davitt always claimed that he had been victimized while serving his term, but he had frequently broken the rules, and was no worse treated than any other prisoner; as a self-recognized 'political' prisoner, Davitt's real source of grievance was that he was treated like any ordinary convict. Davitt was released in December 1877 as a 'ticket-of-leave' man, which authorized his freedom unless he should be convicted of some indictable offence in the United Kingdom, in which case the licence should be forfeited.

Davitt immediately renewed his connections with the IRB. He and other released prisoners were given a hero's welcome on landing in Ireland. His life from now on was one of constant movement, within Ireland and between Ireland and Great Britain. His release was due to the efforts of the Home Rule Party in pressing for an amnesty for Irish nationalist prisoners, and Davitt made contact with the rising star of the home-rule movement, Charles Stewart Parnell. By this time the land question was assuming a new urgency, with Irish agriculture suffering a decline. It was a combination of the land question, Fenianism, and constitutionalism between 1878 and 1880 that created the politics of Parnellism, a unique blend of agrarian agitation and parliamentary leadership.

The Land League In July 1878 Davitt went to the United States of America, where he met the leader of Irish American Fenianism, John Devoy. Here he called for an end to landlordism and for Irish independence, but his orthodox Fenianism was modified when he was attracted to the idea floated by Devoy of a compact with the home-rulers who supported Parnell against the more moderate leadership of Isaac Butt, since the 'end excused the means'. In December 1878 Davitt returned to Ireland, where rural distress was now becoming more acute, and tenants were organizing to defend themselves against high rents and evictions. The first tenant right meeting to develop a strategy, held at Irishtown, co. Mayo, on 20 April 1879, was the result of local initiative; a second meeting at Westport on 8 June was larger, and again locally inspired, but Davitt attended this meeting and called for Irish freedom and an end to the evil of landlordism, ridding Ireland of 'the land robbers who seized it'. Davitt's moment had come. He saw the need to channel the energies of the agitation into some more enduring organization, and in August 1879 he founded the Mayo Land League, with its slogan 'The land of Ireland belongs to the people of Ireland.' Davitt and his colleagues succeeded in persuading Parnell to take the initiative in converting the Mayo league into a national land league. The second 'new departure' combined constitutional and revolutionary agitation, but, unlike that of 1878, it was one that gathered widespread popular support. By now the government was seriously concerned about the revolutionary potential of the league, and Davitt was arrested in Sligo in November 1879. He had become convinced that Parnell must be supported; this cost Davitt his place on the supreme council of the IRB in May 1880, though he remained in its ranks for some years.

Davitt turned to Parnell as the only constitutional politician who could help achieve his aims; privately, he still spoke of the need to arm and prepare for violent conflict.

But his breach with Fenianism widened as he committed himself ever more closely to the 'new departure'. In May 1880 he went to America to organize the American Land League. Here he quarrelled with Fenians who declared that independence must come before land reform. In September 1880 Parnell called on tenants to 'shun' those who broke the Land League's instructions, and on his return to Ireland in November 1880 Davitt embarked on a hectic phase of activity, including a visit to Ulster in January 1881 to address protestant and Presbyterian farmers, warning all tenants not to accept Gladstone's land reforms (including the so-called 'three Fs': fair rent, free sale, and fixity of tenure). But his appeal to the farmers of Ulster was undermined by his nationalist rhetoric, and his references to the 'Irish race'. He was arrested in December 1880 but was released when the jury could not agree. Davitt described the jury as 'packed', even though the trial was manifestly fair and the judge showed him every consideration.

In February 1881 Davitt proposed a rent strike to the league executive in Dublin, arguing long after the event that such a move would have led to a 'kind of civil war' but insisting that the end justified the means, since all 'modern Irish history' showed that 'the only way to obtain reform for Ireland was by insurrection' (Moody, *Davitt*, 458). Whether or not this was the case, the league in October 1881 accepted the rent strike, but declared that it was the 'one constitutional weapon' in its hands. Meanwhile Davitt on 3 February 1881 had his ticket-of-leave revoked, and he was sent to prison in Portland. While there, he was elected MP for County Meath, but disqualified. Davitt was by now developing his ideas on the land question. He had earlier taken an interest in the writings of Henry George, the American economic thinker, and while in prison in Portland he embraced the theory that land nationalization, not peasant proprietorship, was the key to Ireland's prosperity. By the time Davitt was released, in May 1882, Parnell was presiding over the demise of the Land League, and seeking to reach an accommodation with Gladstone. Davitt's supreme moment in Irish politics was now over. He went to America between June and July 1882, after which he produced a plan for a 'National Land and Industrial Union of Ireland', but Parnell opposed this. In September 1882 Davitt met Parnell at the latter's house, Avondale, where Davitt agreed to co-operate in Parnell's plan for a new national organization, and to set aside his plans for land nationalization. The Irish National League was under the official control of the Irish Parliamentary Party, and Davitt later described it as a 'parliamentary substitute' for a 'semi-revolutionary organisation'. When in 1890–91 the Parnell divorce case split the party, Davitt first only asked Parnell to retire from the leadership of the party for six months, but later denounced Parnell on the grounds that he had deceived his colleagues and was morally disgraced. In so doing, he revealed a rather unpleasant talent for personal invective, though he was much provoked by what he now saw as Parnell's attempt to arouse young men to revolution, and by Parnell's taunts over Davitt's inconsistency.

Later life, marriage, travels, death, and reputation Davitt's support of the Irish National League earned him a further, and final, spell in prison in 1883. In 1885 his health broke down, and he toured the Middle East and Italy. He now became a kind of post-revolutionary figure even though he was only in his forties. He lectured on humanitarian issues in Britain, America, New Zealand, and Australia. In December 1886 he married Mary (b. 1861), daughter of John Yore of St Joseph, Michigan; they had two sons and three daughters. In 1887 he visited Wales to support land agitation. In January 1891 at Cork he founded the 'Irish Democratic and Trade and Labour Federation', urging a common interest between the British and Irish working man. He founded and edited a journal, *Labour World*, from September 1890 until May 1891. He visited South Africa in 1900 and denounced British imperialism. In 1903 he investigated Russian antisemitism, and went to Russia again in 1904, when he conversed with Tolstoy at Yasnia. He was returned to parliament for North Meath in 1892, North East Cork in 1893, and Mayo in 1895–9, and welcomed Gladstone's second Home Rule Bill as a 'pact of peace' between England and Ireland. He supported Indian nationalism. He made a brief return to agrarian radicalism in 1898, when the United Irish League was active in the west of Ireland, but he denounced the 1903 Wyndham settlement for land purchase. He strongly supported the British Labour Party in the general election of 1906, mainly because he believed it would deliver Irish self-government. He died at 19 Lower Mount Street, Dublin, of blood poisoning on 31 May 1906, and was buried at Straide, co. Mayo. His wife survived him.

Davitt was at the height of his political influence in the years 1879–82. Thereafter his influence declined, but his version of the land war—that it was a straight fight between landlord and peasant—became the accepted account following the publication of his deeply influential *The Fall of Feudalism in Ireland* (1904). He had the strengths and weaknesses of the revolutionary: he exploited the agrarian crisis of 1879–81, but expected too much from the farmers, whom he described in 1885 as responding to 'self-interest', not 'self-sacrifice'. Davitt was an ascetic man, accepting no tribute for his work other than a house, known as Land League Cottage, at Ballybrack, co. Dublin. He was handsome, brave, and proud, but betrayed a lack of self-confidence and an impatience with those who disagreed with him. Like the old Fenian he was, he harboured suspicions of clerical influence, but, although for a time he ceased to be a communicant, he was an orthodox Roman Catholic, and was never a 'Godless revolutionary' on the continental model.

D. GEORGE BOYCE

Sources T. W. Moody, *Davitt and Irish revolution* (1981) · T. W. Moody, 'Michael Davitt and the British labour movement, 1882–1906', *TRHS*, 5th ser., 3 (1953), 53–76 · P. Bew, *Land and the national question in Ireland, 1858–82* (1978) · F. S. L. Lyons, *Charles Stewart Parnell* (1977) · W. O'Brien and D. Ryan, eds., *Devoy's post bag, 1871–1928*, 2 vols. (1948–53) · M. M. O'Hara, *Chief and tribune: Parnell and Davitt* (1919) · *CGPLA Ire.* (1906) · *DNB*

Archives Catholic University of America, letters · Michael Davitt National Memorial Museum, letters, addresses, police reports, photographs · TCD, corresp. and papers | NL Ire., corresp. with W. M. Colles · NL Ire., corresp. with J. F. X. O'Brien · NL Ire., William O'Brien MSS · NL Ire., letters to John Redmond · TCD, corresp. with John Dillon

Likenesses W. Orpen, portrait, 1906, Hugh Lane Gallery, Dublin [see illus.] · photographs (aged seventeen, thirty-one, thirty-six, and fifty-eight), TCD, Davitt MSS

Wealth at death £151 5s. 2d.: probate, 21 July 1906, *CGPLA Ire.*

Davson, Hugh (1909–1996), physiologist, was born on 25 November 1909 at 203 Maida Vale, Paddington, London, the fifth of eight children of Wilfrid Maynard Davson, general practitioner, and his wife, Mary Louisa, *née* Scott. After schooling at University College School, London, he worked for two years as a clerk at the Baltic Exchange. He found the work extremely boring, and was eventually sacked. He then entered University College, London, and graduated with first-class honours in chemistry in 1931, as did his friend and later colleague James Danielli. On 29 April the same year he married Marjorie Heath (1905/6–1994), portrait painter and daughter of John Heath, general merchant. They had one daughter. In the middle of a national financial crisis jobs were scarce, and somewhat reluctantly Davson accepted the opportunity to remain at University College to undertake research in the chemistry department under Christopher Ingold. Davson found the work tedious and repetitive, and soon transferred to the biochemistry department, where Professor Jack Drummond provided modest living expenses, a laboratory, and a free hand with research. There Davson, often with Danielli, began to investigate the mechanisms whereby the membranes of red blood cells, which were easily and cheaply available from abbatoirs, were selectively permeable, that is some substances could easily and readily cross this barrier, while others could not.

Although financial necessity dictated that Davson apply for, and accept, a position with the Medical Research Council to work on the physiology of the eye and the causation of glaucoma, he continued to be actively interested in membrane permeability. In 1936 a Rockefeller Foundation fellowship permitted him to go to the United States to continue his membrane work, and the following year a Beit memorial fellowship allowed him to return to University College, London, to the department of physiology, to develop his work more fully. Together Davson and Danielli examined the mechanisms whereby electrically charged particles, or ions, of a variety of different chemicals were transported across the membrane. Soon, however, difficulties in finding a position arose once more, and meant that Davson had to move, this time to Dalhousie University in Canada, which he reached on the day the Second World War was declared in 1939. Before leaving Britain he was awarded an MSc degree, which became the basis of a classic physiological text, Davson's and Danielli's *The Permeability of Natural Membranes*, published by the Cambridge University Press in 1943. This book propounded the Davson–Danielli model of the cell membrane, which laid the basis for the understanding of how drugs can enter cells in the treatment of disease, and for much physiological and pharmacological research. In 1940 Davson was made DSc by the University of London and in 1942 he chose to return to Britain with his wife and young daughter, across the U-boat-infested Atlantic, to undertake war work at Porton Down on the effect of mustard gas on the eye, and other projects.

At the end of the war Davson decided against returning to Canada and became involved once again with visual physiology both at University College, London, and from 1947 at the Institute of Ophthalmology, which he helped co-found with Stewart Duke-Elder. But by 1951 personal and intellectual differences between the two men meant that a rupture was inevitable. Davson later described this as the most tragic experience of his life. He decided to leave the institute and return to University College, but having built up a keen young staff working on the physiology of the eye, he felt it was impossible for him to continue to work in the field himself, in opposition to those who had been his colleagues and collaborators. Consequently he started an entirely novel research programme, examining the physiology of the cerebro-spinal fluid that bathes the brain, contained within the blood brain barrier. He remained at University College, London, until his retirement in 1975, and subsequently held visiting professorships and fellowships around the world, being particularly honoured in the United States where, among other honours, in 1993 the American Physiological Society created an eponymous lecture in recognition of his contributions to physiological science. His eminence was less well recognized in his homeland, and Davson's individuality, inability to tolerate scientific bluster and pomposity, and self-acknowledged lack of tact undoubtedly contributed to his comparative lack of British awards. An unusual distinction was his fellowship of the Serbian Academy of Sciences, only the third Englishman after William Ewart Gladstone and the sculptor Henry Moore to be so honoured, because of his active promotion of British–Yugoslav academic exchanges. He delivered his acceptance speech to the academy in Serbo-Croat.

Davson's achievements were not confined to his original research contributions on the physiology of the membrane, in visual physiology, and on the blood brain barrier, but also included his literary distinction as an elegant scholarly writer of textbooks. Among others can be mentioned his *General Physiology*, which first appeared in 1949 (four more editions were to appear, and he was working on the sixth edition when he died); and *The Physiology of the Ocular and Cerebrospinal Fluids*, which first appeared in 1956 (a fourth edition, renamed *The Physiology of the CSF and Blood Brain Barriers*, written with Malcolm Segal, appeared in 1996). Three editions of *Starling's Physiology* appeared under Davson's editorship, and five volumes of *Introduction to Physiology* were co-authored with Malcolm Segal. Each book or edition was meticulously written or revised, Davson typing them all himself and preparing the indices on a vast array of small index cards.

Davson had many interests outside physiological science, and particularly enjoyed reading Johnson, Gibbon,

and Shakespeare, whose sonnets he learned for relaxation. His wife predeceased him in 1994. He died at Rosemary Cottage, Chapel Street, Georgeham, Devon, of a coronary thrombosis, on 2 July 1996. He was survived by his daughter and several grandchildren and great-grandchildren.   E. M. TANSEY

Sources H. Davson, autobiographical fragments · H. Davson, oral history interview, Wellcome L., Physiological Society archives · *The Independent* (8 July 1996) · *The Times* (17 July 1996) · *The Guardian* (15 July 1996) · *Daily Telegraph* (10 July 1996) · b. cert. · m. cert. · d. cert.

Archives Wellcome L., Physiological Society archives, oral history interview

Likenesses photograph, repro. in *The Guardian* · photographs, Wellcome L., Physiological Society archives

Wealth at death £809,836: probate, 18 Dec 1996, *CGPLA Eng. & Wales*

Davy, Adam (*fl.* early 14th cent.), poet, was the author of a verse account of five prophetic dreams (in Bodl. Oxf., MS Laud misc. 622, of the fourteenth century), and describes himself as 'Adam, the marshal', 'of Stratford-atte-bowe' (London) twice, and once as 'Adam Davy'. He claims that he is widely known, but no evidence of this fame has survived, and he is not otherwise known. Perhaps he was the marshal of a household. He says that he dreamt of a great knight, whose name is 'sir Edward þe kyng, Prince of Wales'. It is usually assumed that this is Edward II, the only King Edward of the century to have actually been created prince of Wales (in 1301). If, however, the phrase is not meant as a precise title, the reference could be to Edward I or the young Edward III. In the vision, the king stands in front of the shrine of St Edward, with two knights on either side. They strike him fiercely with their swords, and he suffers the attack in silence, but is not wounded. When they are gone, four beams of light come from his ears, 'off diuers colours, red and white als [also?] hij were' (Davy, 12, l.32), and they spread far and wide in the country. This first dream took place on the Wednesday before the Decollation of John the Baptist (29 August). The second, on the Tuesday before All Saints' day (November 1), promises that the day will come when Edward will be chosen emperor of Christendom. He rides on an ass to Rome as a pilgrim, without hose and shoes; his shanks seem all blood red. In the third dream, on the Wednesday night before St Lucy's day (13 December), the pope crowns Edward emperor in Christendom—May God give him victory over his enemies and the wicked Saracens. In the fourth, on 'worþing-ni₃th' (probably Sunday night), the dreamer goes into a chapel of Our Lady and sees Christ on the cross 'un-nail' his hands and say that he wishes to go with the knight; he asks leave of his mother to accompany their loyal knight:

> in pilerinage he wil gon,
> To bien awreke [avenged] of oure fon [foes].
> (ibid., 14, ll.103–4)

The Virgin grants her son's request, and a voice urges Adam to make his dream known to the king. He sets off eastwards aided by light from heaven. In the final dream, on the Thursday before the feast of the Nativity of the Virgin Mary (8 September), the king stands before the high altar at Canterbury, all clothed in red, and the king is merry 'of þat blee [colour] red as blood' (ibid., 15, l.140). Adam is again urged to make the dream known to King Edward, and he says that he is doing this, not for reward but for fear of almighty God. Perhaps the description of Adam as 'a fanatical rhymer' (*DNB*) is a little harsh. His prophetic visions have the combination of vividness and a tantalizingly enigmatic quality that is characteristic of the genre. On the face of it they might be urging the king to go on crusade, but their context and purpose remain mysterious. Adam was previously supposed to be the author of the other poems in the manuscript, but there is no evidence for this whatsoever. DOUGLAS GRAY

Sources *Adam Davy's 5 dreams about Edward II, The life of St. Alexius, Solomon's book of wisdom, St. Jeremie's 15 tokens before doomsday, The lamentacion of souls*, ed. F. J. Furnivall, EETS, 69 (1878) · **Archives** Bodl. Oxf., MS Laud misc. 622

Davy, Charles (1722/3–1797), Church of England clergyman and writer on music, was born in Norwich, the son of Charles Davy of Hatton Garden, London; his mother may have been Sarah Davy. He was educated at Mr Haslehurst's school at Market Rasen, Lincolnshire, Mr Pigge's school at Watton, Hertfordshire, and Mr Brett's school at Scarning in Norfolk. On 3 May 1739 he matriculated aged sixteen at Gonville and Caius College, Cambridge, where he graduated BA (1742) and MA (1748). In 1764 he was instituted to the rectory of Topcroft, Norfolk, to the rectory of Benacre, Suffolk, two years later, and to that of Onehouse in the same county in 1776.

In 1772 Davy published his *Conjectural Observations on the Origin and Progress of Alphabetical Writing* followed by *Letters Addressed Chiefly to a Young Gentleman* (1787), which included a discussion of Ptolemy's doctrine on music. This work came after his and Christopher Smear's proposed, but unpublished, 'Essay upon the principles and powers of vocal and instrumental music'.

Davy was married to Mary, daughter of Thomas Sheppard; they had two sons, Charles and Frederick. Charles became a fellow of Gonville and Caius College, Cambridge, vicar of Wickham Market, Suffolk (1803), rector of Barking and of Combs, in the same county (1818), and died on 7 March 1836 aged seventy-nine. With Frederick he published a translation of M. T. Bourrit's *A Relation of a Journey to the Glaciers in the Dutchy of Savoy* (1775). The elder Charles Davy died at Onehouse on 8 April 1797 and was buried in the chancel of the parish church.

THOMPSON COOPER, *rev.* PHILIP CARTER

Sources *GM*, 1st ser., 67 (1797), 438 · *GM*, 1st ser., 95/1 (1825), 125 · *GM*, 2nd ser., 5 (1836) · J. Ford, ed., *The Suffolk garland, or, A collection of poems, songs, tales [&c.] relative to that county* (1818) · Foster, *Alum. Oxon.* · Venn, *Alum. Cant.* · IGI

Davy, David Elisha (1769–1851), antiquary, was born on 16 June 1769, son of David Davy (1709–1799), farmer of Rumburgh, near Bungay, Suffolk, and his second wife, Susanna Foyster (c.1743–1800). His uncle Eleazar Davy, of The Grove, Yoxford, high sheriff of Suffolk in 1770, who had no son, educated him to be his heir. After boarding at Bungay grammar school under Thomas Reeve, Davy was sent to Samuel Forster's school at Yoxford about 1782,

then moved with him to Norwich when Forster succeeded Samuel Parr at the grammar school there in 1785. From Pembroke College, Cambridge, he matriculated in 1786 and graduated as sixth senior optime in 1790; two years later he was ordained deacon by the bishop of Norwich. He served curacies at Theberton and Yoxford, but abandoned clerical duties in June 1795 on becoming receiver-general of transferred duties for east Suffolk on Sir John Rous's application to Pitt (Rous, later first earl of Stradbroke, had married Eleazar Davy's stepdaughter). When Eleazar Davy died in 1803, David Elisha had to borrow from Gurney's Bank to pay his uncle's debts and legacies without selling property at a time when land values had slumped. Established at The Grove as a magistrate and deputy lieutenant, he took command of the Blything Hundred Volunteers with the rank of lieutenant-colonel; his friend Henry Jermyn of Sibton (1767–1820) was second in command.

With Jermyn in 1805 Davy began his life's work of gathering materials for a history of Suffolk. They toured together, and in 1810 jointly issued to incumbents a questionnaire as Francis Blomefield did in Norfolk in the 1730s. When in 1820 Jermyn died, Davy feared that his friend's notes might go to a publisher, for each had copied from the other, and Davy still had publication in mind. With mounting debts, he had no alternative but to put The Grove into Gurney's hands, and he resigned his receivership, and retired to a friend's house at Ufford, near Woodbridge. Antiquities now filled his time, and the tours continued, usually with the Revd John Wareyn Darby as companion: his journal records excursions made between 1823 and 1844. With a small circle of like-minded friends including George Bitton Jermyn (Henry's nephew), John Mitford, and Joseph Hunter, he was a regular correspondent, always generous to serious enquirers, but some letters betray the bitterness he felt at having lost the position in society which his uncle intended. He was reluctant to join the many societies that would have welcomed him. He borrowed and transcribed such collections as those of Hervy, Blois, Candler, Martin, and Cullum, but Craven Ord made a cautious response when asked for help, and Davy long mistook this for a rebuff. Eventually he came to realize that publication was less desirable than the amassing of well-ordered collected materials, and his 131 manuscript volumes, mostly folios, are more useful than any printed history.

Davy was the anonymous author of several Suffolk works, and revised Frederic Shoberl's *Beauties of England and Wales* volume for Grieg and Higham's *Excursions* in 1818. He admitted to providing the text for John Sell Cotman's *Suffolk Brasses* (1819), the etchings of which were made from Davy's own rubbings, and for Henry Davy's *Beccles Church and other Suffolk Antiquities* (1818), *Architectural Antiquities of Suffolk* (1827), and *Views of the Seats of the Noblemen and Gentlemen in Suffolk* (1827), as well as writing thirty-five articles in *Gentleman's Magazine* over D.A.Y., the terminals of his names. Carlyle and Edward FitzGerald called him 'Dryasdust', but Davy knew that his collections were invaluable and irreplaceable to those who would later study Suffolk. He died unmarried and intestate at Ufford on 15 August 1851 (having recently recovered The Grove) and was buried at Yoxford on 21 August. Lucy Elizabeth Davy, widow of William Barlee, rector of Wrentham, through John Mitford, offered her brother's Suffolk collections, brass rubbings, and many rare pamphlets to Frederic Madden, keeper of the manuscripts at the British Museum, for £500, but only £200 was forthcoming.

J. M. BLATCHLY

Sources D. E. Davy, *A journal of excursions through the county of Suffolk, 1823–1844*, ed. J. Blatchly, Sussex RS, 24 (1982) • *GM*, 2nd ser., 36 (1851), 543–4 • *DNB* • parish register (burials), Yoxford, Suffolk, 1851

Archives U. Cam., department of plant sciences, *bibliotheca botanica* | BL, collection of brass rubbings, Add. MSS 32483–32484 • BL, corresp., papers, and collections relating to history of Suffolk, Add. MSS 19077–19207, 19209–19210, 19213–19241, 19245–19247 • BL, travel diary, Add. MS 61946 • Bodl. Oxf., corresp. with Sir Thomas Phillipps • Suffolk RO, Bury St Edmunds, collections relating to history of the hundreds of Suffolk [microfilm copies] • Suffolk RO, Ipswich, letters to G. B. Jermyn

Davy, Edmund (1785–1857), chemist, was born at Penzance, the second son of William Davy and his wife, M[ary?] Ann. He obtained his early education in Penzance, where he stayed until moving to London in 1804. With the help of his cousin Humphry *Davy, professor of chemistry at the Royal Institution, he was appointed operator and assistant in the laboratory of the institution in 1807. He was also made responsible for the mineralogical collection in addition to his duties of keeping the laboratory in order. Gaining valuable experience, he held the post until 1813 when, through Humphry Davy's influence, he moved to Ireland, becoming professor of chemistry and secretary at the Royal Cork Institution, founded in 1802, an organization modelled on the Royal Institution. There he obtained a good reputation as a lecturer and research worker.

In 1826 Davy succeeded William Higgins as professor of chemistry at the Royal Dublin Society, where he established a school of practical chemistry and arranged popular courses of lectures in Dublin and in other parts of the country. The lectures were wide-ranging in scope and included agricultural and vegetable chemistry, evening courses on chemistry and, from 1850, lectures on the chemistry of colour pigments. Davy was an excellent teacher and students appreciated the courses, which were well attended. In 1856 he became professor of agricultural chemistry at the Royal Dublin Society, shortly before his retirement from a career spent in teaching, the promotion of scientific education and knowledge, and a great deal of useful, but purely empirical, research.

While at the Royal Institution, Davy published several studies of platinum and its salts. Humphry Davy's research on the miner's safety lamp revealed that a preheated platinum wire continued to glow when held in an inflammable gaseous mixture. This puzzling phenomenon was investigated by Edmund Davy in Dublin. In 1820 he described a finely divided platinum ('platinum black') produced by reducing a solution of platinum sulphate with alcohol. Although he noted its surprising ability to oxidize alcohol at room temperature, Davy failed to grasp the significance of his discovery and it was left to others such as J. W. Döbereiner to exploit the catalytic powers of platinum and other finely divided metals. In 1836 Davy made another important discovery. By the action of water on potassium carbide he obtained an inflammable gas he identified as 'a new bicarburet of hydrogen'. In 1860 it was rediscovered and thoroughly investigated by M. Berthelot, who named it acetylene.

Davy's other researches covered a wide range of subjects. Besides platinum his metallurgical topics included fulminating silver, the detection of metallic poisons using electrochemistry, and tests for manganese. Other publications of agricultural or horticultural interest dealt with the improvement of wheat flour and the detection and prevention of fraud in the sale of skimmed milk, for which Davy designed a lactometer. He also analysed soils and manures. Much of Davy's work at the Royal Dublin Society entailed investigating and solving problems such as the study of bog butter (a tallow-like substance from peat bogs); the state of the Irish soap industry; the use of chloride of lime for fumigation; the comparison of Irish and Virginian tobacco; and a solution to the problem of iron corrosion at Dún Laoghaire harbour. He also published details of experiments on the relative deodorizing powers of peat charcoal, peat, and lime.

Barker's memoir describes Davy as having 'a warm heart and affectionate disposition, ever ready to advise or encourage, tolerant of ignorance, humble even to his inferiors' (Barker, 424). His marriage to Phillis Emma Barry, only daughter of David Barry of Dundulrick, co. Cork, resulted in a family of several children. Their eldest son, Edmund William (1826–c.1900), who assisted his father at the Royal Dublin Society, eventually succeeded him there as professor.

Davy was elected a fellow of the Royal Society in 1826 and was an original member of the Chemical Society of London. He also became a member of the Royal Irish Academy and honorary member of the Société Française Statistique Universelle. In the last year of his life he suffered ill health, and died on 5 November 1857 at his home, Kimmage Lodge, Kimmage, Dublin. He was probably buried in St Mary's churchyard, Crumlin.

CHRISTOPHER F. LINDSEY

Sources W. Barker, 'Memoir of the late Professor Davy', *Journal of the Royal Dublin Society*, 1 (1856–7), 419–25 • H. F. Berry, *A history of the Royal Dublin Society* (1915) • J. Meenan and D. Clarke, *The Royal Dublin Society, 1731–1981* (1981) • Royal Society, *Catalogue of scientific papers*, 2 (1868), 169–70 • 'Biographical notes of Dr. Edmund W. Davy and his father', [n.d.], Royal Institution of Great Britain, London, Edmund Davy file • E. Davy, ledger, 1809–26, Royal Institution of Great Britain, London, Davy MS 22E • H. Davy, letter, 5 Jan 1807, Royal Institution of Great Britain, London, MS HD 26a/6 • *DNB* • private information (2004) [Royal Society of Chemistry] • J. R. Partington, *A history of chemistry*, 4 (1964), 73–4 • J. Russell, 'Edmund Davy', *Journal of Chemical Education*, 30 (1953), 302–4 • M. MacSweney and J. Reilly, 'The Royal Cork Institute', *Journal of Chemical Education*, 32 (1955), 348–52

Archives BL, letters • Royal Institution of Great Britain, London • RS | Royal Institution of Great Britain, London, Humphry Davy archives

Likenesses photograph, repro. in D. Ó. Raghallaigh, *Three centuries of Irish chemists* (1941) · photograph, repro. in *'Africa and the east' CMS missionary exhibition official guide* (1912) · portrait, Royal Dublin Society · sketch, Royal Institution of Great Britain, London; copy, postcard, 1956

Davy, Edward (1806–1885), chemist and promoter of the telegraph, was born on 16 June 1806 at Ottery St Mary, Devon, the eldest son of Thomas Davy, a surgeon, and his wife, Elizabeth Boutflower. He was educated at the Revd Richard Houlditch's school at Ottery St Mary and at the school of his maternal uncle in Tower Street, London. At the age of sixteen he was articled to Charles Wheeler, a house surgeon at St Bartholomew's Hospital, with whom he lived for three years. In 1825 he won the prize for botany, in 1827 gained his licence from the Society of Apothecaries, and in 1828 secured his membership of the Royal College of Surgeons. In 1830 his father bought him a practice at 390 Strand, London, under the impression that it was a medical practice. It was not, and Davy practised as a dispensing and operative chemist under the name of Davy & Co. His interests lay in the general sciences, particularly chemistry and electricity, and a catalogue of instruments, appended to his *Experimental Guide to Chemistry*, published in 1836, includes several devices invented by him in the list of goods and instruments for sale. In 1836 he patented Davy's diamond cement, an adhesive for mending china and glass, from which he gained a small annual income until he sold the rights to the process.

Also in 1836, Davy published *Outline of a New Plan of Telegraphic Communication*, and in 1837 he carried out telegraphic experiments in Regent's Park. He laid down a mile of copper wire in the park and developed his 'electric renewer' or relay system, which renewed the signal with the aid of a local battery to compensate for attenuation of the original signal. He demonstrated a working model of his telegraph that year and a needle telegraph in the Exeter Hall in central London for several months in 1838. He applied for a patent for his telegraph, which was granted on 4 July 1838 after the solicitor-general asked Michael Faraday's advice as to whether it constituted a different mechanism from that of Cooke and Wheatstone, patented on 12 June 1837. Davy managed to interest two railway companies, the Birmingham Railway and the Southampton Railway, in his telegraph, but left England for Australia before developing a practical system or completing negotiations, which he left in the hands of his father and a friend, Thomas Watson, a London dentist. Eventually his patent was bought by the Electric Telegraph Company in 1847 for £600. Although his telegraph was never developed, Davy was important for popularizing to the general public the concept of telegraphy, and was the first to develop a relay system. Without Davy's demonstrations, public awareness of the telegraph would perhaps have been much slower. Moreover, his correspondence with public figures and engineers, such as I. K. Brunel, did much to hasten the adoption of the telegraph. He also devised a block system for recording train movements between stations by means of an electrically operated dial, which would advance when the train passed a milestone, but he never patented this idea. In 1883 J. J. Fahie, a historian of the telegraph, initiated a campaign to have Davy's contribution recognized, and in November 1884 the Society of Telegraph Engineers and Electricians (later the Institution of Electrical Engineers) made him an honorary member.

While in London, Davy married Mary Minshull; they had one son, George Boutflower Davy, who was born before 1837. By 1838 their marriage had irretrievably broken down, and Mary Davy tried unsuccessfully to divorce her husband. Her extravagance and Davy's lack of business sense led to mounting debts, which he settled with help from his father. To free himself from his wife Davy decided to emigrate. He left his son in the care of his family, and in April 1839 set sail for Australia intending to take up a small-holding. He soon abandoned farming to settle in Adelaide, South Australia, where he engaged in various pursuits. He edited the *Adelaide Examiner* from 1843 to 1845, built up a small medical practice, and for a time managed the Yatala copper-smelting works, where he developed a process for copper refining. He patented the process in Australia, and an English patent was granted in 1847 under his brother's name. He also undertook some assay work. In 1852 he was appointed head of the government assay office in Adelaide which he ran very successfully. The following year he was invited to set up the assay office in Melbourne, Victoria, which he also ran very well until a change of government in 1854 led to its abolition. Davy again took up farming near Malmsbury, Victoria, but soon settled in the town itself, where he engaged in local politics, serving for twenty years as a justice of the peace and for three terms as mayor. He developed his medical practice, and acted for twenty years as the first honorary health officer of the borough. When he retired from that position in August 1882, the Malmsbury borough council presented an address of thanks to him at a special evening *conversazione*. He had become a much loved figure in the Malmsbury area.

Davy married twice while in Australia; it is not clear whether his first marriage had ended (by divorce or his wife's death) or whether these marriages were bigamous. By 1845 he had married Rebecca Soper, with whom he had five sons and two daughters. After her death in 1877 he married Arabella Cecil, the daughter of Stephen Tunbridge Hardinge, postmaster-general of Tasmania. They had four children, two of whom, a son and a daughter, survived him. Davy died on 26 January 1885, at Mollison Street East, Malmsbury, and was buried on 27 January in Malmsbury. Efforts to secure a government pension in Australia and England for his widow were unsuccessful, but the Royal Society of Victoria, which had elected Davy an honorary member in March 1883, raised £150 by a subscription among its members for her and her children.

ELEANOR PUTNAM SYMONS

Sources J. J. Fahie, 'Honour to whom honour is due: Edward Davy and the electric telegraph, 1836–1839', *The Electrician*, 11 (1883), 48 · H. Davy, 'Short memoir of Edward Davy', *The Electrician*, 11 (1883), 6 · W. O. Gibberd, 'Davy, Edward (1806–1885)', *AusDB*, vol. 1 · IGI

Archives Inst. EE, corresp. and papers, incl. notes relating to telegraph | Inst. EE, John Joseph Fahie MSS
Likenesses two photographs, c.1884, Inst. EE
Wealth at death not very great

Davy, Henry (1793–1865), artist, was born at The Poplars (later Birketts Farm), Westhall, Suffolk, on 30 May 1793, the fifth son and youngest child of Thomas Davy (1747–1813), farmer, and his second wife, Sarah (1751–1831), eldest daughter of William Gibson, physician, of Willingham Hall, near Beccles. He was apprenticed without prospects to a Halesworth grocer, but with aspirations to art he went instead to John Sell Cotman, then at Great Yarmouth. Within two years of modest beginnings in 1813 he confidently etching his own drawings: in 1818 he published ten prints of Beccles and its environs, *A Set of Etchings Illustrative of Beccles Church and other Suffolk Antiquities*. This was very much in the style he absorbed by helping to etch Cotman's plates of Norfolk antiquities and brasses published in the latter's *A Series of Etchings Illustrative of the Architectural Antiquities of Norfolk* (1818) and *Engravings of the most Remarkable of the Sepulchral Brasses in Norfolk* (1819). With Joseph Lambert's assistance instead of Davy's, the plates illustrative of Cotman's *The Architectural Antiquities of Normandy* (1822) are comparatively dull.

In 1819 Davy continued his training under George Cooke in London, but soon returned to Bury St Edmunds to draw in the area and to seek new patrons. Though not a member, he exhibited twenty-three pictures in all at the Norwich Society of Artists between 1817 and 1823. Back in Southwold in the early 1820s he met Sarah (1801–1854), daughter of James Bardwell, master mariner and stationer, and his wife, Sarah, *née* Critten, whom he married at St Peter's, Ipswich, on 30 November 1824. To boost his income from teaching he opened a public library and reading-room. Davy could now add sixty etchings to the Beccles set for his *Series of Etchings Illustrative of the Architectural Antiquities of Suffolk* (1827), and dedicated one to Cotman. The Suffolk antiquary and genealogist David Elisha Davy of Rumburgh wrote, anonymously, descriptions of the churches, houses, and castles in the three collections Henry published; despite long subscribers' lists (Cotman always included), the books made a loss, and his *Views of the Seats of Noblemen and Gentlemen in Suffolk* (1826) was abandoned after only twenty-two houses had been engraved by Lambert after Davy's exquisite sepia drawings.

After further offers of 'Instructions in Drawing and Sketching from Nature' (Denney, 29) in Southwold, Davy moved the family in 1829 first to Whitton Road and then to 16 Globe Street, Ipswich. That year he exhibited at the Society (later Royal Society) of British Artists, Suffolk Street, London, three small watercolours or prints of Southwold landscapes. On 16 April 1833 Robert Deck, the printer of his two main works, auctioned some of the family's furniture and books to pay himself and other creditors. In Ipswich the Davys always struggled for survival, and of their sixteen children only six survived infancy. Two were artists: Frederick, of Ipswich and later Chesterfield, and Henry George, of Halifax. Still taking

Henry Davy (1793–1865), by C. Osbourne

pupils (notably the daughters of the poet Elizabeth Cobbold), Davy decided to print his own plates and sell them singly for a few shillings each. The influence of Cotman is no longer apparent in the 200 prints etched between 1835 and 1849 and forty-four lithographs executed between 1850 and 1864. Small editions and the destruction of plates on his death make them all rare. The meticulous detail in 134 prints of east Suffolk churches assists architects still. Davy made journalistic illustrations of local events, such as fêtes, bazaars, railway and dock openings, a lifeboat launching, and the laying of the foundation-stone of the new Ipswich grammar school by Prince Albert. When in 1844 Lord William Hill rode head first into an oak, the etched scene was on sale in days. In 1849, for D. E. Davy's Suffolk collections, Davy provided 1300 of his own drawings, and organized the engraved views and portraits of others.

Davy's wife, Sarah, died in 1854, aged fifty-two, leaving him still with two young children to bring up. Slight, unassuming, of few words, but a great walker, he worked on through failing health until he suffered a fatal heart attack on 8 February 1865. After an inquest at The Globe inn, almost next door, he was buried at Ipswich cemetery on the 14th. Sarah's grave in St Matthew's churchyard was unmarked, but Henry Davy's stone has a joint inscription. His later work, always careful, lacked the flair he displayed while Cotman's influence lasted, but the record he made of his half-county over four decades combines charm and delicacy with admirable accuracy.

J. M. BLATCHLY

Sources A. H. Denney, 'Henry Davy, 1793–1865', *Proceedings of the Suffolk Institute of Archaeology*, 29 (1961–3), 78–90 · J. S. Earle, notes, biography, catalogue of etched, lithographed and engraved work of Henry Davy, Suffolk RO, Ipswich, qS 759 Dav • D. E. Davy, *A journal of excursions through the county of Suffolk, 1823–1844*, ed. J. Blatchly, Sussex RS, 24 (1982), 10–12 • M. R. Pidgley, 'John Sell Cotman's patrons and the romantic subject picture in the 1820s and 1830s', PhD diss., University of East Anglia, 1975, 24–8 • S. D. Kitson, *The life of John Sell Cotman* (1937) • M. Rajnai, *The Norwich Society of Artists, 1805–1833: a dictionary of contributors and their work* (1976) • *Ipswich Journal* • Mallalieu, *Watercolour artists* • d. cert. • parish registers, Westhall church, Suffolk, 2 June 1793 • J. Johnson, ed., *Works exhibited at the Royal Society of British Artists, 1824–1893, and the New English Art Club, 1888–1917*, 2 vols. (1975) • d. cert.

Likenesses F. Davy, oils (after J. Pelham), Ipswich Museums and Galleries • C. Osbourne, oils, Ipswich Museums and Galleries • C. Osbourne, watercolour drawing, Ipswich Museums and Galleries [*see illus.*]

Davy, Sir Humphry, baronet (1778–1829), chemist and inventor, was born on 17 December 1778 at 4 The Terrace, Market Jew Street, Penzance, Cornwall, the eldest of five children of Robert Davy, a woodcarver, and his wife, Grace Millett. His father was descended from a line of yeomen, or even gentlemen, but the only property he owned was a small farm at Varfell in Ludgvan, overlooking St Michael's Mount. His mother also came from an old Cornish family. When he was nine, the family moved from Penzance to Varfell, and during school terms Humphry boarded with his godfather John Tonkin, an apothecary–surgeon. After learning to read and write from 'old Mr Bushell', he was sent at the age of six to the grammar school at Penzance, where the schoolmaster, the Revd Mr Coryton, made learning a pain (notably by twisting the boys' ears). Here Davy enjoyed much idleness, which he later felt was fortunate for him, the source indeed of his talents and their application. He became intellectually self-propelled.

Childhood, education, and apprenticeship While at school Davy discovered a talent for writing verses and as a storyteller, and took up fishing and shooting. His first experience of chemistry was when he made fireworks with his sister. Then, at the beginning of 1793, he went at Tonkin's expense to the grammar school in Truro, the county town of Cornwall. There the headmaster was Dr Cardew, whom Davy considered far better than Mr Coryton, but who failed to discover any extraordinary abilities or even any propensity to scientific pursuits. Davy left school in December 1793, just before his sixteenth birthday, and lived with Tonkin, following an informal course of self-education. His father suffered from heart disease and in December 1794, at the age of forty-eight, he died, leaving his widow an income of £150 a year and debts of £1500.

Mrs Davy moved back to Penzance and, with a French refugee, opened a milliner's shop; by 1799 the debts were paid, she had received an unexpected legacy of £300, and she gave up the shop. Davy had told her not to grieve, for he would do all in his power for his brother and sisters, and on 10 February 1795 he was apprenticed to Bingham Borlase, like Tonkin an apothecary–surgeon and prominent citizen of Penzance. He continued with his programme of self-education, which, as well as the chemistry, botany, and anatomy needed for part of his profession, included physics and mechanics.

Davy was a satisfactory apprentice, and clearly also a

Sir Humphry Davy, baronet (1778–1829), by Sir Thomas Lawrence, 1821

rather dreamy young man, declaiming poetry in the wild outdoors but also reading Locke, Berkeley, David Hartley, and other philosophical authors. In 1799 his first poems were published by Robert Southey in the *Annual Anthology*; the best-known of these, 'The sons of genius', was written in 1795–6 and is suffused with both the sublime and the beautiful. Delighting in the rough precipice, in ancient Greece, and in science (then called natural philosophy), Davy saw himself as a son of both nature and genius, hoping:

> To scan the laws of nature, to explore
> The tranquil reign of mild Philosophy;
> Or on Newtonian wings to soar
> Through the bright regions of the starry sky.
> (*Collected Works*, 1.26)

M. Dugast, a French refugee priest from La Vendée, taught him French, but Davy, who had no ear for music, never learned to speak the language without a strong accent.

Davy was, nevertheless, equipped by 1797 to read Lavoisier's *Traité élémentaire de chimie* in French. This book appeared in 1789, and its author and his contemporaries saw it as revolutionary. Its beautifully clear exposition of the idea that oxygen from the air is the crucial agent in combustion, and its new and logical nomenclature, seemed to make chemistry a coherent, and also a French, science. Davy was to make two important amendments to Lavoisier's scheme, and indeed much of his work can be seen as directed against Lavoisier and French hegemony. Sulphuric, nitric, and other acids contain oxygen and it seemed a reasonable inference that this element was the cause of acidity: accordingly, its name (from ancient

Greek) means 'acid-generator'. In addition, Lavoisier saw definite quantities of heat being involved in chemical reactions and in changes of state, and for him heat was a weightless chemical element, 'caloric'. Liquids and gases were thought to be compounds of solid elements with caloric: oxygen and hydrogen were thus for Lavoisier not yet known in elementary form.

Davy began his chemical career by propounding a different idea of heat, and crowned it with a different view of acidity. He aspired to be the Newton of chemistry, and he was attracted to the older view of Bacon, Locke, and Newton that heat was the motion of the particles of matter. Perhaps with adapted instruments from a shipwrecked French surgeon, and certainly with help from Robert Dunkin (a Quaker saddler turned instrument maker), Davy began experiments, notably melting lumps of ice by friction in rubbing them together to prove his theory of heat against Lavoisier's. Swinging one day on Borlase's gate, he caught the attention of Davies Giddy (who changed his name to Gilbert in 1817), a member of parliament with scientific interests, who became his patron and was later his successor as president of the Royal Society. He offered Davy the use of his library and introduced him to Dr Edwards, who later lectured on chemistry at St Bartholomew's Hospital in London. Davy was transported with delight to see Edwards's laboratory, which contained apparatus he knew about only from descriptions and engravings.

As an undergraduate in Oxford, Giddy had attended lectures on chemistry given by Thomas Beddoes, politically a radical whose Oxford career was brought to an end in the reaction against the French revolution. Beddoes visited Cornwall to study its minerals with Giddy at a time when he was proposing to set up in Bristol, with backing from Josiah Wedgwood and help from James Watt, a clinic where the new 'factitious airs', gases discovered by Joseph Priestley, would be administered to the sick. Wedgwood's son Thomas and Watt's son Gregory both suffered from tuberculosis. In the winter of 1797–8 Gregory Watt was sent to Cornwall for its mild climate, and boarded with the Davys, where he was excited by Humphry's offer to demolish the French theory of heat. In April 1798 Beddoes received through the young Watt, and with Giddy's support, Davy's essay on heat and light, and in 1799 published it.

Davy later repudiated this essay, as 'infant chemical speculations', but it helped make his name. While he thought heat was motion, he believed that light was a substance entering into chemical union—Lavoisier's oxygen gas should thus be called 'phosoxygen'. His essay included work on what is now called photosynthesis, and he was the first to establish that pondweeds release oxygen in sunlight; he also connected light with electricity, and with life. The essay ended with the hope that 'chemistry, in its connection with the laws of life, [will] become the most sublime and important of all sciences' (*Collected Works*, 2.86).

Beddoes needed an assistant and with Giddy persuaded Borlase to release Davy from his indentures; Tonkin was

furious that a safe career as a medical practitioner should be abandoned for such quackery, but on 2 October 1798 Davy set out from Penzance for Clifton on his great journey into science and social mobility. Two days later Giddy met him for breakfast at Okehampton, where the mail coach arrived beribboned, bearing news of Nelson's victory over the French on the Nile.

Bristol: laughing gas Bristol was a wealthy city of merchants, much more sophisticated than Cornwall with its mines and fisheries. Beddoes's Pneumatic Institution was eventually set up at Hotwells, in Dowry Square. Finance came from Wedgwood, and also from the coal-owning MP William Henry Lambton, whose sons boarded with Beddoes and got to know Davy; John, the elder, later became earl of Durham. Beddoes's wife was sister to Maria Edgeworth, and they moved in literary circles. Davy soon met Joseph Cottle, who was publishing his essay and also work by William Wordsworth, S. T. Coleridge, and Southey. By early 1799 Davy was doing experiments on gases, following up Priestley's researches, in the well-equipped laboratory.

Davy took up the implausible published claims of a prominent American, Samuel Mitchill, that combinations of oxygen and nitrogen must be poisonous, and that nitrous oxide must be the worst of them, a veritable 'septon' or principle of contagion. Davy tried some experiments with it, and by April could prepare it in sufficient quantity, and pure enough, to breathe it—and thus discovered its effects as laughing gas. The experiment was one of a series of risky trials: with nitric oxide the effects were very painful, and with carbon monoxide nearly fatal, but here was pure pleasure. Davy wrote excellent first-hand accounts of the anaesthetic action of the gas and of its exhilarating effect as he awoke from semi-delirium:

> My emotions were enthusiastic and sublime; and for a minute I walked about the room perfectly regardless of what was said to me. As I recovered my former state of mind, I felt an inclination to communicate the discoveries I had made during the experiment. I endeavoured to recall the ideas, they were feeble and indistinct; one collection of terms, however, presented itself: and with the most intense belief and prophetic manner, I exclaimed … 'Nothing exists but thoughts!—the universe is composed of impressions, ideas, pleasures and pains!' (*Collected Works*, 3.390)

Coleridge became an enthusiastic friend of Davy and collaborated in these experiments; impressive testimony from him and many others on the effects of the gas, with careful chemical analyses of the oxides of nitrogen, were collected into Davy's first book, *Researches, Chemical and Philosophical, Chiefly Concerning Nitrous Oxide*, published in 1800. He recommended the gas as an anaesthetic in minor surgery, but neither he nor anybody else pursued this idea at the time.

Other work Davy did in Bristol included the discovery of silica in grasses, and some researches in electricity. Alessandro Volta had found that when dissimilar metals are piled up with damp pasteboard between them an electric current flows, and his 'pile' is the ancestor of today's electric batteries. This discovery Davy later referred to as an alarm bell: it set him, and many other men of science, off in a new direction. He found that acid in the pile makes it more effective, and believed that its action (which Volta attributed to mere contact) must depend upon a chemical reaction. He made piles with charcoal replacing one metal, and with two fluids and one metal. These were described in the first of his papers to be published in the Royal Society's *Philosophical Transactions*, in 1801.

Meanwhile, Davy also kept up other interests, pursuing his science in bursts of creative activity. He recorded a mystical experience of sympathy with nature, when he would have felt pain in tearing a leaf from a tree. His notebooks, begun from both ends, are full of fragments of verse and prose, doodles, good resolutions, and scientific experiments and jottings. He was asked by Wordsworth to oversee the printing of the second edition of *Lyrical Ballads* and to correct the punctuation; later he visited the Wordsworths at Dove Cottage. He also saw through the press Southey's epic, *Thalaba*. His work on the oxides of nitrogen, where different compounds of the same two elements have very different properties, and on the electric battery, convinced him that nature was no clockwork, but dynamical—based upon polar forces in equilibrium—and not to be explained in material terms alone. He passed through a brief period of religious scepticism to a settled dualism, and a pantheism expressed in a rhapsody of uncertain date:

> Oh, most magnificent and noble nature!
> Have I not worshipped thee with such a love
> As never mortal man before displayed?
> Adored thee in thy majesty of visible creation,
> And searched into thy hidden and mysterious ways
> As Poet, as Philosopher, as Sage?
> (*Fragmentary Remains*, 14)

The Davy family was Anglican, but he seems to have preferred to worship God outdoors rather than belonging to a particular congregation.

The Royal Institution: useful knowledge In September 1800 Davy wrote to his mother about brilliant prospects, and in January 1801 was formally invited by Count von Rumford to a post at the Royal Institution, recently founded in London. Beddoes put no obstacles in his way, and after visiting London in February, Davy moved there to start his new duties in March. Rumford had persuaded landed gentlemen, seeking more efficient ways of raising crops in times of blockade and near famine, to set up this institution where lectures would be given and research carried on. This was a new pattern for London and practical use was expected of it. Rumford had hoped that artisans would come to lectures on mechanics and that new inventions would be displayed there; the lecture theatre, like other theatres, had a separate entrance to the gallery so that the artisans would be segregated from the ladies and gentlemen occupying the best seats. In the event, manufacturers did not want to share their trade secrets but the lectures to the nobility and gentry became a great success during the winters and springs of the London season, while in the laboratory some of the most important experiments of the century were to be performed.

The professor of chemistry was Thomas Garnett, a well-known analyst of mineral waters who disliked London, but he soon died. The managers of the Royal Institution resolved on 28 June 1801 that Davy should in November give a course of lectures on the chemistry of tanning. He spent the summer learning about it, notably with Thomas Poole of Nether Stowey, a lifelong friend, whose tannery embodied the current best practices. Tanning was a disagreeable business which involved much capital because the hides underwent prolonged immersions in various solutions; however, leather, flexible and strong, was a crucial material, and the oak bark and galls necessary to tan it seemed to be becoming scarce. Davy's lectures were supplemented by a major paper, published by the Royal Society in 1803 and largely responsible for his being elected a fellow later that year and awarded its highest honour, the Copley medal, in 1805.

Davy's main conclusion was that the workmen in the best tanneries had arrived at a degree of perfection which could not be very far extended by chemical theory: he provided in essence a rationale for the best practice, which had been arrived at by lengthy trial and error. Poole found tannin in port wine, and Davy in tea, and more promisingly, in catechu from India. Sir Joseph Banks, president of the Royal Society from 1778–1820, who became in effect Davy's patron, supplied samples of the latter, used as an astringent when chewing betel nut, and Davy had a pair of shoes made, one tanned with oak bark and the other with catechu. Here was a promise of replacing oak bark with a cheaper alternative.

Davy gave a general account of the chemistry of tanning which was not significantly improved upon in the next fifty years, and again he moved on. This time it was to agriculture, at the suggestion of his employers and the board of agriculture—again two overlapping groups. He gave a series of lectures year after year, which promised increased production, bringing relief from the wartime food shortages and the pressures of an expanding population (Thomas Malthus's *Essay on Population* had appeared in 1798). If all farms could be brought up to the standard of the best, there would be no problem. Davy urged good practice, beginning with soil analysis: he undertook to do analyses himself, and became a close friend of Thomas Andrew Knight, an eminent plant physiologist and horticulturist on whose estate he went fishing. Davy also supervised a series of experiments at Woburn, under the patronage of the duke of Bedford, on grasses, and on one occasion at the festivities associated with the annual sheep shearing at Woburn, Davy was toasted.

Davy's suggestions were conservative, often providing a scientific basis for practices that had been found empirically to work. Thus he recommended using manure fresh rather than rotted, because it would then still contain much ammonia, and illustrated this with what must have been a rather smelly experiment, in which the fumes rising from dung were conducted beneath a piece of turf, which grew splendidly. He also suggested insecticides, one of which seems to have killed off Lord Egremont's turnip crop, but which generally appear to have been helpful.

The lectures were eventually published, first in a handsome quarto and then in octavo, in 1813, and remained a standard work for a generation. This was essentially science as 'nothing more than the refinement of common sense making use of facts already known to acquire new facts' (*Collected Works*, 9.355), as Davy put it in a phrase later echoed by T. H. Huxley.

It turned out that Davy was a brilliant lecturer and in January 1802 he gave an introductory lecture to a course on chemistry, which created a sensation and led to his being appointed the institution's professor of chemistry in May of that year. He presented a dazzling picture of scientific and technical progress, and this vision of the power of applied science remained with him and his successors at the institution. He became much sought after as a dinner party guest. He spent the time between ten or eleven o'clock in the mornings and three or four in the afternoon in the laboratory, and then dressed for dinner—there were stories of his rushing from the laboratory and putting a clean shirt on top of his dirty one—but on evenings before lectures he dined at home on fish and rehearsed with his assistants. There are messy manuscripts of the lectures, difficult to read; he must have delivered them from memory, maintaining eye-contact with the audience—his eyes were said to be very bright and striking. He was about 5 ft 7 in. in height, but seemed shorter; he soon lost any traces of Cornish accent, and while some found his voice affected, most seem to have delighted in hearing him. The traffic bringing hearers to his lectures was so heavy that Albemarle Street had to be one-way on those nights. He had perfected the art of high-level popularization, and made science attractive and interesting to both men and women.

In 1804 Gregory Watt died, and Davy was desolate, writing about his belief in the individual immortality of the better part of man. In the same year, Coleridge, unhappy in his marriage and addicted to opium, set off for Malta in a desperate bid to regain his health. He was cheered on his way by a splendid letter from Davy, who on his return arranged for him to lecture at the Royal Institution. In 1808 Beddoes died, after writing a melancholy letter to Davy deploring his own lack of definite scientific achievement. By then Davy had moved far beyond his earlier sphere. In 1807 he was elected one of the two secretaries of the Royal Society, with the responsibility of editing its journal, and he had made new friends among the medical and scientific community in London, where he was one of the first to make a living by the practice, or profession, of science. On holidays he studied geology and fished energetically; autumns were his best time for undisturbed research, and in 1806 his work took a new turn, which brought international fame.

Reconstructing chemistry: potassium and chlorine Davy believed that electricity was a force or power, not a substance, and that it would simply decompose substances like water. But the experiments of others revealed acids and alkalis that were apparently generated electrically, so perhaps there were compounds of electricity—'galvanates'. In October 1806, using apparatus of gold, silver, and

agate, and excluding air, Davy verified his conjecture in an excellent example of a goal-directed rather than open-ended experiment: pure water, decomposed by electrical action, yielded nothing but hydrogen and oxygen, in the right proportions. He concluded that electricity and chemical affinity were manifestations of one power. This insight (though not quantitative) seemed appropriate to the would-be Newton of chemistry, and it won him a prize from the Paris Académie des Sciences.

On 19 October 1807 Davy used electricity to decompose caustic potash, in a capital experiment after which he danced about the laboratory in ecstatic delight. The application of electric current to an aqueous solution of the alkali resulted in the water's being decomposed into hydrogen and oxygen. The resulting residue of solid potash did not conduct electricity and so Davy melted it. When he did so, globules of the substance formed at the negative pole and, bursting into flames, threw off bright coruscations. He managed to collect some, and found that they floated on water, catching fire as they decomposed it; he compared his 'potagen' to the alkahest sought by alchemists, but after consultation with other chemists decided that this anomalous substance was in fact a metal, and named it 'potasium', later potassium. Soon he isolated sodium too, and then, using a mercury cathode, calcium and other 'alkaline earth' metals.

Davy's papers describing these researches were chosen as the Bakerian lectures of the Royal Society and marked him as one of the greatest men of science of the day. British science was provincial compared to that in Paris, but now patriots and upholders of freedom could rejoice that a Briton had given chemistry a new direction, making it seem the fundamental science. Davy meanwhile had been consulted about the ventilation of Newgate prison, had visited it, and had then gone down with gaol fever in the hour of his triumph. Medical bulletins were posted at the Royal Institution, but for the first few months of 1808 he was unable to do research or to lecture.

Davy had been a founder of the Geological Society of London, but had promptly resigned under pressure from Banks, who was determined that men of science must hang together in these difficult years in one learned empire and resist anything which looked like fragmentation. Davy was, however, prominent in the Animal Chemistry Club, a subset of the Royal Society where physiology was discussed amid worries about French materialism. He now turned his attention to acidity. It was known that the bad-eggs acid, hydrogen sulphide, contained no oxygen; in research with his friend J. G. Children, Davy proved that the even worse-smelling hydrogen telluride contained none either. Eventually on 12 July 1810 he announced his conclusion that the strong acid from sea salt also contained none: that there was no material basis for acidity. In November of that year, he declared that the green gas contained in this acid was an element, and named it chlorine. For him and his contemporaries, muriatic acid and sulphuric acid had no element in common—Lavoisier had been wrong both about heat and acidity. In triumphant lectures Davy emphasized how the French had been dogmatic about what was in fact the baseless fabric of a vision. He stood at the apex of the scientific world.

Marriage, France, and the safety lamp Davy's income at this point was about £1000 a year, making him a not especially eligible bachelor, but on 2 March 1812 Jane Apreece, *née* Kerr (1780–1855) [*see* Davy, Jane, Lady Davy], a wealthy widow whom he had been pursuing, accepted his proposal of marriage. She had held a salon in Edinburgh and was sophisticated, well-connected, and intellectual. On 8 April 1812 Davy was knighted by the prince regent, and on the 11th he and Jane were married by the bishop of Carlisle at Jane's mother's house in Portland Place. They spent their honeymoon in Scotland, staying with eminent people; Davy took his little apparatus with him, and conducted some researches on gunpowder. He gave up his courses of lectures, and wrote up his *Elements of Chemical Philosophy* the same year. This, dedicated to Jane, dealt with his own work, and was meant to be the first of a multi-volume set, but it did not sell well, for it was not a satisfactory textbook and his researches were accessible in the Royal Society's *Philosophical Transactions*.

Investigating the first high explosive, nitrogen trichloride (which cost its French discoverer an eye and a finger), Davy was disabled in an explosion. As amanuensis he employed Michael Faraday, who had just finished his time as a bookbinder's apprentice. Faraday had read some of the books, and had been given a ticket for what turned out to be Davy's last lecture course, on chlorine. He aspired to a career in science and made a fair copy of his notes, which he presented to Davy. Davy advised him to stick with his trade and smiled at his notion of the nobility of natural philosophers, but nevertheless, on 1 March 1813, on Davy's recommendation, Faraday was given a job at the institution.

On 13 October 1813, the Davys set out for France; passports then came from the country visited, and he had been given one in order to collect his prize. With them, as assistant and sometimes valet, went Faraday. In the enemy capital, Paris, Davy behaved like a Coriolanus fighting alone in science for his country. He refused to be impressed by a tour of the Louvre, which was full of Napoleon's loot, stalked out of an anti-British play, and competed with the leading French chemist, J. L. Gay-Lussac, to elucidate the nature of a curious new substance: recognizing its analogy with chlorine, he called it iodine.

From Paris they went to Italy, which was less of an intellectual hothouse but more congenial, where Davy investigated petrifying springs and carried out some of the first analyses of pigments used in ancient paintings. In Naples, where they observed Vesuvius in eruption, they were planning to go on to Constantinople when they heard of Napoleon's return from Elba; they left on 21 March 1815 and arrived home via the Rhineland on 23 April. On holiday in Scotland in August, Davy received a letter from the Revd Robert Gray of Bishopwearmouth asking him, as Britain's leading man of science, to do something about explosions in coalmines. On 14 August, Davy stopped in

Newcastle and met John Buddle, the leading colliery manager or 'viewer', and another clergyman, the Revd John Hodgson of Jarrow.

Davy went straight to London, declining an invitation to visit Banks, and Buddle sent him samples of the gas, 'firedamp', which issued from the coal and caused the explosions. It was often supposed to be hydrogen, but Davy, working with Faraday as his assistant, proved that it was methane. He found that a mixture of air and methane will explode only at a high temperature, and by 30 October had devised a lamp where the gases entered and left through narrow tubes to cool them down. He went on to enclose the flame in a cylinder of wire gauze in the definitive form of the Davy lamp, which would explode only if white-hot, and which also functioned as a detector of firedamp. Banks wrote Davy a magnificent letter declaring that his work would place the Royal Society higher in popular opinion than all the abstruse discoveries beyond the understanding of ordinary people.

A device developed in the laboratory worked down the mine—this was one of the very first examples of technology as applied science. George Stephenson had developed a similar lamp at the same time, in the older trial-and-error fashion, and there were priority disputes. Davy refused to patent his lamp, and so the matter was never tested in court; understanding the principle, he indignantly rejected Stephenson's claims to have invented a safe lamp, which were pressed sometimes scurrilously by his partisans. Davy was awarded the Royal Society's Rumford medal, a set of plate presented at a public meeting by his old friend Lambton, and a baronetcy: though this was the highest honour yet accorded to a man of science it was an empty honour for a childless man, and was in contrast with the honours showered upon military men for destroying their fellow creatures.

In the course of his work, Davy found that, in the presence of a coil of platinum wire, firedamp and air will combine without explosion, the first example of what came to be known as heterogeneous catalysis. The Davys went for another continental tour, during which they received recognition for the miner's lamp (and tried to unroll papyri from Herculaneum). Then, in 1820, Banks died; he had been president of the Royal Society since a few days before Davy was born, and as the gentleman with the lamp, Davy was the unstoppable candidate to succeed him. The shy W. H. Wollaston, Banks's preferred successor, declined a contest, and on 30 November 1820 Davy was elected to what was then a position of lonely eminence in the world of British science.

President of the Royal Society In the event, Davy's reputation was tarnished by his taking this responsibility: had he died in 1819 it would have been glittering. The society was teetering between remaining a gentlemen's club and becoming an academy of sciences. Davy favoured judicious modernizing and was tolerant of specialisms, and during his presidency the council of the society came to include a majority of men with one or more scientific publications. He made publication an important factor in election, but, lacking the social status of Banks, he was unable to force his will upon the fellows, and found himself between hostile camps, pleasing nobody. Social mobility was recognized then and now as the key to his life, but it had its limits. His patronage secured Children a post at the British Museum, though this weakened confidence in that institution. With Stamford Raffles he set up the London Zoo, as a kind of response to the Museum of Natural History in Paris. He was one of the founders of the Athenaeum, as a real club for intellectual gentlemen.

Davy's relationship with Faraday was a casualty of his elevation. He had in 1816 tactfully propelled Faraday into publication, and eased him through what was in effect an apprenticeship; Faraday's status changed from laboratory assistant, to research student, to junior colleague, and he devotedly preserved and bound Davy's scribbled experimental notes and drafts. There was then no clear point to mark academic coming-of-age, but Faraday by 1821 no longer needed a fatherly supervisor to make helpful suggestions about his papers, for example on the liquefaction of gases; he began independent research, and took up work in electromagnetism which looked a bit like trespassing on Wollaston's territory. Faraday was not good at flattering distinguished elders, and he felt that Davy (whose relationship with Wollaston was respectful but not very close) failed to support him. In 1823, without consulting Davy, he allowed his name to go forward for fellowship of the Royal Society; Davy felt indignant and offended, told him to withdraw, and sulked when he refused. Faraday was elected, and he and Davy were now distanced in a kind of family row which they never really resolved. Two masters of scientific rhetoric found themselves inarticulate, and it was not until after Davy's death that Faraday was able to break fully from his shadow and embark on his own fundamental electrical researches.

In 1823 Davy took upon himself research into the corrosion of the copper bottoms of warships. He showed that this ceased if 'protectors' of a more reactive metal were attached, and these were tried, with Davy going on one of the experimental voyages, to Scandinavia. The protector gave a negative charge to the copper but unfortunately this proved attractive to marine organisms, and protected ships sailed badly. In this case scaling up from the laboratory did not work in the more complex conditions of the outside world and Davy was much mortified.

Last years: contemplating death's shadow At the anniversary meeting of the Royal Society on 30 November 1826 Davy was re-elected unopposed, but his speech was made with such effort that drops of sweat flowed down his countenance and he was unable to attend the dinner which followed. In December he had a stroke; he was forty-eight. His adoring younger brother, John *Davy, who had trained as a doctor at his expense in Edinburgh and was serving with the army, hurried to his bedside, and on 22 January 1827 they set out for Italy. Rides in the woods around Ravenna and a low diet restored Davy's health somewhat but he brooded upon the transience of things. On 30 June he wrote from Salzburg to his wife, and also to his friend Davies Gilbert, that he would resign his presidency at the next anniversary. His favoured candidate was

Robert Peel, whose wealth, influence, and lack of any specific scientific reputation would be very valuable: through Peel, Davy had earlier induced the king to found royal medals for science. He invited Jane to join him for the winter in Italy, but when this proved impossible he resolved unhappily in September to return to England. His love of natural history had not deserted him, and he decided to write a series of dialogues on the subject, entitled *Salmonia, or, Days of Fly-Fishing.*

By the time the book appeared Davy was back on the continent, never to return home. He had set out on 29 March 1828 accompanied by James Tobin, a German-speaking medical student—the son of an old friend of Bristol days—whose long trip in the company of an invalid curmudgeon does not seem to have been much fun. Tobin read endlessly to him, and he fished and shot in solitude. In Slovenia he was consoled by Josephine Detela, whose nickname was Papina, the daughter of an innkeeper in Ljubljana. He loved the Julian alps, fishing and seeking the sources of rivers; a house he took at Podkoren on the Wurzen pass, among beech woods, bears a plaque in his memory. He was delighted about Roman Catholic emancipation, being sympathetic to that church because of his experiences in Italy and Austria, and earlier in his beloved Ireland where he had lectured, and where Trinity College, Dublin, gave him a doctorate in 1811.

Davy's *Salmonia* was a success, and had an enthusiastic review from his friend Walter Scott. He resolved to extend it with general reflections upon life and science. Coming to terms with his prematurely worn-out body, he also began dictating to Tobin a series of dialogues on life, immortality, the pursuit of science, and the nature of time. These were just completed (though had he lived longer he might have added more) on his deathbed, and published posthumously in 1830 as *Consolations in Travel, or, The Last Days of a Philosopher*. The book represents his legacy, and although all the characters clearly represent the author (with some features of Wollaston and other friends), it is a good read and takes us to some extent into his mind, and into the science of his time. We see again the lecturer who had disclosed nature's coyest secrets to those audiences at the Royal Institution, and the participant in the Animal Chemistry Club. Georges Cuvier, in his eulogy of Davy for the Paris Académie des Sciences, described the book as the work of a dying Plato.

Davy wintered in Rome, and there spent his fiftieth birthday hunting in the Campagna, but on 20 February 1829 he had another stroke. He thanked God he had been able to finish all his philosophical labours, and was like to die. His wife and brother were summoned, but he rallied. One day Tobin read Shakespeare to him for nine hours. The party set off for England, but at Geneva, after Tobin had read *Humphry Clinker* until 10 p.m. Davy died peacefully in the early hours of 29 May 1829. Fearful of being buried alive, and squeamish about post-mortems, he had requested that interment be delayed but the laws of Geneva did not permit it. He was given a civic funeral the following Monday, 1 June 1829, and buried at the cemetery of

Plain-Palais. His wife had a memorial tablet put up in Westminster Abbey, for which she was charged £142.

Despite the success of his last works, and his brother's efforts, Davy's reputation was soon eclipsed by that of Faraday. Historians of science concentrating upon positive contributions found little to remark after 1815, but Davy can be seen as one of the first professional men of science, which brought him a high if not always comfortable social position, and tremendous fame. His dialogues, written when he was given time for reflection, moving from science to wisdom, help the reader to enter a world that existed before there were 'two cultures', where the discoverer was becoming a sage.   DAVID KNIGHT

Sources The collected works of Sir Humphry Davy, ed. J. Davy, 9 vols. (1839–40) · J. Z. Fullmer, Sir Humphry Davy's published works (1969) · J. A. Paris, The life of Sir Humphry Davy (1831) · J. Davy, Memoirs of the life of Sir Humphry Davy, 2 vols. (1836) · Fragmentary remains, literary and scientific, of Sir Humphry Davy, ed. J. Davy (1858) · J. J. Tobin, Journal of a tour made in the years 1828–1829 … whilst accompanying the late Sir Humphry Davy (1832) · M. Berman, Social change and scientific organization: the Royal Institution, 1799–1844 (1978) · H. Hartley, Humphry Davy [1966] · A. Treneer, The mercurial chemist: a life of Sir Humphry Davy (1963) · S. Forgan, ed., Science and the sons of genius: studies on Humphry Davy, Davy Bicentenary Symposium [London 1978] (1980) · D. Knight, Humphry Davy: science and power (1992); pbk edn (1998) · J. Golinski, Science as public culture: chemistry and enlightenment in Britain, 1760–1820 (1992) · DNB

Archives NMM, letters and reports relating to ships · NMM · Royal Geological Society of Cornwall, lecture notes and papers · Royal Geological Society of Cornwall Library · Royal Institution of Great Britain, London, corresp. and papers [copies, Keele University] · RS, papers · Sci. Mus., family corresp. | American Philosophical Society, Philadelphia, letters to Alexander Marcet · BL, letters to J. G. Children, Add. MS 38625 · BL, corresp. with Sir Robert Peel, Add. MSS 40356–40389 · Glos. RO, letters to Daniel Ellis · Inst. EE, letters to Michael Faraday · priv. coll., letters to J. Buddle · Royal Swedish Academy of Science, Stockholm, corresp. with Berzelius · RS, corresp. with Sir J. F. W. Herschel

Likenesses J. Gillray, caricature, etching, pubd 1802, BM, NPG · H. Howard, oils, 1803, NPG · A. S. Damer, plaster bust, 1814, Royal Institution of Great Britain, London · T. Lawrence, oils, 1821, RS [see illus.] · S. Joseph, marble bust, 1822, Royal Institution of Great Britain, London · S. W. Reynolds, mezzotint, pubd 1822 (after T. Phillips), BM, NPG · C. Turner, mezzotint, pubd 1835 (after H. Howard), BM, NPG · attrib. J. Jackson, watercolour drawing, NPG · A. B. Joy, plaster medallion, NPG · W. Lane, crayon drawing, Royal Institution of Great Britain, London · T. Phillips, oils · W. Pickersgill, oils (after T. Lawrence), Royal Institution of Great Britain, London · S. Reynolds, mezzotint (after H. Howard, 1804), Royal Institution of Great Britain, London · J. Sharples, pastel drawing, Bristol City Art Gallery and Museum · Walker, stipple (after Jackson, 1830), Royal Institution of Great Britain, London · W. H. Worthington, line engraving (after J. Lonsdale), BM, NPG · bronze bust, Royal Institution of Great Britain, London · oils, Royal Institution of Great Britain, London · statue, Penzance

Wealth at death see will, Paris, Life of Sir Humphry Davy

Davy [née **Kerr**], **Jane**, **Lady Davy** (1780–1855), society figure, was born on 5 February 1780, the only daughter and heir of Charles Kerr (1748–1796) of Kelso and sometime merchant of Antigua, and his wife, Jane Tweedie. Little is known of Jane Kerr's early life. On 3 October 1799 she married Shuckburgh Ashley Apreece, elder son of Sir Thomas Hussey Apreece, bt, of Washingley, Huntingdonshire, but he died (before his father) on 6 October 1807 at Malvern. It was not a happy marriage and in 1802 Jane undertook the first of many journeys abroad, visiting France soon after the peace of Amiens when that country was briefly open to British visitors.

After Apreece died his widow made her mark in society, as her distant cousin Walter Scott said, by taking 'the blue line, and by great tact and management actually established herself as a leader of literary fashion' (Journal, 1.107). A petite and vivacious brunette, she moved to Edinburgh where her house was soon frequented by many literary and scientific celebrities. According to Sir Henry Holland she was young, wealthy, with 'the reputation and fashion of a continental traveller, at a time when few had travelled at all, acquainted with Madame de Staël, and vaguely reported to be the original of Corinne', the beautiful poetess and mysterious genius of de Staël's recently published novel (Holland, Recollections, 87). The elderly mathematician and geologist John Playfair even proposed marriage, and there was no lack of other suitors. She accompanied Scott on his tour of the Western Isles in 1810.

In 1811 she returned to London and entered society there with vigorous determination, soon meeting Humphry *Davy (1778–1829), who hotly pursued her. They were married on 11 April 1812 by the bishop of Carlisle, three days after Davy had received his knighthood. He dedicated Elements of Chemical Philosophy (1812) to his wife. Her wealth enabled Davy to retire from routine work (in 1813 he resigned his Royal Institution professorship) and devote himself, as he hoped, to chemical researches. The marriage, however, was not a happy or comfortable union, each party having been rather too accustomed to adulation. In October 1813 they set out on a continental tour, accompanied by the young Michael Faraday in the anomalous position of both assistant and valet to Davy. This created considerable friction with Jane, and Faraday left a memorable portrait of her bad temper and haughtiness in his letters at this time. They returned in April 1815 and Jane resumed energetic social life in London, interspersed with tours to various parts of Britain. Together with Davy she entertained widely, her guests including Byron, Tom Moore, and Maria Edgeworth, but was more successful with literary or aristocratic guests than with Davy's scientific friends. She accompanied Davy on his second continental tour (1818–20), but from this time travelled more frequently without him, on occasion accompanied by literary minded friends, such as the lords Dudley and Colchester, with whom she visited Nice in 1822. Two years later she set out for the continent again, travelling to Germany, where she called on the aged Goethe, as well as Italy and Switzerland. She remained none the less on good terms with Davy, looking after his literary interests and dealing with his publisher, but did not accompany him on his last travels on the continent. When Davy suffered his final illness she travelled rapidly to Rome to join him in a slow progress northwards until his death in Geneva on 29 May 1829.

Jane continued to travel widely, returning frequently to Italy where she was a well-known figure in Roman society. Nothing pleased her more than to act as guide to the city's ancient monuments, and she had an accomplished knowledge of classical and modern European literature, attested to by Mary Somerville. Her grasp of spoken language was less sure, and her mistakes when speaking Italian were often recounted. While her reputation has suffered at the hands of Davy's brother John and Davy's biographers, who felt that his scientific career suffered after his marriage, she was nevertheless liked by many and carried on a vivacious correspondence with Scott and Sydney Smith among others. Smith indeed implored her not to marry: 'you will be annihilated the moment you do, and, instead of an alkali or an acid, become a neutral salt' (Holland, *Memoir*, 2.91–2). Scott thought that 'though clever and even witty, she had no peculiar accomplishment, and certainly no good taste either for science or letters naturally' (*Journal*, 1.108) yet he remained fond of her and admired her determination. She had little understanding of Davy's scientific work, but was alive to his literary merits and the utility of his invention of the miners' safety lamp, and ensured that his name continued to be remembered. He appointed her his sole executor. She was much appreciated as a hostess, and her conversation was admired for its elegance as well as for amusing anecdotes of her wide acquaintance and foreign travel. Scott wrote of her, 'As a lion-catcher, I would pit her against the world' (ibid.). She also contributed anonymously to charity through her local vicar. She continued to travel and to be seen at every notable social occasion until her death at her home, 26 Park Street, Grosvenor Square, London, on 8 May 1855. SOPHIE FORGAN

Sources The journal of Sir Walter Scott, 1 (1891), 107–9 · The letters of Sir Walter Scott, ed. H. J. C. Grierson and others, centenary edn, 12 vols. (1932–79), vols. 2–3, 8–9 · Fragmentary remains, literary and scientific, of Sir Humphry Davy, ed. J. Davy (1858) · The correspondence of Michael Faraday, ed. F. A. J. L. James, [4 vols.] (1991–) · Burke, Gen. GB (1879) [Keir of the Haie] · W. M. Parker, 'Lady Davy in her letters', QR, 300 (1962), 79–89 · GM, 2nd ser., 44 (1855), 92–3 · H. Holland, Recollections of past life (1872) · M. Somerville, Personal recollections, from early life to old age, of Mary Somerville (1874) · Lady Holland, A memoir of the Reverend Sydney Smith … with a collection from his letters, ed. Mrs Austin, 1 (1855) · The journal of Thomas Moore, ed. W. S. Dowden, 6 vols. (1983–91) · Life, letters, and journals of George Ticknor, ed. G. S. Hillard and others, 2 vols. (1876), vol. 1, pp. 57, 128; vol. 2, p. 179 · Burke, Peerage · Royal Institution of Great Britain, London, Davy MSS · DNB

Archives priv. coll. | John Murray, archives · Royal Institution of Great Britain, London, corresp. with Mrs Apreece

Davy, John (1763–1824), composer, was born at Creedy Bridge, Upton Hellions, near Crediton, Devon, the illegitimate son of Sarah Davie or Davy, on 23 December 1763. He was brought up by his maternal uncle, a blacksmith of Upton Hellions, who played the cello in the church band. When under the age of five Davy could play simple tunes on the fife after one or two hearings. Before he was six, he stole some horseshoes from a neighbouring smith and devised a set of chimes on which he imitated the bells of Crediton church. On hearing of this, the rector, James Carrington, showed him a harpsichord, which he soon learned to play, and he also began the violin. Carrington recommended him to the Revd Richard Eastcott, of Exeter, who gave him piano lessons and persuaded his friends

to article him, by the age of twelve, to William Jackson, organist of Exeter Cathedral. Davy's progress in composition was rapid, and he soon became a competent performer on the organ, violin, viola, and cello. After completing his articles he lived for some years in Exeter as an organist and teacher.

A passion for the stage, which led him to act with William Dowton at the local theatre, caused Davy to move to London, where he played the violin at Covent Garden. About 1790 he had published a set of glees as his op. 1, but theatres were slow to encourage his real gift, which was for instrumental music. He wrote two stage pieces for Sadler's Wells, though success did not come until 1800 with *What a Blunder!* for the Little Theatre, Haymarket. He spent most of his career collaborating with various indifferent theatre composers and contributing songs and numbers to their works and to pasticcios for Covent Garden. A number of his songs were very popular in their day, and he also wrote some successful harp music. But he became depressed, his work deteriorated, and he took to drink. He died, impoverished, in May's Buildings, St Martin's Lane, London, on 22 February 1824, and was buried in the churchyard of St Martin-in-the-Fields on the 28th at the expense of two London tradesmen, one a native of Crediton. JOHN WARRACK

Sources New Grove · Grove, Dict. mus. · Grove, Dict. mus. (1954) · R. Eastcott, Sketches of the origin, progress, and effects of music (1793) · The thespian dictionary, or, Dramatic biography of the present age, 2nd edn (1805) · GM, 1st ser., 94/1 (1824), 280–81 · [Clarke], The Georgian era: memoirs of the most eminent persons, 4 (1834), 267–9 · N&Q, 3rd ser., 4 (1863), 396 · N&Q, 4th ser., 9 (1872), 319 · A. Edwards, 'Crediton musicians', Report and Transactions of the Devonshire Association, 14 (1882), 322–8, esp. 322–5

Davy, John (1790–1868), physiologist and anatomist, was one of the five children of Robert Davy (d. 1794), woodcarver, and Grace Millett. He was the younger brother of Sir Humphry *Davy. John Davy was born at Penzance, Cornwall, on 24 May 1790. In his childhood he appears to have been helped by his brother, and both boys acknowledged the great assistance they received from their mother. Davy was chiefly educated at the preparatory schools of Penzance. About 1810 he went on to study medicine at Edinburgh University, where he took his MD degree in 1814. When Humphry Davy advanced theories as to the constitution of muriatic acid which were opposed to the teaching of Berthollet, and attacked by Dr Murray, John Davy supported his brother's views. He carried out experiments in the laboratory of Edinburgh University and obtained results which entirely confirmed Humphry Davy's theory.

Davy entered the army as a surgeon, saw a great deal of foreign service, and eventually became inspector of hospitals. He usually made careful notes, and studied especially the characters of the local people who came under his notice, and who were often under his medical care. In 1821 he published *An Account of the Interior of Ceylon and of its Inhabitants, with Travels in that Island*. In 1830 Davy married Margaret, daughter of Archibald Fletcher. A daughter,

Grace, married George Rolleston, Linacre professor of anatomy and physiology at Oxford.

Davy visited his brother Humphry during his convalescence at Ravenna in 1827, and was present at his brother's death in 1829. In 1836 he edited the *Memoirs of Sir Humphry Davy*, and in 1839, his collected works. In the same year Davy published *Researches, Physiological and Anatomical*, and in 1842 his *Notes and Observations on the Ionian Islands* (2 vols.). In 1849 he published his *Lectures on Chemistry*, and *Discourses on Agriculture*. He lived in the West Indies for about three years before 1854, and in that year he published a volume entitled *The West Indies before and since Slave Emancipation, Comprising the Windward and Leeward Islands Military Command*. As inspector-general of army hospitals, in 1862 he published *On some of the More Important Diseases of the Army, with Contributions to Pathology*, and in the following year *Physiological Researches*. Up to 1863 Davy had published 152 memoirs and papers in various medical journals and in the *Transactions of the Royal Society*. He was elected a fellow of the Royal Society in 1834. He was a great lover of fishing, and in his *The Angler and his Friends, or, Piscatory Colloquies and Fishing Excursions* (1855) he described the deep delight he took in angling in the Lake District.

Davy died at his home at Lesketh How, near Ambleside, Westmorland, on 24 January 1868. His wife survived him.

ROBERT HUNT, rev. MICHAEL BEVAN

Sources PRS, 18 (1869–70), 112 · Boase & Courtney, *Bibl. Corn.* · *Annals of Philosophy*, new ser., 1 (1821), 144–50 · J. A. Paris, *The life of Sir Humphry Davy* (1831) · *Catalogue of the scientific books in the library of the Royal Society*, Royal Society, 1: *Transactions, journals, observations and reports, surveys, museums* (1881) · GM, 4th ser., 5 (1868), 399–400 · R. Polwhele, *Biographical sketches in Cornwall*, 3 vols. (1831) · H. Bence Jones, *The Royal Institution* (1871) · C. R. Weld, *A history of the Royal Society*, 2 vols. (1848) · CGPLA Eng. & Wales (1868)
Archives Keele University, notebooks and papers · Royal Institution of Great Britain, London, notebooks and papers · University of Toronto, notebook · Wellcome L., journals of travels in Ceylon, Malta, and West Indies | Keele University, Richards MSS · U. St Andr. L., corresp. with James Forbes
Likenesses photograph?, Wellcome L.
Wealth at death under £14,000: probate, 2 April 1868, CGPLA Eng. & Wales · under £14,000: administration with will, 28 Oct 1869, CGPLA Eng. & Wales

Davy, Martin (1763–1839), physician and college head, was the son of William Davy, a country gentleman of moderate estate at Ingoldisthorpe, Norfolk. He was educated first at Lynn School, and was afterwards a pupil of a Yarmouth surgeon. Later he studied medicine at Edinburgh, and adopted the Brunonian system of medicine promoted by John Brown (1735–1788). His taste for classical scholarship had earlier gained him an introduction to Samuel Parr, and through Parr's influence he entered Gonville and Caius College, Cambridge, at the age of twenty-three. There he held a scholarship, 1787–91, and Dr Caius's medical fellowship, 1791–1803; he returned to Edinburgh to complete his medical studies, graduating MB in 1792 and MD in 1797. He was an unsuccessful candidate for the mastership of Caius in 1795, and then spent two years in Europe, travelling for a period as tutor to Lord Ossulston (later the sixth earl of Tankerville), and visiting the antiquities of Rome and Naples. In Cambridge he practised medicine

with considerable success, and continued to do so after his election as master of Caius in 1803. During 1803–4 he was vice-chancellor of the university and became involved in a controversy touching his professional interests when he confirmed a restrictive interpretation placed upon the statute relating to medical study, in order to exclude a capable local practitioner, Frederick Thackeray (1774–1852), from taking a medical degree. He was a strong whig, and on the occasion of Pitt's death he vetoed in the *caput* (21 March 1806) a scheme to erect a statue of him in the Senate House.

Davy's marriage at St George's, Hanover Square, on 16 May 1811, to an heiress, Anne, daughter of William Stevenson of Eccleshall, Staffordshire, coincided with a change in his profession. Having, it was said, been a religious sceptic, he took holy orders in 1810 and was admitted DD in 1811. After his wife's early death, on 9 October 1811, aged thirty-three, he devoted himself to private study in his library, which was well stocked with editions of classical authors. Their sale after his death realized £1130. Elected to the Royal Society in 1801, he was a member of the Linnean Society, and a fellow of the Society of Antiquaries (1812). His only published work was a pamphlet, *Observations upon Mr Fox's Letter to Mr Grey* (1809), which exhaustively discussed C. J. Fox's usage of the word 'merry' in the preface to his *History of the Early Part of the Reign of James the Second*.

Davy served for a second period as vice-chancellor in 1827–8. In 1827 the tory ministry gave him the rectory of Cottenham, Cambridgeshire, and in 1832 he received a non-residentiary canonry at Chichester, but he retained a reputation for religious liberalism, vetoing in the *caput* a petition opposing the bill to admit dissenters to the university (15 May 1834).

Davy was credited with having made his college more open by abolishing restrictions and making academic merit the avenue to college preferment; and the college certainly increased in repute during his time. His own subsequent reputation suffered, however, as a result of the unfavourable accounts of him given in the reminiscences of Henry Gunning, and in the diaries of Joseph Romilly. He died at Cambridge on 18 May 1839, and was buried on 25 May in the antechapel of his college. By his own request his papers were destroyed, which was done by boiling them in the large copper vessel of the college kitchen. He bequeathed his country retreat, an estate of 200 acres at Heacham, Norfolk, to his successors as master of Caius. In 1934 the trust was made over to the college.

G. T. BETTANY, rev. M. C. CURTHOYS

Sources J. Venn and others, eds., *Biographical history of Gonville and Caius College*, 3: *Biographies of the successive masters* (1901), 133–7 · *The Times* (21 May 1839) · GM, 2nd ser., 12 (1839), 88 · *The Athenaeum* (21 Dec 1839), 966 · *The works of Samuel Parr … with memoirs of his life and writings*, ed. J. Johnstone, 8 vols. (1828), vol. 1, pp. 527, 544–6; vol. 2, pp. 189–202, 359–66; vol. 8, p. 406 · H. Gunning, *Reminiscences of the university, town, and county of Cambridge, from the year 1780*, 2 vols. (1854) · C. N. L. Brooke, *A history of Gonville and Caius College* (1985) · D. A. Winstanley, *Early Victorian Cambridge* (1940); repr. (1955)
Archives Linn. Soc., letters to Sir James Smith

Davy [Davys], **Richard** (*d.* 1521?), church musician, is of unknown origins, but rose to be one of the leading composers of his generation. All that is certain about his career is that he was instructor of the choristers at Magdalen College, Oxford, from Michaelmas 1490 until Christmas 1491; he could have held the post as early as Michaelmas 1488 and as late as Christmas 1493. It is probable, however, that he stayed no longer than the many other instructors employed by the college during the 1480s and 1490s; the position was poorly paid, and its occupants tended to move to more lucrative employment. A Richard Davy entered the college as a scholar in 1483, but there is no proof that this was the future instructor. There is, however, no doubt that the instructor and the composer are identical: one copy of Davy's antiphon *O domine caeli terraeque creator* bears the remarkable annotation 'Hanc antiphonam composuit Ricardus Davy uno die collegio magdalene Oxoniis' ('Richard Davy composed this antiphon in one day at Magdalen College, Oxford'). It appears that soon after leaving Magdalen the composer took orders as a priest; in 1495–6 the college paid for the binding of a volume of songs, masses, and antiphons of '*dom.* Richard Davy'. He may possibly have been the Richard Davy of Thorpe Malsor, Northamptonshire, who on 20 September 1494 was ordained priest by the bishop of Lincoln, in whose diocese Oxford lay.

Attempts to trace Davy's post-Magdalen career are impeded by the frequent occurrence of the name and its variants; no later reference unquestionably applies to him. A simple explanation could be that he died or moved to another institution whose archives are lost or await study. A composer of Davy's quality would have been a strong contender for appointment to the household chapel of a magnate; the fact that he produced both sacred and secular music may reflect his activity in an environment that was not exclusively religious.

It is tempting to identify the composer with the Richard Davy who by 1512 was a singer in the choir of Fotheringhay College, Northamptonshire, the prestigious chantry college of the house of York; he was still in place in 1533–4; and dated his will on 31 March 1538. Richard Davy of Fotheringhay, however, was a layman, and therefore cannot be identified with Richard Davy of Magdalen, unless the Magdalen reference to '*dom.* Richard Davy' is to another namesake, or intends *dom*[*inus*] to denote possession of a degree rather than membership of the priesthood. Against the Fotheringay identification, however, is the fact that all of the known music by Richard Davy appears in the Eton choirbook; it would seem odd for him to have composed nothing else during the last thirty-five years of his life.

It is also conceivable that the composer moved from Oxford to Devon, where the *dominus* Richard Davy who revised music books belonging to Ashburton parish church in 1493–4 can probably be identified with the Richard Davy who was admitted as a vicar-choral of the cathedral at Michaelmas 1494. Although such a move might to us appear retrogressive, it need not have seemed so at the time, and there could have been personal or financial reasons for it; a vicarage choral at Exeter was worth more than the instructorship at Magdalen, and the cathedral's requirement that its vicars-choral be priests allowed the prospect of presentation to a benefice. A later instructor at Magdalen, Nicholas Tucker, became clerk of the lady chapel (that is, master of the choristers) at Exeter in 1535. The ordination lists for Exeter diocese reveal two candidates possibly of local origin for identification with the cathedral vicar-choral: a Richard Davy was ordained subdeacon and deacon in 1491 and another was ordained subdeacon in 1492, although neither of these is known to have proceeded to the order of priest.

Richard Davy, vicar-choral of Exeter, vacated this office at some point between summer 1504 and summer 1510, apparently upon his presentation by the dean and chapter to the vicarage of Broadhembury, Devon, on 29 April 1507. While still at the cathedral, this Richard Davy had made a will on 6 July 1501; his date of death is indicated by the grant of probate on 11 July 1521. In 1501 he had appointed two of his fellow vicars-choral as executors, and had made provision for the bequest of a silver cup 'called a nutt' to the sub-prioress of the priory of Polsloe, Devon, and of the remainder of his goods for the maintenance of his mother, Lucy.

The evidence seems therefore to relate to the careers of two or three church musicians named Richard Davy: a composer and instructor of the choristers at Magdalen College, Oxford, in the early 1490s, who may have entered the priesthood and whose later career is obscure; a man active in Devon, who was a priest by 1493–4, became a vicar-choral of Exeter Cathedral in 1494 and held the vicarage of Broadhembury from 1507 until his death in 1521; and a lay-clerk of Fotheringhay College from 1512 or earlier until 1534 or later, who may have died about 1538.

Davy's extant compositions, several of which are now incomplete, include seven votive antiphons, a Magnificat, a setting of the Passion for Palm Sunday, and four songs in English. The Passion, in which he sets only the words of the crowd and the minor characters, is the most ambitious of the four such works known to survive from medieval England. Even more impressive are his antiphons, especially the colossal, virtuosic, and inexhaustibly inventive *In honore summae matris*, in which his sense of colour and flair for effective timing are imaginatively applied to a highly rhetorical text. Here, as in the almost equally ornate *Salve regina*, Davy makes a very large structure coherent by persistently re-using and developing brief musical motifs. Not all Davy's music is so elaborate; the *Stabat mater* is markedly more restrained, allowing him to create the sense of rapt involvement that contemporary devotional manuals prescribe for meditation on the Passion. Davy's devotional songs 'Ah, mine heart', an urgent apology for sin, and 'Ah, blessed Jesu', a vivid anticipation of death, achieve the eloquence and intensity typical of his Latin music.   NICK SANDON

Sources R. Bowers, 'Choral establishments within the English church: their constitution and development, 1340–1542', PhD diss., University of East Anglia, 1976, 6075–80 · N. Orme, 'The early musicians of Exeter Cathedral', *Music and Letters*, 59 (1978), 395–410 · R. Davy, *In honore summe matris*, ed. N. Sandon (1992), i–iii · F. L. Harrison, *Music in medieval Britain*, 2nd edn [1963] · H. Benham, *Latin church music in England, c.1460–1575* (1977) · F. L. Harrison, ed., *The Eton choirbook*, 3 vols., Musica Britannica, 10–12 (1956–61) · J. Stevens, ed., *Early Tudor songs and carols*, Musica Britannica, 36 (1975) · N. Orme, *The minor clergy of Exeter Cathedral, 1300–1548* (1980), 39 · will, PRO, PROB 11/20, sig. 13 · private information (2004) [Dr. D. Skinner and Professor J. Harper]

Archives BL, Add. MS 5465 · BL, Add. MS 34191 · CUL, MS Dd.13.27 · Eton, MS 178 · St John Cam., MS K.31 | BL, Harley MS 1709 · NYPL, Drexel MSS 4180–4185

Wealth at death see will, 6 July 1501, PRO, PROB 11/20, sig. 13

Davy [Devy], **Robert** (*d.* 1793), portrait painter and draughtsman, was born at Cullompton, Devon, and travelled to Rome in 1755. He appears to have made two trips to Italy, in 1755 (remaining until 1760) and again in 1765. As well as painting portraits he seems to have acted as a dealer or agent for British collectors. Ingamells notes that a 'Robert Devy' was exporting marbles from Rome in 1759 (Ingamells, 283). By 1760 he had returned to England and settled in London as a drawing-master at a ladies' school in Queen Square; from 1762 to 1793 he worked as a drawing-master at the Royal Military Academy at Woolwich.

Davy exhibited portrait miniatures at the exhibitions of the Free Society of Artists from 1762 to 1768 and the Royal Academy from 1771 to 1782. His academic *œuvre* also included mythological subjects in paintings such as *Diana Sleeping and Nymphs Bathing* (exh. RA, 1781). He also worked as a professional copyist: a small picture made by him after Benjamin West's *Death of General Wolfe* (1771) attracted attention. Some of his works were engraved, including a portrait of the watchmaker John Arnold, mezzotinted by Susan Esther Reid. In September 1793 he was knocked down and robbed near his home in John Street, Tottenham Court Road, London, and died a few days later on 28 September.

L. H. CUST, *rev.* NATASHA EATON

Sources D. Foskett, *A dictionary of British miniature painters*, 1 (1972) · Waterhouse, *18c painters* · J. Ingamells, ed., *A dictionary of British and Irish travellers in Italy, 1701–1800* (1997) · E. Edwards, *Anecdotes of painters* (1808); facs. edn (1970) · Graves, *Artists*, 1st edn · Redgrave, *Artists*, 2nd edn · G. Reynolds, *English portrait miniatures* (1952); rev. edn (1988) · J. C. Smith, *British mezzotinto portraits*, 4 vols. in 5 (1878–84)

Archives BM, Hayward MSS

Davy, William (*d.* 1780), serjeant-at-law, was the son and heir of William Davy (*d.* before 1741), druggist, of Exeter. Admitted to the Inner Temple on 16 October 1741, he was called to the bar in 1745. According to Lord Eldon's anecdotes he had originally begun in trade and had been made bankrupt, though it is possible that legend had confused the son with the father. Davy was one of a new breed of counsel who made his name at *nisi prius* and in the criminal courts, both on the western circuit and at the Old Bailey, where professional advocacy had once been virtually unknown; and his skill lay in the cut and thrust of trial practice rather than in legal argument. Nevertheless, some manuscript law reports taken by him between 1742 and 1755 survive in Lincoln's Inn, together with some

notebooks on legal subjects and one on Latin grammar. His first important cases came in January 1753, when he defended a forger, who was found guilty, confessed, and was executed at Tyburn. In the same year he was engaged in the famous case of Elizabeth Canning (1734–1773); Davy defended Mary Squires in this trial and afterwards conducted the prosecution of Canning.

Such was Davy's reputation as an advocate that he was created a serjeant-at-law only ten years after call, in 1755, his patrons at the ceremony being the duke of Somerset and the earl of Suffolk. After his appointment as one of the king's serjeants in 1762 he was less involved in defence work, though he was one of the counsel for Elizabeth Chudleigh, duchess of Kingston (1720–1788) in the case against her for bigamy in 1776. He represented the black slave James Somerset in the great slavery case heard by Lord Mansfield in 1772. In his concluding speech Davy reiterated the view that 'this air is too pure for a slave to breathe in. I trust I shall not quit this court without certain conviction of that assertion' (*DNB*). Nevertheless, Davy's efforts were overshadowed by the brilliance of his junior Francis Hargrave. In other prominent cases he found himself supporting arbitrary powers of government against Serjeant Glynn, and in that of the radical politician John Wilkes he was criticized for citing precedents from the time of Charles I. Davy was renowned for his quirky humour and quick repartee, and numerous stories about him circulated at the bar. Two illustrations of his wit may serve. When Lord Mansfield interrupted him in argument, saying, 'If this be law I must burn all my books, I see', Davy instantly replied: 'Your lordship had better read them first' (Woolrych, 2.625–6). On another occasion, when Mansfield proposed to sit on Good Friday, Davy is said to have reminded him that he would be the first judge to do so since Pontius Pilate. For the last three years of his life, by dint of seniority after the death of Mr Serjeant Whitaker in 1777, Davy was leader of the English bar as king's prime serjeant. He died at Hammersmith on 13 December 1780 after a short illness, and was buried at Newington Butts.

J. H. BAKER

Sources Baker, *Serjeants* · H. W. Woolrych, *Lives of eminent serjeants-at-law of the English bar*, 2 vols. (1869) · Sainty, *King's counsel* · *Lord Eldon's anecdote book*, ed. A. L. J. Lincoln and R. L. McEwen (1960) · Inner Temple, London · *GM*, 1st ser., 50 (1780), 591 · W. Musgrave, *Obituary prior to 1800*, ed. G. J. Armytage, 1, Harleian Society, 44 (1899) · *DNB*

Archives Lincoln's Inn, London, law reports and notebooks

Davy, William (1744–1826), theologian, son of Francis and Mary Davy, was born at Downhouse in the parish of Tavistock, Devon, on 4 March 1744. He was baptized on 27 April 1744 at the Presbyterian Abbey Chapel in Tavistock. He was educated at the Exeter Free Grammar School and, from 1762, at Balliol College, Oxford, where he graduated BA on 28 May 1766. After leaving the university he was ordained on the curacy of Moretonhampstead, Devon, where he married Sarah Gilbert, daughter of Mr W. Gilbert of Longbrooke, near Kingsbridge, on 15 June 1768.

They had two daughters and one son. He next became curate of Drewsteignton, and in 1786 was appointed curate of Lustleigh, with a yearly stipend of £40.

In 1785–6 he published a *System of divinity, in a course of sermons, on the being, nature, and attributes of God; on some of the most important articles of the Christian religion; and on the virtues and vices of mankind*, which was printed by R. Trewman of Exeter in six volumes. His systematic compilation of sermons by many different authors was judged to be a practical and acceptable collection by the *Monthly Review*. He had been encouraged to bring out this work by a long list of subscribers, but because many of them neglected to pay their subscriptions, the actual receipts were far less than the expenses, and the author found himself owing the printer more than £100. He none the less determined to extend the work to twenty-six volumes, and being unable to risk a second loss he resolved to print the book himself.

Davy was a skilled mechanic. After the sinking of the *Royal George* in Portsmouth harbour in 1782 he had travelled there with the plan of a diving bell to recover the property sunk in her; but although the plan was afterwards acted upon with considerable success, he received no remuneration. He used his mechanical skills to construct a press of an unusual design; then he bought some old types at a cheap rate from the printer R. Trewman, and in five months, by his own manual labour, produced forty copies of a specimen volume, consisting of 328 pages, besides prefatory matter. He sent twenty-six of these specimen volumes to the universities of Oxford and Cambridge, the Royal Society, the editors of several reviews, and to others who he thought might help him publish the whole work. He was bitterly disappointed. The *British Critic* gave a very favourable notice of the book, but this praise produced no other encouragement. William Enfield, writing in the *Monthly Review*, acknowledged that the project was a laudable undertaking but advised Davy to abandon it because, without financial support, 'his type is too bad, and his skill in the art of printing too defective, to leave him any hope of sending out the work with credit from his own press' (*Monthly Review*, 2nd ser., 18.268–9). Few of those to whom he presented the specimen volume even acknowledged its receipt. He sought in vain the patronage of three successive bishops of Exeter—Ross, Buller, and Courtenay—and of Archbishop Moore and Bishop Porteus, but these prelates sent no financial assistance and declined to accept a dedication from him. Bishop Buller would not look at the specimen volume.

In spite of these discouragements Davy, having fourteen copies remaining, recommended his labours and taught his servant Mary Hole to compose the types; he patiently proceeded, with her assistance, to print fourteen copies of the other twenty-five volumes, each containing about 500 pages, completing the herculean task in 1807. Copies of this extremely curious *System of Divinity* are preserved in the Bodleian Library at Oxford, the Cambridge University Library, the London Institution, and the cathedral library, Exeter. The West Country Studies Library in Exeter has three sets, including Davy's own copy, as well as a three-volume manuscript list of contents (1816) and twelve volumes of 'Sermons on Various Subjects', also in manuscript. At first Davy could only afford sufficient type to print one page at a time. Numerous notes and amendments were accommodated on printed or manuscript slips carefully pasted in and folded. Sir Robert Harry Inglis, who presented a copy of the work to the British Library, considered it to be 'perhaps unparalleled in any age or country, as an effort of the combined skill, industry, and perseverance of one man, undaunted by age, poverty, and forty years of neglect' (R. H. Inglis to A. Panizzi, bound into the British Library copy of *A System of Divinity*, vol. 1, 1795, Cup.408.g.1). From 1818 Davy resided at Willmead, a small farm belonging to his son, but he continued to hold the curacy of Lustleigh.

Besides his great work Davy printed in the same way a volume of extracts from it under the title *Divinity, or, Discourses on the being of God, the divinity of Christ, the personality and divinity of the Holy Ghost, and on the sacred Trinity* (1825). After considerable additions had been made to these discourses, a neat edition of them was published in 1825 at Exeter by Featherstone and Sparke in two volumes. Dr Pelham, bishop of Exeter, now tardily recognized the author's merits, and in December 1825 he presented Davy, then aged eighty-one, to the vicarage of Winkleigh, Devon. He held the benefice only about five months, and died in Winkleigh on 15 June 1826; he was buried in the chancel of Winkleigh church on 17 June. Despite his modest wealth he had presented a set of communion plate to Lustleigh church in 1822 and endowed a school in the parish, which opened in 1825.

THOMPSON COOPER, *rev.* IAN MAXTED

Sources U. Radford, 'William Davy, priest and printer', *Report and Transactions of the Devonshire Association*, 63 (1931), 325–39 · C. Davy, 'Life', in W. Davy, *Divinity* (1827), vol. 1 · *GM*, 1st ser., 95/2 (1825), 441–3, 617 · *GM*, 1st ser., 96/2 (1826), 88–9 · C. Torr, *Small talk at Wreyland*, 1 (1918), 32–35; 3 (1923), 40–41 · S. Baring-Gould, *Devonshire characters and strange events* (1908), 123–7 · Foster, *Alum. Oxon.* · IGI · *Monthly Review*, 76 (1787), 473–4 · *Monthly Review*, new ser., 18 (1795), 268–9 · R. H. Inglis, letter to A. Panizzi, BL, Cup.408.g.1 [bound inside copy of W. Davy, *A system of divinity*, 1 (1795)]
Archives Exeter Central Library, West Country Studies Library, sermons on various subjects, index to *System of divinity*
Likenesses R. Cooper, line engraving (aged eighty-two; after painting by W. Sharland), repro. in Davy, *Divinity*

Davydd. *See* Dafydd, David.

Davydd II. *See* Dafydd ap Llywelyn (*c*.1215–1246).

Davydd III. *See* Dafydd ap Gruffudd (*d*. 1283).

Davys, George (1780–1864), bishop of Peterborough, son of John Davys of Rempstone, Nottinghamshire, and his wife, Sophia, daughter of the Revd B. Wigley of Sawley, Derbyshire, was born at Loughborough, Leicestershire, on 1 October 1780. In 1799 he entered as a sizar at Christ's College, Cambridge, and came out tenth wrangler in 1803. He was elected a fellow of his college in 1806, and in the same year proceeded MA, and became curate, first of Littlebury, Essex, then of Chesterford to 1817, and afterwards of Swaffham Priory. He vacated his fellowship in 1814 on his marriage to Marianne (1789–1858), daughter of the Revd

Edmund Mapletoft, rector of Anstye, Hertfordshire. In 1811 he was presented on his own petition to the small vicarage of Willoughby on the Wolds, Lincolnshire, which he held until 1829.

Davys produced a number of theological works for the instruction of a rustic readership in the principal tenets of the established church. A ninth edition of his *Village Conversations on the Liturgy of the Church of England* (1820) was called for in 1831, while his *Village Conversations on the Principal Offices of the Church* (1824) reached a second edition in 1849. His exposition of the virtues of thrift, *On Savings' Banks* (1824), also adopted the didactic conversational form, in which the prudent Will Wise urged upon his feckless friend Ralph Ragged the benefits of temperance and regular saving.

Davys's simple piety commended him to the duchess of Kent, who in 1827 appointed him tutor to the Princess Victoria, the future queen. Resident at Kensington Palace, he remained the princess's principal master until her accession in 1837, charged particularly with her religious education within the Church of England. She found him a rather monotonous and soporific preacher. In April 1829 he was presented by the crown to the rectory of Allhallows-on-the-Wall, London, which he continued to hold until his elevation to the episcopal bench. He was appointed dean of Chester on 10 January 1831, and at the following commencement at Cambridge was created DD.

On 7 May 1839 Davys was advanced to the bishopric of Peterborough on the recommendation of Lord Melbourne, who was tardy in honouring the custom that the tutor to the reigning sovereign should be raised to the episcopate. Davys's lack of distinction and likely tory sympathies told against him, and Melbourne's reluctance to prefer him was overcome only by pressure from the press and the reflection that the queen would thereby be saved the necessity of paying him a pension. As a bishop he took no active part either in politics or religious controversy, though he was identified as a member of the evangelical wing of the church. He was considered to be fair and liberal towards all religious creeds in his diocese, but was noticed to show a preference towards his relations when making appointments to canonries. Publications of an instructive kind continued to flow from his pen, including *Letters between a Father and his Son on the Roman History* (1848) and *A Plain and Short History of England, for Children* (13th edn, 1859) which also used the epistolary device. He contributed anonymously to the *Cottagers' Monthly Visitor* and the *National School Magazine*. Davys died of bronchitis at the palace, Peterborough, on 18 April 1864, and was buried in the graveyard of the cathedral on 23 April. He was survived by two sons, both clergymen, his eldest son and heir having died in 1836 from the effects of an accident while playing cricket. Davys's career received an ambiguous tribute in *The Times* (19 April 1864, 14): 'His ambition through life was rather to be good than great. Higher praise it is impossible to bestow.' **M. C. CURTHOYS**

Sources Boase, *Mod. Eng. biog.* • Venn, *Alum. Cant.* • O. Chadwick, *The Victorian church*, 1 (1966) • C. Woodham-Smith, *Queen Victoria: her life and times*, 1: *1819–1861* (1972) • R. A. Soloway, *Prelates and people: ecclesiastical social thought in England, 1783–1852* (1969)
Likenesses oils, Christ's College, Cambridge
Wealth at death under £80,000: probate, 26 May 1864, *CGPLA Eng. & Wales*

Davys, John. See Davis, John (*c*.1550–1605).

Davys, Mary (1674–1732), novelist and playwright, was almost certainly born in Ireland, where she became the wife of the Revd Peter Davys, master of the free school of St Patrick's, Dublin, and was widowed on 4 November 1698. The couple had two daughters: Ann, who died in 1695, and Mary, who died in the same year as her birth, 1699. Davys emigrated to London in 1700, in Jonathan Swift's words 'for mere want'. She wrote *The False Friend, or, The Treacherous Portugueze* (published as *The Cousins* in her collected works of 1725) and *The Amours of Alcippus and Lucippe*, published in 1704, the year she moved to York. Sawbridge published *The Fugitive*, an embroidered autobiographical narrative, in 1705—the year he also published Daniel Defoe's *The Storm*. *The Fugitive* was dedicated to Esther Johnson, the woman best known today as Jonathan Swift's Stella. Publication with two different, second-order publishers suggests the difficulties Davys experienced in establishing herself as a writer in London, and it was not until 1716 that she had another publication: a play, *The Northern Heiress*. She moved back to London for its production and by 1718 had earned enough to open a coffee house in Cambridge, where she lived until her death.

York had a lively theatrical culture and was the only provincial theatre to produce its own dramatists. Davys's *The Northern Heiress, or, The Humours of York* was performed in 1715 at the Market House there and in London at Lincoln's Inn Fields in April 1716. The play attacks materialistic marriage and has a familiar but audience-pleasing plot in which the heiress Isabella tests her suitors by pretending to lose her fortune. The play benefits from the contemporary delight in ethnic characters, humour, songs, and dances, and some of Davys's characters, such as Lady Greasy and Sir Loobily Joddrel, are still amusing.

It is as a novelist, however, that Davys is remembered. In 1724 her *The Reform'd Coquet* was published by subscription and carries the names of John Gay and Alexander Pope, a few London actors, and several friends from Cambridge. This delightful novel about a young, independent, somewhat vain, fashionable young lady and the disguised guardian who tries to protect her is filled with comic scenes, lively adventures, adept satire, and well-drawn, popular character types. This novel, rather than Eliza Haywood's *The History of Miss Betsy Thoughtless*, is the true paradigm of the central female tradition in the eighteenth-century novel and contains the key character type: 'the mistaken heroine who reforms' and learns to appreciate a worthy, if sober, man.

The success of this novel led to the publication of Davys's collected works (1725), which includes eight texts. The previously unpublished ones include: *The Modern Poet*, an ironic picture of a poverty-stricken, professionally jealous poet; *The Self-Rival*, a play she labelled as 'should have been acted' at Drury Lane; and *Familiar Letters betwixt a*

Gentleman and a Lady. Some critics have called *Familiar Letters* one of four examples of the highest development of letter fiction before Richardson. In addition to tales of love emphasizing that friendship between a man and a woman should precede marriage, it includes notable political and religious commentary, ranging from gory detail about the Irish uprising to a comic debate between a husband and wife who are fanatically attached to rival political parties. Several pieces are revised, as is *The Merry Wanderer*, an expanded and substantially revised *Fugitive*, and *The Lady's Tale* from her *Amours*. Her final original novel, *The Accomplish'd Rake* (1727), satirizes the fashionable pastimes of the London leisure class and, implicitly, the plots of contemporary novels more harshly than any of her other work. The novel has a number of unpleasant, debauched characters of both sexes and is blunt about consequences; at one point the narrator says of the protagonist, Sir John Galliard, 'His Drinking made him sick, his Gaming made him poor, his Mistresses made him unsound; and his other Faults gave him sometimes, Remorse.' He seduces his best friend's sister, but the brother replaces her with a woman who has venereal disease. In this frank tale, Gaylove repents and proposes to Nancy, whom he has raped, but she makes it clear that her only reason for accepting 'an inferior rascal' is her child's well-being.

Davys was one of a group of novelists that included Daniel Defoe, Eliza Haywood, and Penelope Aubin, who set the direction of the development of the English novel; her ability to construct skilful plots may be the strongest of all. Her sense of humour, her Horatian satire, her lively, sometimes deliberately colloquial, dialogue, and her portrayal of middle- and upper-class life feature in all her writings. At the end of her life, perhaps again experiencing financial distress, she published *The False Friend, or, The Treacherous Portugueze*; it now appeared under the title she had first given it. In that year, 1732, she described herself as in declining health, including being almost blind and having symptoms of palsy. She gave £5 to St Patrick's in Dublin for a large Oxford Bible and died a few months later. She was buried on 3 July 1732 at the church of the Holy Sepulchre, her home parish in Cambridge.

PAULA R. BACKSCHEIDER

Sources M. C. Battestin, ed., *British novelists, 1660–1800*, DLitB, 39/1 (1985) • M. Davys, *The reform'd coquet, or, Memoirs of Amoranda; Familiar letters betwixt a gentleman and lady; and, The accomplish'd rake, or, Modern fine gentleman*, ed. M. F. Bowden (1999) • J. Todd, ed., *A dictionary of British and American women writers, 1660–1800* (1984) • S. Rosenfeld, *Strolling players and drama in the provinces, 1660–1765* (1939) • R. A. Day, *Told in letters* (1966)

Davys, Sarah. *See* Manning, Rosemary Joy (1911–1988).

Dawber, Sir (Edward) Guy (1861–1938), architect, was born at King's Lynn, Norfolk, on 3 August 1861, the younger son of John Stockdale Dawber of King's Lynn and his wife, Lois Ellen Edwards. He was educated at King's Lynn grammar school, and was then articled for four years to William Adams, an architect practising in that town. He subsequently moved to Dublin, where he became an assistant in the office of Thomas Deane. There Dawber spent his spare time measuring and sketching the fine Georgian buildings of the city. He had been there only a year when political troubles caused an interruption in building, and so he moved to London to join the office of Ernest George. George had a reputation as a designer of imposing mansions in the country and picturesque houses in the West End of London; and his office was noted as a nursery of genius. In his evenings, at this period, Dawber attended the Royal Academy Schools. In 1887, however, overwork strained his eyes, and George sent him to be clerk of works on a great house at Batsford in Gloucestershire. This apparent interruption to his career proved, in fact, to be his opportunity; for he applied himself with his usual zest to an intensive study of the beautiful but then little-known architecture of the Cotswolds. Soon he decided to begin practice on his own account there, and for his office hired a room in the village institute at Bourton on the Hill, at a rent of 9*d.* a week. Small commissions began to come to him at once, and in 1891 he opened an office in London. From that date up to the time of his death a steady stream of attractive designs, especially (although not exclusively) for country houses, flowed from his versatile and painstaking pencil. A complete list of them is given in the *Journal of the Royal Institute of British Architects* for 9 May 1938; typical examples include Nether Swell Manor, Burdocks, and Eyford Park in Gloucestershire, Hamptworth Lodge in Wiltshire, and the Foord almshouses at Rochester.

Honours came freely to Dawber in later life. He was elected ARA in 1927 and RA in 1935; he served as president of the Royal Institute of British Architects between 1925 and 1927, having been elected an associate in 1889 and a fellow in 1903; and he was awarded the royal gold medal for architecture in 1928. He was knighted in 1936. He took a prominent part in establishing in 1926 the Council for the Preservation of Rural England, of which he became vice-president and chairman. A friendly, genial man, looking more like a country squire than an artist, he seemed to typify in his person the spirit of rural England which he understood so well; and his charming country houses and gardens invariably melted into their natural surroundings.

Apart from his consummate skill in the English tradition and his sensitive handling of all the building crafts, Dawber was a talented painter in watercolour, whose sketches showed a luminous quality far removed from prosaic architectural drawing. He contributed notes and sketches to two books illustrating *Old Cottages and Farm-Houses in Kent and Sussex* (1900) and *Old Cottages, Farm-Houses, and other Stone Buildings in the Cotswold District* (1905).

In 1896 Dawber married Mary, daughter of Alexander Eccles, of Roby, near Liverpool, who survived him. They had no children. He died at home at 64 Hamilton Terrace, London, on 24 April 1938.

M. S. BRIGGS, *rev.* KAYE BAGSHAW

Sources *The Times* (25 April 1938) • A. S. Gray, *Edwardian architecture: a biographical dictionary* (1985) • *Architect and Building News* (29 April 1938), 112, 114, 155 • *RIBA Journal*, 45 (1937–8), 631, 633, 666–8 •

The Builder, 154 (1938), 827 • personal knowledge (1949) • private information (1949) • *CGPLA Eng. & Wales* (1938)
Archives U. Birm. L., letters to F. Brett Young
Likenesses F. Roe, oils, 1926, NPG • W. Orpen, oils, 1930, RIBA • W. Stoneman, photograph, 1934, NPG • D. Low, caricature, pencil drawing, NPG
Wealth at death £10,471 18s. 2d.: probate, 28 June 1938, *CGPLA Eng. & Wales*

Dawbin [*née* Hadden; *other married name* Baxter], **Anna Maria** (1816–1905), diarist, was born on 24 November 1816 in Exeter, the third of the three children of William Frederick Hadden (*d.* 1822), an army officer, and his wife, Elizabeth Hall. She was educated at a girls' boarding-school, Twyford Abbey, Kensington, London, and on 8 February 1834, when she was seventeen, she married Andrew Baxter (1813–1855). Later that year she opened the first page of a new notebook when she sailed for Van Diemen's Land as wife of the officer in charge of convicts sentenced to transportation. Annie had been keeping a diary, which she called her journal, since childhood. Thirty-two note-books survive, 845,000 words penned across 5500 pages between 1834 and 1868.

The journal constitutes an achievement unmatched in colonial Australian letters and quite remarkable in the broader field of women's writing in English. A detailed and intimate story is told within the broad social narrative of European settlement. Annie was a flamboyant woman of decided opinions and considerable charm who moved in exciting circles, and in the journal she recorded what she saw and heard. She chronicled the world of the 50th regiment stationed in Launceston and Sydney before 1839, when Andrew Baxter sold his commission to take up land in a recently opened district of New South Wales. The Baxters believed that after a few years' hard work in the colony, they could return home to live in style. Annie rev-elled in the squatter's life, and wrote proudly of the inte-gral role she played on the station. Yesabba was not a suc-cess, however, and in 1844 was sold. The Baxters rode on horseback from Sydney to Melbourne, and west along the coast to a new station, Yambuck. There the journal increasingly portrayed marital woe. In 1849 the death of her brother's wife in Hobart provided a socially accept-able reason to leave Baxter: as a childless woman, Annie was accepting the care of her motherless nephew and niece.

Annie accompanied her brother, an officer in the Royal Engineers, on his return to England (where she discovered how changed she had been by her time in Australia) and his posting in Cork. When he remarried, the journal became the account of a superfluous woman, testy and trapped. Escape came with the suicide of Andrew Baxter, who had grown wealthy through investing in Melbourne real estate during the gold rush. In 1857 Annie returned to Australia, sold the property, and on 1 September 1857 mar-ried Robert Dawbin (1826–1913), a young man she had met on the voyage out.

The Dawbins purchased a cattle station in western Vic-toria, where the journal became a record of blighted expectations as Robert Dawbin, the son of a yeoman farmer from Somerset, revealed himself both inept and untruthful. By 1861 he was bankrupt. Unemployable, he sailed for England after his father's death, leaving Annie to board in Melbourne. Increasingly reckless, she culti-vated her genteel social connections while entering into friendships with men met in the borderlands of respect-ability. In 1865 she rejoined Dawbin on a rented farm in Somerset. About this period the journal is silent, begin-ning again when the Dawbins sailed for New Zealand, where Robert had been appointed to breed salmon. On 2 May 1868 upon arrival at Dunedin, Annie stopped writing her journal in mid-word.

After the salmon breeding venture failed, the Dawbins returned to Melbourne, where in 1873 Annie published an anonymous memoir, *Memories of the Past*. In 1888, separ-ated from Dawbin, she purchased a small dairy farm north of Melbourne, where she lived until her death from influ-enza on 22 November 1905. She was buried two days later in the Melbourne general cemetery. *The Journal of Annie Baxter Dawbin, June 1858–May 1868* was edited and pub-lished in 1998. LUCY FROST

Sources A. M. Dawbin, diaries, 1834–68, Mitchell L., NSW, MSQ 181 • *The journal of Annie Baxter Dawbin, 6/1858–5/1868*, ed. L. Frost (1998) • *Memories of the past* (1873) • L. Frost, *A face in the glass: the jour-nal and life of Annie Baxter Dawbin* (1992) • L. Frost, *No place for a nerv-ous lady* (1984)
Archives Mitchell L., NSW | NL Aus., Ferguson collection
Likenesses portrait, priv. coll.
Wealth at death £599 7s. 1d.: probate, Victoria, Australia, 1906

Dawe, George (1781–1829), history and portrait painter, was born on 6 February 1781 in Brewer Street, Golden Square, London, the son of Philip *Dawe (1745?–1809?), a mezzotint engraver, and his wife, Jane (*c.*1752–1832). He was brought up in a creative family: his two younger brothers Henry Edward *Dawe (1790–1848) and James Philip Dawe (1794–1879), and their sister, Mary Margaret Dawe (1785–1871), were all professional artists. Dawe, who was named after his godfather, the genre painter George Morland, started his career as a mezzotint engraver. He practised as an engraver for at least twenty-four years— his first plates after John Graham's originals were pub-lished in 1795 and one of his latest engravings, after his portrait of the duke of Wellington, was made in London in April 1818. In 1794 at the age of thirteen he entered the Royal Academy Schools, and in 1803 received the gold medal for *Achilles, Frantic for the Loss of Patroclus, Rejecting the Consolation of Thetis* (Museum of New Zealand Te Papa Tongarewa, Wellington), which was regarded by con-temporaries as 'the best ever offered to the Academy on a similar occasion' (*Arnold's Library of the Fine Arts*, 1831, 1, 10). In 1804 he sent to the Royal Academy *Naomi and her Daugh-ters* (Tate collection); five years later he was elected an asso-ciate and in 1814 he was elected Royal Academician, sub-mitting *Demoniac* (RA, London) as his diploma work. Dawe had also had strong professional links with the British Institution for the Promotion of the Fine Arts in the United Kingdom since its foundation in 1806. In 1807, for example, he was depicted by A. E. Chalon in a group por-trait of artists in one of the rooms of the British Institu-tion (British Museum), and exhibited there regularly until noteworthy subject picture by Dawe is a huge allegorical panorama or illuminated transparency for Vauxhall (1814), a critical account of which was included by Charles Lamb in his recollections.

One of Dawe's earliest portraits is of Sir Samuel Romilly (c.1806), and as a portrait painter Dawe soon acquired a respectable clientele. Following the appearance of his wonderful portrait of Mrs White (1809; sold by Christies in 1994 at a high price), which was compared by contemporaries with the best works of Sir Thomas Lawrence and Jacques-Louis David, he received commissions for several family portraits from Thomas Hope, and attained wide recognition. His full-length portrait of the actress Eliza O'Neill as Juliet was a great public success. In the summer of 1815 Dawe had briefly employed John Constable, with whom he had been acquainted since 1806, to paint in the background, and this theatrical scene, full of romantic atmosphere achieved by the effect of glittering lamplight, stirred public opinion when exhibited both in London (1816) and later in St Petersburg (1827), where it was taken by Dawe with other good examples of his professional skill. With the execution of portraits of members of the royal family—Princess Charlotte and Prince Leopold, later king of the Belgians, who married in 1816—which became quite popular throughout Europe in engravings, Dawe achieved the status of court painter. Under the patronage of Edward, duke of Kent, Dawe travelled on the continent as part of his retinue visiting Paris, Cambrai, Brussels, and Aix-la-Chapelle, where a congress of representatives of the member states of the grand alliance against France took place. In the autumn of 1818 while working at Aix on a portrait of Prince Volkonsky, Dawe was noticed by Alexander I and invited to go to St Petersburg to paint, on very profitable terms, more than 300 portraits of Russian generals who had distinguished themselves in the war against the emperor Napoleon I. The circumstances of such a flattering invitation were described in a first-hand account in the memoirs of a military historian, Aleksandr Mikhailovsky-Danilevsky, published in Russia in 1897.

Dawe travelled to the Russian capital via Germany, where in Weimar he had portrayed Goethe (Goethe Museum, Weimar) and discussed with him his essay on the theory of colour then in preparation for publication. Staying in Russia for about ten years (from spring 1819 to May 1828, and again briefly in spring 1829) Dawe founded a 'portrait factory', confirming his reputation as an international painter who was prolific and rapid in production. For five years, until the completion of most of the Military Gallery (opened in the Winter Palace in December 1826 and now part of the Hermitage collection), Dawe's studio, including his brother Henry and brother-in-law Thomas Wright (who married Mary Margaret Dawe in St Petersburg in 1825), issued many engravings after the originals which were painted by Dawe himself with the assistance of two Russian apprentices, A. Polyakov and V.-A. Golicke. The engravings were protected by copyright, granted to Dawe by the emperor. About 400 military and not less than 100 high-society portraits associated with the name of Dawe while he was working out of England have been

George Dawe (1781–1829), self-portrait

1813. Dawe's reputation as a history and subject painter began to increase significantly. His *Scene from Cymbeline* (exhibited with the title 'Imogen Found at the Cave of Belarius' (1808; Tate collection; a version in the Museum of New Zealand Te Papa Tongarewa, Wellington) was awarded a special premium at the British Institution and was praised by S. T. Coleridge in a letter to Sir George Beaumont of 7 December 1811 (*Collected Letters of Samuel Taylor Coleridge*, ed. F. L. Griggs, 1959, 3.844–5). Both this painting and *Andromache Imploring Ulysses to Spare the Life of her Son* (1810; sketches in a priv. coll., London, and the Museum of New Zealand Te Papa Tongarewa, Wellington) were bought by the collector Thomas Hope. Dawe's *A Negro Overpowering a Buffalo* also obtained a premium at the British Institution in 1811. The following year his large picture *Genevieve* (now known as 'Lady and the Harper'), signed and dated 1812 (Museum of New Zealand Te Papa Tongarewa, Wellington), based on (in the view of Charles James Fox) 'the most pleasing poem in the English language' by Coleridge entitled 'Love', was exhibited at the Royal Academy (Coburn, ed., *Coleridge*, 3, n. 4142). Paintings exhibited at the Royal Academy in 1811 and 1813 enhanced his reputation. These included: *Philip Howorth as the Infant Hercules Strangling the Serpent* (known through an engraving by Henry Dawe, 1812; impression, V&A), inspired by a work on the same subject by Sir Joshua Reynolds, *Hercules Strangling the Serpent*, painted for Catherine the Great of Russia and delivered to St Petersburg in 1789, where it remains, and *Mother Rescuing her Child from an Eagle's Nest*, based on a Scottish legendary story. A further traced through different sources. Many can be identified in J. Bennet and T. Wright's engraving of 1826 of *The Visit of Emperor Alexander I to the Studio of Dawe*. The artist had an unparalleled success in Russia: in the winter of 1826 he held a solo exhibition in Moscow; Nicholas I chose him as court painter for the coronation ceremony of the same year; in 1820 Dawe was elected an honorary member of the Academy of Fine Arts in St Petersburg, where in 1827 he was allowed to exhibit 150 portraits. The next year he was appointed the first portrait painter at court and in 1829 accompanied Grand Duke Constantine to Warsaw. Among his admirers was the poet Aleksandr Pushkin, who wrote a poem entitled 'To Dawe Esq.' (*The Complete Works of Alexander Pushkin*, 1999–; in English). Dawe's work was widely discussed by the Russian press and public; a reviewer praised 'the effectiveness of his pictorial approach' and capacity 'to seize a likeness' ([N. Gretch], *Syn Otechestva*, 34–40, 1820, 299–300, 302) and criticized for a superficial attitude to the sitter, rough manner, and readiness to paint 'fashionable little portraits for big money' (N. Gogol, *Portret* 1835; N. Gogol, 'The Portrait', in *Selected Works*, 1984, 536). In practice Dawe varied the compositional formulas of military and society portraits employed by contemporary Russian artists such as V. Tropinin, O. Kiprensky, and K. Bryullov. Under the influence of his painting *Mother Rescuing her Child from an Eagle's Nest*, which Dawe brought with him to St Petersburg, A. Orlovsky (in 1828) and M. Markov (in 1833) painted versions of the same subject.

Among the best portraits painted by Dawe in Russia are those of Barclay de Tolly and Admiral Shishkov (both in the State Hermitage Museum, St Petersburg); the young Countess Stroganov (Alupka Palace, Alupka, Crimea), and the Mezhakov family (Vologda Art Gallery, Vologda). Known for his remarkable industry and diverse interests, Dawe studied anatomy, psychology, and languages. He had a fine collection of old masters; studied the theory of colours and the technique of famous artists, and wrote a lively book about George Morland (*The Life of George Morland, with Remarks on his Works*, 1807). While living in Russia, he travelled throughout the country and tried to use the Russian language.

On his first return to England, Dawe brought with him several Russian portraits and in November 1828 showed them at Windsor Castle. From November 1828 to February 1829, during his journey back to Russia, Dawe visited, and was kindly received at, the courts of Germany and France. In August 1829 the artist returned permanently to London, and died, unmarried, a few months later on 15 October at his home, 22 Fortess Terrace, Kentish Town, London. On 27 October he was buried with honours in St Paul's Cathedral. The works of Dawe can be found in many public and private collections in different countries of Europe, as well as in Russia, the United States of America, and New Zealand (where his sister, Caroline Dawe, emigrated with her family following her marriage to Michael Prendergast). G. ANDREEVA

Sources *Artists of USSR: biobibliographical dictionary*, 3 (1976), 451–2 [in Russ.] · V. M. Glinka and A. V. Pomarnatsky, *Military gallery in the Winter Palace, Leningrad* (1981) [in Russ.] · L. A. Dukelskaya and E. P. Renne, *British painting, sixteenth to nineteenth centuries* (1990), vol. 13 of *The Hermitage catalogue of western European painting* (1983–), 45–77, 183–525 · V. N. Makarov, 'George Dawe in Russia', *The Hermitage: proceedings of the department of western art*, 1 (1940), 175–93 [in Russ.] · G. B. Andreeva, 'Russian–English links in painting of the second half of the 18th–first third of the 19th centuries', PhD diss., Moscow University, 1998, chap. 3 [in Russ.] · G. B. Andreeva, 'Russia and the fortune of the artists: the Dawes and Thomas Wright', in G. B. Andreeva and others, *Nezabyvaemaia Rossiia* [Unforgettable Russia] (1997), 103–9 [exhibition catalogue, Tretyakov Gallery and British Council, Moscow] · *DNB* · G. Andreeva, 'Portrait of a painter remembered', *Country Life* (22 April 1993), 62–4 · B. Stewart and M. Cutten, *The dictionary of portrait painters in Britain up to 1920* (1997) · C. R. Leslie, *Memoirs of the life of John Constable*, ed. J. Mayne, 3rd edn (1995), 48–9 · T. Smith, *Recollections of the British Institution* (1860), 25, 50, 60 · W. T. Whitley, *Art in England, 1800–1820* (1928), 156, 163, 184–5, 201, 210, 224 · *Engraved Brit. ports.*, 1.474, 599–600 · E. Renne, 'British artists in Russia in the first half of the nineteenth century', *British art treasures from the Russian imperial collections in the Hermitage*, ed. B. Allen and L. Dukelskaya (1996), 104–15 [exhibition catalogue, Yale U. CBA, 5 Oct 1996 – 5 Jan 1997] · G. Reynolds, *The early paintings and drawings of John Constable*, 2 vols. (1996), vol. 1, pp. 205–14, esp. 213–4; vol. 2, pl. 1255 · PRO, PROB 11/1776, sig. 597 · estate duties, PRO, IR 26/1221, fols. 228v–231r · *Catalogue of prints*, V&A, ed. M. Hardie (1903) · S. C. Hutchison, 'The Royal Academy Schools, 1768–1830', *Walpole Society*, 38 (1960–62), 123–91 · transcript of burial registers from St Paul's Cathedral, Harleian Society, Register Section 26.190 · register, City Westm. AC [baptism]

Archives BM, MSS, catalogues · Courtauld Inst., Witt Library, photographs · NPG, MSS, photographs · priv. coll., MSS, engravings, photographs, pictures · priv. coll., MSS, letters, engravings, pictures · PRO, papers relating to his estate, incl. accounts, corresp., prices of portraits, etc., C 111/102 · RA, MSS, letters · Russian History Archive, St Petersburg, MSS, letters · The Hermitage, St Petersburg, MSS

Likenesses C. C. Vogel, drawing, 1828, Staatliche Kunstsammlungen, Dresden · W. A. Golicke, group portrait, oils, 1834, Russian Museum, St Petersburg · F. Lawrence, drawing, 1842 (after oil painting), RA · A. E. Chalon, group portrait, Indian ink, pen and watercolour (*Study at the British Institution, 1806*), BM · G. Dawe, self-portrait, oils, National Museum of New Zealand, Wellington [*see illus.*] · G. Dawe?, chalk drawing, Castle Museum and Art Gallery, Nottingham · crayon and stipple print, BM

Wealth at death £20,000: PRO, death duty registers, IR 26/1221, fol. 622

Dawe, Henry Edward (1790–1848), painter and printmaker, was born on 24 September 1790 in Kentish Town, London, the second son of Philip *Dawe (1745?–1809?), an engraver and caricaturist. Initially he was taught by his father, and then, like his elder brother George *Dawe (1781–1829) and his younger brother, James Philip (1794–1879), he studied in the Royal Academy Schools. As one of the jobbing engravers employed by Turner in the production of his *Liber Studiorum* he created four prints: *Rievaulx Abbey* (1812), *Mill Near the Grand Chartreuse* (1815), *Twickenham—Pope's Villa* (1819), and *Bonneville, Savoy* (1819).

In 1824 Dawe exhibited two engraved portraits at the newly founded Society of British Artists. These were probably mezzotints of Russian military leaders from a number which were being advertised for sale in London and St Petersburg from 1822 onwards. They were after originals by George Dawe and drawn from the numerous portraits of Russian military men which he was painting for the war gallery in the Winter Palace at St Petersburg. In 1824, when his engravings were exhibited at the Imperial Academy of Arts in that city, Henry Dawe was awarded the title of naznachennyi (associate). The St Petersburg journal *Otechestvenniye Zapiski* (*Home Notes*, no. 206, p. 413) said that such was the strength of his engravings that they seemed to have been drawn in ink with a bold hand.

Keen to maximize his earnings and to establish the copyright monopoly granted him for prints made after his portraits for the war gallery, George Dawe intended to publish a folio of the complete set. To this end, he invited his younger brothers Henry and James Philip and his sister Mary Margaret to settle in the Russian capital, where he had established a large workshop in a house near the palace square and where his collaborator, Thomas Wright, Margaret's husband-to-be, was already in residence. They arrived in 1824. George Dawe's health began to give way and he never finished his commission, so that when the gallery was inaugurated on 25 December 1826 it lacked fourteen portraits. Henry made about twenty-four prints after his brother's depictions of these military men before the project came to an end.

After his return to London in 1827, Henry Dawe continued engraving both in line and mezzotint, producing works after a wide range of artists both past and contemporary. These were mostly shown at the annual exhibitions in Suffolk Street, to which he also contributed several paintings. In 1828, at the British Institution, he showed *The Coronation of George IV*; and in 1832 at the Society of British Artists, of which he had been elected a member two years previously, he exhibited a portrait of the new king, William IV, whom he had previously painted as duke of Clarence. He issued prints of both works. The majority of Dawe's later paintings were genre paintings typical of their time, with subject matter ranging from *The Wreck of George the Fourth, Convict Ship* (1836) to *The Holiday, or, Granny in a Rage* (1845), completed three years before his death. None are preserved in major galleries. He did not use his full name when signing his works, using instead 'Henry Dawe' or 'Hen^y Dawe'.

Dawe was a skilful worker in mezzotint, but unfortunately for him at a time when the laborious and time-consuming medium had been superseded by steel-engraving and lithography. The varied subject matter of his paintings, some of which were engraved by himself or other artists, ensured them a degree of brief popularity among the public at large. Apparently an amiable man, happily married to Mary with whom he had surviving daughters, he lived for many years in Bartholomew Place, Kentish Town. In 1842 he retired to Windsor, where he died six years later, at 13 High Street, on 28 December 1848.   ALAN BIRD

Sources L. A. Dukelskaya and E. P. Renne, *Ermitazh, sobraniye zapadnoevropeiskoi zhivopisi, katalog: Angliiskaya zhivopis, XVI–XIX veka* (1990) · V. M. Glinka and A. V. Pomarnatski, *Voennaia galereia Zimnego dvortsa* [The military gallery of the Winter Palace] (St Petersburg, 1974) · D. A. Rovinskii, *Podrobnyi slovar' russkikh gravirovannykh portretov* [Descriptive dictionary of Russian engraved portraits], [new edn], 4 vols. (St Petersburg, 1886–9) · D. A. Rovinskii, *Podrobnyi slovar' russkikh graverov, XVI–XIX BB* [Descriptive dictionary of Russian engravers, XVI–XIX centuries],

1–11 (1895) · N. G. Saprynkina, *Kollektsiia portretov sobraniia F. F. Vigelia* [The F. F. Vigel collection of portraits] (Moscow, 1980)

Dawe, Philip (1745?–1809?), painter and mezzotint engraver, has been confusingly entangled with an older P. Dawes, painter (*fl.* 1753–1774), who may have been a relation. The earlier figure was a pupil of William Hogarth and exhibited theatrical and historical paintings as well as Hogarthian contemporary satire with the Society of Artists and the Free Society of Artists between 1760 and 1774. Some theatrical pieces signed P. Dawes were published between 1753 and 1764, one of them, *Captain Bobadil Disgraced* (1753), by the painter from his house on the corner of Orange Court, Orange Street, Leicester Fields, London. Later Dawes lived at Mr Brisbayne's in Green Street, Leicester Fields. The younger Philip Dawe might have been the son of William Dawe and his wife, Mary, baptized in London at St Martin-in-the-Fields on 25 August 1745. About 1770, having previously learned to engrave in mezzotint, he was a pupil of the genre painter Henry Morland and he befriended Morland's young son George. He was Henry Morland's principal engraver and scraped a number of his paintings in mezzotint, exhibiting ten with the Free Society from London addresses between 1769 and 1775, at first as 'pupil to Mr Morland' (who lived in Woodstock Street near Bond Street) and later from Goodge Street and Greek Street. These, and other early works such as *Female Lucubration* (1772), are intriguing studies of servant maids and children in artificial light. Dawe also scraped a few portraits, notably of Methodist ministers and of actors, but most of his prints were genre, fancy, and historical subjects after a variety of artists including Richard Cosway, Richard Morton Paye, and George Morland.

Dawe's earliest prints were published first by Morland or by John and Carington Bowles, then by Robert Sayer. As well as scraping mezzotints for the Bowleses and Sayer, Dawe also designed a number of 'droll' satires of current fashion, such as *The Macaroni Courtship Rejected* (1772), *A Hint to the Ladies to Take Care of their Heads* (*c.*1775), and *A New Fashion'd Head Dress for Young Misses of Three Score and Ten* (1777). Once again there is confusion with the older P. Dawes. *Courtship for Money* is listed in the 1769 catalogue as by Mr Dawes of Green Street but was published by Bowles in 1771 as invented and engraved by Philip Dawe. Later plates included a pair of *The Battle of Chevy Chace* (1791) after John Graham and Sawrey Gilpin, published by the Northumbrian Robert Pollard, and six plates after George Morland, among them *Children Fishing* and *Children Gathering Blackberries* (1788), published by William Dickinson. Dawe's marriage to Jane (*c.*1752–1832) produced an artistic family: George *Dawe (1781–1829), Henry Edward *Dawe (1790–1848), James Philip Dawe (1794–1879), and a daughter, Mary Margaret Dawe (1785–1871). He was still engraving in 1808 but is said to have died in 1809.

TIMOTHY CLAYTON and ANITA McCONNELL

Sources G. Meissner, ed., *Allgemeines Künstlerlexikon: die bildenden Künstler aller Zeiten und Völker*, [new edn, 34 vols.] (Leipzig and Munich, 1983–) [George Dawe; Edward Dawe; Philip Dawe] · [M. Arnold], 'Account of George Dawe', *Library of the Fine Arts*, 1 (1831), 9–17 · G. Dawe, *The life of George Morland* (1807) · Redgrave,

Artists • J. C. Smith, *British mezzotinto portraits*, 1 (1878), 152–9 • E. Edwards, *Anecdotes of painters* (1808); facs. edn (1970) • Waterhouse, *18c painters* • M. Postle, *Angels and urchins: the fancy picture in 18th-century British art* (1998) [exhibition catalogue, Djanogly Art Gallery, Nottingham, and Kenwood House, London, 28 March – 9 Aug 1998] • M. D. George, *Hogarth to Cruickshank: social change in graphic satire* (1967), 67

Dawes, Sir Edwyn Sandys (1838–1903), merchant and shipowner, was born at Dilhorne, Staffordshire, on 27 January 1838, the second son of the Revd Charles Thomas Dawes (1793–1863) and his wife, Mary Henrietta (1804–1875), daughter of Captain Henry Sherwood, army officer, and Mrs Mary Martha *Sherwood (1775–1851), the author. Since the late seventeenth century, the Dawes family had lived and owned land at Mount Ephraim, Hernhill, Kent. From 1851 he was educated at King Edward's Grammar School, Birmingham, and in 1854 he went to sea with the Peninsular and Oriental Steam Navigation Company, where he rose to the rank of chief officer.

Dawes served in the Crimea throughout the war against Russia (1854–6), when P. & O. ships were requisitioned as transports, and between 1856 and 1865 he worked in India and China. In 1857 he was shipwrecked off Sumatra and was picked up after five days in an open boat. He became known to William Mackinnon, the leading India merchant and principal partner in the agency house of Mackinnon, Mackenzie & Co. of Calcutta, which was later to come under the leadership of James MacKay, first earl of Inchcape. Dawes transferred ashore and became deeply enmeshed in Mackinnon's affairs; later he worked in Bombay as his representative.

On 21 April 1859 Dawes married Lucy Emily (1835–1921), daughter of William Bagnall of Hamstead Hall, Staffordshire; the marriage produced five sons and five daughters. However, life in India caused his wife's health to fail and they returned home. Mackinnon, who sought a London agency to serve his Indian firm and its associated businesses, in particular the important British India Steam Navigation Company, encouraged Dawes to join his nephew, Archibald Gray, in establishing Gray, Dawes & Co., East India merchants, shipowners, and ship and insurance agents.

Gray found most of the capital while Dawes, who contributed a modest £1800, brought entrepreneurial leadership. As senior partner following Gray's death, his role was vital in developing Gray Dawes into one of London's most important agency houses and in extending Mackinnon's international business, which was based on interlocking family partnerships, beyond its old boundaries of India and the East.

In 1866 Dawes went out to the Persian Gulf to establish Gray, Mackenzie & Co. and Gray, Paul & Co.; he also formed Smith, Mackenzie & Co. at Zanzibar, in 1873, and later at Mombasa. All were Mackinnon vehicles formed to extend the firm's interests in the Persian Gulf and east Africa. By the 1880s Dawes was senior partner in the three firms; his finely tuned entrepreneurship enabled them to prosper through the provision of a wide range of ship, insurance, and other agency services, investment in local businesses, and importing and exporting. His influence grew after Mackinnon's death, when he worked closely with MacKay.

Notwithstanding a potential conflict of interest, in the early 1880s Dawes joined the leading ship and insurance brokers, J. B. Westray & Co., and came to dominate this firm. It brought him influence in New Zealand and Queensland shipping; he became chairman of and a major shareholder in the New Zealand Shipping Company. By 1900 his numerous business interests included the chairmanship of the Australasian United Steam Navigation Company, as well as directorships of the British India Steam Navigation Company, Queensland National Bank Ltd, North Queensland Mortgage and Investment Company, Suez Canal Company, Southern Mahratta Railway Company, and the West of India Portuguese Guaranteed Railway Company. He and his firms took large investments in such businesses and were often active in their promotion.

Dawes had few interests outside business, but he undertook the chairmanship of the Thames Nautical Training College, HMS *Worcester*. About 1876 he occupied the family home, Mount Ephraim, Hernhill, Kent; and he rebuilt it on a much larger scale, acquiring around it an estate on which he practised scientific farming. He supported the local community, its school, and its church.

Dawes, a self-made but modest man, was a leader in London's ship and insurance broking trades, in British shipping, and in the extension of British economic imperialism; his firms provided vital services needed to sustain British trade and commodity production. For such work he was knighted in 1894. Sir Edwyn Dawes died on 21 December 1903 at the Grand Hotel, Puerto, Tenerife, where he had gone to recover from pulmonary tuberculosis; he was survived by his wife. He was buried at Hernhill church on 2 January 1904.　JOHN ORBELL

Sources P. Griffiths, *A history of the Inchcape Group* (privately printed, London, 1977) • A. Fogg, *Westrays: a record of J. B. Westray & Co. Ltd.* (1957) • S. Jones, *Two centuries of overseas trading: the origins and growth of the Inchcape Group* (1986) • WW • *The Times* (24 Dec 1903) • M. Dawes, *Mount Ephraim gardens* (1994) • b. cert. • m. cert. • CGPLA Eng. & Wales (1904)
Archives GL, Gray Dawes & Co. archive
Wealth at death £238,962 1s. 4d.: probate, 20 Feb 1904, CGPLA Eng. & Wales

Dawes, Elizabeth Anna Sophia (1864–1954), classical scholar and teacher, was born on 7 November 1864 at Surbiton, Surrey, the daughter of the Revd John Samuel Dawes, of Newton House, Surbiton, and his wife, Anna Sophia Elizabeth Blasius. Her father, who held a DD degree from Trinity College, Dublin, and a PhD from the University of Jena, was a curate at Petersham, Surrey, from 1864 to 1868 but his main occupation was as a schoolmaster. Elizabeth Dawes was initially educated at home and then attended Bedford College, London, passing in the first division of both the matriculation (1881) and the intermediate examination (1882) of London University, coming first in German and obtaining honours for classics. In 1882 she followed her sister, Mary Clara Dawes

(1861–1939), to Girton College, Cambridge, where she was awarded Lady Stanley's scholarship of £50 tenable for three years. In June 1885 she was placed high in the upper second class in the classical tripos, but as Cambridge degrees remained closed to women could not graduate there. In October 1885 she was placed in the first division of the final examination for the BA degree in the University of London, with honours in Greek and Latin.

In 1886 Dawes spent six months in Greece, studying archaeology and colloquial Greek, in which she became fluent. She spent the academic year 1886–7 as professor of Greek and German at the Bryn Mawr Collegiate School, Baltimore, USA, before returning to take the London University MA examination in classics, in which she was placed fifth in June 1887. In June 1889 she completed her qualification as a candidate for the degree of DLitt (London), being placed first in the examination in medieval and modern French and German. She received her DLitt (the first to a woman) in 1895. Her doctoral thesis, published in 1889 as *The Pronunciation of Greek with Suggestions for a Reform in Teaching that Language*, represented her most important contribution to scholarship; it was followed by works on Attic Greek and Latin vocabularies (1890) and on the pronunciation of Greek aspirates (1894).

Dawes's vigorously argued study of Greek pronunciation supported the approach of revisionist scholars such as John Stuart Blackie and was inspired by her admiration of the nineteenth-century Greek political and cultural revival. It displays a wide scholarly range, analysing Greek literary, philosophical, and theological texts and inscriptions (including discussion of cutting techniques) and shows detailed knowledge of the European classical tradition and the debates from Erasmus (1528) onwards concerning the authenticity or otherwise of traditional pronunciation. She combined assessment of crucial issues such as the pronunciation of diphthongs and the disrupting effect of Latinized approaches with awareness of provincial peculiarities and a belief in the importance of evidence from pronunciation in Greece in her own time. Her method integrated linguistics with anthropological comparisons between ancient and modern Greece. She concluded that there was an unbroken tradition of pronunciation, traceable even from Homeric epic, and that the way to approach ancient literature was therefore to learn to speak the language (as with French and German), treating it as a living language. She attacked teaching methods in the public schools (which she regarded as contributing to the threatened place of classics in the curriculum and distancing people from an understanding of modern Greece) and recommended that Greek staff should be employed to converse and read with the pupils. The book (which was reviewed in the *Classical Review*, 4, 1890, 293–6) was translated into modern Greek by her sister, Mary Dawes (1898).

Dawes was headmistress of the Ladies' School (later Heathlands), Weybridge, from 1889 to 1917 and later taught classics and German privately. After her retirement from teaching her attention turned to translations (in contrast to her earlier scepticism about their value).

Her final work, translating the biographies of three Byzantine saints (1948), was produced in co-operation with Norman Hepburn Baynes, who contributed the introduction and notes, as she was by then unable to travel to libraries from her home in Weybridge. The aim was to produce a 'faithful version'. Her life and work demonstrate how in the late nineteenth century women could achieve scholarly distinction outside the universities when the opportunities to develop an academic career within them remained very limited. She died, unmarried, in Weybridge Hospital, Surrey, on 19 August 1954.

LORNA HARDWICK

Sources K. T. Butler and H. I. McMorran, eds., *Girton College register, 1869–1946* (1948) · qualifications, Girton Cam. [annotated copy with manuscript addition by Dawes] · Crockford (1876)
Archives Girton Cam., qualifications, with MS addition
Wealth at death £17,983 18s. 8d.: probate, 30 Nov 1954, CGPLA Eng. & Wales

Dawes, Geoffrey Sharman (1918–1996), physiologist, was born on 21 January 1918 at the vicarage, Mackworth, Derbyshire, the youngest of the five children of William Dawes, vicar of Mackworth and later of Elveston-with-Thurlaston in Derbyshire, and his wife, Olive Susannah, *née* White. He attended Shardlow Hall, a local preparatory school, and then Repton School, also in Derbyshire. It was planned that he would follow in the footsteps of both his father and grandfather to study at Cambridge, but he won an exhibition at New College, Oxford, where he entered the honours school in physiology in 1936. He took first-class honours in physiology in 1939, and graduated BSc one year later. He graduated BM BCh from the Oxford medical school in 1943, and DM in 1947. After one year as a house physician in the Radcliffe Infirmary he began his scientific career in the pharmacology laboratory in Oxford working on matters related to military questions, such as treatments for gas gangrene or nerve gas exposure. He was precluded from military service because he suffered from asthma. On 15 April 1941 he married Margaret Joan Monk (*b.* 1918/19), daughter of Harold Francis Monk, of the Malay civil service. They had met early in their undergraduate days in Oxford. They had two sons and two daughters.

After the end of the war in 1945 Dawes was elected fellow and tutor in physiology at Worcester College, Oxford. A year later he won a Rockefeller travelling fellowship to work at Harvard University in the department of pharmacology; he also spent some time with the Johnson Foundation in Philadelphia, learning relevant electrophysiological techniques. In 1947 he returned to Oxford, and a Royal Society Foulerton research fellowship.

At the very young age of thirty, in 1948, Dawes was appointed director of the Nuffield Institute of Medical Research in Oxford, where he stayed until he retired in 1985. He at first continued his work on cardiac and pulmonary chemo-reflexes. Among his early DPhil students was John Vane, awarded the Nobel prize for medicine in 1982. In 1950 Dawes redirected his interests to foetal physiology, in particular to the powerful mechanisms, previously undefined, that ensure the massive respiratory and circulatory changes necessary for the first breath taken at birth. This evolved into an interest in foetal asphyxia, where his experiments had clinical implications because of the importance of birth asphyxia as a cause of death or long-term disability. His systematic investigations of methods to improve resuscitation were translated into the worldwide practice of measuring and correcting acidaemia of the newborn after birth asphyxia.

In 1969 Dawes, working with Geoffrey Liggins on sabbatical leave from Auckland, New Zealand, was among the first to establish that the foetus made episodic 'breathing' movements even in the airless environment of the womb, and that these were related to its sleep state. This opened up completely new areas of interest for Dawes, including foetal neurophysiology. He quickly appreciated that spontaneous, cyclical, central nervous system activities (integrated as states of foetal sleep) determine many foetal events, including limb and breathing movements, as well as fluctuations in heart rate variability. In the last five years of his fruitful directorship he translated some of these insights in developing computerized systems for analysing the human foetal heart rate, which depended directly on recognizing changes dependent on foetal sleep state. This system, which he continued to refine until his death, became a clinical standard for assessing the well-being of the unborn child at the turn of the twentieth century.

Dawes published more than 135 scientific papers and 55 reviews. His first publication, in the *Journal of Physiology* in 1941, was on the vasodilator actions of potassium; the last, published posthumously in 1999, was a collaboration with his son Nicholas, and described novel findings on patterns of the human foetal heart rate in labour. After his retirement in 1985 he worked for five years as part-time director of the newly created Sunley Research Centre of London University, located at the Charing Cross and Westminster Hospital. During this time he commuted from his home in Belbroughton Road, north Oxford, the family home from 1953, where he continued to live for the rest of his life.

Dawes received many honours, which reflected his national and international reputation. These included awards from scientific and clinical organizations in the United States, Canada, and Europe. He was made a fellow of the Royal College of Obstetricians and Gynaecologists (1969), the Royal Society (1971), the Royal College of Physicians (1972), the American College of Obstetricians and Gynecologists (1974), and the American Academy of Pediatrics (1976). In 1981 he was appointed CBE. Dawes also had many outside interests. He served on the governing body of Repton School for nearly thirty years, and his leisure activities included fly-fishing and gardening. He died of a sudden and massive stroke, at the John Radcliffe Hospital, Oxford, on 6 May 1996. Three days previously he was discussing the next stage of his research investigations with

his clinical colleagues, retaining an undiminished creativity, curiosity, and enthusiasm for discovery that were the hallmarks of the man and his scientific career. He was survived by his wife and their four children.

C. W. G. REDMAN

Sources G. Liggins, *Memoirs FRS*, 44 (1998), 111–25 · *The Independent* (16 May 1996) · *The Independent* (27 May 1996) · *The Times* (20 May 1996) · *WWW* · private information (2004) [Margaret Dawes, widow; Martin Dawes, son] · personal knowledge (2004) · b. cert. · m. cert. · d. cert.
Likenesses photograph, *c*.1974, repro. in Liggins, *Memoirs FRS* · photograph, repro. in *The Times*
Wealth at death £14,737: probate, 30 Aug 1996, *CGPLA Eng. & Wales*

Dawes [Daus], **John** (*c*.1516–1602), schoolmaster and translator, graduated BA at St John's College, Cambridge, in 1537, and proceeded MA as a fellow of Christ's College in 1541. As chaplain to Thomas, second Lord Wentworth, of Nettlestead in Suffolk, he accompanied him in 1551 when he went to be the last English deputy to Calais. At its fall in 1558 he 'lost all his goodes and one of his sonnes' and from thence 'wente into Germanye to keepe his conscience free from Idolatrie', living there in poverty until Queen Elizabeth succeeded her sister. After returning to Suffolk, he ran a private grammar school in Ipswich where he taught Adam Winthrop of Groton (1548–1623, father of John Winthrop, first governor of Massachusetts), whose autograph 'True narration of the lyfe and deathe of Mr John Daus' is the source of the quotations in this article. Adam Winthrop wrote this on the flyleaf of his own copy of one of Dawes's published translations of Bullinger, *Hundred Sermons upon the Apocalips of Jesu Christe* (1561, dedicated to his patron Wentworth, now in Harvard University Library). Winthrop could not 'shewe where or when [Dawes] was borne, or of what parentage he came' but testified to his being 'very well learned in the latine and greeke tounges and also in the true knowledge of the holy scriptures'. Dawes dedicated another published translation from London the previous year, *A Famouse Cronicle of Oure Time, called Sleidanes Commentaries*, to Francis Russell, second earl of Bedford, whom he probably met in exile. The printer of both books was the Suffolk man John Daye. Winthrop credits him also with 'the Institutions of Mr Calvin in the largest volume, though Mr [Thomas] Norton afterwardes reviewed the same', and the book appeared over Norton's name only. Dawes's translation of 'the Ecclesiasticall storie of Eusebius out of Greeke into Englishe' was 'amongst other thinges he lost at the taking of Calice'.

In 1567 Dawes was appointed master of Ipswich grammar school for life, and through Roger Kelke, master of Magdalene College, Cambridge, and first town preacher of Ipswich from 1560 to 1576, sent many pupils to that college, including Adam Winthrop, and his own sons Joseph and Abraham. In 1574 Kelke and Dawes sold the bequeathed merchant's stock of Roger Barney to support Ipswich scholars at the universities. It was another of Dawes's pupils, John, second son of Sir John Jermy of Brightwell, who presented him to the living of Stutton in

1570, a parish in the Stour valley which was a hotbed of puritanism. Until 1582 he held both the mastership and the living (his son Joseph was his usher, 1577–80). Then John Smith, through the influence of his uncle John Foxe, succeeded him at the school, but only on paying handsome compensation.

For twenty more years Dawes served at Stutton, 'preaching the worde of God and teaching of his flocke', dying 'above fowrescore yeres olde' before 4 May 1602 (when his will was proved); he was buried at Stutton. His successor for the next thirteen years was his son Abraham, just ordained. The following December his widow Alice's will showed how comfortably provided they were; she left money, plate, sheep, and cereal crops, and died some time between 16 January and 10 February 1603.

J. M. BLATCHLY

Sources A. Winthrop, 'True narration of the lyfe and deathe of Mr John Daus', autograph on flyleaf of his copy of J. Dawes, *Hundred sermons upon the apocalips* (1561), Harvard U. · I. E. Gray and W. E. Potter, *Ipswich School, 1450–1950* (1950) · *DNB* · Venn, *Alum. Cant.* · will of Alice Dawes, 29 Dec 1602, Suffolk RO, Ipswich, W38/50 · N. Bacon, *The annalls of Ipswche*, ed. W. H. Richardson (1884), 296–7, 315–16, 323, 330–31 · will, Norfolk RO, 27 Candler

Archives Harvard U., biographical 'true narration' of his life written by Adam Winthrop in flyleaf of J. Dawes, *Hundred sermons upon the apocalips* (1561)

Dawes, Lancelot (1579/80–1655), Church of England clergyman, was born at Barton Kirk, Westmorland. He attended Queen's College, Oxford, first as a poor serving child, then as a taberdar; he matriculated on 14 October 1597, aged seventeen. Despite parental penury, Wood tells us, through 'studious retiredness and a severe discipline' he became an 'ornament' of the college (Wood, 3.349–50). He graduated BA on 30 June 1602 and MA on 6 June 1605; he became a fellow of Queen's in 1605.

In 1608, on the death of John Hudson, Dawes was nominated by John Fetherston to the vicarage of Barton Kirk, and though a second candidate for the living, George Hudson, was presented, it was Dawes who was instituted. He also bought land in the nearby parish of Crosby Ravensworth, including Regill Grange and half the demesne in the manor of Regill. On 25 June 1609 he preached a sermon at Paul's Cross in London. His discourse later appeared as *Gods Mercies and Jerusalems Miseries* (1609) with an epistle, dated 27 June, dedicated to Henry Robinson, bishop of Carlisle. Following his collation to the rectory of Great Asby, Westmorland, in 1617 a complaint led to his being charged with simony and this may have been connected in some way with the contest for the vicarage of Barton. The charge being rejected, he was instituted on 3 July 1619 to the third prebendal stall of Carlisle Cathedral, an appointment widely approved among the clergy of the diocese. At about this time, Wood reports, he was awarded the degree of doctor of divinity at St Andrews University.

Nothing is known of Dawes's life in the 1620s and 1630s. He represented Carlisle at the convocation of April–May 1640 as procurator of the clergy and for the chapter. On 21 April 1642 he was approved by the House of Commons as a representative in the Westminster assembly. His *Sermons Preached upon Severall Occasions* was published in 1653. When, on 23 February 1647, the committee for plundered ministers offered him a choice between the two livings then in his possession he opted to keep the vicarage of Barton. Here, it is thought, he remained until about 1655, when he died, having served there for more than forty-five years.

Walker conceded that Dawes was 'a person of a comprehensive and orthodox judgement, adorned with all variety of learning', recording sadly that he 'submitted to the men of the times; and by that means continued in the possessions of his livings until the time of his death' (Walker, *Sufferings*, 2.10). The date of his death has been the subject of some confusion, understandably since his son of the same name also died about this time and is also known to have had a brother, William, who survived him. A William, brother of Lancelot Dawes, was granted the administration of the latter's estate in March 1654. The deceased was not therefore the vicar of Barton, as Wood assumed, but his son. The father, however, did not live long after, and Le Neve's date of 18 May 1655 is likely to be right either for his death, or burial at Barton Kirk; his will, drawn up in 1650, and unquestionably that of Lancelot senior, was proved on 14 July 1655.

A. C. BICKLEY, *rev.* STEPHEN WRIGHT

Sources *Walker rev.* · J. Walker, *An attempt towards recovering an account of the numbers and sufferings of the clergy of the Church of England*, 2 pts in 1 (1714) · Wood, *Ath. Oxon.*, new edn, 3.349–50 · *Reg. Oxf.*, 2/2.223 · *Fasti Angl.* (Hardy), vol. 3 · will, PRO, PROB 11/248, sig.303 · administration of estate of William Dawes, PRO, PROB 6/29, fol. 556r · J. Nicolson and R. Burn, *The history and antiquities of the counties of Westmorland and Cumberland*, 1 (1777) · L. Dawes, *Sermons preached upon severall occasions* (1653) · J. Davies, *The Caroline captivity of the church: Charles I and the remoulding of Anglicanism, 1625–1641* (1992), 326

Dawes, Manasseh (*d.* 1829), barrister and writer on political and legal subjects, was admitted to the Inner Temple on 30 May 1776, when he was described as 'of Chapel Street in the Parish of St George Hanover Square, gent' (admission register, Inner Temple). He was called to the bar rather later, on 13 May 1789. The Inner Temple proposed him for the readership of Lyon's Inn on 3 June 1791, but it is not known whether he was selected for the post nor whether he carried out the duties, which would have entailed delivering lectures on the common law in the Easter term. Indeed, little is known of his personal or professional life.

Dawes evidently did not practise long at the bar, for he was said by an obituarist in 1829 to have left it 'long since' and to have lived 'in a very retired manner' for the past thirty-six years in Clifford's Inn (*GM*, 1829). The window tax return of 1796 shows him liable for five windows at 12 Clifford's Inn (Inner Temple records, CLI/4/11). The obituarist went on to say:

> He was a gentleman of a very strong mind, and combined with a great knowledge of the law, much general information; and of this he left behind proofs, in several works, published at different periods of his life, of which some bear his name; others were anonymous.

Writing in 1789 a reviewer drily commented of one of his articles: 'This long title explains the writer's design, and his execution displays equal pains and judgement' (*GM*, 1789). The full title was 'A vindication of the proceedings of the Lords and Commons on the regency; in which the right is explained according to the constitution as deduced from the times of the Saxons down to the present. With proofs that the protests are founded in error and that an address to any person to accept the regency would have defeated the end intended to be obtained, be an infringement on the rights of the people, an offence to majesty and an indignity in the Lords and Commons'.

Dawes took the whig side in the war in the American colonies and in 1777 published *Letter to Lord Chatham on American Affairs* in which he claimed to be author of 'several anonymous pieces'. He also sided with the whigs on the law of libels, publishing in 1785 two articles commenting on the Shipley case: 'England's alarm, or, The prevailing doctrine of libels and deformity of the doctrine of libels'. His *Essay on Intellectual Liberty and Tolerance* (1780) criticized Jeremy Bentham's *A Fragment on Government*, and he defended the legal writer Sir William Blackstone against Bentham. He also intervened (1780) in the polemic between Joseph Priestley and Richard Price. His *Essay on Crimes and Punishment* (1782) was a wide-ranging commentary on writings by Beccaria, Rousseau, Voltaire, Montesquieu, Fielding, and Blackstone, while *The Nature and Extent of Supreme Power* commented on John Locke's social compact theory. In 1814 came *Introduction to a Knowledge of the Law on Real Estates*, followed in 1818 by *Epitome of Landed Property*.

Dawes also wrote poetry, notably: 'An Elegy by a Son on the Loss of his Mother; with a Discourse on Selfishness in Sorrow'. A contrasting title was 'The Dying Prostitute'. In 1784 he edited John Stuckey's 'Vanity of All Human Knowledge' which, with typical thoroughness, was 'now corrected, enlarged and arranged with an account of the life of the author'. He died on 2 April 1829 at his home in Clifford's Inn. It appears that he was unmarried: in his will he mentioned a sister, Ann Evans, and two nieces, but no closer relatives. He directed that his library be sold, but left his papers to his 'esteemed acquaintance', the writer Vicesimus Knox. It was his desire to be buried in the Grosvenor chapel, Hyde Park (PROB 11/1754/212).

HUGH MOONEY

Sources admission records, call to bar, window tax return, Inner Temple, London · *GM*, 1st ser., 99/1 (1829), 375–6 · *GM*, 1st ser., 59 (1789), 242 · will of Manasseh Dawes, PRO, PROB 11/1754/212 · death duty register, PRO, IR 26/1184/119 · *DNB*
Archives Inner Temple, London, details of admissions, call to bar, and window tax return for 12 Clifford's Inn, CLI/4/111
Wealth at death under £4000: PRO, death duty registers, IR 26/1184/119; will, PRO, PROB 11/1754/212

Dawes, Richard (*bap.* 1709, *d.* 1766), classical scholar and schoolmaster, was baptized on 27 June 1709 at Market Bosworth, Leicestershire, the son of Richard Dawes, a maltster. He was educated at Market Bosworth grammar school, where the classicist Anthony Blackwell became

headmaster in 1722. He matriculated from Emmanuel College, Cambridge, as sizar, in 1726 and took his BA, as twelfth wrangler, in 1730; he proceeded MA in 1733. Elected fellow in 1731, he resided in his college and built up a reputation as a formidable scholar. His quick temper and eccentricity also gained him a reputation, which may have cost him the election in 1734 for the office of esquire bedell, when he was defeated by Burrowes, of Trinity College. He spent his free time ringing the bells at Great St Mary's and drinking with his fellow bell-ringers. During his time in Cambridge he published two Greek poems on royal subjects: the first on the death of George I, in 1727, and the second on the marriage of Frederick, prince of Wales, in 1734. In 1736 he issued proposals for a translation of Milton's *Paradise Lost* into Greek verse, with a specimen from book 1, but never completed the project.

As Dawes was reluctant to take holy orders he faced losing his fellowship. On 10 July 1738 he accepted the post of master at the grammar school in Newcastle upon Tyne; three months later the corporation appointed him master of the neighbouring St Mary's Hospital. The school had not prospered under the previous headmaster, Edmund Lodge, and pupil numbers initially rose on news of Dawes's appointment. It was not long, however, before Dawes's failings as a teacher and his belligerence towards the corporation affected the school. Though a ready flogger he was unable to maintain discipline; the boys rioted in 1740, and the disorder worsened at the time of the Jacobite rising of 1745. He quarrelled with the corporation when they meddled in school affairs and the two parties traded many insults. Dawes published an extraordinary diatribe against the aldermen in the pamphlet *Extracts from a MS Pamphlet Entitled The Tittle-Tattle Mongers* (1746), in which he attacked his principal foe, the wealthy physician Adam Askew, and his son Anthony Askew, a former pupil. Dawes tendered his resignation on 22 September 1746, but when offered a pension of £80 p.a. he returned to his duties and did not relinquish his post until June 1749, when there were scarcely any pupils left in the school. He accepted the pension of £80 on condition that he was also paid other fees that he was owed, and retired to Heworth Shore, on the south bank of the Tyne.

Despite the failure of his career as headmaster Dawes made his mark as a Greek scholar by the publication in Cambridge of *Miscellanea critica* (1745; new edn, 1781). Although this book contains regrettable, yet characteristic, polemic against Richard Bentley its positive contribution derives from his uncommonly good understanding of the grammar, syntax, and metre of classical Greek, which enabled him to make a number of convincing improvements to the texts of ancient authors. His scholarly labours on this work doubtless had caused him to neglect his school duties. The *Miscellanea critica* earned him a place in Charles Burney's pantheon of seven 'Magnanimi heroes', and he was admired by A. E. Housman for his 'preternatural alertness and insight in the two fields of metre and grammar' (FitzPatrick, 207).

Dawes published nothing more in his retirement and contented himself with rowing on the Tyne, brewing ale, and drinking with the local blacksmith. He may have suffered from mental illness in his last years. He died, unmarried, at his house in Heworth Shore on 21 March 1766, aged fifty-seven, and was buried in the churchyard.

H. R. LUARD, *rev.* S. J. SKEDD

Sources J. Hodgson, *An account of the life and writings of Richard Dawes, AM, late master of the Royal Grammar School, and of the Hospital of St Mary the Virgin, in Newcastle upon Tyne* (1828) • D. R. Laws, *Schola Novocastrensis: a biographical history of the Royal Free Grammar School of Newcastle upon Tyne*, 2 vols. (1932) • P. J. Fitzpatrick, 'Richard Dawes (1708–1766): classical scholar and Tynesider', *Archaeologia Aeliana*, 5th ser., 27 (1999), 145–54; 28 (2000), 205–13 • Venn, *Alum. Cant.*

Dawes, Richard (*bap.* 1793, *d.* 1867), dean of Hereford and educationist, was baptized on 13 April 1793 at Hawes in Yorkshire, the son of James Dawes, who farmed an estate at Hawes, and his wife, Isabella. He had at least three younger brothers. He was educated at the school of the blind Quaker mathematician John Gough at Kendal and proceeded to Trinity College, Cambridge, where he was admitted as a sizar in 1813. He was made a scholar in 1816 and graduated BA as fourth wrangler in 1817, proceeding MA in 1820. From 1818 to 1836 Dawes was mathematical tutor, fellow, and bursar of the newly founded Downing College, Cambridge. He was ordained in 1818 and also held the college living of Tadlow, Cambridgeshire, from 1820 to 1840. At this time Dawes was strongly influenced by the contemporary circle of notable Cambridge scientists, including William Whewell, John Henslow, and Adam Sedgwick.

Dawes was a whig in politics. He believed strongly in religious toleration and supported the conscience clause to withdraw children from denominational religious instruction. In 1834 he signed the petition to parliament in favour of the admission of dissenters to the university, destroying his chances of election to the mastership of Downing, which became vacant in 1836. Despite Dawes's personal popularity as vice-master and meticulous financial management as bursar, the master of Clare College, one of the electors, protested that he would not have supported his candidature for the headship even if Dawes had been his brother (Henry, 10).

Dawes left Cambridge in 1837 to accept the living of the poor rural parish of King's Somborne in Hampshire, to which he was presented by Sir John Barker Mill, bt, a former pupil. In the following year he married Mary Helen, daughter of Alexander Gordon of Logie, Aberdeenshire, and stepdaughter of the surgeon George James *Guthrie. In October 1842 Dawes established the King's Somborne school which soon became an exemplar of nineteenth-century elementary education. Acclaimed by inspectors of schools, notably John Allen, Henry Moseley, and Matthew Arnold, for its efficient management and radical curriculum, the school drew visits from Lord Lansdowne, president of the committee of council on education, and the prime minister, Lord John Russell. Dawes educated children from different social classes and, by charging fees according to means, the school soon became financially self-sufficient.

Dawes should be remembered for his seminal contribution to the development of applied science in elementary education: traditional teaching was replaced with heuristic learning and a rudimentary laboratory was established to promote the use of technical apparatus and simple scientific experiments. Priority was also given to pupils' language development through the use of secular reading material, including the increasingly popular textbooks published by the Irish national board of education. Dawes taught regularly at King's Somborne, as did Edward Frankland, from the nearby Queenwood College, who gave a course of lectures on agricultural chemistry.

In 1849–50 Dawes published two influential pamphlets supporting Kay-Shuttleworth and the committee of council in their struggle with the established church over the management of state schooling. Dawes's other publications included his pioneering manual *Suggestive Hints towards Improved Secular Instruction, Making it Bear upon Practical Life* (1849), which became a prescribed text for teacher training and ran to seven editions. His contribution to elementary education was acknowledged by election to the council of the Society of Arts in 1851. During the next nine years he was the major figure, with Henry Moseley, in the promotion of science in education and participated in the organization of the 1854 Educational Exhibition. He was also a propagandist for competitive examinations for civil service appointments. However, the Newcastle commission on popular education (1859–61) failed to call Dawes as an expert witness.

In 1850, for his work at King's Somborne and his support for the committee of council, Russell nominated Dawes as dean of Hereford. The architect Sir Gilbert Scott was appointed by Dawes to restore the dilapidated cathedral which, under the new dean's financial management, was successfully re-opened in 1863. During this time Dawes remained actively involved in education and science, taking a close interest in the Blue Coat and Foundation schools in Hereford, and in Ledbury's national schools. He was also master of St Catherine's Hospital, Ledbury, and a local magistrate. In 1864 he was vice-president of the Bath meeting of the British Association for the Advancement of Science.

Popular and approachable throughout his life, Dawes was noted at Downing for his generosity towards younger colleagues. George Eliot described his face as 'so intelligent and benignant that children might grow good by looking at it' (Cross, 1.281). Dawes died of paralysis at the deanery, Hereford, on 10 March 1867, and was buried in the Ladye Arbour of the cathedral. He was survived by his wife.

JANET SHEPHERD

Sources W. C. Henry, *A biographical notice of the Very Revd Richard Dawes, dean of Hereford* (1867) • 'Committee of council on education: minutes', *Parl. papers* (1847–8), 50.4–14, no. 998 [schools inspected in southern district] • 'Select committee on scientific instruction', *Parl. papers* (1867–8), 15.39, no. 432 [minutes of evidence] • *GM*, 4th ser., 3 (1867), 674–5 • H. W. Pettit Stevens, *Downing College* (1899) • J. W. Anderson, 'A Hampshire village school', *'The illiterate Anglo-Saxon' and other essays on education, medieval and modern* (1946), 142–54 • *Romilly's Cambridge diary, 1832–42: selected passages from the diary of the Rev. Joseph Romilly*, ed. J. P. T. Bury (1967) •

S. French, *The history of Downing College, Cambridge* (1978) • D. Layton, *Science for the people* (1973) • N. Ball, 'Richard Dawes and the teaching of common things', *Educational Review*, 17/1 (Nov 1964), 59–68 • J. W. Cross, ed., *George Eliot's life as related in her letters and journals*, 1 (1885) • E. Frankland, *Sketches from the life of Edward Frankland*, ed. M. N. W. and S. J. C. (privately printed, London, 1902) • *CGPLA Eng. & Wales* (1867)

Archives National Society RO, King's Somborne school file | Berks. RO, Radnor MSS, D/EP b C 69 • Royal Institution of Great Britain, London, journal of Edward Frankland

Likenesses M. Noble, marble effigy on a monument, 1867, Hereford Cathedral • photograph, Downing College, Cambridge

Wealth at death under £3000: probate, 30 April 1867, *CGPLA Eng. & Wales*

Dawes [*married name* de Feuchères], **Sophie**, Baroness de Feuchères in the French nobility (1792–1841), adventuress and courtesan, was the daughter of Richard Daw or Dawes, a drunken fisherman and smuggler of St Helens, Isle of Wight, and Jane Callaway. Her parents were probably not married, her mother being recorded as a spinster on her death certificate. Sophie was one of ten children, of whom only four grew up, and who were taken into 'public charity' in the house of industry (or workhouse) in Newport, Isle of Wight. As a child she helped her father by picking winkles on the beach. Nine years later she was servant to a local farmer and then seems to have gone to Portsmouth as a chambermaid at the George Hotel. Next she went to London, where she became a milliner's assistant, but was dismissed when she became involved with a water carrier. Like Nell Gwyn, she sold oranges at Covent Garden and is reputed to have appeared briefly on the boards there. Later she became the mistress of an army officer who set her up in a house in Turnham Green, giving her an income of £50 a year when the liaison ended. She sold this annuity to pay for an education at a school in Chelsea. Falling on hard times, she became a servant at a house of ill-repute in Piccadilly, where the servant of Louis Henri Joseph, the duke of Bourbon, pointed her out to his master, who subsequently 'won' her in a bet on a card game with the earl of Winchilsea and the duke of Kent. The liaison with Bourbon began in 1810, and by 1811 he had taken a house for her and her mother, to whom she always remained close, in Gloucester Street, Queen Square, in London. She studied with the Abbé Briant, her lifelong mentor, to make herself acceptable to the society in which she meant to move. Her exercise books, showing great prowess, were still extant when Billault was writing about her about 1870. By 1812 she had £800 a year from Bourbon, who lived in Paris as well as in London. He grew tired of Sophie and departed to Spain to try to be rid of her, allying himself to another Englishwoman, a Miss Harris. Sophie went to Paris to await his return and managed to wheedle her way back into the favour of her 'poor dear' as she called him when speaking both English and French. In 1817 she was baptized a Roman Catholic. The duke then contrived her marriage in London on 6 August 1818 to an officer in the French royal guard, Adrien Victor de Feuchères, Baron de Feuchères, who was led to believe that Sophie was Bourbon's illegitimate daughter. At the time of the marriage, which was conducted in a protestant ceremony in St Martin-in-the-Fields and in a Catholic one at St James's, Spanish Place, she falsely made herself out to be the widow of William Dawes and the daughter of one Richard Clarck, all of which subterfuges were later to make matters of inheritance difficult. Bourbon made a settlement of 214,000 francs on her at the time of the marriage. By 1822 her husband had discovered the true state of affairs and parted from his wife, returning her dowry, a judicial separation following five years later. Louis XVIII, on hearing of the situation from the baron, banned her from court. The liaison with Bourbon continued despite her lowly origins and bullying nature, both parties being said to be 'mediocre in everything' and Sophie being reputed to take coarse lovers of her own original social standing. In order to re-establish herself in court society, Sophie started to ingratiate herself with the king's relatives. First she approached the duke of Berri, who was the king's nephew. When this failed, she approached the duke of Orléans, a nephew of Bourbon's wife, who died about this time. Bourbon was not fond of his relatives, whom he considered renegade, but was by now old and weak and succumbed to Sophie's machinations to accept the son of Orléans, the duke of Aumale, as his godson. But he was not yet prepared to name him his heir, as she wished. However by 30 August 1829 she coerced Bourbon into signing a will which left 2 million francs to herself, along with estates of St Leu, Montmorency, Enghien, Mortefontaine, and le Boissy, the remainder of the estate to go to Aumale. By now Charles X had succeeded his brother Louis, and in February 1830 readmitted Sophie to court, recognizing her liaison with Bourbon unofficially. Bourbon was unhappy, and said he was sure that once Sophie and others had obtained from him all that they wanted his life could be at risk. Sophie was an accepted hostess, known as the Queen of Chantilly and La Montespan of St Leu, with whom Talleyrand often dined; his nephew, the marquess of Chabannes, married Mathilda Dawes, who was Sophie's niece. Her nephew, James Dawes, was given a position in the Bourbon household and the lands and title of baron of Flassons.

The revolution of 1830 altered Bourbon's attitude to his country and he, at the age of seventy-four, made plans to leave for Switzerland, possibly revoking his will. An important letter to Sophie from the new king, Louis Philippe d'Orléans, Aumale's father, begged her to prevent this flight 'at all costs', presumably to ensure the considerable financial succession. On 26 August Bourbon was at St Leu and passed a pleasant evening playing whist, asking his servant to call him at eight the next day. In the morning he was found dead in his room attached to the handle of the french window by two handkerchiefs. Many and various rumours were generated by conflicting evidence at the post-mortem inquiry, where it was proved, for instance, that the duke was by now so feeble that he could not tie his own shoelaces let alone hang himself. To some Sophie was guilty of, if nothing worse, conniving at the death from her room on an adjoining and easily accessible staircase, and she might even have been placed under arrest had not it been for intervention, it was supposed, by the king, the judges deciding that there was no case for prosecution. Whether or not the king's letter played any part is open to speculation, the letter eventually being sent back to the king and later vanishing from the collection of documents about the case in his sister's possession. Bourbon's will was contested by the De Rohans, collateral heirs, on grounds of undue influence, but this also failed. Sophie became estranged from the Orléans when they disregarded a bequest of Bourbon to provide for a charitable institution for old Vendéean soldiers at Écouen, and finding Paris uncomfortable as a residence she moved to a house she had built at Bure Homage in Hampshire, with a leasehold house at 5 Hyde Park Square also. She gradually disposed of her considerable French estates. She became dropsical and died of angina on 2 January 1841 at Great Cumberland Street (later Place), London, worth, it was said, £500,000, although the total of personal assets in the English probate was at one time reckoned at £140,000. There was much disputation about her will and her legitimacy. Eventually James Daw or Dawes, her brother, received £70,000; Mary Ann Clark, her sister, £70,000; and the Paris hospitals to which her husband assigned his share, £13,000. The remainder went to (Mary) Charlotte Thanaron or Tanceron, who had lived with her for some time and who was the daughter of her sister Charlotte, who had become insane, and a retired French army officer.

Sophie's place is more in the history of France than in English society, although *The Times* carried details of her career when reporting a court case of Mary Clark's lawyer suing for his fees in 1843. Sophie was described as being of an inflexible character, seeking only social and financial success, though astute; she was pretty but not beautiful, with flashing dark eyes, tall, and squarely built, with arms and legs which 'could have served as models for a statue of Hercules'.   J. GILLILAND

Sources A. E. Billault de Gérainville, *Histoire de Louis-Philippe*, 3 vols. (1870–85) · Ward, *Men of the reign* · P. Larousse, ed., *Grand dictionnaire universel du XIXe siècle*, 17 vols. (Paris, 1866–90) · M. Bowen, *The scandal of Sophie Dawes* (1935) · A. Deberle, *L'Héritage du prince de Condé* (1872) · V. Montagu, *Sophie Dawes: Queen of Chantilly* (1911) · L. Blanc, *Histoire de dix ans* (1845) · L. André, *Mystérieuse Baronne de Feuchères* (1925) · A. de Bellville, *Les secrets de Saint-Leu: notice curieuse sur ce château et ses propriétaires* (Paris, 1831) · *The Times* (17 Jan 1843) · *The Times* (8 July 1843) · A. de Lassalle, *Histoire et politique de la famille d'Orléans* (Paris, 1853)

Likenesses Huet-Villiers, miniature, 1821, Musée de Condé, Chantilly; repro. in Bowen, *The scandal*, frontispiece · Baron Gérard, portrait, 1829 · Baron Gérard, portrait, 1830 · miniature, Musée de Condé, Chantilly; repro. in Montagu, *Sophie Dawes* · portrait, Chantilly · woodcut, repro. in Bellville, *Les secrets*

Wealth at death approx. £140,000: Bowen, *Scandal of Sophie Dawes*

Dawes, Sir William, third baronet (1671–1724), archbishop of York, was born on 12 September 1671 at Lyons, near Braintree, Essex, the third and youngest son of Sir John Dawes, first baronet (*bap.* 1644, *d.* 1671), and Christian, daughter and heir of William Lyons of Lyons. He

Sir William Dawes, third baronet (1671–1724), by Sir Godfrey Kneller, 1719

entered Merchant Taylors' School, London, on 11 September 1680; he became a good classical scholar and 'a tolerable master of the Hebrew tongue' (*Whole Works*, viii), and produced as his first work a poem, *The Anatomy of Atheisme*. He was elected a scholar of St John's College, Oxford, on 1 July 1687 and seemed destined for the church. He was not deflected from this course, despite becoming heir to the family baronetcy in 1690, following the deaths of his two elder brothers. He migrated from Oxford to Cambridge and entered St Catharine's College as a nobleman in 1689, occupying his eldest brother's former chambers. His next work was devotional in character, *The Duties of the Closet*. Since he was still too young for the ministry he visited his estates and other parts of the kingdom. He married on 1 December 1692, at St Edmund the King, Lombard Street, London, Frances (*c.*1676–1705), eldest daughter of Sir Thomas D'Arcy, first baronet, of Branstead Lodge, Essex. They had five sons and two daughters, of whom only one son and one daughter survived. Dawes was made a fellow and MA of St Catharine's in 1695, received a DD by royal mandate in 1696, was elected master of the college in 1697 (a post that he retained until 1714), and was made vicechancellor of the University of Cambridge in 1698. In 1697 he had been appointed a chaplain to William III, who, following a sermon on 5 November 1697, appointed him 'by way of pledge of his future favour' to a prebend in Worcester Cathedral, to which he was instituted on 26 August 1698 and which he retained until 1708. On 10 November he was appointed rector, and from 19 December dean, of Bocking, in the neighbourhood of the Dawes estates.

With the accession of Queen Anne in 1702 Dawes was

appointed one of her chaplains. He was a renowned preacher, Bishop Nicolson describing one of his sermons, at St James's in November 1702, as 'an excellent discourse' (*London Diaries*, 126). Another bold sermon, preached on 30 January 1705, was reputed to have cost Dawes the bishopric of Lincoln, which went instead to William Wake, but he affected to be unmoved by this, saying that 'he had no manner of concern upon him, because his intention was never to gain one by preaching' (*Whole Works*, xxx). Preferment came in controversial circumstances in 1707–8, following a political struggle in which the queen's determination to appoint him to the see of Chester was threatened by whig pressure on the Godolphin ministry to ensure that candidates for the episcopal bench were more amenable to the whig party line. Though offered the bishopric in April 1707 his appointment was not announced until 6 January 1708; he was consecrated on 8 February by his great supporter and patron John Sharp, archbishop of York.

Dawes was active as a bishop in both pastoral and political matters. He was in Cheshire in the summer of 1708, meeting the notables of his diocese. At dinner with Sir Henry Bunbury on 1 June 1708 he was 'provoked to full discourse on the Prince of Wales [he] is clear in [*sic*] an imposture' (*Diary of Henry Prescott*, 176); on consecutive days in mid-August he had dinner with Mr Cecil Booth, during which he had 'a very warm controversy about nonconformity, my lord affirming he never knew any dissenter that differed from [him] upon a principle, but upon humour, pride, prejudice or the like', followed by a meeting with Peter Legh, a prominent non-juror, 'on the subject of complying with the government and abjuration' (ibid., 185–6). In the 1708–9 session of parliament he attempted to amend the general naturalization bill to ensure that foreign protestants would only be naturalized if they took the Anglican communion, but this was defeated. It was, however, indicative of the tory platform that Dawes would promote from the episcopal bench. In May 1709 he gave a charge to the clergy advising them to 'preserve their people from Atheism, Socinianism to beware of the popish and protestant dissenters, distinguishes betwixt Toleration and Establishment, says schism is schism still … and to observe strictly the state days particularly 5 November as the day of the happy Revolution' (ibid., 238). The summer of 1709 was spent on the primary visitation of his extensive diocese, the second largest in England. He was back at Westminster for the following session, when he voted in March 1710 against the impeachment of Dr Sacheverell, and later played host to this high-flying cleric's triumphal progress through Cheshire. Dawes seems to have steered clear of the type of inflammatory sermons in which Sacheverell specialized. Nicolson recorded that on 30 January 1711 Dawes preached 'a loyal and honest sermon' and in March he reported that Dawes was ashamed that Sacheverell had read the prayers following Dawes's sermon at the celebration of the opening of a London charity school, which had degenerated into a popular demonstration of the tory cause.

Dawes's moderation may explain why he was one of the first tories to break with the ministry of Robert Harley, first earl of Oxford, which had been formed in the wake of the Sacheverell trial in the summer of 1710. Even before the start of the 1713 session Dawes was publicly expressing his concerns over the peace treaty with France, and on the opening day of the session, on 9 April, he entered the opposition lobby on the whig motion for the peace treaties to be laid before the house. He subsequently opposed the commercial treaty with France. He continued to support legislative measures to strengthen the church, such as the bill in 1713 to give the church courts power to imprison offenders, but he remained suspicious of the ministry. However, his concerns over the protestant succession were mirrored by other leading tories and were certainly not a bar to his further promotion. Queen Anne, following the wishes of Sharp, appointed Dawes to succeed him as archbishop of York on 20 February 1714, without consulting her ministers, and he was consecrated on 9 March. From this position Dawes was again able to demonstrate concern over the succession, while supporting measures designed to further the interests of the church, including strengthening the Anglican communion by parliamentary legislation. Thus he chaired the Schism Bill during its progress through committee in the Lords. However, his suspicions of the ministry remained, and he continued to act as a leader of the Hanoverian tories in the Lords. Following the queen's death he acted as a lord justice while the new king was travelling to Britain.

Dawes continued to act as a leader of the Hanoverian tories until his death. As part of George I's determination to conciliate Dawes a bill was passed in 1715 that allowed donors of more than £200 in lands, money, or tithes to a poor living to acquire the right of nominating the incumbent. Dawes remained true to the tory party. He voted on 1 July 1717 for the acquittal of Oxford on charges of impeachment. However, he was keen to defend his reputation against aspersions of Jacobitism, even complaining to the Lords in 1717 about a report in the *St James's Evening Post* that criticized a 'Northern Prelate' for ordaining two men turned out from the excise for disaffection to the government. When in December 1717 the prince of Wales (later George II) was expelled from St James's Palace, Dawes was one of the tories who offered him support and hoped to secure an alliance.

Dawes made a vehement speech against the bill, repealing the Occasional Conformity and Schism Acts in 1718, which led to a clash with Bishop Hoadley. He then supported the clause of Daniel Finch, second earl of Nottingham, aimed at preventing the growth of Socinianism. He opposed the Peerage Bill in 1719 and the South Sea Bill in April 1720. He was also a leading member of the cabal of William, first Earl Cowper, an opposition grouping consisting mainly of tories active from 1721 to 1723, which sought to mobilize those disenchanted with the whig ministry. In the 1721–2 session he seems to have been a kind of whip, responsible in part for five peers and solely responsible for the earls of Nottingham and Rochester. In January 1722 he opposed the Affirmation Bill. Dawes left

London on 11 March 1723 to attend the wedding of his son, an event that also allowed him to dissociate himself from Bishop Francis Atterbury, who was the subject of a bill of pains and penalties for his role in Jacobite conspiracy.

Dawes died in Cecil Street, the Strand, London, of 'inflammation of the bowels' (*Whole Works*, xxxiii), on 30 April 1724 and was buried in St Catharine's College, Cambridge.   STUART HANDLEY

Sources *The whole works of the most reverend father in God, Sir William Dawes, bt*, ed. J. Wilford, 3 vols. (1733) • *The diary of Henry Prescott, LLB, deputy registrar of Chester diocese*, ed. J. Addy and others, 3 vols., Lancashire and Cheshire RS, 127, 132–3 (1987–97) • G. V. Bennett, 'Robert Harley, the Godolphin ministry, and the bishoprics crisis of 1707', *EngHR*, 82 (1967), 726–46 • *The London diaries of William Nicolson, bishop of Carlisle, 1702–1718*, ed. C. Jones and G. Holmes (1985) • C. Jones, 'The new opposition in the House of Lords, 1720–1723', *HJ*, 36 (1993), 309–29 • G. V. Bennett, *The tory crisis in church and state: the career of Francis Atterbury, bishop of Rochester* (1975) • *The manuscripts of his grace the duke of Portland*, 10 vols., HMC, 29 (1891–1931), vol. 7, pp. 150, 178–9, 181–2 • C. Jones, 'The impeachment of the earl of Oxford and the whig schism of 1717: four new lists', *BIHR*, 55 (1982), 66–87 • BL, Sloane 4042, fol. 268 • A. T. Hart, *The life and times of John Sharp, archbishop of York* (1949), 240–42 • *The Wentworth papers, 1705–1739*, ed. J. J. Cartwright (1883), 366–9
Archives Borth. Inst., official corresp. and papers
Likenesses G. Kneller, oils, 1719, Bishopthorpe Palace, York [*see illus.*] • G. Gribelin, line engraving (after J. Closterman), BM, NPG; repro. in W. Dawes, *Sermons* (1707) • G. Vertue, line engraving (after T. Murray), BM, NPG; repro. in Wilford, ed., *Whole works*, appears in BL copy

Dawes, William (1762–1836), astronomer and colonial administrator, probably born at Portsmouth, was the eldest son of Benjamin Dawes, clerk of works in the Office of Ordnance in Portsmouth. He was gazetted second lieutenant of marines in September 1779, and was wounded in the *Resolution* (74 guns) during action against the French in Chesapeake Bay in September 1781. In 1786 he volunteered for service in the first fleet going to New South Wales. He had hoped to get posted ashore but there were no vacancies, so he was appointed to the marine detachment in the *Sirius* (22 guns). However, William Bayly, headmaster of the Royal Naval Academy at Portsmouth, who had been Captain Cook's astronomer, wrote to Sir Joseph Banks recommending Dawes for a similar job, citing his knowledge of languages, botany, mineralogy, and also astronomy. Subsequently the board of longitude appointed him their official astronomical observer and lent him instruments appropriate for setting up an observatory in the new colony. He was asked especially to look out for a comet expected in 1788 or 1789.

The first fleet sailed in May 1787 under the command of the future governor of New South Wales, Captain Arthur Phillip. After leaving the Cape of Good Hope, Dawes and Captain Phillip transferred from the *Sirius* to the armed tender *Supply*, and pushed on ahead of the main fleet to land at Botany Bay on 18 January 1788. Dawes was thus one of the first to land in the new colony. Having decided that Port Jackson a few miles to the north was a better place for the new settlement, Phillip founded the city which he named Sydney on 26 January. Soon after, when news reached Sydney that two French frigates, the *Boussole* and *Astrolabe* under the command of La Pérouse, were anchored in Botany Bay, Dawes accompanied John Hunter, captain of the *Sirius*, from Sydney to Botany Bay to offer any assistance that might be needed, and spent the night in the *Boussole*. The two French ships sailed northwards on 10 March, never to be seen again by white men.

From March 1788 Dawes was employed ashore as engineer and surveyor, and by early July had been discharged from the *Sirius*. He had already begun to build an observatory on what became known as Dawes Point on the west side of Sydney Cove, then known as Point Maskelyne. He saw no comet but made many other observations, principally for settling latitude and longitude. As the new colony's engineer and surveyor—with no extra remuneration—he constructed gun batteries at the entrance to Sydney Cove, and laid out the government farm and the first streets and allotments in Sydney and Parramatta. Often with Watkin Tench, he went on many expeditions in the mountains, where his surveying training and skills were invaluable.

Dawes contemplated settling in Australia but, having fallen out with Governor Phillip, he had to return to England in 1791 and was soon recruited by the anti-slavery evangelicals Wilberforce and Henry Thornton to go to Sierra Leone, where he served as governor in 1792–4 and again in 1795–6. A strong evangelical, he became a member of the Clapham Sect.

In January 1799 he succeeded William Wales as mathematical master at Christ's Hospital. He had married Judith Rutter (d. c.1800) in July 1794, and they had a daughter, Judith, and two sons, William Rutter *Dawes, born in Christ's Hospital on 19 March 1799, who was to become a distinguished astronomer; and Macaulay, who died young (named after Zachary Macaulay, a colleague in Sierra Leone and father of the historian).

Dawes resigned from Christ's Hospital on 7 November 1800 to return to Sierra Leone, where he was again governor from 1801 to 1803. He left William Rutter in the care, first, of his grandfather in Portsmouth, then, from 1807, of Thomas Scott, a colleague at the Church Missionary Society, for whom Dawes worked in England from 1804 to 1808. In 1813, at Wilberforce's suggestion, he went to Antigua to work for the anti-slavery cause, taking his daughter (who later married there) but not his son. Either in Antigua, after 1813, or around 1811, before he left England, he married Grace Gilbert. He died in penury in Antigua in 1836, survived by his second wife. A novel by Jane Rogers based on Dawes's life in Australia, which contains much historical information about him, was published in 1995 under the title *Promised Lands*.

DEREK HOWSE

Sources P. Mander-Jones, 'Dawes, William', *AusDB*, vol. 1 • A. Currer-Jones, *William Dawes R.M., 1762–1836, by his great-granddaughter* (1930) • P. S. Laurie, 'William Dawes and Australia's first observatory', *Quarterly Journal of the Royal Astronomical Society*, 29 (1988), 469–82 • letters to Maskelyne, CUL, Board of Longitude MSS, RGO 14/48 • E. G. Wilson, *John Clarkson and the African adventure*

(1980) • GL, MS 12806, vol. 32, pp. 322–3 [Christ's Hospital] • S. Meacham, *Henry Thornton of Clapham* (1964), 124 • J. Rogers, *Promised lands* (1995)

Archives CUL, Royal Greenwich Observatory archives

Dawes, William Rutter (1799–1868), astronomer, was born on 19 March 1799 at Christ's Hospital, London. His father, William *Dawes (1762–1836), was an officer of marines, the official astronomer with the first fleet to New South Wales in 1787, and governor of Sierra Leone from 1792 to 1796, after which he was appointed mathematics master at Christ's Hospital. His mother, Judith Rutter, died when he was very young, and his father, after working for the abolitionist movement for several years, eventually settled in Antigua, where he ran a sugar plantation employing freed slaves. The young William was sent to Portsmouth to live with his paternal grandfather, Benjamin Dawes, and in 1807 was transferred to the care of Thomas Scott (the author of the biblical commentary) at Aston Sandford, near Haddenham, Buckinghamshire. Here he received his education, which was supplemented by a short period spent at Charterhouse School in 1811.

Although originally destined for an ecclesiastical career, Dawes felt dissatisfied with certain tenets of the Church of England, and he eventually chose to enter medicine. In 1820 he began his training at St Bartholomew's Hospital, and after qualifying as a doctor in 1825 he married Thomas Scott's widow and settled in Haddenham.

Dawes's sister, Judith, had married John Jones, who had business interests in the dockyard at Antigua. However, she died in 1826, and consequent family affairs made it necessary for Dawes to move to the Liverpool area. Here he met one of the leading independent ministers of the day, Dr Raffles, who persuaded him to take charge of a small congregation at Ormskirk. It was a position he retained for only a few years, but it afterwards resulted in his frequently being referred to as Reverend Dawes.

As a young man, Dawes had occasionally observed with a 2 inch refractor, and after moving to Liverpool he used a 1.6 inch refractor to observe double stars, which he identified with a Fortin edition of Flamsteed's *Atlas* that his father had taken to New South Wales. His first observatory, housing a 3.8 inch Dollond refractor, was set up at Ormskirk, and it was here that he began regular and methodical observations.

Dawes was elected fellow of the Royal Astronomical Society in 1830 and was a regular contributor to the *Monthly Notices* and the *Memoirs*. His first published observation was 'Occultation of Aldebaran, 9 Dec 1829', and his first extensive papers, submitted in 1831, were 'Observations of the triple star Zeta Cancri' and 'Observations of double stars'. These were followed by further papers on 126 double stars observed between 1830 and 1833 and by contributions on occultations, planets, comets, the solar eclipse of 1836, photometry, and instruments. He established a considerable reputation within a very short time and soon became a friend and colleague of some of the most eminent astronomers of the day, including Sir John

William Rutter Dawes (1799–1868), by Sir William Huggins, *c.*1865

Herschel and William Lassell, with whom he exchanged books and tested, and observed with, telescopes.

By the late 1830s Dawes had decided to seek a paid position as an astronomer. This was a time when affluent benefactors were setting up well-equipped observatories and employing 'assistants' to carry out the observations. One of these patrons was George Bishop, who had amassed a considerable fortune in the wine trade. Bishop established an observatory, equipped with a 7 inch Dollond refractor, at South Villa, Regent's Park, London, and it was here that Dawes obtained a position in 1839. He continued to concentrate his efforts on the observation and measurement of 250 double stars, the results of which were published in 1852 in *Astronomical Observations at South Villa*. However, he was not credited with making the observations, which led to understandable resentment and his statement that Bishop was incapable of making any observations himself.

Dawes's second marriage, on 28 July 1842, to Ann, *née* Copeland, the widow of John Welsby, a solicitor of Ormskirk, provided him with independent means, and in 1844 he left Bishop's service and moved to Cranbrook, Kent, where he set up a 6⅓ inch refractor by Merz. Here he worked indefatigably for the next few years, but continual headaches (probably migraine) and asthma—both of which afflicted him throughout his life—finally compelled him to move to Torquay in 1849. At this time he seriously considered abandoning his astronomical pursuits, but his interest was revived by a favourable improvement in his health, and in 1850 he moved to Wateringbury, near

Maidstone. He had not long established his observatory there when, at the end of November, he again proved his observational skills by discovering Saturn's crêpe ring, which two weeks earlier had (unknown to him) been independently discovered by W. C. Bond with the 15 inch Merz refractor at Harvard College observatory.

In 1851 Dawes accompanied John Russell Hind (his successor at Bishop's observatory) to Sweden to observe the total solar eclipse of 28 July. This was the first European total eclipse since 1842, and Dawes's description and drawings of solar prominences formed a valuable contribution to the large number of results that were obtained at a time when the true nature of the prominences was still a mystery. The expedition seems to have inspired in him a greater interest in solar observation, and he soon afterwards designed and had made a complex solar eyepiece incorporating a sliding diaphragm-plate pierced with apertures varying from 0.5 to 0.0075 of an inch in diameter. This led to his discovery of the rotation of sunspots and the nature of their nuclei. He also disputed James Nasmyth's description of the pattern of 'willow leaves' on the solar surface, which he considered inapplicable and misleading.

At that time, one of the prime requirements in astronomy was a standard scale for the measurement of stellar magnitudes. For many years Dawes had been carrying out methodical investigations into limiting magnitudes and the resolving power of telescopes. He also invented the wedge photometer, consisting of a sliding wedge of neutral-tint glass, originally incorporated in a later version of his solar eyepiece and afterwards used to estimate the magnitudes of stars. Much of his work formed the basis of Norman R. Pogson's research on the standard photometric scale, which was finally established in the mid-1850s. Charles Pritchard used a variation of his wedge photometer at Oxford observatory between 1881 and 1885.

In 1851 Dawes began corresponding with Alvan Clark, of Cambridgeport, Massachusetts. Clark had written to him to tell him of the double stars that he had discovered with object glasses of his own making, and Dawes was so impressed with their obvious quality that in 1854 he purchased a 7½ inch object glass and tube, which he placed on his Merz mount. Over the next few years he purchased another four—an 8 inch, a 7⅓ inch, another 8 inch, and an 8¼ inch—and sold each of them in turn. All of them subsequently passed through the hands of several eminent owners. The last of them—a complete 8¼ inch refractor which Clark brought with him when he visited Dawes in 1859—finally passed to the Temple Observatory of Rugby School in 1871.

For a few months after the sale of the 8¼ inch refractor in 1863 Dawes possessed no large instrument, but he had already ordered a complete 8 inch refractor from Thomas Cooke of York, and by 1864 he was able to resume his double-star and planetary observations. After his death this instrument belonged to a number of distinguished observers until it found a home at Cambridge observatory,

where it bears the name of its last private owner, William Thorrowgood.

Dawes's contribution to double-star astronomy was enormous, and, although he never attempted to discover new double stars, a list of fifteen discovered by him between 1840 and 1859 was published in 1864. His critical eye was also turned to most solar system objects, although he rarely observed the moon or nebulae, and few variable stars were known at that time. Among his observations of Jupiter were the monitoring of white ovals, satellite phenomena, and features on the satellites. He made many important observations of Saturn, and apart from his discovery of the crêpe ring in 1850 he confirmed the existence of Encke's division in 1843, suggested discontinuity in the rings, and attentively studied the phenomena attending the disappearance of the ring system in 1848. His series of drawings of Mars made during the apparition of 1864–5 are remarkably delicate and accurate, and include features similar to the 'canals' (channels) discovered by Giovanni Schiaparelli in 1877. The other planets were of less interest to him. Dawes observed the transit of Mercury in 1848 and two occultations of Venus, occasionally observed the satellites of Uranus and Neptune, and was involved in the debate concerning the suspected ring of Neptune in 1846. He declared no interest in minor planets.

The nineteenth century was blessed with numerous bright comets, and Dawes observed many of them, notably those of Bremiker in 1840, Biela in 1845, De Vico and Mitchell in 1847, and Donati in 1858. His report on the Leonid meteor storm of 1866 was his single contribution to meteor astronomy.

Dawes was one of the leading observational astronomers of his time and 'by 1860 probably the most skilled visual observer with a refracting telescope in the world … the expanding firms of Clark and Cooke regarded his praise as a warranty for their object glasses' (Chapman, 47). His skill earned him the sobriquet 'eagle-eyed', and his reputation was such that G. B. Airy declared that any telescope tested and approved by him could be guaranteed to be of the highest quality. Throughout his life he owned numerous telescopes, micrometers, and peripheral items of equipment, and many of his 150 or so contributions to scientific journals were major papers. His penultimate paper described his own design for an observing chair especially suited for use with a large refractor.

Dawes appears to have been an amiable and honourable character. He was held in high regard by the people of his neighbourhood, especially the poor, for whom he always provided medical services free of charge. His scientific achievements were rewarded with the highest honours which could be bestowed. In 1855 he was awarded the gold medal of the Royal Astronomical Society, and in 1865 he was elected fellow of the Royal Society.

After the death of his wife in 1860 Dawes's health began to decline. Heart disease and rheumatism were added to the headaches and asthma which had afflicted him throughout his life, and yet he continued to observe until the end of 1867. His most extensive work, 'Catalogue of micrometrical measurements of double stars', covering the period 1839–67, was published shortly before his death. He died at Haddenham on 15 February 1868 and was buried beside his wife in Haddenham churchyard.

R. A. MARRIOTT

Sources letters, Cambridge Observatory · Cambridge Observatory, Neptune MSS · letters, 1841–68, RAS · RAS, Add. MS 69; MSS Hartwell 1, 8, 11; MS Hind I; MS Lassell 16; MS Sheepshanks 1 · RS, Herschel papers, HS6, HS19, HS22, HS25 · Rugby School, Temple Observatory Archive · *Monthly Notices of the Royal Astronomical Society*, 29 (1868–9), 116–21 · *Astronomical Register*, 6 (1869), 73 · W. R. Dawes, 'Letters … to Mr George Knott', *The Observatory*, 33 (1910), 343–59, 383–98, 419–31, 473–8 · CUL, RGO Airy MSS 6/233, 6/235, 6/368, 6/374 · A. Chapman, *The Victorian amateur astronomer: independent astronomical research in Britain, 1820–1920* (1998) · m. cert. · d. cert.
Archives RAS, journals and papers | RAS, letters to Royal Astronomical Society · RAS, letters to Richard Sheepshanks · RS, letters to Sir John Herschel
Likenesses W. Huggins, photograph, c.1865, RAS [*see illus.*]
Wealth at death under £8000: probate, 4 March 1868, *CGPLA Eng. & Wales*

Dawkins, James (1722–1757), antiquary and Jacobite sympathizer, was born in Jamaica, the eldest of four sons of Henry Dawkins (1698–1744) of Clarendon, Jamaica, a wealthy sugar planter, and his wife, Elizabeth (1697?–1757), third daughter of Edward Pennant of Clarendon, chief justice of the island, and his wife, Elizabeth. Educated at Abingdon School in Berkshire under the tory Thomas Woods, Dawkins matriculated at St John's College, Oxford, on 7 December 1739 and graduated DCL in 1749.

After university Dawkins travelled extensively on the continent, moving in Jacobite circles in Paris and Rome. It was in Rome in 1749 that he planned an expedition with an Oxford friend, John Bouverie, around the eastern Mediterranean to the sites of classical antiquity. Robert Wood, seasoned traveller and classical scholar, and Giovanni Borra, an architectural draughtsman, were invited to join them. The party sailed from Naples on 5 May 1750 in a specially equipped ship, the *Matilda*, and during the summer and autumn toured the Aegean and the coast of Asia Minor. Bouverie died at Guzel Hissar on 19 September. The party were in Egypt in November and spent Christmas in Nazareth. In March 1751 they were in Syria, where they visited the ruins of Palmyra and Baalbek (ancient Heliopolis). They arrived on the Greek mainland in May, by way of Tripoli and Cyprus, and embarked for Naples on 7 June 1751.

This was among the first expeditions of its type—a serious journey of archaeological exploration, quite unlike the military, diplomatic, or trading missions which had previously provided the West with accounts of the Levant. 'The combination of wealth, classical scholarship, artistic and architectural talent in this party was truly remarkable' (Harris and Savage); according to Dawkins's nephew, the trip 'cost him no less a sum than £50,000' (J. T. Smith, *Nollekens and his Times*, 1829, 338), much of it supplied by Dawkins himself, but the expedition's journal shows that

he was also an active and dynamic organizer, an accomplished scholar, an observant naturalist, and, perhaps above all, a passionate and apparently tireless measurer and recorder of everything that he saw.

Robert Wood, aided and financially supported by Dawkins, published *The Ruins of Palmyra* (1753) and *The Ruins of Baalbec* (1757), containing detailed engravings of architectural remains previously almost unknown in western Europe. Their effect on classical taste in England and France, based until then on Vitruvian models, was immediate and explosive, scoring 'a triumph such as no architectural books had ever before achieved' (Harris and Savage). Dawkins's generosity also provided financial support for James Stuart and Nicholas Revett in their similar and ultimately more significant enterprise, *The Antiquities of Athens* (1762). In 1755 Dawkins, proposed by Stuart, was elected to the Society of Dilettanti. A collection of manuscripts in the Bodleian Library and of marbles in the Ashmolean Museum in Oxford are the products of his travels.

Dawkins's early contacts with Jacobitism appear to have prompted his journey to Berlin in May 1753 to meet Frederick the Great. This was an attempt to get Prussian support for a Jacobite conspiracy involving William King of Oxford, the earl of Westmorland, and the Earl Marischal, Prussian ambassador in Paris. The meeting was inconclusive, but resulted in the British government issuing a warrant for Dawkins's arrest. This was not executed when, in the following year, 1754, Dawkins returned to England, bought an estate at Laverstoke, Hampshire, and was returned as MP for the open borough of Hindon, Wiltshire, which he held until his death. Dawkins is said to have made highly critical comments about the Pretender (James Stuart) in 1756, yet some contemporaries believed he died a Jacobite.

Dawkins is now thought to be the author of an anonymous 1756 pamphlet, *Reflections physical and moral upon the … numerous phenomena … which have happened from the earthquake at Lima*. This reveals him to have been a fierce opponent of the philosophy of Descartes and Newton. In addition to his Hampshire estate Dawkins owned 25,000 acres (1754) in Jamaica with his brother. It was here, Sutton's Plantation, that Dawkins died, unmarried, on 6 September 1757. He was buried at Old Plantation, Clarendon. In 1922, when the family estates were sold, his remains, together with those of his parents, were re-interred in St Paul's Church, Chapelton, Jamaica.

M. ST JOHN PARKER

Sources U. Lond., Institute of Classical Studies, The Wood Donation [diaries and sketchbooks belonging to Wood, Dawkins, Borra and Bouverie] · R. Wood, *The ruins of Palmyra, otherwise Tedmor in the desart* (1753) · R. Wood, *The ruins of Baalbec, otherwise Heliopolis in Coelosyria* (1757) · J. Stuart, preface, in J. Stuart and N. Revett, *The antiquities of Athens*, 1 (1762), i–viii · C. A. Hutton, 'The travels of "Palmyra" Wood in 1750–51', *Journal of Hellenic Studies*, 47 (1927) · C. Pace, 'Gavin Hamilton's *Wood and Dawkins discovering Palmyra*: the dilettante as hero', *Art History*, 4 (1981) · E. Harris and N. Savage, *British architectural books and writers, 1556–1785* (1990) · W. H. Hutton, *Burford papers: letters of S. Crisp to his sister* (1905) · A. Lang, *Pickle the*

Spy, or, The incognito of Prince Charles (1897) • priv. coll., Dawkins family archive • L. Cust and S. Colvin, eds., *History of the Society of Dilettanti* (1898) • Burke, *Gen. GB* (1900) • Stevenson papers, Bodl. Oxf., Gough MSS, bk 6 • T. D. Kendrick, *The Lisbon earthquake* (1956) • P. Wright, *Monumental inscriptions of Jamaica* (1966)

Archives AM Oxf., gift • Bodl. Oxf., MSS • Institute of Jamaica, Kingston, plantation papers • priv. coll., papers • U. Lond., notebooks relating to tour of the Levant | Bodl. Oxf., Stevenson papers, Gough MSS • U. Lond., Wood donation

Likenesses G. Hamilton, double portrait, oils, 1759 (with R. Wood), NG Scot. • J. Hall, double portrait, line engraving, 1773 (with R. Wood; after G. Hamilton), NPG • R. Carriera, pastel drawing • J. Macardell, mezzotint (after J. Stewart), BM • J. Stewart, pastel drawing, repro. in I. Browning, *Palmyra* (1979) • J. Stuart and N. Revett, double portrait, engraving (with R. Wood), repro. in Stuart, *Antiquities of Athens*, 3 • Zeeman, oils • red chalk drawing, Swansea Art Gallery

Wealth at death with brother owned 25,000 acres in Jamaica; in 1770 this yielded income of £60,000: Dawkins plantation papers, Institute of Jamaica, Kingston, Jamaica, quoted in B. W. Higman, *Jamaica surveyed* (1988)

Dawkins, (Charles John) Massey (1905–1975), anaesthetist, was born on 13 July 1905 at 4 Tanza Road, London, the only child of Charles William Dawkins (1870–1948), European manager of Massey Harris Co. Ltd, and his wife, Eleanor Selina Cranfield. Dawkins, who was known as Jack to his family and friends and as Massey to colleagues, was educated at Mill Hill School (1918–23) and Emmanuel College, Cambridge (1923–6). His father, worried that his own father was a gambler, and knowing Jack was generous with money, had given him the choice of the church or medicine. After Cambridge, Dawkins's clinical training was at the Middlesex Hospital. He married Sylvia Mabel Ransford (1904–1995) secretly on 29 July 1929, when they were both students, and publicly in 1930, after qualifying. They had one son (d. c.1965) and two daughters; the son and younger daughter both became doctors.

Dawkins became resident anaesthetist at the Middlesex, and was anaesthetist to its dental department (1931–8), with honorary posts at Hampstead General Hospital and Paddington Green Children's Hospital. Before the advent of the National Health Service (NHS) it was difficult to support a family solely on the meagre fees for private anaesthetics, so he and his wife went into general practice in the Hampstead area of London, and he combined this work with anaesthetics in several hospitals. In 1936 Dawkins proceeded to MD (Cambridge) and passed the newly founded diploma of anaesthetics. In 1948 he became one of the foundation fellows of the faculty of anaesthetists of the Royal College of Surgeons. From 1941 he was honorary anaesthetist at University College Hospital, and from 1946 until his retirement in 1970 he was the senior anaesthetist. He also held NHS consultant posts at Hampstead General Hospital and Paddington Green Children's Hospital.

Dawkins was a pioneer in the use of epidurals and is credited with administering the first in the UK, in 1942. He kept a casebook of each epidural he administered, in which he recorded all technical details such as the method of finding the epidural space and its distance from the skin. These casebooks were the basis for his many publications. He described the first epidural, together with more than seventy-five epidurals he had performed for surgical operations and for the relief of pain in labour, at a meeting of the section of anaesthetics of the Royal Society of Medicine (RSM) on 8 January 1945. This account appeared in the *Proceedings of the Royal Society of Medicine*, and afterwards he published many more papers, mainly in the journal *Anaesthesia*. The first is a classic: it commemorates the centenary of the first public anaesthetic administered in Europe, for a surgical operation at University College Hospital in December 1846. Other papers were about general anaesthesia for children and for dental surgery, but most concerned epidural block for surgery and the relief of post-operative pain. Dawkins gained an international reputation from these papers, which was reinforced in 1954 when he made a film demonstrating epidural block for caesarean section. This laid the foundations for the use of epidurals for the relief of pain in labour. However, it should be noted that Dawkins was less interested in the relief of pain during labour than in the use of epidurals in major abdominal surgery including caesarean section. In 1963 Dawkins published a critical analysis of methods for overcoming the difficulty of finding the epidural space, in which he described many different techniques collected from worldwide sources.

Dawkins was awarded honorary membership of the Finnish Society of Anaesthetists in November 1958, when he was described as the father of Finnish anaesthesia. During 1966–8 he was honorary secretary of the section of anaesthetics of the RSM, at a time when this was the main forum for research and progress in anaesthesia. In 1969, shortly before he retired, and before the advent of computerized retrieval, he published a detailed and meticulous analysis of 350 publications worldwide relating to epidural and caudal analgesia and its complications. It included his own experience of more than 4000 epidurals over twenty-five years; the paper was still being cited at the end of the twentieth century.

Dawkins was made an honorary member of the Association of Anaesthetists of Great Britain and Ireland in 1974, and in October of that year he became president of the section of anaesthetics at the RSM. His presidential address, 'The relief of post-operative pain with special reference to epidural block', a brilliant review of his own unparalleled experience in the subject, was published as a paper in the *Proceedings of the Royal Society of Medicine* just before his death. He died before completion of his year as president.

Dawkins was of a retiring disposition, and as a result his ideas were not as widely known in the UK as they should have been; otherwise, recent developments for post-operative pain control might have started decades earlier. His advocacy of epidural pain relief for labour was not always welcomed by midwives and also took time to become established. Dawkins did not hesitate to express his own strong and independent views but was never dogmatic and was always prepared to change his methods if convinced by others. He was an enthusiastic and lucid teacher, but his technical expertise could daunt trainees, though he was never critical of their efforts. To his patients and colleagues he was kind and loyal, and he made friends with both. Dawkins was also a perfectionist with no use for self-satisfaction or complacency in anyone else, 'be he surgeon or anaesthetist' (*BMJ*).

Dawkins enjoyed music and reading and possessed a 'puckish sense of humour' (*BMJ*). He and his wife were generous and eccentric hosts at their riverside home in Essex, where they had acquired a collection of disused buildings, including a water tower, a corrugated iron concert hall, and a chapel that was crammed with beachcombing trophies and battered antiques. Dawkins also collected boats, some of which leaked alarmingly. One of his obituarists recalled that 'many generations of anaesthetic registrars have been his crew members, and their more unseamanlike manoeuvres in Essex mud and water are often recounted' (*The Lancet*). Dawkins died of a heart attack at his London home, 27 Well Walk, Hampstead, on 8 August 1975. His body was cremated four days later at Golders Green crematorium.

ADRIAN PADFIELD

Sources *The Times* (12 Aug 1975) · *BMJ* (23 Aug 1975), 2 pts, vol. 3, p. 493 · *The Lancet*, 2 (23 Aug 1975), 373 · E. N. Armitage, 'A medical student's apprenticeship with CJMD', *Proceedings of the History of Anaesthesia Society*, 23 (1998), 52–5 · C. J. M. Dawkins, 'Discussion on extradural spinal block', *Proceedings of the Royal Society of Medicine*, 38 (1945), 299–303 · C. J. M. Dawkins, 'The identification of the epidural space: a critical analysis of the various methods employed', *Anaesthesia*, 18 (1963), 66–77 · C. J. M. Dawkins, 'An analysis of the complications of extradural and caudal block', *Anaesthesia*, 24 (1969), 554–63 · C. J. M. Dawkins, 'The relief of post operative pain with special reference to epidural block', *Proceedings of the Royal Society of Medicine*, 68 (1975), 410–13 · personal knowledge (2004) · private information (2004)
Archives priv. coll., general practice notebook · priv. coll., patient notes | FILM 'Film demonstrating epidural block for Caesarean section' (1954)
Likenesses photograph, priv. coll.
Wealth at death £51,097: probate, 1975, *CGPLA Eng. & Wales*

Dawkins, Richard MacGillivray (1871–1955), classical scholar, was born on 24 October 1871 at Surbiton, Surrey, the eldest child of Richard Dawkins (1828–1896), a captain in the Royal Navy, and his wife, Mary Louisa (*d.* 1897), the daughter of Simon McGillivray (or MacGillivray) and granddaughter of Sir John Easthope. In 1878 his father retired with the rank of rear-admiral and made his home at Stoke Gabriel near Totnes. Dawkins received his schooling at Totnes grammar school (1881–4) and Marlborough College (1884–90). He was an awkward, ungainly, and short-sighted boy with a dislike for all forms of organized games which he retained throughout his life: his schooldays were unhappy, nor did he achieve any distinction in the classroom. He did, however, acquire a taste for botany which enriched his later life. From school he went to King's College, London, to train as an electrical engineer. In 1892, before completing his course, he became apprenticed to Cromptons, a firm of electrical engineers, at Chelmsford. He did not find engineering congenial and

Richard MacGillivray Dawkins (1871–1955), by Walter Stoneman, 1945

these years in lonely lodgings were not happy. As the result of a temporary interest in theosophy, he characteristically determined to teach himself Sanskrit; he continued to read Greek and Latin classics, learned a good deal of Italian and some German, and even started upon Icelandic, Irish, and Finnish.

After the death of his father in 1896 and that of his mother in the following year, a small legacy enabled Dawkins to forsake the engineering profession and enter Emmanuel College, Cambridge, in 1898 at the age of twenty-six. He was a self-taught scholar without the customary grooming in Latin and Greek, but he was fortunate to find himself in the hands of Peter Giles and James Adam. In 1899 the college gave him a scholarship, in 1901 he was placed in the third division of the first class of part one of the classical tripos, in 1902 he obtained a first class with distinction in part two, and an honourable mention in the examination for the Chancellor's medals, and a Craven studentship. In 1904 he became a fellow (and in 1922 an honorary fellow) of Emmanuel College.

Dawkins had first been admitted to the British School at Athens in 1902, during which time he held a Craven studentship. He toured the Greek islands including Karpathos, pursuing his philological interest and in particular the study of Greek dialects. For two years he was in charge of Robert Carr Bosanquet's excavations in eastern Crete at Palaikastro (1904–5). In 1906 he was appointed director of the British School, and was responsible for four seasons of excavations at Sparta, work initiated by his predecessor Bosanquet just before his resignation. This work set a new standard in methods of excavation for Greece, but the outbreak of war delayed publication; *Artemis Orthia*, published by the Hellenic Society, did not appear until 1929. Dawkins, who had hoped to initiate a major excavation at Knidos on the Turkish mainland, conducted a further stratigraphic excavation at Phylakopi on Melos in 1911, a site previously explored by the British School. Further fieldwork was carried out on Crete which included excavation at the Kamares cave (1913). His other achievement from this time at Athens was the book *Modern Greek in Asia Minor* (1916), a study of the curious dialects of Greek spoken by the inhabitants of the Cappadocian plateau, mainly researched in three journeys in 1909, 1910, and 1911.

In 1914 Dawkins resigned the directorship of the British School at Athens; a very substantial legacy from his mother's cousin, J. A. Doyle, who died in 1907, had given him financial independence. The inheritance included a Victorian house, Plas Dulas in Denbighshire, which may have been the inspiration for Llanabba in Evelyn Waugh's *Decline and Fall* (1928); an Oxford rumour suggested that Dawkins had additionally inherited a pack of foxhounds. The outbreak of war saw him at Trebizond. Dawkins returned to Wales and in the early months of the war he noted in a letter to one of the fellows at Emmanuel that he was drilling with what he termed 'the local volunteer corps of old gentlemen'. After six months in censorship at the British legation in Athens, he served from 1916 to 1919 as an intelligence officer, with the rank of temporary lieutenant in the Royal Naval Volunteer Reserve, in eastern Crete, an area well known to him from his days at Palaikastro. His commission was delayed as he insisted on retaining his moustache. In a letter to P. W. Wood, one of the fellows at Emmanuel, Dawkins wrote of how he suffered from seasickness, and how one night in a storm he had been thrown from his hammock onto the deck; but he added, 'I must not grumble'.

In 1920 Dawkins was appointed to the Bywater and Sotheby chair of Byzantine and modern Greek in the University of Oxford and in 1922 Exeter College made him a fellow. Before he was elected to a fellowship he was greatly supported by John Myres, who as a Royal Naval Volunteer Reserve officer had delivered Dawkins to Crete from Athens. His major work during his tenure of the chair was a translation with commentary of the medieval Cypriot *Chronicle of Makhairas* (2 vols., 1932) which records the history of the Lusignan dynasty between 1359 and 1432. In 1939 when he retired under the age limit Exeter College made him an honorary fellow with rooms in college. To the end of his life he kept his zest and interest in young people and he was to generations of Oxford undergraduates a source of real education. He was to act as the senior member of the Hypocrites' Club in Oxford during the

1920s. Osbert Lancaster records, in his lively account of Dawkins in *With an Eye to the Future* (1967), the incident when cackling laughter drew attention to Dawkins perched in a chestnut tree within Exeter College. Except for music, for which he had no ear, his tastes were catholic: he knew about plants, pictures, and European literature.

As a critic, whether of books or men, Dawkins was positive and to the end of his long life, though always intolerant of humbug, enviably receptive to new ideas. He had a wide linguistic knowledge and could talk French, Italian, and modern Greek as rapidly as natives. He knew most parts of the Mediterranean including north Africa and had an unrivalled knowledge at first hand of the Greek-speaking peoples from Pontus in the east to Calabria in the west. In this last period of his life he turned his attention to the subject matter of folk-tales which he had earlier taken down as texts for philological purposes, regularly publishing in *Folklore*. In 1926 he was to become a founder member, with J. R. R. Tolkien, of Kolbítar. In 1950 he published *Forty-Five Stories from the Dodekanese* from manuscripts which had been presented by W. H. D. Rouse to the University of Cambridge. This was followed by *Modern Greek Folktales* (1953) and *More Greek Folktales* (1955), the importance of which was due to the examination of the relative popularity of and the changes undergone by types of Indo-European folk-tales in a definite and exceptionally well-recorded area. In 1947 he broke his thigh, which as it failed to heal required him to walk with an iron brace and sticks, but this did not diminish his incessant industry. Articles and reviews continued to pour out from his somewhat erratic typewriter and his rooms remained a focus of hospitality for promising young men and congenial seniors. Himself an original, he liked originals. His taste in men as in books was catholic. By no means all his friends were academical and his range of acquaintance extended from Norman Douglas, of whom in 1933 he published a perceptive study, to the egregious Baron Corvo (Frederick William Rolfe). Dawkins fell down dead in Parks Road, Oxford, on 4 May 1955 on a visit to Wadham garden. He never married. He was elected FBA in 1933, proceeded DLitt at Oxford in 1942, and was an honorary DPhil of the universities of Athens (1937) and Salonika (1951). A pencil drawing of Dawkins was made by Henry Lamb, whose sister Dorothy had excavated with Dawkins at Phylakopi in 1911. Dawkins himself is recorded as saying of the image, 'The mouth's all wrong. It's the mouth of a liar and a boaster' (Bowra, 252).

W. R. HALLIDAY, rev. DAVID GILL

Sources R. J. H. Jenkins, 'Richard MacGillivray Dawkins, 1871–1955', *PBA*, 41 (1955), 373–88 • *The Times* (6 May 1955) • [N. Coghill and D. W. Phillips], 'Richard MacGillivray Dawkins', *Exeter College Association Register* (1955), 12–15 • *Emmanuel College Magazine*, 37 (1954–5), 90–92 • *Oxford Magazine* (9 June 1955); adapted in *Man*, 56 (1956), 7–8 • O. Lancaster, *With an eye to the future* (1967) • H. Waterhouse, *The British School at Athens: the first hundred years* (1986) • R. M. Dawkins, 'Sir John Myres', *Man*, 54 (1954), 40–41 • G. Stephenson, *The Times* (18 May 1955) • C. M. Bowra, *Memories, 1898–1939* (1966) • F. H. Stubbings, *Forty-nine lives: an anthology of portraits of Emmanuel* men (1983), no. 43 · personal knowledge (1971) · D. Huxley, ed., *Cretan quests: British explorers, excavators, and historians* (2000) · S. Sherratt, *Catalogue of Cycladic antiquities in the Ashmolean Museum: the captive spirit* (2000)

Archives U. Oxf., Taylor Institution, Greek MSS · V&A, embroidery collection incl. notebooks | Bodl. Oxf., corresp. with J. L. Myres

Likenesses W. Stoneman, two photographs, 1933–45, NPG [*see illus.*] · Elliott & Fry, photograph, 1936, repro. in Jenkins, 'Richard MacGillivray Dawkins', pl. 11 · H. Lamb, pencil drawing, 1937, Exeter College, Oxford · W. Roberts, oils, 1949, Emmanuel College, Cambridge; repro. in Stubbings, *Forty-nine lives* · photograph, British School at Athens; repro. in Waterhouse, *The British School at Athens*

Wealth at death £51,387 6s. 5d.: probate, 12 Aug 1955, *CGPLA Eng. & Wales*

Dawkins, Rowland (1618–1691), parliamentarian army officer and deputy major-general, was born at Kilvrough (or Cil-frwch), Pennard, Glamorgan, the eldest son of George Dawkins (*fl.* 1600–1640), a minor gentleman, and Elizabeth, the daughter of the serjeant-at-law William Glyn of Clynnog Fawr, Caernarvonshire. In September 1643, a year after the civil war had broken out, Dawkins suffered the attentions of royalist sequestrators; and he became active on behalf of parliament when Philip Jones became governor of Swansea in 1645. Later that year Dawkins joined the Glamorgan county committee, with the rank of major-general of the garrison troops commanded by Jones. He was present at the battle of St Fagans on 8 May 1648, and became governor of Carmarthen and Tenby the same year. He was unpopular in Haverfordwest for attempting to billet troops there instead of Tenby, which had successfully claimed relief on grounds of its poverty. In 1649 and 1650 Dawkins was added to the Carmarthenshire and Pembrokeshire committees, and he was a commissioner under the Act for the Propagation of the Gospel from February 1650. In this body he was very active in letting tithes to laymen to fund the itinerant ministry of Walter Cradock, Vavasor Powell, and other separatist ministers, and he himself rented the tithes of Bishopston, in the Gower, in 1651. He was also, with others in a joint purchase, able to buy crown lands in Pembrokeshire, Monmouthshire, and Carmarthenshire. These had been made available to Philip Jones's garrison regiment, of which Dawkins was a prominent member.

In June 1651 Dawkins ended a royalist revolt in Cardiganshire, and was appointed a commissioner of the high court of justice to try the rebels. As governor of Carmarthen he was a natural choice as MP for the county in 1654, and shortly after his election he became a commissioner for scandalous ministers in south Wales. Dawkins, Philip Jones, Bussy Mansel, and John Price—all from Glamorgan—in effect ran south Wales for the Commonwealth (and later for the protectorate), by virtue of dominating the various committees appointed to provide governance.

With a high profile in local administration, and a county military background, Dawkins was again naturally chosen for leadership of the militia in March 1655, when the government sought to put in place a higher level of security against royalist insurgency. As commander of its militia, Dawkins was *de facto* major-general for south Wales when in October 1655 no commission was issued specifically for the region. In January 1656, with the rank of colonel, he was confirmed as one of two deputy major-generals under James Berry, whose territory included all Wales and border English counties. Unsurprisingly, in view of the extent of Berry's responsibilities, Dawkins retained his leadership of the military, and was active in supervising the new round of sequestrations and in curbing disorderly meetings in south Wales.

Elected again for Carmarthenshire in 1656, Dawkins proved in parliament a loyal supporter of the protector, but the non-renewal of commissions to the major-generals reduced his power. In 1659 he failed to achieve re-election to parliament at Carmarthen, but sat for Cardigan Boroughs instead. After the collapse of the Protectorate of Richard Cromwell, Dawkins lost his command of the South Wales militia, was temporarily omitted from county committees, and failed to secure a parliamentary seat. After the Restoration he was removed from the corporation of Swansea, where he had been senior alderman from 1656, and was summoned to the consistory court of St David's for not having his children baptized. Unlike some other former 'propagators' such as Philip Jones, Dawkins did not conform to the Church of England after 1660. He had been active in approving ministers for the state church during the interregnum, but was hostile to Quakers and was never, either before or after 1660, a member of the celebrated Baptist congregation at Ilston, Gower, near his home. In 1677 he was listed by Sir Edward Mansel as one who had 'raised his fortune in the late time', worth £250 a year (PRO, SP 29/398, 283–4). During the 1680s he recovered his place on the Glamorgan bench of magistrates, but was detained at Chepstow as a suspect during Monmouth's rising in 1685. The duke of Beaufort, who employed Dawkins as his steward, noted him in 1687 as still a protestant dissenter. He died on 7 May 1691 and was buried at Pennard church. The date of his marriage to Mary Bowen is unknown.   STEPHEN K. ROBERTS

Sources *CSP dom.*, 1649–53; 1655–7 · *JHC*, 4 (1644–6) · G. Williams, ed., *Glamorgan county history, 4: Early modern Glamorgan* (1974) · J. Berry and S. G. Lee, *A Cromwellian major-general: the career of Colonel James Berry* (1938) · T. Richards, *A history of the puritan movement in Wales* (1920) · T. Richards, *Religious developments in Wales, 1654–1662* (1923) · G. T. Clark, *Limbus patrum Morganiae et Glamorganiae* (1886) · A. H. Dodd, *Studies in Stuart Wales*, 2nd edn (1971) · PRO, E 121/3/5/32; E 121/5/6/51 · PRO, SP 29/398, pp. 283–4 · Glamorgan archive service, Fonmon MSS · Thurloe, *State papers* · will, NL Wales, SD 1691/167

Wealth at death over £1000—cash bequests: will, NL Wales, SD 1691/167 · £250 p.a.: PRO, SP 29/398, pp. 283–4

Dawkins, Sir William Boyd (1837–1929), geologist and palaeontologist, was born on 26 December 1837 at the vicarage, Buttington, near Welshpool, the only son of the Revd Richard Dawkins and his wife, Mary Ann Youngman. He was educated at Rossall School, an Anglican public school near Fleetwood, and then went up to Jesus College, Oxford, in 1854. It was there that his career as a geologist began, with a first-class degree in natural sciences (1860) and the encouragement of the professor of geology, John appointment was as curator of natural history at the old Manchester Museum in Peter Street. Founded in 1821, the museum housed both natural history and geological specimens, which by Dawkins's day had fallen into desuetude and were neglected by students and the public alike. Dawkins began cataloguing and sorting the collections, and also lectured in geology at Owens College. In 1872 he became the first lecturer in geology at Owens, when the subject was split from the natural history department of William C. Williamson. He was appointed professor in October 1874 (occupying the chair until his retirement in 1908), though he continued as an adviser to Manchester Museum—which by then had become part of the university—and did what he could to develop its collections and publicize its work with his lectures.

Dawkins's reputation for his work on natural history was still growing, particularly for his researches on English fossil mammals and early man. Between 1875 and 1878, for example, he made further excavations in caves in the Creswell crags, near Worksop, on the border of Derbyshire. He also travelled widely to the continent, Australia, and America. Besides his lecturing and prolific output of papers, he wrote two books, *Cave Hunting* (1874), and *Early Man in Britain and his Place in the Tertiary Period* (1880). The first was a pioneering attempt to correlate within a single volume the growing mass of material which had been unearthed in numerous European countries; the second was intended as a companion to Green's *A Short History of the English People* (1874). Dawkins also collaborated with W. Ayshford Sandford on *British Pleistocene Mammalia*, which was issued in several parts by the Palaeontographical Society between 1866 and 1872.

To his contemporaries Dawkins was an appealing mixture of Victorian man of letters and cave-hunter, a man who was perhaps:

> at his best in the open air at some such place as Arbor Low which, with vivid imagination, he could people with the black-haired, long-headed men of prehistoric times whose every-day life was an open book to him. (*Transactions of the Lancashire and Cheshire Antiquarian Society*, 46, 1929, 141–3)

However his personal papers show that after the 1870s—to the evident dismay of many of his more traditional colleagues—he was increasingly drawn to 'applied' (or engineering) geology. In 1882 he became adviser to one of the pioneering attempts to bore a channel tunnel. That scheme proved abortive, but led to his involvement with the Kent coalfield, which was discovered (through his guidance) in 1890. In the early 1880s he was also a consultant on the Humber Tunnel project. He advised on water supply at Hull, Dover, Eastbourne, Brighton, Worthing, Croydon, and other places and after 1877 also paid particular attention to the water supply from chalk in London by providing consultancy to various private and parliamentary bodies. Apparently, on questions of water supply 'he was more often engaged as an expert witness in the Law Courts than any other geologist of his day' (*Manchester Guardian*, 16 Jan 1929). His work also encompassed environmental damage and in 1892 he supported efforts to obtain compensation for those who suffered the effects of

Sir William Boyd Dawkins (1837–1929), by Sir Benjamin Stone, 1901

Phillips. As an undergraduate he met J. R. Green (later a distinguished historian) and a mutual interest in history led to a pact: Green would deal with the history of Britain in the written record, while Dawkins resolved to explore the prehistory as revealed by geology and archaeology.

At that time there was widespread interest in human prehistory and particularly in the survival of human implements and other remains. As an undergraduate Dawkins turned his attention to cave research. In 1859 he began the excavation of a hyena den at Wookey Hole, near Wells, Somerset, which launched him into a lifetime's interest in extinct mammalia and also a lifelong link with that county. In 1861 he became the first recipient of the Burdett-Coutts scholarship, then recently founded at Oxford to promote the study of geology. Between 1861 and 1869 he was a member of the Geological Survey of Great Britain and became a junior colleague of T. H. Huxley at the Royal School of Mines in Jermyn Street, London. For eight years he mapped parts of the Wealden and other formations in Kent and the Thames valley, which furthered his interest in mammalian remains in the river gravels. This led to the publication of numerous memoirs and papers, exploring subjects as diverse as the dentition of the woolly rhinoceros and the origins of the cave lion, and to his election as a fellow of the Royal Society in 1867.

In 1866 Dawkins married Frances Evans (*d.* 1921), the daughter of a clerk to the Admiralty. Three years later Huxley's recommendation took Dawkins to Manchester, where he was to spend the rest of his working life. His first subsidence due to brine pumping in the Northwich salt district. Abroad he consulted for diamond mining firms in South Africa, oil shale prospectors in Australia, and Italian Carrara marble quarries.

Dawkins's industrial geology reached a peak between 1890 and 1910. His work was an important bridge between academe and industry in Manchester, where after the 1870s a number of academics—for example, Sir Henry Roscoe in chemistry and Sir Arthur Schuster in physics— were busy transforming Owens College into an advanced training and industrial research centre that owed much to the German model. Dawkins used the expertise he gained as a consultant to inform his teaching at the university and at Manchester Museum, where he widened the subject matter and gave it a practical bent. As museum curator he organized free public lectures on Saturday and Sunday afternoons. At the university, as professor of geology, palaeontology, and mining, he was attuned to the opportunities and commitments that stemmed from a location close to the northern coalfields, the salt deposits of Cheshire, the lead mines of Derbyshire, and the iron and copper mines of north Lancashire and Cumberland. In 1905 he instituted teaching classes for mining students and also appointed an assistant lecturer, so that he himself would have more time for the practical side of geology.

Dawkins was a man of great energy, who even at the age of ninety-one insisted on travelling to London to propose a toast at a Geological Society dinner. He also had a taste— some have said weakness—for the limelight of archaeological discovery. A great publicist, he had a number of acrimonious arguments that led to much press reporting. His industrial geology, especially the discovery of the Kent coalfield, brought him to even greater prominence. Among the honours that inevitably followed were the Lyell medal (1889) and the Prestwich medal (1918) awarded by the Geological Society of London, and a knighthood, conferred on him in 1919. He lived in some style (his income doubtless boosted by his engineering consultancy) first in Fallowfield, Manchester, and then at Richmond Lodge in Bowdon, Cheshire, surrounded by books and his collections of antique furniture and *cloisonné* enamels (which he later donated to Manchester City Art Gallery). Dawkins's first wife died in 1921 and the following year he married Mary, *née* Poole, the widow of Hubert Congreve.

He died at Richmond Lodge on 15 January 1929, survived by his daughter, Ella (*d.* 1969), and by his second wife. His remains were cremated at Manchester crematorium. He bequeathed his books and many of his papers to the town of Buxton, which later established a Boyd Dawkins room at its museum.　　　　　　　　　GEOFFREY TWEEDALE

Sources M. J. Bishop, ed., *Cave hunters: biographical sketches of Sir William Boyd Dawkins and Dr. J. Wilfrid Jackson* (1982) • G. Tweedale, 'Geology and industrial consultancy: Sir William Boyd Dawkins, 1837–1929, and the Kent coalfield', *British Journal for the History of Science*, 24 (1991), 435–51 • G. Tweedale and T. Proctor, 'Catalogue of the papers of Professor Sir William Boyd Dawkins in the John Rylands University Library of Manchester', *Bulletin of the John Rylands University Library*, 74 (1992), 3–36 • *Geological Magazine*, 66 (1929), 142 • J. W. Gregory, *Quarterly Journal of the Geological Society*, 85 (1929), lix–lx • 'Eminent living geologists: William Boyd Dawkins', *Geological Magazine*, new ser., 5th decade, 6 (1909), 529–34 • A. S. W. [A. S. Woodward], *PRS*, 107B (1930–31), xxiii–xxvi • W. Gardner, *Archaeological Journal*, 86 (1929) • 'Professor William Boyd Dawkins', *Manchester Faces and Places*, 15 (1904), 297–300 • *Antiquaries Journal*, 9 (1929), 302–3 • Foster, *Alum. Oxon.* • *Manchester Guardian* (16 Jan 1929)

Archives Bodl. Oxf., corresp. • Buxton Museum and Art Gallery, archaeological and palaeontological corresp. and papers • Derbys. RO • GS Lond. • JRL, corresp. and papers • Manchester Museum • Oxf. U. Mus. NH, speleological papers • Som. ARS, papers • Wells Museum, Somerset, exploration diary of Wookey Hole and notes relating to quaternary palaeontology | Oxf. U. Mus. NH, corresp. with James Parker • Oxf. U. Mus. NH, letters to John Phillips • Salisbury and South Wiltshire Museum, letters to A. H. L. F. Pitt-Rivers • Som. ARS, letters to Arthur Bulleid

Likenesses Maull & Fox, photograph, 1893, RS • B. Stone, photograph, 1901, Birmingham Reference Library [*see illus.*] • W. Stoneman, photograph, 1920, NPG • photographs, Buxton Museum, Derbyshire • photographs, repro. in Bishop, ed., *Cave hunters* • two photographs, RS

Wealth at death £24,698 2s.: probate, 23 March 1929, *CGPLA Eng. & Wales*

Dawks, Ichabod (*bap.* 1661, *d.* 1731), printer, was baptized on 22 September 1661 at St Mary's, Westerham, Kent, the eldest son of Thomas *Dawks (1636–1689) [*see under* Dawks, Thomas], printer, and Anne, *née* Brooker (*b.* c.1638/9). By his own account, in 1672 he began to work with his father at John Darby's in Bartholomew Close, London. He continued under his father's supervision when the latter moved in 1673 to join Anne Maxwell's and Elizabeth Flesher's establishments and in 1674 set up on his own in Blackfriars. Ichabod was freed by patrimony on 6 November 1682. On 3 August 1687 he married Sarah (1657?–1737), whose surname is unknown. On his father's death in August 1689, Ichabod and his mother, Anne, succeeded to the business, of which Ichabod became sole proprietor about 1693. Between 1693 and 1725 he kept thirteen apprentices. He became a liveryman of the Stationers' Company on 5 August 1700. His work address in 1705–31 is given as at the west end of Thames Street, near Puddle Dock.

Ichabod is best remembered for his thrice-weekly newspaper *Dawks's News-Letter* (1696–1716). The earliest existing issue, number 23, is dated 13 August 1696, and the latest 22 December 1716 (BL set). Closely modelled on the older manuscript newsletters, Dawks's venture employed a script type whose effect lay between the intimacy of handwriting and the impersonality of newspapers in roman type. The text type, bought from the Grover foundry, was presumably cut to Dawks's order. Identified as the 'Scriptorial english no. 2' displayed in the James's Specimen of 1782 (Mores), it is also shown, recast from the original matrices, in Morison's *Ichabod Dawks*. Foreign news predominated, with the fourth and final page left blank for late news. There were no advertisements. Dawks also published two short-lived news sheets in roman type: the *Philosophical Observator* (first issue 22 January 1695) for John Whitlock, and on his own behalf the *Protestant Mercury, Occurrences Foreign & Domestic* (first issue 9 March 1696). As imprints reveal, he printed many books, often on his own account, especially in the field of popular science and medicine. The copyrights of some of these he had inherited from his father. For many years he also printed two almanacs for the Company of Stationers. Dawks died in London on 27 February 1731, and was buried on 4 March at Low Leyton, Essex. His widow Sarah was still printing in 1736.   Keith Maslen

Sources Nichols, *Lit. anecdotes* · S. Morison, *Ichabod Dawks and his 'News-letter', with an account of the Dawks family of booksellers and stationers, 1635–1731* (1931) · K. Maslen, 'Puritan printers in London: the Dawks family, 1627–1737', *Bibliographical Society of Australia and New Zealand Bulletin*, 25 (2001) · M. Treadwell, 'London printers and printing houses in 1705', *Publishing History*, 7 (1980), 5–44 · D. F. McKenzie, ed., *Stationers' Company apprentices*, 3 vols. (1961–78), vols. 2–3 · E. R. Mores, *A dissertation upon English typographical founders and founderies*, ed. H. Carter and C. Ricks, new edn (1961) · T. B. Reed, *A history of the old English letter foundries*, rev. A. F. Johnson (1952) · *IGI*
Archives BL, diary, Add. MS 42101 · BLPES, notebook, MS collection G 1521
Wealth at death see administration, GL, MS 9050/22, granted 26 March 1731, in Treadwell, 'London printers'

Dawks, Thomas (*bap.* 1611, *d.* 1670), printer, was baptized on 16 June 1611 in Stratford upon Avon, the son of Richard Dawks (*d.* 1626/7), plumber, of Stratford upon Avon; his mother's names are unknown. He was bound on 16 June 1627 to Felix Kingston, printer, of London, and became a freeman of the Stationers' Company on 5 October 1635. In 1649, in his son's school register, he is described as printer, but where he was employed then and later is not known. His grandson Ichabod noted in his diary that his 'Dear Grand Father' died on 11 May 1670 at Low Leyton, Essex, where he owned two houses and land (Morison). Morison confuses Thomas senior with the Puritan divine Thomas Dawks (*b.* 1620, BA Oxford, 1641). Dawks married Frances (*d.* 1667) and their son **Thomas Dawks** (1636–1689), printer, was born at Kelmscott, Oxfordshire, on 8 October 1636. He was admitted on 2 April 1649 to Merchant Taylors' School, London. In 1651 he 'began to Work at Printing at Mr Du Gards' (BL, Add. MS 42101). William Dugard, headmaster of Merchant Taylors' School, was also printer to the council of state. Thomas was freed by patrimony on 6 August 1655. In 1660 he unsuccessfully petitioned to become overseer of the press responsible for suppressing seditious printing.

On 16 February 1661 Dawks married Anne Brooker (*b. c.*1638/9), and Ichabod *Dawks, first of eleven children, was baptized on 22 September 1661. Their daughter Dorothy married the London printer William Bowyer the elder. The family left London during the plague of 1665, and after the 1666 fire retreated temporarily to Low Leyton. On 2 April 1666 Thomas moved to Thomas Roycroft's, Bartholomew Close (too late to work on the polyglot Bible, despite contrary assertions). In 1672–3 he worked successively for John Darby, Anne Maxwell, and Elizabeth Flesher, before setting up for himself in Blackfriars in 1674. He had four apprentices, sons Ichabod and Thomas, and two others bound in 1683.

Thomas the younger had shares in and printed a number of popular medical works, including William Salmon's *Pharmacopeia Londinensis* (3rd edn, 1685). In 1676, having printed in Welsh *The Practice of Piety* (1675), he was appointed king's printer for the British language. In 1679 he projected a short history of printing. Dawks died in August 1689, leaving his printing business to his wife and son Ichabod, and was buried at Low Leyton, where he had died. His wife married one William Ryland on 8 July 1693 in London.   Keith Maslen

Sources Nichols, *Lit. anecdotes* · S. Morison, *Ichabod Dawks and his 'News-letter', with an account of the Dawks family of booksellers and stationers, 1635–1731* (1931) · M. Treadwell, 'London printers and printing houses in 1705', *Publishing History*, 7 (1980), 5–44 · D. F. McKenzie, 'A list of printers' apprentices, 1605–1640', *Studies in Bibliography*, 13 (1960), 109–41 · D. F. McKenzie, ed., *Stationers' Company apprentices*, [2]: *1641–1700* (1974) · *IGI* · *Calamy rev.* · K. Maslen, 'Puritan printers in London: the Dawks family, 1627–1737', *Bibliographical Society of Australia and New Zealand Bulletin*, 25 (2001), 87–106 · Mrs E. P. Hart, ed., *Merchant Taylors' School register, 1561–1934*, 2 vols. (1936) · Foster, *Alum. Oxon.* · P. Morgan, *Warwickshire apprentices in the Stationers' Company of London, 1563–1700*, Dugdale Society, 25 (1978)
Archives BL, diary, Add. MS 42101
Wealth at death family property (houses and land) in Capworth Street, Low Leyton, Essex, valued at £940 in 1670 · ordered Low Leyton property to be sold to pay debts; left his printing house (equipment), also copyrights of works he had printed, jointly to his widow and to his only surviving printer son, Ichabod; enough eventually set aside to provide £30 each to three unmarried daughters; Thomas Dawks the younger: Morison, *Ichabod Dawks*, 6

Dawks, Thomas (1636–1689). *See under* Dawks, Thomas (*bap.* 1611, *d.* 1670).

Dawnay, Guy Payan (1878–1952), army officer and merchant banker, was born on 23 March 1878 at St James's Palace, London, the eldest child of Lieutenant-Colonel the Hon. Lewis Payan Dawnay (1846–1910), MP for Thirsk and Malton from 1880 to 1892, of Beningbrough Hall, Yorkshire, the second son of the seventh Viscount Downe. His mother was Lady Victoria Alexandrina Elizabeth Grey (1853–1922), the daughter of General the Hon. Charles *Grey. He had one brother and two sisters, and was educated at Eton College (1891–5) and Magdalen College, Oxford. He married in 1906 Cecil (1880–1972), the daughter of Francis William Buxton, a merchant banker and former MP for Andover, and the granddaughter of the first Baron Lawrence, army officer and viceroy of India. They had two sons and three daughters.

Dawnay entered the army from the militia, having held a commission in the 3rd battalion of the Yorkshire regiment from 1895. On the outbreak of the Second South African War in 1899, he was gazetted second lieutenant in his father's old regiment, the Coldstream Guards. After fighting in the Transvaal, the Orange Free State, and the Cape, he was posted to railway duties in 1901, and afterwards served on the staff until peace in 1902. He was adjutant of the guards' depot in 1904–6 (MVO 1907), and after attending the Staff College at Camberley in 1908 he spent three years with the committee of imperial defence. Having succeeded his father at Beningbrough, he went onto the reserve of officers in 1911, and entered business.

Dawnay was recalled to service on the outbreak of the First World War, and served at the War Office from September 1914 until March 1915, when he went to the Dardanelles as general staff officer at the headquarters of Sir Ian Hamilton. He planned the attack on Suvla Bay, and played a key role in presenting an unexpurgated analysis of the débâcle to the cabinet in London. It was exceptional for a young staff officer to advise ministers to overrule his own commander-in-chief's authority, and in the event Hamilton was recalled. In 1917 Dawnay was posted to Egypt, where as deputy chief of general staff to Sir Edmund Allenby he devised the Beersheba plan which destroyed the Turkish army on the plain of Armageddon and opened the way for the capture of Jerusalem by the first Christian army since the crusades. He was an outstanding staff officer, although he was, according to T. E. Lawrence, 'the least professional of soldiers, a banker who read Greek history; a strategist unashamed, and a burning poet with strength over daily things' (Lawrence, 383). After Sinai and Palestine, Dawnay served at general headquarters in France until 1919, when he received the honorary rank of major-general. He was mentioned in dispatches eleven times and was decorated CB and CMG in 1918, as well as receiving the French Légion d'honneur, the Russian order of St Anne, the Italian order of St Maurice and St Lazarus, and the American Distinguished Service Medal.

Although Dawnay remained on the reserve list of officers between 1922 and 1933, he returned to business after the war. With Julian C. Day (1905–1978), F. V. Willey (afterwards second Baron Barnby), and N. Stewart Sandeman MP as partners, he formed in 1928 a private merchant bank called Dawnay Day, specializing in investment and finance business, as well as the reconstruction of industrial concerns hit by depression. After 1950 the company operated solely as an investment trust. In association with Brendan Bracken, Dawnay put together the complex financial arrangements involved in forming the Financial News group in 1928, and he became chairman on Bracken's appointment as minister of information in 1941. From 1923 he sat on the London board of Liverpool, London and Globe Insurance, and was chairman in 1925–9 of the troubled British Celanese Company. As chairman (1929–36) of the armaments and engineering company Armstrong Whitworth he had an important role in the industrial rationalization movement. He was chairman of Artillery Mansions Ltd, and a director of other important property companies. In the early 1930s he pioneered unit trusts with the launch of the Security First Trust. He was also chairman of Gordon Hotels (1921–51).

Many of the Dawnays were highly strung, but Guy Dawnay mastered his anxieties effectively. He was a fastidious, charming, and cultured man, interested not only in business and soldiering but also in theology, country life, and politics (after the armistice he planned a new political party in association with Aubrey Herbert and George Lloyd). He loved debate, and was a founder of the Chatham Dining Club. A volume of his verses entitled *Nigella* was privately printed in 1919, and he was an occasional essayist. His discriminating literary tastes brought him the friendship of Maurice Baring and Hilaire Belloc, while his interest in military strategy led him in 1920 to found the *Army Quarterly*, which he edited until 1928. At the age of fifty-five he taught himself classical Greek.

Having in 1916 sold Beningbrough, Dawnay in 1919 bought an estate at Longparish, Whitchurch, Hampshire: 'a delightful, quiet house on the River Test where he fishes', according to Lord Mersey (Mersey, 323). At Longparish he was the quintessential cultivated English country gentleman. During the Second World War he joined the Home Guard there as a private soldier, and took inordinate pride in obtaining a commission. He died at Longparish House, on 19 January 1952, after a cerebral thrombosis. He was buried at Longparish.

RICHARD DAVENPORT-HINES

Sources IWM, Dawnay papers · T. E. Lawrence, *Seven pillars of wisdom: a triumph* (1935), 383 · C. Mackenzie, *Gallipoli memories* (1929), 96 · Viscount Mersey [C. C. Bigham], *A picture of life* (1941), 323 · R. P. T. Davenport-Hines, 'Dawnay, Guy Payan', *DBB* · private information (2004) · d. cert. · b. cert.
Archives IWM, corresp. and papers | CUL, Vickers MSS · IWM, corresp. with P. W. Chetwode
Likenesses H. Lamb, drawing, c.1923, priv. coll. · M. Codner, portrait, priv. coll.
Wealth at death £40,050 6s. 5d.: probate, 24 June 1952, CGPLA Eng. & Wales

Dawson, Abraham (1713?–1789), biblical scholar, was probably born at Horton, near Bradford, into a well-established Yorkshire nonconformist family. His father was Eli Dawson (d. 1744), who served as a Presbyterian minister at Morley, near Halifax, then at Horton, and lastly, from 1728, at Halifax; his mother was Alice Taylor. His grandfather Joseph Dawson (1635/6–1709) had also been a Presbyterian minister and was ejected from Thornton Chapel, near Bradford. Abraham had six brothers, including Benjamin *Dawson (1729–1814) and Thomas *Dawson (c.1725–1782). All but one of his brothers were, like Abraham, educated for and entered the church; all in time left the ministry, Benjamin becoming a philologist, and Thomas a physician.

Abraham Dawson served as a Presbyterian minister for several years before he conformed to the Church of England (as did four of his siblings). In July or August 1754 he was instituted rector of Ringsfield, near Beccles in Suffolk. While there he published *A New English Translation of the First Three Chapters of Genesis* (1763), followed by his translation of the fourth and fifth chapters (1772) and the sixth and eleventh (1786). Dawson, who was married, died at Ringsfield on 3 October 1789 and was buried in the church five days later.

ALEXANDER GORDON, rev. PHILIP CARTER

Sources *The nonconformist's memorial … originally written by … Edmund Calamy*, ed. S. Palmer, [3rd edn], 3 vols. (1802–3) · J. Hunter, *The rise of the old dissent, exemplified by the life of Oliver Heywood* (1842) · *Halifax Northgate End Chapel Magazine* (1886), 15, 46 · A. Dawson, will, PRO, PROB 11/1185, fols. 39v–41r · T. S. James, *The history of the litigation and legislation respecting Presbyterian chapels and charities in England and Ireland between 1816 and 1849* (1867)

Dawson, Agnes (1873–1953), feminist and headteacher, was born on 7 March 1873 at 121 East Surrey Grove, Peckham, London, the daughter of Isaac Dawson, a journeyman carpenter and later master builder, and his wife, Sarah, formerly Burford. On leaving elementary school in Peckham she became a pupil teacher and then trained at Saffron Walden College. She taught first at a school for 'mentally defective' children in east London and then at the John Ruskin School for Physically Disabled Children in Walworth. In 1913 she became headteacher of St Paul's Road infants' school in east London, transferring to Crawford Street infants' school in Camberwell in 1917. She was an enthusiastic supporter of Montessori active education for young children. She called for nursery schools to be built wherever there was a demand to assist working-class women (A. Dawson, *Nursery Schools*, n.d.). She helped establish the Parents' National Educational Union to involve parents in educational matters.

Agnes Dawson was active in the National Federation of Women Teachers (NFWT), a pressure group inside the National Union of Teachers (NUT) before the First World War. Within the NUT she campaigned for the union to support women's suffrage and equal pay, and to oppose mixed elementary schools, since women would be denied status and promotion in male-dominated mixed schools. She was a member of the London Teachers' Association general committee and a regular delegate to the NUT conference. By 1912 she was vice-president of the East Lambeth NUT Association and a member of the London Teachers' Association women's subcommittee and education committee. She stood for the national executive of the NUT unsuccessfully in 1916 and 1917. In 1912 she became the first president of the Women Teachers' Franchise Union. She was a constitutional suffragist, and stated that the only militant act she ever undertook was to sit up all night at a friend's house during census night 1911 (Dawson, 'President, 1919', 3).

Agnes was a member of the central council of the National Federation (later Union) of Women Teachers from 1914 to 1937. She was president of the NFWT in 1919 and helped lead the campaign for the federation to leave the NUT and become an autonomous union, the National Union of Women Teachers. Although a Labour Party member she dissuaded the central council of the NFWT from affiliating, believing that women in the Labour Party would be 'swamped' (Minutes of the central council of the NFWT, 15 Jan 1921). In 1925 she resigned her teaching post and stood successfully for the London county council (LCC) as a Labour Party candidate for North Camberwell. She undertook this post full-time, sustained by money from National Union of Women Teachers' members. She had a difficult time on the LCC, receiving little support from men who were supposed to be representing education (Miss Froud to Miss Turner, 7 May 1925, cited in Kean, 93). She served on the management committee of nursery schools, the special services subcommittee, and the teaching subcommittee of the education committee. She became senior whip of the Labour group, and in 1932 deputy chair of the council. When Labour gained control of the council for the first time in 1934 Agnes became chair of the powerful finance and general purposes subcommittee. After much campaigning she persuaded Herbert Morrison to remove the marriage bar on women teachers in 1935.

In 1937 Agnes left her advisory post with the National Union of Women Teachers, resigned as a joint trustee of the union, and did not stand again for the LCC. She retired to Newport, Essex, where she continued public work as a JP and stood unsuccessfully in 1946 for the parish council. From 1925 she lived with Anne Munns, a former teacher at Crawford Street School, whom she called her 'pal and partner', until Anne's death in 1952 (Dawson to Muriel Pierotti, 13 Dec 1952, National Union of Women Teachers archive, box 112, file 81). She was nevertheless critical of a school atmosphere dominated by celibate teachers ([A. Dawson], 'Married women teachers', *Times Educational Supplement*, 20 July 1935, 257), and this was reflected in her sustained campaign against the marriage bar for women teachers. As a founder member of the NFWT she was a pioneer who evoked not only the admiration but the affection of many people (M. Pierotti to Mrs Tidswell, 28 April 1953, NUWT archive, box 112, file 81). Agnes Dawson died at her home, The Hut, Wicken Road, Newport, Essex, on 20 April 1953, and was cremated at Camberwell.

HILDA KEAN

Sources U. Lond., Institute of Education, National Union of Women Teachers archive · H. Kean, *Deeds not words: the lives of suffragette teachers* (1990) · H. Kean and A. Oram, 'Who would be free herself must strike the blow', *South London Record*, no. 3 (1988) · 'With the NUT at Lowestoft', *London Teacher* (24 April 1914), 316–18 · A. Dawson, 'President, 1919, Miss A. Dawson LCC (London)', *Woman Teacher* (5 Oct 1928), 3 · minutes of the central council of the National Federation of Women Teachers, 15 Jan 1921, U. Lond., Institute of Education, National Union of Women Teachers archive · A. Dawson, 'A foreword from the president, Miss Agnes Dawson', *Woman Teacher* (26 Sept 1919), 2 · Crawford Street School logbook, 1917, LMA · St Paul's Road School logbook, 1913, LMA · b. cert. · d. cert. · CGPLA Eng. & Wales (1953)

Archives U. Lond., Institute of Education, National Union of Women Teachers archive

Likenesses line drawing, repro. in *Time and Tide* (24 Sept 1841), 41 · photograph, U. Lond., Institute of Education Library, National Union of Women Teachers archive, box 470 · photograph, repro. in Kean and Oram, 'Who would be free' · photograph, repro. in H. S. Morrison, *Herbert Morrison: an autobiography* [1960], 33

Wealth at death £3470 8s. 8d.: probate, 8 July 1953, CGPLA Eng. & Wales

Dawson, Ambrose (1705/6–1794), physician, son of William Dawson (c.1677–1762), of Langcliff Hall, Yorkshire, and his wife, Jane, daughter of Ambrose Pudsay, was born at Settle, Yorkshire. William Dawson was an able mathematician and a friend of Isaac Newton. After attending Giggleswick School, Dawson entered Christ's College, Cambridge, in 1724, and he graduated MB in 1730 and MD in 1735. In 1737 he was elected a fellow of the Royal College of Physicians; he was censor four times, and he delivered the Harveian oration in 1744. His oration was printed the following year. He was elected physician to St George's Hospital on 27 April 1745 and held the office until 1760. Dawson lived in Grosvenor Street, London, and was known for his kindness to the poor. When he gave up practice in 1776, the parish of St George's, Hanover Square, presented him with a magnificent tea urn in recognition of his services to the poor of the parish.

Dawson retired to his father's estate at Langcliff Hall, but he did not entirely lose interest in medicine. In 1778 he published *Thoughts on the Hydrocephalus internus* and *Observations on Hydatids in the Heads of Cattle*. Little was known at the time about the anatomical changes which accompany effusion into the cavities of the brain and nothing was known of the natural history of the entozoa. The publications aroused little interest either at the time or in later years. Dawson regretted giving up practising medicine, and the inactivity affected his health. A little later he moved to Liverpool, where he died on 23 December 1794. He was ill for only a few days, and at the time of his death he was the oldest fellow of the Royal College of Physicians. He was buried at Bolton, Craven, Yorkshire, the home of his mother's family.

NORMAN MOORE, rev. CLAIRE L. NUTT

Sources Munk, *Roll* · Venn, *Alum. Cant.* [see also W. Dawson] · S. C. Lawrence, *Charitable knowledge: hospital pupils and practitioners in eighteenth-century London* (1996)

Dawson, Benjamin (1729–1814), Church of England clergyman and philologist, was born in Halifax, the sixth of the seven sons of Eli Dawson (*d.* 1744), Presbyterian minister of Morley, Yorkshire, and his wife, Alice Taylor. He and his brother Thomas *Dawson (*c.*1725–1782), physician, entered the nonconformist academy at Kendal as exhibitioners of the London Presbyterian Board in 1746, and were there taught by Caleb Rotheram. In November 1748 he went to Glasgow University, where he and his brothers Thomas, Abraham *Dawson (1713?–1789), biblical scholar, and Joseph studied as scholars on Dr Williams's foundation. He graduated MA in 1750, and defended a thesis, *De summo bono*, on taking his degree. His thesis, an able disquisition on the relationship between God and human good, was published for the university by the Foulis brothers in 1750.

Dawson was Presbyterian minister at Leek, Staffordshire, in 1754, before moving to Congleton, Cheshire, where he worked as a teacher. He moved from Congleton in 1757 in order to become assistant minister at St Thomas's Presbyterian Church, Southwark. His elder brother Thomas had conformed to the Church of England, and Benjamin followed suit in 1758, the same year that he took the degree of LLD at Glasgow. Their brother Abraham had already conformed and served as rector of Ringsfield, Suffolk, from 1754 until 1789. Obadiah, a merchant in Leeds, was the only brother to remain a dissenter; of the others, Samuel taught at a school, Eli served in the West Indies, and Joseph became rector of Paull, near Hull. Shortly after conforming, Benjamin became rector of Burgh, near Woodbridge, Suffolk, in 1760, a living he held until his death. This did not prevent him from maintaining good relations with dissenters, and in 1763 he accompanied, as his private tutor, Sir Benjamin Ibbetson, a young baronet from Leeds, to Warrington Academy, where Dawson became a member of the active literary society around John Aikin. On 6 June 1776 he married Mary Halsey (1722/3–1803) at Burgh.

All but one of Dawson's works were published after he conformed to the established church. He wrote two essays in defence of Edmund Law's enunciation of the mortalist thesis that the soul slept in the interval between death and the resurrection into eternal life, of which the first appeared in the *Monthly Review* in 1758, and the second in the *Grand Magazine* in 1758. These were later reprinted as an appendix to *An Illustration of Several Texts of Scripture, Particularly those in which the Logos occurs*, which was published by Andrew Millar in 1765. This publication put into print the eight sermons on the Anglican elucidation of trinitarian doctrine which Dawson had preached in 1764 and 1765 on Lady Moyer's foundation. While he was careful not to accuse Arians, Socinians, and Sabellians of being less than Christians, Dawson was determined to demonstrate the flaws in their arguments, thus distancing himself from the Arianism in which he had been reared as a liberal Presbyterian. The lectures were more critical of Arianism than of other anti-trinitarian systems, and he was especially concerned to demonstrate the scriptural and apostolic basis of the Church of England's teaching on the matter. Satisfied though he was of clearing himself from orthodox suspicions, it is notable that a prominent mouthpiece of rational dissent, the *Monthly Repository*, declared in 1810 that, while successful in his assault on Arianism, Dawson's account was, 'in truth, completely Unitarian' (*Monthly Repository*, 1810, 325).

Although the Lady Moyer's sermons were intended to defend the first of the church's Thirty-Nine Articles, Dawson quickly proved himself an ally in the campaign to repeal Anglican subscription to the authority of the Thirty-Nine Articles. He proved a particularly astute defender of Francis Blackburne's major contribution to the campaign, *The Confessional* (1767); Blackburne thought him 'an incomparable writer' (*Monthly Repository*, 1810, 325). Most of the several pamphlets he devoted to the issue criticized point by point the writings produced by the defenders of subscription, notably those by Thomas Rutherforth, John Rotherham, Gloucester Ridley, and Thomas Balguy. Dawson began his campaign with *An Examination of an Essay on Establishments in Religion* (1767), and brought it to an end in *A Letter to the Clergy of the Archdeaconry of Winchester* (1773). The basis of his critique can be found in a pivotal remark in *An Answer to Letters Concerning Established Confessions of Faith* (1769), when he protested that churchmen ought not to subject 'the Gospel, the blessed Gospel of light and truth, to the institutions of fallible man' (p. 36). His was an ultra-protestant position; he argued that the doctrine of men such as Balguy would bring the Church of England '*directly to Popery*' (*A Letter to the Clergy*, 43). Dawson's close association with Blackburne troubled Joseph Priestley, who despised him for having conformed to a church to whose articles he had readily subscribed, paradoxically making of him, as Priestley observed in a letter to Theophilus Lindsey in April 1772, a 'man … living in every contradiction to every principle of the *Confessional*'. He cited Dawson's brother Obadiah, a member of Priestley's congregation, as saying, 'I do not know what my brother meant by attacking you, but I know he hates the Dissenters'. In the same letter Priestley boldly stated, 'I am afraid his case is that of one who hates the light because his deeds are evil' (Rutt, 1.168). Whatever the level of personal antagonism between Dawson and Priestley, Dawson remained on good terms with many dissenters, who appreciated his help in the campaign to alter the terms of subscription required by the Toleration Act in 1779.

Dawson was a firm moralist, as is apparent in his short work *Some Assistance Offered to Parents with Respect to the Religious Education of their Children* (1759). This was confirmed in *National Depravity the Cause and Mark of Divine Judgement upon a Land* (Ipswich, 1780), a fast sermon which he had preached in February 1780 and which he dedicated to Blackburne, 'the Firm, Strenuous, and Consistent Assertor of Religious Freedom'. The sermon espoused an Anglican version of the politics of rational dissent: the country was being judged for sinning against its 'superior principles, both in our Religious and Civil Constitution'. The war with America was described as an 'unhappy, *unnatural* contest with our *fellow-subjects*', hurtful to trade and commerce and, ultimately, to the British constitution; it was, therefore, the duty of Christians to 'throw our *Mite* of Virtue and Piety, as of Taxes, into the public treasure' (*National Depravity*, 14, 16, 21). The sermon he preached as part of the general thanksgiving for the restoration of George III's health in 1789 voiced his conviction that the political constitution had to be preserved, because 'The virtues and vices, the genius, manners, and customs, and also the ease and security of a people, are principally derived hence' (Dawson, *The Benefits of Civil Government, a Ground of Praise to God*, 1789, 7).

In his later years Dawson turned from theology and politico-theology to the fashionable study of language. In 1797 he published at Ipswich *Prolepsis philologiae Anglicanae, or, A Plan of a Philological and Synonymical Dictionary*. He saw synonyms as being introduced into languages in order to register the 'increase and refinement of ideas'; so it was that the conventional method of dictionaries explaining one word by another was 'erroneous': mathematical exactness in definition would only arise by giving the '*general*' and '*special*' import of a word (pp. 9, 34–5, 42). Philology was to be based on the same footing as entomology, ornithology, and botany. He was interested in the literal rather than the figurative use of a word: this was the proper province of the philologist. The *Monthly Repository* of 1810 spoke highly of the *Prolepsis*, describing it as 'a work of great promise, which it is greatly to be wished that the author may live to finish', and attributing its apparent lack of success to its forbidding Latin title. Dawson published the first instalment of his dictionary at Ipswich in 1806, but his *Philologia Anglicana, or, A Philological and Synonymical Dictionary of the English Language* never got beyond 'A–Adornment'. Its style owed much to the example of Johnson's *Dictionary*, complete with citations from English authorities. The first entry, 'A/An', gave

examples from Johnson, Dryden, and Addison, and, significantly for a theologian such as Dawson, from the liberal theologian Richard Watson on Jesus, and Hobbes on the Antichrist. His dictionary plainly served broad educational purposes.

Dawson never produced another volume, and he died at his rectory in Burgh, where he had performed his duties as rector with exemplary care for fifty-four years, on 15 June 1814. He was buried in the chancel of his church on 21 June next to his wife, who had died on 22 June 1803.

B. W. YOUNG

Sources W. I. Addison, ed., *The matriculation albums of the University of Glasgow from 1728 to 1858* (1913) · *Monthly Repository*, 5 (1810), 324–5 · *Monthly Repository*, 9 (1814), 264, 506 · *Life and correspondence of Joseph Priestley*, ed. J. T. Rutt, 2 vols. (1831–2), vol. 1, pp. 140, 167–70, 172–4; vol. 2, p. 209 · B. W. Young, *Religion and Enlightenment in eighteenth-century England: theological debate from Locke to Burke* (1998) · G. E. Noyes, 'The beginnings of the study of synonyms in England', *Publications of the Modern Languages Association of America*, 66 (1951), 951–70, esp. 966–8 · G. E. Noyes, 'The critical reception of Johnson's *Dictionary* in the later eighteenth century', *Modern Philology*, 52 (1954–5), 175–91, esp. 187 · *DNB* · *IGI*

Dawson, Bertrand Edward, Viscount Dawson of Penn (1864–1945), physician, was born at Duppas Hill, Croydon, on 9 March 1864, the fourth son and fifth child of Henry Dawson, architect, and his wife, Frances Emily, daughter of Obadiah Wheeler. He was educated at St Paul's School and University College, London: he lived at University Hall when Henry Morley was principal. In 1884 he entered the London Hospital as a medical student; he graduated BSc in 1888 and qualified in 1890, becoming MRCS in the same year. He became MD and MRCP in 1893, and FRCP in 1903.

Dawson earned his living through hospital appointments and as a lecturer, and in 1896, when he became assistant physician at the London Hospital, he launched himself as a private consultant. He had consulting rooms in Harley Street, and from 1903 in Wimpole Street until the building was bombed in 1940. As was customary at the time, his interests ranged widely. His textbook chapters dealt with diabetes mellitus, diabetes insipidus, influenza, rheumatoid arthritis, and the physical examination of the stomach and intestines. *The Lancet* later described his contribution to clinical medicine as 'respectable rather than remarkable' (*Lancet*, 353). Remembering these years of struggle, with few opportunities for research, in later life he took an active part in the foundation of a postgraduate medical school at London University (pressing that it should be sited at Kenwood, in Hampstead). On 18 December 1900 Dawson married Minnie Ethel Yarrow (*b.* 1878/9), daughter of Alfred Fernandez *Yarrow, shipbuilder and also a principal patron of the London Hospital; they had three daughters. Dawson became full physician at the London Hospital in 1906 and was appointed physician-extraordinary to King Edward VII, a post which he retained with King George V until 1914, when he became physician-in-ordinary. In 1911 he was appointed KCVO.

After the outbreak of the First World War, Dawson, who

Bertrand Edward Dawson, Viscount Dawson of Penn (1864–1945), by Philip A. de Laszlo, 1937

had become commandant of the 2nd London General Hospital in the Territorial Army in 1908, went to France as consulting physician with the acting rank of major-general. He attended the king after he had suffered a serious fall from his horse on a visit to the front in France in 1915, and remained in the country until 1919. Although his time was largely occupied with hospital organization, Dawson used his experiences of war to write on paratyphoid, trench fever, infective gastroenteritis, and influenza; he also organized an official investigation into cases of jaundice in the trenches, which proved to be the newly described Weil's disease. Nor was Dawson oblivious of the manifestations of battle stress in the troops, and he set up four base camps in France at Wimereux, Étaples, Rouen, and Étretat, which were specially concerned with studying and treating 'soldiers' heart'. 'The years in France convinced Dawson that while the "diseases of invasion" were receding before the advance of medical knowledge the "diseases of stress" would multiply with the quickening pace of life' (DNB).

As in the case of recruits for the Second South African War, the First World War also revealed that the British standard of fitness was low. Dawson saw that it was going to become the duty of the medical profession as much to promote national health as to cure sickness in the individual. In particular, whatever the difficulties, the 1911 Insurance Act had to be linked with a universal health service. In July 1918 Dawson developed his ideas in two Cavendish

lectures entitled 'The nation's welfare: the future of the medical profession', given before the West London Medico-Chirurgical Society. Their audiences may have been small, but the influence of the lectures was immense. Widely publicized in both *The Lancet* and the *British Medical Journal*, they were reprinted as a pamphlet (to which Dawson added the term 'health centre', used for the first time). As a result he was drawn into the government consultations concerning the formation of a ministry of health, and in 1919 he was made chairman of the consultative council on medical and allied services set up by Christopher Addison, the first minister of health.

This council was the first body in Britain to focus public opinion on systematized health services. Its report (the *Dawson Report*), published in 1920, foreshadowed by many years a national health service, the recommendations being repeated in the Beveridge report of 1942, the government white paper of 1944, and the National Health Service legislation of 1946. Possibly adopting the terminology from education (provided by Sir Arthur Morant, the first permanent secretary of the Ministry of Health), the report proposed a health service based on primary and secondary health centres (corresponding respectively to subsequent general-practitioner health centres and district general hospitals), with teaching hospitals at their head. Crucially, Morant died of influenza in 1920, financial retrenchment was in the air, and the report received a lukewarm official reception. Dawson was opposed to a compulsory full-time salaried service, and during the 1920s he became increasingly antagonistic towards a state medical service 'which he identified with the threat posed by communism' (Webster, 210). From advocating state collectivism in the provision of medical care he now promoted co-operation between existing agencies (ibid., 221).

In 1920 Dawson was created a baron, taking the title of Lord Dawson of Penn, of Buckinghamshire. In 1936 he became Viscount Dawson. He was the first medical man to enter the Lords as an active member of the profession. As its virtual spokesman he championed the special functions of the teaching hospitals, and in 1936 he opposed the Voluntary Euthanasia (Legalization) Bill in a characteristic speech:

> We do not lay down edicts for these things. It is a gradual growth of thought and feeling that entwines itself into the texture of our thoughts. … This is something which belongs to the wisdom and conscience of the medical profession and not to the realm of law. (DNB)

A man of profound religious conviction, he supported the reform of the prayer book. Dawson was disturbed by what he perceived as a decline in Christian belief and teaching, and saw this reform as a means of reconciling old ideas with new. In 1937 he supported the Matrimonial Causes Bill and a year later was mainly responsible for the Infanticide Bill.

Dawson also continued his private practice and hospital teaching, and his work as examiner for the London Hospital and Royal College of Physicians. In these years he held many hospital appointments; he served (from 1929) on the advisory committee to the Ministry of Health, the council of the King Edward's Hospital Fund, and the Medical Research Council; and he became chairman of the army medical advisory board. From 1928 to 1930 he was president of the Royal Society of Medicine and in 1932 he was elected president of the British Medical Association (BMA) for its centenary year. From 1931 to 1938 he was president of the Royal College of Physicians, and widened its reputation by encouraging active participation by its junior fellows and the election of doctors who were members of the salaried government service rather than clinicians.

Dawson was a freethinker and liberal (so much so that the king had queried his elevation to the Lords), and though he sat on the Liberal benches in the Lords he was not constrained by party opinions. As an undergraduate he had been influenced by Charles Bradlaugh and T. H. Huxley, and he showed an interest in social and political problems that was to persist for the rest of his life; he wrote an early Malthusian pamphlet. He championed sanatoria and spas for preventive health, through the National Fitness Council, and he chose the church congress to promote his advanced views on birth control, which included criticism of the Lambeth conference. At the end of his life he was proselytizing for the formation of an academy of medicine which would represent all its diverse strands (as did his proposal for a national health service and its reliance on health centres); this scheme was many decades ahead of its time.

By the Second World War, Dawson had lost his earlier radicalism and was against significant state intervention in medicine. A member of the medical planning commission (MPC) set up in 1940 by the BMA to consider health service for the nation, Dawson argued that it was essential that voluntary hospitals should be saved and suggested a dual system whereby voluntary and municipal hospitals existed under the aegis of a central hospitals board. However, when he read the MPC draft interim report of 1942 he saw it as too favourable to socialized medicine and urged instead 'the inevitability of gradualness' (Webster, 223). Given his increasing conservatism it was not surprising that he was re-elected president of the BMA in September 1943 following the death of Sir Beckwith Whitehouse, who had himself been 'an uncompromising defender of tradition' (Webster, 225). Dawson was by this time approaching the end of his life and had little involvement in the negotiations between the government and medical profession over the establishment of a national health service. By now, in fact, he had come to see health centres as a step on the road to a full-time salaried service and had thus 'drifted into condemning the institutions of which he was the virtual founder' (Webster, 226).

Much of Dawson's public prominence came from his care of the royal family. Dawson had been called into consultation during the last illness of Edward VII (though he did not sign the authorized account published in *The Lancet*), but his main responsibility was for the health of *George V. In 1929 George V suffered a near fatal illness, developing from a streptococcal infection of the chest into a large abscess. As the king lay seemingly dying, on 12 December, Dawson's syringe found the abscess and he drew off 16 ounces of fluid. Some medical colleagues were nevertheless indignant that Dawson had failed to consult the thoracic specialist Arthur Tudor Edwards in the matter. This was not the only time when Dawson's treatment of his royal patients had angered colleagues. After a dispute over the care of one of the royal children, Lord Moynihan composed the jingle:

> Lord Dawson of Penn
> Has killed lots of men
> So that's why we sing
> God Save the King.
> (Rose, 358)

The king, however, respected Dawson and liked his direct approach. Dawson was by no means unaided when dealing with royal illnesses: during the crisis of 1929 eleven doctors stood round the royal bed. In 1936 Dawson was in continual attendance during the king's final illness. It was Dawson who composed on a menu card the celebrated lines, 'the King's life is moving peacefully towards its close', having modified this from what he described as 'a very commonplace' final bulletin used for Edward VII. Dawson's private Sandringham notebook also shows that he indeed ensured a peaceful conclusion to King George's life; to this end, during the death agony, he injected three-quarters of a grain of morphine and one grain of cocaine into a distended jugular vein.

Like many other famous men, Dawson was a paradox. No more than an ordinary clinician, he yet had far more influence on health care and delivery than many others, though his ideas were rediscovered and developed only many years later. He was a less than consummate politician, but his enthusiasm and commitment were sufficient to persuade people about important issues beyond the delivery of health care, such as contraception. Much of his success in these matters was due to his charm and his capacity to inspire trust in such people as Archbishop Lang and Lloyd George, with whom he visited Hitler at Berchtesgaden in 1936. He also appeared to have time for everybody (he was notoriously unpunctual). Dawson received many honours and appointments: CB (1916), GCVO (1917), KCMG (1919), and KCB (1926); honorary degrees from McGill University and the universities of Pennsylvania, Oxford, Edinburgh, Bristol, Padua, Athens; and honorary fellowships of the American College of Surgeons and the Royal College of Surgeons, London. Dawson died of bronchopneumonia at 2 Weymouth Street, London, on 7 March 1945, and his peerage became extinct. He was survived by his wife.   STEPHEN LOCK

Sources *DNB* · F. Watson, *Dawson of Penn* (1950) · *The Times* (8 March 1945) · *BMJ* (17 March 1945), 389–92 · *The Lancet* (17 March 1945) · F. Watson, 'The death of George V', *History Today*, 36/12 (1986), 21–30 · C. Webster, 'The metamorphosis of Dawson of Penn', *Doctors, politics and society: historical essays*, ed. D. Porter and R. Porter (1993), 212–28 · b. cert. · m. cert. · d. cert. · K. Rose, *King George V* (1983) · *CGPLA Eng. & Wales* (1945)

Archives BL, corresp. with Marie Stopes, Add. MS 58567 · HLRO, letters to David Lloyd George · NA Scot., corresp. with Arthur Balfour · NL Wales, corresp. with Thomas Jones | FILM BFI NFTVA, news footage

Likenesses W. Stoneman, photograph, 1921, NPG • P. A. de Laszlo, oils, 1937, RCP Lond. [*see illus.*] • O. Birley, portrait, priv. coll. • J. Gunn, portrait, priv. coll. • D. Wilding, photograph, NPG • photograph, Wellcome L.

Wealth at death £139,209 18s. 6d.: probate, 21 Aug 1945, *CGPLA Eng. & Wales*

Dawson, Charles (1864–1916), palaeontologist and antiquary, was born on 11 July 1864 at Fulkeith Hall, Lancashire, the second of the four children (he had two brothers and a sister) of Hugh Dawson, barrister, and his wife, Mary Anne Chaffer. By 1873 his father had moved to St Leonards, Sussex. He completed his formal education at the Royal Academy, Gosport, in 1880, and then followed his father into the legal profession, though his real interest always lay in archaeology, historical and industrial. From 1890 until his death he practised as a solicitor in Uckfield, Sussex, where he held several public appointments, and established his own law firm, entering into partnership with Ernest Hart in 1905.

Tall, moustachioed, and prematurely bald, Dawson appeared older than his years and as a long-serving clerk to the magistrates he was an important figure in the life of the town. In 1903 he bought Castle Lodge from the marquess of Abergavenny, a prestigious house under the shadow of Lewes Castle. Until the final stages of the sale the marquess was under the misapprehension that Dawson was purchasing the lodge on behalf of the Sussex Archaeological Society, which had for twenty years rented it to store its collections and records. The purchase soured Dawson's relations with the society, which he had joined in 1892, and they were never properly repaired. On 21 January 1905 he married, at Christ Church, Mayfair, London, Hélène Léonie Elizabeth Postlethwaite (1859–1917), daughter of Barnaby Gaffney of Curzon Street, London, and a widow with two grown children. There were no children from this marriage.

In his time Dawson was viewed as an exemplar of 'that great class of men' who provided 'the driving power to British science—the thinking, observant amateur'. His primary avocation was palaeontology, an interest he had lovingly nurtured since childhood. Indeed, it was a precocious interest in Wealden fossils that led to the assembly of a large and valuable collection that was donated in 1884 to the newly opened Natural History Museum in South Kensington, and which gained him not only the title of honorary collector for the museum but also brought him the coveted fellowship of the London Geological Society at the age of twenty-one. During his lifetime he was responsible for finding several new species of iguanodon, as well as a new species of the Mesozoic mammal *Plagiaulax*.

Dawson also won a reputation in Sussex geology and archaeology, the latter indicated by his election as a fellow of the Society of Antiquaries in 1895. He was a recognized authority on the Sussex iron industry, and his two-volume *History of Hastings Castle* (1909) became a standard work. He wrote many articles about his discoveries which appeared in learned journals such as *The Antiquary*, *Sussex Archaeological Collections*, and the *Geological Magazine*. He was also a

Charles Dawson (1864–1916), by Maull & Fox

highly competent photographer, adept in the preparation and development of glass plates. Although all this assured him a footnote in the history of British science, it was his intimate association with one of the most celebrated scientific forgeries that rescued him from relative obscurity.

Between 1908 and 1912 Dawson recovered the remains of a human skull from a reputedly ancient gravel bed located at Barkham Manor (where he was steward), near Piltdown in Sussex [*see* Piltdown Man]. On 18 December 1912 a reconstruction of these remains was presented to the Geological Society of London by Arthur Smith Woodward, keeper of geology at the Natural History Museum, who was convinced they represented an early human form which he had dubbed *Eoanthropus* ('dawn man') *dawsoni*. In the discussion that followed Professor Arthur Keith hailed the discovery as 'by far the most important ever made in England, and of equal, if not of greater consequence than any other discovery yet made, either at home or abroad' (*Quarterly Journal of the Geological Society of London*, March 1913, 148). During the next forty years, however, it became increasingly difficult to reconcile this hominid with the burgeoning human fossil record from Asia and Africa. In 1953 a detailed examination of the Piltdown remains demonstrated conclusively that they were faked and had been planted as part of an elaborate hoax, evidently aimed at manipulating scientific views on human evolution. Though Dawson may not have masterminded this sophisticated and influential forgery, his complicity in the affair was strongly suspected. But the glory he gained for his 'discoveries' at Piltdown was shortlived. Late in 1915, in a letter to Woodward, Dawson reported that he was ailing from an 'anaemic condition'. He was given serum injections to counteract this, but developed septicaemia and died on 10 August 1916 at his home, Castle Lodge, Lewes.

FRANK SPENCER, rev. MARK POTTLE

Sources J. S. Weiner and others, *The solution to the Piltdown problem* (1953) · J. S. Weiner, *The Piltdown forgery* (1955) · F. Spencer, *Piltdown: a scientific forgery* (1990) · F. Spencer, *The Piltdown papers* (1990) · *Quarterly Journal of the Geological Society of London* (March 1913) · S. Wright, 'Charles Dawson 1864–1916', *Hindsight: Journal of the Uckfield and District Preservation Society*, 6 (summer 2000), 4–18
Likenesses Maull & Fox, photograph, GS Lond., NHM [*see illus.*] · photograph, repro. in Wright, 'Charles Dawson'
Wealth at death £3025 14s. 7d.: probate, 12 Oct 1916, CGPLA Eng. & Wales

Dawson, (Henry) Christopher (1889–1970), cultural historian, was born on 12 October 1889 at Hay, Brecknockshire, the only son and younger child of Colonel Henry Philip Dawson (1850–1933), a Yorkshire landowner, and his wife, Mary Louisa, the eldest daughter of Archdeacon William Latham *Bevan of Hay Castle. He was educated at Winchester College and at Trinity College, Oxford, where he obtained a second class in modern history in 1911. His health prevented active service in the First World War but from 1916 he worked in the war trade intelligence department and in Admiralty research. In that year he married Valery Mary, youngest daughter of Walter Edward Mills, architect, of Oxford. She was the ideal partner for such an unworldly and impractical scholar and thinker, taking all the burdens of daily living off his shoulders. They had two daughters and one son.

Dawson had sufficient private means to be able to follow his own highly original path of historical research and reflection, so that his first book, *The Age of the Gods* (1928), was the result of fourteen years of research. But it was his second, *Progress and Religion* (1929), that first displayed fully the depth of his thought and the astonishing range of his learning. In this, he articulated the theme of all his subsequent writings, that religion is the dynamic of all social culture. *The Making of Europe* (1932) discussed a specific case of this, showing that the 'dark ages' were in fact the most creative period in the culture of the Western world. He developed both these topics further in his Gifford lectures for Edinburgh University, *Religion and Culture* (1948) and *Religion and the Rise of Western Culture* (1950).

Dawson, who had become a Roman Catholic shortly after going down from Oxford, was an influential member of the group of writers which formed around the new Catholic publishing house of Sheed and Ward from the 1930s. For them he edited and contributed to a series of books entitled *Essays in Order*. In 1933 he produced *Enquiries into Religion and Culture*, in 1934 *Medieval Religion*, and in

1943 a very personal socio-political testament, *The Judgment of the Nations*. The admiration which churchmen such as Cardinal Arthur Hinsley and Bishop G. K. A. Bell of Chichester had for Dawson involved him actively as vicepresident in the Sword of the Spirit, a proto-ecumenical movement which, to his disappointment, proved to be too visionary for the Roman authorities of the time.

After the Second World War, Dawson's output of books and articles increasingly stressed the twin themes of Europe and education. He campaigned for an integrated study of Christian philosophy, history, literature, and art in the same way as *literae humaniores* had studied every aspect of classical culture. Only this, he believed, could overcome the schism between religion and culture in the West.

Dawson's achievement owed virtually nothing to the academic world, apart from a short part-time lectureship in the history of culture at the University College in Exeter (1925–33). When he was eventually offered a chair, at the age of sixty-eight, it was not in Britain but in the USA at Harvard. He was professor of Roman Catholic studies there from 1958 to 1962. He was sensitive to this lack of recognition, but at the same time fully understood how much he owed to having been saved from the academic treadmill. In any event, he was physically frail and temperamentally extremely shy and gentle, so that he was unable to do his thought and learning full justice before even small audiences. In contrast, in a one-to-one relationship he was an incomparable teacher. He was elected fellow of the British Academy in 1943.

When his father died in 1933 Dawson inherited the family property in Yorkshire and went to live at Hartlington Hall, but stayed there only a few years because of his frail health. The family then moved to Boars Hill, near Oxford. When his failing health caused his Harvard stay to be cut short, Dawson retired to Fountain Hill House, Budleigh Salterton, Devon; he died in Budleigh Salterton on 25 May 1970 and was buried in St Wilfrid's Church, Burnsall, near Skipton in Yorkshire. WILLIAM KINGSTON, rev.

Sources C. Scott, *A historian and his world: a life of Christopher Dawson, 1889–1970* (1984) · M. D. Knowles, 'Christopher Dawson, 1889–1970', *PBA*, 57 (1971), 439–52 · personal knowledge (1993)
Archives IWM, letters from India and Mesopotamia · U. Lond., Institute of Education, discussion papers · University of St Thomas, St Paul, Minnesota, Center for Catholic Studies
Likenesses photograph, priv. coll.
Wealth at death £53,791: probate, 20 Jan 1971, CGPLA Eng. & Wales

Dawson, Edward (c.1579–1622), Jesuit, was the only son of 'respectable' parents, 'connected with Sir Anthony Staunden', and was born in London. He completed his studies in Spain, and Louvain, in the Spanish Netherlands, and after being ordained priest was sent to the English mission. He was soon apprehended and imprisoned until 1606, when he was sentenced to perpetual exile with forty-seven other priests. He entered the Society of Jesus in Rome the same year. Having been sent back to England on the mission about 1610 he laboured for some time in London and in Lincolnshire. Recalled by his superiors to Ghent he obtained permission to devote himself to the spiritual care of the English and Irish soldiers who were suffering from the plague in the Low Countries. He soon caught the disease, and died at Brussels on 22 December 1622. He was the author of *The Practical Methode of Meditation*, printed in Vicenzo Bruno's *Meditations*, published at St Omer in 1614. THOMPSON COOPER, *rev.* G. BRADLEY

Sources T. M. McCoog, *English and Welsh Jesuits, 1555–1650*, 1, Catholic RS, 74 (1994), 155, 183 · Gillow, *Lit. biog. hist.*, 2.32 · H. Foley, ed., *Records of the English province of the Society of Jesus*, 3 (1878), 300; 6 (1880), 522 · A. F. Allison and D. M. Rogers, 'A catalogue of Catholic books in English printed abroad or secretly in England, 1558–1640', *Biographical Studies*, 3 (1955–6), 161

Dawson [*formerly* Robinson], (**George**) **Geoffrey** (1874–1944), newspaper editor, was born at Skipton in Craven, Yorkshire, on 25 October 1874, the eldest child of George Robinson (*d.* 1907), banker, and his wife, Mary (1847–1903), daughter of William Mosley Perfect. In 1917 he assumed by royal licence the name and arms of Dawson via his mother's eldest sister, Margaret Jane Dawson, the family being descended from a long line of landowners from Langcliffe Hall, Settle.

In 1887 Geoffrey Robinson went to Eton College as a king's scholar, and he found his years there an enjoyable experience (in later life he was to serve as a fellow of the college). He went on to Magdalen College, Oxford, as a demy in 1893, obtaining firsts in classical moderations (1895) and *literae humaniores* (1897). He was later (1926) made an honorary fellow of Magdalen, and the university awarded him an honorary DCL in 1934. In 1898 he entered the civil service by open examination. His first position was in the Post Office, but after only a year he was transferred to the Colonial Office, under Joseph Chamberlain as colonial secretary. In 1898 Robinson was elected to a fellowship at All Souls College, Oxford, an honour which he shared with his lifelong friend Edward Wood, Lord Halifax.

South Africa: Milner's 'kindergarten' When the Second South African War broke out in 1899, Robinson had only a junior position in the South African department of the Colonial Office, but this happy coincidence affected the whole of his future career. In 1901 he was promoted assistant private secretary to Chamberlain, and later in that same year he obtained the same position with the high commissioner for South Africa, the imperialist Alfred Milner. Following the British conquest of the Transvaal and the Orange Free State, the high commissioner became the administrator (later governor) of the two former republics with his headquarters in Johannesburg. There, in a red-brick villa in the suburbs, Robinson was a faithful member of Milner's famous 'kindergarten', whose number also included Robert Brand, Lionel Curtis, Patrick Duncan, Richard Feetham, Lionel Hichens, and later Philip Kerr. The same brotherhood, inspired by Milner's devotion to the British empire, set up the publication *Round Table* in England.

When Milner went back to Britain, he left several of the kindergarten behind in key posts, at a time when South Africa was recovering from years of bitter struggle. In 1905

(George) Geoffrey Dawson (1874–1944), by Sir William Rothenstein, 1923

Robinson left the civil service on being appointed, largely through Milner's influence, editor of the *Johannesburg Star*, and he held the editorship until 1910, during the period of office of William Waldegrave Palmer, second earl of Selborne, Milner's successor as high commissioner. From 1906 onwards he was also the South Africa correspondent of *The Times*, which gave him a platform for a journalistic career in London. For the moment, however, Robinson remained in Johannesburg, a supporter of conciliation with the Boers and the process which culminated in the foundation of the Union of South Africa under Louis Botha in 1910.

Editor of *The Times* under Northcliffe In 1911 Robinson returned to London and became a full-time staff member of *The Times* under its owner, the press magnate Lord Northcliffe. In August 1912, aged only thirty-seven, Robinson was appointed editor on the retirement of George Earle Buckle. At the outset of his editorship, Robinson seems to have 'routinely acquiesced in Northcliffe's views and prejudices' (Koss, 207), though Buckle urged him to stand up to Northcliffe. Others thought that Robinson wrote too many editorials and took too much upon himself. But differences between them emerged with the passage of time: Northcliffe, for example, was far more critical of the government about the Dardanelles fiasco in 1915–16 than was Robinson.

Robinson's successor, Henry Wickham Steed, suggested that Robinson was too much under the influence of his mentor Milner. Although Steed may have overstated this influence, Robinson was a member of the Milnerite 'ginger group', along with Lloyd George, Milner himself, Leo Amery, and Edward Carson, which plotted Asquith's downfall; Robinson's leader of 4 December 1916 was one instance of the important role which *The Times* played in securing Asquith's removal as prime minister in 1916.

During 1918–19 tensions between Dawson (as he had now become) and Northcliffe became acute (he had already offered to resign once), as the owner of the paper became more bombastic and intemperate. Dawson's departure in February 1919 was inevitable, although it seems to have owed as much to Northcliffe's frustrations with the politicians of the day as to any deficiencies in editorship. Somewhat unreasonably, Northcliffe blamed Dawson for the government's alleged flabbiness. Before his departure, Dawson had the opportunity to observe the post-war peace negotiations in Paris with defeated Germany. 'All the world is here', Dawson wrote; 'It's like a gigantic cinema-show of eminent persons' (Dawson, letter of 18 Jan 1919, Dawson papers). But he had found Northcliffe's 'irresponsible Hun-baiting' (Lentin, 152) intolerable, and resigned his post. Already the seeds of Dawson's incarnation as an arch-appeaser had been sown.

As so often in Dawson's life, All Souls College provided a refuge and an encouragement, and on giving up the editor's chair he became estates bursar to the college. On 14 June 1919 he married Margaret Cecilia Lawley, the younger daughter of Sir Arthur Lawley, later sixth Baron Wenlock, who had been lieutenant-governor of the Transvaal from 1902 to 1906. They had one son and two daughters. The South African link was also renewed, as Dawson took up a directorship in the Consolidated Gold Fields of South Africa Company. He was, in addition, secretary to the Rhodes Trust from 1921 to 1922, and became a trustee in 1925. The interest in journalism was maintained by a temporary editorship of the *Round Table*, preserving the links with his Milnerite past.

Second period as editor Northcliffe, whose political machinations had been largely futile, died in August 1922, and this created the opportunity for Dawson to return to *The Times* as editor for a second time in January 1923. The new owners, John Jacob Astor and John Walter, were not interventionists in the Northcliffe mould, and Dawson's second term as editor lasted for nineteen years. A contemporary journalist found him at the peak of his power in the office of *The Times* to be 'urbane and friendly' (Grant Duff, 66). For most of this period, too, he was a pivotal figure in British politics, so that in 'the 1930s it can be said that Dawson was privy to more Cabinet thinking and secrets than most members of the government, whether the Prime Minister was MacDonald, Baldwin, or Chamberlain' (Cockett, 12). During the internal crisis over King Edward VIII's abdication in December 1936, Dawson's opposition to the royal position was crucial, as the other newspapers looked to *The Times* for a lead. Dawson had been concerned before the crisis burst that the contents of the American and foreign press 'have been percolating more and more in this country' (Jones, 289).

Dawson's closest relationship was with Lord Halifax, whose Eton, Oxford, and high Anglican antecedents he shared. Chamberlain shared his outlook on Anglo-German relations, but Dawson's influence over Stanley Baldwin may not have been as great as has sometimes been suggested. In 1936 Dawson wanted Baldwin and Hitler to meet, not in Berlin, but 'in Brussels or on the sea' (Jones, 220). No such meeting ever took place, which supports the more recent view that Baldwin kept his own counsel if advisers like Dawson 'were too unsympathetic to his own opinions, or intruded on sensitive questions' (Williamson, 72).

In reality, Dawson knew little about European affairs, and this weakness was exacerbated by his failure to appoint a foreign editor to succeed Harold Williams at *The Times* on the latter's death in 1928. His world was bounded by 'Printing House Square, Eton, All Souls and the moorland estate he inherited from an aunt in 1917' (Cowling, 128). He was on safer ground with domestic issues, although he could be condescending about Labour politicians like MacDonald and Thomas. He was a friend of leading Conservatives such as William Ormsby-Gore, Samuel Hoare, Thomas Inskip, and Anthony Eden as well of the Astors. A regular visitor to Cliveden, he could be counted upon to share Nancy Astor's pro-appeasement, pro-Chamberlain leanings.

Dawson was a mainstream Conservative. He was suspicious of the Labour Party, but supported Baldwin over reform in India, having toured there and written a series of articles in *The Times* advocating the policy which led to the Government of India Act (1935). Briefly in the later 1930s he seemed to be trying to revive the peace movement of the early thirties in concert with his friend Lord Lothian (the former Philip Kerr), the former member of Milner's kindergarten. But he was unenthusiastic about the League of Nations. Sometimes he could be daring, as when advocating Churchill's inclusion in the 1924 Conservative government, even if 'he was astounded at the use to which he was put' (Middlemas and Barnes, 283) at the exchequer. Yet he rightly saw that Baldwin was the key figure in Conservative politics then, as he was to be in the National Government after 1931. He wrote in a magisterial tone, saying that Baldwin's contribution to the cohesion of the National Government 'was a matter which history will assess and which perhaps only Mr MacDonald can yet appreciate' (*The Times*, 7 June 1935).

Appeasement It would be wrong also to see Dawson as merely a conduit for government opinions. During Italy's invasion of Ethiopia in the Abyssinian crisis of 1935–6, which brought about the resignation of Dawson's friend Samuel Hoare as foreign secretary, *The Times* was critical. It published many letters attacking government policy, and Dawson 'sketched out a leader trying to show the Government the strength of public feeling' (Wrench, 326). The leader duly appeared on 16 December 1935 under the unflattering heading 'A corridor for camels', a devastating critique of the government's attempt to hand over part of Ethiopia to Mussolini in collaboration with the French. Dawson saw no particular need to appease Mussolini, and 'as a Milnerite imperialist, he was suspicious of any attempt to upset the status quo in Africa' (Waley, 57). In this he differed from Chamberlain, who always favoured accommodation with the Italian dictator.

Dawson's views on appeasing Germany, although supported by his long-standing deputy Barrington-Ward, caused divisions in the office of *The Times*. These had already been evident when Dawson had edited the reports of the Berlin correspondent of *The Times*, Norman Ebbutt, whom he deemed too critical of the Nazis. Ultimately, Ebbutt was expelled from Germany in the summer of 1937, despite Dawson's attempt not to upset Nazi susceptibilities. For an anti-appeaser like Churchill's friend Robert Boothby, Dawson then became 'the Secretary General of the Establishment, the fervent advocate of Appeasement' (Rhodes James, 175). Dawson's position has been variously explained: an ignorance of Europe and of European history; too close a rapport with particular politicians; an empirical outlook lacking in principle (Rowse, 115). It is arguable, however, that his support for the Munich agreement stemmed primarily from his imperial concerns; he believed that war with Germany over Czechoslovakia in the autumn of 1938 'would have been misunderstood and resented from end to end of the Empire' (Dawson to Neville Chamberlain, 8 Nov 1940, Dawson papers, 81, fol. 48).

In the later phase of his second editorship, Dawson's leadership of *The Times* underwent a dramatic transformation. Previously stigmatized as a proponent of appeasement, Dawson advocated an energetic war policy and criticized Chamberlain's stewardship in the 'phoney war'. The noted military correspondent B. H. Liddell-Hart was forced to leave *The Times* in October 1939 because of his defeatism.

The damage had been done, however, and *The Times* suffered a considerable loss of prestige. Dawson himself remained unaware of how far his newspaper had been manipulated by Chamberlain and the press office of 10 Downing Street. His health failing, Dawson resigned from his post as editor on 30 September 1941. His last years were spent in retirement in north Yorkshire until his death at one of his homes, 24 Lowndes Street, London, on 7 November 1944.   PETER NEVILLE

Sources Bodl. Oxf., MSS Geoffrey Dawson · I. McDonald, *A man of The Times* (1976) · R. Cockett, *Twilight of truth* (1989) · J. E. Wrench, *Geoffrey Dawson and our Times* (1955) · [S. Morison and others], *The history of The Times*, 4 (1952) · A. Lentin, *Guilt at Versailles: Lloyd George and the pre-history of appeasement* (1985) · T. Jones, *A diary with letters, 1931–1950* (1954) · P. Williamson, *Stanley Baldwin* (1999) · M. Cowling, *The impact of Hitler* (1975) · K. Middlemas and J. Barnes, *Baldwin: a biography* (1969) · R. Rhodes James, *Bob Boothby: a portrait* (1991) · D. Waley, *British public opinion and the Abyssinian War* (1975) · S. Grant Duff, *The parting of ways: a personal account of the thirties* (1982) · S. E. Koss, *The rise and fall of the political press in Britain*, 2 (1984) · W. Nimocks, *Milner's young men: the kindergarten in Edwardian imperial affairs* (1968) · J. Lee Thompson, *Northcliffe: press baron in politics, 1865–1922* (2000) · A. L. Rowse, *All Souls and appeasement* (1961) · L. Heren, *Memories of Times past* (1988) · W. R. Louis, *In the name of God, go! Leo Amery and the British empire in the age of Churchill* (1992) · Burke, *Gen. GB* (1937) · *DNB* · *CGPLA Eng. & Wales* (1945)
Archives Bodl. Oxf., corresp., diaries, and papers · News Int. RO, corresp. and papers | BL, corresp. with Lord Cecil of Chelwood, Add. MS 51156 · BL, corresp. with Lord Northcliffe, Add. MSS 62243–62245 · BL OIOC, letters to Sir B. P. Blackett, MS Eur. E 397 · BL OIOC, corresp. with Sir S. H. Butler, MS Eur. F 116 · BLPES, corresp. with Violet Markham · Bodl. Oxf., corresp. with L. G. Curtis; Round Table corresp. · Bodl. Oxf., letters to Lady Milner · Bodl. Oxf., corresp. with Lord Simon · Bodl. RH, corresp. with J. H. Oldham · CAC Cam., Lord Halifax MSS · CUL, Baldwin MSS · HLRO, letters to Andrew Bonar Law · HLRO, corresp. with J. St L. Strachey · NA Scot., corresp. with Lord Lothian · National Archives of Zimbabwe, corresp. with Sir Francis Chaplin · News Int. RO, *The Times* Archive · NL Scot., corresp. with F. S. Oliver · U. Birm., Neville Chamberlain MSS · U. Reading L., corresp. with Nancy Astor | FILM BFI NFTVA, documentary footage
Likenesses W. Rothenstein, chalk drawing, 1923, NPG [*see illus.*] · O. Birley, group portrait, oils, 1937, News International, London · F. Dodd, oils, 1943, Bodl. RH · O. Birley, oils, Langcliffe Hall, Settle, Yorkshire · J. Gunn, oils, priv. coll.
Wealth at death £76,006 9s. 4d.: probate, except settled land, 3 Feb 1945, *CGPLA Eng. & Wales* · £50,507: further grant limited to settled land, 29 Nov 1945, *CGPLA Eng. & Wales*

Dawson, George (1636?–1700), jurist, was the son of William Dawson, a 'yeoman' of Lotherton, Yorkshire. Dawson was a boy of some promise, as he was educated at Sherborne School under Mr Clarke, and was admitted as a sizar at St John's College, Cambridge, on 16 April 1655, aged eighteen. He gained a BA in 1658–9 and an MA in 1662. His college presented him to the vicarage of Sunninghill, Berkshire, where he remained for the rest of his life.

Dawson was incorporated at Oxford in July 1669, and had married his wife, Anne, before July 1674 when a daughter was baptized at Sunninghill. They had at least five sons, all baptized at Sunninghill, three of whom survived to attend Cambridge University. Dawson wrote *Origo legum, or, A treatise of the origins of laws, and their obliging power; as also their great variety; and why some laws are immutable, and some are not; but may suffer change, or cease to be, or be suspended, or abrogated: in seven books* (1694), which was dedicated to King William and Queen Mary. Dawson was buried at Sunninghill on 5 October 1700, aged sixty-four. His wife died on 26 November 1711.   STUART HANDLEY

Sources Venn, *Alum. Cant.* · Foster, *Alum. Oxon.* · E. Ashmole, *The antiquities of Berkshire*, 2 (1719), 446 · IGI

Dawson, George (1821–1876), preacher and political activist, was born at 36 Hunter Street, London, on 24 February 1821, the son of a radical Baptist schoolmaster, Jonathan Dawson, and his wife, Rachel Biggs. He was educated, and later became a pupil teacher and then classics master, at his father's school, where for a time Charles Dickens was a fellow pupil. He abandoned a course at Marischal College, Aberdeen, in disgust in 1838, but graduated MA at Glasgow University in 1841: here he had been active in the University Liberal Association. He was called to the pastorate of Rickmansworth Baptist Church in 1843 but soon left, driven out, it was said, by the tory squire. In September 1844 he moved to Mount Zion Baptist Chapel, Birmingham, which he soon filled to overflowing by his brilliant, unorthodox addresses in which, among other things, he lauded Voltaire and cast doubts on the Christian character of Calvin. He left Mount Zion in 1846, ostensibly on the open communion issue, but in reality because his advanced teaching conflicted with the evangelical feelings of the older church members. On 24 August 1846 he married Susan Fanny Crompton; their two children were

George Dawson (1821–1876), by Henry John Whitlock

Rachel Anne (1848–1873), who was mentally handicapped, and Bernard (1851–1905), who became a civil engineer.

'To get religion out of the pale of the chapel into the fresh air of heaven and give it full exercise in that world which it came to beautify and animate', the church of the Saviour was built for Dawson by his many admirers and opened in August 1848. Here this handsome, charismatic orator, dressed more like a poet than a preacher, conducted worship from a platform, preaching a gospel of service and brotherhood, based on the example of Christ. But the 'chapel of the doubters', as it was called, was no plain lecture hall. It was brightly painted and adorned with flowers; its musical standards were high—it had a paid choir of twelve singers, and its own book of chants, anthems, and hymns (3rd edn, edited by Dawson and T. H. Gill, 1853). Dawson's prayers were beautifully crafted and the liturgy of the Christian year was observed. Popular Saturday evening concerts were held, as well as lectures for working people, adult classes, and church social gatherings—at that time a startling novelty. In all of these activities Susan Dawson played a prominent role. As a lecturer Dawson was in great demand, both within and outside Birmingham; in Manchester he was particularly popular. He accompanied Carlyle on his first visit to Germany and witnessed with Emerson a phase of the 1848 revolution in Paris. Later his chief significance may have been to popularize Carlyle's and Emerson's thought for the English middle and artisan classes.

Dawson was a friend of many continental radicals, especially Kossuth, the Hungarian nationalist, whom he greeted on his arrival in Britain in 1851. Out of this incident arose the curious Van Beck affair, when Dawson's fervent support for the Hungarian nationalist cause landed him in court, where he incurred a £500 fine. But Dawson was no stranger to controversy. In 1846 he crossed swords with the doughty evangelical Anglican Hugh Stowell of Manchester, who had accused him of spouting 'grandiloquent neologistic nonsense'. He clashed with the archbishop of York in 1847, the same year as the evangelical Congregationalist John Angell James arranged a secret meeting with Dawson in an effort to convert him.

In the life of Birmingham, Dawson's role was diverse. His friends and admirers on three separate occasions backed new local newspapers with Dawson as editor: the *Birmingham Mercury* (1848), the *Daily Free Press* (1855), and the *Birmingham Morning News* (1871). But none of these lasted long, for Dawson, who excelled as a flamboyant, if rather repetitious, orator, was far less at home with the written word. However, his contribution to the public library movement was undeniable: the Birmingham free libraries of the 1860s, the central lending library (1865), and the central reference library (1866) owed their inspiration to him and his friend Sam Timmins, as did the large Shakespeare collection housed in the reference library. He was one of the most active promoters of the Early Closing Association to reduce the excessive hours of Birmingham shop workers, and also of a campaign dubbed 'Lungs for the City', which helped to secure Aston Park as a public recreation area in 1858. It is perhaps as a precursor of Chamberlain and the municipal reform programme of the 1870s that Dawson is chiefly important in Birmingham's history. Most of the political remedies later popularized by Chamberlain he had anticipated—smallholdings (the Midland Freehold Land Association of 1847), secular schooling, extension of the franchise, sanitary reform, and slum clearance—while the Arts Club (1873), which he helped to found, was the forerunner of the Birmingham Liberal Club (1879). More generally it was his vision of God as pitying father and humanity as a prodigal son, and his profound engagement with discerning the mystery of order in the midst of man-made chaos, which gave ideological underpinning to the whole school of municipal reform: the church of the Saviour produced seventeen town councillors during Dawson's pastorate and, of these, six became mayor.

Dawson's fame as an emotional, witty, controversial, and thoroughly compelling speaker reached its climax in 1874 when he went on a lecture tour of the USA. He died suddenly at his home, Watford House, King's Norton, on 30 November 1876, following an aneurism of the larynx. The church of the Saviour struggled on until 1895, when it was sold to the Primitive Methodists. Several of his pamphlets were published in his lifetime, including two on the restoration of the Roman Catholic hierarchy (1850, 1851) in which he strongly upheld voluntaryism and disclaimed any 'no Popery' sentiment on his own part. After his death his wife edited selections from his sermons and lectures from his shorthand notes (4 vols., 1878–82) and two volumes of prayers which appeared in 1878 and 1883. Some of his biographical lectures were also published in two volumes (1886 and 1887). IAN SELLERS

Sources A. Ireland, *Recollections of George Dawson* (1884) · H. W. Crosskey, *Memoir of George Dawson* (1876) · W. Wilson, *The life of George Dawson* (1905) · E. P. Hennock, *Fit and proper persons: ideal and reality in nineteenth-century urban government* (1973) · L. Davidoff and C. Hall, *Family fortunes: men and women of the English middle class, 1780–1850* (1987)
Archives Birm. CA, corresp. and papers | U. Birm. L., corresp. with Thomas Winkworth
Likenesses W. F. Roden, portrait, 1874, Birm. CL · D. J. Pound, stipple and line engraving (after photograph by H. N. King), NPG · H. J. Whitlock, photograph, NPG [*see illus.*] · statue, Birm. CL
Wealth at death under £3000: probate, 15 Dec 1876, *CGPLA Eng. & Wales*

Dawson, George Mercer (1849–1901), geologist and anthropologist, was born in Pictou, Nova Scotia, on 1 August 1849, the son of Sir John William *Dawson (1820–1899), geologist, and Margaret Ann Young Mercer (*b.* 1829/30). His father became principal of McGill College in 1855, and the young Dawson attended Montreal high school in 1858. Tuberculosis of the spine (Pott's disease), which left him with some permanent physical disabilities, then confined his schooling to home. Nevertheless, from 1868 to 1869 Dawson studied at McGill, and in 1870 published a paper on the geographical distribution of foraminifers he had dredged for at Gaspe.

In 1869 Dawson travelled to England and enrolled at the Royal School of Mines, Kensington, where the intensive scientific training included fieldwork with the Geological Survey. Although his father remained notoriously anti-Darwinian, Dawson's studies with Thomas Huxley encouraged a modern evolutionary approach. Graduating with distinction and awards in 1872, he returned to Canada, where he taught at Morrin College, Quebec, before joining the international boundary survey from Lake of the Woods to British Columbia in 1874.

Dawson's *Report* (1875) established him as a brilliant field geologist, and guided future railway building and settlement in western Canada. He illuminated metamorphic and glacial influences upon Pleistocene structures; turned attention to Cretaceous formations, fossiliferous and younger than the Precambrian Shield of central Canada; added hundreds of specimens to the Kew and British Museum collections; mapped Tertiary lignites as crucial fuel sources; and documented locust invasions.

Dawson reaffirmed his remarkable ability to observe and extrapolate over vast expanses of complex terrain when he joined the geological survey of Canada (GSC) in 1875. Through arduous initial explorations in British Columbia and the Red, Assiniboine, Souris, Skeena, and Peace River regions, he related the British Cretaceous to the American Laramie formations. He also linked metamorphism in Canada to volcanic activity elsewhere. While retaining the older hypothesis that drifting icebergs best explained western Canada's surficial geology, Dawson gradually admitted evidence of continental ice sheets, especially in British Columbia. To significant theoretical accomplishments he added invaluable inventories of natural resources in these lands.

In British Columbia, Dawson also conducted important anthropological groundwork. He advocated education and even assimilation of indigenous peoples to prevent their outright extinction. A visit to the Queen Charlotte Islands in 1878 reinforced Dawson's appreciation of Haida culture as highly evolved. The shocking contrast of their diminishing population prompted rich ethnological appendices to his geological report (1879), with warnings that Haida concepts of property demanded government consideration. Further pioneering researches in ethnology brought appointments by the British Association for the Advancement of Science, to direct studies of northwestern tribes in 1884 and to chair an ethnological survey of Canada in 1897.

Dawson also discovered fossil evidence of dinosaurs near Lake of the Woods in 1874, and subsequently along Red Deer River (Alberta). As his anthropological collections called for a national repository that became the Canadian Museum of Civilization, his palaeontological collections grew into the department of vertebrate palaeontology of the National Museum of Natural Sciences. Meanwhile, his geological fieldwork proceeded apace along the Bow and Belly rivers, and into the Rocky and Selkirk mountain ranges. His enthusiasm for exploitation of Albertan coal inspired both entrepreneurs and the House of Commons standing committee on immigration and colonization. Numerous authoritative publications included a cumulative geological map (1887); a study of the mineral wealth of British Columbia (1889), encouraging lode mining in the cordilleras; and an eloquent plea for continued exploration and mapping in Canada (1890).

In 1887 Dawson led a survey into the Yukon territory, long rumoured to harbour placer gold deposits. When glacial patterns supported these hopes, he delineated access routes and a location for the disputed Alaska boundary. Dawson's report sold out two editions, and was widely believed to have heralded the gold rush in the Klondike, which his survey had not actually reached. Dawson City was accordingly named for him in 1898.

Dawson's remarkable field achievements multiplied his administrative responsibilities. He became an assistant director of the GSC in 1883, then acting director while A. R. C. Selwyn travelled abroad in 1885–6. Honours included fellowship in the Royal Society of London and the Geological Society of London's Bigsby medal in 1891; appointment as CMG for aiding Britain in the Bering Sea dispute in 1892; several honorary doctorates; the associate editorship of the *Journal of Geology* (Chicago); and the presidency of the Royal Society of Canada in 1893. He succeeded Selwyn as director of the GSC in 1895.

Dawson's accession fulfilled a long-time ambition. While the GSC's morale and public image required refurbishing, he also hoped to emphasize detailed mapping. The election of Wilfrid Laurier's Liberal government in 1896 and the Klondike gold rush instead intensified public expectations of mineral resources. Like Selwyn, Dawson heeded both scientific and economic calls, suffering criticism for failing to increase funding while his own honours continued to pour in. In 1897 he presided over the geological section of the BAAS in Toronto, led a transcontinental geological excursion by rail, and won the Royal Geographical Society's gold medal. In 1898 he became vice-president of the Canadian Institute of Mining, and in 1900 president of the Geological Society of America.

Allegedly a chain-smoker, Dawson succumbed to bronchitis, dying at Victoria Chambers, Ottawa, on 2 March 1901, shocking many who took his awesome accomplishments for granted; he was buried in Montreal. Although the GSC's internal rivalries and structural difficulties remained unresolved, he had raised the institution to new scientific heights. Eloquent tributes fitted the indefatigable explorer whose work laid the foundation for immense wealth and economic expansion in Canada's new century.   SUZANNE ZELLER

Sources *The Globe* [Toronto] (4 March 1901) · H. M. Ami, *Ottawa Naturalist* (May 1901), 43–52 · R. W. Shannon, *The Commonwealth* (March 1901), 50 · W. J. M. [W. J. McGee], *American Anthropologist*, new ser., 3 (1901), 159–63 · F. D. Adams, *Bulletin of the Geological Society of America*, 13 (1902), 498–509 · B. J. Harrington, *Proceedings and Transactions of the Royal Society of Canada*, 2nd ser., 2 (1902), section 4, pp. 183–92 · M. Reeks, *Register of the associates and old students of the Royal School of Mines* (1920) · P. R. Eakins, 'George Mercer Dawson, 1849–1901, citizen and scientist', *Proceedings of the Geological Association of Canada*, 23 (1971), 19–23 · A. H. Land, 'G. M. Dawson and the economic development of western Canada', *Canadian Public Administration*, 14 (1971), 236–55 · J. van West, 'George Mercer Dawson: an early Canadian anthropologist', *Anthropological Journal of Canada*, 14/4 (1976), 8–12 · M. Zaslow, *Reading the rocks: the story of the geological survey of Canada* (1975) · R. A. Richardson and B. H. MacDonald, *Science and technology in Canadian history: a bibliography of primary sources to 1914* (1987) · H. J. Morgan, ed., *The Canadian men and women of the time* (1898)
Archives Geological Survey of Canada, Ottawa, *Reports of progress* and director's letter-books · McGill University, Montreal
Likenesses photograph, McCord Museum of Canadian History, Montreal, Notman Photographic Archives; repro. in G. Woodcock, *Faces from history* (1973), 15 · photographs, Geological Survey of Canada, Ottawa

Dawson, Grahame George (1895–1944), air force officer, was born in East Finchley, Middlesex, on 18 March 1895, the second of the three children of Albert Dawson (1866–1930), a journalist, editor, and (from 1901 to 1919) principal proprietor of the weekly *Christian Commonwealth*, and his wife, Annie Hutchison Grahame, of Dunbar, East Lothian, Scotland. He was educated first at Tollington School, Muswell Hill, then at the Northern Polytechnic, London, and finally at University College, London, from October 1911, where he graduated BSc (Engineering) in June 1914. He joined the Royal Naval division in October 1914 as a dispatch rider and transferred to the Royal Naval Air Service in February 1915 as a prospective pilot. He learned to fly at Eastchurch, Isle of Sheppey, Kent, was commissioned as a flight sub-lieutenant in June, and acquired the nickname Horse (from his initials GG) which it took him twenty years to suppress.

On 31 August 1915 Dawson went with 2 wing to the island of Imbros in the Aegean to assist the Dardanelles campaign, but he suffered a fractured skull and a severely

Grahame George Dawson (1895–1944), by unknown photographer

injured right hand in a crash landing on 12 October and was invalided home a month later. On 28 April 1916 he was found unfit to resume flying duties and the next day he joined the engineering branch of the Royal Naval Volunteer Reserve as a lieutenant. After service as an instructor, he joined the Admiralty's air department and began his lifelong specialization in aero-engine problems.

Dawson was granted a commission as a captain (technical) in the newly formed Royal Air Force on 1 April 1918. From 1920 to 1925 he served as chief technical officer at the engine repair depot, Abbassia, Cairo. 'This class of work has always appealed to me most,' he recalled in an essay written at the staff college, Andover, Hampshire, in 1930, 'and it was a great interest to build up special tools and all the equipment necessary to enable the depot to operate efficiently' ('Service experiences').

On returning to England in 1925 Dawson learned to fly again and then joined 39 (bomber) squadron at Spittalgate, Lincolnshire. He was promoted squadron leader in July 1927 and seconded in October to the Royal Australian Air Force for two years. He was director of technical services in Melbourne, the home of his brother Albert (Bertie), who had emigrated to Australia. During 1930 he attended the RAF Staff College, where he was taught by Arthur Tedder, later a great commander with whom Dawson formed a vital wartime partnership in Egypt. From 1931 to 1933 he was employed on engineering staff duties at the Uxbridge (west London) headquarters of the air defence of Great Britain. In July 1934 he was promoted wing commander and took charge of the officers' engineering course at the school of aeronautical engineering, Henlow, Bedfordshire.

Dawson was promoted again, to group captain, in November 1938 and appointed Fighter Command's chief engineering officer at Bentley Priory, north London. In April 1940 he went to the Air Ministry as director of the department of repairs and maintenance. His experience, energy, readiness to improvise, disdain for routine, and forthright manner commended him to Lord Beaverbrook, who was appointed to head a new Ministry of Aircraft Production in May 1940. Dawson was transferred to that ministry, promoted to air commodore, given responsibility for engine repairs throughout the rest of that critical year, and promoted air vice-marshal in November.

At Beaverbrook's request Dawson was sent to Cairo in May 1941 to report on aircraft repair, salvage, and maintenance problems. Tedder, now air commander in the Middle East, created for him, despite intense Air Ministry opposition, a new post—chief maintenance and supply officer—independent of the established administrative organization. He supported Dawson's brusque methods because he shared his determination to get every possible aircraft into the sky. Dawson employed thousands of Egyptian civilians, as well as RAF personnel, in numerous small workshops and garages in Cairo to repair and even manufacture spare parts for airframes, engines, and guns. He had ancient caves at Tura, south of Cairo, reopened for major repair and production work in conditions that were safe from aerial attack, spacious, and relatively cool. He also created a transport organization to recover smashed aircraft from the desert and bring them back to Cairo, either for repair or as sources of spares. He established excellent working relations with American suppliers and technical staffs. Not least, he thought of many modifications to equipment that improved performance. Without his efforts, wrote the *Egyptian Mail* on 8 December 1942, 'the air battle of Egypt could never have been won. He is the man responsible for ensuring that the airman has an aircraft to fly and materials to feed it with.' Tedder praised him highly as 'a whirlwind "action this day" man', who 'set up in Egypt a service and repair organisation which literally saved the situation' (Tedder, 416). He was appointed CBE in January 1942 and CB in November the same year.

When Tedder moved to Algiers in January 1943, he took Dawson with him to ensure that he was never short of aircraft during the campaigns of that year in Tunisia, Sicily, and Italy. Harold Macmillan, Churchill's personal representative in north Africa, learned that Dawson was 'responsible for all the wonderful repair organisation of the RAF', and found him 'a most attractive and interesting personality ... the most intelligent man I know out here' (*War Diaries*, 122–3, 380).

Dawson flew from Maison Blanche in Algiers on 14 November 1944 to attend a conference in Paris of maintenance experts and to visit Tedder, now deputy supreme commander under General Eisenhower. His aircraft was a four-engined B-24 Liberator bomber, which he had had repaired after the Americans abandoned it as unserviceable. At about 12.30 p.m., near Autun in eastern France, some 10 miles north of Le Creusot, the Liberator flew into a hillside during a violent snowstorm. All eleven persons aboard were killed, eight servicemen and three French civilians. The servicemen were buried initially in Autun military cemetery, but in September 1950 they were moved to Choloy British cemetery, near Toul. Dawson lies in plot 2A, row A, grave 13. Within the hour of his death, the same storm killed Air Chief Marshal Sir Trafford Leigh-Mallory and all aboard his aircraft in a crash some 15 miles east of Grenoble and 150 miles south of Autun.

Dawson was a small man who carried himself very erect, was always smartly dressed, moved quickly, and spoke bluntly. He had thick black hair, a dark complexion, and strong features, usually set in an expression so severe that few men, even of higher rank in service or civilian life, dared to cross him. It may be that the injuries he suffered to his head and hand on Imbros helped to shorten his temper. On the other hand, he could be perfectly charming to those whom he respected. He married Margery Hope Charles (*b.* 1892), daughter of Thomas Charles, solicitor, of Stow on the Wold, Gloucestershire, in the parish church at Monken Hadley, Middlesex, on 9 September 1916. They had a son, Lindsay Grahame, born on 6 November 1917.

'He rendered services to this country which must give him a place in British history,' wrote Beaverbrook to Dawson's widow on 20 November 1944, 'and there can be no doubt that the record will disclose the vital part he played in the final triumph, both during the Battle of Britain and in his subsequent tasks in the Middle East' (private information). VINCENT ORANGE

Sources private information (2004) [personal collections of M. I. Faid and Anthea Lewis] · [Lord Tedder], *With prejudice: the war memoirs of marshal of the Royal Air Force, Lord Tedder* (1966) · 'Service experiences', 1930, PRO, AIR 1/2391/228/11/141 · *Egyptian Mail* (8 Dec 1942) · *The Times* (5 Dec 1944) · H. Macmillan, *War diaries: politics and war in the Mediterranean, January 1943 – May 1945* (1984) · *Muswell Hill Record and Friern Barnet Journal* (14 Feb 1930) · D. Richard and H. St G. Saunders, *Royal Air Force, 1939–1945*, 2 (1954); rev. edn (1975)
Archives priv. coll.
Likenesses photographs, priv. coll. [*see illus.*]
Wealth at death £2186 1s. 7d.: probate, 1 May 1945, CGPLA Eng. & Wales

Dawson, Henry (1811–1878), landscape painter, was born on 3 April 1811 in Waterhouse Lane, Hull, the second and only surviving child of William Dawson (*d.* 1826), cheesemonger and flax dresser, and his second wife, Hannah Moore, *née* Shardlow (1775–1844). Hull was only a temporary residence, and the year after he was born his parents moved back to Nottingham, where he spent the first half of his life. His father took to drink, and the burden of keeping the household together fell on his mother. Dawson had no formal education—apart from a year and a half at the national school in Nottingham—and at the age of eight was sent out to work, at first in a rope-walk and then in a lace manufactory. He was drawn to painting early but could only practise it in what little spare time he had. In 1835 he took the risk of abandoning the lace industry to become a professional artist. His formal training as a painter was limited to twelve lessons from J. B. Pyne in June 1838; nevertheless, he enjoyed some early success in Nottingham and began to exhibit landscapes in London, at the Royal Academy from 1838 and the British Institution from 1841.

The market for landscape painting in Nottingham proved to be very limited, however, and by the early 1840s Dawson's income had fallen drastically. He had married Elizabeth Whittle (*d.* 1879) on 16 June 1840 and they had already begun a family; the decline of his prospects in Nottingham, together with the death of his mother, determined him in October 1844 to take another gamble and move to Liverpool in the hope of finding a more lucrative market there. He began to exhibit at the Liverpool Academy, becoming an associate in 1846 and a full member the following year. In 1847 he felt confident enough to compete for the decoration of the new houses of parliament, sending in his most ambitious composition to date, *Charles I Raising his Standard, 24 August 1642* (Castle Museum, Nottingham); his entry was not successful, though the painting was sold privately and remains one of his best-known pictures. It was during his Liverpool period that he first began to paint the marine subjects which would become a staple of his repertory.

At the beginning of 1850 Dawson moved south in the hope of establishing his reputation in the London art world. He lived at Croydon until late 1853, at Thorpe Green, near Chertsey, until 1861, and then briefly at Camberwell in London before moving in 1862 to Chiswick, where he lived until his death. At first success still eluded him. He reached a crisis in 1851, when he contemplated giving up art and setting up as a shopkeeper; he sought John Ruskin's advice and received sufficient encouragement to persevere. His work continued to appeal mainly to provincial patrons, and although he exhibited regularly at the Royal Academy, he complained that the hanging committees never did justice to his pictures. In 1868 he was nominated for election as an ARA but only received one vote. He fared much better at the British Institution, where he showed a series of key pictures—*The Wooden Walls of England* (exh. 1854; smaller version 1856, City of Birmingham Museum and Art Gallery), *British Bulwarks* (exh. 1856), and *The New Houses of Parliament, Westminster* (1858, priv. coll.)—and he was certainly hurt by the closure of the institution in 1867. In the 1870s his prices rose sharply and he enjoyed a few years of financial security, though his health had deteriorated by this period. In July 1878 he was honoured by a retrospective exhibition of fifty-seven of his paintings to mark the opening of the Nottingham Castle Museum and Art Gallery.

Dawson's early paintings were in a conservative idiom, much indebted to Richard Wilson. Later, Turner became the dominant influence: some critics considered Dawson one of the main contenders for Turner's mantle after the latter's death in 1851. The work of his middle and later years combines conventional subject matter with often elaborate composition and shows a preference for patriotic or emblematically English motifs and complicated skies. Dawson was always a 'loving admirer of [his] own work'; surveying his retrospective exhibition in 1878, he wrote 'My pictures delighted me; they are a grand show—kings in art. I don't think the work of any landscape painter living or dead could be put in competition with them' (Dawson, 119). His reputation has always lagged behind this glowing self-estimation. Henry Dawson died on 13 December 1878 at his home, The Cedars, Chiswick, and was buried in Brompton cemetery, London. His wife survived him.

The main sources of information on Dawson are the letters and reminiscences which were included in the *Life* published by his son Alfred in 1891; they reveal a man whose unswerving self-belief sustained him in the face of innumerable discouragements. His mixed fortunes did not deter his two eldest sons, Henry Thomas Dawson and Alfred Dawson, from following in his footsteps as artists. (He had seven children altogether, though two of them died young.) Dawson's paintings are in the collections of Nottingham Castle Museum and Art Gallery; the Usher Art Gallery, Lincoln; the Ferens Art Gallery, Hull; and the Yale Center for British Art, New Haven, Connecticut, USA.   NICHOLAS ALFREY

Sources A. Dawson, *The life of Henry Dawson, landscape painter* (1891) · H. Williams, *Henry Dawson, 1811–1878: centenary exhibition* (1978) · H. Williams, 'The lives and work of Nottingham artists from 1750–1914, with special consideration of their association with the lace industry and society at large', PhD diss., U. Nott., 1981 · Graves, *Brit. Inst.* · Graves, *RA exhibitors*, 2 (1905), 274 · H. C. Marillier, *The Liverpool school of painters: an account of the Liverpool Academy from 1810 to 1867, with memoirs of the principal artists* (1904) · B. Webber, *James Orrock: painter, connoisseur, collector* (1903) · *DNB* · *CGPLA Eng. & Wales* (1879)

Likenesses H. Dawson, self-portrait, oils, 1840–52, Nottingham Castle Museum and Art Gallery; version, priv. coll. · H. Dawson, self-portrait, oils, 1840–52, U. Nott. · two photographs, 1860–79, Nottinghamshire County Library, Local Studies Library · S. Redgate, oils, Nottingham Castle Museum and Art Gallery

Wealth at death under £7000: probate, 29 Jan 1879, *CGPLA Eng. & Wales*

Dawson, James (1716/17–1746), Jacobite army officer, was born at Salford, the eldest of the four children of William Dawson, apothecary of Manchester, and his first wife, Elizabeth, daughter of Richard Allen of Redivales in Bury, Lancashire, and a first cousin of the poet and stenographer John Byrom. Educated at Mr Clayton's school, Manchester, he was admitted to Lincoln's Inn on 23 January 1734. Dawson then entered St John's College, Cambridge, on 21 October 1737, at the age of twenty, with the intention of joining the church. He matriculated in the following December. However, his was not a lengthy undergraduate career for, having become 'acquainted with the rakes of the university, he run all manner of lengths with them' until, facing expulsion, he left the college. Nevertheless, there is nothing to show that he had ever been subjected to any punishment for any offence in the university court held by the vice chancellor.

In November 1745, aware that the army of Charles Edward Stuart was approaching Manchester, Dawson joined the Jacobite forces, where he gained a captain's commission. He proved a willing recruit, being:

> so hearty in the cause, that he beat up for voluntiers himself, and took fellows in Manchester to enlist. In all their marches he appeared at the head of his company, and when the young Pretender made a general review of his army at Macclesfield, he passed before him with the usual formalities. He likewise at Carlisle, mounted guard there, and was called captain, and was among the rest of the officers at the surrender of the town [in December 1745]. (*State trials*, 18.374–5)

Dawson was tried and convicted of high treason on 17 July 1746 and was one of eight officers belonging to the

Manchester regiment of volunteers who were hanged, drawn, and quartered on Kennington Common on 30 July 1746. According to a traditional story, had Dawson been pardoned, the day of his execution would have been the day of his marriage to Katherine Norton, 'a young lady of good family and handsome fortune'. She is said to have followed him to the place of execution accompanied by friends and, seeing 'the fire kindled which was to consume the heart she knew so much devoted to her, and all the other dreadful preparations for his fate', drew her head back into the coach, and, crying out, 'My dear, I follow thee—I follow thee! Sweet Jesus, receive both our souls together', expired in the very moment she was speaking (*State trials*, 18.374–5). This incident was made the subject of a popular ballad by William Shenstone.

GORDON GOODWIN, *rev.* DAVIE HORSBURGH

Sources *The private journal and literary remains of John Byrom*, ed. R. Parkinson, 2 vols. in 4 pts, Chetham Society, 32, 34, 40, 44 (1854–7) · T. W. Barlow, ed., *Cheshire and Lancashire Historical Collector*, 2 (1854), 27–9, 32, 33–6 · J. Harland, *Ballads and songs of Lancashire chiefly older than the 19th century* (1865) · *A genuine account of the behaviour, confession and dying words of Francis Townly* (1746) · *True copies of the dying declarations of Arthur, Lord Balmerino* (1750) · BL, Egerton MS 2000, fol. 102 · *State trials* · Venn, *Alum. Cant.*

Dawson, John (*bap.* 1735, *d.* 1820), mathematician and surgeon, was born at Raygill Farm in Garsdale, near Sedbergh in Yorkshire, the younger of the two sons of William Dawson and his wife, Mary, and was baptized on 25 February 1735. Accounts of his life have tended to stress the extreme poverty of his background. But Raygill was, in fact, a rather substantial property, and William Dawson, who was described by Adam Sedgwick as 'a very poor statesman [a small landowner] … with perhaps not more than £10 or £12 a year' (Clark and Hughes, 61), belonged to one of the older and more prosperous families of the dale. After a rudimentary education at the Revd Charles Udal's school in Garsdale, John worked until he was about twenty as a shepherd on his father's freehold, developing an interest in mathematics in his spare time with the aid of books that he bought with the profits from stocking knitting or borrowed from his elder brother, who had become an excise officer. Despite being entirely self-taught he worked up his own system of conic sections and began to establish himself as a teacher of mathematics, often spending two or three months at a time in the houses of his pupils.

What began as a purely local reputation spread quickly, from 1756, when three young men, including the future physician John Haygarth, and Adam Sedgwick's father, Richard Sedgwick, read with him before going up to Cambridge. But the profession on which Dawson embarked was that of a surgeon. In this he was influenced by Henry Bracken, the eminent Lancaster surgeon, with whom he worked as an assistant and pupil. For a year, back in Sedbergh, he practised as a surgeon and then, with his accumulated savings of £100 stitched in his clothing, walked to Edinburgh to study medicine and mathematics. Despite his frugality he could not stay long enough to take a

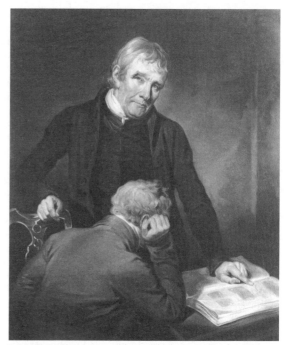

John Dawson (*bap.* 1735, *d.* 1820), by William Whiston Barney, pubd 1809 (after Joseph Allen)

degree and he returned to Sedbergh to resume his practice and save in preparation for another austere period of study, this time in London. His stay in the capital was brief, but he gained experience in the London hospitals, attended surgical and medical lectures, and made a contact, with Edward Waring, the Lucasian professor of mathematics at Cambridge, that was to be important for his future work as a mathematician. Returning to Sedbergh with a diploma, he made his practice the best in the northwestern dales and soon enjoyed security, even prosperity. On 3 March 1767 he married Ann Thirnbeck of Middleton, near Sedbergh. The one daughter of the marriage, Mary, born on 15 January 1768, was to be an important companion to Dawson in his later years, following the death of his wife in 1812.

For over twenty years Dawson maintained his medical practice while also pursuing his work as a mathematician, and it was only from about 1790 that he devoted himself exclusively to mathematical teaching. By then his fame as a teacher was attracting a regular stream of pupils, including Cambridge undergraduates who read with him during the long vacation and others, many, though by no means all of them, from the local area, who were preparing for entry to the university. For a fee of about 5s. a week for unlimited tuition, in addition to the cost of accommodation and food, sometimes in Dawson's house but more commonly in a local inn, pupils were taught in a characteristic peripatetic fashion. As Adam Sedgwick, who read with him in 1804 before going up to Cambridge and subsequently during vacations, recalled, Dawson would seat his pupils, often a dozen or more, at tables about the house and move constantly from one to another, correcting and advising. Dawson's method, developed at a time when the standard of teaching in the ancient universities was at a low ebb, had remarkable results. Between 1781 and 1794, at least seven, possibly eight, of the fourteen senior wranglers at Cambridge had been taught by him, as had four others between 1797 and 1807. Among these eminent Dawsonians were the future chancery barrister John Bell, the Arabist John Palmer, the lawyer and anti-slavery campaigner Thomas Harrison, James Inman, who went on to become professor of mathematics at the Royal Naval College, Portsmouth, and George Butler, later headmaster of Harrow and dean of Peterborough, whose vivid account of the journey of almost five days between London and Sedbergh and his introduction to Dawson was published in *The Sedberghian* for December 1881 (2, 79–80). Pupils who went on to Cambridge and did not achieve the rank of senior wrangler included, in addition to Richard and Adam Sedgwick and Haygarth, the lord chief justice Sir Nicholas Conyngham Tindal, the mathematician Miles Bland, who (like many of Dawson's pupils) was a boy at Sedbergh School, and several bishops. Among those whose medical interests took them to Edinburgh rather than Cambridge were Robert Willan, Thomas Garnett, and George Birkbeck.

Dawson maintained his active engagement in mathematics into his seventies. But from 1812, with his memory and physical strength failing, he took no further pupils. Except through his teaching he left little in the way of a mathematical legacy. An anonymous correspondent writing from Trinity College, Cambridge, in the *European Magazine* (40, 1801, 406–7) urged the university to recognize his status as the first mathematician of England by awarding him an honorary degree. But such an assessment of Dawson's achievements was extravagant. His original contributions to mathematics were not numerous, and while they did not pass unnoticed, the only formal honour they brought him was the very minor one of election as a corresponding member of the Manchester Literary and Philosophical Society.

Dawson, in fact, never fully overcame the handicap of his isolation from the main centres of intellectual life, and he remained a victim both of the limited extent of his work and of the obscurity of the form in which it appeared. His earliest and most substantial publication was his *Four Propositions*, which appeared anonymously in 1769 in an edition that was largely destroyed by fire. In it Dawson identified errors in the calculation that had led Matthew Stewart, the professor of mathematics at Edinburgh, to overestimate the distance between the earth and the sun by more than a quarter. It was characteristic of him that, despite his reputation for modesty and a lack of worldly ambition, he pursued his argument vigorously when he was attacked by Samuel Horley in the *Philosophical Transactions of the Royal Society*; his reply in the *Gentleman's Magazine* (40, 1770, 452–3) made no concessions and reinforced the respect in which he was held by several Edinburgh mathematicians and natural philosophers, including John Playfair, Lord Webb Seymour, and

Henry Lord Brougham, all of whom visited him in Sedbergh. By comparison with *Four Propositions* his other mathematical publications were slight. The most important of them was a series of rather combative letters signed 'Wadson' and published in Charles Hutton's *Miscellanea mathematica* (1775), in which he criticized a paper by Charles Wildbore on the velocity of water emerging from vessels in motion. Less important but more acrimonious in the response that it engendered was an exchange in which Dawson took the side of Thomas Simpson against the cantankerous William Emerson by offering an independent analytical demonstration of the existence of an error in Newton's treatment of precession.

Dawson's interests also embraced metaphysics and theology, subjects that he explored in correspondence with a favourite early pupil, the Revd Thomas Wilson, headmaster of the grammar schools first in Slaidburn and then in Clitheroe. Described by Adam Sedgwick as 'a firm believer and a good sober practical Christian of the old school' (Clark and Hughes, 68), Dawson abhorred the doctrines of David Hume and applauded James Beattie's attack on Humean scepticism. In a similar spirit he wrote against Joseph Priestley's *The Doctrine of Philosophical Necessity* (1777), which he regarded as immoral in tendency and false. His 24-page pamphlet outlining his views on the damaging consequences and unsure foundations of an acceptance of determinism, *The Doctrine of Philosophical Necessity Briefly Invalidated* (1781), elicited a dismissive, unsigned rejoinder in the *Monthly Review* (65, 1781, 66–8), which he answered in an appendix to a second edition of the work in 1803. Although Dawson is said to have retained the respect of Priestley and his other adversaries, his contribution lacked the sophistication that the debate demanded at the highest level and it made little lasting mark.

The impact that Dawson had on those who knew him was heightened by a commanding physical presence well conveyed in the portraits that survive of him. The original of one of the portraits, painted by Joseph Allen in 1809 and showing Dawson teaching a seated pupil, had already been lost by the mid-nineteenth century, but it survived in the form of a copy by the vicar of Sedbergh, the Revd D. M. Peacock, and an engraving by W. W. Barney. The other, a watercolour painted by William Westall in 1817 of a sombre and very elderly Dawson, went to private hands. Striking though Dawson's appearance was, however, he was revered above all for his simplicity of manner and a cheerful, benevolent temperament that left him, in Adam Sedgwick's words, 'without any stiffness or affectation of superiority' (Clark and Hughes, 69). His pupils remained especially loyal to him. In his later life they presented him with a fine set of plate and when he died, on 19 September 1820, they erected a monument high in the nave of St Andrew's Church in Sedbergh, the church where he was buried, in the form of a bust of him by Robert William Sievier, with an eloquent inscription, dated August 1825, by his former pupil John Bell.   ROBERT FOX

Sources J. W. Clark and T. M. Hughes, *The life and letters of the Reverend Adam Sedgwick*, 1 (1890) · *Public characters of 1801–1802* (1802) ·

G. Pryme, *Autobiographic recollections of George Pryme*, ed. A. Bayne (1870) · *A short account of the late Thomas Harrison, Esq.. of Streatham Park, in the county of Surrey* (1825) · *Miscellanies: being a selection from the poems and correspondence of the Rev. Thomas Wilson, with memoirs of his life*, ed. F. R. Raines, Chetham Society, 45 (1857), 105–24 · *N&Q*, 5th ser., 5 (1876), 87, 135, 231, 419 · *N&Q*, 5th ser., 6 (1876), 316 · *N&Q*, 5th ser., 7 (1877), 197 · W. Thompson, *Sedbergh, Garsdale, and Dent: peeps at the past history and present condition of some picturesque Yorkshire dales* (1892) · A. Sedgwick, *Supplement to the memorial of the trustees of Cowgill Chapel* (1870)

Likenesses J. Allen, portrait, 1809; formerly priv. coll. (now lost); D. M. Peacock, copy; formerly priv. coll. · W. W. Barney, mezzotint, pubd 1809 (after J. Allen), BM, NPG, Wellcome L. [*see illus.*] · W. Westall, watercolour, 1817, priv. coll.; repro. in Clark and Hughes, *Life and letters of the Reverend Adam Sedgwick*, facing p. 70 · R. W. Sievier, bust, 1825, St Andrew's Church, Sedbergh, Cumbria

Dawson, John (1827–1903), racehorse trainer, was born at Stamford Hall, Gullane, East Lothian, on 16 December 1827. He was a younger son in the family of seventeen children of George Dawson (*d.* 1846), who had previously trained horses at Bogside, in Ayrshire, and his wife, Jean Alison. Three brothers who survived infancy, Thomas (*d.* 1880), Joseph (*d.* 1880), and Matthew *Dawson, also became successful trainers. All were brought up about their father's training stable at Gullane. Thomas, the eldest, left Gullane in 1830, and settled at Middleham, in Yorkshire, where he trained for Lord Eglinton. In 1838 he was joined by his brother Matthew as head lad, and later Joseph and John also served there.

In 1855 Dawson married Grant Peddie, and two years later he left Middleham and bought Roden House, at Compton, Berkshire, a village which adjoins Ilsley where his brother Joseph trained. In 1861 he moved to Warren House, Newmarket, where he lived for the remainder of his life. Shortly after settling at Newmarket he was appointed private trainer to Prince Batthyany, although others were invited by the prince to keep horses there. When Prince Batthyany died in 1883 his executors sold his horses and John Dawson thus missed the chance to train the outstanding St Simon, that opportunity instead going to his brother Matthew, who trained for the purchaser of the horse, the duke of Portland.

Dawson died at his home on 13 May 1903 and was interred in Newmarket cemetery. He had given up training in 1900 with four classic wins to his credit. His son George took over the Warren House stables. Another son, John Alfred Dawson, was a trainer at Newmarket. A daughter, Helen Rose, married the jockey Fred Archer in 1883 but died in childbirth the following year.

EDWARD MOORHOUSE, *rev.* WRAY VAMPLEW

Sources R. Mortimer, R. Onslow, and P. Willett, *Biographical encyclopedia of British flat racing* (1978) · T. McConnell, *The tartan turf* (1988) · J. Fairfax-Blakeborough, *Northern turf history* (1973) · *Sportsman and Sporting Life* (14 May 1903) · E. M. Humphris, *The life of Matthew Dawson* (1928) · CGPLA Eng. & Wales (1903)

Likenesses G. J. Stodart, engraving, pubd 1908 (after Hills & Saunders), NPG [*see illus.*] · Spy [L. Ward], group portrait, caricature, chromolithograph (*On the heath*), NPG; repro. in *VF* (26 Nov 1896)

Wealth at death £33,188 6s. 9d.: probate, 8 July 1903, CGPLA Eng. & Wales

Dawson, Sir John William (1820–1899), geologist and educationist, was born on 13 October 1820 in Pictou, Nova

John Dawson (1827–1903), by George J. Stodart, pubd 1908 (after Hills & Saunders)

Scotia, the elder of the two sons of James Dawson (1789–1858?), then a merchant and later a bookseller, and Mary Rankine of Stirlingshire. Mary, whose parents had died when she was young, was raised by relatives in Edinburgh, possibly the Boyds of the well-known firm of booksellers Oliver and Boyd. James Dawson was also Scottish, from Ordiquhill, in the north. By the time William (as he was always called by family and friends) was born, James Dawson had embarked on a career as a bookseller, enabling him eventually to discharge earlier debts incurred in maritime trade. William Dawson's intense earnestness and self-reliance were honed in this environment, where his parents constantly struggled to make ends meet. Frugality was probably as important as piety in the Dawson household, both giving him an inescapable and omnipresent seriousness of purpose.

Although lacking in material wealth, Dawson had access to a good education at Pictou Academy, which provided him and his peers with a firm grounding in a range of subjects, especially in the natural sciences. It housed an extensive collection of scientific apparatus, a small natural history museum, and a library with a remarkable assortment of treatises in natural philosophy and natural history. Physically the coastal town was surrounded by rich sandstone and shale rock formations, which contained Carboniferous fossil plants. These provided fertile ground for Dawson's first scientific explorations, and allowed him to put together a respectable collection of geological and palaeontological specimens. When he was

Sir John William Dawson (1820–1899), by unknown engraver, pubd 1886 (after Notman & Sandham)

sixteen he delivered a paper, 'The structure and history of the earth', to the Pictou Literary and Scientific Society.

In 1840, at the age of twenty, Dawson decided to return to his parents' homeland, where he matriculated at the University of Edinburgh and studied natural history. Although he remained fiercely proud of his birthplace and sensitive to any charges of hailing from the backwoods, Canadian life must have seemed impoverished compared to the riches of Edinburgh, a city still riding the fame of its golden years. Financial difficulties called him back to Pictou at the end of the academic year but he subsequently returned to Edinburgh in 1847, to extend his studies and to marry Margaret Ann Young Mercer (b. 1829/30), a distant cousin and the daughter of a lace merchant. (Later, as principal of McGill University, he received an MA from the University of Edinburgh in 1856 and an LLD in 1884.) So smitten was he with Edinburgh and its university that he stood unsuccessfully for posts there on two later occasions.

Dawson's return to Pictou in 1841 to help with the family bookselling business could not have been better timed. The following summer he met William Logan, who was about to become director of the geological survey of Canada, and accompanied him on a geological tour of the Nova Scotian countryside, as he did about the same time with Charles Lyell. Thereafter Dawson maintained a cordial relationship with Logan and became the lifelong protégé, confidant, and disciple of Lyell. On his return to Nova Scotia in 1847 after the completion of a second academic session at the University of Edinburgh (accompanied then by his seventeen-year-old bride), he sought to enlarge the sphere of his business activities beyond bookselling. He was hired by the General Mining Association of London to conduct a geological survey of Cape Breton, and also investigated coal and other mineral deposits for the provincial government and for small mining companies.

Dawson turned his talents, as well, to educational matters, a realm that would increasingly occupy him. During the early 1850s he travelled the length and breadth of Nova Scotia as its first superintendent of education (1850–53). His devotion to the task was so complete that he is credited with single-handedly reforming the public educational system of the province. He managed at the same time to continue his scientific investigations, leading to some of his most important palaeontological discoveries. These included unearthing a fragment of a skeleton of the earliest North American reptile or batrachian (*Dendrerpeton acadianum*), the oldest land snail (*Pupa vetusta*), and the oldest millipede (*Xylobius sigillariae*). His investigations into the geology and mineral deposits of Nova Scotia provided data for his *Acadian Geology* (1855; 4th edn, 1891). This work, the most complete treatment of maritime geology of its day and only slightly modified by the findings of the geological survey of Canada years later, made his reputation as a geologist of the first rank.

In 1855 Dawson left his native province to accept the unanticipated offer of the position of principal of McGill University, Montreal, a post which he held until 1893. He became the indefatigable architect of McGill's rise to educational eminence. Besides his responsibilities as principal, he served as professor of natural science and principal of McGill Normal School (1857–70), which trained teachers for Quebec's protestant schools. After he stepped down from the principalship he continued to serve McGill as emeritus principal and professor, governors' fellow, and honorary curator of the Peter Redpath Museum.

Dawson's vigorous promotion of Canada's scientific institutions extended beyond the boundaries of McGill. He successfully lobbied for the formation of a national scientific organization, resulting in the creation of the Royal Society of Canada in 1882, for which he served as the first president. During the early 1880s, as well, he brought both the American and the British associations for the advancement of science to meet in Montreal. His firm guidance was felt in the affairs of the geological survey of Canada and in myriad scientific societies, especially the Natural History Society of Montreal.

From the 1860s onwards Dawson published an average of ten scientific papers a year, in addition to articles on educational, social, and religious matters. His scientific writings appeared in a wide range of journals and society proceedings, but the *Canadian Naturalist*, *Quarterly Journal of the Geological Society*, and *American Journal of Science* each published more than thirty individual papers.

Dawson's contributions to palaeontology and geology extend beyond publications alone. His unstinting fieldwork, first in Nova Scotia and later in Quebec, increased the number of post-Pliocene fossils known in Canada from about 30 to more than 200. He often chided his scientific adversaries that they should leave their armchairs and cabinets in order to observe specimens *in situ*. He helped to perfect the examination of thin fossil slices using a microscope, a technique that allowed him to describe 125 new species of Palaeozoic plants. His own collection of Canadian rocks and fossils formed the nucleus of the holdings of the Peter Redpath Museum, which was donated to McGill in Dawson's honour in 1882. Dawson discovered the puzzling fossil *Eozoön canadense* in 1864, a fragment that appeared to be a foraminifer. For the rest of his life he argued that the specimen proved the presence of animal life in the Laurentian rocks, despite mounting evidence of its inorganic composition.

Dawson wrote numerous works of popular science. Some of these served polemical purposes in his arguments against the glacial theory (he pushed the efficacy of icebergs or 'floating ice') and evolution (he even took issue with Asa Gray's theistic version), or to promote his views on *Eozoön*. Examples include *The Story of the Earth and Man* (1872), *The Dawn of Life* (1875), and *Modern Ideas of Evolution* (1890). Almost all sought to reconcile scientific truths with religious doctrine, as in *Archaia* (1857), *Nature and the Bible* (1875), and *The Meeting Place of Geology and History* (1894). Because of his devout Presbyterianism, intense anti-evolutionism, and firm commitment to the letter of biblical scripture, he was in great demand as a lecturer at religiously affiliated educational institutions across the United States and Canada. Reflecting his abiding interest in education and lucid scientific exposition, he also wrote textbooks geared towards Canadian students—*Agriculture for Schools* (1864), *Hand-Book of Canadian Zoology* (1871), and *Hand-Book of Canadian Geology* (1889).

Apart from his important role as a popularizer and institution builder, Dawson's scientific reputation rests on his work in palaeobotany. He investigated Canadian formations stretching from the maritime provinces to the west coast, culminating in the *Geological History of Plants* (1888), and published several papers on the subject every year. His more uneven contributions to palaeozoology (the interminable *Eozoön* controversy marred his reputation in this realm) treated a variety of organisms ranging from the lowest forms of life to prehistoric man (in *Fossil Men*, 1880). His scientific legacy includes pioneering work in Canadian geology, particularly for the eastern provinces and the St Lawrence River valley.

Dawson accumulated many scientific honours and awards, both in Canada and abroad. He became a fellow of the Geological Society in 1854 and of the Royal Society in 1862. He presided over the British Association's meeting at Birmingham in 1886, and over the American Association at Montreal in 1882. In 1893 he became president of the American Geological Society. He was knighted in 1884. He also received honorary or corresponding memberships in many other learned societies. Five of his six children survived to adulthood. The eldest son, George Mercer *Dawson, became Canada's leading field geologist and director of the geological survey of Canada. Dawson died at his home, 293 University Street, Montreal, on 19 November 1899 following several years' struggle with chronic pneumonia; he was buried in Mount Royal cemetery in Montreal on 21 November.

SUSAN SHEETS-PYENSON

Sources S. Sheets-Pyenson, *John William Dawson: faith, hope, and science* (1996) • P. R. Eakins and J. S. Eakins, 'Dawson, Sir John William', *DCB*, vol. 12 • W. Dawson, *Fifty years of work in Canada: scientific and educational*, ed. R. Dawson (1901) • C. F. O'Brien, *Sir William Dawson: a life in science and religion* (1971) • F. D. Adams, *Bulletin of the Geological Society of America*, 11 (1899), 550–80 [incl. bibliography] • H. M. Ami, 'Sir John William Dawson: a brief biographical sketch', *American Geologist*, 26 (1900), 1–57 [incl. bibliography]

Archives GS Lond., drawings and maps • McGill University, Montreal, McLennan Library, official papers | CUL, letters to Sir George Stokes • U. Edin. L., special collections division, letters to Sir Charles Lyell

Likenesses wood-engraving, 1886 (after photograph by Notman and Sandham), NPG; repro. in *ILN* (4 Sept 1886) [*see illus.*] • oils, Redpath Museum, Montreal, Canada

Dawson, Leslie [Les] (1931–1993), comedian, was born on 2 February 1931 in Thornton Street, Collyhurst, Manchester, the only child of Leslie Dawson (1905–1970), bricklayer, and his wife, Julia (c.1914–1957), daughter of David and Ellen Nolan. A small, chubby, solitary child, he grew up in some poverty in a Manchester slum. He first sought to make others laugh to stop himself being bullied at school, Moston Lane elementary, where what would become the distinguishing characteristic of his comedy— his sensitivity to the humour inherent in words themselves—was nurtured by a sympathetic teacher. At fourteen he began work in the drapery department of a co-operative store and he was thereafter successively an apprentice electrician, a champion jitterbug dancer, a soldier, a pianist in a Parisian bordello, an insurance representative, a local journalist, and a vacuum-cleaner salesman. His career in the last of these professions was terminated shortly after he walked on stage to compère the strip show in which he was moonlighting to see his manager in the front row of the audience.

Dawson was then performing principally as a comic pianist and he was initially discovered in the early 1950s by Max Wall, who paid for him to have singing lessons; a fellow pupil was Julie Andrews. His first foray into the comedy theatres of London met with little success, and after a spell washing dishes in a Lyons Corner House, he retreated in frustration to Manchester. The turning point of his career came in a trawlermen's club in Hull in 1956. More than usually fortified by drink, Dawson found himself unable to perform his piano routine and instead began to give vent to his weariness at life. The comic persona that emerged was a self-deprecating pessimist whose ill treatment by his wife and his mother-in-law spawned a ready line in cynical patter. Failure was his stock-in-trade, and his constant expectation.

Dawson's humour had its roots in music-hall, the exaggerations of seaside postcards, and a north country world of clogs, shawls, and matronly mill workers that in truth had vanished half a century before. The jokes he told were no more recent either, but Dawson carried them off effortlessly, in part because he gave the impression of not expecting anyone to laugh, and because his lugubrious Lancastrian delivery, laced with pathos and topped with an unexpected punchline, was genuinely funny. Misogyny was a staple of his repertory, the humour saved from unpleasantness by its absurdity. Thus, 'The wife's mother has things many men desire: muscles and a duelling scar', or, 'I'm not saying the wife's ugly, but every time she puts her make-up on, the lipstick backs into the tube.' Dawson derived particular inspiration for this strand of comedy from W. C. Fields. He breathed new life into what was essentially a traditional stand-up routine by garlanding

Leslie Dawson (1931–1993), by R. Poplowski, 1973

his humour with picaresque verbal peregrinations. He had an autodidact's relish of language: 'I was vouchsafed this missive from the gin-sodden lips of a pock-marked lascar in the arms of a frump in a Huddersfield bordello.' The sight of this ornate speech emerging from a face not inaccurately described by its owner as resembling 'a bulldog sucking piss off a nettle' was both incongruous and irresistible.

Dawson steadily built a following in the theatres of the north of England during the 1960s, and he then rapidly achieved national recognition after television appearances on *Opportunity Knocks* and *Blackpool Night Out*. In 1968 he was given his own series by Yorkshire Television, *Sez Les*. It ran for eight years before he moved to the BBC to host *The Les Dawson Show*. His most notable creation in these programmes was, with Roy Barraclough, Cissie and Ada, a pair of stout Lancashire housewives. Much of their time was spent 'mimo-ing' to each other, the northern practice of mouthing vocabulary relating to unmentionably delicate parts of the body or the act of reproduction. Dawson also demonstrated his ability to pull his chin over his nose, the legacy of a broken jaw sustained in a fight.

Dawson's career faltered a little in the early 1980s, despite his creation of what became a well-known troupe of overweight female dancers, the Roly Polys. It was with some reluctance that in 1984 he agreed to succeed Terry Wogan as the host of a game show, *Blankety Blank*, but the programme's inanity proved the perfect target for his subversive humour. In an age when television was rarely held in contempt Dawson gleefully insulted the studio audience ('Good evening, culture hunters'), mocked the celebrity guests ('I've got a picture of you on my mantlepiece; it keeps the children away from the fire'), and derided the cheapness of the prizes.

Despite his success, Dawson hoped to take on straight acting roles, but in fact he was at his best when he did not have to submerge his personality beneath that required by a part. In the mid-1970s he appeared in a trilogy of plays by Alan Plater, *The Loner*, and in 1991 was a centenarian Argentine matriarch in the black farce *Nona*. He was an avid reader and he collected a library of several thousand books at his home, Garth House, Islay Road, Lytham St Anne's. He himself wrote several novels, mainly homages to his favourite authors, such as *Well Fared my Lovely* (1992), a pastiche of Raymond Chandler. The majority of his output was, however, over-written and self-consciously literary.

Dawson married, on 25 June 1960, Margaret Rose Plant (c.1940–1987). Despite the nature of much of his act, he was a proud husband and was overjoyed when, after enduring several miscarriages, they had a son and two daughters. He was devastated by his wife's early death in 1987, but was married again, to the much younger Tracy Roper, in 1989. They had a daughter. A heavy man with too great a fondness for cigarettes and alcohol, Dawson died on 10 June 1993 while receiving treatment for a heart complaint at St Joseph's Hospital, Manchester, and was buried on the 16th. A service of thanksgiving for his life was held in Westminster Abbey on 23 February 1994, attended by more than 2000 guests.　　　　JAMES OWEN

Sources L. Dawson, *A clown too many* (1985) · *Daily Telegraph* (11 June 1993) · *The Times* (11 June 1993) · *The Independent* (11 June 1993) · *CGPLA Eng. & Wales* (1993)
Archives Salford City Archives, school and technical college notebooks, memoirs of service in royal engineers | FILM BFI NFTVA | SOUND BL NSA
Likenesses R. Poplowski, photograph, 1973, Hult. Arch. [*see illus.*] · photographs, 1973, Hult. Arch. · N. Lawn, photograph, 1980, Hult. Arch. · group portrait, photograph, 1980, Hult. Arch. · D. McKenzie, photographs, 1980–82, Hult. Arch. · E. Watson, photograph, 1983–7, NPG · G. Scarfe, cartoon, postage stamp, 1998, NPG · photograph, repro. in *The Times* · photograph, repro. in *The Independent*
Wealth at death £1,434,250: probate, 8 Nov 1993, *CGPLA Eng. & Wales*

Dawson, Margaret Mary Damer (1873–1920), a founder of the Women's Police Service, was born at 1 York Road, Hove, Sussex, on 12 June 1873, the daughter of Richard Dawson, a surgeon, and his wife, Agnes Maria Hemming, Lady Walsingham. Her education in the main was probably private; however, she studied music under Benno Schoenberger and Herbert Sharpe, winning the gold medal and diploma of an institution called the London Academy of Music. Her independent income enabled Margaret Dawson to move in well-to-do circles, and it supported her in her campaigns. In her adult years she became involved with various philanthropic activities. Although she later helped found a home for abandoned babies, her most notable activity at this period was campaigning for the humane treatment of animals, particularly but not exclusively on the continent. She organized the International Congress of Animal Protection Societies which met in London in 1906. For her work she received awards from the Danish and Finnish societies for animal welfare, and she actively participated, together with Louise Lind-af-Hageby, in the Animal Defence and Anti-Vivisection Society.

Dawson was not active in the women's suffrage movement, but she did take an interest in such feminist issues as the campaign against the traffic in women and children, and served on the Criminal Law Amendment Committee in 1914. This led her into the campaign for women police to protect women from sexual exploitation. For some time feminists had become increasingly aware of the shortcomings of the male police in dealing with cases involving women, and especially the sexual abuse of children, and had been considering women's possible role in police work. Nina Boyle of the Women's Freedom League was one of the most prominent in this, but when war came in August 1914 it was Margaret Damer Dawson who took the lead in recruiting women police; she became chief, with Nina Boyle as her deputy. Many of the first recruits, numbering approximately fifty, had experience of being imprisoned as militant suffragists, a point which was stressed by the rival Women's Police Patrols, set up by the National Union of Women Workers (later the National Council of Women). Margaret Damer Dawson's highly respectable non-suffragette background, together with the number of her aristocratic acquaintances, was thus an asset when dealing with figures of authority. Initially the women, all of independent means, called themselves the Women's Police Volunteers, and devised their own version of the police uniform. With the reluctant approval of the metropolitan commissioner they began training with the Metropolitan Police on a purely voluntary basis, in the meantime working with refugees and giving help and advice to women who required it. However, the first call on their services, in November 1914, was from the army at Grantham, to control women 'of bad character', and to enforce the virtual curfew on women in the area. Margaret Damer Dawson agreed to do this, on the grounds that to prove their willingness to accept police discipline 'no order, however distasteful, could be shirked'. As a result of this departure from feminist principles Nina Boyle called for her resignation, but a vote of the members overwhelmingly supported Damer Dawson, and it was Nina Boyle who left, and Mary Allen and Ellen Harburn went to Grantham. At this time Margaret Damer Dawson decided to change her group's name to the Women's Police Service.

In 1916 Lloyd George, then minister of munitions, called upon the Women's Police Service to supervise 'munitionettes' (women munition workers). Margaret Damer Dawson agreed to supply, train, and uniform 140 women, in the first instance without any financial aid, on the undertaking that if they proved successful they would receive some money. The women were sent to munition factories at Chester and Gretna. Meanwhile training continued in London's West End, and the publicity that this received caused displeasure in Scotland Yard and the Home Office. The great drain on the Women's Police Service's financial resources had been offset by a massive anonymous donation. In 1918 Margaret Damer Dawson was one of those consulted over a move to establish a permanent women's police presence under Home Office control; however, largely because of Metropolitan Police hostility to the supposedly more militant Women's Police Service, in the first instance, it was Mrs Sofia Stanley of the rival Women's Police Patrols who was appointed superintendent (again, the Metropolitan Police commissioner's main aim was that of prostitution control).

After the armistice Margaret Damer Dawson, who had been created OBE, got chief constables throughout the country to take on forty-seven of the demobilized munitions women police, but London's commissioner, Sir Nevil Macready, remained hostile. Although the committee on the employment of women on police duties (the Baird committee), to which Margaret Damer Dawson gave evidence, cautiously approved the principle of employing women police, the Home Office did not hide its reluctance to make any concessions. Shortly after the Baird committee heard its last witness, Margaret Damer Dawson died of a heart attack on 18 May 1920 at her home, Danehill Lodge, in Lympne, Kent. She was buried at Lympne four days later.

Margaret Damer Dawson was blonde, blue eyed, and of delicate appearance. Although an obituarist described her as 'singularly unassuming', she was obviously regarded with apprehension by many male officials and magistrates. She inspired great loyalty and affection among the women who served with her. Her successor, Mary Allen, considered that the struggle against the hostility of the male police establishment had contributed to her early death.

DAVID DOUGHAN

Sources J. Lock, *The British policewoman: her story* (1979) • J. Carrier, *The campaign for the employment of women as police officers* (1988) • M. S. Allen, *The pioneer policewoman*, ed. J. H. Heyneman (1925) • *WWW* • *The Times* (20 May 1920) • *Daily Telegraph* (22 May 1920) • H. Kean, *Animal rights: political and social change in Britain since 1800* (1998) • CGPLA Eng. & Wales (1921) • b. cert. • d. cert.

Likenesses Elliott & Fry, photograph, *c.*1918, repro. in Allen, *Pioneer policewoman*, facing p. 26 • photograph, repro. in Kean, *Animal rights*, 151 • photographs, Metropolitan Police archives, London

Wealth at death £385 5s. 1d.: probate, 22 June 1921, CGPLA Eng. & Wales

Dawson, Matthew (1820–1898), racehorse trainer, second son of George Dawson (*d.* 1846), himself a trainer, and his wife, Jean Alison, was born at Stamford Hall, Gullane, East Lothian, on 20 January 1820. After a demanding apprenticeship under his father, in 1838 he became head lad to his eldest brother, Thomas, at Middleham in Yorkshire but returned to Scotland two years later to train on his own account. He married, on 8 July 1844, at Kilwinning, Mary Rose (*d.* 1895). Shortly after the death of his father in November 1846, Dawson left Scotland to train for Lord John Scott and his racing partner, Sir John Don-

and George Blackwell, Felix Leach, William Walters, and Richard Waugh. His brothers Thomas (*d.* 1880), Joseph (*d.* 1880), and John *Dawson were also trainers. As *Baily's Magazine* said of them collectively, 'their manners are courteous, their stable management has passed into a proverb, and their judgement of a yearling is held in as high repute as their irreproachable taste for whisky'. But Matthew was the outstanding figure. Small in stature, immaculate in dress, and autocratic in his training methods, he won twenty-eight classics, including six Derbys.

WRAY VAMPLEW

Sources R. Mortimer, R. Onslow, and P. Willett, *Biographical encyclopedia of British flat racing* (1978) · E. M. Humphris, *The life of Matthew Dawson* (1928) · T. McConnell, *The tartan turf* (1988) · J. Fairfax-Blakeborough, *Northern turf history* (1973) · *The Times* (19 Aug 1898) · *Daily Telegraph* (19 Aug 1898) · *The Field* (20 Aug 1898) · J. Porter, *Kingsclere* (1896) · The Druid [H. H. Dixon], *Scott and Sebright*, rev. edn (1895) · J. Welcome [J. N. H. Brennan], *Fred Archer: his life and times* (1967)

Likenesses Hudson & Kearns, photograph, pubd 1895, National Horseracing Museum, Newmarket [*see illus.*] · Lib [L. Prosperi], caricature, chromolithograph, NPG; repro. in *VF* (4 Dec 1886) · Sedgewick, steel engraving, repro. in Thormanby [W. Willmott Dixon], *Kings of the turf* (1898), facing p. 323 · Spy [L. Ward], group portrait, chromolithograph (*On the heath*), NPG; repro. in *VF* (26 Nov 1896) · portrait, repro. in G. Plumtre, *The fast set* (1895)

Wealth at death £11,994 13s. 7d.: probate, 22 Sept 1898, CGPLA Eng. & Wales

Matthew Dawson (1820–1898), by Hudson & Kearns, pubd 1895

Wauchope. When Lord John gave up racing in 1857 Dawson arranged the sale of his stud to the wealthy Scottish ironmaster James Merry and became Merry's private trainer at Russley, near Lambourn in Berkshire. In 1860 he gained a great success for his master with Thormanby, who won the Derby and cleared £40,000 in bets.

Six years later Dawson left Russley, following differences with Merry (never an easy man to serve), and started as a public trainer at Newmarket, where he bought Heath House. There his principal owners were the heavy-betting dukes of Hamilton and Newcastle, both ultimately forced to leave the turf by their gambling debts. In 1869, however, he secured as a patron the non-gambling Lord Falmouth, who was concerned only with winning important races. Together with the champion jockey Fred Archer, Dawson and Lord Falmouth formed a triumphant trio, winning two Derbys, three Oaks, three St Legers, three One Thousand Guineas, and three Two Thousand Guineas. In 1885, the year after Lord Falmouth retired from the turf, Dawson handed over Heath House to his nephew George H. Dawson and moved to Exning Manor, Suffolk, with just a few horses. Nevertheless, at the age of seventy-five he trained Sir Visto to win both the Derby and St Leger of 1895. That year he retired, but returned to Newmarket two years later to live at Waterloo Lodge, where he died on 18 August 1898.

Although he had no children, Dawson passed on his training skills to many who gained their initial tuition in his yard, including his nephews George and John Dawson,

Dawson, Montague (1895/1898–1973), marine artist, was probably born in Chiswick on 19 September 1895 (or possibly 1898; he claimed he never knew which year), the son of Charles Dawson (*b.* 1860/61), engineer, inventor, and yachtsman, and Florence Bithrey. He had four known siblings, Harold, Horace, Ada, and Eva. His grandfather was the landscape artist Henry *Dawson (1811–1878). Dawson moved with his family to the Smugglers House, Hythe, on Southampton Water, and he passed his childhood drawing and 'messing about in boats'. Educated by tutors at home and never apprenticed to a studio, he learned about painting by studying the work of Dutch and English sea painters. Before the First World War he worked as a commercial artist in Holborn, then enlisted in the Royal Navy, serving as lieutenant on trawlers and minesweepers. He worked with the stage designer Norman Wilkinson on the development of dazzle painting on warships. In Falmouth, Dawson met Charles Napier Hemy RA (1841–1917), the only contemporary artist to influence his work. He regularly submitted to *The Sphere* illustrations of the war at sea, and there recorded the surrender of the German Grand Fleet.

After the war Dawson sailed to the West Indies on a square-rigger and used his sketches years later for such subjects as *Pirates Cove, Cocos Island, Wafer Bay* (1969; priv. coll.). He lived briefly at 8 Percy Street, London, in 1920, then at 2A St Charles Square, Kensington. About 1925 he married Doris Mary Lyle (*c.*1897–1972) and their only daughter, Nyria, was born in 1928. In 1934 the family moved to the New Forest and two years later he bought Hurst, a 1930s property overlooking the Solent.

Dawson's success owed much to his dealer—he sold through Frost and Reed, London, whose astute, energetic managing director, Stanley Wade, created a worldwide market for his paintings and further publicized Dawson's name by selling reproductions of his art. But from early days his work sold easily. He began exhibiting at the Royal Academy in 1917, was elected a fellow of the Royal Society of Arts in 1936, and became a founder member of the Royal Society of Marine Artists in 1939, exhibiting there regularly between 1946 and 1970. By the 1960s Dawson was reputed to be the highest paid living artist after Picasso. His work was certainly the highest priced of any living marine artist of the twentieth century and he was the century's leading exponent of painting clipper ships at sea. His wife and daughter helped cope with his constant stream of fan mail. His work was imitated by many and fakes began to appear even in his lifetime. He enjoyed success, particularly as it brought him the admiration of several members of the royal family and examples of his work entered the Royal Collection.

Dawson's best early works are watercolours, usually yacht races, fishing boats, or clipper ships, but by 1930 Dawson mostly painted in oils. In 1939–45 he again produced monochrome illustrations of the naval war for *The Sphere* and some full-size canvases (several versions) of warships, notably the *Sinking of HMS Kelly*. From the 1930s onwards he depicted named vessels many times over; paintings include *Cutty Sark* and *Lightning* (the famous wool clippers), *Ariel and Taeping* and *Thermopylae* (tea clippers), and *Chesapeake and Shannon* and the *USS Constitution* (battleships). In 1970 he finished a large canvas, *Battle of Trafalgar* (priv. coll.), having uncovered during his research new evidence about Nelson's instructions to the rest of the fleet. He depicted the J-class yachts *Rainbow* and *Endeavour* and pioneering ships such as the *Golden Hind* and *Mayflower*, but few steamships. The heavy brushwork of his early pictures became more refined over the decades, bringing the ability to unite in motion the vessel, waves, and sky in a lifelike though poetic style. He researched his subjects at length and achieved veracity in every detail, the sails and rigging always correctly set for the amount of wind and the tilt of the vessel.

Dawson died at Western Hospital, Southampton, on 21 May 1973 and was buried at Boldre church, Lymington, Hampshire. JULIET M. JOHNSON

Sources L. G. G. Ramsey, *Montague Dawson, RSMA, FRSA* (1967) • private information (2004) • A. Jarman and others, eds., *Royal Academy exhibitors, 1905–1970: a dictionary of artists and their work in the summer exhibitions of the Royal Academy of Arts*, 6 vols. (1973–82), vol. 2 • R. Ranson, *The maritime paintings of Montague Dawson* (1993) • C. B. de Laperrière, *Royal Society of Marine Artists, exhibitors, 1946–1997* (1998) • A. Dawson, *The life of Henry Dawson, landscape painter* (1891) • 'Dawson, Henry', *DNB* • d. cert.
Archives priv. coll., MSS, photographs, press cuttings
Likenesses two photographs, c.1967–c.1970 • photograph

Dawson, Nancy [*real name* Ann Newton] (*bap.* **1728**, *d.* **1767**), dancer, was probably the Ann baptized at Axminster, Devon, on 17 January 1728, the daughter of William Newton. In her will she named her parents as William Newton, a staymaker, of Martlett Court, Covent Garden, and Eleanor Newton, but they may well have followed their daughter to London when she became successful. It seems likely

Nancy Dawson (*bap.* 1728, *d.* 1767), by Michael Jackson

that this is the truth, rather than the colourful, if rather seedy, account given in the anonymous *Authentic Memoirs of the Celebrated Miss Nancy D*ws*n* (n.d. [1765?]). It seems she joined the company of a puppet-showman, Griffin, who taught her to dance, and a figure dancer from Sadler's Wells gained an engagement for her at that theatre. Here, 'as she was extremely agreeable in her figure, and the novelty of her dancing added to it, with her excellent execution, she soon grew to be a favourite with the town' (*N&Q*, 2nd ser., 10, 1860, 195). In her second summer season at Sadler's Wells she was promoted to the part of Columbine. She made her first appearance at Covent Garden on 1 February 1758 as a dancer in Thomas Betterton's dramatic opera *The Prophetess*. It was probably about this time that she became the mistress of the Covent Garden comedian Ned Shuter (1728?–1776); in 1763 George Alexander Stevens published 'a satire upon Edward Shuter, the comedian, and Nancy Dawson, the far-famed toast', *The Dramatic History of Master Edward, Miss Ann, Mr Llwhuddwhydd, and Others*, which was reprinted several times, but copies of which are very scarce.

On 22 May 1758 Nancy Dawson was billed to dance a hornpipe, but her greatest opportunity came in October 1759, when the man who was to dance the hornpipe among the thieves in *The Beggar's Opera* was taken ill. In the manner of Hollywood fantasy, Nancy Dawson was plucked from the chorus to take his place, and from that moment her professional reputation was made. The hornpipe by which she danced into fame was performed to a tune which had various lyrics associated with it, but which was always known as 'The Ballad of Nancy Dawson' (there is no evidence that any words were sung while she danced). The music seems to have been composed by Thomas Arne, and was one of the most popular airs of the day. It was set with variations for the harpsichord as 'Miss Dawson's Hornpipe', and was used in Carey and Bickerstaffe's musical pastiche *Love in a Village* (1762); it was also mentioned by Goldsmith in the epilogue to his *She Stoops to Conquer*. The tune continues to be well known as that to which the nursery rhyme 'Here we go round the mulberry bush' is sung. Dawson's performance (as well as Charlotte Brent's celebrated Polly) contributed to the success of *The Beggar's Opera*, which had an unusually long run, drawing audiences away from Garrick's Drury Lane.

Despite being given her first speaking part (the princess in Shuter's *The English Sailors in America*, 20 March 1760), Dawson was wooed away to Drury Lane by the offer of a higher salary. She danced her hornpipe there, again in *The Beggar's Opera*, on 23 September 1760. She remained there for three years, appearing regularly in revivals of *The Beggar's Opera* and in Christmas entertainments, including *Harlequin's Invasion* (1761–2 season) and *Fortunatus* (1761–2 and 1762–3 seasons). In the summer of 1761 she joined Shuter and Joseph Grimaldi the elder in Lee's company at Winchester. On 26 December 1763 she appeared in a Drury Lane pantomime, *The Rites of Hecate*, and she performed again the following night, but that was the last time she danced on stage. It is not known why she retired, or what she did between then and her death. The Axminster antiquary James Davidson, when preparing his unfinished history of Axminster between 1820 and 1830, learned from his conversations with elderly residents that Dawson made regular visits to Axminster during and after her stage career, where 'she astonished the inhabitants as well by the splendour of her appearances as the boldness of her carriage' (Chapman, 136). Dawson died on 9 June 1767 at Haverstock Hill, Hampstead, Middlesex. She was buried on 12 June in the graveyard of St George the Martyr (later St George's Gardens), Bloomsbury, behind the Foundling Hospital. In her will she made provision for her parents, for her brother and nephew, both named William Newton, and for a niece, Elizabeth Newton, who had been bound to Dawson as an apprentice, suggesting that she might have been involved in some kind of mercantile activity in her last years.

Reputedly 'of shrewish temper' and 'immoral life', Nancy Dawson was included in Edward Thompson's *The Meretriciad* (1761) as one of the most notorious women in London. The size and prominence of her tombstone have prompted speculation about liaisons in her later years; rumours that the stone originally bore a scurrilous eight-line ditty, beginning 'Nancy Dawson was a whore', are unfounded. ALSAGER VIAN, *rev.* K. D. REYNOLDS

Sources Highfill, Burnim & Langhans, *BDA* · *N&Q*, 2nd ser., 10 (1860), 110–11, 126, 195 · *N&Q*, 3rd ser., 9 (1866), 140 · *GM*, 1st ser., 98/1 (1828), 496 · G. M. Chapman, *A history of Axminster to 1910* (1998) · *Authentic memoirs of the celebrated Miss Nancy D*ws*n* [n.d., 1765?] · *Dance Perspectives*, 26 (summer 1966) · private information (2004) [G. M. Chapman] · W. H. Wilkin, 'Some Axminster worthies, part 1', *Report and Transactions of the Devonshire Association*, 65 (1933), 405–24

Likenesses M. Jackson, mezzotint, BM, NPG [*see illus.*] · C. Spooner, mezzotint, BM, NPG · Watson, mezzotint (after C. Spooner), Harvard TC; repro. in Highfill, Burnim & Langhans, *BDA* · oils, Garr. Club · oils (probably Nancy Dawson), Worcester College, Oxford

Wealth at death legacies of £75; clothing, furnishings, and china: will, Highfill, Burnim & Langhans, *BDA*

Dawson, Peter Smith (1882–1961), singer, was born on 31 January 1882 in Adelaide, South Australia, the youngest son and the eighth of the ten children of Thomas Dawson (1842–1919) and Alison, *née* Miller (1841–1916). Both his parents were Scottish; his father, originally from Kirkcaldy and later a seaman, had settled in Adelaide in 1863 and established a plumbing business. Peter was educated at East Adelaide primary school and Pulteney Street grammar school. His mother ensured that all the children had musical training and Peter made his début as a boy soprano at St Peter's town hall, Adelaide, at the age of seven. A keen sportsman, he won medals for running and swimming but music remained an abiding interest and at sixteen he joined the choir of St Andrew's Presbyterian Church, Wakefield Street, Adelaide, studied singing with C. J. Stevens, founder and conductor of the Adelaide Choral Society, and began appearing in singing competitions and concerts. When Dawson left school he joined the family firm as an apprentice plumber but Stevens, convinced that the young man had a future as a singer, persuaded his reluctant father to send him to England to study.

Dawson sailed for England in 1902 and was taken on by the eminent British singer Sir Charles Santley, with whom he studied for three years. Subsequently a Russian singing specialist, Professor Kantorez, extended his range from one of E♭ to D to one of E♭ to A, converting him from a bass to a bass–baritone. Santley persuaded Madame Emma Albani to include Dawson in her touring concert party in 1904 and launched him on his professional career. In 1909 he appeared in *The Mastersingers* at Covent Garden but he disliked opera, considering it 'too much work for too little pay' (Dawson, 22). On the other hand, he enjoyed singing in oratorio, *Messiah* being a particular favourite. He concentrated on his concert career and by the 1920s had established himself as the leading ballad singer in Britain. While the majority of his appearances were in concert halls, he also appeared with success in the music-halls and variety theatres, topping the bill at the London Palladium.

Although he toured the British Isles and the British empire extensively, Dawson himself recognized that he became a household name as a result of his recording career. He made his first recordings for the Edison Bell Company in 1904, the earliest a song called 'Navajo' attributed to Leonard Dawson—the beginning of a continuous recording career stretching from 1904 to 1958. Initially he sang for a wide range of labels and under a variety of names; he recorded most often under his own name but he also sang comic songs as Will Strong, light popular songs as Frank Danby, and Scottish songs as Hector Grant.

Peter Smith Dawson (1882–1961), by unknown photographer

He participated in six full-length Gilbert and Sullivan opera recordings. He signed with HMV in 1906 and sang exclusively for that label from 1912 to 1953. In his autobiography he estimated that he had recorded 3500 songs and sold some 13 million copies, and subsequent estimates suggest sales of 25 million copies during his career. Not only was he performing on stage and gramophone records, but he broadcast regularly on the wireless after making his BBC début on Australia day, 26 January 1923. He also appeared in two films, *Chips* (directed by Edward Godal, 1938), for which he also composed the music, and *Okay for Sound* (directed by Marcel Varnel, 1938).

Dawson was married twice, first on 20 May 1905 to Annie Mortimer (Nan) Noble (1881–1953), who sang professionally as Annette George. She was the daughter of theatre manager Thomas John Noble. She retired after being badly injured in a car accident in 1925. Following Nan's death in 1953, Dawson married her sister, Constance Bedford Noble (*b*. 1897), on 29 April 1954. There were no children of either marriage.

Dawson's forte was the ballad and his singing was always characterized by a clarity of diction, a sincere and robust delivery, and a consistently appropriate and never overstated emotional colouring. His popularity demonstrates the persistence of an essentially Victorian musical sensibility in the British public well into the twentieth century, a sensibility which was sentimental, nostalgic, patriotic, romantic, and religiose. There was no one to equal Dawson in singing 'Glorious Devon', 'The fishermen of England', 'The Cornish Floral Dance', 'The Holy City', or Stanford's setting of Newbolt's *Songs of the Sea* and the various settings of Kipling's *Barrack Room Ballads* (notably his rendering of 'Boots'), all perennial parts of his repertoire. Dawson himself wrote some fifty songs under a variety of pseudonyms, notably J. P. McCall.

Dawson was in Australia in 1914 when war broke out and he returned at once to England to undertake concert work for war charities and the troops. Seeking a more direct involvement he returned to Australia and enlisted as a private in the army, but before he could see active service the armistice was declared. He was in Australia again when the Second World War broke out. Too old for active service, he remained there for the duration, resuming directorial duties at the family firm Thomas Dawson & Sons, then producing tins for military use, but also broadcasting, recording, and touring army camps. He returned to England in 1947 and gave fifty-seven concerts, claiming that he was broke because of tax demands from both England and Australia and poor management of his finances. In 1951 he published his autobiography, *Fifty Years of Song*. In 1954 he made a farewell tour of England and the next year his final English recordings, and in 1955 settled in Australia for good, making his final public appearances and recordings there in 1958. He died of heart failure in Sydney on 27 September 1961 and was buried in Rookwood cemetery, Sydney.

Peter Dawson was 5 feet 6 inches tall, sturdily built, with ruddy complexion, grey eyes, and tattoos on his arms and chest. Personally he was jovial and forthright, an enthusiastic smoker and practical joker, and showed extraordinary generosity to his fellow performers, actively promoting the careers not only of other Australians in England but also of up-and-coming young British singers. His repertoire testified to a deep love of Australia, and his devotion to the Scotland of his forebears and the England where he spent much of his career. His was a true imperial patriotism. As Cunningham Thom, rector of St David's Presbyterian Church, Haberfield, said in his funeral address: 'He belonged to the generation of Kipling and Henley, and of those strong, robust British poets and writers who were the voices of the then invincible British Empire and the then invincible British Army' (Vose, 103).

JEFFREY RICHARDS

Sources P. Dawson, *Fifty years of song* (1951) · P. Burgis, *Ambassador of song* (1981) · J. D. Vose, *Once a jolly swagman* (1987) · G. Moore, *Am I too loud?* (1962) · A. Ziegler and W. Booth, *Duet* (1951) · *AusDB*

Archives NL Aus. · Tate collection, corresp. and MSS | FILM BFI NFTVA, performance footage | SOUND BL NSA, *Talking about music*, 282, 1LP0204751S2 BD1 BBC TRANSC · BL NSA, performance recordings

Likenesses photograph, NPG [*see illus.*] · photographs, Hult. Arch.

Wealth at death £521 9s.—in England: Australian probate sealed in England, 26 Sept 1962, *CGPLA Eng. & Wales*

Dawson, Robert (1771–1860), surveyor and cartographer, was born in Plymouth on 10 November 1771, the seventh of ten children born to Matthew Dawson (*d*. 1783) and his wife, and their only child to live to maturity. He lived with his family in Plymouth Dockyard until he was thirteen when he was taken on as an apprentice by a 'good man' as Dawson described him in a letter, probably William Gardner, chief draughtsman in the drawing office in the Tower of London, who in 1784 was conducting a survey of Plymouth. The same 'good man' secured Dawson's appointment to the Board of Ordnance in 1791. Dawson was to serve with the Ordnance Survey for forty-five years, his technical skill and ability to lead ensuring his rapid promotion. He initially took part in military surveys in the south of England and by 1800 he had gained a reputation as a competent surveyor and an excellent draughtsman and was seconded for two years to teach at the Royal Military Academy at High Wycombe. He proved an outstanding teacher of both military pupils at the academy and, after 1810, of civilian pupils at the East India Company's college at Addiscombe. In 1803 he designed the curriculum for the cadets attached to the developing Ordnance Survey—in six months cadets using his *Course of Instruction* were to become proficient in all practical aspects of surveying and map drawing.

Dawson's early cartographic style owed much to Gardner's teaching, but it changed soon after he left the college at High Wycombe where he had perhaps come under the influence of the French topographical instructor, General François Jarry. He was also influenced by British military cartography and draughtsmanship and by French surveying textbooks. His method of showing relief by a combination of pen and ink shading and soft brushwork hachures developed until, by the 1820s, his technique of using brown colour washes to depict the Welsh landscape conveyed a vivid three-dimensional impression of topography, particularly well suited to rugged areas, which drew praise from contemporaries and continued to command admiration, although his methods were later abandoned. Although Dawson's brushwork was occasionally criticized by engravers as hard to interpret, his maps are unquestionably very pleasing to the eye. His 'model of hills' of 1830 was used to bring more uniformity to the Ordnance board's presentation of relief. He retired about 1836 on a pension, having risen to be chief draughtsman and principal instructor and one of the best paid of the Ordnance board's staff. He married Jane, sister of two well-known ordnance surveyors, Richard and Charles Budgen, in 1794 in Lewes, Sussex. They had eight children, whose various birthplaces reflect the peripatetic life of an ordnance surveyor. Two girls, both Felicia, died in infancy. Matthew and Robert Kearsley *Dawson were commissioned to the Royal Engineers. Charles was a surveyor in the Ordnance Survey. George, a clergyman, was rector of Woodleigh, near Kingsbridge, Devon, where his father was living at the time of his death on 22 June 1860.

ELIZABETH BAIGENT

Sources Y. Hodson, 'Robert Dawson, 1771–1860, ordnance surveyor and draughtsman: a brief note on his early family life', *Map Collector*, 54 (1991), 28–30 • Y. Hodson, *Map making in the Tower of London* (1991) • *The old series ordnance survey maps of England and Wales*, Ordnance Survey, 8 vols. (1975–92), esp. vol. 2 [introduction by J. B. Harley and Y. O'Donoghue] • W. A. Seymour, ed., *A history of the Ordnance Survey* (1980) • CGPLA Eng. & Wales (1860)
Archives BL • PRO
Likenesses oils, priv. coll. • photograph, repro. in Hodson, 'Robert Dawson' • photograph, repro. in Hodson, *Map making*
Wealth at death under £600: probate, 10 July 1860, CGPLA Eng. & Wales

Dawson, Robert Kearsley (1798–1861), surveyor and cartographer, was born in Dover in 1798 while his father, the surveyor and cartographer Robert *Dawson (1771–1860), was employed on the survey of Kent. He was one of eight children born to Robert and his wife, Jane Budgen, and one of three sons to become surveyors. He was educated at the Royal Military Academy, Woolwich, and obtained his first commission in the Royal Engineers in 1818. He was assistant to Thomas Colby on the triangulation of Scotland and later accompanied Colby to Ireland, where, in 1829, he supervised a staff of civil assistants who sketched hills for the one-inch map and collected material for the county memoirs to the six-inch survey. In 1831 he was recalled to England and appointed commissioner under the Reform Bill to settle and map the boundaries of parliamentary boroughs, producing maps mostly at scales of one and two inches to the mile in *Plans of the Cities and Boroughs of England and Wales* (2 vols., 1832). His maps at scales of one and two inches to the mile predate Ordnance Survey maps in the north of the country. In 1836 Dawson became assistant commissioner to the tithe commutation commission, organizing and superintending the surveys on which the permanent commutation of tithes in England and Wales was to be recorded. While employed on this work he also gave advice to the directors of the Wakefield settlements in New Zealand and Australia who were establishing colonies on principles laid out by Edward Gibbon Wakefield. Dawson successfully advocated cheaper but less accurate running surveys in preference to strict trigonometric surveys. Although he favoured the technically superior trigonometric surveys where practicable, as with his own tithe commutation maps, Dawson realized that running surveys would serve the overriding need of the colonists—to prove title to land—without being so costly as to delay settlement. He published his views in a pamphlet *Report on Surveying … with Reference to New Zealand and … the Colonies Generally* (1840). Dawson's experience in Ireland and the Antipodes convinced him of the value of cadastral maps (large-scale maps showing property boundaries) and he argued persuasively that the scope of the English and Welsh tithe survey and mapping should be extended to form a national survey at a scale of one inch to three chains (26.7 inches to a mile, or 1:2376). Despite having won over the tithe and poor law commissioners, his argument found no favour with the exchequer and Britain thus remained without a general cadastral map. None the less, the tithe maps, many drawn to Dawson's specifications, constitute an impressive cartographic achievement. He was appointed assistant commissioner and head of the survey department of the commons enclosure and copyhold commission and for his services was made CB civil division in February 1836. He reached the rank of colonel before his death at 4 Grove Place, Blackheath, on 28 March 1861. He left a widow, Frances Jane, but nothing more is known of his family circumstances.

ELIZABETH BAIGENT

Sources R. J. P. Kain and H. C. Prince, *The tithe surveys of England and Wales* (1985) • R. J. P. Kain and E. Baigent, *The cadastral map in the service of the state: a history of property mapping* (1992) • G. Beech, 'Tithe maps', *Map Collector*, 33 (1985), 20–25 • Y. Hodson, *Map making in the Tower of London* (1991) • *The old series ordnance survey maps of England and Wales*, Ordnance Survey, 8 vols. (1975–92) [introductions to each vol. by J. B. Harley and others] • CGPLA Eng. & Wales (1861) • T. Owen and E. Pilbeam, *Ordnance Survey: map makers to Britain since 1791* (1992)
Archives BL

Likenesses oils, priv. coll. · watercolour on ivory, priv. coll.
Wealth at death £3000: probate, 7 May 1861, *CGPLA Eng. & Wales*

Dawson, Thomas (*c.*1725–1782), physician, was one of the seven sons of Eli Dawson (*d.* 1744), a Presbyterian minister in Yorkshire, and his wife, Alice Taylor. He was the brother of Benjamin *Dawson and Abraham *Dawson. He was educated at Kendal Academy from 1746 and Glasgow College from 1749, and graduated MD at the latter in 1753. In March 1754 he became minister of the Gravel Pit meeting-house in Hackney, but preferring medicine he gave up the pulpit and paid back to the Presbyterian fund what had been granted for his education. He soon began practice in London, occasionally going round the wards of Guy's Hospital. One day he found a Miss Corbett, a patient of his, sitting in her room gazing at the words of 2 Samuel 12: 7: 'Thou art the man'. Taking this to express a wish which she had perhaps suggested less directly before, he made her an offer of marriage and became her husband on 29 May 1758.

Dawson was elected physician to the Middlesex Hospital, London, in 1759, but only held the post for two years. In 1762 he was admitted a licentiate of the Royal College of Physicians, and two years later he was elected physician to the London Hospital, where he remained until 1770. He also saw patients at Batson's coffee house in Cornhill. In 1774 he published *Cases in the Acute Rheumatism and the Gout, with Cursory Remarks and the Method of Treatment*, in which he prescribed half-ounce doses of tincture of guaiacum during the painful stage of both rheumatic fever and gout. His only other work was *An Account of a Safe and Efficient Remedy for Sore Eyes and Eyelids* (1782). Dawson died on 29 April 1782.   NORMAN MOORE, *rev.* CAROLINE OVERY

Sources Munk, *Roll* · Nichols, *Lit. anecdotes*, 9.694 · S. C. Lawrence, *Charitable knowledge: hospital pupils and practitioners in eighteenth-century London* (1996)

Dawson, Sir (Arthur) Trevor, first baronet (1866–1931), armaments manufacturer, was born on 1 May 1866 at Dalkeith House, Richmond, Surrey, son of Hugh Dawson (1836–1884), landowner and barrister, and his wife, formerly Mary Ann Chaffer. Trevor Dawson (as he was always known) became a naval cadet in 1879 and was educated at the Royal Academy, Gosport, and on the training ship *Britannia*. He became a midshipman of the channel squadron in 1881 and subsequently trained at the Royal Naval colleges at Portsmouth and Greenwich, the Royal Artillery College at Woolwich, and the torpedo school on HMS *Vernon*. He was gazetted lieutenant in 1887 (serving on a cruiser in the Mediterranean) and appointed in 1892 as experimental officer at Woolwich arsenal. In that year, he married Louise (1870–1935), daughter of John Miller Grant. They had two sons and two daughters.

Dawson's service career ended in 1896, when he was recruited as ordnance superintendent of the private armaments manufacturers Vickers. In 1898 he was elected to the company's board. He soon familiarized himself with every aspect of its business, and mastered the daily running of each department. Tall, athletic, and dominant, he worked with ferocious energy; the pace and intensity

of his life would have broken most men. Appointed managing director of Vickers in 1906, he was involved in general administration, commercial negotiations, production, and design as well as liaison with the Admiralty, Foreign Office, War Office, and overseas buyers. He had expert knowledge of naval shipbuilding, land and sea guns of all sizes and types, explosives, mines, and other weaponry. The management of Vickers' submarine business after 1902 was a success particularly associated with him. Only two areas of the company were not stamped with his influence: the steelworks (managed by members of the Vickers family) and finance, controlled by Sir Vincent Caillard (1856–1930).

From 1900 Dawson was chairman of Chilworth Gunpowder, a British company set up under the Anglo-German pooling agreement of the explosives trade. He was a director of many of Vickers' overseas companies, such as Canadian-Vickers, Vickers-Terni in Italy, and the Placencia arsenal in Spain. He had numerous associated directorships, notably of Wolseley Motors and of William Beardmore & Co. (both until 1926).

Dawson's knowledge of service needs and contacts with officials were invaluable. His name was restored to the navy list in 1902, by which date he was an important individual in British war preparations. He testified to several government enquiries, sat on departmental committees, was a frequent visitor to the service ministries, and undertook confidential intelligence work. On one occasion he collected evidence for the Admiralty on German naval shipbuilding by skating round the ice-bound dockyards at Kiel to see the ships under construction. He travelled extensively on business and was an adept in all the arcane influences of the international arms trade. Oakeley Arnold-Forster, then secretary of state for war, described him in 1904 as 'this clever but somewhat slippery gentleman' (diary, BL, Add. MS 50342). He was inveterate and ingenious in his efforts to maintain orders. At the height of the Anglo-American naval rivalry Dawson sent Walter Long, first lord of the Admiralty, data 'very secretly obtained from absolutely reliable sources' on US government orders for armour plate, intended to strengthen Long's case in cabinet for large naval spending (T. Dawson to W. Long, 1 Nov 1920, Wilts. & Swindon RO, Long MS 716/1).

Dawson was at the centre of the munitions crisis of 1914–18. 'This Is A Big War! so send Sir Trevor Dawson … [to] New York with carte blanche', Lord Fisher urged Winston Churchill on 2 March 1915. 'You want a "pusher" like Dawson who will go everywhere and buy everything!' (Gilbert, 608). Dawson had the trust of many officials and politicians, and tried to serve the national interest as he perceived it; but the expansion of Vickers' armaments output was so great and conditions so disrupted that misjudgments were inevitable. There were many accusations of overpricing. As Christopher Addison, minister of munitions, noted of a meeting in 1916, 'Trevor Dawson metaphorically shrouded himself in the Union Jack and almost wept as I expostulated that these great patriotic firms were charging too much' (Bodl. Oxf., Addison diary, 8 Feb 1916).

Dawson was a decisive force in Vickers during the company's financial and managerial crisis in 1920–26, and remained a director until his death. Nevertheless the appointment of the ordnance specialist Sir George Buckham to the Vickers board after the war, followed after 1925 by the rise on the naval side of Dawson's protégé Charles Craven and the appointment of Sir J. F. Noel Birch (1865–1939) to take charge of land armaments in 1928, were signs of Dawson's declining powers at Vickers. Several incidents contributed to this decline. In 1915–16 he was involved with the Canadian speculator Grant Morden MP in launching the British Cellulose and Chemical Manufacturing Company. After unscrupulous 'bulling', the company's 6d. shares of 1916 were worth £14 10s. in 1918. This profiteering became notorious as the 'dope scandal' investigated by the select committee on national expenditure in 1918 and by an official enquiry chaired by Lord Sumner in 1919. Dawson's standing was further injured by litigation in 1920 between Admiral Sir Percy Scott and Vickers, caused by Dawson's careless dealings with Scott over royalty payments on his patented naval gun-sights. At one stage the judge, Lord Coleridge, interrupted Dawson's evidence to comment, 'that will not do: I was not born yesterday', and after judgment was given in the admiral's favour, Dawson offered to resign from the Vickers board. His interests continued to seem suspect: the colonial secretary Leo Amery recorded in 1924, 'Trevor Dawson came to see me about oil in Mosul—evidently in connexion with Inverforth's most shady and unpatriotic negotiations with the Turks' (Barnes and Nicholson, 391).

Dawson was a forceful proponent of airships from the inception of Vickers' airship building programme in 1908. He wrote a paper on the subject for *Engineering* (22 October 1920), a letter in *The Times* (11 July 1921), and an article in *Brassey's Naval Annual, 1921–22*. In 1924 he persuaded Vickers to collaborate with Dennistoun Burney's companies in constructing the R100 airship. It was a technical success during flights in 1929–30, but as the British government contributed only £350,000 towards building costs of £460,000 and a base charge of £110,000, Vickers lost £220,000. Dawson was an expansive, ebullient man, and his rumbustiousness, which had so well suited the Edwardian arms race and wartime production crisis, was a liability in the conditions of disarmament and worldwide arms surpluses prevailing in the 1920s.

Dawson received medals from the Royal Society of Arts and the Junior Institution of Engineers (of which he was president in 1912–13). He was prime warden of the Fishmongers' Company in 1920–21 and held decorations from Spain and Japan. He was a strong imperialist. For twenty years he was a knight (latterly knight-president) of the Round Table Club, which fostered inter-imperial trade and held banquets for visiting dominion leaders in London. In 1916 he formed a pressure group called the London Imperialists, intended to secure the election of business-minded MPs for London constituencies; it was later

reorganized and expanded as the British Commonwealth Union, on whose executive committee he sat in 1918–25.

Knighted on 9 November 1909, Dawson was listed to receive a barony in the new year's honours of 1917, but his name was deleted at the last moment (possibly because of the political unpopularity of the big armaments companies). He was consoled with a baronetcy on 5 February 1920. Dawson died very abruptly, of heart failure, on 19 May 1931, at his country home, Edgewarebury House, Elstree, Hertfordshire, and was buried on 21 May in Elstree churchyard. RICHARD DAVENPORT-HINES

Sources *The Times* (20 May 1931), 16 · O. Arnold-Forster, diary, BL, Add. MS 50342, 20 Dec 1904 · Wilts. & Swindon RO, Long MS 716/1 · C. Addison, diary, 8 Feb 1916, Bodl. Oxf. · M. Gilbert, ed., *Winston S. Churchill*, companion vol. 3 (1972) · *The Leo Amery diaries*, ed. J. Barnes and D. Nicholson, 1 (1980) · J. D. Scott, *Vickers: a history* (1962) · C. Trebilcock, *The Vickers brothers* (1977) · R. P. T. Davenport-Hines, 'The British marketing of armaments, 1885–1935', *Markets and bagmen: studies in the history of marketing and British industrial performance, 1830–1939*, ed. R. P. T. Davenport-Hines (1986), 146–91 · R. P. T. Davenport-Hines, 'Vickers as a multinational before 1945', *British multinationals: origins, management and performance*, ed. G. Jones (1986), 43–67 · R. P. T. Davenport-Hines, *Dudley Docker: the life and times of a trade warrior* (1984) · D. C. Coleman, 'War demand and industrial supply: the "dope scandal", 1915–1919', *War and economic development: essays in memory of David Joslin*, ed. J. M. Winter (1975), 205–27 · R. P. T. Davenport-Hines, 'Vickers' Balkan conscience: aspects of Anglo-Romanian armaments, 1918–39', *Business in the age of depression and war*, ed. R. P. T. Davenport-Hines (1990), 253–85 · b. cert. · Burke, *Peerage* · *Debrett's Peerage* · *Kelly's directory* · *Vickers News*

Archives BL, diary of Oakeley Arnold-Forster, Add. MS 50342 · BL, corresp. of Sir Henry Campbell-Bannerman · Bodl. Oxf., Addison deposit · CAC Cam., Reginald McKenna MSS · CUL, Vickers archives · HLRO, Sir Patrick Hannon MSS · PRO, Admiralty MSS · PRO, Air Ministry MSS · PRO, Cabinet Office MSS · PRO, Foreign Office MSS · PRO, Ministry of Munitions MSS · PRO, War Office MSS

Likenesses photograph, 1920–29, repro. in *The Times*, 18 · portrait, *c*.1930, CUL, Vickers archives; repro. in Trebilcock, *Vickers brothers*

Wealth at death £257,589: probate, 7 Aug 1931, *CGPLA Eng. & Wales*

Dawson, William (1773–1841), Wesleyan Methodist preacher, was born on 30 March 1773 at Garforth, near Leeds, the eldest child of Luke Dawson and his wife, Ann Pease. His father was colliery steward to Sir Thomas Gascoigne, bt, of Gawthorpe for twenty-one years. On his father's death in 1791 William succeeded to this post, which included the management of a farm of 150 acres. William, whose parents moved to Barnbow, near Barwick, in his infancy, was educated locally and at the school of a Mr Sanderson at Aberford. His literary ability was noticed by John Graham, curate of Barwick, and others; they hoped to send him to Cambridge with a view to his taking orders in the Church of England. Family and financial reasons put a stop to this plan.

During the Leeds conference of 1793 and subsequently, Dawson heard several eminent Wesleyan ministers, and after long reflection he joined the Wesleyans, becoming an accredited local preacher among them. His popularity steadily increased until he became famous as the eloquent Yorkshire Farmer. He was invited to become an itinerant minister, but his mother and seven young children were dependent upon his income as steward and farmer, and he declined the offer. While working hard as a colliery superintendent and a practical farmer he developed remarkable dramatic powers. On the platform and in the pulpit his natural oratory exercised an unusual charm, moving his audiences to laughter or to tears. He advocated the shortening of the hours of labour in factories and addressed other public issues.

In September 1837 Dawson retired from his employment, and his time became mostly occupied in the opening of chapels, the preaching of anniversary sermons, the advocacy of Christian missions among the heathen, and other charitable objects. From Burmantofts, Leeds, where he now lived, he made preaching tours through the three kingdoms. While at Colne, Lancashire, where he had gone to open a new chapel, he died suddenly on Sunday morning, 4 July 1841. W. B. LOWTHER, *rev.* TIM MACQUIBAN

Sources J. Everett, *Memoirs of the life, character and ministry of William Dawson, late of Barnbow* (1844) · *Selections from the correspondence of William Dawson, late of Barnbow*, ed. J. Everett (1842)
Archives Wesley's Chapel, London, letters

Dawson, William Harbutt (1860–1948), journalist and civil servant, was born on 27 July 1860 at South Field Terrace, Skipton in Craven, Yorkshire, the third of the eight children of John Thomas Dawson (1833–1888), founder and editor of the *Craven Pioneer*, a Liberal newspaper, and his wife, Ann Hurd Harbutt (1828–1893). Brought up in a liberal and nonconformist environment, he attended the Skipton grammar school and Ilkley College before working for his father's paper, which became the *West Yorkshire Pioneer*. After various posts at other papers Dawson went to Berlin in 1885 and worked for a British–German paper to complete his journalistic training. While still contributing articles to his father's *Pioneer* and to other papers, he developed an inexhaustible interest in German social policy. He gave up his job and in October 1886 matriculated at the University of Berlin, where he became a convert to Bismarckian and Lassallean state socialism for a time. These ideas were expressed in his early works, *German socialism and Ferdinand Lassalle: a biographical history of the German socialistic movements during this century* (1888) and above all *Bismarck and state socialism: an exposition of the social and economic legislation of Germany since 1870* (1890), which he pragmatically adapted to British conditions. He considered some sort of state intervention within a free-trade framework to be the crucial innovation to secure the survival of the Liberal Party in the age of the extended franchise.

The sudden death of his father in April 1888 ended Dawson's fruitful time in Berlin as he immediately returned to Skipton to take on the editorship of the *Pioneer*; here he gained importance as a public figure, committed to charitable and educational work, while developing the *Pioneer* as a Liberal forum. On 10 September 1889 he married his first wife, Anna Clara Augusta Gruetz (1862–1912), daughter of Dr A. W. Gruetz, whom he had met during his time in Berlin. They had one son. Dawson turned out a considerable flow of articles for other papers and journals,

including the *Fortnightly Review* and the *National Review*, notably on German social policy, alongside publishing popularist accounts of things German. These were informed by his network of personal contacts in Germany, the most important of whom was Emil Münsterberg, the Berlin city councillor for poor relief and one of the leading authorities in Germany in the field of social policy. In 1906 Dawson published *The German Workman: a Study in National Efficiency*, which paid tribute to the currently popular slogan of national efficiency.

Dawson's expertise on Germany was of interest to the Liberal government, which was about to embark upon a programme of welfare reforms. In February 1906 he was appointed as a temporary investigator at the Board of Trade with the prospect of a permanent position. He sold his newspaper and moved to Beckenham, Kent. His first brief was to examine the functioning of labour exchanges in Germany, and the empirical groundwork which he provided contributed to the ideas of Hubert Llewellyn Smith and later William Beveridge that were embodied in the Labour Exchange Act of 1909 and part two of the National Insurance Act (1911). He also turned out memoranda and reports, gave evidence to commissions, trained other board officials, and was involved in the great statistical inquiries of the Board of Trade on the cost of living of the working classes in Britain and Germany. When, in February 1909, he was promoted to the permanent post of a first-class staff officer in the commercial, labour, and statistical department of the Board of Trade, the board's permanent secretary, Llewellyn Smith, explained to the Treasury that: 'Mr. Dawson's unique knowledge of Germany would in itself be a sufficient reason for retaining his services, for all modern labour problems centre around German experience' (PRO, BT 11/2 C7761, December 1908).

In 1908 Dawson's book on the second empire, *The Evolution of Modern Germany* (1908), was published. Reprinted five times before the First World War, this liberal and progressive interpretation confirmed Dawson's reputation as a matchless authority. It was followed by two further standard reference works: *Social Insurance in Germany* (1912), which included a comparison with the National Insurance Act of 1911, and *Municipal Life and Government in Germany* (1914). His books served a more popular interest as well as the academic demand for systematic knowledge, and reflected the considerable British interest in German ways, especially in the years after the Second South African War. He continued to lend his knowledge to policy makers, notably when Lloyd George became interested in the German precedent of compulsory social insurance after the Old Age Pensions Bill (1908) and began work on a scheme of national insurance following his famous visit to Germany in August of that year. Lloyd George drew upon Dawson's expertise on the German social security system, particularly in the final stages of the legislative process in the spring of 1911.

In February 1912 Dawson was transferred to the National Health Insurance Commission for England, where he remained as a principal clerk until his retirement in 1920. His first wife died in February 1912 and on 8 July 1913 he married Else Münsterberg (1884–1955), the daughter of the late Emil Münsterberg; they had three daughters and one son. The outbreak of war in 1914 came as a profound shock to many British Germanophiles such as Dawson. His resulting booklet, *What is Wrong with Germany?* (1915), contributed to the theory of the two Germanies by separating the 'bad' Germany of Treitschke, Bernhardi, Moltke, and Wilhelm II from the 'good' Germany of Goethe, Kant, vom Stein, and Bismarck. He advocated a fair and democratic peace settlement to support the breakthrough of the 'good' forces within Germany. As a member of the British delegation at the Versailles peace negotiations dealing with the fate of the former German colonies, he argued that Germany should keep its colonies. After his retirement he campaigned for this issue, and continued to write on Germany, urging a revision of the treaty of Versailles in *Germany under the Treaty* (1933). His concept of a 'national character' prevented Dawson from fully recognizing the nature of the new Nazi regime, and led him in 1936 to accept an honorary doctorate from Königsberg University at a ceremony at the German embassy in London. As his appeasing attitude towards Nazi Germany damaged his public reputation, he retreated to his favourite pastime of gardening at his house in Headington, near Oxford.

Dawson, who was 5 feet 6 inches tall, slim, with broad shoulders and deep-set eyes, enjoyed remarkable health and fitness throughout his life. An unsociable personality, constantly preoccupied with his work and with little taste for trivial conversation, he had very few personal friends beyond his immediate family. He died at the Radcliffe Infirmary, Oxford, on 7 March 1948, following surgery after prostate trouble, and was buried in Headington cemetery. The most prominent mediator of German precedents to the British public as well as Whitehall before 1914 was survived by his many publications, some of which were to become textbooks at universities for a new generation of students of Germany.   JÖRG FILTHAUT

Sources U. Birm., W. H. Dawson MSS · J. Filthaut, *Dawson und Deutschland: das deutsche Vorbild und die Reformen im Bildungswesen, in der Stadtverwaltung und in der Sozialversicherung Großbritanniens, 1880–1914* (1994) · private information (2004) · S. Leibfried, '"System" Konkurrenz und Modell "Transfer", oder, Wie kommt eine gehörige Portion "Bismarckismus" zu den englischen sozialen Unterschichten?', *Zeitschrift für Sozialreform*, 34 (1988), 547–89 · G. Hollenberg, *Englisches Interesse am Kaiserreich: die Attraktivität Preußen-Deutschlands für konservative und liberale Kreise in Großbritannien, 1860–1914* (1974) · E. P. Hennock, *British social reform and German precedents: the case of social insurance, 1880–1914* (1987) · PRO, BT 5, 11; T 1 · F. Tennstedt, 'Anfänge sozialpolitischer Intervention in Deutschland und England: einige Hinweise zu wechselseitigen Beziehungen', *Zeitschrift für Sozialreform*, 29 (1983), 631–48 · G. A. Ritter, *Social welfare in Germany and Britain* (1986) · *The Times* (10 March 1948) · S. Berger, 'William Harbutt Dawson: the career and politics of an historian of Germany', *EngHR*, 115 (2000), 76–113
Archives JRL, letters to *Manchester Guardian* · U. Birm., corresp. and papers

Wealth at death £12,575 10s. 6d.: probate, 3 July 1948, *CGPLA Eng. & Wales*

Dawtry, Frank Dalmeny (1902–1968), probation service organizer, was born on 17 January 1902 at 54 Cromwell Street, Walkley, Sheffield, the son of Wycliffe Bright Dawtry, cabinet-maker, and his wife, Alice Jackson Ross. His father was a Unitarian and keen Liberal, who had been apprenticed as a pattern maker by his father, a renowned foundry foreman, when the use of cast iron was at its height. The youngest and most delicate of four brothers, Dawtry won a scholarship to the Sheffield central secondary school, but left at fifteen owing to a breakdown in health. After a period as office boy and later junior clerk in a Sheffield steelworks, he was thrown out of work for almost two years after the trade recession of 1921. This early experience of unemployment made him familiar with the problems faced by the less fortunate members of the community and at this time he became a member of the Independent Labour Party.

In 1923 chance led him to the field of work to which he was to devote his energies for the next forty years. He was appointed clerk bookkeeper to the Sheffield Council of Social Service and within four years became secretary of its personal services committee. At the same time, after a brief apprenticeship with the Wakefield Discharged Prisoners' Aid Society, he was appointed secretary and thus began his close co-operation with the Probation Service. On 19 October 1931 at Port Erin, Isle of Man, Dawtry married Dora Anna, a schoolteacher, whose father, James Robinson Corrin, a local builder and a member of the House of Keys, was appointed MBE on 29 October 1957, the same day as Dawtry, who was advanced to OBE in 1967. They had no children.

Dawtry worked hard to co-ordinate the work of the other local discharged prisoners' aid societies and during this time made weekly visits to both Leeds and Wakefield prisons, where he organized discharge committees and was responsible for the welfare of the prisoners. On the foundation of the National Association of Discharged Prisoners' Aid Societies in 1937 Dawtry was the first to be appointed resident Discharged Prisoners' Aid Society secretary and welfare officer at HM Prison, Wakefield. Additionally he was involved with the first local open prison and the training centre for prison staff. He found a ready acceptance from both prisoners and staff at Wakefield and spent much time visiting and helping prisoners' families. He also travelled extensively, lecturing about prisoners and their needs and enlisting financial support for what was still a voluntary society.

Revised methods of training prisoners were developed, and when the new system was extended to Maidstone prison in 1944 Dawtry was appointed organizer there. However, two years later, feeling that the continued existence of capital punishment in Britain could not be reconciled with his view of the good society, Dawtry resigned and became secretary of the National Council for the Abolition of the Death Penalty. Almost at once he initiated a misleadingly successful campaign, for no sooner had the death penalty been suspended for a trial period than public pressure caused the question to be reconsidered, and it had to be reimposed by the home secretary. However, the number of executions was substantially reduced until the eventual abolition of the death penalty in 1965.

In 1948 Dawtry became general secretary to the National Association of Probation Officers, for which cause he worked untiringly until his retirement in January 1967. He commenced long overdue negotiations on the pay and conditions of service of probation officers. Largely because of his personal influence and his wise and dedicated efforts, the voice of the service was increasingly heard in matters of policy relating to its duties and the prevention and treatment of delinquency. During those years of almost constant change in the scope and nature of its functions, he focused and expressed the view of the service in a way which enabled it to contribute increasingly, from its wealth of practical experience, to the many legislative and other decisions which led to the creation of the modern probation and aftercare service.

For many years, and up to the time of his death, he was on the executive of the Howard League for Penal Reform and an active member of the Institute for the Study and Treatment of Delinquency. He was a founder member of the National Association for the Care and Resettlement of Offenders, was equally involved with the National Association for Mental Health, and was on the council of the National Citizens' Advice Bureaux. He was a convinced pacifist and founded the Sheffield No More War movement, serving as secretary until it amalgamated with the Peace Pledge Union, of whose council he was a member. He was also a fellow of the Royal Society of Arts as well as belonging to many other bodies which reflected his concern for peace, justice, and beauty. In May 1963 the University of Leeds conferred on him the degree of master of arts, *honoris causa*.

After his death at his home, 2 Limes Road, Weybridge, on 5 October 1968, a Frank Dawtry memorial was established whereby a public seminar on a subject in the field of the treatment of offenders, the prevention of crime, and the administration of justice is held regularly in the University of Leeds.

His warmth of personality and love of people, particularly the underdog and the victim of inequality in society, were translated into a life of service without thought of personal reward. To care was to do. He fully understood the importance of political action in furthering the causes for which he was concerned, and had a close association with the House of Commons, where the lord chancellor honoured him with a retirement dinner to express the appreciation of his parliamentary and civil service friends.

He had an intense love of cricket, and for forty years was a keen member of Yorkshire County Cricket Club. His slight figure was familiar and respected on the international scene as well as at the smallest probation branch conference, where his lively mind and imagination were alert to the impact and potential of new ideas. Modest and dedicated, with a keen sense of humour, he was a visionary who translated his visions into achievements, not only for the Probation Service but in the whole field of penology. KENNETH THOMPSON, *rev.*

Sources *The Times* (7 Oct 1968) · *The Times* (9 Oct 1968) · personal knowledge (1981) · private information (1981) · *CGPLA Eng. & Wales* (1968)

Wealth at death £7233: probate, 31 Dec 1968, *CGPLA Eng. & Wales*

Day, Alexander (1745–1841), miniature painter and art dealer, was born in Somerset, the son of John Day. He was the pupil of Ozias Humphry in London, and exhibited miniatures with the Society of Artists in 1768, 1772, and 1773. He was described as 'At Mr Humphrey's, King Street, Covent Garden' in 1768, and as the 'Late Pupil of Mr Humphry's' in 1773 (Graves, *Soc. Artists*). In December 1773 he was at Lyons, travelling to Rome, where Humphry, already resident, obtained a room for him. On his arrival in April 1774 Day was described as a 'scolar to Humphrys' (Stainton). He was to stay more than forty years, practising as a miniaturist, copyist, and dealer.

From 1774 to 1777 Day shared apartments with Humphry in the strada Gregoriana and strada Felice; after Humphry left in April 1777 he continued living in the strada Felice with the Scottish painter James Nevay. He also became the friend of the artist Prince Hoare, who was in Rome between 1776 and 1779, and remained in correspondence with him between 1780 and 1791 (letters in the Beinecke Library, Yale University). On 8 December 1792 Day, described as being forty-two, married Anna Mattei, aged twenty-four, 'an Italian woman who he had secreted in his apartment three years & had children by her'; he had been obliged to marry her 'on it being discovered by an Ecclesiastical authority' (Farington, *Diary*, 4.1380). In 1801 Day and his wife had a son and two daughters aged between one and nine.

Very little is known of Day's work as an artist, though contemporary accounts show he maintained a practice in Rome. A miniature of John, Lord Hervey, dated 1795, is at Ickworth, Suffolk; he copied a portrait of Lady Hamilton in 1792 and painted William Lambton in 1797 (both untraced). His miniatures of Venus and Antinous (ex Sothebys, 11 July 1991) are dated 1793, the year in which Day's miniatures were described as 'much inferior in merit to several in London' (journal of Sir William Forbes, Ingamells, 285), but by that time he was also being employed as a copyist by the fourth earl of Bristol and Philip Hardwicke (later third earl of Hardwicke).

Already in 1779 Day was being described as both a miniature painter and a dealer (Gwynne, 164). In 1787 he was trying to persuade the sculptor Vincenzo Pacetti to sell a marble faun, and in January 1792 he was sending to Sir William Hamilton in Naples 'a Colossal Head & Leg' (Ingamells, 286) cast (presumably) from the celebrated group *Alexander and Bucephalus* on Monte Cavallo (of which Day subsequently assembled a set of casts). When the French invaded Rome in 1798 Day was able to make spectacular acquisitions from apprehensive Italian collectors, in particular from the Aldobrandini, Borghese, and Colunna palaces. At the time he had two French officers billeted on him, 'but they provided for themselves and almost daily invited him to their dinner, thinking it unreasonable to live upon Artists' (Farington, *Diary*, 4.1571); Day meanwhile secreted his pictures 'in walls etc' (Farington, *Diary*, 3.1066).

In 1800 Day returned to London and exhibited his purchases for sale by private contract at 20 Lower Brook Street. There were twenty-nine paintings, including masterpieces now in the National Gallery, London, such as Titian's *Bacchus and Ariadne*, Raphael's *Aldobrandini Madonna* and *St Catherine*, the Michelangelo 'Manchester Madonna' and Annibale Carracci's *Domine quo vadis*, besides Bellini's *Feast of the Gods*, now in the National Gallery, Washington, and the Graeco-Roman bas-relief *The Apotheosis of Homer*, now in the British Museum. It was a remarkable exhibition; whenever he visited it Benjamin West said he 'used to walk home as if he felt himself some inches taller' (Buchanan, 2.9). In July 1801 Day returned to Rome. He sent more pictures to London in 1802 and 1806, and in 1804 he briefly returned with Vincenzo Camuccini, one of two brothers, who were acting as his business partners in Rome. He was again exhibiting pictures in London in 1808.

Although at Easter 1816 Day and his family were listed in the via Sistina (as the strada Felice had become in 1804), in March that year he had already been lodging in London 'for the past six months' with the gem-engraver Nathaniel Marchant (Farington, *Diary*, 14.4805). In February he had appeared before a parliamentary commission as an enthusiastic witness for the purchase of the Elgin marbles. He had also been permitted by the prince regent to adapt the royal stables in the King's Mews for an exhibition of his casts from Monte Cavallo together with further pictures and antiquities. Prince Hoare wrote an explanatory pamphlet for the exhibition which was open at least from February to September. In July, Day was said to have married Mrs Burnage, Marchant's housekeeper, who had been in 'a very poor state of health' on her master's death in March, but had subsequently received more than £9000 in his will (ibid., 4805, 4878); there was then no mention of Day's previous marriage.

There are few facts concerning Day's later years. In 1819 he was offering pictures to the prince regent from an address at the 'Mews Gallery, Charing Cross' (*Letters of George IV*, 2.294–5). He apparently returned to Rome, for in 1821 Farington noted that Day 'who has long been a resident in Rome' had enabled an English artist, Evans, to make copies of Raphael's *Loggie* (Farington, *Diary*, 16.5745). On 21 June 1833 Day held a sale in London at Christies which included pictures from the Aldobrandini collection. He died in Chelsea in his ninety-sixth year on 12 January 1841, by which time, according to his obituarist, he had often been described as 'long since deceased' (*Art Union*, 87). The final dispersal of his collections took place at Christies on 27 May 1843 and 24 May 1845.

When his obituary was reprinted in the *Gentleman's Magazine*, new series, 16 (1841), 101–2, his age was transposed from '96' to '69', which led all his subsequent biographers to assume the existence of at least two, and sometimes three, artists called Day.

JOHN INGAMELLS

Sources J. Ingamells, ed., *A dictionary of British and Irish travellers in Italy, 1701–1800* (1997), 285–6 · Farington, *Diary*, 3.1066; 4.1164, 1380, 1511, 1525, 1571; 14. 4805, 4817, 4878, 4886, 4900; 16.5745 · W. Buchanan, *Memoirs of painting: with a chronological history of the importation of pictures by the great masters into England*, 2 vols. (1824), 2–10 · *Art Union*, 3 (1841), 87 · A. Michaelis, *Ancient marbles in Great Britain*, trans. C. A. M. Fennell (1882), 148 · *The letters of King George IV, 1812–1830*, ed. A. Aspinall, 2 (1938), 294–6 · Graves, *Soc. Artists* · Paul Mellon Centre, London, Brinsley Ford Archive · L. Stainton, 'Hayward's list: British visitors to Rome, 1753–1755', *Walpole Society*, 49 (1983), 3–36, esp. 15 · S. Gwynne, *Memorials of an eighteenth-century painter: James Northcote* (1898), 164 · O. Michel, *Mélanges de l'école française de Rome*, 84 (1972), 2.500, n3
Archives Yale U., letters to Prince Hoare
Likenesses pencil drawing, NPG

Day, Alfred (1810–1849), music theorist, was born in London in January 1810. His father disapproved of his early enthusiasm for music, and he proceeded to study medicine in London and Paris, eventually gaining a diploma from Heidelberg. On his return to London he set up in practice as a homoeopathist, while at the same time nurturing his musical interests. He received instruction from the opera conductor W. H. Kearns and sought the acquaintance of prominent younger musicians such as George Macfarren. Around 1840 he was engaged by Macfarren's father as a critic for the *Musical World*, 'until he could no longer bear with the laconical bitterness of this reviewer' (Banister, 80). He had already begun work on his controversial *Treatise on Harmony*, the work on which his reputation is entirely based; it was eventually published in London in 1845.

In his attempt to explain harmonic practice in a scientific manner, Day was subscribing to a tradition that stretched back to Rameau's treatise of 1722. But he felt dissatisfied with the inconsistencies of earlier theory, and sought to devise a comprehensive and logical system, based on two broad principles. Firstly, he proposed a clear distinction between the ancient and modern styles: the one strict, diatonic, and contrapuntal, with codifiable laws of dissonance preparation; the other free, chromatic, and harmonic (the chromatic notes explicable without recourse to modulation). Secondly, he developed a systematic theory of harmonic progression, based on three fundamental chords of tonic, supertonic, and dominant, all with the possibility of superimposed thirds up to the thirteenth. The novelty and complexity of this seemingly dogmatic system led initially to a cold reception. Macfarren, however, espoused Day's theories at the Royal Academy of Music, even resigning in 1847 when his adherence was questioned; he published a second edition of the *Treatise* in 1885. Day's work was enormously influential on British pedagogy in the later nineteenth century, but his concentration on harmony as a generative procedure has been much criticized, and superseded by a modern view of functional harmony within a contrapuntal context.

Day's intellectual curiosity led him constantly to question established modes of thought, in medicine as well as in music. But he did not live to see his ideas achieve a measure of acceptance during the Victorian era. Following several years of illness he died from consumption at 102 Park Street, Camden, London, on 11 February 1849.

SIMON MCVEIGH

Sources *Musical World* (17 Feb 1849), 97 · J. F. Waller, ed., *The imperial dictionary of universal biography*, new edn, 3 vols. (1877–84) · H. C. Banister, *George Alexander Macfarren* (1891) · Grove, *Dict. mus.* · G. Haydon, 'Alfred Day and the theory of harmony', *Papers read at the International Congress of Musicology* [New York 1939], ed. A. Mendel and others (1944), 233–40 · P. C. Jones, 'Alfred Day and nineteenth-century theory of harmony in England', PhD diss., Rutgers University, 1977 · d. cert.

Day, Angell (*fl.* 1563–1595), stationer and writer, was the son of Thomas Day (Daye), parish clerk. Though little is known of his personal life, Day was apprenticed to Thomas Duxsell, stationer in London, in 1563, beginning his service on Christmas day of that year. By 1575 Day probably had completed his apprenticeship; however, he next distinguished himself as the compiler of a handbook for epistle writing entitled *The English Secretorie*, printed first in 1586 in London by Robert Waldegrave and sold by Richard Jones. Day's book was so successful that it was reprinted in 1592 and again in 1595, 1599, 1607, and 1614. Other subsequent printings occurred: one identified as 'now newly revised', which Pollard and Redgrave dated at 1618, and later printings which are identified as having been printed in 1621, 1625, 1626, and 1635. There also appears to have been a printing of the second part of the book alone in 1614. By the time of its final printing *The English Secretorie* had been in print regularly for almost fifty years. The second printing of the book, entered in the Stationers' register in 1587, but not printed finally until 1592, was dedicated to Sir William Hatton, to whom Day had appealed for patronage in his dedication to *Daphnis and Chloe*, also published in 1587.

Encouraged perhaps by the success of this early work, and urged on by the popularity of pastorals such as Edmund Spenser's *Shepheardes Calendar* (1579), Day produced an adaptation of *Daphnis and Chloe*, a pastoral romance translated from the Greek into French by Jacques Amyot (printed in 1559). Day's version appeared in 1587 (also printed by Robert Waldegrave). Since its republication in a facsimile edition (1890, ed. Joseph Jacobs) literary critics have noted the poem's overt nationalism, with its idealized depiction of Queen Elizabeth as a symbol of England. Today Day's translation of *Daphnis and Chloe* survives in only one copy, now housed in the collection of the British Library.

Day's other literary work was more modest in scope and stature. In 1595 he published commendatory verses, *Nennio, or, A Treatise of Nobility*, a translation of the Italian humanist treatise by William Jones, 'gentleman', printed by Peter Short, who produced the 1599 edition of *The English Secretorie*. Two additional pieces are frequently attributed to Day. The first is the printing of a poem in six-line stanzas entitled *Upon the Life and Death of the most Worthy*

and Thrice Renowned Knight, Sir Phillip Sidney by Robert Waldegrave in 1587 bearing the authorial initials 'A.D.'. The second is a pamphlet (not dated, but thought to be *c*.1585) entitled *Wonderfull Strange Sightes Seene in the Element, over the Citie of London and other Places*.

Nothing is known of Day's life beyond the details of his apprenticeship and his publications. Although biographers have assumed that he gave up a career as a stationer in order to pursue his writing there is, in fact, no evidence to corroborate this. If nothing else, Day's consistent association with printers such as Robert Waldegrave and booksellers such as Cuthbert Burbie and Richard Jones suggests that he retained close ties with the world of printers and booksellers throughout his literary life.

S. P. CERASANO

Sources A. Day, *Daphnis and Chloe*, ed. J. Jacobs (1890) · STC, 1475–1640 · J. P. Collier, ed., *Extracts from the registers of the Stationers' Company of works entered for publication*, 2 vols. (1848–9), vol. 2 · J. Goldberg, *Writing matter* (Stanford, California, 1990) · J. G. McManaway, 'An uncollected poem of John Skeleton (?)', *N&Q*, 196 (1951), 134–5

Day, Charles (1782/3–1836), blacking manufacturer, was born in London, the son of the Yorkshire-born Francis Day, owner of a perfumery and 'hair warehouse' in Tavistock Street, Covent Garden. Charles Day was apprenticed as a barber and, about the turn of the century, plied his trade with Benjamin Martin (*d.* 1834), a native of Doncaster, who had worked as a hairdresser for Francis Day. Then Martin's brother-in-law, a Doncaster innkeeper, obtained—it is said, for a quart of ale—a blacking recipe from the soldier servant of a local recruiting officer, after admiring the high polish on the soldier's boots.

In 1801 Day went into partnership with Martin as blacking manufacturers at 97 High Holborn. There were liquid and paste varieties of their product, mainly sold in pots but later in tins embossed with the prominent number '97'. Society then expected all respectable people to have immaculately polished boots, and demand was brisk. Day and Martin were among the pioneers of advertising. In addition to inserting press notices, they purchased a hundred surplus liveries from Petticoat Lane, hired men to wear them, and sent this posse throughout London to enquire, one after the other, for the blacking in perfumers', oilmen's, and grocers' shops, with encouraging results. In 1808, Day spent £10,000 on buying out Martin, who retired to Doncaster, where he acquired property and died on 9 October 1834, leaving a widow, Hannah.

Day, the wealthier and more entrepreneurial of the two, then became sole proprietor. He had a powerful and accurate mind and paid close attention to detail. He was also overbearing, could not stand contradiction, and required complete obedience from his subordinates. He was highly displeased when in 1816, having brought a case in the court of chancery against a counterfeiter of his products, it was ruled that Day and Martin had no patent rights in their 'real japan blacking'.

Day and his wife, Rebecca, had one daughter. However, his will also mentioned three illegitimate children; it seems likely that his subsequent illness was syphilitic in origin. In 1816 he went blind and for the last two years of his life he was confined to a wheelchair, but he nevertheless retained full control of the firm, thanks to his extraordinary memory and the help of his daughter, who kept the accounts. In August 1836 he suffered an attack of epilepsy and died two months later, on 26 October 1836, at 97 High Holborn, London. His personal estate was assessed at £200,000 and his real estate at £140,000. He expected the firm to be sold at five years' purchase for £69,000, net profit being thus about £14,000 a year. Besides family bequests, he left £100,000 to found an asylum for blind people.

As four codicils dated from after his epileptic seizure, his three executors referred the will to the prerogative court. In mid-1838 the court struck out the final codicil, and that November the case was reopened before the master of the rolls. It was still being heard when Charles Dickens, in August 1853, asked his private secretary, William Henry Wills, for information on the case. Wills reported that its conclusion was as far away as ever (it collapsed in 1854), required thirty or forty counsel to appear at any one time, and had cost £70,000 to date. Dickens referred to it, but not by name, in the preface to *Bleak House* (1853). Day and Martin passed into non-family hands, became a limited company in 1896, and was voluntarily wound up in 1925.

T. A. B. CORLEY

Sources *GM*, 2nd ser., 7 (1837), 101–2 · *GM*, 2nd ser., 8 (1837), 661–2 · *GM*, 2nd ser., 10 (1838), 673–4 · *Croft v. Day* (1838), 1 Curteis 782, 163 ER 271; *Croft v. Day* (1843), 7 Beavan 84, 49 ER 994 [see also other reports, 1838–54] · *The letters of Charles Dickens*, ed. M. House, G. Storey, and others, 7 (1993), 128–9 · *Annual Register* (1836), 215 · *The Times* (19 Aug 1816) · A. Davis, *Package and print* (1967), 30, 41 · T. R. Nevett, *Advertising in Britain: a history* (1982), 36, 132–3 · *The Times* (28 Oct 1836), 4

Wealth at death £350,000–£370,000: *GM*, 2nd ser., 10, p. 673

Day, Daniel (1683–1767), engineer and founder of Fairlop fair, Essex, was born in Southwark, Surrey, where his father was a prosperous brewer. Day never married, and resided all his working life in Wapping, then on the eastern margin of London, where he pursued his trade as an engine, pump, and block maker. He was known as an upright and ingenious mechanic, and was responsible for many improvements and inventions. His modification to the brewers' jigger—a pump used to force beer into vats—was in use for many years. His business prospered and he became sufficiently wealthy to enjoy the pleasures of generosity, endowing his nieces at their marriages, and lending or giving to those in need. Such was his reputation for probity that he was regularly called on to settle local disputes.

Day had many inoffensive eccentricities, some of which he was able to indulge at what became Fairlop fair. He owned a small estate near the Fairlop oak, a venerable and wide-spreading oak in Hainault Forest, Essex, about 10 miles from London, and went there each summer to collect his rent. It became his custom to invite a few neighbours to accompany him, and after his business was done, to partake of a meal of beans and bacon prepared by the nearby public house and consumed under the oak tree's shade. In the course of a few years, this modest beanfeast

expanded into a vast gathering of local people as well as fun-seekers from London, to whom, nevertheless, Day continued to distribute beans and bacon beneath his favourite tree. The event naturally attracted a swarm of hucksters, who set up amusement stalls, giving, by 1725, the appearance of a regular fair.

In his youth, Day walked to Fairlop and back. Later he went on horseback, but after a fall, vowed never to mount a horse again and purchased a mule which, however, also threw him. He next took a post-chaise or cart, but in one of these he also met with an accident and thereafter refused to enter either. He then invented a machine to go by the aid of mechanical power alone, but it too failed on the third journey. His last resort was a jockey cart in which, attended by music, he made his annual trip until July 1767. For some years before his death the pump and block makers of Wapping attended the fair in a boat covered by an awning and mounted on a carriage drawn by six horses. A few years before his death the oak shed a large limb, out of which Day had a coffin made for himself. He died at Wapping on 19 October 1767; the catastrophes which he had suffered on his journeys induced him to direct that his remains be conveyed by water to his place of burial, the churchyard of Barking, Essex.

The roistering that accompanied the fair displeased the authorities, who made several attempts to suppress it, but it survived Day's death, the eventual destruction of Fairlop oak, and even the disafforestation of Hainault. About 1856 the area was enclosed but the fair transferred to various nearby sites before lapsing soon after 1900.

ANITA McCONNELL

Sources *Fairlop and its founder* (1847) · *The history and origin of Fairlop fair* (1808) · *VCH Essex*, 5.218 · G. E. Tasker, *Ilford past and present* (1901), 131–5 · D. Lysons, *The environs of London*, 4 (1796), 646–7

Day, Francis (*fl.* 1625–1652), founder of Madras, is first mentioned in the records of the East India Company as the founder of a factory (trading station) at Armagon, a small port on the Coromandel coast of eastern India, in 1626. The Coromandel coast was important to the European trading companies because it was there that they could purchase Indian textiles, notably chintz, a kind of 'painted' cloth made nowhere else and which was highly sought after in Europe. Diamonds, commonly used as a means of remitting money to Europe, were also available from nearby Golconda. In 1634 he was appointed a factor by the company, and in 1634 chief of Armagon. Owing to the dilapidated state of the Armagon factory, its impoverished trading hinterland, and oppression by both the local Indian ruler and the Dutch at Pulicat, Day had for some time contemplated the establishment of a new factory to the south. In 1637 he made an exploratory voyage from Masulipatam to Pondicherry, and in 1639 he again sailed south. On 23 July of that year he arrived at the coastal village of Madrasipatam, just south of the village of Chinnapatnam and north of the Portuguese settlement of San Thomé. Discovering the area to be a good source of textiles, he negotiated the grant of a plot of coastal land on behalf of the company from Damarla Venkatadri, the local ruler. In February 1640 Armagon was dismantled, and on 20 February the establishment arrived at Madras, where work soon began on building a new fort, later named Fort St George. For this construction Day took on loans on his own account. Finding the financial burden excessive, in August 1640 he proceeded to Surat to plead his case with the governing council, who, although freeing him of the responsibility, dispatched him to England in December 1640 to answer certain charges relating to private trading. Apparently exonerated by the company, Day was re-employed as a merchant for a voyage on the *Hopewell*, commanded by captain Andrew Trumbull, to Madras and Persia. He sailed accompanied by his son, also Francis, and the ship arrived at Madras on 5 July 1642, before proceeding to Balasore. At the end of 1642 he was again at Fort St George, sitting as second on council, before continuing to Persia. In mid-1643 Day and others charged Trumbull with violence and tyranny. In vituperative response, Trumbull accused Day of habitual drunkenness, of stealing a Danish captain's wife and two waiting gentlewomen, and of gaming and illicit private trading. However, Trumbull was dismissed and his allegations remain uncorroborated.

On 27 August 1643 Day took over as chief of Fort St George from Andrew Cogan, but immediately applied to the company to be relieved of the responsibility. He was superseded by Thomas Ivie on 4 August 1644, and on 7 September sailed for Bantam. His subsequent career remains obscure. In 1646, in England, he was fined by the company for private trading, and in 1652 he gave evidence in a case before the court of committee. His death is not recorded.

ANDREW GROUT

Sources H. D. Love, *Vestiges of old Madras, 1640–1800*, 4 vols. (1913) · N. S. Ramaswami, *The founding of Madras* (1977) · H. Furber, *Rival empires of trade in the orient* (1976) · J. J. Higginbotham, *Men whom India has known: biographies of eminent Indian characters*, 8 pts (1870–71)
Archives BL OIOC, factory records

Day, Francis (1829–1889), military surgeon and ichthyologist, was born on 2 March 1829 at Maresfield, Sussex, the third son of William Day (1797–1849) and his wife, Ann, *née* Elliott or Le Blanc. The family moved to Hadlow House in Maresfield about 1833, and farmed an estate of some 2000 acres. Day was educated at Shrewsbury School from 1838 to 1843, and it was here that his interests in natural history developed, revealed in 'boyish observations on the habits of fish' (*Cheltenham Examiner*).

In September 1848 Day enrolled at St George's Hospital in London to study medicine and in 1851 qualified as MRCS. In 1852 he was appointed as an assistant surgeon in the Madras establishment, India, and from 1853 to 1856 he was attached to various regiments at Mercara, Bangalore, and Hyderabad. His interests in Indian natural history began to develop, and subsequently his life was devoted to the people and fauna of India. His twenty-two years in the country were punctuated only by periodic returns to England to recuperate from illness.

Day spent much of 1857 in England on sick leave. He was elected a fellow of the Linnean Society on 16 June 1857; his proposal form indicated that it was his knowledge of ornithology that underpinned his application, rather than ichthyology—the branch of zoology for which he became best known. On 3 November 1857 he married Emma Covey of Basingstoke, Hampshire, and the couple travelled to India in 1858. From 1859 until 1864 they lived in Cochin, where Francis had been appointed civil surgeon. Most of his medical publications—largely accounts of fevers—date from this period. His daughter Fanny Laura was born in Cochin (November 1861), and it was here that he began to study fishes, explored the Nilgiri hills (1863), and wrote *The Land of the Permauls, or, Cochin its Past and Present* (1863).

The family returned to London in 1864, and a son, Francis Meredith, was born in April that year; they moved to Cheltenham in October. In 1865 Day's observations on Cochin fishes were presented at meetings of the Zoological Society—he had been elected a fellow in 1864—and *The Fishes of Malabar* was published. In 1866 Francis and Emma returned to India, leaving their two children in the care of family friends. Day had various posts in Ootacamund, Madras, and Kurnool, began a series of fish stocking experiments, and published on cholera; their second daughter, Edith Mary, was born in October 1867. In 1868 and 1869 Day undertook extensive fishery surveys around Madras, in Orissa, Burma, and the Andaman Islands. He published on new species of fishes and compiled a catalogue of Indian freshwater fishes. Following the death of his wife, Emma, in 1869, Day returned to England in 1870.

Day was appointed inspector-general of fisheries in July 1871. He divided his time between Calcutta and Simla, published extensively on his discoveries, and was promoted to surgeon-major in December. During a brief return to England in 1872 he married Emily Sheepshanks at Coventry on 13 April, the couple travelling together to India where they lived in Simla while Day continued his relentless survey work and published accounts of marine fish and fisheries of India. Sadly, Emily died in 1873, and in 1874 Francis Day left India for the last time, returning to England in May.

Day devoted all his energies to researching and writing about fishes, beginning with *The Fishes of India*. From his home in Richmond-on-Thames he made frequent visits to the British Museum (to examine specimens he had donated between 1864 and 1870), and also journeyed to Paris, Berlin, The Hague, and Leiden in 1875. Part 1 of *The Fishes of India* was published that year, with part 2 appearing in 1876, the same year that Day retired from the army and moved to Cheltenham. Parts 3 and 4 appeared in 1877 and 1878 respectively. Arguably *The Fishes of India* was Day's greatest achievement. While preparing this major publication, Day had been pursuing his interests in British fishes, and a clear indication of his industry was the publication of part 1 of *Fishes of Great Britain* in 1880. Parts 2 to 4 were completed and published between 1881 and 1884. In addition to writing he took an active role in a number of international fisheries exhibitions, including those in Paris (1875), Berlin (1880), and London (1883), and won several medals. His fascination with salmon and trout led to the publication of *British and Irish Salmonidae* in 1887. In the following year a supplement to *Fishes of India* appeared, and his scientific achievements were recognized by the award of an honorary LLD by the University of Edinburgh. In 1889 Day corrected in proof his last major work, the contribution on *Fishes* to the *Fauna of India*. In his journal articles and books Day had described some 328 new species of fishes. He died on 10 July 1889 at his home, Kenilworth House, Cheltenham.

In addition to his published works, Day's major legacy to science was his extensive collections. During his early career in India, he had interests in many aspects of natural history, and made collections of birds, insects, crustaceans, reptiles, and mammals in addition to fishes. Day's large collections of fishes—his own estimate of the number of specimens shipped to England in 1873 was 'about 12,000 specimens in spirit, besides skins'—were distributed among at least twelve institutions. The Indian Museum, Calcutta, the Australian Museum, Sydney, the Rijksmuseum in Leiden, the Zoologisches Museum, Berlin, and the Naturhistorisches Museum in Vienna retain substantial collections, but the largest is that at the Natural History Museum in London, where over five thousand specimens are deposited.   PETER DAVIS

Sources P. J. P. Whitehead and P. K. Talwar, 'Francis Day (1829–1889) and his collections of Indian fishes', *Bulletin of the British Museum (Natural History)* [Historical Series], 5 (1976–7) · *DNB* · *Nature*, 40 (1889), 282 · *Cheltenham Examiner* (17 July 1889)
Archives Australian Museum, Sydney, fishes · Cheltenham Public Library, Day's Natural History Library, letters, MSS, proofs, etc · Field Museum, Chicago, fishes · Harvard U., Museum of Comparative Zoology, fishes · Humbolt University, Berlin, Museum für Naturkunde, bird collection; corresp.; fishes · Indian Museum, Calcutta, fishes · Linn. Soc., corresp.; reprints, scrapbooks · Museo di Fiscia e Storia Naturale, Florence, fishes · NHM, letters and family records [photocopies] · NHM, crustaceans; fishes · NRA, priv. coll., journals, letters, notebooks, photographs · Rijksmuseum, Leiden, fishes · Zoological Museum, St Petersburg, fishes · Zoological Society of London, drawings and MSS · Cambridge, bird collection
Likenesses J. Hughes, photograph, 1865–6, priv. coll.; repro. in Whitehead and Talwar, 'Francis Day' · engraving, 1870–79, priv. coll.; repro. in Whitehead and Talwar, 'Francis Day' · E. White, photographs, 1880–89, priv. coll. · J. C. Egerton, oils, 1893, priv. coll.
Wealth at death £39,540 6s. 7d.: probate, 2 Aug 1889, *CGPLA Eng. & Wales*

Day, George (*c*.1502–1556), bishop of Chichester, was the third son of Richard Day, gentleman, of Newport, Shropshire, and Agnes Osborne, and the elder brother of William *Day (1529–1596). Early in 1521 he graduated BA from St John's College, Cambridge, the centre of humanism in the university. The following year he became a fellow, and in 1523 he had two short Latin verses printed in the treatise *Assertionis Lutheranae confutatio*, published by the university chancellor, John Fisher, bishop of Rochester, a co-founder of his college; these were his only published works. Having proceeded MA in 1524, he became first Linacre professor of medicine in 1525, and then the college praelector in Greek. Early in 1528 he became public orator to the university.

Ordained deacon at Lincoln on 7 March that year, Day

became chaplain to Fisher. The bishop perceptively observed in 1534, however, that Day 'studies to obtain the goodwill of both sides' (*LP Henry VIII*, 8.859). As orator he wrote the university's decree in support of the royal supremacy, and in spite of his connection with Fisher he was appointed a royal chaplain. From 1537, although vice-chancellor that year, he was often at court. Henry VIII gave Day the sapphire ring he later bequeathed to Archbishop Nicholas Heath, and royal influence was responsible for his appointments on 27 July 1537 as master of St John's, in September to the livings of Holsworthy, Devon, and All Hallows-the-Great, London, and then on 5 June 1538 as provost of King's College, Cambridge. Although he held no secular offices, he served on important ecclesiastical commissions. In November 1538 he was one of the theologians nominated to revise the articles in the Bishops' Book on the ten commandments, justification, and purgatory, and the same month was called to express the king's views at the trial for heresy of John Lambert. The following year the king wrote in his name as bishop of the proposed new diocese of Dunstable. In 1540 he was a member of the committee on doctrine, in February 1542 he was among those appointed to correct the New Testament in the short-lived plan to revise the Great Bible, and he was a member of the team responsible for the conservative article on justification in the King's Book (1543). He was further rewarded with prebends in Beverley College, York, and St Stephen's, Westminster, acquiring the latter on 23 March 1543.

When three weeks later, on 15 April, he was nominated as bishop of Chichester, Day resigned all his benefices, but kept the provostship of King's, by royal dispensation. He was installed by proxy but he usually resided and conducted regular visitations. In 1544 he and Bishop Nicholas Heath drew up the statutes for the cathedrals of the new foundation. In July 1545, by now almoner to Queen Katherine, he with others investigated the distribution of funds for the relief of the poor and maintenance of highways, and in the following July he was one of those appointed to nominate the recipients of these funds. In November he participated in a commission to investigate the alleged bigamy of Sir Ralph Sadler's wife. When early in 1546 Archbishop Thomas Cranmer suggested to Henry VIII that Day's endorsement of the abolition of certain ceremonies would make them more generally acceptable, Day duly acquiesced. That February he served on the commission to survey chantries in Sussex, Surrey, and Southwark.

The new reign began well enough for Day when his gift of books to the king earned from the young Edward VI praise for his learning. However, early in 1547 he criticized the fellows of King's for discontinuing private masses, and he resigned as provost before April 1548. He was not present on 9 September when Robert Ferrar became the first bishop to be consecrated according to the rites of the newly introduced English ordinal. His answers to Cranmer's questionnaire of 1548 on the sacraments upheld traditionalist views, except for an ambivalent response about the sacrificial aspect of the mass. Though he had opposed the order of communion of 1548, he enforced its use in his diocese. Later that year he was involved with the draft English prayer book but he objected to parts of it. He regularly attended the Lords, where in opposing most of the religious legislation of the reign he publicly identified himself with the conservative viewpoint, most notably in the debates on the eucharist in December 1548 when he audaciously cited the executed Bishop Fisher and spoke in support of transubstantiation. In January 1549 he voted against the Act of Uniformity and continued to oppose changes in religion except for the Act on Fast Days of 1549. In April 1549 he was appointed to a commission to investigate radical heresies, but he does not seem to have been an active member. In April 1550, possibly in response to the threat of deprivation, he preached a sermon against transubstantiation. Though the following October he cleared himself against a charge of seditious preaching, he was summoned before the council in November and December for his refusal to replace altars with tables in churches in his diocese. He was committed to the Fleet prison on 11 December, and deprived on 10 October 1551. In January 1552 he rejected an offer from the secretary of state William Cecil (another St John's man) to free him if he would accept the removal of altars. In June he was transferred to the custody of the chancellor, Thomas Goodrich, bishop of Ely, possibly through the intervention of Sir John Cheke, his former pupil (his 'bringer-upp … in learning'; Nichols, clxi) and his successor as provost of King's. Cheke, now a royal tutor, had praised Day's learning and loyalty to the crown.

Immediately after Mary's accession, Day was released on 4 August 1553. A distinguished preacher, he was the queen's choice to preach at the funeral of Edward VI on 8 August. His provocative sermon praised the late king but attacked the religious politics of Edward's regime. By 29 September 1553 he was the queen's almoner, and on 1 October he preached at her coronation. In March 1554 he was appointed to the commissions to deprive protestant bishops. In November 1555 during a visit to John Bradford he confessed that fresh from the university, he 'went with the word' but 'it was always against my conscience', although he acknowledged that he approved communion in two kinds for the laity (Acts and Monuments, 7.176 and 178). That year he was involved in the examinations of Bishop John Hooper, John Philpot, and others. The extent of his involvement in the executions for heresy in his diocese is not clear. He died in London on 2 August 1556 and was buried in Chichester Cathedral. In his will, drawn up on 28 July, he placed his hope for salvation on the merits of the blood and death of Jesus Christ, but did not invoke the saints. To his successors at Chichester he left his mitre and crosier, and to the cathedral a new vestment of red silk, chalices and matching pattens, and £40 to buy a silver cross. St John's College library received a copy of the trilingual Complutensian polyglot Bible, and King's the works of Chrysostom and Clement of Alexandria. Apart from Archbishop Heath, other beneficiaries included the bishop of Ely, Day's four brothers, Roger, William,

Thomas of Ford, and Thomas, precentor of Chichester, and his 'mother-in-law' (stepmother), Johane Day, and her daughter Johane. MALCOLM KITCH

Sources PRO, PROB 11/38, fol. 149r–v • G. Burnet, *A history of the reformation of the Church of England*, 1/2 and 2/2 (1816) • *The acts and monuments of John Foxe*, ed. S. R. Cattley, 8 vols. (1837–41), vols. 5–8 • *APC*, 1550–55 • *CSP dom.*, 1547–58 • *CPR*, 1553–6 • *Literary remains of King Edward the Sixth*, ed. J. G. Nichols, 2 vols., Roxburghe Club, 75 (1857) • F. M. Powicke and E. B. Fryde, eds., *Handbook of British chronology*, 2nd edn, Royal Historical Society Guides and Handbooks, 2 (1961) • J. Strype, *Ecclesiastical memorials*, 3 vols. (1822) • J. Strype, *Memorials of the most reverend father in God Thomas Cranmer*, new edn, 2 vols. (1840) • *LP Henry VIII* • Venn, *Alum. Cant.* • D. MacCulloch, *Thomas Cranmer: a life* (1996) • D. MacCulloch, *Tudor church militant: Edward VI and the protestant Reformation* (1999) • C. Haigh, *English reformations* (1993) • R. Tresswell and A. Vincent, *The visitation of Shropshire, taken in the year 1623*, ed. G. Grazebrook and J. P. Rylands, 1, Harleian Society, 28 (1889) • *Sussex Archaeological Collections*, 73 (1936), 131

Day, George Edward (1815–1872), physician, was born on 4 August 1815 at Tenby, Pembrokeshire. He was the son of George Day of Manorabon House, Swansea, who had inherited the fortunes of his father, George Day, physician to the nabob of Arcot, and his uncle Sir John Day, solicitor-general in Bengal. G. E. Day's mother was Mary Hale, a descendant of Sir Matthew Hale, and after his father's ruin by the failure of a bank in 1826 he was brought up by his grandmother, Mrs Hale. Day may have been apprenticed to a general practitioner in Worcestershire before he entered Trinity College, Cambridge, in 1833. After one term he obtained a scholarship at Pembroke College, where he graduated as twenty-ninth wrangler in 1837. He studied medicine in Edinburgh, where he won medals in anatomy, midwifery, and physiological botany. He was awarded the Harveian prize medal for 1843. He took his MA degree at Cambridge in 1840 and was granted a licence to practise by the university in 1842. In 1843 he began practice in 3 Southwick Street, London, becoming a member of the Royal College of Physicians in 1844 and a fellow in 1848. He became FRS in 1850. He was physician to the Western General Dispensary and lecturer on materia medica at the Middlesex Hospital.

Day supplemented his income through reviewing and translating, and was co-editor of the *Monthly Journal of Medical Science* (1845–55), *Monthly Retrospect of Medical Sciences* (1849), and the *Edinburgh Monthly Journal of Medical Sciences* (1848–52). He was also a contributor to many other periodicals. His translations included *Animal Chemistry* (2 vols., 1845–6), from the German of J. F. Simon; *The Pathological Anatomy of the Human Body* (1847), from the German of J. Vogel; and *The Pathological Anatomy of the Organs of Respiration and Circulation* (1852), from the German of C. Rokitansky. In 1849 he became Chandos professor of anatomy and medicine at St Andrews, and quickly obtained the necessary MD degree from Giessen. He was a popular professor, and carried out reforms in the MD examination. Day's own publications include *A Practical Treatise on the Domestic Management and most Important Diseases of Advanced Life* (1849), an early English language textbook on geriatric medicine, an American edition of which also appeared in

1849, and his *Chemistry and its Relation to Physiology and Medicine* (1860). In 1841 he married Ellen Anna, daughter of James Buckton, solicitor, of Doctors' Commons and of Wrexham. They had two sons and four daughters.

Day broke his right arm after falling down a mine shaft on Helvellyn in 1857, as a result of which the arm became virtually useless except for writing 'which he did by lifting the injured arm with his left hand on to a cushion placed on the desk and moving it only from the wrist' (Scott, 833). He soon developed a sinovitis of the right knee which confined him to a wheelchair for the rest of his life. Day retired in 1863 and settled at Torquay in the forlorn hope that it would improve his health. He died at Andersey, Torquay, on 31 January 1872. The council of the St Andrews Medical Graduates Association later organized an appeal in an attempt to provide for his widow.

[ANON.], *rev.* MICHAEL BEVAN

Sources C. J. Scott, 'George Edward Day and "Diseases of advanced life"', *The Practitioner*, 214 (1975), 832–6 · *BMJ* (17 Feb 1872), 198 · *BMJ* (2 March 1872), 247 · *BMJ* (11 May 1872), 514 · C. Marmoy and J. L. Thornton, 'The anatomical and physiological bibliography of George E. Day', *Annals of Science*, 28 (1972), 285–91 · private information (1888) [Ellen Anna Day] · Munk, *Roll* · Venn, *Alum. Cant.* · d. cert. · *CGPLA Eng. & Wales* (1872)
Archives U. St Andr. L., corresp. with James Forbes
Likenesses portrait, repro. in Scott, 'George Edward Day and "Diseases of advanced life"'
Wealth at death under £2000 (in UK): probate, 28 March 1872, *CGPLA Eng. & Wales*

Day, James (*fl.* 1637), poet, is entirely unknown, apart from a volume of devotional verse, entitled *A New Spring of Divine Poetrie*, published in 1637 with an acrostic dedication 'To Mistris Bridget Rudge' and commendatory verses by H. G. and T. J. The two principal poems in the volume are 'The Worldes Metamorphosis' and 'Christ's Birth and Passion'; these are followed by some shorter poems. T. J. may well have been Thomas Jordan, printer and plagiarist. At any rate, Day's work seems not to have sold well, and in 1646 the unsold copies were reissued by Jordan, with a new title-page describing them as the *Divine Raptures* of Jordan himself.

A. H. BULLEN, *rev.* MATTHEW STEGGLE

Sources P. A. Pinsent, 'Plagiarism by Thomas Jordan', *N&Q*, 212 (1967), 336–7 · *STC, 1475–1640*

Day, James Wentworth (1899–1983), journalist, was born on 21 April 1899 at Marsh House, Exning, Suffolk, the elder son of James Thomas Wentworth Day (1862–1906) of Wicken, Cambridgeshire, and his wife, Martha Ethel, daughter of Llewellyn Hatch Staples of Bourn, in Cambridgeshire. Wentworth Day, who was known to his friends as Jim, was educated at Newton College, Newton Abbot, and read English as an extramural student at Cambridge University under Sir Arthur Quiller-Couch. After service in the First World War (in 1917–18) he became a journalist, learning his craft on the *Cambridge Daily News* and then in Fleet Street as a reporter on the *Daily Express*, where in 1923 he was promoted to publicity manager after only five days. From 1924 to 1925 he was make-up sub-editor of both the *Sunday Express* and *Daily Express*. He also

edited a monthly sporting publication called *English Life*, and became Lord Beaverbrook's personal assistant. He was assistant editor of *Country Life* at the age of twenty-six and acting editor of *The Field* (1930–31).

A high tory patriot of extreme right wing views, in 1933 Wentworth Day became the personal representative of the eccentric pro-fascist Lady Houston, and was involved with her sponsorship of the duke of Hamilton's first flight over Mount Everest. Once, when involved with one of Lady Houston's political meetings, he was attacked and received a black eye. A few days later in a West End club Churchill walked in with a friend to whom he introduced Wentworth Day as Lady Houston's kept man—'Observe the love token in his eye'. Although impressed by Mussolini, Wentworth Day persistently warned of the danger posed by German ambitions and criticized the Nazi regime.

After editing the *Illustrated Sporting and Dramatic News* from 1935 to 1937 Wentworth Day made a sudden switch of career to become propaganda adviser to the government of Egypt, providing material for a book, *Sport in Egypt* (1938). He served as a war correspondent in the Second World War but was invalided out in 1943.

Wentworth Day was a self-styled politician though never a member of parliament, having unsuccessfully contested Hornchurch (in 1950 and 1951) and campaigned in seven other by-elections. He listed among his recreations in *Who's Who* 'taking the left wing intelligentsia at its own valuation', and to this end he acted as an *agent provocateur* at a political meeting in Newark during the 1945 general election. While the marxist Harold Laski, then chairman of the Labour Party, was in Newark giving a political address, Wentworth Day put some leading questions to him, making sure that someone from the *Newark Advertiser* reported them. Laski sued the newspaper for suggesting that he had advocated revolution by violent means, but the jury found for the paper and Laski's career was seriously damaged. He also threatened to thrash the Christian socialist vicar of Thaxted, Conrad Noel, if the latter removed a union flag from the church.

Wentworth Day was the author of many books, including biographies of Queen Elizabeth the queen mother (1967), Princess Marina, duchess of Kent (1962), Sir Malcolm Campbell (1931), and Lady Houston (1958). He contributed to various journals such as *Country Life* on ghosts, farming, wildfowling, and on his beloved East Anglia; he also published many books on these topics, including *Essex Ghosts* (1973), *Farming Adventure: a Thousand Miles through England on a Horse* (1975), *The Modern Fowler* (1934), and *Norwich and the Broads* (1953). From 1962 to 1966 he edited *East Anglia Life*, a job for which he was eminently suitable, but quarrelled with the proprietor and resigned.

Wentworth Day was married three times: his first wife was Helen Alexia Gardom, whom he married on 12 December 1925. They were divorced in 1934, and he married Elizabeth Narina Shute on 24 November 1936. This relationship also ended in divorce in 1943, whereupon he married Marion Edith McLean of New Zealand, with whom he had a daughter. Wentworth Day was a caricature of a reactionary English country gentleman of the old school. He was often irascible and difficult to deal with, defects aggravated by old age and near blindness. He died at his splendid house at Ingatestone, in Essex, on 4 January 1983. ROBERT INNES-SMITH

Sources WWW · *The Times* (6 Jan 1983) · *Daily Telegraph* (6 Jan 1983) · Burke, *Gen. GB* (1952) · personal knowledge (2004) · R. Griffiths, *Fellow travellers of the right: British enthusiasts for Nazi Germany, 1933–9*, pbk edn (1983)
Likenesses photograph, 1962, repro. in *East Anglia Life*, 1 (1962), frontispiece
Wealth at death under £25,000: administration, 26 Jan 1983, *CGPLA Eng. & Wales*

Day [Daye], **John** (1521/2–1584), printer and bookseller, may have been born in Dunwich, Suffolk. The capital investment that he brought to his work as a printer and publisher has led some to suppose that he came of a prosperous family, but this may equally be attributed to his business acumen, innovative spirit, and ruthless pursuit of pious opportunity. By 1540 he seems to have been in London, as in that year a John Day was noted in a city deposition as a late servant of the printer and physician Thomas Raynalde. In 1546 Day was very probably one of twenty men freed by redemption (by purchase) into the London Stringers' Company, and, having secured the valuable privilege of the city freedom, he began to print in the same year. From 1547 to 1549 he was based in the parish of St Sepulchre at the sign of the Resurrection; in 1549 he moved into the gatehouse of Aldersgate, rented from the city for £23 a year, which seems to have served as home and printing house for the rest of his career.

Of Day's commitment to the evangelical cause there can be no doubt and from 1546 he worked mostly in partnership with other members of the emerging protestant book trade, principally William Seres. Seres and Day were among the first to grasp the new opportunities afforded by the accession of Edward VI in 1547. A relaxation of the law against heretical books, combined with the positive advocacy of an evangelical agenda by prominent members of the new governing clique, led to a vast increase in the number of books published from 1547 to 1549, an increase entirely accounted for by protestant works. Day found himself in the vanguard of the new movement. Numbered among his publications were books by some of the most prominent authors: John Hooper, Hugh Latimer, John Poynet, and William Turner of the new evangelical establishment; John Calvin of the major continental theologians. Ten of the twenty books published in 1548 by Day and Seres were contributions to the debate over eucharistic doctrine, including works by Luke Shepherd, Robert Crowley, and William Turner. Day also developed a notable speciality in bringing to an English market important works of continental protestantism. His translations included milestone works such as Herman von Wied's *Consultation* on the reform of the diocese of Cologne, a work of obvious relevance to the present debate on the future direction of the English church. Day's editions

John Day (1521/2–1584), by unknown engraver, 1562

were mostly congenial octavos, published in a clear, pleasantly ordered blackletter type with plentiful room for marginal annotation.

In 1550 Day opened a shop in Cheapside, transferred from the Stringers' Company to the Stationers' Company, and dissolved his partnership with Seres. However, he continued to print with or for a number of London publishers, and also under his own name. A steady stream of small-format editions were punctuated by larger, more ambitious projects, most notably an elaborate folio Bible (for which Day seems to have been granted a patent). In all, something like 130 works may be attributed to his press, or were published with his collaboration, during the Edwardian period. In a period when the output of the English printing industry was still markedly less sophisticated than that at most major continental centres, Day's work was also characterized by a notable technical assurance, which may partly be attributed to the extensive use he made of foreign workmen, a professional reliance on foreign expertise that would last for the whole of his career. Day was also closely connected to leading members of the church establishment and political élite, and in 1553 he was granted a patent to publish works by Thomas Becon and John Ponet, a monopoly which became both significant and lucrative when Ponet's *Brief Catechism* was appended to the *ABC*. All of these features of Day's work—typographical sophistication, close connections with the continental printing industries, and official patronage—would underpin his more spectacular success in the Elizabethan period.

For a bookseller so closely associated with the Edwardian regime, the reign of Mary Tudor was bound to be difficult, and Day made little attempt to embrace the new religious principles, though the precise chronology of his activities during the period has been difficult to establish. He did not help his cause by becoming embroiled in the production of clandestine protestant literature. Between October 1553 and May 1554 at least eight works hostile to the new regime appeared, published secretly in England, under the pseudonym Michael Wood of Rouen for which Day may well have been responsible. Although there seems little to connect these grubby, ephemeral tracts with Day's usual quality of workmanship, the distinctive Garamond roman type used by Wood is indeed found in autograph works of Day's press published both before and after. Whether or not responsible for these books, Day certainly did enough to arouse the suspicions of the authorities, and in October 1554 he was arrested and briefly imprisoned. By 1556 he was working again in London, though on a much reduced scale.

With Elizabeth's accession Day's business burst into renewed life. He embarked on a steady production of editions that would continue unabated until his death. His work early in the reign represented partly the re-establishment of patterns established during the Edwardian era: liturgical handbooks for the London Dutch church, sermons and controversial works of the leading figures of the new church establishment. But he also had more ambitious plans. In 1559 he secured a crucial if ambiguous privilege to print Cunningham's *Cosmographical Glass* for life, and any other books 'not repugnant to Holy Scripture or the law' and not covered by other patents, for seven years (*CPR, 1558–60*, 4). Day exploited this to establish control of publication of the *ABC with Little Catechism* (a restoration of his Edwardian privilege), and the period's best-selling book, the English psalter of Sternhold and Hopkins. Even without other prestige projects, such as collected editions of the works of Becon, Latimer, and Tyndale, control of these two staples of English religious life would have made him a rich man. When other aggrieved printers challenged Day's monopoly late in his life, they estimated his annual profit from these two books alone at between £200 and £500. Not surprisingly, the defence of such a lucrative monopoly required powerful protectors at the heart of the regime: in Day's case apparently most crucially Robert Dudley, the queen's favourite and soon to be earl of Leicester.

It was probably only the profits generated by Day's small books which made possible one of the great publishing ventures of the Elizabethan era: John Foxe's *Book of Martyrs*. Foxe returned to England from exile in October 1559, and as he set about gathering the contemporary testimonies that would be the book's enduring claim to greatness, a partnership with Day, who was already engaged in the publication of works by prominent Marian martyrs and whose shop, almost alone in London, had the technical resources to match Foxe's ambitions, seemed a natural choice. In the months leading to the final publication of the *Actes and Monuments* in March 1563 Foxe was a frequent presence at Day's printing house, and indeed received much of his correspondence there. But the burden of making Foxe's vision a practical reality fell on Day.

Remarkably little attention has been paid to the technical aspects of production of this work. This was a project of a complexity seldom before attempted by an English printer. Not only was the book enormous—the first English edition ran to 1800 pages—its complex compositional structure of different typefaces, columns, and marginalia added greatly to the technical difficulties. As news of Foxe's venture spread, new witnesses to the persecutions came forward, and the author was receiving new information up to and after the date of first publication, all of which had to be included. The extent of the interpolations is revealed in the irregularity of the collation, with inserted leaves and extra or irregular gatherings; more modest changes were made possible by the addition of small slips pasted over already set text. Finally, the fifty woodcut illustrations, all new, and all probably cut abroad or by Flemish artists working in England, had to be commissioned and designed. Although one of the great glories of the book, these represented a considerable extra investment; there is some internal evidence that the larger illustrations arrived late in the day, and their incorporation with the text caused further technical difficulties.

Although we lack any precise information about the production process, it is possible to reconstruct in broad outline the impact such an enormous project would have had on Day's press. For the second edition of 1570 Day employed three presses simultaneously. If this were the case for the first edition, a book of 900 folio leaves would still have occupied three presses for almost twelve months, assuming an edition of 1250 copies. That they were indeed so occupied is clearly indicated by the fact that after two busy years the published output of Day's presses slowed to virtually nothing in 1562, when he was described as being forty, with only two works published apart from the valuable psalms. The cost of keeping three presses running, paying the wages of highly skilled Dutch workmen, and buying ink and paper may have amounted to an investment of not far short of £1000—all before a single copy was available for sale.

Having taken such risks, Day reaped his reward. The book was an instant success, helped on its way by official patronage (from the second edition of 1570 it was ordered to be set up in every parish church) and it made Day's reputation. Further editions followed in 1570, 1576, and 1583: Day was still giving pains to this last edition shortly before his death. Foxe and Day remained on good terms throughout, and in the preface to his edition of the works of Tyndale, Barnes, and Frith in 1573 Foxe paid generous tribute to a partner without whom his ambitious plans could scarcely have been realized.

Publication freed Day to return to other projects. In 1564

a smaller-format edition of the letters of the Marian martyrs catered to demand for a cheaper, more accessible version of the martyrology, and works of protestant theology and controversy remained the core of his business. Day also made himself available to publish political tracts helpful to the regime, such as three works by Thomas Norton responding to the papal bull of excommunication (1570) and George Buchanan's polemic against Mary, queen of Scots. In addition, from 1564, Day was the official printer to the city authorities. But the success of the *Actes and Monuments* and steady income from his patents also gave Day room to diversify. Early in the reign Day struck up a relationship with Matthew Parker, to whom he proved a willing foil in the archbishop's cherished antiquarian projects. In 1566 he published for Parker Aelfric's *Testimonie of Antiquitie*, a book which required the design and casting of special Anglo-Saxon characters. The reward for this and other establishment connections was a new and valuable patent: in 1570 Day received the rights to Nowell's *Catechism*, extended to all Nowell's works four years later. Emboldened by the technical success of the *Actes and Monuments*, Day also diversified into other categories of illustrated work, most notably an English translation of Euclid's *Elements of Geometry* (1570), a brilliant deluxe folio.

Day's success was not entirely unalloyed. In 1573, 'one asplyn', either Day's apprentice Thomas Asplin or the stationer Robert Asplin, attempted to murder him and his family (Arber, *Regs. Stationers*, 1.466). About the same time a bold but unsuccessful attempt by Day to build a new shop in the centre of St Paul's Churchyard led to a clash between the city and church authorities; Day eventually secured premises elsewhere in the Churchyard. In the years after 1577 Day became less ambitious, falling back on the reliable best-sellers that were the basis of his wealth. His shop retained a steady output, and in 1583 still operated four presses. His last years were marred by controversy, as competitors in the London trade, led by his former apprentice John Wolfe, made a determined effort to break his stranglehold on such large areas of protestant print. Following a commission of inquiry, Day handed the rights to thirty books to the Stationers' Company in 1584, though not including his most lucrative monopolies. The dispute remained unresolved at his death, leaving a troubled and complex inheritance for his son Richard *Day (*b*. 1552, *d*. in or before 1606).

Day was married twice, and had thirteen children by each marriage; among those from the second marriage was John *Day (1566–1628), Aristotelian scholar and Church of England clergyman. The name of his first wife is unknown; his second, Alice Lehunte (*d*. 1612), a gentlewoman, survived him. He accumulated extensive property in London and Suffolk, and a range of printing types and ornamental materials that would have done justice to a major continental printer. He died at Walden in Essex on 23 July 1584, *en route* to visit his second wife's family in Suffolk. He was buried on 2 August in the parish church of Little Bradley, Suffolk, where a funeral monument was erected; administration of his estate was granted to Alice

on 30 August. His death removed one of the titans of the Elizabethan book world, and one of the London book trade's most innovative and adept members.

ANDREW PETTEGREE

Sources B. P. Davies, 'John Day', *The British literary book trade, 1475–1700*, ed. J. K. Bracken and J. Silver, DLitB, 170 (1996), 78–93 · C. L. Oastler, *John Day, the Elizabethan printer* (1975) · J. Roberts, 'Bibliographical aspects of John Foxe', *John Foxe and the English Reformation*, ed. D. Loades (1997), 36–51 · J. F. Mozley, *John Foxe and his book* (1940); repr. (1970) · R. S. Luborsky and E. Ingram, *A guide to English illustrated books, 1536–1603* (Temple, Arizona, 1998) · H. R. Hoppe, 'John Wolfe: printer and publisher, 1579–1601', *The Library*, 4th ser., 14 (1933–4), 241–88 · F. R. Johnson, 'Notes on English retail bookprices, 1550–1640', *The Library*, 5th ser., 5 (1950–51), 83–112 · R. E. G. Kirk and E. F. Kirk, eds., *Returns of aliens dwelling in the city and suburbs of London, from the reign of Henry VIII to that of James I*, 4 vols., Huguenot Society of London, 10 (1900–08) · H. Andrers, 'The Elizabethan ABC and catechism', *The Library*, 4th ser., 17 (1936–7), 312–32 · R. A. Leaver, *'Goostly psalmes and spirituall songes': English and Dutch metrical psalms from Coverdale to Utenhove, 1535–1566* (1991) · E. J. Baskerville, *A chronological bibliography of propaganda and polemic published in English between 1553 and 1558* (Philadelphia, 1979) · L. P. Fairfield, 'The mysterious press of Michael Wood (1553–1554)', *The Library*, 5th ser., 27 (1972), 220–32 · P. Blayney, 'John Day and the bookshop that never was', *Material London, ca. 1600*, ed. L. C. Orlin (2000), 322–43 · W. W. Greg, ed., *A companion to Arber* (1967) · Arber, *Regs. Stationers* · P. Blayney, 'William Cecil and the stationers', *The Stationers' Company and the book trade, 1550–1990*, ed. R. Myers and M. Harris, St Paul's Bibliographies (1997), 11–34 · administration, PRO, PROB 6/3, fol. 113*v* · *CPR, 1558–60*, 4
Likenesses woodcut, 1562, BM, NPG [*see illus.*] · woodcut, 1563, BM; repro. in J. Foxe, *Actes and monuments* (1563) · funerary monument, Little Bradley, Suffolk; repro. in Oastler, *John Day*, frontispiece · woodcut, repro. in Oastler, *John Day*, 64

Day, John (1566–1628), Aristotelian scholar and Church of England clergyman, was born 'in or over Aldersgate in London' (Wood, *Ath. Oxon.*, 412), the son of John *Day (1521/2–1584), printer, and his wife, Alice Lehunte (*d*. 1612), and brother of Richard *Day (*b*. 1552, *d*. in or before 1606), Lionel, and twenty-four other siblings of whom only Lionel survived him. Admitted to St Alban Hall, Oxford, in 1582, he graduated BA on 15 February 1587. Elected a fellow of Oriel College on 8 May 1588, he was admitted on 23 September, and proceeded MA in 1591. He remained a fellow until his death, holding the offices of senior treasurer (1593/4, 1601/2, 1604/5, 1608/9) and dean (1601, 1611–12, 1616).

Day was a significant exponent of the revived philosophy of Aristotle, taught in Elizabethan Oxford by John Case and John Rainolds. In 1589 he was asked by the fellows of his college to expound the text of Aristotle in the light of modern learning to the scholars of Oriel; the text of his lectures on the *Physics* survives, together with the headings of various arguments for and against numerous Aristotelian propositions, apparently for college disputations. His course must have paralleled that of Rainolds at Corpus Christi College, and his references, inserted in his lecture text, show that he shared the catholic learning of Case. Beside the Latin and Greek classics and modern humanist writers, including his contemporary Joseph Scaliger, he cited with approval numerous scholastic commentators, especially Aquinas, and singled out for praise three contemporary Jesuits. His extremely wide and eclectic reading allowed him, like Rainolds and Case, to relate the teaching of Aristotle to the moral basis of the Elizabethan polity.

In 1605 Day sought leave to study divinity in France, presumably at the new Calvinist academy of Saumur or a similar establishment. On his return, either in college or at St Mary's, Oxford, the college vicarage where he was admitted on 3 December 1609, he aimed to instil a moderate Calvinism in sermons or addresses, frequently refuting Catholic apologists, which were successively printed at the university press. His two English sermons of 1609 expounded the Bible with broad classical and theological learning of a traditional kind. In 1611 he proceeded BD. His Latin address to the heads of houses and doctors of divinity, in 1612, evoked Oxford's academic past and contribution to the commonweal. His twelve sermons in St Mary's on God, the sacraments, and the public virtues (1610–15), published as *Day's Festivals* (1615), were a plain exposition of protestant teaching for a lay congregation, but his best known work, *Day's Dyall* (1614), was like his Aristotelian course delivered to the undergraduates of Oriel in 1612/13, to encourage 'proficiency in both learnings, secular, and celestiall' (Wood, *Ath. Oxon.*, 413), and abounds with references to classical and theological texts from the fathers onwards. His last work was a *Descant* on the first eight psalms, a moral exposition published in 1620. Taken together, they support Wood's description of him as 'well vers'd in the Fathers, schoolmen, and councils', and as 'a plain man, a primitive Christian, and … wholly composed to do good' (Wood, *Ath. Oxon.*, 413).

In 1618, on the death of Provost Anthony Blencowe, Day was an unsuccessful (and absent) candidate for the provostship of Oriel and afterwards challenged the election result before the visitor, but in vain. At the next election, in 1621, he was present and again a candidate, and was once more not elected, whereupon he resigned the living of St Mary's and was preferred in 1622 to that of Little Thurlow, Suffolk, by Sir William Soame, 'not without some discontent at the loss of the said provostship' (Wood, *Ath. Oxon.*, 413). He died at Little Thurlow on 10 January 1628 and was buried there; his brother Lionel's memorial to him, with Latin verses, is in the chancel of Little Thurlow church. Day gave a silver beaker to Oriel on his election, which does not survive, and a book of commentaries on Cicero's orations to the college library.

JEREMY CATTO

Sources J. Day, 'De auscultacione physicae Aristotelis', Bodl. Oxf., MS Rawl. D. 274, fols. 1–125r · J. Day, 'Obiectiones et solutiones Aristotelicae', Bodl. Oxf., MS Rawl. D. 274, fols. 127r–259r · J. Day, *David's desire to goe to church: as it was published in two sermons in St Maries in Oxford* (1612); [another edn] (1615) · J. Day, *Concio ad clerum* (1612); 2nd edn (1615) · *Day's festivals, or, Twelve of his sermons* (1615) · J. Day, *Day's dyall or his twelve howres* (1614) · *Day's descant on Davids psalmes* (1620) · G. C. Richards and H. E. Salter, eds., *The dean's register of Oriel, 1466–1661*, OHS, 84 (1926) · Oriel College Archives, Style MS 158, 1649 (I. C. I.) · G. C. Richards and C. L. Shadwell, *The provosts and fellows of Oriel College, Oxford* (1922) · Wood, *Ath. Oxon.*, new edn, 2.412–14 · BL, MS 19103, fols. 270r–271, 273 · J. K. McConica, 'Humanism and Aristotle in Tudor Oxford', *EngHR*, 94 (1979), 291–

317 · C. B. Schmitt, *John Case and Aristotelianism in Renaissance Oxford* (1983) · memorial inscription, Little Thurlow church, Suffolk
Archives Bodl. Oxf., notebook, MS Rawlinson D. 274 · Oriel College, Oxford

Day, John (1573/4–1638?), playwright, was born at Cawston, Norfolk, the son of Walter Day, husbandman. He attended school at Ely, and on 24 October 1592, at the age of eighteen, entered Gonville and Caius College, Cambridge. Barely six months later, on 4 May 1593, he was expelled for stealing a book.

Day is next heard of in 1598, when he sold a play, 'The Conquest of Brute', to the Admiral's Men for £2. This appears to have been revised by (or with) his older colleague Henry Chettle and performed with some success, since Chettle immediately began work on a sequel. Having got his start with the company, Day wrote regularly for it for the next five years, though of his plays recorded in Philip Henslowe's diary the only one to survive is a further collaboration with Chettle, *The Blind Beggar of Bednal Green* (1600, first printed in 1659). Day apparently called on his Norfolk origins in creating several characters in this play. At one point young Strowd recalls being 'as naked as your *Norfolk*-Dumplin' (sig. D2v), and the play is filled with assertions of regional pride and plain yeoman virtues.

In 1599 Day wrote with William Haughton two domestic murder plays, 'Cox of Collumpton' and 'The Tragedy of Thomas Merry', the latter at least being based on contemporary events. Another lost play of the same year, 'The Orphan's Tragedy', which Day wrote with Chettle and Haughton, may be of similar provenance. This was also the year in which the playwright Henry Porter was killed by 'John Daye of Southwark, yeoman', and although the name is a common one, it is possible that this was the result of a quarrel between two of Henslowe's dramatists—of whom, incidentally, there is no record of collaboration on a play. Day claimed self-defence, was convicted of manslaughter, and apparently pardoned.

'Cox of Collumpton' was seen by Simon Forman at the Rose Theatre in the spring of 1600, and his summary is interesting not only because it supplies the basic plot but also for its account of a stage bear that drives two guilty brothers to suicide. Day collaborated with Thomas Dekker, Chettle, and Haughton on five further plays in 1600, and early in the following year he and Haughton wrote parts 2 and 3 of *The Blind Beggar*, indicating that the first instalment had been judged a winning formula. (The sequels have unfortunately not survived.) Day appears to have made a reasonable living working for Henslowe: he remained an active contributor to the Admiral's repertory after the company moved to the new Fortune Theatre, and was paid over £7 for work on four collaborations between February and May 1601. When Worcester's Men took over the Rose Theatre in 1602, Day wrote for both companies and his earnings rose to a healthy £14 for the season.

The record of Day's lost plays for Henslowe allows glimpses of the playwright's forays into action drama in 'The Conquest of the West Indies' and 'The Conquest of Spain by John of Gaunt' (both 1601), and occasional essays at the history play, in addition to domestic tragedies and city comedies. In 1602–3 he was employed with Chettle to write or revise a play about 'Shore's wife', and a few verse lines in Day's hand dating from about 1601 (preserved in *The Alleyn Papers*, 24) appear to conclude a play about defeated rebellion by 'Percy' and his 'gallant band', one that was perhaps trying to catch the wave of success enjoyed by Shakespeare's *Henry IV* plays.

The first of Day's plays to be printed (and apart from *The Blind Beggar* the earliest to survive) was *The Isle of Gulls* (1606), written for the Children of the Queen's Revels, the boys' company that acted at the Blackfriars playhouse. This appears to have been a new departure for Day, not only in the play's auspices and venue, but also in his cultivation of the kind of topical satire that was fashionable in the private theatres. Day drew on Sir Philip Sidney's *Arcadia* for his plot, and in the prologue protested that a writer seeking to 'ope the vaine of sinne' should not be 'inform'd against for libelling' (sig. A3v). His plea was disregarded: on 7 March 1606 Sir Edward Hoby reported 'much speech of a play in the Black Friars, where, in the Isle of the Gulls, from the highest to the lowest … all men's parts were acted of two divers nations: as I understand sundry were committed to Bridewell' (Birch, 1.60–61). The 'two divers nations' were apparently the English and the Scots, so that the royal circle of King Basilius in the *Arcadia* was transformed by the actors' accents into the confrontational world of James I's court in its early years—a satire made more pointed by the inclusion in the play of a hunting scene, highly redolent of James but nowhere part of King Basilius's leisure activities in Sidney's original. Like another Blackfriars play, *Eastward Ho!*, in the previous year, and for similar reasons, *The Isle of Gulls* apparently got its makers into trouble; and punishment this time meant not only imprisonment of the leading players—though not, as far as is known, of Day himself—but also the loss of Queen Anne's patronage. The company had to drop the word 'Queen's' from their title, as the title-page of the printed quarto of the play shows; and there is evidence of interference during printing of the play, with the publisher's name being removed from the title-page and titles like 'king' and 'queen' substituted by 'duke' and 'duchess'.

The Isle of Gulls is a lively and accomplished satire, and Day composed two further comedies for the boys that have survived: *Law-Trickes, or, Who would have Thought it* (which was probably written with George Wilkins), and *Humour out of Breath*, both published in 1608. All these plays show Day at home in the elegant and witty milieu of the children's theatres, capitalizing on what Shakespeare had added to the comic vocabulary of earlier writers for the boys' companies like John Lyly, and giving it a Jacobean edge. However, Day had not turned his back on the popular stage. His fifth extant play was written for Queen Anne's Men and acted at the Red Bull in Clerkenwell, a playhouse with a reputation for bombast and crowd-pleasing spectacle. *The Travels of the Three English Brothers*, which Day wrote with William Rowley and George Wilkins in 1607, relates a current political story with unusual freedom and directness—Day was clearly not cowed by official dislike of *The Isle of Gulls*, since he risked further censure with this play about the adventures of the Sherley brothers, minor Sussex gentry whose exploits abroad earned them the intense disapproval of the English government. The play's dedication 'To Honour's favourites', however, is a canny appeal to the more militant ethos of Prince Henry and his circle; and its dramatization of the Sherley visit to Persia, and of subsequent efforts to raise support for a Perso-Christian alliance against the Turks, offers a flattering image of English courage and diplomatic skill in the trickiest of contexts. *The Travels* is not a very polished play, but it is one of the most interesting treatments on the early-modern stage of cultural encounter and exotic ordeal.

Day drops out of sight after 1608, apart from an entry in the Stationers' register in August 1610 of 'A Booke called the Madde Prancks of Merry Moll of the Bankside … Written by John Day'. This, if it was a stage work, may have been a Red Bull anticipation of the successful play about Moll Frith, *The Roaring Girl* by Middleton and Dekker, acted at the Fortune in the early summer of 1611. Day is next heard of a decade later, in January 1620, when a play called 'Guy of Warwick' was entered in the Stationers' register under his and Dekker's names. Two more plays followed, both probably collaborations with Dekker: 'The Bellman of Paris' was licensed for performance by the Prince's Men at the Red Bull in July 1623, and 'Come see a wonder' was acted on the same stage in September of that year. None of these works has survived, and there is no further record of Day's activity in the theatre. His stage career, though possibly interrupted, was a long one; for most of it he was a jobbing dramatist invariably collaborating with other writers in all the fashionable genres; but his surviving work for the theatre, nearly all from a brief period between 1605 and 1608 when he also wrote at least two single-authored plays, shows him to have been a writer of distinctive accomplishments.

Day was the author also of two non-dramatic writings. *The Parliament of Bees* survives in manuscript (BL, Lansdowne MS 725) and in a 1641 quarto, of which the title-page describes the work as 'A Bee-hive furnisht with twelve Honycombes, as Pleasant as Profitable. Being an Allegoricall description of the actions of good and bad men in these our daies.' The quarto text is a revision of the manuscript, which must have been composed before 1634, when *The Noble Soldier* by Dekker and Rowley, which borrows several passages from Day's text, was published. Charles Lamb admired the work, and quoted from it in his 'Extracts from the Garrick Plays', thereby giving Day's poetry wider currency than his plays have ever achieved. Lamb and earlier editors cite a 1607 quarto of the *Bees*, but this has not been found. The other work is a manuscript prose tract entitled 'Peregrinatio scholastica, or, Learneinges pillgrimage' (BL, Sloane MS 3150). It appears to belong to Day's later years, since in the epistle the author hopes that his efforts 'may not finde the lesse welcome in reguard I boast not that gawdie spring of credit and youthfull florish of opinion as some other filde in the same rancke with me' (sig. f.2v).

Day's death is the subject of an elegy by his friend and fellow dramatist John Tatham in the latter's *The Fancies Theater* (1640). The poem laboriously puns on Day's name in likening his death to an eclipse ('in that sight was ta'ne away, / Our thrice desir'd refulgent day'; sig. F3v), but it is possible that Tatham was taking advantage of an actual eclipse that 'did late arise' on 11 December 1638. This date is consistent with Day's being the John Dey of Eydolveston, Norfolk, whose will was proved at Norwich in 1639.

ANTHONY PARR

Sources *The Alleyn papers*, Shakespeare Society (1843) · *Henslowe's diary*, ed. R. A. Foakes and R. T. Rickert (1961) · W. W. Greg, *Dramatic documents from the Elizabethan playhouses* (1931) · Venn, *Alum. Cant.* · *John Day's 'Isle of gulls': a critical edition*, ed. R. S. Burns (1980) · N. Carson, *A companion to Henslowe's diary* (1988) · G. E. Bentley, *The Jacobean and Caroline stage*, 7 vols. (1941–68), vol. 3 · J. Tatham, *The fancies theater* (1640) · J. Palmer, *The Catholique planisphaer* (1658) · *Index of wills proved in the consistory court of Norwich, 1604–1686*, Norfolk RS (1958) · W. Peery, 'The noble soldier and The parliament of bees', *Studies in Philology*, 48 (1951), 219–33 · J. Pitcher, 'Fronted with the sight of a bear: Cox of Collumpton and The winter's tale', *N&Q*, 239 (1994), 47–53 · [T. Birch and R. F. Williams], eds., *The court and times of Charles the First*, 2 vols. (1848)

Day, John Barham (1793–1860), jockey and racehorse trainer, was born at Houghton Down, Hampshire, the son of John Day, a local trainer and racing adviser to George, prince of Wales, and his wife, Alice, daughter of a Mr Barham of Stockbridge, Hampshire. Little is known of John Barham Day's education save that from an early stage it took second place to his career as a lightweight jockey. Unusually small, Day was able to weigh in at 7 stone until he retired from race riding about 1840. He began riding at minor tracks near his father's stables. Fees were low as was the standard of the racing, but in 1826 Day was retained by the fourth duke of Grafton on the recommendation of his brother, Lord Henry Fitzroy. In that year Day rode the duke's horses Problem and Devise to win the Two Thousand Guineas and the One Thousand Guineas respectively, for which he was awarded a £20 present and a lecture on the perils of suddenly acquired wealth.

As a lightweight lacking real strength, particularly in a close finish, Day was a useful rather than a great jockey. It was more as a trainer that he was known. In 1835, though still riding competitively, especially in big races, he began training at Danebury, 4 miles north of Stockbridge. The stable's remoteness and its inaccessibility to newspaper touts made it ideal for a trainer fond of a bet. The rewards open to the early nineteenth-century jockey and trainer were limited without recourse to the betting ring; Day's willingness to deceive not only bookmakers but also owners earned him the sarcastic nickname Honest John Day. His first significant patron was Lord George Bentinck who spent lavishly on Danebury in the late 1830s. The pair enjoyed considerable success, especially with the outstanding Crucifix winner of both the One Thousand Guineas and the Two Thousand Guineas and the Oaks in 1840, although their most characteristic success came in the 1836 St Leger with Elis. Beaten in the Derby, though heavily backed by his connections, Elis was a warm favourite for the final classic, his Epsom conqueror being

an absentee. He was priced prohibitively in the betting ring. In 1836 it took about a fortnight to move a horse north to Doncaster and with only a week to go it was known that Elis was still with Bentinck and he began to drift in the market. His owner, however, had been busy constructing one of the first horseboxes, in which he managed to transport the horse to Town Moor in just three days. Elis won the race at 7/2, rather less than the price Bentinck and Day secured.

The association did not, however, last. Midway through the season of 1841 Bentinck discovered, thanks to some carelessly confused letters, that Day was deceiving him about the condition of one of his horses, the better to get a good price on it. With Bentinck gone to Goodwood, Day was left searching for another patron. The first men to fill the post are best known as the Danebury confederacy, a group of professional gamblers including the prizefighter-turned-legislator John Gully, Harry Hill, William Pedley, and Joshua Arnold. In his book *Reminiscences of the Turf*, Day's son William Henry *Day denies that his father knew anything of the activities of these men, but that is unlikely. The formal association, whatever its nature, was ended in 1845 when Day moved to Michel Grove, Findon, Sussex, to act as private trainer to the solicitor, money-lender, and erstwhile confederacy member, Henry Padwick. Day's eldest son, John (1814–1882), took over work at Danebury while William was established as a breeder at Woodyates, Cranborne Chase, Wiltshire, at his father's expense. Day's time at Findon was not without controversy and in 1855 Padwick had to surrender Day's services on finding that his excellent colt St Hubert had lost the Two Thousand Guineas, for which he had been heavily backed, thanks to an arrangement with the trainer's son which allowed William Day's Lord of the Isles to triumph. Day was promptly evicted from Michel Grove and he spent the rest of his life as a guest at Danebury, where he died on 21 March 1860.

Day was known to be as hard on his horses as he was on their owners, always galloping them uphill, often in rugs and blankets. His regime of sweats, drenching, purging, and even bleeding, favoured tough horses and did result in heavy casualties. But Day believed in sending his horses to post fit and with little room for improvement; Danebury runners were unusually successful first time out. Both of his sons who took to training followed his methods. Day was twice married but nothing is known of his wives except that his first wife's name was Goddard. Of his twelve children, all from his first marriage, two more rode professionally: Alfred and Samuel, who won the St Leger on Mango.

Day is, however, significant as more than just an indication of how loose notions of 'honour' could be on the nineteenth-century turf. Along with the Yorkshireman John Scott he was the first trainer to prove himself as a highly skilled professional, not just another groom. He demanded and secured a good wage from influential men too aware of his talent to be overly concerned by his dishonesty. For every patron who left Danebury in disgust, plenty preferred to stay, including Lord Palmerston, whose Iliona won the 1841 Cesarewitch. As the founder of a racing dynasty which later included among its members Lester Piggott, Day is also of some note.

EMMA EADIE

Sources R. Mortimer, R. Onslow, and P. Willett, *Biographical encyclopedia of British flat racing* (1978) · W. Day, *Reminiscences of the turf*, 2nd edn (1886) · M. Seth-Smith, *Lord Paramount of the Turf: Lord George Bentinck, 1802–1848* (1971) · B. Darwin, *John Gully and his times* (1935) · W. Vamplew, *The turf: a social and economic history of horse racing* (1976) · J. Kent, *The racing life of Lord George Cavendish Bentinck*, 2nd edn (1892)
Likenesses H. Hall, portrait, 1841, Tate collection

Day, Sir John Charles Frederic Sigismund (1826–1908), judge, was born at The Hague on 20 June 1826, the eldest son of Captain John Day (1779–1843), a half-pay officer, of Englishbatch, near Bath, and his Dutch wife, Emilie (1789/90–1836), daughter of Jan Caspar Hartsinck. His Roman Catholic parents sent him to school first at St Mary's College, Oscott, then in 1841 to Downside Priory, where he gained his BA from London University in 1845. He also spent time at Freiburg and learned four foreign languages. Admitted to the Middle Temple on 29 October 1845, he was called on 26 January 1849 but, having independent means, did not immediately commence a career at the bar. However, having suffered financial losses and with a growing family to support from his marriage on 1 October 1846 to Henrietta Rosa Mary Brown (1824–1893), a banker's daughter, he began to practise, going the home circuit.

Day's fee earnings grew steadily, from £200 in 1855 to £2000 in 1866, and he increased his income and reputation by his writings. He co-authored an edition of Roscoe's *Nisi prius* and in 1861 brought out an annotated edition of the Common Law Procedure Act of 1852, which became the standard work on a statute of great importance to practitioners. He exploited his lugubrious and highly expressive countenance to great effect with juries and was a masterly cross-examiner whose favoured tactic was to rely wholly on destroying the other side's case and not to call his own evidence at all. Known as Settling Day for his tendency to compromise suits, he did not take silk until 1872 but immediately came to the forefront as the fashionable counsel for breach of promise actions and election petitions; he also became standing counsel to the London Omnibus Company. Pupils, including the future lord chancellor Robert Finlay, testified to his excellence as a pupil master. A bencher of his inn from 1873, he was treasurer in 1896. However, though he had a big and varied practice, he was less effective *in banco* (full court sittings) than at *nisi prius* (where a single judge presided), and seldom appeared before the House of Lords or privy council. Day continued to go on circuit, where his dry wit made him highly popular. He deplored the decay of circuit life and traditions in the railway age and set his own example in upholding them by frequently travelling on horseback between the circuit towns.

Having earlier turned down an offer to go as chief justice to Queensland, Day was made a judge of the Queen's Bench Division on 3 June 1882 and was knighted on 29 June. He was not a great success, for though by no means deficient in learning, he had no deep interest in the law and was indifferent to his reputation among lawyers and public. In civil cases, although speedy and usually correct, he annoyed litigants by often seeming uninterested and occasionally slumbering; in revenue cases in particular his attitude bordered on open contempt for the whole proceedings.

Day had evidently 'decided he would do most good by devoting his main energies to enforcing the moral law' (Day, 117) and now became Judgment Day, the readiness with which he resorted to the severest punishments earning him a fearsome reputation. He took great pains over his sentencing. One of the first judges routinely to provide himself with a full record of the criminal's previous convictions, he acquired first-hand knowledge of conditions in Liverpool by walking the worst streets at night with only his marshal and a single detective. He was a great believer in the efficacy of the lash—he was said to have ordered 3766 lashes on 137 criminals—and his especially fierce retribution for offences of violence made him popular in the northern cities; Liverpool was particularly grateful for his stern handling of the High Rip and Logwood gangs in 1887. However, his severity shocked many lawyers and occasionally outraged public sensibilities, as when he gave penal servitude for life to a seventeen-year-old. It was said that he, Phillimore, and Wills 'judged men by their own high standard of righteousness' (Rowlands, 100) and it was felt that 'where sexual immorality was concerned he knew no compassion, and seemed lost to all sense of proportion' (*DNB*). It was known at the bar, however, that some of his heaviest sentences were pronounced for their deterrent effect and were reduced in private immediately afterwards.

Although he eschewed politics, Day became involved in political controversies because, as one of very few Roman Catholics on the English bench, he was a natural choice for inquiries into Irish affairs. In 1886 he chaired a commission on the recurrent Belfast riots, and though his refusal to allow cross-examination of witnesses brought him into sharp conflict with the leaders of the Irish bar, the general tenor of his report was sufficiently favourable to the Roman Catholics for Lord Salisbury's administration to assume that he would be acceptable to them to investigate (alongside Hannen and A. L. Smith) the charges levelled against Parnell and other Irish nationalist leaders in the pamphlet *Parnellism and Crime*. But the other parties had not been consulted and Day's appointment was bitterly assailed by the nationalists, who cited disparaging remarks about the Irish he had apparently uttered years before on assize. John Morley for the Liberals joined in, quoting a private letter from Judge Adams, one of the Belfast commissioners, which described Day as 'a man of the 17th century in his views, a catholic as strong as Torquemada, a tory of the old high-flier and non-juror type'. Ministers vigorously defended their choice. Throughout the protracted proceedings of the commission Day maintained an almost unbroken silence and an air of profound boredom. He was credited with insisting on early proof of the authenticity of the damning letters attributed to Parnell, the exposure of which as forgeries provided the great sensation of the hearings, but he offered Hannen only half a page of notes towards the report.

Though Day's deadpan witticisms from the bench were relished by lawyers, his eccentric aversion to counsel's moustaches (he continued to affect the full side whiskers fashionable in his early manhood) and increasing deafness were not. He eventually resigned on 2 November 1901 and though sworn of the privy council he never sat on the judicial committee. His first wife had died on 26 March 1893 and on 19 May 1900 he married Edith, daughter of Edmund Westby, who survived him until at least 1921. He retired to Falkland Lodge, near Newbury, where he died on 13 June 1908. He was buried in the Kensal Green Roman Catholic cemetery. Two of his six sons became Jesuit priests and two others entered the law, one of whom became a master of the Supreme Court. His fourth son, Joseph Mary *Day, was a mechanical engineer. One of his three daughters became a nun.

Though his Catholicism was devout and uncompromisingly traditional, Day consorted comfortably with men whose religion and politics differed widely from his. His closest friend was William Willis, a Baptist and radical who as a county court judge was as renowned for his leniency to debtors as Day was for his severity to offenders. Willis was his most frequent companion on the holidays where Day indulged his liking for long walks at a great pace. He was also a fine swimmer and enjoyed yachting.

From an early age Day collected art and displayed a discriminating, if rather narrow, taste. He was among the first to recognize the merits of the Barbizon school and, braving his wife's disapproval, which sometimes led him to smuggle his purchases into the house, he amassed an impressive collection which included a dozen works by Corot and three by Millet. It realized more than £100,000 when it was sold after his death. PATRICK POLDEN

Sources A. F. Day, *John C. F. S. Day, his forebears and himself* (1916) [one of his sons] • W. Willis, *Recollections of Sir J. C. F. Day* (1908) • T. E. Crispe, *Reminiscences of a KC*, 2nd edn (1911) • R. Bosanquet, *The Oxford circuit* (1951) • E. B. Rowlands, *In the light of the law* (1931) • E. D. Purcell, *Forty years at the criminal bar* (1916) • R. Cocks, *Foundations of the modern bar* (1983) • *Hansard 3* (1888), 329.800–23 • *Law Times* (20 June 1908), 196 • C. Biron, *Without prejudice: impressions of life and law* (1936) • A. J. Ashton, *As I went on my way* (1924) • J. Heighton, *Legal life and humour* (1917) • Holdsworth, *Eng. law*, vol. 15 • J. Foster, *Men-at-the-bar: a biographical hand-list of the members of the various inns of court*, 2nd edn (1885) • Sainty, *Judges* • *DNB* • *CGPLA Eng. & Wales* (1911)

Likenesses engraving, 1882 (after photograph), repro. in *ILN* (July 1882) • S. P. Hall, three pencil drawings, NPG • F. Lockwood, pencil sketch, repro. in Alverstone (1914) • F. Pegram, pencil sketch, V&A • Spy [L. Ward], chromolithograph caricature, NPG; repro. in *VF* (27 Oct 1888) • oils, Harvard U.

Wealth at death £143,143 0s. 6d.: resworn probate, March 1911, *CGPLA Eng. & Wales* (1908)

Day, Joseph (*bap.* 1758?, *d.* 1832), lawyer and proposer of reforms, was probably baptized on 19 April 1758 at St Martin-in-the-Fields, London, the son of Joseph Day, attorney, and his wife, Mary. He was articled at the age of about fourteen to his father who then resided in the parish of St Mary-le-Bow in the City of London. Admitted an attorney of the king's bench in 1781, Day was living in Great Bath Street in 1784, but moved during the 1790s and early 1800s, first to Hatton Street, then to Kirby Street, and later still to 66 Lamb's Conduit Street, London.

Little is known of Day's legal practice except that it was secondary to a lifelong, but unsuccessful, devotion to the invention for profit of minor reforms in government. Starting in 1788, when he communicated to the Treasury a scheme for raising revenue by levying stamp duties on probate records, Day tirelessly sought audiences with important people, including the king and the prince of Wales, and on several occasions advertised his ideas by printing pamphlets at his own expense.

Day's most notable project, a plan canvassed during the mid-1790s for reforming the qualifying process for attorneys and solicitors, was in broad outline, and in many of its particulars, an anticipation by more than twenty-five years of the Incorporated Law Society. Arguing that the low reputation of the profession was caused by the failure of the existing system of articled clerkship to guarantee that men of bad character and inadequate training were being excluded from practice, Day proposed that a college of attorneys, under the supervision of the judges, should be established by statute and given the power to examine candidates for admission while serving as a selective society of élite practitioners. Some sixty London attorneys subscribed to the project, and Day was encouraged by interviews he had with the judges and government officials. Although not himself a member, he also consulted with the governing body of the Society of Gentlemen Practisers, the leading club of London attorneys; but, while Day had probably exaggerated from the outset the support he enjoyed, the plan was killed in 1795 when the society turned against it without putting it before its full membership. Fears that the new society would lead to higher taxation, and concern over the role Day saw himself playing in it, were the likely causes of failure, and indeed Day did turn again in 1797 to the creation of new levies on the profession (probably connected with 37 Geo. III c. 90). Then, during the food crisis at the end of the century, he worked on a plan for creating a national inspectorate to survey the available grain stock. His point was that government regulation of the corn trade should be based on accurate information about supply, rather than on the dubious evidence of reported prices, but, although he spoke to government ministers and was invited in early 1802 to appear before London's committee on the high price of provisions, he gained nothing.

Day's last known project, which originated in 1807, was a scheme for improving public access to the information recorded in parish registers by setting up offices in London and York where the records would be made available for consultation and, though it was somewhat more limited in scope than Day's proposal, George Rose steered a bill along these lines through parliament in 1812 (52 Geo. III c. 146). By then suffering severe financial difficulties, Day hoped that a government post arising from the scheme would save him from ruin. Having at some earlier point moved his family from London to Macclesfield, in 1811 he gave up his practice in Cheshire and took accommodation in Frith Street, Soho, London, but his expectations were bitterly disappointed when Rose informed him that no office would be forthcoming. Something of a visionary, and always proud of his service to government and the public, Day's projects evidently left him a broken man. He is last heard from in 1825, when he wrote to Sir Robert Peel from Maldon, Essex, once again begging some reward for all of his past services. He died in 1832.

CHRISTOPHER W. BROOKS

Sources BL, Add. MS 38373, fols. 218–21, 238–42, 256–267v · BL, Add. MS 40372, fol. 240r–240v · BL, Add. MS 38250, fols. 191, 260 · CLRO, Misc. MS 94-24 · PRO, KB 170/1; KB 172/1; CP 70/3 · will of J. Day of Kelvedon, Essex, PRO, PROB 6/208, fol. 208 · IGI

Day, Joseph Mary (1855–1946), mechanical engineer, was born at 14 Albert Terrace, Bayswater, London, on 27 September 1855, the fourth son of the judge Sir John Charles Frederic Sigismund *Day (1826–1908) and his first wife, Henrietta Rosa Mary, née Brown (1824–1893). Day attended Beaumont College, a Catholic school at Windsor, from 1868 to 1873 and then the new Crystal Palace School of Practical Engineering from 1873 to 1874. He was apprenticed at the engineering works of Stothert and Pitt in Bath from 1874 to 1877.

In 1878 Day set up as iron-founder and engineering manufacturer in Bath, making leather-dressing and concrete-making machines (both patented by Day and his then partner, J. W. Lampard) and cranes. Day's firm was clearly then parasitic on the company to which he had been apprenticed, which had a worldwide reputation for such machinery. On 10 May 1879, at Midford Castle near Bath, Day married Margaret Anne (1853–1933), eldest daughter of James John Parfitt of Bruton. They had nine surviving children, at least two of whom were involved with their father's engineering work.

In the 1880s Day became intensely active as an entrepreneur in Bath, in improving that city's water supply, and in devising bread- and ice-making machinery. In April 1891 he applied for his first two-stroke internal combustion engine patent, granted in 1892. The constant litigation in Britain over the validity of the patent for a four-stroke engine, held by the German Dr Nikolaus Otto, had encouraged Day to seek an alternative design. He was thus led to try to simplify existing engine designs, probably drawing on his previous manufacture of valveless air-compressors. His Day engine (as it was soon known) used an enclosed crankcase as a pumping chamber, with two ports controlled by the piston to help charge the cycle. Day could see the possibility of marketing the engine as a portable electricity generator, but his attempts to develop the engine by raising £60,000 on the stock market failed in July 1892. Later that year an employee at Day's Bath works, F. W. C. Cock (1863–1944), suggested another modification of the engine with a third piston-controlled port, which was patented on 15 October 1892. This allowed the cycle to be controlled without the need for valves and with only three moving parts: piston, rod, and crank. The engine

could be run in whichever direction it was started. This ultimate simplification resulted in an internal combustion engine which became the ancestor of all later lightweight, high-speed, high-revving, portable two-stroke engines.

However, any future which might have awaited these inventions had been sabotaged by the legal battles in which Day had become embroiled as a result of his entrepreneurial activities. New legislation to regulate joint-stock companies had encouraged both crusading journalists and predatory lawyers. Day became involved in a flurry of lawsuits, including libel actions, from December 1890, and even though he won all these actions (no doubt helped by his father's connections) the damage to his engineering activities was done. On a visit to the United States in 1894 while trying to sell his engine patents, the British secretary of state even issued instructions for Day's extradition from the USA.

Day and his then partner were declared bankrupt in September 1893 and their manufacturing activities in Bath came to a sudden end. Their works and stock were auctioned in May 1894 and manufacture of Day engines effectively ceased in England until 1905. Engine making passed, via licence deals, to the USA, where an enormous number of engines were made, both legally and illegally, largely to power motor-boats, since the power characteristics of the Day engine proved ideal on water. In 1906 Day discharged his bankruptcy and re-established his engine making, first at Barking in Essex and then beside the Thames at Putney. His business was successful and he supplied motor-boat engines and, during the First World War, portable pumps for dewatering trenches.

This last work brought Day into contact with members of the Ministry of Munitions who were concerned as to how Britain was to maintain its navy in the new era of oil-fuelled warships. Two camps developed, one considering that reserves of overseas oil should be sought, such as those newly discovered in the Middle East. The other, to which Day unfortunately allied himself, supported the uninformed, and ultimately criminal, activities of Dr William Forbes-Leslie (1865–1944), who claimed the answer lay in retorting oil from Jurassic oil-shales exposed in Norfolk and elsewhere in England. Day joined the board of English Oilfields Ltd but was forced to resign in 1923 when it became clear that there was no oil in these shales. Day now sank into the oblivion which surrounded him at his death, at 1 St George's Road, St Margaret's-on-Thames, Middlesex, on Christmas day 1946, aged ninety-one. He was buried on new year's day at Teddington cemetery. His career provides a fine example of the complexities facing the inventor and entrepreneur.

H. S. TORRENS

Sources H. S. Torrens, *Joseph Day, 1855–1946, and the development of the two-stroke internal combustion engine* (1991) · H. S. Torrens, 'A study of "failure" with a "successful innovation": Joseph Day and the two-stroke internal combustion engine', *Social Studies of Science*, 22 (1992), 245–62 · S. H. Day, family papers, 1911 [for private circulation only] · J. Day, 'The two-stroke motor', [*British*] *Motor Boat*, 6 (1903), 294–5, 314, 341, 383 · H. S. Torrens, 'Engineering enterprise in Bath and Bristol', *Industrial Archaeology Review*, 11 (1989), 196–209 · A. T. J. Kersey, *Internal combustion engineering*, 3rd edn (1949) ·

J. Day, 'The retorting of Norfolk Shale', *Petroleum Times*, 9 (9 June 1923), 840 · F. Sass, *Geschichte des Deutschen Verbrennungsmotoren-baues* (1962) · *The Times* (15 May 1879), 1 · *The Times* (1 Oct 1855), 1 · *The Times* (28 Dec 1946), 1 · B. Burke, *A selection of arms authorised by the laws of heraldry* (1860), 132–4 · d. cert.
Archives Bath and North East Somerset RO, Bath, letters · Deutsches Museum, Munich, engine · Sci. Mus., Day engines · Sci. Mus., letters
Likenesses photograph, 1920, repro. in Torrens, *Joseph Day*, p. 2 · M. Mcleod, crayon drawing, 1941, Australia

Day, Lewis Foreman

Day, Lewis Foreman (1845–1910), decorative artist and industrial designer, was born at Peckham Rye, Surrey, on 29 January 1845, the son of Samuel Hulme Day, wine merchant in the City of London, of an old Quaker family of Essex, which claimed descent from John Day (1521/2–1584), the Elizabethan printer. His mother was Mary Ann Lewis. After attending a school in France, he entered Merchant Taylors' School in January 1858, and on leaving continued his education in Germany for eighteen months. After a short time as a clerk he went, at the age of twenty, into the works of Lavers and Barraud, glass painters and designers. Day then moved to the workshops of Clayton and Bell, makers of stained glass, where he remained for two years; his principal work being to design the cartoons. In 1870 he worked for Heaton, Butler and Bayne on the decoration of Eaton Hall, Cheshire, and in the same year he started his own business in London. In 1873 he married Ruth Emma Morrish with whom he had a daughter, Ruth.

Day took from his early training a special interest in stained glass design, gradually acquiring a wider reputation as a designer for textiles, pottery, carpets, wallpapers, silver, and many other branches of manufacture. His designs were always carefully adapted to the material in which they were to be carried out, and to the processes of manufacture which had to be employed. He belonged to the same school of artist-craftsmen as William Morris and Walter Crane, and his influence on contemporary ornament, if not so fully recognized as that of those two artists, was considerable. An important educator in design, many of the best-known designers of his day were taught by him and benefited from his belief in natural forms of ornament and high standards of craftsmanship.

Day was one of the first promoters of the Arts and Crafts Exhibition Society and a founder in 1882 of the Fifteen, a group of artists interested in the role of design in daily life, and of the Art Workers' Guild, of which he was at one time master. He was also seen as a 'forerunner, of a still transitional character' (N. Pevsner, *Pioneers of Modern Design*, 1936, repr. 1991, 26), of the modern movement: Pevsner noted Day's remark that '"whether we like it or no, machinery and steam power and electricity for all we know, will have something to say concerning the ornament of the future"' (ibid.). A course of Cantor lectures at the Royal Society of Arts in 1886, 'Ornamental design', was followed by the publication of many important volumes on ornament and decoration, including *Anatomy of Pattern* (1887), and *The Planning of Ornament* (1887).

From 1897 to his death Day was almost continuously a member of the council of the Royal Society of Arts. His services to the government department, originally that of science and art, and afterwards the Board of Education were much appreciated. From 1890 onwards he examined in painting and ornament, and later with William Morris, Walter Crane, and other decorative artists examined works sent in by schools of art for national competitions. Shortly before 1900 he gave courses of lectures on ornamental art at the Royal College of Art, South Kensington, and he also inspected and reported on provincial schools of art where ornamental work was studied and practised. When the Victoria and Albert Museum was established in its new building (1909) he was a member of the committee appointed to report upon the arrangement of the collections, and he greatly influenced the scheme which was eventually adopted.

Of his published works Day was most satisfied with *Windows* (1897; 3rd edn 1909), the fruit of an exhaustive study of continental stained glass pursued in holiday tours over twenty years. He contributed many articles to the *Magazine of Art*, the *Art Journal*, and the *Journal of Decorative Art*. His monograph on his friend William Morris was published in an extra number of the *Art Journal* in 1899. He was also author of *Instances of Accessory Ornament* (1880); *Every Day Art* (1882; 2nd edn 1894; Dutch trans. 1886); *Alphabets Old and New* (1898; 3rd enlarged edn 1910); (with Mary Buckle) *Art in Needlework* (1900; 3rd edn 1908); *Lettering in Ornament* (1902); *Pattern Design* (1903); the South Kensington handbook *Stained Glass* (1903); *Ornament and its Application* (1904); *Enamelling* (1907); and *Nature and Ornament* (2 vols., 1908–9). He died at his house, 15 Taviton Street, Gordon Square, on 18 April 1910, and is buried in Highgate cemetery.   H. T. WOOD, rev. HELEN CAROLINE JONES

Sources personal knowledge (1912) · Merchant Taylors' School Register, 2.330 · J. Seconds, 'Day, Lewis Foreman', *The dictionary of art* (1996) · private information (1912) · *Manchester Guardian* (19 April 1910) · *Glasgow Herald* (19 April 1910) · D. M. Ross, *Lewis Foreman Day, designer and writer on stained glass* (1929) · E. Rycroft, 'Lewis Foreman Day and the Society of Arts', *RSA Journal*, 140 (1991–2), 333–6 · S. Jervis, *The Penguin dictionary of design and designers* (1984) · *CGPLA Eng. & Wales* (1910)
Likenesses E. R. Hughes, drawing, 1897, Art Workers' Guild, London
Wealth at death £17,017 17s. 11d.: probate, 6 June 1910, *CGPLA Eng. & Wales*

Day, Mabel Katharine

Day, Mabel Katharine (1875–1964), scholar of medieval English, was born at St Leonards House, Linney, Ludlow, Shropshire, on 5 December 1875, the daughter of the Revd Henry George Day (1830–1900), formerly a fellow of St John's College, Cambridge, and headmaster of Sedbergh grammar school, and his wife, Annie Metcalfe. She was educated at Brighton high school and Girton College, Cambridge, where she held a scholarship and in 1899 gained third-class honours in part one of the mathematical tripos. She also studied for a London University degree, graduating BA in 1900 and MA in 1902. From 1900 to 1907 she was an assistant mistress at Monmouth high school, Preston high school, Barnsley high school, and Tiffin Girls' School, Kingston upon Thames, and then from 1907 to 1909 was lecturer in mathematics at Islington Day Training College.

From 1912 Mabel Day was employed as an assistant lecturer in English in evening classes at King's College, London. In 1921 she was awarded the degree of DLitt by the University of London for her (unpublished) thesis 'Early Middle English word-stress investigated on the basis of the unrhymed alliterative poems'. From 1920 to 1936 she was lecturer in English language and literature at King's. She was the invaluable assistant of Sir Israel Gollancz, professor of English at King's and honorary director of the Early English Text Society (EETS).

Mabel Day is remembered for her devoted work for the EETS for an unparalleled twenty-eight years as assistant director and secretary between 1921 and 1949. She not only supervised the society's publications, but was also responsible for dealing with its members. Injunctions to them to send their subscriptions and orders to her at her London address were a standard feature of the society's publications at this period, when its financial position was less than assured. After her resignation she advised the society as a member of council for a further ten years, until her health failed.

Her editorial contributions are characterized by misleading personal modesty: she commonly appears among the society's publications as a co-editor, especially with Gollancz, on whose studies in alliterative poetry she was an indispensable collaborator, most notably on *Sir Gawain and the Green Knight* (1940). The introduction, which she supplied, is regarded as one of her finest pieces of scholarship. She also realized Gollancz's edition of *Mum and the Sothsegger* (1936), with her fellow member of council, Robert Steele, with whom she also edited the English poems of Charles of Orleans (1941, 1946). The edition of *Sir Gawain* had been left incomplete at Gollancz's death, and the demise of other editors also necessitated some of her contributions. In this she showed unfailing tact and attention to detail, as a subsequent director, C. T. Onions, noted in his preface to the *Lyfe of Syr Thomas More by Ro. Ba.* (1950), an edition which had required hours of painstaking work in Lambeth Palace Library 'not seldom in conditions semi-arctic'. Editors for nearly forty years paid tribute to her unselfish generosity and labour in overseeing their work.

Mabel Day's expert knowledge of Middle English texts ranged far beyond her original special interest in alliterative poetry. About 1935 the society embarked on one of its major publishing projects, the issue of diplomatic editions of each of the surviving manuscripts of the *Ancrene Riwle*. Her own edition of the Nero MS version 'on the basis of a transcript by J. A. Herbert' (1952) sets out the principles which have governed all editors of this series, and she advised on others. Her editorial work was distinguished by strong good sense, painstaking attention to detail, and love of the subject. Perhaps her forte was her writing of detailed historical commentary on the texts, in which she pursued enquiries with meticulous thoroughness. Even a passing comment, in *Sir Gawain*, that a precipitous passage at Wetton Mill (Staffordshire), which she proposed as the model for the Green Knight's chapel, was 'still traversable' (p. xx), was based on experiment: as she

remembered in conversation, a countryman was paid to make trial.

Mabel Day died, unmarried, at her home, Bailbrook House, Batheaston, Somerset, on 18 September 1964, and her funeral took place at Bath crematorium on 24 September. Although some of the editions with which she was involved have been revised to take account of recent scholarship, subsequent editors testify to the soundness of the foundations on which they build. She not only did much to maintain the society's high reputation, but made an invaluable contribution to medieval English scholarship at large.   H. L. SPENCER

Sources *The Times* (21 Sept 1964) · private information (2004) · K. T. Butler and H. I. McMorran, eds., *Girton College register, 1869–1946* (1948) · b. cert. · d. cert.
Wealth at death £25,952: probate, 18 Feb 1965, *CGPLA Eng. & Wales*

Day, Matthew (*bap.* **1611**, *d.* **1663**), Church of England clergyman and schoolmaster, was baptized on 24 February 1611 at Windsor, the third son of Matthew Day (1574–1661), mayor of Windsor, and his wife, Mary (1580/81–1667), daughter of George Dowdeswell of Eton. A king's scholar at Eton College between 1624 and 1630, he was then a scholar (1630–33) and fellow (1633–43) at King's College, Cambridge; he graduated BA in 1634 and proceeded MA in 1637. On 9 September 1642 Day, presented by Eton, succeeded David Stokes as rector of Everdon, Northamptonshire; he married Stokes's daughter Elizabeth on 7 May 1645. When parliament's Northampton committee had sought, on 18 May 1644, a reason for his non-appearance before it, Day answered from his home in Windsor that he would not take the covenant. The living's sequestration, for his desertion to royal quarters, was confirmed despite Day's letter of 24 August 1644 explaining his movements (which, he claimed, had included only a day in Oxford). Subsequently his wife was granted a fifth of the revenue (13 April 1647). The committee for advance of money heard on 13 November 1649 that Day—described on this occasion as late minister of Caversham, Oxfordshire, delinquent—had £500 in the keeping of his father and father-in-law.

Undeterred by Day's royalism, Abraham Colfe appointed him master of his Lewisham grammar school, which opened on 10 June 1652. That year Day's only book was published: *Parekbolai, sive, Excerpta in sex priores Homeri Iliados libros*, a selective short commentary for students, dedicated to Colfe. Day resigned his mastership, effective from Michaelmas 1660, after Charles II had made him vicar of Staines, Middlesex, and the bishop of London had collated him to St Paul's prebend of Neasden (17 and 25 August respectively). In 1661 he became DD at Cambridge by royal mandamus. Day's wife died on 31 December that year. He himself died in the autumn of 1663 and was buried at Windsor on 4 October, leaving his mother and father-in-law, the beneficiaries of his will dated 25 September, to care for his four children, Matthew, Mary, Thomas, and Elizabeth.   HUGH DE QUEHEN

Sources W. Sterry, ed., *The Eton College register, 1441–1698* (1943) · L. L. Duncan, *A history of Colfe's Grammar School* (1910) · Venn, *Alum.*

Cant. • *Walker rev.* • J. Bridges, *The history and antiquities of Northamptonshire*, ed. P. Whalley, 1 (1791) • M. A. E. Green, ed., *Calendar of the proceedings of the committee for advance of money, 1642–1656*, 2, PRO (1888) • Register of St John, Windsor, transcript, Society of Genealogists • E. Ashmole, *The antiquities of Berkshire*, 3 (1719) • PRO, PROB 11/312, fols. 190r–190v [Day's will]

Day, Nugent Francis Cachemaille Cachemaille- (1896–1976), architect, was born on 23 July 1896 at St Hiliary, Cleveland Road, South Woodford, Essex, and baptized at Holy Trinity, Hermon Hill, South Woodford, on 16 August that year, the only son of Harvey Francis Day (1864–1906), mechanical engineer, and his wife, Katie Margaret Mary, *née* Cachemaille (1869–1957). He was baptized Nugent Francis Cachemaille Day but in 1924 Day and his mother changed their name by deed poll to Cachemaille-Day, and so Nugent had his mother's maiden name as both first name and surname. He was educated at Westminster School before entering the Architectural Association in 1912 and qualifying in 1920 after the First World War. In 1926 he was made an associate of the Royal Institute of British Architects, becoming a fellow in 1935. Initially Cachemaille-Day worked with Louis de Soissons on the development of Welwyn Garden City and later he became chief assistant to H. S. Goodhart-Rendel. In 1928 he set up in practice with Felix J. Lander (1898–1960) and in 1930 they were joined by Herbert A. Welch (1884–1953), forming the partnership of Welch, Cachemaille-Day, and Lander. In 1935 he established his own practice at 6 Dorset Street, London. On 22 April 1933 he married Marie Anna Luise von Polentz (1900–1983), a German, at which time he was living in St John's Wood. In 1939 the couple moved to Hertfordshire and their only child, Ruth, was born there in 1940. The family returned to London in 1953 before moving to Brighton in 1959.

Cachemaille-Day always had a varied practice, both domestic and commercial, and as a consultant architect to the London county council after the war he was responsible for a number of schools and blocks of flats. However it was as a church architect that he became best-known. As a high Anglican, like his parents, and a keen churchman, he developed a particular interest in church design which, with associated buildings, was to make up by far the largest and most important part of his work. Travelling widely in Europe from the early 1930s, he became well aware of continental developments in church design and was clearly influenced by the ideas of the liturgical movement, the architectural consequences of which emerged in Germany after the First World War. The movement called for the abandonment of traditional architectural styles, for the use of new materials, such as reinforced concrete, for the development of new forms, and, crucially, for changes in planning, particularly the bringing of the altar into the body of the church and the adoption of centralized plans. Cachemaille-Day argued that architectural developments could contribute to a general spiritual revival and that new churches should be at the centre of a complete group of buildings. He rejected any preoccupation with the question of style but he recognized the tenacity of the Gothic tradition and, along with a number of other contemporary stylistic influences, particularly from Germany, can be seen in his work. He recommended brick as a cheaper alternative to stone, citing Albi Cathedral in France as an appropriate model for its simplicity and grandeur, but he also saw the value of reinforced concrete as a means of achieving economy without sacrificing architectural dignity. In terms of planning he believed that the altar should be in the midst of the congregation and not separated from it by a screen or a choir, that the choir itself should be in a side or west gallery, that the pulpit and lectern should be positioned so the word could be clearly heard by all, and that the font should have a dignified setting, preferably at the west end.

Many of these ideas are evident in his remarkably mature first church, St Nicholas's, Burnage, Manchester (1931–2), described by Pevsner as 'a milestone in the history of modern church architecture in England' (Pevsner, 304), which is of brick with a basilican plan and a view of the altar unobstructed by the choir, who were relegated to a side gallery. His next church, St Saviour's, Eltham, Kent (1932–3), which won the RIBA London architectural medal, has a fortress-like exterior with a squat tower over the chancel, strongly reminiscent of Albi. Probably his most important pre-war church is St Michael and All Angels, Wythenshawe, Manchester (1937), 'a sensational church for its country and day' (ibid., 342), which has a centralized star-shaped plan generated from the use of the diagrid reinforced concrete frame system and was originally intended to have a forward altar surrounded on three sides by seating.

With the increased cost of building, Cachemaille-Day's post-war churches are more austere, but continue to develop the use of reinforced concrete and experiment with new plan forms. Perhaps two of the most important are All Saints, Hanworth, Middlesex (1952 and 1958), the main body of which consists of a large square with the altar in a shallow curved apse, and St Richard of Chichester, Crawley, Sussex (1954; dem.), which had a flexible plan, cleverly allowing for congregations of varying sizes. His final church work was to design the extension at the west end of his first church, St Nicholas's, Burnage, in 1963.

Cachemaille-Day was described as a 'large man with an infectious gaiety' (Barnett, 1) and 'a most kind and generous person' (Hill, 25). His sketches reveal this vigorous personality, and he was known to break a pencil in his enthusiasm when illustrating a particular point. He retired in 1963 but failing eyesight prevented him enjoying the painting and modelling in clay which he practised. He continued to live in Brighton until his death at his home there, 7 Chesham Street, on 4 May 1976. He was cremated at Brighton crematorium. Over his career Cachemaille-Day designed, extended, or altered about fifty churches, a body of work of great depth and quality and the product of one of the most talented church architects of the twentieth century.

MICHAEL BULLEN

Sources private information (2004) [Ruth Day, daughter; Anthony Hill] • parish register, Holy Trinity, Hermon Hill, 16 Aug

1896 [baptism] · *CGPLA Eng. & Wales* (1976) · A. Hill, 'N. F. Cachemaille-Day: a search for something more', *Thirties Society Journal*, 7 (1991), 20–27 · L. King, *RIBA Journal*, 83 (1976), 484 · M. Bullen, 'Cachemaille-Day's Manchester churches', MA diss., University of Manchester, 1991 · P. Hammond, *Liturgy and architecture* (1960) · E. Harwood, 'Liturgy and architecture: the development of the centralised eucharistic space', *Twentieth century architecture*, 3: *The twentieth century church* (1998), 50–74 · *South Lancashire*, Pevsner (1969), 304–5, 342 · N. F. Cachemaille-Day, 'Ecclesiastical architecture in the present age', *RIBA Journal*, 40 (1932–3), 825–38 · N. F. Cachemaille-Day, 'Church and community', *Post-war church building*, ed. E. Short (1947), 25–40 · H. A. Barnett, 'Nugent Cachemaille-Day', unpublished notes, May 1978 · M. Bullen, 'Cachemaille-Day's Manchester churches', *The church in Cottonopolis*, ed. C. Ford, M. Powell, and T. Wyke (1997), 144–74

Archives Church of St Michael and All Angels, Wythenshawe, Manchester, vicar and parochial church council, drawings · Church of St Nicholas, Burnage, Manchester, vicar and parochial church council, drawings and corresp. · RIBA
Likenesses photograph, RIBA BAL; repro. in *Architect and Building News* (13 July 1934) · photograph, priv. coll.
Wealth at death £216: probate, 29 June 1976, *CGPLA Eng. & Wales*

Day, Richard (*b.* 1552, *d.* in or before 1606), printer and Church of England clergyman, was born at Aldersgate, London, on 21 December 1552, the son of the printer John *Day (1521/2–1584). Intended by his father for the church, he was educated at Eton College and was admitted as a scholar to King's College, Cambridge, on 24 August 1571. He matriculated in November 1572 and was admitted as fellow on 24 August 1574, proceeding to BA in 1575. He continued his studies, only to give up his fellowship shortly after Michaelmas 1576 without matriculating MA. He later claimed that he had left because of persistent complaints by his stepmother and John Day's second wife, Alice Lehunte, about how much his education was costing and because his father wished him to join the family printing business. In fact, however, it appears that Richard left Cambridge because he had fallen in love with a girl called Ellen Bowles, who lived near Aldersgate. (This was not the woman he married some years later, whose maiden name was Pope.)

In 1576 Day assisted his father in the printing of, and wrote some of the prefixed verses to, the third edition of Foxe's *Actes and Monuments*. The following year, on 28 August 1577, he was named as co-patentee when his father secured the renewal of a lucrative patent for the printing of a number of works including the Psalms in metre and the *ABC with Little Catechism*, although it appears that Richard may have gained his half-share by misleading his father about the terms of the grant. None the less, he was admitted as a freeman of the Stationers' Company at some point before 30 June 1578 when he was elected to the company's livery. In that same year he and his father were part of a patent dispute with William Seres and Henry Denham successfully resolved by the Stationers' Company.

Day entered his first book in the company's registers on 28 May 1578, his own translation of John Foxe's *Christ Jesus Triumphant*. The work was followed by a newly prefaced edition of *A Booke of Christian Prayers, Collected out of the Auncient Writers*, otherwise known as *Queen Elizabeth's Prayer Book*. He also variously edited, translated, registered, and printed a handful of books over the next two years. However, his father evidently did not allow him to produce any works covered by the 1577 patent, as Richard took to pirating the little catechism and the metrical Psalms. As a result, in 1580 his father, then master of the Stationers' Company, assisted by the company's wardens, entered Richard's premises and took from him the bulk of his books, type, and press. No books were issued by Richard Day after this event.

Day was ordained on 1 December 1580, serving as vicar in Mundon, Essex, until about 1583, and occupying Foxe's living at Reigate, Surrey, for a brief period from 24 May 1583 until he resigned at some point during 1584. About this period John Day made a deed of gift to his wife and her family, intended to deprive Richard of his inheritance (worth several thousand pounds) and to force Richard to pay all of his own mounting debts himself. It may well be that, left little option by his father's actions, Richard saw no opening for him other than the church. It is also possible that this was a final attempt to win back his father's approval (and his inheritance), a hope that ended with his father's death on 23 July 1584. The following year Day successfully challenged in chancery the validity of his father's deed of gift. Alice and her brother John Le Hunte counter-sued, and it is this second suit in particular that provides much of the evidence for Richard Day's activities from 1576 onwards.

Despite an attempt by his father in his final years to revoke Richard Day's rights to the 1577 patent, the patent continued in Richard's name until at least 1604 although all printing for it was done by five nominated assigns. In Michaelmas 1585 he and his assigns exhibited a bill of complaint in Star Chamber accusing a number of individuals of infringing the patent. Nothing further is known of his activities after this date, although on 26 February 1591 Verney Alley was granted the reversion to the Day patent on the event of Richard's death. Richard died some time before 13 April 1606, upon which date the court of the Stationers' Company granted 7s. to 'Richard dayes wydowe for her relief' (Jackson, 24). His widow seems to have continued to receive a pension from the company until 1615. The Day patent was eventually passed to the Stationers' Company by Alley's executors in 1614.

ELIZABETH EVENDEN

Sources ints. and deps. *Daye v. Daye*, 1585–6, PRO, Chancery papers, C24/180, 181 · W. Sterry, ed., *The Eton College register, 1441–1698* (1943), 98 · Venn, *Alum. Cant.*, 1/2.23 · C. L. Oastler, *John Day, the Elizabethan printer* (1975), 65–9 · W. W. Greg and E. Boswell, eds., *Records of the court of the Stationers' Company, 1576 to 1602, from register B* (1930) · E. Evenden, 'John Day, Tudor printer', PhD diss., University of York, [forthcoming] · W. A. Jackson, ed., *Records of the court of the Stationers' Company, 1602 to 1640* (1957), 24

Day, Robert (1746–1841), politician and judge, was born on 1 July 1746 at Lohercannon, Tralee, co. Kerry, the third son of the Revd John Day (1711–1781) and his wife, Lucy Fitzgerald, daughter of the knight of Kerry. Educated at Trinity

College, Dublin (1761–9), where he was a scholar and a candidate for fellowship, Day kept terms at the Middle Temple and was called to the Irish bar in Michaelmas term 1774.

A 'bosom friendship' with Henry *Grattan, with whom he shared rooms at the Temple, preceded Day's entry to the Irish House of Commons, where he sat for fifteen years as member successively for Tuam (1783) and Ardfert (1790 and 1797). Although he had been a volunteer Day gently distanced himself in politics from Grattan. Opposing parliamentary reform he defended the existing constitution as approaching 'nearer to perfection than any that the annals of the world could suggest' (1784, *Parliamentary Register*, 3.61–2). Day, however, was an untypical Irish conservative in his advocacy of Catholic emancipation: he supported the measures introduced in 1792 and 1793, and declared himself (22 February 1793) 'friendly to a total emancipation' (ibid., 8.268–70). He befriended the young Daniel O'Connell, who admired in Day 'that smoothness which society bestows on its frequenters' (Houston, 202).

Professionally Day was a 'crown lawyer'. Having obtained silk in 1790 he was appointed chairman of the co. Dublin quarter sessions. As 'Chairman of Kilmainham' (1790–98), he added to his parliamentary reputation as a eulogist of the existing order. Day's *Charges* to the grand jury at Kilmainham, seven of which were published, are models of prose composition, revelatory both of himself and of the growing revolutionary crisis. The 1795 charge, which contained a careful analysis of the nature of evidence, identified Day as a campaigner for the reform of the committal procedure. He was concerned that Irish practice limited grand jury proceedings to 'merely reading the information of an angry and prejudiced witness in his own cause' (Day, *Charge*, 1795, 30). Day wished that he could rule these 'written depositions of witnesses for the Crown, called Informations, sworn before a magistrate, and sent up to the Grand Jury with the bill of indictment' (ibid., 28) illegal and inadmissible. He encouraged grand jurors to adopt the English practice of thorough personal examination of crown witnesses.

Day's appointment to the court of king's bench, the patent for which is dated 28 February 1798, was as amply justified by his intellect and record at Kilmainham as it was appropriate to the times. 'When the very existence of society is at stake', he told his last Dublin grand jury in January 1798, 'it becomes necessary to cloath justice in all its terrors' (Day, *Charge*, 1798, 27). He was a member of the special commission which tried the rebels of 1798, and for the next twenty years he diligently administered the criminal law, in Dublin and on assize, where juries had the opportunity of hearing Day's thoughts on the news from the continent.

At the end of 1818, when he retired from the bench aged seventy-two, Day stood on the threshold of a twenty-two-year retirement. Having attained the 'venerable' age of ninety-four he died at his home at Loughlinstown on 8 February 1841, and was buried in Monkstown churchyard. A mural tablet, erected by his widow in Monkstown parish church, records that 'he was an eloquent advocate, an able lawyer, and a just and merciful judge'.

Day married twice. His first wife, Mary Potts (1746/7–1823) of London, whom he married in London on 8 August 1774, died on 18 April 1823. Their only child, Elizabeth, became the wife of Sir Edward Denny. Day's second wife, whom he married on 21 June 1824, was Mary, daughter of Bartholomew Fitzgerald MD of Bandon, co. Cork, and a Roman Catholic. This lady, ostensibly a companion of his first wife, was the mother of two sons fathered by Day during the currency of his first marriage. These boys, both of whom took Anglican orders, assumed the surname Day in accordance with the terms of their father's will. Their mother, who died on 11 June 1849, was buried in Monkstown churchyard, alongside her husband and his first wife.

Day was a tall man, affable and hospitable, who enjoyed certainty of belief in the providence of an Anglican God, in the common law, and in the British constitution. He was proud of his roots in co. Kerry, which he visited frequently and where his name is commemorated in the Tralee toponym Day Place, a street which he developed. His papers, preserved in the Royal Irish Academy, testify to a cultivated man, thoughtful, orderly, and pious.

KENNETH FERGUSON

Sources E. B. Day, *Mr Justice Day of Kerry, 1745–1841: a discursive memoir* (1938) · R. Day, *Charges delivered to the grand juries, by the honourable Mr. Justice Day* [n.d., 1835?] [incl. the seven pubd Kilmainham addresses, together with that given at Clonmell in 1808 and one further charge delivered in the king's bench in 1810] · J. Porter, P. Byrne, and W. Porter, eds., *The parliamentary register, or, History of the proceedings and debates of the House of Commons of Ireland, 1781–1797*, 17 vols. (1784–1801), vol. 3, pp. 61–2; vol. 4, pp. 294–6; vol. 6, p.176; vol. 7, pp. 461–2; vol. 10, pp. 298–9; vol. 13, pp. 268–70, 553 · *The Proceedings of the Parliament of Ireland*, 3 vols. (1793), 2.160–69, 365, 382–3; 3.395–400 · H. Grattan, *Memoirs of the life and times of the Rt Hon. Henry Grattan*, 5 vols. (1839–46), vol. 1, pp.117–20, 126, 151–2, 154–5, 162, 167–71, 252–5, 259–60; vol. 2, pp.127–8, 248–52; vol. 3, p. 95 · Burke, *Gen. Ire.* (1958), 216–17 · Burke, *Gen. GB* (1858), 301, 462 · V. Bary, *Historical genealogical architectural notes of some houses of Kerry* (1994), 174–5 · H. L. L. Denny, *A handbook of County Kerry family history, biography, &c.* (1923), 20 · Burtchaell & Sadleir, *Alum. Dubl.*, 218 [Robert Day; Edward Fitzgerald; John Robert Fitzgerald] · H. A. C. Sturgess, ed., *Register of admissions to the Honourable Society of the Middle Temple, from the fifteenth century to the year 1944*, 1 (1949), 362 · E. Keane, P. Beryl Phair, and T. U. Sadleir, eds., *King's Inns admission papers, 1607–1867*, IMC (1982), 125 · B. Bannerman and R. R. B. Bannerman, eds., *The registers of marriage of St. Mary le Bone, Middlesex, 1745–1775, Part II* (1918), 155 · Royal Irish Acad., Day papers, MS 12 W 7 · F. E. Ball, *The judges in Ireland, 1221–1921*, 2 (1926), 181–2, 229, 249, 255–7, 271 · R. Lascelles, ed., *Liber munerum publicorum Hiberniae … or, The establishments of Ireland*, later edn, 2 vols. in 7 pts (1852), vol. 1, pt 3, 52d · 'Law changes in Ireland', *The Times* (6 Oct 1818), 3c · *The Times* (11 Feb 1841), 6c · *Journal of the Association for the Preservation of the Memorials of the Dead, Ireland*, 7 (1907–9), 353–4 · F. E. Ball, *A history of the county Dublin*, 6 vols. (1902–20), vol. 1, p. 94 [mural tablet] · grant of arms, 14 Aug 1841, NL Ire., department of manuscripts, Genealogical Office MS 107, fols. 226–7 · J. B. Leslie, *Ardfert and Aghadoe clergy and parishes* (1940), 63, 105, 173–4 · A. Houston, *Daniel O'Connell, his early life, and journal, 1795 to 1802* (1906), 202

Archives Royal Irish Acad., MS history of England · Royal Irish Acad., MSS and diaries · Yale U., Beinecke L., circuit diary with an English travel journal | BL, letters to Sir Robert Peel, Add. MSS 40222–40378 · NA Ire., rebellion and official MSS, corresp. · NL Ire., legal documents bearing on Day property in co. Kerry · NL Ire., letters to second earl of Glandore · NRA, priv. coll., corresp. with Maurice Fitzgerald

Likenesses H. D. Hamilton, oils, 1795, repro. in Day, *Memoir*, facing p. 140 · J. J. Russell, portrait, 1804, RA · E. Orme, engraving, 1807, repro. in R. Day, *Charges* (1808), frontispiece · H. D. Hamilton, oils, King's Inns, Dublin; repro. in W. Ryan-Smolin, *King's Inns portraits* (1992), 22 · Wheatley, group portrait (*Irish House of Commons in 1780*), repro. in Day, *Memoir*, facing p. 135 · miniature, repro. in Day, *Memoir*, facing p. 172

Wealth at death considerable wealth; land in Kerry

Day, Sir Robin (1923–2000), radio and television broadcaster, was born on 24 October 1923 at 84 Oakwood Road, Hampstead Garden Suburb, Middlesex, the youngest of the three children of William Day (*c.*1885–*c.*1948), Post Office telephone engineer, and his wife, Florence, *née* Brown (*c.*1885–*c.*1947). The Day household was intensely political, and William Day (though a Lloyd George Liberal) was an admirer of Winston Churchill long before it became the fashion. After education at Brentwood School in Essex and Bembridge School on the Isle of Wight— where he shone in the school debating society—Day's university education was delayed by the Second World War. After working as a supply teacher in Essex and Suffolk he was called up into the Royal Artillery in 1942, commissioned in 1943, and served until early 1947, the last eighteen months in Africa.

In 1947 Day went up to St Edmund Hall, Oxford, to read law. At first sight this calling lent itself to his talents both for relentless cross-examination and for public speaking. Having undertaken a successful three-month undergraduate speaking tour of America on behalf of the Oxford Union in 1949, he became the union's president for Trinity term 1950. He graduated with a second-class degree in jurisprudence in 1951. In 1952 he was called to the bar of the Middle Temple, having been awarded both a Blackburn and a Harmsworth scholarship. To his and his friends' surprise he did not enjoy life at the bar, despite having secured a place in the chambers of F. H. Lawton, one of the leading common law practitioners of the time. So unhappy was Day that in 1953 he took, instead, a low-paid job with the British Information Service in Washington, and this turned out to be his first tentative step towards journalism.

Into broadcasting Day made sufficient contacts in this post to return home in 1954 and find work as a freelance broadcaster with the BBC and also as a producer of radio programmes. While a producer he wrote a memorandum to the controller of the Home Service in which he outlined a proposal for a breakfast news magazine programme. The idea was rejected, but was revisited in 1957 when the *Today* programme was launched. Day could truly say he was the godfather of what became this institution, and often did.

The BBC, too, Day found unsatisfactory. A friend drew his attention to an advertisement by Independent Television News (ITN) for newscasters for the new commercial television service being launched in 1955. Day applied and, despite his lack of journalistic experience and his

Sir Robin Day (1923–2000), by Godfrey Argent, 1970

somewhat forbidding demeanour, he was hired by Aidan Crawley, ITN's editor. Crawley took a risk on Day because he sensed he had the makings of a formidable television personality, and also because he would contrast with the film-star persona of the other newsreader, the celebrated amateur athlete Christopher Chataway. As a television critic of the time said: 'Hunched forward in close-up, narrowing his eyes behind gleaming spectacles, he delivers the news with such relish that he seems to be daring you to contradict him' (*The Times*, 8 Aug 2000). From the start Day also made a trademark of his spotted bow tie, which became his most recognizable feature to generations of viewers and caricaturists.

There were no strict demarcation lines in the early days of ITN, and Day looked for opportunities to report as well as to read the news. He brought the full weight of his well-developed character to bear on those he had to interview, though he tempered persistence with politeness in seeking answers to difficult questions. This technique seemed to catch the imagination of the public, for it rarely allowed the interviewee to command the viewer's sympathy. When Geoffrey Cox succeeded Crawley in 1956, he recognized in Day the perfect man to develop an art he felt ITN should champion: the political interview. Day made his name in this regard almost overnight in 1957 when, just a few months after Suez, he was dispatched to Cairo with a camera crew to interview Colonel Nasser. The interview showed Nasser as wanting to rebuild relations with Britain and ran for twenty minutes on television. It resulted in Day's being voted television personality of the year. He also interviewed former President Truman, asking him whether he regretted having authorized the dropping of the atomic bombs. Though Day had a detailed knowledge of and interest in foreign affairs, his main impact remained on domestic matters. It was to a large extent thanks to him that, in Britain, television became a key part of the political process.

In February 1959 Day set a new standard for interviewing British politicians in a meeting with the prime minister, Harold Macmillan, on the eve of a trip to Moscow. Day broke the tradition of deference that had distinguished earlier exercises of this nature by questioning Macmillan firmly about the future of his foreign secretary, Selwyn Lloyd. He came to regard this interview as a turning point in his career, marking him out as a broadcaster of distinction. Then, for a moment, Day's ground-breaking work in this line came to an end. He decided, unwisely as he later realized, to stand as Liberal candidate for Hereford at the general election of 1959. He had always been starry-eyed about parliament and, at thirty-six, felt this was the right time to see whether he could be part of it. Taking on a tory majority of 2150, he lost by 7500 votes. He never tried again, partly because the exercise disillusioned him, and partly because he felt the Liberal Party would never again be a satisfactory vehicle for what he regarded as liberal values. Though he kept strictly out of politics for professional reasons thereafter, he had by the end of his life evolved into being a staunch, but non-partisan, tory.

The BBC On his return to television Day accepted an offer of long standing to join the BBC's current affairs department. He worked as a freelance throughout the 1960s and into the early 1970s on *Panorama*, then the BBC's flagship current affairs programme, first as a reporter and interviewer and then, after Richard Dimbleby's death in 1965, as anchorman. His achievement in this job was based on thorough preparation, immersion in politics and the personalities of parliament, and an unfeigned dedication to the pursuit of the truth. Although a showman, he was fundamentally an intensely serious man, well-read, and convinced about the benefits of argument as a way to reach the truth. In the late 1960s he dominated *Panorama* and became synonymous with the broadcast treatment of politics. However, in 1972 he left the programme after complaining of being marginalized by a new generation of producers and executives, who seemed to use confrontations with him as a means of proving their own virility.

Day remained a constant presence on the BBC, always the first choice to conduct a big set-piece political interview or to preside over coverage of election nights, political campaigns, and party conferences. Sir Jeremy Isaacs, with whom Day had a difficult relationship at the BBC, conceded that 'Day is a fair, honest and sharp interviewer. He's quicker to see the point and ask the right question than anyone; the best political interviewer, always was and always will be' (*The Times*, 8 Aug 2000). In 1982, conducting interviews during the Conservative Party conference, Day famously caused the defence secretary, John

Nott, to tear off his microphone and walk out of an interview after Day described him as a 'here today, gone tomorrow politician'. Nott's political career ended soon after the interview: Day suffered no harm, either with the BBC or with the British public.

The BBC found several, mainly unfulfilling, vehicles for Day on television in the 1970s, but he was never especially happy unless handling the cut and thrust of politics. Always by nature a performer, he was thrilled to be asked to appear on the *Morecambe and Wise Show*, then the leading programme in the BBC's light entertainment stable. His rendition of Flanagan and Allen's 'Underneath the Arches' was a staple not just of after-dinner speeches and charity galas but also on several later television variety shows. He wanted to be more than a turn, however: and in 1979 his career revived. He was asked to become anchorman of Radio 4's *The World at One*, to which he brought a new authority and on which he was able to exercise his skill as an interviewer. He also rebuilt his place as a television broadcaster in launching *Question Time*. The show was initially regarded as a temporary filler for the schedules, but became a permanent institution. Day chaired it for its first ten years and came to regret retiring from it when he did. The interaction with an audience showed another side to Day's character, bringing out some of the charm, humour, and kindness that his friends saw in him in private but which had hitherto been unseen in the serious world of political interviewing.

Day's ambitions had always extended beyond the practice of broadcast journalism: spurred on by the considerable ego that made him such an intimidating interviewer, he had longed to become a public figure rather than just a celebrity. As early as 1970 he had been considered for the post of director-general of the Independent Broadcasting Authority, and made no secret of his disappointment when the post went to a former public-school headmaster with no experience of broadcasting, Sir Brian Young. In 1976 he was narrowly beaten for the post of director-general of the BBC by a colleague, Ian Trethowan. He used his weight to campaign for other causes in which he firmly believed, such as televising parliament, on which subject he wrote an authoritative pamphlet for the Hansard Society (of which he was chairman between 1981 and 1983). He would constantly lobby his many friends in the higher echelons of parliament and Whitehall about political and constitutional matters, such as reform of the BBC or electoral reform. He was also an early advocate of a national lottery. At the time of his death he was arranging to be nominated for the first list of 'people's peers', it having long been his ambition to sit in the House of Lords and so, at last, to play a role in parliament.

'Grand inquisitor' Day's seniority as a broadcaster and his contribution to the genre had, however, brought him a knighthood in 1981. Famously, he so irritated Margaret Thatcher (who had recommended him for the honour) in an interview he conducted with her not long afterwards that she pointedly referred to him as Mr Day throughout.

Although some colleagues in broadcasting and journalism had thought it wrong of him to accept the knighthood, the honour was immensely popular with the public, as was Day himself. On his death Baroness Thatcher commented: 'Our paths often crossed and I always enjoyed the joust. He was tough and relentless, but he was also fair, witty and gracious' (*Daily Telegraph*, 8 Aug 2000).

Day's private life had been less smooth. He married late, on 3 April 1965 at the age of forty-one, having always enjoyed the company of a range of younger, attractive women. His wife, Katherine Ainslie (*b*. 1940), an Australian barrister, was one such. They had two sons, but separated in 1982 and were divorced in November 1986. His elder son suffered head injuries in an accident as a child from which he very nearly died and from which he made an incomplete recovery. Day himself suffered heart trouble during his middle age—he had always been heavily built and had occasionally to resort to crash diets to keep his weight under control—and in 1985 he had a major heart bypass. More surgery followed in 1996, when he had to have a valve replacement, and he suffered badly from respiratory problems in the last years of his life. His supposed amorous adventures with younger women made him a frequent target for gossip columnists, whom he from time to time successfully sued as a result.

Day published a well-written autobiography, *Grand Inquisitor*, in 1989, though critics took it and him to task for egotism. By this time his television career was coming to an end, though he continued to work for the BBC during the election campaigns of 1992 and 1997. He became prone to spells of melancholy and loneliness, prompted by his belief that he had not achieved all he could have done in life. To the end he was a fiercely ambitious man, striving to fulfil his potential. Not for nothing did he take from F. E. Smith the superscription for his memoirs: 'The world continues to offer glittering prizes to those who have stout hearts and sharp swords' (Day, v). To an extent, his gregariousness provided some comfort in his blacker moments. He became a pillar of the Garrick Club, where he was in his last years to be found most lunchtimes at the lawyers' table, still cross-examining his circle of friends—mainly senior judges, broadcasting executives, and journalists—as though their lives depended upon it. He was a loyal and generous friend, belying his public persona of sometimes overbearing self-centredness, and took trouble to help in furthering the careers of younger colleagues whom he admired.

Day did not just rewrite the rules of political interviewing in Britain, setting a standard of scrupulous fairness combined with determination to get answers that later generations would desert to their detriment: he sought to conduct himself as a broadcaster in a manner Lord Reith would have considered appropriate. Above all, he sought to maintain what he considered to be one of the most important qualities of the old BBC: its obligation to handle politics with strict impartiality, while properly informing its audience about what was happening. In his own words he was 'counsel for the public' (*The Times*, 8 Aug 2000), asking their elected representatives the questions they themselves would, had they the chance—and being sure to extract the answers. His originality and his dedication to his task made him the finest television journalist of his age.

Day died at the Wellington Hospital, St John's Wood, London, of heart failure on 6 August 2000, having spent much of that day telephoning friends to warn them of his failing health. He was cremated at Mortlake crematorium, London, on 16 August. He was survived by Lady Day, and by their two sons.   SIMON HEFFER

Sources R. Day, *Grand inquisitor* (1989) · *The Times* (8 Aug 2000) · *Daily Telegraph* (8 Aug 2000) · *The Independent* (8 Aug 2000) · *The Independent* (9 Aug 2000) · *The Independent* (12 Aug 2000) · *The Guardian* (8 Aug 2000) · *WWW* · personal knowledge (2004) · private information (2004) [Katherine Day; Sally Stewart, niece] · b. cert.
Archives Bodl. Oxf., corresp. | FILM BBC Library · ITN Library | SOUND BBC Sound Archives
Likenesses photographs, 1959–89, Hult. Arch. · G. Argent, photograph, 1970, NPG [*see illus.*] · R. Beaton, oils, 1985, NPG · J. Mendoza, oils, *c*.1988, priv. coll. · N. Sinclair, photograph, 1991, NPG · C. Willis, photograph, 1991, repro. in *The Independent* (8 Aug 2000) · D. Sillitoe, photograph, repro. in *The Guardian* · photograph, repro. in *The Times* · photograph, repro. in *Daily Telegraph*
Wealth at death £1,382,691 gross, £1,332,030 net: probate, 2000, CGPLA Eng. & Wales

Day [Daye], **Stephen** (1593/4–1668), locksmith and first printer in the British American colonies, was born in England, probably at Cambridge, and married Rebecca, *née* Wright (*bap.* 1588, *d.* 1658), widow of Andrew Bordman, on 24 February 1617 at St Mary-the-Less, Cambridge. He was working as a locksmith in Cambridge on 7 June 1638, when he bound himself and his family to take passage to New England on the *John* of London. The Revd Joseph Glover, who had resigned his cure at Sutton, Surrey, in 1636 rather than read King James's Book of Sports, advanced £51 toward passage and supplies for Day, his wife, their two sons, his stepson William Bordman, and three menservants; Day in return engaged for himself and the servants to work for Glover for two years after their arrival 'in the trade wch the said Stephen … now useth … at such rates … as is usually paid … in the Country there' until the debt of £51 plus interest was worked off (Harvard University archives, Dunster MSS). Glover took along a small press worth £20, fonts of English, Greek, and unpointed Hebrew, and 120 reams of paper, but he died on the way over and the press, together with the services of Day and his workmen, passed to his widow. On 21 June 1641 she married Henry Dunster, president of Harvard College, who controlled the press until 1654, when he resigned from the presidency and sold it to the college.

The *John* arrived in Boston about October 1638 and the press began to operate at Cambridge in 1639, evidently under Day's direction, for the general court granted him 300 acres of land on 10 December 1641 as 'the first that sett upon printing' (N. B. Shurtleff, ed., *Records of the Governor and Company of the Massachusetts Bay in New England*, 5 vols., 1853–4, 1.344). Until 1667 the product was solely dedicated to the church, state, and college, beginning with the freeman's oath of allegiance to the colony (no copy extant) and 1700 copies of the *Bay Psalm Book* (1640), a metrical version by the ministers of Boston and its vicinity. Apart from annual series of Harvard commencement programs (1642–) and possibly of almanacs (1640?–; surviving from 1646) the press produced nothing between 1643 and late 1645, when Governor Winthrop's *Declaration* of his dealings with the Narragansetts appeared, printed in a new pica type probably acquired by Dunster.

Day mortgaged much of his Cambridge property in 1642 and, during the lull in printing, launched upon more congenial but less celebrated enterprises, establishing an ironworks and an Indian trading post with others at Nashaway, and prospecting for graphite and bog iron on behalf of John Winthrop jun. at Tantiusques and Chapnacongoe Pond, all in western Massachusetts. He resented his employment at the press, which had not been envisaged in his bond, and, perhaps because he could have earned more as a locksmith, he later claimed that Dunster owed him £100. Day's eldest son, Stephen, died in 1639 and Matthew (the only Day named in a surviving imprint) probably took over the direction of the press in his father's absence; at Matthew's death, on 10 May 1649, Samuel Green succeeded him as colony printer, leasing the press from Dunster or from Harvard. Day was a shaky speller and neither he, Matthew, nor Green had any regular apprenticeship in printing, but the scanty production of the press required no great competence.

According to Governor Winthrop the Nashaway entrepreneurs were 'most of them poor men, and some of them corrupt in judgment, and others profane' (*Journal of John Winthrop*, 504). Despite 'entertaining both English & Indians at my own house [in Lancaster], from day to day for some yeares together' (Massachusetts Archives, Columbia Point, Boston, 30.135) Day never settled there and forfeited his rights as one of the original company after the plantation was incorporated in 1652. His wife died on 17 October 1658 but there is no evidence that he ever remarried, despite Littlefield's circumstantial assertion (Littlefield, 1.125). He joined the church of Cambridge (where he sat below Samuel Green) on 28 February 1661, and on 22 December 1668 he died, leaving his stepson William, a tailor, about £75 of personal estate, which included his smithy, and land in Cambridge, Lancaster, and Shawshine. A wooden press in the Vermont Historical Society, once hopefully identified as 'the Stephen Daye Press', cannot be dated earlier than 1714.   HUGH AMORY

Sources G. E. Littlefield, *The early Massachusetts press, 1638–1711*, 2 vols. (Boston, MA, 1907) · G. P. Winship, *The Cambridge press, 1638–1692* (1945) · L. R. Paige, ed., *History of Cambridge, Massachusetts, 1630–1877* (1877) · M. I. Gozzaldi, *Supplement and index* (1930) [suppl. to L. R. Paige's *History of Cambridge*] · J. Savage, *A genealogical dictionary of the first settlers of New England*, 4 vols. (1860–62) · *The journal of John Winthrop, 1630–1649*, ed. R. S. Dunn, J. Savage, and L. Yeandle (1996) · S. E. Morison, 'The plantation of Nashaway—an industrial experiment', *Publications of the Colonial Society of Massachusetts*, 27 (1932), 204–22 · G. H. Haynes, '"The tale of Tantiusques": an early mining venture in Massachusetts', *Proceedings of the American Antiquarian Society*, new ser., 14 (1902), 471–97 · M. A. McCorison, 'The old press at the Vermont Historical Society', *Printing and Graphic Arts*, 7 (1959), 84–8 · *IGI* · *Glover v. Dunster*, 2 April 1656, Harvard U., Middlesex county court and probate records · S. P. Sharples, ed., *Records of the Church of Christ at Cambridge* (1906) · T. W. Baldwin, ed., *Vital records of Cambridge, Massachusetts*, 2 vols. (1914–15)
Archives Harvard U., Dunster MSS
Wealth at death approx. £100: Littlefield, *Early Massachusetts press* · approx. £75: inventory of personal estate, 22 Dec 1668, Middlesex probate records, no. 6115

Day, Susanne Rouviere (1875/6–1964), suffragist and writer, was born in Cork city into a family of prosperous merchants; little is known of her early life. She described herself as being 'five-foot seven', and of 'ample proportions … a wild Irishwoman with all the native and national love of a row boiling in my veins' (Day, *Round about Bar-le-Duc*, 205, 218). She was a formative force in organizing a branch of the suffrage organization, the Irish Women's Franchise League (IWFL), in Cork city in 1910. Susanne Day herself did not approve of militant activity and believed originally that the IWFL could remain non-militant. She eventually left the IWFL and formed the Munster Women's Franchise League in 1911, which declared itself to be non-militant. She organized and spoke at meetings on suffrage throughout Munster. Day acknowledged that her suffrage work had raised her awareness of social problems. She stood for election as a poor-law guardian in 1911 and topped the poll in the north-east ward of Cork city. She later wrote a novel based on her experiences as a poor-law guardian, *The Amazing Philanthropists* (1916), a satire on the workhouse system. She described the workhouse as a 'colossal business run by amateurs' (Day, *Amazing Philanthropists*, 89). She believed that the workhouse system 'breeds and perpetuates the very evil it was designed to kill' (ibid., 93). Considered an excellent public speaker, Susanne Day was encouraged by her work as a poor-law guardian to stand as a candidate for the Cork municipal elections in January 1914, but she failed to be elected by six votes.

Susanne Day became involved in relief work during the First World War. She spent fifteen months in northern France with a Society of Friends relief scheme providing aid to refugees in the months surrounding the battle of Verdun. Her experiences are recounted in *Round about Bar-le-Duc* (1918). She also wrote a number of articles on topics such as white slavery, and women and war for the *Irish Citizen*, a suffrage newspaper. Her literary work included co-writing two plays, *Broken Faith*, and *Fox and Geese* with Geraldine Cummins, which were produced in the Abbey Theatre, Dublin, in 1914 and 1917. Her last book, *Where the Mistral Blows*, a travel book about Provence, France, appeared in 1933. Little is known of her life after 1918. She did not marry and is reputed to have worked for the London fire service during the Second World War. A resident of Kensington, London, Susanne Day died on 26 May 1964 in the Cromer and District Hospital, Norfolk.

MARIA LUDDY

Sources A. M. Brady and B. Cleeve, eds., *A biographical dictionary of Irish writers*, rev. edn (1985) · S. Day, *The amazing philanthropists* (1916) · S. Day, *Round about Bar-le-Duc* (1918) · *Cork Examiner* (1910–14) · *Cork Free Press* (1911) · *Irish Citizen* (1912–15) · Irishwomen's Suffrage Federation annual reports (1911–16) [printed by the Irishwomen's Suffrage Federation, Dublin] · d. cert. · *CGPLA Eng. & Wales* (1964)

Likenesses photograph, repro. in *Cork Examiner* (26 May 1911)
Wealth at death £16,170: probate, 3 July 1964, *CGPLA Eng. & Wales*

Day, Thomas (1748–1789), author and political campaigner, was born on 22 June 1748 in Wellclose Square, London, the only child of Thomas Day (c.1690–1749) and his wife, Jane (c.1728–1796), daughter of Samuel Bonham, a City merchant. His father, deputy collector outwards of the customs of the port of London, died when young Thomas was no more than a year old, leaving him with a massive fortune in trust until he came of age. He attended a school at Stoke Newington, Middlesex, but after recovering from smallpox became a boarder at Charterhouse (1757–64). From Charterhouse he went to Corpus Christi College, Oxford, where he studied classics, became a member of a select debating society and close friend of William Jones, but left without a degree in 1767.

While living at Barehill, Berkshire, with his mother and stepfather, Thomas Phillips, Day became great friends with an ardently progressive neighbour, Richard Lovell Edgeworth. Edgeworth, an enthusiastic disciple of Rousseau, had resolved to educate his son Dick in accordance with the precepts of *Émile*, and Day became a kindred spirit in the great experiment. The more he learned of Rousseau, the more excited he became. Were all the world's books destroyed, he declared in 1769, the Bible and *Émile* were the two he would save. He accompanied Edgeworth and young Dick on a trip to Ireland and, later, on a visit to Rousseau.

During all this time, however, Day was also in search of a wife. A large, swarthy, gloomy, heavy-lidded and rather ungainly young man, his face severely pockmarked and his hair rarely combed, Day was not the ideal suitor. In quick succession he fell in love with Edgeworth's sister, with an unknown 'lady of the west', and, during a prolonged stay in Lichfield, with two sisters—each of whom resisted his blandishments. Day decided that, if his ideal woman did not exist, she would have to be created. In 1769 he adopted two girls from foundling hospitals and bore them off to France to see which of them he could educate (in accordance with Rousseau's ideas) into becoming a suitable wife for himself. One (Sabrina) seemed promising, and he brought her back to Lichfield for special tuition. But after conducting some rather extraordinary experiments, which included dropping hot sealing wax on her arm, he concluded that she was insufficiently phlegmatic.

In Lichfield, Day joined the Lunar circle of scientists, chemists, and inventors, presided over by Erasmus Darwin, who included Matthew Boulton (to whom he lent considerable sums of money), Josiah Wedgwood, and James Keir (his first biographer). He also met the leading lady of the town, Anna Seward, a young poet. Initially Anna was a confidante, and recipient of some of his lengthiest letters, but in later years (mainly because of his friendship with Edgeworth) became a violent enemy. In 1804 she wrote a vicious and inaccurate account of him which besmirched his reputation, particularly with regard to his supposed treatment of his wife.

With John Bicknell, in 1773, Day wrote *The Dying Negro*, a long and harrowing poem narrating the tale of a runaway slave, which proved a best-seller. In that same year, after some eighteen months in France, Day began legal studies at the Middle Temple. He shared rooms with William Jones and refused the latter's celebrated command to kill a spider, on the grounds that he had no right to do so and that such instructions created alarming precedents. He was admitted to Lincoln's Inn in 1776 and acquired chambers at Furnival's Inn although his subsequent legal practice, if not totally non-existent, was minimal.

Day's exacting standards for the ideal wife were met in Esther Milnes (1753–1792), an heiress from Chesterfield, the daughter of Richard Milnes (1705–1757), and his wife Elizabeth (d. 1757). Thomas Day and Esther were married at Bath on 7 August 1778. While not totally submerging her own personality, Esther was a satisfactory soulmate, and their marriage was close and loving. They settled in 1779 on a small estate at Stapleford Abbotts, near Abridge in Essex, although it proved singularly dismal and nonproductive. The Days were to have no children, though Thomas Lowndes, Esther's nephew, became for all practical purposes their adopted heir.

Day strongly supported the American colonists in their independence struggle and his poem *The Devoted Legions* (1776) was a scathing indictment of the government's actions. In 1780, caught up in England's short-lived revolutionary movement, he delivered three ringing speeches in favour of an early peace and parliamentary reform. They were published as pamphlets and it seemed that a new John Hampden had appeared on the scene. He declined invitations to stand for parliament and accept a government post, but acted as unpaid private secretary to Henry Laurens, an American congressman involved in the peace negotiations. He continued to publish political reflections including the partial text of a letter written to a plantation owner in 1776. 'If there be an object truly ridiculous in Nature', he declared, 'it is an American patriot signing resolutions of independency with one hand, and with the other brandishing a whip over his affrighted slaves.'

In 1780 Day purchased an estate at Anningsley, in Surrey, where he and Esther took up full-time residence in 1783. They ran it primarily as a philanthropic concern, with the bodily and spiritual welfare of its workers and their families of paramount importance. In desolate surroundings, they laboured to create a new Jerusalem. A pioneer in every sense, Day was not only conscious of the hazards of air pollution, and a campaigner for land reclamation, but an early exponent of afforestation.

Day had meanwhile made an astonishing reputation as a writer of instructive fiction for children. *The History of Little Jack* (1787), a tale for the very young, enjoyed great success. But his most famous production, destined to be a best-seller for eighty years, was *Sandford and Merton*. Published in three volumes (1783, 1786, and 1789), it tells how rebellious Tommy Merton, the spoilt son of a wealthy plantation owner from Jamaica, and his friend Harry Sandford, the poor but worthy son of a local farmer, are patiently educated by the Revd Mr Barlow—and how Master Tommy is brought, by precept and self-discovery, to see the error of his ways. A host of interpolated stories, providing introductions to ancient history, astronomy, biology, science, exploration, and geography, enable facts and figures to be absorbed relatively painlessly but the main narrative easily holds the attention. Rousseau's deductive techniques are deployed to good effect. What comes through is the basic Christian (and early socialist) message that the members of society should be kind not only to each other but also to the poor and the sick, to those of a different race, and to animals, birds, and insects. They should labour to the best of their ability and contribute to a common pool of goods and happiness. But for the idle rich, particularly those who wear fine clothes, play cards, and treat lesser mortals with contempt, the author has no mercy. The book, however sententious, would play a crucial role in moulding the ethos of nineteenth-century England.

A holder and practitioner of strange ideas, a perpetual optimist and a profound pessimist, a philanthropist and a misanthrope, an opponent of organized charity but a soft touch for those on the cadge, a preacher and an iconoclast, and above all a recluse who found it almost impossible to keep out of the limelight, Day was a strange bundle of contradictions. Sometimes lonely and bitter, but endeavouring always to obey the dictates of his conscience, he was a man deeply loved and respected by most of his contemporaries.

Day was thrown from his horse at Barehill, Berkshire, on 28 September 1789 and died almost instantly. He was buried at St Mary's Church, Wargrave, Berkshire, on 6 October 1789. Esther, distraught, survived him by less than three years.   PETER ROWLAND

Sources P. Rowland, *The life and times of Thomas Day, 1748–1789* (1996) [incl. bibliography] · G. W. Gignilliat, *The author of 'Sandford and Merton': a life of Thomas Day, Esq* (1932) · R. L. Edgeworth and M. Edgeworth, *Memoirs of Richard Lovell Edgeworth*, 2nd edn, 2 vols. (1821) · A. Seward, *Memoirs of the life of Dr Darwin* (1804) · J. Keir, *An account of the life and writings of Thomas Day, Esq* (1791) · S. Glover, *The history and gazetteer of the county of Derby*, ed. T. Noble, 2 (1833), 287 **Archives** Birm. CA, corresp. with Boulton family · BL, Hardwicke MSS · BL, corresp. with Walter Pollard, Add. MS 35655 · NL Ire., corresp. with Richard Lovell Edgeworth · Samuel Johnson Birthplace Museum, Lichfield, Seward MSS **Likenesses** J. Wright of Derby, oils, 1770, NPG · H. H. Meyer, stipple, pubd 1820 (after J. Wright of Derby), NPG · J. Condé, stipple, BM, NPG; repro. in *European Magazine* (1794) · J. Wright of Derby, portrait, Yale U. CBA **Wealth at death** £20,000: Gignilliat, *The author of 'Sandford and Merton'*, 317–19; Rowland, *The life and times of Thomas Day*, 340–41

Day, William (1529–1596), bishop of Winchester, was the son of Richard Day of Newport, Shropshire, and Agnes Osborne. He was educated at Eton and King's College, Cambridge, where his elder brother George *Day, future bishop of Chichester, was provost between 1538 and 1547. He was admitted scholar on 14 August 1545 and fellow on 15 August 1548, graduating BA in early 1550 and proceeding MA in 1553.

William Day's conversion to protestantism caused a serious breach between himself and his brother. When he

William Day (1529–1596), by unknown artist, 1593

applied for money to buy books and other necessities the request was sharply refused on the grounds that George was not prepared to assist anyone who was not a member of the true church. Day nevertheless retained his fellowship under Mary and during Cardinal Pole's visitation of the university in January 1557 he appears to have entertained 'all the thirteen seniors' to dinner at his chamber in King's and to have discharged the part of 'Christmas king' (Lamb, 197). Later that year he was chosen proctor.

Early preferment under Elizabeth Day's potential as one of the leaders of a revived protestant regime was at once recognized by Elizabeth's government. He resigned his fellowship in 1559 and, although still a layman, received letters patent, *sede vacante*, for the prebend of Ampleforth in York Minster on 7 November 1559, succeeding the deprived Alban Langdale, and for the archdeaconry of Nottingham on 23 December 1559, succeeding the deprived suffragan bishop of Hull, Robert Pursglove. He was ordained deacon by Edmund Grindal, bishop of London, on 24 March 1560, giving his age as twenty-nine, and priest seven days later by Richard Davies, bishop of St Asaph, acting on Grindal's behalf. He was elected a fellow of Eton later in 1560.

Following the death of the provost of Eton, William Bill, on 15 July 1561 the conservative majority within the fellowship made a futile attempt to thwart the royal prerogative by electing Richard Bruerne as his successor. The election was inevitably declared invalid and Grindal submitted to William Cecil a list of fourteen suitable candidates, many of whom had been in exile under Mary. It was, however, Day who was elected by the fellows on 18 October

1561. He was formally admitted on 5 January 1562. Because of Elizabeth's well-advertised dislike of clerical marriage it has been traditionally assumed that it was Day's celibacy that determined his selection but there is no evidence that the queen took a personal interest in the appointment. The factor which is likely to have most influenced Cecil and the privy council is his lifelong association with Eton and King's. Nor did Day remain celibate. His wife, Elizabeth, whom he married c.1565, was one of the five daughters of William *Barlow, bishop of Chichester, who all married bishops.

In 1562 Day proceeded BTh at Cambridge. His radical views were at the same time forcibly expressed during his early months as provost. The college chapel was transformed with iconoclastic thoroughness. The images were removed, the niches in which they had stood plastered over, and the imposing rood screen demolished. If Sir John Harington is to be believed, he was held in great affection by his scholars. Harington described him as affable and courteous, pleasant in conversation 'yet allwayes sufficiently retaining his gravitie'. He had 'a good and familiar fashion of preaching ... apte to edifie, and easie to remember' (Harington, 2.95–7).

On 13 January 1563 Day preached the sermon that opened the first convocation of the reign since the parliamentary settlement of 1559, on the text 'Feed the flock of God which is among you'. Thereafter he was one of those members of the lower house who attempted to do away with the Catholic ceremonies retained in the Book of Common Prayer. When a modified form of their proposals, summarized in a series of six articles, was eventually accepted for debate they were defeated by a majority of one after proxy votes had been taken into consideration.

At the end of 1563 Day clashed with the French ambassador, Paul de Foix, who had been consigned to Eton under a form of house arrest in retaliation for the French king's similar treatment of Sir Nicholas Throckmorton, English ambassador in Paris. De Foix resented the strictness of college discipline and when on 30 December he was refused the keys for the exit of two guests after the gates had been locked he burst into the provost's chamber, sword in hand, and demanded their surrender. Day complied but not unnaturally dispatched a formal complaint to William Cecil, expatiating on the unacceptable behaviour of the ambassador's entourage and describing their excesses in great detail.

Dean of Windsor On 12 May 1565 Day received letters patent for the canonry at St George's Chapel, Windsor, formerly occupied by Richard Bruerne. Perhaps for that reason he resigned the archdeaconry of Nottingham in June 1565 and the prebend of Ampleforth at the same time or shortly afterwards. He continued to receive special marks of favour from the government and to discharge the duties that went with them. On 11 August 1569 he was granted letters patent for the valuable rectory of Lavenham, Suffolk, and in November 1570 Matthew Parker, archbishop of Canterbury, successfully recommended his appointment as an ecclesiastical commissioner 'for some

causes necessary' (*Correspondence*, 370). In 1572 he was promoted both dean of the Chapel Royal and, on 23 June, dean of Windsor, resigning his canonry but remaining provost of Eton.

The first historian of Windsor College, Thomas Frith, writing within living memory of Day's tenure, dismissed him as a rapacious and unpopular dean who reduced the revenues by overmuch leasing of the estates. He cited a remark by Lord Chancellor Ellesmere that 'Dean Day had excellent skill to creep out of the law' (Ollard, 44). Historians of ancient foundations are, however, notoriously apt to concern themselves with stewardship of estates, and it is possible that Ellesmere was in fact expressing a grudging admiration for Day's ability to preserve, rather than squander, the resources of the deanery by resisting the petitions of importunate suitors for easy pickings from its assets.

Be that as it may, only one serious incident in Day's 24-year sojourn at Windsor survives in the public records. In December 1575, Elizabeth having commanded him to 'permitt no innovacions', he prohibited the catechizing of children in the churches over which, as dean, he exercised ordinary jurisdiction. He was rapped over the knuckles by Cecil (now Lord Burghley), who with consummate diplomacy observed that, catechizing being formally authorized by the Book of Common Prayer, Day must in some way have interpreted the queen's 'spech or admonicion to a wrong sense' (PRO, SP 12/172/1.i).

In 1580 Day served as prolocutor of convocation and was one of many theologians who disputed with Edmund Campion before his execution in 1581. He and Alexander Nowell, dean of St Paul's, thereafter wrote *A true report of the disputation with E. Campion, whereunto is joyned a true report of the other three dayes conferences* (1583).

Bishop in waiting, 1568–1596 The chief interest of Day's long career is his failure to secure a bishopric until the last months of his life. As early as 1568 his brother-in-law William *Overton, future bishop of Coventry and Lichfield, suggested that he succeed their late father-in-law, William Barlow, at Chichester, a diocese in urgent need of protestant evangelization. In March 1570 Archbishop Parker advised Cecil that Day was 'meetest' of the available candidates to follow Grindal as bishop of London (*Correspondence*, 360). The post, however, went to Edwin Sandys. There is no evidence that Day's claims were seriously considered when in 1577 Sandys was elevated to York and John Aylmer promoted in his stead. Yet when in March 1580 Aylmer suggested himself unsuccessfully for vacant Winchester, it was Day whom he recommended as his successor.

At the beginning of his primacy in 1583 John Whitgift renewed the proposal that Day be consecrated to London if Aylmer were to be translated (on this occasion to Ely). After the death of Richard Barnes, bishop of Durham, on 24 August 1587 Burghley vigorously espoused Day's candidacy for the palatine see, in the process opposing that of yet another of his brothers-in-law, Tobie *Matthew, dean of Durham. By the end of November, Burghley had secured Elizabeth's approval of his elevation but, as Day reminded Robert Cecil seven years later, 'the finishing of it was some while put off' when in December Robert Dudley, earl of Leicester, returned from the Low Countries: subsequently Day's nomination was 'clean overthrown' (*Salisbury MSS*, 5.8). In the months that followed Leicester oscillated between the claims of Matthew and those of John Piers, bishop of Salisbury. Deadlock ensued and the disposal of Durham had not been resolved when Leicester died in September 1588. In January 1589 the proposal to translate Aylmer to Ely and promote Day in his place was yet again revived, without success. If Burghley was still privately hoping to secure Day's elevation to Durham he was finally thwarted when Matthew Hutton was elected on 9 June 1589.

When Aylmer died in June 1594 London was finally within Day's grasp: although now sixty-five he remained Burghley's preferred candidate. Day appointed his son-in-law, Thomas Ridley, former headmaster of Eton, to conduct negotiations on his behalf but in the power struggle which followed Burghley and his son Robert Cecil made little headway. London was bestowed on Richard Fletcher, bishop of Worcester, whose candidacy had the backing of Leicester's stepson and political heir, Robert Devereux, second earl of Essex, and (after his failure to secure any support for his protégé Richard Bancroft) of Archbishop Whitgift.

Essex and Whitgift were nevertheless anxious to see Day elevated to the bench at this juncture since another of Essex's protégés, Henry Savile, had his sights firmly set on the provostship of Eton. They therefore suggested Day as Fletcher's successor at Worcester. Burghley, however, once again proposed him for Durham, soon to become vacant with the translation to York of Matthew Hutton. Day formally accepted Durham in a guarded letter of thanks to Robert Cecil on 14 October 1594, dryly observing (as quoted above) that a previous offer of the palatine see had failed in 1587. Perhaps he was already aware that other forces were at work. During the clandestine manoeuvres which followed it seems that, behind his father's back, Robert Cecil entered into secret alliance with Essex to secure Elizabeth's approval of Tobie Matthew. With extreme reluctance Day accepted the bishopric of Worcester instead. Both appointments were announced in council on 1 December.

Although Thomas Ridley twice assured Robert Cecil that he was resolved to proceed to election Day formally withdrew his acceptance of Worcester on 5 January 1595. On 14 January, informed that Elizabeth was displeased at this display of *lèse majesté*, Day explained himself more fully to Robert Cecil. He had made enquiries into his likely income from Worcester and concluded that 'if I should take it, it would utterly beggar me'. He had served the queen at Eton and Windsor 'the greatest part of my life and never sought any further preferment'. He therefore asked that Cecil petition Elizabeth to allow him to remain where he had 'been bred and brought up (child and man) these forty years' rather than, in old age, to be forced 'to seek another country, a strange air, new acquaintance and

another living without sufficient maintenance' (*Salisbury MSS*, 5.84).

Bishop of Winchester Yet when another of his brothers-in-law, William *Wickham, bishop of Winchester, died unexpectedly in June 1595, Day at once succeeded him. In stark contrast to the power struggles of 1594–5 there is not a hint in the records that his candidacy was in any way challenged and indeed he later wrote to Burghley and Robert Cecil that 'you two alone have brought me to the place I am in' (*Salisbury MSS*, 6.64). Day was elected by the Winchester chapter on 3 November 1595 and consecrated on 25 January 1596.

Day was instantly confronted with a demand for an episcopal lease on behalf of Sir Francis Carew, for whom Robert Cecil had been attempting to extract some *douceur* from the late Bishop Wickham. Although Day refused on the usual grounds that he would be despoiling the see to the prejudice of his successors, he was within weeks pressured into offering a lease worth £1000, but only for twenty-one or thirty-one years. Dissatisfied, Carew refused it. Meanwhile, claiming with much melodramatic detail that unless the necessary formalities were expedited he was doomed to financial disaster, Day fought hard for restoration of his temporalities and for favourable terms of composition for Winchester's hefty tax liability. Here he was successful, obtaining on 6 May a royal warrant whereby he received five years to pay off his first fruits, the first instalment not falling due until thirteen months after he had become entitled to his revenues.

Day died on the following 20 September. Thomas Ridley loyally wrote that he 'left behind him a very good remembrance' in Winchester 'for his great housekeeping, painfulness in preaching and diligence in executing his duty in all sorts under her Majesty' (*Salisbury MSS*, 6.408). Perhaps for that reason Elizabeth granted his executors half the profits of the bishopric due at Michaelmas 1596 for the discharging of his funeral expenses.

Day had made a short will on 11 September 1596, from which it would appear that he had already disposed of most of his assets to his family. There were only token bequests to his wife, two sons, and three married daughters Susan Cox, Rachel Barker, and 'Ridley'—Alice, wife of Thomas Ridley. The only substantial legacy was £500 to his unmarried daughter Elizabeth, presumably as a marriage portion. No servants were remembered and there were no charitable bequests. His sons Thomas and William were granted probate as joint executors on 2 October.

Almost nothing survives from Day's pen apart from the volume on Campion. Notes taken from his sermons exist in manuscript in the university libraries of Oxford and Cambridge and a description of the St George's day festivities at Westminster is extant (BL, Harley MS 304, fol. 144).

The failure of William Day The frequent recommendations for Day's further promotion by Parker, Burghley, Aylmer, and Whitgift are clear-cut evidence that he lacked neither energy, administrative ability, nor the queen's goodwill. Why then did he remain bishop of London in waiting for a full quarter of a century after 1570 and twice fail to capture the bishopric of Durham? The steady opposition of Leicester, and then Essex, is a possibility but the ultimate key to Day's failure to prosper perhaps lay in his own temperament. At one point during the struggle for Durham in 1587–8 Tobie Matthew—a consummate ecclesiastical diplomat who on occasion rashly threw diplomacy to the winds—observed to Sir Francis Walsingham's secretary that 'my brother Daye is a good wise man, setting as muche by wealth as by honor, and his old Master [Burghley] no very toughe savior in such maters, when he is well incountred with reason' (BL, Cotton MS Titus B.vii, fol. 424r). Indeed, in 1594 Day's mandarin decision to negotiate for the bishopric of London through the agency of Thomas Ridley seems to have irritated Burghley, who evidently felt that he was not doing enough to win other friends for himself at court. There followed his bold, and potentially fatal, refusal of Worcester. Was it, in sum, Day's apparently patrician stance, in a court where churchmen were expected to be respectful to their Erastian masters, that so frequently cost him promotion? When it came at last it was surely as the result of Burghley's fierce determination to demonstrate his loyalty, in his final months of power, to an old and often disappointed friend.   BRETT USHER

Sources Venn, *Alum. Cant.*, 1/2.24 · Cooper, *Ath. Cantab.*, 2.219 · GL, MS 9535/1, fols. 87r, 88r [ordination in London 1560] · W. P. Haugaard, *Elizabeth and the English Reformation* (1968) · F. O. White, *Lives of the Elizabethan bishops of the Anglican church* (1898) · *Fasti Angl., 1541–1857*, [St Paul's, London] · *Fasti Angl., 1541–1857*, [York] · *Fasti Angl., 1541–1857*, [Canterbury] · *CSP for.*, 1564–5 · BL, Lansdowne MSS, *passim* [letters of Aylmer and Whitgift to William Cecil] · J. Harington, *Nugae antiquae*, ed. T. Park and H. Harington, 2 vols. (1804) · M. R. Pickering, 'Ridley, Thomas', HoP, *Commons, 1558–1603*, 3.291–2 · *Correspondence of Matthew Parker*, ed. J. Bruce and T. T. Perowne, Parker Society, 42 (1853) · will, PRO, PROB 11/88, sig. 72, fol. 163r · *Calendar of the manuscripts of the most hon. the marquis of Salisbury*, 24 vols., HMC, 9 (1883–1976), vols. 5–6 · *CPR, 1563–6*, no. 1816; 1566–9 [Windsor canonry, 1565; Lavenham] · S. L. Ollard, *Fasti Wyndesorienses: the deans and canons of Windsor* (privately printed, Windsor, 1950) · J. Lamb, ed., *A collection of letters, statutes and other documents … illustrative of the history of the University of Cambridge during the Reformation* (1838)
Archives BL, Harley MSS · Bodl. Oxf., Tanner MSS · Hatfield House, Hertfordshire, MSS, letters to Robert Cecil and Lord Burghley · Winchester Cathedral, episcopal register
Likenesses portrait, 1593, King's Cam. [*see illus.*] · M. Gheeraerts senior, etching, BM
Wealth at death assets had been disposed of in lifetime: will, PRO, PROB 11/88, sig. 72, fol. 163r

Day, William (*bap.* 1605, *d.* 1684), Church of England clergyman and biblical commentator, was baptized at Windsor on 23 June 1605, the eldest son of Matthew Day (1574–1661), five times mayor of Windsor, and lord of the manor of Sunninghill, Berkshire, and Mary (1580/81–1667), daughter of George Dowdeswell, gentleman, of Eton, Buckinghamshire, and grandson of his namesake, William *Day (1529–1596), bishop of Winchester; he had five brothers and six sisters, including Matthew *Day (*bap.* 1611, *d.* 1663). He became a king's scholar at Eton, and in 1624 was admitted as a scholar of King's College, Cambridge, where he graduated BA in 1628, proceeded MA in

1632, and was a fellow until 1637. He was also incorporated at Oxford in 1635.

In 1637 Day was presented by Eton College to the vicarage of Mapledurham, Oxfordshire, on the resignation of his prospective father-in-law, Daniel Collins, fellow of Eton and canon of Windsor. He married Mary Collins on new year's day 1638 in St George's Chapel, Windsor, and apparently lived in the town, since his first two sons were baptized at St George's. From late 1643 he was resident at Mapledurham, where five daughters and three more sons were born, several of whom died in infancy. He continued in the parish throughout the Commonwealth. In 1654 he described himself as 'An Unworthy Servant of God in the Gospel, at Mapledurham' when he published *An Exposition of the Book of the Prophet Isaiah*, a scholarly commentary on the text intended for family use, with questions and answers to assist learning, and a glossary of technical vocabulary. In 1660 he was made divinity reader at St George's Chapel, but remained resident at Mapledurham, virtually unassisted, where he also wrote *A Paraphrase and Commentary upon … Romans* (1666); this took a traditional evangelical approach, and argued dispassionately against texts used by Anabaptists and Quakers respectively to support baptism by immersion and personal guidance by the Holy Spirit.

With his eldest son, Matthew, Day helped manage the Sunninghill estate in his father's last years, but sold it in 1668 after his mother's death. After inheriting he gave property to New Windsor parish to endow alms for the poor. He died in 1684, and was buried at Mapledurham church on 20 December; his wife survived him.

ELIZABETH ALLEN

Sources W. Sterry, ed., *The Eton College register, 1441–1698* (1943), 78, 99 · Venn, *Alum. Cant.* · W. Day, *A paraphrase and commentary upon … Romans* (1666), 97–8, 115, 116, 157 · W. Day, *An exposition of the book of the prophet Isaiah* (1654) · Oxfordshire Archives, PAR 164/1/RI/1, 1637–84 · W. H. Rylands, ed., *The four visitations of Berkshire*, 2, Harleian Society, 57 (1908), 83–4 · *VCH Berkshire*, 3.134 · E. Ashmole, *The antiquities of Berkshire*, 3 (1719), 71–2 · Oxfordshire Archives, Oxf. dioc. pprs e. 3, fols. 97, 136r, 158v · E. H. Fellowes and E. R. Poyser, eds., *The baptism, marriage, and burial registers of St George's Chapel, Windsor* (1957), 5–6, 104 · DNB
Wealth at death see administration, Oxon. RO

Day, William (1797–1845), publisher and printer of lithographs, established his business in London in the early nineteenth century. The evidence of trade directories is ambiguous, as there was more than one William Day working as a printer in the 1820s. It is alleged that he was a law writer who turned to printing, and he first appears in a directory running a printing business in London in 1825, at 59 Great Queen Street, Lincoln's Inn Fields. In 1828 he expanded to include bookselling. His earliest recorded imprint is 1824, when he is described as 'Successor to Rowney & Forster'. In 1829 he is listed as having moved to 17 Gate Street, Lincoln's Inn Fields, and is then first described as a 'lithographic-printer and press manuf[ac]turer]'. Yet he must have been engaged in lithographic printing some four years earlier, when he printed with Louis Haghe fourteen of the illustrations in Robert Simpson's book *The Anatomy of the Bones and Muscles* (1825). In

1833 he is styled 'Lithographer to the King', and later he became 'Lithographer to the Queen and the Queen Dowager'.

Haghe, a Belgian artist and lithographer, is said to have moved to England to practise lithography in 1823 at the suggestion of an Englishman called Maxwell, but he met with little success until he became associated with Day by the end of 1825. The next work he and Day printed was *Three Views of Hereford* (1826). There followed a succession of books with lithographic illustrations, and this connection with the firm lasted, even after the death of Day in 1845, until Haghe gave up lithography to concentrate on watercolours in 1852. Haghe was replaced by William Simpson, and the firm was subsequently called Day & Son. The combined talents of Day and Haghe had built up the firm so that it became the most successful and longest lasting business of its kind in the nineteenth century. To the early period belongs a set of twenty-four lithographs by Haghe illustrating *Lays and Legends of the Rhine* (1827–9). The plates of this book, all vignetted and printed on India paper by Day, are among the most delicate and meticulous of early English lithographs. The combination 'Day & Haghe' is not mentioned in the directories until 1834, at least nine years after they had first met. The exact business relationship between them (he was only about nineteen when he met Day) is not clear, yet it is likely that he was always on a paid but not a full partnership basis. Nor is it clear how much, if any, of the lithography in the early period (that is, the drawing on the stone) was actually done by Day.

The firm of Day and Haghe is most famous now for its part in producing the most ambitious lithographic work ever published in England—David Roberts's *The Holy Land, Syria, Idumea, Arabia, Egypt & Nubia* (1842–9). It was issued in parts but is now often found in a set of six folio volumes consisting of 248 lithographs with descriptive text. Haghe, praised by Roberts for the faithful and artistic interpretation of his drawings, must bear most of the credit for the success of this publication. However, it was Day who undertook the very substantial organization for such a large project, which was financed by the publisher F. G. Moon. John Murray, the first publisher who had refused the project, estimated the costs in excess of £10,000, an enormous sum in the 1830s. However, the subscriptions soon amounted to over £20,000. As these lithographs were printed with a series of tint stones with additional hand-colouring, a number of assistants helped Haghe to prepare the total of more than 600 stones. Day and Haghe built up a team of skilled artists and lithographers which eventually included, among others, Charles Haghe (the younger brother of Louis), George Hawkins, Edmund Walker, Robert Carrick, the brothers Andrew and Thomas Picken, Edmond Morin, and William Simpson. Another ambitious and pioneering work was Owen Jones's *Plans, Elevations and Details of the Alhambra* (1842–5). Some of the large plates were printed in several colours and gilt by Day and Haghe to Jones's exacting standards.

Day's eldest son, also named William, with the aid of his two brothers John and Joseph, took over the business at his father's death and completed the printing of *The Holy Land*. William Day the elder died suddenly of apoplexy (presumably a heart attack) at his home at 17 Gate Street on 13 February 1845, and was buried in St Giles-in-the-Fields. A very brief obituary gives virtually the only description of his character: 'gifted with perception almost intuitive, ardent in the pursuit of his object, he saw no difficulties in his path and knew no rest, liberal to those he employed, charitable to the destitute' (*Art Union*, 7.101). William Day the younger (1823–1906) continued to run the firm and printed many sumptuously illustrated books (including the plates for Owen Jones's *Grammar of Ornament*, 1856) until it failed in 1867. Examples of Day's prints are in the British Museum and the Victoria and Albert Museum, London. CHARLES NEWTON

Sources J. R. Abbey, *Travel in aquatint and lithography, 1770–1860*, 2 vols. (1956–7) · *Art Union*, 7 (1845), 100–01 · *Modern Lithographer*, 2 (1906), 535–7 · M. Twyman, *Lithography, 1800–1850* (1970) · M. Twyman, *A directory of London lithographic printers, 1800–1850* (1976) · C. J. Courtney Lewis, *The story of picture printing in England during the nineteenth century* [1928]

Day, William (1797–1849), assistant poor-law commissioner, was born on 15 December 1797, the eldest of the three children of William Day (d. 1807) and his wife, Susannah (d. 1810), of Montague Street, Bloomsbury, Middlesex. He matriculated at Brasenose College, Oxford, on 28 February 1816, graduated BA in 1820, and subsequently read law at Lincoln's Inn. On the death of his father he inherited the Hadlow House estate in Mayfield, Sussex. He was twice married: first, on 18 August 1819, to Caroline, daughter of Dr John Grindley, and second, on 27 September 1825, to Ann Elliott, daughter of W. Le Blanc.

Day published a paper on poor-law reform in 1832 and, as vice-chairman of the newly formed Uckfield union, in 1835 completely restructured the local relief system, devising a scheme of pauper classification which attracted the favourable notice of the poor-law commissioners. Appointed assistant commissioner on 16 January 1836 he was ordered to Shrewsbury with instructions to form unions in Shropshire and north Wales. Between May 1836 and June 1837 he set up thirteen unions in Shropshire and another seventeen in north Wales. In 1841 his district was extended to take in the twenty-seven unions of west and south Wales. He thus had charge of the whole of Wales in addition to an important English county. It was an extensive and volatile district, in which the familiar patterns of protest which greeted the new relief system in England—arising from resentment of central intervention and fear of the workhouses—were complicated by peculiar Welsh factors: differences of language, religion, and nationality, and above all a degree of poverty which was further deepened by the economic depression of 1842–3.

Prominent among the 'Welsh grievances' which touched off the Rebecca riots in 1843 was hatred of the new poor law. A royal commission of inquiry was about to publish its report on the disturbances when, without warning, in January 1844, the poor-law commissioners

(George Cornewall Lewis, Sir Edmund Head, and George Nicholls) ordered Day to send in his resignation. The timing could scarcely have been worse: in the public eye the dismissal unavoidably singled out Day's management of Welsh poor-law matters as a principal cause of the troubles. The report, when it appeared, provided no evidence to support such a judgement. Under pressure, the commissioners produced a series of reasons for Day's removal—evasive, inconsistent, and contradictory, and with one defect in common: none was supported by hard evidence from the board's minutes or correspondence.

With eight years' heavy and blameless service Day had seemed secure in his position as a worthy, though not outstanding, member of the poor-law inspectorate. After his removal he set himself one task: to re-establish his reputation and, in alliance with Edwin Chadwick, to expose the shortcomings of his former chiefs. Their opportunity came in 1846 when an inquiry into a workhouse scandal in the Andover union led to the dismissal for equally dubious reasons of another assistant commissioner, Henry Parker. A House of Commons select committee subsequently found that the poor-law commissioners had 'altogether failed' to justify the removal of their two assistants Day and Parker, and that their proceedings had been 'irregular and arbitrary', and 'such as to shake public confidence in the administration of the law' (Parl. papers, 1846, 5, pt 1, 9–10). In 1847 the Poor Law Board Act replaced that discredited body by a new department headed by a responsible minister (a president) assisted by a parliamentary secretary. The Andover scandal, to which Day's personal tragedy brought an additional measure of odium, had furnished the final clinching demonstration of the need to reshape a department weakened by internal quarrels and inadequately defended against the continual attacks of parliamentary critics.

Day died of 'cerebral disease' at Mayfield on 27 September 1849 and was buried there on 3 October.

R. A. LEWIS

Sources R. A. Lewis, 'William Day and the poor law commissioners', University of Birmingham Historical Journal, 9 (1964), 163–96 · S. E. Finer, The life and times of Sir Edwin Chadwick (1952) · D. J. V. Jones, Rebecca's children (1989) · D. Williams, The Rebecca riots (1971) · d. cert. · E. Sussex RO, SAS/RF 9/94 · Parl. papers (1844), vol. 16 · Parl. papers (1846), vol. 5
Archives NL Wales, NLW 3141–3149 F · PRO, Ministry of Health MSS, corresp. of assistant commissioners, MH 32/14–16 · PRO, Ministry of Health MSS, corresp. with unions, MH 12 · PRO, Ministry of Health MSS, minutes of poor law commissioners, MH 1 · PRO, Home Office MSS, HO 73/52 · PRO, Home Office MSS, HO 45/1611

Day, William Henry (1823–1908), racehorse breeder and trainer, born on 9 August 1823 at Danebury, Hampshire, was a younger son of John Barham *Day (1793–1860) and an Irish woman whose surname was Goddard. His father, known as Honest John, founded the famous Danebury racing stable, where he had for patrons the duke of Grafton, Lord George Bentinck, and Lord Palmerston, among many others. His grandfather John Day of Houghton Down Farm, Stockbridge, was racing adviser to the prince of Wales (later George IV) and acquired the reputation of being able at a sitting to drink two more bottles of wine than any of his companions. He was the Gloomy Day depicted in a celebrated caricature made by Robert Dighton on the Steyne at Brighton in 1801.

William was educated privately with his cousin Russell Day, afterwards a Church of England priest and a master at Eton College, by his uncle Henry Thomas Day LLD, rector of Mendlesham, Suffolk. After entering his father's stable at Danebury, he acquired some fame as a jockey, and rode Lord George Bentinck's horse Grey Momus when it won the Ascot Cup in 1838. His eldest brother, John (1814–1882), was to succeed the father at Danebury; consequently William started training at Woodyates, Cranborne Chase, Dorset. There on the downs he trained many good winners, usually ridden by his brother Alfred. These included James Merry's Lord of the Isles and his own Promised Land, which carried off the Two Thousand Guineas in 1855 and 1859 respectively, Sir F. Johnstone's Brigantine, which won the Oaks and Ascot Cup in 1869, and many good handicap horses. Day also won in 1859 the Goodwood Cup with Promised Land, which finished fourth in the Derby. Day's patrons included Lord Ribblesdale, the marquess of Anglesey, Lord Coventry, and Lord Westmorland. In 1846 he married his cousin Ellen, daughter of James Day, veterinary surgeon, of Kenford, Devon. They had five sons.

In 1873 Day sold off his stud, which realized over £25,000. For a time he gave up training, but resumed operations in 1881, when J. R. Keene sent him some horses, including Foxhall, which won the Grand Prix, the Cesarewitch, and the Cambridgeshire in 1881, and the Ascot Cup in 1882. Day afterwards trained a few horses at Salisbury, but finally retired in 1892. In 1873 he had formed a large breeding stud at Alvediston, near Salisbury, having over sixty thoroughbred brood mares. Cast-off, the dam of Robert-the-Devil, winner of the St Leger in 1880, was bred there, and for a time Flying Duchess, the dam of Galopin, the Derby winner of 1875, was also at Alvediston.

Day used his experiences at Alvediston in writing The Horse: how to Breed and Rear him (1888). He also wrote several articles on turf politics in the Fortnightly Review. His The Racehorse in Training (1880), which was translated into French, was one of the first attempts to treat the subject scientifically; his two volumes of memoirs are rather less reliable.

Of medium height, but tall for a jockey, and possessed of an iron will, Day was a model man of business. Like his father, who, on Sunday evenings, used to read Hugh Blair's sermons to the stable lads until they fell asleep, he was most punctilious in the discharge of his religious duties. He was only too well aware of the temptations which racing presented. For his patrons he won stakes to the value of over £200,000. At one time a comparatively rich man, he lost the bulk of his fortune by speculating in poor land. Day died at Shirley, Southampton, on 29 August 1908, and was buried by the side of his wife at the parish church, Pentridge, near Cranborne Chase, Dorset.

EDWARD MOORHOUSE, rev. EMMA EADIE

Sources W. Day, Reminiscences of the turf, 2nd edn (1886) · W. Day, Turf celebrities I have known (1891) · Sporting Life (31 Aug 1908) · Ruff's

Guide to the Turf (1854) [monthly racing guide] · private information (1912)

Likenesses G. R. Black, lithograph, 1875 (after photograph by Elliott & Fry), NPG · Barraud, photograph, NPG; repro. in *Men and Women of the Day*, 4 (1891)

Daye, Stephen. *See* Day, Stephen (1593/4–1668).

Dayes, Edward (1763–1804), watercolour painter, was born on 6 August 1763 in London. He was apprenticed to the mezzotinter and miniaturist William Pether and entered the Royal Academy Schools on 6 October 1780. He made his début at the academy in 1786, showing in the next few years a mixture of portraits, miniatures, topographical watercolours, and figure subjects, which set the tone for a wide-ranging career encompassing different media and subject types. In all Dayes showed sixty-four works at the Royal Academy, although he was unsuccessful as a candidate for associate membership. He also exhibited at the Society of Artists in 1790 and 1791, and was appointed draughtsman to the duke of York about 1791.

Dayes's work as a miniaturist was confined to the early part of his career and it was as a topographical watercolourist that he made his name. Many of his watercolours were modest in scale and were produced for the print trade. Eleven plates after his works were engraved for the *Copper Plate Magazine* between 1794 and 1797, and he contributed more than forty scenes for John Aiken's *Description of the Country from Thirty to Forty Miles Round Manchester* (1795). However, he also provided more ambitious compositions for *Views on the River Wye* (published by E. Dayes and F. Dukes, 1797–1802), which consisted of sixteen sepia aquatints, while the four watercolours of Oxford scenes for the *Oxford Almanack*, dated 1794 (AM Oxf.), showed that he could exceed the limited brief of architectural publications. Dayes also produced watercolours from the drawings of a number of amateurs. He was commissioned, in 1790, by Lord Stanley to realize views of his trip, in 1789, to Iceland, and he was employed by James Moore to paint watercolours after his drawings of antiquarian subjects; many of these were published in *Twenty Five Views in the Southern Part of Scotland* (1794). Dayes also specialized in producing small-scale watercolours for patrons such as the Wynn family, of Nostell Priory, selling them for a few shillings only. Such works were often carelessly produced, reusing compositions and employing a limited palette of greys and blues, with a little rapid pen work.

At his best, however, in views of the Lake District, such as *Haweswater* (1795; Whitworth Art Gallery), or of architectural subjects, such as *Ely Cathedral* (1792; V&A), Dayes united carefully balanced compositions with a lucid, luminous style of painting. During the mid-1790s such works proved highly influential with a new generation of watercolourists, including his pupil Thomas Girtin (apprenticed in 1789) and J. M. W. Turner. Before they broke away to develop the potential of the medium in ways unimagined by Dayes, these two artists produced works which are sometimes indistinguishable from his. Dayes's *Instructions for Drawing and Colouring Landscapes* (1805) suggests that despite a difficult personality—which

damaged his relationship with Girtin—he was an innovative thinker on professional practice and on the teaching of watercolour techniques, including sketching in colours from nature.

Dayes was also an elegant figure draughtsman, his talent being most apparent in the architectural subjects that he executed for publishers. The fashionably dressed figures in scenes such as *Buckingham House, St. James's Park* (1790; V&A, published 1793) or *Queen's Square* (exh. 1787; Yale U. CBA), one of four views of modern London squares which were published in 1787 and 1789, went far beyond the standard staffage of contemporary watercolourists. Dayes also employed his talents in a number of large-scale watercolours of contemporary events, often with a patriotic theme, which were aimed at the print market. Among the most impressive was *View of the choir of St. Paul's on the day of solemn thanksgiving for the recovery of his majesty, 23 April 1789* (engraved by R. Pollard). Dayes also continued to work occasionally as a mezzotinter and produced two plates, in 1788, after George Morland, *Juvenile Navigation* and *Children Nutting*, and, in 1790, *A Visit to the Grandfather*, after a work by John Raphael Smith.

Dayes illustrated a number of literary texts, including scenes for Bell's *British Theatre*, but these did not satisfy his ambitions as a history painter, and from 1798 he spent an increasing amount of his time painting scenes from the Bible and from the works of Dryden and Milton. His diary for 1798 gives a detailed account of his work on four watercolours, including the striking image of *The Fall of the Angels* (exh. RA, 1798; Tate collection). This work attracted some reviews, albeit mixed, but later works—some in oils—went unnoticed, and there is no evidence that he either attracted sales or succeeded in transforming his status. The extent of Dayes's ambitions was underlined in his theoretical 'Essays on painting', published in the *Philosophical Magazine* for 1801–2, which stressed the importance of the artist's moral role as a teacher. Landscape painting, he urged, must be governed by the intellectual process of selection rather than the mere imitation of nature; his attacks on the landscape of 'effects' marked him out as an opponent of the new generation of artists.

Dayes's last years were marked by a mounting sense of professional failure. He turned more to oils, producing unconvincing works, such as the *View of Welshpool* (1803; exh. Sothebys, 1987) and his one-person exhibition in 1801 seems to have attracted no attention. His 1798 diary underlines the precarious nature of his career, which in that year combined the production of historical watercolours with work for Thomas Barker on the production of a panorama, while earning small sums for colouring prints, painting landscape backgrounds for architectural drawings, and teaching. The unstable state of Dayes's mind is sadly apparent in his account of a *Tour in Yorkshire and Derbyshire* (of 1803), which displays a religious mind, deeply affected by nature but also prone to violent shifts in mood. Dayes committed suicide, in London, late in May 1804. His writings, including the often acerbic *Professional Sketches of Modern Artists*, were collected and edited by E. W. Brayley and were published in 1805 for the benefit of his widow, a miniaturist who exhibited at the Royal Academy from 1797 to 1800, but of whom no further details are known. GREG SMITH

Sources *The works of the late Edward Dayes*, ed. E. W. Brayley (privately printed, London, 1805); facs. edn with new introduction (1971) · D. B. Brown, 'Edward Dayes: historical draughtsman', *Old Water-Colour Society's Club*, 62 (1991), 9–21 · Graves, *RA exhibitors* · J. Turner, ed., *The dictionary of art*, 34 vols. (1996) · M. Hardie, *Watercolour painting in Britain*, ed. D. Snelgrove, J. Mayne, and B. Taylor, 1: *The eighteenth century* (1966), 179–82 · Farington, *Diary*, 28 May 1804 **Archives** V&A NAL, documents relating to him, incl. a work diary · W. Yorks. AS, Leeds, topographical drawings **Likenesses** E. Dayes, self-portrait, oils, 1801, NPG · W. Holl, stipple (after E. Dayes), repro. in Brayley, ed., *Works*

Dayrolles, Solomon (*d.* 1786), courtier and diplomat, was the nephew and heir of James Dayrolles (*d.* 1739), British resident at Geneva, and at The Hague from 1717 to 1739. Nothing is known of his early life until 1730, when his godfather, Lord Chesterfield, tried to obtain for him his first diplomatic posting, though without success. Although Dayrolles received a court position, as master of the revels, on 12 April 1744, he acted as Chesterfield's private secretary on a diplomatic mission to The Hague in 1745 and on his brief visit to Ireland in 1745–6. His persistent patron finally secured him the much coveted diplomatic post on 12 May 1747, when Dayrolles was appointed resident at The Hague. After more than four years he was transferred to Brussels, where he arrived on 30 January 1752. He was recalled late in August 1757 as the French started to take possession of the Austrian Netherlands, seizing Ostend and Nieuport in October.

In 1739 Dayrolles used his inheritance to buy from Sir Richard Child the estate of Henley Park, near Guildford. He returned to London from The Hague to marry Christabella (*d.* 1791), daughter of Colonel Peterson of Ireland, on 4 July 1751. They had one son, Thomas Philip, who became a captain in the 10th dragoons and married a Swiss wife, Mlle H. G. Thomasset. Of their three daughters, the eldest, Christabella, married Townsend Ventry in 1784; Emily married the Baron de Reidezel, aide-de-camp to the duke of Württemberg, on 24 December 1786; and Mary married Richard Croft, a banker, on 5 February 1788. Mary Dayrolles is thought to have inspired Fanny Burney to create the character of Miss Larolles in her novel *Cecilia*.

Dayrolles, who was a member of the Egyptian Club, died in March 1786. His library was sold later that year.

W. P. COURTNEY, rev. S. J. SKEDD

Sources D. B. Horn, ed., *British diplomatic representatives, 1689–1789*, CS, 3rd ser., 46 (1932) · J. C. Sainty and R. Bucholz, eds., *Officials of the royal household, 1660–1837*, 1: *Department of the lord chamberlain and associated offices* (1997), 95 · *The letters of Philip Dormer Stanhope, fourth earl of Chesterfield*, ed. B. Dobrée, 6 vols. (1932) · Nichols, *Lit. anecdotes*, 3.334; 5.663 · *GM*, 1st ser., 9 (1739), 47; 15 (1745), 333; 17 (1747), 248; 21 (1751), 332, 381; 56 (1786), 1146; 58 (1788), 178; 61 (1791), 780; 98/1 (1828); 98/2 (1828), 215–16, 290 · *N&Q*, 1 (1849–50), 219, 373, 476; 7th ser., 2 (1886), 425 **Archives** BL, corresp., Add. MSS 15869–15888 · Bodl. Oxf., corresp. and papers | BL, corresp. with Lord Holdernesse, Egerton MSS 3445, 3455 · BL, letters to Lord Holdernesse and Sir Andrew Mitchell, Add. MSS 6814, 6838 · BL, corresp. with duke of Newcastle, etc., Add. MSS 32706–32957, *passim* · NA Scot., letters to Sir Andrew Mitchell · U. Cal., Berkeley, letters to Lord Chesterfield

De. For names including this prefix *see under* the substantive element of the name; for example, for Guy de Beauchamp *see* Beauchamp, Guy de.

Deacon, (Arthur) Bernard (1903–1927), social anthropologist, was born on 21 January 1903 in Nicolaiev, south Russia, where his father, Arthur Deacon, was the representative of a shipping firm. He came to England in 1916 and attended Nottingham high school, where he was captain of school. An open scholar at Trinity College, Cambridge, where he was admitted on 1 October 1921, he graduated BA in 1924 with a double first in natural sciences and modern languages.

At that time Deacon wished to enter the consular service but was too young to sit the examination. So he chose to remain at Cambridge, and to spend the year at his disposal reading anthropology for amusement. His great ability impressed his tutors so quickly that they persuaded him to read for the tripos, for which he was awarded a first. They then found grants for him to do fieldwork on the island of Malekula in the south Pacific archipelago of the New Hebrides (later Vanuatu).

Deacon arrived on Malekula in January 1926. Working doggedly and successfully, he collected a great deal of information in a relatively short period of time. He found the cultural diversity of this small island (about 20 miles by 10) so rich that he chose not to remain in one village, but toured almost the whole of it, with particular stays in villages on the mid-west and south-west of its coast. A natural and hard-working linguist, he gained a working command of at least three Malekulan languages. In January 1927 he spent six weeks on the neighbouring island of Ambrym. Afterwards he returned to his base in Southwest Bay, Malekula, to collect his things together and await the steamer which would carry him away. Through his Cambridge contacts, he already had a job to go to: a university lectureship in Sydney. But he suddenly fell ill with blackwater fever (malignant malaria) and died within a few days, on 12 March 1927, before the boat had even appeared. He was buried on Malekula.

Deacon is remembered for three main reasons: his ethnography, his work on Ambrym, and his personality. After his death most of his fieldnotes were collected and, together with lengthy comments made in his letters to fellow anthropologists, edited into an ethnography by a persevering peer, Camilla Wedgwood (a scion of the ceramics family). Though the book gives a lopsided account of Malekulan customs (there is, for example, no section on daily life), it remains a richly dense compendium of local beliefs, ceremonies, and forms of social organization. It has proved indispensable to subsequent ethnographers working in the area, and to present-day inhabitants keen to revitalize their traditions or legitimate their land claims. Deacon had thought Malekula, like all the archipelago, destined for imminent depopulation, but his book has become an integral part of the opposite process: the reinvigoration of the islands.

While on Ambrym, Deacon thought he had discovered what anthropologists then called a six-section marriage system. This was of major significance to anthropology at the time. Deacon wrote up his notes on this intricate and intellectually beautiful complex while still in the field and sent the results to several major anthropologists, all of whom were delighted with it. It was mainly because of this work, which leaders of opposed theoretical factions within the discipline sought to annex for their own cause, that Deacon was offered his post in Sydney. It is unfortunate that long-term fieldwork carried out on Ambrym in the early 1970s by the Australian anthropologist Margaret Patterson has shown convincingly that the local marriage system needs to be interpreted in a radically different manner.

All who knew Deacon emphasize the extraordinary nature of his personality: a supremely gifted but unassuming man of very broad interests, a particularly dedicated ethnographer who was unfailingly courteous both to his English acquaintance and (much more unusually for the time) to his Malekulan hosts. His fiancée, Margaret Gardiner (b. 1904), became a noteworthy Hampstead cultural figure and a companion to the scientist J. G. Bernal. Her moving memoir of Deacon, published almost sixty years after his death and containing generous quotations from his fieldwork letters to her, was broadly and very well received. 　　　Jeremy MacClancy

Sources A. B. Deacon, *Malekula: a vanishing people in the New Hebrides*, ed. C. Wedgwood (1934) • M. Gardiner, *Footprints on Malekula: a memoir of Bernard Deacon* (1984) • J. Larcom, 'Following Deacon: the problem of ethnographic reanalysis, 1926–1981', *Observers observed: essays on ethnographic fieldwork* (1983), vol. 1 of *History of anthropology*, ed. G. W. Stocking, 175–95 • I. Langham, *The building of British social anthropology: W. H. R. Rivers and his Cambridge disciples in the development of kinship studies, 1898–1931* (Dordrecht, Holland, 1981) • M. Patterson, 'Kinship, marriage and ritual in north Ambrym', PhD diss., University of Sydney, 1976 • A. B. Deacon, 'The regulation of marriage in Ambrym', *Journal of the Royal Anthropological Institute*, 57 (1927) • admissions book, Trinity Cam.

Archives Royal Anthropological Institute, London, notebooks, corresp., and papers relating to New Hebrides, incl. later contributions from C. H. Wedgwood | CUL, A. C. Haddon papers, corresp. and papers relating to Malekula

Likenesses photographs, repro. in Gardiner, *Footprints on Malekula* • photographs, Royal Anthropological Institute, London, Photo Library

Deacon, Sir George Edward Raven (1906–1984), oceanographer, was born on 21 March 1906 at 81 Bosworth Road, Leicester, the younger child and only son of George Raven Deacon (1866–1954), a boot and shoe factory worker, of Leicester, and his wife, Emma (1868–1957), worker in a hat factory, daughter of David Drinkwater, stone quarrier, from Enderby, near Leicester. He was educated at Newarke secondary school, Leicester; the City of Leicester Boys' School (1919–24); and, as a King's scholar, at King's College, London (1924–7), where he was awarded a first-class honours degree in chemistry in 1926 and a diploma of education in 1927. His parents, who were Strict Baptists, generously supported his studies and those of his sister (who also gained a first-class degree) despite the family's very limited means.

After a brief spell of teaching chemistry and mathematics at Rochdale technical school Deacon was appointed as a hydrographer to the *Discovery* committee which had been established in 1924 to promote research into the hydrography and natural history in a large part of the Southern Ocean. Deacon's post involved making accurate determination of the temperature and salinity of the sea from small research vessels in the stormy Southern Ocean. He worked in the ships *William Scoresby* in 1927–9 and *Discovery II* in 1929–31, 1931–3, and 1935–7 when he served as principal scientist. His observations provided the basis for two important *Discovery* reports (1933 and 1937) on the hydrology of the Southern Ocean, for which he was made DSc of the University of London in 1937.

In 1939 Deacon was seconded by the *Discovery* committee to work for the Admiralty at HMS *Osprey*, a shore establishment at Portland concerned with Asdic (the allied submarine detection investigation committee which gave its name to an echo-sounding device for the detection of submarines) and other anti-submarine equipment. His office was destroyed by a bomb during an air raid and he and his work on underwater sound transferred to Fairlie, Ayrshire, in 1940. In May of that year at Beckenham, Deacon married Margaret Elsa (1903–1966), daughter of Charles David Jeffries (d. 1910), a company secretary. They had met while she was working in the *Discovery* office. Theirs was a very happy marriage and they had one daughter, Margaret Brenda Deacon (b. 1942), a distinguished historian of oceanography. From Fairlie he was sent in 1944 to the Admiralty research laboratory in Teddington, Middlesex, to lead a small group (Group W for waves) that had been set up to study ocean waves and swell.

Deacon encouraged his younger colleagues to combine theory, observations, and analysis (using a specially developed frequency analyser) and rapid progress was made in understanding the propagation of the energy in storm waves over distances as large as thousands of kilometres. Deacon reluctantly left the employment of the *Discovery* committee in 1947 to take up his first permanent post, in the Royal Naval Scientific Service.

By then Deacon's group had branched out into other aspects of physical oceanography and it formed a major component of the National Institute of Oceanography when it was set up in 1949 with Deacon as director. His institute at Wormley, Surrey, rapidly acquired an international reputation in all branches of marine science. His main contribution was to encourage his staff and to shield them from administrative distraction while he struggled to obtain funds for their long-term research.

In 1966 the institute became a component body of the Natural Environment Research Council, which did not please Deacon: he formally retired in 1971 but continued to work in the institute, to publish papers and a book (*The Antarctic Circumpolar Ocean*, 1984), to visit the Southern Ocean again in 1975 and 1979, and to remain active.

Deacon was awarded a Polar medal in 1942, was appointed CBE in 1954, and was knighted in 1971. He was elected FRS in 1944, FRSE in 1957, and a foreign member of the Kungliga Vetenskapsakademien of Sweden in 1958. His elections to honorary membership included those of the Royal Society of New Zealand (1964), the Challenger Society (1971), the Marine Biological Association (1973), the Royal Institute of Navigation (1975), the Scottish Marine Biological Association (1976), and the Royal Meteorological Society (1982). He was made a fellow of King's College in 1948 and given honorary DScs by the universities of Liverpool in 1961 and Leicester in 1970. He was awarded the Alexander Agassiz medal of the US National Academy of Sciences (1962), a Royal medal of the Royal Society (1969), the Albert memorial medal of the Institut Océanographique, Monaco (1970), the founder's medal of the Royal Geographical Society (1971), and a Scottish Geographical Society medal (1972). The American Miscellaneous Society presented him with their coveted Albatross award in 1982. Deacon died in the Royal Surrey County Hospital, Guildford, on 16 November 1984, following a heart attack two days earlier. He was buried on 23 November 1984 at Milford cemetery.

Deacon was a kind man whose modest manner belied his active mind, his determination to succeed, and a proper pride in his achievement. He was a major figure in the modern development of marine science.

H. CHARNOCK, rev. ELIZABETH BAIGENT

Sources M. B. Deacon, 'Sir George Deacon, British oceanographer', *Oceanus*, 28 (1985), 30–34 • H. Charnock, *Memoirs FRS*, 31 (1985), 111–142 • private information (1990) • personal knowledge (1990) • private information (2004) [M. Deacon] • *The Times* (24 Nov 1984) • WWW
Archives Southampton Oceanography Centre, National Oceanographic Library, corresp. and papers, GERD | CAC Cam., corresp. with Sir Edward Bullard • NL Scot., corresp. concerning *Discovery* committee
Likenesses R. J. Manns, photograph, 1971, repro. in Charnock, *Memoirs FRS* • M. Charnock, portrait, 1987, Southampton Oceanography Centre
Wealth at death £288,627: administration, 26 March 1985, *CGPLA Eng. & Wales*

Deacon, George Frederick (1843–1909), civil engineer, was born at Bridgwater, Somerset, on 26 July 1843, the eldest son of Frederick Deacon, a solicitor of that town, who afterwards practised in Preston and was at one time sheriff of Lancashire. His mother was Katharine, third daughter of William H. Charlton, vicar of St Mary's, Bryanston Square, London. He was educated at Heversham grammar school and apprenticed at seventeen to Robert Napier & Sons of Glasgow. During his apprenticeship he studied at Glasgow University under Professor W. J. Macquorn Rankine and Professor William Thomson.

On Thomson's recommendation Deacon was appointed assistant to Cromwell Fleetwood Varley, engineer to the Atlantic Telegraph Company, and under him he took part in 1865 in the laying of the second Atlantic cable by the steamship *Great Eastern*. The cable was lost off Newfoundland and Deacon was subsequently occupied in London on schemes for its recovery. From late 1865 to 1871 he practised at Liverpool as a consulting engineer, making so special a study of the Mersey estuary as to become a recognized authority in regard to it. He also lectured on civil engineering and mechanics at Queen's College, Liverpool.

Between 1871 to 1880 he was borough and water engineer of Liverpool, a dual appointment which he held for eight years.

As borough engineer Deacon was responsible for the construction or reconstruction of about 70 miles of sewerage and he set up a rubbish-disposal system for the town. He laid the inner-circle tramway rails in 1877, on a system of his own, besides introducing wood pavement into Liverpool and improving the method of set paving by adopting a solid concrete foundation for the wearing surface. For this achievement he was awarded the Institution of Civil Engineers' Watt medal and a Telford premium.

As water engineer his work was of even greater importance. In 1873 he invented the Deacon waste-water meter, which enabled sources of leakage and waste to be located. In 1875 he was awarded a second Telford medal and premium. He also devised forms of electrical meters for river currents. In 1880 new sources of water supply for Liverpool became necessary, and Deacon projected a scheme, which was adopted in 1879, for the utilization of the River Vyrnwy in north Wales. Thereupon he resigned the duties of borough engineer in order to devote himself entirely to those of water engineer, which he discharged until 1890.

The works which Deacon designed, in conjunction with Thomas Hawksley, included the fine masonry dam in the valley of the Vyrnwy, forming a lake 1121 acres in extent and having an average depth of 70 feet—the first reservoir in Great Britain closed by a high masonry dam. The dam had a maximum height to the overflow level of 144 feet, and impounded about 13,000 million gallons of water. From this lake the water was conveyed to Liverpool by an aqueduct 76 miles in length, which traversed three mountain tunnels and crossed under or over several railways and beneath a number of canals and rivers, including the Mersey. Hawksley and Deacon were joint engineers of the undertaking until 1885, when Hawksley retired and the undivided responsibility fell upon Deacon. The works, opened by the duke of Connaught in July 1892, gained for Deacon the Institution of Civil Engineers' George Stephenson medal and a Telford premium.

In both branches of his work in Liverpool, Deacon won for himself a high reputation. Every question or problem was studied with the scientific thoroughness with which his former teacher and lifelong friend, William Thomson (who became Lord Kelvin in 1892), had imbued him. He regarded no practical detail as too small for earnest study and attention. He recognized, too, the aesthetic claims of constructional work.

In 1890 Deacon established a consulting practice in Westminster. In that capacity he constructed waterworks for Kendal, Merthyr Tudful, Todmorden, Biggleswade, Milton (Kent), and other places. At his death he was engaged upon the plans of works, subsequently constructed, for supplying Birkenhead from the River Alwen, and of new works for Ebbw Vale. He reported in 1890 to the international Niagara commissioners on the utilization of the falls; in 1897, in conjunction with Sir Benjamin Baker, to the London county council on the water supply of London; and in the same year, in conjunction with Dr

W. C. Unwin and John Carruthers, on the Coolgardie, Australia, water supply scheme.

Deacon was elected an associate of the Institution of Civil Engineers on 3 December 1872, became a full member on 6 January 1874, and was a member of the council from November 1900 until his death. He was also a member of the Institution of Mechanical Engineers and a fellow, from 1893, of the Royal Meteorological Society. He was president of the mechanical science section of the British Association at its Toronto meeting in 1897, as well as of many professional societies. In 1902 the University of Glasgow conferred upon him the honorary degree of LLD.

Deacon had considerable artistic talent and in all his works attempted to combine utility with beauty and harmony with the surroundings. As a parliamentary witness he was in frequent demand and, having taken pains to master his subjects, his evidence carried weight. Indefatigable himself, he drew the best from his assistants.

He married first, on 16 November 1869, at Douglas, Isle of Man, Emily Zoë, eldest daughter of Peter Thomson, of Bombay, and second Ada Emma (d. 1912), eldest daughter of Robert Pearce of Bury St Edmunds. A son and three daughters were born of the first marriage. Deacon died suddenly at his office, 16 Great George Street, Westminster, on 17 June 1909, and was buried at Addington, Surrey, near his country residence. In 1910 two memorial windows were placed in Llanwddyn church, near Vyrnwy Lake, one by members and officials of the corporation of Liverpool, and the other by his family.

W. F. Spear, rev. Anita McConnell

Sources *Nature*, 81 (1909), 16 · *Quarterly Journal of the Royal Meteorological Society*, 36 (1910), 254–5 · *PICE*, 177 (1908–9), 284–7 · IGI
Archives CUL, corresp. with Lord Kelvin
Wealth at death £28,762 5s. 2d.: administration, 4 Aug 1909, CGPLA Eng. & Wales

Henry Deacon (1822–1876), by unknown photographer

Deacon, Henry (1822–1876), chemist and manufacturer, was born on 30 July 1822 in London, the elder son of Henry Deacon, merchant, and his wife and cousin, Esther Deacon. The Deacons belonged to the Sandemanian church, whose most famous member, Michael Faraday, took an interest in their son. When he was fourteen Deacon was apprenticed to Galloway & Sons, a London engineering firm: when it failed, Faraday arranged for him to join Nasmyth and Gaskell at Patricroft, near Manchester. They supplied machinery to Pilkingtons of St Helens, where Deacon moved after completing his apprenticeship in the early 1840s. He became manager of the glass-polishing department and their highest-paid employee, but left in 1851 to work for John Hutchinson, a Widnes alkali manufacturer.

In 1853 Deacon filed his first patent (for an improved sulphuric acid manufacturing process) and established an alkali works in Widnes with William Pilkington. This unhappy partnership was dissolved in 1855, and Deacon, with his former employer Holbrook Gaskell, founded Gaskell, Deacon & Co. He experimented unsuccessfully with the ammonia-soda process (later perfected by others), but for mass production of alkali he relied on the proven method invented by N. Leblanc, which generated quantities of hydrochloric acid. C. Dunlop and Walter Weldon had devised methods for converting this noxious waste to chlorine (which could be profitably combined with lime to make bleaching powder) but they were both expensive and wasteful. About 1867 Deacon, assisted by Ferdinand Hurter, began seeking a better way: in 1870 they claimed success. The Deacon process used a cheaper catalyst (copper chloride) and recovered more chlorine; it remained industrially important for five decades, though its adoption was initially delayed owing to its complexity.

Deacon married Emma Wade of Basford, Nottinghamshire, on 4 December 1851. They had two sons and a daughter. After his first wife's death, Deacon married Caroline Rutt of Islington, London, on 27 November 1866. Deacon accumulated a fortune in excess of £100,000, but his health was weakened by overwork and he died of typhoid on 23 July 1876 at his home, Appleton House, Widnes. He was survived by his widow and seven sons and five daughters, some of whom may have been from his previous marriage.

Michael A. Sutton, rev.

Sources D. W. F. Hardie, *A history of the chemical industry in Widnes* (1950) · D. W. F. Hardie, 'Chemical pioneers 11: Henry Deacon', *Chemical Age*, 78 (1957), 598 · CGPLA Eng. & Wales (1876)
Likenesses photograph, repro. in J. F. Allen, *Some founders of the chemical industry* (1906) [see illus.]
Wealth at death under £120,000: probate, 28 Sept 1876, CGPLA Eng. & Wales

Deacon, James (d. 1750), miniature painter, of whose parents nothing is known, was talented as a painter and a musician. In 1746 the miniature and enamel painter C. F. Zincke was obliged, his sight failing, to give up his house in Tavistock Row, Covent Garden, and retire from his profession. Deacon then took this house and quite probably a proportion of the older painter's business. Horace Walpole noted that he 'painted portraits in miniature in a very masterly manner' (Walpole, 4.183). In the print room of the British Museum there are portraits by Deacon, in Indian ink, of the marine painter Samuel Scott and his wife. Deacon had not long been established in his profession when, attending as a witness at the Old Bailey, apparently at the 'black sessions', he caught gaol fever and died, young, on 21 May 1750.

ERNEST RADFORD, rev. EMMA RUTHERFORD

Sources D. Foskett, *A dictionary of British miniature painters*, 2 vols. (1972) • B. S. Long, *British miniaturists* (1929) • H. Blättel, *International dictionary miniature painters / Internationales Lexikon Miniatur-Maler* (1992) • artist's notes, NPG, Heinz Archive and Library • H. Walpole, *Anecdotes of painting in England: with some account of the principal artists*, ed. J. Dallaway, [rev. and enl. edn], 4 (1827), 183 • Redgrave, *Artists*

Deacon, Pudentiana (1580/81?–1645), Benedictine nun and translator, was the daughter of John Deacon of Middlesex. There are no records of her education but she was received into the Abbey of the Glorious Assumption of Our Lady in Brussels in 1607, so it is likely that her family were Catholics. The English agent for James I in Brussels described the profession:

> Here was yesterday a solemn professing of five Englishwomen to be nuns … [Albert and Isabella] did them honour to assist with their persons and the Pope's nuncio to sing the mass and to put their garments on them. The first in rank was Mrs. Morgan, who sometimes waited on the Countess of Sussex … the fifth one, Mrs. Deacon, that heretofore attended on the Lady Riche.   (PRO, Flanders correspondence, fol. 279)

Pudentiana was undoubtedly from a gentry family, since she attended on Lady Rich, but her social status was the lowest of the five nuns professed that day.

Deacon was received into the abbey on 11 July 1606, invested in holy habit on 23 April 1607, and professed on 29 April 1608, said to be aged thirty-two (though only twenty-seven or twenty-eight if her age given at death is correct). She was described as a 'regular person' (Neville, 9), suggesting her strict adherence to the abbey's rules. In 1623 she was sent with two other nuns to help with a new convent at Cambrai, Our Blessed Lady of Consolation, established directly under the Benedictines. The account of her life, responsibilities, and character is recorded in 'A Catalogue of the names of the religious Dames and Sisters professed of this convent':

> shee being a woman of a very good wit, judgement and understanding, was thought fit by her superiors and others to give help in a business of that consequence as the beginning of a monastery, which shee diligently performed, joyning a great zeal of regular observance with a motherly affection to all and care of all.   (Gillow, 'Records', 77–8)

She held three key administrative roles: cellarer, mistress of the novices, and prioress. The latter two involved giving spiritual direction, and all required effective administrative skills.

The convent was renowned for its translation work and for its manuscript and book collection. Deacon participated in this spiritual literary culture, translating Francis de Sales's *Les vrays entretiens spirituels*, from the French, as *Delicious Entertainments of the Soule*, published at Douai in 1632. Her name is not on the title-page but a seventeenth-century catalogue of the convent's library names her as the translator. Augustine Baker was spiritual director of the convent until 1633, and the nuns engaged in many translations under his direction. It is possible that Deacon was involved in other additional translations; Gillow names her as translator of *The Mantle of the Spouse*, although no supporting evidence confirms this. The prefatory address to *Delicious Entertainments* notes: 'the translatresse, a woman … had not much skill in the Frenche … never intending more than the use of a particular cloister, though God and her superiors have otherwise disposed of it' (sig. a2r). Nevertheless the translation is lucid and professionally finished. De Sales's treatise may have attracted her because it directly addresses sisters for their spiritual direction and education through contemplation.

Having fallen into 'great bodily infirmities which shee suffered with a remarkable patience … Her end was pious and peaceful in the 64 [year] of her age' (Gillow, 'Records', 77–8). Deacon died on 21 December 1645 at Cambrai.

KATE AUGHTERSON

Sources A. Neville, 'English Benedictine nuns in Flanders, 1598–1687', ed. M. J. Rumsey, *Miscellanea, V*, Catholic RS, 6 (1909), 1–72 • J. Gillow, ed., 'Records of the abbey of Our Lady of Consolation at Cambrai, 1620–1793', *Miscellanea, VIII*, Catholic RS, 13 (1913), 1–85, esp. 77–8 • J. S. Hansom, ed., 'The register books of the professions, etc., of the English Benedictine nuns at Brussels and Winchester', *Miscellanea, IX*, Catholic RS, 14 (1914), 174–203, esp. 179 • A. F. Allison and D. M. Rogers, eds., *The contemporary printed literature of the English Counter-Reformation between 1558 and 1640*, 2 (1994), 40 • *Stanbrook Abbey: a sketch of its history* (1925) • *In a great tradition: tribute to Dame Laurentia McLachlan, abbess of Stanbrook*, Benedictines of Stanbrook (1956) • P. Guilday, *The English colleges and convents in the Low Countries, 1558–1795* (1914) • P. Arblaster, 'The infanta and the English Benedictine nuns: Mary Percy's memories in 1634', *Recusant History*, 23 (1996–7), 508–27 • E. Petre, *Notices of the English colleges and convents established on the continent after the dissolution of religious houses in England* (1849) • Gillow, *Lit. biog. hist.*

Archives Stanbrook Abbey, near Worcester, MSS

Deacon, Thomas (1697–1753), bishop of the nonjuring Church of England and physician, was born on 2 September 1697 at Stepney, Middlesex, the son of William Deacon (*d.* 1706), a mariner, and his wife, Cecelia (*fl.* 1697–1733). Lacking a university education, by early adulthood he had become an accomplished writer and had mastered Greek, Latin, French, and possibly Hebrew. The nonjuror George Hickes, who took a paternal interest in Thomas, may have directed his education.

Deacon's mother, who may have married the nonjuring bishop Jeremy *Collier (1716), introduced her son, while still a child, to Jacobitism and such leading nonjurors as Hickes and Collier. Ordained by Collier to the priesthood on 19 March 1716, the eighteen-year-old cleric's first public appearance as a nonjuror came at the execution of William Paul and John Hall in 1716. He denied offering absolution to the two Jacobites, but he did admit to writing the strongly worded Jacobite speeches given by the two men on the gallows. It is most likely that he also ministered to the prisoners in private. After a trip to the Netherlands in 1717 he returned to study medicine with Richard Mead (1673–1754), one of England's most distinguished physicians. In London he served as the minister of the nonjuring congregation at Aldersgate and as assistant at Robert Orme's Trinity Chapel.

Deacon moved to Manchester about 1722, where he became a leading physician. At this time also he married Sarah (b. 1700?, d. 1745), about whom further details are unknown. They resided on Fennel Street, a short distance from the collegiate church and Chetham's Library, and had twelve children, two of whom died in infancy.

While Manchester had a significant Jacobite community and Deacon was the leading nonjuring figure in the city, the extent of his Jacobite activities remains unclear. The Presbyterian Josiah Owen, in a series of letters published in 1746 in the *Gentleman's Magazine*, charged Deacon with having both popish and Jacobite sympathies, offering absolution to William Paul and John Hall on the gallows in 1716, fleeing for the Netherlands with warrants issued against him, and then living 'unmolested' in Manchester. He suggested that three of Deacon's sons had served at their father's behest in the Manchester regiment in 1745, that Deacon himself had received a dispensation from serving from Charles Edward, and that he had been escorted to the 'Pretender's lodgings' (*GM*, 16.69, 579). Of the three sons in question, Thomas Theodorus (c.1723–1746), a captain in the Manchester regiment, was executed at Tyburn; Robert Renatus (c.1725–1746), a lieutenant, died in prison awaiting trial; while Charles Clement (c.1727–1749), ensign, died in Jamaica after being transported. Deacon denied most of Owen's charges in 1748, at which time he replied that he had indeed lived unmolested if by that Owen meant being attacked by mobs, detained by soldiers, and living in fear that his house would be brought down (ibid., 18.206).

Though Jacobite in sympathy, Deacon's primary attention was given to the creation of a separate nonjuring Church of England. He took an extreme view of the church's independence from the state and did not consider reunion with the established Church of England to be possible or desirable. His 'ideal was always the creation of an Orthodox Catholic Church separate from both England and Rome', while his Jacobitism was a 'secondary matter' (Broxap, *Biography*, 140–41, 147). With Thomas Brett, Collier, and Roger Laurence, he was a member of the usagers party, which called for the restoration of four ceremonies: the invocation of the Holy Spirit, the oblation, the mixed chalice, and the prayers for the dead. Believing that these items had been wrongly omitted from the prayer book of 1552, in 1718 Deacon and Thomas Brett drafted a new liturgy. This attempted to be true to the liturgical principles of the early church and to restore the four usages. Though many nonjurors believed that the usages were desirable, they did not wish to obstruct the possibility of a future return to the Church of England. The usagers party, however, insisted that tradition required their inclusion for an efficacious eucharist. Deacon remained adamant about these principles and refused to join in the reunion of the two parties engineered in 1732 by Brett and George Smith of Durham. The usagers party maintained their existence after 1732 when the Scottish bishop Archibald Campbell, acting alone, consecrated Deacon and Laurence as bishops of what had now become the Orthodox British church in 1733. In 1734 Deacon issued his *Compleat Collection of Devotions*, which included a new liturgy, 'The order of the divine offices of the Orthodox British church'. Following Campbell's death in 1744, this replaced the liturgy of 1718. Modelled on the liturgies found in the *Apostolic Constitutions*, it sought to restore even more primitive usages, including infant communion. Thus, Deacon's new liturgy fulfilled the 'warning prophecy' given by the critics of the 1718 session that if one returned to '*some* primitive customs, others would follow' (Grisbrooke, 117–18). Others note that, by attempting to create a liturgy true to the earliest Christian liturgies and by reclaiming for the Anglican tradition the primitive doctrine of eucharistic sacrifice, Deacon's work brought to maturity the work of earlier scholars from Jeremy Taylor to William Whiston (Cuming, 186). The *Compleat Collection* is notable also for its inclusion of excerpts from John Wesley's 'Essay upon the stationary fasts'. John Clayton, a member of Wesley's Oxford group and a native of Manchester, introduced Wesley to Deacon. Deacon requested Wesley's help in the preparation of his collection of devotions and Wesley 'returned from this visit thoroughly fired with zeal both for the ancient church and for the stations' (Baker, 31).

In 1747 Deacon published his most significant work, *A Full, True, and Comprehensive View of Christianity*, which provided two catechisms for teaching the primitive faith and a detailed theological commentary on his *Compleat Collection of Devotions*. Deacon also set out the theological suppositions for his liturgical work and explained the doctrines of the 'Orthodox British Catholic Church'. He also made clear his understanding of the sacraments, which went beyond the Anglican two sacraments, to include twelve offices, such as confirmation, marriage, ordination, and infant communion. His other writings included *The Doctrine of the Church of Rome Concerning Purgatory* (1718), which sought to distinguish between prayers for the dead and the doctrine of purgatory, thereby defending the nonjurors against charges of popery. He also translated two works by the French Jansenist Sebastian le Nain de Tillemont (with whom Deacon had much in common theologically), the translations appearing as *History of the Arians* (1721) and *Ecclesiastical Memoirs of the First Six Centuries* (1733, 1735).

In his later years Deacon encountered financial and physical difficulties. His friend the poet John Byrom wrote to William Law in 1752 noting that Deacon could no longer care for himself or his children. He died on 16 February 1753 and was buried on 19 February in Manchester at St Anne's churchyard alongside his wife, who had predeceased him on 4 July 1745. Deacon was survived by three sons, including Edward Erastus (c.1741–1813), surgeon, and a daughter, Sarah Sophia (1731–1801), who married William Cartwright, nonjuring bishop and Shrewsbury apothecary. ROBERT D. CORNWALL

Sources H. Broxap, *A biography of Thomas Deacon* (1911) · *GM*, 1st ser., 16 (1746), 579–80, 691 · *GM*, 1st ser., 18 (1748), 206 · *GM*, 1st ser., 23 (1753), 100 · *GM*, 1st ser., 91/1 (1821), 232 · H. Broxap, *The later nonjurors* (1924) · S. Hibbert Ware, *Lancashire memorials of the rebellion*, 2 pts in 1, Chetham Society, 5 (1845); repr. (1968) · J. H. Overton, *The nonjurors: their lives, principles, and writings* (New York, 1903) · F. Baker, *John Wesley and the Church of England* (1970) · G. J. Cuming, *A history of Anglican liturgy* (1969) · W. J. Grisbrooke, *Anglican liturgies of the seventeenth and eighteenth centuries* (1958) · A. Livingstone, C. W. H. Aikman, and B. S. Hart, eds., *Muster roll of Prince Charles Edward Stuart's army, 1745–46* (1984) · F. J. McLynn, *The Jacobite army in England, 1745: the final campaign* (1983) · R. Halley, *Lancashire: its puritanism and nonconformity*, 2 vols. (1869) · R. D. Cornwall, 'The later nonjurors and the theological basis of the usages controversy', *Anglican Theological Review*, 75 (1993), 166–86 · R. D. Cornwall, *Visible and apostolic: the constitution of the church in high church Anglican and nonjuror thought, 1688–1745* (1933)
Archives Chetham's Library, Manchester, corresp. relating to his communion | Bodl. Oxf., Brett MSS · Bodl. Oxf., Rawlinson MSS
Likenesses portrait, Chetham's Library, Manchester; repro. in Broxap, *Biography*

Deacon, William Frederick (1799–1845), journalist and author, was born on 26 July 1799 in Caroline Place, Mecklenburgh Square, Bloomsbury, London, the eldest son of William Wranius Deacon, a wealthy merchant, and Caroline Harriet Clayton. At the age of eleven he was sent to Reading School, where the celebrated Dr Richard Valpy instilled in him a love of literature. His senior schoolfellow Thomas Noon Talfourd remembered Deacon as 'tall for his age and naturally graceful, with dark eyes and dirty hands; gay, light-hearted and heedless' (Talfourd, 7). He was apt to neglect lessons for novel-reading and this tendency followed him to Trinity College, Cambridge, where he was admitted as a pensioner in June 1817. He did not reside at Trinity and in the following October he migrated to St Catharine's College and soon, according to Talfourd, became known for his 'fine taste and conversational powers'. He was already composing verse and in 1817 found a publisher in William Hone for *Hacho, or, The Spell of St. Wilten*, a long poem influenced by Sir Walter Scott, which sold well.

Deacon later regretted the 'irregularities' at Cambridge that resulted in his being sent down, and on returning to London he encountered strong disapproval from his father. With this failure went Deacon's hopes of taking holy orders and instead he resolved to enter on a literary career. An annuity of £100 from his grandmother gave him a degree of freedom, and while living in the family home he sought out publishers. He eventually found one in 1820, when the newly established partnership of Joyce Gold and William Northhouse launched its *London Magazine and Monthly Critical and Dramatic Review* as a rival to the better-known *London Magazine* of Baldwin, Cradock, and Joy, which was edited by John Scott. Deacon's connection with Gold's journal probably dates from the first appearance of the Alchymist feature in March 1820, but he may have contributed articles from the outset, in January. From April 1820 until the magazine folded in mid-1821 he

was its sheet anchor, contributing to its pages romantic tales, verse, literary criticism, serio-comic sketches, and parodies under his initials (W. F. D) or using a variety of pseudonyms, including Greville Faulkland, Sam Quiz, and Paul Clutterbuck. Although usually a sound critic, he was less gifted as a writer of romantic fiction and verse, where his immaturity is apparent, but his parodies were mostly accurate and some of them found their way into Deacon's acclaimed *Warreniana* (1824). Of his sketches the best are autobiographical and show the writer drawing heavily on his experiences in and around Reading. 'A day at the mill', for instance, describes Three Mile Cross and interestingly predates by over six months the first sketch by Mary Russell Mitford in her 'Our Village' series.

On 21 October 1820 Deacon launched the *Déjeuné, or, Companion for the Breakfast Table*, a daily miscellany costing 2d. which was modelled on Leigh Hunt's *Indicator*. This venture represented a large commitment for Deacon, who was probably the magazine's sole contributor. The strain told and on 15 December the *Déjeuné* became a thrice-weekly publication and soon afterwards ceased. With the merging in February 1821 of Gold's *London Magazine* with the *Theatrical Inquisitor* Deacon's stint as editor very possibly began. By June, however, a 'sudden and severe illness' had forced him to retire and in the following month the journal was bought out by Taylor and Hessey, the new owners of Baldwin's *London Magazine*. Deacon meanwhile had taken a small cottage near Llangadog in Carmarthenshire, and here he amused himself for several months 'with a few old books and a daily ramble among the Black Mountains' (Deacon, *The Innkeeper's Album*, 424). From Llangadog he wrote to his hero Sir Walter Scott asking for advice and guidance and enclosing samples of his work. In reply Scott praised his writing but strongly recommended that he exchange the insecure and penurious life of a journalist for one of honest toil in a counting-house, according to his father's wishes.

By now Deacon was contemplating a new life in South America, but a partial reconciliation with his father left him free to pursue literature as a career. He became interested in Welsh folklore and for a short while may have been the schoolmaster at Llanwrda, not far from Llangadog. Before long he had returned to London and by late December 1822 was living in Chelsea. In this period he became friendly with the historian Charles Mills, with whom he had much in common, and his first book, *The Innkeeper's Album* (1823), a collection of sketches inspired by his stay in Wales, is dedicated to him. Deacon's next volume, *Warreniana* (1824), was a series of parodies of his contemporaries, including Coleridge, Byron, Scott, and Hunt, in the style of *Rejected Addresses*, and it proved enormously popular. A further collection of tales and sketches, many with a Welsh setting, appeared in 1826 as *November Nights*.

The loss of his annuity in 1829 drove Deacon to depend entirely on his literary efforts. After a short period as an assistant in a school at Dulwich he was without work for a while before joining *The Sun* newspaper as a contributor to its literary criticism. He soon gained a reputation as a critic of taste and scholarship and he became an early champion of Dickens. His own first novel, the two-volume *Exile of Erin* (1835), contained satirical portraits of prominent Irish patriots, such as O'Connell, and was well received both at home and in the United States. Between 1837 and 1839 he wrote a series of papers for *Blackwood's Edinburgh Magazine* under the heading 'The Picture Gallery' (which were much in the style of his earlier sketches), and in doing so realized a long-standing ambition to contribute to a journal he had always admired. These papers were collected in book form in 1858. About 1840 he was appointed editor of *The Sun*, but the extra responsibility weakened an already delicate constitution. He died in London surrounded by his wife Alice and their three children at his home, 2 Malvern Terrace, Islington, on 18 March 1845. He left behind him the manuscript of *Annette*, a novel which was published in three volumes in 1853, with a prefatory memoir by Sir T. N. Talfourd.

R. M. HEALEY

Sources T. N. Talfourd, 'Memoir', in W. F. Deacon, *Annette: a tale*, 3 vols. (1853) • R. M. Healey, 'The other London Magazine: Gold's and its contributors', *Charles Lamb Bulletin*, new ser., 61 (1988), 155–64 • W. F. Deacon, *The innkeeper's album* (1823) • J. Curling, *Janus weathercock* (1938), 396–8 • *The letters of Sir Walter Scott*, ed. H. J. C. Grierson and others, centenary edn, 12 vols. (1932–79), vol. 7, pp. 6–9, 22–4 • B. Dobell, *Sidelights on Charles Lamb* (1903), 258–93 • V. Watson, *Mary Russell Mitford* (1947), 142–3 • probate, 1845, PRO • *DNB* • *IGI* • G. Stones and J. Strachan, eds., *Parodies of the Romantic age*, 4: *Warreniana* (1999)
Archives BL, Add. MSS | NL Scot., letters to William Blackwood & Sons

Deakin, Alfred (1856–1919), prime minister of Australia, was born on 3 August 1856 at 90 George Street, Fitzroy, Melbourne, the younger child of William Deakin (1819–1892), business manager, of Towcester, Northamptonshire, and his wife, Sarah, *née* Bill (1822–1908), of Llanarth, Cardiganshire. Deakin's parents were married in October 1849 and left England for Australia two months later, disembarking at Adelaide, where their daughter, Catherine Sarah, was born in July 1850. When gold was discovered in 1851, William Deakin briefly tried his luck on the Victorian goldfields, but by 1853 the family was living in Melbourne, where Deakin senior became the manager of a coaching business.

Education and entry into politics Deakin was brought up in a small, close-knit family in which he was the centre of attention. His sister, Catherine, was his nurse and mentor, and in later years his confidante and admirer. At the age of four he joined Catherine at a boarding-school in the country, before attending Melbourne Church of England grammar school from 1864 to 1871. A precocious child with a passion for books, he preferred to indulge his own elaborate fantasies rather than pursue his studies, but his talents were recognized and he did well enough to matriculate. At Melbourne University, between 1872 and 1877, he studied law and seized such opportunities as the small academic community offered for intellectual discussion and debate. He also became involved in the spiritualist movement, playing a leading part in its Sunday school, the Progressive

Alfred Deakin (1856–1919), by Swiss Studios, 1900

Lyceum, and becoming president of the Victorian Association of Progressive Spiritualists in 1878. In 1877 he published an extraordinary spiritualist allegory, *A New Pilgrim's Progress*, which was the product of his séance experiments with automatic writing and which he believed, at the time, to have been inspired by the spirit of John Bunyan.

Deakin was admitted to the bar in 1877, but an introduction in 1878 to David Syme, owner of the Melbourne *Age*, deflected him into the much more appealing practice of journalism. Syme persuaded Deakin to forsake the free-trade beliefs he had absorbed at university for the protectionist programme espoused by the *Age*; he also helped Deakin's nomination in the liberal interest for a by-election in 1879 for the Victorian legislative assembly, which he won by a narrow margin. Deakin's début in parliament at the age of twenty-two proved dramatic when he concluded his maiden speech by resigning because of controversy surrounding the conduct of the poll. He lost the second by-election by fifteen votes, but finally won the seat at a general election in 1880.

Deakin was a striking, even handsome, young man, 6 feet tall and slim with dark hair and a trim beard. Always fluent and articulate, he was an eloquent speaker whose versatile, light baritone voice was reinforced by his graceful presence. Many recalled that his dark, glowing eyes contributed to the effect. A bachelor when he entered politics, on 3 April 1882 Deakin married the nineteen-year-old Elizabeth Martha Anne (Pattie; 1862/3–1934), daughter of Hugh Junor Browne, a wealthy distiller, and his wife, Elizabeth. He had met her through the spiritualist movement, but the Brownes, conscious of Deakin's lack of means and uncertain prospects, agreed to the marriage only reluctantly, and there was no dowry. With the beginning of his political career Deakin distanced himself from spiritualist organizations, but he retained an investigative interest in spiritualist phenomena.

Deakin's arrival in parliament coincided with the end of a period of divisive politics involving constitutional conflict between the legislative council, elected on a restricted property franchise, and the popular assembly. At a time when Victoria was entering a phase of heady prosperity, the mood encouraged political compromise, and when a coalition government of conservatives and liberals, led by James Service and Graham Berry, took office in 1883, Deakin, a supporter of Berry, became minister for public works and water supply. In 1885 his rapid rise was confirmed when, with Berry's retirement, he became the leader of the liberals and chief secretary in the government now headed by Duncan Gillies. He and the coalition government remained in office until 1890.

The government's legislative programme was largely uncontroversial, but in 1885 Deakin introduced a Factories and Shops Bill, a basic regulatory measure which drew opposition from the legislative council and was passed only in modified form. Much less contentious was his enthusiasm for irrigation: having chaired a royal commission on water supply in 1884 he led a mission to California to investigate irrigation schemes. Although the state-aided schemes introduced in Victoria were not without their problems, Deakin played a significant part in developing public awareness. In 1885 he published *Irrigation in Western America*, and a later visit to India, sponsored by *The Age*, resulted in *Irrigated India* in 1893.

Relations with the imperial government In 1887 Deakin represented Victoria at the colonial conference which was timed to coincide with Queen Victoria's golden jubilee, and which was seen by the imperial government as an opportunity for coaxing the colonies into making a greater contribution to imperial defence. Deakin attracted attention when, responding to prime minister Salisbury's opening speech, he asserted that Victorians knew no distinction between 'colonial' and 'imperial' interests, and made it clear that Victoria would press its case concerning the empire's role in the Pacific. Deakin was not the only Australasian representative to urge the imperial government to be firm in its negotiations with France over the New Hebrides, but as a native-born colonist he was regarded with particular interest. He returned home to a hero's welcome.

By 1890 Victoria's economic boom had burst, and the national maritime strike of that year ushered in a period of industrial dislocation and depression. Deakin's own financial speculations had been disastrous and he had been associated as chairman or director with several dubious companies. With the defeat of the coalition government he retreated to the back bench for a decade, devoting himself, as a kind of creative penance, to the cause of federation. He emerged through the 1890s as the acknowledged leader of the federal movement in Victoria. Practical concerns about the depression, defence, and Asian immigration all contributed to the growing interest in federation, but Deakin, a member of the Australian Natives' Association (which only native-born colonists were eligible to join), sought to give the movement a higher, national focus. At the conventions of 1891 and 1897–8 he advocated a democratic constitution and sought to limit the powers of the senate as a states' house, but he also played a major role in negotiating the essential compromises between divergent colonial interests. When in 1898 the Victorian government and *The Age* hesitated to endorse the proposed Constitution Bill, Deakin, in a celebrated speech at Bendigo, helped turn the tide, and Victoria voted overwhelmingly for the bill at referendums in 1898 and 1899.

In 1900 Deakin journeyed to England, together with representatives of the other colonies, to negotiate with colonial secretary Joseph Chamberlain points at issue with the imperial government concerning the constitution. Most in contention was a clause preventing appeals to the privy council in matters involving interpretation of the constitution, which Chamberlain proposed to delete. Deakin, together with Edmund Barton of New South Wales and Charles Kingston of South Australia, campaigned vigorously against Chamberlain: a compromise preserved the right of appeal, but by leave of the Australian high court, and left the power further to limit such appeals with the parliament of the Australian commonwealth. Learning of Chamberlain's capitulation, the three leaders joined hands and danced in a gleeful circle. The incident entered political folklore after Deakin recorded it in his history of the federal cause, *The Federal Story* (1944).

In London, Deakin was introduced to the proprietor and the editor of the *Morning Post* and was afterwards invited to act as the newspaper's Australian correspondent. Remarkably, he was to retain this position through the rest of his political career, often commenting on his own successes and failures. As a journalist of old, he probably gained some satisfaction from this well-kept secret, but the £500 a year it earned him also helped the family's finances.

Prime minister When Barton, his colleague and fellow Protectionist, formed the first commonwealth government in 1901, Deakin joined it as attorney-general, and, on Barton's appointment to the high court in 1903, succeeded him as prime minister, holding that office in 1903–4, 1905–8, and 1909–10. During his first two periods of government, when no party commanded a majority in the house of representatives, Deakin and his Protectionists governed with the support of the infant Labor Party. In Victoria the labour movement had been committed to protection, and Labor members in the 1890s had often been regarded as the left wing of the liberal Protectionist Party. Like a number of middle-class liberals and radicals, Deakin had responded to the onset of the depression and mass unemployment by seeking legislative means of addressing 'the social question'. Thus the Protectionists and the Labor Party had found common ground in advancing factory legislation, direct taxation, and old age pensions. In the new commonwealth parliament, however, not all Labor members were supporters of tariff protection, and Deakin had to find new means of cementing the alliance. In promoting what was called the 'new protection', he sought to ensure that protection for the manufacturer was matched by regulated wages and conditions for the worker. Although high court decisions impeded its implementation, the new protection became the slogan of the liberal–Labor alliance.

Deakin is usually seen as the key figure in the first decade of the Australian commonwealth when the nation's institutional structure was created and its founding policies were enshrined in legislation. The establishment of the high court and the commonwealth arbitration court, the introduction of the restrictive immigration policy (commonly known as the white Australia policy), the commitment to defence (including compulsory military training), could, along with tariff protection, all be seen as part of the programme of nation building. If politics were becoming more polarized, there nevertheless appeared to be a degree of consensus underpinning the Deakinite project.

Although the alliance with the Labor Party was productive, Deakin complained of the unsatisfactory state of federal politics with 'three elevens' in the field. In 1908, when Labor withdrew its support from the Protectionists and itself formed a government, Deakin negotiated a fusion with his former enemies, the conservative Free-Traders, and returned to office in 1909. With protection now secure as the national policy, Deakin believed he had won good terms for the merger, but many saw the fusion as a betrayal of his liberal principles, and at the 1910 election the Labor Party was swept into office with majorities in both houses. He had the satisfaction of leading the successful 1911 campaign against Labor's proposed amendments to the constitution extending commonwealth power, but in 1913, his health seriously impaired, he retired from politics.

Assessment and death Deakin was both a nationalist and an imperialist. He had no qualms about supporting Britain in the Second South African War, and during the 'Dreadnought scare' of 1909, when he was briefly in opposition, he was in the forefront of the agitation for Australia to offer Britain a dreadnought. He was also aware of Australia's own defence priorities, and invited the American 'great white fleet' to visit Australian ports in 1908. While attending the Imperial Conference of 1907, Deakin, a supporter in principle of imperial federation, sought a more active role for the self-governing dominions, but his advocacy of imperial preference fell on deaf ears. It was perhaps unfortunate that his views were more appealing to British Conservatives than to the dominant Liberals, so that the publicity he attracted in England cast him as an oppositional figure. While Deakin was not beyond enjoying the attention accorded him, both he and his wife were critical of the social outlook and morality of the Edwardian society which fêted the colonial representatives, and, like many Australian visitors, they were disturbed by the prevalence of urban poverty. Throughout his career his democratic instincts prevented him from accepting any imperial honours.

As a liberal leader at a time when the party system was taking shape, Deakin occupied a strategic position, and his alliance with the emergent Labor Party helped lay the political foundations of the new nation. Deakin was as sincere in his commitment to social reform as he was to federation, yet he was also a consummate politician who was more artful than he cared to admit. He was a man of wide cultural and intellectual interests, whose circle of acquaintances included poets, painters, and musicians. While his public image is suggested by the nickname Affable Alfred, he was an intensely private man who valued the inner life. Some years after his involvement with spiritualism he became interested in theosophy, but for the most part his undogmatic Christianity found expression within the home, which he once described as 'the city of refuge'.

Deakin had been conscious of his declining mental powers as early as 1907. He died on 7 October 1919, at his home, Llanarth, Walsh Street, South Yarra, Melbourne, of meningo-encephalitis. He was given a state funeral and buried on 9 October at St Kilda cemetery, Melbourne, with Anglican rites. He was survived by his wife, Pattie, his three daughters, Ivy, Stella, and Vera, and his sister, Catherine.   JOHN RICKARD

Sources J. A. La Nauze, *Alfred Deakin: a biography*, 2 vols. (1965) · A. Gabay, *The mystic life of Alfred Deakin* (1992) · A. Deakin, *The federal story: the inner history of the federal cause*, ed. H. Brookes (1944); 2nd edn, ed. J. A. La Nauze (1963) · J. Rickard, 'Deakin's ideal of the family', *Voices*, 4/2 (1994), 58–68 · J. Rickard, *Class and politics: New South Wales, Victoria and the early commonwealth, 1890–1910* (1976) · R. Norris, *The emergent commonwealth* (1975) · A. Deakin, *A new pilgrim's progress* (1877) · W. Murdoch, *Alfred Deakin: a sketch* (1923) · *AusDB*

Archives NL Aus., corresp. and papers | BL, corresp. with Sir Charles Dilke, Add. MS 43877 · NA Scot., letters to Sir H. B. Loch · NL Aus., Brookes MSS · NL Aus., Catherine Deakin MSS · NL Aus., letters to second Baron Tennyson

Likenesses Swiss Studios, photograph, 1900, NL Aus. [*see illus.*] · Spy [L. Ward], caricature, mechanical reproduction, NPG; repro. in *VF* (2 Sept 1908) · photographs, NL Aus.

Deakin, Arthur (1890–1955), trade unionist, was born at Holland Street, Sutton Coldfield, Warwickshire, on 11 November 1890, the son of a domestic servant, Annie Deakin. His birth certificate did not record the name of his father. At the age of ten he moved with his mother and stepfather to Dowlais in south Wales, where, when he was thirteen, he started to work for the steel firm Guest, Keen, and Nettlefolds for 4s. a week. He joined the National Union of Gasworkers and came under the influence of Keir Hardie, then member of parliament for Merthyr Tudful, of which Dowlais was a part.

In 1910 Deakin moved to Shotton in north Wales and took a job with another steel firm as a roll turner. While working there he met an active trade unionist, Jack George, whose sister, Annie (1885/6–1970), he married on 30 May 1914. She was the daughter of Robert George of Connah's Quay, Flintshire. They had two sons. For a brief spell Deakin was a member of the Amalgamated Society of Engineers, but in 1911 he moved over to the expanding, heterogeneous Dock, Wharf, Riverside, and General Workers' Union, which gave ample scope to his incipient qualities of leadership. Within three years he was an active lay member, and in 1919 he became a full-time official of the union. Until that year he belonged also to the small British Roll Turners' Society, of which for a brief period he was general secretary. When in 1922 the Dockers' Union became part of the Transport and General

Arthur Deakin (1890–1955), by Bassano, 1947

Workers' Union (TGWU), Deakin was elected assistant district secretary for the north Wales area, where the high unemployment of the next ten years strongly conditioned his attitudes and responses. In 1919 he became an alderman of the Flintshire county council and in 1932 its chairman.

In 1932 Deakin moved to London, where until 1935 he was national secretary of the general workers' trade group of the TGWU. He toured the country examining the problems of his group and so impressed Ernest Bevin, the general secretary of the union, with his organizing ability that in 1935 he was appointed assistant general secretary. He worked closely with Bevin through a difficult time for the union, for in 1938 some of its members seceded to form a union for busmen; and Bevin himself was showing signs of strain from overwork.

When in 1940 Winston Churchill invited Bevin to become minister of labour in the wartime coalition government, Deakin took Bevin's place in the union. He continued as acting general secretary until Bevin retired from union office in March 1946, when Deakin was elected general secretary in his place, with a majority of 59,105 votes over the combined votes of the other five candidates.

Although from 1940 until 1946 Deakin was the formal head of his union, the largest in Britain and one of the largest in the world, his work was done in the shadow of Bevin, whose reputation among the ordinary members was almost legendary and who never effectively relinquished his control of union activities. Deakin himself was essentially a Bevin creation and perhaps the most

loyal supporter of a man upon whom he modelled himself to the extent of copying some of his public mannerisms. On the general council of the Trades Union Congress, where he took Bevin's place, he was a useful but not an influential member. The council had been dominated by Bevin and its general secretary, Sir Walter Citrine; with Bevin's departure Citrine remained firmly in control, unaffected by Deakin's presence. Deakin became a member of the government's war transport council and of the committee established to advise the production executive. In one respect he achieved notoriety during the war. When he visited Sweden in 1943 as a fraternal delegate to the congress of the Swedish Transport Workers' Union he conferred with a Finnish trade union leader on the possibilities of negotiating a peace treaty; for this he received much adverse publicity.

A new phase in Deakin's career began in 1946, when he became leader of the TGWU in his own right. After the resignation of Citrine from the Trades Union Congress and a period of uncertainty in the leadership of the movement, the position gradually clarified and settled. By 1948 Deakin had emerged as the most dominant figure in British trade unionism, influential also in the international movement.

Like so many men who find themselves thrust into positions of power and responsibility, Deakin developed to meet the situation. People who knew him under Bevin could never have imagined his filling the role which he subsequently attained in post-war Britain. A Labour government was in office and the country faced extreme economic difficulties. Both factors demanded that trade unions break with their traditional attitudes. They required a close collaboration with the government and the acceptance of attitudes about productivity and profits which unions had traditionally rejected. After an initial hesitation, Deakin gave the government his unconditional support. He urged unions to try to increase productivity and advocated a policy of wage restraint. He possessed a deep loyalty to the labour movement which was epitomized for him by the Labour government. In his eagerness to support the government he stifled much useful criticism of its activities, for he disliked anything which could be misconstrued by the general public or used for political purposes. He was more than an advocate. As far as he could he applied the policy of wage restraint in his own union and incurred the displeasure of some of his more militant members. But if he thought his policy was right no amount of criticism would deter him. At times he risked the unity of his organization and faced large-scale unofficial strikes rather than make expedient concessions. No government could have had a more loyal supporter.

Deakin travelled widely as a member of the international committee of the Trades Union Congress and as the most prominent representative of his own union. He was a member of the executive board of the World Federation of Trade Unions and did much to heal the breach between its communist and non-communist members. During his tenure as chairman of the board, however, he led a walkout of the non-communist delegates and helped to form the International Confederation of Free Trade Unions in 1949. Thereafter he became uncompromisingly anti-communist in his attitude towards foreign affairs, national domestic affairs, and the running of his own union; in 1949 he persuaded the TGWU to ban communists from holding office.

The attitude of Deakin towards communists was in part a reflection of his attitude towards opposition. He believed in the sanctity of majority decisions and was intolerant of those who opposed them. He attacked minorities in his union and in the Labour Party with invective and organizational measures. He would defy procedures and conventions to get his own way and was often accused by his antagonists of being a dictator. By his public manner—outspoken, brusque, and intolerant—and by his approach to the handling of internal union affairs, he lent support to the accusation. The administrative problems of his union increased as it expanded from 743,349 members in 1940 to 1,305,456 in 1955, and by and large Deakin coped with them. But he disliked delegating authority and maintained a strict control over even the smallest administrative detail in his union's head office. He would sometimes speak on behalf of his union without consulting the general executive council which constitutionally controlled him. Deakin believed in positive leadership. 'I cannot and will not be a cipher', he told his members. Yet he never forgot the source of his power and always made sure that on the major issues he had the majority of his ordinary members behind him. He was sentimental about his relations with the lay members of his union. Nothing hurt him more than the suggestion that he was out of touch with them. A cartoon which depicted him with his head in the clouds caused him considerable anger. He did much to improve contacts between officials and lay members, which he hoped to advance through developing educational provisions within the union. The TGWU introduced pioneering training schemes for shop stewards and branch officials, and under his guidance the education department became large and influential.

The public image of Deakin lent itself to caricature. He dressed flamboyantly, smoked large cigars, and courted publicity. But in essential ways both the public image and the caricatures gave a misleading impression. Deakin was modest and shy. He lived quietly and modestly in a small semi-detached house in a north London suburb where his evenings, when free from union business, were spent at home with his wife. He did not drink alcohol and was a member of the Primitive Methodist church. He did not make friends easily and found communication on an individual level difficult. But those with whom he had a close relationship came from various walks of life and different political affiliations. In this respect he was paradoxical. He tended to distrust Labour Party politicians and his personal relations with them were uneasy, whereas he could get on very well with self-made employers and with Conservative politicians. Thus he found it easy to make the transition from a Labour to a Conservative government in

1951. But he never transferred his distrust of Labour politicians to the party itself, and he disapproved of those trade union leaders who moved into industrial management.

Deakin was often accused of seeking honours, yet he twice refused a knighthood. He was appointed CBE in 1943 and CH in 1949, and was sworn of the privy council in 1954; these he regarded as honours to the labour movement rather than to himself. He retained his trade union and political influence until his death, which took place on 1 May 1955 at the Royal Infirmary, Leicester, after he had been taken ill while addressing a May day rally in that city.   V. L. ALLEN, *rev.*

Sources *The Times* (2 May 1955) · V. L. Allen, *Trade union leadership: based on a study of Arthur Deakin* (1957) · personal knowledge (1971) · *DLB* · *CGPLA Eng. & Wales* (1955) · b. cert. · m. cert.
Archives FILM BFI NFTVA, current affairs footage · BFI NFTVA, documentary footage · BFI NFTVA, news footage · BFI NFTVA, party political footage
Likenesses Bassano, photograph, 1947, NPG [*see illus.*] · two photographs, 1948–52, Hult. Arch. · W. Stoneman, photograph, 1949, NPG · D. Low, pencil caricature, NPG
Wealth at death £8382 2s. 1d.: probate, 9 Aug 1955, *CGPLA Eng. & Wales*

Deakin, John (1912–1972), photographer, was born on the Wirral peninsula at 64 Beaconsfield Road, Lower Bebington, Cheshire, on 8 May 1912, the elder son of John Henry Deakin, a factory checker and later machine minder for Lever Brothers at nearby Port Sunlight, and his wife, Elsie Mary Bond. In 1923 he entered Calday Grange grammar school, West Kirby, where he excelled at swimming and diving, and remained there until 1928. About 1930 he left the Wirral for Ireland and in Dublin took various jobs, including one as a window dresser for a display company. He travelled to Spain to paint its landscape, but returned to Britain in the early 1930s and settled in London. An introduction to Arthur Jeffress, a wealthy American art collector (and later gallery owner), ensured that, as his companion, he could travel the world and paint. He exhibited at the Mayor Gallery, London, during November 1933 to some critical acclaim.

Deakin first picked up a camera in Paris in 1939—it had been left behind in an apartment after a party—and exposed a few frames. 'It was a cheap camera and he'd never taken a picture before', wrote his friend, the poet Elizabeth Smart, 'but his tyrannical eyes took over' (Smart). He took photographs for a living for the next two decades before abandoning it in favour of painting again. His most prolific years—and probably his most creative— were spent as a staff photographer for *Vogue* magazine in the mid-1950s. He enjoyed two periods under contract to the magazine and remains the only photographer in its history to be hired and fired twice by the same editor.

Deakin shot mostly portraits, though he was also obliged to shoot fashion (at which he proved to be mediocre). His subjects were the writers, artists, poets, actors, and popular entertainers of the early post-war years: among them David Lean, John Huston, Yves Montand, Pablo Picasso, Maria Callas, and Dylan Thomas. His best portraits, however, were those of his friends, most of whom inhabited the pubs and clubs of Soho, London's

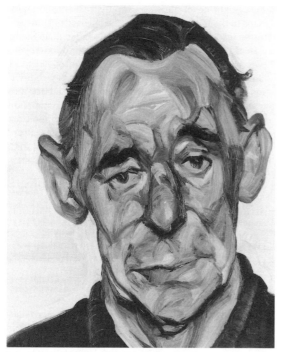

John Deakin (1912–1972), by Lucian Freud, 1963–4

bohemian quarter, the lure of which, in time, led him away from *Vogue*; the Colony Room in Dean Street was a favourite haunt of his until he was barred. These sitters included the painters John Minton and Francis Bacon and the 'two Roberts', Coloquhoun and MacBryde, the poets W. S. Graham and Paul Potts, and the formidable proprietor of the Colony Room, Muriel Belcher. His photographs—typically tightly cropped head shots often greater than life-size—made no concessions to vanity: after pushing the contrast in his prints to its maximum, every pore and blemish was exposed in intimate close-up. His friend Daniel Farson described them as 'prison mugshots taken by a real artist' (Bernard and Noble, 12), and they were frequently found to be too unflattering for *Vogue* to publish. The frontality of his composition and his very lack of 'style' set him apart from his contemporaries and anticipated by at least ten years the fashionable starkness of the portraiture of Richard Avedon and Diane Arbus.

A substantial part of Deakin's *œuvre* was recovered from the floor of Francis Bacon's studio. Dog-eared and splattered with paint, these were portraits of subjects Bacon himself wished to depict; he commissioned from Deakin photographs of Henrietta Moraes, Isabel Rawsthorne, and George Dyer, among others, as *aides-mémoires*, since he was unwilling to paint their likenesses from life.

Before giving up photography in the 1960s, Deakin had completed a book of photographs, *London Today* (1949), and the plate section to Christopher Kininmonth's *Rome Alive* (1951). He had also contributed to *Who Only England Know* (1943) by John Pudney, a book about Malta (where Deakin spent much of the war years as a sergeant in the

army film and photography unit), and completed sample pages for a book on a steelworks and tyre factory in Genoa and one on Paris, which developed out of an exhibition held at David Archer's bookshop in Soho. He had written the text and completed the photographs for an unpublished book, 'Eight Portraits'. In addition, he had photographed examples of children's street art and urban graffiti for two uncompleted projects, 'London Walls' and 'Paris Walls'. A confirmed bachelor, he married in Milan in 1961 not for love but for convenience. In return for citizenship papers, Anna, a stateless Hungarian refugee, financed a replacement for a misplaced Rolleiflex camera.

After his death from heart failure on 25 May 1972 at the Old Ship Hotel, Brighton, Deakin's life's work was retrieved from under his bed in Soho by Bruce Bernard, who later curated a small show of his work, 'John Deakin: the salvage of a photographer', at the Victoria and Albert Museum in London in 1984. At a larger exhibition, 'John Deakin photographs', at the National Portrait Gallery, London, in 1996, many of his rediscovered pictures for *Vogue* were shown and, for the first time, the photographs from the floor of Bacon's studio. He was the subject of a television documentary, *The Salvage of a Soho Photographer* (1991), and appears as a character in the film *Love is the Devil* (1997), played by the actor Karl Johnson. Deakin was also the subject of several character sketches in contemporary fiction, notably Colin Wilson's *Ritual in the Dark* (1960) and Elaine Dundy's *The Old Man and Me* (1964), mostly vitriolic portrayals, for when drunk he was a monster. Barbara Hutton, the Woolworths' heir, called him the 'second nastiest little man she had met in forty years' (Farson, *Sacred Monsters*, 63), but to his peers he was a true original, his professionalism behind the lens, for the most part, unimpeachable.

ROBIN MUIR

Sources R. Muir, *John Deakin photographs* (1996) [exhibition catalogue, NPG] · B. Bernard and A. Noble, eds., *John Deakin: the salvage of a photographer* (1984) [exhibition catalogue, V&A] · D. Farson, *Out of step* (1974) · D. Farson, *The gilded gutter life of Francis Bacon* (1993) · D. Farson, *Soho in the fifties* (1987) · D. Farson, *Sacred monsters* (1988) · E. Smart, 'Introduction', *John Deakin's Paris* (1956) · private information (2004) · Vogue Library, London · b. cert. · CGPLA Eng. & Wales (1974)

Archives IWM · NPG · V&A · Vogue Library, London, James Moores collection

Likenesses attrib. F. Auerbach, photograph, 1950–59, Golden Lion, Soho, London · J. Deakin, self-portrait, photograph, 1952, Condé Nast Library, London · T. Hawkyard, photograph, 1952, Vogue Studio, London · M. Andrews, portrait, 1963, Astrup Feamley Collection, Oslo, Norway · L. Freud, oils, 1963–4, priv. coll. [*see illus.*]

Wealth at death £2623: resworn administration, 11 April 1974, CGPLA Eng. & Wales (1973)

Deakin, Joseph Thomas (1858–1937), railway worker and socialist, was born at Wednesbury, Staffordshire, on 11 August 1858, the son of Charles Deakin, a blacksmith, and his wife, Maria, *née* Middleton, the daughter of a labourer. He was educated at Old Park British School, Wednesbury. On leaving at the age of twelve to start work at Wednesbury goods station, he was awarded the South Staffordshire Coal and Ironmasters' Association prize of a family

Bible. When he transferred to the ticket office at the passenger station in March 1890, his workmates presented him with copies of James Thorold Rogers's *Six Centuries of Work and Wages: the History of English Labour* (1884) and J. J. Jusserand's *English Wayfaring Life in the Middle Ages* (1889), 'in appreciation of his geniality and uniform kindness to all'.

Deakin was an early convert to socialism and in 1887 he became a founder member of the Walsall Socialist Club. He was subsequently elected the club secretary and in this capacity attended the founding conference of the Second Socialist International in Paris in 1889 and its Brussels congress in 1891.

Shortly after returning from Brussels, Deakin became involved with three fellow members of the Socialist Club and two others in the so-called Walsall anarchist plot. This was, in fact, a police trap organized by Inspector William Melville of Scotland Yard. His agent, Auguste Coulon, who claimed anarchist connections in France and England, lured the six men into a bogus scheme to produce bomb making equipment for use in Russia. The six were arrested in January 1892 and following committal hearings in Walsall appeared at Stafford assizes on 30 March 1892, on charges under the Explosive Substances Act of 1883.

The trial was badly flawed. The judge, Mr Justice Hawkins, ruled that the defence could not question Inspector Melville, who was the chief prosecution witness, about his relationship with Coulon and he admitted as evidence a confession by Deakin, which had clearly been made under duress. Consequentially, four of the accused, including Deakin, were convicted. Three of them were sentenced to ten years' imprisonment but the jury recommended clemency for Deakin and he was given a reduced term of five years. He served most of his sentence in Parkhurst prison, where he acted as prison librarian. He earned maximum remission and was discharged on Christmas eve 1895.

On his release Deakin returned to his home, 238 Stafford Street, Walsall, which was a milliner's shop owned by two of his three sisters, Lucy and Elizabeth. His criminal record effectively made him unemployable so he acted as clerk to his sisters' business and supplemented the small income this provided by doing bookkeeping and similar work for friends.

Deakin's belief in socialism remained unshaken and he became the intellectual driving force behind the rise of the labour movement in Walsall. He never held, or even stood for, any office himself but provided those who did with an endless supply of ideas and information, as well as conducting a relentless propaganda campaign in the local press. His reputation as a socialist thinker and advocate soon spread far beyond Walsall and he received a constant stream of requests for advice from all over Britain and from abroad. He always provided a comprehensive answer, either from his own encyclopaedic knowledge or from his cherished book collection.

Deakin died at home on 7 September 1937 and was buried in Ryecroft cemetery three days later. He never married. His closest surviving relatives were his sisters, Lucy and Elizabeth, and a younger brother, Charles. In an obituary, the former Labour MP for Walsall, J. J. McShane, wrote that in all his experience in parliament and elsewhere he had 'never met another comparable with Joe Deakin, in range of knowledge, in ability, and in tenderness of feeling' (*Walsall Observer*, 11 Sept 1937).　　ERIC TAYLOR

Sources *Walsall Advertiser* (1887–1914) [letters from Deakin and reports of his political activities] · *Walsall Free Press* (1887–1903) [letters from Deakin and reports of his political activities] · *Walsall Observer* (1887–1937) [letters from Deakin and reports of his political activities] · *Walsall Times* (1925–37) [letters from Deakin and reports of his political activities] · *Walsall Free Press* (Jan–April 1892) [reports of arrest, committal, and trial] · *Walsall Observer* (Jan–April 1892) [reports of arrest, committal, and trial] · *Wolverhampton Chronicle* (Jan–April 1892) [reports of arrest, committal, and trial] · *Wolverhampton Express & Star* (Jan–April 1892) [reports of arrest, committal, and trial] · *Midland Evening News* (Jan–April 1892) [reports of arrest, committal, and trial] · *The Times* (Jan–April 1892) [reports of arrest, committal, and trial] · D. Nicholl, *The Walsall anarchists: the truth about the Walsall plot* (1892) · *Wolverhampton Express & Star* (9 Sept 1937) · *Walsall Observer* (11 Sept 1937) · *Walsall Times* (11 Sept 1937) · *Railway Review* (1 Oct 1937) · private information (2004) · *Railway Review* (8 Jan 1926) · E. Taylor, 'Deakin, Joseph Thomas', *DLB*, vol. 3 · E. Taylor, 'Deakin, Joseph Thomas', *BDMBR*, vol. 3, pt 1 · K. J. Dean, *Town and Westminster: a political history of Walsall from 1906–1945* (1972) · E. P. Thompson, *William Morris: romantic to revolutionary* (1955) · H. Pelling, *The origins of the labour party, 1880–1900*, revised 2nd edn (1965)

Dealtry, Thomas (1796–1861), bishop of Madras, was born at Knottingley near Pontefract on 19 October 1796, the son of James Dealtry, of the Dealtry family of Lofthouse Hall, Wakefield. He was largely self-taught and from the age of fifteen worked as an usher in a Doncaster school and as a tutor to a private family. In 1819 he married the sister of his pupil 'under romantic circumstances' (Venn, *Alum. Cant.*, pt 2, 1944, 2.263), with whom he had a daughter, Dorothy (1820–1892), but his wife died young and on 22 April 1824 he married a woman whose given names were Jane Brannon (1804–1892).

In 1826 Dealtry entered St Catharine's College, Cambridge, to study law, supporting himself by private tuition. He graduated LLB (first class) in 1828 and in June of the same year was ordained deacon and became officiating minister at St Mary-the-Less, Cambridge. An evangelical but nevertheless catholic in his sympathies, Dealtry was a good preacher and he soon attracted the attention of Cambridge's leading evangelical divine, Charles Simeon, who procured for him an East India Company chaplaincy in Bengal. Dealtry was ordained priest in November 1828 and arrived in Calcutta in early 1829 to take charge of the old mission church. There, as Simeon had hoped, he befriended the missionaries, and eventually he became secretary of the local branch of the Church Missionary Society.

In 1835 Bishop Daniel Wilson appointed Dealtry archdeacon of Calcutta, an administrative post well-suited to his legal abilities. In 1849, when on leave in England, he was appointed third bishop of Madras.

In Madras from January 1850, Dealtry again proved to be an excellent administrator and wisely treated his East

India Company employers with courtesy and understanding. Despite his well-known missionary sympathies he managed to persuade the company to increase its clergy roll in Madras and during his episcopate he ordained forty-four deacons and sixty-one priests, many of whom were Indians. As in Calcutta, Dealtry was occasionally involved in bitter disputes with other churchmen, most notably a long-running feud with Alfred Radford Symonds, secretary of the Madras Society for the Propagation of the Gospel. In 1861 he earned more enemies by making his son Thomas (1825–1882) archdeacon of Madras. Cries of nepotism were raised, though as a former president of the Cambridge Union the younger Thomas may genuinely have been the most able candidate. Dealtry's critics also accused him of lacking talent and intellect. Neither was true, though his long Indian service had cut him off from theological developments in Britain and his religious thinking often appeared naïve to clerics newly arrived from Oxford or Cambridge. His one major publication, *The Divinity of our Lord Jesus Christ Proved from his Own Discourse*, had appeared in 1830. Unlike his critics, however, many of Dealtry's flock appreciated his simple, tolerant evangelicalism and his common-sense approach to church administration. One of his first acts in Madras—to shorten the Sunday morning services—remained one of his most popular.

Dealtry died in Madras from an infected foot on 4 March 1861 and was buried in the burial-ground of St George's Cathedral the following day. A sculpted memorial, funded by public subscription, was placed in the cathedral. He was survived by his wife, Jane; their son Thomas, afterwards rector of Swillington, Yorkshire (1872–8), and vicar of Maidstone, Kent (1878–82); and his daughter from his first marriage, Dorothy, widow of Henry Thomas, East India Company chaplain (1842–59).

A. J. ARBUTHNOT, *rev.* KATHERINE PRIOR

Sources J. J. Higginbotham, *Men whom India has known: biographies of eminent Indian characters*, 2nd edn (1874) · *ILN* (8 Dec 1849), 376 · Boase, *Mod. Eng. biog.* · Venn, *Alum. Cant.* · F. Penny, *The church in Madras*, 3 (1922) · M. E. Gibbs, *The Anglican church in India, 1600–1970* (1972) · E. Chatterton, *A history of the Church of England in India* (1924) · Madras wills, BL OIOC, L/AG/34/29/261, pt 1, fol. 29 · S. J. McNally, 'The chaplains of the East India Company', 1976, BL OIOC, OIR 283.54 · *The Times* (5 April 1861), 7 · *The Times* (30 Jan 1892), 1 · ecclesiastical records, BL OIOC, N/2/42, fol. 44

Archives U. Birm., Church Missionary Society archive, letters

Likenesses E. B. Stephens, bust, 1851, Calcutta Cathedral, India · E. B. Stephens, sculpture, 1861, Madras Cathedral, India; repro. in Penny, *The church in Madras*, facing p. 40 · photograph, repro. in Penny, *The church in Madras*, facing p. 126 · wood-engraving, repro. in *ILN*

Wealth at death £1500: probate, 24 July 1861, *CGPLA Eng. & Wales*

Dealtry, William (1775–1847), Church of England clergyman, was born at Whitgift, Yorkshire, on 20 July 1775, the son of William Dealtry, a small landowner of Swinefleet, Yorkshire. He attended a village school in Swinefleet before going to Hull grammar school (1790–92), where he was one of a number of distinguished pupils during the headmastership of Revd Joseph Milner, a noted evangelical. He was admitted a sizar at St Catharine's College,

Cambridge, in 1792, migrating in the following year to Trinity College. He was elected to a scholarship and graduated BA as second wrangler in the mathematical tripos and second Smith's prizeman in 1796. He spent a year in Clapham as tutor to the sons of Charles Grant, meeting the leading figures in the Clapham Sect. Elected a fellow of Trinity in 1798, he proceeded MA in 1799, and later BD in 1812 and DD in 1829. After his ordination in 1799 he served as curate to Robert Jarratt, rector of Wellington, Somerset, and also a former pupil of Hull grammar school. In 1801 he returned to Cambridge as a college tutor at Trinity, where he became identified as a supporter of Charles Simeon (whose obituary sermon he later delivered). He was an early promoter of the Church Missionary Society, and from 1805 contributed to the *Christian Observer*, an evangelical periodical.

Dealtry was appointed professor of mathematics at the East India College, Haileybury, in 1805, and was among the original members of staff when the college opened early in 1806. There he became a friend of Malthus. Remembered as an effective teacher, he published *The Principles of Fluxions* (1810), which was characteristic of the textbooks produced by Cambridge mathematicians to prepare students for examinations in the period before the adoption of continental differential notation. He laid stress upon developing his pupils' powers of reasoning. He was revered by evangelicals for his courageous pamphlets defending the British and Foreign Bible Society against the criticisms of influential high-churchmen. He published replies to objections by Christopher Wordsworth (1810), Herbert Marsh (1812), and H. H. Norris (1815). His anniversary sermon to the Church Missionary Society in 1813, answering the political objections to missionary activity in India, was published and circulated to members of parliament. He was also active in the anti-slavery movement.

In July 1813, on Simeon's recommendation, the trustees of the rectory of Clapham, Surrey, presented Dealtry to the living made vacant by the death of John Venn. A year later he married Harriet, daughter of Richard Stainforth, with whom he had a son and three daughters. Relinquishing his Trinity College fellowship, he held the college living of Hatfield Broadoak, Essex, from 1814 to 1816. In 1817 his former pupil Abel Smith, the banker and MP, presented him to the rectory of Watton, Hertfordshire, where he occasionally resided. At Clapham he presided over the building of new churches and promoted parochial visitations among the sick and poor. His sermons delivered there, published in 1827, were neither profoundly theological nor particularly spiritual, but of a more practical tone, giving 'clear statements of scriptural truth' (*Christian Observer*, Feb 1848, 135). As a preacher he was noted for the clarity of his exposition. In November 1819, in the period of unrest following Peterloo, he preached a sermon entitled 'The dispositions and conduct required of Christians towards their rulers', drawing a connection between irreligion and disloyalty towards the secular power. During the 1820s he was a correspondent of Thomas Chalmers, whose ideas he disseminated among his Clapham parishioners. His support for church establishments, reiterated in sermons delivered in the early 1830s in response to the campaigns of dissenters against the Church of England's temporal privileges, increasingly aligned him with more orthodox Anglican churchmen. The Society for Promoting Christian Knowledge, of which he became a committee member, published his *Religious Establishments Tried by the Word of God* (1833); membership of the Society for the Propagation of the Gospel also signalled his attachment to the Anglican establishment.

On 25 February 1830 Dealtry was appointed by Charles Sumner, bishop of Winchester, chancellor of the diocese of Winchester with a canonry in the cathedral; he resigned his living at Watton (though he retained Clapham until his death). Energetic in persuading churchwardens to extend accommodation and restore the fabric of churches, he was credited with achieving a general improvement in the decorousness of church interiors in Hampshire. He was appointed archdeacon of Surrey in 1845 and was chosen by Lord John Russell to deliver the sermon to both houses of parliament on the day of national penitence and fasting observed on 24 March 1847 in response to the famines in Ireland and Scotland. By then he was severely ill. Dealtry died at Brighton on 15 October 1847, survived by his wife and three children. Contemporaries knew him as a cheerful man, with a ready wit allied to a natural humility of character. He gave generously to charity in his lifetime with the result that his accumulated wealth was said to amount to no more than the equivalent of a year's income.

M. C. CURTHOYS

Sources *Christian Observer* (1848), 64–5, 133–40 · *GM*, 2nd ser., 29 (1848), 309–10 · C. J. Hoare, *The blessed death of the righteous* (1847) · W. Jowett, *Christ the unchanging and eternal saviour* (1847) · Venn, *Alum. Cant.* · A. Pollard, 'Dealtry, William', *The Blackwell dictionary of evangelical biography, 1730–1860*, ed. D. M. Lewis (1995) · P. James, *Population Malthus* (1979) · B. Hilton, *The age of atonement: the influence of evangelicalism on social and economic thought, 1795–1865* (1988) · *GM*, 1st ser., 84/2 (1814), 288

Archives U. Edin., New Coll. L., letters to Thomas Chalmers

Dean, Basil Herbert (1888–1978), theatre producer, was born on 27 September 1888 in Croydon, Surrey, the second son and second of the four children of Harding Hewar Dean, cigarette manufacturer, of Sanderstead, near Croydon, and his wife, Elizabeth Mary Winton. He was educated at Whitgift Grammar School, Croydon. After leaving school he spent two years in the stock exchange and then joined the repertory company at Manchester run by Annie Horniman. After four years' training as an actor and playwright, in 1911 he directed an experimental theatre season in Liverpool. That year he became the first director of the Liverpool Repertory Theatre (later the Playhouse). In 1913 he became assistant stage director at His Majesty's, London.

On the outbreak of the First World War in 1914 Dean joined the Cheshire regiment. By 1917 he had risen to the rank of captain and the directorship of the entertainment branch of the Navy and Army Canteen Board (later the

Navy, Army, and Air Force Institutes), with control of fifteen theatres and ten touring companies. After the war he began operations in London as managing director of a syndicate—Reandean. With his partner, Alec Lionel Rea, he leased St Martin's Theatre. Under Reandean a series of notable productions was staged, including plays by John Galsworthy, W. Somerset Maugham, Sir James Barrie, and Clemence Dane. Dean had two particular successes: *The Constant Nymph* (1926) by Margaret Kennedy and *Hassan* (1923) by James Elroy Flecker, both of which Dean dramatized with the authors. For the latter, a spectacular oriental drama, he commissioned the music from Frederick Delius, the choreography from Léonide Massine, and the costumes from George Harris. The cast was also illustrious and the production lavish.

Dean was a perfectionist and, because he never learned to suffer fools gladly, he made many enemies. He was meticulous about detail and had a high respect for his technical staff, the importance of whose contribution to a production he always generously acknowledged. He was less loved by actors because of his dictatorial methods as a director. He was a pioneer in the use of stage lighting, importing new equipment from Germany and the United States, as well as devising equipment of his own.

In 1924 he was employed as joint managing director of Drury Lane Theatre in an attempt to revitalize it. In the press he spoke of making Drury Lane a site for a permanent national theatre, but his remarks were greeted with derision, and the idea of a state subsidy for theatre was ignored. Dean, however, was one of the first advocates of a national theatre and for a permanent ensemble of actors as outlined by Harley Granville-Barker. 'There is always better work accomplished', he said in an interview in 1958, 'when it is possible to have corporate effort and a corporate spirit. It is like a football team, the closer and longer you are together, the more goals will be scored'.

Dean's estrangement from Alec Rea led to the breakup of Reandean in 1929. In that year he became first chairman and joint managing director of Associated Talking Pictures, which he had founded (this later became Ealing Studios). During the 1930s Dean's career fluctuated between film and theatre: Gracie Fields always felt indebted to him for making her into 'a real film star'. His first love remained theatre, and in the late 1930s Ealing Studios, feeling that the theatre was claiming too much of his time, forced his resignation. J. B. Priestley at once offered him a lifeline by inviting him to go into management in order to produce mainly Priestley plays, of which three were done: *When we are Married* (1938), *Johnson over Jordan* (1939), and *An Inspector Calls* (1946).

At the approach of the Second World War, Dean wrote pamphlets outlining what could be done by the entertainments industry to sustain national morale not only among the armed services but also among factory workers and the civilian population. When war broke out he became director of entertainments for the Navy, Army, and Air Force Institutes and put forward the name ENSA (Entertainments National Service Association). During six and a half years more than 80 per cent of the entertainments industry gave it service in innumerable performances of plays, revues, and concerts before 3 million people in the services and industry. Richard Llewellyn, Dean's assistant at the time, described him as a 'monolith, a kindly—sometimes—tyrant, a bully ... But his was the influence, the hand on the wheel, that never faltered'.

After the war Dean directed a Priestley play for the Old Vic Company in the West End, organized the first British Repertory Theatre Festival in 1948, and directed revivals of *Hassan* and other plays in various countries. He also wrote a good deal, including an official history of ENSA and two volumes of autobiography.

Dean was thrice married. In 1914 he married Esther, daughter of Albert Henry Van Gruisen, of Oxton, Cheshire; they had three sons. This marriage was dissolved in 1925, the year in which he married Lady Mercy Greville (the actress Nancie Parsons), daughter of Francis Richard Charles Guy Greville, fifth earl of Warwick, MP; they had one daughter. This marriage was dissolved in 1933 and in 1934 Dean married Victoria, daughter of Matthew Garfield Hopper, of Dunston-on-Tyne. This marriage was dissolved in 1948. Dean died at his home, Flat 102, Dorset House, Gloucester Place, London, on 22 April 1978.

JAMES ROOSE-EVANS, rev.

Sources B. Dean, *Seven ages: an autobiography 1888–1927* (1970) · B. Dean, *Mind's eye: an autobiography 1927–1972* (1973) · B. Dean, *The theatre at war* (1956) · R. Fawkes, *Fighting for a laugh: entertaining the British and American armed forces, 1939–1946* (1978) · *The Times* (24 April 1978) · personal knowledge (1986)
Archives BFI, corresp. and papers · JRL, corresp. and papers | Bodl. Oxf., corresp. with Lord Monckton | FILM BFI NFTVA, documentary footage | SOUND BL NSA, documentary recordings · BL NSA, oral history interview · BL NSA, performance recordings
Likenesses H. Coster, photographs, NPG
Wealth at death £114,942: probate, 7 July 1978, *CGPLA Eng. & Wales*

Dean, Sir Maurice Joseph (1906–1978), civil servant, was born in Purley, Surrey, on 16 September 1906, the youngest in the family of two daughters and two sons of William Joseph Dean, a schoolmaster, and his wife, Eleanor Winifred Maurais. Dean went to St Olave's Grammar School, Southwark, from 1918 to 1925 and he then won an open exhibition to Trinity College, Cambridge. He gained firsts in both parts of the mathematical tripos (1926 and 1928), he was senior scholar and a wrangler, and he was awarded the Mayhew prize (in applied mathematics) and the Walker prize. He was president of Trinity Mathematical Society in 1927–8. His brother, W. R. Dean, later became Goldsmid professor of mathematics at University College, London.

Having won first place in the home civil service examination, Dean joined the Air Ministry in October 1929. As resident clerk on Sunday 30 October 1930, soon after midnight, he was faced with dealing with a telephone call from one of the six survivors of the R101 airship crash in which the secretary of state for air and forty-seven others were killed. In 1934 he became private secretary to the chief of the air staff, Edward Ellington, and subsequently to his successor, Cyril Newall. In January 1937 he moved to

the air staff secretariat, of which he became head in 1940 and assistant under-secretary of state in June 1943. On 6 February 1943 he married Anne Emalie, daughter of William Farquhar Gibson, building contractor, of Cardiff. They met as students at Cambridge. They had a daughter and a son.

Dean's period at the Air Ministry proved a long, friendly, and fruitful association, covering the exciting and demanding tasks which produced the Royal Air Force (RAF) of the early days of the war. He made many lasting friendships from working closely with officers who were to lead the RAF throughout the war, particularly Charles Portal and Arthur Harris. This sense of having worked with great men never left him. It extended to the scientists, including Henry Tizard and Harold Hartley, who addressed the problems of aerial warfare. Dean's mathematical education, intellectual stature, sympathy, and understanding enabled him to develop an abiding but not uncritical love for the RAF and a belief in the relevance and efficacy of air power. This is reflected in his book *The Royal Air Force and Two World Wars* (1979) which he completed just before he died.

In 1946 Dean followed his old chief, Arthur Street, to the Control Office for Germany and Austria and the German section of the Foreign Office. He spent roughly a year in each as a deputy secretary. Ernest Bevin, then foreign secretary, made an enduring impression on him. He moved to the Ministry of Defence in 1948, had a brief spell in the Treasury as a third secretary in 1952—where he was head of the overseas co-ordination section—and moved at the end of that year to the Board of Trade as a second secretary. From 1955 to 1963 he was permanent under-secretary of state in the Air Ministry. Nothing could have pleased him more. This was a difficult and challenging period. On the positive side the RAF built up the V-bomber force as the provider of the British nuclear deterrent. More negatively there were the ill-fated Suez campaign and major disagreements among the services. These included controversies over the future of Coastal Command, over aircraft-carriers versus land-based air power, about the army's wish to own and operate larger helicopters, and criticism that the RAF had inadequate numbers of transport aircraft. Equipment costs soared and projects were cancelled. In these and other issues Dean played a major part. It was he, for example, who arranged for a number of eminent scientists, presciently with James Lighthill as their leader, to come together to advise the Air Ministry about strategic policy and weapons. He stood strongly for the maximum use of land-based air power in general and for the RAF retaining Coastal Command. He argued for the transfer of the military supply functions from the Ministry of Supply to the defence ministries. He disagreed with, and was much saddened by, the moves towards the unification of the service departments and their eventual integration into the Ministry of Defence, believing that the result would be a large, cumbersome organization lacking in imagination and motivation. This view and the prospective reorganization took Dean in 1963 away from defence for the remainder of his career. He was appointed an additional second secretary in the Treasury before becoming joint permanent secretary (April–October 1964) of the Ministry of Education. There the main tasks were to co-ordinate the work arising from Lord Robbins's report on higher education and from the report of the committee of inquiry into the organization of civil science. In October 1964 he became permanent secretary of the newly created Ministry of Technology, where he remained until he retired from the civil service at the end of June 1966.

From 1957 to 1960 Dean was a member of the Cambridge University appointments board and from 1963 to 1976 of the Cambridge University women's appointment board. Following his retirement he became a director of the British Printing Corporation, and he was a visiting professor at the University of Strathclyde, which awarded him an honorary LLD (1970). He was a member of the 1972 review committee at the University of Birmingham and of the council of Bedford College, London. From 1966 to 1976 he was chairman of the London advisory board of the Salvation Army.

Dean had outstanding intellectual abilities, a great capacity for meticulous analysis, an enquiring and innovative mind, and absolute integrity. Although there was a certain shyness about him and he carried a strong sense of authority, he was an outgoing man of much humour. He could express himself pungently and directly on occasion but rarely gave offence since his sense of humour was so well developed and his motives never in question. He enjoyed a crisis and on occasion could conjure one up from the thinnest of air—particularly on Friday afternoons. He had the rare gift of combining intellectual enthusiasm for solving problems with an abiding and positive interest in people. Indeed he sought to bring the right person to the right problem. He made a point of encouraging the young especially to extend their horizons and seek the future. He was above all a man of great personal kindness who enjoyed a particularly wide circle of friends. He had many outside interests, including music and golf, and he was no mean cabinet-maker.

Dean was appointed CB in 1946, KCMG in 1949, and KCB in 1957. He died at his home, 27 Bathgate Road, Wimbledon, London, on 7 April 1978, and was buried at Wimbledon parish church.   FRANK COOPER

Sources personal knowledge (2004) · ministry of defence files · *WW* · *WWW* · *Debrett's Peerage* · private information (2004) [P. J. Hudson, J. D. Bryars, K. C. MacDonald, J. Mayne, Lady Wood] · *CGPLA Eng. & Wales* (1978)

Archives King's Lond., Liddell Hart C., corresp. and papers | Nuffield Oxf., corresp. with Lord Cherwell

Wealth at death £64,587: probate, 8 Aug 1978, *CGPLA Eng. & Wales*

Dean, Sir Patrick Henry (1909–1994), lawyer and diplomatist, was born on 16 March 1909 in Berlin, the only son and elder child of Henry Roy Dean (1879–1961), professor of pathology and later master of Trinity Hall, Cambridge, and his wife, Irene (1875–1959), daughter of Charles

Sir Patrick Henry Dean (1909–1994), by Goodchilds, 1969

Arthur Wilson. He was educated at Rugby School and Gonville and Caius College, Cambridge, where he was a classical scholar. He won first-class honours in part one of the classical tripos and in both parts of the law tripos. He was elected a fellow of Clare College in 1932 and then in 1935, having been called to the bar by Lincoln's Inn the previous year, practised as a barrister until 1939. He was a Barstow law scholar at the inns of court in 1934.

On the outbreak of the Second World War, Dean accepted an appointment as assistant legal adviser in the Foreign Office and served throughout the war in that capacity, latterly being responsible for much of the legal preparation required for the war crimes tribunal at Nuremberg. In 1945 he was offered, and accepted, appointment as an established member of the foreign service with the rank of counsellor, and in 1946 he was made head of the German political department of the Foreign Office, an appointment he held until 1950 during an important period of post-war reconstruction. He was appointed CMG in 1947, and on 26 July the same year he married Patricia Wallace, youngest of the four daughters of T. Frame Jackson, of Buenos Aires. Together they had two sons.

Dean was promoted in 1950 and served for two years as minister in the Rome embassy before returning to London as senior civilian instructor at the Imperial Defence College. This led naturally to the post of assistant undersecretary in the Foreign Office responsible for relations with the chiefs of staff and the intelligence services. He became chairman of the joint intelligence committee and remained in that capacity for over six years. In these early years of NATO and with no sign of softening in the attitude of Stalinist Russia, defence aspects of Foreign Office work had become of the greatest importance. Dean's incisive mind and intellectual grasp enabled him to perform the work with widely acknowledged authority, and in the course of his long tenure he was promoted again to be a deputy under-secretary of state in 1956 at the early age of forty-seven.

It was because of his position at the centre of Foreign Office policy making that Dean became involved, albeit involuntarily, in a highly embarrassing episode at a late stage of the Suez affair in 1956. The prime minister, Anthony Eden, had decided to collaborate with a secret French-Israeli plan to attack Egypt and had also attempted to ensure that no word of this should become known beyond a very narrow circle. Thus Dean had no knowledge of the plan discussed by the prime minister with his French counterparts at Chequers on 14 October 1956 and in Paris on 16 October. He first learned of it when he was told by the prime minister on 24 October to go to Paris in order to continue discussions with the French and Israeli ministers begun at Sèvres two days earlier by the foreign secretary, Selwyn *Lloyd. The only instruction given to Dean and his co-emissary, Donald Logan (Lloyd's assistant private secretary), was to make sure that it was understood that British forces would not move unless there was a clear military threat to the canal. The French recorded the discussion in an accurate memorandum which Dean signed *ad referendum*. To his dismay, however, when he showed this to the prime minister that evening, he was ordered to return to Paris the following day and ask that all copies of the record should be destroyed—a request that was refused after Dean and Logan had been incarcerated for some hours in a reception room at the Quai d'Orsay while waiting for the French decision. Dean naturally felt a sense of humiliation over this episode, but in fact he had done his best to carry out the prime minister's instructions. He had had no part in the policy of using force and some years later privately expressed the view that this had been a strange aberration on the part of Eden whom he otherwise much admired.

Dean was advanced to KCMG in 1957 and spent several more years in the Foreign Office before being appointed in September 1960 to be the successor to Sir Pierson Dixon as UK permanent representative at the United Nations (UN). He was aged fifty-one. Dag Hammarskjöld was the UN secretary-general, then at the height of his influence; Kennedy was about to be elected president of the United States; and by the end of that year Adlai Stevenson was to be Dean's colleague in New York as United States ambassador to the UN.

Dean's period of four years in New York was the most successful of his diplomatic career. By the time he arrived the UN—and especially the secretary-general himself—was deeply involved in the civil war in the former Belgian Congo following the grant of independence in July 1960. This, and a series of acutely difficult and dangerous situations elsewhere—Kashmir, Cuba, Kuwait, not to speak of recurrent crises in Arab-Israeli relations—compelled the British representative to play a prominent role in the UN Security Council where as a permanent member Britain enjoyed privileged status. Dean was consistently effective in his handling of Security Council business and he won the admiration and liking of the leading UN personalities of the time—Hammarskjöld, Stevenson, successive French ambassadors, and the representatives of the Commonwealth, especially the Australian ambassador, James Plimsoll. Even the dislikable Zorin, the Soviet representative, whom Dean often worsted in debate, showed grudging respect. Dean was also so bold as to attack Soviet imperialism in general assembly debates at a time when the Russians were with some success cultivating the newly independent African states and trying to instigate them to be as anti-British as possible. However, it was in the Security Council that Dean was most at home. He was appointed GCMG in recognition of his success there in 1963.

Following New York, Dean had hoped to be appointed permanent under-secretary in succession to Sir Harold Caccia. But the newly elected Labour government of 1964 decided that his involvement, however innocent, in the Suez affair was a fatal bar, and with some reluctance they offered him instead the Washington embassy. Dean had been treated with scant courtesy by his former subordinate and newly nominated successor in New York, Sir Hugh Foot (subsequently Lord Caradon), who on being appointed virtually hustled him off the premises. Nevertheless Dean thought that as a public servant he could not refuse the glittering consolation prize of the embassy to the United States and he went to Washington in succession to Lord Harlech in 1965. Washington was not entirely suited to Dean's talents and personality. However, his performance was highly competent and he was both active and successful in the important field of export promotion. While not a natural orator he was a successful speaker on a variety of occasions outside Washington. In 1968 Wilson's government announced his successor a full year before Dean's retirement, thus making him a 'dead duck' ambassador for an unusually long period. While privately chagrined at this discourtesy, possibly unintended, Dean showed no outward sign of resentment.

Dean was a tall, well built man with fair hair and a rubicund complexion. At school and university he had been a fine cricketer and a good all-rounder, and later he found much enjoyment in walking, especially in the mountains. His hobbies were collecting English silver and watercolours. He kept his youthful appearance and continued to enjoy walking until quite a late age and only in later years did he suffer from painful back trouble.

In personality Dean was utterly straightforward and loyal both to his superiors and to his subordinates. But although clear-sighted and sometimes harsh in his judgements of people he was invariably courteous and tolerant of colleagues who fell short of his standards. Throughout his adult life he was sustained by his wife, notable for her elegance and charm. They were very hospitable in both New York and Washington as well as exceptionally considerate to their official staff.

In retirement Dean took on mainly honorary (but also active and responsible) appointments such as chairman of the English-Speaking Union and chairman of the governors of Rugby School. He also served as a trustee of the Harkness fellowship foundation for fifteen years and as chairman of the court of the London School of Hygiene and Tropical Medicine. He was made an honorary fellow of Gonville and Caius College and of Clare College, Cambridge, as well as an honorary bencher of Lincoln's Inn; he was also elected an honorary doctor of law by six American universities. He thought of himself primarily as a lawyer in spite of his outstanding career as a diplomatist. He died at Galsworthy House Nursing Home, Kingston, Surrey, on 5 November 1994, and his remains were cremated at Putney Vale, London, on 11 November. A service of thanksgiving in his memory was held in the chapel at Lincoln's Inn on 25 January 1995.　　ALAN CAMPBELL

Sources WW · annual records, Gon. & Caius Cam. · FO List · private information (2004) [Lady Dean] · personal knowledge (2004) · The Times (8 Nov 1994) · The Independent (8 Nov 1994) · CGPLA Eng. & Wales (1995)
Archives U. Birm. L., corresp. with Lord Avon
Likenesses Goodchilds, photograph, 1969, priv. coll. [see illus.] · A. Freeth, oils, 1980, Rugby School · J. Pannett, crayon drawing, 1980, priv. coll.
Wealth at death £340,947: probate, 16 Feb 1995, CGPLA Eng. & Wales

Dean, Richard (bap. 1726, d. 1778), essayist and Church of England clergyman, was baptized on 8 November 1726 at Kirkby in Craven (or Kirkby Malham) in the West Riding of Yorkshire, the son of Robert Dean (d. 1766) and his wife, Elizabeth King (bap. 1704, d. 1788/9). Nothing is known of his childhood or his upbringing. However, the university education sometimes attributed to him is fictitious. Like many boys of relatively humble origins in the eighteenth century, Dean was destined for the church; his vocation was to be a teacher and a scholar. He became master of Middleton grammar school, near Manchester, the third oldest foundation in Lancashire, receiving his first stipend from the patrons, Brasenose College, Oxford, on Lady day 1753. Licensed by the bishop of Chester on 8 July 1754, Dean was also ordained curate on 15 September, probably serving at St Leonard's parish church in Middleton. He was certainly the first curate at St Paul's in nearby Royton, a chapel established in 1754 as part of the church extension movement in south-east Lancashire. Although not licensed to this post until as late as 7 July 1757, marriage registers at St Leonard's confirm that Dean regularly performed duties in both places until his retirement from Royton in 1760.

By the late 1750s Dean was comfortably ensconced both as schoolmaster and curate of Middleton. His rector was the learned Dr Richard Assheton, kinsman of the lord of the manor and a senior Manchester clergyman with moderately evangelical leanings. Dean now enjoyed several years of professional contentment. His personal life also brought him happiness and further opportunities. On 20 November 1764 he married Hannah Lancashire (1744/5–

1771). In order to supplement his income, he took a small farm on the hill at Hebers, above Middleton, leased from the manor; in 1765 he even advertised lodgings for pupils in the Manchester Mercury (22 January). However, the later 1760s were an unhappy time for Dean. Sir Ralph, the last Assheton lord of Middleton, died in 1765, leaving the estate to his two married daughters and an uncertain future. Dean had been a witness to Sir Ralph's will and was required to pray for the soul of the deceased. The next year Dean's father died. His young wife Hannah also contracted a long and ultimately fatal illness.

It was in this understandably depressing period that Dean composed the text for which he is principally noted, An Essay on the Future Life of Brute Creatures (1767). Published in Manchester by subscription and reprinted in London in 1768, the Essay enjoyed the patronage of the Asshetons and other leaders of regional society. Otherwise just another contribution to an age-old technical debate recently enlivened by Locke and Voltaire, Dean's work displayed two distinctive aspects which accounted for its momentary popularity. First, he volubly attacked the insidious philosophical materialism of the contemporary Enlightenment. Second, he offered a striking depiction of 'natural evil' as the product of moral weakness. Both features must have appealed to Lancashire's landed élite, many of them sympathetic to the revivalist sentiments sweeping through established English religion. Dean savaged those, like Descartes and La Mettrie, who thought animals mere machines, devoid of souls. He spoke of sin and salvation for man and animal alike, appealing emotively to the evangelical mood of the age. He also attacked both determinism and predestination, asserting the absolute primacy of free will in human morality. This was perhaps the most crucial polemical feature of the Essay, which was disparaging of Calvinism in particular. Presbyterianism, after all, was the separatist tradition which, throughout the Manchester area, was the principal rival to the evangelicalism offered by Dr Assheton and his like-minded colleagues from within the Anglican church.

The Essay subsequently fell into an obscurity explicable by its very pertinence to this singular context. James Rothwell, a more conventional Anglican who mistrusted its evangelical flavour, responded with the Letter to the Reverend Mr Dean (1769). But by the early 1770s Dean's work had largely been forgotten. His life now entered its final, dark phase. Dean's wife died on 20 February 1771 and was buried three days later in the churchyard of St Leonard's. Always somewhat irascible, Dean thereafter became embroiled in a property dispute with the manorial steward of the absentee lord, Sir Harbord Harbord of Gunton, Norfolk. Over the next few years, his two surviving children, Ann and Elizabeth, also died. Dean may even have neglected his duties at the grammar school, whose fabric fell into disrepair during the final years of his tenure. Samuel Bamford, recounting local legend, describes the schoolmaster around this time as a superstitious individual, afraid of ghosts and constantly aware of his own mortality (Bamford, 1.29). Such intimations were prescient.

On 8 February 1778, after a period of ill health, Richard Dean died at Middleton; he was buried two days later beside his wife and children in St Leonard's churchyard.

DAVID ALLAN

Sources D. Allan, 'An 18th-century Lancashire minister on animal sentience: Richard Dean's *Essay on the future life of brute creatures*', *Transactions of the Lancashire and Cheshire Antiquarian Society*, 94 (1998), 31–63 • bishop's act book, Chester, 1752–60, Ches. & Chester ALSS, EDA 1/6, fol. 14v; EDA 1/8. fol. 10v • parish register, St Leonard's, Middleton, 1752–1837, Man. CL, Manchester Archives and Local Studies, MFPR 114–115 [marriage, burial] • Greater Manchester RO, Manchester, Assheton MSS, E/7/18–, 20–, 24–, and 25– • C. W. Sutton, *A list of Lancashire authors* (1876), 155 • F. R. Raines, *The rectors of Manchester, and the wardens of the collegiate church of that town*, ed. [J. E. Bailey], 2 vols., Chetham Society, new ser., 5–6 (1885), 171–6 • R. S. Paul and W. J. Smith, *A history of Middleton grammar school, 1412–1964* (1965) • private information (2004) • S. Bamford, *The autobiography of Samuel Bamford*, ed. W. H. Chaloner, new edn (1967), 29 • H. D. Rack, 'The providential moment: church building, Methodism and evangelical entryism in Manchester, 1788–1825', *Transactions of the Historic Society of Lancashire and Cheshire*, 141 (1991), 235–60 • GM, 1st ser., 34 (1764), 602 • *Manchester Mercury* (22 Jan 1765) [item dated 5 Jan]

Dean, (Richmond Leslie) Stansmore (1866–1944). *See under* Glasgow Girls (*act.* 1880–1920).

Dean, Thomas. *See* Deane, Thomas (*b.* 1686/7).

Dean, William (*c.*1557–1588), Roman Catholic priest and martyr, was born at Grassington, Linton in Craven, Yorkshire. He was the son of Thomas Dean, who was a retainer of Richard Norton, one of the principals of the 1569 northern rising. William attended school in Leeds and Clitheroe. Following the collapse of the uprising it appears that he conformed to the Church of England. He matriculated at Magdalene College, Cambridge, in 1575 and was a pensioner at Gonville and Caius College in 1577. He was ordained, and served as a curate at Monk Fryston in the diocese of York. In 1581, however, he was converted to the Roman Catholic church by Thomas Alfield, a Rheims seminarist, and he entered the English College, then at Rheims, in July that year. He was ordained a priest at Soissons on 21 December 1581. Early in 1582 he went back to England and within a month was arrested in London. Dean was imprisoned in Newgate, where he was interrogated by Richard Topcliffe as to where he had said mass. Having spent three years in prison he was at length brought to trial at the queen's bench and was found guilty of high treason, but he was exiled in 1585 with twenty other priests. He went to Rheims and almost immediately, on 21 November, returned to England to continue his work. After less than two years he was again apprehended in London and brought to trial; he and thirteen others were condemned under the New Act of 1585. He was executed by hanging, with great cruelty, at Mile End Green, Middlesex, on 28 August 1588. Dean was beatified by Pius XI in 1929.

G. BRADLEY

Sources E. H. Burton and J. H. Pollen, eds., *Lives of the English martyrs: the martyrs declared venerable, 1583–88*, 2nd ser., 1 (1914), 351–9 • G. Anstruther, *The seminary priests*, 1 (1969), 100 • T. F. Knox and others, eds., *The first and second diaries of the English College, Douay* (1878), 180, 184–5, 208 • R. Challoner, *Memoirs of missionary priests*, ed. J. H. Pollen, rev. edn (1924), 110, 133–5 • Gillow, *Lit. biog. hist.*,

2.37 • J. H. Pollen, ed., *Unpublished documents relating to the English martyrs*, 1, Catholic RS, 5 (1908), 26 • D. A. Bellenger, ed., *English and Welsh priests, 1558–1800* (1984), 54 • Venn, *Alum. Cant.*, 1/2.26

Dean, William Ralph [Dixie] (1907–1980), footballer, was born on 22 January 1907 at his parents' home, 325 Laird Street, Birkenhead, Cheshire, the son of William Dean and his wife, Sarah Emma Brett. There were already four, and soon to be five, sisters. His father was an engine driver on the Great Western Railway and his mother had been in domestic service in Rock Ferry, near Birkenhead. It was there the family moved when Mr Dean got a job on the Wirral Railway. Young Bill seems to have experienced a curious and ineffective schooling. He went to Birkenhead's Laird Street elementary school but at the age of eleven left home voluntarily to enter the Albert Industrial School, a reform school aimed at improving the behaviour of juvenile delinquents which probably became a borstal after legislation in 1907. He was not a juvenile delinquent but he was good at and obsessed by football, for which the facilities and opportunities at Albert Street were better than those at Laird Street.

By the age of twelve Dean had played centre forward for Birkenhead boys and was already establishing his reputation as a footballer of promise. At fourteen he was an apprentice fitter in the engine shop on the Wirral railway and playing with adults in the works' team in the Cheshire league, sometimes against the reserve teams of Football League clubs. A short spell at Pensby in the Wirral combination led to his signing briefly as an amateur and, on reaching the age of sixteen, as a professional for Tranmere Rovers, the local Birkenhead club who had been founder members of the third division (northern section) in 1921. He only played two games in his first season (1923–4) but in 1924–5 he made the breakthrough to regular first team football. His twenty-seven goals in the same number of league games was noticed by several clubs and he was transferred to Everton for £3000, a record fee for an eighteen-year-old, in the spring of 1925.

The next ten years were a good time to be a centre forward. In 1925 the offside law was changed. Before then, a player had been offside if, when receiving the ball in the opposition half of the field, at least three opponents had not been between him and their goal line. In 1925 the three were reduced to two in an attempt to brighten up a game which some critics thought was being spoiled by deliberate offside tactics. The eventual response to the change was even more sophisticated defence but in the transitional stage goals flowed like clichés at a party conference.

It was in this context that Dixie Dean became the most potent goalscorer English football has ever seen. In his first full season for Everton (1925–6) he netted thirty-two goals in thirty-eight matches. A serious motor cycle accident in 1926 restricted his opportunities in 1926–7 but twenty-seven games still produced twenty-one goals. The 1927–8 season was his *annus mirabilis*. Everton won the championship in that year and of their 102 goals in 42 matches Dean scored 60. He actually played in only thirty-nine himself and even more astonishingly scored his

William Ralph [Dixie] **Dean** (1907–1980), by Barker, 1936 [leading Everton out against Arsenal at Highbury, 29 August 1936]

goals in only twenty-nine games. The year before George Camsell of Middlesbrough had established a new record for league goals in a season with fifty-nine. With two games left in 1928 Dean had only scored fifty-three. But he scored seven in the last two matches, four at Burnley and a hat-trick at home to Arsenal in a 3–3 draw in the final game. He was still only twenty-one. If you were a middle-class male it was *Boy's Own Paper* stuff and if you were working-class it was life imitating the art of Roy of the Rovers. For the next ten seasons no one scored goals like Dixie. His average of 0.867 per league game and 0.936 for all games is unlikely ever to be broken.

To mark the sixty-goal feat the people of Birkenhead presented Dean with an illuminated address. Even *The Times* (7 May 1928), which tended to look down on professional football, did not ignore 'that very brilliant player Dean' who was 'largely responsible for Everton winning the championship. A hard, eager player, Dean has had a lot of marking to put up with, but his strength and good humour have carried him through.' He had a strong shot in both feet but was particularly renowned for his heading, which was based on good timing and powerful neck muscles. Twenty of the record sixty goals were headers. He was a physically robust player and perhaps he needed to be, as he suffered fifteen major football injuries. He often played when not fit and it was injury which brought his career to a premature end in 1939 after brief spells with Notts County and Sligo Rovers.

Dean married a local girl, Ethel Fossard, daughter of William Fossard, who worked for an insurance company, in St James's Church, Birkenhead, in 1931. Three sons and a daughter completed the family. Off the field his pleasures included cigarettes, a glass of beer, and a bet. His honeymoon was a tour of the racetracks. At the height of his fame he was filmed by Pathé.

Dixie Dean was not only one of the most celebrated footballers of his generation, but his name remains familiar to many who not only never saw him play but have little interest in football. Some of that notoriety is probably due to the nickname, which Dean himself disliked and whose origins remain obscure. A dixie was a small iron pot or can for boiling tea, rice, or stew used by other ranks in the Indian army. Dixie also refers to the southern United States below the Mason-Dixon line and later became a style of jazz. Several popular songs of the 1920s, the years when Dean first began to play professional football, contained 'Dixie' in the title. Dean himself was tall and swarthy with black, curly hair, which may have influenced some users of the name. The simple alliteration was clearly part of the attraction: perhaps many young men named Dean were nicknamed Dixie in the 1920s. It has also been suggested that it was first used by the supporters of Tranmere Rovers, for whom he signed as a professional at the age of sixteen in 1923. Whether he was the first Dixie or one of many, his footballing achievements have ensured that he remains the best-known.

Dean was never able to transfer his success as a footballer to the wider world. A sports shop he ran in Birkenhead in the 1930s failed, and after war service in the Royal Tank regiment, he became landlord of the Dublin Packet in Chester from 1946 to 1961. The new chairman of Everton, John Moores, head of Littlewoods pools, then found him a job as a security officer, from which he retired in 1972. But his retirement was marred by ill health and he spent his last years confined to a wheelchair after his right leg was amputated following a thrombosis in 1976. His wife died in 1974. Dixie himself collapsed and died at Goodison Park, Everton, a few minutes before the end of the match between Everton and Liverpool on 1 March 1980. He was buried at St James's Church, Birkenhead, six days later.

In 1964 Everton played a testimonial match for Dean twenty-six years after he had left the club. 40,000 people came to watch and pay tribute to a legendary football player.   TONY MASON

Sources N. Walsh, *Dixie Dean* (1977) · *Liverpool Echo* (2 March 1980) · *Liverpool Echo* (4 March 1980) · *Liverpool Echo* (6 March 1980) · *Liverpool Echo* (7 March 1980) · *The Times* (7 May 1928) · *The Times* (2 March 1980) · *The Times* (3 March 1980) · *The Times* (8 March 1980) · b. cert.
Archives FILM Pathé film
Likenesses photographs, 1928–38, Hult. Arch. · Barker, photograph, 1936, Hult. Arch. [*see illus.*]

Deane, Sir Anthony (*c.*1638–1720?), shipbuilder, was born in Harwich, the son of Anthony Deane (*d.* 1659), master mariner. He served his apprenticeship as a shipwright under Christopher Pett, master shipwright at Woolwich and one of the family which dominated the naval dockyards of the period. The distinction between the ship designer, or 'naval architect', and the practical shipbuilder was not clear at that time, but Deane, having been bound to the master shipwright of a naval dockyard, would emerge from his training as more than a mere craftsman. He rose rapidly, and was assistant master shipwright at Woolwich by 1660, at the age of twenty-two.

Two years later Deane first met Samuel Pepys, later his

Sir Anthony Deane (c.1638–1720?), by Sir Godfrey Kneller, 1690

great friend and patron and then a member of the Navy Board, who saw Deane as a possible rival to the Pett family. Pepys found him 'a very able man, and able to do the King's service … [I] will commend his work with skill and vie with others, especially the Petts' (Pepys, *Diary*, 18 Aug 1662). Pepys's diary contains many references to Deane, as he instructed Pepys in the art of shipbuilding. The shipyard at Harwich was reopened in 1664 and Deane was appointed its master shipwright, giving him his first chance to design and build ships. He became an officer in the militia in 1667 and used the title 'Captain' from then until he was knighted in 1675. He was promoted master shipwright of the larger yard at Portsmouth in 1668 and rose to become commissioner at Portsmouth in 1672.

Deane soon gained a reputation for fast vessels, whether building royal yachts or ships of the line carrying 60 to 100 guns. Pepys exulted in the speed of his ships: the seventy-gun *Resolution* of 1667, for example, was 'the best ship by report in all the world' (Pepys, 15 July 1668), and of the sixteen-gun *Greyhound* of 1672 it was said: 'She steers singularly well, keeps a weather helm and never missed staying … We believe she will be as good a sailer as ever built in England' (Johns, 181). Deane built three large ships, first rates of 100 guns and three decks, during his period at Portsmouth, as replacements for ships lost in the Dutch wars. One of these, the *Royal Charles* of 1673, had initial problems of stability, and this seems to have convinced Deane that ships of the line should be made more stable. In all, Deane designed and built twenty-five ships between 1660 and 1675, more than a quarter of the ships added to the navy in those years, and he built sixteen out of forty-four of the larger or 'rated' ships.

Deane's career as an active naval shipbuilder declined when he went to London in 1674 to become a member of the Navy Board as commissioner of the victualling accounts. The duties of his post were light, however, and he designed a few small ships and supervised the construction of thirty new ones ordered by act of parliament in 1677, setting the pattern for naval shipbuilding for the next seventy years. Under his supervision his son, Anthony junior, built two ships of a new type, called galley frigates, intended for use against the Barbary corsairs in the Mediterranean; these combined the advantages of rowing and sailing.

In 1675 Deane visited France on the orders of the king, to build two yachts for Louis XIV. This was held against him in 1679, during the exclusion crisis, when he was accused of giving information to the French and imprisoned in the Tower of London with Pepys. He successfully defended himself but left office in 1680. He was elected to the Royal Society in 1681, serving on its council, and made a substantial living as a commercial shipbuilder for five years, perhaps designing private yachts. In any case he demanded a salary of £1000 to return to the navy as a member of a special commission for the repair of the fleet in 1686. Pepys denigrated the other leading shipwrights in order to ensure that Deane was appointed. The commission appears to have been successful but its term expired in 1688 and Deane was not reappointed after the revolution of that year. He and Pepys were again imprisoned in 1689, but released in 1690. He dined with Evelyn that year, and apparently renounced much of the work he had done since 1664 on the design of ships of the line. He urged their abolition and replacement with small, fast frigates and fireships, reverting to the policies of his youth.

Deane took part in many experiments, for example in building the *Nonsuch* designed by Van Hemskirke, a renegade Dutchman. Pepys later recalled this as 'the ridiculous proposition … of building a ship with regard to the grain of the timber, and laying the roots all one way' (Chappell, appendix II, 301). Deane invented a cannon known from its stout form as Punchinello, and he experimented with the lead sheathing of ships' bottoms. His *Doctrine of Naval Architecture* was written in 1670, and gives the clearest account, before the eighteenth century, of how the hull of a warship was designed. The title page bears the inscription 'written in the year 1670 at the instance of Samuel Pepys', and it had found its way into Pepys's library by 1682, but perhaps that does not tell the whole story. The treatise contains many references to 'the young artist', and also expresses an intention to 'leave nothing unfolded which may advance anything to the meanest capacity'. This was hardly flattering to Pepys, and may suggest that Deane intended it for publication, for the training of young shipwrights.

Little is known about Deane's family life, except that his first wife, Anne, died in childbirth in 1677 and that he married, on 22 July 1678, Christian, widow of Sir John Dawes. He cited his fifteen children as one of the reasons why he needed to be paid £1000 in 1686. In his early days he was often accused of arrogance, having a quarrel with the lord chancellor in 1664 over the felling of timber in his private estate; two years later he was accused by the captain of the *Colchester* of 'having an uncivil tongue … in regard he was a tradesman' (Johns, 171). He died at Charterhouse Square in London, probably in 1720.

Deane's reputation as a ship designer was much boosted by his friendship with Pepys, who lost no opportunity to praise him in his diary and elsewhere. According to Pepys, 'He is the first that has come to any certainty beforehand of foretelling the draught of water of a ship before she is launched' (Pepys, 19 May 1666). Deane mentions the system in his *Doctrine*, but does not claim its invention, and there is evidence that it was in common use by the 1660s. A different view of his qualities was provided by William Sutherland, a shipbuilder of the next generation, who wrote:

> I could never learn that Sir Anthony was much of a mathematical practitioner, or a very great proficient in the practice, but had the art of talking well, and gave good encouragement to those men who was well known to be grounded in the practice part of building ships.
> (Hattendorf, 266)

A more balanced view might suggest that Deane was indeed the best shipbuilder of the early restoration period, but only marginally ahead of rivals such as Sir John Tippets and Christopher, Peter, and Phineas Pett, and not head and shoulders above them as Pepys suggests.

BRIAN LAVERY

Sources A. W. Johns, 'Sir Anthony Deane', *Mariner's Mirror*, 11 (1925), 164–93 · *Deane's doctrine of naval architecture*, ed. B. Lavery (1981) · Pepys, *Diary* · J. R. Tanner, ed., *A descriptive catalogue of the naval manuscripts in the Pepysian Library at Magdalene College, Cambridge*, 1–3, Navy RS, 26–7, 57 (1903–9) · S. Pepys, *Naval minutes*, ed. J. R. Tanner, Navy RS, 60 (1926) · *The Tangier papers of Samuel Pepys*, ed. E. Chappell, Navy RS, 73 (1935) · J. B. Hattendorf and others, eds., *British naval documents, 1204–1960*, Navy RS, 131 (1993) · J. L. Chester and J. Foster, eds., *London marriage licences, 1521–1869* (1887) **Archives** BL · Bodl. Oxf., corresp. and papers · Magd. Cam., papers relating to naval architecture; various letters and MSS · NMM, corresp. · PRO **Likenesses** J. Greenhill, oils, *c*.1670, NMM · G. Kneller, oils, 1690, NPG [*see illus.*]

Deane, Charles Anthony (1796–1848), diver and inventor of diving equipment, was born in September 1796 at 53 Hughes Fields, Deptford, Kent, and was baptized at St Nicholas's Church, Deptford, on 2 October 1796, the son of John Deane (*bap.* 1766, *d.* 1830), a seaman in the East India Company service, and Eleanor Thompson (1769–1846). The family, although much reduced in circumstances in the nineteenth century, was descended from Sir Anthony Deane (*c*.1638–1720?), surveyor to the Royal Navy and a friend of Pepys. This seagoing tradition was maintained and as a result of their father's service with the East India Company both Charles and his brother **John Deane** (1800–1884), who was born on 6 April 1800 at 53 Hughes Fields, Deptford, and baptized on 2 May 1800 at St Nicholas's Church, Deptford, enjoyed a free education at the Royal Hospital School at Greenwich (now the National Maritime Museum). On leaving (Charles in 1810, John in 1813), both were apprenticed to ship's captains; Charles to

a lowly coastal trader, the *Ceres*, and John, more fortunately, to the famous Captain 'Fighting' Tom Larkins of the East Indiaman *Warren Hastings*.

On completing his apprenticeship, Charles Deane married Sophia McIntosh (1794–1836) on 25 May 1817 at St Martin-in-the-Fields, London. In 1822 he found work as a caulker at Barnard's shipyard in Deptford, where his father also worked in the same trade. His last two voyages had been aboard the *Warren Hastings* along with his younger brother, who had recommended him. It is probable that the brothers had benefited from the East India Company custom that allowed those on board to profit from private trade. Charles, who was of an inventive mind, was able to afford to work up the smoke helmet apparatus which he had devised and to patent the design on 4 November 1823. It consisted of a beaten copper helmet with three windows of thick glass, attached to a canvas and leather suit. A supply of air to the helmet was provided by a bellows pump and a second pipe allowed for the escape of the stale air. It is probable that his employer, Edward Barnard, assisted him in the project because some months later he assigned the rights to Barnard for the not inconsiderable sum of £417. The apparatus, demonstrated to several important bodies at home and abroad, was accepted as a useful tool in the days when fire was an ever-present danger in wooden ships and in warehouses and yards storing highly inflammable materials. It was not, however, a commercial success.

Charles's younger brother John had by this time completed his apprenticeship and had found employment with the Thames estuary boatmen from the neighbouring port of Whitstable. This was the centre of an active salvage industry and maintained a flourishing trade in recovering anchors and cargoes in wrecks. It is likely that he took part in bell dives during this work and suffered from the shortcomings of the equipment along with the rest. The principle of the diving bell had been known for centuries but the need for something better was obvious. John Deane had married Agnes Norris (1800–1844) on 9 August 1823, and with a family to support he decided in 1826 to join with his brother to promote and develop the helmet as a diving apparatus. Although in principle it worked in exactly the same way as Smeaton's force pump bell of 1788, the forced air supply helmet's utility lay in its autonomy: it enabled the diver to move freely and work on the sea bed for much longer periods and with comparative ease. This was a tremendous advantage compared with the static nature of the bell.

The adapted 'open helmet dress', as it became known, consisted of the copper helmet with its forced air supply and its heavy glass eyepieces, and stout canvas and leather suit. The used or foul air was now allowed to bubble away at the edge of the breastplate or short jacket. Its major limitation was that the diver was unable to lean too far forward in case the water entered under the breastplate, thereby flooding the suit and helmet. This defect was later rectified by Augustus *Siebe with his 'closed dress'.

Charles and John Deane had already met Siebe who lived and worked in Soho, then the centre of the London metal trade, and had been the manufacturer of Charles's original smoke helmet. In 1830, with Barnard, Charles and John decided to entrust the manufacture and marketing of their apparatus to Siebe as he had—or had local access to—all the necessary engineering skills. He improved the apparatus by the addition of a powerful hand-operated cylinder pump and substituted the newly invented Macintosh waterproof indiarubber material for the less effective canvas and leather. The invention was now in the public eye and Siebe sold some twenty suits over the next few years. Its legal owner, Edward Barnard, seemed content to leave it in the hands of the Deanes and Siebe, although its final development into the standard closed dress apparatus was Siebe's alone.

The Deane brothers used the closed dress apparatus on several famous salvage operations, starting with the East Indiaman *Carn Brea Castle*, lost in August 1829 on the infamous 'back of the Wight'. This project was the first commercial use of the apparatus and many others followed, including dives on the *Royal George* and even on the *Mary Rose*. The brothers recovered guns and many other artefacts from these famous wrecks. Some from the *Royal George* were exhibited at 209 Regent Street, London, in 1835. This led to the publication of the first books on helmet diving methods: *Submarine Researches* (1835) by Charles and *Method of Using Deane's Patent Diving Apparatus* (1836) by John, the world's first helmet diving manual.

It is typical of Charles Deane's difficult and unstable character that in his book, and in general, he refused to acknowledge his brother's contribution to their joint enterprise. John Deane, a far more robust and generous spirit, as his book title suggests, was just the opposite. The brothers finally fell out in 1844 when Charles received a grant from the government of £400 in recognition of his work on the diving dress. He refused to apportion any of the money to John.

Charles, the weaker man physically, gave up his diving activities in 1839 as a possible result of diver's sickness—the bends. Without regular employment he soon fell on hard times. His first wife had died in 1836 and, unable to look after his family of ten children, he was declared insane and confined for a time in Peckham Lunatic Asylum. On 7 November 1845 he married his second wife, Mary Bond (*b.* 1807). The final tragedy came on 7 November 1848 when, after many setbacks in promoting his other inventions, he cut his throat with a razor and died at 5 Providence Place, Commercial Road, in east London.

John Deane meanwhile continued his successful career as Britain's leading submarine engineer. This led in 1854 to his appointment as chief submarine engineer to the Admiralty in the Crimea to undertake the clearance of wrecks sunk by the Russians to block the entrance to Sebastopol harbour during the Crimean War of 1854–6. He was by this time a widower, his wife having died in August 1844. A family friend in Whitstable, Sarah Ann Browning (1827–1865), took on the job of surrogate mother to his five children and on his return from the Crimea they were married on 7 October 1856 in Whitstable parish church. He had earned a rest from his strenuous

labours and decided to retire at the age of fifty-six. He bought several properties in Ramsgate and enjoyed several years of quiet comfort until his death there—at 90 Hardres Street—on 9 July 1884. He had married again, on 10 September 1868; his third wife was his sister-in-law, Ruth Norris (*d.* 1883).

Although the Deane brothers did not reap the full financial benefit of their simple but brilliant invention and for a time suffered from others taking their glory, they have at last been recognized as pioneers in what is now a considerable industry. Their story was told at length in John Bevan's book *The Infernal Diver* (1996), which helped to restore them to their rightful place among the great innovators of the early nineteenth century.

WILLIAM RONALD BRAITHWAITE and JOHN BEVAN

Sources J. Bevan, *The infernal diver* (1996) · H. Slight, *The loss of the Royal George* (1840) · J. Bevan, *Biographical notes on C. A. and J. Deane, 1796–1884* (1994) · C. A. Deane, *Submarine researches* (1835) · J. Deane, *Method of using Deane's patent diving apparatus* (1836) · Whitstable Museum, Whitstable, Kent, archive · Sci. Mus. · m. certs. · d. certs.
Archives Whitstable Museum, Whitstable, Kent, archive | Submex, London, John Bevan collection
Likenesses M. P. Pout, group photograph, *c.*1872 (John Deane) · P. Scoones, photograph, 1996 (John Deane; after M. P. Pout), Submex, London, John Bevan collection
Wealth at death John Deane: will, 1884, LMA; Charles Anthony Deane; value of estate not known, died intestate

Deane, Henry (*c.*1440–1503), administrator and archbishop of Canterbury, is first recorded in 1457 as a canon of Llanthony by Gloucester and a young student there. That he later pursued his studies at Oxford is indicated both by his reference in a letter, years afterwards, to that university as his 'most gracious mother' (Anstey, 675–7), and by the fact that in 1473 and 1488 he is recorded as renting rooms from Exeter College. His parentage and early life are totally obscure, but it is likely that his family came from the Forest of Dean, in Gloucestershire; the subsequent progress of his career suggests that he was born *c.*1440.

In 1467 Deane was elected prior of his community, an office he was to retain, despite his elevation to the episcopate, until 1501. In 1477 he is described, unusually for a religious, as a royal chaplain, and in 1481 he received a papal indult in common form to hold any other benefice with the priory. He proved to be an excellent monastic administrator. In 1481 he obtained from Edward IV, for a fine of 300 marks, the union and subordination to his own community of its ancient mother house of Llanthony Prima in Monmouthshire, where liturgical observance and financial management had sunk to a low ebb. At his own monastery he embarked upon a building programme, of which only the gatehouse survives, decorated (characteristically in this age) with his own arms, a chevron between three birds.

Marks of favour from Henry VII came soon after the king's accession, in the form of grants and confirmations to the priory from December 1485. It is possible that Deane's rise to much greater prominence was through contact with his diocesan Robert Morton (*d.* 1497), from late 1486 bishop of Worcester, and through him with the latter's uncle John Morton (d. 1500), archbishop of Canterbury and chancellor. Deane, whose knowledge of the common law is suggested by his admission to the society of Lincoln's Inn on 30 October 1489, served as a royal councillor, and on 13 September 1494 was appointed chancellor of Ireland (where Llanthony had substantial possessions), to serve under Sir Edward Poynings (d. 1521), the deputy governor acting for Prince Henry. It was Deane who gave the opening speech at the Drogheda parliament of December 1494, where Poynings' law, and other legislation designed to bring Ireland more firmly under the English crown, was enacted. He was in effective control of Irish administration for much of 1495 while Poynings was on campaign further south, and his regime drew forth a protest from the bishop and clergy of Meath. On Poynings' recall in January 1496 Deane was appointed deputy governor and justiciar of Ireland, and engaged in the strengthening of the boundaries of the pale. Soon however, in August 1496, reversion to a policy of government through Anglo-Irish nobles brought about his replacement.

Before his departure from Ireland, Deane had on 13 April 1494 been granted custody of the temporalities of the bishopric of Bangor, to which he was papally provided on 4 July following. The temporalities were restored on 6 October 1496. The diocese was still suffering from the ravages of Owain Glyn Dŵr's rebellion, at the beginning of the century, in which both cathedral and bishop's palace had been severely damaged. Deane inaugurated a process of reconstruction which was completed after his translation. His determined reassertion of episcopal rights is illustrated by his recovery of the bishop's fisheries in the Skerries, now claimed by William Gruffudd. Deane personally led a fishing expedition, successfully repulsed armed resistance, and ultimately re-established the see's control over this lucrative right.

Within less than five years Henry VII signalled his intention of securing ecclesiastical preferment for his 'faithful counsellor' by granting Deane, on 7 December 1499, custody of the vacant see of Salisbury, to which he was provided by the pope on 8 January 1500. Later that year, on 13 October, after the death of Archbishop John Morton, the chancellor, he was appointed keeper of the great seal, an office he held until 27 July 1502. Thomas Langton, bishop of Winchester, was elected to succeed Morton at Canterbury, but died on 27 January 1501, and Deane was in turn elected to the primatial see on 26 April 1501 and translated on 26 May. When Henry VII restored the temporalities of the archbishopric on 2 August, that parsimonious monarch signalled his 'special favour and sincere love' (Rymer, Foedera, 2.773–5) by granting Deane the proceeds of the lordship of Canterbury since Morton's death. He was the first religious to be elevated to Canterbury for 135 years, and he was, of course, the last.

The surviving fragments of Deane's Canterbury register provide information only on routine matters. In his sacramental duties he was represented, as at Salisbury, by John Bell, bishop of Mayo. It appears that there was conflict with the University of Oxford over an unspecified jurisdictional issue. Deane's enthusiasm for architectural refurbishment, so characteristic of late fifteenth-century prelates, was manifested in his rebuilding of the archiepiscopal manor of Otford. On a wider national stage he was chief commissioner in the negotiations that resulted, in January 1502, in the contract of marriage between Henry VII's daughter Margaret and James IV, king of Scots, and in a treaty of perpetual peace between the two kingdoms. The showpiece of his pontificate was his celebration on 14 November 1501, assisted by nineteen bishops, of the marriage between Prince Arthur and Katherine of Aragon.

The extravagance of the royal marriage was matched by that of Deane's own funeral after his death at Lambeth Palace on 15 February 1503. The arrangements specified in his last testament provide an excellent illustration of the late medieval desire for conspicuous commemoration (to be organized in this case by, among others, the archbishop's young chaplain, Thomas Wolsey). Deane's coffin, surmounted by his effigy, was transported by barge from Lambeth to Faversham and thence to Canterbury, surrounded all the way by tapers, accompanied by river-men in mourning livery and on the final stages by an escort of gentlemen tenants. On 24 February he was buried in Canterbury Cathedral near to the site of Thomas Becket's martyrdom, and to the saint's tomb he bequeathed a valuable image of St John the Evangelist. His grave was marked by a monumental brass in the martyrdom (the north-west transept), where mass was to be celebrated for his soul for twenty years. A memorandum in a cathedral priory register suggests that his last wishes were not fulfilled, and that he did not even have his month's mind because of financial exigencies, but that he was betrayed by his executors (of whom the foremost was Sir Reginald Bray). In material terms this alleged neglect is paralleled by the losses of his registers as prior of Llanthony and bishop of Bangor and Salisbury. Because of these lacunae, and because the voices of Henry VII's individual councillors are muted, Deane remains a remarkably obscure figure, whose certain distinction can be illustrated far more often by inference than by evidence. He was obviously an able administrator, in both ecclesiastical and secular spheres, while his probity is surely attested by the plaudit delivered by John Fisher (d. 1535) at the funeral of Queen Elizabeth, the day before Deane's own burial, where the loss of the archbishop is equated with that of the queen and Prince Arthur. However anonymously he was certainly one of the pillars of Henry VII's regime, and at the same time a conscientious prelate.

CHRISTOPHER HARPER-BILL

Sources W. F. Hook, *Lives of the archbishops of Canterbury*, 2nd edn, 12 vols. (1861–84) · Emden, *Oxf.* · A. Conway and E. Curtis, *Henry VII's relations with Scotland and Ireland, 1485–1498* (1932) · W. Campbell, ed., *Materials for a history of the reign of Henry VII*, 2 vols., Rolls Series, 60 (1873–7) · *CPR, 1476–85* · *CEPR letters*, vol. 13 · [H. Wharton], ed., *Anglia sacra*, 1 (1691), 124 · C. E. Woodruff, ed., *Sede vacante wills*, Kent Archaeological Society Records Branch, 3 (1914), 93–100 · A. Hussey, *Kent chantries*, Kent Records Society, 12 (1936), 47–8 · J. B. Deane, 'The will of Henry Deane, archbishop of Canterbury, deceased 15 February 1502-3', *Archaeological Journal*, 18 (1861),

256–67 • Rymer, *Foedera* • H. Anstey, ed., *Epistolae academicae Oxon.*, 2, OHS, 36 (1898) • *The itinerary of John Leland in or about the years 1535–1543*, ed. L. Toulmin Smith, 3: *The itinerary in Wales* (1906), 40
Archives PRO, register, PROB 11/13, fols. 1–16 | LPL, register of John Morton, ii, fols. 169v–171r

Deane, Sir James Parker (1812–1902), judge, the second son of Henry Boyle Deane of Hurst Grove, Berkshire, and his wife, Elizabeth, daughter of James Wyborn of Hull House, Shelden, Kent, was born at Hurst Grove on 25 June 1812. He went to Winchester as a colleger in 1824, and matriculated at St John's College, Oxford, on 29 June 1829, as a law fellow of founder's kin. In 1833 he obtained a second class in the final classical school and a third in the final mathematical school. He graduated BCL on 28 May 1834, proceeded DCL on 10 April 1839, and was admitted a member of the College of Advocates on 2 November following. He had entered the Inner Temple as a student on 8 November 1837, and on 29 January 1841 he was called to the bar by that society. He was made a QC on 16 January 1858, and became a bencher of his inn on 30 April 1858; he served in the office of treasurer in 1878. Deane wrote 'On the exercise of private judgement' for the clergy, produced work on the law of blockade, and edited the Wills Act Amendment Act of 1852.

In 1854 Deane was appointed legal adviser to Admiral Sir Charles Napier, who commanded the British fleet in the Baltic. He was present on board HMS *Duke of Wellington* at the bombardment of Bomarsund, and formed one of the landing party. On the abolition of Doctors' Commons in 1858 Deane transferred to the courts of probate and divorce, where he obtained a large practice. An effective speaker and a vigorous advocate, he adapted himself to juries and to the *viva voce* examination of witnesses more readily than some of his colleagues. His most conspicuous appearances, however, were in the ecclesiastical courts, in which the practice and the traditions of 'the Commons' still flourished, and for a quarter of a century there were few ecclesiastical cases of interest or importance in which Deane was not retained; the most celebrated of these, perhaps, were those of *Boyd* v. *Phillpotts*, in which the legality of the Exeter reredos was challenged, *Rugg* v. *Kingsmill*, and *Rugg* v. *Bishop of Winchester*. He also appeared in the case of *Martin* v. *Mackonochie*, which began in 1867 and lasted until 1882; in its earlier stages he appeared on behalf of the defendant.

Deane was a strong Conservative in politics, and in the general election of November 1868 he contested the City of Oxford against Edward Cardwell and William Vernon Harcourt but was heavily defeated. In 1872 he was appointed vicar-general of the province and diocese of Canterbury on the resignation of Sir Travers Twiss; he had already been made chancellor of the diocese of Salisbury in 1868 by Bishop Hamilton. In 1868 he also became Admiralty advocate-general. From 1872 to 1886, under the title of legal adviser to the Foreign Office, he carried out the duties of the now obsolete office of queen's advocate. In this capacity he prepared the British case in the arbitration between Great Britain and Portugal over the territory south of Delagoa Bay, and he advised the government

throughout the long disputes arising from the action of the *Alabama* and her consorts in the American Civil War.

On 1 August 1885 Deane was knighted and in 1892 he was sworn of the privy council. His duties as vicar-general did not interfere with his forensic work, and he held the leading brief in the famous case of the missing will of the first Lord St Leonards, tried in 1876. He continued to practise at the bar until increasing deafness forced him to retire. In 1890 he sat as vicar-general beside Archbishop Benson and his episcopal assessors in the proceedings against Bishop Edward King of Lincoln, and on the occasion of the confirmation of Winnington Ingram as bishop of London at Bow church on 17 April 1901 the turbulent conduct of the 'opposers' almost got beyond his power of control. His last public appearance was at the confirmation of Dr Francis Paget as bishop of Oxford a few months later.

Deane and Dr T. H. Tristram QC (*d.* 1912) were the last of the 'civilians' trained in 'the Commons' and they were described in Dickens's *David Copperfield* and Warren's *Ten Thousand a Year*. Deane married Isabella Frances (*d.* 1894), daughter of Bargrave Wyborn, at Eastry in 1841. He died at his home, 16 Westbourne Terrace, London, on 3 January 1902, having resigned his offices a few days previously. He was buried at Brookwood cemetery. The only son to survive him was Sir Henry Bargrave Deane, a judge of the Probate, Divorce, and Admiralty Division of the High Court of Justice, and the author of *The Law of Blockade* (1870).

J. B. ATLAY, *rev.* BETH F. WOOD

Sources *The Times* (4 Jan 1902), 6 • *The Times* (18 April 1901), 8 • Allibone, *Dict.* • J. Foster, *Men-at-the-bar: a biographical hand-list of the members of the various inns of court*, 2nd edn (1885) • *Men and women of the time* (1899) • J. E. Martin, ed., *Masters of the bench of the Hon. Society of the Inner Temple, 1450–1883, and masters of the Temple, 1540–1883* (1883) • *Annual Register* (1902) • Foster, *Alum. Oxon.* • WWW
Archives LPL, corresp. with Edward Benson • LPL, corresp. with A. C. Tait, etc.
Wealth at death £44,246 11s. 10d.: probate, 15 Feb 1902, CGPLA Eng. & Wales

Deane, John (*bap.* 1685, *d.* 1761), naval officer in the Russian service and spy, was baptized at St Wilfrid's Church, Wilford, Nottinghamshire, on 21 March 1685, the third of four sons of Jasper Deane, a prosperous farmer, and his first wife (of four), Mary. There is no historical information about Deane's youth, education, or career at sea before 1711. Unfortunately the juvenile fiction writer W. H. G. Kingston (1814–1880), whose *John Deane of Nottingham* appeared in 1870, provided Deane with a Robin Hood-like youth and a career as an officer in the Royal Navy which local historians continue to transmit as historical fact. However, the Admiralty papers demonstrate that he never served as a British naval officer (Warner, 'Captain John Deane and the wreck of the *Nottingham Galley*', 115–16). None the less it is obvious that, as master of the *Nottingham Galley*, he had experience at sea, knew how to navigate, and had made transatlantic crossings. His commission in the Russian navy, rapid promotion, and combat performance suggest possible service in the Royal Navy as a rated seaman or warrant officer or as a privateer.

The pivotal event in Deane's life was the wreck of the

Nottingham Galley in 1711. The mid-winter disaster on the desolate Boon Island off the New England coast has a distinctive place in the annals of shipwreck literature. The crew got ashore but the ship and its cargo were lost. Lacking food and fire, they suffered terribly and were obliged to cannibalize a dead crew member before their rescue. Deane and his mate, Christopher Langman, wrote contradictory accounts of the disaster, which gave the shipwreck enormous notoriety (see Roberts). Although Deane's version prevailed, his reputation was badly damaged and he seized an opportunity to take a commission in the Russian navy, where he disappeared for eleven years in a new career.

Recognizing the need for a deep water fleet, the Russian tsar, Peter the Great, had launched a frantic effort to build ships, to purchase others abroad, and to man them with qualified officers. The timing was perfect for Deane. As a lieutenant in 1714 he brought a 52-gun man-of-war from Archangel around the North Cape to the Baltic on another harrowing late-season voyage. In the following year he was promoted to captain and took command of the frigate *Samson* (32 guns), which earned him a reputation as a successful and daring combat commander. By 1719 he had captured twenty prizes as a commerce raider in the Reval squadron and had won the admiration and patronage of Admiral Apraxin, the head of the Russian admiralty.

In 1717 the *Samson* took two Swedish merchantmen in the Gulf of Danzig, but while Deane was dividing the crew an English frigate and a Dutch man-of-war appeared and demanded the release of the vessels. Out-manned and out-gunned, Deane was compelled to forfeit the prizes. Two years later he was called to account for the Gulf of Danzig incident and was falsely accused of taking a large bribe for yielding the prizes. Although Deane and eleven officers and under-officers of the *Samson* testified that he had not served his own interests, he was found guilty and was demoted to lieutenant, a victim—like many other foreign officers—of the jealousy of Russian junior officers. In 1722 he was formally dismissed from service and expelled from the country. Curiously, Apraxin interceded with a letter and passport, describing him as 'Captain Deane'. This last act of generosity permitted him to make an honourable departure with the rank that he used for the rest of his life.

Deane was penniless when he reached England, but he was rich in the knowledge of the tsar's naval affairs, which he detailed in a manuscript entitled 'A history of the Russian fleet during the reign of Peter the Great'. Using it to promote himself, he caught the attention of the prime minister, Robert Walpole, and Charles Townshend, secretary of state for the northern department. Both were haunted by the spectre of a European-wide Jacobite conspiracy and, after the recall of their ambassador in 1722, felt particularly deficient in intelligence from Russia. Deane was appointed commercial consul at St Petersburg, which Townshend described as 'a colour, [for] his true business is to transmit hither what intelligence he may be able to get for His Majesty's service'. The captain

had entered a new career as a spy and returned to Russia in 1725.

Captain Deane's spy mission lasted only sixteen days before he was expelled, but it yielded two illuminating reports: 'An account of affairs in Russia, June–July 1725', a detailed analysis of the political situation after the death of Peter I, and 'The present state of the maritime power of Russia', an intelligence report on the standing of the Baltic fleet. He also met a Jacobite courier, Edmund O'Conner, whom he persuaded to betray the cause for a promise of a financial reward and a royal pardon. He then intercepted O'Conner in Amsterdam and copied his letters, which confirmed that the Jacobites were planning nefarious activities in the spring. Pleased by Captain Deane's service, Townshend notified him that he could depend on being well rewarded.

In early 1726 Deane was assigned to Sir Charles Wager's squadron, which was dispatched to the Baltic to observe Russian naval activity in the Gulf of Finland. Serving as a political adviser on Russian and Baltic affairs, Deane acquired current intelligence about the Russian fleet and attempted, rather unsuccessfully, to recruit agents to supply future information. He wrote a number of dispatches and seems to have influenced, or to have written, the report (signed by Admiral Wager) entitled 'The present state of the Danes, Swedes and Russians in respect to one another and the English fleet in the Baltic in the yeare 1726'.

In 1728 Townshend rewarded Deane with the post of commercial consul for the ports of Flanders, to be his 'watchful eye' in the suppression of the Ostend East India Company. Deane was placed in Ostend to ensure strict compliance, but the situation was complicated by the large number of British expatriates, most of whom were Irish Jacobites and who were engaged in all forms of trade and smuggling. Many were affiliated with the Ostend company and disguised its trade with their own enterprises, legal and illicit. Captain Deane was a perfect choice for the post—a proven intelligence operative, thoroughly versed in maritime and political affairs, who shared his superiors' obsession with the Jacobite menace. The merchants closed ranks to defend their interests, arguing that the new consul was commissioned to suppress all trade. Deane was offered bribes but stuck to his task, providing information about the movement of Ostend company ships, the business activities of the principal officers of the company, and prominent Scottish merchants who he believed had 'stuck to the cause day and night'.

By 1733 Deane had completed this assignment in Flanders. None the less he continued to see old enemies lurking everywhere in new guises and his over-zealousness became embarrassing. Describing himself as 'beset by enemies', he cast himself as the sole defender of the Hanoverian succession. In the changed circumstances Deane came into conflict with Ambassador Robert Daniels in Brussels who complained of his insufferable nature.

In 1736 Deane retired with a comfortable stipend and returned to Wilford, where he stayed for the rest of his life and died. Enrolled as a Nottingham freeman in 1744, he was among the largest contributors to the duke of Kingston's regiment organized to suppress the Jacobite rising of 1745. The captain and his wife, Sara (of whom further details are unknown), died one day apart in 1761 and were interred in a splendid grave in St Wilfrid's churchyard. They had no children. Captain Deane's shipwreck has lived on in collections on sea disasters and in the popular novel, *Boon Island* (1956), by Kenneth Roberts.

RICHARD H. WARNER

Sources R. H. Warner, 'Captain John Deane: mercenary, diplomat, and spy', *People of the sea*, ed. L. Fischer and W. Minchinton (St Johns, 1992), 157–73 · R. H. Warner, 'Captain John Deane and the wreck of the *Nottingham Galley*', *New England Quarterly*, 68 (1995), 106–17 · K. Roberts, *Boon Island*, ed. J. Bales and R. H. Warner (1997) · S. I. Elagin, ed., *Materialy dlia istorria Russkago flota* [Materials for the history of the Russian fleet], 1–4 (1887) · C. A. G. Bridge, ed., *History of the Russian fleet during the reign of Peter the Great, by a contemporary Englishman*, Navy RS, 15 (1899) · 'The authorship of the *History of the Russian fleet under Peter the Great*', *Mariner's Mirror*, 20 (1934), 333–6 · papers and reports relating to Deane's activity in Russia in 1725 and 1726, PRO, SP 91/9, SP 42/77, SP 84/574 · papers and reports relating to Deane's activity in Flanders, PRO, SP 77/75–86 · map collection, Deane's report, 'The present state of the maritime power of Russia', BL, K Mar. II.51.1, 3–5 · Tsentralnyi gosudarstvennyi arkhiv voenno-morskogo flota[Central government archive of the navy], St Petersburg, Russia, papers of Admiral Apraxin, fol. 233 · Tsentralnyi gosudarstvennyi arkhiv voenno-morskogo flota[Central government archive of the navy], St Petersburg, Russia, papers of the admiralty college, fol. 212
Archives UCL, school of Slavonic and east European studies, MS history of Russian navy · Yale U., Beinecke L., MS observations on Russia and on author's service in Russian navy | PRO, state papers foreign, SP 91/9; 42/77; 84/574; SP 77/75–86

Deane, John (1800–1884). *See under* Deane, Charles Anthony (1796–1848).

Deane, Richard (*bap.* 1610, *d.* 1653), army and naval officer and regicide, was baptized on 8 July 1610 in the parish church of Guiting Power, a younger son of Edward Deane (*d.* before 1653) of Temple Guiting, Gloucestershire, and his second wife, Ann Wass (*d.* 1670). Little is known of his early life. His uncle or great-uncle, Sir Richard Deane, lord mayor of London in 1628–9, was a member of the Skinners' Company, one of the founders of the East India Company, and a member of the Levant, Virginia, and North West Passage companies, and Deane may have begun a mercantile career under his auspices. Though Sir Richard was known as a puritan he gave no help to the merchants who rebelled against impositions during his mayoralty and he received a knighthood from Charles I at the end of his term. There was a Richard Deane at Gray's Inn in 1619—simultaneously with future *regicides—but this was the future general's uncle. Through his mother's family, however, he was related to Cromwell, Hampden, and many future Buckinghamshire parliamentarians. Like George Blake, younger brother of the future general-at-sea, a shipowner called Richard Deane traded out of Plymouth, and had a cargo of deals, ironwork, and timber from Göteborg, on board the *Matthew* of Plymouth, enumerated in the Plymouth customs book under the date 25 November 1633. This is probably the same man who in

1637 is mentioned as having bought a French prize at Plymouth and who was probably the future general. (In June 1653 the council of state ordered the import, customs free, of wines, sugar, and tobacco belonging to Major-General Deane, reinforcing the likelihood of a mercantile background.) As both Blake and Deane were trading with northern Europe in timber there is a strong possibility that they were acquainted and that, through George Blake, Deane was already in contact with his brother Robert.

Military career, 1642–1649 On the outbreak of war Deane served in north-west Kent with a group of parliamentarians headed by Captain Willoughby which secured Woolwich Dockyard, capturing seventy-five pieces of ordnance. Willoughby then occupied Gravesend Fort where Deane became a member of the garrison. He was probably at Edgehill on 23 October 1642, possibly at the first battle of Newbury on 27 September 1643. By August 1644 he was comptroller of the ordnance with Essex's army in Cornwall, waiting on and giving advice to his general, who speaks of him as 'an honest, judicious, and stout man'. When Essex abruptly quitted the army, leaving it to Major-General Philip Skippon to get out of the difficulty the best way he could, Skippon called a council of war, which rejected his proposal to cut their way through the enemy, and determined rather to treat. The negotiation ended in the army of 6000 men laying down their arms and surrendering their guns, of which there were forty-nine, all of brass. Deane, who seems to have been left by the desertion of his seniors in actual command of the artillery, was one of the twenty officers who formed this council and signed the 'attestation' or published report of its proceedings. His involvement in the surrender did him no harm and following parliament's approval for the formation of a siege train for the New Model Army in January 1645 he was again appointed comptroller of the ordnance. He commanded the artillery at Naseby (14 June 1645), where his steady fire broke the force of Rupert's headlong charge. He continued to serve with Fairfax in his conquering march into the west country, and his guns played a particularly important part at the battle of Langport and the capture of Sherborne Castle. At the reduction of Bristol (11 September) his 'dexterity, industry, and resolution' were specially commended. He was one of the commissioners to arrange the terms of Ralph Hopton's surrender at Truro (14 March 1646) and afterwards took part in the siege of Oxford, which surrendered, by the king's orders, on 20 June.

On 21 May 1647, at the Temple Church, Deane married Mary, daughter of John Grymesditch of Knottingley in Yorkshire, the witnesses being Colonel Robert Lilburne, afterwards a fellow regicide, and the Leveller Colonel Thomas Rainborowe. Meanwhile, with the end of active fighting, relations between the army and parliament deteriorated. On 28 May 1647 the parliament appointed Cromwell to be lord-general of the forces in Ireland, and Deane to be with him as lieutenant of the artillery. Their scarcely veiled object was to get Cromwell out of the way, and the association of Deane with him suggests that he was now recognized as one of Cromwell's partisans. Cromwell declined the appointment, choosing to remain in England, as did Deane, now promoted to adjutant-general. The quarrel was rapidly coming to a head. On 4 June the control of the king's person was assumed by George Joyce, who brought him to the army. At Newmarket he was waited on by many of the superior officers, Deane among them, who kissed the king's hand. Joyce asserted that what he had done was by Cromwell's order but this Cromwell denied in the most positive and violent manner, and is said on one occasion to have been prevented from doing Joyce 'some mischief' only by the interposition of Deane and others (*Harleian Miscellany*, 8.304). Throughout this period Deane was a member of the council of officers and on 23 June 1647 signed the remonstrance of the army to parliament. On 5 July he was one of those nominated to draw up propositions to the king and on 16 July was among the officers negotiating with the agitators, drawn from the soldiery. He was present at the Putney debates, where he took only a small part but was placed on the committee appointed to revise the *Agreement of the People* in the light of army resolutions. His stance was that of the less radical element, aligned with Cromwell and Ireton. On the resignation of William Batten in September 1647 Rainborowe was nominated as vice-admiral of the fleet and Deane was immediately given his regiment, much to Rainborowe's annoyance.

When the royalist uprising in 1648 called the army again to the field Deane, in command of a regiment, accompanied Cromwell, first into Wales, where he was actively engaged in the reduction of Pembroke Castle, and afterwards to the north, where in the battle of Preston (17 August) he and Colonel Thomas Pride did good service on the parliamentarian right wing. The army determined to deal with the king. The contribution of Deane's regiment to the remonstrance of the army (20 November 1648) was presumably drawn up by Deane himself, or at any rate in strict accordance with his views; its most important clauses are:

> That the parliament be desired to take a review of their late declaration and charge against the king, as also to consider his own act in taking the guilt of bloodshed upon himself; and accordingly to proceed against him as an enemy to the kingdom.
>
> That strict inquiry be made after the chief fomenters, actors, and abettors of the late war, especially those who were the chief encouragers and inviters of the Scotch army; and that exemplary justice may be accordingly executed, to the terror of evil-doers and the rejoicing of all honest men.

In addition to these, among other matters of detail, was the very practical demand that 'speedy supplies should be sent to the army' so as to put an end to 'that which is so insufferable for us to take and so intolerable for the people to bear, namely, free quarters'. These demands not being met, the army marched on London, and while Pride was instructed to 'purge' the House of Commons, Fairfax wrote (8 December) to the lord mayor and corporation that as the arrears of the assessment due to the army had not been paid as demanded, he had ordered 'Colonel Deane and some others to seize the treasuries of Goldsmiths' Hall and Weavers' Hall'. 'Two regiments of foot and several troops of horse accordingly took up their quarters in Blackfriars and some at Ludgate and Paul's Church. They likewise secured the treasuries … and took away from Weavers' Hall above £20,000' (Rushworth, 2.1356). The proceeding, as Fairfax pointed out to the lord mayor, was the same as 'our forces have been ordered to do by the parliament in the several counties of the kingdom where assessments have not been paid'. And in

Richard Deane (*bap.* 1610, *d.* 1653), by Robert Walker, 1653

carrying out his orders Deane exercised a stern control over his men; two, newly listed, being found by court-martial guilty of extortion on their own account, were sentenced to 'ride the wooden horse for an hour', and 'to run the gantelope through the regiment ... for the example of others who, under colour of being soldiers, care not what knavery they act' (ibid., 2.1369).

Deane played an active part in the trial and execution of the king in January 1649. On 12 January he was on the committee for planning the king's trial and attended fifteen (or possibly nineteen) of the twenty-three sessions of the high court of justice. On 24 January he was appointed one of the committee to examine the witnesses; on the 27th he stood up in approval of the judgment; on the 29th he was one of the committee of five to consider the time and place of execution; and he was the twenty-first out of the fifty-nine who signed the death warrant. His signature is written in his usual firm, bold hand, and his seal of arms is distinctly impressed, without the least sign of hurry or nervousness [see also Regicides].

General-at-sea and major-general, 1649–1653 Cromwell had wanted Deane to succeed Batten as vice-admiral in September 1647, and in December 1648 he appears to have discussed with a deeply discontented earl of Warwick the possibility of Deane's replacing him. No action was taken, however, ahead of the first meeting of the council of state on 17 February 1649, and on the 20th it resolved 'that the commission making the Earl of Warwick lord high admiral be called in', and that the command at sea should be given to commissioners. On the 23rd they named Colonel Edward Popham, Colonel Robert Blake, and Deane as the three commissioners 'to go to sea this summer, to take the command of the fleet'. This appointment of trusted army officers was unquestionably made chiefly from political motives. In the sixteenth and early seventeenth centuries military qualifications always took precedence, it being assumed that the commander would take advice on navigational matters from his council of captains.

In the early part of 1649 the generals-at-sea co-operated in forcing Prince Rupert's privateers to leave the channel, but once he was safely cooped up in Kinsale they separated. Deane concentrated on protecting the army dispatched for the reconquest of Ireland. In August he convoyed Cromwell's army from Milford Haven to Dublin. He was then sent back to London with the marquess of Ormond's intercepted correspondence and missed the siege of Drogheda. He was back in time to command the twenty ships which carried food, siege guns, and ammunition for the attack on Wexford. In the later operations the army suffered much from sickness; Deane, writing from Milford Haven on 8 November 1649, reported: 'I have, ever since my coming out of Ireland, been troubled with the distemper of that country's disease, which brought me into a fever'. He was still sick on 4 December, when orders were sent to Blake 'to go towards Cadiz to seek out Prince Rupert' (Penn, 1.293).

In 1650 Deane commanded in home waters while Blake and Popham chased Rupert to Portugal. His chief task was to cut off communication between the Netherlands and Scotland but he was unable to prevent Charles II's landing. When Cromwell invaded Scotland, Deane sent a squadron under Rear Admiral Hall to assist him but he himself only visited Leith briefly on 15 September. During the winter the squadron in the Forth was commanded by Captain Lionel Lane, and Deane did not return until the spring. On 29 March he arrived at Leith, bringing his own regiment and, among other supplies, a number of large flat-bottomed boats for the transport of the troops across the firth. On 6 May he was ordered by Cromwell to take command on shore as major-general of the army, in which capacity he had a prominent part in the operations of the ensuing summer, the pursuit of the Scottish army into England, and the battle of Worcester (3 September 1651).

Deane returned to Scotland as one of eight commissioners appointed to settle civil government and prepare for a union with England in October 1651; from December 1651 he also shared the chief military command in Scotland with Monck and John Lambert. By March 1652 he was left in sole military command, the departure of the other civil commissioners by the end of the following month leaving him effectively to head the civil and financial administration also. He had been working with Lambert to regulate assessments in Scotland since the previous December, and by November 1652 was empowered to authorize all disbursements of revenue in Scotland. He oversaw the implementation of plans formulated by the commissioners, including the establishment of a high court of judicature consisting of four English and three Scottish judges, to replace the abolished Scottish juridical institutions. In June 1652 he was named as one of the commissioners for the regulation of the universities and the ministry. Deane also managed to get the customs duties between England and Scotland at Carlisle and Berwick abolished. As military commander he secured the three remaining royalist garrisons: Brodick Castle on Arran and the Bass Rock, which commanded the navigation of the Forth and the sea approach to Edinburgh, fell in April 1652, while Dunnottar Castle, the 'last place in Scotland which displayed the standard of Charles II' and the location of the regalia of Scotland, surrendered to Colonel Thomas Morgan in May (Firth, xix). In June Deane issued a proclamation to the clan chiefs and inhabitants of the north-west before launching a two-pronged advance intended to subjugate the highlands. He set out for Inveraray where he finally secured from the marquess of Argyll a submission to the English parliament and acceptance of the union in a series of agreements which allowed Argyll to retain much of his standing.

On 26 November 1652 Deane's commission as general-at-sea was ordered to be renewed, as also was Blake's. Popham had died in August of the previous year, and the vacancy was now filled up by the appointment of Monck. The commission was a matter of routine, and there was probably no immediate intention of calling Deane away from Scotland, but on Blake's representation, after the untoward action off Dungeness on 30 November, both Deane and Monck were ordered to join the fleet as soon as possible. Deane received a grant of £400 'for fitting him with necessary accommodation', and went on board the *Triumph*, in which Blake already had his flag. Thus closely associated with Blake, he took part in the battle off Portland on 18 February 1653 and in the subsequent pursuit of the Dutch fleet. In this obstinate battle the loss on both sides was very great. As Blake was incapacitated by his wound, the letter of 27 February giving the official account of the battle, though signed by the three generals, was probably written by Deane. He and Monck were now left in command of the fleet, and hoisted their flag on board the *Resolution*.

To refit and prepare for new battles was the work of the next two months. Deane had arrived from Scotland too late to take part in framing the articles of war (25 December 1652) but a great number of letters written by him about this time testify to the close attention he was paying to all the details which might ensure efficiency. Similarly, proposals for the encouragement of seamen and increases in their wages had been introduced before his return (20 December 1652) but his correspondence in 1653, together with that of his earlier command, shows the watchful care he had for the welfare and interests of those under his orders. 'We want', he wrote on 30 March:

> an answer to the petition of the officers of the fleet and of the widows of the slain, as we are much importuned by them for some sort of subsistence, and can hardly put them off by telling them it is under consideration.

Or again, he wrote that if possible 'turning men over from one ship to another should be avoided, for it breedeth trouble and discontent', but that when necessary they should be paid their wages in money, for 'a little bit of paper is soon lost' (BL, Add. MS 22546, fol. 103). Appeals of this kind were signed sometimes by Deane alone, sometimes by Popham and Deane, sometimes by Blake and Deane, sometimes by Deane and Monck. His signature is, in the same way, equally affixed to many rules and proposals for the better organization of the naval service, then still in a very crude state. Lieutenants are to be capable seamen; none other will be appointed. Inducements must be offered to seamen; they should be entered for continuous service and kept on continuous pay, the same as soldiers (25 March 1653). A surgeon's mate should be borne in ships having complements of 150 men or upwards; the care is too great for one man (30 March 1649). Other letters, referring to proposed changes in the victualling, in the ordnance stores, and to different matters of detail, with an exactness and intelligence widely different from mere routine, suggest previous experience in equipping and manning ships for sea.

On 20 April 1653 Cromwell dissolved the Rump Parliament. Deane probably knew of the impending step, and agreed with it, but the published *Declaration of the Generals at Sea and the Captains under their Command* (*Resolution*, at Spithead, 22 April 1653), in the drawing up of which he had at least a large share, wisely contains no word of approval or disapproval. 'We have had', they say:

> a very serious consideration of the great changes within this nation … and we find it set upon our spirits that we are

called and entrusted by this nation for the defence of the same against the enemies thereof at sea … and we are resolved, in the strength of God, unanimously to prosecute the same according to the trust reposed in us.

Death and reputation On 30 April the fleet put to sea and, cruising to the northward, was off Aberdeen on 10 May. On the 14th it anchored in Bressa Sound, in Shetland, and after a council sailed again on the 17th. On the 24th the ships were off the mouth of the Scheldt, and they anchored in Solebay on the 31st. They had spent the month vainly looking for the Dutch fleet, but not until the morning of 1 June did they receive any certain intelligence of it. The fleet, increased by successive reinforcements to upwards of a hundred vessels, large and small, immediately put to sea, and sighted the enemy about four o'clock in the afternoon. The next day towards noon the fighting began. As the fleets approached the English appear to have been in three squadrons each in a rough line ahead but the wind dropped and the battle commenced with a cannonade which inflicted great damage on the Dutch. Whether the English intended that to be their final formation is unclear as fleets often turned into a line abreast when they came to close quarters. Later in the day there was heavy fighting which continued until dark, when the two fleets lay by for the night. The battle was renewed the next morning, 3 June; towards afternoon of the second day the Dutch were already retiring when Blake, coming up with a strong reinforcement fresh from the river, completed their rout and put them to the run. The Dutch lost twenty ships sunk or captured, the English none at all. Deane, however, did not live to see this. At the very beginning of the battle a Dutch shot struck him full in the body, cutting it nearly in two. He fell where he stood, and Monck, fearing lest the sailors might be discouraged by the loss, threw a cloak over his mangled remains.

Deane's body was afterwards taken to Greenwich, where it seems to have lain in state, of a sort. The highest honours the government could bestow were granted. A public funeral was ordered. On 24 June the body was taken to Westminster Abbey with great pomp, and buried in the chapel of Henry VII. Deane's widow was granted a pension of £600 a year, secured on estates in Lancashire. Deane left her his property at Hornchurch in Essex and his fee farm rents from the manor of Sydenham and lands at West Court in Ewelme, both in Oxfordshire, but they were burdened with annuities of £25 per annum to his mother and £12 to his sister Jane, whose husband Drue Sparrow had been secretary to Blake and Deane and had been killed standing at their side in the battle of Portland. He was also able to direct that portions of £1000 each should be paid to his two daughters Mary and Hannah, either when they married or reached the age of twenty. On 2 January 1655, being then thirty-two, his widow married Colonel Edward Salmon. After the Restoration Deane's remains were among those ordered to be 'taken up and buried in some place of the churchyard adjoining', but the taking up and reburial were done without either ceremony or solemnity, and it is believed that the remains were thrown promiscuously into a common pit.

A month after Deane's death Cromwell wrote to William Penn, vice-admiral of the fleet, 'I often think of our great loss in your General Deane, my near friend' (Gardiner and Atkinson, 5.266–7). Cromwell had been deeply upset by Deane's death and had gone in person to console his widow. They had worked closely together and shared common political and religious attitudes as well as being distantly related. Deane had been a strong supporter of *The Heads of Proposals*, had signed the king's death warrant, and had sided with Cromwell over the Leveller *Agreement of the People* as against the stance of Rainborowe. He shared Cromwell's strong puritan convictions and his desire for religious toleration, though that did not extend to Roman Catholics. He had a strong mystical streak, being described as a Behmenist (or disciple of Jakob Boehme), and both he and his wife had premonitions of his death. She claimed she had seen it in a vision before it was announced to her, while for him it was foreshadowed in the discovery that part of his doublet had been eaten by rats. Even Clarendon recorded that Deane had 'the reputation of a bold and excellent officer' (Clarendon, *Hist. rebellion*, 5.288). For all his talents he comes across as a fixer and an enabler, the ideal second-in-command. Perhaps, though, such an impression may just be the result of his living in the shadow of two such colleagues as Blake and Monck. If the cannon ball had hit Monck instead perhaps Deane would be thought of differently.

J. K. LAUGHTON, *rev.* MICHAEL BAUMBER

Sources *The writings and speeches of Oliver Cromwell*, ed. W. C. Abbott and C. D. Crane, 4 vols. (1937–47) · J. B. Deane, *The life of Richard Deane* (1870) · *Report on the manuscripts of F. W. Leyborne-Popham*, HMC, 51 (1899) · C. H. Firth, ed., *Scotland and the Commonwealth: letters and papers relating to the military government of Scotland, from August 1651 to December 1653*, Scottish History Society, 18 (1895) · S. R. Gardiner and C. T. Atkinson, eds., *Letters and papers relating to the First Dutch War, 1652–1654*, 4–5, Navy RS, 37–41 (1910–12) · *CSP dom.*, 1637–54 · G. Penn, *Memorials of … Sir William Penn*, 2 vols. (1833) · *The Clarke papers*, ed. C. H. Firth, 4 vols., CS, new ser., 49, 54, 61–2 (1891–1901), vols. 1–2 · BL, Egerton MS 2519 · BL, Add. MS 22546 · T. K. Rabb, *Enterprise and empire: merchant and gentry investment in the expansion of England, 1575–1630* (1967) · J. Foster, *The register of admissions to Gray's Inn, 1521–1889, together with the register of marriages in Gray's Inn chapel, 1695–1754* (privately printed, London, 1889) · A. B. Beaven, ed., *The aldermen of the City of London, temp. Henry III–[1912]*, 2 vols. (1908–13) · D. O. Shilton and R. Holworthy, *High court of admiralty examinations (MS vol. 53): 1637–1638* (1932) · F. D. Dow, *Cromwellian Scotland, 1651–1660* (1979) · B. Capp, *Cromwell's navy: the fleet and the English revolution, 1648–1660* (1989) · W. Oldys and T. Park, eds., *The Harleian miscellany*, 10 vols. (1808–13), vol. 8 · A. Everitt, *The community of Kent and the great rebellion, 1640–60* (1973) · J. Rushworth, *Historical collections*, 5 pts in 8 vols. (1659–1701) · *Herald and Genealogist*, 7 (1873)
Archives Worcester College, Oxford, letters, mainly to Edward Popham
Likenesses R. Walker, oils, 1653, NMM [*see illus.*]

Deane, Richard (*fl.* 1647–1661), government official and Baptist preacher, came from a Gloucestershire family and was a cousin of Richard *Deane (*bap.* 1610, *d.* 1653), regicide and general-at-sea, but his parentage is unknown. Deane served as a captain of foot in Robert Lilburne's regiment, and he was elected to represent his regiment in the general council of the army in 1647. He became secretary

or chief clerk to the army committee of the Rump from 1649 to 1653. His colonel from the winter of 1647 until 1650 was Sir Arthur Hesilrige, one of the most influential politicians of the Commonwealth.

In 1653 Deane followed the more militarily inclined republicans, becoming co-treasurer at war and co-receiver of the assessments with John Blackwell the younger when the army tightened its grip on the fiscal machinery of government. He held this position until the fall of the protectorate in 1659, when he took the republican side. Perhaps thanks to Hesilrige's patronage, he became clerk of the council under the restored Commonwealth of May to October 1659, and again to the committee of safety from October to December 1659. On the latter occasion he chose to serve not Hesilrige, the leading figure in the restored Rump, but the generals, notably Charles Fleetwood and John Lambert. Possibly his religious stance, as a strict Baptist, explains this. He was sent to Scotland on a confidential mission in November 1659, ostensibly to negotiate with General George Monck on behalf of the generals of England, but allegedly to attempt to undermine the loyalty of Monck's army to its commander. He failed to stop the Scottish army's march south in support of a civilian government and, ultimately, of a free parliament. After the return of the secluded members in February 1660, Deane lost his military commissions and other offices.

Following the Restoration, Deane was considered sufficiently dangerous to be listed as one of the twenty-one non-regicides whose property was to be forfeited, and who were excluded from office in perpetuity. He was arrested on 4 January 1661 and placed in the Marshalsea, Canterbury; his wife, Ann, petitioned for his release stating that Deane had sued out a pardon, retired to Lady Scot's house in Kent, and was living quietly. He was released on 16 January 1661 on bond for his good behaviour.

Deane's later career is uncertain. His identification with the Baptist preacher active in and around Bristol from the 1670s to the 1690s is probable, but there were several contemporaneous Richard Deanes with west-country connections. A Richard Deane was credited with the authorship of *A copy of a brief treatise of the proper subject and administration of baptism some years since sent by the author to Thomas late lord bishop of Lincoln*, published in 1693 but written about seven years earlier, possibly in response to James II's policy of religious toleration. In it the writer alludes to having known 'most persons and actions of note' in the years 1649–59. Deane may well have spent his last days in poverty in Foster's almshouses in Michael's parish, Bristol. He may have been the Richard Deane of Bristol whose widow, Hester, was granted administration of his estate on 8 April 1697.

G. E. AYLMER, *rev.* STUART HANDLEY

Sources Greaves & Zaller, *BDBR*, 218–19 · G. E. Aylmer, *The state's servants: the civil service of the English republic, 1649–1660* (1973), 99, 204, 244, 277 · *A copy of a brief treatise of the proper subject and administration of baptism* (1693) · C. H. Firth and G. Davies, *The regimental history of Cromwell's army*, 2 (1940), 456, 460 · *CSP dom.*, 1660–61, 474 · R. Hayden, ed., *The records of a church in Christ in Bristol, 1640–1687*, Bristol RS, 27 (1974), 288 · administration, PRO, PROB 6/73, fol.

62r • T. R. Jamison, *George Monck and the Restoration* (1975), 53 • *The Clarke Papers*, ed. C. H. Firth, 4, CS, new ser., 62 (1901)

Deane [*formerly* Dean], **Silas** (1737–1789), revolutionary politician and diplomat in America, was born on 24 December 1737 in Groton, Connecticut, to Silas Dean (d. 1760), a blacksmith, and Sarah Barker (d. 1761). Upon graduation in 1758 from Yale College, young Silas moved to the thriving commercial community of Weathersfield, Connecticut, where he practised law, added an 'e' to his surname, and assumed responsibility for his six orphaned siblings. In 1763 he married a widow, Mehitable Nott Webb (1732–1767), who brought him five more children in addition to Jesse, whom they had together. Two years after Mehitable's death from tuberculosis Deane married Elizabeth Saltonstall Ebbets (d. 1777), whose membership in New England's powerful Saltonstall family greatly aided her new husband's budding political career.

Deane rose rapidly in Connecticut politics, serving as assemblyman for Weathersfield (1768–9; 1772–5). He was an important member of the Susquehannah Company, which sent settlers to the Wyoming valley to claim what is now northern Pennsylvania for Connecticut. He then became secretary of the Connecticut Committee of Correspondence and, starting in 1774, one of its delegates to the first two continental congresses.

Deane was an active member of congress. He was especially concerned about supplying the forces, earning the nickname Ticonderoga for authorizing the funding that enabled Ethan Allen to capture this British fort and the cannons that ultimately forced the British army out of Boston. In March 1776 the Committee of Secret Correspondence chose him, although he could not speak French, to go to France to solicit arms and supplies and determine if that nation would support an independent United States. Deane remained in France until the spring of 1778; his mission had mixed results. Working with Pierre Augustin Caron de Beaumarchais, the author of *Le barbier de Seville* and *Le mariage de Figaro*, who headed Hortalez & Co., a front established by the French government to supply the Americans, Deane successfully arranged for arms and clothing to reach the American army. Deane was unable, however, to reimburse Beaumarchais for funds he laid out, compromising French government efforts to keep this assistance secret, and leading Arthur Lee, congress's agent in London, to charge that Deane was pocketing the profits. Both Deane's and Beaumarchais's accounts remained unsettled until well after their deaths, with Deane's heirs finally receiving $37,000 in 1841. Deane was criticized further for recommending numerous unemployed French officers to fight with the American army; most of them proved incompetent, arrogant, and unable to speak English. Perhaps his biggest fiasco was an abortive scheme to set fire to the British naval stores in Portsmouth, England, which again compromised French neutrality.

For most of his stay in France, Deane was joined by Arthur Lee and Benjamin Franklin, both of whom suspected him of dishonesty if not disloyalty. They correctly suspected his secretary, Edward Bancroft, of being a British agent. Deane received more criticism from congress, especially from Virginia's Richard Henry Lee (Arthur's brother) and Massachusetts's Samuel Adams, who considered the entanglement of his private commercial ventures with the national accounts to be 'corruption'. Congress unanimously recalled Deane in November 1777, and refused to show him any appreciation when he returned the following spring bearing news of the French alliance he had helped to negotiate. In fact congress refused to explain why he was dismissed and kept him waiting for five months without a chance to speak on his own behalf. A frustrated Deane responded with a public attack on the Lee brothers in the *Pennsylvania Gazette* on 5 December 1778, which split congress into the Lee and Deane factions and ultimately led to Arthur Lee's recall as well.

In 1780 Deane returned to Europe as a private citizen to vindicate his behaviour and settle his accounts. His journey was unfortunate. His scheme to supply the French and Spanish navies with American masts, and his speculations in western land companies, failed. Disillusioned with the America cause, Deane called for the Americans to seek reconciliation with Britain and abandon the duplicitous French. These sentiments, expressed in private letters, were intercepted by the British and published in December 1781, in New York's loyalist press. From this time onward most Americans regarded Deane as a traitor, a judgement historians have by and large shared, although Deane's most serious biographers argue that he was only expressing frustration that his own substantial efforts were unappreciated.

Deane left Paris in 1781, moving to Ghent and in 1783 to London. Still thirsting after commercial success, he began to plan a canal connecting Lake Champlain with the St Lawrence River. Leaving for Canada to recoup his fortunes, he was suddenly taken ill on board ship, and died on 23 September 1789. He was buried in the churchyard at Deal, Kent. The cause of his death his variously been attributed to a stroke, tuberculosis, suicide, or murder: there is speculation that Edward Bancroft may have poisoned his former employer to prevent him from revealing more of Bancroft's role as a double agent during the American War of Independence.

Whether Deane deliberately betrayed the American cause or merely became disgusted with the ingratitude and factional bickering of both his fellow countrymen and the French will always remain a subject of speculation. (Congress ultimately ruled in 1841 that the 1778 audit of his accounts, undertaken by his enemy Richard Henry Lee, was 'a gross injustice'.) What is clear, however, is that many revolutionary American figures such as Deane, Robert Morris, and William Duer did not expect to suffer financially for their patriotism. The line between public service and private business had not yet been established: ultimately, the stricter separation favoured by Deane's opponents prevailed, at least in theory.

WILLIAM PENCAK

Sources C. H. James, *Silas Deane: patriot or traitor?* (1975) • G. L. Clark, *Silas Deane* (1913) • DNB • L. W. Potts, 'Deane, Silas', *ANB* • J. W.

Davidson and M. H. Lytle, *After the fact: the art of historical detection*, 3rd edn, 1 (1997), xiii–xxiv • K. Goldstein, 'Silas Deane: preparation for rascality', *The Historian*, 43 (1980–81), 75–97 • C. Isham, ed., *The Deane papers*, 5 vols. (1887–91) • *The Deane papers: correspondence between Silas Deane, his brothers, and their business and political associates, 1771–95* (Hartford, CT, 1930) • *Paris papers, or, Mr Silas Deane's late interrupted letters* (New York, 1782) • F. Wharton, ed., *The Revolutionary diplomatic correspondence of the U.S.*, 6 vols. (1889)
Likenesses Du Simitière, sketch, repro. in James, *Silas Deane*
Wealth at death insolvent, living on charity from Edward Bancroft

Deane, Thomas (1651–1735), Roman Catholic convert, was the son of Edward Deane of Malden, Kent. He matriculated from University College, Oxford, on 19 October 1669, the same day as his friend and future colleague Nathaniel Boyse, and subscribed the articles and took the oath of supremacy in the following month, when he was probably admitted a servitor. He graduated BA in 1673 and MA in 1676. He became a tutor in the college, of which he was elected fellow on 4 December 1684, and Greek lecturer. He 'declared himself a papist much about the same time that his master, Obadiah Walker, did' in March 1686, 'whose creature and convert he was' (Wood, *Ath. Oxon.*, 4.450). Walker had been his tutor, and Deane, Boyse, and John Massey, future dean of Christ Church, Oxford, were known as Walker's 'three disciples'. Royal permission was given to Deane, Walker, and Boyse to establish a Roman Catholic chapel in May 1686, instead of attending Church of England worship, a development described as 'a propaganda *coup* out of all proportion to the small numbers involved' (Tyacke, 613).

Deane was the author of *The Religion of Mar. Luther neither Catholick nor Protestant, Prov'd from his Own Works*, privately printed in Obadiah Walker's lodgings in Oxford in 1688. He contributed to a volume of congratulatory verse produced by the university for the birth of James II's heir, the prince of Wales, James Stuart, in 1688. To Deane has been attributed 'An essay towards a proposal for Catholick communion' (London, 1704), but the real author was probably Joshua Basset.

After the landing of the prince of Orange in England, Deane and Massey withdrew privately from Oxford (30 November 1688) to avoid the tumult of the mob, and went to London. Deane's fellowship was declared vacant on 4 February 1689. He was once or twice committed to prison in London on suspicion of being a Jesuit or priest. On 18 December 1691 he stood in the pillory at Charing Cross under the name of Thomas Franks, a reputed Jesuit, for concealing a libel or pamphlet against the government, written by a person who lodged in the same house as himself. During the latter part of his life Deane was a prisoner for debt in the Fleet; but he died at Malden on 10 November 1735, having subsisted for some years mostly on charity. THOMPSON COOPER, *rev.* RUTH JORDAN

Sources Wood, *Ath. Oxon.*, new edn, 3.1162; 4.450–51, 665 • *Dodd's Church history of England*, ed. M. A. Tierney, 5 vols. (1839–43), vol. 3, p. 462 • N. Luttrell, *A brief historical relation of state affairs from September 1678 to April 1714*, 4 (1857), 315 • Gillow, *Lit. biog. hist.*, 2.36 • T. Jones, ed., *A catalogue of the collection of tracts for and against popery*, 1, Chetham Society, 48 (1859), 198–9 • N. Tyacke, 'Religious controversy',

Hist. U. Oxf. 4: *17th-cent. Oxf.*, 569–620 • R. A. Beddard, 'James II and the Catholic challenge', *Hist. U. Oxf.* 4: *17th-cent. Oxf.*, 907–54

Deane [Dean], **Thomas** (*b.* 1686/7), musician, was the son of the Revd William Deane of Nottinghamshire. He matriculated at University College, Oxford, the day before taking the degree of DMus on 9 July 1731. He was organist of St Michael's, Coventry, from 1733 to 1749 and of Warwick parish church from 1719 to 1744. This is all that can be asserted positively about him. It is possible that he was the Mr Dean who contributed the 'Allmand by Mr Dean' in *The Second Part of the Division Violin* (1705), and he was almost certainly the violinist who played in several London concerts in 1709 and 1710. A Thomas Deane of Worcester wrote incidental music for Oldmixon's *The Governor of Cyprus* (1703). Whether there were one, two, or three Thomas Dean(e)s active as musicians in the early eighteenth century now seems impossible to ascertain.

W. B. SQUIRE, *rev.* K. D. REYNOLDS

Sources W. Shaw, 'Deane, Thomas', *New Grove* • Foster, *Alum. Oxon.* • W. H. Husk, 'Deane, Thomas', Grove, *Dict. mus.* (1927) • J. Hawkins, *A general history of the science and practice of music*, 5 vols. (1776) • Burney, *Hist. mus.*

Deane, Sir Thomas (1792–1871), builder and architect, was born on 4 June 1792 in Cork, the eldest of the eight surviving children of Alexander Deane (1759/60–1806), builder, and his wife, Elizabeth (*d.* 1828), daughter of Thomas and Elizabeth Sharpe, also of Cork. The Deanes, who had come originally from Scotland, had been involved in the building trade in Cork for several generations. After his father's death in 1806, aged forty-six, his mother took over the business and Deane, who was reputedly self-educated, joined her while still in his teens. In 1809 he married Catherine Connellan, with whom he had two children, John Connellan (1815–1887), assistant secretary to the Dublin Exhibition of 1853 and secretary to the Manchester art treasures exhibition of 1857, and Julia (*d.* 1863).

In 1811 Deane designed the Cork Commercial Buildings in South Mall, won in competition against William Wilkins of London. This had a competent, if unexciting, palace façade in the Regency style. He arranged the education of his siblings, training his brothers Alexander (1796–1847) and Kearns (1804–1847) as architects and sending them to London to study under the drawing master Alfred Nicholson. Kearns, who was particularly talented, designed the Dominican church of St Mary, Pope's Quay, Cork (1832–9). He probably also played a major role in the design of Dromore Castle, near Kenmare, co. Kerry, built by the Deane company in 1831–8. He was jointly responsible for a number of designs with Thomas, including Horsehead, Passage West (1836–7), and Frankfield Chapel, Cork (1838), both in the Gothic style, and the neo-classical Cork Savings Bank on Warren Place (1839–42). The latter superseded Thomas's earlier savings bank on Pembroke Street (1824). Thomas also designed his own residence, Dundanion Castle (1832), the Bank of Ireland in Cork (1838–40; dem.), and the Limerick Savings Bank (1839; executed by W. H. Owen, engineer).

Following the death of his first wife, Deane married, on 13 January 1827, Elizabeth (Eliza) O'Callaghan Newenham (*d.* 1851), with whom he had three children, Sir Thomas Newenham *Deane (1828–1899), who was to join the practice, Susanna, and Olivia. In 1830 he was knighted by the lord lieutenant during his second term in office as high sheriff of Cork. He represented tory merchant interests on the corporation, which seems to have effectively excluded him from architectural practice in the surrounding whig-controlled county. Much of this business went instead to the brothers James and George Richard Pain, to whom the Deanes lost the commission (which they had won in competition) for the city and county court house in Cork (built 1830–35). While Deane's public persona was ebullient (one contemporary described him as a 'ceaseless chatterbox'), he was watchful of professional and political rivals and was ever ready to seize his opportunity. He was also prone to self-doubt, seeking reassurance from friends for his actions.

In addition to his business and political interests, Deane was one of the founders, in 1816, of the Cork Society for the Promotion of the Fine Arts. His protégés included the sculptors John Hogan and Edward Ambrose, and the painter Samuel Forde. Deane's collections included geological specimens, carved marbles from Baalbek and Palmyra, and James Cavanah Murphy's survey drawings of the great Gothic monastery at Batalha in Portugal.

In December 1845 the board of works commissioned Deane to design the new Queen's College, Cork. Firm designs were not, however, prepared until after the board had agreed the following April to purchase a site at Gill Abbey, recommended by Deane for its 'excellent and commanding' situation. Kearns Deane, who was in declining health and died in January 1847, may have had some involvement with the design, which was in the Perpendicular Gothic style. However, much of the credit was due to Deane's new assistant Benjamin Woodward (1816–1861), who joined the practice some time in the first half of 1846.

In April 1847 Deane was awarded a further board of works commission, a new district lunatic asylum at Killarney. The elevations, in the Early English style and much influenced by A. W. N. Pugin, were probably Woodward's, but the planning, which owes much to the writings of Dr John Conolly of Hanwell, was probably largely dictated by the board. The building was opened at the end of 1852.

After the death of his second wife, from breast cancer, in June 1851, Deane fell victim for a time to recurring bouts of depression. The practice was reconstituted with Deane, his son Thomas Newenham Deane (who had graduated from Trinity College, Dublin, in 1849), and Woodward as partners. In the earliest known design of the partnership, an unplaced entry in the Belgic–Gothic style for the Cork town hall competition of 1851, can be seen the origins of their best-known building, the University Museum at Oxford (1854–60). Deane was one of the instigators of the Irish National Exhibition, Cork's answer to the Crystal Palace, which opened in June 1852: his portrait by James Butler Brenan, which was displayed at the exhibition, is now in the collection of the Royal Hibernian Academy. A slightly later lithographic portrait is in the Royal Institute

of the Architects of Ireland. Deane was somewhat stocky in appearance, with striking features and a receding hairline.

In August 1852 Deane and Woodward were invited to submit a design for the new museum building at Trinity College, Dublin, in a limited competition. Following the submission of the working drawings in October 1853, Deane made arrangements to take over the lease of a house on Upper Merrion Street, Dublin, which would serve as both an office and a residence for his son (now married with two children). Deane remarried on 16 November 1853 (in Manchester) and effectively went into semi-retirement, remaining in Cork until 1860. He and his third wife, Harriet Williams (*c.*1814–1881), had one child, Hermann Frederick (1858–1921), later an ordained minister and librarian and chapter clerk of St George's Chapel, Windsor.

While the partnership of Deane and Woodward continued until Woodward's death from tuberculosis in May 1861, there is little evidence that Sir Thomas played any significant role in the design of the buildings that made them famous: the Trinity Museum building (1853–7); the University Museum at Oxford; the Oxford Union (1856–7), decorated by the Pre-Raphaelites; the Kildare Street Club in Dublin (1858–61); and the highly placed competition entry for the government offices in Whitehall (1857). At the Trinity Museum, where they were tied to the plans of the college architect, John McCurdy, the Ruskin-inspired elevations in the Venetian cinquecento style and the use of naturalistic carving can be ascribed to Woodward. The minutes and archives of the University Museum, Oxford, indicate that while Deane attended some early meetings, Woodward was in charge of both the design and execution. When questioned on the matter in 1855, Ruskin wrote: 'Mr. Woodward is, as far as I am concerned, the acting man … I see Woodward and tell him what I want and if [Sir Thomas] Deane does it I am much obliged to him' (*Works of John Ruskin*, 16.xlvi). The main contract was substantially complete by the time Woodward's declining health forced him to spend periods abroad. While Thomas Newenham Deane played an increasing role in running the practice from this time, Woodward managed to continue designing, and can be credited with the bulk of the smaller commissions also, such as houses and schools. Sir Thomas Deane's connections remained useful in securing work and his friendship with the Acland family seems to have been a factor in their entering (and winning) the University Museum competition at Oxford.

Sir Thomas assisted in the revival of the Royal Institute of the Architects of Ireland in 1863: he was elected president in 1868 but offered his resignation at the end of the year on account of advanced age and ill health. In 1860 he was one of the first architects to be admitted to membership of the Royal Hibernian Academy under a new charter and served as its president in 1866–8. He died in his house, 26 Longford Terrace, Monkstown, co. Dublin, on 2 October 1871, at the age of seventy-nine, leaving an estate of almost £14,000, large by Irish standards. He was buried in St Michael's churchyard, Blackrock, co. Cork. Thomas

Newenham Deane continued to run the practice up until his death in 1899, having been joined by his own son Thomas Manly Deane in 1878; both were knighted for their services to the profession.

FREDERICK O'DWYER

Sources F. O'Dwyer, *The architecture of Deane and Woodward* (1997) · E. Blau, *Ruskinian Gothic: the architecture of Deane and Woodward, 1845–61* (1982) · 'Interview with (Sir) Thomas Manly Deane', *Irish Builder*, 43 (1901), 633–5 · 'Interview with Sir Thomas Manly Deane', *Irish Builder*, 43 (1901), 643 · J. C. [J. Coleman], *Journal of the Cork Historical and Archaeological Society*, 2nd ser., 21 (1915), 180–86 · *The works of John Ruskin*, ed. E. T. Cook and A. Wedderburn, library edn, 39 vols. (1903–12) · F. O'Dwyer and J. Williams, 'Benjamin Woodward', *Victorian Dublin*, ed. T. Kennedy (1980), 38–63 · E. Blau, 'The earliest work of Deane and Woodward', *Architectura*, 9/2 (1979), 170–92 · H. W. Acland and J. Ruskin, *The Oxford museum*, rev. edn (1893) · T. Garnham, *The Oxford Museum* (1992) · W. Tuckwell, *Reminiscences of Oxford* (1900); repr. (1901) · *CGPLA Ire.* (1871) · *DNB* · private information (2004)
Archives Bodl. Oxf., Acland MSS, drawings, minute books, and corresp. concerning the University Museum · City Library, Cork, corresp. with Crofton Croker
Likenesses J. B. Brenan, oils, *c*.1852, Royal Hibernian Academy, Dublin · photo-lithograph, *c*.1855, Royal Institute of the Architects of Ireland, Dublin · Hanlon, engraving, repro. in *Dublin Builder* (15 March 1863), 49
Wealth at death under £14,000: probate, 3 Nov 1871, *CGPLA Ire.*

Deane, Sir Thomas Newenham (1828–1899), architect, was born at Dundanion, near Cork, on 15 June 1828. He was the son of Sir Thomas *Deane (1792–1871), architect, and his second wife, Elizabeth O'Callaghan (*d*. 1851), daughter of Robert O'Callaghan Newenham and granddaughter of Sir Edward Newenham, politician. Deane was educated at Rugby School and at Trinity College, Dublin, graduating BA in 1849. He received his early professional training from his father, whose firm he joined in 1850, and was thus concerned in the important buildings carried out at Oxford and elsewhere between 1850 and 1860, largely designed by his father's other partner, Benjamin Woodward. On 29 January 1850 he married Henrietta, daughter of Joseph H. Manly of Ferney, co. Cork; they had several children. On the death of his father in 1871 Deane became the sole member of the firm, Woodward having died in 1861. His work in the 1860s and 1870s included St Mary's Church of Ireland Cathedral at Tuam, co. Galway (1861–78), the restoration of St Canice's Church of Ireland Cathedral, Kilkenny (1864–70), and a number of important additions to Dublin architecture, of which St Ann's Church in Dawson Street (1867) and the Munster and Leinster Bank in Dame Street (1872–4) are perhaps the chief. He also designed the Clarendon Laboratory (1869) and the Meadow Buildings at Christ Church, Oxford (1862–4). In a number of these works he continued the earlier firm's allegiance to the Venetian style. In 1878 he was joined in his practice by his eldest son, Thomas Manly Deane (1850–1933), with whom he remained in partnership until his death. Together with his son he was responsible for such notable buildings as the town hall at Bray, co. Wicklow (1882), and the McArthur Hall at Methodist College, Belfast (1887–91), but unquestionably the work for which Deane will be best remembered is the Science

and Art Museum (known as the National Museum) and National Library of Ireland in Dublin. The result of a public competition, it was begun in 1885, the foundation stone being laid by the prince of Wales (afterwards Edward VII), and it was completed in 1890. At the opening Deane was knighted by the lord lieutenant of Ireland, the earl of Zetland. This work was followed by important additions to the Natural History Museum and the National Gallery of Ireland, and by the building of the Royal Dublin Society's lecture theatre, all of these forming part of the group of buildings of which the eighteenth-century Leinster House (now the seat of the Irish parliament) is the centre. The sustained repute of the firm was shown by its winning second place in the competition for the Imperial Institute at South Kensington, London, and by the submission of its name by the Royal Institute of British Architects to the commissioners of works for selection for the new government buildings in Whitehall and Parliament Street, London.

Deane was keenly interested in the movement for the preservation of the ancient monuments of Ireland, and was appointed to the post of inspector of national and ancient monuments following the Ancient Monuments Protection Acts of 1882 and 1892. He was also a member of the Royal Hibernian Academy and the Royal Institute of the Architects of Ireland. Deane was described by a contemporary as a man of a light and elastic temperament and social disposition, and enjoyed a wide popularity in Dublin. He died suddenly at 37 Stephen's Green, Dublin, on 8 November 1899. After his death his practice was continued by his eldest son, Thomas Manly Deane.

Thomas Manly Deane was born in 1850 at Ferney, co. Cork. He was a pupil of William Burges ARA (1827–1881), of London, and also studied at the Slade School, London, and later in France and Italy. He gained the Royal Academy travelling scholarship in 1876. After his father's death he was joint architect, with Sir Aston Webb RA (1849–1930) of London, for the College of Science and government offices in Dublin (1903–11), and on their opening in 1911 he was knighted by George V. He was a member of the Royal Hibernian Academy but did not join any architectural institutes or societies. Affected by failing eyesight he retired to Wales where he died in 1933.

C. L. FALKINER, rev. PAUL LARMOUR

Sources *Irish Builder*, 41 (1899), 180 · *Irish Builder*, 41 (1899), 196–7 · 'Interview with (Sir) Thomas Manly Deane', *Irish Builder*, 43 (1901), 633–5 · 'Interview with Sir Thomas Manly Deane', *Irish Builder*, 43 (1901), 643 · E. Blau, *Ruskinian Gothic: the architecture of Deane and Woodward, 1845–61* (1982) · F. O'Dwyer, *The architecture of Deane and Woodward* (1997) · M. J. McDermott, 'The Deanes: an Irish architectural dynasty', *RIAI Yearbook* (1975–6) · *CGPLA Eng. & Wales* (1900) · register of deaths, Dublin (district no. 4)
Likenesses J. Hughes, bronze bust (posthumous), NG Ire. · photograph, repro. in Blau, *Ruskinian Gothic*
Wealth at death £873 9*s*. 8*d*. (in England): Irish probate sealed in England, 3 Feb 1900, *CGPLA Eng. & Wales*

Deane, William John (1823–1895), Church of England clergyman and biblical scholar, born on 6 October 1823, was the third son of John Deane of Lymington in Hampshire. After attending Rugby School he matriculated from

Oriel College, Oxford, on 20 October 1843, graduating BA in 1847 and MA in 1872. He was ordained deacon in 1847 and priest in 1849. He was successively curate of Rugby (1847–9), curate of Wick Rissington in Gloucestershire (1849–52), and rector of South Thoresby in Lincolnshire (1852–3). In 1853 he was presented by the chancellor of the duchy of Lancaster to the rectory of Ashen in Essex, which he retained until his death.

Deane was the author of a number of exegetical works, written in a clear and interesting manner. In 1881 he edited the Greek, Latin, and English texts of the Wisdom of Solomon for the Clarendon Press, Oxford, with critical notes, and in 1891 he published *Pseudepigrapha*, a well-written description and estimate of the apocryphal books. He also published biographies of the prophets in the Men of the Bible series and introductions to Old Testament books in the Pulpit Commentary. He was a frequent contributor to *The Thinker*, and published on holy days (1850 and 1864), also editing a volume entitled *Lyon sanctorum* (1850). He died at Ashen rectory on 30 May 1895, leaving a widow, three sons, and three daughters. He was buried on 4 June in Ashen churchyard, under the east window of the chancel.   E. I. CARLYLE, *rev.* H. C. G. MATTHEW

Sources *Suffolk and Essex Free Press* (5 June 1895) • Crockford (1895) • Foster, *Alum. Oxon.* • *CGPLA Eng. & Wales* (1895) • P. Schaff and S. M. Jackson, *Encyclopedia of living divines and Christian workers of all denominations in Europe and America: being a supplement to Schaff-Herzog encyclopedia of religious knowledge* (1887)

Wealth at death £192 13s. 6d.: probate, 21 June 1895, *CGPLA Eng. & Wales*

Deane, William Wood (1825–1873), architect and painter, was born on 3 or 22 March 1825, in Liverpool Road, Islington, London, the third son of John Wood Deane, a bank cashier and painter, and his wife, Anna Maria, *née* Glasse (1784–1859), whose father had been mayor of Barnstaple. He attended the Islington proprietary school until 1842, and won prizes for mathematics, perspective, and French. He showed an early taste for drawing, but as his elder brother Dennis had become an artist, his father determined to make him an architect. On 7 September 1842 he was articled to Herbert Williams, a surveyor. On 13 January 1844 he became an architectural student of the Royal Academy, and in December 1844 he won the academy's silver medal. He continued to exhibit both designs and, later, drawings at the Royal Academy throughout his life. On 21 July 1845 he was awarded the students' book prize for a design at the Institute of British Architects. After completing his articles, in 1846, he became an assistant to David Mocatta (1806–1882) for a short time. He became an associate of the Institute of British Architects in 1848.

In 1844 or thereabouts Deane became involved with private theatricals, and played at Frances Kelly's Royal Soho Theatre at 73 Dean Street, Soho (afterwards the Royalty; dem. 1954), which he subsequently decorated. In 1850 he went to Italy with his brother Dennis and while in Rome became a friend of the painter George H. Mason ARA. He returned to London in late 1851 with his folios full of measured drawings and watercolour sketches. He gave lessons in watercolour drawing to young architects, and started

practising as an architect in partnership with Alfred Bailey, a surveyor, at 13 Great James Street, Bedford Row. Though the partnership broke up in 1855, Deane's early work, including Langham Chambers, showed great promise. He abandoned architecture in 1857, however, for drawing on wood, and making designs and perspectives for architects. He married Ellen Maria, sister of the architect George *Aitchison, who later became president of the Royal Institute of British Architects and acted as Deane's executor.

Deane spent most of his summers sketching in the country: he travelled in 1856 to Normandy, in 1857 to Belgium, and in 1859 to Whitby. On his mother's death in September 1859 he inherited a small sum of money, and determined to devote himself to painting. He moved to 17 Maitland Park Terrace, Haverstock Hill, in 1860, and spent a good part of the year sketching in Cumberland. He was elected an associate of the Institute of Painters in Water Colours in 1862, and became a member in 1867. He also exhibited at the Royal Academy and at the Dudley Gallery, Worcestershire.

In May 1865 Deane left for Venice, intending to settle in Italy, but he returned in October of the same year, and went to live at 64 King Henry's Road, Primrose Hill, London. His watercolours of *The Rialto* and *The Interior of Sta Maria dei Miracoli* showed greater technical ability than his previous sketches. In 1866 he travelled in Spain with the watercolourist Francis William Topham. The oriental character of Spain seems to have acted as a spur to his powers; his drawing of *The Gates of the Alhambra* was one of his most brilliant works. *The Fair at Seville*, with its lines of tents, clouds of dust, and picturesque horsemen, and his *Bull Ring at Seville*, with its brutal crowd in the shade, and the blazing sunshine in the arena, raised his art from the tranquil portraiture of stately buildings and a pearly atmosphere to a higher and more imaginative level. Every year he went to France, Germany, or Italy, and made elaborate studies of the subjects he meant to paint. His drawings were mainly of architectural subjects, and were distinguished by the purity of their colour, their pearly greys, and the effects of sunlight, though he is sometimes considered to have been over-lavish in his use of bodycolour. Among his fellow artists he was called an impressionist.

In 1870 Deane was elected an associate of the Society of Painters in Water Colours. In the autumn of that year poor health caused him to visit Scotland, though in 1871 he still managed to produce drawings of *Sta Maria della Salute*, *Jedburgh Abbey*, and *The North Porch of Chartres*. In 1872 he went to Florence, Verona, and Perugia, and made a beautiful drawing of the basilica of S. Miniato, which was not exhibited until after his death. In 1873 he was posthumously awarded a medal at the Vienna exhibition for *The Bull Ring at Seville*. Examples of his work may be seen in the British Museum, the Victoria and Albert Museum, and the Wakefield Art Gallery, Yorkshire.

Deane died at the age of forty-seven at his home, 64 King Henry's Road, Primrose Hill, on 18 January 1873 of cancer of the liver, and was buried at Kensal Green cemetery.

GEORGE AITCHISON, *rev.* JOHN ELLIOTT

Sources *The Builder*, 31 (1873), 62 · *Dir. Brit. archs.* · Mallalieu, *Watercolour artists* · IGI · J. Johnson, ed., *Works exhibited at the Royal Society of British Artists, 1824–1893, and the New English Art Club, 1888–1917*, 2 vols. (1975) · will, proved 17 March 1873, London · d. cert. **Archives** RIBA, drawing collection · RIBA, nomination papers **Likenesses** woodcut, BM **Wealth at death** under £2000: administration with will, 17 March 1873, *CGPLA Eng. & Wales*

Dearden [*formerly* Dear], **Basil Clive** (1911–1971), film director, was born on 1 January 1911 at St Drostane, Woodfield Road, Southend, Essex, the son of Charles Dear, electrical engineer, and his wife, Dorothy Tripp. He was one of six children brought up in considerable hardship by their mother, following the death of their father at sea during the First World War. Although Basil was sent to work as an office boy with a London insurance firm at an early age, he eventually followed three of his siblings into the theatre. His initial stage experience had been gained during holidays in walk-on parts with the Ben Greet Company, and his theatrical career properly began when he joined the Grand Theatre, Fulham, London, as an assistant stage manager. Back with the Ben Greet troupe he combined acting and administrative roles during its Shakespearian tour of the United States. In 1932 he became production manager for the various theatrical enterprises of impresario Basil Dean, and it was then that he extended his name from Dear to Dearden to avoid confusion with his employer. Dearden's attention switched to cinema in 1937 when he went to work with Dean, who was head of studio at Ealing Studios (having founded Associated Talking Pictures there in 1929). Demonstrating his versatility, Dearden fulfilled numerous functions at the studio: as writer, dialogue director, assistant director, associate producer, and, ultimately, director. By 1938 he was working with Ealing's top comedy stars, co-scripting and producing for George Formby (*Come on George!*, 1939; *Turned out Nice Again*, 1941), and later co-directing with Will Hay (*The Black Sheep of Whitehall*, 1941; *The Goose Steps Out*, 1942). In that year Dean was replaced by Michael Balcon as studio head and the company entered into its most celebrated period of film-making. Dearden married an actress, Melissa Stribling (1927–1992), who appeared in four of his films. They had two sons.

It is well established that Ealing made a distinctive and significant contribution to British cinema during the Second World War, and, as Professor Richards argues, the studio 'found its soul in the concept of "the People's War"' (Burton, O'Sullivan, and Wells, 14). Through such films as *The Foreman Went to France* (1942), *Went the Day Well?* (1943), and *San Demetrio London* (1943), the classic Ealing preoccupations with tolerance, decency, restraint, service, and duty were dramatized within realistic, everyday settings; it was the moment when the people collectively became the heroes of 'their' British films.

Dearden's first work as sole director was a celebration of the wartime Auxiliary Fire Service, *The Bells Go Down* (1943). In this production he worked for the first time with art director Michael Relph, with whom he formed a significant film-making team at Ealing and beyond. Relph continued to supervise art direction on all of Dearden's wartime

Basil Clive Dearden (1911–1971), by unknown photographer

films, and with Ealing's first post-war feature, the prisoner-of-war drama *The Captive Heart* (1946), the duo's characteristic separation of responsibilities emerged: Dearden worked as director and Relph as associate producer, sometimes additionally serving as production designer. Dearden's characteristic thematic concerns evolved out of Ealing Studios' commitment to promoting the 'people's war', and were encompassed within a broadly liberal outlook. Commencing with his wartime films there emerged a consistent faith in this organic notion of society, composed of shared values, traditions, and experience. In addition, the narratives favoured the virtues of public service and civic responsibility, wherein a range of collective heroes struggled tirelessly on behalf of the fire service (*The Bells Go Down*), the police (*The Blue Lamp*, 1950), the probation service (*I Believe in You*, 1952), and juvenile liaison agencies (*Violent Playground*, 1957). Dearden's two remaining wartime features brought these ideals into clarity: *The Halfway House* (1944) charted the redemption of a varied group of disillusioned individuals—black marketeers, embezzlers, estranged couples, an Irish nationalist, and a terminally ill musician—who all rediscover their self-worth and have their faith rekindled in the nation's fight; and *They Came to a City* (1944), a straightforward adaptation of J. B. Priestley's utopian stage play, was a remarkable and uncommercial distillation of such themes as social reconstruction and egalitarianism, effectively portraying comradeship, equality, and decency.

Ealing's most prolific film-makers, Dearden and Relph were given responsibility for Ealing's first Technicolor film, *Saraband for Dead Lovers* (1948), for which top British star Stewart Granger was loaned from Gainsborough. This won Relph an Academy award nomination for art direction. They did not undertake any of the classic comedies for which Ealing Studios became so renowned. Their association with the 'low comedy' of the Formby and Hay years unfortunately partly contributed to a critical downgrading of their film-making. Unlike colleagues Robert Hamer and Alexander Mackendrick they were not praised for their creativity. Instead, their most important work from the late 1940s to the early 1960s was a series of social-problem films. These were works dealing with such issues as rapprochement with Germans (*Frieda*, 1947), law and order (*The Blue Lamp*), the criminal justice system (*I Believe in You*—Dearden's own personal favourite among his films), disaffected youth (*Violent Playground*), race (*Sapphire*, 1959), homosexuality (*Victim*, 1961), and religious tolerance (*Life for Ruth*, 1962). Dearden is now largely remembered for these films, and especially for *The Blue Lamp*, the film that both introduced the iconic presence of PC Dixon (played by Jack Warner, and later a character in a long-running television series) and cast a young Dirk Bogarde as a deranged delinquent. The films sensitively examined social problems within a thriller format: the controversial *Victim* thus focused on the unfortunate tendency of Britain's laws dealing with homosexuality to encourage blackmail—'the blackmailer's charter' as one policeman assesses it in the film. The work filtered the 'social problem' of male homosexuality through the crusade of one determined individual—gay barrister Melville Farr, compassionately played by Dirk Bogarde in an important breakthrough role for him—to expose the malicious blackmailers.

Film critics unfortunately felt Dearden's approach evaded the complexity of the social issues under consideration. Thus in both *Sapphire* and *Victim* the evil perpetrator is revealed as a warped, dysfunctional individual, and once they are removed by the concerned forces of law and order, society recovers its rightness. David Thomson, for example, complained about the 'spurious social alertness' of the films (Thomson, 137). Yet cinemagoers found them both interesting and acceptable; in the event the partnership won its share of honours, with both *The Blue Lamp* and *Sapphire* being awarded British Film Academy awards for best picture of the year.

Dearden and Relph also made a range of other types of film. These included commercial melodramas (*Cage of Gold*, 1950; *Out of the Clouds*, 1955); action films, often with a strong moral dimension (*Pool of London*, 1951; *The Ship that Died of Shame*, 1955); and pictures examining the ethics of sports (*The Square Ring*, 1953; *The Rainbow Jacket*, 1954); and, in 1956, they produced the last comedy made at Ealing Studios, *Who Done It!*, a vehicle for radio and television comedian Benny Hill. Following the sale of Ealing Studios to the BBC and the company's relocation to Borehamwood and the MGM group, Dearden and Relph embarked on a successful period as independent producers. Their first feature outside Ealing, *The Smallest Show on Earth* (1957), ironically, was an archetypal 'Ealing style' comedy, pitting a modern, streamlined, commercial venture—the Grand Cinema, Sloughborough—against a modest fleapit, the

Bijou Kinema. In 1959 Dearden and Relph joined with the other noted British film-makers Richard Attenborough, Bryan Forbes, Jack Hawkins, and Guy Green to form Allied Film Makers (AFM), a consortium of independent film producers that distributed through the Rank Organization. AFM's first release was the Dearden–Relph action-comedy *The League of Gentlemen* (1960), a sizeable box-office hit. During the 1960s Dearden directed a number of large-scale international productions: *Woman of Straw* (1964), *Masquerade* (1965), and *Khartoum* (1966) for United Artists; *Only When I Larf* (1968) for Columbia; and *The Assassination Bureau* (1969) for Paramount. Dearden's last works included a number of episodes of the television series *The Persuaders* for Associated Television. His final feature film, *The Man who Haunted Himself* (1970), was somewhat tragically prophetic in its tale of a man who dies in a road crash. On 23 March 1971 Basil Dearden suffered multiple injuries in an accident on the M4 motorway while driving back from Pinewood Studios to his Belgravia home. He was declared dead at Hillingdon Hospital, Hillingdon.

During the 1960s and 1970s film critics attacked Dearden's works as the product of a naïve, liberal sensibility. According to one view, his films were inextricably bound up with a 'middle-class Establishmentarian ethos' (Durgnat, 27). In *Movie* magazine his films were characterized as 'the unambitious excrescences of the British cinema as a whole' (Perkins, 10). Yet the critics overemphasized the significance of his social-problem films and unfairly underestimated his versatility as a film-maker. Dearden worked impressively across a variety of genres and was a film-maker of meticulous professionalism and integrity.   ALAN BURTON

Sources A. Burton, T. O'Sullivan, and P. Wells, eds., *Liberal directions: Basil Dearden and postwar British film culture* (1997) · R. Durgnat, 'Dearden and Relph: two on a tandem', *Films and Filming* (July 1966), 26–33 · J. Caughie and K. Rockett, eds., *The companion to British and Irish cinema* (1996) · D. Thomson, *A biographical dictionary of the cinema*, rev. edn (1980) · V. Perkins, 'The British cinema', *Movie* (May 1962) [repr. in *Movie Reader*, ed. I. Cameron (1972), 7–11] · *CGPLA Eng. & Wales* (1971) · *The Times* (25 March 1971) · b. cert. · d. cert.
Archives FILM BFI NFTVA, documentary footage
Likenesses photograph, 1951, Hult. Arch. · photograph, BFI [*see illus.*]
Wealth at death £23,883: probate, 12 Nov 1971, *CGPLA Eng. & Wales*

Deare, John (1759–1798), sculptor, was born in Liverpool on 26 October 1759, the son of Thomas Deare (*fl.* 1757–1789), a jeweller and artist in hair of Liverpool, and Esther Molyneaux. He was apprenticed in 1776 to Thomas Carter, a successful London carver, particularly of chimney-pieces. The next year he enrolled at the Royal Academy Schools, and in 1780 he won a gold medal for his model on a subject from Milton. After completing his apprenticeship in 1783 he worked freelance, modelling for other sculptors, notably John Bacon (whom he admired), John Cheere, and Carter. His independent commissions included a plaster relief, *The War of Jupiter and the Titans*, for the pediment of Whitton Park, Hounslow (1783), a relief entitled *The Good Samaritan* (after 1782) for the Liverpool

Dispensary designed by the Liverpool architect John Foster, and a fireplace for a Manchester patron for £63. Contemporary artists, especially Joseph Nollekens, admired his skill. The figures manufactured in ceramic by Derby to decorate clocks by Benjamin Vulliamy—Deare's only surviving early work—are dexterously modelled and derive stylistically from Bacon's decorative neo-classicism and the popular *putti* of Duquesnoy.

In 1785 Deare went to Rome on a three-year pension from the Royal Academy; he remained there until his death. Intoxicated by life in that city, he studied and drew with passion the great collections of antique sculpture in the Villa Albani, Capitoline Museum, and elsewhere. Warm-hearted but quick-tempered, he became the leader of a circle which included the painters Robert Fagan, Charles Grignion, and Samuel Woodforde, and the writer George Cumberland. To discharge his obligation as an academy pensioner—to send a work to the annual exhibition—Deare modelled the largest relief undertaken by a British sculptor in the eighteenth century, *The Judgment of Jupiter*. More than twenty figures of different physical types, in various levels of relief, are woven into a composition emulating contemporary history painting. Owing to a dispute with the academy over its size, the plaster was not sent to London. A marble version (1.48 m x 2.97 m) was commissioned in 1788 by Sir Richard Worsley for £470 (Los Angeles County Museum of Art). For the subject of his next relief, *Edward and Eleanor* (1786), Deare looked to James Thomson's play on this British legend and transposed it from medieval Acre to ancient Greece. Eleanor (modelled in high relief) sucks the poison from her husband's wound—a supreme act of wifely devotion—while he (modelled in shallow relief) sleeps. The marble version (1790, priv. coll.), for Sir Corbet Corbet, dazzles the viewer with its virtuoso carving.

In the marble relief *Marine Venus*, purchased in 1787 by Sir Cecil Bisshop for Parham Park, Sussex, a sensuously carved goddess is borne along by an exuberant sea monster; here Deare blends his devotion to the antique with a new enthusiasm for sixteenth-century mannerist sculpture. He evolves this pictorial style further in the marble *Cupid and Psyche* (1791) for Thomas Hope of Deepdene (plaster version, Lyons House, co. Kildare), and especially in *The Landing of Julius Caesar in Britain* (1791–4; Stoke Manor, Stoke Poges, Buckinghamshire) for John Penn, who had chosen the subject.

Although Deare attracted the patronage of collectors buying from adventurous sculptors such as John Flaxman (Thomas Hope and the earl of Bristol) and Antonio Canova (Henry Blundell and John Latouche), his livelihood, when his academy pension expired, depended on a practical approach to his craft. As in London, he combined the roles of artisan and fine artist. Like many of his contemporaries, he and his workshop carved copies of celebrated antiques for British visitors. Prominent among these were his *Apollo Belvedere*, commissioned in 1792 for Attingham by Lord Berwick (for whom he also restored some antiquities), *Faun with a Kid* (Prado Museum, Madrid), acquired by Lord Cloncurry (priv. coll.), and a bust, *Ariadne* (c.1789, now

in the Capitoline Museum, Rome), for John Latouche. Deare continued to make chimneypieces; the prince of Wales purchased one carved stylishly with masks and festoons (Frogmore House, Windsor). Sometimes Deare employed architects such as Joseph Gandy on chimneypiece design. He also carved a small number of portrait busts, including that of John Penn (Eton College).

Deare, who had married at some time before 3 October 1796, died in Rome on 17 August 1798, apparently from a chill caught while sleeping on a block of marble in the hope of inspiration—not out of character for a man who probably belonged to the Adamiani sect, which held that God should be worshipped naked. He was buried within three days in the protestant cemetery, Rome. Friends including Vincenzo Pacetti and Christopher Hewetson organized the disposal of the contents of his studio for the benefit of his Italian wife and children. Having died young without substantial output, Deare was soon almost forgotten. The high esteem in which his contemporaries held him as a designer and carver of reliefs is well deserved.

John Deare's nephew **Joseph Deare** (*bap.* 1803, *d.* 1835), sculptor, was baptized on 27 May 1803 at the church of St Nicholas, Liverpool, the son of Edward Deare, an attorney, and Margaret Wattleworth of Liverpool. He entered the Royal Academy Schools in London in 1822, and won silver medals in 1823 and 1825, and a gold medal in 1825 for his model *David and Goliath*, which he showed at the Royal Academy in 1826 (the model, formerly at the Walker Art Gallery, Liverpool, is now destroyed). He also twice won the silver Isis medal of the Royal Society of Arts, for his model entitled *Bacchus* in 1823 and a relief the following year.

Deare stayed on in London, exhibiting at the Royal Academy in 1826 and from 1828 to 1832, but from about 1833 he worked also in Liverpool. He exhibited portrait busts, often of local celebrities, such as *Dr Stewart Trail*, at the Liverpool Academy in 1832 and 1834, and posthumously in 1836. He died on 5 August 1835 following an accident while climbing a wall to get into his Liverpool studio. The only work certainly by him traced to date is a sketchbook of portrait studies in Liverpool Public Library.

TIMOTHY STEVENS

Sources J. T. Smith, *Nollekens and his times*, 2nd edn, 2 vols. (1829) · P. Fogelman, P. Fusco, and S. Stock, 'John Deare (1759–1798): a British neo-classical sculptor in Rome', *Sculpture Journal*, 4 (2000), 85–126 · G. Cumberland, *Outlines from the antients: exhibiting their principles of composition in figures and basso-relievos taken chiefly from inedited monuments of Greek and Roman sculpture, with an essay by George Cumberland esq.* (1829) · M. D. Myrone, 'Body-building: British historical artists in London and Rome and the remaking of the heroic ideal, *c.*1760–1800', PhD diss., Courtauld Inst., 1998 · Cumberland MSS, BL, Add. MSS · S. C. Hutchison, 'The Royal Academy Schools, 1768–1830', *Walpole Society*, 38 (1960–62), 123–91 · E. Morris and E. Roberts, *The Liverpool Academy and other exhibitions of contemporary art in Liverpool, 1774–1867* (1998) · Farington, *Diary*, 3.669 · *Liverpool Times* (23 Aug 1835) · *DNB* · *IGI* · *The exhibition of the Royal Academy* [exhibition catalogues] · exhibition catalogues, Liverpool Academy · admission records, 1769–, RA · J. A. Picton, *Memorials of Liverpool* (1903)

Archives Liverpool Central Library, sketchbook, H741.91 DEA D 10617 [Joseph Deare] | Liverpool Central Library, album, riq 920 DEA, Eq 801 [Joseph Deare]

Deare, Joseph (*bap.* 1803, *d.* 1835). *See under* Deare, John (1759–1798).

Dearmer, Geoffrey (1893–1996), writer and radio broadcaster, was born on 21 March 1893 at 59 South Lambeth Road, London, the elder son of Percy *Dearmer (1867–1936), Church of England clergyman and liturgist, and his wife, (Jessie) Mabel Pritchard White (1872–1915), children's writer and illustrator, daughter of Surgeon-Major William White.

Dearmer's early years were portrayed by his mother in *The Noisy Years* (1902), a series of sketches based on the sayings and doings of Geoffrey and his brother, Christopher, his junior by exactly a year. Theirs was a happy childhood, especially after the family's circumstances improved following Percy Dearmer's appointment in 1901 as vicar of St Mary's Church, Primrose Hill, London. Between 1907 and 1910 Dearmer was a day boy at Westminster School, and in Michaelmas term 1912 he went up to Christ Church, Oxford, to read English. However, he left in the spring of 1914 without taking a degree having, as he later admitted, enjoyed a life of pleasure too much.

Dearmer enlisted on the outbreak of war, and was commissioned as a second lieutenant in the 2nd battalion (Royal Fusiliers) of the London regiment on 25 September 1914. He survived what his poem 'Mudros, after the Evacuation' called 'the needless horror of the Dardanelles', and later saw action on the Western front. In August 1916 he was transferred to the Army Service Corps, responsible for transporting supplies of ammunition and stores up to the front line. He was mentioned by the secretary of state for valuable war services in August 1919.

Dearmer had been writing poetry since his schooldays, and his war poems revealed a striking poetic talent. They combined a sensitivity to the beauty of the natural world, even in the midst of battle, with an extraordinary optimism founded on his unshakeable religious belief. His trust in God sustained him when he suffered the devastating blows of the deaths in quick succession of his mother and adored younger brother. Mabel Dearmer died from enteric fever at Kragujevac in Serbia in July 1915 while serving as an orderly with an ambulance unit; three months later came the news of Christopher's death at Gallipoli. He had been mortally wounded at Suvla Bay by a shell which had hit his tent and landed almost in his lap. These were losses which cast a shadow over the rest of Dearmer's life.

Dearmer remained in the army until the summer of 1920. After resigning his commission he went to India for a year as tutor to Lord Lytton's younger son, and then returned to England to write, and to work as a reader of play scripts for the theatrical impresario Maurice Browne. Dearmer's *Poems* (1918) had received critical praise on both sides of the Atlantic, and a second collection, *The Day's Delight*, appeared in 1923. During this period he also published several plays, including a historical drama *St Paul* (1929), and two novels, but he was always extremely diffident about the reception of his work, and made little effort to keep his reputation alive. Among his later poems 'The Blue Whale', comic verses written for children, achieved wide recognition when it was set to music by the American entertainer Hoagy Carmichael and performed throughout the world.

As a member of the committee of the Incorporated Stage Society, Dearmer was responsible for getting R. C. Sherriff's trench drama, *Journey's End*, its first West End production. He had threatened to resign if the society did not accept Sherriff's play. The production, starring Laurence Olivier, opened at the Apollo Theatre in December 1928 to immediate acclaim. On the flyleaf of the copy of the play which he presented to Dearmer, Sherriff wrote

Geoffrey Dearmer (1893–1996), by Tim Bishop, 1993

that 'your name is the only one I shall always couple with *Journey's End*'.

From 1936 to 1950 Dearmer worked as assistant examiner of plays in the lord chamberlain's office, authorizing plays for performance, though, as the least censorious of men, he could not recall having ever recommended that a play be banned. At the same time, he was on the staff of the programme division of the BBC, initially assessing church choirs and preachers for their broadcasting potential and then, from 1939 to 1959, as literary editor of BBC radio's *Children's Hour*. He was appointed MVO in 1955.

Dearmer continued to live with his father and his father's second wife, Nancy (Nan), latterly at their home in Little Cloister, Westminster Abbey, where Percy Dearmer was now a canon, until his marriage on 14 March 1936 to Margaret Helen Procter (1898–1980), elder daughter of Sir Henry Procter. They had one child, a daughter, Juliet, who was later ordained as an Anglican clergywoman.

After his wife's death in 1980 Dearmer moved to a flat in sheltered housing at Birchington on the Kent coast. As he approached his hundredth birthday in 1993, plans were afoot for a new edition of his poetry. Laurence Cotterell, a retired publisher, had been astonished to discover that Dearmer was still alive and had started an appeal for funds to publish a representative selection from his war poems and his later work. Helped by a large donation from the novelist Catherine Cookson, *A Pilgrim's Song* (the title was from a hymn by Dearmer which had been included in *100 Hymns for Today*) was published by John Murray in time for Dearmer's centenary, and launched at a party at the Imperial War Museum in London.

One of the most moving of Dearmer's war poems, 'The Turkish Trench Dog', had been widely anthologized over the years, but much of the rest of his verse had fallen into obscurity. The new selection brought him wide and enthusiastic publicity, and he was hailed as the last surviving published poet of the First World War.

Dearmer died at Birchington on 18 August 1996. His ashes were scattered in the garden of his father's old church, St Mary's, Primrose Hill, London.

MARK BOSTRIDGE

Sources G. Dearmer, *A pilgrim's song: selected poems to mark the poet's birthday* (1993) · N. Dearmer, *The life of Percy Dearmer* (1940) · *Daily Telegraph* (28 Aug 1993) · *The Guardian* (20 Aug 1993) · *The Independent* (25 Aug 1993) · *The Times* (20 Aug 1993) · M. Dearmer, *Letters from a field hospital* (1915) · personal knowledge (2004) · private information (2004) · CGPLA Eng. & Wales (1996)
Archives FILM 'The just peace', pt 4 of *The people's century*, BBC TV (1993)
Likenesses photograph, 1916, repro. in Dearmer, *A pilgrim's song* · T. Bishop, photograph, 1993, News International Syndication, London [*see illus.*]
Wealth at death £215,966: probate, 24 Oct 1996, CGPLA Eng. & Wales

Dearmer, Percy (1867–1936), liturgist and historian of Christian worship, was born in London on 27 February 1867, the younger son of Thomas Dearmer (c.1817–1877), artist and drawing master, who died when Percy was ten years old, and his wife, Caroline Miriam Turner (c.1831–1911), who was proprietor and head of Somerset House, a

school for girls in Maida Vale. He was educated at Streatham School, at Westminster School (1880–81), at a private school at Vevey, Switzerland, and at Christ Church, Oxford (1886–9), where he read modern history.

At Christ Church Dearmer came under the influence of the historian F. York Powell and the future bishop of Oxford T. B. Strong. Powell converted him to socialism, Strong to tractarianism. Further Oxford friendships—with James Adderley, Charles Gore, and others—guided these enthusiasms into a coalescence which was Christian socialism. He threw himself into the work of first the Guild of St Matthew and then the Christian Social Union, of the London branch of which he was secretary from 1891 to 1912. But at heart he was an artist; his most creative work revealed this, and his permanent contribution both to the church and to national life is to be found in his profound understanding of the true relation between religion, particularly worship, and art. He saw art as not merely decoration but an essential and integral component of the worship offered to God by the church. No one did more in his time to raise the standards of art in public worship, and he is one of the few clergymen to have been awarded the distinction of the honorary ARIBA.

Dearmer was ordained deacon in 1891 and priest in 1892 at Rochester and after serving four curacies (which ranged from St Anne's, South Lambeth, to Berkeley Chapel, Mayfair), he was appointed in 1901 to the vicarage of St Mary's, Primrose Hill, where he remained until 1915, and there he was able to put his convictions into practice. Leading artists of all kinds gathered round him, including the designer and stained-glass artist Mark Travers, and St Mary's became known throughout the country through his publications and his establishment in 1912 of the Warham Guild for the design and supply of vestments and ornaments of the type recommended in *The Parson's Handbook* (1899, 12th edn 1931). This, his most important book, was an attempt to recall the church to the native English tradition ('the English Use') in matters of liturgy and ceremonial rather than imitating Roman Catholic usages. His involvement in the Alcuin Club (founded 1897) was another means of advocating that distinctive style of church furnishing adopted in numerous Anglican churches in the first half of the twentieth century. He also made vigorous and imaginative efforts to improve the quality of church music, and was largely responsible for editing the *English Hymnal* (1906), *Songs of Praise* (1925), and the *Oxford Book of Carols* (1928) in which he involved Ralph Vaughan Williams, Martin Shaw, and Gustav Holst, which revolutionized congregational hymn singing.

During the First World War Dearmer was chaplain to the British Red Cross ambulance unit in Serbia where his wife, (Jessie) Mabel Pritchard (1872–1915), daughter of Surgeon-Major William White and his wife, Selina, whom he had married on 26 May 1892, died of enteric fever in 1915. She was a novelist and playwright. On 19 August 1916 he married Nancy (Nan; 1889–1979), only daughter of Arthur and Marian Knowles. With his first wife Dearmer had two sons: the younger, Christopher, died of wounds received at Gallipoli in 1915; his elder son, Geoffrey *Dearmer (1893–1996), lived to 103 and was one of the last First World War poets to survive. With his second wife, who survived him, he had one son, Antony, who was killed in action with the RAF in 1943, and two daughters. After the war Dearmer resided in Chelsea and busied himself in manifold activities, the Church of England not seeming able to harness his talents. He was the first professor of ecclesiastical art at King's College, London (1919–36), and was lecturer in art there (1924–32). In 1920 he became secretary of the recently founded League of Arts (he was chairman from 1921 to 1936), and, along with Miss Maude Royden, with whom he worked until 1924, he established the Guildhouse. To the relief of his many friends, to whom his lack of preferment had become a scandal, in 1931 he was nominated to a canonry at Westminster Abbey, where—perhaps too late in life—his gifts had full scope and opportunity. He made a distinctive contribution to the preaching and ceremonial in the abbey and developed remarkable powers as a broadcaster of services for children. Always striking in appearance and highly individual in speech and manner, Dearmer was an original, independent thinker, informed by a thorough scholarship in his own subjects, although in later life he risked this being dissipated by an over-great and sometimes ephemeral output. He died suddenly, of coronary thrombosis, at his residence at 4 Little Cloister, on 29 May 1936, and his ashes were interred in the Great Cloister, Westminster Abbey, on 3 June.

F. R. SOUTHWELL and F. R. BARRY, *rev.* DONALD GRAY

Sources N. Dearmer, *The life of Percy Dearmer* (1941) · D. Gray, *Percy Dearmer: a parson's pilgrimage* (2000) · J. Shefrin, *Dearmerist Mrs Dearmer*, Friends of the Osborne and Lilian H. Smith Collections, occasional paper, 2 (Toronto, 1999) · M. Dearmer, *Letters from a field hospital* (1915) [with a memoir of the author by S. Gwynne] · S. Fletcher, *Maude Royden: a life* (1989) · m. cert. [Jessie White] · m. cert. [Nancy Knowles] · d. cert.
Archives BL OIOC, diary, letters · Church of England Record Centre, London, corresp. and papers · Oxford University Press, corresp. and papers relating to English hymnal · priv. coll., family papers, photographs, letters, newspaper cuttings · St Mary's, Primrose Hill, parish archives, papers, magazines | BL, corresp. with Albert Mansbridge, Add. MS 65255A · BL, corresp. with Society of Authors, Add. MS 56690 · BL, corresp., incl. with Marie Stopes, Add. MS 58549 · LPL, Davidson, Jonkins, Bell papers, letters · U. Edin. L., corresp. with Charles Sarolea
Likenesses D. Rolt, pencil drawing, 1935, repro. in Dearmer, *Life*, frontispiece; priv. coll.
Wealth at death £5685 11s. 7d.: probate, 26 Aug 1936, *CGPLA Eng. & Wales*

Deas, Sir David (1807–1876), naval medical officer, son of Francis Deas (d. 1857), provost of Falkland, Fife, and his wife, Margaret, daughter of David Moyes, was born at Falkland in September 1807. He was educated at Edinburgh high school and the University of Edinburgh, and became a licentiate of the College of Surgeons of Edinburgh in 1827.

Deas entered the Royal Navy on 7 June 1828 as an assistant surgeon. He saw much service, and in July 1836, at the age of twenty-nine, he was promoted to the rank of surgeon. Before his return to Britain in 1842 he took part in the operations on the coast of Syria and at the Cape of Good Hope. He was promoted to the rank of deputy inspector of hospitals and fleets in June 1854, and was on the *Britannia* during the engagement with the sea defences of Sevastopol on 17 October. In March 1855 he was gazetted inspector-general of the Black sea Fleet and served on the *Royal Albert* until the end of the war with Russia. He served with the fleet on the coast of China, and his attention to the sick and wounded at the capture of Canton (Guangzhou) on 28–9 December 1857 was specially mentioned by the commander-in-chief, Michael Seymour (*London Gazette*, 1858, 1024). On his return to Britain Deas was appointed senior inspector-general of Haslar naval hospital, Portsmouth, a post he retained for eight years, in that time instituting many reforms. In July 1860 he married Margaret Hepburn, daughter of William Hepburn. Deas retired from active service in March 1872.

Deas never rose to the position of director-general, despite predictions to the contrary by contemporaries. He was a respected administrator, had a reputation for singleness of purpose, and showed great compassion for the sick and wounded under his charge. In 1856 he was nominated CB, and in 1867 he was promoted to KCB. He was awarded a good-service pension in 1869. Deas held the Syrian medal, the Crimean medal with Sevastopol clasp, and the Turkish medal, was a chevalier of the Légion d'honneur, and wore the order of the Mejidiye of the fourth class. Deas died on 15 January 1876 at 32 Heriot Row, Edinburgh, the home of his brother, Sir George *Deas, and he was buried in the Warriston cemetery, Edinburgh, four days later. He was survived by his wife.

G. C. BOASE, *rev.* CLAIRE E. J. HERRICK

Sources *BMJ* (29 Jan 1876) · *The Lancet* (29 Jan 1876) · *The Times* (17 Jan 1876) · *The Times* (8 Feb 1876) · *Annual Register* (1876) · *ILN* (22 Jan 1876) · J. Shepherd, *The Crimean doctors: a history of the British medical services in the Crimean War*, 2 (1991), 613 · J. J. Keevil, J. L. S. Coulter, and C. Lloyd, *Medicine and the navy, 1200–1900*, 4: *1815–1900* (1963), 148–9 · O'Byrne, *Naval biog. dict.* · *CCI* (1876)
Wealth at death £35,709 7s. 2d.: confirmation, 17 Feb 1876, *CCI*

Deas, Sir George (1804–1887), judge, was born on 7 January 1804 at Falkland in Fife, the eldest son of Francis Deas (d. 1857), provost of Falkland, Fife, and his wife, Margaret, daughter of David Moyes. Sir David *Deas, naval medical officer, was his brother. His initial schooling took place in Falkland and was then carried on in Perth, probably for some time at the Academy. His father was for some time deputy governor of Perth prison and the family then lived within its walls. Deas may also have attended school at Milnathort, Kinross-shire, during an unsuccessful attempt of his father's at farming there. After an early apprenticeship under Charles Gulland, writer, Deas worked initially for a practice in Cupar, and then moved to Edinburgh. In addition to legal work there he attended classes in logic, moral philosophy, and law at Edinburgh University. His work, marked by talent and great effort, was described by Professor Wilson as 'the perfection of clear, vulgar common sense' (*The Scotsman*, 8 Feb 1887) and was rewarded by class prizes and an honorary MA for one essay. Deas was also a member, and in 1831–2 president, of the Speculative Society. In later years he continued as an extraordinary member, taking an active part in the resolution of disputes between the university and the society over its accommodation in the mid-1860s, for example.

Deas was called to the Scottish bar on 10 June 1828 and quickly built up a large practice. He was helped by his thorough practical training and his extensive contacts with agents. He overcame prejudice about his lack of gentility by earning a reputation for delivering results through effort. He was not graceful or eloquent, but persistent and direct, and his shrewdness and plain talk went down well with juries.

On 14 August 1838 Deas married Margaret (b. 1818), daughter of Silvester Reid, writer to the signet. She died in August 1850. On 29 December 1857 Deas married Sarah (1816–1899), daughter of Joseph Outram, merchant of Glasgow, and widow of Sir Benjamin Fonseca Outram CB MD of London, well known in Indian and medical circles. Among his children, Deas's eldest son, Francis, also became an advocate and wrote a work on railway law.

Deas had friends of influence, notably Admiral Erskine Wemyss, MP for Fife, and Edward Ellice the younger, MP for St Andrews burghs. He was appointed an advocate-depute in 1840, a position he held until the Melbourne ministry fell the following year and to which he was reappointed by the Russell administration in 1846. In 1850 he became sheriff of Ross and Cromarty and in 1851 he was made solicitor-general for Scotland under Lord Advocate James Moncreiff, holding this position until the whigs resigned in 1852. As Lord Aberdeen's whig-Peelite coalition tried to achieve a balance in its Scottish appointments, he was passed over for the same position in early 1853, but was appointed to the court of session as a lord ordinary in May of the same year, taking the courtesy title of Lord Deas. In 1854 he was also given responsibility for criminal cases as a lord of justiciary. On 10 February 1858 he was knighted.

It was as a judge that Deas made his mark. He was reputed to be the last on the bench to use the Scots vernacular. The struggles of his early life were one source of an outwardly hard character, spiced with a good sense of comedy. He avoided an abstract, philosophical approach to the law and approached questions from the practical side. Deas was a self-made man, driven by ambition, and this was reflected in his acerbity and impatience, especially with junior counsel. His opinions could be blunt and crushing, as for example in the Cardross case of the late 1850s and early 1860s when he held that the Free Church had no jurisdiction whatsoever, even ecclesiastical. Through his work as a circuit judge and as a result of press coverage he gained a contemporary reputation for being a voluminous authority on Scottish law and an awe-inspiring, hanging judge, especially when working with Glasgow juries. The trial and sentencing to death of Jessie (or Mary) McLachlan for murder in Glasgow in 1862 provided a controversial example of this. Deas was felt to have summed up the evidence very strongly against the accused and otherwise to have managed the trial unfairly. The resulting widespread calls and petitions in favour of a

reprieve were successful in so far as Sir George Grey, the home secretary, decided in favour of an inquiry. This was carried out by George Young (later lord advocate) and resulted in the commutation of the sentence to penal servitude for life. Generally the case raised serious questions regarding the lack of a review procedure for cases heard in the high court of justiciary. Deas's reputation was also coloured by his apparent over-dependence on expert witnesses in medical matters. Such negative opinions were, however, balanced by examples of what he perhaps meant when he said he would be found to have left more poetry than law behind him. In the 1859 Maciver divorce case, for example, he acquitted a woman of all but indiscretion for visiting an old and dying lover.

Deas also earned a reputation for leniency with those who, because of a sudden temptation or violent emotion, made a single lapse into crime. An otherwise respectable background and good looks were said to help also. This attitude extended to those who could prove that they suffered from a mind temporarily weakened, for instance by a history of ill health. A well-known example of this is Deas's handling of the 1867 trial of Dingwall, an alcoholic, possibly epileptic Aberdeenshire laird who had killed his wife on the previous new year's eve. In his directions to the jury, Deas referred to Dingwall's repeated attacks of delirium tremens and advised them that state of mind could be an extenuating circumstance. Such a case did not, in his opinion, warrant acquittal on the grounds of insanity, but the jury could bring in a verdict of culpable homicide, which they then did. A similar case was that of Andrew Granger in 1878, who was also tried for murder, but found guilty, following Deas's directions, of culpable homicide. Deas was careful to point out before sentencing that simple intoxication would not have been sufficient grounds for such a verdict, but that a weak or diseased state of mind at the time of the act had been. Deas's role in these trials eventually took on a significance beyond Scotland when his attitude was referred to much later, and especially in the 1950s, in support of the introduction of a defence of diminished responsibility in murder trials in England.

An isolated figure in later years, Deas was said to have had more enemies than friends, but was noted for the care he invested in relationships with family and relatives. He was awarded the degree of LLD by Edinburgh University in 1884, the tercentenary of the founding of the university. Increasingly hard of hearing and ill, he resigned in February 1885. Deas died at his Edinburgh home, 32 Heriot Row, on 7 February 1887 and was buried on 11 February in the Warriston cemetery, Edinburgh. He was survived by his second wife.

GORDON F. MILLAR

Sources *The Scotsman* (8 Feb 1887) · *The Times* (8 Feb 1887) · *North British Daily Mail* (8 Feb 1887) · *Journal of Jurisprudence*, 31 (1887), 157–9 · F. J. Grant, ed., *The Faculty of Advocates in Scotland, 1532–1943*, Scottish RS, 145 (1944), 53 · S. P. Walker, *The Faculty of Advocates, 1800–1986* (1987), 41 · N. Walker, *Crime and insanity in England*, 1 (1968) · G. H. Gordon, *The criminal law of Scotland* (1978), 403–7 · *Scottish Law Review*, 1 (1885), 33–6 · *Scottish Law Review*, 3 (1887), 80–82 · C. Sutherland and R. Craik, *Parliament House portraits* (2000), no. 91 · *The Scotsman* (11–12 Feb 1887) · G. W. T. Omond, *The lord advocates* of Scotland, second series, 1834–1880 (1914) · [W. M. Watson], ed., *The history of the Speculative Society, 1764–1904* (1905) · IGI · Irving, *Scots.* · DNB

Archives NRA Scotland, priv. coll., corresp. | NL Scot., Cowan MSS, letters relating to his resignation from the bench and his funeral · NL Scot., letters to Edward Ellice the younger · NL Scot., corresp. with Lord Rutherford
Likenesses J. G. Gilbert, oils, 1864, Faculty of Advocates, Parliament Hall, Edinburgh
Wealth at death £100,329 4s. 2d.: confirmation, 6 April 1887, CCI

Dease, Edmund Gerald (1829–1904), landowner and politician, was the second son of Gerald Dease of Turbotston, co. Westmeath, and his wife, Elizabeth, daughter and coheir of Edmund O'Callaghan of Kilgory, co. Clare. He was born into one of the oldest and most prominent Catholic families in co. Westmeath at Turbotston on 6 September 1829. He succeeded to an uncle's estate in the Queen's county in 1856 and was high sheriff for the county in 1859. On 21 June 1859 he married Mary (d. 2 Feb 1918), a daughter of Henry Grattan MP, and granddaughter of the elder Henry *Grattan, the leading figure in the eighteenth-century Irish parliament. They had two sons and three daughters. He was a magistrate and deputy lieutenant of his county.

Dease fits firmly into the Catholic whig tradition of Irish politics. His local prominence and connection with the Liberal interest made him an obvious candidate for parliamentary honours. Upon securing the support of the clergy and Independent (farmers') clubs, he was returned unopposed on 4 January 1870 at the by-election for the Queen's county. As an MP he pledged support for fixity of tenure with equitable adjustment of rentals, amnesty, the secret ballot, and denomination education, then the usual Catholic liberal platform. Like his fellow Catholics, he was disappointed by William Gladstone's abortive Irish university legislation in 1873. Close relations with the Catholic ecclesiastical hierarchy impelled him to accept a place on the council of the Catholic union created in the aftermath of the University Bill. Dease supported the new self-government movement, and attended the national conference in November 1873 which founded the Home Rule League; he was also a member of the council of the league. At the general election of 1874 he stood as a home-ruler and was re-elected to the House of Commons. He was present at the meeting of home-rule MPs on 3 March 1874 that created a separate Irish party. Though a supporter of Isaac Butt until that leader's death in May 1879, Dease never wholly parted company with the Liberals, and continued to hold moderate views, while giving particular attention to tenant-right and education issues. His notable lack of enthusiasm for the more militant nationalism of Charles Stewart Parnell left him increasingly adrift from popular opinion; finding that his candidacy would meet strong opposition, he decided not to stand at the general election of 1880.

Although he never stood again for parliament, Dease continued to take a part in public life, especially local and county affairs. For many years he was a member of the senate of the Royal University (from which he received an honorary MA) and he was also a long-time commissioner of national education in Ireland. He also gave lengthy service to the grand jury, the infirmary, the asylum, and other local boards. He was a member of the board of governors of the Maryborough District Asylum for forty years and its chairman for an extended period. He was also one of the grand jury representatives on the county council created under the Local Government Act of 1898. After becoming interested in the Irish Renaissance, he allowed his grounds to be used for the annual *feis* and assembled a notable collection of materials concerning the Irish Volunteers of the eighteenth century. He was a fine example of the Catholic landed gentleman who, although squeezed out of parliamentary representation because of his moderation, retained the respect of the local community in which he continued throughout his lifetime to hold a prominent place. He died at Rath, Baleybhittas, Queen's county, on 17 July 1904 and his funeral took place in Rath church on 19 July.   ALAN O'DAY

Sources Burke, *Gen. Ire.* · Walford, *County families* · *Leinster Express* (23 July 1904) · *Freeman's Journal* [Dublin] (18 July 1904) · *The Nation* (22 Nov 1873) · *The Nation* (1 Jan 1874) · *The Nation* (6 Jan 1874) · *The Nation* (21 Feb 1874) · *The Nation* (28 Feb 1874) · *Irish Times* (18 July 1904) · E. Larkin, *The Roman Catholic church and the home rule movement in Ireland, 1870–1874* (1990) · E. Larkin, *The Roman Catholic church and the emergence of the modern Irish political system, 1874–1878* (1996) · M. MacDonagh, *The home rule movement* (1920) · D. Thornley, *Isaac Butt and home rule* (1964) · *Dod's Parliamentary Companion* · WWBMP
Archives NL Ire., Isaac Butt MSS · Roman Catholic archdiocese archive, Dublin, Paul Cardinal Cullen MSS
Wealth at death £6173 10s. 3d.: probate, 8 Sept 1904, CGPLA Ire.

Dease, William (c.1752–1798), surgeon, was born at Lisney, co. Cavan, Ireland. He was sent to Dr Clancy's school in Dublin, and afterwards studied medicine in that city and in Paris. He set up in practice in Dublin, and quickly gained repute as a surgeon, holding good hospital appointments. He took an active part in procuring a charter of incorporation for the Dublin surgeons, and became the first professor of surgery in the new college in 1785, and its president in 1789. He had a good practice, and was much esteemed for his virtues. He married Eliza, daughter of Sir Richard Dowdall. Dease wrote *Observations on Wounds of the Head* (1776; much enlarged, 1778), *Different Methods of Treating the Venereal Diseases* (1779), *Radical Cure of Hydrocele, and on Cutting for the Stone* (1782), and *Observations on Midwifery* (1783).

Dease's death in Sackville Street, Dublin, on 21 January 1798, occurred under circumstances which no coroner's inquest would seem to have cleared up. According to one account he had made the mistake of opening an aneurysm in a patient with a fatal result, taking it for an abscess, and was so appalled by his error that he went to his study and opened his own femoral artery; according to another account, he died from an accidental wound of the femoral artery; and by a third account, from the rupture of an aneurysm. In 1812 the Irish College of Surgeons acquired his bust and placed it in the inner hall; in 1886 a statue of him, presented by his grandson, was placed in the principal hall of the college.

CHARLES CREIGHTON, rev. MICHAEL BEVAN

Sources *GM*, 1st ser., 68 (1798), 89 · C. A. Cameron, *History of the Royal College of Surgeons in Ireland* (1886) · W. Dease, *Radical cure* (1798) [incl. memoir]
Likenesses T. Farrell, statue (posthumous), Royal College of Surgeons, Dublin · J. Smyth, bust (posthumous), Royal College of Surgeons, Dublin

Deasy, Rickard (1812–1883), judge, was born at Clonakilty, co. Cork, on 23 December 1812, the second son of Rickard Deasy (1766–1852), of Clonakilty, brewer, and his wife, Mary Anne, *née* Caller (*d.* 1853). He was educated at Trinity College, Dublin, where he graduated BA in 1833, MA in 1847, and LLB and LLD in 1860. He was called to the Irish bar in the autumn of 1835 and quickly acquired a large practice. In 1849 he was made a queen's counsel, and at once became the leader in the equity courts and on the Munster circuit. On winning a by-election in 1855 Deasy became MP for Cork and held his seat until he was promoted to the bench in January 1861. In 1858 he was elected a bencher of King's Inns, Dublin, and became third serjeant-at-law. He was appointed solicitor-general for Ireland in Lord Palmerston's administration in July 1859. In 1860 he succeeded Lord Fitzgerald as attorney-general for Ireland, and was sworn a member of the Irish privy council. His appointment as baron of the court of exchequer after Baron Greene's resignation in 1861 was one of a number of Liberal appointments of Roman Catholics to the bench. Deasy held the post for seven years and was then promoted by the Conservative government to the post of the lord justice of appeal. In 1861 Deasy married Monica (*d.* 1880), younger daughter of Hugh O'Connor of Sackville Street, Dublin; they had three children, Rickard, Henry, and Mary. Both sons were soldiers; and both Rickard and Mary predeceased their father.

Deasy held the post of lord justice of appeal until his death at his home, 41 Merrion Square East, Dublin, on 6 May 1883. He was buried in Dean's Grange cemetery, Dublin. His death was a great blow to the Court of Appeal, as he was an accomplished lawyer, and a patient and impartial judge. Described by Chief Justice Morris as the Bayard of the Irish bench, Deasy is best remembered for pushing through the Landlord and Tenant Law (Amendment) Act (Ireland) of 1860 (otherwise known as Deasy's Act), which codified and regularized the law in Ireland relating to the duties of landlord and tenant.

G. F. R. BARKER, *rev.* SINÉAD AGNEW

Sources Burke, *Gen. Ire.* (1976), 337 · F. E. Ball, *The judges in Ireland, 1221–1921*, 2 vols. (1926) · *Men of the time* (1875) · Ward, *Men of the reign* · J. Wills and F. Wills, *The Irish nation: its history and its biography*, 4 (1875) · J. R. O'Flanagan, *The Munster circuit: tales, trials and traditions* (1880) · *Annual Register* (1853) · *Irish Law Times and Solicitors' Journal* (12 May 1883) · *Law Times* (12 May 1883) · *Freeman's Journal* [Dublin] (7–10 May 1883) · [J. H. Todd], ed., *A catalogue of graduates who have proceeded to degrees in the University of Dublin, from the earliest recorded commencements to … December 16, 1868* (1869) · CGPLA Ire. (1883)
Wealth at death £37,960 6s. 9d.: probate, 19 June 1883, CGPLA Ire. · £7236: probate, 10 July 1883, CGPLA Eng. & Wales

De Baan, Johannes. *See* Baen, Jan de (1633–1702).

Debbieg, Hugh (1731/2–1810), military engineer and army officer, was educated at the Royal Military Academy, Woolwich (1742–6). Nothing is known of his parentage and birthplace. His ability was manifest at an early age, and he advanced rapidly in the Royal Artillery, becoming matross on 1 April 1742, cadet in May 1744, and cadet gunner in April 1745. During September and October 1746 he served as an engineer in the futile expedition against Point L'Orient, then returned briefly to Woolwich for further study. Appointed engineer-extraordinary in Flanders on 30 January 1747, Debbieg won the praise of William Augustus, duke of Cumberland, for the courage he exhibited at Val, on 2 July 1747. On Cumberland's nomination, he then served at Bergen-op-Zoom during the siege that culminated in a French seizure (17 September). On 2 April 1748 he became a practitioner engineer, and after the cessation of hostilities served on a team of engineers that surveyed the former theatre of war. Early in 1749 he returned to Britain, where he played a major role in surveying the military road which, on completion in 1752, linked Newcastle upon Tyne with Carlisle. He was also engaged in preparing a survey of Scotland, a duty which, he later claimed, awakened superiors to his 'Talent for sketching the Face of a Country' (Debbieg, 13). Newly promoted sub-engineer (2 August 1751), he was assigned to surveying defences at Chatham. He acquired a lieutenancy in the 37th foot on 1 September 1756, but did little if any service with the regiment, and after advancing to the rank of captain-lieutenant on 4 January 1758 he sold his commission (11 March 1761). On 14 May 1757 he was promoted lieutenant in the Royal Engineers, then, in quick succession, captain-lieutenant (4 January 1758) and captain (17 March 1759).

The Seven Years' War and aftermath Ordered to America, Debbieg sailed for Halifax, arriving on 9 May 1758. During the siege of Louisbourg (11 June to 26 July) he served as assistant quartermaster-general under Major-General James Wolfe, continuing in that position throughout the campaign of 1759, except for a brief period when he relinquished it in order to take up duties as an engineer. He participated in the battles of Montmorency (31 July 1759) and the Plains of Abraham (13 September). Debbieg appears to have been with Wolfe when he died, and was so depicted in Benjamin West's *The Death of Wolfe*. During the winter of 1759–60 he remained at Quebec, and he was present at the battle of Sillery (28 April 1760). After the subsequent siege of Quebec (raised on 17 May) and brief service in Boston and Louisbourg, he spent most of the next two years in Halifax, directing the construction of new defensive works. When the French seized Newfoundland during the summer of 1762, he participated in the successful counter-attack, winning praise for his contributions and valour.

Debbieg remained at St John's in 1762–3, supervising work on the defences. On returning to Britain he married Jane (or Janet) Seton (*d.* 1801) in Edinburgh (27 March 1763). His wife may have been a Scottish Presbyterian—as Debbieg may also have been—and their second and third sons, Henry and Hugh, were baptized at Swallow Street Scotch Church, Westminster, on 13 October 1767 and 13 February

1769 respectively. When and where their eldest son, Clement, was baptized is unknown.

Debbieg returned to Newfoundland in 1766, this time as chief engineer, arriving at St John's on 20 August. The following February he submitted an account of the harbours in Newfoundland, and in May he reported to Granby on the condition of the barracks at St John's. His reputation was now sufficient to win him offers of high positions from both the East India Company and Venice. Instead of accepting either offer, he undertook in June 1767, at the request of Richard, fourth Viscount Howe, a secret mission to study harbour defences in France and Spain. Although as he toured he was the object of suspicion, at times confined and ill-treated, he completed the mission, returning to England in March 1768. He subsequently provided the government with plans of Marseilles, Cartagena, Corunna, and Cadiz, as well as with extensive evaluations of the defences of these and other ports. During his travels Debbieg had noted that defences at Gibraltar were weak, and in 1769 he served on a committee of engineers which advised on improving them.

In March 1769, at the instance of his patron, Granby, Debbieg was rewarded for his secret mission with a lifetime pension of £1 per diem. On 23 July 1772 he was breveted major. He expected more, however, and initially directed his anger at Howe, who he claimed had not only failed to provide adequate recompense for his mission but also reneged on a promise, made in November 1770, to win him a brevet as lieutenant-colonel. Furthermore, while on his mission Debbieg was supplanted as senior engineer in North America by an officer who was his junior in service. This switch, which he considered 'almost Petrifying' (Debbieg, 15), he likewise blamed on Howe, claiming the latter had promised that the position would be held for him during the mission.

Political crises in North America and Great Britain Late in 1775 Debbieg was offered a position in America, but he refused to serve under his junior and was incensed by word that his pay while on the service would be cut sharply. At the instance of Sir Guy Carleton, Debbieg was in December 1775 appointed chief engineer in Canada, but he again declined, explaining in a cryptic letter that he had been prevented from going by 'one higher than himself' (Debbieg file, Society of Genealogists). On 29 August 1777 he was breveted lieutenant-colonel, and in May 1778 appointed chief engineer on the staff of Lord Amherst, who had come to know him well when both served in America. By a second appointment (17 March 1778), Debbieg became chief engineer at Chatham, and during the next few years he oversaw improvements to the defences there and elsewhere. He also designed several military bridges and invented an improved pontoon and machinery to defend a breach.

During the Gordon riots of June 1780 Debbieg, on Amherst's orders, organized and participated in the defence of public buildings of London. Twice rioters attacked the Bank of England, and although they were repulsed he later advised the bank on security measures. He also became alarmed at how easily the London water supply could be sabotaged, and recommended safeguards. Both schemes, however, were costly, so neither was pursued. Nevertheless, Debbieg's promotions continued: major and sub-director of the Royal Engineers on 24 January 1781, and colonel on 20 November 1782.

Although Debbieg continued to advance, it was not because he ingratiated himself with those in power. Toward his subordinates he tended to be solicitous. While at Chatham he employed a young recruit, William Cobbett, as his clerk, and instilled in him the importance of reading and grammar. He also strove to protect bargemen on his crew from being pressed for naval duty. His relationship with superiors, however, was often contentious. Bitter towards Howe for the alleged wrongs already noted, he also attacked Lord George Germain in several letters (1775–6), claiming that the latter was duplicitous and was not adequately supporting him in his quest for promotion and preferment. At Chatham he feuded with the commanding officer. A few men in high positions, notably Amherst, may have regarded him with affection, but in general he appealed through his ability, not his personality. A contemporary reported that during the American War of Independence Debbieg 'differed with the ministers … as to their system of conducting their military operations, yet he was consulted by them on many occasions' (GM, 595). Debbieg was aware of his reputation within the high command. In a letter to William Pitt, he acknowledged that he was widely seen as 'a Discordant Spirit', while insisting that in fact he was one:

Whom not the D—l himself can Drive
But Led, the Gentlest thing alive.
(PRO, 30/8/129/1, fol. 8)

Feud with Richmond and quarrel with Pitt Debbieg's fortunes turned when Charles Lennox, third duke of Richmond, became master-general of the ordnance in March 1782. The two men had been at odds since the mid-1770s, and their relationship worsened in 1784 when Richmond obtained a royal warrant to reduce and reorganize the engineers and cut emoluments of colonels in the regiment. Debbieg responded with an angry letter to the duke, and for his temerity he was court-martialled and reprimanded. He was further angered when Richmond blocked his appointment to a board of officers to advise on home defence, then ignored 'the first Principles of a System of Fortification', a plan for fortifying Britain that had occupied Debbieg during much of the 1780s. In March 1789 Debbieg wrote to the duke in contemptuous terms, comparing him to an 'Architect who built an Elegant Town Hall, and left no room for a Stair-case to ascent to it' and challenging him to initiate another court martial (PRO, 30/8/129/1, fols. 5–6). When Richmond did not respond, Debbieg published the letter. The result was the court martial that he had desired, but the court denied him an opportunity to submit his plan of fortification for its review. For having challenged 'good Order and military Discipline' by attacking Richmond, Debbieg was sentenced to be deprived of rank and pay for six months. This penalty was light, which the king attributed 'to the Opinion entertained by the Court Martial of Colonel Debbieg's former Services and professional Merit' (*Proceedings of a General Court Martial*, 103). Both courts martial were widely publicized; after the second a critic of Richmond commented:

Learn thoughtless *Debbeige*, now no more a youth,
The woes unnumber'd that encompass truth.
(*Criticisms on the Rolliad, Part the Second*, 1790, 24)

Debbieg's feud with Richmond coincided with increasing animosity towards Pitt. In this case the issue was mainly financial. He still believed that he had received less than he deserved for his secret mission of 1767–8, and he had spoken or written to various government officials about obtaining further benefits. His bitterness was compounded when in early 1785 he was threatened with imprisonment for debt. On 22 April of that year Pitt, responding to his petition, communicated to him a promise of an additional stipend, plus, as Debbieg interpreted the letter, future preferment. This briefly mollified Debbieg, but he lost patience, and on 16 January 1788 he complained to Pitt, 'Can any Man believe, Sir, that with the Character which I hope I deservedly hold in the Publick Estimation, I should have accepted £290 pr. Annum in lieu of all further Promotion or advantage?' (PRO, 30/8/129/1, fols. 3–4). He appended a list of 'Final Demands', including: companies for two sons in the army and civil employment for a third, 'full compensation for his Disappointments and Losses during the time he was abroad', a doubling of his annual allowance, and assurance that he would be appointed chief engineer in Britain when the position fell vacant. Pitt responded that he had already been amply rewarded for his services (PRO, 30/8/102, fols. 100–01). For the next few years Debbieg submitted further petitions, lacing them with increasingly personal attacks on the prime minister and threatening to make the matter public, through either publication or parliament. When Pitt was unmoved, Debbieg published some correspondence relevant to the aftermath of his mission of 1767–8 and his difficulties with Germain in 1775–7. He appended notes on his career, highlighting alleged mistreatment, and here he referred to Pitt, but not harshly. This work, *Letters to and from Colonel Debbieg, to Several Great Men* (1790), appears to have been published in a very small printing, and to have attracted little notice.

Debbieg's last years were marked by advancement: he was promoted major-general on 12 October 1793, lieutenant-general on 1 January 1798, and general on 25 September 1803. Each promotion, however, came in association with a cohort, and did not reflect special favour. Debbieg was disappointed at being assigned to the invalid engineers (31 August 1799). On 15 March 1800 his pension was augmented, but this did not satisfy him, and he continued to press Pitt for fuller remuneration. Debbieg died at his residence, 52 Margaret Street, Cavendish Square, London, on 27 May 1810, aged seventy-eight. His wife had died on 23 March 1801; their three sons survived him. He died intestate, and his estate was valued at less than £450, suggesting that his complaints of financial distress had not been exaggerated. PAUL E. KOPPERMAN

Sources H. Debbieg, *Letters to and from Colonel Debbieg, to several great men* (1790) · PRO, Chatham MSS, 30/8 · *Authentic copy of the proceedings of a general court martial, held at the Horse-Guards, ... on Hugh Debbieg, esq. one of the colonels of the corps of royal engineers* (1789) · PRO, Amherst MSS, WO 34 · *DNB* · *GM*, 1st ser., 80 (1810), 595 · Society of Genealogists, Debbieg file [typescript notes] · 'Remarks and observations on several seaports in Spain and France during a journey in those countries in 1767–1768', BL, King's MS 41 · *IGI* · J. Redington and R. A. Roberts, eds., *Calendar of home office papers of the reign of George III*, 4 vols., PRO (1878–99) · T. Hayter, *The army and the crowd in mid-Georgian England* (1978) · *Authentic copy of the proceedings of a general court martial, held at the Horse-Guards ... November 1784* (1784)

Archives New York Historical Society, plans for defence of Isle of Wight in form of letter to William Pitt

Likenesses B. West, oils, 1767, National Gallery of Canada, Ottawa; copy, NPG

Wealth at death under £450: Debbieg file, Society of Genealogists, London

Debenham, Sir Ernest Ridley, first baronet (1865–1952), department store owner, was born on 26 May 1865 at 42 Wigmore Street, Marylebone, London, the son of **Frank Debenham** (1837–1917), silk mercer and draper, and his wife, Emma Folkard Ridley.

Frank Debenham inherited a thriving business in Wigmore Street from his father, William Debenham (*d*. 1863). In addition to expanding retail sales, he also developed a considerable wholesale and export trade. A wholesale millinery department was instituted and a factory opened at Luton, as well as departments devoted to costumes, silks, gloves, ribbons, and tulles. Expansion also took place through the acquisition of a number of specialist retailers and manufacturers of fabrics and draperies. From 1851 the firm was known as Debenham and Freebody, the latter being the maiden name of William's wife, Caroline. In 1900 it became Debenham & Co.

The idea of selling small amounts of fabrics to dressmakers was first introduced by Frank Debenham, and almost all the fashionable dressmakers flocked to his store. By the 1850s Debenhams had become the fashionable fabric business; and many of the dresses and hats for royal garden parties and presentations were supplied by it.

As befitted a fashionable London retailer, Frank and Emma Debenham sent their eldest son Ernest to Marlborough College and Trinity College, Cambridge (1883–6). At the age of twenty-seven Ernest joined the family business and brought with him a fresh perspective to the running of the department store. His time at Cambridge had also given him a wide circle of friends which he used to good effect in his business dealings.

At that time Debenhams was developing a lucrative business in the bulk supply of dresses, a factor which was to give it strong buying power with suppliers. However, competition was increasing among London department stores and Ernest reasoned that if Debenhams was to maintain its position it would be necessary to restructure operations and refurbish the London store. In his quest to achieve these ends he was greatly helped by his friend Frederick Oliver, an extremely able barrister, whom he had met at Cambridge. Debenham persuaded Oliver to

Sir Ernest Ridley Debenham, first baronet (1865–1952), by Lafayette, 1930

join the firm and his rapid grasp of business practice proved invaluable.

Ernest, aided by Frederick Oliver, oversaw a number of significant developments in the fortunes of Debenhams. Two separate limited companies were registered in 1905, as the retail and manufacturing operations were split: Debenhams Ltd was formed to own Debenham and Freebody (retailers), along with Debenham & Co. (wholesalers, manufacturers, and shippers). The London store was rebuilt after the architects William Wallace and James Gibson designed a grand new store in 1906. Frank Debenham was chairman until his retirement in 1912. Ernest then took over, with Oliver as his deputy. Frank Debenham died on 15 January 1917 at 1 Fitzjohn's Avenue, Hampstead, London.

The First World War had great impact on the department store trade, especially the fall in the so-called 'luxury' trade. By 1916 a working relationship was established with another London retailer, Marshall and Snelgrove, with the idea of preserving retail operations in the war economy. Such a relationship was to become a basis for a full merger in 1919 when Marshall and Snelgrove were experiencing financial difficulties. In May 1919 Ernest successfully concluded the merger, arguing that competition between Debenhams and Marshall and Snelgrove had been wasteful. Later that year he also began talks with the eighty-year-old Harvey Nichols store which led to a takeover in 1920. Ernest's final years with Debenhams were marked by increasingly complex financial deals. These culminated with his retirement in 1927 when he sold off the bulk of his shares in the company for over £1.8m, effectively ending the family connections.

Ernest Debenham was a paternalistic chairman whose policies materially benefited the working lives of his employees. The firm had for some time run benevolent societies for staff welfare, and in 1921 it went further and pioneered a low-cost dental service. It also established a school for employees. Ernest enlisted help from the Shop Assistants' Union to encourage his staff to participate in further education, and he also sent female employees to working women's colleges. Sadly, not all his activities were so well judged. His letters to his former employees serving at the front in the First World War are illustrative of his insensitive nature. He wrote informing the men that they would be required to have a medical examination on their return before they could be reinstated for work.

In 1892 Debenham married Cecily, daughter of the ironfounder William Kenrick, and they had three sons and four daughters. The family home in London was a fine house in Addison Road, Kensington. Complete with a grand mosaic dome, this had been designed by his friend Halsey Ricardo. Debenham served on the London county council from 1912 to 1919. Away from business, however, his greatest interest was his farm in Dorset. To this he applied the same tireless energy he gave to his business, developing new methods for the intensive production of milk. He also initiated the method of marketing milk in disposable, sealed cartons.

An alert and receptive businessman, Debenham oversaw the transformation of a fashionable London millinery business into a firm composed of a number of large (and still semi-autonomous) department stores. He made the most of his connections, and was created a baronet in 1931. Sir Ernest died on 25 December 1952 at Moor Lane House, Braintspuddle, Dorset. He was succeeded as baronet by his eldest son, Sir Piers Kenrick Debenham.

GARETH SHAW

Sources M. Corina, *Fine silks and oak counters: Debenhams, 1778–1978* (1978) · *The Times* (29 Dec 1952) · G. Havenhand, *Nation of shopkeepers* (1970) · b. cert. · m. cert. · d. cert. · *CGPLA Eng. & Wales* (1917) [Frank Debenham] · *CGPLA Eng. & Wales* (1953) · B. Lancaster, *The department store: a social history* (1995) · Venn, *Alum. Cant.* · WWW
Likenesses Lafayette, photograph, 1930, NPG [*see illus.*] · photograph, repro. in Corina, *Fine silks*
Wealth at death £88,025 9s. 10d.: probate, 1 April 1953, *CGPLA Eng. & Wales* · £207,931 12s. 1d.—Frank Debenham: probate, 1917

Debenham, Frank (1837–1917). *See under* Debenham, Sir Ernest Ridley, first baronet (1865–1952).

Debenham, Frank (1883–1965), geographer and polar scientist, was born at Bowral, New South Wales, on 26 December 1883, the second son of the Revd John Willmott Debenham, vicar of Bowral and schoolmaster, and his wife, Edith Cleveland. He attended the school run by his father and, after his death in 1898, by his mother, and

Frank Debenham (1883–1965), by Herbert George Ponting, 1911

from there went to the King's School, Parramatta (1900–02), and Sydney University (1902–6) from where he graduated BA in arts. He then taught at Armidale School, before re-entering Sydney University in 1908 and graduating BSc in 1910, having majored in geology. Edgeworth David, who was then professor, had been with Sir Ernest Shackleton in the Antarctic between 1907 and 1909. When Robert Falcon Scott was recruiting for his second (*Terra Nova*) expedition in 1910 he wished to associate Australia with it and, having secured Griffith Taylor in London, when in Sydney asked Debenham to join him.

In the Antarctic Debenham's work, geological and cartographical, was done first (1910–11) on the western side of McMurdo Sound. He visited the Koettlitz glacier, the Ferrar glacier, and other features in the foothills of the Royal Society range. An injury to his knee sustained while playing football prevented his going on the ill-fated polar attempt and in 1911–12 he went to Granite harbour and the Mackay glacier. One of his most significant contributions to the work of the expedition, and subsequently to his pupils at Cambridge, was his expertise in plane-table mapping. He convinced Scott and other members of the expedition of its value not only at base camps but also on sledge journeys. Scott in his diary recorded that Debenham was 'a well-trained, sturdy worker, with a quiet meaning that carries conviction; he realizes the conceptions of thoroughness and conscientiousness'.

After leaving the Antarctic in 1913 Debenham went with other members of the expedition to Cambridge to work up his results. He graduated BA in 1919 and MA in 1922. His studies were interrupted by the outbreak of war in 1914.

He joined the 7th battalion, Oxfordshire and Buckinghamshire light infantry, and after service in France and then Salonika, where he was severely wounded and shell-shocked, he was demobilized as a major and returned to Cambridge.

In 1919 Debenham was appointed to the Royal Geographical Society's lectureship in surveying and cartography at Cambridge. In 1919 he was elected into a fellowship at Gonville and Caius College, where he was a tutor (1923–8). In the immediate post-war years the geographical tripos was founded and in addition to continuing his Antarctic work Debenham gave himself wholeheartedly to the building up of the department.

By that time Debenham was the only surviving member of the Antarctic expedition who had both the local knowledge and the cartographic expertise to complete the charts. In 1921 he co-wrote two reports on the geology of Antarctica and later wrote his *Report on the Maps and Surveys* of the *Terra Nova* expedition (1923). His maps were still in use in the late 1950s. His suggestion that some of the Scott Mansion House fund should be used to build an institute for polar research was accepted and he was appointed director in 1926. In 1934 the Scott Polar Research Institute was opened, and it owed much to the enterprise and planning of Debenham. The institute took on its later enlarged form after his death, but he delighted in the gift from the Ford Foundation for the great addition to the original building, although he himself was not wholly reconciled to the fact that polar exploration had ceased to be the preserve of the amateur and had been taken over by sustained government-funded research.

The department of geography expanded continuously from its foundation. Debenham became a reader and head of department in 1928 and was primarily responsible for its move to Downing Place. During its expansion after 1933 Debenham's skill and interest as a planner were again invoked. In 1928 the twelfth international geographical congress was held in part in Cambridge and Debenham acted as secretary of the executive committee. In 1931 he became the first professor of geography in Cambridge. The new department was in full use by 1936, and during the Second World War its activities were numerous. Debenham had a great gift for teaching practical survey methods and making and recording astronomical and other observations. Apart from his normal teaching which still continued, he was notably successful in training a large number of service cadets who were attached for six-month courses. Two of the London departments were also billeted in Cambridge and with Debenham's help and encouragement found a welcome and temporary home there. Meanwhile, the Scott Polar Research Institute housed a section of the naval intelligence division of the Admiralty. He retired as director in 1946.

After the war unprecedented numbers of students came to the department of geography and these years, until Debenham's retirement in 1949, were perhaps the most satisfying of all, because they showed so clearly his role in making Cambridge a leading world centre for both geography and polar research.

After retirement Debenham for some years was very active. He travelled extensively in central Africa and made an interesting study of the water resources of the Bangweulu swamp. Debenham's flair for teaching, planning, and inspiring students and colleagues in their academic work and explorations was universally acknowledged in his lifetime and in the tributes which appeared after his death. Curiously, however, they somehow obscured the significance of his own writing and editorial work which was sustained and solid. He published numerous papers and books of which the most scientifically important were the early reports of his Antarctic work, which appeared at a formative time for glaciology. His books included *The Polar Regions* (1930), *In the Antarctic* (1952), and *Antarctica; the Story of a Continent* (1959), and he edited Bellingshausen's *Antarctic Narrative* for the Hakluyt Society in 1945. He was the founding editor of the *Polar Record* (1913). He also wrote teaching texts in geography and cartography and contributed largely to the high-quality and innovative relief maps in the Reader's Digest *Great World Atlas* (1961).

Lord McNair said that Debenham

> was one of the most modest and unselfregarding persons that I have ever known … He was a good organizer and knew how to get the best out of those working with him—mainly because he was generous in giving credit to others and because he inspired their affection and confidence.
> (address, memorial service)

He respected and encouraged scholarship in others, and the tributes paid after his death show him to have been almost universally liked.

Debenham had an extremely happy domestic life. On 27 January 1917 at St Philip's parish church, Kensington, he married Dorothy Lucy, daughter of J. T. Lempriere of Melbourne; they had two sons and four daughters. He and his wife (Deb and Mrs Deb) were most hospitable and gave a memorable welcome to former colleagues and students. In the last years of his life he suffered from heart trouble and deafness and spent much of his time at his desk, but was always glad to talk to friends for a short time.

In 1919 Debenham was appointed OBE. In 1948 he received the Victoria medal of the Royal Geographical Society of which he was a fellow (from 1914), vice-president (1951–3), and honorary fellow (from 1965). He received the David Livingstone centenary medal of the American Geographical Society in 1948, and he received honorary degrees from the universities of Sydney (1959), Western Australia (1937), and Durham (1952).

Debenham died in the Evelyn Nursing Home, Cambridge, on 23 November 1965. He is commemorated by two buildings at Cambridge, and a mountain and a glacier in Antarctica were named after him. He was survived by his wife.   J. A. STEERS, *rev.* ELIZABETH BAIGENT

Sources personal knowledge (1981) · private information (1981) · *WWW* · *The Times* (25 Nov 1965) · *The Times* (2 Dec 1965), 18f · J. A. Steers, *GJ*, 132 (1966), 173–5 · J. W. Wright and D. Wright, *Geographical Review*, 56 (1966), 596–8 · J. A. Steers, *Geography*, 51 (1966), 150–51 · *Transactions of the Institute of British Geographers*, 40 (1966), 195–8 [incl. bibliography] · G. Manley and others, *Journal of Glaciology*, 6 (1966), 455–9 · G. de Q. R. [G. de Q. Robin], *Polar Record*, 13 (1966–7), 215–21 · *AusDB*, 13.602–3 · *CGPLA Eng. & Wales* (1966)

Archives Scott Polar RI, corresp., journals, and notebooks | NL Scot., corresp. relating to *Discovery* committee · Scott Polar RI, letters to Apsley Cherry-Garrard · Scott Polar RI, letters to Hugh Mill | FILM BFI NFTVA, 'British Antarctic expedition, 1910–1913', 1924 · BFI NFTVA, documentary footage

Likenesses H. G. Ponting, photographs, 1911, Scott Polar RI [*see illus.*] · H. A. Freeth, watercolour drawing, 1961, Scott Polar RI · H. A. Freeth, charcoal and chalk drawing, Scott Polar RI · photograph, repro. in Manley and others, *Journal of Glaciology*, 455 · photograph, repro. in Robin, *Polar Record*, facing p. 216 · photographs, Scott Polar RI

Wealth at death £4201: probate, 11 March 1966, *CGPLA Eng. & Wales*

Debrett, John (d. 1822), publisher and bookseller, took over John Almon's business at 178 Piccadilly, London, in 1781. Debrett inherited some of Almon's whig patronage, and his shop was reputed to be 'much frequented about the middle of the day by fashionable people, and … used as a lounging place for political and literary conversation' (*Picture of London*, 27), especially by those with whiggish sympathies, while those who supported Pitt would visit the neighbouring shop belonging to John Stockdale. Debrett published many works, among them a new edition of *The Foundling Hospital for Wit* (1784), *Asylum for Fugitive Pieces in Prose and Verse* (1785–8), the *European Magazine* (1782–1801), and *The British Imperial Calendar* (1818, 1820–22). During the 1780s he also published a series of pamphlets by John Almon in support of the parliamentary whigs, and in 1797 he published the parliamentary papers. But Debrett is best known for his works on the peerage. The first edition of Debrett's *Peerage of England, Scotland, and Ireland* appeared in 1803. Debrett edited the next fifteen editions (the fifteenth appearing in 1823, after his death). Debrett's *Baronetage of England* began in 1808. Both works, usually published in one volume, still flourish, and Debrett's name is used in a wide variety of reference books.

Despite his fame, Debrett was twice declared bankrupt (in 1801 and 1804). His obituary in the *Gentleman's Magazine* described him as 'a kind, good-natured, friendly, man, who experienced the vicissitudes of life with fortitude. He had full opportunity of acquiring a large fortune, but from too much confidence and easiness of temper, he did not turn it to the best account'. Debrett appears to have given up his shop in 1805, but did not retire from publishing until about 1814. He then lived partly on an annuity from his wife, Sophia, which supplemented the money he earned from the *Peerage* and the *Baronetage*. He died at his lodgings in Upper Gloucester Street, Regent's Park, London, on 15 November 1822, having been ill for some time. He was survived by his wife and four children: John Edward Debrett; Sophia Mirabella, wife of Richard Samuel Butler Sandilands; Maria Amy Debrett; and Henry Symons Debrett.   HANNAH BARKER

Sources I. Maxted, *The London book trades, 1775–1800: a preliminary checklist of members* (1977) · *GM*, 1st ser., 92/2 (1822), 474 · C. H. Timperley, *A dictionary of printers and printing* (1839) · *Annual Biography and Obituary*, 7 (1823), 441 · L. Werkmeister, *The London daily press,*

1772–1792 (1963) · *The picture of London* (1802) · administration, PRO, PROB 6/198, fol. 239*v*
Wealth at death £100: administration, PRO, PROB 6/198, fol. 239*v*

Debus, Heinrich (1824–1915), chemist, was born at Wolfshagen, Hesse, on 13 July 1824, the son of Valentine Debus, a dyer. His mother died when he was two, and although his father then married her sister, Debus was brought up by grandparents in Kassel. There he attended the Bürgerschule and, later, the polytechnic school, where he was inspired by the chemistry teaching of Robert Bunsen (1811–1899). Bunsen moved to the University of Marburg in 1839, and when he was eighteen Debus joined him there, becoming his personal assistant and completing a PhD on madder in 1848. He was the first chemistry student at Marburg to present his thesis in German instead of Latin.

At Marburg, Debus became acquainted with Bunsen's English pupils Edward Frankland, John Tyndall, and Thomas Archer Hirst, with whom he enjoyed lifelong friendships. Through Frankland's influence Debus emigrated to England in 1851 to teach chemistry at Queenwood College in Hampshire. In 1867 he went to teach at Clifton College, Bristol. In 1870 he joined his English friends in London as lecturer in chemistry at Guy's Hospital medical school, and when Hirst became director of the Royal Naval College, Greenwich, in 1873 he invited Debus to become professor of chemistry there. Debus continued in both positions until his retirement in 1888, when he joined his only sister in Kassel. He returned to London each year to see his dwindling number of surviving friends.

Debus joined the Chemical Society in 1859 and was its vice-president in 1871–4. He was elected FRS in 1861 and sat on the Royal Society's council in 1870–72 and 1881–3. He was president of the chemical section of the British Association at Exeter in 1869 and was intermittently the University of London's chief examiner in chemistry from 1864 until retirement. Debus was recognized as an excellent teacher, despite a German accent which he never lost. He was a confirmed bachelor with a quiet dignity and good humour, and was well known for the eccentricity of his dress. He was an ardent clubman and loved to meet and entertain his friends at the Saville or the Athenaeum.

Apart from some experimental work on the law of mass action in 1853, and of the explosion of gunpowder in 1888, all Debus's research was in organic chemistry. In 1856, while at Queenwood, he ingeniously oxidized ethyl alcohol to form the new compounds glyoxal and glyoxylic acid. Over a number of years he made a thorough investigation of the thionic acids and their derivatives. In retirement Debus published (in German) a critical historical study of Avogadro's hypothesis (1894) and some attractive reminiscences of Robert Bunsen (1901).

Debus was one of the last of the Victorian scientific hierarchy that controlled London science. He died at his home, 4 Schlagenweg, Kassel, on 9 December 1915, having remained physically and mentally alert to the end.

W. H. BROCK

Sources *JCS*, 111 (1917), 325–31 · *Nature*, 96 (1915–16), 515–16 · J. Tyndall, journal, Royal Institution of Great Britain, London, Tyndall MSS · T. A. Hirst, journals, Royal Institution of Great Britain, London, Tyndall MSS [5 vols.] · WWW
Archives Royal Institution of Great Britain, London, Tyndall MSS
Likenesses photograph, repro. in R. Anschütz, *August Kekulé*, 1 (1929)

Decker, Sir Matthew, first baronet (1679–1749), political economist and merchant, was born in Amsterdam, the son of Derrick (Dirk) Decker, of Amsterdam, and his wife, Katherina. He received his commercial education under Burgomaster Velters of Amsterdam, but in 1702 travelled to London to establish himself as a merchant, and was naturalized in February 1704, at the second attempt. He then consolidated his business interests, and it was through trader and banker John Drummond that he secured a match on 16 August 1710 with Henrietta (1679–1759), daughter of Richard Watkins DD, rector of Whichford, Warwickshire, a union which produced two sons and four daughters. By that time he had already become a leading figure in Anglo-Dutch commerce, but the change of ministry in the summer of 1710 proved the making of his career, for he quickly established himself as one of Robert Harley's trusted City agents. As early as August 1710 he was ready to loan the government £40,000 to bolster its credit, and during the last three years of the War of the Spanish Succession he advanced several large remittances to keep the forces in the Low Countries supplied. He was also one of the leading backers for Harley's South Sea Company, subscribing for £49,271 worth of stock, and was appointed as one of its original directors. However, he withdrew from the board the following year, and thereafter sought prominence in the East India Company, where he served as a director from 1713 to 1743, as deputy governor in 1720–21 and 1729–30, and as governor in 1725–6 and 1730–33.

By the summer of 1713 Decker was a powerful figure in the City, using his position to advance relations between his native and adopted countries. It was even said that he would 'become a very rich man without risking what he has already got, which is a happiness that few can arrive to' (*Portland MSS*, 5.330). Such good fortune was less apparent the following year, when his patron Harley was dismissed from office, and he found himself 'extremely' pressed for lack of money (*Portland MSS*, 5.497). Although he was never to achieve as close a connection with any Hanoverian ministry, his influence was recognized on 20 July 1716, when he was raised to the dignity of baronet. Three years later he entered parliament as member for Bishops Castle, thanks to the interest of James Brydges, duke of Chandos, a former paymaster of the forces, with whom he had had many financial dealings. In common with the rest of the City, Decker faced great difficulty at the time of the South Sea Bubble, and rumours circulated that he faced bankruptcy. However, his friends moved quickly to quash these reports, observing that he 'had sold out betimes, and had left nothing in any of the stocks but what was pure gains' (*Portland MSS*, 7.282). Decker himself was bullish at this critical moment, writing to assure his Dutch banker Andreas Pels that he could 'draw at sight

£100,000 on him' (ibid.). However, despite his importance in the City and as a former director of the South Sea Company, Decker did not play a prominent parliamentary role in the wake of the bubble, when the regulation of the City was of great national interest, and he declined to seek re-election in 1722.

Although a City magnate, Decker did not covet advancement within the London corporation, and away from East India business his consuming passion was his estate at Richmond, where he entertained George I in 1716. As if to demonstrate his attachment to country life, he was prepared to undertake the onerous position of sheriff of Surrey in 1729–30. He appears to have taken especial care in developing his gardens, and was credited by contemporaries as the first to grow the pineapple in England, although this claim was later refuted. His commercial activities brought other exotic curiosities to Richmond, including a Chinese cock pheasant.

Decker had far from retired from commerce, however, and his principal fame rests with two anonymous treatises of the 1740s which have been attributed to him. The first, *Serious considerations on the several high duties which the nation in general, as well as trade in particular, labour under, with a proposal for preventing the removing of goods, discharging the trader from any search, and raising all the public supplies by one single tax*, appeared in 1743, and went through seven editions by 1756, the last of which named Decker as author. Joseph Massie's pamphlet of 1757, which attacked *The Proposal, Commonly called Sir Matthew Decker's Scheme for one General Tax upon Houses*, also pointed to Decker's involvement, but historians have remained sceptical about such claims. The second work, *An essay on the causes of the decline of the foreign trade, consequently of the value of Britain, and on the means to restore both*, was published in 1744, although 'begun in 1739', and was translated into French by Abbé de Gua de Malves in 1757. Josiah Tucker identified it as Decker's in 1751 (*Townshend MSS*, 376–7), but another contemporary, Francis Fauquier, thought it the work of William Richardson (McCulloch). Such arguments have continued ever since, although it is generally accepted that the *Essay* is Decker's. The principal difficulty in identifying him as the author of both tracts is the irreconcilability of the tax proposals which appear in these writings, with the *Considerations* calling for a single duty on houses, while the *Essay* supports an imposition on luxury consumers. However, there are important similarities between the two works, most notably a proposal for licensing tea consumers.

The treatises attracted considerable comment, particularly for their bold advocacy of free trade and the introduction of an all-embracing single tax. Indeed, the *Considerations* was 'strongly recommended to the electors of Great Britain, that they should, preferably to place and pension bills, or even triennial Parliaments, press their representatives to pass an Act pursuant to the author's scheme' (*GM*, 13.653–5). Both schemes held the plethora of existing customs and excise duties currently as an obstacle to the advancement of trade, an attack meeting the approval of economists such as Fauquier and Malacy Postlethwayt. Equally popular was the expressed concern to alleviate the burden of taxation on the lower orders, and to shift taxes from the merchant to the consumer. Other observers, most notably Joseph Massie, Arthur Young, and Adam Smith, were less convinced by the workability of the schemes, and even the *Considerations* conceded that some prohibitive duties might be needed to regulate trade to protect domestic manufacturers. Such radical proposals had little hope of immediate parliamentary sanction, for eighteenth-century governments remained too timorous to tamper with the customs system in favour of direct taxation.

Decker was still eager to serve the government in June 1747, writing to the duke of Newcastle to enquire whether he could fulfil any services on a forthcoming trip to the Netherlands, or as he still termed it, 'the old fatherland' (BL, Add. MS 32711, fol. 557). However, it was in his adopted country that he died on 18 March 1749, and his body was laid to rest at St Mary Magdalene's Church, Richmond. Estimated by one source to be worth 'upwards of £100,000' at his death, Decker bequeathed his considerable estate to his three surviving daughters (*London Magazine*). His will urged a charitable disposition upon his heirs, for he declared that 'I never have felt so much inward joy as when I gave money or other things in charity, especial[ly] when I was satisfied that it was disposed upon honest, good and industrious Christians' (PRO, PROB 11/769, sig. 103). By the testimony of one obituarist, this was no rhetoric, for he had 'a remarkable evenness of temper, and an uninterrupted tranquillity of mind, … the proofs and rewards of such conscious virtue' (*GM*, 19.141).

PERRY GAUCI

Sources GEC, *Baronetage* · BL, Add. MSS 24120, fol. 241; 32711, fol. 557 · *The manuscripts of his grace the duke of Portland*, 10 vols., HMC, 29 (1891–1931), vol. 5, pp. 111, 307–8, 316–19, 330, 476, 497; vol. 6, p. 164; vol. 7, pp. 16, 280, 282, 364–5 · *The manuscripts of the Marquess Townshend*, HMC, 19 (1887), 346–7, 376–7 · W. A. Shaw, *Calendar of treasury books*, 25/2, PRO (1961), 211; 26/2 (1954), 85, 88, 257, 539; 27/2 (1955), 21, 40–41, 66, 373; 28/2 (1969), 30; 31/2 (1957), 308, 376–7, 498 · J. Carswell, *The South Sea Bubble* (1960); repr. (1961), 57–8, 64, 186, 202, 277 · P. G. M. Dickson, *The financial revolution in England: a study in the development of public credit, 1688–1756* (1967); repr. (1993), 106, 279, 294, 311, 397, 498 · J. Brewer, *The sinews of power: war, money, and the English state* (1989), 216 · *GM*, 1st ser., 13 (1743), 653–5 · *GM*, 1st ser., 19 (1749), 141 · *GM*, 1st ser., 29 (1759), 242 · *London Magazine*, 18 (1749), 145 · J. R. McCulloch, *The literature of political economy: a classified catalogue* (1845), 46–7, 329–30 · E. R. A. Seligman, *The shifting and incidence of taxation*, 5th edn (1927), 84–7, 89–95 · W. R. Ward, *The English land tax in the eighteenth century* (1953), 79, 84 · will, PRO, PROB 11/769, sig. 103 · J. Massie, *The proposal, commonly called Sir Matthew Decker's scheme for one general tax upon houses…* (1757)
Archives Wilts. & Swindon RO, Herbert MSS, journals, F5/1–4
Wealth at death over £100,000; incl. bequests of over £30,000: *London Magazine*; will, PRO, PROB 11/769, sig. 103

Déclán mac Eircc [Declanus] (*fl.* late 5th cent.). *See under* Munster, saints of (*act. c.*450–*c.*700).

Decuman [St Decuman, Decumanus] (*fl.* **6th cent.**), holy man, is the patron of St Decumans, Watchet, Somerset, and of Rhoscrowther (Llanddegyman), Pembrokeshire. The earliest record of him is the Welsh martyrology in BL, Cotton MS Vespasian A.XIV (*c.*1175–1200), recording the feast of 'St Decumannus confessor' for 30 August, and he occurs in later medieval calendars from Muchelney Abbey and Wells Cathedral as 'martyr'. A very late and brief *Vita sancti Decumani*, composed in the fifteenth or early sixteenth century, probably at Wells or Muchelney, describes his alleged origin 'of illustrious stock' in west Wales and his journey over the Bristol Channel on a makeshift raft, alighting near Dunster Castle. Establishing himself as a hermit at a suitably isolated location (Watchet) and being fed milk daily by a cow, he is eventually beheaded by a pagan, but his decapitated body carries the head to a nearby fountain, probably St Decuman's Well near the present church. Of his dedications in Wales, Rhoscrowther was the senior: about 900 it was the main church of the cantref of Penfro and was accordingly considered one of the 'bishop-houses' of Dyfed. His cult is also linked to the churches at Pwllcrochan (also in Penfro) and Llanfihangel Cwm Du in Brecknockshire. In the west country his original church at Watchet was probably located near Dawes Castle (perhaps the site of the Alfredian *burh*) but was moved across the Washford River to the present site before the thirteenth century. Decuman's cult also penetrated Cornwall, perhaps being associated with that of St Petroc, as reflected in Degibma (in Wendron parish) and Decon Downs. Some calendars place his feast day at 27 August. The tradition that he was killed in 706 is probably no earlier than the seventeenth century in origin.

DAVID E. THORNTON

Sources 'Vita sancti Decumani', *Nova legenda Anglie, as collected by John of Tynemouth, J. Capgrave, and others*, ed. C. Horstmann, 1 (1901), 263–5 · G. H. Doble, *Saint Decuman, patron of Watchet (Somerset) and Rhoscrowther (Pembroke)*, Cornish Saints Series, 28 (1932) · J. P. Armitage-Robinson, 'St Cungar and St Decuman', *Journal of Theological Studies*, 29 (1927–8), 137–40 · S. M. Harkis, 'The kalendar of the *Vitae sanctorum Wallensium*', *Journal of the Historical Society of the Church in Wales*, 3 (1953), 3–53 · B. Schofield, ed., *Muchelney Memoranda*, Somerset RS, 42 (1927) · *VCH Somerset*, vol. 5 · F. McAvoy, 'Excavations at Daw's Castle, Watchet, 1982', *Proceedings of the Somersetshire Archaeological and Natural History Society*, 130 (1985–6), 47–60

Dee, Arthur (1579–1651), physician and writer on alchemy, was born on 13 July 1579 at Mortlake, Surrey, the eldest son of the mathematician and astrologer John *Dee (1527–1609) and his second wife, Jane (1555–1605), daughter of Bartholomew Fromonds or Fromond. From 1583 until 1589 he accompanied his father on his travels to Poland and Bohemia; his early initiation into the hermetic sciences and alchemical projection influenced the course of his life. In May 1592 he was placed under the tuition of Edward Grant and William Camden, successive headmasters at Westminster School, and then possibly studied at St Mary's Hall, Oxford, but without taking a degree.

In June 1600 Dee went to Manchester with his father, who assumed the wardenship of Christ's College; Arthur Dee was granted the clerkship of the collegiate church in December. During his time in Manchester Dee began practising medicine. In 1602 he married Isabella (1583–1634), daughter of Edward Prestwich, a Manchester JP. Several of their thirteen children (seven sons and six daughters) were baptized in Manchester. Shortly after his mother

died of the plague in March 1605, his father retired to Mortlake, while Dee settled in London.

At Manchester, Dee had apparently become acquainted with the mathematician Thomas Harriot, who in June 1602 gave him a manuscript by his father's pupil Benjamin Lock, comprising a commentary on John Dee's *Compound of Alchemy* (1591). In London he kept the company of a number of unorthodox medical practitioners, astrologers, and alchemists; among his acquaintances were John Woodall, Francis Anthony, Timothy Willis, and Richard Napier. He was well versed in medical astrology. Between April 1606 and October 1612 he was repeatedly summoned by the College of Physicians for advertising medicines and practising illicitly; in February 1614 he showed the censors his doctoral letters patent of 4 May 1609 from the University of Basel, attesting his linguistic proficiency in German, French, Hungarian, and Polish. By May 1615 he was physician to Queen Anne, James I's wife, having declined a post in July 1614 at Thomas Sutton's newly founded Charterhouse Hospital.

Dee was appointed chief physician by royal recommendation to Tsar Michael Romanov, arriving at Moscow in the autumn of 1621. He received a generous salary, many gifts, and a large house from the tsar, who valued his skill, learning, and practical abilities. He translated for the tsar the notes from his father's 'angelic conversations', as *Divers Curious Narrations of John Dee*, anticipating by four years the execution of Mary, queen of Scots, and the Spanish armada's defeat. On leave in England in December 1626 he recruited, at the tsar's request, John Martin, a jeweller, for the silver chancery, and John Gilbert, chief engraver to the royal mint, as a mining expert and metallurgist, and he arranged for the Society of Apothecaries to supply the Russian court with regular consignments of medicines. Dee's mercantile activities were facilitated by his membership of the Mercers' Company (from 1605) and, with two sons-in-law, of the Muscovy Company. John Dee's characterization of his son Arthur to Camden in 1592 as 'of an exceding great and hauty mynd naturally, ready to revendge rashly' (BL, Cotton MS Julius C.v, art. 41) is borne out by a servant's testimony that, following a heated quarrel at a Moscow supper in 1633, 'Docr Dee did in a great rage take upp his knife from the table and with much furie and passion flung it outreight' (PRO, C 24/610/36, fols. 7–8) at his son-in-law Francis Glover, who ducked in time.

Arthur Dee's wife died at Moscow on 24 July 1634. A year later he left Russia to take up the appointment on 13 November 1635 of physician-extraordinary to Charles I. This was mediated by his friend Sir Theodore Mayerne. He still held this post in 1641.

By his own testimony Dee devoted most of his Russian leisure time to alchemical literature, resulting in his compilation of alchemical writings, *Fasciculus chemicus, abstrusae hermeticae scientiae ingressum*, with the preface dated Moscow, March 1629. While on leave he obtained a pass, in June 1629, from England to France, presumably to negotiate the book's publication by Nicholas de la Vigne (Paris, 1631). The *Fasciculus chemicus* is unusual in that it consists of quotations selected from alchemical authors to form ten short chapters, arranged in the exact order of the operations required to produce the philosopher's stone. Each chapter is summarized by a 'Corollary', and twenty-one 'Observanda' offer general advice at the end. Identification of the sources reveals that Dee would have needed direct access to only fifteen books and two or three manuscripts in order to compile his *opus*. The preface of another edition, dating from 1631, is addressed to the Rosicrucian fraternity. A presentation copy with an additional handwritten title-page displaying alchemical symbols, and inscribed to John Winthrop jun., the first governor of Connecticut, is also extant. Elias Ashmole, under the anagram James Hassolle, made a translation of Dee's work which was published in May 1650 by Richard Mynne as *Fasciculus chemicus, or, Chymical Collections*. A revised, unpublished edition of this work is entitled 'Arca arcanorum, abstrusae hermeticae scientiae' (BL, Sloane MS 1876). Its preface (dated Moscow, 10 August 1634) contains a new dedication to the Bodleian Library (Dee was related to Thomas Bodley). A supplementary title-page depicts hand-coloured symbols, and there are fourteen completely new and informative 'Observanda'.

According to the 'Arca arcanorum', Dee had extracted 2 lb of 'prima materia' from ore brought back to him in May 1618 by the Hungarian Johannes Bánfi Hunyades who performed chemical operations at Gresham College. Dee planned to travel to Hungary in 1646 with Hunyades as his operator, but Hunyades died at Amsterdam before he could join him. At about this time Dee moved to Norwich. John Aubrey, whose grandfather William was John Dee's cousin, relays a local man's remarks that Dee 'was a man of very pleasant conversation and had good practice in Norwich: a great acquaintance of Dr Browne's' (*Brief Lives*, 1.210). Sir Thomas Browne, a literary exponent of the occult philosophy followed by the Dees, wrote to Elias Ashmole on 25 January 1659 that Arthur Dee had 'seen [alchemical] projection made', and had confirmed 'with the highest asseverations ... unto his death that hee had ocularly, undeceavably & frequently beheld it in Bohemia' (*Elias Ashmole*, 2.755). Dee died at Norwich towards the end of September 1651 and was buried at St George Tombland's Church, near Norwich Cathedral. Somewhat overshadowed by his father, Arthur Dee emerges as a fine hermetic philosopher and alchemist, in the Rosicrucian tradition, whose writings have exercised considerable influence. JOHN H. APPLEBY

Sources J. H. Appleby, 'Arthur Dee and Johannes Bánfi Hunyades', *Ambix*, 24 (1977), 96–109 · J. H. Appleby, 'Some of Arthur Dee's associations before visiting Russia clarified, including two letters from Sir Theodore Mayerne', *Ambix*, 26 (1979), 1–15 · J. H. Appleby, 'Dr Arthur Dee: merchant and litigant', *Slavonic and East European Review*, 57 (1979), 32–55 · N. A. Figurovski, 'The alchemist and physician Arthur Dee', *Ambix*, 13 (1965–6), 35–51 · G. M. Phipps, *Britons in 17th-century Russia: a study in the origins of modernization* (1972) · L. Abraham, introduction, in A. Dee, *Fasciculus chemicus, or, Chymical collections*, trans. E. Ashmole, new edn, ed. L. Abraham (1997) · C. Wall, *A history of the Worshipful Society of Apothecaries of London*, ed. H. C. Cameron and E. A. Underwood (1963), 48, 296 · *Elias Ashmole (1617–1692): his autobiographical and historical notes*, ed. C. H. Josten, 5 vols. (1966 [i.e. 1967]), vols. 2, 4–5 · Suffolk RO, Ipswich,

Ashe MSS, MS S1/1/77 · PRO, Russian state papers, MSS SP 91/2 and 91/3 · W. M. von Richter, *Geschichte der Medizin in Russland*, 2 (1815), 30–46 · R. Deacon, *John Dee* (1968) · *Brief lives, chiefly of contemporaries, set down by John Aubrey, between the years 1669 and 1696*, ed. A. Clark, 1 (1898) · BL, Cotton MS Julius C.v, art. 41 · will, PRO, PROB 11/218, sig. 183 [proved 16 Oct 1651]
Archives BL, Sloane MSS 1876, 1881, 1902 · Bodl. Oxf., MSS Ashmole 204, 334 · Suffolk RO, Ipswich, Ashe MSS, MS S1/1/77
Wealth at death property and possessions: will, PRO, PROB 11/218, sig. 183

Dee, Duncan (1657–1720), lawyer, was born on 3 November 1657, a younger son of Rowland Dee (1613–1687), London merchant, and his wife, Jane (*d. c.*1698), and a grandson of Arthur *Dee, physician to Charles I. He was educated at Merchant Taylors' School (1672–3), and went thence in 1673 to St John's College, Oxford. It does not appear that he graduated. He married Mary Everard at St Dionis Backchurch, London, on 4 July 1682 and in the same year was called to the bar at the Inner Temple. He was a common pleader of the City of London (1682–90), a judge of the sheriff's court (1690–1700), and common serjeant of the City of London from 1700 until he died. He was also commissioner of appeals in the excise in 1713–14. Dee defended Dr Sacheverell in his trial before the House of Lords in 1710, speaking on four successive days. He lived in the parish of St Mary Aldermanbury from at least 1684— he and his wife had eight children baptized in the parish church between 1684 and 1696. Dee died in 1720, and was buried on 8 June next to his son Duncan in the great vault in St Mary Aldermanbury.

C. J. ROBINSON, *rev.* S. M. WYNNE

Sources C. J. Robinson, ed., *A register of the scholars admitted into Merchant Taylors' School, from AD 1562 to 1874*, 2 vols. (1882–3) · H. B. Wilson, *The history of Merchant-Taylors' School*, 2 vols. (1812–14) · J. Stow, *A survey of the cities of London and Westminster and the borough of Southwark*, ed. J. Strype, new edn, 2 vols. (1720) · Foster, *Alum. Oxon.* · F. A. Inderwick and R. A. Roberts, eds., *A calendar of the Inner Temple records*, 3 (1901) · W. B. Bannerman, ed., *The registers of St Mary the Virgin, Aldermanbury, London*, 1, Harleian Society, register section, 61 (1931) · IGI

Dee, Francis (*d.* 1638), bishop of Peterborough, was born in London, the eldest son of David Dee and Marcia Roper, who had been licensed to marry on 8 February 1578. A native of Shropshire, David Dee had graduated from Oxford in 1568; he was vicar of Sherborne, Dorset, from 1580 and rector of St Bartholomew-the-Great, London, from 1587 until he was deprived in 1605. Francis was educated at Merchant Taylors' School, London, from 1591 until 1596, when he won a Billingsley scholarship at St John's College, Cambridge, where a conformist style of divinity was developing. He graduated BA in 1600, was ordained a priest on 1 May 1602, proceeded MA in 1603, and became a fellow of St John's. Within a few years Dee married Susan le Poreque; they had two children, Adrian (*b.* 1 December 1606, *d.* 1638) and Mary. The dean (Thomas Neville) and chapter of Canterbury appointed him on 31 January 1607 rector of Holy Trinity-the-Less, Knightrider Street, London, which he resigned in 1620; and on 5 April 1615 of All Hallows, Lombard Street, which he resigned in 1634. He proceeded BD in 1610 and DD in 1617. In 1618 he rose to the chancellorship of Salisbury Cathedral, which

Francis Dee (d. 1638), by unknown artist, 1634–8

he held until 1634, and about 1621–2 he held the living of Sutton-at-Hone, Kent, through the patronage of the dean (Godfrey Goodman) and chapter of Rochester.

In 1629 Dee was chaplain to the English ambassador in Paris and passed to Bishop William Laud a petition from an Englishman imprisoned in the Bastille. In the following year his name appears as one of the founders of Sion College, and on 30 April he became dean of Chichester; he was more assiduous than his predecessors in disciplining the cathedral clergy, and two absentee vicars were forced to resign. Dee was nominated in September 1633 for an anticipated vacancy of the see of Gloucester, but when Bishop Goodman decided not to move he was elevated instead to Peterborough through the influence of Archbishop Laud, who (assisted by Bishop Juxon) carried out the consecration at Lambeth on 18 May 1634. As bishop Dee contributed to a series of Lenten lectures at court. On the death of his first wife he married Elizabeth Winter, who survived him; they did not have children.

By 1634 Dee had evolved into the Laudian prelate *par excellence*. His project was to replace the word-centred piety of the Jacobeans with one which emphasized the necessity of uniform worship and aesthetic, ceremonialized sacraments dominated by the altar. His primary visitation articles were the first episcopal set yet found (Samuel Clarke had done this for the archdeaconry of Derby in 1630) to stipulate the railing-in of communion tables at the east end of the chancel; this insistence even predated the archbishop's own visitation of 1635. Dee's visitation sermon was preached by the zealot Peter Hausted, curate to Laud's chaplain, and in the same year Dee

co-operated with Laud's prosecution of Charles Chauncy's resistance to the altar policy. The regime at Peterborough provoked loud opposition and in 1636 the popular Kettering lecture was abolished. Aware of the need to placate moderate opinion, the bishop contacted the influential moderate puritan Edward, Lord Montagu, eschewing responsibility for this act and claiming to have been a regular preacher himself since 1603. However, his deputies continued to harass the crucial Northampton lecture.

Renewing the drive for conformity in 1637 Dee used the canonical church survey to enforce liturgical practice— the creation of railed, east-end altars and the full Laudian communion in which the priest administered the communion from within the rails to the clergy and laity, who received theirs kneeling. A whole raft of other orders altered the arrangement of parish churches to accommodate the new altar-focused worship, enforced the use of silver communion vessels, promoted the notion of the material church as holy, and even sought to revive the pre-Reformation practice of confession. Dee's friend John Pocklington published apologetic works defending altars and the anti-sabbatarianism of the Book of Sports (enjoined by the bishop in 1633), but Dee still thought it necessary to mollify the moderates, so Edward Reynolds was employed to exhort conscientious waverers to sideline their objections and conform.

Owing primarily to government support and the unusual zeal of his deputies, Sibthorpe and Clarke, Dee achieved a degree of formal conformity and silenced the more vocal opposition, although his report to Laud in 1637 that only three lectures remained in the diocese was hopelessly optimistic. However, he did not live to witness the explosion of resentment which was the consequence of his policies. He died at his bishop's palace on 8 October 1638 and was buried on 12 October close to his throne in the cathedral. By his will he founded two fellowships at St John's and two scholarships for pupils from Merchant Taylors' or Peterborough schools; to the college chapel he bequeathed his library and a gilt communion service. Other beneficiaries included John Towers who, as his successor, was even more draconian.   J. FIELDING

Sources A. J. Fielding, 'Conformists, puritans and the church courts: the diocese of Peterborough, 1603–1642', PhD diss., U. Birm., 1989 • Wood, *Ath. Oxon.*, new edn, 2.300-01 • H. I. Longden, *Northamptonshire and Rutland clergy from 1500*, ed. P. I. King and others, 16 vols. in 6, Northamptonshire RS (1938–52), vol. 4, p. 51 • R. Newcourt, *Repertorium ecclesiasticum parochiale Londinense*, 1 (1708), 144, 255, 556 • will, PRO, PROB 11/178, sig. 134 • PRO, SP16/153/95; 169/65; 247/8, 16; 248/16 • W. D. Peckham, ed., *The acts of the dean and chapter of the cathedral church of Chichester, 1545–1642*, Sussex RS, 58 (1959), 241, 243–5, 249 • *The works of the most reverend father in God, William Laud*, 5/2, ed. J. Bliss (1853), 330, 349 • J. Davies, *The Caroline captivity of the church: Charles I and the remoulding of Anglicanism, 1625–1641* (1992), 41 • *DNB* • K. Fincham, ed., *Visitation articles and injunctions of the early Stuart church*, 2 (1998), xx • K. Fincham, *Prelate as pastor: the episcopate of James I* (1990), 324, n. 10 • H. B. Wilson, *The history of Merchant Taylors' School from its foundation to the present time*, 2 vols. (1814), vol. 2, pp. 1165–76 • Venn, *Alum. Cant.* • Foster, *Alum. Oxon.*

Archives Northants. RO, documents relating to his appointment as bishop of Peterborough

Dee, John (1527–1609), mathematician, astrologer, and antiquary, was born on 13 July 1527 in London, the only child of Rowland Dee and his wife, Joan or Joanna (1508/9–1580), daughter of William Wild.

Antecedents, education, and marriages The Dee family was Welsh and there exist three pedigrees, two of which are heavily annotated by John Dee and are perhaps based on information supplied to him by his cousin Lewis ap Howell Dee in 1567. There he describes his father as 'antesignanus dapiferorum' ('chief sewer') to Henry VIII. Rowland Dee was later a merchant and was admitted to the Mercers' Company of London in 1536. He does not seem to have been a prominent member of the company, and apart from the fact that he was excluded from the pardon issued to those who had taken part in Wyatt's rebellion in 1554 (but was later none the less pardoned), little is known of him; his son does not record his death. The pedigrees, which trace Dee's ancestry through the Lord Rhys (Rhys ap Gruffudd) to Rhodri Mawr and Coel Hen, are unlikely to be accurate for more than three or four generations back. His mother owned houses and land in Mortlake which were surrendered to her son in 1579, and it is possible that her family originated there.

Dee was educated at Chelmsford grammar school, and entered St John's College, Cambridge, in 1542, where he claimed to have studied for up to eighteen hours a day. In 1546 he was elected a fellow and under-reader in Greek at the newly founded Trinity College, and he received his MA in 1548. He is normally styled Doctor Dee, but his only claim to this title seems to be his receiving a doctorate of medicine from the University of Prague in 1584 or 1585. John Chamberlain refers to him as Dr Dee in 1599, and this usage seems to have become accepted after Dee's death.

The date of Dee's first marriage, to Katherine, widow of Thomas Constable, a London grocer with whom he had been in some way associated as early as 1558, is unknown but probably took place in 1565 or 1566, after his return from his third continental journey, and his settling at Mortlake. There were no children of this marriage, and Katherine Dee died in 1575; her burial coincided with a visit by the queen to Mortlake. Dee married for a second time, on 5 February 1578; his new wife was Jane Fromond or Fromonds (1555–1605), daughter of Bartholomew Fromonds of Cheam, Surrey. (In Dee's diary his wife's name is always Fromonds; elsewhere it appears as Fromond.) There were eight children of this marriage, though only Arthur *Dee (1579–1651) and Katherine (*b.* 1581) seem to have survived their father.

First continental visits, and career to 1558 Dee made his first visit to the continent shortly after his election to Trinity College. His own account of his early travels is contained within the 'Compendious rehearsal' which he prepared for the queen's commissioners in 1592 and revised in 1594. This document, supported by written evidence displayed at the time, was designed to emphasize his services to the

John Dee (1527–1609), by unknown artist, 1574–86

state, and, though rhetorical in tone, is accurate in detail. He also made personal entries in printed volumes of ephemerides, though apart from a few entries copied by Elias Ashmole the early volumes have perished. Two volumes, from which J. O. Halliwell published Dee's notes as his *Diary* (1842), are Joannes Stadius's *Ephemerides novae ab anno 1554 usque ad annum 1600* (1570) and Joannes Antonius Maginus's *Ephemerides coelestium motuum ad annos XL* (1582), both in the Bodleian Library. Dee himself normally followed the practice of these works in reckoning the year as beginning on 1 January. The chronological framework is confirmed by Dee's notes of ownership in many of his books.

Dee recorded that he visited the Southern Netherlands in May 1547 'to speake and conferr with some learned men, and chiefly mathematicians' ('Compendious rehearsal', ed. Hearne, 500–01), whom he names as Gemma Frisius, Gerardus Mercator, Gaspar à Mirica, and Antonio Gogava. He returned to Cambridge after a few months, bearing mathematical instruments designed by Gemma and Mercator which were later presented to the college. His only recorded academic achievement at Trinity was a production of Aristophanes' *Pax* in which Trygaeus rode up to the roof of the college hall upon a scarab beetle. This early use of stage machinery caused by his own account 'great wondring' and, combined with his interest in the animation of statues and in mechanical toys, contributed to his enduring (though to him highly unwelcome) reputation as a conjuror.

Dee's return to the Southern Netherlands in the following year may be connected both with his own dissatisfaction with the state of mathematical learning in England

and with proposed curricular changes, favouring mathematics, at Cambridge. He may have been sent by a patron: Sir William Pickering proved to be such in 1549. Dee entered the University of Louvain on 24 June 1548, continuing the studies that he had begun in the previous year, which included mathematics, geography, astrology, astronomical observation, and 'for recreation' civil law. His presence in both Louvain and Antwerp is attested by inscriptions in his growing library. He left Louvain on 15 July 1550, without receiving any further degree, and five days later arrived in Paris. Rheims College was the scene of his lecturing upon Euclid's *Elements*, 'Mathematicé, Physicé, & Pythagoricé', to a vast and eager audience. He also relates that he refused the offer of a professorship of mathematics in the University of Paris at a salary of 200 crowns.

Dee returned to England at the end of 1551 and was so well commended to Edward VI by Sir William Cecil and Sir John Cheke that the king granted him an annual pension of 100 crowns, which was commuted into the rectory of Upton upon Severn, Worcestershire, in May 1553, an income which was later augmented with the rectory of Long Leadenham, Lincolnshire. In 1552 he entered into the service of the earl of Pembroke, and later into that of the duke of Northumberland, to whose son, John, earl of Warwick, he seems to have acted as tutor, and of whose aptitude he later spoke with unusual warmth.

With the accession of Queen Mary in 1553 the Dudleys fell from power; Northumberland was executed in 1553, and Warwick died in 1554. Dee then resorted to the teaching of mathematics in London, but declined an invitation in 1554 from Richard Bruern and Richard Smith to read the mathematical sciences at Oxford; notes in his books show that he was in Oxford in April of that year, and may have acquired his first recorded pupil, Christopher Carye, there. He was in London in the following year, and was admitted by patrimony to the Mercers' Company, thus gaining access to merchants, such as Sir Lionel Duckett and the Loks, who were to make use of his mathematical and navigational skills in trading ventures such as the Russia Company, and in the quest for the north-east and north-west passages.

In May 1555 Dee was arrested on the order of the privy council, together with John Feild (another teacher of mathematics, to whose *Ephemeris* for 1557 he contributed a preface), Sir Thomas Benger, auditor to Princess Elizabeth (and from 1561 her master of the revels), and Christopher Carye who had graduated from Oxford. Their accusers were George Ferrers and John Prideaux, and the charge seems in the first place to have been that of calculating the nativities of the king, the queen, and the Princess Elizabeth, and only later of conjuring and witchcraft. When, immediately upon the accusation, one of Ferrers's children died and a second was stricken with blindness, there were rumours of a familiar spirit. Dee later summed up the charges as 'magic' or conspiring 'by enchantments to destroy Queen Mary' ('Compendious rehearsal', ed. Hearne, 520). But Ferrers, like Dee, had been involved in

theatrical displays, and the antagonism may have originated there. After examination by the lord chief justice of the court of common pleas, they were released on 19 August, Dee into the custody of Edmund Bonner, bishop of London, for enquiry into his religion. He was imprisoned for a while with Barthlet Green, who was burned in 1556, but unlike Green he convinced Bonner of his orthodoxy, and his fate was quite different; a note in one of his books reveals that he was in the house of his 'singularis amicus' ('very good friend') the bishop, at Fulham, by the end of the year. This privileged and assured position is confirmed by John Foxe in the earlier editions of the *Acts and Monuments*, where Dee is named as Bonner's chaplain during the examination of John Philpot on 19 November 1556. Foxe also records Bonner's indignation that Philpot had called his chaplain 'a great conjurer' (J. Foxe, *Acts and Monuments*).

By this time, Dee's unusually positive response to Copernicus's new astronomical system was evident; his preface to Feild's *Ephemeris*, dated 3 July 1556, included lavish praise of Copernicus. Two copies of Copernicus's *De revolutionibus* (1543) were early in his library. There is evidence from his notebooks that at this time he was also reading alchemical books, though there is no record of any alchemical practices at this stage.

In 1558 Dee published his first significant work in natural philosophy, *Propaideumata aphoristica* (2nd edn, 1568). The book brought together two of his long-standing interests, for it consists of a series of propositions in astrological physics. According to one commentator, N. H. Clulee (1988), the propositions set out a naturalistic causality that is constant and uniform, as well as a mathematical method of studying the operation of this causality. All this is informed by a strong commitment to astrology, a belief in the real and natural influence of the heavenly bodies upon terrestrial affairs.

At about this time, Dee also made a brief list of his library, and suffered an illness which caused him to name the Portuguese geographer Pedro Nunes as his heir. On the accession of Queen Elizabeth in November 1558, Dee's Cambridge connections and the favour of the Dudleys eased for him the transition to a protestant regime, and Robert Dudley, later earl of Leicester, sought his astrological advice upon a propitious day for the coronation. Introduction to the royal presence by Dudley and by another former patron, William Herbert, earl of Pembroke, secured for Dee the first of many, if mostly vain, promises of favour from the queen: 'where my brother hath given him a crown I will give him a noble' ('Compendious rehearsal', ed. Hearne, 509). He was also promised the mastership of the hospital of St Katharine by the Tower; this went eventually to Dr Thomas Wilson.

Queen Elizabeth's 'philosopher' Dee's adherence to Bonner may well have made him enemies, and little is known of his activities before the end of 1562, though notes in books suggest that he may have travelled in search of manuscripts. In his *Supplication* to Queen Mary of 1556 and the accompanying *Articles concerning the recovery and preservation of ancient monuments and old excellent writers* he had called for a national effort for the recovery of dispersed manuscripts. It may therefore be significant evidence of animosity towards him that, although Archbishop Matthew Parker and his circle were engaged in just such a recovery of manuscripts as he had advocated, and may have been influenced by his programme, they seem to have been unaware of his own collection. At the end of 1562 he went abroad, evidently with the knowledge and approval of Sir William Cecil. A letter to Cecil from Antwerp on 16 February 1563 seeks approval for his remaining abroad, and recounts his copying of a manuscript version of Trithemius's *Steganographia* (a work which remained unprinted until 1606).

Cecil's support is further indicated by a certificate he issued in May 1563 testifying that Dee's time abroad had been well spent. In April Dee visited Conrad Gesner at Zürich, and went on to cross the Alps into Italy. In May he was in Padua, in June in Venice, and in July in Rome. A meeting with the mathematician Federigo Commandino at Urbino led ultimately to his joint publication with Commandino of the *De superficierum divisionibus* of Machometus Bagdedinus (Pesaro, 1570) from a manuscript copy made by Dee in 1559. He was present at the coronation of Maximilian II as king of Hungary at Pressburg (Bratislava) in September 1563, and it was to Maximilian that his *Monas Hieroglyphica*, printed by Gulielmus Silvius at Antwerp, was dedicated on 14 February 1564. A number of book purchases attest his presence in Antwerp until June, when he escorted Elizabeth Brooke, marchioness of Northampton (1526–1565), from Antwerp to London. The *Monas*, written as Dee claimed in twelve days, is an explication in twenty-four theorems of the symbol of the Monas, a sign which had already appeared on the title-page of the *Propaideumata aphoristica* in 1558. For Dee it was a powerful symbol both of creation and of the unity of the sciences. He was permitted to expound the work to Queen Elizabeth on his return.

Dee, who had been living in London before his travels of 1562–4, now settled at Mortlake in Surrey, only a short distance from the royal residence at Richmond. He was there by September 1566, by which time he was probably already married. The substantial buildings he acquired enabled him both to assemble his extensive and still growing library and to commence the practice of alchemy. Both required financial resources, and he was constantly soliciting preferment, notably the provostship of Eton College. None of these attempts was successful—he made it clear that he did not wish to have a cure of souls—though he was granted dispensations by archbishops Parker and Grindal to hold his two rectories. There is no record that he resided at either, though a now vanished inscription once recorded his presence at Long Leadenham.

The Mortlake period, 1565–1583 The period from his settling in Mortlake about 1565 to his departure for Poland in 1583 was the most prosperous and productive of Dee's life, and the various strands of his activity are intertwined with some complexity. Mathematics remained his most visible interest, though his teaching of the subject must

have been interrupted by his continental journey of 1562–4, and the move to Mortlake no doubt entailed the residence there of his students. The first of many editions by Dee (sixteen survive up to 1607) of Robert Recorde's *Ground of Arts* was published in 1561, though the fact that he lists no copy in his own library suggests that he regarded it as an elementary textbook. His pupil Christopher Carye died in 1563 or 1564, and the only other early recorded pupil is Thomas Digges, to whom he passed a copy of Archimedes in 1559.

The most influential of all Dee's published works was his 'Mathematicall praeface' to Henry Billingsley's English translation of Euclid, *Elements of Geometrie*, printed by John Daye in 1570. The preface is firstly a long encomium of the study of 'thynges mathematicall' as partaking both of the supernatural and of the natural, and of geometry in particular. He goes on to enumerate the practical arts (proper to 'mechanicians') which derive from mathematics, and under one of the last of these, 'thaumaturgike', exculpates himself with some passion from the charge of conjuring. He also defends the use of the vernacular, as not encroaching on the rights of the universities. His concept of 'Archemastrie', which 'procedeth by Experiences' (J. Dee, 'Mathematicall praeface', H. Billingsley, *Elements of Geometrie*, 1570), has been seen by some as foreshadowing the experimental science of the next century, but he also hints at magical interests and practices under this very heading. In general the 'Praeface' is now seen as a retrospective view of his own practice and teaching after his return to England in 1551, but the interest in magic, and possibly in skrying (seeing, or conversing with, spirits), may be a development of the late 1560s.

As a result of his move to Mortlake Dee had more space for the practice of alchemy, and in 1571 he travelled into the duchy of Lorraine to furnish his laboratories (he had three by 1583), bringing back a great cartload of specially made vessels. An inscription in a book shows that he was also in Paris on 31 May. He fell seriously ill on his return, and later recorded it as a mark of royal favour that the queen sent to him two of her physicians, Dr Apsloo (Edward Atslowe) and Mr Balthrop. In November 1572 a supernova appeared in the constellation of Cassiopeia. Dee seems to have concluded that the 'blazing star' was located in the region of the fixed stars, where Aristotelian doctrine taught that nothing might change. The event occasioned many treatises, among them Thomas Digges's *Alae seu scalae mathematicae* of 1573, and Dee's own *Parallaticae commentationis praxeosque nucleus quidam*. The two tracts refer to one another, and often survive bound together. Nevertheless, as an inscription in his copy of Manilius's *Astronomica* shows, the event portended for him the finding of a great treasure or of the philosopher's stone, and quests for gold and silver, whether deliberately buried, to be mined or created by projection, underlay much of his involvement in discovery in the New World, in alchemical pursuits, and ultimately in the 'angelic conversations' with Edward Kelley from 1582. Dee also had, according to his *Diary*, some rights in mining for silver in Devon. His astronomical skills were invoked in reassuring the court about the comet which appeared in 1577, and, more terrestrially, in calming fears about an image of the queen with a pin stuck in its breast, found in Lincoln's Inn Fields.

Enquiries into 'British' history Dee had taken little part in the programme initiated by Archbishop Matthew Parker for the recovery of early English, and particularly Anglo-Saxon, manuscripts. He owned, and often annotated, copies of most of the antiquarian books that resulted from this movement, though with one possible exception, he had no Anglo-Saxon manuscript, and no copy of the Anglo-Saxon gospels printed in 1571. The annotations show that his antiquarian interests were strong, and moreover that he was developing an interest in British (that is Welsh) antiquities, and that this interest was stimulated by an awareness, well documented in his pedigrees, of his Welsh ancestry. In 1574 he undertook a tour of the marches from Chester to Hereford, which also took in some places in eastern Wales. His quest was for 'monuments', a term which embraced both antiquities and manuscripts. He saw some of the latter in the hands of Welsh owners, and may have copied some then, and acquired a few from the family of Sir John Prise (to whom he believed himself related) in Hereford. Some documents were rescued from a decayed chapel at Wigmore.

Like Prise, Dee was a firm believer in the historicity of the 'British history' deriving from Geoffrey of Monmouth, and owned several Brut chronicles in English and Welsh (a language of which he had some reading knowledge and in which he owned several printed books). Arthur (after whom he named his first son) is a frequent subject of annotation in his books and manuscripts. He embroidered upon the British history, adding further realms to King Arthur's conquests, and also interested himself in the story of the voyage of Madog ab Owain Gwynedd to North America, and some of his notes show him seeking evidence for an early 'British' presence in the New World. From these dubious sources he derived not only his own role as a British gentleman, philosopher, and navigator, but also the titles of Queen Elizabeth to large parts of North America.

Navigation and discovery Although Dee claimed, no doubt with justification, early acquaintance with navigators such as Richard and Nicholas Chancellor and Stephen and William Borough who were initiating trade with Russia and seeking a north-east passage to Cathay, precise evidence for his involvement is lacking. From about 1570, however, he emerges, both in manuscript and print, as the advocate of a policy for strengthening England politically and economically, and for imperial expansion into the New World. The first survivor of these manuscript tracts, *Brytannicae reipublicae synopsis* (1570), perhaps a schematic digest of a larger work requested by Dee's friend and patron Edward Dyer, concerns itself with trade, ethics, and national strength. Six years later he began a much more ambitious project, *The Brytish Monarchy*, of which only the first part, *General and Rare Memorials Pertaining to the Perfect Art of Navigation* (1577), achieved print, albeit in a

limited edition. Another volume of great bulk was to consist of *Queen Elizabeth's Tables Gubernautik*, but has not survived; a third volume was destroyed, perhaps by its author, while a fourth, *Of Famous and Rich Discoveries*, remains only in Dee's now very imperfect manuscript. Concurrently with these writings Dee was producing another work, the *Brytanici imperii limites* of 1576–8 (extant only in a manuscript by another hand).

Dee was the first to use the term 'British Impire' (in the *General and Rare Memorials* in English). The *Limites* formed the basis of his 1577 declaration to the queen of her rights in the northern realms, based upon his reconstruction of Arthur's conquests (and in the next year, in a meeting with Daniel Rogers, the conquests of King Malgo were added to the imperial precedents). These rights were further set out in two great rolls presented to the queen and Burghley in October 1580.

English expansion into the New World was supported by a range of motives, including a crudely economic greed for the gold which the Spanish and Portuguese had seized in southern America, and by the desire, both political and religious, to weaken those states. Dee's contribution was not only that of his writings, though the precedent of 'British' conquest was powerful. He also acted as an adviser on navigation to the three voyages of Martin Frobisher in 1576–7, evidently had a financial interest in them, and took some part in the assaying of the ore which Frobisher brought back in the mistaken belief that it was gold.

In the following decade the pace of maritime discovery quickened and there were further calls upon Dee's navigational knowledge. The search for a north-east passage was renewed, and he was among those present at Muscovy House on 17 May 1580 when the intended voyage of Arthur Pet and Charles Jackman was discussed. He provided them with instructions. He was also consulted in July 1582 by Sir George Peckham about the title to Norombega, as the American Indians termed the area roughly covered by Massachusetts and Maine. Peckham had devised a scheme for settling English Catholics in North America, and was naturally concerned about the rights already conferred by the pope upon Spain and Portugal. Dee, assuring Peckham of the priority of Madog's voyage, was promised a generous estate in this new conquest. There was a further meeting with Peckham's men, Clement and David Ingram, in October, but the scheme came to nothing.

More significant than either of these ventures was the initiation of another attempt to discover a north-west passage, with a visit on 23 January 1583 by Sir Francis Walsingham to Dee's house, where Adrian Gilbert, Sir Humphrey Gilbert's younger brother, was already present. The discussions continued on the following day at Robert Beale's house, and now involved John Davys, whom Dee had known since 1579 (and perhaps earlier), and who is thought to have owed much of his theoretical knowledge of navigation to Dee. Adrian Gilbert, Davys, and Dee were subsequently linked in a proposed 'Fellowshippe of New Navigations, Atlanticall and Septentrionall', but in a later draft of the proposal Dee's name was dropped in favour of that of Walter Ralegh.

During this same period Dee was also involved in the debate over the calendar. By the bull *Inter gravissimas* of 24 February 1582, Pope Gregory XIII introduced the reform of the calendar, the main effect of which was the loss of ten days. Dee was consulted, and delivered to Burghley on 26 February 1583 his *Playne discourse … as concerning the needful reformation of the vulgar kalender for the civile yeres and daies accompting*. He recommended the excision of eleven rather than ten days. Harmonization with the Gregorian system was acceptable to him and to the secular authorities, but opposition from Archbishop Grindal and other bishops ensured that England retained the Julian reckoning until 1752.

'Angelic conversations', and journey to Poland Dee had given some hints about magical practice in the 'Mathematicall praeface' of 1570, and these have been plausibly interpreted as 'divination by mirrors, crystals, gems, and other reflecting surfaces' (Clulee, 169). He possessed a number of such objects, such as the distorting mirror (inherited from Sir William Pickering) in which Queen Elizabeth viewed herself in 1575, and the black obsidian mirror and the crystal ball now in the British Museum. Since he was himself unable to see anything in these—except on 25 May 1581 when 'I had sight in *Chrystallō* offerd me, and I sawe'—he employed a series of mediums. Although previous attempts had probably been made, the first recorded session was with Barnabas Saul on 22 December 1581; however, Saul was discredited by March 1582, and was supplanted by 'Mr Talbot', as Dee first knew Edward Kelley.

Dee had seen the nova of 1572 as the augury of some great revelation, and this was realized for him on 10 March 1582, when sessions with Kelley as medium began. The records of the sessions, which ran from May 1583 to May 1587, with some later sessions also recorded, were published in 1659, long after Dee's death, by Meric Casaubon as *A True & Faithful Relation of what Passed for Many Yeers between Dr. John Dee and some Spirits*. Attempts have been made to interpret these writings as the practice of cabbala or even as confidential diplomatic messages. The sessions evidently began with prayer and petitions, and the participants then waited until the medium could see something in the stone; it seems safest to regard them as exercises in crystallomancy. Dee usually records in full the prayer, in Latin or English, with which the action closed.

The ultimate significance of these conversations is of two men linked in mutual dependence on forms of self-deceit: the one, Dee, was led by his own learning to a belief in the possibility of intercourse with a benevolent supernatural world and in the transmutation of baser metals into gold; the other, Kelley, drew upon Dee's learning and substance to feed, perhaps in all sincerity, what must ultimately be judged to be a delusion. As a private record the *True & Faithful Relation* contains not only details of the sessions, but biographical notes supplanting those in the two series of ephemerides, from the time of Dee's departure for Poland to the parting from Kelley. The existence of the sessions must indeed have been known to Dee's contemporaries, since others than he and Kelley were involved, and the angels were at first questioned about the north-west passage, and on 26 March on Adrian Gilbert's task of converting the heathen. When Albrecht Łaski, palatine of Sieradż in Poland, arrived in England and established close relations with Dee, he was admitted to the sessions and occasionally took part in them during the journey to Poland and afterwards.

It is probable that Łaski knew of Dee's fame as an alchemist through Philip Sidney, and that acquaintance with Dee was his principal motive in travelling to England. Łaski arrived on 1 May 1583, and Dee met him on 13 May in Leicester's chambers at Greenwich, and again at Mortlake on 18 May. Łaski returned in greater state to Mortlake in the queen's barge and in the company of Sidney, Lord Russell, and others on 15 June. His acquaintance with Dee was thus being fostered by the more aggressively protestant party at court, which may have seen in Łaski, enriched by alchemical practice and reconverted to protestantism, a counterweight to Catholic and Habsburg power in Europe. Dee's entertainment of Łaski was subsidized by the queen, and his departure with him was no doubt facilitated. The preoccupation with Łaski and with angelic conversations drew Dee away from the planning of the north-west voyage, and the anger that this occasioned among his associates probably lay behind the raid upon his house and library after his departure for Poland. He made over his house to his brother-in-law Nicholas Fromonds, and had his library catalogued (making two fair copies of the catalogue himself) by 6 September. He selected about 800 of his books for the journey.

The party which left Mortlake on 21 September 1583 consisted of Dee, his wife, their three children, Edward Kelley and his wife, Joan, and his step-children, and a retinue of servants. Although Dee took with him his copy of Stadius's *Ephemerides* (one of the two sources of the *Diary*), he made no entries in it until November 1590, some time after his return to England, and evidence for his movements has to be disentangled from the record of 'actions' (as the angelic conversations are normally termed) in the *True & Faithful Relation*. He acquired Maginus's *Ephemerides*, perhaps at the Leipzig fair in 1586; this volume is heavily annotated from September 1586, while the *True & Faithful Relation* provides no biographical information after May 1587.

The party's crossing to the Dutch coast and beyond was hazardous, and once on land its progress in winter was painfully slow. Dee and his family did not reach Łask (near Sieradż) until February 1584. Actions were held (sometimes involving Łaski) on shipboard and at various north German and Polish towns through which Dee and Kelley passed. There were actions at Łask, and many at Cracow, to which Dee and his family moved in March 1584. There he took a house for a year; this probably completed the period of a year and eight months for which he had originally intended to be absent from England, but if his plans had also included the practice of alchemy, nothing of this appears in the actions. Łaski had meanwhile left for Kesmark in Slovakia and seems largely to have lost interest in his guests, though contact and perhaps even payments seem to have been maintained, and Dee records that 'A. L.' (presumably Łaski) was briefly at Třeboň at the end of 1588.

Dee and Kelley, having received angelic bidding to go to the emperor Rudolf, set out for Prague, which they reached on 9 August 1584. Dee wrote to the emperor by Guillermo de San Clemente, the Spanish ambassador, and obtained an hour's audience with Rudolf on 3 September—the only meeting between the two men. Meanwhile Dee received letters from England, dispatched in April, from which he learned of the disasters which had befallen his house and library. The audience with Rudolf had little result, and Dee's contact thereafter was with one of the emperor's counsellors, Jakob Kurtz, though San Clemente proved hospitable, and later acted as godfather to one of Dee's children, Michael. The angel Uriel then instructed Dee to write to the emperor saying he could make the philosopher's stone.

In April 1585 Dee and Kelley (and their families) returned to Cracow and Łaski obtained for Dee audiences with King Stefan Batory. On returning to Prague, Dee and Kelley resumed their angelic conversations, admitting to them Francesco Pucci, a renegade (though ultimately conforming) Catholic. In May 1586 Dee met the Bohemian nobleman Vilém Rožmberk, and at this point Dee's concern with alchemy seems to have revived, and he made a journey to 'Valkenaw glasse-house' and to Leipzig mart. From there he wrote a letter to Walsingham complaining that he had had no answers to his earlier letters, and asking for justice for his house, library, goods, and revenues. Dee and Kelley were banished from the emperor's domains at the instance of the papal nuncio on 29 May, but Rožmberk obtained permission for them to remain on his estates at Třeboň, where, after a confused journey to Erfurt and Kassel, Dee, Kelley, and their families arrived in September 1586.

In December Dee received through Edward Garland an offer of employment from the tsar of Russia. He nevertheless remained with Rožmberk, devoting more time to alchemy, though Kelley increasingly dominated the practice, and even produced what passed for gold. The actions were also resumed, and Dee attempted to 'translate' Kelley's office to his seven-year-old son Arthur. The final recorded actions were in April 1587, during which Kelley received from the spirit Madimi the doctrine that he, Dee, and their wives should hold all things in common. 'It was agreed by us to move the question, whether the sense were of Carnal use (contrary to the law of the Commandment) or of Spiritual love'. The covenant of cross-matching was drawn up and acted upon. Theodore Dee (the name may be significant) was born on 28 February 1588. Although Rožmberk's patronage ensured that the Dees lived in comfort and security at Třeboň, he wrote to Queen Elizabeth in November 1588 to announce the return of himself and Kelley to England. But Kelley did not

return, and Dee made over to him his alchemical materials. For Dee the break was not final; he received letters from Kelley, and continued to hope that he too would return. They parted in February 1589, and Dee left Třeboň at the beginning of a long and occasionally dangerous journey through central Europe to land in England on 23 November 1589.

Dee's library The building up of a large library was a theme that ran through Dee's whole career, and the subject matter of the books in it—insofar as their acquisition can be dated—reflects the themes that preoccupied him throughout his life. At its greatest extent, when the catalogue was compiled immediately before his departure in 1583 for Poland and Bohemia, it was one of the greatest private libraries of sixteenth-century England, rivalled only by those of Andrew Perne and John, Lord Lumley, and it far exceeded in size the libraries in the universities and colleges of Oxford and Cambridge, and such ecclesiastical libraries as had survived the Reformation. There is, however, little evidence for Dee's acquisition of books in the last twenty-five years of his life, and it is also probable that even the 1583 catalogue does not fully record the extent of his collections, particularly of manuscripts.

Dee began to buy books as an undergraduate, and the frequency of the annotations in some of the Latin classical authors which can be attributed to his Cambridge days attest the systematic care with which he read them. The nature of his annotations has in itself been a subject of study; they have been compared to a dialogue between the reader and the text before him. The notes most frequently take the form of underlinings, or of repetition of the words which particularly interested him. These are usually written very neatly in varieties of the elegant italic hand which he developed at Cambridge. Some of the most significant notes, either in the text or on flyleaves, are autobiographical, and are sometimes, to use W. H. Sherman's word, validated with Dee's initials, or with the Greek delta which he used to signify himself. A number of books are recorded in the catalogue in multiple copies, and it has been suggested that, like some university tutors of the time, Dee maintained additional copies for the use of his pupils. A note of exceptional importance records that the book was read in Edmund Bonner's household, and confirms the close association with the bishop which is apparent from a hostile source, the earlier editions of Foxe's *Acts and Monuments*.

Although it was possible to find a wide range of scholarly books in the stock of the Cambridge stationers, the greater range and number of books Dee was able to acquire in Louvain, Antwerp, and Paris is very apparent from the survivors from the years 1548 to 1551. The income he derived from the patronage of Cheke and of Edward VI, and from his aristocratic employers, facilitated the flow of books into his library, until this was halted by the disasters of the Dudleys and his own imprisonment. The introduction to Bonner's household may or may not represent a sincere move to the Catholic position, but the *Supplication* to Queen Mary of 1556 reveals a view common to Catholics and to many protestants, particularly later ones, that the dispersal of the monastic libraries had been a tragedy for learning and a national disgrace. The views that Dee expressed informed the building of his own library for the rest of his life. Most of the recommendations made in the *Supplication* for a royal or national library relate to the rescue, borrowing, and copying of manuscripts from the monasteries, but Dee also envisaged the copying of books in foreign libraries, and the acquisition of large numbers of printed books. In these aims he enjoyed the support of Bonner, but the death of Queen Mary in 1558 and the ejection of Bonner from his see diverted Dee's energy from a national library into the creation of his own, while the books he borrowed, sometimes upon Bonner's security, were not returned. A hastily compiled and possibly incomplete list of his library can also be dated to his time in Bonner's household.

Dee's European travels of 1562–4 ranged more widely than his earlier journeys, and the sources of his books, often the best evidence for his movements, span from Antwerp to Venice; he seems to have employed a copyist in Rome. The dates of publication of his Hebrew books are clustered in these years. Though they survive in relatively large numbers, they are sparsely annotated, which suggests that Dee was not a fluent Hebraist. Although he discussed Paracelsus with Conrad Gesner in 1563, his huge Paracelsian collection seems to be of later date.

For his journey to Poland Dee packed about 800 of his books, and entrusted the care of those remaining at Mortlake to his wife's brother. Within months of his departure the house was raided and many of his books and instruments were stolen or damaged. The culprits can be identified as former associates of Dee—John Davys the navigator and Nicholas Saunder (perhaps a former pupil)—impelled perhaps by Dee's defection from the planning for the north-west passage. It is possible that Adrian Gilbert and Thomas Harriot also received books or instruments. There is no firm evidence for Dee's acquisition of books during his six years of travel in continental Europe. On his return in 1589 he was able, after a dispute, to recover his house and books from Fromonds, and regained some books from Davys, though not from Saunder. During his later years at Mortlake and Manchester there is little evidence for addition to the library, but more for losses, loans, and even sales to alleviate his growing poverty. At some time before his death he seems to have made over his books to John Pontois (1565–1624), a merchant whom he had perhaps met in northern Europe, who retained them until his own death, though both Sir Robert Cotton and John Selden benefited from Pontois's generosity by gift or loan. Since John Woodall and Dee's servant Patrick Saunders were Pontois's heirs, they must have been responsible for the final dispersal of Dee's belongings in 1626 or 1627.

Dee claimed in 1592 that he had owned three thousand books and a thousand manuscripts. The catalogue of 1583, compiled by Andreas Fremonsheim, factor to Birkmanns of Cologne, records a smaller total, though it is possible that in the haste of departure Dee or Fremonsheim under-

recorded the collections, particularly those of manuscripts. Though the library is now widely dispersed, the interests of antiquaries, notably Cotton and Brian Twyne, are responsible for the substantial holdings of manuscripts once owned by Dee now in the British Library and the library of Corpus Christi College, Oxford. The largest single accumulation of his printed books is in the library of the Royal College of Physicians; it derives ultimately from the depredations of Nicholas Saunder in 1583.

Later years and death The five years after Dee's return from Poland in 1589 were spent in attempts to recover his losses and to obtain a place that would provide for the needs of his large and growing household. (Madimi Newton Dee was born in 1590, Frances in 1592, and Margaret in 1595; Michael, however, died in 1594.) He came to an agreement with Nicholas Fromonds about the reoccupation of his house, united the books he had taken abroad with those which still remained at Mortlake, and recovered some of his missing volumes. By a legal oversight he had lost the income from his two rectories, and accordingly petitioned the queen for relief. The 'Compendious rehearsal' laid before the commissioners, Sir Thomas Gorges and Sir John Wolley, on 22 November (and previously before the queen by the countess of Warwick on 9 November) is the most reliable and comprehensive account of his life and works (eight printed and thirty-six in manuscript), and it was updated in 1594. It brought some financial relief from the queen but little redress, and Dee relied for a livelihood on these grants, on loans, and on fees from students. The quest for preferment recommenced, and Dee had hopes of the mastership of St Cross at Winchester, the chancellorship of St Paul's, and, as in 1564, the deanery of Gloucester.

In May 1595 Dee obtained the wardenship of the collegiate church at Manchester, and took up the office in February 1596. He did not, however relinquish his Mortlake house, and seems to have left many of his books there, perhaps under the care of one Bartholomew Hickman, who had been sent to Dee in 1579 by Sir Christopher Hatton. The affairs of the college were in some disorder, and attempts to resolve them caused conflict with the fellows, notably with Oliver Carter, whose conduct was a frequent source of complaint in the *Diary* and in Dee's letters.

Dee was visited by Christopher Saxton in 1596, and in May 1597 conducted a survey of the parish of Manchester. In the latter year Dee gave advice in the case of 'demonic possession' known as the 'Seven in Lancashire', lending books to the justice involved. This is also the year of the last of Dee's political and maritime tracts, the *Thalattokratia Brettanikē*, a treatise on the sea-limits of the British empire written in response to a request in September by Sir Edward Dyer. Dee and his family were hardpressed for money, and perhaps for food also during the famines of the 1590s. Help came in the form of cattle from Dee's Welsh cousins, and in barrels of rye from Pontois, who was to become his final support and his heir. There are no entries in the *Diary* between March 1598 and 18 June 1600; Dee was probably in London, busied about the affairs of the college, since he was able on his return to show the fellows 'the most part of the things that I had browght to pass at London for the College good' (*Private Diary*). He also visited the grammar school on 5 August 1590, finding 'great imperfections' (ibid.) in the scholars. Since the entries cease altogether on 6 April 1601, few details of Dee's later life are known, but the mention of Roger Cook suggests that his old assistant had set up alchemical practice at Manchester.

Dee's poverty was certainly deepening, since he was forced to borrow money from Edmund Chetham in Manchester, and books and manuscripts seem to have been passing into and out of the earl of Northumberland's library at Sion, apparently by the agency of Dee's servant Patrick Saunders. He was presumably also in London for the printing by Peter Short of *A Letter Containing a most Briefe Discourse Apologeticall*, an expanded version of the sixth chapter of the 'Compendious rehearsal' of 1592–4 (in which the list of manuscript works has grown to forty-eight), but addressed to the archbishop of Canterbury. (This tract was reprinted by Short's widow in 1603 as *A Letter, Nine Yeeres since, Written and First Published*.)

After the accession of James I, Dee claims to have become the new king's 'sworne servant' on 9 August 1603, but was nevertheless alarmed by his published opinions on witchcraft. The tract addressed to the archbishop is usually found with a printed petition to the king, and a verse address to the Commons (both dated June 1604) protesting passionately against the slanderous epithet of 'conjurer', and calling for a special act to restrain the slander. Where Dee was at this time is unclear, but his family must have remained in Manchester, since his wife, Jane Dee, died of the plague and was buried there on 23 March 1605. The younger children, and perhaps an older son, Rowland, who had been baptized in 1583, must have perished then, since nothing is known of them thereafter.

Probably some time after 1605, Dee returned to Mortlake with his surviving daughter, Katherine (Arthur had married in 1602), and resumed the angelic actions with Bartholomew Hickman as skryer. An action appended to the *True & Faithful Relation* is dated 9 July 1607, and reveals that he was contemplating another foreign journey, and that he intended, or perhaps had been persuaded, to make Pontois his heir. Dee is traditionally said to have died at Mortlake in December 1608, but Pontois, who inherited Maginus's *Ephemerides* with the other books, noted against the date 26 March 1609 a death's head and 'Jno Δ hor.3.a.m.'. This is confirmed by a note of Anthony Wood to Ashmole that Dee had died in Bishopsgate Street, where Pontois lived. 1609 is also the date given in a letter from Arthur Dee. Neither Pontois nor another informant of Ashmole, John Aubrey, could find a will, but Aubrey was shown the site of Dee's grave in Mortlake church.

Character, religion, and posthumous reputation Aubrey, enquiring on behalf of Ashmole, was told by Goody Faldo of Mortlake, who had as a child known the aged Dee, that 'he was tall (or of good stature & slender) wore a black gowne still with long sleeves, with slitts but without Buttons & loopes & tufts' (J. Aubrey, *Brief Lives*, ed. O. L. Dick, 1949, 89). He was 'a very handsome man', 'a mighty good man: a great Peacemaker'. The course of his life suggests also that he had great charm and persuasiveness. It is hard to categorize his religious views. His profound piety stands out from every page of the *True & Faithful Relation*. 'Protestant humanist' adequately describes the position of his early years, yet in Queen Mary's reign he was able so to persuade Bonner of his Catholic conformity that he was admitted to the bishop's household, and acted as his chaplain. Under Elizabeth he seems to have been aligned with the more militantly protestant party of Leicester, Sidney, and Walsingham, yet in Prague he cultivated the Spanish ambassador, who stood godfather to Michael Dee. He prudently declined Pucci's invitation to Rome. He was certainly perplexed by the angelic teaching on transubstantiation, which emerged from Kelley's mouth as markedly Catholic, at an action of 28 January 1585. There is no ground for supposing that his 'mission' of 1583–9 was in any way ecumenical, nor that his ability to adapt to different religious usages owed anything to the familist doctrine of Hendrik Niclaes.

Dee died in poverty, and in an obscurity perhaps contrived by friends and by his surviving family. Pontois guarded his library, though giving or lending books to scholars such as Selden or Cotton, but his generosity was limited by long absences in Virginia (he was vice-admiral of the colony at the time of his death). Cotton sought older manuscripts, while other collectors were interested in Dee as a mathematician, and it is this aspect of his reputation, based upon the 'Mathematicall praeface', which endured into the seventeenth century. Casaubon's publication of the angelic conversations in 1659, in revealing a 'private' aspect of Dee, in fact distorted the latter's reputation. (There is no better illustration of this than the *Dictionary of National Biography* article on Dee.) If the nadir of Dee's reputation was reached with William Godwin's *Lives of the Necromancers* (1834), serious interest revived with Halliwell's imperfect edition (1842) of the *Diary* and of that part of the library catalogue which listed the manuscripts which he owned.

With M. R. James's *List of Manuscripts Formerly Owned by Dr. John Dee* (1921), the great importance of Dee's part in the preservation of dispersed monastic books began to emerge, and was confirmed by Roberts and Watson's edition of *John Dee's Library Catalogue* (1990), which also listed in full for the first time Dee's printed books. Charlotte Fell Smith's full-length biography, *John Dee* (1909), was a scholarly and sympathetic counter to earlier biographical accounts. Dee's significant part in the education and instructing of Tudor navigators was brought out in E. G. R. Taylor's *Tudor Geography, 1485–1583* (1930), and led to the recognition of his role in planning, and providing precedent for, British settlement in North America.

I. R. F. Calder's London PhD thesis 'John Dee studied as an English Neoplatonist' (1952) was perhaps the first serious study of Dee's thought and led to a revaluation of Dee's place in the English Renaissance by Dame Frances Yates and her colleagues. His influence on the later scientific revolution, his function as a mathematical instructor of artisans, and the strength of his undoubted interest in Neoplatonism and hermeticism were stressed, perhaps to excess. Peter J. French's *John Dee: the World of an Elizabethan Magus* (1972) was the fullest statement of this 'Warburg interpretation'. Subsequent studies concentrated on the elucidation of Dee's (not necessarily consistent) natural philosophy (Nicholas H. Clulee, 1988) and on his relationship with the texts in his library, and his political writings (W. H. Sherman, 1995). *The Diaries of John Dee*, edited by Edward Fenton (1998), includes the early records transcribed by Ashmole and biographical entries from the *True & Faithful Relation* of 1659. A full-length biography, *The Queen's Conjuror: the Science and Magic of Dr Dee*, was published in 2001 by Benjamin Woolley.

R. JULIAN ROBERTS

Sources 'The compendious rehearsal of John Dee', in *Johannis … Glastoniensis Chronica, sive, Historia de rebus Glastoniensibus*, ed. T. Hearne, 2 (1726), 497–556 · J. Dee, annotations to J. Stadius, *Ephemerides novae ab anno 1554 usque ad annum 1600* (1570), Bodl. Oxf., MS Ashmole 487 · J. Dee, annotations to J. A. Maginus, *Ephemerides coelestium motuum ad annos XL* (1582), Bodl. Oxf., MS Ashmole 488 · *The private diary of Dr. John Dee*, ed. J. O. Halliwell (1842) · J. Dee, *Diary for the years 1595–1601*, ed. J. E. Bailey (1880) [privately printed] · J. Dee, 'Conference with angels', BL, MS Sloane 3188 · *A true & faithful relation of what passed for many yeers between Dr John Dee and some spirits*, ed. M. Casaubon (1659) · J. Roberts and A. G. Watson, eds., *John Dee's library catalogue* (1990) · C. Fell Smith, *John Dee, 1527–1608* (1909) · N. H. Clulee, *John Dee's natural philosophy: between science and religion* (1988) · W. H. Sherman, *John Dee: the politics of reading and writing in the English Renaissance* (1995) · P. J. French, *John Dee: the world of an Elizabethan magus* (1972) · J. Roberts, 'John Dee and the matter of Britain', *Transactions of the Honourable Society of Cymmrodorion* (1991), 129–43 · G. A. Williams, *Madoc: the making of a myth* (1979) · G. A. Williams, *Welsh wizard and British empire* (1980) · E. G. R. Taylor, *Tudor geography, 1485–1583* (1930) · J. D. North, 'The western calendar, 12: John Dee as a historian', *Gregorian reform of the calendar*, ed. G. V. Coyne, M. A. Hoskin, and O. Pedersen (1983), 102–4 · G. Lloyd Jones, *The discovery of Hebrew in Tudor England: a third language* (1983) · M. Feingold, *The mathematicians' apprenticeship: science, universities, and society in England, 1560–1640* (1984) · I. R. F. Calder, 'John Dee studied as an English Neoplatonist', PhD diss., U. Lond., 1952 · F. A. Yates, *Theatre of the world* (1969) · F. A. Yates, *The Rosicrucian enlightenment* (1972) · F. A. Yates, *The occult philosophy in the Elizabethan age* (1979)

Archives Bodl. Oxf., alchemical notes · Bodl. Oxf., autobiography · Bodl. Oxf., chemical diary · Bodl. Oxf., commonplace book · Bodl. Oxf., diaries and papers · Bodl. Oxf., library catalogue · Bodl. Oxf., notes on nocturnal visitation · CUL · RCP Lond. · Trinity Cam., library catalogue | BL, Cotton MSS, corresp. and papers · BL, Harley MSS, letters and papers · BL, Lansdowne MSS, letters and papers · BL, Sloane MSS, papers · CCC Oxf., Twyne MSS

Likenesses oils, 1574–86, AM Oxf. [*see illus.*] · J. Dee, self-portrait?, c.1577, BL, MS Cotton Charter XIV.1 · W. P. Sherlock, stipple (after portrait, 1574–86), BM, NPG

Dee, Philip Ivor (1904–1983), physicist, was born on 8 April 1904 in Stroud, the second of three sons (there were no daughters) of Albert John Dee, schoolmaster in Cainscross, and his wife, Maria Kitchen, daughter of William Tiley, a butcher of Ebley. He was educated at Marling School, Stroud, and gained a scholarship to Sidney Sussex College, Cambridge, where he obtained a first class in both parts of the natural sciences tripos (1925 and 1926). In 1929 Dee married Phyllis Elsie, daughter of George Williams Tyte, clockmaker. They had two daughters.

During his years as Stokes student at Pembroke College, Cambridge (1930–33), Dee strongly impressed Lord Rutherford of Nelson, head of the Cavendish Laboratory. He had started research under C. T. R. Wilson and by 1931 was a skilful user of cloud chambers, devices which revealed the tracks of ionizing particles passing through supersaturated water vapour. His mastery of technique meant he could prove with certainty the lack of significant interaction of neutrons with electrons. The great discoveries in 1932 by James Chadwick and by John Cockcroft and E. T. S. Walton persuaded him to switch to study transmutation of atoms by bombardment with accelerated ions. His own early exciting and vivid research concerned the two modes of reaction between deuterons to yield tritium and protons or helium-3 and neutrons. The results of bombardment of lithium-6 with deuterons and of lithium-7 with protons followed, and he proved elegantly that fast protons with boron-11 gave three-helium nuclei. He became a fellow of Sidney Sussex College (honorary fellow, 1948) and university lecturer in 1934 and later a deputy of Lord Rutherford, assuming responsibility for the construction of 1.2 MeV and 2.0 MeV accelerators. Notable researches with these ensued between 1937 and 1939. Dee was a lecturer in physics at the Clarendon Laboratory from 1934 to 1943.

The wartime phase of Dee's work was of great national importance. As a superintendent of the Ministry of Aircraft Production TRE (telecommunications research establishment) from 1939 to 1945 he took charge of most of the work on the generation of energy sources for radar. His team of brilliant young scientists developed new radar equipment for AI (aircraft interception), ASV (anti-surface vessel), and H2S (blind bombing), which gave excellent performance. Dee was eminently practical, and his relations with politicians, service officers of all ranks, and fellow scientists proved equally easy. He was a great catalyst whose unflagging energy inspired all connected with radar to work together as a creative team. Honours came to him, among them fellowship of the Royal Society (1941), appointment OBE (1943) and CBE (1946), and the Hughes medal (1952).

In 1943 Dee was appointed professor of natural philosophy at Glasgow University and after the war he began to modernize physics there. He did much to ensure that the Conseil Européen de Recherches Nucléaires (CERN) at Geneva was created in its university-orientated form and he served important national organizations. Later at the Kelvin Laboratory he built a large linear accelerator yielding electrons of 160 MeV energy. His Glasgow department of physics, from which he retired in 1972, became one of the leaders in nuclear science; both the work done and quality of its graduates testified to his capability. Dee was awarded an honorary DSc by the University of Strathclyde in 1980.

Dee was very dark, over 6 feet tall, and slimly built, and with his commanding presence and direct manner of approach he was held in awe by most of his contemporaries and certainly by his students. Those who came to know him well realized his sincere interest in their well-being. Dee died in the Western Infirmary, Glasgow, on 17 April 1983.   SAMUEL C. CURRAN, *rev.*

Sources S. Curran, *Memoirs FRS*, 30 (1984), 141–66 · P. I. Dee, 'The Rutherford memorial lecture, 1965', *PRS*, 298A (1967), 103–22 · R. V. Jones, *Most secret war* (1978) · private information (1990) · *The Times* (27 April 1983), 12f · *CCI* (1983)
Archives U. Glas., Archives and Business Records Centre, working papers incl. diaries of experiments
Likenesses double portrait, photograph, 1980 (with Sir S. Curran), repro. in Curran, *Memoirs FRS* · C. Kynoch, portrait, repro. in Curran, *Memoirs FRS*
Wealth at death £80,653.67: confirmation, 8 June 1983, *CCI*

Deedes, Sir Wyndham Henry (1883–1956), army officer, civil administrator, and social worker, was born on 10 March 1883 at 19 Westbourne Place, Belgravia, London, the second son of Colonel Herbert George Deedes, assistant under-secretary of state for war, and his wife, Rose Eleanor (*d.* 1940), daughter of Major-General Lousada Barrow of the Madras staff corps. The Deedes family had risen to the ranks of the landed gentry three hundred years before, making its fortune in the woollen trade near Dover. Deedes's own father had inherited two neighbouring properties in Kent, Sandling Park and Saltwood Castle, but had pursued a career in the army.

Deedes's childhood home was Saltwood, but he spent much time in London. He was educated at Eton College from the age of nine, but it was not a happy experience. A gentle, rather grave, little boy, he left school, in his own eyes, 'absolutely uneducated' and joined the army almost at once. In February 1901 he received his commission in the King's Royal Rifle Corps and was soon bound for South Africa, where he impressed his commanding officer. He was a devout Anglican, and his care for the soldiers in his command and an interest in social issues were already evident. He even helped his men dig trenches.

Between 1903 and 1910 Deedes was successively stationed at Bermuda, Ireland (where he was aide-de-camp to his uncle, General Knox), England, and Malta. By 1906 he was a lieutenant. In February 1908 he was dispatched to Malta, there serving as aide-de-camp to the governor, Sir Harry Grant. A gifted linguist, he had already taught himself Dutch and German; and it was in Malta that he began to learn the language which would change his life: Turkish. He applied to join the gendarmerie in the British district of Macedonia, and he arrived in Constantinople in February 1910. There Deedes made the acquaintance of as many Turks as he could and perfected his knowledge of their language. At this time he also met the young Robert Graves. He was subsequently transferred, first to Smyrna, then to Tripoli, superintending an area stretching from the Mediterranean to the southern fringe of the Libyan desert: four times the size of France. Here he found the gendarmerie in a desperate state. They were only a handful. They had few clothes and no barracks. They had not been paid. Deedes himself had no money and no maps. He was only twenty-seven. But still he relished the challenge.

Sir Wyndham Henry Deedes (1883–1956), by Elliott & Fry, 1944

By the time he left, in July 1911, and returned to Smyrna the gendarmerie was 1500 strong and impressively efficient.

At this time Deedes was profoundly influenced by reading the *Prevention of Destitution* (1911), by Sidney and Beatrice Webb, and he wrote to his mother from Smyrna that he could think of no better way to live than to spend himself in charity organization work. Nevertheless, he was placed on a government commission in the east of Anatolia, landing at Samsun in July 1913 and taking the works of John Stuart Mill, Thomas Huxley, and Charles Darwin with him into the Anatolian highlands. In 1913 he was seconded by the Foreign Office to the Turkish government to assist Talaat, minister of the interior. He went gladly, beginning to write articles on Turkey for the *Nineteenth Century*. He then became a civil inspector, a position granted by the sultan, and worked on a scheme to resettle refugees in Bursa. However, the outbreak of the First World War forced his return to Britain. Highly respected for his knowledge of Turkish, he was reunited with the intelligence department at the War Office, visiting the Turkish embassy frequently, and watching the effects of British diplomacy critically as Turkey swung into the German camp.

Deedes was still at the War Office when the Gallipoli campaign was first drafted and he was pessimistic about its prospects. Between February 1915 and January 1916 he served on the expedition as a staff captain. He was given his own section, I(B), with a brief to keep an eye open on guides, interpreters, and dubious characters, and also to hunt for spies. An outstanding officer who saw issues with a rare clarity, he had the courage to press, with a number of junior officers, for strategic change. When, after twelve futile months, withdrawal took place, I(B) played a valuable part in ensuring the secrecy, and the success, of the evacuation. Deedes himself was three times mentioned in dispatches and in January 1916 was awarded the DSO.

By now Deedes had been transferred to the intelligence service in Cairo and Alexandria. In Cairo he joined forces with those who were planning the Arab revolt, among them T. E. Lawrence, with whom he worked closely but apparently without any personal rapport. In 1916 he became a major; in 1917 brevet lieutenant-colonel. When General Allenby entered Jerusalem on 11 December Deedes was one of the party. Shortly afterwards he was stationed there to help administer the city, conciliate in disputes, work for displaced peoples, and orchestrate the efforts of relief agencies in the city. It was here he encountered, perhaps for the first time, the aspirations of the Zionist movement (with which he was later to identify) and in April 1918 he met Chaim Weizmann. In that year the two became firm friends, discussing ideals and collaborating in saving a Jewish settlement scheduled for eviction as a security hazard.

In 1918 Deedes was made temporary brigadier-general, one of the youngest in the army. In 1919 he was seconded to the Foreign Office for work in Egypt. His distinctive gifts for sympathetic but dispassionate diplomacy, and his rare linguistic expertise, had earned him a reputation in influential quarters. After the armistice with Turkey it was intended that he should join the allied commission at Constantinople. However, while on home leave after four and a half years spent abroad, he was approached to join the administration to run Palestine under the new British mandate. Despite a feeling of unworthiness, and still committed to the idea of doing social work, Deedes was persuaded by Herbert Samuel, the first high commissioner, to become chief secretary in the Palestine administration. Samuel later wrote in his memoirs that he had asked for Deedes in April 1920 not only because he was by profession a soldier of great administrative capacity, but because 'there was in him a strong strain of idealism which drew him powerfully to the Holy Land' (DNB). However, Deedes undertook to serve for only two years. On arrival in Jerusalem in May 1920 he recruited an energetic staff of young men, Arabs as well as Jews, who established a model of collaboration and enterprise. He was deeply interested in both the Arab desire for freedom from foreign rule and the Jewish claim on Palestine as a national home.

Deedes believed in personal relations more than political and official relationships: essentially he was driven not by politics, but by his religion. He sought to reconcile Arab and Zionist aspirations, but opposed centralization and ventured into the provinces to see matters for himself. He grew popular and was warmly praised by Jews and Arabs alike. A leading Arab newspaper commented: 'Every element in the country, as far as we can observe, seems to think that he is their friend' (DNB). Both communities sensed that his was a distinctive and unusual presence among them and knew how to value it. His mother joined him in Jerusalem, creating a home in which people of different faiths and opinions could meet together and talk. But the situation was increasingly volatile. Deedes struggled to control the May Day riots in Jaffa in 1921, decisively allowing Jews to defend themselves, standing on a lorry, unarmed and virtually alone, and exhorting the crowds around him to disperse. He saved a Jewish settlement at Rehoboth from an assault by a crowd of ten thousand, not by deploying soldiers, but by instructing an aeroplane to dive low over their heads.

In 1921 Deedes was knighted. Early in 1923 he resigned. Some thought him worn down by administration. In reality he was troubled by the gulf which separated him as chief secretary from humble people: he had no interest in material advantages, and the trappings of office and authority seemed only a hindrance to spiritual life. He had always practised stern self-denial and cultivated the great grace of humility, and he argued that there were plenty of abler men to replace him. He transferred to the Highland light infantry in 1923 and retired with the rank of colonel and honorary rank of brigadier-general. In April 1923 he finally returned to live in England, refusing all official ceremonies, preferring to say his farewells quietly and personally.

At the age of forty Wyndham Deedes began a new career in social work. He moved into two rooms in University House, Bethnal Green, a poor suburb of London, much inhabited by immigrants. There he became absorbed in social work for several organizations, pursuing the solitary, devout life of a Christian ascetic. He worked assiduously for the National Council of Social Service and chaired its London council. He helped to establish a bookshop where public talks took place. He slept little, rose at 5.30, and dealt with correspondence before breakfast. Usually, he ate only a biscuit for lunch. Much of his income he gave away. He read a great deal, often theology, in the evenings, and also translated Turkish novels into English.

The world beyond Bethnal Green was not cast aside. Deedes broadcast once a week over the BBC, in Turkish which now seemed a little dated, though it had a rare elegance. He still travelled abroad, to promote Zionism in Europe and the United States. He made himself useful in the new representative bodies of the Church of England. Instinctively he strongly opposed national socialism and visited Germany twice on missions of protest or assistance. Deedes was often a guest of the Weizmanns, who lived in Kensington. He revisited Turkey towards the end of 1939 after a violent earthquake had occurred there. He was a founder of the Turkish Centre in Fitzhardinge Street in London. In 1943 he was instrumental in creating, in Bedford Square, the British Association for the Jewish National Home in Palestine; a year later he was chiefly responsible for acquiring the house in Manchester Square which became Palestine House. (On 30 September 1948 it became the legation of Israel.)

When war broke out again in September 1939 Deedes chose to serve in the civil defence. He became a conscientious chief air-raid warden for the borough. When bombed out of University House he moved into a neighbouring tenement. In 1941 his work assumed a more explicitly political character when he became Labour member of the London county council for North-East Bethnal Green, remaining such until 1946. He also became a member of the education committee.

A succession of operations—three in 1946 alone—diminished Deedes's physical powers and his stamina. His mother had died in 1940, and Saltwood Castle was sold. He was advised to leave London on health grounds, and in 1950 he returned to Hythe, near the family home of Saltwood, living simply in a single bed-sitting room in a boarding-house, often passing the night deep in meditation and noting his reflections, as he had for years, on little scraps of paper. Visitors were struck by the spiritual side of his nature. Eliahu Elath, the Israeli ambassador, who met him in 1950, noted that 'the strength which was so visibly deserting his body could, in some mysterious way, be transmuting itself into moral and spiritual vitality' (Elath, Bentwich, and May, 82). The creation of the state of Israel proved to be the fulfilment of his hopes, and Deedes reflected that perhaps he had been allowed to live only to see it happen. Sir Wyndham Deedes died on 2 September 1956 in St Bartholomew's Hospital, London.

ANDREW CHANDLER

Sources J. Presland [G. Bendit], *Deedes Bey* (1941) · Anglo-Israel Association, *Memories of Sir Wyndham Deedes*, ed. E. Elath, N. Bentwich, and D. May (1958) · Viscount Samuel [H. L. S. Samuel], *Memoirs* (1945) · B. Wasserstein, *Wyndham Deedes in Palestine* (1973) · B. Wasserstein, *The British in Palestine: the mandatory government and the Arab–Jewish conflict, 1917–1929*, 2nd edn (1991) · B. Wasserstein, *Herbert Samuel: a political life* (1992) · b. cert. · d. cert. · *CGPLA Eng. & Wales* (1956) · *The Times* (4 Sept 1956)
Archives Canterbury Cathedral, archives, corresp. and papers, mainly relating to Middle East · Queen's College, Birmingham, MSS · St Ant. Oxf., Middle East Centre, corresp. | Bodl. Oxf., corresp. for British Association for the Jewish National Home in Palestine · Bodl. Oxf., corresp. for the co-ordinating committee for refugees · Wellcome L., corresp. with Charles Singer | FILM BFI NFTVA, propaganda film footage
Likenesses Elliott & Fry, photograph, 1944, NPG [*see illus.*] · Elliott & Fry, photograph, *c.*1945, Anglo-Israel Association; repro. in *Memories*
Wealth at death £1238 15*s.* 1*d.*: administration, 6 Dec 1956, *CGPLA Eng. & Wales*

Deeping, (George) Warwick (1877–1950), novelist, was born on 28 May 1877 at Prospect House, High Street, Southend-on-Sea, Essex, the only son and eldest of the three children of George Davidson Deeping (1848–1909), surgeon, and his wife, Marianne (1843–1920), daughter of William Rollinson Warwick MD of Southend-on-Sea and his wife, Anne. Warwick Deeping came from a medical family. His father, born in Lincolnshire, had joined the medical practice of Warwick and Philips in Prospect House about 1874, and held the offices of Admiralty surgeon, medical officer of health, and magistrate. Deeping's maternal grandfather, William Rollinson Warwick MD, who was born in Newark, Nottinghamshire, had practised

(George) Warwick Deeping (1877–1950), by Howard Coster, 1937

in Southend from the early 1840s. The Deepings and the Warwicks were closely involved in the life of St John's Church, Southend, although Warwick Deeping was baptized in the neighbouring parish of Southchurch. By 1881 Warwick Deeping's family had moved to 8 Royal Terrace, and by 1891 to 19 Royal Terrace, Southend, and it was here, overlooking the Thames estuary, that Deeping spent his childhood and youth. The family was comfortably off, with three servants. In his recollections of St John's Church, written in 1945, Deeping gives an amusing and lively description of his childhood. He was a happy child and enjoyed simple outdoor pursuits such as cricket, blackberrying, 'playing ... games in the Shrubbery, and running wild on the somewhat wild cliffs, and paddling and digging on the beach, and being much nearer to Nature than many modern children' (Deeping). His childhood was not without sadness, however, for his small sister Constance Eleanor died at home in 1885 aged seven months. He described himself as a 'shy and sensitive youth', and as far as girls were concerned 'romance seemed frustrated' (ibid.). Warwick Deeping was educated by private tutors, and at the Merchant Taylors' School in London, but he claimed he was bored and idle at school, and 'escaped some of the repressions and futilities of a merely academic education' (Kunitz and Haycraft, 361). He went on to read science and medicine at Trinity College, Cambridge, gaining a BA in 1898 and MB, MA in 1902. He continued his medical training at the Middlesex Hospital, London, and was awarded his MD in 1912.

The Deeping family moved to Hastings in Sussex when Dr Deeping retired in 1900. There on 21 September 1904 Warwick Deeping married Maude Phyllis Merrill (1882/3–1971), daughter of Captain Jacob Merrill, late of the hussars (Deeping's first novel, the Arthurian *Uther and Igraine*, 1903, was dedicated to 'Maude Merrill with the author's homage'). They began married life in rooms in Sedlescombe in Sussex, and by 1908 had moved to Gate Farm, Battle. From 1911 to 1919 they lived in a small house, Green Gore, in Whatlington Road, Battle, which they had built for themselves.

Warwick Deeping began to write poetry at the age of twenty. Becoming 'infected with medievalism of the romantic school' (Kunitz and Haycraft), he then wrote a series of historical novels, including *Uther and Igraine*, *Bertrand of Brittany* (1908), and *The Red Scout* (1909). These early works were successful enough to persuade Deeping to take up writing full-time, having practised as a doctor in Hastings for just one year. It was *Sorrell and Son* (1925) which made Deeping famous. Inspired by the novelist's experiences in the First World War, it tells the moving story of Captain Stephen Sorrell, who, having found life hard since demobilization, struggles to make a living in order to give his son Kit a private education and send him to medical school. Deeping had joined the Royal Army Medical Corps in April 1915; he saw active service in the Gallipoli campaign, and afterwards in Egypt, France, and Belgium. He stated later: 'The war, as a great human experience, launched me on deeper seas. Inevitably *Sorrell and Son* was a product of the war. One realized that a nice culture was less important than courage and character' (Kunitz and Haycraft). The developing relationship between Stephen Sorrell and his son is at the centre of the story, and reflects the love and admiration which Deeping felt for his own father:

> Kit's most convincing hero was his father. Convincing because his heroism was not too obvious; it had that quality of steadfastness … as Christopher matured, his father became to him—not quite a great man—but something more human, a very lovable one.

Sorrell and Son was a best-seller, and was made into a film in 1933 directed by Jack Raymond and starring H. B. Warner as Sorrell and Hugh Williams as Kit (a silent version had been made in 1927).

Deeping was a skilful and entertaining story-teller, basing many of his novels on his own life and experiences, and drawing particularly on his medical background and training. The central characters of *Sorrell and Son*, *Roper's Row* (1929), *Sincerity* (1912), and *The Dark House* (1941) are doctors, and Deeping uses medical terms with ease and describes operations in detail. Several of his novels, including *The Road* (1931), *No Hero This* (1936), and *Blind Man's Year* (1937), are set in Sussex, where he lived for twenty years; four are based on his childhood recollections. *The Dark House*, *Slade* (1943), *Mr Gurney and Mr Slade* (1944), and *Caroline Terrace* (1955) are set in Southend (alias Southfleet) in the period from 1890 to the First World War.

Warwick Deeping has been criticized for sentimentality. 'His gift was very much for the sentimental and all too human narrative. He was content to make recognizable emotional symbols rather than individual men and women' (*The Times*, 21 April 1950). His novels, however, deal with some serious themes, including the role of women and marriage in *Sorrell and Son*. Deeping was a prolific writer, producing a collection of short stories and more than seventy novels, published by Cassell. His books were translated into other languages, notably German (*Sorrell and Son* sold more than 230,000 copies in Germany), and were also published in North America, where Deeping enjoyed a large following. The *New York Times*, on 21 April 1950, described his novels as possessing 'British solidity, and gentlemanly goodness and fun, and well-woven plots'. Deeping may not now be seen as a major literary figure, but he was an extremely popular novelist in his day.

Deeping and his wife, Maude, moved to Surrey in 1919, purchasing Eastlands in Brooklands Lane, Weybridge, from Hugh Locke-King. They had a very happy marriage, and Deeping described his wife as 'the sort of comrade a man dreams of and so rarely finds' (Kunitz and Haycraft). There were no children. Deeping remained at Eastlands until his death, writing most of his novels there. He extended the estate and redesigned the gardens, which he opened for charity. His interests included tennis, golf, motoring, gardening, and carpentry. Deeping died on 20 April 1950, at Weybridge Hospital, Surrey, and was cremated at Woking crematorium on 24 April 1950. A memorial plaque to him was placed in St John's churchyard, Southend.

JENNIFER BUTLER

Sources Venn, *Alum. Cant.* · S. J. Kunitz and H. Haycraft, eds., *Twentieth century authors: a biographical dictionary of modern literature* (1942) · W. Deeping, *The parish church of St John's, Southend* (1950) · parish register, Southend, St John's, Essex RO, D/P 534/1/1, 2, 7, 10 · parish register, Southchurch, Essex RO, D/P 120/1/5 · L. Titman, 'Warwick Deeping and Southend', *Essex Countryside*, 2/5–6 (1953–4) [with associated letter] · *The Times* (21 April 1950) · *Southend Standard* (27 April 1950) · *WW* (1914) · *WW* (1933) · *WW* (1937) · *WW* (1948) · b. cert. · m. cert. · d. cert. · trade directories for Southend-on-Sea, 1839–1905, Essex RO, Southend · electoral registers and trade directories, E. Sussex RO · electoral registers, Surrey RO · local history cuttings, Southend Central Library, local studies library, books 5–8, 12, 15, 1936–70 · reference files on Deeping and Eastlands, Elmbridge Museum · B. Jacobs, *A history of Eastlands* (c.1984) · Woking crematorium · census returns, 1891

Archives Boston University, Warwick Deeping collection · Essex RO, Southend, typescript draft history of St John's, Southend, and associated corresp., D/P 534/28/8, 9 | BL, corresp. with Society of Authors, Add. MSS 63231–63233 · King's Lond., corresp. with Basil Liddell Hart

Likenesses K. Shackleton, chalk drawing, 1936, NPG · Bassano Studios, photographs, 1937, NPG · H. Coster, photograph, 1937, NPG [*see illus.*] · H. Coster, photographs, c.1939, NPG · J. T. May, photographs, repro. in *Surrey County Journal* · photograph, repro. in *The Times* · photograph, repro. in Kunitz and Haycraft, eds., *Twentieth-century authors* (1942) · photographs (in youth), repro. in Deeping, *The parish church*

Wealth at death £33,675 9s. 6d.: probate, 2 Sept 1950, *CGPLA Eng. & Wales*

Deering, George Charles [*formerly* Georg Karl Dering] **(1695?–1749)**, botanist, was born in Saxony and educated at the Hamburg Gymnasium and the University of Leiden (1708–10), where he studied under Boerhaave but did not proceed to a degree. After extensive travel in Europe he moved to London in 1713 as secretary to Baron Schach, envoy-extraordinary from Peter the Great to Queen Anne. He decided to stay on in Britain and obtained a series of posts as a tutor until he married, in November 1718; his wife's name is not known. Three days after the wedding he returned to the continent to qualify in medicine. He acquired a degree at Rheims, then proceeded to Paris, where he studied midwifery, anatomy, and botany. He then returned to England in 1719 and set up in medical practice in a poor part of London. Having developed a keenness for field botany while in Paris, he joined a small botanical society, established by John Martyn, which existed from 1721 to 1726.

By 1736 Deering was no longer married (his wife having died or parted from him), and he thought to improve his position by moving to Nottingham, with a letter of recommendation from Sloane. After two years there he published a list of plants which he had observed in the neighbourhood, one of the earliest British local floras. For some of the cryptogamic coverage in this he was aided by his fellow countryman Dillenius, whose acquaintance he had made in Martyn's botanical society and who afterwards acknowledged the help received from Deering in the preface to his classic work, *Historia muscorum*.

At first Deering was successful in his new practice in Nottingham, especially in treating smallpox, on which he published a small tract setting out his method; but an unfortunate temper seems to have been his undoing and reduced him to something like poverty. Friends bought him 'an electrical machine' (doubtless a Leyden jar, for the treatment of rheumatic conditions) by which he was able to earn a little money, but service as an ensign in 1745 in a company of foot raised in Nottingham to counter the Young Pretender's advance proved more expense to him than profit. Then, again by the good offices of friends, the materials collected by John Plumptre for a history of Nottingham were placed in his hands; these he prepared for publication, and the work appeared posthumously in 1751 as *Nottinghamia vetus et nova*. Through much of his life Deering suffered from gout, and in later life he became asthmatic. He died on 12 April 1749. He was saved at the last minute from a pauper's burial and laid to rest in St Peter's churchyard, Nottingham, opposite the house he lived in. He is commemorated by a genus of Indo-Malaysian plants, *Deeringia*, named in his honour in 1810 by Robert Brown.   B. D. JACKSON, *rev.* D. E. ALLEN

Sources Nichols, *Illustrations*, 1.211–20 · R. Pulteney, *Historical and biographical sketches of the progress of botany in England*, 2 (1790), 257–64 · D. E. Allen, 'John Martyn's botanical society: a biographical analysis of the membership', *Proceedings of the Botanical Society of the British Isles*, 6 (1967), 305–24

Deering [*formerly* Gandy], **John Peter** (1787–1850), architect, was the youngest child in the family of six sons and four daughters of Thomas Gandy (*d.* 1814), who worked at White's Club, St James's, London, and his wife, Sophia, *née* Adams. His older brothers included the painter Joseph

Michael *Gandy ARA (1771–1843) and the architect Michael *Gandy (*bap.* 1773, *d.* 1862). John Peter Gandy was a pupil of James Wyatt from 1805 to 1808. In 1805 he was admitted to the Royal Academy Schools. He exhibited at the Royal Academy between 1805 and 1833, and was awarded the silver medal in 1806. His early exhibits included *A Design for the Royal Academy* (1807) and two drawings, *An Ancient City* and *The Environs of an Ancient City* (1810). In 1810 he won first prize in a competition for a design for the new Bethlem Hospital, but it was never carried out.

When he left James Wyatt's office, Gandy took a job at the barrack office, from which he was granted leave from 1811 to 1813, when he accompanied Sir William Gell on an expedition to Greece on behalf of the Society of Dilettanti, acting as architectural draughtsman. This trip was written up in 1817 as *The Unedited Antiquities of Attica*, and in 1840 as the third volume of *Antiquities of Ionia*, edited by William Wilkins. With Sir William Gell, Gandy also published *Pompeiana* (1817–19), which became the standard work on the excavations at Pompeii. He was elected a member of the Society of Dilettanti in 1830. He then began to establish himself as an architect. To begin with he collaborated with William Wilkins, and together in 1817 they designed a 280 foot tower to commemorate the battle of Waterloo, to be erected in Portland Place, but the project fell through because of the economic recession. He worked with Wilkins on the University Club, Pall Mall (1822–6), and was runner-up to Wilkins in the competition for a design for University College, London, and then acted as Wilkins's assistant in its construction. Other buildings in London included St Mark's Church, North Audley Street (1825–8), a Greek revival church, and Exeter Hall, in the Strand (1830–31). He also remodelled the courtyard of Burghley House, Northamptonshire (1828), and made alterations at Shrubland Park, Suffolk (1831–3). Most of his designs were neo-classical in style, and he was regarded as an authority on Greek architecture, although there were exceptions, such as the hospital at Stamford, in Tudor Gothic style.

In 1828 Gandy inherited the Lee estate, near Great Missenden, Buckinghamshire, from his friend Henry Deering, and took the name of Deering. With the support of Wilkins, he had been elected ARA in 1826 and RA in 1838, an honour scarcely justified by his subsequent professional inactivity. Deering gradually gave up his profession as an architect, and spent the rest of his life as a country gentleman. He was elected MP for Aylesbury in 1847, and high sheriff of Buckinghamshire in 1840. He died in Hanover Square, London, on 2 March 1850.

G. W. BURNET, *rev.* ANNE PIMLOTT BAKER

Sources 'Gandy afterwards Deering, John Peter', Colvin, *Archs.*, 387–8 · *Dir. Brit. archs.* · R. Windsor Liscombe, *William Wilkins, 1778–1839* (1980) · *IGI* · Graves, *Artists*, 76, 107 · *The Builder*, 8 (1850), 130 · S. C. Hutchison, 'The Royal Academy Schools, 1768–1830', *Walpole Society*, 38 (1960–62), 123–91 · 'Gandy-Deering (Peter John, also known as J. P. Gandy, Gandy Deering and J. P. Deering from 1828', *The dictionary of architecture*, ed. [W. Papworth] (1853–92) · *GM*, 2nd ser., 33 (1850), 448
Archives RIBA BAL, biography file | BL, letters to Sir William Gell, Add. MS 63617

Defoe, Daniel (1660?–1731), writer and businessman, was the youngest of the three children of James Foe (d. 1706), a prosperous tallow chandler in the parish of Cripplegate and a freeman of the City of London, and Alice Foe, who died some time between 1668 and 1671. His sisters, Mary and Elizabeth, were born on 13 November 1657 and 19 June 1659. Defoe was probably born in London or just outside the city during autumn 1660. During this time of political unrest many citizens' lives were disrupted and records were lost. Carefully educated at the Revd Charles Morton's dissenting academy in Newington Green, Defoe was intended for the nonconformist ministry, but in 1681 he chose to follow his father in trade and the political life of the city. As he said, 'the pulpit is none of my office'.

Early ambitions and commitments After leaving Morton's academy, Defoe established a home and business in Freeman's Yard, Cornhill, and became a wholesale hosier. On 1 January 1684 he married Mary Tuffley (1665–1732), who brought him a dowry of £3700; they had six daughters (Mary, Maria, Hannah, Henrietta, Sophia, and Martha) and two sons (Benjamin and Daniel), all but two of whom, Mary and Martha, lived into adulthood. Defoe shared the persecution of the nonconformists and was a lifelong supporter of freedom of religion and the press. He had joined Monmouth's revolt in June 1685, fought at Sedgemoor under the banner 'Fear nothing but God', and managed to escape capture after the defeat. In January 1686 he made bail for two widows arrested at a conventicle meeting and soon began to write political essays. He was pardoned for taking part in the uprising in May 1687.

In the late 1680s Defoe began investing in ships and expanding into the export-import business with tobacco, logwood, wine, spirits, and cloth goods. He opened a brick and pantile factory on land in Tilbury that he had leased years before. In the early 1690s he invested in highly speculative ventures such as civet cats and a diving bell. Ruined by misfortunes in shipping, risk taking, and overextension, Defoe went bankrupt in 1692 for an astonishing £17,000, approximately £680,000 in modern money, and was committed to Fleet prison and transferred immediately to king's bench prison on 29 October. He found recognizances, appeared to answer the charges in court, and was discharged. More creditors came forward, and he was committed to king's bench prison again on 12 February 1693. Some of his creditors never bothered to add their debts to the charges against him, and once again men willing to be recognizants stepped forward. Defoe negotiated terms with his prosecutors and received employment as an accountant from men with connections to King William; he worked with a lottery and as an accountant for the commissioner for the glass duty, among other things. His brick and pantile factory continued to clear about £600 per year, and he had contracts with such prestigious projects as the building of the Greenwich Hospital for sailors and mariners. Defoe also began to write for money and to submit 'projects' to the government and private investors. His *Essay upon Projects* (1697) included the kinds of ideas that were making other

Daniel Defoe (1660?–1731), by Michael Vandergucht, pubd 1706 (after Jeremiah Taverner, 1706)

men rich. One of them, on naval recruitment and maintenance, eventually helped lead to his invitation to speak to a parliamentary committee. Several show an early, acute understanding of banks, the new credit economy, and the transportation system necessary for increasing trade. Others reveal an acute awareness of social problems and groups of needy human beings, among them widows and 'idiots'.

Not only did Defoe write political pamphlets and poetry in support of his hero King William, but he began to exhibit some signs of literary ambition. His poem *The Pacificator* joins the ancient/modern controversy and engages such then respected poets as Samuel Garth and Richard Blackmore. His timely satiric poem *The True-Born Englishman* required fifty editions by mid-century, and about 1701 he embarked on what he intended to be the great defence of the revolution settlement of 1688 and the poem to establish his reputation as an important poet. *Jure divino* is a philosophical verse essay in 12 books, running to 375 pages of heroic couplets. According to Defoe, he never published most of the part composed before his arrest for seditious libel in 1703 because he feared it would give dangerous offence; what has survived was mostly written in prison and was completed during the time of insecurity and distress immediately thereafter. Published in 1706 after delays during which he tried to secure more subscribers and waited out political situations that might have embroiled his poem in new and threatening controversy, it was immediately pirated by a former printer of Defoe's and was even abridged into a chapbook; Defoe claimed that he lost £1500 because of the piracy. His hopes for poetic fame were not quite spent, however. His *Caledonia*, a sixty-page poem published in 1706 with a grant from the Scottish privy council, celebrates Scottish history and a number of its most illustrious and historically important families.

Fight for religious freedom and the pillory Between 1688 and 1706 Defoe often wrote about and questioned the practice of occasional conformity, the dissenters' 'occasional' taking of communion in the Church of England, which qualified them for employment and government office. In fact, both Defoe's contemporaries and modern historians sometimes blame Defoe for beginning the controversy over occasional conformity. Roger Thomas, for instance, credits Defoe with 'the earliest shot in the agitation' (R. Thomas, *The English Presbyterians*, 1968, 124). When the nonconformist lord mayor Sir Humphrey Edwin attended St Paul's in the morning and the Pinners' Hall conventicle in the afternoon in his official robes and with his sword of office, Defoe published *An Inquiry into Occasional Conformity* (1698) that included inflammatory phrases such as 'playing Bo-peep with God Almighty'. When the next lord mayor, Sir Thomas Abney, also a dissenter, repeated the act, Defoe reissued his pamphlet and added a preface in which he demanded that John How, the prominent minister whose meeting-house Abney attended, either defend occasional conformity or declare against it. How responded with a personal admonition, reminding Defoe that the heart of dissent was the individual conscience and that he was not to set up as 'the Conscience-general of Mankind' (Backscheider, *Defoe*, 89).

A full-scale controversy over occasional conformity broke out, during which the moderate King William died unexpectedly. The proposal of the bill to prevent occasional conformity at the beginning of Queen Anne's reign seriously threatened the nonconformists. Even bailiffs, foresters, and scavengers would have to conform, lose their offices, or pay heavy, escalating fines. Nonconformists would be banned from supplying hospitals, workhouses, and prisons with such necessities as bread and firewood. There was general agreement that the intent of the bill was to 'incapacitate'. Although Defoe continued to oppose occasional conformity, he recognized the prejudice and extreme desire to oppress that the bill represented and began a print campaign to hold a mirror to the faces of those supporting the bill. The result, his *Shortest Way with the Dissenters* (December 1702), collected the key phrases and major arguments of the high-church party and used them in a mock recommendation to 'root out this cursed Race from the World'. Defoe was already one of the best-known men in London because of his *The True-Born Englishman* and his address to parliament demanding the freeing of the Kentish petitioners, *Legion's Memorial*

(1701). *The Original Power of the Collective Body of the People of England* (1702) is one of the most eloquent defences of the rights of the people and most militant about their relationship to government written in the century. Actually written before King William dismissed parliament in November 1701, it portrayed the king as listening to the people, attacked hereditary monarchy, and with great rhetorical power asserted many of Locke's arguments for contract theory and the supreme power of the people. It 'vindicates' the 'original right' of 'all men' to live under a government dedicated to their benefit: 'the People remain … Original Power endures to the same Eternity the World endures to … Nor have I advanced any new Doctrine, nothing but what is ancient as Nature, and born into the world with our Reason' (dedication).

When Defoe's authorship of *The Shortest Way* was finally discovered, he hid and attempted to negotiate with the government but was arrested for seditious libel in May and brought before the secretary of state for the southern region, the earl of Nottingham, and then imprisoned in Newgate until 5 June, when he made the £1500 bail. He was sentenced to a large fine, to stand in the pillory three times, and to remain in Newgate until he could find 'sureties of good behaviour' for seven years. After a delay of the original sentence to stand in the pillory beginning on 19 July during which Nottingham tried to get Defoe to reveal his 'Accomplices' and Defoe was brought before the queen, he stood in the pillory on 29, 30, and 31 July. The pillory was ringed with Defoe's protective supporters, and he appeared as Alexander Pope described him, 'unabashed on high'. His *Hymn to the Pillory* was sold in the streets and declared defiantly that he was 'an Example made,/To make Men of their Honesty afraid'. He spent the next four months in Newgate.

Imprisoned during the critical season for brick making, responsible for a large, mostly female family, and run into greater debt because unable to work, Defoe left Newgate in November with his finances and his reputation—critical for businessmen, who must have credit—severely damaged. By summer 1706 he was in trouble again. He owed over £2000, feared imprisonment for debt again, and chose to submit to a commission of bankrupts. A settlement was reached in August. Defoe was seldom entirely free from debt, and future claims came from all over Great Britain. For instance, in 1713 a Yarmouth man renewed a suit of 1706, and in 1728 some of his London debts were prosecuted anew.

Although Defoe's release from Newgate was arranged by Lord Treasurer Sidney Godolphin and Speaker Robert Harley and he was later pardoned by the queen on 31 July 1704, for the rest of his life Defoe was a marked political agitator, best-known as the writer who was pilloried, and was subject to whimsical, politically motivated arrests. He was often threatened with arrest in 1705 and 1706 for violating the 'good behaviour' terms of his conviction and occasionally had to rush to London to defend himself. Immediately after Queen Anne's death in 1714 Defoe was indicted for seditious libel again and arrested on 28 August. Brought before a friendly judge, Defoe accepted a plea bargain in 1715 that secretly pledged him to work for the new secretary of state Charles Townshend, specifically to begin a new moderate tory paper, *Mercurius Politicus*, and to infiltrate as many tory presses and periodicals as he could.

Writing career and work for the government, 1703–1713 After his release from Newgate in 1703 Defoe published *A True Collection of the Author of the True Born English-Man*, which attempted to set the record of his writing straight, to remind people of his popular *True-Born Englishman*, and to make money from his notoriety, and *The Second Volume of the Writings of the Author of the True-Born Englishman*, both important in establishing the canon of Defoe's writing. *The Consolidator*, *The Storm*, and *A True Relation of the Apparition of Mrs. Veal* were also commercial enterprises, although each has important spiritual and political elements. His great achievement of 1704 was to launch *The Review*, the ground-breaking periodical that moved English journalism in new directions. Before Defoe, what news was printed was without elaboration, interpretation, or even context. *The Review* demonstrated the possibilities of using history and news for propaganda purposes, and pointed out the advantages of a sense of discrete audiences. His first great biographer, James Sutherland, wrote, 'If *Robinson Crusoe* is indisputably Defoe's greatest work, the *Review* can at least claim to be his most astonishing performance' (Sutherland, 106). Defoe wrote nearly every word of it, regardless of where he was or his personal situation, from the first number on 19 February 1704 to the last on 11 June 1713. As Maximillian E. Novak has said:

> There were a number of one-man editorial sheets that ran for a while, but Defoe raises the level of debate over politics, foreign affairs, and economics. In a sense, he places the *Review* in the 'public sphere' of the coffee house where ideas that will ultimately transform the politics of a nation may be debated—and all of this five to six years before the *Tatler* and *Spectator*. (private communication)

Charles Leslie, a rival journalist, complained that 'the greatest part of the *people* ... cannot read at all, but they will gather about one that can *read*, and listen to ... [a] *Review* (as I have seen them in the streets)' (C. Leslie, preface, *The Rehearsal*, 1704–8, iv). In March 1705, *The Review* began appearing three rather than two times a week. The popularity of the Scandal Club section led first to a monthly supplement, which began in October 1704 and lasted for five numbers, and then to the *Little Review*, which he began in June 1705 and of which he wrote twenty-three numbers before he tired of it. Dialogue, satires of the press, dramatic irony, and families of characters became regular features of the Club, and both political parties began to take notice of the popularity and influence of the news commentaries.

From the beginning, the paper criticized the press, morals, manners, and the government, especially its conduct of the war with the French. On 29 June 1704 Godolphin demanded that Harley, by then one of the secretaries of state, 'find out the author' (*Bath MSS*, 1.58–9). Early in July *The Review* changed direction, and Defoe defended himself against charges of being pro-France and began to write about Charles XII of Sweden, a subject related to Harley's responsibilities as secretary of state for the northern region. Letters show that Defoe and Harley had been meeting since at least mid-April, that the specifics of what Defoe would do were being discussed but had not been decided, but by late June they were taking firm shape.

Defoe became one of Harley's agents and an opinion sampler. Over the next three years he extended the possibilities of counter-insurgency, invented practices that survive to the present day, and earned the reputation of master spy. A modern historian has called him 'one of the great professionals in all these centuries of secret service ... in himself almost a complete secret service' (R. Rowan, *Thirty-Three Centuries of Espionage*, completed R. Deindorfer, 1967, 102). He set up an unrivalled intelligence network and through his journalistic and pamphlet writing became, in the words of a rival journalist, 'the Goliath of his party' (anonymous tory writer, *The Moderator*, 2 June 1710). In summer 1704 he took two trips that covered most of England, taking note of opinions, reporting objections and reservations about the ministry's actions, infiltrating groups, identifying influential men and faction leaders, and writing essays designed to win over the suspicious or uncommitted. His network of acquaintances and friends began sending him information and distributing his political poems, pamphlets, and individual issues of *The Review*. Some numbers, such as that for 17 April 1705, were also bought and distributed by other political leaders and agents. Scattered records survive: for instance, of individuals asking for 100 copies of each *Review* and lists of men responsible for delivering nearly 2000 copies of one of Defoe's pamphlets. In this time of ferocious political party activity, Harley had embarked on a campaign summarized by the word 'Moderation', and, although Defoe was certainly motivated by his extravagant gratitude to Harley, he believed in moderation and the ministry's domestic and foreign policies and propagated them wholeheartedly.

In autumn 1706 Defoe was one of the agents sent to Scotland to work for the union, and his service there was energetic. He infiltrated some of the most influential groups in Edinburgh and came to control all of the newspapers. As a cover and also as speculation to provide for the future, he invested in the linen and weaving industries and explored the salt trade, among others. He soon had sources in the Scottish parliament, the Church of Scotland, and major business and civic groups. Exposed to numerous dangers in the volatile city, Defoe acted with discretion, courage, and resolution and left a variety of moving, important records of the time. In addition to *The Review*, a little over half his letters giving reports to Harley survive, as do his series of pamphlets, all but one beginning with the title *An Essay at Removing National Prejudices Against a Union with Scotland*; other occasional essays were designed to explain, persuade, and address what today seem ephemeral details of the treaty of union, and his *History of the Union of Great Britain* (1709) was on-the-scene description, commentary, and propaganda. After fifteen months Defoe returned to

London, but Godolphin sent him back at the end of March 1708, shortly after the Pretender attempted to land in Scotland and just before the first Scottish elections. Defoe described his job as to provide 'plain, naked, and unbyasst accounts both of persons and things' (*Letters*, 256) and sent reports to both Godolphin and the earl of Sunderland, now secretary of state for the southern region. Defoe continued to sample opinion, discuss issues eloquently with his Edinburgh friends, write often impassioned propaganda, and attempt to avoid the danger from random mobs and personal enemies.

His work completed, Defoe returned to London in December 1708, but decided to go back to try to develop his business and newspaper interests in autumn 1709. He took his son Benjamin to study at the University of Edinburgh. The renewed attacks on the dissenters, often seen to have been triggered by the Revd Henry Sacheverell's sermon *The Perils of False Brethren*, brought Defoe back to London. Defoe once called Sacheverell the 'Foundation of my Destruction' (*The Review*, 6.462), and his joining the battle with such vigour was personal, religious, and political. He saw Sacheverell's arguments as being aimed not only at the dissenters but at the revolution settlement, and he used extreme rhetoric to alarm people about Sacheverell and his opinions and to urge Sacheverell's conviction for seditious libel. On 23 March, however, Sacheverell received what was widely described as a 'derisory sentence' of having two of his sermons burnt by the common hangman and being forbidden to preach for three years. Riotous celebrations that included the burning of dissenting chapels all over the country broke out, and Sacheverell enjoyed a royal procession to his new living (clerical appointment) in Selattyn, just inside the English border in Shropshire. Defoe recognized this as the outbreak of long hidden, deep prejudices, and his response was a return to tempered essays on moderation and satires of party extremism that he had hoped the country had repudiated.

Harley returned to power, becoming chancellor of the exchequer in August 1710, and Defoe began to work for him again. Through the next few years of political turmoil Defoe continued his journalistic and other propagandistic writing, and from at least 1707 until the accession of George I he received an income of between £400 and £500 per year from the government. His final trip to Scotland was in autumn 1712, another time of severe Scottish discontent over the imposition of oaths, a bill to tolerate episcopal communion in Scotland, and the decision to extend the malt tax to Scotland when the peace with France was made. His reports were largely optimistic. On 20 September he reports, 'An Inclination to Moderation Appeares Among the best men Every where' (*Letters*, 386–7).

During this time and in the aftermath of the dismissal by George I of Harley and his ministry, Defoe expanded his writing strategies. He began to create increasingly distinctive voices and to hone his ability to reach specific groups of readers. In his campaign to explain the new credit economy and to make ending the War of the Spanish Succession acceptable, he designed essays for general readers and for the range of political stances from moderate tory to opposition whig. For instance, a pamphlet of his published by John Morphew, publisher of the tory *Examiner*, treated England's separate negotiations with France more favourably than those printed by the whig bookseller John Baker. Some of them, such as *Some Thoughts upon the Subject of Commerce with France* (1713), carried an identification of his authorship, 'By the Author of the Review', and, therefore, the assurance that the same point of view and expertise that many readers appreciated would reward their purchase. Others, such as his series on the articles of the treaty with France, are of a piece with his earlier publications for the ministry, some of which are known to have been suggested to him by Harley or other insiders. His writings kept up a running commentary on domestic and foreign events, an evaluation of the performance of the government, and almost unbelievably cocksure advice to his fellow Britons. In his first publication after George's landing, *Advice to the People of Great Britain*, for example, he urges everyone to 'ease … foolish strife, forget the Wrongs done to one another, and bury … Resentment'. He encourages them to have faith in harmonious happy times and never forgets to assess and admonish the Scots.

Experimental fictions and conduct books Defoe is usually described as an unprincipled man who would write on any side of any question for money. As P. N. Furbank and W. R. Owens have written, 'It was a favourite theme of his enemies that he was a mercenary hack … and he was frequently provoked into complaining both at specific attributions to him and at the general tendency to father all ownerless pamphlets on him' (Furbank and Owens, xiv). Although over his long life he certainly contradicted himself now and then and changed his mind, he is not guilty of these charges. All serious Defoe scholars agree that a set of core principles and opinions runs through all his works regardless of the reader being addressed. The general opinion is that he was a whig and a moderate by nature, a thorough supporter of the revolution of 1688, and, like most of the people of his generation, suspicious of political parties and reluctant to be identified entirely with one. Unfortunately there is no standard edition of Defoe's works; indeed, fewer than a quarter are in print. Recent biographies that are 'full' rather than 'critical' (devoted primarily to his 'literary' writings) have begun slowly to correct this misconception with scholars, if not with the general public. But several factors continue to obscure the principles for which he stood and sacrificed much: his gift for assuming voices in order to address different groups of people; his ability to select different aspects of an issue to discuss; the untidy, inflated canon that included works that contradicted a great deal that Defoe stood for; his periods of acute economic distress; and the unexamined acceptance of the often heated words of his contemporaries.

Since at least Procopius, political writers had used scandalous memoirs, fake journals and letters, and other forms borrowed from prose fiction to stigmatize the people and actions on the opposite side, and Defoe began to use these forms more frequently. Although Delarivière Manley is the best-known of these writers during Defoe's lifetime, almost all journalists and propagandists resorted to them at some time or another. Although there were anecdotes, some exaggerated and some fictional, in some of Defoe's pamphlets and *The Review*, his *Memoirs of Count Tariff* published in 1713 is the most important sign of the novelist to come. J. Paul Hunter and Geoffrey Sill have located this political satire in the puritan allegorical and emblematic traditions in which characters are social types and representatives of ideologies that reveal dangerous social and moral truths obscured by appearances and complacent thinking. The characters in *Memoirs* are the parts Defoe saw behind the parliamentary vote on the Bill of Commerce, and he tells a story of groups, such as merchants represented by Alderman Traffick and manufacturers represented by Harry Woolpack, who share interests being set against each other. The characters act in a well-developed fictional structure, and the text is particularly interesting for the ways Defoe illustrates the dynamic relationship among individuals, public opinions, and events, a theme that is especially obvious in his *Col. Jack*.

In the year after Queen Anne's death Defoe wrote secret histories, fictional memoirs, histories, and epistles and called his works 'accounts', 'reflections', 'expostulations', 'appeals', 'rebukes', 'apologies', and half a dozen other forms of address. Fully realized dialogues between friends, husbands and wives, and parents and children were used to dramatize his arguments but sometimes also to create individualized, lively mini-personalities existing in a world of intrigue and self-interest. Maximillian Novak characterizes the period between 1715 and 1724 as 'the great creative period' of Defoe's life that 'produced a literal explosion of fiction' (Novak, 42).

The *Minutes of the Negotiations of Monsr. Mesnager* (1717) is one of Defoe's cleverest and most informed secret histories. Defoe makes his narrator the lowly under-secretary to Louis XIV who has worked his way up to become an important agent in the negotiation of the 'separate peace' that ended the War of the Spanish Succession. One of the earliest French contacts with the Harley ministry, Mesnager was well known to Harley, and the *Minutes* exhibit Defoe's inside knowledge. This devastating critique of the treaty of Utrecht (a treaty universally acknowledged to be unworthy of England's military achievement), of a queen determined to have peace at any price, and of a set of ministers doing Mesnager's work by calling the war too costly in men and money supported Robert Harley by portraying him as the only minister who could not be manipulated by the French. The 325-page book was reprinted in 1736 as fiction, and Defoe indeed included many unusual fictional elements. For example, Mesnager is made to react to some English customs and events as though he were as foreign as *The Spectator*'s Indians or Oliver Goldsmith's commentator in his 'Chinese letters'. Defoe's sense of humour is also

in evidence, as he has Mesnager comment on things that Defoe had found enormously frustrating, such as:

> I have heard of some who have waited upon him [Harley], by his own appointment, on Business of the Greatest Consequence, and have been entertained by him, from one Hour to another, on some Trifle, 'till at last the main Affair has been confin'd to a Minute or two, or perhaps deferred to another Occasion. (D. Defoe, *Minutes of the Negotiations of Monsr. Mesnager*, 1717, 183)

With the publication of *The Family Instructor* in 1715 Defoe began a series of practical divinity or domestic conduct books that eventually covered every stage of life and all classes. These books, especially the first, were enormously popular. Defoe had *The Family Instructor* printed by his Newcastle printer John Button to avoid having his reputation as an immoral, hack political writer tarnish its reception; it went through eight editions in five years and twenty by the end of the century. Although the dialogue form had been used in conduct books before, Defoe's was highly original in its leisurely creation of characters, relationships, and stories. Most conduct books were composed of brief essays, summary 'morals', and lists of maxims; Defoe's relatively long, developed narratives with commentary broke new ground. He divided the book in ways that emphasized the form's concentration on marriage, moral relationships, and household governance: 'I. Relating to fathers and children. II. To masters and servants. III. To husbands and wives'. Within each, however, are developed characters and suspenseful stories, and in the third part Defoe traces the rebellion, fall, death, and presumed damnation of part one's eldest brother.

The prefatory letter written by the Revd Samuel Wright claimed for the three dialogues what came to be the commonplace claim for the truth of the English novel: 'The Substance of each Narrative is *Real*. And there are some whole Dialogues which, with very little Alteration, I my self could put *Names* and *Families*'. This conduct book (and many of the political essays written about the same time) explores 'temper and constitution'—what might now be called personality—and their effect on people and their relationships, especially as they affect how people respond to situations. Defoe also broke new ground in directing his conduct book to mature readers rather than to the usual audience, those on the brink of adulthood. The conduct books that followed continued to concentrate on mature married people, although children and even black servants are important, often morally superior and reforming characters. In the second volume of *The Family Instructor* (1718) Defoe turned to the adjustments newly married people must make, the establishment of virtuous households, and the behaviour of fathers, especially in their responsibility for the spiritual guidance in their extended households and for learning to balance business and domestic obligations. *Religious Courtship* (1722) is a lively set of stories advising young couples on avoiding cheats and selecting virtuous partners. In it a father formerly 'hurried in the world' has retired to his home with his three unmarried daughters, and his business is to marry them well. Defoe develops a list of questions that young women should ask, because, as he says in most of the conduct books and several novels, the 'hazard' is chiefly on the woman's side. This word and his plots highlight the gamble that marriage is, and Defoe's questions are an attempt to increase the rationality of the decision. Published a month after *Moll Flanders* and eleven months before *Col. Jack*, it outlines marriage themes and recommendations that the novels dramatize. Also extremely popular, it was serialized in 1729 in the Philadelphia *Universal Instructor and Family Gazette*. *Conjugal Lewdness* (1727) explains the purposes of marriage and condemns such things as intercourse during pregnancy.

The Complete English Tradesman (1726) is a highly original conduct book, one that offered 'useful instructions for a young Tradesman', and prefigured the better-known *Apprentice's Vade Mecum* (1734) by Samuel Richardson. Defoe defines the complete tradesman as one who understands all the inland trade, knows where raw materials and manufactured items come from, and knows all 'methods' of correspondence, payment, shipping, and other transactions. One of Defoe's most passionate and personal books, it describes trade as a 'calling' in which hands, head, and heart must be applied to business. He covers in detail everything from the diligent, patient, personable demeanour required of the 'tradesman behind his counter' to the maintaining of credit and keeping of good accounts. The description of the feelings of the failed bankrupt tradesman is justly famous, but his reflective passages on the growing taste for luxuries and show without substance are even more important social history. About a pastry shop set up for £300, he broods that:

> the gilding and painting may go a little way, but 'tis the having a shop well fill'd with goods, having good choice to sell, and selling reasonable, these are the things that bring a trade, and a trade thus brought will stand by you and last.
> (D. Defoe, *The Complete English Tradesman*, 1726, 1.317)

Tradesmen, their families, and customers take the stage, are given feelings and personalities, and exit.

More and more Defoe gave free rein to the creation of fictional worlds, and the flow into fantasy in whatever he wrote became more common. Swept away into a family's tensions, a palace intrigue, a battle, or a person's vexed musings, he published longer and longer works of a more dramatic nature, and he increasingly depicted the flow between the private and public spheres that the scandalous memoirs had always argued and the conduct books allegorized.

The novels Defoe's first novel, *Robinson Crusoe*, published in 1719 when he was about fifty-nine, brings all his interests together. Crusoe is a disobedient son, arguing with his father, representing opinions of a new world—one where life in England is uncertain but global opportunity beckons, and children are increasingly torn between traditional obedience to family and individual self-satisfaction. Drawn to the sea regardless of parental and what appear to be providential warnings of catastrophe, he finds unbounded economic opportunity in Brazil. Defoe's fascination with travel narratives and with Great Britain as an international trading nation shapes the book and especially its sequel. Defoe also writes out of his engagement with religious controversies of the time, especially the Bangorian and Salters' Hall controversies. When Crusoe instructs Friday in the Christian faith, he is demonstrating the adequacy of scripture and revelation alone. Also inscribed are Defoe's theories of government and of colonization. Crusoe sets himself up as monarch, prince, generalissimo, and finally colonial governor, and perhaps ironically his abandonment of his island is emblematic of the neglect of which Great Britain was often guilty with its Caribbean colonies. In fact, this novel can be placed within Defoe's propaganda for the settlement of the New World and especially his writings about the doctrinal controversies splitting and embarrassing dissenters as well as Anglicans. Above all, however, it is the greatest mythic fantasy ever written of the solitary survivor who will never succumb. He will not starve, and he will not give in to his paralysing fear or extended isolation. Physically, mentally, and spiritually he survives and grows stronger.

Defoe's work always displayed a keen understanding of the reading public, and *Robinson Crusoe* is no exception. The best-selling books of this time were sermons and travel literature, and Defoe probably conceived *Robinson Crusoe* along the lines of travel books. Peace and optimism about open seas inspired new books like Daniel Beeckman's *Voyage to and from the Island of Borneo* and new editions of a number of earlier works such as Woodes Rogers's *Cruising Voyage Round the World* (both 1718). Travel books often began with a restless son and gave prominence to religious elements. Defoe's special contributions to travel literature were the power of his protagonist's personality and the previously unmatched evocation of states of mind—the extended presentations of a person reasoning, choosing, struggling for, if not understanding, acceptance of his fate.

An initial edition of 1000 was printed near the end of April 1719, followed by a second edition on 9 May, a third about 6 June, and a fourth shortly before the publication of the sequel, *Farther Adventures of Robinson Crusoe*, in August 1719. By the end of the year, the two parts were published together with a map and six plates. The *Original London Post* serialized it in 164 parts. Within a year the book had been translated into French, German, and Dutch. Other writers took note, and books such as Ambrose Evans's *The Adventures and Surprizing Deliverances of James Dubourdieu and his Wife* and William Chetwood's *The Voyages, Dangerous Adventures and Imminent Escapes of Captain Richard Falconer* began to appear. Six months after *Crusoe* was published novels such as *The Adventures ... of Dubourdieu and his Wife* were being advertised as 'very proper to be bound up with *Robinson Crusoe*' (*Daily Post*, 8 Oct 1719). By 1820 at least two different masters of children's schools had translated it into simple Latin with fake words such as '*tormenta*' for 'guns' when modern inventions required them, and in 1869 Lucy Aikin published the ghastly *Robinson Crusoe in Words of one Syllable*, which was so popular that it enjoyed a second edition in that same year.

Penelope Aubin specifically related her travel adventure and island fiction *The Adventures of the Count de Vinevil and his Family* to *Robinson Crusoe* in her preface and recognized it as a new way to instruct and delight. By 1724 there were at least three more female Robinsonades: Aubin's *The Life of Charlotta Du Pont* and the anonymous *Jungfer Robinsone, oder, Die verschmitzte Junge-Magd* and *Madame Robunse mit ihrer Tochter, Jungfer Robinsgen*. In 1731 the first of the great German Robinsonades, Johann Gottfried Schnabel's *Die Insel Felsenberg*, appeared.

Defoe gave free rein to his imagination and exulted in the evidence that his analysis of 'the modern Vice of the reading Palate' was correct. He believed that novelty sold books, and he provided it. In a time when, as Crusoe said, 'The whole World is in Motion', Defoe's travel books captured his readers' imaginations. In the preface to *Farther Adventures* Defoe claimed that the success of *Robinson Crusoe* came from 'the surprising variety of the subject' and 'the agreeable manner of the performance'. He promised more 'novel' incidents than those in *Robinson Crusoe*, and he did indeed provide more 'incidents'. Within the first hundred pages Crusoe's ship had rescued another ship (with a passenger who had stayed alive partly by eating gloves), Crusoe had heard the stories of battles among the survivors on his island, of wars between cannibal bands, and of an invasion of the island by cannibals. In the last hundred pages Crusoe went by land from the coast of China, through Peking (Beijing) to Archangel where he took a ship to Hamburg, travelled by land to The Hague, and finally arrived in London. During this odyssey he saw the Great Wall, battled Tartar raiders, burnt an idol before the eyes of enraged priests, and rescued a royal political prisoner. Drawn-out tales of elaborate ruses stood next to brief, funny descriptions of people met on the road. Defoe described two 'amazing' houses (one of wicker and one of china), defined irony as 'speaking in colours', and had a boatload of natives defiantly bare their bottoms at the English seamen.

The Life, Adventures, and Pyracies, of the Famous Captain Singleton was published in June 1720 and covers the part of the known world that Crusoe missed. The idea for *Singleton* may have been in the back of Defoe's mind as he wrote *Robinson Crusoe* because he has Crusoe list among his blessings: 'But I am cast on an Island, where I see no wild Beasts to hurt me, as I saw on the Coast of Africa: And what if I had been Shipwreck'd there?' Singleton sails to Newfoundland and the East Indies before he is marooned on Madagascar for his part in a mutiny. He and his fellow conspirators then walk across the wide part of Africa from Mozambique to Guinea. Lions, tigers, leopards, crocodiles, and elephants appear, and Defoe is artful enough to make them both beautiful and menacing. The waterfalls, jungles, and deserts amaze and horrify the men, and Defoe again renders extreme states of mind. At one point Singleton says:

> Having with infinite Labour mounted these Hills [we saw] a vast howling Wilderness, not a Tree, a River, or a Green thing to be seen, for as far as the Eye could look; nothing but a

scalding Sand, which as the Wind blew, drove about in Clouds, enough to overwhelm Man and Beast.

The last half of the book traces Singleton's career as a pirate in the West Indies, along the coast of South America, on Madagascar, in the Red Sea, Persian Gulf, Moluccas, the Philippines, and then below Australia and concludes with his retirement in England.

Captain Singleton is a transition to Defoe's writing about crime and the development of criminal minds. When he wrote *Captain Singleton* pirates were a national concern, for they discouraged trade and colonization and put individuals at risk. Defoe's *Col. Jack* records the booty taken by a French privateer and comments in the words of many of his creator's contemporaries, 'This was a Terrible Loss among the *English* Merchants'. The state papers include numerous petitions from merchants, shipmasters, traders, and planters for military protection. In 1718 Captain Woodes Rogers had defeated a huge pirate colony in the Bahamas and, in the aftermath, some 2000 had surrendered and received the royal pardon. As Defoe noticed, the centre of pirate operations shifted to Madagascar, and by 1721 the English dispatched navy squadrons to protect the East India Company ships. Reports of the capture and subsequent trials of pirates appeared almost daily in the papers.

In *Mercurius Politicus* (1716–20) and *A Plan for the English Commerce* (1728), Defoe had argued that the destruction of the pirates on the coasts of Africa would be a worthy work for a great, far-sighted king like George I; he had envisioned the European nations joining together to make the seas safe and open to merchants of every nation. Because of the War of the Quadruple Alliance privateers were again being licensed in large numbers and joined the hoard of pirates already in the sea lanes. Moreover, some of the Madagascan pirates were negotiating with the Hanoverian enemy Sweden to become their privateers. In contrast to the opinions he expressed in his non-fiction, Defoe gives a more complex and sympathetic portrayal of pirates in the novels. Crusoe is in danger of being mistaken for a pirate simply because of the ship he has bought. Singleton has nowhere to go and no way of making a living and seems a drifter more than a predator. Descriptions of sailing 'up and down', chasing ships, and deciding more on whim than anything else to try another part of the world alternate with brief and often bloody fights and lists of prizes that give the men wealth they seem unable to enjoy. Quaker William, the witty resourceful Quaker who becomes Singleton's friend, lightens the novel's tone and distracts the reader from the pirates' cruelty and destructiveness so much that even the multiple violent deaths of men who sail with Singleton and Singleton's suicidal despair and paranoid retirement in England make little impression.

Although not his next published novel, *Col. Jack* (1722) is the natural extension of these travel novels, as is his *A New Voyage Round the World* (1724). Jack, like Crusoe and Singleton, is a citizen of the world and a man on the make in a predatory economy. Like Singleton, he is left on his own in childhood. Over his long life he is a thief, a soldier in northern England, a kidnapped bondservant, a plantation owner and colonial trader, a gentleman traveller, a soldier in France and Italy on the side of France and Spain, a Jacobite who witnesses the battle at Preston (and is, therefore, a rebel), a captive of privateers, and a smuggler. As violent a novel as any written by Tobias Smollett, *Col. Jack* depicts a society in which only the legal system works efficiently, and all Jack's occupations seem to be based on warfare, military or economic. His ships are sunk, captured, and confiscated, and in this crazy, evil world he fights for France and is robbed by French privateers, is a traitor because he prefers a former king over a present king, and experiences brutality in the streets, in London, in Edinburgh, on ships, on the plantations, and even in private homes regardless of his wealth, status, or citizenship. Something of a romantic in his individuality and especially in his yearnings for a home, a country, and happiness, Jack is never truly at home in the sombre violent societies in which he tries to operate. Defoe once called gangs, which proliferated as vigorously as pirates in the 1720s, 'land pirates', and Jack briefly belonged to one. Here, as in *Moll Flanders* (1722) and *Captain Singleton*, Defoe's fascination with the formation of criminal minds is evident. Denied a calling, religious or familial, Jack is a vehicle for new psychological and historical variations on Defoe's religious and economic themes.

The first part of *Col. Jack* shows how the homeless boys in London become gangs of 'naked, ragged Rogues' who progress to adult gangs that terrorize travellers and then come to threaten inland trade to the extent that pirates did the import-export business. Their random crimes and their willingness to commit violence, their youth and lack of principles, and the number of men like them in the population made them especially frightening. In *Moll Flanders*, the novel often paired with *Col. Jack*, the first part shows Moll trying to succeed in the occupation that religion and society told her was her destiny and calling—marriage. What she learns, of course, is that:

> What makes a homely Woman fair?
> About Five Hundred Pounds a Year
> (*The Commentator*, 1 Aug 1720)

She happens to be 'fair', compliant, and talented in all the arts, such as music, dancing, and conversation, that made women pleasing, but she has no money and no family. What the reader learns is that the marriage market and the thieves' underworld are mirror images—deceit, opportunism, economic motives, and even the class system are the same. Of these novels a contemporary newspaper (*Flying Post*, 1 March 1729) reported on their immediate and continuing popularity:

> Down in the kitchen, honest Dick and Doll
> Are studying Colonel Jack and Flanders Moll
> (Sutherland)

In this novel Defoe's belief that he should 'contribute … to the publick Welfare' is especially clear. Both in his exposure of the abuses inherent in the marriage market mentality of his time and in his warnings about underworld practices and their roots he exhibited the same keen interest and almost compulsive imagining of policy

making apparent in his *Essay upon Projects*. In a small way he used *Moll Flanders* to serve national policy, specifically the somewhat controversial Transportation Act of 1718, which allowed courts to sentence even clergied felons to transportation to America. On a very limited scale transportation had been used since before the Restoration as an alternative to capital punishment, and by 1700 had become a fairly common form of conditional pardon. The judge could pronounce it or the criminal could petition as Moll Flanders did for transportation. By 1722, the year *Moll Flanders* was published, about 60 per cent of the convicted male clergiable felons and 46 per cent of the women were transported. As resistance began to form on both sides of the Atlantic, Defoe presents transportation as opportunity for the nation and individual criminals who can start afresh and prosper.

Of *Moll Flanders* James Joyce wrote, 'The first English author to write without imitating or adapting foreign works, … to devise for himself an artistic form which is perhaps without precedent … is Daniel Defoe, father of the English novel' (J. Joyce, 'Daniel Defoe', ed. and trans. J. Prescott, *Buffalo Studies*, 1, 1964, 7). In *The Rise of the Novel* Ian Watt concluded of *Moll Flanders*: 'Very few writers have created for themselves both a new subject and a new literary form to embody it' (Watt, 134). Holding both literary and mass appeal, the novel is one of the most popular of all eighteenth-century novels. Its resilient optimistic heroine with her myriad adventures, griefs, and escapes and the story's happy ending appeal to all kinds of readers. An important portrayal of Defoe's time, the novel continues to challenge readers to confront enduring moral, economic, and social questions. Like all Defoe's novels, it is haunted by questions about evil: What is evil? What is its source? Of what are humans capable? Is a person good or evil, or just the person's words or actions? Is evil part of human nature, as basic as hunger or thirst? How does evil grow in the human heart? Why do the 'evils' in a society, such as ignorance and want, result in moral evil for the ignorant and wanting? Is Moll guilty or her society?

Journal of the Plague Year, published in the same year as *Moll Flanders* and *Col. Jack*, may be Defoe's most underappreciated great novel. H. F., the protagonist, lives in London throughout the plague, and he is torn between fleeing and staying, between pragmatic, even crass economic motives, and spiritual impulses, and, even more importantly, is obsessed with determining the reasons individuals get the plague. Very much a man of the time when the world was poised between the religious certainties of the sixteenth and seventeenth centuries and modern scepticism and secularism, H. F. collects evidence, ponders, sorts, and entertains or rejects hypotheses about the cause of the plague even as he seeks to understand God's will and occasionally succumbs to superstitions such as bibliomancy. That H. F.'s research is hopeless (the cause of plague was not identified until 1894 as the bacillus *Yersinia pestis*, which is primarily an internal parasite of rodents and carried initially by fleas) does nothing to detract from the energy of his mind and the questions

Defoe raises about ethical conduct, public policy, and human limits. In this new way to cast the questions of the nature of the universe and the individual's relationship to God and his world, Defoe has, in the words of Maximillian Novak, created an innovative character distinguished by his 'general sympathy for the human condition' (M. Novak, 'Defoe and the disordered city', *Publications of the Modern Language Association of America*, 92, 1977).

Absorbing contemporary concerns about society can easily be located as major themes or even motivating forces in all Defoe's novels. Just as the plague in Marseilles and the ways it had been used in the debates over restricting the import of calicoes as well as over the Quarantine Act of 1721 helped shape *Due Preparations for the Plague* and *A Journal of the Plague Year*, so the South Sea and stock company schemes and his reports of crimes and trials contributed to *Moll Flanders* and *Col. Jack*. Always the critical and independent thinker, Defoe could support the ship quarantine in the Quarantine Act but oppose shutting up houses and point relentlessly at the possible consequences of quarantining entire towns. Defoe's novels demonstrate new ways for literature to participate in immediate debates and to become an instrument of social persuasion but also portray the eternal struggle of the individual against the 'wilderness of this world'. Every novel not only records but contributes to the thinking of his contemporaries, and some influenced public policy, as did *Plague Year*, which contributed to the repeal of the Quarantine Act (1721) and to the reshaped act of 1722. The issues, large and small—*Robinson Crusoe* and Salters' Hall, *Roxana* and the increase in fashionable gambling houses, *Moll Flanders* and transportation, and *Col. Jack* and the need for schools for the Blackguard boys—are too numerous to identify. And yet the novels also explore the most enduring themes of life and literature: survival; the search for happiness; man against nature; the desire to escape urban complexity. Defoe's fictions gave literary history the defining characteristics of the novel, those characteristics that set it apart from, for instance, poetry and drama: its 'loose and baggy shape' and its 'obsession' with the mind, with identity. In fact, the form serves this kind of exploration of character and becomes a source of radical power because it is the structure of the mind and experiences of the character.

With the profits from his novels and his daughter Hannah's profits from her South Sea stock, Defoe paid £1000 to the corporation of the city of Colchester in August 1722 for a ninety-nine-year lease on hundreds of acres of land that belonged to the city and for the timber rights which had never been granted to previous leaseholders. The beautiful healthy oak, ash, and elm trees, if carefully managed, were worth thousands of pounds. Located in the parish of St Michael, Mile End (now Myland), Essex, the land included Kingswood, the Severalls Brinkley farms (sometimes called Kingswood Heath), Tubswick in Lexden Hundred, and Pound Marsh. About the same time Defoe leased Broomfield in nearby Earlscolne parish. Also known as Pound Farm, it was located on the Colne River

and had rich clay soil—brick and tile clay soil. These properties already had buildings, fences, houses, and cultivated fields. Defoe reverted to the ambitions of his young manhood. He believed, as he said in *Roxana*, that a merchant was:

> the best Gentleman in the Nation; that in Knowledge, Manners, in Judgment of things ... out-did many of the Nobility ... able to spend more Money than a Gentleman of 5000 l. a Year Estate ... [for] an Estate is a Pond; but ... Trade was a Spring.

He bred cattle and raised corn, sold some of the corn as well as cheese, butter, veal, and beef, all established Colchester products. Over the next few years Defoe added honey and oysters to the commodities he sold from Colchester and even began to sell metal buttons, tanned leather, cloth, and imported anchovies in London, St Neots, Lichfield, Coventry, and other Cambridgeshire towns. So intent was Defoe on a second chance that he began to plan a tile factory on the Colchester land. Late in 1723 or early in 1724, he began to try to persuade John Ward, a Nuneaton mercer and linen draper, to become his partner.

Economist and global citizen, 1722–1728 Also in 1722 Defoe began writing a series of respected books that changed his reputation again. He began *Atlas maritimus*, a huge economic geography with maps protected by a royal patent, and *A Tour thro' the Whole Island of Great Britain*, the only book written by Defoe that has consistently been described as approaching *belles-lettres*. As Pat Rogers says, *A Tour* 'has been lauded by the most eminent historians as a prime source of understanding for Britain', both in the eighteenth century and in 'the birth of the modern on a global scale' (Rogers, 11). As Defoe said in *The Great Law of Subordination Consider'd*, 'I made myself Master of the History, and *ancient State of England*, I resolv'd in the next Place, to make my self Master of its *Present State* also' (P. Rogers, introduction to D. Defoe, *A Tour thro' the Whole Island of Great Britain*, 1971, 34). Defoe's love for his country is everywhere in this survey of the entire nation. He begins his *Tour* with the statement that his subject is 'the most flourishing and opulent Country in the World', and exults,

> Like *Eden* Fruitful, like *Arabia* Gay,
> So blest, they scarcely know for what to pray:
> ENGLAND in native Glory springs.
> (D. Defoe, *A Tour thro' the Whole Island of Great Britain*, 1724, 1.1)

Alive to landscape as he had seldom shown himself to be before *Captain Singleton*, he described scene after scene in books written in this period and invested these descriptions with the expansiveness and harmony of his vision for his country. He remarked on 'the glorious interspersing of capital Cities', the 'safe and capacious Havens', 'magnificent Buildings', 'innumerable Beauties [that] render the ... View desirable and pleasant, and that in the most solid and significant manner'. He was simultaneously alive to history, to commercial produce and possibilities, and to the new tourist industry. The result was that he was the first to compose a book equally useful for those who wanted to view historical antiquities, to tour stately homes, to study agricultural and estate improvements, and to take a picturesque tour (in Rogers's words, 'a kind of aesthetic adventure' for persons of sensibility; Rogers, 40).

Defoe began to invent an astonishingly detailed, carefully ordered construct towards which Great Britain might aspire. This construct is worked out primarily in *A Tour*, *The Royal Progress* (both 1724), *The Complete English Tradesman*, *A General History of Discoveries and Improvements* (both 1726), *Plan of the English Commerce*, *Atlas maritimus and commercialis* (both 1728), and several shorter works such as *An humble proposal to the people of England, for the encrease of their trade, and encouragement of their manufactures* (1729). In these books Defoe characterized the English people, identified their strengths and advantages, and charted their course to greatness. Typically, he began with surveys—of the present state of England (*A Tour*) and of their place in worldwide commercial history (*A General History of Discoveries and Improvements*)—and with guides for the most basic cogs in the machine (*The Great Law of Subordination Consider'd* and *The Complete English Tradesman*). All of them have the spoke and wheel model that made London the centre—goods flowing in to this great port from all over the world and all over Great Britain and then being redistributed throughout the world from this great collection centre. He insisted that London was the only port in the world on which every sea captain could depend to buy his cargo and then reload his ship, and he used homely examples to prove how dependent the country and the world were on the exchange of goods. For example, in a series of lists in *Complete English Tradesman*, Defoe shows how ordinary household furnishings and daily attire prove his point; he counts, for instance, eleven regions that contributed to a man's everyday outfit.

Defoe's plan for his country was nothing less than world domination. Trade, not military might, would make this conquest. In *Plan of the English Commerce* he wrote, 'Trade is the Foundation of Wealth, and Wealth of Power' and in *The Advantages of Peace and Commerce* (1729) he said, 'if any one Nation could govern Trade, that Nation would govern the World'. He challenged his countrymen to duplicate the pattern of English commerce in their foreign trade. *A Plan of the English Commerce* and *Atlas maritimus* target countries and products and urge Englishmen to develop trade with them. His plan included establishing England's independence; very high on his list of priorities, therefore, is getting timber, hemp, turpentine, resin, and masts from the American colonies rather than from the Baltic and Scandinavian countries. That shipbuilding and repair had to depend on these fractious countries alarmed him. Another part of the plan was to identify the imports which worked against a favourable balance of trade or were, in his opinion, exorbitantly expensive. He argued that by studying climate as Crusoe had done Englishmen could plant more effectively and, for example, bring the price of coffee and spices down. He saw Africa as the most promising place for this endeavour. England's west coast territory, the part he called 'Guinea', was but two weeks away from London; in contrast, Jamaica with its similar climate was six to ten weeks over the treacherous open sea of the Atlantic. Defoe compared such things as latitude and chided the British for letting 'fruitful Soil [lie] waste'. He reminded them that even the slothful Portuguese now grew coffee in Brazil and their arch-rivals the Dutch in Java.

Last years Defoe's last years were not happy. By 1728 he was being sued for debt by John Ward, his tenant and manager of some of the Colchester property, and by Elizabeth Stancliffe and Mary Brooke, who were claiming £800 that Defoe had allegedly owed since 1692. In order to save the Colchester property, Defoe transferred it to his son Daniel, who was forced to mortgage it rapidly and repeatedly. His son Benjamin had quit studying for the law, become a journalist and hack writer, and had already been arrested and sent to Newgate for seditious writing. In October 1729 Defoe lost the Stancliffe–Brooke case in the court of exchequer. Were he not to pay, he could be prosecuted and gaoled for debt. Brooke, who survived Stancliffe, pursued her money until she was granted administration of Defoe's estate in 1733. By that time he had given his daughter Sophia's husband, Henry Baker, a 34 and a half year mortgage on his Stoke Newington house as pledge for her £500 dowry, and on 30 May 1730 Baker took possession. In the final year of his life Defoe moved among various London lodgings and a village in Kent. In his last surviving letter he describes himself as 'sinking under the Weight' of 'Insupportable Sorrows'. He writes about missing his family and being unable even to have them visit and the special pain from his (correct) belief that he would never see Sophia's first baby.

On 24 April 1731 Defoe died in lodgings on Rope Makers' Alley, a winding street in the heart of the old City of London, and his death was recorded in the St Giles Cripplegate general registry, the registry holding his sisters' baptismal records. The cause of death was listed as a lethargy, what would now be called a stroke. He was buried in Bunhill Fields, the great cemetery for nonconformists, on 26 April 1731. His wife, Mary, was buried beside him on 19 December 1732.

Contributions and legacies Even the most conservative lists of Defoe's works include 318 titles, and most Defoe scholars would credit him with at least 50 more. His greatest contributions to his contemporaries were his conception of what Great Britain could become and a style of writing effective for its propagation. His late economic writings offered England the most detailed description of what became England's vision of herself for 150 years and drove her imperial ambitions—championing the settlement of North America when European attention was on South America and the Caribbean, for example. At the time he wrote, Walpole and Bolingbroke debated domestic economic policies, but Defoe made the globe his study. A protectionist like Walpole, Defoe differed from the prime minister in casting a critical eye on the great companies' monopolies and in defending high wages. An enemy like Bolingbroke of stockjobbing and the political liaison with the great companies, he had no patience with

Bolingbroke's idealized picture of *laissez-faire* or with his complaints about the rising power of the Commons. Even as Defoe applauded the measures Walpole took to lessen manufacturers' costs, encourage exports of manufactured goods, and raise the prices of imported goods not used as raw materials, he chafed over the lack of colonial investment and encouragement. None of these men was an original economist and each in his own way was conservative, but Defoe grasped the global reverberations of historical and contemporary actions and saw how symbiotic world trade was better than either of them.

Defoe's immortality will always rest on a few of his novels, and especially on *Robinson Crusoe*, that immensely subtle, complex book with its simple plot and a character of compelling reality who appears in one archetypal incident after another. Embedded in world cultural consciousness, *Robinson Crusoe* has never been out of print. Most people still encounter Crusoe in childhood and never forget him. Only the Bible has been printed in more languages. From the very beginning Defoe's impact was international, as was the recognition that *Robinson Crusoe* was a new *literary* form with revolutionary power to 'instruct and delight'. The earliest experts celebrate it as such, as did Ludwig Vischer, who wrote the preface to the 1721 German translation. *Moll Flanders*, once considered coarse and low, now rivals *Crusoe* in classrooms, and *Roxana*, whose title character was described by Charles Lamb as 'harlot and something worse', has attracted some of the most sophisticated criticism of the eighteenth-century novel. Students in a range of courses and programmes, including humanities in medicine, are reading *The Journal of the Plague Year*, and scholars study *Col. Jack* for early attitudes towards slavery and even alcoholism.

Defoe's novels have always led a double life. The greatest writers and thinkers of the eighteenth century praised him, and his novels were notoriously read in kitchens and hovels. Samuel Johnson named *Robinson Crusoe* as one of only three books readers ever wished longer, and Charles Gildon noted, 'Not an old Woman that can go the Price of it, but buys thy Life and Adventures' (C. Gildon, *The Life and Strange Surprizing Adventures of Mr. D— De F—*, 1917, ix–x). The same bifurcation continues today. Critics and students study the art of *Moll Flanders*, and movies and television films have fixed its reputation as 'a novel of lust, survival and protofeminist spirit' (*Newsweek*, 14 Nov 1996, 83). Whether readers emphasize Defoe's intelligent brooding over the problem of crime or over women's situation in the world, see Moll as an example of capitalism run amok or of woman in a man's world, or simply celebrate her resilient spirit, the novel speaks eloquently to every generation. Important theorists indicate why. For instance, Pierre Machery finds Moll 'the eloquent, simple critic of love, commerce and marriage, those basic categories of … society' (P. Machery, *A Theory of Literary Production*, 1978, 247). Hubert Damish says of *Robinson Crusoe* what is also true of *Moll Flanders*, that Defoe forces us 'to judge our needs, our productions, our values, our cultural heritage, by the sole light of necessity' (H. Damish, 'Robinsonnades I: the Allegory', *October*, 85, 1998, 19).

Roxana is universally described as 'disturbing'. Its technical and psychological mastery heightens portrayals of the situation of individuals, especially women, in modern society and themes such as the enquiry into the nature of evil.

In the television production of *Moll Flanders* (1996), Moll occasionally turns full face to the camera and asks the audience directly, 'What would you do?' *Roxana* asks that question in even more complex troubling situations. Indisputably Defoe has created two of the strongest and most important women characters in the history of literature. Both are compelling individuals but they are also 'sites' that reveal the forces of history and society. John Richetti points out that Roxana 'aspires to a new category and actually declares that her ultimate ambition lies in a powerful androgyny' (J. Richetti, *Defoe's Narratives*, 1975, 195). Critics have turned the most powerful tools of modern theory—psychoanalytic, Foucauldian, feminist—on the novel. And yet *Roxana* sells in airports with cover illustrations depicting Roxana gazing in a mirror or emerging from a curtain in her Turkish costume.

Critical interest in *Robinson Crusoe* has never diminished, and sophisticated work on the novel can be found in chapters in wide-ranging thematic studies and at special conferences. No history or discussion of the English novel is now written without considerable space devoted to Defoe's work. And the novel continues to inspire countless Robinsonade novels, stories, movies, and even television series, and some of the greatest writers, producers, and directors in dozens of countries have adapted it to their times. In the twentieth century Michael Tournier's *Vendredi* (1985) and J. M. Coetzee's *Foe* (1986) earned critical acclaim, and they indicate the international appeal of the story. Unlike Defoe's novel, many Robinsonades are utopian fictions, such as the influential *Der schweizerische Robinson* (1812–13) by Johann David Wyss. Each author reaccentuates different parts of the novel to meet cultural needs and immediate concerns, as *Castaway* (2000) did. In this film Friday is a volleyball, and he has also been depicted as robots, fairies, and almost anything imaginable. Directed by Robert Zemeckis and starring Tom Hanks, *Castaway* was the top film in January 2001, and, like all good Robinsonades, it captured a nation's obsessions, once again testing an Everyman within the myth. Luis Buñuel's *The Adventures of Robinson Crusoe* (1952) features Crusoe alone for seven of the ten reels of the film, a daring experiment that *Castaway* repeats. Buñuel, the master of horror and surrealism, explained that he was attracted to Crusoe's struggle with despair, a theme in a number of his best-known films (A. Corvin, 'The celluloid Crusoe', PhD diss., University of Wisconsin, 1989, 20–21). *Robinson Crusoe* has inspired a line of science-fiction films, again written, directed, or produced by the most distinguished people in the field. For instance, Byron Haskin, who directed *The War of the Worlds* and Disney's first live-action film, maintained that *Robinson Crusoe on Mars* (1964) was the best film he ever directed, and it has been named one of the twenty best science-fiction films ever produced (ibid., 132–3, 141–2). Dozens of intriguing movies not of this calibre have been made—*Little Robinson Corkscrew* (1924), *Mr Robinson Crusoe* (1931; Crusoe, Douglas Fairbanks, swings through trees like Tarzan and is rescued by a boatload of pin-up girls), *Sex Family Robinson* (1968), and *Mickey Mouse: Mickey's Man Friday* (1935), one of six Robinsonade movies Walt Disney made. Movies and made-for-television films are shown frequently, and the 1960 television series *Gilligan's Island* is still shown in America. Cartoons such as *Molly Moo Cow and Robinson Crusoe* adapt the story creatively. Molly washes up on Crusoe's island and wants to be his friend. He is rude and finally manages to drive her away, but when some stereotypical savages land and Crusoe calls for help Molly returns, rescues him, and becomes his Friday—a bizarre twist to 'girl Friday'.

In a time when fewer and fewer eighteenth-century novels are being read or even taught, most of Defoe's have become fashionable and significant again as they speak to modern post-colonial concerns and contribute to an understanding of public-health decisions, crime, cities, the family, and political economy. Again and again Defoe seems not just timely, but prescient.

Defoe's greatest bequests to posterity are his contributions to modern journalism and his place in the development of the English novel and novelistic discourse. From the beginning of his career he worked to design a prose style that would communicate clearly. He wanted to write so that he could not be misunderstood; he wrote

> the best Rule in all Tongues (viz) to make the Language plain, artless, and honest, suitable to the Story, and in a Stile easie and free … that the meanest Reader may meet with no Difficulty in the Reading and may have no Obstruction to his searching the History of things by their being obscurely represented. (Backscheider, *Defoe*, 532)

Although Defoe's style is not praised as often as that of Addison, Swift, or Johnson, it has far more versatility and has always attracted admirers. James Joyce described the style of *A Journal of the Plague Year* as 'masterly' and even 'orchestral', and countless other novelists have cited Defoe's influence. That Joyce would select for special praise what is perhaps Defoe's most journalistic novel is fitting. The energetic combination of fact, narrative, and editorial commentary that Defoe developed in *The Review* serves the novel well. Writing at a time when novels by William Chetwood, Penelope Aubin, Charles Gildon, Eliza Haywood, and Jane Barker wavered wildly among the prose styles of the pastoral romance, the southern European novella, Renaissance euphuism, and 'plain' English discourse, Defoe calmly developed a narrative voice that did more to establish the perimeters of novelistic discourse than any other writer. The idea that the phrase 'immethodical homespun garrulity' characterizes his writing and that he wrote without much self-consciousness, art, or revision has long been discredited. The manuscript of *The Compleat English Gentleman* (first published in 1890, ed. K. D. Bülbring) shows many corrections, additions, deletions, and revisions as well as a substantial number of the tricks of an experienced, confident, voluminous, and somewhat repetitious writer (abbreviations, sketched or shorthand sections). One of

the few novelists who has consistently appealed to the intellectual and the masses, Defoe has never lost his appeal. Several of his novels have never been out of print, and understanding of his importance to the history of the novel continues to grow. PAULA R. BACKSCHEIDER

Sources P. R. Backscheider, *Daniel Defoe: his life* (Baltimore, 1989) · J. Sutherland, *Defoe* (1937); repr. (1971) · *The letters of Daniel Defoe*, ed. G. Healey (1955) · G. Sill, *Defoe and the idea of fiction* (E. Brunswick, N. J., 1983) · P. Rogers, *The text of Great Britain* (Newark, 1998) · P. N. Furbank and W. Owens, *Defoe de-attributions* (1994) · P. R. Backscheider, 'Daniel Defoe and early modern intelligence', *Journal of Intelligence and National Security*, 11 (1996), 1–21 · M. E. Novak, 'Defoe as an innovator of fictional form', *Cambridge companion to the eighteenth-century novel*, ed. J. J. Richetti (1996) · I. Watt, *The rise of the novel*, 6th edn (1967) · *Calendar of the manuscripts of the marquis of Bath preserved at Longleat, Wiltshire*, 5 vols., HMC, 58 (1904–80)

Archives NA Scot. · NL Scot. · PRO, letters, mostly to Charles Delafaye | BL, corresp. with Harley · BL, letters to Lord Oxford, Add. MS 70291

Likenesses G. Bickham, group portrait, caricature, line engraving, 1711 (*The Whigs Medley*), BL; repro. in *Whig's Medley* (July 1711) · M. Vandergucht, line engraving (after J. Taverner, 1706), BM, NPG; repro. in D. Defoe, *Jure divino* (1706) [*see illus.*] · satirical prints

Wealth at death virtually nothing: exchequer records of last law suits

Degge, Sir Simon (1612?–1703), judge, was probably born on 5 January 1612, the eldest son of Thomas Degge (d. 1628) of Strangsall, Uttoxeter, Staffordshire, and Dorothy, daughter of George Crichlow of Wolscote, Staffordshire. He was admitted to the Inner Temple in 1639, but the civil war interrupted his studies. As a royalist he was present at the siege of Lichfield in 1643 and was captured at Stafford. Eventually he received a licence from the Stafford county committee to reside at home in Callowhill, Kingston. He compounded for delinquency in November 1645. Degge had married Jane (1609/10–1652), daughter of Thomas Orrell, but following her death in July 1652, on 7 December 1652 he married Alice Oldfield (1614–1696), relict of James Trollope (d. 1649), of Spalding, Lincolnshire.

Degge resumed his legal studies and was called to the bar on 24 November 1653. He practised as a civilian lawyer in Doctors' Commons. In 1660 he became puisne judge of Carmarthen circuit and two years later a justice of the Welsh marches. Both places he retained until 1674. In 1661 he became recorder of Derby and in 1662 steward of the court of the manor of Peverel. He was elected a bencher of the Inner Temple on 7 November 1668, but he was 'disbenched' in 1674 for refusing to read at the next Lent vacation. He was knighted on 2 March 1670. Degge served as high sheriff of Derbyshire in 1674–5 and the following year published *The Parson's Counsellor, with Law of Tithes or Tithing*, a leading textbook on the subject for many years. Degge was a committed tory and during the reign of James II freely consented to the 'three questions' posed by the king's agents. This led to some royal support for a parliamentary candidature in 1688, but it did not lead to Degge having any truck with dissenters as he refused to let Derby's dissenters meet despite the declaration of indulgence.

In his later years Degge seems to have pursued his antiquarian interests, providing William Woolley with information for his *History of Derbyshire*. Degge's 'Observations upon the possessions of monastery-lands in Staffordshire' was included in Sampson Erdeswick's *A Survey of Staffordshire* (1717). Degge died on 10 February 1703, having recently made his will in which he declared his wish to be buried in the 'little chapel I lately built adjoining to the parish church of Kingston'. STUART HANDLEY

Sources S. Erdeswick, *A survey of Staffordshire*, ed. T. Harwood, new edn (1844), lx, liv · W. R. Williams, *The history of the great sessions in Wales, 1542–1830* (privately printed, Brecon, 1899), 175 · IGI · will, PRO, PROB 11/469, sig. 65 · *William Woolley's History of Derbyshire*, ed. C. Glover and P. Riden, Derbyshire RS, 6 (1981), 4, 31, 41, 211 · W. H. Cooke, ed., *Students admitted to the Inner Temple, 1547–1660* [1878], 302 · G. Duckett, ed., *Penal laws and Test Act*, 2 (1883), 197, 284, 294 · M. A. E. Green, ed., *Calendar of the proceedings of the committee for compounding … 1643–1660*, 5 vols., PRO (1889–92), 89, 1016 · *CSP dom., 1687–9*, 329 · HoP, *Commons, 1660–90*, 1.189 · F. A. Inderwick and R. A. Roberts, eds., *A calendar of the Inner Temple records*, 3 (1901), 63, 99, 283 · J. Le Neve, *Monumenta Anglicana*, 4 (1717), 53

Archives U. Birm. L., commonplace books

Dehn, Paul Edward (1912–1976), writer and film critic, was born on 5 November 1912 at 13 Belfield Road, Didsbury, Manchester, the eldest of the three children of Frederick Edward Dehn (*fl.* 1882–1947), cotton merchant, and Helen Susman (1880–1976). His parents were British of German Jewish descent. His godfather was James Agate, the drama critic, a close friend of his father. Known as Fritz (his original name before Anglicization), Dehn's father was very musical and was remembered by Agate for his panache and high spirits, along with a tendency to launch out into political tirades in inappropriate places.

Dehn was educated at Shrewsbury School (1925–30), for which he retained an affection, and at Brasenose College, Oxford (1930–34). After a brief spell on the *Birmingham Post*, in 1936 he joined the *Sunday Referee* as a film critic and columnist. At the start of the Second World War he went into intelligence, and is said to have worked for a while as personal assistant to General Gubbins. His talent as a linguist resulted in his being transferred to the Special Operations Executive (SOE) at Beaulieu, where his task—along with Kim Philby—was to teach propaganda (including 'black') warfare. He delighted everyone with his entertaining manner and piano playing, and could put on a 'good nightclub act'. He is also recorded as having been a 'serious thinker', with a warm and romantic nature, not to mention an outstanding instructor. In America it was said that listening to him was more exciting than reading a spy novel. The story goes that once he lay in his bath learning by heart how to deliver a lecture in Polish to Polish students. The talk went off perfectly, but the students were perplexed when he was unable to answer their questions.

In the winter of 1942 Dehn was posted as chief instructor to Camp X at Oshawa, Ontario, Canada. Then in the summer of 1943 he went to the United States to read propaganda warfare to members of the office of strategic services. After the German surrender he went to Norway on an interrogation mission; he also compiled an agent's handbook. It was in 1944 that he met James Michael (Jimmy) Bernard (*b.* 1925), later to become a well-known composer of film music, and they lived together until Dehn's death. After leaving the army as a major he worked as a film critic of considerable distinction on the *Sunday Chronicle*, then on the *News Chronicle*, and from 1960 to 1963 on the *Daily Herald*. He contributed lyrics to many of the very successful theatre revues of the early 1950s: *The Lyric Revue*, *The Globe Revue*, *Penny Plain*, *At the Lyric*, and so on. In 1952 he wrote a masque for Shrewsbury School's 400th anniversary and a verse commentary for an award-winning film on the Thames, *Waters of Time*. In the same year both he and James Bernard were awarded Hollywood Oscars as joint authors for the film *Seven Days to Noon*. An adaptation of Wilde's *A Woman of No Importance* ran at the Savoy in 1953, and in 1954 Lennox Berkeley's opera *A Dinner Engagement*, for which Paul had written the libretto, was presented at the Aldeburgh festival and later ran at Sadler's Wells. He was also a critic on the BBC, and in 1956 president of the Critics' Council. Meanwhile he had published two books of poetry, *The Day's Alarm* (1949) and *The Romantic Landscape* (1952), which included one of his best poems, 'The Sunken Cathedral'. *For Love and Money* (1956) was a miscellaneous collection of articles, essays, poems, and light verse, mostly already published in *Punch*, *The Listener*, *The Observer*, and elsewhere.

In 1958 Dehn received the British Film Academy award for the script of *Orders to Kill*. His collaboration with Terence Rattigan in *Joie de vivre* (1960), a musical version of *French without Tears*, was not a success, but the musical version of Vanbrugh's *Virtue in Danger* (1963, with James Bernard), for which he wrote the book and lyrics, was better received. In 1967 he wrote the librettos for William Walton's *The Bear* and Lennox Berkeley's *The Castaway*. After giving up film criticism, he concentrated on screenplays, for which he gained a brilliant reputation. These included *Goldfinger* (1964, as co-author), *The Spy who Came in from the Cold* (1966), *The Deadly Affair* (1966), Zeffirelli's version of *The Taming of the Shrew* (1967), three of the *Planet of the Apes* films (1969, 1971, 1972), and most notably *Murder on the Orient Express* (1974). This last received an Oscar nomination, and Agatha Christie declared that it was the best film adaptation of any of her books. There were two more books of poems: *Quake, Quake, Quake* (1961), written with ghoulish wit, and with drawings to match by Edward Gorey; and *The Fern on the Rock* (1965).

It is not surprising that with all this tremendous literary activity friends were periodically told that 'Paul is in purdah'. Nevertheless there were many lavish dinner parties at 19 Bramerton Street, Chelsea, where he and Bernard lived for twenty-five years. A menu book was kept so that guests would not have the same dishes twice. Colour schemes were mostly strong, and in a corner there might be a large pot of flowering orchids. Paintings by Ivon Hitchens and Keith Vaughan were special features. Among the most famous of Dehn's and Bernard's friends were Terence Rattigan, John Gielgud, Lennox and Freda Berkeley, Michael Redgrave, William Walton, and Arthur Marshall. Dehn's earnings were of course considerable at times, but taxation in the 1950s was punitive. In one year

Dehn wrote to *The Times* gently pointing out that he had had to pay £80,000 in tax. Slightly built, good-looking with pale skin and long black eyelashes, a splendid host, witty and affectionate, Paul Dehn in obituaries was chiefly remembered as a superb writer of screenplays and lyricist; his work in the Special Operations Executive during the Second World War was virtually overlooked. Dehn would give ornithology as his hobby. He was a heavy smoker and developed lung cancer, from which he suffered for nearly two years. In the last year of his life he and Bernard moved to 18 Tite Street, Chelsea, London, where he died on 30 September 1976. He bequeathed his body to the Westminster Hospital for cancer research.

RALEIGH TREVELYAN

Sources personal knowledge (2004) · private information (2004) · *The Times* (1 Oct 1976) · M. R. D. Foot, *S. O. E.* (1984) · J. Parker, ed., *Who's who in the theatre*, 15th edn (1972)
Archives priv. coll. | FILM BFI NFTVA
Likenesses photographs, priv. colls.
Wealth at death £130,860: probate, 27 April 1977, *CGPLA Eng. & Wales*

D'Eichthal, Gustave (1804–1886), visionary and social observer, was born in Nancy, the son of Louis D'Eichthal (1780–1840), a Jewish banker, and his wife, Fleurette, *née* Lévy (d. 1837). Raised as a Catholic from 1817, when he was baptized at Deüil, near Versailles, he was educated in Paris, first at a Catholic boarding-school and then at the Lycée Henri IV. Late in 1822 he became the young Auguste Comte's first disciple, and was responsible for introducing Comte's work to Hegel and other German philosophers in 1824. During the next few years, while working in commerce, he began to drift away from Comte and was drawn instead to the Saint-Simonians; he was fully converted in 1829, and for the next three years was a leading member and benefactor of the Saint-Simonian sect. Comte regarded this as a betrayal.

D'Eichthal made an extended visit to Britain in 1828, and recorded his observations in the form of extensive notes, which were first published by his son some three-quarters of a century later. These notes have been unduly neglected, perhaps, by historians of nineteenth-century Britain. D'Eichthal stayed for eight months, mostly in London, but he also made a two-month trip to the industrial north and to Scotland. The title under which his notes were published in 1902 implied that he was primarily interested in working-class life, but that bias is not apparent in the full text of his notes; neither is there much justification for the assertion that he was shocked by what he saw of working-class living standards in industrial Britain. He recorded his observations in a matter-of-fact tone. D'Eichthal's main interest, then and for the rest of his life, was religion, and his notes are peppered with observations on religious practice. He was not greatly impressed by 'the apparent respect the English show for religious matters', which he thought a matter of habit rather than conviction (Ratcliffe and Chaloner, 31).

It is sometimes said that D'Eichthal was interested in Britain because, as a Saint-Simonian, he regarded the birthplace of the industrial revolution as being in the vanguard of history. This interpretation is open to dispute. He saw Britain in 1828 as an *ancien régime* in its last years. 'Privilege and monopoly', he thought, 'are the basis of the entire constitution', and he was thinking not just of the privileges of the aristocracy and the gentry, of the clergy and the municipalities, rather, 'the keystone of this whole edifice of privilege, which in my opinion has made its survival possible for so long, is the privilege enjoyed by the poor who *have a right* to relief from the rich, according to the level of their wages and the number of children in their families' (Ratcliffe and Chaloner, 40–41). He drew an explicit comparison between the situation in England in 1828 and the state of France on the eve of the revolution of 1789. D'Eichthal did not think of England as the epitome of modernity in all respects; he did see it as a society ripe for conversion to Saint-Simonism, and that belief was to account for his next visit in 1832.

Conversations with bankers and economists in England influenced the monograph on government finance which D'Eichthal completed on his return to France in 1829. Influenced by the work of the House of Commons finance committee, he argued for the desirability of government loans and stressed the absurdity of a sinking fund. He was also impressed by the savings bank movement, and proposed the creation of similar institutions in France as a means of improving the working-class standard of living.

During the visit to Britain D'Eichthal had met J. S. Mill, who became perhaps his closest English friend. He introduced Mill to Comte's work, and Mill and D'Eichthal began a lengthy correspondence. Another of his notable English contacts was Francis Place, with whom he had lengthy conversations about the machinery question. On his return to France D'Eichthal had planned to write a book on Britain, and he wrote to Place and Mill about it. The project never came to fruition. It was during this period that he also began to correspond with Thomas Carlyle, who had come to his attention as the author of 'Signs of the times' in the *Edinburgh Review*. He viewed Carlyle as a likely convert: somewhat optimistically, since Carlyle, though sympathetic to Saint-Simonian social and historical philosophy, was unable to see it as a religion.

D'Eichthal visited England again in January 1832, when with Duveyrier he undertook a Saint-Simonian 'mission'. On the eve of the visit he wrote that Britain—in the midst of reform agitation—was ripe for conversion: the last bastions of feudalism were on the point of collapse, and circumstances were propitious for the new Saint-Simonian doctrine to take hold. In the event the apostles were spectacularly unsuccessful in winning converts, though they attracted press attention and reinforced the celebrity, or notoriety, of the Saint-Simonian sect. Carlyle, who finally met his correspondent, thought the two missionaries 'the greatest Babblers I have ever heard' (*Collected Letters*, 6.127). The sect was denounced in *The Times*, and in organs as different as the *Quarterly Review* and the *Westminster Review*. In the same year the new religion collapsed as several of its leaders were successfully prosecuted in Paris. D'Eichthal was one of the last of the leaders to abandon the sect, in

November 1832, and the Saint-Simonian conception of history exercised a lifelong influence on his thinking.

Thereafter, D'Eichthal's active interest in Britain subsided, although he continued to correspond with Mill. D'Eichthal also pinned his hopes on Greece for a while, and in 1834–5 served in the new state's political economy office, which had been set up at his suggestion to look into the land question. He was an enthusiast for the promotion of Greek as an international language, and thought that its adoption as the official language could be a solution to the nationality question in the Habsburg monarchy. But his chief interest was religion: he published a number of penetrating works of biblical criticism, both on the gospels and on the Pentateuch. He also devoted himself to promoting the unity of the human race through a new synthesis of the three great 'Mediterranean' religions. This project was not successful. He married a Jewess, Félicité Rodrigues-Henriques, who came from a Sephardic family of stockbrokers who had converted to Catholicism. Their eldest son, Eugène, became director of the École Libre des Sciences Politiques in Paris. D'Eichthal died in Paris on 9 April 1886.   H. S. JONES

Sources J. Balteau and others, eds., *Dictionnaire de biographie française*, [19 vols.] (Paris, 1933–) • E. D'Eichthal, ed., 'Condition de la classe ouvrière en Angleterre (1828), notes prises par Gustave d'Eichthal', *Revue historique*, 79 (1902), 63–95 • B. M. Ratcliffe and W. H. Chaloner, eds., *A French sociologist looks at Britain: Gustave d'Eichthal and British society in 1828* (1977) • E. D'Eichthal, ed., *John Stuart Mill: correspondance avec Gustave d'Eichthal (1828–1842, 1864–1871)* (1898) • R. K. P. Pankhurst, *The Saint Simonians, Mill and Carlyle: a preface to modern thought* (1957) • *The collected letters of Thomas and Jane Welsh Carlyle*, ed. C. R. Sanders and K. J. Fielding, 5–6 (1976–7)
Archives Bibliothèque de l'Arsenal, Paris • Bibliothèque Thiers, Paris | BL, Francis Place MSS • Maison d'Auguste Comte, Paris, Auguste Comte MSS
Likenesses statues and busts

Deicolus [St Deicolus, Deicola] (*d. c.*625), Benedictine monk and hermit, was allegedly a companion of St Columbanus of Luxeuil and Bobbio (*d.* 615), and a half-brother of Gall of St Gallen. His feast day is 18 January.

According to his life, written about 965, sickness prevented Deicolus from following Columbanus when the Irish missionary and his followers were expelled from Burgundy about 611 by King Theuderic II and his grandmother, Queen Brunechildis. Since the departing Columbanus forbade Deicolus to return to the former's foundation of Luxeuil (north of Besançon, in what is now eastern France), he founded a hermitage nearby at a church dedicated to St Martin. After some initial resistance, Deicolus obtained royal privileges and, during a visit to Rome, the protection of the pope. Thus the foundation was laid for what was later to become the monastery of Lure, a few miles south of Luxeuil. At the end of his life Deicolus retreated to a little oratory and died there on 18 January, about 625. He was buried at Lure.

Although he is not in the list of companions of Columbanus known by name, claims to Deicolus's historicity may have some justification. He is mentioned as a disciple of Colmán in the martyrology of Donegal on the same feast day as in continental documents. The life of Germanus, monk of Luxeuil and first abbot of the neighbouring monastery of Granfelden (Grandval), is dedicated to a Deicolus, who may be identical with the one of Lure. The name appears repeatedly in Irish texts, and is also borne by the Carolingian teacher and astronomer Dicuil, who flourished at the beginning of the ninth century.

Some episodes of Deicolus's biography, however, seem to derive from the earlier life of his alleged half-brother St Gall. The visit to Rome in order to obtain privileges from the pope also indicates the late date of Deicolus's life. The fact that 'Dícuill' is also the name of one of the companions of Fursa, whose feast day occurs on 16 January, may point to some confusion between the two. But some credence may be given to the statement that Deicolus handed over his monastery at Lure to a 'Columbinus' (*sic*), as a 'Columbanus' is also mentioned as one of the disciples of the St Columbanus in Jonas's contemporary life of the latter.

DAGMAR Ó RIAIN-RAEDEL

Sources J. Colgan, *Acta sanctorum veteris et majoris Scotiae seu Hiberniae* (1645) • 'Vita sancti Deicoli', *Acta sanctorum: Januarius*, 2, 199–210 • 'Vita sancti Deicoli', [*Supplementa tomorum I–XII, pars III*], ed. G. Waitz and W. Wattenbach, MGH Scriptores [folio], 15/2 (Stuttgart, 1888) • M. O'Clery, *The martyrology of Donegal: a calendar of the saints of Ireland*, ed. J. H. Todd and W. Reeves, trans. J. O'Donovan (1864) • J. F. Kenney, *The sources for the early history of Ireland* (1929); repr. (1979)

Deighton, John (1747/8–1828), bookseller and publisher, is of unknown origins. By the time that he announced his arrival in Cambridge from London, in April 1778, he was a bookseller and master bookbinder, although no record of his apprenticeship has been found. He purchased the stock of Richard Matthews, a relatively minor bookseller with premises on Regent Walk, at the heart of the university, and quickly expanded the business, adding to the stock and supplying, binding, and repairing many books for the university library. On 11 February 1779 he married Mary Readhead (1758/9–1819) of Cambridge, and in November of that year he purchased the stock of the bankrupt John Woodyer, who, in partnership with William Thurlbourne, had once been the pre-eminent Cambridge bookseller. Deighton moved to Woodyer's premises on Trinity Street, opposite the Senate House, a prominent location long occupied by booksellers. He also began publishing books by Cambridge authors, and by 1785 his imprint had appeared on at least thirty books. At the end of that year Deighton left Cambridge to take over the bookselling business of William Cater in Holborn, London; in 1792 he moved further up Holborn, having purchased the valuable stock of Lockyer Davis. His move to London coincided with a marked increase in his publishing activity, and in the nine years that he stayed there over 200 works appeared with his imprint.

In October 1794 Deighton returned to Cambridge to take over the stock of John and Joseph Merrill, at the same time taking on the mantle of the university's leading copyholding bookseller, a position which he maintained to his death. He purchased prominent premises on Trinity Street—situated between the Senate House and the two largest colleges, Trinity and St John's—and rapidly made his shop a central focus of university life, where students enrolled for professorial lectures and learned of their preliminary ranking into classes after the oral disputations. As a bookseller he continued to supply most of the needs of the university library as well as of students and scholars, both in Cambridge and further afield. He issued regular catalogues of retail stock and acquired a particular reputation for his ability to obtain foreign works. In addition he established the first publishing house in Cambridge that could boast a national reputation, exploiting the expanding local and national markets for educational works. Reflecting the interests of the university, his list was particularly strong in mathematical and classical works. He issued a popular guide to the university and town, a glossary of university slang, and the annual *Cambridge University Calendar*. Most of Deighton's publications were printed at the university press, and his contracts provided the press with a significant proportion of its income. When the university printer, John Burges, died unexpectedly in 1802 Deighton was temporarily appointed until a suitable replacement could be found. In addition he succeeded the Merrills as the Cambridge agent for the bibles and prayer books published by the university press. Deighton apprenticed his two children, John (1791–1854) and Joseph Jonathan (1792–1848), as printers, and in January 1813 he took them into partnership. Suffering ill health he retired in 1827, the business being continued by his sons. He died, aged eighty, at his home in Market Street, Cambridge, on 16 January 1828 and was buried at St Michael's Church, Trinity Street, on 23 January. Though the lack of personal references suggests that he was not a man of great charisma, Deighton was clearly a man of great energy and ability, and he wielded significant power within the university.   JONATHAN R. TOPHAM

Sources J. R. Topham, 'Two centuries of Cambridge bookselling and publishing: a brief history of Deighton, Bell and Co., 1778–1998, with a checklist of the archive', *Transactions of the Cambridge Bibliographical Society*, 11 (1996–9), 350–403 · J. R. Topham, 'A textbook revolution', *Books and the sciences in history*, ed. M. Frasca-Spada and N. Jardine (2000), 317–37 · D. McKitterick, *Cambridge University Library, a history: the eighteenth and nineteenth centuries* (1986) · D. McKitterick, *A history of Cambridge University Press*, 2 (1998) · parish register, Cambridge, Great St Mary's, Cambs. AS, 11 Feb 1779 [marriage] · *GM*, 1st ser., 98/1 (1828), 188 · parish register, Cambridge, St Michael's, Cambs. AS, 23 Jan 1828 [burial] · *Cambridge Chronicle and Journal* (6 Aug 1819)
Archives Cambs. AS · CUL, Cambridge University Press archive | CUL, Deighton, Bell & Co. archives
Wealth at death a shop; probably a house; £344 19s. in monetary bequests: will, PRO, PROB 11/1737

Deiniol [St Deiniol, Daniel] (d. **584**), bishop of Bangor and founder of monasteries, is first recorded in the early ninth-century Irish martyrology of Tallaght, where his feast day is given as 11 September; this agrees with almost all the later Welsh calendars. In the martyrology of Tallaght he is given as 'Deiniol, bishop of Bangor', but in his obit in the *Annales Cambriae*, s.a. 584, he is 'Daniel of the Bangors'. This suggests that he was already known as the patron saint of his foundation, Bangor Is-coed, the monastery mentioned in a famous story in Bede's *Historia*

ecclesiastica, about the battle of Chester, assigned by the *Annales Cambriae* to 613, nearly thirty years after Deiniol's death. According to the story as it reached Bede, the number of monks was so great that the community had been divided into seven sections, with no section having fewer than 300 members. Entries in Irish annals referring to Bangor in Britain and the fact that he was one of only three Welsh saints to be included in the martyrology of Tallaght also indicate the importance of his foundations in the pre-viking period.

There is, however, no narrative account of Deiniol surviving other than the brief résumé in the lections for his feast, copied by a prominent north Welsh antiquarian, Sir Thomas Wiliems, between 1594 and 1610. The version given in these lections corresponds closely to the story in a poem in praise of Deiniol by Sir Dafydd Trefor in 1527. The important aspect of the lections is that they show Deiniol as a hermit close to Pembroke before he became a bishop. George Owen's *Description of Pembrokeshire* mentions 'St Daniells chappell neere Penbrok' (Owen, 1.108). In 1620 a 'Cae Ffynnon Daniel' ('Field of Daniel's field') was recorded at Bangor Is-coed. It appears, therefore, that, although Deiniol came to be predominantly associated with the cathedral church of Bangor, his cult remained active in south-west and north-east Wales right up to the Reformation. The wide range of the cult is also echoed by the importance and range of his supposed saintly kinsmen: his father, Dunod (Donatus), is said to have been a son of *Pabo Post Prydain, ancestor of a number of saints, including St *Asaf and St *Tysilio (the principal saint of Powys). Through his mother, Dwywai, he may have been linked with further saints, predominantly in the north. His name is commemorated in the national monument to W. E. Gladstone at Hawarden, Flintshire: St Deiniol's Library.   T. M. CHARLES-EDWARDS

Sources E. Phillimore, ed., 'The *Annales Cambriae* and Old Welsh genealogies', *Y Cymmrodor*, 9 (1888), 141–83 [version A], esp. 152–69 · R. I. Best and H. J. Lawlor, eds., *The martyrology of Tallaght*, HBS, 68 (1931) · P. C. Bartrum, ed., *Early Welsh genealogical tracts* (1966) · D. Trefor, *cywydd* to Deiniol, 1527 · S. Harris, ed., 'Liturgical commemorations of the Welsh saints [pt 1]', *Journal of the Historical Society of the Church in Wales*, 5 (1955), 5–22 [copied by T. Wiliems, 1594–1619, into Peniarth MS 225, fols. 155–60] · J. E. Caerwyn Williams, 'Buchedd Ddeiniol Sant', *Transactions of the Caernarvonshire Historical Society*, 10 (1949), 123–35 [Welsh edn and trans. of *Legenda novem lectionum…*] · G. Owen, *The description of Penbrokshire*, ed. H. Owen, 4 vols., Honourable Society of Cymmrodorion, Cymmrodorion Record Series, 1 (1892–1936), pts 1–3 · S. Baring-Gould and J. Fisher, *The lives of the British saints*, Honourable Society of Cymmrodorion, Cymmrodorion Record Series, 2 (1908), 325–31 · E. R. Henken, *Traditions of the Welsh saints* (1987) · E. R. Henken, *The Welsh saints: a study in patterned lives* (1991)

Deios, Laurence (d. **1618**), Church of England clergyman, was a native of Shropshire. He matriculated from St John's College, Cambridge, in Easter 1571, graduated BA in January 1573, became a fellow in March 1573, and proceeded MA in 1576 and BD in 1583. Deios won preferments from the Elizabethan episcopate, being a chaplain to both John Aylmer, bishop of London, and John Whitgift, archbishop of Canterbury, and was collated by the latter to the rectory of Chiddingstone, Kent, on 16 April 1585, to the rectory of

East Horsley, Surrey, on 14 June 1590, and to the rectory of Brasted, Kent, on 13 November 1591. The series of records collected under the heading of the Remembrancia relate how in 1581 Deios had demonstrated both his sacerdotal-ism and his anti-puritanism when clashing with the alder-men of London over the scheme to increase the number of preachers in the city: according to them he had asserted in a sermon 'that if the appointing of preachers was commit-ted to them, they would [appoint] such as would defend usury, the family of love and puritanism' (Overall and Overall, 355–6). Deios was loyal to the Church of England as by law established and defended its doctrine and discip-line in his chief printed work, published in 1591 and entitled *That the pope is that Antichrist; and an answer to the objections of sectaries, which condemn this Church of England*, which contained two sermons, one of which had been preached at Paul's Cross. It is likely that Deios resided at his Chiddingstone living in Kent, for he was buried there on 27 December 1618.   WILL ALLEN

Sources Venn, *Alum. Cant.* · Register Whitgift, LPL, i. fols. 461v, 487v, 495v · Extracts from dispensation rolls at the PRO, BL, Add. MS 39402, fol. 20v · *Analytical index, to the series of records known as Remembrancia, preserved among the archives of the City of London*, Corporation of London, ed. [W. H. Overall and H. C. Overall] (1878), 355–6

Dekker, Thomas (*c.*1572–1632), playwright and pamphlet-eer, is of obscure origins, and his own words are often the only source for personal details. Nothing is known of his parents, though his name suggests that he was of Dutch descent. His date of birth is generally given as about 1572 from the epistle dedicatory to *English Villainies* (1632) in which Dekker refers to 'my three-score years'. He had already hinted at his declining years in the dedication to *Match mee in London* (1631), claiming: 'I have been a priest in Apollo's temple many years; my voice is decaying with my age'. In all probability he was born in London, where he lived all his life. Dekker consistently presented himself as the city's devoted and nurtured son. Writing about Lon-don in *The Seven Deadly Sinnes* (1606), Dekker claimed that 'from thy womb received I my being, from thy brests my nourishment' (sig. A3v). Years later, in *A Rod for Run-Awayes* (1625), he still presented himself as one of London's sons: 'O London! (thou Mother of my life, Nurse of my being)' (sig. Bv).

There is no evidence regarding Dekker's education; no reference that he attended university, or any sign that he had any special familiarity with the inns of court. How-ever, his writing strongly suggests that he had a grammar school education. An accomplished Latin scholar, he translated Fredriech Dedekind's Latin poem *Grobianus* as *The Guls Horne-Book* (1609). Dekker had an extensive work-ing knowledge of the classics, including Ovid, Horace, Vir-gil, and Martial. He was an avid reader of contemporary authors, and Stow, Holinshed, and Harrington were all sources for his writing. In *A Knight's Conjuring* (1607) he writes of an authors' Elysium, where he pays special trib-ute to 'old Chaucer' and 'his son', 'grave Spenser'. Among the others who were there, but 'in another company', were Thomas Kyd, Christopher Marlowe, Robert Greene,

George Peele, and his old friend and collaborator Henry Chettle, all of whom watch as Thomas Nashe arrives denouncing 'dry-fisted patrons'. Dekker's sole livelihood was writing. He was principally a playwright, though he later turned his hand to non-dramatic pamphlets, may-oral pageants and public entertainments, satires, com-mendatory verse, and other poetry. That Dekker, unlike many of his contemporary writers, had no consistent pat-ron, no financial investments in either the theatre or the printing industry, and was not an actor, meant that he was constantly shadowed by debt. From topical and thematic issues in his writing to moments of personal crisis, debt had a marked effect upon his career. Sometimes it over-whelmed him. He was imprisoned for debt in 1598 and 1599, and he spent seven years from 1612 to 1619 in the king's bench prison, during which time his first wife, Mary, died. She was buried in St James, Clerkenwell, on 24 July 1616. The couple had three daughters whose baptisms are all recorded in the register of St Giles, Cripplegate: Dorcas, baptized on 27 October 1594; Elizabeth, on 29 November 1598; and Anne, on 24 October 1602.

Early years as a playwright, 1594–1602 In January 1598 Dek-ker makes his first appearance in Henslowe's diary. The record shows that Philip Henslowe, on behalf of the Lord Admiral's Men, laid out £4 'to bye a boocke of mr dicker called fayeton' (*Henslowe's Diary*, ed. Foakes and Rickert, 86), a play Dekker later revised for the court for a further 30s. Henslowe's accounts reveal that between the begin-ning of 1598 and the end of 1602, Dekker had a hand in over forty plays, including script doctoring and revising both his own plays and those of other writers. All but a handful of these plays are lost. Involved in at least fifteen plays in 1598 alone—the year in which Henslowe began keeping details of the dramatists responsible for each play—Dekker may be considered an accomplished play-wright at this stage. In his literary review published in that year, *Palladis tamia*, Francis Mere names Dekker alongside William Shakespeare, Michael Drayton, George Chapman, and Ben Jonson as 'our best for Tragedy'. The best evidence of Dekker's experience as a writer prior to 1598 is his involvement in the play *Sir Thomas More*, the manuscript of which is in the British Library. Never staged, the play was written about 1593–4 for the Lord Strange's Men and the Admiral's Men who acted together at that time. It seems likely that Anthony Munday wrote the lion's share of the original play, possibly with Chettle and Dekker (with Dekker writing the 'prentices scene'). The play then ran into problems with both the theatre company and the master of the revels, Edmund Tilney, who seemed unwilling to give it a licence. Dekker is among those brought in to revise the play, and thirty-one lines in his own handwriting have been identified. Other hands also distinguished are those of Shakespeare, Chettle, and, possibly, Thomas Heywood.

According to Henslowe's diary, until the end of 1602 Dekker was sole author of just seven plays: 'Phaeton' (January 1598, and altered for the court in 1601); 'The Trip-licity of Cuckolds' (March 1598); 'The Gentle Craft' (July 1599), published in 1600 as *The Shomakers Holiday* after being played before Elizabeth I at court on new year's night; 'Bear a Brain' (August 1599); 'The Whole History of Fortunatus' (November 1599), published in 1600 as *The Pleasant Comedie of Old Fortunatus* (which Dekker also altered for the court in December 1599); 'Medicine for a Curst Wife' (September 1602); and 'Fortune's Tennis' (September 1600). *The Shoemaker's Holiday* has become Dekker's most famous play. Although the play concludes with a feast and the eponymous holiday, it carefully depicts some of the cultural tensions of contemporary London society. It combines much which marks Dekker's style, including a compassionate and sensitive presentation of lower-class characters and an intimate depiction of London.

Writing for Henslowe was predominantly a collaborative business. During this period Dekker mainly worked with Drayton, Chettle, and Robert Wilson, in a variety of configurations, and in association with other playwrights. In just over two months, Dekker, Chettle, Drayton, and Wilson produced five plays: 'The Famous Wars of Henry I' (March 1598), 'Godwin and his Three Sons' (March 1598), 'Pierce of Exton' (April 1598), 'Black Batman of the North' (May 1598), and 'Godwin, part II' (June 1598). For the rest of 1598 Dekker worked with Drayton and Wilson, producing: 'Madman's Morris' (July 1598), 'Hannibal and Hermes' (July 1598), 'Pierce of Winchester' (August 1598), 'Hannibal and Hermes, part II', otherwise called, by Henslowe, 'Worse Afeared than Hurt' (September 1598). With Drayton alone, Dekker wrote: 'The First Civil Wars of France' (September 1598), 'Conan, Prince of Cornwall' (October 1598), 'The Civil Wars of France, part II' (November 1598), and 'The Civil Wars of France, part III' (December 1598). Early in the new year he joined Henry Chettle to write: 'Troilus and Cressida' (April 1599), of which a plot fragment survives; 'The Tragedy of Agamemnon, or, Orestes Furious' (May 1599); 'The Stepmother's Tragedy' (October 1599). Towards the end of 1599 Dekker and Chettle worked with Jonson '& other Jentellman' (probably John Marston) to produce 'Robert II, or, The Scot's tragedy' (September 1599); and with William Haughton for *Patient Grissill* (November–December 1599), published in 1603. Amid the period with Chettle, Dekker co-authored 'The Lamentable Tragedy of Page of Plymouth' (August 1599) solely with Jonson.

About this time Dekker's collaborations became more varied. In early 1600 he joined Haughton and John Day to write 'The Spanish Moor's tragedy' (February 1600), which possibly appeared later as *Lusts Dominion*, published in 1657. Chettle joined Haughton, Day, and Dekker for 'The Seven Wise Masters' (March 1600); and Dekker, Chettle, and Day wrote 'The Golden Ass, [or], Cupid and Psyche' (April–May 1600). A month later he worked with four other writers—Drayton, Richard Hathway, Anthony Munday, and Wilson—to produce 'The Fair Constance of Rome' (June 1600). After this play Dekker's prodigious output for Henslowe and the Admiral's Men tapered off; and the only play recorded in Henslowe's diary for the whole of 1601 is 'King Sebastian of Portugal' (May 1601), written

with Chettle. Apart from those which were published, all of these plays are lost.

Towards the end of 1600 Dekker's exclusive relationship with Henslowe and the Admiral's Men came to an end as his pen was employed by other companies. How much this change was a consequence of his involvement in the so-called 'war of the theatres' is difficult to say. The first play identified as Dekker's after his departure from Henslowe is *Satiro-mastix* (entered in the Stationers' register, 11 November 1601), published in 1602. The play appears to be located on the cusp of the stage quarrel, being produced by both the Paul's Boys (boy actors were in vogue at the time) in a private theatre (Paul's), and by adult actors of the Chamberlain's Men at a traditional public theatre (Globe). Competition between public and private theatres, and rivalry between the companies, underpinned the 'war'.

Satiro-mastix was, in part, a response to Jonson's attack on Marston and Dekker which seems to have begun in *Every Man out of His Humour* (1599), and culminated in *Cynthia's Revels* (1600) and *Poetaster* (1601). In *Poetaster*, Marston is represented as Crispinus, a dilettante and impecunious poet who turns to writing for players, whereupon he encounters Demetrius Fannius, representing Dekker, a hack writer, 'a dresser of plays about the town', one who will slander any man for money—not least the poet Horace, in whom Jonson thinly disguises himself. With possible assistance from Marston, Dekker's responding mockery in *Satiro-mastix* recasts Crispinus and Demetrius as reputable young men who see Horace as a pompous, selfish, and sycophantic hypocrite. Although some of the mud stuck in this slanging match, Dekker's play was the last salvo in the writers' conflict and they became friends again soon after.

Not directly part of the quarrel, Dekker wrote another play at this time for the Paul's Boys: *Blurt Master-Constable* (1602), hitherto thought to have been the work of Thomas Middleton. This means that Dekker wrote only four plays between September 1600 and January 1602, whereupon he resumed working for Henslowe. And, although published in 1602, it is possible that his commendatory verses for Anthony Munday, *The Third and Last Part of Palmerin of England*, were written in 1601. Such little writing appears to be anomalous, and would have hardly constituted a living for the playwright. However, if Dekker wrote anything else for the Paul's Boys or another non-Henslowe company there are no records.

Dekker's return to Henslowe was as a play dresser. He supplied the prologue and epilogue to 'Pontius Pilate' (January 1602); and provided alterations to 'Tasso's Melancholy' (c.1602) which had appeared previously in 1594. With Munday he wrote 'Jeptha' (May 1602); and in collaboration with Munday, Drayton, Middleton, and Webster, he produced 'Caesar's Fall, or, The Two Shapes' (May 1602). But his relationship with the company with whom he had worked for at least the last four years was starting to unravel. In July 1602 Dekker was paid £4 on behalf of the Admiral's Men in part payment for 'Medicine for a Curst Wife' (July–September 1602); Henslowe cancelled these payments, only to restore them later. By September, Dekker had been paid £6 in full for the play on behalf of the Lord Worcester's Men, in whose employ he remained for the rest of the year. For them he revamped the 1599 Admiral's Men's play *Sir John Oldcastle* by writing additions to it for *Sir John Oldcastle, Part II* (September 1602). With Webster, Chettle, Heywood, and Wentworth Smith, he wrote 'Lady Jane, or, The Overthrow of Rebels, part I' (October 1602); and a few weeks later he alone was contracted to write 'Lady Jane, part II' (October 1602). Whether the latter was completed is unclear; however, the 'Lady Jane' plays survive in an abridged and modified form as *The Famous History of Sir Thomas Wyatt*, published in 1607 with Dekker and Webster cited as the authors. Dekker's last play prior to Elizabeth's death was written with Webster, Chettle, and Heywood: 'Christmas Comes but Once a Year' (November 1602). Apart from *Sir Thomas Wyatt*, all his 1602 output is lost.

Dekker's time as a prolific writer of plays within Henslowe's circle of playwrights was coming to a close. Only Chettle, his old friend and collaborator, appears in Henslowe's accounts to have been more productive. More than once Henslowe lent Dekker money to discharge his debts, though keeping his writers out of gaol was good business practice as much as beneficence.

Other writing, 1603–1619 Until the end of 1602 Dekker could be considered the consummate Elizabethan playwright: writing popular plays for a broad audience across a range of topics and genres, often lacing them with the prosaic aspects of London life. Yet Elizabeth's passing, initially at least, appeared to provide increased opportunities for the versatile and established writer. In 1603 Dekker and his old rival Jonson were commissioned to write London's official greeting of the new king: *The Magnificent Entertainment Given to King James*, published in 1604. Following this Dekker wrote commendatory verses for Stephen Harrison's *The Arches of Triumph Erected in Honour of James I* (1604). Unfortunately the virulent plague which delayed *The Magnificent Entertainment* kept returning and closing the theatres; and it was the stage which provided Dekker's main source of income. In response Dekker turned to writing pamphlets for London's increasing book trade. His first was a eulogy for Elizabeth, written through images of the plague, entitled *The Wonderfull Yeare* (1603). Plague as a topic proved to be surprisingly popular and this pamphlet was followed by *Newes from Gravesend* (1604).

But working for London's pamphlet publishers and booksellers did not pay as well as writing plays and as soon as the theatres reopened Dekker returned to producing for the stage. On the accession of James I, his old company came under new management: the Admiral's Men became Prince Henry's Men. For the new company Dekker joined Middleton to write *The Honest Whore, Part I* (1604); this was followed by *The Honest Whore, Part II* (1605) which he wrote alone. At the same time, with Webster, he also found employment with the Paul's Boys, producing *Westward Hoe* (1604) and *Northward Hoe* (1605), both published in 1607. It is likely that *The Roaring Girle* (1605?), in

collaboration with Middleton, was Dekker's last happy experience with playwriting for some time.

About 1606 the Paul's Boys collapsed, and soon after Dekker fell out with Prince Henry's Men. *The Whore of Babylon* (1607), an anti-papist jibe, was not a dramatic success, and he did not write another play for the next four years. In 1611 he wrote *If this be not Good the Divel is in it* for Prince Henry's Men, but they turned it down. Bitter and upset, Dekker touted the play around until it was taken up by the Queen's Majesty's Company at the Red Bull Theatre. Many theatre companies were experiencing difficulties through plague and competition, and Dekker found it difficult to gauge the audiences' taste which seemed to prefer sharp satires and gory tragedies—genres which, in the main, Dekker eschewed.

As Dekker's dramatic production tapered off, so his pamphlet writing increased. He cast his literary net wide looking for a readership to sustain him. His non-dramatic writing of this period began with *The Double PP* (1606) which, like *The Whore of Babylon*, attempted to cash in on anti-Catholic sentiment following the discovery of the Gunpowder Plot. More viable was *The Seven Deadly Sinnes of London* (1606), a lively satire on city life. Dekker returned to writing plague texts in his homage to Thomas Nashe's *Pierce Penilesse, his Supplication to the Divell* entitled *Newes from Hell* (1606). Both tracts are predicated upon the precarious status of authorship at this time. Dekker expanded *Newes from Hell* to produce *A Knight's Conjuring* (1607). Not least of the pamphlet writer's discontent was the fact that, without copyright or royalties, authors got a one-off fee for their work. Consequently much of the writing was produced in haste, which often had deleterious effects on its literary merit. *Jests to Make you Merie*, with George Wilkins (1607), *The Dead Tearme* (1607), and *The Great Frost: Cold Doings in London, Except it be at the Lotterie* (1608) suffer from these effects to a certain degree.

A more productive method, deployed by Dekker, consisted of reworking his own writing and that of others, to generate a 'new' pamphlet for the publisher and reader. In so doing Dekker drew upon and updated Elizabethan writers such as John Awdeley, Thomas Harman, Robert Greene, and Nashe, for his cony-catching and canting literature. The first of these was *The Belman of London* (1608); a sequel, *Lanthorn and Candle-Light, or, The Bell-Mans Second Nights Walke* (1608) became one of Dekker's most popular pamphlets, and went through at least nine editions in the next forty years. Notable among those editions are *O per se O … being an Addition, or Lengthening, of the Bell-Mans Second Night-Walke* (1612) and *Villainies Discovered … Being an Addition to the Bell-Mans Second Night-Walke* (1616). His best-known non-dramatic work, *The Guls Horne-Book* (1608), was published in 1609, and remained popular into the Restoration. Also published about this time were *The Ravens Almanacke* (1609), *Worke for Armourers* (1609), and *Foure Birds of Noahs Ark* (1609).

Between 1610 and 1612 Dekker's output is very thin, and the reasons for this are not as clear as the consequences. Apart from the troubled *If this be not Good* and a pamphlet, *A Strange Horse-Race* (1613), Dekker's only other work was a commission for Sir John Swinerton's mayoral pageant: *Troia-Nova triumphans* (October 1612). Whatever money he received for this, it was not enough to keep him from being arrested for debt later that year. He owed £40 to the coach maker John Webster (the playwright's father), who began a suit against him in the king's bench in 1613. Dekker spent the next seven years in the king's bench prison.

If imprisonment effectively stopped Dekker's dramatic output, it did not arrest his writing altogether—although it certainly hampered its quality. In 1615 he reworked an earlier tract, *The Great Frost*, to produce *The Cold Yeare 1614*. About the same time he wrote *The Artillery Garden*, published in 1616, and commendatory verses for John Taylor's *Taylor's Urania, or, His Heavenly Muse*. Attempting to profit as much as possible from his situation, Dekker looked to expand the writing on prisons and prisoners which he had begun in *Villainies Discovered* (1616). He proceeded to add six 'prison characters' to those published under *Sir Thomas Overburie his Wife* (1616), and in 1617 he contributed to Geoffrey Mynshull's *Certain Characters and Essays of Prisons and Prisoners*, published in 1618. Dekker was finally released some time in 1619, and in October that year he completed *Dekker his Dreame*—a disturbing and disjointed poem which bears the marks of his traumatic 'long sleep' in prison. He wrote that his hair had

> turn'd *white*
> More through the *Ghastly Objects* of this *Night*,
> Then with the *Snow* of *Age*.
> (*Dekker his Dreame*, 1620, 37)

The later years, 1620–1632 On release from gaol Dekker quickly re-established himself as a playwright by producing *Match mee in London* (1620, published 1631), to be played at the Red Bull Theatre. The up-and-coming Philip Massinger joined him to write *The Virgin Martyr* (1620). Based on current events, *The Witch of Edmonton* (1621, published 1658), with William Rowley and John Ford, became one of his more popular works. Dekker joined John Day to write three plays: *The Noble Spanish Souldier* (1622?); 'The Bellman of Paris' (1623), now lost; and *The Wonder of a Kingdom* (1623?). 'A Moral Masque' was the subtitle of *The Sun's-Darling* (1624, published 1656) which he co-wrote with Ford. The same team produced another 'masque', 'The Fairy Knight' (1624), and 'The Bristow Merchant' (1624), both lost. Dekker alone may have been responsible for reworking *The Noble Spanish Souldier* into 'The Welsh Ambassador' (1624). With Ford, Rowley, and Webster, Dekker put together 'The Late Murder in Whitechapel, or, Keep the Widow Waking' (1624), now lost. The play was based on two notorious crimes which had caught the contemporary imagination. Records survive of Dekker's testimony, given when a relative of one depicted in the play brought the matter to court.

London's 1625 plague took its toll on life, theatre, and, in all probability, Dekker's livelihood. Charges of recusancy brought against him in 1626 and 1628 are almost certainly due to the fact that he avoided church in order to escape arrest for debt. He did pick up some work at this time, writing the inaugural pageants for various incoming mayors of London: a pageant for Sir Hugh Hamersley (1627),

now lost; *Brittannia's Honour* (1628) for R. Deane; and *Londons Tempe* (1629) for J. Campbell. In the second half of the 1620s Dekker turned to pamphleteering once again. His non-dramatic writing of this period includes: *A Rod for Run-Awayes* (1625), *Looke Up and See Wonders* (1628), *Warres, Warres, Warres* (1628), *London Looke Backe* (1630), *The Blacke Rod: and the White Rod* (1630), and *Penny-Wise, Pound-Foolish* (1630). The commendatory verses which Dekker wrote for Richard Brome's play *The Northern Lasse* (1632) could well have been his last piece of work, although it is tempting to think that his last written words were those in the 1632 epistle to his most popular tract, *The Belman of London* (now called *English Villainies*) in which he claimed to be sixty years old.

Dekker's output ceased in 1632 and it seems probable that the 'Thomas Decker, householder' who was buried at St James, Clerkenwell, on 25 August that year is the author. His widow, Elizabeth, renounced the administration of his estate on 4 September 1632, a sure sign that Dekker died in debt.

Jonson's accusation that Dekker was a hack, Charles Lamb's backhanded compliment that he had 'poetry enough for anything', and Swinburne's dislike of his carelessness, were all pointed at a someone whose writing was predominantly driven by financial pressure. From comments such as these a strand of criticism developed which depicted Dekker as a good-natured and versatile journeyman writer—jack of all trades, master of none—operating in the shadow of Shakespeare, Jonson, Middleton, and others. Often charged with being sentimental, Dekker's writing does reveal a sustained compassion for society's misfits and casualties. Perhaps Hazlitt had this in mind when he called him 'gentle-hearted' and 'honest'. More recent scholarship has been less condescending, seeing in Dekker's work an incisive commentary on the social, political, and religious structure of London. That Dekker's work encompasses such a wide range of views and genres bears testimony to a writer whose career spanned more than thirty-five years, who was continuously productive under three monarchs, and who survived poverty, plague, and prison.

JOHN TWYNING

Sources G. Melchion, ed., *Sir Thomas More* (1990) · M. Edmond, 'In search of John Webster', *TLS* (24 Dec 1976), 1622 · parish register, Clerkenwell, St James's, 24 July 1616 [burial: Mary Dekker, wife] · parish register, Clerkenwell, St James's, 25 August 1632 [burial] · *The non-dramatic works of Thomas Dekker*, ed. A. B. Grosart, 5 vols. (1885) · *The dramatic works of Thomas Dekker*, ed. F. Bowers (1953–61) · *The plague pamphlets of Thomas Dekker*, ed. F. P. Wilson (1925) · F. P. Wilson, 'Three notes on Thomas Dekker', *Modern Language Review*, 15 (1920), 82–5 · K. L. Gregg, *Thomas Dekker: a study in economic and social backgrounds* (1924) · M. Eccles, 'Thomas Dekker: burial place', *N&Q*, 177 (1939), 157 · E. K. Chambers, *The Elizabethan stage*, 4 vols. (1923) · A. F. Allison, *Thomas Dekker c.1572–1632: a bibliographical catalogue of early editions* (1972) · P. Shaw, 'Dekker's position in prison literature', *Proceedings of the Modern Languages Association*, 62 (1947), 366–91 · *Henslowe's diary*, ed. R. A. Foakes and R. T. Rickert (1961) · *Henslowe's diary*, ed. W. W. Greg, 2 vols. (1904–8) · M. T. Jones-Davies, *Un peintre de la vie Londonienne: Thomas Dekker circa 1572–1632*, 2 vols. (1958) · G. R. Price, *Thomas Dekker* (1969) · J. Twyning, *London dispossessed: literature and social space in the early modern city* (1998) · M. L. Hunt, *Thomas Dekker: a study* (1911) · F. O. Waage, *Thomas Dekker's pamphlets, 1603–1609, and Jacobean popular literature*, 2 vols. (1977) ·

J. Gasper, *The dragon and the dove: the plays of Thomas Dekker* (1980) • C. H. Hoy, *Introduction, notes, and commentaries to texts in 'The dramatic works of Thomas Dekker, edited by Fredson Bowers'*, 4 vols. (1980) • D. R. Adler, *Thomas Dekker: a reference guide* (1983) • G. E. Bentley, *The Jacobean and Caroline stage*, 3 (1956)
Archives PRO, deposition, 3 Feb 1625 | Dulwich College, London, letters to Edward Alleyn
Likenesses line engraving (after woodcut), NPG • woodcut, BL; repro. in T. Dekker, *Dekker his dreame*
Wealth at death None—in debt; widow renounced administration of estate: Clerkenwell records

De la. For most names including this prefix *see under* the substantive element of the name; for example, for Richard de la Pole *see* Pole, Richard de la. For a very few subjects whose names were not Anglicized *see under* La; for example, La Cloche, Jacques de.

Delafaye, Charles (1677–1762), public servant, was born on 25 July 1677 in Paris, probably the eldest of the three children of Lewis and Mary Delafaye. His father, whose family originated in Dijon, abjured the Roman Catholic faith, moved to England, and entered the service of the duke of Ormond; he later became the French translator of the *London Gazette*. Nothing is known of Charles's early education. In 1692 he matriculated at All Souls College, Oxford, and in 1696 received the degree of BA. A year later he was appointed secretary to Sir Joseph Williamson, ambassador to the United Provinces. Shortly after Williamson's return to England in March 1699 Delafaye secured employment as a clerk in the secretary of state's office through the influence of his father. He served in the southern department successively under the earl of Jersey, James Vernon, and the earl of Nottingham. By 1701 he had married Elizabeth (*d.* 1742), whose maiden name has not been established.

In 1702 Delafaye was given the additional post of writer of the *London Gazette*. In this capacity he was summoned before the House of Lords in 1704 to explain how a notice reflecting on the instructions of the lord high admiral had come to be inserted in the *Gazette*. Despite this apparent setback Delafaye's career did not suffer. On the removal of the earl of Nottingham in April 1704 he passed first into the service of Sir Charles Hedges and then into that of the earl of Sunderland, who appointed him chief clerk, a position of special trust. He continued in this office under the next secretary of state, Lord Dartmouth.

In August 1713 Delafaye was selected by the duke of Shrewsbury, lord lieutenant of Ireland, to be his second or Ulster secretary. In accepting this office Delafaye abandoned the relative security and obscurity of a clerk for the greater prominence and responsibility of a secretary, whose fortunes were closely bound up with those of his political masters. He accompanied Shrewsbury to Dublin for the meeting of the Irish parliament and was rewarded with the post of gentleman sewer in the royal household. Following the death of Queen Anne in August 1714 Shrewsbury was replaced as lord lieutenant by Delafaye's former master Sunderland, who continued him in his post. When in August 1715 the Irish administration was placed in the hands of the duke of Grafton and the earl of Galway, Delafaye was made one of their joint secretaries, and he continued as such under their successor, Viscount Townshend. In order to strengthen the official representation in the Irish House of Commons Delafaye was found a seat as one of the members for Belturbet, co. Cavan, which he held until 1727.

In April 1717, when Sunderland became once more secretary of state, Delafaye was appointed one of his under-secretaries. Thereupon he left Ireland to begin the final phase of his official life. At first he served in the northern department under Sunderland, Viscount Stanhope, and Townshend. Delafaye appears to have left the bulk of foreign business to his colleague as under-secretary and to have concentrated on home affairs. In particular he was employed in the delicate and confidential business of managing the press on behalf of the government. In April 1724 he was transferred to the southern department to become one of the under-secretaries to the newly appointed duke of Newcastle. In addition to his strictly departmental duties he developed an interest in colonial affairs, and acted as agent for the colony of Jamaica between 1728 and 1734. Between 1719 and 1727 Delafaye was called upon to act as secretary to the lords justices of England during the absence of the king in Hanover. In 1728 he obtained the sinecure office of one of the clerks of the signet, which he held until his death. In 1725 he was elected a fellow of the Royal Society. He was an active freemason.

Delafaye suffered a serious illness in 1733 and resigned as under-secretary in July of the following year, being then aged fifty-seven. His career was remarkable in a number of respects. His introduction to government service was due to family influence and he was sustained throughout his career by powerful patrons. At no point did he enjoy permanent status in a formal sense. Nevertheless his abilities were such that he remained continuously in the service of the government for nearly forty years. Aided by a good education and linguistic proficiency, he was able to work his way up from the clerical to the secretarial level of government service. His responsibilities in Ireland provided him with invaluable experience and led directly to his appointment as an under-secretary. In this office he was able to place his skills at the disposal of four secretaries of state for a period of seventeen years, providing continuity at the intermediate level which made an essential contribution to the orderly processes of administration.

Delafaye retired to the village of Whitsbury in Wiltshire, where he died on 11 December 1762 at the advanced age of eighty-five. None of his children survived him.

J. C. SAINTY

Sources J. C. Sainty, 'A Huguenot civil servant: the career of Charles Delafaye, 1677–1762', *Proceedings of the Huguenot Society*, 22 (1970–76), 398–413 • W. A. Shaw, ed., *Letters of denization and acts of naturalization for aliens in England and Ireland, 1603–1700*, Huguenot Society of London, 18 (1911) • Foster, *Alum. Oxon.* • R. C. Hoare, *The history of modern Wiltshire*, 3 (1834–5), 70
Archives BL, letters to John Ellis, Add. MSS 28893–28900 • BL, letters to Lord Hardwicke, Add. MSS 35585–36139 • BL, corresp. with

duke of Newcastle, etc., Add. MSS 32686–33067 · BL, letters to Thomas Robinson, Add. MSS 23782–23791 · BL, corresp. with Charles Whitworth · CUL, letters to Sir Robert Walpole · NL Scot., corresp. with Duncan Forbes · NRA, priv. coll., letters to Earl Waldegrave · PRO

Delafield, E. M. *See* Dashwood, Edmée Elizabeth Monica (1890–1943).

Delamain, Richard, the elder (*d.* 1644?), mathematician, began his career as master of a writing-school in Drury Lane in the early 1620s, according to William Oughtred (Oughtred, sig. B2, recto). At the same time he attended lectures at Gresham College, thus gaining a knowledge of mathematics. He referred to Edmund Gunter (who resided in London from 1615 to his death in 1626) as his tutor, and was taught astronomy by Oughtred. He established himself as a mathematics teacher during the late 1620s. Nothing is known of his birth, origins, and early life.

In 1629 Delamain sent the manuscript of *Grammelogia, or, The Mathematical Ring* to Charles I, together with the instrument, a circular slide rule. The king granted him a monopoly on the instrument and the book was published in January 1631. In the same year Delamain produced *The Making, Description and Use of … a Horizontall Quadrant*, which described an instrument inscribed with a projection of the celestial sphere onto the plane of the horizon. These books involved him in a bitter dispute with Oughtred, who claimed both instruments as his invention, saying that Delamain had stolen the designs.

On 4 March 1633 a royal warrant was issued granting Delamain the right to teach the use of his ring and all other mathematical instruments in London and elsewhere. He was also employed for £40 a year as quartermaster-general and tutor to the king. He worked on surveying forts and castles with Sir John Heydon, the master of the ordnance, but petitions for a position as royal engineer were unsuccessful. Delamain was commissioned by the king to oversee the making of a number of instruments, including a 'great Octans', and a 'great Universal Concave' (perhaps the concave dial at Whitehall), besides pieces for the king's bedchamber and the 'Great Ship'. It is probable that the silver sundial sent to the duke of York by the king just before his death was one of Delamain's horizontal quadrants.

At some time in the early 1620s Delamain married Sarah (*d.* in or after 1645); they had at least eleven children, of whom four attended the Merchant Taylors' School. The clergyman Richard *Delamaine the younger (*bap.* 1627, *d.* 1657) and the Muggletonian Alexander *Delamaine (*bap.* 1631, *d.* 1685) were his sons. Delamain was still working for the king early in 1644 but presumably died shortly thereafter, since his widow petitioned the House of Lords for relief the following year.   H. K. HIGTON

Sources E. G. R. Taylor, *The mathematical practitioners of Tudor and Stuart England* (1954) · *CSP dom.*, 1629–45 · W. Oughtred, *The circles of proportion and the horizontal instrument*, trans. W. Forster, another edn (1633) · R. Delamain, *Grammelogia, or, The mathematical ring* (1631) · *Lords journals*, 1645 · Wood, *Ath. Oxon.*

Delamaine, Alexander (*bap.* 1631, *d.* 1685), Muggletonian, was baptized at St Andrew's, Holborn, London, on 3 October 1631, the son of the mathematician Richard *Delamain (*d.* 1644?) and his wife, Sarah (*d.* in or after 1645). His name appears in the register of Merchant Taylors' School, London, in September 1642, alongside three of his brothers, including his elder brother Richard *Delamaine.

Delamaine's brother Edward became a Baptist preacher, and Alexander may at some point have shared his brother's beliefs. By June 1654 he had become a Quaker, and as an apprentice in London came into conflict with his master: when challenged as to why he failed to attend family prayers, Delamaine accused his employer of being a hypocrite. His master struck him and summoned a minister—whom Delamaine called a hireling—to reason with him. The master threatened to tear up his indentures and so forfeit Delamaine's right to become a freeman and citizen of the City. The master was further aggrieved with his spiritually rebellious apprentice because he was driving customers away by 'my not speaking to them, as to tell them of what they ask me, or bidding them welcome' (Barclay, 327). How this quarrel—known through a letter Delamaine wrote to a fellow Quaker in the north—ended is uncertain. However, Delamaine did in due course become free of the Salters' Company, establishing himself as a wealthy London tobacconist who carried on his business at the sign of the Three Tobacco Pipes on Bread Street Hill. Moreover Alexander, his son with his first wife, Martha, was baptized in the parish church of St James Garlickhithe on 12 December 1661.

It may have been Delamaine's second marriage in 1667 to Anne Lowe, *née* Hall (*d.* 1688), which served as the catalyst to Delamaine's conversion to Muggletonianism. On 5 July Lodowicke Muggleton wrote to Anne as 'now the wife of Alexander Delamaine, senior', giving her the formal blessing that she had requested from him; he wrote of the good influence upon her of her dead aunt. There was to be a more striking tribute to her from Muggleton on 3 February 1687, when he addressed her as Delamaine's widow. Even Muggleton's own daughter Sarah could not match her fidelity, prompting Sarah to say in a company of women that 'you, when your name was Anne Hall, were the beloved disciple of her father of all the women in London' (Delamaine, *Spiritual Epistles*, 223, 585).

By 1668, the year after his marriage to Anne, Delamaine was clearly committed to her beliefs, to the extent that he passed on to his prophet a remonstrating letter to himself from his brother Edward, the Baptist preacher. Muggleton had urged Delamaine, on the receipt of his first letter, to damn his brother to eternity. Because of the closeness of their relation, Alexander could not bring himself to do it. In a long letter to Edward, Muggleton with some relish repaired the omission on 16 June 1668. Alexander Delamaine went on, however, to be one of the most trusted of Muggleton's confidants. It was to Delamaine that Muggleton turned for help in poor relief for a former servant of the dead co-prophet, John Reeve. And it was to Delamaine that he turned for transmitting the joyous news to believers in Ireland of his release from prison on 19 July 1677. Delamaine chose another way of marking the occasion by bursting into verse, including this couplet:

> This, this was the day (19th July) fate sparkled disdain
> That a dungeon should longer God's prophet detain.
> (Frost and Frost, *Divine Songs*, 268)

19 July—along with the February celebrations of the anniversary of God's commission to Reeve—became the regular 'holidays' celebrated by the sect into the twentieth century. On one such dinner, at the Green Man in Holloway, Middlesex, on 19 July 1682, Delamaine, his wife, and daughter paid 5s. each; the prophet and Mrs Muggleton went free. Delamaine's greatest contribution was to complete in 1682 the transcription of the letters of Muggleton (and a few by Reeve) into one large folio book (BL, Add. MS 60171). He began on 19 April 1682 a second volume of additional letters that 'would not goe into my grate book'. The importance of the 'Great book', as it came to be known to believers, cannot be underrated. The movement survived by letters; Muggleton was a gifted, as well as prolific, writer. Towards the end of his life a blessing entered into the 'Great book' from Muggleton counted more with followers than oral blessings from him (despite the prophet's gentle remonstrances to the contrary). There is a certain fitness in the fact that the last recorded of these unnecessary written supplements to the oral blessings previously conferred was from Muggleton to Delamaine's daughter Sarah and her husband, Robert, on 14 December 1691. There are two gaps in Delamaine's collection, where letters were later torn out, for the periods September 1673 to August 1676 and October 1680 to May 1681.

Delamaine left behind no published writings; however, he and Thomas Greenhill from Harrow Weald celebrated their recent conversions to the faith in an exchange of letters in March 1669. He also contributed to an interesting debate with his fellow believer John Ladd in 1676 on how far 'Reason' (the bad seed, compared with the good seed 'Faith') should be denigrated. Delamaine scorned 'reasons wiles' categorically; Ladd sought 'a middle way' (BL, Add. MS 60138, fols. 26–32v).

Delamaine died in the second half of December 1685: he made his will on 16 December and it was proved on the 30th. By it he requested to be interred in 'the Common buriall in Bethlehem burial place in Moorfields', where three years later his widow also requested to be buried. He left various small bequests to Muggleton and his wife, and to his own son Alexander, daughter Mary, and son-in-law Robert. To his wife, Anne—Muggleton's favourite woman disciple—Delamaine left a staggering bequest of £1685. Tobacco was a lucrative trade indeed.

WILLIAM LAMONT

Sources A. Delamaine, 'Great book', BL, Muggletonian archives, Add. MS 60171 · index to Delamaine's 'Great book', BL, Muggletonian archives, Add. MS 60172 · J. Frost and I. Frost, *Divine songs of the Muggletonians* (1829) · C. Hill, B. Reay, and W. Lamont, *The world of the Muggletonians* (1983) · L. Muggleton, *The acts of the witnesses*, ed. T. L. Underwood (1999) · J. Frost and L. Muggleton, *Works*, ed. J. Frost and I. Frost, 3 vols. (1832) · A. Delamaine, ed., *A volume of spiritual epistles* (1755) · J. Reeve, *Sacred remains*, ed. J. Frost (1856) · J. Reeve and L. Muggleton, *A stream from the tree of life*, ed.

J. Peat (1758) · J. Frost and I. Frost, eds., *Supplement to the book of letters* (1831) · IGI · will, PRO, PROB 11/381, sig. 149 · will of Anne Delamaine, PRO, PROB 11/393, sig. 161 · W. C. Braithwaite, *The beginnings of Quakerism*, ed. H. J. Cadbury, 2nd edn (1955) · A. R. Barclay, ed., *Letters … of early Friends* (1847), vol. 11 of *The Friends' library*, ed. W. Evans and T. Evans, 326–7 · BL, Muggletonian MSS, Add. MSS 60232, 60168, 60138 · C. J. Robinson, ed., *A register of the scholars admitted into Merchant Taylors' School, from AD 1562 to 1874*, 1 (1882) · DNB

Archives BL, Muggletonian archives, Add. MSS 60168–60256

Wealth at death left wife £1685; small legacies to others: will, PRO, PROB 11/381, sig. 149

Delamaine, Richard, the elder. *See* Delamain, Richard, the elder (d. 1644?).

Delamaine [Delamain], **Richard, the younger** (*bap.* 1627, *d.* 1657), clergyman, was baptized on 7 or 8 March 1627 at St Andrew's, Holborn, in London, the eldest son of Richard *Delamain the elder (*d.* 1644?), mathematician, and his wife, Sarah (*d.* in or after 1645). The Muggletonian Alexander *Delamaine (*bap.* 1631, *d.* 1685) was his younger brother. He once reportedly claimed to have attended Oxford University, but there is no evidence for this, and confidence is not strengthened by the tale that when asked which college he attended, he replied Emmanuel. Delamaine made his first fleeting entrance on the public stage with the presentation to the House of Lords, early in 1642, of a tabulated ready-reckoner setting out the rates at which investments might be made in land in the respective provinces of Ireland, by the terms of the recently passed act for the Irish adventure. This the Lords authorized for publication.

Like his father, who appears to have had a hand in the fortification of London during the civil war, Richard the younger supported the parliamentarians, but he made no real mark on affairs until 1648, whereafter he became established as a preacher in Herefordshire. In 1654 his behaviour there came under fire from an anonymous writer in a pamphlet entitled *Impostor magnus: the legerdemain of Richard Delamain, now preacher in the city of Hereford. Being a narrative of his life and doctrine since his first coming into that county*. Its author lambasted Delamaine's ignorance of gospel, deriding his 'notional frenzy' and 'familistical carriages' (*Impostor magnus*, 15). He also decried the dangers to which heretics such as Delamaine exposed government, property, and civil society itself. Much of the tract is taken up with allegations about moral incontinence, hypocrisy, and aggressive nest-feathering which were a commonplace of parliamentarian factional infighting in the period. Despite its full title, little is revealed concerning the details of Delamaine's life except that he had apparently undergone some sort of conversion experience, had been 'brought' to Herefordshire by one Mr Hill, whose religion the author considered heretical, and that he had then enjoyed the patronage of several godly women in Bredwardine. Mention is made of an interlude at Worcester. But it was in the city of Hereford itself that he came good. Becoming an intimate of the governor, Lieutenant-Colonel Wroth Rogers, Delamaine appears to have taken some sort of responsibility for the ordnance of the castle. He was also said to have won favour in the eyes of Major-

General Thomas Harrison. He had promises of employment as muster-master and either clerk or trooper in the horse troop of the county, and may have seen action during the Worcester emergency. He made several attempts to secure himself ministerial livings around Herefordshire. In 1652 he got himself one of the three posts at Hereford Cathedral maintained by an ordinance of parliament since 1646. It was alleged that he had to be 'shamed' into surrendering the other parishes for which he was responsible. With the support of Wroth Rogers, Delamaine obtained the mastership of St Ethelbert's Hospital in Hereford and the control of a charitable foundation there in 1653. The same year, and possibly on the same account, he was also in receipt of a clerical augmentation.

Whatever the truth of the various allegations levelled at him in 1654, there can be little doubt that Delamaine was deeply implicated in a vigorous struggle for dominance in Hereford during the 1650s. While there he married a woman called Mary, whom his detractor described as a serving woman to the wife of Wroth Rogers. Their son was christened Wroth. Delamaine made his will on 26 April 1657 and died some time between then and 14 August when the document was proved. He left a daughter, Elizabeth, as well as his son, neither of whom had attained majority by the time of their father's death.

C. J. ROBINSON, rev. SEAN KELSEY

Sources The humble presentation of Richard Delamain the yonger (1642) · Impostor magnus: the legerdemain of Richard Delamain, now preacher in the city of Hereford. Being a narrative of his life and doctrine since his first coming into that county (1654) · PRO, PROB 11/267, fol. 47 · DNB · CSP dom., 1644; 1653–4 · Calamy rev., 504 · IGI · JHC, 4 (1644–6)
Wealth at death Left property in Herefordshire and Buckinghamshire, on which he devised a £200 legacy for his daughter: PRO, PROB 11/267, fol. 47

De La Mare, Walter John. See Mare, Walter John de la (1873–1956).

Delamer [Delamere]. For this title name see Booth, George, first Baron Delamer (1622–1684); Cholmondeley, Hugh, third Baron Delamere (1870–1931).

Delamotte, Freeman Gage (1813/14–1862). See under Delamotte, William (1775–1863).

Delamotte, Philip Henry (1821–1889), photographer and illustrator, was born in Sandhurst, Surrey, on 21 April 1821, the fifth son in the family of five sons and four daughters of William *Delamotte (1775–1863), a drawing-master and watercolour painter, and his wife, Mary Anne Gage. His family was of Huguenot ancestry. Tutored by his father, who served as drawing-master at the Royal Military College, Sandhurst, Delamotte became skilful at drawing and engraving. Among his earliest recorded works were the illustrations to the catalogue of the objects shown at the 1850 exhibition of ancient and medieval art at the Society of Arts. On 4 August 1846, at Paddington, where he was then resident, he had married Ellen Maria, the daughter of Thomas George, a farmer. They had five daughters and a son.

Perhaps Delamotte's greatest contribution to the arts was as a pioneer photographer and photographic instructor, and he established himself as one of the most accomplished artists turned photographers of his generation. He was a main contributor to the photographic exhibition held in the great room of the Society of Arts in London in 1852, which was the first of its kind. In 1853 his manual The Practice of Photography was published by his sometime photographic collaborator Joseph Cundall, at whose Bond Street premises Delamotte held some of the first ever commercial photographic exhibitions and gave photographic instruction. The next year he displayed photographs of Ireland at the Society of Antiquaries. Delamotte was made a fellow of that society (6 May 1852) and also belonged to the Society of Arts and the Society of Artists, having exhibited a number of architectural drawings at the Royal Academy.

Among Delamotte's best-known commissions was the photography (undertaken weekly from 1851 to 1854) of the reconstruction of the Crystal Palace at Sydenham, where he displayed his skills of composition and perspective, applying the objectivity of the camera to produce masterly photographs that were artistically sound. The results were published in Photographic Views of the Progress of the Crystal Palace, Sydenham (2 vols., 1855). His landscape and portrait studies were equally successful. However, in 1855 he took up the post of professor of drawing at King's College, London, the duties of which he combined with book illustration. Over the next thirty years he wrote or illustrated more than seventy books. He also continued to give drawing lessons, and the grandchildren of Queen Victoria were among his pupils. In 1873 he published The Art of Sketching from Nature, a manual where he described the watercolour sketching technique, which he illustrated with his own lithographs; 1874 saw the publication of the History of Holland House, which was illustrated by his own carbon photographic prints. His versatility was shown in 1876 with the publication of the Buckland edition of Natural History and Antiquities of Selborne by Gilbert White, to which he contributed a charming series of bird and animal illustrations.

Delamotte was appointed to the chair of fine art at King's College, London, in 1879 and is remembered for introducing the admission of women to the art lectures. He continued to practise photography as a hobby until 1887, taking an 'unalloyed enjoyment of the art', much as he had done with his drawing and engraving.

Delamotte died of heart disease at the home of his son-in-law, Bromley Park School, Bromley, Kent, on 24 February 1889; he was recorded as having been latterly resident at Headley, Liphook, Hampshire.   A. J. STIRLING, rev.

Sources family archives, priv. coll. · A. J. Stirling, 'Philip Henry Delamotte: artist and photographer', RSA Journal, 138 (June 1990) · archives, RSA · King's Lond., archives · m. cert. · d. cert. · CGPLA Eng. & Wales (1889) · Boase, Mod. Eng. biog. · C. Bloure, 'Delamotte, P(hilip) H(enry)', The dictionary of art, ed. J. Turner (1996)
Archives priv. coll., family archives | King's Lond., archives · RSA, archives
Wealth at death £2111 0s. 6d.: probate, 7 Aug 1889, CGPLA Eng. & Wales

Delamotte, William (1718–1743), Moravian evangelist, born on 11 June 1718 in Greenwich, Kent, was the fourth of five surviving children (out of thirteen) of Peter Delamotte (d. 1749), a sugar merchant and JP, and his wife, Elizabeth (1685–1771). His brother Charles (1714–1796) accompanied the Wesleys and Benjamin Ingham to Georgia in 1735.

William matriculated as a sizar of St Catharine's College, Cambridge, in May 1736. During a serious illness he resolved to lead a better life. At home at Blendon Hall, Bexley, Kent, during the 1737 summer vacation he was 'struck to the heart' by Ingham's preaching (*Journal of the Rev. Charles Wesley*, 74). Back in Cambridge he began a fellowship group whose members were soon 'stigmatized for Methodists' (Walsh, 257). When Charles Wesley expounded the Moravians' emphasis on justification by faith at Blendon in 1738 Delamotte initially resisted, but on 29 June he experienced the gift of the Spirit.

Delamotte's Cambridge group coalesced with another centred on Francis Okely. Visiting in December, Ingham found a vigorous group of five students and a society for townspeople. Delamotte supplemented Ingham's preaching in Bedford by expounding scripture in private houses, and may have continued to visit and advise the society which resulted. Having preached to huge crowds in London in 1739, at the Moravians' suggestion he assisted Ingham in the burgeoning Yorkshire revival from November. Delamotte's preaching was long remembered as producing many conversions. Back in Cambridge in October 1740, debts forced him to sell his books and furniture. By November 200 people were attending his thrice-weekly biblical exposition to the town society. However, only two fellow Cambridge Methodists remained in Cambridge, and one of these withdrew, rejecting lay exposition.

Delamotte was now asked to return to London, probably to fill the vacuum caused by the Wesleys' withdrawal from the Fetter Lane society. He was reluctant to leave his successful work among townspeople, but other undergraduates had begun to disrupt meetings and he felt isolated in college. He removed his name from the college books, but then illness intervened. A swelling which did not respond to treatment kept him at Blendon, and he became gravely ill. He was in London from August 1741, but improvements in his health proved only temporary.

In June 1742 Delamotte was received into membership of the Moravians' first English congregation, founded to take over Ingham's Yorkshire work. Despite continuing weakness, he travelled north that August. Living in a Moravian community house in the area of his earlier activity, he was deeply contented. He preached again, copied, and translated, helping to prepare the Moravians' 1743 *Watchwords* for publication. However, his running sore refused to heal. In January 1743 he returned to London, dying there on 22 February. He was buried at St Dunstan-in-the-East on 27 February. His sisters Elizabeth Holland (1710–1780) and Esther Kinchin, later Schlicht (1712–1779), remained prominent English Moravians.

C. J. PODMORE

Sources Moravian Church House, London, AB86.A3.6 · Unitätsarchiv, Herrnhut, Germany, R13.A7.8 · JRL, Eng. MS 1076.23 · F. Okely, *Dawnings of the everlasting gospel light* (1775) · J. D. Walsh, 'The Cambridge Methodists', *Christian spirituality: essays in honour of Gordon Rupp*, ed. P. Brooks (1975), 249–83 · *The journal of the Rev. Charles Wesley*, ed. T. Jackson, 2 vols. [1849] · diary, Unitätsarchiv, Herrnhut, Germany, R13.C1.6 · Fetter Lane congregational diary, Moravian Church House, London · daily helpers conference minutes, Moravian Church House, London · 'Extracts from the archives of United Brethren', 1850, Moravian Church House, London · 'Memoirs', Fulneck Moravian Church, Fulneck, Yorkshire · parish register (baptism), Greenwich, St Alfege, 15 June 1718 · parish register (burial), London, St Dunstan-in-the-East, 27 Feb 1743 · Venn, *Alum. Cant.* · D. Benham, *Memoirs of James Hutton* (1856)

Archives Moravian Church House, London, letters, AB86.A3.6

Delamotte [de la Motte], **William** (1775–1863), landscape artist, was born at Weymouth, Dorset, on 2 August 1775, the eldest son of Peter De la Motte and his wife, Sarah, daughter of the Revd Digby Cotes of Abbey Dore, Herefordshire. His father was of Huguenot extraction and was postal agent at Weymouth, where he established a library with assembly rooms over it on the esplanade. William is said to have attracted the notice of George III, a frequent visitor to Weymouth, and to have been placed by him as a pupil of Benjamin West, president of the Royal Academy, the king's favourite artist. Delamotte entered the Royal Academy Schools in 1794, having first exhibited at the Royal Academy in the previous year. He continued to exhibit paintings and watercolours each year until 1805, and from 1809 at irregular intervals until 1850. In his early watercolours Delamotte was influenced by Thomas Girtin, but he soon established his own reputation, especially with his Welsh watercolours, and developed a more personal manner, in which the washes were very lightly applied over delicate pen or pencil outlines. He was an excellent architectural draughtsman, and also a sympathetic recorder of the landscape, at first in and around Oxford, on the Thames, in Wales, Cumberland, and Derbyshire, and later also on the continent. In the early years of the nineteenth century he was one of a group of pioneering younger British artists that included Constable and Turner, who sketched landscape in the open in oils.

Delamotte lived in Oxford for a period from 1798, where he briefly took over J. B. Malchair's practice as a drawing-master, and where he restored the Streater ceiling decoration in the Sheldonian Theatre. In 1802, at the time of the peace of Amiens, he was one of the many British artists to visit Paris, where he spent ten weeks. In the following year he was appointed an assistant drawing-master at the Royal Military College at (first at Marlow, then from 1812 at Sandhurst), where he remained, ultimately as drawing-master, for some forty years. According to Joseph Farington, whose *Diary* provides what little personal information there is about Delamotte, he was 'not liked' (8.2936). He married on 28 August 1804, Mary Anne, eldest daughter of Thomas Gage, with whom he had five sons and four daughters. Delamotte became an associate member of the newly formed Society of Painters in Water Colours in 1806, but exhibited only for three years and was never elected a full member. After 1815 he travelled more extensively on the continent, and he exhibited views of Belgium, France, and Switzerland. A few of his topographical drawings were engraved, and in 1816 he published *Thirty Etchings of Rural Subjects*. His work is well represented in the Ashmolean Museum, Oxford, and there are drawings in the print rooms of the British Museum, the Victoria and Albert Museum, and elsewhere. A sale of William Delamotte's drawings and sketches took place at Sothebys in May 1864.

Delamotte died of old age at his daughter's house, The Lawn, St Giles' Fields, near Oxford, on 13 March 1863. His youngest son, Philip Henry *Delamotte (1821–1889), was a pioneer photographer and a successful drawing-master, who was appointed professor of fine art at King's College, London, in 1879. Another son, **Freeman Gage Delamotte** (1813/14–1862), was a wood-engraver who published several works on alphabets and illumination. He died apparently unmarried, at 15 Beaufort Buildings, Strand, Middlesex, on 16 July 1862, aged forty-eight. Another son, Alfred William, who is sometimes confused with his father, was also a watercolour artist. A cousin, Lieutenant-Colonel **Philip de la Motte** (d. 1805), was the author of *The principal historical and allusive arms borne by families of the United Kingdom of Great Britain and Ireland … collected by an antiquary, with biographical memoirs … and copper-plates*, published in 1803. He died at Batsford, Gloucestershire, on 11 March 1805.   LUKE HERRMANN

Sources Farington, *Diary*, vols. 4–5, 7–9 · J. L. Roget, *A history of the 'Old Water-Colour' Society*, 2 vols. (1891) · Redgrave, *Artists* · *DNB* · M. Hardie, *Water-colour painting in Britain*, ed. D. Snelgrove, J. Mayne, and B. Taylor, 3: *The Victorian period* (1968) · personal knowledge (2004) · *CGPLA Eng. & Wales* (1863) · d. cert. [William De la Motte] · d. cert. [Freeman Gage Delamotte] · *IGI* · R. K. Engen, *Dictionary of Victorian wood engravers* (1985)
Wealth at death under £2000: probate, Oct 1863, *CGPLA Eng. & Wales*

DeLancey, James (1703–1760), politician and lawyer in America, was born in New York city on 27 November 1703. He was the son of Stephen DeLancey (1663–1741), a French Huguenot who emigrated to New York in 1686 and in 1700 married Anne Van Cortlandt (*b.* 1674?), one of the local Dutch notables. His father was a merchant, landowner, and politician. James was educated in England, studying at Corpus Christi College, Cambridge, from 1721 and at Lincoln's Inn from 1723. When he returned to New York in 1725 he was one of only a handful of New Yorkers who possessed both a university education and membership in one of the English inns of court. He began a successful law practice and married Anne, daughter of Caleb Heathcote, a wealthy Westchester county landowner and lord of the manor of Scarsdale. His family connections secured DeLancey appointment to the council in 1729 by Governor John Montgomerie, whom he assisted in drawing up the 1730 charter which governed New York city until the revolution. The next year Montgomerie named him to the supreme court.

In 1732 the new governor, William Cosby, demanded of Rip Van Dam, president of the council, half of the salary

and perquisites Van Dam had earned during the year between Cosby's appointment and his arrival in New York. Van Dam refused. Cosby, fearing his unpopularity would cause him to lose before a jury, and unable to bring a suit in chancery because he himself would have to sit as chancellor, had the supreme court constituted as a court of exchequer to hear the suit. Chief Justice Lewis Morris declined this jurisdiction, whereupon Cosby dismissed him and put DeLancey in his place.

The case soon became a political issue, as Morris organized an opposition party to the governor and started a new newspaper, the *New-York Weekly Journal*, which began publishing virulent criticisms of Cosby. The governor ordered the printer, John Peter Zenger, to be charged with seditious libel. The case was heard in the supreme court. When Zenger's attorneys challenged the commissions of the justices, DeLancey dismissed them. A new attorney argued that Zenger's criticisms of the governor were true. DeLancey instructed the jury to decide only whether Zenger had printed the offending material, on the existing legal ground that 'the greater the truth, the greater the libel'. The jury ignored DeLancey's instructions and acquitted Zenger.

The famous Zenger trial was hardly a set-back for DeLancey, who became the confidant of Cosby and frustrated his successor, George Clarke, by gaining control of the assembly and opposing Clarke's efforts to secure a long-term revenue. When a new governor, George Clinton, arrived in 1743, he, too, turned to DeLancey as his political adviser, rewarding him with a new commission as chief justice, now 'on good behavior' instead of 'at pleasure', and naming several of his friends to the council. DeLancey now controlled both houses of the legislature and the judiciary. Clinton soon realized his impotence when DeLancey refused to support a militia bill Clinton wanted passed, and he broke with DeLancey in 1746. He sought to get rid of the chief justice only to learn, to his mortification, that DeLancey was named lieutenant-governor in 1747.

Clinton came to detest DeLancey personally, but they differed on matters of substance as well. Clinton had been instructed to pursue King George's War (1744–8) vigorously, but DeLancey, to satisfy his mercantile constituents who profited from the trade between Albany and Montreal, was lukewarm on the subject. Clinton had also been ordered to secure long-term support from the assembly and the right to appoint executive officers whose salaries would be paid by the assembly. That DeLancey-controlled body offered only a one-year support, and insisted on naming the officers whose salaries they would pay. In the contest that continued the governor learned that DeLancey's 'interest' among the British government at Westminster made him invulnerable to Clinton's efforts to get rid of him. DeLancey's father-in-law was brother to Sir Gilbert Heathcote, a founder and governor of the Bank of England. His son, Sir John, who succeeded him, was an MP and one of Sir Robert Walpole's managers. The influential English merchants William and Samuel Baker were the DeLanceys' mercantile correspondents and financiers to the government. William was also a London alderman, an MP, and a friend of the duke of Newcastle. DeLancey's former tutor at Cambridge, Thomas Herring, was now archbishop of Canterbury, and DeLancey's sister Susannah was married to Sir Peter Warren, an MP, an admiral of the fleet, a knight of the Bath, and one of the wealthiest men in England. Additionally, New York's agent at Westminster, Robert Charles, was Sir Peter's private secretary.

For the rest of his administration Clinton contested in vain with DeLancey and out of spite refused to give him his commission as lieutenant-governor until the last day of his term. His successor, Sir Danvers Osborne, arrived on 7 October 1753, only to commit suicide five days later, leaving DeLancey in charge of the government. Except for two years (1755–7) when Sir Charles Hardy served as governor, DeLancey remained the chief executive of the colony until his death. During his administration DeLancey trod a fine line, striving to please the ministry and at the same time retain the loyalty of his local supporters. He presided over the Albany congress of 1754 but did nothing to promote the intercolonial union it proposed. He supported the French and Indian War (1754–63) to protect the security of New York, but did little to assist New England in its campaigns against Canada. He persuaded the ministry to accept an annual grant from the assembly and to allow it to name executive officers, thus satisfying the assembly. He pleased Anglican churchmen by granting a charter in 1754 to King's College in the face of objections from dissenters who wanted a less sectarian institution. Despite determined opposition from the Livingston faction, the DeLanceys remained in control of the government almost until DeLancey's death, of a heart attack, in New York city on 30 July 1760. He was buried at the city's Trinity Church on 31 July.

A man of considerable learning and talent, a poor public speaker and an indifferent writer, DeLancey managed to build a party that enlisted the support of both upper and lower classes. His chief vice, even his supporters conceded, was his 'indolence'. Critics claimed that his own ambition was his chief interest, but his supporters eulogized him as one who had 'more the love and confidence of the people' than any man 'before or since' (De Lancey, 1056), surely an exaggeration. However, even one of his contemporary critics, years later, conceded that he was 'an ornament to the country which gave him birth' (Smith, 2.247). One thing is certain: as a self-interested Anglo-American politician, DeLancey was a brilliant success.   MILTON M. KLEIN

Sources E. F. De Lancey, 'Memoir of the Hon. James De Lancey, lieutenant governor of the province of New York', *The documentary history of the state of New York*, ed. E. B. O'Callaghan, 4 (1851), 1037–59 • S. Katz, 'Between Scylla and Charybdis: James De Lancey and Anglo-American politics in early eighteenth-century New York', *Anglo-American political relations, 1675–1775*, ed. A. G. Olson and R. M. Brown (1970), 92–108 • P. U. Bonomi, *A factious people: politics and society in colonial New York* (1971) • S. Katz, *Newcastle's New York: Anglo-American politics, 1732–1753* (1968) • W. Smith, *The history of the province of New-York* (1757); repr. M. Kammen, ed., 2 (New York, 1972) • M. L. Lustig, *Privilege and prerogative: New York's provincial elite, 1710–1776* (1995) • D. A. Story, *The deLanceys: a romance of a great family* (1931) • R. Herbert, 'James De Lancey and New York provincial politics, 1729–1760', MA diss., St John's University, New York, 1971 • L. S. Launitz-Schurer, 'Whig-loyalists: the De Lanceys of New York', *New-York Historical Society Quarterly*, 56 (1972), 179–98 • N. Varga, 'New York government and politics during the mid-eighteenth century', PhD diss., Fordham University, 1960 • B. McAnear, 'Politics in provincial New York, 1689–1761', PhD diss., Stanford University, 1935 • J. Alexander, *A brief narrative of the case and trial of John Peter Zenger*, ed. S. N. Katz, 2nd edn (Cambridge, MA, 1972) • J. Judd, 'De Lancey, James', *ANB* • J. G. Wilson, *Memorial history of the city of New York*, 2 vols. (1892–3), 2.300–01

Archives Museum of the City of New York, family MSS | probably Lincs. Arch., Ancaster MSS, letters to Sir John Heathcote • New York Historical Society, Colden MSS

Delane [Delany], **Dennis** (1694/5?–1750), actor, was born in Ireland and educated at Trinity College, Dublin. Burtchaell and Sadleir identified him as the Dennis Delany who was the son of Solomon Delany, a clergyman, and who was educated at Mr Griffin's school, Elphin, before his matriculation at Trinity on 16 December 1711 at the age of sixteen. Originally intended for the bar, Delane made his acting début in 1729 at the Smock Alley Theatre in Dublin, under Thomas Elrington's management. There he developed a sizeable repertory of mostly tragic major roles, his principal parts being Alexander in Nathaniel Lee's *The Rival Queens* and Bevil in Richard Steele's *The Conscious Lovers*. Delane negotiated for a London engagement at Drury Lane but the company was 'brimful' (Chetwood, 131) and he was employed instead by Henry Giffard at Goodman's Fields. He made his first appearance on 24 November 1731 as Chalmont in Thomas Otway's *The Orphan*, and in his first three seasons he played at least thirty-five different roles, including Othello, Oroonoko, Richard III, Bevil, Alexander, Tamerlane, Aimwell in George Farquhar's *The Stratagem*, Hotspur, Manly in *The Provok'd Husband* by John Vanbrugh and Colley Cibber, Brutus, Piercy in John Banks's *Virtue Betray'd*, Macbeth, Lear, and Cato. With his 'good person' (Highfill, Burnim & Langhans, *BDA*) and rich repertory, Delane was an immediate and conspicuous success in London.

Delane's first appearance at Covent Garden, where he had been recommended by James Quin, was as Alexander in *The Rival Queens* on 25 October 1735, under the management of John Rich. Delane was one of the original twenty-four members of the Sublime Society of Beefsteaks, formed by Rich in 1735. At Covent Garden he reprised many of his old parts and added Antony, Lothario, Falstaff, King John, Richard II, Henry V, Volpone, and Herod. On 10 September 1741 he made his first appearance, as Othello, at Drury Lane, where he remained until the end of the 1747–8 season, creating the characters of Mahomet, King Henry, and Osmond in James Thomson's *Tancred and Sigismunda*, as well as adding Comus, Antonio in *The Merchant of Venice*, Silvio in John Fletcher's *Women Pleased*, and a number of other new roles to his repertory.

Delane married Margaretta Horsington at St Paul's, Covent Garden, on 9 November 1745, when both declared themselves residents of the parish of St Martin-in-the-Fields, and buried a daughter there on 11 July 1746. Delane moved lodgings frequently in London, living at various addresses in the Strand and Covent Garden. He often returned to Ireland for summer seasons, where he inherited a small paternal estate. Upon his death *Faulkner's Dublin Journal* described him as 'of Killinough in the County of Roscommon, a Gentleman of exceeding good character'.

In the *Apology for the Life of Mr. T[heophilus] C[ibber], Comedian*, ascribed to Henry Fielding, Delane is compared favourably to James Quin, his mentor. While admitting that Delane 'has a Sameness of Tone and Expression, and drawls out his Lines to a displeasing Length' the author concedes that 'that loud Violence of Voice is useful to him when Anger, Indignation, or such enrag'd Passions are to be expres'd' (Highfill, Burnim & Langhans, *BDA*). Not all critics, however, were impressed by Delane's loud voice, described by Thomas Gray in 1746 as 'deep-mouth'd' and 'like a Passing Bell' (Walpole, *Corr.*, 14.6).

Delane's friendship with David Garrick ended irrevocably after the summer of 1748, when Delane recommended Mrs Ward to Rich at Covent Garden. Garrick resented this as disloyalty and was furious. Delane left Drury Lane and played at Covent Garden for the remainder of his career, beginning with Hotspur on 17 October 1748. Faced with the ridicule of Garrick, who mimicked his style when portraying Bayes in *The Rehearsal*, he turned to alcohol 'for relief to his hurt mind' and 'continued to use it with such excess that he was never himself again' (Wilkinson, 1.83).

Delane, however, played a heavy schedule during his 1748–9 season, and for the first time in his career he acted with Quin. He put in a special appearance at Twickenham on 21 September 1749 as Manly in William Wycherley's *The Plain Dealer*, a part considered ideal for him due to his 'easy and polite' manner. John Hill suggested in *The Actor*, shortly after Delane's death, that his reputation would unquestionably have been much higher had he only played characters with 'strength of voice and dignity of figure' (Highfill, Burnim & Langhans, *BDA*), such as Aimwell, rather than the heroic parts that brought him to prominence. It is commonly agreed that Delane achieved success before he had matured as an actor and that he simply couldn't compete with Garrick and Spranger Barry at Drury Lane, both of whom played similar lines. Delane gradually turned more to comedy and was given fewer opportunities to play good leading roles. According to Davies 'his attachment to the bottle prevented his rising to any degree of excellence' (Davies, *Life of Garrick*, 1.27). Delane was a well-built, good-looking, graceful man but, by 1749, 'inclining to the bulky' (Chetwood, 131).

Delane's last appearance was at a benefit on 17 March 1750. He died on 31 March and was buried at St Paul's, Covent Garden, on 6 April. He had written an undated will in which he bequeathed his entire estate, including land in co. Roscommon and co. Galway, to his wife.

ROBERTA MOCK

Sources W. R. Chetwood, *A general history of the stage, from its origin in Greece to the present time* (1749) · A. Murphy, *The life of Garrick* (1801) · [J. Hill], *The actor, or, A treatise on the art of playing* (1755) ·

T. Davies, *Dramatic miscellanies*, new edn, 3 vols. (1785) · T. Davies, *Memoirs of the life of David Garrick*, 2 vols. (1808) · B. Victor, *The history of the theatres of London and Dublin*, 3 vols. (1761–71); repr. (1969) · [H. Fielding?], *An apology for the life of Mr. T[heophilus] C[ibber], comedian, being a proper sequel to The apology for the life of Mr. Colley Cibber, comedian* (1740) · R. Hitchcock, *An historical view of the Irish stage from the earliest period down to the close of the season 1788*, 2 vols. (1788–94) · W. C. Russell, *Representative actors* [1888] · Genest, *Eng. stage*, vols. 2–3 · A. H. Scouten, ed., *The London stage, 1660–1800*, pt 3: *1729–1747* (1961) · G. W. Stone, ed., *The London stage, 1660–1800*, pt 4: *1747–1776* (1962) · T. Wilkinson, *Memoirs of his own life*, 4 vols. (1790) · Burtchaell & Sadleir, *Alum. Dubl.*, 2nd edn · Highfill, Burnim & Langhans, *BDA*

Likenesses engraving, Folger; repro. in Highfill, Burnim & Langhans, *BDA*

Wealth at death land in co. Roscommon and co. Galway: Highfill, Burnim & Langhans, *BDA*

Delane, John Thadeus (1817–1879), newspaper editor, was born on 11 October 1817 at South Molton Street, London, the second of the nine children of William Delane (1793–1857), barrister and treasurer of *The Times*, and his wife, Mary Ann White (*d.* 1869), niece of Colonel John Babington. The family was descended from the Delaneys of Mountreth, Queen's county, Ireland. Delane's childhood was spent at his father's house at Easthampstead, Berkshire, within a united family. After early education at private schools, Delane attended King's College, London, from 1833 to 1835, and then received private tuition from Dr Jeremiah Bowles at Faringdon Hall, Oxfordshire, before entering Magdalen Hall, Oxford, in 1836. At Oxford Delane's exploitation of his natural talents, especially his quickness of apprehension and resourcefulness, compensated for some lack of application to his studies. He enjoyed many forms of sport, and once got the better of a former prizefighter, 'the Chicken of Wheatley', in a confrontation between students and quarrymen. At Oxford, as throughout his life, horse-riding was Delane's favourite exercise, to the extent that his tutor once remarked: 'We must remember that he, like the centaurs of old, is part and parcel of his horse' (Dasent, 1.18). Delane was attracted at this time to the Oxford Movement and, though he never discussed his religion, he was throughout his life a sincere and tolerant Anglican.

Delane graduated BA in July 1840 and was immediately employed by *The Times*, for which his father had been treasurer since 1831. There was also social contact between the Delane and Walter families, who were neighbours in Berkshire. John Walter (1776–1847), chief proprietor of *The Times*, had recognized John Delane's potential and now took steps to develop it through experience in a range of reporting and editorial tasks under the direction of the editor, Thomas Barnes. Barnes was in failing health, and died in May 1841 without an obvious successor. Walter appointed Delane to the vacancy, causing an elated twenty-three year old to exclaim to his fellow lodger, the publisher John Blackwood, 'By Jove, John, what do you think has happened? I am editor of *The Times*' (Dasent, 1.26). He was to retain the position for thirty-six years.

At first Delane was merely the chief editorial lieutenant,

John Thadeus Delane (1817–1879), by Herbert Watkins, late 1850s

supervising matters already defined by the chief proprietor. However, the title of 'editor' soon gained Delane's admission to circles where political intelligence could be gathered. Delane had superlative abilities in this regard, as well as a sharp eye for good news stories. He quickly won the confidence and loyalty of the old guard of reporters and established good working relationships with his leader writers, though he directed from above whereas Barnes had done so from within. After only two years of Delane's editorship a former editor noted that *The Times* had become mild, argumentative, and discriminating, in contrast to its thundering reputation under Barnes.

Delane had quickly learned that moderation is strength, but in 1847 the strength of his own position was seriously threatened by a fracture in the relationship of trust between the chief proprietor and his father. The cause was a misleading financial statement prepared by the treasurer. John Walter, terminally ill, decided that William Delane must go, and that he must surrender his *Times* shares. Delane's father would not accept the terms offered, and the continuance of the dispute over several months placed Delane in a very difficult position. His call to the bar in May 1847 suggests private doubts as to the outcome. Eventually William Delane was persuaded, for the sake of his son's future, to agree to Walter's terms. Within a few days Walter was dead.

The new chief proprietor was his eldest son, also John Walter (1818–1894), a year younger than Delane, who wished to combine control of *The Times* with his duties as a landowner and member of parliament. He needed Delane to take full editorial responsibility, but this did not stop Walter, especially in the early years, from taking a close interest in the paper's content and editorial direction, which Delane sometimes resented. Nevertheless there ensued a relationship of mutual respect shading into friendship, in which Walter played the role of constitutional monarch to Delane's prime minister. Delane ran *The Times* like a great department of state, and managed the editorial side brilliantly. A measure of Delane's achievement is in the circulation figures. These progressed from about 20,000 copies in 1842 to a sustained level of more than 60,000 copies throughout the last decade of Delane's editorship, despite pressure from cheaper competing titles.

Delane's first major exclusive was published in December 1845, when *The Times* announced the imminent repeal of the corn laws on the basis of information from Lord Aberdeen, Peel's foreign secretary. The close understanding which developed between Delane and Aberdeen provided a valuable political tutelage. Delane greatly respected Aberdeen as his mentor during this early stage of his editorial career. The later close relationship with Palmerston developed only after a long period during which *The Times* had generally opposed his policies. An intuitive ability to see 'how it will look tomorrow' was an important factor in Delane's success as a journalist. He was particularly adept in the art of 'journalistic curvature', the process by which the editor steered opinions into new directions which his finely tuned political antennae told him governments would presently follow. Although this practice led to criticism of *The Times* for vacillation, it was also crucial to the paper's reputation and influence. In its implementation Delane was ever careful not to require leader writers to write in support of views and policies with which they did not agree.

Under Delane's editorship *The Times* was loosely identified with Liberalism, but his main concern was always to maintain the paper's independence, so as to be able to support governments without being their organ. This support was lent rather than given, and could at any time be replaced by criticism or outright opposition. The power of *The Times* in opposition to government was seen very clearly during the Crimean War, when Delane felt it was his duty to condemn those directing the war. Kinglake wrote of the great journal using its leadership 'to speak, nay, almost one may say to act, in the name of a united people' (Kinglake, 203).

That Delane was 'the man who worked *The Times*' was universally known, but in exercising this role he maintained the closest anonymity. Only once was 'the man in the mask' forced to break cover. During an acrimonious dispute with Richard Cobden in 1863—over views expressed by John Bright and Cobden respecting the distribution of landed property—Delane argued, in a letter which Cobden published, that public questions were 'best discussed, not between Mr Cobden and Mr Delane, but as it has always been the practice of the English press to discuss them—anonymously' (Dasent, 2.89). In certain directions Delane enhanced the editor's reputation at the paper's expense, and the man became inseparable, in the world's eyes, from the paper. A late twentieth-century assessment, by Stephen Koss, is that it was Delane who formulated a principle that 'the duty of the press is to speak; of the statesman to be silent' (*The Times*, 6 Feb 1852), in which privilege was mistaken for duty and abused. In his lifetime Delane was widely regarded as the unquestioned head of the journalistic profession, who had done much to raise the tone of journalism. Some of his innovative methods of reporting news, which included the use of interviews, and his Crimean and other 'crusades', foreshadowed the 'new journalism' of the later nineteenth century. In a centennial tribute William Stebbing referred to the extraordinary degree to which Delane won the admiration of rival journalists and concluded that he had been the ideal editor.

In the social circles which Delane frequented, constantly on the alert for political intelligence, he was welcomed as a delightful companion. He was observant, critical, somewhat reserved, and imperturbably calm, but among friends he would talk animatedly and without restraint. When other men opened their minds, Delane measured them, but all who confided in him knew he would scrupulously respect their trust. As editor Delane was seen as a proud, harsh man, a hard taskmaster who was also true, sincere, and kind-hearted. His idea of dignified happiness was that of a country gentleman, and in mid-life this robust man, with his florid complexion, bright eyes, and genial smile between mutton-chop whiskers, looked the part. In the 1860s Delane still paid his morning calls on horseback before riding to the House of Commons. He claimed to have been the last man to ride through Fleet Street to the West End, on one occasion with a duke walking on either side as he proceeded slowly down Whitehall. He was elected to the Reform Club (1857) and to the Athenaeum (1862). In 1874 he was appointed deputy lieutenant for Berkshire.

Although Delane wrote little for publication—his peculiar facility as a journalist was in polishing and sharpening articles written by others—he was a prolific letter and note writer. Every day he wrote terse and vigorous directions to his leader writers, letters of advice, instruction and criticism to foreign and war correspondents, letters to friends, and an account of the day's activities to his mother. Few Indian mails failed to include letters to two brothers, who were army officers there. All these were written with a quill pen dipped in an inkstand formed from the hoof of a favourite horse. Letters written on holidays show a persistent interest in distances, speeds, and prices. Delane expected all leading articles to be written, like his own notes of instruction, in good simple English, without slang or technicality. He watched with the utmost care every detail of expression, and thereby exerted a valuable influence on the standard of correct English writing. Henry Wace, a regular contributor to *The Times* and

dean of Canterbury, considered Delane a good scholar, lawyer, and doctor—he had studied for a time in Paris under François Magendie, an eminent physiologist. But politics was what really interested him.

Delane married, on 9 August 1842, Fanny Horatia Serle Bacon, *née* Twiss (1818–1874), widow of Francis Bacon, assistant editor under Barnes, and daughter of Horace Twiss (1787–1849), barrister. Her grandfather was Francis *Twiss. There were no children from the marriage. Fanny Delane became mentally ill, and from 1853 until her death in 1874 had to be confined. Throughout this period of 'married widowhood' Delane wrote constantly to his wife and kept all her letters to him. His personal correspondence during these years not surprisingly hints at loneliness and frustration, and he often comments on beautiful women he met in society. When first appointed editor Delane lived at 4 Chatham Place, Blackfriars, 'to be near his work', then at 22 New Bridge Street, before settling from about 1847 at 16 Serjeant's Inn, Temple. In 1858 he bought a property at Ascot Heath, to which he retreated whenever possible.

The editor's daily routine was both arduous—a sixteen-hour working day seems to have been usual—and stressful, demanding a peak of mental effort in the small hours. Delane's hand was firmly on all departments. Although he took regular holidays during parliamentary recesses, these were often largely spent in meetings with foreign correspondents and statesmen. Delane's commitment to *The Times* was total. He told John Walter, following an illness in 1861, 'My whole life is bound up with the paper—I must either work for it or not at all' (Dasent, 2.27).

His mother's death in 1869 affected Delane very much, and after 1870 he was often seriously ill from overwork, asthma, bronchitis, and gout. W. H. Russell found him in April 1877 'thin, old, bowed, speaking slowly, with glassy eye' (Cook, 259). Even before Delane retired, after attending to the issue for 9 November 1877, effective control had been discreetly and informally assumed by others. Delane's final months were spent at Ascot Heath, cared for by his unmarried sister. He died on 22 November 1879 and was buried in Easthampstead churchyard, Berkshire, on 29 November 1879.   GEOFFREY HAMILTON

Sources A. I. Dasent, *John Thadeus Delane*, 2 vols. (1908) · E. Cook, *Delane of The Times* (1915) · [S. Morison and others], *The history of The Times*, 2 (1939) · H. Wace, *John Thadeus Delane* (1908) [repr. in *Cornhill Magazine*, Jan 1909, 93–100] · G. W. Smalley, *London letters*, 1 (1890) · *The Athenaeum* (29 Nov 1879), 695 · *Macmillan's Magazine*, 41 (1880), 267–72 · *The Standard* (25 Nov 1879) · *The Times* (25 Nov 1879) · A. W. Kinglake, *The invasion of the Crimea*, [new edn], 7 (1883) · S. E. Koss, *The rise and fall of the political press in Britain*, 1 (1981) · H. R. Fox Bourne, *English newspapers: chapters in the history of journalism*, 2 (1887) · [T. H. S. Escott], 'John Delane and modern journalism', *QR*, 209 (1908), 524–48 · W. Stebbing, *The Times* (11 Oct 1917) · P. Brendon, *The life and death of the press barons* (1982) · *The Times* (1 Dec 1879) · m. cert.

Archives News Int. RO, corresp. and papers | BL, corresp. with Lord Aberdeen, Add. MSS 43244–43252 · BL, corresp. with Lord Carnarvon, Add. MS 60776 · BL, corresp. with W. E. Gladstone, Add. MSS 44359–44454 · BL, letters to Sir A. H. Layard, Add. MSS 38983–39111 · BL, letters to Sir Robert Peel, Add. MSS 40519–

40588 • Bodl. Oxf., corresp. with Benjamin Disraeli • Bodl. Oxf., letters to Sir William Harcourt • Bodl. Oxf., corresp. mainly with Sir William Napier • GS Lond., letters to Roderick Impey Murchison • Herefs. RO, letters to George Moffat • LPL, corresp. with A. C. Tait • NA Scot., letters to G. W. Hope • NL Ire., letters to G. C. Brodrick • NL Scot., corresp. with Blackwoods • PRO, letters to Lord Granville, PRO 30/29 • Ransom HRC, letters to Stebbing • U. Southampton, corresp. mainly with Lord Palmerston • U. Southampton L., Temple MSS • UCL, corresp. with Sir Edwin Chadwick; letters to Joseph Parkes
Likenesses double portrait, photograph, c.1850 (with his wife), News Int. RO • H. Watkins, two albumen prints, 1850–59, NPG [*see illus.*] • Mayall, photograph, 1861, repro. in Dasent, *John Thadeus Delane* • H. A. G. Schiött, oils, 1862, NPG • C. Spencelayh, miniature on copper, 1862 (after oil painting by H. A. G. Schiött), NPG • E. Edwards, carte-de-visite, NPG • photograph, repro. in S. V. Makover, *Some notes on the history of The Times* (1904) • portraits, News Int. RO • three photographs, News Int. RO
Wealth at death under £30,000: probate, 19 Dec 1879, *CGPLA Eng. & Wales*

Delane, Solomon (1727–1812), landscape painter, was born probably in Dublin, the son of Richard Delane, a clergyman. He trained under the artist Robert West in the school in George's Lane, Dublin, and was awarded a premium by the Dublin Society in 1750. His first recorded work is a portrait of a famous Dublin comedian, *The Right Comical L.C.J.I. Sparks*, of which he made a folio-sized etching inscribed 'S. Delane pinxit ex fecit' in 1752. He spent some twenty years in Rome, where he was well regarded as a landscape painter. In 1763 he was elected to the Society of Arts and sent landscapes from Italy to exhibitions in 1773 and 1776 as well as to the Royal Academy in 1777 and 1782–4. During these years Ingamells noted his travels in Italy, including his election to the Accademia di Belle Arti, Florence in 1777 (Ingamells, 290). In 1781 he travelled near Augsburg, Germany, and in the following year reached London, before returning to Dublin where he married. Although he no longer exhibited in London after 1784, his name appears among the exhibitors at Parliament House in 1802 and at Hawkins Street, Dublin, in 1812.

Delane worked in the classical manner of Claude Lorrain and many of his pictures were sold in London as Claude originals. This landscape idiom had been popularized by the Welsh-born painter Richard Wilson and Delane found many aristocratic clients in Rome who had developed a taste for such pictures. One patron, James Irvine, admired his composition but found his colouring 'a little too cold' (Ingamells, 290). Although principally renowned for his views of the Roman campagna, Delane also depicted Dublin in this grand manner and examples of his work are in the National Gallery of Ireland. Delane died in Dublin in 1812.

L. H. Cust, *rev.* Natasha Eaton

Sources J. Ingamells, ed., *A dictionary of British and Irish travellers in Italy, 1701–1800* (1997) • A. Crookshank and the Knight of Glin [D. Fitzgerald], *The painters of Ireland, c.1660–1920* (1978) • W. G. Strickland, *A dictionary of Irish artists*, 2 vols. (1913); repr. with introduction by T. J. Snoddy (1989) • Waterhouse, *18c painters* • Redgrave, *Artists* • Graves, *RA exhibitors*, vol. 1 • G. Meissner, ed., *Allgemeines Künstlerlexikon: die bildenden Künstler aller Zeiten und Völker*, [new edn, 34 vols.] (Leipzig and Munich, 1983–)

Archives BM, department of prints and drawings • Courtauld Inst., Witt Library | BM, department of prints and drawings, Hayward MSS • RA, Ozias Humphry MSS
Likenesses G. Dance, drawing, 1795, Castle Museum and Art Gallery, Nottingham; repro. in Strickland, *Dictionary*, vol. 1, p. 274

Delany [*née* Granville; *other married name* Pendarves], **Mary** (1700–1788), court favourite and artist, was born at Coulston, Wiltshire, on 14 May 1700. The elder daughter of Bernard Granville (1671–1723) and his wife, Mary Westcomb (d. 1747), she was widely connected in court and political circles. Her father's elder brother was George Granville, Lord Lansdowne; his sister Ann, the wife of Sir John Stanley, who held a court appointment, had been maid of honour to Queen Mary.

The family moved to London shortly after Mary's birth. Educated at home and at an exclusive school run by a Huguenot refugee, she became fluent in French, well read in history and the classics in translation as well as English literature, a good musician, and a superb needlewoman. She showed early talent for drawing, cutting, and design. When she was eight she went to live with her aunt Stanley at Whitehall, presumably to be groomed for a place at court. However, the death of Queen Anne in 1714 and the subsequent whig supremacy reversed the family fortunes. Lord Lansdowne was held in the Tower for nearly two years. Bernard Granville was detained briefly; he then retired with his family to Benchland, near Camden, Gloucestershire. There Mary attracted the attention of a young man, Robert Twyford, who was as penniless as she. An invitation for her to join the Lansdowne household at Longleat in September 1717 was a welcome solution to this unsuitable courtship.

At Longleat Mary Granville met Alexander Pendarves (1660–1725) of Roscrow, near Falmouth, Cornwall. The wealthy and childless 57-year-old MP welcomed a match that would possibly bring him an heir in addition to furthering his political alliance with Lansdowne. Since her family was entirely dependent on her uncle's generosity, Mary Granville had little choice but to accept Pendarves's proposal. They were married at Longleat on 17 February 1718. The marriage was unhappy for both partners. They first lived at Roscrow, where Mary was kept in nearly total seclusion, as he was jealous of any attention she received. Removed from her family and friends, she experienced the greatest despair of her life. The situation improved somewhat after 1721, when they returned to London, although Pendarves drank heavily and brought in his sister to keep an eye on his wife. Mary, however, was able to make visits to her family and to sample the delights of London society. Pendarves died unexpectedly on 8 March 1725. His widow was left with no resources beyond her jointure, but she was freed from his unpredictable presence.

For the next eighteen years Mary Pendarves lived in London. The first years of her widowhood were spent under the protection of the Stanleys, and from 1733 she occupied a house in Lower Brook Street. She was a participant at court functions, and attended the opera and theatre as well as private social events. Despite her lack of fortune

Mary Delany (1700–1788), by John Opie, 1782

her charm and vivacity brought her a number of suitors, including Lord Baltimore and Lord Clare, but she showed no inclination to marry again. Many of her most important friendships were cemented in this period, especially that with Margaret, duchess of Portland. The great collection of letters to these friends, and to her mother and sister, began during her widowhood; her autobiographical fragment, in the form of letters to the duchess, was written about 1740.

In 1731 Pendarves and her friend Anne Donnellan, the daughter of an Irish judge, went to Ireland for a visit of eighteen months. They were widely entertained in Dublin and the country and introduced to most of Anglo-Irish society. Pendarves met Jonathan Swift, with whom she afterwards corresponded. More important was her meeting with Patrick *Delany (1685/6–1768), an Irish Anglican cleric. The two were clearly attracted to each other, but he was already engaged to a rich widow, whom he married in 1732. In 1743, after his wife's death, Delany went to England to propose to Pendarves. Her male relations opposed the match, for Delany had neither fortune nor gentle birth. But she ignored these protests, and the marriage took place in London in early June 1743.

The Delanys lived principally at Delville, his house in Dublin. After his appointment as dean of Down in 1744 they spent some time there each year when in Ireland. Every two to three years they made an extended visit to family and friends in England. Mary Delany entered fully into her husband's life in Ireland, entertaining, decorating and embellishing his houses, and improving the gardens. She approached her important relations such as Lord Carteret for a higher place in the church for her husband, but with no success. They were frequently worried

by a lawsuit over his first wife's property, which was finally settled in his favour. Patrick Delany died at Bath in May 1768.

Mary Delany returned to London, and lived first at Thatched House Court and then at St James's Place. She spent most summers at Bulstrode in Buckinghamshire, the favourite country house of the duchess of Portland. There the friends improved the gardens, collected shells and botanical specimens, indulged in various arts and crafts, and entertained poets, scientists, theologians, friends, and royalty. It was there in 1774 that Delany began what she called her paper mosaics, the cut-paper illustrations of flowers and plants that were her most important artistic achievement. Using various shadings of coloured tissue, she cut freehand all the parts of the plant, which were then pasted on black paper to make a perfect specimen. Nearly a thousand pages of her *Hortus siccus* were completed by 1784, when she had to give up the work because of failing eyesight; these are now in the British Library.

Among the visitors to Bulstrode were George III and Queen Charlotte. Delany and the royal pair had many tastes in common, including botany and the music of Handel. After the duchess's death in 1785, the king gave Delany a house at Windsor and a pension of £300. She enjoyed her last years as a royal favourite, and died at Windsor Castle, probably of pneumonia, on 15 April 1788. She was buried at St James's, Piccadilly.

Although the flower collages were Delany's major work of art, she left other evidence of her talents. She designed and embroidered panels for clothing, chair covers, bed hangings and coverings, and other furnishings. She was a fine copyist of paintings, a maker of silhouettes, and a creative crafter of shellwork. Her most important legacy is the extensive correspondence that she carried on with members of her family and her friends. These letters contain information about every aspect of the life of the propertied class in England and Ireland from about 1725 to 1788. Cultural figures including Swift, Handel, and Rousseau make an appearance, as do prominent women writers such as Frances Burney, Elizabeth Montagu, Frances Boscawen, and Hannah More. The greatest number of the letters are to and from Delany's sister Ann Granville Dewes, her daughter Mary Dewes Port, and her daughter Mary Ann Port Waddington. The letters were edited and published in six volumes in 1861–2 by Lady Llanover, Waddington's daughter. Although much personal detail is omitted in this edition, the letters are nevertheless a major source for contemporary information about such varied topics as medicine, servants, food, costume, reading, marriage, gardening, and collecting.

BARBARA BRANDON SCHNORRENBERG

Sources *The autobiography and correspondence of Mary Granville, Mrs Delany*, ed. Lady Llanover, 1st ser., 3 vols. (1861) · *The autobiography and correspondence of Mary Granville, Mrs Delany*, ed. Lady Llanover, 2nd ser., 3 vols. (1862) · R. Hayden, *Mrs Delany: her life and flowers* (1980) · J. F. Thaddens, 'Mary Delany: model to the age', *History, gender, and eighteenth century literature*, ed. B. F. Tobin (1994), 113–40 ·

Letters from Mrs Delany to Mrs Frances Hamilton (1820) • B. Rizzo, *Companions without vows: relationships among eighteenth-century British women* (1994)

Archives BM • NL Wales, corresp. and papers • Royal Arch. • Yale U., Farmington, Lewis Walpole Library | Bodl. Oxf., letters to first earl of Guilford

Likenesses Barber, enamel miniature, *c.*1760 • J. Opie, oils, *c.*1782, Royal Collection • J. Opie, oils, second version, 1782, Beningbrough Hall, Yorkshire; on loan from NPG [*see illus.*] • attrib. J. Hoppner, pencil drawing, V&A • oils, Man. City Gall.

Wealth at death probably *c.*£500–£600 in cash; many possessions; books; pictures; vases: will, described in Llanover, ed., *Autobiography and correspondence*, 2nd ser., 3.483ff

Delany, Patrick (1685/6–1768), Church of Ireland dean of Down and writer, was born at Rathkreagh in Queen's county, a younger son of Denis Delany, a small farmer. He was educated at the popular school run by Dalton at Athy in co. Kildare, whence he proceeded to Trinity College, Dublin, in 1701. He was elected a scholar of the foundation in 1704. Later Delany paid tribute to the excellent grounding he received there from the then provost, Peter Browne. To Browne he traced his taste in the classics, his style in preaching, and perhaps his concern with charity. He continued beyond his BA (taken in 1706) and MA (1709) to prepare for ordination. In 1709 he was elected to a fellowship of the college. At this stage his political leanings towards the tories assisted his ascent. By 1713 he was a chaplain to the intemperate tory lord chancellor, Sir Constantine Phipps. Delany's toryism proved less helpful after 1714 but his reputation as the foremost tutor in the college and one of the best preachers in Dublin protected him. In 1724 he was appointed professor of oratory and history. The following year Archbishop Hugh Boulter calculated that Delany earned £600 or £700 from his pupils. Boulter, keen to see Delany's influence within the college diminished, refused to allow him to combine a fellowship with the incumbency of a Dublin parish (St John's). However in 1728, backed by Dean Swift and the lord lieutenant, Carteret, he received the chancellorship of Christ Church Cathedral in the capital. Within two years he added the chancellorship of Dublin's second cathedral, St Patrick's. He was also inducted into a college living in co. Fermanagh.

With access to these prominent pulpits Delany was able to consolidate his position as a leading preacher. Concurrently he was active in the cultural and social life of protestant Dublin. Friendly with Swift, even before his formal link with the cathedral of which the latter was dean, Delany turned his hand to verse and periodic journalism as well as to sermons. Later, in 1754, he published a refutation of Lord Orrery's criticisms of Swift. With a colleague from Trinity, Dr Richard Helsham, Delany built a suburban retreat outside Dublin, subsequently renamed Delville. There sociability was consciously (even self-consciously) cultivated. Delany, a byword for hospitality, managed his ample emoluments badly. Difficulties were eased by a timely marriage in 1732 to Margaret Tenison, *née* Barton, the rich widow of a co. Louth landowner. She brought her new husband an annual income of £1600. After her death in 1742 problems over her will involved

Patrick Delany (1685/6–1768), by Andrea Soldi, 1750s

Delany in protracted litigation, which had not been resolved by the time he died. Earlier his expansive tastes could be indulged not just at Delville but in his Dublin town house in Stafford Street. Each Thursday seven or eight friends would gather. Both the conversation and the restrained refreshment were remembered affectionately. Here he practised those virtues, such as contentment and happiness, that he extolled in print. Integral to his philosophy was an ideal of moderation. Virtue and piety, he firmly believed, were most likely to be found among those 'in the middle state' (P. Delany, *Sixteen Discourses*, 1754, 235).

From the 1730s Delany wrote more ambitious works than the slight verses that he had previously published. In 1732 he published an attack on contemporary education, *The Present State of Learning*, under an easily penetrated pseudonym. He lamented the neglect of classical literature and contempt for the scriptures among feeble imitators of Newton. He feared that this attitude had affected some clergy who no longer behaved as if they were addressing 'corrupt, unruly mortals' but 'pure, unbodied intelligences' (P. Delany, *The Present State of Learning*, 1732, 7–8). 'Profane scurrility' was instead the favoured mode. At the same time fashionable lay people treated church services as a kind of entertainment. This assault was incorporated into a more comprehensive restatement of the tenets of orthodox Christianity in *Revelation Examined with Candour*, which appeared in three volumes between 1732 and 1763. Despite the persisting doubts about his political reliability Delany was invited to preach on state occasions. His sermon in 1738 on the anniversary of Charles I's execution was acclaimed by Swift for its refusal to compromise. Delany urged all Christians to obey the current sovereign and warned that republican ideas 'must end, as they are intended, in popery and arbitrary power' (P. Delany, *A Sermon Preach'd in Christ-Church, Dublin, … on Monday, January 30, 1737* [8], 1737 [8], 19). In the same decade he was tempted to examine and attack the practice of polygamy. He analysed both ancient and modern empires to disprove the contention that the habit increased population more rapidly than monogamy; he had been aided in demonstrating this by the demographic calculations of his friend Dr Helsham. He also published a three-volume life of King David (Dublin, 1743), whom he promoted as the exemplar of friendship, an attribute to which he often reverted. Characteristically the study was designed to improve, entertain, and inform.

On 9 June 1743 Delany married, as his second wife, Mary, *née* Granville (1700–1788), widow of Alexander Pendarves and the elder daughter of Bernard and Mary Granville [*see* Delany, Mary]; her mother was an artist with wide court and society connections. Thanks to her persistence and connections Delany was advanced in 1744 to the deanery of Down, where (to his wife's chagrin) he stuck. Vacant bishoprics eluded him. The revenues of the deanery were reckoned to be £2300 per annum, however, and Delany's wish to retain his other preferments irritated his superiors. It was part of an attitude to the clerical calling, idealistic in the abstract but personally lax, notably over the question of residence. He spent long periods in England and, as his health worsened in the 1760s, so he contracted his circuit to Dublin and its environs. Yet he publicly espoused a number of causes dear to the interests of the established Church of Ireland. A noted educationist himself, he often adverted to the importance of proper schooling. Good schoolmasters, he contended, were among the most useful members of any society. He reminded the young at Trinity College of the value of early industry. He inveighed against parents who neglected the education of their children or entrusted them to ignorant servants and foreign tutors. He wanted women to be educated so that they were better prepared for becoming faithful friends and amiable companions of their husbands (in the mode—no doubt—of his own wife). He backed the Incorporated Society and its charter schools as helps to the poor. More contentiously he upheld the rights of the clergy to their tithes. At Down he became embroiled in a battle to extract tithes from the local linen weavers; although he contended that only disinterested zeal for the rights of the church motivated him he found himself opposed not just by the weavers but also by the official linen board and powerful landowners.

On entering into the deanery of Down Delany tried to rectify the neglects of his predecessors and planned to visit all the families within the district. He wanted to build new churches and a fitting residence for himself and his successors. In his rented house at Mount Panther, outside Downpatrick, as well as at Delville, he and his wife personified the social virtues that he so frequently recommended. In manner of life, avoiding ostentation, he continued to merit Swift's tribute that he made 'no parade'

and was 'one of the very few within my knowledge on whom a great access of fortune hath made no manner of change' (*Correspondence*, 4.104). He continued to combat vicious habits common among the leaders of society; thus duelling, gambling, excess in dress, diet, and drink, cheating, avarice, envy, and pride were all attacked in his publications. On occasion too he voiced something of the patriotism increasing among aggrieved Irish protestants. In a sermon of 1744 he regretted the deluded English policies that had led to constant economic discrimination against Ireland. He insisted that the interests of the protestants of Ireland were inseparable from those of their co-religionists in Great Britain. He wanted this fact to be recognized in more generous treatment of Ireland by the Westminster parliament. Ironically, in view of his own lineage (seemingly of native Irish stock), he insisted that there were not ten notable families in Ireland 'who are not originally British' (P. Delany, *A Sermon Preach'd before the Society Corresponding with the Incorporated Society in Dublin … March 13th, 1743/4*, 1744, 15). His voluminous writings, economical and direct in style, convey something of the reasons why he was so esteemed as mentor and preacher.

In a quest for restoratives Delany revisited England, where—at Bath—he died on 6 May 1768. His body was returned to Ireland to be interred at Glasnevin, close to his favourite haunt of Delville. TOBY BARNARD

Sources *The autobiography and correspondence of Mary Granville, Mrs Delany*, ed. Lady Llanover, 1st ser., 3 vols. (1861) • Newport Public Library, Monmouthshire, Delany MSS • PRO NIre., Castle Ward MSS, D 2092/1/7, 130, 133, 139, 141, 169 • *The correspondence of Jonathan Swift*, ed. H. Williams, 5 vols. (1963–5) • pedigree of Delany, Genealogical Office, Dublin, MS 176, 411–12, 481–2 • *Letters written by … Hugh Boulter … to several ministers of state*, ed. [A. Philips and G. Faulkner], 2 vols. (1769–70); repr. (1770) • *Manuscripts of the earl of Egmont: diary of Viscount Percival, afterwards first earl of Egmont*, 3 vols., HMC, 63 (1920–23), vol. 3, p. 301 • Burtchaell & Sadleir, *Alum. Dubl.*

Likenesses A. Soldi, painting, 1750–59, priv. coll. [*see illus.*] • attrib. J. van Nost junior, marble bust, *c.*1768, TCD • attrib. R. Barber, enamel on copper miniature, NG Ire.; repro. in A. Day, ed., *Letters from Georgian Ireland* (1991), 18

Delap, John (1724/5–1812), poet and playwright, the son of John Delap, gentleman, of Gainsborough, Lincolnshire, was born at Spilsby in that county. After schooling at Beverley, Yorkshire, he was originally entered at Trinity College, Cambridge, but transferred to Magdalene College and was admitted pensioner on 15 March 1744. He took the degrees of BA in 1747, MA in 1750, and DD in 1762. On 30 December 1748 he was elected to a fellowship at Magdalene, and on 4 March 1749 was admitted into its emoluments. He was ordained a priest in the Church of England on 23 December 1750 and was once curate to William Mason the poet. His thesis for his divinity degree (12 April 1762), entitled 'Mundi perpetuus administrator Christus', was published in 1763. He was vicar of Ilford and Kingston, near Lewes in Sussex, from 1765 to 1812 and of Woolavington from 1774 to 1812. He may have been rector of Ousby, Cumberland from 1759 to 1766.

Delap's first publication was *Marcellus: a Monody* (1751), which was inspired by the death of George II's eldest son, and was inscribed to his widow, the princess of Wales. This was followed by his *Elegies* (1760) in which the author who 'very feelingly lamented his want of health' is heavily influenced by Gray. Later poems include *An Elegy on the Death of the Duke of Rutland* (1788), *Sedition, an Ode Occasioned by his Majesty's Late Proclamation* (1792), and *The Lord of the Nile, an Elegy* (1799).

Delap's great love was writing tragedies and while he met with little dramatic success, he remained undaunted both in his attempts to promote his own efforts and to curry favour and fame. He also conferred and disputed endlessly with friends and colleagues over the merits of his own writings. David Garrick and Frances Burney were both recipients of Delap's almost obsessive preoccupation with his dramatic works. Burney described Delap's fondness for talking about his own work to the point of tedium and impoliteness: 'he returned to the same thing a million times, asked the same questions, enacted the same compliments, and worked at the same passages, till I almost fell asleep with the sound of the same words'. Burney also claims that Delap's thirst for reputation was such that he preferred to 'make a general rout and reform' of his plays rather than miss the chance of production—an intention which he communicated to Garrick 'at portentous length' (Parsons, 186). Burney summed up Delap as 'a man of deep learning, but totally ignorant of life and manners'.

Hecuba (1761), a tragedy in three acts, was Delap's first dramatic success. The play was produced by Garrick at Drury Lane on 11 December 1761. In a letter to George Coleman, manager of Drury Lane, Garrick claims that: 'We might steal it on to Six Nights with much loss, but I hope, that the Author will be reasonable, & satisfy'd with what We have already done, without insisting upon our losing more to *force* a Reputation' (*Letters*, 1.348). While Garrick also alludes to the performance as resulting from a personal favour to the author it seems unlikely that he would have produced, spoken the prologue, and written the epilogue if he considered it to be totally without merit. Stone states that the play was produced four times between its first night and 8 January 1762 while Baker claims that 'it only ran for three nights'. Genest asserts that the play is derivative from West's *Hecuba* but also describes it as 'not void of merit, but it cannot by any means be called a good play' (Genest, *Eng. stage*, 4.638). Baker confirms this assessment pointing to the play's lack of dramatic action, a tendency for too much declamatory statement, its 'indifferent success', but he does concede that it contains certain merits in its use of poetic language (Baker, 2.287). As a tragedy *Hecuba* stays faithful to its classical model in its emphasis on representing Hecuba as the most unfortunate of mothers. While little action takes place on stage the text is of interest for its rendition of a model of feminine passivity (Hecuba's maternal suffering and Polyxena's sacrifice) and how this signifies definitions of male heroism (ghostly Achilles's decree, Ulysses's justification for the Greeks' actions and Polydore's suicide for honour's sake). The potential within the play to offer a reading of the codification of gender roles was not missed

by Garrick whose epilogue (spoken by Miss Bride) draws a contemporary analogy:

> Do you not shudder parents, at this tale?
> You sacrifice a daughter now and then,
> To rich, old, wither'd half-departed men.

The play was published in 1762 at a price of 11s. 6d. and dedicated to Thomas Barrett of Lee, near Canterbury, where it appears Delap was living. A number of Dublin editions followed.

Delap's next play, *Panthea*, was rejected by Garrick and never produced, though this fact did not deter the author, who stated his intention to rewrite the play (*Letters*, 3.933). Delap was again in correspondence with Garrick concerning his attempt to get his next play *The Royal Suppliants* produced. Garrick advised Delap to make a number of changes to give the play dramatic interest and was most perturbed by the last act which he described as being the 'worst, & ought to be the best' (ibid., 3.932). The subject of this neoclassical five-act tragedy is a dynastic power struggle. Baker praises the play for 'two very affecting scenes between the mother and daughter, which are genuine pictures from nature' (Baker, 3.231). The play, which is based on Euripides's *Heraclidae* and *The Suppliants* of Aeschylus, was finally produced at Drury Lane on 17 February 1781 and thereafter eight times. The performance announced in the playbill for 1 March 1781 did not occur owing to the illness of the actress Miss Crawford. The play was published in 1781 with two further editions in the same year.

Delap was again in correspondence with Garrick over his next play *Royal Exiles*, which, though rejected, was finally produced in a revised form and with the new title *The Captives* on 9 March 1786 at Drury Lane where it ran for three nights. It was published in the same year. The play was not a success: Baker refers to it as being withdrawn 'after dragging through three nights' (Baker, 2.82). Kemble in a letter to Malone offers a contemporary review, caustically describing the play as being 'set at liberty last night, amidst roars of laughter' (Hogan, 10.870). A further play, *Gunilda*, which was never acted, was published in 1786. This play, together with other unacted plays, was published in Delap's *Dramatic Poems: Gunilda, Usurper, Matilda, and Abdalla* (1803).

Delap appears to have lived for most of his literary life in South Street, Lewes, in Sussex. He was nevertheless acquainted with literary circles of the day, visiting the Thrales at Brighton and Tunbridge Wells. Through the Thrales he became acquainted with Samuel Johnson as well as David Garrick and Frances Burney. His acquaintance with important literary figures of the day does not seem greatly to have enhanced his own dramatic abilities. Delap died at Lewes in 1812 aged eighty-seven. He was unmarried.

                                       GAIL BAYLIS

Sources C. J. Stratman, ed., *Bibliography of English printed tragedy, 1565–1900* [1966], 154–5 • G. W. Stone, ed., *The London stage, 1660–1800*, pt 4: *1747–1776* (1962), 907–8, 911 • C. B. Hogan, ed., *The London stage, 1660–1800*, pt 5: *1776–1800* (1968), 409, 411–12, 423, 868, 870 • G. Watson, I. R. Willison, and J. D. Pickles, eds., *The new Cambridge bibliography of English literature*, 5 vols. (1969–77) • *GM*, 1st ser., 83/1 (1813), 89 • *The letters of David Garrick*, ed. D. M. Little and G. M. Kahrl, 3 vols. (1963) • Genest, *Eng. stage*, 4.637–8 • F. M. Parsons, *Garrick and*

his circle (1906), 186 · *The diary of Fanny Burney*, ed. L. Gibbs (1940), 29, 30, 32, 35–6 · D. E. Baker, *Biographia dramatica, or, A companion to the playhouse*, rev. I. Reed, new edn, rev. S. Jones, 3 vols. in 4 (1812)
Archives JRL, letters to Hester Piozzi · V&A NAL, corresp. with David Garrick
Wealth at death see *GM*, 89

Delaram, Francis (*fl.* 1615–1624), engraver, was a contemporary of Simon de Passe, with whom he dominated the London engraving trade in the second half of the reign of James I, putting an end to the near monopoly that had previously been held by Renold Elstrack. Nothing is known about his life apart from what can be deduced from his forty-seven surviving prints. The earliest of them is a portrait of James's botanist Matthias de Lobel, dated 1615, which is fully developed in style and among the best of his plates. This, and the fact that other plates are lettered 'Londini', suggests that Delaram had been trained abroad and had recently arrived in London. But if he was (as seems most likely on stylistic grounds) a Netherlander, no trace of his activity has been recorded in the Low Countries either before or after his time in London.

Most of Delaram's plates are title-pages and portraits, apparently after his own designs. He also made some of the first English books of flowers, beasts, and birds, and probably the first English drawing-book (of which no copy survives). Delaram worked for all the main London publishers of the day, including Compton Holland, Sudbury and Humble, Thomas Jenner, Roger Daniell, and Maurice Blount; he never published anything himself. His most interesting works are a portrait of Queen Elizabeth after Nicholas Hilliard, published with a royal privilege; this has always been linked with a licence that Hilliard was given in 1617 that gave him a monopoly of printed portraits of James I. Delaram's major plate, a very large portrait of James, published by Edward Pierson, is dated 1619, the year of Hilliard's death, and therefore after the expiry of his monopoly. Only one impression of it survives and is now in the British Museum. ANTONY GRIFFITHS

Sources A. M. Hind, *Engraving in England in the sixteenth and seventeenth centuries*, 2 (1955), 215–42 · A. Griffiths and R. A. Gerard, *The print in Stuart Britain, 1603–1689* (1998), 53–6 [exhibition catalogue, BM, 8 May – 20 Sept 1998]

Delattre [Delatre], **Jean Marie** (1745–1840), engraver, was born at Abbeville, France. He was a pupil of J. P. Le Bas and had already composed some small portrait engravings in Paris before coming to England in 1770 to work for William Wynne Ryland. He showed with the Society of Arts in that year when he was living opposite the Mother Red Cap in Kentish Town, London—François Ravenet's address—and a year later was publishing in partnership with Ravenet's son-in-law Victor Marie Picot. He apparently returned to Paris shortly before 1773, where he produced two portraits and worked for the printsellers Esnauts and Rapilly, but after this date he settled in London, and on 18 February 1773 married Ann Davis (*d.* 1834) at St Anne, Soho. Two daughters survived him: Charlotte May (1780–1851) and Juliet Ann (*b.* 1783).

From 1779 Delattre engraved for a variety of printsellers including Anne Bryer, and also for Francis Bartolozzi.

Early prints after Kaufmann for Bartolozzi are signed 'Delattre sculps. Bartolozzi direxit'. Later he became Bartolozzi's principal assistant and was responsible for much of the work bearing Bartolozzi's signature. He also worked for booksellers, making portraits and vignettes for *London Theatre* (1776) and portraits for Samuel Johnson's *Works of the English Poets* (1779). Occasionally he engraved in line rather than in stipple, as in his work for Bell's *British Theatre*.

About 1800 the American painter John Singleton Copley commissioned Delattre to produce a line-engraving at a reduced scale of Bartolozzi's large plate *Death of the Earl of Chatham*, which depicted fifty-six members of the House of Lords, and for which Bartolozzi had received £2000. Copley agreed to pay £800, with an advance of £220, but he was dissatisfied with the resulting print and refused further payment. Delattre brought an action in king's bench to recover the balance. The trial on 2 July 1801 occupied the entire day; Delattre called fourteen witnesses, who declared that the sixty portraits depicted were all good likenesses, and that the print was worth at least £800. Copley's twelve witnesses considered the likenesses to be poor. The jury found for Delattre, who received the outstanding £580. *The Times* later commented that the real defect of the print was that it depicted equally strong likenesses in all lights and at all distances.

Delattre and his family resided in one of the small houses known as St John's Villas, on North End Road, Fulham, London. A watercolour, now in the British Museum, was made of Delattre one year before his death on 30 June 1840. The inscription on his tomb in Fulham churchyard declares that he was in his ninety-eighth year, which would have brought his birth forward to 1742 or 1743. His wife, who died in 1834 aged eighty-four, and his eldest daughter, who died in 1851 aged seventy-one, are also commemorated on this tomb.

F. T. MARZIALS, *rev.* TIMOTHY CLAYTON and ANITA MCCONNELL

Sources Redgrave, *Artists* · A. W. Tuer, *Bartolozzi and his works*, 2 vols. [1882] · *Dictionnaire biographique française*, fasc. 57 (1963), 733–4 · *The Times* (3 July 1801), 3b · *The Times* (4 July 1801), 4d · C. J. Feret, *Fulham old and new*, 3 vols. (1900), vols. 1 and 2 · *Memoirs and recollections of the late Abraham Raimbach*, ed. M. T. S. Raimbach (1843) · tombstone, Fulham churchyard, London
Likenesses E. Bell, watercolour drawing, BM

Delaune, Gideon (1564/5–1659), apothecary, was born in Nîmes, France, the eldest of the ten children of William *Delaune (*c.*1530–1611), physician and Reformed protestant minister, and Katherine des Loges (*d.* 1607). Paul *Delaune was a younger brother. The family moved to England in 1572–3, to escape the persecution of Huguenots in France, and settled in the Blackfriars precinct in London some time about 1575. Although it is not known where he received his medical training, by 1590 Delaune was established as an apothecary in Blackfriars and was married to another French immigrant, Judith Chamberlen. This marriage and his sister Sarah's subsequent marriage to Judith's cousin, Pierre Chamberlen, tightly connected Delaune to this other prominent

Huguenot refugee medical family, whose members were principally known for their contributions to obstetrics. Judith died in 1631, and Delaune remained a widower for eighteen years before he married Jane Johnson on 31 May 1649. Jane was still living at the time of his death in 1659.

Some time between 1606 and 1610 Delaune was appointed apothecary for Anne of Denmark, James I's queen. Together with the king's physician, Théodore Turquet de Mayerne, another Huguenot refugee, Delaune pressed for the formation of a separate guild or society for apothecaries, who at that time were subsumed within the Grocers' Company. In 1610 he was the foremost advocate of a parliamentary bill that would have distinguished apothecaries from grocers. That bill failed, but in December 1617 James I did grant a charter incorporating apothecaries into a separate society, placing them, however, under the ultimate supervision of the College of Physicians. Delaune, one of the original members of the new society named in the charter, immediately took an active and prominent part in the life of the new body. He headed the first court of assistants of the society, and in 1618 oversaw the revision of the *Pharmacoepia Londoniensis*, which set out the proper ingredients of the goods which members of the society could make and sell. After the City of London made him a freeman in 1623, Delaune served as underwarden of the society in 1624–5, upper-warden in 1627, and master in 1628–9 and again in 1636–7. In 1632 he provided the property for the building of Apothecaries' Hall in Blackfriars, the area of London where he resided throughout his life in England. An entry in the court minutes of the society in 1648 acknowledged Delaune as 'a principal means for the procuring of the said company to be made a corporation and for the purchasing of the capital messuage now belonging to the said company called Apothecaries' Hall'.

Delaune was also one of the foremost members of the Huguenot immigrant community in the capital, which gathered together in the autonomous French church in Threadneedle Street, London. The minister of this church, Nathaniel Marie, was his brother-in-law, while Delaune's own brother Pierre was minister to the Huguenot congregation in Norwich. Delaune himself served as a deacon of the London church from 1593 to 1596, and as elder from at least 1614 and throughout the 1620s. In 1621 he served on its delegations, which called on the archbishop of Canterbury and the privy council to argue for the preservation of the church's distinct Calvinist ecclesiastical discipline.

Delaune's alien birth at times impeded his participation in the political and economic life of London. In January 1626 he had to step down from the office of alderman of Dowgate Ward, to which he had been elected, because he was a 'stranger'. Although he only became a 'denizen' of the realm in April 1635, Delaune largely overcame the disabilities connected with his alien birth and was able to enter the circles of the native English élite. In 1613 the College of Arms awarded him and his brothers a coat 'of the arms of the family of Delaune of Belmesnil in Normandy, from which they were descended'. He owned the manor of Sharsted in Kent, an estate at Roxted in Bedfordshire,

shares of land in Virginia and Bermuda, and a mansion and ten tenements in Blackfriars, London. The two children from the twelve born to him who grew to adulthood both married into the English gentry. His daughter, Anne Delaune, married Sir Richard Sprignell, baronet, of Coppenthorpe, Yorkshire; his son, Abraham Delaune, married Anne Sandys, the daughter of Sir Edwin Sandys of Northbourne Court, Kent.

A kinsman, Thomas Delaune, claims with a good deal of hyperbole in his *The Present State of London* (1681) that Delaune was worth £90,000 at the time of his death at Blackfriars in 1659 (p. 330). Much of this great wealth probably came from the sales of 'Delaune's pill', which Thomas Delaune claimed 'is in great request to this day, notwithstanding the swarms of pretenders to pill-making' (ibid.). Gideon Delaune's will and a funeral certificate from the College of Arms both claim that he was aged ninety-four years at his death. He left £1000 for his burial and was buried on 3 March 1659 in the churchyard of St Anne Blackfriars; the funeral was conducted by the College of Arms and followed the ceremony usually reserved for an alderman of London.

CHARLES G. D. LITTLETON

Sources F. N. L. Poynter, *Gideon Delaune and his family circle* (1965) · C. Wall and H. Cameron, *History of the worshipful society of apothecaries*, ed. E. A. Underwood, 1 (1963) · L. G. Matthews, 'London's immigrant apothecaries, 1600–1800', *Medical History*, 18 (1974), 262–74 · L. G. Matthews, *History of pharmacy in Britain* (1962), 49–55 · L. G. Matthews, *The royal apothecaries* (1967), 98–100 · B. Burch, 'The parish of St Anne's Blackfriars, London, to 1665', *Guildhall Miscellany*, 3 (1969–71), 1–54 · *The registers of the French church, Threadneedle Street, London*, 1, ed. W. J. C. Moens, Huguenot Society of London, 9 (1896) · I. Scouloudi, *Returns of strangers in the metropolis, 1593, 1627, 1635, 1639: a study of an active minority*, Huguenot Society of London, 57 (1985) · R. E. G. Kirk and E. F. Kirk, eds., *Returns of aliens dwelling in the city and suburbs of London, from the reign of Henry VIII to that of James I*, 4 vols., Huguenot Society of London, 10 (1900–08) · Consistory 'Actes', 1588–1615, French Protestant Church of London, Soho Square, MS 4 · 'Actes', 1615–80, French Protestant Church of London, Soho Square, MS 5 · parish register, St Ann Blackfriars, GL, manuscripts section, MSS 4508–10 · A. B. Beaven, ed., *The aldermen of the City of London, temp. Henry III–[1912]*, 2 (1913), 59 · PRO, PROB 11/293, fols. 239–41 · PRO, PROB 11/286, fol. 45v

Likenesses attrib. C. Johnson, oils, 1640, Apothecaries' Hall, Blackfriars, London · N. Young, marble bust, c.1676, Apothecaries' Hall, Blackfriars, London

Wealth at death approx. £90,000: Thomas Delaune, *The present state of London* (1681)

Delaune, Paul (c.1585–1655?), medical practitioner, was born in the parish of St Anne Blackfriars, London, the youngest of the four surviving sons of the Huguenot immigrant William *Delaune (c.1530–1611), physician and Reformed minister, and Katherine des Loges (d. 1607). He was thus the youngest brother of the wealthy Blackfriars apothecary Gideon *Delaune.

Paul Delaune was educated at Emmanuel College, Cambridge, where he proceeded MA in 1610. He graduated MD at the University of Padua on 13 October 1614, the degree being incorporated at Cambridge on 4 November 1615. He was examined before the censors' board of the College of Physicians on 8 September 1615, was admitted a candidate of the college on 25 June 1616, and became a fellow on 21

April 1618. During the previous year (22 November 1617) he married, in his parish of St Anne Blackfriars, Sarah Argent the sister of John Argent who was to be eight times president of the College of Physicians (1625–33).

When Lord Falkland was appointed lord deputy of Ireland in 1622, Delaune accompanied him as his physician, and lived in Dublin for many years. There he worked for the formation of a college of physicians in Dublin, modelled on that in London, but this project was not realized until 1654, well after Delaune had left Ireland. By 24 May 1642 (by which time his wife had died) he was in London again, when he was made an elect, and in 1643 senior censor, of the College of Physicians. On 13 June 1643, after the withdrawal of Thomas Winston to the continent, Delaune was appointed professor of physic in Gresham College through the influence of Thomas Chamberlane, a member of the Mercers' Company. For over nine years Delaune carried out his professorial duties with efficiency and success. On 27 June 1643 he volunteered to act as one of three college physicians serving the parliamentary army under the earl of Essex. Delaune's involvement in the parliamentary cause, his education at Emmanuel College, and his service as an elder of the French church of London from 1651 to 1654 strongly suggest that he was of puritan religious inclinations.

In 1652 Thomas Winston returned to England and was restored to the Gresham professorship. For some time after his compulsory resignation of the chair of physic Delaune was in straitened circumstances. In 1654 he accepted from Cromwell the appointment of physician-general to the fleet that was about to embark to capture Hispaniola as part of the 'western design'. He was probably present at the capture of Jamaica in 1655, but appears to have been been lost at sea shortly thereafter, as the fleet on its return could give no information regarding his whereabouts.

John Ward, in his *Lives of the Professors of Gresham College* (1740), writes of Delaune that 'He was naturally of an easy temper, and chearful with a small fortune, temperate and frugal himself, tho indulgent to his children some of whom probably survived him' (Ward, 268–9). His will of 13 December 1654 mentions three children: his son and heir, Benjamin Delaune, a merchant of the East India Company, and his daughters, Elizabeth and Olave.

A. W. RENTON, *rev.* CHARLES G. D. LITTLETON

Sources F. N. L. Poynter, *Gideon Delaune and his family circle* (1965) · Munk, *Roll* · J. Ward, *The lives of the professors of Gresham College* (1740), 268–9 · A. H. T. Robb-Smith, 'Cambridge medicine', *Medicine in seventeenth century England: a symposium held … in honor of C. D. O'Malley* [Berkeley 1974], ed. A. G. Debus (1974), 327–69, esp. 359–66 · J. D. H. Widdess, *A history of the Royal College of Physicians of Ireland, 1654–1963* (1963), 4–6 · Venn, *Alum. Cant.* · parish register, St Ann Blackfriars, GL, MSS 4508–4510 · will, PRO, PROB 11/117, sig. 23 · G. Clark and A. M. Cooke, *A history of the Royal College of Physicians of London*, 1 (1964) · I. Scouloudi, *Returns of strangers in the metropolis, 1593, 1627, 1635, 1639: a study of an active minority*, Huguenot Society of London, 57 (1985)
Archives BL, medical diary and pharmacopoeia, Sloane MS 890
Wealth at death not wealthy: 6 June 1657, will, PRO, PROB 11/265, fol. 329v

Delaune, Thomas (d. 1685), religious writer, was born at Brinny in co. Cork, Ireland. His parents were poor Roman Catholics who rented a farm from Major Edward Riggs, a wealthy Cromwellian soldier who had settled on a large estate about 7 miles from the town of Cork in 1651 and who also had a partnership in a nearby fishery. Riggs, who was the founder of Cork Baptist Church, was sufficiently impressed with Delaune's intellectual giftedness that he provided for his education until Delaune was about sixteen. The young Catholic became a Baptist largely through the influence of Riggs. For several years Delaune was the clerk of a pilchard fishery near Kinsale, which may very well have been the one in which Riggs had a share. Delaune's embrace of protestantism, though, brought upon him obloquy from his Catholic neighbours and this eventually compelled him to settle in England.

Not long after his arrival Delaune made the acquaintance of Edward Hutchinson, a Baptist minister with experience in Ireland, whose daughter Hanna he subsequently married. The couple made their home in London, where Delaune provided a livelihood for his family by keeping a grammar school and publishing religious works. A number of theological tracts and treatises came from his pen during the 1670s and early 1680s. Some of them took up the defence of Baptist principles against various paedobaptist authors, including the prominent nonconformist Richard Baxter. Delaune was clearly highly regarded by the leadership of the London Particular Baptist community. In July 1675, for instance, he co-authored a book with Hanserd Knollys, William Kiffin, and three others that defended believers' baptism. Six years later Delaune and Benjamin Keach co-authored the monumental *Tropologia: a Key to Open Scripture Metaphors* (1682), which sought to give the interpreter of scripture a solid grasp of the various tropes, metaphors, and similes in the Bible. In it Keach owned his debt of gratitude to Delaune, whom he called his 'Friend', for the work was far 'too heavy for a single Undertaker' (foreword, *Tropologia*, book 2). It is clear from *Tropologia* that Delaune was fully conversant with Hebrew, Greek, and Latin, and that he had read widely in classical authors such as Virgil and Pliny the younger, a number of church fathers including Tertullian and Gregory of Nazianzus, and various Reformed divines. By his own admission, he was never ordained.

Other writings, better known, defended nonconformity. Delaune's *A Plea for the Non-Conformists* (1683) was issued in response to a sermon by the Anglican minister Benjamin Calamy about the 'scrupulous conscience' of dissent. Calamy maintained that dissenters had no just cause to separate from the Church of England. In fact, he argued, their separation was about 'mere niceties' and thus their 'wayward skittish Consciences ought to be well bridled and restrained' (B. Calamy, *A Discourse about a Scrupulous Conscience*, 1683). In response Delaune's tract argued that the dissenters had as much reason to separate from the Church of England as the latter did from Rome. Moreover, they did not separate over trivial matters, but profound spiritual issues. Delaune also defended religious toleration. 'I cannot find', he wrote, 'that Christ or his disciples, ever … *Newgated* scrupulous consciences to conformity' (*Plea*, pt 3). Convinced that *A Plea* 'contained things dangerous to the government' (*Plea*, pt 3), government authorities ordered Delaune's arrest on 29 November 1683. He was tried in January 1684 at the Old Bailey on a charge of sedition and found guilty, despite the fact that nothing seditious had been said in his book. He was fined 100 marks (just under £67), but because he was unable to pay he was kept in Newgate prison. Delaune's books were also publicly burnt in front of the Royal Exchange, London. His wife and two children soon joined him in prison. The utterly miserable conditions in the prison broke their health and the entire family perished there, Delaune dying last, in 1685.

Tropologia and Delaune's *Plea* were the two literary pieces by which posterity would remember Delaune. The *Plea* became something of a standard nonconformist apology, reprinted up to the beginning of the nineteenth century. Daniel Defoe, who wrote the preface to a 1706 edition, noted something of the irony in this: surely, he asked, the dissenters, whose 'champion' Delaune was, could have raised the money to have paid his fine and thus freed him.　　　　　　　MICHAEL A. G. HAYKIN

Sources T. Crosby, *The history of the English Baptists, from the Reformation to the beginning of the reign of King George I*, 4 vols. (1738–40), vol. 2 · C. Thompson, *Delaune: the English Baptist martyr* (Philadelphia, 1870) · K. Herlihy, '"A gay and flattering world": Irish Baptist piety and perspective, 1650–1780', *The religion of Irish dissent, 1650–1800* (Dublin, 1996) · St J. D. Seymour, *The puritans in Ireland, 1647–1661* (1912) · *Calendar of the correspondence of Richard Baxter*, ed. N. H. Keeble and G. F. Nuttall, 2 vols. (1991)

Delaune, William [*formerly* Guillaume de Laune] (*c.*1530–1611), Reformed minister and physician, was born at 'Bellenewell', near Dieppe, but little else is known about his background. In 1582 he said that he was aged fifty-two. He studied medicine for eight years at Paris and Montpellier, under Duretus and Rondelet. About 1558, having completed his medical training, he became a Reformed minister, most probably at Montpellier, combining this with the practice of medicine. He married Katherine des Loges (*d.* 1607) from Rouen, probably the daughter of a fellow minister, M. des Loges (*d.* 1570), at Uzès. In 1564 or 1565 their first son, Gideon *Delaune (*d.* 1659), was born at Nîmes; Isaac, Peter, Nathaniel, Paul *Delaune (*c.*1585–1655?), Sara, Ester, and Elizabeth were born subsequently.

Delaune initially served the churches of Générac and Beauvoisin in Lower Languedoc. On des Loges's death, Delaune took responsibility for his family, and in 1570 asked to be relieved of his church due to his extreme poverty. He seems to have returned to Normandy, where he may have had property, but in the wake of the St Bartholomew's day massacre (1572) took refuge in England, initially at Rye where he served as a minister. By 1575 he had moved to London, where he became an assistant minister in the French church. He also had contacts with Cambridge, corresponding with the professor of divinity, Peter Baro, but, with the support of the French church,

continued to practise medicine and as a result was summoned to appear before the College of Physicians in December 1582. He petitioned the college for permission to continue to practise as he depended upon it for his livelihood; the college agreed and he was made a licentiate. The following year he asked for permission to be released from his preaching duties in order to concentrate on medicine.

However, Delaune continued to be involved in religious matters. In 1583 he published an abridged version of Calvin's *Institutes*, entitled *Institutionis Christianae religionis a Joannes Calvins conscriptae epistome*; a second edition was published in 1584 and an English translation in 1585. He also retained his links with the continent. In 1599 he arranged for his son Nathaniel to be sponsored in his studies for the ministry by the Reformed church in Dieppe. Delaune died in London early in 1611; he was buried on 19 February at St Anne Blackfriars beside his wife, who had predeceased him.　　　　　　ANDREW SPICER

Sources D. C. A. Agnew, *Protestant exiles from France, chiefly in the reign of Louis XIV, or, The Huguenot refugees and their descendants in Great Britain and Ireland*, 3rd edn, 2 vols. (1886) · F. de Schickler, *Les églises du réfuge en Angleterre*, 3 vols. (Paris, 1892) · 'Les pasteurs d'une église des Cévennes au XVIe siècle (1561–1605)', *Bulletin Historique et Littéraire* [Société de l'Histoire du Protestantisme Français], 49 (1900) · G. Mayhew, *Tudor Rye* (1987) · R. R. James, 'A sixteenth century London physician's bond, 1585', *BMJ* (29 Oct 1927), 793 · I. Scouloudi, *Returns of strangers in the metropolis, 1593, 1627, 1635, 1639: a study of an active minority*, Huguenot Society of London, 57 (1985) · Munk, *Roll* · will, PRO, PROB 11/117, sig. 23 · annals, RCP Lond. · G. Daval and J. Daval, *Histoire de la Réformation à Dieppe, 1557–1657*, ed. E. Lesens, 2 vols. (Rouen, 1878–9) · F. N. L. Poynter, 'Gideon De Laune and his family circle', the Gideon De Laune lecture, 1964, 1965, Wellcome L.

Wealth at death property in Blackfriars, London: will, 1611, PRO, PROB 11/117, sig. 23

Delaune, William (1659–1728), college head, was born on 14 April 1659 and baptized on 26 April at St Stephen, Coleman Street, London, the son of Benjamin Delaune of London, and Margaret, daughter of George Coney, a wealthy London merchant, and possibly grandson of Paul *Delaune (*c.*1585–1655?). Educated at Merchant Taylors' School, London, from 1672, he proceeded to St John's College, Oxford, in 1675. He graduated BA in 1679, and proceeded MA in 1683 and BD in 1688. Once ordained he became chaplain to Peter Mews, bishop of Winchester, who presented him to the living of Chilbolton, Hampshire, in 1689.

In 1697 Delaune proceeded DD, and on 12 March 1698 was elected president of St John's, allegedly on account of his inherited wealth. Installed as a canon of Winchester in 1701, he was appointed vice-chancellor of the University of Oxford in October of the following year. As vice-chancellor, Delaune was chairman of the delegates to the university press. During his tenure of this office, which lasted until October 1706, the press's income (including the profits from the first two editions of Clarendon's *History of the Great Rebellion*) was calculated to be £2773 3*s.* 9*d.* Only £493 of this sum had been paid into the university chest, Delaune borrowing much of the remainder, probably to finance gambling debts. Thomas Hearne charged him, perhaps unfairly, with embezzlement. Delaune admitted making advances to himself out of the university exchequer but claimed he had every intention of repaying. When he was sued in 1709 by the chancellor's court for £231 1s. 2d., Delaune appears to have agreed to pay £300 in two portions. Canon William Stratford claimed that when Delaune admitted that he was unable to pay, the income from his college presidency was sequestered, but there is no evidence to confirm this. However, Delaune did default, and his successor to the vice-chancellorship, William Lancaster, determined to recover the debt in full. He charged Delaune with owing £2280 3s. 9d., the difference between the press's income during Delaune's delegacy and the amount actually paid to the university. Lancaster met with no success, so obtained an order from the chancellor's court to sequester both Delaune's rectory of Long Hanborough, Oxfordshire, and his Winchester prebend. Between 1711 and 1720 a sum of £2590 2s. was recovered.

Hearne suggested that an affection for cards and dice was the vice which contributed principally to Delaune's financial difficulties, and the outburst against the vice-chancellor by the 'terrae filius' at the Act (encaenia) in 1703 confirmed that there were scandals attributable to Delaune. Nicholas Amhurst, expelled from St John's in 1719 by the president and fellows, printed a revengeful account of the encaenia incident in his series of pamphlets, *Terrae filius*, first published in 1721. Amhurst is also thought to have written the accusatory *Letter from a Student in Grubb Street* (1720).

Delaune is said to have lost his considerable fortune, as well as the money borrowed from the university chest and from colleagues. His financial situation was perilous; in 1711 his tory friends, notably the future lord chancellor, Simon Harcourt, were pressed to help. Harcourt planned to obtain for Delaune the lucrative bishopric of Raphoe. Two years later another attempt was made to secure for him the see of Derry. In spite of the chancellor's influence, Delaune was appointed to neither.

In 1715 Delaune successfully stood for election to the Lady Margaret divinity professorship. It was said that Delaune had swung the election in his favour by calling in all the bachelors of divinity who had left the university in debt; only two heads of houses and six doctors of divinity voted for him. Ironically, he was also appointed a delegate of the press and of accounts in 1721. The publication in 1728 of *Twelve Sermons upon Several Subjects and Occasions* (fulsomely dedicated to Lord Abingdon) was also an attempt to relieve his deep debts.

Delaune, of tory persuasion, did not allow his personal politics to interfere with potential advancement. In 1704 he had allied himself to the rising Robert Harley and developed close relations with Harcourt, Henry Sacheverell, and Francis Atterbury, but when times changed Delaune changed with them. Although chaplain to Queen Anne from 1703, during which time he acquired some reputation as a preacher (although Thomas Wagstaff declared that Delaune knew little of theology or patristics), Delaune determined that the queen's death in 1714 would not jeopardize his future; in spite of his personal politics he made sure to be seen praying for the new king some hours before it was announced that Anne had died, and was quick to dissociate himself from Harley in decline.

Delaune died, unmarried, on 23 May 1728, and was buried without the usual eulogistic epitaph in St John's College chapel. Wagstaff's humorous epitaph suggests that Delaune's appearance, with his broad-brimmed hat which put him into perpetual shade, his wide and flapping collars, and his agitated hand movements, were sufficient to make him both very noticeable and, apparently, distressing to young ladies. J. H. CURTHOYS

Sources W. C. Costin, *The history of St John's College, Oxford, 1598–1860*, OHS, new ser., 12 (1958) · H. Carter, *A history of the Oxford University Press*, 1: *To the year 1780* (1975) · Foster, *Alum. Oxon.* · N. Amhurst, *Terrae filius* (1721) · [N. Amhurst], *Letter from a student in Grubb Street* (1720) · Nichols, *Lit. anecdotes*, vol. 1

Delaval family (*per. c.*1520–1752), landowners and industrialists of Hartley and Seaton Delaval, Northumberland, were descended from immigrants who arrived in England at or just after the Norman conquest and acquired land in the area of Hartley in the twelfth century. Thus by about 1219 Gilbert Delaval, lord of Callerton, owned an estate there, probably of about 100 acres of land, a coalmine, and some cottages. The township would appear to have been quite prosperous by the end of the thirteenth century, with a fishery and salt pans—natural bedfellows for a coastal township with shallow coals. Coal and salt were, indeed, the spurs to the industrial development of the Hartley area, and in the sixteenth century the salt pans of **Sir John Delaval** (1498–1562) were said to produce salt which was 'esteemed by sutche as buye the same to be better than any other white salt' (Earnshaw, 4). Evidently the salt and coal trades were already considerable revenue earners for the family, and it was said of Sir John a few years after his death that he 'hath been a patron of worship and hospitality, most like a famous gentleman during many years, and powdreth no man by the salt of extortion of oppressing his neighbour, but liberally spendeth his salt, wheat and malt like a gentleman' (Hedley, 150). Knighted by 1519, he was five times high sheriff of Northumberland between 1527 and 1554, a position which many of his descendants were to occupy. He married Mary, daughter of Thomas Carey of Chilton, Wiltshire.

The lands in Hartley in the early sixteenth century were held by the crown and by other families besides the Delavals, but much of the township was being leased to the latter and Sir Robert Delaval (*c.*1541–1607), grandson of Sir John, bought out all the freeholders between 1574 and 1577. He converted the tillage lands to pasture and effectively annexed the manor of Hartley to that of his manor of Seaton Delaval in 1578. Thereafter Hartley and Seaton Delaval remained with the Delavals until the early nineteenth century.

Sir Robert had married Dorothy Grey (*d.* before 1600) and was succeeded by his eldest son, **Sir Ralph Delaval** (*c.*1576–1628), who married Jane Hilton (*d.* 1645). Little is known about his public life other than that he was high sheriff for Northumberland in 1604, 1608, and 1621, and that he was knighted in 1608. However, his youngest son, Thomas, wrote an affectionate portrait of his father as a man who:

> kept an open, great and plentiful house for entertainment, his own family consisting daily in his house of threescore persons and above … His life was religious. He kept a chaplain ever in his house that read public prayers daily in his house and preached each Sunday commonly in his chapel and taught and educated his children. He governed his people in excellent order, and stocked and managed his whole estate himself, directing his servants daily their several labours. He kept also the books of his cattle, corn, etc., and how they were disposed. He never rid to any public assembly without five or six men in liveries and two or three of his sons to attend him. He never affected drinking. Cards nor dice, he never could abide them … His apparel ever decent not rich. He was a man of voluble tongue, excellent discourse and of good memory. He understood the Latin and Greek tongues, and in his younger days did write of several subjects. He understood the laws of the land expertly. His times of private devotions were daily—at morn, noon and night. He loved hunting but left it off long ere he died. He was very zealous in religion which he openly professed to the last, and, having settled his estate … taken the communion, blessed his wife and children and desiring absolution of his sins from the minister, which done, within 24 hours he made a calm and quiet period of his life. (Hedley, 152)

The annual rental of Sir Ralph's estates amounted to £1991 13s. 8d. by the 1620s, and against this the yearly outlay in family annuities, rents, and wages amounted to £311 6s. 4d. At his death, on 24 November 1628, his personal estate was valued at £2934 6s. 9d.

Sir Ralph was succeeded by his son Sir Robert Delaval (1600–1623), who had married Barbara Selby (d. 1679), and then by their only son, **Sir Ralph Delaval**, first baronet (1622–1691). Until this time any potential expansion of the coal and salt trades was limited by the fact that seagoing trading vessels could not use the small haven at Hartley, so that coal and salt had to be carried from Hartley to the Blyth or the Tyne for shipment. About 1670 this disadvantageous situation was rectified by Sir Ralph by the building of a pier—after two unsuccessful attempts—at the mouth of the burn, 'and so it stood', noted Sir Francis North in 1676, 'and was very useful to him in his trade of Salt and Coal' (Emsley, 16). The building of the pier was followed by the creation of a tidal sluicing system to clear the harbour of river-borne silt and tide-washed sand, also seen by North. Thereafter the harbour became known as Seaton Sluice, and this harbour sluicing system so impressed John Smeaton, who examined it some eighty years later, that he recommended a similar system in his famous harbour plan for Ramsgate. The £7000 which Sir Ralph had spent on his harbour works persuaded Charles II to make him collector and surveyor of his own port, and it would seem that he then built a second pier, presumably on the opposite side of the mouth of the burn to the first, having been offered a £1500 grant towards its construction by the king. One-third of this grant had been paid at the time of Charles's death in 1685, but the remainder was never forthcoming.

On 2 April 1646 Sir Ralph had married the widowed Lady Anne Fraser (d. 1696), daughter of General Alexander Leslie, earl of Leven, commander of the Scottish army which had stormed and taken Newcastle only two years before; one month after the marriage Leslie was holding Charles I prisoner in the town. In 1649 Sir Ralph became the first high sheriff of Northumberland appointed by the Commonwealth, and he entered Richard Cromwell's parliament as a knight of the shire for Northumberland in 1659, being re-elected after the Restoration. He was made a baronet on 29 June 1660 and, after a fifteen-year absence from the house, he was elected to the long-lasting Cavalier Parliament at a by-election in 1677, subsequently supporting the court party; he was re-elected to the three subsequent parliaments.

In spite of the success of the harbour at Seaton Sluice the Delaval estates around Hartley seem to have been in a parlous state by the late 1680s and Sir Ralph attempted to amend this situation by making advantageous marriage arrangements for his sons—he and his wife had seven sons and three daughters. His first son, Robert (1647–1682), apparently a sickly young man, was married to Lady Elizabeth Livingston (1648?–1717), daughter of James, earl of Newburgh, in 1670 [see Delaval, Lady Elizabeth]; Lady Elizabeth was a noted beauty at the court of Charles II but the marriage was not a success and had effectively ended before Robert's death without an heir. In 1684 Sir Ralph arranged the marriage of his eldest surviving son, another Sir Ralph (1649–1696), to Diana Booth (d. 1713), daughter of Lord Delamere. He settled the succession of the estates on this son and his heirs male, and failing any, upon the next surviving son **Sir John Delaval**, third baronet (bap. 1654, d. 1729), subject to a payment of £8000 for any daughters born to Ralph and Diana. Sir John had married Mary Goodyer (1659/60–1683) in 1683, but she died after a few months of marriage; he later had a daughter, Ann (c.1689–1723), but there is no evidence for a second marriage. He had a distinguished military career, served in many campaigns in Flanders, and rose to become colonel in the guards; he was elected MP for Morpeth, Northumberland, in 1701 and 1702.

His brother Sir Ralph died five years after their father, leaving only a daughter, Diana (1686–1710). His personal estate went to pay his creditors, while the Seaton Delaval and Hartley estates devolved upon his widow, Diana, under the terms of their marriage settlement, and Sir John came into possession of Seaton Sluice, the coalmines, quarries, and salt pans. Diana married again in October 1699; her husband, Sir Edward *Blackett (1649–1718) [see under Blackett, Sir William] of Newby in Yorkshire, tightened his grip on the £8000 portion by marrying his stepdaughter Diana to his own eldest son, William, within two months of his own marriage. The younger Diana was only thirteen years old at the time, but there was a clear advantage to Sir Edward in having her both as stepdaughter and daughter-in-law. At the same time Blackett ensured that the £8000 should be paid to him rather than to his son, and in 1709 he secured an agreement from the sole surviving trustee for the settlement, that 6 per cent interest should be charged on the £8000 from 1691.

Meanwhile Sir John Delaval was facing familiar problems with the deterioration of a pier at the harbour, and he attempted to recoup his £500 outlay on its repair by seeking to recover the remainder of Charles II's earlier offer of a grant to his father. In his unsuccessful argument Sir John noted the great benefits that had accrued from Sir Ralph's work; eight salt pans were now at work, the excise on salt alone averaging £5000 per annum, and during the year 1704 some 1400 chaldrons (nearly 3700 tons) of coal had been exported. But even greater financial problems faced Sir John as he was presented with his brother-in-law's claim arising from the marriage settlement, the sum at issue having increased through interest charges to £14,624 by the time of the former Lady Delaval's death in 1713. Sir John put forward his own claims to Seaton Delaval and Hartley on Diana's death, but faced with Blackett's claim, which was confirmed by a court order of 1715, and which amounted to a sum well beyond his means, it was inevitable that he should have to sell off a large portion of his property, namely the manor of Seaton.

The only member of the family in a position to rescue the situation was Admiral **George Delaval** (*bap.* 1668, *d.* 1723), of a branch of the family settled at Dissington in Northumberland. The third son of George Delaval (*c.*1628–1695) and Margaret Grey (*d.* 1709), the admiral became MP for West Looe in 1715 and 1722, but it was his combined naval and diplomatic careers—he had been employed in embassies in Morocco and Portugal—that brought him sufficient wealth to pay off various fractious and impoverished members of the family. During 1718 he bought Sir John out of Seaton and Hartley, paid off Blackett, purchased the Bavington estate in Northumberland, and commissioned Vanbrugh to design Seaton Delaval Hall as a replacement for the old Delaval Castle; Sir John was left with a life interest in Hartley and Seaton Sluice. Admiral Delaval, who never married, gained little of the fruits of his enterprise for he was thrown from his horse and promptly died of his injuries in 1723; Seaton Delaval Hall was still six years from completion, and Vanbrugh himself died three years later and was, therefore, never to see his finest work completed. Gutted by fire in the early nineteenth century, its shell survives as a dramatically angular conflation of differing elements—classical, medieval, and contemporary—all tightly bound together in a startling unity.

The admiral's will, made a few weeks before his death, devised Bavington to his sister's son George Shafto and the remainder of his estates to his brother's son, **Francis Blake Delaval** (*bap.* 1692, *d.* 1752), the son of Edward Delaval of South Dissington (*bap.* 1664, *d.* 1744) and Mary Ord, *née* Blake (*c.*1664–1711). Francis, a naval captain in the impress service, had inherited the Ford estate in north Northumberland from his maternal grandfather, Francis Blake, in 1718, and under the terms of that will he replaced his Delaval surname with that of Blake. On succeeding to Admiral Delaval's estates Francis also added his original

surname. In 1729 he inherited Sir John Delaval's possessions, including Seaton Sluice. In 1724 Francis had married Rhoda Apreece (*d.* 1759), heir of Sir Thomas Hussey of Doddington, Lincolnshire, her maternal grandfather, and she brought the Doddington estate to the marriage as part of her dowry; Francis could now afford to finish off the building of Seaton Delaval Hall. The income from the estates was perhaps £6000 per annum when Francis inherited, and it seems to have remained at about that level until he died. All of his properties were settled on his eldest son, Sir Francis (1727–1771), of a family of eight sons and four daughters, but the future fortunes of the Delavals were to rest upon the second son, John Hussey *Delaval, Baron Delaval (1728–1808), industrialist and politician. The third son was Edward Hussey *Delaval (*bap.* 1729, *d.* 1814), natural philosopher.   STAFFORD M. LINSLEY

Sources *A history of Northumberland*, Northumberland County History Committee, 15 vols. (1893–1940) · W. P. Hedley, *Northumberland families*, 2 vols., Society of Antiquaries of Newcastle upon Tyne, Record Series (1968–70) · E. Mackenzie, *An historical, topographical, and descriptive view of the county of Northumberland*, 2nd edn, 2 vols. (1825) · K. Emsley, 'A circuit judge in Northumberland', *Tyne & Tweed*, 31 (spring 1978), 13–18 · F. Askham, *The gay Delavals* (1955) · T. S. Earnshaw, *Hartley and old Seaton Sluice* (1957)

Archives Northumbd RO, Newcastle upon Tyne, family MSS
Wealth at death £2934 6s. 9d.—Sir Ralph Delaval (*d.* 1628)

Delaval, Edward Hussey (*bap.* **1729**, *d.* **1814**), natural philosopher, was baptized at Newburn, Northumberland, on 12 June 1729, the third son of Francis Blake *Delaval (*bap.* 1692, *d.* 1752) [*see under* Delaval family], landowner of Seaton Delaval and Ford Castle, Northumberland, and of Doddington, Lincolnshire, and his wife, Rhoda (*d.* 1759), daughter of Robert Apreece of Washingley, Huntingdonshire. He was admitted a fellow-commoner at Pembroke College, Cambridge, on 4 July 1747; he graduated BA in 1750 and MA in 1754, and was elected a fellow in 1755. When his eldest brother, Sir Francis Blake Delaval, died in 1771, his elder brother, John Hussey *Delaval (1728–1808), succeeded to the Northumberland estates; he was made Baron Delaval of Seaton Delaval in 1786. When the latter died childless in 1808 the barony was extinguished, and Edward Delaval succeeded to the entailed estates at Seaton Delaval, having already inherited Doddington in 1774. On 22 December 1808 he married Sarah, daughter of George Scott of Methley, Yorkshire; they had no children.

Delaval was an accomplished musician and classicist, with a knowledge of French, German, and Italian. At Cambridge, under the influence of John Mickleburgh, professor of chemistry, he became interested in Newtonian natural philosophy and the experimental ramifications of Newton's work in chemistry, electricity, and optics. His family patronized the portrait painter and electrician Benjamin Wilson, and in 1759 Delaval supported Wilson's theory of two electric fluids with some ingenious experiments on conductivity, which were published in the Royal Society's *Philosophical Transactions* (51, 1759, 83–8; 52, 1761, 353–6). This led to a dispute with John Canton, who supported a one fluid theory. Delaval was elected a fellow of the Royal Society on 6 December 1759 (his certificate was signed by Wilson and Benjamin Franklin), and in 1764 he contributed an illustrated account of the effects of lightning on St Bride's, Fleet Street, London, to the *Philosophical Transactions*. In 1769 he was appointed with Franklin, Wilson, and William Watson to report to the society on the means of securing St Paul's against danger from lightning. When the cathedral was struck by lightning on 22 March 1772, Delaval gave an account of the damage. In the subsequent controversy between Franklin and Wilson on the merits of pointed or blunt lightning conductors to protect the powder works at Purfleet, Delaval sided with Wilson.

Following up Newton's *Opticks* (3rd edn, 1721), Delaval experimented on the specific gravities of gold, lead, silver, copper, and iron and their colours when united to glass or in solutions; for his paper on the subject, published in the *Philosophical Transactions* in 1765, he received the Royal Society's Copley medal. He believed that the 'bigness' (size) of the ultimate particles of metals might be deduced from their colours. He developed the subject in *An Experimental Inquiry into the Cause of the Changes of Colours in Opake and Coloured Bodies* (1777), the first fifty pages of which had been printed 'some years ago' (p. 55) and translated into French in 1774. A complete French translation was made by the dyer Quatremère Dijonval in 1778, and an Italian version appeared in 1779. Delaval's classical scholarship was revealed in a long historical preface on the dyeing and textile technologies of the ancients, his argument being that since a practical skill in dyeing depended upon the separation of matter into its smallest parts, the ancients were aware of the atomic nature of matter. The treatise was packed with interesting experiments on the colours of plant extracts, animal materials, and minerals, and Delaval suggested that the sky is blue because blue is the most refrangible colour and air is more minutely divided than any other medium (p. 92). In 1785 he was awarded the gold medal of the Manchester Literary and Philosophical Society for *An Experimental Inquiry into the Cause of the Permanent Colours of Opake Bodies*, which detailed his investigations of reflected and transmitted light. Implicit in all of his work on colours was a corpuscular theory of light; he also adhered to the phlogiston theory of chemical composition. Although he lived through the chemical revolution he published nothing after 1785; before then his writings were well known on the continent, and he was a member of the royal societies of Göttingen and Uppsala, and of the Institute of Bologna.

Among Delaval's minor achievements was the manufacture, under his direction, of an elaborate set of musical glasses. These inspired Franklin to design the armonica in 1761. Delaval also made artificial gems, and devised a method of extracting fluor (calcium fluoride) from glass, of which he left various coloured samples. His Gothic-styled house in Parliament Place, Westminster, London, was fireproofed with artificial stones made under his direction. He died in Parliament Place on 14 August 1814, and was buried in the nave of Westminster Abbey. His estates were inherited by a nephew, Sir Jacob Henry Astley, MP for Norfolk. W. H. BROCK

Sources DNB · C. Taylor, 'Biographical memoranda respecting Edward Hussey Delaval', *Philosophical Magazine*, 45 (1815), 29–32 · GM, 1st ser., 84/2 (1814), 293 · Venn, *Alum. Cant.* · E. H. Delaval, 'A letter … on the agreement between the specific gravities of the several metals and their colours', *PTRS*, 55 (1765), 10–38 · E. H. Delaval, *An experimental inquiry into the cause of the changes of colours in opake and coloured bodies* (1777) · E. H. Delaval, *An experimental inquiry into the cause of the permanent colours of opake bodies*, [another edn] (1785) · GEC, *Peerage*, new edn · J. Priestley, *The history and present state of electricity*, 3rd edn, 2 vols. (1775), 237–45 · *The papers of Benjamin Franklin*, 8, ed. L. W. Labaree (1965), 359–60; 10, ed. L. W. Labaree (1966), 74, 118–19; 16, ed. W. B. Willcox (1972), 145–51; 19, ed. W. B. Willcox (1975), 260 · I. B. Cohen, *Franklin and Newton* (1956) · L. J. M. Coleby, 'John Mickleburgh', *Annals of Science*, 8 (1952), 165–74

Likenesses portraits, Doddington Hall, Lincolnshire

Wealth at death inherited family estates in 1808; always man of independent means

Delaval [*née* Livingston], **Lady Elizabeth** (1648?–1717), memoirist and Jacobite agent, was the only child of James *Livingston, first earl of Newburgh (1621/2–1670), nobleman, and his first wife, Catherine (d. 1650), eldest daughter of Theophilus Howard, second earl of Suffolk, and widow of George Stuart, ninth seigneur d'Aubigny. Her parents were supporters of Charles I during the civil war and fled from Bagshot, Surrey, to The Hague in 1649. After the death of her mother in 1650, Lady Elizabeth was brought up by her father's sister, Dorothy, wife of the second Lord Stanhope, at Nocton, Lincolnshire, before being appointed in 1662, when she was fourteen, a maid of the privy chamber to Catherine of Braganza through the offices of her half-brother Charles *Stuart, third duke of Richmond.

Lady Elizabeth is of interest as the writer of a manuscript volume of memoirs and meditations, now in the Bodleian Library, whose entries cover events in her personal life between 1663 and 1672. The volume itself appears to have been created many years after the events described, a fair copy transcribed from notes and loose documents. Its contents, which were mistakenly classified by Kirchberger as a 'religious diary' (Kirchberger, 59) and by Craster as a 'common place book' (Craster, 'Notes', 149), consist of a series of long prose entries, prayers, transcribed letters, and a poem. The reader is assisted with dated, descriptive headings and helpful marginal glosses identifying various people mentioned, which suggests the volume was intended for a wider readership than just the author herself. Through her narration of her childhood and her romantic misadventures, the volume sheds light on the upbringing and marriage arrangements of a girl belonging to a prominent royalist family and documents the range and nature of the reading and writing habits of a late seventeenth-century Englishwoman composing her autobiography.

The early entries, written when Lady Elizabeth was fourteen, described selected events from her childhood that she saw as having shaped her character. She noted that she was very fond of reading romances, and that by the age of ten she had 'red severall great volumns of them; all Casander, the Grand Cyrus, Cleopatra and Astrea' (Bodl. Oxf., MS Rawl. D. 78, fol. 15). As a child she also appeared in several theatrical performances staged at Nocton, even persuading the family servants to act in a performance of Guarini's *Il pastor fido* with herself as Amaryllis. Interspersed among her accounts of the secular events of her life are prayers and meditations on her attempts to control her passions. Her rendering of the events of her life, however, is shaped more by the conventions of romance fiction than religious meditation.

After becoming a maid in the queen's household Lady Elizabeth quickly became disillusioned with court life, castigating herself for contracting debts she could not pay and flirting with attractive young men. She noted, without apparent irony, that the men behaved and spoke just like her favourite romance characters and described falling in love with James, Lord Annesley, son of the earl of Anglesey; according to her memoirs, it was her aunt and not her father who objected to this match. The conclusion of their relationship resembled a typically tangled seventeenth-century romance plot: Annesley gave way to pressure from his father and in 1669 married Lady Elizabeth Manners, sister of Lord Roos. Roos had, apparently, combined with Lady Stanhope to engineer the marriage with the design of removing Annesley from the scene and marrying Lady Elizabeth himself. The final entries of the memoir chronicled Lady Elizabeth's bitter disappointment with the fickleness of her lover, described her lack of interest in her father's choice for her marriage partner, Robert (1647–1682), son of Sir Ralph *Delaval of Seaton Delaval, Northumberland [*see under* Delaval family], and their subsequent lacklustre marriage, which commenced about July 1670. They had no children.

Lady Elizabeth did not complete her personal history, leaving the final third of the volume blank, but she lived on for many years. In November 1677 she unsuccessfully sought an appointment with the newly married Mary, princess of Orange, and in January 1682 she was reported to be in London but 'looks very plaine' (*Rutland MSS*, 2.64). Her husband died on 1 August 1682 and by a licence of 1 April 1686 Lady Elizabeth married Henry Hatcher of Kirby, Lincolnshire, who was aged about twenty-two. In 1689 she was involved in the so-called Pewter pot plot and a warrant was issued for her arrest for carrying correspondence from the exiled court of James II; the leader of this plot was Edward, Lord Griffin, the husband of her cousin Essex, both of whom are mentioned with affection in her memoirs. Abandoning England for France, Lady Elizabeth is said to have died in Rouen in 1717.

MARGARET J. M. EZELL

Sources M. Ezell, 'Elizabeth Delaval's spiritual heroine: thoughts on redefining manuscript texts by early women writers', *English manuscript studies, 1100–1700*, 3 (1992), 216–37 · *The meditations of Lady Elizabeth Delaval written between 1662 and 1671*, ed. D. Greene (1978) · H. Craster, 'Notes from a Delaval diary', *Proceedings of the Society of Antiquarians of Newcastle-upon-Tyne*, 3rd ser. (1903–4), 149–53 · J. L. Chester and G. J. Armytage, eds., *Allegations for marriage licences issued from the faculty office of the archbishop of Canterbury at London, 1543 to 1869*, Harleian Society, 24 (1886) · Bodl. Oxf., MS Rawl. D. 78 · L. Stone, *The family, sex, and marriage, 1500–1800* (1977) · M. Ezell, *The patriarch's wife: literary evidence and the history of the family* (1987) · Clarendon, *Hist. rebellion* · A. Hamilton, *Memoirs of the comte de Gramont*, trans. P. Quennell (1930) · *The manuscripts of his grace the duke of Rutland*, 4 vols., HMC, 24 (1888–1905), vols. 2, 4 · *The manuscripts of Sir William Fitzherbert … and others*, HMC, 32 (1893) · *A history of Northumberland*, Northumberland County History Committee, 15 vols. (1893–1940), vol. 10 · W. P. Hedley, *Northumberland families*, 1, Society of Antiquaries of Newcastle upon Tyne, Record Series (1968) · C. Kirchberger, 'A catalogue of Bodleian manuscripts relating to mystical theology, 16th–18th century', Bodl. Oxf., MS Eng. misc. d. 312, 59

Archives BL, letters, Add. MSS 21947–21948 · Bodl. Oxf., MS Rawl. D. 78

Delaval, Francis Blake (*bap.* 1692, *d.* 1752). *See under* Delaval family (*per.* c.1520–1752).

Delaval, George (*bap.* 1668, *d.* 1723). *See under* Delaval family (*per.* c.1520–1752).

Delaval, Sir John (1498–1562). *See under* Delaval family (*per.* c.1520–1752).

Delaval, Sir John, third baronet (*bap.* 1654, *d.* 1729). *See under* Delaval family (*per.* c.1520–1752).

Delaval, John Hussey, Baron Delaval (1728–1808), industrialist and politician, was born on 17 March 1728, the second of twelve children of Captain Francis Blake *Delaval RN (*bap.* 1692, *d.* 1752) [*see under* Delaval family] and his wife, Rhoda Apreece (*d.* 1759), heiress, of Doddington, Lincolnshire [*see* Delaval family (*per.* c.1520–1752)]. His father, born Francis Delaval, changed his name to Francis Blake on inheriting the Ford estate in north Northumberland in 1718, and then to Francis Blake Delaval in 1729, on inheriting the coal-rich coastal estates at Seaton Delaval and at Hartley in south-east Northumberland. His younger brother was Edward Hussey *Delaval. John Delaval was educated at Westminster School and Eton College. He went to Pembroke College, Cambridge, in 1746, but his academic career was curtailed when the 'Captain Hargreaves' living with him proved to be female. He married Susanna Potter, *née* Robinson (*d.* 1783), widow of John Potter, on 2 April 1750, thereby acquiring property in Soho and Mayfair, Westminster. By 1756 he had effectively superseded his hedonistic and profligate elder brother Francis as head of the family, and the fortunes of the estates, then carrying debts of £45,000, thereafter depended upon him.

Ford, a rural and largely barren estate of about 7000 acres, was enclosed and divided by Delaval. By 1794 plantations had been established, and farmsteads extended or rebuilt, at a cost of £9000; another £10,500 was devoted to remodelling the castle. Delaval favoured improving farm leases and having 'practical' farmers as tenants—having a known dislike of gentlemen farmers—and was able to increase the estate rental from about £1000 to nearly £5000 by 1794. Existing collieries and limeworks were extended, and a brick and tile works and an iron forge were established. As an industrial centre Hartley was always more significant than Ford. Because of its natural harbour, there had been fishing, coalmining, and salt making since the thirteenth century, but Delaval added considerably to these activities. Under skilled agents, pumping engines and wagon-ways were introduced at the pits. The increased coal outputs, together with the establishment of a glass-bottle works in 1762, then required an improved harbour, and this was achieved in 1764 at a reputed cost of £10,000.

The improved harbour at Seaton Sluice allowed faster turnaround times for the collier brigs, thereby increasing the vend and market price of Hartley coals. It also facilitated the import of raw materials for the glassworks, and the export of its products. By 1788, Delaval's Royal Northumberland Bottle Works had become the largest such enterprise in the country, a position it held until the 1800s, its output having reached 200,000 dozen bottles per year. Copperas production was also begun, using iron pyrites found in some coals, to provide a colouring agent for the glassworks, and also for export. The glass and copperas works, like the salt works before them, utilized the almost unsaleable small coals from the Hartley pits.

Delaval encouraged his agents to be innovative in these developments, but he maintained close overall control, except for a period after 1764 when family disagreements saw his younger brother Thomas assume responsibility for the Hartley enterprises. Thomas was no businessman, however, and his financial difficulties enabled John to resume control in 1771. This was a prelude to further family upsets. John had succeeded to the Doddington estate in 1759 (adding Hussey to his name), only to lose it to his brother Edward in 1774. Having spent £17,000 on improvements there, John sought revenge by ordering every tree on the estate to be felled. He was created a baronet on 1 July 1761.

By 1770 the Hartley pits alone employed 300 hands, and in 1777 some 48,000 tons of coal were shipped coastwise, about 180 ships cleared the harbour, and around £24,000 was paid in port revenues. Such success did not enamour Delaval to the Tyneside coal traders, especially when he refused to be bound by their cartel arrangements. Another development was the industrial village alongside the harbour. By 1790 Seaton Sluice, with forty-three cottage houses in the predictably named John, Hussey, and Delaval streets, also had a market square, a school, a brewery, and public houses, so that 'no man should have an opportunity of gaining money here, and spending it elsewhere' (Askham, 128).

As a politician Delaval defeated the young John Wilkes at Berwick in the general election of 1754, and when Wilkes subsequently disputed the result, Delaval made a flippant speech 'full of wit, humour, and buffoonery, which kept the House in a roar' (HoP, Commons), but which brought harsh words from William Pitt (1759–1806). Delaval lost the seat in 1761, regained it at a by-election in 1765, and held it in 1768. Failing to win the Berwick freemen's support for Wilkes's plans for electoral reform, Delaval lost a county seat in the election of 1774 but was returned for Berwick as a whig in 1780. Initially he supported Charles James Fox's plan to regulate the East India Company; but he later changed his party. On 24 May 1784 Delaval:

astonished a great many by a very warm, explicit declaration that he had, in the last Parliament, opposed Mr Pitt as a

supposed minister of secret influence, but having now heard so unequivocally from the people themselves that he was *their* minister, he should most heartily obey their voice, and give him all the support he deserved. (HoP, Commons)

Delaval had received an Irish peerage in 1783, and Pitt rewarded him with an English peerage in 1786 to strengthen tory support in the Lords. Delaval's elevation led to his being mentioned in 'The Rolliad', and he was the butt of an opposition satire, 'The Delavaliad'.

Susanna died in 1783, and Delaval took the sixteen-year-old Elizabeth Hicks as his mistress in 1786, spending lavishly on her. Miss Hicks died in 1796, having from 1795 shared Delaval's affections with Susanna Elizabeth Knight (c.1762–1822), whom he finally married on 5 January 1803.

Delaval banked with Surtees and Burdon in Newcastle, but also with Hoares & Co. in London, and when the former crashed in 1803 he faced a degree of financial embarrassment. His losses are uncertain, but he asked Newcastle tradesmen to accept payment in coal rather than money, and sold the contents of his wine cellar. However, presumably cushioned by his deposits with Hoares & Co., he was able to maintain a family even keel, the housekeeping expenses at Seaton Delaval for 1807 amounting to £2,390.

Delaval died without a male heir on 17 May 1808 at Seaton Delaval Hall and was buried in June 1808 in St Paul's Chapel at Westminster Abbey. The Ford estate, the Hartley glassworks, and his personal possessions passed to his widow for life. His entailed estates at Seaton Delaval and Hartley devolved upon his brother Edward Hussey *Delaval, on whose death in 1814 the Delaval family became extinct in the male line.

STAFFORD M. LINSLEY

Sources F. Askham, *The gay Delavals* (1955) · R. Welford, *Men of mark 'twixt Tyne and Tweed*, 3 vols. (1895) · Northumbd RO, Delaval papers · Venn, *Alum. Cant.* · *A history of Northumberland*, Northumberland County History Committee, 15 vols. (1893–1940), vol. 9 · L. Namier, 'Delaval, John (1728–1808)', HoP, *Commons* · *Old Westminsters*, vol. 1
Archives Northumbd RO, Newcastle upon Tyne, corresp. and papers; family corresp., corresp. relating to estates and elections | BL, corresp. Newcastle, Add. MSS
Likenesses W. Bell, oils, 1771, probably Seaton Delaval Hall, Northumberland · W. A. Rainger, mezzotint, pubd 1864 (after J. Reynolds), BM, NPG

Delaval, Sir Ralph (c.1576–1628). *See under* Delaval family (*per. c.*1520–1752).

Delaval, Sir Ralph, first baronet (1622–1691). *See under* Delaval family (*per. c.*1520–1752).

Delavall, Sir Ralph (d. 1707), naval officer, was the eldest son of William Delavall (1616–1667) of Newcastle and his wife, Mary (d. 1675), daughter of Sir Peter Riddell of Newcastle. Delavall was probably educated locally and his spelling in later life was bad and phonetic. He was appointed lieutenant of the *Cambridge* on 23 August 1666 and served in the *Henrietta* from October 1666 to December 1667 before being appointed a lieutenant on the *Tiger* from March 1668 to May 1669. As part of retrenchment he was then dismissed, and not employed again until January 1671 when he was appointed lieutenant of the *Adventure*. In January 1672 he moved to the *Advice* as lieutenant, but seems to have missed the battle of Solebay on 28 May 1672 as the *Advice* had been sent out cruising. On 6 January the next year he was promoted to captain of the *Eagle* and ordered to sail to Guinea, so missing the battles of Schooneveld and the Texel. When he returned early in 1674 he was sent out with a convoy to Helsingor where he seized a Dutch cannon. When asked why he had seized the Dutch property, Delavall replied that the Dutch were 'professed Enemies to my Nation and that my Prince had declared them to be so, it was my duty to do them all the prejudice I could' (PRO, ADM 51/4177/1, *Eagle*). When Delavall returned to England he was among the captains dismissed from the service at the end of the Third Anglo-Dutch War and in December 1674 he was commissioned a lieutenant in the regiment of foot guards; in 1685 he was promoted to captain and in 1687 to lieutenant-colonel.

Delavall was appointed captain of the *Constant Warwick* on 9 April 1677, having been given permission to leave his regiment. In June 1677 he clashed with Balthazar St Michel, muster-master at Deal, over his refusal to sign the ship's muster-books, Delavall 'alleging his not being enjoined thereto by his instructions' (PRO, ADM 106/326, fols. 238–9; Cat. iv 446). Delavall was in the West Indies in 1678; he had returned to England by May the next year, when he appeared before the parliamentary committee investigating miscarriage in the navy, concerning his seizing several ships on the pretence of their trading to Guinea. He also had to justify his religion, as it had been publicly suggested he was a Roman Catholic. He was discharged from his commission in July 1679 and rejoined the foot guards.

On 1 October 1688 Delavall was appointed captain of the *York*. He told the Navy Board on 3 November 1688 that he had not yet fitted his ship out because Portsmouth was 'barren of saylers … esteeming myself extremely unfortunate under this unhappy delay' (PRO, ADM 106/383, fol. 275). As part of the fleet commanded by Arthur Herbert he took part in the battle of Bantry Bay on 1 May 1689. A year later, on 31 May 1690, he presented a loyal address from the fleet to the queen, who knighted him. Promoted to vice-admiral of the blue he raised his flag in the *Coronation* and commanded the Blue squadron, the rear squadron at the battle of Beachy Head on 30 June 1690: he and his squadron fought the French for five hours and at the inquiry made by the lords commissioners sent to investigate the action he blamed the large Dutch losses on the Dutch themselves. Delavall was allegedly no friend of Torrington's and was president of Torrington's court martial in December 1690 (which acquitted him).

From the end of 1690 until the summer of 1691 Delavall commanded a powerful squadron in the channel, cruising off Dunkirk and attacking the port. He captured a French ship and seized papers relating to Viscount Preston's plots in England, but as he could not understand French he did not know what he had found until one of his captains told him. In December 1691 he commanded a squadron off Cadiz and in January 1692 convoyed the Mediterranean Fleet to the straits and continued cruising in the channel to protect trade. In March 1692 when Delavall arrived at Plymouth he was said to have £2.5 million of bullion aboard, though this was later said to be exaggerated. On 13 May, with his flag in the *Royal Sovereign*, Delavall served under Russell as vice-admiral of the Red squadron, and at the battle of Barfleur/La Hougue he commanded the detached squadron which on 22 May burnt the *Soleil Royal* and two other French ships in Cherbourg. Afterwards Delavall complained bitterly and constantly about Russell's conduct before and after the battle. In November 1692 it was reported that Delavall had fallen off his horse while on his way to Portsmouth and had broken his arm. In 1693 Delavall, Killigrew, and Shovell were appointed jointly as admirals of the fleet. Following the loss of the merchant convoy destined for Smyrna, it was suggested that Killigrew and Delavall were acting in the interest of King James. Delavall bitterly denied this, declaring 'I … should be ashamed were I guilty of intended ill to my country' (*CSP dom.*, *1693*, 201). William none the less dismissed him from all his military offices, including his command of the 1st foot regiment, and he did not serve at sea again although in July 1693 he was appointed a prize commissioner for Jamaica and Barbados and promoted to admiral of the blue. Appointed an Admiralty commissioner in April 1693, Delavall, because of his service at sea, attended only two meetings. Following his dismissal as admiral later that year William ordered him not to attend any further meetings and he was removed at the next renewal in May 1694. At the end of 1694 Delavall kissed William's hand and it was said he would command the fleet in 1695, but this did not happen.

Delavall sat as MP for Great Bedwyn as a tory in 1695–8. In 1699 he was granted a pension 'for good service at sea' (*CSP dom.*, *1699–1700*, 197) and as admiral of the blue 'by a dormant commission' he was included on a list presented to William on 30 March 1700 of flag officers 'unemployed at sea' (*CSP dom.*, *1700–02*, 283). Delavall married Hester Major of London. They had at least four children, two sons who died young and two daughters, Hester and Mary, who survived him. He possibly retired to Seaton Delaval in Northumberland, and may have died in London at his house in St Margaret's Westminster. He was buried on 23 January 1707 in the upper end of the west aisle of Westminster Abbey; his wife died six months later, on 10 July.

PETER LE FEVRE

Sources A history of Northumberland, Northumberland County History Committee, 15 vols. (1893–1940), vol. 9 · admiralty papers: list of commissioned officers services, 1660–85, PRO, ADM 10/15 · journal, captain's log, *Eagle*, PRO, ADM 51/4177 · letters to navy board misc. 'S', 1677, PRO, ADM 106/326 · letters to navy board misc. 'D', 1688, PRO, ADM 106/388 · Magd. Cam., Pepys Library, Pepys MS 2856 · CSP dom., 1693; 1699–1702 · W. A. Aiken, ed., *The conduct of the earl of Nottingham* (1941) · N. Luttrell, *A brief historical relation of state affairs from September 1678 to April 1714*, 2 (1857); repr. (1969) · admiralty minute book, PRO, ADM 3/9 · *The parliamentary diary of Narcissus Luttrell, 1691–1693*, ed. H. Horwitz (1972) · *Report on the manuscripts of Allan George Finch*, 5 vols., HMC, 71 (1913–2003), vols. 3–4 · admon, Sir Ralph Delavall, 11 March 1707, PRO, PROB 6/83, fol. 45 · D. B. Smith and Royal Navy College, eds., *The commissioned sea officers of* the Royal Navy, 1660–1815, 3 vols. [n.d., c.1954] • J. R. Tanner, ed., A descriptive catalogue of the naval manuscripts in the Pepysian Library at Magdalene College, Cambridge, 4 vols., Navy RS, 26–7, 36, 57 (1903–23)

Archives Magd. Cam. | CKS, corresp. with Shovell and Killigrew and Admiralty copies of his orders • Leics. RO, corresp. with earl of Nottingham • NYPL, logbook of Royal Sovereign • PRO, Admiralty papers

Likenesses group portrait, oils, c.1692, NMM • M. Dahl, oils, Seaton Delaval Hall, Northumberland

---

Delderfield, Ronald Frederick (1912–1972), writer and playwright, was born on 12 February 1912 at 37 Waller Road, New Cross, south London, the third of the four children of William James Delderfield (1873–1956), a meat sales manager at Smithfield market and later a Devon newspaper proprietor, and his wife, Alice Emma, née Jones, the only daughter of a Welsh tea trader, whose family had moved to London from Aberystwyth in the 1850s. In 1918 the Delderfield family moved from south London to 22 Ashburton Avenue in Addiscombe, near Croydon, then a quiet rural suburb on the Kent–Surrey border. When he was eleven Delderfield was briefly enrolled at Selhurst grammar school, Croydon, which he disliked. The suburban world of Addiscombe would later provide the backdrop for Delderfield's first two major novels, The Dreaming Suburb and The Avenue Goes to War (1958). In 1923 the volatile James Delderfield inexplicably purchased the Exmouth Chronicle. The family moved to Devon and Delderfield was sent to complete his education at West Buckland, a nearby boys' boarding-school. This school was to be affectionately portrayed as Bamfylde, at the end of Delderfield's life, in his novel To Serve them All my Days (1972).

After a course at Fulford's Business School Delderfield, aged seventeen, became editor of his father's newspaper in 1929. Eleven years of journalism taught him his craft as a writer. At the same time, always prolific, he began writing full-length and one-act plays, some of which were staged for short provincial runs. On 14 March 1936 he married May (Marnie) Evans (b. 1905/6), a Manchester laboratory assistant whom he met on holiday in Wales. The couple adopted two children.

Delderfield did five years of peripatetic desk work in the RAF from 1940 because, severely short-sighted, he was deemed unfit for active service. Worm's Eye View, having been written in 1943, was staged in London in 1945. A comedy about the sufferings of wartime British servicemen at the hands of civilians, it ran in London for over five years until 1951. Of Delderfield's thirty or so published plays only Worm's Eye View is now remembered.

After the war the Delderfield family returned to Devon. There in 1956 he turned from writing plays to concentrate on novels and non-fiction. A lifelong fascination with Napoleonic times had already led to Farewell the Tranquil Mind (1950). Napoleon in Love was published in 1959, and there were several other books on this theme. Bird's Eye View, the first of four autobiographical works, appeared in 1954. He published a total of twenty-two miscellaneous short volumes of fiction and non-fiction.

But it is for his ambitious multi-volume sagas—straightforward Dickensian or Galsworthian story-telling in which the historical and geographical setting is as vital as the characterization—that Delderfield is best-known. Published from 1966 to 1968, the three-volume A Horseman Riding By tells the story of a Devon valley, its inhabitants, and its squire during the first two-thirds of the twentieth century.

Delderfield's final and finest work, the Swann saga, began with God is an Englishman (1970), continued with Theirs was the Kingdom (1971), and ended with the posthumous publication Give us this Day (1973.) The Swann books tell the story of Adam Swann, who steals a valuable necklace from a dead Indian mutineer in 1857 and uses the capital to start a London-based nationwide haulage business. The narrative sweeps epic-like through all the major events of history as the nineteenth century gives way to the twentieth and the Swann children grow up and move, somewhat implausibly, around the world.

Never athletic, Delderfield was a heavy-set, myopic man who wore thick-lensed spectacles and who smoked heavily. He died from lung cancer at his home, Dove Cottage, Manor Road, Sidmouth, Devon, on 24 June 1972.

A number of Delderfield's novels were serialized for television. A Horseman Riding By was produced in 1977 and starred Nigel Havers as Paul Craddock. To Serve them All my Days, dramatized for the BBC by Andrew Davies and broadcast in 1981, featured Frank Middlemass as the headmaster Algy Herries. Delderfield's two-book love story Diana (1960 and 1962) was also serialized by the BBC in 1984.

Delderfield is remembered and respected as a storyteller rather than as a great novelist: 'as a purveyor of quality, classic realistic fiction for popular consumption, R. F. Delderfield has few peers' (Sternlicht, 134).

SUSAN ELKIN

Sources S. Sternlicht, R. F. Delderfield (Boston, MA, 1988) • R. F. Delderfield, Bird's eye view (1954) • R. F. Delderfield, For my own amuseument (1968) • R. F. Delderfield, Overture for beginners (1970) • b. cert. • m. cert. • CGPLA Eng. & Wales (1972)

Archives BBC WAC, corresp. and literary papers • Boston University, literary MSS and papers • GL, corresp. with publishers

Wealth at death £83,260: probate, 7 Dec 1972, CGPLA Eng. & Wales

---

Delenus, Gualter (c.1500–1563), theologian, was born at Balen, near Antwerp. He studied at Louvain, and quickly acquired a reputation as a distinguished scholar: his particular fame rests on the fact that he was the first teacher of Hebrew in the northern Netherlands, first at Haarlem (1523–7) and then in Amsterdam (1533–5). By this time he was already a convert to the Reformation. His interest in the new doctrines was evident from the time of a brief visit to Wittenberg in 1522, and his lectures in Amsterdam soon raised the suspicions of the authorities. In September 1534 the stadhouder of Holland, Graf Hoogstraten, ordered that Delenus's contract should be terminated the following June; by this time, however, Delenus had also come under investigation for some unspecified role in the attempted Anabaptist coup in the city, inspired by the contemporary events in Münster. Delenus wisely left

Amsterdam without waiting for the results of the inquiry; he returned to Haarlem (1535–7) and then moved to England, where he quickly obtained employment in royal service.

In England, Delenus enjoyed a markedly successful career, all the more remarkable given the accusations of unorthodoxy that had dogged his years in Holland. He arrived in England at precisely the moment when the English authorities were engaged on a major effort to harass Anabaptist refugees. Delenus's suspicious past must either have been unknown in England or, in view of his scholarly distinction, judged irrelevant. He was employed as the king's 'biblioscopus': an obscure term which may indicate a specific function connected with the registration and cataloguing of books which came into the Royal Collection from the dissolution of the monasteries. He also had time to pursue his studies. In 1540 he published his *Novum Testamentum* (*STC*, 1475–1640, 2799), a reworking of the Erasmus New Testament which shows the influence of the work of Guillaume Budé. Several manuscripts from these years in Delenus's hand survive in English collections. These texts show him to have been an enthusiastic supporter of the royal supremacy and the dissolution of the monasteries; and, perhaps more significant in terms of his earlier experiences, a fierce critic of Anabaptism. He took out letters of denization in 1539; the royal accounts for this same year show payment of quarterly wages of £5 6s. 8d. The alien tax registers of 1541–7 attest to the fact that Delenus had by the last years of Henry's reign succeeded in building a comfortable prosperity.

On the death of Henry VIII, Delenus initially continued in royal service, but in 1550 he was named in the foundation charter as one of the first ministers of London's new Dutch church. He was something of an outsider in the otherwise tightly knit group that formed the leadership of the church; his association with the church must have been a deliberate act of royal patronage. In the first days Delenus shared with John à Lasco, the church's superintendent, responsibility for the twice weekly public lectures: À Lasco preached on the New Testament, Delenus on the Old Testament. But his unorthodox beliefs led to disputes with his colleagues over doctrine and practice. He took exception to three aspects of the new discipline: the insistence on godparents at baptism, kneeling at communion, and the article on Christ's descent into hell, which he wished to be omitted from the confession of faith. After sharp exchanges with his colleagues, Delenus was brought to admit that he had erred; but the Latin lectures were from this point discontinued.

With the accession of Mary the church was soon shut up and the congregation dispersed. Delenus and his son Pieter [*see below*] were the last of the leaders of the church to leave London, and they may indeed have attempted to keep some kind of informal congregation alive. But in February 1554 the two men and thirty-two of their followers left to join the rest of the church in Emden. Here Delenus took a more retiring role; although named at one point an elder of the church, he mostly devoted himself to study. He played an important part in the collective venture orchestrated by Jan Utenhove to publish a new Dutch translation of the New Testament (1556). Two years later he published his own translation of Johann Sleidanus's *De religionis statu* (*Commentaries on the State of Religion during the Reign of Charles V*), *Waerachtige beschrivinge hoe dattet met de religie gestaen heeft* (1558). With the accession of Elizabeth, however, Delenus was soon lured back to London to assist the restoration of the church, and in November 1559 he joined leading members of the community as signatories to a letter requesting that his son Pieter be dispatched to serve the church as minister. In his old age Delenus was himself spared this demanding role and, comfortably settled in London, he seems to have maintained his wife and five children (Pieter and four siblings, Carolus, Hendrik, Martinus, and Maria) by private tuition. He died in 1563, a victim of the plague epidemic that ravaged the Dutch community and also claimed the life of both its ministers. He was survived by his wife, Christyne (possibly this was a second marriage), who died some time after 1569.

Pieter Delenus (*c*.1530–1563) followed his father into the ministry. As one of the first to take advantage of the formidable educational institutions of the Dutch church, he was marked out for office from an early age, and seems to have become a minister in that church shortly before its dissolution in 1553. Arriving in Emden with his father early the following year, Pieter Delenus soon drew both admiration and controversy for his preaching. Although briefly forbidden the pulpit in Emden by the local authorities, he was much in demand as a minister: in 1556 he took part in a debate with Anabaptists in Norden, and the following years brought invitations to serve as minister from the churches in Antwerp, Aachen, and Frankfurt. Delenus also made a number of missionary sorties to the incipient congregation at Groningen. But having avoided a fixed charge at any of the continental exile congregations, in 1559 Pieter Delenus was the natural choice to take command of the restored Dutch church in London, a calling he accepted early in 1560. This second London ministry was a decisive but turbulent period in Delenus's career. He had been preceded in London by the distinguished preacher and martyrologist Adriaan van Haemstede. Having played a part of some importance in securing a place of meeting for the church in the first year of the new reign, Haemstede was keen to have a continuing role, but he and Delenus soon fell out. In the ensuing quarrel, Delenus, as the officially appointed minister, inevitably emerged the victor, particularly as Haemstede further muddied the waters by suggesting that the hand of brotherhood should be extended to members of the Anabaptist sects. An extended disciplinary procedure resulted in Haemstede's excommunication (17 November 1560) and eventual disgrace, but it also took its toll on Delenus's already delicate health. On 24 August 1563 he died of plague. He left a widow, Anna de Buson, whom he had married in London on 26 January 1561.

ANDREW PETTEGREE

Sources D. Nauta and others, eds., *Biografisch lexicon voor de geschiedenis van het Nederlandse protestantisme*, 3 vols. (Kampen,

1978–88) · A. Pettegree, *Foreign protestant communities in sixteenth-century London* (1986) · A. Pettegree, *Emden and the Dutch revolt: exile and the development of reformed protestantism* (1992) · R. E. G. Kirk and E. F. Kirk, eds., *Returns of aliens dwelling in the city and suburbs of London, from the reign of Henry VIII to that of James I*, Huguenot Society of London, 10/1 (1900), 40, 280 · A. A. van Schelven, ed., *Kerkeraads-protocollen der Nederduitsche vluchtelingenkerk te Londen, 1560–1563*, Historisch Genootschap te Utrecht, 3rd ser., 43 (1921) · H. F. Wijnman, 'Wouter Deelen, de eerste professor in het hebreeuwsch te Amsterdam', *Jaarboek Amstelodamun*, 27 (1930), 43–65 · H. J. de Jonge, 'Caro in Spiritum', *De geest in het geding*, ed. I. B. Horst (1978) · J. Trapman, 'Delenus en de bijbel', *Nederlands Archief voor Kerkgeschiedenis*, 56 (1975), 95–113 · *LP Henry VIII*, vol. 14 · *STC, 1475–1640*, no. 2799 · will, London Comm. 1563/4, vol. 15, fol. 186v
Archives BL, Royal MSS 12 A 32, 12 B 2, 12 B 13, 8 B II, Royal Appendix 80, Royal 7 D XX · Bodl. Oxf., MS New College 136

Delenus, Pieter (*c*.1530–1563). *See under* Delenus, Gualter (*c*.1500–1563).

Delepierre, Joseph Octave (1802–1879), author and antiquary, was born at Bruges on 12 March 1802, the son of Joseph Delepierre, for many years receiver-general of West Flanders. His mother was a Penaranda, descended from a Spanish family long established in the Netherlands. By the age of twelve he had been taught neither to read nor to write, but when at last he was sent to school he made rapid progress and soon qualified for the University of Ghent. Having obtained the degree of doctor of laws, he became an *avocat*, and was appointed archivist of West Flanders in Bruges and at once set himself to bring the chaotic archive into better order.

Delepierre was a keen antiquary and his *Précis des annales de Bruges* (1835) was the first of many volumes devoted to the antiquities of his native city. He also collected books and works of art. When the prince consort and his brother visited Bruges in 1839, Delepierre was their cicerone. In 1840 he compiled the first volume of a *Précis analytique* of the contents of the archives under his care. From 1841 he also edited several volumes for the Société d'Émulation.

Denied promotion in the archive, Delepierre was persuaded by Van de Weyer, afterwards Belgian minister in Britain, to go to London in 1843; in August 1849 Van de Weyer appointed Delepierre a secretary of legation, and obtained for him the post of Belgian consul. During his first years in Britain official duties and an active participation in literary circles occupied him so completely that he published little until 1849, when he drew up an account of a collection of early French farces and moralities in the British Museum. In 1852 he produced *Macaronéana*, followed in 1862 by *Macaronéana Andra*, well-reviewed descriptions of macaronic writings.

When the duc d'Aumale, Van de Weyer, Lord Houghton, and others founded the Philobiblon in 1853 (then limited to thirty-six members), Delepierre was appointed one of the honorary secretaries. He contributed twenty-two papers to its *Miscellanies*, many of which he later enlarged and republished separately. Delepierre was a fellow of the Society of Antiquaries of London, and a member of many other British, Belgian, and French societies. He was decorated with several foreign orders of knighthood. For more than thirty-five years he acted as Belgian secretary of legation, and, until 1877, when he resigned, he was consul-general for Belgium in London. He was twice married, first to Emily, the sister of Sir Robert Cornelius Napier, the first Lord Napier of Magdala, and daughter of Major Charles Frederick Napier (*d.* 1812); they had two daughters. One of these died young; the other married Johannes Nicholas Trübner, who wrote a memoir of Delepierre in 1880. His second wife, who survived him, was the widow of Captain Jasper Trowce. Delepierre died on 18 August 1879 at the house of his son-in-law J. N. Trübner at 29 Upper Hamilton Terrace, London, and was buried in Highgate cemetery on 22 August.

Delepierre was a prolific author, mainly on topics related to Belgium and particularly Bruges, and in many fields of antiquarian studies. His works were mainly in French and were published in Belgium. They extend to translations and editions of the works of others as well as his own writings. Tall and dignified, Delepierre was a good companion, who enjoyed conversation and chess. Although he became quite English in habits and speech, he never lost his attachment to his native land.

H. R. Tedder, *rev.* Elizabeth Baigent

Sources N. T. [N. Trübner], *Joseph Octave Delepierre: ... in memoriam, for friends only* (1880) · *The Athenaeum* (30 Aug 1879), 272 · *The Times* (19 Aug 1879) · *The Times* (20 Aug 1879) · Burke, *Peerage*
Likenesses portrait, repro. in Trübner, *Joseph Octave Delepierre*

Delépine, Auguste Sheridan (1855–1921), pathologist and bacteriologist, was born on 1 January 1855 at Rolle, Switzerland, the eldest son of Antoine Delépine, a Parisian landowner, and Henriette, formerly Mennet, a Swiss from the Canton de Vaud. Delépine was educated at the Collège Charlemagne, Paris until 1870, and then at the Académie de Lausanne, Switzerland, where he obtained a BSc in 1872. He then worked in Alsace and studied at the University of Geneva before electing in 1877 to study medicine in Edinburgh, where he graduated MB, CM, in 1882, with first-class honours. He served as assistant to several of the leading medical figures of the day, including D. J. Hamilton, William Rutherford Sanders, and Sir William Turner, in Edinburgh, and then Sir Andrew Clark at St George's Hospital, London. Between 1882 and 1891 Delépine undertook much of Clark's routine pathological work, and was appointed pathologist and lecturer in physiology and pathology at St George's Hospital. During this period Delépine established his reputation in pathology, working on the lungs, the liver, and septic infections. He also published on cell division. In 1891 he was appointed to the new Proctor chair of pathology and morbid anatomy at Owens College, Manchester, soon to be the University of Manchester. While teaching pathology to undergraduates Delépine developed an expertise in bacteriology and from 1894 he began to teach practical bacteriology as part of the course for the diploma in public health, in newly built laboratories.

In 1892 Delépine was first approached by local sanitary authorities to provide diagnostic and investigative services and in 1895 these were made routine when the payment of fees for service was allowed by the college. The erratic demand for investigations and uneven flow of income made it difficult to provide a comprehensive service and for many years the work relied on Delépine's efforts and the work of unpaid assistants. However, by the early 1900s the laboratory was working for more than sixty local authorities across the north of England and the enterprise had expanded so rapidly that it had to move to new accommodation in 1903, and to its own building in 1905. In 1904 Delépine became professor of public health and bacteriology and in 1908 director of the Public Health Laboratory. The laboratory in York Place, which Delépine designed, was staffed by a dedicated group of full- and part-time staff, most of whom had been trained in the department. Delépine was a prime mover in the institutionalization of bacteriology and experimental pathology nationally as well as regionally, being active in the creation of the *Journal of Pathology and Bacteriology* in 1892 and of the Pathological Society of Great Britain and Northern Ireland, whose first meeting was held in Manchester in 1906.

After 1900 Delépine's published works were increasingly based on investigations undertaken on behalf of local authorities. The most famous were those on arsenic in beer (1900), summer diarrhoea (1903), anthrax in Chester (1905), tubercular bacilli in cow's milk (1908–9), disinfection (1910–11), and water filtration (1914). During the First World War he made a valuable study of trench foot. He was renowned locally as an inspiring teacher, a painstaking investigator, and a reliable expert adviser, who according to Sir George Newman exemplified the new model of public health officer. Delépine was liked and respected by all who knew him. He was loyal and courteous in an old-fashioned way, and firm on matters of principle.

Delépine married Florence, the daughter of Frederick Rose of London. They had a daughter and son, whose death in the First World War cast a shadow over Delépine's final years. He died on 13 November 1921 at his home, Ellerslie, 41 Palatine Road, Withington, Manchester. His body was cremated and his ashes placed in the York Street laboratory. He was survived by his wife.

MICHAEL WORBOYS

Sources G. Sims Woodhead, 'Sheridan Delépine', *Journal of Pathology and Bacteriology*, 25 (1922), 113–17 · R. M. Stirland, 'Auguste Sheridan Delepine', *Some Manchester doctors: a biographical collection to mark the 150th anniversary of the Manchester Medical Society, 1834–1984*, ed. W. J. Elwood and A. F. Tuxford (1984) · *Manchester Guardian* (14 Nov 1921), 12 · 'Memorial to Professor Delépine', *BMJ* (22 Dec 1923), 1233 · *CGPLA Eng. & Wales* (1921) · *WWW* · *The medical who's who* (1915)
Archives JRL, Manchester medical collection
Likenesses Millard, bust, University of Manchester, Stopford Building · photograph, repro. in Woodhead, 'Sheridan Delépine', pl. ix
Wealth at death £5503 3s. 7d.: probate, 24 Dec 1921, *CGPLA Eng. & Wales*

Delevingne, Sir Malcolm (1868–1950), civil servant, was born on 11 October 1868 at Oxford Street, London, the second child of Ernest Thomas Shaw Delevingne, wine, spirit, and liquor merchant, and his wife, Hannah Gresswell. His paternal family was of Huguenot descent and his father, though a British subject from birth, was born in Paris. Between 1877 and 1887 he attended the City of London School, where he was school captain (1885–7) and won a scholarship at Trinity College, Oxford, which he entered in October 1887. He gained first-class honours in classical moderations in 1889 and in *literae humaniores* in 1891. In 1892 he passed the civil service examination for 'first division' clerkships and, after a brief period at the Local Government Board, was transferred to the Home Office. He remained there for the rest of his career. Initially private secretary to the secretary of state, he rose by stages to the position of permanent under-secretary of state in 1922. He retained this rank until his retirement in 1932.

Although Delevingne was involved in many aspects of the work of the Home Office, he was particularly associated with two questions: occupational health, welfare, and safety and—especially towards the end of his career—the control of dangerous drugs. He brought to this work both profound religious faith and a strong social conscience, and soon acquired an encyclopaedic knowledge of factory legislation 'not only on its practical but also on its historical side' (*The Times*, 1 Dec 1950). He was the unobtrusive force behind moves to improve employment conditions in the first quarter of the twentieth century. In particular, he was instrumental in bringing about the Police, Factories, etc. (Miscellaneous Provisions) Act, 1916, which allowed the home secretary to order the provision of amenities such as seats, canteens, washrooms, drinking water, and first aid without the need for a full-scale revision of the Factory Act. In addition he was influential in reorganizing the work of the factory department and establishing the Home Office Industrial Museum as a permanent exhibition of methods for promoting safety, health, and welfare. He was also much involved with mining regulation and did much of the preliminary work which led to the Coal Mines Act of 1911.

Delevingne was also active on the international stage. In 1905, 1906, and 1913 he was a British government delegate to the international conferences on labour regulations at Bern. As such he was a party to several important agreements, including for prohibitions on the use of white phosphorus in matches and on night work for women. In 1919, as the British representative on the labour commission of the Versailles peace conference, he was one of the architects of the International Labour Organization, whose original constitution he did much to draft. Subsequently he participated in the international labour conferences at Washington (1919) and Geneva (1923, 1928, and 1929). Even in retirement he remained actively involved in questions of industrial welfare. In 1933 he chaired a Home Office committee on shift work for women and young people. Subsequently he served on the royal commission on safety in coal mines (1936) and chaired the Safety in Mines Research Board (1939–47). He was also, again in 1936, chairman of an inter-departmental committee on the rehabilitation of persons injured by accidents.

Delevingne's work for international controls on dangerous drugs took him repeatedly to Geneva and even as far afield as Bangkok, mainly as the British delegate at opium conferences. Convinced that the drug trade was 'a great evil which must be fought', 'he never spared himself in the combat' (Martindale, 34). Responsible for co-ordinating and representing the views of all government departments, he rapidly gained a global reputation as an authority on the subject. As such he served as chairman of the supervisory body under the international convention of 1931 for the limitation of the manufacture of dangerous drugs, and was Great Britain's representative on the League of Nations's advisory committee on opium traffic, 1921–34. After his retirement—indeed, up to the age of seventy-nine—he continued to represent the United Kingdom at the international opium conferences. In 1932 the privy council nominated him a member of the council of the Pharmaceutical Society. In recognition of his services Delevingne was appointed CB in 1911, KCB (1919), and KCVO (1932).

Delevingne was imaginative, innovative, 'clever and able' (Martindale, 35), and was imbued with drive, determination, and a 'remorseless quest for precision' (Butler, 157). Senior colleagues also regarded him as courteous, kind, loyal, and even lovable. Yet his methods sometimes attracted criticism. This was partly because he was something of an autocrat who preferred to deal with a matter personally rather than to delegate, and partly because he 'sometimes gave the impression of being too much the bureaucrat who thought that to settle a matter you had only to tie it up in a bundle of regulations, preferably of his own drafting' (The Times, 1 Dec 1950). He also fought tenaciously and, for the duration of his career, successfully, to prevent the transfer of industrial administration from his beloved Home Office to the 'upstart' Ministry of Labour. This brought, in comparison to other countries, a certain irrationality into labour administration in Britain, which it was one of Bevin's first actions as minister of labour to remedy.

Delevingne never married. Of his siblings, Walter Norman Delevingne (1870–1937) had a distinguished career in the Indian Civil Service, and his elder brother, Edgar Constant Delevingne (b. 1867), spent some forty years as a master at the City of London School. During his working years his chief recreations were travelling and walking—especially in Norway and Italy. In retirement, until his health deteriorated, he undertook various kinds of social work, especially for Dr Barnardo's Homes. Elected a member of the charity in 1903, he joined its council in 1934. Delevingne died at his home, 20 FitzGeorge Avenue, West Kensington, London, on 30 November 1950.

P. W. J. BARTRIP

Sources H. Martindale, *Some Victorian portraits and others* (1948) · *The Times* (1 Dec 1950) · *The Times* (8 Dec 1950) · *DNB* · R. A. S. Redmayne, *Men, mines and memories* (1942) · H. Butler, *Confident morning* (1950) · *WWW, 1941–50* · admission register, Trinity College Archives, Oxford · census returns, 1871, 1881 · *City of London School Magazine* (Easter 1951) · private information (2004) [City of London School archivist]
Likenesses W. Stoneman, photograph, 1919, NPG

Wealth at death £44,911 4s. 2d.: probate, 19 Feb 1951, *CGPLA Eng. & Wales*

Delfont, Bernard [*formerly* Boris Winogradsky], **Baron Delfont** (1909–1994), theatrical impresario and leisure executive, was born on 5 September 1909, at Tokmak, Ukraine, Russia, the second son of Isaac Winogradsky (1879–1935) and Golda (later Olga) Izenstadt (c.1887–1981). His father ran a drapery store in Tokmak before emigrating to England, where, in London's East End, he worked successively as tailor's presser, embroiderer, and (unsuccessful) cinema exhibitor. Boris had two brothers, Louis, later Lew *Grade, Lord Grade, and Lazarus, later Leslie Grade, and a sister, Rita. Boris's father was by all accounts a failure in worldly matters; his mother was a woman of remarkable character, fiercely devoted to and proud of her children's achievements. To avoid the failure of the former and gratify the hopes of the latter appear to have been motor impulses in the spectacular rise of the three sons. The daughter also brought joy to the long-lived Mrs Winogradsky by marrying a distinguished Jewish doctor, Joseph Freeman; though the family was not religious, their Jewish East End background remained important.

The family's earliest years are not easy to chart, because there are no documents such as birth certificates and because Isaac Winogradsky did not take out British citizenship, the cost of which would have been prohibitive. Its absence meant that Bernard (Boris first changed his name to Barnet, then Bernard) was not eligible for service in the Second World War; this also meant that his career did not suffer the interruption experienced by many men of his age. (He was naturalized as a British subject in July 1961.) The least scholastically inclined of the three brothers, he received only a rudimentary education at the Rochelle Street and the Stepney Jewish schools, before leaving when barely into his teens to take up his first work as office boy in a chinaware company—but not before already exhibiting his entrepreneurial proclivities as organizer of a farthing sweepstake, which drew the wrath of his teachers.

Not content for long with the chinaware company, Bernard followed Lew's footsteps, literally in that he too became a highly proficient Charleston dancer, winning competitions, first with Albert Sutan (later the comedian Hal Monty) as partner, and the two were christened the Delfont Boys by their agent, the name sticking in Bernard's case. His second partner was a half-Japanese girl, Toko, and they were billed as 'Delfont and Toko: Syncopated Steps-Appeal'. After considerable experience in Europe and the variety halls of Britain, Delfont realized that his dancing days were numbered and made his final stage appearance at the Wood Green Empire in 1937.

Lew Grade (he changed his name as a performer, and Leslie and Rita also adopted the name Grade) was by this time established as a theatrical agent with Joe Collins, and for a short time Delfont joined the Collins and Grade agency in 1937. However, by 1939 he had left to become exclusive booking agent for Mecca, a move partly instigated by the fact that he and Lew were not close (each got

Bernard Delfont, Baron Delfont (1909–1994), by unknown photographer, 1981

on better with the more retiring, business-orientated Leslie), partly because he aspired towards management. More than the other brothers, he always wanted to be associated with the creative side of theatrical management, and in 1943 he acquired his first theatre, the Wimbledon, following this quickly with two West End houses, the St Martin's and the Whitehall.

Delfont's first staged show was *Hello America* (1939), a pot-pourri of available American acts, but his taste moved away from variety in the direction of light plays and musical theatre, and during the Second World War he staged popular operettas such as *Rose Marie* (1942) and comedies such as *The Admirable Crichton* (1943). By the war's end Delfont controlled seven theatres, and by early 1947 his name was on fourteen West End and touring shows. During the war he met the musical-comedy star, Helen Violet Carolyn, *née* Haymen (*b.* 1918), who acted under the name Carole Lynne; she was then married to the actor Derek Farr. This marriage had suffered the fate of many contracted in wartime; when the Farrs' divorce was final, Delfont and she were married on 22 January 1946. Throughout the rest of their lives together she was a strong and discerning supporter of his theatrical enterprises, eventually relinquishing her own career. The marriage produced three children, Susan (*b.* 1947), Jennifer (*b.* 1949), and Daniel (*b.* 1953), none of whom went into show business.

After the war Delfont's became a big name in London theatre. He co-presented with Laurence Olivier the American comedy hit *Born Yesterday*; on several occasions brought the Folies Bergères to London, touring them overseas in the 1950s; had enormous success with the musical *Bless the Bride*; and was also willing to take risks on European arthouse fare such as *The Madwoman of Chaillot* and *The Visit*. He was associated particularly with three London theatres. First was the Casino (now Prince Edward), which

he had to close in the later 1940s because it could not compete with the Palladium, run by Val Parnell. Later he and Parnell became associates, and he presented shows at the Palladium for twenty years, starring major comics such as Norman Wisdom. Second, he renovated the Hippodrome, near Leicester Square, and established it in 1958 as the home of a dinner-theatre entertainment called *The Talk of the Town*, joining forces with the catering magnate Charles Forte to create an institution which would last for several decades. Third was the more intimate Prince of Wales, which was Delfont's favourite theatre.

The history of Delfont's fortunes in Britain's entertainment world is a complicated saga of amalgamations and deals, as he and his brothers gradually assumed preeminence over the theatrical and leisure scene. Delfont was responsible for bringing some of the biggest names, including Barbra Streisand, Sophie Tucker, and Yves Montand, to London to perform either in his own or in other theatres, becoming Britain's leading impresario. He joined the Grade Organisation in 1964 (Leslie was managing director, Lew the major shareholder), and in 1967 the organization was sold to EMI. EMI invited Delfont to build up and run its leisure division, and this took him into the world of film, though he still continued to present plays. He bought the Associated British Picture Corporation, its Elstree studios, and its cinema chain, and appointed Bryan Forbes as head of production. However, there were difficult labour relations and, despite odd hits in the 1970s such as *Murder on the Orient Express* (1974), the company had continued financial difficulties and was bought in 1979 by Thorn, the electrical conglomerate. In 1980 Trusthouse Forte bought EMI's leisure interests and Delfont became chief executive of the new Trust House Forte (THF) leisure division, whose interests included West End theatres, the Leicester Square Empire ballroom, sports centres, and the Blackpool Tower. In 1983, leading a management buy-out from THF, he became chairman of the First Leisure Corporation, and in this capacity oversaw the refurbishment of two theatres important to him: the Prince of Wales and the Prince Edward.

In 1974 Delfont was knighted for services to the entertainment industry, and in 1976 was created a life peer as Baron Delfont of Stepney in recognition of his involvement with many show-business charities. For twenty-one years he presented the Royal Variety Performance, the proceeds of which assisted such charities, and he held major posts of responsibility with other such organizations as the Entertainment Artistes' Benevolent Fund (president, 1978–94) and the Actors' Benevolent Fund. A man of probity who loved his work (only his wife's pertinacity ensured adequate respite), he never ceased to be grateful for the opportunities his adopted country had given him. He died on 28 July 1994 at his country home, Tall Trees, High Street, Angmering, Littlehampton, Sussex.　　　　　　　　　　　　BRIAN MCFARLANE

Sources B. Delfont and B. Turner, *East End, West End* (1990) · H. Davies, *The Grades: the first family of British entertainment* (1981) · L. Grade, *Still dancing: my story* (1987) · private information (2004)

[Lady Delfont] · *The Times* (29 July 1994); (6 Oct 1994) · *The Independent* (29 July 1994) · *International who's who* (1993) · A. Walker, *Hollywood, England* (1974) · A. Walker, *National heroes* (1985) · P. Noble, ed., *1980–81 screen international film and TV year book* (1981) · m. cert. · d. cert. · naturalization cert., PRO, HO334/345/BNA 67419

Archives FILM BFI NFTVA, 'A full life', ITV, 16 June 1985 · BFI NFTVA, documentary footage | SOUND BL NSA, performance recordings

Likenesses photograph, 1981, Hult. Arch. [*see illus.*] · caricatures · photographs · portrait (when made a peer)

Wealth at death £3,944,487: probate, 11 Nov 1994, *CGPLA Eng. & Wales*

Delius, Frederick Theodor Albert (1862–1934), composer, was born on 29 January 1862 at Claremont, Horton Lane, Bradford, Yorkshire, the grandson of Ernst Friedrich Delius (1790–1831) and the fourth of the fourteen children of Julius Delius (1822–1901) and his wife, Elise Pauline Krönig (1838–1929). Both his parents were born in Bielefeld, Germany. His father moved to Bradford to work in the wool trade; he was naturalized in 1850, and married in 1856. Delius's younger sister Clare in her *Memories* (1935) recalled their father as a disciplinarian, with 'a ledger mind' (Delius, *Memories*, 96) whose 'guiding influence … was fear' (ibid., 22). He was, however, a just man, and not averse to the arts: Joseph Joachim and Alfredo Carlo Piatti made music at the Delius home. Little Fritz (the name with which he was baptized and which he used until he was about forty) played the piano and the violin, improvising with ease. Hearing Chopin's posthumous E minor waltz opened an 'entirely new world' (ibid., 48) for him.

Early life Delius was a strong, athletic boy who delighted in roaming the Yorkshire moors. He attended the Bradford grammar school (1874–8), then the International College at Isleworth (1878–80). The family took it for granted that he should enter his father's trade. He was sent first as the firm's representative to Stroud in Gloucestershire, where his handsome appearance and charming manners won him friends and business success. For Delius, however, it meant that he could slip up to London for concerts. Next he was sent to Chemnitz, but neglected his duties in favour of trips to Dresden, Leipzig, and Berlin (where he heard Wagner's *Die Meistersinger*). Then it was Scandinavia, where, as his sister put it, he associated with 'such figures in the textile world as Ibsen and [another Norwegian dramatist] Gunnar Heiberg' (Delius, 63). Ibsen's revolt against the conventions that hinder self-expression, together with the majestic Norwegian mountains, fortified Delius's self-reliance. Next his father tried him in France. Three years passed (1880–83) before Delius senior admitted that his son was a black sheep in the wool trade and set him up as a citrus fruit farmer in Florida (1884).

The old Spanish plantation called Solana Grove was run down. In a wooden chalet, alone, amid lush vegetation on the banks of the broad St Johns River, Delius dreamed and found himself. He laid musical foundations unexpectedly. One summer night, while he was sitting on his veranda, there came to him the distant sound of the plantation workers singing. He experienced a 'state of illumination';

Frederick Theodor Albert Delius (1862–1934), by Ernest Procter, 1929

and the memory haunts some of his greatest works. Christopher Palmer (*Delius: Portrait of a Cosmopolitan*, 1976) suggests that Delius's idiom was influenced by the strange untutored harmonies of the black labourers and their longing for the 'promis' land'. Also, by chance Delius met Thomas Ward, a Brooklyn organist convalescing in Jacksonville; Ward taught him for six months, and Delius later claimed that Ward's were the only lessons from which he derived benefit.

Delius earned his keep by teaching music in Danville, Virginia (1885–6), and briefly in New York, and then, with his father's support, he studied at the Leipzig Conservatory (1886–8), working under Hans Sitt, Carl Reinecke, and Salomon Jadassohn (though according to Patrick Hadley no trace of this formal instruction can be found 'except in certain of his weaker passages'; *DNB*).

At Leipzig Delius met Christian Sinding, a fellow student, and Edvard Grieg. A walking tour in Norway (1887), the first of many, confirmed the 'profound, mystical and indelible' (Beecham, 2) influence of that country. Grieg intervened on his behalf with his father, who grudgingly granted Delius a minimal allowance but never came to accept his son's distinction.

Delius's father's brother Theodor, living in Paris, became his friend, mentor, and benefactor. In 1888 Delius settled near him, and by 1894 he belonged to a circle of artists and writers, among them Paul Gauguin, August Strindberg, and Edvard Munch (described by Lionel Carley in *Delius: the Paris Years*, 1975). He was found to be attractive, warm-hearted, spontaneous, and amorous. He was also industrious. As well as short pieces, he had already composed (1886–7) the *Florida Suite*, privately performed in Leipzig in 1888. His symphonic poem *Paa Vidderne* was performed in Christiania (Oslo) in 1891, and Gunnar Heiberg commissioned incidental music for his play *Folkeraadet*, a political satire, produced there with some controversy in 1897. Hans Haym in Elberfeld conducted *Over the Hills and Far Away* in 1897. The operas *Irmelin* (1890–92, first performed in Oxford, 1953) and *The Magic Fountain* (1894–5, first performance by the BBC, 1977) were composed; and *Koanga* was begun in 1896.

Innovation and audacity Delius met the artist Helena Sophie Emilie Rosen (1868–1935), known as Jelka, the granddaughter of the composer and pianist Ignaz Moscheles, in 1896. She was no Sunday painter, but worked in her studio up to ten hours a day and exhibited in the Salon des Indépendants. Later she impressed Beecham by her 'gravity of thought and a quiet intensity of emotion' (Beecham, 79). She and Delius were brought together by their shared passion for Nietzsche. She had been given permission to paint in the romantic garden running down to the River Loing of a house in Grez-sur-Loing, a village 40 miles outside Paris on the edge of Fontainebleau. Delius visited her there, and in 1897 she bought the house. He returned to Florida on business, and she wondered if she had lost him. On his return he simply took up residence at Grez, which became his home until he died. In 1903 Delius and Jelka were married.

From then on Delius's life, apart from visits to Paris, Germany, Norway, and London, was spent in those calm and idyllic surroundings. There were no children. Marriage did not curtail his affairs with other women: Jelka was often distressed, but remained devoted. Supported by his father, then by his wife, Delius never had need to earn. His uncle's death in 1898 brought him a legacy: he used part to buy Gauguin's painting *Nevermore* (now in the Courtauld Inst.). The rest allowed him to mount a concert of his music in London on 30 May 1899, conducted by Alfred Hertz. The second half comprised excerpts from *Koanga*. All the music was new to the country of his birth. Some critics were baffled, but many commented on the innovation, the audacity, and above all the vitality of the music—estimates which might surprise later generations who came to regard Delius as a languorous sensualist.

Delius then promoted his music in Germany, where interest was rising. Jelka's German painter friend Ida Gerhardi (her portraits include several of Delius and Jelka) became his fervent ambassador. Haym produced *Paris* in Elberfeld in 1901, and in 1904 there were first performances there of *Koanga* (under Fritz Cassirer) and *Appalachia* (variations on an old plantation song), and the piano concerto, and in Düsseldorf of *Lebenstanz*. In *A Village Romeo and Juliet* (1899–1901, first performed in Berlin, 1907) influences of Grieg, Strauss, and Wagner were banished or fully absorbed. Delius found his authentic voice: passionate, regretful, individual, introspective. The tale is of idealistic adolescent love, shadowed by the sinister, seductive Dark Fiddler and ending in an ecstatic double *Liebestod*. The interlude, *Walk to the Paradise Garden* (composed later, and popular in concerts), sums up the opera's beauty and pathos. In *Sea Drift* (1903–4, first performed in Essen, 1906) an adult relives in memory a boy's first anguished experience of bereavement, through the seabird's loss of his mate. Delius described how 'the shape of it was taken out of my hands … as I worked' (Fenby, 36), and was 'bred' from Whitman's poetical and his musical ideas. Of course there are thematic allusions and balances, tonal and rhythmic relationships, but the sensations seem to arise spontaneously from the melting chromaticisms and colours.

In 1907 Thomas Beecham, then aged twenty-eight, heard *Appalachia* under Cassirer in London and instantly became a sympathetic advocate. (Delius, still a prodigious walker, exhausted poor Beecham on a Norwegian holiday in 1908.) Granville Bantock, Norman O'Neill, Percy Grainger, and Ernest Newman also admired Delius's music, which began to make headway in England. He briefly became involved in the Musical League, one of his few excursions into musical politics. Bantock conducted the première of *Brigg Fair* at Liverpool in 1908. That year Delius himself conducted *Appalachia* at Hanley in Staffordshire; he was an infrequent and inept conductor, though he did conduct the première of the first *Dance Rhapsody* at the 1909 Three Choirs festival—strange context for a composer who in 1912 defiantly declared 'I believe … in no doctrine whatever … in complete annihilation as far as our personal consciousness goes' (Carley, *Letters*, 2.86).

Energy and contemplation In the *Mass of Life* (1904–5) Delius testified to his atheism. With Cassirer's assistance, he selected the words from Nietzsche's prose-poem *Also sprach Zarathustra* (part of the closing section, 'Mitternachtslied', had been performed at his 1899 London concert). The larger part of the mass was produced in 1908 in Munich, and Beecham conducted the complete work in London in 1909. It is the grandest and most ambitious of Delius's concert works, needing four soloists, a double choir, and a large orchestra. In music that touches extreme poles of physical energy and rapt contemplation, Delius celebrates the human 'Will' and the 'Individual', and the 'Eternal Recurrence of Nature'. If there is a weakness, it is (as in all Delius's output) occasional rhythmic monotony.

A group of shorter orchestral works—concert favourites—shows characteristic features. In *Brigg Fair* (1907), variations on a Lincolnshire folk-song collected by Grainger, the simple modal melody is supported by sliding and juxtaposed chromatic chords; often in Delius a chord has an instant rather than long-term function. In *a Summer Garden* (1908, revised 1911) and *Summer Night on the River* (1911) are refined examples of his orchestral pointillism, and of the way in which he seems to improvise a structure. In fact, the music—condensed and elliptical—is made from evolving motifs and groups of chords. Delius generally avoids symmetry and stable tonal centres; he creates a continuous harmonic flow of tension and delayed resolution, mirroring a stream of high emotional experience. In *On Hearing the First Cuckoo in Spring* (1912) the spacing and placing of even the diatonic chords, let alone their chromatic alterations, make for a mood almost hypnotic in its poignancy. These exquisite idylls, for all their composer's German descent and French domicile, spell 'England' for most listeners. Their influence is felt in many an evocative piece of comparable length by composers of the English pastoral school, though not all Delius's followers achieve his concentration.

Songs of Sunset (1906–7) carries the sweetness almost to swooning point, apt for Ernest Dowson's world-weary verse. In writing for voices Delius concentrates little on the energy and imagery of words, more on what mood the words evoke. His unaccompanied partsong *On Craig Ddu* (first performed in 1907) shows this. The choruses of *Song of the High Hills* (1911–12, first performed in London, 1920) are wordless: human voices paradoxically increase the sense of solitude. To this cooler period belong *North Country Sketches* (1913–14), consisting of evocations of his still-loved Yorkshire moors, and *Eventyr* (1917). If not austere, they are certainly bleaker. In 1909–10 Delius composed *Fennimore and Gerda*, his sixth and last opera (first performed in Frankfurt am Main, 1919), to a libretto drawn from Jens Peter Jacobsen's novel *Niels Lyhne*: it deals with the division between romantic dreaming and reality, though Delius oddly gave the opera a happy ending. Awkward in shape and in length, laconic compared with *A Village Romeo*, it has been called a contemporary conversation piece. Delius's operas, often deemed undramatic, respond to sensitive treatment which sustains their atmosphere.

In 1911 the young Philip Heseltine (Peter Warlock) wrote to Delius, beginning an exchange of letters which, together with his book (1923), give an insight into Delius's views on morality and on his obligations to his gifts. He scorned the bourgeoisie, the common herd, and despised conventional ties which inhibit the artist. He distrusted academic learning which killed instinct, and stressed the value of perseverance, application, and concentration of energy.

Between 1913 and 1916 Delius composed his Requiem, dedicated 'to the memory of all young Artists fallen in the war'. Again he took the text from Nietzsche—how wryly he must have smiled at using the titles 'mass' and 'requiem'! When Eric Coates produced it in London in 1922 it offended recently bereaved Christians, denying as it does an afterlife and offering instead the pantheistic renewal of Nature. Shorter than the mass and continuous, it is—until the final ecstatic affirmative return of spring—Delius's sternest work. Together with the sinister *Arabesque* (1911, 1915; first performed in Newport, Wales, 1920) to a text by Jacobsen—'Knowest thou Pan?'—the *Mass* and the Requiem present Delius's 'creed'.

In 1914 Delius was at the height of his fame. As the Germans advanced, the Deliuses retreated to England, where he was by now much fêted. Osbert Sitwell thought he might more easily be taken for a great lawyer than a great composer. Beecham in his biography (1959) wrote of the 'mingled cast of asceticism and shrewdness' (Beecham, 146) that one might find in a cardinal. Eugene Goossens remarked on Delius's querulous and penetrating voice (he

was always a polemical conversationalist). Grainger discerned in his speech half-Yorkshire, half-German peculiarities. Delius wrote letters in English, German, French, and Norwegian; but as time passed Jelka took on more of his correspondence.

Hearing May and Beatrice Harrison play Brahms's double concerto in 1914 prompted Delius, now back in Grez after a visit to Norway, to compose a similar work for them (1915). It was the first of his mature instrumental works in the traditional classical forms that were not quite second nature to him (Deryck Cooke's 1962 articles, reprinted in *A Delius Companion*, 1976, offered analyses based on organic development). As well as chamber music, there are concertos for violin (1916) and cello (1921). In 1920 came a commission from the impresario Basil Dean to compose incidental music for Flecker's oriental drama *Hassan*. When the lavish production came out in London in 1923 it ran for 281 performances. The serenade became a hit, and the closing chorus, sung as the caravan passes out of sight, is incantatory.

Final years During 1917 Delius began to show symptoms of the syphilis that he had contracted in 1895; but in 1921 the Deliuses built themselves a chalet in Norway. Despite treatment at sanatoria across Europe, by 1922 he was walking with two sticks; and by 1928 he was paralysed and blind. A young Yorkshireman called Eric Fenby heard of his condition, and that he was trying to dictate to Jelka, as he still wished to compose. For five years Fenby acted as his unpaid amanuensis, variously revising, completing, and composing *Cynara* (a setting of Ernest Dowson), *A Late Lark* (a setting of W. E. Henley), *A Song of Summer*, a third violin sonata, the *Irmelin* prelude, and *Idyll* (1932; a reworking from the *verismo* one-act opera *Margot la rouge*, 1901–2; first performed in St Louis, USA, 1983). Their greatest combined achievement, *Songs of Farewell*, settings of Walt Whitman's poems for eight-part chorus and orchestra, was dedicated to Jelka. It was first performed in 1932. By now Delius's self-reliance had hardened into egotism. Racked with pain and frustration, he became an intolerant, tyrannical figure. He loved to taunt and provoke Fenby, a sensitive and devout young man. Despite this, Fenby's devotion to Delius's music, his skill—telepathy, almost—and his compassion for the two lonely old people are frankly and movingly described in his *Delius as I Knew Him* (1936; the 1981 revision details the Delius–Fenby legacy). In 1968 Fenby acted as consultant to Ken Russell's 'disturbingly life-like' (Fenby, 178) BBC television film, *A Song of Summer*, in which Max Adrian played Delius, Christopher Gable Fenby himself. There are no recordings of Delius's voice or person.

In 1929 Delius was appointed Companion of Honour, and in October that year Beecham mounted a magnificent six-day Delius Festival in London. Delius, in his bath chair, was present, and people who saw with sentimental pity that emaciated immobile figure gained a false impression, for his stoicism, mental acuity, and sardonic wit remained unimpaired.

Back at Grez the darkness was lightened by visits from

Delius's many devoted friends, among them the composer Henry Balfour Gardiner, who had bought the Deliuses' house in 1923, allowing them to live there free (the war reduced their royalties, and Delius's malady brought extra expenses). The wireless and the gramophone now became valuable links to the musical world, though he listened to little music other than his own. In 1933 Elgar, in France to conduct his violin concerto with Menuhin, spent an afternoon at Grez. Delius, who not surprisingly rated *The Dream of Gerontius* a 'nauseating work' though he admired *Falstaff*, welcomed him warmly, and the two great composers chatted animatedly. 'A poet and a visionary' Elgar called Delius in his account of their meeting (Redwood, 94).

That summer Fenby, near breakdown, had to leave the Deliuses. 'What he suffered and what she endured' (Fenby, 103), he later recorded. In May 1934 Jelka sent for him to take charge of the household, as she had to be operated on for bowel cancer. Delius began to sink, and Jelka was brought from her hospital bed to sit at his side until he died on 10 June 1934.

Delius wished to be buried in his garden; failing that, in some country churchyard in the south of England, where people could 'place wild flowers' (Fenby, 227) on his grave—strange request for an exile and an unbeliever. As Jelka was too ill to travel, he was buried at Grez, then exhumed and reinterred at St Peter's, Limpsfield, Surrey, on 26 May 1935. Jelka died a few days later and was buried beside him.

At Beecham's suggestion Jelka had set up a trust from royalties which, together with the society founded in 1962, has promoted Delius's work. Beecham edited, propagated, and interpreted Delius's scores with unique understanding; above all, he recorded most of the concert works in performances which had been enthusiastically endorsed by the composer himself. His conducting at the Royal College of Music in 1934 of *A Village Romeo and Juliet* fully revealed the opera's seductive power. The Bradford Festival of 1962 and the fourth Delius Festival of 1982 encouraged scholarly reassessment of a composer whose professionalism, if highly individual, has tended to be underestimated. Delius's music is not everyday fare, but it enshrines his sense of bliss and aching loss at its passing. 'I have seen the best of the earth and have done everything that is worth doing; I am content' (Fenby, 73). The sentiment is worthy of the man who in his Requiem set the words 'I honour the man who can love life'.

DIANA MCVEAGH

Sources L. Carley, *Delius: a life in letters*, 1 (1983); 2 (1988) · R. Lowe, *Frederick Delius: a catalogue of the music archive of the Delius Trust, London* (1974) · R. Threlfall, *A catalogue of the compositions of Frederick Delius* (1977) · R. Threlfall, *Frederick Delius: a supplementary catalogue* (1986) · C. Delius, *Frederick Delius: memories of my brother* (1935) · E. Fenby, *Delius as I knew him* (1936) · E. Fenby, *Delius as I knew him*, rev. edn (1981) · T. Beecham, *Frederick Delius* (1959) · L. Carley, *Delius: the Paris years* (1975) · C. Redwood, ed., *A Delius companion* (1976) · L. Carley, ed., *Frederick Delius: music, art and literature* (1998) · C. Palmer, *Delius: portrait of a cosmopolitan* (1976) · *CGPLA Eng. & Wales* (1935)

Archives 16 Ogle Street, London, archive | BL, corresp. with Philip Heseltine, Add. MSS 52547–52549 · BL, letters to Sydney Schiff and Violet Schiff, Add. MS 52917 | SOUND BL NSA, 'Delius as I knew him', 10 June 1974, T695R C1 · BL NSA, *Talking about music*, 18, NP 6888WR TR1 C2 · BL NSA, 'Basil Dean on Delius', BBC Radio 3, 20 Sept 1977; *Talking about music*, 284, BBC, 1982; documentary recordings
Likenesses E. Munch, drawing, c.1890, Munch Museum, Oslo · I. Gerhardi, oils, 1903, Frau Malve Steinweg collection · J. Delius, oils, 1912, University of Melbourne, Percy Grainger Museum · I. Gerhardi, oils, 1912, Gerhardi/Steinweg collection · E. Munch, lithograph, 1920, Munch Museum, Oslo · E. Riccardi, bronze bust, c.1920, Royal College of Music, London · E. Munch, lithograph, 1922, NPG, Toledo Museum of Art, Ohio · A. John, pencil drawing, 1929, Birmingham Museums and Art Gallery · E. Procter, oils, 1929, Royal Albert Hall, London · E. Procter, pencil sketches, 1929, NPG · E. Procter, study, 1929 (for his portrait), NPG [see illus.] · J. Gunn, oils, 1932, Bradford City Art Gallery · E. Kapp, crayon drawing, 1932, BM · E. Kapp, drawing, 1932, Barber Institute of Fine Arts, Birmingham · J. Kramer, oils, 1932, Leeds City Art Gallery · photographs, repro. in L. Carley and R. Threlfall, eds., *Delius: a life in pictures* (1977) · photographs, Frederick Delius Trust, London · photographs, University of Melbourne, Percy Grainger Museum · portraits, repro. in Carley, *Letters*, 2, pl. 12 and 13
Wealth at death £2053 11s. 9d.—in England: administration with will, 27 March 1935, *CGPLA Eng. & Wales*

Dell, Edmund Emanuel (1921–1999), historian and politician, was born on 15 August 1921 at 288 Amhurst Road, Hackney, London, the third of the three gifted children of Reuben Dell, formerly Deligtisch, a manufacturer of carnival goods, and his wife, Frances (Fanny), *née* Wahl. He was educated at Owen's School, London. While there he became the London boys' chess champion. He won an open scholarship to Queen's College, Oxford, to read history, but his career there was interrupted by his war service. When he went before the army commissioning board his studies in history were commented on. He was asked who he thought was the greatest English general. He knew that the expected answer was Wellington or Marlborough. He replied, 'Cromwell'. Surprised by this answer, the board asked for his explanation. 'Cromwell', he said, 'had to create his model army. He did not inherit one. And from nothing he created an army which beat the King' (private information). He duly received his commission, as a lieutenant in the Royal Artillery.

After demobilization Dell returned to Oxford and won a first-class honours degree in 1947, following the similar distinction of his elder brother Sidney. Queen's College offered, and he accepted, the position of lecturer in modern history. In 1949 he published, with Christopher Hill, *The Good Old Cause: the English Revolution of 1640–1660*, a selection of documents from the period. Also in 1949 he was asked to join ICI at their dyestuffs division in Manchester and so began his industrial career. Throughout this period he retained an interest in politics. He served on Manchester city council from 1953 to 1960 and was secretary of the Labour group. In 1955 he was the unsuccessful Labour candidate in Blackley, Manchester, a seat Labour had held before 1951. In 1958 he was elected president of the Manchester and Salford Trades Council, an indication of his appeal to all parts of the labour movement.

Following a twelve-month visit to South America for ICI,

Dell was in 1963 faced with the opportunity of becoming a senior figure in the company if he were to abandon his political career. His friends insisted that he would be missing an important opportunity to play a prominent role in parliament and government, and this advice influenced his decision not to accept ICI's tempting offer. He was offered and accepted a one-year Simon research fellowship at Manchester University, and published articles and a Fabian pamphlet, *Brazil: the Dilemma of Reform* (1964). In his later work at the Department of Trade he was able to visit South America and impressed British exporters with his fluency in both Spanish and Portuguese. Before the general election of 1964 he became the parliamentary candidate for the safe Labour seat of Birkenhead, following the retirement of Percy Collick. Nineteen sixty-three was also an important year for him for more personal reasons, since on 5 July that year he married Susanne Regina (Susi) Gottschalk, whom he knew from his Oxford days and with whom he had continued a long and eventually successful courtship. She was a factory inspector and daughter of Henry Gottschalk, electrical engineer. Following their marriage they lived in her house in Reynolds Close, Hampstead Garden Suburb. There were no children of the marriage.

In October 1964 Dell retained Birkenhead for Labour and on arriving at the House of Commons became parliamentary private secretary to John Diamond, chief secretary to the Treasury. Nevertheless he soon realized that this position, while giving him an insight into the working of government and the Treasury, meant that he could not take part in economic or financial debates, and so resigned. At a time of acute interest in all matters concerning the new government, his talent for avoiding publicity was well demonstrated: his resignation was not noticed. He had realized that a new and wide-ranging Finance Bill would provide an opportunity to intervene with useful effect. He took part in the debate, and made good use of his industrial and commercial experience. This was noted, and the general election of 1966 brought about his appointment as parliamentary secretary at the Ministry of Technology and, in the following year, at the Department of Economic Affairs. In 1968 he became minister of state at the Board of Trade. In the latter year Robert Maxwell, desperate for recognition, began the 'I'm backing Britain' campaign. This was an attempt to persuade everyone to buy or support British products and ideas. The means he used were populist and extravagant. Harold Wilson decided to provide public support for this campaign and chose Dell to co-ordinate government assistance from the Department of Trade. Dell's participation in this campaign was supremely successful: at a time when the campaign was littering the front pages he used his special talents to conceal his involvement. In 1969 he moved to the Department of Employment and Productivity, again as minister of state.

After the general election of 1970 Dell was front-bench spokesman on industry matters, but resigned after joining sixty-eight other Labour MPs in defying a three-line whip against Britain's joining the European Economic Community, on 28 October 1971. He became a member of the public accounts committee. Following the illness of Harold Lever in 1972 he became chairman. He realized that the benefit the country was going to receive from the taxation of North Sea oil would be quite inadequate. Unusually for those days, he used his position to begin a full inquiry. The subsequent report of the committee led to the revenue petroleum tax, which he introduced when he became paymaster-general at the Treasury in the 1974 Labour government. This ensured that Britain received a proper contribution from the oil companies for the North Sea exploitation. When he was appointed paymaster-general he recalled the actions of an earlier holder of the office, Henry Fox, who was reputed to have made over £1 million by using the office to benefit himself. Recalling this, Dell did not follow custom by immediately signing away his rights to civil servants, but instead went to bed that night indulging himself with the power he still retained.

When James Callaghan replaced Harold Wilson as prime minister in April 1976, Dell became secretary of state for trade and played an important part in supporting Denis Healey's negotiations with the International Monetary Fund, particularly in the lengthy cabinet discussions. Nevertheless he became increasingly disillusioned with Labour policy, and encountered difficulties with left-wingers in his Birkenhead constituency. In the autumn of 1978 he was offered, and decided to accept, the position of chairman and chief executive of the merchant bank Guinness Peat. Callaghan insisted that he resign his cabinet post immediately, and in November 1978 he was succeeded by John Smith. He retired from parliament at the election of 1979.

Dell stepped down as chairman and chief executive of Guinness Peat in 1982, following a disagreement with Lord Kissin, the group's president. Nevertheless his presidency of the London chamber of commerce (1991–2) as well as his work in various working parties and committees on finance confirmed his reputation in commerce and finance. He was a director of Shell Transport and Trading Co. from 1979 to 1992. In 1980 he was named as the founder chairman of Channel 4 television. In that position (which he retained until 1987) he established the channel as an important and innovative addition to the medium which, many years later, still bore some of the impressions from his founding years. Following the formation of the Social Democratic Party in 1981 Dell became a trustee of the new party and a member of its finance committee. Although ambivalent about the merger with the Liberals, he led the SDP negotiating team and became a Liberal Democrat trustee. Nevertheless he later allied himself to no political party. He was involved in prison reform, where he was much influenced by the work and publications of his wife, Susi. In 1988 he became chairman of the Prison Reform Trust. He loved opera and was chairman of the finance committee of the English National Opera. He was one of the 'three wise men' appointed in 1978 by the European council to review the procedures of the EC. This extended his already considerable interest in the development of the EC.

The last years of Dell's life were taken up by his writings, and he devoted many hours to research at the Public Record Office. He was exacting in his requirement that assertions made in his writings should be properly footnoted. His publications included *The Politics of Economic Interdependence* (1987), *A Hard Pounding: Politics and Economic Crisis, 1974–76* (1991), *The Schuman Plan and the British Abdication of Leadership in Europe* (1995) (the definitive account of those unhappy years), *The Chancellors: a History of the Chancellors of the Exchequer, 1945–90* (1996), and *A Strange Eventful History: Democratic Socialism in Britain* (2000). His book *The Chancellors* provided a deep understanding of the problems facing holders of that office. Many contemporaries regarded it as a lost opportunity that his talents were not employed in the office itself.

Dell died of cancer at the North London Hospice, 47 Woodside Avenue, Finchley, on 31 October 1999, and was cremated at Golders Green crematorium. He was survived by his wife, Susi. After his death Peter Hennessy, professor of contemporary history, and Graham Zellick, vice-chancellor of the University of London, wrote that Dell possessed

> qualities of mind and character that can be, but too rarely are, found in those called to high office in our country's governance. He combined strong convictions rooted in principle with fearlessness, a formidable intellect and complete integrity. He brought an almost scholarly detachment to public policy—a respect for the primacy of evidence over prejudice; and in retirement, this made him a valued and respected member of the scholarly community. Those of us privileged to know him will always remember him as an exemplar of standards and qualities in public life. (*The Times*, 8 Nov 1999)

ROBERT SHELDON

Sources *The Guardian* (4 Nov 1999) · *The Independent* (4 Nov 1999) · *The Times* (5 Nov 1999) · *The Times* (8 Nov 1999) · *Daily Telegraph* (5 Nov 1999) · WWW · personal knowledge (2004) · private information (2004) · b. cert. · m. cert. · d. cert.
Archives Bodl. Oxf., papers · priv. coll. | Bodl. Oxf., corresp. with his brother Sidney
Likenesses photograph, 1966, repro. in *The Independent* · P. Cade, double portrait, photograph, 1978 (with Kirillin), Hult. Arch. · photograph, 1989, repro. in *Daily Telegraph* · photograph, 1996, repro. in *The Times* (5 Nov 1999) · photograph, repro. in *The Guardian*
Wealth at death £903,730—gross; £902,124—net: probate, 31 Jan 2000, CGPLA Eng. & Wales

Dell [*married name* Savage], **Ethel Mary** (1881–1939), novelist, was born on 2 August 1881 at 61 Hayter Road, Brixton, London, the third and last child of John Vincent Dell (*d.* 1913) and his wife, Irene Parrott (*d.* 1918), daughter of John Parrott, a solicitor of Stony Stratford, Buckinghamshire, and his wife, Irene Smith. Her father had followed his father into the Equitable Life Assurance Company, and the family were comfortable but not affluent. The children were initially educated at home by their mother; in 1890 the family moved to Polworth Road, Streatham, London, and in 1893 Ethel and her sister Ella were sent to

Streatham College for Girls, where they remained until 1898.

Ethel M. Dell originally began to write stories at school to amuse her friends, and her father had some privately printed. After she left school, and the family moved first to Knockholt, Kent, and (in 1907) to Ashford, Surrey, writing became a full-time obsession. Some stories were taken by magazines such as the *Universal and Ludgate* and the *Red Magazine*, but she went through years of discouragement before she managed to place a novel. Her first and best known, *The Way of an Eagle*, went through many refusals and redraftings before being accepted by T. Fisher Unwin for his First Novel Library in 1912. It became an immediate best-seller, and she subsequently published thirty-two more novels, eight volumes of short stories, and a book of poems, her last novel being published in the year of her death. In 1921 she met Lieutenant-Colonel Gerald Tahourdin Savage (*b.* 1883) of the Royal Army Service Corps, whom she married on 7 June 1922. They had no children, and she is said to have disliked them, much preferring her dogs.

Ethel M. Dell spans interestingly the period between the sensation novelists of the late nineteenth century, such as Rhoda Broughton and M. E. Braddon, and the twentieth-century mass women's fiction market of writers such as Georgette Heyer and Catherine Cookson. She never aspired to any intellectual qualities, but she knew her public and supplied her readers with melodrama, romance, purity, and happy endings, preferably in that order and in a genteel setting. Originally a comment by Rebecca West, it became commonly held that 'she rode the Tosh Horse hell for leather'. Her language was often banal and her plots stereotyped, but she was adept at producing the tense situation and the twist in the action which would delay the ending for another hundred pages. Her heroines were spirited but virtuous, her heroes faithful, chivalrous, and steely (though often small and insignificant in appearance, as her own husband was), her villains thoroughly villainous. The children which resulted from the villainy are usually eliminated by contrived accidents in order not to impede the happy ending. Many of her novels have a background in India, a country she never visited, though she read about it obsessively. Running through all of them is a heavy emphasis on religiosity and a disturbingly sadistic undertone. Although she had no literary pretensions, there is evidence that she resented the patronizing reviews she frequently received, and that she could mock her own reputation. 'Now we really shall see what the brainy Blanche reads in her leisure moments', says the heroine of *The Juice of the Pomegranate* (1938). 'Great Scott! It's an Ethel M. Dell'.

For a celebrated writer, Ethel M. Dell led a private, almost reclusive life. After her parents' deaths she lived quietly with her sister in Guildford. After her marriage she lived in the country, avoiding her fans and leading a life of almost ascetic industry, in which she frequently got out of bed to write through the night in her bathroom. She earned vast sums of money with which she was generous to her family and to charity, but was notoriously indifferent to what she wore or ate, and she disliked foreign holidays. Her servants and friends all bore witness to her considerable charm of manner. In 1929 she was operated on for breast cancer, and in 1930 she and her husband moved from Ewhurst in Hampshire, where they were living, to a less remote house in Winchester. When war was imminent in 1939 her husband, who was on the reserve list, was called up, and the couple moved to Hertford; it was here that she found that cancer had recurred. She died in the Hertfordshire County Hospital in Hertford on 17 September 1939 and was buried in Hertford cemetery. Her will left everything to her husband.　　HARRIET HARVEY WOOD

Sources *The Times* (19 Sept 1939) · P. Dell, *Nettie and Sissie: a biography of best selling novelist Ethel M. Dell and her sister Ella* (1977) · BL, Society of Authors Archive, Add. MS 56690 · *News Chronicle* (19 Sept 1939) · P. Braybrooke, *Some goddesses of the pen* (1927) · CGPLA Eng. & Wales (1939)
Archives BL, corresp. with Society of Authors, Add. MS 56690
Likenesses photographs, repro. in Dell, *Nettie and Sissie*
Wealth at death £32,937 5s. 10d.: probate, 19 Sept 1939, CGPLA Eng. & Wales

Dell, Henry (*b.* in or before **1733**), bookseller and playwright, was the son of Henry Dell, a tailor in St Peters Chalfont, Buckinghamshire. He was apprenticed to the London stationer James Penny on 6 March 1750 and was freed as a member of the Stationers' Company on 5 July 1757. As a bookseller, Dell first appears trading in Tower Street, London, possibly from the same premises as his former master; he served as master to Edward Barker between 6 December 1757 (when the apprentice was turned over to Dell from Kenrick Peck) and 12 June 1759 when Barker was freed. On 6 June 1758 Jonathan Turner Dell, probably Dell's brother, was also bound to Dell but he never seems to have completed his term. By 1765 Dell was trading as Dell & Co. at the corner of Brooke Street and Holborn, London, and appears to have been mostly concerned with the peddling of secondhand books.

As a bookseller Dell forged a less than distinguished career, although he did continue to issue catalogues until 1793, but it was his association with the London stage which dominates his reputation. His acting career seems restricted to a curious attempt to perform the part of Mrs Termagant at Covent Garden Theatre in Thomas Shadwell's popular play *The Squire of Alsatia*. Dell appears to be the only man to take the role of Mrs Termagant during the eighty-year history of the play, and not surprisingly his performance was, by all accounts, without success. He was also the author or adapter of four plays, the first of which was *The Spouter, or, The Double Revenge*, an original comic farce produced in 1756. Although there is no record of performance, it seems that Dell's play was the inspiration for Arthur Murphy's *The Spouter, or, The Triple Revenge*, which was performed at Covent Garden Theatre on 26 April 1756. That same year Dell wrote a tragedy called *Minorca* which was 'printed just when the place from which it is named was taken. Nothing can be more contemptible than it is in every point of view' (*New Theatrical Dictionary*,

186). The untimely nature of the play prevented its performance; however, a second edition was printed in 1756 in which Dell responded to 'what obscure hackney writers have been pleased to say concerning a few mistakes' (*DNB*). Dell also adapted Cibber's *Comical Lovers* as a two-act comedy called *The Frenchified Lady Never in Paris*, which was first performed at Covent Garden Theatre on 23 March 1756 and regularly revived there and at Drury Lane Theatre until 1773. The following year another adaptation by Dell called *The Mirror*, from Thomas Randolph's *The Muses' Looking-Glass*, appeared but it was never acted.

Some years later Dell wrote and published *The Bookseller: a Poem* (1766), which one reviewer in the *Gentleman's Magazine* described as 'mere prose in rhyme' and which another critic denounced as 'a wretched, rhyming list of Booksellers in London and Westminster, with silly commendation of some, and stupid abuse of others' (*GM*; Nichols, *Lit. anecdotes*, 3.641). Nothing further is known about Dell's life or career and he reputedly died in poverty at his place in Holborn but no record of his death or estate can be found. He does not seem to have been the Henry Dell, bachelor, formerly of Kew, whose estate was administered on 11 March 1795.　　MICHAEL T. DAVIS

Sources *DNB* · T. Gilliland, *The dramatic mirror, containing the history of the stage from the earliest period, to the present time*, 2 vols. (1808) · S. O. Jones, *Biographia dramatica* (1812) · *The new theatrical dictionary* (1792) · B. R. Schneider, *Index to 'The London stage, 1660–1800'* (1979) · H. R. Plomer and others, *A dictionary of the printers and booksellers who were at work in England, Scotland, and Ireland from 1726 to 1775* (1932) · D. F. McKenzie, ed., *Stationers' Company apprentices*, [3]: *1701–1800* (1978) · *GM*, 1st ser., 36 (1766), 241 · Nichols, *Lit. anecdotes*, vol. 3 · I. Maxted, *The London book trades, 1775–1800: a preliminary checklist of members* (1977) · administration, PRO, PROB 6/171, fol. 32v · T. Belanger, 'A directory of the London booktrade, 1766', *Publishing History*, 1 (1977), 7–48
Wealth at death administration, PRO, PROB 6/171, fol. 32v · died in poverty: Nichols, *Lit. anecdotes*, 641

Dell, Jonas (*d.* **1665?**), soldier and religious writer, may have fought in the parliamentarian army in the civil war. Nothing is known about his origins or early life, but in 1658 he attacked a corrupt establishment thus: 'I did not think at Marston Moor fight, nor several other engagements since, that ever any of the innocent lambs of God should have been beaten and put into prison … for crying out against the ministers of Antichrist' (Dell, *A Voyce*, 44). Certainly, his *Christ Held Forth by the Word*, dedicated before September 1646 to 'my honourable Collonel Rich', suggests he was by then a soldier. This work concluded that 'Christ is so our liberty, to redeem us from the bondage of the law, from the bondage of ceremonies, and from the bondage of human ordinances' (sig. D2). Such views were common in radical circles, and soon the Quakers provided organization for many of those that shared them. Dell later recalled that 'till Christ was made manifest in me I was not saved, nor had no life as to God, though I was high in profession and knowledge outwardly' (Dell, *Forms*, 48). He may himself have been earlier a Baptist, for he argued against them in 1657 that 'I am come out of your ground, and I cannot observe your fashions', and was forced therefore to 'disown you ... who are degenerated from what you were' (Dell, *A Voyce*, 38, 95).

It seems that Dell joined the Quakers in 1655–6, certainly before George Fox's arrival in the country in 1657. When serving in Scotland at the garrison of 'Holmdell' (perhaps Helmsdale) in Sutherland, he tells us, he had argued with a group of Baptists who held the doctrines of free will and falling away, and with another Baptist officer, one W. P. (probably William Packer, later deputy to Major-General Fleetwood), who had written a 'scandalous paper which was handed up and down in the regiment, from one to another, making a scorn of me' (Dell, *Forms*, 11). W. P. accused him of antinomianism (which he denied) and of opposing the literal truth of the resurrection (a view he vigorously defended). Dell may have earlier been attached to the free-will group, for he confessed of them that 'you do something more resemble the true church than they in outward things' (ibid., 11). He wrote *Forms the Pillars* in 1656; the work would have been longer 'but that this great marsh [march] out of this onked [unkind] nation of Scotland into England, hath prevented me' (ibid., 72). In December 1657 he was resident in the capital, referring to 'my neighbour anabaptists in the city and suburbs of London' (Dell, *A Voyce*, 92). Though *A Voyce* was 'written and published to go abroad in the army', Dell seems by now to have been at the point of leaving it, disillusioned with the Cromwellian establishment, resentful of ceremonious respect for rank, and contemptuous of 'carnal weapons'. Spiritual warfare, however, was another matter: on 28 December 1657, 'in the night upon the Guard in Paul's that great cathedral, when as I was reproving the souldiers for sin in the power of God, and directing them to the light', Dell was engaged in polemical combat by John Mercer, a Baptist officer (ibid., 89).

Jonas Dell is reported to have died at Stepney in 1665. Perhaps, many years earlier, he had married and had children. The administration of the will of a Jane Dell of Stepney was granted to her son John in November 1667, but in February the following year, probate of the estate of John Dell of Stepney was granted to his principal creditor, Maria Haffnaile.   STEPHEN WRIGHT

Sources C. H. Firth and G. Davies, *The regimental history of Cromwell's army*, 2 vols. (1940) · J. Dell, *A voyce from the temple* (1658) · J. Dell, *Forms the pillars of Antichrist* (1656) · J. Dell, *Christ held forth by the word, the onely way to the father* (1646) · *DNB*

Dell, William (d. 1669), ejected minister and educational reformer, was admitted sizar at Emmanuel College, Cambridge, in April 1624; there is no reliable information about his early life. He graduated BA in 1628 and MA in 1631, subsequently becoming a fellow. With the support of Oliver St John, first earl of Bolingbroke, on 20 February 1641 he was instituted rector of Yielden (sometimes Yelden), Bedfordshire, a benefice worth some £200 a year. His first published work, *Power from on High* (1645), was dedicated to Elizabeth St John, countess of Bolingbroke, whom he thanked for supporting him through an earlier crisis, perhaps a serious illness.

During the early 1640s Dell was most prominent as chaplain to Sir Thomas Fairfax and the New Model Army, at which time the earliest signs of Dell's controversial nature became apparent: in November 1644 he was sent home as part of Oliver Cromwell's attempt at conciliating the earl of Manchester. He was subsequently recalled, however, and he accompanied the New Model on its key campaigns from Naseby (June 1645) onwards, first as minister to Colonel Sir Miles Hobart's regiment and later as personal chaplain to Fairfax. His contribution climaxed with a sermon to the triumphant army before Oxford, published as *The Building and Glory of the Truely Christian and Spiritual Church* (1646), in which the army was his principal example of the lively, spiritual church as opposed to 'the forms of the former age'. He officiated at the marriage of General Ireton and Bridget Cromwell at Holton, Oxfordshire, on 15 June 1646. He was awarded £50 by the Commons on 22 June for bringing the news of the surrender of the city of Oxford and went back to consolidate the ideological victory in the pulpits of the city. However, on 27 June he was ordered to appear before the House of Lords to answer accusations made in a paper they had received relating to his sermon at Marston earlier in the month. In July he successfully argued that the charges were too general to stick, but he continued to be the butt of presbyterian attacks. He preached the November 1646 fast sermon to the House of Commons, published as *Right Reformation*, complete with an attack on Christopher Love, the presbyterian who had also been preaching that day. He resigned as chaplain to Fairfax in March 1648, but he continued to defend the army 'in its ways of Justice and Righteousness' (title-page) in *The City Ministers Unmask'd* (1649).

At the height of his influence Dell was one of the puritan ministers offering spiritual consolation to Charles I before his execution—though his offer was turned down. That year he dedicated to the House of Commons his sermon *The Way of True Peace and Unity in the Churches*, in which he argued that congregations should choose their ministers, and the state should keep out of church and theological matters. Dell disliked uniformity in church practice, and made a clear distinction between unity and uniformity, regarding the latter as an inappropriate exercise of power in spiritual matters. This brought him into regular controversy with the presbyterians, most notably Thomas Edwards, who in the third part of *Gangraena* accused him of sedition, and Samuel Rutherford, whose *Survey of the Spirituall Antichrist* (1648) argued that Dell's emphasis on inward religion was antinomian: 'Come and learn at Mr Del, to keepe the heart right, and violate all the ten commandments' (p. 31). Dell's tract *The Doctrine of Baptisms* (1652), for example, argues that any kind of water baptism is irrelevant to the spiritual baptism of Christ; as late as 1832 this was being republished by Quakers, though Dell had no leanings towards Quakerism himself. It is not clear how thorough-going he was in putting his convictions into practice. By the early 1650s he had married Martha (d. 1681), whose other name is unknown. Of their seven children the names of Anne (16 December 1653), Nathaniel (16 May 1655), and Mercy (16 February 1657) appear in the baptismal registers of Yielden, while that of John (*b*. 1652/3) does not. This may indicate that he changed his mind, or simply that baptismal registers in the Commonwealth were used as records of births. Dell's indifference to ceremony is illustrated by the complaint his parishioners made to the House of Lords on 20 June 1660 that in 1659 he had not celebrated communion at Christmas, but had let John Bunyan, a tinker, preach to them; this is of a piece with his earlier encouragement of 'mechanic preachers' in the army. Yet his policy on baptism was not the only one vulnerable to charges of hypocrisy: he preached against tithes but still took them, and the same ambivalence characterized his second university career.

On 7 May 1649 Dell was intruded as master of Gonville and Caius College, Cambridge. During his early years he appears to have been active in managing the college, including the chapel, but less so as his term progressed. On the evidence of the college gesta book, he appears to have been present at key moments in the college's life, but not ordinarily resident, although he managed to get his salary augmented. In the early 1650s he preached controversial sermons in the university church and town on the role of learning, arguing that understanding scripture was a spiritual gift, and that 'humane learning' was a positive hindrance, involving the corrupting study of pagan authors. This was in response to a commencement sermon by his fellow Independent Sydrach Simpson, now master of Pembroke, who had argued for a learned ministry. Dell argued that universities should stop awarding divinity degrees; the syllabus led its candidates astray, the concept of degrees was unacceptably hierarchical in the church, and their existence served to mislead people who took them as marks of holiness. In *The Stumbling Stone* (1653) he argues 'there needs nothing to the ministry of the New Testament but only God's pouring out his Spirit' (p. 24). In an appendix to *The Tryal of Spirits* (1653), 'The right reformation of learning', he made further proposals for the reformation of education: that the civil power should provide schools in every town and village in the Commonwealth, and that there should be a university in each major town to reduce the hold of Oxford and Cambridge, teaching the liberal arts, mathematics, medicine, and law (though not divinity, of course) to a much wider constituency. Dell's emphasis, like that of many of the antinomian commentators on education at the time, such as John Webster, Gerard Winstanley, and George Fox, is on learning that might be useful to the Commonwealth. For these views he was attacked by Simpson, and in an appendix to Seth Ward's *Vindiciae academiarum* (1654). In 1657 he was active, along with John Donne, the minister of Pertenhall in Bedfordshire, in collecting a petition against the second protectorate parliament, published as *The Humble and Serious Testimony*. Dell's disappointment with his onetime allies was thus political as well as spiritual.

Dell resigned his mastership on 11 May 1660, just before the Restoration. Following the hostile petition of his Yielden parishioners on 20 June, he was ejected from his living; his successor was instituted on 4 January 1661. While there were some disputes over college property near his lands in Westoning, south of Bedford, where he lived in retirement, his correspondence from that period seems genial and cheerful. He died on 5 November 1669 and was buried in his own land two days later. He was survived by his wife, Martha, and six of his children. Some years later, during the exclusion crisis of 1681, his *Increase of Popery* was published.

Dell was a key figure in the development of antinomian religion in the 1640s and 50s, though he quotes most often from Luther, and regarded himself as the heir of Wycliff and Hus as well. His influence lasted more than a century after his death, though ironically among Quakers rather than the heirs of the Independents with whom he was most closely associated. Richard Baxter, who had earlier been alarmed at Dell's influence in the army, wrote that he was 'one, who took reason, sound doctrine, order and concord to be the intolerable maladies of Church and State, because they were the greatest strangers to his mind' (quoted in Walker). The evidence of his writing, and what survives of his charismatic preaching, suggests that his reforming ideas were more substantial than that verdict suggests; but it does show Dell's talent for making enemies.   ROGER POOLEY

Sources *Calamy rev.*, 161–2 · E. C. Walker, *William Dell, master puritan* (1970) · C. N. L. Brooke, *A history of Gonville and Caius College* (1985) · L. F. Solt, *Saints in arms* (1959) · C. Webster, 'William Dell and the idea of university', *Changing perspectives in the history of science*, ed. M. Teich and R. Young (1973), 110–26 · J. Venn and others, eds., *Biographical history of Gonville and Caius College*, 3: *Biographies of the successive masters* (1901), 93–104 · Venn, *Alum. Cant.* · P. Burke, 'William Dell, the universities and the radical tradition', *Reviving the English revolution*, ed. G. Eley and W. Hunt (1988), 181–9 · R. L. Greaves, *The puritan revolution and educational thought* (1969) · F. G. Emmison, ed., *Bedfordshire parish registers*, 7 (1933); 20 (1939) · *The letter books of Sir Samuel Luke, 1644–45*, ed. H. G. Tibbutt, Bedfordshire Historical RS, 42 (1963) · R. Schlatter, 'The higher learning in puritan England', *Historical Magazine of the Protestant Episcopal Church*, 23 (1954), 167–87 · A. Laurence, *Parliamentary army chaplains, 1642–1651*, Royal Historical Society Studies in History, 59 (1990)
Archives Gon. & Caius Cam., College Gesta Book (minute book) and letters, MS 714, fols. 143–51
Likenesses oils, Gon. & Caius Cam.; repro. in Walker, *William Dell*
Wealth at death £25 p.a. for seven years, manor of Aynells and freehold of Sampshill, and library bequeathed to wife and children: will

Deller, Alfred George (1912–1979), singer, was born on 31 May 1912 at 42 Clifton Terrace, Margate, Kent, the son of Thomas William Deller (1871–1951), a physical training instructor, and his wife, Mary Ann Cave (1874–1946). He was the sixth of seven children. He was educated at the Central School, Margate, before finding employment in 1927 as an apprentice in the furniture shop of Munro Cobb in Margate. When that job was discontinued he went to work in 1929 for the Hastings firm of Elijah Gray & Sons Ltd, house furnishers and undertakers, as a furniture salesman. There he met the owner's daughter, Kathleen Margaret Lowe (*b*. 1913/14), whom he married on 5 June 1937; they had two sons and a daughter. His wife became a firm supporter of his desire to sing and to give that precedence over his other employment.

Alfred George Deller (1912–1979), by Erich Auerbach, 1960
[rehearsing as Oberon in *A Midsummer Night's Dream* by Benjamin Britten]

Deller's earliest singing experience was as a boy chorister at St John's Church, Margate, where he sang the treble solos until he was sixteen. His first position as a counter-tenor was at Christ Church, St Leonards, where he sang from 1930; he moved to Canterbury Cathedral as a lay clerk in 1939. A firm pacifist, after appearing at a conscription tribunal in October 1940 he was registered as a conscientious objector. Deller was fortunate enough to find work on a farm within cycling distance of Canterbury which allowed him to continue with his cathedral duties.

Deller's solo career was launched in 1943 when Michael Tippett was in Canterbury prior to the first performance of his *Plebs angelica*. Tippett was encouraged to hear him sing Purcell's 'Music for a while', at which, Tippett wrote later, 'the centuries rolled back. For I recognised absolutely that this was the voice for which Purcell had written' (Tippett, Bergmann, and Spencer, 43). In a testimonial dated 15 July 1946 Tippett further wrote: 'It is the most remarkable male alto voice that I have ever heard, with an unrivalled purity of diction added—I can only imagine by hard work' (private information). Tippett and Walter Bergmann together decided to take Deller's voice to London, where Deller made his début singing Purcell's ''Tis nature's voice' from the ode to St Cecilia of 1694 at the Friends' meeting-house in Euston Road on 31 December 1943, a concert promoted to raise funds for Morley College. Tippett then asked Deller to perform the 'Esurientes' from J. S. Bach's Magnificat with the Morley College choir. Many engagements followed, including an invitation to sing Purcell's *Come ye Sons of Art* in the BBC Third Programme's inaugural concert in 1946. Deller soon moved to

London after this, turning fully professional when he joined the choir of St Paul's Cathedral in 1947 as a vicar-choral, a post that he held until 1961. Although his career was to require him to live in London, and to travel all over the world, he never lost touch with Kent, eventually settling in Ashford.

Deller's reputation rests principally on his performances of English lute songs, most importantly those of Dowland, and as an unrivalled interpreter of Purcell: it was his artistry that caused both these repertories to be recognized for their full worth for the first time. In addition he had a limited but significant career as an opera singer, culminating in the role of Oberon in *A Midsummer Night's Dream*, which Benjamin Britten wrote for him. This received its first performance in 1960 at Aldeburgh: Deller sang both on this occasion and on the subsequent recording. He founded the Deller Consort in 1950, primarily to specialize in the English madrigal repertory, and the group toured widely in North America, Europe, Australasia, and the Far East. In addition, in 1963 he started the Stour Music Festival in Kent, where he directed performances of larger works. His regular accompanists included Walter Bergmann, Desmond Dupré, and later Robert Spencer.

Deller's reputation also rests on the fact that he was the first falsetto singer to bring the counter-tenor voice to prominence. Indeed he did more than this, since when he started his career the counter-tenor sound was scarcely known outside cathedral circles and, when it became known, was treated with suspicion. Bergmann remembered that:

> audiences in the 1940s did not know what to make of a man who sang in a female voice's tessitura. At its best they held it for a gimmick, at its worst for 'unnatural', even for a castrato's voice. And was there any music composed for that strange voice, and if so was it not outdated? ... At each concert [Deller] had first to overcome the antipathy of 75 per cent of his audience. (Tippett, Bergmann, and Spencer, 44)

Deller himself liked to tell the story of an agent who, at the beginning of his career, broke out in indignation, 'What? A Purcell programme? A dead loss' (ibid.). Yet such was Deller's talent and tenacity of purpose that works which had once been bypassed because they contained complicated counter-tenor solo parts were eventually searched out and performed for the same reason.

As the first counter-tenor to become an international star, Deller created the platform on which many younger singers were able to perform; yet none of them made a sound to resemble his. The explanation is that Deller trained in cathedral choirs and retained the essentially vibrato-less, almost white tone of the ideal cathedral singer. Later it became customary for counter-tenor soloists to develop a fuller tone, even in lute songs, which by comparison gives Deller's performances—described at various times as being 'sweet', 'flexible', 'agile', and with the sound 'focussed to a pin-point'—a rare quality. Unusual also was the intensity of his conviction that singing was nothing if not communication with an audience, in modern concert conditions. Unlike many later singers of the earlier repertories Deller had no interest in musicological knowledge or analysis, but relied on a vivid artistic imagination which left everything to the performance. Robert Spencer recalled:

> Alfred disliked rehearsal … The first time I accompanied him he reluctantly went through every song with me, and I was feeling reasonably confident. Fortunately his son Mark warned me that the performance might not be so predictable, but I was flabbergasted when the evening bore so little resemblance to the afternoon. (Tippett, Bergmann, and Spencer, 45)

Deller has occasionally been criticized for vocal mannerisms—the colouring of a high note, the drawing back of a rhythm—yet the artlessness of his vocal sound conveys a straightforward sincerity. However involved the search for authenticity in early music becomes it will never find a way of replacing Deller's concern for the inspiration of the moment.

Despite suffering from angina, Deller continued to sing, 'albeit with diminishing range and power' (Steane). He was appointed OBE in 1970. He had a heart attack while in Bologna in Italy, and died there at the Ospedale S. Orsola on 16 July 1979; he was buried in the churchyard of All Saints', Boughton Aluph, Kent. His wife, Kathleen, survived him. His son Mark Deller continued to perform with and direct the Deller Consort.   PETER PHILLIPS

Sources M. Tippett, W. Bergmann, and R. Spencer, 'Alfred Deller', *Early Music*, 8 (1980), 43–5 · *MT*, 120 (1979), 762 · private information (2004) [Mark Deller, son; incl. Michael Tippett's testimonial, 15 July 1946] · M. Hardwick and M. Hardwick, *Alfred Deller: a singularity of voice* (1980) · D. Scott, 'Deller, Alfred (George)', *The new Grove dictionary of opera*, ed. S. Sadie, 1 (1992) · J. B. Steane, 'Deller, Alfred (George)', *New Grove* · P. Giles, *The history and technique of the countertenor* (1994) · *WWW* · b. cert. · m. cert. · d. cert.

Archives BL NSA, performance recordings | SOUND BL NSA, performance recordings

Likenesses E. Auerbach, photograph, 1960, Hult. Arch. [see illus.]

Wealth at death £5129: probate, 2 Nov 1979, *CGPLA Eng. & Wales*

Deller, Sir Edwin (1883–1936), university administrator, was born at Paignton, Devon, on 16 March 1883, the son of Edwin Deller, carpenter, of Paignton, and his wife, Mary Ann Stone. He was educated at local schools up to the age of fourteen, when he began work as a clerk for an uncle at Paignton. He went to London at the age of about twenty and worked as a clerk in various offices. He was then employed by Kent education committee until 1912, when he became a secretary in the academic department of London University. He was already a member of the university, for he had matriculated in 1908 as an evening student at King's College, graduating LLB in 1911. He obtained the degree of LLD in 1916 with a thesis entitled 'The liberty of the subject', as a student of University College. He also studied at the London School of Economics. In 1914 he married Winifred Lilian (Betty), eldest daughter of Benjamin Willey Betts, embosser and chaser, of Hornsey; they had a son.

Deller's career on the staff of London University was rapid. In 1921 he became academic registrar and in 1929 he was elected principal of the university in succession to the geologist Sir Franklin Sibly, whose period of office had not been entirely successful. He was a born administrator and

Sir Edwin Deller (1883–1936), by Gilbert Spencer, 1922

a man of great culture and knowledge of the world, while his quickness of intuition made him skilful in handling men and situations. He seldom intervened in debate, but when he did, he would settle a point by a few brief words, wise and tactful, and often touched with a quiet and irresistible humour. He had a quick eye for the heart of any problem, and an equability of temper which was of great value in handling the often heated controversies that confronted him during his term of office. Above all, he was a man of striking personality and charm, whose open-hearted friendliness and quiet wisdom spread a much-needed spirit of goodwill and co-operation in the university, upon which the erection of the central buildings in Bloomsbury set the crown. In the organization of these buildings, the commissioning of an architect (Charles Holden), and the general policy of the development of the site Deller made a great contribution, often working closely with William Beveridge. He was not destined to see the buildings' completion, however. He died in University College Hospital, London, on 30 November 1936 from the effects of an accident which had occurred three days earlier when he was visiting the great tower, then in the course of construction. He was survived by his wife.

Outside the university, Deller played a great part in founding the British Institute in Paris. In 1926 he visited the United States of America, and on his return wrote an excellent book, *Universities in the United States* (1927). He was made a chevalier of the Légion d'honneur in 1932 and was knighted in 1935. Among other distinctions he was elected an honorary bencher of the Inner Temple in 1933.

H. E. BUTLER, *rev.* M. C. CURTHOYS

Sources *The Times* (1–2 Dec 1936) · *The Times* (2 Dec 1936) · *The Times* (4–5 Dec 1936) · *The Times* (5 Dec 1936) · personal knowledge (1949) · N. B. Harte, *The University of London, 1836–1986: an illustrated history* (1986) · *CGPLA Eng. & Wales* (1936)

Likenesses G. Spencer, drawing, 1922, U. Lond. [*see illus.*] · H. M. Campbell, pencil drawing, U. Lond.

Wealth at death £4001 6s. 9d.: administration with will, 6 Jan 1937, *CGPLA Eng. & Wales*

Delmer, (Denis) Sefton (1904–1979), journalist, was born in Germany at Berlin on 24 May 1904, the only son and elder child of Professor Frederick Sefton Delmer and his wife, Mabel Hook. His father was an Australian lecturer in English at Berlin University and author of a standard textbook for German schools, *English Literature from Beowulf to Bernard Shaw* (1913). His mother was also Australian. He was brought up to speak German and as late as 1939 still spoke English with a slight accent. At the outbreak of the First World War his father was interned, and Delmer had the highly unusual experience of going to school in Berlin as an enemy alien. But Tom, as he was known, was not subjected to much persecution, and on the whole enjoyed himself. Professor Delmer was released in May 1917 and given permission to go to England. Delmer was then sent to St Paul's School, Hammersmith, London, and from there won a scholarship to Lincoln College, Oxford, where he obtained a second class in German in 1927.

After the war Delmer's father returned to Germany and by 1927 was earning a living as a stringer for a number of English newspapers in Berlin. It was here in that year while helping his father out that Delmer first caught the eye of Lord Beaverbrook, who gave him a job on the *Daily Express*. Within a year he was back in Berlin as head of the paper's new bureau. He was only twenty-four and was destined to remain in Lord Beaverbrook's employment for another thirty years—something of a record.

Delmer, like many young Englishmen, threw himself into the social life of the Weimar republic, reporting with relish the stories of political scandal and corruption. He later laid great stress on the number of charlatans of one kind or another who at that time flourished in Germany and how when he first attended a Nazi meeting in Berlin in 1929 and heard Hitler exhorting his audience not to eat foreign fruit such as oranges, he dismissed him as yet another crackpot. Later, however, he became friendly with Ernst Röhm and as a result was the first British reporter to interview Hitler at his Brown House headquarters in Munich. Eventually he became so familiar with the Nazis that the Foreign Office suspected him of being a German agent. In 1932 he travelled in Hitler's aeroplane during his election campaign and in the following year secured his most famous scoop when he walked through the burning Reichstag at Hitler's side. (He used to remark ruefully that when he phoned his story through to the *Daily Express*, the sub-editor was only interested in the details of the fire.) Delmer was later criticized in some

quarters for his close Nazi contacts, but he regarded it as all part of a reporter's job. Besides which there is no doubt that he enjoyed himself immensely. In 1933 he was sent to Paris for a year as *Daily Express* correspondent, and in 1936 to Spain to report the civil war. He spent two years in Spain and at the outbreak of the war was in Poland and subsequently in Paris.

Delmer married in 1935 Isabel, daughter of Captain Philip Llewellyn Nicholas, master mariner. She was a model for the sculptor Jacob Epstein. Delmer claimed that he had determined to marry her after first seeing a bust of her in an exhibition. The marriage was dissolved in 1946 and Isabel Delmer subsequently married the composer Alan Rawsthorne.

In September 1940 Delmer, who had been engaged to broadcast on the German Service of the BBC, was recruited by Special Operations Executive to organize what were known as 'black propaganda' broadcasts to Germany. The object was to sabotage the German war effort by spreading rumours and false reports. Delmer could not have had a job better suited to his background and talents. He began in May 1941 by inventing Der Chef, a right-wing German patriot opposed to the Nazis broadcasting to members of his secret organization apparently from within Germany. This was followed by several other RUs (research units) which ranged from bona fide Roman Catholic propaganda to astrology. Following the construction of the new 500 kW transmitter (Aspidistra) at Crowborough in 1942 Delmer launched his most successful project, a pseudo-German forces programme, *Soldatensender Calais*, a 'grey' station as opposed to 'black' which relied on its snappy presentation and especially its popular music to attract listeners among the German forces, even though many of them would know or suspect it to be an enemy wavelength. Though it was never possible precisely to estimate the effect of these various propaganda exercises, post-war research suggests that they did, in fact, contribute a great deal to the undermining of enemy morale. For his war work, Delmer was appointed OBE in 1946.

At the end of the war, after a short spell in Germany working for the Allied Control Commission, Delmer rejoined the *Daily Express* as chief foreign affairs reporter. In 1948 he married Zoë Ursula (Peggy), daughter of Thomas Stubley Black, printer. They had one son and one daughter.

Delmer covered virtually every major foreign news story until his departure from the paper in 1959, becoming an almost legendary Fleet Street figure, famous for his knack of being in the right place at the right time. In 1956 he was the only British reporter in Poland at the time of the Poznań riots. In the same year he was expelled from Egypt after he described President Nasser as a 'frightened Pharaoh'. Two months later he marched with Hungarian rebels in Budapest and secured an exclusive interview with Colonel Pal Maleter, leader of the insurgents who was later executed by the Russians. Germany, however, remained his chief interest and he was always quick to point out any sign of Nazi resurgence.

Delmer's eventual departure from the *Daily Express* was

blamed by colleagues on his increasingly extravagant expenses claims, which were by then very much part of the legend. 'I can only think clearly in a five-star hotel' (private information, 1986), he once said. He liked to have a suite at his disposal and lavish hospitality laid on to entertain his guests. In 1959 Lord Beaverbrook dismissed him and he retired to his idyllic farmhouse in Suffolk, where he wrote two volumes of autobiography which contain a great deal of valuable historical material, though he never managed to shed his reporter's style. In 1963–4 he returned to Germany and spent a year as editorial adviser to *Der Spiegel*. He also published *The Counterfeit Spy* (1973), an account of the successful attempt to deceive the Germans about allied invasion plans, as well as a short historical survey, *Weimar Germany* (1972).

In later life Delmer was a huge Falstaffian figure of benign and monk-like appearance. It was hard to picture him as a sleuth or to imagine that in his youth he had been famous for his Byronic good looks. Unlike many of his Fleet Street colleagues, he was essentially a humble man who inspired deep affection and loyalty from a wide variety of people. Some fellow journalists saw him as a guru or prophet. He liked to clown, but his strength as a reporter lay in his shrewdness and his down-to-earth approach. Delmer died on 4 September 1979 at his home at Lamarsh, Suffolk, after many years of ill health.

RICHARD INGRAMS, *rev.*

Sources S. Delmer, *Trail sinister* (1961) · S. Delmer, *Black boomerang* (1962) · E. Howe, *The black game* (1982) · private information (1986) · *The Times* (6 Sept 1979) · WWW
Archives SOUND BL NSA, performance recording
Likenesses R. Dumont, photograph, 1956, Hult. Arch.

Deloitte, William Welch (1818–1898), accountant, was born in London. Although his family background is not well documented, it is known that his father was a secretary to a well-known firm of provision merchants and his mother was the daughter of a West Indies planter named Welch. Reputedly, his paternal grandfather was a Count de Loitte, who had fled from the revolutionary reign of terror in France during 1793 and found refuge in Hull.

Having spent twelve years on the staff of the official assignee in bankruptcy, Deloitte in 1845, at the age of twenty-seven, set up his own practice. His experience proved invaluable, for at this time the most lucrative assignments that an accountant could win fell in the field of insolvency. His first office, at 11 Basinghall Street, London, was close to his former employers and, significantly, to the bankruptcy courts. Living over the premises, Deloitte gathered some eighty-seven clients (mostly individuals or partnerships) by the end of his first year in practice, and was soon employing ten clerks. Under his leadership the firm continued to grow, so that by 1897 it comprised seventy staff and, by 1900, shortly after his death, its fee income had reached £41,193, having risen from £7597 in 1874.

A crucial event in the long-term success of the practice was the appointment in 1849 of Deloitte to assist the shareholder auditors of the Great Western Railway (GWR). Not the least advantage of this was that Deloitte

William Welch Deloitte (1818–1898), by unknown engraver

could then mention the assignment as a measure of his integrity when writing to bankrupts named in the *London Gazette*, offering to prepare their statements of account prior to a court appearance. The shares of the GWR had been falling in value, and the proprietors, increasingly concerned for the company's well-being, recorded in February 1850 that 'the auditors have been assisted for the first time throughout the laborious examination of all books, accounts and documents of the company by a public account [Deloitte] whom they appointed without previous communication with any individual connected with the company' (PRO, RAIL 250/65, 166). Although surprised by this action by the shareholders, the directors concurred with the arrangement once they were satisfied, in August 1849, that the 'sole object [of the auditors] was to strengthen their hands and inspire general confidence in the management' (ibid., 250/127, 2). In the event, Deloitte continued to advise the shareholder auditors until 1887, when he was personally elected to one of these posts, which he retained until his retirement in 1897. The appointment, of considerable importance in terms of both status and fee income, then passed to his firm.

Deloitte (who audited the Langham Hotel from 1883 and the Savoy from 1890) was said to have been the originator of a system of hotel accounting which was later widely adopted. Unlike some City practices, he built up a strong industrial base among his clientele, and audited not only railway companies (Lancashire and Yorkshire, West London Extension, and the South Wales Railway, as well as the GWR and a large number in South America) but also docks, collieries, and ironworks, including the Vulcan

Foundry Company, Powell Duffryn (from 1864), and the Ocean Coal Company. Deloitte was closely associated with Sir Daniel Gooch, Sir John Pender, Sir George Elliot, and Cyrus Field and the other pioneers of submarine telegraphy, so that his firm secured the audit of almost all the large cable companies, including the Telegraph Construction and Maintenance Company. However, his practice was not exclusively industrial: from 1889 Deloittes audited the Prudential, from 1882 were joint auditors of the London Stock Bank, and had many newspaper assignments, with, among others, *The Observer* from 1886.

His standing within the profession led to Deloitte being called upon to investigate frauds—one committed against the Great Northern Railway in 1857, and another at the Great Eastern Steamship Company in 1870. The inroads that financing the employment of his many staff made on his capital encouraged him to seek a partner in March 1857, and he sold a 50 per cent share in the firm to Thomas Greenwood, who was then share registrar of the GWR. When Greenwood left the partnership in 1867, his share of the capital was worth £6000. Deloitte then admitted a succession of partners, all of whom had trained in the firm: Henry Dever (1867–97), Alfred Richard Hollebone (1867–73), and John George Griffiths (1869–1902).

An important aspect of Deloitte's career concerned his involvement with the Institute of Chartered Accountants in England and Wales, of which he served as fourth president in 1888–9, having been the vice-president from 1884. He had been an original council member of its predecessor, the Institute of Accountants in London, and on its foundation in 1880 became a council member of the English Institute. In addition he had been a member of the Manchester Society of Accountants, having joined because of his office in that city, which practised under the style of Deloitte and Halliday. Yet the partnership with James Halliday ceased in 1877 and no further branches were opened in the UK until one was established at Cardiff in 1912.

About 1858 Deloitte settled at Hill House, Mount Pleasant, Southall, Middlesex, where he lived until his death. He was married twice and had at least one child, a daughter. A freemason for more than fifty years, he was also a benefactor of the Church of England, funding the construction of Holy Trinity Church, Southall, and six almshouses for the poor. He did not retire until 1897 when, aged seventy-nine, he was said to be the oldest practising accountant in London. One of those who had worked for his firm described him as 'an alert, decisive little man with just a touch of austerity in his manner; this, however, covered a kind heart' (Kettle, 6). He died at his home, Hill House, on 23 August 1898.   EDGAR JONES

Sources R. Kettle, *Deloitte & Co., 1845–1956* (privately printed, Oxford, c.1958) · E. Jones, 'Deloitte, William Welch', *DBB* · *The Accountant* (27 Aug 1898) · H. Howitt and others, eds., *The history of the Institute of Chartered Accountants in England and Wales, 1880–1965, and of its founder accountancy bodies, 1870–1880* (1966) · R. H. Parker, ed., *British accountants: a biographical sourcebook* (1980) · d. cert. · *CGPLA Eng. & Wales* (1898)

Archives PRO, company records of Great Western Railway, RAIL 250

Likenesses engraving, Coopers and Lybrand, London · lithograph, priv. coll. [*see illus.*]

Wealth at death £74,707 12s. 2d.: probate, 26 Sept 1898, *CGPLA Eng. & Wales*

Deloney, Thomas (*d.* in or before **1600**), silkweaver and writer, is thought to have been born in Norwich; his surname is of French origin, and Flemish and French protestant refugees had been settling in Norfolk in the fifteenth and sixteenth centuries, working in the cloth trades. In addition, the first known ballad by Deloney was published in Norwich. There is, however, no clear evidence to confirm his place of birth. Deloney began publishing in the early 1580s and may well have been born any time between about 1540 and 1560. He evidently received a grammar school education, given that he published translations from Latin. He may also have translated Bonaventure Des Périers's *Les contes ou les nouvelles récréations et joyeux devis*; the English version, *The Mirror of Mirth and Pleasant Conceits*, is signed T. D. (*Novels*, xxiv). Deloney's trade was silkweaving, although it is not certain where he practised it. In October 1586 he was living in London, as the baptism of his son Richard at St Giles Cripplegate indicates.

By the early 1590s Deloney was famous for his ballads; Thomas Nashe, in *Have with You to Saffron Walden* (1596), describes him as 'Thomas Deloney, the Balleting Silkweaver' who:

> hath rime inough for all myracles, & wit to make a *Garland of Good will* more than the premisses, with an Epistle of *Momus* and *Zoylus*; whereas his Muse, from the first peeping foorth, hath stood at Livery at an Ale-house wispe, never exceeding a penny a quart, day or night, and this deare yeare, together with the silencing of his looms, scarce that; he being constrained to betake him to carded Ale: whence it proceedeth that, since *Candlemas* or his Jigge of *John for the King*, not one merrie Dittie will come from him, but *The Thunder-bolt against Swearers, Repent, England, repent, & The strange judgements of God.* (*Works of Thomas Nashe*, 3.84)

The Garland of Good Will was a popular collection of Deloney's ballads, entered in the Stationers' register in 1593 (like the rest of his works, early editions have been read out of existence and the earliest surviving is that of 1626). Many of Deloney's ballads consist of what might be called topical reportage, such as *The Queenes Visiting of the Campe at Tilsburie with her Entertainment there* of 1588, one of several ballads about incidents surrounding the Spanish Armada. As well as political news, he wrote about sensational events, as in *The lamentation of Mastr Pages wife of Plimmouth, who being enforced by her parents to wed him against her will, did most wickedly consent to his murther, for the love of George Strangwidge*. There is also a series of ballads on historical subjects (for example, Edward II, Edward III, Henry I, Henry II, and John).

In the 1590s Deloney became caught up in political protest by the London weavers, who believed that French and Dutch workers relocating in England were ignoring the rules of apprenticeship laid down by the Weavers' Company. The weavers wrote to the pastors of the French and Dutch churches in London in 1595, asking that their parishioners obey the rules, but the pastors had the weavers' three ringleaders (including Deloney) jailed in Newgate. They were later released, after petitioning the lord chief justice (*Novels*, xxvii–xxviii; Consitt, 146–52). In 1596 the mayor of London objected to a ballad (now lost) in which Deloney complained of the scarcity of grain in England, giving rise to 'discontent' (*Novels*, xxviii). The mayor took into custody the publisher and printer of the ballad, but was apparently unable to apprehend Deloney.

It was during this time, in the late 1590s, that Deloney turned to the genre of prose fiction, producing four works between 1597 and 1600. While some of his ballads are powerful and many are of considerable historical interest, his fiction is a remarkable achievement, given the paucity of models for what was virtually a new genre. In 1597 he published *The Pleasant History of John Winchcomb, in his Younger Years called Jack of Newbury* (often referred to as *Jack of Newbury*). Deloney dedicated this work 'To all famous cloth workers in England', praising the 'long honoured trade of English Clothiers'. The narrative is based on a historical figure and is set in the reign of Henry VIII. The rags to riches story follows the fortunes of Jack, who begins as an exemplary workman, marries his master's widow, and becomes master himself of a massive (for the times) weaving establishment. Reflecting the tension in the late 1590s between the increasing economic power of the merchant class and the lack of a defined social position for its members, Deloney's text is a mixture of archaic forms and social realism. Jack's achievements as a master weaver are capped by his response to a summons to arms from the king, when he is able to provide a more impressive contingent of men for the French campaign than many a powerful nobleman. Despite this, Jack does not want to change his social status (unlike the social climber Wolsey), but he is a ruler within his own world and his 'kingdom' is, in some ways, more impressive and certainly more orderly than the king's. In chapter 2, in a set-piece description (in rhyming couplets for greater effect), the reader is shown Jack's workroom with its 200 looms, 100 carders, and 200 spinners, right through to the dye-house. The episodic tale consists mostly of events which prove just how superior a figure Jack is.

In his next work Deloney turned to a different trade: shoemaking. *The Gentle Craft* was published in two parts, probably in 1597 and 1598. The first part is dedicated to the shoemakers, the second to the Company of Cordwainers. Both narratives are more fragmented than *Jack of Newbury*, though the first part has the clear purpose of offering a mythologized ancestry for the 'gentle-craft' of shoemaking, with the stories of St Hugh, sons of the king of Powys, and Crispin and Crispianus, sons of the king of Logria. The concluding episode in part 1 is an account of Simon Eyre, the shoemaker who became mayor of London. The second part of *The Gentle Craft* is something of a pot-pourri, held together by the theme, once again, of the glory and worthiness of shoemakers. Like in Deloney's other fiction, broad knockabout comedy is a feature, and there is a considerable amount of jest-book fare, including material

centred on Long Meg of Westminster (legendary subject of other jest-books).

Symbolically, *Thomas of Reading, or, The Six Worthy Yeomen of the West* may be seen as Deloney's last work of fiction because it reveals a new, sombre side to his vision; it may well have been published before the second part of *The Gentle Craft*, but the exact date is unknown. In contrast to his other fiction, this narrative seems to question the exuberant success stories and benign association of aristocrats and tradesmen. In particular, the grim account of the murder of Thomas Cole (one of the worthy yeomen) for his money by a marauding host and hostess of an inn serves to question the prosperity that is so celebrated elsewhere in Deloney's work.

All four of Deloney's pieces of prose fiction proved to be extremely popular: *Jack of Newbury* had some sixteen editions by 1700, *The Gentle Craft*, part 1, at least thirteen, and *Thomas of Reading* eight. Further testimony to Deloney's popularity is found in 1599, when Thomas Dekker used the first part of *The Gentle Craft* as a source for his play *The Shoemaker's Holiday*. In 1598 Deloney's last published work was entered in the Stationers' register: *Canaan's Calamity, Jerusalem's Misery* (first extant edition, 1618), an ambitious poem on the destruction of Jerusalem derived from Josephus and from Nashe's *Christ's Tears over Jerusalem*. Deloney uses this theme to offer some sharp social commentary on contemporary England:

> Seeke not your neighbors lasting spoyle
> By greedy sute in lawe.
> (*Deloney's Works*, 459)

The only detailed reference to Deloney's death is in Will Kemp's *Kemp's Nine Days' Wonder* (1600), which concludes with a prose comment headed: 'To the tune of Thomas Delonies Epitaph'. Kemp describes Deloney as:

> the great Ballet-maker T. D., alias Tho. Deloney, Chronicler of the 6. yeomen of the west, Jack of Newbery, the Gentle-craft, and such like honest men, omitted by Stow, Hollinshead, Grafton, Hal, froysart, and the rest of those wel deserving writers; but I was given since to understand your late generall Tho. dyed poorely, as ye all must do, and was honestly buried. (Kemp, 21)

The exact circumstances of Deloney's death are unknown and no will has been traced. PAUL SALZMAN

Sources The novels of Thomas Deloney, ed. M. E. Lawlis (1961) · Deloney's works, ed. F. O. Mann (1912) · The works of Thomas Nashe, ed. R. B. McKerrow, 5 vols. (1904–10); repr. with corrections and notes by F. P. Wilson (1958), vol. 3 · Kemps nine daies wonder, ed. A. Dyce (1840) · E. P. Wright, Thomas Deloney (1981) · F. Consitt, The London Weavers' Company, 1 (1933) · A. Halasz, 'Thomas Deloney', Sixteenth-century British nondramatic writers: third series, ed. D. A. Richardson, DLitB, 167 (1996), 41–7

Deloraine. For this title name *see* Scott, Henry, first earl of Deloraine (1676–1730); Scott, Mary, countess of Deloraine (*bap.* 1703, *d.* 1744).

Delpini, Carlo Antonio (*c.*1740–1828), pantomimist, was born in Rome, possibly in the parish of San Martino, and was a pupil of Nicolini. His first London engagement was apparently with David Garrick at Drury Lane in 1774, although two years later, on 26 December 1776 at Covent Garden, the playbills announced his 'first appearance on an English stage' when he performed in the pantomime *Harlequin's Frolics*, in the role of Pierrot. His attention then turned to behind-the-scenes work, particularly with respect to mechanical arrangements for the 1777–8 season at Covent Garden. However, he continued to act in pantomimes both there (1778–9, 1789, 1796–7, 1799–1800) and at various other London theatres, including the Haymarket (1780, 1784–5, 1788, 1794–5, 1795–6, 1806), Drury Lane (1779–80), and the Royal Theatre (1787–8, 1782), where his wife, whom he married in 1784, also acted. With his expertise in scenic invention and his stress on character acting, Delpini is credited with having invented the Regency pantomime. In 1788 he worked as acting manager at Hughes's Royal Circus, producing pantomimes alongside the entertainment provided by the theatre's horses, tigers, leopards, and other animals. In the following year he was seriously hurt in an accident at the Haymarket. He appeared in 1798 at Astley's Amphitheatre, the main rival of the Royal Circus, but the production was not well received. Delpini had failed to subscribe to a theatrical fund which acted as a friendly society providing for death and sickness; as a result, he lay on his sickbed in old age with no relief, except for the £200 granted to him by his patron, 'The Prince—his Present Majesty', George IV, for whom he had once organized a grand masquerade at the Pantheon and arranged entertainments at the Pavilion in Brighton. Delpini had a superstitious fear of the number eight and predicted that he would die in 1788; instead, he died early in 1828 at the age of eighty-eight, either on 20 January or on 13 February (according to different sources), in Lancaster Court, Strand, London.

BRENDA ASSAEL

Sources Highfill, Burnim & Langhans, *BDA* · S. D'Amico, ed., *Enciclopedia dello spettacolo*, 11 vols. (Rome, 1954–68) · *The thespian dictionary, or, Dramatic biography of the present age*, 2nd edn (1805) · D. Pickering, ed., *Encyclopaedia of pantomime* (1993) · M. Banham, ed., *The Cambridge guide to theatre*, rev. edn (1992), 273 · *DNB*
Likenesses portrait, 1782 · J. Sayers, etching, pubd 1785, BM, NPG · J. Nixon, etching, pubd 1789, BM · B. Rebecca, engraving, 1798 · W. Hincks, drawing or engraving · engraving · prints, BM, Harvard TC

Deluc, Jean-André (1727–1817), natural philosopher and politician, was born on 8 February 1727 in Geneva, the elder of the two children of François Deluc, a wealthy watch manufacturer. He was educated by his father, who had published defences of Christianity against Mandeville and other rationalistic writers, and was active in the stormy arena of Genevan politics. François Deluc had been 'one of the most terrible of the [bourgeois] party in our troubles of 1734 and 1737', complained Charles Bonnet; the 'two sons suckled demagogy with their milk and are, with their father, at the head of the party' (Wolf, 4.194–5). Bonnet's assessment of the Deluc family's political leadership is just, though the implications as to Deluc's character are not. In 1763, after the republic's aristocratic ruling council had burned Rousseau's *Social Contract* and banned its author, Deluc was chosen, along with forty-one others, to submit a representation protesting

against the act. This inaugurated Geneva's bourgeois revolution. He continued to lead the party of *représantants* in negotiations with Rousseau and played a key role in difficult and dangerous negotiations with Geneva's guarantor powers, France, Bern, and Zürich, and with the aristocratic ruling party. At the eleventh hour these negotiations secured a peaceable solution: a new constitution, the edict of 1768, that granted the bourgeoisie significant powers. A contemporary observed that during the crisis Deluc frequently cooled heated spirits: 'always calm in the midst of peril, in the greatest dangers he never lacked expedients, and rendered distinguished service to his fellow citizens' (Gür, 170).

A trade embargo imposed by France during the crisis caused the failure of Deluc's business, and in 1773 he emigrated to England, a refuge for liberal bourgeois Genevans. There he secured a post as reader to Queen Charlotte and lived at Windsor. The queen found him 'philosophe comme il faut, for … all his works are full of admiration for the Supreme Being' (Tunbridge, 18). He was elected FRS in 1773. In the 1790s, as Geneva fell increasingly under threat from France, he received letters requesting his intercession with George III in favour of British intervention; many Genevans hoped for his return. In 1797, under cover of an appointment as honorary professor of natural history and geology to the University of Göttingen, he was sent by the British government on a secret mission to enlist the duke of Brunswick's support for the entry of Prussia into a Quadruple Alliance; Deluc also met Frederick William III, king of Prussia. The mission, however, was unsuccessful.

'The elder is made for better things', Bonnet had urged (Wolf, 4.194–5). Deluc had acquired early on a taste for natural philosophy. Already at seventeen years of age he began nearly annual explorations of the alps of the Faucigny, at the time an unknown region. His brother, Guillaume Antoine, accompanied him on these journeys and continued to supply him with observations for the duration of his lifetime. His alpine travels led Deluc to the two fields to which he was to make important contributions: meteorology and geology, both terms which he used himself. His mountain observations of fogs and clouds convinced him of the incorrectness of the accepted solution theory of evaporation, according to which evaporating water dissolves into the air. In his *Idées sur la météorologie* (2 vols., 1786–7) and in several articles he maintained instead that heat causes evaporation and that water vapour is an expansible fluid (a gas) that fills space independently of the presence of any other gases. This principle was extended to all gases by John Dalton some fifteen years later, to form what was later known as Dalton's law of partial pressures. Long awaited, and regarded as revolutionary by his contemporaries, Deluc's *Recherches sur les modifications de l'atmosphère* (2 vols., 1772) was the product of his search for a reliable method to measure mountain heights with a barometer. His approach to the problem generated exemplary designs for accurate barometers and thermometers, along with rigorous methods for using them in precise measurement. Deluc also arrived at a clear statement of such principles of instrumentation as comparability among instrument scales, their linearity, and the role of the fixed point.

Deluc published his geological investigations in numerous treatises, articles, and letters, among which the most important are *Lettres … sur l'histoire de la terre* (1779), *Lettres à Delamétherie* (1790–93), and *Geological Letters, Addressed to Professor Blumenbach* (1793–4). His early interest in the subject sprang from a youthful appreciation of the beauties of mountain scenery; later he came to view the earth's history as necessary background for an understanding of the origin, history, and nature of man—which he viewed as a pious Christian of Calvinist origin.

Deluc sought to establish a chronology of the earth's history based on the character of the rock strata and the fossils they contained: 'two parallel histories', as he put it, 'that of rock layers and that of organized beings' (Ellenberger and Gohau, 248). These histories recorded a succession of forms through time, with the more recent fauna being closer to present forms. The way in which these alterations occurred, according to Deluc, was as follows: in the beginning God created a chaotic fluid. From this fluid the successive rock strata precipitated, the precipitate changing as expansible fluids (gases) periodically erupted from the interior of the earth, altering the chemical composition of the original fluid. The fluid's changing composition induced modifications among the fauna as well. Shells and skeletons were deposited in successive strata. The eruptions of gases also deformed previously laid down strata. In this way he bound together fauna, lithology, and orientation of strata.

Deluc recognized the high antiquity of the earth and correlated long epochs, punctuated by eruptions of expansible fluids, with the six days of the account in Genesis—to the defence of which he devoted himself unremittingly. The six epochs terminated with the deluge, since which time, some 5000–6000 years ago, creative geological processes ceased; the earth was now quiescent, under the operation of 'present-day causes'—a term that he coined (Deluc, '8e Lettre', *Observations sur la physique*, 37, 1790, 202–9).

Deluc's religious convictions, his belief that the earth had experienced transformations too great to allow for the operation of present-day causes in the distant past, and his determined opposition to Hutton—whose theory seemed to him not only to threaten Christianity, but also to lack sufficient historical sense—have earned him harsh criticism from historians of geology from Lyell onwards. His great prolixity did not lighten the task of his advocates; Priestley complained that 'he could barely comprehend' the *Idées sur la météorologie* (Bickerton, 94). Nor did his vigorous opposition to the new chemistry of Lavoisier help, although his opposition was shared by many British and Germans who associated French chemistry with the French Revolution and its conquests. Two other controversies in which he became embroiled further reduced his credit: with Horace Bénédict de Saussure over the relative merits of their respective hygrometers (Saussure's was

superior), and over his claim to be the discoverer of the principle of latent heat. Nevertheless, contemporaries held him in universally high regard. Hutton considered him his most redoubtable adversary, and Cuvier, who borrowed extensively from him, placed him in the first rank among geologists of the late eighteenth century.

Historians of geology began to re-evaluate Deluc's work at the end of the twentieth century. Far from having engaged in baseless speculations, he supported his theories with an immense fund of observations gathered on his extensive travels. His correlation of fossils with rock strata was an important early contribution to the notion of palaeontological dating of strata. His appreciation of the close relation between palaeontological and tectonic changes influenced the later work of Elie de Beaumont and Croizet and Jobert, and he recognized the long-term formation of mountains, requiring successive periods of orogenic activity or, as he put it, 'revolution upon revolution' (Gohau, 227). If he was not first to use the term 'geology' in its modern sense, he was one of its earliest advocates. His principal weakness in geology lay in his focus on a grand theory of the earth and his relative lack of interest in the prosaic, methodical description of local strata.

Deluc married twice: the name of his first wife is not known; his second wife, Mary, he married after settling in England. He suffered a painful and lingering illness during the last years of his life, which confined him to his room but did not prevent him from pursuing research in electrochemistry. He developed a galvanic pile, which he called a dry pile but has more often been called the Zamboni pile after its later improver. The pile consisted of a large number of discs of zinc foil and of paper silvered on one side. By eliminating the wet conductor between the two metal conductors he believed he had succeeded in separating the electrical from the chemical aspects of the pile.

Besides works in meteorology and geology Deluc published treatises on a wide range of subjects: a work showing that Bacon's French translator had omitted passages favourable to religion (*Bacon tel qu'il est*, 1800); on Christian education (*Lettres sur l'education religieuse de l'enfance*, 1799); and an apologetic work, *Lettres sur le christianisme adressées à M. le pasteur Teller*, 1801.

Deluc died at Windsor on 7 November 1817 and was buried in the churchyard at Clewer, Somerset. Contemporaries praised the mildness of his character, 'the warmth of his feelings, and the habitual gentleness and urbanity of his manners' (*Philosophical Magazine*, 393). Much loved at court, he was described by Fanny Burney as the queen's philosopher. THEODORE S. FELDMAN

Sources A. Gür, 'La négociation de l'édit du 11 mars 1768, d'après le journal de Jean-André Deluc et la correspondance de Gédéon Turrettini', *Revue Suisse d'Histoire*, 17 (1967), 166–217 · F. Ellenberger and G. Gohau, 'Á l'aurore de la stratigraphie paléontologique: Jean-André De Luc, son influence sur Cuvier', *Revue d'Histoire des Sciences et de leurs Applications*, 34 (1981), 218–57 · P. Tunbridge, 'Jean André Deluc, FRS, 1727–1817', *Notes and Records of the Royal Society*, 26 (1971), 15–33 · T. Feldman, 'The history of meteorology, 1750–1800: a study in the quantification of experimental physics', PhD diss., U. Cal., Berkeley, 1983 · R. Porter, *The making of geology: earth science* *in Britain, 1660–1815* (1977) • D. R. Oldroyd, 'Historicism and the rise of historical geology', *History of Science*, 17 (1979), 191–213, 227–57 • G. Gohau, *History of geology*, ed. and trans. A. V. Carozzi and M. Carozzi (1991) • T. Feldman, 'Applied mathematics and the quantification of experimental physics: the example of barometric hypsometry', *Historical Studies in the Physical Sciences*, 15 (1984–5), 127–97 • R. Wolf, *Biographien zur Kulturgeschichte der Schweiz*, 4 vols. (1858–62) • *Philosophical Magazine*, 50 (1817), 392–4 • *DSB* • D. M. Bickerton, *Marc-Auguste and Charles Pictet, the Bibliothèque britannique (1796–1815), and the dissemination of British literature and science on the continent* (1986)

Archives Bibliothèque Publique et Universitaire, Geneva • NHM, diary of travels in England • UCL, Huguenot Library, family corresp. and papers • UCL • Yale U., Sterling Memorial Library, corresp. and papers | Birm. CA, letters to the Boulton family • Birm. CA, letters to James Watt • BL, letters to Lord Grenville, Add. MS 59030

Likenesses C. Penny, stipple, BM, NPG • Schroeder, mezzotint (after W. de Stetten), BM • engraving, RS • portrait, repro. in *Dictionnaire historique et biographique de la Suisse*, 7 vols. (1921–33)

Delvaux, Laurent (1696–1778), sculptor, was born in Ghent on 17 January 1696, the son of Godefroid Delvaux (d. 1743), a cornet in the Austrian cavalry, and his wife, Françoise Chasselat. There were no sculptors in his immediate family: his early training was with Gery Helderenberg (1651–1739) in Ghent and in 1713 or 1714 he joined the Brussels workshop of Pierre-Denis Plumier (1688–1721). In 1721 he accompanied his master to London, where Plumier died leaving designs and models for a major monument to John Sheffield, duke of Buckingham, in Westminster Abbey. Delvaux and Peter Scheemakers completed this in 1722, Delvaux carving the figure of Time, according to George Vertue. In 1722 he was also responsible for a life-sized Hercules (Waddesdon Manor, Buckinghamshire) for Lord Castlemaine's gardens at Wanstead, a companion to Scheemakers's Omphale; also for Wanstead he carved two vases (Anglesey Abbey) for a set of four, using as models the antique Borghese and Medici vases.

After working briefly for Francis Bird, Delvaux joined forces about 1723 with Scheemakers, working from premises at Millbank, Westminster. Together they provided the wall monument to Sir Thomas Grantham (*c*.1723?) in Bicester church, Oxfordshire, and large standing monuments to Lewis Watson, first earl of Rockingham at Rockingham church, Northamptonshire, 1724–5 and Sir Samuel Ongley at Old Warden church, Bedfordshire, 1727–8. After 1725 Delvaux carved a group, *Vertumnus and Pomona* (V&A) for Cannons, Middlesex, a companion to Scheemakers's *Apollo and Venus*. Delvaux provided a life-sized marble statue of George I (1727; Royal Courts of Justice, London) for the Rolls House and, for an unknown garden, figures of Four Seasons (West Wycombe Park). He and Scheemakers also turned out a number of small recumbent Venus statuettes, including one for Sir Andrew Fountaine.

On 27 May 1726 Delvaux went briefly to Antwerp, where he married Plumier's widow, Madeleine (*née* Pauwels), in Sint Jacobskerk; she died shortly after in childbirth. In 1728 Fountaine gave Delvaux an introduction to Cardinal Corsini (later Pope Clement XII) and, with Scheemakers,

he auctioned their stock, announcing that they were going to Italy: they sold several classically inspired models, probably for garden figures. Papal protection led to commissions in Rome, including two colossal angels completed in 1730 as part of a large project for the basilica of the royal palace in Mafra, Portugal. Around 1730 Delvaux carved marble copies of the *Nymph with a Shell*, *Crouching Venus*, *Hermaphrodite*, and *Biblis and Caunus*; in 1732 he signed and dated a bust of Caracalla, which evidently pleased him since it featured in a portrait of the strong-featured, portly sculptor in formal dress painted by Isaac Whood in 1733. These works were all sold to the duke of Bedford, together with a lion after Flaminio Vacca and a David, after Bernini; all are now at Woburn Abbey, Bedfordshire. Payments were received between 1733 and 1736.

Delvaux probably carved *Longevity* for Hugh Chamberlen's monument in Westminster Abbey—otherwise the work of Scheemakers—before leaving London. However, he did return there briefly in 1733; thereafter he maintained English contacts through Scheemakers, who negotiated the sale of the Woburn marbles. In 1732 Delvaux moved to the Austrian Netherlands with a papal introduction to the regent, the archduchess Marie-Elisabeth, who appointed him court sculptor in 1733. He established a workshop in Nivelles, where he remained until his death. In 1734 he married a silk and lace merchant, Marie-Agnès Colas (1698–1764), with whom he had three children, two of whom survived: Jean Godefroid (1737–1813) and Anne-Françoise (1740–85). During the 1740s Delvaux carved his masterpieces, which were narrative compositions, largely of oak, for religious institutions: they include a *Conversion of St Paul* (1735–6) for St Paul's, Nivelles, a pulpit for the Carmelite church, Nivelles (1743–4; now St Gertrude's Collegiale), and the magnificent marble and oak pulpit in Ghent Cathedral (1741–5) which graphically presents Time and Truth, surrounded by naturalistic foliage. His interest in the antique was displayed in the monument to Leonard Vandernoot, for the Carmelite church in Brussels (1746; Rijksmuseum, Amsterdam), with its grieving Minerva. These works illustrate his transitional style, which hovered between the rococo and neo-classicism.

After Charles of Lorraine's succession as governor of the Netherlands in 1750, Delvaux worked on decorative schemes for the royal palaces at Tervuren, Mariemont, and particularly Brussels, where he carved allegorical reliefs for the façade and staircase and free-standing statues, including an imposing Hercules (1768–70) at the staircase foot. He died on 24 February 1778 and was buried near his pulpit in the Carmelite church. Among his many workshop assistants were Joseph Wilton, employed in the early 1740s, A.-J. Anrion, Laurent Tamine, P.-F. le Roy, and G.-L. Godecharle. A notebook relating to his practice between 1738 and 1742 survives in the Delvaux family archive and a sketchbook of studies from baroque sculpture made in Rome is in the Bibliothèque Royale, Brussels. Several of his delicate terracotta models can be found in Belgian museums.

INGRID ROSCOE

Sources A. Jacobs, *Laurent Delvaux (1696–1778)* (1999) · M. Whinney, *Sculpture in Britain, 1530 to 1830*, rev. J. Physick, 2nd edn (1988), 157, 182–6, illustrations 101–2, 124 · G. Willame, *Laurent Delvaux* (1914) · I. M. Roscoe, 'Peter Scheemakers', *Walpole Society*, 61 (1999), 163–404 · Vertue, *Note books*, 1.101; 3.36, 44, 53, 66 · C. Avery, 'Laurent Delvaux's sculpture at Woburn Abbey', *Apollo*, 118 (1983), 253–64 · A. Jacobs, 'Joseph Wilton's Nivelles years and the influence of Laurent Delvaux', *Church Monuments*, 12 (1997), 58–66 · J. L. Delattre and R. Laurent, *Laurent Delvaux, 1696–1778* (1978) [exhibition catalogue, Collégiale Sainte-Gertrude, Nivelles, Belgium] · F. Popelier, ed., *Laurent Delvaux: les terres cuites dans les collections publiques belges* (1975) [exhibition catalogue, Nivelles, Belgium] · A. W. Moore, *Norfolk and the grand tour: eighteenth-century travellers abroad and their souvenirs* (1985), 77, 109–11, 137 [exhibition catalogue, Norwich Castle Museum, 5 Oct – 24 Nov 1985] · M. Devigne, *Laurent Delvaux et ses élèves* (1928) · A. Jacobs, 'L'Archange Raphael et l'ange tutélaire du royaume du Portugal sculptés à Rome vers 1730–1732 par Laurent Delvaux', *Gazette des Beaux-Arts*, 6th ser., 128 (1996), 71–90 · London ratebooks, St Margaret, Westminster, City Westm. AC, E.344–E.348

Likenesses I. Whood, oils, 1735; [now lost] · F. L. Godecharle, plaster bust, 1824; in the Academy at Ghent, 1888 · F. L. Godecharle, bust, reduced version, 1826, Musées des Beaux-Arts, Brussels · A. van Haecken, mezzotint (after I. Whood, 1735), BM, NPG; repro. in Avery, 'Laurent Delvaux's sculpture at Woburn Abbey', 254 · W. Hibbart, etching (after I. Whood), BM, NPG; repro. in H. Walpole, *Anecdotes of painting in England … collected by the late George Vertue, and now digested and published*, 3 vols. (1762)

Wealth at death first will, 3 May 1764, document no. 19, notariat général de Brabant, minutes of notary, A. L. Detraux, no. 21848 · bequests incl. gold snuffbox, diamond ring, sword with silver sheath, gold watch, works in marble, medal with portrait of the archduchess, seals, and extensive chattels: second will, 12 Sept 1777

Delvin. For this title name *see* Nugent, Richard, first Baron Delvin and baron of Delvin (d. 1475); Nugent, Richard, third Baron Delvin (d. 1538); Nugent, Christopher, fifth Baron Delvin (1544–1602).

Delysia, Alice [*real name* Alice Henriette Lapize] (**1889–1979**), actress, was born on 3 March 1889 in Paris, the daughter of Henri Lapize, sculptor. She made her first appearance as a chorus girl at the age of fourteen in *The Belle of New York* by Hugh Morton at the Théâtre du Moulin Rouge in Paris in 1903, and in 1905 went to New York as one of the chorus of French 'Gibson girls' in the Broadway production of *The Catch of the Season* by Seymour Hicks and Cosmo Hamilton. In 1909, after working for several years in London, she left the stage. She was at that time married to Harry Fragson (born Victor Philippe Pot), singer and composer of the famous song 'Hello! Hello! Who's your lady friend?' The couple parted—a year before Fragson was murdered by his father following a quarrel over his mistress—and Alice returned to the Paris theatre in 1912.

Alice Delysia was discovered by C. B. Cochran at the Olympia variety theatre in Paris in 1913 when he was looking for talent for a revue he wanted to stage on the lines of those he had seen in the small variety theatres in Paris. Cochran took her to London in 1914 to star in his first revue, *Odds and Ends* by Harry Grattan at the Ambassadors Theatre. Her rendition of the recruiting song 'We don't want to lose you, but we think you ought to go' was a triumph, and only after more than 500 performances was

Odds and Ends replaced by a new revue, *More*, also by Grattan, another great success, starring Delysia and the French actor Léon Morton. After the success of *Pell Mell* by Fred Thompson and Morris Harvey in 1916, again starring Delysia and Morton, Cochran left the Ambassadors for a larger theatre and in 1917 put on the operetta *Carminetta*, with music by Emile Lassailly, at the Prince of Wales Theatre with Delysia, despite her lack of training as a singer. Her warm and effervescent personality contributed to her popularity in London, and she sang in many charity performances during the First World War. She entertained wounded troops, and took many French refugees and orphans into her home. In 1918 she returned to revue in *As you were* by Arthur Wimperis (from the French) at the London Pavilion, which Cochran had refurbished and reopened: in this she played Helen of Troy, Queen Elizabeth, and Cleopatra, and the skin-tight black costume in which she appeared as Lucifer had to be modified after attracting the attention of the lord chamberlain.

After the war Delysia remained in London to play in *Afgar* by Fred Thompson and Worton David, a musical comedy set in a Moorish harem, staged by Cochran at the London Pavilion in 1919; this ran for 300 performances and she went to New York at the end of 1920 for the Broadway production. She returned to the London stage in 1922 in Cochran's *Mayfair and Montmartre*, which flopped after Delysia had to withdraw with a throat infection. She continued to delight London audiences throughout the 1920s, mainly in revues and musicals staged by Cochran, including Noel Coward's *On with the Dance* in 1925 at the London Pavilion, in which she played a French lady's maid and with Hermione Baddeley sang the duet 'Poor little rich girl', Noel Coward's first song hit. She was in Jerome Kern's *The Cat and the Fiddle* in 1932 at the Palace Theatre, and her last big London success was at the Gaiety Theatre in 1933, in *Mother of Pearl*, adapted for the English stage with Delysia in mind by A. P. Herbert (1890–1971) from Oscar Straus's *Eine Frau, die weiss was sie will*: she played an ageing actress whose lover is stolen by her daughter and her song 'Every woman thinks she wants to wander' was a big hit. On 8 November 1928 she had married her second husband, Georges Emile Denis, the general manager of a newspaper; the marriage ended in divorce in 1938.

Believing that the only hope for France lay in Britain and General de Gaulle, Delysia joined the Entertainments National Service Association in May 1941, and served until the end of the war entertaining troops in north Africa, the Middle East, Normandy, Belgium, and the Netherlands: she was awarded the African Star of the Eighth Army. On 10 January 1944 she married her third husband, Commander (Joseph Marie Antoine) René Kolb-Bernard of the Free French navy, who had heard her sing after Dunkirk and had asked to her to adopt the crew of the French submarine he was commanding. After the war she retired from the stage. Kolb-Bernard was appointed French minister in Nicaragua, and went on to hold a number of diplomatic posts, including that of French consul in the Canary Islands, where Delysia spent much of her retirement. He predeceased her. Alice Delysia died from cancer on 10 February 1979 in the French Convalescent Home, De Courcel Road, Brighton.   ANNE PIMLOTT BAKER

Sources C. B. Cochran, *The secrets of a showman* (1925) · K. Gänzl, *The British musical theatre*, 2 (1986) · J. Harding, *Cochran* (1988) · J. P. Wearing, *The London stage, 1890–1959* (1976–93) · *The Times* (16 Nov 1979) · *Sunday Telegraph* (11 Feb 1979) · m. cert. [Georges Emile Denis] · d. cert. · m. cert. [René Kolb-Bernard]
Likenesses photograph, repro. in Cochran, *Secrets of a showman*, facing p. 196

Demainbray, Stephen Charles Triboudet (1710–1782), natural philosopher and astronomer, was born on 20 February 1710 in the parish of St Martin-in-the-Fields, Westminster, London, the son of Stephen Triboudet Demainbray of that parish and his wife, Marie Rigaud, daughter of Alexandre de Schivac, minister of the French church in Bristol. Demainbray's parents were Huguenots who had come to Britain with William III. They died when he was a small child, and he was subsequently brought up by his uncle, and then in the family of John Theophilus Desaguliers. He was educated at Westminster School and by Desaguliers, and as the latter was then the most influential lecturer in natural philosophy in England, Demainbray became familiar with the business of lecturing. In 1727, at the age of seventeen, he married Mary Warshare (*d.* before 1755) of Embden, and left England to study at the University of Leiden, in the Netherlands. About 1731 he became a freemason, and joined a French lodge in London.

In the 1740s Demainbray ran a school in Edinburgh for young ladies learning French and English. His teaching career was interrupted when he volunteered for the English army and took part in the battle of Prestonpans on 21 September 1745. By 1747 he had experimented on the effect of electricity on plant growth and published letters on the subject in the *Caledonian Mercury* and *Gentleman's Magazine*. Although he did not pursue this work further, these letters brought him to the attention of savants such as Stephen Hales and Abbé Nollet. During the winter of 1748–9 he took up lecturing on natural philosophy. Having left Edinburgh in early 1749, he gave courses of lectures in Newcastle, Durham, and Sunderland. By December he was in York, where he met the instrument maker Henry Hindley, from whom he acquired a pyrometer to demonstrate in his lectures. Demainbray lectured next in Leeds in April 1750. His growing reputation led to his being awarded an LLD degree by King's College, Aberdeen, the following July.

By August 1751 Demainbray was in Dublin. There, through James Simon, a wine merchant and antiquarian, he made contact with Henry Baker, a teacher of deaf people and writer on the microscope, in London. In 1753 he left Dublin for France, and during the next year he travelled to Bordeaux, Montpellier, where his wife died, Lyons, and Toulouse. In each of these towns he lectured to the local academy and became an associate member in recognition of his work. His success was in part due to the fact that the members of these academies had a growing interest in Newtonian philosophy. In Lyons he collected models of machines, including some he copied from

Stephen Charles Triboudet Demainbray (1710–1782), by unknown artist

M. De Grollier's collection, which he later demonstrated in his lectures in London. In the autumn of 1754, on the eve of the outbreak of the Seven Years' War, he returned to London, having visited Paris on the way.

In London, on 1 February 1755, Demainbray remarried. His new wife was Sarah Tooke, whose father was the royal poulterer. Later that month Demainbray offered a course of lectures on natural and experimental philosophy at his house in Panton Street, near the Haymarket. Soon afterwards he lectured to the prince of Wales, later George III, and Prince Edward. One consequence of this royal patronage was that Demainbray introduced his brother-in-law, John Horne (later John Horne *Tooke), to the prince of Wales, a connection that eventually caused much embarrassment for Demainbray when Horne became a staunch supporter of John Wilkes and opponent of the king.

Unfortunately for Demainbray and others, lecturing on natural philosophy could not provide sufficient income in the later 1750s. In an attempt to increase his audience, Demainbray offered a course on natural history. During 1758 he moved from Panton Street to an 'experiment-room' in Carey Street, but his fortunes did not improve and he gave up these premises early in 1759. He made a last attempt to give a 'Popular and practical course of experimental philosophy' in 1761, but it was not a success. During a visit to Britain two years later the French astronomer Lalande heard that Demainbray had abandoned physics and could not even be bothered to show his instruments to Benjamin Franklin.

When George III, his old pupil, came to the throne in 1760, Demainbray's hopes of royal patronage rose. He became an official of the customs, and eventually found a sinecure connected with natural philosophy. In 1768 he was appointed superintendent of the king's new observatory at Richmond. Kew observatory, as it was known, was built for the king to observe the transit of Venus that occurred on 4 June 1769. The significance of this rare event was that it was possible, from measurements made at different places on earth as Venus crossed the disc of the sun, to calculate the size of the solar system; numerous expeditions were mounted to observe the transit in remote parts of the world.

In the years following the transit Demainbray spent his time recording the weather, perhaps giving a few lectures, and checking the clocks that provided time for parliament. He died on 20 February 1782 at Northolt, Middlesex, where he was living at the time and where he was buried. His son, **Stephen George Francis Triboudet Demainbray** (c.1759–1854), succeeded him as superintendent at Kew. The younger Demainbray was also a royal chaplain. He was assisted at the observatory by his brother-in-law Stephen Rigaud, and then by his nephew S. P. *Rigaud (1774–1839), who later became professor of astronomy at Oxford and a historian of science.   ALAN Q. MORTON

Sources A. Q. Morton and J. A. Wess, *Public and private science: the King George III collection* (1993), 89–120 · G. Rigaud, 'Dr Demainbray and the king's observatory at Kew', *The Observatory*, 5 (1882), 279–85 · S. C. T. Demainbray, *Scots Magazine*, 9 (1747), 40, 93 [letter to the *Caledonian Mercury*] · *GM*, 2nd ser., 42 (1854), 193 · D. Lysons, *The environs of London*, 3 (1795), 317–81 · *Old Westminsters*, 1.259 · P. J. Anderson, ed., *Officers and graduates of University and King's College, Aberdeen, MVD–MDCCCLX*, New Spalding Club, 11 (1893), 111 · PRO, PROB 8/175/2960 · *DNB*
Archives Sci. Mus., apparatus · U. Aberdeen L., special libraries and archives, papers and diplomas
Likenesses silhouette, Sci. Mus. [*see illus.*] · silhouette, Radcliffe Observatory, Oxford

Demainbray, Stephen George Francis Triboudet (c.1759–1854). *See under* Demainbray, Stephen Charles Triboudet (1710–1782).

Demant, Vigo Auguste (1893–1983), theologian and social commentator, was born on 8 November 1893 in Newcastle upon Tyne, the eldest of three children and only son of Thorvald Conrad Frederick Demant, a professional linguist and translator, who started a language school in Newcastle, and his wife, Emilie Thora Wildemann. On the paternal side he came from a line of Huguenot organ builders and piano makers who had worked their way northwards to settle in Denmark. T. C. F. Demant was a Unitarian and a follower of Auguste Comte.

After school in Newcastle Demant was sent on a six-month exchange to Tournan, to finish his schooling in France. He spent some time at the Sorbonne then returned to the north-east to study engineering at Armstrong College (later to become Durham University). Having obtained his BSc and wishing to enter the Unitarian ministry, he moved to Oxford in 1916 as a member of Exeter and Manchester colleges, taking the diploma in anthropology. He briefly ministered to a Unitarian congregation in Newbury, but meanwhile had met Charles Gore. Gore was a major influence, and through him Demant was converted to the Church of England and Anglo-Catholicism. After a short time at Ely Theological College he was ordained deacon in 1919 and priest in 1920. He became a curate at St Thomas's in Oxford (1919–23), St Michael's in Summertown, Oxford (1923–4), and the mission of St Nicholas, Plumstead, Norfolk (1924–6).

In 1926 Demant met M. B. Reckitt, a prominent Anglican layman and author. He and Reckitt formed a close association which continued for the rest of their lives. Through Reckitt's patronage he was introduced into membership of the exclusive Chandos circle, which met regularly from 1926, surviving to the 1970s. Reckitt also encouraged him to use his abilities within a wider sphere than the parochial ministry, and in 1929, while based at St Silas's, Kentish Town, he became director of research for the Christian Social Council, which had emerged from the Conference on Politics, Economics, and Citizenship. He produced as reports *The Miners' Distress and the Coal Problem* (1929), *The Just Price* (1930), and *This Unemployment: Disaster or Opportunity?* (1931). In 1933 he became vicar of St John's, Richmond, Surrey, moving to St Paul's as canon residentiary in 1942. In 1949 he returned to Oxford as canon of Christ Church and regius professor of moral and pastoral theology, retiring to Headington in 1971.

Demant was the major theoretician in the Christendom Group of Anglican Catholic thinkers, whose concern was to establish the centrality of what they termed 'Christian sociology', an analysis of society fundamentally rooted in a Catholic and incarnational theology. The group included Reckitt, W. G. Peck, and P. E. T. Widdrington, and in addition to numerous books their ideas were propounded in a quarterly journal, *Christendom*, which ran from 1931 to 1950. Annual summer schools sought to extend their influence further. William Temple was often an ally, but the Christendom Group placed greater emphasis on the need to derive Christian principles about society from Christian doctrine. Demant was one of the speakers at Temple's 1941 Malvern conference, and Malvern probably marked the high point of the Christendom Group's influence on the Church of England.

Demant was at home across a range of subjects and languages unusual in the Church of England of his time. His upbringing had been Darwinian. He had received an early training in Henri Bergson's philosophy. Much of this he rejected, but it gave him an access to continental thought. He helped introduce the work of Nikolay Berdyaev and Jacques Maritain to Anglican circles, and he also brought the thought of Søren Kierkegaard before an English audience. His reading embraced anthropology, economics, sociology, philosophy, and theology, in French, German, and Danish. His clarity of mind fed on this varied diet and produced a coherent theology which carried forward an Anglican Catholic tradition of social thought.

Demant's conviction that an incarnational theology cannot be separated from the condition of human beings in society, and that the problems of society are structural rather than individual, can be seen in some of the titles of books written in the London years: *This Unemployment* (1931), *God, Man and Society* (1933), and *Theology of Society* (1947). One of the most influential was *Religion and the Decline of Capitalism*, the Scott Holland lectures for 1949, broadcast in 1950 and published in 1952. Taking up the theme earlier expounded by R. H. Tawney, he examined contemporary religion and society to argue that capitalism was inherently self-destructive, being inimical to organic association, and thus contrary to human nature and needs. In 1957–8 he delivered the Gifford lectures at St Andrews, surveying Christian ethics, but he chose not to publish them.

Demant was a sensitive and kindly priest, and an approachable and helpful figure to students and other scholars. He much valued Christ Church life, and became subdean of the cathedral. He was made DLitt of Oxford (1940) and an honorary DD of Durham University.

In 1925 Demant married Marjorie, daughter of George Tickner, a zoologist; they had one son and two daughters. Demant's programme of reading and writing, in tandem with his priestly duties, required a rigid daily timetable but within this ordered framework he was much involved in family life. This setting also provided an outlet for his considerable practical talents, such as carpentry and kite making. A persistent interest was the authorship of the works of Shakespeare: Demant urged the claims of Edward de Vere, earl of Oxford, even travelling to the USA to lecture on the theme. He died on 3 March 1983 in the John Radcliffe Hospital, Oxford.

ANGELA CUNNINGHAM, *rev.*

Sources *The Times* (17 March 1983) · private information (1990) **Archives** GL, corresp. with publishers, Hodder and Stoughton · University of Bristol Library, special collections, corresp. and statement relating to trial of *Lady Chatterley's lover*

Demaus, Robert (1829–1874), schoolmaster and biographer, was educated at Edinburgh University, where he was signet medallist and graduated MA on 13 February 1850. He became master of the Breadalbane School at Aberfeldy in Perthshire, and in 1856 addressed a *Letter to the Right Hon. Earl Granville, Lord President of the Council* criticizing recent regulations enacted by the committee of council on education for improving the efficiency of teachers in government schools. In the same year he was appointed principal of the grammar school at Alnwick; in 1857 he became a fellow of the Educational Institute of Scotland, and in 1858 master at the West End Academy in Aberdeen. In 1860 he was ordained deacon by the bishop of Down and Connor, and in 1862 priest by the same prelate. From 1860 to 1865 he was chaplain to Thomas George Suther, bishop of Aberdeen, and in 1865 he became senior curate of St Luke's, Chelsea, where he remained until his death. In 1869 he was also appointed principal of Whitelands Training College, an institution founded by the National Society for training school mistresses for church schools.

The author of a considerable number of textbooks, including *A Class-Book of English Prose* (1859) and *The Young Scholar's Guide* (1860), Demaus is best remembered for his biographies of Latimer and Tyndale. His *Hugh Latimer* appeared in 1869, a new and revised edition being published in 1881. In 1871 he issued *William Tyndale: a Contribution to the Early History of the English Bible*; a new edition, slightly revised by Richard Lovett, appeared in 1886. His work for these biographies was careful and critical. He carried out extensive research among state papers and in archives in Brussels and other Belgian towns. The subsequent publication of the *Letters and Papers of Henry VIII* added little factually to Demaus's biography of Tyndale,

which remained the standard work for many years, despite its unhelpful system of referencing; even after it was superseded it continued to be regarded as a real contribution to Tyndale scholarship. Demaus died, apparently of apoplexy, at 11 St Leonard's Terrace, Chelsea, on 15 March 1874. His wife, Jane, survived him.

E. I. CARLYLE, *rev.* ROSEMARY MITCHELL

Sources Crockford (1874) · Boase, *Mod. Eng. biog.* · C. H. William, *William Tyndale* (1969), 157–8

Wealth at death under £4000: probate, 21 April 1874, *CGPLA Eng. & Wales*

Demon Barber of Fleet Street, the. *See* Todd, Sweeney (*supp. fl.* 1784).

De Morgan, William Frend. *See* Morgan, William Frend De (1839–1917).

Dempsey, Sir Miles Christopher (1896–1969), army officer, was born in New Brighton, Cheshire, on 15 December 1896, son of Arthur Francis Dempsey, a marine insurance broker, and his wife, Margaret Maud De la Fosse. He was educated at Shrewsbury School and the Royal Military College, Sandhurst, and was commissioned into the Royal Berkshire regiment in 1915. He served with his regiment in France from 1916, when he commanded a company at the age of nineteen, to 1918; he was wounded, mentioned in dispatches, and awarded the MC. He subsequently took part in operations in Iraq (1919–20). Between the wars he served both with his regiment and on the staff, at one time with Archibald Wavell as his divisional commander. At the outbreak of war in 1939, Dempsey was lieutenant-colonel in command of the 1st battalion of his regiment. During the battle for France he took command of 13th infantry brigade, which played a major part in the British counter-attack at Arras in May 1940; as a result of its contribution in a three-day battle in the Ypres and Comines Canal area, the British expeditionary force gained time for its withdrawal to Dunkirk. Dempsey was appointed to the DSO.

The next action which Dempsey saw was in the Middle East. Having been promoted lieutenant-general, he took command of 13th corps of the Eighth Army after the battle of El Alamein, and helped Sir Bernard Montgomery to plan the invasion of Sicily. His corps landed at Syracuse on 10 July 1943 and took part in the hard battle for Catania. During the descent on Italy itself, on 3 September 1943, his corps was in the spearhead, and Dempsey conducted the winter battles in southern Italy in a masterly fashion. But he did not remain there for long. Montgomery needed him for the coming invasion of western Europe, and in January 1944 he returned home to command the Second Army. His part in the battle for Normandy and the subsequent breakout, closing up to the Rhine, and finally advancing to the Elbe, was a model of how to conduct operations soundly and successfully. He was in many ways the ideal subordinate to Montgomery: never seeking the limelight, nor able (from the nature of Montgomery's directives) to indulge in bold strokes of initiative, he always fully understood what Montgomery's purpose was, and quietly and steadily got on with it. He would spend much of his time visiting his subordinate commanders and their troops, assessing the situation, listening to their problems, and giving instructions clearly and succinctly. He had profound understanding of the soldiers under his command and firm control over operations, so he inspired both subordinates and superior commanders with confidence in his judgement and leadership. Yet he remained relatively unknown to the public.

Dempsey was very good at understanding a battlefield; a map became a relief map in his hand. His sound, albeit cautious establishment of the initial bridgehead was followed by the application of ever-growing pressure in the Caen sector. His conduct of the battle was governed by the knowledge that the breakout was to be by the Americans in the western flank of the bridgehead; he therefore went on hitting away at the Germans, drawing more and more of their strength against his own army. He was determined to take Caen, since its capture would, as he put it, 'loosen the enemy's hinge and provide us with a firm hinge'. During the subsequent operations in the latter part of July 1944, which led to the American breakout and the subsequent Falaise and Argentan battles which broke the German positions in Normandy, Dempsey was always ready to take advantage of the opportunity to exploit success, but never tried to reinforce stalemate. He would also wholeheartedly accept responsibility for taking critical decisions, without worrying if the efforts of the army were misinterpreted by the press or senior allied commanders. He was quite unperturbed when there were suggestions that operation Goodwood (which was designed to draw more German Panzers away from General Omar Bradley's First Army) had been a failure, and he merely pointed out that such misunderstandings would help with the deception plan. After the breakout in Normandy, Dempsey's army conducted difficult and deliberate winter operations in Belgium (it was during a visit to the front at this time that George VI dubbed him KCB, an appointment which had been gazetted in June 1944), and established itself at the Rhine by March 1945; in the subsequent advance to the Elbe his army was in the forefront, and he himself received the surrender of Hamburg on 3 May 1945.

When the European war was over Dempsey was appointed commander of the Fourteenth Army for the reoccupation of Singapore and Malaya, in succession to Sir William Slim, whom he also followed as commander-in-chief, allied land forces, south-east Asia, until 1946 when he was promoted to the rank of general. He was appointed KBE in 1945. In 1946–7 he was commander-in-chief Middle East, and he retired in July 1947 at his own request. In 1948 he married Viola Mary Vivien, youngest daughter of Captain Percy O'Reilly, of Colamber, co. Westmeath; they had no children.

After his retirement Dempsey joined a number of companies: he was a director of H. and G. Simonds, and chairman in 1953–63; he was also chairman of Greene, King & Sons in 1955–67, and deputy chairman of Courage, Barclay, and Simonds in 1961–6. But he derived especial pleasure from chairing the Racecourse Betting Control Board

(1947–51). He had always been an excellent horseman, and was very fond of hunting and racing; he bred and raced his own horses, and once commented that his position on the Racecourse Betting Control Board enhanced his enjoyment of racing all the more for knowing that it was also his duty to be there. Nor did he sever his connection with the army: he was colonel commandant of the corps of Royal Military Police in 1947–57, and of the Special Air Service in 1951–60. He was also colonel of his regiment, the Royal Berkshires, in 1946–56, and a deputy lieutenant for Berkshire from 1950. He was commander-in-chief (designate), UK land forces, in 1951–6, and was appointed GBE on his retirement from this post.

Dempsey, who was nicknamed Bimbo, had many interests: he was a student of military history with a remarkable memory, and he loved music, both playing the piano and singing. At Shrewsbury School he had captained the first eleven, and later at Staff College he had played cricket—he was left-handed—with Thomas Troubridge, who was afterwards his naval colleague for the invasion of Sicily. Tall, lean, and tough, a man of considerable charm and modesty, young-looking and always immaculately turned out, he radiated confidence and authority. Dempsey died at his home, Coombe House, Yattendon, near Newbury, Berkshire, on 5 June 1969.

JOHN STRAWSON, rev.

Sources *The Times* (7 June 1969) · L. F. Ellis and others, *Victory in the West*, 2 vols. (1962–8) · personal knowledge (1981) · *WWW* · J. Keegan, *Six armies in Normandy. From D-day to the liberation of Paris, June 6th–August 25th 1944* (1982) · M. Hastings, *Overlord: D-day and the battle for Normandy* (1989) · *CGPLA Eng. & Wales* (1969)
Archives King's Lond., Liddell Hart C., military papers · PRO, military papers, WO 285 | King's Lond., Liddell Hart C., corresp. with Sir B. H. Liddell Hart · King's Lond., Liddell Hart C., corresp. with Sir Harold Pyman | FILM BFI NFTVA, news footage · IWM FVA, 'H.M. the king', Army film and photographic section, 15 Oct 1944, A 700/177/5 | Dempsey being awarded the KCB by the king| · IWM FVA, actuality footage · IWM FVA, home footage · IWM FVA, news footage |SOUND IWM SA, oral history interview
Likenesses W. Stoneman, photograph, 1944, NPG · B. Hailstone, oils, 1946, IWM
Wealth at death £29,304: probate, 11 Aug 1969, *CGPLA Eng. & Wales*

Dempster, George, of Dunnichen (1732–1818), agriculturist and politician, was born at Alexander Kyd's Close, Dundee, Forfarshire, on 8 December 1732, the eldest son of John Dempster (1700–1754), landowner and grain merchant, and his first wife, Isabel Ogilvie (1700x10–c.1738).

Early life Dempster was educated at Dundee grammar school (c.1739–c.1748) and possibly also at the small parish school at Leuchars, Fife. On 24 February 1748 he entered the University of St Andrews and studied there until about 1750, when he left without taking a degree and moved to Edinburgh, to study law at the university. Edinburgh at this time was entering upon its greatest period of social and intellectual glory, and Dempster, by nature gregarious and convivial, took full advantage of the opportunities offered. He became one of the first members of the Select Society and later became a member of the *Poker Club.

On the death of his father in November 1754 Dempster

George Dempster of Dunnichen (1732–1818), by John Opie

exceeded by only 16 MPs out of the total of 692), he was not a natural politician. Although he called himself a whig, party politics and the need to vote with a party against his principles were distasteful to him, and he almost invariably followed an independent line. He wrote:

> I have long thought … that unless one preserves a little freedom and independency in Parliament to act in every question and to vote agreeably to the suggestions of one's mind, a seat in Parliament is a seat on thorns and rusty nails. (*Letters*, 84–5)

His insistence on speaking and voting in accordance with his conscience rather than with his party gained him a reputation for incorruptibility and independence, and the sobriquet Honest George. Dempster readily presented petitions on behalf of his constituents, and regularly championed Scottish economic causes. Although this led to his being viewed as a Scottish patriot, he resented any accusation of partiality, saying that 'the sooner all national distinctions between the two kingdoms were forgot the better it would be for both' (Debrett, 10.125).

Early in his career Dempster was recruited as a government supporter, but he soon became restive and withdrew his support in December 1762. In 1765 he spoke and voted against the Stamp Act, and thus began a long involvement with American affairs in which he unwaveringly supported the colonists and opposed government attempts to oppress them. The American question led Dempster to become a supporter of the marquess of Rockingham, whose views on America accorded with his own, and he remained a Rockinghamite for almost the whole of the remainder of his parliamentary career. When Rockingham became prime minister in August 1765, Dempster's support earned him the appointment of secretary to the Order of the Thistle, of which he was immensely proud. His unwillingness to place party above personal integrity, however, resulted in this being the only office he was ever granted.

India also became a major interest, both in and out of parliament. Dempster became a 'proprietor' (shareholder) in the East India Company in 1763, and was elected a director in 1769 and 1772. He was very active, opposing government attempts to remove the company's independence, instead favouring internal reform of the company to eliminate fraud, corruption, and other abuses. He argued against colonization, believing that relations with India, as with China, should be purely commercial, and in 1787 he proposed a new type of government for India made up of a viceroy, council, and, in an echo of his views on America, an elected assembly of resident Europeans to which native Indians could make representations. Dempster strongly defended Warren Hastings against Edmund Burke's campaign of impeachment, believing Hastings to be unfairly blamed for many of the scandals involving the company.

Other issues that Dempster vigorously supported included proposals for a Scottish militia, freedom of the press and the right of newspapers to report parliamentary proceedings, and reduction of the national debt, the last being a theme to which he returned regularly. He backed

inherited the family estates, which comprised some 6000 acres, yielding £769 per annum, and thereby became moderately wealthy. Four months later he completed his legal studies, being admitted as a member of the Faculty of Advocates on 4 March 1755. The following year he set off on the grand tour of Europe, but was recalled suddenly to Scotland because of the illness of his eldest sister. Although she recovered, Dempster never managed to complete his grand tour. His role as family head occupied the next few years, dealing with estate and family affairs in Dundee and looking after the education of his younger brothers and sisters. The record of Dempster's career as an advocate has not survived, though it appears that he did practise during these years.

Political career In 1760 Dempster turned his back on the legal profession and decided to enter parliament, offering himself as a candidate for the Perth district of burghs (comprising Perth, St Andrews, Dundee, Forfar, and Cupar), which were notorious for corruption and venality. Against the odds Dempster succeeded at his first attempt, albeit at a crippling cost, estimated at £10,000. He contested four more general elections, on each occasion strengthening his popularity and support. He faced serious opposition in 1768 and 1780, but by 1784 had become virtually unassailable, remaining unchallenged despite his whig sympathies, while over 160 whigs lost their seats. The enormous cost of his first two elections forced Dempster to sell some 2500 acres—all his land apart from the family estate at Dunnichen—which he regretted for the rest of his life.

Dempster was an MP for 28 years, but though from the start a frequent and passionate speaker (between 1768 and 1774, for example, he spoke on 193 occasions, a record the younger Pitt's proposed sinking fund, but managed to find fault with every one of the taxes with which Pitt intended to finance it. On reform of the parliamentary franchise Dempster was ambivalent. He was by nature a democrat and champion of the common man, but while supporting extension of the franchise in the counties he repeatedly surprised his colleagues by resisting that of the burghs, apparently to avoid betraying his electors; he was placing friendship, in this case to his constituents, above political principle.

In London Dempster married, on 24 September 1774, Rose Heming (c.1748–1810), daughter of a Jamaica sugar planter. The marriage produced no children, but from the start was a very happy one. Dempster commented to Sir Adam Fergusson's brother, Charles, 'as for happiness I protest to you I did not know what it was till I was married' (*Letters*, 87). After his marriage he became increasingly disillusioned with parliament and spoke often of settling down as a farmer. This resulted, in the summer of 1788, in his resolving not to stand again for parliament, and though he participated in the 1788–9 session he did not attend the final session the following year. His last major parliamentary activity was in autumn 1788 during the regency debates, when he opposed Pitt's proposed limitations on the prince of Wales's powers as regent. Dempster's last recorded speech was on 22 July 1789, in support of famine relief for Revolutionary France.

Trade and industry Dempster gained great fame among his Scottish countrymen for striving to advance Scottish commerce and manufactures. He tirelessly promoted the textile industry, first linen and later also cotton. In 1763, realizing that the lack of proper banking facilities was hampering trade in his native Forfarshire, Dempster founded the first bank in Dundee, under the name George Dempster & Co., and it prospered sufficiently for a second bank to be established in Dundee in 1792. Despite the leading role he played in founding the bank, once it was established he withdrew from active involvement.

Dempster's greatest period of activity in the cause of the Scottish economy was in the 1780s, when he attempted to stem the growing tide of emigration to North America by transforming the wealth of the highlands and islands. Inspired by the reports of John Knox and James Anderson, Dempster conducted his own tour of the west highlands in January 1785, and became convinced that with encouragement the highland economy was capable of considerable advancement.

Improvements to the fisheries came first, and Dempster was instrumental in the setting up of a parliamentary inquiry, which led to two Fisheries Acts, of 1785 and 1786. These reformed the salt laws and other antiquated fisheries legislation, and established an incorporated company, the British Fisheries Society, to encourage the industry. Other measures included acts promoted by Dempster in 1787 and 1789 to found lighthouses on the Scottish coasts and to establish the Northern Lighthouse Board, and, about 1785, Dempster's suggestion of transporting fish preserved in ice rather than salt as hitherto, thus laying the foundation of the vast modern frozen food industry.

As one of the directors he was from the outset a leading light in the British Fisheries Society, which established villages at Tobermory and Ullapool, and at Stein in Skye, to support fishermen and act as centres of economic growth. He took a particular interest in Ullapool and Stein, and also in another site not in the end selected, on Canna.

In the same period Dempster vigorously promoted the textile industry. In 1783 he encountered Richard Arkwright, the great cotton pioneer, and was so impressed with the mills at Cromford that he invited Arkwright to join him in establishing a mill in Scotland. Arkwright agreed to build mills at New Lanark in partnership with Dempster and the Glasgow merchant and manufacturer David Dale (1739–1806). Building started in April 1785 and spinning commenced in March 1786. However, Dempster withdrew in December 1786 to concentrate on another venture, a cotton mill at Stanley, Perthshire, involving Arkwright and some Perth merchants. Construction here commenced in 1785 with production beginning early in 1786. The company experienced mixed fortunes and was finally dissolved in December 1799, with heavy losses for the partners.

Perceiving that the lack of good roads was an impediment to economic prosperity, in his later years Dempster promoted road building in both the highlands and the lowlands. The Ullapool to Dingwall road, built by the British Fisheries Society and connecting the east and west coasts, was the first such project in which Dempster was involved. He successfully steered the proposal through parliament in 1789, and the road was constructed between 1792 and 1794. In the 1780s and 1790s he campaigned for turnpike roads in Forfarshire, and he was instrumental in the proprietors' obtaining a Turnpike Act in 1789. By 1790 he was delightedly informing his correspondents of the commencement of the Arbroath to Forfar turnpike; during the next ten years further turnpikes were constructed linking all the main settlements of the region.

Dempster's efforts on behalf of the Scottish economy were recognized on 13 July 1786 by his being voted a piece of silver plate by the convention of royal burghs of Scotland.

Agricultural improvements From the time of his inheritance in 1754 Dempster displayed great interest and enjoyment in the management and improvement of his estate at Dunnichen. He found the tenants, as elsewhere in Scotland, in a state of wretched poverty, still bound by medieval codes of loyalty and servitude to their landlords, and the land divided up and farmed in accordance with the antiquated and inefficient runrig system. Reflecting contemporary enlightened opinion, he was determined to provide greater prosperity for both tenant and landlord by a reform of agricultural practices and the conditions under which tenants worked, and by the introduction of manufacturing industry.

Dempster commenced his improvements in 1761, and in the following year gave his tenants greater security by granting them leases for life, at the same time abolishing all personal services: thirlage to the mill and blacksmith's shop, carriage, and bonnage. These he felt especially strongly about, frequently inveighing against them in his correspondence. He substituted money rent for payment in kind, enclosed farms with freestone walls, and built proper houses to replace the hovels that existed formerly. The runrig system was replaced by crop rotation, and turnips and other crops were introduced for winter feed for cattle and horses, the breeds of both being progressively improved. Dempster's early efforts were driven more by enthusiasm than prudence, which forced him to retrench for a while, but by 1764 he was ready to start again. In 1768 he wrote to Edmund Burke:

> I am a farmer and a very serious one myself. … Of late the spirit of agriculture has gain'd ground amongst us [in Scotland]. I have been employ'd in it these last four years and hope in as many more to Quadruple the value of my six thousand Patrimonial Acres. (Dempster to Burke, 26 Sept 1768, Wentworth Woodhouse MS MF/76, 1/223)

Dempster planted trees in vast numbers, hoping thereby to derive significant income. He devised incentives for the tenants to protect and nurture them, and this policy was very successful, the tenants even planting replacement trees when necessary. In January 1788 he commenced draining Loch Restenneth in order to extract shell-marl, a form of lime that was extremely valuable as fertilizer. The operation was completed in July, exposing a vast area of marl: Dempster, after meeting his own needs, profited hugely from sales—estimated at £14,000 over fourteen years.

Another ambitious project was the founding, in 1788, of a village at Letham, intended as a market town and centre for linen manufacture. In 1803 Dempster pioneered there a system of self-government based on a nine-member feuars' committee, which was to adjudicate in disputes and the affairs of the village. The members were to be chosen by a surprisingly modern method of secret voting invented by Dempster. This used grooved voting sticks in which a sliding tongue could be moved to indicate a 'yes' or 'no' vote; the system apparently survived until well into the twentieth century.

In July 1786 Dempster purchased the run-down estate of Skibo in Sutherland, 18,000 acres in area, and later added a number of smaller contiguous estates. He intended Skibo to be run by his half-brother, John Hamilton Dempster, a sea captain in the East India Company's service, on John's retirement from the sea. He also expected that Captain Dempster's son, on whom Dempster doted, would eventually inherit the estate.

These purchases also gave Dempster the opportunity to try out his agricultural improvements on a larger scale, and to demonstrate their viability and worth in the more extreme climatic conditions of the highlands. He hoped by his example to encourage other landowners to do likewise, thus complementing the British Fisheries Society's work. The basic strategy was the same as at Dunnichen: the tenants were granted long leases and relieved of personal services, and agricultural practices were reformed. As at Letham, Dempster granted his Skibo tenants a constitution and encouraged new settlers to become tenants of the estate, and devised a system of concessions and incentives to that end.

Dempster was eager to establish villages at Skibo, and having selected two sites, he established a small linen-weaving business at one and the more ambitious project of a cotton mill at the other. Both projects failed: the linen-weaving concern never amounted to much while the mill, completed in 1794, was burdened with heavy debts from the start and suffered from its remote location, and the highlanders found it difficult to adjust to long hours of mill work alien to their traditional life. In 1805 it was sold to a Glasgow cotton spinner and in 1806 was destroyed by fire and never rebuilt. However, the agricultural innovations were much more successful, enabling rents to be raised dramatically while Dempster gained great esteem from his reforming zeal.

Later years In the 1790s Dempster suffered severe personal setbacks. His half-brother's wife and son both died of tuberculosis in the period 1798–1801, and the captain himself drowned at sea in 1800. Skibo passed to John Hamilton Dempster's natural daughter, who returned from India with her husband to claim it. Dempster henceforth increasingly confined himself to Dunnichen and its environs, though this may have been from increasing infirmity due to age as much as from loss of spirit. At Dunnichen he remained energetic, in 1802 rebuilding the church there and in 1803 founding the Lunan and Vinney Farming Society, named after the two principal burns on the Dunnichen estate. The society was modelled on others founded at the same time, its only activity being the holding of an annual meeting, which involved a formal meal followed by speeches and convivial discussion on a wide range of matters relating to agricultural improvement. The membership, which reached a peak of about eighty, tended to be Dempster's friends and neighbours in the local farming and landowning community. He was elected president in perpetuity at the first meeting, and remained so until the society's eventual demise about 1815.

Dempster's wife, Rose, died on 10 July 1810, following which he began spending time at Broughty Ferry and St Andrews, at the latter encountering to his delight an old friend from his Edinburgh days, the philosopher Adam Ferguson. In St Andrews Dempster also befriended some old ladies with whom he played whist, a game of which he had always been fond. Nevertheless, by this time the deaths of most of his lifelong friends (Ferguson himself died in 1816) made his last years increasingly lonely. Towards the end of 1817 Dempster suffered a stroke, and he died at Dunnichen House on 13 February 1818. He was buried that month at Restenneth Priory, near Forfar.

Dempster is remembered best as an agricultural improver, but he spent half his adult life as a popular, very active, and conscientious independent whig MP, and gained great public renown through his efforts to promote Scottish trade and industry. His attractive and outgoing personality was marked by candour, enthusiasm for the causes he espoused, and a willingness to help others. He placed personal merit above rank and wealth, and commanded much affection, partly from his charming personality and partly from the altruism and integrity he displayed in public life. His reputation survived the use of bribery during elections—which was, however, a normal part of public life in the eighteenth century.

ANDREW M. LANG

Sources A. M. Lang, *A life of George Dempster, Scottish M.P., of Dunnichen (1732–1818)* (1998) • *Letters of George Dempster to Sir Adam Fergusson, 1756–1813, with some account of his life*, ed. J. Fergusson (1934) • E. H. Guest, 'Dempster, George', HoP, *Commons* • *Public characters of 1809–10* (1809) • P. D. G. Thomas, 'The debates of the House of Commons, 1768–1774', PhD diss., U. Lond., 1958 • J. Debrett, ed., *The parliamentary register, or, History of the proceedings and debates of the House of Commons*, 83 vols. (1775–1804) • T. C. Smout, 'The landowner and the planned village in Scotland, 1730–1830', *Scotland in the age of improvement*, ed. N. Phillipson and R. Mitchison (1970), 73–106 • S. B. Calder, 'The industrial archaeology of Sutherland: a Scottish highland economy, 1700–1900', MLitt diss., University of Strathclyde, 1974 • J. Dunlop, *The British Fisheries Society, 1786–1893* (1978) • R. S. Fitton, *The Arkwrights: spinners of fortune* (1989) • R. W. Munro, *Scottish lighthouses* (1979) • *Scotland and Scotsmen in the eighteenth century: from the MSS of John Ramsay, esq., of Ochtertyre*, ed. A. Allardyce, 2 vols. (1888) • *Scots Magazine* (1754–1818) • C. W. Boase, *A century of banking in Dundee*, 2nd edn (1867) • S. G. Checkland, *Scottish banking: a history, 1695–1973* (1975) • A. Jervise, *Memorials of Angus and the Mearns: an account historical, antiquarian & traditionary*, 2 vols. (1885) • J. M. Anderson, ed., *The matriculation roll of the University of St Andrews, 1747–1897* (1905) • J. Malcolm, *The parish of Monifieth in ancient and modern times with a history of the landed estates and lives of eminent men* (1910) • A. Lowson, *Portrait gallery of Forfar notables* (1893) • C. Mackie, 'Alphabetical list of those who attended the prelections on history and Roman antiquitys from 1719 to 1744 inclusive: collected 1 July, 1746', U. Edin. L., MS Dc.5.24² • Wentworth-Fitzwilliam papers, Sheff. Arch., Wentworth Woodhouse muniments, WWM/MF/76, 1/223, WWM R1 • NA Scot., Blair Adam MSS • small purchases, NL Scot., MS 5319 • old parish registers, Dundee register of baptisms and marriages, General Register Office for Scotland, Edinburgh, 282/4, 282/3 • Brechin commissary court records, NA Scot., CC 3/5 • University of Toronto, Thomas Fisher Rare Book Library, Dempster MSS

Archives University of Toronto, Thomas Fisher Rare Book Library, corresp. and MSS, MS 126 | BL, corresp. with first earl of Liverpool, Add. MSS 38211–38222, 38308–38311 • Bodl. Oxf., letters to Sir James Bland Burges • Hunt. L., letters to William Pulteney • NL Scot., corresp. • NRA Scotland, priv. coll., letters to Sir John Sinclair • NRA, priv. coll., letters to Sir Adam Ferguson and Sir James Fergusson, sixth baronet • priv. coll., letters to Robert Graham of Fintry • Sheff. Arch., Wentworth Woodhouse MSS, corresp. with Edmund Burke • Sheff. Arch., letters to Charles, second marquess of Rockingham • U. Edin. L., special collections division, letters to Grímur Thorkelin • Yale U., Beinecke L., corresp. with James Boswell

Likenesses G. Willison, oils, 1786, Dundee Museum and Art Galleries • Birrell, line engraving, 1788 (after J. Tassie), Scot. NPG • J. Tassie, paste medallion, 1788, Scot. NPG • line engraving, 1793, Scot. NPG • line engraving, Dec 1808, repro. in *Public characters of 1809–10*, facing p. 523 • J. S. Copley, oils • J. T. Nairn, oils, Scot. NPG • J. Opie, oils, Scot. NPG [*see illus.*] • Raeburn, oils, priv. coll.; repro. in *Letters*, ed. Fergusson, frontispiece • J. Young, line engraving, repro. in A. Lowson, *Portrait gallery of Forfar notables* (1893), facing p. 1 • line engraving (after medallion by J. Tassie), NL Scot.; repro. in *European Magazine* (Sept 1793) • line engraving, Scot. NPG • oils, County Hall, Forfar; copy, Feuars' Hall, Letham, Perthshire

Dempster, Thomas (1579–1625), writer, was, by his own account, born on 23 August 1579, a date which has been accepted by those authorities who have written about him. The place of his birth was Cliftbog in Aberdeenshire, an estate belonging to his father, Thomas Dempster, laird of Muiresk, Auchterless, and Killesmont, who also seems to have held the office of lieutenant (*prorex*) of Banff and Buchan. His mother was Jean Leslie, daughter of William Leslie, ninth baron of Balquain. The couple, according to Dempster's autobiography, had twenty-nine children, of which he was the twenty-fourth. This statement has been taken at face value by Irving (Irving, *Lives*, 1.347), but it is possible that Dempster was only the third son of three (Leslie, vol. 3).

Early life and education in Scotland Dempster—again by his own account—learned the alphabet in one hour at the age of three. Whatever the truth of this, he was sent at an early age to school in Turreff, under the care of the schoolmaster Andrew Ogston. After this, he continued his education in the classics at Aberdeen, under Thomas Cargill, who later became rector of the grammar school there.

While Dempster was receiving this early education, his family became embroiled in an internal feud. This was caused by James, his eldest brother, marrying his father's mistress, Isabella Gordon, for which his father disinherited him. James sought revenge by gathering some Gordon associates and attacking his father as he rode about his business one morning. In the resultant battle several men on both sides were killed, and James Dempster fled Scotland. That he was disinherited is confirmed by a charter of 6 January 1592, which gives the barony of Muiresk to the elder Dempster's second son, Robert. If Thomas Dempster was only the third son, and his brother Robert died during his lifetime, he would have been justified in calling himself baron of Muiresk, as he did in later life. If, however, he was the twenty-fourth child as he claimed, it is highly unlikely that he ever inherited the honour. It was in any case an empty one, as the Muiresk estate was impoverished, and would have brought him no financial benefit even if he had legitimately been the tenth baron.

Further education: England and Europe This family chaos caused Dempster's uncle, John Dempster, an Edinburgh lawyer, to advise his nephew to leave Scotland. Taking this advice, Dempster went to Cambridge about 1589, and became a student at Pembroke College under a tutor called Walter Whalley. How long he stayed at Cambridge is uncertain, but he soon left for France, being robbed of all his money and most of his clothes on the journey and, with difficulty, eventually reaching Paris. Here he was assisted by some fellow Scots, and planned to continue his studies. He was prevented from doing this by a severe outbreak of plague, which killed many Parisians and which nearly killed him as well. When he recovered, he left for Louvain and entered the university there, but did not stay long. He was selected along with other Scottish students by the Jesuit William Crichton, principal of the Scottish College at Louvain, to be sent for further education in Rome. He reached that city after a hazardous journey through Germany and Italy, which were ravaged by war and plague at the time.

At Rome Dempster attracted the attention of Cardinal Cajetan, on whose recommendation he was admitted into the Roman seminary. Unfortunately, he again fell seriously ill, and doctors advised a change of climate. Accordingly, he set off for the Netherlands, travelling via Switzerland, in the company of another Scot, Andrew Crichton. At Tournai he met his fellow countryman James Cheyne, who had been professor at both Paris and Douai, and it was by Cheyne's advice that Dempster entered the latter university. He soon became disenchanted and planned to leave, but Cheyne persuaded him to complete the three-year course, and Dempster took the degree of MA at Douai. He was maintained during his studies by a pension from the king of Spain, and Archduke Albert, who governed the Spanish Netherlands. Following this, he taught briefly at Tournai, but soon left for Paris. Here he took a doctorate in canon law, and became a regent in the Collège de Navarre. Dempster asserts that he was seventeen at this time, which would mean that he took up his college position in 1596. This is unlikely, but not impossible in the seventeenth century when it was feasible for a precocious young man to attain academic distinctions that today would be associated with people much older. Dempster also seems to have become a doctor of civil law at about this time, but at what university is unknown. In later life, he described himself as a doctor of both branches of law.

Academic career: travels and conflict in France and Scotland

Dempster soon continued his travels, visiting St Maixent in Poitou and becoming professor of humanities at Toulouse, a city which his involvement in 'town and gown' battles soon obliged him to leave. He considered becoming professor of philosophy at Montpellier, on the invitation of two Scots, Adam Abernethy and Andrew Currie, but instead went to Nîmes, where he became professor of eloquence as the result of a competition for the post, which he won. As Nîmes was a Huguenot college, it is probable that Dempster concealed his Catholicism, although he usually presented himself in Europe as one who had abandoned a great estate in Scotland for the sake of his religion.

Dempster was not allowed to pursue his career in peace. One of the defeated competitors in the contest for the professorship, the Swiss Jacob Grasser, attacked him in print and tried to have him suspended from his duties. However, Dempster fought back successfully, and managed to have Grasser imprisoned at Nîmes, and, when he escaped, in Paris. A two-year lawsuit followed, which the *parlement* of Toulouse eventually decided in Dempster's favour.

Despite this vindication, Dempster started travelling again. He made a brief visit to Spain, and, on his return to France, accepted a position as tutor to Arthur l'Espinay, the son of the famous soldier Marshal de Saint-Luc and later bishop of Marseilles. He lost this post almost immediately by quarrelling with one of his charge's relations at Brissac, and decided to return to his homeland. Here, however, he found that most of his relations were too poor to be of any assistance to him, and that his Catholicism was a severe drawback. The Scottish protestant clergy appear to have harassed him, and, according to his autobiography, he engaged in a three-day theological dispute with William Cowper, later bishop of Galloway, which he claims he won. The truth of this story is uncertain, but Dempster certainly seems to have had a grudge against Cowper, whom he treated abusively in his *Historia* and damned as a heretic.

As Scotland had nothing to offer, Dempster returned to Europe about 1608, and was employed for seven years as regent in the four Paris colleges of Lisieux, Grassins, Du Plessis, and Beauvais. While at Paris, he published in 1613 his edition of Rosinus's *Antiquitatum Romanorum corpus*, which he dedicated to James VI and I of Scotland and England.

It was while at the Collège de Beauvais that Dempster became involved in an affair which caused him to leave France again. His own version of the story is that he left because a Norman called Jean Robillard tried to assassinate him for some unspecified reason. A more circumstantial account, repeated by Irving (Irving, *Lives*, 1.353), states that the trouble was caused by Dempster's public flogging of a student who had challenged another to a duel. The young man tried to avenge this humiliation by bringing three soldier relations to the college in order to attack Dempster, who armed his servants, ordered the killing of his assailants' horses to prevent their escape, and led a counter-attack so successful that he overpowered his adversaries and locked them up in the college bell-tower. Legal proceedings would certainly have followed this episode, and as Dempster was unsure as to what the outcome of these would be, he left France.

England: royal favour and marriage

Dempster went to England, where he had been previously invited by King James, who considered himself a scholar and who had been flattered by the dedication in the *Antiquitatum Romanorum corpus*. He arrived there in 1615 or early 1616. The king awarded him the sum of £200 on 19 February 1616, and seems to have appointed him historiographer royal for England. This arguably makes Dempster the first holder of this office, although the unbroken line of English historiographers royal only begins in 1661 (Hay, 24, 31). While in London, he married Susanna Waller. The couple later had one child, a daughter, who lived only a few days after her birth. Dempster might have begun a successful career in England, but once again his religion proved a stumbling block. The English clergy, led by Dr Montagu, the bishop of Bath and Wells, criticized him to the king and convinced him that it was improper for the king of a protestant country to show such favour to a professed Catholic. Realizing that he would never prosper with such opposition, Dempster left England, having stayed only a short time.

Return to Europe and success in Italy

Dempster made his way to Rome where he was arrested on suspicion of espionage, and briefly imprisoned. He easily proved this suspicion baseless and soon left for Florence. In Rome he had become friendly with Gucciardini, the Tuscan ambassador to the papal court, and it was on Gucciardini's recommendation, supported by that of the pope, that he was appointed professor of the pandects at the University of Pisa by the grand duke of Tuscany, Cosimo II, in 1616.

Shortly after his appointment, Dempster went back to England to fetch his wife. The couple travelled to Pisa by way of France, where Mrs Dempster caused commotion by appearing with more flesh exposed than was normally the case in France. The crowd she attracted grew so dense and disorderly that the Dempsters were obliged to take refuge in a house. The rest of the journey, however, was uneventful, and they reached Pisa in time for Dempster to deliver his inaugural lecture on 2 November. Their short-lived daughter was born soon after they arrived in Italy.

Dempster at last showed signs of prospering. His salary was increased to 400 ducats a year, and he began work on his *De Etruria regali*, a project which pleased the grand duke as it dealt with the history of the part of Italy which formed his duchy. Dempster appears to have been an enthusiastic and dedicated scholar, who wrote and studied for fourteen hours a day, when possible, and had so powerful a memory that he was known as the Living Library. He was equally fluent in Latin and Greek, and dictated in these languages so rapidly that no pen could keep up. He also seems to have been thorough about research, and in 1617 again visited Britain, in order to obtain books for use in writing the *Etruria*.

In 1619 Dempster's career at Pisa came to an end. He became involved in a dispute with an unnamed English ecclesiastic, who seems to have had the ear of the grand duke, and who managed to convince that ruler that Dempster was in the wrong. The duke gave Dempster a choice of apologizing or of leaving Tuscany. Refusing to apologize, Dempster left Pisa on 21 July 1619. His intention appears to have been to try his luck in Scotland again, but on his way he stopped at Bologna to visit Cardinal Capponi, who convinced him to stay in Italy. The cardinal also managed to obtain for him within twelve days the professorship of humanities at the University of Bologna, at that time the most prestigious seat of learning in Italy.

Accusations of heresy Trouble, however, continued to follow Dempster. The English priest with whom he had clashed at Pisa renewed his attacks, accusing Dempster of being a doubtful Catholic and of possessing heretical books. Dempster did not help his case by writing the Englishman a furious letter, which his enemy had translated into Italian and presented as evidence against its writer. He succeeded in gaining the support of several cardinals, and Dempster was obliged to go to Rome personally in order to defend himself in audience with the pope. A reconciliation was eventually staged between Dempster and the English foe, but the accusations caused the Inquisition in Rome to regard Dempster with continued suspicion. A decree dated 16 March 1621 condemned his edition of Rosinus, and a further one of December 1623 prohibited another of his works.

Bologna: family problems and death Dempster's career now flourished. He attracted many students to Bologna, and evidently lost his urge to wander, as he turned down the offer of a professorship of civil law at Padua, although the salary there was larger than that which he received at Bologna. A new pope, Urban VIII, himself a keen Latinist,

knighted him and granted him an annual pension. He was also made a member of the distinguished Academia della Notte.

In 1625 Dempster's wife eloped with a lover, assisted by some of Dempster's own students and taking with her some of her husband's property. He set off in pursuit, and got as far as Vicenza, where he learned that the fugitives had crossed the Alps and were out of Italy. Abandoning the chase, he went to Butri, near Bologna, to rest. Here he caught a fever, which made it necessary to move him to his home in Bologna, where he died on 6 September 1625. He was buried in St Dominic's Church in that city, where his fellow members of the Academia della Notte erected a monumental stone with a Latin inscription in his memory.

The *Historia ecclesiastica gentis Scotorum* Dempster listed fifty of his own works, a list which is reproduced by Irving (Irving, *Lives*, 1.363–70), who also admitted that there is no confirmation for items twenty-nine to forty-seven on the list except Dempster himself. Considering his working habits, it is certainly possible that Dempster produced a large volume of work, but when and where he wrote most of the items on his list is unknown. The work for which he is most famous, or notorious, is the *Historia ecclesiastica gentis Scotorum*, first published in Bologna in 1627, two years after his death. Despite the title, this is not an ecclesiastical history of Scotland, but a descriptive catalogue of supposedly Scottish writers and saints. It includes people whose existence is doubtful, and lists books which are almost certainly fictitious. Dempster claimed as Scots many early figures who were more likely Irish, but this might be the result of genuine confusion, because the term Scotia was used to describe both Ireland and Scotland until at least the eleventh century, after which its use was increasingly limited to Scotland. Besides this, Dempster also claimed as Scots such unarguably non-Scottish figures as Alcuin, the noted Carolingian scholar, St Boniface, and even Boudicca (Boadicea), the Icenic queen who fought the Romans in the first century AD. Not only is she made out to be Scottish, but she is also attributed with the authorship of several books. His descriptions of other historical figures have been considered more valuable, although they are sometimes distorted by Catholic prejudice; Dempster invented an imaginary work attacking Wyclif by a fourteenth-century Scottish hermit called Grant, and plainly thought that the early Scottish protestants Patrick Hamilton and George Wishart were justly burned at the stake.

Dempster's reasons for exaggerating the number of early Scottish writers were almost certainly patriotic. As David Allan has pointed out (Allan, *Virtue*, 197, 222), he is only one of a number of Scottish historians who, over the centuries, have tried to present the dark ages as an era of learning in Scotland.

Other works Charges of fraud have not been levelled against Dempster's other writings. These, even if half his list is disregarded for lack of evidence, are numerous and varied. His *De Etruria regali* was much admired and is regarded by Irving as his best work (Irving, *Lives*, 1.360). His edition of Rosinus was also commended, and subsequent writers on Roman antiquities used it as a source. Dempster also produced some small works on Roman law, commentaries on the works of the late Roman poets Claudian and Corippus, and some original Latin verse, which was highly regarded by his contemporaries.

Reputation to the present day In the seventeenth century Scots seem to have regarded Dempster as a writer of whom to be proud, and an example of the once-great literary tradition from which late seventeenth-century Scotland was seen to have fallen (Allan, 'Prudence', 473). At the same time, however, non-Scots such as Towers and Bishop Lloyd denounced him for the exaggerations and lies of the *Historia*. In the eighteenth century Dempster appears to have vanished into the obscurity created by Scottish enlightenment belief that the seventeenth century was a dark age for Scottish letters, a belief to which the lamentations of late seventeenth-century Scottish writers had contributed. He resurfaced briefly in the nineteenth century during the period of Scottish antiquarian enthusiasm associated with Sir Walter Scott, and his *Historia*, edited by David Irving, was published for the Bannatyne Club in Edinburgh in 1829. Irving also included Dempster among the illustrious Scots he described in his *Lives of Scotish Writers*, published in 1839. Irving's account takes Dempster to task for the falsifications of the *Historia*, and these features of Dempster's work are what subsequent writers have concentrated upon, when they mention Dempster at all. This reputation for dishonesty, or, more charitably, incredulity, and the fact that Dempster wrote entirely in Greek or Latin, is probably largely responsible for his not having received much in the way of serious scholarly attention. ALEXANDER DU TOIT

Sources D. Irving, *Lives of Scotish writers*, 1 (1839), 347–70 · *Thomae Dempsteri Historia ecclesiastica gentis Scotorum, sive, De scriptoribus Scotis*, ed. D. Irving, rev. edn, 2 vols., Bannatyne Club, 21 (1829), vol. 1, pp. 193–5; vol. 2, pp. 672–80 · F. Michel, *Les écossais en France, les français en Écosse*, 2 vols. (1862), vol. 2, pp. 215–21 · J. F. Waller, ed., *The imperial dictionary of universal biography*, 3 vols. (1857–63), vol. 2, p. 66 · Chambers, *Scots.* (1855), 2.67–9 · W. Anderson, *The Scottish nation*, 2 (1868), 29 · J. Michaud and L. G. Michaud, eds., *Biographie universelle ancienne et moderne*, 84 vols. (1811–62), vol. 2, pp. 68–70 · *The dictionary historical and critical of Mr Peter Boyle*, 5 vols. (1734), vol. 2, pp. 645–6 · R. Goring, ed., *Chambers Scottish biographical dictionary* (1992), 115 · Colonel Leslie [C. J. Leslie], *Historical records of the family of Leslie, from 1067 to 1868–9*, 3 (1869) · D. Allan, *Virtue, learning and the Scottish Enlightenment: ideas of scholarship in early modern history* (1993), 19, 197, 222 · D. Allan, 'Prudence and patronage: the politics of culture in seventeenth-century Scotland', *History of European Ideas*, 18 (1994), 467–80, 473 · R. Douglas and others, *The baronage of Scotland* (1798), 532 · Venn, *Alum. Cant.*, 1/2.30 · D. Hay, 'The historiographer royal in England and Scotland', *Renaissance essays* (1988), 24, 31 · J. G. Wallace-James, 'Order of the Star of Bethlehem', *SHR*, 9 (1911–12), 109–11 · J. H. Baxter, 'Four "new" mediaeval Scottish authors', *SHR*, 25 (1927–8), 90–97
Archives NL Scot., Advocates' Library · NL Scot., Antiquaries MSS

Denbigh. For this title name *see* Feilding, William, first earl of Denbigh (*c*.1587–1643); Feilding, Basil, second earl of Denbigh (*c*.1608–1675).

Denby, Elizabeth Marion (1894–1965), urban reformer, was born on 20 May 1894 at 95 Horton Road, Bradford, the second of the four daughters of Walter Denby (*d.* 1944), a doctor, and his wife, Clara Emma Bassett, a nurse. She was educated privately and at Bradford Girls' Grammar School (1906–13), where she excelled in drawing and music. Her recollections of the slums of industrial Bradford and the contrastingly pretty stone-built villages of the Yorkshire countryside never left her and served as motive and model for her later rethinking of urban environments.

During the First World War Denby studied in the department of social science and administration at the London School of Economics, taking a certificate in social science in 1916–17; this laid the foundations for her assiduous research methods and sociological approach to urban problems. After a period at the Ministry of Labour (1917–21) and co-ordinating volunteer work in Kensington (1923–5), she was appointed organizing secretary of the Kensington Housing Association (and Trust, founded 1926) from 1925 to 1933. In the slums of North Kensington she had responsibility for administration and fundraising publicity and, most importantly, got to know the tenants and their problems, dealing daily with the practical and social implications of bad housing.

Following the Housing Act of 1930—which supported slum clearance and the provision of low-rent housing—Denby and her colleagues in the voluntary housing association movement publicized their agenda for urban reform through 'New Homes for Old' (1931), the first in a series of campaigning exhibitions. Denby was its organizing chairman, a role which she repeated in the larger landmark exhibition of 1932 at Olympia; she wrote the new building section (planning and equipment) of the exhibition catalogue. The exhibition featured a typical Denby argument using charts of statistics based on the 1931 census to address local authority and government policymakers on overcrowding, population numbers, and housing needs. It also used a typical Denby contrast to reach a wider audience: a model of a slum room juxtaposed with a spacious, brightly furnished flat, designed by two women architects. It caused a sensation and contributed momentum to the public housing programme, which by 1936 was completing 5000 dwellings every month.

For Denby, 'New Homes for Old' proved a watershed: she wrote that 'My life, my interest, enjoyment and heart, [now] lay with new building, with construction and everything it meant' (autobiographical notes, Elizabeth Denby collection). She argued unrelentingly for cities rather than suburban estates or garden cities; the designing of communities rather than individual buildings; the rehabilitation of old properties instead of blanket demolitions; and especially for the provision of small terraced houses with gardens for families, rather than blocks of flats. With her own statistics on housing densities, she put her case forcefully but ultimately unsuccessfully in a talk in the Royal Institute of British Architects in 1936 (she was the first woman to address that body and later became an honorary associate member in 1942). However, she recognized the inevitability of flats in city centres, as well as their appropriateness for single people and childless couples; with Mozelle Sassoon as patron, she collaborated with the architect Maxwell Fry on the design of Sassoon House in Peckham (1933–4), a block of architecturally and socially innovative flats. In her self-invented role as housing consultant Denby represented the users' perspective and provided design suggestions and revisions based on her experience of tenants' needs.

Although she operated better as a campaigner, Elizabeth Denby became a tireless committee member, serving on committees for the Pioneer Health Centre (1934–48), the Peckham Health Centre (1934–5), the London county council's housing committee (1936), the Council for Art and Industry (1936–7), the utility furniture committee at the Board of Trade (1941–6), and the Modern Architecture Research Group. She was a catalyst for the social programme of modernism, advising the leading modernist architects Wells Coates (1935), Erno Goldfinger (1938), and Godfrey Samuel (c.1938), as well as local authorities and government agencies.

Denby's Leverhulme fellowship (1933) to study interwar housing in eight European countries resulted in her most influential publication, *Europe Re-Housed* (1938). Her travels informed much of her housing practice, including Kensal House (1933–7), a scheme in North Kensington. With Fry as chief executive architect, they designed homes (albeit flats) as communities with new standards of light, fresh air, and equipment. In this urban village, Denby's user-centred approach challenged class-bound professional attitudes which assumed that tenants could not be entrusted with extra features and amenities. Designed into the project were clubs for teenagers and for parents, a sheltered garden for older people, allotments, ground-floor storage for prams and cycles and, most progressively, a nursery school with its own playground. Two balconies, one for family activities and one for clothes-drying, became a hallmark of Denby's planning. She was one of the founders of House Furnishing Ltd (1936–41), a shop near Euston, which supplied well-designed curtains and furnishings—a benefit normally reserved for middle-class clients—at a price Kensal residents could afford.

To promote her ideal of the terraced house and garden Denby turned architect, designing the All Europe House for the Ideal Home Exhibition in 1939. Although the Second World War intervened and limited its impact (only a few examples were built), her intention was to provide a prototype which could be tailored to all purses, built alongside flats if necessary, and scaled up and down according to need and purpose. During the war, Denby ran a small architectural practice from her home at 11 Princes Street, London, which undertook this and several other jobs, most importantly the planning of prefabricated housing using the Tarran system. Although she had no formal architectural training, Denby designed her own work, making the plans, elevations, and sections herself, while she collaborated with qualified architects who checked the drawings and supervised construction.

Maxwell Fry, who knew her well, described Denby as a 'passionate, combative, mercurial, but utterly devoted

noble woman' (*The Times*, 9 Nov 1965). Now greatly esteemed and seen as an originator of tenants' participation and interdisciplinary collaboration, after the war and in spite of good connections with the Labour Party, she had difficulty making a place for her work. Although she designed a room for the important 'Britain can make it' exhibition of 1946, and intervened in the overspill debate of the mid-1950s on the side of tighter density planning in cities, her ideas were generally dismissed as unfeasible. She moved to Hythe in Kent in the 1960s, and died unmarried at Hythe Nursing Home on 3 November 1965. She was cremated and her ashes were scattered at Charing crematorium, Kent.

LYNNE WALKER

Sources Building Research Establishment Library, Garston, Watford, Elizabeth Denby collection · E. Darling, 'Elizabeth Denby, housing consultant: social reform and cultural politics in the inter-war period', PhD diss., U. Lond., 2000 · *The Times* (8 Nov 1965) · *The Times* (9 Nov 1965) · RIBA BAL, Godfrey Samuel MSS · P. Rathbone, *The housing centre* (1938) · biography file, RIBA BAL · E. Denby, drawing of All Europe House, 1939, RIBA BAL, Drawings Collection · E. Darling, '"Enriching and enlarging the whole sphere of human activities": the work of the voluntary sector in housing reform in inter-war Britain', *Regenerating England: science, medicine and culture in inter-war Britain*, ed. C. Lawrence and A.-K. Meyer [forthcoming] · b. cert. · d. cert. · *Catalogue of the drawings collection of the Royal Institute of British Architects: C–F* (1972) · M. Fry, 'Housing', *Architects' Journal* (9 Dec 1937), 947–8 · C. Johnson, 'Elizabeth Denby', BA diss., Sheffield Polytechnic, 1989 · Lady Pedlen, 'The evolution of the housing centre', *Housing Review*, 33 (Sept–Oct 1984), 158

Archives Building Research Establishment Library, Garston, Watford · Housing Centre Archive, London · NRA, priv. coll., papers · RIBA BAL, Godfrey Samuel MSS

Likenesses photograph, repro. in *Architects' Journal* (11 June 1942)

Dence, Marjorie Lillian (1901–1966), actress and theatre manager, was born on 14 June 1901 at Fairhaven, Park Road, Teddington, Middlesex, the daughter of Ernest Martin Dence (d. 1937), brass-founder and company director, and his wife, Annie Eleanor Searle. Dence studied for an arts degree at London University. Her love of drama drew her to the University Dramatic Society, where she met David Steuart who was to become a lifelong friend and artistic partner.

After working as a theatre secretary and on the staff of a London theatre magazine, Marjorie Dence became an actress herself. In 1934 she joined the Greater London Theatre Company where she found David Steuart in the same cast. In the railway station, going home after a performance in Ilford, Steuart pointed to Perth on a large map, and suggested that it would be an ideal place to start a repertory theatre. By a strange coincidence, the following week the sale of Perth Theatre was advertised in *The Stage*. Ernest Dence purchased it for £4000 and appointed his daughter as manager.

Marjorie Dence and David Steuart set off for Perth and with £1000 of their own money and a great deal of hard work they refurbished the old theatre and assembled a company. On 23 September 1935 their first season began successfully with a performance of *The Rose without a Thorn* by Clifford Bax. The audience response was most encouraging. A further eighteen plays were presented in weekly repertory. This exacting schedule took a lot of stamina. Marjorie herself acted in several productions and at one time a warming-pan, which she held in the character of an innkeeper's wife, was used to hide the script for the next play which she had been studying in the wings. As well as being artistic director, Steuart acted in most productions.

Snow and icy roads during the first three months of 1936 resulted in depleted audiences and strained finances. The company gallantly accepted a cut in salaries and Dence tentatively asked the people of Perth for a guarantee of £500. Donations, to be no less than 2s. 6d. and no more than £10, flooded in. The sum was reached in a fortnight. Admirably the guarantee was never called upon. In October 1938 an invitation to give a command performance was received from Balmoral. The play chosen was a thriller, *The Fourth Wall*, by A. A. Milne and the actors played on a small stage specially erected in the ballroom. The audience included King George VI and Queen Elizabeth as well as members of the royal household, guests, and tenants from the estate. Supper and an overnight stay were enjoyed by the company. The resulting publicity was invaluable.

In June 1939 the city of Perth provided a lovely setting for Scotland's first theatre festival. Marjorie Dence devised the programme and James Bridie not only agreed to be patron but contributed a new comedy, *The Golden Legend of Shults*. The event was a huge success and there was even a small profit. Despite the outbreak of war in September Dence and Steuart kept the theatre going, realizing the importance of entertainment for the community. The actors got board and lodging; some slept in the theatre itself, and rations were pooled to make their evening meal, served well before the audience came in. Salaries came from equal division of any box-office profits.

In 1941 the Council for the Encouragement of Music and the Arts (CEMA) announced that grants would be made to any company prepared to take plays to remote areas of Scotland. As a result, Perth Theatre began annual tours of villages throughout Scotland, taking plays to the highlands and islands, the borders, and Orkney and Shetland. The company visited over 120 different venues from 1941 onwards as well as 20 in Northern Ireland, in addition to maintaining the regular season in Perth. In 1946 Perth and Kinross councils took on the financial responsibility, thus creating a civic theatre, putting Dence and Steuart on generous salaries as business manager and artistic director.

The theatre established by Marjorie Dence has remained a distinguished centre for the arts in Scotland. Her work was first recognized by her appointment as MBE in 1952, and in 1957 the twenty-first anniversary of the theatre was commemorated with a presentation plaque from the Scottish Arts Council. During Marjorie's tenure in Perth Theatre many eminent artistes played there. These included such theatrical luminaries as Alec Guinness, James Cairncross, Sophie Stewart, Gordon Jackson, John Laurie, Russell Hunter, Una McLean, Walter Carr, Edith MacArthur, and Martyn James. Plays presented included works by Shakespeare, G. B. Shaw, J. M. Barrie, and James Bridie, as well as some culled from the current

West End successes. Among the assistants who trained there was Joan Knight, who later became a distinguished incumbent of the director's post.

Marjorie Dence was a highly respected figure in Perth, where she served as a JP. Her annual garden party, given at the beginning of each season, was a popular event with the Theatre Club. Just before the season began in August 1966 Marjorie hosted the party from a wheelchair because of a broken ankle. The next day she held a dinner party for some actors from the company. Sadly an unexpected complication set in and she died suddenly the following evening, 23 August 1966, at her home, Boatland, Isla Road, Perth. Her body was cremated on 26 August. Her will stated that the theatre was to be sold to the city of Perth for £5000, the exact initial outlay. The money she had lost throughout the years she dismissed with the typical remark, 'That money brought me much happiness' (*Perth Advertiser*, 31 Aug 1966, 1).   HELEN MURDOCH

Sources A. K. Bell Library, Perth, Perth Theatre archive [on indefinite loan] · R. Boutcher and W. G. Kemp, *The theatre in Perth* (1975) [A. K. Bell Library] · M. Dence and D. Steuart, *The actors are come hither: souvenir book* (1935–56) · D. Campbell, *Playing for Scotland* (1996) · B. Findlay, *A history of Scottish theatre* (1998) · *Perth Theatre, 1935–1985* (1985) · b. cert. · d. cert. · *The Times* (25 Aug 1966) · private information (2004) · *Stage and Television Today*, no. 4455 (1 Sept 1966)

Archives A. K. Bell Library, Perth, Perth Theatre archive

Likenesses photograph, Perth Theatre, Perthshire · presentation plaque, Perth Theatre, Perthshire

Dendy, Edward (*bap.* 1613, *d.* 1674), government official, was baptized on 25 September 1613 at St Martin-in-the-Fields, London, the son of Edward Dendy, serjeant-at-arms. The family originated from west Sussex; Edward's father acted for parliament and in its absence the court of Star Chamber to carry out judicial orders and hold prisoners. The Long Parliament fined him in December 1640 for excessive force in executing a Star Chamber warrant on Henry Burton in 1636. The younger Dendy inherited his father's position during the civil war and on 16 January 1644 he married Elizabeth Gouldsmor(e) at St Pancras, Soper Lane, in the City; there were at least nine children of the marriage.

Willing to act for the purged parliament, on 8 January 1649 Dendy was chosen to proclaim the king's trial in London and thus became implicated in regicide. In reward the council of state made him their serjeant-at-arms on 27 March, in which capacity he supervised running Whitehall Palace and in his ceremonial role proclaimed council edicts such as the establishment of the high court of justice in March 1650 and made search for illegal copies of Lilburne's *England's New Chains Discovered*. He took custody of the council's prisoners and took fees from them for their maintenance; in June 1650 he was unsuccessfully accused of extortion. In August 1651 he was commissioned captain to raise a troop of horse in Westminster against Charles II's invasion. He had trouble extracting pay and expenses from the council, but was compensated with Irish lands in Castleknock and Rathdowney baronies, secure territory near Dublin.

Dendy was kept on when the Rump was dissolved, and

in July 1653 was given the management of the Marshalsea prison, replacing Sir John Lenthall (the previous speaker's brother) though Lenthall maintained legal challenges. Dendy proclaimed Cromwell as protector in London on 19 December 'with sound of trumpets and in the most solemn manner', and continued to take charge of prisoners for the new council, including Vavasour Powell, Christopher Feake, and, in 1656, Sir Henry Vane and Edmund Ludlow. The judges ruled that Dendy's tenure of the Marshalsea had expired with the dissolution of the parliament that appointed him and approved Lenthall's life patent. Refusing to resign until reimbursed Dendy was still in possession in 1655 when Lenthall petitioned parliament and accused Dendy of lecturing him on obedience to the authorities. The council, however, voted Dendy a share in the proceeds of the sale of four state forests in August 1654 and £106 7s. due from the time of the Rump in May 1655. On 6 September he complained that he had received little benefit in office as the council sent richer prisoners to the Tower and others could not pay him; he had received only £80 fees in two and a half years and had to support a wife and eight children on a salary of £365. The council, however, prevented legal challenges to his landholding in Ireland succeeding as against the state's interest.

Dendy remained in office under Cromwell's successors, and in October 1659 relayed the generals' orders to the guards at the Parliament House to readmit the evicted Rump. In January 1660 his Whitehall lodgings were seized for Colonel Okey. He was excluded from pardon in June 1660 for his part in the king's trial and fled abroad; his Irish lands were granted in early 1661 to the earl of Kingston and others. In July 1661 he was at Rotterdam, and was warned to escape before the English ambassador Downing could get an arrest warrant issued. Joining up with other republicans to take refuge in Switzerland, in September–October 1662 he settled at Lausanne with Ludlow's group. He may have acted as Ludlow's amanuensis when the latter was preparing his memoirs. He stayed on after Ludlow's departure and Lisle's assassination, and died in obscurity in April 1674. A minor but highly visible participant in great events, the extent of his venality and idealism is uncertain.   TIMOTHY VENNING

Sources T. Mason, ed., *A register of baptisms, marriages, and burials in the parish of St Martin in the Fields … from 1550 to 1619*, Harleian Society, register section, 25 (1898) • W. B. Bannerman, ed., *The registers of St Mary le Bowe, Cheapside, All Hallows, Honey Lane, and of St Pancras, Soper Lane, London*, 2 vols., Harleian Society, register section, 44–5 (1914–15) • *CSP Ire.*, 1660–62 • *CSP dom.*, 1649–55; 1659–61 • E. Ludlow, *A voyce from the watch tower*, ed. A. B. Worden, CS, 4th ser., 21 (1978) • *The memoirs of Edmund Ludlow*, ed. C. H. Firth, 2 vols. (1894) • *JHC*, 2 (1640–42) • *The journal of Sir Simonds D'Ewes from the beginning of the Long Parliament to the opening of the trial of the earl of Strafford*, ed. W. Notestein (1923) • *The diary of Bulstrode Whitelocke, 1605–1675*, ed. R. Spalding, British Academy, Records of Social and Economic History, new ser., 13 (1990) • Bodl. Oxf., Godwin pamphlets no. 1040 • A. M. Burke, ed., *Memorials of St Margaret's Church, Westminster* (1914)
Archives PRO, Protectorate Council of State records, petitions for pay arrears and relating to Irish lands, esp. Council papers for

14 June 1654, 11 May and 6 Sept 1655, 15 Feb 1656, in Council of State records for 1650s, SP 18
Wealth at death in exile after attainder; complained of financial difficulties

Dendy, Helen. *See* Bosanquet, Helen (1860–1925).

Dendy, Mary (1855–1933), promoter of residential schools for mentally handicapped people, was born on 28 January 1855 at Bryncelyn, Mold, Flintshire, the second child of John Dendy (1828–1894), Unitarian minister, and his wife, Sarah Beard (1831–1922), eldest daughter of John Relly *Beard. Her siblings included Helen *Bosanquet, who worked for many years for the Charity Organization Society, and Arthur Dendy (1865–1925), a biologist. Mary was educated at home in Patricroft, near Manchester, and at Bedford College, London. In 1882, having taught in the Sunday school at Monton for several years, she became a companion to Miss Sarah Ann Cawston, the adopted daughter of Samuel Courtauld, in High Garrett, near Braintree, Essex. In 1891, following Miss Cawston's death (1889), she returned to Manchester where she lived and worked until her appointment to the Board of Control in 1913.

Mary Dendy first became aware of what she referred to as 'the problem of the feeble-minded' while working in the Collyhurst Recreation Rooms, founded in Manchester by her uncle James Rait Beard. After her election to the Manchester school board in 1896 she began a detailed mental and physical assessment of nearly 40,000 schoolchildren in Manchester. Her subsequent report, prepared with the help of Dr Henry Ashby, convinced the board to establish special classes and schools for mentally handicapped children in Manchester.

During her work for the school board (later the Manchester education committee) Mary Dendy became convinced that mentally handicapped young adults continued to pose a threat to the community after they left school. She therefore began to advocate lifelong institutional care for the mentally handicapped. In 1898 she established the Lancashire and Cheshire Society for the Permanent Care of the Feeble-Minded, to which she was secretary for many years. Utilizing the support of influential Unitarian friends and relatives, she campaigned to raise money for the society, which, in 1902, opened the Sandlebridge Boarding-Schools and Colony near Alderley Edge in Cheshire.

Miss Dendy travelled extensively throughout England, Scotland, and North America in order to raise public awareness of the social problems associated with the mentally handicapped and to secure financial support for Sandlebridge. Many of her public addresses were published as pamphlets or journal articles. In *Feeble-Minded Children* (1898), *The Importance of Permanence in the Care of the Feeble-Minded* (1901), *Feebleness of Mind, Pauperism and Crime* (1901), and *The Problem of the Feeble-Minded* (1910), and in articles in *The Lancet* (1902) and the *Medical Magazine* (1911), she argued that 'feeble-mindedness' was the cause of crime, poverty, and drunkenness, and that such 'evils' would be transmitted to subsequent generations unless immediate action were taken. In an address to the Manchester and Salford Sanitary Association (1911), in an appendix to Charles Paget Lapage's *Feeblemindedness in Children of School-Age* (1911), and in the *Journal of State Medicine* (1914), she outlined the nature of the work used to occupy and train residents at Sandlebridge. She also campaigned vigorously for legislation to compel education committees to provide special schools and to allow local authorities to detain the mentally handicapped beyond the age of sixteen, objectives that were realized with the passage of the Mental Deficiency Act in 1913 and the Elementary Education Act in 1914.

Dendy's opinions did not pass unchallenged. Some contemporary commentators disagreed with her principle of permanent segregation, and feminists were concerned that women in particular would be treated harshly under the terms of the Mental Deficiency Act. However, her work at Sandlebridge generally met with approval from prominent doctors, such as Alfred Tredgold, and from others working in the field, such as Ellen Pinsent. Her knowledge and expertise were acknowledged both in the report of the royal commission on the care and control of the feeble-minded, published in 1908, and in her appointment as a commissioner of the newly created Board of Control in 1913.

Late Victorian and Edwardian schemes to institutionalize people classified as 'mentally deficient' have sometimes been dismissed entirely as the product of contemporary anxieties about degeneration and as manifestations of eugenic strategies to control the lower classes. While much of Mary Dendy's rhetoric was clearly influenced by eugenics, her contribution to the care of the mentally handicapped was more complex. Her writings and her work at Sandlebridge demonstrate her genuine commitment to improving the lives of children admitted to the Colony. In addition, by drawing attention to the problems associated with training people with what are now referred to as learning difficulties, she contributed to the development of the concept of 'special needs' in education.

In 1910 Dendy was awarded an honorary degree by the University of Manchester in recognition of her contribution to the education of the mentally handicapped. However, her involvement in civic and philanthropic work was not restricted to the care of the mentally handicapped. During her years in Manchester she was also secretary of the South Manchester Women's Liberal Association, secretary to the Women Guardians Society, a governor of the Manchester High School for Girls, and served on the Manchester Distress Committee. Although she supported women's suffrage she was wary of militant suffragettes, and opposed the employment of married women as teachers on the grounds that the combination of home duties and work caused breakdowns in women.

In addition to contributing to local and national newspapers, such as the *Manchester Guardian*, Dendy also published poems, stories, and novels, including *Lesson Stories for the Little Ones* (1888) and *Only a Business Man* (1910). She maintained close connections with Unitarianism throughout her life, speaking in chapels and regularly contributing to Unitarian publications, such as the *Sunday School Helper* and *The Inquirer*.

Mary Dendy did not marry. A bequest from Miss Cawston allowed her sufficient financial independence not only to pursue her work with the mentally handicapped but also to indulge her broader interests, such as travel and the theatre. She retired from the Board of Control in 1921, when she returned to live at Greencote, close to Sandlebridge, at Alderley Edge, Cheshire. She continued to take an active part in the Boarding-Schools and Colony until her death. Mary Dendy died at her home on 9 May 1933 and was buried on 12 May at Alderley Edge cemetery.   MARK JACKSON

Sources H. McLachlan, *Records of a family, 1800–1933: pioneers in education, social service and liberal religion* (1935) · M. Cruikshank, 'Mary Dendy, 1855–1933, pioneer of residential schools for the feeble minded', *Journal of Educational Administration and History*, 8 (Jan 1976), 26–9 · 'Miss Dendy', *Lancashire Faces and Places*, 12 (Jan 1901), 8–10 · 'Miss Dendy', *Health Guardian*, 1 (1903), 10–12 · J. McLachlan, 'Mary Dendy and the care of the mentally handicapped', *Learning as Unitarians, our heritage at work*, 1st ser., 5 · *Manchester Guardian* (10 May 1933), 18 · *The Times* (11 May 1933), 16 · P. Hollis, *Ladies elect: women in English local government, 1865–1914* (1987)
Likenesses photograph, repro. in *Health Guardian*, 11 · photograph, repro. in *Lancashire Faces and Places* · photograph, repro. in McLachlan, *Records of a family*, pl. IX, facing p. 135
Wealth at death £13,789 6s. 5d.: resworn probate, 28 June 1933, *CGPLA Eng. & Wales*

Dendy, Walter Cooper (1794–1871), surgeon, was born at or near Horsham in Sussex. After an apprenticeship in that area he moved to London about 1811 and entered himself as a student at Guy's and St Thomas's hospitals. He became a member of the Royal College of Surgeons in 1814 and commenced practice in Stamford Street, Blackfriars; soon after he moved to 6 Great Eastcheap. He was made a fellow of the Medical Society of London, of which he became president.

Dendy was noted for his cultivated taste and polished manners; he was also an excellent speaker. He held some unusual religious views but he was considered too much of an enthusiast to be a materialist. He was the author of many books, including *On the Phenomenon of Dreams* (1832), *The Philosophy of Mystery* (1841), and *Psyche: a Discourse on the Birth and Pilgrimage of Thought* (1853). His other writings included works on medical and geographical topics. Dendy was a skilled draughtsman and illustrated his own works. He also contributed to medical journals and published a number of papers in the *Psychological Journal*. For many years he acted as senior surgeon to the Royal Infirmary for Children, in the Waterloo Road. On 2 April 1867 he was nominated a fellow of the Anthropological Society of London; on 3 November 1868 he read a paper 'Anthropogenesis' before the society, which contained a trenchant attack on Darwinian theories.

Dendy was somewhat retiring by nature and, with the exception of the annual dinner of the Medical Society and the biennial festival of the students of Guy's Hospital, he seldom appeared at the profession's social events. Having retired from practice he spent much of his time in the reading-room of the British Museum, where his eccentric costume made him a well-known character. After a short illness he died at his home, 25 Suffolk Street, Pall Mall, London, on 10 December 1871.

G. C. BOASE, *rev.* SUSAN SNOXALL

Sources *Medical Circular* (1 March 1854), 155 · J. F. C., *Medical Times and Gazette* (16 Dec 1871), 756–7 · T. S., letter, *Medical Times and Gazette* (23 Dec 1871), 780–81 · J. Hogg, letter, *Medical Times and Gazette* (6 Jan 1872), 23 · J. F. Clarke, *Autobiographical recollections of the medical profession* (1874), 441–9 · *Journal of the Anthropological Institute* (1872), 1.398–9 · *CGPLA Eng. & Wales* (1872)
Wealth at death under £12,000: probate, 29 Jan 1872, *CGPLA Eng. & Wales*

Dene, Peter (*d.* in or after **1334**), canon lawyer and monk, no doubt derived from one of the villages called Dean in Sussex. A secular priest of the Chichester diocese, he began to acquire benefices in Sussex by the late 1280s and, later, benefices elsewhere. By 1287 Dene was a master of arts and, probably by the century's end, a *doctor utriusque iuris*, though his university is unknown. In the meantime he had become a royal clerk and several times travelled overseas on the king's business for both Edward I and Edward II, while in 1297 he was a member of the regency council governing England in Prince Edward's name. In 1300, for a retaining fee of £10 yearly, he became legal adviser to the monastery of St Augustine at Canterbury, whose rights he undertook to uphold against the archbishop of Canterbury, among others. No doubt this contributed to the dispute in which he became embroiled with Archbishop Winchelsey, whose visitation of his province in 1302 found Dene's possession of East Tangmere church to be irregular. In 1302, and again in 1305, Winchelsey deprived him of all his benefices in the province of Canterbury, including canonries at Wells Cathedral and at St Paul's, London.

A man of abundant enterprise and talent, Dene was soon in the service of the archbishop of York, acting, at different times, as his chancellor, commissary-general, and vicar-general. As a canon of York, he accompanied the archbishop on a visitation of St Mary's Abbey, York, whose chronicler called him (using Ovid's words) 'a dreadful snake' (*serpente diro*; *Chronicle of St Mary's*, 71). His wealth permitted him not only to donate the heraldic window in the north nave of York Minster but also to make generous gifts to St Augustine's, where he built houses within the monastic enclosure, presumably for his own use and for the use of his household when they were in Canterbury.

Involvement in support of Thomas, earl of Lancaster, in his unsuccessful rebellion against Edward II in 1322, ended his career in the north. Within two weeks of the defeat at Boroughbridge, and within a week of the execution of Lancaster at Pontefract, Dene fled south, 'being threatened with arrest, imprisonment, loss of position, the seizure of all his property, and even with death' ('Chronica Guillielmi Thorne' col. 2055). (His fears were probably not without foundation, for Sir Bartholomew Badlesmere, with whom Dene may have been connected in his ill-fated adventure, was executed at Bleen near Canterbury on 14 April 1322.) He appeared at the gates of St

Peter Dene (*d.* in or after 1334), stained glass

Augustine's in Canterbury on 31 March 1322, begging admission to the community, and was instantly given the habit of a Benedictine monk. Three days later, without observing the usual year of probation, he made solemn profession, and Dr Peter Dene, became Brother Peter, monk of St Augustine's. His profession, as he later claimed, may have lacked canonical validity. In a hastily drafted will he left all his goods to the abbey, on the condition that he could have continued use of them until his death. He also remitted debts owed him by the monastery and bequeathed to the house a considerable amount of money and silver. The profession itself, he later claimed and the monastic chronicler seems to have concurred, was at best conditional: he would wear the habit and live at the monastery, but he would not live in the monastic dormitory, rather with his household in his own dwellings. Also, he would not join the other monks in church, chapter, refectory, or elsewhere for community exercises. 'He was free to act as the Lord inspired him and as it pleased him' (*prout sibi dominus inspiraret et de ipsius Petri libera procederet voluntate*; 'Chronica Guillielmi Thorne' col. 2055). Dene made a public statement before the community in chapter to the effect that by his profession he had no intention of leading the regular life.

Eight—or possibly nine—years later, when the political climate had cooled, Dene asked for permission to leave and return to his former life. When the abbot paid no serious attention to his request, Dene, on a wintry night in December 1331, dressed in secular garb, climbed over the wall and, with the assistance of the rector of St Martin's, fled into what the monks considered apostasy. Three monks of St Augustine's snatched their apostate from a royal official, who had captured him and was removing him to prison at Maidstone. Dene subsequently claimed that upon his return he was forced to make a statement that his profession was absolute and that he was truly a monk. Dene's situation was complicated even further when he learned that Henry, the new earl of Lancaster, suspected him of stealing from his late brother's treasury and of concealing the stolen goods at St Augustine's. Nothing further is heard of this.

Meanwhile, the canonist Dene secretly appealed to the pope at Avignon. Of the three papally appointed commissioners only Richard Oxenden, prior of neighbouring Christ Church Priory, entered St Augustine's on 23 and 24 November 1332 to determine the facts in the case. The reluctance of the community to co-operate led to Oxenden's excommunication of the prior and another monk. When at length Dene was allowed to be interviewed, he replied *alto voce* for the benefit of his fellow monks that he was truly a monk and *sotto voce* for the benefit of Prior Oxenden that he was too old in years and broken in body to pursue the matter. He remained at St Augustine's, perhaps not altogether unhappily, for in the following year he was selected to serve on a committee to choose a new abbot. He died some time after June 1334.

Dene's library included the canon law texts of Gratian's *Decretum* and the *Decretals* of Gregory IX, and canonical commentaries by Hostiensis, Innocent IV, Guido de Baysio, William Durandus, Johannes Monachus, and Giovanni d'Andreae, as well as a five-volume collection of Roman law texts. He is depicted prominently as a kneeling figure in the heraldic window in York Minster.

F. DONALD LOGAN

Sources F. D. Logan, *Runaway religious in medieval England, c.1240–1540*, Cambridge Studies in Medieval Life and Thought, 4th ser., 32 (1996) · Emden, *Oxf.* · 'Chronica Guillielmi Thorne', *Historiae Anglicanae scriptores X*, ed. R. Twysden (1652) · *William Thorne's chronicle of St Augustine's Abbey, Canterbury*, trans. A. H. Davis (1934) · J. B. Sheppard, ed., *Literae Cantuarienses: the letter books of the monastery of Christ Church, Canterbury*, 2, Rolls Series, 85 (1888) · J. H. Denton, *Robert Winchelsey and the crown, 1294–1313: a study in the defence of ecclesiastical liberty*, Cambridge Studies in Medieval Life and Thought, 3rd ser., 14 (1980) · H. H. E. Craster and M. E. Thornton, eds., *The chronicle of St Mary's Abbey, York*, SurtS, 148 (1934)
Likenesses stained-glass window, York Minster [*see illus.*]

Dene, William (*fl.* 1317–1354), supposed chronicler, may have been the author of BL, Cotton MS Faustina B.v, which comprises the *Registrum Roffense*, the author of which declares himself to be a public notary (BL, Cotton MS Faustina B.v, fol. 12v), and the *Historia Roffensis*. The former contains a detailed account of the disputed election of Hamo Hythe (*d.* in or after 1357) as bishop of Rochester. William Dene, a public notary, was one of those sent by the bishop-elect to cardinals Gaucelin and Luca at Durham in August 1317 with a papal commission to confirm his election. When the cardinals then remitted the case to the papal curia, Hythe sent William Dene and Dr Michael Berham as his proctors to prosecute his claim there. At Avignon Dene was physically threatened by Jean de Jargeau, the proctor of Queen Isabella, who was supporting another candidate. Back in England, after his election had been confirmed, Hythe handed the papal bulls confirming his election to Dene on 29 November 1319; and Dene was present when Hythe made his profession to Walter Reynolds, archbishop of Canterbury (*d.* 1327), and when he performed homage to the king at York in early December 1319. Dene's name occurs in the long series of documents arising out of the dispute between Hythe and Walter Reynolds over sums due to Hythe from the long vacancy of the latter's see; but so does that of another public notary, Gilbert Sedgeford, who has therefore also been considered a possible author of the manuscript. John Joscelyn (*d.* 1603) did not differentiate between the *Registrum* and the *Historia* when asserting that William Dene was the author of the manuscript.

The *Historia Roffensis* provides a chronological narrative moving between information of local interest and national importance from 1320 to 1350. Part of it was printed by Henry Wharton, *Anglia sacra* (1691), while folios 34v to 36v, describing the events of the Westminster parliament of 1321, have been published in *Parliamentary Texts of the Later Middle Ages* (ed. N. Pronay and J. Taylor, 1980). Other passages provide insight into the diplomatic activity resulting from the War of St Sardos. The revolution that led to Edward II's deposition, the deposition itself, and the coronation of Edward III are well covered. The chronicle is one of the richest sources for the career of the little-known Archbishop Simon Mepham (*d.* 1333), about whom Dene is critical, probably reflecting Bishop Hamo's attitude. Despite Hythe's reluctance to attend parliaments in the 1330s, the chronicle provides valuable information about Edward III's wars in Scotland from Dupplin Moor and Halidon Hill to Nevilles Cross. Concern that Scottish campaigns were making the realm vulnerable to French attack is at times discernible. Events leading to the Hundred Years' War and the burden of taxation that the war brought with it are detailed, as are major military and naval events: Sluys; the siege of Tournai (about which the chronicler incorporates an extensive news bulletin); Crécy; and the siege of Calais. Other lengthy insertions include evidence pertaining to the bishop of Rochester's claim to jurisdiction over the church of Isleham in the diocese of Norwich; a sympathetic account of the assumption of power in Rome by Rienzi, whose death in 1354 is the last securely dated event to be referred to; and legislation consequent upon the black death.

Like the *Registrum*, the *Historia* was almost certainly written by someone who was in the entourage of Hamo Hythe while he was bishop of Rochester between 1319 and 1352, and who was alive in 1354. It is possible therefore that the William Dene who was provided to the archdeaconry of Rochester at the bishop's request in September 1323, and who resigned that office in June 1359, was the author. However, in Bishop Hamo's register, this William Dene is described as *magister* when instituted to the church of Maplescombe, Kent, in September 1321, whereas the William Dene in the *Registrum Roffense* is never so described.

M. C. BUCK

Sources BL, Cotton MS Faustina B.v · *Registrum Hamonis Hethe, diocesis Roffensis, AD 1319–1352*, ed. C. Johnson, 2 vols., CYS, 48–9 (1948) · Robert of Avesbury, *Historia de mirabilibus gestis Edwardi III*, ed. T. Hearne (1720) [incl. notes by John Joscelyn] · *Fasti Angl., 1300–1541*, [Monastic cathedrals], 41 · N. Pronay and J. Taylor, *Parliamentary texts of the later middle ages* (1980) · [H. Wharton], ed., *Anglia sacra*, 2 vols. (1691)

Archives BL, Cotton MS Faustina B.v

Deneke, Helena Clara (1878–1973), German scholar, was born on 19 May 1878 at 89 Denmark Hill, London, the oldest child and elder of the two surviving daughters of Philip Maurice Deneke (1842–1925), a wealthy London merchant banker born in Germany, and his wife, Clara Sophia Overweg (1847–1933), who came from a landed Westphalian family. She was educated at home and at St Hugh's Hall, Oxford, then still a very small society. In 1903 she was placed in the first class of the new honour school of English language and literature, and in October 1904 she became librarian of St Hugh's, where she first taught English, changing to German at the suggestion of Ernest de Selincourt and becoming tutor in German in 1909. What were later described as her 'precise linguistic standards … and her extraordinary familiarity with a wide range of literature' (*The Times*, 4 Oct 1973) had their origin in this early experience of moving with ease from philology to English literature to German, possible in the days before more restricted academic specialism became the norm. Her broad interests had been fostered too during her stimulating younger years in the family's London homes, where music predominated and a succession of distinguished musicians visited and played, the celebrated violinist Joseph Joachim among them.

Helena Deneke was an enthusiastic supporter of the first principal of St Hugh's, Annie Moberly, but soon developed an uneasy relationship with her vice-principal, Eleanor Jourdain, whose inevitable election to the principalship she saw as being potentially disastrous. She was also unhappy with the events surrounding the publication, in 1911, of *An Adventure*, an account by Moberly and Jourdain of their supposedly supernatural experiences in the grounds of Versailles during a trip they made there in 1901, and was unconvinced by Jourdain's evidence of the experience. This doubt lent further weight to her decision to resign 'with a heartache' from the society she had so loved, lest she become 'unwillingly a sort of centre of disaffection' (H. Deneke to Kathleen Kenyon, 16 Aug 1966, Deneke MSS). During the 'row' at St Hugh's in 1923/4 Deneke, accused of 'German rancour' by Miss Jourdain, rallied support for Cecilia Ady, the dismissed tutor, with whom she had a close and affectionate relationship.

In 1913 Helena Deneke became bursar and tutor in German at Lady Margaret Hall, Oxford, and was a fellow from 1926 until her retirement in 1938. She was a popular and energetic Oxford tutor ('exacting but genial and constructive') who inspired an enduring affection in her pupils. The famous music room at Gunfield, the Gothic villa in Norham Gardens where she lived for five decades with her sister, the musicologist Margaret Deneke (1882–1969), witnessed 'much music making, not a little of it memorable' (M. Deneke, *Ernest Walker*). Generations of Oxford undergraduates, colleagues, and friends enjoyed the Denekes' hospitality at the many Gunfield concerts. For some twenty-seven years the Oxford Chamber Music Society met there free of charge, with Margaret Deneke making up any deficits; the society owed its survival, particularly during the Second World War, to the generosity of the Deneke sisters. Marga Deneke, herself a talented

Helena Clara Deneke (1878–1973), by Hubert Andrew Freeth [left, with her sister, Margaret Deneke]

pianist, was choirmaster at Lady Margaret Hall and, raising considerable sums of money through concerts and lecture recitals, became one of the college's benefactors. Among Helena Deneke's enduring achievements at Lady Margaret Hall was the design of the college gardens; she became garden steward in 1924 and held the post for over forty years.

Helena Deneke's scholarly efforts went into teaching rather than research, and she wrote little: a piece on Jean Paul in the *Festschrift* to H. G. Fiedler (1938) and a popular biography (1946) of her contemporary Grace Hadow, principal of the Society of Oxford Home-Students, together with various articles on her post-war work in Germany, including an important report, *Women in Germany* (1947), written with Betty Norris.

Helena Deneke had become involved with the work of Women's Institutes following her resignation as treasurer of the National Union of Women's Suffrage Societies after the First World War, and she was to serve at various times as secretary, chair, and president of the Oxfordshire Federation of Women's Institutes. It was this involvement with women's groups that led to her being invited to play a part in the democratic development of women's organizations in Germany. In the considerable task of educational 'reconstruction' in Germany after the Second World War the help of public-spirited figures with a deep knowledge of Germany and its institutions was actively sought, and from 1946 to 1951 Helena Deneke made many official visits to the country, addressing women's groups, attending meetings under the aegis of the Allied Control Commission, and broadcasting in German. Hers was a robust, common-sense approach to the encouragement of democracy among the women of Germany, fully cognizant as she was of the dilemma faced by an occupying power in having the right to impose procedures which by their nature challenge the notion of imposition. In promoting the development of non-party-political, non-sectarian groups she did much to shape the future development of women's organizations in Germany. Following the closure of the department for women's affairs in 1951, she served on the academic council of Wilton Park, and so was able to continue an involvement with Anglo-German exchanges. Helena Deneke died, following a stroke, on 26 September 1973, at Freeland House, Freeland, Oxfordshire.   D. PHILLIPS

Sources H. C. Deneke, memoirs, 5 vols., Lady Margaret Hall, Oxford · Bodl. Oxf., MSS Deneke · C. Anson, 'Helena Clara Deneke', *Brown Book* (1974), 26–30 · *The Times* (1 Oct 1973) · A. E. Armstrong, *The Times* (4 Oct 1973) · M. Deneke, memoirs, 2 vols., Lady Margaret Hall, Oxford · M. Deneke, *Ernest Walker* (1951) · P. Griffin, ed., *St Hugh's: one hundred years of women's education in Oxford* (1986) · b. cert. · d. cert. · register, St Hugh's Hall, Oxford, 1886–1918, St Hugh's College, Oxford · Deneke MSS, St Hugh's College, Oxford

Archives Bodl. Oxf. · Lady Margaret Hall, Oxford · St Hugh's College, Oxford

Likenesses H. A. Freeth, double portrait, watercolour drawing (with her sister), Lady Margaret Hall, Oxford [*see illus.*] · photographs, Bodl. Oxf., MS Eng. misc. c. 701

Wealth at death £77,473: probate, 21 Feb 1974, *CGPLA Eng. & Wales*

Denewulf (*d.* 908), bishop of Winchester, has a bad reputation which does not seem to have been fully deserved. In the period of the tenth-century reformation he was castigated for allowing estates belonging to his cathedral (Old Minster) in Winchester to fall into lay hands. His denigration in Winchester tradition is epitomized by the legend, reported by William of Malmesbury, that he was in origin a swineherd whom Alfred had met in a wood while on the run from the vikings. It is true that a number of Winchester estates were either leased to laymen or lost during Denewulf's episcopate (878/9–908), but it would appear that Denewulf had little choice in the matter and that considerable pressure was placed on him by Alfred and his son and successor, Edward the Elder, to surrender estates to them. When King Edward compelled the community of Old Minster to lease him an estate at Beddington (Surrey), the bishop felt obliged to request that 'you desire no more land of that foundation for it seems to them an unwelcome demand; so that God need blame neither you nor us for the diminishing in our days' (AS chart., S 1444).

Even when Winchester had a seemingly inviolate claim to an estate, the kings could drive a hard bargain. Before Denewulf's episcopacy an estate belonging to Old Minster at Alresford had been leased to the family of a nobleman called Alfred. In the reign of King Alfred this nobleman was found guilty of adultery and his possessions were forfeit to the crown. In spite of Old Minster's prior claim, Denewulf was able to recover Alresford from the king only by payment of the very substantial sum of 120 mancuses of gold. The bishop was also unsuccessful in obtaining lands left to Old Minster in the will of King Æthelwulf, in spite of surrendering another large estate to Alfred to secure the reversion. King Edward subsequently used one of the reversionary estates to endow his foundation of New Minster in Winchester and Old Minster had to take a rather smaller estate instead. Land in Winchester also had to be sold to the king for the new foundation, which was built immediately adjacent to the Old Minster church. However, Denewulf was not always so unfortunate in his dealings with the royal house. An exchange with the king of the episcopal estate at Portchester (probably desired by the king for its defensive potential) for the former monastic site at Bishop's Waltham was a transfer of estates of very similar size and Denewulf received the gift of an estate at Ruishton (Somerset) from King Alfred with no apparent strings attached.

Of Denewulf's other activities as bishop little is known. He was presumably meant to be included in Alfred's criticisms of his bishops in the preface of his translation to Pope Gregory's *Pastoral Care*, and the absence of any specific benefaction to Denewulf or Winchester in Alfred's will could be seen as another indication that Denewulf was not closely involved with Alfred's reforming policies. The Anglo-Saxon Chronicle records his death in 908; he presumably died and was buried at Winchester.

BARBARA YORKE

Sources AS chart., S 352, 354, 372, 385, 1284–7, 1443–4 · *Willelmi Malmesbiriensis monachi de gestis pontificum Anglorum libri quinque*, ed.

N. E. S. A. Hamilton, Rolls Series, 52 (1870), 162 • *English historical documents*, 1, ed. D. Whitelock (1955), 543–4 • *Alfred the Great: Asser's Life of King Alfred and other contemporary sources*, ed. and trans. S. Keynes and M. Lapidge (1983) • H. P. R. Finberg, *The early charters of Wessex* (1964), 214–48 • B. A. E. Yorke, 'The bishops of Winchester, the kings of Wessex and the development of Winchester in the ninth and early tenth centuries', *Proceedings of the Hampshire Field Club and Archaeological Society*, 40 (1984), 61–70 • S. Keynes, 'The West Saxon charters of King Æthelwulf and his sons', *EngHR*, 109 (1994), 1109–49 • *ASC*, s.a. 908 [text A]

Denham. For this title name *see* Bowyer, George Edward Wentworth, first Baron Denham (1886–1948).

Denham, Dixon (1786–1828), explorer in Africa, born in London on 1 January 1786, was the son of James Denham and his wife, Eleanor, *née* Symonds. He was educated from 1793 at Merchant Taylors' School. After being briefly articled to a London solicitor, he joined the army as a volunteer in 1811 and served in the Peninsula, where he was promoted lieutenant, and in Belgium. In Lisbon he married Harriet Hawkins, a widow, a marriage he solemnized in London on 20 February 1815 but never again seems to have referred to publicly. He was placed on half pay in 1818 and appointed an instructor at the Royal Military College, Sandhurst, where he ingratiated himself with the authorities.

The course of the Niger was still untraced. Attempts to trace it from west Africa, begun originally by Mungo Park, had ended in disaster, and it was proposed instead to approach it from Tripoli, where the British consul-general, Hanmer Warrington, had established friendly relations with the ruling Turkish pasha, Yusuf Karamanlı. In 1818 Joseph Ritchie set out but died after a few months. To replace him, the Colonial Office recruited a Scottish doctor, Walter Oudney, and his Edinburgh neighbour Hugh Clapperton, a half-pay naval officer. Denham then wrote to the Colonial Office proposing his own services. He seems to have had influential supporters, for he was not only accepted but given command of the expedition. This was to prove disastrous. Pushy, self-important, and malicious, Denham treated his colleagues with a scarcely veiled contempt that from the start soured relations between them.

In April 1822 they left Tripoli for Murzuq, the capital of the Fezzan. The success of their journey depended on the pasha's support. At Murzuq they found that no further arrangements had been made, so Denham returned to Tripoli and, after fruitless arguments with the pasha, set off impulsively for London. At Marseilles, however, he heard that the necessary military escort would be provided and rejoined his colleagues; in November 1822 they set out southwards.

They travelled across the desert along the long-established Sahara trade route to the kingdom of Bornu (later Nigeria), a route littered with the skeletons of thousands of slaves abandoned there over the centuries. At the pasha's suggestion they wore European clothes (consular uniforms), since they were in no danger under his protection. In February, having sighted Lake Chad, they reached Kuka (later Kukawa), the capital of Bornu, where to their

Dixon Denham (1786–1828), by Thomas Phillips, 1826

amazement they were welcomed by a spectacular array of some five thousand horsemen, many of them wearing chain-mail armour, sent by Sheikh Muhammad el Kanemi, the Muslim prophet who ruled Bornu in the king's name. Though delighted to meet them, he refused to let them leave Bornu, lest they meet some misadventure for which he would be blamed. Unwillingly he let Denham accompany a campaign against some neighbouring Fulani. The Bornu forces were routed, Denham was wounded and nearly captured. During the rains Denham and his companions stayed in Kuka, Denham secretly sending home malicious reports about Clapperton's sexual behaviour (which he was later to admit he had never believed). They then separated. Oudney and Clapperton made for Kano, but Oudney died on the way. Denham investigated Lake Chad, but was prevented by warfare from reaching its eastern shore. Once Clapperton was back from Kano they returned to Tripoli, suffering a terrible desert crossing. They reached England in June 1825, having failed to find the Niger, but having opened much of north central Africa to European knowledge.

Unlike his companions, Denham retained his health throughout the expedition. Clapperton, despite his broken condition, immediately embarked again on the Niger quest, where he died. Denham, fêted in London as the hero of the expedition, and elected a fellow of the Royal Society, published his *Narrative of Travels and Discoveries in Northern and Central Africa* (1826), in which he suppressed as much as possible all mention of his companions, and took the credit for some of their discoveries. Written in a lively style, and embellished with engravings of his own sketches, it became one of the classics of its genre.

A new appointment was found for Denham in Sierra Leone, to reorganize the Liberated African department, which cared for the slaves rescued by the British naval squadron and liberated in Freetown. He arrived in January 1827 with the rank of lieutenant-colonel to find that the newly appointed governor, Sir Neil Campbell, was busy reorganizing every aspect of government, including his own department. Not until Campbell died in August was Denham able to take full charge. He travelled round the villages where the liberated people were settled, and sent detailed, well-thought-out descriptions and recommendations to the Colonial Office—not in formal dispatches, but in private letters to the under-secretary, where he could safely indulge malicious comment. In January he went on a cruise for his health to Fernando Po, where he heard, and sent home, the news that his erstwhile colleague Clapperton had died.

Meanwhile Denham had secured for himself the post of lieutenant-governor, and was soon quarrelling with the officer commanding the troops, his senior in age and rank. But his term of office was brief. In Sierra Leone his customary good health failed. A contemporary wrote, 'he took to physicking himself, became soft and fleshy, and gradually sank under the fever' (Alexander, 111–12), and he died in Freetown on 9 June 1828. He was buried on 15 June at the city's Circular Road cemetery.

CHRISTOPHER FYFE

Sources E. W. Bovill, ed., *Missions to the Niger*, 4 vols., Hakluyt Society, 2nd ser., 123, 128–30 (1964–6) · E. W. Bovill, *The Niger explored* (1968) · PRO, CO267/81–83, 94; CO323/148 · C. Fyfe, *A history of Sierra Leone* (1962) · J. E. Alexander, *Narrative of a voyage…* (1837) · IGI · letter from John Charles Denham to the Colonial Office, PRO, CO267/101 · C. J. Robinson, ed., *A register of the scholars admitted into Merchant Taylors' School, from AD 1562 to 1874*, 2 (1883) · parish register (marriage), St Paul Covent Garden, London, 20 Feb 1815 · d. cert.
Archives Bodl. Oxf., accounts and notes of African travels · PRO, CO2/13, 14, FO 76/14–19, CO267/81–83, 94, CO323/148 · RGS, corresp., journals, and papers relating to north Africa
Likenesses T. Phillips, oils, 1826, NPG [*see illus.*]
Wealth at death died in debt; owed several thousand pounds to brother: John Charles Denham to Colonial Office, 21 March 1829, PRO, CO267/101

Denham, Henry (*fl.* 1556–1590), printer, of whose parents and family nothing is known, was apprenticed to the London printer and bookseller Richard Tottel on 14 October 1556 and was made free of the Company of Stationers on 30 August 1560. He set up his own printing house in White Cross Street, London, in 1564 but from 1565 was at the sign of the Star in Paternoster Row. Denham was involved in several controversies concerning printing privileges and in 1564–5 he was fined for illicit printing. He was fined again in 1564–5 for employing someone without informing the master and wardens of the company. The following year he was fined for 'mysvsying' one of the wardens (Arber, *Regs. Stationers*, 1.316). He was admitted into the livery of the Stationers' Company on 20 July 1573, and held several posts within the company. He acted as an official searcher on several occasions and served as renter warden in successive years for 1579–80 and 1580–81, and as underwarden for 1586–7 and 1588–9. On 6 January 1579 he failed to attend before the lord mayor and incurred a fine of 12*d.*, and in August he was fined for arresting a freeman of the company without a licence. However, a 20*s.* fine in April 1584 for using indecent speech to the upper warden was remitted.

Despite signing a petition against printing privileges in 1577, Denham benefited the following year when William Seres, no longer able to continue his own business, assigned his privilege for the printing of all psalters, primers, and prayers to Denham together with 'all his presses letters stock and copies' for a yearly rent (Arber, *Regs. Stationers*, 2.771). Denham duly took seven young men from the Stationers' Company to assist him. By 1583 he was noted as operating four printing presses and in the same year, as executor with Ralph Newbery for Henry Bynneman, he also inherited Bynneman's privilege for printing dictionaries, chronicles, and histories. In January 1584 he was among several printers who made over their privilege in certain books for the benefit of the poor of the company. In 1585 he moved to Aldersgate Street where he remained until at least 1587; another survey of London printing presses, in 1586, recorded that he had three in operation. In 1587–8 he was one of a number of senior members of the company who contributed towards the cost of the drawing up of the 1586 Star Chamber decrees concerning printing. In November 1589 he gave a gift to the company of a gilt spoon, about 3 oz in weight, engraved with his name.

Denham 'had a large and varied assortment of letters' and his blacks were noted for their beauty (McKerrow, 88–9). His woodcut initials belonged to those known as the AS series which are attributed to Anton Sylvius, an Antwerp engraver. His mark was a star surrounded with the inscription *Os homini sublime dedit*. Among the many books to appear under this sign was the New Testament in Welsh which he printed for Humphrey Toy in 1567, four years after a bill was passed in parliament for the Bible to be translated into Welsh. He also printed *Bullokar's Booke at Large* (1580), the first attempt to establish orthography for English to appear in print. As an assignee of Henry Bynneman he was able to print the second edition of Holinshed's *Chronicles* which Clair suggests was probably the edition which Shakespeare used.

We do not know the date of Denham's death, but he was last recorded in attendance at the court of the Stationers' Company on 4 July 1590. No book was printed under his sign after 1590.

PATRICIA BREWERTON

Sources W. W. Greg and E. Boswell, eds., *Records of the court of the Stationers' Company, 1576 to 1602, from register B* (1930) · Arber, *Regs. Stationers*, vols. 1–2 · J. Ames, *Typographical antiquities, or, An historical account of the origin and progress of printing in Great Britain and Ireland*, ed. W. Herbert, 3 vols. (1785–90) · H. G. Aldis and others, *A dictionary of printers and booksellers in England, Scotland and Ireland, and of foreign printers of English books, 1557–1640*, ed. R. B. McKerrow (1910) · C. Clair, *A chronology of printing* (1969) · C. Clair, *A history of European printing* (1976) · E. C. Bigmore and C. W. H. Wyman, *A bibliography of printing*, 1 (1880) · STC, 1475–1640 · BL cat. · C. Blagden, *The Stationers' Company: a history, 1403–1959* (1960) · C. H. Timperley, *Encyclopaedia* *of literary and typographical anecdote*, 2nd edn (1842); repr. (1977), vol. 1 · J. P. Berjeu, *Early Dutch, German and English printers' marks* (1866)

Denham, Henry Mangles (1897–1993), naval officer and author, was born on 9 September 1897 at 7 Kenton Avenue, Harrow, Middlesex, the son of Henry Mangles Denham, civil engineer, and his wife, Helen Clara, *née* Lowndes. He joined the navy as a cadet in 1910, going to the Royal Naval College at Osborne and Dartmouth. He went to sea at the outbreak of the First World War in 1914, joining the pre-dreadnought battleship *Agamemnon*, and served in her in the Dardanelles campaign, commanding a steam picket boat during the landings at Suvla Bay in August 1915. He later published his diaries and notes from this period, *Dardanelles: a Midshipman's Diary, 1915–16* (1981). After service in the destroyers *Racoon* and *Sylph*, he was one of the young officers sent by the Admiralty to Cambridge. He went up to Magdalene College in 1919 for what he recalled as one of the happiest years of his life.

In 1920 Denham served in the battle cruiser *Renown* during the prince of Wales's cruise to Australia and New Zealand. He then spent two years in the Rhine flotilla commanding a small armed motor launch as part of the Rhine army of occupation. Next he served in the battleship *Centurion* in the Mediterranean before going to Austria to learn German. On 3 May 1924 he married Estelle Margaret Sibbald (Madge; 1898/9–1979), daughter of Charles Sibbald Currie, of independent means. There were one son and two daughters of the marriage. Following his marriage, Denham was a divisional officer in the boys' training ship *Impregnable* at Devonport from 1924 to 1926 and was then invited by Admiral Sir Osmond Brock, commander-in-chief, Portsmouth, to be his flag lieutenant. In 1927 he went to the Mediterranean for more than five years, serving in the fleet flagships *Queen Elizabeth* and *Warspite* as boats officer and as 'snotties' nurse', in charge of the midshipmen. In 1937 he was appointed executive officer of the new light cruiser *Penelope* and served in her during the Spanish Civil War and the Munich crisis.

Denham first joined naval intelligence in 1939, when he created an 'information section', recruiting civilians from many walks of life to gather intelligence about enemy and potential enemy coastlines through discreet surveys by yachtsmen and disguised fishermen. He was then appointed naval attaché in Copenhagen and arrived in the Danish capital on new year's day 1940. Hearing of increased German mine-sweeping activity in the Great Belt, he went down to the coast to look and he was actually sitting on the beach with a pair of binoculars on 7 April when the German cruiser *Blücher* and other ships passed by. Denham hurried to signal the Admiralty that it was probable that the Germans were about to move against Norway. But his warning, like other intelligence pointing the same way, was ignored, and the German landings, forty-eight hours later, caught the Home Fleet off balance. When the Germans entered Copenhagen, Denham and the rest of the legation staff went by special train to Ostend and thence to London. He was then appointed naval attaché in Stockholm, where he arrived early in June 1940 to find

himself plunged into a diplomatic furore over four destroyers which the Swedish navy had bought from Italy and which had reached the Faeroes, where they were illegally seized by the British. Denham's tactful handling of the head of the Swedish navy defused a tense situation but Great Britain had to pay Skr 1 million in damages.

It was Denham who first warned the Admiralty by 'most immediate' signal on 20 May 1941 that 'two large warships', escorted by destroyers and aircraft, had been sighted at sea in the Kattegat off Göteborg that afternoon. They proved to be the German battleship *Bismarck* and the heavy cruiser *Prinz Eugen*, about to sail on their Atlantic sortie. Denham heard the news from the Norwegian military attaché, Colonel Roscherlund, but doubted its authenticity. It seemed to him unlikely that the sighting could have been reported so quickly and he gave it only a modest reliability grading. But the German ships had indeed been sighted and reported by a Swedish cruiser. Denham's signal set in train the dramatic series of events which led to the destruction of *Bismarck* on 27 May. Denham was gratified to receive an Admiralty acknowledgement of the crucial part his signal had played. Through such friends as Colonel Björnstjerna, the director of Swedish combined intelligence, and Ebbe Munck, the Danish Arctic explorer and journalist, Denham was able to gather many other valuable pieces of information. He also played an important part in helping George Binney to organize the smuggling of special steels, ballbearings, and tools to England.

The Swedes were always suspicious of Denham and kept a close watch on him. At dinner in his flat one evening a noise was heard overhead. A man was discovered in the loft, eavesdropping with a microphone. The Swedes were much impressed, however, when, in a dark period for the allies, they heard that Denham had sent a telegram to England, ordering a yacht to be built for him to sail after the war. In 1945 Denham was appointed CMG, a rare award for a naval officer in the Second World War. He also received decorations from the Dutch, the Danes, and the Norwegians. Even the Swedes—though they tapped his telephone, bugged his flat, and tried constantly to have him expelled as *persona non grata*—offered him a decoration which the British government refused him permission to accept.

After retiring from the navy in 1947 Denham was able to indulge his love of sailing, and he embarked on another career as a nautical travel writer. He published a series of Sea Guides, *The Aegean* (1963); *The Eastern Mediterranean* (1964); *The Adriatic* (1967); *The Tyrrhenian Sea* (1969); *The Ionian Islands to Rhodes* (1972); *Southern Turkey, the Levant and Cyprus* (1973); and *The Ionian Islands to the Anatolian Coast* (1982). These were a most readable blend of practical seamanship, navigational tips, history, and mythology. In 1981 he published the diary he had kept (contrary to regulations) as a midshipman in the Dardanelles, containing many caustic remarks about his senior officers. His war memoirs, *Inside the Nazi Ring: a Naval Attaché in Sweden, 1940–1945*, appeared in 1984.

As a naval attaché, Denham was outstanding. With his

experience of *Renown*'s royal cruise and as a flag lieutenant, he was socially very accomplished. With his height and his fine-drawn features, he looked like a distinguished diplomat. Urbane and discreet, he made friends easily and had a gift for making and keeping contacts. He was a member of the Royal Automobile and Royal Cruising clubs, and of the Royal Yacht Squadron. He died at his home, 8 Carlyle Square, Chelsea, London, on 15 July 1993, of bronchopneumonia. He was survived by his son and two daughters. JOHN WINTON

Sources WWW, 1991–5 · *The Independent* (23 July 1993) · *The Times* (29 July 1993) · *Daily Telegraph* (22 July 1993) · H. Denham, *Dardanelles: a midshipman's diary, 1915–16* (1981) · H. Denham, *Inside the Nazi ring: a naval attaché in Sweden, 1940–1945* (1984) · b. cert. · m. cert. · d. cert.
Archives CAC Cam., corresp. and papers relating to service as naval attaché in Stockholm
Likenesses photograph, repro. in *Daily Telegraph* · photograph, repro. in *The Independent* · photograph, repro. in *The Times*
Wealth at death £360,068: probate, 8 Sept 1993, CGPLA Eng. & Wales

Denham, Sir James Steuart, the elder. *See* Steuart, Sir James, of Coltness and Westshield, third baronet (1713–1780).

Denham, Sir James Steuart, of Coltness and Westshield, eighth baronet and fourth baronet (1744–1839), army officer, was born James Steuart on 7 August 1744 at Goodtrees, near Edinburgh, only son of Sir James *Steuart of Coltness and Westshield, seventh and third baronet (1713–1780), political economist, and his wife, Lady Frances (1722–1789), daughter of James Wemyss, fifth earl of Wemyss. A year after his birth James was left in the care of relatives on his father's political exile, but he later joined his parents in Angoulême, France. On the outbreak of war between Britain and France in 1755 the family removed itself from Paris, first to Flanders and then, in 1757, to Tübingen in Württemberg, where young James enrolled in the university. He studied there until 1761, when, through the good offices of the secretary at war, Lord Barrington, he was given a cornetcy in the 1st dragoons; he subsequently served with his regiment throughout the Westphalian campaign of 1762. On 13 January 1763 he purchased a captaincy in the 105th foot, went on half pay when his regiment was reduced a year later, and then spent two years travelling on the continent until the opportunity arose for him to purchase a troop in the 5th dragoons. Posted in consequence to Ireland, in 1769 he was appointed aide-de-camp to the lord lieutenant, Lord Townshend, and in 1772 he married Alicia (d. 1840), daughter of William Blacker of Carrick, co. Antrim. The same year he purchased a majority in the 13th dragoons and, in 1776, after a brief spell with the 1st Irish horse, returned to the 13th dragoons as lieutenant-colonel.

Steuart succeeded to his father's titles and the seat at Coltness, Lanarkshire, in 1780 and took the additional surname of Denham, which his father had adopted upon inheriting Westshield (also in Lanarkshire) four years earlier. Promoted brevet-colonel (1782), he entered parliament as member for Lanark county in 1784, a seat which

he held for the next eighteen years. In 1788, while stationed in Dublin, he was entrusted with improving the training of the cavalry in Ireland; the changes which he introduced to its system of field movements was much commended by headquarters. However, neither this achievement nor the support that he gave to the Pitt administration in parliament sufficed to win him the colonelcy of a regiment of foot, something which he earnestly sought: he was given instead the colonelcy of the 12th dragoons (9 November 1791). In October 1793 he was promoted major-general, which had the effect of making him too senior to join the siege at Toulon, where he had previously been ordered. He was also disappointed when, in 1794, having been given command of the cavalry intended to accompany Lord Cornwallis's mission to the Prussian army, the enterprise was cancelled. That September he accepted Henry Dundas's offer of a post on the staff in Scotland with a brief to superintend the fencible cavalry.

In March 1798, as a newly promoted lieutenant-general, Steuart Denham arrived to take command of Ireland's southern district. Major-General John Moore found him to be suffering from a nervous complaint 'which … completely unfitted him for business' (*Diary*, 1.275). None the less, Steuart Denham persisted and, in the months before the outbreak of the Irish rising, pursued a conciliatory policy. During the Wexford rising he took credit to himself for his subordinate General Henry Johnson's victory at New Ross (5 June 1798). But within a fortnight he received an official reprimand from the commander-in-chief, General Lake, for failing—until the order was repeated—to send troops from Munster against Wexford from the west. In response Steuart Denham claimed that he had possessed discretionary powers to withhold the troops, and resigned from the Irish staff in protest a month later. He received no further employment.

Steuart Denham was promoted full general in 1803 and exchanged the colonelcy of the 12th dragoons for that of the 2nd dragoons on 12 January 1815. He was made a knight grand cross of the Royal Guelphic Order in 1830. Although never rich, Steuart Denham expended his fortune on hospitality and improvements to the neighbourhood, 'leaving to his latter days a pittance barely adequate for comfortable subsistence, and that, ere his death, his heritage had passed to strangers' (Dennistoun, 390). He died at Cheltenham on 12 August 1839; his baronetcies fell to a cousin. ALASTAIR W. MASSIE

Sources J. Dennistoun, ed., *The Coltness collections, MDCVIII–MDCCCXL*, Maitland Club, [58] (1842) · J. Philippart, ed., *The royal military calendar*, 3rd edn, 5 vols. (1820) · *The works, poetical, metaphisical, and chronological of the late Sir James Steuart of Coltness, bart*, 6 (1805) · Irish rebellion papers, 1796–8, NAM, 5910–198 · *The diary of Sir John Moore*, ed. J. F. Maurice, 1 (1904) · E. Haden-Guest, 'Steuart-Denham, Sir James', HoP, *Commons, 1754–90* · D. G. Henry, 'Steuart Denham, Sir James', HoP, *Commons, 1790–1820* · GM, 2nd ser., 12 (1839), 541–2 · DNB · W. Fraser, *Memorials of the family of Wemyss of Wemyss*, 3 vols. (1888), vol. 1, pp. 359–60
Likenesses R. Dighton, watercolour drawing, 1836–7, NPG · H. Raeburn, oils, NG Ire. · oils, Arniston House, Lothian

Wealth at death a pittance: Dennistoun, ed., *Coltness collections*, 390

Denham, Sir John (1559–1639), judge, was the second son of William Denham (*d.* 1583), a goldsmith of St Matthew's, Friday Street, London, and later of Thorpe, Surrey, and his wife, Joan (*d.* 1589), perhaps a Prideaux. Nothing is known of his schooling; he entered Lincoln's Inn from Furnival's Inn in August 1579. Called to the bar on 29 June 1587, Denham was appointed with two fellow barristers in 1602 to refurbish the house library (which might link him with the John Denham who owned a fifteenth-century English verse life of St Cuthbert, now BL, Egerton MS 3309). Promoted bencher the following year, in 1604 he purchased the mansion of Imworth at Egham, Surrey, which he subsequently rebuilt. Having delivered his reading in Lent 1607 on the statute 31 Eliz. c. 6 (elections to colleges), he was created serjeant in May 1609 (naming the earl of Salisbury and Lord Chancellor Ellesmere as his patrons) and also knighted, preparatory to being sworn chief baron of the exchequer in Ireland.

In 1612 Denham succeeded Humphrey Winch, another Lincoln's Inn lawyer, as chief justice of Ireland. Following the death that year of his first wife, Cicely Kellefet (*née* Farr), who herself had been twice widowed before she married Denham in 1596, he married Eleanor Moore, the daughter of an Irish peer, about 1614; she was the mother of his first acknowledged child, the future poet John *Denham, at Dublin in 1614 or 1615. After serving as one of the lords justices during a vacancy in the viceroyalty from November 1615 until July 1616 Denham returned to England early the next year, and was appointed baron of the exchequer in May 1617. Eleanor died in childbed two years later; a monument erected by her husband in Egham church depicts her with a 'beautiful and ingenious visage' (Aubrey, *Natural History*, 3.157).

Denham remained on the judicial bench for another twenty years. Commended by the godly divine Richard Bernard as 'reverend and religious' (Bernard, sig. A4), Denham was nevertheless appointed to the ecclesiastical high commission in 1633, although he also joined Chief Justice Richardson in a celebrated attempt to suppress Somerset church ales. His written decision against the crown in the ship money trial was delivered shortly before his much anticipated death, which occurred at Egham on 6 January 1639. He was buried at Egham on 10 January. A long-time colleague memorialized Denham as 'an able, prudent, and good judge, of great integrity and honesty … who died with [the] good applause of all good and pious men' (*Diary of Sir Richard Hutton*, 113), but in 1637 a barrister characterized him as 'the old absurd Baron' (Bulstrode Whitelock to Edward Heath, BL, Add. MS 37343, fol. 147). His wealthy estate included lands in Essex, Suffolk, and Surrey, '2000 or 1500 pounds in ready money, two houses well furnished, and much plate' (*Brief Lives*, 182).

WILFRID PREST

Sources B. O'Hehir, 'The family of Denham of Egham', *Surrey Archaeological Collections*, 65 (1968), 71–85 · W. P. Baildon, ed., *The records of the Honorable Society of Lincoln's Inn: the black books*, 1–2

(1897–8) · W. P. Baildon, ed., *The records of the Honorable Society of Lincoln's Inn: admissions*, 1 (1896) · Baker, *Serjeants* · W. R. Prest, *The rise of the barristers: a social history of the English bar, 1590–1640* (1986) · *The diary of Sir Richard Hutton, 1614–1639*, ed. W. R. Prest, SeldS, suppl. ser., 9 (1991) · *Aubrey's Brief lives*, ed. O. L. Dick (1949) · C. Kenny, *King's Inns and the kingdom of Ireland* (1992) · J. Aubrey, *The natural history and antiquities of the county of Surrey*, 3 (1718) · *VCH Surrey*, vol. 3 · O. Manning and W. Bray, *The history and antiquities of the county of Surrey*, 3 (1814) · *DNB* · R. Bernard, *A guide for grand-iury men* (1627)

Archives BL, northern dialogue life of St Cuthbert (possibly owned by subject), MS Egerton 3309 · Surrey HC, marriage settlement of his son Denham, 1634, ACC 922 Add. Box 2

Likenesses portrait, Kirtlington Park, Oxfordshire

Wealth at death substantial landholdings in Surrey and Essex: will, PRO, PROB 11/79, sig. 41; C 142/786/59

Denham, Sir John (1614/15–1669), poet and courtier, was probably born in Dublin, the only son of Sir John *Denham (1559–1639), judge, and his second wife, Eleanor (*d.* 1619), daughter of Gerald, or Garret, Moore, Baron Moore of Mellefont and first Viscount Drogheda. His father, some fifty-six years his senior, was then serving as chief justice of the king's bench in Ireland. In October 1619, two years after their return to England, Lady Denham died after giving birth to a stillborn daughter and was buried at Egham in Surrey.

Early life and works, 1631–1640 On 26 April 1631 Denham was enrolled at Lincoln's Inn and on 18 November following matriculated as fellow-commoner from Trinity College, Oxford, aged sixteen; his autograph subscription describes him as a son of Sir John of Little Horseley, Essex. John Aubrey, to whom is owed most of the surviving anecdotal information about Denham, was told by his college contemporary Josias Howe that he had been 'the dreamingst young fellow; he never expected such things from him as he haz left the world' (*Brief Lives*, 1.217). Denham's great vice was to 'game extremely' (ibid.), and he was rebuked in chapel by the president of the college, Ralph Kettel, for not repaying a loan from the recorder of Oxford. Wood asserts that he performed the exercises for the BA, but did not graduate. On 25 June 1634 he married, at St Bride's, Fleet Street, Anne (*d. c.*1647), one of the two daughters of Don Cotton and coheir of her grandfather Ralph Cotton of Whittington, Gloucestershire. She brought with her the Buckinghamshire manor of Horsenden. They had at least two sons and two daughters.

Denham then applied himself to the study of common law. Judge Wadham Windham, his senior by three years at Lincoln's Inn, recalled that he was 'as good a student as any in the house', though 'not suspected to be a witt' (*Brief Lives*, 1.217). A drunken prank of painting out all the signs between Temple Bar and Charing Cross, which 'cost him … some moneys', was recalled by 'R. Estcott, esq., that carried the inke-pott' (ibid.). Aubrey records that parental disapproval of his addiction to cards and dice led him to write the brief tract that was printed anonymously in April 1651 as *The anatomy of play: written by a worthy and learned gent.: dedicated to his father, to shew his detestation of it*. His earliest known literary venture is the translation of books 2–6 of Virgil's *Aeneid* that he made in 1636, which was not published until 1656.

Sir John Denham (1614/15–1669), by unknown artist, c.1661

Denham and his family lived with his father at the manor house of Imworth in Egham. The burial of one of Denham's sons in Egham on 28 August 1638 was followed by the death of Denham's father on 6 January 1639. On 29 January that year Denham was called to the bar. Despite the income from eight inherited estates in Surrey, Essex, and Suffolk worth upwards of £10,000, in less than twelve months he had run up gambling debts of £4500 and over the next four years sold or mortgaged several properties.

Royalist writer and agent, 1641–1659 In March 1641 Denham was called upon as a witness for the defence of Thomas Wentworth, earl of Strafford, on whose death in May he wrote, but did not publish, an elegy. His true début as poet and dramatist came about on the very eve of civil war with *Cooper's Hill* and *The sophy*, issued anonymously early in August 1642, of which the poet Edmund Waller famously remarked that he 'broke-out like the Irish Rebellion— threescore thousand strong before anybody was aware' (*Brief Lives*, 1.217). *The sophy*, a verse tragedy based on events in Persia under the tyrannic Shah Abbas I (*d.* 1628), was advertised as having been acted 'with success' (*DNB*) by the king's company at Blackfriars. In *Cooper's Hill* the prospect from a Thames-side viewpoint at Egham is made the occasion for historical and moral reflections on kingship at a critical juncture in English history. The poem, which shows the influence of some then unprinted verses by Waller, was praised by fellow poet Robert Herrick and pronounced by John Dryden 'the exact Standard of good Writing' (Wood, *Ath. Oxon.*, 3.825). As an early instance of the topographical reflective genre and in its development of the closed couplet it looks forward to the Augustans. It was progressively revised, translated into Latin in 1667 by

Moses Pengry, and long remained one of the most famous poems in the language.

On 10 November 1642 Denham, then sheriff of Surrey, briefly took possession of Farnham Castle for the king, following withdrawal of the parliamentary garrison under the aged poet George Wither. The removal of goods allegedly worth £2000 from Wither's house by members of the occupying force led the older poet to spend fifteen years seeking reparation from the younger. Farnham surrendered after three weeks and Denham was sent prisoner to London. On his release in March 1643 he published *Mr Hampdens speech occasioned upon the Londoners petition for peace*, a satire in rhyming verse, and, leaving his wife about to give birth at Imworth, he joined the cavaliers in Oxford where he brought out a new edition of *Cooper's Hill* and wrote anti-parliamentary ballads. Articles of peace drawn up in November 1644 stipulated his removal from the royal counsels. While his creditors continued to pursue him and parliament early in 1645 ordered the sale of his goods he persisted in his old habits, losing £200 at 'New-cutt' in a single night (*Brief Lives*, 1.218). Taken in January 1646 at the surrender of Dartmouth, on the journey to London he managed to impress the Independent minister Hugh Peters. The Commons exchanged him for a prisoner held at Exeter, but although discharged from the king's bench he was briefly re-arrested for debt.

Following his release in May 1646 Denham retired to the continent and spent some months in Paris with Henrietta Maria, who sent him to attend Charles I in captivity: the Lords' pass for him to return to compound for his estates is dated 24 March 1647. At some time before May his wife died, and in July through the influence of Peters he obtained access to the king at Caversham. Charles, who had seen his commendatory verses in Richard Fanshawe's *Il pastor fido*, urged him to give up poetry now that he was 'thought fit for more serious Employments' (J. Denham, 'Epistle', *Poems*, 1668). Later in the month Denham was one of the eleven-member council convened at Woburn to answer the army's proposals, but when the king fled from Hampton Court in November he had orders to remain in London as agent for royal correspondence, being 'furnisht with nine several Cyphers in order to it' (Kelliher, 5). Then and for some years afterwards he figured in royalist documents under various pseudonyms. In December he delivered his petition to compound, and parliament left him relatively unmolested in London until about August 1648, when his role was 'discovered by their knowledge of Mr. Cowleys hand' (J. Denham, 'Epistle', *Poems*, 1668). He fled to The Hague to join the prince of Wales, who soon afterwards appointed him to negotiate for the aid of the Scots. In the spring he was acting as courier between Charles, now king, and his mother: Henrietta Maria's signed instructions to him of 10 May 1649 are copied in Abraham Cowley's hand. In June he contributed an elegy to the *Lachrymae musarum* published in England on the death of Lord Hastings, and at the Louvre until mid-September wrote verses 'to divert and put off the evil hours of our banishment' (ibid.) on subjects proposed by Charles.

In April 1650 one fifth of Denham's estate was ordered

to be paid to Colonel John Fielder as guardian to his two daughters, Elizabeth and Anne, and son John, who is last heard of as enrolling at Wadham College, Oxford, in July 1654. About June Denham left the exiled court at Breda with William, Lord Crofts, on a mission to raise money from Charles's Scottish subjects resident in Poland. By their return in autumn 1651 they had collected £10,000; disposal of the money was discussed in two letters that Denham wrote to Lady Isabella Thynne at Paris that winter. He continued to lose at play, wrote ribald ballads on his fellow exiles Thomas Killigrew and Sir John Mennes, and may have been cured of disfiguring venereal disease. Lack of money drove him to return to England in March 1653 to face a committee of the council of state, a member of which, Philip Herbert, sixth earl of Pembroke, entertained him over the year that followed in London and at Wilton, where Aubrey first made his acquaintance. By September his new found favour with the regime was known in Paris, where a spy of Thurloe's could write of him as 'the state's poet' (Thurloe, State papers, 1.471). In April appeared Certain verses written by severall of the authors friends, a series of mock commendatory poems on Sir William Davenant's Gondibert (1651), of which eight were the unsigned work of Denham. Along with a new version of Cooper's Hill (1653, 1655), emended to suit the changing political climate, he published a revised translation of book 2 of The Aeneid as The Destruction of Troy (February 1656), claiming it to represent a 'new way of translating this Author' (J. Denham, preface, Destruction of Troy, 1656) in the non-literal manner which he had praised in Fanshawe, and according to Aubrey wrote and then burnt a burlesque of Virgil. On 9 June 1655 he was banished from London on suspicion of conspiracy, but three days later John Evelyn was asked by his friend Thomas Henshaw to endorse Denham as 'the fittest man … in England' for a post in the household of the earl of Northumberland (BL, Add. MS 78311). In October 1656 Denham and his son called on Sir Richard Browne in Paris and in June 1657 he was at Brussels with the duke of Buckingham. The following March he obtained a licence from Cromwell to live at Bury St Edmunds, and on 24 September was granted a passport to go abroad with Pembroke's heir, William, Lord Herbert. By mid-November he was attempting to mediate between Charles II and the new protector, later joining Aubrey de Vere, earl of Oxford, in opposition to Lord Mordaunt's attempts to promote conspiracy. In May 1659 he published in broadside a scurrilous anti-Quaker ballad later reprinted as 'News from Colchester'. Although Sir Edward Hyde's lingering suspicion of his connections with Henrietta Maria's party still stood in the way of complete trust, Denham's correspondence with the king early the next year shows him trying to form a party to restore the king, and he was still negotiating with parliamentary factions on the eve of the Restoration.

Surveyor of the works and MP In May 1660 Denham was confirmed in the post, which had been spontaneously offered to him at St Germain in 1649, of surveyor of works, despite a petition from John Webb, nephew and assistant of the previous holder, Inigo Jones. It thus fell to him in April 1661 to make the physical arrangements for the coronation, at which he figured among sixty-eight new knights of the Bath. In the same month Pembroke's interest secured him a seat for the borough of Old Sarum in the new parliament, and on 20 May 1663 he was elected as one of the first fellows of the Royal Society. As surveyor he lacked the practical skills of an architect: in the dedication to Denham of his translation of Fréart's Parallel (1664) Evelyn, whose advice on the siting of the new Greenwich Palace he rejected, praised him merely for paving the streets of Holborn. Yet he proved an active and competent administrator and left Webb to superintend building work on the royal palaces. In March 1661 he leased land adjoining his office in Scotland Yard for a building of twenty rooms that he let out for rent, and in 1665 built Burlington House. Aubrey reports that he 'gott seaven thousand pounds, as Sir Christopher Wren told me of, to his owne knowledge' (Brief Lives, 2.219) on an official salary of only £382. In the Commons, which he attended regularly over eleven sessions as an adherent of the court party, he sat on sixty-two committees, though none of any political importance. Wither's committal to the Tower in April 1662 for publishing a seditious pamphlet may have given rise to the story of Denham's seeking his pardon on the ground that while Wither lived he himself 'should not be the worst poet in England' (ibid., 221).

On 25 May 1665 in Westminster Abbey Denham, then fifty years of age, 'ancient and limping' (Brief Lives, 1.219), married Margaret (1641/2–1667), daughter of Sir William Brooke, and a beauty some twenty-seven years his junior. Six days earlier, as coheir of the last lord Cobham, she had been granted the precedency due to a baron's daughter. From summer, when the great plague struck London, to October, when parliament convened at Oxford, the couple may have been absent from the capital. Early in the following March Denham's lameness led him to be summoned by the king to test the healing abilities of Valentine Greatrakes. Soon after, while in the west country to inspect the Portland stone quarries, he fell dangerously ill; Lady Denham left London on 7 April to be with him. By the 14th it was said that the 'great master of wit and reason, is fallen quite mad, and he who despised religion, now in his distraction raves of nothing else' (Ormonde MSS, new ser., 3.217). Rumour attributed his derangement to jealousy at his wife's very public affair with the duke of York, whom Pepys on 10 June reported to be already 'wholly given up' to it (Pepys, 7.158), visiting her with his retinue at Scotland Yard. By 22 September Denham had resumed his official duties, and though said not to have 'recovered his former understanding in any measure, yet spoke very good sense' in debate on 13 October (Bodl. Oxf., Carte MS 35, fol. 101). In his mock 'Panegyric upon Sir John Denham's recovery from his madness', Samuel Butler savagely attacked him for literary plagiarism, peculation, gambling, and faults of character. By November, when the duke's passion had abated, Lady Denham in turn was sick. Pepys noted that she 'says, and everybody else discourses, that she is poysoned' (Pepys, 7.365), while gossip fastened on a cup of 'mortal Chocolate' (A. Marvell, Last Instructions,

1667, 1.342) administered through the duchess of York's agency (*CSP dom.*, *1666–7*, 262–3). After rallying awhile Lady Denham died on 6 January 1667, when an autopsy performed by her own wish found her free from venom (*A Collection of the State Letters of … Roger Boyle, First Earl of Orrery*, ed. T. Morrice, 1742, 219), and, as Pepys sceptically added, still a virgin. She was buried three days later in Westminster Abbey. No credence need be given to the fanciful account in Anthony Hamilton's *Memoirs of the comte de Grammont* (1713) or to the scurrilous story preserved by Oldys that Denham contracted syphilis in order to pass it on to the duke.

In September 1667 it was reported that like his friend and fellow courtier Edmund Waller, 'poor Sir John Denham is fallen to the ladies also. He is at many of the meetings at dinner, talks more than ever he did, and is extremely pleased with those that seem willing to hear him' (W. Temple, *The Works of Sir William Temple*, new edn, 4 vols., 1814, 1.459). When the Commons reconvened in October, besides allegedly proclaiming the merits of the newly published *Paradise Lost* there, Denham opposed the bill for further penalties on recusants by citing a tale of Boccaccio, and on 7 November, during the attack on the lord chancellor, Clarendon, made 'a most rational and excellent speech' (*Diary of John Milward*, 104–5, 116). Late in the year appeared a pamphlet entitled *Directions to a painter … being the last works of Sir John Denham*. This included four pieces in the advice-to-a-painter mode recently introduced by Waller. Denham's authorship of the *Second advice* (c.June 1666), an attack on the conduct of the Second Anglo-Dutch War that alluded in passing to his wife's affair, was strenuously denied in his friend Christopher Wase's poem 'Divination', and he is not nowadays thought to have had a hand in any of them. His pen, however, had not been idle. By the time that he registered his elegy on Cowley, a mere twelve days after the latter's funeral on 3 August 1667, plans for a collected edition of his poems were already forming. The project did not come to fruition until the following February, a month in which the court witnessed a sumptuous performance of Corneille's *Horace* in a translation by Katherine Phillips that Denham had been persuaded to complete. In *Poems and Translations* (1668), which comprised twenty-five pieces, fourteen of them printed for the first time, he claimed that, true to his promise to Charles I, he had not taken up writing poetry until the previous summer at 'the Wells', instancing his translation of two fifteenth-century Latin moralizing poems. These, with another didactic piece, 'The progress of learning', and a revised version of *The sophy* conclude the incomplete and oddly haphazard collection that remained the basis for all editions until that of T. H. Banks in 1928, revised in 1969. Denham's own copy incorporates autograph texts of an elegy on Davenant's death on 7 April 1668, along with eleven satires of which eight had been printed anonymously in the *Gondibert* volume. In the same year his *Version of the Psalms of David*, unprinted until 1714, came to the notice of Samuel Woodford, a former contemporary of Denham's son at

Wadham. The final months of his life saw the publication of his *Cato Major of old age* (1669), a loose verse translation of Cicero's *De senectute*, while some mock commendatory verses appeared in Edward Howard's *British princes* in Easter term. A century later Johnson summed him up as, by virtue of *Cooper's Hill*, one of the founding fathers of English poetry, commenting on his talent for 'grave burlesque' and reflective poetry (Johnson).

Denham's last official act, on 6 March 1669, was to ensure the appointment of Wren as his successor in the surveyorship. He died in Scotland Yard on 19 March and was buried four days later among the poets in the abbey, 'at night and without pomp' (BL, Add. MS 36988, fol. 91). His passing was strangely unlamented, the sole known elegy, by Wase, surviving only in manuscript. Aubrey described him as 'of the tallest' but slightly bent at the shoulders, not very robust, with a stalking gait and piercing grey eyes that 'look't into your very thoughts' (*Brief Lives*, 1.220). His will, dated 13 March 1669, affirmed his Anglican faith and named as one of its overseers Sir John Birkenhead, the 'J. B.' of the address printed in the 1655 edition of *Cooper's Hill*. The will was proved on 9 May by his unmarried daughter Elizabeth, to whom he left the lease of Scotland Yard, worth about £440 a year, from which sums were to be set aside for the education of his eldest grandson, John Morley (d. 1683), child of his daughter Anne and her husband Sir William Morley. To the new St Paul's he donated £100 and all the fees that he had received for rebuilding the old cathedral before the fire. Other grandchildren also received bequests, but all dying without issue his line became extinct. An inventory taken on 24 June records, besides almost £1000 owing to his estate, household goods and money estimated at £382 and 'bookes valued at £5-0-0'.   W. H. KELLIHER

Sources B. O Hehir, *Harmony from discords: a life of Sir John Denham* (1968) · B. O Hehir, *Expans'd hieroglyphics: a critical edition of Sir John Denham's Cooper's Hill* (1969) · *The poetical works of Sir John Denham*, ed. T. H. Banks, 2nd edn (1969) · *Brief lives, chiefly of contemporaries, set down by John Aubrey, between the years 1669 and 1696*, ed. A. Clark, 2 vols. (1898) · Wood, *Ath. Oxon.*, new edn · G. Langbaine, *An account of the English dramatick poets* (1691), annotated copy, BL, C.45.d.14 · H. Berry, 'Sir John Denham at law', *Modern Philology*, 71 (1974), 266–76 · W. H. Kelliher, 'John Denham: new letters and documents', *British Library Journal* (spring 1986), 1–20 · J. G. Nichols and J. Bruce, eds., *Wills from Doctors' Commons*, CS, old ser., 83 (1863) · J. P. Ferris, 'Denham, John', HoP, *Commons, 1660–90* · *The diary of John Milward*, ed. C. Robbins (1938) · P. Beal and others, *Index of English literary manuscripts*, ed. P. J. Croft and others, [4 vols. in 11 pts] (1980–) · J. Maclean and W. C. Heane, eds., *The visitation of the county of Gloucester taken in the year 1623*, Harleian Society, 21 (1885) · H. M. Colvin and others, eds., *The history of the king's works*, 6 vols. (1963–82) · S. Johnson, *Life of Denham* (1779) · R. Fréart, *A parallel of the antient architecture with the modern*, ed. and trans. J. Evelyn (1664) · Pepys, *Diary* · Thurloe, *State papers*, vol. 1 · *Calendar of the manuscripts of the marquess of Ormonde*, new ser., 8 vols., HMC, 36 (1902–20), vol. 3 · GEC, *Peerage*, new edn · BL, Add. MS 36988, fol. 91; Add. MS 78200 · inventory, PRO, PROB 32 8/45

Archives NRA, letters and literary MSS · Yale U., MS poems

Likenesses portrait, c.1661, U. Lond., Sterling Library [*see illus.*] · J. Collyer, line engraving, 1779, BM, NPG; repro. in Johnson, *Life of Denham* · L. Legouse, stipple, 1808, BM, NPG; repro. in J. Denham, *Memoirs of Count Garamont* (1808) · Restoration artist, oils, NPG

Denham, Michael Aislabie (1800/01–1859), collector of folklore, was a native of Bowes, Yorkshire, who worked at Hull in the early part of his life and ultimately settled as a general merchant at Piercebridge, near Gainford, co. Durham, where he was a member of the Society of Friends.

From 1825 Denham industriously collected local proverbial lore, beginning with *A collection of proverbs and popular sayings relating to the seasons, the weather, and agricultural pursuits, gathered chiefly from oral tradition* (1846), printed by the Percy Society. Other folklore compilations included *Cumberland Rhymes, Proverbs, and Sayings* (published in four parts, the last in 1854); *Folklore of the North* (six parts, the last in 1856), a similar work relating to Westmorland (two parts, 1858); and *Folklore, or, A collection of local rhymes, proverbs, sayings, prophecies, slogans, &c., relating to Northumberland, Newcastle-on-Tyne, and Berwick-on-Tweed* (1858). From 1849 to about 1854 twenty *Minor Tracts on Folklore* were published; a distinctive volume was *The Slogans, and War and Gathering Cries of the North of England* (1850, 1851). Denham listed his works in *A Classified Catalogue of the Antiquarian Tomes, Tracts, and Trifles* (1859). He died at Piercebridge on 10 September 1859, aged fifty-eight.

THOMPSON COOPER, *rev.* JOHN D. HAIGH

Sources *GM*, 3rd ser., 7 (1859), 539 · *N&Q*, 4th ser., 11 (1873), 163 · *N&Q*, 5th ser., 3 (1875), 170 · W. T. Lowndes, *The bibliographer's manual of English literature*, ed. H. G. Bohn, [new edn], 6 vols. (1864) · d. cert. · Allibone, *Dict.*, suppl.
Archives Durham RO, notebooks | U. Edin. L., letters to James Halliwell-Phillipps
Wealth at death under £450: probate, 1 Nov 1859, *CGPLA Eng. & Wales*

Denholm, James (1772–1818), topographer and painter, was born in Glasgow, where he painted miniatures and landscapes. A member of the Glasgow Academy, he was taught drawing and geography. He made his publishing début in 1797, with *An Historical and Topographical Description of the City of Glasgow*. An enlarged edition appeared in 1789 and a third edition followed in 1804, with 'a sketch of a tour of the principal Scotch and English lakes' appended. The *Sketch* was also published separately in the same year.

In 1803 Denholm became a member of the Philosophical Society of Glasgow, founded in 1802; he was president from 1811 to 1814. He was also a member of the Philotechnical Society of Glasgow and the Manchester Literary and Philosophical Society. Denholm was married with children; he died in Glasgow on 20 April 1818. Although now fallen into obscurity, his artistic work was valued by his contemporaries. Compilers of nineteenth-century local histories and guidebooks paid him the compliment of plundering his *Description*; in *Glasgow, Past and Present* (2nd edn, 1884) he was described as 'one of the most interesting and able of our local chroniclers' (Pagan and Robertson, 1.62).

JOANNE POTIER

Sources DNB · *Glasgow Herald* (27 April 1818) · D. Foskett, *A dictionary of British miniature painters*, 1 (1972) · [J. Pagan], ed., *Glasgow, past and present: illustrated in dean of guild court reports and in the reminiscences and communications of Senex, Aliquis, J.B., &c*, 3 vols. (1851–6); rev. D. R. [D. Robertson], 3 vols. (1884), vol.1, p. 62
Likenesses J. Denholm, self-portrait; formerly in Glasgow, 1984

Denis, Sir Peter, baronet (*c.*1713–1778), naval officer, was born at Chester, the eleventh of twelve children of Revd Jacob Denis, or Dennis as he was known in England (*b.* *c.*1667, *d.* before 1746), a Huguenot who had fled from France after the revocation of the edict of Nantes, and Martha Leach (*c.*1669–1746), originally from Manchester. His father became a naval chaplain in 1718, and Peter, who retained the surname Denis, entered the navy as chaplain's servant to his father on 9 June 1724 in the *Success* (Captain Isaac Townshend), succeeding Robert Denis, probably a brother, who seems later to have become a purser. In 1728 he entered the *Tartar* as able seaman and became midshipman ordinary and then midshipman. After spells in the *York*, he became mate in the *Hound*, but he left her 'for preferment' in May 1734. Although he passed for lieutenant on 16 October 1734 he next appears only in 1739 when appointed lieutenant to the *Centurion* and then the *Wager*, both ships being in the squadron dispatched under George Anson against Spanish possessions in South America. Anson brought Denis back to the *Centurion*, where he proved a useful officer, his activities including detached services. As with most of the *Centurion*'s officers, he was promoted soon after his return, becoming captain on 9 February 1745 at a time when Anson was called to the Board of Admiralty; Denis also became Anson's political follower.

In 1746 Denis commanded the *Windsor* (60 guns) and in 1747 his old ship, the *Centurion*, with a reduced armament of 50 guns. In her he took part in Anson's action with De la Jonquière, and afterwards carried home Anson's dispatches. In the autumn he joined the fleet under Rear-Admiral Edward Hawke, but not until after the defeat of L'Etenduère. On 2 September 1750 he married Elizabeth (*c.*1721–1765), illegitimate daughter of John James Heidegger; they had no children. In 1754 he was elected MP for the borough of Hedon in Yorkshire, but he was to attend only rarely. Early in the following year he was appointed to command the *Medway* (60 guns). In her he continued on the home station during 1756, and he sat as a member of the court martial which tried and condemned Admiral John Byng. In 1757 he had command of the *Namur* (90 guns) which formed part of the fleet under Hawke in the unsuccessful expedition against Rochefort, Denis being one of those appointed to survey the coast. In 1758 he commanded the *Dorsetshire* (70 guns), in which he captured, after a sharp action, the French ship *Raisonnable* (64 guns) on 19 April, and the following year shared in the great victory in Quiberon Bay, the *Dorsetshire* being the first to engage. In March 1760 he was moved to the *Thunderer*, and in August 1761 he commanded the yacht *Charlotte* as flag-captain to Lord Anson, on the voyage which took to England George III's bride, Princess Charlotte of Mecklenburg. He continued to command the yacht until 18 October 1770, when he was promoted rear-admiral of the blue, having been made a baronet on 19 September 1767. In the spring of 1771 he was commander-in-chief of the *Medway*, and in the summer he went out to the Mediterranean, with his flag in the *Trident*. His command there was uneventful. After his return he was advanced to vice-admiral of the blue on 31 March 1775. Sir Peter lived with his wife in Queen Square, London, and later at Valence, near Westerham. Following Elizabeth's death on 30 December 1765 he moved to Maze Hill House, Greenwich. He died vice-admiral of the red on 12 June 1778 at his Greenwich home. At the time of his death Denis also had a house in Percy Street, London, and land in Romney Marsh. His will shows him to have had considerable means—he made bequests of £12,600, to numerous friends and also to many charities, as well as his property, much of which he left to his sister Anne, and he had shares in the Pantheon and the opera house in London and the public assembly rooms, Bath. Unfortunately nothing comes through of his character, though he was clearly a competent commander. J. K. LAUGHTON, *rev.* A. W. H. PEARSALL

Sources G. Williams, ed., *Documents relating to Anson's voyage round the world, 1740–1744*, Navy RS, 109 (1967) · *The Hawke papers: a selection, 1743–1771*, ed. R. F. Mackay, Navy RS, 129 (1990) · R. F. Mackay, *Admiral Hawke* (1965) · H. W. Richmond, *The navy in the war of 1739–48*, 3 vols. (1920) · J. S. Corbett, *England in the Seven Years' War: a study in combined strategy*, 2 vols. (1907) · [earl of Bristol], *Augustus Hervey's journal*, ed. D. Erskine (1953) · J. Charnock, ed., *Biographia navalis*, 5 (1797), 369 · J. Brooke, 'Denis, Peter', HoP, *Commons, 1754–90* · logs, PRO, ADM MSS, ADM 51/262 *Dorsetshire* · letters, PRO, ADM MSS, ADM 1/1699 · muster books, PRO, ADM MSS, ADM 36/1268, *Grafton*; 1503, 1505 *Hound*; 3965 *Success*; 4179 *Tartar* · passing certificate, PRO, ADM MSS, ADM 107/3, p. 264 · GEC, *Peerage*

Archives PRO, ADM MS 51/262, 1/1699, 36/1268, 1503, 1505, 3965, 4179, 107/3, p. 264

Likenesses N. Dance, oils, 1767–70, NMM

Wealth at death bequests of over £12,000; at least two houses and other property; investments

Denison [*formerly* Conyngham], **Albert**, **first Baron Londesborough** (1805–1860), connoisseur of the arts and politician, was born Albert Conyngham at 8 Stanhope Street, Piccadilly, London, on 21 October 1805, the third son of Henry Conyngham, first Marquess Conyngham (1766–1832), and his wife, Elizabeth *Conyngham (1769–1861), eldest daughter of Joseph *Denison, banker, of St Mary Axe, London; later rumours that he was a natural son of George IV appear to be unfounded. He was educated at Eton College and in 1820 was gazetted a half-pay cornet in the (disbanded) 22nd dragoons. He served in the Horse Guards in 1823–4, but resigned and joined the diplomatic service as attaché at Berlin, May 1824, and at Vienna from May 1825, then was secretary of legation at Florence, February 1828, and secretary at Berlin, January 1829 to June 1831. He was created KCH (civil) in August 1829. He sat as the MP (Liberal) for Canterbury 1835–1841 and 1847–50, but on 4 March 1850 was created Baron Londesborough, in the East Riding of Yorkshire. On 4 September 1849 he had taken the sole name of Denison, in lieu of that of Conyngham, to comply with the will of his uncle the banker and MP William Joseph *Denison, whose enormous wealth he inherited. He acquired estates in Yorkshire at Selby (bought from the Hon. Mrs E. R. Petre), Londesborough near Market Weighton (bought from George Hudson MP), and Grimston Park, near Tadcaster (bought from Lord Howden), and he owned over 60,000 acres, producing an income of about £100,000 per annum.

Albert Denison, first Baron Londesborough (1805–1860), by Sir Francis Grant, 1851

Londesborough was an enthusiastic antiquary, and was elected FSA on 26 March 1840 and FRS on 13 June 1850. He became first president of the British Archaeological Association in 1843 but resigned in 1849 and later became a vice-president of the Archaeological Institute and president of the London and Middlesex Archaeological Society in 1855. He served also as president of the Numismatic Society and was a vice-president of the British Association at its Hull meeting in 1853. He took an active role in tumular excavations, in Kent and the East Riding, for example those near Driffield, which he reported in the *Archaeologia* in 1852; and he frequently displayed examples from his extensive collections to fellow enthusiasts at the antiquaries' meetings and at special receptions. His collections of armour, plate, and other objects (including John Dee's famous mirror, French furniture from the Petit Trianon, and also Landseer's *The Monarch of the Glen*) were of wide range and high quality. A quarto catalogue, *Miscellanea graphica*, compiled by F. W. Fairholt and introduced by Thomas Wright, was issued in 1857, and one (also by Fairholt) of his antique silver plate in 1860, after his death. His antiquities were dispersed mainly in four London sales in 1879, 1884, and 1888. In 1835, as Lord Albert Conyngham, he had published *The Natural Son*, a translation of Carl Spindler's *Der Bastard*, and in 1849 a journal of his travels in Greece and Italy, *Wanderings in Search of Health*.

Lord Londesborough, in the portrait by Sir Francis Grant, formerly at Blankney, is depicted as an imposing figure of 6 feet 4 or 5 inches, tall and thin and dark, and (in the words of his grandson Sir Osbert Sitwell) 'like a comb, all teeth and backbone' (Sitwell, 60). He is shown, in recognition of his antiquarian tastes, with his hand resting beside a great helm. He had the reputation of being highly strung, and did not wish to see his servants, who had to attend to his many houses invisibly. He married first, on 6 July 1833, Henrietta Maria (1809–1841), fourth daughter of Cecil Weld-Forester, first Baron Forester, with whom he had two sons and four daughters; and second, on 21 December 1847, Ursula Lucy Grace (1823–1883), eldest daughter of Vice-Admiral the Hon. Charles Orlando Bridgeman, with whom he had a further four sons and two daughters. Having latterly, for the benefit of his health, spent much time at his villa at Cannes, he wintered in 1859 at St Leonards, but returned to his London house, 4 Carlton House Terrace, where he died on 15 January 1860. He was buried on 24 January in Grimston, Yorkshire. He was succeeded by his eldest son, who became first earl of Londesborough in the jubilee creations of 1887.   ALAN BELL

Sources DNB · GEC, *Peerage*, new edn · Sir O. Sitwell, *Left hand right hand* (1944)
Archives Surrey HC, corresp. concerning sale of shares in Guildford Public Hall · U. Edin. L., letters to James Halliwell-Phillipps · Yale U., Beinecke L., letters to T. J. Pettigrew
Likenesses F. Grant, portrait, 1851; Sothebys, 26 July 1978 [*see illus.*] · J. Faed, mezzotint (after portrait by F. Grant), BM · portrait, repro. in *ILN* (17 Sept 1853), 225
Wealth at death under £180,000: probate, 1860, CGPLA Eng. & Wales

Denison, Edmund. *See* Beckett, Sir Edmund, fourth baronet (1787–1874).

Denison, Edmund Beckett. *See* Beckett, Edmund, first Baron Grimthorpe (1816–1905).

Denison, Edward (1801–1854), bishop of Salisbury, was born at 34 Harley Street, London, on 13 March 1801, son of John Denison, formerly Wilkinson (1758?–1820), of Ossington, Nottinghamshire, a merchant and politician, and Charlotte, his second wife, daughter of Samuel Estwick, a West India planter and MP for Westbury. (John) Evelyn *Denison (1800–1873), speaker of the House of Commons, George Anthony *Denison (1805–1896), archdeacon of Taunton, and Sir William Thomas *Denison (1804–1871), colonial governor, were his brothers. He was educated at Esher and Eton College, matriculated at Oriel College, Oxford, in 1818, graduated BA with first-class honours in 1822, and entered the Middle Temple. Regarded as one of the most promising men of his generation at Oxford, he was elected fellow of Merton College, Oxford, in 1826, and proceeded MA in 1827. Ordained on 23 December 1827 as assistant curate successively of Wolvercote, near Oxford, and Radcliffe, Nottinghamshire, he became vicar of St Peter-in-the-East, Oxford, and a prebendary of Southwell in 1834. He was a traditional high-churchman of liberal whig sympathies. Lord Melbourne nominated him bishop of Salisbury in 1836. Joseph Blanco White alleged he was appointed because, although learned, he never published, and was passive in theology, and it was difficult to find a sympathetic Oxford whig to prefer.

On 27 June 1839 Denison married Louisa Mary (b. 1812),

daughter of Henry Ker Seymer of Hanford, Dorset, who died on 22 September 1841. It was of this first marriage that Edward *Denison (1840–1870) was born. He married secondly, on 10 July 1845, Clementina (b. 1812), daughter of Charles Baillie-Hamilton, archdeacon of Cleveland, who died on 12 May 1894.

Denison supported reform in the church, but criticized the legislation for merely diverting revenues to purposes deemed of greater utility. In the Lords he amended the Cathedrals Bill to retain prebendal stalls and their titles after the alienation of their endowments. In appointing new prebendaries at Salisbury he preferred senior clergy from the diocese, and encouraged residentiaries to become involved in diocesan work. He was an early advocate of the revival of synodical government in the Church of England.

Denison criticized the Tractarians for their exaggerated views, declining to support Pusey and Newman's projected Library of the Fathers in 1838 and joining in the condemnation of Tract 90. He did not always see eye to eye with his Tractarian brother George Anthony Denison, most notably at the outset of the controversy over eucharistic doctrine sparked by the latter in 1853–4. However, he presented Walter Kerr Hamilton, his Tractarian successor at St Peter-in-the-East, to a canonry of Salisbury and encouraged him to 'improve' worship in the cathedral. Later he recommended Hamilton to Lord Aberdeen as his successor, and he was duly appointed.

As a reforming bishop Denison established a church building society and discouraged pluralism. He gave concomitant encouragement to clerical residence, despite the smallness of the population in many parishes. He noted a steady increase in the number of parishes where there were two Sunday services and monthly holy communions. He used the new railways to visit his clergy regularly and to conduct confirmations in more parishes, confirming in sixty-four places compared with his predecessor's nine confirmation centres.

In the alarm over government grants to denominational schools based on satisfactory inspection reports, Denison, along with bishops Blomfield and Kaye, sought to avoid confrontation with the government, and persuaded Archbishop Howley to a compromise, giving the archbishop of Canterbury a veto in the appointment of inspectors. Denison feared that lack of provision of education contributed to the restlessness of the poor in industrial towns. In many parishes too small to support day schools, he encouraged Sunday schools when evening schools were unsuccessful. He established a diocesan board of education, a system for inspecting schools, and an institution for training schoolmistresses.

Denison criticized the new poor law, rejecting as self-righteous the individuality of political economy. He saw the poor as victims of the faults of their betters, including the church. He discouraged clergy from serving as guardians, and regretted the church's identification with the new workhouses, believing the church was becoming cut off from the poor. He encouraged the establishment of friendly societies to assist the poor to save money. In the

Salisbury cholera epidemic of 1849 he was reputed to have visited many of the sufferers. He was reckoned to have given away more than £17,000 to charitable causes in his lifetime. Denison died on 6 March 1854 at the bishop's palace, in Salisbury, aged fifty-two, and was buried in the cathedral cloister garth on 15 March.   W. M. JACOB

Sources DNB • R. A. Soloway, *Prelates and people: ecclesiastical social thought in England, 1783–1852* (1969) • P. Barrett, *Barchester: English cathedral life in the nineteenth century* (1993) • E. R. Norman, *Church and society in England, 1770–1970* (1976) • C. F. Brown, *A history of the English clergy, 1800–1900* (1953) • O. Chadwick, *The Victorian church*, 1 (1966) • H. P. Liddon, *The life of Edward Bouverie Pusey*, ed. J. O. Johnston and others, 4 vols. (1893–7), vol. 1
Archives U. Nott. L., corresp. | BL, corresp. with W. E. Gladstone and others • Bodl. Oxf., letters to Samuel Wilberforce • Borth. Inst., corresp. with second Viscount Halifax • NL Scot., corresp. with J. R. Hope-Scott • NL Wales, corresp. with earl of Powis • Pusey Oxf., letters to G. A. Denison
Likenesses J. H. Lynch, print (after F. Sandys), BM • H. W. Pickersgill, oils, Merton Oxf. • wax portrait, Salisbury Cathedral

Denison, Edward (1840–1870), philanthropist, born at the palace, Salisbury, Wiltshire, on 8 September 1840, was the son of Edward *Denison (1801–1854), bishop of Salisbury, and his first wife, Louisa Mary (1812–1841), second daughter of Henry Ker Seymer of Hanford, Dorset. After some education at home Denison went to Eton College and to Christ Church, Oxford. Unfortunately, while at Eton, when training for a boat race, he overtaxed his strength and brought on congestion of the lungs, from which he never really recovered. He matriculated in 1858 from Christ Church, and in 1861 obtained a second-class degree in law and history, missing a first solely as a consequence of his bad health. From 1862 to 1866 he read for the bar at Lincoln's Inn, being called in 1868.

In the spring of 1864 Denison travelled through Italy and the south of France to Madeira and Tangier. While at St Moritz in Switzerland on his way back, he was deeply impressed with the habits and condition of the peasantry there. On his return to England he showed great interest in the state of the poor in the East End of London, and became almoner of the Society for the Relief of Distress in the District of Stepney. With a view to studying social questions from a practical point of view, he moved in the autumn of 1867 to a lodging in Philpot Street, Mile End Road, where he stayed for eight months, only occasionally visiting his friends in the West End. During that time he built and endowed a school, in which he himself taught Bible classes and gave lectures to working men.

Denison was one of the earliest members of the committees formed in 1869 by the Society for Organising Charitable Relief and Repressing Mendicity (or the Charity Organization Society). Though he represented the moral rather than the political economy tradition in the society he favoured treating destitutes harshly and believed that charity was a chief cause of the housing crisis in London. In 1868 he went to Paris, and later to Edinburgh, to study the working of the poor law. In November 1868 he was elected for Newark, where his uncle (John) Evelyn *Denison, the speaker, lived. (He was his uncle's heir presumptive.) In May 1869, with his health declining, he visited the

Channel Islands, whose political constitution he studied with great interest. In Guernsey he had an interview with Victor Hugo, who 'ranted' at him for half an hour, and convinced him that 'with all his sublimity of imagination he was a bad politician and a worse reasoner'. Further difficulties with his lungs forced him to abandon a projected visit with Sir Michael Hicks Beach to the United States, and he decided to make a voyage to Melbourne, where he hoped to study the questions of emigration and colonization. He left England in October 1869; the voyage made his health worse rather than better, and he died at Melbourne on 26 January 1870, within a fortnight of landing. He never married.

Denison's letters and other writings, edited by Sir Baldwyn Leighton, were published in 1872 (repr. 1875); they had considerable impact and he posthumously obtained something of the much greater influence attached to Arnold Toynbee. Denison House, the headquarters of the Charity Organization Society, perpetuated his name.

ROBERT HARRISON, rev. H. C. G. MATTHEW

Sources *Letters and writings of Edward Denison*, ed. B. Leighton (1875) • *The Times* (22 March 1870) • Boase, *Mod. Eng. biog.* • Foster, *Alum. Oxon.* • G. Stedman Jones, *Outcast London* (1971) • C. L. Mowat, *The Charity Organisation Society, 1869–1913* (1961) • J. R. Green, *Stray studies* (1876)
Likenesses J. Hayter, chalk drawing, 1845, NPG

Denison, (John) Evelyn, Viscount Ossington (1800–1873), speaker of the House of Commons, was the eldest of the nine sons of John Denison MP (1758?–1820), of Ossington Hall, Nottinghamshire, and his second wife, Charlotte, daughter of Samuel Estwick MP. One of his sisters, Lucy, married Charles Manners-*Sutton, speaker of the House of Commons. His brothers included Edward *Denison (1801–1854), Sir William Thomas *Denison (1804–1871), and George Anthony *Denison (1805–1896). He was born at Ossington on 27 January 1800, and was educated at Eton College from 1811 to 1817. He then went to Christ Church, Oxford, where he graduated BA in June 1823, MA in May 1828, and honorary DCL in June 1870. In July 1823 he entered parliament as one of the members for the borough of Newcastle under Lyme, and in the following year went on a lengthy tour through Canada and the United States, in company with lords Derby, Taunton, and Wharncliffe. At a by-election in December 1826 he was returned unopposed for Hastings. Though seen as a whig, his maiden speech opposed Lord John Russell's motion for parliamentary reform. On 2 May 1827 he was appointed one of the council of the duke of Clarence, the lord high admiral in Canning's administration. When Wellington became prime minister in 1828, Denison resigned the post and never again took office. On 14 July 1827 he married Lady Charlotte Cavendish-Scott-Bentinck (1806–1889), third daughter of William Cavendish-Scott-Bentinck, fourth duke of Portland, and his wife, Henrietta. At the general election of 1830 he unsuccessfully contested his old constituency of Newcastle under Lyme, and in November that year was defeated at the by-election at Liverpool consequent on Huskisson's death. At the general election of 1831 he was elected for both Liverpool and the then

Denison was fairly well regarded as speaker. A consolidator rather than an innovator (he prevented, for example, the introduction of printed notice of questions to ministers), he none the less defended the financial rights of the Commons against the Lords, deploring the latter's action in rejecting the bill of 1860 repealing the paper duty, and opposing the Lords' introduction of a financial provision into a divorce bill (Laundy, 307). The tories in 1862 hoped he might be encouraged to retire and be replaced by Spencer Walpole. Denison was the last speaker to speak and vote in committee, and he voted against the government on the budget on 9 June 1870. He was a dignified speaker but was thought by contemporaries sometimes lacking in firmness. *The Times* noted on his death: 'On the occasions which called for his active interposition with the House we do not care to dwell' (Laundy, 310). Denison was a cultivated man who thought the speaker should have a general influence on national life: thus he sponsored the Speaker's Commentary on the Bible (published in ten volumes between 1871 and 1881).

The fast pace of legislation in Gladstone's first government exhausted Denison and he retired in February 1872, being succeeded by H. B. W. Brand. Denison was created Viscount Ossington of Ossington on 13 February 1872, but declined the usual substantial speaker's pension on the grounds that he had 'a private fortune which will suffice, and for the few years of life that remain to me I should be happier in feeling that I am not a burden to my fellow-countrymen'. Denison kept a discreet diary between 1857 and 1872, which shows him to have had an unsubtle but competent mind; it was published posthumously as *Notes from my Journal when Speaker of the House of Commons* (1900), edited by his widow. He was president of the Royal Agricultural Society in 1856-7 and was a trustee of the British Museum from 1872. He died at Ossington Hall on 7 March 1873, aged seventy-three, and was buried on the 13th in the family vault there. He had no heir. His widow, on the death of her brother the fifth duke of Portland, succeeded to part of the Portland estates and in 1882 took the surname of Scott instead of Denison, leaving over £400,000 when she died in 1889.

G. F. R. BARKER, *rev.* H. C. G. MATTHEW

Sources *The Times* (8 March 1873) · J. E. Denison, *Notes from my journal when speaker of the House of Commons* (1900) · P. A. C. Laundy, *The office of speaker* (1964) · A. I. Dasent, *The speakers of the House of Commons* (1911) · Gladstone, *Diaries* · *Daily News* (8 March 1873) · *Daily News* (14 March 1873) · E. G. Blackmore, *The decisions of the Rt. Hon. Evelyn Denison, speaker of the House of Commons* (1881) · GEC, *Peerage*

Archives Bodl. Oxf., notebook · U. Nott. L., corresp. and papers | BL, corresp. with Gladstone, Add. MS 44261 · BL, letters to William Huskisson, Add. MSS 38750-38758 · BL, letters to Sir Anthony Panizzi, Add. MSS 36718-36726 · Bodl. Oxf., corresp. with Benjamin Disraeli · Bodl. Oxf., letters to Samuel Wilberforce · Borth. Inst., letters to Lord Halifax · Chatsworth House, Derbyshire, letters to dukes of Devonshire · Derbys. RO, letters to Sir R. J. Wilmot-Horton · Harrowby Manuscript Trust, Sandon Hall, Staffordshire, corresp. with Lord Harrowby · LPL, corresp. with A. C. Tait on speaker's commentary on the Bible · Lpool RO, letters to fourteenth earl of Derby · PRO, corresp. with Lord John Russell, PRO 30/22 · St Deiniol's Library, Hawarden, corresp. with Sir John Gladstone · U. Durham L., letters to third Earl Grey · U. Nott. L., corresp. with duke of Newcastle; letters to duke of Portland

(John) Evelyn Denison, Viscount Ossington (1800-1873), by John & Charles Watkins

undivided county of Nottinghamshire, where his family had some, but not great, influence. He chose to sit for the latter, and in the two following parliaments of 1833 and 1835 was returned for South Nottinghamshire without opposition. He supported the reform bills of 1831-2. Denison was a whiggish Liberal, and the chief influence in the constituency was the tory duke of Newcastle. In 1837 Denison did not contest the constituency, which returned two tories. After being out of the house for four years, he was returned unopposed at the general election of 1841 for the borough of Malton, which constituency he continued to represent in the two following parliaments of 1847 and 1852. In March 1857, the Newcastle influence having become more Liberal, he was elected without opposition for North Nottinghamshire, holding the seat until his retirement from the Commons. Denison played some part, but not a significant one, in the private and public business of the house, and it was with some surprise—to himself as well as his contemporaries—that Palmerston, on J. T. Delane's recommendation, suggested to him that he be the government's candidate for the speakership on the retirement of Charles Shaw Lefevre. He was unanimously elected on 30 April 1857 and sworn of the privy council on 1 May. Denison was three times re-elected to the chair unopposed, on 3 May 1859, 1 February 1866, and 10 December 1868.

Likenesses Aτη [A. Thompson], caricature, chromolithograph, NPG; repro. in *VF* (12 March 1870) • Caldesi, Blandford & Co., carte-de-visite, NPG • W. and D. Downey, carte-de-visite, NPG • W. P. Frith, group portrait, oils (*Marriage of the prince of Wales, 1863*), Royal Collection • J. Hawkins, oils (after F. Grant, 1862), Palace of Westminster, London • G. Hayter, group portrait, oils (*The House of Commons, 1833*), NPG • J. & C. Watkins, two cartes-de-visite, NPG [*see illus.*] • F. C. Lewis, stipple (after J. Slater), BM • J. Phillip, group portrait, oils (*The House of Commons, 1860*), Palace of Westminster, London • oils, Eton • oils (after F. Grant), Hughenden Manor, Buckinghamshire • woodcut (as Speaker), BM

Wealth at death under £120,000: probate, 3 April 1873, *CGPLA Eng. & Wales*

Denison, George Anthony (1805–1896), Church of England clergyman, born at Ossington, Nottinghamshire, on 11 December 1805, was the fourth son of John Denison (1758?–1820), merchant, of Leeds, MP for Colchester (1802–6) and for Minehead (1807–12), and his second wife, Charlotte Estwick. His siblings included Edward *Denison (1801–1854), bishop of Salisbury, (John) Evelyn *Denison, Viscount Ossington (1800–1873), and Sir William Thomas *Denison (1804–1871), colonial governor. Denison was educated at private schools, at Eton College from 1817 to 1823, and at Oxford, for which he was prepared by a private tutor, Charles Drury, whose severe discipline he described as the most salutary experience of his life. He matriculated from Christ Church on 14 November 1823, graduated BA (with a first class in *literae humaniores*) in 1827, and proceeded MA in 1830. He twice gained the chancellor's prize—by his Latin essay in 1828, in which year he was elected fellow of Oriel College, and by his English essay in 1829.

In 1832 Denison took holy orders and served as curate of Cuddesdon. In 1830 he was elected to a college tutorship at Oriel, which he retained until 1836, when he exchanged it for the office of treasurer. He found Oriel society extremely uncongenial, and in 1838 accepted from his brother Edward, bishop of Salisbury, the vicarage of Broadwinsor, Dorset. On 4 September of that year he married Georgiana (1819–1908), eldest daughter of Joseph Warner *Henley. He was collated on 10 August 1841 to the prebend of Wilsford and Woodford in the church of Sarum, and on 28 April 1849 to the ninth prebend of Combe in the church of Wells. This he exchanged for the two prebends of Milverton in the same church on his appointment in September 1851 to the archdeaconry of Taunton. In 1845 he had been appointed vicar of East Brent in Somerset.

From the first a strong high-churchman, and subsequently very sympathetic to the teachings and practices of the Tractarians, Denison united with Henry Edward Manning in organizing resistance to the regulation of parochial schools by the state, on which subject he wrote extensively from 1847, becoming a champion of the National Society. He also joined in the protests against the preferment of the broad-churchman R. D. Hampden to the see of Hereford in 1847 and against the final judgment of 1850 in the Gorham case. He was himself defendant in another ecclesiastical *cause célèbre*. The high-church doctrine of the eucharist which, as examining chaplain to the

George Anthony Denison (1805–1896), by Hennah & Kent, 1855

bishop of Bath and Wells, he set before the candidates for ordination led to a disagreement with the bishop's commissary, in which Denison was so poorly supported by the bishop, Richard Bagot, that he resigned (June 1853). He then defined his doctrinal position with precision in three sermons preached in Wells Cathedral (7 August 1853, 6 November 1853, and 14 May 1854). In these sermons Denison affirmed a real (though non-material) presence of Christ in the elements by virtue of consecration and prior to their reception. All communicants thus received the inward grace of the sacrament (though not necessarily its spiritual benefit) together with the outward sign. Such a view seemed to contradict article twenty-nine of the Thirty-Nine Articles and, moreover, to encourage devotion to the sacramental species. The terminology which he employed reflected that of other Tractarians, especially R. I. Wilberforce in his *The Doctrine of the Holy Eucharist* of 1853. Denison's position was also explicitly supported by John Keble in the latter's *On Eucharistical Adoration* (1857) when the Evangelical Alliance, on the basis of Denison's sermons, instituted proceedings in the ecclesiastical courts. The prosecution, initiated ostensibly by the Revd Joseph Ditcher, vicar of South Brent, was pursued with vigour, and met with firm resistance from Denison. The result, as in the Gorham case, served only to illustrate the uncertainty of the law. Denison's views were declared contrary to the twenty-eighth and twenty-ninth of the articles of religion by Archbishop J. B. Sumner, sitting with assessors at Bath on 12 August 1856, and as Denison declined to recant he was sentenced to deprivation on 22 October. However, the execution of the sentence was deferred, pending an appeal to the court of arches, which resulted in its reversal on a technical point on 23 April

1857. An appeal from this decision was dismissed by the judicial committee of the privy council on 6 February 1858 without any decision on the substantive question, but to the relief of most Tractarians.

Denison was editor of the *Church and State Review*, published from 1862 until 1865. For many years he was a potent conservative voice in the convocation of Canterbury, which he succeeded in committing in 1863 to a censure (20 May) of J. W. Colenso's *Pentateuch and the Book of Joshua Critically Examined*, and in the following year to a more formal condemnation (24 June) of the controversial *Essays and Reviews* (1861). He also led opposition to the endowment of the regius chair of Greek at Oxford, apparently for no other reason than that it was held by the heterodox Benjamin Jowett (1817–1893), and in December 1869 entered his protest against Frederick Temple's consecration to the see of Exeter. He was also a consistent opponent of any change in the law of divorce. Denison remained staunchly opposed to any form of state intervention in Church of England schools and viewed the 1870 Education Act with disgust. His attempt to foreclose the discussion on the Athanasian creed, in the course of Dean Stanley's speech in the lower house of the convocation of Canterbury, on 24 April 1872, caused a dramatic scene which terminated in his temporary secession from the assembly.

The one issue upon which Denison himself admitted to a change of opinion was that of ritualism. His eucharistic beliefs gradually led to his support for more ceremonial, a fact signalled by his joining the Society of the Holy Cross in 1877. He remained entirely unreceptive to development of biblical criticism, and his disapproval of *Lux mundi* (1889), a series of essays by more liberally inclined younger Anglo-Catholics, caused his secession in 1892 from the English Church Union, of which he had been one of the founders. He was resolutely opposed to the policies of the Gladstonian Liberal Party in the 1880s and 1890s, and his vehement denunciations in print of Gladstone's character and opinions attracted much public attention. Embittered by the progress of the social, political, and religious change which he had vainly but vigorously opposed, he spent his last years in comparative seclusion at East Brent, where he died on 21 March 1896. He was buried in East Brent churchyard on 26 March.

Although an unsparing opponent in public controversies, Denison's private character was an appealing one. He reserved his *odium theologicum* exclusively for public use: despite the depth of his public differences he always maintained harmonious private relations with Dean Stanley. As a parish priest he shared in the Tractarian desire to restore the neglected aspects of worship, and had a keen eye to the temporal as well as the spiritual needs of his parishioners. With him the popular harvest festival is said to have originated, and he improved the water supply at East Brent at his own expense.

J. M. RIGG, *rev.* GEORGE HERRING

Sources G. A. Denison, *Notes of my life, 1805–1878* (1878) · A. Härdelin, *The Tractarian understanding of the eucharist* (1965) · O. Chadwick, *The Victorian church*, 2nd edn, 1 (1971), 491–5 · B. R. Marshall, 'The theology of church and state with reference to the concern for popular education in England, 1800–1870', DPhil diss., U. Oxf., 1956 · J. W. Burgon, *Lives of twelve good men*, new edn (1891) · Burke, *Gen. GB* (1914) · *The Times* (23 March 1896) · *The Guardian* (25 March 1896) · *The Guardian* (1 April 1896)
Archives Pusey Oxf., corresp. and papers · U. Nott. L., letters and leaflets | BL, corresp. with Lord Carnarvon, Add. MS 60836 · BL, corresp. with W. E. Gladstone, Add. MS 44140 · Bodl. Oxf., corresp. with Benjamin Disraeli · Borth. Inst., corresp. with second Viscount Halifax · Lancing College, letters to Nathaniel Woodard · LPL, letters to William Scott · LPL, corresp. with A. C. Tait, etc. · LPL, letters to Cecil Wray · Sion College, London, Scott MSS · Suffolk RO, Ipswich, letters to Lord Cranbrook
Likenesses Hennah & Kent, photograph, 1855, NPG [*see illus.*] · Lock & Whitfield, woodburytype photograph, pubd 1876, NPG · Bassano, carte-de-visite, NPG · H. Hering, carte-de-visite, NPG · Hills & Saunders, cabinet photograph, NPG · D. J. Pound, stipple and line engraving (after photograph by Mayall), BM, NPG · S. A. Walker, carte-de-visite, NPG · photographs, NPG
Wealth at death £13,842 0s. 7d.: probate, 16 May 1896, *CGPLA Eng. & Wales*

Denison, John (1569/70–1629), Church of England clergyman, from a Warwickshire family, matriculated at Oxford from Magdalen Hall in May 1590, when he was twenty, graduated BA from Balliol College in 1594, and proceeded MA in 1600. After holding the headmastership of the free school in Reading, Berkshire, he was then successively vicar of the three churches in the town, being instituted to St Laurence's in 1604, St Giles's in 1612, and St Mary's in 1614. Between November 1610 and the spring of 1613 he held concurrently the rectory of Woodmansterne, Surrey, to which he had been presented by the king. Meanwhile he returned to Oxford to take his BD in 1607 and DD in 1611.

Having been licensed in 1606, he was, according to Wood, highly regarded as a preacher, and was chaplain to the duke of Buckingham, whose father Denison described in 1619 as 'my much honoured friend' (*Heavenly Banquet*, dedication), and to James I. Between 1608 and 1624 he published a number of sermons, several subsequently reissued in various editions, and *De confessionis auricularis vanitate* (1621), a treatise countering Cardinal Bellarmine's views on auricular confession, dedicated to the king. Dedications to such works as *The Heavenly Banquet, or, The Doctrine of the Lords Supper* (1619), *The Sinne Against the Holy Ghost* (1620), and *The Blessednesse of Peace-Makers* (1620) reveal that he had long enjoyed the friendship and patronage of a variety of eminent men including Lord Chancellor Ellesmere, Bishop John King of London, and the earl of Kelly. The works themselves combine thoroughgoing antipopery, approval of sabbath observance, and quotation of Calvin and Beza, Cartwright and Reynolds, with justification of kneeling at communion as 'most consonant to comeliness and order' (*Heavenly Banquet*), exhortation to 'study to make our election sure by good works' (*Blessednesse of Peacemakers*, 79) and denunciations of 'peace-breakers' (42) who object to surplices—'they have the zeale of God, though not according to knowledge' (ibid., 42).

According to a letter from Sir Thomas Bodley to Dr John King, vice-chancellor of Oxford University, read in convocation in July 1628, Denison presented 'several valuable books to the Bodleian Library' (Coates, 336–7). He died in Reading at the end of January 1629, leaving money for the poor in the three Reading parishes, a study of books to his eldest son, John, legacies to him, to another son, and to three daughters, and property in Fryers Street, Reading, to his wife, Mary. He was buried in St Mary's Church, Reading, on 1 February.

THOMPSON COOPER, *rev.* VIVIENNE LARMINIE

Sources Foster, *Alum. Oxon.* • Wood, *Ath. Oxon.*, new edn, 2.439 • *BL cat.* • J. Denison, *Foure sermons: viz 1. The blessednesse of peace-makers, 2. The advancement of Gods children, 3. The sinne against the Holy Ghost ...,* 4. *The Christian petitioner* (1620) • J. Denison, *The heavenly banquet, or, The doctrine of the Lords Supper, set forth in seven sermons ... and a iustification of kneeling in the act of receiving* (1619) • J. Denison, *De confessionis auricularis vanitate* (1621) • PRO, PROB 11/155, fol. 279 [35 Ridley] • C. Coates, *The history and antiquities of Reading* (1802), 336–7 • O. Manning and W. Bray, *The history and antiquities of the county of Surrey,* 2 (1809), 466

Likenesses R. Sawyer, line print, pubd 1820, BM, NPG • line print, BM, NPG

Wealth at death £600—left to four children; also house in Fryers Street, Reading, and other property: will, PRO, PROB 11/155, fol. 279

Denison, Joseph (*c.*1726–1806), banker, was probably the elder son of Joseph Denison, cloth merchant, of Burmantofts Hall, Leeds, and his first wife, Rebecca, *née* Wainman. Nineteenth-century accounts of Denison's life, seeking to contrast his great wealth in later life and the fine marriages of his daughters with his humble origins, went so far as to assert he was 'a parish boy, ignorant of reading and writing, who made his way from Yorkshire up to London on foot' (Taylor, 231). Certainly, identification is not made easier by the fact that the name of Denison was extremely common in the Leeds area, and no evidence of Denison's baptism there has been unearthed. Nevertheless, given that rags to riches was a rare phenomenon in Georgian England, a mercantile background seems more plausible.

Reputedly, Denison became a clerk in the counting-house of an Irish Catholic merchant (Dillon) before starting out on his own account. He was connected with the Liverpool banking firm of Heywood, acting as their London agent and eventual partner, as well as handling the accounts of other large-scale north-country merchants and bankers. By the 1780s he had made a very considerable fortune, the reward, according to Taylor, of 'unabated industry and the most rigid frugality' (Taylor, 231). In fact, little is known of Denison's banking activities. But his success was evident enough. In 1787 he purchased Denbies in Surrey, built by Jonathan Tyers, the celebrated proprietor of Vauxhall Gardens; five years later he acquired, for around £100,000, the east Yorkshire estates of the duke of Leeds.

Joseph Denison was twice married. His first wife, Sarah, was the daughter of William Sykes of Salford. After her death in 1768 he married Elizabeth (1738/9–1771), the daughter of William Butler, variously described as merchant of Lisbon and Southwark hatter. The second marriage produced a son and two daughters, before Elizabeth's early death. Their son, William Joseph *Denison

(1770–1849), continued his father's banking business, becoming senior partner in Denison, Heywood, and Kennard. W. J. Denison was high sheriff of Yorkshire in 1808, MP for Camelford (1796–1802), Kingston upon Hull (1806–7) and, surviving eight elections to become father of the house, MP for the western division of Surrey from 1818 until his death in 1849. His estate, reckoned to be worth a colossal £2.3 million, and realizing £80,000 a year, passed to his nephew, Lord Albert Denison Conyngham (created Baron Londesborough in 1850). By 1883 the latter's son, who became the first earl of Londesborough in 1887, was the largest landowner in the East Riding of Yorkshire, with 52,655 acres.

However, the fame of Joseph Denison's elder daughter surpassed that of her brother. Elizabeth Denison [see Conyngham, Elizabeth] married Henry Burton Conyngham: she achieved notoriety as George IV's avaricious, over-weight mistress, acquiring a marquessate for her husband (lord steward of the king's household), a barony (Wenlock) for the husband of her younger sister, Anna Maria, and a peerage (which he declined) for her brother, William Joseph. By the early nineteenth century, the wealth and social range of the Denisons was a byword in Regency England. Both were founded on Joseph Denison's extraordinary assiduity as a banker. He died at home in the parish of St Mary Axe, London, on 12 December 1806, aged, according to his obituary in *Gentleman's Magazine,* about eighty. He was buried in Bunhill Fields, just outside the City of London.

R. G. WILSON

Sources G. D. Lumb, 'The Denison family', *Publications of the Thoresby Society,* 26 (1924), 102–5 • *GM,* 2nd ser., 32 (1849), 422–3 • *GM,* 1st ser., 76 (1806), 181–2 • *The Times* (3 Aug 1849), 3d, 4d • *The Times* (11 Sept 1849), 8a • GEC, *Peerage,* new edn • G. D. Lumb, 'The family of Denison of Great Woodhouse and their residences in Leeds', *Thoresby Society Miscellanea,* 15 (1909), 251–73 • G. D. Lumb, 'The Old Hall, Burmantofts', *Publications of the Thoresby Society,* 26 (1924), 106–12 • R. V. Taylor, ed., *The biographia Leodiensis, or, Biographical sketches of the worthies of Leeds* (1865)

Denison, Sir Thomas (1699–1765), judge, was one of at least two sons of Joseph Denison, a merchant of Leeds. His elder brother William resided at Ossington Hall, Nottinghamshire, and was the grandfather of John Evelyn Denison (1800–1873), speaker of the House of Commons. However, the records of the Inner Temple state that Thomas was admitted in February 1719 as the son and heir apparent of Joseph Denison, gentleman. He had been educated at Leeds grammar school. From the Inner Temple, Denison migrated in 1721 to Gray's Inn, and thence in 1727 to Lincoln's Inn where he was called to the bar in 1733. These facts suggest a difficulty in gaining a foothold in the law, and it may be that he practised for some years below the bar. Nevertheless, by 1740 he was the leader of the king's bench bar, in terms of the number of causes which he handled there, and, in 1742, within ten years of call, he was appointed one of the justices of that court. According to his epitaph, allegedly written by Lord Mansfield, he had been 'pressed, and at last prevailed upon', to accept this office, and 'discharged the important trust of that high office with unsuspected integrity, and uncommon ability', steadily adhering to 'a religious application of the inflexible rule of law to all questions concerning the power of the crown, and privileges of the subject' (Foss, *Judges*). He married Anne (d. 1785), daughter of Robert Smithson.

Denison was knighted in 1745, on the occasion of the presentation by the judges of their loyal address after the Jacobite rising, and remained in office until 14 February 1765, when he resigned on grounds of ill health. He died on 8 September 1765, and was buried in Harewood church, Yorkshire, near the tomb of Chief Justice Gascoigne. His monument is surmounted by a bust in judicial robes, and there is a painting in robes by Thomas Hudson which has been engraved in mezzotint. Denison left a useful series of judicial notebooks, which are now in the Harvard law school. Denison's wife, Anne, survived him by twenty years. As they had no children the estates passed to Anne's grand-niece, who married Edmund, the fifth son of Sir John Beckett, baronet. **J. H. BAKER**

Sources Sainty, *Judges* · J. H. Baker, *English legal MSS in USA* (1998) · Baker, *Serjeants* · Foss, *Judges* · Inner Temple, London · W. Musgrave, *Obituary prior to 1800*, ed. G. J. Armytage, 1, Harleian Society, 44 (1899) · will, PRO, E 403/2547 · R. V. Taylor, ed., *The biographia Leodiensis, or, Biographical sketches of the worthies of Leeds* (1865) · D. Lemmings, *Professors of the law* (2000), 346–50

Archives Harvard U., law school, legal notebooks

Likenesses bust, c.1765, Harewood, Yorkshire · T. Hudson, oils, Harvard U., law school · engraving (after T. Hudson)

Denison, William (1713/14–1782), merchant, born in Leeds, was the eldest son of John Denison of Old Hall, Great Woodhouse, near Leeds. He was a member of a prolific cloth-making and merchanting clan which produced four of the wealthiest commercial dynasties in late Georgian Yorkshire. Indeed the Denisons were so numerous in Leeds that compilers of genealogies and biographical notes thoroughly confused their origins and relationships. Taylor wrote despairingly (although it induced little caution): 'even to the present time the name of Denison is nearly as common about Leeds, as Smith in London, or Jones in Wales, or Campbell in Scotland, though it is rarely met with in other parts of her Majesty's dominions' (Taylor, 231). William and his two brothers, Robert (1719/20–1785) and Matthew (1725–1758), also merchants in Leeds, were the descendants of a long line of Great Woodhouse cloth makers, although their father had probably become a merchant. Certainly they boasted more prosperous kinsmen: Sir Thomas Denison (1699–1765), justice of the king's bench, and the merchant brothers Thomas (1687–1757) and Robert Denison (1689–1766), the latter mayor of Leeds in 1727 and 1737.

Almost all the evidence about William Denison's extraordinary success in becoming the senior partner of the largest and most prosperous merchant house in Georgian Leeds comes from the end of his life and is derived from two letter-books covering the years 1779–81 and the testamentary papers of him and his brothers. His schooling and early career are obscure. He was probably educated at

Leeds grammar school and doubtless served an apprenticeship in the Leeds cloth trade. He first came to prominence in the 1750s, when he refused to serve the office of mayor of Leeds on no fewer than four occasions (he had been elected to the corporation in 1750). The corporation brought a case at York assizes in 1759, settled on condition that Denison agree to pay its costs and his brother Robert act in his place. The correspondence of his last years reveal him to have been an awkward, outspoken, and influential man, immensely shrewd, immensely proud of his vast wealth and northernness. His fortune, largely self-made, appears to have been based on the export of Yorkshire cloth primarily to the Italian market. Clearly it was already substantial by the late 1750s, when he began to buy land on a large scale, a passion which by the 1770s left him with many thousands of acres scattered across Yorkshire, Durham, Lincolnshire, and Nottinghamshire.

Certainly Denison's interests were never confined to the cloth export trade. A reference in the *Leeds Intelligencer* (3 October 1773) suggests he joined Sir George Colebrooke, the well-known London banker, MP, and chairman of the East India Company, along with Josiah Smith, in a city merchant partnership. However, since Colebrooke was on the verge of bankruptcy, his affairs stretched by well-published raw material speculations, it seems unlikely that Denison would have been unwise enough to make any attempt to rescue him. If he did join him in 1773, he emerged unscathed. By the end of the 1770s, when the Mediterranean trade was at a standstill, he was dealing extensively (and unprofitably) in annuities for some of the more extravagant members of the aristocracy, buying government stock (grumbling mightily about Lord North and those government insiders who scaled down his sizeable applications—£12,000 in 1780, £20,000 in the following year), and threatening to sell some of his landed property because the returns on it were inferior to those he could make in the funds.

In 1779 Denison served office as high sheriff of Nottinghamshire with great reluctance, claiming he never spent more than a fortnight a year on his Ossington estate. On all his properties he was an exacting landlord and a keen agricultural improver, revealing a good knowledge of up-to-date farming practices and woodland management. Although he appears to have visited them each year, he was firmly based in Kirkgate, Leeds, in a house surrounded by the bustle of an industrial town, with his work and packing shops crowded into the yard behind. Short on public spirit, he was generous to the poor. In the winter of 1775–6 he provided the poor of Kirkgate with thirty loads of corn and 400 corves of coal.

Denison's brother Robert seems to have possessed a more civilized veneer. He furnished Ossington from the best London cabinet-makers; he entertained smart shooting parties there; he was painted by Francis Coates for a life-size portrait. Neither William nor Robert Denison married, and when the latter died in 1785 their enormous fortunes—the Leeds newspapers estimated William's to have been in the range of £500,000–£700,000—passed principally to their young nephew John Wilkinson, the son of their only sister, Anne. Her husband, also John, is variously described as a dyer, packer, and London factor. His direct involvement in the Leeds firm is unclear, although he clearly benefited enormously from the fortunes of his Denison brothers-in-law, and sat to Gainsborough for a full-length portrait. The younger John Wilkinson happily changed his name to Denison in 1785, settled at Ossington, brought up a large family, and sent his nine sons to Eton. They were a byword in Victorian England for their achievements—a speaker of the House of Commons (Viscount Ossington), a bishop of Salisbury, a governor-general of Australia (Sir William Thomas Denison), and 'three others, first-class men at Oxford' (Taylor, 230).

William Denison died at Bath on 11 April 1782 and was buried at Ossington. Under the terms of his brother's will, two superb life-size statues of them both were erected in Ossington church (built by Robert to John Carr's designs). They were carved by England's leading sculptor, John Nollekens, at the enormous cost of £921. The base of William's statue is a fine relief with a ship, wool bales, and sheep—a fitting allusion to his life and riches.

R. G. WILSON

Sources R. G. Wilson, *Gentleman merchants: the merchant community in Leeds, 1700–1830* (1971) · R. G. Wilson, 'Ossington and the Denisons', *History Today*, 18 (1968), 164–72 · R. G. Wilson, 'The Denisons and Milneses: eighteenth century merchant landowners', *Land and industry*, ed. J. T. Ward and R. G. Wilson (1971), 145–72 · R. V. Taylor, ed., *The biographia Leodiensis, or, Biographical sketches of the worthies of Leeds* (1865) · G. D. Lumb, *The family of Denison of Great Woodhouse and their residences in Leeds*, Thoresby Society, 15 (1909), 251–73 · R. G. Thorne, 'Denison, William Joseph', HoP, *Commons* · Burke, *Gen. GB* · will, PRO, PROB 11/1091, sig. 277
Archives U. Nott., MSS
Likenesses J. Nollekens, monument, marble, 1787 (full length), Ossington church, Nottinghamshire
Wealth at death £500,000: *Leeds Intelligencer*, 16 April 1782 · £700,000: *Leeds Mercury*, 30 April 1782

Denison, William Joseph (1770–1849), banker and politician, was born in Prince's Street, Lothbury, London, in May 1770, the only son of Joseph *Denison (c.1726–1806), a cloth merchant and banker of St Mary Axe, London, and Denbies, near Dorking, Surrey, and his wife, Elizabeth (1738/9–1771), daughter of William Butler, a hat maker of Tooley Street, Southwark. Denison's paternal grandfather had been a woollen cloth maker and dissenter in Leeds, and his father had amassed a considerable fortune in London, purchasing, in 1787, the Denbies estate in Surrey from Lord King, and also the Seamore estate, near Scarborough, from the duke of Leeds for £100,000. Little is known of Denison's early life. He spent his business career in his father's bank, Denison, Heywood, and Kennard of Lombard Street, becoming senior partner upon his father's death. The bank, which dealt in both domestic and foreign loans, prospered exceedingly under his direction, and Denison was probably among the eight or ten wealthiest British businessmen at the time of his death.

Upon the advice of George Rose, the MP and Pittite minister, Denison entered parliament, successfully contesting Camelford in 1796, and holding the seat until 1802. After unsuccessfully contesting Hull in 1802, he was elected for this seat in 1806, but failed to stand at the 1807 election. He was elected for Surrey in 1818, remaining its member until 1832; after the Reform Act he was elected for Surrey West, holding the seat until his death. He was thus a member of parliament for thirty-eight years. Although a keen supporter of Pitt recommended his entry into politics, Denison was, from the first, a staunch whig, joining Brooks's Club in 1797 and speaking regularly on behalf of the whig opposition in parliament. Denison was a strong supporter of parliamentary reform, voting in its favour in 1797 and subsequently. He was, however, opposed to the repeal of the corn laws in 1846. Denison was one of the founders of the Reform Club, and his portrait occupies a prominent place in the club's main room.

Denison also became a major landowner in Yorkshire and Surrey. He served as a lieutenant in the Middlesex Volunteers and, in 1808–9, as high sheriff of Yorkshire; he was a patron of two livings. In 1794 Denison's sister Elizabeth (d. 1861) married Henry Conyngham, third Baron and first Marquess Conyngham. Owing to the influence of his sister, a friend of George IV, Denison was offered—and declined—a peerage at some time in the 1820s.

Denison left the whole of his fortune, estimated by contemporaries at £2.3 million, to his nephew Lord Albert Conyngham (1805–1860) [see Denison, Albert, first Baron Londesborough], the second surviving son of the first Marquess Conyngham, on the condition that he alter his name to Denison. Although the younger son of an aristocrat could normally expect neither title nor estate, through this highly unusual arrangement Denison's nephew received both. In 1850 he was created Baron Londesborough, and he used his inherited wealth to add substantially to the landed acreage he inherited from his uncle. In 1883 the second Baron Londesborough owned nearly 53,000 acres in Yorkshire, worth £68,000 per annum in rental income, one of the very greatest examples of the use of business wealth to purchase land on a grand scale in modern British history.

Denison, who was unmarried, died at his home at 90 Pall Mall on 2 August 1849. He was the author of a patriotic poem on Napoleon's threatened invasion of 1803.

W. D. RUBINSTEIN

Sources HoP, *Commons* · F. M. L. Thompson, 'Life after death: how successful nineteenth century businessmen disposed of their fortunes', *Economic History Review*, 2nd ser., 43 (1990) · GM, 2nd ser., 32 (1849), 422–3 · Burke, *Peerage* [Londesborough] · d. cert.
Archives Sheff. Arch., corresp. with Earl Fitzwilliam
Likenesses W. Giller, mezzotint (after F. R. Say), BM, NPG · portrait, Reform Club
Wealth at death est. at £2,300,000 by contemporaries

Denison, Sir William Thomas (1804–1871), army officer and colonial governor, the third son of John Denison (1758?–1820), of Ossington, Nottinghamshire, and his second wife, Charlotte Estwick, was born in London on 3 May 1804. (John) Evelyn *Denison (1800–1873), Edward *Denison (1801–1854), and George Anthony *Denison (1805–1896) were his brothers. After attending a private school at Sunbury he spent four years at Eton College, and then

Sir William Thomas Denison (1804–1871), by James John Chant, pubd 1863 (after Richard Buckner)

studied under a private tutor, the Revd C. Drury. In February 1819 he entered the Royal Military Academy at Woolwich. He passed for the Royal Engineers in 1823, but did not receive his commission as lieutenant until 1826, having spent part of the interval in working at the Ordnance Survey.

Following instruction at Chatham, Denison was sent in 1827 to Canada, where during the following four years he was employed with a company of sappers in the construction of the Rideau Canal. While on this duty he made experiments to test the strength of various kinds of American timber, as a result of which the Institution of Civil Engineers voted him the Telford medal and appointed him an associate. After returning to England at the end of 1831 he served at Woolwich, and in February 1833 was appointed instructor of the engineer cadets at Chatham, where he established a small observatory. In 1835 he was appointed a member of the municipal corporation boundary commission, and the following year he was employed at Greenwich in making observations with Ramsden's zenith sector. In the autumn of 1837 he was appointed engineer in charge of the works at Woolwich Dockyard, and in 1841 was promoted captain. He worked for the

Admiralty at Woolwich and Portsmouth, and in 1842 visited Bermuda to inspect the dockyard works; in all three places he gained experience in dealing with convict labour. During these years Denison paid considerable attention to scientific and professional studies; at Woolwich he originated the publication of the professional papers of the Royal Engineers in 1837, and edited them until he left. In 1844–5 he served as an engineer on the royal commission on the health of towns, whose report was the basis of British health legislation for twenty-five years.

In June 1846 Denison was nominated lieutenant-governor of Van Diemen's Land on the recommendation of Sir John Burgoyne, inspector-general of fortifications, whom the colonial secretary, W. E. Gladstone, had asked to nominate an officer of engineers qualified for the post. Gladstone's successor, Lord Grey, confirmed the appointment, and Denison, knighted that year for his services under the Admiralty, sailed for Hobart Town on 13 October; he arrived there on 25 January 1847.

The colony was in a somewhat disorganized condition. The excessive number of convicts transported between 1842 and 1845 had caused a large deficit in the Treasury, a crisis in the convict department, and the recall of Sir John Eardley-Wilmot for his incompetent administration. Denison was told that no convicts would be sent for two years, which would give him time to reform the department (helped by a new controller, Dr. J. S. Hampton). But Grey wanted to resume transportation in 1848 and was delighted to find Denison then convinced that convict labour was desirable to undertake the public works he wanted to carry out, to relieve the labour shortage, and to keep down wages. However, Denison faced strong and growing opposition from members of the Anti-Transportation League, which he foolishly described as 'a farce'. Led by the Revd John West, whom Denison intolerantly described in a letter to Deas Thomson in Sydney as 'a dirty dog with whom no gentleman would associate' (West, xvii), in 1851 the league's supporters won every elective seat in the legislative council. However, the discovery of gold on the mainland, together with prison building and less perceived crime at home, convinced Lord Stanley's tory administration in 1852 that imperial convicts should no longer be transported to Van Diemen's Land. Denison was disappointed, but the decision removed a major source of opposition to him, and in 1854 he earned further praise by closing the much criticized penal establishment on Norfolk Island.

Denison had been criticized for high-handedness in making appointments to the legislative council, in trying to dismiss Chief Justice Pedder after the supreme court had declared the Dog Tax Act invalid in 1847, and the following year in authorizing expenditure which the legislative council had rejected. He was fortunate in that, although Grey censured him for acting 'rashly and unadvisedly', he tempered his criticism of these 'errors of judgment' by praise for Denison's 'zeal and ability' (Denison, 1.98). This he had shown in dealing with the convicts, by successfully asserting over Bishop Nixon the crown's right to nominate Anglican clergy as convict chaplains, and by establishing in 1853 a board of education to control undenominational schools. These he thought should be based on 'religious principles' but not necessarily on 'religious opinions', and they would supplement the existing denominational schools—though he was unable to persuade the legislative council to authorize local rates to pay for them. He paid great attention to the orphan school and he established local councils in Hobart Town and Launceston. When the Crimean War broke out in 1854 he ordered the construction of batteries for the defence of Hobart's harbour and trained the police to act as gunners. He continued to show an interest in science, succeeded in negotiating a union between the rival Royal and Tasmanian societies, became the patron of the new Royal Society, and contributed six papers to the first volume of the latter's journal. In the 1854 debates on the new constitution to be granted to Van Diemen's Land he criticized the prevailing 'democratic spirit' and the character of the colonists and pressed for a nominated upper house; this was rejected, but he gained agreement for a very restrictive franchise for an elective council and a not very liberal one for the legislative assembly.

On 29 November 1838 Denison had married Caroline Lucy (d. 1899), the daughter of Admiral Sir Phipps *Hornby. She accompanied him on all his postings, and over the years they had thirteen children; domestic life at Government House contrasted favourably with that of his predecessor, Sir John Eardley-Wilmot, whose conduct had occasioned gossip in Hobart and concern at the Colonial Office. But Denison's strength lay in his administrative ability, which also contrasted sharply with Eardley-Wilmot's, and it was that which brought him promotion to New South Wales, where he assumed office as governor-general in January 1855—described in his journal as 'a very great appointment for so *young a Governor*' (Denison, 1.256).

The title of governor-general of Australia which went with the governorship of New South Wales was nothing more than a name. Denison himself opposed it, and his lack of power was shown in the limited role he was able to play in the inter-colonial negotiations about tariffs, the Murray River border convention of 1855, and the subsidizing of a steam postal service to the United Kingdom. He did nothing to prevent New South Wales and Victoria adopting different railway gauges, and he opposed Lord Grey's proposals to establish a federal system in Australia, telling the secretary of state that if 'a general assembly' of the local colonies were established it 'would have nothing to do' (Denison, 1.262). But being governor of New South Wales was a different matter, and Denison retained this office until 1861. Shortly after his arrival in Sydney he had introduced the new system of constitutional or responsible government there. He did not like it, and complained on 31 October 1859 that during three and a half years he had had five sets of ministers, by whom 'not one measure of social improvement had been passed, and the only acts of importance that had stood the ordeal were those of very questionable advantage' (Denison, 1.467). He wanted to diminish what he thought were the evils of a low qualification by dividing the country into large electoral districts, each returning several members, and limiting the right of voting to one vote so as to give more scope for the representation of various interests and of property.

Denison emphatically deprecated the disposition to regard the colonies rather as an encumbrance than as a benefit to the empire. He was opposed to the formation of a colonial military force as likely to be expensive and ill disciplined, but in 1855 hastened the building of Fort Denison in Sydney harbour and installed other batteries for its defence. He was happy to send some of its imperial troops both to India during the mutiny and to New Zealand during the wars there—though he was sympathetic to the Maori grievances after his visit to New Zealand in 1857. He held that the prevention of crime was the main object of punishment, and objected to 'maudlin sentimentality' in dealing with criminals; he considered that sentences should be fully and strictly enforced, and that imprisonment should invariably, even in the case of prisoners awaiting trial, be accompanied by labour. In this, in 1858, the New South Wales government adopted his views at least partially. Denison took much personal interest in the return of the Pitcairn islanders, the descendants of the mutineers of the *Bounty*, to Norfolk Island, twice visiting it and investigating various matters connected with the well-being of the islanders. In 1856 he was created a civil KCB.

In September 1860 the imperial government decided to appoint Denison governor of the Madras presidency, and in January 1861 he left for this post. Immediately on assuming office, on 18 February, he had to consider a plan for reorganizing the Sepoy army. He thought it radically unsound, and predicted that the proposal to link promotion to length of service would lead before long to an excessive proportion of field officers, while the irregular system, depending for its efficiency on exceptional capacity in the officers, was utterly unsuitable for an entire army. Five years later he thought it had been 'in every way injurious'. He also opposed the retention of separate armies for Bengal, Madras, and Bombay, and here he anticipated a report of the Indian army commission, but the home government rejected it. He was against the establishment of legislative councils in the minor presidencies and provinces and the introduction of Indians into those councils, holding that these measures would lead to demands for representation and were not really desired by the Indians. He deprecated the cry of 'India for the Indians', and emphatically condemned 'the theory that we are acting as tutors to teach the Hindoos to govern themselves', which he characterized as 'sentimental trash'. He speedily formed an unduly low opinion of the native character. He was opposed to the recently introduced system of open competition for admission into the covenanted civil service, insisting that, above all else, officers should be gentlemen, and he disapproved of the settlement of Europeans in India, as they were likely to get into trouble with the Indians.

Denison again gave much attention to public works. He

recognized the great value of irrigation and of improved communications, although he deemed the railways being built needlessly expensive. He reorganized the public works department, and took issue with the employment of officers of the Royal Engineers on civil duties. He passed a town improvement act in 1865 and tried to promote the improvement of agriculture and the revision of the principles on which the land revenue should be assessed.

Following the death of Lord Elgin, in the latter part of 1863, Denison was called on to assume temporarily the office of governor-general; he was then able to recall an order for the withdrawal of the troops then engaged on the Sitana expedition, a measure which he thought could not have failed to affect injuriously Britain's military prestige.

Denison retired from the Madras government in March 1866. In 1868 he was appointed chairman of a royal commission to consider the pollution of British rivers, a position he held until his death, at Observatory House, Mortlake, East Sheen, Surrey, on 19 January 1871.

His abilities were solid rather than brilliant, but his great industry and unimpeachable integrity made him a distinguished public servant. A keen scientist, in Sydney he had urged the imperial government to compile a natural history of the British colonies; in Madras he wanted a natural history of India. He corresponded with Sir Roderick Murchison on geography and population. With the strong religious convictions of a fundamentalist Anglican, he decidedly rejected the theories of Charles Darwin and wrote a criticism of *Essays and Reviews* and an essay on the antiquity of man; he showed little interest in 'humane' disciplines which might have modified his severe judgements, though a tendency towards arrogance was modified in his private life, where he was warm-hearted and generous.

A. J. ARBUTHNOT, *rev.* A. G. L. SHAW

Sources W. T. Denison, *Varieties of vice-regal life*, 2 vols. (1870) · J. West, *The history of Tasmania*, ed. A. G. L. Shaw, [new edn] (1971), 200–43 · L. Robson, *A history of Tasmania*, 1: *Van Diemen's Land from the earliest times to 1855* (1983), pt 4 · A. G. L. Shaw, *Convicts and the colonies: a study of penal transportation from Great Britain and Ireland* (1966), chap. 15 · W. A. Townsley, *The struggle for self-government in Tasmania, 1841–46* (1951) · A. C. V. Melbourne, *Early constitutional development in Australia*, ed. R. B. Joyce, 2nd edn (1963), 417–32 · J. M. Ward, *Earl Grey and the Australian colonies, 1846–1857: a study of self-government and self-interest* (1958), chaps. 6, 9, 10 · R. Therry, *Reminiscences of thirty years' residence in New South Wales and Victoria*, 2nd edn (1863), 449–69 · C. H. Currey, 'Denison, Sir William Thomas', *AusDB*, vol. 4 · H. H. Dodwell, ed., *The Indian empire, 1858–1918* (1932), vol. 6 of *The Cambridge history of India* · m. cert. · d. cert.
Archives Mitchell L., NSW · NL Aus., corresp. · priv. coll. · PRO, CO 201/453–526 (NSW); CO 280/191–322 | BL OIOC, letters to Lord Elgin, MS Eur. F 83 · BL OIOC, corresp. with John Lawrence, MS Eur. F 90 · U. Durham L., corresp. with third Earl Grey · U. Nott. L., letters to J. E. Denison · U. Nott. L., corresp. with duke of Newcastle · W. Yorks. AS, Leeds, letters to Lord Canning
Likenesses J. J. Chant, engraving, pubd 1863 (after R. Buckner), NL Aus. [*see illus.*]
Wealth at death under £4000: resworn probate, Jan 1872, *CGPLA Eng. & Wales*

Denisot, Nicolas (1515–1559), French poet and tutor, was born at Le Mans, the son of Jean Denisot (*d.* 1539), bailiff of Assé and advocate in the provincial court of Le Mans. He learned the arts of engraving and cartography and produced maps of Maine and Peru. In 1540 he was a member of the entourage of Cardinal Philippe de Luxemburg at Le Mans. He also figured in a group of Le Mans poets who became involved in a literary argument between Clement Marot and François Sagon. Denisot's verses in defence of Sagon were so clumsy that his name was used by his opponents to imply that he was a fool (*sot*). Most of his subsequent works were written under a pseudonym, usually Le conte d'Alsinois, an anagram of his name. In 1545 he composed a series of religious songs, the *Noëls*. In the course of that year he left Maine for Paris, entering the service of François I where he was given a post in the household 'for his good qualities and merits' (Jugé, 42). During this period his poetic style was refined by his contact with the Renaissance poets of the Pléiade.

Between 1547 and 1549 Denisot was in England and became a tutor to the three daughters of the duke of Somerset, lord protector during the minority of Edward VI. He may have ingratiated himself by writing poems in praise of the new king and his father, Henry VIII. These survive in the British Library, in an exquisite little vellum book probably made by Denisot. On his return to France he edited a collection of Latin poems by the daughters of Somerset and a number of French poets, which paid tribute to Marguerite de Navarre, who had recently died. The following year, 1551, he brought out another edition with translations in Greek, French, and Italian by members of the Pléiade; it was prefaced by an engraving of Marguerite de Navarre by Denisot. He may have left England under a cloud; subsequently Dr Wotton, England's ambassador in France, expressed the opinion that he had forged letters and was 'a crafty child' (*CSP for.*, 1553–8, 267).

It was probably on his return from England that Denisot had been appointed valet of the chamber to Henri II. In 1553 he distanced himself from the Pléiade by publishing the devout *Cantiques du premier advenement de Jésus Christ*, which condemned both paganism and the laxity of priests. Yet he does not seem to have inclined towards protestantism. Indeed, in 1556 he was probably asked by Henri to go to Calais under the pretext of tutoring the children of the controller, again ingratiating himself by exploiting his handsome appearance and pleasing manner. He drew a plan of the town which he sent to the French king; he was identified as a spy and imprisoned but managed to escape. His efforts probably contributed to the French capture of Calais in 1558. He may subsequently have married, as his second wife, a peasant girl who assisted his escape, Michelle Mesnil; in 1567 she was involved in a dispute with his heirs over her dowry.

In 1557, under the name Théodose Valentinian, Denisot composed his largest work, *Amant resuscité de la mort d'amour*. This sentimental novel subverts the cult of carnal love in favour of the duty owed to God and Christian marriage. In September 1559 he died of a fever while residing in the faubourg St Marceau in Paris and was buried in the church of St Étienne-du-Mont. His reputation as a poet remained high during the sixteenth century but was subsequently eclipsed; he was later seen as occupying an 'eccentric' position in French literature outside the circle of Pléiade poets (Balmas, 21).

MARGARET LUCILLE KEKEWICH

Sources C. Jugé, *Nicolas Denisot du Mans (1515–1559): essai sur sa vie et ses œuvres* (Paris, 1907) • [J. C. F. Hoefer], ed., *Nouvelle biographie générale*, 13 (1855), 643 • M. Harris, *A study of Théodose Valentinian's 'Amant resuscité de la mort d'amour'* (1966) • V. Duché-Gavet, ed., *L'amant resuscité de la mort d'amour en cinq livres* (1558) (1998) • *CSP for.*, 1553–8 • E. Balmas, 'Un poeta francese in Inghilterra nel Cinquecento', *Critical dimensions: English, German and comparative literature essays in honour of Aurelio Zanco*, ed. M. Curreli and A. Martino (1978), 21–38 • G. Marcel, 'Le conte d'Alsinoys géographe', *Revue de Géographie* (1894), 1–7 [extract] • N. Denisot, *Annae, Margaritae, Janae, sororum virginum heroidum Anglarum 'In Mortem Divae Margaritae Valesiae, Navarrorum Reginae Hecatodisticon'* (1550) • É. Picot and P. Lacombe, eds., *Querelle de Marot et Sagon* (1920) • N. Denisot, *Le tombeau de Marguerite de Valois, royne de Navarre* (1551) • G. Corrozet, *Le Parnasse des poets françois* (1571) • G. Reynier, *Le roman sentimental avant l'Astrée* (Paris, 1908); repr. (1971)
Archives BL, MS Royal 12 A VII, fols. 1–34r
Likenesses portrait, Society of Agriculture, Science and Arts of the Sarthe at Le Mans

Deniz, José William [Joe] (1913–1994), guitarist, was born on 10 September 1913 at 9 Christina Street, Cardiff, the second of three guitarist sons of Antoni Francisco Deniz, formerly Diniz (1878–*c*.1931), merchant seaman, and his wife, Gertrude Blanch, *née* Boston (1886–1974); the others were Francisco Antonio (Frank) Deniz (*b*. 1912) and Laurence Richard (Laurie) *Deniz (1924–1996). A sister died in infancy and a half-brother, John, died of meningitis aged fourteen. Their father was an African from the Cape Verde Islands and their mother was Welsh, of African American and English parentage. The family's Portuguese surname, correctly pronounced Dinish, was also spelt Dennis, and although it was eventually changed to Deniz (and wrongly pronounced Denise) the two elder brothers continued to use the spelling Dennis during their early days in the musical profession.

Deniz attended South Church Street School in the bay area of Cardiff's Butetown, and sold newspapers on finishing his education. The family was musical: his mother and half-sister played piano and he learned Portuguese *fado* from his father, who played violin and guitar. He also heard calypsos played by the Bay's West Indian guitarists and African seamen and by his mid-teens was playing ukelele and Hawaiian guitar in a trio with George Glossop and Victor Parker. At Christmas, they operated as strolling players for 'rounds' and local community dances, joined by Trinidadian seaman Brylo Forde playing quatro and Don Johnson on mandolin. With his comrades he also found occasional stage jobs at Cardiff's Playhouse Theatre, then when aged twenty he went to sea as a messboy. He travelled to Russia via Norway, but was soon back in Cardiff, playing dances with his brother Frank. Because their father had died at sea, he did not want to follow a seafaring life and travelled to London to join Glossop and Parker who were working in a ramshackle Soho dive. The job was disrupted by ruffians who broke up the club, and

after a period of living rough he was forced to send for his fare home.

Deniz's mother tried to discourage him from a life in music but he was determined not to return to sea. He tried his luck in London again, and at the Nest, a favourite venue with visiting Americans, found work as a drummer. He was back on guitar in 1936 when he joined Trinidadian drummer Happy Blake at the Cuba, one of the first London nightclubs to feature a Latin-American ambience. A few casual Soho jobs followed, before he joined the new all-black band formed by trumpeter Leslie Thompson for the dancer Ken Johnson. Now, in addition to his acoustic rhythm instrument, he played the amplified Hawaiian guitar and was featured on this for the band's recording of 'My buddy' (1938). He also continued to frequent the Nest, where he met Bernard Addison, the American guitarist and Mills Brothers' accompanist, and in 1938 Django Reinhardt, his lifelong hero: from both he absorbed techniques and instrumental lore, through watching them and playing with them. Apart from a break when he joined a touring show and a short wartime period at sea, he remained with Ken Johnson until the leader's death at the Café de Paris in the German blitz on London. His leg was badly injured in the bombing of 8 March 1941, but he recovered sufficiently to join clarinettist Carl Barriteau when the latter reformed Johnson's enterprise.

Deniz reached public prominence during the war years, broadcasting and recording with clarinettist Harry Parry and his Radio Rhythm Club Sextet. Now playing electric plectrum guitar, he took part in the epochal first English public jam session of 1941, which was recorded for posterity, and became a fixture at sessions held regularly at London jazz clubs such as the Bag O'Nails and Feldman's. His most notable jazz engagements were with saxophonist Harry Hayes, violinist Stephane Grappelli, and progressive trumpeter Johnny Claes, but he also worked in such nightclub bands as Felix Mendelssohn's Hawaiian Serenaders. He was the father of Barry Laurence (surname unknown), born in 1943 or 1944. On 18 November 1943 he married Betty Madeleine Blanche Bradshaw (*b*. 1917/18), daughter of William Arthur Bradshaw, wine merchant. (The marriage was dissolved *c*.1950/1951.) The following year he joined Leslie 'Jiver' Hutchinson's All-Coloured Band but left soon after when touring exacerbated the severe ankle injury he sustained in the blitz.

A reliable rhythm player and competent soloist who switched successfully from acoustic to the electric guitar, Deniz was a stalwart of British jazz and dance music at a time when popular music was in transition. While swing music was his natural milieu, he could also acquit himself well in the post-war bebop idiom and improvising on the chord changes of a tune. Nevertheless, as the jazz climate altered, he became more comfortable playing with his brothers in the 'Latin-American' manner. Both he and Frank Deniz had visited South America with the merchant navy and this experience and their early musical upbringing attracted them to the authentic Spanish and Afro-Cuban rhythms. They formed Hermanos Deniz, sometimes with younger brother Laurie also on guitar, and while maintaining prestigious residencies at the Grosvenor House Hotel and the Talk of the Town, played music for films and recorded.

A dedicated do-it-yourself fanatic who built amplifiers for other guitarists and made his own furniture, Deniz was alert and resourceful. He remained active in musical circles after retiring in 1976, fraternizing with his former associates and recording his story for posterity. He died in the Middlesex Hospital, London, on 24 April 1994, following a stroke.   VAL WILMER

Sources J. Green, 'Joe Deniz: a guitarist from Cardiff', *Keskidee*, 1 (autumn 1986), 13–17 · *The Guardian* (3 May 1994) · J. Deniz, 'Personal call', *Fanfare* (Feb 1945), 15–17 · L. Henshaw, 'Joe Deniz', *B. M. G.: a Journal Devoted to the Banjo, Mandoline, and Guitar* (March 1946), 107 · V. Wilmer and J. Deniz, interview, BL NSA · personal knowledge (2004) · private information (2004) · b. cert. · m. cert. · d. cert.

Archives SOUND BL NSA, oral history

Likenesses photographs, 1923–50, priv. coll. · V. Wilmer, photographs, 1980–89, BL NSA

Deniz, Laurence Richard [Laurie] (1924–1996), guitarist, was born on 17 August 1924 at 7 Christina Street, Cardiff, the youngest of three surviving sons of Antoni Francisco Deniz, formerly Diniz (1878–c.1931), merchant seaman, and his wife, Gertrude Blanch, *née* Boston (1886–1974). His elder brothers were Francisco Antonio (Frank) Deniz (b. 1912) and José William (Joe) *Deniz (1913–1994). All three played the guitar.

Deniz attended South Church Street School in Cardiff's Butetown and played the piano at first, then acquired a Spanish guitar. He played this in the classical manner until he heard the great French Gypsy guitarist Django Reinhardt, but remained self-taught on this instrument apart from a few lessons from Victor Parker. For two years from the age of twelve he travelled on the variety circuit with the Harlem Pages, a group of twelve black Cardiff boys; he received educational tuition while touring, then at fourteen commenced full-time work. From seamen who lived in the docks area of Butetown he learned to play calypsos and, while continuing to hold labouring jobs, teamed up with accordionist Tony Chadgidakis to play this popular Caribbean music at pubs and for parties.

About 1942 Deniz travelled to London with Chadgidakis, a Welshman of Greek descent already familiar with the Soho milieu. They formed a cabaret act to play at bottle parties and the many clip joints that had sprung up in London's West End during wartime. They also found work together at American servicemen's dances held at United States camps, before Deniz returned briefly to Wales for a tour with Trinidadian pianist Clarie Wears. On his return to London, and in common with most black musicians based there, he was drawn into the burgeoning Latin-American scene, where having a dark skin was an advantage. He sometimes adopted the name Lorenda, and worked with the trumpeter Denis Walton and others. He also played jazz, and, until war service claimed him, toured in violinist Stephane Grappelli's band with his brother Joe Deniz on second guitar and George Shearing

on piano. Stationed in Sheffield with the Royal Army Service Corps, he drove lorries, but after nine months without playing his guitar he suffered a breakdown. He was invalided out of the army and recommenced work in Latin circles, joining Don Marino Barreto's band in which Eddie Calvert, later to be a popular figure, played the trumpet.

Deniz's association with Barreto continued intermittently during the late 1940s, but by April 1945 he had also started to make an impact in progressive modern jazz circles. He worked with the young vibraphonist Victor Feldman, then in the summer of 1946 replaced Lauderic Caton at the Caribbean Club in its eponymous trio. He then divided his time between the Latin-American outfit of Santiago Lopez and more demanding jazz work with saxophonist Buddy Featherstonhaugh and others. On 7 August 1947 he married Lydia May Wilson (1914–1991), a London-born dancer and occasional singer who subsequently worked as a nurse; she was the divorced wife of William Wilson, and the daughter of Henry Mahomet Taibe, merchant seaman. They had two sons: Laurence Anthony (b. 1949) and (Howard) Martin (b. 1951). The latter later played guitar, keyboards, bass, and drums, and was a member of the award-winning Australian rock band Max Merritt and the Meteors.

In 1949 Deniz again replaced Lauderic Caton, this time in the radical Ray Ellington quartet, a move that brought nationwide exposure. Where his predecessor excelled in providing this sophisticated group with its rhythmic drive, Deniz brought beautiful melodic guitar lines. He became a popular figure in his own right, but his period in the limelight was short-lived. The pressures of touring contributed to him becoming unwell, and after suffering two car accidents in 1950 he became severely depressed. He temporarily gave up music and opened a garage business in partnership with Douglas Ferriday, who was prominent also as a sound recordist. Nevertheless, when this venture failed, he resumed playing the guitar. In 1953 he was a featured jazz soloist at Manchester's Club 43, and he continued to develop his considerable talent for improvisation while working with the band leaders Vic Ash, Johnny Franks, and Cab Quaye. He joined his two brothers in their Latin-American group Hermanos Deniz, and his musical arrangements contributed greatly to the band's success; apart from lengthy residencies, the brothers played for American servicemen's dances and other functions. With Frank Deniz he composed background music for the film *Our Man in Havana* (1959), then in 1961 he formed his own trio.

At a time when the techniques of playing the electric guitar were still quite basic, Deniz was a progressive. In the early 1950s he experimented with lighter gauge strings than were the norm and set up his amplification carefully to avoid feedback. He also played the electric guitar with his thumb in preference to using a plectrum, more than ten years before the American guitarist Wes Montgomery surprised the guitar world by adapting this older acoustic technique to the modern instrument. Like many black British players of his generation, he earned his living in nightclubs and rumba bands, where, before the days of universal amplification, a strong rhythm was required. This way of life in no way damaged his capacity to play jazz. His worth as an improviser was well known among musicians.

Deniz continued to freelance into the 1970s until the illness which had disabled him intermittently for several years prevented him from playing. He died of heart disease at his home, 206C Shirland Road, West Kilburn, London, on 23 February 1996. He was survived by his two sons, his wife, Lydia, having predeceased him.

VAL WILMER

Sources *The Guardian* (28 March 1996) · T. Brown, 'A rehearsal with the Ray Ellington quartet', *Melody Maker* (19 May 1951) · V. Wilmer and J. Deniz, interview, BL NSA · personal knowledge (2004) · private information (2004) · b. cert. · m. cert. · d. cert. · *CGPLA Eng. & Wales* (1996)
Archives SOUND BL NSA, oral history
Likenesses V. Wilmer, photographs, BL NSA · photograph, priv. coll.
Wealth at death under £145,000: administration, 1 May 1996, *CGPLA Eng. & Wales*

Denman, Edmund (1753/4–1827), bassoonist, who was born in England, may have been a son of Edmund Denman and Elizabeth Voutron, who married at St Paul's, Covent Garden, London, in 1736 (Highfill, Burnim & Langhans, *BDA*). Nothing is known of his life before his application for membership of the Royal Society of Musicians on 1 February 1784. The deposition states that Denman had 'practic'd music upwards of seven years, is in the first troop of Grenadier Guards, plays the Bassoon, Clarinett & French Horn, is a married man, has two children, one 10 and the other 8 years old, [and he is] about 30 years of age' (ibid.). At some time before 1774 he married Margaret, with whom he had at least four children: Henry [*see below*] and James (*b.* 14 Sept 1791), who were both musicians, and two others who died in infancy. Both Edmund and Henry appear in Joseph Doane's *Musical Directory*, where, despite his declaration to the Royal Society of Musicians, Edmund is listed only as a bassoonist, while Henry appears as an organist, bassoonist, bass singer, and composer. Both are listed as participants in the Portland Chapel Society (who performed anthems, services, and oratorios at the Portland Chapel, Marylebone) and the Handel commemorations in Westminster Abbey, and the mention of a 'Mr Denman' (Burney, 18) in Burney's list of instrumental performers at the 1784 commemoration suggests that Edmund had been participating in these since their inception. He likewise participated in the annual May charity concerts at St Paul's Cathedral in 1790 and 1792–8. Significantly Doane does not list Edmund Denman as a member of the Grenadier Guards, perhaps suggesting that he had left military service by 1794.

Born on 30 April 1774, **Henry Denman** (1774–1816) was baptized at St Marylebone on 29 May. On 3 May 1795 Edmund Denman had proposed his son as a member of the Royal Society of Musicians, his deposition stating that Henry played 'the Piano Forte, Violin and Tenor [i.e. viola]', although not the bassoon or organ as mentioned by Doane. In addition it notes: 'His Engagements at present are, at Drury Lane Theatre as Chorus Singer, and at Miss Olivers school on Bloomsbury Square as a Performer on the Violin' (Highfill, Burnim & Langhans, *BDA*). His position at Drury Lane appears to have dated from 23 May 1792, when he sang in Stephen Storace's production of *Dido, Queen of Carthage*, and by 2 April 1800 he had become one of the 'principal singers' for a performance of Haydn's *Creation*. Given that the other principals on this occasion included Gertrude Elizabeth Mara, Sophia Dussek, and James Bartleman, it is clear that his voice had some merit, and Sainsbury describes him as a 'celebrated English bass singer' (Sainsbury, 1.207). From the title-pages of a number of James Hook's song collections it is clear that he also participated as a singer in the musical entertainments at Vauxhall between about 1796 and 1800.

Henry Denman seems to have been a reasonably accomplished composer. His four sets of extant sonatas are all relatively simple, while his other instrumental works include rondos based on popular melodies and *Two Grand Marches*, all for harpsichord or piano. His extant vocal works, which include *Six Glees* and several ballads, were popular but are less interesting compositionally.

On 28 February 1794 at St Marylebone Henry married Jane Burgess, with whom he had a daughter, Rose Charlotte, on 1 December 1802. About the same time the Royal Society of Musicians records note his participation as a violinist in their May charity concerts. Records of Henry Denman's later life are primarily contained within the archive of the Royal Society of Musicians, who began assisting him financially 'for relief' on 5 July 1812. By 4 February 1815 Denman was 'ill & needed medical aid' (Highfill, Burnim & Langhans, *BDA*). On 3 August 1816 he went into St Bartholomew's Hospital, and by 6 October 1816 he had died there; he was buried in London on that day, the payment of his funeral expenses of £8 being met by the society. His widow was housekeeper to the Royal Society of Musicians from 1 May 1825 to 6 August 1826, and died in 1827.

Like his son, Edmund Denman seems to have suffered from illness periodically between early 1800 and his death in London in 1827, and virtually all records of his life in this period are found in the of the Royal Society of Musicians. With the exception of his inclusion in the list of instrumentalists for the Concerts of Ancient Music in 1813, it is unclear what his musical activities were in the last third of his life. Having granted him an allowance of £5 5*s.* per month in 1807, the society altered its assistance to a pension on 1 September 1822, in which year he was aged sixty-eight, and finally his funeral expenses of £6 2*s.* were paid on 2 December 1827. CLAIRE M. NELSON

Sources C. Burney, *An account of the musical performances … in commemoration of Handel* (1785) · J. Doane, ed., *A musical directory for the year 1794* [1794]; facs. edn (1993) · B. Matthews, ed., *The Royal Society of Musicians of Great Britain: list of members, 1738–1984* (1985) · H. D. Johnstone and R. Fiske, eds., *Music in Britain: the eighteenth century* (1990) · [J. S. Sainsbury], ed., *A dictionary of musicians*, 2 vols. (1824);

2nd edn (1827) · Highfill, Burnim & Langhans, *BDA* · *Répertoire international des sources musicales*, ser. A/I, 9 vols. (Munich and Duisburg, 1971–81); addenda and corrigenda, 4 vols. (1986–99) · E. B. Schnapper, ed., *The British union-catalogue of early music printed before the year 1801*, 2 vols. (1957) · L. Baillie and R. Balchin, eds., *The catalogue of printed music in the British Library to 1980*, 62 vols. (1981–7)

Wealth at death Henry Denman; pension for widow and funeral expenses met by Royal Society of Musicians: Highfill, Burnim & Langhans, *BDA*, 4.324–5

Denman, George (1819–1896), judge and politician, was born on 23 December 1819 at 50 Russell Square, London, the twelfth child and seventh son of Thomas *Denman, first Baron Denman (1779–1854), and his wife, Theodosia Anne (1779–1852), eldest daughter of the Revd Richard Vevers, rector of Kettering. Thomas Aitchison *Denman, second Baron Denman, was his brother. He was educated first at Felsted and then at Repton School, before entering Trinity College, Cambridge, in October 1838, where he obtained a scholarship in 1840. As the son of a peer he was permitted to study classics without having to pass an examination in mathematics and distinguished himself as senior classic in 1842. He also rowed in the Oxford and Cambridge boat races of 1841 and 1842, and won the Colquhoun sculls in October 1842. He graduated BA in 1842 and was elected fellow of Trinity College on 10 October 1843. He became MA in 1854, and acted as auditor of Trinity College from 1852 to 1865.

On 19 February 1852 Denman married Charlotte, daughter of Samuel Hope, banker, of Liverpool; they had six children. Their eldest son, G. L. Denman, was appointed a Metropolitan Police magistrate in 1890.

Encouraged by his father to choose the bar as a profession Denman became a student at Lincoln's Inn in November 1843, entering the chambers of a well-known conveyancer, Peter Bellinger Brodie. In November 1844 he became a pupil of Barnes Peacock, then a junior in a large practice, staying with him until he was called to the bar at Lincoln's Inn on 24 November 1846. He joined the home circuit on 2 March 1849, and gradually acquired a practice there. During his early years at the bar he also acted as a law reporter on the staff of the *Law Journal*.

In 1856 Denman stood, unsuccessfully, as parliamentary candidate for Cambridge University as a Liberal after the death of Henry Goulburn. In the following year he was appointed counsel to the university. He became queen's counsel in 1861. At the general election in May 1859 Denman was elected MP for Tiverton as Lord Palmerston's colleague, and held the seat until 1872, except for a short interval in 1865–6. In parliament he became interested in the reform of the law of evidence in criminal trials. The Evidence Further Amendment Act of 1869, popularly known as Denman's Act, was entirely due to his efforts. This allowed witnesses of no religious belief to affirm in place of taking the oath in courts of justice, so that parties who previously could not be heard could give evidence.

On 3 May 1864 Denman seconded a motion for a select committee to inquire into the retention of the death penalty (*Hansard 3*, 1864, 174.2069). He was always in favour of enlarging the operation of the various reform bills and took an active part in the debate on the Representation of the People Bill of 1867. He also showed great interest in parliament in all questions affecting public schools and universities, and supported the University Tests Bill of 23 May 1870 (*Hansard 3*, 1870, 201.1280).

In October 1872 Denman was chosen to succeed Sir James Shaw Willes in the court of common pleas. As the son of a peer he did not accept the customary knighthood. In November 1875, by virtue of the Judicature Act, he became justice of the Common Pleas Division of the High Court. From 1881 to 1892, when he retired from the bench, he acted as judge of the High Court of Justice, Queen's Bench Division. After retirement he became a privy councillor in January 1893, and occasionally sat on the judicial committee of the privy council.

Denman was popular on the bench, but was more distinguished as a graceful scholar than as a strong lawyer. He was said to have a fine presence and a beautiful voice. From his schooldays he had found writing verses easy and continued to read Greek and Latin classics for pleasure. In 1871 he published a translation of Gray's *Elegy* in Greek elegiac verse, which he dedicated to Sir Alexander Cockburn, the lord chief justice, and in 1873 the first book of Pope's translation of the *Iliad* in Latin elegiacs, which he dedicated to W. E. Gladstone. In 1896 he printed for private circulation a translation of *Prometheus Bound* in English verse. *Intervalla*, a selection of his verses in Greek, Latin, and English, was printed for private circulation in 1898.

Denman died on 21 September 1896 at his London home, 8 Cranley Gardens, South Kensington, and was buried in the churchyard at Willian, near Hitchin. A brass was placed in the chapel of Repton School to commemorate him and a memorial scholarship founded in his name.

WILLIAM CARR, *rev.* HUGH MOONEY

Sources *The Times* (22 Sept 1896) · J. E. Sandys, *Cambridge Review* (5 Nov 1896) · G. Denman, *Autobiographical notes of George Denman, 1819–47* (1897)

Archives RCP Lond., legal opinions | UCL, letters to Lord Brougham, Lord Denman, and Sir Benjamin Brodie

Likenesses W. Walker & Sons, carte-de-visite, c.1860–1869, NPG · H. T. Wells, oils, exh. RA 1893, East Sussex county council; repro. in *Royal Academy*, 51 (1893); version, Trinity Cam. · S. Carter, oils, Repton School, Derbyshire · Lock & Whitfield, woodburytype photograph, NPG; repro. in T. Cooper, *Men of mark: a gallery of contemporary portraits*, 6 (1882), 16 · Stuff [Wright], watercolour, NPG; repro. in *VF* (19 Nov 1892) · portrait, repro. in *ILN*, 101 (29 Oct 1892), 542 · portrait, repro. in *ILN*, 109 (26 Sept 1896), 392 · wood-engraving (after photograph by J. Watkins), NPG; repro. in *ILN*, 61 (16 Nov 1872), 460

Wealth at death £12,527 7*s*. 10*d*.: probate, 24 Oct 1896, *CGPLA Eng. & Wales*

Denman [*née* Pearson], **Gertrude Mary**, Lady Denman (1884–1954), public servant, was born on 7 November 1884 at 4 Durham Villas, London, the second of the four children and only daughter of Weetman Dickinson *Pearson (1856–1927), contractor, Liberal MP, and afterwards first Viscount Cowdray, and his wife, Annie Cass (1862–1932), charitable worker and political hostess. Between attending day school in Queen's Gate, London (1894?–1897), and

Gertrude Mary Denman, Lady Denman (1884–1954), by
Bassano, 1918

finishing school in Dresden in 1901, she supplemented the
educational attentions of governesses by wide reading,
especially of books on economics and philosophy in her
father's library. Her father's business ventures frequently
took her parents abroad, and her somewhat isolated childhood fostered both an independence of mind and a shyness which she nearly always overcame by sheer hard
work, enthusiasm, and concentration. Slim and boyish in
appearance, Trudie, as she was known, was described as
characterful rather than pretty, a broken nose sustained
in childhood depriving her of claims to great beauty.

On 26 November 1903 she married Thomas Denman,
third Baron Denman (1874–1954), army officer and Liberal
peer. A son and daughter were born in 1905 and 1907, and
in 1911 she accompanied her husband to Australia on his
appointment as governor-general. The marriage was not a
success, and although remaining on friendly terms they
lived largely separate lives after their return to England in
1914.

Born to great wealth, Lady Denman believed that the
only justification for such an inheritance was service to
the community. A brief period as a member of the executive committee of the Women's Liberal Federation (1908–
10) gave her an invaluable introduction to the machinery
and business of a large organization, and throughout her
life she was involved not only in family concerns—as a director of the Westminster Press Ltd and the Cowdray Trust,
and a board member of S. Pearson & Son Ltd—but also in
numerous philanthropic activities—as chair of the
Smokes for Wounded Soldiers and Sailors Society (1916–

17) and the Cowdray Club for Nurses and Professional
Women (1937–52), as an executive committee member of
the Land Settlement Association (1934–9), and as a trustee
of the Carnegie United Kingdom Trust (1938–48). An
enthusiastic games player, she particularly enjoyed tennis
and golf, and was president of the Ladies' Golf Union from
1932 to 1938.

In October 1916 Lady Denman became chairman of the
subcommittee of the Agricultural Organization Society
which, on the suggestion of Margaret Rose Watt, had
undertaken to found Women's Institutes. On 4 October
1917 the 137 institutes transferred to the Board of Agriculture and Fisheries and she became honorary assistant director of the women's branch of the food production
department, responsible for the newly created Women's
Institute section. She insisted that the institutes must be
self-governing and on the formation on 16 October of the
National Federation of Women's Institutes she was
elected chairman, a post to which she was re-elected
annually until she retired in 1946, wishing to make way
for someone younger. She saw in the Women's Institute
movement a great opportunity for social reform; a means
for democratic training in citizenship for countrywomen,
for widening their knowledge, and for improving their
standards of life. The remarkable achievements of the
movement are the fruit of her talent for administration,
her foresight, and the principles of good procedure and
democracy on which she based its early organization.
When she died there were over 8000 institutes with a
membership of 450,000. The Women's Institute Residential College, founded in September 1948 at Marcham, near
Abingdon, Berkshire, was called Denman College in recognition of her services.

In 1930 Lady Denman helped to found and became
chairman of the National Birth Control (later Family Planning) Association, an office which she held until her
death. Having witnessed in Australia the suffering caused
to women by too-frequent childbirth, she was convinced
they should be given the means to plan their families so as
to avoid poverty and ill health. Her unstinting support for
this controversial cause needed considerable courage and
forthrightness, and she considered it to be the most difficult job she had ever undertaken.

As head of the women's branch of the Ministry of Agriculture from April 1938 Lady Denman co-ordinated the
re-establishment of the Women's Land Army, becoming
its honorary director in 1939, and lending her home, Balcombe Place in Sussex, as its administrative headquarters.
She brought to the task initiative and good sense, always
seeing the work of the land army in relation to the needs
of the nation at war, yet she realized that there were many
obstacles to be overcome and her powers of leadership
were greatly needed to reconcile conflicting demands.
She waged constant battles for proper recognition of the
land army, and succeeded in securing conditions of
employment which were of lasting benefit to agricultural
workers as a whole. However, the government ultimately

refused to award the land army the grants, gratuities, and benefits which it accorded to women in the civil defence and armed services, and she resigned in protest on 15 February 1945.

As a chairman Lady Denman excelled, her contemporaries praising her genius for organization and the impartiality, quick understanding, and sense of humour which enabled her to handle with success any meeting, however large or difficult. She could be formidable in opposition—which she enjoyed—but was fair and generous to those whose opinions differed from hers. Underlying the administrative drive, the penetrating eye in committee, the often gloriously caustic comment, and the intolerance of dishonesty, pomposity, and pretension, there was deep affection for those whose cause she championed, for succeeding generations of her own family, and for her many friends whom she welcomed to Balcombe Place.

In 1920 Lady Denman was appointed CBE, in 1933 DBE, and in 1951 GBE. Taken ill with appendicitis while on holiday in France in February 1936, mismanagement of her condition by local doctors nearly cost her her life. In early 1954 a period of ill health was traced to the displacement of an organ, a legacy of 1936, and although she survived the major operation this necessitated, her heart subsequently failed and she died at 20 Devonshire Place, London, on 2 June 1954. A memorial service was held in Balcombe parish church, although as the bishop of Chichester pointed out in his address, she personally eschewed dogma, refusing to call herself a member of the church. Her body was cremated and the ashes scattered at Balcombe Place.   TESSA STONE

Sources DNB · G. Huxley, *Lady Denman, G.B.E., 1884–1954* (1961) · *The Times* (16 April 1932) · *The Times* (3 June 1954) · *The Times* (4 June 1954) · *The Times* (8 June 1954) · *The Times* (10 June 1954) · *The Times* (14 June 1954) · *The Times* (27 Nov 1903) · N. Tyrer, *They fought in the fields: the women's land army, the story of a forgotten victory* (1996) · I. Jenkins, *The history of the Women's Institute movement of England and Wales* (1953) · R. K. Middlemas, *The master builders* (1963) · 'Denman, Thomas', *AusDB*, 8.285 · O. Banks, *The biographical dictionary of British feminists*, 2 (1990), 61–5
Archives BBC WAC, broadcast transcripts and corresp. · Denman College, Marcham, Oxfordshire (formerly in Berkshire), National Federation of Women's Institutes archives · King's Lond., Liddell Hart C., papers · priv. coll. · W. Sussex RO, papers relating to women's land army | FILM BFI NFTVA, documentary recording | SOUND BBC WAC, documentary footage
Likenesses W. Nicholson, portrait, 1909, priv. coll. · W. G. Phillips, photograph, 13 April 1910, Hult. Arch. · Bassano, photograph, 1918, NPG [*see illus.*] · E. Hodgkin, portrait, 1933, Knepp Castle · A. Devas, oils, 1951, Denman College, Marcham, Oxfordshire · photograph, National Federation of Women's Institutes, London
Wealth at death £156,481 3s. 11d.: English probate, resealed Southern Rhodesia, 1 April 1955, CGPLA Eng. & Wales (1954)

Denman, Henry (1774–1816). *See under* Denman, Edmund (1753/4–1827).

Denman, Thomas (*d.* 1500/01), physician, was of obscure origins. Although his brother, William, became a monk of Lenton Abbey, Nottinghamshire, references in Thomas's

will of 1500 to property in Easton, and bequests to religious houses in the nearby town of Stamford, might suggest that he came from Northamptonshire. However, this connection may have been forged later, in response to the needs of his patron, Lady Margaret Beaufort (*d.* 1509), who lived only a short distance from Easton at Collyweston, where Denman ended his life as a parishioner, probably so that he could remain in regular attendance as she grew increasingly arthritic.

Denman's academic background made him an appropriate choice as physician (and perhaps also astrologer) to such a learned patient, not least because the royal court favoured medical practitioners who had trained in France or Italy, where standards of medical education were generally higher than in England. On becoming a fellow of Peterhouse, Cambridge, in 1473, Denman was allowed to incept as a master of arts, because he had already graduated as a bachelor of medicine at an unspecified continental university. By 1486 he had been awarded a doctorate from the faculty of medicine at Cambridge, choosing to remain in lodgings provided by his college rather than escaping at the first opportunity to establish a more lucrative practice in London. Peterhouse had traditional connections with the Beaufort family, and Lady Margaret may have helped to support him on the understanding that he stayed in Cambridge (within a day's ride of her home). He certainly maintained a lifelong attachment to the college, becoming a senior fellow and serving intermittently between 1481 and 1494 as keeper and stationer of the loan chest (from which he himself borrowed until his medical practice made him rich as well as successful). He was rewarded for services given 'both to us and our dearest mother' by Henry VII in 1494 with a grant for life of the mastership of the London hospital of St Mary Bethlehem (*CPR, 1485–94*, 471).

The mastership of St Mary's, then the only specialist institution for the insane in England, was regarded as a sinecure, but Denman appears to have taken his duties seriously. In the event of his dying in London, he asked to be buried in the hospital chapel; and he left a gold chain and cross decorated with marguerites (which had probably been given to him by Lady Margaret) to adorn the statue of the Virgin there. On a more practical level, he bequeathed mattresses and linen for the beds and generous doles to the poor inmates.

Despite these commitments, Denman never allowed his links with Peterhouse to lapse. He was the first physician to be elected master, in 1500, possibly because of his influential connections. His death, at some time between 19 November 1500 and 17 March 1501, must have come as a blow to the fellows, although he left the college twenty of his 'better' books and various items from an impressive collection of hangings and plate. Eight of these volumes have been identified, all being conventional medical and astrological texts which betray little evidence of early years spent in a less conservative milieu. He did, however, own a commentary on Avicenna, whose works were not included in the English university syllabus. Since the fellows of Peterhouse purchased candles for his funeral, it appears that Denman died in Cambridge, where he was buried at Peterhouse, rather than in London as he had expected. He left a brother and two sisters.

CAROLE RAWCLIFFE

Sources C. H. Talbot and E. A. Hammond, *The medical practitioners in medieval England: a biographical register* (1965) · Emden, *Cam.* · M. K. Jones and M. G. Underwood, *The king's mother: Lady Margaret Beaufort, countess of Richmond and Derby* (1992) · *Chancery records* · Canterbury, Chapter Library, Cathedral Priory Register, MS F, fols. 25r–25v · T. A. Walker, *A biographical register of Peterhouse men*, 2 vols. (1927–30) · P. Zutshi, ed., *Medieval Cambridge: essays on the pre-Reformation university* (1993)
Likenesses portrait, Peterhouse, Cambridge
Wealth at death approx. £24—extensive collection of plate, books, clothing, and jewels: Canterbury, Chapter Library, Cathedral Priory Register, MS F, fols. 25r–25v

Denman, Thomas (1733–1815), man-midwife, was born at Bakewell, Derbyshire, on 27 June 1733, the second son and third child of John Denman, apothecary, and his wife, Elizabeth. After early education at the free school in Bakewell, Denman became assistant to his elder brother, who had succeeded to their father's business. In 1753 Denman went to London and began to study medicine at St George's Hospital, but within six months his savings had run out. He then decided to apply for the post of surgeon's mate in the navy. During the next nine years Denman led an adventurous life as surgeon's mate and surgeon. On leaving service in 1763, he returned to Bakewell, but he soon decided to move to London and resume his medical studies. Midwifery in particular attracted him. The male practice of midwifery had been steadily increasing since the first quarter of the eighteenth century, and many were the medical men who had made their fame and fortune in this field. Once in London, Denman continued his study of anatomy, and attended William Smellie's midwifery lectures. On 13 July 1764 Denman gained an MD from Aberdeen University. After a short but unsuccessful attempt to set up practice in Winchester, Denman returned to London, where he lodged at first with Mr Norton, apothecary in the Strand. Denman took on any job, however small, but progress was so slow that he tried to resume his previous position in the navy.

Denman was unable to procure a warrant, but he had the luck to be granted £70 a year for occasional duties as a surgeon on one of the royal yachts. This enabled him to rent a small house in Oxenden Street, off the Haymarket, which helped increase his professional visibility. His practice began to grow rapidly, boosted also by two publications that were well received in medical circles. The collection of *Essays on the Puerperal Fever, and on Puerperal convulsion* (1768) was followed in the same year by a short publication on the *Construction and Use of Vapour Baths*, which appeared in the form of a letter to Dr Huck. Denman recommended the use of an apparatus in which steam from the spout of a kettle was introduced within the envelope of blankets enclosing the patient.

As a man-midwife Denman faced strong competition in London. William Hunter enjoyed the most extensive and lucrative practice in the West End of town, and it was not until his death in 1783 that Denman was able to make

rapid progress. Denman was appointed physician–accoucheur to the Middlesex Hospital in 1769. About this time Dr Cooper, a teacher of midwifery of no great reputation, died, and Denman agreed to give lectures in conjunction with William Osborn, a fellow student at St George's Hospital. Denman and Osborn purchased Cooper's apparatus for £120 and in 1770 they began to lecture. The lectures flourished, as did Denman's business. Denman married at St James, Westminster, on 1 November 1770, Elizabeth (1747–1833), younger daughter of Alexander Brodie, an army linen-draper; they had one son, Thomas *Denman (1779–1854), who became lord chief justice of England, and twin daughters; one married Matthew *Baillie, the other Sir Richard *Croft. In 1772 Denman moved to Queen Street, Golden Square, where he lectured and practised. By 1778 he was making £600 a year from his practice and £150 from the lectures, but as he found that his income was not increasing as rapidly as he hoped, he took six pupils. In 1781 the house in Queen Street burnt down and Denman then moved to Old Burlington Street, where he lived for many years.

By the mid-1780s Denman had established his reputation as one of the leading man-midwives in London. In 1783, when the Royal College of Physicians resolved to grant a licence in midwifery, Denman was one of three practitioners who successfully applied for it. By now his practice was so extensive that he was forced to resign his post at the Middlesex Hospital. In 1791 he purchased a house at Feltham, Middlesex, and began to limit himself to consultations, while his son-in-law Richard Croft carried out the more laborious part of the practice. When Croft was established Denman moved to a smaller house in Old Burlington Street, and afterwards to Mount Street.

Denman's reputation rests on two works: *Aphorisms on the application and use of the forceps, and vectis; on preternatural labours, on labours attended with haemorrhage, and with convulsions* (1783); and *An Introduction to the Practice of Midwifery* (2 vols., 1794, 1795). The latter ran through seven editions. Denman advocated the induction of premature labour in cases of contracted pelvis. It was chiefly due to his adoption of the procedure that the practice became established in Britain long before it was accepted abroad. In cases requiring the use of instruments, Denman favoured the vectis over the forceps. This suggests that he may have been connected with John Bamber, a London man-midwife who had acquired the vectis from the Chamberlen family and kept its use a secret for a long time. Denman's use of instruments was limited, however. Like Smellie and Hunter he trusted and admired nature, arguing that too much confidence in one's dexterity and too little dependence on the natural resources of the organism caused more errors in the practice of midwifery than ignorance of the art.

Denman had a cheerful and amiable disposition. He was a well-cultivated and entertaining man, of remarkably simple habits and unassuming manners. He had a firm belief in religion and took an active interest in public charities, especially the Society for the Relief of Widows and Orphans of Medical Men. Denman died suddenly at Mount Street on 25 November 1815 and was buried in London at St James's Church, Piccadilly.

ORNELLA MOSCUCCI

Sources T. Denman, *An introduction to the practice of midwifery*, 7th edn (1832) · Munk, *Roll* · *DNB* · A. Wilson, *The making of man-midwifery: childbirth in England, 1660–1770* (1995) · *IGI*
Archives RCP Lond. · University of Kansas Medical Center, Kansas City, Clendening History of Medicine Library and Museum, lecture notes · Wellcome L., lecture notes
Likenesses stipple, 1788, Wellcome L. · W. Skelton, line engraving, pubd 1792 (after L. F. Abbott), BM, Wellcome L. · oils, RCP Lond. · stipple, Wellcome L.

Denman, Thomas, first Baron Denman (1779–1854), judge, was born on 23 February 1779 in Queen Street, Golden Square, London, the only son and youngest of the three children of Thomas *Denman (1733–1815), a distinguished physician whose textbook on midwifery was an eighteenth-century best-seller, and his wife, Elizabeth (1747–1833), daughter of Alexander Brodie, an army accoutrement maker. Denman remained close to his parents and twin sisters throughout their lives. His moral rectitude, the hallmark of his character, owed much to his mother's stern example and training (Arnould, 1.8). His biblical knowledge was built on his promise to her to read one chapter of the Bible each day, a promise which he fulfilled even during the busiest period of his life. It was she who inspired his love of music and literature. His letters reveal him constantly turning to such favourites as Shakespeare, Dante (in a translation by his son-in-law, Ichabod Wright), Byron, whose obscene conversation repelled him however, and Wordsworth. Jane Austen's *Emma*, by contrast, he dismissed as a 'very silly book' (ibid., 1.114).

Education Denman's love of the classics was just as great and his knowledge as profound. His classical education was a traditional one. From the age of three he was at Mrs Barbauld's school at Palgrave, Suffolk, and from seven at Dr Thompson's, Kensington. At the age of nine he was sent to Eton College where he remained until he was sixteen. At Eton he first expressed his ultra-liberal views, and was consequently bullied by most of his peers who were vehement Peelites or anti-Jacobins. But this ragging did not dilute his regard for the school; he sent three sons, Thomas, Joseph, and Richard, there, and presided at its 400th anniversary festival.

Denman's health was indifferent, and his father concluded that he should spend a year with his uncle the Revd Peter Brodie, rector of Winterslow, Wiltshire, before going up in 1796 to St John's College, Cambridge. At Cambridge he read 'classics and general literature'. For pure mathematics he had nothing but contempt; so, unable to take the mathematical tripos, he was debarred from competing for such major classical prizes as the chancellor's medals and left Cambridge with an ordinary degree. But unlike most 'ordinaries' he did not give himself over to idleness and pleasure. His Cambridge companions were the intellectual élite and he contributed a translation of the song of Callistratus to their *Collections from the Greek*

Thomas Denman, first Baron Denman (1779–1854), by Sir Martin Archer Shee, *c.*1832

Anthology, which Byron said was 'the best English translation' (Byron, *Childe Harold*, III.20). Cambridge strengthened his liberal views; like his father Denman venerated Fox and remained a Foxite until he died.

The Denman who left Cambridge in 1800 was no longer a sickly youth.

> His countenance was very expressive; the features high and strongly marked, but well formed and handsome, the whole face conveying an expression of sweetness combined with power. He was about five feet eleven inches in height, spare and strong in frame, capable and fond of vigorous exertion, as is proved by his having more than once while at Cambridge walked thence to London … in little more than twelve hours. (Arnould, 1.25)

He had intelligence, presence, and a mellifluous voice, which have been the hallmarks of many a successful barrister, as he was determined to be.

Early years at the bar Success at the bar came slowly. From 1800 Denman spent three years in London as a pupil successively to Charles Butler, the eminent real property lawyer, Henry Dampier, who became a judge of the king's bench, and the special pleader, William Tidd, whose pupils included John Singleton Copley (later Lord Lyndhurst), Christopher Charles Pepys, and John Campbell, all future lord chancellors. In 1803 he began practising as special pleader and a year later, on 18 October 1804, married the sister of a college friend, Theodosia Anne Vevers (1779–1852), 'a young lady rich in virtues and graces … but with little or no fortune' (Arnould, 1.42). They lived modestly on an allowance of £400 from Denman's father and on Denman's occasional articles for the *Monthly Review*, a whig magazine. Their marriage was an exceptionally happy and united one; of their fifteen children, five sons (among them Thomas Aitchison *Denman, second baron, and George *Denman) and six daughters survived to adulthood.

Denman was called to the bar by Lincoln's Inn on 9 May 1806, the same year as Campbell and two years after Copley, and joined the midland circuit and the Lincolnshire sessions. Denman claimed that on circuit he and Copley were drawn together by their 'sentiments … of extreme political Liberalism' (Arnould, 1.62). When Copley became solicitor-general in the Liverpool administration in 1819 Denman publicly accused him of apostasy, but Copley always denied ever having held radical views. Thereafter their relationship was formal—Greville once saw them shake hands 'with much politeness and grimace' (Greville, 2.331). Denman 'never could forget or forgive this dereliction of principle' (Arnould, 1.63).

Denman was never without a certain amount of practice but, like many young barristers, he had to find other means of financial support, so he turned to literary journalism; for example, he reviewed John Marshall's *Life of Washington*. However, he rejected his father's suggestion that he become, like Copley and Campbell, a law reporter; Campbell's *Nisi prius Reports* proved wrong his prediction that 'the office of reporter is much oftener a bar than an introduction to general business' (Arnould, 1.69–71). During these years his family was growing and on occasions his wife found herself 'distressed for money'. Generous to a fault, he did not number prudence and economy among his many virtues. He enjoyed the social pleasures of circuit life which first brought him into contact with Brougham, who was to become an intimate friend. His uncle, Dr Joseph Denman, died in 1812 leaving him estates in Lynn, Norfolk, and Stoney Middleton in Derbyshire. This munificent device did not immediately relieve him of his financial worries since his interest was a reversionary one. But these did not deter him from leaving 5 Queen Square in Bloomsbury and moving to 50 Russell Square, then in 'point of residence, the "ne plus ultra" of a successful barrister's ambition' (Arnould, 1.58).

Entry into parliament and Queen Caroline's trial After five years Denman's practice began to increase, but at the bar he never earned the large fees which Campbell, Scarlett, or Pollock commanded. It was his eloquent defence in 1817 of Luddites, charged with high treason, which first brought him to the attention of the whig grandees who had few able lawyers in the House of Commons. His political views were well known, and in 1818 he was brought in as the member for the close borough of Wareham in Dorset, taking his seat on 14 January 1819. But he was never a committed parliamentarian and his interventions in

debate were ponderous and uninspiring, disappointing his political patrons. In 1820, in the election following the death of George III, he was compelled to incur the considerable expense of contesting the open borough of Nottingham which, although he won the election, threw him further into debt.

1820 was for Denman a momentous year. Brougham and he were appointed respectively Queen Caroline's attorney- and solicitor-general. They were then made benchers of Lincoln's Inn, but Eldon, who never forgave them for attacking his court of chancery, refused to make either of them a king's counsel. Denman believed the queen to be 'the most wronged and insulted of womankind' (Arnould, 1.137). But, following Brougham's example, he forbade his wife to call on her, a decision which he later regretted. Soon after the queen's arrival in England Denman urged the House of Lords select committee to delay its report on the queen's conduct until the witnesses called by the Milan commission arrived in England. This was refused, and Lord Liverpool introduced a bill of pains and penalties in the House of Lords. Copley led for the crown and Brougham for the queen. Denman was the most prominent of Brougham's juniors. His final speech (24–25 October 1820), which lasted ten hours, made him a popular Liberal hero. It was histrionic, passionate, emotional oratory which moved everyone who heard it but which does not have the same impact in print. Denman made two tactless aspersions. His sarcastic parallel between Caroline and the innocent Octavia, the wife of Nero, whose servants were tortured in an attempt to prove her adultery with a slave, enraged George IV who would not hear Denman's name spoken and refused him a silk gown. It was only after Denman's memorial, denying that he intended to compare the king to Nero, and Wellington's personal intervention at the insistence of Lyndhurst, that the king relented in 1828. The future William IV, who did not conceal his belief that Caroline was an adulteress, was equally incensed by Denman's famous apostrophe addressed to him, 'Come forth, thou slanderer'; but, more magnanimous than his brother, he did not oppose Denman's appointment either as attorney-general (1830) or as lord chief justice two years later. The public loved what they saw as Denman's Hanoverian jibes, and Carlton House became known as Nero's Hotel. What passed unnoticed at that time in the packed and emotional House of Lords was his inapposite appeal to their lordships to imitate 'that Divine Authority' who would not condemn the woman taken in adultery but said 'Go and sin no more'—which prompted the epigram

Most gracious Queen we thee implore
To go away and sin no more;
Or, if that effort be too great,
To go away at any rate.

Political views Denman's popular success led to his election in 1822 as common serjeant of the City of London, defeating Bolland, later a baron of the exchequer. He was still a junior, so the stipend of £1200 as common serjeant was a most welcome addition to his income. Among Denman's papers there is an autobiographical fragment which recorded his political credo while a member of the House of Commons. He opposed the policy of repression in Ireland, and was committed to the interest of 'freedom, justice and truth', to free trade, political and legal reform, to the purgation of corruption and abuse, and above all else to the abolition of slavery in every corner of the world. Between 1818 and 1826, in a hostile House of Commons, he introduced a motion for black emancipation, supported Brougham's motion for an inquiry into slavery in the West Indies, and spoke feelingly of the plight of individuals who had fallen foul of the repressive legislation forbidding seditious meetings and blasphemous libels, two of the infamous Six Acts. Both he and Campbell supported whig motions condemning Eldon's steadfast opposition to any proposal to remove the chancery arrears or to the reform of common-law procedure. He was very anxious to soften the rigour of the bloody criminal law, attempting to secure the abolition of the death penalty for forgery and counsel for those accused of felonies. Both proposals were later to be adopted.

Denman's campaign for legal reform was conducted outside the house as well as within it. It was probably he—speaking fluent French as he did—who wrote the critical, if complacent, review-essays in the *Edinburgh Review* (40, 1824, 169–207) of Dumont's French edition of Bentham's *Traité des preuves judiciares* advocating the adoption of the French system of investigation and interrogation of witnesses. For Denman, as for Blackstone, it was a matter of pride that an Englishman enjoyed the security of trial by a lawful jury of his county. Interrogation, he argued, was unfair to the prisoner: 'the mere fact of being accused is, in itself, an overwhelming calamity to an innocent man' (*O'Connell* v. *R.*, House of Lords appeal, D. Leady). Moreover, in France the 'keen encounter of wits between judge and culprit ... have a direct tendency to degrade the dignity of justice, because they always disturb its calmness and serenity'.

Attorney-general: the Reform Bill In the election of 1826 Denman decided not to stand; his finances were not equal 'even to an undisputed election' (Arnould, 1.204). However, after he became a king's counsel his practice increased; so in 1830 he stood again, and was elected for Nottingham. Denman was saddened that Wellington, whom he personally respected, remained obdurately opposed to parliamentary reform. But Wellington soon resigned, to be succeeded by Grey. In 1831 the cabinet resolved to introduce the first Reform Bill, and Denman, who had been appointed attorney-general in the previous November, was instructed to draft its complex provisions. In his speech following the introduction of the first Reform Bill he took the opportunity to confess 'some sense of shame that he had not had virtue' to refuse the invitation to stand for the rotten borough of Wareham in 1818 (*Hansard 3*, 2, 2 March 1831, 1247). His speeches, on the second reading, were largely devoted to the refutation of the special objections to its clauses. On the dissolution of parliament, after Grey's defeat on Gascoyne's motion against the bill, Denman was returned for Nottingham unopposed.

When the Reform Bill was reintroduced the considerable burden of defending its schedules in committee fell on Denman. Like Campbell, Denman considered that the paramount question was parliamentary reform. But, also like him, he was no republican, describing himself as a 'Conservative reformer' (Arnould, 1.393).

> For to hazard all the secured benefits of an established order, from a distaste for those forms which fools alone contest; to reject the freedom which may be enjoyed under a constitutional monarchy for the purpose of an experiment ... this is a course which would no doubt deserve many other names, but certainly that of folly in a pre-eminent degree. (ibid., 1.389)

He reflected on the impact of the bill in a letter to his close friend Merivale:

> For my part I could have been well pleased to follow the great work of Parliamentary Reform with a long repose, that we may set our House in order, not as on the eve of dissolution, but to ensure its being safely and comfortably and socially inhabited. (ibid., 1.394)

In March 1832 the bill passed the Commons, only for the Lords, led by Lyndhurst, to resolve to postpone discussion of the disenfranchising clauses until the enfranchising clauses had been debated. Grey immediately resigned and Wellington was invited to form an administration. Denman's prospects were now bleak. But he wrote cheerfully to his eldest daughter that, despite the loss of the common serjeantship, which he had resigned on becoming attorney-general, and the fact that the etiquette of the bar prevented him going on circuit again, he could not doubt that he should 'hold a good station at the Bar'; his wife was not so optimistic, being a 'little hard to pacify just at first' but was now 'a very Portia' (Arnould, 1.362). Denman's fears were not realized. Wellington found it impossible to form a government, and Grey once more became prime minister. On 4 June the House of Lords passed the Reform Bill, the majority of tory peers having accepted Wellington's advice to give up the struggle.

It was not until early September 1832 that the parliamentary session ended and Denman was able to escape to the grange (or small manor house) at Stoney Middleton, near Bakewell, Derbyshire, which he had lovingly improved over the years. Some thought it unprepossessing; Wensleydale said that Denman 'must be very fond of ancestral property to like such a house' (Arnould, 1.384 n.). Denman was very tired. The Reform Bill debates had been prolonged. Moreover, he had the burden of prosecuting the agrarian and Bristol rioters and was induced to issue *ex officio* informations against William Cobbett and Richard Carlile, the atheistic publisher, who were, he considered, more guilty than the rioters, having encouraged them to violence. But he resisted royal pressure to initiate further *ex officio* informations for libels on the royal family. Shocked as he was by their content and tone, he concluded that further prosecutions might be seen by juries as an attack on the freedom of the press.

Lord chief justice of England The execution of rioters in Nottingham in January 1832 led to Denman's being vilified at a public meeting in August that year. However, at the general election following the Reform Bill's enactment he was again elected, having refused an invitation from the county of Derby. On 3 November 1832 Lord Tenterden died. On Brougham's suggestion, Grey proposed Denman as his successor and, 'after a short struggle' (*Life and Times*, 3.224), William IV assented to the appointment which was enthusiastically greeted by the profession and the press. Denman was sworn in as lord chief justice of England on 9 November 1832, and presided over that most influential common-law court for the next seventeen years.

As an advocate Denman could not be compared to Scarlett, and as a lawyer he was much inferior to Campbell and Parke. Nor was he as intelligent as his contemporaries, Lyndhurst and Brougham. But his tenure as a judge was a successful one. His relationship with the other judges was one of 'uninterrupted harmony' (Arnould, 1.420–21), the bar respected him, and the public regarded him as the personification of judicial dignity. When he took office there was a substantial volume of business in arrears in the king's bench. The exchequer was relatively moribund and the work of the court of common pleas was restricted by the fact that only serjeants-at-law could practise before it. Denman resolved to destroy what he called 'that gigantic monster called Arrear' (ibid., 1.423). He did so by working 'like a dragon' (ibid.) and requiring the court to sit from early in the morning until late in the evening; remarkably he did so without alienating either the profession or their clients. Denman was a distinguished trial judge. Although he quickly reached a decision, he had the capacity '[to wind himself] up to the state of patience and quiet which alone can guide [him] through [the heavy calendar] with the least possible annoyance' (ibid., 2.140). He was impartial and unfailingly courteous. Like Lyndhurst, Denman was a judge for the parties, fair, scrupulous, and temperate.

Greville's judgement was very different. He wrote in his journal that Denman was a 'very bad judge but much respected' (Greville, 2.331). It is true that he left few memorable judgments. Denman thought that his reputation as a lawyer would depend on his judgment in *Stockdale* v. *Hansard* in 1839, which the distinguished American judge and jurist Joseph Story had praised (Arnould, 2.110–11). The court of king's bench held that the existence of a privilege claimed by either of the houses of parliament and, in particular, the House of Commons was a matter of law for the courts and was not determined by a resolution of either house. To decide otherwise would make the judge 'an accomplice in the destruction of the liberties of his country, and expose every individual who lived in it to a tyranny no man ought to submit to'. 'In truth, no practical distinction can be drawn between the right to sanction all things under the name of privilege, and the right to sanction all things whatever, by merely ordering them to be done'. Denman never forgave Campbell, then attorney-general, for his intemperate expression of disapproval and portrayal of Denman as a vainglorious champion of the people.

In *O'Connell's case* Denman joined Cottenham and Campbell in quashing O'Connell's conviction for conspiracy and sedition. They upheld two objections to the validity of the sentence, rejecting the advice of the great majority of the judges. Some of the counts in the indictment were bad. Moreover, the omission of names from the list of jurors was fatal. If this latter objection were rejected, 'trial by jury itself, instead of being a security to persons who are accused, will be a Mockery, A Delusion and a Snare'. The reports contain other well-known judgments: for example, *Eastwood* v. *Kenyon* (1840), which established that moral consideration was not consideration necessary to found a binding contract; and *Williams* v. *Carwardine* (1833), which held that the motive for an act which amounts to an act of acceptance in law of an offer to contract is immaterial.

Denman as a law reformer In 1834 Brougham persuaded Grey to strengthen the judicial membership of the House of Lords. Denman was the obvious candidate; on 22 March his title was duly gazetted as Baron Denman of Dovedale. His belief in the rights of the individual was one of the moral principles central to his life. Unlike Lyndhurst, Denman was not a man who would sacrifice principle for party dogma. After the passing of the Reform Bill, he wrote:

> The greatest of all political evils I have always thought was this—injustice deliberately perpetrated or wilfully persisted in by the State. My own opinion has uniformly been that injustice and wrong, whenever detected, ought to be instantly swept away. Like everything that prevails, it will by degrees strengthen itself by inveterate habits and factitious interests … Let, then, the first moment be taken when you can bring a sufficient force to bear upon mischief. Shake off the bad principle while you may, and scan not too nicely the inconsistencies or even dangers that may result from the success of your exertions. (Arnould, 1.388–93)

He was alive to the connection between ignorance and crime, and 'doubted how far the State was justified in inflicting punishment for offences against which it had taken no means to guard' (*Hansard 3*, 27, 21 May 1835, 1335). In order to 'shake off bad principle' he was ready to support tory bills for the repeal of the Test Acts and the passing of the Catholic Emancipation Bill.

Denman and Lyndhurst persuaded the House of Lords to pass, despite the opposition of most of the judges, Campbell's Prisoners' Counsel Act of 1837 which allowed counsel for a person accused of felony to address the jury and the accused to inspect and take copies of the deposition against him. Its 'practical execution' was essential for 'the honour of the laws, for the due administration of justice, for the realisation of truth, and for the protection of innocence' (*Hansard 3*, 34.760–78); and in the same year a bill abolishing the death penalty for all cases of forgery passed through both houses—two measures which he had fought for when first elected to the House of Commons. In 1838, this time supported by his fellow judges, Denman unsuccessfully sought to persuade the house to allow witnesses to affirm instead of taking the oath; he thought a witness should be sworn according to the form which was binding on his conscience. The Law of Evidence (Amendment) Act of 1842 which Denman introduced embodied the Benthamite principles that all interested persons should be allowed to give evidence, leaving it to the jury to estimate its value. In 1841, moved by the appeal of Caroline Norton, Denman supported the Custody of Infants Bill which gave a wife separated from her husband access to her children. Denman was one of the few whig peers to attack the government over its treatment of Mazzini, who was said to be a dangerous foreigner, spreading sedition. His letters had been opened at the Post Office under the warrant of Peel's home secretary, Sir James Graham. In the debate in 1844 Denman condemned that so-called right as 'new, and … dangerous and utterly unknown to the people of England'. It is no surprise that Denman supported every Liberal measure. What is surprising is that he regarded his successful proposal that the courts could sit *in banco* outside the brief legal terms as so significant that he asked for it to be recorded on his tombstone.

Campaign against the slave trade The abolition of all manifestations of the slave trade was, for Denman, the most important of reforms. Slavery was 'the foulest stain that ever rested on the character of the country' (*Hansard 3*, 3, 1831, 1408–96). His first major speech in the House of Lords was in the debate on the Bill for the Better Suppression of the Slave Trade of 15 August 1839. Before speaking he was in a 'state of the utmost anxiety' (Arnould, 2.101), as he always was when he spoke on slavery. The bill gave the crown power to seize vessels suspected of engaging in the slave trade. Denman dismissed fears that this would lead the country into war with France. Suppression of the slave trade must be a fact as well as a name: 'There must be a right of visitation and search'. It was true that mistakes would inevitably be made by raiding parties; therefore it was necessary to 'indemnify the officers of Her Majesty in the discharge of the duty imposed on them' (*Hansard 3*, 50.331–4). The judgment in *R. v. Serva* in 1845 shocked him. The *Felicidade* was a slave-trading vessel, whose crew had killed a boarding party from a Royal Navy cruiser and had been convicted of murder. But the judges gathered to consider crown cases concluded that their convictions could not stand. Denman and Baron Platt dissented. The majority gave no reasons for their decision, and in a pamphlet Denman proposed that in future they should do so.

Denman's son, Joseph, became the captain of a similar cruiser on the west African coast. He had released slaves from, and set fire to, barracoons where they had been incarcerated. Captain Denman was unsuccessfully sued for the loss suffered by the slave owner. The court of exchequer held that, although the slave owner had property in his slaves and could sue in trespass for their seizure, the ratification by the ministers of state of Captain Denman's act rendered it an act of state, for which the crown alone was liable. Denman bitterly commented that it was the first time that the claim of an owner of slaves had been recognized in an English court of justice.

Denman sensed with alarm that many politicians and members of the public were becoming antipathetic to the anti-slavery movement. The Sugar Duties Bill of 1846 proposed to equalize the duties on British colonial and slave-produced sugar. Denman spoke fervently against it, arguing that its enactment would increase the slave traffic. But the appeal to free trade prevailed and the bill reached the statute book. In 1848 a committee of the House of Commons, chaired by Benjamin Hutt, who had slave-trading interests, concluded that the posting of naval squadrons was ineffectual and counter-productive, increasing the suffering of black people. The slave trade should be left to itself. On 22 and 28 August Denman made two powerful speeches in the house which swayed public opinion and significantly contributed to the decision not to withdraw the squadrons. Denman's speeches on the slave trade were highly emotional, and he admitted that it was 'utterly impossible to talk of slavery and the Slave Trade with any degree of moderation,—or indeed with any other feeling than that of the most perfect abhorrence' (*Hansard 3*, 88, 1848, 511). Anxious to appeal to the country, he published a number of pamphlets, including *The Slave Trade and the Press*, published anonymously in 1847, and *Letters to Lord Brougham on the Extinction of the Trade* (1848).

Final years In 1849 Denman was seventy. On circuit and in London he sat very long hours in court; twelve-hour sittings were frequent. The strain was great and he suffered his first stroke the day before the beginning of the Easter term. But, ignoring medical advice, he was determined to sit in the Trinity term and to speak in the house, not only on the slave trade (which his doctors knew would excite him), but also on the motion to enable witnesses who had religious scruples to affirm rather than to take the oath. But the house again rejected the motion. In July 1849 Denman suffered his second stroke. He could now barely sign his name. Friends, including Brougham, and the eminent physicians, Sir Benjamin Brodie and Dr Thomas Watson, urged him to resign. But the prospect of Campbell succeeding him increased his determination to struggle on. Campbell's bitter attack on his motives in deciding *Stockdale v. Hansard* still rankled ten years later. But Denman was mollified by the letter of Russell, the prime minister: 'No one can be more persuaded than I am that in the decisions given on Privilege, as in all other cases, none but a conscientious sense of duty was allowed to prevail'. Russell concluded with an assurance that Denman's name stood as a

> model of uprightness and independence in the judicial office. If, as I infer, you are about to resign, it would surely be better to carry an undivided homage with you into retirement than to raise a question as to your successor, in which many may think you right, but many others may think you wrong. (Arnould, 2.290–91)

In March 1850 Denman resigned.

For a short period Denman's health improved. In a letter to Brougham, later published in the *Law Review*, he chided his judicial brethren for their reluctance to embrace reform and their belief in the perfection of the legal system, 'whereas in truth the existing system is for the most part the neglected growth of time and accident' (Arnould,

2.319–21). His final speech in the house, in May 1852, supported Truro's Common Law Procedure Bill. The 'one subject and one subject only, beyond the limits of his private grief [the death of his wife]' which 'had still power to move him deeply … was the terrible, ever-haunting subject of slavery and the slave trade' (ibid., 2.332). The publication in England of Harriet Beecher Stowe's *Uncle Tom's Cabin* aroused Denman's pity and horror. It led him to attack bitterly, through a series of articles in *The Standard*, his old friend Dickens, for his caricature of philanthropy run mad, personified by Mrs Jellaby in *Bleak House*, which he believed would undermine the anti-slavery movement. Dickens realized that Denman was a sick man, and wrote to his daughter, Margaret (Mrs Cropper), to say that he had 'cleared [his] mind of Lord Denman's last opinions of me' (ibid., 2.333).

Denman never recovered from his wife's death on 28 June 1852, and his final stroke occurred in Nice in early December of the same year. He comprehended what was said to him, but he would never speak again and could copy only what others had written. Denman died on 22 September 1854 at Stoke Albany, Northamptonshire, and was buried in the churchyard there.

GARETH H. JONES and VIVIENNE JONES

Sources J. Arnould, *Memoir of Thomas, 1st Lord Denman*, 2 vols. (1873) · Holdsworth, *Eng. law*, vol. 15 · E. W. D. Manson, *The builders of our law*, 2nd edn (1904) · Foss, *Judges* · C. C. F. Greville, *A journal of the reign of King George IV and King William IV*, ed. G. G. Moore, 2 vols. (1875) · E. Foss, *Biographia juridica: a biographical dictionary of the judges of England … 1066–1870* (1870) · D. Le Marchant, *Memoir of John Charles, Viscount Althorp, third Earl Spencer*, ed. H. D. Le Marchant (1876) · *The life and times of Henry, Lord Brougham*, ed. W. Brougham, 3 vols. (1871) · *The Times* (27 Sept 1854) · *EdinR*, 40 (1824) · *Hansard 3* (1831), 2.1247, 3.1408–96; (1835), 27.1335; (1836), 34.760–78; (1839), 50.331–4; (1848), 88.511 · W. Ballantine, *Some experiences of a barrister's life* (1873)
Archives Derbys. RO, letters · Lincoln's Inn, London, judicial papers · NRA, priv. coll., corresp. | BL, corresp. with Lord Holland, Add. MS 51813 · Glamorgan RO, Cardiff, corresp. with Lord Lyndhurst · PRO, corresp. with Lord John Russell, PRO 30/22 · W. Sussex RO, letters and papers relating to Queen Caroline and legal career · W. Sussex RO, letters to duke of Richmond
Likenesses M. A. Shee, oils, c.1832, NPG [*see illus.*] · J. E. Jones, marble bust, exh. RA 1845, Lincoln's Inn, London · J. Doyle, pen and pencil drawing, c.1851, BM · W. Walker, mezzotint, pubd 1852 (after E. U. Eddis), BM, NPG · T. Barber, oils, Castle Art Gallery, Nottingham · J. J. Halls, oils, NPG · G. Hayter, group portrait, oils (*The trial of Queen Caroline, 1820*), NPG · G. Hayter, pen and wash drawing, NPG · T. Hodgetts, mezzotint (after T. Barber), BM, NPG · D. Wilkie, group portrait, oils (*The first council of Queen Victoria, 1837*), Royal Collection · marble bust, Eton

Denman, Thomas Aitchison, **second Baron Denman** (1805–1894), politician, born in London on 30 July 1805, was the first son of Thomas *Denman, first Baron Denman (1779–1854), and his wife, Theodosia Anne (1779–1852), the eldest daughter of Richard Vevers, rector of Kettering. George *Denman was his brother. He was educated at Eton College and at Brasenose College, Oxford. He matriculated on 17 May 1823. He was called to the bar at Lincoln's Inn in 1833, and for eighteen years acted as associate to his father as chief justice of England.

Denman succeeded to the peerage on the death of his father on 22 September 1854. He was always concerned rather with politics than law. During his long life as a peer he was a regular frequenter of the House of Lords, but won notoriety rather from his eccentricities than any eminent qualifications. Though described by Dod as a Liberal until 1884, he frequently voted against major Liberal bills. Limitation of the duration of speeches in the House of Lords and the granting of female suffrage were subjects to which he unsuccessfully devoted his support. Year after year with unfailing regularity, from 1886 to 1894, he brought in bills to secure these objects, and, despite his inability on any occasion to secure even a second reading, he was not deterred from making fresh efforts in each succeeding year.

Denman married, on 12 August 1829, Georgina, eldest daughter of Thomas Roe; she died on 25 April 1871. He then married, on 10 October 1871, Maria, the eldest daughter of James Aitchison of Alderston, co. Haddington, and by royal licence on 20 December 1879 assumed the additional surname of Aitchison under the will of his wife's mother. With neither of his wives had he any children. He died of heart failure at the King's Arms, Berwick upon Tweed, on 9 August 1894 and was buried at Alderston.

WILLIAM CARR, *rev.* H. C. G. MATTHEW

Sources GEC, *Peerage* · *The Times* (11 Aug 1894)
Archives U. Nott. L., letters to Em Wrench
Likenesses Walton, lithograph · wood-engraving (after photograph by J. Horsburgh), NPG; repro. in *ILN* (18 Aug 1894)
Wealth at death £11,831 15s. 10d.: probate, 24 Dec 1894, *CGPLA Eng. & Wales*

Denne, Henry (1605/6?–1666), General Baptist minister and religious controversialist, was born at Well, Ickham, in Kent, the son of David Denne, gentleman. He matriculated at Sidney Sussex College, Cambridge, in 1621, graduated BA in 1625, and proceeded MA in 1628. At an unknown date he married Roberta, whose surname is unknown; they had four sons and a daughter. After ordination in 1630 at St David's Denne was curate at Pirton, Hertfordshire, for about ten years. Latterly Denne's disputatious printed works led to controversy with other ministers. His *Grace, Mercy, and Peace* (c.1640) and *Seven Arguments to Prove … God Doth Justifie his Elect* (1643), evoked a charge of antinomianism from 'D. H.' in *An Antidote Against Antinomianism* (1644). His visitation sermon at Baldock, Hertfordshire, on 9 December 1641, critical of fellow clergy (*The Doctrine and Conversation of John Baptist*, 1642, to which was added *A Conference between a Sick Man and a Minister*), brought similar charges from Thomas Rotherham in *A Den of Theeves Discovered* (1643) and Samuel Rutherford in *A Modest Survey* (1648). The heresiographer Thomas Edwards also considered Denne 'a great Antinomian, a desperate Arminian' (*Gangraena*, 1645, 1.76).

By 1643 Denne had adopted Baptist views and joined the Bell Alley General Baptist Church in London under the ministry of Thomas Lamb the soap boiler and future Leveller. The church sent Denne as an evangelist into Bedfordshire, Cambridgeshire, and Huntingdonshire, where he established congregations at Fenstanton and Warboys. He was presented to the living at Eltisley, Cambridgeshire, probably in 1643, by the family of Major-General John Desborough, the brother-in-law and associate of Cromwell. In the following year, however, the Cambridge committee for providing preaching ministers had him imprisoned for preaching against infant baptism, but he was removed to London, detained at the Peter-house (Lord Petre's house in Aldersgate Street), and released. In spite of his experience, Denne's *Antichrist Unmasked in Two Treatises* (1645), included not only *The Man of Sin Discovered*, who was said to fill English pulpits, but also *The Foundation of Christian Baptism Discovered and Rased*, which attacked paedobaptist works by Stephen Marshall and Daniel Featly, a fellow detainee at Peter-house.

In 1645 Denne preached in London and at Rochester, Chatham, and Canterbury in Kent, and the next year he was arrested in Spalding, Lincolnshire, for baptizing four persons in the river. On this occasion he identified his home as at Caxton near Eltisley and admitted to preaching four times, but not baptizing, at Spalding. In 1646 he added *The Drag-Net of the Kingdome of Heaven* to his earlier work to produce *Antichrist Unmasked in Three Treatises*. Denne's argument in *Drag-Net* that Christ died for all, and his use of the New Testament concept of 'light' have been seen as advancing the Quaker doctrine of the inner light two years before George Fox did, but this now appears doubtful.

In 1647 Denne joined the parliamentary army as cornet in Colonel Adrian Scrope's regiment of horse. He participated with Levellers in the mutiny of May 1649, marching from Salisbury to Burford, where Cromwell crushed the uprising. Denne and three others were to be executed, but upon his recantation he was spared. As with his earlier release from Peter-house, Denne's association with the Desboroughs perhaps contributed to his pardon. In *The Levellers Designe Discovered* (1649) he criticized impetuous actions of mutinous Levellers who then responded by denouncing 'the most Trayterous assertions' of 'that wretched *Judas Den*' (*The Levellers … Vindicated*, 1649, 8). By 1653 Denne was again active at Fenstanton but the next year was sent by the congregation to live and minister in Canterbury at the request of Baptists there. In London in 1658 he publicly debated with Peter Gunning on infant baptism, but also displayed wider concerns. In *The Quaker No Papist* (1659) he came to the defence of Friends, arguing against Cambridge University librarian Thomas Smith (who later rebutted him in *A Gagg for the Quakers*, 1659) that they were papists because they refused oaths. Denne also defended John Bunyan's right to preach and urged greater toleration for Roman Catholics. Finally, in *An Epistle Recommended to All the Prisons* (1660) he argued that Christians could lawfully take oaths and thus many needlessly languished in prisons, provoking counter-arguments from the Baptist Henry Adis in *A Fanaticks Testimony Against Swearing* (1661) and the Quaker Samuel Fisher in *One Antidote More* (1660).

Denne was among thirty Baptist signatories to *The Humble Apology* (1661) denouncing Venner's Fifth Monarchist rebellion. He eventually settled in Rochester where in 1666 he died and was buried at St Margaret's Church. His will of 1 June 1666, which gives his age as sixty-one, provided 1s. for each of twenty poor widows, 10s. to his oldest son John (church elder at Fenstanton), 5s. to each of John's four children, 10s. to each child of Denne's deceased son, David, £100 and half his goods to his wife, and his books to his youngest son, Thomas, who was named executor. As a Church of England priest turned Baptist, Denne had, with unusually broad sympathies, supported some of the principles or practices of Levellers, Quakers, and Roman Catholics, and in such a manner as to justify his own conclusion of 1645 that 'The Lord hath sent me *as* a man of contention' (*The Man of Sin Discovered*, A2v). His epitaph, however, read only:

> To tell his wisdom, learning, goodness, unto men,
> I need to say no more; but, Here lies Henry Denne.
> (Taylor, 1.222)

T. L. UNDERWOOD

Sources T. Crosby, *The history of the English Baptists, from the Reformation to the beginning of the reign of King George I*, 4 vols. (1738–40), vol. 1 · A. Taylor, *The history of the English General Baptists*, 1: *The English General Baptists of the seventeenth century* (1818) · E. B. Underhill, ed., *Records of the Churches of Christ, gathered at Fenstanton, Warboys, and Hexham, 1644–1720*, Hanserd Knollys Society (1854) · Venn, *Alum. Cant.* · PRO, PROB 11/321, fol. 17v · T. L. Underwood, 'The Baptist Henry Denne and the Quaker doctrine of the inner light', *Quaker History*, 56 (1967), 34–40 · J. Ivimey, *A history of the English Baptists*, 4 vols. (1811–30), vols. 1–2 · Greaves & Zaller, *BDBR* · A. C. Underwood, *A history of the English Baptists* (1947) · B. R. White, *The English Baptists of the seventeenth century* (1983) · D. Neal, *The history of the puritans or protestant nonconformists*, trans. J. Toulmin, new edn, 2–3 (1837) · M. Spufford, *Contrasting communities* (1974) · M. Tolmie, *The triumph of the saints: the separate churches of London, 1616–1649* (1977)

Wealth at death £103 plus goods: will, PRO, PROB 11/321, fol. 17v

Denne, John (1693–1767), Church of England clergyman and antiquary, was born on 25 May 1693 at Littlebourne, Kent, the eldest son of John Denne, woodreeve to the see of Canterbury. He was educated at the grammar school, Sandwich; the King's School, Canterbury; and at Corpus Christi College, Cambridge, whence he matriculated in 1709. He graduated BA (1713), MA (1716), and DD (1728). He was tutor and fellow of his college from 1716 to 1721. Following ordination in 1716, he was presented to the perpetual curacy of St Benedict's Church, Cambridge. In 1721 he became rector of Norton by Daventry, Northamptonshire, exchanging that living in 1723 for the vicarage of St Leonard, Shoreditch.

In 1724 Denne married Susannah (1703–1780), youngest daughter of Samuel *Bradford (1652–1731), bishop of Rochester, to whom he was domestic chaplain for many years. They had three children: John (d. 1800), chaplain of Maidstone gaol; Samuel *Denne (1730–1799), the antiquary; and Susannah. While Denne was vicar St Leonard's was rebuilt by George Dance, between 1736 and 1740. From 1725 to 1728 Denne delivered (but did not publish) the Boyle lectures. In 1728 he was appointed archdeacon and prebendary of Rochester and was vicar of St Margaret's, Rochester, until 1731 when he resigned for the rectory of St Mary, Lambeth, which he held until his death. He was for some time prolocutor of the lower house of convocation.

As an antiquary Denne arranged and bound up the archives of Rochester Cathedral and the acts of the courts of the bishop and archdeacon. He collated Hearne's edition of the Textus Roffensis with the original at Rochester. He compiled 'A history of the chancellors of the diocese of Rochester' and made collections for a history of the cathedral, including transcribing from the registers entries of burials from over 100 years. Manuscripts relating chiefly to Rochester made by him and continued by his son Samuel Denne were rescued from destruction when purchased by the British Museum in 1841 (BL, Add. MSS 11819–11826). Denne was especially learned in ecclesiastical history and contributed materials to John Lewis's *The History of the Life and Sufferings of John Wicliffe* (1720). He published three other historical works and fifteen sermons, including *The Blessing of a Protestant King and Royal Family to the Nation* (1727). Having suffered from ill health since 1759, he died on 5 August 1767 at Rochester and was buried in the cathedral there. W. W. WROTH, *rev.* JOHN WHYMAN

Sources A. Winnifrith, *Men of Kent and Kentish Men: biographical notices of 680 worthies of Kent* (1913), 152–3 • E. Hasted, *The history and topographical survey of the county of Kent*, 2nd edn, 4 (1798), 153 • E. Hawkins, 'Notes on some monuments in Rochester Cathedral', *Archaeologia Cantiana*, 11 (1877), 1–9, esp. 7 • W. B. Rye, 'The ancient episcopal palace at Rochester, and Bishop Fisher', *Archaeologia Cantiana*, 17 (1887), 66–76, esp. 66 • A. A. Arnold, 'The chancellors of the diocese of Rochester', *Archaeologia Cantiana*, 24 (1900), 160–74, esp. 160 • A. W. B. Messenger, 'Rochester Cathedral heraldry before AD 1800', *Archaeologia Cantiana*, 39 (1927), 113–29, esp. 115, 120 • F. W. Cook, 'A few letters from my scrapbook chiefly of Kentish historians', *Archaeologia Cantiana*, 48 (1936), 1–10, esp. 2 • Nichols, *Lit. anecdotes*, 1.590, 694; 3.213, 524–8, 531; 6.388, 454; 8.218; 9.297 • Nichols, *Illustrations*, 4.610–18; 6.782–9 • *GM*, 1st ser., 37 (1767), 430 • *GM*, 1st ser., 69 (1799), 723 • Venn, *Alum. Cant.* • H. Ellis, *The history and antiquities of the parish of St Leonard, Shoreditch, and liberty of Norton Folgate* (1798) • A. Chalmers, ed., *The general biographical dictionary*, new edn, 32 vols. (1812–17) • J. S. Sidebotham, *Memorials of the King's School, Canterbury* (1865), 55, 56

Archives BL, papers relating to ecclesiastical affairs, Add. MSS 11819–11826 • Bodl. Oxf., papers, mainly relating to Rochester Cathedral | SOAS, corresp. with Society for Promoting Christian Knowledge

Denne, Samuel (1730–1799), antiquary, was born at the deanery, Westminster, on 13 January 1730, the second of the two sons of John *Denne (1693–1767), archdeacon of Rochester and antiquary, and Susannah Bradford (1703–1780). He was educated at Streatham and at the King's School, Canterbury, and was admitted to Corpus Christi College, Cambridge, in 1748; he graduated BA in 1753 and MA in 1756. In 1754 he was presented to the vicarage of Lamberhurst in Kent, but he resigned the living in 1767 when he became vicar of the parishes of Wilmington and Darenth, both near Dartford. In 1783 he became a fellow of the Society of Antiquaries.

Denne was described in his obituary as a 'loyal son', and demonstrated this loyalty in maintaining his father's interest in antiquarianism. His first publication on the subject in 1772 was a history of Rochester and its environs, which was published by the local bookseller Thomas Fisher, but to which Denne contributed most of the content. He also assisted Fisher in his revision of the *Kentish Traveller's Companion*. Denne senior had at one time been vicar of St Leonard, Shoreditch, and Samuel continued the family interest in the parish of Shoreditch, providing Henry Ellis with considerable assistance in his parochial history. He also maintained the family connection with Lambeth, of which his father had been rector, with his *Historical Particulars of Lambeth Parish and Lambeth Palace*, published in 1795. In addition he made significant contributions to other publications, notably John Thorpe's *Custumale Roffense*, Richard Gough's *Sepulchral Monuments*, the *Bibliotheca Topographica Britannica*, and the *Illustrations of the Manners and Expences of Antient Times in England* (1797). He corresponded regularly with the *Gentleman's Magazine* using the signature W & D (Wilmington and Darenth) and was a prolific contributor of papers to the Society of Antiquaries, many of which were published in *Archaeologia*, notably on the introduction of arabic numerals, on water marks, and on stone fonts in England. Like many other antiquaries of his time he entertained a keen interest in Anglo-Saxon antiquities and literature, but was handicapped by having no real command of the language. Denne was somewhat pedantic and not an original thinker but his interests were diverse and wide-ranging.

Denne appears as a somewhat lonely figure (he never married) and clearly drew immense pleasure from his antiquarian researches and the contacts it brought him with like-minded people. Settled in rural Kent, he felt isolated and often complained of the lack of antiquarian interest in the local town of Dartford. His correspondence with other antiquaries and in particular with his fellow 'Benedictine', Richard Gough, was something of an intellectual lifeline. His circle also included the other Kentish antiquaries William Boys, John Thorpe, and John Latham, but he rather disapproved of the county's historian Edward Hasted whose private life and publications, in Denne's view, both left something to be desired. He was close to his family, particularly his brother and sister. The former, chaplain of the gaol at Maidstone, suffered periods of mental instability from 1777, which Denne blamed on his having to cope with the insurrection at Maidstone gaol, when the prisoners attempted to blow it up. He was very supportive of both him and his sister-in-law, and when she died in 1798 he estimated that he had written over a thousand letters to his brother to amuse him. His brother's experiences as chaplain may account for Denne's own interest in prison reform, which formed the subject of a letter to Sir Robert Ladbroke published in 1771. To his sister, Susannah, who had lived with him, he left his entire estate when he died. In politics he professed great admiration for Walpole, bitterly regretted the loss of the American colonies, and was fiercely critical of the prosecution of the war against France during the 1790s. He appears to have performed his duties as vicar conscientiously and his obituary described him as devoted to the poor and needy of his parish.

Denne died on 3 August 1799, at Wilmington, in his library, having suffered from a bilious complaint for over forty years, and was buried near his father in the south transept of Rochester Cathedral on 10 August.

R. H. SWEET

Sources *GM*, 1st ser., 69 (1799), 722–3 · Nichols, *Lit. anecdotes*, 3.528–31 · Nichols, *Illustrations*, 6.609–787 · Bodl. Oxf., MS Gough Gen Top 39 · BL, Egerton MS 926 · J. S. Sidebotham, *Memorials of the King's School, Canterbury* (1865), 69 · *DNB* · IGI
Archives BL, papers and list of sermons, Add. MSS 11819, 11826 · Bodl. Oxf., incomplete copy of his history of Rochester with MS additions and corrections | BL, letters to Sir Henry Ellis, Add. MS 38626 · BL, letters to Thomas Fisher, Egerton MS 926 · Bodl. Oxf., corresp. with John Charles Brooke · Bodl. Oxf., corresp. with Richard Gough
Wealth at death estate at Northwood: will, PRO, PROB 11/1332, sig. 769

Dennett, John (1790–1852), inventor of a life-saving rocket, and antiquary, lived in Newport, Isle of Wight. In or about 1830 he invented a life-saving rocket apparatus (known as 'Dennett's') for conveying a rope from the shore to a shipwrecked crew. George William Manby had previously used a grappling shot fired from a mortar for the same purpose. Dennett's apparatus resembled a sky-rocket, but had an iron casing rather than a paper one, and a pole 8 feet long. It weighed 23 lb, was propelled by a 9 lb charge, and had a range of 250 yards. Dennett subsequently increased the range to 400 yards by placing two rockets side by side on the same pole, but the action of these parallel rockets proved to be unsatisfactory.

A ship's crew off Bembridge, in the Isle of Wight, having been saved by means of Dennett's rocket, the board of customs in 1834 had the apparatus supplied to several coastguard stations. Its official use was superseded by the adoption of Boxer's rocket in 1865. Dennett's rockets are said to have been sent to all parts of the world, and to have won for their inventor several overseas honours. A short time before his death, Dennett was appointed custodian of Carisbrooke Castle. It would appear that this was a form of recognition for his services as an inventor. He had a practical knowledge of antiquities, and was a corresponding member of the British Archaeological Association. He contributed to its journal short accounts of various antiquities found in England, and read a paper on the barrows of the Isle of Wight at the Winchester congress of the association in 1845. He died on 10 July 1852.

W. W. WROTH, *rev.* R. C. COX

Sources *GM*, 2nd ser., 38 (1852), 319–20 · 'Rocket and mortar apparatus for saving life from shipwreck and volunteer life brigades', *Cornhill Magazine*, 28 (1873), 72–87

Denney, James (1856–1917), United Free Church of Scotland minister and theologian, was born on 5 February 1856 in Paisley, the eldest son of John Denney and his wife, Mary Barr. His parents belonged to the Reformed Presbyterian church (the Cameronians), in which his father, a joiner, was a deacon. When he was four months old his parents moved to Greenock. He attended the Highlanders Academy in the town before studying at the University of Glasgow (1874–9), graduating with a double first in classics and philosophy. Denney then studied theology at the Free Church college in Glasgow, the Reformed Presbyterians having joined with the Free Church of Scotland while he was at university. He graduated in 1883 and then spent three years in the East Hill Street Mission of Free St John's Church, Glasgow. In 1886, at the age of thirty, he was ordained and inducted to the charge of East Free Church in Broughty Ferry. A few months later, on 1 July 1886, he married Mary Carmichael Brown of Glasgow: they had no children and she predeceased him in 1907. During his time as a parish minister he published several books, including *The Epistles to the Thessalonians* (1892) and *The Second Epistle to the Corinthians* (1894).

Denney remained in Broughty Ferry until 1897, when he was appointed to the chair of systematic and pastoral theology at the Free Church college in Glasgow. His theological acumen had by this date already been widely recognized, as evidenced by the invitation to give a series of lectures at the Chicago Theological Seminary in 1894, later published as *Studies in Theology* (1895). As a teacher Denney was a hard taskmaster, always demanding the very highest quality of work from his students. His manner could be curt and even abrasive, and sometimes, to those who did not know him, he appeared remote, even cold. This, however, was countered by another side to his character, as witnessed by the admiration and loyalty he inspired in successive generations of students, and the warmth and humour he displayed among close friends such as J. P. Struthers, W. R. Thomson, and W. Robertson Nicoll. On the death of A. B. Bruce in 1899, Denney succeeded to the chair of New Testament language, literature, and theology. He held this chair until his untimely death in 1917, also serving as principal of the college from 1915. He was awarded honorary doctorates in divinity by Chicago Theological Seminary, Glasgow University, and Aberdeen University.

Theologically Denney was, on the whole, conservative. This was apparent in his critique of the prevailing liberal theology of his day: he objected to Harnack's treatment of miracle and the supernatural, and he highlighted the consequences of Ritschl's denial of the bodily resurrection of Jesus Christ. However, on some issues, Denney was decidedly on the liberal wing of his church, revealing an original and creative theological mind and anticipating Karl Barth and the neo-orthodox movement. His position on the doctrine of scripture caused considerable anguish among the evangelicals (with whom, on so many theological issues, he was at one). In one of the lectures given in Chicago, revised heavily before publication, he denied verbal inspiration. Denney continued to promote his views on this subject and, indeed, on several occasions, at both presbytery and general assembly, he publicly denied the infallibility of scripture and the doctrine of verbal inerrancy. Liberal tendencies were also noticeable in his desire for the abandonment of credal subscription: he argued for the replacement of subscription to the Westminster confession of faith with the simple formula, 'I believe in God through Jesus Christ, His only Son our Saviour'.

As a theologian, Denney's great theme was the cross of Christ. He was passionately committed to the doctrine of substitutionary atonement, and increasingly viewed the cross as the heart and centre of all theology. It has been argued that this position, developed much more fully in his later work, was the result of his wife's having introduced him to the sermons of C. H. Spurgeon. Whether or not this is so, it is certainly true that the forgiveness of sins through the atoning death of Christ became for Denney the prevailing theme of all his writing and preaching. His most important writings in this area were *The Death of Christ* (1902), *The Atonement and the Modern Mind* (1903), and the posthumously published *The Christian Doctrine of Reconciliation* (1917). As a scholar he was precise and thorough, with a meticulous eye for detail. He had a sharply critical intellect which, combined with his gift for clear and forthright speech, gave him a great advantage in debate and discussion. Denney also had a wide knowledge of classical and other literature. T. H. Walker quotes him as having said that if Shakespeare's tragedies were lost he could replace them from memory. His critical contributions in print and speech were much appreciated.

Denney was a prolific writer, producing fourteen books as well as co-writing another. In addition, two volumes of his letters were published posthumously: *Letters of Principal Denney to W. Robertson Nicoll, 1893–1917* (1920) and *Letters of Principal Denney to his Family and Friends* (1921). He also wrote many short pieces for dictionaries, journals, and newspapers, notably numerous articles for James Hastings's *Dictionary of the Bible*, including 'Ascension', 'Creed', 'Knowledge', and 'Promise'. His contributions to Hastings's *Dictionary of the Gospels* included 'Authority of Christ' and 'Regeneration'. His magazine articles were mostly for *The Expositor*, including: 'Caesar and God' (January 1896), 'Adam and Christ in St Paul' (February 1904), and 'A commentary on St Matthew' (March 1915). His newspaper writing was, with very few exceptions, for the *British Weekly*, to which he contributed dozens of articles between 1898 and 1917. Topics included: 'The everlasting gospel' (3 February 1898), 'Faith and science' (11 April 1907), 'Why was Jesus sent to the cross?' (29 December 1910), 'Religions and the true religion' (21 August 1913), 'The Christian community and the war' (13 August 1914), 'The war and the national conscience' (20 August 1914), and 'Prohibition' (15 February 1917).

Denney, however, was no ivory-tower theologian, but was deeply concerned with the work of the gospel and the advancement of the kingdom of God. His remark that, 'If evangelists were our theologians and theologians our evangelists we should be nearer the ideal' was never more truly witnessed than in his own ministry. He said on a number of occasions that he had no interest in a theology which did not help in the work of evangelization or in a theology which could not be preached. Denney proved himself an active and devoted churchman. In 1900, when the Free Church of Scotland united with the United Presbyterian Church of Scotland to form the United Free Church of Scotland, Denney took part in the talks leading to the union. He was also involved in discussions about a further union with the Church of Scotland, which ultimately took place in 1929, after his death. He also played a role on the administrative side of the church as convener of the central fund, which was concerned with financial matters, in particular the stipend of ministers. He served

in this capacity from 1913 to 1917, and just before his death had agreed to continue as convener for another four years. Denney could be a crusader, too: his involvement with the temperance movement led to his virulent attack on the drink trade during the First World War. The last thing he wrote before he died was an article on Robert Burns and the dangers of drink.

Denney became ill in February 1917 and died on 11 June 1917 in Glasgow. His funeral took place on Friday 15 June. After a private service at his home, 15 Lilybank Gardens, there was a public service in the Free Church college. He was buried in the western necropolis, Glasgow.

A. T. B. McGowan

Sources T. H. Walker, *Principal James Denney D. D.* (1918) • J. R. Taylor, *God loves like that! the theology of James Denney* (1962) • A. P. F. Sell, *Defending and declaring the faith: some Scottish examples, 1860–1920* (1987), 195–220 • d. cert.
Archives U. Edin., New Coll. L., lectures, sermons, and papers
Wealth at death £3,942 14s. 0d.: confirmation, 25 July 1917, CCI

Dennie, William Henry (1789–1842), army officer, was born at Deptford, Kent, on 22 June 1789, the son of Henry Dennie, barrister, of London, and his wife, Grace, daughter of William Steele and granddaughter of Laurence Steele of Rathbride, co. Kildare. Through General the Hon. Edward Fox, Dennie's widowed mother obtained for him an ensigncy in the 22nd foot, dated 1 January 1800. He became lieutenant in August 1804 and captain on 4 October 1810. He first joined the regiment after its arrival in India in 1802, and won Lord Lake's approval by his conduct during a minor regimental mutiny. Dennie served with the regiment throughout Lake's campaigns in India in 1804–5, at the capture of Mauritius in 1810, and afterwards in Mauritius, the Channel Islands, and Ireland. After obtaining his majority in April 1821 he exchanged to the 13th foot (soon made light infantry) and went to India. With the 13th light infantry he served during the First Anglo-Burmese War, in which he distinguished himself and was severely wounded; he was awarded a brevet lieutenant-colonelcy and a CB. He served with his regiment in the army of the Indus in 1838–9.

When General Nott was appointed to the 2nd division of the army, Dennie succeeded to the command of Nott's sepoy brigade, and was employed in Sind, Baluchistan, and Lower Afghanistan. He quarrelled with General Keane early in the Afghan campaign and General Nott took an instant dislike to him. His services were unacknowledged at headquarters, where there appears to have been a desire to make him a scapegoat for the administrative blundering of the Afghan campaign. He led the storming party at the capture of Ghazni but, as he was at the time in disfavour at headquarters, the Ghazni honours conferred on some of his juniors were withheld from him. He complained respectfully but bitterly to the Indian authorities and the Horse Guards, without redress. Fiery and romantically chivalrous, as a writer in the *Bombay Gazette* described him, Dennie appears to have been irritably impatient of acts of injustice which would scarcely have moved a less sensitive man. During the occupation of

Kabul, Dennie was dispatched with a small force in September 1840 against part of the army of Dost Muhammad, which, after a series of brilliant manoeuvres and though greatly outnumbered, he decisively defeated at Bamian on 18 September. Dost Muhammad surrendered immediately afterwards and the campaign ended.

In October 1841 a brigade under Sir Robert Sale was sent from Kabul against Afghan insurgents who had occupied the Khurd Kabul Pass. This brigade, which included the 13th light infantry, seized the ruined fortress of Jalalabad and rendered themselves 'illustrious' by its subsequent defence from November 1841 to April 1842. Dennie commanded the rear-guard in the operations in the Khurd Kabul between 9 and 30 October, and, when Sir Robert Sale was wounded, succeeded to the command of the force, which he held during the greater part of the defence of Jalalabad. In the sortie of 7 April 1842 Dennie was shot through the body when riding at the head of his regiment and died soon after. He was buried in a bastion used as a graveyard by the garrison. He was unmarried. His services had been recognized by his appointment as aide-de-camp to the queen. He died after forty-two years' military service, mostly in India, during which he had purchased every step of regimental rank. After his death, Dennie's letters from the Anglo-Afghan War were published as *Personal Narrative of Campaigns in Affghanistan, Sinde, Beloochistan* (1843); they reveal that his courage and military qualities notwithstanding, Dennie was quick to take offence and frequently at odds with his superiors. He appears to have been assertive, sometimes obstructive, and often quarrelsome, but a fine fighting soldier.

H. M. CHICHESTER, *rev.* JAMES LUNT

Sources Burke, *Gen. GB* [Steele of Rathbride] · *Hart's Army List* · *The path of glory: being the memoirs of the extraordinary military career of John Shipp*, ed. C. J. Stranks (1969) · T. Seaton, *From cadet to colonel: the record of a life of active service*, 2 vols. (1866) · W. Broadfoot, *The career of Major George Broadfoot … in Afghanistan and the Punjab* (1888) · J. C. Pollock, *Way to glory: the life of Havelock of Lucknow* (1957) · W. H. Dennie, *Personal narrative of campaigns in Affghanistan, Sinde, Beloochistan*, ed. W. E. Steele (1843) · J. W. Kaye, *History of the war in Afghanistan*, 3rd edn, 3 vols. (1874) · G. R. Gleig, *Sale's brigade in Afghanistan: with an account of the seisure and defence of Jellalabad* (1846) · J. H. Stocqueler, *Memoirs and correspondence of Major-General Sir William Nott*, 2 vols. (1854) · T. Carter, ed., *Historical record of the thirteenth, first Somersetshire, or Prince Albert's regiment of light infantry* (1867) · J. Shipp, *Extraordinary military career of John Shipp*, 1 (1843) · *GM*, 2nd ser., 18 (1842), 95 · *N&Q*, 146 (1924), 394

Archives BL OIOC, MSS connected with Sale's brigade, HM 534–4S · PRO, Edenborough MSS, 30.12 · PRO NIre., Pottinger MSS, D1584A · Nicolls MSS, vols. 39, 40

Denning, Alfred Thompson [Tom], **Baron Denning** (**1899–1999**), judge, was born on 23 January 1899 in Newbury Street, Whitchurch, Hampshire. He was the fourth of five sons and the fifth among the six children of Charles Denning (1859–1941), draper, and his wife, Clara (1865–1947), the eldest daughter of John Thomas Thompson, coal merchant, of Lincoln. He was born prematurely, and was not expected to live long.

Family and education Denning's birthplace, Whitchurch, was (and still is) a small community in north Hampshire, in size between a large village and a small town, where his

Alfred Thompson Denning, Baron Denning (1899–1999), by Bryan Organ, 1982

father kept a draper's shop. Photographs have survived which reveal the small scale of the shop, with very few goods displayed in a tiny window; and Denning later described how his father used to go out in his horse and trap to deliver goods, wrapped up in brown paper and string, to customers in the surrounding villages. Denning provided a proud and vivid account of his family in his book *The Family Story* (1981). There was indeed cause for pride. The family consisted of one girl, Marjorie (*b.* 1891), and five boys. Two of the boys, Jack (1892–1916) and Gordon (1897–1918), died on active service in the First World War; astonishingly, of the surviving three, the eldest, Sir Reginald Francis Stewart Denning (1894–1990), became a general, the second, Denning himself, became a great judge, while the third, Sir Norman Egbert *Denning (1904–1979), became an admiral. The strength of character seems to have come from the mother's side. Denning epitomized the qualities of his parents in his book: 'Father kind and thoughtful, beloved by all. Mother strong and determined, standing no nonsense' (Denning, *Family Story*, 21). She is said to have nursed an unconcealed ambition for her children. Denning retained his affection for Whitchurch, and eventually was able to buy a handsome white house there called The Lawn, with the River Test running through the garden. He was proud to describe himself as a Hampshire man; he retained his distinctive Hampshire burr throughout his life; indeed, to some it seemed to become more pronounced as he grew older.

After attending a small private school run by a friend of the family in Whitchurch, Denning went to Andover grammar school; he entered the school in 1909 with his brother Gordon after both had won free places. From there he won a demyship to Magdalen College, Oxford. He went up to Oxford in 1916, and took a first in mathematical moderations in 1917, but his university career was interrupted by the First World War, in which he served with the Royal Engineers from 1917 to 1919, seeing active service on the Western Front. He then returned to Oxford, where he graduated with a first in mathematics in 1920. He then taught mathematics at Winchester for a year; but after a visit to the assizes at Winchester Castle he decided that his career did not lie in schoolmastering but in the law. He returned to Magdalen, where, in one year, he obtained another first, in jurisprudence. These achievements were capped by his joining the very select group of those who tried but failed to achieve a fellowship at All Souls College, Oxford (the fellows appear to have preferred Cyril Radcliffe, one of the most successful lawyers of his generation, who was awarded a fellowship in law). 'I joined the distinguished company of "Failed All Souls"' (Denning, *Family Story*, 39), as he wrote. His academic successes nevertheless provide early evidence of his brilliant intellect and his capacity for hard work, which in due course provided the foundation for his successful legal career.

His career at the bar and his marriages Denning was awarded an Eldon law scholarship in 1921, and a prize studentship of the inns of court, and was called to the bar in 1923 by Lincoln's Inn, the oldest and most magnificent of the four inns of court. He gave the inn a lifetime's loyalty and affection. For many years he rented a flat there, up many stairs in one of its most ancient buildings.

Meanwhile, in September 1922, before he had been called to the bar, Denning became the pupil of Henry O'Hagan in 4 Brick Court, in the Temple. The only other member of chambers was Stephen Henn-Collins, but between them they had a wide range of work. Denning was later recruited as a member of these chambers, where he continued to practise during his professional career as a barrister, gradually building up a solid, wide-ranging practice, in London and on the western circuit, to which he naturally gravitated. This he succeeded in doing not only because he was very clever but also because he worked hard and prepared his cases with scrupulous care. One of his principal clients was the Southern Railway Company; his task was to enforce the terms of the company's railway tickets which, as a judge, he later regarded with some disfavour. He took silk in 1938. Just over a year later the Second World War broke out; and it was in the difficult wartime years that he practised as a king's counsel.

Denning was twice married. He married first, on 28 December 1932, (Hilda) Mary Josephine Harvey (*b.* 1899/1900), daughter of the Revd Frank Northam Harvey, rector of Fawley, Hampshire. This marriage took place after a long courtship, during which Denning was deeply in love with Mary, but she did not at first feel able to return his affection. But in the end she did so, and their marriage was very happy. They had one child, Robert (*b.* 1938), who followed in Denning's footsteps to Magdalen College, Oxford, where he became a fellow and professor of inorganic chemistry. Denning was devoted to Mary, and her death in November 1941 was a great blow. Fortunately, however, he married again, on 27 December 1945. His second wife was Joan Daria Stuart (1899/1900–1992), the daughter of John Vinings Elliott Taylor, publisher, and widow of John Matthew Blackwood Stuart, engineer. She was a wonderful wife to Denning, gentle and kind but a tower of strength. Through her he was the inheritor of an extended family, including her daughter Hazel Fox (*b.* 1928), a brilliant lawyer in her own right who became a fellow of Somerville College, Oxford, and as a leading international lawyer became director of the British Institute of International and Comparative Law, of which Denning was chairman. Her husband, Sir Michael Fox (*b.* 1921), was himself to become a distinguished appellate judge.

Appointment to the bench In 1944 Denning became recorder of Plymouth; later in the same year he was appointed a justice of the High Court. He was then the youngest judge on the High Court bench. It was said that he had attracted the attention of the lord chancellor, Viscount Simon, when he appeared before the appellate committee of the House of Lords in *United Australia Ltd* v. *Barclays Bank Ltd* (1941).

When appointed to the bench, Denning (who was knighted the same year) was first assigned to the Probate, Divorce, and Admiralty Division of the High Court. Most, if not all, of his work in London was in divorce. Having regard to his strict views on the sanctity of the marriage vow, this cannot have been congenial work for him; but he discharged his duty with great humanity. Indeed, shortly after his transfer to the King's Bench Division of the High Court in 1945, he was invited by the lord chancellor to chair a committee to inquire into the administration of the divorce law, with special reference to expediting the hearing of suits and reducing costs, and to considering whether machinery should be available for the purpose of attempting reconciliation between the parties. With characteristic speed and efficiency he guided his committee to present its report within six months. The report was very well received: and two years later Denning was invited to become president of the National Marriage Guidance Council.

When he was transferred to the King's Bench Division in 1945, Denning also inherited the position of judge for pensions appeals, on whom fell the duty to adjudicate on war pensions—a matter of great importance in the aftermath of the Second World War. There was no appeal from his decisions, a fact of which he took full advantage. At that time there was great dissatisfaction because the burden of proof rested on the applicant to prove that his disability or injury was due to war service. Early in 1946 Denning removed the grievance by holding that, if a man was fit for service when he joined up and was discharged on medical grounds, this raised a presumption that his disability was due to war service: in other words, he reversed the burden of proof. This was an act of great judicial courage, the precursor of many others yet to come; and it was followed by a ruling which had the effect of allowing appeals out of time. The result was little less than a revolution in the handling of these claims, a remarkable achievement for a judge of first instance who had only recently been appointed to the bench. The decisions must have been well received. They did not in any way harm his prospects of promotion, since he was promoted to the Court of Appeal in 1948, before he was fifty.

Appellate judge Denning served as a lord justice of appeal from 1948 to 1957, when he was promoted to the House of Lords as a lord of appeal in ordinary, with the title Baron Denning of Whitchurch. His time in the appellate committee of the House of Lords was not altogether happy. This was partly because, in such a substantial group, of which he was the junior member (the law lords habitually sit in a committee of five) he could not dominate the committee; but principally because it was in the House of Lords that he found most opposition to his desire to mould and develop the common law in order to achieve practical justice. The opposition was expressed principally by Viscount Simonds, who felt deeply that Denning's approach to his judicial work conflicted with the doctrine of precedent by which all judges are bound. In one case, *Rahimtoola* v. *Nizam of Hyderabad* (1958), the disagreement between Denning and Simonds entered the public domain through a magisterial rebuke administered by Simonds, which Denning must not only have regarded as uncalled for, but also have seen as very wounding. The specific ground for complaint on this occasion was that Denning had proceeded on the basis of arguments and cases cited neither by counsel in argument nor by the judges in the courts below. However, the opinion expressed by Denning in that case, that a sovereign state engaged in commerce should not be entitled to invoke the protection of the principle of sovereign immunity, subsequently gained acceptance, both judicially and in due course by statute; on this occasion, as on many others, Denning was ahead of his time.

Master of the rolls All this must have added to Denning's pleasure in returning to the Court of Appeal in 1962 as master of the rolls, where he sat in a court of three over which he presided and which he could more easily persuade to his point of view; where he could influence the choice of cases to be decided by his court; and where his court could proceed with greater speed than in the more stately House of Lords, so that he could give judgment in a greater number of cases. He was reported as having said (no doubt with his tongue at least partially in his cheek) that, in the Court of Appeal, where he sat with two colleagues as opposed to sitting as a member of a committee of five in the House of Lords, the odds against justice being done had been shortened from 4–1 to 2–1. He served as master of the rolls, in which capacity he presided over the civil division of the Court of Appeal, for the astonishing period of twenty years, until his retirement from the bench in 1982.

It was during his time as master of the rolls that Denning really caught the popular imagination. 'Lord Denning decides …', shouted the banner headlines. His colleagues who sat with him were ignored, and if his decision was reversed by the House of Lords—as from time to time his decisions were (indeed at one time no fewer than nine of his decisions in a row were reversed)—the newspapers were not interested. It was Lord Denning who interested them, partly because he was seen as the champion of the man in the street against those in authority, partly because he expressed himself in language which ordinary people could understand, but mainly because, with his passion for justice, his unique personality, and his command of language, he had simply caught the popular imagination. In 1983, in a foreword to a book published after Denning's retirement, Lord Devlin wrote that 'the secret of Lord Denning's attraction—for the profession as well as for the general public—is … the belief that he opens the door to the law above the law' (Jowell and McAuslan, vii).

Denning's judicial qualities In practical terms Denning's essential qualities were his brilliant intellect, coupled with an astonishing memory—he appears to have had almost total recall—and boundless energy. With these remarkable gifts he produced, over his long judicial career, a remarkable number of judgments. Very frequently his judgments were delivered extempore, which speeded up his court in dealing with cases, and so also the number of cases in which he gave judgment. As his colleagues who sat with him observed, the notes he took during argument were of the most exiguous kind: he was able to rely on his superb memory. His summaries of the facts and issues were vivid, economical, and lucid in the extreme; he must have been the greatest master of relevance ever to sit on the English bench. There are memorable examples in the pages of the law reports. Perhaps the most famous is in *Beswick* v. *Beswick* (1966), in which his judgment opened with words which became immortal: 'Old Peter Beswick was a coal merchant in Eccles, Lancashire. He had no business premises. All he had was a lorry, scales and weights …' (Denning, *Family Story*, 208). There are many other examples, almost as vivid. In *Lloyds Bank* v. *Bundy* (1975), for example, his judgment began:

> Broadchalke is one of the most pleasing villages in England. Old Herbert Bundy, the defendant, was a farmer there. His home was at Yew Tree Farm. It went back for three hundred years. His family had been there for generations. It was his only asset. But he did a very foolish thing. He mortgaged it to the bank. Up to the very hilt … (ibid., 210)

His statement of the facts in each case was followed by an equally concise and lucid statement of the legal issues, in which complexity was reduced to simplicity; and his conclusion was expressed in words which left no one in doubt as to the reasons for his decision.

In the Court of Appeal Denning dominated his court. This was not so much a matter of his prestige. It was rather that his grasp of the case was from the outset so secure, and that his mind operated with such speed and accuracy, that it must have been difficult to keep pace with him. In particular few, if any, of the judges who sat with him could prepare to give an extempore judgment with his speed and skill.

Denning's relationship with the advocates who appeared before him was friendly and courteous. It was a pleasure as well as a privilege to present a case before him. He was never overbearing. He was always deeply interested in the case, however arid the point of law, however small the sum at stake. He always listened with care and courtesy to the argument of counsel, however junior and inexperienced he or she might be; though his reactions were so quick that pages of counsel's notes seemed to melt away like the snow in summer, and rapidly had to be discarded as irrelevant. His conclusion was always expressed in such simple and compelling language that the unsuccessful advocate sometimes wondered how he had had the temerity to argue to the contrary.

Denning was famous for the skill and tact with which he dealt with cases presented by litigants in person. Many litigants in person lack the competence to present a case in a court of law; and some judges have found their patience tried to breaking point when a hopeless argument is presented with such persistence that it seems impossible to bring the case to any reasonable conclusion. But somehow Denning had litigants in person eating out of his hand. The combination of innate courtesy and natural friendliness, his total lack of any pomposity, and his remarkable accent, coupled with his complete grasp of the case and his evident interest in it, had the effect that the litigant left the court convinced that he had had a fair hearing, even though he may have come away empty-handed.

Denning was a lion for work. His concentration seemed never to flag. At the conclusion of each case he habitually gave the first judgment, usually, if not always, unreserved, scarcely seeming to refer to his sparse notes. And hardly a gap used to separate one case from another. It was always: 'Next case please'. Almost before counsel in the last appeal had left the court Denning began to hear the next appeal with the same care and consideration as he had given to the one just completed. His enthusiasm for his judicial work never faded.

That Denning was a great master of the common law, there can be no doubt. How did he achieve that mastery? It cannot have been the product of his study of the law for one year at Oxford University. Of course, he must have learned a good deal from his practice at the bar; but knowledge of that kind tends to be scattered and disorganized. It seems that he must have learned most from his work as one of the three editors of the thirteenth edition of *Smith's Leading Cases* (1929). This was a remarkable book which in the days before legal textbooks was much used by practising lawyers and was described as 'a work of incalculable benefit for the student'. Denning himself recognized that he must have learned a great deal about the fundamental principles of the common law from his work as editor, when he said of the book that 'it taught me most of the law I ever knew' (Denning, *Family Story*, 94).

Some important cases Perhaps the first of Denning's famous cases was the High Trees case (*Central London Property Trust Ltd* v. *High Trees House Ltd*, 1947), decided when he was a judge of first instance. This case was concerned with the doctrine of equitable estoppel, but in his judgment Denning appeared to be undermining a much criticized fundamental principle of the law of contract called the doctrine of consideration; and all the lawyers, especially perhaps the academic lawyers, speculated whether the days of that doctrine were numbered—there were certainly parts of Denning's judgment which appeared, and perhaps were intended, to point in that direction. But after an exciting period of speculation, the case settled down as one which revived the doctrine of equitable estoppel which, as a result, acquired new prominence as a principle of great utility.

One of Denning's most admired judgments was his dissenting judgment in *Candler* v. *Crane Christmas & Co.* (1951). This case raised the question whether a person can be held liable in tort for damage caused by a negligent misstatement. Of the Court of Appeal, only Denning held, in his dissenting judgment, that a person could be so held liable. The principles stated by him in his judgment were expounded with such extraordinary clarity and simplicity, and with such prophetic accuracy, that nearly forty years later they were accepted by the House of Lords without amendment in *Caparo Industries plc* v. *Dickman* (1990).

Other influential judgments were concerned with controlling the abuse of power. Two early cases in this line, in which Denning gave judgments of which he was particularly proud, were *R* v. *Northumberland Compensation Tribunal, ex parte Shaw* (1952) and *Barnard* v. *National Dock Labour Board* (1953). These followed on his remarkable treatment of the subject in the first series of Hamlyn lectures, delivered by him in 1949. It was cases such as these which persuaded the press, and therefore the public, that Denning was protecting ordinary people from those in authority. This was particularly true of his judgment in the later case of *Congreve* v. *Home Office* (1976), known as the 'television licence case', decided when he was master of the rolls. There the plaintiff, faced, like many thousands of other licence holders, with an impending increase in the cost of his licence, applied for a new licence before his old one had expired, in order to beat the date of the rise. The Home Office demanded the increase of £6; and, when the plaintiff refused to pay, revoked his licence. The plaintiff asked for a declaration that the home secretary had acted unlawfully. With Denning presiding, the Court of Appeal granted the application. Bernard Levin's comment on this decision was: 'Blow the trumpets of victory for US over THEM in the TV Licence War' (*The Times*, 5 Dec 1976). Even more memorable was his injunction to the attorney-general, in *Gouriet* v. *Union of Post Office Workers* (1977), reported in 1978, to bear in mind the words of Thomas Fuller: 'Be you ever so high, the law is always above you'. Denning's judicial work in this field paved the way for the most welcome development by the House of Lords of a rational and effective system of judicial review of executive and administrative action.

In *Conway* v. *Rimmer* (1967) Denning, in a dissenting judgment in the Court of Appeal, declined to follow a ruling of the House of Lords that an objection by a minister to the admissibility of evidence in a court on the ground of crown privilege was conclusive and could not be overridden by the court. The House of Lords then exercised the power recently acquired by it to depart from an earlier decision and unanimously upheld the opinion expressed by Denning in his dissenting judgment. The practical effect was that Denning, sitting in the Court of Appeal, had overturned a decision of the House of Lords.

One of Denning's great campaigns was to promote a purposive, rather than a literal, approach to the construction of statutes and documents. This campaign, which at first provoked opposition but ultimately achieved considerable success, is associated with a vivid metaphor coined by him in his judgment in *Seaford Court Estates Ltd* v. *Asher* (1949), when he stated that the judge must not alter the material of which the statute is woven, but that he can and should iron out the creases. In a dissenting judgment shortly after, in *Magor* v. *Newport Corporation*, reported in 1952, he adopted a similar approach, which, however, provoked the wrath of Viscount Simonds in the House of Lords. In the same year, in a case which attracted much attention at the time, *British Movietone News Ltd* v. *London & District Cinemas Ltd* (1952), concerned with the construction of a contract, Denning went further. He said that the courts should not always follow the literal meaning of the words in a contract but should consider the background against which the contract was made and changed circumstances, not in the contemplation of the parties, in order to do therein what is just and reasonable: 'The court qualifies the literal meaning of the words so as to bring them into accord with the contemplated scope of the contract' (Freeman, 222). This statement of the law was criticized by Viscount Simon in the House of Lords; but gradually the courts adopted a purposive approach, doing their best to give effect to the evident intention of the contracting parties.

Another campaign of Denning's which proved to be less successful was for the recognition of a 'deserted wife's equity', that is, for her right to remain in the matrimonial home, as against any successor to the husband's title, unless he neither knew, nor should have known, of the wife's situation. This, however, ran into difficulties because it failed to take proper account of the rights of other persons in the relevant property, and in *National Provincial Bank* v. *Ainsworth* (1965) the deserted wife's equity was, in Denning's words, 'blown to smithereens' (Heward, 52) by the House of Lords. More successful was his exploitation of injunctive relief to restrain the transfer by defendants of their assets out of the jurisdiction pending judgment in legal proceedings in this country. This much needed power came to be christened the 'Mareva injunction' after one of the early cases (*Mareva Compania Naviera S.A. of Panama* v. *International Bulk Carriers S.A.*, 1975) in which the relief was granted by Denning and his colleagues in the Court of Appeal. It was criticized at the time as an illegitimate extension of the use of injunctive relief;

but it proved to be so useful in practice and was so frequently invoked that it was legitimized by statute, in the Supreme Court Act (1981).

One subject in which Denning was deeply interested was the development of a coherent law of restitution, to provide for adequate remedies in cases in which the defendant had been unjustly enriched at the expense of the plaintiff. At one time he started to gather together the relevant material with a view to writing a book on the subject but had to leave the task to others, warmly encouraged by him. Even so, some of his decisions betrayed his interest in, and knowledge of, this subject: in particular, *Nelson* v. *Larholt* (1948) and *Larner* v. *L.C.C.* (1949).

When European law appeared on the scene Denning, who must have regretted the inevitable downgrading of the common law, nevertheless adopted a realistic attitude. Characteristically, he spoke in vivid language: 'The treaty is like an incoming tide. It flows into the estuaries and up the rivers. It cannot be held back' (Freeman, 369).

Other activities Denning was involved in a great range of activities outside his judicial work. His friendship with Professor Geoffrey Cheshire, Vinerian professor of English law at Oxford University, led to his appointment as chairman of the trustees of the Cheshire Homes for Incurables, founded by Cheshire's son Wing Commander Leonard Cheshire VC. He was also the first chairman (from 1959 to 1986) of the British Institute of International and Comparative Law, an institute of great importance which grew out of two other institutions. Not only was he a highly effective chairman, but his great reputation proved a magnet for endowments for the institute. Among the numerous other bodies to which he gave his support were Magdalen College, Oxford, Birkbeck College, London, and the University of Buckingham; the Law Society, the Magistrates' Association, and the Lawyers' Christian Fellowship; the Historical Manuscripts Commission and the English Association; the National Association of Parish Councils; and the Drapers' Company. He was also chancellor of two dioceses, London and Southwark.

In 1963 Denning conducted the inquiry into the Profumo affair, an exercise which he performed in only three months and in a highly effective, if unorthodox, manner which deprived the media of the opportunity to rake over the ashes of a much exaggerated scandal and was infinitely less expensive than the more cumbrous inquiries of later years (though it has to be said that his report was criticized as showing signs of naïvety).

Denning was always ready to meet students and to address them, and he gave up much time to them. They were fascinated by his judgments: exciting, not too long, vivid, and easy to understand. They loved his tilting at authority, his passion for justice, sometimes at the expense of the doctrine of precedent, and his protection of the little man from overbearing authority. But especially they loved the man himself: approachable, warm, friendly, informal, and lacking in condescension. The master of the rolls' court in the Royal Courts of Justice always had a sprinkling, sometimes a substantial gathering, of people in attendance. They were mostly law students, but also some unemployed young barristers and even some members of the public. They used to come just to watch, and to listen to, Lord Denning.

Denning's overseas tours took him all over the common law world (often with his wife) and he visited many countries outside it. He was preceded by his great reputation; but as always the magic of his personality, and his deep interest in the activities of his hosts, combined with his natural courtesy, made a profound impression. These long journeys, and the many engagements at his destinations, must have been very exhausting yet his energy enabled him to cope. He was deeply admired by the lawyers who practised in the Commonwealth. Lord Bingham later recalled that he once met a Guyanese advocate who practised from Denning Chambers in Georgetown and who had christened his eldest son Alfred Thompson.

On these tours Denning must have had many speaking engagements. Although diffident at first, he acquired great skill, and his own special style, as a public speaker. He usually spoke without notes, and had a great sense of drama; his Hampshire accent reinforced the dramatic effect of his delivery. Everybody enjoyed his speeches. He had a number of favourite stories: it did not seem to matter that his audience had heard them before—they enjoyed hearing them again and again. In his speeches he spoke of his deep affection for his country, its history and traditions, for Shakespeare (from whose works he could quote long passages by heart), and above all for the common law and its greatest offspring, the rule of law. It was when he spoke in public that his audience had a vision of his personality, rounded and complete despite its extraordinary contradictions: the combination of simplicity and shrewdness in his character, and of tradition and modernity in his outlook.

Publications During the later part of his judicial career and after he retired, Denning published a number of books. The first was *The Discipline of the Law* (1978). It began with a consideration of the construction of documents, in which he contrasted the approach of the 'strict constructionists' with that of the 'intention seekers'. The reader was left in no doubt to which school Denning himself belonged. In the second part he considered 'misuse of ministerial powers'. This reflected his determination that the exercise of these powers should be subject to review by judges. In 1981 he published *The Family Story*, his proud and affectionate account of his remarkable family. This was followed in 1982 by *What Next in the Law*.

Sadly, two passages in the latter book, relating to the suitability of black jurors, caused great offence to the black community and led to adverse press comment. The *Daily Mirror* spoke to Lady Denning. She replied: 'He is very distressed. He has done more for the black people in this country than any other judge. He is very upset. He realises that he has made a mistake' (Denning, *Closing Chapter*, 11). Denning wrote to the lord chancellor, offering to retire at once. The lord chancellor persuaded him that he should not retire until the end of the long vacation. Meanwhile,

however, two black jurors who had participated in a trial at Bristol threatened proceedings against Denning for libel. He took legal advice from a very experienced solicitor, and from leading and junior counsel. Agreement was reached. No writ was issued, and no damages were sought. The book was withdrawn, the offending passages were removed, and Denning made a public apology in terms which were agreed. It was a sad end to a great career. A man who had been accustomed to speak his mind with impunity had gone too far. The blow was, however, softened by a generous letter written to *The Times* by Rudy Narayan, the secretary of the Society of Black Lawyers, in which he wrote:

> The remarks are clearly wrong and it is good to read Lady Denning's quoted remarks. Lord and Lady Denning have thousands of friends in Africa, Asia and the Caribbean who will be surprised at his remarks, and his own and Lady Denning's distress is plain to see. A great judge has erred greatly in the intellectual loneliness of advanced years; while his remarks should be rejected and rebutted he is yet, in a personal way, entitled to draw on that reservoir of community regard which he has in many quarters and to seek understanding, if not forgiveness. (*The Times*, 26 May 1982)

In 1983 Denning published his fourth and last book, *The Closing Chapter*. In it he recounted, with engaging frankness, the sad story of his retirement from judicial office. It has to be admitted, even by his warmest admirers, that this unfortunate episode revealed a flaw in his character: a streak of hubris which led him to believe that he was not as other men were, and in particular that he was not subject to the same restraints as other judges. It was this trait in his character which led him not merely to develop the common law in an acceptable manner to achieve practical justice, but on occasion to decide individual cases simply on the merits as he saw them, without troubling too much about settled legal principle which might point in another direction. It was this aspect of his work which most upset judges who heard appeals from his decisions, and which led to many of his decisions being reversed by the House of Lords, with consequent waste of judicial time and of legal costs. For his successors on the bench, however, his great achievement stands: that he taught the English judiciary that the common law cannot stand still. It must be capable of development, on a case-by-case basis, to ensure that the principles of the common law are apt to do practical justice in a living society; even so, it is recognized that this must be done within the confines of a doctrine of precedent, the function of which is to ensure stability in the law and consistency in its administration, but which must not be construed too strictly to preclude the organic development of the common law.

Retirement In 1982 Denning retired to Whitchurch, where he had many visitors. He usually received them in his study, filled with mementoes of his career, including the desk of his most distinguished predecessor, Sir George Jessel, at which he used to sit. The mantelpiece and the top of his bookcase provided a home to many gifts from overseas, including carved elephants and other animals from Africa. Some of his visitors came to fish, at his invitation, in the River Test as it ran through his garden; among them was Viscount Simonds, whose deep and public disagreement with Denning's more revolutionary judgments seems to have left no trace of rancour.

For some years after his retirement Denning continued to go up to London. He spoke in the chamber of the House of Lords on many topics. But sadly both his eyesight and his hearing became gravely impaired and increasingly he was confined to his home, where he had the benefit of an effective apparatus, involving a microphone and large ear-muffs, to overcome his deafness. He spent a good deal of his time offering free advice on the law, of dubious practicality, to all sorts of people. He even himself embarked on litigation on local issues from time to time. But his greatest pleasure was derived from his family, and especially from his grandchildren. The death of his second wife, Joan, in 1992 was a great blow.

Denning received many honours, including honorary doctorates from numerous universities in Britain, Europe, and United States, and the Commonwealth, and honorary fellowship of the British Academy. Very late in his life he received the great honour of being admitted to the Order of Merit, a unique distinction for a judge. The award gave great pleasure, not only to himself but also to his many admirers in the country. Unfortunately he was by then no longer able to travel to London to receive the insignia from the queen; instead her representative made the presentation to Denning in his home at Whitchurch.

Denning's 100th birthday was an occasion for great rejoicing, at his home in Whitchurch and by his many admirers in the country at large. A family party was held at The Lawn. Outside, the church bells were ringing—including a new tenor bell, Great Tom, cast in his honour and making up a peal of ten bells, unusual for the church of so small a community. Inside the house, a section of the Basingstoke male voice choir sang 'Happy birthday to you'. Robert Denning opened and read his telegram from the queen; Denning had already received on the previous day a telegram from the queen mother. He died only a few weeks later, on 5 March 1999; he was taken ill at home in Whitchurch, and was rushed by ambulance to the Royal Hampshire County Hospital, Winchester, where he died of an internal haemorrhage combined with old age. He was buried in the graveyard at Whitchurch, beside the grave of his second wife, Joan.

Denning's great career was recalled by an enormous congregation at a memorial service in Westminster Abbey on 17 June 1999, at which his extraordinary character and achievements were extolled by Lord Bingham of Cornhill, who described Denning as 'the best-known and best loved judge in our history' (*The Times*, 18 June 1999). The size of the congregation reflected not only the vast range of his activities and the number of organizations in which Denning was involved, but also the deep affection in which he was held by the whole legal profession.

Character and assessment Tom Denning, as he was known in his family and to all his many friends, was a tall man of considerable presence, though he habitually appeared to be half-smiling. When he removed his judicial wig, his head was revealed to be surprisingly bald, fringed with grey hair.

In pursuing his great aim of modernizing the law, Denning came to be regarded by some as a revolutionary. Yet it is a curious, even paradoxical, fact that, at heart, he held views of the most conventional, indeed old-fashioned, nature. He was a devout member of the Church of England, and described religion as 'perhaps the chiefest influence [on him] of all' (Denning, *Family Story*, vi). He was deeply patriotic in his love for his country and its history and culture. He was a lifelong teetotaller and non-smoker—principles adopted by him when he was a university student and very short of money, but observed by him rigorously throughout his long life, except that he took a small glass of port for toasts. His morality was strictly conventional and his views on topics such as capital punishment and homosexuality could be, and were, regarded as reactionary. That these aspects of his ethos did not diminish the esteem in which he was held by the general public was largely due to his simplicity of character, his evident courage and public spirit, his personal charm and great charisma, and his passionate belief in freedom under the law and in fair play. Also his evident determination to protect the little man from overbearing authority made him very attractive to the media, so that they seem to have been inclined to forgive the more extreme expressions of his old-fashioned morality.

Denning's great achievement was that he reminded a whole generation of lawyers that the duty of a judge is not merely to apply the law but to do justice; and that, if justice was to be done according to law, the common law could not stand still—it must be developed to respond to the needs of justice in a living society. The path he chose was the path of justice; he once wrote, 'so long as I did what I thought was just, I … could sleep at night. But if I did what was unjust, I stayed awake worrying' (Denning, *Family Story*, 183). It is difficult to imagine more fundamental lessons than those he taught: and so effectively were the lessons reinforced by the example of his own judicial work that by the time of his death their precepts were regarded as axiomatic, throughout the common law world. Yet in the earlier years of the twentieth century many influential judges regarded their function as being simply to apply the principles of the common law as then understood, and as laid down in the decided cases. They regarded it as an abuse of judicial power to 'change' the law as Denning sought to do; that, they thought, could only be achieved by legislation. One of his principal critics, Viscount Simonds, spoke of 'a naked usurpation of the legislative function under the thin disguise of interpretation' (Freeman, 220). This philosophy, although espoused in all good faith, was stultifying in its effect. Even so, it required great courage on the part of Denning to challenge it and great perseverance on his part to overcome it, in the face of considerable opposition from a number of the older judges. He gradually acquired allies, not only on the bench but also, and perhaps especially, in the academic world, in support of his campaign, and in the end his view prevailed.

With the wisdom of hindsight Denning's victory can be seen to have been entirely justified. It may from time to time cause some temporary instability in the law; but in the long term practical justice has been the beneficiary. Indeed, it can be said that the common law, based as it is upon a case law system, was ideally suited for Denning's purpose; it is surely much more difficult for judges to change a codified system, or indeed to identify an intellectual justification for doing so, than it is to develop by judicial decision a system of law which consists of previous decisions by the judges themselves.

Denning was one of the greatest and most influential judges ever to sit on the English bench. Some would maintain that the title of this country's greatest judge of all time should still be awarded to Lord Mansfield (who, in the age of the Enlightenment, transformed its medieval common law and procedure into a modern system which has survived through the centuries, and who was also the father of commercial law). Nevertheless, few would dispute that Denning was the greatest English judge of the twentieth century.   ROBERT GOFF

Sources Lord Denning, *The family story* (1981) · Lord Denning, *The closing chapter* (1983) · I. Freeman, *Lord Denning: a life* (1993) · E. Heward, *Lord Denning: a biography*, 2nd edn (1997) · J. L. Jowell and I. D. W. B. McAuslan, *Lord Denning: the judge and the law* (1984) · S. Krebs, *Lord Denning et le droit communautaire* (1983) · P. Robson and P. Watchman, *Justice, Lord Denning and the constitution* (1981) · *The Times* (6 March 1999) · *Daily Telegraph* (6 March 1999) · *The Guardian* (6 March 1999) · *The Independent* (6 March 1999) · Lord Goff of Chieveley, 'Lord Denning: a memoir', *Denning Law Journal* (1999), xxiii–xxxiii · *Denning Law Journal* (1999) [special issue] · Lord Bingham of Cornhill, 'Address at the service of thanksgiving for the Rt Hon Lord Denning OM', *Denning Law Journal* (2000), 1–6 · Burke, *Peerage* · WWW · b. cert. · m. certs. · d. cert. · personal knowledge (2004) · private information (2004)
Archives Bodl. RH, papers relating to conference on the future of law in Africa · Hants. RO, corresp., diaries, personal and family papers | Bodl. Oxf., letters to A. L. Goodhart
Likenesses W. Stoneman, photograph, 1945, NPG · N. Hepple, group portrait, oils, 1958 (*A short adjournment*), Lincoln's Inn, London · photographs, 1963–80, Hult. Arch. · W. Bird, photograph, 1964, NPG · E. Halliday, oils, 1974, Lincoln's Inn, London · A. Newman, colour print, 1978?, NPG · A. Newman, photograph, 1978, NPG · J. Ward, oils, 1978, Birkbeck College, London · photograph, 1980, repro. in *The Independent* · B. Organ, oils, 1982, NPG [*see illus.*] · photograph, 1987, repro. in *The Times* · photograph, repro. in *The Times* · photograph, repro. in *Daily Telegraph* · photograph, repro. in *The Guardian* · photographs, repro. in Denning, *Family story* · photographs, repro. in Freeman, *Lord Denning* · photographs, repro. in Heward, *Lord Denning*

Denning, Sir Norman Egbert (1904–1979), naval officer, was born at Whitchurch, Hampshire, on 19 November 1904, the youngest in the family of one daughter and five sons of Charles Denning (1859–1941), a draper, and his wife, Clara Thompson (1865–1947). Two of the sons died during the First World War and Denning's other two brothers were Lieutenant-General Sir Reginald Francis Stewart Denning (1894–1990) and Alfred Thompson (Tom) *Denning, Baron Denning (1899–1999), later an eminent master of the rolls.

Norman Denning, who was always known as Ned, joined the navy from Andover grammar school as a special entry cadet in 1921. As indifferent eyesight prevented him

from becoming an executive officer he joined the paymaster (later supply and secretariat) branch—in which he quickly showed outstanding ability, being several times appointed secretary to senior executive officers. In 1933 he married Iris, daughter of Captain Richard James Curtis, master mariner, of Singapore; they had two sons, one of whom died in 1977, and a daughter.

As a paymaster lieutenant-commander Denning was appointed to the Admiralty's intelligence division in 1937 and quickly realized its unreadiness for the war with Germany which was plainly approaching. He therefore studied the records of the First World War, and especially the accomplishments of the cryptographic office known as Room 40 OB. He appreciated the fundamental weakness which lay in the separation of the work of that office from the operational conduct of the war at sea—which produced disastrous results, notably on the night following the battle of Jutland (31 May–1 June 1916), and so began to plan and organize an operational intelligence centre (OIC) in which the two functions would be totally integrated. Encouraged by rear-admirals J. H. Godfrey and J. A. G. Troup, the directors of naval intelligence of the period, he soon got the principles on which the new centre was to work accepted; but on the outbreak of the Second World War the staff allocated to it was tiny. Admiral Godfrey used the author Charles Morgan to recruit suitable outsiders and gradually built up a brilliant team which manned and operated the OIC throughout the war. From 1941 it was situated deep underground in the heavily reinforced concrete citadel built on the west side of the main Admiralty building.

In the OIC large-scale plots were maintained showing the course and position of all allied warships and of every mercantile convoy or independently routed merchant ship, and the positions and probable movements of all enemy units derived from every form of intelligence but especially from the decrypts produced by the Government Code and Cypher School, the name by which the cryptographic and cryptanalytical centre at Bletchley Park was known. This became increasingly important after the German machine cipher known as Enigma had been broken in 1941. The OIC thus became the brain centre for the conduct of the war at sea, and in it the responsible officers, and Winston Churchill when first lord of the Admiralty, could see at a glance the position (or presumed position) of the forces of both sides.

At first Denning was in charge of all the OIC's work including the U-boat plot and tracking room, but after Captain C. R. N. Winn RNVR had taken over that responsibility he devoted his whole energies to the surface ship plot on which the movements of enemy warships and disguised raiders were recorded. From those two plots, which were manned continuously, the operational authorities were able to initiate the measures necessary to improve the safety of allied shipping and, if possible, direct forces to intercept the enemy. Denning thus became the chief adviser to the first lord and first sea lord on the conduct of that aspect of the conflict. He also acted as the link between the OIC and other sections of the naval intelligence division, with the Ministry of Economic Warfare, the army, Fighter and Bomber commands of the RAF, the Secret Intelligence Service, and the Special Operations Executive.

Denning was promoted paymaster-commander in 1941 and paymaster-captain in 1951; but it was not until the establishment of the general list for officers at the beginning of 1956 that the invidious distinction between the executive and non-executive branches was abolished. Denning then dropped his paymaster title and in 1958 became a rear-admiral on the general list—a position which his abilities had always merited.

After the war Denning's first appointment was as director of administrative planning in the Admiralty, but in 1956 he moved to the Royal Naval College, Greenwich, as its director. Two years later he became deputy chief of naval personnel and in 1959 director of manpower in the Admiralty. Earl Mountbatten of Burma related how he selected Denning to be director of naval intelligence—the first non-executive officer to be appointed to that important post. He held it in 1960–64 very successfully, and it was again Mountbatten's confidence in him and appreciation of his abilities which brought him to the top of the tree as deputy chief of defence staff (intelligence) from 1964 to 1965.

Denning was appointed OBE in 1945, CB in 1961, and KBE in 1963. After his retirement in 1967 he became secretary of the services, press, and broadcasting committee (known as the 'D Notice Committee'), in which capacity his wide experience of security problems and his tactful handling of the press proved invaluable. He died at Micheldever, Hampshire, on 27 December 1979.

STEPHEN W. ROSKILL, rev.

Sources F. H. Hinsley and others, *British intelligence in the Second World War*, 5 vols. in 6 (1979–90) · P. Beesly, *Very special intelligence: the story of the admiralty's operational intelligence centre, 1939–1945* (1977) · P. Beesly, *Very special admiral: the life of Admiral J. H. Godfrey* (1980) · D. McLachlan, *Room 39: naval intelligence in action, 1939–1945* (1968) · S. W. Roskill, *The war at sea, 1939–1945*, 3 vols. in 4 (1954–61) · A. T. Denning, *The family story* (1981) · *The Times* (28 Dec 1979) · personal information (1986) · *CGPLA Eng. & Wales* (1980)

Archives NMM, papers | SOUND BL NSA, current affairs recording

Wealth at death £60,171: probate, 27 Feb 1980, *CGPLA Eng. & Wales*

Denning, William Frederick (1848–1931), astronomer, was born on 25 November 1848 at Wellow, near Radstock, Somerset, the son of Isaac Poyntz Denning, a public accountant, and his wife, Lydia, *née* Padfield. Denning, who attended various schools in Bristol, became interested in natural history as a boy. In his late teens he began to concentrate on astronomy, possibly motivated by his observation of the great meteor shower of 1866. In 1869 his new enthusiasm led him to found a Society of Young Amateur Observers, and he began to submit notes on meteor observations for publication.

It was known that meteor showers represented clusters of particles orbiting the sun. About the time Denning first became interested in them, a comparison of cometary orbits with those of meteor showers showed that some might be connected. Determining the orbit of a meteor shower depends on finding a 'radiant' point in the sky from which the meteors appear to emanate. Denning set about determining radiants for as many showers as he could find. By 1890 he was able to publish a list of several hundred radiants from the observations he had made in the preceding two decades. Mainly as a consequence of this work he was awarded the gold medal of the Royal Astronomical Society in 1898. He published further lists in later years, including data from other observers. He also drew attention to the varied appearances of meteors from different showers, suggesting that this might indicate differing physical properties. These studies led Denning into one continuing controversy. Because of the relative motions involved, the apparent position of a radiant in the sky changes from night to night. Denning claimed that he had found some meteor showers where this did not occur. He defended the existence of such 'stationary' radiants for the rest of his life, though most of his colleagues remained unconvinced.

Denning's knowledge of the night sky, derived from his meteor observing, helped him discover two novae—one in 1918 and the other in 1920. He was also a leading discoverer of comets, finding four between 1881 and 1894. Perhaps his most important non-meteor work, however, was his planetary observations, especially of Jupiter. He took a particular interest in the Great Red Spot, showing that, though its appearance changed with time, it had been present in the Jovian atmosphere for many years. His observations of Saturn allowed him to derive a new period, close to the currently accepted value, for its rate of rotation.

Denning, like his father, was trained as an accountant, but he gave up a business career in order to pursue his astronomical interests. In his earlier years he was a keen cricketer. At one stage he was invited by W. G. Grace to keep wicket for Gloucestershire, but he declined. He was granted a civil pension in 1904. Denning never married, and, in later years became something of a recluse. This may have been as a result of the ill health that dogged him for much of his life: he nevertheless maintained a considerable correspondence with other astronomers. He died at his home, 44 Egerton Road, Bishopston, Bristol, on 9 June 1931.

A. J. MEADOWS

Sources *The Observatory*, 54 (1931), 276–83 · *Monthly Notices of the Royal Astronomical Society*, 92 (1931–2), 248–50 · *WWW* · b. cert. · d. cert.

Wealth at death £65 17s. 6d.: administration, 8 July 1931, *CGPLA Eng. & Wales*

Dennis. *See also* Denis, Denys.

Dennis, George (1814–1898), archaeologist, was born on 21 July 1814 in Ash Grove, Hackney, Middlesex, the fourth child of John Dennis (1779–1864), an official in the Excise Office, and his wife, Mary Hull. In 1828 Dennis was sent to Charterhouse School, but in the following year his father took him away from school and put him to work in his own office as a clerk, and he received no further formal education. Feeling the urge to travel, he went on a walking tour of Scotland in 1834. In 1836 he sailed from London to Portugal and southern Spain. The result of this trip was his first book, *A Summer in Andalucia*, which was published anonymously by Richard Bentley and received favourable reviews. Dennis left home again in July 1839 and travelled to Switzerland, Milan, and Venice; he returned via Zürich. In July 1840 he went to Paris and on to northern Spain, where he visited Madrid, Toledo, and Saragossa. In 1841 he decided to begin exploring ancient Etruria, and he left England in April 1842. His most constant travelling companion through Etruria was the artist Samuel Ainsley (*c*.1810–1874). They made three tours together between June 1842 and July 1843, exploring Tarquinia and most of the other important Etruscan sites, as well as spending a considerable time in Rome. Ainsley made many other visits to Italy without Dennis, and held two exhibitions of his paintings at the Royal Academy. Dennis himself was also a competent artist of pencil drawings. In 1845 Dennis published a short book, *The Cid: a Short Chronicle, Founded on the Early Poetry of Spain*. More lengthy visits to Italy were carried out by Dennis between 1844, when he obtained the agreement of John Murray to publish his book, and 1848, when it at last appeared. *The Cities and Cemeteries of Etruria*, in two volumes, consisted of 114 plus 1085 pages of text, and gave the most detailed descriptions that had yet appeared in any language of all recorded Etruscan sites. It was heavily illustrated with Dennis's own drawings.

Dennis's humble post at the Excise Office having come to an end, he was interviewed by the Colonial Office and offered a position as private secretary to the governor of British Guiana, a part of the world which was destined to be most uncongenial to him. He sailed from England in January 1849 and was in Georgetown from the following month until the winter of 1862, though he made several return trips to Europe on leave. At some time during this period of his life he married a woman whose first name was Honoria or Nora: nothing more is known about her and there were no children. The only piece of writing from his pen concerning South America was a lecture given by him many years later, in 1892, entitled 'The Aborigines of South America and speculations on their origin'.

In the spring of 1863 Dennis and his wife arrived in Sicily, his fourth visit to the island. He carried out archaeological research at Girgenti and Gela, and from then on he was hard at work on a *Handbook for Travellers in Sicily*, a book of over 500 pages published by Murray in 1864.

Dennis was then appointed vice-consul at Benghazi, where he arrived in February 1864. He hated the place, and his official duties there were uninteresting, but he made every effort to carry out at least some archaeological excavations in the neighbourhood, at Teucheira, Cyrene, and Ptolemais. In these he was in the main disappointed. He and his wife were able to leave Benghazi about the end of April 1868, having been transferred to Smyrna. In Turkey between 1868 and 1870 Dennis threw himself with renewed vigour into archaeological research, at Sardis, but he never produced a book on Turkey. As far as possible he worked for the British Museum, sending back consignments of terracotta figurines and other objects. He always enjoyed the support of Charles (later Sir Charles) Newton, keeper of Greek and Roman antiquities at the museum, but he frequently expressed his frustration at what he considered the lack of financial aid offered him by the trustees. In 1869 he was promoted consul for the island of Crete, but did not go there, and in 1870 he moved on to Palermo, a much happier posting. He resumed excavations in Sicily and Etruria, and in 1878, thirty years after its first appearance, a revised edition of *The Cities and Cemeteries of Etruria* was published, this time with a dedication to Sir Henry Layard, whom he had known since 1839, and to whom he often wrote asking for advice or assistance. Having been appointed to Smyrna as consul in June 1879, he arrived there with his wife in May 1880, and whenever possible worked at Sardis and Bin Tépé. From time to time on these sites he met and entertained the archaeologists Sir W. M. Ramsay (1851–1939) and Professor A. H. Sayce (1845–1933), both from Oxford, and the Frenchman Salomon Reinach (1858–1932), with whom he exchanged many letters. In 1885, on a visit to England, Dennis received the honorary degree of doctor of civil law at Oxford, arranged for him by Sayce.

Mrs Dennis died in Smyrna on 1 April 1888, and Dennis officially retired a month later, being in the same year appointed CMG. His last, lonely years were spent between London and Rome, with visits to Spain and Tangier. In Rome he gave several lectures on his past experiences in various countries. He died on 15 November 1898, in South Kensington, and was buried in Hampstead cemetery. In 1888 there was a reissue of *The Cities and Cemeteries of Etruria*, and in 1907 the great work was again published by Dent in a cheap edition as part of Everyman's Library. The book has been translated into Italian, but so far only a few extracts from it have been published in that language.

Dennis's younger brother John Dennis (1825–1911), with whom he kept on permanently good terms, was a prolific author and critic of English literature. Dennis had seven sisters, most of whom continued to write to him with family news during his long life spent mainly overseas.

DENNIS E. RHODES

Sources D. E. Rhodes, *Dennis of Etruria: the life of George Dennis* (1973) · D. E. Rhodes, *Dennis d'Etruria*, trans. D. Mantovani (1992) · T. W. Potter, 'Dennis of Etruria: a celebration', *Antiquity*, 72 (1998), 916–21 · John Murray, London, archives, Dennis MSS · BL, Layard MSS, Add. MSS 38993–39133 · *FO List* (1891)
Archives BL, letters to family, Add. MS 62114 | BL, corresp. with Sir Austin Layard, Add. MSS 38993–39133
Wealth at death £1888 1s. 5d.: administration, 10 May 1899

Dennis, James Blatch Piggott (1815–1861), palaeontologist and natural historian, was born, possibly at Colchester, on 4 August 1815, the son of Philip Dennis, an army officer. After attending Bedford School from 1830 to 1833 he was admitted to Queen's College, Oxford, in 1835. He graduated in 1839 and was ordained a minister in the Church of England. Two years later, on 30 November 1841, at Heworth, co. Durham, he married a minor, Eliza Potts, daughter of Mathew Potts.

During 1848 James Dennis produced two pamphlets under the pseudonym Lucius debating Lord John Russell's ecclesiastical policy. He also wrote a tract in his own name, *Rites and Ceremonies in the Church and the Apostolic Succession*. In 1850 he was appointed curate at St James's Church in Bury St Edmunds, Suffolk, but resigned his curacy two years later to become a master at the local King Edward VI Grammar School. An active figure in local intellectual life, he organized geological and natural history displays with lectures and study groups in the town's museum.

From Bury St Edmunds Dennis frequently visited the Norfolk broads to study bird life. In accordance with the ornithological attitudes of the time he shot and stuffed many birds; he sent fifty specimens to the Great Exhibition. At Stonesfield in Oxfordshire he discovered the fossil jawbone of *Stereognathus ooliticus*, a previously unknown Jurassic mammal. Richard Owen's subsequent study of the jawbone, published in the *Journal of the Geological Society* in 1856, led to Dennis's election as a fellow of the Geological Society.

In 1856 and 1857 Dennis published articles on the microscopic study of bones and fossils in the *Quarterly Journal of Microscopic Science*. A paper on the origin of mammals, based on investigations of fossils from Lyme Regis in Dorset, put forward a theory on the bone structure of animals with the power of springing movement. Other contributions discussed cetacean fossils from Felixstowe in Suffolk, and evidence for the origin of birds from fossils found at Stonesfield. In 1860, at the Oxford meeting of the British Association for the Advancement of Science, he delivered a paper on pterodactyl flight, based on researches into fossils from the Cambridgeshire coprolite beds.

Dennis retired from his post at the Bury St Edmunds grammar school in 1857. In the following year he published *An Answer to Mr. Ballie* (a member of the Church of England who had converted to Roman Catholicism), arguing the two churches' relative merits. He died of 'brain disease' at his house in Garland Street, Bury St Edmunds, on 13 January 1861, and was buried in the town cemetery. His wife survived him, and after his death the trustees of the town's museum organized a subscription and exhibition to purchase his ornithological collections and provide for his family.   ROBERT HALLIDAY

Sources R. Halliday, 'The early history of the Bury St Edmunds museum', *Suffolk Review*, new ser., 22 (1994), 1–17 · H. Stevenson, *The birds of Norfolk*, 2 vols. (1866) · King Edward VI Grammar School, Bury St Edmunds, governors' registers, 1831–58, Suffolk RO, Bury St Edmunds, GD 502/2 · Foster, *Alum. Oxon.* · *Bury and Norwich Post* (15 Jan 1861) · *GM*, 3rd ser., 10 (1861), 225 · *Bury and Norwich Post* (30 April 1851) · *Bury and Norwich Post* (11 Oct 1854) · *Bury and Norwich Post* (12 Nov 1856) · *Bury and Norwich Post* (2 Dec 1856) · *Bury and Norwich Post* (30 June 1857) · Ely diocesan records, curates' licences, CUL, department of manuscripts and university archives, G 3/6 · admission list and headmaster's list of registrations, Bedford School · CGPLA Eng. & Wales (1861) · cemetery register, Bury St Edmunds, Suffolk RO, Bury St Edmunds, J 700/1 · m. cert. · d. cert.
Archives NHM, letters to Richard Owen
Wealth at death £6000: probate, 6 March 1861, CGPLA Eng. & Wales

Dennis, John (1658–1734), literary critic, was born on 16 September 1658 in the parish of St Andrew's, Holborn, London, the only child of Francis Dennis (d. 1663), a saddler, and Sarah Dennis (d. 1709/10), who later married Thomas Sanderson, who was also a saddler, with whom she had a daughter, Dennis's half-sister Elizabeth.

Education Dennis was educated at Harrow School under Dr William Horne. He was elected orator in 1674. On 13 January 1676 he matriculated from Gonville and Caius College, Cambridge, where he held one of Harrow's two founder's exhibitions, and took his BA in 1679. On reaching his majority, Dennis inherited a bequest of £500 from Simon Eve, his paternal uncle, an alderman of London. He remained in residence but his career at the college came to an end following an incident with a fellow student: on 4 March 1680, he was mulcted £3, deprived of his scholarship, and obliged to leave after attacking and wounding Charles Glenham. Dennis moved to Trinity Hall in 1681. There, in 1683, he took his MA, and with that qualification, but not on the foundation of the college, it is probable that he worked as a tutor until 1686.

In that year Dennis brought a chancery suit against his mother. She had defrauded him, he claimed, of the interest on his uncle's bequest. Her son had become an unfilial spendthrift, his mother countered. It is likely that the family arrived at an out-of-court settlement. By 1688 he could afford to accompany one of his former Harrow schoolmates, Lord Francis Seymour, on the grand tour. Theirs was the traditional itinerary; the letter in which Dennis describes crossing the Alps into Italy is an early expression of the romantic sublime. The record of his travels is coloured, however, by a hostility to absolutist, Catholic Europe which permanently darkened his political thought. 'I mortally hate them', he wrote of the French (J. Dennis, *Miscellanies in Verse and Prose*, 1693, 126).

Embarks on a literary career On his return Dennis determined on a literary career. Supported by his private income, he established himself in London as a modish man of letters, publishing occasional verse (fables, translations, and self-conscious exercises in wit, some of which were collected in *Poems in Burlesque*, 1692, and his *Miscellanies*) and several Pindaric odes, including *The Court of Death* (1695), dedicated to the memory of Queen Mary, and *The Nuptials of Britain's Genius and Fame* (1697), on the conclusion of the Nine Years' War. He cultivated the leading literary figures, Dryden, Wycherley, and Congreve among them. At the same time, and with an eye on his dwindling fortune, Dennis also courted statesmen. A committed but independent whig, he was proud that his literary works had been favourably received by 'the late Earls of *Godolphin* and *Halifax*, Mr. *Maynwaring* and others among the Whigs', he recalled in 1719, 'and by the present Duke of *Buckingham* and my Lord *Lansdown* among the Tories' (*Critical Works*, 2.173). Rewards were none the less modest and infrequent. His greatest success followed the publication of *Britannia triumphans* (1704), a celebration of the victory at Blenheim: the duke of Marlborough gave Dennis 100

John Dennis (1658–1734), by John Vandergucht, pubd 1734

him, however; 'indeed he had taken no Care to get himself exempted in the Articles of Peace', John Mottley's drily aristocratic account relates, 'and he could not help thinking, that he had done the *French* almost as much Damage as Mr. *Dennis* himself' (Mottley, 214). A year later *Gibraltar* (1705), Dennis's weakest play, fell after two performances. *The Masque of Orpheus and Euridice* (published 1707) was probably never performed. For the production of *Appius and Virginia* (1709), which ran for three noisy nights, Dennis improved the mustard bowl device in which stage managers created claps of thunder. His advance is remembered in English idiom. At a performance of *Macbeth* shortly after his own play had closed, tradition tells that Dennis heard deep rumbling off-stage. 'Damn them!', he is said to have exclaimed, 'they will not let my play run, but they steal my thunder'. According to the *Oxford English Dictionary* this was the origin of the figurative expression, but the incident is more likely to be apocryphal, a story Pope put about to further his own image of the critic. Dennis wrote one more play in 1710, but it was not performed for several years.

Decline in fortune The second decade of the eighteenth century marked a decline in Dennis's fortunes. Frequently ill (he suffered from gout, fevers, stones, increasing weight, and deteriorating sight), he retired from the metropolitan world of clubs and coffee houses in 1705. His finances remained uncertain. Since at least 1710 Dennis had found work as a notary public, empowered to act as an agent and banker. Although he had taken the cause of Royal Navy ratings before parliament (*The Seamens Case*, 1699?) and had published a couple of pamphlets on naval affairs (*An Essay on the Navy*, 1702, and *A Proposal for Putting a Speedy End to the War*, 1703), in which he reveals an impressive command of detail and sympathy for the sailor's plight, he was twice accused of defrauding seamen of their wages. At some date after May 1711, insolvent, he left the capital. An examining commission declared him bankrupt in August 1711; days later Granville wrote to Robert, earl of Oxford, the lord high treasurer, reminding him that Dennis had made various proposals for raising revenue, including a new tax calculated to assist merchant shipping, and recommending that he be helped. Dennis acknowledged Granville, who stepped in when the ministry failed to act, in the dedication to *An Essay on the Genius and Writings of Shakespear* (1712) but relief was temporary; corporation records show that he was discharged from the Fleet, where he had been imprisoned for debt, in January 1713 (he may even have been held there as a debtor as early as 1696, but identification is not certain). At times during this period Dennis lived within the verges of the court, where he was safe from arrest, but in March 1716 he sold his waitership to Benjamin Hudson for £600, to which he attached a fifteen-year reversion (he was fifty-seven at the time of the sale), and for at least four years he 'lodg'd continually in the Neighbourhood of *White-hall*' (*Critical Works*, 2.212). He continued to divide his year between the capital and the country. Throughout his life, for months at a time, Dennis sought seclusion, particularly in Northamptonshire and at Cobham, in Surrey;

guineas and obtained for him the position of queen's waiter at the Port of London, a sinecure worth £52 a year.

A place, however exiguous, compensated for the inheritance Dennis had spent. With neither vocation nor profession to fall back on, he had also turned to the theatre. Dennis wrote several plays which achieved, at best, modest success: *A Plot, and No Plot* (1697), a farcical comedy; *Rinaldo and Armida* (1698), a dramatic opera with musical passages written mainly by John Eccles, which freely adapted Tasso's *Gerusalemme liberata* (1575); *Iphigenia* (1699), based on Euripides and supported by Colonel Christopher Codrington, who encouraged his friends to attend the author's benefit; and *The Comical Gallant* (1702), a farcical adaptation of *The Merry Wives of Windsor*, which quickly closed (Dennis was the first to record the tradition that Shakespeare wrote the play at Queen Elizabeth's command). With *Liberty Asserted* (1704) Dennis achieved his one theatrical success, an anti-French story set in Canada so successful (it was performed ten times between 24 February and 16 March 1704, and again on 27 March) that the author—it is claimed—feared the French would seek his extradition under the terms of the treaty of Utrecht. He sought Marlborough's help. The duke could not assist 'who that has Quails and *Burgundy* before him', he asked Thomas Sergeant, 'would leave them for *Porter* and Ram Mutton?' (Dennis, *Original Letters*, 127).

The critic Dennis is now best remembered as a critic. His first substantial works, *The Impartial Critick* (1693), a Socratic dialogue in five conversational parts, and *Remarks on a Book, Entitul'd Prince Arthur* (1696), were both directed at opponents of Dryden. *Letters upon Several Occasions* (1696) gathered correspondence on a variety of literary and critical topics, including a couple of thoughtful letters to Congreve on Ben Jonson and dramatic comedy. Dennis also wrote political defences of the theatre. *The Usefulness of the Stage to Religion* (1698) was a subtle first reply to the Revd Jeremy Collier's principled, anti-Williamite attacks, and in both 'The causes of the decay and defects of dramatick poetry' (1725?), one of a number of manuscripts held by the printer against money borrowed and unpublished in the author's life, and *The Stage Defended* (1726), he argued that government regulation of the theatres had social, political, and religious benefits.

The works Dennis published in the first years of the eighteenth century established his reputation. *The Advancement and Reformation of Modern Poetry* (1701) revisits the ancients and moderns controversy to propose a return to verse inspired by, and responsive to, Christian precepts. *The Grounds of Criticism in Poetry* (1704) invokes and amplifies many of the principles aired in the earlier account, including Horatian senses of Aristotelian good order (at some point before 1702 Dennis had translated the *Ars poetica* into verse), passion, the sublime, and the place of religion in literature, but it was no mere recapitulation; the contents of the volume were a small part of what had been intended to be an ambitious subscription which would formulate the rules for each genre and include critical biographies of selected English poets. Fewer than eighty readers underwrote the edition, however, and Dennis was obliged to publish only what he had gathered.

In 1711 an occasional series of articles appeared in *The Spectator* which disparaged critics. Dennis was particularly angered by no. 40 (16 April 1711), which attacked the theory of poetic justice (the idea that characters' fortunes should be determined by their moral conduct), a notion which Dennis had attempted to dramatize in his own plays and whose inclusion in the article he took as a personal affront. He replied in numerous letters to the periodical; a selection was first published as an appendix to his essay on Shakespeare. Addison kept his counsel. With relations strained, and in the face of the greatest dramatic success of the day, it was an act of critical independence, and courage, for Dennis to publish his *Remarks upon Cato* (1713), a formal account of how Addison's play suffers from its strict adherence to the dramatic unities. Johnson reprinted approvingly long extracts in his life of the essayist. Dennis was eventually reconciled to Addison but remained suspicious of Richard Steele's (blameless) hand in the articles.

Worse was to come. In a political act, Colley Cibber was deprived of his position at the Theatre Royal. Steele, the patentee of Drury Lane since 1715, wrote in his defence, in favour of the actor–managers whom Dennis blamed for the year-long delays in the production of his final play, *The Invader of his Country* (1719), an adaptation of *Coriolanus*, and its brief run. The four letters which form the two parts of *The Characters and Conduct of Sir John Edgar* (1720) turn from a libel of Cibber to a vigorously *ad hominem* attack on Steele, on his humble birth, his financial imprudence, his plagiarism, and dishonesty. In his *A Defence of Sir Fopling Flutter* (1722) and *Remarks on a Play, Call'd The Conscious Lovers* (1723), Dennis maintained the virtues of robustly realistic comedy against the type of sentimental romance Steele had sedulously promoted.

Pope was scarcely on nodding acquaintance with Dennis when he included him in *An Essay on Criticism* (1711):

> *Appius* reddens at each Word you speak,
> And *stares, Tremendous!* with a *threatning Eye*,
> Like some *fierce Tyrant* in *Old Tapestry*.
> (ll. 585–7)

Dennis unwittingly confirmed Pope's compression of insight and association in his *Reflections Critical and Satyrical, upon a Late Rhapsody, Call'd, An Essay on Criticism* (1711). The cumulative effect of Pope's subsequent literary and personal ridicule in, among others, *The Narrative of Dr Robert Norris* (1713), the Scriblerian collaborations *Three Hours after Marriage* (1717), in which Dennis appears briefly as Sir Tremendous Longinus, and *Peri Bathous* (1728), and, further, *The Dunciad: An Heroic Poem, in Three Books* (1728), was to suggest that the critic was lunatic: 'And all the Mighty Mad in Dennis rage' (A. Pope, *Dunciad variorum*, 1729, 1.104). In his own replies, *A True Character of Mr Pope and his Writings* (1716), printed without his permission, *Remarks upon Mr. Pope's Translation of Homer* (1717), and *Remarks on Mr Pope's Rape of the Lock* (1728), to which he added a preface on the attacks of 1728, Dennis let indignation get the better of him; acute close readings of individual lines (later editions of *An Essay on Criticism* silently incorporated several changes as a result) often give way to abuse of his adversary's physique and disabilities, his religion, politics, and commercial success. Only in *Remarks upon Several Passages in the Preliminaries to the Dunciad* (1729), a much cooler and more various response, did Dennis arrive at a winningly disinterested tone. Few noticed.

Non-literary writings Throughout his career Dennis commented on topics of public interest. His non-literary prose includes works on morality; both *An Essay on the Opera's after the Italian Manner* (1706) and *An Essay upon Publick Spirit* (1711) denigrate foreign influences on the nation; *Julius Caesar Acquitted* (1722) was Dennis's reply to a republican advocate of political murder, and *Vice and Luxury Publick Mischiefs* (1724) reacted to a new, expanded edition of Bernard Mandeville's *The Fable of the Bees* (1714; 1723). Dennis's religious tracts (*The Danger of Priestcraft to Religion and Government* (1702), the first of his works to sell widely, and *Priestcraft Distinguish'd from Christianity* (1715), a very popular anti-Jacobite pamphlet which had run to a third edition by 1718) were broadly protestant in their sympathies, as were two later works, *The Faith and Duties of Christians* (1728), a translation of the Revd Thomas Burnet's *De fide et officiis Christianorum*, and *A Treatise Concerning the State of*

Departed Souls (1730), which rendered Burnet's *De statu mortuorum et resurgentium*.

These translations, composed at the request of Burnet's literary executor, were completed in poor health and with failing sight. Dennis's final years, spent in blind infirmity, were wretched. He did not marry, although one story uniquely records 'the son of the critic' threatening violent revenge on the poet (*The Works of Alexander Pope*, ed. W. Elwin and W. J. Courthope, 10 vols., 1871–86, 8.237, n. 3). In old age, for Dennis, therefore, having outlived the reversion on the sale of his waitership, patronage became alms: since 1724 the earl of Pembroke had remembered the critic with occasional presents of 5 or 10 guineas, Atterbury sent £100 from his French exile in 1730, and, although he had never been a hired pen, Walpole found £20 for him for several years. In January 1725 and January 1731 benefit performances of *The Old Bachelor* and *Volpone* were staged for Dennis; on 18 December 1733 a performance of *The Provoked Husband* at the Haymarket, organized by Thomson, Mallet, Martin, and Pope (who anonymously supplied an equivocal prologue), was given for his benefit.

By his own admission, Dennis almost always wrote in haste. He revised little and left the transmission of what were often first and only drafts to the discretion of the printer. For a time, though, in the first decade of the eighteenth century, Dennis was England's leading critic, an elegant prose stylist possessed of a shrewd and perceptive literary intelligence. Subsequent generations have always acknowledged his abilities but his reputation gradually dwindled in the face of what others, Pope especially, said he had done. In his early championing of Milton, however, his emphasis on the psychological effects of the sublime, and in his contribution to the development of Wordsworth's and Coleridge's critical thought, Dennis's importance has begun to be recognized. And at his best, Dennis was capable of searchingly acute observation: the blank verse of Shakespeare's tragedies, he noticed, was complicated by polysyllabic line endings which paradoxically domesticate the speech of the characters, close reading he demonstrates at once: 'Such Verse we make when we are writing Prose; we make such Verse in common Conversation' (*Critical Works*, 2.5). The pity of his life was the moment he looked up from his studies at the world, and more particularly the people, around him. Dennis died on 6 January 1734 and was buried in the parish church of St Martin-in-the-Fields.

JONATHAN PRITCHARD

Sources H. G. Paul, *John Dennis: his life and criticism* (1911) • *The critical works of John Dennis*, ed. E. N. Hooker, 2 vols. (1939–43) • J. Dennis, *Original letters, familiar, moral and critical*, 2 vols. (1721) • F. S. Tupper, 'Notes on the life of John Dennis', *ELH: a Journal of English Literary History*, 5 (1938), 211–17 • A. N. Wilkins, 'John Dennis' stolen thunder', *N&Q*, 201 (1956), 425–8 • P. Rogers, 'New light on Dennis', *N&Q*, 217 (1972), 217–18 • J. Dennis, *Letters upon several occasions* (1696) • [J. Mottley], *A compleat list of all the English dramatic poets*, pubd with T. Whincop, *Scanderbeg* (1747) • W. Van Lennep and others, eds., *The London stage, 1660–1800*, 5 pts in 11 vols. (1960–68) • *The life of Mr John Dennis* (1734) • E. N. Hooker, 'Pope and Dennis', *ELH: a Journal of English Literary History*, 7 (1940), 188–98 • R. B. Kline, 'Prior and Dennis', *N&Q*, 211 (1966), 214–16 • W. T. J. Gun, ed., *The Harrow School register, 1571–1800* (1934) • J. Venn and others, eds., *Biographical history of Gonville and Caius College*, 1: 1349–1713 (1897) • J. Redington, ed., *Calendar of Treasury papers*, 4, PRO (1879) • E. N. Hooker, 'An unpublished autograph manuscript of John Dennis', *ELH: a Journal of English Literary History*, 1 (1934), 156–62 • S. Johnson, *Lives of the English poets*, ed. G. B. Hill, [new edn], 2 (1905) • J. Spence, *Observations, anecdotes, and characters, of books and men*, ed. J. M. Osborn, new edn, 2 vols. (1966) • J. Dennis, *Priestcraft distinguish'd from Christianity* (1715)

Likenesses S. Ireland, etching, 1799 (after W. Hogarth), BM, NPG • J. Vandergucht, line engraving, BM, NPG; repro. in *Life of Mr John Dennis* [see illus.]

Dennis, John Henry Cawsey (1871–1939), engineer and motor vehicle manufacturer, was born on 20 February 1871 at Huntshaw, near Torrington, Devon, the third son of William Henry Dennis, farmer, and his wife, Susanna, *née* Cawsey. After education at Taunton College, he followed his early interest in machinery and became apprenticed to a repairing ironmonger in Bideford, against his parents' wishes. He then secretly took up a post as an ironmonger's assistant in Guildford in 1894, and as a sideline he began to build and sell bicycles. For a short time he gained further experience with Brown Brothers, the well-known component factors, in London.

In early 1895 John Dennis returned to Guildford and opened his own shop, the Universal Athletic Stores, in the High Street. Here he sold cycles mainly of his own manufacture, with parts supplied by Brown Brothers. Like his contemporary William Morris (1877–1963), Dennis subsequently transferred his engineering skills from cycles to motor vehicles. Morris, however, went on to create a mass car-manufacturing concern, whereas Dennis chose to specialize in commercial vehicles.

Later in 1895 Dennis was joined by his younger brother, **Sir (Herbert) Raymond Dennis** (1878–1939), motor vehicle manufacturer. The fourth son, Raymond was born on 25 June 1878 at Huntshaw. Educated at Wellington School, Somerset, his initial contribution to their joint venture included his success as a competitive cyclist. In 1898 production of the brothers' first motorized vehicle, a tricycle with a De Dion engine, was added to that of their Speed King and Speed Queen bicycles. Quadricycles followed, and in 1901 cycle production gave way to the manufacture of motor vehicles, initially cars. John Dennis married Dora Annie, daughter of Stephen Baker, in 1903. There was one son of the marriage. Following Dora's death in 1934, he subsequently married her sister, Julia Elizabeth. In 1922 Raymond married Sybil Margaret, daughter of Sir Leonard Llewelyn, a government minister in charge of non-ferrous metals in the First World War. They had four sons and a daughter.

The first commercial vehicle from the Dennis works, a van for Harrods (followed by repeat orders), was delivered in 1904. A range of commercial vehicles was then built up; fire engines were added in 1908 (and remained a Dennis speciality). Car manufacture ceased in 1913, though not before inroads had been made into the taxi market, with such users as the General Motor Cab Company.

1913 had a double significance for Dennis Brothers, for

in this year the private company of 1901, which had replaced the original partnership, with the two brothers alternating as chairman, was itself relaunched as a public company with an authorized capital of £300,000. Dennis Brothers was by then a leading lorry manufacturer. By producing vehicles under the government's subvention scheme (whereby the purchasers of lorries which were accepted as suitable for subsequent military use would receive an annual subvention in peacetime), the company further strengthened its position as a significant producer of commercial vehicles. Orders from such major Post Office contractors and carriers as McNamara and Carter Paterson had helped to establish this position in the decade between the introduction of commercial vehicles and the First World War. This expansion of production and a larger product necessitated a move to Woodbridge Hill, Guildford, where the firm had room to grow.

John Dennis was a paternalistic employer; he established a non-contributory benevolent fund and developed extensive company housing, including 102 houses (Dennisville) built to accommodate the workforce associated with the White and Poppe engine company of Coventry, acquired in 1919 and transferred to Guildford in 1932. Lawnmower manufacture was introduced in the early 1920s as part of a diversification programme which included the production of industrial pumps (in addition to those for fire-fighting) and municipal vehicles. The latter proved commercially beneficial, as public expectations of local authority services grew and the physical growth of suburbia and housing estates created extra demand. Bus, coach, and ambulance designs, and new commercial vehicles, were developed in the 1920s and 1930s. It was the success of the bus, coach, and municipal vehicle ranges which provided momentum for the firm in the middle years of this period.

The partnership of the two brothers, who were actively involved in the firm as joint managing directors, combined John's engineering aptitude with Raymond's marketing skills. (Raymond Dennis was knighted in 1920 in recognition of the firm's wartime production effort.) Less well-known than the collaboration of the Rootes brothers, the lifelong working partnership of John and Raymond Dennis, which ended only with their deaths in the same year, is an equally impressive example of sibling co-operation in the development of a business. Alfred White and Peter Poppe provided the board with further engineering expertise when the White and Poppe engine firm was absorbed in 1919. Sir Raymond Dennis died at Gratham Grange, Gratham, Surrey, on 20 May 1939. The death of John Dennis occurred on 27 August 1939, at Down Place, Compton, Guildford, Surrey, only three months later; he was survived by his second wife. Both brothers enjoyed outdoor recreational pursuits, such as fishing. John Dennis served as a JP. RICHARD A. STOREY

Sources C. Gulvin, 'Dennis, John Cawsey, and Dennis, Sir Herbert Raymond', *DBB* · P. Kennett, *Dennis*, World Trucks, 6 (1979) · J. C. R. Dennis, 'A brief encounter. Twelve years of Dennis motor cars', *Veteran Car Handbook* (1973), 17–21 · *Commercial Motor* (1 Sept 1939), 84 · *CGPLA Eng. & Wales* (1939) · *WWW* · m. cert. [John Cawsey Dennis and Dora Annie Baker] · d. cert. [John Cawsey Dennis]

Archives Castle Arch Museum, Guildford, business records

Wealth at death £215,442 3s. 11d.: probate, 11 Nov 1939, *CGPLA Eng. & Wales* · £282,043 19s. 4d.—H. R. Dennis: probate, 26 July 1939, *CGPLA Eng. & Wales*

Dennis, Nigel Forbes (1912–1989), writer, was born on 16 January 1912 in Bletchingley, Surrey, the younger child and only son of Lieutenant-Colonel Michael Frederick Beauchamp Dennis (*d.* 1918) and his wife, Louise Marguerite Jermyn, youngest daughter of Theodore and Merelina Bosanquet, whose family were descendants of Huguenots from the Languedoc region of France. His parents lived in north Devon. As a young man Michael Dennis had tried his fortune in South Africa, fought in the Second South African War, and then settled in Southern Rhodesia, where Nigel's sister, Dorothy, was born. He returned to Britain on the outbreak of the First World War and enlisted in the King's Own Scottish Borderers; he was killed in 1918. In 1920 his widow married his best friend, Fitzroy Griffin, and the whole family returned to Rhodesia. Nigel was sent first to Plumtree School, Southern Rhodesia, and then to St Andrew's, Grahamstown, South Africa, which he had to leave early on account of attacks of epilepsy, an affliction which had struck him at the age of about eleven and against which he bore up courageously for the rest of his life. He had a half-brother and a half-sister.

From South Africa, Dennis was dispatched to Kitzbühel in Austria, where an uncle, A. Ernan Forbes Dennis, husband of the novelist Phyllis Bottome and friend of the psychologist Alfred Adler, was running a sort of crammer for would-be entrants to the Foreign Office (Peter and Ian Fleming were fellow pupils in Dennis's time) and also acting as British consul. From there he moved on, at his uncle's suggestion, to the Odenwaldschule in Bavaria, a progressive, co-educational establishment at the opposite pole, educationally speaking, to Plumtree and St Andrew's. Dennis, whose youthful literary ambitions had been expressed in stories contributed to the *Boy's Own Paper* (until a hot one from the Odenwaldschule caused the editor to disengage), was very soon writing a novel about this experience. Called *Chalk and Cheese*, it was published a few years later, in 1934, under the pseudonym Richard Vaughan. Dennis later chose to disown it.

After a further unsettled period (more tutoring, this time in Wales; helping his family, by now repatriated, to run a small hotel in Chipping Campden in the Cotswolds called 'The Live and Let Live', where the young Graham Greenes were neighbours; and selling ladies' garments door-to-door) Dennis got his lucky break. A legacy enabled him to travel steerage to New York and a dockers' strike prevented him from returning on the appointed date. He stayed eighteen years, working first as an assiduous freelance, writing stories and articles and helping to translate the writings of Adler, then landing salaried jobs. He became (improbably) secretary of the national board of the *Review of Motion Pictures* (1935) and was assistant editor and book reviewer of the *New Republic* (1937–8) and staff reviewer of *Time* magazine (from 1940). In 1949 he published his first acknowledged novel, *Boys and Girls Come out to Play* (*A Sea Change* in the USA), which won the Anglo-American novel award for that year (shared with Anthony West). It starts very personally, with a description of a young man having an epileptic fit.

Dennis returned to England in 1950 and five years later published *Cards of Identity*, the novel which made his name. Its theme—the ease with which modern man, uncertain of who he is, can be manipulated by charlatans—was advanced and piquant. At the request of George Devine, of the English Stage Company, Dennis turned it into a play; it was produced in London at the Royal Court Theatre in 1956. A second play, *The Making of Moo*, an anti-religious send-up which caused protests in the stalls, followed a year later and in 1958 both were published in book form as *Two Plays and Preface*—the preface being a Voltairean swipe at theologians such as St Augustine and a paean of praise for satirists such as Aristophanes. His last play, *August for the People*, was produced in 1961.

Dennis's books were few but distinguished: *Dramatic Essays* (1962), a collection worth pondering for its radical approach; *Jonathan Swift* (1964), a study of one of his heroes, which won the Royal Society of Literature award under the W. H. Heinemann bequest (1966); and a haunting last novel, *A House in Order* (1966), which showed the influence of Franz Kafka and the author's passion for gardening. In 1967 he moved to Malta and two final volumes—*Exotics* (1970), a book of Mediterranean poems, and the short, quirky, bellicose *An Essay on Malta* (1972), with illustrations by Osbert Lancaster—were inspired by this new scene.

From its launch in February 1961 until his retirement twenty years later Dennis was lead reviewer of the *Sunday Telegraph*. His admixture of wit, acuteness, and common sense made him an unfailing draw. Between 1963 and 1970 he was drama critic, contributor, and finally co-editor of *Encounter* magazine, but this association ended in acrimony. He wrote for, and read on, radio.

Dennis was tall, somewhat sardonic-looking, and with facial corrugations in his later years which rivalled, but could not quite match, those of his admired W. H. Auden. A fine conversationalist when the mood took him, he could also be elusive and tortuous: not for nothing had he fielded in boyhood for B. J. T. Bosanquet, the famous cricketer who invented the googly. He was twice married: first, probably in 1934, 1935, or 1936, to Marie-Madeleine, daughter of Avit (Jean) Massias, a peasant farmer from the Charente in France; the couple had two daughters. The marriage was dissolved and in 1959 he married Beatrice Ann Hewart Matthew, a most spirited support and scribe. She was the daughter of William Alexander Matthew, a director of his family's shipping firm in Cardiff. Dennis died on 19 July 1989 in Little Compton, near Moreton in Marsh, Warwickshire, at the home of his elder daughter.

RIVERS SCOTT, *rev.*

Sources R. Verrecchia, 'Westdown to Mosali: the diaries of Louise Bosanquet', BA diss., Manchester Metropolitan University, 1993 ·

The Times (21 July 1989) · personal knowledge (1996) · private information (1996)

Dennis, Sir (Herbert) Raymond (1878–1939). *See under* Dennis, John Henry Cawsey (1871–1939).

Dennis, Sir Thomas. *See* Denys, Sir Thomas (*c.*1477–1561).

Dennison, Stanley Raymond (1912–1992), economist and university administrator, was born in a small terrace flat at 49 Trevor Terrace in North Shields on 15 June 1912, son of Stanley Dennison (1884–1943) and his wife, Florence Ann Smythe (*d.* 1984). His father worked in the office of the local gas company, first as a clerk and then as cashier. The boy went to Tynemouth Municipal High School, in the first year in which economics was taught there. He then went to Armstrong College, Newcastle, part of Durham University, where he so impressed his teachers that they arranged for his admission to Trinity College, Cambridge. From 1935 to 1939 he was lecturer in economics at Manchester University, years which saw the completion of *The Location of Industry and the Depressed Areas* (1939), an influential book on a theme which had interested him since Armstrong College days. In 1939, when only twenty-seven, he was appointed professor of economics at University College, Swansea, but in 1940 became chief economic assistant in the war cabinet secretariat, one of a team responsible for mobilizing the industrial war effort. For this work he was made a CBE. In 1945 he became a fellow of Gonville and Caius College, and university lecturer in economics, at Cambridge. His lectures on the structure of industry were informed by deep practical knowledge of the subject gained during the war, and were very popular with students.

In post-war decades Dennison encountered conflicts both in college and in the university's economics faculty. At Caius, discontent was aimed at reforming an old-fashioned system of college government. Dennison was on the side of the reformers; as senior tutor from 1952 he did much to modernize the college's administrative procedures. Among Cambridge economists, differing views on economic policy polarized into disputes maintained with a rancour which astonished visiting scholars. Some of the disciples of J. M. Keynes, convinced of the competence of the state as an economic manager, and gullible about contemporary communist regimes, enjoyed a dominant position among Cambridge economists in these years. Those who disagreed with them, like D. H. Robertson and Dennison, were treated with an intolerance which made rational argument difficult. In his writings and teaching Dennison never wavered from his reasoned exposition of more liberal economic doctrines.

In 1958 Dennison left Cambridge to become professor of economics at Queen's University, Belfast. Four years later he was appointed to the prestigious David Dale chair of economics at Newcastle. He modernized the department, expanding staff and student numbers and encouraging a programme of research and publication which greatly enhanced its standing. He also served for six years as pro-vice-chancellor, making a major contribution to the administration of the newly independent University of Newcastle.

In 1972 Dennison became vice-chancellor of the University of Hull, where he secured significant improvements in staffing and subject coverage. He was less happy in dealing with militant students encouraged by a disaffected minority of left-wing academic staff. Dennison was angered by what he saw as unjustified disruption of the university's affairs, and this was reflected in his sometimes abrasive handling of the malcontents. When he retired in 1979 he returned to Tyneside, spending his last years in a flat with views of the sea and the mouth of the Tyne. He continued for some years to chair the governing body of Newcastle's Royal Grammar School. Throughout his career he was in demand for committee work; for example, he served on the review body on remuneration of doctors and dentists, on the University Grants Committee, and as vice-chairman of the Committee of Vice-Chancellors and Principals. He died, unmarried, on 22 November 1992 at Greenacres Nursing Home, Coast Road, Wallsend, and was cremated on 1 December at Tynemouth crematorium.

Among twentieth-century economists, Dennison was an influential champion of a kind of liberal economic thought which, though overshadowed for a while by post-Keynesian collectivist doctrines, had before the century's end revived to exercise an effective influence on both economic thinking and public policy. He never courted popularity, and expressed profound scepticism about the economic competence of the state at times when to do so was unfashionable. Although his lucid writings and his participation in public inquiries were significant, much of his personal influence was exercised in ways which were less visible, which may account for the limited public recognition which he received. He was always willing to welcome and support visiting scholars who espoused beliefs similar to his own. For example, in Milton Friedman's *Memoirs*, Dennison appears repeatedly not only as 'a first-rate economist', but also as someone who had warmly but unobtrusively supported Friedman on his early visits to Britain. The Institute of Economic Affairs was one of the most influential think-tanks in twentieth-century Britain, paving the way in its publications and other activities for what came to be seen as the Thatcherite era. For many years, as a member of its council, Dennison played an important role in shaping the institute's work. He was an active early participant in the Mont Pelerin Society, an international group of considerable standing inspired by the work of Hayek.   NORMAN McCORD

Sources *Daily Telegraph* (26 Nov 1992) · *The Independent* (26 Nov 1992) · *The Independent* (28 Nov 1992) · *The Times* (24 Nov 1992) · M. Friedman and R. D. Friedman, *Two lucky people: memoirs* (1998) · personal knowledge (2004) · *Evening News* [North Shields] (27 May 1943) · private information (2004) [Lord Harris of High Cross; Peter Cropper; William Scott] · b. cert. · d. cert. · *CGPLA Eng. & Wales* (1993)

Likenesses J. Gilroy, portrait (as vice-chancellor), Jubilee Room, U. Hull · photograph, repro. in *Daily Telegraph* · photograph, repro. in *The Independent* · photograph, repro. in *The Times* · photographs, U. Hull

Wealth at death £372,819: probate, 19 Feb 1993, *CGPLA Eng. & Wales*

Denniston, Alexander Guthrie [Alastair] (1881–1961), cryptanalyst and intelligence officer, was born on 1 December 1881 at Greenock, the eldest child of James Denniston, a medical practitioner, and his wife, Agnes Guthrie. He was educated at Bowdon College, Cheshire, and at the universities of Bonn and Paris.

From 1906 to 1909 Denniston taught at Merchiston Castle School. He then went to teach foreign languages at the Royal Naval College at Osborne, Isle of Wight. A considerable athlete, he played hockey for Scotland in the pre-war Olympic games. When war broke out in 1914, he was one of the few men in the service of the Admiralty who were fluent in German, and he played a leading part in the hasty establishment of Room 40 OB. Taking its name from the office in which it operated (Room 40, Old Buildings, Admiralty), this organization intercepted, decrypted, and interpreted on behalf of the naval staff German and other enemy wireless and cable communications. For its wartime exploits—and most of all, perhaps, for its success in decrypting the notorious Zimmermann telegram—Room 40 OB subsequently became internationally known. The fame did not extend to Denniston, nor (though he was at the centre of the cryptanalytical process) did he contribute to the publicity on which it rested: he was by nature reticent, and in 1919 he had been selected to lead the country's peacetime cryptanalytical effort as head of the Government Code and Cypher School (GCCS). In 1917 Denniston married Dorothy Mary Gilliat, who worked at the time with him in Room 40 OB. She was the daughter of Arthur Gilliat, a businessman; they had one son and one daughter. Their son, Robin, made his career in publishing and became the academic publisher at Oxford University Press.

Denniston served as the operational head of GCCS from 1919 to February 1942. He supervised its formation as a small interdepartmental organization of twenty-five people recruited from Room 40 OB and its equivalent section in the War Office, MI1B. It included defectors from Russia, linguists, and talented amateurs of all kinds. Denniston, appointed CBE in 1933, presided over its slow inter-war expansion. In those years it had to cope with the continuously increasing sophistication of cipher security and with a decline in wireless communications, as well as with a shortage of funds. Yet he succeeded in the important task of preserving continuity of expertise and experience, and also presided over GCCS's rapid expansion and transfer to Bletchley Park on the outbreak of the Second World War in 1939.

In 1937 Denniston had begun to recruit a number of dons who were to join GCCS on the outbreak of war. His contacts with academics who had been members of Room 40 OB helped him to choose such men as Alan Turing and Gordon Welchman, who subsequently led the attack on Wehrmacht Enigma. Denniston's foresight, and his wise selection of the new staff, who for the first time included mathematicians, were the basis for many of GCCS's outstanding wartime successes, especially against Enigma. In

Alexander Guthrie Denniston (1881–1961), by Lafayette, 1933

the first half of 1940 Denniston had the satisfaction of knowing that, reinforced by the wartime staff which he had recruited and with the aid of vital information supplied by Polish cryptanalysts who had solved Wehrmacht Enigma many years earlier, GCCS was beginning to solve the problem which had most stubbornly defied all its efforts. This was the problem posed by Germany's adoption of the Enigma cipher machine in various versions for the secret communications of the armed forces, the railways, the secret service, and other government organizations.

Yet Denniston knew that GCCS could not hope to tackle the ciphers of the axis powers on its own. From early 1941 onwards he strove to promote full co-operation between GCCS and the United States' army and navy code-breaking units, urging the Americans to attack Japanese traffic, with GCCS concentrating on German and Italian signals. Although some senior figures both inside and outside GCCS were initially very reluctant to share GCCS's Enigma secrets with the Americans, his views were implemented in the Holden agreement of October 1942 on naval ciphers and the BRUSA (Britain–United States of America) agreement of May 1943 on the army, air force, and secret service ciphers of Germany, Italy, and Japan. Both Britain and America benefited immeasurably from the resulting co-operation, which later led to similar far-ranging post-war agreements between the two countries.

GCCS achieved a substantial mastery of Enigma in the second half of 1941, reading from then until the end of the

war many of the ciphers it employed. In the course of doing so, it increased its staff from about 200 in September 1939 to 10,500 (including its out-stations in England) by January 1945. GCCS also encountered new administrative requirements, and to an ever greater extent came to rely for its operation on specialized apparatus and machinery. Although Denniston recognized that these developments called for a major reorganization, he was not himself the man to carry it out: he had always been a reluctant administrator, preferring to concentrate on technical matters. Nor was he forceful enough in pressing GCCS's case for priority in obtaining junior staff and vital code-breaking machinery. In October 1941 four cryptanalysts, including Turing and Welchman, became so frustrated with the resulting delays in breaking Enigma that they appealed for help directly to Winston Churchill, who immediately ordered that they were to 'have all they want on extreme priority' (minute, 22 Oct 1941, PRO, HW 1/155). A reorganization in February 1942 divided GCCS into a services and a civil, and much smaller, wing, which had only about 250 staff (including its commercial section) by March 1944. As head of the services division Denniston was succeeded by Commander Edward W. Travis; he himself, having been appointed CMG in 1941, remained the head of the civil division, moving to London (to above Madame Riché, 'couturier des dames' in Berkeley Street), where, on seven floors, he and his team dealt with the diplomatic traffic of Germany, Italy, Japan, and many neutral countries—the commercial section, which had fifty staff in May 1943, worked in the nearby Aldford House.

The department worked eighteen hours a day, seven days a week, and achieved many successes. Colonel Alfred McCormack, the influential deputy head of the US army's special branch, which supervised signal intelligence in the US war department, was extremely impressed by Berkeley Street during a lengthy visit to GCCS in 1943. He informed the department that it would be 'absolutely astonished' by the 'resources of intelligence … here in Denniston's show, waiting for somebody to tap them' (cable 4952, 2 June 1943, 'Colonel McCormack's trip to London'). Denniston, continuing his policy of co-operating fully with the United States, had 'turned his people over to us [McCormack's team] for questioning and given us a free run of his place' more than anybody else in GCCS ('Conversations with Denniston', Colonel McCormack's trip to London, 63). Although Denniston was bitterly disappointed at no longer being sole head of GCCS, he headed the Berkeley Street section most effectively. He retired in 1945 and thereafter taught French and Latin at a Leatherhead preparatory school.

Throughout his long period of office as operational head of an undivided GCCS, directly responsible to the chief of the secret service, Denniston brought unusual distinction and expertise, as well as devotion, to his work. If he had little liking for questions of administration, he had even less for the ways of bureaucracy and the demands of hierarchy. By his willingness to delegate, his trust in subordinates, his informality, and his charm he set his stamp on the character of the place, particularly in the early war years in Bletchley Park. More than any other man, he helped it to maintain both the creative atmosphere which underlay its great contribution to British intelligence during the Second World War and the complete security which was no less an important precondition of its achievement.

Alastair Denniston, as he was known, was a small man, with a strong, craggy-featured face—indeed, colleagues referred to him as 'the little man'. With his athletic figure, he was always very neatly turned out. He died at the Memorial Hospital, Milford-on-Sea, Hampshire, on 1 January 1961.   F. H. HINSLEY, *rev.* RALPH ERSKINE

Sources F. H. Hinsley and others, *British intelligence in the Second World War*, 1 (1979) · P. Seale and M. McConville, *Philby: the long road to Moscow* (1973) · C. Andrew, *Secret service: the making of the British intelligence community* (1986) · A. G. Denniston, 'The Code and Cypher School between the wars', *Codebreaking and signals intelligence*, ed. C. Andrew (1986), 47–70 · private information (1981) · *CGPLA Eng. & Wales* (1961) · R. Denniston, 'The professional career of A. G. Denniston', *British and American approaches to intelligence*, ed. K. Robertson (1987), 104–29 · R. Erskine and M. Smith, eds., *Action this day: Bletchley Park from the breaking of the Enigma code to the birth of the modern computer* (2001) · R. Erskine, 'What did the Sinkov mission receive from Bletchley Park?', *Cryptologia*, 24 (2000), 97–109 · R. Erskine, 'The Holden agreement on naval sigint: the first BRUSA?', *Intelligence and National Security*, 14/2 (1999), 187–97 · Colonel McCormack's trip to London, May–June 1943, National Archives and Records Administration, College Park, Maryland, Historic Cryptographic Collection, RG 457, nos. 3443, 3600 · F. L. Birch, 'British sigint, 1914–1945', PRO, HW 43/1 to 3 · PRO, HW 1, HW 3, and HW 14 files

Archives CAC Cam., corresp. and papers

Likenesses Lafayette, photograph, 1933, NPG [*see illus.*]

Wealth at death £3054 13*s.* 10*d.*: probate, 16 Feb 1961, *CGPLA Eng. & Wales*

Denniston, John Dewar (1887–1949), classical scholar, was born on 4 March 1887, at Bareilly, India, the younger surviving son of James Lawson Denniston, of the Bengal civil service, and his wife, Laura Mary Davies. He attended the Dragon School, Oxford, and was a scholar of Winchester College and of New College, Oxford, where he gained a first class in classical moderations in 1908 and a second class in *literae humaniores* in 1910. He was Craven scholar in 1909 and in 1913 was elected a fellow of Hertford College, where he remained for the rest of his life with the exception of the war years. In 1914 he was commissioned in the King's Own Scottish Borderers, served in France, and was twice wounded. He later transferred to the War Office and was appointed OBE for his services; he returned to the War Office again for the duration of the Second World War. He married on 5 July 1919 Mary Grace, daughter of Joseph John Morgan, solicitor, of London; there were no children.

Denniston ranked among the most gifted and distinguished classical scholars of his time. His principal publications include *Greek Literary Criticism* (1924), Cicero's *Philippics I and II* (1926), *The Greek Particles* (1934; 2nd rev. edn, 1954; reprinted 1981); and Euripides' *Electra* (1939), one of the best extant editions of a Greek tragedy. *Greek Prose Style* appeared posthumously in 1952, and was reprinted in 1997; an Italian version by Enrico Renna, with excellent indexes, came out in 1993.

The quality of all Denniston's work was very high; but his greatest contribution to knowledge was his monumental book on the Greek particles. This is a work which bears comparison with the achievements of the great scholars of the past. It represents the exercise of an original and penetrating mind in a field of vast extent. The whole of classical Greek literature is explored; the examples (which number over 20,000) depend on Denniston's own reading and judgement, and their complexity is made intelligible by a lucid and accurate intellect, the myriad interpretations each the result of fresh and fine meditation. The style is vigorous, and the ideal humane. Denniston was concerned much less with linguistic schematism than with niceties of meaning: the Greek particles are keys to the undertones of meaning, and Denniston was the first to detect and interpret the undertones in thousands of passages of Greek prose and poetry. The book is indispensable in all fields of Greek literature, and it is difficult to see how it can ever be superseded.

Denniston was a joint editor of the first edition of the *Oxford Classical Dictionary* (1949), to which he contributed a masterly survey of Greek metre. His draft of an edition of Aeschylus's *Agamemnon* was completed after his death by Denys Page and appeared in 1957.

Denniston was among the most successful classical tutors of his time at Oxford, and tutors from other colleges sent their best students to him for final preparation before university scholarships. He required of his pupils keenness and honesty in their work and it then seemed no effort to him to treat them on terms of equality, whatever their intellectual gifts. He came to regard the tutorial hour as a matter of importance, almost of urgency, and could be outspoken in praise or blame, but always strove to impart something of his own love and understanding of the ancient world, and of his high ideals of scholarship. A considerable part of the work which he did with his pupils was published in *Some Oxford Compositions* (1949) of which he was a joint editor and a principal contributor. He was unsurpassed in the art of rendering English prose into classical Greek.

From his schooldays Denniston was devoted to music, and enjoyed playing tennis and, later, watching cricket, but his chief delight was in good conversation and in the happy home which was for many years a centre of lively entertainment in Oxford. For him, conversation meant argument on a stated theme. Through smaller talk he would growl absently; then a phrase would attract him, and with much brushing of the coat-lapel and lightening of the eyes he would attack. His mind was singularly clear and quick, his speech candid and forceful, almost violent. No quarter was given, nor yet offence. Ironical but not sarcastic, subtle but not sophistical, he left in the mind of the listener the impression of a powerful intellect controlled by good humour, a warm heart, and a profound inner modesty. He was a lifelong Liberal and an active and proselytizing member of the League of Nations Union. He watched with horror the rise of the dictators and was among the first to offer refuge in his home to exiles from Austria.

When the regius chair of Greek became vacant on the retirement of Gilbert Murray in 1936, Denniston was passed over in favour of E. R. Dodds. He was elected FBA in 1937 and proceeded DLitt at Oxford in 1949, shortly before his death, at The Beeches, Church Stretton, Shropshire, on 2 May 1949.   D. L. PAGE, *rev.* MARK POTTLE

Sources C. M. Bowra, *PBA*, 35 (1949), 219–32 · personal knowledge (1959) · private information (1959, 2004) [Sir Hugh Lloyd-Jones] · *The Times* (9 May 1949) · *CGPLA Eng. & Wales* (1949)
Archives AM Oxf., notebooks and papers on Greek metre | Bodl. Oxf., corresp. with Gilbert Murray
Likenesses W. Stoneman, photograph, 1938, NPG; repro. in Bowra, *PBA*
Wealth at death £6316 8s. 9d.: probate, 19 Aug 1949, *CGPLA Eng. & Wales*

Denniston, Sir Robert, of Montjoy (1546/7–1625), government official and diplomat, was the eldest son of James Denniston, provost of Linlithgow, and Margaret, daughter of Sir Thomas Bellenden of Auchnoull, justice-clerk. His mother later married Robert Hamilton of Ecclesmachan. Denniston matriculated from St Mary's College at the University of St Andrews in 1566 and graduated BA in 1570 and MA in 1571, apparently having studied law. On 4 September 1578 he was appointed procurator fiscal for the king for all royal causes before the commissary court of Edinburgh. He shared this office from 1584 with John Leirmonth, and resigned it on 6 January 1587 in favour of Thomas Rollock. Before 5 April 1586 he married Helen Myrtoun (or Mortoun; *d.* 1608), widow of Colonel Andrew Traill.

On 1 May 1589 Denniston officially succeeded his paternal kinsman George Halkheid in the office of conservator of the Scottish nation at Campveere. A statement in Halkheid's will suggests that this succession had been earlier endorsed by James VI, and Denniston probably served in an unofficial capacity from 1587. Campveere was the principal Scottish trading port and staple in the Low Countries, allowed to Scotland by treaty. In 1591 the privy council passed an act making the conservator directly responsible to the council, rather than answering to the council of royal burghs, as was the tradition. This change enhanced James VI's consolidation of central power. From 1597, to help collect customs duties, a coquet customs seal from the conservator's office attesting to goods loaded on all ships bound for Scotland was required. More importantly Denniston was Scotland's only resident ambassador in Europe at a time when embassies, even to England, were otherwise funded only for specific purposes.

Following the agreement with George Halkheid regarding his succession as conservator, Denniston sold 164 acres in Linlithgow inherited from his father. The buyer was his cousin, Sir Lewis Bellenden of Auchnoull, justice-clerk, who paid 10,000 merks. However, Denniston used the style 'of Cardmondlawes' in 1586 and 'of Montjoy' from 1600; both these lands were apparently reserved as a liferent from his estate, an unusual arrangement. In reality Denniston owned no land, though he was permitted the designation customary to a laird.

Denniston was officially suspended from his duties from September to November 1596 after the earl of Erroll escaped from his custody. Erroll had been an exiled fugitive from Scotland since March 1595, following his involvement with the Roman Catholic earls Huntly and Angus in the Spanish plot and related events in summer 1594. Well-meaning officials of the estates of Zealand recognized Erroll in early 1596 and arrested him, thinking it would please James VI, and promptly turned the earl over to the custody of Denniston, though the Scots had neither requested nor encouraged these actions. Nevertheless, news of Erroll's capture and subsequent 'escape' caused an outcry among segments of the Scottish population (and particularly among the more strident members of the protestant ministry) and James VI made a show of recalling Denniston. The English ambassador, Robert Bowes, expressed his view that the king never intended to punish Denniston. It is unclear whether Denniston had secret instruction from the king or whether he permitted the escape on his own initiative, though both possibilities were suspected by contemporaries and appear more likely than Erroll's escape by his own means. There is every likelihood that the king was relieved that Erroll's escape obviated the need to bring him to trial for treason. Denniston continued to enjoy the king's confidence and was subsequently employed in matters involving delicate 'real politic', including the role of third-party peace negotiator in the Low Countries between England and Spain in 1600; his letters about these negotiations are in the Moray muniments and the De L'Isle and Salisbury papers. He was knighted at the celebration of Prince Charles's baptism on 25 December 1600.

A member of the congregation at Greyfriars Church, Edinburgh, Denniston actively supported the king's efforts to assert the crown's authority over the kirk, including the extension of episcopal power. Calderwood records that when William Cranston, a minister of the Melvillian party, refused to demit his pulpit at the August 1607 synod of Fife, as ordered by the lords commissioners, Denniston went to Cranston 'and rounded his ear, desiring him to desist, for the Lords had appointed another to preach' (Calderwood, 6.674). Appointed to the privy council in 1602, Denniston was active there until June 1607. His wife died on 13 February 1608 and was buried in the churchyard of St Andrew's Cathedral; there is no record of any children. After a second period abroad, Denniston was reappointed to council in 1617 and from 1619 to 1624 served on several council committees concerning commercial matters as diverse as the loading of ships to the tanning of hides and the making of soap. Owing to his age and inability to travel, from 30 December 1623 he shared the office of conservator with Nathaniel Udwart, burgess of Edinburgh.

Denniston died in Edinburgh on 15 June 1625, aged seventy-eight, leaving an estate of more than £12,600 Scots (including debts owed to him of £9705 Scots); he was buried in Greyfriars churchyard, where a splendid monument, constructed with 1200 merks (£800 Scots) provided for the purpose in his will, survives by the east wall. He left legacies to two hospitals: 500 merks (£330 Scots) for Linlithgow Hospital and 100 merks to Stirling Hospital. He also endowed a bursary of 500 merks to the College of Edinburgh, with preference to students of the Denniston surname. Denniston was survived by his second wife, Christian (d. 1641), daughter of George Gibson (d. c.1590), clerk of session, and previously widow of Martin Shoner, physician to the king, with whom she had had at least four children. Each of these children was a beneficiary of Denniston's will, and his widow was provided with a maintenance of 10,000 merks (£6600 Scots) to be administered by her brother, Lord Alexander *Gibson of Durie, a lord of session and one of Denniston's executors. She subsequently bought the lands of Caskberrie in Fife from James Weymss of Caskberrie in 1627, and enjoyed the style of Lady Caskberrie until her death on 31 July 1641.

R. R. ZULAGER

Sources A. I. Dunlop, ed., *Acta facultatis artium universitatis Sanctiandree, 1413–1588*, St Andrews University Publications, 56 (1964) · D. Calderwood, *The history of the Kirk of Scotland*, ed. T. Thomson and D. Laing, 8 vols., Wodrow Society, 7 (1842–9) · *CSP Scot., 1547–1603* · T. Thomson, ed., *Inquisitionum ad capellam domini regis retornatarum … abbreviatio*, 3 vols. (1811–16) · J. M. Thomson and others, eds., *Registrum magni sigilli regum Scotorum / The register of the great seal of Scotland*, 11 vols. (1882–1914) · *Reg. PCS*, 1st ser. · *Reg. PCS*, 2nd ser. · M. Livingstone, D. Hay Fleming, and others, eds., *Registrum secreti sigilli regum Scotorum / The register of the privy seal of Scotland*, 8 vols. (1908–82) · J. M. Anderson, ed., *Early records of the University of St Andrews*, Scottish History Society, 3rd ser., 8 (1926) · *Proceedings of the Society of Antiquaries of Scotland*, 70 (1935–6), 114 · *An inventory of the ancient and historical monuments of the city of Edinburgh, with the thirteenth report of the commission*, Royal Commission on the Ancient and Historical Monuments in Scotland (1951), 49–50 · R. Monteith, *An theatre of mortality, or, The illustrious inscriptions extant upon the several monuments erected over the dead bodies (of the sometime honourable persons) buried within the Grayfriars Church yard; and other churches and burial-places within the city of Edinburgh and suburbs* (1704), 11–12 · R. Zulager, 'A study of the middle-rank administrators in the government of King James VI of Scotland, 1580–1603', PhD diss., U. Aberdeen, 1991, 263–71 · NRA Scotland, SRO, RD1/xxxv/153b–158 [lands of Montjoy] · NRA Scotland, SRO, CC8/8/liii/142–46; SRO, CC8/8/xxii/271b–272b [Edinburgh testaments] · NRA Scotland, Moray muniments, SRO, 217, vol. XII, box 43, items 259, 260, and 263 · Edinburgh City Archives, ECA, Moses bundles, documents 7607–11, 7616 · J. Davidson and A. Gray, *The Scottish staple at Veere* (1909), 186–95
Wealth at death £12,600: NA Scot., CC 8/8/liii/142–46 [Edinburgh testaments]

Dennistoun, James, of Dennistoun (1803–1855), antiquary and art collector, eldest son of James Dennistoun of Colgrain and Camiseskan (d. 1834) and his wife, Mary Ramsay, daughter of George Oswald of Auchencruive and Scotston, was born in Dunbartonshire on 17 March 1803—one of fourteen children. He was descended from the lords of Danzielstoun who traced their ancestry to the reign of Alexander III. After receiving his education at the universities of Edinburgh and Glasgow he became a member of the Faculty of Advocates in 1824 but never practised.

Dennistoun early developed a taste for legal and historical antiquities, and made some progress in the collection of materials for a history of Dunbartonshire. During a continental tour in 1825 and 1826, in which his companions were Mark Napier, John Hamilton Gray of Camtyne, and Alexander Dunlop of Keppoch, the art and literature of Italy first attracted his attention. After his father's death he was obliged to part with the family estate on the shores of the Clyde, but with part of his remaining fortune he was able to purchase the farm of Dennistoun Mains in Renfrewshire, the centre of the original possessions of his family in that county.

A second visit abroad in 1836–9, to the Netherlands, Germany, Switzerland, and Italy, was devoted mainly to literary research and to the examination of the monuments of art. It was at this stage that Dennistoun began to form a small, but choice, collection of early Italian pictures and illuminated miniatures from manuscripts, as well as items of the applied arts, which was added to during further visits to the continent in 1843–6, 1851, and 1853. His declared intention was to illustrate 'the progress of painting from the 13th century through the successive schools down to modern times—but my favourite style goes back to the 14th and 15th' (Dennistoun to D. Laing, 3 December 1848, Brigstocke, 'James Dennistoun's second European tour', 247). He did not in fact achieve his wider aim, but was one of the first acknowledged collectors of early Italian and Netherlandish painting. He also seems to have acquired pictures with his scholarly interests in mind; they included, for example, the portrait of Guidobaldo da Montefeltro attributed to Piero della Francesca (Museo Thyssen-Bornemisza, Madrid). Although Dennistoun bought extensively abroad, he also attended sales in Britain and correspondingly his taste widened to include Spanish seventeenth-century painting and, somewhat surprisingly, the work of Sir Joseph Noël Paton, whose *The Reconciliation of Oberon and Titania* (National Gallery of Scotland, Edinburgh) he owned. The collection was assembled at Dennistoun's house, 119 George Street, Edinburgh, his permanent home from 1846, and a brief account of it was published in the third volume of G. F. Waagen's *Treasures of Art in Great Britain* (1854).

Dennistoun was a magistrate and deputy lieutenant for the county of Renfrew, and became a member of most of the societies formed for collecting materials for illustrating the history of Scotland, with a particular interest, for example, in the history of Dunbartonshire. For the Bannatyne Club he edited David Moysie's *Memoirs of the Affairs of Scotland from 1577 to 1603* (1830). For the Maitland Club he prepared *Cartularium comitatus de Levenax, ab initio seculi decimi tertii usque ad annum MCCCXCVIII* (1833), *Cochrane Correspondence Regarding the Affairs of Glasgow, 1745–6* (1836), *Coltness Collections, 1608–1840* (1842), and, as co-editor with Alexander Macdonald, *Miscellany, consisting of original papers illustrative of the history and literature of Scotland* (3 vols., 1834). He also wrote *Letter on the Scotish [sic] Reform Bill by a conservative* (1832) and *Memoirs of Sir Robert Strange, engraver, and of his brother-in-law, Andrew Lumisden, private secretary to the Stuart princes* (2 vols., 1855). His most significant work, however, was *Memoirs of the dukes of Urbino, illustrating the arms, arts, and literature of Italy from 1440 to 1630* (3 vols., 1851), which combined his interest in early Italian history, art, and literature. It was notable, for example, for the attention devoted to Piero della Francesca. Dedicated to Lord Lindsay, twenty-fifth earl of Crawford, author of *Sketches of the History of Christian Art* (3 vols., 1847), the *Memoirs of the Dukes of Urbino* was issued in a second edition in 1909 with a short biography of the author by Edward Hutton. For the *Quarterly Review* of December 1846 Dennistoun wrote an article entitled 'The Stuarts in Italy', and in the *Edinburgh Review* of October 1854 a review of J. H. Burton's *History of Scotland*. After a highly critical article in the *Edinburgh Review* in April 1853 (pp. 390–420) Dennistoun gave valuable evidence before the committee of the House of Commons on the National Gallery in London in the same year, and furnished an analysis of the report of the committee to the *Edinburgh Review* of April 1854.

Dennistoun married, on 2 March 1835, in Bern, Isabella Katharina, eldest daughter of James Wolfe Murray, Lord Cringletie. He died at his home at 119 George Street, Edinburgh, on 13 February 1855, aged fifty-two. The greater portion of Dennistoun's collection was sold at Christies on 14 June 1855 (list reprinted in the first volume of the 1909 edition of *Memoirs of the Dukes of Urbino*, pp. xix–xxviii). Several of the paintings are now in public collections. Of the illuminated manuscripts, the Ghislieri book of hours is in the British Library (Yates Thompson MS 29), and several items were in the collection of Kenneth, Lord Clark, and were sold at Christies on 3 July 1984.

G. C. BOASE, *rev.* CHRISTOPHER LLOYD

Sources H. Brigstocke, 'James Dennistoun—as a collector and traveller', *The Connoisseur*, 184 (1973), 90–97 · H. Brigstocke, 'James Dennistoun's second European tour, 1836–1839', *The Connoisseur*, 184 (1973), 240–49 · H. Brigstocke, 'Memoirs of 'the duke of Urbino', James Dennistoun: collector and traveller', *The Connoisseur* (1975), 316–22 · A. N. L. Munby, *Connoisseurs and medieval miniatures, 1750–1850* (1972), 158 · J. W. Dennistoun, *Some account of the family of Dennistoun of Dennistoun and Colgrain* (1906) · 'Dennistoun, James', *The dictionary of art*, ed. J. Turner (1996) · *GM*, 2nd ser., 43 (1855), 647–8 · *Fraser's Magazine*, 51 (1855), 643–4 · G. F. Waagen, *Treasures of art in Great Britain*, 3 (1854), 281–2

Archives NL Scot., corresp. and MSS · NL Scot., papers relating to Dunbartonshire · U. Edin. L., corresp. | NL Scot., letters to William Mure · NL Scot., corresp. and MSS relating to Sir Robert Strange

Likenesses A. Edouart, silhouette, Scot. NPG

Denny, Alexandra Elene MacLean [Sandy] (1947–1978), singer and songwriter, was born at Nelson Hospital, Merton, Surrey, on 6 January 1947, the youngest child of Neil MacLean Denny, a civil servant, and his wife, Edna Marjorie, *née* Jones, of Wimbledon, Surrey. She attended nearby Cottenham Park infants' school in Raynes Park and then, having passed her eleven-plus exam, went to a local grammar school. After leaving school with two A levels, she worked briefly as a nurse at the Brompton Chest Hospital, before going on to study at Kingston Art College. While still in her teens she began singing and accompanying herself on guitar in the folk clubs that were springing up around the capital in the mid-1960s, such as The Barge at Kingston, The Troubadour in Earls

Court, and Bunjies and Les Cousins in Soho. Blonde and photogenic, she cultivated a tough image in order to make her way on the male-dominated live music circuit.

On the folk-club circuit Sandy Denny was close to a number of other fledgeling singer–songwriters, including Al Stewart, Bert Jansch, and Cat Stevens, as well as visiting Americans such as Jackson C. Frank and Paul Simon. Like most of her contemporaries, her early repertory was based around the traditional folk catalogue and the work of American singer–songwriters such as Tom Paxton and Bob Dylan, but she soon began to write her own songs. By the age of twenty she was appearing regularly on the folk programmes broadcast by the BBC's Light Programme and World Service; and in 1967 she made her recording début, performing a number of traditional folk ballads on the album *Alex Campbell & Friends*. Later that year she was asked to join The Strawbs, and they recorded one album together in Denmark—*All our Own Work*—which contained the first version of her best-known song, 'Who knows where the time goes', although the album remained unreleased until 1973.

The folk-rock group Fairport Convention recruited Sandy Denny in 1968 and, although she stayed with them for only eighteen months, it was undeniably their most creatively fertile period. During 1969 alone they recorded *What we did on our Holidays*, *Unhalfbricking* (which included another version of 'Who knows where the time goes'), and *Liege & Lief*. The latter was one of the most innovative and influential LPs ever released by a British group, uniting traditional folk material with electric rock and roll instrumentation to produce the first true 'folk-rock' fusion. With her exhaustive knowledge of the folk tradition, it was Sandy Denny who helped transform Fairport from just another north London band covering predominantly American material into the first electric rock and roll band to reinterpret the traditional folk repertory. But ironically it was Fairport's decision to persevere with their folk-rock innovations that caused her to quit: she was now keen to work up her own songs rather than researching and interpreting the traditional material that she had already been singing for years.

A glittering solo career beckoned—Sandy Denny won *Melody Maker*'s prestigious best female vocalist award two years running (1970 and 1971)—but rather than working alone, she formed Fotheringay with her future husband, Australian musician Trevor Lucas. The group recorded just one album, *Fotheringay* (1970), but a chance encounter with Led Zeppelin, the most successful British group of the era, led her to sing with them on 'The battle of evermore', which appeared on the following year's *Led Zeppelin IV*, giving her the distinction of being the only guest vocalist ever to feature on a Led Zeppelin album. She eventually married Lucas on 20 September 1973; they had a daughter, Georgia Rose (*b.* 1977).

By the time Sandy Denny began her solo career in earnest, with 1971's *The North Star Grassman & the Ravens*, the momentum seemed to have been lost. Island Records invested substantial sums in recording *Sandy* (1972), which was seen as a make-or-break album, but although it contained some of Sandy's best songs—'Listen, listen', 'It suits me well', and 'It'll take a long time'—sales were poor. *Like an Old Fashioned Waltz* (1973) was another pristine album, with notable cuts including the title track, 'Solo', 'Friends', and 'At the end of the day'. A short-lived reunion with Fairport followed, producing a live album and the over-ambitious *Rising for the Moon* (1975), before she left once again. The solo outing *Rendezvous* (1977) proved to be her final album. Alcohol and drug abuse had been a feature of her life for some time and her marriage failed to provide the stability which she needed. In April 1978 Lucas left for Australia, taking their daughter with him. Sandy went to stay with a friend in Barnes, south-west London. There she was found collapsed on 17 April with what turned out to be a brain haemorrhage; she died on 21 April at Atkinson Morley's Hospital, Wimbledon. She was buried in Putney Vale cemetery.

Only posthumously was Sandy Denny's talent fully appreciated: during her lifetime her only gold record was awarded for a brief appearance on the 1972 album of the rock opera *Tommy*. Of her own four albums only her début—*The North Star Grassman & the Ravens*—achieved a chart placing, reaching number thirty-one in the UK. In 1986 a box-set, *Who Knows Where the Time Goes*, containing many demos and unreleased performances, was released to commemorate her music. Since then, a number of retrospective collections have kept her name prominent and testified to the stature of her work: *Sandy Denny: the BBC Sessions, 1971–1973* (1997), *Gold Dust: Live at the Royalty* (1998), *Listen, Listen: an Introduction to Sandy Denny* (1999), and a two-CD compilation, *No More Sad Refrains* (2000), released to coincide with the first biography of Sandy. Among those who recorded her songs are Griffith, Julie Covington, Linda Thompson, and Emmylou Harris; and many others, including Kate Bush, The Bangles, Beth Orton, and Don Henley, hailed her work as inspirational. Led Zeppelin's Robert Plant called Sandy Denny 'my favourite singer out of all the British girls that ever were', and The Who's Pete Townshend rated hers 'the perfect British folk voice. Not a trace of vibrato. Pure and easy' (Heylin, dust jacket). PATRICK HUMPHRIES

Sources P. Humphries, *Meet on the ledge: Fairport Convention the classic years* (1997) · C. Heylin, *No more sad refrains: the life & times of Sandy Denny* (2000) · b. cert. · d. cert.

Likenesses M. Stroud, double portrait, photograph, 1970 (with Robert Plant), Hult. Arch. · S. Wood, photograph, 1970, Hult. Arch. · double portrait, photograph, 1970 (with John Peel), Hult. Arch. · photograph, 1970, Hult. Arch. · J. Minihan, photograph, 1971, Hult. Arch.

Wealth at death £14,000: probate, 25 Sept 1978, *CGPLA Eng. & Wales*

Denny, Sir Anthony (1501–1549), courtier, was born on 16 January 1501 at Cheshunt, the second son of Sir Edmund Denny (d. 1520), a Hertfordshire landowner who became a baron of the exchequer in the early years of Henry VIII, and his second wife, Mary (d. 1507), daughter of Robert Troutbeck of Bridge Trafford, Cheshire. He was educated at St Paul's School, London, and at St John's College, Cambridge, where he does not seem to have graduated. He

began his public career in the service of Sir Francis Bryan, a favourite of the king, on diplomatic missions to France, and in the late 1520s found a modest informal employment in the royal household. His formal connection with the privy chamber can be traced as early as May 1533; an indenture of 28 May 1536 identified him as 'of the privy chamber', and a grant of 9 September described him as groom. He became a yeoman of the wardrobe in 1536 and was entrusted with the privy purse informally in the same year. He is recorded as gentleman of the privy chamber about the beginning of 1539, when he replaced Bryan as the second chief gentleman, and as deputy groom of the stool. A client of Thomas Cromwell's, Denny was informally entrusted with the keepership of Westminster Palace at least two years before his formal appointment on 20 September 1538. He was named keeper of the privy purse on 24 April 1542. As keeper of the privy purse Denny handled substantial amounts of royal money, making massive withdrawals from and deposits in the king's coffers. He may have represented Ipswich in the parliament of 1535–6.

As the 1540s progressed Denny became ever closer to King Henry. He was one of the first courtiers whom Henry took into his confidence in lamenting his nuptial contract with Anne of Cleves. In 1544 he accompanied the king to Boulogne, and was knighted there on 30 September, after the city's capitulation. Denny had hitherto been junior to Sir Thomas Heneage in the privy chamber, but henceforward his influence exceeded Heneage's, especially after 20 September 1545 when Denny, along with John Gates (the husband of his sister Mary) and their assistant William Clerk, was licensed by the king to affix the royal stamp—the sign manual—on all documents emanating from the monarch. Occasioned by Henry's growing infirmity, this was a transfer of authority which gave great influence to the men who wielded it. Then in October 1546 Heneage retired from service and Denny replaced him as first chief gentleman and groom of the stool. Denny often exchanged gifts with the king. On new year's day 1537 Queen Jane Seymour gave him a gold brooch (presumably intended for his wife), and at the beginning of 1545 Denny presented the king with a clock designed by Hans Holbein.

In the context of the last months of Henry's reign it was of considerable importance that Denny was a patron of humanist letters and a firm friend to religious reformation, praised as such by men like Nicholas Wentworth and Roger Ascham. A pupil of John Colet at St Paul's, he recovered and restored the lands and buildings of Sedbergh School in Yorkshire, which belonged to his alma mater of St John's, Cambridge, and saved part of the library of Waltham Abbey from destruction. Most of his associates were humanists, committed to Erasmian pietism and the cause of learning, and Denny himself was moderate in the expression of his religious views, which never conflicted with his loyalty to and friendship with the king. His sympathy with the reformed faith did not prevent his taking notice of heretical books as a loyal government servant. Both the protestant humanist Sir John Cheke and the Catholic Henry Howard, earl of Surrey, wrote in his praise. But of Denny's own protestant allegiance there can be no doubt. In 1544 he and the king's physician, William Butts, saved Richard Turner of Canterbury, accused of 'free and bold preaching against popish errors' (Sil, 'King's men', 22), from prosecution. A friend of Archbishop Thomas Cranmer and a supporter of the evangelically inclined Edward Seymour, earl of Hertford, in 1546 Denny supported the archbishop's recommendations against the 'vain ceremonies' of traditional religion, and after his death was hailed as 'an enemy to the Pope and his superstition' (Dowling, 63).

In his religious stance Denny undoubtedly had the support of his wife. **Joan Denny**, Lady Denny (d. 1553), was the daughter of Sir Philip Champernon of Modbury, Devon, and his wife, Katherine Carew. She married Anthony Denny on 9 February 1538, and with him had five sons, including Sir Edward *Denny (1547–1600), and four daughters. She herself had a position in the households of queens Anne of Cleves and Katherine Parr, while her sister-in-law Lady Berkeley was governess to Princess Elizabeth. A committed protestant, with her sister Katherine Raleigh she is reported to have protected the persecuted reformers in Devon. In the summer of 1546 Lady Denny (and by extension her husband) was one of the court protestants whom religious conservatives tried to incriminate through accusations wrung from Anne Askew, a distant relative of Joan's uncle Sir Gawain Carew; Anne would admit only that Lady Denny's servant had brought her money, and Sir Anthony survived as a leading figure among Seymour's associates at the close of the reign. It is a sign of his personal intimacy with Henry VIII that according to John Foxe it was Denny who at the very end advised the dying king 'to prepare himself to death … and to call upon God … for grace and mercy' (Sil, 'Sir Anthony Denny', 196). An executor of Henry's will, he also received a substantial bequest, quite possibly arranged by Denny himself after the king's death. During Henry's funeral procession 'then were set at the head and feet of the said corpse Sir Anthony Denny and Sir William Herbert, two of the chief of his privy chamber', and six months later a royal patent recognized Denny as 'the most intimate of Henry VIII's council and chamber' (ibid., 197–8).

Denny's influence continued into the following reign. He was named to the privy council on 31 January 1547, and to the privy chamber as groom of the stool on 30 April. That four months later he was replaced by Sir Michael Stanhope as keeper of the privy purse and first gentleman of the privy chamber may, paradoxically, have represented promotion, the desire of Seymour, now protector and duke of Somerset, to utilize the services of a veteran for more important affairs. During the Scottish campaign of 1547 Denny was appointed by Somerset to remain with the king in London, thus acting as a surrogate for the protector. In the same year he represented Hertfordshire in parliament. In January 1549 he was one of the MPs on the parliamentary committee which examined the protector's brother, Lord Seymour of Sudeley, accused of treason,

and signed the council's order for his execution. In late July he and John Gates accompanied the marquess of Northampton on his unsuccessful expedition to suppress Robert Ket's Norfolk rebellion. But he was taken ill shortly afterwards, and died at Cheshunt on 10 September 1549. He was buried in St Mary's Church there.

Denny's lands, which were principally concentrated in the counties of Essex, Hertfordshire, and Suffolk, consisted mainly of former monastic properties, notably those of Hertford and Cheshunt priories and Waltham and St Albans abbeys. His Hertfordshire lands, which had once belonged to St Albans, covered some 20,000 acres. His revenues from his estates amounted to over £700, while his income from his offices amounted to at least £200. His will made provision for five sons and four daughters (and also named an illegitimate son, William). It also shows his concern for humanistic principles of education, in his instructions to his wife that she should bring up their children so that 'the commonwealth may find them profitable members and not burdens as idle drones be to the hive' (HoP, *Commons, 1509–58*, 2.28). His heir was his eldest son, Henry, who married Honora, daughter of William Grey, thirteenth Lord Grey of Wilton, and was the father of **Edward Denny**, first earl of Norwich (1569–1637). Educated at Cambridge, Edward became a groom of Elizabeth's privy chamber, and in 1590 or 1591 married Mary, daughter of Thomas Cecil, first earl of Exeter, Burghley's eldest son. In 1602/3 he was high sheriff of Hertfordshire, and in that capacity welcomed James I at Royston in 1603. His demeanour so pleased the new monarch that James presented Denny with the gloves from his own hands, as an earnest of future favour. Knight of the shire for Essex in the first session of parliament of 1604, on 27 October he was made Baron Denny of Waltham. His only child was his daughter, Honora, who in 1607 married James Hay, second earl of Carlisle; the marriage was said to have been arranged by the king, while the bride was regarded as a great heiress. No doubt it is a sign of her father's wealth that in 1617 he entered into a contract to collect heriots and reliefs falling due to the crown. On 17 October 1626 Denny became first earl of Norwich. He died on 24 October 1637, and was buried at Waltham Abbey.

NARASINGHA P. SIL

Sources H. L. L. Denny, 'Biography of the Right Honourable Sir Anthony Denny, PC, MP', *Transactions of the East Hertfordshire Archaeological Society*, 3/2 (1906), 197–215 • N. P. Sil, 'Sir Anthony Denny: a Tudor servant in office', *Renaissance and Reformation*, new ser., 8 (1984), 190–201 • N. P. Sil, 'King's men, queen's men, and statesmen: a study of the careers of Sir Anthony Denny, Sir William Herbert, and Sir John Gate, gentlemen of the Tudor privy chamber', PhD diss., University of Oregon, 1978 • R. E. Brock, 'The courtier in early Tudor society: illustrated from select examples', PhD diss., U. Lond., 1963 • D. R. Starkey, 'The king's privy chamber, 1485–1547', PhD diss., U. Cam., 1973 • D. Starkey, *The reign of Henry VIII: personalities and politics* (1985) • M. Dowling, *Humanism in the age of Henry VIII* (1986) • P. Swensen, 'Patronage from the privy chamber: Sir Anthony Denny and religious reform', *Journal of British Studies*, 27 (1988), 25–44 • R. C. Braddock, 'The royal household, 1540–1560: a study of office holding in Tudor England', PhD diss., Northwestern University, 1971 • HoP, *Commons, 1509–58*, 2.27–9 • H. L. L. Denny, 'Pedigrees of some East-Anglian Dennys', *The Genealogist*, new ser., 38 (1921–2), 15–28 · J. Murphy, 'The illusion of decline: the privy chamber, 1547–1558', *The English court: from the Wars of the Roses to the civil war*, ed. D. R. Starkey and others (1987), 119–46 · M. C. D. Dixon and E. C. D. Vann, *Denny genealogy: first book* (1944) · E. W. Ives, 'Henry VIII's will—a forensic conundrum', *HJ*, 35 (1992), 779–804 · *Selected works of John Bale (1495–1563), containing the examinations of Lord Cobham, William Thorpe, and Anne Askewe and the image of both churches*, ed. H. Christmas, Parker Society, 37 (1849) · *The acts and monuments of John Foxe*, ed. S. R. Cattley, 8 vols. (1837–41), vol. 5 · D. Wilson, *A Tudor tapestry: men, women and society in Reformation England* (1972) · S. Brigden, *London and the Reformation* (1989) · GEC, *Peerage*, new edn, 9.767–9 · L. Stone, *The crisis of the aristocracy, 1558–1641* (1965), 439–40

Likenesses attrib. H. Holbein, portrait, V&A

Wealth at death £700—total income from landed properties: Sil, 'King's men, queen's men, and statesmen'; Brock, 'The courtier'

Denny [*née* Fitzmaurice], **Lady Arabella** (1707–1792), philanthropist, was the second daughter of Thomas Fitzmaurice (*d.* 1741), twenty-first lord of Kerry, and his wife, Anne (*d.* 1737), the daughter of Sir William Petty. She grew up at Lixnaw Castle, Tralee, becoming Lady Arabella on her father's creation as first earl of Kerry on 17 January 1722. On 26 August 1727 she married Colonel Arthur Denny, MP for County Kerry; they had no children and she was widowed on 8 August 1742. In 1748 she settled in Blackrock, co. Dublin, in a house leased from Lord Fitzwilliam. In 1751 she made a continental tour and returned to Dublin some time in the following year.

Denny began to visit the Dublin Foundling Hospital with other women in November 1759. The hospital was part of the Dublin workhouse, and the mortality rates among the infants and children abandoned there were extremely high. Denny hired the wet-nurses for the institution and paid a bounty from her own funds to nurses in the country who provided good care. In addition, she spent over £4000 enlarging and improving the hospital buildings. The changes she instituted went some way to reducing the mortality rate, and in 1761 a committee of the Irish House of Commons recognized the success of her work. A contemporary noted that she 'had put a stop to barbarity and murder and saved the lives of thousands' (Robins, 25). In recognition of her work she was awarded the freedom of the city of Dublin in 1765. She remained a visitor at the hospital until 1778.

Denny's work in the foundling hospital also brought to her attention the plight of young women who were at risk of becoming prostitutes. In consequence she opened the first Magdalen asylum, a rescue home for such women, in Dublin in 1767. A chapel attached to the asylum was opened in 1768 and served to raise funds for the institution. Denny was also a member of the ladies' committee of the Rotunda Lying-In Hospital, and used her social standing and family connections to promote her charitable schemes. Some of her activities caused controversy. During the 1770s she exerted her influence by having the archbishop of Dublin silence Lady Huntingdon's chaplain, Henry Peckwell, for views she considered subversive to the church establishment. This was to cause some division between herself and Lady Moira, Peckwell's influential patron and the daughter of Lady Huntingdon.

In 1765 Denny was appointed a patroness of the silk warehouse of the Royal Dublin Society, and in the following year was the first woman to be elected a member (honorary) of the society. She took a keen interest in damask manufacture and gave advice about damask patterns through the society. She was also attributed with introducing carpet weaving into Ireland and bred silkworms at her Blackrock home. Described by her cousin William, first marquess of Lansdowne, as 'the only example I had before me of the two qualities of mind which most adorn and dignify life—amiability and independence'. She was thanked by the society in 1770 'for her humane and constant attention to the welfare of this Kingdom' (Butler, 1.15). Denny died on 18 March 1792 at her home, Peafield Cliff, Blackrock, and was buried in the family vault beneath the chancel of the church at Tralee.

MARIA LUDDY

Sources B. B. Butler, 'Lady Arbella Denny, 1707–92', *Dublin Historical Record*, 9/1 (1946–8), 1–20 · *Life of William, earl of Shelburne … with extracts from his papers and correspondence*, ed. E. G. P. Fitzmaurice, 3 vols. (1875–6) · J. A. Robins, *The lost children: a study of charity children in Ireland, 1700–1900* (1980) · GEC, *Peerage*

Archives Bowood House, Wiltshire, Lansdowne MSS

Wealth at death approx. £900: Butler, 'Lady Arbella Denny', 18–19

Denny, Sir Archibald, first baronet (1860–1936), shipbuilder and engineer, was born at Dumbarton on 7 February 1860. He was the fourth son of Peter *Denny (1821–1895), of Helenslee, Dumbarton, shipbuilder, and his wife, Helen (*d.* 1905), the eldest daughter of James Leslie, of Dumbarton. Educated at Dumbarton Academy until the age of fourteen, he then went to the *école cantonale* at Lausanne, Switzerland, where he spent two years on the study of science, mathematics, and languages.

Denny began his apprenticeship in the shipbuilding department of the family business of William Denny & Brothers, during which time he qualified for entry to the Royal Naval College, Greenwich, where for three years he combined the academic study of naval architecture with the practical training of the shipyard. On completion of this training he served for a short time at the Liverpool office of Lloyd's Register of Shipping. In 1883 Denny became a partner in his father's firm. He assumed responsibility for the technical side of the undertaking, filling the gap left on the death of his brother William *Denny (1847–1887) [*see under* Denny, Peter]. He was involved in the development of the ship model experiment tank at the Leven shipyard, which commenced operation in 1883 as the world's first hydromechanics laboratory set up by a commercial shipyard, and remains in operation.

Denny became best known for the leadership which took the shipyard to a position recognized worldwide as second to none for technical excellence. The yard produced high-quality ships, many of which were destined for the high-speed and cross-channel routes. In 1901 it delivered the pioneer passenger turbine steamer *King Edward* using its vast experience coupled with the knowledge gained from research and experimentation in the ship model tank. Denny was consulted regularly by government departments and other interests, he played a prominent part in the council of the Institution of Naval Architects, and for many years was chairman of the technical committee of the British Corporation Register of Shipping, the Glasgow-based rival to Lloyd's Register of Shipping. He chaired the British Engineering Standards Institution for nine years, the Board of Trade committee on the subdivision of ships from 1920 to 1924, the *Titanic* disaster investigation committee (1912–15), and the International Conference on the Safety of Life at Sea. He served on many government and official commissions and committees, either as chairman or as a committee member.

In 1885 Denny married Margaret, second daughter of John Tulloch, engineer, of Dumbarton, a partner in the engineering department of the firm. They had five sons and one daughter. Denny served for many years in the volunteers, becoming second in command of a battalion of the Argyll and Sutherland Highlanders. He was created a baronet in 1913, and in 1911 and 1927 received the honorary degree of LLD from the universities of Glasgow and of Cambridge respectively. He was elected a fellow of the Royal Society of Edinburgh in 1894, but recognition by his peers took the form of election as president of the Institution of Engineers and Shipbuilders in Scotland, for the sessions 1903–5. In 1921 he took up residence in London and for the remaining fifteen years of his life represented the shipyard interests in the City. He died in London on 29 May 1936, and was succeeded as second baronet by his eldest son, Maurice Edward *Denny (1886–1955), who also chaired the company board for thirty years. He was survived by his wife.

MAURICE DENNY, *rev.* FRED M. WALKER

Sources *Transactions of the Institution of Engineers and Shipbuilders in Scotland*, 79 (1935–6) · William Denny & Brothers Ltd, *Denny Dumbarton, 1844–1932*, 2nd edn (privately printed, London, [1933]) · *DSBB* · D. J. Lyon, ed., *The Denny list*, 4 vols. (1975–6), vol. 1 · F. M. Walker, *Song of the Clyde* (1984) · A. B. Bruce, *The life of William Denny, shipbuilder*, 2nd edn (1889) · *CGPLA Eng. & Wales* (1936)
Archives Denny Ship Model Tank, Dumbarton · NMM · U. Glas.
Likenesses M. Greiffenhagen, portrait, priv. coll.
Wealth at death £103,523 16s. 10d.: confirmation, 25 Sept 1936, *CCI*

Denny, Sir Edward (1547–1600), soldier, was the fifth son of Sir Anthony *Denny (1501–1549), privy councillor and royal favourite, and his wife, Joan *Denny (d. 1553) [*see under* Denny, Sir Anthony], daughter of Sir Philip Champernon of Modbury, Devon. Brought up by John Tamworth, executor to his mother's will, little is known of Denny's early years, although in 1564 he is recorded at Merton College, Oxford, and by 1573 he had been appointed receiver-general of the counties of Southampton, Wiltshire, and Gloucestershire.

In 1574 Denny took part in the ill-fated expedition of Walter Devereux, first earl of Essex, to Ireland and in the late 1570s engaged in privateering on his own account in the English Channel. In July 1580 Denny again left for Ireland, this time with his cousin Walter Ralegh and 200 soldiers to participate in the suppression of the uprising of the earl of Desmond. In a letter of 8 September to his

cousin Sir Francis Walsingham, Denny complained bitterly of Ireland, which 'happens still in bogs, glinnes and woods, as in my opinion it might better fit mastives than brave gentlemen that desier to win honour' (Denny, 249), but in November he took part in the siege and capture of the Spanish encampment 'Fort del Ore' near Dingle, for which action he was personally commended to the queen by his commander, Lord Grey of Wilton, lord deputy of Ireland. In autumn 1581 Denny was again in active service, in command of an expedition against the O'Tooles near Dublin, whose revolt he had crushed by the end of the year.

In 1583, by which time he was a groom of the privy chamber, Denny married Margaret (1560–1648), eldest daughter of Piers and Margaret Edgcumbe of Mount Edgcumbe in Cornwall, with whom he had seven sons and three daughters. In 1584, having stood unsuccessfully as the earl of Leicester's candidate in Hertfordshire, Denny was returned with his father-in-law as one of the two MPs for Liskeard. But by 1587 he was again in Ireland, in March being granted the castle, town, and 6000 acres of land adjoining Tralee, co. Kerry, on which to establish English settlers, a venture in which he was particularly successful. Denny was knighted in October 1588 and seems to have entered an agreement with Sir Richard Bingham to succeed him as governor of Connaught. Despite having the support of the lord deputy, Sir William Fitzwilliam, nothing came of this proposal and in December Denny was in Ulster as part of a force against an uprising there.

In summer 1589, following his appointment in May as clerk of recognizances in the courts of the chief justices of the queen's bench and common pleas, a post he was to hold until his death, Denny and his family returned to England. The following April it was agreed that his 'charge' in Ireland might be filled by a deputy, owing to his engagement in royal service. It was probably about this time that he bought back the estate of the former Benedictine nunnery of Cheshunt, Hertfordshire, which his father had transformed into a country house after the dissolution and which had then been sold in 1564. Denny probably carried out further remodelling there before selling it to Lord Burghley in 1592. His time at Cheshunt is recorded in the verse 'A Tale of Two Swannes' by William Vallans:

> From thence to Broxbourne, and to Wormley wood
> And so salute the holy house of Nunnes,
> That late belong'd to captaine Edward Dennie,
> A knight in Ireland of the best accompt
> Who late made execution on our foes,
> I mean of Spanyardes, that with open armes
> Attempted both against our Queene and us.

In April 1591 Denny was given command of a relief of ships sent to assist Admiral Lord Thomas Howard off the Azores, apparently his last military mission. Returned as MP for Tregony, Cornwall, in October 1597, Denny lost his possessions in co. Kerry following the successes of Hugh O'Neill, earl of Tyrone, against the English in 1598, and died on 12 February 1600. He was buried at Waltham Abbey, Essex, two days later. NICHOLAS DOGGETT

Sources H. L. L. Denny, 'Biography of Sir Edward Denny', *Transactions of the East Hertfordshire Archaeological Society*, 2/3 (1904), 247–60 · HoP, *Commons, 1558–1603*, 2.29–30 · *CSP Ire., 1574–1600* · *CSP dom., 1547–80; 1598–1601* · *Calendar of the manuscripts of the most hon. the marquis of Salisbury*, 3, HMC, 9 (1889); 7–8 (1899); 10 (1904); 15 (1930) · *APC, 1582–2, 12; 1591–2, 364–5* · G. H. Johnson, *Waltham Abbey* (1919), 19–20, 45 · S. D'Ewes, *A complete journal … of the Lords and … Commons* (1682), 496, 575 · BL, Lansdowne MS 44, fol. 198 · W. Vallans, 'A tale of two swannes (1590)', in *The itinerary of John Leland the antiquary*, ed. T. Hearne, 3rd edn, 5 (1769) [contained in the same writer's 'Account of several parts of Hartfordshire', prefix to T. Hearne's 1769 edn] · Foster, *Alum. Oxon.*
Likenesses F. Zuccaro, oils, priv. coll.

Denny, Edward, first earl of Norwich (1569–1637). *See under* Denny, Sir Anthony (1501–1549).

Denny, Henry (1803–1871), entomologist, was for forty-five years curator of the museum of the Literary and Philosophical Society in Leeds. Before his appointment he had published on the genus *Pselaphus* (*Monographia Pselaphorum et Scydmaenorum Britanniae, or, An essay on the British species of the genera Pselaphus of Herbst, and Scydmaenus of Latreille*, 1825). His studies were to follow this direction for the rest of his life, and, while performing his duties as curator, he made himself a leading authority on the subject of parasitic insects.

Denny was the first salaried curator of the Leeds museum, and was dedicated to the institution. The entomologist William Kirby (1759–1850), to whom Denny dedicated his first monograph, tried unsuccessfully to secure for the latter employment as illustrator on a serial entomological publication. In 1842 the British Association for the Advancement of Science made a grant to Denny of 50 guineas for the purpose of assisting him in the study of British *Anoplura*. That year he published *Monographia Anoplurorum Britanniae, or, An essay on the British species of parasitic insects belonging to the order Anoplura of Leach*. He died at Leeds on 7 March 1871, and a fund amounting to £883 was raised by subscription for the benefit of his widow, Ann, and their younger children.

ROBERT HARRISON, *rev.* YOLANDA FOOTE

Sources *The Athenaeum* (18 March 1871), 340 · *Reports of Leeds Philosophical Society* (1870–72) · J. Freeman, *Life of the Rev. William Kirby* (1852), 403, 428 · *Report of the British Association for the Advancement of Science* (1842) · *CGPLA Eng. & Wales* (1871)
Archives Oxf. U. Mus. NH, Hope Library, corresp. and papers relating to *Anoplura* | Bath Royal Literary and Scientific Institution, letters to Leonard Blomefield · Museum of Scotland, Edinburgh, letters to Sir William Jardine
Wealth at death under £1500: probate, 13 July 1871, *CGPLA Eng. & Wales*

Denny, Joan, Lady Denny (d. 1553). *See under* Denny, Sir Anthony (1501–1549).

Denny, Sir Maurice Edward, second baronet (1886–1955), engineer and shipbuilder, was born at Braehead, Dumbarton, on 11 February 1886, the eldest son of Archibald *Denny (1860–1936) and Margaret Tulloch. Maurice Denny was the third generation of the family in control of

Sir Maurice Edward Denny, second baronet (1886–1955), by Walter Stoneman, 1947

shipbuilding at Dumbarton, but, unlike his father and grandfather, did not go to the local school. He was educated first at Tonbridge School, Kent, and then spent two years in Switzerland and one in Germany at the universities of Lausanne and Heidelberg. He then embarked upon an apprenticeship in the firm, combining it in a sandwich course with four years at the Massachusetts Institute of Technology, where he studied naval architecture under Professor C. H. Peabody, graduating with first-class honours as BSc in 1909. This was followed by a further year in the drawing office of Wm Doxford & Sons Ltd, Sunderland, learning about the new diesel engine. On his return to the Leven shipyard in 1911 he became a partner in the business at the age of twenty-four. In 1916 Denny married Marjorie, daughter of William Royse Lysaght, steelmaker, of Castleford, Chepstow, Monmouthshire; they had two sons and two daughters.

When the family firm became a limited company in 1918, the two sides of the business, the Leven shipyard of William Denny & Brothers and the marine engineering works of Denny & Co., were united in the single business of Wm Denny & Co.; Maurice Denny was appointed a director. He was elected vice-chairman in 1920, and in 1922 succeeded his uncle, Colonel John M. Denny, as chairman. He was then thirty-six years old and held that office for the next, troubled, thirty years until 1952, when he retired and became president.

Naval architecture, especially in areas of the design, stability, and propulsion of ships, was the consuming interest of the young and technically expert Denny. He co-operated with Charles Parsons in 1911 to produce Dennys' first set of geared turbines, to engine the destroyers *Badger* and *Beaver*, the first to be fitted with this type of engine. His experimentation was cut short by the First World War, during which Denny rose to the rank of major in the machine-gun corps in France. However, on account of the pressure on shipbuilding, and his experience, he was recalled to take up the post of deputy director of designs under the controller-general for merchant shipbuilding at the Admiralty, and was appointed CBE in 1918.

After the war Denny was keen to apply his scientific brain and well-trained mind to the many shipbuilding problems, but there was a deep depression in world trade, and the need for rigid economies had to have priority. But even in these very difficult years he enhanced his company's reputation, particularly in the construction of fast cross-channel ships with turbine propulsion. He also developed a 'vane-wheel' system for powering flat-bottomed riverboats, and produced two types of torsion meters, the Denny-Johnstone and the Denny-Edgecumbe. His company also built the first all-welded ship in Scotland in 1934, the *Robert the Bruce*, which was in addition the first diesel–electric paddler constructed in Britain. Even more significant was his collaboration with William Wallace (1881–1963) of Brown Brothers to produce the Denny-Brown stabilizer. This was first fitted extensively during the Second World War to give greater stability for gunnery. After the war it was widely used in ships all over the world.

Denny made a lasting contribution to the progress of the industry, particularly in promoting research. He became chairman of the Shipbuilding Conference in 1940, and also served on the advisory committee on merchant shipbuilding, working closely with Sir Henry Lithgow in co-ordinating the shipbuilders' work during the war. In spite of heavy demands on his time he was instrumental in the foundation of the British Shipbuilding Research Association in 1944; and he was a member of its research council and served as chairman of its research board from its inception until his death. It was largely due to his driving force that the *Lucy Ashton* trials to measure the power and speed of ships were carried out. The modification of this old Clyde paddle-steamer, fitted with four jet engines, permitted full-scale self-propelled experiments, delivering valuable hydrodynamic data. His services in administration during the war earned him the KBE in 1946.

Among many appointments, Denny was chairman of the technical committee of the British Corporation Register of Shipping and Aircraft, the Glasgow-based registration company, which was eventually amalgamated with Lloyd's Register. He also played a prominent role in the Air Registration Board, being chairman for many years. On Clydeside he was president of the Clyde Shipbuilders'

Association, and nationally the president of the Shipbuilding Employers' Federation. He was a valued supporter of many of the professional institutions and notably president in 1935 of the Institute of Marine Engineers, as his father and grandfather had been. He received an honorary LLD from Glasgow in 1949. Denny's business interests also involved him in many directorships, notably of shipping companies, mainly the Irrawaddy Flotilla Company, the India General Navigation and Railway Company, and the British and Burmese Steam Navigation Company. He was also a director of the Union Bank of Scotland, of Guest, Keen, and Nettlefolds, and of Lloyds British Testing Company.

In his approach to his business Denny was driven by a meticulous integrity, which was the outstanding quality of his character. He was a man of wide interests, and a witty and genial personality. He found his recreation in country life—he was a golfer, a keen gardener, and an ornithologist of wide knowledge with an almost complete egg collection of birds of the British Isles. In ship model-making he was a skilled craftsman and he presented to the Science Museum his handmade model of the *Cutty Sark*, a famous clipper ship completed by Denny Brothers. Following a coronary thrombosis, Denny died at Drymen, Stirlingshire, on 2 February 1955. His eldest son, Alistair Maurice Archibald Denny, succeeded to the baronetcy.

BILSLAND, rev. ANTHONY SLAVEN

Sources *DSBB* · J. Shields, *Clyde built: a history of ship-building on the River Clyde* (1949) · b. cert. · d. cert.
Archives U. Glas., Archives and Business Records Centre, letter-books and corresp.
Likenesses J. Gaiger, group portrait, photograph, 1930, Hult. Arch. · W. Stoneman, photograph, 1947, NPG [*see illus.*] · D. S. Ewart, oils, 1953, NMM
Wealth at death £150,253 15s. 9d.: confirmation, 7 May 1956, *CCI*

Denny, Sir Michael Maynard (1896–1972), naval officer, was born at the vicarage in Kempley, Gloucestershire, on 3 October 1896, the seventh son and thirteenth and youngest child of Edward Denny, vicar of Kempley, and his wife, Alona Mary Chesshyre. He entered the Royal Naval College, Osborne, in 1909 and then Dartmouth, and was appointed midshipman in the *Neptune* before the outbreak of the First World War. He served throughout the war in this and, later, the *Royal Sovereign*. In 1923 he married Sarah Annie Esmé (d. 1971), the daughter of Colonel Loftus Welman, of the Royal Irish Rifles. There were no children.

After specializing in gunnery in 1920 and gaining the Egerton memorial prize for the top student of his year Denny took the advanced 'G' course and alternated his service from lieutenant to commander between experimental work and G in the *Emperor of India* (which under his tutelage demolished two battle-practice targets and won the commander-in-chief's prize) and the *Nelson*. He was promoted commander in 1930, and served as experimental commander and then fleet gunnery officer in the Mediterranean Fleet; he was made captain in 1936 after being second-in-command of the *Shropshire*. Denny served in the naval ordnance department until 1940 during a time of hectic rearmament, when his capacity for work and for mastering technical detail played a dominant part in design and in encouraging industry to provide the capacity needed.

The end of the 'phoney' war found him in the thick of the landings and then the evacuation around Trondheim, from which he was the last to leave. He was sent to Dover as chief staff officer to organize the evacuation from Dunkirk and was created CB (1940), awarded the Norwegian order of St Olaf (1st class), and mentioned in dispatches for gallantry and distinguished service in these operations.

Denny commanded two ships in the war, the cruiser *Kenya* and the aircraft-carrier *Victorious*, and was chief of staff of the Home Fleet during much of the time that convoys were being fought through to Russia. *Kenya* escorted Arctic and Mediterranean convoys and operated against German raiders and in raids on the Norwegian coast. *Victorious*, which he joined at the end of 1943, took part in raids against the *Tirpitz* and against Japanese-held islands in the East Indies, and then joined the Pacific Fleet. Denny's skilful handling avoided damage from the kamikaze attacks. He was appointed to the DSO and promoted rear-admiral in July 1945.

Then followed a new role for Denny in the department of the chief of naval personnel. Here his amazing grasp of detail and his ability to sustain long hours of work seven days a week while needing only three or four hours' sleep a night proved what was needed for the rapid but orderly demobilization of the fleet, which was accomplished without organizational breakdown.

After commanding the small ship flotillas in the Mediterranean for sixteen months, Denny returned to the Admiralty as third sea lord and controller of the navy for the years 1949–53, having been promoted vice-admiral in 1948. As the board member responsible for *matériel* and weapons, he introduced the Daring-class destroyers and Ton-class minesweepers and did much to rationalize the naval shipbuilding capacity swollen by the needs of war. His hours of work remained long and his need for sleep seemed to diminish. He was appointed KCB in 1950 and promoted admiral in 1952.

Denny's last naval appointment was to the Home Fleet and to the command of the NATO eastern Atlantic area from 1954 to 1956. He was appointed GCB in 1954. In 1956 he was made chairman of the British joint services mission in Washington and British representative on the NATO military committee. He held this double post for three years and impressed his colleagues as much by his complete grasp of military affairs as by his stamina for work and recreation.

Denny's application to his work seldom allowed his wife to take part in his life. His only hobby was to form a collection of dolls. He sailed service boats occasionally and as a lieutenant led a rugger side well, but later displayed no special bent for sport. He showed no interest in religion. He was shy and reserved with his colleagues and unnecessarily feared for his knowledge and efficiency. And with it he maintained an energetic social life ashore wherever he went.

Denny was placed on the retired list in July 1959. He became chairman of Cammell Laird, shipbuilders and engineers, on retirement but resigned after six years as his health was deteriorating. From then his health and memory became steadily worse, and in 1970 he had to enter a hospital from which he did not emerge. His wife predeceased him in 1971. He died at Gloucester on 7 April 1972.

H. R. LAW, *rev.*

Sources The Times (11 April 1972) · S. W. Roskill, *The war at sea, 1939–1945*, 3 vols. in 4 (1954–61) · WWW · private information (1986) · personal knowledge (1986) · CGPLA Eng. & Wales (1972) **Archives** FILM IWM FVA, actuality footage **Wealth at death** £59,359: probate, 11 Oct 1972, CGPLA Eng. & Wales

Denny, Peter (1821–1895), shipbuilder and shipowner, was born in Dumbarton on 25 October 1821, the fifth son of William Denny (1779–1833) and his wife, Christeanne, formerly McIntyre. The Denny family had been involved in boat-building in the town since at least the mid-eighteenth century and were then engaged in developing steamships. Denny was apprenticed at first to a local lawyer and then at the Dumbarton glassworks. At the age of twenty-one he joined his brothers in the shipbuilding trade, gaining experience in bookkeeping in the counting house of Robert Napier & Sons. When his brothers established their own shipbuilding firm at Dumbarton in 1844 he became a junior partner, using his commercial knowledge to organize the office. On 26 January 1846 he married Helen Leslie, with whom he had eight sons, including the shipbuilder and engineer Sir Archibald *Denny, and seven daughters.

In 1850 Denny went into partnership with two engineers, John McAusland and John Tulloch, to form the marine engineering business of Tulloch and Denny, to operate in parallel with, but independently of, the shipyard. His eldest brother, William, after whom the business was named, died four years later, leaving Peter virtually in sole charge as his other brother James had more or less withdrawn from the firm. Learning from Napiers, he saw the advantage of investing in shipping ventures to secure a market for the yard. At the time of the Disruption in the Church of Scotland in 1843, he had joined the Free Church of Scotland, which brought him in touch with the partners in the shipping firm of Paddy Henderson & Co. He began to build ships for them and to take shares in their various ventures, including support for the Free Church colony on the south island of New Zealand. The business grew rapidly and in 1859 a new shipyard, the North yard, was acquired and the engine works extended. His brother James and John Tulloch retired in 1862; Peter Denny took sole charge of the shipyard, and the engine works was renamed Denny & Co. An enlightened employer, he laid out at the same time a model factory village—Dennistoun—for the workforce of both businesses at a cost of almost £3300. A completely new shipyard was constructed in 1866–7. Despite his commercial background he served on the parliamentary committee on the design of warships in 1871 and on the royal commission on the loss of life and property at sea in 1876.

Using profits made from building blockade runners and speculating in Confederate bonds during the American Civil War, Denny began to invest very heavily with the Hendersons in new shipping companies, personally buying large blocks of shares in 1868 in the Albion Shipping Company and the Irrawaddy Flotilla Company. Building vessels for the latter, which provided services on the shallow winding Irrawaddy River in Burma, was a considerable technical challenge that demanded not only the development of special hull shapes but also lightly constructed engines with well-distributed weight. The firm's success in overcoming these obstacles yielded a flood of orders and profits from the flotilla company. Technical improvements, particularly in hull forms, along with the management of the yard and engine works were increasingly the responsibility of Peter's eldest son, **William Denny** (1847–1887), who became a partner in 1868. Born on 25 May 1847, he was educated at St Helier's School in Jersey and the Royal High School in Edinburgh before serving an apprenticeship in the family firm. He continued his general education by reading widely, particularly on theological subjects, coming to dislike the repressive Calvinism of the Free Church of Scotland.

In 1870 William Denny began to experiment with piecework for the iron trades in the yards to improve productivity, which was eventually extended to all the firm's trades. He also established an awards scheme—the first of its kind in Britain—to encourage members of the workforce to suggest improvements in working practices, methods, and equipment. At the same time he introduced progressive speed trials over a measured mile for all vessels built in the yards. This led to an interest in hull forms and contact with the well-known naval architect William Froude. Denny published many papers on this subject and on the techniques of construction. He designed revolutionary shallow-draught vessels for the Irrawaddy and other estuarial navigations and from 1876 pioneered steel shipbuilding, culminating in the construction of the *Rotomahana* (1879)—the first ocean-going steel ship. To enhance even further the quality and efficiency of the firm's hull shapes, he persuaded his father to build the first commercial test tank in the world at Dumbarton in 1881, with assistance from Froude's son, superintendent of the Admiralty test tank in Torquay. This investment was part of a massive extension of the yard, which included a new wet dock, longer berths, and heavier cranes. Critical of Lloyd's rules for the construction of iron steamships, William Denny was appointed a member of the Board of Trade load-line committee in 1884.

By handing over much of the day-to-day management of the business to his son, Peter Denny had more time to devote to his other business interests and to winning custom for the yard. He became chairman or a director of twelve companies, mostly enterprises connected with the Henderson family, including Paddy Henderson itself, the Albion Steamship Company, the British and Burmese

Steam Navigation Company, and Rio Tinto Mines, earning during his career over £20,000 in fees. He cultivated orders from foreign governments, particularly Spain, Portugal, and Belgium, all of which honoured him for his services. He also willingly loaned money to local firms either to get them out of difficulty or to help them develop. Befitting his wealth and status he built an impressive home—Helenslee, named after his wife—overlooking the Clyde at Dumbarton, between 1866 and 1868. He gave large sums to charitable bodies such as Glasgow Western Infirmary and the Glasgow home for incurables, and, deeply committed to education, he established scholarships at Dumbarton schools and at the University of Glasgow. His services to education were recognized with the award of an LLD by the university in 1890.

In an attempt to repeat their success on the Irrawaddy, the Denny and the Henderson families took a large stake in La Platense Flotilla Company in 1882 to operate river steamers in Argentina and Uruguay. William Denny was appointed a director to represent the families' interests on the board. Repeatedly troubled with bouts of ill-health, put down to overwork, he suffered a breakdown in the autumn of 1882. Having returned home after a long convalescence on the continent, he and his wife were taken seriously ill with typhoid in 1883. During his recuperation his Dumbarton home, Bellfield, with its valuable library, was destroyed by fire, encouraging a morbid fascination with the medico-religious philosophy of James Hinton. Although he had already left the Free Church of Scotland in 1873 and joined the more liberal United Presbyterians, this did not prevent him from believing that he was destined to die young.

When he returned to the yard William Denny threw himself into work unsparingly. Determined to prevent stoppages and strikes, he pioneered a works council in 1884, first to discuss the charitable giving of the workforce but soon to negotiate new rules and to settle demarcation and other disputes before they became a problem. The rules, which unusually applied to the management as well as to the workforce, embraced the novel concept that all fines for infringements would be returned to the employees. The La Platense venture never lived up to its promise and was taken over in its entirety by the Dennys and Hendersons in 1885–6. In the face of severe local competition, matters went from bad to worse. William Denny recommended that the local opposition should be bought out at the huge cost of £720,000, a decision which proved ill-advised. Deeply troubled by this experience, he sailed for South America in June 1886 in an attempt to save the business. Conscience-stricken by the scale of the catastrophe, he committed suicide in Buenos Aires on 17 March 1887. He was survived by his wife, Lelia, eldest daughter of Leon Serena of Venice, with whom he had a son and three daughters. La Platense was wound up three years later at a total loss.

The effect of this tragedy on Peter Denny was devastating. Already more or less retired, he withdrew from the business. He died at Helenslee on 22 August 1895, leaving about £200,000—only a fraction of his net drawings during his career, which have been estimated at nearly £1.5 million. His wife survived him and died on 5 March 1905.

MICHAEL S. MOSS

Sources N. J. Morgan and M. S. Moss, '"Wealthy and titled persons": the accumulation of riches in Victorian Britain; the case of Peter Denny', *Business History*, 31/3 (1989), 28–47 · A. B. Bruce, *The life of William Denny, shipbuilder*, 2nd edn (1889) · P. L. Robertson, 'Shipping and shipbuilding, the case of William Denny and Brothers', *Business History*, 16 (1974), 36–47 · A. Slaven, 'Denny, Peter', *DSBB* · D. J. Lyon, ed., *The Denny list*, 4 vols. (1975–6), vol. 4, appx 8 · J. Ward, 'Memoir of the late William Denny FRSE', *Transactions of the Institution of Engineers and Shipbuilders of Glasgow* (1887), 257–83 · J. Irving, *The history of Dumbartonshire*, rev. edn, 3, ed. J. Irving (1917) · b. cert. · m. cert. · d. cert.
Archives NMM · U. Glas., Archives and Business Records Centre
Likenesses portrait (William Denny), repro. in Irving, *History of Dumbartonshire*
Wealth at death £190,979 14s.: confirmation, 6 Jan 1896, *CCI* · £17,287 12s. 10d.: eik additional estate, 12 March 1897, *CCI*

Denny, Sir William, baronet (*d.* **1676**), poet, was born in Norwich, the son of Sir William Denny (*d.* 1642), who was recorder there, and his wife (*d.* 1631). He was educated at Norwich School, Norfolk, and at Gonville and Caius College, Cambridge, where he matriculated on 17 February 1620 and was a fellow commoner in 1621, before graduating BA in 1623. On 2 November 1621 he was admitted to Gray's Inn. In his youth Denny contributed to a range of literary works. Ralph Knevet's *Rhodon and Iris*, first acted at Norwich at the Florists' Fête on 3 May 1631, included his introductory verses. His 'Encomiastick to his worthy friend Mr Robert Dover' of 151 lines, the fourth poem in *Annalia Dubrensia* (1636), provides a lively detailed account, supported by appropriate and accurate classical allusions, of the Cotswold Olimpick games which he had attended. Later he contributed to Edward Benlowes's *Theophila* (1652).

On 3 June 1642, on the death of his father, Denny was created a baronet by Charles I. However, the following year he was imprisoned at Windsor Castle by parliament for plotting in the royalist cause. By 1649 he had married Catherine Young. In 1653 his *Pelecanicidium, or, The Christian adviser against self murder together with a guide and the pilgrims passe to the land of the living* was published. This treatise of 318 pages sets out in a serious manner how to lead a worthy life. The same year he drafted 'The Shepheards Holiday', a pastoral poem first published in Henry Huth's *Inedited Poetical Miscellanies* (1870). In 1654 there was a proposal that he should become governor of Yarmouth, Norfolk, but his fortunes did not improve and he died in great poverty in June 1676. He was buried on 19 June at St Giles Cripplegate, London.

F. D. A. BURNS

Sources *DNB* · F. Blomefield, *An essay towards a topographical history of the county of Norfolk* (1736–9), 3.377, 11.34 · C. Whitfield, *Robert Dover and the Cotswold Games* (1962), 114 · J. Foster, *Admissions to Gray's Inn*, 164 · Venn, *Alum. Cant.*, 1/2.33

Denny, William (**1709–1765**), army officer and colonial governor, was born at Eastwick, Hertfordshire, on 9 March 1709, the only surviving son of the Revd Hill Denny (1678–1719) and his wife, Abigail, *née* Berners (*b.* 1683). He received his BA from Oriel College, Oxford, in 1730. In the mid-1730s he became one of the first members of the Society of Dilettanti, devoted to the appreciation of the arts of antiquity. He married Mary Hill, daughter of a Hertfordshire squire. They had no children. While in Pennsylvania, Denny would keep his wife a virtual prisoner as he spent her money and entertained a mistress, named Drage. On return to England when his appointment concluded, his wife fled and took refuge with friends.

In 1743 Denny was a cornet in the duke of Montague's horse regiment, and by 1746 a captain. He may have fought at the battle of Dettingen, and in opposition to the Jacobite rising. The commanding general, the duke of Cumberland, recommended Denny to Thomas Penn, chief proprietor of Pennsylvania, and promoted him to lieutenant-colonel.

Soon after Denny arrived in Philadelphia in August 1756 he alienated the proprietors' supporters in the province by not conducting business conscientiously and by accommodating the traditionally contentious assembly. Denny preferred to retreat to his library and immerse himself in books about ancient Greece and Rome. He proved similarly unaccomplished when dealing with the Native American community, his success at Indian treaties being primarily due to a reliance on experienced negotiators. At a major peace treaty at Easton in October 1758 Denny lost his temper at trivial slights, behaved very irresponsibly, insulted the American Indian negotiators, and caused them to mock him. While doing no harm to Indian policy, he showed that he lacked the temperament for serious business.

Denny and the assembly were jointly responsible for the quartering crisis of the winter of 1756–7 in Philadelphia. On 8 December 1756 Denny approved a quartering bill that he thought inadequate. However, he never made it clear to the assembly how quartering could best be achieved. When the available quarters became overcrowded and smallpox was spreading, Denny and the house could not agree on action. Only when the British commander-general threatened to seize quarters did the assembly give in.

Denny soon learned that passing the bills on which the house insisted, and thereby violating the instructions of the proprietors, would earn him rewards. In March 1757, urged by the British commander, the earl of Loudoun, he approved a bill appropriating £100,000 for emergency military reasons, disregarding his instructions by allowing the assembly to control disbursement. Thereupon the house paid the governor £600. The assembly had awarded Denny's obstinate predecessor only £500 during his two years as governor. In late March 1759 the assembly presented another £100,000 appropriation bill for war support, but this time insisted on both control of disbursement and taxation of the Penn family's proprietary lands. General Jeffrey Amherst wrote to Denny in mid-April to waive his instructions, as Denny had done at Loudoun's behest in 1757. He agreed to the bill on 16 April 1759, and the house presented him with £1000. In June, General

John Stanwix requested funds and Denny obliged by signing an additional money bill; he was immediately paid another £1000. A third such payment came on 7 July, when he approved a bill giving the assembly more control of land sales. The house paid Denny at a higher rate than any earlier Pennsylvania governor had received. Beginning in May 1759 he also sold flags of truce, intended for prisoner exchange, to merchants to use for illegal trade with enemy ports. In sum, his governorship garnered him over £5000.

In November 1759 Denny was replaced by the proprietors. He went to London in the summer of 1760, where, after separating from his wife, Denny lived a life of leisure, continuing his activities in the Society of Dilettanti. He was never prosecuted for his sale of flags of truce or sued for breaking the Penns' instructions. He died at Westminster in late 1765.   BENJAMIN H. NEWCOMB

Sources N. B. Wainwright, 'Governor William Denny in Pennsylvania', *Pennsylvania Magazine of History and Biography*, 81 (1957), 170–98 · H. L. Denny, 'Memoir of His Excellency Colonel William Denny, lieutenant-governor of Pennsylvania', *Pennsylvania Magazine of History and Biography*, 44 (1920), 97–121 · J. J. Kelley, *Pennsylvania: the colonial years, 1681–1776* (1980) · J. H. Hutson, *Pennsylvania politics, 1746–1770: the movement for royal government and its consequences* (1972) · *The papers of Benjamin Franklin*, 6–7, ed. L. W. Labaree and R. L. Ketcham (1963); 8, ed. L. W. Labaree (1965) · G. Mackinney and C. F. Hoban, eds., *Votes and proceedings of the house of representatives of the province of Pennsylvania*, 8 vols. (1754–76), vols. 4–5 [Oct 1744 – Sept 1767] · T. Thayer, *Pennsylvania politics and the growth of democracy, 1740–1776* (1953) · J. E. Illick, *Colonial Pennsylvania: a history* (1976) · *Minutes of the provincial council of Pennsylvania* (1851–3)
Archives Hist. Soc. Penn., Gratz collection · Hist. Soc. Penn., Penn MSS, official corresp. · Hist. Soc. Penn., Thomas Penn MSS [microform] · Hist. Soc. Penn., Richard Peters letter-book
Likenesses G. Knapton, oils, Brooks's Club Society of Dilettanti, London
Wealth at death some property; Pennsylvania estates: Denny, 'Memoir'

Denny, William (1847–1887). *See under* Denny, Peter (1821–1895).

Dennys, John (d. 1609), poet, was the son of Hugh Dennys (d. 1559?) and Katherine (d. 1583), daughter of Edward Trye of Hardwick, Gloucestershire. He is known to have resided in the neighbourhood of Pucklechurch, Gloucestershire, in 1572 and was married to Elianor (or Helena), daughter of Thomas Millet of Warwickshire, with whom he had a son, Henry.

Dennys was author of *The Secrets of Angling*, the first extant fishing poem in English, which was published posthumously in 1613. Before the publication of Sir Henry Ellis's *A Catalogue of Books on Angling* (1811) and the investigations of Thomas Westwood and Canon Ellacombe, the author of *Secrets* was known only by the initials I. D. (from the title-page), which resulted in various attributions of authorship. Six stanzas of the poem (B7r–v) were quoted with inaccuracy of both text and authorship by Izaak Walton in *The Compleat Angler* (1653–76). In the first edition, the author is identified as 'Jo. Da'. This error was absorbed into the text in the second edition (1655), and wrongly expanded to 'Jo. Davors Esq.' in the third edition (1661), as it remained in subsequent editions. Dennys's poem was

prefaced by commendatory verses 'In due praise of this praiseworthy skill and worke' by 'Jo. Daues'. This man was probably a relative of Dennys, whose great-grandmother was Agnes, daughter and coheir of Sir Robert Davers, Danvers, or Daues.

In *The Angler's Sure Guide* (1706), Robert Howlett ascribed *The Secrets of Angling* to 'that great practitioner, master and patron of it [angling], Dr. *Donne*' (Howlett, iii). Sir John Hawkins, who knew of the existence of Dennys's poem but had 'never been able to get a sight of it', was attracted to this particular attribution, but rejected it as erroneous (Walton, 152–3). Authorship was settled when the entry for *The Secrets of Angling* by John Dennys was found in the Stationers' registers (23 March 1613). The poem's reference to 'sweet *Boyd*', a brook fed by a rivulet that runs through the parish of Pucklechurch, provides collateral evidence for Dennys's authorship (Ellacombe, 1).

There seem to have been four editions of *The Secrets of Angling* between 1613 and 1652. In 1614 Gervase Markham published a prose paraphrase of the poem in *The Pleasures of Princes*, an appendix to *The English Husbandman*. Initially, Markham made no mention of his debt to Dennys; however, in later reprints (for example, *Country Contentments*, 4th edn, 1631) he acknowledged that this work was originally 'written in a small Treatise in Rime, and now for the better understanding of the Reader, put into Prose, and adorned and inlarged' (Poynter, 117–18; French, vi). Dennys's work proved popular in the nineteenth century, when extracts from it were frequently republished, with a new edition of the whole text published in 1883 by Thomas Westwood (reissued in 1970).

John Dennys died in 1609 and was buried at St Thomas's, Pucklechurch. The burial place of the Dennys family is at the upper end of the north aisle.   NICHOLAS D. SMITH

Sources *DNB* · J. Dennys, *The secrets of angling*, repr. (1883) [with introduction by T. Westwood] · T. Westwood and T. Satchell, *Bibliotheca piscatoria* (1883) · Arber, *Regs. Stationers* · J. M. French, *Three books on angling* (1962) · F. N. L. Poynter, *Bibliography of Gervase Markham, 1568?–1637* (1962) · I. Walton and C. Cotton, *The complete angler, or, The contemplative man's recreation*, ed. J. Hawkins (1760) · R. Howlett, *The angler's sure guide, or, Angling improved* (1706) · R. Atkyns, *The ancient and present state of Glostershire*, 2 pts in 1 (1712); repr. in 2 vols. (1974) [incl. new introduction by B. S. Smith] · H. T. Ellacombe, *The history of the parish of Bitton in the county of Gloucester* (1881) · *N&Q*, 4th ser., 4 (1869), 91–3, 177

Densell, John (d. 1536), serjeant-at-law, came of a Cornish family whose name derived from Densell or Denzil in the parish of Mawgan in Pydar. He was admitted to Lincoln's Inn in 1504 at the instance of John Skewes, and was elected a bencher in 1520, four years before his first reading (which was on the Statute of Westminster II c. 45). His signature appears frequently on bills in chancery during Wolsey's chancellorship, and he also practised in the requests. By 1526 he was counsel to Dartmouth corporation, and in 1530 became a justice of the peace for Cornwall. At an unknown date he married Mary (d. 1540).

Densell achieved some fame in the profession by reason of his second reading, given in Lent 1530, on the 1489 Statute of Fines (4 Hen. VII c. 24). This circulated very widely over the next century, and at least ten manuscript texts still survive. It was printed in 1662, to accompany Coke's reading on fines, as *Le reading del Monsieur Denshall, sur l'estatute de finibus fait anno 4. H. 7*. The year after delivering this reading, on 12 or 13 November 1531, he was chosen to be a serjeant-at-law, and delivered a third reading (on an unknown subject) as serjeant-elect. He did not, however, live long enough to secure a major appointment. He died on 3 January 1536, and in accordance with his instructions was buried in the chancel of St Giles-in-the-Fields, Middlesex.

Family tradition had it that Densell 'was no corrupt or griping lawyer, for he made no improvement at all of his estate' (Holles, 54). He did, nevertheless, add to his Cornish properties an estate at Hendon in Middlesex and a house in St Giles's parish. He appointed his wife as his sole executor, 'to whom', he said, 'I commyt all my truste to do for my sowle as hir kynde harte shall thinke meate'. They had two daughters. Anne married Sir William Holles (*d.* 1591), and their eldest son was named Denzil after her father; their great-grandson was the well-known parliamentarian Denzil *Holles. Alys married the Cornishman William Reskymer.   J. H. BAKER

Sources W. P. Baildon, ed., *The records of the Honorable Society of Lincoln's Inn: the black books*, 1 (1897) · Baker, *Serjeants* · J. H. Baker and J. S. Ringrose, *A catalogue of English legal manuscripts in Cambridge University Library* (1996), 313 · will, PRO, PROB 11/25, sig. 31 · PRO, C142/57/32 · H. R. Watkin, *Dartmouth*, 264, 269 · G. Holles, *Memorials of the Holles family, 1493–1656*, ed. A. C. Wood, CS, 3rd ser., 55 (1937), 54 · HoP, *Commons, 1558–1603*, 2.330 · PRO, CP 40/1144A, m. 638 · will of Mary Densell, PRO, PROB 11/28, sig. 17

Dent family (*per. c.*1820–1927), Far East merchants, came to prominence with the brothers Thomas, Lancelot, and Wilkinson Dent, respectively the third, fifth, and sixth sons of William Dent (1762–1801), merchant, and Jane Wilkinson (*bap.* 1763, *d.* 1840), of Trainlands, Crosby Ravensworth, Westmorland, who had married in 1791; there were in all six sons and one daughter. There is a suggestion that William and his brother Robert were in Canton (Guangzhou) at some point between 1787 and 1796. The Dent family had a financially solid background and provided substantial benefactions locally, including funds for the rebuilding and endowment of Crosby Ravensworth village school in 1784. Links with the Wilkinson family were particularly strong and when William died, leaving an extremely young and large family, Thomas Wilkinson, possibly a London insurance broker and agent, took at least some of the boys under his wing.

The third son, **Thomas Dent** (1796–1872), was born on 21 December 1796 at Crosby Ravensworth, Westmorland, and was schooled in London. After three terms at Christ's College, Cambridge, in 1815–16, he went to Canton, where by 1820 he was exercising powers of attorney on behalf of the absent merchant W. S. Davidson. By 1823 he had formally joined forces with Davidson and an American, William Blight, to trade as W. S. Davidson & Co. Following Davidson's retirement to London, Dent became the senior partner and by 1824 the firm had changed its name to

Thomas Dent & Co. In order to legitimize his trade as a private merchant in Canton in the face of the East India Company's monopoly, Dent followed a well-established practice and between 1824 and 1829 he acted as the Sardinian consul. With his younger brother now entrenched in the business he left Canton for London in 1830 to develop the family interest in Rickards, Mackintosh & Co. He finally abandoned his residual role in the Canton partnership when he joined the London firm known from 1835 as Palmer, Mackillop, Dent & Co. Consorting in business with the impressive Horsley Palmer, a governor of the Bank of England (1830–33), Dent clearly aspired to the role of a City grandee himself but was not to be accorded the laurels he sought. His attempt to become a director of the Bank of England when he assumed leadership of Dent, Palmer & Co. in 1858 was frustrated. He was married to Sabine Ellen Robarts, and they had eight sons. He died on 19 November 1872, at 12 Hyde Park Gardens, London, and was survived by his wife.

The fifth son, **Lancelot Dent** (1799–1853), was born on 4 August 1799 at Crosby Ravensworth, Westmorland, and appears to have been engaged initially in the wine trade. He is recorded in 1824 as a partner in Messrs Keirs & Co. of Madeira, yet by 1827 he had arrived in Canton. Under his leadership the firm evolved from its status as a barely tolerated participant in the 'country trade', on the fringes of the East India Company's monopoly, to that of the second largest China trading house making its constructive contribution to the institutions of local commerce and society. He successfully navigated the firm through the uncertainties resulting from the ending of the East India Company's monopoly of the China trade in 1834 and ensured that it exploited the main chance then presented. By the late 1830s, following the return to Britain of William Jardine, Lancelot Dent was regarded as the senior British merchant in Canton. From no. 6 Pao shun hong he presided over a burgeoning trade which included imports of raw cotton, manufactured goods, and, most famously and illegally, opium; exports of tea and silk; and the range of attendant insurance and banking services typical of an agency house.

Lancelot Dent combined an unusual attention to detail bordering on pedantry, with sufficient large-mindedness and affability to secure greater popularity than his brother Thomas. His moderate temperament, finding expression in the firm's mouthpiece, *The Canton Press*, sprang from a tory political sympathy, a respect for the stable framework provided by the East India Company, and a practical recognition that coercive measures against the Chinese to expand trading opportunities could be counter-productive. As a prime mover in the establishment of the Canton general chamber of commerce in 1836 he helped to reduce divisiveness within the merchant community, and his leadership of and benefaction to the Morrison Education Society (founded in the same year) fostered, in a modest way, greater mutual understanding between Chinese and Western cultures.

The painting by George Chinnery *On Dent's Verandah*,

executed about 1840, well evokes the languorous interludes between the Canton trading seasons when Dent would decamp for his well-appointed residence on Macão's Praya Grande. This pattern was to be rudely interrupted when the Chinese imperial government intensified its intermittent attempts to end the opium trade with the appointment in 1838 of Lin Zexu as high commissioner for Canton. Faced with Lin's summons to an interview at Canton's city gates, urgently reinforced on 23 March 1839 by the appearance of two leading Chinese Cohong merchants in chains, Dent would have acceded if not prevented by fellow merchants afraid both for his safety and for the possible surrender of opium stocks. The situation was saved only by the arrival in Canton of Captain Elliot, the British government's superintendent of trade. With the disruption of trade caused by the ensuing First Opium War (1839–42), Lancelot Dent possibly moved at least a part of his operations to Manila, where he had acquired a house. As the firm became established in Hong Kong, gaining a substantial foothold near Pedders Wharf in the first land sale of 1841, and extending its operations into the newly acquired treaty ports, Dent's role diminished. On his return to England by 1842, he retired to the Skersgill estate in Cumberland. He died, unmarried, at the Plough Hotel, Cheltenham, on 28 November 1853. Reporting his death the *Gentleman's Magazine* noted he was the head of an eminent house in China which bore his name, and added that 'He was the type of a true English merchant' (*GM*, 217). He was buried in St Lawrence's churchyard, Crosby Ravensworth.

Born on 24 December 1800 at Crosby Ravensworth, **Wilkinson Dent** (1800–1886) was in many respects a lesser man of business than his elder brothers, and his arrival in Canton was by a more circuitous route. Unsuccessful in Europe, he showed no greater promise in Calcutta. He departed in 1835 for Canton where by the year end Lancelot Dent had secured a partnership for him in Daniell & Co., hoping ultimately to effect a takeover (which never materialized). Present at Lancelot's discomfiture of 23 March 1839, Wilkinson Dent was a key restraining influence on his brother's readiness to leave the factories and face Lin. It was the Hong Kong branch of the firm which subsequently became his base. On his return to England, Wilkinson Dent lived at Flass House, Maulds Meaburn, Westmorland, which he and Lancelot had reconstructed with the fruits of their Far Eastern endeavours. The nearby church of St Lawrence, Crosby Ravensworth, was equipped with a chapel dedicated to the Dent family in 1871, funded by Wilkinson. He too died a bachelor, on 10 May 1886, at the family residence, 8 Fitzroy Square, London. He was buried near his brother in St Lawrence's churchyard.

Unfortunately a degree of complacency set in after the death or retirement of the three brothers, and the firm collapsed in 1867. A nephew, John Dent (1821–1892), had a lifestyle that certainly suggested extravagance (he was reported to have spent £10,000 on a racehorse to win the Hong Kong cup) but the firm's achievements, principally in the leading role it played in the establishment of the

Hongkong and Shanghai Bank, were still registered and failure was poignant when it came.

'It was a bitter moment when we had to haul down the old house flag' (Lubbock, 373), recalled **Sir Alfred Dent** (1844–1927), who was responsible for restoring the family fortunes. Born on 12 December 1844, the third son of Thomas Dent, he was educated at Eton College between 1858 and 1862, and was in the firm's employ on the China coast by 1864. Soon after the crash he had the business, reconstituted as Alfred Dent & Co., operational once more in the old Shanghai premises. He was, however, to make a spectacular departure from the time-honoured Dent career path. With Alfred's financial backing the Austro-Hungarian Herr van Overbeek, a former manager of Dent & Brothers in Hong Kong, succeeded in extracting commercial concessions from the sultan of Brunei and the Pangiran Temanggong in the face of American, Spanish, and Italian competition. The treaty sealing these arrangements in 1877 resulted in Overbeek's becoming maharaja of Saba and raja of Gaya and Sandakan. It was Dent's longstanding friendship with Sir Julian Pauncefote, permanent under-secretary at the Foreign Office, which provided support against the resulting complaints of Raja Brooke to which the colonial secretary, Sir Michael Hicks Beach, had lent a sympathetic ear. Dent bought out Overbeek's interest in 1880 and, following the grant of a royal charter the following year, the North Borneo Company was created with sovereign rights over the territories formerly in Overbeek's charge. For £120,000 Dent transferred all his rights to it. One of the provinces created for administrative purposes was named Dent.

Sir Alfred Dent was to broaden his activities even further. Head of the City firm of Dent Brothers & Co., merchants and commission agents, he also became chairman of the Caledonian (Ceylon) Tea Estates, and the Shanghai Electric Construction Company, and held directorships of the Chartered Bank of India, Australia, and China, the London County and Westminster Bank, and the Royal Exchange Assurance Corporation. In 1898 he was appointed to the Indian silver currency commission. His wide-ranging achievements were recognized by his knighthood (KCMG) in 1892 and his appointment as high sheriff of Sussex in 1908.

Something of a sportsman Dent pursued recreations such as rowing, tennis, hunting, and shooting. He married late, in 1896, Margaret, the daughter of Charles Aird; they had one son, Lesley. Dent's London addresses included Belgrave Mansions, Grosvenor Gardens, and, later, 10 Cambridge Gate, Regent's Park; he also favoured his country house, Ravensworth, in Eastbourne. Sir Alfred died on 23 November 1927 at his home in Cambridge Gate, and he was buried in Ocklynge cemetery, Eastbourne. He was survived by his wife.

Managers of a business partnership which played a major role in the expansion of British trade in the Far East, the Dent family provided an outstanding example of economic imperialism at work. At its height the firm rivalled the now better-known Jardine Matheson partnership for supremacy of the old China trade. Unfortunately, the presumed loss of the Dent business records has radically distorted historical accounts of the opening of trade with China in favour of Jardines, whose archive is still largely intact and readily accessible to scholars.

PHILIP K. LAW

Sources Burke, *Gen. GB* (1965–72), vol. 2 · d. certs. [Lancelot Dent, Sir Alfred Dent] · *WW* · *Canton Press* (1835–44) · M. Greenberg, *British trade and the opening of China, 1800–42* (1951) · F. Welsh, *A history of Hong Kong* (1993) · W. E. Cheong, *Mandarins and merchants: Jardine Matheson & Co., a China agency of the early nineteenth century* (1979) · B. Lubbock, *The opium clippers* (1933) · *The Times* (24 Nov 1927) · J. Orange, *The Chater collection: pictures relating to China, Hong Kong, Macao, 1655–1860* (1924) · S. Runciman, *The white rajahs: a history of Sarawak from 1841 to 1946* (1960) · M. Keswick, ed., *The thistle and the jade: a celebration of 150 years of Jardine, Matheson & Co.* (1982) · J. K. Fairbank, *Trade and diplomacy on the China coast: the opening of the treaty ports, 1842–1854*, 2 vols. (1953) · *GM*, 2nd ser., 41 (1854), 217 [Lancelot Dent] · J. H. Haswell, ed., *The parish registers of Crosby Ravensworth, 1568–1812* (1937) · tombstones [Wilkinson Dent, Lancelot Dent] · *CGPLA Eng. & Wales* (1872) · *CGPLA Eng. & Wales* (1896) · *CGPLA Eng. & Wales* (1928) · *CGPLA Eng. & Wales* (1834)

Archives Cumbria AS, Kendal, family papers

Likenesses portraits (Lancelot Dent and Wilkinson Dent), repro. in Lubbock, *The opium clippers*, facing p. 158 · portraits (Thomas Dent and Alfred Dent), repro. in Lubbock, *The opium clippers*, facing p. 374

Wealth at death under £500,000—Thomas Dent: probate, 1872, *CGPLA Eng. & Wales* · £183,386 9s. 10d.—Wilkinson Dent: probate, 1886, *CGPLA Eng. & Wales* · £61,962 6s. 9d.—Sir Alfred Dent: probate, 23 Jan 1928, *CGPLA Eng. & Wales* · £500,000—Lancelot Dent: *GM*, (1854), 217

Dent, Abraham (*bap.* 1729, *d.* 1803), shopkeeper, was baptized on 4 February 1729 at Kirkby Stephen, Westmorland, the elder child and only son of William Dent (1698–1774), a shopkeeper and wine merchant of Kirkby Stephen. A sister, Isabel, was baptized in 1732. Little is known of Dent's early life, but since he and his father were in partnership for a time, being addressed as Messrs W. Dent & Son, it might be conjectured that Abraham received his business training from his parent.

On 19 August 1754 Dent married Elizabeth Grainger. Their first two children died shortly after birth, but in 1761 a daughter, Elizabeth, survived, to be followed by sons Thomas and Abraham in 1765 and 1767. Letters and burial records show that a second wife, Anne, about whom nothing is known, died in 1781. Dent's third marriage, two years later, was to a widow, Isabel Metcalfe (*d.* 1807), of Sedbusk in Wensleydale, where the couple eventually lived.

What is known of Dent's life is gained almost entirely from surviving records of his business, between the years 1756 and 1780: one ledger of purchases for the shop from 1756 to 1777 with names and addresses of suppliers; a daybook of credit sales from the shop from 1762 to 1765; and another of sales from 1767 to 1780 dealing predominantly with stockings. There are also some loose papers, letters, and a letter-book covering the period from 1780 to 1789.

Although they sold goods which can be categorized as groceries, the Dents, father and son, were not called grocers but were variously described as mercers, merchants, and wine merchants. Their stocks were in the tradition of the mercers—who initially sold imported and slightly exotic wares alongside their cloth and other luxury goods. Tea, sugar, dried fruits, tobacco, and spices featured prominently in the Dents' shop, together with a good range of household necessities such as flour, hops, soap, and starch, patent medicines, paper, books, and magazines. A wide variety of individual items, from gardening and building equipment to items of clothing and cutlery, attest to Abraham Dent's willingness to arrange specific commissions for his customers; he also regularly supplied gunpowder to several companies.

Dent stocked everything needed for making clothes, and his records are informative about the quantities and materials required for particular garments. In 1764, for example, we see the same elements of superfine black cloth, shalloon, dimity, buckram, pocket fustian, canvas, thread, tape, twist, and coat and breast buttons being purchased in different quantities for two clerical gentlemen, at a cost of around £3 5s. 11d., while thick-set, shalloon, and flannel were bought for making servants' clothing at a total of £1 15s. 7d.

Again in the tradition of the mercers, Dent sold small items of ready-made clothing: gloves, assorted handkerchiefs, and knitted stockings. He was both manufacturer and retailer of hosiery; he took specific orders for hose, bought wool with which to supply the local hand-knitters with yarn, then collected and dispatched the finished work. Most of his orders came from two main army contractors in London, and were for different types of military stockings—soldiers' and sergeants' hose, marching regiments' hose, and guards' hose—although other types, such as ribbed yarn hose and loop worsted hose, were also supplied. Quantities varied, but the prices Dent charged remained fairly constant over twenty years. Business was brisk in the 1770s, when an individual order could be for as many as 7000 pairs of marching regiments' hose at 12d. a pair, but sales declined considerably in the 1780s.

Dent's daybook of credit sales shows that his shop customers came from a wide social range. The middle class predominates, with a number of clergy, doctors, and schoolmasters, but purchases were made by consumers from both ends of the social spectrum: tea and paper were bought by Sir George Dalston of Smarldale Hall, while sugar, treacle, flour, and candles were bought by labourer James Petty.

Dent was also a brewer, and owned a small acreage of land. His position as a propertied tradesman in a country township conferred a degree of public responsibility: his property qualified him to be a voter in the county elections, he sat on the jury of the local manorial court, and was a churchwarden. For the year 1767–8 he shared the job of overseer of the poor for the township, keeping the accounts in his ledger book, and some years later shared the position of surveyor of the highways.

It might be true to say, as Willan (147) suggests, that Dent was 'too versatile', combining 'too many roles', and that his connections were too wide and his social contacts too broad for him to be viewed as typical of a small town shopkeeper in the 1700s. It may be, however, that his energetic hard work and his innovative diversification make Dent particularly representative of the rising class of retailers whose entrepreneurial spirit made new demands of their suppliers—demands which stimulated and fuelled the growth of consumerism and industrialization.

Dent was buried at Hardraw on 3 March 1803 and was survived by his third wife. Although evidence suggests that during his lifetime Dent's private, public, and business activities had only local impact, his records provide invaluable information: they demonstrate methods of wholesale, retail, and dealership practices; show the social interaction, purchasing customs, and employment of a small community; and provide details of the wares themselves, their range, qualities, and values. They cast light on an extremely important, but historically underrepresented group—the small town shopkeepers of eighteenth-century England. POLLY HAMILTON

Sources T. S. Willan, *An eighteenth-century shopkeeper, Abraham Dent of Kirkby Stephen* (1970)
Archives Cumbria AS, Kendal, MSS of Isabel Dent, WDB/63/55–68, (Acc.1474) WDB/63/1–68
Wealth at death see administration of widow's will (1807–10), incl. correspondence and bids and accounts relating to the sale of estate by auction, Cumbria AS, Kendal, WDB/63/55–68

Dent, Sir Alfred (1844–1927). *See under* Dent family (*per. c.*1820–1927).

Dent, Arthur (1552/3–1603), Church of England clergyman and religious writer, was born at Melton Mowbray, Leicestershire, son of William Dent. William's brother John was a London merchant whose widow married Sir Julius Caesar. Having matriculated as a pensioner at Christ's College, Cambridge, in November 1571, Dent graduated BA in 1576 and proceeded MA in 1579. He was ordained deacon at Peterborough in March 1577 and priest, by John Aylmer, bishop of London, the following May, when he gave his age as twenty-four.

Immediately engaged as curate by George Withers, rector of Danbury, Essex, and archdeacon of Colchester, Dent was in the curious position of being protected by one of Aylmer's officials while subject to the unfriendly authority of another, John Walker, archdeacon of Essex. He was cited before Walker for refusing to church women in December 1577, and for conducting an irregular marriage in May 1578, but both charges seem to have been dropped. He received Aylmer's licence to preach throughout London diocese in October 1579.

On 17 December 1580 Aylmer instituted Dent to the rectory of South Shoebury, Essex, on the presentation of Robert, second Lord Rich, who had been showing increasing sympathy towards radical preachers since the mid-1570s. Yet when Rich and Aylmer clashed during the following months over quasi-congregational meetings at Rochford Hall, orchestrated by Robert Wright, Dent appears to have been unsympathetic towards his patron's proceedings.

Thus the evidence for Dent's involvement in the politico-religious agitation of the 1580s is conflicting. During Aylmer's visitation of 1583 he produced his preaching licence and was not further troubled. Yet in March 1584 he was one of seven preachers, including George Gifford, whom Aylmer interviewed about Whitgift's demand for unqualified subscription to the Book of Common Prayer. Given fourteen days to deliberate, Dent was one of twenty-seven Essex ministers who petitioned the privy council for protection. In July 1584 he was again before Archdeacon Walker on charges of ritual nonconformity, and it was later claimed that he had been 'sundry times troubled for omitting the cross and the surplice' (Peel, 2.164). Yet he escaped prosecution during the visitation of 1586, is not found among those Essex clergy suspended during Aylmer's 'last visitation and since for the surplice' (ibid., 2.261), and was appointed one of six commissioners to oversee exercises for the instruction of the less able clergy in Rochford deanery. Not until 1589 did his persistent failure to wear the surplice receive attention at an episcopal visitation, but again that charge, and the lesser one of omitting weekday services, appears to have been dropped after a routine period of excommunication.

Altogether, once Whitgift had been forced to moderate his original demand for unqualified subscription, Dent was not singled out, like Gifford, as one of the 'ringleaders' against whom further measures were to be taken. Yet a ringleader in some sense Dent certainly was: he was involved in discussions about the Book of Discipline (1585–7), and was nominated one of seven Essex delegates to the proposed provincial synod designed to follow the setting up of 'presbytery in episcopacy' during the winter of 1586–7.

Aylmer's leniency was no doubt dictated in part by the belligerent support which Dent could expect from his patron, but also, perhaps, by the fact that Dent's temperament was essentially eirenic. His ability to edify rural congregations was legendary, and, like many who abandoned political for pastoral courses after 1590, he translated this skill into print, becoming one of the most popular protestant authors of his generation. His *Sermon of Repentance*, preached at Leigh in March 1582, was reprinted at least twenty-two times up to 1638. Dent's third published work, *The Plaine-Mans Pathway to Heaven* (1601)—'wherein every man may clearly see whether he shall be saved or damned'—was dedicated to Julius Caesar and enjoyed unparalleled success. Reaching a twenty-fifth edition by 1640, it thus became one of the most frequently reprinted English books of its time. A forty-first edition appeared as late as 1831. It profoundly influenced John Bunyan and also Richard Baxter, who recast it in 1674 as *The Poor Man's Family Book*, abandoning Dent's homely dialogue for connected prose.

Dent's fourth work, *The Ruine of Rome, or, An Exposition upon the Whole Revelation*, was with the printer when its author succumbed to fever, dying within three days, on about 10 January 1603. His will, dated 7 January, is thus a brief document which left everything to his wife, Margery, 'for the education of all my children' (DL/C/359, fol. 389r). Ezekiel Culverwell, one of its witnesses, saw *The Ruine of Rome* through the press, adding a dedicatory epistle to Robert, third Lord Rich. Although his reference to his 'near conjunction' with his 'late brother' led to the erroneous assumption that Margery Dent was Culverwell's sister, it is possible that the first Mrs Culverwell (*d. c.*1597), otherwise unidentifiable, was the sister of Dent.

Culverwell extolled Dent's 'diligence, yea extreme and unwearied pains in his ministry publicly, privately, at home and abroad for four and twenty years at least'. *The Ruine of Rome* appeared only days before Elizabeth's death in 1603, reached a tenth edition by 1656, and seems to have found favour with the eighteenth-century evangelical movement: it was reprinted five more times between 1798 and 1841. Seven posthumous works bearing Dent's name were in print by the end of 1614, some perhaps representing spurious attempts by unscrupulous printers to profit from his popularity.

In 1972 Dent was paid the curious tribute of providing the name of the anti-hero—just as his most influential work informed the title—of Douglas Adams's *The Hitchhiker's Guide to the Galaxy*.   BRETT USHER

Sources Venn, *Alum. Cant.*, 1/2.33 · act books of archdeacon of Essex, Essex RO, D/AEA 10 and 12 · call-books of episcopal visitation, 1583, 1586, 1589, GL, MS 9537/5–7 · LMA, DL/C/333, fol. 179v; DL/C/334, fol. 19r · A. Peel, ed., *The seconde parte of a register*, 2 vols. (1915) · R. G. Usher, ed., *The presbyterian movement in the reign of Queen Elizabeth, as illustrated by the minute book of the Dedham classis, 1582–1589*, CS, 3rd ser., 8 (1905) · M. Hussey, 'Arthur Dent, rector of South Shoebury (1553–1603)', *Essex Review*, 57 (1948), 196–201 · registered will, LMA, DL/C/359, fol. 389r · [R. Bancroft], *Daungerous positions and proceedings* (1593) · P. Collinson, *The Elizabethan puritan movement* (1967) · A. Dent, preface, *The ruine of Rome, or, An exposition upon the whole Revelation* (1603)

Wealth at death see will, LMA, DL/C/359, fol. 389r

Dent, Charles Enrique (1911–1976), physician and biochemist, was born in Burgos, Spain, on 25 August 1911, the second son and youngest of the three children of Dr Frankland Dent, chemist and analyst, who worked in the Rio Tinto Mining Company, and his wife, Carmen Colsa de Mira y Perceval (1876–1976), daughter of Colsa de Mira, who held judicial office. Dent's paternal grandfather was a Church of England parson, but his father became a Roman Catholic on his marriage and all the children were brought up in the Catholic faith. In 1912 the family went to Singapore, but returned to Britain on the outbreak of war in 1914. Dent received his early education first at Bedford School and later at Wimbledon College, a Jesuit foundation. After leaving school in 1927 he worked first as a bank clerk and then as a laboratory technician, while taking evening classes at the Regent Street Polytechnic. In 1930 he passed the intermediate BSc examination and entered Imperial College as a student in chemistry. He graduated in 1932 with first-class honours and proceeded immediately to a PhD, which was awarded in June 1934, whereupon he obtained employment as a chemist in the dyestuffs division of Imperial Chemical Industries in Manchester. In 1937 Dent decided to study medicine at University College, London. After passing his second MB examination he transferred to University College medical school.

Dent's clinical studies were interrupted several times by the Second World War. He had been in the Territorial

Army since 1929, had become involved in intelligence work, and was an expert on secret writing. He went to France with the British expeditionary force in 1939, and participated in the retreat to Dunkirk. For his work as a dispatch rider he was mentioned in dispatches. Later he spent two years in Bermuda and was promoted to captain in the intelligence corps. He finally completed his medical course in 1944 and became the last house officer of the distinguished physician Sir Thomas Lewis. In the same year he became MRCP and was appointed assistant to the medical unit of University College Hospital medical school under Harold Himsworth. In 1944 he married Margaret Ruth, daughter of the Revd William Samuel Coad, a residentiary canon of Chester Cathedral. They had met while working in intelligence in Bermuda. They had six children, five daughters and one son, of whom two took up medicine.

In 1945 Dent was a member of the medical team involved in the investigation and treatment of survivors of the Belsen concentration camp. The rest of his professional career was spent at University College Hospital medical school; he was appointed reader in medicine in 1951 and professor of human metabolism in 1956.

Dent's early scientific work, carried out with R. P. Linstead, was on phthalocyanines. In 1946 he applied the newly discovered method of paper chromatography to an investigation of the metabolism of amino acids in man. He studied the pattern of amino acid excretion in the urine and applied these methods to an investigation of metabolic disorders such as hypophosphatasia and cystinuria. He established that the latter was not an error of metabolism *per se*, but was caused by a malfunction of a transport mechanism. Dent's later work was more oriented towards clinical medicine and he became an outstanding expert on diseases affecting the metabolism of calcium, phosphorus, and magnesium, as well as the pathology of bone. He also worked extensively on the pathology of vitamin D metabolism.

Dent had unusually high standards of personal behaviour, largely based on his complete loyalty to the Roman Catholic church, and he did not believe that there was any conflict between science and religion. He was always very keen on games, particularly rugby football. Another favourite hobby was wine making from his own vines.

Dent was made FRCP in 1954, elected FRS in 1962, gave the Humphry Davy Rolleston lecture in 1962, received the Gairdner Foundation award in 1965, and was made honorary MD of Louvain in 1966, and of Uppsala in 1974. He was appointed CBE in 1976. Dent died of leukaemia in London on 19 September 1976.   ALBERT NEUBERGER, *rev.*

Sources A. Neuberger, *Memoirs FRS*, 24 (1978), 15–31 · private information (1986) · personal knowledge (1986)

Archives Wellcome L., corresp. and papers

Likenesses photograph, repro. in *Memoirs FRS*, 24 (1978)

Wealth at death £59,659: probate, 1 Dec 1976, *CGPLA Eng. & Wales*

Dent, Edward John (1790–1853), chronometer maker, was born on 19 August 1790 in Portugal Street, Westminster, the elder of two sons of John Dent (*b.* 1767), an officer of the East India Company, and his first wife, Elizabeth, formerly Chapman (d. 1793), of Bedford. The younger son, William (1792–1858), became a printer's clerk, working in London and Bedford before returning to Islington where he died.

Edward Dent was apprenticed in 1804 to his grandfather John Wright Dent, a tallow chandler. Lodgings were to be provided for him under this agreement and he lived with his cousin Richard Rippon (1767–1835), watchmaker, of 46 King Street, Westminster. Dent became fascinated by the craft of watchmaking and in 1807 persuaded his grandfather to turn him over for the remainder of his apprenticeship to Edward Gaudin, watchmaker in Clerkenwell. At the end of his term Dent returned to live in Rippon's house, by then 43 King Street. He was employed by several of the leading watchmakers, acquiring from Barraud & Son a good knowledge of chronometers. He began making these for himself and in 1829 his no. 114 won the Royal Observatory's premium award.

In September 1830 Dent entered into partnership with John Roger Arnold, then one of the foremost chronometer makers. Arnold had a small factory at Chigwell, Essex, but he and his foreman were elderly and Dent offered both new ideas and proven business ability. Dent was made free of the Clockmakers' Company in 1831 and he moved into Arnold's house at 84 Strand. At this time one cause of error in timekeepers arose from extremes of temperature acting on the metals composing the balance springs. The properties of these various metals, and how magnetism affected them, were poorly understood. Arnold and Dent, probably with Richard Rippon's son, Frederick William Rippon (1808–1860), experimented with glass balance springs, though these did not live up to their early promise. Dent also experimented with mercury-filled clock pendulums (another temperature-compensating device) and lectured on this subject to the British Association for the Advancement of Science meeting at Newcastle in 1838. By that time Dent's own reputation was assured. He was a fellow of the Royal Astronomical Society, an associate of the Institution of Civil Engineers from 1833, and in 1838 Arnold and Dent received the royal warrant.

During 1837–9 Dent, urged on by the astronomer royal, George Biddell Airy, began estimating the longitudes of certain observatories by sending groups of chronometers, set to Greenwich time, to compare with local time there. Such journeys, by sea and in the rough land transport of the period, challenged the best chronometers, but their successful outcome was a valuable advertisement. Dent sent chronometers to Paris—their journey vividly described in the *Nautical Magazine* of 1838 and subsequently as a publicity booklet; to Scotland (Sir Thomas Brisbane's observatory at Makerstoun, and Edinburgh); to Dublin and Armagh; to Oxford, Bedford (Admiral Smyth's observatory), and Cambridge; to Portsmouth and Hamburg; and to New York. It is not clear how many of these expeditions Dent accompanied. He had agents in many ports and was a frequent visitor to the continent.

Relations with Arnold deteriorated from 1838 and the partnership ended in 1840. Dent went to live at The Mall, Kensington, but he also bought 82 Strand, where he installed a roof-top observatory, a temperature-controlled chronometer testing room, and fully equipped workshop. Frederick Rippon accompanied him, and he traded from 1 October 1840 as E. J. Dent, London, obtaining the royal warrant in 1841. Fortunately Airy and Captain Beaufort, the hydrographer, continued to pass Dent a share of the jobs formerly sent to Arnold and Dent, and after Arnold's death in 1843 he secured the entire business.

Dent continued to experiment with balance springs and filed his most important patent in 1842, though it was worded loosely enough for him to continue to develop his ideas in subsequent months. As with Dent's other patents, a similar patent was applied for in Paris. In 1843 Dent was asked to send chronometers to ascertain the difference in longitude between the observatories of Altona, near Hamburg, and Pulkovo, in Ukraine. In view of their satisfactory performance, the Russian emperor awarded him a gold medal and the title of chronometer maker to his imperial majesty. He also provided regulator clocks for observatories at Pulkovo, Geneva, Turin, and Venice.

At the late age of fifty-two Dent married, on 1 July 1843, Elizabeth Rippon, formerly Davis (1789–1865), the widow of his cousin Richard Rippon. Her two sons Frederick and Richard Edward Rippon (1817–1856) were also watchmakers, Frederick being employed by Dent. Both subsequently took the name of Dent. Elizabeth also had two daughters, Mary Elizabeth (1813–1892), married to Thomas Buckney, and Amelia Lydia Sophia (1814–1881), married to Henry Gardner. At about the time of his marriage Dent became involved in the manufacture of the dipleidoscope and two other instruments, the aneroid barometer and the marine compass, whose mechanisms bore similarities to those of watchwork. The dipleidoscope, the idea of his watchmaker friend P. M. Bloxham and patented in 1843, was based on the principle of double reflection. It consisted basically of a prism, though larger models had a small telescope and compass, and it enabled the meridian passage of the sun to be timed with great accuracy. Thus it could be used to set a watch, or if the time were known, to calculate the longitude.

The aneroid barometer was invented in France by Lucien Vidie, but was dismissed by French scientists as unworkable. Vidie went to London, where an example was constructed and tested, and patented in 1844. Vidie called on Dent as a possible maker, but found Dent unwell and in pessimistic mood. He did, however, allow Vidie to hang three aneroids in his shop window where they were seen and bought by a naval officer who tested them and returned to order thirty more. From this first sale, the aneroid gained in popularity, helped by its small size, portability, and cheapness (Dent sold 6 in. diameter aneroids for 3 guineas). It is unclear whether those bearing Dent's name had mechanisms made in Vidie's workshop in Paris or were built entirely in London.

Dent's improvements to the marine compass, patented in 1844 and 1850, consisted in suspending the card on a vertical needle carried at both ends in jewelled bearings, and in weighting the card in such a way as to prevent it from ceaselessly oscillating with the ship's motion.

Dent had recently begun to take an interest in turret clocks when in 1843 tenders were invited for a chiming clock for the newly built Royal Exchange. He submitted the lowest tender and it was accepted in August that year. Dent went to examine turret clocks in France and Belgium, acquired a factory at Somerset Wharf, off the Strand, and purchased the necessary machine tools. Airy contributed ideas for the clock's design but Dent had to put these into practice and he was particularly exercised over the choice of metal for the wheels and the method of cutting the teeth. These difficulties were overcome, however, and Airy declared the clockwork satisfactory on 31 August 1844. Dent already had another shop at 33 Cockspur Street for the Westminster trade, run by his stepson Richard; now he rented 34 Royal Exchange, one of the tiny shops fronting the Exchange building.

When the Palace of Westminster was to be rebuilt, following its destruction by fire in 1834, Dent applied to tender for the clock to be installed in the tower (now known as Big Ben). He was strongly supported by Airy but had to compete against Benjamin Lewis Vulliamy and John Whitehurst of Derby. Relations between these three rapidly soured, and in 1847 Dent withdrew his tender and departed to St Petersburg. After much deliberation between Airy, the architect Charles Barry, and various other officials and representatives of government, Dent agreed to retender and on 25 February 1852 his estimate was accepted. However, he died, at The Mall, Kensington, on 8 March 1852, and so Frederick Dent, who had inherited this part of the business, continued with the clock's construction. This was not to the liking of some of the officials concerned and legal advice was sought; Airy resigned from the committee overseeing the progress of the clock after conflicting with Edward Beckett Denison (later Baron Grimthorpe), a barrister known for his competence in horology, but eventually by 1859 the clock was installed and running.

Edward John Dent had divided his business interests between Richard, who inherited the Cockspur Street premises but died, intestate, of a brain disease in 1856, and Frederick. Before he died on 25 April 1860, Frederick destroyed the will and codicils that Denison had drawn up for him, triggering a lengthy legal dispute which was won by his widow. Elizabeth Dent continued to trade, assisted by her sons-in-law, as E. Dent & Co. After her death the firm was controlled by members of the Buckney and Gardner families, descended from Frederick's two sisters, and employed other members of the extended Dent family. In 1968 the last Buckney emigrated, turning the business over to the managing director. In 1975 it became a subsidiary of Toye & Co. Ltd.

G. C. BOASE, rev. ANITA McCONNELL

Sources V. Mercer, *The life and letters of Edward John Dent, chronometer maker, and some account of his successors* (1977) · A. E. Fanning, *Steady as she goes: a history of the compass department of the admiralty* (1986) · A. McConnell, 'The aneroid barometer comes to London', *Bulletin of the Scientific Instrument Society*, 38 (1993), 20–22 · d. cert.

Likenesses portrait, c.1844, repro. in Mercer, *Life and letters*, 258 · drawing, 1853, repro. in Mercer, *Life and letters*, frontispiece
Wealth at death £70,000: Mercer, *Life and letters*, 419

Dent, Edward Joseph (1876–1957), musicologist, was born at Ribston Hall, Wetherby, Yorkshire, on 16 July 1876, the fourth and youngest son of John Dent, barrister and for many years an MP, and his wife, Mary Hebden, daughter of John Woodall, of Scarborough. A scholar at Eton College and at King's College, Cambridge, Dent gained a third class in part one of the classical tripos in 1898. However, he had studied music, at which he excelled, at Eton under C. H. Lloyd; and at Cambridge, where he was a pupil of Charles Wood and Charles Stanford, he gained the MusB in 1899. From 1902 to 1908 he was a fellow of King's College, Cambridge, and lectured on music history, also teaching harmony, counterpoint, and composition. During this time he became absorbed in research on Alessandro Scarlatti, who was the subject of *Alessandro Scarlatti* (1905), his first book and perhaps his most notable achievement. This research was based largely on the study of manuscripts, involving travel throughout Italy, and was followed soon afterwards by major articles on Leonardo Leo, eighteenth-century Italian opera in general, and Orazio Vecchi's *Amfiparnaso*. These publications established Dent as the leading British musicologist of his day, and the first to gain an international reputation.

Following Charles Wood's death in 1926, Dent was appointed professor of music at Cambridge University, a post which he held until 1941. He was responsible for reorganizing the teaching of music on a broader basis, as the prerogative not only of organists and organ scholars but of those interested in all branches of music. He particularly encouraged performances of early music, especially baroque. His interests focused on Scarlatti; seventeenth- and eighteenth-century Italian opera, on which he published articles in the *Encyclopaedia Britannica*, the second edition of *Grove's Dictionary of Music and Musicians*, and the Riemann Festschrift of 1909; and Mozart. His *Mozart's Operas* (1913), published at a time when most of Mozart's operas were still almost completely unknown in England, became the standard work in any language on this subject and demonstrated Dent's ability to form keen critical judgements on the basis of close scholarship. Opera meant more to Dent than any other form of music. He made new translations of Mozart's *Le nozze di Figaro*, *Don Giovanni*, and *Die Zauberflöte*, and supervised a celebrated student production of the last of these at Cambridge in 1911. His later translations included several of Verdi's operas, Berlioz's *Les Troyens*, and Beethoven's *Fidelio*. He also edited many of Purcell's works and produced these at Cambridge, the Old Vic, the Glastonbury festival, and elsewhere; he made a new edition of *Dido and Aeneas* in 1924.

From 1919 Dent was the music critic of *The Athenaeum*, remaining after its amalgamation in 1921 into *The Nation and Athenaeum* (until 1924). He was also active in the formation of the British Music Society. But he remained essentially international in outlook. He was responsible for the fact that the International Festival of Contemporary

Chamber Music, held in 1922 at Salzburg, developed into the International Society of Contemporary Music; this body has branches in many countries and gives annual festivals of modern music. He became its first president, a post he held until 1938 and again in 1945–7. In 1927 he became vice-president of the newly formed International Society for Musicology, of which he later became president. He also served on the board of directors of Sadler's Wells Theatre, of which he became a governor. When the Covent Garden Opera Trust was set up in 1946 he became a director and showed a very active interest in presenting opera of all kinds in English. In 1950 he became the first president of the Liszt Society.

Dent had a strong rebellious streak, and delighted in expressing outrageous opinions about music that he felt had been accepted with unthinking reverence. His chapter on modern English music in Guido Adler's *Handbuch der Musikgeschichte* (1924; 2nd edn, 1930) caused some controversy, as he devoted considerably more space to the music of Sir Hubert Parry and Sir Charles Stanford than to that of Sir Edward Elgar, writing that 'for English ears Elgar's music is too emotional and not quite free from vulgarity'. In 1931 a protest against Dent's remarks, signed by many well-known musicians and others, was sent to the Press Association, leading to a flood of highly charged correspondence in various papers. For the 1929 edition of the *Oxford History of Music* Dent wrote a chapter entitled 'Social aspects of music in the middle ages', and he later served on the editorial board of the *New Oxford History of Music*. He was an honorary doctor of music of Oxford (1932), Harvard (1936), and Cambridge (1947) universities. He was also, in 1953, one of the first two musicians elected a fellow of the British Academy. His other books include *Foundations of English Opera* (1928) and a masterly biography of Ferruccio Busoni (1933), a composer whom he knew well as a personal friend. His prolific writings included many articles, forewords to books, and programme notes.

Dent composed a few original works, of which the most important are a set of polyphonic motets. He also made an arrangement of John Gay's *The Beggar's Opera* and a practical edition of one of the earliest oratorios, the sacred drama *La rappresentatione di Anima, et di Corpo* of Emilio de' Cavalieri. His scholarship was a living activity; he was always interested in promoting live performances of music which interested him, not merely in writing articles about it in learned journals. He revived a great deal of early music at a time when there was relatively little interest in it, while at the same time being keenly involved in contemporary music. He left his mark on many fields of music, not only in Cambridge, but in the whole international scene. In recognition of his contribution to musicology the Royal Musical Association, of which he was president from 1928 to 1935, instituted the Dent medal, which is awarded annually to recipients selected for outstanding achievement in this field. Dent, who was unmarried, died at his London home, 17 Cromwell Place, on 22 August 1957.   NIGEL SCAIFE

Sources P. Radcliffe, *E. J. Dent* (1976) · *Duet for two voices: an informal biography of Edward Dent compiled from his letters to Clive Carey*, ed. H. Carey (1979) · L. Haward, *Edward J. Dent, a bibliography* (1956) · W. Dean, 'Edward J. Dent, a centenary tribute', *Music and Letters*, 57 (1976), 353–61 · *DNB* · *CGPLA Eng. & Wales* (1957) · G. Adler, *Handbuch der Musikgeschichte* (Frankfurt am Main, 1924) · A. Lewis and N. Fortune, 'Dent, Edward J.', *New Grove*
Archives BL, annotated copy of Edmund Spenser's *Faerie queene* · CUL, corresp. · King's AC Cam., corresp., diaries, papers | CUL, letters to W. Hill · King's AC Cam., letters to Oscar Browning · King's AC Cam., letters to W. J. H. Sprott · NL Scot., letters to D. C. Parker
Likenesses S. Waterlow, pencil drawing, 1900, FM Cam. · A. P. Thompson, caricature, c.1901, King's Cam. · E. Kapp, lampblack and stump drawing, 1941, FM Cam. · L. Gowing, oils, 1948, King's Cam.
Wealth at death £37,751 9s. 1d.: probate, 18 Nov 1957, *CGPLA Eng. & Wales*

Dent, Frederick James (1905–1973), research chemist, was born on 12 October 1905 at Horbury in Yorkshire, the son of Frederick Dent and his wife, Sarah Liddle Pearson. His father had been a talented and inventive professional photographer who, after his business failed, became an engineer supervising the installation of telephone exchanges; later he was an engineering inspector in the civil service based in Leeds. Dent's mother came from a seafaring family; she won a scholarship and became a teacher.

Dent had an outstanding school career at the Leeds Boys' Modern School, where he became head boy. He had intended to follow an artistic career, but towards the end of his time at school he was persuaded to turn towards science with such good effect that he was awarded two scholarships, enabling him to enter the department of fuel at Leeds University. In 1927 he obtained first-class honours, the LeBlanc medal, and a postgraduate scholarship. As there had been close links between the university and the gas industry since the early years of the century, it was natural that Dent should undertake research on carbonization for his PhD, which was awarded in 1929.

Following this, Dent was appointed research chemist by the joint research board of Leeds University and the Institution of Gas Engineers. He spent several years investigating the cyclical water–gas process of making gas from coke. Hearing in 1935 of the new German Lurgi process for gasification of lignite, Dent turned his attention to the direct gasification of coal under high pressure. This work progressed well but was interrupted by the war and he had to turn his attention to the synthesis of methane. On 1 January 1942 he married Jean Marie Macvean, and they had one son and one daughter.

Dent's prospects were transformed by the nationalization of the gas industry in 1949. He was appointed head of one of the industry's research stations, with both staff and resources, and was responsible for work on high-pressure gasification. This was the start of an extremely fruitful period of research under his inspiration, at first into coal gasification and later, when oil supplies became widely available, into the direct conversion of oil into gas. Processes developed under his leadership include the catalytic rich gas (CRG) process, using naphtha, and the gas recycle hydrogenator (GRH), which could use other oil fractions. These processes were flexible and cheap and could produce either a coal-gas equivalent or a substitute natural gas (SNG). They were therefore of great interest wherever gas was supplied. At the time of his death, Dent's CRG process was being used widely in the USA, Japan, and South America, as well as in the UK, incidentally earning substantial royalties for the British gas industry. Dent and his team, to whom he gave generous credit, were responsible for numerous scientific papers and patent specifications for gas-making processes.

Dent was notable for his ability not only to visualize chemical processes but also to design the hardware to transform them into process technology on an industrial scale. He was a prodigious worker and hard taskmaster who nevertheless managed to endue his colleagues with his own unbounded enthusiasm for the tasks in hand. Despite having spent much of his life working on coal, in his fifties he had the vision to be able to turn with equal success to oil gasification, producing results that were of even greater significance to the industry. By nature a hands-on researcher, he was less at home with the routines of managing a large research establishment. He was appointed OBE in 1958 and was elected FRS in 1967, the year of his retirement.

Dent's enthusiastic nature was manifested not only in his work but also in the leisure activities into which he threw himself. He was an accomplished photographer, and gained an abiding love of the sea after he was introduced to sailing by a colleague at Poole during the war. Family holidays were spent in his *Blue Jay*, a cutter built in 1926, exploring the south coast and, later, Normandy and Brittany. After his retirement he severed all connections with the gas industry. He left Britain and sailed past Gibraltar into the Mediterranean, to Malta, where he set up home, and to the Greek islands. He returned only briefly in 1971 to receive the prestigious MacRobert award from Prince Philip at Buckingham Palace. He died on 5 October 1973 at his home, 13 Valley View Court, Zaccheus Street, Maida, Malta, shortly after being taken ill while cruising round Greece. His wife survived him.

FRANCIS GOODALL

Sources K. Hutchinson and D. Hebden, *Memoirs FRS*, 20 (1974), 155–80 · *The Times* (12 Oct 1973)
Likenesses photograph, repro. in Hutchinson and Hebden, *Memoirs FRS*

Dent, John (*b.* in or after **1761**, *d.* **1826**), politician and book collector, was the son of Robert Dent (1731–1805), of Child & Co.'s bank, Temple Bar, London, and his wife, Jane Bainbridge (*c.*1726–1800), who married at St James's, Piccadilly, on 11 October 1760. His younger brother Robert entered Gray's Inn on 2 February 1785, and died on 20 November 1788. His father, who came from an old Westmorland family, rose from a clerkship with Child's to a partnership in 1763, and bought a house at Clapham, Surrey, and a share in the manor of Cockerham, near Lancaster. John Dent joined the bank and became a partner in 1795. On 29 October 1800 he married Anne Jane (*d.* 1856), the daughter and coheir of John Williamson, a brewer, of Roby, near Liverpool. They had five sons and five daughters.

In 1790 Dent successfully contested the parliamentary seat of Lancaster, where he established an interest strong enough to enable him to retain the seat at the next four general elections. He gave general but independent support to Pitt's first ministry, opposed abolition of the slave trade, as befitted the member for a slaving port, and spoke frequently on a variety of financial and commercial subjects. By proposing a tax on dogs and vehemently denouncing the species in 1796 he saddled himself with the nickname of Dog Dent. Unimpressed by Addington as Pitt's successor, he and his brother-in-law Isaac Gascoyne, MP for Liverpool, acted with the 'new' Grenvillite opposition from 1802. By the next year he had attached himself to Canning, whose devoted acolyte and unwitting butt he remained for the rest of his days. He supported Pitt's second administration and tried in vain to promote a junction with the Foxite whigs in 1805, when he turned down the baronetcy offered him at Canning's instigation, supposedly because his wife was averse to it. He opposed the Grenville ministry and was one of the eighteen die-hards who voted against the abolition of the slave trade in 1807. He supported the Portland government until Canning resigned from it in October 1809, and, until his retirement from the expensive Lancaster seat at the dissolution three years later, was one of Canning's 'little senate' of personal followers. He canvassed Poole, which lay a few miles along the channel coast from his Hampshire villa at Barton, between Christchurch and Lymington, but made no headway against the inimical influence of the new Liverpool ministry and the prince regent. He apparently declined Canning's offer of a seat for Petersfield.

After Canning's reconciliation with the government in 1814 Dent applied for a baronetcy, but to no avail. Canning asked Huskisson, 'How could I guess the Dog's wish to be Sir Dogby, when he so positively denied it [in 1805]. Has Mrs dog changed her mind, I wonder?' (Port and Fisher, 590). Dent won a seat for Poole at the 1818 general election and was returned unopposed in 1820. He gave general support to the ministry as a friend of Canning, to whose sensibilities he deferred after his resignation from the cabinet over the prosecution of Queen Caroline in December 1820. By the time Canning became foreign secretary in September 1822 Dent, who had suffered from poor health for several years, was a virtual cipher in the Commons. Tortured by tic douloureux, he threw himself off a cliff near his villa in 1825, but survived. He retired from parliament at the dissolution in 1826.

Dent was a voracious book collector, and at considerable cost assembled one of the finest private libraries of his day, which included a 1462 Latin Bible, the first three Shakespeare folios and many quartos, and a fine collection of Aldines and Elzeviers. He died at his London house, 10 Hertford Street, Mayfair, on 14 November 1826. His widow survived him for almost thirty years. His books and manuscripts were dispersed in two sales of 2976 lots in March and April 1827, which realized over £15,000.

D. R. FISHER

Sources M. H. Port and D. R. Fisher, 'Dent, John', HoP, *Commons, 1790–1820* · D. R. Fisher, 'Dent, John', HoP, *Commons, 1820–32* [draft] · *GM*, 1st ser., 58 (1788), 1034 · *GM*, 1st ser., 70 (1800), 491,

1286 · *GM*, 1st ser., 97/1 (1827), 179 · *GM*, 3rd ser., 1 (1856), 123 · S. De Ricci, *English collectors of books and manuscripts* (1930), 99 · W. Y. Fletcher, *English book collectors* (1902), 278–80 · J. Dent, *A catalogue of the library of John Dent* (1825) · *Catalogue of the splendid, curious, and extensive library of the late John Dent* (1827) [sale catalogues, R. H. Evans, London, 29 March – 7 April 1827 and 25 April – 6 May 1827] · *IGI* · Burke, *Gen. GB* (1906)

Archives BL, letters, Add. MSS 28653, fols. 107–8; 38321, fols. 128, 135; 38739, fols. 29, 40

Wealth at death under £35,000: PRO, death duty registers, IR 26/1118/124

Joseph Malaby Dent (1849–1926), by unknown photographer

Dent, Joseph Malaby (1849–1926), publisher, was born at 3 Archer Street, Darlington, on 30 August 1849, the tenth child of George Dent, a house-painter, and his wife, Isabella, *née* Railton. Joseph Dent attended a Wesleyan school until the age of thirteen. He was briefly an apprentice printer, but proved so inept at that trade that he turned to bookbinding. Dent was a product of the autodidact culture that flourished among self-improving Victorian artisans. His own father had taught music and sold musical instruments as a sideline, and Dent himself discovered Walter Scott's novels while still at school; at the age of fifteen he became enamoured of literature when he spoke before a chapel mutual improvement society on Boswell's *Life of Samuel Johnson*. That book would become the first volume in Dent's great series of cheap classics, Everyman's Library. In August 1867 Dent moved to London, where he worked for a bookbinder in Bucklersbury, out of Cheapside. He married Hannah (1840/41–1887), daughter of George Wiggins, on 1 October 1870: they had four sons and two daughters. After the death of his first wife, he married Alexandra Campbell, daughter of Thomas Burnett Main, on 13 April 1889; they had four daughters and two sons.

Dent set up his own London shop in Hoxton in 1872, and in 1881 he moved to larger premises at 69 Great Eastern Street, but that plant burnt down on new year's day 1888. The insurance money allowed him to rebuild, and the following autumn J. M. Dent & Co. ventured into publishing. Dent had often been struck by the contrast between his handsome leather bindings and the spindly Victorian type on the pages they enclosed; he now embarked on a crusade to raise standards of book production. He published the Temple Library, starting with Charles Lamb's *Essays of Elia*, edited by Augustine Birrell, with etchings by Herbert Railton. This series of limited editions, produced on handmade paper, won both commercial success and the endorsement of the antiquarian bookseller Bernard Quaritch. In 1889 Dent put out an edition of *The Canterbury Tales* with hand-coloured illustrations; then he turned to uniform editions of the great English novelists. A trip to Florence and Siena in 1890 inspired the Mediaeval Towns series: illustrated books about the historic cities of Europe. There followed in 1893–4 a magnificent edition of Sir Thomas Malory's *The Birth, Life and Acts of King Arthur*, with about 300 illustrations by the nineteen-year-old Aubrey Beardsley.

Dent recognized an enormous potential demand for cheap classics among self-educated readers. He was secretary of the Shakespeare Society at the Toynbee Hall settlement house, where the members had to cope with a confusing variety of editions, most of them badly edited and without helpful critical apparatus. Between 1894 and 1896 he produced the forty-volume Temple Shakespeare, edited by Israel Gollancz, with title-pages by Walter Crane, all for 1s. a volume; the series was to sell 5 million copies over the next forty years. There followed the Temple Dramatists, editions of other Elizabethan and Jacobean playwrights; the Temple Biographies; the Temple Greek and Latin Classics; English Men of Science; a forty-volume translation of Balzac's *Comédie humaine*; as well as multi-volume Temple editions of Fielding, Scott, Dickens, Hugo, Thackeray, and Hazlitt. There was even a Temple Bible in thirty-one volumes. Dent's list was not, however, limited to the classics. He also published contemporary writing by Maurice Hewlett, H. G. Wells, Henryk Sienkiewicz, Bernhard Berenson, Edward Thomas, John Masefield, Henry James, Padraic Colum, George Santayana, Mary Webb, and the later works of Joseph Conrad and W. H. Hudson, as well as children's books by Kate Greenaway and Edith Nesbit. The Temple Primers series popularized academic subjects for lay readers.

In 1906 Dent began his greatest project, a 1000-volume uniform edition of world literature, selling for 1s. a volume. His editor was Ernest Rhys, who proposed the name Everyman's Library. Cheap classic reprints were by no means a new concept—Rhys himself had earlier edited the 1s. Camelot Classics for the Newcastle publisher Walter Scott—but Everyman's Library was unprecedented in its breadth, coherence, and beautiful design. Reginald Knowles designed the bindings, endpapers, and title-pages in the manner of William Morris. A hand-lettered title and a distinctive floral ornament were stamped on the spine in gold. The demand for Everyman's Library was so great that Dent had to build the Temple Press, a vast new production facility at Letchworth Garden City. In 1911 the firm moved to imposing new offices at 10–13 Bedford Street, Covent Garden, London. Having invested so much capital in his Letchworth plant, Dent could be stingy with his workers, authors, and editors. Rhys, for instance, had to work at breakneck speed to prepare new volumes for publication (152 in the first year), and at first earned only 3 guineas per volume. But Dent was a capitalist with an entirely genuine commitment to quality: when one of the first Everyman volumes, Lamb's *Essays of Elia*, fell short of his aesthetic standards, he had the entire print run destroyed.

Dent has been criticized for his over-reverent, conservative, petit bourgeois tastes in literature. (He always pronounced it *litterchah*, his employee Frank Swinnerton recalled.) Since the early Everyman volumes were reprints of out-of-copyright texts, they inevitably represented the standard canon of Greek, Roman, English, American, and western European classics. By 1956 the firm's editorial director admitted that many of the Victorian war-horses had already become anachronisms. With puritanical fastidiousness, Dent blocked the admission of Tobias Smollett and *Moll Flanders* to Everyman's Library. Yet in other respects the series was remarkably inclusive, embracing the Russian classics, the great books of India, and an impressive range of female novelists. (Dent himself wrote the introduction to Elizabeth Gaskell's *Cranford*, one of his personal favourites.) A Liberal nonconformist, Dent was inspired by an almost religious mission to bring culture to the masses. As a member of the Toynbee Hall education committee, he organized a Sunday afternoon concert series that ran in Whitechapel for thirty years. From 1902 he served on the council of the British and Foreign School Society, and he was a strong supporter of Margaret McMillan's nursery school movement.

In 1912 Dent launched *Everyman*, a penny literary weekly. It was a failure, partly as a result of quarrels with the editor, Charles Sarolea. The First World War slowed the publication of new Everyman's Library volumes to a near standstill, and wartime inflation forced the series to raise its prices and economize on ornamentation. Dent was devastated by the loss of two sons, Paxton and Austen, in the war; significantly, the first work of twentieth-century literature published in Everyman's Library was Henri Barbusse's devastating war novel *Le feu*, translated as *Under Fire*.

J. M. Dent's sons Hugh and Jack Dent and Jack's son, F. J. Martin Dent, all assumed managerial roles in the family firm. J. M. Dent retired in 1924, and died of heart failure at his home, Cromhamleigh, Harewood Road, south Croydon, on 9 May 1926. He was buried in Sanderstead churchyard, Surrey. Everyman's Library did not reach volume 1000 until 1956, but Dent had lived to see total sales exceed 20 million.   JONATHAN ROSE

Sources J. M. Dent, *The house of Dent, 1888–1938* (1938) · D. A. Ross, *The reader's guide to Everyman's Library*, 4th edn (1976) · E. Rhys, *Everyman remembers* (1931) · J. M. Dent archives, University of North Carolina, Chapel Hill, Wilson Library · U. Edin. L., Charles Sarolea

MSS · J. Rose, 'J. M. Dent and Sons', *British literary publishing houses, 1881–1965*, ed. J. Rose and P. J. Anderson, DLitB, 112 (1991) · b. cert. · m. cert. · d. cert.
Archives University of North Carolina, Chapel Hill, Wilson Library, MSS | U. Edin. L., business corresp. with Charles Sarolea
Likenesses D. Noyes, sketch, repro. in Dent, *The house of Dent* · photograph; Sothebys, 18 July 1991, lot 348 [*see illus.*]
Wealth at death £14,276 13s. 8d.: probate, 22 June 1926, CGPLA Eng. & Wales

Dent, Lancelot (1799–1853). *See under* Dent family (*per.* c.1820–1927).

Dent, Peter (1628/9–1689), apothecary and naturalist, the son of Peter Dent of Cambridge, was admitted to Trinity College, Cambridge, in 1649/50. He acquired properties in the parish of St Sepulchre, Cambridge, soon after 1650 and was in practice there by 1657. These properties, which he improved during his tenure, included a small leasehold shop at Bridge Street with adjoining house, warehouse, and other premises, and a separate leasehold garden behind the church, occupied by a house and two or three cottages. Dent's first wife, Katherine, died in 1659 giving birth to their second child, who died shortly afterwards. He married, within fifteen months, Elizabeth Pleys. She was buried on 2 March 1709. From these two marriages, thirteen children were baptized at St Sepulchre, including three named Peter, two of whom died in infancy.

Dent obtained a Lambeth MB degree in 1678, probably on the strength of recommendations from his friends and patients; in the custom of the time, he practised both as apothecary and physician, and may have taken patients into his home for treatment. He obtained a Cambridge degree by incorporation in 1680. Through his interest in botany he became a member of John Ray's (1627–1705) circle of friends. He contributed to Ray's *English Catalogues* of 1670 and 1677, and was singled out for mention in the introduction to the latter edition as having recorded nine plants not included in Ray's *Catalogus plantarum circa Cantabrigiam nascentium* (1660). He also contributed to Ray's great *Historia plantarum* (3 vols., 1686–1704). In its preface Ray expressed his obligation to Dent for many observations. In 1685 a second *Appendix* to Ray's Cambridge catalogue appeared anonymously, its sixty plants having been principally communicated by Dent. Raven states that this appendix was not Ray's work, and was uncertain whether it was due to Dent (Raven, 122), but since Ray would not have sought the credit in these circumstances it is likely to have been Dent's work.

Dent's observations on the structure of the trachea in the male of most ducks were credited by Ray in *The Ornithology* (1678), where Ray described Dent as 'an ingenious observer' (Willughby and Ray, *Ornithology*, 9). It was the contemporary compliment and Raven remarked that this 'is a nice point to find noticed so early' (Raven, 317). Ray also acknowledged 'Dominus Petrus Dent' in his preface to Willughby's *Historia piscium* (1686). In English, his acknowledgement reads 'Master Peter Dent communicated several observations concerning cartilaginous flat fish, especially of the uterus and eggs of rays, and fine sketches, first of the fish themselves, and then of their inner parts'.

Dent died on 3 September 1689 and was buried two days later at the church of St Sepulchre, Cambridge. He was survived by his widow, at least two sons, Pierce (1663–1727) and William (1665–1694), and three daughters. Pierce Dent inherited his father's practice as apothecary, together with his property, and like his father was interested in botany and entomology, and a friend of Ray. He married Deborah Ewin in 1692 and they had seven children before she died in 1702. There were no children from his second marriage, to Bridgett, who survived him.

Peter Dent (1637/8–1717) was probably a cousin; he joined Dent in Cambridge about 1663, and was admitted to Trinity College in 1671/2. By about 1691 he was described as a 'cook', meaning a catering contractor, probably to one of the Cambridge colleges. He was twice married, and had five children between 1671 and 1708, during which time he lived in one of Dent's houses.   F. HORSMAN

Sources J. D. Whittet and M. Newbold, 'Apothecaries in the diary of Samuel Newton, alderman of Cambridge', *Pharmaceutical Journal*, 221 (1978), 115–18 • C. E. Raven, *John Ray, naturalist: his life and works*, 2nd edn (1950); repr. with new introduction by S. M. Walters (1986) • Venn, *Alum. Cant.* • J. Petiver, 'An account of divers rare plants', *PTRS*, 27 (1710–12), 375–94, esp. 385 • P. Dent, *Appendix ad catalogum plantarum circa Cantabrigiam nascentium* (1685) • J. Ray, *Historia plantarum*, 3 vols. (1686–1704) • J. Ray, *Catalogus plantarum Angliae* (1670); 2nd edn (1677) • F. Willughby and J. Ray, *The ornithology* (1678) • F. Willughby and J. Ray, *Historia piscium* (1686) [preface] • *The diary of Samuel Newton, alderman of Cambridge (1662–1717)*, ed. J. E. Foster, Cambridge Antiquarian RS, 23 (1890) • J. Ray, *Catalogus plantarum circa Cantabrigiam nascentium* (1660) • parish registers, St Sepulchre, Cambridge, Cambs. AS • title deeds, St John Cam. • lease books, CCC Cam. • will, CUL, department of manuscripts and university archives, vice-chancellor's court, reg. IV, 309

Dent, Thomas (1796–1872). *See under* Dent family (*per. c.*1820–1927).

Dent, Wilkinson (1800–1886). *See under* Dent family (*per. c.*1820–1927).

Denton, Alexander (*bap.* 1679, *d.* 1740), judge, was baptized at Hillesden, near Buckingham, on 25 August 1679, the second son of Alexander Denton and his wife, Hester, daughter and heir of Nicholas Herman of Middleton Stoney, Oxfordshire. His father was elected MP for Buckingham in 1689. His elder brother was Edmund Denton, first baronet, also member for Buckingham. Denton was admitted to St Edmund Hall, Oxford, in April 1697, and the following year to the Middle Temple, by which inn he was called to the bar in 1704 and to the bench in 1720.

The year after his call Denton was the victim of a serious threat to the independence of the bar. As one of the counsel representing the prisoners in the Aylesbury election case, on their application for habeas corpus, he was himself committed to prison by the House of Commons for a supposed breach of privilege. The case resulted in a major conflict between the two houses of parliament. It may, however, have served Denton well by bringing him to the

attention of Lord Wharton, who probably supported him when he was elected to succeed his brother as member of parliament for Buckingham in 1708; he served in parliament from 1708 to 1710, and in the Irish parliament from 1709 to 1710, and then again (as king's counsel) in the English parliament from 1715 until 1722. On 3 March 1716 Denton married Catherine, daughter and heir of John Bond of Sundridge, Kent, with a fortune of £20,000.

Denton's local connections secured his election as recorder of Buckingham, and as early as 1710 the duke of Devonshire wrote to Chief Justice Parker asking for 'your favour at the bar for him' (BL, Stowe MS 750, fol. 13); but his eminence in the profession was firmly secured when he was appointed attorney-general to the duchy of Lancaster in 1714, and king's counsel in 1715. He was considered for the position of solicitor-general in 1720, but passed over in favour of Philip Yorke (subsequently Lord Hardwicke). In 1722 he was appointed to the bench as one of the justices of the common pleas, the patrons at his serjeant's call being Viscount Townshend and Robert Walpole. A puisne judgeship was not the summit of his ambition, and in 1729 he secured the courtly position of chancellor to Frederick, prince of Wales, but his further aspirations were thwarted. In 1735 he wrote to Hardwicke, now lord chancellor, seeking the chief justiceship of the common pleas, offering to resign as prince's chancellor, but Hardwicke tactfully questioned whether his health would withstand the strain. In the event Thomas Reeve was appointed. On Reeve's death in 1737 Denton applied again to Walpole, alleging some 'court promises' to support him; but Walpole thought him 'too old and infirm to discharge the duty' (HoP, *Commons*). The following year he was offered the office of chief baron of the exchequer when James Reynolds indicated his wish to retire, turned it down in a letter to Hardwicke on 2 July, suggesting Edmund Probyn instead, and then changed his mind almost immediately but too late. Mr Justice Abney wrote privately that he was unfit for either office, 'for he wanted spirit and rediness to preside in any court, and was a total stranger to the practice of the Exchequer' (Abney's reports, MS IHR 976(2), University of London).

Thomas Abney considered that these disappointments 'sat so heavy on his spirits that they contributed much to shorten his days' (Abney's reports), which ended at Bath on 22 March 1740. The final cause of death was 'a tedious complicated distemper of consumption and gout' (ibid.). A monument, with a bust in judicial robes, was erected at Hillesden, which suggests that he might have been buried there. A painting by Jonathan Richardson, in scarlet judicial robes, with the embroidered purse of Prince Frederick, was engraved in quarter length by George Vertue in 1731.

It is known that Denton wrote law reports, which were cited by contemporaries but have not yet been discovered. The obituary by Abney epitomizes his character by saying that 'though his parts were low and his manner heavy, yet he had taken great pains in his profession and had really more knowledge in it than those who were not intimate with him conceiv'd'. As Denton and his wife had no children the estates devolved on the judge's nephew, George Chamberlayne, who also succeeded him as MP for Buckingham.   J. H. BAKER

Sources R. S. Lea, 'Denton, Alexander', HoP, Commons, 1715–54, 1.610–11 · Baker, Serjeants · Sainty, King's counsel · Sainty, Judges · Foss, Judges · Foster, Alum. Oxon. · J. H. Baker, English legal MSS in USA (1998) · Sir Thomas Abney's reports, U. Lond., MS IHR 976 · Yorke corresp., BL, Add. MSS 35585–35586 · Newcastle correspondence, BL, Add. MS 32691, fol. 103 · BL, MS Stowe 750, fol. 13 · W. Musgrave, Obituary prior to 1800, ed. G. J. Armytage, 1, Harleian Society, 44 (1899) · IGI
Archives BL, corresp. with Sir John Bridgeman, Eg MS 1974
Likenesses G. Vertue, engraving, 1731 (after J. Richardson) · bust on monument, c.1740, Hillesden, Buckinghamshire · oils, Harvard U.

Denton, Henry (c.1640–1681), Church of England clergyman and translator, was the second son of Thomas Denton (1612–1643), from an old Cumberland family living at Warnell Hall, Warnell Denton, south of Carlisle, and Lettis (d. 1678), daughter of John Lougher, of Perton, Staffordshire, and Mary *Fitton, maid of honour to Elizabeth I. On 24 June 1653 he matriculated at Queen's College, Oxford, together with his elder brother Thomas [see under Denton, John]. At Queen's he had as his chamber fellow, and perhaps tutor, William Lamplugh, afterwards archbishop of York. He graduated BA on 21 March 1656 and MA on 25 June 1659. He had also proved himself an accomplished violinist. In 1660 he became a fellow of Queen's College, succeeding to the rooms of his friend Joseph Williamson, who had left academic for political life.

In autumn 1664, on the recommendation of Sir Heneage Finch, the Levant Company appointed Denton chaplain to the English ambassador in Constantinople, Sir Heneage's cousin Heneage Finch, earl of Winchilsea. Denton set out early in 1665, stopped to preach in Smyrna, and favourably impressed Winchilsea, who described him as 'a modest, ingenious person' (Finch MSS, 389). In Constantinople, Denton is said to have mastered Arabic, Syriac, and Slavonic, and the Turkish-Latin grammar by the Polish interpreter Albert Bobowski (known as Ali Bey) which Denton brought back to Oxford (Bodl. Oxf., Hyde MS 43) suggests that he was well advanced in the study of Turkish. On his return to England after Winchilsea's recall late in 1668 Denton took up residence at Queen's College. In 1673, the year in which he seems to have married an Oxford woman whose surname was Ellis and with whom he had at least one son, baptized on 22 March 1681, the provost and fellows gave him the nearby living of Bletchingdon.

Like his successors at the embassy in Constantinople, Thomas Smith (his friend and near contemporary at Queen's) and John Covel, Denton took an interest in the Greek Orthodox church when he was in the Levant. He befriended Joseph Georgirenes, archbishop of Samos, and their friendship continued when Georgirenes came to England in 1676 to have a liturgical work printed for his parishioners. Georgirenes soon became involved in the plan to build a church for the Greek colony in London. (The church in Soho Fields was to give its name to Greek

Street.) Hoping to raise money for it, he wrote his *Description of the Present State of Samos, Nicaria, Patmos, and Mount Athos* (1678). Dedicated to the duke of York (later James II) and strongly anti-Turkish and anti-Venetian, the text was translated into English by Denton, who added explanatory notes and an epistle to the reader emphasizing the points of agreement between the Greek church and the Church of England.

Denton died at Bletchingdon on 18 August 1681 and was buried in the parish church two days later.

                                              ALASTAIR HAMILTON

Sources S. Runciman, The great church in captivity: a study of the patriarchate of Constantinople from the eve of the Turkish conquest to the Greek War of Independence (1968) · Report on the manuscripts of Allan George Finch, 5 vols., HMC, 71 (1913–2003), vol. 1 · Foster, Alum. Oxon. · J. B. Pearson, A biographical sketch of the chaplains to the Levant Company, maintained at Constantinople, Aleppo and Smyrna, 1611–1706 (1883) · DNB · A. N. Pippidi, 'Knowledge of the Ottoman empire in late seventeenth-century England: Thomas Smith and some of his friends', DPhil diss., U. Oxf., 1983 · parish register, Bletchingdon, Oxfordshire [baptismal, burial] · Denton family pedigree, Manx National Heritage Library, Douglas, Isle of Man, MS 5A, fol. 7

Denton, James (d. 1533), dean of Lichfield, was educated at Eton College, before in 1486 going as a king's scholar to King's College, Cambridge, where he proceeded BA in 1489, and MA in 1492, becoming in due course a fellow in 1489 and bursar of the college in 1496/7 and 1498/1500. He subsequently studied canon law at Valence, where he earned a doctorate in that faculty. In 1505 he obtained licence to stand in the same degree at Cambridge. He became a royal chaplain, and was rewarded with various preferments, including a canonry at Windsor (1509), and prebends at Lichfield (1509), Salisbury (1510), and Lincoln (1514). He was also rector of several parishes, including St Olave's, Southwark.

In 1514 Denton went to France as almoner with Mary, the sister of Henry VIII, on her marriage to Louis XII, and attended her in France until her husband's death and her own return to England. He afterwards acted as her chancellor, and in 1525 visited France on some mission about her dowry. She showed great anxiety to promote him, and informed Wolsey that he had done her much service. In 1520 he was one of the royal chaplains, 'clothed in damask and satin', at the Field of Cloth of Gold. In 1522 his contribution of £200 to the clerical subsidy-loan to the king attested both his loyalty and his wealth. In 1524 he formed part of a commission with Sir Ralph Egerton and Sir Anthony Fitzherbert, justice of the king's bench, to reform the government in the Irish pale on the cheap, and to settle Ireland's many internal disputes, particularly the feud between the earls of Ormond and Kildare. The commission worked diligently and apparently effectively to pacify the pale, and it replaced Ormond with Kildare as lord deputy. But their hopes of securing order without having to commit additional English resources proved vain, Kildare's personal ambitions and the chronically volatile situation in Ireland soon frustrating their ambitions.

Denton's next public employment was as chancellor to the council of Princess Mary, which, on the analogy of the previous councils of Prince Edward, son of Edward IV, and of Prince Arthur, was established in 1526, immediately with a view to the superintendence of her education, but also with the wider object of governing her 'principality' and marches of Wales, and of repressing the chronic disorders of a disturbed district. The council usually sat at Ludlow, where Mary herself most often was, and Denton was one of the few permanent councillors in residence. He frequently also acted on commissions of the peace for the border counties. He retained his position in the Ludlow council until his death, and was also master of the College of St John the Evangelist in Ludlow town. In 1531 he proposed converting the Welsh lordships into English-style shires, a plan which Henry VIII found to be sensible although no action was taken until the Act of Union in 1536 and subsequent related statutes.

Denton's ecclesiastical preferments were numerous. From 1523 to his death he was archdeacon of Cleveland. On 7 January 1522 he became dean of Lichfield. He was a man of great liberality. At Lichfield he 'environed the fair old cross with eight fair arches of stone', and 'made a round vault over them for poor people to sit dry', at an expense of £160 (*Itinerary of John Leland*, 2.100). He was also a benefactor of King's College and of St George's Chapel, Windsor. At Lichfield he increased the number of choristers and provided for their maintenance. Between 1517 and 1520 he built, furnished, and endowed a house at Windsor for the chantrists and choristers, situated on the north side of the collegiate church, at a cost of nearly £500. In his will, dated 1 August 1526 (Bodl. Oxf., MS Ashmole 1123, fols. 104–5), he further endowed them with property in Windsor, giving them the reversion of property there, and directing that its issues should be used to finance distributions of bread and clothes to the poor of the town. Denton was also concerned for the preservation of the muniments of King's College, and had them transcribed into at least one large volume, known as the Liber Denton. Extracts from it survive in the Bodleian Library (Bodl. Oxf., MSS Ashmole 1124, fols. 47–82, and 1125, fols. 90–107). He was also generous to his servants, and especially in providing for the education of their sons. He died at Ludlow on 23 February 1533, and was buried in St Lawrence's Church there.

T. F. TOUT, *rev.* RONALD H. FRITZE

Sources Emden, *Cam.*, 182–3 · G. Williams, ed., *Glamorgan county history*, 3: *The middle ages*, ed. T. B. Pugh (1971) · Wood, *Ath. Oxon.*: *Fasti* (1815), 16 · Cooper, *Ath. Cantab.*, 1.45, 529 · *The itinerary of John Leland in or about the years 1535–1543*, ed. L. Toulmin Smith, 11 pts in 5 vols. (1906–10), vol. 2, pp. 77, 100 · T. Harwood, *The history and antiquities of the church and city of Lichfield* (1806) · *LP Henry VIII* · *State papers published under ... Henry VIII*, 11 vols. (1830–52) · R. R. Tighe and J. E. Davis, *Annals of Windsor*, 2 vols. (1858) · Bodl. Oxf., MSS Ashmole 1123–1125 · S. G. Ellis, *Ireland in the age of the Tudors* (1998) **Archives** Bodl. Oxf., MSS Ashmole

Denton, John (*b.* in or before **1561**, *d.* **1617**), antiquary, was the son of Henry Denton (*c.*1535–1584) of Cardew, in the parish of Dalston, Cumberland, and his wife, Mary (*d.* 1588), daughter of John Lamplugh. The Dentons had held Cardew since the fourteenth century and also held land in Northumberland. As country gentlemen holding their Cardew estate of the bishops of Carlisle and living close to the episcopal seat at Rose Castle the Dentons had frequent contact with the diocesan officials, and the young John Denton served as a page in the household of Richard Barnes, bishop between 1570 and 1577. He subsequently had training in law, although he is not mentioned in inns of court registers. In 1584 he was described as 'aged 23 years and more' (Dendy, 189). Before 1585 he married Elizabeth, daughter of Sir John Dalston of Dalston. They had at least eight children, of whom two sons and two daughters appear to have survived their father. Elizabeth Denton died, probably soon after the birth of their last child, and was buried on 3 July 1595.

After his wife's death Denton was appointed as a crown agent in Cumberland for the discovery of concealed lands, a role which enabled him to gain an extensive knowledge of landownership in his native county, particularly as it gave him access to the records in the Tower of London, where he spent time in 1600 and 1601. He also gained entrance to the diocesan records in Carlisle through his kinsman Henry Robinson, bishop of Carlisle from 1598 to 1616. By 1600 Denton had written parts of an antiquarian tract on Cumberland, tracing the pedigrees and arms of the gentry families, and he offered to make his notes available to William Camden for his *Britannia*. Reginald Bainbrigg, Camden's correspondent in Cumberland, thought highly of Denton's work. He was, he wrote, 'a man well reed in antiquities in his owne contrie, as anie one man in the northe', who took great pains. He 'dailie traveleth from plaice to place about this busyness, ... he goes by no hearesaies but by ancient records' (Haverfield, 369–70). Denton's assiduous archival research caused suspicion and resentment among the local gentry, however. A hostile witness claimed that he had had 'the secrett fingering' of all the diocesan records, had 'insinuated' himself into private estate archives, and had accumulated 'whole loads of old evidences gotten heere and there' (Wilson, 12).

By about 1603 Denton had completed 'An accompt of the most considerable estates and families in the county of Cumberland', a manuscript which is regarded as the first attempt to compile a history of the county. No fewer than fifteen copies of Denton's 'Accompt' are known, dating from the seventeenth and eighteenth centuries, and his work formed the basis of many later antiquarian accounts of Cumberland, including the first printed county history by Joseph Nicolson and Richard Burn, published in 1777.

John Denton died on 26 November 1617 and was buried at Dalston on the same day. There can be no doubt that his work stimulated the development of antiquarian studies in Cumberland and Westmorland later in the seventeenth century by men like Sir Daniel Fleming of Rydal and Bishop William Nicolson, and also by the topographer **Thomas Denton** (1637–1698). Thomas was born at Warnell Hall, Sebergham, Cumberland, on 24 August 1637, the eldest son of Thomas Denton (1612–1643) and his wife, Letitia, or Lettis (*d.* 1678), the daughter of John Lougher of Perton, Staffordshire, and his wife, Mary *Fitton (*bap.* 1578, *d.* 1641); the translator Henry *Denton (*d.* 1681) was his younger brother. The Dentons of Warnell were distantly connected to the Dentons of Cardew, sharing common ancestry in the fourteenth century.

Thomas Denton's early life was disrupted by the civil war. His father's death in 1643, from wounds received as a royalist officer in the siege of Hull, and war damage to Warnell Hall led the family to live with an uncle in Reading, Berkshire. Denton entered Queen's College, Oxford, in 1653, graduating BA in 1656. He had already, on 1 November 1655, been admitted to Gray's Inn, and was called to the bar in 1660. In 1659 or 1660 he married Letitia (*bap.* 1639, *d.* 1678), daughter of Thomas Vachell of Coley Hall, Reading. Four of their children survived infancy. They lived in Chertsey, Surrey, for five years, returning to Cumberland in 1664 when Denton took up the post of recorder of Carlisle, an office he filled until 1679. He also held other legal appointments, including the stewardship of the royal honour of Penrith and Inglewood Forest, and of the manors of the bishop of Carlisle and other landowners in Cumberland. He lived at Penrith until 1668, when he appears to have returned to Warnell. After the death of his wife in 1678, Denton married Dorothy Dale (1660–1683), daughter of Lancelot Threlkeld of Melmerby, Cumberland.

Denton's role as a manorial steward gave him an extensive knowledge of estates in his native county. In the 1680s Sir John Lowther of Lowther commissioned him to prepare surveys of the honour of Penrith and Inglewood Forest and, later, the whole county of Cumberland. The latter manuscript, compiled in 1687–8, provides a detailed topographical description of Cumberland, including population estimates for each parish and valuations of many estates, built around John Denton's historical 'Accompt', which he borrowed without acknowledgement. Denton confessed to having been 'more particular then did befitt me in putting a yearly estimate upon most gentlemen's estates' fearing that this 'might give greate occasion of offence, if some had the purusall hereof' (T. Denton, 'Description of Cumberland', preface). To his description of Cumberland, Denton added briefer accounts of Westmorland, the Isle of Man, and Ireland, the last two drawn largely from Camden but containing a first-hand description of Dublin. Denton's manuscript remains in the Lowther archive. It was used without acknowledgement by Joseph Nicolson and Richard Burn for their account of the two Allerdale wards of Cumberland in their *History and Antiquities of the Counties of Westmorland and Cumberland* (1777) and was used in 1808 (with due acknowledgement) by the Lysons for their *Magna Britannia*. For most of the nineteenth century it was thought to be lost until rediscovered in 1892 in Lord Lonsdale's house in Carlton Gardens.

Thomas Denton died at Harby Brow, a family property near Aspatria to which he had moved about 1680, on 6 February 1698 and was buried in Allhallows Old Church, Cumberland, two days later.

MARY WANE and ANGUS J. L. WINCHESTER

Sources J. Wilson, 'The first historian of Cumberland', *SHR*, 8 (1910–11), 5–21 • F. W. Dendy, 'The Heton–Fenwick–Denton line of descent', *Archaeologia Aeliana*, 3rd ser., 14 (1917), 173–90 • F. Haverfield, 'Cotton Julius F.VI', *Transactions of the Cumberland and Westmorland Antiquarian and Archaeological Society*, new ser., 11 (1911) • M. E. Kuper, 'Seven volumes of Dalston parish registers', *Transactions of the Cumberland and Westmorland Antiquarian and Archaeological Society*, old ser., 7 (1884), 156–200 • *An accompt of the most considerable estates and families in the county of Cumberland … by John Denton of Cardew*, ed. R. S. Ferguson (1887) • D. J. W. Mawson, 'Another important copy of John Denton's manuscript', *Transactions of the Cumberland and Westmorland Antiquarian and Archaeological Society*, new ser., 78 (1978), 97–103 • private information (2004) • autobiographical note, in Thomas Denton's own hand, in a bound manuscript, Manx National Heritage Library, MS 5A • T. Denton, 'Perambulation of Cumberland and Westmorland, containing the discription, hystory, and customes of those counties: written in the yeares 1687 and 1688 by TD', Cumbria AS, D/LonsL12/4/2 • parish registers, Sebergham, Allhallows, Newbiggin, and Melmerby, Cumbria AS • T. H. B. Graham, 'The family of Denton', *Transactions of the Cumberland and Westmorland Antiquarian and Archaeological Society*, new ser., 16 (1915–16), 40–56 • J. Foster, *The register of admissions to Gray's Inn, 1521–1889, together with the register of marriages in Gray's Inn chapel, 1695–1754* (privately printed, London, 1889), 274 • memorial, Allhallows Old Church, near Wigton, Cumberland [Thomas Denton] • parish register, Sebergham, 10 Nov 1678, Cumbria AS [burial: Letitia Crackenthorpe, mother of Thomas Denton; Letitia Denton, wife of Thomas Denton] • parish register, London, St Lawrence Jewry, 4 April 1639 [baptism: Letitia Vachell] • parish register, Dalston, Cumberland, 3 July 1595 [burial: Elizabeth Denton, wife of John Denton] • parish register, Allhallows Old Church, near Wigton, Cumberland [burial: Thomas Denton]

Archives Manx National Heritage Library, Douglas, Isle of Man, mainly in Denton's hand, MS 5A | Cumbria AS, Carlisle, Lonsdale family archives, 'Perambulation of Cumberland and Westmorland', D/LonsL12/4/2

Likenesses oils, *c.*1700–1750 (Thomas Denton; after unknown portrait attrib. to P. Lely, *c.*1660–1679), Tullie House Museum, Carlisle

Denton, John (*c.*1626–1709), Church of England clergyman, was born in the parish of Bradford, in the West Riding of Yorkshire. He was probably the son of John Denton (*fl.* 1613–1642) of Manningham in the same parish, a clothier, who held 18 acres of land at Lilliecroft, Manningham, in 1613, and who signed the protestation oath to maintain the king, parliament, and the protestant religion in Bradford parish on 28 March 1642. On 4 May 1646 Denton was admitted as a sizar to Clare College, Cambridge, where he studied under David Clarkson. He matriculated later that year, graduated BA in 1649, proceeded MA in 1653, and became a fellow of Clare.

At Cambridge, Denton befriended John Tillotson, a subsequent archbishop of Canterbury, defending Tillotson's reputation in a letter to a friend, and tending him during a dangerous illness. They maintained a frequent correspondence thereafter, 'having contracted a most intimate friendship' (*Life of … Tillotson*, 436). In 1653 Denton's degrees were incorporated at Oxford, but by the following year he was the rector of Oswaldkirk, in the North Riding of Yorkshire, the parish in which Tillotson shortly preached his first sermon. On 8 May 1654 he married Elizabeth (*bap.* 1622, *d.* 1669), sister-in-law to the autobiographer Alice Thornton and eldest daughter of Robert Thornton of East Newton, Yorkshire, and his second wife,

Elizabeth, daughter of Sir Richard Darley of Buttercrambe. Their eldest son and heir, John, was baptized at Oswaldkirk on 5 September 1655. In November 1657 Denton was also described as vicar of Sherburn in the North Riding of Yorkshire.

In 1662 Denton was ejected from Oswaldkirk for nonconformity; Edmund Calamy lauded him as 'a very pious Man and a profitable Preacher' (Calamy, *Abridgement*, 2.818). After the death of his first wife he married about 1670 Elizabeth (*d.* 1715), whose surname is unknown. The couple had four children, three of whose names are known—John, Robert (*b.* 1676), and Ellen. On 16 May 1672 Denton was licensed as a presbyterian at Osgodby Grange in the North Riding of Yorkshire; he also applied, unsuccessfully, for a licence at East Newton, in the parish of Stonegrave. However, in June 1690 he was reordained in the Church of England by Thomas Barlow, bishop of Lincoln. Residing in East Newton by this time, he initially officiated as curate under Dr Thomas Comber, but was rector of Stonegrave by December 1690. In that year he began a volume, continued by his successors at Stonegrave, accounting for the yearly receipts and disbursements of the offertory. He was installed as prebendary of Husthwaite in York Minster on 1 December 1694 and was succeeded by his son Robert as rector of Stonegrave on 27 May 1700. Denton remained a close friend of the Thorntons, and on Alice Thornton's death in 1707 she bequeathed 'to my good brother Mr. John Denton' (*Autobiography of Mrs Alice Thornton*, 338) £5 in her will, requesting that he preach her funeral sermon. He died on 14 January 1709, in his eighty-third year, and was buried in Stonegrave parish church two days later, where his monumental tablet remains. He was survived by his wife.

ROBERT HARRISON, *rev.* ANDREW J. HOPPER

Sources *The autobiography of Mrs Alice Thornton*, ed. [C. Jackson], SurtS, 62 (1875) • Venn, *Alum. Cant.*, 1/2 • *The life of the most Reverend Dr John Tillotson, lord archbishop of Canterbury compiled chiefly from his papers and letters*, ed. T. Birch (1752) • *Fasti Angl., 1541–1857*, [York] • will, Borth. Inst., vol. 65, fol. 207 • Stonegrave parish register transcripts, 1598–1856, Borth. Inst., microfilm 507 • P. Rowley, ed., *Parish register of Oswaldkirk, vols. 1–10, 1538–1837*, Yorkshire Parish Register Society, 135 (1970) • E. Calamy, ed., *An abridgement of Mr. Baxter's history of his life and times, with an account of the ministers, &c., who were ejected after the Restauration of King Charles II*, 2nd edn, 2 vols. (1713) • W. Robertshaw, ed., 'The township of Manningham in the seventeenth century', *Bradford Antiquary*, 27 (1935), 57–89 • H. Rook, ed., 'The protestation of the commons, 1641', *Bradford Antiquary*, new ser., 47 (1982), 135–45 • *Calamy rev.* • Foster, *Alum. Oxon.*

Wealth at death rents of £64 17s. in Temple Hirst, from which daughter's portion of £250 was to be paid: will, Borth. Inst., vol. 65, fol. 207

Denton, John Bailey (1814–1893), surveyor and civil engineer, was born on 26 November 1814, the second son of Samuel Denton, a solicitor of Gray's Inn, London, and his wife, Helena Cornelia. After limited schooling he was articled in 1830 to Anthony Jackson of Barkway, Hertfordshire, surveyor and agent to Lord Dacre. Denton was instructed in estate management and field surveying, and under Jackson's direction he surveyed the inclosure of much common land in south-east England. He acquired a

reputation for the accuracy and detail of his plotted surveys, skills which he publicized in his *Outline of a Method of Model Mapping* (1841). In London in 1843 he organized an Association of Surveyors, arising from a protest against the proposed use of the Ordnance Survey in mapping the metropolis, and he was a founder member of the Surveyors' Institution in 1868.

In 1842 Denton published *What Can now be Done for British Agriculture?*, turning his interests to agriculture. He argued that by investment in under-draining and farm building, agricultural productivity could be so increased as to offset low prices and the loss of protection. He also became one of the promoters of the application of collective capital to the improvement of landed property. He was elected a director of the first drainage company, the Yorkshire Land Drainage Company, founded in 1843 for that purpose. The company failed because of difficulties raised by mortgagees and other claimants with interests in entailed estates. Jointly with the duke of Richmond and Philip Pusey, he succeeded in obtaining an act of parliament in 1845 which recognized the principle of priority for improvement charges over all other mortgages and encumbrances. This principle was employed in the Public Money Drainage Acts of 1846 and 1850, by which £4 million of public money was made available for under-draining purposes. To augment these funds, Denton promoted and was chiefly responsible for the General Land Drainage and Improvement Company's Act of 1849, by which companies were empowered to lend to landowners to undertake agricultural improvement in general. Denton acted as his company's principal engineer from its inception until 1892, in which time he saw more than £3 million advanced for agricultural improvement. In his extensive writing on the subject, especially *Agricultural Drainage* (1883) and *The Farm Homesteads of England* (1863), and in his evidence in 1873 to the select committee on the improvement of land and in 1881 to the royal commission on the agricultural interest, he presented an absolute view of agricultural improvement: the progress of under-draining was assessed in terms of the total wetland area, irrespective of land quality, and farm building provision was measured in terms of the number of totally new farmsteads constructed. Denton was essentially a propagandist for best-practice agricultural improvement, oblivious of the constraints involved in its on-estate adoption.

Denton's interest in civil engineering also developed in the early 1840s. From 1842 he was involved in the railway movement and was associated with the construction of the Great Northern, the London and South Western, the Midland, and other railways. His commitment to under-draining led to studies of the impact of the discharge from drains on arterial channels and outfalls (*On the Discharge from under-Drainage*, 1864), and from these he made a series of proposals for the storage of surplus water for human consumption, especially in London (*The Water Question*, 1866). Denton further addressed the related problem of sewage disposal (*Sanitary Engineering*, 1877, and *Sewage Disposal*, 1881). In 1849 his design for the sewerage of London had been placed second out of 150 plans submitted (*Sewerage of London*, 1849). In 1871 he was asked to apply his experience to the purification of sewage at Merthyr Tudful. So successful was the scheme that other local authorities sought his advice; examples of sewage farms laid out under his guidance included projects in Barnsley, Kendal, Great Malvern, and Northampton. He made a further attempt to deal with sewage disposal in London in 1885, proposing the purchase of Canvey Island for its conversion into a sewage farm.

Failing health forced Denton to retire in 1892 to Orchard Court, Stevenage, Hertfordshire, where he had lived since the middle of the century. He died there on 19 November 1893, at the age of seventy-eight, of a brain haemorrhage. In a career spanning sixty years, Denton had established himself as a noted land surveyor; as an agricultural engineer involved in the development and application of the mid-century land improvement legislation; as a civil engineer concerned with railway construction, water supply, and sewage disposal; and as a prolific author on all these activities. A. D. M. PHILLIPS

Sources *PICE*, 115 (1893–4), 368–9 · d. cert. · 'Select committee of the House of Lords to inquire into … the improvement of land', *Parl. papers* (1873), 16.534–885, no. 326 · 'Royal commission on the depressed condition of agricultural interests', *Parl. papers* (1881), 15.162–8, 217–25, C. 2778 · 'Select committee of the House of Lords on entailed estates', *Parl. papers* (1845), 12.163–7, no. 490 [charges for drainage] · A. D. M. Phillips, *The underdraining of farmland in England during the nineteenth century* (1989), 5–8, 27–31 · F. M. L. Thompson, *Chartered surveyors: the growth of a profession* (1968), 119–20 · *CGPLA Eng. & Wales* (1894) · *IGI*

Wealth at death £13,597 10s.: resworn probate, Nov 1894, *CGPLA Eng. & Wales*

Denton, Nathan (*bap.* 1635, *d.* 1720), clergyman and ejected minister, was born in Bradfield in the parish of Ecclesfield, West Riding of Yorkshire, the son of Francis Denton, and baptized at Bradfield Chapel on 8 January 1635. From the grammar school at Worsborough he went to University College, Oxford, where he matriculated in 1654 and graduated BA in 1657. After university he returned to the corner of Yorkshire where he had been raised and where he was to spend most of the rest of his life. First he taught at the grammar school at Cawthorne, preaching alternately at Cawthorne and High Hoyland. He was ordained in 1658 at Hemsworth by the West Riding presbytery as minister of High Hoyland. From there he moved to Derwent chapel, Derbyshire, and early in 1660 to the perpetual curacy of Bolton upon Dearne in the West Riding (his predecessor was buried on 27 March 1660). At Bolton on 6 February 1662 he married Anne Burley (*d.* 1715), with whom he had five children: Daniel, John, Hannah, Ruth, and Joseph.

Denton was ejected from Bolton upon Dearne under the Act of Uniformity of 1662 but continued to live in the parish, except for two periods of about two years each during the enforcement of the Five Mile Act (1665). For a year after his ejection he preached in the parish church of Hickleton, West Riding, where he was maintained as lecturer by Lady Jackson, sister of George Booth, Baron Delamer. Thomas Vincent (*d.* 1667) of Barnborough Grange

near Bolton upon Dearne offered Denton an Anglican living worth £100 p.a. but he refused this and all other offers of preferment, which Edmund Calamy noted he 'could not accept with Satisfaction to his Conscience, and declared he never yet repented his Nonconformity' (Calamy, *Continuation*, 2.950–51). In 1669 he was reported as again preaching at Hickleton, formerly at Jackson's house and now at another house. On 8 May 1672 he was licensed as a presbyterian to preach at the house of Silvanus Rich, near Penistone, West Riding. Under the Toleration Act he was granted a certificate at the Barnsley sessions on 15 October 1689 to use his house at Bolton upon Dearne as a place of worship. From 1690 onwards he appears to have preached at various places in Yorkshire and Derbyshire, including to a presbyterian congregation at Great Houghton, a township in the parish of Darfield which lay adjacent to Bolton. From 1693 to 1720 he was in receipt of a grant from the Common Fund.

Calamy, writing in August 1713 when Denton was in his eightieth year, says that he still preached sometimes at Great Houghton. To Calamy he was 'the picture of an old puritan', who led 'an unblameable life, and maintained his integrity' (Calamy, *Continuation*, 2.951). When he died in 1720 Denton had outlived all those who had been ejected with him fifty-eight years before. He was buried at Bolton upon Dearne on 12 or 13 October 1720. His eldest son, Daniel Denton (1663–1721), followed him in his ministry and connections and for twenty-eight years was chaplain to the Riches of Bull House, Penistone, and ministered to a congregation there.

ALEXANDER GORDON, *rev.* CAROLINE L. LEACHMAN

Sources *Calamy rev.*, 163 · E. Calamy, *A continuation of the account of the ministers … who were ejected and silenced after the Restoration in 1660*, 2 vols. (1727), vol. 2, pp. 950–51 · A. Gordon, ed., *Freedom after ejection: a review (1690–1692) of presbyterian and congregational nonconformity in England and Wales* (1917) · *The nonconformist's memorial … originally written by … Edmund Calamy*, ed. S. Palmer, 2 (1775), 556–7

Denton, Richard (1586–1662), Church of England clergyman and colonist, was born in Yorkshire. Nothing is known of his parents or of his life before he graduated BA from St Catharine's College, Cambridge, in 1623. Before 1626 he married Helen Windlbank, about whom nothing is known, and by 1631 was installed as curate of Coley Chapel, near Halifax. In the late 1630s Denton migrated to New England, staying briefly at Watertown, Massachusetts, before moving to Wethersfield, Connecticut. Dissension in that congregation led him to move on to the Connecticut town of Stamford in 1644. This was merely a stopping place, however, for Denton and a group of fellow Englishmen soon received a grant from the Dutch authorities in New Netherland to settle on Long Island, where they founded the town of Hempstead. This community of Englishmen stayed neutral during the First Anglo-Dutch War, and the New Netherland's director, Peter Stuyvesant, expressed his appreciation of Denton in a letter to the Hempstead magistrates in 1657. In that same year the Dutch ministers J. Megapolensis and S. Driius wrote to the classis of Amsterdam that Denton was 'sound in faith, of a friendly disposition, and beloved by all'. Denton had presbyterian convictions but the Dutch visitors reported that his congregation also included congregationalists, who absented themselves from the services when children of the parish were to be baptized.

In 1659 Denton returned to England to claim a large legacy left him by a friend. He settled in Essex, where he lived until his death there in 1662. His son Daniel remained in the colonies and became a local official and author of *A Brief Description of New York* (1670). FRANCIS J. BREMER

Sources F. M. Kerr, 'The Reverend Richard Denton and the coming of the presbyterians', *New York History*, 21 (1940), 180–86 · *DNB* · K. J. Hayes, 'Denton, Daniel', *ANB* · H. Hastings, ed., *Ecclesiastical records of the state of New York*, 1 (1901)

Denton, Thomas (1637–1698). *See under* Denton, John (*b.* in or before 1561, *d.* 1617).

Denton, Thomas (*bap.* 1723, *d.* 1777), Church of England clergyman and writer, was born at Sebergham, Cumberland, and baptized in the parish church there on 2 December 1723, the fourth of five children of Isaac Denton (*d.* 1739), yeoman, of Greenfoot in Sebergham and his wife, Matilda, *née* Stanwix (*d.* 1762/3). He was educated by the Revd Joseph Relph (1712–1743) at the village school, and edited his master's poems, which were published by subscription in 1747. Denton matriculated at Queen's College, Oxford, on 7 July 1740 and graduated BA on 4 March 1746, and MA in 1752.

Denton was left a small amount of property by his father but had to make his own way in the world. He took holy orders, being ordained deacon by Bishop George Fleming of Carlisle on 15 March 1746 and priest by Fleming's successor, Bishop Richard Osbaldeston, at Rose Castle on 26 June 1747. Having served as curate at Irthington, Denton went on to become curate to the Revd Robert Graham at Arthuret near by. There he resumed his minor literary career by privately printing a local poem entitled 'Gariston'. In 1753, when Graham settled at Netherby on his family's estate, Denton became Graham's curate at St Giles's Church, Ashtead, Surrey. Here he became chaplain to Graham's aged and infirm relative Catharine, Lady Widdrington, last surviving joint heir to Charles Graham, third and last Viscount Preston (*d.* 1739), who persuaded Graham to resign the rectory in Denton's favour. He was duly presented by the Hon. Thomas Howard (later fourteenth earl of Suffolk and seventh earl of Berkshire) of Ashtead Park on 7 November and instituted on 14 November 1754. In 1755 or 1756 he married a Mrs Ann Clubbe, a Yorkshire woman, who was companion to Lady Widdrington on her death in 1757, and received a legacy from her mistress.

Denton continued to apply himself to literary studies. He edited a manual of meditations on central Christian themes entitled *Religious retirement for one day in every month; freed from the peculiarities of the Romish superstition; and fitted for the use of protestants* (London, 1758). This was based on the work of the seventeenth-century English Catholic convert John Gother. 'If, in any one instance', Denton opined in the advertisement, 'a sinner is brought

by them to serious reflection and amendment of life, he will think his trouble amply compensated'. He was also a minor poet in Spenserian vein though, as William Hutchinson tactfully put it, 'Fastidious criticism' might say it is 'correct even to coldness' (Hutchinson, 420). Denton brought out *Immortality, or, The Consolation of Human Life: a Monody* (1754) and *The House of Superstition: a Vision* (ten pages, 1762), prefixed to William Gilpin's *Lives of the Reformers*. Both are poems in imitation of Spenser. Denton also compiled the supplemental volume to the first edition of the *General Biographical Dictionary* (1761).

Denton became corpulent and unwieldy in later life and died at Ashtead on 27 June 1777. He was buried in St Giles's Church on 1 July, leaving a widow and seven surviving children (three sons and four daughters). Thomas Howard gave the next presentation to Mrs Denton and by judicious management she turned the gift into a comfortable annuity. NIGEL ASTON

Sources W. Hutchinson, *The history of the county of Cumberland*, 2 (1794), 419–21, 533 · J. Nicolson and R. Burn, *The history and antiquities of the counties of Westmorland and Cumberland*, 2 (1777), 325–6, 464–9 · Foster, *Alum. Oxon.* · episcopal register, Cumbria AS, DRC1/7, fols. 131, 139 · O. Manning and W. Bray, *The history and antiquities of the county of Surrey*, 2 (1809), 635 · parish transcripts, Ashtead, Surrey Record Centre · Surrey presentation deeds, Hants. RO, 21M65/E2/1194 · G. J. Gollin, *Bygone Ashtead* (1987), 45–7 · *VCH Surrey*, 3.251 · *DNB* · private information (2004) [Mary Wane]
Likenesses memorial, Ashtead

Denton, Thomas (*d.* 1789), coiner, was born in the North Riding of Yorkshire and originally made a living as a tinman. He kept a bookseller's shop in York for about ten years and moved to London about 1780. There he is said to have made a copy of a 'speaking figure made by some foreigners' (*GM*, 757), the precise nature of which remains unknown. Denton exhibited his mechanism about the country, and followed this by constructing a 'writing figure'. Apparently active as an amateur chemist, in 1784 Denton published *Physical Amusements and Diverting Experiments*, translated from the work in French by Giuseppe Pinetti de Wildalle, a book of elementary parlour magic. In addition he made pentagraphs and other mathematical instruments, and carried on the business of silver plating alongside his ownership of a bookshop in Holborn. He became associated with a well-known coiner, and was himself tried and convicted of possessing coining implements. He was hanged before Newgate prison, with his accomplice, John Jones, and two others on 1 July 1789. H. R. TEDDER, *rev.* PHILIP CARTER

Sources *GM*, 1st ser., 59 (1789), 757–8 · *European Magazine and London Review*, 16 (1789), 86 · *Annual Register* (1789) · C. H. Timperley, *Encyclopaedia of literary and typographical anecdote*, 2nd edn (1842) · A. Knapp and W. Baldwin, *The Newgate calendar, comprising interesting memoirs of the most notorious characters*, 4 vols. (1824–6)

Denton, William (*bap.* 1605, *d.* 1691), physician, born at Stowe, Buckinghamshire, and baptized at Hillesden on 14 April 1605, was the youngest son of Sir Thomas Denton (*d.* 1633), a lawyer and landowner, and his wife, Susan Temple (*d.* 1641). He matriculated at Magdalen Hall, Oxford, in 1621, graduating BA (1624) and MA (1627). The Denton men had traditionally been lawyers, but William took up medicine, studying with Henry Ashworth in Oxford and taking his DM on 10 October 1634. In April 1636 he was appointed court physician to Charles I, and in 1639 was with the king and the army during the Scots war. The Dentons' large families over several generations brought William a wide range of kinship connections in the south midlands and in London. He fostered these from his house in Covent Garden, where he lived and entertained for much of his life. His reputation for wit and polite conversation at court, particularly among the ladies, brought him the nickname of 'speaker of the Parliament of Women' (*The Genealogist*, 47). This and his position at court made him privy to a wide range of information, some of it sensitive. He married three times, but little is known of his first two wives, except that the second may have been Lady Muschamp of Yorkshire. His third wife, whom he married during the 1630s, was Catherine (*d.* 1675), daughter of Bostock Fuller of Tandridge Court, Surrey; they had one daughter, Anne (*b.* 1640). She married George Nicholas, son of the king's secretary, Sir Edward Nicholas, in 1664.

Denton attended the king throughout the civil war, but was quickly able to make his peace with parliament, compounding in December 1646 for £55. During the interregnum he practised in London and the surgeon Richard Wiseman often and respectfully mentioned his professional skills. At the Restoration, Nicholas and the earl of Ormond worked to restore him to the position of royal physician, which he duly achieved on 24 January 1661. He was elected an honorary fellow of the College of Physicians in 1664, and was at one point mentioned as a physician to the duke of York.

Although William Denton was a respected physician with a large and diverse practice, his busy life covered a much wider range of activities. The trials and tribulations of his extended family meant that he spent much time sorting out their business affairs. He was close to his nephew Sir Ralph Verney (less than eight years younger than himself) and was devoted to Verney's wife, Mary. He corresponded with Verney more than once a week except when they were together in London or Buckinghamshire; the letters span more than fifty years, and are a great record of seventeenth-century male friendship. Denton played a vital part in securing the Verney estates while Sir Ralph was in self-imposed exile from 1643 to 1653, acted as foster parent to the Verney children when they were alone in England, and managed much of Verney's business. Like Verney he found himself assisting his own wider family affairs after his eldest brother, Sir Alexander Denton, died in prison in 1644 and his sister-in-law died the year after. Denton's role as trustee for the estates involved him in finding husbands for his nieces, and places for his nephews, all of which took up much of his time. With the early death of the young head of the next generation in 1658, many of the same problems ensued.

These activities nevertheless left the energetic Denton time for wide reading especially in history, philosophy, and current affairs. The lists of books he sent the exiled Sir Ralph Verney in France give some indication of the range.

After the Restoration, Denton wrote five treatises between 1664 and 1690. These reflected the Erastian and anti-papist protestant views he held as a member of the Church of England, and drew on a wide range of primarily historical material. He also published a translation of an Italian work of Pietro Sarpi, *A Treatise of Matters Beneficiary* (1680), which he dedicated to Charles II. His final works, published in 1689 and 1690, wholeheartedly supported the revolution of 1688 and religious toleration. He passed his love of languages and learning on to his daughter Anne, whom Denton considered very like him, and whose godfather, Sir Ralph Verney, teased her as a bluestocking.

Denton's wide range of interests was often practical as well as intellectual. He learned much of estate management, passing shrewd judgements on the land market and enclosure, and showing an up-to-date knowledge of trends in agricultural thinking when, for instance, advocating turning estates over to dairy farming. His lively commentaries on current events, court machinations, and social scandals are a vital strand of the seventeenth-century Verney correspondence. Denton died at his house in Covent Garden, London on 9 May 1691. His lifelong friend Sir Ralph Verney had hurried from the country to his bedside. Denton was buried at Hillesden, Buckinghamshire. His epitaph in Hillesden church captures his personality: 'He was blessed with that happy composition of Body and Mind that preserved him chearfull, easy and agreeable to the last, and endeared him to all that knew him'.

JOHN BROAD

Sources F. P. Verney and M. M. Verney, *Memoirs of the Verney family*, 4 vols. (1892–9) • A. L. Rowse, *The English past* (1951) • Foster, *Alum. Oxon.* • Wood, *Ath. Oxon.*, new edn, 4.307 • *CSP dom.*, 1640–67 • M. A. E. Green, ed., *Calendar of the proceedings of the committee for compounding … 1643–1660*, 5 vols., PRO (1889–92) • R. Wiseman, *Severall chirurgicall treatises* (1676) • 'Notes on the life of Sir George Wheler, knight [pt 2]', *The Genealogist*, new ser., 3 (1886), 41–9, esp. 47 • *DNB* • Munk, *Roll*

Archives BL, letters [microfilm] • Bucks. RLSS, letters [microfilm] | Claydon House, Buckinghamshire, Verney MSS, letters and other documents

Likenesses portrait, Claydon House, Buckinghamshire

Wealth at death property in various parts of London at the time of the great fire; endowed daughter with income of £100 p.a. at her marriage: Claydon House, Buckinghamshire, Verney MSS, letters and other documents

Denton, William (1815–1888), Church of England clergyman, born in March 1815 at Newport in the Isle of Wight, was the eldest son of James Denton of that town. He matriculated from Worcester College, Oxford, in 1841, graduating BA in 1844 and MA in 1848. Influenced by the Tractarian movement he was ordained deacon in 1844, as curate of St Andrew's, Bradfield, in Berkshire, where Thomas Stevens was rector, and priest in 1845, as curate of Barking. In 1847 he became curate of Shoreditch, and on 22 June 1848 married Jane, youngest daughter of William Hurst *Ashpitel, architect, of Clapton Square. They had at least two sons.

In 1850 Denton was presented to the vicarage of St Bartholomew, Little Moorfields, Cripplegate, a crown living, which he retained until his death. As the incumbent of an inner-London parish, he took up the cause of the poor whose homes were demolished to make way for new railways. His *Observations on the displacement of the poor by metropolitan railways and other public improvements* (1861), which pointed out that railway companies chose routes through working-class areas because tenants there had fewer legal rights, and that the problems of overcrowding were increased by the tendency for housing adjoining railways to be turned over to warehouses, attracted considerable attention. On 28 February 1861 the earl of Derby presented a petition from Denton to the House of Lords, and the question was debated for two nights. He later gave evidence to the royal commission on the housing of the working classes (1884–5), advocating that industries should be moved out of city centres into suburbs, where workers could be rehoused in healthy surroundings.

Denton had personal contacts with members of the Orthodox church in the Near East, and produced in 1862 *Servia and the Servians*, one of the first well-informed books in English on Serbia. He subsequently produced an edition of Chedomil Miyatović's *Serbian Folklore* (1874) and a work on Montenegro (1877). His *The Christians in Turkey* (1863), which alleged that British diplomats had carried out a conspiracy of silence about the sufferings of Christians under Ottoman rule, initially attracted little notice, but in 1876, when the 'Bulgarian atrocities' had aroused public outrage, the original edition sold out and a new and enlarged edition appeared. A third edition was reached in 1877, and was translated into German and Serbian. He was on the platform of the National Convention on the Eastern Question, chaired by the duke of Westminster and Lord Shaftesbury, at St James's Hall, London, in December 1876. In recognition of his campaigning on behalf of Balkan Christians he was created a knight commander of the Serbian order of St Saviour of Takhova, and awarded a grand cross of the order of St Saba.

Apart from occasional sermons, Denton published commentaries on the gospels for Sundays and holy days (3 vols., 1861–3), the Lord's prayer (1864), the Epistles (2 vols., 1869–71), and the Acts of the Apostles (2 vols., 1874–6). In 1863 he published an edition based on the original manuscripts of the *Sacra privata* of Thomas Wilson (1663–1755), bishop of Sodor and Man. His last work was a study of England in the fifteenth century (1888). Denton died at his home, 22 Westbourne Square, Paddington, London, on 2 January 1888.   M. C. CURTHOYS

Sources *Men of the time* (1887) · Foster, *Alum. Oxon.* · Boase, *Mod. Eng. biog.* · R. W. Seton-Watson, *Disraeli, Gladstone and the eastern question: a study in diplomacy and party politics* (1935) · J. R. Kellett, *Railways and Victorian cities* (1979) · *GM*, 2nd ser., 30 (1848), 200

Archives BL, letters to W. E. Gladstone, Add. MSS 44407–44786, passim

Wealth at death £1166 14s.: probate, 30 Jan 1888, *CGPLA Eng. & Wales*

Denys, Sir Thomas (*c.*1477–1561), administrator, was the eldest son of Thomas Denys (*d.* 1498) of Holcombe Burnell, Devon, and Janera, daughter of Philip Loveday of Sneston, Suffolk. Long established in a minor way in Devon, the family was destined to prosper under the younger Thomas, whose legal studies prepared him for a lifetime

of crown service. His greatest impact was upon the administration of his own shire. Denys was appointed to the peace commission in Devon in 1504, an honour which he retained until his death, and he assiduously attended quarter sessions. He served as sheriff of Devon no fewer than nine times between 1507–8 and 1553–4, and sat on commissions responsible for musters, the collection of subsidies, and the assessment of church and chantry wealth. His legal advice was valued by many of Devon's monasteries and boroughs, particularly the city of Exeter, which retained Denys for two lengthy stints as its recorder. He was also employed directly by the crown, being thrice auditor of the duchy of Cornwall, and deputy warden of the stannaries by 1512.

For a man like Denys, whose career rested more upon his own wit than on inherited status, the route to such local preferment began at Westminster. Lacking a university education, the ambitious Denys cultivated the law instead. He was probably a member of Lyon's Inn before his admission to the Inner Temple, where he was elected marshal in 1511 and 1514. It was also important for the aspiring shire gentleman to see some military action, and Denys took part in the Tournai campaign of 1513 (which earned him a knighthood the following year); he would return to France in 1544. But real advancement demanded a patron, and for this he turned to the court. By the time of Henry VII's death Denys was a gentleman usher and esquire of the body; but these were relatively lowly positions, and so by 1515 he had found his way into Cardinal Wolsey's household, where he rose to be chamberlain. From 1526 he was also serving the Princess Mary as comptroller, and in due course was retained by Thomas Cromwell, a friendship that was cemented by the marriage of Denys's stepdaughter Francis Murfyn to Cromwell's nephew Richard. Proximity to the monarchy gained him access to the ceremonial display of Tudor royal power. Having borne a banner at Jane Seymour's funeral Denys was among the party that welcomed Anne of Cleves to English soil, and became chancellor of the new queen's household. His growing status was recognized in his election as one of Devon's knights of the shire in 1529, 1539, and 1553 (although details of his time in the Commons are scant) and in orders, subsequently withdrawn, to muster 200 men against the northern insurgents in 1536.

But it is as an administrator in his native shire, and especially as a correspondent of Cromwell, that it is easiest to trace the public career of Sir Thomas Denys. His duties ranged from the mundane (supplying the names of those who had unlawfully constructed weirs) to the politically sensitive, as when in 1538 he examined Gulphinus Abevan, a Breton priest supposedly in the employ of Reginald Pole, who made the alarming claim that the renegade cardinal was at large in England. In 1537 his career almost suffered a major reverse: the government was furious that Denys had concealed a robbery in Devon, and the attorney-general even cited him before Star Chamber. But this was not the case of corruption that it appeared to be. Denys had characteristically opted for local arbitration over the full process of law, and Cromwell accepted his apology. Denys was soon back at work hunting down speakers of seditious words, and was a natural choice to serve on Cromwell's brief council of the west.

By Edward VI's reign Denys was ageing, but he proved a staunch opponent of the south-western rebels of 1549, albeit more conciliatory and less hot-headed than Sir Peter Carew; Denys may have exceeded his brief by promising an end to religious change in order to pacify the commons. His last great act of crown service came when Carew led his own conspiracy against Queen Mary in January 1554. As he had in summer 1553, Denys stood firm for Mary, disproving rumours that he, too, had plotted to prevent Philip of Spain from landing in the west country. But the suspicion remains that his attempts to arrest Carew were calculatedly half-hearted, and that he suffered his countryman and fellow knight of the shire to steal away to France and exile.

As might be expected, Thomas Denys married shrewdly. By 1506 he had selected Anne, twice widowed; one of her previous husbands, Thomas Warley, had been an exchequer official. In 1524 he married another widow, Elizabeth, daughter of Sir Angel Donne and previously married to Sir Thomas Murfyn, mayor of London. They had three daughters and five sons, the eldest being Sir Robert (d. 1592), who succeeded his father as MP for Devon in 1555, and served both Mary and Elizabeth as sheriff of Devon. Robert's first marriage, to Mary, daughter of William Blount, fourth Baron Mountjoy, indicates how the standing of the Denys family had risen in Thomas's lifetime.

Denys's religious faith is difficult to pin down. Slandered in Henry VIII's reign as a papist who hung at the sleeves of the conservative marquess of Exeter, Denys nevertheless profited from the dissolution of monasteries and chantries alike, and bought up land in Essex as well as in Devon. In 1536 it was equally his task to examine the bizarre protestant beliefs of the Axminster shoemaker Philip Gammon, and to question the Exeter women whose stout defence of St Nicholas's Priory had ended in a minor riot; Denys ordered that the women be released, perhaps out of sympathy. In religious terms, his most noteworthy act was to supervise the burning for heresy of the Exeter schoolmaster Thomas Benet in January 1532. Benet, whose crime was to post a scroll on the cathedral door identifying the pope as Antichrist, has his place in Foxe's *Actes and Monuments* courtesy of the protestant Exonian John Hooker. In sum, Denys's long life witnessed the religious settlements of four Tudor monarchs, and he was loyal to all of them.

Sir Thomas made his will on 13 December 1558; his wife, Elizabeth, was his executor. Since he was by this time an octogenarian, his deputy lieutenancy of Devon and Cornwall that year can have been little more than a titular recognition of his many years of service. Denys died on 18 February 1561, and asked to be buried with neither feasting nor lights, 'by cause I will avoide all pompe used aboute my ded corps'. A Devonian to the last, he bequeathed 20s. to the prisoners in Exeter gaol.

J. P. D. COOPER

Sources HoP, *Commons, 1509–58* · *LP Henry VIII* · PRO, SP 11/3/10 · PRO, STAC 2/2, fols.183–7, 267–72 · J. P. D. Cooper, 'Propaganda, allegiance and sedition in the Tudor south-west, c.1497–1570', DPhil diss., U. Oxf., 1999 · H. M. Speight, 'Local government and politics in Devon and Cornwall, 1509–49, with special reference to the south-western rebellion of 1549', PhD diss., U. Sussex, 1991 · will, PRO, PROB 11/44, fol. 156 · J. Foxe, *The seconde volume of the ecclesiastical historie, conteining the acts and monuments of martyrs*, 4th edn (1583), 1037–40 · R. Whiting, *The blind devotion of the people: popular religion and the English Reformation* (1989) · D. M. Loades, *Two Tudor conspiracies* (1965) · DNB

D'Éon de Beaumont, Charles Geneviève Louis Auguste André Timothée, Chevalier D'Éon in the French nobility (1728–1810), diplomatist and transvestite, was born at the Hotel d'Uzès, Tonnerre, Burgundy, on 5 October 1728. He came of an old noble family, possibly of Breton origin, though, like much else about this extraordinary personage, his genealogical pretensions later gave rise to judicial proceedings. His father, Louis D'Éon de Beaumont (1695–1749), was a lawyer who became mayor of Tonnerre and a sub-delegate of the intendant of the generality of Paris; he married Françoise de Chavanson (d. 1792) in 1723, and the couple also had a daughter. Charles's grandfather Louis D'Éon (1656–1720), styled 'écuyer, avocat, bailli de Tanlay, St Vincent, Quincy, Molosmes, St Martin, etc', had also been the intendant's sub-delegate. Louis D'Éon had close links with the comte d'Argenson, intendant of Paris, sending him presents of game on his appointment as minister of war in 1743. The young D'Éon studied law at the Collège des Quatre-Nations in Paris, obtaining several degrees. At nineteen he was already a lawyer at the *parlement*. His brilliance, as well as his family background, helped him to become secretary to Bertier de Sauvigny, intendant of Paris. He showed early signs of the prolific writer that he was to become. In 1753 he published an *Essay historique sur les différentes situations de la France par rapport aux finances sous le règne de Louis XIV et sous la régence de M. le duc d'Orléans*, which was praised by Controller-General Machault and by the historian President Hénault. He became a friend of Malesherbes, who appointed him as a royal censor for history and literature in 1758.

Russian mission and military career, 1755–1763 In a letter of 5 June 1774 to his brother-in-law, the Chevalier O'Gorman, D'Éon claimed that in 1755 he had attended a ball at Versailles disguised as a woman and, briefly revealing his masculinity, had seduced Madame de Pompadour. Having resumed his feminine role, he had then been the object of Louis XV's pressing attentions (F. Gaillardet and H. Gaillardet, 302–3). Although epicene in appearance, D'Éon was indisputably male. Moreover, his well-established court and country connections provide a more reliable explanation to the origins of his career than his alleged nocturnal and possibly transvestite activities. In 1755 he was already well known to Louis XV's cousin the prince de Conti, who was in charge of the king's private diplomatic system known as the *secret du roi*. The *secret* involved recruiting clandestine agents to work alongside unsuspecting official French diplomats, particularly in eastern Europe. That year D'Éon was probably recruited by Conti to accompany a Scots Jacobite, Alexander Peter

Charles Geneviève Louis Auguste André Timothée D'Éon de Beaumont, Chevalier D'Éon in the French nobility (1728–1810), by George Dance, 1793

Mackensie of Kildin, known as the Chevalier Douglas, on a secret mission to Russia aimed at establishing private lines of communication between Louis XV and the Empress Elizabeth. No written proof of D'Éon's presence on this mission, or of his having adopted female attire, has been found (Cox, 23). Douglas's mission was a success, and the empress asked Louis XV to accredit a minister to her court. Douglas was chosen, and from 4 August 1756 he was joined by D'Éon, now definitely in male attire, as embassy secretary, a position which he retained under the subsequent French ambassador, the marquis de l'Hôpital, until 20 August 1760. When Russia adhered to the Franco-Austrian alliance against Prussia, Douglas unwittingly nullified a clause protecting France's ally Turkey from the warlike attentions of the Russians by accepting a secret agreement between the three powers to that effect. France ratified the treaty but not the secret agreement. D'Éon saved the situation, though not Douglas's position, in May 1757 by using his influence with the empress to set aside the secret agreement. D'Éon served Louis XV's clandestine intentions in 1759 when he persuaded Elizabeth and the Russian chancellor, Vorontsov, to withdraw an offer of mediation which the French foreign minister, the duc de Choiseul, had prevailed upon her to make, and to continue the war.

D'Éon left Russia in 1760 to follow his natural calling as a soldier, and after his arrival at Versailles in October (bringing with him the empress's adherence to the anti-British maritime convention) he was granted a pension of 2000 livres. He asked the count of Broglie, who had succeeded Conti at the head of the *secret*, whether he could serve under his orders and those of his brother, the maréchal de Broglie, in the forthcoming campaign. Choiseul, then minister of war, agreed to this request, and on 18 May 1761 D'Éon was transferred from his first regiment, the colonel-general dragoons, to the régiment d'Autichamp. He was present at the costly engagement of Villinghausen, where the marshal's army lost the advantage through the failure of the army under Soubise to lend it timely support. After Broglie's army crossed the Weser on 19 August 1761 D'Éon was sent with an order to a lieutenant-general, the count of Guerchy, who refused to execute it. D'Éon little knew the role Guerchy was later to play in his career, but he had become aware of the way French court factions and antagonisms had fatal repercussions on military operations. Guerchy, like Soubise, was part of the circle of Madame de Pompadour, whereas the Broglie brothers were not in favour with her. D'Éon was wounded in an engagement at Ulstrop, where a troop of cavalry passed over him, an event which may have had an effect on his mental state, though it did not prevent him from displaying courage and initiative at Einbeck and, in October, capturing a force of several hundred Prussians who had tried to sever French lines of communication at Osterwick.

Brilliant as it had been, D'Éon's military career was brief. After the death of the Empress Elizabeth in January 1762 the comte de Broglie asked him for a memorandum on the state of the Russian court and wanted to send him back to St Petersburg, especially after the *coup d'état* which placed Catherine II on the throne on 9 July. The new minister of foreign affairs, the comte de Choiseul (later duc de Praslin), had other plans for the young dragoon, whom he had befriended in Vienna while D'Éon was recovering from a broken leg on his earlier return from Russia. Despite D'Éon's reluctance, he was appointed on 29 August 1762 secretary to the duc de Nivernais, who was sent to negotiate the peace in London. Louis XV ordered Tercier, the acolyte of Broglie in the *secret*, to pay the young man a gratuity of 1000 livres. It was a timely payment as he had already incurred considerable expenditure both in the army and in anticipation of returning to Russia. Although reckless financial extravagance was a charge to which D'Éon laid himself open over the years, it is worth noting that the French court acted on the principle that expected lavish expenditure should precede irregular and parsimonious reimbursement.

London, 1763–1764 In London, Nivernais was in no position to negotiate from strength, but he obtained the best terms he could for his country and was ably seconded by 'le petit D'Éon', who laboured assiduously on the paperwork and knew how to exploit situations and indiscretions. Much to Praslin's surprise, Nivernais even persuaded George III to allow D'Éon to take the English ratification of the treaty of Paris back to France, an unusual privilege for a foreigner. He delivered the instrument of ratification to the duke of Bedford in Paris on 26 February 1763. D'Éon was at the apogee of his career, earning the praise of Praslin and a verbal commendation from Louis XV at Versailles. Upon his return to London, Nivernais invested him, on 30 March, with the insignia of the royal and military order of St Louis. He was henceforth known as the Chevalier D'Éon. In addition he received a gratuity of 6000 livres.

If 1763 was D'Éon's year of personal success, it also marked the beginning of his downfall. Louis XV was understandably angered by the humiliating terms of the treaty of Paris and he sought revenge against Britain. Through the agency of the *secret* he began to gather information that would facilitate an eventual invasion of the British Isles. An officer called Carlet de la Rozière was sent over in June 1763 to reconnoitre the English coastline. Nivernais had left England in May at the end of his embassy. D'Éon, who had been made resident chargé d'affaires on 17 April, was promoted in July to the rank of minister-plenipotentiary until the arrival of the next ambassador. The arrangement was convenient for Louis XV, and the chevalier, who had already worked for him in Russia, was now brought fully into the *secret* by a letter of 3 June from the king. He was informed about La Rozière's mission and told that his secret correspondents would be Broglie and Tercier. Broglie also asked him to spy on the new ambassador, who turned out to be the insubordinate officer whom the chevalier had encountered before, the comte de Guerchy. For greater security, D'Éon was to move out of the embassy into lodgings with a cousin, D'Éon de Mouloize, who was sent over for the purpose, and with La Rozière. According to the chevalier, Madame de Pompadour discovered his role in the elusive chain of the *secret*. The story is plausible. Choiseul and Praslin, supported by Madame de Pompadour and Guerchy, were opposed to the influence of the Broglie brothers and actively sought to neutralize the network of the *secret*.

D'Éon was caught between the factions. Moreover he lived on a lavish scale in London, entertaining Horace Walpole, David Hume, and others. His pension was still only 2000 livres, and he had never been adequately reimbursed for his earlier expenditure in Russia. Yet he bought fine clothes and collected books and rare manuscripts. Creditors began to press their demands on the chevalier, who pestered Praslin for payment of his debts but without success. He also wanted to retain the title of minister-plenipotentiary after Guerchy had taken up his post. From France, Nivernais, his only friend in the Choiseul circle, warned him that his conduct was unreasonable. With Guerchy's arrival on 16 October, D'Éon became unhinged. Praslin's reply to his request about his title was offensive, though understandable, and D'Éon's rejoinder to it was insulting. He soon picked a quarrel with Guerchy. The ambassador had brought with him D'Éon's letters of recall, but at the same time the chevalier received a private note from the king implying that the signature on the letters was only a clerk's manual and not his own, thus rendering them technically invalid. On 23 October D'Éon dined with Guerchy at the latter's residence, Monmouth House, in Soho Square, and subsequently claimed that the ambassador had tried to poison and kidnap him. Louis XV

yielded to Praslin's demand to have him extradited, while at the same time sending word to him to go into hiding and to take good care of his secret papers. By this stage D'Éon had moved into 38 Brewer Street, where he was armed and barricaded himself in with his cousin. Although he had complied with an order to hand over official papers to Guerchy, he had kept back those relating to the *secret*, which, as Broglie pointed out to the king, he was prepared to defend at all costs. The papers which had not already been returned to the king through La Rozière were now carefully hidden in the recesses of his lodgings.

The British government refused the request for his extradition. D'Éon was not prepared to return to France unless he had positive guarantees of freedom and safety from Praslin. In February he learned from the banker Thomas Walpole that payment of his French pension had been discontinued because of a new law suspending payment on all pensions granted after April 1759. As the king did nothing to help him, the chevalier took the outrageous step in March 1764 of publishing the correspondence between himself, Nivernais, Guerchy, Choiseul, and Praslin concerning his disputes with them. Horace Walpole wrote that the book 'had an immense circulation, and the attempts to suppress it at Paris, of course, served to make it more sought after' (Walpole, 3.393). The publication by J. Dixwell of the *Lettres, mémoires et négociations particulières du Chevalier D'Éon, ministre plénipotentiaire auprès du roi de Grande-Bretagne* had made the French government a laughing stock. His official pension was stopped. However, it is worth noting that D'Éon had printed no documents relating to the *secret*. He began to apply pressure on the king through Broglie, claiming that the opposition was offering him £40,000 for his remaining papers. He demanded redress against Guerchy by 22 April, otherwise he would be forced to clear his name by further revelations. Louis XV took the threat calmly, but arranged for him to receive a secret pension of 12,000 livres (paid in two half-yearly instalments and backdated to 1 April 1762) in exchange for the return of compromising documents. An intermediary, de Nort, returned to France without the papers, D'Éon having indicated that he wanted a further payment of 116,341 livres to clear all his debts.

London, 1764–1777 Following the publication of the *Lettres, mémoires et négociations* Guerchy sued D'Éon for libel, and the case was heard in the court of the king's bench on 3 July 1764. D'Éon did not present himself and was found guilty by default. Sentence was postponed until he could be brought to court. He was subsequently outlawed. He had disappeared, adopting female attire as a disguise. He hid himself at Byfleet, Surrey, in the house of an opposition MP, Humphrey Cotes, a friend of John Wilkes. On 12 February 1765, on the evidence of an adventurer called Treyssac de Vergy, originally an acolyte of Guerchy but now an ally of D'Éon, the French ambassador was indicted in the court of common pleas of having incited Treyssac to kill D'Éon. The case went through several stages. Guerchy's residence was stoned by a Wilkite mob. The ambassador was recalled, and the chief cause of D'Éon's agitation was removed. Broglie, who found the chevalier's reports on the British political scene extremely useful, urged the king to make another conciliatory gesture towards a man whose personal loyalty to the monarch had not wavered. Guerchy was replaced by Durand, a member of the *secret*, as minister-plenipotentiary, and in July 1766 Durand handed over to D'Éon a handwritten letter from the king bestowing upon him the pension of 12,000 livres, to be paid 'wherever he may be, except in time of war amongst my enemies and until such time as I think proper to appoint him to some post, the salary of which shall exceed the amount of this pension' (Louis XV to D'Éon, 1 April 1766, Boutaric, 1.350). The chevalier handed over some papers to Durand, but the threat remained that, under the pressure of his creditors, he might reluctantly be forced to sell the rest to the earl of Chatham or to others.

However, D'Éon was still an outlaw, though no further proceedings had been taken against him in the English courts. In 1769 he left Brewer Street temporarily for Petty France, Westminster. The summer he spent at Staunton Harold, the seat of his friend the fifth Earl Ferrers, working on a massive treatise on public administration which was eventually published in thirteen volumes at Amsterdam in 1774 under the title of *Les loisirs du Chevalier d'Éon*. His wide circle of friends, which now included Wilkes, enabled him to keep Louis XV informed about the British political scene. In 1772, for instance, he reported the claim that Bute and Mansfield were plotting to restore the Pretender on condition that he converted to Anglicanism. A year later Broglie was seeking information from him about the identity of Junius after an Englishman, probably Thomas Mante, had been presented as the pamphleteer at Versailles. Doubts were expressed at this time about D'Éon's sex, and wagers were made, although he himself professed to be indignant at the suggestion that he was not a man. Yet, according to a document cited by the duc de Broglie (2. 468–9), D'Éon had confided to Drouet, another agent of the *secret*, that he was in reality a woman. This admission was communicated by the comte de Broglie to Louis XV in July 1772. The chevalier's situation remained desperate because his secret royal pension was paid irregularly and his debts had not been expunged. His reports were accompanied by requests for money and reminders that he still held compromising documents, which he had entrusted to Lord Ferrers and Humphrey Cotes, partly for safekeeping and partly in pawn for advances of money.

With Louis XV's death in May 1774 the *secret du roi* came to an end, as the new king wished to conduct diplomacy through regular channels. D'Éon was offered a deal: the return of his papers and an undertaking to remain silent on the disputes with Praslin and the now deceased Guerchy in exchange for a confirmation of his pension and a safe-conduct to return to France. D'Éon held out for a reimbursement of debts amounting to 250,000 livres, public vindication of his past conduct, and the new post he had been promised by Louis XV. The king refused these terms, and his pension was stopped. With the approach of war, however, his services were even more in demand. During October and November 1775 an agreement was reached between him and Beaumarchais, whom Vergennes, the new minister of foreign affairs, had sent over to London for the purpose. In addition to handing over his papers, D'Éon was required to adopt female attire, though he was to be allowed to continue wearing the cross of the order of St Louis. Louis XVI would treat his debts as a capital sum invested towards a lifelong annuity of 12,000 livres to be paid in lieu of his pension. There was also a recognizance by Beaumarchais that D'Éon had contracted debts of unspecified 'plus fortes sommes' which Beaumarchais undertook to repay (F. Gaillardet and H. Gaillardet, 338; Boutaric, 2.445). The new 'chevalière' was also to be paid a trousseau. It is likely that the requirement about female attire was viewed at Versailles as reasonable in the light of D'Éon's earlier admission as to his sex, and also as a means of controlling an unruly individual who had often provoked his opponents to duels.

Later years, 1777–1810 Sensing rightly that the slippery Beaumarchais would not honour all the financial agreements, D'Éon kept back some papers (of which, it now appears, he had made copies). The payment of the 'plus fortes sommes' gave rise to bitter disputes between the two. In August 1777 he returned to France. Upon presenting himself at Versailles in military uniform, he was promptly ordered to resume female dress. The chevalier found himself ill at ease in female garb, despite the services of Marie Antoinette's modiste, Mlle Bertin. His requests to be allowed to don his uniform and to serve in the war were turned down, and he was refused permission to return to London in 1778 to look after his financial interests after the death of Lord Ferrers. D'Éon settled on his family estates at Tonnerre. After a few months imprisonment at Dijon in 1779 for wearing his uniform in public, he again took up residence at Versailles before being finally allowed to return to England in November 1785. His unpaid landlord in Brewer Street was threatening to sell his library and collections. D'Éon was also pursuing the successive heirs of Lord Ferrers for £5000 which the earl had received from Beaumarchais on his behalf. He resumed his social life, dining frequently with Wilkes and his daughter; he stayed with the duke of Dorset at Knole and saw Lord Chancellor Loughborough (who had been his lawyer in 1763). James Boswell met 'Madame D'Éon' on 5 March 1786 and was shocked by her appearance: 'she appeared to me a man in woman's clothes, like Hecate on the stage' (*English Experiment*, 48). The *chevalière* took to fencing as a source of revenue. On 9 April 1787 he appeared in an 'assault of arms' with Saint-Georges at Carlton House in the presence of the prince of Wales, his female dress adding panache to his dexterity.

The collapse of the *ancien régime* freed D'Éon from any bonds of loyalty to a system which had treated him badly, but it also had disastrous consequences for him. He may have celebrated the 14 July in 1790 but he also found that his annuity fell into arrears and was later stopped. He twice offered his military services to his country without success. He had to sell his collection of books and manuscripts (including those of Vauban) in 1791. A public subscription in the City of London provided him with £475, but by 1792 he had to sell his jewellery and plate. Several of his relatives were guillotined. After the deaths of his mother and sister, the estates at Tonnerre were confiscated, although he was not technically an émigré.

In partnership with Mrs Bateman, an actress and female fencer, D'Éon gave displays of his skill at the Haymarket Theatre and at Ranelagh in 1793. Though sixty-five years old, the *chevalière* fenced 'as though in the vigour of youth' (Cox, 132). At Southampton on 26 August 1796 he was seriously wounded in the armpit during an assault of arms and was thereafter unable to fence. He had left his lodgings in Brewer Street in 1793 and was then living with Mrs Mary Cole, a native of Lorraine and the widow of a Royal Navy pump-maker, at 26 New Milman Street. She kept house for him for fourteen years believing him to be a woman. He spent five months in prison for debt in 1804. That year he signed a contract with Messrs Richardson for the publication of his memoirs, which were to be written by Thomas William Plummer. The work was never completed, though the material was assembled for it. He finally had to sell his cross of St Louis. D'Éon died peacefully on 21 May 1810 at 26 New Milman Street. A medical examination carried out by several doctors, including the surgeon Thomas Copeland, in the presence of Sir Sidney Smith and others, found that his male organs were 'in every respect perfectly formed' (F. Gaillardet and H. Gaillardet, 406). Mrs Cole 'did not recover from the shock for many hours' (Cox, 135). According to his wishes, D'Éon was buried, on 28 May, in the graveyard of St Pancras Old Church with, between his hands, a crucifix and a copy of the *Imitation of Christ*, 'which I have so badly imitated' (ibid., 136). His grave disappeared when the Midland Railway destroyed the churchyard. He had made a will but had not signed it, and administration of the estate was entrusted to Plummer. His belongings, including Richard Mead's collection of editions of Horace's works, were sold by Christies on 19 February 1813. Plummer retained many papers of D'Éon, including some relating to his role in the *secret du roi*, which were unfortunately dispersed in 1966.

The Chevalier D'Éon's outrageous, though understandable, behaviour in 1763–4 and his extraordinary career as a transvestite have overshadowed his remarkable prowess as a soldier, his undoubted skills as a diplomat, informant, and secret agent, and his qualities as a scholar and writer.

J. M. J. ROGISTER

Sources correspondance politique, Angleterre, Archives du Ministère des Affaires Étrangères, Paris, 450–593; suppls. 13, 16, 17 · Bibliothèque municipale de Tonnerre, Yonne, France, Papiers D'Éon · Archives Nationales, Paris, Papiers D'Éon, K157, 159, 164; 277 AP · BL, D'Éon MSS, Add. MSS 11, 339–11, 341; 29993–29994 · F. Gaillardet and H. Gaillardet, *Mémoires du Chevalier D'Éon* (1935) · C. d'Éon de Beaumont, *The maiden of Tonnerre: the vicissitudes of the Chevalier and the Chevalière d'Éon*, ed. and trans. R. A. Champagne, N. Ekstein, and G. Kates (2001) · E. Boutaric, ed., *Correspondance secrète inédite de Louis XV sur la politique étrangère avec le comte de Broglie, Tercier, etc.*, 2 vols. (1866) · D. Ozanam and M. Antoine, eds., *Correspondance secrète du comte de Broglie avec Louis XV (1756–1774)*, 2 vols. (1956) · *Catalogue of valuable printed books, music, autograph letters, and historical documents* (1966) [sale catalogue, Sotheby & Co., 13 June 1966] · J. B. Telfer, *The strange career of the Chevalier D'Éon de Beaumont* (1885) · Duc de Broglie, *Le secret du roi: correspondance secrète de Louis XV avec ses agents diplomatiques, 1752–1774*, 2 vols., 4th edn (1888) · *Lettres, mémoires et négociations particulières du Chevalier D'Éon, ministre plénipotentiaire auprès du roi de Grande-Bretagne* (1764) · E. A. Vizetelly, *The true story of the Chevalier d'Éon* (1895) · *Boswell: the English experiment, 1785–1789*, ed. I. S. Lustig and F. A. Pottle (1986), vol. 13 of *The Yale editions of the private papers of James Boswell*, trade edn (1950–89) · C. Cox, *The enigma of the age: the strange story of the Chevalier D'Éon* (1966) · H. Walpole, *Memoirs of the reign of King George the Third*, ed. D. Le Marchant, 4 vols. (1845) · P. Pinsseau, *L'étrange destinée du Chevalier D'Éon, 1728–1810*, 2nd edn (1945) · G. Kates, *Monsieur d'Éon is a woman: a tale of political intrigue and social masquerade* (2001)

Archives Archives Nationales, Paris, 277 AP · Bibliothèque Municipale de Tonnerre, Yonne, France · BL, journal, corresp., etc., Add. MSS 29993–29994 · U. Leeds, Brotherton L., corresp. and papers | Archives du Ministère des Affaires Étrangères, Paris, correspondance politique, Angleterre 450–593, suppls. 13, 16, 17 · BL, collection of the comte de Bastard, Add. MSS 11339–11341 · BL, Wilkes MSS, Add. MS 30877

Likenesses Vispré, engraving, 1764, repro. in F. Gaillardet, ed., *The memoirs of the Chevalier D'Éon*, trans. A. White (1970) · T. Burke, mezzotint, pubd 1771 (after J. G. Huguieur), BM · S. Hooper, print, 1771 (*A policy … on the Chevr. D'Éon, man or woman*), Bibliothèque Municipale, Auxerre · J.-B. Bradel, engraving, 1779, repro. in F. Gaillardet, *The memoirs of the Chevalier D'Éon*, trans. A. White (1970) · J.-B. Bradel, engraving, 1783 (as a woman), repro. in A. Angremy and others, *Beaumarchais* (1966) [exhibition catalogue, Bibliothèque Nationale, Paris, 28 Oct 1966 – 8 Jan 1967] · T. Chambars, stipple, pubd 1787 (after R. Cosway), BM · F. Haward, stipple, pubd 1788 (after A. Kauffmann; after Latour), BM, NPG · J. Condé, stipple, pubd 1791, BM, NPG; repro. in Cox, *Enigma of the age* · G. Dance, chalk and watercolour, 1793, BM [*see illus.*] · R. Cooper, portrait, 1821 (after J. Condé) · Robineau, group portrait, engraving (*Assault of arms at Carlton House in the presence of the prince of Wales, 9 April 1787*), repro. in Cox, *Enigma of the age* · four prints, Bibliothèque Municipale, Auxerre; repro. in Pinsseau, *L'étrange destinée* · prints, BM, NPG; repro. in Pinsseau, *L'étrange destinée*

Wealth at death most belongings auctioned at Christies, 19 Feb 1813

Deorman (*fl.* 1119–1141), moneyer and merchant, was a member of the first London family of moneyers for whom biographical details can be assembled, and his importance lies in what they reveal about the prominent but largely unknown class of men responsible for organizing and running the Anglo-Saxon and Anglo-Norman mints. The name of Deorman appears on the coins of London struck in the reigns of Æthelred II, Harold I, and Edward the Confessor, and it is likely that the family held the royal office of moneyer by long descent. The repeated use by successive generations of the names Deorman and Theoderic, long after Saxon names had become unfashionable, hints at the pride they took in their descent. It would appear from the family's connections with the church of St Antonin in Watling Street, most probably built by Deorman's grandfather at the end of the eleventh century, that the church was close to their mint. If this was so, the mint was situated on what seems to have been the main street of King Alfred's London.

The first documentary references to Deorman's family occur in Domesday Book, and show that his grandfather, also Deorman, held land in Islington, Essex, and Hertfordshire as a tenant-in-chief—some of it by petty serjeanty—apparently as remuneration for his important office of supervising the mints. He was also one of the knights of the archbishop of Canterbury's fee, no doubt because of the financial services which he could render. Four of the elder Deorman's sons were also London moneyers and were prominent among the aldermanic families in the city. One of them, Theoderic, had at least four sons of his own. They included Walter (an alderman in 1132), and the second Deorman.

This Deorman first appears in the documents in 1119, when he claimed the church of St Antonin by hereditary right. He was described elsewhere as a moneyer, and his name, like those of three of his brothers, appears on coins of the London mint—in his case between 1134 and 1141. It seems clear, though, from the family's high social standing that its members were not actively engaged in the work of striking and exchanging coins, work which was probably supervised by goldsmiths. But moneyers were well placed to accumulate trading capital, as they were exempt from royal taxation and could also make use of the deposits of bullion temporarily left in their charge. Moreover they had close contact with foreign merchants, who were obliged to exchange their own coin and bullion at the mints for English coins. Moneyers had the capital to provide hostels for alien merchants, and inevitably these contacts encouraged them to make their own ventures in foreign trade. The unusual dedication of St Antonin's Church suggests that the family of Deorman had trading links with the Castilian town of Palencia, of which St Antonin was patron; here they could profitably acquire gold. It is also likely that they were the founders of the group of London pepperers who by 1180 had their own guild and specialized in selling spices and other luxury goods imported from the Mediterranean.

Confirmation that Deorman dealt in imported luxuries comes from a book of miracles written by Osbert de Clare, the mid-twelfth-century prior of Westminster Abbey, which included a story about a very rich merchant of London called Deorman. This was undoubtedly the London moneyer, whose family the prior must have known well since Deorman's three aunts had given lands to Westminster Abbey in return for rights of burial and confraternity. Abbeys were also used as storehouses of bullion and valuables, and there is considerable evidence for close links between them and moneyers. A later version of the same story by Abbot Samson of Bury (d. 1211), who must also have known Deorman, says that he dealt in expensive spices, silks, and rich fabrics which he took to the fair at Bury St Edmunds. On one occasion, while Deorman was praying in the abbey church, a bag containing jewels and gold was stolen from him. By a miracle he recovered his valuables, and out of compassion for the penitent thief he let her go unpunished. According to the story it was this experience which led Deorman (presumably after 1141, when his name last appears on London coins) to abandon his successful life as a moneyer and merchant to become a monk at Bury, where he lived to a good old age.

Deorman's son, **Theoderic Fitzdeorman** (d. in or before 1162), carried on the family mint from 1141 until 1158, when Henry II closed down all the established London mints, dismissed the hereditary moneyers, and apparently established a central workshop in their place. But before then Theoderic had raised his family to even greater heights by his marriage to Matilda, a relation of Gilbert de Clare, earl of Pembroke (d. 1148), one of the most powerful barons in England. The earl was one of Stephen's supporters until 1147, and he held Montfichet Castle in London during the civil war. It would seem that the marriage was Theoderic's reward for assisting Stephen, and this would account for his appointment as justiciar of London between 1143 and 1152. Theoderic died in or before 1162, by when his son Bertram had granted 80 acres of lands at Stoke Newington to St Mary's, Clerkenwell, for the soul of his father. Bertram's son Thomas confirmed the grant shortly before 1187. After this the family's links with London became tenuous and soon untraceable. PAMELA NIGHTINGALE

Sources P. Nightingale, *A medieval mercantile community: the Grocers' Company and the politics and trade of London, 1000–1485* (1995), 26–30 · P. Nightingale, 'Some London moneyers and reflections on the organisation of English mints in the eleventh and twelfth centuries', *Numismatic Chronicle*, 142 (1982), 34–50 · C. Horstman, ed., *Nova legenda Anglie, as collected by John of Tynemouth, J. Capgrave, and others*, 2 vols. (1901) · T. Arnold, ed., *Memorials of St Edmund's Abbey*, 1, Rolls Series, 96 (1890), 183–5 · C. N. L. Brooke and G. Keir, *London, 800–1216: the shaping of a city* (1975), 219 · St Paul's Cathedral, London, 1883, Historical Manuscripts Commission, London, 61a, 66b, 67b · D. C. Douglas, ed., *The Domesday Monachorum of Christ Church, Canterbury* (1944), 58–62 · *Calendar of the charter rolls*, 6 vols., PRO (1903–27), vol. 2, pp. 71–2 · G. C. Brooke, *Catalogue of English coins in the British Museum: the Norman Kings*, 1 (1916) · H. W. C. Davis, 'London lands and liberties of St Paul's, 1066–1135', *Essays in medieval history presented to T. F. Tout*, ed. A. G. Little and F. M. Powicke (1925), 57 · *Reg. RAN*, 3.198

Derby. For this title name *see* Ferrers, Robert de, first Earl Ferrers [earl of Derby] (d. 1139); Ferrers, Robert de, sixth earl of Derby (c.1239–1279); Stanley, Thomas, first earl of Derby (c.1433–1504); Beaufort, Margaret, countess of Richmond and Derby (1443–1509); Stanley, Edward, third earl of Derby (1509–1572); Stanley, Henry, fourth earl of Derby (1531–1593); Stanley, Ferdinando, fifth earl of Derby (1559?–1594); Spencer, Alice, countess of Derby (1559–1637); Stanley, William, sixth earl of Derby (*bap.* 1561, d. 1642); Stanley, Charlotte, countess of Derby (1599–1664); Stanley, James, seventh earl of Derby (1607–1651); Stanley, William George Richard, ninth earl of Derby (1655–1702); Stanley, James, tenth earl of Derby (1664–1736); Stanley, Edward Smith, twelfth earl of Derby (1752–1834); Farren, Elizabeth [Elizabeth Smith Stanley, countess of Derby] (1759×62–1829); Stanley, Edward Smith, thirteenth earl of Derby (1775–1851); Stanley, Edward George Geoffrey Smith, fourteenth earl of Derby (1799–1869); Stanley, Mary Catherine, countess of Derby (1824–1900); Stanley, Edward Henry, fifteenth earl of Derby (1826–1893); Stanley, Frederick Arthur, sixteenth earl of Derby (1841–1908); Stanley, Edward George Villiers, seventeenth earl of Derby (1865–1948).

Derby, Alfred Thomas (1821–1873), watercolour painter, was born on 21 January 1821 in London, the eldest son among the eight children of William *Derby (1786–1847), watercolourist. He was educated at Mr Wyand's school in Hampstead Road, London. After studying at the Royal Academy Schools he painted portraits and scenes from the novels of Walter Scott. In 1838 his father had a stroke, and until his father's death he helped him to carry on producing watercolour copies of paintings by Landseer and others, including Landseer's *Return from the Highlands*. After that he continued to paint watercolours, mainly producing copies, including a copy of Gainsborough's portrait of the Hon. Mrs Thomas Graham. He exhibited twenty-two pictures, mainly portraits, at the Royal Academy between 1848 and 1872, and also exhibited at the British Institution and the Suffolk Street Gallery.

For almost thirty years Derby lived in Osnaburgh Street, Regent's Park, until in the late 1860s he moved to Hammersmith. He died on 19 April 1873 at his home, 11 Hammersmith Terrace, London, after a long illness; he left a widow, Maria, but no children. His collection of drawings from portraits was sold at Christies on 23 February 1874.

R. E. GRAVES, rev. ANNE PIMLOTT BAKER

Sources B. Stewart and M. Cutten, *The dictionary of portrait painters in Britain up to 1920* (1997) · Wood, *Vic. painters*, 3rd edn · *Art Journal*, 35 (1873), 208 · Boase, *Mod. Eng. biog.* · J. Johnson, ed., *Works exhibited at the Royal Society of British Artists, 1824–1893, and the New English Art Club, 1888–1917*, 2 vols. (1975) · Graves, *RA exhibitors*
Wealth at death under £3000: probate, 20 April 1873, *CGPLA Eng. & Wales*

Derby, Elias Hasket (1739–1799), merchant in America, was born in Salem, Massachusetts, on 16 August 1739, the son of Richard *Derby (1712–1783), an established merchant and shipmaster, and Mary Hodges (d. 1770). In 1761 he married Elizabeth Crowninshield, daughter of another leading merchant. They had four sons and three daughters. During the American War of Independence he managed the eighty privateers his father outfitted that captured 144 British ships, as against only 19 losses, and employed 8000 men. Derby ships—the *Quero* and *Astraea* respectively—carried news to Europe in 1775 that hostilities had broken out at Lexington and Concord, and that peace had been signed at Paris in 1783.

After the revolution the American economy slumped as the British attempted to cut off the new nation's traditional trade with the West Indies. Derby responded by sending vessels all over the world in search of new markets. In 1784 Derby's *Light Horse* took West Indian sugar to St Petersburg, the first American vessel to trade with Russia or be seen in the Baltic. The next year he sent the *Grand Turk* to the Cape of Good Hope, and in 1786 dispatched the same ship to the Indian Ocean. Commanded by his 21-year-old son Hasket, it inaugurated a trade with the Isle de France (Mauritius) and Bombay in India, the first American ship to sail to India. The silks and spices which had formerly come to the western hemisphere through foreign hands were now accessible without an additional middleman. To exchange these products Derby's crews picked up and traded for cargo all over the globe.

Derby preferred to employ daring young mariners—he once launched a 'boys' voyage' where the captain was nineteen and only one crew member was over twenty-one. He lost only one ship in his career. Derby's vessels were the first American ones in Bombay, Calcutta, Mocha, Rangoon, Manila, Ceylon, Sumatra, and Siam. He sent five ships to Canton (Guangzhou) in the 1780s as well, though Robert Morris's *Empress of China* had the honour of being the first to arrive there in 1785, but withdrew from the China trade as it proved less lucrative than that of the Indian Ocean.

Derby's quest for novelty was not limited to trade. He bought a farm outside Salem where he experimented with growing exotic plants brought by his ships. Derby's crews also returned with the first elephant, zebra, and inhabitant of India to be seen in the United States. Derby was among the first American merchants to use copper-bottomed rapid sailing vessels, and was influential in persuading the federal government to build warehouses where goods could be bonded and quality assured.

By the time of his death in Salem on 8 September 1799, King Derby, who had done so much to expand American commerce throughout the world, was one of the few men in the nation estimated to be worth a million dollars. Unfortunately his sons and sons-in-law, who inherited his fortune, quarrelled among themselves and lost it during the embargo President Jefferson imposed on American shipping overseas between 1806 and 1809. Elias Hasket junior, the principal heir, was unable even to keep up Salem's most magnificent mansion, built by his father in 1797, which has been restored and survives as a reminder of the family's former wealth. WILLIAM PENCAK

Sources R. McKey, 'Elias Hasket Derby: merchant of Salem Massachusetts, 1739–1799', PhD diss., Clark University, 1961 · R. McKey, 'Elias Hasket Derby and the American Revolution', *Essex Institute Historical Collections*, 97 (1961), 166–96 · R. McKey, 'Elias Hasket Derby and the founding of the eastern trade', *Essex Institute Historical Collections*, 98 (1962), 1–25, 65–83 · *DNB* · D. A. Morrison, 'Derby, Elias Hasket', *ANB*
Archives Peabody Essex Museum, Salem, Massachusetts, papers
Wealth at death $1,000,000; considered one of the wealthiest (if not the wealthiest) men in America: McKey, 'Elias Hasket Derby'

Derby, Richard (1712–1783), merchant in America, was born in Salem, Massachusetts, on 16 September 1712 to ship's captain Richard Derby (d. 1716) and Martha Hasket. His mother raised him, as his father died when he was four. By the age of twenty-four the younger Richard Derby had served as a ship's captain on a voyage to Spain. He began buying ships of his own, made frequent trips to Europe and the West Indies, and in 1735 married Mary Hodges (d. 1770), also of Salem. They had three daughters, and three sons who joined their father as leaders of the revolutionary cause in Salem. In 1771 Richard married the widow Sarah Hersey, *née* Langley.

Derby became one of the richest men in Salem. In 1755 he built Derby Wharf and a warehouse, and two years later was at the head of a subscription list to pay back wages to Salem's soldiers fighting in the French and Indian War whom the province had failed to reimburse.

During the war Derby engaged in privateering and supplied the British West Indies with New England timber and foodstuffs. Like most New Englanders trading to the Sugar Islands, he also traded with the French and Spanish colonies, and at least four of his ships were confiscated by the British government for illegal commerce during the war. Despite these setbacks, by 1760 he was Salem's leading merchant and built the fine mansion that still stands on what is now Derby Street.

Derby continued to lose vessels for illegal trade in the 1760s; he responded by leading Salem, which was the second largest town in Massachusetts, in resisting British trade regulations and taxation. He put up the money for the *Essex Gazette*, Massachusetts's first newspaper outside Boston, which began publication on 2 August 1768. The printer Benjamin Hall wasted no time in condemning the five members of the house of representatives from Essex county who supported British policy. The following May four of them were defeated, and Richard Derby was chosen to represent Salem. He held this post for six of the next seven years, when he was elevated to the Massachusetts council.

Derby himself held no major political office, but he was clearly Salem's political boss. A son-in-law, Dr John Prince, probably represented the clan at the Boston Tea Party in 1773. The American War of Independence almost broke out in Salem in February 1775, when British soldiers hoping to seize the town's munitions were met by a crowd of citizens under Derby's lead. When ordered to surrender the guns he replied: 'Find them if you can, take them if you can, they will never be surrendered.' Unlike at Lexington and Concord two months later, the British backed down.

Derby enjoyed the honour that one of his ships, the *Quero*, commanded by his son John, was the first to reach Europe with news that hostilities had broken out. In consequence the *Essex Gazette*'s pro-American version of events was reprinted throughout the British press for two weeks before the British version was known. Another Derby vessel, the *Astraea*, also informed America that peace had been concluded and independence recognized in 1783. In the interim Derby put up the capital that allowed his son Elias Hasket *Derby to equip over eighty privateers (half Salem's contingent) that employed 8000 men and captured 144 British vessels.

Although Derby barely survived past the news of the American victory, dying in Salem on 9 November 1783, his contribution in the War of Independence had been critical. British interference with his trade made Salem's leading merchant its leading revolutionary. And the estate of over £20,000 in cash plus ships and real estate that he left to his son Elias Hasket laid the foundation for an even greater fortune, earned through worldwide commerce, that contributed significantly to the rise of the United States as a maritime power.   WILLIAM PENCAK

Sources J. D. Philips, 'The life and times of Richard Derby, merchant of Salem', *Essex Institute Historical Collections*, 65 (1929), 243–89 · R. L. Tagney, *The world turned upside down: Essex county during*

America's turbulent years, 1763–1790 (West Newbury, MA, 1989) · *DNB* · W. Pencak, 'Derby, Richard', *ANB*
Archives Massachusetts Archives, Boston · Peabody Essex Museum, Salem, Massachusetts, papers
Wealth at death £20,000 in cash; plus ships and real estate: Philips, 'The life and times'

Derby, William (1786–1847), watercolour and miniature painter, was born on 10 January 1786 in Birmingham and studied drawing with the landscape painter Joseph Barber. In 1808 he settled in London, where he painted portraits in oil and watercolour, and miniatures. He also made watercolour copies of paintings by other artists. In 1825 he took over the copying of images for Edmund Lodge's *Portraits of Illustrious Personages of Great Britain* from William Hilton; these were completed in 1834. He was then commissioned by the earl of Derby, whose portrait he painted in 1837, to make a series of watercolour drawings of the portraits of his ancestors from the reign of Henry VII onward, which were scattered around the country. William Derby exhibited forty-nine paintings, mainly portraits, at the Royal Academy between 1811 and 1837, and also exhibited at the Society of British Artists.

In 1838 Derby was disabled by a stroke and was only able to carry on his work with the help of his son Alfred Thomas *Derby (1821–1873). One of the best of his drawings from this period was a watercolour copy of Edwin Landseer's *Return from the Highlands*. Derby died on 1 January 1847 at his residence in Osnaburgh Street, Regent's Park, London, leaving a widow and eight children. Two of his daughters, Emma Maria and Caroline, were miniature painters, winning several prizes from the Society of Arts. Two of his watercolours, *A Fisherman* (1834) and *A Man Holding a Book*, are in the Victoria and Albert Museum, and his paintings are also in the National Portrait Gallery, the British Museum, and the Wallace Collection, London. Six of his miniatures were lent to the South Kensington Museum Exhibition in 1865.

R. E. GRAVES, rev. ANNE PIMLOTT BAKER

Sources D. Foskett, *Miniatures: dictionary and guide* (1987), 527 · P. Hollins, 'Memoir', *Art Union*, 9 (1847), 88 [repr. *GM*, 2nd ser., 27 (1847), 668] · Mallalieu, *Watercolour artists*, vols. 1–2 · L. Lambourne and J. Hamilton, eds., *British watercolours in the Victoria and Albert Museum* (1980) · B. Stewart and M. Cutten, *The dictionary of portrait painters in Britain up to 1920* (1997) · Graves, *RA exhibitors* · R. Ormond, *Early Victorian portraits*, 2 vols. (1973)

Dereham, Elias of (d. 1245), ecclesiastical administrator, was a native of West Dereham, Norfolk. His earliest patron was Hubert Walter (d. 1205), later archbishop of Canterbury, a fellow native of West Dereham and founder there of a Premonstratensian abbey whose charters are witnessed by Master Elias, perhaps as early as 1188. Between 1193 and 1201 it is possible that he is to be identified with a Master Elias, steward to Gilbert de Glanville, bishop of Rochester (d. 1214), a close friend and kinsman of Hubert Walter. Less likely, but by no means impossible, is the suggestion that he is to be identified with a man named Master Elias the Engineer, or Elias of Oxford, who before 1201 had charge of the king's houses in Oxford and of various castle-building operations across southern England. The only certainty is that by 1201 Dereham was attached to the household of Hubert Walter at Canterbury, being credited at least once with the title of archbishop's steward. At about this time he acquired the churches of Brightwalton, Berkshire, and Melton Mowbray, Leicestershire, gifts from the monks of Battle and Lewes.

Hubert Walter's death in 1205 forced Dereham to transfer to the household of Bishop Jocelin of Wells (d. 1242), again as steward. With the imposition of the papal interdict in 1208 Jocelin and Elias went into exile in France, together with Jocelin's brother, Bishop Hugh of Lincoln (d. 1235). Hugh promoted Elias to the Lincoln prebend of Lafford and in November 1212 appointed him executor of his will. The most important of Dereham's contacts made in exile was with Archbishop Stephen Langton (d. 1228). He was twice employed as Langton's envoy to England, and in 1213, at the end of the interdict, returned to Canterbury as Langton's steward. In the next year he had custody of Rochester Castle. Following the award of Magna Carta in 1215 Dereham helped distribute the charter around the shires, becoming an enthusiastic adherent of the rebel barons and preaching their cause at Paul's Cross in London. As a result he was despoiled of his various churches and exiled to France when the royalist party triumphed in 1217. By 1220 he was pardoned and allowed to return to Langton's household; he assisted in the construction of a new shrine to Thomas Becket in Canterbury, in which context he is described by the chronicler Matthew Paris as an 'incomparable artificer'.

Before 1222 Dereham had acquired the prebend of Potterne in Salisbury under Langton's pupil, Bishop Richard Poor (d. 1235). For the remainder of his life he was to be closely associated with the building of Salisbury's new cathedral. He is said to have served for twenty-five years as rector of the cathedral fabric fund, and is undoubtedly found in association with the cathedral's masons and workshops. Before 1234 he had supervised the construction of a model dwelling place for himself within the cathedral close, the profits from whose sale he later put towards Salisbury's fabric fund. Elsewhere he renewed his contacts with Bishop Jocelin of Wells, then in the process of rebuilding the cathedral church in Wells. He served three successive archbishops of Canterbury—Langton, Richard Grant (d. 1231), and Edmund of Abingdon (d. 1240)—either as steward or executor. In 1228 Bishop Richard Poor was translated from Salisbury to Durham, whereafter Dereham is found witnessing deeds relating to both these sees. He was later to serve as Poor's executor and, perhaps as proxy for Poor, as the executor of William (I) Marshal, earl of Pembroke (d. 1219). He also found service with Peter des Roches, bishop of Winchester (d. 1238), a leading political rival of Langton and Poor, whom Elias none the less assisted with the foundation of monastic houses in Selborne and Titchfield, both in Hampshire, and for whom he subsequently acted as executor. Probably under Archbishop Edmund he was promoted to the Canterbury peculiar of Harrow, Middlesex, the chancel of whose church he was repairing in 1242.

Throughout these years Dereham's services were much in demand at court. Between 1233 and 1238 he had charge of royal building work at the great hall of Winchester Castle, besides supervising the installation of windows and pavements at Clarendon Palace, Wiltshire, helping to construct a tomb used for the burial of Joan, queen of Scots (who died in 1238, and was buried at Tarrant in Dorset), and being sent to direct the enclosure of an anchoress in Britford, Wiltshire.

Inevitably, given his association with building projects, his work on Becket's shrine, the fact that Matthew Paris preserved Dereham's drawing of a wind-rose, and since most of his employers were renowned as patrons of cathedral or monastic architecture, Elias of Dereham has been canvassed as one of the principal influences in the development of early thirteenth-century English Gothic. Specifically, an attempt has been made to present him as the architect of Salisbury Cathedral. The attempt has failed, through scepticism that one man could have supervised such a major project while still discharging Dereham's functions as steward and administrator elsewhere. The best that can be said is that to appeal to such a wide diversity of patrons he clearly possessed some very rare talent indeed. It is more likely that such a talent lay in site administration and the guidance of taste rather than in any practical work as craftsman, architect, or mason. Dereham died shortly after April 1245, whereupon his benefices were seized for the use of a papal nuncio.

NICHOLAS VINCENT, rev.

Sources A. H. Thompson, 'Marter Elias of Dereham and the king's works', *Archaeological Journal*, 98 (1941), 1–35 · J. Harvey and A. Oswald, *English mediaeval architects: a biographical dictionary down to 1550*, 2nd edn (1984) · C. R. Cheney and E. John, eds., *Canterbury, 1193–1205*, English Episcopal Acta, 3 (1986) · J. Thorpe, ed., *Registrum Roffense, or, A collection of antient records, charters and instruments … illustrating the ecclesiastical history and antiquities of the diocese and cathedral church of Rochester* (1769) · H. M. Colvin and others, eds., *The history of the king's works*, 6 vols. (1963–82) · *Fasti Angl., 1066–1300*, [Lincoln] · *Fasti Angl., 1066–1300*, [Salisbury] · Paris, *Chron.*, vols. 4, 6

Derfel, Robert Jones [*formerly* Robert Jones] (1824–1905), Welsh nationalist and socialist, was born Robert Jones at Y Foty, his grandfather's farm, near Bethel, Merioneth, on 24 July 1824, the second son of Edward Jones, a farmer and cattle dealer, and his wife, Catherine. His childhood was unremarkable save for his choosing to run away from home at the age of ten to live with his uncle, Jonah Roberts, a master weaver, near Corwen. From the age of twelve, he worked at a factory in Llangollen, and at twenty-one, uneducated beyond what he had learned at Sunday school, and still entirely ignorant of the English language, he moved to England. For several years he was unable to find permanent work but, around 1850, he was taken on at the drapery warehouses of J. F. and H. Roberts in Manchester. Employed first as an odd-job man, he quickly worked his way up to being a successful travelling salesman, his territory extending from the midlands to north Wales.

From this point Derfel's life settled down and he quickly came to occupy a prominent place within the Welsh community in Manchester. After a tragically short first marriage to the daughter of Jonas Lee, a leading Mancunian

Welshman, he married Mary Griffith of Ruthin in 1853 and together they had eleven children. Long a popular lay preacher with the Baptists, he was formally ordained in 1862. Above all, he won recognition as a man of letters. An active member of the Manchester Cambrian Society, and close friend of such notable Mancunian Welsh poets as William Williams (Creuddynfab; 1814–1869) and John Jones (Idrys Fychan; 1825–1887), he won several prizes for his poetry at the national eisteddfod. By the early 1860s he had become so well known by his bardic name that he adopted Derfel as his formal surname, a measure also influenced by a belief that the Welsh possessed an insufficient variety of surnames.

While much of Derfel's early poetry dealt with standard themes from religion and nature, he also celebrated the idea of patriotism. His first volume of poetry, *Rhosyn Meirion* (1853), contained a prize-winning poem on the Hungarian nationalist, Kossuth, while the distinctively Welsh inflection of this idea that typified his work first became evident in a play, *Brad y llyfrau gleision* (1854). The play satirized the infamous royal commission on education in Wales (1847) which made many disparaging observations on Welsh culture and religion. It created a sensation when it originally appeared, serialized anonymously in the Liverpool newspaper, *Yr Amserau*, because the commissioners threatened to take legal action against the proprietor if publication did not cease. Undaunted, Derfel published the complete play privately.

Themes of national pride, together with condemnation of those who betrayed their nation (by implication, those who had given evidence to the 1847 commission) reappeared continually in Derfel's poetry during the 1860s in volumes such as *Caneuon min y ffordd* (1861), *Mynudau segur* (1863), *Caneuon gwladgarol Cymru* (1864), and *Songs for Welshmen* (1865). Derfel was also a competent essayist, however, and this medium gave him greater scope to elaborate his views regarding the Welsh nation. In 'What I would do if I had the money' (from *Traethodau ac areithiau*, 1864), for example, he advocated the creation of an education system of schools and universities with instruction through the medium of Welsh; and the foundation of a national library, a national museum, a national school of arts and crafts, a national observatory, and a daily Welsh-language newspaper. He urged the reform of the national eisteddfod on similar lines, pressing for the inclusion of a science section alongside the traditional disciplines of music and literature.

In addition to his Welsh interests, Derfel was active in radical politics. He published a lecture entitled *The Enfranchisement of Women* in 1867 and also joined the Manchester branch of the Reform League, becoming a member of the executive council and a strong supporter of Ernest Jones, the former Chartist who stood for Manchester at the general election of 1868.

By this time, however, the peak of Derfel's material fortunes had passed. In 1865 he gave up travelling and invested his savings in a Welsh bookshop in Manchester which quickly collapsed. Already middle-aged, and with a growing family, he began to seek his livelihood as a printer. From the late 1860s until the 1880s he published nothing. The struggle to establish his new business undoubtedly contributed to this, but it also coincided with a crisis of faith. Inspired by Ernest Jones, Derfel turned to the works of Robert Owen, and became a convert to socialism: 'the light burst on me suddenly', he wrote, '[and] I saw clearly that the source of the world's evils and suffering was in the social system, and not in sin or in the dispensation of Providence' (I. ap Nicholas, 28). He joined the Social Democratic Federation and toured the country giving lectures; simultaneously, he renounced religion, abandoning the Baptists to embrace secularism. He joined the Rationalist Press Association and contributed to various journals such as *Freethinker*. In 1890 he helped organize the Manchester branch of the Fabians, though he remained in essence an Owenite: he even suggested in 1903 that Robert Owen should replace St David as the patron saint of Wales.

Derfel's change of heart was reflected in his poetry and essays. Between 1889 and 1904 came a second flood of publications, including *Common Misconceptions about Socialism* (1889), *Hymns and Songs for the Church of Man* (1890), *Of the Importance of Right Methods in Teaching Socialism* (1891), *Socialism* (1892), *An Unauthorised Programme* (1895), and *Musings for the Masses* (1897). In addition, he wrote the first articles in Welsh on socialism for newspapers like *Y Cymro* and *Llais Llafur*. His earlier nationalism was now, however, superseded by a championship of internationalism.

In the course of his career, Derfel published 800 poems in Welsh and another 500 in English, in addition to over 50 other publications. He died at 17 Bremner Street, Manchester, after a short illness, on 16 December 1905, and was cremated at Barlow Moor Road crematorium in Manchester later that month. MATTHEW CRAGOE

Sources I. ap Nicholas, *Derfel: Welsh rebel, poet, and preacher* (1945) • I. Jenkyns, 'R. J. Derfel, Manceinion', *Y Celt* (24 Feb 1888) • R. J. Derfel, *Songs for Welshmen* (1865) • R. J. Derfel, *Traethodau ac areithiau* (1864) • T. R. Roberts, *Eminent Welshmen: a short biographical dictionary* (1908) • *DWB* • d. cert.
Archives NL Wales, corresp. and papers
Likenesses J. Thomas, photograph, *c.*1866, NL Wales • sketch, *c.*1888, repro. in *Y Celt* • photograph (in old age), repro. in I. ap Nicholas, *Derfel*

Derham, Samuel (1652x5–1689), physician, the son of William Derham of Weston, near Chipping Campden, Gloucestershire, was born, probably at Weston, between 1652 and 1655. In Michaelmas term 1672 he entered Magdalen Hall, Oxford, where he pursued a long academic career which included disputations on topics as diverse as the role of the imagination in causing disease and the nature of scurvy. He graduated BA on 13 June 1676, MA on 3 May 1679, BM on 9 February 1681, and DM on 18 January 1687.

Although there are no extant records to show that Derham practised medicine before his final qualification, it is likely that he had begun to do so, for in 1685 he published *Hydrologia philosophica, or, An account of Ilmington waters in Warwick-shire, with directions for drinking of the same*. Dedicated to William Lenthall of Haseley, the work gave an account of the waters at Ilmington and recommended them for a variety of scrofulous complaints. Derham's recommendation and the investment of Lord Capell, the local landowner, made the spa a place of significant resort in the late seventeenth and early eighteenth centuries.

In his book Derham exhibited strong support for experimental philosophy and considerable familiarity with chemical and iatrochemical developments in medicine. He was not, however, to develop his medical career, for he was struck down by smallpox and died at his house in Oxford on 26 August 1689. He was buried in his parish of residence, at the church of St Michael-at-the-Northgate, Oxford, on the following day.   MARK S. R. JENNER

Sources Wood, *Ath. Oxon.* · registers of St Michael, Oxfordshire Archives, DD Par Oxford, St Michael b2 · churchwardens' accounts, St Michael Northgate, 1660–1709, Oxfordshire Archives, DD Par Oxford, St Michael a4 · W. Dugdale, *The antiquities of Warwickshire illustrated*, rev. W. Thomas, 2nd edn, 2 vols. (1730) · R. Frank, 'Medicine', *Hist. U. Oxf.* 4: *17th-cent. Oxf.*, 505–58 · P. Henbry, *The English spa, 1560–1815* (1990) · parish register, Chipping Campden, Glos. RO, PMF 81/1, and 81u 1/1 · IGI

Derham, William (1657–1735), Church of England clergyman and natural philosopher, was born at Stoulton, near Worcester, on 26 November 1657. His father's name was Thomas, but no other information is available about his parents. He went to school at Blockley, Gloucestershire, and was admitted to Trinity College, Oxford, as a servitor on 14 May 1675; he graduated BA on 28 January 1679. Dr Ralph Bathurst, president of Trinity, recommended him to Dr Seth Ward, bishop of Salisbury, who in turn recommended him as chaplain to dowager Lady Catherine Grey of Werke. He was ordained deacon by Dr Henry Compton, bishop of London, on 29 May 1681 and priest by Seth Ward on 9 July 1682. That same month he was presented with the living of Wargrave, Berkshire, by Richard Neville, son-in-law to Lady Grey. He received his MA degree from Trinity on 4 July 1683. He took out a licence to marry Isabella Darrell (*bap.* 1655) of Kingsclere on 17 January 1684, but nothing more is known about this union.

Derham left Wargrave in 1689 when he became rector at Upminster, Essex, at £200 a year. For the rest of his life he lived at High House, a two-storeyed house 100 yards from the church. As a widower he married Anna Scott (*b. c.*1675) of Woolstan Hall, Chigwell, on 2 June 1699. They had five children: Anna (1700–1710), Elizabeth (1701–1780), William (1702–1757), Thomas (1704–1738), and Jane (1709–1735); William *Derham became president of St John's College, Oxford. On the accession of George I in 1714 Derham became chaplain to the prince of Wales, the future George II, who procured a canonry of Windsor for him in 1716, which obliged him to spend part of the year at Windsor. Derham always sailed a middle course in religion and did not play a part in the theological controversies of his times. The University of Oxford awarded him his degree of DD by diploma in June 1730.

Apart from his parochial duties Derham was also an amateur scientist interested in nature, mathematics, and philosophy. In 1696 he published *The Artificial Clockmaker: a*

Treatise of Watch and Clock-Work, which included a short history of horology. The treatise was translated into German (1708) and French (1731). Derham knew many of the leading scientists of his time, among them Isaac Newton and the astronomer Edmond Halley, and was himself elected to the Royal Society on 3 February 1703. He contributed thirty-eight articles to the society's *Philosophical Transactions* on a wide range of subjects, including meteorology, natural history (examples are the migration of birds, death-watch beetles, and wasps), and, in later years, astronomy. In one of these, published in 1733, he expressed an opposite view to that of Halley on the nature of nebulous objects. An example of Derham's practical scientific work can still be seen in the sundial, for which he did the calculations, attached to the Lincoln chapel of St George's Chapel in Windsor Castle. He was also interested in medicine and seems to have acted as a physician to his family and parishioners. He frequently asked Hans Sloane for medical advice.

In 1711 and 1712 Derham delivered the Boyle lectures at St Mary-le-Bow, London, in the spirit of Boyle's intention to refute anti-Christian philosophies by using natural history to promote and prove a natural theology. The lectures were subsequently published as *Physico-Theology, or, A Demonstration of the Being and Attributes of God from his Works of Creation* (1713). The book became a popular work on natural theology and was reprinted frequently (12th edn, 1754) and translated into several languages, among them Italian (1719), French (1726), and Dutch (1728). In 1715 he published another book on the same lines, his *Astro-Theology* (14th edn, 1777), which was also translated into several languages. He edited various books, among them Eleazer Albin's *Natural History of English Insects* (1724) and Robert Hooke's *Philosophical Experiments and Observations* (1726). He also edited works by his friend John Ray: his *Synopsis methodica avium et piscum* (1713), later editions of his *Wisdom of God* (1714), and the *Three Physico-Theological Discourses* (1713, 1721, and 1732), a book on the same subject as Derham's own Boyle lectures. He published some of Ray's correspondence as *Philosophical Letters* in 1718, and wrote a short biography that was published posthumously by George Scott, Derham's nephew-in-law, in *The Select Remains of the Learned John Ray* (1760).

According to the editors of the *Biographia Britannica*, who claimed to have received their information from his son William, Derham was a fairly tall, strong, healthy, and amiable man. He died on 5 April 1735 at his home, High House, in Upminster. He was buried at Upminster church; no memorial marks his grave. On 8 July of that same year probate was granted to his widow, to whom Derham left the remainder of his estate after bequeathing £1000 each to three of his children (Thomas had apparently already received his part of the inheritance). His books, instruments, and papers were left to his son William.

MARJA SMOLENAARS

Sources *Biographia Britannica, or, The lives of the most eminent persons who have flourished in Great Britain and Ireland*, 3 (1750) · A. D. Atkinson, 'William Derham', *Annals of Science*, 8 (1952), 368–92 · C. K.

Aked, 'William Derham and *The artificial clockmaker* [pts 1–3]', *Antiquarian Horology and the Proceedings of the Antiquarian Horological Society*, 6 (1968–70), 362–72, 416–27, 495–505 · Foster, *Alum. Oxon.*

Archives Essex RO, MSS · RS, letters to RS · U. Oxf., Taylor Institution, papers | BL, letters mainly to Sir Hans Sloane, Sloane MSS 4025–4053, *passim* · BL, Stowe MSS, letters

Likenesses J. Baker, engraving, RS; repro. in Aked, 'William Derham' · J. Green, line print, BM, NPG · R. K., portrait, Trinity College, Oxford · G. White, oils, RS · portrait, Bodl. Oxf.

Wealth at death over £3000; incl. £1000 each to three children; residue to wife: will, Essex RO, probate copy D/DA F56

Derham, William (1702–1757), college head, was born at Upminster, Essex, on 5 October 1702, the eldest son of William Derham (1657–1735), canon of Windsor, and his wife, Anna Scott (*b. c.*1675). He entered Merchant Taylors' School in 1714 and proceeded to St John's College, Oxford, in 1721, where he was elected a fellow in 1724. He graduated BA in 1725 and MA in 1729. He was junior proctor of the university in 1736, elected Whyte's professor of moral philosophy on 7 February 1737, and graduated BD the same year. He was ordained and made a DD in 1742, and in 1748 was elected president of St John's, where his income was supplemented by £120 p.a. as rector of Hanborough. His term of office was uneventful. He spent his leisure in making a neat transcript of the college's earlier records, which perhaps indicates a taste for antiquarian research. He died on 17 July 1757, and was buried in the college chapel, where his epitaph credits him with most of the virtues. He did not marry and bequeathed all of his estate to his mother. J. M. RIGG, rev. JOHN D. HAIGH

Sources C. J. Robinson, ed., *A register of the scholars admitted into Merchant Taylors' School, from AD 1562 to 1874*, 2 (1883), 40 · A. Wood, *The history and antiquities of the colleges and halls in the University of Oxford*, ed. J. Gutch (1786), 546, 559, 634 n. 10 · private information (1888) · Foster, *Alum. Oxon.* · J. Foster, *Oxford men and their colleges* (1893) · J. Chambers, *Biographical illustrations of Worcestershire* (1820) · *Hist. U. Oxf.* 5: *18th-cent. Oxf.*, 239, 860, 864 · will, PRO, PROB 11/833, fol. 117

Archives St John's College, Oxford, notes and lectures on ethics

Dering, Edward (c.1540–1576), Church of England clergyman and evangelical preacher, was the third son of John Dering of Surrenden Dering, Kent, and of Margaret, daughter of John Brent of Charing in the same county.

Early career The Derings were an ancient family, predating the conquest. The seventeenth-century MP and antiquary Sir Edward *Dering, first baronet (1598–1644), was a great-nephew of Dering, and named for him. Dering entered Christ's College, Cambridge, and commenced BA in 1560, and MA in 1563. He took his BTh in 1568 and was expected to proceed to the doctorate. He was a fellow of Christ's from 1560 to 1570, and ordained deacon by Bishop Cox of Ely in 1561. There is no record of his ordination to the priesthood.

Dering laid the foundations for a notable ecclesiastical career. He gained a reputation as a Greek scholar—'the greatest learned man (so thought) in England', Archbishop Parker later caustically recalled (Bruce and Perowne, 410)—and he was chosen to make the Greek oration on the occasion of Queen Elizabeth's visit to the university in 1564. In 1566 he was proctor, and in 1567 Lady Margaret preacher. Dering spent time in Archbishop Parker's

household, perhaps as a chaplain, and in 1567 Parker collated him to the rectory of Pluckley, which included his family seat of Surrenden Dering. He was non-resident, and it is not clear that his curate was licensed to preach. Later a different and perhaps converted Dering would condemn the life which he himself had led: 'While they are clothed in scarlet, ther flockes perishe for colde; and while they fare deliciouslie, ther people are faint with a most miserable hunger' (BL, Lansdowne MS 12, fols. 190–191v). Meanwhile, Dering was chaplain to England's premier nobleman, Thomas Howard, fourth duke of Norfolk, and held another chaplaincy in the Tower of London. The greater preferments which might have followed were not altogether absent from his mind. He told Burghley that he was well known in Cambridge, in London, and at court. He was disappointed when Parker passed him over for the profitable peculiar of Bocking in Essex: 'If my necessarie wants were supplyed, I wold not desire great things ...; if that had byn bestowed upon me, it should not have bene unwillinglie accepted' (BL, Stowe MS 743/1, fols. 1–2).

Administering reproofs That was in 1570, a year which seems to have been marked by a moral climacteric, which may have been connected with the radical presbyterian lectures delivered by Thomas Cartwright in the spring of that year, or with some deterioration in his own health, or with the downfall of his master, the duke of Norfolk. In 1572 Dering would write to the duke as he awaited execution, regretting that his 'high calling' had caused him to bridle his words in taking him to task for his wicked servants, popish friends, and 'your adulterous woman'. (Was this Mary, queen of Scots?) 'Why should I have tarried in your Lordship's house except these things had bin amended?' (Dering, 'Certaine godly and comfortable letters', *Workes*, 1597, sigs. D3–E2v). At the very end, Dering wrote to Norfolk as to his 'Christian brother'. Dering's tongue was not bridled when he read the book to the Kentish magnate Henry Neville, sixth Lord Abergavenny, whom he described as 'a lothesome example ... an evell man'; 'I love you in the Lorde and therfore I speak so playne' (Kent Archives Office, MS Dering C1/2). In March 1570 he resigned Pluckley and decided to unbridle his tongue to none other than William Cecil, Lord Burghley, and to Archbishop Parker. Burghley was charged with maladministration of the university of which he was chancellor. Parker was reprimanded for the lax administration of his province and for the religious condition of Kent, in which only two parishes out of six hundred enjoyed adequate instruction. He was also rebuked for swearing, and for allowing his sons and retainers to wear 'monstrous great breeches' (BL, Stowe MS 743/1, fols. 1–2).

As if this was not to burn bridges enough, Dering took the queen herself to task in the most outspoken Lenten sermon she ever heard. This should have presented a decisive career opportunity. Instead, Dering held Elizabeth personally responsible for the deplorable state of the ministry of her church:

> And yet you in the meane while that all these whordoms are committed, you at whose hands God will require it, you sit still and are carelesse, let men doe as they list. It toucheth

not belike your common wealth, and therfore you are so well contented to let all alone. (*Derings Workes*, 27)

No Elizabethan sermon was more often reprinted, with sixteen editions by the year of Elizabeth's death, 1603, sponsored, it appears, by John Field. As for its repercussions, Dering later told the queen that it was 'a great many yeeres ..., and they have passed exceeding slowlie' since he first heard how much she misliked him (*Derings Workes*, sigs. *1–3). What did he expect?

Puritan spokesman Clearly Dering was now some kind of puritan, if he had not been one before, and Christ's was a college which bred puritans, but it may be asked, what kind of puritan? In 1568, in a book written in defence of Bishop John Jewel and against the Catholic Thomas Harding, he wrote: 'Our service is good and godly, everie tittle grounded on holie scriptures' (Dering, *A Sparing Restraint*, pt 1.5). He claimed to have always been a conformist, and he told Burghley: 'I have never broken the peace of the Churche, nether for cappe nor surplesse, for archbyshop nor byshop.' He was critical of Cartwright for standing 'so stiffly' on indifferent matters. But he defended the nonconformist conscience. There was a proverb that the man who had been struck with the sword was afraid of the scabbard. Burghley was told: 'I would yow had seene the horror of sinne; I am sure yow woold also be afrayde of the shadow' (BL, Lansdowne MS 12, fols. 190–191v). Ceremonies and ecclesiastical dignities were shadows of the sin and corruption which were eating out the heart of the church. But Dering's own puritanism was a limitless concern with the substance of sin and with its remedy, preaching of the gospel. He was unique in insisting, in an unpublished treatise, 'Of the viseble Church, how it may be known' (CKS, MS Dering U 350, C1/2), written by Archbishop Parker's commission against Nicholas Sander's *De visibili monarchia ecclesiae*, that preaching was an essential mark of the church. The preacher was nothing less than 'the minister by whom the people doe beleeve' (Edward Dering and John More, 'A briefe and necessarie catechisme', *Derings Workes*, sig. A3). This conviction enforced the jettisoning of worldly learning, and Dering condemned so-called preachers who 'use the pulpit like a philosopher's chaire' (Dering, 'XXVII lectures or readinges upon part of the epistle written to the Hebrues', ibid., sig. T5v). Parker thought that such sentiments contained 'too much childishness' (Bruce and Perowne, 409–10).

Dering might have defined himself as a mere Christian, but he could not escape the ecclesiastical storm which struck in the early 1570s, with Cartwrightian presbyterianism popularized in the *Admonition to the Parliament* published by John Field and Thomas Wilcox. Dering was compromised when he visited Field and Wilcox in prison. But Bishop Edwin Sandys of London either still approved of Dering or found it expedient to seem to, and in 1572, the year of the *Admonition*, he appointed him reader of the divinity lecture in St Paul's Cathedral. At about the same time Dering secured (nominally from the crown) the prebend of Chardstock in Salisbury Cathedral. At St Paul's he delivered a celebrated course of lectures on the epistle to the Hebrews and enjoyed a huge reputation; not only with those whom in a dedicatory epistle he called 'the godly in London' but also with such patrons as Henry Killigrew and Catherine his wife, Burghley's sister-in-law, and the earl of Leicester. But the most popular preacher of the day was not popular with the queen. There followed a curious series of judicial charades, one of them conducted in Star Chamber, in which bishops and privy councillors vied with each other in trying not to seem to be Dering's accusers. Burghley and Sandys fell out over Dering. On 28 June 1573 the privy council ruled that Dering could continue his lectures, but a month later ordered him to 'surcease'. Eventually, according to Dering himself, he was 'forbidden to preach any more openly' in her majesty's dominions (Dering, 'A sermon preached before the queenes maiestie', *Derings Workes*, sig. *). Yet a full year later Archbishop Parker was told that the queen 'disliked Deering's reading' (Bruce and Perowne, 476). In February 1575 there was a plan for Dering to succeed Thomas Sampson as the Clothworkers' lecturer at Whittington College, but it seems to have failed.

Through all these almost comic proceedings, Dering dealt with the burning issue of hierarchy like a vegetarian who occasionally eats meat. Jocular words spoken at a dinner party about Parker being the last archbishop of Canterbury were uttered 'merrily', although much was made of them. Dering declared that he loved the bishops as brethren and honoured them as elders, but confessed that he would not have chosen to be a bishop himself. His chequered, but for the most part protected, career is striking evidence of the powerlessness of the bishops, and even of the queen, to suppress a preacher who enjoyed the support of the great and the good in court, country, and city.

Marriage, death, and afterlife In 1572 Dering married Anne *Locke (*née* Vaughan, later Prowse), a wealthy city widow who, of all the many female friends of the Scottish reformer John Knox, had most equally matched the latter in intellect. Dering's letter of proposal to this 'good possession' (Dering to Mrs Locke, n.d., Kent Archives Office, MS Dering C1/2) is surely the earliest surviving document of its kind to have been penned by a clergyman of the Church of England. To Mrs Locke, Dering must have seemed to be Knox reborn, a point which also occurred to John Field, who later stretched propriety in obtaining from Dering's widow and sending to the printer works by both Knox and Dering. But Anne Dering had to share her husband with many other ladies who depended on him for spiritual sustenance, among them Mrs Killigrew and the formidable Kentish matriarch and religious depressive Mrs Mary Honywood. Fourteen spiritual letters from Dering to women friends survive, notable examples of a distinct literary and religious genre, and about 1590 most of them were printed by Richard Schilders in Middelburg as *Certaine Godly and Verie Comfortable Letters, Full of Christian Consolation*. The women responded with reciprocal ministrations to a man who was by now in the late stages of pulmonary tuberculosis. He told Mrs Killigrew:

I weigh not all the world a feather, and with as glad a minde I spit blood (I trust) as cleare spittle. To those that love God all things are for the best. He hath a hard hart that beleeveth not this. (Dering, 'Certaine godly and comfortable letters', *Derings Workes*, sig. C4)

Dering died on 26 June 1576 at Thobie Priory in Essex, in a stylized deathbed scene, surrounded by preachers and others who recorded his last words.

Dering's affecting and early death helped to make him a living legend, a mirror of exemplary godliness and evangelical ardour. He was one of the first godly divines to have his collected works posthumously published. It is possible to infer from a letter to his widow that John Field was primarily responsible. The works consisted of set-piece sermons, including the sermon before the queen, the lectures on Hebrews, collections of prayers and of letters, and a catechism, jointly written with his Christ's contemporary John More, the 'apostle' of Norwich, which achieved as a separate publication and in two versions at least forty-two editions. The almost clandestine 1590 Schilders edition of the *Workes* was succeeded by the more respectable and enlarged London editions of 1597 and 1614, an indication of how far the religious spirit of Elizabethan puritanism came to be accommodated within the Jacobean church. Dering's engraved portrait appeared in Henry Holland's *Herōologia Anglica* (1620) and Thomas Fuller included his deathbed speeches in *Abel redevivus* (1652). PATRICK COLLINSON

Sources R. Hovenden, ed., *The visitation of Kent, taken in the years 1619–1621*, Harleian Society, 42 (1898) · P. Collinson, *A mirror of Elizabethan puritanism: the life and letters of godly Master Dering* (1964); repr. in P. Collinson, *Godly people: essays on English protestantism and puritanism* (1983), 288–324 · M. Derings workes: more at large than euer hath heere-to-fore been printed in any one volume (1614) · E. Dering, *A sparing restraint of many lauishe vntruthes, which M. doctor Harding dothe chalenge* (1568) · E. Dering, 'Of the viseble Churche, how it may be known', CKS, MS Dering U 350 C1/2 · E. Dering, letters, CKS, MS Dering U 350 C/1, 2 · E. Dering, *Certaine godly and verie comfortable letters, full of Christian consolation* (1590?) · BL, Lansdowne MS 12, fols. 98, 190–191v · BL, Lansdowne MS 15, fols. 154–5 · BL, Lansdowne MS 17, fols. 195, 197–200v · BL, Lansdowne MS 19, fol. 161 · BL, Stowe MS 743/1, fols. 1–2 · *The works of John Knox*, ed. D. Laing, 6 vols., Bannatyne Club, 112 (1846–64), vol. 4, pp. 92–3 · BL, Harl. MS 6992, fol. 21 · Cooper, *Ath. Cantab.*, 1.354–7 · *APC*, 1571–5 · *Correspondence of Matthew Parker*, ed. J. Bruce and T. T. Perowne, Parker Society, 42 (1853) · Venn, *Alum. Cant.*, 1/2.36 · *DNB*

Archives CKS, letter-books, U 350 C1/2

Likenesses Passe, line engraving, BM, NPG; repro. in H. Holland, *Herōologia Anglica* (1620)

Dering, Sir Edward, first baronet (1598–1644), antiquary and religious controversialist, was born on 28 January 1598, and baptized on 9 February, the eldest son of Sir Anthony Dering (1557/8–1636), landowner and JP, of Surrenden Dering in Pluckley, Kent, and his second wife, Frances (1577–1657), daughter of Robert Bell. He was born in the Tower of London, where his father may have been acting as deputy for his mother's stepfather, who was lieutenant of the Tower. Dering was apparently educated at Westminster School, and was a fellow-commoner of Magdalene College, Cambridge, from January 1615 to September 1617 (typically for one of his social station, he did not proceed to a degree); he was admitted to the Middle Temple on 23 October 1617. He paid a very brief visit to Calais

Sir Edward Dering, first baronet (1598–1644), by Cornelius Johnson, 1630s?

and Gravelines in 1620 and he visited a cousin in Ireland in 1621.

Aspiring courtier, 1619–c.1635, and local governor, c.1625–1640 Dering's father enjoyed the patronage of his relative Edward, first Lord Wotton, and it may have been through friendship with the Wottons that Edward was introduced to the court: in January 1619, suggestively close to his twenty-first birthday, he was, as he recorded in one of his notebooks, 'knighted at Newmarket through the meanes and favor of the Marquesse of Buckingham' (Bodl. Oxf., MS Gough Kent 20, p. 4). His first marriage, on 25 November 1619, to Elizabeth (1602–1622), daughter of a Kentish neighbour, Sir Nicholas Tufton, the future first earl of Thanet, may have strengthened his links with the court. Certainly Dering's second marriage, following his first wife's early death, to Anne Ashburnham (1604/5–1628), is evidence both of his continued ambition and of his success in attaching himself directly to the circle around the duke of Buckingham. The marriage took place on 1 January 1625 in Buckingham's lodgings at Whitehall; Anne's mother was a destitute widow, but she was related to the duke, and Dering accepted Anne without any marriage portion on the understanding that her mother would use her connections to his advantage. In May 1625 Dering travelled to Boulogne in the company of Buckingham's mother and elder brother, presumably in the hope of meeting Charles I's queen, whom the favourite was escorting from France, although Dering returned to England before the queen set sail.

In 1625 Dering was returned to parliament as a member for the Cinque Port of Hythe in Kent—Buckingham had become lord warden of the Cinque Ports in 1624 and, although Dering was not Buckingham's nominee, his connections with the favourite were invoked on his behalf in the election; the backing of Buckingham and of other courtiers was obtained for Dering's unsuccessful attempts to find a parliamentary seat in 1626 and in 1628. On 1 February 1627 Dering became the fifth baronet to be created by Charles I, something in which his mother-in-law claimed to have been instrumental. It was also in early 1627 that Dering took the oath of a gentleman-extraordinary of the king's privy chamber. This was not a position of great importance, although it gave him access at court. The only office of potential profit that Dering obtained was the lieutenancy of Dover Castle in Kent, effectively the post of local deputy to the lord warden of the Cinque Ports, which had been held by a Dering in the early sixteenth century. Sir Edward enjoyed Buckingham's support in his efforts to gain the lieutenancy, although the favourite was killed while Dering was negotiating for the post and he had to pay the existing holder in order to obtain the office, which he finally entered in March 1629. In practice the lieutenancy proved both frustrating and unprofitable; although Dering continued to enjoy the support of courtiers, in particular the earl of Dorset after Buckingham's death, he was to claim in 1635 that he 'was never gratified or benefitted by anie of the greate friends and kindred' of Anne Ashburnham's mother, as had been promised at the time of his marriage (PRO, C2/Charles I/D.31/40). In 1634–5 he left the lieutenancy; although he remained active in local government until 1640, he wrote in the mid-1630s that 'the circumference which a Statesman must fill, is a larger Orbe then my ambition doth stretch unto … so (beside proteccion generally due to all subjectes) I have no neede of the State' (Folger Shakespeare Library, V.b.307, p. 71). Dering's court connections fade into the background in the later 1630s; he declined a summons to attend the king at York during the first bishops' war and his name does not feature among the extraordinary gentlemen of the privy chamber listed in the household establishment of 1641, perhaps as a result of this.

Dering's motivation for the pursuit of office was probably in part financial: when he declared that he had 'no neede of the State', he added the rider that 'my fortunes are not now to make' (Folger Shakespeare Library, V.b.307, p. 71). Although his father had already transferred some of the family estate to him, he had been over £1400 in debt in midsummer 1629, just after assuming the lieutenancy of Dover Castle. Following his second wife's death in 1628 he had again sought a profitable marriage, albeit this time by the more conventional means of courting a wealthy widow. The possibility of increasing his income from office may therefore have been important for Dering in 1628–9. Indeed, it is less clear why he felt that his finances were more secure in the mid-1630s. When he did remarry, on 16 July 1629, it was to Unton Gibbes (d. 1676), the daughter of a Warwickshire gentry family, who brought a portion of £2000, but he appears to have inherited a debt of some £3000 on his father's death in 1636, and net sales of

land in 1636–8 were necessary in order to reduce his debts to just over £1000 by May 1638, although this situation did not prevent him rebuilding the family seat.

Even in the later 1620s, while pursuing his court career, Dering took his duties as a magistrate and as a militia officer seriously. His court connections had enabled him to succeed his father as a JP in 1626 while retaining his father's precedence on the bench. Dering became notorious in Kent for his zeal in response to the commissions issued in 1630–31 to compound for failure to take up knighthood and he was said to have ensured the success of ship money in the county, probably as a result of his contributions at the initial rating meeting. Yet Dering was not undiscriminating in the implementation of central initiatives in the localities: for example, he appears to have connived at the Cinque Ports' petition for exemption from the knighthood compositions. Indeed, in his conduct as a magistrate and as lieutenant of Dover Castle there are signs of religious preoccupations which would also be evident in his later career as a member of the Long Parliament and the hope of promoting them may even have played a part in his pursuit of office. His anti-Catholicism is apparent in his activity as a JP while, as lieutenant, he sought to tighten the regulation of Roman Catholics passing to and from the continent. However, Sir Roger Twysden recalled that Dering had once wondered whether a 'Puritane' (by which Dering probably meant separatist) was more likely to be saved than a 'papist' (BL, Stowe MS 184, fol. 10), and Dering's opposition to separatism is also evident both in his conduct as a JP and in his denunciation of separatists at Dover in his capacity as lieutenant.

Antiquarianism and theology, c.1625–1640 Another concern apparent in Dering's later career, his antiquarian interests, was also present in the later 1620s, and also interacted with his connections at court. It was by Buckingham's 'especiall favor' that Dering obtained in 1627 a warrant authorizing him to consult public records without paying any fees (CKS, U.1107, Z.3). It may have been envisaged that Dering would apply his antiquarian researches to political questions on Buckingham's behalf, in the way that, for example, Sir Robert Cotton had done on behalf of the earl of Northampton earlier in the century. Dering's extensive collections and compilations of records were concerned, however, with the more limited spheres of his county and his family. In 1638 Dering formed an association with three other antiquaries (William Dugdale, Sir Christopher Hatton, and Sir Thomas Shirley), called Antiquitas Rediviva; the members were to collect 'all memorable notes for historicall illustration of this kingdome', but 'especially' those concerning the four counties in which they resided (Larking, 'Antiquaries', 5). However, the only connected historical writings to survive from the 1630s are drafts of the preface to, and of some early entries in, a history of the Dering family. Dugdale described Dering as 'an excellent Antiquarye' (Wright, 373); in recognizing the importance of mastering Old English, Dering was in tune with leading scholars of his generation. Yet he also adjusted names on documents in his collection in order to support his claims for the antiquity and importance of his family; Dering may have seen himself as reconstructing what must once have existed, for he alleged that an antiquary employed by his father had stolen many family records.

Dering had other interests in the mid-1630s: apart from his rebuilding of Surrenden Dering, he interested himself in garden design and he apparently remained interested in drama (he had earlier produced a shortened version of Shakespeare's *Henry IV* for private performance). However, according to his son Sir Edward *Dering, Dering 'wholly addicted himself' to 'the study of Divinity' from the late 1630s onward (CKS, U.1107, Z.3). He became involved in 1639–40 in controversy with the Carmelite Thomas Doughty (Father Simon Stock), at least in part as a result of attempts to convert Roman Catholic acquaintances, one of them a recent convert. Two of Dering's polemical works were later published (*The Foure Cardinall-Vertues of a Carmelite-Fryar*, 1641; *A Discourse of Proper Sacrifice*, 1644). Dering made some use of his knowledge of English history to expose the novelty of papist doctrines, although this was far from being the principal source for his arguments, in which the church fathers figured largely. He appears to have come to believe, in the course of his theological researches, that Church of England divines such as Peter Heylyn and John Pocklington were expounding views that were indistinguishable from popery, especially on the sacrament of the eucharist; the publication with official sanction of 'Libelling Pamphlets against true Religion' would become a major plank of Dering's argument against the ecclesiastical hierarchy in the Long Parliament (Dering, *Speeches*, 13).

Dering wrote, with regard to the Short Parliament election in the spring of 1640, that 'in times so desperate I would contribute no help to any privy councillor or deputy lieutenant' (Jessup, 2). There can be little doubt that Dering's perception of popish tendencies in the church contributed to this conviction and fed, in turn, into his dogged pursuit of one of the seats for Kent in both of the 1640 elections, unsuccessfully in the spring but successfully in the election for the Long Parliament. In the spring he pursued the parliamentary seat despite warnings that his opposition to the privy councillor Sir Henry Vane was badly taken at court; his wife was able to remind him that his candidature for the Long Parliament had been 'only assumed for God's Glory' (CKS, U.350, C.2/82).

The Long Parliament and the church, 1640–1642 Dering's election to the Long Parliament opened the most conspicuous phase of his career; as Dering himself later put it, his first speech, which presented the petition of a deprived Kentish minister and denounced Archbishop Laud as the 'Center' of 'our miseries' (Dering, *Speeches*, 11), 'did beget me … many new friends' (ibid., 162). His speech on 23 November 1640 complaining of the authorization of crypto-popish publications was followed by his nomination to the chair of a subcommittee (later a committee in its own right) to deal with ministers' grievances and the licensing of books. Numerous manuscript copies of his early speeches survive, and some were published as 'separates', before Dering produced his own editions. Even a

hostile contemporary admired Dering's oratory and he appears by May 1641 to have become an important member of the Commons. In addition to his speeches on ecclesiastical matters he made several procedural motions, including an important and successful one in May 1641 for a committee to determine what matters should be brought to a conclusion before the recess. It is not surprising, therefore, that Sir Arthur Hesilrige placed the root and branch bill for the abolition of episcopacy in Dering's hands on 27 May 1641, prompting Dering to introduce the bill.

However, the alliance between Dering and the leading supporters of root and branch proved short-lived. On 21 June, Dering launched a scheme to replace the existing bishops with a new structure under which the ecclesiastical affairs of each shire would be managed by a presbytery, in each of which a 'moderatour' or 'President' would be established (Bodl. Oxf., Rawlinson MS D1099, fol. 80v; BL, Harley MS 5047, fol. 30). Although he was almost certainly propounding the 'constant presidents' whom he would describe as bishops when he published the speech in 1642, contemporary diarists did not interpret the speech as a plea for episcopacy, and Dering would claim in 1642 that his intention had been to encourage the 'rooters' and the would-be reformers of episcopacy to coalesce around a model of what would replace the existing hierarchy. However, if this was his intention, he was unsuccessful; the question of what would replace the existing hierarchy was postponed in favour of a plan to put ecclesiastical government into the hands of interim commissioners.

Dering left the Commons in early August and did not return until after the recess. The reasons for this absence may well not have been political: attendance at Westminster kept him away from his estates, from his library, and from his wife, to whom he complained that he might not have patience to sit the session out as early as May 1641. What is certain is that after the recess Dering adopted an openly partisan position. On 21 October 1641 he impugned the force of the orders that the Commons had issued on religious matters prior to the recess. He was aware of feeling in Kent on this issue, but he probably realized that his speech would touch a raw nerve in some quarters: Henry Marten suggested that Dering should withdraw while the offence given by his remarks was considered. In November, Dering attacked the content of the grand remonstrance and, indeed, the very principle of a document addressed by the Commons to the people rather than to the king. Furthermore, in January 1642 he took the step of publishing a collection of his speeches in the Long Parliament, in vindication of his own conduct, but also as a condemnation of the factionalism of others. While bemoaning others' partisanship, he depicted his opponents in the blackest of terms: he alleged that one member of the Commons had told him privately that he wished to 'bring the Lords down into our House' (Dering, *Speeches*, 166). Dering spoke as the voice of 'moderation' (ibid.), but his political tactics were far from moderate. The result was, on 2 February 1642, the condemnation of

Dering's published speeches, which were ordered by the Commons to be burnt by the common hangman, and his own expulsion from the Commons; on a division he was sent to the Tower, where he remained until discharged on his own petition on 11 February.

Dering's opposition to the grand remonstrance brought him into line with future royalists such as John Colepeper, Edward Hyde, and Lucius Cary, Viscount Falkland, with whom he had disagreed on ecclesiastical matters before the recess, but his views on episcopacy still did not accord with theirs. By January 1642 Dering was certainly using the word 'bishop' to describe the 'constant presidents' he favoured, and he had slightly softened some of the presbyterian aspects of his proposals; his views on the relative roles of the laity and of the clergy in determining religious matters had shifted somewhat in favour of the clergy. However, he was still propounding the extirpation of the existing bishops and their replacement by county-based sees in which bishops would be assisted by presbyteries. According to one critic, Dering was no better than a presbyterian. Indeed, Dering may have felt himself to be isolated in the Commons: he was nominated to barely any committees in November and December 1641. This may explain his decision to make an appeal to opinion outside the house by publishing his speeches, thus doing exactly what he had condemned in the grand remonstrance.

The part that Dering took in the drafting of the Kentish petition of March 1642 perhaps reflects a realization that to have an impact politically he would have to identify more closely with the more conservative defenders of episcopacy. He now became involved with a petition that asked, not that episcopacy should be uprooted and replanted, but merely that it should be 'preserved'. The petition's assertive defence of the prayer book— 'celebrious by the Piety of holy Bishops and Martyrs who composed it'—contrasts with Dering's sponsorship in late 1641 of a petition which, while defending the prayer book, had entertained its 'severe Reformation' (Woods, 141–2; Larking, *Proceedings*, 61). Contemporaries described the March 1642 petition as Dering's, although they probably exaggerated his importance in its making on account of his existing notoriety. None the less his involvement with this petition identified him with the royalist side of (and, indeed, exacerbated) the paper war being conducted between the king and his advisers on the one hand, and the two houses at Westminster on the other. Furthermore, by linking together the question of ecclesiastical government and the dispute over control of the militia, the petition reflects a process (first apparent in Dering's condemnation of the Commons' orders on religious questions) by which, in order to defend his ecclesiastical ideals, Dering adopted constitutional positions at variance with the majority in the Commons. It was on these constitutional positions, rather than on ecclesiastical matters, that the Commons dwelt in the impeachment drawn up against Dering in April 1642.

Dering was, therefore, as contemporaries argued, inconsistent. Yet underlying his shifting proposals for church government was surely his desire to see proper order restored to the church as soon as possible: he had written in May 1641 of 'the necessity of composing the state and church in those things wherein [the Commons] had (upon just groundes) disjoynted them' (Larking, *Proceedings*, 47). In part this 'necessity of composing' resulted from the radicalism apparent both in London and in Kent following the collapse of ecclesiastical authority in 1640–41. However, Dering did show throughout his career a concern for a uniform church with a set liturgy: as has been seen, he had opposed separatism in Kent prior to 1640 and he had also seen the Church of England's 'devout and pious' liturgy as a point in its favour when combating popery (CKS, U.2479, Z.1); in 1640 he removed attacks on the liturgy from the Kentish petition against episcopacy before presenting it to the Commons; though he supported, in 1641, reform of the prayer book, he could still, in his *Collection of Speeches*, praise Laud's 'intent of publike uniformity', while accepting that 'in the way of his pursuit thereof he was extreamly faulty' (p. 4). The retention of a set liturgy was more important to Dering than the precise nature of ecclesiastical government; no form of government had a *jure divino* claim, he argued, and, in proposing the root and branch bill, he argued that it was necessary because the hierarchy was incapable of reform (not because it was essential, on principle, to return the church to a primitive state)—indeed, his later claim that his chief purpose in introducing the bill was to expedite the bill against the bishops' secular jurisdiction may have some foundation.

By early 1642 Dering appears to have had little confidence in the parliamentary leaders' ability to establish a speedy settlement in the church, or even in the sincerity of their professions on the matter, studiedly moderate though these were in late 1641 and early 1642. In forming this judgement he may have been influenced by his involvement in the unsuccessful attempt to condemn Henry Burton's radical *Protestation Protested*, which was reportedly blocked in committee by a number of leading supporters of root and branch. In contrast, Dering was aware that his views were finding a ready ear at court, through the agency of one of his Ashburnham relatives; a copy of his collected speeches was given to the king, who was reported to have smiled at the preface and conclusion of the work. In such a context the king's efforts in late 1641 and early 1642 to claim the middle ground by dissociating himself from the religious policies of the 1630s must have seemed convincing to Dering. Dering could see no grounds for the fear of popish plotting which both energized and held together the parliamentary leadership in late 1641 and early 1642: as the Commons took measures to defend themselves in January 1642, following the attempted arrest of the five members, Dering complained that they had voted a guard 'against no enemy'; he thought that the king intended 'to pursue the five gentlemen in a legal way' (Larking, *Proceedings*, 69, xliii).

Summer 1642 – June 1644 Following the affair of the Kentish petition in March 1642, Dering was summoned before the Commons but slipped away and returned to Kent. Unsurprisingly after his role in the March petition, he was placed by the king on the commission of array for Kent, and his later claim that his move toward active royalism was reluctant may be called into question by reports that he had undertaken a 'circuit' to raise support for it (N. Payne, *A True Relation of a Brave Exploit Performed by Captain Richard Dawks*, 1642, 7). Both Dering and his eldest son were with the king when the royal standard was raised at Nottingham. None the less, Dering sought a rapprochement with the two houses at Westminster in October 1642: a 'Mr P.' (who may have been Pym, but was perhaps Purefoy) was said to be 'much joyed' by Dering's approaches (CKS, U.350, C.2/99), but the existence of earlier votes of delinquency against Dering was deemed to necessitate some formal submission from him, and perhaps he baulked at making this. None the less, it was apparently only in July 1643 that Dering was commissioned to raise a regiment for the king and, if a later account is to be trusted, he resigned his commission the following November. Military activity may have been less uncongenial to him than has been supposed, as there are signs that he had been an enthusiastic militia officer in the 1620s, and he had his portrait painted in armour against a military background, probably in the 1630s; but allegations that he encouraged a royalist drive towards Kent, promising a rising in the county in response, should probably be treated with caution.

The circumstances of Dering's final defection from royalism at the beginning of 1644 are confused. He was widely reported to be among the royalists besieged from December 1643 to January 1644 in Arundel Castle, but he escaped before the castle fell and appears to have returned to the court at Oxford. Newsletters reported that articles were being drawn up against him there, but Dering himself alleged that he was thought at Oxford to be the least likely person to defect. What is certain is that Dering had contacts who gave him advance notice of the declaration of both kingdoms; on 7 February he became the first person to petition the Commons at Westminster for a pardon according to its terms.

Dering's petition exists in two somewhat differing printed versions, one of them published with some additional remarks at the behest of the Kent county committee, which insisted that Dering produce it to 'satisfie the vulger' whom he had 'misled' (BL, Stowe MS 184, fol. 73). The explanations of Dering's decision to make his peace with the parliament which these publications contained related partly to recent events: he claimed, for example, that he was scandalized by the king's attempt to assemble a parliament at Oxford; he also pointed to the 'cessation' in September 1643 between the king and the Irish rebels, explaining that the popish plot was now 'explicited unto me' (Dering, *Declaration*, 8, 9). Experience of religious services at Oxford may explain the complaints that he subjoined to the petition, which are not anticipated in his earlier writings, about the excessive use of music in church services, although the very general terms in which he denounced the royalist clergy's love of 'externall pomp' (ibid., 11) contrast somewhat with his more discriminating treatment of ceremonial matters in 1642;

Dering's tone in 1644 was probably somewhat adapted to his parliamentarian audience. Yet continuity with his earlier views is definitely apparent in his complaint against the continuing attachment of some clergy around the king to hierarchy. In 1641 Dering had found that he had common ground with the 'rooters' in his desire to remove the existing hierarchy, but that this common ground was insufficient to sustain agreement on how the church should be rebuilt; by the end of 1643 he had discovered, it appears, that the common ground of support for liturgy and episcopacy (broadly understood) was insufficient to enable him to live in the royalist camp.

Yet Dering's writings in 1644 were not simply a denunciation of the royalists. There was a warning for the houses at Westminster that if the conflict were continued it might end in military tyranny. Dering's insistence that the king should return to London, but that this should be arranged in a way that would be honourable to the king, may also have contained an implied call for greater moderation at Westminster. Indeed, hostile observers said that Dering had left Oxford simply because the king had refused to give him office. They were probably right that Dering's departure from Oxford is not to be explained simply in ideological terms. As on previous occasions in his career, separation from his wife and family may have been a factor in his behaviour, especially as Dering was already in pain from an 'imposthume in his head' (possibly a brain tumour), which proved fatal on 22 June 1644 (*Diaries*, 109).

Dering had spent the preceding months in conflict with the county committee over the sequestration of his estate. According to tradition he died in extreme poverty on a farmhouse on his estate; his correspondence in his last months certainly alleges poverty, but is dated from Surrenden Dering, and presumably he died there. He appears to have died intestate (although his widow alleged that a will had been concealed); he was buried in St Nicholas's Church, Pluckley. His fine was finally fixed by the Commons on 27 July and his heir, Edward, was able to obtain the remission of the fine and the discharge of the estate in the following month. Edward was a child of Dering's second marriage, a son of Elizabeth Tufton's having died in 1634. However, Dering's third marriage, to Unton Gibbes, had been one of great mutual affection (he once called her 'my most comfortable Numpes' (Larking, *Proceedings*, 55); Dering had settled on her a life interest in the family seat and made generous provision for the sons born of his marriage to her.

Reputation Dering's final defection to the protection of the parliament ensured that he was harshly treated by royalist writers: Clarendon called him 'a man of levity and vanity' (Clarendon, *Hist. rebellion*, 1.314). The incumbent at Pluckley, during a dispute with Dering in the 1630s, allegedly called him 'the proudest man in the world' (CKS, U.350, Q.1). Yet such judgements, especially those made in the light of Dering's 'defections' in 1641–2 and 1644, should not obscure the extent of Dering's reputation in mid-1641; in May he wrote to his wife of being shaken by the hand by 'many ... whom I knew not; many said to one another "There goes Sir Edward Dering"' (Larking, *Proceedings*, 47–8). Furthermore, even at the end of his career some parliamentarian writers thought it worth trying to rehabilitate his reputation, in order to claim the defection of a man of 'singular Wit and Learning', as evidence of the frustration felt by the 'moderate partie about the King' (*Mercurius Anglicus*, 1, 31 Jan–7 Feb 1644, 5; *A Declaration wherein is Full Satisfaction Given Concerning Sir Edward Deering*, 1644, sig. A2v).

Recent writers have emphasized Dering's connections with Kentish opinion, seeing him as driven by 'service to the county and its desire for moderation' (A. Everitt, *The Community of Kent and the Great Rebellion, 1640–60*, 1966, 207; cf. Hirst). Yet what is perhaps most striking about Dering's career is the range of his connections and interests; thanks to his concern to record (and often to justify) his own life, and the survival of so many of his papers, it is possible to trace not only Dering's relationships with the gentry and clergy of Kent, but also how those relationships intermeshed with his theological and antiquarian researches, and with his links to the court. Dering's career—eccentric though its particular course may have been—can therefore provide useful insights into the world of the early and mid-seventeenth-century political élite.   S. P. SALT

Sources CKS, Dering papers, U.133, U.275, U.350, U.570, U.1107, U.1256, U.1311, U.1364, U.1551, U.2479 · Canterbury consistory court act book, 1641–63, CKS, PRC 22/19, fol. 66v · BL, Dering letters, Stowe MSS 184, 743–744 · Dering notes and papers, Folger, V.b.97, V.b.296–7, V.b.307, X.d.488, Z.e.27 · L. B. Larking, ed., *Proceedings principally in the county of Kent in connection with the parliaments called in 1640, and especially with the committee of religion appointed in that year*, CS, old ser., 80 (1862) · E. Dering, *A collection of speeches ... in matter of religion* (1642) · E. Dering, *A declaration by Sir Edward Dering ... with his petition to the honourable House of Commons* (1644) · Gough's notes from a Dering memorandum book, Bodl. Oxf., MS Gough Kent 20 · *The diaries and papers of Sir Edward Dering, second baronet, 1644 to 1684*, ed. M. F. Bond (1976), 108–9 [incl. genealogical table by P. H. Blake] · F. W. Jessup, 'The Kentish election of March 1640', *Archaeologia Cantiana*, 86 (1971), 1–10 [prints Dering's narrative from Bodl. Oxf., MS Top. Kent e. 6] · T. P. S. Woods, *Prelude to civil war, 1642: Mr Justice Malet and the Kentish petitions* (1980) · D. Hirst, 'The defection of Sir Edward Dering, 1640–1641', *HJ*, 15 (1972), 193–208 · C. E. Wright, 'Sir Edward Dering: a seventeenth-century antiquary and his "Saxon" charters', *The early cultures of north-west Europe*, ed. C. Fox and B. Dickins (1950), 369–93 · L. B. L. [L. B. Larking], 'An early society of antiquaries', *N&Q*, 11 (1855), 5–6 · P. H. Blake, 'Sir Edward Dering, first baronet, a factual biography', incomplete unpublished MS, covering Dering's life up to c.1630 · R. Priestley, 'Marriage and family life in the seventeenth century: a study of the gentry families of England', PhD diss., University of Sydney, 1988 · S. P. Salt, 'The origin of Sir Edward Dering's attack on the ecclesiastical hierarchy, c.1625–40', *HJ*, 30 (1987), 21–52 · *The journal of Sir Simonds D'Ewes from the beginning of the Long Parliament to the opening of the trial of the earl of Strafford*, ed. W. Notestein (1923) · *The journal of Sir Simonds D'Ewes from the first recess of the Long Parliament to the withdrawal of King Charles from London*, ed. W. H. Coates (1942) · W. H. Coates, A. Steele Young, and V. F. Snow, eds., *The private journals of the Long Parliament*, 1: *3 January to 5 March 1642* (1982) · BL, Harley MSS 162–164, 477, 5047 · unpublished sections of Dering's journals of the Long Parliament, Bodl. Oxf., MS Rawl. D.

1099 · BL, Add. MS 4180, fol. 173v · Dering's report (never delivered) from the Commons licensing committee on Burton's *Protestation protested* [draft or holograph copy], 1641, BL, Stowe MS 354, fols. 111–12 · *JHC*, 2–3 (1640–44) · *JHL*, 5 (1642–3), 17–18 · P. R. Newman, *Royalist officers in England and Wales, 1642–1660: a biographical dictionary* (1981), 107 · M. A. E. Green, ed., *Calendar of the proceedings of the committee for compounding ... 1643–1660*, 5 vols., PRO (1889–92), 2.831–2 · S. Brown, ed., *Women's writing in Stuart England* (1999), 144–50 · G. Wilks, *The barons of the Cinque Ports and the parliamentary representation of Hythe* (1892), 76–9 · Dering's letter-books relating to Cinque Ports business, 1629–35, BL, Add. MSS 47788–47789, 52798A · Dering's memorandum book, 1637, BL, Add. MS 47787 · Dering MSS formerly in the possession of (and seen by kind permission of) the late P. H. Blake · 'Observations on Sir Edward Dering's methods of reforming the Church of England', [1642], TCD, MS 537 · list of members of the royal household, 1641, PRO, LC3/1, fols. 24–5 · Venn, *Alum. Cant.*, 1/2.36 · W. Shakespeare, *The history of King Henry IV*, rev. E. Dering, ed. G. W. Williams and G. B. Evans (1974) · G. B. Evans, ed., *Shakespearean prompt books of the seventeenth century*, 1, pt. 1 (1960), 5–8 [partly corrected by G. B. Evans, 'New evidence on the provenance of the Padua prompt books', *Studies in Bibliography*, 20 (1967) 239–42] · J. Finberg, 'A chronological list of portraits by Cornelius Johnson, or Jonson', *Walpole Society*, 10 (1922), 1–37 · GEC, *Peerage* · Keeler, *Long Parliament*, 155 · N. M. Sutherland, 'Dering, Anthony', HoP, *Commons, 1558–1603*, 2.33 · PRO, C/231/1, fol. 109r; C231/4, fol. 209v · H. A. C. Sturgess, ed., *Register of admissions to the Honourable Society of the Middle Temple, from the fifteenth century to the year 1944*, 1 (1949), 107 · F. S. A. Haslewood, *The parish of Pluckley, Kent: monumental inscriptions* (1899), 12 · PRO, C2/Charles I/D.15/66 · J. J. Howard and F. Haslewood, eds., 'Philpott's visitation of Kent in 1619: the Dering pedigree', *Archaeologia Cantiana*, 10 (1876), 327–8 · E. Hasted, *The history and topographical survey of the county of Kent*, 3 (1790), 229n. · J. Peacey, 'Tactical organization in a contested election: Sir Edward Dering and the spring election at Kent, 1640', *Parliament, politics and elections, 1604–1648*, ed. C. R. Kyle, CS, 5th ser., 17 (2001), 237–72 [prints poll bk from Bodl. Oxf., MS Top. Kent e.6] · PRO, C5/395/78; C5/404/83 · PRO, PROB 6/23, fol. 119r

Archives BL, antiquarian and historical transcripts, Add. MSS 5481, 37688, 43471 · BL, antiquarian and historical transcripts, Stowe MSS 543, 763, 853, 924, 927 · BL, classification scheme of library, Add. MS 50130 · BL, corresp. relating to the 1640 elections and to the Long Parliament, Add. MS 26785 · BL, corresp. and papers, RP 2162 [copies] · BL, letters, Stowe MSS 184, 743–744 · BL, letter-books relating to Cinque Ports business, Add. MSS 24113, 47788–47789, 52798A · BL, MSS, Add. MS 34147–34151, 34156–34160 [transcripts] · BL, memorandum book, Add. MS 47787 · BL, notes as chairman of the Long Parliament subcommittee on ministers' grievances etc., Add. MS 26786 · BL, papers, Add. MS 34195, fols. 20–33 · BL, reports (never delivered) from the Commons licensing committee on Burton's *Protestation protested*, 1641, Stowe MS 354, fols. 111–12 [draft or holograph copy] · Bodl. Oxf., antiquarian and historical transcripts, MS Gough Kent 1, MS Rawl., B.18 · Bodl. Oxf., poll book and narrative of the Kent Short Parliament election, MS Top. Kent e.6 · CKS, antiquarian and historical transcripts, U.1823/3 Z1 · CKS, MSS, U.133, U.275, U.350, U.570, U.715, U.1107, U.1256, U.1311, U.1364, U.1392, U.1551, U.1579, U.1769, U.1808, U.2479 · CKS, MSS, U.1823 Acc. 2960 [transcripts] · CKS, Dover Borough MSS, papers relating to Cinque Ports affairs, Do/ZCPW.1–7 · Folger, notes and papers, V.b.34 · LPL, reports (never delivered) from Commons licensing committee on the petition of Philip Chetwin, MS 943, pp. 735–7 [draft or holograph copy] · S. Antiquaries, Lond., antiquarian and historical transcripts, MS 350 · S. Antiquaries, Lond., notes on Kentish churches, MS 497A | BL, corresp. and papers of Sir John Coke, secretary of state, Add. MSS 64870–64924 · BL, memorandum of agreement between Sir Edward Dering and the earl of Suffolk as lord warden of the Cinque Ports, Add. MS 49977, fol. 51 · Bodl. Oxf., Gough's notes from a Dering memorandum book, MS Gough Kent 20 · Lincs. Arch., Dering to

Mr Bruges, captain of Warwick Castle, Lincoln 10 Anc./347 [photo-copy]

Likenesses oils, 1625 · C. Johnson, oils, 1630–1639?, Parham House, Sussex [*see illus.*] · G. Glover, line engraving, pubd 1640 (after C. Johnson), BM, NPG; repro. in A. M. Hind, *Studies in English engraving* (1933) · H. L. Smith, engraving, *c.*1862 (after C. Johnson), repro. in Larking, *Proceedings* · attrib. W. Dobson, oils (Edward Dering?), The South Wales Borderers and Monmouthshire Regimental Museum of the Royal Regiment of Wales, Brecon · W. Hollar, line engraving (after C. Johnson), BM · C. Johnson, oils, other versions; recorded in NPG archives · line engraving (after C. Johnson), BM

Wealth at death estates in sequestration; income assessed by parliament as £800 p.a.: PRO, C2/Charles I/D.15/66; C5/395/78; C5/404/83; cf. Canterbury consistory court act book, 1641–63, CKS, PRC 22/19, fol. 66v; administration, PRO, PROB 6/23, fol. 119r · had settled estates through deeds entered into before end of 1640: JHC, 3.572 (27 July 1644)

Dering, Sir Edward, second baronet (1625–1684), politician, was born on 12 November 1625 at Surrenden Dering, Kent, and baptized on 8 December at Pluckley in the same county, the only son of Sir Edward *Dering, first baronet (1598–1644), antiquary and religious controversialist, of Surrenden Dering, and his second wife, Anne (1604/5–1628), daughter of Sir John Ashburnham. He was educated at schools in Kent and London, and at Sidney Sussex College and Emmanuel College, Cambridge; he entered the Middle Temple in 1641. Dering joined his father with the king at the raising of the royal standard in Nottingham, but returned to Cambridge, from where he graduated BA in 1643. He planned to continue his studies at Leiden, where he learned of the death of his father and thus succeeded to his title in 1644, but after two more years' travelling in France and the Netherlands he returned to England and an estate encumbered by debts and a dispute with his stepmother, Unton.

On 5 April 1648 Dering married Mary (*bap.* 1629, *d.* 1704) [*see* Dering, Mary, Lady Dering], daughter of Daniel Harvey, a wealthy Turkey merchant; another of Harvey's daughters married Heneage Finch, the lawyer, and for a time all four seem to have lived together at the mother-in-law's home in Lambeth. During the 1650s Dering seems deliberately to have sought obscurity while pursuing literary interests, in part as a member of the circle of Katherine Philips. But having, in his own words, 'most carefully and resolutely refused during all the time of the usurped powers all manner of public employments' (*Diaries*, 110), on the eve of the Restoration he became a militia commissioner in Kent and secured election as knight for the shire to the Convention Parliament.

At the Restoration, Heneage Finch became solicitor-general, and Dering profited from the connection. In July 1662 he was appointed as one of seven commissioners to execute the Act for the Settlement of Ireland. He was returned to the Irish House of Commons that year for Lismore. The activities of the commission in sorting out land rights after the various forfeitures of the previous two decades brought opportunities both to please the powerful and for personal gain. Dering was regarded as one of the commissioners closest to the English court; in 1667 he was

sworn of the Irish privy council. His work under the commission, and under a second court of claims appointed under the 1665 Act of Explanation, occupied him until 1669, when the court's work was complete. Soon after his return to England he was made one of the three commissioners of the privy seal and in 1670 he was returned to parliament for East Retford in Nottinghamshire. The appointment of Arthur Annesley, first earl of Anglesey, as lord privy seal in 1673 superseded the commission and was a setback for Dering's finances. Yet the appointment of Sir Thomas Osborne (later earl of Danby) as lord treasurer, and Heneage Finch as lord keeper the same year helped to draw him into the inner circle of the court's system of parliamentary management, and to secure for him (eventually) a pension to compensate for his loss of office. By 1675 Dering was acting regularly in the Commons as a court spokesman, particularly in the debates on supply in October–November 1675 and in Danby's bill of 1677 for bringing up the children of the duke of York as protestants. In December 1675 he was appointed one of the commissioners of the customs: two years later he was also made a commissioner to inquire into abuses in the Royal Mint. His parliamentary role continued to grow: in early 1678 he chaired committees of the whole house on supply and on ways and means.

Following the emergence of the Popish Plot allegations and the dissolution of the Cavalier Parliament at the end of 1678 Dering found his court role more difficult. He was elected in 1679 and 1681 for the local Kentish borough of Hythe, and shortly after the beginning of the 1679 parliament, in March, was appointed one of the five commissioners who replaced Danby at the Treasury. Dering sought awkwardly to articulate a middle position: he urged the unity of protestants in the face of the popish threat and promoted measures for the removal of penalties from protestant nonconformists, but he voted against the exclusion of the duke of York from the throne. Towards the end of the parliament of 1680–81, perhaps shaken by an absurd accusation of popery from Israel Tonge, he signalled his acceptance of exclusion. He suffered little royal displeasure for it. An uncomfortable interview with the king in August 1681 concerning the activities and whiggish opinions of his eldest son may have been an oblique indication of disapproval, but Dering retained his office in the Treasury and was encouraged by the king to work up proposals for a new form of the Irish revenue, although these were ultimately abandoned after Dering expended enormous effort on them.

Dering died in London, probably in his house in Gerard Street, on 24 June 1684. He was buried at Pluckley four days later. He had inherited from his antiquary father not only an interest in religious controversy, but also an inveterate habit of note taking: he compiled detailed notes and diaries of proceedings at the court of claims, in parliament, and before the Treasury commission. He was survived by his wife, with whom he had eight sons (of whom four died in infancy) and nine daughters (three of whom did not survive childhood). PAUL SEAWARD

Sources *The diaries and papers of Sir Edward Dering, second baronet, 1644 to 1684*, ed. M. F. Bond (1976) · B. D. Henning, 'Dering, Sir Edward', HoP, *Commons, 1660–90*, 2.208–12 · *The parliamentary diary of Sir Edward Dering, 1670–1673*, ed. B. D. Henning (1940) · *CSP Ire.*, 1662–9

Archives BL, household account book and parliamentary journal, Add. MSS 22466–22467 · BL, household book, Add. MS 70887 · CKS, corresp. and papers · CKS, corresp., diary, parliamentary journal, and household accounts · HLRO, historical collections, papers · Hunt. L., diary and commonplace book · NRA, priv. coll., memoranda book | BL, corresp. with Sir John Perceval, Add. MSS 46957–46960 · CKS, letters to Sir Robert Southwell, U1713 · NL Ire., notebook relating to the Act of Settlement in Ireland

Likenesses Le Neve, miniature, *c*.1648–1649; at Emo Court, co. Laois in 1976 · P. Lely, oils, 1651, repro. in Bond, ed., *Diaries and papers*, frontispiece; Parham Park, Sussex, 1976 · G. Kneller, oils, 1683, repro. in Bond, ed., *Diaries and papers*, frontispiece; Beechwood Park, Nenagh, co. Tipperary, 1976 · portrait, 1687 (after unknown portrait); County Hall, Maidstone

Wealth at death see will, 24 Feb 1683, *Diaries and papers*, ed. Bond, 208–10

Dering, Heneage (1665–1750), dean of Ripon and Latin poet, was born in St Bride's parish, London, on 7 February 1665 and baptized on 14 February, the eldest of four sons and five daughters of Christopher Dering (1625–1693), barrister of the Inner Temple, of Wickins in Charing parish, Kent, and Elizabeth (*d*. 1724), daughter and heir of Thomas Spackman of Wiltshire. Heneage was named after his father's friend and patron, Heneage Finch, later earl of Nottingham, who was also his godfather; from 1673 Christopher Dering acted as Finch's secretary. He was educated at St Edward's Grammar School in St Albans (1674–8), where he was taught by Charles James, a former pupil of Richard Busby at Westminster School. He was admitted to the Inner Temple in 1678, and as a pensioner to Clare College, Cambridge, in 1680, leaving in 1682 without taking a degree. In February 1683 his father bought him a set of chambers in Figtree Court, Inner Temple, for £140, and Heneage was called to the bar in 1689 (Inderwick, 260) or 1690 (Dering, 338). In 1691 he became secretary to John Sharp, chaplain to Heneage Finch, on his promotion to the archbishopric of York, and in 1692 took up residence at Bishopthorpe Palace.

Early in 1701 Dering decided to take holy orders and, with this object in mind, he was created LLD of Clare College, *per literas regias*, in January 1701. On 9 February he was appointed Sharp's chaplain on being ordained deacon in Bishopthorpe Chapel, and was ordained priest on 20 July. Preferment after preferment now followed through Sharp's patronage. He was archdeacon of the East Riding (1702–50) and a canon of York Minster, holding the prebend of Grindal from 1705 and the richer one of Fridaythorpe from 1708. He was instituted to the rich rectory of Scrayingham, East Riding, where he rebuilt the parsonage house for the resident curates, in 1704, and to the deanery of Ripon on 3 March 1711. In June 1712 Sharp appointed him master of the hospitals of St Mary Magdalene and St John the Baptist in Ripon. Since, on his father's death, he had inherited the manor of Wickins, and the family estates in Westwell, Kent, he had become one of the wealthiest clergymen in England. He married, at Bishopthorpe Chapel on 9 January 1712, Anne Sharp (*bap*. 1691),

eldest daughter of Archbishop Sharp and his wife, Elizabeth Palmer, whom he had known all her life. Their eldest son, John (1715–1774), became rector of Hilgay, Norfolk, and prebendary and subdean of Ripon; Heneage was born and died in 1718; the third son, also Heneage (1719–1802), was successively vicar of Tadcaster, West Riding, and of Burley on the Hill, Rutland, perpetual curate of Wye, Kent, rector of Milton Keynes, Buckinghamshire, and finally prebendary of Canterbury. Two of their five daughters, Elizabeth (1713–1777) and Mary (1721–1798), married, respectively, Charles Elsley of Patrick Brompton, North Riding, and Dr John Sharp, archdeacon of Northumberland. Anne (1716–1780), Philadelphia (1723–1806), and Judith (1730–1813) did not marry.

Dering was conscientious in performing his duties as dean and, though installed by proxy, he came to Ripon a few months later and thereafter resided continually at the deanery with only brief absences on ecclesiastical or family business. Punctilious in his care for the church, he was solicitous in securing the best vicars-choral for the choir and ensuring the welfare of his clergy and parishes. He regularly conducted visitations of his archdeaconry and arranged for confirmations to be held in Ripon in 1723 and 1737. He also ensured that the church registers, which had fallen into some neglect, were properly made up. He made additions to the deanery and alterations to the minster: the font was moved to make room for a new ecclesiastical court (1722), a clock was erected (1723), the surviving fragments of medieval glass from the east window were restored (1724), and the monument to the last wakeman of Ripon, Hugh Ripley (1637), which had been defaced during the civil war, was repaired (1730). He agreed to give Edward Harley, earl of Oxford, a fifteenth-century miscellany manuscript from Dean Anthony Higgin's collection in the minster library and received in exchange a number of valuable printed books.

Dering published two poems in Latin hexameters. The first, *Reliquiae Eboracenses* (1743), was a ninety-five page history of Yorkshire under Roman rule, which was originally intended to cover the period of Saxon and Danish rule as well. An English translation in heroic couplets was made by the York printer Thomas Gent 'for his private amusement' in the winter of 1760–61 or 1761–2 and survives interleaved in a copy of the Latin text in York Minster Library. Gent proposed to issue his translation in eight or so sheets if he succeeded in attracting a hundred subscribers. The proposal evidently failed but Gent produced a few copies in octavo in 104 pages on his usual coarse paper, without title-page or introduction, but with over fifty crude woodcuts. Dering's other publication was a slender folio entitled *De senectute* (1746). While the *Reliquiae* is a fragment of pseudo-historical epic, ostensibly the later work is purely fanciful and is the lament of one of a pair of oak trees in Studley Royal Park about their approaching doom of being felled. This poem may have been an oblique criticism of the drastic remodelling of the park carried out by the Aislabies.

Dering lived to a great old age and even in 1739, eleven years before his death, he remarked that he was the oldest member of the York chapter and the oldest dean and archdeacon in the northern province. He died at the deanery on 8 April 1750 and on 14 April was buried at the east end of the north choir aisle in Ripon Minster, where a marble wall tablet was placed in his memory. His widow was buried beside him on 19 November 1771.

C. BERNARD L. BARR

Sources DNB · Old Westminsters · E. Brunskill, ed., The parish register of Bishopthorpe, Yorkshire Archaeological Society, parish register section, 150 (1986) · R. Davies, A memoir of the York press: with notices of authors, printers, and stationers, in the sixteenth, seventeenth, and eighteenth centuries (1868); facs. edn, ed. B. Barr (1988) · H. Dering, 'Autobiographical memoranda', Yorkshire diaries and autobiographies, ed. C. Jackson, [1], 333–50, nn. 464–71, SurtS, 65 (1877) · Foster, Alum. Oxon. · [J. T. Fowler], ed., Memorials of the church of SS Peter and Wilfrid, Ripon, 2, SurtS, 78 (1886) · J. T. Fowler, 'Ripon Minster library and its founders', Yorkshire Archaeological and Topographical Journal, 2 (1871–2), 371–402 · D. F. Foxon, ed., English verse, 1701–1750: a catalogue of separately printed poems with notes on contemporary collected editions, 2 vols. (1975) · The life of Mr Thomas Gent … written by himself, ed. J. Hunter (1832); repr. (1974) · A. T. Hart, The life and times of John Sharp, archbishop of York (1949) · E. Hasted, The history and topographical survey of the county of Kent, 4 vols. (1778–99) · J. Philipott, ed., 'The visitation of the county of Kent, taken in the year 1619 [pt 4]', Archaeologia Cantiana, 10 (1876), 325–51 · J. Hunter, Hallamshire: the history and topography of the parish of Sheffield in the county of York, new edn, ed. A. Gatty (1869) · F. A. Inderwick and R. A. Roberts, eds., A calendar of the Inner Temple records, 3 (1901) · G. Lipscomb, The history and antiquities of the county of Buckingham, 4 vols. (1831–47) · N&Q, 7th ser., 1 (1886), 189, 276, 308, 356–7, 392–3, 436, 471 · S. L. Ollard and P. C. Walker, eds., Archbishop Herring's visitation returns, 1743, 5 vols., Yorkshire Archaeological Society, 71–2, 75, 77, 79 (1928–31) · Ripon millenary: a record (1892) · R. F. Scott, ed., Admissions to the College of St John the Evangelist in the University of Cambridge, 3: July 1715 – November 1767 (1903) · T. Sharp, The life of John Sharp, D.D., lord archbishop of York, ed. T. Newcome, 2 vols. (1825) · R. H. Skaife, 'The register of burials in York Minster', Yorkshire Archaeological and Topographical Journal, 1 (1869–70), 226–330 · L. Smith, The story of Ripon Minster (1914) · Venn, Alum. Cant. · The diary of Humfrey Wanley, 1715–1726, ed. C. E. Wright and R. C. Wright, 2 vols. (1966) · J. R. Walbran, A guide to Ripon, etc., 12th edn (1875) · J. Welch, The list of the queen's scholars of St Peter's College, Westminster, ed. [C. B. Phillimore], new edn (1852)

Archives Leeds Leisure Services, papers relating to archdeaconry of East Riding | U. Leeds, Ripon Minster archives

Wealth at death administration bond for £1000; bequests totalling considerably more: 'Autobiographical memoranda', Jackson, ed., 470–71

Dering [née Harvey], **Mary**, Lady Dering (bap. **1629**, d. **1704**), composer, was baptized at St Laurence Pountney, London, on 3 September 1629, the daughter of Daniel Harvey (1587–1647), merchant, and his wife, Elizabeth, née Kynnersley (bap. 1601, d. 1655). Her father was described by his son-in-law as 'a Turkey merchant of very eminent loyaltie, prudence, integritie and generositie' (Diaries and Papers, 109); her uncle William Harvey was the discoverer of the circulation of blood. Mary attended Mrs Salmon's boarding-school in Hackney, where Katherine Fowler (later Mrs Philips, 'the matchless Orinda') and Mary Aubrey, niece of the antiquary John Aubrey, were among her friends. About 1645 she made a clandestine marriage to her cousin William Hauke (b. c.1625), who had been her father's apprentice. According to one account Hauke 'had bedded with her twelve months before the marriage was

Mary Dering, Lady Dering (bap. 1629, d. 1704), by Sir Peter Lely, 1651

discovered' (Hasted, 7.469) but Sir Roger Twysden's near-contemporary account tells of her 'the very day returning him his ring, and disclayming it, and never suffering him to come neere her' (Twysden, fol. 95v). An annulment was obtained, and on 5 April 1648 Mary married Sir Edward *Dering (1625–1684) of Surrenden Dering, Pluckley, Kent.

In 1649 Mary was taking lessons with the composer Henry Lawes, who had known Dering's father and who, during the civil war, 'betook himself to the teaching of ladies to sing' (Hawkins, 4.56). When Lawes published his Second Book of Ayres, and Dialogues in 1655 he dedicated it to Lady Dering:

> Not only in regard of that honour and esteem you have for Musick, but because those Songs which fill this Book have receiv'd much lustre by your excellent performance of them; and (which I confess I rejoice to speak of) some which I esteem the best of these Ayres, were of your own Composition, after your Noble Husband was pleased to give the Words. (Lawes, a2)

Three charming airs in the style of her master—'When first I saw fair Doris eyes', 'And is this all? what one poor kisse?', and 'In vain, fair Cloris, you design'—bear the words 'The Lady Deerings Composing'. All the other works in the book are by Lawes himself. Sir Edward, who wrote the words for all three of his wife's songs, was an accomplished poet and was known in the Katherine Philips circle as 'the noble Sylvander'. It was rare for well-born amateurs to allow works to be published under their own names, and this is the first time that a woman composer is thus credited, so it is remarkable that in this Lawes volume the work of the Derings is so clearly acknowledged.

The marriage of the Derings proved a notably happy one. No more compositions by Lady Mary Dering were published, but she had seventeen children, ten of whom survived childhood. On his wedding anniversary in April 1684, two months before his death, Sir Edward wrote: 'after 36 years I believe we are not weary of one another, nor our children weary of either of us' (*Diaries and Papers*, 28). Lady Dering died at Surrenden Dering on 7 February 1704 and was buried in the family vault at Pluckley on 12 February.　　　　OLIVE BALDWIN and THELMA WILSON

Sources J. M. Kerr, 'Mary Harvey—the Lady Dering', *Music and Letters*, 25 (1944), 23–33 • H. Lawes, *The second book of ayres, and dialogues* (1655) • *The diaries and papers of Sir Edward Dering, second baronet, 1644 to 1684*, ed. M. F. Bond (1976) • *The parliamentary diary of Sir Edward Dering, 1670–1673*, ed. B. D. Henning (1940) • R. Twysden, notebook, BL, Add. MS 34164 • E. F. Rimbault, 'Sir Edward Dering's household book, AD 1648–52', *N&Q*, 1 (1849–50), 161–2 • F. Haslewood, *The parish of Pluckley, Kent: monumental inscriptions* (1899) • W. M. Evans, *Henry Lawes, musician and friend of poets* (1941) • G. Keynes, *The life of William Harvey* (1966) • GEC, *Baronetage*, vol. 2 • W. J. Harvey, 'Genealogy of the family of Hervey', *Miscellanea Genealogica et Heraldica*, 2nd ser., 3 (1890), 332 • parish register, London, St Laurence Pountney, 3 Sept 1629 [baptism] • J. Hawkins, *A general history of the science and practice of music*, 4 (1776) • E. Hasted, *The history and topographical survey of the county of Kent*, 2nd edn, 7 (1798)

Likenesses C. Neve, portrait, 1649 • P. Lely, oils, 1651, Parham House, Sussex [*see illus.*] • T. Hawker, oils, 1683, repro. in *Diaries and papers*, ed. Bond

Dering, Richard (*c*.1580–1630), organist and composer, was the illegitimate son of Henry Dering of Liss, Hampshire, and, according to one source, of Lady Elizabeth Grey, sister of Henry Grey, earl of Kent (1547–1614) (BL, Add. MS 5534). He was educated at Christ Church, Oxford, where he supplicated for the degree of BMus on 26 April 1610 stating that he had studied music for ten years. This is at odds with Anthony Wood's statement that Dering 'was bred up in Italy where he obtained the name of a most admirable musician' (Wood, fol. 41v–42). However, it seems likely that Dering did indeed visit Italy in his early adulthood, for a 'Mr Dering'—very likely the composer—is noted as being present in Rome, having visited Venice and 'now gone to see more of Italy', in a letter from Sir Dudley Carleton (the king's envoy in Venice) to Sir John Harrington (PRO, SP 99/10, no. 62; 26 June 1612). He probably converted to Catholicism about this time and by 1617 he was organist to the English nuns of the convent of the Blessed Virgin Mary at Brussels. While he was in the Low Countries he published two sets of motets: *Cantiones sacrae quinque vocum* and *Cantica sacra … senis vocibus* (P. Phalèse, Antwerp, 1617 and 1618 respectively); and two sets of canzonettas: *Canzonette a tre voci* and *Canzonette a quattro voci* (both P. Phalèse, Antwerp, 1620).

In 1625 Dering returned to England and by 22 December was listed among the 'lutes, viols and voices' at the English court; he was paid a salary of £40 per annum. When he was later succeeded by Giles Tomkins, his place was described as 'for the virginals with the voices in ordinary'. Dering also became organist to Queen Henrietta Maria and in a warrant of 23 October 1626 he is listed as one of eleven musicians who had served the queen from the previous 25 March. His salary for this appointment was £120 per annum.

Dering's English music, none of which was published in his lifetime, consists of anthems (full and verse) for the Anglican church, fantasias and dances for viols, two madrigals, and the *City Cries* and *Country Cries* for voices and viols which incorporate popular melodies of the time. His Italianate works, nearly all of which were published, include Catholic church music (Latin motets) and Italian canzonettas and madrigals. These all include a part for continuo instruments and show a complete assimilation of the techniques of contemporary Italian *concertato* music (which he probably studied during his travels in Italy or from printed Italian music circulating in the Low Countries). A number of his small-scale motets may have been written during his time in Brussels, but most were probably composed in England specifically for Queen Henrietta Maria's Roman Catholic services in her private chapel. One large collection of Catholic liturgical organ music often associated with him (Christ Church, Oxford, MS 89) may not be his work.

Dering died, unmarried, and was buried at St Mary Savoy, London, on 22 March 1630. His motets remained popular after his death and appear in manuscripts throughout the civil war, Commonwealth, and Restoration periods. Thomas Mace reports that, in the days before the civil war, after he and his friends had finished playing consort music, they 'did *Conclude All*, with some *Vocal Musick*, to the *Organ*, or (for want of *That*) to the *Theorboe* … viz. Mr *Deering's Gloria patri* and other of *His Latin Songs* … *Wonderfully Rare*, *Sublime* and *Divine*, beyond all Expression' (Mace, 235). Anthony Wood (Wood, s.v. 'Hingston') records that the motets were popular with Oliver Cromwell, and their appeal was such that John Playford published a substantial number of them in his two books of *Cantica sacra* (1662 and 1674). The diarist Samuel Pepys noted that on Saturday 22 November 1662 on 'meeting Mr. Playford, he did give me his Latin Songs of Mr Deerings, which he lately printed' (Pepys, 3.263) and on Sunday 10 May 1668 he notes that he taught Mary Mercer to sing 'Canite Jehovæ', presumably Dering's setting (ibid., 9.194). Dering is important in the history of seventeenth-century English music as one of the first pre-Commonwealth composers to show a commitment to the Italianate *stile nuovo*.

JONATHAN P. WAINWRIGHT

Sources P. Platt, 'Richard Dering: an account of his life and work', BLitt diss., U. Oxf., 1952 • P. Platt, 'Dering's life and training', *Music and Letters*, 33 (1952), 41–9 • A. Ashbee, ed., *Records of English court music*, 3 (1988) • A. Ashbee, ed., *Records of English court music*, 5 (1991) • A. Ashbee, ed., *Records of English court music*, 8 (1995) • A. Ashbee and D. Lasocki, eds., *A biographical dictionary of English court musicians, 1485–1714*, 1 (1998), 344–5 • A. Wood, 'Lives of the musicians', *c*.1688, Bodl. Oxf., MS Wood D. 19/4, fols. 41v–42 [incl. later additions] • BL, Add. MS 5534 • T. Mace, *Musick's monument* (1676), 235 • Foster, *Alum. Oxon.* • Pepys, *Diary*, 3.263; 9.194 • I. Spink, 'The musicians of Queen Henrietta-Maria: some notes and references in English state papers', *Acta Musicologica*, 36 (1964), 177–82 • P. Platt, 'Perspectives of Richard Dering's vocal music', *Studies in*

Music, 1 (1967), 56–66 • J. P. Wainwright, *Musical patronage in seventeenth-century England: Christopher, first Baron Hatton (1605–70)* (1997), 178–85

Wealth at death numerous bequests of monies: will, PRO, PROB 11/157, sig. 34, proved 27 March 1630, quoted in Ashbee and Lasocki, eds., *Biographical dictionary*, 345

D'Erlanger, Baron Emile Beaumont (1866–1939), merchant banker, was born on 4 July 1866 in rue Taitbout, Paris, the second son of **Baron Frederic Emile D'Erlanger** (1832–1911), merchant banker, and Matilda (*née* Slidell). Frederic D'Erlanger was one of the most buccaneering and successful financiers of the second half of the nineteenth century; born of Jewish ancestry in Frankfurt, where his father, Rafael Erlanger, was a banker, he had converted to Christianity in order to marry. Frederic entered the family firm in 1849, aged seventeen. Ten years later, in 1859, he established his own private banking house in Paris. D'Erlanger's firm was very active as a manager of international bond issues in the bull market of the mid-1860s. He was awarded the title of baron in 1864 as a reward for successfully bringing out a loan on behalf of the government of Sweden to finance railway construction. Other sovereign clients were of rather more doubtful creditworthiness, such as those in Egypt and Tunis, for whom he raised funds in 1862 and 1864 respectively.

Frederic D'Erlanger's most controversial coup was the successful issue of a large loan in Paris and London in 1863, in the middle of the American Civil War, on behalf of the Confederacy. The bonds carried a novel right of conversion into cargoes of cotton, which made them attractive counters for speculators. The Confederate envoy with whom D'Erlanger negotiated the loan was James Slidell, a Southern landowner and politician. In 1864 D'Erlanger married Slidell's daughter Matilda. Her sister also wedded a prominent international financier, August Belmont, Rothschilds' representative in New York, strengthening D'Erlanger's transatlantic connections.

Emile Beaumont D'Erlanger was born in the mansion built for his parents in the rue Taitbout, in the style of the Second Empire, by the fashionable architect Bouvens. When Emile was four the family moved to London because of the Franco-Prussian War, and took up residence in Belgrave Square. His mother being a fervent Roman Catholic he was educated at Catholic schools, partly in England and partly in France. As a result he was bilingual in English and French; he was also fluent in German and Spanish. He took a degree in science in France.

In 1870 Frederic D'Erlanger established a new firm in London, Erlanger & Co., which henceforth was his principal business, though he maintained a Paris office at 35 boulevard Haussmann. He resumed his securities-issuing activities in London, which included involvement in a notorious loan for Costa Rica in 1872 that promptly defaulted on interest payments. This episode resulted in his being summoned to appear as a witness before the royal commission on foreign loans of 1875. In the second half of the 1870s, he became heavily involved in North American railroads, controlling a network of lines that served Alabama and Louisiana that was known colloquially as the Erlanger system. There was even a town called Erlangerville, where the repair workshops were sited.

Emile D'Erlanger's commercial training began in 1885, when he was nineteen. First of all he was dispatched on a grand tour overseas to meet family and business associates and to familiarize himself with the firm's interests, the usual preliminary for the son of a senior partner of a merchant bank. When the boat docked in New York, where his trip began, he was mobbed by reporters as the son of the famous financier. His uncle, James Slidell, and his father's business associate, Charles Schiff, brother of the partners in the leading Wall Street brokerage firm Schiff & Co., introduced him to the luminaries of American finance. Accompanied by Schiff he toured his father's extensive American railroad interests.

After his return to Europe, Emile D'Erlanger worked initially in the Paris office. He then moved back to London, where he learned the workings of the City as an unpaid 'volunteer', first in a stock-exchange firm and then with accountants Deloitte, Griffiths & Co. He entered Erlanger & Co. in 1888, at the same time as his younger brother Frederic, though their elder brother Raphael did not join them. At that time, he recalled, it was a small undertaking, comprising just ten people. In the following year his father sent him to Chile and Bolivia to report on the Antofagasta railway system and the Huanchaca nitrate mines, in whose development he was the leading financier.

D'Erlanger adopted British citizenship by naturalization in 1901. He was an enthusiastic 'imperialist', a label which for him meant a global horizon and economic modernization. He described as a task after his own heart his exertions to raise funds for railway building in such a remote corner of the empire as British North Borneo. His association with southern Africa began in 1892, when his father was approached by Cecil Rhodes about financing the consolidation of the Kimberley diamond industry. But it was in railway building that D'Erlanger made his mark; the family firm managed the financing of nearly all the railways of the British South African Company and of the construction of Rhodesia's railway system. He also raised capital for the Victoria Falls and Transvaal Power Company, the New Transvaal Chemical Company, and for building the port of Beira.

In 1895 D'Erlanger met in Normandy (Marie Rose Antoinette) Catherine de Robert d'Aqueria, daughter of the marquis de Rochegude. They married in the following year and spent their honeymoon in Egypt. The couple set up home in Rutland Gate, London, two doors away from his father; they had a son and a daughter. In 1910, at Catherine's behest, they moved to 139 Piccadilly, Lord Byron's former residence. Here the D'Erlangers entertained extensively and lavishly, Catherine becoming one of London's leading hostesses.

The fifteen years before the First World War saw Emile and his brother Baron Frederic A. D'Erlanger (1868–1943) in their prime. Their father, now in his seventies, left the running of the business to his sons; he died in 1911 and they both assumed the title of baron. Building on their father's achievements they developed the bond-issuing side of the business but also built up a substantial accepting business, making the firm a fully-fledged City merchant bank. Business was brisk in both the London and the Paris offices, and Emile was constantly on the move between the two.

These years saw the development of varied new interests. D'Erlanger became chairman of the New General Traction Company, a promoter of electric tramways in Coventry, Norwich, and elsewhere. He was also closely involved with the Forestal Land Timber and Railways Company, which cultivated the Argentinian *quebracho*, a forest hardwood, abundant in tan, that was much in demand from the local leather industry. Greece, a country with which the D'Erlanger family's Frankfurt firm had long-standing connections, became a focus of business in these years. D'Erlanger was active in raising finance for railway construction and loans for the Greek government. He also devised a price-support scheme for Greek currant-producers, which successfully stabilized prices and saved the currant farmers of the Peloponnese from ruin.

The 1920s saw a resumption of Erlangers' management of issues on behalf of foreign sovereign borrowers and municipalities, and also a revival of the firm's accepting activity. In the 1930s Erlangers refocused on serving British corporate clients, assembling an outstanding client list. In 1927 Emile D'Erlanger was joined in the partnership by his nephew Leo *D'Erlanger (1898–1978). Emile's only son, Gerard *D'Erlanger (1906–1962), pursued an eventful business career in the upper echelons of the aviation industry.

Given his Anglo-French schooling and outlook—his memoirs are written half in English and half in French—it was natural that D'Erlanger should be a supporter of the channel tunnel scheme. He was a director of the pioneering Channel Tunnel Company and its chairman from 1911 until his death, and he missed no opportunity to promote the project. Yet there was also a romantic side to D'Erlanger's nature. He authored several volumes of poetry and translated numerous English poems into French. He enjoyed physical pastimes, exercising daily, and was keen on golf and shooting, no doubt favourite topics of conversation at his club, Whites.

Baron Emile D'Erlanger died at 'Sydney', Cliff Road, Hythe, Kent, on 24 July 1939.   RICHARD ROBERTS

Sources private information (2004) · *WWW* · *The Times* (25 July 1939) · *CGPLA Eng. & Wales* (1939) · d. cert.
Archives CAC Cam., corresp. with Channel Tunnel Company and drafts of lectures · Derbys. RO, papers relating to British South Africa Company
Wealth at death £460,213 12s. 11d.: probate, 19 Aug 1939, *CGPLA Eng. & Wales*

D'Erlanger, Baron Frederic Emile (1832–1911). *See under* D'Erlanger, Baron Emile Beaumont (1866–1939).

D'Erlanger, Sir Gerard John Regis Leo (1906–1962), airline company director and financier, was born at Hall Place, Bexley, Kent, on 1 June 1906. He was the only son and the elder of the two children of Baron Emile Beaumont *D'Erlanger (1866–1939), international banker and

chairman of Erlangers Ltd, and his wife, (Marie Rose Antoinette) Catherine de Robert d'Aqueria, daughter of the marquis de Rochegude of Bollène in Vaucluse, France. He was educated at Eton College where he acquired the nickname 'Pop' by which he was known to his friends for the rest of his life. As a member of a family which had as many links with France as with England, D'Erlanger completed his education in Paris and then qualified in London as a chartered accountant in 1933. At the same time he took up private flying with enthusiasm and gained a pilot's 'A licence' (Royal Aero Club aviator's certificate no. 9730) at the Airwork Flying School at Heston in Middlesex on 11 March 1931. In company with two wealthy friends, Gordon Selfridge the younger and Whitney Straight, he acquired a taste for continental touring by air and, on a business visit to Argentina in 1932, flew himself around in a single-seat Composer Swift. He started a career in the family tradition when he joined Myers & Co. in 1934 and, in the following year, became a member of the London stock exchange.

Already D'Erlanger's flying interests had begun to extend beyond the sporting field. In 1934 he joined the board of the privately owned Hillman's Airways. No more incongruous—or successful—association could be imagined than that of the tough, self-made businessman, Edward Hillman, and the young, urbane, Etonian accountant. Hillman died in December 1934 just as the company went public, and D'Erlanger took a leading part in bringing his father's banking house to invest in the company. There was already one other financial institution entering the field of air transport—Whitehall Securities, founded by the first Lord Cowdray, managed by Clive Pearson, and including on its board Harold Balfour MP. In 1935, thanks largely to D'Erlanger and Balfour, Hillman's Airways merged with United Air Lines, owned by Whitehall Securities, and was renamed British Airways in 1936. The result was a powerful independent airline with substantial financial backing which could challenge the state-supported Imperial Airways.

D'Erlanger became a director of British Airways on its formation and in 1937 he married Gladys Florence, daughter of H. J. Sammut; they had one son and two daughters, one of whom, Mary Caroline (Minnie), was the first wife of Winston Churchill (b. 1940). On 1 April 1940, following the report of the committee chaired by Lord Cadman, Imperial Airways and British Airways were merged to form the state-owned British Overseas Airways Corporation (BOAC), with D'Erlanger on the board of BOAC from its official beginning.

Before this, when war was clearly imminent, D'Erlanger began negotiations in 1938 with the Air Council member for development and production, Air Marshal Sir Wilfrid Freeman, for an auxiliary force of private pilots, too old or unfit for military service, who might be used to ferry aircraft from manufacturers to squadrons in time of war. At first the Air Ministry was lukewarm but, when war was declared in September 1939, Air Transport Auxiliary rapidly came into being at White Waltham, near Maidenhead, Berkshire, with D'Erlanger as commandant. During the next six years 1215 men and women from fourteen nations ferried some 308,000 aircraft of 147 different types in all weathers and often in the most difficult conditions, with the loss of 173 lives, sixteen of whom were women. A memorial was set up in St Paul's Cathedral with their motto: *Aetheris avidi* ('Eager for the air'). For this contribution to the war effort D'Erlanger was made a CBE in 1943.

Before the war ended, D'Erlanger began discussions with Sir Harold Hartley, chairman of the Railway Air Services, about the formation of a new airline for domestic and European services. The result was the formation on 1 August 1946 of British European Airways (BEA), a second nationalized corporation. It took over the former services of the independent airlines, including those of Railway Air Services and BOAC's European routes, under Hartley's chairmanship and with D'Erlanger as managing director. When Hartley became chairman of BOAC in July 1947, D'Erlanger took the chair of BEA but—following a dispute about the level of subsidy with the minister of civil aviation, Lord Pakenham—he resigned on 14 March 1949 and returned to the City. He was succeeded as chairman of BEA by Lord Douglas of Kirtleside. D'Erlanger was a member (from 1952) and deputy chairman (from 1954) of the Air Transport Advisory Council, resigning in 1955.

Early in 1956, after the resignation of Sir Miles Thomas in the wake of the disasters involving the early jet airliner Comet I, D'Erlanger was appointed chairman of BOAC. It was a very difficult time, with BOAC having to use obsolescent equipment in the face of its competitors' more modern aircraft and having to fight the ministry and the Treasury over the shortage of dollars needed to buy American equipment and costs generally, which neither understood. D'Erlanger's tenure was made the more difficult both because he was a part-time, unpaid chairman who operated from his flat in London, and because the government pressed for purchase of the VC-10 and Super VC-10 jet airliners rather than allowing BOAC to buy all Boeing 707s. D'Erlanger signed the contract despite the protests of incoming chairman, Sir Matthew Slattery.

D'Erlanger was knighted in 1958. He retired from BOAC in 1960 to devote himself to City affairs as chairman of City and International Trust, of the General and Consolidated Investment Trust, and of the Moorgate Investment Company. He was also deputy chairman of the Provident Mutual Life Association, and a director of John Mackintosh & Sons and of Philip Hill Investment Trust, with which Erlangers had merged. He settled down to enjoy a less onerous life at his home at 11 Hyde Park Street in London. Surrounded by a circle of friends, he had wide interests, which included the Royal Yacht Squadron. Two years after his retirement he died suddenly on 15 December 1962, at his home in London. He was survived by his wife.

Pop D'Erlanger's chief contribution to British aviation was to bring together early commercial airline interests and adequate finance in the years before the war of 1939–45, and to help consolidate their scattered remnants to form BEA under state ownership in 1946. His imaginative formation of the Air Transport Auxiliary in 1939 provided

a valuable source of flying experience which might otherwise have remained untapped. This was a contribution to the war effort which, because it fitted no service mould, went largely unrecognized. Always pleasant, often worried, never happy with officialdom, D'Erlanger had an innate reserve which, combined with difficulty in communication, kept him from still greater attainments. In aviation he was a gifted amateur in a tough professional field and a political amateur in a highly politicized industry; in finance he was very much the professional who was often among amateurs.

Peter G. Masefield, *rev.* Robin Higham

Sources *The Times* (17 Dec 1962) · *WW* (1950) · *WW* (1960) · BOAC archives and oral histories in connection with R. Higham, unpublished history of BOAC, British Airways · R. Higham, *Britain's imperial air routes, 1918–1939* (1960) · L. Curtis, *The forgotten pilots* (1971) · *DBB* · R. E. G. Davies, *A history of the world's airlines* (1964) · *CGPLA Eng. & Wales* (1963) · d. cert.

Likenesses photographs, possibly *Flight International* archives · photographs, British Airways Photographic Section, Heathrow

Wealth at death £317,043 14s.: probate, 5 March 1963, *CGPLA Eng. & Wales*

D'Erlanger, Leo Frederic Alfred (1898–1978), merchant banker and air transport promoter, was born on 2 July 1898 at 6 Hamilton Place, London, the elder of the two children of Baron François Rodolphe D'Erlanger (1872–1932), writer on Arab music and painter, and his wife, Elisabetta Barbiellini-Amidie (1875–1961), the daughter of the chamberlain of Pope Leo XIII, who became his godfather. His father was half-German, half-American, and his mother was Italian. Leo was one of the first members of this remarkable family of European bankers to be born in England. After schooling in France and at St Leonards in England he went to Eton College, living during his formative years with his uncle Baron Frederic (1868–1943) who, with his brother Emile (1866–1939) [see D'Erlanger, Baron Emile Beaumont], ran the family bank, Erlangers Ltd, in London. His father was never involved in the family business.

Leaving Eton in 1916, D'Erlanger went to Sandhurst for a year, subsequently serving with the Grenadier Guards in the last year of the First World War under Gort in France, where he suffered shell-shock. On his return to England D'Erlanger in 1919 joined the family bank, which his great-grandfather had formed in Frankfurt in 1840 (it later moved to Paris while the London branch, founded 1870, became the heart of the bank). He steadily rose through a number of senior positions, becoming a partner in the bank in 1927, a director in 1939, and finally chairman in 1944. The house specialized in corporate finance, acceptance credit business, and foreign exchange, and while D'Erlanger became an experienced banker, he remained an entrepreneur. In the 1920s the bank's main business was in the arrangement of international bond issues for foreign municipalities and governments, but the scope for expansion was severely curtailed by the German financial crisis of the early 1930s. Through the subsequent refocusing of its strategy, Erlangers became one of the first merchant banks to invest in British industrial organizations, and built up a valuable list of corporate clients.

Although D'Erlanger never learned to fly, the aviation industry became one of his major areas of involvement. He was a substantial shareholder, albeit through nominees, in Imperial Airways Ltd, formed in 1924. He shared this interest with one of his best friends from Eton days, Esmond Cecil Harmsworth (later second Viscount Rothermere), who joined the airline's board in 1934. However, the prospects of playing a role in international negotiations eluded him. At the beginning of 1935 a small and recently publicly floated airline, Hillman's Airways, came on the market following the death of its founder, Edward Hillman (1889–1934), and D'Erlanger purchased it. Putting his younger cousin, Gerard *D'Erlanger, onto its board, he some months later merged Hillman's Airways Ltd with the airline interests of Whitehall Securities Ltd to form British Airways Ltd. The latter airline subsequently became the government's second chosen instrument in developing civil aviation with the aid of subsidies and mail contracts. He avoided direct personal involvement in pioneering businesses in case their demise might compromise him; instead he used nominees to represent his interests, although many years later he doubted whether this had been the wisest policy. In 1935 he was involved in proposals for a British air service to South America together with Harmsworth and Whitehall Securities, but international politics prevented the plans being implemented.

D'Erlanger was to play a greater role on the manufacturing side of the airline industry. He helped to raise capital for the De Havilland Aircraft Company, and others who benefited from his advice included Short Brothers, as well as the flying boat manufacturers Saunders Roe. He participated in a series of meetings between Roy Fedden of the Bristol Aeroplane Company, Colonel Devereux of High Duty Alloys Ltd, and Ernest Hives of Rolls Royce, at which plans were laid for the production of the Merlin engine which was successfully installed in the Spitfire, Lancaster, and Mosquito aircraft. With Devereux he realized the importance of reprocessing scrap aluminium and other metals in short supply and they set up International Alloys for the purpose. He also played a crucial part in saving the chemical firm Alginate Industries Ltd.

On the fall of France in 1940 D'Erlanger asked F. W. Winterbotham of MI5 to rescue the principal French aeronautical engineers and their plans for heavy undercarriage hydraulics, which were ahead of Britain's. After this was accomplished the French worked with the staff of the aircraft component manufacturers, Dowty, subsequently providing the undercarriage for the successful Lancaster bomber. D'Erlanger's war work was later recognized by the French when he became an officer of the Légion d'honneur. He also brought his influence to bear on the efforts of Winterbotham to obtain authorization for experimental work by Barnes Wallis that culminated in the bouncing bomb. In addition he had a great interest in motor cars and was a friend and admirer of Bugatti. He later backed Roy Fedden in developing a new car but it proved disastrous.

D'Erlanger's long involvement with the channel tunnel scheme dated from the death in 1939 of his uncle Baron Emile, who had been chairman of the Channel Tunnel Company since 1911. Believing that he had a duty to shareholders to keep the company alive until the tunnel was built D'Erlanger gave the scheme his support. He and Sir Herbert Walker, the newly appointed chairman of the company, who had been general manager of the Southern Railway until 1937, became powerful advocates of the tunnel. A major milestone appeared to have been reached in 1956 when the Suez Canal Company became interested: they saw it as a possible successor business to the canal, on which their lease would run out in 1968. However, in the event the canal was nationalized by the Egyptian government that summer.

The formation of the channel tunnel study group in July 1957 resulted in the inclusion of French and American interests. The group's scheme was later adopted by the British and French governments, and although no longer at the centre of negotiations, D'Erlanger continued to be occupied in lobbying, lecturing, and explaining the need for a tunnel to a variety of audiences. He ceased to be the principal financier associated with the scheme well before an agreement was signed in 1972 between the British and French governments and the Channel Tunnel and financing companies, though he played some part in the British government's decision. He resigned from Channel Tunnel Investment Ltd (as the company had become) in 1974. D'Erlanger was reported as having said that he would have a reserved seat in the first train to travel through the tunnel. If he were then dead, his coffin was to be dug up and placed in the train, but in the event this did not happen when the first passenger train went through the tunnel in 1994.

D'Erlanger's active involvement in banking also came to an end in the early 1960s. In 1959 Erlangers Ltd merged with Philip Hill, Higginson & Co., an investment bank specializing in new issues. D'Erlanger served as vice-chairman of a new house, Philip Hill Higginson Erlangers Ltd; however, he stepped down from this position and also gave up his seat on the board of Philip Hill Investment Trust in 1961.

D'Erlanger married in 1930 Edwina Louise Prue (1906–1994), an American whom he had earlier pursued across the world; they had two children, a daughter, and a son who also became a merchant banker. In some ways Leo D'Erlanger was a paradox: a disciplined creature of habit who ignored convention; always sensitive, a champion of national causes who abhorred publicity; a devout Catholic given to the quaintest superstitious practices; and a man born to wealth who lived off toast. A man of immense courtesy and charm, he was consequently very persuasive. In 1974 he left England to become a tax exile at the exquisite Arab palace his father had rebuilt in Tunisia.

Leo D'Erlanger died in Geneva on 25 October 1978 after a stroke, and was buried at Glion sur Montreux, Switzerland. He was survived by his wife, Edwina.

JOHN KING

Sources J. King, 'D'Erlanger, Leo Frederic Alfred', *DBB* • personal knowledge (2004) • private information (2004) • A. Hilton, 'A light at the end of the Chunnel', *Sunday Express* (25 June 1972) · *Daily Telegraph* (26 Oct 1978) · *The Times* (26 Oct 1978)

Archives PRO, Air Ministry records

Likenesses photograph, 1972, Hult. Arch. · photograph, repro. in King, 'D'Erlanger, Leo Frederic Alfred' · photographs, priv. coll.

Dermody, Thomas (1775–1802), poet, was born at Ennis, co. Clare, on 15 January 1775, the eldest of the three sons of Nicholas Dermody, himself the sixth son of a wealthy farmer. Nicholas Dermody was a bright but alcoholic rural schoolmaster, and Dermody revealed himself to be his father's son, showing a precocious talent for drinking, poetry, and scholarship. A child prodigy, he learned Latin and Greek from the age of four, and was employed as classical assistant in his father's school at the age of nine.

At the age of fifteen, inspired by his reading of *Tom Jones*, Dermody resolved to seek his fortune, and ran away to Dublin. Penniless on arrival, he initially accepted employment from a bookstall keeper, who discovered him reading Anacreon. Word about his poetic gifts and classical ability soon spread, and he won the patronage of various civic dignitaries and aristocrats, including Henry Grattan, Lady Moira, who convened a well-known literary salon, and the translator and anthologist Charlotte Brooke. In 1792 a small volume of his poems was published at the expense of one of his patrons, the Revd Gilbert Austin. Dermody went on to publish two more volumes, some critical essays, and, inspired by events in France in 1793, a pamphlet on the revolution.

Increasingly concerned about Dermody's behaviour, defiantly articulated in his poetic declarations such as 'I am vicious because I like it', his patrons consigned him for a brief spell to the guardianship of a priest in Killeigh, but to little avail. Dermody remained a committed and unrepentant drinker, pawning his clothes, being collared by the watch, and increasingly resembling a vagrant. His patrons finally abandoned him to his fate when he refused a scholarship at Trinity College, Dublin.

Having nearly been press-ganged into the army on two previous occasions, Dermody had little choice but to enlist voluntarily in the 108th regiment as a private, and, benefiting from the strict regime, obtained a commission in the wagon corps, having served with distinction in France. Later wounded and living on half pay in London, Dermody however quickly returned to drinking, finally dying in poverty in a hovel near Sydenham, Kent, on 15 July 1802, aged twenty-seven. He was buried in Lewisham churchyard which contains a monument to his memory. James Grant Raymond published a biography in 1807, containing all of Dermody's poems. Dermody's allusive, occasionally brilliant satiric verse has often been reprinted and anthologized, even well into the twentieth century. For instance, two of his most famous poems, 'An Ode to Myself' and 'John Baynam's Epitaph' appeared in the *Field Day Anthology of Irish Writing* (1991).   JASON EDWARDS

Sources J. G. Raymond, *The life of Thomas Dermody*, 2 vols. (1806) · R. Hogan and others, eds., *The Macmillan dictionary of Irish literature* (1980), 343–6 · A. M. Brady and B. Cleeve, eds., *A biographical dictionary of Irish writers*, rev. edn (1985), 58 · R. Welch, ed., *The Oxford companion to Irish literature* (1996), 142 · S. Deane, A. Carpenter, and J. Williams, eds., *The Field Day anthology of Irish Writing*, 1 (1991), 399,

401–3, 418, 492, 495 · P. Somerville-Large, *Irish eccentrics: a selection* (1975), 127–36 · R. Ryan, *Biographica Hibernica: a biographical dictionary of the worthies of Ireland* (1819–21)

Likenesses C. Allingham, oils, 1802, NG Ire. · W. Ridley, stipple, pubd 1802 (after C. Allingham), NG Ire.

Dermot [later MacDermot], **Anthony** (c.1708–1784), merchant and Roman Catholic activist, was born probably in the parish of St Michan, Dublin, the son of Christopher Dermot (d. 1727), merchant, and his wife, Mary. No information has been discovered with regard to his education. He married Mary Tobin (d. in or before 1777) and his will mentions three sons and a daughter, but there were probably other children. With the death of his father in 1727 Dermot had perforce, at an early age, to take over the running of a merchant business. Later, with his three sons, he went on to develop a large and lucrative provisions trade as well as a shipping business.

The setting up of the Catholic Committee in Dublin in 1756 offered prominent merchants such as Dermot a chance to play a public role, and he was an early secretary of that body. He was also a prime mover in organizing an address by the Catholic gentry, merchants, and citizens of Dublin to the lord lieutenant, the duke of Bedford, in December 1759. This address proved so welcome to a government beset by fears of a French invasion that the lord lieutenant ordered the speaker to call Dermot before the Irish House of Commons and to hand him a written reply assuring Catholics that, as long as they conducted themselves with duty and affection, they could not fail to obtain his majesty's protection.

In 1761 the Society of Merchants, which consisted of both Catholic and protestant merchants, was set up in Dublin. It largely replaced the long-established merchants' guild in that city which had discriminated against Catholic merchants. The aims of the new society were to promote laws beneficial to merchants and to defend their trade. Dermot was a member of the executive committee of the society, along with three or four other Catholic merchants, and he occasionally acted as chairman. He was also active in forming fire and general insurance companies. The Society of Merchants ceased to exist when a chamber of commerce was set up for the city in 1783. Dermot was elected a vice-chairman of the council of the new body.

Meanwhile the Catholic Committee, which had been dormant for several years, had been revived in the early 1770s, with Dermot again prominent at meetings. He was a member of a sub-committee which sought in vain amendments to the special oath for Catholics contained in a bill passed into law in June 1774. Although there was bitter opposition to this oath from some Catholics, Dermot was among those who accepted it. The act of 1774 was a sort of curtain-raiser for the Catholic Relief Acts of 1778 and 1782 but Dermot, who now assumed the old and proper form of his name, MacDermot, was not to live long enough to enjoy the benefits of these. He died in Dublin in January 1784 and was buried there, in St James's churchyard, on 1 February.   PATRICK FAGAN

Sources L. M. Cullen, *Princes and pirates: the Dublin chamber of commerce, 1783–1983* (1983), 38–54 • P. Fagan, *Catholics in a protestant country: the papist constituency in eighteenth-century Dublin* (1998), 168–73 • M. Wall, *Catholic Ireland in the eighteenth century* (1989) • R. D. Edwards, ed., 'The minute book of the Catholic Committee, 1773–1792', *Archivium Hibernicum*, 9 (1942), 1–172 • minute book of the Committee of Merchants, Royal Irish Acad., MS 12.D.29 • Betham's abstracts of wills, NA Ire. • *Wilson's Dublin directory* (1752–84) • parish register, Dublin, St James, 1 Feb 1784 [burial] • K. W. Nicholls, 'The Lynch Blosse papers', *Analecta Hibernica*, 29 (1980), 113–218, esp. 191

Dermott, Laurence (1720–1791), freemason, was born in Ireland but further details of his place of birth and parentage are unknown. He was initiated into the masons in Dublin in 1740, and went to London about 1750. He was elected grand secretary of the 'Antient' masons in 1752. Little is known of Dermott's life apart from his masonic activities. He is thought to have been in the employment of a master painter shortly after his arrival in London and later to have set himself up as a wine merchant in the City of London. He married, presumably before June 1770 when he drew up his will, naming his wife, Elizabeth Dermott, as the sole beneficiary. In 1756 he published *Ahiman Rezon, or, A Help to a Brother*, an influential law book the format of which was copied by other lodges. In 1771 the duke of Atholl appointed him deputy grand master of the Antient masons, an office he held until December 1787. He died in June 1791 at Mile End Old Town, London, where he was living at that time. His place of burial remains unknown.   PHILIP CARTER

Sources W. M. Bywater, *Notes on Laurence Dermott G.S. and his work* (1884) • R. A. Wells, *Freemasonry in London, from 1785* (1984) • R. F. Gould, *The history of freemasonry: its antiquities, symbols, constitutions, customs*, 3 vols. (1884–7)
Wealth at death everything to wife: will, 15 July 1791, reprinted in Bywater, *Notes on Laurence Dermott*, 56

Derrick, Samuel (1724–1769), author, was born in Dublin; his family had held land near Carlow, but had lost it as a result of the disturbances of the seventeenth century. Derrick was apprenticed to a linen draper, but fled to London to become an actor, at which he was unsuccessful. He therefore turned his hand to writing, publishing a number of works, notably *The dramatic censor; being remarks upon the conduct, characters, and catastrophe of our most celebrated plays* (1752); *A Voyage to the Moon* (1753), translated from the work by Cyrano de Bergerac; *The Battle of Lora* (1762), attributed to Ossian; and an edition of Dryden, *Works, with a Life and Notes* (1760). He also published a collection of his letters, entitled *Letters Written from Leverpoole, Chester, Corke …* (1767), in two volumes, with his portrait included as a frontispiece. His association with the theatre continued in spite of his acting failures, and he contributed the prologue to a production of *The Miser* performed on 17 December 1756 as a benefit for raising money for 'friendless and deserted boys for the Sea'.

For a time in the 1750s or 1760s Derrick lived with the actress Jane *Lessingham (1738/9–1783) as his wife, although she was already married. He was acquainted with both Samuel Johnson and James Boswell, whose opinion of him was somewhat ambivalent. Johnson, while having 'a kindness' for him, on being asked which was the finer poet, Derrick or Christopher Smart, replied that there was 'no settling the point of precedency between a louse and a flea' (Boswell, 272, 1214). Boswell, though an associate of Derrick during his first trip to London in 1760, later turned against this 'little blackguard pimping dog' (28 March 1763, *Boswell's London Journal, 1762–3*, ed. F. A. Pottle, 1950). Derrick also appears to have been acquainted with John Wilkes, publishing *A View of the Stage* (1759) under his name. A correspondent of Derrick's wrote to him from Dublin about 1763 to mention that 'a Mr Wilkes has latterly enjoyed every body's attention here. Pray, is it the same I have heard you mention as a man of wit and spirit?' (Derrick, *Letters*). Certainly the subscription list for Derrick's volume of poems includes names familiar in Wilkes's circle, such as Sir Francis Dashwood, David Garrick, Samuel Johnson, Colley Cibber, Samuel Foote, Tobias Smollett, and Richard 'Beau' Nash.

In January 1763 Derrick succeeded James Collet (Jacques Colet) as master of ceremonies at Bath and Tunbridge Wells, an appointment which Johnson attributed less to his social skills than to his being a 'literary man' (Boswell, 327). Some have suggested that his appointment was originally intended as a joke, and *The New Bath Guide* for 1798 reports that Derrick kept the position 'notwithstanding great opposition'. Certainly his reputation suffered during the nostalgic reminiscences which followed the death in 1761 of Bath's greatest master, Beau Nash, compared to whom Derrick was 'so small and pusillanimous in his appearance, that it was next to impossible for him to command respect' (*The Original Bath Guide*, 1811, 97). To others, by the very nature of his position he embodied the triviality of Bath society, being a 'puny monarch' in Tobias Smollett's *Humphrey Clinker* (1771, letter of 6 May), and 'an insignificant puppy' to the Cornish visitor John Penrose. None the less, as *The New Bath Guide* for 1766 suggests, Derrick did enjoy popularity among the company, if never that of Nash in his prime; Penrose's criticism, for example, followed a benefit ball which raised £150 for the master, while more impressionable visitors looked favourably on a man described by Smollett's Lydia Melford as 'so sweet, so fine, so civil, and polite, that in our country he might pass for the prince of Wales' (letter of 26 April). Derrick lost or squandered an inheritance in 1755, and died in Bath on 28 March 1769. A compilation entitled *Derrick's Jests, or, The Wits Chronicle* was published soon after.

     R. D. E. EAGLES

Sources S. Derrick, *The dramatic censor*, ed. J. Aikins (1985) • L. Melville, *Bath under Beau Nash* (1926) • S. Derrick, *Letters written from Leverpoole, Chester, Corke, the Lake of Kilarney, Dublin, Tunbridge-Wells, and Bath*, 2 vols. (1767) • *The new Bath guide* (1970) [with an introduction by K. G. Ponting] • *The new Bath guide* (1798) • G. W. Stone, ed., *The London stage, 1660–1800*, pt 4: *1747–1776* (1962) • T. Smollet, *Humphry Clinker*, ed. Ross (1967) • S. Derrick, *A view of the stage* (1759) • *GM*, 1st ser., 39 (1769), 215 • J. Boswell, *Life of Johnson*, ed. P. Rogers (1980)
Archives BL, translation of third satire of Juvenal • V&A, account of Bath • V&A NAL, corresp. and papers • Yale U., Beinecke L., autograph of his translation of Juvenal's third satire
Likenesses Hibbart, engraving, repro. in Derrick, *Letters from Leverpoole* • W. Hibbert, etching (after Vespris), BM, NPG

Derricke, John (*fl.* 1578–1581), author, was probably a follower of Sir Henry Sidney. It is possible but unlikely that he was the Mr Derricke who, in 1557, was employed to make the great seal for Ireland by direction of Mr Secretary Sir John Bourne. It is more plausible that he was the John Derick appointed as a collector of the custom duty on wine imported into Ireland on 11 November 1569 when Sir Henry Sidney was granted the right to collect such revenue after an act of the Irish parliament (October 1569). It is likely that Derricke remained in Ireland from that date until 1578 when Sir Henry Sidney finally returned to England. He signed the dedication of his *Image of Irelande* (1581) to Sir Philip Sidney at Dublin on 16 June 1578.

Derricke's profession is not known for certain. *The Image of Irelande* contains twelve plates which he advertises as 'Made and devised by him'. This may mean he was an engraver, or possibly he simply drew the originals. It is most likely that the plates were made in London after Derricke's return, possibly by the author and his family as they are similar in style, four being signed 'FD' and two 'ID'. These six designs are probably the finest woodcuts made in a sixteenth-century English book.

Derricke's work, a mixture of verse and prose, is a staunch defence of Henry Sidney's deputyship, detailing his military triumphs against the native Irish. The book was published by John Day, the most important publisher of illustrated books in the second half of the sixteenth century. It is likely that Derricke witnessed many of the scenes he depicted, further indicating his work's value. It consists of three parts: the first and second detail the evils of the Irish wood kerne; an apparently appended third section narrates the fate of the rebel Rory Oge O'More. *The Image of Irelande* is one of the most valuable records of Elizabethan Ireland. ANDREW HADFIELD

Sources J. Derricke, *The image of Irelande*, ed. D. B. Quinn (1985) · J. Derricke, *The image of Irelande*, ed. J. Small (1883) · E. Hodnett, *Image and text: studies in the illustration of English literature* (1982) · *CSP Ire.*, 1509–73, 138

Derwentwater. For this title name *see* Radcliffe, James, styled third earl of Derwentwater (1689–1716); Radcliffe, Charles, styled fifth earl of Derwentwater (1693–1746) [*see under* Radcliffe, James, styled third earl of Derwentwater (1689–1716)].

Desaguliers, John Theophilus (1683–1744), natural philosopher and engineer, was born on 12 March 1683 at Aytré, near La Rochelle, France, the only surviving child of Jean Desaguliers (1644–1699), minister and schoolmaster, and Marguerite Thomas la Chapelle (*c.*1640–1722). His parents were French Huguenots who emigrated separately after the revocation of the edict of Nantes in 1685. His father smuggled him to Guernsey, then took him to London in 1690. Two years later his father became an Anglican minister of the Swallow Street French Chapel, and subsequently opened the French School in Islington, Middlesex. Desaguliers was a pupil in this school until his father's death, and was then taught by William Saunders in Sutton Coldfield, Warwickshire. After a period teaching in the French School, he matriculated at Christ Church,

John Theophilus Desaguliers (1683–1744), by Peter Pelham, 1725 (after Hans Hysing)

Oxford, in 1705. He graduated bachelor of arts in 1709 and lectured on natural philosophy at Hart Hall, Oxford, from 1710 to 1712, when he proceeded MA. In 1719 he received the Oxford degrees of bachelor and doctor of laws, and these were incorporated at Cambridge in 1726.

In 1712 Desaguliers moved back to London, where he lived for the rest of his life. On 14 October 1712 he married Joanna Pudsey (1690x95–1753), daughter of William and Anne Pudsey of Kidlington, near Oxford. They had four sons and three daughters, for most of whom they acquired aristocratic godparents, but only two children survived beyond infancy: John Theophilus (1718–1751) graduated from Oxford, became a clergyman, and died childless, while Thomas *Desaguliers (1721–1780) led a distinguished scientific military career. From 1715 Desaguliers advertised lectures at his home in Channel Row, where the family lived until about 1739, when the construction of Westminster Bridge—on which Desaguliers had advised—resulted in the demolition of their house. Desaguliers then moved his home and his classes to Bedford Coffee House, Covent Garden, a popular venue for whig lecturers of natural philosophy.

Cultivating patronage Desaguliers took deacon's orders in Fulham in 1710 and priest's orders in Ely in 1717. In 1716 he was appointed chaplain to James Brydges (later the duke of Chandos) who became his most valuable patron and made him rector of Stanmore Parva, Middlesex, in 1719; between 1717 and 1738 Desaguliers acquired two further livings (running consecutively in Bridgeham, Norfolk, and Little Warley, Essex) from George I and George II, and two more chaplaincies (to Frederick, prince of Wales, and to a military regiment). These appointments testify less to Desaguliers's religious commitment than to his skill at acquiring sources of income. His major interests were scientific rather than theological, and his failure to fulfil his clerical duties exacerbated the decline in his profitable relationship with Chandos. Scanty evidence of his faith survives: a sermon he preached before the king in 1717 based on his own entrepreneurial misfortunes, and his physicotheological preface to *The Religious Philosopher* (1718–19), John Chamberlayne's translation from the Dutch of Bernard Nieuwentyt or Nieuwentijt.

The protégé of Isaac Newton, Desaguliers rapidly became well known in élite metropolitan circles and was adept at cultivating aristocratic patronage. One example of his diplomatic expertise is *The Newtonian System* of 1728, a long allegorical poem written for the accession of George II, which helped to ensure the continuation of his royal support. Flatteringly dedicating it to Queen Caroline, for whom he had already performed experiments, Desaguliers deftly wove together praise for Newton's genius, English liberty, and royal splendour by comparing Newtonian astronomical certitude with Hanoverian stability. In addition, Desaguliers's social mobility was greatly facilitated by his prominent role as an innovative freemason. He was closely involved with James Anderson in establishing the new constitution of speculative masonry in 1717, and belonged to the influential and prestigious lodge that met at the Rummer and Grapes inn close to his home in Channel Row. Desaguliers became grand master in 1719, was deputy grand master three times, and remained actively involved in masonic activities for most of his adult life. Like other members of London society, many fellows of the Royal Society were masons during this period. Desaguliers and his peers doubtless arranged many valuable acquaintanceships during meetings: in 1737, for example, he presided over the ceremonies in which Prince Frederick was initiated.

With his Huguenot origins, Desaguliers had many foreign contacts, and often travelled on masonic business: for instance, in 1721 he became a mason in Edinburgh; in 1731 he visited several cities in the Netherlands; and in 1735, on his only return to France, he attended an aristocratic initiation ceremony. However, the significance of his masonic allegiances for the promulgation of scientific ideas or for religious and political subversion is debatable. William Hogarth, also a freemason, is judged to have portrayed Desaguliers three times: in the background of a conversation piece packed with Newtonian references showing John Conduitt's town house, and in two satirical caricatures with masonic implications (as a pedantic preacher and as an old woman riding a donkey). In Hogarth's unflattering representations, confirmed by more conventional portraits, Desaguliers appears stocky and myopic.

Promoting Newtonianism Through his lectures, books, and activities at the Royal Society, Desaguliers contributed to the international consolidation of Newtonian natural philosophy and its establishment as a vital component of English polite culture. Fluent in English, French, and

Latin, he facilitated English familiarity with continental innovations through his translations, lectures, and books; conversely, by publishing in French, travelling to Europe, and maintaining international contacts, he helped to spread Newtonian ideas abroad. Enmeshed in a metropolitan network of instrument makers, natural philosophers, and experimental engineers, Desaguliers utilized his patronage relationships—particularly with Chandos—to gain financial backing for his technological innovations. Formerly appraised mainly for his role in developing and promoting Newton's ideas, Desaguliers is now also interpreted as a key figure in the rise of science as a public enterprise during the first half of the eighteenth century. By demonstrating the valuable contribution natural philosophy could make to England's material and commercial welfare, he helped to forge a mutually profitable alliance between Newtonian philosophy, public benefit, and private gain that facilitated the nation's future scientific, industrial, and economic transformation.

At Oxford, Desaguliers had attended John Keill's university course, on which his own lectures in Oxford and London were at first closely modelled. Soon after coming to London in 1712 he entered the competitive commercial world of popular lecturing. Benefiting from the death of Francis Hauksbee the elder in 1713, Desaguliers ran courses for Hauksbee's widow and—perhaps with Keill's backing—gradually took over Hauksbee's role as Newton's experimental assistant. Desaguliers was elected a fellow of the Royal Society in 1714, and from 1716 to 1743 filled Hauksbee's former post as curator of experiments. For several years he received Godfrey Copley's benefaction of £100, and was later awarded the society's annual Copley medal three times (1734, 1736, and 1741). The fact that his salary ranged between £30 and £50 a year according to the number of experiments and lectures he produced is reflected in his prolific output of over fifty papers in the society's *Philosophical Transactions*. These covered a huge variety of topics, most importantly optics, mechanics, and electricity, and relied on his great skill as an experimental demonstrator. This practical approach underpinned his theoretical work and his popular success, as well as his entrepreneurial engineering projects.

Practical experiments Before Newton's death in 1727, most of Desaguliers's activities at the Royal Society were dedicated to defending contested items of Newtonian doctrine in mechanics and optics. For example, he replicated older experiments and devised new ones to demonstrate the existence of a vacuum dispersed throughout apparently solid matter, a central tenet of Newtonian theory. His explanations of how he repeated some of Newton's optical experiments were designed specifically to refute French criticisms that Newton had left insufficient instructions to permit verification of his results. In 1727 he published four articles to counter important French claims that Newton had incorrectly described the shape of the earth. Other papers of this period described how he tested air resistance by dropping balls in St Paul's Cathedral, melted substances with a lens, and analysed perpetual motion machines.

Desaguliers was greatly influenced by Stephen Hales's *Vegetable Staticks* of 1727, a study of plant respiration informed by the lengthy suggestions Newton had articulated as queries in his *Opticks*. Having immediately welcomed this book in a laudatory review, in subsequent papers Desaguliers developed some of Hales's practical devices and explored the implications his conjectures raised about the repulsive and attractive properties of particles of matter. Spread over about fifteen years, Desaguliers's studies of elasticity (expansion and compression) and evaporation offered important contributions to the continuing eighteenth-century debate about whether repulsive phenomena were best accommodated within a Newtonian framework by corpuscles—as Desaguliers tried unsuccessfully to show—or by an aether, or subtle fluid, the solution favoured by English natural philosophers after about 1740.

Desaguliers's most radical conjecture about repulsive particles was to relate the elasticity of fluids and vapours to electricity. Although he had investigated electricity since at least 1716, when Stephen Gray came to live with him at Westminster for three years and assist at his lectures, Desaguliers started performing and describing experiments at the Royal Society only after Gray's death in 1736. Electricity was rapidly becoming the most exciting topic in natural philosophy, and Desaguliers studied and demonstrated phenomena such as conduction, discharge, and attraction and repulsion. Drawing on French research, he revised existing terminology and suggested that air consists of permanently electrified attractive and repulsive particles. His short *Dissertation Concerning Electricity* (1742), comprising accounts of twenty-nine experiments and his theoretical suggestions, won a prize offered by the Bordeaux Academy.

Lectures and demonstrations Outside the Royal Society, Desaguliers continued his commercial lecturing activities. These were extremely influential among the international community of natural philosophers as well as at a less scholarly level. Like that of other lecturers, his success owed much to his dramatic performances with instruments intended for demonstration rather than experimental research; many of these instruments he designed himself, including working models of engineering equipment he had invented and a planetarium, a mechanical device for displaying the movement of the planets round the sun, which he claimed was more accurate than elaborate orreries. In London men and women came to hear Desaguliers's frequent lectures at Channel Row, where his house must have been crammed with instruments, teaching materials, student boarders, and new inventions such as model engines and an 8 foot wide centrifugal bellows. Advertising his ability to lecture in three languages, Desaguliers went on lecturing tours to provincial cities like Bath and visited the Netherlands several times during the 1730s. In addition, he entertained

members of the royal family with philosophical experiments at Hampton Court and at Kew, where Prince Frederick had a room full of Desaguliers's instruments. In 1734 he boasted that he was embarking on his 121st course, and that, of the dozen or so other experimental lecturers in the world, eight had been his students. These included William 'sGravesande, who subsequently became a prominent professor interpreting and teaching Newtonian natural philosophy at Leiden, and Stephen Demainbray, a popular international lecturer who later worked for George III.

Writing and publishing Desaguliers reached still wider audiences by publishing his lectures, some versions appearing in French as well as English. His earlier publications, such as his *Physico-Mechanical Lectures* (1717) and a couple of syllabuses of the 1720s, were abstracts designed primarily as advertising material. Paul Dawson compiled *Lectures on Experimental Philosophy* (1719) from notes, opportunistically placing Desaguliers's name on the title page, but Desaguliers ensured that a critical preface was included. The first volume of his own far more substantial *Course of Experimental Philosophy* did not appear until 1734; there was a further delay of ten years before the appearance of the second volume, reportedly because Desaguliers was grappling with the international *vis viva* debate between Leibnizians and Newtonians about the mathematical relationship between the force and velocity of a moving object. The two volumes contain twelve separate lectures, many of them on mechanical topics, and each carrying detailed annotations for further study. Aiming at a wide market, Desaguliers deliberately avoided mathematical explanations. In a characteristically chauvinistic assault on René Descartes's 'philosophical Romance', he stressed that it was through Newton's experimental and observational approach that 'we owe the routing of this Army of Goths and Vandals in the Philosophical World' (preface, *Course of Experimental Philosophy*, 1734). With their fine illustrations these books—particularly the second—visually demonstrate the inseparability of Desaguliers's theoretical and experimental work at the Royal Society from the many schemes of practical engineering in which he was involved. As well as standard philosophical apparatus such as air-pumps, thermometers, and magnets, he built and described working models of technical inventions, including a watermill, steam engines, and carts. To explain physical principles he often used non-technical examples familiar to his popular audiences; for example, he showed labelled drawings of fairground performers displaying feats of strength.

In addition to his own writing and teaching, Desaguliers was involved in other publishing projects. For instance, he contributed pieces on topics such as the reflecting telescope and Hadley's quadrant. As a fluent linguist, in the early stages of his career he earned money through translations, though some arguments with publishers and authors did ensue. His choice of texts reflects his own interests, and sometimes he added Newtonian editorial notes. His translations from French included a detailed practical book on military fortification (1711), an instruction manual for building better chimneys (1715), a text on hydrostatics and water fountains (1718), and a short account of mechanical automata and wind instruments (1742). From Latin he translated Archibald Pitcairne's pro-Newtonian iatro-mechanical physiology (1715) and in 1720 'sGravesande's *Physices elementa mathematica* as *Mathematical Elements of Natural Philosophy*, thus influentially importing Dutch versions of Newtonian ideas into England.

Desaguliers was obsessed with experimentation. When some of his spectacular water rockets unfortunately exploded underneath a passing barge and nearly sank it, he immediately converted this disastrous experience into underwater trials of gunpowder. Constantly spending beyond his means, he sought ways to supplement his income by using his skills in natural philosophy to solve practical problems. For example, in collaboration with the instrument maker William Vream, he focused on the ventilation and heating deficiencies plaguing buildings, ships, and mines, and redesigned chimneys, bellows, and air heaters. Relying on his international connections with other engineers, he built new types of water-wheels and steam engines that could more efficiently drain water from mines or supply ornamental fountains. He constructed improved versions of other devices, including a pyrometer, a barometer, a crane, and various pumps.

In the competitive and financially unstable environment of early eighteenth-century London, Desaguliers became involved in patent disputes, forged temporary alliances with other entrepreneurs, denounced fraudsters, and used his social connections to win profitable contracts. Most importantly, between 1716 and about 1740, he was embroiled in an increasingly stormy patronage relationship with Chandos, initially visiting the latter's Middlesex estate every week. In exchange for clerical sinecures, Chandos deployed Desaguliers's technological expertise to improve his own property and involved him in numerous financial ventures, such as soap manufacture, ore refinement, and mine development. Desaguliers reported many of the inventions he developed for Chandos in the *Philosophical Transactions*. He showed the fellows experiments on working models to explain his innovations, and discussed the difficulties he had encountered in schemes to measure depth at sea, purify the air, or install piped water systems.

Desaguliers had long suffered from gout every winter, and died after several months of severe illness at his home in the Bedford Coffee House on 29 February 1744; he was buried on 6 March in the Savoy Chapel, Savoy Street, London. Mainly on the basis of a satirical verse by James Cawthorn in his poem 'The Vanity of Human Enjoyments', some biographers have claimed that Desaguliers died impoverished, but this seems unlikely since he made a will in favour of his elder son shortly before his death.

PATRICIA FARA

Sources M. E. Rowbottom, 'John Theophilus Desaguliers (1683–1744)', *Proceedings of the Huguenot Society*, 21 (1965–70), 196–218 • L. R. Stewart, *The rise of public science: rhetoric, technology, and natural philosophy in Newtonian Britain, 1660–1750* (1992) • J. Torlais, *Un rochelais grand-maître de la franc-maçonnerie et physicien au XVIII^esiècle, le Révérend J.-T. Desaguliers* (1937) • W. R. Hurst, *An outline of the career of John Theophilus Desaguliers, M.A., LL.D., F.R.S.* (1928) • J. Harland, *The house and farm accounts of the Shuttleworths of Gawthorpe Hall … from September 1582 to October 1621*, 4 vols., Chetham Society, 35, 41, 43, 46 (1856–8), 276–8 • J. Barles, 'Le schisme maçonnique anglais de 1717: autres notes sur Desaguliers', *Les Archives de Trans-en-Provence*, 61 (1937), 281–8 • J. Barles, 'Le schisme maçonnique anglais de 1717: autres notes sur Desaguliers', *Les Archives de Trans-en-Provence*, 62 (1938), 331–6 • R. Paulson, *Hogarth*, 2 (1992) • D. L. Lee, *Desaguliers of no. 4 and his services to freemasonry* (1932)

Archives BL, papers, Add. MSS 4432–4437 • RS, papers • U. Cam., scientific periodicals library, mathematical notebooks

Likenesses P. Pelham, mezzotint, 1725 (after H. Hysing), BM, NPG [*see illus.*] • W. Hogarth, group portrait, 1736 (*The sleeping congregation*) • J. Tookey, line print, 1815 (after H. Hysing), BM, NPG; repro. in Nichols, *Lit. anecdotes*, 9 • W. Hogarth, group portrait (*Scene from 'The conquest of Mexico'*) • W. Hogarth, group portrait (*The mystery of masonry brought to light*) • R. Scaddon, engraving (after T. Frye, 1743) • oils, NMM • portrait, repro. in J. Anderson, *Constitutions of the free masons* (1723), frontispiece

Wealth at death several livings; everything to elder son: will, 29 Nov 1743, PRO • died a pauper: Nichols, *Lit. anecdotes*, vol. 9, p. 641

Desaguliers, Thomas (1721–1780), army officer and military engineer, was born on 5 January 1721, and baptized on 20 January at St Mary's, Westminster, the fourth (but second surviving) son and fifth child of John Theophilus *Desaguliers (1683–1744), natural philosopher and engineer, and his wife, Joanna Pudsey (1690x95–1753). Pursuing his father's interest in the military applications of advances in mechanics, he entered the regiment of Royal Artillery as a cadet on 1 January 1740, and was promoted second lieutenant on 1 September 1741, first lieutenant on 1 February 1742, captain-lieutenant on 3 April 1743, and captain on 1 January 1745. He first saw service in Flanders in 1744, when he joined the Royal Artillery train under Colonel William Belford, and spent most of the period, until the close of the War of the Austrian Succession in 1748, on continental Europe. He was present at the battle of Fontenoy, as well as many minor engagements. On 18 March 1746 at St George, Mayfair, he married Mary Blackwood (*bap.* 23 June 1727), daughter of John Blackwood of Charlton, Kent, and his wife, Anne Mavel. They had three children: Mary Catherine (d. 1814), who married Thomas Cartwright of Aynho, Northamptonshire, and second Sir Stephen Cotterel, master of the ceremonies; Anne (1748–1801), who married Robert Shuttleworth of Gawthorpe, Lancashire; and Frederick (*bap.* 1749), who was killed in North America c.1775.

Desaguliers was made chief firemaster at Woolwich on 1 April 1748, a post which he held for thirty-two years, until his death in 1780. The chief firemaster was the superintendent of Woolwich arsenal, and Desaguliers was the first scientific maker of cannon and the first regular investigator into the powers of gunnery in the English army. He was promoted lieutenant-colonel on 5 February 1757, and in 1761 was summoned from his experiments and manufactures to take command of the siege train and the force of artillerymen intended to accompany the expedition to the island of Belleisle, off the west coast of France. This was the first opportunity for testing on a large scale the improvements made in siege artillery since the days of

Marlborough, and Desaguliers was able to put his ideas into practice. General Studholme Hodgson was in command, with generals Crauford, William Howe, John Burgoyne, and Guy Carleton under him, and when Desaguliers arrived at Belleisle on 12 April with the temporary rank of brigadier-general, one unsuccessful attempt had already been made to disembark. Desaguliers at once volunteered to reconnoitre, and, by putting some of his heavy guns into ship's boats, managed to cover the landing of the army. The island soon submitted, and General Hodgson directed Desaguliers to form the siege of the citadel. The manuscript journal which he kept during the siege of all his operations forms the basis of the account given of the siege by Francis Duncan in his *History of the Royal Regiment of Artillery*. Desaguliers got thirty guns and thirty mortars into battery, fired seventeen thousand shot and twelve thousand shells into the citadel, had great difficulties to contend with owing to the flooding of the trenches, and was wounded five days before the capitulation of the fortress on 7 June.

On his return to England Desaguliers was promoted colonel on 19 February 1762, and made colonel-commandant of a battalion of the Royal Artillery on 10 March the same year. He devoted himself for the rest of his life to his work at Woolwich. His work there was most valuable; he invented a method of firing small shot from mortars, and made the earliest experiments with rockets. Desaguliers's instrument was for many years in use at the royal gun factories for examining and verifying the bores of cannon. In recognition of his scientific work he was elected a fellow of the Royal Society in 1780, being the first officer of Royal Artillery who won that distinction. He was promoted major-general on 25 May 1772, and lieutenant-general on 29 August 1777, and died at Woolwich on 1 March 1780. His daughter Mary Catherine Cotterel was his sole executor and residuary legatee.

H. M. STEPHENS, rev. JONATHAN SPAIN

Sources F. Duncan, ed., *History of the royal regiment of artillery*, 2 vols. (1872–3) · J. Kane, *List of officers of the royal regiment of artillery from the year 1716 to the year 1899*, rev. W. H. Askwith, 4th edn (1900) · *Army List* (1772–8) · J. Balteau and others, eds., *Dictionnaire de biographie française*, [19 vols.] (Paris, 1933–) · H. Wagner, 'Descendants of Jean Desaguliers (Huguenot refugee)', *The Genealogist*, 5 (1881), 117–22 · M. E. Rowbottom, 'John Theophilus Desaguliers (1683–1744)', *Proceedings of the Huguenot Society*, 21 (1965–70), 196–218

Archives Royal Artillery Institution, Woolwich, London, papers, MD/80

Desart. For this title name *see* Cuffe, Hamilton John Agmondesham, fifth earl of Desart (1848–1934).

Des Barres, Joseph Frederick Wallet (1721–1824), hydrographer and colonial official, was born in November 1721, either in Basel, Switzerland, or in Paris, the eldest child of Joseph-Léonard Vallet des Barres, a Huguenot, and his wife, Anne-Catherine, *née* Cuvier. He was baptized Joseph-Frédéric Vallet and was educated at Basel under the Bernouillis. In 1752 or 1753, under the patronage of William Augustus, duke of Cumberland, he entered the Royal Military Academy, Woolwich. In February 1756 he

was commissioned lieutenant in the Royal Americans (62nd, later 60th foot), and that March embarked for North America. In 1758 he served as an assistant engineer at the siege of Louisbourg, Cape Breton Island, where he impressed his superior officers. He prepared a chart of the St Lawrence River, which was used by James Wolfe. He served as an assistant engineer in the 1759 and 1760 campaigns and worked on the Halifax defences in 1761. In 1762 he was an assistant engineer at the recapture of St John's, and after the French surrender he surveyed in Newfoundland with James Cook.

Recommended by the commanding officer of the Royal Navy in North America, from 1764 to 1773 Des Barres, with a small team and risking drowning, painstakingly surveyed the coast of Nova Scotia and beyond. He returned to England in 1774, and for several years prepared his and other charts and views for publication. His *The Atlantic Neptune, Published for the Use of the Royal Navy of Great Britain* (1774–84) comprised charts and views of Nova Scotia, New England, the Gulf of St Lawrence including Cape Breton and Prince Edward Island, and the coast south of New York. Largely accurate and aesthetically pleasing, these continued to be standard works well into the nineteenth century. Des Barres had a protracted dispute with the Admiralty over payment for the *Atlantic Neptune*. His other publications included *Nautical Remarks and Observations on the Coasts and Harbours of Nova Scotia* (1778).

Des Barres acquired by grant and purchase much land in the maritime colonies, becoming one of their largest landowners. He was promoted captain in September 1775 and major in March 1783. In August 1784 he was appointed lieutenant-governor of Cape Breton, where he arrived in January 1785. He encouraged immigration and economic development, including coalmining and whaling, and founded and planned the colony's capital, Sydney. However, he quarrelled with the military commander and others, largely over supplies. In November 1786 Thomas Townshend, Viscount Sydney, the home secretary, recalled Des Barres, and in 1787 the latter handed over to his successor, left Cape Breton, and returned to England. Following the appointment in 1794 of his friend William Windham as secretary at war, the government paid most of the expenses he claimed for the *Atlantic Neptune* and Cape Breton. He was promoted lieutenant-colonel in March 1794 and colonel in January 1798. He pressed for another colonial appointment and in May 1804, aged eighty-two, was appointed lieutenant-governor of Prince Edward Island, where he arrived in July 1805. Though hampered by the legislature's unwillingness to provide revenue, he built roads and public buildings and improved defence, but became involved in local political disputes, being associated with James Bardin Palmer and his 'loyal electors' against the rival 'old party'. Pressed by the landed proprietors, in August 1812 Henry, third Earl Bathurst, the colonial secretary, recalled Des Barres.

Des Barres moved to Amherst, Nova Scotia, and in 1817 to Halifax. He had six children with a mistress, Mary Cannon, whom he met in 1764 and whom in 1776 he made agent for his estates. Later they were estranged, and in

1809, alleging she had 'fraudulently and corruptly betrayed [his] trust and confidence' (*DCB*, 196), he sued her in the court of chancery in Halifax, but the case was still undecided when he died. He also had eleven children with Martha Williams of Shrewsbury, whom he may have married. He was a man of ability and vision, but pushy, selfish, and callous. His greatest achievement was the *Atlantic Neptune*. He died, aged 102, on 27 October 1824 at Halifax, Nova Scotia, and was buried there.   ROGER T. STEARN

Sources *DCB*, vol. 6 · G. N. D. Evans, *Uncommon obdurate: the several public careers of J. F. W. Des Barres* (1969) · J. C. Webster, *The life of Joseph Frederick Wallet Des Barres* (1933) · J. F. W. Des Barres, *A statement submitted by Lieutenant Colonel Desbarres, for consideration, respecting his services* (1795) · J. Philippart, ed., *The royal military calendar*, 3rd edn, 4 (1820), 138 · D. Campbell, *History of Prince Edward Island* (1875) · J. Knox, *An historical journal of the campaigns in North America for the years 1757–1760*, 2 vols. (1769) · J. Holland Rose and others, eds., *Canada and Newfoundland* (1930), vol. 6 of *The Cambridge history of the British empire* (1929–59) · J. B. Brebner, *Canada: a modern history* (1960)

Archives BL, letters and papers · NA Canada, corresp. and papers

Likenesses oils, NA Canada

Desborough. For this title name *see* Grenfell, William Henry, Baron Desborough (1855–1945); Grenfell, Ethel Anne Priscilla, Lady Desborough (1867–1952).

Desborough [Disbrowe], **Samuel** (1619–1690), politician and administrator, was born in November 1619 at Eltisley, Cambridgeshire, probably at the Old House, built in 1612 on the site of the rectory for his father, James Desborough, or Disbrowe (1582–1638), landowner and lord of the manor of Eltisley, and his wife, Elizabeth Marshall (d. 1628/9). Samuel seems not to have attended university or the inns of court. He developed strongly puritan religious views, and it was probably these which led him to emigrate to America.

After arriving at New Haven in July 1639, Desborough was one of the founders of Guilford, Connecticut. Despite his youth, he was named as one of the seven pillars of the Independent church there on 19 April 1643. On 27 October 1646 he was chosen magistrate for Guilford for the following year, and he became a leading figure in the settlement. In October 1649 he was chosen as one of the arbitrators in a boundary dispute between New Haven and Totoket. At an unknown date he married Dorothy (d. 1654), daughter of Henry *Whitfield of Ockley, Surrey, the first minister of Guilford, who too had emigrated to New Haven in 1639. The couple had at least one daughter, Sarah, who died in March 1649, and a son, James, who married Abigail Marsh of St Albans, Hertfordshire, on 9 March 1679, was admitted to the Royal College of Physicians in 1688, and died at Stepney Causeway between November 1690 and January 1691.

Desborough was still at Guilford early in November 1650, but returned to England soon afterwards, accompanied by his wife, children, and father-in-law. He quickly obtained state employment, perhaps through the influence of his brother John *Disbrowe or of George Fenwick, a fellow settler in Connecticut who had returned in 1645; both were then colonels in the parliamentary army. About

20 September 1651, before the completion of the conquest of Scotland, it was reported that there had been a 'great dispute between the officers and Comm[issioner] Desborow about the ships taken at Dundee. He claimed them in the right of the state, which they denied, and went on in the sale of them' (Firth, *Scotland and the Commonwealth*, 16). The following month, Desborough accompanied troops to arrest relations of the governor of Bass Island, who were threatened with the sequestration of their estates should the governor continue recalcitrant. By June 1652 Desborough had been made a parliamentary commissioner in Scotland; on 4 June he and his five fellow commissioners issued an order which named themselves and three others as visitors of the universities and schools in Scotland, and promised 'in convenient time, to alter and abolish all such lawes in the same, as shall be found inconsistent with the Government of the Commonwealth of England' (ibid., 44–5). Under an order of 11 November 1652, which placed the revenues of Scotland under military authority, Desborough served as one of the three commissioners for sequestrations, sitting at Leith, a post he continued to hold under the protectorate. His wife having died of smallpox in 1654, in the following year Desborough married Rose, *née* Hobson (1616/17–1699), widow of Samuel Penoyer, merchant of London.

During the protectorate Desborough was also an MP. In 1654 he was returned to Cromwell's parliament at Westminster, in which he sat for Edinburgh. During the elections of 1656 Lord Broghill reported that 'I shall engage the interest I have in Mid-Lothian for Mr Disborough'; on 30 August Monck reported his election for that seat (Thurloe, *State papers*, 5.295). Desborough became increasingly prominent in the administration of Scotland. On 30 March 1655 instructions were issued by Cromwell to nine persons, including Desborough, 'appointed his Highness's Council in Scotland, for the government of that nation' (*CSP dom.*, 1655, 108). Also in 1655 Desborough was appointed keeper of the great seal of Scotland. The seal appears not to have arrived for many months, for a letter from Broghill dated 25 June 1656 specified that he was now to discontinue the practice of signing his name to orders issued under its authority, and should use the seal instead. The warrant of authority formally vesting the office in him was dated even later, on 16 September 1657. Desborough continued to hold this office during the brief government of Richard Cromwell.

Meanwhile, early in 1656 a new Scottish version of the court of exchequer was set up to deal with forfeited estates, and Desborough was named as one of the presiding judges. But despite its narrowly defined jurisdiction, the court's activities aroused resentment, and by September 1657 Desborough was warning against efforts to expand the authority of what was widely seen as an executive instrument of foreign rule. Revenue commissioners, he thought, should pursue cases through the ordinary civil courts, despite the probability that these might be swayed by pressure from powerful Scottish vested interests. In May 1658 the court of sessions, renamed the commission for the administration of justice, was ordered to set aside time for issues arising from forfeited properties, and as a means to strengthen the authority of the court, Desborough was ordered to sit with the judges. In July 1658 he became their president and sat as chancellor, 'haiffing his mace borne befoir him' (Nicoll, 218).

Desborough's moderation must have met with the approval of George Monck, and they collaborated in efforts to have government sympathizers elected to Richard's parliament at the end of 1658, underestimating the determination of the duke of Argyll to frustrate this goal. Elected for the shire of Edinburgh, Desborough wrote to Monck that, though ill, he intended to make the long journey soon after the new year. Little is known of Desborough's political stance in 1659, but in spring 1660, with the Restoration increasingly certain, he grasped at the opportunity offered by the declaration of Breda and promised unswerving loyalty to Charles II: 'I do lay hold of and accept of his majesties grace favour and pardon in the said declaration held forth' (BL, Egerton MS 2519, fol. 32). His submission was signed on 21 May and personally witnessed by Monck.

Desborough obtained a full pardon, with restitution of goods and lands, on 12 December 1660. He retired to the manor of Elsworth, Cambridgeshire, purchased from Thomas Wendy in 1655 by trustees acting on his behalf, where he seems to have lived in complete obscurity, abstaining from politics. Pevsner suggests that the manor house there can be dated to the later seventeenth century and was probably built for Samuel Desborough. Desborough died at Elsworth on 10 December 1690 and was buried there. His will, proved on 16 April 1691, indicates great affection for his second wife, who was clearly not on good terms with her stepson James, and made elaborate provisions to ensure that she could enjoy her jointure and an income of £100 a year, measures apparently stemming from suspicion of his son's intentions. The young man, however, seems not to have long outlived his father. Rose died on 4 March 1699, aged eighty-two, and was buried next to her husband. STEPHEN WRIGHT

Sources F. D. Dow, *Cromwellian Scotland, 1651–1660* (1979) · BL, Egerton MS 2519 · H. Waters, *Genealogical gleanings in England* (Boston, 1886–9), vol. 1, pt 1 · C. H. Firth, *Scotland and the Commonwealth*, Publications of the Scottish History Society, 18 (1895) · C. H. Firth, ed., *Scotland and the protectorate: letters and papers relating to the military government of Scotland from January 1654 to June 1659*, Scottish History Society, 31 (1899) · C. Hoadly, ed., *Records of the colony and plantation of New Haven*, 2 vols. (1857) · J. Savage, *A genealogical dictionary of the first settlers*, 4 vols. (Boston, 1860–62) · Thurloe, *State papers*, vols. 5, 7 · J. Nicoll, *A diary of public transactions and other occurrences, chiefly in Scotland, from January 1650 to June 1667*, ed. D. Laing, Bannatyne Club, 52 (1836) · will, PRO, PROB 11/404, sig. 66 · *VCH Cambridgeshire and the Isle of Ely*, vols. 5, 9 · *Ancient town records: New Haven town records, 1649–1662*, New Haven Historical Society (1917) · *Cambridgeshire*, Pevsner (1970) · J. Felt, *The ecclesiastical history of New England* (1855) · will, PRO, PROB 11/450, sig. 56 [Rose Desborough, second wife] · IGI

Archives BL, corresp. and papers, Egerton MS 2519

Wealth at death substantial lands at Elsworth: will, PRO, PROB 11/404, sig. 66

Desch, Cecil Henry (1874–1958), metallurgist, was born at 99 Hemingford Road, Islington, London, on 7 September 1874, the eldest child in the family of two sons and one daughter of Henry Thomas Desch, surveyor, and his wife, Harriet Ingerson, of Pilton, Devon. Desch was educated at Birkbeck School, Kingsland, Middlesex, and at the age of fifteen entered Finsbury Technical College, London, where Silvanus Thompson was principal. He spent two years studying organic chemistry and a further year as a research student in the laboratory of Raphael Meldola. He then joined F. Kendall & Son, a firm of industrial chemists, in Stratford upon Avon, as assistant chemist, and took an external London BSc degree. He obtained a PhD at Würzburg University in 1902, and then studied under Sir William Ramsay at University College, London, and was awarded a DSc.

Desch's first academic appointment in 1902 was to the metallurgy department of King's College, London. While there, Sir Flinders Petrie asked him to work on metal implements found during the excavations at Ur. From 1908 until 1918 he was lecturer in metallurgy at Glasgow University, and became professor of metallurgy at the Royal Technical College, Glasgow, in 1918. In 1909 Desch married Elison Ann, the daughter of Professor Ivison Macadam, professor of chemistry at the Royal College of Surgeons, Edinburgh. They had two daughters.

From 1920 to 1932 Desch was professor of metallurgy at Sheffield University. In 1932 he became superintendent of the department of metallurgy at the National Physical Laboratory at Teddington, Middlesex. He retired in 1939, but with the outbreak of the Second World War he became scientific adviser to the Iron and Steel Research Council and then entered the steel industry, becoming, in 1943, director of research of Richard Thomas & Co. Ltd and, following reorganization, a director of the Whitehead Iron and Steel Company.

In 1923 Desch was elected FRS. He was president of the Faraday Society in 1926–8. President of the Institute of Metals in 1938–40, he was awarded their platinum medal in 1941. He was president of the Iron and Steel Institute (1946–8), having received the Bessemer gold medal in 1938. He thus achieved distinction in both ferrous and non-ferrous metallurgy.

As the author of many papers and books on metallurgical topics, Desch's most notable contribution was his book *Metallography*, which ran to six editions between 1910 and 1942. It was read with awe by generations of students who wondered how he succeeded in making such an interesting topic so boring. He was the forerunner of the modern professor of materials in that he wrote, with F. M. Lea, *The Chemistry of Cement and Concrete* (1956). He also published papers on social topics and had a great interest in historical metallurgy. Desch was a lithe man of military bearing whose presence commanded immediate respect. He died on 19 June 1958 in the General Hospital, Amersham, Buckinghamshire. He was survived by his wife.

J. NUTTING, *rev.*

Sources A. McCance, *Memoirs FRS*, 5 (1959), 49–68 · *Journal of the Iron and Steel Institute*, 155 (1947) · personal knowledge (1993) · *The Times* (21 June 1958), 8e · *The Times* (25 June 1958), 12b · CGPLA Eng. & Wales (1958) · b. cert. · d. cert. · *The Engineer* (27 June 1958), 972 ·

Engineering (27 June 1958), 804 · *Mining Engineering*, 11 (1959), 842 · *Nature*, 182 (1958), 223–4
Archives NRA, corresp. and notebooks · University of Sheffield Library, corresp., diaries, and papers | Sci. Mus., corresp. with Oswald John Silberrad
Likenesses photograph, repro. in McCance, *Memoirs FRS*
Wealth at death £16,373 2s. 7d.: probate, 22 Oct 1958, *CGPLA Eng. & Wales*

Desenfans, Noel Joseph (1744–1807), art dealer, was born at Avesnes-sur-Helpe, near St Quentin, France, in December 1744. Educated at the universities of Douai and Paris, he published the Rousseauesque *L'élève de la nature* (1763), and a stage comedy. At Douai he met the future actor John Philip Kemble and Charles-Alexandre de Calonne, first minister of France in the 1780s and a noted collector. He settled in London as a language tutor in 1769; on 10 June 1776 he married Margaret Morris (1731–1813), a wealthy woman and sister to Sir John Morris, bt, of Clasemont, Glamorgan.

Socially ambitious, financially secure, but inexperienced, Desenfans began picture dealing, and in 1784 he moved to a large house, 38 and 39 Charlotte Street, Portland Place (now demolished). He forged close links with Jean-Baptiste-Pierre Lebrun (1748–1813) of Paris, a remarkable connoisseur and dealer, with whom he worked for over thirty years, and whose example he followed of using his private house to display his personal collection, preferring to seem a gentleman-dealer. He lavishly entertained the world of art and literature but not high society. About 1776 Desenfans 'adopted' (informally) Peter Francis Bourgeois (1756–1811), who had been abandoned by his Swiss watchmaker father, and who, although an indifferent painter, by the 1780s assisted Desenfans in his business.

Lebrun helped Desenfans to obtain major masterpieces such as Murillo's *Flower Girl* (c.1670), Poussin's *Triumph of David* (c.1631–3; both from the Calonne collection), and Watteau's *Les plaisirs du bal* (c.1716–17), all now in Dulwich Picture Gallery, London. Lebrun's paintings were sold by Desenfans privately or at auction, with proceeds divided equally between them. Desenfans became well known, if not well liked, and in 1790 Prince Michael Poniatowski, brother of Stanisław August, king of Poland, asked him to abandon commerce so as to 'promote the progress of the fine arts in Poland' (Taylor). The king's tastes are reflected in the purchases made by Desenfans; Stanisław wished to found a Polish national gallery in Warsaw, and appointed Desenfans consul-general of Poland in London.

There were rich pickings from the dispersal of French and Italian noble collections. Rembrandt's *A Young Man, perhaps the Artist's Son Titus* (1663; possibly from the Calonne collection), Veronese's *St Jerome and a Donor* (c.1580), Claude-Joseph Vernet's *Italian Landscape* (1738; from the Calonne collection), Raphael's *St Francis of Assisi* and *St Anthony of Padua* (1540–45; from the Colonna altarpiece), and Rubens's *Venus, Mars, and Cupid* (c.1636–8; both from the Orléans collection) were among the principal masterpieces Desenfans bought for the king and which are now at Dulwich. For in 1795 Poland was partitioned for the third time in twenty-two years, and Stanisław abdicated. His death in 1798 extinguished any hope that Desenfans would be paid for the 180 paintings he had acquired for Poland, and three applications to the tsars for payment proved fruitless. Desenfans claimed to have spent £9000 on paintings for Poland between 1790 and 1795, and to have given up other valuable business. He wrote *A Plan for Establishing a National Gallery* in 1799, proposing, unsuccessfully, that the British government should add his paintings to the British Museum's collection, as part of a more general campaign to establish a national gallery in London.

In February and March 1802 Desenfans held an auction of the 'Polish' paintings at Skinner and Dyke, Berners Street, London, publishing a two-volume catalogue in which he extolled French connoisseurship and damned the mediocrity and jealousy of British dealers—a foolish exercise which earned him lasting animosity. Many of the attributions were very optimistic and the sale was a failure. By 1803 Bourgeois seems to have taken over the running of Desenfans's affairs—Desenfans now suffering from a nervous illness—and added major works such as Guercino's *Woman Taken in Adultery* (c.1621) to the collection, which he wished to preserve intact. Desenfans died at his home in London on 8 July 1807; by his will of 8 October 1803 he bequeathed his property jointly to his widow and Bourgeois, but his paintings to Bourgeois only. His remains, later moved to Dulwich, were housed in a mausoleum designed by Sir John Soane and erected behind his Charlotte Street house. Although the will does not require that the collection of 350 paintings be kept together, Bourgeois knew of his friend's wishes and in his own will of 20 December 1810 bequeathed it to Mrs Desenfans on condition that it went to Dulwich College after her death. Soane designed the Dulwich Picture Gallery and a mausoleum within, which houses the remains of Mr and Mrs Desenfans and Sir Francis Bourgeois. DENNIS FARR

Sources will, 8 Oct 1803, PRO, PROB 11/1465, sig. 655 · J. T. [J. Taylor], *Memoir of Noel Desenfans* (1810) · G. Waterfield, 'A history of Dulwich Picture Gallery', in G. Waterfield and others, *Rembrandt to Gainsborough: masterpieces from Dulwich Picture Gallery* (1999), 11–22 · P. Murray, *The Dulwich Picture Gallery: a catalogue* (1980)
Archives Dulwich College, London, letters and memoranda · Dulwich Picture Gallery, London, MSS
Likenesses J. Northcote, oils, 1796, Dulwich Picture Gallery, London · P. Sandby, watercolour, c.1805 (with P. F. Bourgeois), Dulwich Picture Gallery, London · C. Prosperi, bust, Dulwich Picture Gallery, London · oils, Dulwich Picture Gallery, London
Wealth at death clearly wealthy: will, PRO, PROB 11/1465, sig. 655

Des Granges, David (*bap.* 1611, *d.* in or before 1672?), miniature painter, was baptized on 24 March 1611 at the French church in Threadneedle Street, in the City of London, and again at the church of St Anne Blackfriars. He was the first of five children of Samson Des Granges (*d.* 1636) and his wife, Marie, *née* Bouvier, who had married, also at the French church, on 2 November 1609. Among the witnesses of David's baptism and the baptism of the second son, Francis (10 June 1613), were the maternal aunt Esther, a silkwoman to the queen, and George Heriot, the king's goldsmith and jeweller. The family continued to live in the parish of St Anne Blackfriars, close to the family of Isaac Oliver, Cornelius Jonson, and Anthony Van Dyck, until David's marriage at the church of St Martin-in-the-Fields, on 7 January 1636, to Judith Hoskins. Her family is not known but the name suggests a relationship with the household of John *Hoskins, and hence with Samuel and Alexander Cooper, all miniaturists. David and Judith Des Granges had at least four children whose names are identifiable: David (d. 1648), John (1643–1685/6), Mary (b. 1646), and Esther (d. 1690). The family lived on Elm Street, Long Acre, in the parish of St Martin-in-the-Fields, where David is documented until 1672 (Edmond, 'Limners and picturemakers', 123–4). In 1671 he petitioned the king for payment of money owed to him. In 1672, though three people with the name Degrange (John, Magdalen, and Katherine) were mentioned in Samuel Cooper's will, he himself was not, and was presumably dead.

Des Granges's earliest miniatures date from the later 1620s and show a strong consciousness of the style and technical practice of both Peter Oliver and John Hoskins. Like Alexander Cooper he may have been taught by Peter Oliver. During the 1630s he seems to have worked in some sort of association, possibly arising out of a family relationship with Hoskins, helping in particular with the multiplication of Hoskins's images, after Van Dyck, of the king and the future Charles II (versions are in the Buccleuch collection, Scotland, the National Portrait Gallery, and the Victoria and Albert Museum, London). This period culminates in the painting in 1640 of the so-called *Allegory of the Marchese del Vasto*, after the Titian then in the Royal Collection (now in the Musée du Louvre, Paris). Des Granges's miniature, which is in the collection of the Victoria and Albert Museum at Ham House in Surrey, would have been copied via an *editio princeps* by Peter Oliver of 1629 (Royal Collection), which was borrowed from the Royal Collection in that year to be copied also by Richard Gibson, 'My Ld Chamberleine's Page' (the Gibson miniature is dated 1640 and is now at Welbeck Abbey in Nottinghamshire).

At the outbreak of the civil wars Des Granges seems to have followed the court out of London. During the interregnum he was with Charles II in Scotland, producing batches of a Charles II likeness after Adriaen Hanneman (versions in the National Portrait Gallery and at Ham House), on which Nathaniel Thach also worked (versions of the Thach copy are in the Mauritshuis in The Hague and on loan at the Victoria and Albert Museum). It was this work that gave rise to Des Granges's petition to the king in 1671 for payment due, in which he claims, perhaps plausibly but in the language usual in such petitions, to be 'old and infirm, and his sight and his labour failing him … forced to rely on the charity of well-disposed persons' (Goulding, 29). The schedule to the same document specifies the distribution of thirteen miniatures:

> one to a French Marquess who came to Your Majesty at St Johnston's in 1651 pretending raising a troop of horse for Your Majesty; one to Mr Oudart … one to Mr Seymour … one to Lady Balcarris … one for Lady Annandale … one for Major

> Boswel … which Your Majesty gave with your own hands; one to Mr Harding, attendant upon Your majesty, given the same night; three to Sir James Erskine … One to my Lord of Newburgh; one to my Lady Tullibardin, and one to Mr Rainsford employed in a message to Your majesty on the 6th of July 1651. (ibid.)

The list shows how important the portrait miniature was in acquiring and maintaining the loyalty of those in the inner circle of the exiled king, at this time especially.

After the Restoration there is some fine, sophisticated work by Des Granges showing that he responded to the influence of the new court portraitists such as Jacob Huysmans (*Catherine of Braganza as a Shepherdess*, formerly in the collection of Mrs Daphne Foskett) and some evidence (a so-called *Brian Duppa* in the Victoria and Albert Museum) that he experimented with the red-brown hatching style associated with Samuel Cooper. This stylistic variability, and the existence of some poor-quality work that bears the DDG monogram, has led to the use of Des Granges's name as a portmanteau attribution, especially in the salerooms. That in turn has inflated the apparent size of his *œuvre* in miniature, which may well now distort our sense of the main field in which he was active. George Vertue saw an engraving by him: 'St. George on horseback—after Raphael—David des Granges Sculpsit 1628. I have before remarkt. this print. dedicated to Wm. Earl of Pembroke—and afterwards done by L. Vorstermans, much like it' (Vertue, *Note books*, 4.194). He is also reputed to have been a painter in oils: the well-known large oil painting *The Saltonstall Family* (Tate collection), a composition that defies the Renaissance science of perspective, is attributed to him. In 1658 William Sanderson, a court loyalist like Des Granges, citing the leading artists of the British school, referred to him alongside Robert Walker, Gerard Soest, John Michael Wright, Sir Peter Lely, and John Hales (or Hayls) as 'rare Artizans' (*Graphice*, 1658, 20), but no substantial or certain *œuvre* in oils survives on which to base any sense of his achievement in that medium. He was not mentioned by Sanderson among the miniaturists, nor as an engraver.　　　　JOHN MURDOCH

Sources Vertue, *Note books* · R. W. Goulding, 'The Welbeck Abbey miniatures', *Walpole Society*, 4 (1914–15) [whole issue] · M. Edmond, 'Limners and picturemakers', *Walpole Society*, 47 (1978–80), 60–242, esp. 123–4 · M. Edmond, *Hilliard and Oliver: the lives and works of two great miniaturists* (1983) · J. Murdoch, *Seventeenth-century English miniatures in the collection of the Victoria and Albert Museum* (1997)

Des Maizeaux, Pierre (1672/3–1745), biographer and journalist, was born at Paillat in the Auvergne, France, the only child of Louis Des Maizeaux (d. 1701), protestant pastor, and Marie Dumonteil (d. 1726). In 1685, after his father was indicted for sedition for an incautious remark in a sermon about Louis XIV and the revocation of the edict of Nantes, the family fled to Switzerland. Des Maizeaux was educated at the lyceum in Bern (1690–95) and the academy in Geneva (1695–9), where he studied theology. He had an early reputation for independence of mind and left for England in 1699 before completing his studies, never to return. His father, who expected him to become a pastor, found his son's abandonment of a ministerial career hard to forgive.

Des Maizeaux passed through the Netherlands where he made contacts in the book trade and met the great Huguenot religious philosopher Pierre Bayle. In England he at first made a living as a tutor and writer, but soon began to search for a secure patronage appointment, which constantly eluded him, although he obtained timely, if modest, help from Anthony Ashley Cooper, third earl of Shaftesbury, Joseph Addison, Lord Halifax, and Thomas Parker, lord chancellor. His legal position in England was secured when he was naturalized in 1708, and his finances improved enough for him to abandon tutoring when he gained an Irish pension, through Addison's patronage, in 1710. He lived in rented accommodation in London, mostly in or near Soho, near St Martin's Lane.

In 1700 Des Maizeaux began to contribute articles and literary news on English books and their authors to French-language journals in the Netherlands and France. This became a staple for more than four decades through which he made a wide range of English writing and thought better known on the continent. He was an early theorist of the literary journal, and recognized its significance for realizing the ideal of the republic of letters. His friends and acquaintances in England included Hans Sloane, secretary of the Royal Society; the freethinkers John Toland and Anthony Collins, whose friendship and intellectual compatibility was significant; Richard Steele and Joseph Addison; Dr Richard Mead, celebrated physician and antiquarian book collector; the French booksellers in the Strand; and the Huguenot intellectuals who regularly met at the Rainbow Coffee House and later at Slaughter's in St Martin's Lane. He befriended the Epicurean satirist and exile Charles de Saint-Evremond, then living in London, and jointly edited his works and wrote his biography (Œuvres mêlées de Saint-Evremond, 2 vols., 1705, and Mélanges curieux, 2 vols., 1706).

Bayle, however, is the central figure in Des Maizeaux's literary career. Des Maizeaux won Bayle's respect and friendship while sending him material for the second edition of Bayle's Dictionnaire historique et critique (3 vols., 1702) and defended the philosopher's reputation against slanderous attacks in England. His early journalism, including his critique of Cartesian proofs of God's existence and a draft criticism of Leibniz, was favourably received by Bayle. Des Maizeaux wrote two lives of Bayle, the first, The Life of Mr. Bayle (1708), appeared soon after Bayle's death in 1706, while the other, La vie de l'auteur (1730), is often viewed as his best biographical writing, notwithstanding its hagiographic treatment of its subject. He portrayed Bayle less as a systematic sceptic and more as a freethinker acutely aware of the limits of human reason. He collected and edited Bayle's correspondence twice. The first time his edition was appropriated by Prosper Marchand (Lettres choisies de Mr. Bayle, 3 vols., 1714), which provoked a protracted literary quarrel between the rival claimants to Bayle's literary heritage; the second edition was Lettres de Bayle (3 vols., 1729). He extended Bayle's historical-critical method to English lives, and published lives of two seventeenth-century latitudinarians, John

Hales and William Chillingworth. The model was later adopted and extended in the General Dictionary Historical and Critical (10 vols., 1734–41), with which he was associated and to which he contributed lives of Addison and materials for its life of Collins. Several of its other articles rely on his biographies. A set of rare lives in French that he had collected was published, but not as a collection, in Dutch periodicals. The most controversial was La vie de Spinose, which had previously circulated clandestinely in manuscript; its publication in Nouvelles littéraires (10, 1719, 40–74) provoked strong critical reaction. His antiquarian interests were also reflected in his edition of a volume of rare sixteenth-century Latin love poetry by Jean Bonnefons, from a book he borrowed from the earl of Sunderland; it was published as Johannis Bonefonii Arverni carmina (1720).

Des Maizeaux edited two significant collections. The first, Collection of Several Pieces of John Locke (1720), used materials largely supplied by his friend Anthony Collins. The second, Recueil de diverses pièces (2 vols., 1720), includes Samuel Clarke's celebrated correspondence with Leibniz and Anthony Collins's dispute with Clarke on human liberty, as well as shorter pieces on the dispute between Newton and Leibniz on the discovery of the calculus and other Leibnizian material. Newton tried to delay or divert the publication of the correspondence on the calculus which, as he anticipated, reignited a dispute he did not wish to see revived. For his publication of Receuil, Des Maizeaux was made a fellow of the Royal Society (1720), an honour he highly valued. He also edited John Toland's posthumous papers, Collection of Several Pieces of Mr. John Toland (2 vols., 1726), to which he added a biographical sketch. When Collins died, it was expected that Des Maizeaux would do the same for him, but he sold the manuscripts Collins had left him to Collins's widow, an action he regretted, but was unable to undo.

Not all of Des Maizeaux's writings were well received. His Life of Boileau (1712) provoked Warburton's witticism that Des Maizeaux seemed to believe that 'every Life must be a Book; and, what is worse, it seems a Book without a Life' (Nichols, Lit. anecdotes, 5.546). He was attracted to individuals such as the latitudinarians and freethinkers with an adventurous cast of mind who challenged orthodoxy, but he became increasingly cautious about revealing much of himself, particularly when not writing anonymously. In his life of Hales he declared he would give no basis to the charges made against Bayle of writing obscenely or undermining religion. Lord Molesworth thought he would do better 'if he would imitate Monsr. Bayle more' (BL, Add. MS 4465, fol. 36, undated letter, John Toland to Molesworth). Nevertheless, the free examination of ideas and toleration are themes which inform his writing. Some 1300 letters from more than 200 correspondents sent to Des Maizeaux survive in the British Library. They include one from the young David Hume in 1739 soliciting Des Maizeaux's opinion of his philosophical writing. Collectively they illuminate the state of the republic of letters of which Des Maizeaux viewed himself a citizen.

For much of his life Des Maizeaux was in financial need and poor health, both of which impeded his literary projects. Nevertheless, he was generous and provided money to his mother, to John Toland, and to Richard Steele. He was a rotund figure, and a French visitor to London in 1724 described him in appearance as 'un pauvre cancre' ('a poor wretch'; *Journal et mémoires de Matthieu Marais*, 3.272). In the 1730s he was living with a common-law wife, Ann Brown, and her young daughter, of whom he was possibly the father. They married at St Paul's, Covent Garden, on 2 February 1740 to facilitate the transfer of his pension in anticipation of his death, which took place on 11 July 1745.　　　　　　　　　　J. DYBIKOWSKI

Sources J. Almagor, *Pierre Des Maizeaux (1673-1754): journalist and English correspondent for Franco-Dutch periodicals, 1700-1720* (1989) · P. Bayle, *Œuvres diverses*, ed. E. Labrousse, 4 vols. (1968), 4 · C. Berkvens-Stevelinck, *Prosper Marchand et l'histoire du livre* (1978) · BL, Birch MSS, Add. MSS 4282, fols. 204-5; 4283, fols. 239-40; 4289, fols. 37-8, 83, 336 · J. Toland, letter to Robert Molesworth, [n.d.], BL, Add. MS 4465, fol. 36 · J. H. Broome, 'An agent in Anglo-French relationships: Pierre Des Maizeaux (1673-1745)', PhD diss., U. Lond. · E. Carayol, 'Père et fils: deux lettres de Louis Desmaizeaux à son fils Pierre', *Bulletin* [Société de l'Histoire du Protestantisme Français], 104 (1958), 186-93 · *Bulletin* [Société de l'Histoire du Protestantisme Français], 87 (1938), esp. 198 · *Bulletin Historique et Littéraire* [Société de l'Histoire du Protestantisme Français], 47 (1898), esp. 462-3 · *The correspondence of Isaac Newton*, ed. H. W. Turnbull and others, 6-7 (1976-7) · *GM*, 1st ser., 15 (1745), 388 · A. Goldgar, *Impolite learning* (1995) · *Journal et mémoires de Matthieu Marais*, 4 vols. (1863-8), vol. 3, p. 272 · Nichols, *Lit. anecdotes* · *The record of the Royal Society of London*, 4th edn (1940), 396 · S. Stelling-Michaud, ed., *Le livre du recteur de l'Académie de Genève, 1559-1878*, 6 vols. (Geneva, 1959-80), vol. 3, pp. 94-5; vol. 6, p. 366 · *DNB*

Archives BL, Add. MSS 4281-4289; 4470 · BL, MSS, Add. MS 4226 | BL, letters, mainly to Sir Hans Sloane, Sloane MSS 4037-4066 · PRO, Shaftesbury MSS · Société de l'Histoire du Protestantisme Français, Paris, Charles de la Motte corresp. · University of Leiden, Marchand MSS

Desmond. For this title name *see* Fitzgerald, Maurice fitz Thomas, first earl of Desmond (*c*.1293-1356); Fitzgerald, Gerald fitz Maurice, third earl of Desmond (1338?-1398); Fitzgerald, Thomas, seventh earl of Desmond (1426?-1468); Fitzgerald, James fitz Maurice, *de jure* twelfth earl of Desmond (*d.* 1540); Fitzgerald, James fitz John, thirteenth earl of Desmond (*d.* 1558); Fitzgerald, Gerald fitz James, fourteenth earl of Desmond (*c*.1533-1583); Fitzgerald, Katherine, countess of Desmond (*d.* 1604); Fitzgerald, James fitz Thomas, *styled* fifteenth earl of Desmond (*d.* 1608?); Fitzgerald, James fitz Gerald, fifteenth earl of Desmond (*c*.1570-1601).

Desmond, Florrie [*real name* Florence Elizabeth Dawson] (1905-1993), actor and impersonator, was born Florence Elizabeth Dawson on 31 May 1905 at 64 Bride Street, Lower Holloway, London, the daughter of George Dawson, a bootmaker who loved the theatre, and his wife, Ada Baker, a barmaid. She was educated at Dame Alice Owen's School in Islington until the age of fourteen.

Having attended many productions at nearby Sadler's Wells, at the age of ten Florrie Dawson won a role in a touring pantomime, *Babes in the Woods*, earning £5 weekly. At twelve, already blessed with a deep, husky voice, she

Florrie Desmond (1905-1993), by Dorothy Wilding, 1930s

began calling herself Desmond (no reason for the choice has emerged). After leaving school she began a full-time professional career, as Florrie Desmond, in variety, a genre engaged in distancing itself from its working-class parent, music-hall. In a turn she later categorized as 'low comedy', Desmond played two distinct characters—a male dude and a pretty little girl. She continued thus for several years, working briefly with Marie Lloyd before Lloyd's death in 1922.

The tiny, blonde Desmond bloomed in her era's more sophisticated new entertainment genres—cabaret, revue, and radio. Eventually she became the best-known 'impressionist' (as such artistes were then called) of her era. In 1925 she was dancing in the Piccadilly Hotel's cabaret when she was selected by the impresario Charles B. Cochran to join the first troupe of Mr Cochran's Young Ladies. This revue chorus, patterned upon the intelligent, multi-talented small choruses of André Charlot, became a springboard for many future stars.

Working for Cochran, Desmond also understudied the revue star Hermione Baddeley from 1925 to 1926. After diction and singing sessions with Geraldine Ullmar, an American who had in the 1890s sung Gilbert and Sullivan in London, Desmond went to New York with Cochran and Noël Coward's *This Year of Grace* (1928). There she understudied the comedienne Beatrice Lillie. Upon her return and apparently on the advice of Coward, Desmond decided to specialize, incorporating what she had seen and heard on Broadway into a cabaret act based upon mimicry.

Impressions of famous people (usually very broad, partly through fear of litigation) had long been a staple of theatrical entertainment, but Desmond raised the level of the genre, employing the quick strokes of a caricaturist. The variety historian Roger Wilmut praised the wickedness of her observation: 'just enough exaggeration without becoming a caricature' (Wilmut, 28). Desmond later confessed to a certain puzzlement at her own skill, saying she started 'with the shape of the face … it took no more than three sightings' (private information).

Desmond's new act emphasized impressions of stage stars—Alice Delysia (Cochran's long-time French leading lady), Jessie Matthews (a Charlot and Cochran star), Tallulah Bankhead (the outrageous American), and Coward himself. When Charlot hired her for his 1930 revue, which opened London's art deco Cambridge Theatre, she raised her impression of Bankhead to new heights, as attested after the performance by Bankhead herself: 'She speaks like me off stage—the bitch!' (Desmond, 49).

The rise of talking motion pictures, alongside the increasing popularity of the wireless (an estimated 12 million listeners by 1930), made Desmond a star. She had made her first appearance in film in 1931 with Gracie Fields in *Sally in our Alley*, and for a 1933 BBC broadcast Desmond wrote a sketch called 'Hollywood Party', a *tour de force* in which she impersonated Janet Gaynor entertaining Fields, Bankhead, Greta Garbo, Marie Dressler, ZaSu Pitts, Marlene Dietrich, and even Jimmy Durante. HMV quickly signed her to repeat it—the recording became a best-seller—and it was incorporated into the revue *Savoy Follies*. Onstage, Desmond recalled, she changed character simply by pushing her hair around.

The success of 'Hollywood Party' brought Desmond a contract with Fox Films in the USA. She appeared in the 1933 *Mr Skitch* alongside Will Rogers and Pitts (in one scene she impersonates Pitts while standing alongside her) but though she gained some fame on the vaudeville stage, her American film career never blossomed. Back in Britain in 1934, she appeared with Sophie Tucker and the dance bands of Maurice Winnick and Howard Jacobs in the film *Gay Love* and expanded her repertory to include John Gilbert, Katharine Hepburn, Lionel Barrymore, and Mae West in the revue *Why not Tonight?* In the 1935 musical comedy *Seeing Stars* she added Bing Crosby and tragedienne Elisabeth Bergner.

A particular peak came in 1934 when, in Cochran's revue *Streamline*, Desmond demolished the overstated, commercialized heroics of the famous errant aviator Amy Johnson. In the same year Desmond met the pilot Tom Campbell Black, who proceeded to win the 1934 England–Australia air race. They married in 1935, but eighteen months later Black was killed in a collision on the ground in Liverpool. They had no children. She soon met Charles Hughesdon, another pilot who was also an insurance salesman, and they married in 1937. They adopted a son, Christopher, and remained married until Desmond's death.

Desmond's film career continued in a variety of roles and with varied co-stars: George Formby jun., Douglas Fairbanks jun., Harry Richman. In 1937 she was added (Desmond claimed, by the queen herself) to the royal variety performance. The Second World War brought a number of Entertainments National Service Association tours, a great deal of radio work aimed directly at the armed forces, regular stints at the Café de Paris (until it was bombed out), a series of Palladium revues alongside the Crazy Gang, pantomimes—always as the glamorous principal boy—and her best-known recording, the *risqué* 'I've got the deepest shelter in town'.

Desmond became much better known in the USA after an engagement at New York's Blue Angel Club in 1946 and continued in similarly upmarket venues, including the Persian Room of the Plaza Hotel and El Rancho Vegas in Las Vegas, Nevada. During her Blue Angel residency she appeared on Broadway in *If the Shoe Fits*, a pastiche Cinderella tale in which she added Claudette Colbert to her repertory. Desmond toured South Africa and made another royal variety performance appearance in 1951. In the early 1950s she was a frequent guest on the American television series *Your Show of Shows*. In 1952 Desmond's West End comeback, playing seven roles in a comedy written for her called *The Apples of Eve*, lasted only two weeks. Her 1958 swansong was much more satisfactory. Playing opposite Beatrice Lillie in *Auntie Mame* as best friend Vera Charles, she was part of a happy 301-performance run.

Desmond gradually withdrew from performing. She and Hughesdon retired to Surrey; as 'Mrs C. Hughesdon' Desmond was patron to the Ambassadors Theatre in Woking. After St Luke's Hospital in Guildford closed in 1983, the name of a ward there, which she had endowed, was revived in 1985 as the Florence Desmond Day Hospital of the Royal Surrey County Hospital, specializing in the care of the elderly.

Desmond retained her gift for impersonation well into old age. In an interview given when aged seventy-six she suddenly slipped into an imitation of Bette Davis: 'from four feet away [she] was hilariously accurate in both voice and appearance' (Wilmut, 28). She died in Guildford on 16 January 1993.   JAMES ROSS MOORE

Sources [F. Desmond], *Florence Desmond by herself* (1953) · *Variety* (25 Jan 1993) · R. Wilmut, *Kindly leave the stage! The story of variety, 1919–1960* (1985) · D. Gilford, *The golden age of radio* (1985) · B. Dean, *Mind's eye* (1973) · private information (2004) [D. Drummond] · private information (2004) [S. Fisher, Royal Surrey County Hospital, Guildford] · *CGPLA Eng. & Wales* (1993) · b. cert.
Archives Theatre Museum, London, papers | Trinity College of Music, London, Mander and Mitchenson Theatre Collection, papers | FILM BFI NFTVA, performance footage | SOUND BL NSA, 'The leading ladies: Florence Desmond', T3736BWBD1 · BL NSA, 'Recollections of her life and career', P704RBD1 · BL NSA, documentary recordings · BL NSA, performance recordings
Likenesses D. Wilding, photograph, 1930–39, NPG [see illus.]
Wealth at death £175,525: probate, 7 April 1993, *CGPLA Eng. & Wales*

Desoutter, André Marcel (1894–1952), aviator and airport manager, was born on 31 January 1894 at 1 Maddox Street,

London, the second of six children of Louis Albert Desoutter and his wife, Philomène. His parents were French immigrants, his father being a skilled watchmaker and jeweller. After education at the London Polytechnic in Regent Street, Desoutter was trained as a watchmaker, endowing him with a craftsman's belief in accuracy, application, and rectitude.

In 1911 Desoutter took flying lessons at Hendon aerodrome but after passing the tests had to wait until his eighteenth birthday before he could be issued with pilot's licence no. 186. Within a few weeks he became a flying instructor. His life changed dramatically on Easter Sunday 1913 when he lost control of his monoplane and crashed before a large audience, breaking a leg. The fracture proved difficult to repair, and after tetanus set in, the leg was amputated above the knee. With intensive nursing, large doses of drugs, and a determination to live, he made a remarkable recovery, earning a lengthy report in *The Lancet* (1.308–9).

Desoutter received the standard clumsy peg leg, but with the help of his younger brother Charles, an articulated leg made of duralumin was successfully assembled to enable him to resume many of his activities, including flying. With Marcel as managing director, Desoutter Bros. Ltd was formed in 1914 to manufacture artificial legs. Greatly expanding during the First World War, the company also developed the production of pneumatic handdrills which Charles had invented, initially for making the artificial legs.

In 1929 Desoutter sold his interest in the family firm to his brothers. Forming the Desoutter Aircraft Company, he began building at Croydon airport, under licence, a threeseat, cabin monoplane. A number of orders were obtained, and success seemed to be achievable, but the demise of a major customer led to the closure of the company in 1932 after forty-one machines had been built. The aeroplane manufactured by the firm had a good reputation and two were later preserved in museum collections.

Desoutter became technical consultant to the Artificial Limb Company at Roehampton, but returned to aviation again in 1934. He became business manager of Airports Ltd, which the previous year had been formed by Morris Jackaman to develop Gatwick aerodrome into a passenger airport. Desoutter and Jackaman both recognized Gatwick's great potential, as it was on a main-line railway near London; and they eventually persuaded Hillman's Airways, a new airline, to transfer to Gatwick after the Southern Railway had been induced to open a new station. They initiated major improvements to the airport while architects were engaged to design a terminal. More capital was obtained by Airports Ltd and it became a public company in 1935, with Jackaman and Desoutter as joint managing directors. In the meantime, the airline had merged with others to become British Airways Ltd, transferring to Gatwick with its services in the spring of 1936. When Jackaman resigned, Desoutter became sole managing director of Airports Ltd in 1937.

The future for Gatwick may have looked bright at first, with several features including the first circular airport terminal and its own railway station; but, after the airport became water-logged in 1937, it lost its passenger services. Desoutter again displayed his determination when he persuaded the military authorities to set up an RAF air training school. This was followed by the establishment of aviation companies (Airwork Ltd and Southern Aircraft Ltd) associated with defence activities.

During the Second World War the airport was requisitioned for the RAF. Desoutter still believed that Gatwick had a potential for passenger services, however, and in 1943 commissioned a report to indicate how the airport could be developed after the war. Unfortunately, he did not receive encouragement from government departments and worse followed after the war, when Gatwick was nearly lost to the air transport world. A change in official policy did not occur until 1950, when the Ministry of Civil Aviation decided that Gatwick should be retained for use as a diversionary airport for Heathrow.

In spite of the pressures and worries of Gatwick, Desoutter enjoyed sailing and skiing throughout his life. By nature he was quiet, gentle, courteous, and a romantic. At the same time, he was full of fun and life, and on 19 October 1919 married Margaret Rust. The couple had three children, including Denis Desoutter, an aviation and sailing writer.

Desoutter did not live to see the fruition of his plans for Gatwick as a great passenger airport. He died at his home, White Hatch, Oldfield Road, Horley, Surrey, on 13 April 1952 and was cremated at Reigate on 19 April. He was survived by his wife.   JOHN KING

Sources D. M. Desoutter, *The Desoutter story*, unpublished address to Croydon Airport Society, 1991, RAF Museum Library · J. King, *Gatwick: the evolution of an airport* (1986) · D. Evernden, 'The Desoutter family', *Prop-Swing: Shuttleworth Vintage Aeroplane Society Journal* (1986), 13–23 · D. Evernden, 'The Desoutter Aircraft Company', *Prop-Swing: Shuttleworth Vintage Aeroplane Society Journal* (1987), 19–24 · *Aeronautics* (June 1952) · *Indian Skyways* (May 1952) · *Flight* (25 April 1952) · *Engineering* (18 April 1952) · *The Aeroplane* (18 April 1952) · *The Aeroplane* (25 April 1952) · *The Times* (16 April 1952) · *Manchester Guardian* (15 April 1952) · *Royal Aero Club Gazette* (June 1952) · private information (2004) · V. E. Negus, 'A case of acute tetanus with recovery', *The Lancet* (31 Jan 1914), 308–9 · E. R. Desoutter, 'Back to activity', promotional booklet of Desoutter Bros. Ltd, 1938, Wellcome L. · *CGPLA Eng. & Wales* (1952)

Archives PRO, Air Ministry Gatwick airport corresp. files, corresp. with Air Ministry, Avia 2/1679, 2/2145

Likenesses photographs, 1912–52, repro. in *Flight* · photographs, 1912–52, repro. in *The Aeroplane* · photographs, priv. coll.

Wealth at death £61,611 1s. 0d.: administration, 13 June 1952, *CGPLA Eng. & Wales*

Despagne [D'Espagne], **Jean** [John] (1591–1659), Reformed minister and theologian, was born in Mizoën, Dauphiné, France, one of several children of Henri D'Espagne (*d.* in or after 1626), protestant pastor there and subsequently at Bourg d'Oisans. His will placed the beginning of his ministerial career about 1611, but he seems to have been ordained in 1617. His first charge was at Orange in Dauphiné, but by 1626 he had moved to The Hague. In 1629, however, he was excluded from every pulpit in the

Netherlands, possibly in the wake of unproven but still damaging allegations of sexual immorality, possibly because, as a staunch Calvinist, he had spoken out too forcefully against Arminianism, or possibly because he had politically embarrassed the prince of Orange by an ill-timed denunciation of Louis XIII and Richelieu's campaign against the Huguenots at La Rochelle.

Despagne went to England, where he had or soon found alternative patrons. He may already have formed a connection with Horace Vere, Lord Vere, commander of English forces in the Netherlands. Just before leaving The Hague he published a treatise on ecclesiastical ceremonial and its historical evolution into superstition, *Traité des anciennes cérémonies* (1629), dedicated somewhat inappropriately to Charles I. In 1630 he wrote in French to Dudley Carleton, Viscount Dorchester (from 1626 to 1628 envoy to The Hague, but by this time secretary of state), requesting an introduction to the king and 'a little benefice or prebend of moderate revenue' (*CSP dom.*, addenda, 1625–49, 392) in order to fund books and research assistance for a major scholarly work. Perhaps this was *Antiduello … the Lawfulnesse and Unlawfulnesse of Single Combats*, published in 1632 both anonymously and under his name: this topical exploration of royal authority over duels exhibited a surprising knowledge of English history and probably rested on the services of a translator. More likely the subsidy was for a theological project, of which the first manifestation, *Les erreurs populaires … qui concernent l'intelligence de la religion*, appeared at The Hague in 1639: the English translation, *Popular Errors* (1648), referred in its dedication to 'king Charles' to a command 'from the deceased king' (James I unless the date is actually February or March 1649, in which case the address is daringly royalist) for 'the Manuscript which was the first fruits of my Pen'.

Despagne spent a year in the Netherlands from about 1636 and continued to publish at The Hague, but seems to have made England his home for most of the 1630s, becoming chaplain to Benjamin de Rohan, duc de Soubise, the Huguenot military leader in exile. His attractive preaching and effective writing, evident in *La manducation du corps de Christ* (1640), an exposition of eucharistic doctrine which combined a reverence for the sacrament with orthodox Calvinist theology, won him the approval of Gilbert Primrose, one of the ministers of the French church in Threadneedle Street, London. However, Soubise's influence was insufficient to prevail against the hostile reaction of other members of the consistory and to secure Despagne a pastorate there. Following the duc's death in 1642, Despagne served briefly as pastor at the French church at Sandtoft, Lincolnshire. On his return to London the Threadneedle Street consistory complained to the House of Lords about his 'unauthorised' preaching, but the latter concluded on 21 January 1643 that his sermons delivered at the house of Lady Annandale (presumably Elizabeth Shaw, widow of John Murray, first earl of Annandale) were 'rather an Advantage than any Inconvenience' (*JHL*, 5.566) and declined to silence him.

As before Despagne had well-placed patrons. Within a few months he was preaching to a congregation at Durham House, the London residence of Philip Herbert, earl of Pembroke. It prospered, attracting the social and intellectual élite among French (and English) residents of Westminster who found it geographically convenient and personally congenial, but drew the enmity and envy of the divided and less financially favoured official City church. As early as December 1643 the Threadneedle Street consistory requested from their Amsterdam equivalent a copy of the 1629 proceedings against Despagne. Their reiterated complaints that he was splitting their congregation were finally formalized in 1646, when Despagne was formally pronounced schismatic and his adherents barred from attending communion at the City church.

Apparently little affected, Despagne continued to publish. Works on the creed, the Lord's prayer, the ten commandments, and other cornerstones of Christian doctrine with dedications to Pembroke and (once) to the House of Lords appeared regularly from 1646, first in French and rapidly translated by others into English. Between May 1648 and June 1650 John Egerton, second earl of Bridgewater, heard him preach four sermons and twenty-four catechitical expositions, the latter clear elucidations of Calvin, on whom he was a recognized authority. His sermons took a robustly moderate political line. *An Abridgement of a Sermon* (1648), preached on 12 September 1648, a fast day for the proposed treaty between king and parliament, stressed their mutual duties and mutual faults and exhorted 'both sides [to] endeavour to out-goe one another in benignitie, honour and pietie' in order to 'restore the Church to its lustre, to the Lawes their vigour, to the Common-weal an happy peace' (p. 21). In March 1649 parliament employed him to translate some of the treaty documents into French.

Pembroke's death on 23 January 1650 left the Durham House congregation secure: in his funeral sermon Despagne celebrated 'nostre Philippe', a reliable and responsive benefactor who had carefully left the church in the care of his son. That year he ordained his disciple Théodore Crespin to serve a secessionist wing of the French church at Canterbury, and in January 1651 he tried unsuccessfully to set up a colloquy with the churches at Sandtoft and Southampton rivalling the authority of that of London. Such controversial activities hampered attempts by the Westminster congregation to reach a compromise with their London co-religionists late the same year, but helped by members of the council of state and others Despagne's flock moved in 1653 to the chapel of the Savoy at Somerset House. This became their permanent home and the basis of the future conformist French church of London, using in time the translated liturgy of the prayer book. Early members such as Isaac de Caus (d. 1648), the designer and architect, and Nicholas Briot (d. 1646), the engraver, and later members such as the physicians Sir Théodore Turquet de Mayerne, Jean Colladon, and Théophilus de Garencières point to a conservative political outlook, and the fact that the diarist John Evelyn worshipped there is suggestive. Yet Despagne retained favour under the protectorate and was in tune with its intellectual cutting edge. His *Shibboleth ou réformation de quelques passages … de la Bible* (1653) was dedicated to Oliver Cromwell, and in April 1657 the council of state approved an augmentation of his salary. His *Examen de XVII maximes judaiques* (1657) (dedicated to Edward Lawrence, son of John Lawrence, lawyer and sometime MP), *Essay des merveilles de Dieu* (1657) (dedicated to John Holles, earl of Clare and son-in-law of Lord Vere), and *The Joyfull Convert* (1658) reveal debate with Jewish scholars and an interest in cabbalism.

This context both nurtured the continuing hostility of the Threadneedle Street church to Despagne and ensured his survival unscathed. The most devastating attack on him yet was mounted by 'Guillaume Herbert', sometimes identified as a scion of Pembroke's family but from his own remarks more probably not English, in *Réponse aux questions de Mr Espagne, addressées à l'eglise françoise de Londres* (1657). Furious insults of the perceived schismatic and crypto-Catholic—a wolf, fox, calumnist, 'Pape de Somerset' (p. 46), 'Romane ridicule' (p. 64)—are accompanied by quotation from damagingly vivid testimonies in the 1629 adultery case supplied by the Amsterdam consistory. The synodical verdict of unproven should be, says Herbert, a source of shame and regret: Despagne is in effect a moral bankrupt.

By November 1658 Despagne was ill and the Savoy elders asked their Threadneedle Street brothers to supply a substitute preacher. He died on 25 April 1659, aged sixty-eight, and was probably buried in the Savoy Chapel, as he had wished; Garencières supplied an admiring epitaph there. Although Haag mentions a funeral sermon for his wife delivered on 31 October 1647, there is no trace of this or of a marriage; one of Herbert's complaints was that he was a hedonistic childless bachelor. In his will dated 13 April 1659 Despagne named as his heirs his two sisters in Dauphiné, Suzanne and Magdalen, and their families. His executor, Henry Browne, oversaw at least one of the many subsequent editions of Despagne's works. In the preface to *An Essay of the Wonders of God* (1662) Browne explained that he had frequented Despagne's chapel 'to be a partaker of those excellent Sermons and Doctrines of our Author, who was then followed by many of the Nobility, and the best of the Gentry, who rendered both to God and Ceasar their due'; as an ode by Garencières in the same volume proclaimed, he was the 'Belle lumière des Pasteurs'.

VIVIENNE LARMINIE

Sources E. Haag and E. Haag, *La France protestante*, 2nd edn, 6 vols. (Paris, 1877–88), vol. 6, pp. 86–90 · R. D. Gwynn, ed., *A calendar of the letter books of the French church of London … 1643–1659*, Huguenot Society of London, 54 (1979) · R. D. Gwynne, 'The French churches in England in the 1640s and 1650s', *Proceedings of the Huguenot Society*, 23 (1977–82), 256–61 · E. R. Briggs, 'Reflexions upon the first century of the Huguenot churches in England', *Proceedings of the Huguenot Society*, 23 (1977–82), 114–19 · E. R. Briggs, 'The London French churches, 1640–1660', *Proceedings of the Huguenot Society*, 23 (1977–82), 414–19 · C. L. Hamilton, 'Jean d'Espagne and the second earl of Bridgewater (1622–1686)', *Proceedings of the Huguenot Society*, 24 (1983–8), 232–9 · *CSP dom., addenda, 1625–49*, 392; *1648–9*, 28; *1652–3*, 343; *1656–7*, 331 · *JHL*, 5 (1642–3), 566, 570 · will, PRO, PROB 11/291, fol. 195r–v · [W. Herbert], *Réponse aux questions de Mr Espagne, addressées à l'eglise françoise de Londres* (1657) · 'Communion cups from the Huguenot–Walloon church at Canterbury', *Proceedings of the Huguenot Society*, 17 (1942–6), 473 · B. Cottret, *The Huguenots in England: immigration and settlement, c.1550–1700* (1991), 131–2, 147–8

Likenesses J. C. Böcklin, line engraving, BM · line engraving, NPG

Wealth at death see will, PRO, PROB 11/291, fol. 195r–v

Despard [*née* French], **Charlotte** (1844–1939), feminist and socialist reformer, was born on the family estate at Ripple Vale in Kent on 15 June 1844, the third child and third daughter of the family of five daughters and one son of Captain John Tracey William French (*d.* 1854), retired naval officer, and his wife, Margaret, *née* Eccles (*d. c.*1865). Her brother was John *French, later field marshal and first earl of Ypres. Charlotte French had a conventional Victorian young lady's upbringing, and frequently lamented her lack of a thorough education.

> There were moments in my hot youth, when I would rail against Heaven for having made me a woman. What might I not have been; what might I not have done had I the freedom and intellectual advantages so largely accorded to men? (Despard, 'Suffragette')

Her father died in 1854 and within a few years her fragile mother was confined to a mental home. In 1863 the family moved to London, where Charlotte French attended a finishing school. For several years she toured the continent with her unmarried sisters. Then, on 20 December 1870, she married Maximilian Carden Despard (1839–1890), an Anglo-Irish businessman who had made a fortune in the Far East. They had no children, probably because of Maximilian's poor health, on account of which they spent every winter cruising in the Mediterranean or visiting India and North America. With her husband's encouragement, Mrs Despard occupied herself by writing romantic novels (including *Chaste as Ice, Pure as Snow*, 1874) with high-minded heroines, exotic settings, and happy endings.

In 1890 Max Despard died, and after months of seclusion Charlotte Despard emerged as an unusually engaged philanthropic widow. Her chosen slum was the Nine Elms district of Battersea in south London, one of Victorian England's 'little Irelands'. There she funded and staffed a health clinic, as well as organizing youth and working men's clubs, and a soup kitchen for the local unemployed. During the week she lived above one of her welfare 'shops' and her identification with the local community was sealed by her conversion to Catholicism. At the end of 1894 she was elected as a guardian for the Vauxhall board of the Lambeth poor-law union. She proved herself a brilliant committee woman, bringing a rare combination of informed compassion, practical experience, and military efficiency to the board's deliberations. She was especially committed to the welfare of the most vulnerable 'paupers': children, mothers, and old people. She supported campaigns for free school meals and medical inspections for poor children, and in 1902 she toured Canada to see what had become of the Lambeth union's boy emigrants.

Mrs Despard's charitable efforts were paralleled by her

political commitments. She was an active and vocal supporter of the Social Democratic Federation and the Independent Labour Party. By 1906, the year in which the suffragette organization, the Women's Social and Political Union (WSPU), moved from Manchester to London, she was a familiar figure on progressive platforms. Mrs Despard wore a simple black chiffon mantilla instead of the large hat of a conventional Edwardian lady, and open sandals instead of tight boots. Although she never lost the bearing of a Victorian *grande dame* and was, by all accounts, a generous hostess, her own lifestyle was famously austere: 'In her settlement in Nine Elms she *lived* the life of a socialist' ('Mrs Despard's birthday party', *The Vote*, 15 July 1932). The suffragette activists Annie Kenney and Tessa Billington-Greig who went to Battersea to woo her for 'the cause' knew that the venerable and incorruptible Mrs Despard could not be dismissed as a hysterical self-seeker.

Charlotte Despard was more than happy to become the WSPU's honorary secretary:

> I had sought and found comradeship of some sort with men. I had marched with great processions of the unemployed. I had stood on the platforms of Labour men and Socialists. I had tried to stir up the people to a sense of shame about the misery of their homes, and the degradation of their women and children. I had listened with sympathy to fiery denunciations of Governments and the Capitalist systems to which they belong. Amongst all these experiences, I had not found what I met on the threshold of this young, vigorous Union of Hearts.   (Despard, 'Suffragette')

With those two other great widows, Millicent Fawcett and Emmeline Pankhurst, Charlotte Despard was soon recognized as one of the leaders of the struggle for votes for women. In 1907 she was imprisoned twice in Holloway gaol, where her courage and good humour were an inspiration to other suffragette prisoners. However, later in that year the suffragette movement split, and Mrs Despard left the WSPU, eventually to become president of the Women's Freedom League (WFL).

Women's Freedom Leaguers were self-styled 'constitutional militants'. Unlike the WSPU, which was run like an army, the WFL was democratically organized. It concentrated on 'moral' tactics, rather than campaigns against property or individual politicians. The sensational grille protest, in which women chained themselves to the metal grating (now in the Museum of London) that fenced off the Ladies' Gallery in the House of Commons, was a WFL initiative. Mrs Despard, whose household furniture was repeatedly seized in lieu of taxes refused on grounds of 'no taxation without representation', was closely identified with such passive resistance strategies.

After the outbreak of the First World War, Charlotte Despard's immediate concern was distress on the 'home front'. Since her beloved only brother, Sir John French, was commander-in-chief of the British expeditionary force, she might have been expected to take a jingoistic line on that conflict. Instead, to her brother's mortification, she joined Sylvia Pankhurst in the socialist pacifist movement. After the Bolshevik revolution of 1917, her commitment to international socialism intensified. In the spring of 1918, soon after the vote was granted to women over thirty, she resigned from the WFL presidency in order to concentrate on a variety of other issues, including Save the Children, the Indian independence movement, theosophy, the Labour Party and the early British Communist Party, the London Vegetarian Society, and the Irish Self Determination League.

In the general election of 1918 Charlotte Despard stood, unsuccessfully, as a pacifist Labour parliamentary candidate for Battersea. However, she was delighted by Sinn Féin's victory in the same election. Among the suffragette leaders she had stood out as a supporter of Irish home rule, and when that movement gave way to the struggle for complete independence she became an active supporter of the British solidarity organization the Irish Self Determination League. Her sympathy for the Irish republican movement brought her into direct conflict with her brother, who in 1918 had been sworn in as lord lieutenant of Ireland. While he set about crushing the 'rebels', his sister was supporting them.

Soon after the Anglo-Irish treaty was signed in 1921, Charlotte Despard wound up her London life and moved to Ireland. Her ancestors on her father's side had been Irish, and she was fond of her Despard in-laws as well as her Irish friends in Battersea. Now she hoped to play a part in the setting up of a brave new state, but, as Ireland collapsed into a bitter civil war, she found herself back at work as a campaigner for civil rights and the relief of distress. In Dublin she became the president of the Women's Prisoners' Defence League. The house she shared with Maud Gonne was at the centre of radical Irish campaigns in the 1920s. Like other republican women, who found the English 'Mrs' odious, but baulked at the Irish equivalent, *Bean*, which translates as 'woman of', she took Madame as her Dublin title and was nicknamed Madame Desperate. In spite of that nickname, and her great age, she was active enough to be classified as a dangerous subversive under the terms of the Irish Free State's 1927 Public Safety Act. When Maud Gonne was imprisoned she kept a constant vigil, for twenty days and nights, outside Kilmainham gaol.

Charlotte Despard continued to visit London for her summer birthday parties, around which the WFL organized its annual gatherings. At the celebrations to mark the Equal Franchise Act of 1928 she was fêted as an honoured veteran of the struggle for female suffrage. By then, however, communism was her main cause. In 1930, at the age of eighty-six, she toured Soviet Russia, taking a particular interest in schools, nurseries, and the general status of women.

In 1933, soon after her house in central Dublin had been attacked by an anti-communist mob, Charlotte Despard moved north. In Belfast she hoped to involve herself in a campaign that, briefly, had united unemployed protestant and Catholic workers. Then, as the international fascist menace grew, she supported anti-appeasement campaigns. She was too infirm to go to Spain for a show of solidarity with the republicans fighting against Franco, but in 1937 she did journey to London for the WFL's celebration of her ninety-third birthday. Two years later, on 10 November 1939, she died after a fall in her new house, Neadna-Gaoithe, Whitehead, near Belfast. Madame Charlotte Despard was buried on 13 November, with republican honours, at Glasnevin cemetery in Dublin, near the grave of her good friend Constance Markievicz.

MARGARET MULVIHILL

Sources C. Despard, 'In the days of my youth', Belfast PRO · C. Despard, 'Why I became a "suffragette"', *Women's Franchise* (4 July 1907), 1 · *The Vote* (1909–33) · C. Booth, *Life and labour of the people in London*, 3rd ser., 5 (1902) · R. M. Fox, *Rebel Irishwomen* (1935) · A. Linklater, *An unhusbanded life* (1980) · M. Mulvihill, *Charlotte Despard: a biography* (1989) · m. cert. · private information (2004)
Archives PRO NIre., corresp., diaries, and papers · Women's Library, London, letters and diary | LMA, minutes of the Lambeth Board of Guardians · Women's Library, London, Billington-Greig MSS · Women's Library, London, letters to Charles Wilson
Likenesses M. Edis, exh. 1916, NPG · Broom, photograph, NPG · attrib. C. M. Horsfall, oils, NPG · J. Jarché, photograph, NPG; repro. in *Daily Herald* (1933) · photograph, BL · photograph, Mary Evans/Fawcett Library · photograph, NPG · photograph, Syndication International Ltd · photograph, National Museum of Photography, Film and Television, Bradford
Wealth at death £3218 2s. 8d.: Irish probate sealed in London, 6 March 1940, *CGPLA NIre.*

Despard, Edward Marcus (1751–1803), army officer and revolutionary, was born into a military family in Queen's county, Ireland, on 6 March 1751; the youngest of six sons of William Despard and his wife, Jane. John *Despard (1743/4–1829) was his brother. He joined the army as an ensign in 1766 and was promoted lieutenant in 1772, while stationed in Jamaica. He was a skilled military engineer and, working closely with Horatio Nelson, particularly distinguished himself in an expedition to capture Fort San Juan from Spain in 1779. Promoted captain in 1780 he continued to work as an engineer until his appointment in 1781 as commandant, first of the island of Roatan, off the Honduran coast, and then of British possessions in the Gulf of Honduras. In 1782, having overseen the defence of Jamaica against France and Spain, Despard headed an expedition of Jamaican settlers, assisted by British artillery, to recapture Spanish-occupied Black River territory in south-western Jamaica. For this he received royal commendation and was made a colonel of provincials.

In June 1786 Despard took up an appointment as superintendent of Honduras. Though he handled relations with the Spanish authorities well he was notably less adept as a civilian governor. His unswerving support for settlers displaced from territories recently ceded to Spain (many of whom he knew from San Juan and the Black River) led him into repeated conflict with the established British settler community, who complained repeatedly to London of his 'visible Spirit of Self-importance and uncontrollable Domination' (PRO, CO 123/6, 21 Feb 1788). Events culminated in his annulment (June 1789) of the colony's police and magistracy; Despard ruled by direct decree until, suspended on half pay, he was ordered to return to Britain, where he arrived in May 1790.

Despard had to wait until October 1791 to learn that, while complaints against him were dismissed, he was not to be reinstated as superintendent of Honduras. In pursuit

Edward Marcus Despard (1751–1803), by John Chapman, pubd 1804

of compensation he grew increasingly irascible, while the combination of enforced idleness and grievance against authority led him to both the London Corresponding Society and the overtly revolutionary United Irishmen (UI). He quickly became an intimate of the leading United Irishman and French secret agent William Duckett and in 1797 was reported to be co-ordinator of a proposed rising in London planned to coincide with one in Ireland and a French landing there. In 1798 Despard was pivotal in negotiations between the United Irishmen and a broader conspiratorial group, the United Britons, to foment simultaneous English and Irish risings to assist a French invasion. When O'Connor and O'Coighley, the principal leaders of the conspiracy, were apprehended in February, while hiring a boat to take them to France, habeas corpus was suspended and further arrests followed. Despard's was predictably among them.

Despard seems to have been aware that the revolutionary threat had been contained by the government when, in June 1799, he petitioned for his release in return for voluntary transportation. Among political prisoners at this time he seems to have received the harshest treatment—'more like a common vagabond than a gentleman or State Prisoner', complained his wife, Catherine (PRO, HO 42/43)—and Sir Francis Burdett made Despard's case the centre of a campaign against the 'English Bastille'.

When Despard was finally released, in March 1801, he returned to his family's Irish estate, apparently intending to take no further part in politics. However, in February 1802 he returned to London at the behest of the UI leader William Dowdall. After the collapse of the Irish rising of 1798 the United Irishmen had reconstituted itself as a small, centralized military body. Though Britain was now at peace with France food shortages and industrial unrest created a climate in which talk of revolution flourished. Despard now concentrated on enlisting the support of militant Irish labourers and guardsmen stationed in Windsor and London but intelligence sources also show him to have been in contact with Irish and French emissaries during the summer. Disaffected guardsmen tried to force the issue with a rising on 6 September but Despard restrained them, arguing that such action could be effective only if it coincided with an Irish rising and a French invasion; but then, on 16 November, Despard was arrested at the Oakly Arms, Lambeth, apparently planning a *coup d'état* to coincide with the opening of parliament later that month.

The circumstances behind Despard's arrest have been variously interpreted. The popular contemporary view that he was himself victim of a government conspiracy can be safely dismissed. At his trial in February 1803, before a special commission of the lord chief justice and other judges, the prosecution simply claimed that he was a psychotic maverick who had enticed a small band of unfortunates into supporting a futile plot. The prosecution, however, was restricted in the evidence that it could use; aside from issues of legal admissibility, public confidence might have suffered if the full extent of any conspiracy was revealed. Nor was it in the state's interest to reveal more than was absolutely necessary of its intelligence sources; records from the latter implicate a significant number of London Jacobins in the conspiracy, of whom the motley dozen soldiers and workmen tried with Despard were far from typical. Leeds magistrates had been told as early as June that 'Major General Despot' would become 'commander in Chief of the Union' (Wells, 238–9). The United Irish and Britons maintained separate structures and it appears to have been Despard's task to co-ordinate them. The only incriminating evidence found at his arrest was a printed card calling for 'the independence of Great Britain and Ireland. An equalization of Civil, Political, and Religious Rights; [and] an ample Provision for the families of the Heroes who shall fall in the contest'. An oath of allegiance to the United Britons was appended (*Trial of Edward Marcus Despard*, 64). Identical cards circulated in Lancashire and Yorkshire. Such points led Edward Thompson to argue, in *The Making of the English Working Class* (1963), that Despard was the leader of a nationwide revolutionary conspiracy. However it has also been suggested that 'there was no general *coup* planned for the opening of Parliament on 23rd November' (Elliott, 'Despard conspiracy', 57) and that Despard was a marginal figure in a rising actually intended for 1803. His arrest was simply an opportunist move by a government acting on fragmentary evidence.

Despard's defence was circumspect, wishing perhaps not to incriminate others but also aware that the prosecution case was uneven. He enjoyed wide popularity and Nelson himself gave evidence as to his good character: 'no man could have shewn more zealous attachment to his Sovereign and his Country' (*Trial of Edward Marcus Despard*,

174). Though finding him guilty the jury recommended mercy 'on account of his former services' (*BDMBR*, 119). The government, however, was not inclined to clemency. Whatever the truth of the conspiracy an exemplary verdict had been secured and punishment was enacted accordingly. On 21 February 1803, having taken leave of his wife and refusing all religious consolation, Despard was drawn on a hurdle to the Surrey county gaol, Newington, where, before a crowd reportedly of 20,000, he delivered from the scaffold a speech that was loudly cheered. Along with six co-conspirators he was hanged and his corpse decapitated, whereupon the executioner held up the head, declaring: 'This is the head of a traitor' (*GM*). His widow received the remains, which on 1 March were buried in the churchyard by St Paul's Cathedral. Troops drafted into the area in anticipation of rioting were not needed. In his address from the scaffold Despard denied all charges of treason and claimed to be 'a friend to truth, to liberty, and to justice … to the poor and the oppressed' (*Full and Accurate Report*, 74). How far his politics stemmed from intellectual conviction and how far from personal resentment remains a moot point but in a letter to James Mill in 1817 Francis Place described Despard as an 'extraordinary' man 'to whom I was indebted for some portion of the knowledge I possess and for whom I shall always maintain strong feelings of regard' (BL, Add. MS 35152, fol. 1).

MALCOLM CHASE

Sources *The trial of Edward Marcus Despard, esquire, for high treason* (1803) · *Full and accurate report of the whole proceedings upon the trial of Colonel M. E. Despard* (1803) · PRO, CO 123/4–123/12; CO 137/50; CO 137/86; CO 137/88; HO 42/43; HO 42/66 · J. A. Burdon, ed., *Archives of British Honduras*, 1 (1931) · BL, Place papers, Add. MS 35152 · M. Elliott, 'The Despard conspiracy reconsidered', *Past and Present*, 75 (1977) · R. Wells, *Insurrection: the British experience, 1795–1803* (1983) · M. Elliott, *Partners in revolution: the United Irishmen and France* (1982) · J. Bannantine, *Memoirs of Edward Marcus Despard* (1799) · C. Oman, *The unfortunate Colonel Despard and other studies* (1922) · *GM*, 1st ser., 73 (1803), 276 · R. H. Condon, 'Despard, Col. Edward Marcus', *BDMBR*, vol. 1 · *DCB*, vol. 6
Archives PRO, 'A narrative of the publick transactions in the Bay of Honduras from 1784 to 1790, by Edward Marcus Despard', CO 123/10 · PRO, 'Appendix to Mr Despard's narrative', CO 123/11
Likenesses Barlow, etching, pubd 1803, BM · J. Chapman, engraving, pubd 1804, NPG [*see illus.*] · engraving, repro. in Elliott, *Partners in revolution* · line engraving (*On the gallows*; after unknown portrait), BM, NPG; repro. in *The new wonderful museum, and extraordinary magazine* (1804), 2

Despard, John (1743/4–1829), army officer and colonial administrator, was born in Ireland and baptized on 4 August 1744 at St Peter and St Kevin in Dublin, the fifth of six sons of William and Jane Despard. He was the brother of Edward Marcus *Despard. He began his military career at the age of sixteen as an ensign in the 12th foot during the Seven Years' War, when, at the battle of Warburg, the colours were shot from his hand. After service in the battle of Vellinghausen he was promoted lieutenant on 12 July 1762. Placed on half pay following the war, in 1767 he was appointed lieutenant in the 7th Royal Fusiliers. In 1773 he sailed with his regiment for Quebec, returned to England to recruit in 1774, and in May 1775 was sent from Quebec to the Canadian frontier at Fort St Johns, where he was later forced to surrender by insurgent Americans. In December 1776 he was exchanged and joined Sir William Howe in New York, where he was promoted captain on 25 March 1777. In October 1777 Despard served at the assault on Fort Montgomery, and in June 1778, as major, he organized Lord Rawdon's new loyalist corps, the Volunteers of Ireland. He then served as the army's deputy adjutant-general at the capture of Charles Town, South Carolina (1780), and acted in the same capacity with Lord Cornwallis's army in the south until the surrender at Yorktown. With the peace in 1783 he rejoined the fusiliers and had risen to the rank of lieutenant-colonel by 1791.

On 6 March 1793 Despard married Harriot Anne (1772–1848), daughter of Thomas Hesketh and Jacintha Dalrymple, and the sister of Sir Thomas Dalrymple Hesketh, third baronet, of Rufford Hall, Lancashire. They had at least one daughter, Harriot Dorothea (b. 1795), who married Henry Francis Greville in 1816. Despard served as commander of the regiment at Quebec at some point during 1793 but in 1794 Prince Edward, commander of the forces in the Maritime provinces, ordered him to England where he again successfully recruited for the regiment. He returned to serve under the prince at Halifax, Nova Scotia, and was promoted to the rank of colonel on 21 June 1795. In 1799 he was appointed, as major-general (from 21 June 1798), to the military command of Dorset; and it was while there, in August 1799, that Edward, now duke of Kent, offered him the post of military commander and civil administrator of the colony of Cape Breton, which Despard accepted.

The appointment to Cape Breton presented many challenges. The colony was governed through an executive council riven by power struggles. Despard's appointment was challenged by some council members, but he suppressed this faction by threatening to call out the militia. Turning to the development of the colony's potentially rich coal mines, he privatized them and improved wharf facilities so that production and shipments both increased. Since the colony had no house of assembly, taxes were not being collected. He persuaded the Treasury board to allow the collection of taxes by local ordinance, thereby giving the colony resources for internal improvements. With the concurrence of the home authorities he then organized an escheats court and seized large tracts of unoccupied properties, thus opening land to settlement. Shortly after, in August 1802, the first boatload of highland Scots sailing directly to Cape Breton found free land and assistance, which led to an eventual immigration of 25,000 highlanders to the island. Throughout Despard had to contend with political factions arguing for and against a house of assembly. The frustration of lacking the authority to decide this question and declining health, probably exacerbated by his brother's execution for treason, led to his departure in July 1807.

The remainder of Despard's life was spent in semi-retirement in England. On 25 June 1808 he was appointed colonel of the 12th Royal Veteran battalion, colonel of the 5th West India regiment in 1809, and, on 4 June 1814, general. He died on 3 September 1829, in his eighty-sixth year, at Swan Hill, Oswestry, from 'ulcerated intestines' (Oswestry church records), which had plagued him for many years. He was buried on 9 September in St Oswald's churchyard, Oswestry. Despard was a distinguished, resourceful, and brave soldier who demonstrated surprising governing abilities, all undertaken with a 'mild and chearful … disposition' (William Woodfall to Adam Gordon, 25 July 1805, CO 217, vol. 123, fol. 175).

R. J. Morgan

Sources PRO, CO 217, vols. 117–25 · *DNB* · R. J. Morgan, 'Despard, John', *DCB*, vol. 6 · R. J. Morgan, 'Orphan outpost, Cape Breton colony, 1784–1820', PhD diss., University of Ottawa, 1972 · R. J. Morgan, 'Sydney's debt to John Despard', *Essays in Cape Breton history*, ed. B. D. Tennyson (1973) · *GM*, 1st ser., 99/2 (1829), 369–70 · J. Philippart, ed., *The royal military calendar*, 3 vols. (1815–16), 1.369–70 · Public Archives of Nova Scotia, Halifax, Nova Scotia, Sir John Wentworth MSS, vol. 53 · Public Archives of Nova Scotia, Halifax, Nova Scotia, Archibald Charles Dodd MSS, MG. 1, 262 B · St Oswald's Church records and tombstone, Oswestry · St George's Church records, Sydney, Nova Scotia, University College of Cape Breton, Beaton Institute, MG 13, 4 (MB 19) · GEC, *Baronetage* · IGI

Despenser, Constance, Lady Despenser (*c.*1375–1416), noblewoman, was the daughter of *Edmund of Langley, first duke of York (1341–1402), and Isabella (d. 1392), daughter of Pedro the Cruel of Castile and his mistress Maria de Padilla. Her parents were married in July 1372 and Constance was their second child. On 16 April 1378 Edmund was granted the marriage of Thomas, Lord *Despenser (1373–1400), who had married Constance by November 1379. Thomas, who became earl of Gloucester in 1397 but lost his new title following the deposition of Richard II, took part in the 'Epiphany rising' of 1400 against Henry IV and was executed at Bristol on 13 January. On 11 February Constance was granted specified goods of her dead husband to the value of £200, with various items of jewellery and plate which had been regarded as her own during his lifetime. Eight days later she was granted specified manors worth 1000 marks, and on 3 March she was granted custody of her son Richard. She received a further mark of favour in January 1404 when she sued for, and was granted, dower rights notwithstanding her dead husband's forfeiture.

In spite of these marks of favour, Constance conspired against the crown. On 15 February 1405 it became known that Constance had fled with the Mortimer children and was making for the Despenser lordship of Cardiff, presumably with the intention of joining Owain Glyn Dŵr. The pursuing royal forces caught up with them near Cheltenham, and Constance was brought before a great council at Westminster, where she denounced her brother *Edward, duke of York, as instigator of the plot. When the duke denied his involvement she called for a champion, and an esquire, William Maidstone, challenged the duke to combat. York accepted, but at that point Thomas of Lancaster intervened and brother and sister were imprisoned, Constance at Kenilworth. On 12 March her lands and goods were seized. Partial restitution was made in January 1406, but the king took the precaution of keeping her Welsh lands in his own hands, and order was not given for their restoration until June 1407. Little is heard of Constance thereafter. She was among the landowners ordered to remain on their Welsh estates in May 1409 to resist the rebels. She died on 28 November 1416, and writs of *diem clausit extremum* were issued on the same day, which perhaps implies that she died in or near Westminster. She was buried before the high altar of Reading Abbey.

Constance had three children with Thomas Despenser: Richard, their heir, who was born on 30 November 1396 and had died by 16 April 1414; and two daughters, Elizabeth and Isabella. Both sisters were still alive in 1404, when they were in the care of the king's yeoman John Grove, but Elizabeth may have died soon after. She is said to have died young and to have been buried in St Mary's Church, Cardiff. Isabella, who was born on 26 July 1400, became heir to the Despenser lands after her brother died childless. She married, first, Richard Beauchamp, earl of Worcester (d. 1422), and, second, his cousin Richard *Beauchamp, earl of Warwick (d. 1439).

After Thomas Despenser's death Constance was the mistress of Edmund *Holland, seventh earl of Kent (1383–1408), and had a daughter with him, Eleanor, who later married James Audley (d. 1459). Eleanor's later claim (which was rejected) that Constance had married Kent and that she was therefore the earl's heir dates the liaison to before Kent's marriage to Lucia Visconti in January 1407. On 10 January 1405 Kent had been granted royal licence to marry whom he pleased of the king's lieges. If the grant had been secured with Constance in mind her involvement in treason presumably rendered the alliance inexpedient. ROSEMARY HORROX

Sources GEC, *Peerage* · *Chancery records* · *RotP* · *The itinerary of John Leland in or about the years 1535–1543*, ed. L. Toulmin Smith, 11 pts in 5 vols. (1906–10) · J. H. Wylie, *History of England under Henry the Fourth*, 4 vols. (1884–98) · F. Devon, ed. and trans., *Issues of the exchequer: being payments made out of his majesty's revenue, from King Henry III to King Henry VI inclusive*, RC (1837) · J. L. Kirby, ed., *Calendar of signet letters of Henry IV and Henry V* (1978) · *Thys rol was laburd and finished by Master John Rows of Warrewyk*, ed. W. Courthope (1859); repr. as *The Rous roll* (1980) [with historical introduction by C. Ross]

Despenser, Edward, first Lord Despenser (1336–1375), magnate and soldier, was born at Essendine, Rutland, on 24 March 1336, the son and heir of Sir Edward Despenser (d. 1342)—the second son of Hugh *Despenser the younger (d. 1326)—and his wife, Anne (d. 1367), the daughter of William, Lord Ferrers of Groby. Henry *Despenser was his brother. From his father, who died in 1342, Edward Despenser inherited substantial estates, including nine manors, mostly in the midlands, and in 1349 he succeeded his childless uncle, Hugh, second Lord Despenser (of the first creation), in the principal estates of the family. A profitable marriage was arranged, probably in 1346, between Despenser and Elizabeth (d. 1409), granddaughter of Bartholomew Burghersh, the elder (d. 1355), a wealthy magnate who was the king's chamberlain. Elizabeth was the sole heir of her father, the younger Bartholomew *Burghersh, and his first wife, Cecily Weyland. This marriage, which took place before 2 August 1354, ultimately enabled Despenser, after his father-in-law's death in

1369, to acquire his wife's valuable estates, which comprised ten manors in Suffolk and half of the Welsh marcher lordship of Ewias Lacy.

Throughout Edward Despenser's minority the greater part of his lands was administered by his kinsfolk and officials on his behalf. After dower had been assigned to Hugh's widow, Elizabeth, the residue of the Despenser estates was farmed, on 8 February 1350, to Bartholomew Burghersh, the elder, and the young heir, for the probably undervalued sum of £1000 a year. This custody was subsequently transferred to the Despenser heir and his mother, Lady Anne, on the same terms. Although he came of age in 1357, Edward Despenser did not have full possession of his family inheritance until after the death of the dowager, Elizabeth, in 1359.

Despenser's military career began before his coming of age in March 1357. With his father-in-law, Lord Burghersh, he was in the retinue of the Black Prince on his first expedition to Gascony in 1355, and he fought at Poitiers on 19 September 1356, when the French king, John II, was captured. He was still in Gascony in March 1357, and he probably returned to London with the prince of Wales during the following month. He was summoned to parliament in December 1357. When Edward III invaded France for the last time in October 1359, Despenser was one of the English magnates who served with the king, and he was still in France two years later. In 1361 he was made a knight of the Garter and given the stall next to the king's in St George's Chapel, Windsor. Meanwhile the treaty of Brétigny, made in May 1360, had ended the most profitable phase of the French war.

Although Despenser was one of the Irish landowners who were commanded in February 1362 to go to Ireland to assist the king's third son, Lionel, to restore order in that land, it seems unlikely that he left England again until 1368. He was present in London when Lionel was created duke of Clarence on 13 November 1362, and it was in his service that he later enlisted. Despenser was the most important of the followers who accompanied Duke Lionel on his journey to Milan to marry Violante Visconti in May 1368, and he remained in Italy for over four years. After Lionel died suddenly on 17 October 1368, Despenser believed that his patron's death had been brought about by poison, and in revenge he took service with the pope, Urban V, in his war against the Visconti of Milan. On 10 March 1370 the pope wrote to John of Gaunt commending Despenser, who had won a great reputation by his prowess in battles in Lombardy. Despenser's prolonged sojourn in Italy appears to be commemorated in the fresco of the church militant and triumphant painted by Andrea da Firenze (Andrea Bonaiuti) and others in the Spanish chapel of Santa Maria Novella in Florence. This fresco depicts the meeting at Viterbo of Urban V and the emperor, Charles IV, on 17 October 1368; conspicuous in the group standing near the emperor is a knight of the Garter, clad in white, gold-embroidered garments. This figure, which portrays in profile a good-looking man with a short, reddish, pointed beard, has been identified as Edward, Lord Despenser, who was the only knight of the Garter in Italy at that time. If this identification is correct, he was the first Englishman to be portrayed in Italian art since Thomas Becket.

Despenser's exploits in Italy made him a renowned hero of chivalry. Froissart, who knew him personally and benefited from his patronage, eulogizes him as the most handsome, most courteous, and most honourable knight of his time in England, and relates that it was at the request of John of Gaunt that Despenser returned home in the summer of 1372. He was constable of Gaunt's army in the great *chevauchée* of 1373, when Gaunt marched across France from Calais to Bordeaux, losing half his troops on the way. The Breton expedition in the spring of 1375 was the last successful English undertaking in France in the late fourteenth century; Despenser, in company with Edmund of Langley, earl of Cambridge (afterwards duke of York), and Edmund Mortimer, earl of March, was attacking Quimperlé when this campaign was cut short by the truce of Bruges. After his return home Despenser visited Cardiff in September 1375; he died a few weeks later at his manor of Llanblethian, near Cowbridge, on 11 November, aged thirty-nine. His effigy on his tomb in Tewkesbury Abbey shows him in full armour, kneeling in prayer. His death was followed by another prolonged minority, since his surviving son, Thomas *Despenser, was only two years old when his father died. The Despensers were an unlucky family; if Edward Despenser's career had not been prematurely cut short, his knightly prowess might well have earned him promotion to an earldom, a rank merited by his great landed possessions and his prestige as a famous military hero.

T. B. PUGH

Sources Adae Murimuth continuatio chronicarum. Robertus de Avesbury de gestis mirabilibus regis Edwardi tertii, ed. E. M. Thompson, Rolls Series, 93 (1889) · Œuvres de Froissart: chroniques, ed. K. de Lettenhove, 25 vols. (Brussels, 1867–77) · CEPR letters, vol. 4 · Dugdale, Monasticon, new edn · W. Dugdale, The baronage of England, 2 vols. (1675–6) · H. J. Hewitt, The Black Prince's expedition of 1355–1357 (1958) · G. Williams, ed., Glamorgan county history, 3: The middle ages, ed. T. B. Pugh (1971) · GEC, Peerage · G. Andres, J. M. Hunisak, and J. R. Turner, The art of Florence (1988) · M. A. Devlin, 'An English knight of the garter in the Spanish chapel in Florence', Speculum, 4 (1929), 270–81 · A. Gardner, English medieval sculpture, rev. edn (1951) · G. B. Parks, The English traveler to Italy (1954) · CIPM
Likenesses A. da Firenze and others, fresco, c.1368, Spanish chapel of Santa Maria Novella, Florence, Italy · effigy, Tewkesbury Abbey, Gloucestershire

Despenser, Henry (d. 1406), bishop of Norwich, was the fourth son of Sir Edward Despenser, killed at the siege of Vannes in 1342, and his wife, Anne (d. 1367), daughter of William, Lord Ferrers of Groby. His father was the second son of Hugh *Despenser the younger, the notorious favourite of Edward II. Although said by the pope on 2 August 1354 to be in his tenth year, Henry Despenser was obviously older than that; the papacy had consistent difficulty with his age. His nephew Thomas *Despenser was briefly earl of Gloucester (1398–9). An aunt Isabella was married to Richard (II) Fitzalan, earl of Arundel, but repudiated. Through his second marriage Fitzalan was the father of Archbishop Thomas Arundel.

Henry Despenser (d. 1406), seal

Early career and elevation to Norwich The future bishop's brother, Edward *Despenser, Lord Despenser, petitioned the pope and secured for Henry Despenser a canonry with expectation (never made good) of a prebend in Salisbury Cathedral on 2 August 1354. On 20 January 1361 the pope gave him licence to acquire a cure of souls at the age of nineteen; he was admitted to the rectory of Bosworth, Leicestershire, on 22 December. He was a master at Oxford University by February 1361, when he was studying civil law, of which he was a bachelor and licentiate by the time of his promotion. He was ordained, even as a subdeacon, only on 17 December 1362. By 20 April 1364 he was archdeacon of Llandaff (the family had estates in south Wales), an office that the pope allowed him to keep with either a canonry in Lincoln Cathedral or the rectory of Elsworth, Cambridgeshire.

By then Despenser was a long-term resident at the papal curia and actually took part in military activity on behalf of Urban V, presumably alongside his brother Edward against the city of Milan. On 8 August 1369 the see of Norwich fell vacant on the death of Thomas Percy, whose sister Margaret was married to Despenser's maternal cousin, William Ferrers. Although a licence to elect was granted promptly on 20 August, the ageing Edward III was consistently indecisive in nominating to bishoprics at this time, which allowed several families of the higher nobility to intrude their own kin. Encouraged by Henry's intimacy and that of Lord Despenser with the curia, and also by their own with the late bishop, the Despensers saw their chance. Nothing is known of any election or other manoeuvring, but on 3 April 1370 Henry Despenser was papally provided with a dispensation because (the pope understood) he was still only in his twenty-seventh year. He was consecrated at Rome on 20 April. It cannot be assumed that the English government had already been persuaded to agree, because although Despenser was able to return home and have Archbishop Simon Sudbury accept his profession of obedience on 4 June, his spiritualities were only given to him on 12 July and his temporalities as late as 14 August.

Despenser took to his diocese and played no part in government. He never did impress some, especially the bitter monk–chronicler of St Albans, Thomas Walsingham (whose sole, brief, and admittedly unsuccessful period in broad administrative office was as prior of Wymondham in Despenser's diocese): immature, unlearned, lacking in discretion, undisciplined, arrogant, unmindful of making or keeping friends, was how Walsingham saw him. It is no real evidence to the contrary that on 9 May 1376 he was named by the Commons to be on an intercommuning committee with them from the Lords, which was composed strongly in favour of those leading the impeachment of several leading members of Edward III's court. After John of Gaunt, duke of Lancaster, had reacted furiously by singling out Bishop William Wykeham as a scapegoat and having his temporalities seized, Despenser was to the fore alongside Bishop William Courtenay in defending Wykeham in the convocation of Canterbury, and leading the opposition to any grant of a subsidy in February 1377. Thereafter he returned to diocesan administration.

The peasants' revolt and the Flemish crusade About June 1377 Despenser was involved in a riot in Bishop's Lynn, Norfolk, and even wounded, while trying to exert episcopal rights of lordship over the town by having a mace borne before him. Richard II's regency council was obliged to intervene. This was a well-established feud which was still violent and bitter in the middle of the next century, so the outburst should not be attributed unequivocally to Despenser's belligerent gesture. In April 1379 Despenser was appointed overseer of the will of Sir William Morley, and in such mundane diocesan duties he spent his time. However, in June and July 1381 he sprang into action to repress the widespread peasant agitation in his diocese, dashing back from Burley, Rutland, gathering forces, and leading them personally into a violent rout of the reluctant rebels at North Walsham. He hanged the leader, Geoffrey Lister, having (according to a swiftly developed legend) shriven him first. This vigour and severity was much admired in conservative circles, especially in contrast to the feeble response of the authorities to revolt in other counties. On the other hand, an abortive revolt in Norfolk in 1382 unsurprisingly had his death among its ambitions.

All this had whetted Despenser's appetite and he offered, perhaps at Pope Urban VI's instigation, to lead a military expedition into Flanders, with the aim of putting pressure on France, against whom frontal attacks had been very unsuccessful in recent years. The Commons in parliament in October 1382 were very enthusiastic, especially because the bishop could have this declared a crusade by the pope against his schismatic opponents and thus shift most of the costs onto the clergy, the laity simply redirecting a previous subsidy. They rejected the Lords' support for John of Gaunt's alternative proposal to lead a campaign against France's Spanish allies, which the laity would have to underwrite. Besides, Despenser was a

current hero, Gaunt decidedly was not. On 17 May 1383 the bishop crossed to Calais with an army of 8000 and enjoyed an initial success against a mixed force of Frenchmen and Flemings near Dunkirk on 25 May and the surrender of nearby towns. On 9 June he besieged Ypres. This proved disastrous and had to be abandoned on 8 August. Despenser's proposal to invade Picardy was opposed by his professional lieutenants, headed by the experienced Sir Hugh Calveley, who set up a separate campaign. The bishop still attempted his invasion, to no avail, and the appearance of a French army under Charles VI himself at the end of August forced a humiliating settlement at Gravelines in mid-September.

On his return to England, Despenser found out that the greater the enthusiasm, the more bitter the recrimination; he was impeached in parliament on 28 October for his mishandling of the campaign, and suffered forfeiture of his temporalities, although with no loss of liberty or episcopal authority. It has to be supposed that many around the government were delighted that his unwanted interference had ended as a fiasco, and the Commons were too disappointed to defend him. John Wyclif and his followers used the fiasco repeatedly as a warning in their writings. Even now, though, there were some who blamed his lieutenants' disloyalty rather than his own performance. In July 1385 Richard II let the bishop accompany his own military campaign into Scotland, perhaps to alarm Bishop Thomas Rossy of Galloway, who had recently challenged any English bishop to dispute the matter of the papal schism with him by single combat, singling out Despenser, 'who takes such delight in deeds of arms' (Baxter, 219–20). It is worth noting, too, that it was Bishop Thomas Arundel who on 24 October 1385 secured the restitution of Despenser's temporalities.

Diocesan and political business Despenser played no special role in the political crisis of 1386–8 and, perhaps despondently, confined himself to local business. For ten years he was one of the least mobile of contemporary diocesans. Apart from 1388, when he preferred his manor of Hoxne, Suffolk, he rarely left his palace in Norwich from 1385 to 1395, save to attend parliaments and convocations and, in some years, to spend part of October on a visitation. From 1395 he began to use South Elmham, Suffolk, as his main base and to travel around much more. 1397, as will appear, was an unusual year. In May and June 1399 Despenser moved around his diocese as never before, possibly more concerned on the king's behalf than his own. From 1390 he had conducted drawn-out litigation with Walter, Lord Hilton, in the court of chivalry. In 1399 he secured the recantation of a heretic, William Sawtre, perhaps none too gently, and is even said to have threatened him with burning when this punishment was not yet legal in England.

From May 1397 to February 1398 Despenser resided entirely in his London inn. There are two possible reasons, perhaps both valid. Firstly, Richard II was conducting his coup against his political opponents. The king can hardly have looked to Despenser for political wisdom and authority, but the bishop's loyalty to him was to prove devoted. Secondly, Despenser had taken up from early in his episcopate an ancient dispute with the cathedral priory about the bishop's authority over them, their monastic life and estates, and, in defiance of the pope's directives, Richard II had just commanded that this be decided by the archbishop of Canterbury. In March 1398 Despenser was given almost all he wanted.

In July 1399 Despenser reverted to type. His family were much in favour with Richard II, and he was one of the few to put up a show of defiance to Henry Bolingbroke's invasion. He was arrested at Berkeley Castle when refusing, unlike the duke of York (Richard's deputy in England), to come to terms. He was allowed to take his place in parliament in October 1399, staying at that time with Sir Robert Fulmer, and returned to his diocese at the end of November. Despite remaining at South Elmham from mid-December, he was implicated, perhaps through his nephew Thomas, in the abortive 'Epiphany plot' of 1400. He suffered no formal punishment, possibly because on 5 February 1400 he appointed John Derlington, archdeacon of Norwich, as his vicar-general at South Elmham and submitted himself to the custody of Archbishop Arundel, who seems to have shown him favour and affection over the years. He lived at Canterbury, playing effectually no part in administering his diocese until he was granted a pardon in parliament in February 1401. He was in London at that time, so may even have attended. It was perhaps through this unusual custody arrangement that Arundel had learned of the case of William Sawtre and brought it to convocation's notice in that month. Despenser did not attend but sent a written memorandum on 23 February. Sawtre, whom the bishop had held in prison, now became the show-piece demonstration that church and crown intended fully to utilize the capital punishment being brought in as a penalty against heretics and seditious preachers.

Last years and death Despenser returned once more to his diocese shortly after 19 March 1401. There is some evidence that he caught up on visitation duties (or perhaps rights and profits) during the rest of the year. Meantime, the monks of the cathedral had challenged his rights once more with the pope, and even secured a prohibition on Archbishop Arundel's hearing the case on the grounds that he was too friendly towards the bishop. The judge appointed by the pope indeed decided for them. Notwithstanding, Arundel took the bishop's side and cowed the monks into accepting his arbitration, which reverted to the verdict of 1398 in Despenser's favour. The monks decided to give up and make a composition with Despenser to enjoy their privileges.

On 14 July 1402 Despenser was ordered to array his clergy against a possible invasion of the Suffolk coast. No doubt to his disappointment, this threat vanished. In 1403–4 the feud with Lynn flared up once more, but on 14 July 1404 the king told him to stay his litigation. In the previous month there were rumours in Flanders that he was to lead another campaign, but even though Henry IV faced a crisis on many fronts at that time, it is impossible to believe that he and Arundel would have let the bishop

kick over the traces yet again. None the less, it is a striking illustration of the reputation the bishop had (quite accurately) acquired. He was now almost entirely resident at North Elmham, Norfolk, then switching in March 1405 to his palace in Norwich. All he did of note in his last years was to secure the recantation of one John Edward, a chaplain charged with heresy, on 12 April 1405. It was said shortly afterwards that there was considerable heresy in his diocese, but there is no sign that Despenser hunted it with any of the gusto one might expect of him.

It is perhaps of note that Despenser, who now rarely travelled, took himself to Lynn via North Elmham in the second week of August 1406, returned to Norwich by the 21st, and then moved yet again to North Elmham on the very next day. Perhaps something had roused him to confront the Lynn corporation yet again, but the exertion proved too much. He died on 23 August 1406. It is a matter of regret that he was declared intestate, for his will, if he made one and was not caught out by his apparently sudden death, could have been fascinating. Predictably, he had failed to prepare a chantry chapel, but was accorded burial immediately before the high altar in the cathedral. The monks had had their quarrel with him, but they appreciated him at the end. It is greatly to be doubted whether he really had wanted to be a bishop, at least one confined to a diocesan role. There was something of the bovine about him, but clearly he was in no way wanting in courage and loyalty. Even those in authority with whom he came into contact seem to have recognized that there was nothing malignant about him, and tried to tame, not destroy, him.

R. G. DAVIES

Sources Emden, *Oxf.*, 3.2169–70 · R. G. Davies, 'The episcopate in England and Wales, 1375–1443', PhD diss., University of Manchester, 1974, cix–cxi · episcopal register, Norfolk RO, Reg/3/6 · M. D. Legge, ed., *Anglo-Norman letters and petitions from All Souls MS 182*, Anglo-Norman Texts, 3 (1941) · N. Housley, 'The bishop of Norwich's crusade, May 1383', *History Today*, 33/5 (1983), 15–20 · N. Saul, *Richard II* (1997), 102–7 · M. Aston, 'The impeachment of Bishop Despenser', *BIHR*, 38 (1965), 127–48, esp. 138–41 · [J. Haldenston], *Copiale prioratus Sanctiandree: the letter-book of James Haldenstone, prior of St Andrews, 1418–1443*, ed. J. H. Baxter, St Andrews University Publications, 31 (1930), 219–20 · A. Hudson, *The premature reformation: Wycliffite texts and Lollard history* (1988) · I. Atherton and others, eds., *Norwich Cathedral: church, city and diocese, 1096–1996* (1996) · [T. Walsingham], *Chronicon Angliae, ab anno Domini 1328 usque ad annum 1388*, ed. E. M. Thompson, Rolls Series, 64 (1874)
Archives Norfolk RO, episcopal register, Reg /3/6
Likenesses seal, BL; Birch, *Seals*, 2047 [*see illus.*]

Despenser, Sir Hugh (*c.*1223–1265), justiciar, was a middle-ranking baron who became a leading supporter of Simon de Montfort, earl of Leicester, and the last holder of the office of justiciar of England re-established after the baronial seizure of power in 1258. He inherited his estates, which were mainly in Leicestershire, from his father, Hugh Despenser (*d.* 1238), who was a hereditary officer of Earl Ranulf of Chester, and high in the favour of Henry III. In recognition of his father's faithful service, the king in February 1238 permitted Despenser to marry as his friends thought best for his advancement. His wardship was bestowed on his uncle Geoffrey Despenser, he was given respite of knighthood in July 1244, and in the following January he received two casks of wine for the feast to celebrate his knighthood. Other marks of royal goodwill included gifts of timber in 1247 and 1249, and of free warren on an estate in Rutland in 1253.

From the late 1250s Despenser began to figure increasingly prominently in public affairs. In 1255 he was appointed constable of the royal castle at Horston, Derbyshire, for five years, and between April and September 1257 he was a member of the retinue of the king's brother Richard of Cornwall on his visit to Aachen for his coronation as king of the Romans. Next year he was included in the baronial twelve appointed to help draw up the provisions of Oxford, and under its terms he became a member of the committee of twelve chosen to represent the baronage at parliaments, and was reappointed constable of Horston Castle. He had been a friend of Simon de Montfort since at least 1256 when the two men undertook with others to arrange the politically sensitive marriage of Henry, son and heir of Edmund de Lacy, and on 1 January 1259 Montfort named him as an associate executor of his will, but this is not necessarily evidence of firm political loyalties. By early 1260 Despenser was married to Alina, daughter of Philip *Basset, an influential magnate also involved in the Lacy covenant and a member of the parliamentary committee of twelve, who increasingly sided with the king. Moreover in August 1260 Despenser was one of the nobles summoned to London even though known supporters of Montfort were omitted, and the following month he was a member of the Lord Edward's household. His son and heir Hugh *Despenser, the ill-starred favourite of Edward II, was born on 1 March 1261.

For unexplained reasons Despenser never took up his duties as justice on the special eyre in Wiltshire, Oxfordshire, and Berkshire in November 1259. Nevertheless about 20 October 1260 a committee of five chosen by the royal council rejected the king's own nominee and chose instead Despenser to replace Hugh Bigod, the brother of the earl of Norfolk, as justiciar and keeper of the Tower of London, with an annual salary of 1000 marks. He thus became the chief administrative and judicial officer of the king, one of the appointments that caused Henry III to complain that the new baronial officials 'were wholly ignorant of their offices' (Treharne and Sanders no. 30, 215). Regardless of this Despenser discharged the omnicompetent duties of his predecessor and was particularly active trying cases on the special eyre in Sussex in the winter of 1260–61. Together with Philip Basset, his father-in-law, he was also retained as a member of the king's household in December 1260. About 12 June 1261 however, after Henry III had regained his authority, he was dismissed as justiciar and keeper of the Tower, despite his protests that he could not be removed against the wishes of the barons, and replaced by Basset. He was not among the king's tenants-in-chief summoned to London in October 1261, and in June 1262 he was deprived of Horston Castle. By then Despenser's family was irreconcilably divided. Basset sided with the king, but Despenser himself, his brother-in-law *John fitz John (who was also the nephew

of Hugh Bigod), his cousin John Despenser (son of his former guardian), and John's half-brother, Roger de St John (who was probably married to Hugh Despenser's sister), supported Simon de Montfort.

When Montfort regained the ascendancy, Despenser was reappointed justiciar and keeper of the Tower, between 15 and 18 July 1263, on the usual salary, and later that year, between 23 September and 7 October, acted as regent during the king's visit to France. By the end of October, however, as disorder spread, he ceased to function as justiciar, although he seems to have kept control of the Tower. On 13 December 1263 he was one of the king's opponents who agreed to submit the baronial cause to the arbitration of Louis IX, but he rejected the king's abrogation of the provisions of Oxford. In March 1264, as keeper of the Tower, he led an angry crowd of Londoners who sacked Richard of Cornwall's manor of Isleworth, Middlesex, but in April he gave refuge in the Tower to the City's Jewish community which was being despoiled by, among others, John fitz John. At the battle of Lewes on 14 May 1264 Despenser fought in the front rank of the victorious rebel army, and forced his wounded father-in-law to surrender. No doubt it was at the request of his solicitous sons-in-law that Basset received a royal grant of venison and conies three weeks later. Despenser was also probably behind moves to secure the release of his cousin John, who had been captured fighting the king at Northampton.

With Montfort's triumph Despenser became a leading figure in the new government. He resumed his duties as justiciar on the customary salary, and was promised a staff of a hundred knights or serjeants to distrain offenders against the church. Although not formally a member of the new ruling Council of Nine, which included Roger de St John, he participated in its discussions, attended parliaments, authorized writs, and witnessed numerous royal charters. He was present at Westminster on 3 November 1264, when Henry, prior of St Radegund, took up his duties as treasurer, and on 25 February 1265, when Thomas de Cantilupe was appointed chancellor, the king himself folding the writ. He was also in attendance at Hereford on 7 May 1265 when special arrangements were approved for Cantilupe's absence from court.

Despenser was given a key role in co-ordinating the defences of the country to meet the threat of invasion by the king's supporters who had fled abroad. He assembled troops at London and ships at Sandwich, had custody at different times of the castles of Devizes, Oxford (later committed to Roger de St John), Orford, and Nottingham, and was given special responsibility for the defence of the coastline of East Anglia. As the threat of invasion passed he became increasingly active in the desperate search for a settlement with the king. On 11 and 15 September 1264 his name was included in panels to amend the new form of government, and on 24 September he went to France as a baronial envoy to inform the papal legate Guy Foulquois, cardinal-bishop of Sabina, that the barons were prepared to modify the Provisons of Oxford if the king would promise to expel aliens and rule through natives.

Despenser was among those who were excommunicated on 20 October when they refused to submit.

Despenser profited considerably from his alliance with Montfort, despite the view of some that he was never fully rewarded for his support. In September 1264, eight years after the Lacy agreement, he was allowed to purchase the wardship on preferential terms. Robert de Pierpoint, who had been captured at Lewes, was kept in Despenser's prison until he undertook to pay a ransom of 700 marks, and Marmaduke Thweng, another of his prisoners, also had to be ransomed. Despenser, for his part, could be relied on to use his authority in favour of the Montfort family. On 30 June 1264 he headed a court that awarded vindictive damages of 10,000 marks, to be paid within ten days, against William (VI) de Briouze for allegedly ravaging one of the younger Simon de Montfort's manors, and on 18 November he was an obvious choice for the committee to adjudicate on the difficult problem of Eleanor de Montfort's dower.

Leaving his wife in the Tower, Despenser accompanied Montfort on his last campaign in the marches in the summer of 1265, and with John fitz John and others tried unsuccessfully to resolve the dispute between the earl and his fellow triumvir Gilbert de Clare, earl of Gloucester. The collapse of Montfort's power brought disaster for Despenser and most of his relatives. John Despenser was captured at Kenilworth, and in the battle of Evesham on 4 August 1265 Roger de St John was slain, and Despenser himself, having refused to flee, was killed, reportedly by the thrust of a dagger. With the king's permission, his body was buried, with that of Montfort, at the foot of the steps before the high altar of the abbey church, where his remains were reported to have performed miracles, curing blind and disabled people. His widow surrendered the Tower before seeking the protection of her father, who was given Despenser's lands for his services to the king. Alina married as her second husband, by October 1271, Roger (III) Bigod, earl of Norfolk, the brother of the man Despenser had replaced as justiciar in 1260. She died in 1281.

CLIVE H. KNOWLES

Sources Chancery records · Ann. mon., vols. 2, 4 · T. Stapleton, ed., De antiquis legibus liber: cronica majorum et vicecomitum Londoniarum, CS, 34 (1846) · [W. Rishanger], The chronicle of William de Rishanger, of the barons' wars, ed. J. O. Halliwell, CS, 15 (1840) · The historical works of Gervase of Canterbury, ed. W. Stubbs, 2 vols., Rolls Series, 73 (1879–80) · H. R. Luard, ed., Flores historiarum, 3 vols., Rolls Series, 95 (1890), vols. 2–3 · J. Stevenson, ed., Chronica de Mailros, Bannatyne Club, 49 (1835) · E. B. Fryde and others, eds., Handbook of British chronology, 3rd edn, Royal Historical Society Guides and Handbooks, 2 (1986) · C. H. Knowles, 'The justiciarship in England, 1258–65', British government and administration: studies presented to S. B. Chrimes, ed. H. Hearder and H. R. Loyn (1974) · R. F. Treharne and I. J. Sanders, eds., Documents of the baronial movement of reform and rebellion, 1258–1267 (1973) · GEC, Peerage
Wealth at death lands seized: CIPM, 1, nos. 769, 771, 772, 798, 856

Despenser, Hugh, the elder, earl of Winchester (1261–1326), administrator and courtier, was the son of Sir Hugh *Despenser, the justiciar who was killed at Evesham in 1265, and his wife, Alina, daughter of Philip Basset. Born on 1 March 1261, in May 1281 he was granted full administration of his father's forfeited lands, and in August received livery of his mother's lands, although he was not yet of age. In March 1282 he received the manor of Martley in Worcester as heir to his uncle John Despenser. Later in 1282 Despenser paid 1600 marks to William de Beauchamp, earl of Warwick (d. 1296), for his own marriage. In 1287 he was fined 2000 marks by the king for his marriage without licence to Isabel (d. 1306), daughter of William de Beauchamp and widow of Payn Chaworth. Despenser might be said to have recovered this sum in 1306, when the king paid £2000 for the marriage of his only son, the younger Hugh *Despenser, who became the husband of the king's eldest granddaughter, Eleanor de Clare, sister of the earl of Gloucester.

In the reign of Edward I, Despenser made a career for himself through service both at home and abroad, where he was frequently employed on diplomatic missions. In 1287 he was with the king in Gascony, and in 1289 he went abroad with Roger (IV) Bigod, earl of Norfolk and marshal (d. 1306). In June 1294 he was appointed constable of Odiham Castle, and at about the same time was named one of the king's envoys to the German king, Adolf of Nassau, and the archbishop of Cologne. Late in 1294 he served in Gascony, and in 1295 he was summoned for the first time to parliament. In 1296–7 Despenser again served as a diplomat, and was one of the king's proxies to the treaty sealed with the count of Flanders on 5 February 1297. A week later he was appointed justice of the forest south of Trent, and in June of that year was named as a member of the royal council. In the summer of 1300 he accompanied the king on his Scottish campaign, one of only three men of baronial status to do so, and in November he went on an embassy to Rome with the earl of Lincoln. He was one of the envoys sent to France to restore peace in April 1302. In January 1303 he was made keeper of all rivers in defence on this side of Trent (north, at this time), while he continued to serve as justice of the forest. In October 1305 he was sent to Clement V (r. 1305–14) at Lyons to treat with the pope both for a possible crusade and concerning relations between the kings of England and France. He obtained a bull absolving the king from the oaths that he had taken to his people in 1297 and later. Interspersed with these various diplomatic missions were periods of service with the king in Scotland in 1303, 1304, and 1306. Despenser was rewarded for his constant service by Edward I with the Oxfordshire manors of Kirtlington (1296) and Great Haselese (1301), and with numerous lesser favours such as permission to enclose 30 acres of forest on one estate, and a weekly market and annual fair for another.

From the outset of Edward II's reign the elder Despenser was an ardent royalist. Indeed, even before the prince became king, as early as 1301, he referred to Despenser as 'one of our friends' (Johnstone, 102). It should not therefore be surprising to find that in the first year of the reign alone he appears in the charter rolls as a witness to some twenty-one of the thirty-eight acts enrolled there. At the coronation he carried part of the royal insignia. During the baronial crisis of 1308 Despenser was granted custody of Devizes, Marlborough, and Striguil castles, as well as of the town of Chepstow. In March 1308 he was again appointed a justice of the forest south of Trent, an appointment that was renewed for life in August 1309. In the later attacks on Piers Gaveston (d. 1312) he stood virtually alone in defending the Gascon favourite. For this reason he had been one of the courtiers singled out at the Northampton parliament of October 1307 who were to be dismissed from the council. His support for Gaveston was undoubtedly an important cause of the king's growing reliance on Despenser, as well as of the personal animosity increasingly felt for him by Thomas of Lancaster and others of the king's antagonists, not to mention Queen Isabella, throughout the reign.

Nevertheless, by November 1308 Despenser was back at court, as attested by his ubiquitous presence in the charter rolls throughout the rest of the second year of the reign, and indeed until the summer of 1314. In May 1313 he accompanied the king to France for the knighting of the sons of Philippe IV, a service for which he drew wages of 100s. a day, and he again accompanied the king to his meeting with Philippe IV at Montreuil in December of the same year. By that time he was considered to be an enemy of Thomas of Lancaster who had emerged as the leader of the baronial opposition. In the period of Lancaster's ascendancy following Bannockburn, Despenser, who had been present at the disastrous battle, is seldom if ever found at court, although he continued to serve as justice of the forest and in other capacities. He was among those present at the burial of Gaveston at Kings Langley on 3 January 1315, but shortly afterward was removed from the council by the king's enemies. In July 1315 a commission was appointed to hear complaints regarding his conduct as keeper of the forest south of Trent.

In the spring of 1316 Despenser once again became prominent at court and in the royal council, this time alongside his son and namesake. In 1317 he served with the king in Scotland. At this point, as record sources demonstrate even more clearly than earlier in the reign, he was at odds with the earl of Lancaster. Ironically, the appointment of the younger Despenser as chamberlain of the household was arranged in 1318 as part of the settlement between the king and Lancaster, and this appointment seems to have propelled the Despensers into the period of their greatest prominence. While the younger Despenser became ever more powerful at court and consolidated his territorial holdings in the Welsh march, his father continued his career of royal service. In 1320 he was sent to Gascony with Bartholomew Badlesmere (d. 1322) in order to consider reforms there and to visit the curia. From there he travelled to Amiens to join the king. By the following year, however, animosity towards the Despensers had grown to such a degree among the marcher lords and their ally Lancaster that even the king was unable to prevent the outbreak of violence.

On 4 May 1321 the ravaging of Despenser lands began. In August the baronial opposition met with the king in parliament and laid their charges against the Despensers, father and son. On 14 August the king capitulated to baronial demands for the exile of the Despensers, and on 20 August he pardoned those involved for their attacks on the royal favourites. The elder Despenser spent his exile in Bordeaux, within relatively close reach in the event of a recall. The king duly engineered this through a convocation held at Canterbury, which agreed on 1 December 1321 that the exile was invalid and should be annulled. A formal announcement to that effect was made on 1 January 1322, by which time a safe conduct had already been sent to Despenser. In the most effective military undertaking of his reign, in late 1321 and early 1322 Edward II routed the baronial opposition, the final blow being delivered at Boroughbridge on 16 March 1322. The earl of Hereford was killed in the battle, and the earl of Lancaster was executed six days later. Despenser is said to have been present at the latter's trial.

The period from 1322 to 1326 saw the Despensers rise to an unprecedented level of wealth and power. On 10 May 1322 the father was elevated to the peerage as earl of Winchester. Along with centres of power in the midlands and Wiltshire, Despenser now also built up a substantial holding near London based on the manor of Kennington. He received numerous grants of lands recently forfeited by the king's enemies, by members of the Bohun, Badlesmere, Damory, Giffard, and other families. From the great Lacy lordship he acquired the manor of Denbigh. In all, his lands were valued at £3884 at his death. The elder Despenser may not have been as aggressively acquisitive as his son, but an accumulation of other men's property on this scale ensured that he came to share the hatred felt for the latter. Opposition to their regime became widespread and reached to the highest levels of English society, in the person of the queen. By 1326 the queen, who was in France on a diplomatic mission to her brother Charles IV, refused to return to England until the Despensers had been removed from the court. In the event she led an armed invasion in September of that year, and the king and his favourites were driven westward before her. On 26 October the garrison at Bristol capitulated to Queen Isabella, and the elder Despenser was forced to surrender. He was tried in a court of chivalry before William Trussell on the following day. He was denounced, and sentenced to death, for offences that included usurpation of royal power, depriving the church of its rights, and complicity in the illegal execution of Thomas of Lancaster. He was condemned to be drawn for treason, hanged for robbery, and decapitated for his crimes against the church, his head to be taken to Winchester, 'where you were earl against law and reason' (Stubbs, 1.317).

J. S. HAMILTON

Sources J. R. S. Phillips, *Aymer de Valence, earl of Pembroke, 1307–1324: baronial politics in the reign of Edward II* (1972) · N. Fryde, *The tyranny and fall of Edward II, 1321–1326* (1979) · PRO, esp. charter rolls C 53 · N. Denholm-Young, ed. and trans., *Vita Edwardi secundi* (1957) · *Chancery records* · M. Prestwich, *Edward I* (1988) · GEC, *Peerage* · N. Saul, 'The Despensers and the downfall of Edward II', *EngHR*, 99 (1984), 1–33 · W. Stubbs, ed., *Chronicles of the reigns of Edward I and Edward II*, 2 vols., Rolls Series, 76 (1882–3) · H. Johnstone, *Edward of Carnarvon, 1284–1307* (1946) · exchequer, king's remembrancer, extents, PRO, E 142/33

Archives PRO, exchequer, king's remembrancer, extents, E 142/33

Likenesses portrait (identification uncertain), Tewkesbury Abbey, Gloucestershire

Wealth at death £3884 10s 10¼d. in estates; £1600 in cash; £4364 19s, 7d. in goods: Fryde, *Tyranny*, Appendix 1

Despenser, Hugh, the younger, first Lord Despenser

(*d.* 1326), administrator and royal favourite, was the son of Hugh *Despenser the elder (1261–1326) and his wife, Isabel (*d.* 1306), widow of Payn Chaworth and daughter of William de Beauchamp, earl of Warwick (*d.* 1296). His parents had married by 1287, and Hugh was old enough to be knighted by the prince of Wales on 22 May 1306. In the same year Edward I purchased his marriage for £2000 and arranged for him to wed Eleanor de Clare (*d.* 1337), eldest daughter of Gilbert de *Clare, earl of Gloucester (*d.* 1295), and the king's own granddaughter. At the outset of the reign of Edward II the younger Despenser does not seem to have possessed substantial property—on 14 May 1309 Edward II granted him the manor of Sutton in Norfolk, formerly a templar property, in order to make up his income to £200 per annum. In the following year his father provided him with several manors in Cambridgeshire, Suffolk, and Essex from the inheritance of his own mother, Alina Basset. In 1313 he accompanied the king to France, and at this time he received the wardship and marriage of William Huntingfield, a grant that was contested unsuccessfully by Thomas of Lancaster (*d.* 1322), and that may have been one source of their later enmity. His prospects were greatly enhanced by the death of his brother-in-law, Gilbert de Clare, earl of Gloucester, at Bannockburn on 24 June 1314. But although the earl's widow, Matilda, received her dower lands in December, the division of the Clare lands among the earl's three sisters could not take place immediately as the widowed countess claimed to be pregnant. In May 1315, tired of waiting, Despenser seized Tonbridge Castle in Kent. The castle was held by the Clares of the archbishop of Canterbury, and, despite equivocation on Despenser's part, it had to be returned to the archbishop. Nevertheless, this episode seems to be indicative of the avaricious and violent tendencies that Despenser was later to demonstrate so frequently.

Surprisingly, perhaps, the younger Despenser makes his first appearance as a witness in the charter rolls of Edward II only on 14 May 1316 (although as early as 17 July 1314 his father is specifically referred to therein as Hugh Despenser, senior), after which date he appears occasionally until February 1319. Thereafter he and the king were virtually inseparable until July 1321, when the Despensers, father and son, were sent into exile. In part Despenser's increased proximity to the king can be attributed to his appointment as chamberlain of the king's household at the York parliament of October 1318. The office of chamberlain was associated by contemporaries with Edward II's earlier favourite, Piers Gaveston, who had been executed by a coalition of barons in 1312. Certainly this office provided Despenser with ready access to the

Hugh Despenser the younger, first Lord Despenser (*d.* 1326), stained glass [centre, with Gilbert de Clare and Robert fitz Haimon]

king, and, like Gaveston, Despenser would soon be accused of denying others, including the queen herself, access to the king. There seems to be far less basis for suspecting any homosexual relationship between the king and Despenser than had been the case with Gaveston, but there can be little doubt of Edward's growing confidence in and dependence upon his new favourite. In any case, by 1317 the younger Despenser had become an important magnate by virtue of his wife's inheritance. The apportionment had been long delayed, first by the rising of Llywelyn Bren in Glamorgan in 1316, and later by the need to find suitable husbands for Eleanor de Clare's younger sisters. Margaret, widow of Piers Gaveston, married Hugh Audley in April 1317, and Elizabeth, widow of John de Burgh, son of the earl of Ulster, married Roger Damory in May 1317. In November 1317 the settlement of the Clare lands was at last finalized, the Despenser share being valued at some £1500, the vast majority of which was located in Wales. Almost at once Despenser set about consolidating his hold over the Clare lands, and not only his own. Before Hugh Audley could obtain formal seisin of Gwynllŵg, Despenser had already taken the homage and fealty of tenants there, and despite royal intervention on Audley's behalf, Despenser managed to hold on to this valuable parcel of land. Indeed, within a year he was able to obtain confirmation of his lordship in exchange for some less valuable manors elsewhere, and he was also confirmed in a life interest in the castle of Dryslwyn and the lordship of Cantref Mawr.

Despenser's acquisitive tendencies soon led to war. Tensions in the kingdom mounted between 1318 and 1321, aided by the ignominious failure of the Scottish campaign of 1319, but largely fuelled by Despenser's activity in the Welsh march. A confrontation was occasioned by Despenser's entry into the dispute over the lordship of Gower, which William (VII) de Briouze was proposing to sell. In this he aroused the enmity of a broad coalition of marcher lords, including Humphrey (VII) de Bohun, earl of Hereford, Roger Mortimer of Wigmore, John (I) Mowbray, Maurice Berkeley, and Hugh Audley. In October 1320 Mowbray, the son-in-law of William de Briouze, entered Gower without royal licence and was challenged by Despenser. Hereford took the lead for the marcher lords, defending the custom of the marches, but Edward took Gower into his own hands in December. Despite injunctions from the king to abstain from illegal assemblies, the marchers and other disgruntled magnates, including the earl of Lancaster, met to weigh their options, and on 4 May 1321 they attacked the Despenser lands. On 8 May 1321 Newport fell, followed by Cardiff on the 9th, and Gower on the 13th. The devastation of the Despenser lands was thorough. In August the marchers met with the king in parliament in London and laid their charges against the Despensers. The catalogue of charges is reminiscent of those brought against Piers Gaveston earlier in the reign: encroaching on the royal power; denying access to the king except in their presence; replacing good officials with corrupt ones; misappropriating templar properties. The younger Despenser was even charged with murder, in the execution of Llwelyn Bren after his rebellion. On 14 August, having been advised by the earl of Pembroke that there was no alternative, Edward II agreed in parliament to the exile of the Despensers, and on 20 August he pardoned the barons for their attack on them.

Rather than ending hostilities, the exile from England of the Despensers led to far greater bloodshed. While the younger Despenser tried his hand at piracy in the channel, attacking a Genoese ship, killing its crew and seizing its cargo, and attacking Southampton, the king opened an offensive against the baronial opposition by besieging Bartholomew Badlesmere's castle of Leeds in Kent. The marchers did not relieve it, and when it fell on 31 October the king had the garrison and its commander executed. Next he sought the recall of the Despensers through a convocation summoned to Canterbury in December. He obtained the answer he sought, and on 8 December he recalled the Despensers. Soon afterwards he set out for the Welsh march, supported by the earls of Pembroke, Arundel, Warenne, and Richmond, and a coalition of Welsh lords. This was perhaps the most successful military undertaking of Edward II's entire reign. In January and February 1322 many of the marchers surrendered. The rest retreated to join their ally the earl of Lancaster. As the king moved north, joined by Despenser at Lichfield on 2 March, the barons retreated before him, and on 16 March 1322 were defeated by royalist forces at Boroughbridge. Hereford was killed in the battle, and Lancaster was captured the next day. On 22 March he was executed, and many more were to follow. The baronial opposition was crushed, while royal power was correspondingly reasserted.

The period between 1322 and 1326 saw Despenser's wealth, power, and influence reach their zenith. Both son and father were ubiquitous at court, as is apparent in the charter rolls, which also attest to their territorial aggrandizement during this period of confiscations, fines, and near anarchy at the local level. During these years—and in this they acted as they had done before the crisis of 1321—the Despensers, and particularly the younger Hugh, built up a network of retainers who also served as royal officers, and by exploiting the potentialities of this 'double allegiance' they were able to exert tremendous influence across the realm. Their victims could have little hope of redress, when royal agents of justice were also agents of the Despensers. This revealed itself most clearly in the seizure and subsequent administration of lands forfeited by the king's opponents. The younger Despenser used a combination of royal favour, legal manipulation, and outright force to consolidate his holdings in Wales and the marches, so that by the time of his death his lands were valued at no less than £7000. The bullying tactics he employed against such vulnerable victims as Elizabeth Damory (widow of Hugh Audley), Alice, countess of Lancaster (widow of Thomas, earl of Lancaster), and Mary, countess of Pembroke (widow of Aymer de Valence), are well documented. His lavish expenditures at Caerphilly Castle and Tewkesbury Abbey have left enduring monuments to his exalted stature during these years. Even so, the contrariants continued to seek redress against Despenser's aggressive policy of self-advancement, and with the continuing failure of English arms, both in Scotland and in Gascony, discontent with the royal government continued to grow. Despenser himself seems to have been aware of the hatred increasingly felt for him, since he complained to the pope that he was being threatened by black magic.

Militarily the so-called War of St Sardos in 1323-5 may have been a minor affair, but for Edward II and the Despensers it turned out to have incalculable consequences. The king's inability or unwillingness to leave the country prevented a negotiated settlement to this conflict. In March 1325 he sent his wife, Isabella, sister of the French king, Charles IV, as his mediator. The author of the contemporary *Vita Edwardi secundi* sagely remarked that 'she will not (so many think) return until Hugh Despenser is wholly removed from the king's side' (*Vita*, 135). The settlement arranged by the queen called for Edward II to perform homage for English lands in France, but he was afterwards allowed to send his heir in his stead. However, neither the queen nor the prince returned to England following his performance of homage. In January 1326 Queen Isabella wrote to Bishop John Stratford (d. 1348) saying that she would not return until the Despensers had been removed from the court. In May 1326 two legates arrived in England with a pair of papal letters for the younger Despenser. The first called on him to assist in reconciling the king and queen, while the second, more generally, asked that he seek to foster better relations. Essentially, the letters were calling for Despenser to step aside in order to facilitate Isabella's return. But Edward II had the legates arrested, and after he had interviewed them in Dover Castle, they left the country without publishing their letters.

Despite elaborate preparations for defence of the realm on the king's behalf, the queen's invasion in September 1326 was virtually unopposed. The earl of Norfolk, Edward II's half-brother, was charged with the defence of the east coast, but he went over at once to the queen's side. His actions may have been prompted by a personal grievance against Despenser, who had coerced him into surrendering the lordship of Chepstow on very poor terms. But Norfolk's defection was representative of a much larger problem for Despenser and the king. As recent studies by Saul and Waugh have convincingly demonstrated, the Despenser administrative machine was widespread, but thinly rooted. The value of the sheriff's office, for instance, appears to have been insufficiently appreciated, and oaths of allegiance, when taken only as a means of obtaining access to crown patronage, did little to strengthen the Despensers' cause once it began to fail. The king and Despenser abandoned London on 2 October and headed west, towards Despenser's lands and the Welsh allies who had served Edward so well in 1321–2. Bristol fell to Isabella on 26 October, when king and favourite were at Cardiff. From there they travelled to Caerphilly, which was left in charge of Despenser's eldest son, Hugh. After moving west to Margam and then Neath, on 16 November the king and Despenser with a small entourage were taken prisoner near Neath, or perhaps Llantrisant, by Henry of Lancaster, earl of Leicester, and Rhys ap Howel, a marcher lord connected to the Bohun earls of Hereford. Despenser was taken to Hereford. Outside the city he was stripped and then reclothed with his arms reversed, and he was crowned with stinging nettles. Condemned to death as a traitor, on 24 November 1326 he was drawn on a hurdle to the gallows, and then hanged from a height of 50 feet. Still alive, he was cut down and eviscerated before finally being beheaded. His head was displayed on London Bridge; his quarters were sent to Bristol, Dover, York, and Newcastle. In December 1330 Eleanor de Clare received royal permission to collect her husband's bones and inter them in Tewkesbury Abbey.

The younger Despenser was responsible for the remodelling of Tewkesbury Abbey church, work subsequently completed by his widow and their son Hugh. It has been convincingly argued that this building programme was meant to produce a grandiose family mausoleum that would glorify the house of Despenser. The younger Despenser is represented in stained glass in the north window of the west bay between Robert fitz Hamon (d. 1107), founder of the abbey, and on the other side Gilbert de Clare, first earl of Gloucester (d. 1230) in the Clare family, and Henry I's illegitimate son Robert, the first lord of Tewkesbury to bear the title earl of Gloucester. Even more impressive as a symbol of his aspirations is the depiction of Despenser among the lords of Tewkesbury in paradise, in the arch of the choir and sanctuary.

J. S. HAMILTON

Sources N. Fryde, *The tyranny and fall of Edward II, 1321–1326* (1979) • N. Saul, 'The Despensers and the downfall of Edward II', *EngHR*, 99 (1984), 1–33 • S. Waugh, *For king, country, and patron: the Despensers and local administration, 1321–22* • R. Morris, 'Tewkesbury Abbey: the Despenser mausoleum', *Transactions of the Bristol and Gloucestershire Archaeological Society*, 93 (1974), 142–55 • PRO, C 53; E 142/33 • J. R. S. Phillips, *Aymer de Valence, earl of Pembroke, 1307–1324: baronial politics in the reign of Edward II* (1972) • N. Denholm-Young, ed. and trans., *Vita Edwardi secundi* (1957) • W. Stubbs, ed., *Chronicles of the reigns of Edward I and Edward II*, 2 vols., Rolls Series, 76 (1882–3) • GEC, *Peerage* • CPR • CClR • *Calendar of the charter rolls*, 6 vols., PRO (1903–27)
Likenesses stained-glass window, Tewkesbury Abbey, Gloucestershire [*see illus.*]
Wealth at death £7000: Fryde, *Tyranny*; PRO, E 142/33

Despenser, Thomas, second Lord Despenser (1373–1400), nobleman, was the sole surviving son of Edward *Despenser, first Lord Despenser (1336–1375), and his wife, Elizabeth Burghersh (d. 1409). Born on 22 September 1373 he was two years old when his father died in 1375, and he remained in royal wardship until 1394. His marriage was granted on 16 April 1378 to Richard II's uncle Edmund of Langley, earl of Cambridge (afterwards duke of York; 1341–1402), whose only daughter, Constance [*see* Despenser, Constance, Lady Despenser (*c*.1375–1416)], Despenser married before he was seven years old. As a royal ward he became one of the young king's personal friends and gained influence at court. He also had links with two of Richard II's opponents; at the age of fifteen he was serving with Richard (III) Fitzalan, earl of Arundel (d. 1397), who was admiral of England, and in 1391 he joined the king's youngest uncle, Thomas of Woodstock, duke of Gloucester, on his unlucky crusade to Prussia, an expedition which got no further than the coast of Norway.

The political power enjoyed by the house of York in the later years of Richard II's reign was a consequence of the king's affection for his cousin, Edmund of Langley's elder son, Edward, earl of Rutland (*c*.1373–1415). It was as Rutland's brother-in-law that Despenser joined the court party of young nobles whose support enabled Richard II to carry out his successful *coup d'état* in July 1397. When parliament met at Westminster on 21 September, Despenser was one of a group of eight courtier lords who appealed of treason the king's enemies, Gloucester, Arundel, and Warwick. Despenser's reward was the title of earl of Gloucester (29 September); his great-grandmother Eleanor (d. 1337), who married Hugh Despenser the younger, was the eldest sister and coheiress of Gilbert de Clare, earl of Gloucester (d. 1314). He also received a large share of the forfeited estates of the vanquished. His spoils included Elmley Castle, six manors in Worcestershire, and the Welsh marcher lordship of Elfael, all formerly belonging to the earl of Warwick. He was granted for life the constableship of Gloucester Castle and the wardenship of the Forest of Dean. In the Shrewsbury parliament of January 1398, Despenser obtained the reversal of the judgements passed in 1321 and 1327 on his ancestors, the two Hugh Despensers.

Despenser's gains gave him reason to uphold Richard II's autocracy during the last two years of his reign. He was one of the king's chief lieutenants when his second expedition to Ireland took place early in the summer of 1399, and he commanded the rearguard of the royal army. He was sent to treat with the Irish king of Leinster, Art Mór mac Murchadha, but he failed to bring him to terms; their meeting in a glen in Wicklow is depicted in one of the well-known illustrations to the manuscript of Jean Creton's chronicle of the deposition of Richard II. The outbreak of the revolution in England, which followed Henry Bolingbroke's landing at Ravenspur in Yorkshire late in June, compelled the king to abandon his Irish campaign. According to Adam Usk, after Richard disembarked at Pembroke on 22 July he sent Despenser to rally the men of Glamorgan on the king's behalf, but the inhabitants refused to obey the summons of their marcher lord. When the fallen king met Henry Percy, earl of Northumberland, at Conwy Castle, Despenser was one of the eight persons for whose safety Richard stipulated, but, like the rest of the king's former courtiers, he deserted once Richard's cause was lost. He was one of the seven commissioners appointed to pronounce the sentence of Richard II's deposition on 30 September 1399. In the first parliament of Henry IV's reign Despenser was one of five lords who had appealed the king's enemies of treason in 1397 now called upon to answer for their conduct two years earlier; Despenser denied that he had had any share in the responsibility for the death of the duke of Gloucester. He was punished by degradation from his earldom (3 November), the loss of the lands and offices granted to him in 1397, and a short spell of imprisonment in the Tower of London. He evidently contemplated withdrawing from English politics and going on a new crusading venture, either to Prussia or to Rhodes, and it would have been better for him if he had kept to that resolution.

Early in January 1400 Despenser joined the earls of Kent, Huntingdon, and Salisbury in a bid to restore the deposed Richard II to the throne. Popular support for Henry IV soon made the attempted rising a fiasco, and, having narrowly escaped capture at Cirencester, Despenser fled to Glamorgan, where he took ship at Cardiff, intending to seek refuge abroad. Instead the captain of the ship took him to Bristol, where he was seized and afterwards summarily executed on 13 January. He was buried at Tewkesbury Abbey. His unpopularity is reflected in the rumour that he had poisoned the late duke of Gloucester's young son, Humphrey, who had died in August 1399, shortly after Despenser's return from Richard II's Irish expedition.

Despenser had three children with his wife, Constance; his only son, Richard, born on 30 November 1396, married c.1408 Eleanor Neville (d. c.1472), one of the four daughters of Ralph, first earl of Westmorland (d. 1425), and his second wife, Joan Beaufort. Richard Despenser died childless possibly on 7 October 1413 (and certainly by 16 April 1414) while still a minor in royal wardship, and with his death

the male line of his family was extinguished. Thomas Despenser's eventual heir was his posthumous child, Isabel (d. 1439), born at Cardiff on 26 July 1400; she married first Richard Beauchamp (1396–1422), who was created earl of Worcester in 1421, and second his cousin, Richard Beauchamp, earl of Warwick (1382–1439).   T. B. Pugh

Sources 'Annales Ricardi secundi et Henrici quarti, regum Angliae', *Johannis de Trokelowe et Henrici de Blaneforde … chronica et annales*, ed. H. T. Riley, pt 3 of *Chronica monasterii S. Albani*, Rolls Series, 28 (1866), 155–420 · *Thomae Walsingham, quondam monachi S. Albani, historia Anglicana*, ed. H. T. Riley, 2 vols., pt 1 of *Chronica monasterii S. Albani*, Rolls Series, 28 (1863–4) · G. B. Stow, ed., *Historia vitae et regni Ricardi Secundi* (1977) · *Chronicon Adae de Usk*, ed. and trans. E. M. Thompson, 2nd edn (1904) · [J. Creton], 'Translation of a French metrical history of the deposition of King Richard the Second … with a copy of the original', ed. and trans. J. Webb, *Archaeologia*, 20 (1824), 1–423, esp. 295–423 · *RotP*, vols. 3–4 · Dugdale, *Monasticon*, new edn · W. Dugdale, *The baronage of England*, 2 vols. (1675–6) · J. H. Wylie, *History of England under Henry the Fourth*, 4 vols. (1884–98) · GEC, *Peerage* · G. Williams, ed., *Glamorgan county history*, 3: *The middle ages*, ed. T. B. Pugh (1971), 180, 607 (n.93) · C. Given-Wilson, ed. and trans., *Chronicles of the revolution, 1397–1400: the reign of Richard II* (1993) · CIPM
Likenesses portraits, repro. in *Burlington Magazine*

D'Este, Sir Augustus Frederick (1794–1848), peerage claimant, was born on 13 January 1794, the son of *Augustus Frederick, duke of Sussex (1773–1843), and Lady Augusta Murray (*bap.* 1761, *d.* 1830), second daughter of the fourth earl of Dunmore. Their marriage, which took place in Rome and was repeated in London in 1793, was declared invalid under the terms of the Royal Marriages Act, and the relationship ended late in 1801. Lady Augusta (who was deeply chagrined at her treatment by the royal family) brought up her son to think of himself as a prince and as a possible suitor for his cousin Princess Charlotte of Wales. Sussex brought actions against her to prevent her calling herself duchess of Sussex, and accepted the illegitimacy of Augustus and his sister Ellen Augusta (later Lady Truro) with apparent equanimity. Augustus was sent to Harrow School in 1807, under the surname Douglas, but in 1809 Sussex claimed custody of his children, gave them the surname D'Este (a family name of the house of Brunswick), and placed his son at Winchester College. In practice the D'Este children appear to have continued living with their mother, who was given the title Lady D'Ameland.

Like other royal bastards D'Este suffered from the uncertainty of his status: his mother had heightened his pretensions but could not make the world accept him. In 1812 he joined the 7th Royal Fusiliers as a lieutenant, and served with them in Jersey (where he annoyed his superiors); in 1814 he went with them to America, where as aide-de-camp to Sir John Lambert he participated in the ill-fated attack on New Orleans in January 1815. In 1817 he received the command of a troop in the 9th lancers, and in 1822 he was appointed major in the 4th Royal Irish Dragoons. He was promoted lieutenant-colonel in 1824 and colonel in 1838, but his active career in the army had long since ended.

In the winter of 1825 D'Este fell in love with the half-sister of Princess Victoria of Kent, Princess Feodora of Lei-ningen. Their romance had the assistance of a lady-in-waiting, but when it was discovered by the duchess of Kent, Sussex wrote 'purposely to insult, to torture and to outrage every sentiment of Honor, of moral principle and of integrity of his son' (Firth, 22), insisting that the inappropriate relationship end at once. Shortly after-wards D'Este suffered the first serious attack of a disease that dominated the rest of his life—disseminated, or mul-tiple, sclerosis. He kept a detailed account of his symp-toms, which included numbness in his legs, unsteadiness in walking, problems with his eyes, general debility and weakness, twitching in his limbs, and, as the years passed, bouts of giddiness and increasing pain. He also recorded in detail the various cures and remedies that he sought at spas and seaside resorts throughout England and Europe; he tried baths, douching, massages, changes of air, elec-trical therapy, and constantly evolving prescriptions of drugs and exercise regimens. In March 1843, for example, 'I went to Brighton, where I took some Vapor-baths and was shampoo'd at Mahomets' (ibid., 35). The various cures had no effect on the progression of the disease, and he was increasingly confined to a wheelchair.

D'Este's great preoccupation was with his status. From William IV (already hard pressed by his own extensive illegitimate family) he received in 1830 a knight com-mandership of the Royal Guelphic order, a civil-list pen-sion, and the appointment of deputy ranger of St James's Park and Hyde Park. This was not enough to dissuade D'Este from pursuing his claim to a peerage, and in 1831, according to Greville, he 'filed a bill in chancery, into which he had put all his father's love letters, written thirty years ago, to perpetuate evidence' (DNB), having received a legal opinion that the Royal Marriages Act did not apply abroad, and that in consequence his birth was legitimate. In 1834 he petitioned the duke of Cambridge to intercede with the king for recognition of his legitimacy, and on the duke of Sussex's death, in 1843, he made a claim to suc-ceed to his father's honours. In neither attempt was he successful.

D'Este was an active member of the Aborigines Protec-tion Society, particularly interested in native Americans. In 1833 he gave material assistance to Maconse, an Ojibwa, stranded in Britain. When Peter Jones, the Missassauga missionary and leader, visited Britain in 1838 to argue for the title of his people to their lands in Upper Canada, D'Este was one of his patrons; it was possibly through his good offices (and those of his cousin Sir Charles Murray, the master of the queen's household) that Jones was granted an audience with Queen Victoria in September 1838. Jones visited D'Este again in 1845, finding him 'as kind and as much interested for the welfare of the Abori-gines of our country as ever' but 'quite an invalid' and 'not able to walk without assistance' (Smith, 200). It was per-haps Jones who sent D'Este a 'Present of Indian Moccassins' in December 1846, which enabled him to walk without a steel bar to support his ankle (Firth, 54). D'Este offered thanks for this 'decided Improvement' in the last entry in the casebook of his condition. He lived for another two years, and died, unmarried, in London on 28 December 1848. He was buried next to his mother at St Laurence, on the Isle of Thanet. D'Este's record of his ill-ness, written with some detachment and great powers of self-observation, is probably the 'earliest clinical account of disseminated sclerosis', albeit written by a layman (Firth, preface); the first pathological description dates from 1836.   K. D. REYNOLDS

Sources D. Firth, *The case of Augustus D'Este* (1948) · GEC, *Peerage* · *GM*, 2nd ser., 31 (1849), 203–4 · *The correspondence of George, prince of Wales, 1770–1812*, ed. A. Aspinall, 8 vols. (1963–71) · D. B. Smith, *Sac-red feathers: the Reverend Peter Jones (Kahkewaquonaby) and the Missassauga Indians* (1999)
Archives PRO, corresp., diary, etc., PRO 30/93 · RCP Lond., diaries
Likenesses R. Cosway, miniature, 1799 ('A boy, said to be Sir Augustus Frederick d'Este (1794–1848)'), V&A; repro. in D. Firth, *The case of Augustus D'Este* (1948)

Des Vœux, Sir (George) William (1834–1909), colonial governor, was born on 22 September 1834, the eighth of the nine children of Henry Des Vœux (1786–1857) of Baden-Baden, Germany, a clergyman who spent his time in foreign travel, and his second wife, Fanny Elizabeth, daughter of George Hutton of Carlton, Nottinghamshire. His grandfather was Sir Charles Des Vœux, first baronet (d. 1814), who had held office in the government of India. His mother died when he was two years old; his father remarried in 1839 and returned to settle in England, first in London, then at Leamington Spa. William was educated at Charterhouse School (1845–53) and Balliol College, Oxford (from 1854), which he left in his third year without taking a degree, as he could not meet his father's wishes that he take holy orders.

Des Vœux went to Canada in 1856, originally intending to farm, but instead settled at Toronto. He graduated BA from the university there, and also passed in law. After practising briefly at the Canadian bar, to which he was admitted in 1861, in 1863 he became a stipendiary magis-trate and superintendent of rivers and creeks in an upriver district of British Guiana. Having been transferred to a coastal district including extensive sugar estates, which were worked largely by means of Indian and Chi-nese indentured labourers, Des Vœux, an ardent liberal, formed the opinion that the 'coolies' were grievously oppressed by the planters. He was reluctant, as magis-trate, to enforce 'the Draconic laws against the coolie indentured labourers', and rather demonstratively took the part of the labourer against the employer, thereby incurring—though not to the extent which he imagined—the hostility of the planters and the distrust of the government. Relations became so strained that he asked for a transfer to another colony, and in 1869 was sent as administrator to St Lucia. From his new post he at once wrote to Lord Granville of what he regarded as the grievances of the indentured labourers in Guiana. He him-self afterwards characterized his letter as 'defective', 'written in great haste', and 'without notes to refresh his memory'. *The Times* described it as 'the severest indict-ment of public officers since Hastings was impeached'. A royal commission of inquiry was appointed and Des

Vœux was recalled to Guiana to prove his case. The commission corrected certain abuses in the labour system, but Des Vœux failed to prove what he later described as an exaggerated view.

Des Vœux returned to his duties in St Lucia, 'depressed by a sense of personal failure', although the Colonial Office did not condemn him. At St Lucia he reorganized and codified the old French system of law in force there, put right the island finances, and started a central sugar factory. While on sick leave in 1875 he married, on 24 July, Marion Denison, the daughter of the pioneer of submarine telegraphy Sir John *Pender. They had two daughters and five sons, three of whom died in infancy.

During 1877–8 Des Vœux was acting governor of Trinidad, and in 1878 he left St Lucia and acted for about a year as governor of Fiji during the absence on leave of Sir Arthur Gordon (afterwards Lord Stanmore). Des Vœux successfully carried on the task of creating the first British crown colony in the south sea islands. After a visit home, during which he was appointed governor of the Bahamas but did not take up the post, in 1880 he returned to Fiji as actual governor and as high commissioner of the Western Pacific, where he remained until 1885. He was made KCMG in 1883. He was governor of Newfoundland in 1886 and of Hong Kong from 1887 until his final retirement from the service in 1891. He was made GCMG in 1893.

Thereafter Des Vœux lived quietly in England, chiefly in London. He published his autobiography, *My Colonial Service*, in 1903, a pleasant, gossipy book in two volumes containing much of interest on colonial administration. He died in Brighton on 15 December 1909, survived by his wife.   E. F. IM THURN, *rev.* LYNN MILNE

Sources G. W. Des Vœux, *My colonial service* (1903) • *WWW* • *Australian Graphic* (Dec 1883) • Burke, *Peerage* • private information (1912) • personal knowledge (1912) • *CGPLA Eng. & Wales* (1910) • Foster, *Alum. Oxon.*
Archives Mitchell L., NSW | BL, letters to Lord Stanmore, Add. MS 49205 • Bodl. Oxf., corresp. with Lord Kimberley
Likenesses etching, repro. in *Australian Graphic* • photographs, repro. in Des Vœux, *My colonial service*
Wealth at death £4669 2s. 3d.: probate, 27 Jan 1910, *CGPLA Eng. & Wales*

Deterding, Henri Wilhelm August (1866–1939), oil magnate, was born in Amsterdam on 19 April 1866, the youngest but one of the five children of Philip Jacob Deterding, captain in the merchant navy, and his wife, Catherina Adolphina Geertruida Kayser. Deterding's father died at sea in 1870, leaving the family in financial straits. His education at the Higher Citizens' School in Amsterdam ceased in 1882, when he was sixteen. He then joined the Twentsche Bank as its youngest employee, where he developed a skill in figures and in reading balance sheets which served him throughout his life. After enduring the tedium of this job for six years, he sat a competitive examination for posts in the Dutch East Indies.

Having come top in this examination, Deterding went east as an employee of the Netherlands Trading Company. He made his mark by disentangling the confused accounts of a branch which was in difficulties; he was later appointed sub-agent in the important Penang branch. More significantly for the future, he became involved in the affairs of the Royal Dutch Petroleum Company, gaining its directors' goodwill by granting it a loan after all other sources had refused one.

In 1894 Deterding married Catherina Louisa Neubronner (d. 1916); they were to have two sons and a daughter. Three years later he accepted a management post with Royal Dutch, and he and his family moved to The Hague. In 1900, when only thirty-four, he was appointed the company's managing director.

Since the output of Royal Dutch then accounted for only about 2 per cent of the world's oil production, Deterding at once evolved a strategy for building the company up into a major oil enterprise. This meant arriving at understandings with rival companies, on the proverbial principle that 'unity gives strength'. He therefore made overtures to Marcus Samuel (first Viscount Bearsted), founder of Shell Transport and Trading which also owned substantial oilfields in the Far East. In 1903 the two men agreed to set up—together with the Rothschilds, who had oil interests in Russia—a joint distribution organization for their eastern output, to be named the Asiatic Petroleum Company. Appointed the first managing director of the London-based Asiatic, he took up residence in England and acquired a country house, Kelling Hall, in Norfolk.

Owing to Samuel's multifarious outside interests and to poor corporate management, Shell a little later ran into grave financial problems, and in 1907 Deterding compelled him to merge Shell into the newly created Royal Dutch–Shell group. Samuel had to accept a minority stake of 40 per cent and the non-executive chairmanship. Deterding held the reins of power with 60 per cent of the shares and the post of managing director; his chief assistant was the very able Robert Waley Cohen. The commercial side of the business was situated in London and the technical side in The Hague.

Although Deterding maintained a very clear vision of striving for global co-operation over oil, so as to avoid price wars, he was not so successful with his American rival, the Standard Oil Company of New Jersey. He sought understandings over security of supply, and for Asiatic to have a half-share in all oil product markets outside the United States. Standard Oil responded to this audacious proposal by launching a sequence of price wars; in retaliation Deterding acquired a number of oilfields in the western hemisphere, including in California (1913), Venezuela (1913), and Mexico (1918).

Deterding reached an agreement with the Burmah Oil Company, based in Britain, about oil sales in India. In 1909, the year after oil was discovered in Persia, the Anglo-Persian Oil Company—the future British Petroleum—was floated in London, and Deterding undertook the marketing of its products. He was therefore incensed when in 1914 the British government acquired a controlling interest in Anglo-Persian. Meanwhile, he had secured for the Shell group a quarter share in the consortium prospecting for oil in Mesopotamia (later Iraq).

Notwithstanding these events, on the outbreak of the First World War, Deterding unreservedly placed the group's oil and tanker fleet at Britain's disposal. From 1916 onwards he worked hard to create an all-British oil combine, to be made up of (British) Shell, Anglo-Persian, and Burmah Oil, as a counterweight to Standard Oil. In 1920 his public wartime service to the allied cause was recognized when he was created an honorary KBE. He thereafter used the title Sir Henri in Britain, though not entitled to do so as he never became a British citizen. Soon afterwards, as his scheme for an oil combine unravelled in the face of widespread hostility in the UK, and with ministers having second thoughts, Deterding suffered a nervous breakdown and lost some of his entrepreneurial dynamism.

Deterding's first wife had died in 1916, and in 1924 he married Lidiya Pavlovna, daughter of the tsarist general Pavel Kudoyarov; they had two daughters. He then bought a residence in Ascot. As a White Russian émigrée, Lidiya helped to fuel his intense anti-communism, caused in large part by the company's loss of its Russian oilfields because of the Russian Revolution. However, that did not deter the company from later buying up large quantities of Soviet oil, which were used to destabilize the Americans' efforts in the Far East.

During much of the inter-war period, the global oil industry was in constant travail, with growth in demand held back by economic depressions and with supplies rising as new oilfields came on stream. To curb the resulting beggar-my-neighbour rivalry, in 1928 Deterding invited the chairmen of Anglo-Persian and Standard Oil of New Jersey to join him at Achnacarry Castle in Scotland. There the 'big three' in world oil hammered out a secret 'as is' agreement that froze the oil market as it then stood; this laid down a global price structure and encouraged co-operation where appropriate to minimize costs. The cartel agreed at Achnacarry was the last great *coup* of Deterding's career, and by the 1930s he appeared to have lost the sense of direction that had earlier led John, first Baron Fisher, to refer to him as 'Napoleonic in his audacity; Cromwellian in his thoroughness' (R. S. Churchill, p. 1951). To his cost, Deterding possessed no political antennae; his only declared aim was to make money.

Deterding at this time was progressively coming under the influence of his German personal assistant, Charlotte Minna Knaak, and in 1936 he divorced Lidiya and married Charlotte; they had two daughters. After retiring from Royal Dutch–Shell at the end of 1936, he then spent much time at his new residence in Mecklenburg, Germany. Although the evidence is weak that he actively supported the Nazi regime, he did propose certain schemes which conveyed that impression—for instance, that the group should aid the German economy by providing a year's supply of oil on credit. Whether or not he had the power to make such arrangements, consternation ensued in both The Hague and Whitehall; in fact, Deterding's attitude to the German authorities cooled when he discovered that they were buying from Mexico oil that he

regarded as 'stolen' from the group (Shell had earlier seen its Mexican oilfields nationalized).

Deterding was remembered as a mercurial man, his flashing smile turning in an instant into violent temper. Of no more than average height, he put great faith in physical fitness, regularly swimming in cold water before breakfast and enjoying long walks and skiing. Deterding died suddenly of angina pectoris while wintering at the Villa Olga, St Moritz, in Switzerland, on 4 February 1939, and was buried a week later in Mecklenburg; he was survived by his wife. The British Foreign Office became agitated in case his company shares might fall into German hands, but the fear proved groundless.

T. A. B. CORLEY

Sources H. W. A. Deterding, *An international oilman* (1934) · P. Hendrix, *Sir Henri Deterding and Royal Dutch–Shell: changing control of world oil, 1900–1940* (2002) · R. D. Q. Henriques, *Marcus Samuel: first Viscount Bearsted and founder of the Shell Trading and Transport Company* (c.1960) · K. Beaton, *Enterprise in oil: a history of Shell in the United States* (1957) · D. Yergin, *The prize: the epic quest for oil, money and power* (1991) · *The Times* (6 Feb 1939) · *The Times* (12 Feb 1939) [burial] · private information (2004) · R. W. Ferrier, *The history of the British Petroleum Company*, 1: *The developing years, 1901–1932* (1982) · F. C. Gerretson, *The history of the Royal Dutch*, 1–4 (1953–7) · R. S. Churchill, ed., *Winston S. Churchill*, companion vol. 2/3 (1969) · W. S. Churchill, *Great contemporaries* (1941), 250 · CGPLA Eng. & Wales (1939)

Archives Royal Dutch–Shell archives, The Hague | FILM BFI NFTVA, documentary footage

Likenesses photographs, Royal Dutch–Shell archives, The Hague

Wealth at death £370,400 19s. 3d. effects in England: probate, 16 June 1939, CGPLA Eng. & Wales

Dethick, Sir Gilbert (1499/1500–1584), herald and diplomat, was the grandson of Robert Derrick (d. 1525) of the king's armoury at Greenwich, a German armourer brought to England by Erasmus Kyrkener, and Agatha, daughter of Matthis Leyendecker, a barber of Aachen. His grandparents had three sons, Derick, Gilbert, and Matthew. The latter two were made denizens by act of parliament in 1542–3, making the unlikely claim that their father had been born in England and was descended from the Dethicks of Dethick Hall, Derbyshire, whose arms they used. Matthew Dethick (d. 1572) became an armourer at Greenwich; his brother Gilbert married the daughter of Leonard, a Dutch shoemaker at the sign of the Red Cock, St Martin's Lane, and had children who included Gilbert, the future herald, and Matthew, who was buried in York Minster in August 1583.

The younger Gilbert Dethick became Hampnes pursuivant-extraordinary on 16 June 1536 and rose rapidly, becoming Rouge Croix pursuivant in December 1540, Richmond herald on Christmas day 1540, and Norroy king of arms by patent dated 16 August 1547. He accompanied Lord Protector Somerset on his expedition against the Scots the same year, and was nearly shot by the Scots at the siege of Musselburgh. In 1549 he was sent to demand the surrender of the rebels in Kent, Essex, Suffolk, and Norfolk. There is a story that he stood at the 'tree of pardon' in Norwich and announced a free pardon to the rebels if they would disperse, and that he narrowly escaped being hanged by their leader, Robert Kett, although it has also been claimed that the herald concerned was York herald, not Dethick. Dethick became Garter king of arms on 20 April 1550 and was knighted on 14 April 1551.

Dethick was popular with his sovereigns. Henry VIII gave him a house and an acre of land in Poplar, where his family remained for 200 years, and he regularly exchanged new year presents with Elizabeth I. He invested Philip II of Spain, consort of Queen Mary; Emanuele-Philiberto, duke of Savoy; Frederick II of Denmark; Adolphus, duke of Holstein; Charles IX of France; François, duke of Montmorency; Johann Casimir, the son of the elector palatine of the Rhine; the duke of Bavaria; the earl of Rutland; and Henry, Lord Scrope of Bolton, with the Garter, and assisted in the investitures of Henri II of France, of which he wrote an account (Harl. MS 1355, art. 6), and of Emperor Maximilian II at Vienna. The latter expedition, made with the earl of Sussex in 1568, was followed by a tour of Carinthia with Archduke Karl. Dethick proclaimed several declarations of peace and war and, because he knew German and Dutch, was also sent on diplomatic expeditions, fulfilling the role of an effective rather than of a purely ceremonial envoy. Henry VIII sent him several times to Denmark to claim ships, and he is alleged to have attended the diet of Regensburg in 1546. He was involved in negotiations for three marriages for Edward VI, with a Cleves princess, Mary, queen of Scots, and Elisabeth de Valois of France. In 1554 he went on an embassy to Flanders.

When Dethick became Garter the heralds were still without a base, so from 1554 they met at Dethick's house in Poplar. In 1555 he secured the grant of a house occupied by Sir Richard Sackville in Derby Place, Sts Benet and Peter, from Queen Mary. Sackville left eleven years later, and the heralds moved into what became the College of Arms on 25 January 1565. Dethick complained that he was allotted only four rooms. As Garter he made over 140 grants of arms, and forty more in conjunction with the provincial kings of arms. Collections of his work survive at the British Library and Gonville and Caius College, particularly BL, Harley MS 5826, Add. MS 10110, and 'Dethickes guiftes' (his grants and confirmations, 1549–84), Add. MS 12454 (see too Harley MS 5847). He trained several heralds, including Nicholas Paddy, Lancaster, and Hugh Cotgrave, Richmond, who began their careers as his servants, and also his son William *Dethick. Dethick was a sound genealogist and heraldist, and a member of the original Society of Antiquaries.

A handsome man, Dethick married twice. His first wife was Alice, daughter of Leonard Peterson, a Dutchman. They had three sons: Nicholas (1539–1596), later Windsor herald; William (1543–1612); and Henry *Dethick, who became chancellor of the diocese of Carlisle, and whose son Henry (1623–1707) became Richmond herald. Alice died on 13 January 1572, and Dethick was remarried; his new wife was Jane, daughter of Richard Duncomb of Moreton, Buckinghamshire, the widow of William Naylor. They had further children: Robert (b. 1561, d.

before 1583), godson to Elizabeth I; and Mary, to whom her father bequeathed £500, and who married Thomas Butler, barrister, of Orwell, Cambridgeshire. Dethick died in London on 3 October 1584 and was buried in the church of St Benet Paul's Wharf; he was survived by his second wife. He is commemorated on his son's memorial in St Paul's Cathedral, which states that he died aged eighty-four.

ANTHONY R. J. S. ADOLPH

Sources M. Noble, *A history of the College of Arms* (1805) · W. H. Godfrey, A. Wagner, and H. Stanford London, *The College of Arms, Queen Victoria Street* (1963) · A. Wagner, *Heralds of England: a history of the office and College of Arms* (1967) · prerogative court of Canterbury, wills, PRO, PROB 11/67, fols. 274r–274v · F. W. Russell, *Kett's rebellion in Norfolk* (1859) · J. Evans, *A history of the Society of Antiquaries* (1956) · BL, Add. MSS 10110, 12454 · BL, Harley MSS 1355, 5826, 5847 · J. Anstis, ed., *The register of the most noble order of the Garter*, 1 (1724), 381–6 · W. Dugdale, *The history of St Paul's Cathedral in London* (1658) · J. Weever, *Ancient funerall monuments* (1631) · J. Dallaway, *Inquiries into the origin and progress of the science of heraldry in England* (1793) · *DNB*

Archives BL, papers relating to order of the Garter, grants of arms, and other papers, Add. MSS 10110, 12454, 14293, 15215 · Bodl. Oxf., heraldic papers · Coll. Arms, MSS · Gon. & Caius Cam., MSS | BL, heraldic papers, incl. some of Sir William Dethick, and grants of arms, Harley MSS 5826, 5847

Likenesses M. Gheeraerts senior, etching (*Procession of knights of Garter, 1576*), BM · portrait, Coll. Arms; repro. in Wagner, *Heralds*, pl. 15, 176 · portrait (from MS initial letter), repro. in Dallaway, *Inquiries*

Wealth at death approx. £500—bequest to daughter: will, PRO, PROB 11/67, fols. 274r–274v

Dethick, Henry (1547/8–c.1613), Latin poet and writer on poetic theory, was the third son of Sir Gilbert *Dethick (1499/1500–1584), Garter king of arms under Queen Elizabeth, and Alice Peterson (d. 1572), and the brother of Sir William *Dethick, who succeeded Sir Gilbert as Garter in 1586. He was admitted to Winchester College in 1560 at the age of twelve. From Winchester he passed to Oxford, where he was admitted BA on 16 February 1569 and was licensed for his MA on 14 June 1572, being incorporated MA a month later, on 14 July. He supplicated for the degree of BCL on 16 January 1574 and was admitted to the degree on 2 July 1578. He supplicated for the degree of DCL on 12 December 1581, but it does not seem to have been awarded. His college is not known, but it was quite likely Corpus Christi, since the friends who wrote liminary poems to Dethick's *Feriae sacrae* in 1577 were mainly from that college.

Dethick's *Oratio in laudem poëseos*, dedicated to Lord Burghley and printed c.1574, is one of the earliest formal defences of poetry in Elizabethan England. It is not a sophisticated work, and was probably not well known. It was printed only once and is extant in only two copies. The treatise does, however, maintain that poetry is a divine gift, aiming to civilize humanity, and operating through mythological allegory. It evokes Dethick's youthful enthusiasm for poetry. Christopher Jonson, headmaster of Winchester College and himself a Latin poet, contributed prefatory verses to this work.

Dethick's main work was the *Feriae sacrae libri octo* (1577), a lengthy collection of biblical paraphrases and verses on biblical incident, a popular Elizabethan genre. It contains poems on Adam, Noah's ark, the ten commandments, John the Baptist, Herod, the temptation of Christ, and numerous other topics, not all of them biblical. The *Feriae sacrae* is carefully constructed within a framework deriving, first, from the threefold division of Christian history into the time of natural law, the time of Mosaic law, and the time of grace after the coming of Christ, and, second, from the Augustinian division into 'six ages of the world'. The work is dedicated to Lord Burghley and contains prefatory verses by, among others, Laurence Humphrey, the president of Magdalen College, Oxford, and biographer of Bishop Jewel, and Stephen Gosson, the puritan opponent of the stage and Dethick's contemporary at Oxford.

Dethick himself wrote commendatory verses to a Latin translation of Castiglione's *Courtier* (1571 and 1577) by Bartholomew Clerke, and to Richard Stanyhurst's work on logic, *Harmonia, seu, Catena dialectica* (1570). He also edited and wrote Latin commendatory verses to *The Gardener's Labyrinth* (1577) by Thomas Hill (Didymus Mountaine). Dethick again dedicated this work to Lord Burghley.

After leaving Oxford, Dethick became master of Greetham Hospital, in Cumberland, and then successively chancellor and, in 1588, archdeacon of Carlisle. He ended his career as chancellor of the diocese of Carlisle and died c.1613. J. W. BINNS

Sources J. W. Binns, ed., *Latin treatises on poetry from Renaissance England* (1999) [incl. text and trans. of Dethick's *Oratio in laudem poëseos*] • J. W. Binns, *Intellectual culture in Elizabethan and Jacobean England: the Latin writings of the age* (1990) • 'Dethick, Sir Gilbert', *DNB* • T. F. Kirby, *Winchester scholars: a list of the wardens, fellows, and scholars of … Winchester College* (1888), 136 • *Reg. Oxf.*, 2/3.20 • Foster, *Alum. Oxon.* • Wood, *Ath. Oxon.: Fasti* (1815), 208–9 • G. D. Squibb, *Doctors' Commons: a history of the College of Advocates and Doctors of Law* (1977)

Dethick, Sir William (1543–1612), herald and antiquary, was the second son of Sir Gilbert *Dethick (1499/1500–1584) and Alice Peterson (d. 1572). The Latin poet Henry *Dethick was a younger brother. He was educated at St John's College, Cambridge, and was later a member of Gray's Inn, but his principal education came from his father, who obtained for him the post of Rouge Croix pursuivant on 9 February 1567, and whom he accompanied to the Garter investitures of Charles IX (1564) and Emperor Maximilian (1568). He left the latter expedition to travel independently in Italy in order to increase his considerable knowledge of Roman antiquities.

William Dethick became York herald by patent dated 24 March 1570. Displaying early signs of arrogance, probably fostered by his father's position, he made three grants of arms under his own seal. Eighteen months after his father died he succeeded him as Garter king of arms. He bribed the signet clerk to add a clause to his patent, dated 21 April 1586, allowing him to make visitations and grant arms, thus breaching the rights of Norroy, Ulster, and Clarenceux kings of arms. He then proceeded to abort Clarenceux's visitation of Lincolnshire, consequently earning a severe reprimand from Lord Burghley. He surrendered the patent, which was regranted without the new rights, but following Burghley's death in 1598 he produced a copy of the original one. He never interfered with visitations again, but continued to make grants himself, including one to William Shakespeare's father, which was criticized by his fellow herald Ralph Brooke for being too similar to Lord Mauley's. In 1595 Dethick was cited in Star Chamber for having granted George Rotheram the arms of Lord Grey of Ruthin on the basis of a false pedigree. He blamed this on Rotheram, but there were other charges of pedigree forgery too.

Dethick's integrity as a genealogist was no worse than that of his contemporaries, at a time when the discipline of using original records to prove pedigrees was still in its infancy. John Anstis, in his account of the Order of the Garter, published in 1724, praised Dethick for his diligence. The old Society of Antiquaries, of which he was an active member, used to meet in his rooms; he himself contributed papers (printed by Hearne in 1771) on such subjects as mottes, epitaphs, and the antiquity of Christianity in England. None of his other writings, which survive in collections in the British Library, the College of Arms, and Gonville and Caius College, Cambridge, have been printed. They include some fine heraldic manuscripts, notably 'A booke of the armes of the noblemen in Henry the Fifts tyme' (BL, Harley MS 1864), and works on such subjects as Germany and its principal families, and the Swiss grisons.

More serious than bad pedigree work was Dethick's apparent support of the prospective marriage of the duke of Norfolk and Mary, queen of Scots, in 1571, demonstrated by his marshalling their arms together on a manuscript pedigree and in some stained glass. For this treasonous act he was suspended from office, but Queen Elizabeth forgave him, and in due course he oversaw Mary's funeral at Peterborough in 1587. In 1596 he accompanied the earl of Shrewsbury for the presentation of the Garter to Henri IV of France, who gave him 500 crowns. His account of his mission survives in BL, Add. MS 6298, fol. 280. In 1601, when the earl of Essex rebelled in London, Dethick accompanied Thomas Cecil, Lord Burghley, into the city to proclaim the earl a traitor and to persuade him to desist. Essex later claimed 'I saw no herald but that branded fellow, whom I took not for an herald'. To this, the answer was that 'an herald, though a wicked man, is nevertheless an herald' (Noble, 199–200).

James I knighted Dethick on 13 May 1603. His popularity with the king was matched by his unpopularity with his fellow heralds, who presented many charges of his atrocious behaviour. In 1573 he attacked the Chester herald's wife, pushing her head into the fireplace with his boot, and pouring hot ashes, alcohol, and the contents of her chamber pot over her head, and was only prevented from killing her by his cousin Richard Dethick of Polstead, Suffolk. According to Brooke, he punched his own father (who cursed him for it), wounded his brother with a dagger at Windsor Castle, and beat and slandered many of his fellow heralds, writing, for example, of 'Clarentius the drunkard, Mr Wade the vainglorious, Chester the tavern haunter' and 'Richmond herald that should have been executed at Berwick' (Wagner, 201). He interrupted the funeral of Sir Henry Sidney at Penshurst by hitting the minister, and that of the countess of Sussex in Westminster Abbey by striking two people with his dagger, for which he was indicted at Newgate, though he escaped being charged because he knew the recorder and because one of the victims did not attend to present evidence.

Responding to an allegation that Dethick had disparaged the Stuarts' right to the crown, James I gave William Segar, Somerset herald, a signet bill to be Garter. Remembering Dethick's good offices to his mother, Mary, queen of Scots, however, James I sent Dethick, still with his title of Garter, in August 1603 to place a pall of state on her tomb, and the next month he was sent, again as Garter, to invest the duke of Württemberg, for which he was rewarded richly. Dethick's enemies persisted, alleging irregularities in the investiture, and James I capitulated, allowing a warrant for Dethick's dismissal to pass the great seal on 1 January 1604. Dethick refused to yield, wearing his tabard defiantly at court that Christmas, but the marshal's court on 26 January 1605 confirmed the dismissal. He still refused to abandon his office, and sought redress from parliament and the court of common pleas, but finally the king persuaded him to give up his office in return for an annuity increased from £40 to £200 and exemption from all taxes. Once this was granted, he finally surrendered his office to Segar in December 1606. Even then his bad behaviour continued, and he was fined and sentenced to imprisonment by a church court for calling a clergyman 'a bald, rascally priest' and striking him (Noble, 201).

Dethick wrote his will on 21 April 1612, and it was proved on 26 October that year. He was buried in St Paul's Cathedral. He had married Thomasine (whose burial took place on 18 July 1633 at Stepney), only daughter of Robert Young, citizen and fishmonger of London. They had three sons: George of Gray's Inn, to whom he left his house in Poplar; Gilbert, who became registrar of the court of chivalry (d. 1639), and whose daughter Ann married John Watson, Bluemantle; and Henry (d. 1639), to whom he left his papers, and who was the father of Henry Dethick, Richmond herald, and of Elizabeth, wife of Everard Exton, Rouge Dragon.　　　　　　　　ANTHONY R. J. S. ADOLPH

Sources M. Noble, *A history of the College of Arms* (1805) · W. H. Godfrey, A. Wagner, and H. Stanford London, *The College of Arms, Queen Victoria Street* (1963) · A. Wagner, *Heralds of England: a history of the office and College of Arms* (1967) · Rymer, *Foedera*, 1st edn, 15.679 · J. Anstis, ed., *The register of the most noble order of the Garter*, 1 (1724), 386–99 · T. Hearne, *A collection of curious discourses*, 2 vols. (1771) · J. Nichols, *The progresses, processions, and magnificent festivities of King James I, his royal consort, family and court*, 4 vols. (1828) · BL, Add. MS 25247, fols. 291b–296 · BL, Harley MS 1864 · PRO, PROB 11/120, fols. 173r–173v · BL, Add. MS 6298, fol. 280 · *DNB*
Archives Bodl. Oxf., collections of arms | BL, account of Germany, Norfolk pedigrees, heraldic papers, incl. some of Sir Gilbert Dethick, and papers relating to order of the Garter, Harley MSS 2287, 5826; Add. MSS 10110, 17434, 19816; King's MS 417 · Northants. RO, arms and pedigree of Hatton family
Likenesses portrait, Coll. Arms; repro. in Wagner, *Heralds*, pl. 17

Detmold, Edward Julius (1883–1957). *See under* Detmold, (Charles) Maurice (1883–1908).

Detmold, (Charles) Maurice (1883–1908), painter and printmaker, was born in Putney, London, on 21 November 1883, the son of Edward Detmold, electrical engineer, and his wife, Mary Agnes Luck. His mother may have died in childbirth as Maurice and his twin brother, **Edward Julius Detmold** (1883–1957), also a painter and printmaker, were raised as orphans and entrusted into the care of an uncle, Dr E. B. Shuldham, who lived in Hampstead. From the age of five both boys showed an interest in drawing animals in the zoological gardens and in the British Museum (Natural History) in London, and shortly after this time they spent six months drawing at the Hampstead Conservatoire, thereby receiving what is likely to have been their only formal artistic training. They showed a precocious artistic talent, being deeply influenced in their work by both Shuldham's knowledge of natural history and his collection of Japanese prints. In 1897, aged thirteen, the pair exhibited at the Royal Academy, attracting the attention of Edward Burne-Jones who advised them to abandon any future plans for artistic training. They then went on to exhibit at the Royal Institute of Painters in Water Colour and began to experiment with etching.

Maurice Detmold's first attempt at mezzotint was made in 1898 but he only once returned to this technique of printmaking and henceforth experimented mainly with colour printing. In that year the brothers exhibited at the Royal Institute of Painters in Water Colours, the English Art Club, and the International Exhibition at Kensington, London. In 1898 they produced a small portfolio, *Eight Proof Etchings by Maurice and Edward Detmold*, this edition selling out almost immediately. In 1899 the brothers learned the use of aquatint, which they applied to their work with some success. Also in 1899 a volume of coloured reproductions of the brothers' drawings, *Pictures from Birdland*, was published by Dent. In 1900 they held an exhibition of drawings and prints in a variety of techniques at the galleries of the Fine Art Society. They continued to work together, painting large watercolours illustrating an edition of Rudyard Kipling's *Jungle Book* which was published in 1903. In 1904 Maurice exhibited at the Royal Academy, and the brothers contributed a joint etching, *The Falcon*, to the *Artist Engraver*. On 12 January 1905 the brothers were elected associates of the Royal Society of Painter-Etchers and Engravers. Although they later resigned their membership, they contributed some of their best work to that year's exhibition. During August and September of the same year, the Arts and Crafts Exhibition at Leicester included designs for stained glass by both brothers. These designs added to the increasing evidence in Maurice's work that he in particular wished to escape from the label of 'animal artist' and move into more imaginative fields of art.

Two plates produced late in 1905 were Maurice Detmold's last etched works. He had produced in total ten etchings and two woodcuts in collaboration with Edward and twenty-five etchings done by himself, though in part from drawings by his brother. Many of the works produced separately by the brothers are almost indistinguishable from each other, but it is the collaboration involved in producing the single-plate etchings that is the most remarkable. 'They seemed as one soul divided between two bodies, inspired by the same ideal, using the same means of expression, possessing the same quickness of eye and deftness of hand' (Dodgson, 'Maurice and Edward Detmold', 373).

For several years the brothers had resided in West Hampstead but had spent periods at Ditchling in Sussex. On 9 April 1908, prior to one of these visits to Sussex, Maurice Detmold committed suicide—at his home in Inglewood Road—by inhaling chloroform. A suicide note found near his side read: 'This is not the end of a life. I have expressed through my physical means all that they are capable of expressing, and I am about to lay them aside' (Art Journal). He was unmarried.

Although Maurice Detmold was generally considered to be the more talented of the pair, both brothers' later works in particular show a remarkable technical ability which a combination of lack of training and experience did not allow to mature and develop. These works are distinguished by their personal interpretations of the subject matter and are heavily influenced by the works of Japanese masters (notably Hiroshige and Hokusai) while adhering to the conventions of art nouveau. Their animal paintings and illustrations show refined naturalistic features, with plumes and feathers subordinated to decorative arrangement, giving the subject an exaggerated and stylized appearance.

For over a decade after Maurice's death Edward Detmold continued to produce prints and watercolours and was perceived as a notable British printmaker. In the 1930s he retired into virtual obscurity, creating mainly saleable watercolours and prints depicting birds and flowers. Becoming increasingly disillusioned with the world around him, which he referred to as 'this blood-drenched civilisation', he, as did his brother nearly half a century earlier, took his own life, by shooting himself in Montgomery, Wales, in 1957. An exhibition of his work was held at the Keyser Gallery in 1979. Examples of the brothers' work are in the collections of the National Art Library of the Victoria and Albert Museum and the British Museum's department of prints and drawings, London.

CAMPBELL DODGSON, rev. CHANTAL SERHAN

Sources N. Alfrey and R. Verdi, *Charles Maurice (1883–1908) and Edward Julius (1883–1957) Detmold: a centenary exhibition* (1983) [exhibition catalogue, Heslington Hall, University of York, 17 Oct – 21 Nov 1983; University Art Gallery, U. Nott., 25 Nov – 17 Dec 1983; Natural History Museum, London, 6 Jan – 4 Feb 1984] · C. Dodgson, 'Maurice und Edward Detmold', *Die Graphischen Künste*, 33 (1910), 17–24 [trans. as 'Maurice and Edward Detmold', *Print Collector's Quarterly*, 9/4 (Dec 1922), 373–405] · M. H. Spielmann, 'Two boys—Maurice and Edward Detmold', *Magazine of Art*, 24 (1899–1900), 112–18 · 'Inquests', *The Times* (14 April 1908) · *Art Journal*, new ser., 28 (1908), 186, 224, 370 · review of illustrations for Rudyard Kipling's *Jungle book*, *The Studio*, 30 (1903–4), 252 · *The Studio*, 33 (1904–5), 80 · *The Studio*, 38 (1906), 244 · D. Larkin, *The fantastic creatures of Edward Julius Detmold* (1979) · *CGPLA Eng. & Wales* (1909) · private information (1912)

Likenesses E. J. Detmold, pencil drawing, 1899, NPG

Wealth at death £14: administration, 23 March 1909, *CGPLA Eng. & Wales*

Detrosier, Rowland [*formerly* Rowley Barnes] (1800?–1834), freethinking radical and popular lecturer, was born in London, the son of a Manchester merchant, Robert Norris, and a Frenchwoman named Detrosier. His parents abandoned him soon after his birth and he was adopted by a Swedenborgian tailor from Hulme in Manchester, Charles Barnes, who brought him up as his own son, naming him Rowley Barnes. Following only rudimentary education (at Sunday school and the Manchester Benevolent Vegetarian Institute) he began work in a warehouse at the age of nine. Aged twelve, he was apprenticed to a fustian cutter but six years later, in 1818, gave up this trade to work first at a cotton factory as a maker-up of twist, then at a throstle mill as a reeler and bookkeeper. Despite the ravages of a trade depression and the expense of a wife (whom he married when he was nineteen) and a growing family, he saved enough to buy books, pamphlets, and apparatus and taught himself grammar, rhetoric, French, Latin, mathematics, astronomy, physics, chemistry, botany, and geology. However, by 1821 he was in severe distress and was saved only by the patronage of John Shuttleworth, a local Unitarian and radical, who secured work for him as a salesman and clerk at Benjamin Naylor's cotton-spinning factory. The upturn in his fortunes coincided with his parents' decision to reveal the truth about his upbringing, and Rowley Barnes became Rowland Detrosier.

Shuttleworth's intervention opened up the opportunity for Detrosier to indulge in his passion for education. His great natural talents for speaking and writing had already been displayed at Hulme and Salford Swedenborgian Sunday schools, where he taught science from the age of sixteen. During the early 1820s he lectured widely across the north of England, and especially at Hulme and Salford Mechanics' Institutes, promoting independent working-class self-education to his artisanal audiences. The period 1824–6 also saw him briefly successful in partnership with Marshall, a manufacturing chemist. When the business failed, Detrosier was forced to return to his earlier career, this time as a clerk and buyer to a foreign house in the cotton-twist trade.

Detrosier had been brought up in the Swedenborgian Chapel of the New Jerusalem but as a young man joined the strict vegetarian and teetotal Bible Christian movement of Joseph Brotherton. Recognizing his didactic talents, Brotherton sought Detrosier a position and installed him as minister in the recently raised Brinksway Chapel, near Stockport (ironically nicknamed the Beefsteak Chapel for its adherents' vegetarianism). The ground had been prepared by his earlier lecturing and Detrosier's following became enormous. Encouraged by this, he issued his first publication, *A Form of Public Worship on the Principles of Pure Deism* (1827). In this work he proclaimed the utility of morality and the need for a society of universal benevolence.

Detrosier owed his conversion to deism to the strong local presence of Richard Carlile's freethinking movement and it was in the course of debate with militant zetetics some time between 1820 and 1822 that he embraced Paineite radical politics. Although he quickly moved to the centre of working-class radical and republican politics, Detrosier did not become an atheist. Nevertheless, his enlightenment deism was strong enough to lead Brotherton to eject him from his ministry at the Brinksway Chapel in September 1827.

Detrosier returned to working-class education and accepted the presidency of the self-governing and self-financed New Mechanics' Institution, in Poole Street, Manchester, in March 1829. Although he was not an Owenite, Detrosier's help was sought by the fledgeling Owenite trade union movement under John Doherty and its *Co-Operative Journal* records many of his lectures on science and morality in 1829–30.

Detrosier's work at Poole Street also attracted the interest of Francis Place and members of the Place–Bentham circle. He was encouraged to take up lecturing as a full-time career, with a stipend collected for him by Place; and Shuttleworth arranged to have his lecture *On the Necessity of an Extension of Moral and Political Instruction among the Working Classes* published in 1831, attracting attention from Lady Byron and Jeremy Bentham. Bentham sent letters and books, encouraging Detrosier in his new belief that moral progress must precede political progress and schooling him in the dangers of untutored democracy. Place chose Detrosier, a Lockean and now a convert to political economy, to serve as secretary of the National Political Union in October 1831, thus confirming his entry into middle-class radical politics. This new milieu secured Detrosier the friendship of John Stuart Mill and introductions to Carlyle, the Saint-Simonian Gustave d'Eichtal, George Birkbeck, and J. A. Roebuck. It also resulted in Detrosier being asked to appear before the factory commission in 1833. He assisted in the preparation of Southwood Smith's report.

Although not a Saint-Simonian, Detrosier accompanied Gregorio Fontana and Gioacchino Prati on their English mission of 1834, as interpreter. This ensured his removal from his lectureship at the London Mechanics' Institution, where he had taught meteorology and pneumatics. A new benefactor, Robert Mordan, found him a position at the New Mechanical Hall of Science in Finsbury, and Detrosier supplemented this by paid writing. He caught a cold returning from his inaugural lecture at the New Stratford Institute, rapidly weakened, and died at his home, in Seymour Street, near Euston Road, London, on 23 November 1834, leaving his body to science.

Detrosier was a child of the Enlightenment, valuing reason above demagoguery. Although he was drawn into ultra-radicalism, popular education and science, not politics, was his sphere, and deism, not atheism, his creed.

MATTHEW LEE

Sources G. A. Williams, *Rowland Detrosier* (1965) · W. E. Styler, 'Rowland Detrosier', *Adult Education*, 21 (1949), 133–8 · J. Shuttleworth, in R. Detrosier, *On the necessity of an extension of moral and political instruction among the working classes* (1834) [a memoir of Detrosier appended to] · N. J. Gossman, 'Detrosier, Rowland', *BDMBR*, vol. 2 · 'Report … inquiring into the employment of children in factories', *Parl. papers* (1833), 20.12–21, no. 450 [R. Detrosier's evidence; royal commission] · G. J. Holyoake, *Sixty years of an agitator's life*, 3rd edn, 2 vols. (1893), 187–8; repr. (1906) · *The earlier letters of John Stuart Mill, 1812–1848*, ed. F. E. Mineka (1963), vol. 12 of *The Collected Works of John Stuart Mill*, ed. J. M. Robson (1963–91), 165, 171, 183, appx · *Letters of Thomas Carlyle*, ed. C. E. Norton, 2 (1888), 5 · T. Kelly, *George Birkbeck* (1987), 138–40

Wealth at death J. S. Mill supported Detrosier's wife and family for a number of years: Williams, *Rowland Detrosier*

Deuchar, James (1849–1927), brewer, was born on 30 August 1849 in Guthrie, Forfar, Scotland, the son of David Deuchar, farmer, and his wife, Jane Wilson. Nothing is known of his early life until, as a young man, he moved to Tyneside with his three older brothers, Alexander, George, and Robert. Deuchar began as a publican at the Argyle Hotel, High Street, Gateshead, and in 1868, with his brother George, joined a partnership with John and James Meikle as wine, spirit, ale, and porter merchants at the Half Moon inn in Newcastle. In 1870 the firm diversified when Deuchar and Meikle purchased the Arthurs Hill brewery, Westgate Road, Newcastle. From a modest start the venture grew until it had taken over a number of other public houses on Tyneside.

In 1872 Deuchar became the licensee of the Ridley Arms, in Pilgrim Street, Newcastle, and in 1874 he became its owner. He married Lizzie Henderson (*d.* 1926), on 19 October 1875, in Birmingham; they had four daughters and three sons, one of whom, James Wilson Deuchar, succeeded his father as chairman of the firm. During 1875, extensions and alterations at the rear of the brewery were carried out, with further improvements being made in 1882. Deuchar rapidly built up a prosperous trade, and, benefiting from the 'brewery boom' of that decade, expanded his business to such an extent that in 1888 he was able to purchase the Monkwearmouth brewery and maltings of J. J. and W. H. Allison in Sunderland, at the same time acquiring more public houses. In 1893 the plant at the Ridley Arms was dismantled and brewing operations were concentrated in Sunderland.

The firm adopted limited liability in July 1894 when the company's assets were valued at £227,000. The capital was restructured two years later. The authorized share capital was £350,000, but only £100,000 in debentures were sold to the public, all of the ordinary shares being retained by the Deuchar family. The assets of the company at that time were given in the prospectus as £616,000, including forty-five freehold hotels and public houses (among these, several hotels in Newcastle, Sunderland, and Tynemouth) and thirty-one leasehold pubs. Profits in the three years to 1898 had averaged over £30,000. Deuchar became chairman and managing director; his brother Robert was another of the directors. Robert had followed his younger brother into the industry by purchasing the Sandyford Stone brewery, in Newcastle. His own company of Robert

Deuchar Ltd, registered in 1897, also built up a substantial trade on Tyneside and Wearside.

While strong ale was always the mainstay of the Tyneside beer market, there was growing demand for pale ales of the kind brewed in Edinburgh and Burton upon Trent, and in 1900 this led Deuchar to acquire the Lochside brewery of William Ross & Co., Montrose. Despite this company's distance from Newcastle, it continued to do considerable trade in Scottish pale ale in that city, and maintained a large warehouse on Quayside by the Tyne, to which beer from north of the border was shipped in the firm's own steamships, *Lochside* and *Lochside II*. Later, in 1922, the Union mills in Montrose were purchased for use as maltings. Partly to secure his own barley supplies, Deuchar began to farm extensively and to acquire land at Middleton and Ilderton in Northumberland (a total of 7000 acres), and at Stichill, near Kelso, Roxburghshire (an estate of 6000 acres). He was more enterprising than others in his Scottish ventures, which enabled him to import Scottish ales into the Tyne area, and to make inroads into the Scottish market itself.

From modest beginnings in the licensed trade Deuchar had, by the time of his death, built up an extensive portfolio of 150 public houses and hotels, including some of the best in Newcastle, supplied by his own breweries. Even after the end of the boom in 1902, when many breweries were struggling, the business continued to prosper, and was paying dividends of 12 per cent and upwards during most of the period before 1914. Such returns were far exceeded in the decade after 1918, when the firm declared dividends ranging from 20 to 40 per cent.

Deuchar died at Stichill House, near Kelso, on 12 December 1927. He left an estate of over £1,200,000, a substantial sum for the time, and some measure of his acumen in the volatile business of brewing. The firm he founded was eventually taken over by Newcastle Breweries Ltd in 1956. IAN DONNACHIE

Sources D. J. Rowe, 'Deuchar, James', *DBB* · B. Bennison, 'Concentration in the brewing industry of Northumberland and Durham, 1890–1914', *Northern History*, 30 (1994), 161–78 · I. Donnachie, *A history of the brewing industry in Scotland* (1979) · B. Bennison, *Brewers and bottlers of Newcastle upon Tyne: from 1850 to the present day* (1995) · *Newcastle Daily Chronicle* (1894) · *Newcastle Daily Chronicle* (1898) · *Stock Exchange Official Intelligence* · *Newcastle Daily Journal* (1927) · private information (2004) · d. cert.

Archives U. Glas., Archives and Business Records Centre, Scottish Brewing Archive | Durham RO, records of James Deuchar Breweries

Wealth at death £1,207,726: probate, 3 May 1928, *CGPLA Eng. & Wales*

Deuchar, John James Walker (1851–1911), actuary and insurance company manager, was born on 24 September 1851 in Edinburgh, the youngest of five sons of John Deuchar (1786–1863), lecturer in chemistry at Edinburgh University, and his wife, Jane, daughter of James Walker, a publisher in Edinburgh. The family were Presbyterians who owned Morningside House, a modest mansion within its own park, and were well known in Edinburgh for their artistic and scientific talents. J. J. W. Deuchar studied at the Edinburgh Institute of Glasgow University

until 1868, when he joined Standard Life Insurance Company as an actuarial trainee. After qualifying as a fellow of the Faculty of Actuaries, the professional body for Scotland, in 1876 he became assistant actuary for City of Glasgow Life. Public responsibilities followed. He took a leading part in founding the Insurance and Actuarial Society of Glasgow in 1881, and was an examiner for the city's Institute of Actuaries and Accountants. Unlike many actuaries, he became interested in business organization and also attended early morning lectures in law at Glasgow University. Wider professional recognition came with his election as fellow of the Institute of Actuaries, London, in 1883, followed by his appointment as actuary and secretary to Norwich Union Life Insurance Society in 1887. Norwich Union had previously given these responsibilities to two officials; Deuchar was their first joint appointment and he remained chief executive until 1910 when ill health forced him to retire.

When Deuchar joined Norwich Union Life it was under threat of take-over because the sixty-year-old society was languishing in a market dominated by new sales methods. Its directors refused to accept the need for change until Deuchar spelt out the options logically for the first time. He was fortunate to have an ally in George Forrester, a director keen for change, who was the society's president from 1888 to 1898; his was clearly the influence behind Deuchar, but it remained for Deuchar to transform practices. Adopting Scottish insurance company methods, he persuaded the directors to work in subcommittees so as to focus attention on crucial issues at their main board. He then produced meticulously planned proposals for expansion. Sensitive to the directors' conservatism, he initially avoided rapid overseas growth and focused on the home market, switching from old-fashioned 'whole-life' policies to an imaginative variety of endowment schemes. These reached the key growth sector and he managed the subsequent expansion with immense skill. Tighter controls kept costs low, and he eschewed expensive press advertising, preferring to gain new business by offering better bonuses. The results proved his point. When he arrived annual new business was tottering around £200,000 insured, which barely covered what was lost through claims; by 1890 it was £1 million and it continued rising, to reach £5 million when he retired. Initial scepticism in the insurance press turned to unqualified praise. From a ranking below at least twenty other British life-insurance firms in 1887, Deuchar took Norwich Union's new business to second place behind only the massive Prudential.

Deuchar's personal and social life remained more out of public view than was usual for such a prominent insurance official. He married and had two sons and two daughters; his wife died before him. From 1907 he reluctantly served as a Conservative councillor in Norwich, taking a special interest in local education. Other activities included golf, freemasonry, and the Norwich Scots Society, and he remained a Presbyterian. However, he was preoccupied with his heavy professional responsibilities, which probably caused the breakdown of his health (he suffered at different times from blood poisoning and pneumonia) and forced him to resign. A grateful board elected him a director, and he visited Egypt, hoping to regain his strength, but he died in Norwich on 6 June 1911. Despite his immense reputation as a financier, his annual salary never rose much above £3000, and his total estate, shared with characteristic fairness and attention to detail in his will, was a modest £14,287.   ROGER RYAN

Sources *Eastern Daily Press* (7 June 1911) · *Eastern Daily Press* (10 June 1911) · *Norwich Mercury* (10 June 1911) · *Norwich News* (10 June 1911) · W. Mair, *Historic Morningside* (1947) · C. J. Smith, *Historic South Edinburgh*, 4 vols. (1978–88) · R. Blake, *Esto perpetua: the Norwich Union Life Insurance Society* (1958) · R. Ryan, 'A history of the Norwich Union Fire and Life Insurance Societies from 1797–1914', PhD diss., University of East Anglia, 1984 · R. Ryan, 'Deuchar, John James Walker', *DBB* · private information (2004) · probate, John Deuchar (1786–1863), NA Scot., SC 70/1/118, SCO 70/4/88 · *CGPLA Eng. & Wales* (1911)
Archives Norwich Union Museum, Norwich, Norwich Union MSS
Likenesses J. C. Michie, portrait, 1908, Norwich Union Museum, Norwich
Wealth at death £14,287 2s. 6d.: probate, 12 Aug 1911, *CGPLA Eng. & Wales*

Deusdedit [St Deusdedit, Frithona] (*d.* 664), archbishop of Canterbury, succeeded Honorius in March 655, after a vacancy of almost eighteen months. A West Saxon, consecrated by Ithamar, bishop of Rochester, he was the first English holder of the see. His Latin name, like that of his immediate predecessor, was that of a recent pope. It was clearly an adopted one, and in this he followed the practice of other early native English bishops. According to Goscelin of Canterbury in the late eleventh century, followed by Thomas of Elmham in the early fifteenth, Deusdedit's English name was Frithona.

Deusdedit consecrated Ithamar's successor, the South Saxon Damian, bishop of Rochester. He died on the same day, 14 July 664, as King Eorcenberht of Kent, probably as a result of an epidemic of plague. Little else is known about him. His episcopate seems to have coincided with a low point in Canterbury's influence, and it is not even certain that he was represented at the important Synod of Whitby, held to settle a uniform method for the calculation of Easter. Apart from Damian, Deusdedit seems to have consecrated few if any bishops; candidates for important sees such as Wine at Winchester and Wilfrid at York sought consecration abroad. At his death there remained only one English bishop who had been canonically ordained. Bede's statement that Theodore, who acceded to Canterbury in 669, was the first archbishop whom the whole English church consented to obey, clearly implies that Deusdedit's authority was limited. Such influence as he had was probably largely confined to Canterbury, where his successor Wigheard was drawn from his clergy, and to Canterbury's dependent see of Rochester.

Deusdedit was buried with his predecessors in the *porticus* of St Gregory in the abbey church of St Peter and St Paul, Canterbury (later St Augustine's). There are limited signs of a cult. He was commemorated on 15 July in the calendar of the Bosworth psalter (almost certainly produced at St Augustine's between 988 and 1022). His remains, and those of his five predecessors, were translated to new tombs at the east end of the new abbey church of St Augustine in 1091. Goscelin composed a life of Deusdedit based on Bede as part of the literature associated with the 1091 translations, and mass propers for the feast day were probably also compiled at this time.   ALAN THACKER

Sources Bede, *Hist. eccl.*, 3.20, 28–9; 4.1–2 · Thomas of Elmham, *Historia monasterii S. Augustini Cantuariensis*, ed. C. Hardwick, Rolls Series, 8 (1858), 7.18 (pp. 192–3) · *Venerabilis Baedae opera historica*, ed. C. Plummer, 2 (1896), 174, 195 · Goscelin, 'Translatio S. Augustini Anglorum apostoli et sociorum eius', *Acta sanctorum: Maius*, 6 (Antwerp, 1688), 411–43 · R. Sharpe, 'The setting to St Augustine's translation, 1091', *Canterbury and the Norman conquest*, ed. R. Eales and R. Sharpe (1995), 1–13 · N. Orchard, 'The Bosworth psalter and the St Augustine's missal', *Canterbury and the Norman conquest*, ed. R. Eales and R. Sharpe (1995), 87–94 · R. Sharpe, 'The naming of Bishop Ithamar', *EngHR*, 117 (2002), 889–94 · BL, Cotton MS Vespasian B.xx, fol. 222r
Archives BL, Cotton MS Vespasian B.xx, fol. 222r

Deutsch, André (1917–2000), publisher, was born on 15 November 1917 in Budapest, Hungary, the only child of Bruno Deutsch, dental surgeon, and his wife, Maria, *née* Havas. His father was Jewish and his mother partly so. Deutsch was educated at various schools in Budapest, Vienna, and Zürich; the atmosphere at home was Anglophile and he learned to speak English at an early age. In 1939 when he was twenty-two he went to London aiming to become a student at the London School of Economics. But with the outbreak of war, funding from his parents, who remained in Hungary, ceased and he was forced to take a job at the Dorchester Hotel.

As a Hungarian citizen Deutsch was rounded up under the Defence of the Realm Act and interned on the Isle of Man. He was soon released, however, and returned to the wartime London of the blitz. He became a fire-watcher and joined the Home Guard. An introduction from a fellow internee to John Roberts, the volatile Welsh managing director of the publishers Nicholson and Watson, resulted in Deutsch's joining its staff as sales representative and soon after becoming sales manager. He acquired a thorough grounding in all aspects of the book trade and became convinced that publishing was his vocation.

Deutsch belonged to a circle of gifted refugees from Europe. He was a friend of George Weidenfeld who, exiled from his native Vienna, was then working for the BBC with plans to publish *Contact*, a high-level miscellany that would serve as a forum for the cultural and political life of post-war Britain. Thanks to Deutsch this compilation, which ran for several numbers, appeared under the imprint of Nicholson and Watson. As the war in Europe drew to an end Deutsch decided it was the time to found his own publishing company. With an initial capital of only £3000, the firm Allan Wingate, a name he conjured out of the air, was born. It was saved many times from bankruptcy by the irrepressible buoyancy of its founder and his knack of finding people prepared to inject fresh capital into the company in exchange for directorships.

Deutsch had a nose for the kind of book that, in journalistic parlance, is called a 'scoop'. It led him to go to Turkey

André Deutsch (1917–2000), by Leonard Rosoman, 1987

after the Second World War in pursuit of the spy Elyesa Bazna (Cicero), valet at the British embassy, who had sold allied secrets to the Germans. This led to two books Deutsch published at an interval of ten years: *Operation Cicero* by Bazna's German contact L. C. Moyzich, and a later one by Bazna himself, *I was Cicero*. While on the trail of Cicero, Deutsch met Franz von Papen, Germany's wartime ambassador in Turkey. Deutsch quickly realized that here was an even bigger potential catch for his list. He persuaded von Papen to write a volume of memoirs to be published by Wingate. Unfortunately by 1951 when these were written the company was in total disarray. Deutsch lost control to his fellow directors and had to resign.

Deutsch soon set about forming a new publishing company, André Deutsch Ltd. He persuaded Diana Athill (*b*. 1918), who had been with him at his former firm since its outset in 1945, to join it. Athill, an Oxford English literature graduate, became Deutsch's business partner for the rest of their publishing careers. Her cool sound judgement and skill as an editor were the perfect complement to Deutsch's initiative and flair. At the start for a short time they became lovers, or, as Athill explains in her entertaining memoir *Stet: an Editor's Life* (2000), 'we ate an omelette and went to bed together, without—as I remember it—much excitement on either side'. Excitement often came to them but in a different form, as colleagues in the two publishing houses that Deutsch founded. Deutsch exploited Athill, but she put up with it because she loved her work. 'So while it is true that André took advantage of my nature', she wrote, 'in getting me cheap and having to bother so little about my feelings, it cannot be said that *in relation to the job* he did any violence to those feelings' (ibid.).

Deutsch regarded the rights to the von Papen book as his and planned to publish it. His former director-colleagues took a different view of the matter and made

an approach to the author to keep the book on the Wingate list. A puzzled von Papen telephoned Deutsch to find out what was going on and after talking to him at some length affirmed his loyalty to Deutsch and his right to be the publisher of the book. Deutsch then sold the serialization rights to *The People*, the Sunday newspaper, for £30,000. The book was successfully published by Deutsch's new company in 1952 and was the means of its early survival.

In seeking authors Deutsch made an annual trip to the USA where he signed up Philip Roth and John Updike before either was known in Britain. Back home on his expanding fiction list he published Roy Fuller, the war-time poet turned novelist; Brian Moore, the Belfast writer whose first novel, *Judith Hearne*, appeared in 1955; and Wolf Mankowitz, whose novella about the antique business *Make me an Offer* struck a refreshingly new note of Anglo-Jewish humour. Even more successful in the comic field was a short book, *How to be an Alien*, by Deutsch's fellow Hungarian George Mikes, destined to remain in print for many years. Illustrations for it by the artist Nicolas Bentley resulted in Bentley's becoming a working director of the company.

A meeting in London between Athill and V. S. Naipaul led to the publication of *The Mystic Masseur* (1957) and many of Deutsch's subsequent books. His appreciation of Athill as an editor was shared by many of the firm's authors. The Trinidad historian and politician Eric Williams was another Caribbean writer published by Deutsch. The discovery of Jean Rhys's prequel to Charlotte Brontë's *Jane Eyre*, *Wide Sargasso Sea* (1966), set in Dominica (where the author was born) and Jamaica heralded a revival of interest in a hitherto unjustly neglected writer. In 1962 Deutsch founded the African Universities Press in Lagos, Nigeria, and in 1964 the East Africa Publishing House, Nairobi, Kenya. During the 1970s his friendship with Harold Evans, the editor of the *Sunday Times*, resulted in Deutsch publishing the work of the paper's Insight team, investigative journalism in book form. Deutsch's love of travel made him an ideal ambassador for his profession. He would head missions promoting British publishing in central Europe or throughout the Indian subcontinent.

At sixty-five Deutsch had no thought of retirement but he realized, albeit reluctantly, that the company could not continue solely under his leadership for ever. In 1984 he received an approach from T. G. (Tom) Rosenthal (*b*. 1935), the former chairman of William Heinemann Ltd, to take over André Deutsch Ltd. Somewhat unwisely Deutsch tried to conclude a deal with Rosenthal whereby he would still retain a large measure of control of the company. After protracted negotiations conducted for Deutsch by Lord Goodman, Rosenthal acquired 50.1 per cent of the company, with the two men as joint chairmen and joint managing directors. An unhappy time ensued for Deutsch who was reluctant to cede any form of authority to the younger man. He lingered on with an office and various titles until he was seventy-two, when in considerable bitterness he retired completely from active involvement in the company. In 1989 he was awarded the CBE for his contribution to publishing. In 1991 he became a director of Libra, an imprint in his native Budapest.

Deutsch was a popular member of the Garrick Club and had a wide circle of friends who enjoyed his lively talk with its insights into politics and people uttered in what always remained a distinctly Hungarian accent. His boyish good looks never deserted him even in old age. Until he became crippled by the debilitating illness Crohn's disease, he was a keen skier, going to Davos every year.

On one of these holidays when he was still young Deutsch met Gwen, an English woman ten years his senior and the wife of Francis Winham. There was instant rapport; the two of them formed an attachment that proved lifelong. Gwen survived the death of her husband by many years but she and Deutsch never married and always had separate residences. It was, however, recognized among their circle that they were a devoted couple. Deutsch died of heart failure at the Chelsea and Westminster Hospital on 11 April 2000 aged eighty-two and was cremated.   ANTHONY CURTIS

Sources personal knowledge (2004) · private information (2004) [Miss Diana Athill, T. G. (Tom) Rosenthal] · G. Weidenfeld, *Remembering my good friends: an autobiography* (1994) · *WW* · *The Guardian* (12 April 2000) · *The Times* (12 April 2000) · D. Athill, *Stet: an editor's life* (2004)
Archives BLPES, corresp. with Lady Rhys Williams · SOAS, corresp. with Frances Moraes | SOUND BL NSA, documentary recordings
Likenesses F. Godwin, photographs, *c*.1960–1970 · A. Newman, bromide print, 1978, NPG · L. Rosoman, oils, 1987, NPG [*see illus.*]
Wealth at death £2,479,868—gross; £2,450,336—net: probate, 10 Nov 2000, *CGPLA Eng. & Wales*

Deutsch, Emanuel Oscar Menahem (1829–1873), Semitic scholar and orientalist, was born of Jewish parents in Neisse in Prussian Silesia on 28 October 1829, and at the age of six entered the local *Gymnasium*. Two years later he was sent to study with his uncle, Rabbi David Deutsch of Mislowitz (1810–1873), a distinguished Talmudist and author of an annotated translation of the book of Habakkuk (1837). A strong opponent of Reform Judaism, Rabbi Deutsch held his nephew to a rigorous schedule. Winter and summer he had to rise at 5 a.m. and his whole day was devoted to the study of Hebrew and Aramaic literature, except for half an hour for exercise and recreation. At thirteen he returned to Neisse, where, since he had attained the necessary standard for his final examination at the *Gymnasium* before the prescribed period, the rules were relaxed in his favour, and he was allowed to matriculate at the University of Berlin at sixteen. Unable to secure a teaching position at a *Gymnasium* or university without conversion to Christianity, Deutsch supported himself by giving lessons and later by contributing Jewish tales and poems to German magazines.

In 1855 Deutsch was appointed, on the recommendation of the publishers Asher, first-class assistant in the library of the British Museum at a salary of £295 per annum. Seldom has the department of printed books acquired the services of so variously accomplished a man. A Hebrew scholar of the first rank, he was also an excellent classicist. In Berlin he had studied ancient Greece with Boeckh, Latin with Meineke, history with Ranke, while Von Hagen had taught him folklore and German mythology. Despite his impressive credentials, for fifteen years he was largely confined to helot's work as a cataloguer of books. His major professional achievement as a consultant on oriental culture at the British Museum was his important assistance to W. S. W. Vaux (1818–1885) in publishing in 1863 Phoenician inscriptions discovered on Carthaginian votive tablets in 1856–8 by Nathan Davis (1812–1882). Deciphering the Phoenician letters provided a standard of reference for determining inscriptions discovered thereafter.

Deutsch gradually perfected his grasp of colloquial English and achieved a unique prose style, an English version of Heine's ironic blending of satire and lyricism. In 1861 he published an anonymous piece on the purported literary plagiarisms of Robert Bulwer-Lytton (Owen Meredith) in the *Literary Gazette* (165.180–85). Throughout the early years of the decade his independent scholarship included learned articles in Smith's *Dictionary of the Bible* ('Targums', 'Samaritan Pentateuch'), Kitto's *Cyclopedia of Biblical Literature* ('Lamentations', 'Phoenicia', 'Semitic languages'), and a long series of unsigned contributions to Chambers's *Cyclopedia*.

By 1867 Deutsch's growing self-confidence as a popular writer and speaker of English joined with his erudition in religious and cultural history to produce a great success: the famous essay on the Talmud, in the *Quarterly Review* of October 1867 (123.246). This created an extraordinary sensation, as much by the vigour and richness of its language as by the novelty of its subject. It helped to correct the biased view of the Talmud that many English readers of the previous generation had imbibed from Isaac D'Israeli's dismissive approach in *The Genius of Judaism* (1833) and that was being promulgated even more strongly in the conversionist literature of the day. In the same year the British Museum was prepared to allow Deutsch to accompany the Abyssinian expedition, but he was discouraged from going by his friend the philologist Viscount Strangford (Percy Smythe), who thought this adventure would provide little if any archaeological results relevant to Deutsch's interest in the Middle East. His career at the British Museum, unsatisfactory in many ways, was coming into conflict with his reputation as a writer, lecturer, and epigraphist specializing in Semitic culture.

Throughout the rest of the decade Deutsch was besieged with applications for lectures and articles; he delivered courses of lectures at the Royal Institution (in 1868), the Midland Institute, and elsewhere, and his excessive labours, joined to habitual neglect of ordinary precautions of health, undermined a naturally robust constitution. Among those with whom he dined was the prime minister, Gladstone, who in February 1869 wrote that he 'had much interesting conversation with Mr Deutsch on Phoenicia' (Gladstone, *Diaries*, 7.29). Invited by Nubar Pasha to be present at the opening of the Suez Canal in the spring of 1869, he was unable to receive official leave from his cataloguing duties. He did, however, manage to arrange a two-month journey to Egypt, Lebanon, and Palestine in March and April that year, and explored antiquities near Sidon. At the request of George Grove (1820–1900), founder of the Palestine Exploration Fund, he called on Charles Warren (1840–1927), who was in charge of excavations in Jerusalem, and verified Phoenician stone-cutters' markings at the base of the outer wall of the Temple Mount. The distinguished archaeologist Charles Newton (1816–1894) praised the report Deutsch filed with the trustees at the British Museum, but it was mysteriously misplaced. The 'Talmud Man', as he was now called by the press and public, chafed under what he felt was contempt by his superiors for his new status as a public figure and for his hopes of instituting a department of Semitic studies.

After Deutsch's return, renewed activity in lecturing and writing aggravated the stomach cancer which was slowly killing him. It was at this time that he wrote his article on Islam in the *Quarterly* for October 1869 (27.254), which, despite the epigrammatic brilliance of the style and the imaginative glow which were inseparable from his writings, struck many of his readers as less effective than his Talmud essay. Like too many 'sequels' it failed to sustain the reputation which the earlier article had created. The main reason for the falling off from the Talmud essay was thought to be Deutsch's lack of sufficient expertise in Arabic matters, but the real 'fault' of the essay was its relentless exposure of Islam's indebtedness to Judaism, a position that older readers who remembered Carlyle's 'The hero as prophet. Mahomet: Islam' (1840) had difficulty in accepting. From September to November 1869 Deutsch contributed a series of striking articles on the Ecumenical Council to *The Times*. He wrote with the bitter memories of a Jew, and his retrospect of papal history at once startled and fascinated by its wealth of imagery and its unsparing irony. He championed the unsuccessful efforts of liberal delegates to block the campaign to establish papal infallibility.

In 1870 Deutsch's health visibly broke down. The dull routine of cataloguing in poorly ventilated rooms, and the close scrutiny of officious and hostile superiors augmented by private study at night, destroyed what little health remained. In this period many of the library staff were bitter and frustrated at their treatment, and after Deutsch's death a polemical pamphlet by Stephan Poles, *The Actual Condition of the British Museum* (1875), accused museum officials of causing the death of Deutsch, 'slowly murdered by the studied malice, and the petty jealousy of officials' (Miller, 287). Hugh Reginald Haweis (1838–1901), perpetual curate of St James, Marylebone, London, and popular preacher and lecturer, and his wife, Mary, were Deutsch's neighbours; she took him into their home and nursed him until he was strong enough to undertake a last despairing journey to Egypt.

Deutsch died of stomach cancer at the Prussian Deaconesses' Hospital, Alexandria, on 12 May 1873, and was buried on 13 May in the Jewish cemetery, Alexandria. He had died still young, with the promise of his life unfulfilled.

His true place in Hebrew scholarship was to have been decisively established by a great work, never completed, on the Talmud, of which the *Quarterly* article was but the foretaste. Nevertheless, his numerous articles and reviews on Semitic subjects reveal extensive reading and a wide grasp of oriental history, philosophy, and world literature. In whatever he wrote, his vividly poetic nature asserted itself. At the time of his death he was credited with having enlightened gentile attitudes toward Jewish culture. His executor, Emily Anne, Viscountess Strangford, published a representative collection of his work, *Literary Remains of Emanuel Deutsch, with a Brief Memoir* (1874).

Although Deutsch did not live to write a work which he hoped would allow the Talmud to enter the general discussion of antiquity in Western intellectual circles, his devotion to Jewish heritage greatly impressed George Eliot. She befriended him in the mid-1860s and encouraged his scholarship. In 1869 she went to Oxford primarily to hear his lecture on the Moabite stone. Deutsch gave her lessons in Hebrew and recommended important Jewish books. Gradually Eliot caught the fire of Deutsch's pre-Zionist vision and, shortly after he died, dedicated her last major novel, *Daniel Deronda* (1876), to the Jewish quest for a homeland. Her novel is his principal monument.

PETER BRIER

Sources E. A. Strangford, ed., *Literary remains of Emanuel Deutsch, with a brief memoir* (1874) · B. L. Abrahams, 'Emanuel Deutsch of "the Talmud" fame', *Transactions of the Jewish Historical Society of England*, 23 (1969–70), 53–63 · *Jewish Chronicle* (1867–73) · *Jewish Chronicle* (30 May 1873) · J. Rodenberg, *Erinnerungen aus der Jugendzeit*, 2 vols. (Berlin, 1899) · H. R. Haweis, 'Emanuel Deutsch: a memorial', *Contemporary Review*, 23 (1873–4), 779–98 · H. M. Rabinowicz, *Treasures of Judaica* (1971) · B. Howe, *Arbiter of elegance* (1967) · J. Irwin, ed., *George Eliot's Daniel Deronda notebooks* (1996) · W. Baker, *George Eliot and Judaism* (1975) · *The George Eliot letters*, ed. G. S. Haight, 9 vols. (1954–78) · P. M. Young, *George Grove, 1820–1900: a biography* (1980) · E. Alexander, 'George Eliot's rabbi', *Commentary Magazine*, 92 (July 1991), 28–31 · I. Singer and others, eds., *The Jewish encyclopedia*, 12 vols. (1901–6) · E. Miller, *That noble cabinet: a history of the British Museum* (1974) · Gladstone, *Diaries* · Boase, *Mod. Eng. biog.* · CGPLA *Eng. & Wales* (1873)

Archives BL, letters to Gladstone · BL, letters to Layard

Likenesses R. Lehmann, pencil drawing, 1868, BM · M. Haweis, sculptured head

Wealth at death under £450: resworn probate, Feb 1874, CGPLA *Eng. & Wales* (1873)

Deutsch, Oscar (1893–1941), cinema owner and film exhibitor, was born on 12 August 1893 at Balsall Heath, Birmingham, the son of Leopold Deutsch (d. 1904), a scrap metal merchant, and his wife, Leah Cohen. His parents were both Jewish, and immigrants: his mother from Poland, and his father from Betzho, Transchener Komitat, in Hungary. Leopold Deutsch died in an accident in 1904, but the business was continued by his brother, Adolf Brenner, under the name of Deutsch and Brenner. Deutsch was educated at the King Edward VI Grammar School, Birmingham, where he developed a fascination for the cinema shared by two other pupils, Michael Balcon and Victor Saville. At the age of seventeen he joined Deutsch and Brenner, but found it dull and in 1920 he formed a local film distribution company with Balcon and Saville which acted as the midlands representative for C. M. Woolf's film company. Deutsch then provided some of the financial backing when his two friends went into film production in 1923, but stayed in Birmingham himself, continuing to work for the family firm. He now had a family of his own: in 1918 he married Lily Tanchan; they had three sons.

In 1925 Deutsch moved into cinema ownership. In partnership with Reginald Noakes he bought three cinemas, including the Globe and Crown in Coventry. He built and opened his first cinema, the Picture House at Brierley, Staffordshire, in association with several other businessmen. This was followed in 1930 by a cinema at Perry Barr, Birmingham, which was named Odeon and introduced the distinctive, straight-edged lettering of the name that was to become a well-known trademark. By 1931 Deutsch was chairman of the midlands branch of the Cinematograph Exhibitors' Association of Great Britain and Ireland.

In 1932 in partnership with W. G. Elcock and Stanley Bates Deutsch drew up plans to open a circuit of cinemas using the Odeon name. These were concentrated initially in south-east England and the London suburbs and set up as separate companies with a local partner who usually supplied the site or was the builder of the cinema. The first five Odeons opened in 1933, followed by another seventeen in 1934. By 1936 Deutsch's circuit comprised 142 cinemas and was the fourth largest in the country.

The Odeon South Harrow was the first of several designed for the circuit by A. P. Starkey with simple, modern façades covered in yellow faience tiles, relieved by colour bands, which made them stand out among other buildings in the high street. The Odeon Worthing was the first to have a tower feature, while the Odeon Haverstock Hill, in north London, was the first flagship cinema. The early 1930s saw widespread new cinema construction as many circuits sought to expand, but the speed at which Deutsch enlarged the Odeon chain was phenomenal: 136 new cinemas were opened before the Second World War forced the suspension of further development. By building so many new, clearly recognizable Odeons, Deutsch cleverly established a brand image.

Deutsch relied on the architectural practice of Harry Weedon in Birmingham and the London practices of George Coles and Andrew Mather to design most of his new Odeons, which usually followed a house style of distinctive, streamlined exteriors using yellow or cream faience tiles and slab towers, although many were schemes already in progress that could not be revised to have the same look. When work began in 1937 on the Odeon Leicester Square, a coal-black exterior was deliberately chosen to distinguish it as the new flagship cinema from the rest of the circuit.

Deutsch also took over many existing cinemas, renaming them Odeons. By 1939 his circuit had built or planned cinemas in virtually every large city in England and had begun operating in Scotland. When Deutsch arranged to take over the small but well-placed Paramount chain just before the Second World War, he made Odeon without doubt equal to the two longer-established national circuits, Gaumont and ABC.

Deutsch was most concerned that his Odeons should be eye-catching externally, especially when outlined in neon at night. Internally, the cinemas were more functional, without the design frills of many rivals. Deutsch did not believe in organs and supporting stage shows but simply in providing films in comfortable surroundings. His wife, Lily, was a consultant on the colour schemes. There were, however, many standard features inside the cinemas, including carpets, clocks, settees, and ash-stands, all with a distinctive art deco design.

Deutsch gave the American distributor United Artists a substantial holding in Odeon to ensure a supply of top-quality British films, especially the productions of Alexander Korda. However, he made a specific point of not involving the company in film production, where huge losses had been incurred by other groups.

The growth of Odeon was all the more remarkable as Deutsch had serious health problems which were, however, a well-kept secret. He had a major operation for cancer in the late 1920s and followed a strict diet. In 1935 the head office of the Odeon circuit was moved to London and Deutsch lived close by at the Dorchester Hotel. He nevertheless returned home to Birmingham on Friday afternoons to be with his family, and to attend Singer's Hill Synagogue (of which he was warden and president) on the sabbath. A strong supporter of rearmament in the late 1930s, he was able, through the help of Sir Michael Bruce, to help significant numbers of German Jews to escape the Nazi threat.

Deutsch incurred considerable stress in 1938 when he set about consolidating the various local Odeon companies into one: only the assistance of his accountant, John Davis, enabled proper accounts to be produced, quashing rumours that Odeon was in financial difficulty.

A courteous, considerate employer, a man of great charm and charisma who readily delegated authority, Deutsch was much admired by his colleagues and staff. His early death from cancer in the London Clinic on 5 December 1941 may have been precipitated by injuries after a bomb explosion hurled him out of bed. His unachieved ambitions, left to his successor as chairman of Odeon Theatres, J. Arthur Rank, had been to take over the rival Gaumont chain and to expand abroad. He was buried in Birmingham and the funeral procession detoured to pass his first Odeon at Perry Barr. Deutsch was survived by his wife.

ALLEN EYLES

Sources A. Eyles, 'Oscar and the Odeons', *Focus on Film*, 22 (1975), 38–57 · *Variety* (10 Dec 1941) · R. Murphy, 'Deutsch, Oscar', *DBB* · *CGPLA Eng. & Wales* (1942) · d. cert.
Likenesses photograph, BFI
Wealth at death £285,601 7s. 3d.: probate, 15 Sept 1942, *CGPLA Eng. & Wales*

Deutscher, Isaac (1907–1967), biographer and historian, was born in Chrzanow, near Cracow, Galicia, in Austro-Hungarian Poland on 3 April 1907, the eldest among the three children of Jacob Kopel Deutscher, who owned his own printing business, and his second wife, Gustawa, *née* Jolles. The family were prosperous, cultured Jews whose ancestors had emigrated to Galicia from Nuremberg, Germany, in the sixteenth century. An uncle represented the Jewish party, Agudsh, in the Polish upper house and his father, a Germanophile who admired Spinoza, Heine, Goethe, and Lasalle, was a strong influence on the young Deutscher. He was brought up in the Hasidic sect, although he attended both the *kheder*, the Jewish religious academy, and Polish Catholic schools. His horizons were broadened and his intellectual development stimulated by the conflict of cultures, for Cracow stood at the intersection of Austrian, German, and Russian Poland. In 1918 he witnessed the fall of the three emperors and the emergence of the new nation state which he always associated with the pogroms which his family narrowly escaped. The progress of the Russian Revolution was a matter of intense local interest; he remembered the Hungarian soviet and the Russian march on Warsaw in 1920.

Polish communist Deutscher was a brilliant, largely self-educated scholar. He developed a passion for Polish literature and at seventeen was reading his poems to the Cracow literati at the Jagiellonian University, where he took extramural courses. He rejected his father's ambition to make him a rabbi. Instead he became an atheist and, following in the footsteps of Marx, Trotsky, and his countrywoman Rosa Luxemburg, a lifelong 'non-Jewish Jew' (*Non-Jewish Jew*, ed. Deutscher). In 1925 he moved to Warsaw, where he became a proof-reader on *Nasz Przeglad* ('Our Review') and a freelance journalist. He published literary criticism, interviews with writers, and theatre reviews, and encountered socialist intellectuals. Reading Marx and Lenin was an epiphany. At nineteen, early in 1927, he joined the outlawed Communist Party of Poland (CPP). He worked for its underground publications centre, which produced legal and illegal material, and was a member of the editorial boards of its 'front' journals *Miesięcznik Literati* ('Literary Monthly') and the Yiddish-language *Literashe Trybune* ('Literary Tribune').

National service in the Polish army 1928–9 and a long visit to the USSR sponsored by the CPP in 1931 strengthened Deutscher's self-confidence and enhanced his ability to think for himself. He did not like what he saw in Russia. He related his experiences to his existing concerns about the politics of the Comintern's sectarian, ultra-left Third Period, the CPP's designation of social democrats as social fascists, and its anathema on a united front between revolutionaries and reformists. Influenced by Trotskyist literature, he joined a broad-based opposition group comprising supporters of Trotsky and Bukharin which was critical of Comintern policy. In spring 1932 he published two articles in the CPP press, 'The danger of a new barbarism' and 'The twelfth hour'. They criticized Stalin's underestimation of Nazism, its totalitarianism, and its drive to war, and called for a coalition of communists and social democrats to oppose both Hitler and Pilsudski. In June 1932 he was expelled from the CPP as 'an agent of the social fascists'.

Deutscher became the leading thinker of the Union of Communist Internationalists of Poland (UCIP), which was affiliated to Trotsky's International Left Opposition. Living for politics and donating half his earnings to the group, he was absorbed in producing its underground journals. He was subjected to sustained harassment from the police and the CPP, suffering serious assault by the Stalinists in the Journalists' Union Club. Two of his pamphlets, *Current Problems of the Workers' Movement* and *The Moscow Trial*, were widely circulated and influential on the Polish left. When Trotsky called on his supporters to 'enter' the social democratic organizations, the UCIP was dissolved and Deutscher joined the Polish Socialist Party. 'Entrism' achieved little; by 1937 he was once more playing a leading part in an openly Trotskyist organization, the Bolshevik Leninist group. Twelve years as a revolutionary activist and six years in the Trotskyist movement came to an end with the formation of the Fourth International in September 1938. Deutscher had long opposed this initiative as premature. He believed that the basis of a new International did not exist in the tiny groups adhering to Trotskyism, while its declaration was unlikely to mobilize significant new support in a period of reaction. At the founding conference at Périgny, near Paris, the Polish delegates argued for this position. But it was defeated and they accepted the majority verdict. When the Polish Bolshevik Leninists ratified their action, Deutscher led a small group out of the organization.

This did not save Deutscher from the intensifying repression of the Trotskyists after Stalin dissolved the CPP and executed its leaders in 1938. He escaped arrest in the police raids of February 1939 but learned that, in the event of war, he would be interned. War was in the air. Other Trotskyist leaders had already left for Paris and *Nasz Przeglad* agreed, in April 1939, that he could go to London as their correspondent. Many of his comrades died in the gulag or the Warsaw ghetto. Both his parents, his brother, Salek, and his sister, Manya, perished at Auschwitz.

Émigré writer: Trotsky and Stalin Deutscher spent some weeks in Paris before embarking for London. He arrived in Britain, where he spent his maturity and fulfilled his promise, in summer 1939. A young British socialist remembered encountering him in London on successive Sundays that summer at Speakers' Corner in Hyde Park. Despite having only a few words of English, he enjoyed the extravagant disputation. The German invasion of Poland in September 1939 left him jobless, penniless, and stateless. Given his lack of English, he possessed few prospects. Searching for bearings, he became involved with a small London-based Trotskyist group, the Revolutionary Workers' League, which also stood outside the Fourth International. As he taught himself a new language, some of his earliest writing in English appeared under the pseudonym Josef Bren in its paper *Workers' Fight*, although he was soon able to place articles in other journals, notably *The Economist*.

In 1940 Deutscher enlisted in General Sikorski's Polish army-in-exile. He was initially regarded as a subversive, not least because of his complaints against antisemitism, and spent most of his stint in uniform as a corporal in a camp near Kirkcaldy in Scotland. He later worked for Sikorski's ministry of information in London, his earlier critical stance on the war having given way to support after Hitler's attack on the USSR in June 1941. He persevered with his English, devouring dictionaries, grammars, newspapers, and Hazlitt. He was rewarded when, in 1942, its editor, Donald Tyerman, offered him a job on *The Economist*. His brief was to cover the war in Russia. But he was soon reporting on the European theatre of operations and beyond. Through the good offices of a colleague, Barbara Ward, he secured an additional appointment with *The Observer*, where as Peregrine he wrote an influential column.

Deutscher's war ended in Europe. As a roving correspondent for *The Observer*, he followed the allied troops into Germany and Austria. He travelled with his fellow contributor to *Tribune* George Orwell, whose Manichaean antagonism to Stalinism he always derided as simplistic and unduly pessimistic. Deutscher had overcome the devastating personal crisis that had confronted him in 1939–40 and established a niche in the Fleet Street firmament. He determined to make London his home rather than undergo the renewed vicissitudes that awaited him in Stalinist Warsaw. During his sojourn with the Polish army he had met Tamara Frimer (1913–1990), a journalist. She was the daughter of Samuel Lebenhaft, and was the divorced wife of Hilary Frimer. Born in Łódź and educated in Brussels, she had been caught up in the conflagration and arrived in London with the Polish forces after the fall of France. They quickly became companions and married at Hampstead register office, London, on 6 June 1947. They lived at Haverstock Hill, Hampstead. She was instrumental in his decision in 1946 to forsake journalism and turn himself into a contemporary historian. In this endeavour she acted as his intellectual partner, joint researcher, critic, and typist.

Deutscher's reputation was established by, and still centrally rests on, his *Stalin* (1949) and his three-volume biography of Trotsky: *The Prophet Armed* (1954), *The Prophet Unarmed* (1959), and *The Prophet Outcast* (1963). He prepared by immersing himself in Gibbon, Macaulay, and modern historiography. Yet he reached a wider public than most historians through the slightly regarded genre of political biography. By the end of the 1940s he had assembled the stock of ideas that permeated all his future work. They were based on a dialogue between his Polish past and the post-war world. They centred on his credo that revolution was natural and inevitable, his continuing critical identification with 1917, and his sustained interrogation of Trotsky's analysis of the Russian Revolution and its resurgent fortunes in a new era of cold war and global *realpolitik*. Neither Auschwitz nor high Stalinism could dent Deutscher's optimism about the future of Russia's great experiment, which Trotsky had believed was, in the absence of international revolution, unlikely to survive the war. In the benign, deterministic vision which informed Deutscher's biographies and essays, history was a progressive process moving inevitably, if gradually and unevenly, towards socialism. Fascism had been a temporary aberration, Stalinism a necessary, barbarous prelude to an assured, emancipatory dénouement.

For Deutscher revolutions—all revolutions thus far—followed fundamental laws. Stalin as much as Napoleon or Cromwell was the instrument of historical necessity, the custodian of the revolution in its conservative phase, decidedly not its gravedigger. Stalin represented not the annulment of Lenin and Trotsky's achievement but its affirmation through revolution from above. For Deutscher the revolution could not have been sustained in any other way. Socialism did not necessarily require the working class as its architect. He followed Trotsky in insisting that, because of its statified property relations (state ownership of means of production), the USSR remained a 'workers' state'. He parted company with him over the necessity for a political revolution to transcend 'autocratic socialism' and restore workers' democracy. The Soviet bureaucracy, he believed, could reform itself: destalinization was as fated as Stalinism. As early as 1942 he had seen the war producing democracy and equality in Russia and, in his calculations, war was soon replaced as the agent of necessity by economic advance. If the working class was a questionable transformative force, he now argued, in a further break with his activist past, that the realm of the socialist intellectual lay neither in political action, as the class struggle resolved itself into the 'Great contest' (the title of his study of Russia and the West, 1960) between capitalism and 'actually existing socialism', nor in the literary anti-communism of Koestler or Orwell. The socialist intellectual should, rather, withdraw to 'the watchtower' and 'study the world and interpret it *sine ira et studio* [that is, dispassionately]' (I. Deutscher, *Heretics and Renegades and other Essays*, 1955, 20).

For Deutscher his protagonists—his anti-hero Stalin, the favoured child of Clio; and his tragic hero, Trotsky, whom he compared in the trilogy with Sisyphus, Hamlet, and Lear—were little more than the puppets of history. Yet in the Trotsky trilogy he not only redeemed reputations and dismantled myths: he evoked both the complex, talented man and the panorama of revolutionary modernity of the first forty years of the twentieth century. The further irony was that, in the case of Trotsky, Deutscher's extraordinary literary gifts—he stood comparison with his countryman Joseph Conrad in his ability to write majestically in a foreign language—his powers of historical imagination, dramatization, and metaphor invested his protagonist with a humanity and human agency which engaged readers emotionally and impelled some, at least, into political activity. Perhaps the final irony came when he was taken to task for exaggerating the role of Stalin as an individual.

Deutscher was branded by *Pravda* 'an inveterate enemy of Marxism'. He was none the less criticized on both the right and the left as a subtle apologist for the USSR. He certainly provided sections of the Stalinist and fellow travelling left with an intellectual rationale for supporting it. But he also influenced a section of the Trotskyist movement which sought to transcend its impotence in a period of working-class quiescence by fastening upon substitute agencies for socialist change. His views were welcomed in the conservative and liberal as well as the radical press. And he was popular among the new left of the 1950s and 1960s, although some of its youthful adherents disagreed with his prognostications. Perhaps the grandeur of his style, and his comforting message that a happy ending was guaranteed, transcended differences in analysis.

Despite his advocacy of retreat to the watchtower, Deutscher never denied himself the prophet's mantle. However, his pronouncements were sometimes ambivalent and questionable. He idealized the virtues of centralized planning and the dynamism of the Soviet economy. *Russia after Stalin* (1953), written in the immediate aftermath of the tyrant's death, promised democratic regeneration. But when an element of change did come, vindicating him against other commentators who presented the USSR as a frozen, completely immobile society, Deutscher, who harboured illusions about Malenkov and then Khrushchov, exaggerated the change as 'a deep and radical break'. And he admonished those who sought to meddle with history by taking matters further, depicting the East German rising of 1953 and the Hungarian revolt of 1956 as counter-revolution and capitalist restoration, an attempt 'to wind the clock back' (see his *Ironies of History: Essays on Contemporary Communism*, 1966; *Russia, China and the West, 1953–1966*, ed. F. Halliday, 1970; and *Marxism, Wars and Revolutions*, ed. T. Deutscher, 1984).

Life and influence in Britain The decade from 1947, when Deutscher broke the back of the biographical project, was a time of isolation and pressure. It was enriched by the birth of his only child, Martin Charles, in August 1950, the success of *Stalin*, rewarding work in the Trotsky archives at Harvard University, despite initial difficulties in securing a visa, and an unlikely but enduring friendship with E. H. Carr, who held distinct but similarly 'progressive' views on the USSR. However, the former Talmudic scholar drew the line in his friendship with the Cambridge-educated scion of the Foreign Office, invoking *amicus Plato sed magis amica veritas* ('Plato is dear to me, but dearer still is truth') when defending a critical review of Carr's *History of Soviet Russia*. He was reunited with his old friends from Warsaw, the Singer family. He befriended and subsequently conducted an extended correspondence with Heinrich Brandler, the former leader of the German Communist Party, while another close intellectual support was Jon Kimche, Middle East expert, *Guardian* correspondent, and former Independent Labour Party Marxist.

Deutscher became a British citizen in May 1949. The family moved to Coulsdon, Surrey, in 1951 and in 1956 further out into suburbia in a move to Wokingham. But the tensions and insecurities, mental and financial, of an independent existence were brought home in 1953 when he suffered problems with his heart. In the late 1950s he expanded what had always remained a significant output of analytical journalism. He spoke at new left meetings in Britain, looking forward to 'the Red Sixties'. He lectured in

North America and finally received permission from Natalia Trotsky and the lawyers to work on the closed section of the Harvard archive.

Deutscher became increasingly well known as an opinion-maker among Britain's left-wing intelligentsia, while the miners' leader Lawrence Daly testified to his impact on thinking trade unionists. He was praised by Bertrand Russell, and in 1961 *Tribune* acclaimed him 'the most eminent, accurate and informative of all commentators on Soviet affairs' (*Tribune*, 20 Oct 1961). But his influence extended beyond the left into the liberal sections of the establishment, a development which attracted irritation and concern on the anti-Soviet right. His articles and reviews appeared in *The Times*, *The Observer*, the *Times Literary Supplement*, *The Economist*, *The Listener*, and the *New Statesman*, and were syndicated worldwide. He broadcast on the Third Programme and the BBC Overseas Service, and even addressed British military analysts.

Among fellow historians Deutscher influenced not only Carr but also the historian of the English revolution Christopher Hill. His ideas acted as challenge and stimulus to a coming cohort of historians of the Russian Revolution such as Leonard Schapiro and Robert Conquest, who profoundly disagreed with them. Intellectually he was at the zenith of his powers. About 5 feet 6 inches in height, balding with greying moustache and dark goatee beard, his warm, penetrating brown eyes undiminished by severe black-rimmed glasses, he resembled the popular idea of the *Mitteleuropa* professor or, perhaps, the older Trotsky. His work was his life. But he relaxed listening to music, occasionally attending concerts and the theatre and playing chess. He smoked a pipe and enjoyed a glass of vodka.

The Trotsky trilogy was completed in July 1962. The final volume, *The Prophet Outcast*, appeared to critical acclaim in the following year. It represented a tremendous achievement for an independent scholar lacking the resources and *cachet* of an academic institution. Re-entering the thick of things, the Deutschers moved back to Hampstead and at fifty-six he sought the recognition and security which a university post offered. There was a possibility of a chair in history at Sussex University in 1963. His hopes were thwarted by the intervention of the philosopher and historian of ideas Isaiah Berlin. They had clashed as long ago as 1954, when Deutscher addressed Carr's seminar at Balliol College, Oxford. Berlin, from an émigré family, took a keen interest in Soviet studies: he was critical of the USSR and had little sympathy with Deutscher's views. As a member of the advisory committee, he successfully made his opposition felt.

Despite Deutscher's high profile in political culture, the incident affirmed that, unlike so many of his contemporaries in the European intellectual diaspora of the 1930s and 1940s, he was never fully accepted in British academic life. There were compensations. His influence on *New Left Review*, particularly on its analysis of the USSR, was enduring: its editor described him as 'the greatest Marxist historian in the world' (Anderson, 'Components', 234; preface, i). Vacating the watchtower, he was caught up in the agitation against the Vietnam War; in 1965 he spoke to

15,000 at the 'teach-in' in Washington and at packed student meetings in Berkeley. With his powerful delivery, authoritative aura, range of reference, and contagious conviction, he was becoming a cult figure for a new generation. In 1966 he lectured at Berkeley and New York, urging students to turn from the ivory tower to the slumbering working class, and addressed the American Socialist Scholars' Conference. His open letter to the Polish prime minister, Wladislaw Gomulka, protesting against the trial and imprisonment of his old Trotskyist comrade Ludwik Hass, and the young dissidents Jacek Kuron and Karol Modzelewski, attracted worldwide publicity. He was a member of the International War Crimes Tribunal, convened by Bertrand Russell and chaired by Jean-Paul Sartre, and prominent in its deliberations in Stockholm in 1967. In that year he received belated academic recognition in Britain when he delivered the G. M. Trevelyan lectures at Cambridge University, published, with a title which encapsulated his lifelong preoccupations, as *The Unfinished Revolution: Russia, 1917–1967* (1967). And there was a sustained output of articles, essays, and collections.

Isaac Deutscher died from a heart attack on 19 August 1967 while on holiday in Rome. He was laid to rest in London at Golders Green crematorium. He was a man of modesty, warmth, humanity, and immense erudition, as well as a writer of power and luminosity. His life can be understood only in the context of his generation, its political longings to realize socialism, and the indelible imprint which 1917 left on his consciousness. He remained implacably dedicated to the socialism he embraced in his youth. His faith in Marxism and his own understanding of it remained unshakeable. His insights enriched our comprehension of the Russian Revolution and its protagonists. History, in whom he invested such hopes, dismissed his prophecies. Adjudicating the 'great contest', she unmasked the inadequacies of authoritarian, bureaucratic planning and affirmed the dynamism of capitalism. She judged Stalin a failure, without vindicating Trotsky or Deutscher. Deutscher never properly grasped the limitations of Soviet economy and society, and he underestimated the central significance of democracy in its analysis. He was an optimistic fatalist who, if he was no prophet, endures as a great political biographer. His *Stalin* has stood up well to the opening of the Moscow archives. His *Trotsky* remains a historical masterpiece and an unsurpassed introduction to classical Marxism.

JOHN MCILROY

Sources D. Horowitz, ed., *Isaac Deutscher: the man and his work* (1971) [incl. D. Singer, 'Armed with a pen'; L. Menashe, 'The dilemma of de-Stalinization'; L. Daly, 'A working class tribute'] · L. Syre, *Isaac Deutscher: Marxist, Publizist, Historiker* (1984) · T. Deutscher, 'Isaac Deutscher, 1907–67', in I. Deutscher, *The non-Jewish Jew*, ed. T. Deutscher (1968) · T. Deutscher, 'The education of a Jewish child', in I. Deutscher, *The non-Jewish Jew*, ed. T. Deutscher (1968) · *The Times* (21 Aug 1967) · *WWW* · m. cert. · J. Jacobson, 'Isaac Deutscher: the anatomy of an apologist', *New Politics* (autumn 1964) · J. Jacobson, 'Isaac Deutscher as a theoretician', *New Politics* (spring 1966); repr. in J. Jacobson, *Soviet communism and the socialist vision* (1972) · L. Labedz, 'Isaac Deutscher: historian and prophet', *Survey* (1962); repr. with L. Labedz, 'Deutscher's Stalin', *Survey*, 30 (March 1988) · P. Beilharz, 'Isaac Deutscher: history and necessity', *History of Political Thought*, 7 (1982) · H. Weber, ed., *Unabhängige Kommunisten: der Briefwechsel zwischen Heinrich Brandler und Isaac Deutscher, 1947 bis 1967* (1981) [excerpted in *New Left Review*, 105 (Sept 1977)] · J. Rosenberg, 'Isaac Deutscher and the lost history of international relations', *New Left Review*, 215 (Jan 1996) · P. Anderson, preface, in I. Deutscher, *Marxism, wars and revolutions*, ed. T. Deutscher (1984) · P. Anderson, 'Components of the national culture', *Student power*, ed. A. Cockburn and R. Blackburn (1969) · L. Hass, 'Trotskyism in Poland up to 1945', *Revolutionary History*, 6 (1995) · S. Bornstein and A. Richardson, *The war and the International: a history of the Trotskyist movement in Britain, 1937–1949* (1986) · J. Getty, *Origins of the great purges* (1985) · J. Haslam, *The vices of integrity: E. H. Carr, 1892–1982* (1999) · M. Ignatieff, *Isaiah Berlin: a life* (1998)

Archives Internationaal Instituut voor Sociale Geschiedenis, Amsterdam, corresp., drafts of articles, books, broadcasts, press clippings | JRL, letters to the *Manchester Guardian* · U. Birm., E. H. Carr MSS

Likenesses photograph, repro. in Horowitz, ed., *Isaac Deutscher*, jacket · photograph, repro. in *The Times* · photographs, priv. coll.

Wealth at death £10,763: probate, 9 Aug 1968, *CGPLA Eng. & Wales*

Devant, David [*real name* David Wighton] (1868–1941), conjuror and illusionist, was born on 22 February 1868 at 4 Boston Terrace, Holloway, London, eldest of the seven children of James Wighton, a Scottish artist, and his wife, Mary Ansell. After attending local schools he worked at several jobs before becoming a professional entertainer. His interest in magic was aroused when he was about twelve and was fuelled by visits to Maskelyne and Cooke's *Mysteries* at the Egyptian Hall, Piccadilly, London. At seventeen he gave his first public performance as David Devant, the surname being adopted from a French painting of David and Goliath entitled *David devant Goliath*. About 1888 he married Annie Marion Melville (1864/5–1928), who as his stage assistant was known as Marion Melville; they had a daughter, Vida (*d.* 1954), but apparently neither marriage nor birth was registered. Soon Devant was appearing at music-halls, where John Nevil Maskelyne saw and engaged him. For his début at the Egyptian Hall in 1893 he devised a new illusion, 'The Artist's Dream', in which the portrait of a young woman came to life. There followed more than two decades of highly productive continuous association with Maskelyne, with whom he went into partnership as Maskelyne and Devant at St George's Hall, London, from 1905 until 1915.

Devant's formative years were influenced by the inventive French magician Buatier de Kolta and by the gentlemanly, humorous presentation of Charles Bertram, the leading society magician of the time. Indeed, a characteristic of Devant's presentation was his 'drawing-room' style and his tremendous success undoubtedly derived from personal charm and a refreshingly new approach to the art. Thus he discarded the magic wand and any apparatus which might appear to have been made especially for conjuring purposes, reasoning that suspicion would thereby be allayed. He created numerous small tricks and more than twenty ingenious illusions, probably the finest being 'The Mascot Moth' (1905), the disappearance in full view of a woman, dressed as a moth with wings, when Devant approached her with a lighted candle. Another was 'Biff' (1913), in which a motor cycle and rider vanished

David Devant (1868–1941), by unknown photographer [detail]

from a wooden crate hoisted in the air. An outstanding feature of his illusions was that none involved the theme of mutilation: the element of horror was banished and his slogan of 'all done by kindness' never dispelled.

When the Lumière brothers' films were first demonstrated in London in 1896, Devant immediately realized their potential. He purchased a theatrograph machine from R. W. Paul, becoming the first independent operator in Britain, with three provincial touring companies besides exhibiting films at the Egyptian Hall. Devant toured with versions of the Maskelyne and Cooke entertainment during the late 1890s and early 1900s, extending his popularity to the provinces. Later, in 1912–13, when managing director of Maskelyne and Devant, he toured the music-halls, and he returned to this activity in 1915 after severing his connection with Maskelyne.

When the Magic Circle was founded in London in 1905 Devant became its first president and donated his personal library to the society, but he retired from office after one year due to pressure of work. As a consequence of magazine articles he wrote exposing magical secrets, contrary to the society's rules, his resignation was tendered in 1910, and requested in 1936; after the first time he was reinstated in 1912, and after the second he was elected to honorary life membership in 1937.

Throughout his active performing days Devant was the subject of numerous magazine and newspaper articles as well as himself being a prolific contributor. Additionally he was the author of eight substantial books, including *Our Magic* (1911), written in collaboration with Nevil Maskelyne (J. N. Maskelyne's eldest son). He appeared in the first royal command variety performance at the Palace Theatre, London, in 1912, assisted by his daughter, Vida, and Nevil Maskelyne's son Jasper. Such now was his reputation that he received a testimonial address and silver plate from magicians worldwide at St George's Hall on 3 February the next year.

At the height of his powers Devant was stricken with a progressive palsy and retired from public performing at the end of 1919. In retirement he gave lessons on conjuring and continued to write magazine articles and books,

including his autobiography, *My Magic Life* (1931), and *Secrets of my Magic* (1936), an important work on illusions. Devant's wife died in 1928 and his daughter in 1954. Progressive incapacitation, throughout which he was tended by his companion, William Curtis, led in June 1937 to Devant's admission to the Royal Hospital for Incurables, Putney, where he died (of paralysis agitans according to the death certificate) on 13 October 1941, aged seventy-three, acclaimed 'the foremost magician of all time' by *The Times* obituary. He was buried on 17 October at Highgate old (west) cemetery.   EDWIN A. DAWES

Sources D. Devant, *My magic life* (1931) · D. Devant, *Secrets of my magic* (1936) · S. H. Sharpe, *Devant's delightful delusions* (1990) · J. Fisher, 'All done by kindness', *Paul Daniels and the story of magic* (1987), 118–33 · E. A. Dawes, *The great illusionists* (1979), 165–8, 189, 191 · M. Christopher, *The illustrated history of magic* (1973), 167–79 · *The Magic Circular* [Devant memorial number, December 1941], 36 (1941–2), 32–3, 41–58 · *Genii* [David Devant issue], 38 (1974), 184–94, 199–205 · *The Times* (14 Oct 1941) · CGPLA Eng. & Wales (1941) · b. cert. · d. cert. · census returns for Fulham, 1891

Archives Centre for the Magic Arts, London, Magic Circle Museum, original artwork (incl. John Hassall) for some posters | FILM BFI NFTVA, performance footage | SOUND BBC WAC

Likenesses F. Winter, bronze bust, Centre for the Magic Arts, London · oils · photograph, Theatre Museum, London [*see illus.*] · photographs, Centre for the Magic Arts, London

Wealth at death £222 13s.: probate, 11 Nov 1941, CGPLA Eng. & Wales

Devas, (Thomas) Anthony (1911–1958), portrait, still-life, and landscape painter, was born on 8 January 1911 in Bromley, Kent, the second son of the four children of Thomas Gronow Devas, chairman of the City of London wholesale textile firm Devas Routledge, and his wife, Marjorie Cecilia Wilson. While at Repton School, Devas sought solace from his unhappiness there in the school art studio, and he was encouraged by the art master, Arthur Norris, to leave at sixteen to pursue his painting at the Slade School of Fine Art in London. From 1927 he studied there under Henry Tonks and Philip Wilson Steer, made lifelong friends with Rodrigo Moynihan, Robin Darwin, and William Coldstream, and fell in love with Nicolette Macnamara (1911–1987) [*see* Devas, Nicolette], daughter of the Irish poet–philosopher Francis Macnamara and sister of Caitlin, the future wife of Dylan Thomas.

The pattern of both Devas's artistic and personal life was thus effectively already established by the time he left the Slade and married Nicolette, on 25 June 1931. Through her he was drawn into the orbit of Augustus John, in whose ménage the Macnamara girls had been raised, and whose influence can be felt in the portraits of both Nicolette and Caitlin (Tate collection), painted during the war years when, owing to ill health, Devas was serving as an air raid warden in Chelsea. Like portraits of close friends from this period, such as the poet Laurie Lee (1944 version on loan to the National Portrait Gallery, London), they are now generally accepted as being among his best work.

Devas had initially been associated in the public mind with his friends in the Euston Road School, partly because of shared subject matter such as gently realist portraits and figure subjects, but also through the subdued colours and soft focus of his early work. By 1941, when he had his first major exhibition at Thomas Agnew & Sons Ltd, he had built up a small but enlightened portrait clientele who favoured the informality of his approach and greater freedom of brushwork than that offered by other members of the Royal Society of Portrait Painters, of which he became a member in 1945. Official commissions included portraits for the War Artists' Advisory Committee and one of Sir George Dyson for the Royal College of Music in 1952. That same year his portrait of Count Benckendorff helped to secure his election as associate of the Royal Academy, where he had been exhibiting regularly since showing *Flowers in a Yellow Jug* there in 1940.

Portraits of Devas's three children, including *Emma Dressed Up* (Museum and Art Gallery, Derby), were influential in securing a demand for child portraits, but the undeniable charm which he brought to these and to portraits of fashionable women became increasingly decorative as his approach became correspondingly conservative. The portrait of Camilla and Mark Sykes (1947, Bradford Art Galleries and Museums) and subject pictures such as *At the Couturier* (1955, Harris Museum and Art Gallery, Preston) are typical of the fashionable chic which won him a popular following, and in 1953 he painted a series of 'Aero' girls for Rowntrees chocolate. His portrait of Elizabeth II, painted for the Royal Artillery company in 1957, now has little more than period charm to recommend it, though his last commission, *Peggy Ashcroft as Imogen*, painted for the Royal Shakespeare Theatre and exhibited posthumously at the Royal Academy in 1959, has a freshness and originality which are said to have reduced Augustus John to tears.

Following two years of heart trouble, Anthony Devas died suddenly after a stroke on 21 December 1958 at his home, Flat 3, 86 Elm Park Gardens, Chelsea. Nicolette Devas, in her excellent autobiography *Two Flamboyant Fathers* (1966), described her husband's stammer, his 'oversensitive face' and 'extreme good looks in the romantic Rupert Brooke style', and included an invaluable account both of his portrait practice and of their life and friendships in the Chelsea of the 1940s and 1950s.

ROBIN GIBSON

Sources N. Devas, *Two flamboyant fathers* (1966) · H. Brooke, '"A lonely furrow", Anthony Devas: a reappraisal', *Country Life*, 168 (1980), 658–9 · *The Times* (22 Dec 1958) · *WWW* · *Anthony Devas, ARA, memorial exhibition* (1959) [exhibition catalogue, Thomas Agnew & Sons Ltd, London] · *Devas: a family circle* (1991) [Graves Art Gallery, Sheffield, exhibition] · *Anthony Devas: family and friends at Tenby* (1992) [exhibition catalogue, Tenby Museum and Picture Gallery] · A. Jarman and others, eds., *Royal Academy exhibitors, 1905–1970: a dictionary of artists and their work in the summer exhibitions of the Royal Academy of Arts*, 6 vols. (1973–82) · *Catalogue*, Royal Society of Portrait Painters (1934–59) [annual exhibition catalogues, London] · *CGPLA Eng. & Wales* (1959) · b. cert.

Likenesses R. Shephard, oils, 1940, priv. coll. · A. Devas, self-portrait, oils, priv. coll. · photographs, priv. coll.

Wealth at death £8680 8s. 7d.: probate, 1 April 1959, *CGPLA Eng. & Wales*

Devas, Charles Stanton (1848–1906), political economist, was born on 26 August 1848 at Long Ditton, Surrey, the second son of William Devas (*d.* 1870), a merchant, later of Old Windsor, Berkshire, and his wife, Martha Anne (*d.* 1894), daughter of Charles Stanton of Upfield, Stroud, Gloucestershire. He was educated at Eton College and from 1867 at Balliol College, Oxford, where he graduated in 1871 with first-class honours in the school of law and modern history. He entered Lincoln's Inn (1870) but was never called to the bar. The rest of his life was devoted to study, writing, and lecturing. He had become a Roman Catholic in 1867 and in 1876 was appointed as tutor in constitutional history and political economy at the short-lived Catholic University College in Kensington, founded by Cardinal Manning. He remained there until 1878 but did not obtain a professorship, although he is usually referred to as being professor of political economy. It seems that his only other salaried post was as external examiner in political economy at the Royal University of Ireland, a position he held for nine years. In 1874 he married Eliza Mary Katherine, daughter of Francis Ridout Ward of 26 Hyde Park Street, Westminster; they lived in London at 8 Inverness Gardens, Kensington, and had six sons and two daughters. Three of the sons became Roman Catholic priests and served as chaplains in the First World War, during which they won awards for gallantry; all three were appointed OBE after the war. A fourth son, Bertrand, became a writer and was for a time assistant editor of the *Dublin Review*.

Devas's most ambitious work was his *Groundwork of Economics*, published in 1883; the most influential was his *Political Economy*, published in 1892. This went into a third, revised, edition in 1907 (prepared by the author just before his death) and was also translated into German; it was recommended for many years by the Catholic Social Guild. Other subjects covered in his books and pamphlets included the Christian family, the historical importance of the Catholic church, the relationship between labour and capital, socialism, Christian democracy, and free trade. He contributed articles and reviews to the *Dublin Review*, the *International Journal of Ethics*, and the *Economic Journal*, and presented papers to the British Association (in 1894 and 1901), the Manchester Statistical Society, and various Catholic conferences.

Devas was concerned to find an alternative to both socialism and *laissez-faire* individualism. He admitted that socialism had a number of attractive features, and there is a welcome absence from his writings of the simplistic dismissal of it frequently found in contemporary Catholic writings. He was no dreamy-eyed medievalist and welcomed modern industrialized society; the challenge was to structure it so as to benefit all its citizens. Socialism was not the answer: its view of humanity was fundamentally unhistorical, its programmes would be unworkable, and, above all, there was total incompatibility between it and the family. The family was the basic unit of society, with rights and duties anterior to those of the state, to be protected at all costs. The solution lay in the establishment of a Christian democracy. This would not provide easy answers, but would protect labour by supporting trade unions and end cut-throat competition among employers:

'there must be regulated trading and collective bargaining' (C. S. Devas, *The Meaning and Aims of Christian Democracy*, 1899, 13). He condemned international free trade as a 'vampire [that] sucked the very life-blood of the nation' (introduction to J. Byles, *Sophisms of Free Trade*, 1904). Economics, he insisted, must be essentially ethical. There was some criticism of the dogmatism of his more overtly Catholic writings, but all praised the fairness with which he treated the views of opponents.

Devas died suddenly of a heart attack on 6 November 1906 at Mount Pleasant, Farningham, Kent, while visiting his elder brother. PETER DOYLE

Sources G. McEntee, *The Social Catholic movement in Great Britain* (1927), 102–6 · E. R. A. Seligman, ed., *Encyclopaedia of the social sciences*, 15 vols. (1930–35) · *Catholic Directory* (1876–9) · W. G. Gorman, *Converts to Rome* (1910), 84 · I. Elliott, ed., *The Balliol College register, 1833–1933*, 2nd edn (privately printed, Oxford, 1934) · *The Times* (8 Nov 1906) · *The Tablet* (17 Nov 1906) · *Economic Journal*, 16 (1906), 637–8 · b. cert. · C. Merell, 'The late Victorian Roman Catholic periodical press and attitudes to the problem of the poor', PhD diss., De Montfort University, Leicester, 2001

Wealth at death £17,261 14s. 4d.: resworn probate, 29 Dec 1906, CGPLA Eng. & Wales

Devas [*née* Macnamara; *other married name* Shephard], **Nicolette** (1911–1987), author and artist, was born on 1 February 1911 in London. She was the eldest of the four children of Francis Macnamara (1884–1946), an Irish eccentric, poet, and landowner, of Ennistymon House, co. Clare, and his wife, Mary Yvonne Majolier (1886–1973), who was of French and Anglo-Irish extraction. Her youngest sister became Caitlin *Thomas (1913–1994) upon her marriage to Dylan Thomas (1914–1953). When Nicolette was five Macnamara, committed to his freethinking ideas, deserted his family, who then for several years moved as refugees from one household to another. But primarily the lives of the Macnamaras became united with the large and unorthodox household of the painter Augustus John and his mistress Dorelia McNeil. In 1917 they were sharing the same house as the John family, Alderney Manor in Dorset. Then followed years of wandering from one place to another, and for a few years with grandmother Majolier in France. In 1923 Yvonne Majolier bought the family a home of their own, New Inn House at Blashford on the borders of the New Forest, only 7 miles from where the John family settled at Fryern Court near Fordingbridge in Hampshire. Later Nicolette was to give an account of her extraordinary childhood in her classic biography, *Two Flamboyant Fathers* (1966). This highly unconventional upbringing meant that she had almost no formal education and could not read until she was twelve. However, she learned other things: an appreciation of painting and a great love of the outdoor world, which led to an intimate knowledge of natural history. She had a particular interest in and love of birds, an interest which was to develop throughout her life. For a short time she attended schools in France, first the *lycée* in Cannes, then in Paris, where she began her art training.

At the age of sixteen Nicolette went to the Slade School of Fine Art, where she studied under Henry Tonks but refused to conform to his stringent ideas on art. She became part of a group of students which included William Coldstream, Rodrigo Moynihan, Elinor Bellingham-Smith, and Rupert Norman *Shephard (1909–1992), who was later to become her second husband. At the Slade she met, and married on 25 June 1931, the portrait painter (Thomas) Anthony *Devas (1911–1958). She was now on the way to making a successful career as a painter herself, exhibiting her work at the New English Art Club, the Royal Academy, and the London Group, and at a one-woman show at the Storran Gallery. But the outbreak of war in 1939, and her family of three children, made the pursuit of her career increasingly difficult. She also found it almost impossible for two artists to work happily under the same roof, so it was a sensible decision to turn her creative energies to writing. She published four successful novels, *Bonfire* (1958), *Nightwatch* (1961), *Black Eggs* (1970), and *Pegeen Crybaby* (1986; illustrated by Shephard), and also a life of her mother's family, *Susanna's Nightingales* (1978). *Bonfire* was read for the publishers by C. Day Lewis, who wrote, 'The untidiest, worst spelt manuscript I have ever read. PUBLISH'. It was also reviewed in the *Daily Telegraph* by John Betjeman, who called it 'a refreshing and bold experiment'.

Throughout her life Nicolette Devas never lost her love of nature, and ornithology became a major interest and study. For some years she worked in the Natural History Museum sorting birds' eggs and studying British and exotic birds in their cases. She became friends with the ornithologist James Fisher, and painted pictures of birds in the London Zoo.

Anthony Devas died in 1958; seven years later, on 24 April 1965, Nicolette Devas married the artist Rupert Shephard, her friend from her Slade days. He was a widower, and the two families (Rupert Shephard also had three children) joined up in a large house at 68 Limerston Street in Chelsea. This house became a centre for the meeting of artists and writers. Nicolette Devas had a great gift for friendship and conversation, and all her life she was an exceptionally beautiful and attractive woman, and was always ready to help and encourage any friend who might be going through a difficult time. She was an active member of the International Association of Poets, Playwrights, Editors, Essayists, and Novelists (PEN) and for many years she served on the executive committee, and travelled abroad to many international PEN conferences.

Nicolette Devas's last years were clouded by Alzheimer's disease. She died in London on 10 May 1987. A memorial service was held for her on 18 May at Chelsea Old Church, London, and she was buried on the 19th at the church of St Mary and All Saints at Ellingham, near Ringwood in Hampshire. Shortly after her death a very successful one-woman show of her work was held at the gallery of Sally Hunter Fine Art (July 1987). CATHERINE DUPRÉ

Sources N. Devas, *Two flamboyant fathers* (1966) · P. Elstob, 'Nicolette Devas: a personal memory', *PEN Broadsheet* (autumn 1988) · introduction, *Nicolette Devas (1911–1987) with three friends from the Slade* (1987) [exhibition catalogue, Sally Hunter Fine Art, 15 July – 17 Aug 1987] · *Daily Telegraph* (14 May 1987) · *The Times* (20 May 1987) · S. Chilvers, address, given at Nicolette Devas's memorial service,

Chelsea Old Church, London, 18 May 1987 [priv. coll.] • J. Betjeman, 'Review of *Bonfire*', *Daily Telegraph* (1958)
Likenesses A. Devas, oils, 1942, priv. coll. • A. Devas, oils, 1943–4, priv. coll.
Wealth at death £193,193: probate, 7 July 1987, *CGPLA Eng. & Wales*

Deverell, Sir Cyril John (1874–1947), army officer, was born in St Peter Port, Guernsey, on 9 November 1874, the son of Lieutenant (later Major) John Baines Seddon Deverell and his wife, Harriet Strappini Roberts. He was educated at Bedford School and in 1895 was gazetted a second lieutenant in the 2nd battalion, the West Yorkshire regiment. In autumn 1895 he accompanied the regiment to west Africa where he took part in the bloodless Asante expedition. Shortly afterwards he transferred to the 1st battalion in India and as a result missed involvement in the Second South African War of 1899–1902. On 31 March 1902 he married Hilda, daughter of Lieutenant-Colonel Gerald Grant-Dalton, who was then his commanding officer. In 1906 he was chosen to attend the Staff College at Quetta; afterwards he held a number of staff appointments in India in which he was judged to have performed well.

At the outbreak of war in 1914 Deverell was back in England. He was appointed a brigade major in the 28th division, one of the first of the 'Kitchener's Army' divisions. Deverell proceeded to France with this division early in 1915. He was constitutionally and temperamentally well suited to meeting the challenge of war, and on the western front his career flourished. Tall, broad-shouldered, and therefore physically imposing, he was also decisive and mentally robust. This combination of qualities inspired confidence in those around him and he rose from captain to major-general in two years. During the war as a whole he received three brevets and seven mentions in dispatches.

After serving as a brigade major throughout the second battle of Ypres in the spring of 1915, Deverell was given command of the 4th battalion of the East Yorkshire regiment with which he served for four months before being given command of the 20th brigade of the 4th division. He commanded this brigade in the early stages of the great Somme offensive of 1916 before being promoted once again—this time to command the 3rd division, an appointment he held until the armistice. The 3rd division fought under his command in the latter part of the 1916 Somme offensive. It also took part in the battle of Arras (1917), in the third battle of Ypres (1917), and at Cambrai in the following year. In the last year of the war it fought in Picardy and Flanders during the German spring offensives and with General Sir Julian Byng's Third Army in the allied offensives of August to November 1918, which brought the war to an end. The 3rd division was generally regarded as a good division and Deverell as an excellent divisional commander. The 3rd division and Deverell personally particularly distinguished themselves during the final campaign.

After the armistice Deverell, who was appointed CB in 1918 and KBE in 1926, commanded the Welsh division of

Sir Cyril John Deverell (1874–1947), by Elliott & Fry

the Territorial Army for two years before going to India, where he commanded the United Provinces district for four years. In 1927 he was appointed quartermaster-general in India, and after three years in that post he was appointed chief of the general staff in Delhi. In 1931 he returned to England to take over the western command. Two years later he was promoted general and transferred to the eastern command. Deverell thus had even more experience of senior staff appointments in peacetime than he had of field commands in war. His success in both kinds of employment made it increasingly likely that he would rise to the very top of his profession. His success in commanding one of two opposing corps in large scale manoeuvres held in 1935, winning his victory by a particularly subtle operation, made him the obvious candidate to succeed Sir Archibald Montgomery-Massingberd as chief of the Imperial General Staff (CIGS). In 1936 he thus rose to the most senior position in the British army and was promoted field marshal. He was appointed KCB in 1929 and GCB in 1935.

The army in which Deverell now held the top post was in a somewhat dilapidated condition. Both regular and territorial units were desperately short of recruits and much of the equipment was obsolete. The international situation was increasingly threatening and the army of National Socialist Germany was growing fast. A rearmament programme for the regular army (though not for the Territorial Army) had been approved by the cabinet before Deverell took office. This programme had been conceived by the general staff under Montgomery-Massingberd on the basis that the British army was likely to have to fight alongside the French against the Germans, as in 1914–18. But Neville Chamberlain, then chancellor of the exchequer, wished to place the main emphasis on developing British airpower, considering that this might deter war. When Chamberlain became prime minister in May 1937 he appointed a new secretary of state for war, Leslie Hore-Belisha, and Deverell came under pressure to make fundamental changes in military policy. The government decided to give a much lower priority to preparing the British army to fight on the continent, making it almost exclusively a force for home and imperial defence. A large part of the object of this new army policy was to limit expenditure on the army, particularly on tanks. As a good soldier Deverell could not and did not refuse to implement the military policy of his government. But he did not believe that it was realistic to try to check German expansion on the continent without preparing the British army to fight there. Because of Deverell's evident lack of enthusiasm for the new policy, and reluctance to contemplate radical changes in army organization, Hore-Belisha sacked him in December 1937.

Few would now doubt that Deverell was in the right on the policy issue at stake. Indeed the government tacitly admitted as much when it began actively preparing a field force for the continent a little over a year later. The dismissal, moreover, was handled shabbily. In public Hore-Belisha indicated that he was sacking Deverell because the ageing CIGS had become a drag on the army's rearmament. The secretary of state for war made no public reference to the fundamental difference over strategic policy which, as he admitted in private correspondence with the prime minister, was the real motive for the dismissal. Deverell was furious at the contemptuous tone which Hore-Belisha adopted in the letter dismissing him. In a written reply he indicated that his conscience was clear as to his duty to the army and as to its rearmament, and that he regarded Hore-Belisha's comments on his performance as both unjust and cruel.

In retirement Deverell lived at Lymington, Hampshire, where he took a prominent part in local affairs, serving on the borough council and chairing the local defence committee during the Second World War. He died at Court Lodge, Lymington, on 12 May 1947. His wife and a son and a daughter survived him. For thirteen years before his death he had been colonel of his old regiment, the west Yorkshire. J. P. HARRIS

Sources B. Bond, *British military policy between the two world wars* (1980) · B. H. Liddell Hart, *The memoirs of Captain Liddell Hart*, 2 vols. (1965) · *The private papers of Hore-Belisha*, ed. R. Minney (1960) · *Chief of staff: the diaries of Lieutenant-General Sir Henry Pownall*, ed. B. Bond, 1 (1972) · J. P. Harris, *Men, ideas and tanks: British military thought and amoured forces, 1903–1939* (1995) · *DNB* · *The Times* (13 May 1947) · *CGPLA Eng. & Wales* (1947)

Archives IWM, notebook, western front · King's Lond., Liddell Hart C., letters · PRO, war office MSS | King's Lond., Liddell Hart C., corresp. with Sir B. H. Liddell Hart

Likenesses W. Stoneman, two photographs, 1920–36, NPG · Elliott & Fry, photograph, NPG [*see illus.*] · R. Marientrey, portrait, priv. coll. · A. P. W. Smith, portrait, priv. coll.

Wealth at death £27,012 13s. 8d.: probate, 16 Oct 1947, *CGPLA Eng. & Wales*

Deverell, Edith Mary. *See* Marvin, Edith Mary (1872–1958).

Deverell, Mary (*fl.* 1774–1797), moral and religious writer, was born probably at Minchinhampton, Gloucestershire. She described herself as 'a person of obscure and undistinguished rank' (Deverell, *Sermons*, 3rd edn, iv) and may have come from a clothing family. She was possibly related to the family of John Deverell, esquire, of Clifton, who are listed as subscribers to her *Miscellanies* (1781). She was probably unmarried.

Deverell's *Sermons on the Following Subjects* (1774) was published in Bristol by the newspaper owner Sarah Farley. Anticipating criticism of her choice of subject, Deverell explained in her preface (pp. iii–v) that she would have changed the title but for the pleas of her subscribers. The list of these published in the first edition shows that she had strong support among the aristocracy and the Bristol clergy; they include the duke of Dorset and the earl of Coventry, and the rector of Minchinhampton, who subscribed for twenty volumes. The duchess of Queensberry and the marchioness of Rockingham subscribed to the second edition for four and eight copies respectively. The sermons dealt with moral issues in a conventional fashion.

Between the publication of the first and second editions of her sermons Deverell went to London and was present at Garrick's final performance, on 10 June 1776. She also found that the clergy 'approve of my writings … But the title of *Sermons* from a woman startles them! and must not be encouraged in our sex' (Deverell, *Miscellanies*, 1.110); however, she received permission to dedicate the third edition (1777) to Charlotte, princess royal. In London she may have met Samuel Johnson, who subscribed to her *Miscellanies*, along with his friend Dr William Adams, master of Pembroke College, Oxford. The *Miscellanies*, which was printed for the author, was a much more polemical work than the *Sermons* and contained trenchant criticism of the treatment of literary women. Deverell complained that 'the world in general have a very illiberal opinion of the conduct and manners of women who are deemed *learned*' (ibid., 1.228). She declared herself 'something of a rebel' against the belief that 'the female sphere is domestic, and the practice of our duty in that province should be our highest ambition' (ibid., 1.43) and described a woman trapped in an unhappy marriage as 'the legal slave of a despotic sovereign' (ibid., 2.119–20). She recognized that women were disadvantaged by exclusion from men's 'useful clubs and friendly associations' (ibid., 1.113), though she was able to use the public space of the pump rooms at Bath and the Bristol Hotwells to collect subscriptions.

Mary Deverell's career parallels that of Hannah More. Both were protégées of the Bristol heiress Ann Lovell Gwatkin and both went to London about the same time (1774) to further their literary careers. The Mrs More in Bristol who is listed as subscriber to Deverell's *Sermons* may have been Hannah More's mother. However, More herself did not subscribe and referred to Deverell derisively as '*parsoness* and *poetess*' (Roberts, 1.192). In 1782 she wrote from Bristol to Ann Kennicott, widow of Dr Benjamin Kennicott, following a visit from Deverell:

> I think I never saw her in such a fit of poetical phrenzy before, mad as the Cumoean maid, and bursting with the inspiring God, she repeated without stopping to take breath … *eighteen hundred lines*, being a Poem she has just finished, and to which she has modestly prefixed the title of *Epic*. (More MSS)

This must be a reference to *Theodora and Dydimus* (1784), a heroic poem in three cantos in praise of female heroism. It was not well received. Her play, *Mary Queen of Scots* (1792), was apparently never performed.

Deverell's career demonstrates that, given the right connections, it was possible for a woman to establish a literary reputation. However, her writings show a strong awareness of the precariousness of the career of a literary woman. With the failure of her later works she lapsed into obscurity, though in 1797 she subscribed 5 guineas for the widows and orphans of the men killed at the naval battle of Camperdown. It is not known when or where she died.

ANNE STOTT

Sources J. Todd, ed., *A dictionary of British and American women writers, 1660–1800* (1984) · M. Deverell, *Sermons on the following subjects*, 1st edn (1774) · M. Deverell, *Sermons on the following subjects*, 3rd edn (1777) · M. Deverell, *Miscellanies in prose and verse*, 2 vols. (1781) · H. More, letter to A. Kennicott, 10 Oct 1782, U. Cal., Los Angeles, William Andrews Clark Memorial Library, Hannah More MSS [uncatalogued] · *N&Q*, 3rd ser., 5 (1864), 379, 446 · W. Roberts, *Memoirs of the life and correspondence of Mrs Hannah More*, 2nd edn, 4 vols. (1834) · *Bonner and Middleton's Bristol Journal* (11 Nov 1797)

Deverell [*formerly* Pedley], **Robert** (1760–1841), author and classical scholar, was born in May or June 1760, the second son of Simon Pedley of St Stephen's, Bristol, and his wife, a daughter of Robert Deverell, a merchant of Bristol. He was educated in Bristol in a school run by a Mr Lee, and matriculated in April 1777 at Brasenose College, Oxford, whence he migrated to St John's College, Cambridge, in June of that year. In 1782 he won the college's Latin essay prize, and he held a fellowship from 1784 to 1791. Having been recommended by Nathaniel Ryder, Lord Harrowby, he acted as tutor to the future politician and diarist Sir Robert Heron, who later recalled that Pedley had 'some learning and much ignorance, but being a little mad, his strange ideas taught me to think for myself. We spent two summers together in France, Germany and Holland' (Heron, 291).

Having been admitted to Lincoln's Inn in June 1784, Pedley was called to the bar (19 April 1788) and practised at 2 Lincoln's Inn Stone Buildings, though his name disappears from the *Law List* at some point after 1805. He adopted his mother's family name in lieu of his father's by royal licence on 25 June 1793. At the general election of 1802 he was brought in for Saltash by William Beckford, the politician and art connoisseur, for whom his brother John Pedley acted as estate manager in the West Indies. In line with his patron, he generally supported the administration, but occasionally displayed a streak of independence, as exemplified by his vote against the Additional

Force Bill promoted by Pitt, the prime minister (8 June 1804). In 1806 he published *Two Letters … to … William Pitt on the Ancient Aries, or Battering Ram*, which suggested a strategy for destroying the French fleet at Boulogne, and advanced a claim *en passant* that the ancient civilizations had possessed a knowledge of firearms, but had 'concealed all their knowledge under aenigmatical disguises' (p. 15): similar suppositions informed many of his other writings. A despondent footnote adds that after Pitt's death he had laid his scheme before 'a highly distinguished person' (ibid.), but had received no reply after 'many months' (ibid.). His interventions in Commons debate were apparently less arcane, and were made chiefly in support of the slave trade, the continuance of which was decidedly in Beckford's interest: Deverell claimed once to have been as keen a champion of abolition as Wilberforce himself, but to have undergone a very convenient Damascene conversion. On the same subject he published *A Letter to Samuel Whitbread* (1807) in which he frankly admitted that any defence of the trade rested on 'political expediency'. In the meantime his parliamentary career had come to an end at the dissolution in October 1806.

Deverell's posthumous repute rested on his other extraordinary publications, which made him a regular subject of enquiry for incredulous correspondents of *Notes and Queries*. *Alter et idem, a New Review* (1794) was apparently intended, but not pursued, as a series. It featured poetry, an ingenious scheme for printing script backwards (to be read with the aid of a mirror), as well as plans for steering a hot air balloon, riot prevention, savings banks, and the construction of a single-wheel chaise, only the last of which was plainly intended as a joke. His subsequent works found the sort of esoteric meanings in text that would leave most modern literary scholars standing. *Andalusia, or, Notes tending to show that the yellow fever of the West Indies, and of Andalusia … was a disease well known to the ancients* (1805) used heavily annotated extracts from the classics to support his main contention—that the ancients not only knew about yellow fever, but of a cure. He expatiated in *A Supplement*, published the following year, in which he offered supporting evidence in the shape of an interpretation of the hieroglyphic inscriptions on a mummy preserved at Cambridge. *A new view of the classics and ancient arts; tending to shew their invariable connexion with the sciences* (1806) took Homer's *Odyssey* as its main text, and discovered in it complex geographical allusions which indicated that its author possessed an intimate knowledge of world geography, including that of Japan and of the interior of Africa. Perhaps his most celebrated work was the six-volume *Discoveries in hieroglyphics, and other antiquities, in progress of which many compositions are put in a light entirely new* (1813). Herein, with the aid of copious notes, a multitude of classical allusions, and 196 engraved illustrations, he sought to prove that the characters, plots, and events described in several literary classics, including works by Shakespeare (among them *Hamlet*, *Othello*, and *The Merchant of Venice*), Samuel Butler (*Hudibras*), Milton, and Homer, were nothing more than allusions to the phases of the moon. It was later claimed, doubtfully, that he attempted to have the book withdrawn from sale (Watt, *Bibl. Brit.*). One correspondent to *Notes and Queries* denominated it 'one of the most extraordinary works ever published' (*N&Q,* 10, 236); another thought that 'the whole affair seems to afford indications of insanity' (*N&Q,* 2, 61). Heron, who spoke from personal experience, noted by way of elegy that Deverell 'wrote works which decidedly proved insanity, and his conduct was also, sometimes, such as to admit of no other excuse; yet, he was also the best tutor I could have had; for, with a private education, without companions of any ability, I was in need of his strange and active imagination to excite my reasoning faculties' (Heron, 263–4).

Deverell certainly appears to have inhabited a strange parallel universe; perhaps unsurprisingly, he never married. He died on 29 November 1841 in New Norfolk Street, London, having directed that his sizeable personal estate be divided among the children of his niece Mary Couthard. A bequest of £100 was paid to the Hon. Mrs Carpenter of Bowness, Westmorland. H. J. SPENCER

Sources DNB · M. H. Port, 'Deverell, Robert', HoP, *Commons, 1790–1820* · R. Heron, *Notes by Sir Robert Heron*, 2nd edn (1851) · *N&Q,* 2 (1850), 469 · *N&Q,* 2 (1850), 61 · *N&Q,* 10 (1854), 236 · *N&Q,* 2nd ser., 5 (1858), 466 · *N&Q,* 3rd ser., 4 (1863), 503–4 · will, PRO, PROB 11/1962/322 · death duty register, PRO, IR 26/1603/317 · *Browne's General Law List* (1797) · *New Law List* (1798) · *Clarke's New Law List* (1805) · Foster, *Alum. Oxon.* · Venn, *Alum. Cant.* · W. P. Baildon, ed., *The records of the Honorable Society of Lincoln's Inn: admissions*, 2 vols. (1896) · Watt, *Bibl. Brit.*

Archives Bodl. Oxf., corresp. with William Beckford, MS Beckford c29, fols. 78–88

Wealth at death under £30,000—personal estate: PRO, death duty register, IR 26/1603/317; will, PRO, PROB 11/1962/322

Devereux, Frances. *See* Howard, Frances, countess of Somerset (1590–1632).

Devereux, John, Baron Devereux (d. 1393), soldier and royal councillor, of Dinton, Buckinghamshire, was reputedly a younger son of William Devereux of Bodenham, Herefordshire, but his background remains obscure. The foundations of his reputation for military prowess were already laid before 1366 (by when he was certainly a knight), the year he was recruited by the great Breton commander Bertrand du Guesclin to fight on behalf of Enrique da Trastamara in his bid for the throne of Castile. Devereux and his fellow countrymen were, however, ordered to change sides by Edward, the Black Prince, who backed his kinsman by marriage, King Pedro the Cruel. The latter's supporters won a notable victory at Nájera in 1367, when Devereux rode in the van of the English contingent. 'Then, of a surety', wrote the Chandos herald, 'was no heart in the world so bold as not to be amazed at the mighty blows they dealt with the great axes they bore, and the swords and daggers' (*Life of the Black Prince*, ll. 3286–91). A period of energetic campaigning, during which he served as seneschal of the Limousin (1369–71) and of Rochelle (1372), and was present when Limoges fell to Prince Edward, ended abruptly with his capture by du Guesclin at Chize in 1373. He had been ransomed by 1375, and two years later the prince recompensed him with an annual pension of 200 marks payable for life in recognition of his services overseas.

The accession of Prince Edward's son, Richard II, allowed Devereux to assume a more political role as a member of the royal council and intimate of the young king's surviving uncles. He became constable of Leeds Castle, Kent, in March 1378, and—of far greater strategic importance—captain of Calais (1380), with additional responsibility for the defences of Calais pale and Guînes (1381). These appointments brought with them onerous diplomatic duties, involving seven separate missions to treat with the French and the Flemings between then and 1390. There were many rewards, too. The duke of Brittany, under whom he had fought in Poitou, gave him 100 marks a year for life (although payment often fell into arrears), and he was well placed to secure the lease of valuable property confiscated by the government in wartime. Most of the rent of £246 a year which he contracted to pay was remitted after his summons to parliament as Lord Devereux, in September 1384, and his creation as a banneret by King Richard.

Evidence of Devereux's dramatic rise up the social ladder may be found in his marriage, by 1379, to Margaret (d. 1398), daughter of John de Vere, earl of Oxford (d. 1360), and Maud, daughter of Bartholomew, Lord Badlesmere (d. 1322). A rich widow to boot, she had previously been married to Henry, Lord Beaumont (d. 1369), and Sir Nicholas Loveyn (d. 1375), who left her in possession of the manor of Penshurst, Kent. Devereux was, moreover, able to purchase outright, in 1385, the castle and lordship of Kilpeck in Herefordshire. Further preferment followed, with his promotion to the stewardship of the royal household, which he held from February 1388 until his death, his appointment as constable of Dover Castle and warden of the Cinque Ports one year later, and his elevation as a knight of the Garter by April 1389. The fall of Sir Simon Burley and other unpopular royal favourites in 1388 not only strengthened his own position, but also brought him Lyonshall in Herefordshire as a share of the spoils.

Devereux died suddenly at his London inn, Le Coldeherberwe (Coldharbour), on 22 February 1393, while preparing to leave England on another diplomatic mission. He was buried, according to his wishes, at the church of the London Greyfriars. In his will of 1385 he had left large quantities of plate and 2000 marks to find a bride for his son, John, but by 1390 the boy had already married Philippa, granddaughter and coheir of Guy, Lord Brian (d. 1390). He died childless in 1396, and was succeeded in his estates by his sister, Joan (1379–1409), wife of Walter *Fitzwalter, Lord Fitzwalter (d. 1406) [*see under* Fitzwalter family (*per. c.*1200–*c.*1500)], and then of Hugh, Lord Burnell (d. 1420). CAROLE RAWCLIFFE

Sources Chancery records · GEC, *Peerage* · Rymer, *Foedera* · Chandos herald, *Life of the Black Prince by the herald of Sir John Chandos*, ed. M. K. Pope and E. C. Lodge (1910) · PRO, PROB 11/1, sig. 3 · *Chroniques de J. Froissart*, ed. S. Luce and others, 15 vols. (Paris, 1869–1975) · *Œuvres de Froissart: chroniques*, ed. K. de Lettenhove, 25 vols. (Brussels, 1867–77) · *CIPM*, 17, no. 332 · GEC, *Peerage* · J. Stow, *A survey of London*, rev. edn (1603); repr. with introduction by C. L. Kingsford as *A survey of London*, 2 vols. (1908), vol. 1, p. 320

Wealth at death left 2000 marks for son's marriage: will, PRO, PROB 11/1, sig. 3, fols, 18*r*–19*v* · £21 Dinton, Buckinghamshire: *CIPM*, 17, no. 332

Devereux, Lettice. *See* Dudley, Lettice, countess of Essex and countess of Leicester (*b.* after 1540, *d.* 1634).

Devereux, Robert, second earl of Essex (1565–1601), soldier and politician, was born on 10 November 1565. He was the elder son and heir of Walter *Devereux, first earl of Essex (1539–1576). Through his mother, Lettice (Laetitia; *b.* after 1540, *d.* 1634), he was a member of Elizabeth I's extended Boleyn–Carey cousinage [*see* Dudley, Lettice, countess of Leicester]. He was presumably named after his godfather, Robert *Dudley, earl of Leicester, the queen's great favourite. He had two older sisters, Penelope [*see* Rich, Penelope, Lady Rich (1563–1607)] and Dorothy (*b.* 1564?). His younger brother, Walter, was born in 1569.

Little is known of Devereux's early childhood. Sir Henry Wotton later claimed that Devereux's father had had a 'cold conceit' of him and preferred his younger son and namesake (Wotton, 8). However, Wotton constitutes a poor source for these early years. His story clearly reflects later assumptions deriving from the notorious dislike which arose between the first earl of Essex and the earl of Leicester by the 1570s. Wotton's 'constant information' is probably only oft-repeated speculation that Essex had harboured doubts about the paternity of his elder son, based upon rumours that Leicester had had an affair with Essex's wife (a story which was widely publicized from the mid-1580s by scurrilous Catholic propaganda such as *Leicester's Commonwealth*).

Devereux's childhood companions included a son of Nicholas White, master of the rolls in Ireland, and Gabriel Montgommery, son of the Huguenot leader, Count Montgommery, who had been executed in France in 1574. His upbringing was therefore Francophile and strongly protestant from the start. His earliest known teacher was Thomas Ashton, headmaster of Shrewsbury School, fellow of Trinity College, Cambridge, and a trusted family servant. Ashton was succeeded as Devereux's 'scolemaster' by his protégé Robert Wright, who had been a pupil at Shrewsbury before becoming a fellow of Trinity. This appointment, undoubtedly made at Ashton's urging, perhaps signified Essex's intention that his son should also go to Trinity College.

Royal ward, 1576–1586 At the time of his father's death in September 1576, the new earl of Essex was living with his brother and sisters at Chartley, the family seat in Staffordshire. By virtue of succeeding to his title as a minor, Essex became a ward of the crown. Although Essex's siblings went to live under the supervision of the earl and countess of Huntingdon in Leicestershire, the chief responsibility for the young earl himself (as for many other aristocratic minors during the reign of Elizabeth) was taken by William Cecil, Lord Burghley, the lord treasurer and master of the court of wards. According to a report of November 1576, Essex showed great promise: 'he can express his mind in Latin & French as well as in Englishe, verie curteus and modest, rather disposed to heare than to

Robert Devereux, second earl of Essex (1565–1601), by Marcus Gheeraerts the younger, *c.*1597

aunswer, given greatly to learning, weake & tender, but very comly & bewtifull' (BL, Lansdowne MS 23, fol. 190*r*). He was also, however, a young nobleman whose estate was very heavily encumbered by debts. Earl Walter's efforts to seize territory in Ulster had destroyed the family finances, leaving his heir some £18,000 in debt, much of it owed to the crown. The responsibility for overseeing this estate during the earl's minority, and for reducing as much of the debt as possible, lay with Richard Broughton, a lawyer who had been a servant and trustee of Earl Walter.

Essex left Chartley in January 1577 and travelled to London, where he stayed briefly at Cecil House. He also spent time at Burghley's Hertfordshire estate of Theobalds, often under the supervision of Lady Burghley or the countess of Oxford, Burghley's elder daughter. Burghley's younger son, Robert Cecil, was undoubtedly one of the 'children' who mixed with Essex during these months. Early in May, Essex went up to Trinity College, Cambridge, accompanied by Robert Wright, who now became his tutor there. Despite Wotton's assertion that Essex came under 'the oversight' of John Whitgift, the future archbishop of Canterbury, at Trinity (Wotton, 8), the mastership of the college had already passed to John Still by the time the earl arrived. Essex's initial arrangements for life at Trinity were overseen by Gervase Babington. Among the many significant scholarly and clerical contacts which Essex made during his time at Cambridge were Gabriel and Richard Harvey, William Whitaker (for whom Essex became his 'verie good lord'; Baker, 2.604), John Overall (a fellow student at Trinity), and Hugh Broughton, brother of his estate manager Richard.

Essex's studies at Cambridge nourished his propensity towards 'bookishnesse' (Devereux, *Apologie*, sig. A1v) and made him almost as eager for the company of scholars as for the company of soldiers. Nevertheless he spent a considerable amount of time away from Cambridge. In 1578, for example, the threat of plague ensured that he spent fully half the year at Keyston, a family estate in Huntingdonshire which had been leased to his uncle by marriage, Henry Clifford. In August 1578 he visited Staffordshire and received the stewardship of Tamworth in person. Essex's life was now also increasingly influenced by the earl of Leicester, who secretly married Essex's mother in September 1578. At the new year Essex visited London and the court to watch Elizabeth's reception of Duke Casimir, whose visit was largely stage-managed by Leicester. The oft-repeated, but erroneous, story that Essex met the queen on this occasion and refused to let her kiss him is based upon a conflation of Casimir's behaviour with that of the young earl. Essex also visited Leicester's house in London and stayed at Kenilworth during the summer of 1581, following his graduation as an MA. Essex returned to Trinity for the celebration of the queen's accession day (17 November), before going to live with his maternal grandfather, Sir Francis *Knollys, until February 1582. At the end of that month he went to join the earl of Huntingdon, who was based at York as lord president of the council of the north. It was hoped that life in the north would reduce Essex's expenditure, which had mounted rapidly during his time at Cambridge: the two suits of clothes which he bought for the wedding of his sister Penelope to Lord Rich in November 1581, for example, cost more than £40.

Essex remained in the north with Huntingdon until the end of 1583, when he went to stay with Leicester in London. During the following summer he accompanied Leicester on a grand progress across the midlands, before it was terminated by the sudden death of Leicester's infant son (and Essex's half-brother), Robert Dudley, Lord Denbigh, in mid-July. Essex subsequently travelled to south Wales, where he met and established strong ties with his family's numerous followers and servants in the region. His base over the autumn and winter of 1584–5 was Lamphey in Pembrokeshire, at a house which was usually occupied by his uncle George Devereux. Essex headed back to Chartley in April 1585 and remained there until late in August. During this visit, and perhaps for several months before, it seems that Essex came under pressure from his mother to forsake his life in the country and go to court. Now he finally did so. Travelling to Leicester's seat at Kenilworth, he joined his stepfather for the journey south. Despite his later success as a royal favourite, Essex's arrival at court early in September 1585 apparently

attracted little notice. The queen's attention, like that of Leicester and the other leading courtiers, was anxiously focused upon the war in the Netherlands, where an English army was about to be dispatched to aid the Dutch against the forces of Spain. Essex himself later claimed that he found 'small grace and new friends' when he first attended the court (Devereux, *Apologie*, sig. A2v). He was also unable to prevent his chief estate of Chartley, which he had so recently left, being chosen as the new prison for Mary, queen of Scots.

Following Leicester's appointment to command the army going to the Netherlands, Essex was granted permission (presumably by the queen, since he was still a royal ward) to accompany his stepfather to war. Essex sailed with Leicester's entourage from Harwich on 8 December 1585. A month later, when the army was mustered for service, Essex was appointed colonel-general of the cavalry, paralleling Sir John Norris's appointment as colonel-general of the foot. Because Essex himself was undergoing a military apprenticeship, much of the routine administration of the cavalry was carried out by Sir William Russell. Command of the cavalry was not only socially prestigious but also politically significant, for many of the horsemen were provided by Leicester's own extended Dudley following. Although Leicester's nephew Sir Philip Sidney won the high-profile job of governor of Flushing, Essex's command of the cavalry declared his status as Leicester's new political protégé and a potential future leader for his supporters. Leicester's backing for his stepson was also signalled in the extravagant celebration of St George's day at Utrecht, where Essex made his public début as a jouster. Essex loyally supported his stepfather in the bitter feud between Leicester and Sir John Norris which plagued the English army throughout 1586–7, but deeply regretted its occurrence. In his subsequent military career Essex devoted much effort to avoiding a repetition of such internecine quarrels among his own officers. In September 1586 he participated in Leicester's capture of Doesburg and in the famous skirmish at Zutphen, where he and a small body of other horsemen repeatedly charged a much larger Spanish force with almost foolhardy bravery. Essex was later dubbed a knight banneret by Leicester for his courage in the fight.

The aftermath of Zutphen also sealed Essex's connection with Sir Philip Sidney, who was mortally wounded in the battle. Sidney had once been intended to marry the earl's sister Penelope and later wrote sonnets about her as the 'Stella' to his 'Astrophel'. Leicester had also once planned to marry Sidney to Essex's other sister, Dorothy. Both matches failed, but the dying Sidney made a last-minute bequest to Essex of one of his two 'best' swords, symbolically transferring to Essex his twin roles as Leicester's right-hand man and knightly champion of England's participation in the defence of international protestantism. The conjunction of Sidney's death and Essex's knighthood—which released him from wardship and gave him full control of his estates—cemented the bond between them to a profound degree. Many of Essex's subsequent actions can be seen (and were meant to be seen) as allusions to Sidney and to the myth created about his death, especially the idea that he transcended mortality by the fame which he had earned during his lifetime. Essex clearly sought to win a similarly transcendent knightly renown, which gave added fuel to his martial ambitions.

The queen's new favourite, 1587–1592 Essex returned to England late in October 1586 as a war hero and free from the bonds of wardship. He quickly caught the queen's eye. To Elizabeth, Essex seemed a handsome, intellectual, and intriguing distraction from the agonizing business of consenting to the death of Mary, queen of Scots. Moreover, he was backed by Leicester, who knew better than anyone else how to win the queen's favour. As Lord Henry Howard later observed of Essex's career, 'the greatest enemie to his father was his meane to rise' (Durham University Library, Howard MS 2, fol. 117r). Leicester pushed Essex forward not only because he was his stepson and because Zutphen had dashed whatever hopes he may have harboured for Sidney, but also because Essex's advancement would weaken the position of Sir Walter Ralegh. Ralegh had begun to win a hold on the queen's favour in recent years, especially during Leicester's absence in the Netherlands. Leicester believed that Ralegh had tried to take advantage of his absence to undermine his relationship with the queen, and regarded him as a grasping outsider who failed to show sufficient gratitude for the favours which Leicester had shown him. Essex instinctively shared his stepfather's antagonism towards Ralegh, sharpened further by a recognition that he and Ralegh were direct competitors for the queen's favour. Leicester's success in renewing his old rapport with the queen late in 1586 and early in 1587 temporarily stifled Ralegh's hopes and gave Essex a decisive advantage.

By May 1587 Essex had become established as Elizabeth's constant young companion. As one of his servants boasted, even at night, 'my lord is at cardes or one game or another with her, that he commeth not to his owne lodginge tyll the birdes singe in the morninge' (Folger Shakespeare Library, L.a.39). Leicester built upon this success by dealing with Elizabeth to become lord steward on condition that his office as master of the horse, which he had held since the start of the reign, should pass to Essex. The mastership of the horse guaranteed Essex's close attendance upon the queen and boosted his crippled finances by about £1500 per annum. These twin promotions were confirmed (on 18 June) shortly before Leicester returned to the Netherlands, leaving Essex to defend his interests at court. Leicester's trust in Essex pointed the way towards a growing reliance upon his stepson in the future, but it also sparked open rivalry between Essex and Ralegh. Perhaps the most spectacular manifestation of this rivalry was the furious row which developed between Essex and the queen at Northaw, Hertfordshire, at the end of July. Essex blamed Ralegh for the queen's hostility towards one of his sisters and remonstrated with her at length about Ralegh's unworthiness until 'I saw she was resolved to defend him and to crosse me' (Bodl. Oxf., Tanner MS 76, fol. 29v). Essex then rode off to join the defence

of Sluys, only to be stopped at the coast by Robert Carey, whom the queen had sent after him. Essex apparently suffered no serious consequences for his defiance of the queen. He was back at court within a few days, urging Elizabeth not to blame his stepfather for the fall of Sluys.

The bitter competition between Essex and Ralegh was cooled only by the final return of Leicester from the Netherlands in December. Leicester's support soon helped Essex to acquire a whole string of new rewards. Early in 1588 or late in 1587 the queen granted Essex the use of York House (paralleling Ralegh's access to Durham House), presumably because it no longer seemed convenient or appropriate for the earl's London base to consist only of a suite of rooms at Leicester House. On 11 April Essex and a group of friends and old comrades from the Netherlands were created honorary MAs of Oxford University, where Leicester was chancellor. On 23 April 1588 Essex was elected a knight of the Garter. In June Elizabeth granted him the lands of Sir Francis Englefield, who had been attainted for treason. Essex was even given special treatment when he was reunited in military service with his stepfather during the crisis of July and August, when the realm faced invasion by Spain's Armada. Although the cavalry commanders had already been named, Elizabeth appointed Essex as overall commander of the horse in Leicester's army because 'she wold not have me discontented' (BL, Harley MS 286, fol. 144r). As befitted a man who aspired to prove himself a great captain, Essex brought with him the largest and most lavishly equipped of all the private contingents of soldiers which joined the army. When Elizabeth paid her famous visit to Leicester's troops at Tilbury, Essex attended upon her as both general of the horse and master of the horse. At the end of August, when the emergency had passed and Leicester retired to the country for a rest, Elizabeth asked Essex to move into his stepfather's lodgings at court.

Leicester's sudden death on 4 September 1588 came as an unexpected blow to Essex. Leicester's grooming of his stepson had been too brief for Essex to extract the full benefit of his stepfather's influence, leaving him burdened with political expectations which he lacked the resources and experience to fulfil. Many of Leicester's former clients apparently looked elsewhere for patronage. The chaotic state of Leicester's finances also left Essex's mother exposed financially, especially as Elizabeth was determined to ensure repayment of the huge debts which the late earl owed to the crown. Ultimately, Essex proved a major beneficiary from the seizure of Leicester's assets. In January 1589 he took over Leicester's lucrative farm of the customs on sweet wines, which became the linchpin of his finances over the next decade, being renewed in 1593 and 1597. Essex also later negotiated leases for Leicester's estate at Wanstead, Essex, and for Leicester House, which was renamed Essex House by 1593. More immediately, Leicester's death triggered a fresh round of competition between Essex and Ralegh over who would dominate the queen's favour. This rivalry was fought out through poetry and even portraiture—a portrait of Ralegh wearing pearls under a crescent moon set against Nicholas Hilliard's miniature of Essex as the *Young Man among Roses*. At times the rivalry also came close to being fought out with swords. At Christmas 1588, and again a few days later, Essex and Ralegh apparently came to the very brink of duelling at Richmond, only to be thwarted by the intervention of the queen and the privy council.

Despite his determination to establish himself in the queen's favour at Ralegh's expense, Essex remained deeply ambivalent about life at court. On the one hand he needed the material rewards which only royal favour could bring. He also aspired to become an arbiter of his country's future, believing that Elizabeth and her aged councillors could not live beyond a few more years. It was in this spirit that Essex and his sister Lady Rich made secret overtures during the second half of 1589 to James VI of Scotland, the queen's likeliest successor. This initiative proved an embarrassing failure when Essex's letters were compromised. Even so, Essex's desire to shape England's future direction remained undiminished. On the other hand Essex often felt uncomfortable at court and increasingly resented the restrictions which pleasing the queen put upon his behaviour. He also despised the sort of calculated smoothness and outright dissimulation of courtly life, of which Leicester had been a master. Instead of the gilded cage of court, Essex pined for the more straightforward life of military service and of virtues demonstrated on the battlefield, where all could see. Military service would not only prove his right to be regarded as the new Sidney but also help to defend his country from foreign enemies—Spain, the papacy, and the Catholic League of France—which he regarded as cruel, unprincipled, and genuinely threatening. Characteristically such thinking reflected an almost inseparable mix of altruism and self-aggrandizement. It also encapsulated the belief that shaped Essex's whole career: that deeds upon the battlefield were more important for the safety of the queen and the realm than actions at court, and merited greater reward from the queen than any other possible royal service. Any reverse which he might suffer at court could therefore be made good, and more, by the active display of his martial virtues on campaign. This fundamental misapprehension about the relationship between war and politics, which he sustained in the face of repeated disappointments, later proved to be a consistent political failing. In the early years of his career, however, events seemed to bear out his belief that soldiering was the highest form of royal service, and merited appropriately lofty rewards.

Essex consistently angled for opportunities to practise his profession of arms. In 1587, even though his desire to abandon court for the siege of Sluys was thwarted, he prepared the way for new possibilities by informing Henri of Navarre (later Henri IV) and the vicomte de Turenne (later duc de Bouillon) that he hoped to join them in fighting for the protestant cause in France. By February 1588 Essex also looked to the sea. He secretly invested in a naval expedition to be led by Sir Francis Drake and clearly planned to sail with the fleet himself. Although this scheming was overtaken by events, Essex's covert dealings with Drake bore fruit in 1589 when Drake and Sir John Norris commanded England's counter-Armada to attack Spain and Portugal.

Although Elizabeth denied him permission to join this force, Essex secretly left London on the evening of 3 April 1589 and rode hard for Falmouth, where he boarded the queen's ship *Swiftsure*, under the command of his friend Sir Roger Williams. Faced with the queen's fury about Essex's blatant disregard for her prohibition, Drake and Norris denied any knowledge of the earl's actions—almost certainly a lie. Essex apparently invested several thousand pounds in the voyage and later claimed that he had played a major part in naming the officers in Norris's army. He and Williams also knew precisely where to rendezvous with the fleet when it prepared to land troops in Portugal. Indeed, the fleet rejoiced at Essex's arrival and Norris allowed him to lead the vanguard ashore at Peniche, where Essex and Williams landed in shoulder-high surf to face enemy troops waiting on the beach. Such conspicuous bravery helped to inspire the army and he sought to repeat the effort when Norris's troops found themselves thwarted in their efforts to capture Lisbon. Essex pursued enemy soldiers into the suburbs of the city, challenged the governor to a duel (which was declined), and finally rode up and drove a lance into the city gates as a symbolic act of defiance when the siege could be sustained no longer. He also threw his own belongings out of a carriage in order to carry English wounded back to the fleet. However, such bravado could not disguise the failure of the expedition or delay any longer his return to face the queen. He arrived in Plymouth about 24–5 June and, having sent his brother ahead to test the waters, returned to court on 9 July.

Essex's defiance of Elizabeth to join the Portugal expedition might have been fatal to his chances of retaining royal favour. Wotton later opined that 'all his hopes had like to bee strangled almost in the very cradle' (Wotton, 3). However, Essex quickly regained his hold on the queen's affections. In addition to Elizabeth's own warm, almost maternal, feelings towards him, and his ability to play upon them, Essex's return to favour was assisted by the support which he enjoyed from many of the queen's most trusted courtiers, such as Burghley, Lord Hunsdon, Sir Francis Knollys, Sir Francis Walsingham, Sir Christopher Hatton, and influential women like the countess of Warwick. These senior courtiers regarded him as a young nobleman whose commitment to virtuous behaviour warranted approbation, albeit mixed with a certain degree of tempering. Essex also had the overwhelming attraction of being an insider—literally a blood relative of many of them, including Elizabeth herself—whereas Ralegh was a pushy outsider who threatened to disturb their relations with the queen. Essex was therefore 'mightelie backt by the greatest in opposition to Sir Walter Ralegh, who had offended manie and was maligned of most' (BL, Egerton MS 2026, fol. 32r).

Essex's rapid recovery of favour in mid-1589 effectively betokened victory in his bitter rivalry with Ralegh. Within six weeks of his return from the Portugal expedition, Essex's dominance seemed so obvious that his followers boasted he 'hath chassed Mr Rauly from the coart and hath confined him in to Irland' (LPL, MS 647, fol. 247r). In this light, it seemed that military service had indeed paid large dividends. Although he and Ralegh continued to snipe at each other during 1590, Essex felt sufficiently confident of his hold on royal favour to contract a secret marriage with Frances (1567–1632), the widow of Sir Philip Sidney and daughter of Sir Francis Walsingham, the secretary of state. The precise date of this marriage remains uncertain, but it became publicly known in October 1590, when the countess's pregnancy could be hidden no longer. The birth of a son, Robert *Devereux, Lord Hereford (later third earl of Essex), in January 1591 indicates that Essex and Lady Sidney had probably become lovers before the death of her father in April 1590. It seems likely that the marriage took place either in the early months of 1590, with the blessing of the dying Walsingham, or during the summer, after the secretary's death and when it had become apparent that Lady Sidney was pregnant. As Essex had expected, Elizabeth was initially furious about his marriage, both because it had been kept secret from her and because it reflected a triumph of Essex's romanticism over political calculation—Lady Sidney brought him the Sidney name and a stepdaughter (Elizabeth Sidney, later countess of Rutland), but neither the money which he needed nor blue blood. Elizabeth's anger soon cooled, but her lingering disapproval of his choice of wife and the new countess's own apparent wariness of politics meant that Essex lacked the support of having a wife at court. The resultant long periods of separation from his wife also perhaps help to explain Essex's dalliances with other women, including Elizabeth Southwell, a maid of honour (which resulted in the birth of his illegitimate son, Walter Devereux, at the end of 1591), and Elizabeth Stanley, countess of Derby, in 1596–7. Early in 1598 he was also reported as having revived a relationship with 'his fairest B', who was perhaps Elizabeth Brydges, the elder daughter of Giles Brydges, third Lord Chandos. Although sufficiently scandalous to infuriate the queen, it is unclear whether this was a sexual liaison. However, despite such behaviour by Essex at court, his wife apparently remained devoted to him and experienced pregnancies throughout the 1590s: Walter (*bap.* 21 January, *bur.* 19 Feb 1592), Penelope (*b.* 1593/4, *bur.* 27 June 1599), Henry (*bap.* 14 April 1595, *d.* 7 May 1596), Frances (*b.* 30 September 1599), later duchess of Somerset, and Dorothy (*b. c.*20 Dec 1600), later Lady Shirley, as well as stillbirths in 1596 and 1598.

The cooling animosity between Essex and Ralegh was also reflected in the way that they both supported Burghley's unsuccessful attempts in 1591 to shield leading presbyterians from Archbishop Whitgift's drive for ecclesiastical conformity. In the period after Leicester's death Essex had flirted with the idea of setting himself up as the new political champion of puritanism, but Whitgift's success in 1591–2—with the backing of Elizabeth—and his own concern to become involved in events overseas soon swayed him against this option. Although puritans continued to dedicate books to him throughout the 1590s, Essex restricted his support for puritanism after 1591

largely to low-key patronage of individuals such as William Hubbock, Nicholas Bownd, and Stephen Egerton. With the queen's encouragement he began to cultivate Whitgift, who was eager to woo him from unduly open support for the puritan cause and saw him, in the longer term, as a potentially useful ally in his own struggle with Burghley.

In 1590–91 relations between Essex and his former guardian remained strong. Even Essex's unsuccessful effort to persuade Elizabeth to recall the disgraced William Davison to replace Walsingham as secretary of state—which cut across Burghley's own plans for his son, Robert Cecil—failed to disturb the bond between them for long. In the spring of 1591 Essex looked to Burghley and Hatton, the two most senior lay councillors, for support in his bid to command an expeditionary force being sent to Normandy. Essex had tried to secure a similar command when troops were sent to Brittany in the previous year, but his private deal with Sir John Norris had fallen apart in the face of Elizabeth's intransigence. Now Burghley, in particular, had to persuade the queen to let her young favourite leave the court and lead an English army in an important joint operation with the forces of Henri IV. Essex had prepared the ground on the French side through his frequent correspondence with the king, his intimacy with the French ambassador in England, and his lavish hospitality for the visiting vicomte de Turenne in November 1590. However, Essex's appointment was not secured until Burghley convinced Elizabeth that the earl was the best choice to command the expedition. Appropriately, Essex mustered his cavalry for the queen on the day of his departure from London at Burghley's house in Covent Garden.

Essex's commission as lieutenant-general of the queen's army in Normandy was initially restricted to two months' duration and his instructions required him to heed the advice of hand-picked old advisers like Sir Thomas Leighton and Henry Killigrew. Nevertheless, this first independent command demonstrated that Essex was no longer merely a royal favourite who harboured military pretensions. From the start he was faced with delays and problems which lay beyond his control and was burdened by Elizabeth's unrealistic expectations about how quickly and easily the campaign could be conducted. Essex's army of 4000 men landed at Dieppe on 2 August 1591 but Henri IV did not move to join him, as promised. Instead, Essex and his cavalry were forced to traverse enemy territory on a four-day journey to meet the king near Compiègne on 19 August. Essex and his men feasted, talked, and competed in sports with the king and his entourage for several days. This meeting cemented a lifelong bond between the two men and confirmed Essex's deep Francophilia, but it also infuriated Elizabeth, who suspected that Essex would rather serve a king than a queen and might ignore her commands. Although the earl's willingness to strain the limits of his instructions also reflected the impracticality of her efforts to run the war from a distance, the queen's suspicions proved well-founded. Throughout his career, whenever he was frustrated by her chronic indecisiveness or her failure to heed his advice on military matters, Essex blamed Elizabeth's behaviour on the fact that she was a woman. For her part, Elizabeth resented Essex's absences from court. When he sought to extend his service in Normandy, she 'collecteth his so small desire to see her as shee doth requite him accordingly with crossing him in his most earnest desire' (UCL, Ogden MS 7/41, fol. 4v).

Essex did not rejoin his army and begin offensive operations until early September. Almost immediately he suffered a shattering blow when his younger brother, Walter, was killed in a skirmish near Rouen on 8 September. This tragedy was compounded by a series of stinging letters from Elizabeth, who wrote to vent her frustration at the slow pace of the campaign and her mistrust of Henri and his influence upon the earl. These criticisms hit Essex hard, especially as the army was wilting from the effects of sickness and was only being preserved from disintegration by the force of his personality and subsidies from his own over-stretched purse. For a few days he was on the point of complete physical and mental collapse. However, he soon regained a sense of purpose with the arrival of French forces under Marshal Biron and the capture of Gournai. Essex subsequently made two trips back to England early in October and in late November / early December to plead with Elizabeth for permission to continue the campaign and for additional men and resources. Both trips proved successful. In effect Elizabeth was forced to acknowledge that Essex needed freedom of action if he was to campaign effectively—and hence that her attempts to continue treating him like an errant young favourite, instead of a real general, must end. However, although politically necessary, Essex's absences also demoralized the army. His subsequent efforts to galvanize his men by fresh acts of heroism—despite Elizabeth's strict injunction to stay away from the front lines—proved unavailing. As the winter set in, it was obvious that the Normandy campaign was an utter failure.

Essex finally returned to court on 14 January 1592. Although he learned much, his first independent command had been a very painful and costly ordeal. His faith in the political and moral value of military service had also been dented. During his time away the death of Sir Christopher Hatton had thrown open the chancellorship of the University of Oxford. Essex had been mooted by some puritan dons as a potential chancellor after Leicester's death in 1588, but he had rejected the overture in favour of supporting the candidacy of his friend Hatton. On Hatton's death in November 1591 Essex clearly had enough support within the university to be elected as chancellor, especially as his secretary, Thomas Smith, the university orator, was busily canvassing fellows on his behalf. However, Elizabeth intervened to ensure that Thomas Sackville, Lord Buckhurst, was appointed instead, allegedly to punish Essex for his continuing desire to fight in France. Essex was also aggrieved that his efforts had brought him nothing but debts and discomfort, whereas the unsoldierly Sir Robert Cecil had become

a privy councillor. He also believed, unfairly, that Burghley had not done enough to support him during the campaign. These grievances, nourished by dismay at his failure to score a military triumph, were the seeds of Essex's increasingly awkward relations with Burghley and Cecil. Essex's efforts to escape being regarded again as merely the queen's favourite now put him on a collision course with the Cecils: he 'resolved to give this satisfaction to the queen, as to desist for a tyme from his cowrse of the warrs and to intend matters of state' (LPL, MS 653, fol. 3r). Accordingly he increased his involvement in intelligence-gathering, into which Francis Bacon and Thomas Phelippes had introduced him in early 1591. His recruitment of Francis's older brother, Anthony Bacon, to organize a spy network for him in 1592 was both a signal of his intent 'to intend matters of state' and a direct challenge to Burghley, for whom Bacon had previously worked. The harder Essex worked to prove his worth to join the privy council, the more convinced he became that Burghley's influence on Elizabeth was holding him back. On the other hand, he felt sufficiently forgiving towards Ralegh to treat him as a friend and stand as godfather to his son, Damerei, in April 1592. Such generosity helps to explain why even Essex's rivals usually regretted being on bad terms with him.

Privy councillor, 1593–1595 Essex was sworn of the privy council on 25 February 1593, just as a new parliament came into session. He immediately threw himself into committee work and the other meetings and paperwork which dominated council business. Having tried to make himself the perfect soldier, he now sought to become the perfect councillor. This conscientiousness reflected his usual mix of altruism and self-advancement: unable to do what he thought was necessary for England's future upon the battlefield, he instead sought to equip himself for influencing matters at the council table—while boosting his standing with Elizabeth in the process. Essex's goal was clearly to take over Burghley's role as the queen's chief adviser. Indeed Burghley's ill health during 1593 gave his efforts a sense of urgency: 'their chief hour glass [that is, Burghley] hath little sand left in it and doth run out still' (*Salisbury MSS*, 4.116). Inevitably Burghley resented the earl's aggressive manner and disliked his efforts to redirect policy towards more wholehearted support for Henri IV in France. Sparks flew between them in June when, at Anthony Bacon's urging, Essex displaced Burghley as employer of the spy Anthony Standen. Tensions peaked again in January 1594 when Essex accused one of the court physicians, Roderigo Lopez, of plotting to murder the queen. Burghley dismissed the idea out of hand and Elizabeth ridiculed Essex for suggesting it. The earl suffered another of his acute crises of confidence, shutting himself in his chamber for two days. However, he was soon able to produce new evidence against Lopez and the doctor was arrested, interrogated, condemned, and ultimately executed. This triumph put Burghley on the back foot and earned Essex much popular acclaim. It also helped to create the conditions for a *modus vivendi* between Essex and Burghley, in which Sir Robert Cecil—

loyal to his father, desperate to win the still-vacant post of secretary of state, and yet also eager to co-operate with the queen's undisputed favourite—played the part of a bridge-builder.

The basis of this accommodation was a rough division of political interests. Essex largely accepted Burghley's dominating influence in domestic politics and patronage and in matters relating to Ireland. He recognized that, after more than thirty years in power, Burghley's hold on the levers of patronage was too well encrusted to be challenged without a struggle and that this could only distract from what he regarded as more pressing events overseas. Essex also believed that Burghley would soon die and calculated that the political weight which he gained by focusing on foreign and military affairs would inevitably enable him to succeed to the lord treasurer's influence when the time came. Essex therefore threw himself into military administration, the appointment of army officers, intelligence-gathering, and an ever-growing number of foreign correspondences—areas of often frenetic activity which reflected his conviction that confronting Spain was England's most urgent task and which provided him with a steady supply of the political ammunition which he needed to impress this view upon a reluctant queen. For his part, Burghley was apparently happy to scale back his involvement in European affairs beyond those regions nearest to England, content to be rid of the expense involved and feeling increasingly out of sympathy with constant foreign demands for more English aid.

Although Essex took over correspondence with Florence (through James Guicciardini) in 1593 and invested much time and money in intelligence-gathering from 1592, the full extent of his ambition to become a statesman of truly international significance emerged only in 1595. In that year he took advantage of Thomas Smith's entry into royal service to expand his secretariat from two to four, his 'confident' secretary Edward Reynoldes being joined by three high-powered new men: Henry Wotton, William Temple, and Henry Cuffe. The return to France of Antonio Perez, the former secretary of Philip II of Spain whom Essex had hosted and regularly debriefed over the preceding eighteen months, also gave him the opportunity to win royal approval to station his own semi-diplomatic agent at Venice. Dr Henry Hawkyns served there as Essex's—and Elizabeth's—chargé d'affaires from December 1595 until March 1598. Essex subsequently employed Sir Thomas Chaloner to perform a similar function in Florence. Although the evidence is thin, it seems that he also employed resident agents in various parts of the Holy Roman empire, including a Monsieur le Douz at Vienna in 1596. As well as sending regular intelligence reports, such men were required to create elaborate dossiers to brief Essex on the intricacies of individual foreign states. Young gentlemen whom he sponsored during their continental tours, such as Francis Davison, were encouraged to do the same. Essex was not only anxious for information to help him better understand European politics but also believed that such work would train men who could administer the more expansive foreign policy

which he envisaged himself as presiding over in the future: 'the cheife ende of my employinge yow be rather your inablynge hereafter then your present service' (Hammer, 'Essex and Europe', 374). Essex made similar promises to Robert Naunton, who served as his intermediary with Perez in France between 1596 and 1598.

Part of the reason for Essex's success in projecting himself upon what he often called 'the stage of Christendom' was the belief abroad—which his agents diligently fostered—that he was the obvious choice to succeed Burghley as Elizabeth's dominant councillor and that he was committed to making England play a full part in European affairs. Another reason was that Essex supported the idea of toleration for Catholics in England—as long as they opposed Spain and Spanish influence over the papacy. Although Essex remained resolutely protestant, even puritan, in his own religious beliefs, he began to position himself as a champion of toleration from at least the time of Standen's return to England in 1593. Despite his bellicosity towards Spanish 'tyranny', many of Essex's friends leaned towards the old religion, as did many of the foreign visitors whom he hosted on the queen's behalf: Perez, for example, was quietly allowed to hold mass in Essex House. By 1595 Essex's reputation was such that the Jesuit Thomas Wright surrendered himself into the earl's protection in June, and poet and Catholic convert Henry Constable was moved to begin corresponding with him about toleration from France.

Essex also played an increasingly dominant role in military matters, although he never attained the monopoly which he might have wanted. At times of crisis he was dispatched to oversee preparations at the coast, often in tandem with the lord admiral, Charles Howard, Lord Howard of Effingham. Organizing major military operations entailed much paperwork and taxed his stamina to the limit. In March 1596 one of his servants complained that 'he is in continewall labour. I thinke the husbandman endureth not more toyle' (LPL, MS 656, fol. 75r). Essex deliberately set out to become the 'great patron of the warrs' (Hatfield House, Cecil MS 62/71), encouraging army officers to regard him as their chief advocate and the key to securing new commands. When new armies were raised or fresh amphibious expeditions were launched, as in 1595, Essex was also able to draw out hundreds of gentlemen volunteers who served as unpaid soldiers and gave English forces an added cutting edge. Essex supplemented his own judgement and experience in military matters with expert advice from Sir Roger Williams (until his death in late 1595) and Sir Francis Vere (until he fell out with Essex in mid-1597), as well as aristocratic friends like Charles Blount, Lord Mountjoy, and Lord Willoughby. He also received advice on the laws of war from Alberico Gentili and Matthew Sutcliffe. However, Essex's relationship with Norris never recovered from the collapse of their private arrangement concerning the command of troops sent to Brittany in 1590.

One of Essex's few serious ventures into the field of high-level domestic patronage was his consistent support for Francis Bacon's unsuccessful attempts to secure high legal office between 1593 and 1596. Essex repeatedly sought Burghley's backing for these suits, recognizing the lord treasurer's influence in such matters and believing that a united front would overcome Elizabeth's lingering doubts about Bacon. Burghley ultimately rebuffed Bacon when he sought to become attorney-general in 1593–4, fuelling fresh recriminations with Essex. However, both men agreed to support Bacon's subsequent suit to become solicitor-general—until the queen declared her refusal to fill the post if their united front was maintained. Elizabeth complained that acceding to their request would make it seem that she was governed by her two councillors and would undermine her princely authority. Burghley promptly withdrew his backing for Bacon. Essex fumed at Burghley's defection and, characteristically, redoubled his own efforts for Bacon because he believed that he was honour-bound to support his friend, despite the faint chance of success. Essex's repeated efforts to urge the queen into appointing Bacon salved his own conscience, but merely delayed the inevitable and underlined Burghley's continuing mastery of court politics. It was equally characteristic of Essex that he compensated Bacon for his failure from his own pocket—even though he remained chronically short of money—and continued to believe that he would one day be properly rewarded for his principled conduct, in contrast to what he regarded as the selfish expediency of other courtiers. For her part, the queen was irritated by Essex's deliberate tactic of harping on about Bacon, but was prepared to forgive him much because of the zeal which he showed in her service.

Although Essex believed that Elizabeth herself would heap riches and responsibility upon him once Burghley died, his actions were also partly conditioned by the belief that he had a secret trump card. During the early 1590s James VI of Scotland became increasingly angry at Elizabeth's blatant interference in his realm, and especially at her support for the troublesome earl of Bothwell in 1593–4. Since this policy was pursued on the queen's orders by Burghley and Cecil, the king regarded them as his enemies. By contrast, Essex's well-known rivalry with Burghley, more cosmopolitan outlook, and concern for events which would follow Elizabeth's death made him the obvious choice to become the champion of James's claim to the English throne. At least as early as June 1593 Anthony Bacon was exploiting his contacts in Scotland to open indirect communication with the king on Essex's behalf. By early 1594 this 'mutuelle intelligence' (BL, Add. MS 4125, fol. 38r) had clearly expanded to encompass Essex's commitment to support the king as Elizabeth's successor and the king's promise of substantial rewards for Essex in return. This alignment—orchestrated through third parties like Bacon, David Foulis, and James Hudson—endured to the end of Essex's life and gradually became an open secret within the British Isles and abroad.

Although the details of his political manoeuvrings were known to only a few close associates, Essex enjoyed a public profile at home and abroad during the 1590s which was second only to that of the queen. One index of the power

of his name—and of his deliberate cultivation of a reputation for aristocratic munificence—was the half-dozen or so printed works which were dedicated to him each year after he had established himself as Leicester's successor as royal favourite. Not even Elizabeth herself received as many dedications as Essex during the 1590s. These works included manuals on war and honour, translations of foreign or classical texts, and numerous puritan religious tracts. Among the latter were three separate works by George Gifford, Nicholas Bownd's classic sabbatarian tract *The Doctrine of the Sabbath* (1595), and John Rainolds's monumental *De Romanae ecclesiae idolatria* (1596). In at least one instance Essex may also have contributed to a published work. Some contemporaries claimed that he was the real author of the epistle to the reader in Henry Savile's *The Ende of Nero and Beginninge of Galba* (1591), a landmark translation of key works by the classical Roman historian Tacitus. Even if this claim is erroneous, Essex was certainly an eager student of the new 'politic' history which was being derived from the works of Tacitus and sought to apply its insights to his own political actions. He also had a long and close relationship with the polymathic Savile, whom he helped to become provost of Eton and who in turn provided the earl with expert scholarly advice and perhaps acted as a talent scout for him at Oxford. Thanks to Savile and Thomas Smith and various contacts at Cambridge, such as William Whitaker, Essex had a very high reputation at the universities and was a regular recruiter of promising students and dons. In addition to performing research services or undergoing 'inablynge' overseas, Essex's patronage of university men included employment among his chaplains. More than thirty of his chaplains have been identified, including William Alabaster, John Buckeridge, George Downham, Richard Harris, Samuel Hieron, George Montaigne, Leonell Sharpe, John Spencer, Owen Wood, and Anthony Wotton. By the mid-1590s, thanks to his burgeoning relationship with Archbishop Whitgift, Essex's patronage of clergymen also extended to winning advancement for men who sought to become bishops. Beneficiaries of his support included Richard Fletcher, Anthony Rudd, Thomas Bilson, Gervase Babington, and Richard Vaughan, while his endorsement of Martin Heton and Robert Some proved unsuccessful. In late 1596 Essex also joined Whitgift in backing Richard Bancroft to succeed Fletcher as bishop of London. Given Bancroft's reputation as a notorious anti-puritan crusader, Essex's willingness to see him take control of the key diocese of London reflected his own desire to side with Whitgift against Burghley over this appointment and his belief that Bancroft would keep his promise not to persecute puritans under the earl's protection. It was characteristic of Essex's high political ambitions that he entered into such an arrangement with Whitgift and Bancroft, and testimony to his success that the deal stuck until the time of Essex's own final downfall.

'A man of great designs', 1595–1597 Essex's grand political designs were based upon the expectation that he would soon simply take over from Burghley and persuade Elizabeth, using his charm and intellect, to commit more resources to war on the continent. Events in 1595 proved these assumptions naïve. Although Burghley (as chancellor of the university) presumably approved the grand bestowing of honorary MAs at Cambridge which Essex arranged in February 1595, they clashed repeatedly during the remainder of the year. In May, when news finally broke that Essex was the father of Elizabeth Southwell's son, an attempt was made to capitalize on Elizabeth's fury by pushing for Cecil to become secretary of state. Although the appointment was stopped at the last minute, it demonstrated that Cecil was now a genuine rival to Essex for Burghley's political mantle. In response Essex launched a propaganda campaign later in the year to demonstrate his own credentials to succeed Burghley. This effort included a remarkable display at the accession day tournament at Whitehall in November, where he risked outshining the queen by staging an entertainment (perhaps written for him by Francis Bacon) which dramatized his talents for the crowd. Early in 1596 Essex began to circulate a letter of travel advice for the earl of Rutland which was also designed to highlight his statesmanlike qualities. This proved highly successful and ultimately migrated into print in 1633. Although Essex himself wrote a series of private letters of travel advice to Rutland in late 1595, this document was probably edited for public consumption by his newly enlarged secretariat or by Bacon.

Essex's campaign to win broad support for his claim to become the queen's next chief minister was both encouraged and complicated by a deepening disagreement over policy. During 1595 his continuing commitment to Henri IV put him increasingly at odds with the queen, who was now determined to withdraw all remaining English troops from France. In Essex's mind the growing antipathy of Elizabeth and Burghley towards the French king was blinding them to the vital necessity of sustaining the war abroad. Only by genuinely pooling resources with its French and Dutch allies, he believed, could England ensure that the Spanish menace was kept at arm's length and, ultimately, defeated. Essex was so upset by the queen's stance that he secretly instructed his friend Sir Henry Unton, who went to France as ambassador in December 1595, to exaggerate the difficulties faced by the French king in order to force Elizabeth to change her mind. However, even this had little impact upon the queen.

Essex was also dismayed in the middle of 1595 when Elizabeth and the Cecils expressed scepticism about his intelligence reports from Spain, which seemed to show that a new invasion of England was being prepared. Essex's interpretation of the intelligence was actually incorrect, but this became irrelevant after a minor Spanish raid on Cornwall late in July encouraged unanimous support for a pre-emptive strike against Spain. The operation was initiated by Lord Admiral Howard but it expanded dramatically in size when Essex was appointed to share the command early in 1596. Essex poured his resources—and those of his friends and followers—into the venture because he not only intended to neutralize the Spanish fleet but also harboured the secret intention

to forestall Elizabeth's steady disengagement from the continent by seizing a Spanish port and garrisoning it. Essex spelt out this intention—which ran directly contrary to the queen's orders—in a letter which he left behind to be delivered to the council only when the fleet was beyond recall. When Elizabeth decided to cancel the expedition in May, Essex was mortified, especially as preparations had already been delayed during April by a bungled effort to relieve the French garrison at Calais. Essex took the lead in this operation (much to the lord admiral's dismay), but Elizabeth's dithering ensured the port's loss to the Spanish and cast a stain upon the earl's honour. This made him more determined than ever to make the most of any opportunity for action. His attitude towards the queen and her direction of the war was now one of acute frustration: 'I know I shall never do her service butt against her will' (LPL, MS 657, fol. 140r).

Elizabeth ultimately permitted the expedition to proceed and it finally sailed from Plymouth on 3 June 1596. The fleet headed straight for Cadiz. On 21 June it destroyed a Spanish fleet anchored in the bay and landed troops who stormed the city. Essex helped to lead the naval assault before landing in the first boat ashore and leading his troops over the city walls and through the streets. This day's action was the most complete and dramatic English victory of the war against Spain. However, Essex failed to convince the lord admiral that Cadiz should be held in defiance of the queen's instructions. The vast riches which were plundered from the city also made many officers anxious to return home. With great reluctance Essex agreed that Cadiz should be burned and abandoned. The fleet subsequently raided the town of Faro, where the plunder included 178 books from the bishop's library. Essex later donated many of these books to Thomas Bodley's new library at Oxford. Delayed by ensuring the safe return of two captured Spanish warships, Essex did not return to Plymouth until 8 August. By then the queen was already furious about how much of the plunder had been hidden from royal officials. When Burghley and Cecil (newly appointed as secretary of state) launched an investigation, Essex despaired at Elizabeth's lack of gratitude for the victory, especially as he had himself spent so much and taken so little. Ultimately, a political explosion was averted and the earl's conduct on the voyage was vindicated. However, the failure of his plan to garrison Cadiz meant that the expedition had wounded Spanish national pride without inflicting long-term damage. Philip II's determination to avenge the humiliation of Cadiz resulted in the hasty dispatch of a fleet towards England in October. Although this was soon overwhelmed by an autumn storm England was shocked by the unexpected danger and remained in the grip of invasion fever until the end of November. Essex played a key role in the realm's preparations for defence, confirming his new status as the queen's chief military commander.

Essex's frustration at Cadiz did not mark the end of his efforts to redirect the queen's war policy. Thwarted in his hopes of holding the city, he tried to whip up public support for his plans—and bolster his own reputation as what

Edmund Spenser now called 'great England's glory and the world's wide wonder' (*Prothalamion*, 1.146)—by directing Henry Cuffe to write a 'True relacion' of the victory at Cadiz. Elizabeth prevented this tract from being printed in London, but related documents were circulated in manuscript within England and abroad. Essex also unsuccessfully tried to use his contacts with the Dutch and French, and with the City of London, to press Elizabeth into using the returning army for an assault on Calais. More subtly Essex retained the beard which he had grown on the voyage, which henceforth became a trademark feature of his appearance. The new image—in effect, the 'face of Cadiz'—was formalized in portraits painted by Marcus Gheeraerts the younger and Isaac Oliver, and in various later engravings which closely followed the Oliver pattern. These paintings confirm the description of Essex given by a Venetian visitor in late 1596: 'fair-skinned, tall, but wiry', sporting a beard, 'which he used not to wear', and 'right modest, courteous, and humane' (*CSP Venice, 1592–1603*, 9.238).

Although he had finally established himself as the central figure in England's war effort, Essex succumbed to another bout of severe depression during the early months of 1597, alternately seeking to abandon the court and shutting himself in his chamber there for days on end. Despite all his efforts and all he had achieved in 1596, he had still failed to commit Elizabeth to wholehearted war on the continent. His ambition of being seen as the only viable successor to Burghley had also been thoroughly dented by Cecil's appointment as secretary of state. Worse, despite the superficial amity which had reappeared by the end of the year, a growing coalition of councillors and courtiers was now clearly determined to oppose Essex, while he himself was virtually alone. This disparity soon became obvious when Henry Brooke, eighth Lord Cobham, sought to succeed his father as warden of the Cinque Ports. Essex despised Cobham, but his best efforts to support the rival candidacy of Sir Robert Sidney could do no more than delay Cobham's appointment. Although he apparently still considered withdrawing from politics as late as the end of March, Essex could not abandon the path to which he had committed himself: to do so would be a craven submission to despair and a betrayal of honour and of those who counted upon his support. He was also attracted by Elizabeth's offer to appoint him master of the ordnance, especially as the realm's whole military administration was thrown into crisis when Sir Thomas Sherley 'broke credit' on 8 March. Essex was appointed to the post on 18 March, with a remit to tackle the rampant corruption which he had repeatedly claimed was impeding the war effort. In a letter of 4 October 1596, which has been much quoted by modern scholars, Francis Bacon had explictly warned Essex about the political dangers of accepting any military post:

> keep it in substance, but abolish it in shows to the Queen. For her Majesty loveth peace. Next, she loveth not charge. Thirdly, that kind of dependence maketh a suspected greatness ... Let that be a sleeping honour awhile, and cure the Queen's mind in that point.　(Spedding, 2.43)

Essex's acceptance of the mastership of the ordnance showed that he could not adapt himself to the sort of calculated political manoeuvring which Bacon suggested. Even though he spent fully eight days haggling with Elizabeth over the terms of his patent, his own self-identity as a soldier, the urging of friends such as Lord Willoughby, and the obvious need for drastic action compelled him to accept the office.

Although his eagerness to be seen as a soldier dismayed Bacon, Essex returned to the political fray with a specific agenda. Dealing with Cecil and Ralegh, he struck a bargain which would allow him to execute his illicit strategy of 1596 with a fresh fleet and army and full royal approval in 1597. The final terms of the arrangement—which Elizabeth was prevailed upon to implement—were thrashed out after a dinner at Essex House on 18 April. Essex was assigned the task of neutralizing the continuing threat from Spain and given the chance to put into practice his strategy of seizing and holding a port in Spain. This would not only force the Spanish to pull many of their forces home but also serve as a base for English ships to blockade the Spanish coast, cutting off the vital supply of New World silver and diverting it into Elizabeth's coffers. Ralegh would serve as one of Essex's subordinates on the new expedition and be restored to his old position as captain of the queen's guard. Cecil was to receive the office of chancellor of the duchy of Lancaster, while the lord admiral ceded command of the expedition to Essex and received lucrative grants from the queen. Essex gambled that he could achieve sufficient military success abroad to counter—and overmatch—the benefits which he was yielding to his rivals at home.

Essex sought to give himself the best possible chance of succeeding in this gamble. As well as reorganizing the militia to improve its ability to counter a Spanish landing, he readied a fleet and army which were superior to those of the previous year. The expedition sailed from Plymouth on 10 July, but was battered by a storm and driven back to port. Essex was so determined not to abandon the voyage that he pushed his ship almost to breaking point, barely making it back to Falmouth. Despite Essex's fears that she would cancel the operation after this near-disaster, Elizabeth grudgingly agreed to continue. However, adverse winds kept the fleet from sailing and the soldiers began to fall sick in large numbers. Ultimately Essex was forced to disband all but a small part of his army. When the fleet finally departed on 17 August Essex's planned strategy had therefore already been rendered impracticable. It soon became clear that the fleet lacked even the resources necessary for attacking the Spanish fleet at Ferrol, the primary purpose for which Elizabeth approved the expedition. Instead, Essex and his subordinates decided to sail to the Azores and lie in wait for the Spanish silver fleet. Essex himself had dismissed this sort of hit-or-miss enterprise in the previous year as merely 'idle wanderings upon the sea' (BL, Add. MS 74287, fol. 13*v*). Now he was forced to gamble all on the hope of capturing enough Spanish silver to encourage Elizabeth to give him another chance at attacking Spain in the following year. Unfortunately, a purely naval venture placed an overwhelming burden on Essex's very limited experience of command at sea. His shortcomings as an admiral contributed to a showdown with Ralegh at Fayal in September, when partisans of the earl demanded that Ralegh be charged with mutiny for landing troops before Essex arrived to oversee the operation. The fleet also suffered the cruel misfortune of failing to intercept the Spanish silver fleet at Terceira by a mere three hours. The final indignity occurred when Essex's exhausted fleet straggled home at the end of October only to discover that the Spanish fleet—which had not been drawn from Ferrol to help defend the Azores—was almost on the point of assaulting Falmouth. Once again England was plunged into an invasion scare and Essex was forced to improvise defensive measures with extreme speed. However, it soon emerged that the same wind which had scattered Essex's returning fleet had also dispersed the Spanish. The alarm was quickly over, but it underlined the utter failure of Essex's Azores or 'Islands' voyage. Many of his followers were ruined by the costs of taking part in the expedition and his military reputation was severely dented.

Essex's dismay at his failure and at the advantages gained by his rivals who had stayed at home made him acutely sensitive about his personal honour. This sensitivity soon turned to fury when he learned that the lord admiral had been created earl of Nottingham and that the new earl's patent of creation seemed to credit him with the victory at Cadiz. To Essex it appeared that his triumph of 1596 was being stolen from him. He insisted that Elizabeth amend the patent or that Nottingham surrender it. When these demands produced no result Essex withdrew from court by 9 November. Although he initially pleaded ill health, it soon became clear that he would not return to the queen's service until she gave him some form of public reward to salve his wounded pride. Such behaviour reinforced the claims of his rivals that he was a dangerous maverick and undermined the queen's trust in his judgement and commitment to her service. However, in Essex's mind, the terrible political cost of defending his honour actually made it all the more virtuous for him to take this stand. By risking so much, he showed his true commitment to honour and should be rewarded accordingly. Although the lord admiral resigned the lord stewardship in protest at Essex's behaviour, Elizabeth ultimately gave way in this test of wills. After more than a week of argument about the wording of the patent she appointed Essex to the vacant office of earl marshal on 28 December 1597. This post ensured that Essex regained precedence over the lord admiral and made him the queen's chief arbiter of honour.

The fall of Essex, 1598–1601 By the start of 1598 Essex was still 'a man of great designs' (De Maisse, 7), but his ambitions to bestride the European stage seemed increasingly at odds with his deteriorating position in domestic politics. His ability to sway the queen on matters of importance now appeared highly questionable, and the resolve of his opponents—including Burghley, Cecil, Nottingham,

Cobham, Ralegh, and Buckhurst—had been strengthened by recent events. More importantly, his commitment to waging aggressive war against Spain in partnership with the French and the Dutch now risked leaving him stranded by the changing tide of European politics. By late 1597 Essex's old comrade in arms, Henri IV of France, was determined to secure peace with Spain. This decision meant the final abandonment of the triple alliance with England and the Dutch, and heightened tensions between the king and his protestant subjects. Both the Dutch and the Huguenots looked to Essex, their chief supporter in England, to lobby Elizabeth to ensure that Henri's action would not endanger their interests. For his part, unlike Elizabeth or Burghley, Essex had lived his entire life under the shadow of Spanish 'tyranny'. He believed that Spain simply could not be trusted to maintain a peace unless it had first been driven into submission by force of arms. Elizabeth's strong interest in following Henri's lead therefore challenged Essex on a number of levels.

The need to confer with England's French and Dutch allies kept Cecil, the key figure among Essex's rivals, overseas between mid-February and the end of April. Essex even took over Cecil's duties as secretary of state for part of this period. However, he also promised not to take any action which would harm Cecil's interests during his absence. Despite the regularity with which Cecil and others had profited from his own absences abroad and despite urging from Francis Bacon 'to put your sickle into another's harvest' (Spedding, 2.96), Essex refused to breach this arrangement. Instead, he sought to pacify the queen's notorious dislike for his mother—with very limited success. Cecil's return and the signing of the Franco-Spanish peace at Vervins on 2 May 1598 (os) effectively removed Essex's room for manoeuvre. Already Essex had been accused of preventing England from making peace. According to William Camden, Burghley had become so infuriated with the earl's stance that on one occasion he had pulled out a psalm book and quoted at him the verse that 'men of blood shall not live out half their days' (Camden, 555). The queen was also incensed that opposition from the Dutch, whom Essex defended, was tying her hands. In response to such criticisms Essex once again sought to influence political debate by appealing over the heads of the queen and his opponents at court to a broader public audience. He wrote an impassioned and lengthy rebuttal of the 'ugly and odious aspersion' that he sought 'to keepe the state of England in continuall warre', defending his own past actions and arguing the terrible dangers of making peace with an enemy which had consistently acted with perfidy and malice (Devereux, *Apologie*, sig. A1r). Written in the deniable format of a private letter to Anthony Bacon, this 'Apologie' was secretly disseminated in manuscript form. When the circulation of the document was brought into question, Essex denied all knowledge and blamed its spread on the excessive enthusiasm of his friend Fulke Greville and unnamed servants. Essex's 'Apologie' proved immensely successful and enjoyed very wide circulation, although many of the manuscript copies which survive may actually have been made after his death. An authorized printed edition of the 'Apologie' was published in 1603 and quickly spawned a Dutch translation.

The increasingly acrimonious debate about future royal policy came to a head at a meeting on 30 June or 1 July 1598 when Elizabeth sought to choose a new lord deputy for Ireland. When the queen suggested that Essex's uncle Sir William Knollys should fill the vacant post Essex sought to prevent the loss of a key ally at court by nominating Cecil's friend Sir George Carew. Angered at Elizabeth's scornful response, Essex turned his back on her. This breach of protocol infuriated Elizabeth and she struck him across the head. He instinctively reached for his sword, only to be held back by the lord admiral. Before leaving the room, Essex told the queen and his dumbfounded colleagues that 'he neither could nor would put up so great an afront and indignity, neither would he have taken it at King Henry the Eighth his hands' (Camden, 556). He may have compounded the disaster—if the oral tradition reported by the young Edward Hyde (later earl of Clarendon) is accurate—by rebuking the queen with the comment that 'she was as crooked in her disposition as in her carcass' (Hyde, 192). Although none of the sources for the confrontation is precisely contemporary, it is clear that his explosion arose from frustrations and anger which had been building for several years. In Essex's mind everything which he had done to advance the queen's service had been met with rejection or quibbling while rewards had flowed in profusion to those men who carped at him from the safety of the court and ventured nothing of their own. Unwilling to see the true nature of his own failings, he believed that this injustice ultimately stemmed from the queen, whose female qualities made her unduly sympathetic to the inglorious counsels of his adversaries and unable, or unwilling, to recognize the conspicuous virtue of his actions.

Essex's angry withdrawal from the court punctured for ever the notion of his indispensability to government which he had cultivated so painfully during the first half of the decade. However, the council could not yet function fully effectively without him. More importantly, despite his outrageous behaviour, Elizabeth was not yet sure how to live without him. Less than a fortnight after Essex had withdrawn to his country estate at Wanstead messengers were sent to sound him out about returning to court. Friends of Essex wrote letters urging him to make his peace with the queen. Most famously the lord keeper, Sir Thomas Egerton, urged him to conquer his false pride and show the obedience owed by all the queen's subjects. Essex, however, rejected the suggestion that he should simply submit, raising dangerous questions about royal power in the process: 'what, cannot princes err? cannot subjects receive wrong? is an earthly power or authority infinite?' (Birch, 2.387). Manuscript copies of this epistolary exchange (many of them redated from 15 and 18 July to 15 and 18 October) were subsequently disseminated among Essex's friends and gradually followed his 'Apologie' into wider circulation. Together these documents formed a kind of political manifesto, which continued to attract interest, and recopying, during the first half of the seventeenth century.

Such prideful behaviour made it impossible for Essex to share fully in the great redistribution of offices which followed Burghley's death on 4 August 1598. Although chosen as chancellor of Cambridge University in Burghley's place on 25 August, he refused to return to council meetings until Elizabeth gave him a private audience at which he could air his grievances. News of the disaster at Blackwater on 14 August, which seemed to herald the complete loss of Ireland, and of the death of Philip II of Spain a month later, made Essex's participation in council business even more urgent than before. However, although he was willing to tender his advice directly to the queen in writing he would not rejoin his colleagues at the council table until Elizabeth demonstrated to him—and them—that she was once again willing to place special trust in him and allow him the kind of latitude she would not permit to any other subject. Essex clearly recognized that the military emergency in Ireland put him in a strong position, for he was not only master of the ordnance, but also the leading patron of army officers and the realm's most famous soldier. This calculation proved correct. Despite the complications caused by the queen's fury about the secret marriage between Henry Wriothesley, earl of Southampton, and Elizabeth Vernon (respectively, Essex's friend and cousin), concerted efforts were made to arrange his return to court by early September. In the end, the breakthrough came when Essex succumbed to a bout of fever, which allowed Elizabeth to put aside her fury and play the role of concerned sovereign. She sent her own physician to treat him and a succession of messengers to gather reports on his progress. By 10 September Essex was sufficiently recovered to attend a council meeting for the first time since the end of June. He met the queen two days later.

Although it seemed that Essex had again succeeded in bending the queen to his will, the remarkable favour which she had always displayed towards him was now distinctly brittle. Although he expected to be given Burghley's old mastership of the court of wards, the office was never granted to him. The fact that many observers of the court believed that Essex would receive the post made the queen's failure to confer it upon him all the more unsettling. During late October and early November, Essex was able to win more positive comment from the revelation of the so-called Squire plot. This conspiracy allegedly involved separate attempts to kill both Elizabeth and Essex by smearing poison on, respectively, a saddle and a chair. The attempt on Essex's life supposedly occurred during the Azores expedition, while the fleet was near Fayal. Like the Lopez plot of 1594, the sensational charges against Edward Squire excited public outrage against Spain and dealt a severe blow to any prospect of peace talks. The news also gave a fresh boost to popular perceptions of Essex's status as a hero of the war against Spain and as the queen's most loyal lieutenant. However, despite his apparent recovery of royal favour, Essex remained at odds with the queen and most of his conciliar colleagues over the issue of Ireland. Anxious to preserve his own status as the indisputable colossus in English military affairs, he criticized previous campaigns in Ireland and stubbornly rejected the idea that anyone else was suitable for such a command, even his friend Lord Mountjoy. Inevitably this constant belittling of others and boasting of his own capabilities soon put him in the position of having to accept the command in Ireland himself or backing down and allowing another to take the lead in what was to be England's greatest military effort since 1588. As a soldier who still dreamed of winning martial glory and the political rewards which he believed this would bring, Essex could not bear to let the opportunity pass to another. He also recognized that this was also his only chance to recapture the political initiative from his rivals.

Although it was clear that Essex would go to Ireland by early November, Elizabeth did not confirm his appointment there—as lord lieutenant, rather than merely lord deputy—until 30 December. The size of his army and details of his commission remained under debate almost until he left London on 27 March 1599. He arrived in Dublin on 14 April, having almost drowned during his crossing of the Irish Sea. Essex intended a short, sharp campaign. He planned a three-pronged assault to crush the earl of Tyrone's forces in Ulster and ensure his own speedy return to England. However, it was soon clear that neither the resources at hand nor the state of the countryside would permit an immediate attack on Tyrone. Essex and his advisers therefore postponed the Ulster operation until June and instead launched a sweep through Leinster, which began on 9 May. Essex continued this expedition into Munster, capturing the supposedly impregnable Cahir Castle on 30 May and relieving a fort at Askeaton in early June. These operations safeguarded southern Ireland from the rumoured threat of a Spanish landing, but consumed time, money, and supplies. By the time Essex returned to Dublin on 11 July he was exhausted, sick, and disillusioned by the tenacity of Irish resistance. He could envisage victory only by a long and costly war of attrition—precisely the sort of struggle which he wanted to avoid, given his earlier promises of rapid success and his growing belief that his opponents at home were poisoning the queen against him. Elizabeth needed little prompting to lash out at Essex. Already angry over the vast cost of his expedition, she was further enraged by Essex's profligacy in bestowing knighthoods, demands for more men and supplies, and lack of action against Tyrone. In fact, Essex had concluded that he lacked the numbers to attack Tyrone, even before Sir Conyers Clifford led his troops into a bloody ambush in the Curlew Mountains on 5 August. Believing that he was being stabbed in the back by his enemies at home, Essex's thoughts increasingly focused on leaving Ireland and settling matters at court as quickly as possible. Secret overtures were made to Tyrone through Captain Thomas Lee, while Essex himself even considered shipping his army to Wales and taking the field against his domestic enemies. Ultimately, such open treason proved too large a step to take. Despite his continuing protestations about the impossibility of confronting Tyrone, Essex finally obeyed the queen's command to march north at the end of August. Outnumbered and unable to outflank the enemy, he agreed to Tyrone's request for a parley on 7 September. The two earls met at Bellaclynthe ford, near Drumconragh, and talked privately for half an hour, their horses standing belly-deep in the water. Tyrone later told a Spanish priest that he almost convinced Essex to turn against Elizabeth, but Essex could not reconcile himself to becoming an ally of Spain (*CSP Spain*, 1587–1603, 4.685). In the absence of testimony from a third party it is difficult to judge whether Tyrone's claim was merely empty boasting. Nevertheless, the two leaders subsequently agreed a truce and Essex dispersed his army and began medical treatment. However, it was soon apparent that Elizabeth would not accept Essex's actions. Alarmed by the furious tone of her letters, he decided to return to court immediately, despite her recent order to the contrary.

Trusting in speed rather than numbers Essex sailed for England with only a few companions on 24 September 1599, reaching the court at Nonsuch on the morning of 28 September. Still muddied from the ride, he rushed into the queen's chamber. Famously, he found her incompletely dressed and with her hair in disarray. A more formal meeting occurred about 11 a.m., by which time both were more suitably attired. All seemed to be going well. However, at their third meeting, after lunch, Elizabeth began reproving Essex and ordered him to explain his behaviour to members of the council. This was the last time that Essex and Elizabeth ever saw each other. He was confined to his chamber late that evening. The next afternoon he spent several hours defending himself before his conciliar colleagues, before being sent to York House as a prisoner. While the council began drawing up charges against him, Essex began to collapse mentally and physically. Not only was he drained by his efforts in Ireland, but the sense of mission which had sustained him for so long now deserted him and he began to realize that his career might be ending in abject failure. On 29 November the council excoriated Essex's proceedings in Ireland in Star Chamber and publicly justified his imprisonment, but more serious action was put on hold until it was clear whether his sickness would prove terminal. On 18–19 December and at Christmas it seemed that Essex was on the verge of death, prompting several churches in London to ring their bells or offer special prayers for him—infuriating both the queen and the council. Essex survived and gradually recovered, but he was only a shadow of the man who had been such a dynamic figure in the mid-1590s.

In early February 1600—in the wake of a new scandal involving the sale of an equestrian portrait of Essex, engraved by Thomas Cockson, which described him as 'Vertue's honor', 'Grace's servant', and, most ominously, 'God's elected'—it was finally decided that Essex would be tried in Star Chamber on 13 February. However, when the earl sent her a submissive letter Elizabeth cancelled the trial and a long-running effort to frame charges of treason against him was also put aside. On the evening of 20 March he was allowed to return to Essex House, albeit under the oversight of Sir Richard Berkeley. Early in May, a printer's attempt to publish a pirate edition of the 'Apologie'—which Essex immediately disowned—attracted further attention to his anomalous status as an uncondemned detainee in his own house. A special hearing was therefore arranged at York House on 5 June, at which Essex was charged with various acts of insubordination during his time in Ireland. The hearing lasted from 9 a.m. until 8 p.m. Those speaking against Essex included Francis Bacon, whose attack on the earl seemed to suggest that he positively relished the task. Although Essex's fortitude in enduring the speeches against him drew general admiration, his detailed rebuttal of the charges angered the commissioners even as it cheered his supporters in the audience. Essex was sequestered from all his offices and ordered to remain under house arrest during the queen's pleasure. Although the sentence brought tears from many in the audience, Elizabeth soon began to loosen the shackles. Essex was allowed to spend time at his wife's country house at Barn Elms and, on 1 July, was relieved of Berkeley's presence. Despite Elizabeth's continuing fury over his prodigality with knighthoods in Ireland and fresh efforts by his enemies on the council during July to find evidence of treason (especially involving John Hayward's dedication to Essex of *The First Part of the Life and Reign of King Henry the III* in February 1599), he was finally granted his liberty on 26 August.

Essex's release prohibited him from going to court, which meant that his political career was finished—and that his enemies were determined to prevent him from using his old charm to regain favour with the queen. However, Essex's huge debts meant that he simply could not afford to retire. Unless Elizabeth agreed to renew his lease of the customs on sweet wines in October, he would be ruined. The recent opening of peace talks with Spain also fuelled his fears that his rivals were about to sell out to the enemy. In Essex's eyes, his opponents not only lacked the moral courage to continue the war but even sought a Spanish successor to Elizabeth because they feared that James VI of Scotland would promote Essex to a dominant position in a new Jacobean regime. These fears provoked contradictory responses among Essex's followers and reflected divergent impulses within his own mind. On the one hand, the renewal of the wines lease depended upon favour from the queen and support from key members of the council, which required sincere displays of penitence and humility. This accorded with Essex's belief, which had been strongly evident since his return from Ireland, that he was a wretched sinner who was being chastised and tested by God, to which the only proper response was repentance and self-abasement. On the other hand, Essex also resented the success of his rivals and feared its consequences for England. In this view, Essex could not allow Elizabeth to remain the puppet of men who had apparently proved their traitorous intent by dealing with Spain and by besmirching men of honour and action such as

himself and his friends. The diehard Essexians who espoused these views, especially Southampton and Henry Cuffe, had plotted ineffectually to rescue Essex from York House and subsequently encouraged him in covert dealings with Mountjoy (who had succeeded him in Ireland), James VI, and probably also leading figures in France. Such half-hearted conspiracies produced no result, but effectively undermined the efforts of his more moderate supporters to encourage reconciliation and win him an audience with Elizabeth.

The battle for, and within, Essex's mind was settled when Elizabeth refused to renew his sweet wines lease on 30 October. Essex was ruined and all that remained was desperation. An appeal for help was sent to James VI and preparations began for some kind of action. Essex House became a centre for disaffected aristocrats, unemployed army officers, and noisy puritan preaching. The council's efforts to monitor and control developments at Essex House over the next few months merely heightened fears among Essex's followers that he was at risk from some precipitate action by his enemies. Rumours swirled that Ralegh and Cobham meant to murder him. On Tuesday 3 February 1601 a group of Essex's most ardent partisans met at Drury House—deliberately removed from Essex House and the earl himself—to consider how he could pre-empt his enemies and denounce them to the queen: should he attempt to seize control of the court, the Tower, or the City? Chaired by Southampton, the meeting proved inconclusive. When Essex received a summons to appear before the council on Saturday 7 February the result was panic and the adoption of a half-baked plan to appeal for assistance from the City. One group of Essex's gentlemen friends spent the afternoon at the Globe Theatre, where they had paid Shakespeare's company to revive an old play about Richard II to steel themselves for action. On the morning of Sunday 8 February three councillors and the earl of Worcester arrived at Essex House to demand an explanation for his failure to appear on the previous day. Although all four men were well disposed towards him, Essex had them locked up. He then led about 300 men on a march into the City, wearing swords and doublets, but no armour, and carrying few firearms. Essex's companions included the earls of Southampton, Bedford, and Rutland, lords Cromwell, Sandys, and Mounteagle, Sir Charles Danvers, Sir Christopher Blount, and two brothers of the earl of Northumberland. Calling for help from the citizens as they walked, Essex's procession arrived at the house of Sir Thomas Smythe, sheriff of London, about midday. However, Smythe proved evasive and all hope of City support quickly disappeared. Indeed, the lord mayor ordered the gates shut, and troops loyal to enemies of Essex, such as Thomas Cecil, second Lord Burghley, began to surround the demonstrators. By 3 p.m., with fewer than 100 men remaining by his side, Essex headed back to Essex House. Stiff opposition at Ludgate forced him to take to the river and only a hard core managed to reach Essex House, where they were promptly besieged by troops commanded by the lord admiral. Two cannon arrived from the Tower about 9 p.m. and Essex finally decided to surrender.

He spent the night as a prisoner in Lambeth Palace before being moved to the Tower in the morning. Scores of his followers were also arrested.

While Essex contemplated his failure, Captain Thomas Lee tried to force his way into Elizabeth's presence on the evening of 12 February and compel her to summon Essex to an audience. He failed and was swiftly condemned and executed. On the Sunday following Essex's insurrection the preachers of London were required to sermonize against him. The intention was to blacken his public reputation, which remained high. On 19 February Essex and Southampton were tried for treason at Westminster Hall. By then the council had uncovered information about the plotting of the last few months and the meeting at Drury House. The trial generated enormous interest and details are preserved in a mass of manuscript copies of the proceedings. For the prosecution Sir Edward Coke delivered a typically bullying performance, while Francis Bacon again publicly turned the knife in the wound of his old patron. Essex defended himself energetically, but the result was a foregone conclusion and both earls were condemned to death. Nevertheless, the council remained suspicious about Essex's earlier actions in Ireland and following his return, and sent a preacher, Dr Thomas Dove, to urge him to confess. Dove failed but one of Essex's chaplains, Abdias Assheton, succeeded. Assheton's spiritual bludgeoning demolished Essex's sense of heroic failure and encouraged a self-abasement which prompted an outpouring of critical evidence which helped to condemn friends and servants such as Sir Christopher Blount, Gelly Meyrick, and Henry Cuffe. Assheton's efforts also ensured that Essex went to his death with his mind focused upon godly penitence rather than defiance. Essex was beheaded before a small audience in the courtyard of the Tower on 25 February 1601. Characteristically, he sought to die a model death. His pious behaviour during his last hours was recorded in several different accounts of his execution which were widely circulated and copied during the years after his death. He was buried in the chapel of St Peter ad Vincula on Tower Green.

Essex's posthumous reputation Elizabeth remained extremely sensitive about Essex's memory for the remaining two years of her reign. Men who were too closely associated with his death, such as William Barlow, who had delivered a high-profile sermon against Essex at Paul's Cross in February 1601, were barred from her presence. Elizabeth's death and the succession of James I in March 1603 permitted the public expression of grief over Essex's fate. In addition to his *Apologie*, a variety of ballads and other remembrances of Essex were published in the early years of James's reign. Southampton's prompt release from the Tower, the restoration of the earldom to Essex's son, and early marks of favour towards his sister, Lady Rich, reflected a rehabilitation of Essex's memory. Sir Francis Bacon felt it necessary to issue a public defence of his actions towards Essex in 1604 and Sir Walter Ralegh was forced to do the same when he himself went to the scaffold in 1618. However, there was no 'Essexian revival' in politics, and pamphlets or plays which explored the causes of Essex's fall attracted immediate action from James's privy council, as Ben Jonson discovered with his *Sejanus* and Samuel Daniel with his *Philotas*. Essex's widow helped to ensure that there would be no political grouping of former Essexians by marrying Richard de Burgh, fourth earl of Clanricarde, an Irish nobleman who had been a protégé of her late husband and who looked like a younger version of him, in April 1603. Although she survived until February 1632, she spent relatively little time at court. In the 1620s the memory of Essex was used to exemplify militant Elizabethan Hispanophobia and thus implicitly to criticize the policies of James I and Charles I. Essex's image as the champion of aristocratic martial honour and defender of protestantism received a fresh boost in the early 1640s, when his son became a leader of the parliamentarian forces against Charles I. Manuscript copies of Essex's writings also seem to have enjoyed considerable currency during the decades following his death, reflecting both a nostalgia for the Elizabethan era and the continuing appeal of his political stance.

Writing during the reign of James I, William Camden portrayed Essex as a tragically flawed figure, endowed with great talent and potential, but 'not a man made for the court' (Camden, 624). Sir Henry Wotton and Sir Robert Naunton produced broadly similar portrayals in their accounts of Essex written in the early years of Charles I's reign. In contrast to these retrospective political analyses by men who had known him, writers on the continent traded upon Essex's international reputation to construct fictional dramas about his fall which portray him as a romantic hero and the tragic victim of a plot to deceive the queen. A Dutch play on this theme was perhaps staged in the 1620s, while the anonymous Spanish play *Dar la vida por su dama* and Gauthier de Costes de la Calprenède's *Le comte d'Essex* date from the 1630s. La Calprenède's work plays upon the idea that Essex would have been spared if he had not been prevented from sending a ring to Elizabeth. This romantic invention was eschewed in Thomas Corneille's *Le conte d'Essex* of 1678, but repeated in John Banks's play *The Unhappy Favourite* (1681) and many other works.

The modern historiographical image of Essex is still emerging from the caricature to which it was reduced by the nineteenth- and early twentieth-century prejudice against male royal favourites, who were frequently treated as no more than parasitic playboys whose prominence rested solely upon their ability to win and retain the sovereign's affections. Essex was perhaps especially vulnerable to such criticism because of his erratic behaviour during the last two years of his life and because belittling Essex helped to confirm the prevailing rose-tinted views about Elizabeth I and the Cecils. However, a more complex understanding of Essex (and of late Elizabethan politics) began to emerge in the 1950s. New research showed that Essex developed a coherent military strategy for the war against Spain and examined the broader cultural context which helped to shape his career. More recent works have illuminated his role in intelligence-gathering and his patronage of university scholars, whose research helped to serve his political needs. Essex even wrote (or at least edited and approved for circulation) a letter to Fulke Greville which explains how such research should be conducted. Essex was also the greatest cultural patron of the 1590s and various studies have explored his involvement with portraiture, music, and printed works. A scholarly edition of Essex's own poetry was published by S. W. May in 1980.

PAUL E. J. HAMMER

Sources Cecil MSS, Hatfield House, Hertfordshire · papers of Anthony Bacon, LPL, MSS 647–662 · State papers domestic, Elizabeth I, PRO, SP12 · State papers domestic, addenda, Edward VI to James I, PRO, SP15 · State papers Ireland, PRO, SP63 · State papers foreign, Flanders, PRO, SP77 · State papers foreign, France, PRO, SP78 · State papers foreign, Holland, PRO, SP84 · State papers foreign, Spain, PRO, SP94 · *Calendar of the manuscripts of the most hon. the marquis of Salisbury*, 24 vols., HMC, 9 (1883–1976) · *Report on the manuscripts of Lord De L'Isle and Dudley*, 6 vols., HMC, 77 (1925–66) · H. Sydney and others, *Letters and memorials of state*, ed. A. Collins, 2 vols. (1746) · *The letters of John Chamberlain*, ed. N. E. McClure, 2 vols. (1939) · Folger, Bagot papers, L.a.1–1076 · inventories relating to Essex, Folger, G.b.4 · [R. Devereux, second earl of Essex], *An apologie of the earle of Essex … penned by himselfe in anno 1598* (1603) · W. Camden, *The history of the most renowned and victorious Princess Elizabeth*, 4th edn (1688) · P. E. J. Hammer, *The polarisation of Elizabethan politics: the political career of Robert Devereux, 2nd earl of Essex, 1585–1597* (1999) · BL, Lansdowne MSS 17, 23, 25, 27–8, 30 · *The manuscripts of his grace the duke of Rutland*, 4 vols., HMC, 24 (1888–1905) · J. Stow, *The annales of England … untill this present yeere, 1601* (1601) · T. Birch, *Memoirs of the reign of Queen Elizabeth*, 2 vols. (1754) · *The letters and life of Francis Bacon*, ed. J. Spedding, 7 vols. (1861–74) · G. Ungerer, *A Spaniard in Elizabethan England: the correspondence of Antonio Perez's exile*, 2 vols. (1974–6) · BL, Add. MSS 4125, 33769, 48014, 48152, 64081, 74286–74287 · H. Wotton, *A parallel betweene Robert late earle of Essex and George late duke of Buckingham* (1641) · BL, Harley MSS 36, 167–168, 285–288, 290, 296, 4762, 6992–6997 · Bodl. Oxf., MSS Tanner 76, 78–79, 82, 338 · BL, Egerton MSS 6, 8, 1943, 2026 · UCL, Ogden MS 7/41 · *State trials*, vol. 1 · L. W. Henry, 'Essex as strategist and military organiser, 1596–7', *EngHR*, 68 (1953), 363–93 · *De Maisse: a journal*, ed. G. B. Harrison and R. A. Jones (1931) · U. Durham L., archives and special collections, Howard MS 2 · H. A. Lloyd, 'The Essex inheritance', *Welsh History Review / Cylchgrawn Hanes Cymru*, 7 (1974–5), 13–39 · *The memoirs of Robert Carey*, ed. F. H. Mares (1972) · E. Hyde, 'The difference and disparity between the estate and the conditions of George duke of Buckingham and Robert earl of Essex', *Reliquiae Wottonianae, or, A collection of lives, letters [and] poems*, 4th edn (1685), 184–202 · *CSP Spain, 1580–86* · T. Coningsby, 'Journal of the siege of Rouen, 1591', ed. J. G. Nichols, *Camden miscellany, I*, CS, 39 (1847) · P. E. J. Hammer, 'Essex and Europe: evidence from confidential instructions by the earl of Essex, 1595–6', *EngHR*, 111 (1996), 357–81 · P. E. J. Hammer, 'Myth-making: politics, propaganda and the capture of Cadiz in 1596', *HJ*, 40 (1997), 621–42 · *CSP Venice, 1581–1603* · T. Baker, *History of the college of St John the Evangelist, Cambridge*, ed. J. E. B. Mayor, 2 vols. (1869) · S. W. May, 'The poems of Edward de Vere, seventeenth earl of Oxford, and of Robert Devereux, second earl of Essex', *Studies in Philology*, 77 [special fifth number] (1980) · GEC, *Peerage* · W. B. Devereux, *Lives and letters of the Devereux, earls of Essex … 1540–1646*, 2 vols. (1853) · *The Yale edition of the shorter poems of Edmund Spenser*, ed. W. A. Oram and E. Bjorvand (1989) · C. Read, *Mr Secretary Walsingham and the policy of Queen Elizabeth*, 3 (1925) · L. M. Ruff and D. A. Wilson, 'The madrigal, the lute song and Elizabethan politics', *Past and Present*, 44 (1969), 3–51 · D. Piper, 'The 1590 Lumley inventory: Hilliard, Segar and the earl of Essex', *Burlington Magazine*, 99 (1957), 224–31, 299–303 · R. Strong, 'The courtier: Hilliard's *Young man amongst roses*', *The cult of Elizabeth: Elizabethan portraiture and pageantry* (1977), 56–83 · R. Strong, 'Queen Elizabeth, the earl of Essex and Nicholas Hilliard', *Burlington Magazine*, 101 (1959), 145–9 · R. Strong, 'My weeping stagg I crowne: the Persian lady reconsidered', *The Tudor and Stuart monarchy: pageantry, painting, iconography*, 2: *Elizabethan* (1996), 303–24

Archives BL, incomplete treatise on strategy, Add. MS 74287 · Bodl. Oxf., accounts relating to his minority, Douce MS 171 · Bodl. Oxf., corresp. · Bodl. Oxf., household accounts · CUL, corresp. relating to University of Cambridge · Hatfield House, Hertfordshire, letters and papers · Inner Temple, London, papers · Longleat House, Wiltshire, notes and evidence, papers relating to financial and estates management · LPL, corresp. and papers, incl. sermon delivered on death · NRA, priv. coll., corresp. · PRO, state papers, letters, SP 12 and 78 · Warks. CRO, letters | BL, corresp. and papers, Cotton MSS · BL, letters to Elizabeth I and account of the Cadiz expedition, Add. MSS 74286–74287 · BL, Harley MSS · BL, papers relating to expedition to Ireland, Add. MS 46369 · BL, letters, King's MSS · BL, letters to his sister Lady Penelope Rich, Add. MS 64081 · Folger, letters to Richard Bagot, L.a.1–1076 · LPL, corresp. with Anthony Bacon, Francis Bacon, and others, MSS 647–662

Likenesses attrib. N. Hilliard, miniature, *c.*1587, NPG · N. Hilliard, miniature, *c.*1588, V&A · W. Segar, oils, 1590, NG Ire. · attrib. W. Segar, oils, 1590–92, Museum of Fine Arts, Boston · W. Segar?, oils, *c.*1591, priv. coll. · N. Hilliard, miniature, 1593–5, Wrest Park, Bedfordshire · I. Oliver, miniature, after 1596, NPG; version, Royal Collection · M. Gheeraerts the younger, oils, 1596–7, Woburn Abbey, Bedfordshire; version, Trinity Cam. · I. Oliver, miniature, 1596–7, Yale U. CBA, Paul Mellon collection · oils, 1596–7 (after M. Gheeraerts the younger), NPG · M. Gheeraerts the younger, oils, *c.*1597, NPG [*see illus.*] · R. Peake, oils, *c.*1598; sold by Weiss Gallery, London, 1991 · W. Rogers, line engraving, 1599, BM; repro. in A. M. Hind, *Engraving in England in the sixteenth and seventeenth centuries*, 3 vols. (1952–64), vol. 1, pl. 138 · R. Boissard, line engraving, 1600, BM; repro. in A. M. Hind, *Engraving in England in the sixteenth and seventeenth centuries*, 3 vols. (1952–64), vol. 1, pl. 109 · T. Cockson, line engraving, 1600, BM; repro. in A. M. Hind, *Engraving in England in the sixteenth and seventeenth centuries*, 3 vols. (1952–64), vol. 1, pl. 126

Wealth at death thousands of pounds in debt

Devereux, Robert, third earl of Essex (1591–1646), parliamentarian army officer, was born on 11 January 1591 at Walsingham House in Hart Street, London, and baptized there in the chapel on 22 January by Lancelot Andrewes. He was the first-born son of Robert *Devereux, second earl of Essex and stormy petrel of late Elizabethan politics (1565–1601), and his wife, Frances (1567–1632), daughter of Elizabeth's puritan secretary Sir Francis *Walsingham, and widow of Sir Philip *Sidney, the protestant poet and military hero. Essex grew up in a profoundly dysfunctional family. His father hardly ever saw him, being either on military campaign against the Spaniards or the Catholic Irish, or on political campaign against his detractors at court. He had five more children with Frances—although only one son and two daughters survived infancy—yet he and his countess led largely separate lives and both had lovers. Frances—who had married both Sidney and Devereux without the queen's knowledge or consent—was banned from court. Then in 1601 the second earl was beheaded for rebellion and treason. With indecent haste the countess married her lover Richard *Burke (or de Burgh), fourth earl of Clanricarde, and decamped for the west of Ireland. Robert was suddenly stripped of his parents, his title, and his wealth. He was sent to Eton College to study under the ascetic protestant

Robert Devereux, third earl of Essex (1591–1646), by unknown artist, *c.*1620

humanist Henry Savile. (He subsequently transferred in 1602 with him to Oxford, living with him in the warden's lodge at Merton College.) At twelve he was a penniless, escheated orphan.

A failed apprenticeship at court, 1603–1619 Devereux's fortunes were transformed by the accession of James VI of Scotland to the English throne. James immediately showed that he remembered fondly the loyalty to his reversionary right shown by the second earl of Essex. The young Robert Devereux was invited to bear James's sword before him as he entered London at the end of April 1603 and at his coronation on 25 July. James proceeded to restore him to his titles—Baron Bourchier, Viscount Hereford, and earl of Essex—and to his estates and made him a page to Prince Henry. A succession of token honours (such as an Oxford MA *honoris causa* conferred simultaneously on Robert Cecil's son and heir and on Essex in August 1605) marked him out as a man of promise, and the Howards, earls of Suffolk and Nottingham, insecure in their dominant position at court, were keen to take advantage of this. They persuaded the king to sponsor a marriage between the Devereux and Howard families. On 5

January 1606 Robert, not yet fifteen, was married to Frances *Howard (1590–1632), Suffolk's daughter, herself only eight months his elder. Cohabitation at that age was out of the question, and so Robert was sent on a 21-month grand tour (1607–9), albeit one restricted to France and the Netherlands. He returned just before his eighteenth birthday to begin married life. His wife was now a noted beauty, and strong rumours linked her to the amorous attentions of Prince Henry and of the king's new favourite Robert Carr. A severe bout of smallpox, which left Essex badly scarred, was untimely. The relationship of husband and wife quickly became, first from her side and then from his, one of bitter distaste. He felt a sense of duty to his line to have heirs and persisted in seeking a sexual dimension to a loveless match. She lacked his willingness to make the best of a bad job.

Essex had an equally trying return to court life. In 1610 and 1611 he fell out with Prince Henry and hit him with a tennis racquet after the prince called him the son of a traitor, drawing blood. Then a card game in his chambers at Whitehall led to a brawl and a duel, in which he was not a principal but became involved. In 1612 he fought and wounded William Herbert, earl of Montgomery, during an argument while they were hunting with the king at Woodstock. He was clearly a very insecure young man. After this he took Frances to Chartley, his favourite house in the midlands, in a determined attempt to secure an heir. The countess sulked and refused his attentions. It later became clear that her first attempt to poison him occurred at this time. When they returned to court she all too publicly took up a sexual liaison with Carr, now earl of Somerset.

A public cuckold with thin skin and a pock-marked face, Essex had lost all prospects at court. With the death of Prince Henry and the inexorable rise of his estranged wife's family Essex faced a bleak future. And it quickly got worse. In 1613 the Howards persuaded the king to establish a commission to grant Frances an annulment of her marriage on the ground of her husband's impotence. Some members of the commission treated with contempt the long-drawn-out process, with dozens of witnesses and a stark statement by Essex himself that:

> he hath found an ability of body to know any other woman, and hath oftentimes felt motions and provocations of the flesh … but that he hath lain by the lady Frances two or three years last past, and hath no motion to know her, and he believes never shall. (*State trials,* 2.787)

After the king had appointed additional and compliant judges the inevitable decree was granted to Frances on 25 September 1613. To twist the knife in the wound the judicial commission ordered Essex to return Frances's dowry. And if the humiliation of that—and the proliferation of salacious manuscript accounts of it all—was not enough Essex was briefly imprisoned for attempting to fight a duel with Charles Howard, his brother-in-law, after the latter had mocked his honour and his manhood.

Shortly after this Essex took his seat in the parliament of 1614, and unsurprisingly sided with the earl of Southampton in criticism of the crown over impositions and of royal ministers like Sir Francis Bacon, Sir Thomas Parry, and Bishop Richard Neile for overreaching themselves. One newsletter writer spoke of the king as being 'very angry' with many of the peers: Essex was named second after Southampton (Snow, *Essex the Rebel*, 77).

Essex then retreated to his estates at Chartley, Staffordshire, and remained there for five years, except for a brief visit to London to observe the trial and conviction of his former wife and her new husband for having murdered Sir Thomas Overbury as a lethal by-product of their plots against him. Otherwise he discharged faithfully his duties as a lord lieutenant of Staffordshire and busied himself with the marriages of his sisters. It is noteworthy that when James passed within a mile or two of Chartley on his return journey from Scotland in 1617 he did not call. Essex did however return to London for the funeral of James's queen, Anne of Denmark, in 1619. While he was there the elector palatine, Frederick V, called for volunteers to assist him to secure the throne of Bohemia. Essex immediately agreed to lead 300 men and raised them easily.

A successful apprenticeship in war, 1619–1624 In every year from 1620 to 1624 Essex served in protestant armies in the Rhineland. His experience was one of stalemate alternating with defeat. Thus he served in 1620 under Sir Horace Vere, when he and his fellows were toyed with by the wily Spinola. A game of cat and mouse lasted until heavy frost, starvation, and demoralization caused the campaign to be abandoned. James now called on him to join his council of war for the recovery of the palatinate, and over a five-week period in January and February 1621 Essex took part in drawing up a plan involving the deployment of 20,000 foot and 5000 horse at a cost of £900,000. This proposal was rejected by the king, but James continued to look for volunteers to assist Frederick, and in each of the four summers from 1621 Essex raised men and took them to join the army of Prince Maurice of Nassau. Every time he returned to England he personally led appeals for volunteers, and on each occasion sufficient men answered the call in quick time. His limited self-esteem was bolstered by this evidence of the prestige of, and trust in, his name.

Every summer Essex crossed to the Low Countries. Every summer there was frustration and privation, and then each winter he returned home with his sense of the messiness of war further reinforced. In 1621 he spent the second half of the year entrenched around the small town of Rees in Cleves, seeing little action. Neither Prince Maurice of Nassau nor Spinola made any headway. Disease was the only winner. In 1622 he again served as a colonel under Maurice in the same Rhineland stalemate. In 1623 Essex and his men were part of a strong defensive force in Arnheim, the capital of Nassau, anticipating an assault from the imperial general John Tzerklaes, Count Tilly. But Tilly was deflected and the assault never came. Essex had seen no significant action, but had won the respect of his men. In his encomium on Essex published at his death Robert Codrington wrote: 'he first trailed a pike and refused no service in the field which every ordinary gentleman is accustomed to perform. This did much to endear him to his soldiers, and his liberality and humanity did the more

advance him' (Codrington, 9). There is a ring of truth to this. It fits in with his demonstrable practice in England when war broke out in 1642.

In 1624 Essex saw rather more action. James I committed himself to raising four regiments each of 1500 men and commissioned the grumblers in the House of Lords—the earls of Essex, Oxford, and Southampton—as colonels of three of them. Once more Essex was the first to raise his men: 'his name still possessed magnetic qualities' (Snow, *Essex the Rebel*, 119). By late August all four regiments were in The Hague, where they joined up with 4000 Dutch troops. Their assignment was the relief of the siege of Breda. Since they were heavily outnumbered by Spinola's men this was to be achieved by harrying the latter's supply lines and picking off convoys. Something, but in truth very little, was gained by these manoeuvres; and disease carried off many of the English, including both Southampton and his son Lord Wriothesley. This time, Essex stayed on over the winter and right through to the final surrender of Breda on 4 June 1625. He thus played no part in the obsequies for James VI and I, who had died on 27 March. He returned, flushed with defeat, to find a new and more hostile atmosphere at court.

Essex's military apprenticeship had one final humiliation to endure. Charles I and the duke of Buckingham were determined to take the war of honour against the king of Spain into his own heartland. They planned to repeat the great triumph won by Essex's father at Cadiz in 1596. Thirty years on his son was a key player in a repeat performance. The third earl was named as vice-admiral under Sir Edward Cecil, with personal command of a whole squadron and the command of a regiment of foot. It was to be the greatest ever English armada, comprising almost a hundred vessels and some 15,000 fighting men. But it was a disaster. The fleet sailed too close to the shoreline and was spotted, ruining the element of surprise. There were then delays, problems in ensuring all the captains had the same instructions, poor co-ordination (this cost Essex dear), and very inadequate leadership by all those with whom Essex had to work. The Spaniards were able to block the entrance to the harbour and ward off an attempted direct assault and several attempts to take outlying defences. The one success was ruined when Cecil's men got drunk on plundered wine. Savage autumn storms disrupted any further action. The fleet limped home. Only six vessels were lost, but many more were severely damaged. Half the men were dead, booty was small, and the whole sorry expedition cost more than £300,000 (the equivalent of five parliamentary subsidies). Nobody blamed Essex for the catastrophe. But the men he knew to be guilty of failed and incompetent leadership—the duke of Buckingham and Sir Edward Cecil (grandson of Lord Burghley and therefore a scion of the family that was the second earl's nemesis)—were exonerated in a conciliar cover-up. Cecil was even rewarded by a peerage, and not just a peerage, but a viscountcy (of Wimbledon).

Essex's military achievements in the 1620s were therefore modest. From them he learned that outright victory was rarely attainable and the cost in human life was high.

It made him a negative and reactive commander, which helps to explain his failings in the civil wars. In addition it reinforced his estrangement from the political establishment. As he accumulated experience he anticipated recognition and promotion. But royal distrust always kept him in a subordinate position. When the king offered the command of an expeditionary force to assist the king of Denmark in 1627 to junior members of the English and then the Scottish peerage and then to a commoner—Colonel Sir Charles Morgan—Essex resigned his commission in disgust ('being offended and not without reason' as the Venetian ambassador noted; *CSP Venice, 1626–8*, 62). He had overreacted to slights on his honour before, and did so throughout his life. But at the same time he had received the constant reassurance that his men revered him. Every year he had to recruit new men, and his name caused his regiments to fill immediately. He was a good commander, showing concern and compassion for his men, and they followed him loyally. It was balm to his damaged self-esteem that away from court and from the sneers of courtiers he was recognized as the scion of a great house.

Political apprenticeship, 1621–1629 Whenever parliament was in session in the 1620s Essex was its most assiduous attender. He hardly missed a day, and he hardly ever spoke. As his secretary, Arthur Wilson, put it: 'he had an honest heart, and though nature had not given him eloquence, he had a strong reason that did express him better' (A. Wilson, *The History of Great Britain being the Life and Reign of King James the First*, 1653, 162). He was more comfortable on committees and in small groups drafting reports, and soon became an inveterate member of the grand committees of privileges and of petitions. In every parliament he was a thorn in the royal flesh, stubbornly defending the honour of the house and consistently supporting parliamentary investigation of the ministers upon whom the monarch most relied. In 1621 he led a protest against the Scottish invasion of the English peerage and took a taciturn but relentless part in the Lords investigation of three royal ministers accused of corruption: the lord chancellor, Sir Francis Bacon, Sir Henry Yelverton, and Sir John Bennet. In 1624 he took up a number of privilege cases, including the freedom from arrest during the session of his own chaplain William Hulbocke, and was restrained but unrelenting in the house's investigations of the lord treasurer, Lionel Cranfield, earl of Middlesex. He was present but unobtrusive in 1625, but in 1626, following the fiasco of the Cadiz expedition, he was prominent in defending the rights of peers to be free from arrest even on a direct order from the king, and in the escalating crisis that began with the duke of Buckingham and the earl of Bristol accusing each other of treason and ended in the impeachment of the former. For Essex there was no doubt, as far as the Cadiz fiasco was concerned, that the buck stopped with Buckingham. Although—unlike the earls of Bristol and Arundel—he was not arrested for his part in these events, it was at this point that Charles denied him the command of the expeditionary force that was to assist the king of Denmark. This ended his continental soldiering and brought him home in a malcontent

mood. In 1627 he was one of those who not only refused the forced loan, but made his refusal public. His name appears at the head of a list of fifteen 'refractory lords'—ahead of the earls of Warwick, Lincoln, Bolingbroke, and Clare, and Viscount Saye and Sele (*CSP dom., 1625–6*, 485). A proposal for their imprisonment was debated in the privy council, but no action was taken. In spring 1627 he was invited to lead a regiment in the La Rochelle expedition, but declined to do so and retreated rather sulkily to Chartley.

When Charles's third parliament met in 1628 Essex followed his usual course. He attended almost every day and was appointed to and attended the grand committees of privileges and of petitions; he spoke little but used his taciturn influence in the lobbies. Once again he was ultra-sensitive on matters relating to the honour of individual peers and the privileges of the House of Lords. He played a leading part in the attempted impeachment of Roger Manwaring, a preacher who had published two sermons in which he had defended the king's right to require payment of the forced loan and in which he had castigated the 'refusers' like Essex. Essex was the first to respond to John Pym's demand for a Lords investigation and he (with Bishop John Williams) was deputed to interrogate the printer of Manwaring's two pamphlets. During the great debates that led to the petition of right 'Essex sided with Saye but said little. He did however engage in some significant parliamentary manoeuvres' (Snow, *Essex the Rebel*, 170–71), such as moving to transfer discussion into a committee of the whole house to allow opponents to speak as often as they wished. When parliament was prorogued Essex returned to the country until it reconvened on 20 January 1629. Again he was the most assiduous attender, missing only one day, and he was appointed to the committee that drew up the petition for the redress of grievance.

By 1629 Essex was seriously malcontent. He resented the slights he had received from the king, he had a visceral dislike of (the now dead) Buckingham, and he had been sickened by the way the king had protected Buckingham and those who fawned upon him. He was ashamed at the incompetence and maladministration that had caused the failure of one attempt after another to further the protestant cause on the continent. He had supported, quietly but resolutely, every attempt of successive parliaments to remonstrate with the king about these matters. He (rightly) discerned that as far as King Charles was concerned he represented a bad smell on the margins of the court.

The personal rule Throughout the decade from 1629 Essex remained in the country and concentrated on his estates and on family matters. The death of both his grandmother Lettice *Dudley, countess of Leicester, and his mother brought their jointures back to him, more than doubling his annual income, from £3000 to £7000, placing him in the upper middle range of aristocracy. The coalmines at Merevale, Warwickshire, promised further long-term enhancements. In 1633 he travelled to Ireland to view and arrange the management of the Irish estates that had come back to him. He was welcomed into Dublin with a formal progress that exceeded that afforded to the lord deputy, Sir Thomas Wentworth, a few weeks later. It reminded him that his family name still carried a great weight. He leased out Essex House in the Strand to his brother-in-law William *Seymour, earl of Hertford, for a large sum that cleared his debts (he retained the use of one wing).

But Essex also contracted a disastrous second marriage. At the end of the 1629 parliament he sought out Bishop John Williams and consulted him about the morality of remarriage during the lifetime of his first wife. If she had been given a divorce on the grounds of his impotence, and he was not impotent, how would God view the status of that union? Williams declared him free to remarry, and in some haste Essex married, on 11 March 1630, a notable beauty he had met at the home of his sister Frances, countess of Hertford. She was Elizabeth (d. 1656), the daughter of Sir William Paulet, a bastard son of the marquess of Winchester.

For a while all went well. Essex became more cheerful and sociable. He entertained regularly and spent much time with his relatives—he hunted with Hertford in Wiltshire, and played bowls with his popish half-brother Clanricarde in Kent. He played backgammon and cards with family members. He took on a librarian and began to accumulate a fine library. He became an aficionado of the spa towns. He avoided, mentally as much as physically, the court. He tried to become the model rural aristocrat. But new tragedy lay just round the corner. His second marriage collapsed, less spectacularly but just as cruelly as his first marriage had done. By 1636 he and Elizabeth were living largely separate lives, and she was implicated in an adulterous relationship with Sir William Uvedale, an unctuous courtier and treasurer of the king's chamber, the epitome of all that Essex despised. Rumours of the adultery became significant when the countess became pregnant, and the situation had its farcical side, with Essex's brother, Walter, spending long hours on a rickety ladder peering through bedroom windows. Consulting his calendar Essex announced that if she gave birth before 5 November 1636 he would own the child; if after 5 November, he would disown child and countess. Polite society took sides and placed bets. Once more Essex was the butt of humiliating humour. The baby duly arrived on 5 November itself. Essex bit the bullet, owned the child, and forgave the countess. And then, a month later, the infant, Viscount Hereford, succumbed to plague. Essex retreated into a deeper bitterness and despair. Henceforth 'he shunned women and put aside all hopes of a successful marriage and an heir. He relegated the Countess to a small and inconspicuous place in his life' (Snow, *Essex the Rebel*, 194). He undertook the provincial duties entrusted to him (he was reappointed lord lieutenant of Staffordshire in 1629, and he was appointed a member of the council in the marches at the same time as his mother's death restored to him the family holdings in south Wales). He was conscientious and uncontentious in his discharge of these duties.

Into the fray, 1638–1642 By the late 1630s, then, Essex was a stranger to court, someone the king remembered with distaste, but he had not been a trouble-maker in recent years. And he had more military experience than anyone of his rank in the English peerage. So when Charles decided to use English force to impose his Scottish policies he appointed Thomas Howard, earl of Arundel (an earl marshal who had no experience of war), as lord-general and Essex as his second-in-command. But then the queen prevailed upon the king to give Essex's post to her favourite, Henry Rich, earl of Holland. Essex was demoted to lieutenant-general in command of the horse. Yet again he felt the smart more than the honour. It cannot have been easy, either, for him to have to put all his requests for supplies and money through Sir William Uvedale, treasurer at war and lover of his estranged wife. He carried out his duties scrupulously and effectively, and when the Scottish covenanting lords wrote to him, in an attempt to persuade him to stand down and use his influence to halt the planned invasion of their country, Essex forwarded the letters, unopened, to Charles. Unhappily the king chose to interpret the fact of the approach as evidence of his unsoundness and when honours were lavished on those who had led the king to a humiliating pacification, Essex was passed over. Three men he considered his inferiors received the Garter. The result was a deepening of the mutual ill will. In the second Scottish campaign of 1640 he was replaced as lieutenant-general by Thomas Wentworth, now earl of Strafford. By then Essex had attended every day of the Short Parliament and he had been prominent among the minority of twenty-five peers who had voted against voting supply before a consideration of grievances.

In summer 1640, for the first time in more than a decade, Essex remained in London, in the quarters he retained in the Strand, and he was almost certainly involved in secret discussions with the covenanters. He let John Pym have a tenement nearby and he was fully involved in the petition of the twelve peers who listed their and the people's grievances and called for a parliament and for a treaty with the Scots. Within a month Charles found himself unable to prevent a Scottish invasion and the occupation of Northumberland. He called a great council to York which Essex attended. He renewed his call for a parliament and a treaty, and he was one of several of the twelve to be appointed to the team of sixteen negotiators Charles sent to treat with the covenanters.

When the Long Parliament assembled on 3 November 1640 Essex was immediately prominent. As many as twelve members of the Commons owed their selection in significant part to him and could be counted on to amplify his views in the lower house; and he held two (at one time three) proxies as well as his own vote in the Lords. As in the previous six parliaments he was the most assiduous of all attenders. He played an important and restrained part in the prosecution of Strafford (though when Sir Edward Hyde appealed to him that Strafford deserved dismissal and imprisonment for life but not death, Essex replied 'stone-dead hath no fellow'; Clarendon, *Hist. rebellion*, 1.343), and he put his weight behind the dismantling of the instruments of personal rule and the reconstruction of royal government. He was thus a key figure in seeing the Triennial Bill through the Lords, but he showed precocious alarm at the demands for a reconstruction of the church settlement, clearly fearing the political and social consequences of root and branch reform. Charles may have disliked him, but he recognized both that he carried huge moral and political authority and that he did not look much beyond a change of the personnel of government: as the earl of Clarendon later wrote, 'Essex was rather displeased with the person of the archbishop and some other bishops than indevoted to their function' (ibid., 1.328). He was one of the seven men whom Charles appointed to the privy council on 19 February 1641 (as were his closest friend and brother-in-law, now marquess of Hertford, and other long-term political allies). Essex worked hard to secure the addition of those whom he trusted, and most of those in the second round of appointments were close to him by blood or marriage, most remarkably his Irish Catholic half-brother, Ulick de Burgh (or *Burke), fifth earl of Clanricarde (appointed under his English title of earl of St Albans). For a few months down to the summer recess (September–November 1641) he bestrode the political world, notable as one of the 'popular lords' but also as one whose advice the king sullenly followed. His key role was as chair of the committee charged with disbanding the English and Scottish armies. Still, it took Charles too long to offer him office and responsibility. He resisted appointing Essex lord lieutenant of Yorkshire (a key post during the Scottish occupation of the north-east). Too late—at the end of July 1641—Charles appointed him lord chamberlain and on 9 August appointed him commander of all the armed forces south of the Trent in case of an emergency while he was up in Scotland. But whereas Hertford was admitted more and more into the king's confidence Essex was kept at arm's length. In the end, his sense of public duty and slighted honour would count for more than the ties of blood.

Essex was resigned to childlessness, and the death of his brother, Walter, from plague in July resigned him to the extinction of his title and family name. Perhaps in the years to come this made him less anxious about how his actions might ruin his family. He had nothing left to offer but his life and his honour and he clearly valued the latter more than the former.

Essex was prominent—as spokesman for the Lords—in seeking in August 1641 to delay the king's departure for Scotland, and he also tried to prevent the queen from keeping the prince of Wales (he attempted in vain to place the prince under the protection of a group of protestant lords and chaplains at Richmond Palace). As general he had to deal with a number of scares of plots to assassinate MPs, by strengthening the forces under his personal control in Westminster and Whitehall. He was prominent among the sixteen commissioners who governed England during Charles's absence. On 6 November 1641, as news of

the Irish uprising created panic in London, Oliver Cromwell moved an ordinance for Essex to mobilize all the forces of the southern half of England; and in an embryonic version of the militia ordinance Denzil Holles moved on 15 November that all the trained bands be 'put in a posture of defence and … the command [be given] to the earl of Essex' (*The Journal of Sir Simonds D'Ewes*, ed. W. H. Coates, 1942, 147). It is not therefore surprising that on the day after his return from Scotland to London the king revoked Essex's commission and stood down the guards which the earl had provided for the houses of parliament. For much of December the houses sought to assert a right to reorganize national defence under generals whom they nominated to the king. Essex's name was always prominent in these proposals. Distrust and distaste reinforced one another. Charles felt betrayed and therefore would not give Essex the honour and trust he craved. But Essex feeling keenly and resenting this lack of trust and recognition constantly rubbed salt into Charles's wounds. They were two thin-skinned men jabbing fingers into one another's flesh.

When on the morning of 5 January 1642 Essex was told by the countess of Carlisle, from gossip at the queen's table, that Charles intended to seize five members of the Commons whom he intended to put on trial for treason, he tipped off the MPs concerned. Charles, humiliated, withdrew from London and made his way, gradually, to York. Essex refused all commands to join him there, pleading the order of the parliament that he attend to the business of the realm there. In doing so he broke decisively from his brother-in-law and confidant Hertford, who, after a bout of diplomatic illness, made his way to the itinerant king. On 9 April Essex was dismissed from the post of lord chamberlain that he had possessed but barely held. He was the first peer to surrender his royal warrants as lord lieutenant and to accept new ones under the militia ordinance. He was drifting into treason.

Essex spent the spring and early summer months in the parliamentary administrative arrangements for the expeditionary force raised to put down the Irish uprising. But as the king escalated the political rhetoric and the preparations for war, the houses responded and all their military plans centred on Essex. On 12 July the Commons

> resolved that an army shall be forthwith raised for the safety of the king's person, the defence of both houses of parliament, and of those who have obeyed their orders and commands; and for the preservation of the true religion, the laws, liberties and peace of the kingdom. [And] resolved, that the Earl of Essex be named general thereof. (Snow, *Essex the Rebel*, 307)

He never wavered about accepting this office with its risks and responsibilities. He took it on fearlessly and resolutely. He drew up his will, dispersing his estates among his sisters and their children with generous provision for his servants and for the poor, and, providing himself with a coffin and a winding sheet, he set out to make war in the name of king and parliament against a king ensnared, body and mind, by evil counsellors. Any doubt that he had done the right thing was removed by the discovery that the odious Sir William Uvedale was one of the five commissioners appointed to bring peace proposals from the king to the houses.

Captain-general: the first campaign, 1642 Essex was captain-general of the English parliament's forces for thirty months. In that time he did not win a single battle outright, but he did not lose a pitched battle outright either. He was meticulous in planning his campaigns, technically correct and effective in carrying out military manoeuvres—forced marches, sieges, battlefield dispositions—but such caution made him slow, and technical effectiveness also made him predictable. He never took his enemies by surprise. His experience of the Thirty Years' War made him pessimistic about the possibility of knock-out blows, gloomy about the prospects of keeping poorly paid and supplied bodies of men together for a sustained campaign, determined to see the war in defensive terms, and constantly seeking to promote the deadlock out of which he and others could squeeze a negotiated settlement. And he craved absolute power as general over all other commanders and over the peace process. Thus he sought appointment as constable of England, with plenipotentiary powers of war and peace (a post with fourteenth-century precedents). And when he was denied the freedom of action he craved he chafed as much as ever, and was as thin-skinned towards the parliament as he had hitherto been towards the king.

Essex began his campaign by gathering a remarkable life guard of one hundred men, including many future major-generals and republicans (Charles Fleetwood, Henry Ireton, Thomas Harrison, and Edmund Ludlow) as well as the sons of the lords Bedford, Holland, and Saye and Sele, serving under the motto 'God with us'. He built up a strong commissariat and selected his general officers from those with noble blood and those with strong continental experience. By 9 September he was ready for war, and he took his leave of the houses. As he rode in his coach from the Strand towards Watling Street thousands flocked out to cheer him on: 'no rebel had received such a royal farewell before' (Snow, *Essex the Rebel*, 325). He went to war a hero in September 1642, and from then on it was downhill all the way.

Essex's troops were mustered at Northampton, and there he raised his standard on 14 September. The king was trying to bring his army up to strength in the upper Severn valley, and Essex set as his first task to take Worcester and cut off the royalist supply lines. His troops lost a skirmish at Powick Bridge (23 September) but succeeded in occupying the town and thus secured control of the river. Essex then wasted three weeks securing control of the hinterland of Worcester, delivering the initiative to the king. As the latter moved south-east in a straight line from Shrewsbury to London, Essex had to force march his troops so as to intercept them. The result was the great drawn battle of Edgehill, near Banbury, on 23 October. Each side thought it was lower on ammunition and morale than the other, and so declined to resume the battle and set off on parallel quick marches towards London. Essex won the race and, reinforced by the London militia,

interposed himself between the king and the City at Turnham Green.

Despite having twice as many men as the king (24,000 : 12,000) Essex's council of war decided to await the king's attack. After a tense stand-off the king retreated to Oxford. The chance for a quick end to the war was lost.

Lord-general, 1643 Essex spent the bitter winter of 1642–3 quartered in and around Windsor. As a result his army melted away with the winter snows. And so more time was spent recruiting back up to strength. He spent most of 1643 seeking to secure complete control of the Thames valley. His strategic purposes were to capture the king or at least to knock out his headquarters at Oxford. With the exception of a march to relieve Gloucester—which he unwillingly undertook after repeated orders from the houses—his army was never more than 30 miles from Oxford from the time that he captured Reading on 26 April. In unspectacular fashion he did take control of the surrounding towns, and he did tighten the noose around Oxford, but it seemed little return for all the investment of men and money that parliament put at his disposal. A sharp letter from Pym led to his tendering his resignation on 28 June, but it was not accepted. He was, however, speaking openly of making peace, and that is probably why the houses appointed Sir William Waller (who had had a number of spectacular successes blunted by heavy defeat at Roundway Down) to a semi-autonomous command. Essex reacted with fury to this slight, and called the bluff of Pym and his allies: they backed off their support for his rival. Essex's relief of the siege of Gloucester (8 September) and skilful deployment of troops in a running battle through the suburbs of Newark (20 September) restored his name somewhat. Indeed many historians see this battle as the turning point of the war: as the king's last realistic prospect of victory. Slow, cautious, and unimaginative Essex may have been. But with far deeper pockets and more solid control of a less scattered heartland, parliament was always going to win a long war.

The politics of attrition, October 1643 to May 1644 Essex spent most of the next seven months at Westminster losing a war of attrition to shore up his personal authority and to maintain an army worthy of the name under his command. The simplest struggle was for resources. His army was a national army but as a result it had no regional base, no bloc of counties from which to raise the men and supplies to keep itself going. In the winter months, with no pay coming in and in quarters that were cold, damp, and miserable, most of his army—all but 2000 of his foot and more than half his cavalry—drifted away, taking their weapons. Such ammunition as was available was procured by Waller, the earl of Manchester, and other commanders who were actively engaged in the field. At one point, meditating on his inability to protect London if there was a lightning strike, Essex even commissioned one Thomas Taylor to raise a company of archers to help defend the capital. New men were recruited, but were then put into the dispiriting winter quarters. They then just melted away. Essex made a whole series of visits to raise morale to promise more cash and supplies. But it was not until May 1644 that he had put together a fighting force large enough to undertake a campaign.

Inactivity bred demoralization and prevented all thought of a winter campaign. And in any case Essex was preoccupied with the politics of war. He spent much of October 1643 trying to get the houses to remove Sir William Waller from his command for having refused point blank an order to bring his southern association army to join him on his return from Gloucester. Waller simply refused to accept that he was Essex's subordinate. Essex even threatened to resign. According to a clerk's account of Essex's ultimatum at a conference of the houses: 'the Lord General desired of this House, and the House of Commons, leave to deliver up his commission, and go beyond the seas, in regard of the commission to Sr Wm Waller, which is inconsistent with his, and in regard of the many discouragements he hath received in being General' (*JHL*, 1643–4, 246). In the end there was the inevitable uneasy compromise. Waller resigned, but was immediately recommissioned by Essex as commander of the London trained bands, and spent a hectic winter besieging Basing House and Arundel and mopping up pockets of royalist resistance in the south coast counties from Kent to Hampshire. Much of December 1643 was taken up with the court martial of Nathaniel Fiennes for surrendering Bristol long before its defence was impossible (he was convicted and sentenced to death and then reprieved by Essex). Essex's time was wasted with processing the demand from Lord Willoughby of Parham that his commission to command troops in Lincolnshire be upheld in the face of the ordinance placing Lincolnshire in the eastern association and its troops under the command of the earl of Manchester. In January and February Essex fought a losing battle to prevent the creation of the committee of both kingdoms, which would give Westminster politicians (including many of his critics) control of military strategy and the authority to direct scarce resources to the detriment of his honour, authority, and commission (very much in that order). And (at a time when the king was pretending that the meeting of some eighty peers and a hundred members at the Commons at Oxford was the real parliament and the assembly at Westminster a rebellious remnant) Essex was the recipient of a series of peace initiatives from Oxford, which he dutifully handed on unopened to the speakers of the houses. Each letter led to many hours of committees. By late spring Essex was caught up in a thirteen-day stand-off between Lords and Commons over the renewal of the eastern association ordinance and a briefer, blunter, nastier exchange between the houses over the extension of the life of the committee of both kingdoms. He lost both arguments. By now most of the regional commanders—the Fairfaxes in Yorkshire, Sir William Brereton in the north midlands, Sir Thomas Myddleton in north Wales, Manchester in the eastern counties, above all the Scots—never thought to ask his advice or tell him their plans. They reported and negotiated directly with the committee of both kingdoms. Waller was directly answerable to him, but that did not stop him appealing over Essex's head or behind his back when he did not feel like co-operating. For a man of Essex's pride and self-importance this was intolerable. But the blunt fact is that he was doing nothing to earn the respect and goodwill of the other generals.

Disaster in the west, May to September 1644 Not until mid-May did Essex launch his new campaign. Having interrupted a meeting of the Westminster assembly and persuaded it to suspend church reform for a day and to devote itself to prayers for his success, he found it necessary neither to change his will nor to repack his coffin. A campaign that was to end in catastrophe began in hope. He decided to strike at the very heart of the king's territory by an assault on Oxford. Within three weeks he had retaken Reading and Abingdon and had almost encircled the king's headquarters, but, as Essex secured the last of the Cherwell bridges in a fierce fight involving 4000 men, the king, with almost 6000 men, punched his way out of Oxford to the north. Although Essex gave chase the king was in no hurry to fight, and kept slipping away from him. Meanwhile reports reached Essex that Lyme Regis was likely to fall, opening up Dorset and the southern counties to the western royalists. At a crucial and contested council of war on 6 June it was decided that Waller with his light cavalry should harry the king (this led three weeks later to Waller's crushing defeat at Cropredy Bridge), while Essex went to the relief of Lyme and the liberation of the southwest.

It was not in itself a foolish strategy. This was a brilliantly managed operation, with the army marching along a southerly route, its movements co-ordinated with those of the main part of the navy: as Bulstrode Whitelocke put it, 'the Earl of Warwick with his fleet sailed along the coast as the Lord General marched, and carried his ammunition, and sent ships to keep off the enemy' (Whitelocke, *Memorials*, 88). For eight weeks all was well managed, and Essex relentlessly recaptured garrison towns and fortified manor houses throughout Somerset and Devon, culminating in the relief of Plymouth. This was important of itself, and it also meant that Essex had now trapped the queen in Cornwall. The crushing defeat of the royalist armies at Marston Moor on 2 July paradoxically released the king from thoughts of combining with his northern armies. Now Charles *had* to prioritize the west. His defeat of Waller freed him to chase Essex and to join up with Hopton's army, which was in Bristol. And the plight of the queen ensured that Charles would focus all his energies on rescuing her. So Essex finished up trapped between the queen and Sir Richard Grenville in Cornwall and the king and Hopton hot on his heels. The tension was showing: he condoned the execution of Irish prisoners at Dorchester, in clear breach of his own articles of war. He had assumed both that Waller would regroup and come to join him and that, as a last resort, he could embark his army on Warwick's ships and sail to safety. But he chased Grenville too far and for too long and he found himself surrounded by vastly superior numbers of royalists at Lostwithiel. On 31 August his cavalry broke through the royalist lines, and the infantry marched through a summer storm to Fowey.

But strong winds prevented Warwick from coming inshore to transport them away, and they were faced by surrender or a massacre. Essex sailed away in a fishing boat, leaving Philip Skippon to negotiate surrender articles.

'It is the greatest blow that ever befell our party,' Essex wrote to Sir Philip Stapilton on 3 September, 'I desire nothing more than to come to the Tryal, such losses as these must not be smothered up' (J. Rushworth, *Historical Collections*, 8 vols., 1721–2, 5.703–4). Although Independent divines were quick to denounce him from London pulpits the houses closed ranks for once as they sought to mitigate the disaster. They ordered the earl of Manchester to join Waller and such troops as Essex could assemble and reassemble and to interpose themselves between the king and London. Essex had lost the moral right to command this joint force, and the houses were not yet ready to fight over the succession, and so on 14 October day-to-day management of the joint army was entrusted to a council of war consisting of the three generals, together with Lord Robartes, Lieutenant-General Oliver Cromwell, Sir Arthur Hesilrige, and two members of the Commons attending the army. This camel of a committee secured a victory at Newbury on 23 October but botched the aftermath. Since Essex and Waller were unable to be in the same room together it was perhaps as well that for more than a fortnight from 15 October Essex was *hors de combat* with 'excessive flux and vomiting' (*Portland MSS*, 1.189) and under medical supervision in Reading.

Eclipse, 1645–1646 In the ensuing months the recriminations between Manchester and Cromwell dominated the political scene, but behind that were two deeper struggles. The first was between those who were willing to seek a negotiated settlement to the civil war, and those determined to impose a settlement in the wake of a complete victory. Essex was for the best peace that could be secured, not least because the willingness of men like Cromwell to promote low-born men within the army made him fear for social order. The second struggle was over how far the English parliamentarians had to honour to the letter the terms of the solemn league and covenant which had tied the English to the vision of the Scots for the erection of a new confessional state drawing heavily on the Scottish model.

Essex was no rigid presbyterian, and indeed his own preferred system of church governance was probably a lame, Erastian episcopalianism, but he disliked sects and sectarianism, and if presbyterianism would safeguard the virtues of the old Calvinist international he would accept it. All these issues made him detest and suspect Oliver Cromwell, and on 3 December 1644 he called a meeting of all his allies and of the Scottish commissioners in Essex House. The Scots were proposing to denounce Cromwell to the parliament as an 'incendiary' and Essex wanted to know if his friends thought an impeachment on such a charge could succeed. The weathervane lawyers, Bulstrode Whitelocke and John Maynard, thought not, and Essex let the matter drop. But in the months that followed, as Essex and his friends fought the self-denying ordinance all the

way, it is clear that they cared almost as much about ensuring that Cromwell was subject to its provisions as that they should be exempt. After four months of procedural foot-dragging they were completely defeated. So desperate was Essex to prevent Fairfax from getting the very powers he had so jealously guarded—the power to choose the officers of his army—that on 17 March 1645 he even tried (in vain) to use the proxy of his Irish Catholic half-brother, the earl of Clanricarde, to block Fairfax's nominations. Having clung to his commissions long after he had lost all the parliamentary battles Essex finally resigned them in a dignified statement ('a well phrased and restrained statement [in which] he accepted his eclipse and stepped aside like a gentleman', as his twentieth-century biographer put it; Snow, *Essex the Rebel*, 479).

The remaining eighteen months of Essex's life were spent in the half-light. Once he had left the army, his record was looked at by many through rose-tinted spectacles. Josiah Ricraft put together, as a best-selling broadside, *A perfect list of the many victories obtained (through the blessing of God) by the parliaments forces under the command of his excellency, Robert earl of Essex*; and, after his death, early in 1647 Ricraft would be even more specific in highlighting his victories in *A Survey of England's Champions*. There was little opposition in parliament to the showering of financial rewards on Essex—most notably an annuity of £10,000 a year out of confiscated royalist land voted to him, without a division in either house. He became a venerable figure in semi-retirement, regularly attending the Lords, but saying little. He remained a figurehead for those who supported the broad peace strategy known as the Newcastle propositions, and he did all he could quietly to impede the military career of Oliver Cromwell. But then at the end of his life he seems to have planned a major comeback. He had asked, in 1642, to be appointed to the old medieval post of constable, guardian of the realm at a time of crisis. In summer 1646, after Charles had surrendered himself to the Scots, Essex began to reassert the claim, affecting the symbols of vice-regal, protectoral rank, attended as he came and went to the Lords by heralds in their tabards. Whether this would have provoked some kind of crisis can never be known—for at precisely this juncture he died quite suddenly. He suffered a stroke on 10 September 1646 after a strenuous day's stag-hunting in Windsor Forest and died four days later at Essex House.

Funeral and reputation Essex was accorded the greatest state funeral of any non-royal personage for many decades. More than 3000 people were marshalled by the officers of the College of Arms for a funeral based on that of Henry, prince of Wales, to whom Essex had been companion in his teenage years: 'almost all the details of the composition of the cortege seem to have been copied copiously from accounts of Henry's funeral' (Adamson, 'Chivalry and political culture', 191).

So Essex was buried, on 22 October 1646, with the pomp so long denied him in life, and was laid to rest in Westminster Abbey. Richard Vines, an old friend and minister of the parish within which Essex House lay, preached a funeral oration on a text from the second book of Samuel, about how Abner had delivered the Israelites from the tyranny of Saul (explicitly, Charles I) and subjected them to the sceptre of David (explicitly, parliament). A month later the new tomb was vandalized and Essex's effigy beheaded by an axe-wielding former royalist soldier. And at the Restoration his refurbished effigy was destroyed on the orders of Charles II. But his corpse was left undisturbed on both occasions, and is still in the abbey, marked by a modest plaque installed by Dean Stanley in mid-Victorian times.

Essex died without male heirs. The title was extinguished and his property was divided among his sisters and cousins, each fighting like a tiger to get more than their fair share. His life was dominated by the circumstances of his birth: by a desperate concern for the good name put at risk by his father's treason. He was the child of an adulterer (though also of a cuckold), and he twice became an infamous cuckold himself. He was a man of conventional godly piety. He was totally out of sympathy with both the new piety of the court of Charles I and the 'teeming liberty' of zealous men who attached themselves to the movement which he led as a movement of ancient aristocratic virtue. He was a soldier who cared more for honour than for victory, a general who expected to create the conditions for negotiation, not to win outright. He was a devoted but mute parliamentarian, a man who yearned for a king who would take his counsel, but who did nothing to earn the trust that would make that possible. He lacked his father's flamboyance and arrogance, but not his capacity for self-immolation. He was an inverted Midas: all that was golden in his inheritance and circumstance he turned to dust. Only in the false bombast of his funeral was the recognition he craved ever accorded him. His was a life of unfulfilled promise.

JOHN MORRILL

Sources R. Codrington, *The life and death of the illustrious Robert, earl of Essex* (1646) · A. Wilson, 'Autobiography', *Desiderata curiosa*, ed. F. Peck, new edn, 2 vols. in 1 (1779) · W. B. Devereux, *Lives and letters of the Devereux, earls of Essex … 1540–1646*, 2 vols. (1853) · Clarendon, *Hist. rebellion* · C. H. Firth and R. S. Rait, eds., *Acts and ordinances of the interregnum, 1642–1660*, 3 vols. (1911) · *The list of the army raised under the command of his excellency Robert earl of Essex* (1642) · *The earl of Essex his speech to the soldiers on Tuesday last* (1642) · *The lawes and ordinances of war established for the better conduct of the army* (1642) · *The mannor and forme of the proceeding to the funerall of the right honourable Robert earl of Essex* (1646) · R. Vines, *The hearse of the renowned right honourable Robert earl of Essex* (1646) · V. Snow, *Essex the rebel: the life of Robert Devereux, the third earl of Essex, 1591–1646* (1970) · S. R. Gardiner, *History of the great civil war, 1642–1649*, new edn, 4 vols. (1893) · G. Davies, 'The parliamentary army under the earl of Essex, 1642–5', *EngHR*, 49 (1934), 34–54 · V. Snow, 'Essex and the aristocratic opposition to the early Stuarts', *Journal of Modern History*, 32 (1960), 3–44 · V. Snow, 'The lord general's library, 1646', *Transactions of the Bibliographical Society*, 21 (1966), 115–23 · A. Somerset, *Unnatural murder: poison at the court of James I* (1992) · E. Le Conte, *The notorious Lady Essex* (1969) · C. L. Kingsford, 'Essex House', *Archaeologia*, 2nd ser., 23 (1922–3) · T. Pape, *Newcastle-under-Lyme in Tudor and Stuart times* (1938) · D. L. Smith, *Constitutional royalism and the search for settlement, 1640–1649* (1994) · J. H. Hexter, *The reign of King Pym* (1941) · J. S. A. Adamson, 'The baronial context of the English civil war', *TRHS*, 5th ser., 40 (1990), 93–120 · J. S. A. Adamson, 'Parliamentary management, men-of-business and the House of Lords, 1640–

1649', *A pillar of the constitution: the House of Lords in British politics, 1640–1784*, ed. C. Jones (1989), 21–50 · J. S. A. Adamson, 'Chivalry and political culture in Caroline England', *Culture and politics in early Stuart England*, ed. P. Lake and K. Sharpe (1994), 161–98 · W. B. Bannerman, ed., *The registers of St Olave, Hart Street, London, 1563–1700*, Harleian Society, register section, 46 (1916) · GEC, *Peerage* · [B. Whitelocke], *Memorials of the English affairs* (1682) · will, PRO, PROB 11/198, sig. 185 · A. P. Stanley, *Historical memorials of Westminster Abbey* (1888), 1.206 · *The manuscripts of his grace the duke of Portland*, 10 vols., HMC, 29 (1891–1931), vol. 1

Archives BL, corresp. and papers, Add. MSS 11692, 46188–46193 · Bodl. Oxf., corresp. · Derbys. RO, Matlock, corresp.

Likenesses D. Mytens, oils, 1616–24; in possession of the duke of Portland in 1970; on loan to NPG · R. Elstrack, line engraving, *c*.1620, BM · oils, *c*.1620, priv. coll.; on loan to NPG, on display at Montacute House, Somerset [*see illus.*] · R. Walker, oils, *c*.1642, NPG · line engraving and etching, 1643, NPG · W. Hollar, etching, pubd 1644, BM, NPG · T. A. Dean, stipple, pubd 1827 (after R. Walker), NPG · S. Cooper, miniature, Royal Collection · R. Elstrack, line engraving, BM, NPG · W. Hollar, etching, BM, NPG · W. Marshall, line engraving, BM, NPG; repro. in D. Evance, *Justa honoraria, or, Funeral rite in honor to the great memorial of my deceased matter* (1646) · attrib. R. Peake, double portrait, oils (*The earl of Essex and Henry prince of Wales*), Royal Collection · H. T. Ryall, stipple (after R. Walker), BM, NPG · T. Simon, gold and silver medal, BM · medals and badges, BM

Devereux, Sir Walter (1411–1459). *See under* Devereux, Walter, first Baron Ferrers of Chartley (*c*.1432–1485).

Devereux, Walter, **first Baron Ferrers of Chartley** (*c*.1432–1485), landowner and soldier, was of Herefordshire stock (at Weobley and Bodenham); his father was a retainer of Richard, duke of York, and he himself became Edward IV's councillor. The son of **Sir Walter Devereux** (1411–1459) (with whom historians sometimes confuse him) and Elizabeth (*d*. 1438), daughter and heir of John Merbury, another Herefordshire landowner, he grew up as his father and William *Herbert (his sister's husband) strove to dominate south-east Wales and Herefordshire, partly in the Yorkist interest. The elder Walter had become York's tenant, retainer, and councillor by the 1440s: he joined the duke's expedition to Normandy in 1441 and held several captaincies there, and he was knighted about 1441–2. One of the most prominent of Herefordshire landowners and county officials, he was involved in York's protests against the government in 1450–52, sought to strengthen the duke's influence in Hereford itself, and was indicted of treason for his pains (though pardoned in 1452). After he and William Herbert led a force to west Wales in August 1456 to enforce York's authority in the principality shires, he was arrested and placed for a time in the Tower of London. Young Walter was involved in such disturbances in the spring of 1456, exploiting civic factions to control Hereford—though he later claimed that he was falsely accused. When his father died on 22 or 23 April 1459, Walter inherited his estates in Herefordshire and Leicestershire; the Lincolnshire lands had been conveyed to him and his wife, Anne (1438–1469), daughter and heir of Sir William Ferrers of Chartley, Staffordshire, when they married in 1446. Much of Ferrers's estate was entailed to Lady Ferrers (*d*. 1471), but the rest had been conveyed to Anne in March 1453, even though she was only fifteen.

Walter Devereux continued to serve the house of York, even though he was overshadowed in Wales and the marches and at court by his brother-in-law, Herbert. He was with York at Ludford Bridge in October 1459, but threw himself on the king's mercy to save his life; though attainted in the Coventry parliament, he was able to recover his properties for a fine of 500 marks, and in March 1460 secured a pardon. Once Richard Neville, earl of Warwick, had captured Henry VI at Northampton in July, Devereux returned publicly to his Yorkist allegiance: he was appointed JP in Herefordshire and, along with Sir William Herbert, represented the county in parliament in 1460–61. After the duke of York's death in December 1460 he acted as steward of Duchess Cecily's Herefordshire estates. When her son, Edward, earl of March, gathered an army before the battle of Mortimer's Cross (2–3 February 1461), Devereux probably joined him; he certainly was among the group that proclaimed him king at Baynard's Castle in London on 3 March. He fought at Towton on 29 March and was knighted after Edward's victory. Edward IV summoned him on 26 July to his first parliament, Devereux taking his father-in-law's title as Baron Ferrers of Chartley. A few days earlier, the king granted him a brewhouse in London, appropriately named Le Walsheman. But Ferrers's new dignity required more substantial support, and in February 1462 he received forfeited Lancastrian estates of the earls of Devon and Wiltshire in the midlands and Welsh border shires. These grants were extended in March 1466 to Ferrers's heirs general, presumably because his son John was barely two years old.

Ferrers was associated with Herbert in restoring order in Wales and the marches between the capture of Pembroke Castle in September 1461 and the fall of Harlech in 1468; in June 1463 he was appointed constable of Aberystwyth Castle for life. He was also active elsewhere: in February 1462 he foiled the earl of Oxford's plot against the king, and he accompanied Edward to the north later in the year. He was one of the king's councillors. At the time of the rebellion led by Warwick and Clarence in 1469–70 Ferrers was summoned to support the king, and, when Edward recovered his authority in the autumn, Ferrers, now that Herbert was dead, went to south Wales to suppress disorder. In November he was given control of the lordships of Brecon, Hay, and Huntington during the duke of Buckingham's minority, and in July 1470 became sheriff of Caernarvonshire and master forester of Snowdon for life. He offered protection at Weobley to his sister Anne, countess of Pembroke, and her young wards, Henry Tudor, earl of Richmond, and Henry Percy, earl of Northumberland; and although Lady Margaret Beaufort took steps to recover her son, it seems that Anne kept Richmond at Weobley until the readeption of Henry VI, in October 1470, when the boy was handed over to his uncle Jasper Tudor. Northumberland, however, was moved to the Tower of London, though he was granted his freedom on swearing allegiance to Edward IV and offering bonds, partly provided by Ferrers, in October 1469.

At the readeption Ferrers lost not only his Tudor guest, but possibly also the manors he had enjoyed since 1462; he

was removed, too, as JP in Herefordshire. When Edward IV regained his throne in April 1471, Ferrers returned to royal service, especially in Wales and the marches. He was among the lords who swore on 3 July to accept Prince Edward as the king's heir, and was made responsible for imposing order in Wales following the battle of Tewkesbury. In August he and Herbert's son, the earl of Pembroke, whom he presumably advised, pursued Jasper Tudor and his nephew; he was in Carmarthen by October, only to hear of the fugitives' escape to France. In September 1471 he was appointed steward of Elfael by the duke of Clarence. Ferrers's military experience earned him election as a knight of the Garter in 1472, and he was well qualified to join the prince of Wales's council, to which Edward IV gradually assigned governmental responsibilities in the marches and English borderland: on 20 February 1473 he became the prince's tutor as well as a councillor, and was active on numerous commissions in the region.

The king's expedition to France in July 1475 mustered many nobles, including Ferrers, but there was no opportunity to display valour. In 1478 he was a trier of petitions in the parliament of January–February that condemned the duke of Clarence. In September that year he was nominated to investigate treasons and insurrections in Yorkshire, renewing an acquaintance with Richard, duke of Gloucester, that had been formed in Wales in 1470. Ferrers's rewards seem comparatively modest, but they included, in January 1476, the earl of Oxford's forfeited estates in Leicestershire to augment his own holdings. And trust between Ferrers and Edward IV may be indicated by the sale of the marriage of the former's son and heir, John (c.1463/4–1501), to the king in 1478–9. Ferrers himself, having been widowed in 1469, married in 1482 Joan, widow of Thomas Ilam, who outlived him.

Ferrers attended Edward IV's funeral at Windsor in April 1483. His attitude to Richard III is not known, though he attended his coronation in July. But when Buckingham rebelled in October, the duke and his family made for Weobley to raise men, perhaps hoping to exploit Anne Ferrers's Tudor connection; it was while they were hiding in the neighbourhood that the duke was captured and subsequently executed. Richard III's treatment of Ferrers may therefore have been cautious. He gave him an annuity of 100 marks, and in August 1484, for life, the manor of Cheshunt, Hertfordshire, which, as part of the earldom of Richmond, may represent an attempt to induce Ferrers to oppose Henry Tudor. He turned out for the king in 1485 and fell at Bosworth on 22 August. He was attainted in Henry VII's first parliament and his estates were forfeited. In 1486 his son John was allowed to acquire the lands of his mother but had to wait until 1489 for the recovery of the Devereux and Merbury estates. R. A. GRIFFITHS

Sources PRO [esp. Chancery, inquisitions post mortem, C139/176 no. 22] · *Chancery records* · Longleat House, Wiltshire, Devereux MSS · *RotP*, vols. 4–5 · A. F. Sutton and P. W. Hammond, eds., *The coronation of Richard III: the extant documents* (New York, 1984) · R. Horrox and P. W. Hammond, eds., *British Library Harleian manuscript 433*, 4 vols. (1979–83) · A. Wright, 'Public order and private violence in Herefordshire, 1413–61', MA diss., U. Wales, 1978 · M. A.

Hicks, 'False, fleeting, perjur'd Clarence': George, duke of Clarence, 1449–78 (1980) · F. P. Barnard, Edward IV's French expedition of 1475: the leaders and their badges (1925) · D. H. Thomas, 'The Herberts of Raglan as supporters of the house of York in the second half of the fifteenth century', MA diss., U. Wales, 1967 · M. K. Jones, 'Richard III and Lady Margaret Beaufort: a re-assessment', Richard III: loyalty, lordship and law, ed. P. W. Hammond (1986), 25–37 · N. Pronay and J. Cox, eds., The Crowland chronicle continuations, 1459–1486 (1986) · visitation of Warwickshire · GEC, Peerage
Archives Longleat House, Wiltshire, papers

Devereux, Walter, first Viscount Hereford (c.1489–1558), administrator and nobleman, was the son and heir of John Devereux, second Baron Ferrers of Chartley (c.1463/4–1501), and his wife, Cecily (d. 1493), heir of the houses of Bourchier and de Bohun and niece of Edward IV. Succeeding his father as third Lord Ferrers in 1501, Walter had, while still under age, married Lady Mary, daughter of Thomas *Grey, first marquess of Dorset and great-grandfather of Lady Jane Grey. Having been a ward in the royal household, he was summoned to Henry VIII's first parliament in January 1510 and soon afterwards became steward of several royal manors and joint constable of Warwick Castle. In 1512 he joined his brother-in-law Thomas *Grey, second marquess of Dorset, on an Anglo-Spanish expedition intended to recover Aquitaine, and in 1513 was nominated by the king himself to captain the Gryt Herry Imperyall, serving also in that year at the battle of Flodden. When in June 1520 King Henry met François I of France at the Field of Cloth of Gold and then the recently elected Emperor Charles V at Gravelines, Devereux was present on both occasions. In 1521 he sat with other peers in judgment on Edward Stafford, duke of Buckingham, and two years later served again in France, returning there once more for the campaign of 1544 when the king himself took charge.

Meanwhile Devereux became increasingly active in the government of Wales and the Welsh marches, location of much of his landed estate. Already a member of the council originally formed to administer the lands of the prince of Wales and then developed into a vehicle of provincial law enforcement, he was appointed to that body as reconstituted by Wolsey in 1525, holding at the same time the office of steward in the Princess Mary's household at Ludlow. Further appointments to offices of profit rapidly followed, culminating in 1545 in that of chamberlain of the recently established court of general surveyors, and punctuated along the way by more stewardships of crown lordships and manors as well as regular service on administrative and judicial commissions in Wales, the marches, and the west midlands. By comparison, Devereux's gains in terms of land were relatively modest. In 1548 his gross annual income from rents amounted to approximately £870, while his heir eventually took possession of a landed estate valued at a mere £400 per annum.

Even so, in the turbulent politics of the mid-sixteenth century Devereux was manifestly significant. Allied through his first marriage to the family of Grey, he was also linked from 1536 to that of Hastings when his second son, Richard, married Dorothy, daughter of the first earl of Huntingdon. The second earl of Huntingdon and the

third marquess of Dorset emerged as prominent supporters of John Dudley, earl of Warwick, when, from October 1549, he carried through his coup against the lord protector, Somerset. In January 1550 Devereux was sworn of the privy council; in February he was created Viscount Hereford. Seasoned in the ways of provincial government, this well-connected marcher lord was a valuable asset in Warwick's stratagems, even though his role in the subsequent progress of the Reformation and other events of Edward VI's reign remains obscure. Briefly imprisoned on Mary Tudor's succession to the throne, he lost not only his place at the centre of affairs, but also many of his offices. Yet, by one of the last grants of her reign, and within two months of the viscount's death, the queen granted stewardships of lands and courts in several shires of Wales to his heir. That heir, again named Walter and again a minor, was the viscount's grandson by his second son, the eldest of his three sons by his first marriage, to Mary Grey, having also predeceased him. Following Mary's death in 1538 Devereux had taken as his second wife Margaret (d. 1599), daughter of John Garneys of Kenton in Suffolk, with whom he had a daughter, Katherine, and a fourth son, Edward, father of the fifth Viscount Hereford. Devereux died on 17 September 1558 at his home, Chartley, Staffordshire, and was buried in Stowe church under a monument.   HOWELL A. LLOYD

Sources H. A. Lloyd, 'The Essex inheritance', Welsh History Review / Cylchgrawn Hanes Cymru, 7 (1974–5), 13–39 · GEC, Peerage, new edn · Longleat House, Wiltshire, Devereux MSS · LP Henry VIII · CPR, 1485–1509 · CIPM, Henry VII, 1–3 · Report on the manuscripts of the late Reginald Rawdon Hastings, 4 vols., HMC, 78 (1928–47), vol. 1, p. 313 · J. G. Nichols, ed., The chronicle of Queen Jane, and of two years of Queen Mary, CS, old ser., 48 (1850) · DNB · D. E. Hoak, The king's council in the reign of Edward VI (1976) · P. Williams, The council in the marches of Wales under Elizabeth I (1958)
Archives Longleat House, Wiltshire, MSS
Wealth at death approx. £1000 p.a. in land, with personal and other assets of uncertain value: Devereux MSS, Longleat House, Wiltshire, box I, no. 32, vol. IX, fol. 55; will, PRO, PROB 11/41, sig. 47

Devereux, Walter, first earl of Essex (1539–1576), nobleman and adventurer, was born on 16 September 1539 at Chartley, Staffordshire, the eldest son of Sir Richard Devereux and his wife, Dorothy, daughter of George *Hastings, first earl of Huntingdon. Sir Richard, who was created a knight of the Order of the Garter on 20 February 1548, died the same year, in the lifetime of his father, Walter *Devereux, first Viscount Hereford. The family was descended from Robert d'Evreux, a companion of William the Conqueror who settled in Herefordshire. Walter *Devereux, first Baron Ferrers of Chartley, met his death fighting for Richard III at Bosworth. His son John succeeded as Lord Ferrers, and married Cecily, heir of her brother Henry Bourchier, earl of Essex. The offspring of this marriage, Walter, Lord Bourchier and Lord Lovaine through his mother, Lord Ferrers of Chartley through his father, and Viscount Hereford by creation in 1550, was, on his death in 1558, succeeded in all his dignities by his grandson Walter. Biographical verses written on the life of this Walter Devereux and an elegy on his death collected

Walter Devereux, first earl of Essex (1539–1576), by unknown artist, 1575? [after original, 1572]

by J. Payne Collier indicate that he spent his youth on the large family estates at Lamphey in Pembrokeshire.

Loyalty during the rising of the northern earls On Elizabeth I's accession Walter, Lord Hereford, went up to court, and about 1561 married Lettice (b. after 1540, d. 1634) [see Dudley, Lettice], eldest daughter of Sir Francis *Knollys; both were in their early twenties. For the next seven years they lived at Chartley Hall in Staffordshire. It was during this period that their eldest child, Penelope *Rich, was born. His first call to public service came in 1568 when ordered to keep a body of horse in readiness to prevent any attempt to release Mary, queen of Scots, from Tutbury, then under the charge of the earl of Shrewsbury. John Leslie, the Scottish queen's envoy and historian of Scotland, spread rumours about the young Lord Hereford to poison Queen Elizabeth's mind against him, in particular that Hereford had slandered Leicester, her favourite. Later events would divide Leicester and Hereford but at this time, on 29 September 1569, Hereford protested to William Cecil that he bore no grudge against Leicester. From his letter to the queen on 27 November 1569 it is clear that Hereford had raised troops to aid the suppression of the northern uprising under the earls of Northumberland and Westmorland, and joined the earl of Warwick's army at Leicester where he was appointed 'high marshal of the field'. He was commended for his decisive part in the suppression of the rising. On St George's day (23 April) 1572 Hereford was made a knight of the Garter, and on 4 May

was created earl of Essex, his great-granduncle's title. Such rewards were indicative of his steady and efficient loyalty to the queen and to the reformed religion.

The Ulster background to Essex's Irish career In 1573 Essex undertook as a partial adventurer to colonize Ulster, then the *ultima Thule* of Gaeldom, a province known to statesmen as 'the gall and misery of all evil men in Ireland' (Essex to Burghley, 23 June 1574). Previous efforts to settle Ulster had failed. Turlough Luineach O'Neill then held sway over what is now co. Tyrone, the senior O'Neill Gaelic lordship, and in south Derry and north Armagh. He also occasionally controlled the influential vassal chief (uriath) Turlough mac Henry O'Neill of the Fews in south Armagh, and was betimes in alliance with Sir Brian mac Phelim O'Neill, ruler of Clandeboye (most of south Antrim). The O'Neills also had formidable support from the mercenaries of Sorley Boy MacDonnell, the brother of James McDonnell, lord of north Antrim, of Rathlin Island, and of Kintyre and the isles in Scotland.

Confident of success in Ireland, Essex hoped to further his credibility at court and to move to centre stage in political life. By formal agreement with Queen Elizabeth in July 1573 he was to take over Clandeboye, the present co. Antrim, save for the fortress of Carrickfergus and its hinterland. When secured, the territory was to be free of tax for seven years and enjoy free trade with England and all manorial rights, but not to benefit from fines of the crown courts. An army of 1200 men was to be raised jointly by Essex and the queen, and costs of fortifications were to be shared equally between them: 'the Earl shall fortify as occasion shall require before division at the equal charges of her Majesty and the Earl' (Calendar of the Carew Manuscripts, 1.444). Elizabeth loaned Essex £10,000 on mortgage of his properties in Buckinghamshire and Essex. If the sum was not repaid within three years these pledged properties—about a third of all his property—would be forfeited. In sanguine mood Essex reckoned that his Ulster plantation would yield an annual rental of £5000 which would offset any outlay the crown was prepared to make in its support. In 1572 similar arrangements had been granted to Thomas Smith, the natural son of Sir Thomas Smith, to colonize the Ards peninsula between Belfast and Strangford Lough in co. Down. That project had been a failure, but Essex's new scheme was heartily supported. Lord Rich, Sir Peter Carew, William and John Norris of Rycot, William Morgan, Francis Kellaway, Sir Arthur Champernowne, Henry Knollys (Essex's brother-in-law), Michael and John Carey, the sons of Lord Hunsdon, and Henry Sydenham all raised volunteer bands. Essex wanted each adventurer to 'build a small castle with a bawn of stone and intrench a town' (BL, Add. MS 48015, fols. 296–300). He prudently employed officers who had previous Irish experience such as Nicholas and John Malby, Edward Barkeley, Thomas Chatterton, and Francis Drake, captain of the Falcon. Early in July 1573 the queen advised him to avoid bloodshed as far as possible and not to make any hasty enforced changes in religion.

Essex sailed from Liverpool in good spirits with part of his expedition on 19 July 1573. The small fleet was soon storm-scattered; some ships were blown on to the Isle of Man and others as far south as Cork. Essex landed with difficulty at Carrickfergus where he took command of the garrison and where Hugh O'Neill (later second earl of Tyrone) joined his force. He wintered at Belfast where an earthen fort at Skegoneill, near the present city, is associated with Essex. Thence he issued a proclamation to Turlough Luineach O'Neill to the effect that his sole aim was to rid Ulster of the Scots and that all who helped him to do so would be well received. Sir Brian mac Phelim O'Neill initially made feint submission by sending in supplies of cattle to Carrickfergus, but a few days later withdrew his forces to join Turlough Luineach O'Neill's, and at the same time managed to recover his cattle from Essex. The problem for Essex was to prevent the O'Neills, Turlough and Brian, acting together with their Scottish allies and mercenaries; rather his aim was to have them at each other's throats. One fierce attack was made on Sir Brian MacPhelim at Masereene, near Antrim town, but simultaneously a raid by the Scots on the Ards resulted on 18 October 1573 in the death of Thomas Smith, on whom Essex had relied for support. Essex's difficulties increased as his men began to desert, some to England and some to the pale; he lacked a steady stream of supplies and to compound his ill luck the plague broke out—twin factors which accounted for the failure of many Elizabethan colonial ventures. Some of his volunteers openly declared their intention of going home so that Essex was left to depend on the support of drafted men, and was forced to plead for further financial aid from the queen who loaned him additional money against further mortgages. 'I will not leave this enterprize as long as I have any foot of land in England unsold', he wrote to the council in March 1574 (PRO, SP 63/45/7). Contrary to his original plans, Essex now suggested winning the support of Sorley Boy and his Scots to use against the O'Neills.

Difficulties with Fitzwilliam, the lord deputy The lord deputy, William Fitzwilliam, who had been against the project from the beginning, now declined to help Essex, who promptly sent his secretary, Edward Waterhouse, to report his situation to queen and council. Orders were sent directly to Fitzwilliam to succour Essex in Ulster. A proposal to recall Fitzwilliam and have him replaced by Essex was aborted by the intervention of Leicester, to whom the queen listened. Instead, to satisfy Essex, he was promised the titles of governor of Ulster and earl marshal of Ireland. Early in March 1574 he appealed to Fitzwilliam for help in an excursion against Turlough Luineach O'Neill; he got but a handful of men from the pale. Again, desertions and want of supplies stopped the attempt; instead a truce was negotiated with Turlough before the end of the month.

The whole enterprise was manifestly failing, and the queen contemplated recalling Essex out of Ireland. Essex foresaw the ruin of his fortunes unless the terms of his contracts could be altered. He first asked the queen for another 700 men while he continued to support 100 himself, and asked her to grant him Island Magee at a nominal rent; alternatively he asked her to take £250 a year in discharge of the £10,000 debt. Elizabeth graciously acceded to his first request. These reinforcements arrived but once more disease, desertions, and famine became rampant in Carrickfergus; old and new soldiers were dying at the rate of fifteen or twenty a day. With heroic fortitude Essex shared in their sufferings and although his forces were weakened they did manage to persuade Sir Brian mac Phelim O'Neill to consider surrendering his territory of Clandeboye to the queen in May 1574. In June 1574, at Fitzwilliam's request, Essex moved south to ask the earl of Desmond to negotiate with the deputy and council in Dublin. In this he was temporarily successful. On his return north Essex mustered what soldiers he could, and with the help of Hugh O'Neill, baron of Dungannon (and second earl of Tyrone *de jure*, 1562), carried out a murderous raid on a Clandeboye O'Neill crannog (a fortified island in a lake) near Banbridge, co. Down. From there he marched through Turlough Luineach O'Neill's lordship from Benburb in co. Tyrone to the River Foyle, burning a bountiful harvest as he went. At Lifford in Tyrconnell he placed a loyalist O'Donnell in charge instead of a dissident one.

However, this show of strength failed to bring Turlough Luineach to submission. The trail of damage was quickly repaired since in a pastoral economy no towns and few substantial houses existed. Essex could see that only permanent forts garrisoned by paid government troops could effectively bring the province under English control. He also would have liked coastal fortifications to keep the Scots out of Ulster. His frustration at his perceived lack of progress in carrying out his project drove him to desperate measures. In November 1574 he invited MacPhelim to conference and to spend Christmas with him at Belfast, at that time but a cluster of houses around a church and small fort at a ford on the Lagan River. A rich banquet was prepared for the Irish chief, his wife, his brother, and their retainers. At a signal his troops treacherously slaughtered Sir Brian's company, seized the three chief guests, and had them sent to Dublin Castle and there executed, presumably for treachery. Essex boasted that this little execution broke the faction and struck terror into the rest. No justification was given for the atrocity.

Continued troubles between Essex and Fitzwilliam Differences and difficulties with the Dublin administration led to confusion of authority as Essex and Fitzwilliam were frequently at cross purposes. Fitzwilliam regarded Essex and his prospective colonists with suspicion. The Irish enemy made capital on the confusion by claiming they were 'no rebels', but acting in self-defence against predators; that if indeed it was the queen's war, then the lord deputy and not Essex would have been appointed to lead it. When Fitzwilliam had to reduce the forces in Ireland to about 2000 soldiers, Essex's army was threatened with extinction. Hence he resigned. The queen praised his earlier efforts and declared that the enterprise was not to be abandoned. And yet she informed Essex that she was not prepared to continue support for the colonization of Ulster. By June 1575, as part of his evacuation plans, he moved his headquarters from Carrickfergus to Drogheda and there opened negotiations with Turlough Luineach O'Neill. The queen now ordered Essex to retire as soon as he could. By the end of June 1575 he threw up a fort and bridge across the Blackwater, north of Armagh, but in his haste that work was unfinished because his men were continually harassed by followers of Sorley Boy Mac-Donnell and Turlough Luineach O'Neill. However, he came to terms with Turlough Luineach, who undertook to confine himself to his Tyrone lands and to relinquish claims over his neighbours. Essex then drove the Scots under Sorley Boy out of Clandeboye and handed it over to a minor Irish chieftain, Brian Fertagh O'Neill.

The Rathlin Island massacre An essay in frightfulness followed when Essex sent a naval expedition under John Norris and Francis Drake to Rathlin Island where Sorley Boy had sent his own family and those of his chief followers for safety. Robert Bruce's former castle on the island was stormed and 200 defenders killed in a siege that lasted four days (22–6 July 1575). No quarter was given, and some 300 to possibly 400 people, including women and children, were hunted down and slaughtered in the caves where they had taken refuge. Rathlin proved easy to sack but difficult to hold, being a staging post on the way to and from the south Hebrides. Drake and Norris were forced to abandon the island under pressure from Sorley Boy who in retaliation sacked Carrickfergus.

The massacre of Rathlin Island was the last act in Essex's Ulster tragedy. The whole venture had been a costly failure, the queen having spent over £130,000 in Ireland in the two and a half years to September 1575. In November 1575, once Sir Henry Sidney had returned to Ireland as lord deputy to replace Fitzwilliam, he visited Ulster and found it 'utterly disinhabited'. Modern research would seem to confirm Froude's description of the massacre on Rathlin Island, some aspects of which were questioned by Brewer in letters to *The Athenaeum* in 1870, particularly that Sorley Boy had witnessed the murder of his children from the mainland, and that Essex and the queen regarded the operation with satisfaction. Contemporary reports would appear to support Froude's views rather than Brewer's. The massacre is long remembered in the catalogue of English outrages and Irish grievances as recorded by the Gaelic annalists. Little had been achieved by Essex in Ulster. At best Turlough Luineach O'Neill was restrained from exercising authority over his neighbours and from bringing in undue forces of Scottish mercenaries, but fears of Scots-Irish intrigues continued until the execution of Mary, queen of Scots, in 1587.

Essex's final years In October 1575 Essex arrived at his house in Lamphey, Pembrokeshire. The queen had eased his anxieties by writing on 2 September:

> You may think it has been a dear conquest to you, in respect of the great care of mind, toil of body, and intolerable charges you have sustained to the consumption of some good portion of your patrimony, but you have invested yourself with immortal renown. (*Calendar of the Carew Manuscripts*, 2.24)

By 29 December 1575 he was at Durham House in London

petitioning for compensation from the privy council for the loss of his fortune in Ireland and to pay off his creditors. Negotiations dragged as offers were made and rejected by Essex, and Lord Burghley became irritable. At length, on 9 March 1576 the queen signed a warrant reappointing Essex 'earl marshal of Ireland' and on 9 May confirmed the grant of the Farney in co. Monaghan, about one-fifth of that shire. He then defrayed debts amounting to about £35,473 by selling off land in Staffordshire, Cornwall, Essex, Wiltshire, and Yorkshire. He left Chartley Hall, Staffordshire, in mid-July 1576 and arrived in Dublin on the 23rd where, in the absence of Sir Henry Sidney, he was welcomed by the chancellor, William Gerard, and by Adam Loftus, the archbishop of Dublin. After visiting his lands in Monaghan, Sidney invested him in the office of earl marshal of Ireland.

By September Essex was ill with dysentery. On 20 September he wrote to the queen that he was on his deathbed and begged her to favour his elder son, Robert. He died in Dublin on 22 September 1576, aged thirty-seven, and was buried in Carmarthen on 26 November. In his will, drawn up on 14 June 1575, Essex left moneys to be expended on fortifying the pale at the discretion of the lord deputy. A funeral sermon (published in London in 1577) was preached by Richard Davies, bishop of St David's, and an epitaph was entered in the Stationers' Company register in 1575/6 which is identical with 'The Death of Devoreux' printed by J. Payne Collier from a manuscript in his possession in his *Extracts from the Stationers' Company Registers*. Thomas Churchyard published an elegy in his *Generall Rehearsall of Warres* (1579), which may in fact have been issued separately at the time of the earl's death.

Controversy on cause of death A rumour that the earl had been poisoned proved groundless, as attested by the post-mortem examination ordered by Sir Henry Sidney. Sidney's report to Walsingham gives a detailed description of Essex's last days, and likewise his secretary, Edward Waterhouse, wrote a sad account, printed in William Camden's *Annales* (as edited by Thomas Hearne, 1717). A manuscript copy of the latter, erroneously attributed to Thomas Churchyard's hand and once belonging to William Cole, the Cambridge antiquary, is now in the British Library (BL, Add. MS 5845, fols. 337–49). *Leicester's Commonwealth*, an attack on Leicester's character written in 1584, wrongly ascribes to Robert Parsons the allegation that Leicester was responsible for Essex's death, motivated, as he may well have been, by his adulterous relations with Essex's wife. A contemporary ballad, 'Leicester's Ghost', repeats the story, but it was not published until 1641. Certainly Lady Essex did not accompany her husband to Ireland. In 1575 she was at Kenilworth when Leicester entertained the queen there, and on 6 August the countess of Essex received the queen at Chartley Hall in the absence of the earl. We know that Leicester was anxious in March 1576 to have Essex return to Ireland, and there is no proof that the countess intrigued with Leicester in her husband's lifetime. She married Leicester on 21 September 1578. By her second marriage she had a son who died in

1584. After Leicester's death (4 September 1588) she married Sir Christopher *Blount in July 1589. He was executed in 1601 for his part in the treason plot of her son Robert *Devereux, second earl of Essex, and she lived a widow until her death at the age of ninety-four on 25 December 1634. She was buried at the side of her second husband at Warwick.

Assessment All who knew Essex, and especially those who served with him in Ulster, testify to his exceptional courage in sharing all the hardships of the campaign to which his men were subjected. But his Ulster enterprise was ill-conceived and incompetently executed, and its inexorable failure was due as much to his lack of judgement as to the vacillating policy of the queen and the rivalry of William Fitzwilliam. The wanton atrocities committed on the O'Neills and the Scots on Rathlin Island precipitated a further deterioration in Anglo-Gaelic relations.

Richard Davies, the preacher of his funeral panegyric, said that Essex was learned in history and genealogy and heraldry. According to Waterhouse, Essex's secretary, he sang a hymn of his own composition on his deathbed. A poem attributed to Essex exists in two copies in the British Library, and another in the Bodleian. These verses are printed as 'The Compleynt of a Sinner' in *The Paradise of Dainty Devices* (1576) above the initials F. K. (Francis Kinwelmersh, friend of the Elizabethan writer and poet George Gascoigne). J. J. N. McGurk

Sources W. B. Devereux, *Lives and letters of the Devereux, earls of Essex … 1540–1646*, 2 vols. (1853) · *CSP Ire.*, 1573–6 · J. S. Brewer and W. Bullen, eds., *Calendar of the Carew manuscripts*, 1–2, PRO (1867–9) · G. Hill, *An historical account of the MacDonnells of Antrim* (1873) · H. A. Lloyd, 'The Essex inheritance', *Welsh History Review / Cylchgrawn Hanes Cymru*, 7 (1974–5), 13–39 · E. P. Shirley, *History of Monaghan* (1879) · N. P. Canny, *The Elizabethan conquest of Ireland: a pattern established, 1565–76* (1976) · C. Brady, *The chief governors: the rise and fall of reform government in Tudor Ireland, 1536–1588* (1994) · T. Ó'Flaich, 'The O'Neills of the Fews', *Seanchas Ardmhacha*, 7 (1973–4), 1–64, 263–315 · J. A. Froude, *The reign of Elizabeth*, 4 (1909) · T. W. Moody and others, eds., *A new history of Ireland*, 3–9 (1976–84) · R. C. Morton, 'The enterprise of Ulster', *History Today*, 17 (1967), 114–21 · S. G. Ellis, *Ireland in the age of the Tudors* (1998), 302–10 · G. A. Hayes-McCoy, *Scots mercenary forces in Ireland (1565–1603)* (1937) · R. Dunlop, 'Sixteenth century schemes for the plantation of Ulster', *SHR*, 22 (1924–5), 50–60, 115–26, 197–212 · H. Morgan, 'The colonial venture of Sir Thomas Smith in Ulster, 1571–1575', *HJ*, 28 (1985), 261–78 · will, PRO, PROB 11/58, sig. 34 · *DNB* · A. F. Kinney, *Titled Elizabethans: a directory of Elizabethan state and church officers* (1973)

Archives BL, corresp. · BL, copies of a poem attrib. to Essex, Add. MS 5830, fol. 122 · Staffs. RO, household inventory | BL, Sloane MS 1896, fol. 58 · Bodl. Oxf., Gough MS

Likenesses oils, 1572, Christchurch Mansion, Ipswich · oils, 1572, Metropolitan Museum of Art, New York · oils, 1573–4, Ulster Museum, Belfast · oils, 1575? (after portrait, 1572), NPG [*see illus.*] · M. Gheeraerts, etching (*Procession of knights of the Garter*, 1576), BM · Passe, line engraving, NPG; repro. in H. Holland, *Herōologia Anglica* (1620) · oils, NPG

Wealth at death approx. £20,000—held manors in three Welsh shires and eight English shires, and property in London and the Farney, co. Monaghan, Ireland: will, PRO, PROB 11/58, sig. 34

Devey, George (1820–1886), architect and painter, was born on 23 February 1820 at 34 Ely Place, London, the second of four children of Frederick Nicholls Devey (1786–1862), a solicitor, and his wife, Ann (*b.* 1785), daughter of

George Devey (1820–1886), by unknown photographer

Durs Egg, a Swiss gunmaker who had emigrated to England. It was probably the artistic interests of his mother's family—her younger brother was the painter Augustus *Egg—which encouraged Devey's early enthusiasm for painting and sketching. He was educated first at a private school in Stanmore, Middlesex, and then, from 1832 to 1835, at King's College School, London, where he was taught drawing by John Sell Cotman. In 1837 he was articled to the architect Thomas Little in Northumberland Street, London. Little appreciated his skill at draughtsmanship, and employed him in his office after his pupillage had ended.

Although Devey exhibited designs for buildings under his own name at the Royal Academy on four occasions between 1841 and 1848, he does not appear to have set up in practice by himself until about 1846, after his return from a tour of Germany and Italy. His first office was at 16 Great Marlborough Street, London, where he remained until 1880, when he moved to 123 Bond Street. In 1856 he became a fellow of the Royal Institute of British Architects. His career was established slowly. In 1848 he was introduced to Lord De L'Isle, for whom he restored and extended a group of cottages known as Leicester Square at the entrance to Penshurst Place in Kent. Devey's sensitive handling of these modest tile-hung buildings reveals his close examination of the vernacular architecture of the Kentish Weald, a study unexceptional for an artist at that date but unprecedented for an architect.

This was the beginning of a busy country house practice, although it was not until 1866 that Devey received his first commission for an entirely new house, the half-timbered Akeley Wood, Buckinghamshire. His main work was remodelling old houses and designing estate buildings. Many were for Liberal politicians, as a result of Devey's friendship with Sir Walter James (later first Baron Northbourne), like Devey an accomplished watercolour painter and skilled horseman. Devey remodelled Bettes-hanger, James's seat near Deal in Kent, for which he also provided garden designs. The Liberal connection proved most profitable for Devey in an introduction to the Roths-childs, on whose Buckinghamshire estates he worked for many years, beginning with new estate buildings for Sir Anthony de Rothschild at Aston Clinton in 1863. His major documented works for the Rothschilds were the pavilion at Eythrope (1876–9) for Alice de Rothschild and the enlargement for Leopold de Rothschild of Ascott from 1874 onwards, to create what Mary Gladstone called 'a palace-like cottage' (L. Masterson, ed., *Mary Gladstone: her Diaries and Letters*, 1930, 196).

Although Devey's genius was for modest picturesque buildings, he received many commissions for large houses. Among them are Hall Place, Leigh, Kent (1871–4), for the hosiery manufacturer and Liberal MP Samuel Morley, which at £70,913 was Devey's most expensive building; and Goldings, near Hertford, for the banker Robert Smith, which was the biggest (1871–4). Devey's sensitivity to materials is perhaps shown to better effect in his many extensions and alterations to old houses, most notably his additions to Walmer Castle, Kent, for the second Earl Granville (1872–5) and to Melbury House, Dorset, for the fifth earl of Ilchester (1884–6). His concern for the external harmony of his buildings was not matched by any interest in interior design.

Devey was a solitary man, who did not encourage publication of his designs; since they were almost exclusively for domestic buildings, and so out of the public eye, few were noticed by his contemporaries. Not until his rediscovery by H. S. Goodhart-Rendel in 1957—'one of three most influential domestic architects in England of the 19th century'—did Devey's reputation begin to rise (P. Ferriday, ed., *Victorian Architecture*, 1963, 67). And it was not until the publication of Jill Allibone's biography in 1991 that it became clear that Devey was not only a prolific country house architect but also a pioneer of the revived interest in English vernacular models. His cottages at Penshurst were seen and sketched by W. E. Nesfield and Richard Norman Shaw in 1860 and so probably influenced their creation of the 'Old English' style in the late 1860s and 1870s, which had a decisive impact on English domestic architecture.

Devey never married. Although he fell in love with a clergyman's daughter, Flora Hoskins, and proposed to her twice—before she married in 1857 and after she was widowed in 1866—he was rejected both times, probably because of his heterodox religious beliefs. He was a member of the Theistic church founded by the Revd Charles Voysey, thanks to which Voysey's architect son Charles Francis Annesley Voysey worked in Devey's office for two years. Voysey later recalled that 'When asked by his client to join a house-party, Devey would make the most fascinating catch-penny sketches while dressing for dinner and present them during dessert, charming everyone' (J. Brandon-Jones, 'C. F. A. Voysey: a memoir', *Architectural Association Journal*, 72, 1957, 241–62).

Devey's practice was wound up after his death. There is a large collection of his drawings in the drawings collection of the Royal Institute of British Architects, together with a substantial number of photographs commissioned by him; he was a pioneer in the use of photography to record buildings, including his own under construction as well as completed. Devey lived with his parents first at Ely Place and subsequently at Ealing. After they died he moved to Elm Park House in Chelsea and then, at some point between 1881 and 1884, to Ashley House in Lavender Hill, Clapham, where he was living at the time of his death. He died of bronchitis on 4 November 1886 at his brother's house, Devonshire House, Pelham Crescent, Hastings (where he had bought a house intended for his retirement), and was buried in the borough council's cemetery at Ore, in Kent. His estate was valued at £32,531, 'a pretty large sum, as times go, for a man to have accumulated by his own exertions in a profession the emoluments of which are not over-liberal' (*The Builder*, 25 June 1887, 931). MICHAEL HALL

Sources J. Allibone, *George Devey: architect, 1820–1886* (1991) [incl. work list] · A. Saint, *Richard Norman Shaw* (1976) · *CGPLA Eng. & Wales* (1887)

Archives RIBA, account book · RIBA, MSS and drawings · RIBA BAL, specification of works and account book

Likenesses photograph, RIBA [*see illus.*]

Wealth at death £32,531 1s. 7d.: probate, 2 June 1887, *CGPLA Eng. & Wales*

Device, Alizon (d. 1612). *See under* Pendle witches (act. 1612).

Device, Elizabeth (b. before 1572, d. 1612). *See under* Pendle witches (act. 1612).

Device, James (d. 1612). *See under* Pendle witches (act. 1612).

Device, Jennet (b. 1602/3). *See under* Pendle witches (act. 1612).

Devine, George Alexander Cassady (1910–1966), actor and theatre director, was born on 20 November 1910 in Hendon, near London, the only child of Giorgios Devine, bank clerk, of Hendon, and his wife, Ruth Eleanor Cassady. He was educated at Clayesmore School, of which the founder and headmaster was his uncle Alexander Devine, and at Wadham College, Oxford, where he read modern history. One of his tutors was Lord David Cecil. As president of the Oxford University Dramatic Society in his last year, he established a foothold in the professional theatre by inviting John Gielgud to direct the society's 1932 production of *Romeo and Juliet*, in which Devine played Mercutio in company with Peggy Ashcroft's Juliet and Edith Evans's Nurse, and Christopher Hassall's Romeo.

Devine left Oxford without taking schools to embark on a London acting career. At the same time, he attached himself as business manager to the firm of *Motley, the stage design partnership of Elizabeth Montgomery, Margaret

Harris, and her sister (Audrey) Sophia Harris (1900–1966), who on 27 October 1939 became Devine's wife, and was the mother of his only child, Harriet.

It was in the Motley studio that he first met Michel Saint-Denis, director of the Compagnie des Quinze, whom for the rest of his life he acknowledged as his master. With Saint-Denis and others he set up the London Theatre Studio (1936–9) which attempted a revolution in British stage training. After the war (which Devine spent mostly in Burma as a captain in the Royal Artillery, and during which he was twice mentioned in dispatches), he resumed his alliance with Saint-Denis at the Old Vic Centre: a tripartite offshoot of the Old Vic Company, comprising a school (directed by Glen Byam Shaw), the Young Vic touring troupe (directed by Devine), and a never-completed experimental theatre (in the charge of Saint-Denis). From its opening in 1947 the centre produced an astounding crop of young actors, directors, and designers, and when the governors of the Old Vic closed it down in 1952 their action provoked a storm of professional outrage and parliamentary criticism.

Up to this time Devine had spent most of his working life as a teacher–administrator, but with the break-up of the Vic Centre, he turned to freelance directing: partly of opera at Sadler's Wells and Covent Garden (where he directed the première of Sir William Walton's *Troilus and Cressida*, 1954), and partly of the Shakespeare repertory at Stratford upon Avon (collaborating with Gielgud and Isamu Noguchi in the 'Japanese' *King Lear* in 1955). In 1956 he resumed his reformist mission as artistic director of the newly formed English Stage Company at the Royal Court Theatre. The company's original policy was to persuade established novelists to write for the stage, a policy abandoned after the production of John Osborne's *Look Back in Anger* (1956) which released a tidal wave of new plays by hitherto unknown young playwrights including John Arden and Arnold Wesker. Until the end of the decade the Court was the spearhead of the so-called 'breakthrough' movement, challenging the reigning conventions of dramatic craftsmanship and reasserting the theatre's role as a platform for radical opinion.

Throughout this spectacular period Devine remained personally inconspicuous. After the first season he directed very few new plays himself (excepting those by his close friend Samuel Beckett); and when he acted on the Court stage it was usually to save money. His purpose was to create a free space where the best talents could collaborate in pushing the theatre from the periphery to the centre of English cultural life: a purpose partly acknowledged in 1958 when he was appointed CBE 'for services to drama'.

Devine's 'writers' theatre' was a place where material of a kind formerly restricted to club performances found a public outlet. He was not the originator of this idea, but he was the first English director to make it work. He succeeded through an unshakeable determination, entirely untouched by narrow obsessiveness. In opening his doors to unknown writers and directors he also kept them open to eminent pre-war colleagues such as Ashcroft and Laurence Olivier: and in keeping an open space for the rebel artists under his roof he took great care not to play the rebel with his own management committee. He remained a dedicated teacher, and the creator of an exemplary theatre in which the technician was respected no less than the actor and the writer. His final years were spent with his former London Theatre Studio pupil the designer Jocelyn, daughter of Sir Alan *Herbert. In her company he died in London on 20 January 1966.

IRVING WARDLE, *rev.*

George Alexander Cassady Devine (1910–1966), by Howard Coster, 1934

Sources I. Wardle, *The theatres of George Devine* (1975) · *CGPLA Eng. & Wales* (1966) · m. cert. · **Archives** SOUND BL NSA, documentary recordings · BL NSA, performance recordings · **Likenesses** H. Coster, photograph, 1934, NPG [*see illus.*] · **Wealth at death** £18,146: probate, 17 June 1966, *CGPLA Eng. & Wales*

Devine [*née* Blackley], **Rachel** (1875–1960), weaver and trade unionist, was born on 13 February 1875 at Dudhope Crescent, Dundee, the daughter of John Blackley, yarn dresser, and his wife, Rachel McClellan. She became a weaver, and married John Devine, a cabinet-maker.

Active as a trade unionist, Rachel Devine was neither the best-known nor the longest-serving executive member of the Dundee and District Union of Jute and Flax Workers, but she was certainly among the most outspoken. At the 1929 joint trade union women's conference, held in Dundee, delegates from outside the city complained of the lack of representation of women in the trade union leadership, that organized male workers were failing to recruit women, and that female workers were too often silent at union meetings. To a great deal of laughter, Mrs Devine remarked, with typical bluntness, that 'the difficulty in Dundee was not getting their women to speak, but in getting them to speak and to hold their tongues at the right time' (newspaper cuttings book, Lamb Collection, Dundee Central Library).

Rachel Devine was present at the founding meeting of the union in 1906. The constitution that was then adopted stated that half of its executive should consist of women, an important feature for a union seeking to represent workers in an industry that employed large numbers of females. Elected to the executive as a representative from the Heathfield works in 1909, Rachel Devine was to hold a number of positions on the union's management committee up to at least the 1940s.

In 1911 Rachel Devine was one of the union executive signatories to the Scottish Trade Union Congress (STUC) affiliation document. She was a regular delegate to the STUC, and appeared along with Jeannie Spence and Mary McArthur in a photograph of a group of women delegates to the congress in 1911. She represented the union on the local trades council and Dundee's Labour Representative Committee before the First World War. By early 1915 disagreements within the executive, and her criticism of the full-time secretary, John F. Sime, resulted in her dismissal as its representative. She returned to the executive in October 1915, and successfully moved a resolution for the union to support the provision of legal assistance to rent strikers.

Against a background of industrial action in 1923, Rachel Devine was elected vice-president of the union with one of the largest recorded votes. A year later she was elected president, and held the position until 1930 when she was replaced by another founding and long-serving member, Jeannie Spence. As president of the union, Rachel Devine, along with the secretary, John F. Sime, negotiated wages and conditions with the employers' Association of Jute Spinners and Manufacturers after the First World War. The association minutes suggest that she was both an aggressive and a capable negotiator.

Rachel Devine again served as vice-president, up to 1934, when both the positions of president and vice-president began to be taken by men. She lost her place on the executive after she found employment in another factory in 1935, but returned to the Heathfield works and was again elected as a representative in 1937. In 1938 she became a trustee of the union and a delegate to the trades council and Labour Party. In 1940 she made the presentation, on behalf of the union, to John F. Sime on his retirement as secretary. In her speech she recalled the low wages and long hours that had been a central feature of the pre-1914 jute industry, and the progress that the union had made. She was still active, as a trustee, in the 1940s. She died on 13 April 1960 at Maryfield Hospital, Dundee, and was cremated at Dundee crematorium on 16 April. She was survived by her husband. GRAHAM R. SMITH

Sources Dundee and District Union of Jute and Flax Workers minute books, 1906–66, Dundee City Archive and Record Centre, Dundee, GD/JF/1–21 · *Dundee Courier and Advertiser* (15 April 1960) · newspaper cutting book, Dundee Central Library, Lamb Collection, vol. 1B, 222 · I. McDougall, *A catalogue of some labour records in Scotland and some Scots records outside Scotland* (1978), 234 (2) · University of Dundee, Dundee, MS 84/5 · **Archives** McManus Galleries, Dundee, union certificates and photographs, incl. certificate of affiliation, 1911 · University of Dundee, MS 84 | Dundee City Archive and Record Centre, Dundee and District Union of Jute and Flax Workers minute books, GD/JF · **Likenesses** group portrait, photograph, 1911, repro. in *Dundee Courier and Advertiser* · photograph, 1933 (delegation to royal commission?)

Devis, Anthony (1729–1816/17). *See under* Devis, Arthur (1712–1787).

Devis, Arthur (1712–1787), portrait painter, was born on 19 February 1712 in Preston, Lancashire, and baptized there on 22 February, the eldest of the four sons of Anthony Devis (*b. c.*1682, *d.* after 1761), carpenter and town councillor, and his wife, Ellin, *née* Rauthmell (*d.* 1727). After his mother's death his father married, in 1728, Anne Blackburne (*bap.* 1695?), with whom he had two sons, the elder of whom was Anthony Devis [*see below*].

Arthur Devis trained with the sporting and topographical landscape artist Peter Tillemans, whose sale in London in 1733 included nine of Devis's Italianate landscapes with ruins. His earliest documented work is a bird's-eye view, *Hoghton Tower, Lancashire* (1735, priv. coll.), for which he was paid £6 6*s.* Soon thereafter he began to produce portraits in the conversation piece genre. In 1742, when he was described in the Preston guild roll as 'of London, Painter', he married, on 20 July, Elizabeth Faulkner (1723–1788) at St Katharine by the Tower, London. By 1747 the couple had moved to Great Queen Street, where they lived until moving to Brighton in 1783. Of their twenty-two children only six survived, including Ellin Devis (1746–1820), author and a headmistress of a girls' school, and Thomas Anthony Devis (1757–1810) and Arthur William *Devis (1762–1822), both painters.

Devis's speciality, the conversation piece, is described as

a painting of one or more full-length figures in small scale, frequently accompanied by family members with their possessions, furnishings, and domestic animals, in compositions set within proprietary interiors or landscapes. Taken up in England during the 1720s by William Hogarth and used by Thomas Gainsborough and George Romney (early in their careers), the genre was popular with numbers of unnamed provincial artists whose works have been attributed wrongly to Devis. The most prolific of the eighteenth-century conversation piece artists, Devis produced more than 300 paintings in the format for members of the established, and largely tory, landed gentry and professional classes. For several years after he moved to London he relied on commissions which drew him back to Lancashire and adjacent counties. Thereafter he travelled less frequently, and attracted sitters to his studio in London where he refined his craft to produce, from 1745 until the early 1760s, his most important works.

Devis exhibited at the Free Society of Artists between 1761 and 1763, between 1767 and 1770, in 1775, and in 1780, and was elected president of the organization in 1768. He restored paintings for Sir Roger Newdigate in 1762–4 and was hired by the commissioners of the Royal Naval Hospital, Greenwich, in 1777 to clean and repair the Painted Hall for £1000. Devis also supplemented his income by producing paintings on glass. He had an apprentice, George Senhouse, from 1752 to 1755, and his pupils included Robert Marris and his sons Arthur William and Thomas Anthony. In 1783, the year in which Devis moved to Brighton, the London auctioneer Barford offered for sale, on 10 and 11 April, 'Pictures belonging to Mr. Devis of Great Queen Street, Portrait Painter and Picture-Cleaner'.

Untrained in academic study from the live human model, Devis frequently used a small wooden manikin, or lay figure (Harris Museum and Art Gallery, Preston), and occasionally clothed it in costumes kept to hand. Although the practice made apparent his deficiencies in anatomical rendering, he was valued by his clients for his ability to describe a wealth of information and to place his figures within legible interior spaces or landscapes. His use of layered glazes and his meticulous handling of the brush, the result of a study of seventeenth-century Dutch masters and his own occasional work as a miniature painter, gave his canvases a highly crafted finish which increased their visual appeal. In such compositions as *William Atherton, Mayor of Preston, and his Wife Lucy* (c.1743–4, Walker Art Gallery, Liverpool) and *Gentleman and Lady at a Harpsichord* (1749, Victoria and Albert Museum, London) he demonstrates a topographer's eye for describing the sheen of satin dresses and waistcoats, and the glowing polish on furnishings and floorboards, and for placing his sitters within the vertical and horizontal planes of an interior. In his landscape conversation pieces he also defined with clarity of detail the natural features of a setting. For example, in *Sir George and Lady Strickland* (1751, Ferens Art Gallery, Hull) the burdock weeds, tree trunks, and winding river are so distributed as to present the figures within an ordered scheme. Only a few of Devis's compositions represent actual locations, among them the interior in *Sir Roger Newdigate in his Gothic Library at Arbury, Warwickshire* (1756–8, priv. coll.) and the river scenery in *Philip Howard of Corby Castle, Cumbria* (1759, priv. coll.). Within his restrained and carefully planned group compositions each figure is spaced at wide intervals, isolated by local detail and defined contours rather than assembling into an integrated pictorial whole. Interpreted as a visual allusion to his patrons' codes of behaviour, his conversation pieces record hierarchies of age, gender, and property. His sitters, such as *Mr and Mrs Hill* (c.1750–51, Yale U. CBA), comport themselves in a range of polite attitudes illustrated in contemporary etiquette manuals. Later in his career Devis attempted to give his figures greater mobility and several of his landscapes allude to the picturesque or summon up wilder aspects of the English countryside. But most of his tableaux remain static owing to their smooth finish, graphic precision, and pervasive reliance on displays of decorum. His work was criticized by those for whom such displays betrayed the sitter's social aspirations. After the Royal Academy's founding in 1768 (the year in which Devis became president of the far less prestigious Free Society of Artists), English artists were no longer marginalized by connoisseurs, and many enjoyed international reputations. In this competitive milieu, Devis's modest reputation suffered a steep decline, not to be reassessed until the 1930s. He has since been recognized as a master of his special craft, that of describing, in small compass, the ideals of a privileged society.

Arthur Devis died in Brighton on 25 July 1787 and was buried in the churchyard of St Mary's, Paddington, Middlesex. His wife died in London on 15 March 1788.

Arthur Devis's half-brother **Anthony Devis** (1729–1816/17), landscape painter, was born on 18 March 1729 in Preston, Lancashire, and baptized in April in Preston, the elder son of Anthony Devis and his second wife, Anne Blackburne, who was from Yorkshire and was born at a house called Frier Head. In 1742 he was described in the Preston guild roll as 'of London, Painter'. He exhibited landscapes at the Free Society of Artists in 1761 and 1763, and at the Royal Academy in 1772 and 1781. He was in 1764:

> at the Hon. Mr. Vernon's, Newick Park Sussex; 1770 Sept at Robert Child's Esq., Osterley Park; 1771 Robert Child's Esq. Upton; Sir John Chichester's, Youlton near Barnstaple; 1773, June, Duke of Manchester's, Kimbolton; Sept, John Peploe Birch Esq. Garnston, Herefordshire; Oct., the Hon. Mr. Vernon's, Britton Ferry, Glamorganshire; 1775, July, Lord Ducie's, Woodchester Park; 1776, May, Lord Peters; June, Sir Rich. Worsley's, Appuldercomb, Isle of Wight. (*N&Q*, 416)

In 1780 he purchased Albury House, Guildford, Surrey, of which he made many paintings, drawings, and watercolours (1792, Harris Museum and Art Gallery, Preston; undated, British Museum, London). He travelled widely to sketch and paint English scenery. He died, unmarried, at Guildford on 26 April 1816 or 1817.

ELLEN G. D'OENCH

Sources E. D'Oench, 'Arthur Devis (1712–1787): master of the Georgian conversation piece', PhD diss., Yale U., 1979 • E. G. D'Oench, *The conversation piece: Arthur Devis and his contemporaries* (1980) [exhibition catalogue, Yale U. CBA, 1 Oct – 30 Nov 1980] •

S. Sartin, *Polite society by Arthur Devis, 1712–1787: portraits of the English country gentleman and his family* (1983) [exhibition catalogue, Preston and London, 1 Oct 1983 – 29 Jan 1984] • S. H. Pavière, *The Devis family of painters* (1950) • E. D'Oench, 'Arthur Devis and an idle apprentice, 1752–1755', *Eighteenth-Century Life*, 6 (1980–81), 60–78 • E. Waterhouse, *Painting in Britain, 1530–1790*, 4th edn (1978) • *N&Q*, 3rd ser., 1 (1862), 416

Archives Harris Museum and Art Gallery, Preston, Lancashire, family archive • PRO, MS minutes of the directors of Greenwich Hospital, ADM 67/11, fol. 226, 67/26, fols. 105–6, 143, 176 | Cumbria AS, Senhouse MSS, D/Sen Add. letters • GL, George Senhouse, IRA, book 19, fol. 32 • Warks. CRO, Newdigate MSS 1762, 1764

Likenesses A. Devis, self-portrait, oils, *c.*1737–1738, Harris Museum and Art Gallery, Preston, Lancashire • A. Devis, oils, *c.*1742 (Anthony Devis), priv. coll. • A. Devis, self-portrait, oils, 1742, Harris Museum and Art Gallery, Preston, Lancashire • A. Devis, self-portrait, oils, 1742–4, NPG • A. Devis, self-portrait, oils, *c.*1754–1755, Harris Museum and Art Gallery, Preston, Lancashire • A. Devis, self-portrait, drawing, *c.*1787 (after A. Devis), Harris Museum and Art Gallery, Preston, Lancashire • three miniatures, Harris Museum and Art Gallery, Preston, Lancashire

Devis, Arthur William (1762–1822), portrait painter, was born in London on 10 August 1762, the nineteenth child of the portrait painter Arthur *Devis (1712–1787) and his wife, Elizabeth Faulkner (1723–1788), and the nephew of the landscape painter Anthony *Devis (1729–1816/17) [*see under* Devis, Arthur].

Early career Arthur William Devis received his early art education from his father but was enrolled in the Royal Academy Schools at the age of only twelve. Although he exhibited a handful of works at the Free Society and the Royal Academy, little is known of Devis's early career until his father obtained for him the post of draughtsman aboard the *Antelope*, a messenger ship commissioned to sail to China by the East India Company. Devis was to be paid 100 guineas to make maps of the islands in the South China Sea. On the outward journey he was wounded in the chest and jaw when the *Antelope* stopped off the coast of New Guinea to trade with natives who had paddled out to them. The ship's captain, Henry Wilson, recorded in his log that 'suddenly the people in the boats discharged a flight of arrows at us' (MS log of the *Antelope*, 1 April 1783, BL OIOC, L/Mar/B/570A). Devis was not severely injured but the face wound caused him 'a locked jaw, by which he suffered to the last moment of his life' (undated appeal, *c.*1822, Biddulph papers).

The *Antelope* reached Macao in June 1783. After repairs had been made and sixteen Chinese sailors engaged to supplement the crew, the *Antelope* began the return journey. In early August the ship ran aground on an uncharted coral reef close to a group of islands now known as Palau, or Belau more locally. All but one of the crew survived and Devis, who evidently had salvaged his drawing materials, recorded the construction of a smaller ship made from the wreck of the *Antelope*. Captain Wilson described the extraordinary adventures of the crew, in which Devis figured prominently, as they made the acquaintance of the 'Pelew' islanders and assisted them to conquer the neighbouring islands. Devis's studies of the king of Pelew and his wives were used to illustrate George Keate's *Account of the Pelew Islands*, first published in 1788. Several Pelew landscapes and portraits were exhibited at the Royal Academy and the British Institution between 1796 and 1807.

India, 1784–1795 In their newly constructed ship, the *Oroolong*, named after the small island on which they had landed, the crew returned to Macao and eventually to England, except for Devis, who sailed from there for Calcutta in September 1784. Johann Zoffany and Thomas Hickey were both well-established portrait painters in Calcutta at that time but Devis nevertheless found himself initially in great demand. He received lucrative portrait commissions from the departing governor-general, Warren Hastings, and from the high court judge Sir Robert Chambers and his wife, whose portraits are in the Yale Center for British Art, New Haven, Connecticut. His portrait of John Addison, the resident judge at Moorshadabad (Harris Museum and Art Gallery, Preston), is an excellent example of Devis's early portrait style. Addison's elongated limbs and bold outline are reminiscent of Arthur Devis senior's portraits, which were dependent on the use of the lay figure. Placed in such an exotic setting, and contrasted with the bulk of the elephants behind him and a naturalistic group of Indian servants, the figure emanates a sense of classical poise and elegance.

Devis was at the centre of a scandal involving a fellow artist, John Alefounder. When in 1785 Alefounder fell ill, Devis sold many of Alefounder's paintings and materials to pay off his friend's immediate creditors. Alefounder publicly accused Devis of acting maliciously and years later, when Alefounder committed suicide in 1794, the rumours resurfaced and followed Devis home. Devis was unable to obtain sufficient patronage as a portrait painter in Calcutta to support himself. While travelling around Madras and Bengal in search of patrons he began collecting material for an ambitious series of subject paintings depicting 'the arts, manufactures, and agriculture of Bengal', which was to be engraved in colour and dedicated to the orientalist Sir William Jones, who was painted by Devis in 1793 (BL). Only four of the engravings were ever published but the thirty paintings provide a unique record of life in rural Bengal, combining loosely painted, delicately coloured landscapes, a naturalistic figure style with occasional touches of classicism, and finely observed still-life elements. These paintings are dispersed among the collections of the Victoria and Albert Museum, London, the Ashmolean Museum, Oxford, and the Yale Center for British Art, New Haven, and a number of private collections.

Devis was back in Calcutta in 1792, when he was commissioned to paint the portrait of Governor-General Cornwallis following his military victory over Tipu Sultan, the 'tiger of Mysore'. Two of Tipu's sons were taken hostage by Cornwallis and Devis painted the elaborate handing-over ceremony in his most ambitious work to date (*Lord Cornwallis Receiving the Sons of Tipu Sultan as Hostages*). At least three versions of the event were completed (all priv. colls.), the largest, measuring over 4 metres in length, has over sixty portraits of officers and Indian dignitaries.

Despite receiving astronomically high fees, notably

£2530 for his portrait of Cornwallis, Devis struggled financially and eventually decided to return to England, setting sail in January 1795. He had recently made what was generally considered to be an unwise marriage to an actress, Mrs Coombes. Instead of returning with him to England, she travelled first to Lisbon, then to Paris, and finally to Verdun, where she died in 1805, shortly after her release from a debtors' prison.

London c.1795–1822 In the late 1790s Devis struggled to establish himself as an artist in London, relying on portrait commissions from his Indian connections but also exhibiting landscapes, animal paintings, and theatrical subjects. His full-length portrait *Sir William Pitt Amherst* (Harris Museum and Art Gallery, Preston), dating from 1803, shows Devis competing in scale, drama, and the bravura handling of paint with Thomas Lawrence's portraits in the grand manner. By 1800, however, he was bankrupt and was saved from prison only through the intervention of John Biddulph, a friend and long-term patron whom Devis had probably met in India. Biddulph bought up many of the paintings seized by Devis's creditors following his bankruptcy. By 1803 Devis owed over £2000 to Biddulph, who was forced to refuse further financial help. Devis contracted still more debts on behalf of a failing dressmaking business owned by his sister and Margaret Lanchester, who was to become his second wife.

Devis was imprisoned in 1804, gaining his release in November or December the following year to gather material for what would be his most famous work, *The Death of Nelson* (c.1805–7; NMM). A prize of £500 had been offered by the engraver Josiah Boydell in November 1805 for the best representation of the subject and Devis saw this as a major opportunity to clear his debts and establish his reputation as a painter of modern history. He joined the *Victory* at Spithead in December, and made sketches of Nelson's body (he was present when 'the fatal ball' was removed from his body) as well as portrait studies of all those who had been present, after determining precisely where each one had stood at the moment of Nelson's death. Devis's documentary approach prompted a hostile response from Benjamin West, who complained that the painting was not an 'Epic representation' and that Nelson should not have been pictured 'like a sick man in a Prison Hole' (Farington, *Diary*, 3.150). Following the popular success of the painting (oil sketch exh. by Boydell, 1807; Royal Collection; finished painting exh. British Institution, 1809) and Boydell's engraving, Devis applied for associate status of the Royal Academy. He was summarily rejected for 'irregular living'—the circumstances of his first marriage, the Alefounder scandal, and his bankruptcy all telling against him.

From 1807 until his death in 1822 Devis managed to stay ahead of his creditors and resumed his friendship with the Biddulph family. He established a reputation as a painter of child portraits, many of which were engraved. He also produced several history paintings, collaborating with John Augustus Atkinson on *The Battle of Waterloo* (watercolour and engraving, c.1816–1818; BM), which was engraved by Boydell in 1819. In his later years he painted a number of large-scale group portraits and ambitious single-figure portraits such as his portrait of the actress Eliza O'Neill as *Belvidera … a Greek Courtesan* (exh. British Institution, 1816; Wolverhampton Art Gallery), which compares favourably with William Beechey's large-scale portraits.

In his final years Devis received royal patronage. *The Apotheosis of Princess Charlotte* (c.1819; Belgian Royal Collection), complete with swirling drapery and flying cherubs, was painted for the bereaved Prince Leopold, and demonstrates the continuing influence of a Reynoldsian neo-classical influence throughout Devis's career. A mezzotint after the work was published in 1820, as was an engraving after his portrait of Queen Caroline (1820; Ashmolean Museum, Oxford), the wife of George IV.

Devis died suddenly on 11 February 1822 at his home at Caroline Street, Bedford Square, London, and was buried in the churchyard of St Giles-in-the-Fields. He left his wife, children, and sisters unprovided for. His studio contained numerous unfinished portraits of titled sitters, as well as Indian, religious, and genre subjects and over 4000 fashion plates, for many of which Devis had provided the designs.

With the majority of his paintings in private collections, many in India and America, Devis's reputation quickly dwindled, resting almost entirely on *The Death of Nelson*, which remained a national icon well into the twentieth century. Since the 1970s several important works have appeared in the salerooms, including works from the Indian Manufactures series, helping to re-establish Devis as one of the more gifted and innovative followers of Reynolds. The Harris Museum and Art Gallery, Preston, the British Museum, London, and the Yale Center for British Art, New Haven, Connecticut, have large collections of his work.   STEPHEN WHITTLE

Sources S. H. Pavière, *The Devis family of painters* (1950) · M. Archer, *India and British portraiture, 1770–1825* (1979) · U. De, 'The economy of human life: Arthur William Devis' images of Indian arts, agriculture and manufacture', unpublished paper, 1998, priv. coll. · W. Foster, 'British artists in India, 1760–1820', *Walpole Society*, 19 (1930–31), 1–88 · S. Whittle, *Arthur William Devis* (2000) [exhibition catalogue, Harris Museum and Art Gallery, Preston, 2000] · D. J. Peacock, *Lee Boo of Belau: a prince in London* (Hawaii, 1987) · G. Keate, *An account of the Pelew islands composed from the journals of Captain Henry Wilson* (1783) · undated appeal, 1822?, Herefs. RO, Biddulph papers · R. Walker, *The Nelson portraits* (1998)
Archives Herefs. RO, Biddulph MSS
Likenesses A. W. Devis, self-portrait, watercolours, c.1790, Harris Museum and Art Gallery, Preston · A. W. Devis, self-portrait, pencil drawing, c.1808, AM Oxf. · T. Cheesman, stipple (after self-portrait; in *Elizabeth … detecting Babington's conspiracy*), Harris Museum and Art Gallery, Preston · T. Cheesman, stipple (after A. W. Davis, c.1808), NPG
Wealth at death see catalogue of contents of house and studio in Biddulph papers, Herefs. RO; Pavière, *Devis family*, 110

Devisme, Louis. See Vismes, Louis de (1720–1776).

Devizes, Richard of (c.1150–c.1200), Benedictine monk and chronicler, was a monk of the cathedral priory of St Swithun, Winchester. The convent is thinly documented in his time, and the details of his life are largely inferential. Nothing is known of his family, but his name connects him with Wiltshire, while his apparent familiarity with Master Robert, son of Henry, prior of Winchester from 1187 to 1191, implies that he was of some seniority in Robert's time, and was perhaps born before 1150. His chronicle survives in the form of a draft, and was probably not revised after 1198. It has been suggested that he contributed to the Winchester annals between 1196 and 1210, but on balance it seems likely that he had ceased to write, and was probably dead, before the end of Richard I's reign. He was buried at Winchester.

The general tone of Richard's chronicle is aristocratic. Winchester was a major see, uncomfortably involved in high politics during the long episcopate of Henry de Blois (1129–71), and still close to the court under Richard of Ilchester (1173–88) and Godfrey de Lucy (1189–1204). The latter's dispute with William de Longchamp, the chancellor, was composed at Winchester in 1191. Richard of Devizes is an important witness to that episode, but he probably also had his own sources of information. Although he was a firm champion of his house and of Benedictine monasticism, and consequently critical of other orders and of the secular clergy, his apparent familiarity with the life of the court, and with the literary conventions of romance, is suggestive of wider, worldly, contacts, as is his taste for scenes of battle and knightly prowess. His detailed and enthusiastic account of the first stages of Richard I's crusade seems to derive from some participant in the expedition who returned to England after the army left Sicily.

The chronicle of Richard of Devizes begins with a bantering dedication to Master Robert, who in 1191 had resigned the priorate of Canterbury to become a Carthusian monk at Witham, Somerset. Witham was the first Carthusian foundation in England, and a celebrated focus of spiritual endeavour, but the Benedictines had their own traditions. Two of Robert's predecessors had been elected to major Benedictine abbacies, at Glastonbury and Westminster, and his own migration to another order was not wholly pleasing to Winchester. Richard notes wryly that the Carthusians regale their visitors with a blessing rather than a dinner, and that despite their rule of silence they are better and more promptly informed than anyone else about events in the wider world, to which they are far from indifferent. He hopes that his work may help his friend further to appreciate his privileged seclusion.

The chronicle describes both Richard I's progress through the Mediterranean to Acre and the Holy Land, and the dissension raised in England during his absence by the conduct of his chancellor, William de Longchamp, and the ambitions of his brother Prince John. The narrative is dramatic and lively, with pungent reflections upon all the principal characters. On occasion Devizes preserves fragments of conversation, as with the king's aside, when raising funds for his expedition, that he would be willing to sell London if he could find a buyer. Even in such set pieces as Longchamp's formal defence of his conduct he may be embellishing rather than inventing, though he

adorned his script with classical tags, and sought to match his style to the dignity of the occasion. There is something of the romance in his dramatic presentation of individuals and events. He makes a curious excursus, having earlier referred to the massacre of Jews in various places that accompanied Richard I's coronation, by describing an alarm in Winchester over the suspected murder of a Christian boy. The story is clearly related to the alleged murder of William of Norwich in 1144 and similar fantasies elsewhere, but its real purpose is to present an account, attributed to a French Jew, of the principal towns in England, which culminates in an encomium of Winchester as the most favoured of all.

First and last Devizes' stock-in-trade is irony; he is well informed about the world, and he views it with an amused detachment. He writes for an informed audience, one that can be presumed to share his interests, enjoy his style, and appreciate his classical allusions. In many respects he invites comparison with Walter Map, for the setting of his drama is the court, and its echoes of romance emphasize that connection. Map, however, was a secular, and Richard was a Benedictine with a strong pride in his house and his order. He represents monastic learning in the last phase of its pre-eminence, immediately before the emergence of the universities. It is unlikely that he had any sense of such a threat, but he may well have been aware that Winchester itself, which he praised, was losing ground to London, to which the royal treasury had already moved, and which soon came to house the principal courts and administrative records.

There are two manuscripts of the *Gesta Ricardi I*: the author's holograph in Cambridge, Corpus Christi, MS 337, and a copy in BL, Cotton MS Domitian A.xiii, which may have been made at Witham. Both also contain the Winchester annals, a chronicle of English history which Richard probably began, and which was later continued to 1210, and subsequently beyond. The *Gesta* has been printed three times, by Joseph Stevenson in 1838, by Richard Howlett for the Rolls Series in 1886, and most recently by J. T. Appleby, as *The Chronicle of Richard of Devizes of the Time of King Richard I* (1963).   G. H. MARTIN

Sources *Chronicon Richardi Divisensis / The Chronicle of Richard of Devizes*, ed. J. T. Appleby (1963) · J. T. Appleby, 'Richard of Devizes and the annals of Winchester', *BIHR*, 36 (1963), 70–77 · A. Gransden, *Historical writing in England*, 1 (1974), 248–52 · R. Howlett, ed., *Chronicles of the reigns of Stephen, Henry II, and Richard I*, 3, Rolls Series, 82 (1886) · *Ann. mon.*, 2.3–125
Archives BL, Cotton MS Domitian A.xiii · CCC Cam., MS 337

Devlin [*married name* Campbell], **Anne** (1781–1851), Irish nationalist, the daughter of Winifred Dwyer and her husband, Bryan Devlin, a dairy farmer, was born at Cronebeg, near Aughrim, co. Wicklow. Her father moved the family to a 30 acre property at Corballis, near Rathdrum, when Anne was a girl. She had one elder sister, Mary, three younger brothers, and two younger sisters. Although virtually uneducated, Anne proved herself intelligent and exceptionally diligent in all aspects of her life.

The Devlins supported the republican United Irishmen from the spring of 1797 and both Anne's father and younger brother 'Little' Arthur were members of the illegal organization. While reputedly inactive during the rising of 1798, the Devlins harboured men wounded at the battle of Newtownmountkennedy on 30 May 1798 and had their house burnt in consequence by the yeomanry. The Devlins were again persecuted on 16 October 1798 when Anne's first cousin Michael Dwyer of Imaal attacked yeomanry residences around Rathdrum. Her father was arrested but Rathdrum cavalryman Thomas Darby, their landlord, prevented the home being razed for the second time. Anne frequently carried messages and provisions to the fugitive rebels who held out in the Wicklow Mountains under Dwyer and another first cousin, 'Big' Arthur Devlin of Crone. In late February 1799 she assisted in the reburial of three insurgents in the rebel plot at Kilranelagh cemetery.

The Devlins moved to a dairy farm in Rathfarnham, co. Dublin, upon the release of Anne's father from prison in September 1801. Anne remained there until April 1803 when she took work in nearby Butterfield Lane as housekeeper to Robert Emmet. She was present when prominent United Irish leaders conferred with Emmet, not least Thomas Russell, Thomas Cloney, and Dwyer. When the rising plans miscarried on 23 July 1803 she visited Emmet's party at their hiding place in the Dublin Mountains but was arrested in Butterfield Lane on the 26th. She was tortured by the military for refusing to answer their questions by means of 'half hanging' (repeated partial strangulation) and the infliction of numerous shallow bayonet wounds.

Most of the extended Devlin family were soon committed to Dublin's Kilmainham prison where Anne's nine-year-old brother, James, died of extreme neglect. Edward Trevor, the prison doctor, and Dublin's police chief, Major Henry Charles Sirr, pressed Devlin for details of the Emmet plot and responded to her remarkable obstinacy by holding her in some of the wettest cells. She was forced to view Emmet's mutilated corpse shortly after his execution on 20 September 1803. When her health deteriorated to the point that her life was in danger, brief visits to Lucan spa were arranged. Her relocation to Dublin Castle in early 1806 was motivated by Trevor's wish to keep her under lock and key lest she be released along with other 'state prisoners' by the more liberal incoming Westminster government. Anne was kindly treated in the castle by a Mrs Hanlon, who helped take advantage of the moderate political climate to secure her release after a short period.

Anne married a Mr Campbell (d. 1845), who may have been called William, soon after being freed and lived with him and their two children, William and Catherine, in John's Lane West until about 1845, when she was widowed. It had long been thought that the extreme poverty into which she sank in later life was her lot from 1806, but later research indicates that she was employed as a maid for friends of the Emmet family until 1810. More importantly, it appears that the master of St Patrick's Hospital, where Emmet's physician father had worked for over thirty years, was a close relative of her husband. She

was very probably the laundress of that name who was paid an inflated salary of £63 per annum between 1825 and the late 1830s when that much criticized institution was reformed.

The loss of steady work impacted severely on Anne's lifestyle, and occasional small gifts of money from nationalist historians R. R. Madden and Luke Cullen after 1842 did not offset a sharp decline into poverty. She died at 2 Little Elbow Lane, in the Coombe district, on 18 September 1851 and was buried in a pauper's grave in Glasnevin. On hearing of her death Madden organized her reinterment in a more prestigious part of the cemetery and erected a tombstone detailing her loyalty to Emmet.

RUÁN O'DONNELL

Sources NL Ire., Luke Cullen MSS, 9761, 9762, 8339 · C. Dickson, *The life of Michael Dwyer* (1944) · J. Finegan, ed., *Anne Devlin, patriot and heroine* (1992) · E. Malcolm, 'Anne Devlin: the heroine as laundress', *History Ireland*, 6/4 (1998), 9–10 · R. O'Donnell, *Insurgent Wicklow, 1798, the story as written by Luke Cullen, O. D. C.*, 3rd edn (1998)

Devlin, Joseph (1871–1934), Irish nationalist and politician, was born at 10 Hamill Street, in the lower Falls area of Belfast, on 13 February 1871. He was the fifth child of Charles Devlin (d. 1906), a jarvey (hackney cab owner), and his wife, Eliza King (d. 1902), an illiterate who sold groceries from the house; rural migrants and Roman Catholics, they had married in Belfast in 1858. Until he was twelve Devlin attended the nearby Christian Brothers' schools, where the curriculum presented a more 'national' view of Ireland's history and culture than was offered by the diocesan schools or the state system. After a brief period as a clerk, concerning which he later alleged discrimination, he worked in a pub. He showed an early aptitude for public speaking, becoming chairman of a debating society formed in 1886 to commemorate the first nationalist election victory in West Belfast. Between 1891 and 1893 he was a journalist on the *Irish News* and the *Freeman's Journal*. He then managed a Belfast pub for the nationalist MP Sam Young, which sustained him until he became a full-time politician in 1902, affording him the flexible working conditions needed to organize the anti-Parnellite Irish National Federation in eastern Ulster. Notwithstanding nationalist reunion in 1900 Devlin's local party remained in bitter conflict until 1905 with the bishop's Catholic Association, which wanted city politics to be based on Catholic rights and episcopal leadership rather than nationalism. In 1901 his aspiration was still to acquire a pub in Glasgow or London as the base for a future political career. His early experiences convinced Devlin that priests and publicans, properly managed, could underpin nationalist organization in a way that class-based or cross-communal appeals could not.

In 1902 Devlin's career took off: the Irish party sent him to Irish America on the first of many successful fund-raising tours; in February he entered parliament unopposed following a by-election in Kilkenny North; and on his return he accepted a paid position in the nationalist movement (which he once vowed he would never do) as London-based secretary of the United Irish League of Great Britain (UIL), moving in 1905 to Dublin as general secretary. Devlin's special skills lay in the arousal and organization of minority and emigrant nationalists, initially in Belfast and Glasgow. Thus the Ancient Order of Hibernians (AOH) came to interest him. The AOH was a benefit society for Irish American Catholics; it also existed in Ireland and Britain, but was discouraged by the Catholic church because of its paraphernalia of oaths and secrecy, although these practices resembled modern freemasonry more than any traditional secret society. Devlin encountered the order's power in America in 1902–3, and on return set out to claim it for constitutional nationalism. From 1905 until his death he was national president of the AOH 'board of Erin', developing it as a grass-roots movement under his personal control, but in harness with the UIL: it was attractive to nationalists with no interest in land agitation, to small businessmen seeking advantage, and to workers seeking insurance benefits. The AOH continued the O'Connellite link between Catholicism and nationalism, but through an organization under lay control. To the Irish party's opponents, both nationalist and unionist, the order was symptomatic of the party's corruption, jobbery, and Catholic exclusivism.

After the 1906 general election Devlin sat for West Belfast, which he regained from the Unionists by sixteen votes. He became a distinguished parliamentarian, though his best oratorical performances continued to be on the public platform. He took up labour issues effectively, especially conditions in the linen mills and sweating in the textile trades. He came to parliamentary prominence after 1910, when home rule dominated politics: Winston Churchill thought him 'the one new figure of distinction in the Irish Party' (R. S. Churchill, *Winston Spencer Churchill*, 2, companion, pt 2, 1969, 1035). Conservatives feared that he would oppose compromise on Ulster, but loyalty to the party leadership remained his touchstone. He followed John Redmond in supporting wartime recruiting. After Easter 1916 he procured for the party a self-denying ordinance from nationalist Ulster to assist Lloyd George's abortive home rule negotiations, organizing a convention which endorsed temporary six-county exclusion from home rule by a vote of 475 to 265. Although his reputation never entirely recovered from this episode Devlin easily retained his Belfast seat in 1918, against Eamon de Valera of Sinn Féin, when elsewhere the Irish party was annihilated. Never again did he go out on a political limb: in the Irish convention of 1918 he sided with the bishops in blocking Redmond's compromise with the southern unionists over customs; during the 1919–22 period, reduced to the leadership of six MPs, he avoided any policy involvement, believing that the popular mandate had passed to Sinn Féin.

Partition left Devlin in depressed personal and political circumstances. He ruled out escape into southern politics; he lost West Belfast through boundary changes in October 1922, when he also failed to become Independent Labour MP for Liverpool Exchange. In 1929 he was returned for Tyrone and Fermanagh, but made little impact. He was elected to the new parliament of Northern Ireland in 1921, and led his small party out of abstention in 1925. In 1928,

at the instigation of former pro-treaty Sinn Féiner Cahir Healy, he founded the National League of the North, an attempt to create a united and formally structured nationalist movement in Northern Ireland, drawing in all but the irreconcilable IRA element, but the movement had expired by the time of his death. He won amendments to the Northern Ireland Education Act of 1930 which improved the funding of Catholic schools, but these were years of demoralization for northern Catholics, and his party abstained after 1932.

Devlin was a small man, known affectionately as Wee Joe by his constituents. Though sneeringly dubbed the 'duodecimo Demosthenes' by T. M. Healy he was a charming and effervescent personality, and widely loved. For twenty-five years his existence was nomadic and, like one in four of his Irish male contemporaries, he never married. He spent much of his leisure time with priests and with families, where he was especially popular with children. He organized seaside 'days of delight' for thousands of Belfast children, and in 1920 opened a holiday hotel in Bangor for mill girls. Though nervous he was a fluent and powerful orator. One contemporary characterized his approach as 'getting there', without too much concern as to the destination (F. Cruise O'Brien in *The Leader*, 19 Feb 1910): the archetypal party secretary, his energies were devoted less to the formulation than to the implementation of policy. Devlin acquired the image of a political 'boss' in some quarters, and critics alleged that he surrounded himself with people less sincere and dedicated than he was. Perhaps because for so much of his career he served a leadership which was superior in both age and social status, and which to some extent patronized him, he tended in turn to surround himself with sycophants rather than with challenging or innovative minds. Arising from his formative experience during the Parnell split, party loyalty became a prime characteristic of his own career, and a quality which he perhaps prized too greatly in others.

Devlin's main residence was in Belfast with his parents until 1902; then in London and Dublin; then, during the First World War, alongside professionals at 3 College Square North, Belfast; and, after 1926, at Ard-Righ, 362 Antrim Road, Belfast, formerly the home of F. J. Bigger. In later years he was comfortably off, as a director of the Distillers Company and chairman of the *Irish News*. He died at St John's Nursing Home, Belfast, on 18 January 1934 of a gastric haemorrhage, following several years of failing health. He was buried at Milltown cemetery, Belfast, two days later. His funeral at St Peter's Pro-Cathedral, Belfast, was attended by leading members of both Irish governments. A. C. HEPBURN

Sources E. Phoenix, *Northern nationalism* (1994) · F. S. L. Lyons, *John Dillon* (1968) · D. Gwynn, *The life of John Redmond* (1932) · A. C. Hepburn, *A past apart: studies in the history of Catholic Belfast, 1850–1950* (1996) · *Belfast Telegraph* (18 Jan 1934) · *Irish Weekly & Ulster Examiner* (27 Jan 1934) · *The Leader* (19 Feb 1910) · *Review of Reviews*, 43 (1911), 235–7 · *Christian Brothers' Souvenir* (1927) · *Hibernian Journal* (June 1959) · *DNB* · d. cert.

Archives PRO NIre., papers | NL Ire., letters to John Redmond · NL Ire., letters to Alice Stopford Green · NL Ire., letters to John

Horgan · Plunkett Foundation, Long Hanborough, Oxfordshire, corresp. with Sir Horace Plunkett · TCD, corresp. with John Dillon
Likenesses J. Lavery, oils, 1928, Ulster Museum, Belfast · F. Doyle-Jones, bronze head, 1932, Charlemont House, Dublin · photograph, repro. in Gwynn, *Life of John Redmond*, facing p. 260
Wealth at death £47: probate, 5 Nov 1934, *CGPLA Éire*

Devlin, Patrick Arthur, Baron Devlin (1905–1992), judge and legal philosopher, was born at Chislehurst, Kent, on 25 November 1905, the eldest of three sons and second of five children of William John Devlin (*d.* 1932), architect, and his wife, Frances Evelyn (Fanny), *née* Crombie. His father, William, came from a Catholic family from co. Tyrone in Ulster but had left Ireland for London to train as an architect. His mother, Frances, was a member of a wealthy Aberdeen family of cloth manufacturers who were protestants. His father's practice did not prosper and in 1909 the family moved from Chislehurst to Aberdeen where Devlin's mother had many relatives and where his father, as the only Catholic architect, might hope to improve his earnings. The hope was disappointed but, with his Crombie relatives, Devlin had a happy childhood. He and his siblings were brought up as Catholics. His brother Christopher (1907–1961) subsequently became a Jesuit priest and writer, and his two sisters, Joan (*b.* 1904) and Frances (1909–1941), became nuns; his youngest brother, William (*b.* 1911), was a Shakespearian actor.

Education and career at the bar Devlin was sent to school at Stonyhurst College (1914–22). He did not excel academically but he learned to speak clearly and enjoyed debating, for which he won a joint first prize. He left school early to join the Dominican order as a novice, but after a year abandoned the idea. His enquiring mind had developed a distaste for unthinking acceptance of dogma. Subsidized by his uncle George Crombie he went instead to Christ's College, Cambridge (1923–7). There his talent for debating flowered. He represented the university on a debating tour of the American middle west in 1925 and became president of the Cambridge Union in 1926. With striking red hair and a clear, resonant voice, he possessed both wit and charm. He made some good friends, notably the Butlers (R. A. and Sir Geoffrey) and Arthur Goodhart. He read first history and then law, in both of which he acquired a lifelong interest. His mind was not however attuned to examinations. Their unpredictable questions left no time for serious thought, and he was twice placed in the second half of the second class. All his life he needed time for reflection. He ceased at Cambridge to be a practising Catholic, though his cast of mind continued in the Jesuit mould.

In 1925 Devlin committed himself to a career at the bar but, as it was a choice not a vocation, he did not mean to let it prevent his enjoying life. Enjoyment meant not idleness, which he dreaded, but a life of occupation and congenial work that allowed for the pursuit of virtue. The virtue he preferred to pursue, if he had to choose between compassion and justice, was justice, 'the root of which is a love of the order that moves the universe' (P. Devlin, *Taken*

Patrick Arthur Devlin, Baron Devlin (1905–1992), by John Ward, 1972

at the Flood, 74). The 'planetary pleasures', high among which he ranked good wine, contributed to enjoyment but for them money was needed. £400 a year was the figure he aimed at when starting at the bar, and with the generous help of Uncle George and Arthur Goodhart, whom he helped with editing the *Law Quarterly Review*, he managed to secure it. He joined Gray's Inn in 1927 and took lodgings first in Half Moon Street, Mayfair, then at the Savile Club, the centre more of a literary than a legal circle. In 1928 he was marshal to Mr Justice Charles on the northern circuit. He passed the bar examination in 1929. His pupillages with Cartwright Sharp and St John Field did not lead to many briefs, but he soon had the good luck to be interviewed by William Jowitt, the Labour attorney-general, with a view to becoming his devil. At the end of the interview 'with my hand on the door handle I turned around and said that I was very keen to get the job' (ibid., 104). He was taken on and worked for Jowitt while he was attorney-general from 1929 to 1931 and later shared his chambers when in 1932 Jowitt returned to private practice. In the meantime Devlin had become known as junior counsel for the prosecution in the Annie Hearn case, a *cause célèbre* of murder by poisoning tried in 1931. His career was however solidly established only after a commercial brief in 1935, for which he was chosen because, of the juniors in practice at the time, his name sounded most Irish. He took the chance, which led to a good deal of work for Shell, and soon became a leading commercial lawyer. 'Luck at the bar is opportunity. It is a try that can be converted into a goal' (ibid., 160).

Devlin had already, on 12 February 1932, married Madeleine Hilda Oppenheimer (b. 1909), younger daughter of Sir Bernard Oppenheimer, the diamond magnate. They had six children, four boys and twin girls, and, in due course, dozens of grandchildren. His wife and all six children became Catholic converts. His family life was notably happy. What with that and his powerful intellect, he was largely able to brush off the criticism that he later attracted.

By the outbreak of the Second World War, Devlin had a lucrative commercial practice. From 1931 to 1939 he was prosecuting counsel to the mint. During the war he served as junior counsel to the ministries of War, Transport, Food, and Supply, and in the legal department of the Ministry of Supply (1940–45). He took silk in 1945, was attorney-general for the duchy of Cornwall in 1947–8, and became a master of Gray's Inn in 1947. But he did not practise as senior counsel for long. Jowitt, now lord chancellor, appointed him a judge in the King's Bench Division in October 1948 at the age of forty-two. He was the second youngest person to be appointed to the High Court bench in the twentieth century. The appointment was not political, for Devlin was not a Labour supporter. He was conservative by temperament. But like Lord Goddard, a friend and admirer, he would not tolerate injustice, and was often critical of the legal establishment. He was knighted in 1948.

Devlin as a judge As a judge Devlin soon established himself as a sound commercial and maritime lawyer. He became a successful president of the restrictive practices court from its creation in 1956 until 1960. He did not share the reservations of those who thought that the work of the court would involve too much economic and political controversy. In this he turned out to be correct. Unlike Lord Denning, Devlin did not regard it as the judge's duty to bring the law into line with contemporary views of justice. That role was for parliament and the jury. The judge should analyse the law carefully and administer it as it stood.

Devlin also made a mark, unexpectedly, as a judge in criminal cases. He was prepared to probe the principles underlying criminal law with a rare insight and attention to detail. As an assize judge in 1949 he gave a direction to the jury on the law of provocation that was much admired. In 1957 he tried Bodkin Adams, an Eastbourne doctor who was popularly supposed to have murdered up to 400 elderly patients from whom he expected legacies. The charge was confined to one alleged murder, supposedly the one best supported by the evidence. The evidence unearthed by the defence, however, weakened the prosecution case. On Devlin's direction, which drew a distinction between alleviating pain and deliberately cutting short life, the jury acquitted the bumbling doctor. Thirty years later, when the persons concerned were all dead, Devlin wrote a brilliant account of the trial in *Easing the Passing* (1985). In it he lambasted the prosecutor, Sir Reginald Manningham-Buller, attorney-general at the time of the trial and later lord chancellor, as clumsy, stupid, and

perverse. Devlin was not throwing doubt on the jury's verdict, though in his view Bodkin Adams was probably a mercy killer greedy for legacies. He was criticized for expressing this view of Dr Adams, but he combined respect for the due process of law with a zeal for truth, even harsh truths.

After the trial Devlin and Manningham-Buller were both regarded as candidates for the vacant post of lord chief justice, to which in the event neither was appointed. Two years later, in 1959, Devlin was chairman of a commission of inquiry into the declaration by the governor of a state of emergency in Nyasaland. The commission concluded that there were grounds for declaring the state of emergency but that the supposed plot by Dr Hastings Banda and others to murder the governor, his officials, and all the Europeans in Nyasaland was a figment of an informer's imagination. Manningham-Buller ridiculed this conclusion in a speech, much applauded, in the House of Commons. The statement in the commission's report that Nyasaland was 'a police state, no doubt temporarily' was true but caused offence in governing circles. But despite what Devlin, tongue-in-cheek, referred to as his 'incompetence in finding the elementary facts' (Devlin, *Easing the Passing*, 191) the prime minister promoted him to the Court of Appeal in 1960 and the House of Lords (as Baron Devlin of West Wick) in 1961.

Devlin was not happy as an appellate judge. He found the work dreary and was frustrated by the time-wasting procedures and lack of office and secretarial facilities for appeal judges, especially in the House of Lords. The United States supreme court seemed to him more effectively organized. He gave some interesting judgments, taking the view that the civil law of torts should only rarely be used to punish a defendant who had deliberately behaved badly, but that it could properly be used to give remedies for economic as well as physical losses. He did not have time to make the sort of impact on the law made by his contemporary Denning. Whether, as many thought, he would have made a great mark had he held the office of lord chief justice or master of the rolls can only be surmised. The incumbents staying on longer than expected, he was not appointed to either post and, after fifteen years on the bench, he resigned in 1964 at the early age of fifty-eight.

Devlin as a writer After his resignation Devlin secured interesting and lucrative work as an arbitrator. He was also judge of the administrative tribunal of the International Labour Office (ILO) in Geneva from 1964 to 1986 and greatly enjoyed his visits there. From 1969 to 1971 he chaired the ILO inquiry into freedom of association in Greece. From 1964 to 1969 he was the first non-journalist chairman of the Press Council and in that capacity was diplomatic enough to establish easy relations with the press. He sat as chairman of the Wiltshire quarter sessions from 1957 until 1971, his informal manner, free from any hint of the pompous, being much appreciated. But he resisted attempts to lure him back to the judiciary.

Instead the latter part of Devlin's career was devoted mainly to writing about law and history, which he now saw as not only a pleasure but a duty. He had the knack of presenting a closely reasoned and professionally accurate argument in a form that was intelligible and of interest to non-lawyers. Many of his lectures and addresses were published in *Samples of Lawmaking* (1962), *The Enforcement of Morals* (1965), and *The Judge* (1979). Keenly interested in the relation between law and morals, he saw the criminal jury as the body with the power, though not the right, to refuse to apply laws that were politically oppressive or that the ordinary person found unjust, for instance the law of bigamy as it applied to those who could not afford a divorce. Only in this way could criminal justice take account not merely of the law but of the merits of a case. Devlin first expounded this theme in his incisive Hamlyn lectures, *Trial by Jury* (1956). He elaborated it in later works, right up to an article, 'The conscience of the jury', published in the *Law Quarterly Review* in 1991. It was not that he thought juries particularly shrewd, except in deciding who was telling the truth. But judges, having conferred on juries the power to decide guilt or innocence, should respect that power. He therefore criticized decisions of the Court of Appeal and the House of Lords in which judges, when new evidence had come to light after a conviction, took it on themselves to decide its cogency without referring it to a jury.

This was one reason why Devlin joined Ludovic Kennedy, Lord Scarman, Basil Hume, and others in campaigns to secure a further review of the convictions first in the Luton post office murder trial (*R. v. Cooper and McMahon*, 1969), then in that of the Guildford four, convicted in 1975. The Guildford case arose from an IRA bombing in which the police arrested and forced confessions from four innocent people, though by the time of the appeal in 1977 it was known who had in fact carried out the bombing and how. The campaigns were in the end successful and the convictions were quashed, those of the Guildford four in 1989. Despite increasing deafness, Devlin continued to campaign for a review of some other dubious convictions that undermined respect for English criminal justice. In the upshot an independent body was set up to review convictions that were alleged in the light of new evidence to be wrongful.

Devlin's interest in the relation of law to morality led to a famous controversy with Professor Herbert *Hart. The context was the recommendation of the Wolfenden committee in 1957 that homosexuality between consenting adults should cease to be criminal. Devlin favoured a modest degree of reform, but in his Maccabaean lecture of 1959 was driven to dig deeper. He argued that the ordinary person's sense of what was morally unacceptable was not valuable merely in inducing juries to frustrate the enforcement of bad laws. If sufficiently strong, popular morality could justify making conduct a criminal offence. It was not true, as Wolfenden had argued, that there was a sphere of private morality into which the criminal law should not enter. Devlin's argument, as he later discovered, was along lines similar to that advanced by a previous judge, Fitzjames Stephen, in *Liberty, Equality, Fraternity* (1873). Though Devlin clearly had in mind the sort of

sub-Christian morality that prevailed in Britain at the time, his argument was open to the objection that it appeared to justify the enforcement of any morality strongly supported by public opinion, however corrupt—for example that of the Nazis. Hart, in reply, renewed a theme developed by John Stuart Mill, arguing that only the avoidance of harm to others could justify making conduct criminal. He failed, however, to explain satisfactorily how differences of opinion about what was harmful could be resolved, and how far the state was justified in preventing vulnerable people from harming themselves. The debate, though inconclusive, was conducted at a high level of eloquence and has been educative to generations of students. Devlin revised and extended his views on the subject in *The Enforcement of Morals* (1965).

Old age In retirement Devlin lived at West Wick House and Farm in Pewsey, Wiltshire, which he had bought in 1943. He also had a property in the Algarve in Portugal. He now had more time to think. One of the topics he thought about more deeply was the personality of Woodrow Wilson, in whom he had become interested during the debating tour of America in 1925. In *Too Proud to Fight* (1974), a patient and well-marshalled but over-long book, he concluded that Wilson entered the war in 1917, despite having just been re-elected on a policy of neutrality, in order to have a dominating place at the peace conference that would follow when the war was won.

In recognition of his status as a writer on law Devlin was made a fellow of the British Academy in 1963. Between 1962 and 1980 he received honorary degrees from the universities of Glasgow, Toronto, Oxford, Cambridge, Leicester, Sussex, Durham, Liverpool, and St Louis, Missouri. He was high steward of Cambridge University from 1966 to 1991. Though increasingly deaf, he continued to help the campaign against the unjust convictions of supposed terrorists, such as the Maguire seven. In 1988 he began a fascinating autobiography, *Taken at the Flood* (1996), which was aimed at budding lawyers and which he carried, as intended, up to 1935, the year in which his practice became firmly established. Of medium height and latterly with a stoop, he was not physically a commanding figure. But his charm, sense of humour, and informality endeared him to people of all sorts. He enjoyed life and brought enjoyment to others. When near death he asked after careful reflection to see a priest. He died peacefully at West Wick on 9 August 1992, fortified by the rites of the Catholic church, and was buried in Pewsey cemetery on 11 August. He was survived by his wife and six children. A memorial mass was held at St James's, Spanish Place, on 28 October 1992.

Devlin was a complex character. His rigorous conscience and eloquence made him a thoughtful and effective enemy of untruth and injustice. At the same time he admired and skilfully defended the common-law tradition of organic growth, even if it involved tolerating anomalies. He and Denning, also appointed to the bench in his early forties by Lord Chancellor Jowitt, combined judicial and juristic work in a way that had no parallel among English judges since the time of James Fitzjames

Stephen. If Denning was the more influential judge, Devlin was the more powerful writer, indeed the most impressive produced by the English bench in the twentieth century.   TONY HONORÉ

Sources P. Devlin, *Taken at the flood*, ed. M. Devlin, T. Devlin, and A. Devlin (1996) · R. F. V. Heuston, 'Patrick Arthur Devlin, 1905–1992', *PBA*, 84 (1994), 247–62 · P. Devlin, *Easing the passing: the trial of Dr John Bodkin Adams* (1985); another edn (1986) · P. Devlin, prefaces [to pubd works] · *The Times* (11 Aug 1992) · *The Times* (13 Aug 1992) · *The Times* (20 Aug 1992) · *The Times* (29 Oct 1992) · *The Independent* (11 Aug 1992) · *The Independent* (13 Aug 1992) · *The Independent* (22 Aug 1992) · *The Independent* (2 Sept 1992) · *The Independent* (10 Sept 1992) · *The Guardian* (11 Aug 1992) · L. Kennedy, 'Introduction', in P. Devlin, *Taken at the flood*, ed. M. Devlin, T. Devlin, and A. Devlin (1996), 5–11 · B. Hume, 'Epilogue', in P. Devlin, *Taken at the flood*, ed. M. Devlin, T. Devlin, and A. Devlin (1996), 161–2 · Burke, *Peerage* · *WWW*, 1991–5 · private information (2004)
Archives Bodl. Oxf., corresp. with A. L. Goodhart · Bodl. RH, papers relating to Nyasaland inquiry commission · CAC Cam., corresp. with Monty Belgion |SOUND BL NSA, recorded talk
Likenesses J. Ward, oils, 1972, Gray's Inn, London [*see illus.*] · photograph, repro. in Heuston, 'Patrick Arthur Devlin', 246 · photograph, repro. in Devlin, *Easing the passing* · photograph, repro. in *The Times* (11 Aug 1992) · photograph, repro. in *The Times* (13 Aug 1992) · photograph, repro. in *The Times* (20 Aug 1992) · photograph, repro. in *The Independent* (11 Aug 1992) · photograph, repro. in *The Independent* (22 Aug 1992)
Wealth at death £5735: probate, 3 Sept 1993, *CGPLA Eng. & Wales*

Devlin, Patrick Joseph [Paddy] (1925–1999), politician, was born on 8 March 1925 at 46 Lady Street in the Falls Road area of Belfast, the eldest of the seven children of Thomas Devlin (*b.* 1891), a flour mill worker, and his wife, Anna Lillis (1902–1974), a spinner. After a rudimentary education in local Catholic schools he began work at fourteen, having joined the youth wing of the IRA, Na Fianna Éireann, at eleven. He graduated into the IRA in 1940, and gathered information about military and strategic installations which was passed to Berlin and used to plan German bombing raids on Belfast. This caused him great anguish in later life. He was interned in Crumlin Road prison from 1942 until the end of the war, where he rethought his commitment to armed struggle and became a socialist. In 1948 he moved to England, where he found employment in the car industry. A trial with Coventry City Football Club led to the offer of a contract for the 1949–50 season, but for family reasons he returned to Belfast where he became a storeman in the mill where his father worked.

In 1949 Devlin broke with the IRA and became a trade unionist, attending trade-union education courses and joining the Irish Labour Party. On 26 October 1950 he married Teresa Gertrude Duffy (*b.* 1925/6), a clerk, with whom he had three daughters and two sons; the family lived in Andersonstown, west Belfast. He was elected to Belfast city council in 1956, but lost his seat two years later. He then joined the non-sectarian Northern Ireland Labour Party (NILP), and was a founder member of the Northern Ireland Civil Rights Association. In 1969 he was elected to the Stormont parliament to represent the Falls, and continued to campaign for civil rights. Sectarian tensions were running high in Ulster in the summer of 1969, and Belfast's Roman Catholics bore the brunt of the violence

that broke out in August; many hundreds were burnt out of their homes. At a public meeting in Dublin, Devlin rashly appealed for guns to defend the nationalist community. The remark came back to haunt him, as the Provisional IRA began procuring weapons.

In 1970 Devlin was among the six Stormont MPs who set up the Social Democratic and Labour Party (SDLP), a cross-community party whose members shared a loathing for sectarian violence. He faced persistent harassment from the IRA, and he carried (legally) a pistol to defend himself and his family. In March 1972, as Northern Ireland became dangerously polarized, the Stormont parliament was prorogued and direct rule was imposed. Devlin brokered an IRA ceasefire and in July the secretary of state, William Whitelaw, met a Provisional IRA delegation in London. Hard-liners ended the ceasefire and reverted to terrorism.

Devlin became a member of the Northern Ireland assembly, and in 1973 played a leading role in forming the power-sharing executive in which he served as minister for health and social services. Notwithstanding the executive's collapse under the weight of Unionist opposition, he persevered with efforts to secure an agreement between the SDLP and the Unionists. His efforts were aborted when the convention (1975–6) that had been mandated to devise a form of government acceptable to both nationalists and Unionists was dissolved. In 1975 he was appointed Northern Ireland organizer of the Dublin-based Irish Transport and General Workers' Union. A measure of his success in this post was a fourfold increase in membership in ten years.

From the mid-1970s Devlin became increasingly disenchanted by the SDLP's steady drift towards communal nationalism. Stripped of his membership in 1977, he made several unsuccessful attempts to launch a non-sectarian socialist party. He suffered another setback when he lost his deposit in the European parliamentary election of 1979. In 1981 he was forced to move house after repeated attacks were made on his home when he resisted IRA pressure to support the hunger strikes in the H-block.

As a member of Belfast city council from 1973 to 1985 Devlin strongly supported the arts. He wrote several plays himself, and in 1981 was awarded an MSc by Cranfield College of Technology. His thesis, on the joint efforts by Catholics and protestants to fight poverty, formed the basis of a book, *Yes we Have No Bananas: Outdoor Relief in Belfast, 1920–1939* (1981). He wrote a weekly newspaper column until failing eyesight caused him to abandon journalism. His autobiography, *Straight Left* (1993), was awarded the *Irish Times* literature prize for non-fiction. His contribution to politics and community service was acknowledged in 1996 when he was awarded honorary degrees by Queen's University, Belfast, and by the University of Ulster. He was appointed CBE in the 1999 new year's honours list, which he accepted as recognition of the labour and trade union movement in Northern Ireland. Devlin, who suffered from diabetes, died later that year, on 15 August 1999, in the Mater Infirmorum Hospital, Belfast. His remains were cremated at Roselawn cemetery in east Belfast on 17 August.

Paddy Devlin was a big, burly man, who forcefully argued his case in colourful language, occasionally resorting to fisticuffs to bolster his argument. A senior civil servant once described him as 'the coarsest man who ever faced the British government' (*The Guardian*), but his principled politics and social concern won him widespread respect. PATRICK GILLAN

Sources P. Devlin, *Straight left: an autobiography* (1993) · *Daily Telegraph* (16 Aug 1999) · *Irish Times* (21 Aug 1999) · *The Independent* (17 Aug 1999) · *The Guardian* (16 Aug 1999) · *The Times* (17 Aug 1999) · b. cert. · m. cert. · d. cert.
Archives priv. coll., papers
Likenesses photograph, repro. in *The Guardian* · photograph, repro. in *Daily Telegraph*
Wealth at death £40,000: probate, 23 Sept 1999, CGPLA NIre.

Devon. For this title name *see* Revières, Baldwin de, earl of Devon (*c*.1095–1155); Forz, Isabella de, *suo jure* countess of Devon, and countess of Aumale (1237–1293); Courtenay, Thomas, thirteenth earl of Devon (1414–1458); Courtenay, Thomas, fourteenth earl of Devon (1432–1461) [*see under* Courtenay, Thomas, thirteenth earl of Devon (1414–1458)]; Stafford, Humphrey, earl of Devon (*c*.1439–1469); Courtenay, Edward, first earl of Devon (*d*. 1509); Courtenay, William, first earl of Devon (*c*.1475–1511) [*see under* Courtenay, Edward, first earl of Devon (*d*. 1509)]; Katherine, countess of Devon (1479–1527); Courtenay, Edward, first earl of Devon (1526–1556); Courtenay, William Reginald, eleventh earl of Devon (1807–1888).

Devon, James (1866–1939), prison medical officer and criminologist, was born on 25 October 1866 at 18 James Street, Calton, Glasgow, the son of John Devon, a journeyman iron-moulder, and his wife, Margaret, *née* Arthur. His family was poor working class—his mother signed his birth certificate with a cross—and he left school aged eleven. Devon was ambitious to be a doctor and studied part time at Anderson's and St Mungo's colleges, Glasgow. In 1893, aged twenty-seven, he obtained the Scottish triple qualification in medicine. Initially Devon had worked as a clinical clerk in Glasgow Eye Infirmary and as demonstrator and assistant to the pathologist at Glasgow Royal Infirmary. Thereafter he was appointed resident house surgeon and assistant to the professor of clinical surgery in Glasgow Royal Infirmary and resident assistant medical officer at Glasgow poorhouse and Town's Hospital in Glasgow. On 1 April 1895 he was appointed medical officer at Glasgow prison (Duke Street), where he remained until appointed medical commissioner to the Scottish Prison Commission on 10 April 1913. In 1902 he had been nominated a medico-legal examiner for the crown in criminal cases. Throughout his period as Scottish prison commissioner his chairman was Lord Polwarth, and Devon retired on 31 March 1929.

Glasgow's Duke Street prison had been a showcase house of correction for Scotland when it opened in 1823. However, by the end of the nineteenth century it was an overcrowded, under-funded, down-at-heel, poor-quality prison for short sentence and remand prisoners. In 1900 there was a total of 20,000 admissions, with a daily average of around 140 men and 260 women. In 1912 Devon described an unstimulating, dismal regime of plank beds, prohibition on speaking, exercise by prisoners walking a ring, and drab corduroy or moleskin uniform. He was concerned that reforms advocated for England by the 1895 Gladstone committee on prisons were not being implemented in the sixteen penal institutions overseen by the Scottish Prison Commission. Indeed he gave evidence to the 1900 departmental committee on Scottish prisons that at Duke Street there lacked adequate nursing provision and infirmary care. At this time Devon was instituting nurse training for prison staff while urging that this, albeit an improvement, was not a proper substitute for fully qualified professional nurses. Not until very recently had an assistant medical officer been appointed at Duke Street, and Devon's evidence to this committee was cited several times in its final report.

Devon was responsible for advising the Scottish Prison Commission on all health matters from 1913 to 1929. He oversaw the force-feeding of imprisoned suffragettes in Scotland in 1913, and was attacked with a dog whip on one occasion in this connection. He also oversaw the implementation of the so-called Cat and Mouse Act, under which hunger-striking suffragettes were released and later reimprisoned when their health was restored. Between 1916 and 1918 the prison system was faced with conscientious objectors, some of whom were Marxist revolutionaries, such as the 'Red Clydesiders' John Maclean, James Maxton, and William Gallacher—all sentenced for sedition under the Defence of the Realm Act. The issue of force-feeding conscientious objectors who went on hunger strike was testing and controversial for the medical commissioner. Also, prisons in the 1920s were greatly influenced by the work of Alexander Paterson of the English Prison Commission regarding reform of the Borstal system for young prisoners. New training systems for these required careful medical supervision with frequent calls upon the medical commissioner.

Devon wrote *The Criminal in the Community* (1912) and *Some Causes of Crime* (1908). His work was also described or published in medical journals such as the *British Medical Journal* and in more general ones such as the *Hibbert Journal*. By his death he was well known as a writer, criminologist, lecturer, and radio broadcaster. He repudiated the Lombrosian positivistic criminology, which held that heredity determines the bulk of criminality, and argued for careful understanding of the social context of the individual. However, he rejected one-dimensional explanations of crime as oversimplified and was, for example, well aware that policing and sentencing could act in a biased and discriminatory manner. Notwithstanding, Devon believed that crime flourished in overcrowded, neglected neighbourhoods which politicians ignored and profiteers exploited, and he argued that real concern for, and interest in, such neighbourhoods would restore bonds of social obligation and charity throughout the whole of society.

Although not an abolitionist Devon was highly critical of both capital and corporal punishment and of the regimes generally in Scottish prisons. He wanted drab and demoralizing routines of punishment for, in the main, trivial offenders to be replaced by individualized sympathy, guidance, and commitment. He strongly believed in the personal interest represented by the Probation Service and wanted young and first-time offenders diverted from custody. For many prisoners, he was convinced that prison was merely a warehouse, returning them to society with their lives and capacities severely disrupted: the former prisoner was therefore less fitted for self-maintenance than prior to sentence, with other criminals often their only recourse. None the less, Devon was suspicious of a tendency in the 1930s among some penal reformers to ascribe all criminality to environment and he insisted that deterrence was essential to criminal disposal. Thus Devon, initially a humanitarian prison reformer in an age of penal severity, found himself at odds with the later fashionable notion of the prison as essentially a moral reformatory.

Devon was twice married and was survived by his second wife and two daughters, one of whom entered the medical profession. He died on 25 February 1939, having lived his retirement at 67 Great King Street, Edinburgh; he was survived by his second wife, Jane Shiel, formerly Buchan. He was a member of the Scottish Liberal and Scottish Arts clubs until his death, and in his later years was in much demand as a speaker at Burns festivals.

BILL FORSYTHE

Sources *The Times* (2 March 1939), 19c · *Annual reports of the Scottish prison commission* (1895–1929) · departmental committee on Scottish prisons: report, *Parl. papers* (1900), vol. 42, Cd 218–19 · *WWW* · J. Cameron, *Prisons and punishment in Scotland* (1983) · L. Radzinowicz and R. Hood, *A history of English criminal law and its administration from 1750*, rev. edn, 5: *The emergence of penal policy in Victorian and Edwardian England* (1990) · *The Lancet* (4 March 1939), 547 · *BMJ* (11 March 1939), 538 · L. Leneman, *A guid cause: the women's suffrage movement in Scotland* (1995) · b. cert. · *CCI* (1939)
Archives U. Aberdeen L., special libraries and archives, letters to A. J. Keith
Wealth at death £503 9s. 1d.: confirmation, 10 May 1939, *CCI*

Devonport. For this title name *see* Kearley, Hudson Ewbanke, first Viscount Devonport (1856–1934).

Devons, Ely (1913–1967), statistician and economist, was born in Bangor, north Wales, on 29 July 1913, the second eldest in a family of three boys and three girls of David Isaac Devons, a Jewish minister from Vilna who had arrived in Britain in 1902 on a Russian passport at the age of twenty-one, and his wife, Edith Edelstein, who was from Ireland and ten years younger than her husband. A younger brother, Samuel, was professor of physics at the University of Manchester in the 1950s when Devons held the chair of applied economics.

Devons attended a number of different schools as his family moved to Stoke-on-Trent, Portsmouth, and then Manchester, ending up at North Manchester Municipal High School before entering the University of Manchester. In the course of a chance encounter in the street he was persuaded by Harold Laski to study economics and graduated in 1934 with first-class honours in the school of economics, politics, and modern history. As Drummond Fraser research fellow he read for the MA degree at Manchester, researching British production statistics and producing his first article, 'Output per head in Great Britain, 1924–33' (*Economic Journal*). He married in 1939 Estelle Wine, a concert pianist from Dublin and a pupil of Solomon. They had two sons and one daughter.

Devons's career as a statistician began in 1935 with a post under Glyn Hughes as economic assistant to the Joint Committee of Cotton Trades Organizations in Manchester. In March 1940 he joined the Central Economic Information Service—a small group of economists and statisticians from which developed at the end of the year both the economic section of the war cabinet secretariat and the Central Statistical Office. Devons quickly made his mark as one of a number of Manchester men, including John Jewkes, D. N. Chester, and Harry Campion, who played a major part in the early days of these bodies. His special responsibility was to assemble the secret statistics accumulating in various parts of Whitehall and issue them in a form convenient for the central direction of policy. In this he was extremely successful and the work he initiated in 1940–41 had a revolutionary effect on the presentation of official statistics. Government statistics never afterwards looked so dull, discontinuous, and inaccessible. It was a job which he repeated in the Ministry of Aircraft Production and again for the Organization for European Economic Co-operation in 1950 when he took a hand in the first issue of its statistical bulletins.

Devons did not steep himself in statistics without considering the lessons they pointed. He had a chance to combine the two when Jewkes, now in charge of aircraft planning, asked him to join him as chief statistician. In the next four years Devons came to exercise an increasingly dominant role in the Ministry of Aircraft Production, taking over from Jewkes as head of planning in 1944. His experience in the planning of aircraft and aircraft components formed the background to much of his later thinking about economic and administrative problems and provided the material for his *Planning in Practice* (1950), a classic of its kind.

At the end of the war, after some hesitation, Devons returned to Manchester as reader and later professor of applied economics. He remained there for much of the time as dean of the faculty of economic and social studies, until appointed in 1959 to the chair of commerce at the London School of Economics. Nearly all Devons's published work was composed during his years in Manchester. His *Introduction to British Economic Statistics* (1956), a critical guide displaying an unrivalled knowledge of official statistics, was followed by *Essays in Economics* (1961). But his main contribution was the stimulus he provided to his distinguished colleagues. The staff seminar which he conducted with Arthur Lewis has been described by Professor Harry Johnson as 'the most devastatingly critical forum in the country into which a careless economist could blunder'.

The move to London was not altogether a success since

international trade was not Devons's normal field of interest. But as convener of the economics department he was an initiator of structural change, able to think and plan in terms of the institution as a whole. He was largely responsible for the new MSc degrees in economics and econometrics and helped to raise money for graduate fellowships in support of them. In 1965 the title of his chair was changed from commerce to economics. While at the LSE he served from 1959 to 1965 as a member of the Local Government Commission for England and acted as consultant to the British and foreign governments.

A victim of insomnia, Devons was an omnivorous reader and had a particular appetite for government publications, especially minutes of evidence. He declared his leisure activities to be fell-walking, tree-felling, and disputing (*WWW*). He loved debating and was given to paradox and skittishness. This put off many people who failed to notice how right even his more extravagant forecasts proved to be. He was always in command of the relevant facts, never bowed without question to received opinion, and was possessed of an acute and firm judgement rooted in common sense. He hated arrogance, dogmatism, and—most of all—humbug. He had an eye for the weakness of an argument and for the workable solution to a problem. To a rare combination of administrative skill and intellectual power was added an impressive firmness of character which made him incorruptible even in small matters.

Devons's published work seems slight and his career disappointing in relation to his intellectual gifts. This partly reflects his disenchantment with technical economic analysis, partly his preference for administrative tasks, but perhaps most of all a detachment which sprang from lack of ambition. He was not a natural writer or man of action. But he had a capacity for leadership which in the post-war years never found full expression.

Devons had to contend throughout the last twelve years of his life with repeated bouts of illness in the middle of arduous administrative duties. He died, survived by his wife, in St Thomas's Hospital, Lambeth, on 28 December 1967 after two years of almost continuous ill health.

ALEC CAIRNCROSS, rev.

Sources 'Memoir', *Papers on planning and economic management*, ed. A. Cairncross (1970) · *The Times* (29 Dec 1967), 8f · *The Times* (4 Jan 1968), 10h · *WWW* · d. cert. · personal knowledge (1981) · private information (1981) · C. Roth, ed., *Encyclopaedia Judaica*, 16 vols. (Jerusalem, 1971–2) · H. Cohen, ed., *Jews in the world of science* (1956), 49

Archives BLPES, papers · JRL, letters to *Manchester Guardian*

Wealth at death £13,911: probate, 7 May 1968, CGPLA Eng. & Wales

Devonshire. For this title name *see* Cavendish, William, first earl of Devonshire (1551–1626); Blount, Charles, eighth Baron Mountjoy and earl of Devonshire (1563–1606); Cavendish, William, second earl of Devonshire (1590–1628); Cavendish, Christian, countess of Devonshire (1595–1675); Cavendish, William, third earl of Devonshire (1617–1684); Cavendish, William, first duke of Devonshire (1641–1707); Cavendish, William, fourth duke of Devonshire (*bap.* 1720, *d.* 1764); Cavendish, William,

fifth duke of Devonshire (1748–1811); Cavendish, Georgiana, duchess of Devonshire (1757–1806); Cavendish, Elizabeth Christiana, duchess of Devonshire (1757–1824); Cavendish, William George Spencer, sixth duke of Devonshire (1790–1858); Cavendish, William, seventh duke of Devonshire (1808–1891); Cavendish, Louise Frederica Augusta, duchess of Devonshire (1832–1911); Cavendish, Spencer Compton, marquess of Hartington and eighth duke of Devonshire (1833–1908); Cavendish, Victor Christian William, ninth duke of Devonshire (1868–1938).

Devoto, John (*fl.* 1708–1752), painter and scene designer, was referred to as being French during his lifetime, but his parents were probably Italian and the name has Genoese connections. It is circumstantially probable that he was related to the John Devoto who made properties for the court masque *Callisto* (1675), and possibly also to Antonio Devoto, an Italian puppet showman, who performed at a booth in Charing Cross between 1662 and 1675.

In 1708 Devoto worked as an assistant to the Flemish painter Gerard Lanscroon (*d.* 1737), painting the 'great room' at Burley on the Hill in Rutland for Daniel Finch, second earl of Nottingham. Devoto seems to have established himself as a decorative painter by 1718, and drawings of 1719 show similarities to the work of James Thornhill (1675–1734). There are clear links between the techniques and subject matter of the decorative and architectural painter and the scenic artist: 'ingenious foreshortening, play of perspective, and painting of false architecture and sculpture … the same classical themes did duty both for ceilings and walls, and for the arguments of *opera seria* and heroic drama' (Croft-Murray, 7). Early scenic commissions of 1719–20 suggest that Devoto may have additionally established his reputation by producing work in the style of, or indeed copies of, the Italian designers: the Bibiena family, Filippo Juvarra (1676–1736), and Pietro Righini (1683–1743). His first recorded theatre work was to produce designs for *Julius Caesar* at the Drury Lane theatre, 'With an entire Sett of Scenes representing Ancient Rome, painted by Mons. Devoto' (*Daily Courant*, 24 Sept 1723). The following year, for John Thurmond's *Harlequin Sheppard* at Drury Lane, the playbill (28 November 1724) records, 'A New Night Scene. The Scenes being all painted from the real Place of Action'. His work must have been sufficiently well recognized by audiences for Hogarth to include the reference, in his *A Just View of the British Stage* (1725), to 'Scene Newgate, by M D–V–to'.

Devoto prepared scenes for Thurmond's *The Miser, or, Wagner and Abericock—a Grotesque Entertainment* (30 December 1726); for *Perseus and Andromeda* (15 November 1728); for *Othello* (15 November 1731) at Drury Lane, whose playbill offered 'a new set of Scenes being a prospect of the Ponte Rialto at Venice painted by Mr Devoto'; and for Theophilus Cibber's *The Harlot's Progress, or, The Ridotto al' Fresco: a Grotesque Pantomime Entertainment* (31 March 1733). There is, however, insufficient recorded work to indicate that Devoto was a resident painter at Drury Lane. Henry Angelo, in his *Reminiscences* (1823), indicates that he may have worked for John Rich at Lincoln's Inn Fields Theatre after 1732, although Rich moved into his newly built Covent Garden theatre in 1732 and the playbills make no mention of Devoto.

At Henry Giffard's new theatre in Ayliffe Street, Goodman's Fields, Devoto designed scenes for Vanbrugh's *The Mistake* and 'a New Dramatick Entertainment, call'd Jupiter and Io … in which will be Introduc'd, a new Pantomime Interlude, call'd Mother Shipton's Wish; or Harlequin's Origin' (24 January 1735). Referring to Dryden's *King Arthur*, the *Daily Post and General Advertiser* said:

> We hear the Designs of Merlin's Cave, that were presented last week to Her Majesty by Mr Giffard, have been so well approv'd of, by many Persons of Quality, that Mr Devoto, who made the Draughts, has had several Copies bespoke by the Nobility. (*Daily Post and General Advertiser*, 27 Jan 1736)

In a theatre world where scenes were taken from stock and their precise relationship with the play may only have been circumstantial, artists would frequently provide generic scenes, or rework earlier scenes, for new theatrical circumstances. In this way Devoto, for example, provided scenes for the White Swan Theatre in Norwich, where it was reported 'the fine Sett of Scenes painted by the famous French Painter Devoto are arriv'd' (*Norwich Gazette*, 20–27 Jan 1739). But there is also evidence to suggest that Devoto was providing for the growing taste for topographical scenes that could be recognized by their audiences. For the New Wells Theatre, London Spa, Clerkenwell, in June 1740 he was responsible for scenes for *A Hint to the Theatres, or, Merlin in Labour*. This included a view of Merlin's Cave, one of Queen Caroline's features in the royal gardens at Richmond. Given the reference to the queen's satisfaction with this topic, it is likely that this was either a reworking of the scene from *King Arthur* or simply the original set of scenes hired from Ayliffe Street.

Spectacle and pantomime provided an opportunity for theatres such as Ayliffe Street and the New Wells to evade the 1737 Stage Licensing Act, which permitted only Drury Lane and Covent Garden to present 'legitimate' drama. At Goodman's Fields, Devoto prepared the scenes and their associated machinery for *Harlequin Student, or, The Fall of Pantomime* (3 March 1741). These included a magician's cave which broke open to reveal Pierrot, views of Covent Garden, the Tower of London, the Hermitage in Richmond (another of the queen's garden follies), and a court of Cupid which disappeared while a stage descended representing a heathen heaven. As Harlequin is banished with Mercury's song

> Sink Sink, Dishonour of the Age
> Disgrace and Scandal of the Stage
> Ye Worthless Crew, away,

the stage direction reads, 'The Scene draws, and discovers the Monument of Shakespear, exactly represented, as lately erected in Westminster Abbey.' The following year the *Daily Post* (3 July 1742) advertised 'A Grand Representation of Water Works, as in the Doge's Gardens at Venice' with scenes by Devoto at the New Wells Theatre.

In 1744 David Garrick, whose London début had taken place at Ayliffe Street in 1741, engaged Devoto to provide

'one Flat Scene and 4 Wings' for the private theatricals of John Russell, fourth duke of Bedford, at Woburn, for which the painter received £10 10s. On 29 January 1746 a benefit was planned for Devoto at the New Wells Theatre in Lemon Street, Goodman's Fields. The occasion was additionally intended to mark the début of his daughter in Thomas Otway's *The Orphan*, but the play was changed and there are no further references to his daughter's acting career.

The few references to Devoto's career after this date make no mention of continued scenic work. However, for the Covent Garden Lenten oratorio season in 1752 he designed theatrically inspired admission tickets for performances of Handel's *Samson* and *The Choice of Hercules*. Also in 1752 he provided a satirical frontispiece for an edition of *Twelve English Songs, Serious and Humorous* by Barnabas Gunn.

There are no later references to the life or work of the artist and there is no evidence of a will being made, or of the date of Devoto's death. However, a John Devoto, possibly his son, living in Bedford Street, Covent Garden, established a drawing school at 139 Longacre in 1775 and exhibited at the Society of Artists of Great Britain in 1776.

John Devoto was painted by the Venetian Vincenzo Damini some time before 1730 (when Damini left the country), and a mezzotint, after Damini, was made by John Faber the younger and published in 1738, inscribed, *Johannes Devoto: historicus scenicusque pictor*. Ninety-one designs, which represent Devoto's principal theatrical and decorative work, are to be found in the print room of the British Museum. CHRISTOPHER BAUGH

Sources Highfill, Burnim & Langhans, *BDA*, vol. 4 · E. Croft-Murray, *John Devoto: a baroque scene painter* (1953) · S. Rosenfeld, *Georgian scene painters & scene painting* (1981) · S. Rosenfeld and E. Croft-Murray, 'A checklist of scene painters working in Great Britain and Ireland in the 18th century [pt 2]', *Theatre Notebook*, 19 (1964–5), 49–64, esp. 51–2 · A. H. Scouten, ed., *The London stage, 1660–1800*, pt 3: *1729–1747* (1961) · G. W. Stone, ed., *The London stage, 1660–1800*, pt 4: *1747–1776* (1962) · S. Rosenfeld, *A short history of scene design in Great Britain* (1973)

Likenesses J. Faber jun., engraving, pubd 1738 (after V. Damini, c.1730), BM

Devoy, John (1842–1928), Irish nationalist, was born on 3 September 1842, at Kill, co. Kildare, the son of William Devoy (1807–1880) and Elizabeth Dunne, who were married about 1833 and lived in a cottage on half an acre given by Elizabeth's family. A literate and able man, William came of a family with an inheritance of some self-esteem as tenant farmers and well-placed servants of titled families. He played a prominent local role in the O'Connellite and temperance mobilizations of the 1820s, 1830s, and 1840s. He took occasional jobs in canal, road, and railway construction, cultivated his little holding intensively, and improved his cabin to accommodate a growing family. However, the famine crisis undermined this economy and in 1849 he moved his household to Dublin, where, through connections, he obtained full-time employment, eventually becoming managing clerk of Watkins's Brewery in Ardee Street. John, who had briefly attended Kill national school, continued his formal education in Dublin at O'Connell's (Christian Brothers) schools, Marlborough Street model school, a small private school off the South Circular Road, and School Street model school. Although at the last-named institution he was a paid monitor from the age of fourteen for two and a half years, his disciplinary record was not unblemished; by his own account he was dismissed from Marlborough Street for kicking a teacher on the shin, and he records a number of other altercations with teachers. After leaving school he obtained an office job.

Devoy soon took up the learning of Irish (a task which he never completed) at evening classes, where he was also introduced to nationalist movements, firstly the national petition campaign of 1859–61, and then the Fenians, into whose organization he was sworn in 1861. His father, conscious of having himself invested too much in patriotic endeavours, put pressure on Devoy to attend to his further education and his prospects in life. The eighteen-year-old responded by leaving home to join the French Foreign Legion. After a year in Algeria he returned to Dublin and then moved to Naas, co. Kildare, to promote the Fenian organization in the town and surrounding area. In September 1865 James Stephens put him in charge of Fenian recruitment among Irishmen in British army regiments. After Stephens himself had been arrested on a charge of treason two months later, Devoy was a key figure in planning and effecting his rescue from Richmond prison, which occurred on 24 November 1865. On 20 and 21 February 1866 Devoy attended a council of war at which Stephens effectively backed away from an immediate rising. Devoy was himself arrested on 22 February 1866 and after a year of detention was formally charged with treason felony. Unlike the line of Fenian leaders who had preceded him into the dock, he pleaded guilty, pragmatically estimating that this might produce a more lenient sentence. In the event he was given fifteen years of penal servitude. He subsequently served almost four years in various English prisons—Millbank, Portland, and Chatham—before being released in January 1871, whereupon he went into exile in the United States.

Finding the Irish-American movement in a chaotic state, Devoy and other released Irish prisoners threw their weight behind a new organization, the Irish Confederation. This proved to be a disappointment and around 1873 Devoy joined Clan na Gael, which dated from 1867. Thanks largely to Devoy it became the premier Irish-American nationalist association; despite explosive internal conflicts it was to be his principal vehicle for fifty years of purposeful endeavour on behalf of Irish independence. Through the Clan he masterminded the rescue of six Fenian prisoners from Western Australia in 1876, a spectacular achievement. The resulting prestige helped Devoy to secure an arrangement with the supreme council of the Irish Republican Brotherhood (IRB) under which Clan na Gael influence over the home movement was copper-fastened and a joint revolutionary directory created. These successes encouraged Devoy to think of taking advantage of the prospective conflict between Britain and Russia over the Balkans: a Clan delegation met the Russian ambassador in Washington in November 1876. Devoy was still planning for an imminent Irish revolution when Michael Davitt, the recently released IRB leader, arrived in New York in August 1878. Following consultations with Davitt, in October 1878 Devoy launched the 'new departure': this was intended to link the IRB and Clan na Gael with the 'obstructionist' section of home-rule MPs supporting Charles Stewart Parnell, in a campaign that would draw on the rising sense of anxiety caused by agricultural depression. In furtherance of his objective, Devoy attended a gathering of the IRB supreme council in Paris in January 1879 and held meetings with Parnell and Davitt in Dublin. The understandings achieved contributed greatly to the emergence of the Land League by October 1879 and to the character of the ensuing land war. Devoy and the Clan contributed massively to the political and financial success of Parnell's triumphant US tour in early 1880. However, the political

John Devoy (1842–1928), by unknown photographer, 1871 [standing, left, with: (seated, left to right) Captain Charles Underwood O'Connell and Jeremiah O'Donovan Rossa; (standing) Harry Mulleda and Captain John McClure]

effect of the land war was to advance constitutional 'home rule' nationalism rather than the radical separatism which Devoy wished to promote.

There ensued decades of conflict within and around Clan na Gael as Devoy and others struggled for control of militant Irish nationalism in the USA, and for influence over Irish nationalism at home. But, largely under the influence of Devoy, Clan na Gael was available to support Irish radicals and militants at crucial moments. He gave significant encouragement to the Gaelic Athletic Association and the Gaelic League. He was a vital supporter of the military council within the IRB, which planned the rising of Easter Week 1916, and he was a key figure behind the Friends of Irish Freedom, an open organization backed by Clan na Gael which by late 1919 had raised a million dollars in support of the independence movement. Relations between the Friends of Irish Freedom and the Sinn Féin leadership subsequently became very sour and very complicated, and Devoy acquired another batch of bitter enemies, this time including Eamon de Valera. With division rampant on both sides of the Atlantic, Devoy gave his support to the Anglo-Irish treaty of December 1921 and to the new Irish Free State. He visited the country in August 1924, when the Tailteann games in Croke Park, Dublin, provided an opportunity for formal public expression of respect and gratitude. He also made sentimental visits to the haunts of his early life. Back in the United States, he gathered together his memoirs in a volume which appeared in 1929 as *Recollections of an Irish Rebel*. He died on 30 September 1928 in Atlantic City, New Jersey, and was interred temporarily in New York before final burial in Glasnevin cemetery, Dublin.

Small and pugnacious, Devoy was the most able, tenacious, and pragmatic individual to devote his life to the cause of Irish separatism. Journalism, and especially the weekly *Gaelic American*, had been throughout his American career at once a source of income and a means to his political ends; he died unmarried and with little money.   R. V. COMERFORD

Sources J. Devoy, *Recollections of an Irish rebel* (1929) · D. Ryan, *The phoenix flame: a study of Fenianism and John Devoy* (1937) · W. O'Brien and D. Ryan, eds., *Devoy's post bag, 1871–1928*, 2 vols. (1948–53) · M. F. Funchion, *Irish American voluntary organizations* (1983) · R. V. Comerford, *The Fenians in context: Irish politics and society, 1848–82* (1985)
Archives NL Ire., corresp. and papers
Likenesses group portrait, photograph, 1871, repro. in O'Brien and Ryan, eds., *Devoy's post bag* [*see illus.*] · S. Keating, charcoal drawing, NG Ire. · photograph, repro. in Devoy, *Recollections of an Irish rebel*, frontispiece · photographs, repro. in O'Brien and Ryan, *Devoy's post bag*

Dewar, De Courcy Lewthwaite (1878–1959). *See under* Glasgow Girls (*act.* 1880–1920).

Dewar, Donald Campbell (1937–2000), first minister of Scotland, was born on 21 August 1937 at 194 Renfrew Street, Glasgow, the only child of Dr Alisdair Campbell Dewar, a consultant dermatologist, and his wife, Mary Howat, *née* Bennett.

Education Dewar's parents were both unwell soon after his birth—his father had tuberculosis and spent long

Donald Campbell Dewar (1937–2000), by Michael Powell, 1998

periods in a sanatorium, and his mother suffered a brain tumour—so he had a lonely and self-reliant life from a very early age. From the time he was two he was sent to preparatory schools, first in Perthshire, then in Hawick, where, as he said, 'I was in care—organised by my parents.' Throughout his life his accent reflected the borders (with maybe a hint of his first constituency in Aberdeen) and not his native Glasgow. When he was nine he went to Moss Park primary school in Glasgow, and at the age of ten to Glasgow Academy. At both schools he felt lonely and unloved; at Glasgow Academy he starred neither at studies nor at sport. His school reports were littered with faint praise, such as 'a good worker … sound … works hard'. He stayed on an extra year to retake his higher leaving certificate, and at the second attempt obtained good enough grades to proceed to Glasgow University. On his leaving record, Glasgow Academy listed his 'probable occupation or profession' as '??'.

Dewar started to blossom only on arriving at Glasgow University to study history in 1957. He graduated MA with honours in 1961, then took a second degree in law, and graduated with a second-class LLB in 1964. On 20 July of the latter year he married a fellow Glasgow student, six years his junior, Alison Mary, daughter of Dr James Shaw McNair, a medical practitioner, and his wife, Agnes McCrae Anthony, *née* Murray. They had a daughter, Marion, and a son, Ian.

Humanities students in the old Scottish universities had a distinctive culture in the 1950s. Maintenance grants from the Scottish education department were not tenable in English universities. Few Scottish students, except the children of wealthy parents and those educated in public schools, went to university outside Scotland. Their teachers were probably themselves Scots or Ulstermen, educated in the same Scottish universities a generation before. This reinforced the climate of cultural nationalism that was probably strongest in law. Law students, of course, studied Scots law, whose teachers assert its technical superiority to English law. This period in Dewar's life solidified his own intense cultural (but never political) nationalism, which he may have imbibed from his mother, who was the secretary of the Scottish Culture Society. Like Sir Walter Scott, he combined cultural nationalism with fierce opposition to Scottish independence. Throughout his life he retained an intense interest in Scottish history and culture. He had an expert knowledge of the highland clearances, of the Disruption of the Church of Scotland, and of the paintings of the Scottish colourists. He rarely left Scotland except when national business took him to London. When, in later life, he had to go abroad as shadow Scottish secretary, his aides discovered that he did not possess a passport.

Glasgow University, in Dewar's time, was at the peak of its reputation for student debating. In the rough house of the Glasgow University men's union, Dewar learned the debating skills that friend and foe came to admire in his political career. He also formed the close political friendships across party divides that stayed with him throughout his life. He succeeded John Smith (later leader of the Labour Party) as chairman of the university Labour Club and president of the union; he and Smith won *The Scotsman* debating trophy in 1961. Other close associates from university days were the Liberal politician Menzies Campbell and the Conservative lawyer Ross Harper. Dewar's own political commitment was Scottish Gaitskellite. On the right wing of the Labour Party, he was never tempted to join the Social Democrat breakaway in 1981, perhaps because the breakaways were weaker in Scotland than in the rest of the UK.

In and out of parliament On leaving university, Dewar became a solicitor, though he also pursued a political career, having in 1962 been selected as Labour candidate for Aberdeen South. In 1964 he was defeated by the sitting Conservative, Lady Tweedsmuir, the daughter-in-law of John Buchan; she had told him that he would not 'need to interrupt his studies' (*The Scotsman*, 12 Oct 2000). Nevertheless, in 1966 he won the seat, defeating Lady Tweedsmuir by 1799 votes. In the parliament of 1966–70 he served on the public accounts committee (a highly unusual posting for a first-term MP) and from 1967 to 1969 was parliamentary private secretary to Anthony Crosland, president of the Board of Trade, although he and Crosland did not become close. Roy Jenkins unsuccessfully proposed him for junior ministerial office in April 1968. However, in the general election of 1970 he lost his seat.

1970 was Dewar's *annus horribilis*, since in that year he also lost his wife, who left him for a life in London with another Scottish Labour lawyer, and formerly a friend of Dewar, Alexander (Derry) Irvine (later the patron of Tony Blair and, as Lord Irvine of Lairg, lord chancellor in the Labour governments of 1997 and 2001). They were divorced in 1973. Although he never talked about it, this was a shattering blow to Dewar. He never remarried, and lived alone for the rest of his life in the former matrimonial home in Cleveden Crescent, Glasgow. He would call, unannounced, on friends, who always enjoyed entertaining him. Menzies Campbell and his wife, Elspeth, regularly invited him for Christmas dinner until he said that he would rather eat fish fingers at home. Also in 1970 Dewar started to suffer the back trouble that left him stooped and in pain in later life.

Dewar's political allies assumed that he would soon return to parliament. However, he was not selected for a Scottish Labour-held seat until 1978, probably because his opinions were too right-wing for selection committees; possibly also because he was unsympathetic to the bitterly anti-devolutionist leadership of Willie Ross, secretary of state for Scotland in 1964–70 and 1974–6. After losing his seat he took the new quasi-judicial post of reporter to a children's panel. These panels were intended to be tribunals, less adversarial than traditional courts, for dealing with juvenile offenders. Friends attributed Dewar's choice of this career to his own disturbed and lonely childhood. He also hosted a political discussion programme on Radio Clyde called *Clyde Comment*. In the early 1970s he moved into private practice at the instigation of his university friend Ross Harper, becoming a partner in Harper's firm, Ross Harper Murphy, in 1975. Although his personal disorganization tried his colleagues sorely, he remained popular for his integrity and energizing pessimism.

Return to parliament The Scottish National Party (SNP) did well in the two general elections of 1974. In October of that year they won eleven seats and obtained 30 per cent of the Scottish vote. The Conservatives, with fewer votes, won more seats; and Labour retained its customary majority of the seats on a minority of the vote. Nevertheless, it was clear to all parties that the SNP was very close to a tipping point. If its vote were to rise to 35 per cent or beyond, it would tip suddenly from underrepresentation in seats to overrepresentation, and win more than half the seats in Scotland. It had announced that it would take this as its cue for starting independence negotiations. The Labour Party, however strong or weak its commitment to the union of the United Kingdom, could not tolerate such a threat to its own base. Not only the Labour government of October 1974, but most Labour governments, depended on Scottish Labour seats for their majorities. Therefore, something had to be done about Scottish devolution. However, the 1974–9 government's efforts were incompetent. It was common knowledge that ministers were proposing a Scotland and Wales Bill (later split into separate bills after the first had been defeated in an English backbench revolt), not for its own sake but in order to preserve the UK government's majority. John Smith was the only minister who believed in it.

Early in 1978 the death of the sitting member, Willie Small, forced a by-election in Glasgow Garscadden, a constituency dominated by the huge and multiply deprived Drumchapel estate in the north-west of the city. Dewar won the Labour nomination, but everyone, including Dewar himself, expected the SNP to gain the seat. Instead, he won with a majority of 4552 over the nationalists. Some instant pundits attributed the upset to the fact that the SNP candidate, Keith Bovey, was an active supporter of the Campaign for Nuclear Disarmament in a constituency where the naval shipyards were one of the largest employers. Dewar retained the seat (later renamed Anniesland) for the rest of his life. The SNP faded fast after the Garscadden by-election. At the general election of 1979 they were reduced to two seats. The incoming prime minister, Margaret Thatcher, abandoned Scottish devolution, and the issue disappeared from the UK agenda for eighteen years. Even in Scotland it did not resurface until the late 1980s.

Dewar became an opposition Scottish spokesman in 1980 and shadow secretary of state for Scotland in 1983. He joined the shadow cabinet in 1984. He remained shadow secretary of state for Scotland until his friend John Smith became Labour leader in 1992. Smith made Dewar shadow secretary of state for social security, a post he retained after Smith's death in 1994 until Tony Blair made him Labour chief whip in 1996.

Dewar was highly effective in both shadow secretary of state posts. Although he was a solicitor, not an advocate, his personal disorganization had forced on him the advocate's skill of mastering a very complex brief in a very short time. His university debating skills made him one of the few MPs who could actually debate, with wit and savagery. As shadow secretary of state for Scotland, he had an ambiguous triumph in getting some clauses deleted from the Conservative government's Law Reform (Miscellaneous Provisions) (Scotland) Bill in 1990. 'The Law Society', an unselfconscious tribute stated, 'was forever grateful to Donald Dewar for assisting in the deletion of many of the worst parts of the Act [sic]—including conveyancing by banks and building societies' (Scots Law Times). As shadow social security secretary, he created a party commission on social justice that began the transition from old to new Labour in that policy area. As chief whip, his absent-minded professorial manner hid an efficient, not to say ruthless, operation, despite which he made no lasting enemies.

Devolution Dewar supported devolution to Scotland within the United Kingdom throughout his political career. In the 1960s and 1970s this was unfashionable for a Labour politician. Most of his contemporaries were firm unionists for two reasons, one good and one bad. The good reason was that, if Labour was committed to equality, then that implied redistributing resources from the rich, wherever they were, to the poor, wherever they were. Devolution could cut across this. Labour's most fervent egalitarian, Aneurin Bevan, opposed devolution for this reason, and so did his disciple Neil Kinnock until a late conversion as Labour leader. (Unsurprisingly, relations between Dewar and Kinnock were sometimes strained.) The bad reason was that Labour normally needed the votes of its Welsh and Scottish MPs to govern England. The bad came to undermine the good. It blunted Dewar's attack on legislation that Conservative governments imposed on Scotland while holding very few seats there. Although all the opposition parties denounced the Law Reform Bill in 1990 and, even more, the bill to impose the poll tax on Scotland in 1987, Dewar could not play the legitimacy card. It would give hostages both to the Scottish nationalists, who decried what they called the 'feeble fifty' Scottish Labour MPs, and to the Conservatives, who could point out that, although the Conservative

government held a minority of seats in Scotland, most Labour governments also held a minority of seats in England, and had not hesitated to pass English legislation with Scottish votes.

Unionist politicians were terrified at the prospect of Scottish independence, federalism, or even devolution—Conservatives because they loved the union in and of itself, Labour politicians because of the threat to their capacity to govern England. Therefore, since at least 1918 and perhaps since 1886, they bought off Scottish sentiment by allowing higher public spending per head there. Throughout Dewar's political career, public spending per head in Scotland was higher than in the deprived regions of England. Devolution impaired equality, not because the devolved regions got less, but because they got more, than comparable regions elsewhere in the UK. This was one anomaly that Dewar did not tackle.

The devolution bills of the 1970s had enumerated powers that were to go to the devolved assemblies; the list was bitterly contested between the Scottish and Welsh offices and the 'English' departments, which won most of the battles. Most lawyers believe that, if they had not been abandoned, the Scotland and Wales Acts of 1978 would have been unworkable because of constant disputes about the powers of the devolved and Westminster administrations. To prevent a repetition, Dewar was one of those who initiated the Scottish Constitutional Convention in 1989. The convention brought together the Labour and Liberal parties, some churches, and other civil society organizations; its chairman was an Episcopalian clergyman, Canon Kenyon Wright. The SNP and Conservatives, for opposite reasons, did not take part. The convention was, of course, self-appointed, but it enabled Smith and Dewar to insist that devolution was, in Smith's phrase, 'the settled will of the Scottish people'.

On Labour's victory in the general election of 1997 Dewar became secretary of state for Scotland. He led the referendum campaign for a double yes, which in September 1997 legitimized both a Scottish parliament and its power to vary tax rates, both by substantial majorities. He largely wrote, and piloted through the Commons, the Scotland Bill. Launching the bill in December 1997, he read its opening words: '"There shall be a Scottish Parliament" [slight pause]. I like that' (The Scotsman, 12 Oct 2000). The bill duly became the Scotland Act of 1998. As soon as he announced that he would run for the Scottish parliament created by that act, it was assumed on all sides that Dewar would be the first Labour leader and (assuming, as everyone did, that Labour became the largest party) the first first minister of Scotland. So it came to pass.

The arrangements proposed by the Scottish Constitutional Convention were copied with few alterations into the Scotland Act. Whereas the bills of the 1970s had provided a list of devolved powers reluctantly conceded by the Cabinet Office, the convention and the act of 1998 provided a list of powers reserved to Westminster, proposed and defended by Dewar. In cabinet committee bargaining with his old adversary Lord Irvine, who (like English ministers in the 1970s) wanted to restrict the powers of the

Scottish parliament, Dewar won many of his battles. He could use the 'settled will of the Scottish people' as his bargaining counter.

One arrangement carried over from the convention to the act provided for proportional representation in the Scottish parliament. As Labour would probably have easily won an outright majority of its seats on a minority vote had the Westminster system applied there, Dewar called this 'the best example of charitable giving this century in politics' (*Parliamentary Debates*, vol. 312, 6 May 1998, col. 803). However, it guaranteed the legitimacy of the Scottish parliament and made it harder for the SNP to gain a majority in it. The first devolved administration was, as everybody had expected, a coalition between the two constitutional convention parties, Labour and the Liberal Democrats. Likewise, the double referendum was the result of tortuous negotiation through bad-tempered Labour committees, and it attracted some derision when it was proposed. In retrospect, though, it was another triumph for Dewar, because it sealed the legitimacy of the Scottish parliament's power to tax.

On becoming first minister of Scotland in May 1999, Dewar wrote, 'The people of Scotland rightly have high hopes and expectations for their Parliament; they already feel a sense of ownership and of connection to it and we must not let them down.' But within less than a year the euphoria had faded, as Dewar became embroiled in both policy and personality disputes, including a scandal surrounding the behaviour of two special advisers, and another derived from the escalating costs of the new Scottish parliament building. He seemed less successful as first minister than he had been as father of the nation (the title instantly bestowed by all the obituaries).

In April 2000 Dewar was diagnosed as suffering from heart trouble. He retired temporarily in order to undergo surgery to repair a damaged aortic valve. However, he resumed office too soon that summer, and he suffered a brain haemorrhage after a fall outside his official residence on 10 October 2000; he died in the Western General Hospital, Edinburgh, on 11 October. He was cremated at Clydebank on 18 October and his ashes scattered at Lochgilphead in Argyll. Notorious for his frugal lifestyle, he reserved one last surprise for his will, which revealed that he had left over £2 million. Most of this was in inherited equities and three houses, but it also reflected his acute tastes in art. A storm over his alleged hypocrisy in holding shares in companies privatized by Conservative governments quickly subsided when it became clear that the shares had been held in a blind trust, and the property comprised one inherited house, the former matrimonial home, and a flat to which he had been intending to move after his convalescence.

A modest and self-deprecating man, Dewar was noted for his acerbic wit and generally gloomy features. 'I'm not dour and horrid', he once protested, 'but people do say that I am the most melancholic man in politics. I can usually find some reason to take a very dim view of the prospects' (*The Times*, 12 Oct 2000). He was a very hard worker, and many contemporaries believed that he literally worked himself to death for his beloved country. Nevertheless, the heartfelt tributes that poured out at his death showed that he had triumphantly secured the legitimacy of the Scottish parliament and had wrong-footed both of the parties that had stayed out of its creation, the SNP and the Conservatives. They clambered on board, but the SNP could not, in Dewar's lifetime, use the parliament as their lever to extract more concessions from the English, and Dewar's wrong-footing of them may have contributed to their poor performance in the general election of 2001. Indeed, at the time of Dewar's death it seemed likely that, if the arrangements were to unravel, it would probably be from England rather than from Scotland. The existence of the Scottish parliament forced the issues of regional taxing and spending into the open as never before. But Dewar, described at his death as 'a throwback to the Scottish Enlightenment' (*The Scotsman*, 12 Oct 2000), would not have objected to that.   IAIN McLEAN

Sources T. Dalyell, *The Independent* (12 Oct 2000) • *The Times* (12 Oct 2000) • E. MacAskill and B. Wilson, *The Guardian* (12 Oct 2000) • *The Scotsman* (12 Oct 2000) • *Daily Telegraph* (12 Oct 2000) • *Financial Times* (12 Oct 2000) • *Scots Law Times* (27 Oct 2000) • *Parliamentary debates*, Commons, 6th ser. • *Glasgow Academy Chronicle* (1950–57) • *Glasgow University Guardian* (1957–64) • *Glasgow University Magazine* (1957–64) • R. H. S. Crossman, *The diaries of a cabinet minister*, 3 (1977) • *A guide to the Scottish parliament*, Centre for Scottish Public Policy (1999) • private information (2004) • WWW • b. cert. • m. cert. • d. cert.
Archives NA Scot., departmental records • PRO, departmental records • U. Glas., Archives and Business Records Centre, papers relating to his student career
Likenesses M. Clarke, group portrait, photograph, 1978 (*Devolution*?), Hult. Arch. • group portrait, photograph, 1978, Hult. Arch. • M. Powell, photograph, 1998, News International Syndication, London [*see illus.*] • photographs, repro. in *The Scotsman*
Wealth at death £2,060,456.40: confirmation, 2001, *CCI*

Dewar, James (1793–1846), conductor and composer, was born on 26 July 1793 in Edinburgh, the son of Daniel Dewar, a violinist and composer of reels, and his wife, Catharine, *née* Ballantyne. His brother John Dewar was a composer. In 1817 he succeeded his teacher, William Penson, as conductor of the band of the Theatre Royal, Edinburgh, where he remained until his death. He was also organist at St George's Episcopal Church in the city from 1815 to 1835. He was one of the founders of the Edinburgh Professional Society of Musicians, and conducted their concerts. In 1821 he conducted a four-day orchestral and vocal festival at the Theatre Royal, Glasgow, and from 1826 to 1827 organized a season of subscription concerts in Glasgow.

Dewar composed several glees, one of which, 'The Goldfinch', was awarded first prize in a competition by Sir George Mackenzie in 1843. He arranged Scottish airs for piano and orchestra, and wrote music for some of the plays based on Sir Walter Scott's novels, including *Waverley* (1823), and *The Antiquary* (overture only). In 1826 he published six books of *Popular National Melodies Adapted for the Pianoforte*, and about 1829 edited *The Border Garland*, with poems by Hogg. Dewar died in Edinburgh on 4 January 1846.   ANNE PIMLOTT BAKER

Sources H. G. Farmer, *A history of music in Scotland* (1947) · D. Baptie, ed., *Musical Scotland, past and present: being a dictionary of Scottish musicians from about 1400 till the present time* (1894) · Brown & Stratton, *Brit. mus.* · b. cert.

Dewar, Sir James (1842–1923), chemist and physicist, was born at Kincardine-on-Forth, Scotland, on 20 September 1842, the youngest son of Thomas Dewar, vintner, and his wife, Ann Eadie, daughter of a shipowner. At the age of ten his schooling was interrupted by an attack of rheumatic fever, and during the period of incapacity that followed he occupied himself in making fiddles—an exercise to which he was wont to attribute his manipulative skill. On recovering he was sent to Dollar Academy, and thence, about 1858, to Edinburgh University. There he worked successively under James David Forbes, the professor of natural philosophy, Lyon Playfair, the professor of chemistry, whose demonstrator he was, and, on Playfair's resignation in 1869, under his successor Alexander Crum Brown. In 1869 he was appointed lecturer on chemistry in the Royal (Dick) Veterinary College, where he later became professor. From 1873 he was also assistant chemist to the Highland and Agricultural Society, with the duty of delivering what he called 'peripatetic lectures'. In 1875 he left Edinburgh for Cambridge, having been elected to the Jacksonian chair of natural experimental philosophy. Two years later he was elected Fullerian professor of chemistry at the Royal Institution of Great Britain, London. Both these chairs he held until his death. While at Edinburgh he married in 1871 Helen Rose, daughter of William Banks, of that city. They had no children.

During his time at Edinburgh Dewar worked on both organic and inorganic chemistry. His first published paper, presented to the Royal Society of Edinburgh in 1867, described a 'simple mechanical arrangement' for illustrating the structure of the non-saturated hydrocarbons, and showed how it could be used to represent seven different formulae for benzene, including the well-known Dewar formula. The device was sent by Playfair to the German chemist F. A. Kekulé, who conceived the widely recognized ring formula for benzene. Kekulé then invited Dewar to spend the summer of 1867 in his laboratory at Ghent. Dewar went on to do work on chlorosulphuric acid, the oxidation products of picoline, the thermal equivalents of the oxides of chlorine, and the temperature of the sun and of the electric spark. Of some interest is his work on the specific heat of Graham's hydrogenium, thought of as a volatile metal associated with hydrogen. During this investigation, in order to prevent the influx of heat into his calorimeter, he employed, in 1872, the vacuum jacket which later proved indispensable for the liquefaction of gases, and became, though not in his hands, the silver coated 'Thermos' flask. Similarly, the use of coconut charcoal for absorbing gases, which also played a most important part in his later work, was mentioned in a paper he published with P. G. Tait in 1874, entitled 'On a new method of obtaining very perfect vacua' (*Transactions of the Royal Society of Edinburgh*, 8, 1875,

Sir James Dewar (1842–1923), by Alexander Scott or Ethel Glazebrook, 1902

348–9). During this period Dewar's complementary interest in biological subjects, which repeatedly appeared in his subsequent researches, was shown by his investigation with Dr Arthur Gamgee in 1871 of the constitution and physiological relations of cystine, and by elaborate studies conducted from 1873 onwards with John Gray M'Kendrick, professor of physiology in Glasgow University from 1876 to 1906, on the physiological action of light on the eye.

Soon after moving south, in 1875, Dewar joined George Downing Liveing, then the professor of chemistry at Cambridge, in a series of spectroscopic investigations the results of which were published at intervals over a quarter of a century. Much of this research was designed to controvert Norman Lockyer's speculations on the dissociation of elements at very high temperatures. Some of the work was done at Cambridge, but the Royal Institution, where he had better laboratory facilities, became the chief centre of Dewar's experimental activities, and, indeed, of his whole life.

At the Royal Institution, Dewar implemented the extensive research programme into cryogenics for which he is best known. In 1878, at a Friday evening lecture, he showed in operation the apparatus by which L. P. Cailletet had effected the partial liquefaction of oxygen; at another lecture, in 1884, he exhibited the gas in the form of a true liquid by the aid of a modification of the apparatus of Z. F. Wróblewski and K. S. Olszewski. In 1891, using essentially improved methods, he discovered that both liquid oxygen and liquid ozone are attracted by the magnet. Hydrogen, the only one of Faraday's 'permanent' gases which had not been liquefied, was for the first time collected by Dewar as a liquid in an open vessel in 1898, and in the following year he obtained it as a transparent ice. This brought him into a dispute over priority with William Hampson, consultant to Brin's Oxygen Company (later British Oxygen Company). For his work on hydrogen Dewar built a large machine, weighing a couple of tons, in which he made use of the Joule–Thomson effect by continuously expanding the highly compressed gas through a fine orifice on a cascade principle. His success was largely due to the inclusion of two novel features—the vacuum jacket as a means of heat insulation, and a device consisting of a coiled tube which gave sufficient elasticity to enable the liquid gas to be drawn off without fracture of the glass by the intense cold. He also attempted the liquefaction of helium, the only known gas not reduced to the liquid state, but had not succeeded when, in 1908, H. Kamerlingh Onnes, working in his cryogenic laboratory at Leiden, obtained the liquid.

Dewar's research facilities were greatly improved in 1896 when Ludwig Mond generously gave £100,000 to found and equip the Davy–Faraday Laboratory next door to the Royal Institution. He became its first director. In 1902, the year in which he was president at Belfast of the British Association, Dewar again turned his attention to charcoal, studying the conditions under which it must be prepared in order to develop the greatest activity, and finding that its power of absorbing gases is enormously increased by cold. He used it for the liquefaction of gases, the analysis of gaseous mixtures without liquefaction, and, above all, for the production of very high vacua; this last application probably contributed more than any other single agency to the advances made by atomic physics in immediately succeeding years. Charcoal also enabled him to make vacuum storage vessels of metal larger and stronger than was possible with glass, for he found that a portion of charcoal placed in the vacuous space absorbed occluded gas escaping from the metal and thus maintained the vacuum.

In producing liquid gases Dewar always had in view their utilization in opening up new fields to research. Thus as soon as he obtained them in sufficient quantity, as well as devising methods for their thermometry and making determinations of their physical constants, he applied them to a wide range of pioneer explorations of the properties of matter at very low temperatures—chemical and photographic action, phosphorescence, the cohesion and strength of materials, and, with Professor John Ambrose Fleming, of University College, London, electric and magnetic effects such as conduction, thermoelectricity, dielectric constants, and magnetic permeability. With Henri Moissan, Dewar liquefied fluorine in 1897 and in 1903 solidified it. Between 1903 and 1908 he made several researches on radium, investigating with Sir William Crookes the effect of extreme cold on its emanations, examining with Pierre Curie the gases occluded or given off by it, and determining the rate at which it evolves

helium. A notable piece of research, which he published in 1913, showed that the mean atomic specific heats of the elements between the boiling-points of liquid nitrogen and hydrogen, when plotted in terms of their atomic weights, exhibit a definite periodic variation instead of being approximately uniform as they are at ordinary temperatures. Similar observations, published posthumously, of the molecular specific heats of many series or homologous groups of inorganic and organic compounds revealed some striking relations.

During the First World War, in the restricted time left for research after meeting the demands of government departments, Dewar paid attention to the chemistry of the soap bubble, which in 1878–9 had been the subject of the first of the nine courses of Christmas lectures for young people which he delivered at the Royal Institution. He elucidated the conditions necessary for the production of long-lived bubbles and flat films, and studied the interference colours displayed when a jet of air was made to play upon their surface. At this period also he made from the roof of the institution a series of observations of sky radiation with a delicate charcoal thermoscope.

The papers recording the spectroscopic researches which Dewar made with Liveing were published in collected form in 1915, and the rest of his papers in 1927. In addition to the research recorded in his journal papers, he also engaged in a number of other scientific projects. These included, for example, the experiments resulting in the invention of cordite which he and Sir Frederick Augustus *Abel carried out as members of the government committee on explosives (1888–91), one of the special chemical and other researches entailed by his large practice as an expert witness. The work on cordite involved him and Abel in prolonged litigation with Alfred Nobel, who believed that their patent for cordite infringed his own for ballistite. The case eventually went to the House of Lords, where Nobel finally lost. It cost him £28,000 and left him permanently embittered. Dewar was also an authority on sewage disposal and water supply, and a member of the Balfour commission on London water supply (1893–4); for many years he and Crookes made daily chemical and bacteriological analyses of the water distributed to the metropolis. He was elected FRS in 1877, knighted in 1904, and received many honours from scientific societies in Europe and America.

Well read in English literature, especially poetry, Dewar was devoted to music; a little violin playing, with his wife as accompanist, often ended the day's work in the small hours of the morning. His rooms at the Royal Institution and his house at Cambridge were filled with *objets d'art* of all kinds, and he was a fine judge of wine and tobacco. To many contemporaries, Dewar was seen as quarrelsome, litigious, and impatient, with few close friends in the scientific community. To others, while sometimes choleric and prone to vigour of expression, he was seen as a kindly and generous man. His contributions to science lay rather in the discovery of new facts than in the elaboration of theory; he published no theoretical papers. As an experimenter he was unsurpassed, as daring and imaginative in conception as he was brilliant and sure in execution. Dewar died at his home in the Royal Institution, 21 Albemarle Street, on 27 March 1923.

H. M. ROSS, *rev.* TREVOR I. WILLIAMS

Sources A. Findlay and W. H. Mills, eds., *British chemists* (1947) · H. E. Armstrong, *PRS*, 111A (1926), xiii–xxiii · H. E. Armstrong, *JCS* (1928), 1066–1706 · *DSB* · *Nature*, 111 (1923), 472–4 · R. Cory, 'Fifty years at the Royal Institution', *Nature*, 166 (1950), 1049–53 · A. M. Clerke, 'Low temperature research at the Royal Institution, 1898–1900', *Notices of the Proceedings at the Meetings of the Members of the Royal Institution*, 16 (1899–1901), 698–718 · H. E. Armstrong, 'Low temperature research at the Royal Institution, 1900–07', *Notices of the Proceedings at the Meetings of the Members of the Royal Institution*, 19 (1908–10), 354–412 · H. E. Armstrong, 'Low temperature research at the Royal Institution, 1908–16', *Notices of the Proceedings at the Meetings of the Members of the Royal Institution*, 21 (1914–16), 735–85 · H. E. Armstrong, *James Dewar, 1842–1923: a Friday evening lecture to the members of the Royal Institution* (1924) · J. R. Partington, *A history of chemistry*, 4 (1964), 904–6 · personal knowledge (1937)
Archives Royal Institution of Great Britain, London, corresp. and papers · Sci. Mus., corresp. relating to experiments concerning vacuum flask | California Institute of Technology, Pasadena, corresp. with G. E. Hale · CUL, corresp. with Lord Kelvin · CUL, letters to Lord Rutherford · CUL, letters to Sir George Stokes · CUL, letters to Sir Joseph Thomson · ICL, letters to H. E. Armstrong · ICL, letters to Lord Playfair · RGS, letters to Sir David Gill · RS, letters to Sir Joseph Thomson
Likenesses W. Q. Orchardson, oils, exh. RA 1894, Peterhouse, Cambridge · T. W. Dewar, oils, 1900, Scot. NPG · A. Scott or E. Glazebrook, photograph, 1902, NPG [*see illus.*] · C. Melilli, bronze statuette, 1906, NPG · G. D. Macdougald, bronze bust, 1910, NPG · O. Edis, photograph, *c.*1920, NPG · H. J. Brooks, group portrait, oils (*Sir James Dewar lecturing on liquid hydrogen at the Royal Institution, 1904*), Royal Institution of Great Britain, London · R. De l'Hôpital, oils, Chemical Society, London · E. Dyer, oils (after W. Q. Orchardson), Scot. NPG · B. McKennal, bronze panel, Royal Institution of Great Britain, London · photograph, repro. in Findlay and Mills, eds., *British chemists*
Wealth at death £124,555 1s. 9d.: probate, 16 May 1923, CGPLA Eng. & Wales

Dewar, John Alexander, first Baron Forteviot (1856–1929), whisky blender and philanthropist, was born at Perth on 6 June 1856, the second surviving son in a family of five sons and two daughters of John Dewar (1806–1880), wine and spirit merchant, and his wife, Jane (1820–1900), daughter of John Gow, farmer at Pittendynie, Perthshire. His youngest surviving brother, born at Perth on 6 January 1864, was **Thomas Robert Dewar**, Baron Dewar (1864–1930), whisky blender and politician.

During the last quarter of the nineteenth century a number of highly successful firms developed in the Scotch whisky industry. One of the most successful was John Dewar & Sons Ltd of Perth. The firm had been founded in 1846 by John Dewar, the son of a crofter. Born in Aberfeldy in 1806 and educated at the parish school, he trained as a joiner but in 1828 moved to Perth to take up an offer of employment from a relative, James Macdonald, a wine merchant. They formed a partnership in 1837 which was dissolved nine years later when Dewar decided to begin his own business. When he died in 1880 the business was still mainly local though it made sufficient profit for him to leave an estate worth over £30,000.

John Alexander Dewar, first Baron Forteviot (1856–1929), by Bassano, early 1900s

John Alexander and Thomas Robert Dewar joined the firm in 1879 and 1881 respectively. Both had been educated at Perth Academy and had served the customary apprenticeship in other wine and spirit firms, John with Condamine & Co. of Leith, Thomas with Forrest and Turnbull of Leith and later with Robertson and Baxter of Glasgow. Together the brothers created a firm whose product became a household name. Profit figures indicate their achievement. When their father died annual profits were a mere £1321. By 1900 they were £59,000 and by 1925, when the firm merged with the Distillers Company, profits were over £1 million.

The brothers' characters were very different. John was a cautious, dour individual, very much absorbed by finance and administration. As older brother he was acutely aware of the family's dependence on the firm and yet wanted it to expand. His main priority was not heavy advertising expenditure but a gradual expansion of sales, coupled with the reinvestment of available profits in mature whisky stocks. He was twice married. His first wife, whom he married in 1884, was Joan, daughter of William Tod, farmer; they had five daughters and one son. She died in 1899, and in 1905 he married Margaret, daughter of Henry Holland, merchant; they had one daughter and one son. Thomas Dewar, who never married, was by contrast an extrovert and an extremely effective whisky salesman. John's career was spent in Perth while Thomas pioneered new markets in England and overseas. Their attributes thus complemented one another where business was concerned. Their political beliefs, however, were a very different matter, with John a Liberal and Thomas an active Conservative and Unionist. As Liberal MP for Inverness-shire from 1900 to 1916, John was to find himself in opposition to his party over the people's budget of 1909 with its increased taxation on spirits, and subsequently became a prominent spokesman for the whisky trade.

John became a partner in 1879, the year before his father's death, and his brother in 1885 when the firm was styled John Dewar & Sons. The firm made modest progress until June 1890 when John obtained a credit of £12,000 from the Distillers Company (DCL) in exchange for Dewars tying their purchases of grain whisky to the DCL. The credit, soon increased to over £75,000, freed resources for investment in whisky stocks and branch offices, and allowed T. R. Dewar to make an international sales tour between 1891 and 1893, during which he visited twenty-six countries, appointed thirty-two agents, and arranged for opening consignments to each country he had visited. The tour cost £14,000, a hefty increase in costs when current profits were less than £7000 a year, but it established Dewars on a worldwide basis. Such sales trips became a hallmark of the firm's approach to exporting. T. R. Dewar undertook another in 1898 and by 1914 the firm's representatives had made five such campaigns.

Dewars' 'take-off' was greatly assisted by DCL and by 1896, when Dewars' debts to DCL were in excess of stock in bond at £76,790, the board of DCL noted that 'Although this was considered a very large risk to have with any single firm, it was not deemed necessary to take any steps to reduce it as the firm … were thought to be of undoubted stability' (United Distillers archive, DCL, board minute book 8, 15 Oct 1896). Reliance on DCL diminished after 1897 when Dewars made a public share issue to provide resources for further expansion. Significantly, though, John Dewar advised DCL that Dewars would continue 'to give the DCL a preference in their grain spirit orders' (ibid., 9 May 1897). His close relationship with DCL and its managing director, William Ross, later proved crucially important.

Although Dewars' home sales continued to expand, despite the declining demand for spirits in Britain after 1900, exports were much more important for they were three times as profitable as home sales. With the largest volume of export sales among the 'big three' blending firms (Buchanan, Dewars, and Walkers), Dewars were well placed in the amalgamation discussions which began in April 1909. An amalgamation of the 'big three' proved unattainable in the pre-war years but the Dewar brothers joined forces with James Buchanan in a holding company, Scotch Whisky Brands, in 1915. This was subsequently renamed Buchanan-Dewar in 1919, and merged along with John Walker & Sons in the Distillers Company in 1925.

John Dewar played a greater role in the merger discussions than his brother on account of his mastery of financial detail and because of his friendship with William Ross, DCL's managing director. Dewar and Ross came to share a common set of beliefs about the problems facing the Scotch whisky industry. They wished to see greater stability in the trade, a reduction in the influence of speculators, and an end to certain 'unbusiness like methods', especially 'the very extravagant distribution of advertising material' (United Distillers archive, John Dewar & Sons Ltd, letter-book, 18 Aug 1900).

Persuading the Walker family that an amalgamation between the 'big three' and the DCL was desirable proved extremely difficult. John Dewar's contribution was to urge that it was the future earning power of the combine that was vital, not the precise value put on family interests. He also persuaded the other participants that Ross should be the chairman of the combine. His only major disagreement with Ross was over the location of the head office. Dewar, following his financial adviser, Sir Gilbert Garnsey, argued that London was essential if the company was to have the confidence of the City. Ross thought it inconceivable that the leading firm in the Scotch whisky industry should be based outside Scotland, a view that ultimately prevailed.

John and Thomas Dewar were appointed to the board of Distillers, but were too far advanced in their careers to play a significant part in shaping future developments, as DCL became increasingly drawn into the industrial alcohol and chemical trades in response to the decline in whisky consumption. For them the amalgamation was more important as a means of rearranging their financial interests.

John Dewar had many other interests as a politician, town and county councillor, landowner, and agriculturalist. He became a member of Perth town council in 1883, was elected treasurer in 1888, and served as lord provost from 1893 to 1899, pushing through local housing and sanitary reforms. In 1907 he was created a baronet and in 1916 was elevated to the peerage as Baron Forteviot of Dupplin, the first of the 'whisky barons'. His title derived from the estate of Dupplin which he purchased from the earl of Kinnoull in 1910 for £249,000. As a landowner, Lord Forteviot set about the task of rural regeneration, building the model village of Forteviot in the style of a small Dutch township. He held directorships in Longmorn–Glenlivet Distilleries, the Dundee, Perth and London Shipping Company, and the Bank of Scotland, and was chairman of John Shields & Co.

Part of John Dewar's fortune was used for philanthropic purposes. An estimated £50,000 was devoted to projects in Perth such as the restoration of St John's Church as a war memorial, the building and equipping of a maternity ward at Perth Royal Infirmary, and the building of a new model lodging house in Skinnergate. He also founded the Forteviot Charitable Trust with an endowment of £60,000 for the benefit of the city of Perth and its inhabitants. Other public service included chairing two commissions of inquiry into medical conditions in the highlands and islands of Scotland, membership of Perth county council and education authority, chairmanship of the Territorial Force Association, and deputy lord lieutenancy of Perthshire.

Thomas Dewar was active in civic and political life in London: he served on the London county council for West Marylebone from 1892 to 1895, and was Conservative MP for the St George's division of Tower Hamlets in London from 1900 to 1906. He became lieutenant of the City of London. Knighted in 1902, he received a baronetcy in 1917, and was created Baron Dewar of Homestall in 1919. His interests included painting, shooting, racing, and coursing.

Lord Forteviot died at Perth on 23 November 1929 leaving an estate worth £4.4 million. His heir, John Dewar MC, had been appointed to the board of the DCL in 1925 and became chairman in September 1937. His brother, Lord Dewar, died on 11 April 1930 at his Sussex home, The Homestall, East Grinstead, leaving an estate valued at over £5 million.   RONALD B. WEIR

Sources R. B. Weir, 'The development of the distilling industry in Scotland in the nineteenth and early twentieth centuries', PhD diss., U. Edin., 1974, vol. 2, pp. 527–51 · R. B. Weir, *The history of the Distillers Company, 1877–1939* (1995) · J. L. Anderson, 'History of the house of Dewar', *DCL Gazette* (April 1929–Jan 1930) · *DSBB* · *Glasgow Herald* (25 Nov 1929) [obit.] · *CGPLA Eng. & Wales* (1930) [Thomas Robert Dewar] · *WWW* · *WWBMP*, vol. 2

Archives United Distillers, Balfour Building, Banbeath, Leven, Fife, records of John Dewar & Sons Ltd, Brands Publicity, Scotland

Likenesses T. Graham, portrait, 1900, repro. in Anderson, 'History of the house of Dewar', 63 · Bassano, photograph, 1900–04 [see illus.]

Wealth at death £4,405,347 12s. 10d.: confirmation, 13 Feb 1930, *CCI* · £5,000,000—Thomas Robert Dewar: probate, 30 May 1930, *CGPLA Eng. & Wales*

Dewar, Thomas Robert, Baron Dewar (1864–1930). *See under* Dewar, John Alexander, first Baron Forteviot (1856–1929).

PICTURE CREDITS

Daly, Denis (1747–1791)—unknown collection / Christie's; photograph National Portrait Gallery, London

Dalyell, Sir John Graham, sixth baronet (1775–1851)—photograph by kind permission of The National Trust for Scotland

Dalzel, Andrew (1742–1806)—Scottish National Portrait Gallery

Damer, Anne Seymour (1749–1828)—© reserved

Damm, Sheila Van (1922–1987)—© Lewis Morley, courtesy of The Akehurst Bureau; collection National Portrait Gallery, London

Dampier, William (1651–1715)—© National Portrait Gallery, London

Danby, Francis (1793–1861)—The Maas Gallery Ltd

Dance, Charles (1794–1863)—© National Portrait Gallery, London

Dance, George, the younger (1741–1825)—© National Portrait Gallery, London

Dance, William (1755–1840)—© National Portrait Gallery, London

Dancer, Daniel (1716–1794)—© National Portrait Gallery, London

Dancer, John Benjamin (1812–1887)—Gernsheim Collection, Harry Ransom Humanities Research Center, the University of Texas at Austin

Danckwerts, Peter Victor (1916–1984)—Godfrey Argent Studios / Royal Society

Daniel, Glyn Edmund (1914–1986)—by permission of the Master and Fellows of St John's College, Cambridge

Daniel, Samuel (1562/3–1619)—© National Portrait Gallery, London

Dannreuther, Edward George (1844–1905)—© National Portrait Gallery, London

Dansey, Sir Claude Edward Marjoribanks (1876–1947)—© National Portrait Gallery, London

Darbishire, Helen (1881–1961)—© National Portrait Gallery, London

Darby, John Nelson (1800–1882)—© National Portrait Gallery, London

D'Arcy, Martin Cyril (1888–1976)—with the permission of the Master of Campion Hall, University of Oxford

D'Arcy, Robert, fourth earl of Holdernesse (1718–1778)—© Leeds Museums & Galleries (Temple Newsam House)

Dare, Zena (1886–1975)—Public Record Office

Darling, Charles John, first Baron Darling (1849–1936)—© National Portrait Gallery, London

Darling, Sir Ralph (1772–1858)—by permission of the National Library of Australia

Darnton, (Philip) Christian (1905–1981)—© National Portrait Gallery, London

Dart, John (d. 1730)—© National Portrait Gallery, London

Dart, (Robert) Thurston (1921–1971)—© reserved

Dartiquenave, Charles (bap. 1664?, d. 1737)—© National Portrait Gallery, London

Darwin, Sir Charles Galton (1887–1962)—© National Portrait Gallery, London

Darwin, Charles Robert (1809–1882)—by permission of the Linnean Society of London

Darwin, Erasmus (1731–1802)—private collection; photograph National Portrait Gallery, London

Darwin, Sir Francis (1848–1925)—by courtesy of the Department of Plant Sciences in the University of Cambridge

Darwin, Sir George Howard (1845–1912)—© National Portrait Gallery, London

Darwin, Sir Robert Vere [Robin] (1910–1974)—© courtesy the Artist's Estate / Bridgeman Art Library; photograph Royal College of Art

Dashwood, Edmée Elizabeth Monica [E. M. Delafield] (1890–1943)—© National Portrait Gallery, London

Dashwood, Francis, eleventh Baron Le Despencer (1708–1781)—The Dashwood Heirloom Collection. Photograph: Photographic Survey, Courtauld Institute of Art, London

Daubeney, Giles, first Baron Daubeney (1451/2–1508)—© Dean and Chapter of Westminster

Daunt, William Joseph O'Neill (1807–1894)—© National Portrait Gallery, London

Davenant, John (bap. 1572, d. 1641)—© The President and Fellows of Queens' College, Cambridge

Davenant, Sir William (1606–1668)—© National Portrait Gallery, London

Davenport, Harold (1907–1969)—© National Portrait Gallery, London

Davenport, Mary Ann (1759–1843)—Garrick Club / the art archive

David I (c.1085–1153)—© The Duke of Roxburghe, Floors Castle, Kelso; Trustees of the National Library of Scotland

David II (1324–1371)—The British Library

David, Albert Augustus (1867–1950)—© National Portrait Gallery, London

David, Elizabeth (1913–1992)—© reserved; estate of Elizabeth David

Davidson, John Colin Campbell, first Viscount Davidson (1889–1970)—© National Portrait Gallery, London

Davidson, Sir John Humphrey (1876–1954)—© National Portrait Gallery, London

Davidson, Randall Thomas, Baron Davidson of Lambeth (1848–1930)—reproduced by kind permission of His Grace the Archbishop of Canterbury and the Church Commissioners. Photograph:

Photographic Survey, Courtauld Institute of Art, London

Davidson, William (1786–1820)—Ashmolean Museum, Oxford

Davies, Clement Edward (1884–1962)—© National Portrait Gallery, London

Davies, (Sarah) Emily (1830–1921)—The Mistress and Fellows, Girton College, Cambridge

Davies, Frances Mary Jemima Woodhill (1861–1934)—Getty Images – Sasha; collection Royal College of Music, London

Davies, Dame Gwen Lucy Ffrangcon- (1891–1992)—© Estate of Walter R. Sickert 2004. All rights reserved, DACS. Collection Browse & Darby

Davies, John (1564/5–1618)—© National Portrait Gallery, London

Davies, Margaret Caroline Llewelyn (1861–1944)—Hull University Archives

Davies, Rhys (1901–1978)—© National Portrait Gallery, London

Davies, (William) Robertson (1913–1995)—Paddy Cook

Davies, Sneyd (1709–1769)—© National Portrait Gallery, London

Davies, Sir (Henry) Walford (1869–1941)—© National Portrait Gallery, London

Davies, William Henry (1871–1940)—© Elizabeth Banks; collection National Portrait Gallery, London

Davies, Sir William Llewelyn (1887–1952)—© National Portrait Gallery, London

Davis, Arthur Joseph (1878–1951)—© National Portrait Gallery, London

Davis, Brian [Michael ffolkes] (1925–1988)—© National Portrait Gallery, London

Davis, Elizabeth [Betsy] (1789–1860)—© National Portrait Gallery, London

Davis, Henry William Carless (1874–1928)—© National Portrait Gallery, London

Davis, Sir John Henry Harris (1906–1993)—© National Portrait Gallery, London

Davis, Joseph [Joe] (1901–1978)—Getty Images – A. J. O'Brien

Davis, Sir Rupert Charles Hart- (1907–1999)—Camera Press

Davis, Thomas Osborne (1814–1845)—National Gallery of Ireland

Davis, William (1771/2–1807)—© National Portrait Gallery, London

Davison, Emily Wilding (1872–1913)—© reserved; collection National Portrait Gallery, London

Davison, Maria Rebecca (1780x83–1858)—Garrick Club / the art archive

Davitt, Michael (1846–1906)—courtesy the Hugh Lane Municipal Gallery of Modern Art, Dublin

Davy, Henry (1793–1865)—Ipswich Borough Council Museums and Galleries

Davy, Sir Humphry, baronet (1778–1829)—© The Royal Society

Dawe, George (1781–1829)—Collection of the Museum of New Zealand, Te Papa Tongarewa (B.042007)

Dawes, Sir William, third baronet (1671–1724)—by kind permission of the Archbishop of York and the Church Commissioners

Dawes, William Rutter (1799–1868)—© Royal Astronomical Society Library

Dawkins, Richard MacGillivray (1871–1955)—© National Portrait Gallery, London

Dawkins, Sir William Boyd (1837–1929)—reproduced by permission of Birmingham Library Services

Dawson, Bertrand Edward, Viscount Dawson of Penn (1864–1945)—The de László Foundation / by permission of the Royal College of Physicians, London

Dawson, Charles (1864–1916)—© The Natural History Museum, London

Dawson, (George) Geoffrey (1874–1944)—© Estate of Sir William Rothenstein / National Portrait Gallery, London

Dawson, George (1821–1876)—© National Portrait Gallery, London

Dawson, Grahame George (1895–1944)—© reserved; private collection

Dawson, John (bap. 1735, d. 1820)—© National Portrait Gallery, London

Dawson, John (1827–1903)—© National Portrait Gallery, London

Dawson, Sir John William (1820–1899)—© National Portrait Gallery, London

Dawson, Leslie (1931–1993)—Getty Images – R. Poplowski

Dawson, Matthew (1820–1898)—National Horseracing Museum

Dawson, Nancy (bap. 1728, d. 1767)—© National Portrait Gallery, London

Dawson, Peter Smith (1882–1961)—© National Portrait Gallery, London

Day, John (1521/2–1584)—© National Portrait Gallery, London

Day, Sir Robin (1923–2000)—© National Portrait Gallery, London

Day, William (1529–1596)—by kind permission of the Provost and Fellows of King's College, Cambridge

Deacon, Henry (1822–1876)—© National Portrait Gallery, London

Deakin, Alfred (1856–1919)—by permission of the National Library of Australia

Deakin, Arthur (1890–1955)—© National Portrait Gallery, London

Deakin, John (1912–1972)—© Lucian Freud

Dean, Sir Patrick Henry (1909–1994)—private collection

Dean, William Ralph [Dixie] (1907–1980)—Getty Images – Barker

Deane, Sir Anthony (c.1638–1720?)—© National Portrait Gallery, London

Deane, Richard (bap. 1610, d. 1653)—© National Maritime Museum, London